Occupational Outlook Handbook

2010-11 Edition

U.S. Department of Labor
Hilda L. Solis, Secretary

U.S. Bureau of Labor Statistics
Keith Hall, Commissioner

January 2010

Bulletin 2800

Suggested citation: U.S. Bureau of Labor Statistics, U.S. Department of Labor, *Occupational Outlook Handbook, 2010-11 Library Edition,* Bulletin 2800. Superintendent of Documents, U.S. Government Printing Office, Washington, DC.

To order additional print copies of this title,
please contact Bernan directly at 800-865-3457

Published by Bernan
A wholly owned subsidiary of The Rowman & Littlefield Publishing Group, Inc.
4501 Forbes Boulevard, Suite 200, Lanham, Maryland 20706
http://www.bernan.com
800-865-3457; info@bernan.com

ISBN Paperback: 978-1-60175-805-7
ISBN Casebound: 978-1-60175-804-0

Acknowledgments

The Bureau of Labor Statistics produced the *Handbook* under the general guidance and direction of Dixie Sommers, Associate Commissioner for Occupational Statistics and Employment Projections, and Kristina J. Bartsch, Chief, Division of Occupational Outlook, Office of Occupational Statistics and Employment Projections. Chester C. Levine and Roger J. Moncarz, Managers of Occupational Outlook Studies, provided planning and day-to-day direction.

Supervisors overseeing the research and preparation of material were Douglas Braddock, Arlene Dohm, Teresa L. Morisi, Henry T. Kasper, Sheryl Konigsberg, Terry Schau, and Michael Wolf. Occupational analysts who contributed material were Phillip C. Bastian, Adam Bibler, Diana Gehlhaus Carew, Lauren Csorny, Tamara Dillon, Tom DiVincenzo, Jonathan Kelinson, Bradley Kunz, William Lawhorn, Kevin M. McCarron, Colleen D. Teixeira Moffat, Alice Ramey, Mike Rieley, Brian Roberts, Patricia Tate, Dalton B. Terrell, Benjamin Wright, and Ian Wyatt.

Editorial work was provided by Kathleen Green, Drew Liming, John Mullins, and Elka Maria Torpey, Office of Occupational Statistics and Employment Projections. Editorial work also was provided by Brian Baker, Edith Baker, Monica Gabor, Casey Homan, Lawrence H. Leith, and Maureen Soyars, Office of Publications and Special Studies, and Eugene Becker and Richard M. Devens, formerly with BLS, all under the supervision of William Parks II, Division Chief, BLS Publishing, and Leslie Brown Joyner, Branch Chief, Editorial Services. Technical and computer programming support was provided by T. Alan Lacey, C. Brett Lockard, Erik A. Savisaar, and D. Terkanian, under the supervision of Eric Figueroa. Ryan Buffkin and Megan Sweitzer also provided technical support. The cover and other art were designed by Keith Tapscott. Drew Liming also contributed art.

Photographs were provided by the Department of Labor Photographic Services. The Bureau of Labor Statistics also wishes to express its appreciation for the cooperation and assistance of the many organizations and individuals who either contributed photographs or made their facilities available to photographers working for or under contract to the Department of Labor. Situations portrayed in the photographs may not be free of every possible safety or health hazard. Depiction of company or trade name in no way constitutes endorsement by the Department of Labor.

Dedication

This edition of the *Occupational Outlook Handbook* is dedicated to the memory of **Michael J. Pilot**, who retired in 2005 after 42 years of Federal Government service. Mike's leadership significantly contributed to the quality of many editions of the *Handbook*.

Contents

v

Additional Information About the 2008–18 Projections

Readers interested in more information about the projections; about the methods and assumptions that underlie them; or about details on economic growth, the labor force, or industry and occupational employment, should consult the November 2009 *Monthly Labor Review*, or the Winter 2009–10 *Occupational Outlook Quarterly*.

More information about employment change, job openings, earnings, and training requirements by occupation is available on the Bureau's Employment Projections homepage at **http://www.bls.gov/emp**. The *Career Guide to Industries*, which presents occupational information from an industry perspective, is also accessible.

Overview of the 2008–2018 Projections

Job openings result from the relationship between the population, labor force, and demand for goods and services. The population restricts the size of the labor force, which consists of working individuals and those looking for work. The size and productivity of the labor force limits the quantity of goods and services that can be produced. In addition, changes in the demand for goods and services influence which industries expand or contract. Industries respond by hiring the workers necessary to produce goods and provide services. However, improvements to technology and productivity, changes in which occupations perform certain tasks, and changes to the supply of workers all affect which occupations will be employed by those industries. Examining past and present changes to these relationships in order to project future shifts is the foundation of the Employment Projections Program. This chapter presents highlights of population, labor force, and occupational and industry employment projections for 2008–2018. Sources of additional information about the projections appear on the preceding page.

Population

Shifts in the size and composition of the population can create a number of changes to the U.S. economy. Most importantly, population trends produce corresponding changes in the size and composition of the labor force. The U.S. civilian noninstitutional population, including individuals aged 16 and older, is expected to increase by 25.1 million from 2008 to 2018 (chart 1). The projected 2008–18 growth rate of 10.7 percent is less than the 11.2-percent growth rate for the 1988–98 period and the 13.9-percent rate for the 1998–2008 period. As in the past few decades, population growth will vary by age group, race, and ethnicity.

As the baby boomers continue to age, the 55 and older age group is projected to increase by 29.7 percent, more than any other age group. Meanwhile, the 45 to 54 age group is expected to decrease by 4.4 percent, reflecting the slower birth rate following the baby-boom generation. The 35 to 44 age group is anticipated to experience little change, with a growth rate of 0.2 percent, while the population aged 16 to 24 will grow 3.4 percent over the projection period. Minorities and immigrants are expected to constitute a larger share of the U.S. population in 2018. The numbers of Asians and people of Hispanic origin are projected to continue to grow much faster than other racial and ethnic groups.

Labor force

Population is the single most important factor in determining the size and composition of the labor force. The civilian labor force is projected to reach 166.9 million by 2018, which is an increase of 8.2 percent.

The U.S. workforce is expected to become more diverse by 2018. Among racial groups, Whites are expected to make up a decreasing share of the labor force, while Blacks, Asians, and

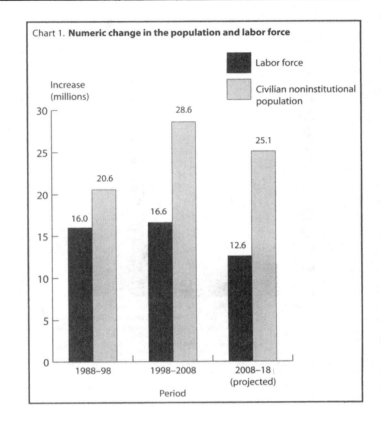

Chart 1. **Numeric change in the population and labor force**

all other groups will increase their share (chart 2). Among ethnic groups, persons of Hispanic origin are projected to increase their share of the labor force from 14.3 percent to 17.6 percent, reflecting 33.1 percent growth.

The number of women in the labor force will grow at a slightly faster rate than the number of men. The male labor force is projected to grow by 7.5 percent from 2008 to 2018, compared with 9.0 percent for the female labor force.

The share of the youth labor force, workers aged 16 to 24, is expected to decrease from 14.3 percent in 2008 to 12.7 percent by 2018. The primary working-age group, those between 25 and 54 years old, is projected to decline from 67.7 percent of the labor force in 2008 to 63.5 percent by 2018. Workers aged 55 years and older, by contrast, are anticipated to leap from 18.1 percent to 23.9 percent of the labor force during the same period (chart 3).

Employment

Total employment is expected to increase by 10 percent from 2008 to 2018. However, the 15.3 million jobs expected to be added by 2018 will not be evenly distributed across major industry and occupational groups. Changes in consumer demand, improvements in technology, and many other factors will contribute to the continually changing employment structure of the U.S. economy.

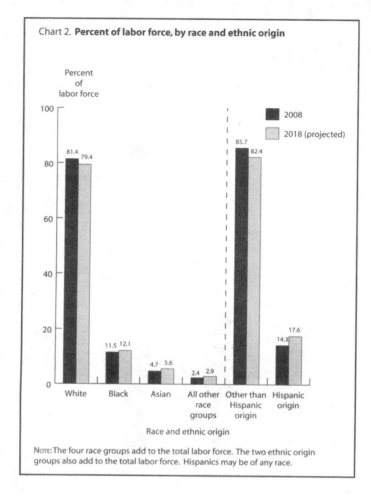

Chart 2. **Percent of labor force, by race and ethnic origin**

Note: The four race groups add to the total labor force. The two ethnic origin groups also add to the total labor force. Hispanics may be of any race.

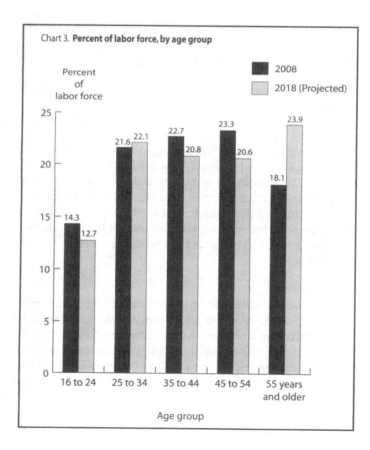

Chart 3. **Percent of labor force, by age group**

The next two sections examine projected employment change within industries and occupations. The industry perspective is discussed in terms of wage and salary employment. The exception is employment in agriculture, which includes the self-employed and unpaid family workers in addition to wage and salary workers. The occupational profile is viewed in terms of total employment—including wage and salary, self-employed, and unpaid family workers.

Employment change by industry

Goods-producing industries. Employment in goods-producing industries has declined since the 1990s. Although overall employment is expected to change little, projected growth among goods-producing industries varies considerably (chart 4).

Mining, quarrying, and oil and gas extraction. Employment in mining, quarrying, and oil and gas extraction is expected to decrease by 14 percent by 2018. Employment in support activities for mining will be responsible for most of the job loss in this industry with a decline of 23 percent. Other mining industries, such as nonmetallic mineral mining and quarrying and coal mining, are expected to see little or no change or a small increase in employment. Employment stagnation in these industries is attributable mainly to strict environmental regulations and technology gains that boost worker productivity.

Construction. Employment in construction is expected to rise 19 percent. Demand for commercial construction and an increase in road, bridge, and tunnel construction will account for the bulk of job growth.

Manufacturing. Overall employment in this sector will decline by 9 percent as productivity gains, automation, and international competition adversely affect employment in most manufacturing industries. Employment in household appliance manufacturing is expected to decline by 24 percent over the decade. Similarly, employment in machinery manufacturing, apparel manufacturing, and computer and electronic product

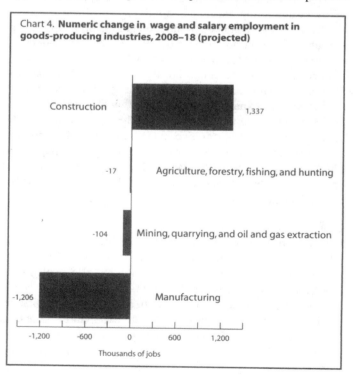

Chart 4. **Numeric change in wage and salary employment in goods-producing industries, 2008–18 (projected)**

manufacturing will decline as well. However, employment in a few manufacturing industries will increase. For example, employment in pharmaceutical and medicine manufacturing is expected to grow by 6 percent by 2018; however, this increase is expected to add only 17,600 new jobs.

Agriculture, forestry, fishing, and hunting. Overall employment in agriculture, forestry, fishing, and hunting is expected to decrease by 1 percent. Employment is projected to continue to decline because of rising costs of production, increasing consolidation, and more imports of food and lumber. Within this sector, the only industry that is expected to add jobs is support activities for agriculture and forestry, which includes farm labor contractors and farm management services. This industry is anticipated to grow by 13 percent, but this corresponds to an increase of only 13,800 new jobs.

Service-providing industries. The shift in the U.S. economy away from goods-producing in favor of service-providing is expected to continue. Service-providing industries are anticipated to generate approximately 14.5 million new wage and salary jobs. As with goods-producing industries, growth among service-providing industries will vary (chart 5).

Utilities. Employment in utilities is projected to decrease by 11 percent through 2018. Despite increased output, employment in electric power generation, transmission, and distribution and in natural gas distribution is expected to decline because of improved technology that will increase worker productivity. However, employment in the water, sewage, and other systems industry is anticipated to increase 13 percent by 2018. As the population continues to grow, more water treatment facilities are being built. Further, changing Federal and State Government water quality regulations may require more workers to ensure that water is safe to drink and to release into the environment.

Wholesale trade. The number of workers in wholesale trade is expected to increase by 4 percent, adding about 255,900 jobs. The consolidation of wholesale trade firms into fewer and larger companies will contribute to slower-than-average employment growth in the industry.

Retail trade. Employment in retail trade is expected to increase by 4 percent. Despite slower-than-average growth, this industry is projected to add about 654,000 new jobs over the 2008–18 period. Slower job growth reflects both continued consolidation and slower growth in personal consumption than in the previous decade.

Transportation and warehousing. Employment in transportation and warehousing is expected to increase by 10 percent, adding about 445,500 jobs to the industry total. Truck transportation is anticipated to grow by 10 percent, and the warehousing and storage sector is projected to grow by 12 percent. Demand for truck transportation and warehousing services will expand as many manufacturers concentrate on their core competencies and contract out their product transportation and storage functions.

Information. Employment in the information sector is expected to increase by 4 percent, adding 118,100 jobs by 2018. The sector contains fast-growing computer-related industries. The data-processing, hosting, and related services industry, which is expected to grow by 53 percent, includes establishments that provide Web and application hosting and streaming services. Internet publishing and broadcasting is expected to grow rapidly as it gains market share from newspapers and other more traditional media. Software publishing is projected to grow by 30 percent as organizations of all types continue to adopt the newest software products.

The information sector also includes the telecommunications industry, whose employment is projected to decline 9 percent. Despite an increase in demand for telecommunications services, more reliable networks along with consolidation among organizations will lead to productivity gains, reducing the need for workers. In addition, employment in the publishing industry is expected to decline by 5 percent, which is the result of increased efficiency in production, declining newspaper revenues, and a trend towards using more freelance workers.

Finance and insurance. The finance and insurance industry is expected to increase by 5 percent from 2008 to 2018. Employment in the securities, commodity contracts, and other financial investments and related activities industry is projected to expand 12 percent by 2018, which reflects the number of baby boomers in their peak savings years, the growth of tax-favorable retirement plans, and the globalization of securities markets. Employment in the credit intermediation and related activities industry, which includes banks, will grow by about 5 percent, adding 42 percent of all new jobs within the finance and insurance sector. Employment in the insurance carriers and related activities industry is expected to grow by 3 percent, translating into 67,600 new jobs by 2018. The number of jobs in the agencies, brokerages, and other insurance-related activities industry is expected to grow by 14 percent. Growth will stem from both the needs of an increasing population and new insurance products on the market.

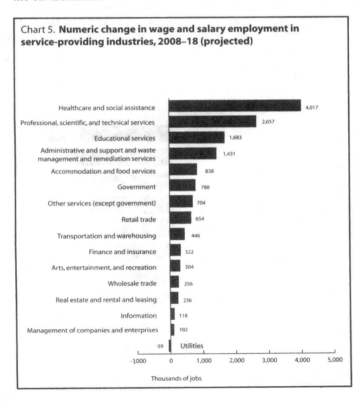

Chart 5. **Numeric change in wage and salary employment in service-providing industries, 2008–18 (projected)**

Industry	Thousands of jobs
Healthcare and social assistance	4,017
Professional, scientific, and technical services	2,657
Educational services	1,683
Administrative and support and waste management and remediation services	1,431
Accommodation and food services	838
Government	788
Other services (except government)	704
Retail trade	654
Transportation and warehousing	446
Finance and insurance	322
Arts, entertainment, and recreation	304
Wholesale trade	256
Real estate and rental and leasing	236
Information	118
Management of companies and enterprises	102
Utilities	-59

Real estate and rental and leasing. The real estate and rental and leasing industry is expected to grow by 11 percent through 2018. Growth will be due, in part, to increased demand for housing as the population expands. The fastest growing industry in the real estate and rental and leasing services sector will be lessors of nonfinancial intangible assets (except copyrighted works), increasing by 34 percent over the projection period.

Professional, scientific, and techncal services. Employment in professional, scientific, and technical services is projected to grow by 34 percent, adding about 2.7 million new jobs by 2018. Employment in computer systems design and related services is expected to increase by 45 percent, accounting for nearly one-fourth of all new jobs in this industry sector. Employment growth will be driven by growing demand for the design and integration of sophisticated networks and Internet and intranet sites. Employment in management, scientific, and technical consulting services is anticipated to expand at a staggering 83 percent, making up about 31 percent of job growth in this sector. Demand for these services will be spurred by businesses' continued need for advice on planning and logistics, the implementation of new technologies, and compliance with workplace safety, environmental, and employment regulations.

Management of companies and enterprises. Management of companies and enterprises is projected to grow relatively slowly, by 5 percent, as companies focus on reorganization to increase efficiency.

Administrative and support and waste management and remediation services. Employment in this sector is expected to grow by 18 percent by 2018. The largest growth will occur in employment services, an industry that is anticipated to account for 42 percent of all new jobs in the administrative and support and waste management and remediation services sector. The employment services industry ranks fifth among industries with the most new employment opportunities in the Nation over the 2008–18 period and is expected to grow faster than the average for all industries. Projected growth stems from the strong need for seasonal and temporary workers and for specialized human resources services.

Educational services. Employment in public and private educational services is anticipated to grow by 12 percent, adding about 1.7 million new jobs through 2018. Rising student enrollments at all levels of education will create demand for educational services.

Healthcare and social assistance. About 26 percent of all new jobs created in the U.S. economy will be in the healthcare and social assistance industry. This industry—which includes public and private hospitals, nursing and residential care facilities, and individual and family services—is expected to grow by 24 percent, or 4 million new jobs. Employment growth will be driven by an aging population and longer life expectancies.

Arts, entertainment, and recreation. The arts, entertainment, and recreation industry is expected to grow by 15 percent by 2018. Most of the growth will be in the amusement, gambling, and recreation sector. Job growth will stem from public participation in arts, entertainment, and recreation activities—reflecting increasing incomes, leisure time, and awareness of the health benefits of physical fitness.

Accommodation and food services. Employment in accommodation and food services is expected to grow by 7 percent, adding about 838,200 new jobs through 2018. Job growth will be concentrated in food services and drinking places, reflecting an increase in the population and the convenience of many new food establishments.

Other services (except government and private households). Employment is expected to grow by 13 percent in other services. Personal care services comprise the fastest growing industry in this sector, at 32 percent. This industry includes barbers, salons, and spas, which have experienced growing demand as individuals increasingly are seeking to improve their personal appearance.

Government. Between 2008 and 2018, government employment, excluding employment in public education and hospitals, is expected to increase by 7 percent. Growth in government employment will be fueled by expanding demand for public safety services and assistance provided to the elderly, but dampened by budgetary constraints and the outsourcing of government jobs to the private sector. State and local governments, excluding education and hospitals, are anticipated to grow by 8 percent as a result of the continued shift of responsibilities from the Federal Government to State and local governments. Federal Government employment, including the Postal Service, is expected to increase by 3 percent.

Employment change by occupation

Industry growth or decline will affect demand for occupations. However, job growth is projected to vary among major occupational groups (chart 6).

Management, business, and financial occupations. Workers in management, business, and financial occupations plan and direct the activities of business, government, and other organizations. Their employment is expected to increase by 11 percent by 2018. These workers will be needed to help organizations navigate the increasingly complex and competitive business

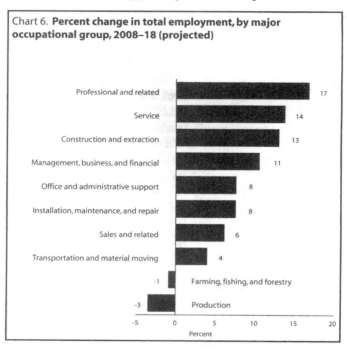

Chart 6. **Percent change in total employment, by major occupational group, 2008–18 (projected)**

Occupational group	Percent
Professional and related	17
Service	14
Construction and extraction	13
Management, business, and financial	11
Office and administrative support	8
Installation, maintenance, and repair	8
Sales and related	6
Transportation and material moving	4
Farming, fishing, and forestry	-1
Production	-3

environment. A large portion of these jobs will arise in the management, scientific, and technical consulting industry sector. A substantial number, in addition, are expected in several other large or rapidly growing industries, including government, healthcare and social assistance, finance and insurance, and construction.

Employment in management occupations is projected to grow slowly over the projection period, increasing by 5 percent, an addition of 454,300 new jobs. Growth is being affected by declines in several occupations, including farmers and ranchers. Employment of farmers and ranchers is projected to decline as the agricultural industry produces more output with fewer workers.

Employment in business and financial operations occupations is projected to grow by 18 percent, resulting in 1.2 million new jobs. Increasing financial regulations and the need for greater accountability will drive demand for accountants and auditors, adding roughly 279,400 jobs to this occupation from 2008 to 2018. Further, an increasingly competitive business environment will grow demand for management analysts, an occupation that is expected to add 178,300 jobs. Together, these two occupations are anticipated to account for 38 percent of new business and financial operations jobs.

Professional and related occupations. This occupational group, which includes a wide variety of skilled professions, is expected to be the fastest growing major occupational group, at 17 percent, and is projected to add the most new jobs—about 5.2 million.

Employment among healthcare practitioners and technical occupations, a subgroup of the professional and related category, is expected to increase by 21 percent. This growth, resulting in a projected 1.6 million new jobs, will be driven by increasing demand for healthcare services. As the number of older people continues to grow, and as new developments allow for the treatment of more medical conditions, more healthcare professionals will be needed.

Education, training, and library occupations are anticipated to add more than 1.3 million jobs, representing a growth rate of more than 14 percent. As the U.S. population increases, and as a larger share of adults seeks educational services, demand for these workers will increase.

Computer and mathematical science occupations are projected to add almost 785,700 new jobs from 2008 to 2018. As a group, these occupations are expected to grow more than twice as fast as the average for all occupations in the economy. Demand for workers in computer and mathematical occupations will be driven by the continuing need for businesses, government agencies, and other organizations to adopt and utilize the latest technologies.

Employment in community and social services occupations is projected to increase by 16 percent, growing by roughly 448,400 jobs. As health insurance providers increasingly cover mental and behavioral health treatment, and as a growing number of elderly individuals seek social services, demand for these workers will increase.

Employment in arts, design, entertainment, sports, and media occupations is expected to grow by 12 percent from 2008 to 2018, resulting in almost 332,600 new jobs. Growth will be spread broadly across different occupations within the group. Media and communications occupations will add a substantial number of jobs, led by rapid growth among public relations specialists, who will be needed in greater numbers as firms place a greater emphasis on managing their public image. Employment among entertainers and performers and those in sports and related occupations also will increase, partly as a result of increasing demand for coaches and scouts. Furthermore, art and design occupations will see substantial growth, with demand increasing for graphic and interior designers. As more advertising is conducted over the Internet, a medium that generally includes many graphics, and as businesses and households increasingly seek professional design services, a greater number of these workers will be needed.

Employment in life, physical, and social science occupations is projected to increase by nearly 277,200 jobs over the 2008–18 projection period. This increase represents a growth rate of 19 percent, almost twice the average for all occupations across the economy. About 116,700 of these jobs are expected to be created among social science and related occupations, led by strong growth among market and survey researchers, as businesses increase their marketing efforts in order to remain competitive and as public policy firms and government agencies utilize more public opinion research. Employment in life science occupations, in addition, will increase rapidly as developments from biotechnology research continue to be used to create new medical technologies, treatments, and pharmaceuticals.

Architecture and engineering occupations are projected to add roughly 270,600 jobs, representing a growth rate of 10 percent. Much of this growth will occur among engineering occupations, especially civil engineers. As greater emphasis is placed on improving the Nation's infrastructure, these specialists will be needed to design, implement, or upgrade municipal transportation, water supply, and pollution control systems.

Legal occupations will add the fewest new jobs among all professional and related subgroups, increasing by about 188,400. However, with a growth rate of 15 percent, this group will grow faster than the average for all occupations in the economy. Of the new jobs created, lawyers will account for 98,500 while paralegals and legal assistants will account for 74,100. Paralegals and legal assistants are expected to grow by 28 percent as legal establishments begin to expand the role of these workers and assign them more tasks once performed by lawyers.

Service occupations. The duties of service workers range from fighting fires to cooking meals. Employment in service occupations is projected to increase by 4.1 million, or 14 percent, which is both the second-largest numerical gain and the second-largest growth rate among the major occupational groups.

Among service occupation subgroups, the largest number of new jobs will occur in healthcare support occupations. With more than 1.1 million new jobs, employment in this subgroup is expected to increase by 29 percent. Much of the growth will be the result of increased demand for healthcare services as the expanding elderly population requires more care.

Employment in personal care and service occupations is anticipated to grow by 20 percent over the projection period, adding more than 1 million jobs. As consumers become more concerned with health, beauty, and fitness, the number of cosmetic and health spas will increase, causing an increase in demand for workers in this group. However, the personal care and service group contains a wide variety of occupations, and two of them—personal and home care aides, and child care workers—will account for most of this group's new jobs. Personal and home care aides will experience increased demand as a growing number of elderly individuals require assistance with daily tasks. Child care workers, in addition, will add jobs as formal preschool programs, which employ child care workers alongside preschool teachers, become more prevalent.

Employment in food preparation and serving and related occupations is projected to increase by roughly 1 million jobs from 2008 to 2018, representing a growth rate of 9 percent. Growth will stem from time-conscious consumers patronizing fast-food establishments and full-service restaurants.

Employment in building and grounds cleaning and maintenance occupations is expected to grow by almost 483,900 jobs over the projection period, representing a growth rate of 8 percent. As businesses place a larger emphasis on grounds aesthetics, and as households increasingly rely on contract workers to maintain their yards, grounds maintenance workers will see rapid growth. In addition, more building cleaning workers will be needed to maintain an increasing number of residential and commercial structures.

Protective service occupations are expected to gain the fewest new jobs among all service subgroups: about 400,100, or 12-percent growth. These workers protect businesses and other organizations from crime and vandalism. In addition, there will be increased demand for law enforcement officers to support the growing U.S. population.

Sales and related occupations. Sales and related workers solicit goods and services for businesses and consumers. Sales and related occupations are expected to add 980,400 new jobs by 2018, growing by 6 percent. As organizations offer a wider array of products and devote an increasing share of their resources to customer service, many new retail salesworkers will be needed. Job growth in this group will be spread across a wide variety of industries, but almost half will occur in retail sales establishments.

Office and administrative support occupations. Office and administrative support workers perform the day-to-day activities of the office, such as preparing and filing documents, dealing with the public, and distributing information. Employment in these occupations is expected to grow by 8 percent, adding 1.8 million new jobs by 2018. Customer service representatives are anticipated to add the most new jobs, 399,500, as businesses put an increased emphasis on building customer relationships. Other office and administrative support occupations will experience declines as advanced technology improves productivity, decreasing the number of workers necessary to perform some duties.

Farming, fishing, and forestry occupations. Farming, fishing, and forestry workers cultivate plants, breed and raise livestock, and catch animals. These occupations are projected to decline by about 1 percent, losing 9,100 jobs, by 2018. Productivity increases in agriculture will lead to declining employment among agricultural workers, offsetting small gains among forest, conservation, and logging workers.

Construction and extraction occupations. Construction and extraction workers build new residential and commercial buildings and also work in mines, quarries, and oil and gas fields. Employment of these workers is expected to grow 13 percent, adding about 1 million new jobs. Construction trades and related workers will account for about 808,400 of these jobs. Growth will result from increased construction of homes, office buildings, and infrastructure projects. Declines in extraction occupations will reflect overall employment stagnation in the mining and oil and gas extraction industries.

Installation, maintenance, and repair occupations. Workers in installation, maintenance, and repair occupations install new equipment and maintain and repair older equipment. These occupations are projected to add 440,200 jobs by 2018, growing by 8 percent. More than 1 in 3 new jobs in this group will occur in the construction industry, because these workers are integral to the development of buildings, communication structures, transportation systems, and other types of infrastructure. As construction on these types of projects increases over the projection period, installation, maintenance and repair workers will be needed in greater numbers.

Production occupations. Production workers are employed mainly in manufacturing, where they assemble goods and operate plants. Production occupations are expected to decline by 3 percent, losing 349,200 jobs by 2018. As productivity improvements reduce the need for workers, and as a growing number of these jobs are offshored, demand for production workers will decline. Some jobs will be created in production occupations, mostly in food processing and woodworking.

Transportation and material moving occupations. Transportation and material moving workers transport people and materials by land, sea, or air. Employment of these workers is anticipated to increase by 4 percent, accounting for 391,100 new jobs. As the economy grows over the projection period, and the demand for goods increases, truck drivers will be needed to transport those goods to businesses, consumers, and other entities. In addition, a substantial number of jobs will arise among bus drivers, as well as taxi drivers and chauffeurs, as a growing number of people utilize public transportation.

Employment change by detailed occupation

Occupational growth can be considered in two ways: by the rate of growth and by the number of new jobs created by growth. Some occupations both have a fast growth rate and create a large number of new jobs. However, an occupation that employs few workers may experience rapid growth, although the resulting number of new jobs may be small. For example, a small occupation that employs just 1,000 workers and is projected to grow 50 percent over a 10-year period will add only 500 jobs. By contrast, a large occupation that employs 1.5 million workers may experience only 10 percent growth, but will add 150,000 jobs. As a result, in order to get a complete picture of employment growth, both measures must be considered.

Occupations with the fastest growth. Of the 20 fastest growing occupations in the economy (table 1), half are related to healthcare. Healthcare is experiencing rapid growth, due in large part to the aging of the baby-boom generation, which will require more medical care. In addition, some healthcare occupations will be in greater demand for other reasons. As health-

Table 1. Occupations with the fastest growth

Occupations	Percent change	Number of new jobs (in thousands)	Wages (May 2008 median)	Education/training category
Biomedical engineers	72	11.6	$77,400	Bachelor's degree
Network systems and data communications analysts	53	155.8	71,100	Bachelor's degree
Home health aides	50	460.9	20,460	Short-term on-the-job training
Personal and home care aides	46	375.8	19,180	Short-term on-the-job training
Financial examiners	41	11.1	70,930	Bachelor's degree
Medical scientists, except epidemiologists	40	44.2	72,590	Doctoral degree
Physician assistants	39	29.2	81,230	Master's degree
Skin care specialists	38	14.7	28,730	Postsecondary vocational award
Biochemists and biophysicists	37	8.7	82,840	Doctoral degree
Athletic trainers	37	6.0	39,640	Bachelor's degree
Physical therapist aides	36	16.7	23,760	Short-term on-the-job training
Dental hygienists	36	62.9	66,570	Associate degree
Veterinary technologists and technicians	36	28.5	28,900	Associate degree
Dental assistants	36	105.6	32,380	Moderate-term on-the-job training
Computer software engineers, applications	34	175.1	85,430	Bachelor's degree
Medical assistants	34	163.9	28,300	Moderate-term on-the-job training
Physical therapist assistants	33	21.2	46,140	Associate degree
Veterinarians	33	19.7	79,050	First professional degree
Self-enrichment education teachers	32	81.3	35,720	Work experience in a related occupation
Compliance officers, except agriculture, construction, health and safety, and transportation	31	80.8	48,890	Long-term on-the-job training

care costs continue to rise, work is increasingly being delegated to lower paid workers in order to cut costs. For example, tasks that were previously performed by doctors, nurses, dentists, or other healthcare professionals increasingly are being performed by physician assistants, medical assistants, dental hygienists, and physical therapist aides. In addition, patients increasingly are seeking home care as an alternative to costly stays in hospitals or residential care facilities, causing a significant increase in demand for home health aides. Although not classified as healthcare workers, personal and home care aides are being affected by this demand for home care as well.

Two of the fastest growing detailed occupations are in the computer specialist occupational group. Network systems and data communications analysts are projected to be the second-fastest-growing occupation in the economy. Demand for these workers will increase as organizations continue to upgrade their information technology capacity and incorporate the newest technologies. The growing reliance on wireless networks will result in a need for more network systems and data communications analysts as well. Computer applications software engineers also are expected to grow rapidly from 2008 to 2018. Expanding Internet technologies have spurred demand for these workers, who can develop Internet, intranet, and Web applications.

Developments from biotechnology research will continue to be used to create new medical technologies, treatments, and pharmaceuticals. As a result, demand for medical scientists and for biochemists and biophysicists will increase. However,

although employment of biochemists and biophysicists is projected to grow rapidly, this corresponds to only 8,700 new jobs over the projection period. Increased medical research and demand for new medical technologies also will affect biomedical engineers. The aging of the population and a growing focus on health issues will drive demand for better medical devices and equipment designed by these workers. In fact, biomedical engineers are projected to be the fastest growing occupation in the economy. However, because of its small size, the occupation is projected to add only about 11,600 jobs.

Increasing financial regulations will spur employment growth both of financial examiners and of compliance officers, except agriculture, construction, health and safety, and transportation.

Self-enrichment teachers and skin care specialists will experience growth as consumers become more concerned with self-improvement. Self-enrichment teachers are growing rapidly as more individuals seek additional training to make themselves more appealing to prospective employers. Skin care specialists will experience growth as consumers increasingly care about their personal appearance.

Of the 20 fastest growing occupations, 12 are in the associate degree or higher category. Of the remaining 8, 6 are in an on-the-job training category, 1 is in the work experience in a related occupation category, and 1 is in the postsecondary vocational degree category. Eleven of these occupations earn at least $10,000 more than the National annual median wage,

Table 2. Occupations with the largest numerical growth

Occupations	Number of new jobs (in thousands)	Percent change	Wages (May 2008 median)	Education/training category
Registered nurses	581.5	22	$62,450	Associate degree
Home health aides	460.9	50	20,460	Short-term on-the-job training
Customer service representatives	399.5	18	29,860	Moderate-term on-the-job training
Combined food preparation and serving workers, including fast food	394.3	15	16,430	Short-term on-the-job training
Personal and home care aides	375.8	46	19,180	Short-term on-the-job training
Retail salespersons	374.7	8	20,510	Short-term on-the-job training
Office clerks, general	358.7	12	25,320	Short-term on-the-job training
Accountants and auditors	279.4	22	59,430	Bachelor's degree
Nursing aides, orderlies, and attendants	276.0	19	23,850	Postsecondary vocational award
Postsecondary teachers	256.9	15	58,830	Doctoral degree
Construction laborers	255.9	20	28,520	Moderate-term on-the-job training
Elementary school teachers, except special education	244.2	16	49,330	Bachelor's degree
Truck drivers, heavy and tractor-trailer	232.9	13	37,270	Short-term on-the-job training
Landscaping and groundskeeping workers	217.1	18	23,150	Short-term on-the-job training
Bookkeeping, accounting, and auditing clerks	212.4	10	32,510	Moderate-term on-the-job training
Executive secretaries and administrative assistants	204.4	13	40,030	Work experience in a related occupation
Management analysts	178.3	24	73,570	Bachelor's or higher degree, plus work experience
Computer software engineers, applications	175.1	34	85,430	Bachelor's degree
Receptionists and information clerks	172.9	15	24,550	Short-term on-the-job training
Carpenters	165.4	13	38,940	Long-term on-the-job training

which was $32,390 as of May 2008. In fact, 9 of the occupations earned at least twice the National median in May 2008.

Occupations with the largest numerical growth. The 20 occupations listed in table 2 are projected to account for more than one-third of all new jobs—5.8 million combined—over the 2008–18 period. The occupations with the largest numerical increases cover a wider range of occupational categories than do those occupations with the fastest growth rates. Health occupations will account for some of these increases in employment, as will occupations in education, sales, and food service. Office and administrative support services occupations are expected to grow by 1.3 million jobs, accounting for about one-fifth of the job growth among the 20 occupations with the largest growth. Many of the occupations listed in the table are very large and will create more new jobs than occupations with high growth rates. Only 3 out of the 20 fastest growing occupations—home health aides, personal and home care aides, and computer software application engineers—also are projected to be among the 20 occupations with the largest numerical increases in employment.

The education or training categories and wages of the occupations with the largest numbers of new jobs are significantly different than those of the fastest growing occupations. Twelve of these occupations are in an on-the-job training category, and just 7 are in a category that indicates any postsecondary education. Ten of the 20 occupations with the largest numbers of new jobs earned less than the National median wage in May 2008.

Occupations with the fastest decline. Declining occupational employment stems from falling industry employment, technological advances, changes in business practices, and other factors. For example, technological developments and the continued movement of textile production abroad are expected to contribute to a decline of 71,500 sewing machine operators over the projection period (table 3). Fifteen of the 20 occupations with the largest numerical decreases are either production occupations or office and administrative support occupations, both of which are adversely affected by increasing plant and factory automation or the implementation of office technology, reducing the need for workers in those occupations. The difference between the office and administrative support occupations that are expected to experience the largest declines and those which are expected to see the largest increases is the extent to which job functions can be easily automated or performed by

Table 3. Occupations with the fastest decline

Occupation	Percent change	Number of jobs lost (in thousands)	Wages (May 2008 median)	Education/training category
Textile bleaching and dyeing machine operators and tenders	-45	-7.2	$23,680	Moderate-term on-the-job training
Textile winding, twisting, and drawing out machine setters, operators, and tenders	-41	-14.2	23,970	Moderate-term on-the-job training
Textile knitting and weaving machine setters, operators, and tenders	-39	-11.5	25,400	Long-term on-the-job training
Shoe machine operators and tenders	-35	-1.7	25,090	Moderate-term on-the-job training
Extruding and forming machine setters, operators, and tenders, synthetic and glass fibers	-34	-4.8	31,160	Moderate-term on-the-job training
Sewing machine operators	-34	-71.5	19,870	Moderate-term on-the-job training
Semiconductor processors	-32	-10.0	32,230	Postsecondary vocational award
Textile cutting machine setters, operators, and tenders	-31	-6.0	22,620	Moderate-term on-the-job training
Postal Service mail sorters, processors, and processing machine operators	-30	-54.5	50,020	Short-term on-the-job training
Fabric menders, except garment	-30	-0.3	28,470	Moderate-term on-the-job training
Wellhead pumpers	-28	-5.3	37,860	Moderate-term on-the-job training
Fabric and apparel patternmakers	-27	-2.2	37,760	Long-term on-the-job training
Drilling and boring machine tool setters, operators, and tenders, metal and plastic	-27	-8.9	30,850	Moderate-term on-the-job training
Lathe and turning machine tool setters, operators, and tenders, metal and plastic	-27	-14.9	32,940	Moderate-term on-the-job training
Order clerks	-26	-64.2	27,990	Short-term on-the-job training
Coil winders, tapers, and finishers	-25	-5.6	27,730	Short-term on-the-job training
Photographic processing machine operators	-24	-12.5	20,360	Short-term on-the-job training
File clerks	-23	-49.6	23,800	Short-term on-the-job training
Derrick operators, oil and gas	-23	-5.8	41,920	Moderate-term on-the-job training
Desktop publishers	-23	-5.9	36,600	Postsecondary vocational award

other workers. For instance, the duties of executive secretaries and administrative assistants involve a great deal of personal interaction that cannot be automated, whereas the duties of file clerks—adding, locating, and removing business records—can be automated or performed by other workers.

Only 2 of the occupations with the fastest percent decline are in a category that indicates workers have any postsecondary education, while the rest are in an on-the-job training category. Eleven of these occupations earned less than $30,000 in May 2008, below the National median wage of $32,390.

Employment change by education and training category

In general, occupations in a category with some postsecondary education are expected to experience higher rates of growth than those in an on-the-job training category. Occupations in the associate degree category are projected to grow the fastest, at about 19 percent. In addition, occupations in the master's and first professional degree categories are anticipated to grow by about 18 percent each, and occupations in the bachelor's and doctoral degree categories are expected to grow by about 17 percent each. However, occupations in the on-the-job training categories are expected to grow by 8 percent each (chart 7).

Total job openings

Job openings stem from both employment growth and replacement needs (chart 8). Replacement needs arise as workers leave occupations. Some transfer to other occupations, while others retire, return to school, or quit to assume household responsibilities. Replacement needs are projected to account for 67 percent of the approximately 50.9 million job openings between 2008 and 2018. Thus, even occupations that are projected to experi-

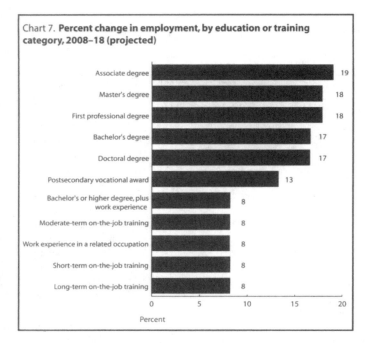

Chart 7. **Percent change in employment, by education or training category, 2008–18 (projected)**

Category	Percent
Associate degree	19
Master's degree	18
First professional degree	18
Bachelor's degree	17
Doctoral degree	17
Postsecondary vocational award	13
Bachelor's or higher degree, plus work experience	8
Moderate-term on-the-job training	8
Work experience in a related occupation	8
Short-term on-the-job training	8
Long-term on-the-job training	8

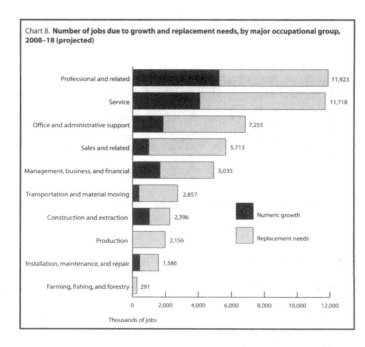

Chart 8. **Number of jobs due to growth and replacement needs, by major occupational group, 2008–18 (projected)**

Occupational group	Thousands of jobs
Professional and related	11,923
Service	11,718
Office and administrative support	7,255
Sales and related	5,713
Management, business, and financial	5,035
Transportation and material moving	2,857
Construction and extraction	2,396
Production	2,156
Installation, maintenance, and repair	1,586
Farming, fishing, and forestry	291

Numeric growth

Replacement needs

ence slower-than-average growth or to decline in employment still may offer many job openings.

Professional and related occupations are projected to have the largest number of total job openings, 11.9 million, and 56 percent of those will be due to replacement needs. Replacement needs generally are greatest in the largest occupations and in those with relatively low pay or limited training requirements. As a result, service occupations are projected to have the greatest number of job openings due to replacements, about 7.6 million.

Office automation will significantly affect many individual office and administrative support occupations. Although these occupations are projected to grow about as fast as average, some are projected to decline rapidly. Office and administrative support occupations are expected to create 7.3 million total job openings from 2008 to 2018, ranking third behind professional and related occupations and service occupations.

Farming, fishing, and forestry occupations and production occupations should offer job opportunities despite overall declines in employment. These occupations will lose 9,100 and 349,200 jobs, respectively, but are expected to provide more than 2.4 million total job openings. Job openings will be due solely to the replacement needs of a workforce characterized by high levels of retirement and job turnover.

The analysis underlying BLS employment projections uses currently available information to focus on long-term structural changes in the economy. The 2008–18 projections assume a full-employment economy in 2018. The impact of the recent recession, which began in December of 2007, on long-term structural changes in the economy will not be fully known until some point during or after the recovery. Because the 2008 starting point is a recession year, the projected growth to an assumed full-employment economy in 2018 will generally be stronger than if the starting point were not a recession year.

Classification of occupations by most significant source of education or training

Postsecondary awards

First professional degree. Completion of the degree usually requires at least 3 years of full-time academic study beyond a bachelor's degree. Examples are lawyers; and physicians and surgeons.

Doctoral degree. Completion of a Ph.D. or other doctoral degree usually requires at least 3 years of full-time academic study beyond a bachelor's degree. Examples are postsecondary teachers; and medical scientists, except epidemiologists.

Master's degree. Completion of the degree usually requires 1 or 2 years of full-time academic study beyond a bachelor's degree. Examples are educational, vocational, and school counselors; and clergy.

Bachelor's or higher degree, plus work experience. Most occupations in this category are management occupations. All require experience in a related nonmanagement position for which a bachelor's or higher degree is usually required. Examples are general and operations managers; and judges, magistrate judges, and magistrates.

Bachelor's degree. Completion of the degree generally requires at least 4 years, but not more than 5 years, of full-time academic study. Examples are accountants and auditors; and elementary school teachers, except special education.

Associate degree. Completion of the degree usually requires at least 2 years of full-time academic study. Examples are paralegals and legal assistants; and medical records and health information technicians.

Postsecondary vocational award. Some programs last only a few weeks, others more than a year. Programs lead to a certificate or other award, but not a degree. Examples are nursing aides, orderlies, and attendants; and hairdressers, hairstylists, and cosmetologists.

Work-related training

Work experience in a related occupation. Most of the occupations in this category are first-line supervisors or managers of service, sales and related, production, or other occupations; or are management occupations.

Long-term on-the-job training. Occupations in this category generally require more than 12 months of on-the-job training or combined work experience and formal classroom instruction for workers to develop the skills necessary to be fully qualified in the occupation. These occupations include formal and informal apprenticeships that may last up to 5 years. Long-term on-the-job training also includes intensive occupation-specific, employer-sponsored programs that workers must complete. Among such programs are those conducted by fire and police academies and by schools for air traffic controllers and flight attendants. In other occupations—insurance sales and securities sales, for example—trainees take formal courses, often provided on the jobsite, to prepare for the required licensing exams. Individuals undergoing training generally are considered to be employed in the occupation. Also included in this category is the development of a natural ability—such as that possessed by musicians, athletes, actors, and other entertainers—that must be cultivated over several years, frequently in a non-work setting.

Moderate-term on-the-job training. In this category of occupations, the skills needed to be fully qualified in the occupation can be acquired during 1 to 12 months of combined on-the-job experience and informal training. Examples are truckdrivers, heavy and tractor-trailer; and secretaries, except legal, medical, and executive.

Short-term on-the-job training. In occupations in this category, the skills needed to be fully qualified in the occupation can be acquired during a short demonstration of job duties or during 1 month or less of on-the-job experience or instruction. Examples of these occupations are retail salespersons; and waiters and waitresses.

Sources of Career Information

This section identifies some major sources of information on careers. These sources are meant to be used in addition to those listed at the end of each *Handbook* statement, and they may provide additional information.

How to best use this information. The sources mentioned in this section offer different types of information. For example, people you know may provide very specific information because they have knowledge of you, your abilities and interests, and your qualifications. Other sources, such as those found in the State Sources below, provide information on occupations in each State. Gathering information from a wide range of sources is the best way to determine what occupations may be appropriate for you, and in what geographic regions these occupations are found. The sources of information discussed in this section are not exhaustive, and other sources could prove equally valuable in your career search.

Career information

Like any major decision, selecting a career involves a lot of fact finding. Fortunately, some of the best informational resources are easily accessible. You should assess career guidance materials carefully. Information that seems out of date or glamorizes an occupation—overstates its earnings or exaggerates the demand for workers, for example—should be evaluated with skepticism. Gathering as much information as possible will help you make a more informed decision.

People you know. One of the best resources can be your friends and family. They may answer some questions about a particular occupation or put you in touch with someone who has some experience in the field. This personal networking can be invaluable in evaluating an occupation or an employer. These people will be able to tell you about their specific duties and training, as well as what they did or did not like about a job. People who have worked in an occupation locally also may be able to give you a recommendation and get you in touch with specific employers.

Employers. This is the primary source of information on specific jobs. Employers may post lists of job openings and application requirements, including the exact training and experience required, starting wages and benefits, and advancement opportunities and career paths.

Informational interviews. People already working in a particular field often are willing to speak with people interested in joining their field. An informational interview will allow you to get good information from experts in a specific career without the pressure of a job interview. These interviews allow you to determine how a certain career may appeal to you while helping you build a network of personal contacts.

Professional societies, trade groups, and labor unions. These groups have information on an occupation or various related occupations with which they are associated or which they ac-

tively represent. This information may cover training requirements, earnings, and listings of local employers. These groups may train members or potential members themselves, or they may be able to put you in contact with organizations or individuals who perform such training.

Each occupational statement in the *Handbook* concludes with a "Sources of Additional Information" section, which lists organizations that may be contacted for more information. Another valuable source for finding organizations associated with occupations is the *Encyclopedia of Associations*, an annual publication that lists trade associations, professional societies, labor unions, and other organizations.

Guidance and career counselors. Counselors can help you make choices about which careers might suit you best. They can help you establish what occupations suit your skills by testing your aptitude for various types of work and determining your strengths and interests. Counselors can help you evaluate your options and search for a job in your field or help you select a new field altogether. They can also help you determine which educational or training institutions best fit your goals, and then assist you in finding ways to finance them. Some counselors offer other services such as interview coaching, résumé building, and help in filling out various forms. Counselors in secondary schools and postsecondary institutions may arrange guest speakers, field trips, or job fairs.

You can find guidance and career counselors at many common institutions, including:

- High school guidance offices
- College career planning and placement offices
- Placement offices in private vocational or technical schools and institutions
- Vocational rehabilitation agencies
- Counseling services offered by community organizations
- Private counseling agencies and private practices
- State employment service offices

When using a private counselor, check to see that the counselor is experienced. One way to do so is to ask people who have used their services in the past. The National Board of Certified Counselors and Affiliates is an institution which accredits career counselors. To verify the credentials of a career counselor and to find a career counselor in your area, contact:

➤ National Board for Certified Counselor and Affiliates, 3 Terrace Way, Suite D, Greensboro, NC 27403-3660. Internet: **http://www.nbcc.org/directory/FindCounselors.aspx**

Postsecondary institutions. Colleges, universities, and other postsecondary institutions typically put a lot of effort into helping place their graduates in good jobs, because the success of their graduates may indicate the quality of their institution and may affect the institution's ability to attract new students. Postsecondary institutions commonly have career centers with libraries of information on different careers, listings of related jobs, and alumni contacts in various professions. Career centers frequently employ career counselors who generally provide their services only to their students and alumni. Career centers can help you build your résumé, find internships and co-ops—which can lead to full-time positions—and tailor your course selection or program to make you a more attractive job applicant.

Local libraries. Libraries can be an invaluable source of information. Since most areas have libraries, they can be a convenient place to look for information. Also, many libraries provide access to the Internet and email.

Libraries may have information on job openings, locally and nationally; potential contacts within occupations or industries; colleges and financial aid; vocational training; individual businesses or careers; and writing résumés. Libraries frequently have subscriptions to various trade magazines that can provide information on occupations and industries. Your local library also may have video materials. These sources often have references to organizations that can provide additional information about training and employment opportunities.

If you need help getting started or finding a resource, ask your librarian for assistance.

Internet resources. A wide variety of career information is easily accessible on the Internet. Many online resources include job listings, résumé posting services, and information on job fairs, training, and local wages. Many of the resources listed elsewhere in this section have Internet sites that include valuable information on potential careers. No single source contains all information on an occupation, field, or employer; therefore you will likely need to use a variety of sources.

When using Internet resources, be sure that the organization is a credible, established source of information on the particular occupation. Individual companies may include job listings on their Web sites, and may include information about required credentials, wages and benefits, and the job's location. Contact information, such as whom to call or where to send a résumé, is usually included.

Some sources exist primarily as a Web service. These services often have information on specific jobs, and can greatly aid in the job hunting process. Some commercial sites offer these services, as do Federal, State, and some local governments. *Career OneStop*, a joint program by the Department of Labor and the States as well as local agencies, provides these services free of charge.

Online Sources from the Department of Labor. A major portion of the U.S. Department of Labor's Labor Market Information System is the *Career OneStop* site. This site includes links to the following:

• *State job banks* allow you to search over a million job openings listed with State employment agencies.
• *America's Career InfoNet* provides data on employment growth and wages by occupation; the knowledge, skills, and abilities required by an occupation; and links to employers.
• *America's Service Locator* is a comprehensive database of career centers and information on unemployment benefits, job training, youth programs, seminars, educational opportunities, and disabled or older worker programs.

Career OneStop, along with the National Toll-Free Jobs Helpline (877-USA-JOBS) and the local One-Stop Career Centers in each State, combine to provide a wide range of workforce assistance and resources:

➤ Career OneStop. Internet: **http://www.careeronestop.org**

Use the O*NET numbers at the start of each *Handbook* statement to find more information on specific occupations:

➤ O*NET Online. Internet: **http://www.onetcenter.org**

Provided in collaboration with the U.S. Department of Education, *Career Voyages* has information on certain high-demand occupations:

➤ Career Voyages. Internet: **http://www.careervoyages.gov**

The Department of Labor's Bureau of Labor Statistics publishes a wide range of labor market information, from regional wages for specific occupations to statistics on National, State, and area employment.

➤ Bureau of Labor Statistics. Internet: **http://www.bls.gov**

While the *Handbook* discusses careers from an occupational perspective, a companion publication—*Career Guide to Industries*—discusses careers from an industry perspective. The *Career Guide* is also available at your local career center and library:

➤ *Career Guide to Industries.* Internet: **http://www.bls.gov/oco/cg**

For information on occupational wages:

➤ Wage Data. Internet: **http://www.bls.gov/bls/blswage.htm**

For information on training, workers' rights, and job listings:

➤ Employment and Training Administration.
Internet: **http://www.doleta.gov/jobseekers**

Organizations for specific groups. Some organizations provide information designed to help specific groups of people. Consult directories in your library's reference center or a career guidance office for information on additional organizations associated with specific groups.

Disabled workers:
Information on employment opportunities, transportation, and other considerations for people with a wide variety of disabilities is available from:

➤ National Organization on Disability, 888 Sixteenth St. NW., Suite 800, Washington, DC 20006. Telephone: (202) 293-5960. TTY: (202) 293-5968. Internet: **http://www.nod.org/economic**

For information on making accommodations in the work place for people with disabilities:

➤ Job Accommodation Network (JAN), P.O. Box 6080, Morgantown, WV 26506. Internet: **http://www.jan.wvu.edu**

A comprehensive Federal Web site of disability-related resources is accessible at:

➤ **http://www.disability.gov**

Blind workers:

Information on the free national reference and referral service for the blind can be obtained by contacting:

➤ National Federation of the Blind, Job Opportunities for the Blind (JOB), 1800 Johnson St., Baltimore, MD 21230. Telephone: (410) 659-9314. Internet: **http://www.nfb.org**

Older workers:

➤ National Council on the Aging, 1901 L St. NW., 4th Floor., Washington, DC 20036. Telephone: (202) 479-1200. Internet: **http://www.ncoa.org**

➤ National Caucus and Center on Black Aged, Inc., Senior Employment Programs, 1220 L St. NW., Suite 800, Washington, DC 20005. Telephone: (202) 637-8400. Fax: (202) 347-0895. Internet: **http://www.ncba-aged.org**

Veterans:

Contact the nearest regional office of the U.S. Department of Labor's Veterans Employment and Training Service or:

➤ Credentialing Opportunities Online (COOL), which explains how military personnel can meet civilian certification and license requirements related to their Military Occupational Specialty (MOS). Internet: **http://www.cool.army.mil**

Women:

➤ Department of Labor, Women's Bureau, 200 Constitution Ave. NW., Washington, DC 20210. Telephone: (800) 827-5335. Internet: **http://www.dol.gov/wb**

Federal laws, executive orders, and selected Federal grant programs bar discrimination in employment based on race, color, religion, sex, national origin, age, and handicap. Information on how to file a charge of discrimination is available from U.S. Equal Employment Opportunity Commission offices around the country. Their addresses and telephone numbers are listed in telephone directories under U.S. Government, EEOC. Telephone: (800) 669-4000. TTY: (800) 669-6820. Internet: **http://www.eeoc.gov**

Office of Personnel Management. Information on obtaining civilian positions within the Federal Government is available from the U.S. Office of Personnel Management through USA-Jobs, the Federal Government's official employment information system. This resource for locating and applying for job opportunities can be accessed through the Internet or through an interactive voice response telephone system at (703) 724-1850 or TDD (978) 461-8404.

➤ USA Jobs: **http://www.usajobs.opm.gov**

Military. The military employs and has information on hundreds of occupations. Information is available on tuition assistance programs, which provide money for school and educational debt repayments. Information on military service can be provided by your local recruiting office. Also see the *Handbook* statement on Job Opportunities in the Armed Forces. You can find more information on careers in the military at:

➤ Today's Military. Internet: **http://www.todaysmilitary.com**

State Sources. Most States have career information delivery systems (CIDS), which may be found in secondary and post-secondary institutions, as well as libraries, job training sites, vocational-technical schools, and employment offices. A wide range of information is provided, from employment opportunities to unemployment insurance claims.

Whereas the *Handbook* provides information for occupations on a national level, each State has detailed information on occupations and labor markets within their respective jurisdictions. State occupational projections are available at:

➤ **http://www.projectionscentral.com**

Alabama
Labor Market Information Division, Alabama Department of Industrial Relations, 649 Monroe St., Room 422, Montgomery, AL 36131. Telephone: (334) 242-8859. Internet: **http://dir.alabama.gov**

Alaska
Research and Analysis Section, Department of Labor and Workforce Development, P.O. Box 25501, Juneau, AK 99802-5501. Telephone: (907) 465-4500. Internet: **http://almis.labor.state.ak.us**

Arizona
Arizona Department of Economic Security, P.O. Box 6123 SC 733A, Phoenix, AZ 85005-6123. Telephone: (602) 542-5984. Internet: **https://www.azdes.gov**

Arkansas
Labor Market Information, Department of Workforce Services, #2 Capital Mall, Little Rock, AR 72201. Telephone: (501) 682-3198. Internet: **http://www.discoverarkansas.net**

California
State of California Employment Development Department, Labor Market Information Division, P.O. Box 826880, Sacramento, CA 94280-0001. Telephone: (916) 262-2162. Internet: **http://www.labormarketinfo.edd.ca.gov**

Colorado
Labor Market Information, Colorado Department of Labor and Employment, 633 17th St., Suite 600, Denver, CO 80202-3660. Telephone: (303) 318-8850. Internet: **http://lmigateway.coworkforce.com**

Connecticut
Office of Research, Connecticut Department of Labor, 200 Folly Brook Blvd., Wethersfield, CT 06109-1114. Telephone: (860) 263-6275. Internet: **http://www.ctdol.state.ct.us/lmi**

Delaware
Office of Occupational and Labor Market Information, Department of Labor, 19 West Lea Blvd., Wilmington, DE 19802. Telephone: (302) 761-8069. Internet: **http://www.delawareworks.com/oolmi/**

District of Columbia
DC Department of Employment Services, 64 New York Ave. NE., Suite 3000, Washington, D.C. 20002. Telephone: (202) 724-7000. Internet: **http://www.does.dc.gov/does**

Florida
Labor Market Statistics, Agency for Workforce Innovation, 107 E. Madison St., MSC 110 - Caldwell Building, Tallahassee, FL 32399-4111. Telephone: (850) 245-7105.
Internet: **http://www.labormarketinfo.com**

Georgia
Workforce Information and Analysis, Room 300, Department of Labor, 223 Courtland St., CWC Building, Atlanta, GA 30303. Telephone: (404) 232-3875. Internet:
http://www.dol.state.ga.us/em/get_labor_market_information.htm

Guam
Guam Department of Labor, 504 D St., Tiyan, Guam 96910. Telephone: (671) 475-0101. Internet: **http://guamdol.net**

Hawaii
Research and Statistics Office, Department of Labor and Industrial Relations, 830 Punchbowl St., Room 304, Honolulu, HI 96813. Telephone: (808) 586-9013. Internet: **http://www.hiwi.org**

Idaho
Research and Analysis Bureau, Department of Commerce and Labor, 317 West Main St., Boise, ID 83735-0670. Telephone: (208) 332-3570. Internet: **http://lmi.idaho.gov**

Illinois
Illinois Department of Employment Security, Economic Information and Analysis Division, 33 S. State St., 9th Floor, Chicago, IL 60603. Telephone: (312) 793-6521. Internet: **http://lmi.ides.state.il.us**

Indiana
Research and Analysis—Indiana Workforce Development, Indiana Government Center South, 10 North Senate Ave., Indianapolis, IN 46204. Telephone: (800) 891-6499. Internet: **http://www.in.gov/dwd**

Iowa
Policy and Information Division, Iowa Workforce Development, 1000 East Grand Ave., Des Moines, IA 50319-0209. Telephone: (515) 281-5387. Internet: **http://www.iowaworkforce.org/lmi**

Kansas
Kansas Department of Labor, Labor Market Information Services, 401 SW Topeka Blvd., Topeka, KS 66603-3182. Telephone: (785) 296-5000. Internet: **http://laborstats.dol.ks.gov**

Kentucky
Research and Statistics Branch, Office of Employment and Training, 275 East Main St., Frankfort, KY 40621. Telephone: (502) 564-7976. Internet: **http://www.workforcekentucky.ky.gov**

Louisiana
Research and Statistics Division, Department of Labor, 1001 North 23rd St., Baton Rouge, LA 70802-3338. Telephone: (225) 342-3111. Internet: **http://www.laworks.net**

Maine
Labor Market Information Services Division, Maine Department of Labor, 45 Commerce Dr., State House Station 118, Augusta, ME 04330. Telephone: (207) 623-7900. Internet: **http://maine.gov/labor/lmis**

Maryland
Maryland Department of Labor Licensing and Regulation, Office of Labor Market Analysis and Information, 1100 N. Eutaw, Baltimore, MD 21201. Telephone: (410) 767-2250.
Internet: **http://www.dllr.state.md.us/lmi/index.shtml**

Massachusetts
Executive Office of Labor and Workforce Development, Division of Career Services, 19 Staniford St., Boston, MA 02114. Telephone: (617) 626-5300. Internet: **http://www.detma.org/LMIdataprog.htm**

Michigan
Bureau of Labor Market Information and Strategic Initiatives, Department of Labor and Economic Growth, 3032 West Grand Blvd., Suite 9-100, Detroit, MI 48202. Telephone: (313) 456-3100. Internet: **http://www.milmi.org**

Minnesota
Department of Employment and Economic Development, Labor Market Information Office, 1st National Bank Building, 332 Minnesota St., Suite E200, St. Paul, MN 55101-1351. Telephone: (888) 234-1114. Internet: **http://www.deed.state.mn.us/lmi**

Mississippi
Labor Market Information Division, Mississippi Department of Employment Security, 1235 Echelon Pkwy., P.O. Box 1699, Jackson, MS 39215. Telephone: (601) 321-6000. Internet: **http://mdes.ms.gov**

Missouri
Missouri Economic Research and Information Center, P.O. Box 3150, Jefferson City, MO 65102-3150. Telephone: (866) 225-8113. Internet: **http://www.missourieconomy.org**

Montana
Research and Analysis Bureau, P.O. Box 1728, Helena, MT 59624. Telephone: (800) 541-3904.
Internet: **http://www.ourfactsyourfuture.org**

Nebraska
Nebraska Workforce Development—Labor Market Information, Nebraska Department of Labor, 550 South 16th St., P.O. Box 94600, Lincoln, NE 68509. Telephone: (402) 471-2600. Internet: **www.dol.nebraska.gov/nwd/center.cfm?PRICAT=3&SUBCAT=4Z0**

Nevada
Research and Analysis, Department of Employment Training and Rehabilitation, 500 East Third St., Carson City, NV 89713. Telephone: (775) 684-0450. Internet: **http://www.nevadaworkforce.com**

New Hampshire
Economic and Labor Market Information Bureau, New Hampshire Employment Security, 32 South Main St., Concord, NH 03301-4857. Telephone: (603) 228-4124. Internet: **http://www.nh.gov/nhes/elmi**

New Jersey
Division of Labor Market and Demographic Research, Department of Labor and Workforce Development, P.O. Box 388, Trenton, NJ 08625-0388. Telephone: (609) 984-2593. Internet: **http://www.wnjpin.net**

New Mexico
New Mexico Department of Labor , Economic Research and Analysis, 401 Broadway NE., Albuquerque, NM 87102. Telephone: (505) 222-4683. Internet: **http://www.dws.state.nm.us/dws-lmi.html**

New York
Research and Statistics, New York State Department of Labor, W. Averell Harriman State Office Campus, Building 12, Albany, NY 12240. Telephone: (518) 457-9000.
Internet: **http://www.labor.state.ny.us**

North Carolina
Labor Market Information Division, Employment Security Commission, 700 Wade Ave., Raleigh, NC 27605. Telephone: (919) 733-2936. Internet: **http://www.ncesc.com**

North Dakota
Labor Market Information Manager, Job Service North Dakota, 1000 East Divide Ave., Bismarck, ND 58506. Telephone: (800) 732-9787. Internet: **http://www.ndworkforceintelligence.com**

Ohio
Bureau of Labor Market Information, Ohio Department of Job and Family Services, 420 East 5th Ave., Columbus, OH 43219. Telephone: (614) 752-9494. Internet: **http://ohiolmi.com**

Oklahoma
Labor Market Information, Oklahoma Employment Security Commission, P.O. Box 52003., Oklahoma City, OK 73152. Telephone: (405) 557-7172. Internet:
http://www.ok.gov/oesc_web/Services/Find_Labor_Market_Statistics/index.html

Oregon
Oregon Employment Department, Research Division, 875 Union St. NE., Salem, OR 97311. Telephone: (503) 947-1200. Internet: **http://www.qualityinfo.org/olmisj/OlmisZine**

Pennsylvania
Center for Workforce Information & Analysis, Pennsylvania Department of Labor and Industry, 220 Labor and Industry Building, Seventh and Forster Sts., Harrisburg, PA 17121. Telephone: (877) 493-3282. Internet: **http://www.paworkstats.state.pa.us**

Puerto Rico
Department of Work and Human Resources, Ave. Muñoz Rivera 505, Hato Rey, PR 00918. Telephone: (787) 754-5353. Internet: **http://www.dtrh.gobierno.pr**

Rhode Island
Labor Market Information, Rhode Island Department of Labor and Training, 1511 Pontiac Ave., Cranston, RI 02920. Telephone: (401) 462-8740. Internet: **http://www.dlt.ri.gov/lmi**

South Carolina
Labor Market Information Department, South Carolina Employment Security Commission, 631 Hampton St., Columbia, SC 29202. Telephone: (803) 737-2660. Internet: **http://www.sces.org/lmi/index.asp**

South Dakota
Labor Market Information Center, Department of Labor, P.O. Box 4730, Aberdeen, SD 57402-4730. Telephone: (605) 626-2314. Internet: **http://dol.sd.gov/lmic**

Tennessee
Research and Statistics Division, Department of Labor and Workforce Development, 220 French Landing Dr., Nashville, TN 37245. Telephone: (615) 741-1729. Internet: **http://www.state.tn.us/labor-wfd/lmi.htm**

Texas
Labor Market Information, Texas Workforce Commission, 9001 North IH-35, Suite 103A, Austin, TX 75753. Telephone: (866) 938-4444. Internet: **http://www.tracer2.com**

Utah
Director of Workforce Information, Utah Department of Workforce Services, P.O. Box 45249, Salt Lake City, UT 84145-0249. Telephone: (801) 526-9675. Internet: **http://jobs.utah.gov/opencms/wi**

Vermont
Economic and Labor Market Information, Vermont Department of Labor, P.O. Box 488, Montpelier, VT 05601-0488. Telephone: (802) 828-4000. Internet: **http://www.vtlmi.info**

Virgin Islands
Bureau of Labor Statistics, Department of Labor, 53A & 54AB Kronprindsens Gade, St Thomas, VI 00803-2608. Telephone: (340) 776-3700. Internet: **http://www.vidol.gov**

Virginia
Virginia Employment Commission, P.O. Box 1358, Richmond, VA 23218-1358. Telephone: (800) 828-1140. Internet: **http://www.vec.virginia.gov/vecportal/index.cfm**

Washington
Labor Market and Economic Analysis, Washington Employment Security Department, P.O. Box 9046, Olympia, WA 98507-9046. Telephone: (360) 438-4833. Internet: **http://www.workforceexplorer.com**

West Virginia
Workforce West Virginia, Research, Information and Analysis Division, 112 California Ave., Charleston, WV 25303-0112. Telephone: (304) 558-2660. Internet: **http://workforcewv.org/lmi**

Wisconsin
Bureau of Workforce Information, Department of Workforce Development, P.O. Box 7944, Madison, WI 53707-7944. Telephone: (608) 266-7034. Internet: **http://worknet.wisconsin.gov/worknet**

Wyoming
Research and Planning, Wyoming Department of Employment, 246 S. Center St., Casper, WY 82602. Telephone: (307) 473-3807. Internet: **http://doe.state.wy.us/lmi**

Sources of Education, Training, and Financial Aid

Education can present opportunities for those looking to start a new career or change specialty within their current occupation. This section outlines some major sources of education and training required to enter many occupations, as well as some ways to finance that education or training.

For information on the specific training and educational requirements for a particular occupation, and what training is typically provided by an employer, consult the "Training, Other Qualifications, and Advancement" section of the appropriate *Handbook* statement.

Sources of Education and Training

Four-year colleges and universities. These institutions provide detailed information on theory and practice for a wide variety of subjects. Colleges and universities can provide students with the knowledge and background necessary to be successful in many fields. They also can help to place students in cooperative education programs (often called "co-ops") or internships. Co-ops and internships are short-term jobs with firms related to a student's field of study that lead to college credit. In co-ops and internships, students learn the specifics of a job while making valuable contacts that can lead to a permanent position.

For more information on colleges and universities, go to your local library, consult your high school guidance counselor, or contact individual colleges. Also check with your State's higher education agency. A list of these agencies is available on the Internet: **http://www.ed.gov/erod**.

Junior and community colleges. Junior and community colleges offer a variety of programs that lead to associate degrees and training certificates. Community colleges tend to be less expensive than 4-year colleges and universities. They usually are more willing to accommodate part-time students than colleges and universities, and their programs are more tailored to the needs of local employers. Many community colleges have an open admissions policy, and they often offer weekend and night classes.

Community colleges often form partnerships with local businesses that allow students to gain job-specific training. Many students may not be able to enroll in a college or university because of their academic record, limited finances, or distance from such an institution, so they attend junior or community colleges to earn credits that can be applied toward a degree at a 4-year college. Junior and community colleges also are noted for their extensive role in continuing and adult education.

For more information on junior and community colleges, go to your local library, consult your high school guidance counselor, or contact individual schools. Also check with your State's higher education agency. A list of these agencies is available on the Internet: **http://www.ed.gov/erod**.

Online colleges and universities. Online colleges and universities cover most of the same material as their traditional classroom counterparts, but they offer classes over the Internet. Offering classes on the Internet provides a great deal of flexibility to students, allowing many who work, travel frequently, or lack the ability or means to attend a traditional university to earn a degree from an accredited institution.

A prospective student should talk to a guidance counselor or advisor before deciding to enroll in an online college or university. Additionally, the prospective student should check the college or university's accreditation with the U.S. Department of Education. This can be done online at: **http://ope.ed.gov/accreditation**.

Vocational and trade schools. These institutions train people in specific trades. They offer courses designed to provide hands-on experience. Vocational and trade schools tend to concentrate on trades, services, and other types of skilled work.

Vocational and trade schools frequently engage students in real-world projects, allowing them to apply field methods while learning theory in classrooms. Graduates of vocational and trade schools have an advantage over informally trained or self-trained jobseekers because graduates have an independent organization certifying that they have the knowledge, skills, and abilities necessary to perform the duties of a particular occupation. These schools also help students to acquire any license or other credentials needed to enter the job market.

For more information on vocational and trade schools, go to your local library, consult your high school guidance counselor, or contact individual schools. Also check with your State's director of vocational-technical education. A list of State directors of vocational-technical education is available on the Internet: **http://www.ed.gov/erod**.

Apprenticeships. An apprenticeship provides work experience as well as education and training for people entering certain occupations. Apprenticeships are offered by sponsors, who employ and train the apprentice. The apprentice follows a training course under close supervision and receives some formal education to learn the theory related to the job.

Apprenticeships, which generally last between 1 and 4 years, are a way for inexperienced people to become skilled workers. Some apprenticeships allow the apprentice to earn an associate degree. An *Apprenticeship Completion Certificate* is granted to those completing programs. This certificate is administered by federally approved State agencies.

For more information on apprenticeships and for assistance finding a program, go to the Office of Apprenticeship Training, Employer, and Labor Services on the Internet: **http://www.doleta.gov/atels_bat**.

Professional societies, trade associations, and labor unions. These groups are made up of people with common interests, usually in related occupations or industries. The groups frequently are able to provide training, access to training through their affiliates, or information on acceptable sources of training for their field. If licensing or certification is required, they also may be able to assist you in meeting those requirements.

For a listing of professional societies, trade associations, and labor unions related to an occupation, check the "Sources of Additional Information" section at the end of that occupational statement in the *Handbook*.

Employers. Many employers provide on-the-job training, which can range from spending a few minutes watching another employee demonstrate a task to participating in formal training programs that may last for several months. In some jobs, employees may continually undergo training to stay up to date with new developments and technologies or to add new skills.

Military. The United States Armed Forces trains and employs people in more than 4,100 different occupations. For more information, see the *Handbook* statement on "Job Opportunities in The Armed Forces." For detailed answers to specific questions, contact your local recruiting office. Valuable resources also are available on the Internet: **http://www.todaysmilitary.com**.

Sources of Financial Aid
Many people fund their education or training through financial aid or tuition assistance programs. Federal student aid comes in three forms: grants, work-study programs, and loans. All Federal student aid applicants must first fill out a Free Application for Federal Student Aid (FAFSA), which provides a Student Aid Report (SAR) and eligibility rating. Forms must be submitted to desired institutions of study, which determine the amount of aid you will receive.

For information on applying for Federal financial aid, visit the FAFSA Internet site: **http://www.fafsa.ed.gov**.

A U.S. Department of Education publication describing Federal financial aid programs, called *Funding Education Beyond High School: The Guide to Federal Student Aid*, is available at **http://www.studentaid.ed.gov/students/publications/student_guide/index.html**.

Information on Federal programs is available from **http://www.studentaid.ed.gov** and **www.students.gov**.

Information on State programs is available from your State's higher education agency. A list of these agencies is available at **http://www.ed.gov/erod**.

Grants. A grant is money that is given to students or the institution they are attending to pay for the student's education or training and any associated expenses. Grants are usually given on the basis of financial need. Grants are considered gifts and are not paid back. Federal grants are almost exclusively for undergraduate students. They include Pell Grants, which can be worth up to $5,350 annually. The maximum amount given out can change each year, however. Federal Supplemental Educational Opportunity Grants (FSEOG) can be worth up to $4,000 annually. Priority for FSEOG awards is given to those who have also received the Pell Grant and have exceptional financial need.

Additional information on grants is available on the Internet: **http://www.studentaid.ed.gov**. Information also is available from your State Higher Education agency. A list of these agencies is available at **http://www.ed.gov/erod**.

Federal Work-Study program. The Federal Work-Study program is offered at most institutions and consists of Federal sponsorship of a student who works part time at the institution he or she is attending. The money a student earns through this program goes directly toward the cost of attending the institution. There are no set minimum or maximum amounts for this type of aid, although, on average, a student can expect to earn about $2,000 per school year.

For additional information on work-study opportunities offered, check with individual institutions. General information on the Federal Work-Study program is available at **http://studentaid.ed.gov/PORTALSWebApp/students/english/campusaid.jsp**.

Scholarships. A scholarship is a sum of money donated to a student to help pay for his or her education or training and any associated costs. Scholarships can range from small amounts up to the full cost of schooling. They are based on financial need, academic merit, athletic ability, or a wide variety of other criteria set by the organizations that provide the scholarships. Frequently, students must meet minimum academic requirements to be considered for a scholarship. Other qualifying requirements—such as intended major field of study, heritage, or group membership—may be added by the organization providing the scholarship.

Scholarships are provided by a wide variety of institutions, including educational institutions, State and local governments, private associations, social groups, and individuals. There are no federally awarded scholarships based on academic merit. Most large scholarships are awarded to students by the institution they plan to attend. Students who have received State scholarships and plan to attend a school in another State should check with their State to see if the scholarship can be transferred.

Information on scholarships is typically available from high school guidance counselors and local libraries. Additional scholarship information is available from State higher education agencies. A list of these agencies is available at **http://www.ed.gov/erod**. The College Board has information on available scholarships at **http://www.collegeboard.com/pay**.

Student loans. Many institutions, both public and private, provide low-interest loans to students and their parents or guardians. The Federal Government also provides several types of student loans based on the applicant's level of financial need. The amount of money a student can receive in loans varies by the distributing institution and depends on whether the student is claimed by a parent or guardian as a dependent. Since the process of applying for a loan may take several months, it is a good idea to start applying for Federal student loans well in advance.

The available Federal loan programs can accommodate prospective undergraduate, graduate, vocational, and disabled students. Federal loans can be distributed through the school that the student is attending, from the Federal Government directly, or from a third-party private lender or bank. Perkins loans are distributed through the school the student is attending. Loans coming from the Federal Government directly from the William D. Ford Federal Direct Loan Program are dispersed by the Department of Education. Third-party loans through a private lender or bank are from the Federal Family Education Loan (FFEL) program. For all federally funded loans, payments are made to the institution that originally dispersed the funds.

For those with financial need, Federal Perkins loans and both Direct and FFEL-subsidized Stafford loans are available. Perkins loans have no minimum amount; they are capped at $5,500 per year for undergraduates. Students should visit the Department of Education's Web site (**http://www.studentaid.ed.gov/ PORTALSWebApp/students/english/fafsa.jsp**) to learn about the current level of aid available because it will vary by year and a student's status (married, single, dependent, or independent). Subsidized Stafford loans vary in size and can increase as a student completes more years of undergraduate, graduate, or professional education. Interest rates for both loans will be gradually decreasing until 2012. Information on specific interest rates is available through the school's financial aid officer or the Department of Education's Web site. Individuals who receive Perkins loans are not responsible for starting to repay the loan until they have been out of school for 9 months. Those with subsidized Stafford loans must begin payments within 6 to 9 months of leaving school but are not charged monthly interest while in school.

For those who do not demonstrate financial need, Direct and FFEL-unsubsidized Stafford Loans and Federal Parent Loans for Students (PLUS) are available. Unsubsidized Stafford loans vary in value and are capped at the cost of attendance. With Federal unsubsidized Stafford Loans, interest payments start almost immediately and can be paid monthly or accrued until the completion of studies. The latter option results in a larger total loan cost but may be more convenient for some students. With PLUS loans, the parent must pay interest and principal payments while the student is enrolled in school and must continue payments after completion. Check with your lender for available repayment schedules. Students usually have 10 years to repay Perkins loans and from 10 to 30 years for unsubsidized Stafford loans.

Subsidized and unsubsidized Stafford loans are only available to students who are enrolled in an academic program at least half time. As with any loan, be sure to investigate different lenders, and understand what your loan contract requires of you before agreeing to any loan. Check with established financial institutions to compare the terms of available private student loans. Comparisons of the various types of loans are available on the Internet: **http://www.studentaid.ed.gov/students/publications/ student_guide/index.html**. The College Board has information on available loans at **http://www.collegeboard.com/pay**.

Employer tuition support programs. Some employers offer tuition assistance programs as part of their employee benefits package. The terms of these programs depend on the firm and can vary by the type and amount of training subsidized, as well as by eligibility requirements. Consult your human resources department for information on tuition support programs offered by your employer.

Military tuition support programs. The United States Armed Forces offer various tuition assistance and loan repayment programs for military personnel. See the *Handbook* statement on "Job Opportunities in the Armed Forces" for more information, or go to **http://www.todaysmilitary.com/benefits/tuition-support**.

Finding and Applying for Jobs and Evaluating Offers

Finding—and getting—the job you want can be a challenging process, but knowing more about job search methods and application techniques can increase your chances of success. And knowing how to judge the job offers you receive makes it more likely that you will end up with the best possible job.

Where to learn about job openings

Personal contacts
School career planning and placement offices
Employers
Classified ads
   —National and local newspapers
   —Professional journals
   —Trade magazines
Internet resources
Professional associations
Labor unions
State employment service offices
Federal Government
Community agencies
Private employment agencies and career consultants
Internships

Job search methods

Finding a job can take months of time and effort. But you can speed the process by using many methods to find job openings. Data from the Bureau of Labor Statistics suggest that people who use many job search methods find jobs faster than people who use only one or two.

In the box above, some sources of job openings are listed. Those sources are described more fully below.

Personal contacts. Many jobs are never advertised. People get them by talking to friends, family, neighbors, acquaintances, teachers, former coworkers, and others who know of an opening. Be sure to tell people that you are looking for a job because the people you know may be some of the most effective resources for your search. To develop new contacts, join student, community, or professional organizations.

School career planning and placement offices. High school and college placement services help their students and alumni find jobs. Some invite recruiters to use their facilities for interviews or career fairs. They also may have lists of open jobs. Most also offer career counseling, career testing, and job search advice. Some have career resource libraries; host workshops on job search strategy, resume writing, letter writing, and effective interviewing; critique drafts of resumes; conduct mock interviews; and sponsor job fairs.

Employers. Directly contacting employers is one of the most successful means of job hunting. Through library and Internet research, develop a list of potential employers in your desired career field. Then call these employers and check their Web sites for job openings. Web sites and business directories can tell you how to apply for a position or whom to contact. Even if no open positions are posted, do not hesitate to contact the employer: You never know when a job might become available. Consider asking for an informational interview with people working in the career you want to learn more about. Ask them how they got started, what they like and dislike about the work, what type of qualifications are necessary for the job, and what type of personality succeeds in that position. In addition to giving you career information, they may be able to put you in contact with other employers who may be hiring, and they can keep you in mind if a position opens up.

Classified ads. The "Help Wanted" ads in newspapers and the Internet list numerous jobs, and many people find work by responding to these ads. But when using classified ads, keep the following in mind:

- Follow all leads to find a job; do not rely solely on the classifieds.
- Answer ads promptly, because openings may be filled quickly, even before the ad stops appearing in the paper.
- Read the ads every day, particularly the Sunday edition, which usually includes the most listings.
- Keep a record of all ads to which you have responded, including the specific skills, educational background, and personal qualifications required for the position. You may want to follow up on your initial inquiry.

Internet resources. The Internet includes many job hunting Web sites with job listings. Some job boards provide National listings of all kinds; others are local. Some relate to a specific type of work; others are general. To find good prospects, begin with an Internet search using keywords related to the job you want. Also look for the Web sites of related professional associations.

Also consider checking Internet forums, also called message boards. These are online discussion groups where anyone may post and read messages. Use forums specific to your profession or to career-related topics to post questions or messages and to read about the job searches or career experiences of other people. Although these message boards may seem helpful, carefully evaluate all advice before acting; it can be difficult to determine the reliability of information posted on message boards.

In online job databases, remember that job listings may be posted by field or discipline, so begin your search using keywords. Many Web sites allow job seekers to post their resumes online for free.

Professional associations. Many professions have associations that offer employment information, including career planning, educational programs, job listings, and job placement. Information can be obtained directly from most professional associations through the Internet, by telephone, or by mail. Associations usually require that you be a member to use these services.

Labor unions. Labor unions provide various employment services to members and potential members, including apprenticeship programs that teach a specific trade or skill. Contact the appropriate labor union or State apprenticeship council for more information.

State employment service offices. The State employment service, sometimes called the Job Service, operates in coordination with the U.S. Department of Labor's Employment and Training Administration. Local offices, found nationwide, help job seekers to find jobs and help employers to find qualified workers at no cost to either. To find the office nearest you, look in the State government telephone listings under "Job Service" or "Employment."

Job matching and referral. At the State employment service office, an interviewer will determine if you are "job ready" or if you need help from counseling and testing services to assess your occupational aptitudes and interests and to help you choose and prepare for a career. After you are job ready, you may examine available job listings and select openings that interest you. A staff member can then describe the job openings in detail and arrange for interviews with prospective employers.

Services for special groups. By law, veterans are entitled to priority job placement at State employment service centers. If you are a veteran, a veterans' employment representative can inform you of available assistance and help you to deal with problems.

State employment service offices also refer people to opportunities available under the Workforce Investment Act (WIA) of 1998. Educational and career services and referrals are provided to employers and job seekers, including adults, dislocated workers, and youth. These programs help to prepare people to participate in the State's workforce, increase their employment and earnings potential, improve their educational and occupational skills, and reduce their dependency on welfare.

Federal Government. Information on obtaining a position with the Federal Government is available from the U.S. Office of Personnel Management (OPM) through USAJOBS, the Federal Government's official employment information system. This resource for locating and applying for job opportunities can be accessed through the Internet at **http://www.usajobs.gov** or through an interactive voice response telephone system at (703) 724-1850, (866) 204-2858, or TDD (978) 461-8404. These numbers are not all toll free, and telephone charges may result.

Community agencies. Many nonprofit organizations, including religious institutions and vocational rehabilitation agencies, offer counseling, career development, and job placement services, generally targeted to a particular group, such as women, youths, minorities, ex-offenders, or older workers.

Private employment agencies and career consultants. Private agencies can save you time and they will contact employers who otherwise might be difficult to locate. Such agencies may be called recruiters, head hunters, or employment placement agencies. These agencies may charge for their services. Most operate on a commission basis, charging a percentage of the first-year salary paid to a successful applicant. You or the hiring company will pay the fee. Find out the exact cost and who is responsible for paying associated fees before using the service. When determining if the service is worth the cost, consider any guarantees that the agency offers.

Internships. Many people find jobs with business and organizations with whom they have interned or volunteered. Look for internships and volunteer opportunities on job boards, school career centers, and company and association Web sites, but also check community service organizations and volunteer opportunity databases. Some internships and long-term volunteer positions come with stipends and all provide experience and the chance to meet employers and other good networking contacts.

Applying for a job

After you have found some jobs that interest you, the next step is to apply for them. Many potential employers require complete resumes or application forms and cover letters. Later, you will probably need to go on interviews to meet with employers face to face.

Resumes and application forms. Resumes and application forms give employers written evidence of your qualifications and skills. The goal of these documents is to prove—as clearly and directly as possible—how your qualifications match the job's requirements. Do this by highlighting the experience, accomplishments, education, and skills that most closely fit the job you want.

Gathering information. Resumes and application forms both include the same information. As a first step, gather the following facts:

- Contact information, including your name, mailing address, e-mail address (if you have one you check often), and telephone number.
- Type of work or specific job you are seeking or a qualifications summary, which describes your best skills and experience in just a few lines.
- Education, including school name and its city and State, months and years of attendance, highest grade completed or diploma or degree awarded, and major subject or subjects studied. Also consider listing courses and awards that might be relevant to the position. Include a grade point average if you think it would help in getting the job.
- Experience, paid and volunteer. For each job, include the job title, name and location of employer, and dates of employment. Briefly describe your job duties and major accomplishments. In a resume, use phrases instead of sentences to describe your work; write, for example, "Supervised 10 children" instead of writing "I supervised 10 children."
- Special skills. You might list computer skills, proficiency in foreign languages, achievements, or membership in organizations in a separate section.
- References. Be ready to provide references if requested. Good references could be former employers, coworkers, or teachers or anyone else who can describe your abilities and job-related traits. You will be asked to provide contact information for the people you choose.

Throughout the application or resume, focus on accomplishments that relate most closely to the job you want. You can even use the job announcement as a guide, using some of the same words and phrases to describe your work and education.

Look for concrete examples that show your skills. When describing your work experience, for instance, you might say that you increased sales by 10 percent, finished a task in half the usual time, or received three letters of appreciation from customers.

Choosing a format. After gathering the information you want to present, the next step is to put it in the proper format. In an application form, the format is set. Just fill in the blanks. But make sure you fill it out completely and follow all instructions. Do not omit any requested information. Consider making a copy of the form before filling it out, in case you make a mistake and have to start over. If possible, have someone else look over the form before submitting it.

In a resume, there are several acceptable ways of organizing the information you want to include. It is common to place the most important information first. One format is to list the applicant's past jobs in reverse chronological order, describing the most recent employment first and working backward. But some applicants use a functional format, organizing their work experience under headings that describe their major skills. They then include a brief work history section that lists only job titles, employers, and dates of employment. Still other applicants choose a format that combines these two approaches in some way. Choose the style that best showcases your skills and experience. Examples of resume formats can be found on the Web sites of career centers, job boards, and State employment services.

Whatever format you choose, keep your resume short. Many experts recommend that new workers use a one-page resume. Avoid long blocks of text and italicized material. Consider using bullets to highlight duties or key accomplishments.

Before submitting your resume, make sure that it is easy to read. Are the headings clear and consistently formatted with bold or some other style of type? Is the type face large enough? Much like application forms, it is useful to ask someone to proofread your resume for spelling and other errors. In addition, use your computer's spell checker.

Keep in mind that some employers scan resumes into databases, which they then search for specific keywords or phrases. The keywords are usually nouns referring to experience, education, personal characteristics, or industry buzz words. Identify keywords by reading the job description and qualifications in the job ad; use these same words in your resume. For example, if the job description includes customer service tasks, use the words "customer service" on your resume. Scanners sometimes misread paper resumes, which could mean some of your keywords don't get into the database. So, if you know that your resume will be scanned, and you have the option, e-mail an electronic version. If you must submit a paper resume, make it scannable by using a simple font and avoiding underlines, italics, and graphics. It is also a good idea to send a traditionally formatted resume along with your scannable resume, with a note on each marking its purpose.

Cover letters. When sending a resume, most people include a cover letter to introduce themselves to the prospective employer.

Most cover letters are no more than three short paragraphs. Your cover letter should capture the employer's attention, follow a business letter format, and usually should include the following information:

- Name and address of the specific person to whom the letter is addressed.
- Reason for your interest in the company or position.
- Your main qualifications for the position.
- Request for an interview.
- Your home and work telephone numbers.

If you send a scannable resume, you should also include a scannable cover letter, which avoids graphics, fancy fonts, italics, and underlines.

As with your resume, it may be helpful to look for examples and common formats of cover letters on the Internet or in books at your local library or bookstore, but do not copy letters directly from other sources.

Interviewing. An interview gives you the opportunity to showcase your qualifications to an employer, so it pays to be well prepared. The accompanying box provides some helpful hints.

Job interview tips

Preparation:
Learn about the organization.
Have a specific job or jobs in mind.
Review your qualifications for the job.
Be ready to briefly describe your experience, showing how it relates it the job.
Be ready to answer broad questions, such as "Why should I hire you?" "Why do you want this job?" "What are your strengths and weaknesses?"
Practice an interview with a friend or relative.

Personal appearance:
Be well groomed.
Dress appropriately.
Do not chew gum or smoke.

The interview:
Be early.
Learn the name of your interviewer and greet him or her with a firm handshake.
Use good manners with everyone you meet.
Relax and answer each question concisely.
Use proper English—avoid slang.
Be cooperative and enthusiastic.
Use body language to show interest—use eye contact and don't slouch.
Ask questions about the position and the organization, but avoid questions whose answers can easily be found on the company Web site.
Also avoid asking questions about salary and benefits unless a job offer is made.
Thank the interviewer when you leave and shake hands.
Send a short thank you note following the interview.

Information to bring to an interview:

Social Security card.

Government-issued identification (driver's license).

Resume or application. Although not all employers require a resume, you should be able to furnish the interviewer information about your education, training, and previous employment.

References. Employers typically require three references. Get permission before using anyone as a reference. Make sure that they will give you a good reference. Try to avoid using relatives as references.

Transcripts. Employers may require an official copy of transcripts to verify grades, coursework, dates of attendance, and highest grade completed or degree awarded.

Evaluating a job offer

Once you receive a job offer, you must decide if you want the job. Fortunately, most organizations will give you a few days to accept or reject an offer.

There are many issues to consider when assessing a job offer. Will the organization be a good place to work? Will the job be interesting? Are there opportunities for advancement? Is the salary fair? Does the employer offer good benefits? Now is the time to ask the potential employer about these issues—and to do some checking on your own.

The organization. Background information on an organization can help you to decide whether it is a good place for you to work. Factors to consider include the organization's business or activity, financial condition, age, size, and location.

You generally can get background information on an organization, particularly a large organization, on its Web site or by telephoning its public relations office. A public company's annual report to the stockholders tells about its corporate philosophy, history, products or services, goals, and financial status. Most government agencies can furnish reports that describe their programs and missions. Press releases, company newsletters or magazines, and recruitment brochures also can be useful. Ask the organization for any other items that might interest a prospective employee. If possible, speak to current or former employees of the organization.

Background information on the organization may be available at your public or school library. If you cannot get an annual report, check the library for reference directories that may provide basic facts about the company, such as earnings, products and services, and number of employees. Some directories widely available in libraries either in print or as online databases include:

- *Dun & Bradstreet's Million Dollar Directory*
- *Standard and Poor's Register of Corporations*
- *Mergent's Industry Review* (formerly *Moody's Industrial Manual*)
- *Thomas Register of American Manufacturers*
- *Ward's Business Directory*

Stories about an organization in magazines and newspapers can tell a great deal about its successes, failures, and plans for the future. You can identify articles on a company by looking under its name in periodical or computerized indexes in libraries, or by using one of the Internet's search engines. However, it probably will not be useful to look back more than 2 or 3 years.

The library also may have government publications that present projections of growth for the industry in which the organization is classified. Long-term projections of employment and output for detailed industries, covering the entire U.S. economy, are developed by the Bureau of Labor Statistics and revised every 2 years. (See the *Career Guide to Industries*, online at **http://www.bls.gov/oco/cg**.) Trade magazines also may include articles on the trends for specific industries.

Career centers at colleges and universities often have information on employers that is not available in libraries. Ask a career center representative how to find out about a particular organization.

During your research consider the following questions:

Does the organization's business or activity match your own interests and beliefs?

It is easier to apply yourself to the work if you are enthusiastic about what the organization does.

How will the size of the organization affect you?

Large firms generally offer a greater variety of training programs and career paths, more managerial levels for advancement, and better employee benefits than do small firms. Large employers also may have more advanced technologies. However, many jobs in large firms tend to be highly specialized.

Jobs in small firms may offer broader authority and responsibility, a closer working relationship with top management, and a chance to clearly see your contribution to the success of the organization.

Should you work for a relatively new organization or one that is well established?

New businesses have a high failure rate, but for many people, the excitement of helping to create a company and the potential for sharing in its success more than offset the risk of job loss. However, it may be just as exciting and rewarding to work for a young firm that already has a foothold on success.

The job. Even if everything else about the job is attractive, you will be unhappy if you dislike the day-to-day work. Determining in advance whether you will like the work may be difficult. However, the more you find out about the job before accepting or rejecting the offer, the more likely you are to make the right choice. Consider the following questions:

Where is the job located?

If the job is in another section of the country, you need to consider the cost of living, the availability of housing and transportation, and the quality of educational and recreational facilities in that section of the country. Even if the job location is in your area, you should consider the time and expense of commuting.

Does the work match your interests and make good use of your skills?

The duties and responsibilities of the job should be explained in enough detail to answer this question.

How important is the job to the company or organization?

An explanation of where you fit in the organization and how you are supposed to contribute to its overall goals should give you an idea of the job's importance.

What will the hours be?

Most jobs involve regular hours—for example, 40 hours a week, during the day, Monday through Friday. Other jobs require night, weekend, or holiday work. In addition, some jobs routinely require overtime to meet deadlines or sales or production goals, or to better serve customers. Consider the effect that the work hours will have on your personal life.

How long do most people who enter this job stay with the company?

High turnover can mean dissatisfaction with the nature of the work or something else about the job.

Opportunities offered by employers. A good job offers you opportunities to learn new skills, increase your earnings, and rise to positions of greater authority, responsibility, and prestige. A lack of opportunities can dampen interest in the work and result in frustration and boredom.

Some companies develop training plans for their employees. What valuable new skills does the company plan to teach you?

The employer should give you some idea of promotion possibilities within the organization. What is the next step on the career ladder? If you have to wait for a job to become vacant before you can be promoted, how long does this usually take? When opportunities for advancement do arise, will you compete with applicants from outside the company? Can you apply for jobs for which you qualify elsewhere within the organization, or is mobility within the firm limited?

Salaries and benefits. When an employer makes a job offer, information about earnings and benefits are usually included. You will want to research to determine if the offer is fair. If you choose to negotiate for higher pay and better benefits, objective research will help you strengthen your case.

You may have to go to several sources for information. One of the best places to start is the information from the Bureau of Labor Statistics. Data on earnings by detailed occupation from the Occupational Employment Statistics (OES) Survey are available from:

➤ Bureau of Labor Statistics, Office of Occupational Statistics and Employment Projections, 2 Massachusetts Ave. NE., Room 2135, Washington, DC 20212-0001. Telephone: (202) 691-6569. Internet: **http://www.bls.gov/OES**.

Data from the Bureau's National Compensation Survey are available from:

➤ Bureau of Labor Statistics, Office of Compensation Levels and Trends, 2 Massachusetts Ave. NE., Room 4175, Washington, DC 20212-0001. Telephone: (202) 691-6199. Internet: **http://www.bls.gov/eci**.

You should also look for additional information, specifically tailored to your job offer and circumstances. Try to find family, friends, or acquaintances who recently were hired in similar jobs. Ask your teachers and the staff in placement offices about starting pay for graduates with your qualifications. Help-wanted ads in newspapers sometimes give salary ranges for similar positions. Check the library or your school's career center for salary surveys such as those conducted by the National Association of Colleges and Employers or various professional associations.

If you are considering the salary and benefits for a job in another geographic area, make allowances for differences in the cost of living, which may be significantly higher in a large metropolitan area than in a smaller city, town, or rural area.

You also should learn the organization's policy regarding overtime. Depending on the job, you may or may not be exempt from laws requiring the employer to compensate you for overtime. Find out how many hours you will be expected to work each week and whether you receive overtime pay or compensatory time off for working more than the specified number of hours in a week.

Also take into account that the starting salary is just that—the start. Your salary should be reviewed on a regular basis; many organizations do it every year. How much can you expect to earn after 1, 2, or 3 or more years? An employer may be unable to be specific about the amount of pay if it includes commissions and bonuses.

Benefits also can add a lot to your base pay, but they vary widely. Find out exactly what the benefit package includes and how much of the cost you must bear.

For more information

To learn more about finding and applying for jobs, visit your local library and career center. You can find career centers that are part of the U.S. Department of Labor One-Stop Career system by calling toll free (877) 348-0502 or visiting their Web site at **http://www.careeronestop.org**.

The *Occupational Outlook Quarterly*, a career magazine published by the Bureau of Labor Statistics, is one of the resources available at many libraries and career centers. The magazine includes many articles about finding, applying for, and choosing jobs. See, for example:

➤ "Career myths and how to debunk them," online at **http://www.bls.gov/opub/ooq/2005/fall/art01.pdf**.

➤ "Getting back to work: Returning to the labor force after an absence," online at **http://www.bls.gov/opub/ooq/2004/winter/art03.pdf**.

➤ "Job search in the age of the Internet: Six job seekers in search of employers," online at **http://www.bls.gov/opub/ooq/2003/summer/art01.pdf**.

➤ "Internships: Previewing a profession," online at **http://www.bls.gov/opub/ooq/2006/summer/art02.pdf**.

➤ "Resumes, applications, and cover letters," online at **http://www.bls.gov/opub/ooq/2009/summer/art03.pdf**.

Occupational Information Included in the *Handbook*

The *Occupational Outlook Handbook* is a career guidance resource that provides information on hundreds of occupations that provide the overwhelming majority of jobs in the United States. Each occupation is presented in its own chapter, or "statement," that discusses the type of work performed, the work environment, the education and training requirements, the possibilities for advancement, job outlook, and the typical earnings. Each statement is presented in a standard format, making it easy to compare occupations.

Because the *Handbook* covers so many occupations, it is best used as a reference, and is not meant to be read from cover to cover. Readers can navigate the *Handbook* by browsing the table of contents, in which similar occupations are grouped in clusters, or the reader can look at the index to find specific occupations.

About the Occupational Information Network

The Occupational Information Network (O*NET) is a system used by State employment service offices to classify applicants and job openings, and by some career information centers and libraries to file occupational information. At the end of each detailed occupational statement, the *Handbook* provides the Internet address of the online version of the statement. This online version provides links to O*NET information related to the particular occupation.

You can use O*NET to search for occupations that match your skills, or you may search by keyword or O*NET code. For each occupation, O*NET reports information about different aspects of the job, including tasks performed, knowledge, skills, abilities, and work activities. It also lists interests, work styles, such as independence, and work values, such as achievement, that are well suited to the occupation. O*NET ranks and scores the descriptors in each category by their importance to the occupation.

The *Handbook* chapter on "Occupational Information Network Coverage" cross-references O*NET codes to occupations covered in the *Handbook*. You can access O*NET on the Internet at **http://www.online.onetcenter.org**.

Sections of Occupational Statements

Significant Points
This section highlights key occupational characteristics discussed in the statement.

Nature of the Work
This section describes the typical tasks and responsibilities of workers in the occupation, including what tools and equipment they use and how closely they are supervised. The statement on fire fighting occupations, for example, gives a detailed account of the responsibilities of a fire fighter, which include operating the fire hose, providing emergency medical care, and cleaning and maintaining equipment. Some statements mention common alternative job titles or occupational specialties. The statement on accountants and auditors, for example, discusses several specialties, including public accountants, management accountants, and internal auditors.

The *Handbook* is revised every 2 years. This section may be revised for several reasons. One is the emergence of occupational specialties. For instance, webmasters—who are responsible for the technical aspects of operating a Web site—constitute a specialty within computer scientists and database administrators. Another reason for revision is a change in technology that affects the way in which a job is performed. The Internet, for example, allows purchasers to acquire supplies with a click of the mouse, saving time and money. Furthermore, job duties may be affected by modifications to business practices, such as organizational restructuring or changes in response to new government regulations. An example is paralegals and legal assistants, who increasingly are being used by law firms in order to lower costs and increase the efficiency of legal services.

Work environment. This subsection describes the workplace, the level of physical activity expected, and typical hours of workers in the occupation. It may also describe opportunities for part-time work, the extent of travel required, any special equipment that is used, and the risk of injury that workers may face.

In some occupations, people work regular business hours—40 hours a week, Monday through Friday. However, many establishments like restaurants, stores, and hospitals are open evenings, weekends, and in some cases 24 hours a day, seven days a week. The work settings can range from indoors at a comfortable desk to outdoors in every kind of weather. For example, radiologic technologists and technicians may use protective clothing or equipment, some construction laborers do physically demanding work, truck drivers might be susceptible to injury on the road, and paramedics have high job-related stress.

Information on various worker characteristics, such as the average number of hours worked per week, is obtained from the Current Population Survey (CPS)—a survey of households conducted by the U.S. Census Bureau for the Bureau of Labor Statistics (BLS).

Economists in BLS consult many sources before making changes to the nature of the work section, or any other section, of a *Handbook* statement. Usual sources include articles from newspapers, magazines, and professional journals, as well as the Web sites of professional associations, unions, and trade groups. Information found on the Internet or in periodicals is verified through interviews with individuals employed in the occupation, professional associations, unions, and others with occupational knowledge, such as university professors and career counselors.

Training, Other qualifications, and Advancement

After gathering your initial impressions of what a job is all about, it is important to understand how to prepare for it. The training, other qualifications, and advancement section explains typical paths to entry and advancement in each occupation.

Education and training. This subsection describes the most significant sources of education and training, the type education or training preferred by employers, and the typical length of training. Some common forms of education and training include a high school diploma, informal on-the-job training, previous work experience, formal training (including internships), and various postsecondary awards and degrees. The type of education or training required for each occupation in the *Handbook* varies, and two seemingly similar occupations can have very different requirements. For example, respiratory therapists typically need an associate degree for entry-level employment while occupational therapists typically need a master's degree or higher for entry-level employment.

Licensure. Some States regulate the practice of certain occupations, typically through licensure. This subsection discusses the number of States that regulate a given occupation and some of the typical requirements for such licenses. The requirements for licensure vary according to State law. Some common requirements for licensure are some minimum level of education, passage of an occupation-specific examination that demonstrates competency, and continuing education credits to maintain valid licensure. Examples of occupations that may require State licensure include child care workers, cosmetologists, electricians, occupational therapists, architects, and lawyers.

Credentialing is discussed in this subsection when it is a mandatory requirement for an occupation, much like licensure. For example, accountants who file reports with the Securities and Exchange Commission are required by law to be a Certified Public Accountant (CPA). A number of occupations have voluntary credentialing, often offered by professional organizations. If credentialing is voluntary, it may be addressed in this subsection or under the other qualifications or advancement subsections. When voluntary credentialing is relevant, the statement typically includes information on the type of credential, the credentialing organization, and some typical requirements for credentialing.

Other qualifications. Any additional qualifications that are not included in the previous subsections, such as the desirable skills, aptitudes, and personal characteristics that employers look for would be discussed in this section. For example, meeting and convention planners must have excellent interpersonal and organizational skills, the ability to work under pressure, and must pay attention to detail. For some entry-level jobs, personal characteristics are more important than formal training. Employers generally seek people who read, write, and speak well; compute accurately; think logically; learn quickly; get along with others; and demonstrate dependability. This subsec-

tion may also include information about voluntary, entry-level credentialing.

Advancement. This subsection details possible advancement opportunities after gaining experience in an occupation. Advancement can come in several forms, including advancement within the occupation, such as promotion to a management position; advancement into other occupations, such as leaving a job as a lawyer to become a judge; and advancement to self-employment, such as an automotive technician opening his or her own repair shop.

Certain types of certification can also serve as a form of advancement. Voluntary certification often demonstrates a level of competency to employers, and can result in more responsibility, higher pay, or a new job. Radiologic technologists may, for example, become specialists in magnetic resonance imaging (MRI) with voluntary certification.

Information in the training, other qualifications, and advancement section comes from personal interviews with individuals employed in the occupation, Web sites, published training materials, and interviews with the organizations that grant degrees, certifications, or licenses, or are otherwise associated with the occupation.

Employment

This section reports the number of jobs that the occupation provided in 2008, the key industries in which those jobs were found, and, if significant, the number or proportion of self-employed workers in the occupation.

The source of estimated employment in a particular occupation in the *Handbook* is the Bureau's National Employment Matrix, which presents current and projected employment for 276 industries and 750 occupations over the 2008–2018 period. Data in the matrix come primarily from the establishment-based Occupational Employment Statistics (OES) Survey, which reports employment of wage and salary workers for each occupation in every industry except agriculture and private households. The household-based Current Population Survey (CPS) provides input for matrix data on the number of self-employed and unpaid family workers in each occupation. The matrix also incorporates CPS data on total employment—wage and salary, self-employed, and unpaid family workers—in the agriculture and private household industries.

The estimate of total employment in each *Handbook* occupation thus combines data from several different sources. Furthermore, some *Handbook* occupations combine several matrix occupations. For these reasons, employment numbers cited in the *Handbook* may differ from employment data provided by OES, CPS, and other employment surveys.

When significant, the geographic distribution of jobs is mentioned, reflecting CPS data. On the basis of OES survey data, some *Handbook* statements, such as textile, apparel, and furnishings occupations, list States that employ substantial numbers of workers in the occupation.

Job Outlook

In planning for the future, it is important to consider potential job growth and job opportunities. This section describes the factors that affect employment growth or decline, and in some instances, describes the relationship between the number of job seekers and the number of job openings.

Employment change. This subsection reflects the occupational projections in the National Employment Matrix. Each occupation is assigned a descriptive phrase based on its projected percent change in employment over the 2008–2018 period. This phrase describes the occupation's projected employment change relative to the projected average employment change for all occupations combined. (These phrases are listed at the end of this chapter.)

Many factors are examined in projecting the employment change for each occupation. One such factor is changes in technology. New technology can either create new job opportunities or eliminate jobs by making an occupation obsolete. The Internet has increased the demand for workers in the computer and information technology fields, such as computer support specialists and systems administrators. However, the Internet also has adversely affected travel agents, because many people now book tickets, hotels, and rental cars online.

Another factor that influences employment trends is demographic change. By affecting the services demanded, demographic change can influence occupational growth or decline. For example, an aging population will demand more healthcare services, leading to occupational growth in healthcare occupations.

Another factor affecting job growth or decline is changes in business practices, such as restructuring businesses or outsourcing (contracting out) work. Corporate restructuring has made many organizations "flatter," resulting in fewer middle management positions. Also, in the past few years, insurance carriers have been outsourcing sales and claims adjuster jobs to large, 24-hour call centers in order to reduce costs. Jobs in some occupations, such as computer programmers and customer service representatives, have been "offshored"—moved to lower-wage foreign countries.

The substitution of one product or service for another can also affect employment projections. For example, consumption of plastic products has grown as they have been substituted for metal goods in consumer and manufactured products in recent years. The process is likely to continue and should result in stronger demand for machine operators in plastics than in metal.

Competition from foreign trade usually has a negative affect on employment. Often, foreign manufacturers can produce goods more cheaply than they can be produced in the United States, and the cost savings can be passed on in the form of lower prices with which U.S. manufacturers cannot compete. Increased international competition is a major reason for the decline in employment among textile, apparel, and furnishings workers.

Another factor is job growth or decline in key industries. If an occupation is concentrated in an industry that is growing rapidly, it is likely that that occupation will grow rapidly as well. For example, the growing need for business expertise is fueling demand for consulting services. This is expected to cause rapid growth in the management, scientific, and technical consulting services industry, which, in turn, will lead to rapid growth in the employment of management analysts.

Job prospects. In some cases, the *Handbook* mentions that an occupation is likely to provide numerous job openings or,

in others, that an occupation likely will have relatively few openings. This information reflects the projected change in employment, as well as replacement needs. Large occupations in which workers frequently enter and leave, such as food and beverage serving occupations, generally provide the most job openings—reflecting the need to replace workers who transfer to other occupations or who stop working.

Some *Handbook* statements discuss the relationship between the number of job seekers and the number of job openings. Job opportunities are affected by several factors, including the creation of new jobs, the number of people who apply for jobs, and the number of people who leave the occupation. In some occupations, there is a rough balance between job seekers and job openings, resulting in *good* opportunities. In other occupations, employers may report difficulty finding qualified applicants, resulting in *excellent* job opportunities. Still other occupations are characterized by a surplus of applicants, leading to *keen* competition for jobs. (These phrases used to describe the relationship between job seekers and job opportunities appear at the end of this section.) Variation in job opportunities by industry, educational attainment, size of firm, or geographic location also may be discussed. Even in crowded occupations, job openings do exist. Good students or highly qualified individuals should not be deterred from undertaking training for, or seeking entry into, those occupations.

Employment projections table. The employment projections table lists employment statistics from the National Employment Matrix. It includes 2008 employment, projected 2018 employment, and the 2008–2018 change in employment in both numerical and percent forms. Current and projected employment and the numerical change in employment are rounded to the nearest hundred, and the percent change in employment is rounded to the nearest whole number. Numerical and percent changes are calculated using non-rounded 2008 and 2018 employment figures, and then are rounded for presentation in the employment projections table.

Earnings

This section discusses typical earnings and how workers are compensated—annual salaries, hourly wages, commissions, piece rates, tips, or bonuses. Within every occupation, earnings vary by experience, responsibility, performance, tenure, and geographic area. Almost every statement in the *Handbook* contains 2008 OES-survey wage estimates for wage and salary workers. Information on earnings in the major industries in which the occupation is employed, also supplied by the OES survey, may be given as well.

In addition to presenting earnings data from the OES survey, some statements contain additional earnings data from non-BLS sources. Starting and average salaries of Federal workers are based on 2009 data from the U.S. Office of Personnel Management. The National Association of Colleges and Employers supplies information on average salary offers in 2009 for students graduating with a bachelor's, master's, or Ph.D. degree in certain fields. A few statements contain additional earnings information from other sources, such as unions, professional associations, and private companies. These data sources are cited in the text.

Benefits account for a significant portion of total compensation costs to employers. Benefits such as paid vacation, health insurance, and sick leave might not be mentioned, because they are widespread. In some occupational statements, the absence of these traditional benefits is pointed out. Although not as common as traditional benefits, flexible hours and profit-sharing plans may be offered to attract and retain highly qualified workers. Less common benefits also include child care, tuition for dependents, housing assistance, summers off, and free or discounted merchandise or services. For certain occupations, the percentage of workers affiliated with a union is listed. These data come from the CPS survey.

Unless otherwise noted, the source of employment and earnings data presented in the *Handbook* is the Bureau of Labor Statistics. Nearly all *Handbook* statements cite employment and wage estimates from the OES survey, and some include data from outside sources. OES data may be used to compare wages among occupations; outside data, however, may not be used in this manner, because characteristics of these data vary widely.

Related occupations

Occupations involving similar duties, skills, interests, education, and training are listed.

Sources of additional information

No single publication can describe all aspects of an occupation. Thus, the *Handbook* lists the mailing addresses of associations, government agencies, unions, and other organizations that can provide occupational information. In some cases, toll free telephone numbers and Internet addresses also are listed. Free or relatively inexpensive publications offering more information may be mentioned; some of these publications also may be available in libraries, in school career centers, in guidance offices, or on the Internet. Most of the organizations listed in this section were sources of information on the nature of the work, training, and job outlook discussed in the *Handbook*.

For additional sources of information, also read the earlier chapters, "Sources of Career Information" and "Sources of Education, Training, and Financial Aid."

Abbreviated occupational statements

At the end of some major occupational groups—office and administrative support occupations, for example—the *Handbook* includes selected occupational statements under headings such as "other office and administrative support occupations" or "other professional and related occupations." These statements provide the same career guidance information as the more-detailed occupational statements, but in an abbreviated format.

Key phrases in the *Handbook*

This box explains how to interpret key phrases used to describe projected changes in employment. Also explained are the terms used to describe the relationship between the number of job openings and the number of job seekers. The description of this relationship in a particular occupation reflects the knowledge and judgment of economists in the BLS Office of Occupational Statistics and Employment Projections.

Changing employment between 2008 and 2018

If the statement reads:	Employment is projected to:
Grow much faster than average	Increase 20 percent or more
Grow faster than average	Increase 14 to 19 percent
Grow about as fast as average	Increase 7 to 13 percent
Grow more slowly than average	Increase 3 to 6 percent
Little or no change	Decrease 2 percent to increase 2 percent
Decline slowly or moderately	Decrease 3 to 9 percent
Decline rapidly	Decrease 10 percent or more

Opportunities and competition for jobs

If the statement reads:	Job openings compared with job seekers may be:
Very good to excellent opportunities	More numerous
Good or favorable opportunities	In rough balance
May face, or can expect, keen competition	Fewer

Management, Business, and Financial Occupations

Management Occupations

Administrative Services Managers

Significant Points

- Applicants for the limited number of higher-level management jobs will face keen competition; less severe competition is expected for lower-level management jobs.

- Administrative services managers work throughout private industry and government and have a wide range of responsibilities, experience, earnings, and education.

- Like other managers, administrative services managers should be analytical, detail-oriented, flexible, decisive, and have good leadership and communication skills.

Nature of the Work

Administrative services managers plan, coordinate, and direct a broad range of services that allow organizations to operate efficiently. They might, for example, coordinate space allocation, facilities maintenance and operations, and major property and equipment procurement. They also may oversee centralized operations that meet the needs of multiple departments, such as information and data processing, mail, materials scheduling and distribution, printing and reproduction, records management, telecommunications management, security, recycling, wellness, and transportation services. Administrative services managers also ensure that contracts, insurance requirements, and government regulations and safety standards are followed and up to date. They may examine energy consumption patterns, technology usage, and personal property needs to plan for their long-term maintenance, modernization, and replacement.

Specific duties for these managers vary by size of company or office and degree of responsibility and authority. In small organizations, a single administrative services manager, sometimes called an *office manager*, may oversee all support services. (See the statement on office and administrative support worker supervisors and managers elsewhere in the *Handbook*.) In larger ones, however, there may be several layers of administrative services managers that may specialize in different areas and report to directors of administration, or vice presidents of administration who oversee all administrative services.

The nature of these managerial jobs varies as significantly as the range of administrative services required by organizations. For example, administrative services managers who work as *contract administrators* oversee the preparation, analysis,

negotiation, and review of contracts related to the purchase or sale of equipment, materials, supplies, products, or services. Other administrative services managers handle the acquisition, distribution, and storage of equipment and supplies, while others oversee the disposal of surplus or unclaimed property.

Administrative services managers who work as *facility managers* plan, design, and manage buildings, grounds, equipment, and supplies. Increasingly, they develop and implement plans that incorporate energy efficiency into a facility's operations and structures. These tasks require integrating the principles of business administration, information technology, architecture, and engineering. Although the specific tasks assigned to facility managers vary substantially depending on the organization, the duties fall into several categories, relating to operations and maintenance, real estate, project planning and management, communication, finance, facility function, technology integration, and environmental factors. Tasks within these broad categories may include space and workplace planning, budgeting, purchase and sale of real estate, lease management, renovations, or architectural planning and design. Facility managers

Administrative services managers review plans and contracts to ensure smooth implementation.

may oversee renovation projects to improve efficiency or ensure that facilities meet government regulations and environmental, health, and security standards. For example, they may influence building renovation projects by recommending energy-saving alternatives or production efficiencies that reduce waste. Additionally, facility managers continually monitor the facility to ensure that it remains safe, secure, and well-maintained. Often, facility managers are responsible for directing staff, including maintenance, grounds, and custodial workers.

Work environment. Administrative services managers spend much of their day in an office, but site visits around the building, outdoors to supervise groundskeeping activities, or to other facilities under their management are common. If overseeing a construction project, travel to the construction site is typical. Technology allows many facility managers to monitor equipment remotely and teleconferencing has reduced the need to travel as frequently to meet with off-site staff and vendors.

About half of administrative services managers work a standard 40-hour week; most of the remaining workforce work longer hours. However, uncompensated overtime frequently is required to resolve problems and meet deadlines. Facility managers often are "on call" to address a variety of problems that can arise in a facility during nonworking hours.

Training, Other Qualifications, and Advancement

Education and experience requirements for these managers vary widely, depending on the size and complexity of the organization. In small organizations, experience may be the only requirement. In large organizations, however, administrative services managers may need a bachelor's degree and appropriate experience.

Education and training. Specific education and training requirements vary by job responsibility. Office mangers in smaller operations or lower-level administrative services managers with fewer responsibilities may only need a high school diploma combined with appropriate experience, but an associate degree is increasingly preferred.

In larger companies with multiple locations, equipment, and technologies to coordinate, higher-level administrative services managers need at least a bachelor's degree. Managers of highly complex services, such as contract, insurance, and regulatory compliance, generally need at least a bachelor's degree in business administration, human resources, accounting, or finance. Lower-level managers may also need a bachelor's degree, but related postsecondary technical training may also be substituted for managers of printing, security, communications, or information technology. Those involved in building management should take a drafting class. Regardless of major, courses in office technology, accounting, computer applications, human resources, and business law are highly recommended.

Most facility managers have an undergraduate or graduate degree in engineering, architecture, construction management, business administration, or facility management. Many also have backgrounds in real estate, construction, or interior design, in addition to managerial experience. Whatever the educational background, it must be accompanied by related work experience reflecting managerial and leadership abilities. Many administrative services managers obtained their experience by specializing in one area at first, then augmenting their qualifications by acquiring work experience in other specialties before assuming managerial duties.

Managers of property acquisition and disposal need experience in purchasing and sales, and knowledge of the variety of supplies, machinery, and equipment used by the organization. Managers concerned with supply, inventory, and distribution should be experienced in receiving, warehousing, packaging, shipping, transportation, and related operations. Contract administrators may have worked as contract specialists, cost analysts, or procurement specialists.

Other qualifications. Persons interested in becoming administrative services managers should have good leadership and communication skills and be able to establish effective working relationships with many different people, ranging from managers, supervisors, and professionals, to clerks and blue-collar workers. They should be analytical, detail-oriented, flexible, and decisive. They must be able to coordinate several activities at once, quickly analyze and resolve specific problems, and cope with deadlines.

Certification and advancement. Most administrative services managers in small organizations advance by moving to other management positions or to larger organizations. The Association of Professional Office Managers offers online training geared towards small businesses that indicate a level of professionalism and commitment to office management.

Advancement is easier in large firms that employ several levels and types of administrative services managers. A master's degree in business administration or a related field can enhance a manager's opportunities to advance to higher-level positions, such as director of administrative services. Some experienced managers may join or establish a management consulting firm to provide administrative management services to other companies on a contract basis.

Advancement of facility managers is based on the practices and size of individual companies. Some facility managers transfer among departments within an organization or work their way up from technical positions. Others advance through a progression of facility management positions that offer additional responsibilities. Completion of the competency-based professional certification program offered by the International Facility Management Association can give prospective candidates an advantage. In order to qualify for the Certified Facility Manager (CFM) designation, applicants must meet certain educational and experience requirements. People entering the profession also may obtain the Facility Management Professional (FMP) credential, a stepping stone to the CFM.

Employment

Administrative services managers held about 259,400 jobs in 2008. They are found in all industries, but several industries have a greater share of these managers than others. They are the education services industry with 15 percent, the health care industry with 12 percent, State and local government with 12 percent, and finance and insurance with 9 percent.

Job Outlook

The number of jobs is projected to grow about as fast as average. Applicants for the limited number of higher-level management jobs will face keen competition; less severe competition is

Projections data from the National Employment Matrix

Occupational Title	SOC Code	Employment, 2008	Projected Employment, 2018	Change, 2008-2018	
				Number	Percent
Administrative services managers	11-3011	259,400	291,700	32,300	12

(NOTE) Data in this table are rounded. See the discussion of the employment projections table in the *Handbook* introductory chapter on *Occupational Information Included in the Handbook.*

expected for lower-level management jobs. Demand should be strong for facility managers.

Employment change. Employment of administrative services managers is projected to grow by 12 percent over the 2008-18 decade, about as fast as the average for all occupations. Continued downsizing by companies and increasing use of office technology may result in a more streamlined organizational structure with fewer levels of management, reducing the need for some positions. Demand should be strong for facility managers because businesses increasingly realize the importance of maintaining, securing, and efficiently operating their facilities. Cost-cutting measures to improve profitability, streamline operations, and compete globally will continue to be addressed by many organizations, resulting in more firms outsourcing facility management services or hiring qualified facility managers who are capable of achieving these goals in-house.

Administrative services managers employed in management services and management consulting should grow as companies increasingly look to outside specialists to handle a myriad of administrative tasks that have become increasingly complex and expensive. Administrative services managers specializing in contract administration will also be in demand as outsourcing of administrative tasks becomes increasingly prevalent for activities such as food and janitorial services, space planning and design, energy, telecommunications, and grounds and equipment maintenance and repair. Other areas that administrative services managers will increasingly plan and coordinate include information technology, data and personal security, records management, wellness, and energy conservation.

Job prospects. Applicants will face keen competition for the limited number of higher-level administrative services management jobs; competition should be less severe for lower-level management jobs. Job prospects will also be better for those who can manage a wide range of responsibilities, than for those who specialize in particular functions. In addition to the new administrative services management jobs due to growth in the occupation, many job openings will stem from the need to replace workers who transfer to other jobs, retire, or leave the occupation for other reasons.

Job opportunities may vary from year to year because the strength of the economy affects demand for administrative services managers. Industries least likely to be affected by economic fluctuations tend to be the most stable places for employment.

Earnings

Wages of administrative services managers vary greatly depending on the employer, the specialty, and the geographic area. In general, however, median annual wages of salaried administrative services managers in May 2008 were $73,520. The middle 50 per-

cent earned between $52,240 and $98,980. The lowest 10 percent earned less than $37,430, and the highest 10 percent earned more than $129,770. Median annual wages in the industries employing the largest numbers of these managers were:

Management of companies and enterprises	$85,980
General medical and surgical hospitals	77,870
Local government	74,860
Colleges, universities, and professional schools	72,460
State government	65,690

In the Federal Government, industrial specialists averaged $82,169 a year in March 2009. Corresponding averages were $78,995 for facility operations services managers, $79,457 for industrial property managers, $70,386 for property disposal specialists, $78,562 for administrative officers, and $71,049 for support services administrators.

Related Occupations

Administrative services managers direct and coordinate support services and oversee the purchase, use, and disposal of personal property. Occupations with similar functions include:

	Page
Cost estimators	100
Office and administrative support worker supervisors and managers	594
Property, real estate, and community association managers	76
Purchasing managers, buyers, and purchasing agents	79
Top executives	83

Sources of Additional Information

For information about careers and education and degree programs in facility management, as well as the Certified Facility Manager designation, contact:
➤ International Facility Management Association, 1 East Greenway Plaza, Suite 1100, Houston, TX 77046-0194. Internet: **http://www.ifma.org**

For information on training and classes for professional office management personnel, contact:
➤ Association of Professional Office Managers, P. O. Box 1926, Rockville, MD 20849. Internet: **http://www.apomonline.org**

The Occupational Information Network (O*NET) provides information on a wide range of occupational characteristics. Links to O*NET appear at the end of the Internet version of this occupational statement, accessible at **http://www.bls.gov/ooh/ocos002.htm**

Advertising, Marketing, Promotions, Public Relations, and Sales Managers

Significant Points

- Keen competition is expected for these highly coveted jobs.

- College graduates with related experience, a high level of creativity, and strong communication and computer skills should have the best job opportunities.

- High earnings, substantial travel, and long hours, including evenings and weekends, are common.

- Because of the importance and high visibility of their jobs, these managers often are prime candidates for advancement to the highest ranks.

Nature of the Work

Advertising, marketing, promotions, public relations, and sales managers coordinate their companies' market research, marketing strategy, sales, advertising, promotion, pricing, product development, and public relations activities. In small firms the owner or chief executive officer might assume all advertising, promotions, marketing, sales, and public relations responsibilities. In large firms, which may offer numerous products and services nationally or even worldwide, an executive vice president directs overall advertising, marketing, promotions, sales, and public relations policies. (Executive vice presidents are included in the *Handbook* statement on top executives.)

Advertising managers. Advertising managers direct a firm's or group's advertising and promotional campaign. They can be found in advertising agencies that put together advertising campaigns for clients, in media firms that sell advertising space or time, and in companies that advertise heavily. They work with sales staff and others to generate ideas for the campaign, oversee a creative staff that develops the advertising, and work with the finance department to prepare a budget and cost estimates for the campaign. Often, these managers serve as liaisons between the firm requiring the advertising and an advertising or promotion agency that actually develops and places the ads. In larger firms with an extensive advertising department, different advertising managers may oversee in-house accounts and creative and media services departments. The *account executive* manages account services departments in companies and assesses the need for advertising. In advertising agencies, account executives maintain the accounts of clients whereas the creative services department develops the subject matter and presentation of advertising. The *creative director* oversees the copy chief, art director, and associated staff. The *media director* oversees planning groups that select the communication medium—for example, radio, television, newspapers, magazines, the Internet, or outdoor signs—that will disseminate the advertising.

Marketing managers. Marketing managers work with advertising and promotion managers to promote the firm's or organization's products and services. With the help of lower level managers, including *product development managers* and *market research managers*, marketing managers estimate the

Advertising, marketing, promotions, public relations, and sales managers often serve as liaisons between the firm requiring the advertising and an advertising or promotion agency that develops and places the ads.

demand for products and services offered by the firm and its competitors and identify potential markets for the firm's products. Marketing managers also develop pricing strategies to help firms maximize profits and market share while ensuring that the firms' customers are satisfied. In collaboration with sales, product development, and other managers, they monitor trends that indicate the need for new products and services and they oversee product development.

Promotions managers. Promotions managers direct promotions programs that combine advertising with purchasing incentives to increase sales. Often, the programs are executed through the use of direct mail, inserts in newspapers, Internet advertisements, in-store displays, product endorsements, or other special events. Purchasing incentives may include discounts, samples, gifts, rebates, coupons, sweepstakes, and contests.

Public relations managers. Public relations managers plan and direct public relations programs designed to create and maintain a favorable public image for the employer or client. For example, they might write press releases or sponsor corporate events to help maintain and improve the image and identity of the company or client. They also help to clarify the organization's point of view to their main constituency. They observe social, economic, and political trends that might ultimately affect the firm, and they make recommendations to enhance the firm's image on the basis of those trends. Public relations managers often specialize in a specific area, such as crisis management, or in a specific industry, such as healthcare.

In large organizations, public relations managers may supervise a staff of public relations specialists. (See the *Handbook* statement on public relations specialists.) They also work with advertising and marketing staffs to make sure that the advertising campaigns are compatible with the image the company or client is trying to portray. In addition, public relations managers may handle internal company communications, such as company newsletters, and may help financial managers produce company reports. They may assist company executives in drafting speeches, arranging interviews, and maintaining other forms of public contact; oversee company archives; and respond to requests for information. Some of these managers handle special events as well, such as the sponsorship of races, parties introducing new products, or other activities that the firm supports in order to gain public attention through the press without advertising directly.

Sales managers. Sales managers direct the distribution of the product or service to the customer. They assign sales territories, set sales goals, and establish training programs for the organization's sales representatives. (See the *Handbook* statement on sales representatives, wholesale and manufacturing). Sales managers advise the sales representatives on ways to improve their sales performance. In large multiproduct firms, they oversee regional and local sales managers and their staffs. Sales managers maintain contact with dealers and distributors, and analyze sales statistics gathered by their staffs to determine sales potential and inventory requirements and to monitor customers' preferences. Such information is vital in the development of products and the maximization of profits.

Work environment. Advertising, marketing, promotions, public relations, and sales managers work in offices close to those of top managers. Working under pressure is unavoidable when schedules change and problems arise, but deadlines and goals still must be met.

Substantial travel may be required in order to meet with customers and consult with others in the industry. Sales managers travel to national, regional, and local offices and to the offices of various dealers and distributors. Advertising and promotions managers may travel to meet with clients or representatives of communications media. At times, public relations managers travel to meet with special-interest groups or government officials. Job transfers between headquarters and regional offices are common, particularly among sales managers.

Long hours, including evenings and weekends are common. In 2008, over 80 percent of advertising, marketing, promotions, public relations, and sales managers worked 40 hours or more a week.

Training, Other Qualifications, and Advancement

A wide range of educational backgrounds is suitable for entry into advertising, marketing, promotions, public relations, and sales manager jobs, but many employers prefer college graduates with experience in related occupations.

Education and training. For marketing, sales, and promotions management positions, employers often prefer a bachelor's or master's degree in business administration with an emphasis on marketing. Courses in business law, management,

economics, accounting, finance, mathematics, and statistics are advantageous. In addition, the completion of an internship while the candidate is in school is highly recommended. In highly technical industries, such as computer and electronics manufacturing, a bachelor's degree in engineering or science, combined with a master's degree in business administration, is preferred.

For advertising management positions, some employers prefer a bachelor's degree in advertising or journalism. A relevant course of study might include classes in marketing, consumer behavior, market research, sales, communication methods and technology, visual arts, art history, and photography.

For public relations management positions, some employers prefer a bachelor's or master's degree in public relations or journalism. The applicant's curriculum should include courses in advertising, business administration, public affairs, public speaking, political science, and creative and technical writing.

Most advertising, marketing, promotions, public relations, and sales management positions are filled through promotions of experienced staff or related professional personnel. For example, many managers are former sales representatives; purchasing agents; buyers; or product, advertising, promotions, or public relations specialists. In small firms, in which the number of positions is limited, advancement to a management position usually comes slowly. In large firms, promotion may occur more quickly.

Other qualifications. Computer skills are necessary for recordkeeping and data management, and the ability to work in an Internet environment is becoming increasingly vital as more marketing, product promotion, and advertising is done through the Internet. Also, the ability to communicate in a foreign language may open up employment opportunities in many rapidly growing areas around the country, especially cities with large Spanish-speaking populations.

Persons interested in becoming advertising, marketing, promotions, public relations, and sales managers should be mature, creative, highly motivated, resistant to stress, flexible, and decisive. The ability to communicate persuasively, both orally and in writing, with other managers, staff, and the public is vital. These managers also need tact, good judgment, and exceptional ability to establish and maintain effective personal relationships with supervisory and professional staff members and client firms.

Certification and advancement. Some associations offer certification programs for these managers. Certification—an indication of competence and achievement—is particularly important in a competitive job market. Although relatively few advertising, marketing, promotions, public relations, and sales managers currently are certified, the number of managers who seek certification is expected to grow. Today, there are numerous management certification programs based on education and job performance. In addition, the Public Relations Society of America offers a certification program for public relations practitioners that is based on years of experience and performance on an examination.

Although experience, ability, and leadership are emphasized for promotion, advancement can be accelerated by participation in management training programs conducted by larger firms. Many firms also provide their employees with continuing education opportunities—either in-house or at local colleges and universities—and encourage employee participation in seminars and conferences, often held by professional societies. In collaboration with colleges and universities, numerous marketing and related associations sponsor national or local management training programs. Course subjects include brand and product management; international marketing; sales management evaluation; telemarketing and direct sales; interactive marketing; product promotion; marketing communication; market research; organizational communication; and data-processing systems, procedures, and management. Many firms pay all or part of the cost for employees who complete courses.

Because of the importance and high visibility of their jobs, advertising, marketing, promotions, public relations, and sales managers often are prime candidates for advancement to the highest ranks. Well-trained, experienced, and successful managers may be promoted to higher positions in their own or another firm; some become top executives. Managers with extensive experience and sufficient capital may open their own businesses.

Employment

Advertising, marketing, promotions, public relations, and sales managers held about 623,800 jobs in 2008. The following tabulation shows the distribution of jobs by occupational specialty:

Sales managers 346,900
Marketing managers 175,600
Public relations managers 56,700
Advertising and promotions managers 44,600

These managers were found in virtually every industry. Sales managers held about 56 percent of the jobs; about 62 percent of sales managers were employed in wholesale trade, retail trade, manufacturing, and the finance and insurance industries. Marketing managers held approximately 28 percent of the jobs; the professional, scientific, and technical services, and the finance and insurance industries employed around 32 percent of marketing managers. About 27 percent of advertising and promotions managers worked in the professional, scientific, and technical services industries and wholesale trade. Around 48 percent of public relations managers were employed in service-providing industries, such as professional, scientific, and technical services; public and private educational services; finance and insurance; and healthcare and social assistance.

Job Outlook

Employment is projected to grow about as fast as average. As with most managerial jobs, keen competition is expected for these highly coveted positions.

Employment change. Overall employment of advertising, marketing, promotions, public relations, and sales managers is expected to increase by 13 percent through 2018. Job growth will be spurred by competition for a growing number of goods and services, both foreign and domestic, and the need to make one's product or service stand out in the crowd. In addition, as the influence of traditional advertising in newspapers, radio, and network television wanes, marketing professionals are being asked to develop new and different ways to advertise and promote products and services to better reach potential customers.

Sales and marketing managers and their departments constitute some of the most important personnel in an organization and are less subject to downsizing or outsourcing than are other types of managers, except in the case of companies that are consolidating. Employment of these managers, therefore, will vary primarily on the basis of the growth or contraction in the industries that employ them. For example, if, as is expected, the number of automobile dealers declines over the next decade, these major employers of sales managers will need fewer of them. Employment of marketing managers will grow 12 percent between 2008 and 2018, and that of sales managers will grow 15 percent over the same period.

Advertising and promotions managers are expected to experience little or no change in employment from 2008 to 2018. Despite large declines in the number of advertising managers in recent years, due mainly to the sharp reduction in the number of advertising agencies and newspaper and periodical publishers, which employ the greatest numbers of these managers, advertising and promotions managers are not expected to experience similar declines in the future. Because advertising is the primary source of revenue for most media, advertising departments are less affected in a downturn. An expected increase in the number of television and radio stations and a sharp increase in the amount of advertising in digital media, such as the Internet and wireless devices will generate a need for advertising managers to oversee new and innovative advertising programs. A number of these advertising managers will be self-employed.

Public relations managers are expected to see an increase in employment of 13 percent between 2008 and 2018, as organizations increasingly emphasize community outreach and

Projections data from the National Employment Matrix

Occupational Title	SOC Code	Employment, 2008	Projected Employment, 2018	Change, 2008-2018	
				Number	Percent
Advertising, marketing, promotions, public relations, and sales managers	11-2000	623,800	704,100	80,300	13
Advertising and promotions managers	11-2011	44,600	43,900	-800	-2
Marketing and sales managers	11-2020	522,400	596,200	73,700	14
Marketing managers	11-2021	175,600	197,500	21,900	12
Sales managers	11-2022	346,900	398,700	51,800	15
Public relations managers	11-2031	56,700	64,100	7,300	13

(NOTE) Data in this table are rounded. See the discussion of the employment projections table in the *Handbook* introductory chapter on *Occupational Information Included in the Handbook.*

customer relations as a way to enhance their reputation and visibility. Especially among the growing number of nonprofit organizations, such as education services, business and professional associations, and hospitals, where many of these workers are employed, public relations managers will be charged with promoting the mission of the organization and encouraging membership or use of the organization's services.

Job prospects. Most job openings for this occupation will be due to the need to replace workers who leave the occupation or retire. However, advertising, marketing, promotions, public relations, and sales manager jobs are highly coveted and are often sought by other managers or highly experienced professionals, resulting in keen competition. College graduates with related experience, a high level of creativity, and strong communication and computer skills should have the best job opportunities. In particular, employers will seek those who have the skills to conduct new types of advertising, marketing, promotions, public relations, and sales campaigns involving new media, particularly the Internet.

Earnings

Median annual wages in May 2008 were $80,220 for advertising and promotions managers, $108,580 for marketing managers, $97,260 for sales managers, and $89,430 for public relations managers.

Median annual wages of advertising and promotions managers in May 2008 in the advertising, public relations, and related services industry were $105,960.

Median annual wages in the industries employing the largest numbers of marketing managers were as follows:

Computer systems design and related services $127,870
Management of companies and enterprises 115,650
Management, scientific, and technical
    consulting services 111,130
Insurance carriers 103,210
Depository credit intermediation.................................98,510

Median annual wages in the industries employing the largest numbers of sales managers were as follows:

Professional and commercial equipment
    and supplies merchant wholesalers $125,130
Wholesale, electronic markets,
    and agents and brokers 114,670
Automobile dealers 107,500
Management of companies and enterprises 106,980
Department stores...54,560

Wages vary substantially, depending upon the employee's level of managerial responsibility, length of service, and education; the size and location of the firm; and the industry in which the firm operates. For example, manufacturing firms usually pay these managers higher salaries than nonmanufacturing firms. For sales managers, the size of their sales territory is another important determinant of salary. Many managers earn bonuses equal to 10 percent or more of their salaries.

According to a survey by the National Association of Colleges and Employers, starting salaries for marketing majors graduating in 2009 averaged $43,325.

Related Occupations

Advertising, marketing, promotions, public relations, and sales managers direct the sale of products and services offered by their firms and communicate information about their firm's activities. Other workers involved with advertising, marketing, promotions, public relations, and sales include the following:

Sources of Additional Information

For information about careers in advertising management, contact:
➤ American Association of Advertising Agencies, 405 Lexington Ave., 18th Floor, New York, NY 10174-1801. Internet: **http://www.aaaa.org**

Information about careers and professional certification in public relations management is available from:
➤ Public Relations Society of America, 33 Maiden Lane, 11th Floor, New York, NY 10038-5150. Internet: **http://www.prsa.org**

The Occupational Information Network (O*NET) provides information on a wide range of occupational characteristics. Links to O*NET appear at the end of the Internet version of this occupational statement, accessible at **http://www.bls.gov/ooh/ocos020.htm**

Computer and Information Systems Managers

Significant Points

- Employment is expected to grow faster than the average for all occupations.

- A bachelor's degree in a computer-related field usually is required for management positions, although employers often prefer a graduate degree, especially an MBA with technology as a core component.

- Many managers possess advanced technical knowledge gained from working in a computer occupation.

- Job prospects should be excellent.

Nature of the Work

In the modern workplace, it is imperative that Information Technology (IT) works both effectively and reliably. *Computer and information systems managers* play a vital role in the implementation and administration of technology within their organizations. They plan, coordinate, and direct research on the computer-related activities of firms. In consultation with other managers, they help determine the goals of an organization and then implement technology to meet those goals. They oversee all technical aspect of an organization, such as software development, network security, and Internet operations.

Computer and information systems managers direct the work of other IT professionals, such as computer software engineers and computer programmers, computer systems analysts, and computer support specialists (information on these occupations can be found elsewhere in the *Handbook*). They plan and coordinate activities such as installing and upgrading hardware and software, programming and systems design, the implementation of computer networks, and the development of Internet and intranet sites. They are increasingly involved with the upkeep, maintenance, and security of networks. They analyze the computer and information needs of their organizations from an operational and strategic perspective and determine immediate and long-range personnel and equipment requirements. They assign and review the work of their subordinates and stay abreast of the latest technology to ensure that the organization remains competitive.

Computer and information systems managers can have additional duties, depending on their role within an organization. *Chief technology officers (CTOs),* for example, evaluate the newest and most innovative technologies and determine how these can help their organizations. They develop technical standards, deploy technology, and supervise workers who deal with the daily information technology issues of the firm. When a useful new tool has been identified, the CTO determines one or more possible implementation strategies, including cost-benefit and return on investment analyses, and presents those strategies to top management, such as the *chief information officer* (CIO). (Chief information officers are covered in a separate *Handbook* section on top executives.)

Management information systems (MIS) directors or *information technology (IT) directors* manage computing resources for their organizations. They often work under the chief information officer and plan and direct the work of subordinate information technology employees. These managers ensure the availability, continuity, and security of data and information technology services in their organizations. In this capacity, they oversee a variety of technical departments, develop and monitor performance standards, and implement new projects.

IT project managers develop requirements, budgets, and schedules for their firm's information technology projects. They coordinate such projects from development through implementation, working with their organization's IT workers, as well as clients, vendors, and consultants. These managers are increasingly involved in projects that upgrade the information security of an organization.

Work environment. Computer and information systems managers generally work in clean, comfortable offices. Long hours are common, and some may have to work evenings and weekends to meet deadlines or solve unexpected problems; in 2008, about 25 percent worked more than 50 hours per week. Some computer and information systems managers may experience considerable pressure in meeting technical goals with short deadlines or tight budgets. As networks continue to expand and more work is done remotely, computer and information systems managers have to communicate with and oversee offsite employees using laptops, e-mail, and the Internet.

Computer and information systems managers oversee a variety of workers, including systems analysts, support specialists, and software engineers.

Injuries in this occupation are uncommon, but like other workers who spend considerable time using computers, computer and information systems managers are susceptible to eyestrain, back discomfort, and hand and wrist problems such as carpal tunnel syndrome.

Training, Other Qualifications, and Advancement
Computer and information systems managers generally have technical expertise from working in a computer occupation, as well as an understanding of business and management principles. A strong educational background and experience in a variety of technical fields is needed.

Education and training. A bachelor's degree in a computer-related field usually is required for management positions, although employers often prefer a graduate degree, especially an MBA with technology as a core component. Common majors for undergraduate degrees are computer science, information science, or management information systems (MIS).

A bachelor's degree in a computer-related field generally takes 4 years to complete, and includes courses in computer science, computer programming, computer engineering, mathematics, and statistics. Most also include general education courses such as English and communications. MIS programs usually are part of the business school or college, and contain courses such as finance, marketing, accounting, and management, as well as systems design, networking, database management, and systems security.

MBA programs usually require 2 years of study beyond the undergraduate degree, and, like undergraduate business programs, include courses on finance, marketing, accounting, and management, as well as database management, electronic business, and systems management and design.

A few computer and information systems managers attain their positions with only an associate or trade school degree, but they must have sufficient experience and must have acquired additional skills on the job. To aid their professional advancement, many managers with an associate degree eventually earn a bachelor's or master's degree while working.

Projections data from the National Employment Matrix

Occupational Title	SOC Code	Employment, 2008	Projected Employment, 2018	Change, 2008-2018	
				Number	Percent
Computer and information systems managers...................................	11-3021	293,000	342,500	49,500	17

(NOTE) Data in this table are rounded. See the discussion of the employment projections table in the *Handbook* introductory chapter on *Occupational Information Included in the Handbook.*

Certification and other qualifications. Computer and information systems managers need a broad range of skills. Employers look for individuals who can demonstrate an understanding of the specific software or technology used on the job. Generally, this knowledge is gained through years of experience working with that particular product. Another way to demonstrate this trait is with professional certification. Although not required for most computer and information system management positions, certification demonstrates an area of expertise, and can increase an applicant's chances of employment. These high-level certifications are often product-specific, and are generally administered by software or hardware companies rather than independent organizations.

Computer and information systems managers also need a thorough understanding of business practices. Because information technology is a central component of many organizations, these workers often must make important business decisions. Consequently, many firms seek managers with a background in business management, consulting, or sales. These workers also must possess good leadership and communication skills, as one of their main duties is to assign work and monitor employee performance. They also must be able to explain technical subjects to people without technical expertise, such as clients or managers of other departments.

Advancement. Computer and information systems managers may advance to progressively higher leadership positions in an information technology department. A project manager, for instance, might be promoted to the chief technology officer position and then to chief information officer. On occasion, some may become managers in non-technical areas such as marketing, human resources, or sales because in high technology firms an understanding of technical issues is helpful in those areas.

Employment

Computer and information systems managers held about 293,000 jobs in 2008. About 16 percent worked in the computer systems design and related services industry. This industry provides IT services on a contract basis, including custom computer programming services; computer systems design and integration services; and computer facilities management services. Other large employers include insurance and financial firms, government agencies, business management organizations, and manufacturers.

Job Outlook

Faster than average employment growth is expected, and job prospects should be excellent.

Employment change. Employment of computer and information systems managers is expected to grow 17 percent over the 2008-18 decade, which is faster than the average for all occupations. New applications of technology in the workplace will continue to drive demand for workers, fueling the need for more managers. To remain competitive, firms will continue to

install sophisticated computer networks and set up more complex intranets and websites. They will need to adopt the most efficient software and systems and troubleshoot problems when they occur. Computer and information systems managers will be needed to oversee these functions.

Because so much business is carried out over computer networks, security will continue to be an important issue for businesses and other organizations, and will lead to strong growth for computer managers. Firms will increasingly hire security experts to fill key leadership roles in their information technology departments because the integrity of their computing environments is of utmost importance.

The growth of computer and information systems managers should be closely related to the growth of the occupations they supervise. For information on these occupations, see the *Handbook* sections on computer software engineers and computer programmers; computer systems analysts; computer network, systems, and database administrators; computer scientists; and computer support specialists.

Among computer and information systems managers, job growth is expected to be the fastest in computer systems design establishments; software publishing firms; data processing and hosting companies; management, scientific, and technical consulting services; and healthcare organizations. Increased consolidation of IT services may reduce growth to some extent in other industries.

Job prospects. Prospects for qualified computer and information systems managers should be excellent. Workers with specialized technical knowledge and strong communications and business skills, as well as those with an MBA with a concentration in information systems, will have the best prospects. Job openings will be the result of employment growth and the need to replace workers who transfer to other occupations or leave the labor force.

Earnings

Wages of computer and information systems managers vary by specialty and level of responsibility. Median annual wages of these managers in May 2008 were $112,210. The middle 50 percent earned between $88,240 and $141,890. Median annual wages in the industries employing the largest numbers of computer and information systems managers in May 2008 were as follows:

Software publishers..	$126,840
Computer systems design and related services..........	118,120
Management of companies and enterprises...............	115,150
Depository credit intermediation...............................	113,380
Insurance carriers..	109,810

In addition to salaries, computer and information systems managers, especially those at higher levels, often receive employment-related benefits, such as expense accounts, stock-option plans, and bonuses.

Related Occupations

Other occupations that manage workers, deal with information technology, or make business or technical decisions include:

Sources of Additional Information

Additional information on a career in information technology is available from the following organizations:

➤ Association for Computing Machinery (ACM), 2 Penn Plaza, Suite 701, New York, NY 10121-0701. Internet: **http://www.computingcareers.acm.org**

➤ Institute of Electrical and Electronics Engineers Computer Society, Headquarters Office, 2001 L St. NW., Suite 700 Washington, DC 20036-4910. Internet: **http://www.computer.org**

➤ National Workforce Center for Emerging Technologies, 3000 Landerholm Circle SE., Bellevue, WA 98007. Internet: **http://www.nwcet.org**

➤ University of Washington Computer Science and Engineering Department, AC101 Paul G. Allen Center, Box 352350, 185 Stevens Way, Seattle, WA 98195-2350. Internet: **http://www.cs.washington.edu/WhyCSE**

➤ National Center for Women and Information Technology, University of Colorado, Campus Box 322 UCB, Boulder, CO 80309-0322. Internet: **http://www.ncwit.org**

The Occupational Information Network (O*NET) provides information on a wide range of occupational characteristics. Links to O*NET appear at the end of the Internet version of this occupational statement, accessible at **http://www.bls.gov/ooh/ocos258.htm**

Construction Managers

Significant Points

- About 61 percent of construction managers are self-employed.

- Jobseekers who combine construction work experience with a bachelor's degree in a construction-related field should enjoy the best prospects.

- Certification, although not required, is increasingly important for construction managers.

Nature of the Work

Construction managers plan, direct, coordinate, and budget a wide variety of construction projects, including the building of all types of residential, commercial, and industrial structures, roads, bridges, wastewater treatment plants, and schools and hospitals. Construction managers may supervise an entire project or just part of one. They schedule and coordinate all design and construction processes, including the selection, hiring, and oversight of specialty trade contractors, such as carpentry, plumbing, or electrical, but they usually do not do any actual construction of the structure.

Construction managers are salaried or self-employed managers who oversee construction supervisors and personnel. They are often called *project managers, constructors, construction superintendents, project engineers, construction supervisors,* or *general contractors*. Construction managers may be owners or salaried employees of a construction management or contracting firm, or they may work under contract or as a salaried employee of the property owner, developer, or contracting firm managing the construction project.

These managers coordinate and supervise the construction process from the conceptual development stage through final construction, making sure that the project gets completed on time and within budget. They often work with owners, engineers, architects, and others who are involved in the process. Given the designs for buildings, roads, bridges, or other projects, construction managers supervise the planning, scheduling, and implementation of those designs.

Large construction projects, such as an office building or an industrial complex, are often too complicated for one person to manage. Accordingly, these projects are divided into various segments: site preparation, including clearing and excavation of the land, installing sewage systems, and landscaping and road construction; building construction, including laying foundations and erecting the structural framework, floors, walls, and roofs; and building systems, including protecting against fire and installing electrical, plumbing, air-conditioning, and heating systems. Construction managers may be in charge of one or several of these activities.

Construction managers determine the best way to get materials to the building site and the most cost-effective plan and schedule for completing the project. They divide all required construction site activities into logical steps, estimating and budgeting the time required to meet established deadlines. Doing this may require sophisticated scheduling and cost-estimating techniques using computers with specialized software. (See the section on cost estimators elsewhere in the *Handbook*.)

Construction managers also manage the selection of general contractors and trade contractors to complete specific phases of the project—which could include everything from structural metalworking and plumbing, to painting, to installing electricity and carpeting. Construction managers determine the labor requirements of the project and, in some cases, supervise or monitor the hiring and dismissal of workers. They oversee the performance of all trade contractors and are responsible for ensuring that all work is completed on schedule.

Construction managers direct and monitor the progress of construction activities, occasionally through construction su-

Construction managers direct and monitor the progress of construction activities, occasionally through construction supervisors or other construction managers.

pervisors or other construction managers. They are responsible for obtaining all necessary permits and licenses and, depending upon the contractual arrangements, for directing or monitoring compliance with building and safety codes, other regulations, and requirements set by the project's insurers. They also oversee the delivery and use of materials, tools, and equipment; worker safety and productivity; and the quality of the construction.

Work environment. Working out of a main office or out of a field office at the construction site, construction managers monitor the overall construction project. Decisions regarding daily construction activities generally are made at the jobsite. Managers might travel considerably when the construction site is not close to their main office or when they are responsible for activities at two or more sites. Management of overseas construction projects usually entails temporary residence in the country in which the project is being carried out.

Often on call 24 hours a day, construction managers deal with delays, such as the effects of bad weather, or emergencies at the jobsite. More than one-third worked a standard 40-hour week in 2008, and some construction projects continue around the clock. Construction managers may need to work this type of

schedule for days or weeks to meet special project deadlines, especially if there are delays.

Although the work usually is not inherently dangerous, injuries can occur and construction managers must be careful while performing onsite services.

Training, Other Qualifications, and Advancement

Employers increasingly are hiring construction managers with a bachelor's degree in a construction-related field, although it is also possible for construction workers to become construction managers after many years of experience. Construction managers must understand contracts, plans, specifications, and regulations. Certification, although not required, is increasingly important.

Education and training. For construction manager jobs, a bachelor's degree in construction science, construction management, building science, or civil engineering, plus work experience, is becoming the norm. However, years of experience, in addition to taking classes in the field or getting an associate's degree, can substitute for a bachelor's degree. Practical construction experience is very important for entering this occupation, whether earned through an internship, a cooperative education program, a job in the construction trades, or another job in the industry. Some people advance to construction management positions after having substantial experience as construction craftworkers—carpenters, masons, plumbers, or electricians, for example—or after having worked as construction supervisors or as owners of independent specialty contracting firms. However, as construction processes become increasingly complex, employers are placing more importance on specialized education after high school.

More than 100 colleges and universities offer bachelor's degree programs in construction science, building science, and construction engineering. These programs include courses in project control and development, site planning, design, construction methods, construction materials, value analysis, cost estimating, scheduling, contract administration, accounting, business and financial management, safety, building codes and standards, inspection procedures, engineering and architectural sciences, mathematics, statistics, and information technology. Graduates from 4-year degree programs usually are hired as assistants to project managers, field engineers, schedulers, or cost estimators. An increasing number of graduates in related fields—engineering or architecture, for example—also enter construction management, often after acquiring substantial experience on construction projects.

Several colleges and universities offer a master's degree program in construction management or construction science. Master's degree recipients, especially those with work experience in construction, typically become construction managers in very large construction or construction management companies. Often, individuals who hold a bachelor's degree in an unrelated field seek a master's degree in construction management or construction science to work in the construction industry. Some construction managers obtain a master's degree in business administration or finance to further their career prospects.

A number of 2-year colleges throughout the country offer construction management or construction technology programs.

Many individuals also attend training and educational programs sponsored by industry associations, often in collaboration with postsecondary institutions.

Other qualifications. Construction managers should be flexible and work effectively in a fast-paced environment. They should be decisive and work well under pressure, particularly when faced with unexpected events or delays. The ability to manage several major activities at once, while analyzing and resolving specific problems, is essential, as is an understanding of engineering, architectural, and other construction drawings. Familiarity with computers and software programs for job costing, online collaboration, scheduling, and estimating also is important.

Good oral and written communication skills are important as well, as are leadership skills. Managers must be able to establish a good working relationship with many different people, including owners, other managers, designers, supervisors, and craftworkers. The ability to converse fluently in Spanish is increasingly becoming an asset, because Spanish is the first language of many workers in the construction industry.

Certification and advancement. There is a growing movement toward certification of construction managers. Although certification is not required to work in the construction industry, it can be valuable because it provides evidence of competence and experience. Both the American Institute of Constructors and the Construction Management Association of America have established voluntary certification programs for construction managers. Requirements combine written examinations with verification of education and professional experience. The American Institute of Constructors awards the Associate Constructor (AC) and Certified Professional Constructor (CPC) designations to candidates who meet its requirements and pass the appropriate construction examinations. The Construction Management Association of America awards the Certified Construction Manager (CCM) designation to workers who have the required experience and who pass a technical examination. Applicants for this designation also must complete a self-study course that covers the professional role of a construction manager, legal issues, the allocation of risk, and other topics related to construction management.

Advancement opportunities for construction managers vary with the individual's performance and the size and type of company for which the person works. Within large firms, managers may eventually become top-level managers or executives. Highly experienced individuals may become independent consultants; some serve as expert witnesses in court or as arbitrators in disputes. Those with the required capital may establish their own construction management services, specialty contracting, or general contracting firms.

Employment

Construction managers held 551,000 jobs in 2008. About 61 percent were self-employed, many as owners of general or specialty trade construction firms. Most salaried construction managers were employed in the construction industry—11 percent by specialty trade contractor businesses (for example, plumbing, heating, air-conditioning, and electrical contractors), 10 percent in nonresidential building construction, and 7 percent in residential building construction. Others were employed by architectural, engineering, and related services firms.

Job Outlook

Faster than average employment growth is expected. Jobseekers who combine construction work experience with a bachelor's degree in a construction-related field should enjoy the best prospects.

Employment change. Employment of construction managers is projected to increase by 17 percent during the 2008–18 decade, faster than average for all occupations. Construction managers will be needed as the level and variety of construction activity expands, but at a slower rate than in the past. Modest population and business growth will result in new and renovated construction of residential dwellings, office buildings, retail outlets, hospitals, schools, restaurants, and other structures that require construction managers. A growing emphasis on making buildings more energy efficient should create additional jobs for construction managers involved in retrofitting buildings. In addition, the need to replace portions of the Nation's infrastructure, such as roads, bridges, and water and sewer pipes, along with the need to increase energy supply lines, will further increase demand for construction managers.

The increasing complexity of construction projects requires specialized management-level personnel within the construction industry. Sophisticated technology; the proliferation of laws setting standards for buildings and construction materials, worker safety, energy efficiency, and environmental protection; and the potential for adverse litigation have complicated the construction process. In addition, advances in building materials, technology, and construction methods requires continual learning and expertise.

Job prospects. Prospects should be best for people who have a bachelor's or higher degree in construction science, construction management, or civil engineering, plus practical work experience in construction. A strong background in building technology is beneficial as well. Construction managers also will have many opportunities to start their own firms.

In addition to job openings arising from employment growth, many openings should result annually from the need to replace workers who transfer to other occupations or leave the labor force for other reasons. A number of seasoned managers are

Projections data from the National Employment Matrix

Occupational Title	SOC Code	Employment, 2008	Projected Employment, 2018	Change, 2008-2018	
				Number	Percent
Construction managers..	11-9021	551,000	645,800	94,800	17

(NOTE) Data in this table are rounded. See the discussion of the employment projections table in the *Handbook* introductory chapter on *Occupational Information Included in the Handbook.*

expected to retire over the next decade, resulting in a number of job openings.

Employment of construction managers, like that of many other construction workers, is sensitive to the fluctuations of the economy. On the one hand, workers in these trades may experience periods of unemployment when the overall level of construction falls. On the other hand, shortages of these workers may occur in some areas during peak periods of building activity.

Earnings

Wages of salaried construction managers and self-employed independent construction contractors vary with the size and nature of the construction project, its geographic location, and economic conditions. In addition to receiving typical benefits, many salaried construction managers earn bonuses and are allowed the use of company motor vehicles.

Median annual wages of salaried construction managers in May 2008 were $79,860. The middle 50 percent earned between $60,650 and $107,140. The lowest paid 10 percent earned less than $47,000, and the highest paid 10 percent earned more than $145,920. Median annual wages in the industries employing the largest numbers of construction managers were as follows:

Building equipment contractors	$81,590
Nonresidential building construction	79,950
Other specialty trade contractors	78,410
Foundation, structure, and building exterior contractors	76,880
Residential building construction	74,770

The earnings of self-employed workers are not included in these numbers.

According to a July 2009 salary survey by the National Association of Colleges and Employers, people with a bachelor's degree in construction science or construction management received job offers averaging $53,199 a year.

Related Occupations

Construction managers participate in the conceptual development of a construction project and oversee its organization, scheduling, and implementation. Other workers who perform similar functions include the following:

	Page
Architects, except landscape and naval	151
Civil engineers	161
Cost estimators	100
Engineering and natural sciences managers	46
Landscape architects	154

Sources of Additional Information

For information about constructor certification, contact:
➤ American Institute of Constructors, P.O. Box 26334, Alexandria, VA 22314. Internet: **http://www.aicnet.org**

For information about construction management and construction manager certification, contact:
➤ Construction Management Association of America, 7926 Jones Branch Dr., Suite 800, McLean, VA 22102. Internet: **http://www.cmaanet.org**

Information on accredited construction science and management educational programs is available from:
➤ American Council for Construction Education, 1717 North Loop 1604 E, Suite 320, San Antonio, TX 78232. Internet: **http://www.acce-hq.org**

➤ National Center for Construction Education and Research, 3600 NW. 43rd St., Building G, Gainesville, FL 32606. Internet: **http://www.nccer.org**

The Occupational Information Network (O*NET) provides information on a wide range of occupational characteristics. Links to O*NET appear at the end of the Internet version of this occupational statement, accessible at **http://www.bls.gov/ooh/ocos005.htm**

Education Administrators

Significant Points

- Many jobs require a master's or doctoral degree and experience in a related occupation, such as teaching or admissions counseling.

- Strong interpersonal and communication skills are essential because much of an administrator's job involves working and collaborating with others.

- Excellent opportunities are expected for most jobs.

Nature of the Work

Successful operation of an educational institution requires competent administrators. *Education administrators* provide instructional leadership and manage the day-to-day activities in schools, preschools, day care centers, and colleges and universities. They also direct the educational programs of businesses, correctional institutions, museums, and job training and community service organizations. (College presidents and school superintendents are covered in the *Handbook* statement on general managers and top executives.)

Education administrators set educational standards and goals and establish the policies and procedures required to achieve them. They also supervise managers, support staff, teachers, counselors, librarians, coaches, and other employees. They develop academic programs, monitor students' educational progress, train and motivate teachers and other staff, manage career counseling and other student services, administer recordkeeping, prepare budgets, and perform many other duties. They also handle relations with parents, prospective and current students, employers, and the community. In a smaller organization such as a small day care center, one administrator may handle all these functions. In universities or large school systems, responsibilities are divided among many administrators, each with a specific function.

Educational administrators who manage elementary, middle, and secondary schools are called *principals*. They set the academic tone and work actively with teachers to develop and maintain high curriculum standards, formulate mission statements, and establish performance goals and objectives. Principals confer with staff to advise, explain, or answer procedural questions. They hire and evaluate teachers and other staff. They visit classrooms, observe teaching methods, review instructional objectives, and examine learning materials. Principals must use clear, objective guidelines for teacher appraisals, because principals' pay often is based on performance ratings.

Principals also meet with other administrators and students, parents, and representatives of community organizations. Decisionmaking authority increasingly has shifted from school district central offices to individual schools. School principals have greater flexibility in setting school policies and goals, but when making administrative decisions, they must pay attention to the concerns of parents, teachers, and other members of the community.

Principals also are responsible for preparing budgets and reports on various subjects, such as finances, attendance and student performance. As school budgets become tighter, many principals have become more involved in public relations and fundraising to secure financial support for their schools from local businesses and the community.

Principals ensure that students meet national, State, and local academic standards. Many principals develop partnerships with local businesses and school-to-work transition programs for students. Principals must be sensitive to the needs of a rising number of non-English-speaking students and a culturally diverse student body. In some areas, growing enrollments are a cause for concern, because they lead to overcrowding at many schools. When addressing problems of inadequate resources, administrators serve as advocates for the building of new schools or the repair of existing ones. During the summer months, principals are responsible for planning for the upcoming year, overseeing summer school, participating in workshops for teachers and administrators, supervising building repairs and improvements, and working to make sure that the school has adequate staff for the upcoming school year.

Schools continue to be involved with students' emotional welfare as well as their academic achievement. As a result, principals face responsibilities outside of academics. For example, many schools have a large number of students from single-parent families, families in which both parents work outside the home or students who are teenage parents. To support these students and their families, some schools have established before- and after-school child care programs or family resource centers, which also may offer parenting classes and social service referrals. With the help of community organizations, some principals have established programs to combat increases in crime, drug and alcohol abuse, and sexually transmitted diseases among students.

Assistant principals aid the principal in the overall administration of the school. Some assistant principals hold the position for only a few years, during which time they prepare for advancement to principal; others are assistant principals throughout their careers. They are primarily responsible for scheduling student classes and ordering textbooks and supplies. They also coordinate transportation, custodial, cafeteria, and other support services. They usually handle student discipline and attendance problems, social and recreational programs, and matters of health and safety. In addition, they may counsel students on personal, educational, or vocational matters. With the advent of site-based management, assistant principals play a greater role in academic planning by helping to develop new curricula, evaluating teachers, and dealing with school-community relations—responsibilities previously assumed solely by the principal. The number of assistant principals that a school employs may vary with the number of students.

Administrators in school district central offices oversee public schools under their jurisdiction. This group of administrators includes those who direct subject-area programs such as English, music, vocational education, special education, and mathematics. They supervise instructional coordinators and curriculum specialists and work with them to evaluate curricula and teaching techniques and to develop programs and strategies to improve them. (Instructional coordinators are covered elsewhere in the *Handbook*.) Some administrators may oversee career counseling programs. Others may administer testing that measures students' abilities and helps to place them in appropriate classes. Some may direct programs such as school psychology, athletics, curriculum and instruction, and professional development. With site-based management, administrators have transferred the primary responsibility for many of these programs to the principals, assistant principals, teachers, instructional coordinators, and other staff in the schools.

In preschools and child care centers, which are usually much smaller than other educational institutions, the *director* or *supervisor* of the school or center often serves as the sole administrator. The director's or supervisor's job is similar to that of other school administrators in that he or she oversees the school's daily activities and operation, hires and develops staff, and ensures that the school meets required regulations and educational standards.

In colleges and universities, *provosts*, also known as *chief academic officers*, assist presidents, make faculty appointments and tenure decisions, develop budgets, and establish academic

Education administrators manage the day-to-day activities in schools, preschools, day care centers, and colleges and universities.

policies and programs. With the assistance of *academic deans* and *deans of faculty*, provosts also direct and coordinate the activities of deans of individual colleges and chairpersons of academic departments. Fundraising is the chief responsibility of the *director of development* and also is becoming an essential part of the job for all administrators.

College or university department heads or *chairpersons* are in charge of departments that specialize in particular fields of study, such as English, biological science, or mathematics. In addition to teaching, they coordinate schedules of classes and teaching assignments; propose budgets; recruit, interview, and hire applicants for teaching positions; evaluate faculty members; encourage faculty development; serve on committees; and perform other administrative duties. In overseeing their departments, chairpersons must consider and balance the concerns of faculty, administrators, and students.

Higher education administrators also direct and coordinate the provision of student services. *Vice presidents of student affairs or student life, deans of students*, and *directors of student services* may direct and coordinate admissions, foreign student services, health and counseling services, career services, financial aid, and housing and residential life, as well as social, recreational, and related programs. In small colleges, they may counsel students. In larger colleges and universities, separate administrators may handle each of these services. *Registrars* are custodians of students' records. They register students, record grades, prepare student transcripts, evaluate academic records, assess and collect tuition and fees, plan and implement commencement exercises, oversee the preparation of college catalogs and schedules of classes, and analyze enrollment and demographic statistics. *Directors of admissions* manage the process of recruiting, evaluating, and admitting students, and work closely with *financial aid directors*, who oversee scholarship, fellowship, and loan programs. Registrars and admissions officers at most institutions need computer skills because they use electronic student information systems. For example, for those whose institutions present college catalogs, schedules, and other information on the Internet, knowledge of online resources, imaging, and other computer skills is important. *Athletic directors* plan and direct intramural and intercollegiate athletic activities, overseeing the publicity for athletic events, preparing budgets, and supervising coaches. Other increasingly important administrators direct public relations, distance learning, and technology.

Work environment. Education administrators hold leadership positions with significant responsibility. Most find working with students extremely rewarding, but as the responsibilities of administrators have increased in recent years, so has the stress. Coordinating and interacting with faculty, parents, students, community members, business leaders, and State and local policymakers can be fast paced and stimulating, but also stressful and demanding. Principals and assistant principals, whose duties include disciplining students, may find working with difficult students challenging. They also are increasingly being held accountable for their schools meeting State and Federal guidelines for student performance and teacher qualifications.

About 35 percent of education administrators worked more than 40 hours a week in 2008; they often supervise school ac-

tivities at night and on weekends. Most administrators work year round, although some work only during the academic year.

Training, Other Qualifications, and Advancement

Most education administrators begin their careers as teachers and prepare for advancement into education administration by completing a master's or doctoral degree. Because of the diversity of duties and levels of responsibility, educational backgrounds and experience vary considerably among these workers.

Education and training. Principals, assistant principals, central office administrators, academic deans, and preschool directors usually have held teaching positions before moving into administration. Some teachers move directly into principal positions; others first become assistant principals or gain experience in other administrative jobs at either the school or district level in positions such as department head, curriculum specialist, or subject matter advisor.

In most public schools, principals, assistant principals, and school district administrators need a master's degree in education administration or educational leadership. Some principals and central office administrators have a doctorate or specialized degree in education administration. In private schools, some principals and assistant principals hold only a bachelor's degree, but the majority of principals have a master's or doctoral degree.

Educational requirements for administrators of preschools and child care centers vary with the setting of the program and the State of employment. Administrators who oversee preschool programs in public schools often are required to have at least a bachelor's degree. Child care directors who supervise private programs typically are not required to have a degree; however, most States require a preschool education credential, which often includes some postsecondary coursework.

College and university academic deans and chairpersons usually advance from professorships in their departments, for which they need a master's or doctoral degree; further education is not typically necessary. Admissions, student affairs, and financial aid directors and registrars sometimes start in related staff jobs with bachelor's degrees—any field usually is acceptable—and obtain advanced degrees in college student affairs, counseling, or higher education administration. A Ph.D. or Ed.D. usually is necessary for top student affairs positions. Computer literacy and a background in accounting or statistics may be assets in admissions, records, and financial work.

Advanced degrees in higher education administration, educational leadership, and college student affairs are offered in many colleges and universities. Education administration degree programs include courses in school leadership, school law, school finance and budgeting, curriculum development and evaluation, research design and data analysis, community relations, politics in education, and counseling. The National Council for Accreditation of Teacher Education (NCATE) and the Educational Leadership Constituent Council (ELCC) accredit programs designed for elementary and secondary school administrators. Although completion of an accredited program is not required, it may assist in fulfilling licensure requirements.

Licensure and certification. Most States require principals to be licensed as school administrators. License requirements vary by State, but nearly all States require either a master's degree or some other graduate-level training. Some States also require candidates for licensure to pass a test. On-the-job training, often with a mentor, is increasingly required or recommended for new school leaders. Some States require administrators to take continuing education courses to keep their license, thus ensuring that administrators have the most up-to-date skills. The number and types of courses required to maintain licensure vary by State. Principals in private schools are not subject to State licensure requirements.

Nearly all States require child care and preschool center directors to be licensed. Licensing usually requires a number of years of experience or hours of coursework or both. Sometimes, it requires a college degree. Often, directors also are required to earn a general preschool education credential, such as the Child Development Associate credential (CDA) sponsored by the Council for Professional Recognition, or some other credential designed specifically for directors. One credential designed specifically for directors is the National Administration Credential, offered by the National Child Care Association. The credential requires experience and training in child care center management.

There usually are no licensing requirements for administrators at postsecondary institutions.

Other qualifications. To be considered for education administrator positions, workers must first prove themselves in their current jobs. In evaluating candidates, supervisors look for leadership, determination, confidence, innovativeness, and motivation. The ability to make sound decisions and to organize and coordinate work efficiently is essential. Because much of an administrator's job involves interacting with others, a person in such a position must have strong interpersonal skills and be an effective communicator and motivator. Knowledge of leadership principles and practices, gained through work experience and formal education, is important. A familiarity with computer technology is a necessity for many of these workers as computers are used to perform their basic job duties and they may be responsible for coordinating technical resources for students, teachers, and classrooms.

Advancement. Education administrators advance through promotion to higher level administrative positions or by transferring to comparable positions at larger schools or systems.

They also may become superintendents of school systems or presidents of educational institutions.

Employment

Education administrators held about 445,400 jobs in 2008. Of these, about 58,900 were held by preschool or child care administrators, about 230,600 by elementary or secondary school administrators, and 124,600 by postsecondary administrators. The great majority—more than 81 percent—worked in public or private educational institutions. Most of the remainder worked in child day care centers.

Job Outlook

Employment is projected to grow about as fast as the average for all occupations. Job opportunities should be excellent due to a large number of expected retirements and fewer applicants for some positions.

Employment change. Employment of education administrators is expected to grow by about 8 percent between 2008 and 2018, which is about as fast as the average for all occupations. Expected growth is primarily the result of growth in enrollments of school-aged children. Enrollment of students in elementary and secondary schools is expected to grow relatively slowly over the next decade, limiting the growth of principals and other administrators in these schools. However, the number of administrative positions will continue to increase as more administrative responsibilities are placed on individual schools, particularly with regard to monitoring student achievement. Preschool and child care center administrators are expected to experience substantial growth because of increasing enrollments in formal child care programs as fewer young children are cared for in private homes. In addition, as more States implement or expand public preschool programs, more preschool directors will be needed.

The number of students at the postsecondary level is projected to grow more rapidly than other student populations. Many of these schools cater to working adults who might not ordinarily participate in postsecondary education. Such schools allow students to earn a degree, receive job-specific training, or update their skills in a convenient manner, such as through part-time programs or distance learning. As the number of these schools continues to grow, more administrators will be needed to oversee them.

Job prospects. Job opportunities should be excellent due to a large number of expected retirements and fewer applicants for some positions. Principals and assistant principals should have

Projections data from the National Employment Matrix

Occupational Title	SOC Code	Employment, 2008	Projected Employment, 2018	Change, 2008-2018	
				Number	Percent
Education administrators	11-9030	445,400	482,500	37,000	8
Education administrators, preschool and child care center/ program...	11-9031	58,900	65,800	6,900	12
Education administrators, elementary and secondary school	11-9032	230,600	250,400	19,800	9
Education administrators, postsecondary....................................	11-9033	124,600	127,400	2,800	2
Education administrators, all other...	11-9039	31,400	38,900	7,500	24

(NOTE) Data in this table are rounded. See the discussion of the employment projections table in the *Handbook* introductory chapter on *Occupational Information Included in the Handbook.*

excellent job prospects because a sharp increase in responsibilities in recent years has made the job more stressful and has discouraged some teachers from taking positions in administration. Principals are now being held more accountable for the performance of students and teachers, while at the same time they are required to adhere to a growing number of government regulations. In addition, overcrowded classrooms, safety issues, budgetary concerns, and teacher shortages in some areas are creating additional stress for administrators. Many teachers feel that the increase in pay for becoming an administrator is not high enough to compensate for the greater responsibilities.

Opportunities may vary by region of the country. Enrollments are expected to increase the fastest in the West and South, where the population is growing faster, and to decline or remain stable in the Northeast and the Midwest. School administrators also are in greater demand in rural and urban areas, where pay is generally lower than in the suburbs.

Fewer applicants are expected for nonacademic administrative jobs, such as director of admissions or director of student affairs. Furthermore, many people are discouraged from seeking administrator jobs by the requirement that they have a master's or doctoral degree in education administration—as well as by the opportunity to earn higher salaries in other occupations.

Earnings

In May 2008, preschool and child care program administrators had median annual wages of $39,940. The middle 50 percent earned between $31,290 and $54,680. The lowest 10 percent earned less than $25,910 and the highest 10 percent earned more than $77,150.

In May 2008, elementary and secondary school administrators had median annual wages of $83,880. The middle 50 percent earned between $68,360 and $102,830. The lowest 10 percent earned less than $55,580 and the highest 10 percent earned more than $124,250.

In May 2008, postsecondary school administrators had median annual wages of $80,670. The middle 50 percent earned between $58,940 and $113,860. The lowest 10 percent earned less than $45,050 and the highest 10 percent earned more than $160,500.

Salaries of education administrators depend on several factors, including the location and enrollment level of the school or school district.

According to a survey of public schools conducted by Educational Research Service, average salaries for principals and assistant principals in the 2007-2008 school year were as follows:

Principals:
Senior high school $97,486
Jr. high/middle school 91,334
Elementary school..85,907

Assistant principals:
Senior high school..79,391
Jr. high/middle school 76,053
Elementary school...71,192

According to the College and University Professional Association for Human Resources, median annual salaries for selected administrators in higher education during the 2008–2009 school year were as follows:

Chief academic officer $158,000

Academic deans:
Business...150,000
Arts and sciences..134,632
Graduate programs..130,000
Education..128,550
Nursing..125,400
Health-related professions..120,980
Continuing education 109,925
Occupational studies/vocational education 92,622

Other administrators:
Chief development officer 141,712
Dean of students...88,280
Director, student financial aid 74,261
Registrar 71,764
Director, student activities..54,931

Benefits for education administrators are generally very good. Many get 4 or 5 weeks of vacation every year and have generous health and pension packages. Many colleges and universities offer free tuition to employees and their families.

Related Occupations

Education administrators apply organizational and leadership skills to provide services to individuals. Workers in related occupations include:

Education administrators also work with students and have backgrounds similar to those of :

Sources of Additional Information

For information on principals, contact:
➤ The National Association of Elementary School Principals, 1615 Duke St., Alexandria, VA 22314-3483. Internet: **http://www.naesp.org**

➤ The National Association of Secondary School Principals, 1904 Association Dr., Reston, VA 20191-1537. Internet: **http://www.nassp.org**

For a list of nationally recognized programs in elementary and secondary educational administration, contact:

➤ The Educational Leadership Constituent Council, 1904 Association Dr., Reston, VA 20191. Internet: **http://www.npbea.org/ncate.php**

For information on collegiate registrars and admissions officers, contact:

➤ American Association of Collegiate Registrars and Admissions Officers, One Dupont Circle NW., Suite 520, Washington, DC 20036-1171. Internet: **http://www.aacrao.org**

For information on professional development and graduate programs for college student affairs administrators, contact:

➤ NASPA, Student Affairs Administrators in Higher Education, 1875 Connecticut Ave. NW., Suite 418, Washington, DC 20009. Internet: **http://www.naspa.org**

For information on the National Administrator Credential for child care directors, contact:

➤ National Child Care Association, 1325 G St. NW., Suite 500, Washington, DC 20005. Internet: **http://www.nccanet.org**

For information on the Child Development Associate Credential, contact:

➤ Council for Professional Recognition, 2460 16th St. NW., Washington, DC 20009. Internet: **http://www.cdacouncil.org**

The Occupational Information Network (O*NET) provides information on a wide range of occupational characteristics. Links to O*NET appear at the end of the Internet version of this occupational statement, accessible at **http://www.bls.gov/ooh/ocos007.htm**

Engineering and Natural Sciences Managers

Significant Points

- Most engineering and natural sciences managers have formal education and work experience as engineers, scientists, or mathematicians.

- Opportunities will be best for scientists and engineers with strong communication and business management skills.

- Thirty-six percent of jobs are in manufacturing industries, and 33 percent are in professional, scientific, and technical services.

Nature of the Work

Engineering and natural sciences managers plan, coordinate, and direct research, design, and production activities. They may supervise engineers, scientists, and technicians, along with support personnel. These managers use their knowledge of engineering and natural sciences to oversee a variety of activities. They determine scientific and technical goals within broad outlines provided by top executives, who are discussed elsewhere in the *Handbook*. These goals may include improving manufacturing processes, advancing scientific research, or developing new products. Managers make detailed plans to accomplish these goals. For example, they may develop the overall concepts of a new product or identify technical problems preventing the completion of a project.

To perform effectively, these managers also must apply knowledge of administrative procedures, such as budgeting, hiring, and supervision. They propose budgets for projects and programs and determine staff, training, and equipment needs. They hire and assign scientists, engineers, and support personnel to carry out specific parts of each project. They also supervise the work of these employees, check the technical accuracy of their work and the soundness of their methods, review their output, and establish administrative procedures, policies or standards—such as environmental standards, for example.

In addition, engineering and natural science managers use communication skills extensively. They spend a great deal of time coordinating the activities of their unit with those of other units or organizations. They confer with higher levels of management; with financial, production, marketing, and other managers; and with contractors and equipment and materials suppliers.

Engineering managers may supervise people who design and develop machinery, products, systems, and processes. They might also direct and coordinate production, operations, quality assurance, testing, or maintenance in industrial plants. Many manage research and development teams that produce new products and processes or improve existing ones. Others are plant engineers, who direct and coordinate the design, installation, operation, and maintenance of equipment and machinery in industrial plants.

Natural sciences managers oversee the work of life and physical scientists, including agricultural scientists, chemists, biologists, geologists, medical scientists, and physicists. These managers direct research and development projects and coordinate activities such as testing, quality control, and production. They may work on basic research projects or on com-

In addition to technical knowledge, engineering and natural sciences managers need administrative and communication skills.

mercial activities. Science managers sometimes conduct their own research in addition to managing the work of others.

Work environment. Engineering and natural sciences managers spend most of their time in an office. Some managers, however, also may work in laboratories, where they may be exposed to the same conditions as research scientists, or in industrial plants, where they may be exposed to the same conditions as production workers. Managers tend to work long hours in order to meet project deadlines; in 2008, almost half worked over 40 hours per week. They may also experience considerable pressure to meet technical or scientific goals on a short deadline or within a tight budget.

Training, Other Qualifications, and Advancement

Strong technical knowledge is essential for engineering and natural sciences managers, who must understand and guide the work of their subordinates and explain the work in nontechnical terms to senior management and potential customers. Therefore, most managers have formal education and work experience as an engineer, scientist, or mathematician.

Education and training. Engineering and natural sciences managers usually advance to management positions after years of employment as engineers or scientists. Nearly all engineering managers therefore have at least a bachelor's degree in some specialty of engineering. Many also gain business management skills by completing a master's degree in engineering management (MEM) or business administration (MBA), either before or after advancing to management positions. Employers often pay for such training. In large firms, some courses required in these degree programs may be offered onsite. Typically, engineers who prefer to manage in technical areas pursue an MEM, and those interested in less technical management earn an MBA.

Similarly, since most science managers begin their careers as scientists, they may have a bachelor's, master's or Ph.D. degree in a scientific discipline. Graduate programs allow scientists to augment their undergraduate training with instruction in other fields, such as management or computer technology. Future natural science managers interested in more technical management may earn traditional master's or Ph.D. degrees in natural sciences or master's degrees in science that incorporate business management skills. Those interested in more general management may pursue an MBA. Given the rapid pace of scientific developments, science managers must continuously up-- grade their knowledge.

Other qualifications. Engineering and natural sciences managers must be specialists in the work they supervise. To advance to these positions, engineers and scientists generally must gain experience and assume management responsibil-

ity. To fill management positions, employers seek engineers and scientists who possess administrative and communication skills in addition to technical knowledge in their specialty, since they must effectively lead groups and coordinate projects.

Advancement. Engineering and natural sciences managers may advance to progressively higher leadership positions within their disciplines. Some may become managers in nontechnical areas such as marketing, human resources, or sales. In high-technology firms, managers in nontechnical areas often must possess the same specialized knowledge as do managers in technical areas. For example, employers in an engineering firm may prefer to hire experienced engineers as sales workers because the complex services offered by the firm can be marketed only by someone with specialized engineering knowledge. Such sales workers can eventually advance to jobs as sales managers.

Employment

Engineering and natural sciences managers held about 228,700 jobs in 2008. Manufacturing industries employed 36 percent of engineering and natural sciences managers. Another 33 percent worked in professional, scientific, and technical services industries, primarily for firms providing architectural, engineering, and related services, and scientific research and development services. Other large employers include Federal, State, and local government agencies.

Job Outlook

Employment of engineering and natural sciences managers is projected to grow as fast as the average for all occupations. Opportunities will be best for engineers and scientists with strong communication and business management skills.

Employment change. Employment of engineering and natural sciences managers is expected to grow 8 percent over the 2008–18 decade, as fast as the average for all occupations. Employment growth should be affected by many of the same factors that affect the growth of the engineers and scientists that these managers supervise. However, job growth for managers will be somewhat slower than for engineers and scientists because the increasing tendency to outsource research and development to specialized engineering and scientific research services firms will lead to some consolidation of management.

Job prospects. Opportunities for engineering managers should be better in rapidly growing areas of engineering, such as environmental and biomedical engineering, than in more slowly growing areas, such as electrical and mechanical engineering. Opportunities for natural sciences managers should be best in the rapidly growing medical and environmental sci-

Projections data from the National Employment Matrix

Occupational Title	SOC Code	Employment, 2008	Projected Employment, 2018	Change, 2008-2018	
				Number	Percent
Engineering and natural sciences managers	–	228,700	246,900	18,200	8
Engineering managers...	11-9041	184,000	195,400	11,300	6
Natural sciences managers..	11-9121	44,600	51,500	6,900	15

(NOTE) Data in this table are rounded. See the discussion of the employment projections table in the *Handbook* introductory chapter on *Occupational Information Included in the Handbook.*

ences. (See the statements on engineers and life and physical scientists elsewhere in the *Handbook*.) Engineers and scientists with advanced technical knowledge and strong communication skills will be in the best position to become managers. Because engineering and natural sciences managers are involved in the financial, production, and marketing activities of their firm, business management skills are also advantageous for those seeking management positions. In addition to those openings resulting from employment growth, job openings will result from the need to replace managers who retire or move into other occupations.

Earnings

Earnings for engineering and natural sciences managers vary by specialty and by level of responsibility. Median annual wages of engineering managers were $115,270 in May 2008. The middle 50 percent earned between $91,870 and $141,730. Median annual wages in the industries employing the largest numbers of engineering managers were:

Scientific research and development services $141,030
Navigational, measuring, electromedical,
   and control instruments manufacturing 128,630
Semiconductor and other electronic
   component manufacturing 127,790
Aerospace product and parts manufacturing 118,430
Architectural, engineering, and related services 114,110

Median annual wages of natural sciences managers were $112,800 in May 2008. The middle 50 percent earned between $85,910 and $151,400. Median annual wages in the industries employing the largest numbers of natural sciences managers were:

Pharmaceutical and medicine manufacturing $144,640
Scientific research and development services 136,310
Federal Executive Branch 102,410
Architectural, engineering, and related services 98,980
State government 69,220

In addition, engineering and natural sciences managers, especially those at higher levels, often receive more benefits—such as expense accounts, stock-option plans, and bonuses—than do nonmanagerial workers in their organizations.

Related Occupations

The work of engineering and natural sciences managers is closely related to that of:

Sources of Additional Information

For information about a career as an engineering and natural sciences manager, contact the sources of additional information for engineers, life scientists, and physical scientists that are listed at the end of the statements on these occupations elsewhere in the *Handbook*.

Information on engineering management programs accredited by the Accreditation Board for Engineering and Technology is available from:
➤ ABET, Inc., 111 Market Place, Suite 1050, Baltimore, MD 21202. Internet: **http://www.abet.org**

To learn more about managing scientists and engineers in research and development, see the *Occupational Outlook Quarterly* article, "Careers for scientists—and others—in scientific research and development," online at **http://www.bls.gov/opub/ooq/2005/summer/art04.htm** and in print at many libraries and career centers.

The Occupational Information Network (O*NET) provides information on a wide range of occupational characteristics. Links to O*NET appear at the end of the Internet version of this occupational statement, accessible at **http://www.bls.gov/ooh/ocos009.htm**

Farmers, Ranchers, and Agricultural Managers

Significant Points

- Modern farming requires knowledge of new developments in agriculture, often gained through growing up on a farm or through postsecondary education.

- Overall employment is projected to decline because of increasing productivity and consolidation of farms.

- Small-scale, local farming, particularly horticulture and organic farming, offer the best opportunities for entering the occupation.

Nature of the Work

American farmers, ranchers, and agricultural managers direct the activities of one of the world's largest and most productive agricultural sectors. They produce enough food and fiber to meet the needs of the United States and for export. *Farmers and ranchers* own and operate mainly family-owned farms. They also may lease land from a landowner and operate it as a working farm. *Agricultural managers* manage the day-to-day activities of one or more farms, ranches, nurseries, timber tracts, greenhouses, or other agricultural establishments for farmers, absentee landowners, or corporations. While their duties and responsibilities vary widely, all farmers, ranchers, and agricultural managers focus on the business aspects of running a farm. On small farms, they may oversee the entire operation; on larger farms, they may oversee a single activity, such as marketing.

Farm output and income are strongly influenced by the weather, disease, fluctuations in prices of domestic farm products, and Federal farm programs. In crop-production operations, farmers and managers usually determine the best time to plant seed, apply fertilizer and chemicals, and harvest and market the crops. Many carefully plan the combination of crops they grow, so that if the price of one crop drops, they will have sufficient income from another crop to make up the loss. Farmers, ranchers, and managers monitor the constantly changing prices for their products. They use different strategies to protect themselves from unpredictable changes in the markets for agricultural products. If they plan ahead, they may be able to store their crops or keep their livestock to take advantage of higher prices later in the year. Those who participate in the futures market enter contracts on future delivery of agricultural goods. These contracts can minimize the risk of sudden price changes by guaranteeing a certain price for farmers' and ranchers' agricultural goods when they are ready to sell.

While most farm output is sold to food-processing companies, some farmers—particularly operators of smaller farms—may choose to sell their goods directly to consumers through farmers' markets. Some use cooperatives to reduce their financial risk and to gain a larger share of the prices consumers pay. For example, in community-supported agriculture, cooperatives sell shares of a harvest to consumers prior to the planting season. This frees the farmer from having to bear all the financial risks and ensures a market for the produce of the coming season. Farmers, ranchers, and agricultural managers also negotiate with banks and other credit lenders to get the best financing deals for their equipment, livestock, and seed.

Like other businesses, farming operations have become more complex in recent years, so many farmers use computers to keep financial and inventory records. They also use computer databases and spreadsheets to manage breeding, dairy, and other farm operations.

The type of farm managers operate determines their specific tasks. On crop farms—farms growing grain, cotton, other fibers, fruit, and vegetables—farmers are responsible for preparing, tilling, planting, fertilizing, cultivating, spraying, and harvesting. After the harvest, they make sure that the crops are properly packaged, stored, and marketed. Livestock, dairy, and poultry farmers and ranchers feed and care for animals and keep barns, pens, coops, and other farm buildings clean and in good condition. They also plan and oversee breeding and marketing activities. Both farmers and ranchers operate machinery and maintain equipment and facilities, and both track technological improvements in animal breeding and seeds, and choose new or existing products.

The size of the farm or ranch often determines which of these tasks farmers and ranchers handle themselves. Operators of small farms usually perform all tasks, physical and administrative. They keep records for management and tax purposes, service machinery, maintain buildings, and grow vegetables and raise animals. Operators of large farms, by contrast, have employees who help with the physical work. Although employment on most farms is limited to the farmer and one or two family workers or hired employees, some large farms have 100 or more full-time and seasonal workers. Some of these employees are in nonfarm occupations, working as truck drivers, sales representatives, bookkeepers, and computer specialists.

Agricultural managers usually do not plant, harvest, or perform other production activities; instead, they hire and supervise farm and livestock workers, who perform most daily production tasks. Managers may establish output goals; determine financial constraints; monitor production and marketing; hire, assign, and supervise workers; determine crop transportation and storage requirements; and oversee maintenance of the property and equipment.

Horticultural specialty farmers oversee the production of fruits, vegetables, flowers, and ornamental plants used in landscaping, including turf. They also grow nuts, berries, and grapes for wine. *Aquaculture farmers* raise fish and shellfish in marine, brackish, or fresh water, usually in ponds, floating net pens, raceways, or recirculating systems. They stock, feed, protect, and otherwise manage aquatic life sold for consumption or used for recreational fishing.

Work environment.   Farmers and farm managers on crop farms usually work from sunrise to sunset during the planting and harvesting seasons. The rest of the year, they plan next season's crops, market their output, and repair machinery.

On livestock-producing farms and ranches, work goes on throughout the year. Animals, unless they are grazing, must be fed and watered every day, and dairy cows must be milked two or three times a day. Many livestock and dairy farmers monitor and attend to the health of their herds, which may include assisting in the birthing of animals. Such farmers and farm managers rarely get the chance to get away, unless they hire an assistant or arrange for a temporary substitute.

Farmers and farm managers who grow produce and perishables have different demands on their time depending on the crop grown and the season. They may work very long hours during planting and harvesting season, but shorter hours at other times. Some farmers maintain cover crops during the cold months, which keep them busy beyond the typical growing season.

On very large farms, farmers and farm managers spend substantial time meeting farm supervisors in charge of various activities. Professional farm managers overseeing several farms may divide their time between traveling to meet farmers or

A farmer bails hay for feeding cows during the winter.

landowners and planning the farm operations in their offices. As farming practices and agricultural technology become more sophisticated, farmers and farm managers are spending more time in offices and on computers, where they electronically manage many aspects of their businesses. Some farmers also attend conferences exchanging information, particularly during the winter months.

Farm work can be hazardous. Tractors and other farm machinery can cause serious injury, and workers must be constantly alert on the job. The proper operation of equipment and handling of chemicals are necessary to avoid accidents, safeguard health, and protect the environment.

Training, Other Qualifications, and Advancement

Experience gained from growing up on or working on a family farm is the most common way farmers learn their trade. However, modern farming requires making increasingly complex scientific, business, and financial decisions, so postsecondary education in agriculture is important, even for people who were raised on farms.

Education and training. Most farmers receive their training on the job, often by being raised on a farm. However, the completion of a 2-year associate degree or a 4-year bachelor's degree at a college of agriculture is becoming increasingly important for farm managers and for farmers and ranchers who expect to make a living at farming.

Students should select the college most appropriate to their interests and location. All State university systems have at least one land-grant college or university with a school of agriculture. Common programs of study include business with a concentration in agriculture, farm management, agronomy, dairy science, agricultural economics and business, horticulture, crop and fruit science, and animal science. For students interested in aquaculture, formal programs are available and include coursework in fisheries biology, fish culture, hatchery management and maintenance, and hydrology.

Agricultural colleges teach technical knowledge of crops, growing conditions, and plant diseases. They also teach prospective ranchers and dairy farmers the basics of veterinary science and animal husbandry. Students also study how the environment is affected by farm operations, such as the impact of various pesticides on local animals.

New farmers, ranchers, and agricultural managers often spend time working under an experienced farmer to learn how to apply the skills learned through academic training. Those without academic training often take many years to learn how weather, fertilizers, seed, feeding or breeding affect the growth of crops or the raising of animals in addition to other aspects of farming. A small number of farms offer formal apprenticeships to help young people learn the practical skills of farming and ranching.

Other qualifications. Farmers, ranchers, and agricultural managers need managerial skills to organize and operate a business. A basic knowledge of accounting and bookkeeping is essential in keeping financial records, and knowledge of credit sources is vital for buying seed, fertilizer, and other needed inputs. Workers must also be familiar with safety regulations and requirements of governmental agricultural support programs. Computer skills are becoming increasingly important,

especially on large farms, where they are widely used for recordkeeping and business analysis. In addition, skills in personnel management, communication, and conflict resolution are important in the operation of a farm or ranch business.

Mechanical aptitude and the ability to work with tools of all kinds also are valuable skills for a small-farm operator, who often maintains and repairs machinery or farm structures.

Certification and advancement. Because of rapid changes in the industry, farmers, ranchers, and agricultural managers need to stay informed about continuing advances in agricultural methods, both in the United States and abroad. They need to monitor changes in governmental regulations that may affect production methods or markets for particular crops. Agricultural managers can enhance their professional status through voluntary certification as an Accredited Farm Manager (AFM) by the American Society of Farm Managers and Rural Appraisers. Accreditation requires several years of farm management experience, the appropriate academic background—a bachelor's degree or, preferably, a master's degree in a field of agricultural science—and passing courses and examinations related to the business, financial, and legal aspects of farm and ranch management.

Employment

Farmers, ranchers, and agricultural managers held more than 1.2 million jobs in 2008. Nearly 80 percent were self-employed farmers and ranchers, and the remainder were wage and salary agricultural managers. Most farmers, ranchers, and agricultural managers oversee crop production activities, while others manage livestock and dairy production.

The soil, topography of the land, and climate often determine the type of farming and ranching done in a particular area. California, Texas, Iowa, Nebraska, and Minnesota are the leading agricultural States in terms of agricultural output measured in dollars. Texas, Missouri, Iowa, Oklahoma, and Kentucky are the leading agricultural States in terms of numbers of farms.

Job Outlook

Overall employment is projected to decline, reflecting the decline of self-employed farmers because of the consolidation of farms and increasing productivity; however, employment of salaried agricultural managers is expected to increase.

Employment change. Employment of self-employed farmers is expected to decline moderately by 8 percent over the 2008–18 decade. The continuing ability of the agriculture sector to produce more with fewer workers will cause some farmers to go out of business as market pressures leave little room for the marginally successful farmer. As land, machinery, seed, and chemicals become more expensive, only well-capitalized farmers and corporations will be able to buy many of the farms that become available. These larger, more productive farms are better able to withstand the adverse effects of climate and price fluctuations on farm output and income. Larger farms also have advantages in obtaining government subsidies and payments because these payments are usually based on acreage owned and per-unit production.

In contrast, agricultural managers are projected to gain jobs, growing by about 6 percent, slower than the average for all occupations. Owners of large tracts of land, who often do not live

Projections data from the National Employment Matrix

Occupational Title	SOC Code	Employment, 2008	Projected Employment, 2018	Change, 2008-2018	
				Number	Percent
Agricultural managers..	11-9010	1,234,000	1,169,400	-64,600	-5
Farm, ranch, and other agricultural managers.............................	11-9011	248,100	262,700	14,600	6
Farmers and ranchers	11-9012	985,900	906,700	-79,200	-8

(NOTE) Data in this table are rounded. See the discussion of the employment projections table in the *Handbook* introductory chapter on *Occupational Information Included in the Handbook.*

on the property they own, increasingly will seek the expertise of agricultural managers to run their farms and ranches in a business-like manner.

Despite the expected continued consolidation of farmland and the projected decline in overall employment of this occupation, an increasing number of small-scale farmers have developed successful market niches that involve personalized, direct contact with their customers. Many are finding opportunities in horticulture and organic food production, which are among the fastest growing segments of agriculture. Others use farmers' markets that cater directly to urban and suburban consumers, allowing the farmers to capture a greater share of consumers' food dollars. Some small-scale farmers belong to collectively owned marketing cooperatives that process and sell their product. Other farmers participate in community-supported agriculture cooperatives that allow consumers to buy a share of the farmer's harvest directly.

Job prospects. Fewer jobs are expected for farmers and ranchers than in the past; better prospects are expected for wage and salary agricultural managers. Small-scale, local farming, particularly horticulture and organic farming, offer the best opportunities for entering the occupation. With fewer people wanting to become farmers and a large number of farmers expected to retire or give up their farms in the next decade, there will be some opportunities to own or lease a farm. Additionally, the market for agricultural products is projected to be good for most products over the next decade, so many farmers who retire will need to be replaced. Farmers who grow crops used in landscaping, such as trees, shrubs, turf, and other ornamentals, also will have better job prospects, as people put more money into landscaping their homes and businesses.

Some private organizations are helping to make farmland available and affordable for new farmers through a variety of institutional innovations. Land Link programs, coordinated by the International Farm Transition Network, operate in 20 States. They help match up young farmers with farmers approaching retirement so that arrangements can be made to pass along their land to young farmers wishing to keep the land under cultivation. Often beginning farmers lease some or all of their farmland. Sometimes, a new farmer will work on a farm for a few years, while the farm owner gradually transfers ownership to the new farmer.

Earnings

Incomes of farmers and ranchers vary greatly from year to year, because prices of farm products fluctuate with weather conditions and other factors that influence the quantity and quality of farm output and the demand for those products. In addition to farm business income, farmers often receive government subsidies or other payments that supplement their incomes and

reduce some of the risk of farming. Many farmers—primarily operators of small farms—have recently been relying more and more on off-farm sources of income.

Full-time, salaried agricultural managers had median weekly earnings of $775 in 2008. The middle half earned between $570 and $1,269 per week. The lowest paid 10 percent earned less than $358, and the highest paid 10 percent earned more than $1,735 per week.

Self-employed farmers must procure their own health and life insurance. As members of farm organizations, they may receive group discounts on health and life insurance premiums.

Related Occupations

Farmers, ranchers, and agricultural managers strive to improve the quality of agricultural products and the efficiency of farms. Others whose work relates to agriculture include:

	Page
Agricultural and food scientists	177
Agricultural inspectors...	612
Agricultural workers, other...	609
Engineers..	161
Farm and home management advisors.....................................	824
Purchasing managers, buyers, and purchasing agents	79

Sources of Additional Information

For general information about farming and agricultural occupations, contact:

➤ National FFA Organization, Attention: Career Information Requests, P.O. Box 68690, Indianapolis, IN 46268-0960. Internet: **http://www.ffa.org**

For information about certification as an accredited farm manager, contact:

➤ American Society of Farm Managers and Rural Appraisers, 950 Cherry St., Suite 508, Denver, CO 80246- 2664. Internet: **http://www.asfmra.org**

For information on the USDA's program to help small farmers get started, contact:

➤ Small Farm Program, U.S. Department of Agriculture, National Institute of Food and Agriculture, 1400 Independence Avenue SW, Stop 2201, Washington, DC 20250-2201. Internet: **http://www.csrees.usda.gov/smallfarms.cfm**

For information on Land Link Programs, contact:

➤ The Beginning Farm Center, 10861 Douglas Avenue, Suite B, Urbandale, IA 50322-2042. Internet: **http://www.farmtransition.org/netwpart.html**

➤ Center for Rural Affairs, 145 Main Street PO Box 136, Lyons, NE 68038-2677. Internet: **http://www.cfra.org/resources/beginning_farmer**

For information on organic farming, horticulture, and internships, contact:

➤ Alternative Farming System Information Center, NAL, 10301 Baltimore Ave., Room 132, Beltsville, MD 20705-2326. Internet: **http://www.nal.usda.gov**

➤ ATTRA, National Sustainable Agriculture Information Service, P.O. Box 3657, Fayetteville, AR 72702-3657. Internet: **http://www.attra.ncat.org**

The Occupational Information Network (O*NET) provides information on a wide range of occupational characteristics. Links to O*NET appear at the end of the Internet version of this occupational statement, accessible at **http://www.bls.gov/ooh/ocos176.htm**

Financial Managers

Significant Points

- Jobseekers are likely to face competition.

- About 3 out of 10 work in finance and insurance industries.

- Most financial managers need a bachelor's degree, and many have a master's degree or professional certification.

- Experience may be more important than formal education for some financial manager positions—most notably, branch managers in banks.

Nature of the Work
Almost every firm, government agency, and other type of organization employs one or more financial managers. *Financial managers* oversee the preparation of financial reports, direct investment activities, and implement cash management strategies. Managers also develop strategies and implement the long-term goals of their organization.

The duties of financial managers vary with their specific titles, which include controller, treasurer or finance officer, credit manager, cash manager, risk and insurance manager, and manager of international banking. *Controllers* direct the preparation of financial reports, such as income statements, balance sheets, and analyses of future earnings or expenses, that summarize and forecast the organization's financial position. Controllers also are in charge of preparing special reports required by regulatory authorities. Often, controllers oversee the accounting, audit, and budget departments. *Treasurers* and *finance officers* direct their organization's budgets to meet its financial goals. They oversee the investment of funds, manage associated risks, supervise cash management activities, execute capital-raising strategies to support the firm's expansion, and deal with mergers and acquisitions. *Credit managers* oversee the firm's issuance of credit, establishing credit-rating criteria, determining credit ceilings, and monitoring the collections of past-due accounts.

Cash managers monitor and control the flow of cash receipts and disbursements to meet the business and investment needs of their firm. For example, cash flow projections are needed to determine whether loans must be obtained to meet cash requirements or whether surplus cash can be invested. *Risk and insurance managers* oversee programs to minimize risks and losses that might arise from financial transactions and business operations. Insurance managers decide how best to limit a company's losses by obtaining insurance against risks such as the need to make disability payments for an employee who gets hurt on the job or costs imposed by a lawsuit against the company. Risk managers control financial risk by using hedging and other techniques to limit a company's exposure to currency or commodity price changes. Managers specializing in international finance develop financial and accounting systems for the banking transactions of multinational organizations. Risk managers are also responsible for calculating and limiting potential operations risk. Operations risk includes a wide range of risks, such as a rogue employee damaging the company's finances or a hurricane damaging an important factory. (Chief financial officers and other executives are included with top executives elsewhere in the *Handbook*.)

Financial institutions—such as commercial banks, savings and loan associations, credit unions, and mortgage and finance companies—employ additional financial managers who oversee various functions, such as lending, trusts, mortgages, and investments, or programs, including sales, operations, or electronic financial services. These managers may solicit business, authorize loans, and direct the investment of funds, always adhering to Federal and State laws and regulations.

Branch managers of financial institutions administer and manage all of the functions of a branch office. Job duties may include hiring personnel, approving loans and lines of credit, establishing a rapport with the community to attract business, and assisting customers with account problems. Branch mangers also are becoming more oriented toward sales and marketing. As a result, it is important that they have substantial knowledge about the types of products that the bank sells. Financial managers who work for financial institutions must keep abreast of the rapidly growing array of financial services and products.

In addition to the preceding duties, financial managers perform tasks unique to their organization or industry. For example, government financial managers must be experts on the government appropriations and budgeting processes, whereas healthcare financial managers must be knowledgeable about issues surrounding health care financing. Moreover, financial managers must be aware of special tax laws and regulations that affect their industry.

Financial managers play an important role in mergers and consolidations and in global expansion and related financing. These areas require extensive, specialized knowledge to reduce risks and maximize profit. Financial managers increasingly are hired on a temporary basis to advise senior managers on these and other matters. In fact, some small firms contract out all their accounting and financial functions to companies that provide such services.

The role of the financial manager, particularly in business, is changing in response to technological advances that have sig-

Financial managers oversee the preparation of financial reports and investment activities.

nificantly reduced the amount of time it takes to produce financial reports. Technological improvements have made it easier to produce financial reports, and, as a consequence, financial managers now perform more data analysis that allows them to offer senior managers profit-maximizing ideas. They often work on teams, acting as business advisors to top management.

Work environment. Working in comfortable offices, often close to top managers and with departments that develop the financial data those managers need, financial managers typically have direct access to state-of-the-art computer systems and information services. They commonly work long hours, often up to 50 or 60 per week. Financial managers generally are required to attend meetings of financial and economic associations and may travel to visit subsidiary firms or to meet customers.

Training, Other Qualifications, and Advancement

Most financial managers need a bachelor's degree, and many have a master's degree or professional certification. Bank managers often have experience as loan officers or in other sales positions. Financial managers also need strong interpersonal, math, and business skills.

Education and training. A bachelor's degree in finance, accounting, economics, or business administration is the minimum academic preparation for financial managers. However,

many employers now seek graduates with a master's degree, preferably in business administration, finance, or economics. These academic programs develop analytical skills and teach financial analysis methods and technology.

Experience may be more important than formal education for some financial manager positions—most notably, branch managers in banks. Banks typically fill branch manager positions by promoting experienced loan officers and other professionals who excel at their jobs. Other financial managers may enter the profession through formal management training programs offered by the company.

Licensure. Many financial managers work in accounting departments. Accounting positions normally require workers to be certified public accountants (CPAs). (See the statement on accountants and auditors elsewhere in the *Handbook*.)

Other qualifications. Candidates for financial management positions need many different skills. Interpersonal skills are important because these jobs involve managing people and working as part of a team to solve problems. Financial managers must have excellent communication skills to explain complex financial data. Because financial managers work extensively with various departments in their firm, a broad understanding of business is essential.

Financial managers should be creative thinkers and problem-solvers, applying their analytical skills to business. Financial managers must have knowledge of international finance because financial operations are increasingly being affected by the global economy. In addition, a good knowledge of regulatory compliance procedures is essential.

Certification and advancement. Financial managers may broaden their skills and exhibit their competency by attaining professional certification. Many associations offer professional certification programs. For example, the CFA Institute confers the Chartered Financial Analyst designation on investment professionals who have at least a bachelor's degree, work experience, and pass three difficult exams. The Association for Financial Professionals confers the Certified Treasury Professional credentials to those who pass a computer-based exam and have a minimum of 2 years of relevant experience. Continuing education is required to maintain these credentials. Also, financial managers who specialize in accounting or budgeting sometimes earn the Certified Management Accountant (CMA) designation. The CMA is offered by the Institute of Management Accountants to its members who have a bachelor's degree, at least 2 years of work experience, pass the institute's four-part examination, and fulfill continuing education requirements. (See accountants and auditors elsewhere in the *Handbook* for additional information on the CMA designation.)

Continuing education is vital to financial managers, who must cope with the growing complexity of global trade, changes in Federal and State laws and regulations, and the proliferation of new and complex financial instruments. Firms often provide opportunities for workers to broaden their knowledge and skills by encouraging them to take graduate courses and attend conferences related to their specialty. Financial management, banking, and credit union associations, often in cooperation with colleges and universities, sponsor numerous national and local training programs. Subjects covered by training programs include accounting management, budget management, corporate cash management, financial analysis, international banking, and information systems. Many firms pay all or part of the costs for employees who successfully complete the courses. Although experience, ability, and leadership are emphasized for promotion, advancement may be accelerated by this type of special study.

Because financial management is so important to efficient business operations, well-trained, experienced financial managers who display a strong grasp of the operations of various departments within their organization are prime candidates for promotion to top management positions. Some financial managers transfer to closely related positions in other industries. Those with extensive experience and access to sufficient capital may start their own consulting firms.

Employment

Financial managers held about 539,300 jobs in 2008. Although they can be found in every industry, approximately 31 percent were employed by finance and insurance establishments, such as banks, savings institutions, finance companies, credit unions, insurance carriers, and securities dealers. About 7 percent worked for Federal, State, or local government.

Job Outlook

Employment growth for financial managers is expected is to be as fast as the average for all occupations. However, applicants will likely face keen competition for jobs. Those with a master's degree and certification will have the best opportunities.

Employment change. Employment of financial managers over the 2008–18 decade is expected to grow by 8 percent, which is as fast as the average for all occupations. Regulatory changes and the expansion and globalization of finance and companies will increase the need for financial expertise and drive job growth. As the economy expands, both the growth of established companies and the creation of new businesses will spur demand for financial managers. Employment of bank branch managers is expected to increase because banks are creating new branches. However, mergers, acquisitions, and corporate downsizing are likely to restrict the employment growth of financial managers to some extent.

Long-run demand for financial managers in the securities and commodities industry will continue to be driven by the need to handle increasingly complex financial transactions and manage a growing amount of investments. Financial managers also will be needed to handle mergers and acquisitions, raise capital, and assess global financial transactions. Employment of risk managers, who assess risks for insurance and investment purposes, also will grow.

Some companies may hire financial managers on a temporary basis, to see the organization through a short-term crisis or to offer suggestions for boosting profits. Other companies may contract out all accounting and financial operations. Even in these cases, however, financial managers may be needed to oversee the contracts.

Job prospects. As with other managerial occupations, jobseekers are likely to face competition because the number of job openings is expected to be less than the number of applicants. Candidates with expertise in accounting and finance—particularly those with a master's degree or certification—should enjoy the best job prospects. An understanding of international finance, derivatives, and complex financial instruments is important. Excellent communication skills are essential because financial managers must explain and justify complex financial transactions.

As banks expand the range of products and services they offer to include wealth management, insurance, and investment products, branch managers with knowledge in these areas will be needed. As a result, candidates who are licensed to sell insurance or securities will have more favorable prospects. (See the *Handbook* statements on insurance sales agents; personal financial advisors; and securities, commodities, and financial services sales agents.)

Earnings

Median annual wages, excluding annual bonuses and stock options, of wage and salary financial managers were $99,330 in May 2008. The middle 50 percent earned between $72,030 and $135,070. Median annual wages in the industries employing the largest numbers of financial managers were:

Securities and commodity contracts
  intermediation and brokerage...............................$134,940
Management of companies and enterprises 115,520
Insurance carriers 110,750
Local government..78,650
Depository credit intermediation.................................77,280

Large organizations often pay more than small ones, and salary levels also can depend on the type of industry and location. Many financial managers in both public and private industry receive additional compensation in the form of bonuses which, like salaries, vary substantially by size of firm. Deferred compensation in the form of stock options is common, especially for senior-level executives.

Related Occupations

Financial managers combine formal education with experience in one or more areas of finance, such as asset management, lending, credit operations, securities investment, or insurance

Projections data from the National Employment Matrix

Occupational Title	SOC Code	Employment, 2008	Projected Employment, 2018	Change, 2008-2018	
				Number	Percent
Financial managers	11-3031	539,300	580,500	41,200	8

(NOTE) Data in this table are rounded. See the discussion of the employment projections table in the *Handbook* introductory chapter on *Occupational Information Included in the Handbook.*

risk and loss control. Workers in other occupations requiring similar training and skills include:

Sources of Additional Information

For information about careers and certification in financial management, contact:

➤ Financial Management Association International, College of Business Administration, University of South Florida, 4202 East Fowler Ave., BSN 3331, Tampa, FL 33620. Internet: **http://www.fma.org**

For information about careers in financial and treasury management and the Certified Treasury Professional program, contact:
➤ Association for Financial Professionals, 4520 East-West Hwy., Suite 750, Bethesda, MD 20814. Internet: **http://www.afponline.org**

For information about the Chartered Financial Analyst program, contact:
➤ CFA Institute, 560 Ray Hunt Dr., Charlottesville, VA 22903. Internet: **http://www.cfainstitute.org**

For information on The American Institute of Banking and its programs, contact:
➤ American Bankers Association, 1120 Connecticut Ave. NW, Washington, DC 20036. Internet: **http://www.aba.com**

For information about the Certified in Management Accounting designation, contact:
➤ Institute of Management Accountants, 10 Paragon Dr., Montvale, NJ 07645. Internet: **http://www.imanet.org**

The Occupational Information Network (O*NET) provides information on a wide range of occupational characteristics. Links to O*NET appear at the end of the Internet version of this occupational statement, accessible at **http://www.bls.gov/ooh/ocos010.htm**

Food Service Managers

Significant Points

- Although most food service managers qualify for their position based on their restaurant-related experience, an increasing number of employers prefer managers with a 2- or 4-year degree in a related field.

- Food service managers coordinate a wide range of activities, but their most difficult tasks may be dealing with irate customers and motivating employees.

- Job opportunities for food service managers should be good, as the number of managers who change jobs or leave this occupation is typically high and, in the long run, as more are hired to meet the growing demand for convenient food service.

Nature of the Work

Food service managers are responsible for the daily operations of restaurants and other establishments that prepare and serve meals and beverages to customers. Besides coordinating activities among various departments, such as kitchen, dining room, and banquet operations, food service managers ensure that customers are satisfied with their dining experience. In addition, they oversee the inventory and ordering of food, equipment, and supplies and arrange for the routine maintenance and upkeep of the restaurant's equipment and facilities. Managers are generally responsible for all administrative and human-resource functions of the business, including recruiting new employees and monitoring employee performance and training.

Managers interview, hire, train, and when necessary, fire employees. Retaining good employees is a major challenge facing food service managers. Managers recruit employees at career fairs and at schools that offer academic programs in hospitality management or culinary arts, and arrange for newspaper advertising to attract additional applicants. Managers oversee the training of new employees and explain the establishment's policies and practices. They schedule work hours, making sure that enough workers are present to cover each shift. If employees are unable to work, managers may have to call in alternates to cover for them or fill in themselves. Some managers may help with cooking, clearing tables, or other tasks when the restaurant becomes extremely busy.

Food service managers ensure that diners are served properly and in a timely manner. They investigate and resolve customers' complaints about food quality and service. They monitor orders in the kitchen to determine where backups may occur, and they work with the chef to remedy any delays in service. Managers direct the cleaning of the dining areas and the washing of tableware, kitchen utensils, and equipment to comply with company and government sanitation standards. Managers also monitor the actions of their employees and patrons on a continual basis to ensure the personal safety of everyone. They make sure that health and safety standards and local liquor regulations are obeyed.

In addition to their regular duties, food service managers perform a variety of administrative assignments, such as keeping employee work records, preparing the payroll, and completing paperwork to comply with licensing, tax, wage and hour, unemployment compensation, and Social Security laws. Some of this work may be delegated to an assistant manager or bookkeeper, or it may be contracted out, but most general managers retain responsibility for the accuracy of business records. Managers also maintain records of supply and equipment purchases and ensure that accounts with suppliers are paid.

Managers tally the cash and charge receipts received and balance them against the record of sales, securing them in a safe place. Finally, managers are responsible for locking up the establishment, checking that ovens, grills, and lights are off, and switching on alarm systems.

Technology influences the jobs of food service managers in many ways, enhancing efficiency and productivity. Many restaurants use computers and business software to place orders and track inventory and sales. They also allow food service managers to monitor expenses, employee schedules, and payroll matters more efficiently.

In most full-service restaurants and institutional food service facilities, the management team consists of a *general manager*, one or more *assistant managers*, and an *executive chef*. The executive chef is responsible for all food preparation activities, including running kitchen operations, planning menus, and maintaining quality standards for food service. In some cases, the executive chef is also the general manager or owner of the restaurant. General managers may employ several assistant managers that oversee certain areas, such as the dining or banquet rooms, or supervise different shifts of workers. In limited-service eating places, such as sandwich and coffee shops or fast-food restaurants, managers or food preparation or serving supervisors, not executive chefs, are responsible for supervising routine food preparation operations. (For additional information on these other workers, see material on top executives or on chefs, head cooks, and food preparation and serving supervisors elsewhere in the *Handbook*.)

In restaurants, mainly full-service independent ones where there are both food service managers and executive chefs, the managers often help the chefs select menu items. Managers or executive chefs at independent restaurants select menu items, taking into account the past popularity of dishes, the ability to

Food service managers ensure that food is in adequate supply and stored at the appropriate temperature.

reuse any food not served the previous day, the need for variety, and the seasonal availability of foods. Managers or executive chefs analyze the recipes of the dishes to determine food, labor, and overhead costs, work out the portion size and nutritional content of each plate, and assign prices to various menu items. Menus must be developed far enough in advance that supplies can be ordered and received in time.

Managers or executive chefs estimate food needs, place orders with distributors, and schedule the delivery of fresh food and supplies. They plan for routine services or deliveries, such as linen services or the heavy cleaning of dining rooms or kitchen equipment, to occur during slow times or when the dining room is closed. Managers also arrange for equipment maintenance and repairs, and coordinate a variety of services such as waste removal and pest control. Managers or executive chefs receive deliveries and check the contents against order records. They inspect the quality of fresh meats, poultry, fish, fruits, vegetables, and baked goods to ensure that expectations are met. They meet with representatives from restaurant supply companies and place orders to replenish stocks of tableware, linens, paper products, cleaning supplies, cooking utensils, and furniture and fixtures.

Work environment. Many food service managers work long hours—12 to 15 per day, 50 or more per week, and sometimes 7 days a week. Such schedules are common for fine dining restaurants and those, such as fast-food restaurants, that operate extended hours. Managers of institutional food service facilities, such as school, factory, or office cafeterias, work more regular hours because the operating hours of these establishments usually conform to the operating hours of the business or facility they serve. However, many managers oversee multiple locations of a chain or franchise or may be called in on short notice, making hours unpredictable.

Managers should be calm, flexible, and able to work through emergencies, such as a fire or flood, to ensure everyone's safety. They also should be able to fill in for absent workers on short notice. Managers often experience the pressures of simultaneously coordinating a wide range of activities. When problems occur, it is the manager's responsibility to resolve them with minimal disruption to customers. The job can be hectic, and dealing with irate customers or uncooperative employees can be stressful.

Managers also may experience the typical minor injuries of other restaurant workers, such as muscle aches, cuts, or burns. Although injuries generally do not require prolonged absences from work, the incidence of injuries requiring at least one day's absence from work exceeds that of about 60 percent of all occupations.

Training, Other Qualifications, and Advancement
Experience in the food services industry, whether as a cook, waiter or waitress, or counter attendant, is the most common training for food service managers. Many restaurant and food service manager positions, particularly self-service and fast-food, are filled by promoting experienced food and beverage preparation and service workers.

Education and training. Most food service managers have less than a bachelor's degree; however, some postsecondary education, including a college degree, is increasingly preferred for many food service manager positions. Many food service management companies and national or regional restaurant chains recruit management trainees from 2- and 4-year college hospitality or food service management programs, which require internships and real-life experience to graduate. While these specialized degrees are often preferred, graduates with degrees in other fields who have demonstrated experience, interest, and aptitude are also recruited.

Most restaurant chains and food service management companies have rigorous training programs for management positions. Through a combination of classroom and on-the-job training, trainees receive instruction and gain work experience in all aspects of the operation of a restaurant or institutional food service facility. Areas include food preparation, nutrition, sanitation, security, company policies and procedures, personnel management, recordkeeping, and preparation of reports. Training on the use of the restaurant's computer system is increasingly important as well. Usually, after several months of training, trainees receive their first permanent assignment as an assistant manager.

Almost 1,000 colleges and universities offer 4-year programs in restaurant and hospitality management or institutional food service management; a growing number of university programs offer graduate degrees in hospitality management or similar fields. For those not interested in pursuing a 4-year degree, community and junior colleges, technical institutes, and other institutions offer programs in the field leading to an associate degree or other formal certification.

Both 2- and 4-year programs provide instruction in subjects such as nutrition, sanitation, and food planning and preparation, as well as accounting, business law and management, and computer science. Some programs combine classroom and laboratory study with internships providing on-the-job experience. In addition, many educational institutions offer culinary programs in food preparation. Such training can lead to careers as cooks or chefs and provide a foundation for advancement to executive chef positions.

Many larger food service operations will provide or offer to pay for technical training, such as computer or business courses, so that employees can acquire the business skills necessary to read spreadsheets or understand the concepts and practices of running a business. Generally, this requires a long-term commitment on the employee's part to both the employer and to the profession.

Other qualifications.   Most employers emphasize personal qualities when hiring managers. Workers who are reliable, show initiative, and have leadership qualities are highly sought after for promotion. Other qualities that managers look for are good problem-solving skills and the ability to concentrate on details. A neat and clean appearance is important, because food service managers must convey self-confidence and show respect in dealing with the public. Because food service management can be physically demanding, good health and stamina are important.

Managers must be good communicators as they deal with customers, employees, and suppliers for most of the day. They must be able to motivate employees to work as a team, to ensure that food and service meet appropriate standards. Additionally, the ability to speak multiple languages is helpful to communicate with staff and patrons.

Certification and advancement.   The certified Foodservice Management Professional (FMP) designation is a measure of professional achievement for food service managers. Although not a requirement for employment or necessary for advancement, voluntary certification can provide recognition of professional competence, particularly for managers who acquired their skills largely on the job. The National Restaurant Association Educational Foundation awards the FMP designation to managers who achieve a qualifying score on a written examination, complete a series of courses that cover a range of food service management topics, and meet standards of work experience in the field.

Willingness to relocate is often essential for advancement to positions with greater responsibility. Managers typically advance to larger or more prominent establishments or regional management positions within restaurant chains. Some may open their own food service establishments or franchise operation.

Employment

Food service managers held about 338,700 jobs in 2008. The majority of managers are salaried, but 42 percent are self-employed as owners of independent restaurants or other small food service establishments. Forty-one percent of all salaried jobs for food service managers are in full-service restaurants or limited-service eating places, such as fast-food restaurants and cafeterias. Other salaried jobs are in special food services— an industry that includes food service contractors who supply food services at institutional, governmental, commercial, or industrial locations, and educational services, which primarily supply elementary and secondary schools. A smaller number of salaried jobs are in hotels; amusement, gambling, and recreation industries; nursing care facilities; and hospitals. Jobs are located throughout the country, with large cities and resort areas providing more opportunities for full-service dining positions.

Job Outlook

Food service manager jobs are expected to grow 5 percent, or more slowly than the average for all occupations through 2018. However, job opportunities should be good because many openings will arise from the need to replace managers who leave the occupation.

Projections data from the National Employment Matrix

Occupational Title	SOC Code	Employment, 2008	Projected Employment, 2018	Change, 2008-2018	
				Number	Percent
Food service managers..	11-9051	338,700	356,700	18,000	5

(NOTE) Data in this table are rounded. See the discussion of the employment projections table in the *Handbook* introductory chapter on *Occupational Information Included in the Handbook.*

Employment change. Employment of food service managers is expected to grow 5 percent, or more slowly than the average for all occupations, during the 2008-18 decade, as the number of eating and drinking establishments opening is expected to decline from the previous decade. Despite these reductions in the number of new eating and drinking places, new employment opportunities for food service managers will emerge in grocery and convenience stores and other retail and recreation industries to meet the growing demand for quick food in a variety of settings. Employment growth is projected to vary by industry. Most new jobs will be in full-service restaurants and limited service eating places. Manager jobs will also increase in healthcare and elder care facilities. Self-employment of these workers will generate nearly 40 percent of new jobs.

Job prospects. In addition to job openings from employment growth, the need to replace managers who transfer to other occupations or stop working will create good job opportunities. Although practical experience is an integral part of finding a food service management position, applicants with a degree in restaurant, hospitality, or institutional food service management will have an edge when competing for jobs at upscale restaurants and for advancement in a restaurant chain or into corporate management.

Earnings

Median annual wages of salaried food service managers were $46,320 in May 2008. The middle 50 percent earned between $36,670 and $59,580. The lowest 10 percent earned less than $29,450, and the highest 10 percent earned more than $76,940. Median annual wages in the industries employing the largest numbers of food service managers were as follows:

Traveler accommodation	$54,710
Special food services	52,680
Full-service restaurants	49,420
Limited-service eating places	41,320

In addition to receiving typical benefits, most salaried food service managers are provided free meals and the opportunity for additional training, depending on their length of service. Some food service managers, especially those in full-service restaurants, may earn bonuses depending on sales volume or revenue.

Related Occupations

Other managers and supervisors in hospitality-related businesses include:

Sources of Additional Information

Information about a career as a food service manager, 2- and 4-year college programs in restaurant and food service manage-

ment, and certification as a Foodservice Management Professional is available from:

➤ National Restaurant Association Educational Foundation, 175 West Jackson Blvd., Suite 1500, Chicago, IL 60604-2702. Internet: **http://www.nraef.org**

Career information about food service managers, as well as a directory of 2- and 4-year colleges that offer courses or programs that prepare persons for food service careers is available from:
➤ National Restaurant Association, 1200 17th St. NW., Washington, DC 20036-3097. Internet: **http://www.restaurant.org**

General information on hospitality careers may be obtained from:
➤ The International Council on Hotel, Restaurant, and Institutional Education, 2810 North Parham Rd., Suite 230, Richmond, VA 23294. Internet: **http://www.chrie.org**

Additional information about job opportunities in food service management may be obtained from local employers and from local offices of State employment services agencies.

The Occupational Information Network (O*NET) provides information on a wide range of occupational characteristics. Links to O*NET appear at the end of the Internet version of this occupational statement, accessible at **http://www.bls.gov/ooh/ocos024.htm**

Funeral Directors

Significant Points

- Job opportunities should be good, particularly for those who also embalm.

- Some mortuary science graduates relocate to get a job.

- Funeral directors are licensed by the State in which they practice.

- Funeral directors need the ability to communicate easily and compassionately and to comfort people in a time of sorrow.

Nature of the Work

Funeral practices and rites vary greatly among cultures and religions. However, funeral practices usually share some common elements—removing the deceased to a mortuary, preparing the remains, performing a ceremony that honors the deceased and addresses the spiritual needs of the family, and carrying out final disposition of the deceased. *Funeral directors* arrange and direct these tasks for grieving families, taking great pride in their ability to provide comfort to family and friends of the deceased and in providing appropriate services.

Funeral directors, also called *morticians* and *undertakers*, arrange the details and handle the logistics of funerals, taking into account the wishes of the deceased and family members. Together with the family, funeral directors establish the location, dates, and times of wakes, memorial services, and burials. They arrange for a hearse to carry the body to the funeral home or mortuary.

Funeral directors prepare obituary notices and have them placed in newspapers, arrange for pallbearers and clergy, schedule the opening and closing of a grave with a representative of the cemetery, decorate and prepare the sites of all services, and provide transportation for the deceased, mourners, and flowers between sites. They also direct preparation and shipment of bodies for out-of-State burial.

Most funeral directors also are trained, licensed, and practicing *embalmers*. Embalming is a sanitary, cosmetic, and preservative process through which the body is prepared for interment. If more than 24 hours elapse between death and interment, State laws usually require that the remains be refrigerated or embalmed.

When embalming a body, funeral directors wash the body with germicidal soap and replace the blood with embalming fluid to preserve the tissues. They may reshape and reconstruct bodies using materials such as clay, cotton, plaster of Paris, and wax. They also may apply cosmetics to provide a natural appearance, dress the body, and place it in a casket. Funeral directors maintain records such as embalming reports and itemized lists of clothing or valuables delivered with the body. In large funeral homes, an embalming staff of two or more, plus several apprentices may be employed.

Funeral services may take place in a home, house of worship, funeral home, or at the gravesite or crematory. Some services are not religious, but many are. Funeral directors must be familiar with the funeral and burial customs of many faiths, ethnic groups, and fraternal organizations. For example, members of some religions seldom have the deceased embalmed or cremated.

Burial in a casket is the most common method of disposing of remains in the United States, although entombment also occurs. Cremation, which is the burning of the body in a special furnace, is increasingly selected because it can be less expensive and allows for the memorial service to be held at a more convenient time in the future when relatives and friends can come together. A funeral service followed by cremation need not be any different from a funeral service followed by a burial. Usually, cremated remains are placed in some type of permanent receptacle, or urn, before being committed to a final resting place. The urn may be buried, placed in an indoor or outdoor mausoleum or columbarium, or interred in a special urn garden that many cemeteries provide for cremated remains.

Funeral directors handle the paperwork involved with the person's death, including submitting papers to State authorities so that a formal death certificate may be issued and copies distributed to the heirs. They may help family members apply for veterans' burial benefits or notify the Social Security Administration of the death. Also, funeral directors may apply for the transfer of any pensions, insurance policies, or annuities on behalf of survivors.

Funeral directors also work with those who want to plan their own funerals in advance. This ensures that the client's wishes will be taken care of to their satisfaction.

Most funeral homes are small, family-run businesses, and many funeral directors are owner-operators or employees with managerial responsibilities. Funeral directors, therefore, are responsible for the success and the profitability of their businesses. Directors must keep records of expenses, purchases, and services rendered; prepare and send invoices for services; and file all required State and Federal employment reports and tax forms. Funeral directors increasingly use computers for billing, bookkeeping, and marketing. Some are beginning to use the Internet to communicate with clients who are planning their funerals in advance or to assist them by developing electronic obituaries and guest books. Directors strive to foster a cooperative spirit and friendly attitude among employees and a compassionate demeanor toward the families. Increasingly, funeral directors also help individuals adapt to changes in their lives following a death through aftercare services and support groups.

Work environment. Most funeral directors work in funeral homes that have one or more viewing rooms, a casket-selection room, a preparation room, and sometimes a chapel. Some may also have a crematory on the premises.

In general, the occupation is safe, but funeral directors occasionally come into contact with bodies that had contagious diseases, but when the appropriate safety and health regulations are followed the possibility of infection is remote.

Funeral directors often work long, irregular hours, and the occupation can be highly stressful. Many are on call at all hours because they may be needed to remove remains in the middle of the night. Shift work sometimes is necessary because funeral home hours include evenings and weekends. In smaller funeral homes, working hours vary, but in larger establishments, employees usually work 8 hours a day, 5 or 6 days a week.

Training, Other Qualifications, and Advancement
Funeral directors are licensed in all States. State licensing laws vary, but most require applicants to be 21 years old, have 2 years of formal education, serve a 1-year apprenticeship, and pass an examination.

Education and training. College programs in mortuary science usually last from 2 to 4 years. The American Board of Funeral Service Education accredits about 60 mortuary science programs. The majority are two-year associate degree programs offered at community colleges. About 6 colleges and universities offer programs that culminate in a bachelor's degree. In ad-

Funeral directors, also called morticians and undertakers, arrange the details of funerals, taking into account the wishes of the deceased and family members.

dition, many specialized, stand alone funeral service institutions offer two-year programs, although some are 4 years in length. Mortuary science programs include courses in anatomy, physiology, pathology, embalming techniques, restorative art, business management, accounting and use of computers in funeral home management, and client services. They also include courses in the social sciences and in legal, ethical, and regulatory subjects such as psychology, grief counseling, oral and written communication, funeral service law, business law, and ethics.

Many State and national associations offer continuing education programs designed for licensed funeral directors. These programs address issues in communications, counseling, and management. More than 30 States have requirements that funeral directors receive continuing education credits to maintain their licenses.

Apprenticeships must be completed under the direction of an experienced and licensed funeral director. Some States require apprenticeships. Depending on State regulations, apprenticeships last from 1 to 3 years and may be served before, during, or after mortuary school. Apprenticeships provide practical experience in all facets of the funeral service, from embalming to transporting remains.

High school students can start preparing for a career as a funeral director by taking courses in biology and chemistry and participating in public speaking or debate clubs. Part-time or summer jobs in funeral homes also provide good experience. These jobs consist mostly of maintenance and cleanup tasks, such as washing and polishing limousines and hearses, but they can help students become familiar with the operation of funeral homes.

Licensure. All States require funeral directors to be licensed. Licensing laws vary by State, but most require applicants to be 21 years old, have 2 years of formal education that includes studies in mortuary science, serve a 1-year apprenticeship, and pass a qualifying examination. After becoming licensed, new funeral directors may join the staff of a funeral home.

Some States require all funeral directors to be licensed in embalming. Others have separate licenses for directors and embalmers, but in those States funeral directors who embalm need to be licensed in embalming, and most of these professionals obtain both licenses.

State board licensing examinations vary, but they usually consist of written and oral parts and include a demonstration of practical skills. People who want to work in another State may have to pass the examination for that State; however, some States have reciprocity arrangements and will grant licenses to funeral directors from another State without further examination. People interested in a career as a funeral director should contact their State licensing board for specific requirements.

Other qualifications. Funeral directors need composure, tact, and the ability to communicate easily and compassionately with the public. Funeral directors also should have the desire and ability to comfort people in a time of sorrow.

To show proper respect and consideration for the families and the dead, funeral directors must dress appropriately. The professions usually require short, neat haircuts and trim beards, if any, for men. Suits and ties for men and comparable business attire, for women are customary.

Advancement. Advancement opportunities generally are best in companies with multiple funeral homes. Funeral directors working for these companies may earn promotions to higher paying positions such as branch manager or general manager. Some directors eventually acquire enough money and experience to establish their own funeral home businesses.

Employment

Funeral directors held about 30,000 jobs in 2008. About 13 percent were self-employed. Nearly all worked in the death care services industry.

Job Outlook

Employment growth is expected to be as fast as average for all occupations. Job opportunities are expected to be good, particularly for funeral directors who also embalm.

Employment change. Employment of funeral directors is expected to increase by 12 percent during the 2008–18 decade, about as fast as the average for all occupations. Projected job growth reflects growth in the death care services industry overall due to the aging of the population.

Job prospects. In addition to employment growth, the need to replace funeral directors who retire or leave the occupation for other reasons will result in good job opportunities. Funeral directors are older, on average, than workers in most other occupations and are expected to retire in greater numbers over the coming decade. In addition, some funeral directors leave the profession because of the long and irregular hours. Job prospects may also be better for some mortuary science graduates who can relocate to get a job.

Earnings

Median annual wages for funeral directors were $52,210 in May 2008. The middle 50 percent earned between $38,980 and $69,680. The lowest 10 percent earned less than $29,910 and the top 10 percent earned more than $92,940.

Salaries of funeral directors depend on the number of years of experience in funeral service, the number of services performed, the number of facilities operated, the area of the country, and the director's level of formal education. Funeral directors in large cities usually earn more than their counterparts in small towns and rural areas.

Projections data from the National Employment Matrix

Occupational Title	SOC Code	Employment, 2008	Projected Employment, 2018	Change, 2008-2018	
				Number	Percent
Funeral directors	11-9061	30,000	33,600	3,600	12

(NOTE) Data in this table are rounded. See the discussion of the employment projections table in the *Handbook* introductory chapter on *Occupational Information Included in the Handbook.*

Related Occupations

The job of a funeral director requires tact, discretion, and compassion when dealing with grieving people. Others who need these qualities include:

Sources of Additional Information

For a list of accredited mortuary science programs and information on the funeral service profession, write to:

➤ The National Funeral Directors Association, 13625 Bishop's Dr., Brookfield, WI 53005. Internet: **http://www.nfda.org**

For information about scholarships and educational programs in funeral service and mortuary science, contact:

➤ The American Board of Funeral Service Education, 3414 Ashland Ave., Suite G, St. Joseph, MO 64506. Internet: **http://www.abfse.org**

For information on specific State licensing requirements, contact the State's licensing board.

For more information about funeral directors and their work, see the *Occupational Outlook Quarterly* article, "Jobs in weddings and funerals: Working with the betrothed and the bereaved," available in many libraries and career centers and online at **http://www.bls.gov/opub/ooq/2006/winter/art03.pdf.**

The Occupational Information Network (O*NET) provides information on a wide range of occupational characteristics. Links to O*NET appear at the end of the Internet version of this occupational statement, accessible at **http://www.bls.gov/ooh/ocos011.htm**

Human Resources, Training, and Labor Relations Managers and Specialists

Significant Points

- The educational backgrounds of these workers vary considerably, reflecting the diversity of duties and levels of responsibility.

- College graduates and those who have earned certification should have the best job and advancement opportunities.

- Human resources occupations require strong interpersonal skills.

- Much faster than average growth is expected during the projection period.

Nature of the Work

Every organization wants to attract, motivate, and retain the most qualified employees and match them to jobs for which they are best suited. Human resources, training, and labor relations managers and specialists provide this connection. In the past, these workers performed the administrative function of an organization, such as handling employee benefits questions or recruiting, interviewing, and hiring new staff in accordance with policies established by top management. Today's human resources workers manage these tasks, but, increasingly, they consult with top executives regarding strategic planning. They have moved from behind-the-scenes staff work to leading the company in suggesting and changing policies.

In an effort to enhance morale and productivity, limit job turnover, and help organizations increase performance and improve results, these workers also help their companies effectively use employee skills, provide training and development opportunities to improve those skills, and increase employees' satisfaction with their jobs and working conditions. Although some jobs in the human resources field require only limited contact with people outside the human resources office, dealing with people is an important part of the job.

There are many types of human resources, training, and labor relations managers and specialists. In a small organization, a *human resources generalist* may handle all aspects of human resources work, and thus require an extensive range of knowledge. The responsibilities of human resources generalists can vary widely, depending on their employer's needs.

In a large corporation, the *director of human resources* may supervise several departments, each headed by an experienced manager who most likely specializes in one human resources activity, such as employment and placement, compensation and benefits, training and development, or labor relations. The director may report to a top human resources executive. (See top executives elsewhere in the *Handbook.*)

Employment and placement. *Employment and placement managers* supervise the recruitment, hiring, and separation of employees. They also supervise employment, recruitment, and placement specialists, including employment interviewers. *Employment, recruitment, and placement specialists* recruit and place workers.

Recruitment specialists maintain contacts within the community and may travel considerably, often to job fairs and college campuses, to search for promising job applicants. Recruiters screen, interview, and occasionally test applicants. They also may check references and extend job offers. These workers must be thoroughly familiar with their organization, the work that is done, and the human resources policies of their company in order to discuss wages, working conditions and advancement opportunities with prospective employees. They also must stay informed about equal employment opportunity (EEO) and affirmative action guidelines and laws, such as the Americans with Disabilities Act.

Employment interviewers—whose many job titles include *human resources consultants, human resources development specialists,* and *human resources coordinators*—help to match employers with qualified jobseekers. Similarly, *employer relations representatives*, who usually work in government agencies or college career centers, maintain working relationships with prospective employers and promote the use of public employment programs and services.

Compensation, benefits, and job analysis. *Compensation, benefits, and job analysis specialists* administer compensation

Human resources, training, and labor relations managers and specialists explain company procedures and benefits to new employees.

programs for employers and may specialize in specific areas such as pensions or position classifications. For example, *job analysts*, occasionally called *position classifiers*, collect and examine detailed information about job duties in order to prepare job descriptions. These descriptions explain the duties, training, and skills that each job requires. Whenever a large organization introduces a new job or reviews existing jobs, it calls upon the expert knowledge of job analysts.

Occupational analysts research occupational classification systems and study the effects of industry and occupational trends on worker relationships. They may serve as technical liaisons between companies or departments, government, and labor unions.

Establishing and maintaining a firm's pay structure is the principal job of *compensation managers*. Assisted by compensation analysts or specialists, compensation managers devise ways to ensure fair and equitable pay rates. They may participate in or purchase salary surveys to see how their firm's pay compares with others, and they ensure that the firm's pay scale complies with changing laws and regulations. In addition, compensation managers often oversee the compensation side of their company's performance management system. They may design reward systems such as pay-for-performance plans, which might include setting merit pay guidelines and bonus or incentive pay criteria. Compensation managers also might administer executive compensation programs or determine commission rates and other incentives for corporate sales staffs.

Employee benefits managers and specialists administer a company's employee benefits program, notably its health insurance and retirement plans. Expertise in designing, negotiating, and administering benefits programs continues to take on importance as employer-provided benefits account for a growing proportion of overall compensation costs, and as benefit plans increase in number and complexity. For example, retirement benefits might include defined benefit pension plans, defined contribution plans, such as 401(k) or thrift savings plans and profit-sharing or stock ownership plans. Health benefits might include medical, dental, and vision insurance and protection against catastrophic illness. Familiarity with health benefits

is a top priority for employee benefits managers and specialists, because of the rising cost of providing healthcare benefits to employees and retirees. In addition to health insurance and retirement coverage, many firms offer employees life and accidental death and dismemberment insurance, disability insurance, and benefits designed to meet the needs of a changing workforce, such as parental leave, long-term nursing or home care insurance, wellness programs, and flexible benefits plans. Benefits managers must keep abreast of changing Federal and State regulations and legislation that may affect employee benefits. Working with employee assistance plan managers or work-life coordinators, many benefits managers work to integrate the growing number of programs that deal with mental and physical health, such as employee assistance, obesity, and smoking cessation, into their health benefits programs.

Employee assistance plan managers, also called *employee welfare managers* or *work-life managers*, are responsible for a wide array of programs to enhance employee safety and wellness and improve work-life balance. These may include occupational safety and health standards and practices, health promotion and physical fitness, medical examinations and minor health treatment, such as first aid, flexible work schedules, food service and recreation activities, carpooling and transportation programs such as transit subsidies, employee suggestion systems, child care and elder care, and counseling services. Child care and elder care are increasingly significant because of growth in the number of dual-income households and the older population. Counseling may help employees deal with emotional disorders, alcoholism, or marital, family, consumer, legal, and financial problems. Some employers offer career counseling and outplacement services. In some companies, certain programs, such as those dealing with physical security or information technology, may be coordinated in separate departments by other managers. (See administrative services managers elsewhere in the *Handbook*.)

Training and development. *Training and development managers and specialists* create, procure, and conduct training and development programs for employees. Managers typically supervise specialists and make budget-impacting decisions in exchange for a reduced training portfolio. Increasingly, executives recognize that training offers a way of developing skills, enhancing productivity and quality of work, and building worker loyalty. Enhancing employee skills can increase individual and organizational performance and help to achieve business results. Increasingly, executives realize that developing the skills and knowledge of its workforce is a business imperative that can give them a competitive edge in recruiting and retaining high quality employees and can lead to business growth.

Other factors involved in determining whether training is needed include the complexity of the work environment, the rapid pace of organizational and technological change, and the growing number of jobs in fields that constantly generate new knowledge and, thus, require new skills. In addition, advances in learning theory have provided insights into how people learn and how training can be organized most effectively.

Training managers oversee development of training programs, contracts, and budgets. They may perform needs assessments of the types of training needed, determine the best means of delivering training, and create the content. They may provide employee training in a classroom, computer laboratory, or on-site production facility, or through a training film, Web video-on-demand, or self-paced or self-guided instructional guides. For live or in-person training, training managers ensure that teaching materials are prepared and the space appropriately set, training and instruction stimulate the class, and completion certificates are issued at the end of training. For computer-assisted or recorded training, trainers ensure that cameras, microphones, and other necessary technology platforms are functioning properly and that individual computers or other learning devices are configured for training purposes. They also have the responsibility for the entire learning process, and its environment, to ensure that the course meets its objectives and is measured and evaluated to understand how learning impacts performance.

Training specialists plan, organize, and direct a wide range of training activities. Trainers consult with training managers and employee supervisors to develop performance improvement measures, conduct orientation sessions, and arrange on-the-job training for new employees. They help employees maintain and improve their job skills and prepare for jobs requiring greater skill. They work with supervisors to improve their interpersonal skills and to deal effectively with employees. They may set up individualized training plans to strengthen employees' existing skills or teach new ones. Training specialists also may set up leadership or executive development programs for employees who aspire to move up in the organization. These programs are designed to develop or "groom" leaders to replace those leaving the organization and as part of a corporate succession plan. Trainers also lead programs to assist employees with job transitions as a result of mergers or consolidation, as well as retraining programs to develop new skills that may result from technological changes in the work place. In government-supported job-training programs, training specialists serve as case managers and provide basic job skills to prepare participants to function in the labor force. They assess the training needs of clients and guide them through the most appropriate training. After training, clients may either be referred to employer relations representatives or receive job placement assistance.

Planning and program development is an essential part of the training specialist's job. In order to identify and assess training needs, trainers may confer with managers and supervisors or conduct surveys. They also evaluate training effectiveness to ensure that employees actually learn and that the training they receive helps the organization meet its strategic goals and achieve results.

Depending on the size, goals, and nature of the organization, trainers may differ considerably in their responsibilities and in the methods they use. Training methods also vary by whether the training predominantly is knowledge-based or skill-based or sometimes a combination of the two. For example, much knowledge-based training is conducted in a classroom setting. Most skill training provides some combination of hands-on instruction, demonstration, and practice at doing something and usually is conducted on a shop floor, studio, or laboratory where trainees gain experience and confidence. Some on-the-job training methods could apply equally to knowledge or skill training and formal apprenticeship training programs combine classroom training and work experience. Increasingly, training programs involve interactive Internet-based training modules that can be downloaded for either individual or group instruction, for dissemination to a geographically dispersed class, or to be coordinated with other multimedia programs. These technologies allow participants to take advantage of distance learning alternatives and to attend conferences and seminars through satellite or Internet communications hookups, or use other computer-aided instructional technologies, such as those for the hearing-impaired or sight-impaired.

Employee relations. An organization's *director of industrial relations* forms labor policy, oversees industrial labor relations, negotiates collective bargaining agreements, and coordinates grievance procedures to handle complaints resulting from management disputes with employees. The director of industrial relations also advises and collaborates with the director of human resources, other managers, and members of their staffs, because all aspects of human resources policy—such as wages, benefits, pensions, and work practices—may be involved in drawing up a new or revised work rules that comply with a union contract.

Labor relations managers and their staffs implement industrial labor relations programs. Labor relations specialists prepare information for management to use during collective bargaining agreement negotiations, a process that requires the specialist to be familiar with economic and wage data and to have extensive knowledge of labor law and collective bargaining procedures. The labor relations staff interprets and administers the contract with respect to grievances, wages and salaries, employee welfare, healthcare, pensions, union and management practices, and other contractual stipulations. In the absence of a union, industrial relations personnel may work with employees individually or with employee association representatives.

Dispute resolution—attaining tacit or contractual agreements—has become increasingly significant as parties to a dispute attempt to avoid costly litigation, strikes, or other disruptions. Dispute resolution also has become more complex, involving employees, management, unions, other firms, and government agencies. Specialists involved in dispute resolution must be highly knowledgeable and experienced, and often report to the director of industrial relations. *Mediators* advise and counsel labor and management to prevent and, when necessary, resolve disputes over labor agreements or other labor relations issues. *Arbitrators*, occasionally called umpires or referees, decide disputes that bind both labor and management to specific terms and conditions of labor contracts. Labor relations specialists who work for unions perform many of the same functions on behalf of the union and its members.

EEO officers, representatives, or *affirmative action coordinators* handle equal employment opportunity matters. They investigate and resolve EEO grievances, examine corporate practices for possible violations, and compile and submit EEO statistical reports.

Other emerging specialties in human resources include *international human resources managers*, who handle human resources issues related to a company's overseas operations and *human resources information system specialists*, who develop and apply computer programs to process human resources information, match jobseekers with job openings, and handle other human resources matters; and *total compensation* or *total rewards specialists*, who determine an appropriate mix of compensation, benefits, and incentives.

Work environment. Human resources personnel usually work in clean, pleasant, and comfortable office settings. Arbitrators and mediators many of whom work independently may work out of home offices. Although most human resources, training, and labor relations managers and specialists work in the office, some travel extensively. For example, recruiters regularly attend professional meetings, participate in job fairs, and visit college campuses to interview prospective employees. Arbitrators and mediators often must travel to the site chosen for negotiations. Trainers and other specialists may travel to regional, satellite, or international offices of a company to meet with employees who work outside of the main corporate office.

Many human resources, training, and labor relations managers and specialists work a standard 40-hour week. However, longer hours might be necessary for some workers—for example, labor relations managers and specialists, arbitrators, and mediators—when contract agreements or dispute resolutions are being negotiated.

Training, Other Qualifications, and Advancement

The educational backgrounds of human resources, training, and labor relations managers and specialists vary considerably, reflecting the diversity of duties and levels of responsibility. In filling entry-level jobs, many employers seek college graduates who have majored in human resources, human resources administration, or industrial and labor relations. Other employers look for college graduates with a technical or business background or a well-rounded liberal arts education.

Education and training. Although a bachelor's degree is a typical path of entry into these occupations, many colleges and universities do not offer degree programs in personnel administration, human resources, or labor relations until the graduate degree level. However, many offer individual courses in these subjects at the undergraduate level in addition to concentrations in human resources administration or human resources management, training and development, organizational development, and compensation and benefits.

Because an interdisciplinary background is appropriate in this field, a combination of courses in the social sciences, business administration, and behavioral sciences is useful. Some jobs may require more technical or specialized backgrounds in engineering, science, finance, or law. Most prospective human resources specialists should take courses in principles of management, organizational structure, and industrial psychology; however, courses in accounting or finance are becoming increasingly important. Courses in labor law, collective bargaining, labor economics, and labor history also provide a valuable background for the prospective labor relations specialist. As in many other fields, knowledge of computers and information systems is useful.

An advanced degree is increasingly important for some jobs. Many labor relations jobs require graduate study in industrial or labor relations. A strong background in industrial relations and law is highly desirable for contract negotiators, mediators, and arbitrators; in fact, many people in these specialties have law degrees. A master's degree in human resources, labor relations, or in business administration with a concentration in human resources management is highly recommended for those seeking general and top management positions.

The duties given to entry-level workers will vary, depending on whether the new workers have a degree in human resource management, have completed an internship, or have some other type of human resources-related experience. Entry-level employees commonly learn by performing administrative duties—helping to enter data into computer systems, compiling employee handbooks, researching information for a supervisor, or answering phone calls and handling routine questions. Entry-level workers often enter on-the-job training programs in which they learn how to classify jobs, interview applicants, or administer employee benefits; they then are assigned to specific areas in the human resources department to gain experience. Later, they may advance to supervisory positions, overseeing a major element of the human resources program—compensation or training, for example.

Other qualifications. Experience is an asset for many specialties in the human resources area, and is essential for advancement to senior-level positions, including managers, arbitrators, and mediators. Many employers prefer entry-level workers who have gained some experience through an internship or work-study program while in school. Employees in human resources administration and human resources development need the ability to work well with individuals and a commitment to organizational goals. This field demands skills that people may have developed elsewhere—teaching, supervising, and volunteering, among others. Human resources work also offers clerical workers opportunities to advance to more responsible or professional positions. Some positions occasionally are filled by experienced individuals from other backgrounds, including business, government, education, social services administration, and the military.

The human resources field demands a range of personal qualities and skills. Human resources, training, and labor relations managers and specialists must speak and write effectively. Ever-changing technologies and the growing complexities inherent to the many services human resources personnel provide require that they be knowledgeable about computer systems, storage and retrieval software, and how to use a wide array of digital communications devices.

The growing diversity of the workforce requires that human resources managers and specialists work with or supervise people of various ages, cultural backgrounds, levels of education, and experience. Ability to speak a foreign language is an asset, especially if working in an industry with a large immigrant workforce or for a company with many overseas operations. Human resources employees must be able to cope with conflicting points of view, function under pressure, and demonstrate discretion, integrity, fair-mindedness, and a persuasive, genial personality. Because much of the information collected by these employees is confidential, they must also show the character and responsibility of dealing with sensitive employee information.

Certification and advancement. Most professional associations that specialize in human resources offer classes intended to enhance the skills of their members. Some organizations offer certification programs, which are signs of competence and credibility and can enhance advancement opportunities. For example, the International Foundation of Employee Benefit Plans confers a designation in three distinct areas of specialization—group benefit, retirement, and compensation—to persons who complete a series of college-level courses and pass exams. Candidates can earn a designation in each of the specialty tracks and, simultaneously, receive credit toward becoming a Certified Employee Benefits Specialist (CEBS). The American Society for Training and Development (ASTD) Certification Institute offers professional certification in the learning and performance field. Addressing nine areas of expertise, certification requires passing a knowledge-based exam and successful work experience. In addition, ASTD offers 16 short-term certificate and workshop programs covering a broad range of professional training and development topics. The Society for Human Resource Management offers two levels of certification, including the Professional in Human Resources (PHR) and the Senior Professional in Human Resources (SPHR). Additionally, the organization offers the Global Professional in Human Resources certification for those with international and cross-border responsibilities and the California Certification in Human Resources for those who plan to work in that State and become familiar with California's labor and human resources laws. All designations require experience and a passing score on a comprehensive exam. The WorldatWork Society of Certified Professionals offers four distinct designations in the areas of compensation, benefits, work-life, and global remuneration that comprise the total rewards management practice. Candidates obtain the designation of Certified Compensation Professional (CCP), Certified Benefits Professional (CBP), Global Remuneration Professional (GRP), and Work-Life Certified Professional (WLCP). Certification is achieved after passing a series of knowledge-based exams within each designation. Additionally, WorldatWork offers online and classroom education covering a broad range of total rewards topics.

Exceptional human resources workers may be promoted to director of human resources or industrial relations, which can eventually lead to a top managerial or executive position. Others may join a consulting or outsourcing firm or open their own business. A Ph.D. is an asset for teaching, writing, or consulting work.

Employment

Human resources, training, and labor relations managers and specialists held about 904,900 jobs in 2008. The following tabulation shows the distribution of jobs by occupational specialty:

Training and development specialists	216,600
Employment, recruitment, and placement specialists	207,900
Compensation, benefits, and job analysis specialists	121,900
Compensation and benefits managers	40,500
Training and development managers	30,400
Human resources, training, and labor relations specialists, all other	224,600
Human resources managers, all other	63,100

Human resources, training, and labor relations managers and specialists were employed in virtually every industry. About 13 percent of human resources, training, and labor relations managers and specialists were employed in administrative and support services, 11 percent in professional, scientific, and technical services, 10 percent in healthcare and social assistance, and 9 percent in finance and insurance firms. About 12,900 managers and specialists were self-employed, working as consultants to public and private employers.

Job Outlook

Employment is expected to grow much faster than the average for all human resources, training, and labor relations managers and specialists occupations. College graduates and those who have earned certification should have the best job opportunities.

Employment change. Overall employment is projected to grow by 22 percent between 2008 and 2018, much faster than the average for all occupations. Legislation and court rulings revising standards in various areas—occupational safety and health, equal employment opportunity, wages, healthcare, retirement plans, and family leave, among others—will increase demand for human resources, training, and labor relations experts. Rising healthcare costs and a growing number of healthcare coverage options should continue to spur demand for specialists to develop creative compensation and benefits packages that companies can offer prospective employees.

Projections data from the National Employment Matrix

Occupational Title	SOC Code	Employment, 2008	Projected Employment, 2018	Change, 2008-2018	
				Number	Percent
Human resources, training, and labor relations managers and specialists	—	904,900	1,102,300	197,400	22
Human resources managers	11-3040	133,900	146,800	12,900	10
Compensation and benefits managers	11-3041	40,500	43,900	3,400	9
Training and development managers	11-3042	30,400	34,000	3,600	12
All other human resources managers	11-3049	63,100	68,900	5,800	9
Human resources, training, and labor relations specialists	13-1070	770,900	955,500	184,500	24
Employment, recruitment, and placement specialists	13-1071	207,900	265,900	58,000	28
Compensation, benefits, and job analysis specialists	13-1072	121,900	150,600	28,700	24
Training and development specialists	13-1073	216,600	267,100	50,500	23
Human resources, training, and labor relations specialists, all other	13-1079	224,600	271,900	47,200	21

(NOTE) Data in this table are rounded. See the discussion of the employment projections table in the *Handbook* introductory chapter on *Occupational Information Included in the Handbook.*

Employment of labor relations staff, including arbitrators and mediators, should grow as companies attempt to resolve potentially costly labor-management disputes out of court. Additional job growth may stem from increasing demand for specialists in international human resources management and human resources information systems.

Job growth could be limited by the widespread use of computerized human resources information systems that make workers more productive. Like other workers, employment of human resources, training, and labor relations managers and specialists, particularly in larger companies, may be adversely affected by corporate downsizing, restructuring, and mergers; however, as companies once again expand operations, additional workers may be needed to manage company growth.

Demand may be particularly strong for certain specialists. For example, employers are expected to devote greater resources to job-specific training programs in response to the increasing complexity of many jobs and technological advances that can leave employees with obsolete skills. Additionally, as highly trained and skilled baby boomers retire, there should be strong demand for training and development specialists to impart needed skills to their replacements. In addition, increasing efforts throughout industry to recruit and retain quality employees should create many jobs for employment, recruitment, and placement specialists.

Among industries, firms involved in management, consulting, and employment services should offer many job opportunities, as businesses increasingly contract out human resources functions or hire human resources specialists on a temporary basis to deal with increasing costs and complexity of training and development programs. Demand for specialists also should increase in outsourcing firms that develop and administer complex employee benefits and compensation packages for other organizations.

Job prospects. College graduates and those who have earned certification should have the best job opportunities, particularly graduates with a bachelor's degree in human resources, human resources administration, or industrial and labor relations. Those with a technical or business background or a well-rounded liberal arts education also should find opportunities. Demand for human resources, training, and labor relations managers and specialists depends on general economic conditions and the business cycle as well as staffing needs of the companies in which they work. A rapidly expanding business is likely to hire additional human resources workers—either as permanent employees or consultants—while businesses that have consolidated operations or merged with another company may require fewer of these workers. Also, as human resources management becomes increasingly important to the success of an organization, some small and medium-size businesses that do not have separate human resources departments may assign various human resources responsibilities to some employees in addition to their usual responsibilities; others may contract with consulting firms to establish formal procedures and train current employees to administer programs on a long-term basis.

In addition to new human resources management and specialist jobs created over the 2008-2018 projection period, many job openings will arise from the need to replace workers who transfer to other occupations, retire, or leave the labor force for other reasons.

Earnings

Annual salary rates for human resources workers vary according to occupation, level of experience, training, location, and firm size.

Median annual wages of compensation and benefits managers were $86,500 in May 2008. The middle 50 percent earned between $64,930 and $113,480. The lowest 10 percent earned less than $49,350, and the highest 10 percent earned more than $147,050. Median annual wages in the industries employing the largest numbers of compensation and benefits managers were:

Computer systems design and related services	$97,630
Insurance carriers	94,340
Management of companies and enterprises	94,230
General medical and surgical hospitals	86,060
Depository credit intermediation	84,980

Median annual wages of training and development managers were $87,700 in May 2008. The middle 50 percent earned between $64,770 and $115,570. The lowest 10 percent earned less than $48,280, and the highest 10 percent earned more than $149,050. Median annual wages in the industries employing the largest numbers of training and development managers were:

Management of companies and enterprises	$93,140
Insurance carriers	92,210
General medical and surgical hospitals	86,820
Local government	70,430
Employment services	69,170

Median annual wages of human resources managers, all other were $96,130 in May 2008. The middle 50 percent earned between $73,480 and $126,050. The lowest 10 percent earned less than $56,770, and the highest 10 percent earned more than $163,220. Median annual wages in the industries employing the largest numbers of human resources managers, all other were:

Management of companies and enterprises	$107,280
General medical and surgical hospitals	91,580
Local government	89,240
Colleges, universities, and professional schools	86,920
State government	76,570

Median annual wages of employment, recruitment, and placement specialists were $45,470 in May 2008. The middle 50 percent earned between $35,020 and $63,110. The lowest 10 percent earned less than $28,030, and the highest 10 percent earned more than $85,760. Median annual wages in the industries employing the largest numbers of employment, recruitment, and placement specialists were:

Management, scientific, and technical consulting services	$56,110
Computer systems design and related services	55,600
Management of companies and enterprises	51,320
Local government	42,950
Employment services	42,670
State government	38,970

Median annual wages of compensation, benefits, and job analysis specialists were $53,860 in May 2008. The middle 50 percent earned between $42,050 and $67,730. The lowest 10 percent earned less than $34,080, and the highest 10 percent earned more than $84,310. Median annual wages in the industries employing the largest numbers of compensation, benefits, and job analysis specialists were:

Management, scientific, and technical consulting services	$59,810
Local government	56,930
Management of companies and enterprises	54,930
Agencies, brokerages, and other insurance related activities	53,490
Insurance carriers	51,890
State government	43,880

Median annual wages of training and development specialists were $51,450 in May 2008. The middle 50 percent earned between $38,550 and $67,450. The lowest 10 percent earned less than $29,470, and the highest 10 percent earned more than $85,160. Median annual wages in the industries employing the largest numbers of training and development specialists were:

Computer systems design and related services	$61,110
General medical and surgical hospitals	56,540
Insurance carriers	55,190
Management of companies and enterprises	54,800
Local government	52,080
State government	48,480

According to a July 2009 salary survey conducted by the National Association of Colleges and Employers, bachelor's degree candidates majoring in human resources, including labor and industrial relations, received starting offers averaging $45,170 a year.

Related Occupations

Human resources occupations require strong interpersonal skills. Other occupations that demand these skills include:

	Page
Counselors	234
Education administrators	41
Lawyers	257
Psychologists	215
Public relations specialists	350
Social and human service assistants	244
Social workers	246

Sources of Additional Information

For information about human resource management careers and certification, contact:

➤ Society for Human Resource Management, 1800 Duke St., Alexandria, VA 22314. Internet: **http://www.shrm.org**

For information about careers in employee training and development and certification, contact:

➤ American Society for Training and Development, 1640 King St., Box 1443, Alexandria, VA 22313-2043. Internet: **http://www.astd.org**

For information about careers and certification in employee compensation and benefits, contact:

➤ International Foundation of Employee Benefit Plans, 18700 W. Bluemound Rd., Brookfield, WI 53045. Internet: **http://www.ifebp.org**

➤ WorldatWork, 14040 N. Northsight Blvd., Scottsdale, AZ 85260. Internet: **http://www.worldatwork.org**

The Occupational Information Network (O*NET) provides information on a wide range of occupational characteristics. Links to O*NET appear at the end of the Internet version of this occupational statement, accessible at **http://www.bls.gov/ooh/ocos021.htm**

Industrial Production Managers

Significant Points

- Industrial production managers coordinate all the people and equipment involved in the manufacturing process.

- Most employers prefer to hire workers with a college degree; experience in some part of production operations usually is required as well.

- Employment is expected to decline as overall employment in manufacturing declines.

Nature of the Work

Industrial production managers plan, direct, and coordinate the production activities required to produce the vast array of goods manufactured every year in the United States. They make sure that production meets output and quality goals while remaining within budget. Depending on the size of the manufacturing plant, industrial production managers may oversee the entire plant or just one area of it.

Industrial production managers devise methods to use the plant's personnel and capital resources to best meet production goals. They may determine which machines will be used, whether new machines need to be purchased, whether overtime or extra shifts are necessary, and what the sequence of production will be. They monitor the production run to make sure that it stays on schedule, and they correct any problems that may arise.

Part of an industrial production manager's job is to come up with ways to make the production process more efficient. Traditional factory methods, such as mass assembly lines, have given way to "lean" production techniques, which give managers more flexibility. In a traditional assembly line, each worker was responsible for only a small portion of the assembly, repeating that task on every product. Lean production, by contrast, employs teams to build and assemble products in stations or cells. Thus, rather than specializing in a specific task, workers are capable of performing all jobs within a team. Without the constraints of the traditional assembly line, industrial production managers can more easily change production levels and staffing on different product lines to minimize inventory levels and more quickly react to changing customer demands.

Industrial production managers oversee all stages of the production process.

Industrial production managers also monitor product standards and implement quality control programs. They make sure that the finished product meets a certain level of quality, and if it doesn't, they try to find out what the problem is and solve it. Although traditional quality control programs reacted only to problems that reached a certain significant level, newer management techniques and programs, such as ISO 9000, Total Quality Management (TQM), or Six Sigma, emphasize continuous quality improvement. If the problem relates to the quality of work performed in the plant, the manager may implement better training programs or reorganize the manufacturing process, often on the basis of the suggestions of employee teams. If the cause is substandard materials or parts from outside suppliers, the industrial production manager may work with the supplier to improve their quality.

Industrial production managers work closely with other managers of the firm to implement the company's policies and goals. They also must work with the firm's financial departments in order to come up with a budget and spending plan. They work the closest with the heads of the sales, procurement, and logistics departments. Sales managers relay the client's needs and the price the client is willing to pay to the production department, which must then fill the order. The logistics or distribution department handles the delivery of the goods, often coordinating with the production department. The procurement department orders the supplies that the production department needs to make its products. The procurement department also is responsible for making sure that the inventories of supplies are maintained at proper levels so that production proceeds without interruption. A breakdown in communications between the production manager and the procurement department can cause slowdowns and a failure to meet production schedules. Just-in-time production techniques have reduced inventory levels, making constant communication among managers, suppliers, and procurement departments even more important.

Work environment. Most industrial production managers divide their time between production areas and their offices. While in the production area, they must follow established health and safety practices and wear the required protective clothing and equipment. The time in the office, which often is located near production areas, usually is spent meeting with subordinates or other department managers, analyzing production data, and writing and reviewing reports.

Many industrial production managers work extended hours, especially when production deadlines must be met. In 2008, about a third of all workers worked more than 50 hours a week, on average. In facilities that operate around the clock, managers often work late shifts and may be called at any hour to deal with emergencies. This could mean going to the plant to resolve the problem, regardless of the hour, and staying until the situation is under control. Dealing with production workers as well as superiors when working under the pressure of production deadlines or emergency situations can be stressful. Corporate restructuring has eliminated levels of management and support staff, thus shifting more responsibilities to production managers and compounding the stress.

Training, Other Qualifications, and Advancement

Because of the diversity of manufacturing operations and job requirements, there is no standard preparation for this occupation. Most employers prefer to hire workers with a college degree. Experience in some part of production operations is also usually is required also.

Education and training. Many industrial production managers have a college degree in business administration, management, industrial technology, or industrial engineering. However, although employers may prefer candidates with a business or engineering background, some companies will hire well-rounded graduates from other fields who are willing to spend time in a production-related job, because experience in some aspect of production operations is needed before one advances to upper management positions.

Some industrial production managers enter the occupation after working their way up through the ranks, starting as production workers and then advancing to supervisory positions before being selected for management. These workers already have an intimate knowledge of the production process and the firm's organization. To increase one's chances of promotion, workers can expand their skills by obtaining a college degree, demonstrating leadership qualities, or taking company-sponsored courses to learn the additional skills needed in management positions.

As production operations become more sophisticated, an increasing number of employers are looking for candidates with graduate degrees in industrial management or business administration, particularly for positions at larger plants where managers have more oversight responsibilities. Combined with an undergraduate degree in engineering, either of these graduate degrees is considered particularly good preparation. Managers who do not have graduate degrees often take courses in decision sciences, which provide them with techniques and statistical formulas that can be used to maximize efficiency and improve quality.

Those who enter the field directly from college or graduate school often are unfamiliar with the firm's production process. As a result, they may spend their first few months in the company's training program. These programs familiarize trainees with the production process, company policies, and the requirements of the job. In larger companies, they also may include assignments to other departments, such as purchasing and accounting. A number of companies hire college graduates as first-line supervisors and promote them to management positions later.

Other qualifications. Today, companies are placing greater importance on a candidate's interpersonal skills. Because the job requires the ability to compromise, persuade, and negotiate, successful production managers must be well rounded and have excellent communication skills. Strong computer skills also are essential.

Industrial production managers must continually keep informed of new production technologies and management practices. Many belong to professional organizations and attend trade shows or industry conferences where new equipment is displayed and new production methods and technologies discussed.

Certification and advancement. Some industrial production managers earn certifications that show their competency in various quality and management systems. Although certification is not required for industrial production manager jobs, it may improve job prospects.

One credential, Certified in Production and Inventory Management (CPIM), is offered by APICS, the Association for Operations Management, and requires passing a series of exams that cover supply chain management, resource planning, scheduling, production operations, and strategic planning. Those certified must complete a set number of professional development activities every 3 years to maintain their certification.

The American Society for Quality offers the Certified Manager of Quality/Organizational Excellence (CMQ/OE) credential. This certification is open to managers who pass an exam and who have at least 10 years of experience or education, 5 of which must be in a decisionmaking position. It is intended for managers who lead process improvement initiatives. To maintain certification, workers must complete a set number of professional development units every 3 years.

Industrial production managers with a proven record of superior performance may advance to plant manager or vice president of manufacturing. Others transfer to jobs with more responsibilities at larger firms. Opportunities also exist for managers to become consultants. (For more information, see the statement on management analysts elsewhere in the *Handbook*.)

Employment

Industrial production managers held about 156,100 jobs in 2008. About 80 percent are employed in manufacturing industries, including fabricated metal product, transportation equipment, and computer and electronic product manufacturing. Production managers work in all parts of the country, but jobs are most plentiful in areas where manufacturing is concentrated.

Job Outlook

Employment is expected to decline moderately. Applicants with experience in production occupations, along with a college degree in industrial engineering, management, or a related field, will enjoy the best job prospects.

Employment change. Employment of industrial production managers is expected to decline moderately by 8 percent over the 2008–18 decade. Overall manufacturing employment is expected to decline as the production process becomes more automated. However, because industrial production managers coordinate the use of both workers and machines in the production process, they will not be as affected as other occupations by automation. Nevertheless, the employment decline will result from improved productivity and increased imports of manufactured goods.

Efforts to increase efficiency at the management level have led companies to ask production managers to assume more responsibilities, particularly as computers and production management software allow managers to coordinate scheduling, planning, and communication more easily among departments. In addition, more emphasis on quality in the production process has redistributed some of the production manager's oversight responsibilities to supervisors and workers on the production line. However, most of the decisionmaking work of production managers cannot be automated, a factor that will limit the decline in their employment.

Job prospects. Despite the projected employment decline, a number of jobs are expected to open because of the need to replace workers who retire or transfer to other occupations. Applicants with experience in production occupations, along with a college degree in industrial engineering, management, or business administration (particularly those with an undergraduate engineering degree and a master's degree in business

Projections data from the National Employment Matrix

Occupational Title	SOC Code	Employment, 2008	Projected Employment, 2018	Change, 2008-2018	
				Number	Percent
Industrial production managers..	11-3051	156,100	144,100	-11,900	-8

(NOTE) Data in this table are rounded. See the discussion of the employment projections table in the *Handbook* introductory chapter on *Occupational Information Included in the Handbook*.

administration or industrial management), will enjoy the best job prospects. Employers also are likely to seek candidates who have excellent communication skills and related work experience and who are personable, flexible, and eager to enhance their knowledge and skills through ongoing training.

Earnings

Median annual wages for industrial production managers were $83,290 in May 2008. The middle 50 percent earned between $64,390 and $108,710. The lowest 10 percent earned less than $50,330, and the highest 10 percent earned more than $140,530. Median annual wages in the manufacturing industries employing the largest numbers of industrial production managers were as follows:

Navigational, measuring, electromedical,
    and control instruments manufacturing..................$97,860
Pharmaceutical and medicine manufacturing 96,620
Motor vehicle parts manufacturing 83,720
Printing and related support activities.........................80,080
Plastics product manufacturing...................................78,090

Related Occupations

Industrial production managers oversee production staff and equipment, ensure that production goals and quality standards are met, and implement company policies. Other managerial occupations with similar responsibilities include the following:

Occupations requiring comparable training and problem-solving skills include the following:

Sources of Additional Information

General information on careers in industrial production management is available from local manufacturers and schools with programs in industrial management.

For more information on careers in production management and information on the CPIM certification, contact:
➤ APICS, the Association for Operations Management, 8430 West Bryn Mawr Ave., Suite 1000, Chicago, IL 60631. Internet: **http://www.apics.org**

For more information on quality management and the CMQ/OE certification, contact:
➤ American Society for Quality, 600 North Plankinton Ave., Milwaukee, WI 53203. Internet: **http://www.asq.org**

The Occupational Information Network (O*NET) provides information on a wide range of occupational characteristics. Links to O*NET appear at the end of the Internet version of this occupational statement, accessible at **http://www.bls.gov/ooh/ocos016.htm**

Lodging Managers

Significant Points

- Long hours, including night and weekend work, are common.

- Employment is projected to grow more slowly than the average for all occupations.

- College graduates with degrees in hotel or hospitality management should have better opportunities for jobs at full-service hotels and for advancement than those without a degree.

Nature of the Work

A comfortable room, good food, and a helpful staff can make being away from home an enjoyable experience for both vacationing families and business travelers. *Lodging managers* make sure that these conveniences are provided, while also ensuring that the establishments are run efficiently and profitably. Most lodging managers work in traditional hotels and motels, but some work in other lodging establishments, such as recreational camps and RV parks, inns, boardinghouses, and youth hostels.

Lodging establishments can vary significantly in size and in the number of services they provide, which can range from supplying a simple in-room television and a continental breakfast to operating a casino and accommodating conventions. These factors affect the number and type of lodging managers employed at each property.

The one person who oversees all lodging operations at a property is usually called a *general manager*. At larger hotels with several departments and multiple layers of management, the general manager and multiple *assistant managers* coordinate the activities of separate departments. (See related sections elsewhere in the *Handbook* on supervisors and managers of housekeeping and janitorial workers; human resources, training, and labor relations managers and specialists; financial managers; advertising, marketing, promotions, public relations, and sales managers; and food service managers.) In smaller limited-service hotels—mainly those without food and beverage service—one lodging manager may direct all the activities of the property.

Lodging managers have overall responsibility for the operation and profitability of the hotel. Depending on the hotel and the size of its staff, lodging managers may either perform or direct housekeeping, personnel, office administration, marketing and sales, purchasing, security, maintenance, oversight of recreation facilities, and other activities. They may hire and train staff, set schedules, and lend a hand when needed.

Within guidelines established by the owners of the hotel or executives of the hotel chain, lodging managers set room rates, allocate funds to departments, approve expenditures, and ensure that standards for guest service, decor, housekeeping, food quality, and banquet operations are met. Increasingly, lodging managers also are responsible for ensuring that the information technology common in today's hotels is operational. Some lodging managers, often called *revenue managers*, work in financial management, monitoring room sales and reservations, overseeing accounting and cash-flow matters at the hotel, projecting occupancy levels, and deciding which rooms to discount and when to offer rate specials.

Front office managers, a category of lodging manager, coordinate reservations and room assignments and train and direct the hotel's front desk staff. They ensure that guests are treated courteously, complaints and problems are resolved, and requests for special services are carried out. At some hotels, they may greet the guests personally and provide them individual attention to see their needs are met. Any adjustments to bills often are referred to front office managers for resolution.

Convention services managers coordinate the activities of various departments to accommodate meetings, conventions, and special events. They meet with representatives of groups or organizations to plan the number of conference rooms to reserve, the configuration of the meeting space, and determine what other services the group will need, such as catering or banquets and audio, visual, or other electronic requirements. During the meeting or event, they resolve unexpected problems and monitor activities to ensure that hotel operations conform to the group's expectations.

Lodging managers may work with hotel sales and marketing directors and public relations directors to manage and coordinate the advertising and promotion of the hotel. They help develop lodging and dining specials and coordinate special events, such as holiday or seasonal specials. They may direct their staff to purchase advertising and to market their property to organizations or groups seeking a venue for conferences, conventions, business meetings, trade shows, and special events.

Lodging managers who oversee the personnel functions of a hotel or serve as human resource directors ensure that all accounting, payroll, and employee relations matters are handled in compliance with hotel policy and applicable laws. They also oversee hiring practices and standards and ensure that training and promotion programs reflect appropriate employee development guidelines.

Computers are used extensively by lodging managers and their assistants to keep track of guests' bills, reservations, room assignments, meetings, and special events. In addition, computers are used to order food, beverages, and supplies, as well as to prepare reports for hotel owners and top-level managers. Many

Lodging managers may oversee individual departments, such as housekeeping.

hotels also provide extensive information technology services for their guests. Managers work with computer specialists and other information technology specialists to ensure that the hotel's computer systems, Internet, and communications networks function properly.

Work environment. Because hotels are open around the clock, night and weekend work is common. Many lodging managers work more than 40 hours per week and are often on-call, which means they may be called back to work at any time. In some hotels and resort properties where work is seasonal, managers may have other duties less related to guest services during the off season or they may find work in other hotels or occupations.

The pressures of coordinating a wide range of activities, turning a profit for investors, and dealing with guests who sometimes are angry can be stressful. Managing conferences and working at the front desk during check-in and check-out times can be particularly hectic.

Training, Other Qualifications, and Advancement

Management trainees for larger upscale hotel chains almost always need a bachelor's or master's degree, preferably in hospitality or hotel management. If not coming from such a college background, experience working at a hotel is generally required to get a position as a lodging manager.

Education and training. Most large, full-service hotel chains usually hire people who have a bachelor's degree in business, hotel, or hospitality management for management trainee positions; however, a liberal arts degree coupled with experience in the hospitality field may be sufficient. At other hotels, especially those with fewer services, employers look for applicants with an associate degree or certificate in hotel, restaurant, or hospitality management along with experience. Formal internships or part-time or summer work in a hotel are an asset. Most degree programs include work-study opportunities.

Community colleges, junior colleges, and many universities offer certificate or degree programs in hotel, restaurant, or hospitality management leading to an associate, bachelor, or graduate degree. Technical institutes, vocational and trade schools, and other academic institutions also offer courses leading to formal recognition in hospitality management. More than 500 educational facilities across the United States provide academic training for prospective lodging managers. About 100 hospitality management programs are accredited by the Accreditation Commission for Programs in Hospitality Administration. Hotel management programs include instruction in hotel administration, accounting, economics, marketing, housekeeping, food service management and catering, and hotel maintenance and engineering. Computer training also is an integral part of hotel management training due to the widespread use of computers and hospitality-specific software in reservations, billing, and housekeeping management. Lodging managers also need to know how to generate and read profit-and-loss reports and other business and economic data.

More than 450 high schools in 45 States offer the Lodging Management Program created by the Educational Institute of the American Hotel and Lodging Association. This 2-year program offered to high school juniors and seniors teaches management principles and leads to a professional certification called

Projections data from the National Employment Matrix

Occupational Title	SOC Code	Employment, 2008	Projected Employment, 2018	Change, 2008-2018	
				Number	Percent
Lodging managers..	11-9081	59,800	62,600	2,800	5

(NOTE) Data in this table are rounded. See the discussion of the employment projections table in the *Handbook* introductory chapter on *Occupational Information Included in the Handbook.*

the "Certified Rooms Division Specialist." Many colleges and universities grant participants in this program credit towards a postsecondary degree in hotel management.

Hotel employees who do not have hospitality training or a college degree but who do demonstrate leadership potential and possess sufficient experience may be invited to participate in a management training program sponsored by the hotel or a hotel chain's corporate parent. Those who already possess the people skills and service orientation needed to succeed in hotel management can usually train for technical expertise in areas such as computer use and accounting principles while on the job. Trainees usually begin as assistant managers and may rotate assignments among the hotel's departments to gain a wide range of experiences. Relocation to another property may be required to help round out the experience and to help a trainee grow into a more responsible management position in a larger or busier hotel.

Other qualifications. Lodging managers must be able to get along with many different types of people, even in stressful situations. They must be able to solve problems quickly and concentrate on details. Initiative, self-discipline, effective communication skills, and the ability to organize and direct the work of others are essential for lodging managers. Managers must have a good knowledge of hotel operations, including safety and security measures, repair and maintenance, and personnel practices. Knowledge of hotel financing is essential to operate a hotel profitably.

Certification and advancement. Large hotel chains may offer better opportunities for advancement than small, independently owned establishments, but relocation every several years often is necessary for advancement. Large chains have more extensive career ladder programs and offer managers the opportunity to transfer to another hotel in the chain or to a regional or central office. Career advancement can be accelerated by the completion of certification programs offered by various hotel and lodging associations. Certification usually requires a combination of course work, examinations, and experience.

Employment

Most lodging managers work in the traveler accommodation industry, including hotels and motels, although they can work for any business that provides room or shelter for people. Companies that manage hotels under contract also employ lodging managers. Lodging managers held about 59,800 jobs in 2008. Most lodging managers—almost half—worked in hotels and motels; almost as many lodging managers were self-employed, primarily as owners of small hotels and bed-and-breakfast inns.

Job Outlook

Slower than average growth in employment will result as the lodging industry shifts to building more limited service hotels

and fewer full-service properties that have more departments to manage. Those seeking jobs at hotels with the highest level of guest services will face keen competition as these jobs are highly sought after by people trained in hospitality.

Employment change. Employment of lodging managers is expected to grow 5 percent from 2008 to 2018, which is slower than the average for all occupations. Over the decade, travel and tourism is expected to grow, however, more new hotels will be smaller limited-service hotels that will not have large staffs or need many managers. In addition, in order to cut expenses, some lodging places are streamlining operations and either eliminating some managers or requiring fewer to be available at all times. Chain hotels are increasingly assigning a single manager to oversee multiple properties within a region. Despite these cutbacks in management, larger full-service hotels, including resort, casino, and convention hotels that provide a wider range of services to a much larger customer base will continue to generate job openings for experienced managers and management trainees.

Job prospects. Job openings are expected to occur as experienced managers leave the labor force or transfer to other occupations, in part because of the long hours and stressful working conditions. Job opportunities are expected to be best for people with good customer service skills and experience in the food service or hospitality industries. People with a college degree in hotel or hospitality management are expected to have better opportunities, particularly at upscale and luxury hotels.

Earnings

Median annual wages of lodging managers were $45,800 in May 2008. The middle 50 percent earned between $34,970 and $62,880. The lowest 10 percent earned less than $28,160 and the highest 10 percent earned more than $84,270. Median annual wages for lodging managers in traveler accommodations were $45,380.

Salaries of lodging managers vary greatly according to their responsibilities, location, and the segment of the hotel industry in which they work. Managers may earn bonuses of up to 25 percent of their basic salary in some hotels and also may be furnished with meals, parking, laundry, and other services. In addition to providing typical benefits, some hotels offer profit-sharing plans and educational assistance to their employees.

Related Occupations

Other workers who supervise or manage a business focused on customer service include:

Sources of Additional Information

For information on the hotel and lodging industry, contact:
➤ American Hotel and Lodging Association, 1201 New York Ave. NW., Suite 600, Washington, DC 20005. Internet: **http://www.ahla.com**

Information on careers in the lodging industry and professional development and training programs may be obtained from:
➤ Educational Institute of the American Hotel and Lodging Association, 800 N. Magnolia Ave., Suite 300, Orlando, FL 32803. Internet: **http://www.ei-ahla.org**

For information on educational programs in hotel and restaurant management, including correspondence courses, write to:
➤ International Council on Hotel, Restaurant, and Institutional Education, 2810 North Parham Rd., Suite 230, Richmond, VA 23294. Internet: **http://www.chrie.org**

Information on accreditation standards and a list of accredited educational programs in hospitality administration may be obtained from:
➤ Accreditation Commission for Programs in Hospitality Administration, PO Box 400, Oxford, MD 21654. Internet: **http://www.acpha-cahm.org/**

The Occupational Information Network (O*NET) provides information on a wide range of occupational characteristics. Links to O*NET appear at the end of the Internet version of this occupational statement, accessible at **http://www.bls.gov/ooh/ocos015.htm**

Medical and Health Services Managers

Significant Points

- Job opportunities will be good, especially for applicants with work experience in healthcare and strong business and management skills.

- A master's degree is the standard credential, although a bachelor's degree is adequate for some entry-level positions.

- Medical and health services managers typically work long hours and may be called at all hours to deal with problems.

Nature of the Work

Healthcare is a business and, like every business, it needs good management to keep the business running smoothly. *Medical and health services managers*, also referred to as healthcare executives or healthcare administrators, plan, direct, coordinate, and supervise the delivery of healthcare. These workers are either specialists in charge of a specific clinical department or generalists who manage an entire facility or system.

The structure and financing of healthcare are changing rapidly. Future medical and health services managers must be prepared to deal with the integration of healthcare delivery systems, technological innovations, an increasingly complex regulatory environment, restructuring of work, and an increased focus on preventive care. They will be called on to improve efficiency in healthcare facilities and the quality of the care provided.

Large facilities usually have several *assistant administrators* who aid the top administrator and handle daily decisions. Assistant administrators direct activities in clinical areas, such as nursing, surgery, therapy, medical records, and health information.

In smaller facilities, top administrators handle more of the details of daily operations. For example, many *nursing home administrators* manage personnel, finances, facility operations, and admissions, while also providing resident care.

Clinical managers have training or experience in a specific clinical area and, accordingly, have more specific responsibilities than do generalists. For example, directors of physical therapy are experienced physical therapists, and most health information and medical record administrators have a bachelor's degree in health information or medical record administration. Clinical managers establish and implement policies, objectives, and procedures for their departments; evaluate personnel and work quality; develop reports and budgets; and coordinate activities with other managers.

Health information managers are responsible for the maintenance and security of all patient records. Recent regulations enacted by the Federal Government require that all healthcare providers maintain electronic patient records and that these records be secure. As a result, health information managers must keep up with current computer and software technology, as well as with legislative requirements. In addition, as patient data become more frequently used for quality management and in medical research, health information managers must ensure that databases are complete, accurate, and available only to authorized personnel.

In group medical practices, managers work closely with physicians. Whereas an office manager might handle business affairs in small medical groups, leaving policy decisions to the physicians themselves, larger groups usually employ a full-time administrator to help formulate business strategies and coordinate day-to-day business.

A small group of 10 to 15 physicians might employ 1 administrator to oversee personnel matters, billing and collection, budgeting, planning, equipment outlays, and patient flow. A large practice of 40 to 50 physicians might have a chief administrator and several assistants, each responsible for a different area of expertise.

Medical and health services managers in managed care settings perform functions similar to those of their counterparts in large group practices, except that they could have larger staffs to manage. In addition, they might do more community outreach and preventive care than do managers of a group practice.

Some medical and health services managers oversee the activities of a number of facilities in health systems. Such systems might contain both inpatient and outpatient facilities and offer a wide range of patient services.

Work environment. Some managers work in comfortable, private offices; others share space with other staff. Many medical and health services managers work long hours. Nursing care facilities and hospitals operate around the clock; administrators

Large healthcare facilities usually have several assistant administrators who aid the top administrator and handle daily decisions.

and managers may be called at all hours to deal with problems. They also travel to attend meetings or to inspect satellite facilities.

Training, Other Qualifications, and Advancement

A master's degree in one of a number of fields is the standard credential for most generalist positions as a medical or healthcare manager. A bachelor's degree is sometimes adequate for entry-level positions in smaller facilities and departments. In physicians' offices and some other facilities, on-the-job experience may substitute for formal education.

Education and training. Medical and health services managers must be familiar with management principles and practices. A master's degree in health services administration, long-term care administration, health sciences, public health, public administration, or business administration is the standard credential for most generalist positions in this field. However, a bachelor's degree is adequate for some entry-level positions in smaller facilities, at the departmental level within healthcare organizations, and in health information management. Physicians' offices and some other facilities hire those with on-the-job experience instead of formal education.

Bachelor's, master's, and doctoral degree programs in health administration are offered by colleges; universities; and schools of public health, medicine, allied health, public administration, and business administration. In 2008, according to the Commission on Accreditation of Healthcare Management Education, there were 72 schools that had accredited programs leading to the master's degree in health services administration.

For people seeking to become heads of clinical departments, a degree in the appropriate field and work experience may be sufficient early in their career. However, a master's degree in health services administration or a related field might be required to advance. For example, nursing service administrators usually are chosen from among supervisory registered nurses with administrative abilities and graduate degrees in nursing or health services administration.

Health information managers require a bachelor's degree from an accredited program. In 2008, there were 48 accredited bachelor's degree programs and 5 master's degree programs in health information management, according to the Commission

on Accreditation for Health Informatics and Information Management Education.

Some graduate programs seek students with undergraduate degrees in business or health administration; however, many graduate programs prefer students with a liberal arts or health profession background. Candidates with previous work experience in healthcare also may have an advantage. Competition for entry into these programs is keen, and applicants need above-average grades to gain admission. Graduate programs usually last between 2 and 3 years. They may include up to 1 year of supervised administrative experience and coursework in areas such as hospital organization and management, marketing, accounting and budgeting, human resources administration, strategic planning, law and ethics, biostatistics or epidemiology, health economics, and health information systems. Some programs allow students to specialize in one type of facility—hospitals, nursing care facilities, mental health facilities, or medical groups. Other programs encourage a generalist approach to health administration education.

Licensure. All States and the District of Columbia require nursing care facility administrators to have a bachelor's degree, pass a licensing examination, complete a State-approved training program, and pursue continuing education. Some States also require licenses for administrators in assisted-living facilities. A license is not required in other areas of medical and health services management.

Certification and other qualifications. Medical and health services managers often are responsible for facilities and equipment worth millions of dollars, and for hundreds of employees. To make effective decisions, they need to be open to different opinions and good at analyzing contradictory information. They must understand finance and information systems and be able to interpret data. Motivating others to implement their decisions requires strong leadership abilities. Tact, diplomacy, flexibility, and communication skills are essential because medical and health services managers spend most of their time interacting with others.

Health information managers who have a bachelor's degree or post baccalaureate degree from an approved program and who pass an exam can earn certification as a Registered Health Information Administrator from the American Health Information Management Association.

Advancement. Medical and health services managers advance by moving into more responsible and higher paying positions, such as assistant or associate administrator, department head, or chief executive officer, or by moving to larger facilities. Some experienced managers also may become consultants or professors of health care management.

New graduates with master's degrees in health services administration may start as department managers or as supervisory staff. The level of the starting position varies with the experience of the applicant and the size of the organization. Hospitals and other health facilities offer postgraduate residencies and fellowships, which usually are staff positions. Graduates from master's degree programs also take jobs in large medical group practices, clinics, mental health facilities, nursing care corporations, and consulting firms.

Projections data from the National Employment Matrix

Occupational Title	SOC Code	Employment, 2008	Projected Employment, 2018	Change, 2008-2018	
				Number	Percent
Medical and health services managers..	11-9111	283,500	328,800	45,400	16

(NOTE) Data in this table are rounded. See the discussion of the employment projections table in the *Handbook* introductory chapter on *Occupational Information Included in the Handbook.*

Graduates with bachelor's degrees in health administration usually begin as administrative assistants or assistant department heads in larger hospitals. They also may begin as department heads or assistant administrators in small hospitals or nursing care facilities.

Employment

Medical and health services managers held about 283,500 jobs in 2008. About 38 percent worked in hospitals, and another 19 percent worked in offices of physicians or in nursing and residential care facilities. Many of the remainder worked in home healthcare services, Federal Government health care facilities, outpatient care centers, insurance carriers, and community care facilities for the elderly.

Job Outlook

Employment is projected to grow faster than the average. Job opportunities should be good, especially for applicants with work experience in healthcare and strong business management skills.

Employment change. Employment of medical and health services managers is expected to grow 16 percent from 2008 to 2018, faster than the average for all occupations. The healthcare industry will continue to expand and diversify, requiring managers to help ensure smooth business operations.

Managers in all settings will be needed to improve quality and efficiency of healthcare, while controlling costs, as insurance companies and Medicare demand higher levels of accountability. Managers also will be needed to oversee the computerization of patient records and to ensure their security as required by law. Additional demand for managers will stem from the need to recruit workers and increase employee retention, to comply with changing regulations, to implement new technology, and to help improve the health of their communities by emphasizing preventive care.

Hospitals will continue to employ the most medical and health services managers over the 2008–18 decade. However, the number of new jobs created is expected to increase at a slower rate in hospitals than in many other industries because of the growing use of clinics and other outpatient care sites. Despite relatively slow employment growth in hospitals, a large number of new jobs will be created because of the industry's large size.

Employment will grow fast in offices of health practitioners. Many services previously provided in hospitals will continue to shift to these settings, especially as medical technologies improve. Demand in medical group practice management will grow as medical group practices become larger and more complex.

Medical and health services managers also will be employed by healthcare management companies that provide manage-ment services to hospitals and other organizations and to specific departments such as emergency, information management systems, managed care contract negotiations, and physician recruiting.

Job prospects. Job opportunities will be good, especially for applicants with work experience in healthcare and strong business management skills. Medical and health services managers with experience in large hospital facilities will enjoy an advantage in the job market, as hospitals become larger and more complex. Competition for jobs at the highest management levels will be keen because of the high pay and prestige.

Earnings

Median annual wages of wage and salary medical and health services managers were $80,240 in May 2008. The middle 50 percent earned between $62,170 and $104,120. The lowest 10 percent earned less than $48,300, and the highest 10 percent earned more than $137,800. Median annual wages in the industries employing the largest numbers of medical and health services managers in May 2008 were:

General medical and surgical hospitals	$87,040
Outpatient care centers	74,130
Offices of physicians	74,060
Home health care services	71,450
Nursing care facilities	71,190

Earnings of medical and health services managers vary by type and size of the facility and by level of responsibility. For example, the Medical Group Management Association reported that, in 2007, median salaries for administrators were $82,423 in practices with 6 or fewer physicians; $105,710 in practices with 7 to 25 physicians; and $119,000 in practices with 26 or more physicians.

According to a survey by the Professional Association of Health Care Office Management, 2009 average total compensation for office managers in specialty physicians' practices was $54,314 in gastroenterology; $54,201 in dermatology; $58,899 in cardiology; $48,793 in ophthalmology; $44,910 in obstetrics and gynecology; $51,263 in orthopedics; $51,466 in pediatrics; $48,814 in internal medicine; and $47,152 in family practice.

Related Occupations

Medical and health services managers have training or experience in both health and management. Other occupations requiring knowledge of both fields include:

Sources of Additional Information

Information about undergraduate and graduate academic programs in this field is available from:

➤ Association of University Programs in Health Administration, 2000 North 14th St., Suite 780, Arlington, VA 22201. Internet: **http://www.aupha.org**

For a list of accredited graduate programs in medical and health services administration, contact:

➤ Commission on Accreditation of Healthcare Management Education, 2111 Wilson Blvd., Suite 700, Arlington, VA 22201. Internet: **http://www.cahme.org**

For information about career opportunities in healthcare management, contact:

➤ American College of Healthcare Executives, One N. Franklin St., Suite 1700, Chicago, IL 60606. Internet: **http://www.healthmanagementcareers.org**

For information about career opportunities in long-term care administration, contact:

➤ American College of Healthcare Administrators, 1321 Duke St., Suite 400, Alexandria, VA 22314. Internet: **http://www.achca.org**

For information about career opportunities in medical group practices and ambulatory care management, contact:

➤ Medical Group Management Association, 104 Inverness Terrace East, Englewood, CO 80112. Internet: **http://www.mgma.org**

For information about medical and healthcare office managers, contact:

➤ Professional Association of Health Care Office Management, 3755 Avocado Blvd., Suite 306, La Mesa, CA 91941. Internet: **http://www.pahcom.com**

For information about career opportunities in health information management, contact:

➤ American Health Information Management Association, 233 N. Michigan Ave., 21st Floor, Chicago, IL 60601. Internet: **http://www.ahima.org**

The Occupational Information Network (O*NET) provides information on a wide range of occupational characteristics. Links to O*NET appear at the end of the Internet version of this occupational statement, accessible at **http://www.bls.gov/ooh/ocos014.htm**

Property, Real Estate, and Community Association Managers

Significant Points

- Opportunities should be best for those with college degrees in business administration, real estate, or related fields and for those with professional designations.

- Particularly good opportunities are expected for those with experience managing housing for older people or with experience running a healthcare facility.

- About 46 percent of property, real estate, and community association managers are self-employed.

Nature of the Work

To homeowners, a well-managed property looks nice, operates smoothly, and preserves the resale value of the property. To businesses and investors, properly managed real estate may result in greater income and profits. *Property, real estate, and community association managers* maintain and raise the value of real estate investments by handling the logistics of running a property. *Property and real estate managers* oversee the operation of income-producing commercial or residential properties and ensure that real estate investments achieve their expected revenues. *Community association managers* manage the communal property and services of condominiums, cooperatives, and planned communities through their homeowner or community associations.

When owners of residential homes, apartments, office buildings, or retail or industrial properties lack the time or expertise needed for the day-to-day management of their real estate investments or homeowner associations, they often hire a property or real estate manager or a community association manager. Managers are employed either directly by the owner or indirectly through a contract with a property management firm.

Generally, property and real estate managers handle the financial operations of the property, making certain that rent is collected and that mortgages, taxes, insurance premiums, payroll, and maintenance bills are paid on time. Some oversee the preparation of financial statements and periodically report to the owners on the status of the property, occupancy rates, expiration dates of leases, and other matters. When vacancies occur, property managers may advertise the property or hire a leasing agent to find a tenant. They also may suggest to the owners what rent to charge. In community associations, homeowners pay no rent and pay their own real estate taxes and mortgages, but community association managers collect association fees that help pay for a variety of services such as playground, clubhouse, and swimming pool maintenance.

Often, property managers negotiate contracts for janitorial, security, landscaping, trash removal, and other services. They monitor the performance of contractors and investigate and resolve complaints from residents and tenants when services are not properly provided. Managers also purchase supplies and equipment for the property and make arrangements with professionals for repairs that cannot be handled by regular property maintenance staff.

In addition to fulfilling these duties, property managers must understand and comply with pertinent legislation, such as the Americans with Disabilities Act, the Federal Fair Housing Amendment Act, and local fair housing laws. They must make certain that their renting and advertising practices are not discriminatory and that the property itself acts in accordance with all of the local, State, and Federal regulatory and building codes.

Onsite property managers are responsible for the day-to-day operations of a single property, such as an apartment complex, an office building, a shopping center, or a community association. To ensure that the property is safe and properly maintained, onsite managers routinely inspect the grounds, facilities, and equipment to determine whether repairs or maintenance is needed. In handling requests for repairs or trying to resolve

When vacancies occur, property, real estate, and community association managers may advertise the property or hire a leasing agent to find a tenant.

complaints, they meet not only with current residents, but also with prospective residents or tenants to show vacant apartments or office space. Onsite managers also are responsible for enforcing the terms of rental or lease contracts, such as rent collection, parking and pet restrictions, and termination-of-lease procedures. Other important duties of onsite managers include keeping accurate, up-to-date records of income and expenditures from property operations and submitting regular expense reports to the senior-level property manager or the owner(s).

Some property and real estate managers, often called *real estate asset managers*, plan and direct the purchase, sale, and development of real estate properties on behalf of businesses and investors. These managers focus on long-term strategic financial planning, rather than on day-to-day operations of the property. In deciding to acquire property, real estate asset managers consider several factors, such as property values, taxes, zoning, population growth, transportation, and traffic volume and patterns. Once a site is selected, they negotiate contracts for the purchase or lease of the property, securing the most favorable terms. Real estate asset managers review their company's real estate holdings periodically and identify properties that are no longer financially profitable. They then negotiate the sale of, or terminate the lease on, such properties.

Community association managers, by contrast, do work that more closely compares to that of onsite property managers. They collect monthly assessments, prepare financial statements and budgets, negotiate with contractors, and help to resolve complaints. Usually hired by a volunteer board of directors of the association, they manage the daily affairs, and supervise the maintenance, of property and facilities that the homeowners own and use jointly through the association. Community association managers also assist the board and owners in complying with association and government rules and regulations.

Some associations cover thousands of homes and employ their own onsite staff and managers. In addition to administering an association's financial records and budget, managers may be responsible for the operation of community pools, golf courses, and community centers and for the maintenance of landscaping and parking areas. Community association managers regularly meet with the elected boards of directors to discuss and resolve legal issues or disputes that may have an effect on the owners, as well as to review any proposed changes or improvements by homeowners to their properties, to make sure that they comply with community guidelines. They may also meet to address association finances or discuss long-term planning.

Work environment. Nearly all property, real estate, and community association managers work out of an office. However, many managers spend a significant portion of their time away from their desks. Onsite managers, in particular, may spend a large part of their workday away from their offices, visiting the building engineer, showing apartments, checking on the janitorial and maintenance staff, or investigating problems reported by residents. Real estate asset managers may spend time away from home while traveling to company real estate holdings or searching for properties to purchase.

Property, real estate, and community association managers often must attend evening meetings with residents, property owners, community association boards of directors, or civic groups. Not surprisingly, many managers put in long workdays, especially before financial and tax reports are due and before board and annual meetings. Some apartment managers are required to live in the apartment complexes where they work, so that they are available to handle emergencies, even when they are off duty. They usually receive compensatory time off for working nights or weekends. Many apartment managers receive time off during the week so that they may be available on weekends to show apartments to prospective residents.

Training, Other Qualifications, and Advancement

For the most part, onsite property managers who primarily oversee the rental and maintenance of properties learn on the job or have experience in the real estate or maintenance field. Managers of commercial properties and those dealing with a property's finances and contract management increasingly are needing a bachelor's or master's degree in business administration, accounting, finance, or real estate management, especially if they do not have much practical experience.

Education and training. Most employers prefer to hire college graduates for property management positions, particularly for offsite positions dealing with a property's finances and contract management and for most commercial properties. A bachelor's or master's degree in business administration, accounting, finance, real estate, or public administration is preferred for these positions. Those with degrees in the liberal arts also may qualify, especially if they have relevant coursework. In addition, most new managers participate in on-the-job training.

Many people entering jobs such as assistant property manager have onsite management experience.

Licensure.   Real estate managers who buy or sell property are required to be licensed by the State in which they practice. In a few States, property association managers must be licensed. Managers of public housing subsidized by the Federal Government are required to be certified.

Other qualifications.   Previous employment as a real estate sales agent may be an asset to onsite managers, because it provides experience that is useful in showing apartments or office space. In the past, those with backgrounds in building maintenance have advanced to onsite management positions on the depth of their knowledge of mechanical systems in buildings, but this path is becoming less common as employers place greater emphasis on administrative, financial, and communication abilities for managerial jobs.

People most commonly enter real estate asset manager jobs by transferring from positions as property managers or real estate brokers. Real estate asset managers must be good negotiators, adept at persuading and working with people, and good at analyzing data in order to assess the fair-market value of property or its development potential. Resourcefulness and creativity in arranging financing are essential for managers who specialize in land development.

Good speaking, writing, computer, and financial skills, as well as an ability to deal tactfully with people, are essential in all areas of property management.

Certification and advancement.   Many people begin property management careers as assistants, working closely with a property manager and learning how to prepare budgets, analyze insurance coverage and risk options, market property to prospective tenants, and collect overdue rent payments. In time, many assistants advance to property manager positions.

Some people start as onsite managers of apartment buildings, office complexes, or community associations. As they gain experience, often working under the supervision of a more experienced property manager, they may advance to positions of greater responsibility. Those who excel as onsite managers often transfer to assistant offsite property manager positions, in which they can gain experience handling a broad range of property management responsibilities.

The responsibilities and compensation of property, real estate, and community association managers increase as these workers manage more and larger properties. Property managers are responsible for several properties at a time. As their careers advance, they gradually are entrusted with larger properties that are more complex to manage. Many specialize in the management of one type of property, such as apartments, office buildings, condominiums, cooperatives, homeowners' associations, or retail properties. Managers who do well at marketing properties to tenants might specialize in managing new properties, while those who are specifically knowledgeable about buildings and their mechanical systems might specialize in the management of older properties requiring renovation or more frequent repairs. Some experienced managers open their own property management firms.

Many employers encourage managers to attend short-term formal training programs conducted by various professional and trade associations that are active in the real estate field. Employers send managers to these programs to develop their management skills and expand their knowledge of specialized fields, such as the operation and maintenance of mechanical systems in buildings, the improvement of property values, insurance and risk management, personnel management, business and real estate law, community association risks and liabilities, tenant relations, communications, accounting and financial concepts, and reserve funding. Managers also participate in these programs to prepare themselves for positions of greater responsibility in property management. The completion of such programs, plus related job experience and a satisfactory score on a written examination, can lead to certification, or the formal award of a professional designation, by the sponsoring association. (Some organizations offering certifications are listed as sources of additional information at the end of this statement.) A number of associations also require their members to adhere to a specific code of ethics.

Employment

Property, real estate, and community association managers held about 304,100 jobs in 2008. About 46 percent of these managers are self-employed. Another 21 percent worked for lessors of real estate and in offices of real estate agents and brokers. Others worked for government agencies that manage public buildings.

Job Outlook

As fast as average employment growth is expected. Opportunities should be best for jobseekers with a college degree in business administration, real estate, or a related field and for those who attain a professional designation. Particularly good opportunities are expected for those with experience managing housing for older people or with experience running health care facilities.

Employment change.   Employment of property, real estate, and community association managers is projected to increase by 8 percent during the 2008–18 decade, about as fast as average for all occupations. Job growth will be attributable to a growing population that will increasingly live in developments managed by third-party property management companies. These developments include apartment buildings, condomini-

Projections data from the National Employment Matrix

Occupational Title	SOC Code	Employment, 2008	Projected Employment, 2018	Change, 2008-2018	
				Number	Percent
Property, real estate, and community association managers.............	11-9141	304,100	329,700	25,600	8

(NOTE) Data in this table are rounded. See the discussion of the employment projections table in the *Handbook* introductory chapter on *Occupational Information Included in the Handbook.*

ums, homeowner associations, and the fast-growing amount of senior housing. Developments of new homes are increasingly being organized with community or homeowner associations that provide community services and oversee jointly owned common areas requiring professional management. There is also increasing awareness that property management firms help make properties more profitable and improve the resale value of homes and commercial property.

To cater to the increasing population, a small rise in the number of commercial and retail buildings that will need to be managed also will generate jobs for property managers.

Job prospects. In addition to openings from job growth, a number of openings are expected as managers transfer to other occupations or leave the labor force. Opportunities should be best for jobseekers with a college degree in business administration, real estate, or a related field and for those who attain a professional designation. Because of the projected increase in the elderly population, particularly good opportunities are expected for those with experience managing housing for older people and with experience managing healthcare facilities.

Earnings

Median annual wages of salaried property, real estate, and community association managers were $46,130 in May 2008. The middle 50 percent earned between $31,730 and $68,770 a year. The lowest 10 percent earned less than $21,860, and the highest 10 percent earned more than $102,250 a year. Median annual wages of salaried property, real estate, and community association managers in the largest industries that employed them in May 2008 were as follows:

Management of companies and enterprises	$74,010
Local government	59,480
Offices of real estate agents and brokers	44,160
Activities related to real estate	43,430
Lessors of real estate	40,180

Many resident apartment managers and onsite association managers receive the use of an apartment as part of their compensation package. In addition, managers often are reimbursed for the use of their personal vehicles.

Related Occupations

Property, real estate, and community association managers plan, organize, staff, and manage the real estate operations of businesses. Workers who perform similar functions in other fields include the following:

Sources of Additional Information

For information about education and careers in property management, as well as information about professional designation and certification programs in both residential and commercial property management, contact:

➤ Institute of Real Estate Management, 430 N. Michigan Ave., Chicago, IL 60611. Internet: **http://www.irem.org**

For information on careers and certification programs in commercial property management, asset management, facility management, and building systems maintenance, contact:

➤ Building Owners and Managers Institute, One Park Place, Suite 475, Annapolis, MD 21401. Internet: **http://www.bomi.org**

For information on careers and professional designation and certification programs in residential property management and community association management, contact:

➤ Community Associations Institute, 225 Reinekers Ln., Suite 300, Alexandria, VA 22314. Internet: **http://www.caionline.org**

➤ National Board of Certification for Community Association Managers, 225 Reinekers Ln., Suite 310, Alexandria, VA 22314. Internet: **http://www.nbccam.org**

The Occupational Information Network (O*NET) provides information on a wide range of occupational characteristics. Links to O*NET appear at the end of the Internet version of this occupational statement, accessible at **http://www.bls.gov/ooh/ocos022.htm**

Purchasing Managers, Buyers, and Purchasing Agents

Significant Points

- About 42 percent of purchasing managers, buyers, and purchasing agents are employed in wholesale trade or manufacturing establishments.

- Employment is projected to grow 7 percent, which is as fast as the average.

- Opportunities should be best for those with a college degree in engineering, business, economics, or one of the applied sciences.

- Prospects often need continuing education or certification to advance.

Nature of the Work

Purchasing managers, buyers, and *purchasing agents* buy a vast array of farm products, durable and nondurable goods, and services for companies and institutions. They attempt to get the best deal for their company—the highest quality goods and services at the lowest possible cost. They accomplish this by studying sales records and inventory levels of current stock, identifying foreign and domestic suppliers, and keeping abreast of changes affecting both the supply of, and demand for, needed products and materials. Purchasing professionals consider price, quality, availability, reliability, and technical support when choosing suppliers and merchandise. To be effective,

Purchasing professionals use many resources to gather information about potential suppliers.

purchasing professionals must have a working technical knowledge of the goods or services to be purchased.

There are several major types of purchasing managers, buyers, and purchasing agents. *Wholesale and retail buyers* purchase goods, such as clothing or electronics, for resale. Purchasing agents buy goods and services for use by their own company or organization. *Purchasing agents and buyers of farm products* purchase goods such as grain, Christmas trees, and tobacco for further processing or resale. Purchasing managers usually handle more complicated purchases and may supervise a group of purchasing agents. Purchasing professionals employed by government agencies or manufacturing firms usually are called purchasing directors, managers, or agents; sometimes they are known as contract specialists. Purchasing professionals in government place solicitations for services and accept bids and offers through the Internet. Some purchasing managers, called contract or supply managers, specialize in negotiating and supervising supply contracts.

Purchasing specialists who buy finished goods for resale are employed by wholesale and retail establishments, where they commonly are known as buyers or *merchandise managers.* Wholesale and retail buyers are an integral part of a complex system of distribution and merchandising that caters to the vast array of consumer needs and desires. Wholesale buyers purchase goods directly from manufacturers or from other wholesale firms for resale to retail firms, commercial establishments, and other organizations. In retail firms, buyers purchase goods from wholesale firms or directly from manufacturers for resale to the public.

Buyers largely determine which products their establishment will sell. Therefore, it is essential that they have the ability to predict what will appeal to consumers. If they fail to purchase the right products for resale, buyers jeopardize the profits and reputation of their company. They keep track of inventories and sales levels, check competitors' sales activities, and watch general economic conditions to anticipate consumer buying patterns. Buyers working for large and medium-sized firms usually specialize in acquiring one or two lines of merchandise, whereas buyers working for small stores may purchase the establishment's complete inventory.

Evaluating suppliers is one of the most critical functions of a purchasing manager, buyer, or purchasing agent. Many firms now run on a lean manufacturing schedule and use just-in-time inventories so any delays in the supply chain can shut down production and potentially cost the firm its customers. Purchasing professionals use many resources to find out all they can about potential suppliers. The Internet has become an effective tool for searching catalogs, trade journals, industry and company publications, and directories. Purchasing professionals attend meetings, trade shows, and conferences to learn of new industry trends and make contacts with suppliers. They often interview prospective suppliers and visit their plants and distribution centers to assess their capabilities. It is important to make certain that the supplier is capable of delivering the desired goods or services on time, in the correct quantities, and without sacrificing quality. Once all of the necessary information on suppliers is gathered, orders are placed, and contracts are awarded to those suppliers who meet the purchaser's needs. Most of the transaction process is now automated through use of the Internet.

Purchasing professionals often work closely with other employees in a process called "team buying." For example, before submitting an order, the team may discuss the design of custom-made products with company design engineers, the problems involving the quality of purchased goods with production supervisors, or the issues in shipping with managers in the receiving department. This additional interaction improves the quality of buying by adding different perspectives to the process.

Work environment. Most purchasing managers, buyers, and purchasing agents work in comfortable offices. They frequently work more than the standard 40-hour week, because of special sales, conferences, or production deadlines. Evening and weekend work also is common before holiday and back-to-school seasons for those working in retail trade. Consequently, many retail firms discourage the use of vacation time during peak periods. Travel is sometimes necessary. Purchasers for worldwide companies may even travel outside the United States.

Training, Other Qualifications, and Advancement

Workers may begin as trainees, purchasing clerks, junior buyers, or assistant buyers. Most employers prefer to hire applicants who have a college degree and who are familiar with the merchandise they sell and with wholesaling and retailing practices. Prospects often need continuing education or certification to advance.

Education and training. Educational requirements tend to vary with the size of the organization. Large stores and distributors prefer applicants who have completed a bachelor's degree program with a business emphasis. Many manufacturing firms put an even greater emphasis on formal training, preferring applicants with a bachelor's or master's degree in engineering, business, economics, or one of the applied sciences. A master's degree is essential for advancement to many top-level purchasing manager jobs.

Regardless of academic preparation, new employees must learn the specifics of their employer's business. Training periods vary in length, with most lasting 1 to 5 years. In manufacturing, new employees work with experienced purchasers to learn about commodities, prices, suppliers, and markets. In addition, they may be assigned to the production planning department to learn about the material requirements system and the inventory system the company uses to keep production and replenishment functions working smoothly.

In wholesale and retail establishments, most trainees begin by selling merchandise, checking invoices on material received, and keeping track of stock. As they progress, trainees are given increased buying-related responsibilities.

Other qualifications. Purchasing managers, buyers, and purchasing agents must know how to use various software packages and the Internet. Other important qualities include the ability to analyze technical data in suppliers' proposals; good communication, negotiation, and mathematical skills; knowledge of supply-chain management; and the ability to perform financial analyses.

People who wish to become wholesale or retail buyers should be good at planning and decision making. They also should have an interest in merchandising. In addition, marketing skills and the ability to identify products that will sell are very important. Employers often look for leadership ability, too, because buyers spend a large portion of their time supervising assistant buyers and dealing with manufacturers' representatives and store executives.

Certification and advancement. An experienced purchasing agent or buyer may become an assistant purchasing manager before advancing to purchasing manager, supply manager, or director of materials management. At the top levels, duties may overlap with other management functions, such as production, planning, logistics, and marketing.

Regardless of industry, continuing education is essential for advancement. Many purchasing managers, buyers, and purchasing agents participate in seminars offered by professional societies and take college courses in supply management. Professional certification is becoming increasingly important, especially for those just entering the occupation.

There are several recognized credentials for purchasing agents and purchasing managers. The Certified Purchasing Manager (C.P.M.) designation was conferred by the Institute for Supply Management. In 2008, this certification was replaced by the Certified Professional in Supply Management (CPSM) credential, covering the wider scope of duties now performed by purchasing professionals. The Certified Purchasing Professional (CPP) and Certified Professional Purchasing

Manager (CPPM) designations are conferred by the American Purchasing Society. The Certified Supply Chain Professional (CSCP) credential is conferred by APICS, the Association for Operations Management. For workers in Federal, State, and local government, the National Institute of Governmental Purchasing offers the designations of Certified Professional Public Buyer (CPPB) and Certified Public Purchasing Officer (CPPO). These certifications are awarded only after work-related experience and education requirements are met and written or oral exams are successfully completed.

Employment

Purchasing managers, buyers, and purchasing agents held about 527,400 jobs in 2008. About 42 percent worked in the wholesale trade and manufacturing industries and another 10 percent worked in retail trade. The remainder worked mostly in service establishments, such as management of companies and enterprises or professional, scientific, and technical services. A small number were self-employed.

The following tabulation shows the distribution of employment by occupational specialty:

Purchasing agents, except wholesale, retail,
    and farm products..295,200
Wholesale and retail buyers, except farm products....147,700
Purchasing managers...70,300
Purchasing agents and buyers, farm products..............14,100

Job Outlook

Employment of purchasing managers, buyers, and purchasing agents is expected to increase 7 percent through the year 2018. Job growth and opportunities, however, will differ among different occupations in this category.

Employment change. Overall employment of purchasing managers, buyers, and purchasing agents is expected to increase 7 percent during the 2008-18 decade, which is as fast as the average for all occupations. Employment of purchasing agents, except wholesale, retail, and farm products—the largest employment group in the industry—will experience faster than average growth as more companies demand a greater number of purchased goods and services. Additionally, large companies are increasing the size of their purchasing departments to accommodate purchasing services contracts from smaller companies. Also, many purchasing agents are now charged with procuring services that traditionally had been done in-house,

Projections data from the National Employment Matrix

Occupational Title	SOC Code	Employment, 2008	Projected Employment, 2018	Change, 2008-2018	
				Number	Percent
Purchasing managers, buyers, and purchasing agents	–	527,400	565,900	38,500	7
Purchasing managers	11-3061	70,300	71,400	1,100	2
Buyers and purchasing agents..	13-1020	457,100	494,500	37,400	8
Purchasing agents and buyers, farm products...........................	13-1021	14,100	14,000	-200	-1
Wholesale and retail buyers, except farm products	13-1022	147,700	144,400	-3,300	-2
Purchasing agents, except wholesale, retail, and farm products..	13-1023	295,200	336,100	40,900	14

(NOTE) Data in this table are rounded. See the discussion of the employment projections table in the *Handbook* introductory chapter on *Occupational Information Included in the Handbook.*

such as computer and IT (information technology) support in addition to traditionally contracted services such as advertising. Nonetheless, demand for workers may be somewhat limited by technological improvements such as software that has eliminated much of the paperwork involved in ordering and procuring supplies, and the growing number of purchases being made electronically through the Internet and electronic data interchange (EDI). Demand will also be limited by offshoring of routine purchasing actions to other countries.

Employment of purchasing managers is expected to have little or no change. The use of the Internet to conduct electronic commerce has made information easier to obtain, thus increasing the productivity of purchasing managers. The Internet also allows both large and small companies to bid on contracts. Exclusive supply contracts and long-term contracting have allowed companies to negotiate with fewer suppliers less frequently. Still, purchasing managers will be needed to oversee large consolidated purchasing networks, thus spurring some employment growth.

Employment of purchasing agents and buyers of farm products is also projected to have little or no change, as overall growth in agricultural industries and retailers in the grocery-related industries consolidate. Furthermore, automation, offshoring, and the outsourcing of more services is expected to further impede employment growth.

Finally, little or no change in employment of wholesale and retail buyers, except farm products, is expected. In the retail industry, mergers and acquisitions have caused buying departments to consolidate. In addition, larger retail stores are eliminating local buying departments and creating a centralized buying department at their headquarters.

Job prospects. Persons who have a bachelor's degree in engineering, business, economics, or one of the applied sciences should have the best chance of obtaining a buyer position. Industry experience and knowledge of a technical field will be an advantage for those interested in working for a manufacturing or industrial company. Government agencies and larger companies usually require a master's degree in business or public administration for top-level purchasing positions. Most managers need experience in their respective field.

Earnings

Median annual wages of purchasing managers were $89,160 in May 2008. The middle 50 percent earned between $67,370 and $115,830. The lowest 10 percent earned less than $51,490, and the highest 10 percent earned more than $142,550.

Median annual wages of purchasing agents and buyers of farm products were $49,670 in May 2008. The middle 50 percent earned between $37,930 and $67,440. The lowest 10 percent earned less than $28,990, and the highest 10 percent earned more than $96,220.

Median annual wages of wholesale and retail buyers, except farm products, were $48,710 in May 2008. The middle 50 percent earned between $36,460 and $66,090. The lowest 10 percent earned less than $28,710, and the highest 10 percent earned more than $90,100. Median annual wages in the indus-

tries employing the largest numbers of wholesale and retail buyers, except farm products, were:

Management of companies and enterprises $56,400
Wholesale electronic markets and
    agents and brokers...53,650
Grocery and related product
    merchant wholesalers 49,770
Machinery, equipment, and supplies
    merchant wholesalers 46,250
Grocery stores 35,700

Median annual wages of purchasing agents, except wholesale, retail, and farm products, were $53,940 in May 2008. The middle 50 percent earned between $41,670 and $70,910. The lowest 10 percent earned less than $33,650, and the highest 10 percent earned more than $88,790. Median annual wages in the industries employing the largest numbers of purchasing agents, except wholesale, retail, and farm products, were:

Federal Executive Branch $73,520
Aerospace product and parts manufacturing................64,220
Navigational, measuring, electromedical,
    and control instruments manufacturing....................59,040
Management of companies and enterprises 58,420
Local government..51,870

Purchasing managers, buyers, and purchasing agents receive the same benefits package as other workers, including vacations, sick leave, life and health insurance, and pension plans. In addition to receiving standard benefits, retail buyers often earn cash bonuses based on their performance and may receive discounts on merchandise bought from their employer.

Related Occupations

Another occupation that obtains materials and goods for businesses:

Other occupations that need knowledge of marketing and the ability to assess consumer demand include:

Sources of Additional Information

Further information about education, training, employment, and certification for purchasing careers is available from:

➤ American Purchasing Society, P.O. Box 256, Aurora, IL 60506.

➤ APICS the Association for Operations Management, 8430 West Bryn Mawr Avenue, Suite 1000, Chicago, IL 60631. Internet: **http://www.apics.org**

➤ Institute for Supply Management, P.O. Box 22160, Tempe, AZ 85285-2160. Internet: **http://www.ism.ws**

➤ National Institute of Governmental Purchasing, Inc., 151 Spring St., Suite 300, Herndon, VA 20170-5223. Internet: **http://www.nigp.org**

The Occupational Information Network (O*NET) provides information on a wide range of occupational characteristics. Links to O*NET appear at the end of the Internet version of this occupational statement, accessible at **http://www.bls.gov/ooh/ocos023.htm**

Top Executives

Significant Points

- Keen competition is expected because the prestige and high compensation of these jobs attract a substantial number of applicants.

- Top executives are among the highest paid workers; however, long hours, considerable travel, and intense pressure to succeed are common.

- The formal education and experience of top executives vary as extensively as the nature of their responsibilities, but many of these workers have at least a bachelor's degree and considerable experience.

Nature of the Work

All organizations have specific goals and objectives that they strive to meet. *Top executives* devise strategies and formulate policies to ensure that these goals and objectives are met. Although they have a wide range of titles—such as *chief executive officer, chief operating officer, general manager, president, vice president,* school superintendent, county administrator, and mayor—all formulate policies and direct the overall operations of businesses and corporations, public-sector organizations, nonprofit institutions, and other organizations.

A corporation's goals and policies are established by the chief executive officer in collaboration with other top executives. All of these principals are closely monitored by a board of directors. In a large corporation, the chief executive officer meets frequently with the other top executives to ensure that the overall operation of the corporation is conducted in accordance with these goals and policies. In a governmental or nonprofit organization, top executives oversee budgets and ensure that resources are used properly and that programs are carried out as planned. Chief executive officers in government often nominate citizens to boards and commissions, encourage business investment, and promote economic development in their communities. To do all of these varied tasks effectively, top executives rely on a staff of highly skilled personnel.

Although the chief executive officer of a corporation retains overall accountability, a chief operating officer may be delegated several responsibilities, including the authority to oversee other executives who direct the activities of various departments and implement the organization's guidelines on a day-to-day basis. In publicly held and nonprofit corporations, the board of directors or a similar governing body ultimately is accountable for the success or failure of the enterprise and the chief executive officer reports to the board. In addition to being responsible for the operational success of a company, top executives, particularly *chief financial officers*, are accountable for the accuracy of their financial reporting, especially among publicly traded companies.

The nature of the responsibilities of other high-level executives depends on an organization's size. In small organizations, such as independent retail stores or small manufacturers, a partner, an owner, or a general manager often is responsible for purchasing, hiring, training, quality control, and day-to-day supervisory duties. In large organizations, top executives not only direct the overall organization, but also may be responsible for implementing strategies and setting the overall direction of a certain area of the company or organization. For example, chief financial officers direct the organization's financial goals, objectives, and budgets. They oversee the investment of funds and manage associated risks, supervise cash management activities, execute capital-raising strategies to support a firm's expansion, and deal with mergers and acquisitions.

Chief information officers are responsible for the overall technological direction of their organizations. Today, these officers are playing a more important role in organizations and are increasingly becoming part of the executive team. To perform effectively, they need knowledge of the workings of the total organization. These managers propose budgets for projects and programs and make decisions about staff training and purchases of equipment. They hire and assign computer specialists, information technology workers, and support personnel to carry out information-technology-related projects. They manage the work of these employees, review their output, and establish administrative procedures and policies. Chief information officers also provide organizations with the vision to master information technology as a competitive tool.

General and operations managers plan, direct, or coordinate the operations of companies and other public- or private-sector organizations. Their duties and responsibilities include formulating policies, managing daily operations, and planning the use of materials and human resources that are too diverse and general in nature to be classified into any one area of management or administration, such as personnel, purchasing, or administrative services. In some organizations, the tasks of general and operations managers may overlap those of chief executive officers.

Work environment. Top executives of large organizations typically have spacious offices and numerous support staff. Long hours, including evenings and weekends are standard for most top executives and general managers, although their schedules may be flexible.

To monitor operations and meet with customers, staff, and other executives, general managers and executives travel considerably among international, national, regional, and local offices. Many top executives also attend meetings and conferences sponsored by various associations. In large organizations, job transfers between local offices or subsidiaries are common for those on an executive career track.

Top executives are under intense pressure to succeed; depending on the organization, success may mean earning higher

Top executives need highly developed management skills and the ability to communicate clearly and persuasively.

profits, providing better service, or attaining fundraising and charitable goals. Executives in charge of poorly performing organizations or departments usually find their jobs in jeopardy.

Training, Other Qualifications, and Advancement

The formal education and experience required by top executives vary as extensively as their responsibilities do, but many of these workers have at least a bachelor's degree and considerable experience.

Education and training. Many top executives have a bachelor's or master's degree in business administration, liberal arts, or a more specialized discipline. The specific type and level of education required often depends on the type of organization for which top executives work. College presidents and school superintendents, for example, typically have a doctoral degree in the field in which they originally taught or in education administration. (For information on lower level managers in educational services, see the *Handbook* statement on education administrators.)

Some top executives in the public sector have a degree in public administration or liberal arts. Others might have a more specific educational background related to their jobs. (For information on lower level managers in health services, see the *Handbook* statement on medical and health services managers.)

Many top executive positions are filled from within the organization by promoting experienced lower level managers when an opening arises. In industries such as retail trade or transportation, for example, individuals without a college degree may work their way up within the company and become executives or general managers. When hiring top executives from outside the organization, those doing the hiring often prefer managers with extensive managerial experience.

Other qualifications. Top executives must have highly developed personal qualities and be able to communicate clearly and persuasively. An analytical mind, the ability to analyze large amounts of information and data quickly, and the ability to evaluate the relationships among numerous factors, also are important qualities. For managers to succeed, they need other important qualities as well, including leadership, self-confidence, motivation, decisiveness, flexibility, sound business judgment, and determination.

Certification and advancement. Advancement may be accelerated by participation in company training programs that impart a broader knowledge of company policy and operations. Participation in conferences and seminars can expand one's knowledge of national and international issues that influence the organization and can help the participants develop a network of useful contacts. To facilitate their promotion to an even higher level, managers who have experience in a particular field, such as accounting or engineering, may attend executive development programs geared toward their backgrounds.

Managers also can help their careers by becoming familiar with the latest trends in management and by attending national or local training programs sponsored by various executive training organizations. For example, the Institute of Certified Professional Managers offers the Certified Manager (CM) credential, which is earned by completing training and passing an exam. This certification is held by individuals at all experience levels, from those seeking to enter management careers to those who are already senior executives. Certification is not necessary for advancement, but may be helpful in developing and demonstrating valuable management skills.

General managers may advance to a top executive position, such as executive vice president, in their own firm, or they may take a corresponding position in another firm. They may even advance to peak corporate positions, such as chief operating officer or chief executive officer. Chief executive officers often become members of the board of directors of one or more firms, typically as a director of their own firm and often as chair of its board of directors. Some top executives establish their own firms or become independent consultants.

Employment

Top executives held about 2.1 million jobs in 2008. Employment by detailed occupation was distributed as follows:

General and operations managers 1,733,100
Chief executives 400,400

Job Outlook

Little to no change in employment of top executives is expected. Keen competition for jobs is expected because the prestige and high pay of these positions attract many applicants.

Employment change. Employment of top executives—including chief executives and general and operations managers—is expected to experience little to no change from 2008 to 2018. However, because these workers are essential to running companies and organizations, projected employment of top executives will vary by industry and will generally reflect the growth or decline of that industry. For example, job growth

Projections data from the National Employment Matrix

Occupational Title	SOC Code	Employment, 2008	Projected Employment, 2018	Change, 2008-2018	
				Number	Percent
Top executives..	–	2,133,500	2,125,700	-7,800	0
Chief executives	11-1011	400,400	394,900	-5,500	-1
General and operations managers	11-1021	1,733,100	1,730,800	-2,300	0

(NOTE) Data in this table are rounded. See the discussion of the employment projections table in the *Handbook* introductory chapter on *Occupational Information Included in the Handbook.*

is expected in the fast-growing health services industry, while employment declines for top executives are projected for many manufacturing industries.

Employment of top executives also will be affected by the amount of consolidation occurring in a particular industry, because some management jobs typically are lost after a merger with another company. As a business grows, the number of top executives changes less than the number of employees. Therefore, top executives are not expected to experience as much employment growth as workers in the occupations they oversee.

Job prospects. Keen competition is expected for top executive positions because the prestige and high pay attract a substantial number of qualified applicants. Because this is a large occupation, numerous openings will occur each year as executives transfer to other positions, start their own businesses, or retire. However, many executives who leave their jobs transfer to other executive positions, a pattern that limits the number of job openings for new entrants to the occupation.

Experienced managers whose accomplishments reflect strong leadership qualities and the ability to improve the efficiency or competitive position of an organization will have the best opportunities. In an increasingly global economy, experience in international economics, marketing, and information systems, as well as knowledge of several languages also may be beneficial.

Earnings

Top executives are among the highest paid workers in the United States. However, salary levels vary substantially, depending on level of executive responsibility; length of service; and type, size, and location of the firm, organization, or government agency. For example, a top manager in a very large corporation can earn significantly more than the mayor of a small town.

Median annual wages of general and operations managers in May 2008 were $91,570. The middle 50 percent earned between $62,900 and $137,020. Because the specific responsibilities of general and operations managers vary significantly within industries, earnings also tend to vary considerably. Median annual wages in the industries employing the largest numbers of general and operations managers were as follows:

Computer systems design and related services........	$133,140
Management, scientific, and technical consulting services	130,390
Management of companies and enterprises	113,690
Building equipment contractors	91,370
Local government..	82,150

Median annual wages of wage and salary chief executives in May 2008 were $158,560. Some top executives of large companies earn hundreds of thousands of dollars to more than $1 million annually, although salaries vary substantially by type and level of responsibilities and by industry. Government executives often earn considerably less.

In addition to salaries, total compensation for corporate executives often includes stock options and other performance bonuses. Among other benefits commonly enjoyed by top executives in private industry are the use of executive dining rooms and company-owned aircraft and cars, access to expense allowances, and company-paid insurance premiums and physical examinations. A number of chief executive officers also are provided with company-paid club memberships and other amenities. Nonprofit and government executives usually get fewer benefits.

Related Occupations

Top executives plan, organize, direct, control, and coordinate the operations of an organization and its major departments or programs. Many other management occupations have similar responsibilities, but are concentrated in specific industries or are responsible for a specific department within an organization that assigns them to another occupation. Other managerial occupations that are discussed elsewhere in the *Handbook* include the following:

Sources of Additional Information

For more information on top executives, including educational programs, contact:

➤ American Management Association, 1601 Broadway, 6th Floor, New York, NY 10019. Internet: **http://www.amanet.org**

➤ National Management Association, 2210 Arbor Blvd., Dayton, OH 45439. Internet: **http://www.nma1.org**

For more information on executive financial management careers, contact:

➤ Financial Executives International, 200 Campus Dr., Florham Park, NJ 07932. Internet: **http://www.financialexecutives.org**

➤ Financial Management Association International, College of Business Administration, University of South Florida, 4202 East Fowler Ave., BSN 3331, Tampa, FL 33620. Internet: **http://www.fma.org**

For information about management skills development, including the Certified Manager (CM) credential, contact:

➤ Institute for Certified Professional Managers, James Madison University, MSC 5504, Harrisonburg, VA 22807. Internet: **http://www.icpm.biz**

The Occupational Information Network (O*NET) provides information on a wide range of occupational characteristics. Links to O*NET appear at the end of the Internet version of this occupational statement, accessible at **http://www.bls.gov/ooh/ocos012.htm**

Business and Financial Operations Occupations

Accountants and Auditors

Significant Points

- Most jobs require at least a bachelor's degree in accounting or a related field.

- Job opportunities should be favorable; those who have earned professional recognition through certification or licensure, especially a CPA, should enjoy the best prospects.

- Much faster than average employment growth will result from an increase in the number of businesses, changing financial laws and regulations, and greater scrutiny of company finances.

Nature of the Work

Accountants and auditors help to ensure that firms are run efficiently, public records kept accurately, and taxes paid properly and on time. They analyze and communicate financial information for various entities such as companies, individual clients, and Federal, State, and local governments. Beyond carrying out the fundamental tasks of the occupation—providing information to clients by preparing, analyzing, and verifying financial documents—many accountants also offer budget analysis, financial and investment planning, information technology consulting, and limited legal services.

Specific job duties vary widely among the four major fields of accounting and auditing: *public accounting*, *management accounting*, *government accounting*, and *internal auditing*.

Public accountants perform a broad range of accounting, auditing, tax, and consulting activities for their clients, which may be corporations, governments, nonprofit organizations, or individuals. For example, some public accountants concentrate on tax matters, such as advising companies about the tax advantages and disadvantages of certain business decisions and preparing individual income tax returns. Others offer advice in areas such as compensation or employee healthcare benefits, the design of accounting and data processing systems, and the selection of controls to safeguard assets. Still others audit clients' financial statements and inform investors and authorities that the statements have been correctly prepared and reported.

These accountants are also referred to as *external auditors*. Public accountants, many of whom are *Certified Public Accountants* (CPAs), generally have their own businesses or work for public accounting firms.

Some public accountants specialize in forensic accounting—investigating and interpreting white-collar crimes such as securities fraud and embezzlement, bankruptcies and contract disputes, and other complex and possibly criminal financial transactions, including money laundering by organized criminals. *Forensic accountants* combine their knowledge of accounting and finance with law and investigative techniques to determine whether an activity is illegal. Many forensic accountants work closely with law enforcement personnel and lawyers during investigations and often appear as expert witnesses during trials.

Management accountants—also called *cost, managerial, industrial, corporate, or private accountants*—record and analyze the financial information of the companies for which they work. Among their other responsibilities are budgeting, performance evaluation, cost management, and asset management. Usually, management accountants are part of executive teams involved in strategic planning or the development of new products. They analyze and interpret the financial information that corporate executives need to make sound business decisions. They also prepare financial reports for other groups, including stockholders, creditors, regulatory agencies, and tax authorities. Within accounting departments, management accountants may work in various areas, including financial analysis, planning and budgeting, and cost accounting.

Government accountants and auditors work in the public sector, maintaining and examining the records of government agencies and auditing private businesses and individuals whose activities are subject to government regulations or taxation. Accountants employed by Federal, State, and local governments ensure that revenues are received and expenditures are made in accordance with laws and regulations. Those employed by the Federal Government may work as Internal Revenue Service agents or in financial management, financial institution examination, or budget analysis and administration.

Internal auditors verify the effectiveness of their organization's internal controls and check for mismanagement, waste, or fraud. They examine and evaluate their firms' financial and information systems, management procedures, and internal

Accountants and auditors analyze and interpret financial information.

controls to ensure that records are accurate and controls are adequate. They also review company operations, evaluating their efficiency, effectiveness, and compliance with corporate policies and government regulations. Because computer systems commonly automate transactions and make information readily available, internal auditors may also help management evaluate the effectiveness of their controls based on real-time data, rather than personal observation. They may recommend and review controls for their organization's computer systems, to ensure their reliability and integrity of the data. Internal auditors may also have specialty titles, such as *information technology auditors, environmental auditors, and compliance auditors.*

Technology is rapidly changing the nature of the work of most accountants and auditors. With the aid of special software packages, accountants summarize transactions in the standard formats of financial records and organize data in special formats employed in financial analysis. These accounting packages greatly reduce the tedious work associated with data management and recordkeeping. Computers enable accountants and auditors to be more mobile and to use their clients' computer systems to extract information from databases and the Internet. As a result, a growing number of accountants and auditors with extensive computer skills specialize in correcting problems with software or in developing software to meet unique data management and analytical needs. Accountants also are beginning to perform more technical duties, such as implementing, controlling, and auditing computer systems and networks and developing technology plans.

Work environment. Most accountants and auditors work in a typical office setting. Some may be able to do part of their work at home. Accountants and auditors employed by public accounting firms, government agencies, and organizations with multiple locations may travel frequently to perform audits at branches, clients' places of business, or government facilities.

Almost half of all accountants and auditors worked a standard 40-hour week in 2008, but many worked longer hours, particularly if they are self-employed and have numerous clients. Tax specialists often work long hours during the tax season.

Training, Other Qualifications, and Advancement

Most accountants and auditors need at least a bachelor's degree in accounting or a related field. Many accountants and auditors choose to obtain certification to help advance their careers, such as becoming a Certified Public Accountant (CPA).

Education and training. Most accountant and auditor positions require at least a bachelor's degree in accounting or a related field. Some employers prefer applicants with a master's degree in accounting, or with a master's degree in business administration with a concentration in accounting. Some universities and colleges are now offering programs to prepare students to work in growing specialty professions such as internal auditing. Many professional associations offer continuing professional education courses, conferences, and seminars.

Some graduates of junior colleges or business or correspondence schools, as well as bookkeepers and accounting clerks who meet the education and experience requirements set by their employers, can obtain junior accounting positions and advance to accountant positions by demonstrating their accounting skills on the job.

Most beginning accountants and auditors may work under supervision or closely with an experienced accountant or auditor before gaining more independence and responsibility.

Licensure and certification. Any accountant filing a report with the Securities and Exchange Commission (SEC) is required by law to be a Certified Public Accountant (CPA). This may include senior level accountants working for or on behalf of public companies that are registered with the SEC. CPAs are licensed by their State Board of Accountancy. Any accountant who passes a national exam and meets the other requirements of the State where they practice can become a CPA. The vast majority of States require CPA candidates to be college graduates, but a few States will substitute a number of years of public accounting experience for a college degree.

As of 2009, 46 States and the District of Columbia required CPA candidates to complete 150 semester hours of college coursework—an additional 30 hours beyond the usual 4-year bachelor's degree. California, Colorado, New Hampshire, and Vermont are the only States that do not require 150 semester hours for certification. Many schools offer a 5-year combined bachelor's and master's degree to meet the 150 semester hour requirement, but a master's degree is not required. Prospective accounting majors should carefully research accounting curricula and the requirements of any States in which they hope to become licensed.

All States use the four-part Uniform CPA Examination prepared by the American Institute of Certified Public Accountants (AICPA). The CPA examination is rigorous, and less than one-half of those who take it each year pass every part on the first try. Candidates are not required to pass all four parts at once, but most States require candidates to pass all four sections within 18 months of passing their first section. The CPA exam is now computerized and is offered 2 months out of every quarter at various testing centers throughout the United States. Most States also require applicants for a CPA license to have some accounting experience; however requirements vary by State or jurisdiction.

Nearly all States require CPAs and other public accountants to complete a certain number of hours of continuing professional education before their licenses can be renewed. The professional associations representing accountants sponsor numerous courses, seminars, group study programs, and other forms of continuing education.

Other qualifications. Previous experience in accounting or auditing can help an applicant get a job. Many colleges offer students the opportunity to gain experience through summer or part-time internship programs conducted by public accounting or business firms. In addition, as many business processes are now automated, practical knowledge of computers and their applications is a great asset for jobseekers in the accounting and auditing fields.

People planning a career in accounting and auditing should have an aptitude for mathematics and be able to analyze, compare, and interpret facts and figures quickly. They must be able to clearly communicate the results of their work to clients and managers both verbally and in writing. Accountants and auditors must be good at working with people, business systems, and computers. At a minimum, accountants and auditors should be familiar with basic accounting and computer software packages. Because financial decisions are made on the basis of their statements and services, accountants and auditors should have high standards of integrity.

Certification and advancement. Professional recognition through certification or other designation provides a distinct advantage in the job market. Certification can attest to professional competence in a specialized field of accounting and auditing. Accountants and auditors can seek credentials from a wide variety of professional societies.

The Institute of Management Accountants confers the Certified Management Accountant (CMA) designation upon applicants who complete a bachelor's degree or who attain a minimum score or higher on specified graduate school entrance exams. Applicants must have worked at least 2 years in management accounting, pass a four-part examination, agree to meet continuing education requirements, and comply with standards of professional conduct. The exam covers areas such as financial statement analysis, working-capital policy, capital structure, valuation issues, and risk management.

The Institute of Internal Auditors offers the Certified Internal Auditor (CIA) designation to graduates from accredited colleges and universities who have worked for 2 years as in-

ternal auditors and have passed a four-part examination. The IIA also offers the designations of Certified in Control Self-Assessment (CCSA), Certified Government Auditing Professional (CGAP), and Certified Financial Services Auditor (CFSA) to those who pass the exams and meet educational and experience requirements.

ISACA confers the Certified Information Systems Auditor (CISA) designation upon candidates who pass an examination and have 5 years of experience auditing information systems. Information systems experience, financial or operational auditing experience, or related college credit hours can be substituted for up to 2 years of information systems auditing, control or security experience.

For those accountants with their CPA, the AICPA offers the option to receive any or all of the Accredited in Business Valuation (ABV), Certified Information Technology Professional (CITP), or Personal Financial Specialist (PFS) designations. CPAs with these designations demonstrate a level of expertise in these areas in which accountants practice ever more frequently. The business valuation designation requires a written exam and the completion of a minimum of 10 business valuation projects that demonstrate a candidate's experience and competence. The technology designation requires the achievement of a set number of points awarded for business technology experience and education. Candidates for the personal financial specialist designation also must achieve a certain level of points based on experience and education, pass a written exam, and submit references.

Many senior corporation executives have a background in accounting, internal auditing, or finance. Beginning public accountants often advance to positions with more responsibility in 1 or 2 years and to senior positions within another few years. Those who excel may become supervisors, managers, or partners; open their own public accounting firm; or transfer to executive positions in management accounting or internal auditing in private firms.

Management accountants often start as cost accountants, junior internal auditors, or trainees for other accounting positions. As they rise through the organization, they may advance to accounting manager, chief cost accountant, budget director, or manager of internal auditing. Some become controllers, treasurers, financial vice presidents, chief financial officers, or corporation presidents.

Public accountants, management accountants, and internal auditors usually have much occupational mobility. Practitioners often shift into management accounting or internal auditing from public accounting, or between internal auditing and management accounting. It is less common for accountants and auditors to move from either management accounting or internal auditing into public accounting. Additionally, because they learn about and review the internal controls of various business units within a company, internal auditors often gain the experience needed to become upper-level managers.

Employment

Accountants and auditors held about 1.3 million jobs in 2008. They worked throughout private industry and government, but 24 percent of accountants and auditors worked for accounting, tax preparation, bookkeeping, and payroll services firms. Approximately 8 percent of accountants and auditors were self-employed.

Most accountants and auditors work in urban areas, where public accounting firms and central or regional offices of businesses are concentrated.

Some individuals with backgrounds in accounting and auditing are full-time college and university faculty; others teach part time while working as self-employed accountants or as accountants for private industry or in government. (See teachers—postsecondary elsewhere in the *Handbook*.)

Job Outlook

Accountants and auditors are expected to experience much faster than average employment growth from 2008-18. Job opportunities should be favorable; accountants and auditors who have a professional certification, especially CPAs, should have the best prospects.

Employment change. Employment of accountants and auditors is expected to grow by 22 percent between 2008 and 2018, which is much faster than the average for all occupations. This occupation will have a very large number of new jobs arise, about 279,400 over the projections decade. An increase in the number of businesses, changing financial laws and corporate governance regulations, and increased accountability for protecting an organization's stakeholders will drive job growth.

As the economy grows, the number of business establishments will increase, requiring more accountants and auditors to set up books, prepare taxes, and provide management advice. As these businesses grow, the volume and complexity of information reviewed by accountants and auditors regarding costs, expenditures, taxes, and internal controls will expand as well. The continued globalization of business also will lead to more demand for accounting expertise and services related to international trade and accounting rules and international mergers and acquisitions. Additionally, there is a growing movement towards International Financial Reporting Standards (IFRS), which uses a judgment-based system to determine the fair-market value of assets and liabilities, which should increase demand for accountants and auditors because of their specialized expertise.

An increased need for accountants and auditors also will arise from a greater emphasis on accountability, transparency, and controls in financial reporting. Increased scrutiny of company finances and accounting procedures will create opportunities for accountants and auditors, particularly CPAs, to audit financial records more thoroughly and completely. Management accountants and internal auditors increasingly will be needed to discover and eliminate fraud before audits, and ensure that important processes and procedures are documented accurately and thoroughly. Forensic accountants also will be needed to detect illegal financial activity by individuals, companies, and organized crime rings.

Job prospects. Job opportunities should be favorable. Accountants and auditors who have earned professional recognition through certification or other designation, especially a CPA, should have the best job prospects. Applicants with a master's degree in accounting or a master's degree in business administration with a concentration in accounting also may have an advantage.

Individuals who are proficient in accounting and auditing computer software and information systems or have expertise in specialized areas—such as international business, international financial reporting standards, or current legislation—may have an advantage in getting some accounting and auditing jobs. In addition, employers increasingly seek applicants with strong interpersonal and communication skills. Many accountants work on teams with others who have different backgrounds, so they must be able to communicate accounting and financial information clearly and concisely. Regardless of qualifications, however, competition will remain keen for the most prestigious jobs in major accounting and business firms.

In addition to openings from job growth, the need to replace accountants and auditors who retire or transfer to other occupations will produce numerous job openings in this large occupation.

Earnings

Median annual wages of wage and salary accountants and auditors were $59,430 in May 2008. The middle half of the occupation earned between $45,900 and $78,210. The bottom 10 percent earned less than $36,720, and the top 10 percent earned more than $102,380. Median annual wages in the industries employing the largest numbers of accountants and auditors were as follows:

Accounting, tax preparation, bookkeeping,
    and payroll services $61,480
Management of companies and enterprises 59,820
Insurance carriers 59,550
Local government...53,660
State government..51,250

According to a salary survey conducted by the National Association of Colleges and Employers, bachelor's degree candidates in accounting received starting offers averaging $48,993 a year in July 2009; master's degree candidates in accounting were offered $49,786 initially.

Wage and salary accountants and auditors usually receive standard benefits, including health and medical insurance, life insurance, a 401(k) plan, and paid annual leave. High-level se-

Projections data from the National Employment Matrix

Occupational Title	SOC Code	Employment, 2008	Projected Employment, 2018	Change, 2008-2018	
				Number	Percent
Accountants and auditors..	13-2011	1,290,600	1,570,000	279,400	22

(NOTE) Data in this table are rounded. See the discussion of the employment projections table in the *Handbook* introductory chapter on *Occupational Information Included in the Handbook.*

nior accountants may receive additional benefits, such as the use of a company car and an expense account.

Related Occupations

Accountants and auditors design internal control systems and analyze financial data. Others for whom training in accounting is valuable include

Some accountants have assumed the role of management analysts and are involved in the design, implementation, and maintenance of accounting software systems. Others who perform similar work include

Sources of Additional Information

Information on accredited accounting programs can be obtained from:

➤ AACSB International—Association to Advance Collegiate Schools of Business, 777 South Harbour Island Blvd., Suite 750, Tampa FL 33602. Internet: **http://www.aacsb.edu/accreditation/ AccreditedMembers.asp**

Information about careers in certified public accounting and CPA standards and examinations may be obtained from:

➤ American Institute of Certified Public Accountants, 1211 Avenue of the Americas, New York, NY 10036. Internet: **http://www.aicpa.org**

➤ AICPA Examinations Team, Parkway Corporate Center, 1230 Parkway Ave., Suite 311, Ewing, NJ 08628-3018. Internet: **http://www.cpa-exam.org**

Information on CPA licensure requirements by State may be obtained from:

➤ National Association of State Boards of Accountancy, 150 Fourth Ave. North, Suite 700, Nashville, TN 37219-2417. Internet: **http://www.nasba.org**

Information on careers in management accounting and the CMA designation may be obtained from:

➤ Institute of Management Accountants, 10 Paragon Dr., Montvale, NJ 07645-1718. Internet: **http://www.imanet.org**

Information on careers in internal auditing and the CIA designation may be obtained from:

➤ The Institute of Internal Auditors, 247 Maitland Ave., Altamonte Springs, FL 32701-4201. Internet: **http://www.theiia.org**

Information on careers in information systems auditing and the CISA designation may be obtained from:

➤ ISACA, 3701 Algonquin Rd., Suite 1010, Rolling Meadows, IL 60008. Internet: **http://www.isaca.org**

The Occupational Information Network (O*NET) provides information on a wide range of occupational characteristics. Links to O*NET appear at the end of the Internet version of this occupational statement, accessible at **http://www.bls.gov/ooh/ocos001.htm**

Appraisers and Assessors of Real Estate

Significant Points

- Workers generally must be licensed or certified, but State requirements vary.

- About 27 percent were self-employed.

- Employment is expected to grow more slowly than the average over the 2008-18 decade.

- During recessions, demand for appraisers declines; demand for assessors is less affected by economic and real estate market fluctuations.

Nature of the Work

Appraisers and assessors of real estate estimate the value of real property whenever it is sold, mortgaged, taxed, insured, or developed. They work in localities they are familiar with, so they have knowledge of any environmental or other concerns that may affect the value of a property. They note any unique characteristics of the property and of the surrounding area, such as a specific architectural style of a building or a major highway located next to the parcel. They also take into account additional aspects of a property such as the condition of the foundation and roof of a building or any renovations that may have been done. They might take pictures to document a certain room or feature, in addition to photographing the exterior of the building. After visiting the property, the appraiser or assessor will estimate the value of the property by taking into consideration such things as comparable home sales, lease records, location, view, previous appraisals, and income potential. During the entire process, appraisers and assessors keep a meticulous record of their research, observations, and methods used in calculating the property valuation.

Appraisers have independent clients and typically focus on valuing one property at a time. They often specialize in a certain type of real estate. For example, *commercial appraisers* specialize in property used for commercial purposes, such as stores or hotels. *Residential appraisers* focus on appraising homes or other residences and only provide appraisals for those that house 1 to 4 families. Other appraisers have a general practice and are willing to appraise the value of any type of real property.

Assessors predominately work for local governments and are responsible for valuing properties for property tax assessment purposes. Unlike appraisers, who generally focus on one property at a time, assessors often value entire neighborhoods using mass appraisal techniques and computer-assisted mass appraisal systems to value all the homes in a local neighborhood at once. Although they do not usually focus on a single property, they

Appraisers play an important role in the purchasing and selling of real estate.

may use single property methods if the property owner challenges the assessment. Revaluations of assessed properties are performed cyclically on a schedule established by State statute or local practice Depending on the size of the jurisdiction and the number of staff in an assessor's office, a mass appraisal firm or a revaluation firm may do much of the work of valuing the properties in the jurisdiction. These results are then officially certified by the assessor.

When properties are reassessed, assessors issue notices to property owners indicating the new assessment. Assessors must be current on tax assessment procedures and must be able to defend the accuracy of their property assessments, either to the owner directly or at a public hearing, since assessors are responsible for dealing with taxpayers who want to contest their assigned property assessments. Assessors also keep a database of every parcel in their jurisdiction, labeling the property owner, assessment history, and size of the property, as well as property maps of the jurisdiction detailing the property distribution of the jurisdiction.

Work environment. Appraisers and assessors spend much of their time researching data and writing reports. However, with the advancement of computers and other technologies, such as wireless Internet, time spent in the office has decreased because research can now be done in less time and at site locations. Records that once required a visit to a courthouse or city hall often can be found online. On-site visits usually occur during daylight hours, and according to the client's schedule. Time spent on-site rather than in the office also depends on the specialty. For example, residential appraisers tend to spend less time on office work than commercial appraisers, who could spend up to several weeks on one property analyzing information and writing reports. Appraisers who work for private institutions generally spend most of their time inside the office, making on-site visits when necessary. Appraisers and assessors usually conduct on-site appraisal work alone.

Assessors and privately employed appraisers usually work a standard 40-hour work week. However, self-employed appraisers, often called "independent fee appraisers," tend to work more than a standard 40-hour work week, including spending their evenings and weekends writing reports. Approximately 13 percent of appraisers and assessors worked part time in 2008.

The offices of most independent-fee appraisers are relatively small, occupied by either the appraisers alone or by them and a small staff. However, private institutions such as banks and mortgage companies often employ several appraisers within one establishment. The size of offices of assessors depends mostly on the size of the local jurisdiction and the amount of work for which a particular office is responsible.

Training, Other Qualifications, and Advancement

The requirements to become a fully qualified appraiser or assessor are complex and vary by State and, sometimes, by the value or type of property. In general, both appraisers and assessors must be licensed or certified. Prospective appraisers and assessors should check with their State to determine the specific requirements.

Education and training. Many practicing appraisers and assessors have at least a bachelor's degree. Coursework in related subjects such as economics, finance, mathematics, computer science, English, and business or real estate law can be very useful for prospective appraisers and assessors.

Federal law mandates that most appraisers hold State certification. Requirements for these certifications vary by State, but there are certain minimum standards that appraisers must meet. Most appraisers of residential real property must have at least an associate degree, while appraisers of commercial real property are required to have at least a bachelor's degree.

Unlike appraisers, there are no federally mandated education and training requirements for assessors. In most States, the State assessor board sets education and experience requirements that must be met to obtain a certificate to practice as an assessor. A few States have no Statewide requirements, with standards instead set by each locality.

In States that mandate certification for assessors, the requirements are usually similar to those for appraisers. Some States also have more than one level of certification. All candidates must attend State-approved schools and facilities and take basic appraisal courses. Although appraisers generally value one property at a time while assessors value many at once, both occupations use similar methods and techniques. As a result, assessors and appraisers tend to take the same basic courses. In addition to passing a Statewide examination, candidates are usually required to have a set number of on-the-job hours that must be completed. For those States not requiring certificates for assessors, the hiring office usually will require the candidate to take basic appraisal courses, complete on-the-job training, and accrue a sufficient number of work hours to meet the requirements for obtaining appraisal licenses or certificates. Many assessors also possess a State appraisal license.

Assessors tend to start out in an assessor's office that is willing to provide on-the-job training; smaller municipalities are often unable to provide this experience. An alternate source of experience for aspiring assessors is through a revaluation firm.

Licensure. Being a Certified Residential Real Property Appraiser is the minimum qualification for valuing any residential property with a loan amount exceeding $250,000 and for valuing any other type of real property with a loan value of less than $250,000. Candidates for this certification must have at least an associate degree or in lieu of the degree, 21 units of specified college-level education. In addition, this certification requires 200 hours of appraiser-specific classroom training and 2,500 hours of work experience accrued over at least 2 years.

Certified General Real Property Appraisers have no restrictions on the types or values of real property for which they can give valuations. Candidates for this certification must have at least a bachelor's degree, or in lieu of the degree, 30 units of specified college-level education. In addition to a degree, this certification requires 300 hours of appraiser-specific classroom training and 3,000 hours of work experience accrued over at least 30 months. At least half of these hours must be in nonresidential appraisal work.

In addition to the Federally required Certified Residential and Certified General Real Property Appraiser classifications, most States also have the Licensed Residential Real Property Appraiser classification. Holders of this license are permitted to appraise noncomplex one-to-four residential units having a transaction value of less than $1,000,000, and complex one-to-four residential units having a transaction value of less than $250,000. For the Licensed Residential Appraiser classification, candidates must obtain 150 qualifying education hours and at least 2,000 hours of on-the-job training obtained over a period of no less than 1 year. In addition, all candidates must pass an examination.

In many States, those working on their appraiser requirements for licensure or certification are classified as a "trainee." Training programs vary by State but usually require at least 75 hours of specified appraisal education before one can apply for a trainee position. The number of additional courses trainees must take depends on the State requirements and the kind of license they wish to obtain.

Across all levels of certification and licensure, 15 hours of classroom education must be devoted to the Uniform Standards of Professional Appraisal Practice (USPAP), which are set forth by the Appraisal Standards Board (ASB) of the Appraisal Foundation. Additionally, the Licensed Residential, Certified Residential, and the General Real Property Appraiser designations each have an associated examination that must be passed before these credentials are awarded.

For both appraisers and assessors, continuing education is necessary to maintain a license or certification. The minimum continuing education requirement for appraisers is 14 hours per year. Appraisers must also complete a 7-hour National USPAP Update Course every 2 years. Some States have further requirements. Continuing education may be obtained in any State-approved school or facility, as well as in recognized seminars and conferences held by associations or related organizations. Assessors also must fulfill a continuing education requirement in most States, but the amount varies by State.

Other qualifications. Appraisers and assessors must possess good analytical skills, mathematical skills, and the ability to pay attention to detail. They also must be able to work alone as well as with other people. Because they work with the public, appraisers and assessors must be polite and have the ability to listen and thoroughly answer any questions from clients about their work.

Certification and advancement. Many appraisers and assessors choose to become a designated member of a regional or nationally recognized appraiser or assessor association. Designations are a way for appraisers or assessors to establish themselves in the profession, and are recognizable credentials to show employers and potential clients a higher level of education and experience. Obtaining a designation usually requires 5 to 10 years of training and experience, which is more than the minimum licensing requirements. Many appraisal associations have a membership category specifically for trainees, who then can receive full membership after licensure. Since States differ greatly on the requirements to become an assessor, licensure is not necessarily required for membership or designations; however, the imposed designation qualifications tend to be very stringent.

Advancement within the occupation comes with experience. The higher the level of appraiser licensure, for example, the higher the fees an independent fee appraiser may charge. Staying in one particular region or focusing on one type of appraising specialty also will help to establish one's business, reputation, and expertise. Assessors often have a career progression within their office, starting as a trainee and eventually ending up appointed or elected as a senior appraiser or supervisor.

Employment

In 2008, appraisers and assessors of real estate held about 92,400 jobs. About 27 percent were self-employed; virtually all were appraisers. Employment was concentrated in areas with high levels of real estate activity, such as major metropolitan areas. Assessors are more uniformly spread throughout the country than appraisers because every locality has at least one assessor.

About 29 percent of appraisers and assessors worked in local government; nearly all were assessors. Another 31 percent, mainly appraisers, worked for real estate firms.

Job Outlook

Employment is expected to grow more slowly than the average. Job opportunities should be best in areas with active real estate markets, and most job openings will result from the need to replace appraisers and assessors who retire or otherwise leave the occupation permanently.

Employment change. Employment of appraisers and assessors of real estate is expected to grow more slowly than the average over the 2008-18 decade, increasing by 5 percent. Demand for appraisal services is strongly tied to the real estate market,

Projections data from the National Employment Matrix

Occupational Title	SOC Code	Employment, 2008	Projected Employment, 2018	Change, 2008-2018	
				Number	Percent
Appraisers and assessors of real estate	13-2021	92,400	96,600	4,200	5

(NOTE) Data in this table are rounded. See the discussion of the employment projections table in the *Handbook* introductory chapter on *Occupational Information Included in the Handbook.*

which can fluctuate in the short term. Over the long term, employment growth will be driven by economic expansion and population increases—factors that generate demand for real property. However, employment will be held down to a certain extent by productivity increases brought about by the increased use of computers and other technologies, which allow appraisers and assessors to deal with more properties. The increased use of automated valuation models to conduct appraisals for mortgage purposes might also shift work away from appraisers.

Job prospects. Most job openings will result from the need to replace appraisers and assessors who retire or otherwise leave the occupation permanently. Employment opportunities should be best in areas with active real estate markets. Although opportunities for established certified appraisers are expected to be available in these areas, aspiring entrants to this occupation may have difficulty locating a trainee position because traditional sources of training positions, such as real estate offices and financial institutions, increasingly prefer not to take on new trainees.

The cyclical nature of the real estate market will have a direct effect on the job prospects of appraisers, especially those who appraise residential properties. In times of recession, fewer people buy or sell real estate, causing a decrease in the demand for appraisers. As a result, opportunities will be best for appraisers who are able to switch specialties and appraise different types of properties.

Because assessors are needed in every local or State jurisdiction to make assessments for property tax purposes regardless of the state of the local economy, assessors generally are less affected by economic and real estate market fluctuations than are appraisers.

Earnings

Median annual wages of appraisers and assessors of real estate were $47,370 in May 2008. The middle 50 percent earned between $34,330 and $66,640. The lowest 10 percent earned less than $25,900, and the highest 10 percent earned more than $88,680. Median annual wages of those working for local governments were $43,550. Median annual wages of those working in activities related to real estate were $47,890. Earnings for independent-fee appraisers can vary significantly because they are paid fees on a per appraisal basis.

Related Occupations

Other occupations that involve the inspection of real estate include the following:

	Page
Construction and building inspectors	628
Real estate brokers and sales agents	540

Another occupation involved in determining the value of items is:

Claims adjusters, appraisers, examiners, and investigators	96

Sources of Additional Information

For more information on licensure requirements, contact
➤ The Appraisal Foundation, 1155 15th St. NW., Suite 1111, Washington, DC 20005. Internet: **http://www.appraisalfoundation.org**

For more information on individual State licensure requirements, contact
➤ Appraisal Subcommittee (ASC), 1401 St. NW., Suite 760, Washington, D.C. 20005. Internet: **http://www.asc.gov**

For more information on appraisers of real estate, contact
➤ American Society of Appraisers, 555 Herndon Pkwy., Suite 125, Herndon, VA 20170. Internet: **http://www.appraisers.org**

➤ Appraisal Institute, 550 W. Van Buren St., Suite 1000, Chicago, IL 60607. Internet: **http://www.appraisalinstitute.org**

➤ National Association of Independent Fee Appraisers, 401 N. Michigan Ave., Suite 2200, Chicago, IL 60611. Internet: **http://www.naifa.com**

For more information on assessors of real estate, contact
➤ International Association of Assessing Officers, 314 W. 10th St., Kansas City, MO 64105. Internet: **http://www.iaao.org**

The Occupational Information Network (O*NET) provides information on a wide range of occupational characteristics. Links to O*NET appear at the end of the Internet version of this occupational statement, accessible at **http://www.bls.gov/ooh/ocos300.htm**

Budget Analysts

Significant Points

- The need for sound financial analysis will spur job growth for budget analysts.

- A bachelor's degree generally is the minimum educational requirement, but some employers prefer or require a master's degree.

- Candidates with a master's degree are expected to have the best opportunities.

- About 41 percent of all budget analysts work in government.

Nature of the Work

Budget analysts help organizations allocate their financial resources. They develop, analyze, and execute budgets, as well as estimate future financial needs for private businesses, nonprofit organizations, and government agencies. In private sector firms, a budget analyst's main responsibility is to examine the budget and seek new ways to improve efficiency and increase profits. In nonprofit and governmental organizations, which usually are not concerned with profits, analysts try to find the most efficient way to distribute funds and other resources among various departments and programs.

In addition to managing an organization's budget, analysts are often involved in program performance evaluation, policy analysis, and the drafting of budget-related legislation. At times, they also conduct training sessions for company or government personnel regarding new budget procedures.

At the beginning of each budget cycle, managers and department heads submit operational and financial proposals to budget analysts for review. These plans outline the organization's programs, estimate the financial needs of these programs, and propose funding initiatives to meet those needs. Analysts then examine these budget estimates and proposals for completeness, accuracy, and conformance with established procedures, regulations, and organizational objectives. Sometimes they employ cost-benefit analyses to review financial requests, assess program tradeoffs, and explore alternative funding methods. They also examine past budgets and research economic and financial developments that affect the organization's income and expenditures.

After the initial review process, budget analysts consolidate individual departmental budgets into operating and capital budget summaries. These summaries contain statements that argue for or against funding requests. Budget summaries are then submitted to senior management, or as is often the case in government organizations, to appointed or elected officials. Budget analysts then help the chief operating officer, agency head, or other top managers analyze the proposed plan and devise possible alternatives if the projected results are unsatisfactory. The final decision to approve the budget usually is made by the organization head in a private firm, or by elected officials, such as State legislators, in government.

Throughout the year, analysts periodically monitor the budget by reviewing reports and accounting records to determine if allocated funds have been spent as specified. If deviations appear between the approved budget and actual spending, budget analysts may write a report explaining the variations and recommending revised procedures. To avoid or alleviate deficits, budget analysts may recommend program cuts or a reallocation of excess funds. They also inform program managers and others within the organization of the status and availability of funds in different accounts.

Data and statistical analysis software has greatly increased the amount of data and information that budget analysts can compile, review, and produce. Analysts use spreadsheet, database, and financial analysis software to improve their understanding of different budgeting options and to provide accurate, up-to-date information to agency leaders. In addition, many organizations are beginning to incorporate Enterprise Resource Planning (ERP) programs into their budget-making process. ERP programs can consolidate all of an organization's operating information into a single computer system, which helps analysts estimate the effects that a budget alteration will have on each part of an organization.

Work environment. Budget analysts usually work in a comfortable office setting. They spend the majority of their time working independently, compiling and analyzing data and preparing budget proposals. Some budget analysts travel to obtain budget details first-hand or to personally verify funding allocation.

The schedules of budget analysts vary throughout the budget cycle, and many are required to work additional hours during the initial development, mid-year reviews, and final reviews of budgets. The pressures of deadlines and tight work schedules can be stressful. In 2008, about 48 percent of budget analysts worked 40 hours per week, while about 11 percent worked more than 50 hours per week.

Training, Other Qualifications, and Advancement

A bachelor's degree usually is the minimum educational requirement for budget analyst jobs, but some organizations prefer or require a master's degree. Entry-level budget analysts usually begin with limited responsibilities but can be promoted to intermediate-level positions within 1 to 2 years, and to senior positions with additional experience.

Education and training. Employers generally require budget analysts to have at least a bachelor's degree, but some prefer or require a master's degree. Within the Federal Government, a bachelor's degree in any field is sufficient for an entry-level budget analyst position. State and local governments have varying requirements, but usually require a bachelor's degree in one of many areas, including accounting, finance, business, public administration, economics, statistics, political science, or sociology. Because developing a budget requires strong numerical and analytical skills, courses in statistics or accounting are helpful, regardless of the prospective budget analyst's major field of study. Some States may require a master's degree. Occasionally, budget-related or finance-related work experience can be substituted for formal education.

In most organizations, budget analysts usually learn the job by working through one complete budget cycle. During the cycle, which typically lasts 1 year, analysts become familiar with the various steps involved in the budgeting process. Many budget analysts also take professional development classes throughout their careers.

Other qualifications. Budget analysts must abide by strict ethical standards. Integrity, objectivity, and confidentiality are all essential when dealing with financial information, and budget analysts must avoid any personal conflicts of interest. Most

Budget analysts help organizations determine the best use of financial resources.

Projections data from the National Employment Matrix

Occupational Title	SOC Code	Employment, 2008	Projected Employment, 2018	Change, 2008-2018	
				Number	Percent
Budget analysts	13-2031	67,200	77,400	10,100	15

(NOTE) Data in this table are rounded. See the discussion of the employment projections table in the *Handbook* introductory chapter on *Occupational Information Included in the Handbook.*

budget analysts also need mathematical skills and should be able to use software packages, including spreadsheet, database, data-mining, and financial analysis programs. Strong oral and written communication skills also are essential, because budget analysts must prepare, present, and defend budget proposals to decision makers. In addition, budget analysts must be able to work under strict time constraints.

Certification and advancement. Entry-level budget analysts usually begin with limited responsibilities, working under close supervision. Capable analysts can be promoted to intermediate-level positions within 1 to 2 years, and to senior positions with additional experience. Because of the importance and high visibility of their jobs, senior budget analysts may be promoted to management positions in various parts of their organizations, or with other organizations with which they have worked.

Government budget analysts employed at the Federal, State, or local level may earn the Certified Government Financial Manager designation granted by Advancing Government Accountability, an organization that represents government accountability officers. To earn this designation, candidates must have a minimum of a bachelor's degree, 24 credit hours of study in financial management, and 2 years of professional-level experience in governmental financial management. They also must pass a series of three exams that cover topics on the governmental environment; governmental accounting, financial reporting, and budgeting; and governmental financial management and control. To maintain the designation, individuals must complete 80 hours of continuing professional education every 2 years.

Employment

Budget analysts held 67,200 jobs in 2008. Government is a major employer, accounting for 41 percent of budget analyst jobs. Budget analysts were also employed in manufacturing; management services; professional, scientific, and technical services; and schools.

Job Outlook

Budget analyst jobs are expected to increase faster than average. Candidates with a master's degree are expected to have the best opportunities.

Employment change. Employment of budget analysts is expected to increase by 15 percent between 2008 and 2018, faster than the average for all occupations. Employment growth will be driven by the continuing demand for sound financial analysis in both the public and the private sectors.

As businesses and other organizations become more complex and specialized, budget planning and financial control will demand greater attention. In recent years, computer applications used in budget analysis have become increasingly sophisticated, allowing more data to be analyzed and processed in a short-er amount of time. As a result, agency leaders have begun to demand more data, analyses, and other types of information relevant to the budgeting process. This has increased the workload of budget analysts, and created the need for more workers. As this process continues, demand for budget analysts will grow.

Job prospects. Job openings will result from employment growth and from the need to replace workers who retire or leave the occupation for other reasons. Candidates with a master's degree are expected to have the best opportunities. Familiarity with spreadsheet, database, data-mining, financial-analysis, and Enterprise Resource Planning software packages also should enhance a jobseeker's prospects.

Earnings

Wages of budget analysts vary by experience, education, and employer. Median annual wages of budget analysts in May 2008 were $65,320. The middle 50 percent earned between $52,290 and $82,150. The lowest 10 percent earned less than $42,470, and the highest 10 percent earned more than $100,360. Median annual wages in the industries employing the largest numbers of budget analysts were:

Aerospace product and parts manufacturing	$70,830
Federal Executive Branch	70,650
Management of companies and enterprises	70,460
Colleges, universities, and professional schools	58,190
Elementary and secondary schools	57,700

The average annual salary in March 2009 for budget analysts employed by the Federal Government was $80,456.

Related Occupations

Other workers involved in financial analysis include:

Sources of Additional Information

Information about career opportunities as a budget analyst may be available from your State or local employment service.

Information on careers and certification in government financial management may be obtained from:
➤ Advancing of Government Accountability, 2208 Mount Vernon Ave., Alexandria, VA 22301. Internet: **http://www.agacgfm.org**

Information on careers in budget analysis at the State government level may be obtained from:

➤ National Association of State Budget Officers, Hall of the States Building, Suite 642, 444 North Capitol St. NW., Washington, DC 20001. Internet: **http://www.nasbo.org**

Information on obtaining budget analyst positions with the Federal Government is available from the Office of Personnel Management through USAJOBS, the Federal Government's official employment information system. This resource for locating and applying for job opportunities can be accessed through the Internet at **http://www.usajobs.gov/** or through an interactive voice response telephone system at (703) 724-1850. This number is not toll free, and charges may result. For advice on how to find and apply for Federal jobs, see the *Occupational Outlook Quarterly* article "How to get a job in the Federal Government," online at **http://www.bls.gov/opub/ooq/2004/summer/art01.pdf.**

The Occupational Information Network (O*NET) provides information on a wide range of occupational characteristics. Links to O*NET appear at the end of the Internet version of this occupational statement, accessible at **http://www.bls.gov/ooh/ocos003.htm**

Claims Adjusters, Appraisers, Examiners, and Investigators

Significant Points

- Employment is concentrated in insurance-related industries.

- Training and entry requirements vary widely.

- College graduates and those with related experience should have the best opportunities for most types of jobs; competition will be keen for jobs as investigators.

- Job opportunities should be best in health insurance companies, and in regions susceptible to natural disasters.

Nature of the Work

Individuals and businesses purchase insurance policies to protect against monetary losses. In the event of a loss, policyholders submit claims, or requests for payment, seeking compensation for their loss. Adjusters, appraisers, examiners, and investigators deal with those claims. They work primarily for property and casualty insurance companies, for whom they handle a wide variety of claims alleging property damage, liability, or bodily injury. Their main role is to investigate claims, negotiate settlements, and authorize payments to claimants, who are the policyholders who make a claim. They must be mindful not to violate their rights under Federal and State privacy laws. They must determine whether the customer's insurance policy covers the loss and how much of the loss should be paid. Although many adjusters, appraisers, examiners, and investigators have overlapping functions and may even perform the same tasks,

the insurance industry generally assigns specific roles to each of these claims workers.

Adjusters plan and schedule the work required to process a claim. They might, for example, handle the claim filed after an automobile accident or after a storm damages a customer's home. Adjusters investigate claims by interviewing the claimant and witnesses, consulting police and hospital records, and inspecting property damage to determine how much the company should pay for the loss. Adjusters may consult with other professionals, such as accountants, architects, construction workers, engineers, lawyers, and physicians, who can offer a more expert evaluation of a claim. The information gathered—including photographs and statements, either written, or recorded audio or video—is set down in a report that is then used to evaluate the claim. When the policyholder's claim is approved, the claims adjuster negotiates with the claimant and settles the claim. When claims are contested, adjusters will work with attorneys and expert witnesses to defend the insurer's position.

Some large insurance companies centralize claims adjustment in a claims center, where the payout amount is estimated and a check is issued immediately. However, cases handled by independent adjusters, or those involving business losses or homeowner claims, such as hurricane or fire damage, all require a senior adjuster to physically inspect the damage and determine proper compensation.

When it comes to business or residential loss caused by, for example, vandalism or flooding, claimants can opt not to rely on the insurance company's adjuster and may instead choose to hire a public adjuster. Public adjusters are self employed and work in the best interest of the client, rather than the insurance company. In doing so, the adjuster prepares and presents claims to insurance companies, looking to negotiate the best possible settlement for the claimant. Insurance carriers also use the service of independent adjusters on a freelance basis, often in lieu of hiring them as regular employees. In this case the independent adjusters work in the interest of the insurance company.

Claims examiners within property and casualty insurance firms may have duties similar to those of an adjuster, but often their primary job is to review claims after they are submitted in order to ensure that proper guidelines have been followed. They may assist adjusters with complicated claims or when, for instance, a natural disaster suddenly greatly increases the volume of claims.

Most claims examiners work for life or health insurance companies. In health insurance companies, examiners review health-related claims to see whether costs are reasonable given the diagnosis. They use guides that have information on the average period of disability, expected treatments, and average hospital stays for various ailments. Examiners check claim applications for completeness and accuracy, interview medical specialists, and consult policy files to verify the information reported in a claim. They then authorize appropriate payment, deny the claim, or refer the claim to an investigator for a more thorough review. Claims examiners usually specialize in group or individual insurance plans and in hospital, dental, or prescription drug claims.

In life insurance, claims examiners review the causes of death, particularly in the case of an accident, since most life insurance policies pay additional benefits if a death is accidental. Claims examiners also may review new applications for life insurance to make sure that the applicants have no serious illnesses that would make them a high risk to insure.

Another occupation that plays an important role in the accurate settlement of claims is that of the *appraiser*, whose role is to estimate the cost or value of an insured item. The majority of appraisers employed by insurance companies and independent adjusting firms are *auto damage appraisers*. These appraisers inspect damaged vehicles after an accident and estimate the cost of repairs. This information is then relayed to the adjuster, who incorporates the appraisal into the settlement.

Many claims adjusters and auto damage appraisers are equipped with laptop computers from which they can download the necessary forms and files from insurance company databases. Specialized software then generates estimates on standard forms. Adjusters also utilize digital cameras, which allow photographs of the damage to be sent to the company, allowing for faster and more efficient processing of claims.

When adjusters or examiners suspect fraud, they refer the claim to an investigator. *Insurance investigators* handle claims in which the company suspects fraudulent or criminal activity, such as arson, falsified workers' disability claims, staged accidents, or unnecessary medical treatments. The severity of insurance fraud cases can vary greatly, from claimants simply overstating damage to a vehicle to complicated fraud rings supported by dishonest doctors, lawyers, and even insurance personnel.

Investigators usually start with a database search to obtain background information on claimants and witnesses. Investigators can access personal information and identify Social Security numbers, aliases, driver's license numbers, addresses, phone numbers, criminal records, and past claims histories to establish whether a claimant has ever attempted insurance fraud. Then, investigators may visit claimants and witnesses to obtain an oral statement, take photographs, and inspect facilities, such as doctors' offices, to determine, for example, whether the doctors have a proper license. Investigators often consult with legal counsel and can be expert witnesses in court cases.

Often, investigators also perform surveillance work. For example, in a case involving fraudulent workers' compensation claims, an investigator may covertly observe the claimant for several days or even weeks. If the investigator observes the subject performing an activity that is ruled out by injuries stated in a workers' compensation claim, the investigator will take photos to document the activity and report it to the insurance company.

Work environment. Working environments of claims adjusters, appraisers, examiners, and investigators vary greatly. Many claims adjusters and auto damage appraisers often work outside the office, inspecting damaged buildings and automobiles. Adjusters who inspect damaged buildings must be wary of potential hazards, such as collapsed roofs and floors, as well as weakened structures.

Some adjusters report to the office every morning to get their assignments, while others simply call in from home and spend their days traveling to claim sites. Occasionally, experienced adjusters must be away from home for days—for example,

when they travel to the scene of a disaster such as a tornado, hurricane, or flood—to work with local adjusters and government officials.

Most claims examiners employed by life and health insurance companies work a standard 5-day, 40-hour week in a typical office environment. In contrast, adjusters often must arrange their work schedules to accommodate evening and weekend appointments with clients. This sometimes results in adjusters working irregular schedules, especially when they have a lot of claims to scrutinize. Adjusters are often called to work in the event of emergencies and may have to work 50 or 60 hours a week until all claims are resolved.

Appraisers spend much of their time offsite at automotive body shops estimating vehicle damage costs. The remaining time may be spent working in the office. Many independent appraisers work from home, as continually improving valuation software has made estimating damage easier and more routine. Auto damage appraisers typically work regular hours, and rarely work on the weekends. Self employed appraisers also have the flexibility to make their own hours, as many appraisals are done by appointment.

Some days, investigators will spend all day in the office, searching databases, making telephone calls, and writing reports. Other times, they may be away, performing surveillance activities or interviewing witnesses. Some of the work can involve disagreements with claimants, so the job can be stressful and potentially confrontational. Insurance investigators often work irregular hours because of the need to conduct surveillance and contact people who are not available during normal working hours. Early morning, evening, and weekend work is common.

Training, Other Qualifications, and Advancement

Training and entry requirements vary widely. Although many in these occupations do not have a college degree, most companies prefer to hire college graduates, or those with some insurance-related work experience or vocational training.

Education and training. There are no formal education requirements for any of these occupations, and a high school degree is typically the minimal requirement needed to obtain employment. However, most employers prefer to hire college

Claims adjusters evaluate insurance claims, report their findings, and make recommendations.

graduates or people who have some insurance-related work experience or vocational training.

While a variety of degrees can be an asset, no specific college major is recommended. For example, a claims adjuster who has a business or an accounting background might be suited to specialize in claims of financial loss due to strikes, breakdowns of equipment, or damage to merchandise. College training in architecture or engineering is helpful in adjusting industrial claims, such as those involving damage from fires or other accidents. A legal background can be beneficial to someone handling workers' compensation and product liability cases. A medical background is useful for those examiners working on medical and life insurance claims.

While auto damage appraisers are not required to have a college education, most companies prefer to hire persons with formal training, previous experience, or those with knowledge and technical skills who can identify and estimate the cost of repair. Many vocational colleges offer 2-year programs in auto body repair and teach students how to estimate the costs to repair damaged vehicles.

For investigator jobs, most insurance companies prefer to hire people trained as law enforcement officers, private investigators, claims adjusters, or examiners because these workers have good interviewing and interrogation skills.

Beginning claims adjusters, appraisers, examiners, and investigators work on small claims under the supervision of an experienced worker. As they learn more about claims investigation and settlement, they are assigned larger, more complex claims. Trainees take on more responsibility as they demonstrate competence in handling assignments and progress in their coursework. Auto damage appraisers typically receive on-the-job training, which may last several months. This training usually involves of working under close supervision while estimating damage costs until the employer decides the trainee is ready to perform estimates on their own.

Continuing education is very important for claims adjusters, appraisers, examiners, and investigators because Federal and State laws and court decisions affect how claims are handled and the scope of insurance policies. Also, examiners working on life and health claims must be familiar with new medical procedures and prescription drugs. Examiners working on auto claims must be familiar with new car models and repair techniques.

Many companies offer training sessions to inform their employees of industry changes, and a number of schools and associations give courses and seminars on various topics having to do with claims. Online courses are also making distance learning possible.

Licensure. Licensing requirements for claims adjusters, appraisers, examiners, and investigators vary by State. Some States have few requirements, while others require either the completion of pre-licensing education, a satisfactory score on a licensing exam, or both. Earning a voluntary professional designation can sometimes substitute for completing an exam. In some States, claims adjusters employed by insurance companies can work under the company license and need not become licensed themselves. Public adjusters may need to meet separate or additional requirements. For example, some States

require public adjusters to file a surety bond—a unique contract between at least three parties.

Some States that require licensing also require a certain number of continuing education credits per year in order to renew the license. Workers can fulfill their continuing education requirements by attending classes or workshops, by writing articles for claims publications, or by giving lectures and presentations.

Other qualifications. Claims adjusters, appraisers, and examiners often work closely with claimants, witnesses, and other insurance professionals, so they must be able to communicate effectively with others. Knowledge of computer applications also is very helpful. In addition, a valid driver's license and a good driving record are required for workers who must travel on the job. Some companies require applicants to pass a series of written tests designed to measure their communication, analytical, and general mathematical skills.

When hiring investigators, employers look for individuals who have ingenuity and who are persistent and assertive. Investigators should not be afraid of confrontation, should communicate well, and should be able to think on their feet. Good interviewing and interrogation skills also are important and usually are acquired in earlier careers in law enforcement.

Certification and advancement. Employees who demonstrate competence in claims work or administrative skills may be promoted to more responsible managerial or administrative jobs. Similarly, claims investigators may rise to become supervisor or manager of the investigations department. Once they achieve expertise, many choose to start their own independent adjusting or auto damage appraising firms.

Numerous examiners and adjusters choose to earn professional certifications and designations to demonstrate their expertise. Although requirements for these designations vary, some entail a minimum number of years of experience and the successful completion of an examination; in addition, a certain number of continuing education credits must be earned each year to retain the designation.

Employment

Adjusters, appraisers, examiners, and investigators held about 306,300 jobs in 2008. Insurance carriers employed 49 percent of claims adjusters, appraisers, examiners, and investigators; agencies, brokerages, and other insurance related activities, such as private claims adjusting companies, employed another 24 percent. Less than 4 percent of these jobs were held by auto damage insurance appraisers. About 2 percent of adjusters, appraisers, examiners, and investigators were self-employed.

Job Outlook

Overall employment is expected to increase as fast as average. For claims adjusters and examiners, opportunities will be best with health insurance companies. For appraiser jobs, opportunities will be best for those who have some vocational training and previous auto body repair experience. Keen competition is expected for investigator jobs as the number of applicants typically outnumbers the number of positions available.

Employment change. Employment of claims adjusters, appraisers, examiners, and investigators is expected to grow by 7 percent over the 2008–18 decade, as fast as average for all occupations. Employment growth of adjusters and claims ex-

Projections data from the National Employment Matrix

Occupational Title	SOC Code	Employment, 2008	Projected Employment, 2018	Change, 2008-2018	
				Number	Percent
Claims adjusters, appraisers, examiners, and investigators	13-1030	306,300	327,200	20,900	7
Claims adjusters, examiners, and investigators............................	13-1031	294,600	315,500	20,900	7
Insurance appraisers, auto damage	13-1032	11,700	11,700	100	1

(NOTE) Data in this table are rounded. See the discussion of the employment projections table in the *Handbook* introductory chapter on *Occupational Information Included in the Handbook*.

aminers will primarily stem from the growth of the health insurance industry. Rising health care premiums and attempts by large insurance carriers to minimize costs will result in a greater need for claims examiners to more scrupulously review a growing number of medical claims. More claims being made by a growing elderly population also should spur demand for adjusters and claims examiners. Although technology is reducing the amount of time it takes for an adjuster to complete a claim, thereby increasing the number of claims that one adjuster can handle, demand for these jobs will increase anyway because many tasks cannot be easily automated.

Employment of insurance investigators is not expected to grow significantly, despite the expected increase in the number of claims in litigation and complexity of insurance fraud cases. Efficiencies gained through the Internet will continue to reduce the amount of time it takes investigators to perform background checks, allowing them to handle more cases.

Little to no change in employment of auto damage appraisers is expected. Despite a growing number of drivers and auto insurance policies being sold by insurance companies, the number of claims being filed is not expected to increase as much as the number of policies as efforts to make vehicles, roads, and highways safer will yield a decrease in the number of claims per policy.

Job prospects. Job opportunities for claims adjusters and examiners will be best in the health insurance industry as the industry seeks to minimize the number of paid claims, and in areas susceptible to natural disasters, such as the Gulf coast or West coast. Hurricanes in Florida or wild fires in California, for example, will continue to spur demand, and opportunities with smaller independent firms will be particularly good. And while technology has made the work more efficient, workers will still be needed to contact policyholders, inspect damaged property, and consult with experts. Numerous job openings also will result from the need to replace workers who transfer to other occupations or leave the labor force. College graduates and those with previous related experience should have the best opportunities for jobs as claims adjusters, examiners, and investigators. Auto damage appraisers with related vocational training and auto body shop experience should have the best prospects. People entering these occupations with no formal training may find more opportunities with large insurance companies rather than small independent firms who prefer to hire experienced workers.

Competition for investigator jobs will remain keen because the occupation attracts many qualified people, including retirees from law enforcement, the military, and experienced claims adjusters and examiners who choose to get an investigator license.

Heightened media and public awareness of insurance fraud also may attract qualified candidates to this occupation.

Earnings

Median annual wages of wage and salary claims adjusters, examiners, and investigators were $55,760 in May 2008. The middle 50 percent earned between $42,400 and $70,860. The lowest 10 percent earned less than $34,140, and the highest 10 percent earned more than $84,260.

Median annual wages of wage and salary auto damage insurance appraisers were $53,440 in May 2008. The middle 50 percent earned between $43,990 and $63,180. The lowest 10 percent earned less than $36,500, and the highest 10 percent earned more than $73,210.

Many claims adjusters, especially those who work for insurance companies, receive additional bonuses or benefits as part of their job. Adjusters are often furnished with a laptop computer, a smart phone, and a company car, or are reimbursed for the use of their own vehicle for business purposes.

Related Occupations

Property-casualty insurance adjusters and life and health insurance examiners must determine the validity of a claim and negotiate a settlement. They also are responsible for determining how much to reimburse the client. Occupations whose duties are related include:

In determining the validity of a claim, insurance adjusters must inspect the damage to assess the magnitude of the loss. Workers who perform similar duties include:

To ensure that company practices and procedures are followed, property and casualty examiners review insurance claims to which a claims adjuster has already proposed a settlement. Other workers who review documents for accuracy and compliance with a given set of rules and regulations are:

Auto damage appraisers must be familiar with the structure and functions of various automobiles and their parts. They must also be familiar with techniques to estimate value. The following workers have similar duties:

Insurance investigators detect and investigate fraudulent claims and criminal activity. Their work is similar to that of:

Sources of Additional Information

General information about a career as a claims adjuster, appraiser, examiner, or investigator is available from the home offices of many insurance companies. Information about licensing requirements for claims adjusters may be obtained from the department of insurance in each State.

Information about the property-casualty insurance field can be obtained by contacting:

➤ Insurance Information Institute, 110 William St., New York, NY 10038. Internet: **http://www.iii.org**

For information about professional designation and training programs, contact any of the following organizations:

➤ American Institute for Chartered Property Casualty Underwriters and the Insurance Institute of America, 720 Providence Rd., Suite 100, Malvern, PA 19355–3433. Internet: **http://www.aicpcu.org**

➤ International Claim Association, 1155 15th St. NW., Suite 500, Washington, DC 20005. Internet: **http://www.claim.org**

➤ National Association of Public Insurance Adjusters, 21165 Whitfield Place, Suite 105, Potomac Falls, VA 20165. Internet: **http://www.napia.com**

Information on careers in auto damage appraising can be obtained from:

➤ Independent Automotive Damage Appraisers Association, P.O. Box 12291 Columbus, GA 31917–2291. Internet: **http://www.iada.org**

The Occupational Information Network (O*NET) provides information on a wide range of occupational characteristics. Links to O*NET appear at the end of the Internet version of this occupational statement, accessible at **http://www.bls.gov/ooh/ocos125.htm**

Cost Estimators

Significant Points

- About 59 percent of cost estimators work in the construction industry, and another 15 percent are employed by manufacturers.

- Good job opportunities are expected; those with industry work experience and a bachelor's degree in a related field will have the best prospects.

- Voluntary certification can be beneficial to cost estimators; some employers may require professional certification for employment.

Nature of the Work

Accurately forecasting the cost, size, and duration of future projects is vital to the survival of any business. *Cost estimators* develop the cost information that business owners and managers need to make a bid for a contract or to decide on the profitability of a proposed new project or product. They also determine which endeavors are making a profit.

Regardless of the industry in which they work, estimators collect and analyze data on all of the factors that can affect costs, such as materials, labor, location, duration of the project, and special machinery requirements, including computer hardware and software. Job duties vary widely depending on the type and size of the project.

The methods for estimating costs can also differ greatly by industry. On a large construction project, for example, the estimating process begins with the decision to submit a bid. After reviewing various preliminary drawings and specifications, the estimator visits the site of the proposed project. The estimator gathers information on access to the site; surface topography and drainage, and the availability of electricity, water, and other services. The estimator records this information, which may go in the final project estimate.

After the site visit, the estimator determines the quantity of materials and the labor required to complete the firm's part of the project. This process, called the quantity survey or "take-off," involves completing standard estimating forms, filling in dimensions, numbers of units, and other information. A cost estimator working for a general contractor, for example, estimates the costs of all of the items that the contractor must provide. Although subcontractors estimate their costs as part of their own bidding process, the general contractor's cost estimator often analyzes bids made by subcontractors. Also during the takeoff process, the estimator must make decisions concerning equipment needs, the sequence of operations, the size of the crew required, and physical constraints at the site. Allowances for wasted materials, inclement weather, shipping delays, and other factors that may increase costs also must be incorporated in the estimate.

After completing the quantity surveys, the estimator prepares a cost summary for the entire project, which includes the costs of labor, equipment, materials, subcontractors, overhead, taxes, insurance, markup, and any additional costs that may affect the project. The chief estimator then prepares the bid proposal for submission to the owner. On large construction projects, there may be several estimators, each specializing in one area, such as electrical work or excavation, concrete, and forms.

Construction cost estimators also may be employed by the project's architect, engineering firm, or owner to help establish a budget, manage and control project costs, and to track actual costs relative to bid specifications as the project develops. During construction, estimators may be employed to manage the cost of change orders and negotiate and settle and extra costs or mitigate potential claims. Estimators may also be called upon as expert witness on cost in a construction dispute case.

In manufacturing, cost estimators usually are assigned to the engineering, cost, or pricing department. The estimator's goal is to accurately estimate the costs associated with developing and producing products. The job may begin when management

Cost estimators develop information that business owners and managers need to determine the potential profitability of a new project or product.

requests an estimate of the costs associated with a major redesign of an existing product or the development of a new product or production process. For example, when estimating the cost of manufacturing a new product, the estimator works with engineers, first reviewing blueprints or conceptual drawings to determine the machining operations, tools, gauges, and materials that will be required. The estimator then prepares a parts list and determines whether it would be more efficient to produce or to purchase the parts. To do this, the estimator asks for price information from potential suppliers. The next step is to determine the cost of manufacturing each component of the product. Some high-technology products require a considerable amount of computer programming during the design phase. The cost of software development is one of the fastest growing and most difficult activities to estimate. As a result, some cost estimators now specialize in estimating only computer software development and related costs.

Thereafter, the cost estimator prepares time-phase charts and learning curves. Time-phase charts indicate the time required for tool design and fabrication, tool "debugging"—finding and correcting all problems—manufacturing of parts, assembly, and testing. Learning curves graphically represent the rate at which the performance of workers producing parts for the new product improves with practice. These curves are commonly called "cost reduction" curves, because many problems—such as engineering changes, rework, shortages of parts, and lack of operator skills—diminish as the number of units produced increases, resulting in lower unit costs.

Using all of this information, the estimator then calculates the standard labor hours necessary to produce a specified number of units. Standard labor hours are then converted to dollar values, to which are added factors for waste, overhead, and profit to yield the unit cost in dollars. The estimator compares the cost of purchasing parts with the firm's estimated cost of manufacturing them to determine which is less expensive.

Computers play a vital role in cost estimation because the process often involves complex mathematical calculations and requires advanced mathematical techniques. For example, to undertake a parametric analysis (a process used to estimate costs per unit based on square footage or other specific requirements of a project), cost estimators use a computer database containing information on the costs and conditions of many other similar projects. Although computers cannot be used for the entire estimating process, they can relieve estimators of much of the drudgery associated with routine, repetitive, and time-consuming calculations. New and improved cost estimating software has lead to more efficient computations, leaving estimators more time to visit and analyze projects.

Operations research, production control, cost, and price analysts who work for government agencies may do significant amounts of cost estimating in the course of their usual duties. In addition, the duties of construction managers may include estimating costs. (For more information, see the statements on operations research analysts and construction managers elsewhere in the *Handbook*.)

Work environment. Estimators spend most of their time in offices, but visits to construction worksites and factory floors are often needed for their work. In some industries, there may be frequent travel between a firm's headquarters, its subsidiaries, and subcontractors.

Estimators usually work a 40-hour week, but overtime is common. Cost estimators often work under pressure and stress, especially when facing bid deadlines. Inaccurate estimating can cause a firm to lose a bid or to lose money on a job that was not accurately estimated.

Training, Other Qualifications, and Advancement

Job entry requirements for cost estimators will vary by industry. In the construction and manufacturing industries, employers increasingly prefer to hire cost estimators with a bachelor's degree in a related field, although it is also possible for experienced construction workers to become cost estimators. Voluntary certification can be beneficial to cost estimators; some employers, including the Federal Government, may require professional certification for employment.

Education and training. In the construction industry, employers increasingly prefer individuals with a degree in construction management, building science, or construction science, all of which usually include several courses in cost estimating. Most construction estimators also have considerable construction experience, gained through work in the industry, internships, or cooperative education programs; and for some estimators, years of experience can substitute for a degree in addition to taking classes in the field or getting an associate degree. Applicants with a thorough knowledge of construction materials, costs, and procedures in areas ranging from heavy construction to electrical work, plumbing systems, or masonry work have a competitive edge.

In manufacturing industries, employers prefer to hire individuals with a degree in engineering, physical science, operations research, mathematics, or statistics or in accounting, finance, business, economics, or a related subject. In most industries, experience in quantitative techniques is important.

Many colleges and universities include cost estimating as part of bachelor's and associate degree curriculums in civil engineering, industrial engineering, information systems development, and construction management or construction engineering technology. In addition, cost estimating is often part of master's degree programs in construction science or construction management. Organizations representing cost estimators, such as the American Society of Professional Estimators (ASPE), the Association for the Advancement of Cost Engineering (AACE International) and the Society of Cost Estimating and Analysis (SCEA), also sponsor educational and professional development programs. These programs help students, estimators-in-training, and experienced estimators learn about changes affecting the profession. Specialized courses and programs in cost-estimating techniques and procedures also are offered by many technical schools, community colleges, and universities.

Estimators also receive long-term training on the job because every company has its own way of handling estimates. Working with an experienced estimator, newcomers become familiar with each step in the process. Those with no experience reading construction specifications or blueprints first learn that aspect of the work. Subsequently, they may accompany an experienced estimator to the construction site or shop floor, where they observe the work being done, take measurements, or perform other routine tasks. As they become more knowledgeable, estimators learn how to tabulate quantities and dimensions from drawings and how to select the appropriate prices for materials.

Other qualifications.   Cost estimators need to have an aptitude for mathematics, be able to analyze, compare, and interpret detailed but sometimes poorly defined information, and be able to make sound and accurate judgments based on this information. The ability to focus on details, while analyzing and managing larger obstacles, is vital. Assertiveness and self-assurance in presenting and supporting conclusions are also important, as are strong communications and interpersonal skills, because estimators may work as part of a team alongside managers, owners, engineers, and design professionals. Cost estimators also need to be proficient with computers and have skills in programming. Familiarity with cost estimation software, including commercial, and Building Information Modeling (BIM) software is beneficial. BIM software technology takes standard blueprints and creates three-dimensional models on the computer, allowing for better estimates of the building process. Proficiency in project management and the ability to incorporate work breakdown structure (WBS) techniques are increasingly important in cost estimating complex development projects.

Certification and advancement.   Voluntary certification can be beneficial to cost estimators because it provides professional recognition of the estimator's competence and experience. In some instances, individual employers may even require professional certification for employment. The ASPE, AACE International, and SCEA administer certification programs. To become certified, estimators usually must have between 2 and 8 years of estimating experience and must pass a written examination. In addition, certification requirements may include the publication of at least one article or paper in the field.

For most estimators, advancement takes the form of higher pay and prestige. Some move into management positions, such as project manager for a construction firm, program manager for a government contractor, or manager of the industrial engineering department for a manufacturer. Others may go into business for themselves as consultants, providing estimating services for a fee to government or to construction or manufacturing firms.

Employment
Cost estimators held about 217,800 jobs in 2008. About 59 percent of estimators were in the construction industry and another 15 percent were employed in manufacturing. The remainder worked in a wide range of other industries.

Cost estimators work throughout the country, usually in or near major industrial, commercial, and government centers and in cities and suburban areas experiencing rapid change or development.

Job Outlook
Employment is projected to grow much faster than average. Overall, good job opportunities are expected; those with industry work experience and a bachelor's degree in a related field will have the best prospects.

Employment change.   Employment of cost estimators is expected to grow by 25 percent between 2008 and 2018, much faster than average for all occupations. Growth in the construction industry will account for most new jobs in this occupation. In particular, construction and repair of highways, streets, bridges, subway systems, airports, water and sewage systems, and electric power plants and transmission lines will stimulate the need for more cost estimators. Similarly, an increasing population will result in more construction of residential homes, hospitals, schools, restaurants, and other structures that require cost estimators. As the population ages, the demand for nursing and extended-care facilities will also increase. The growing complexity of construction projects will also boost demand for cost estimators as more workers specialize in a particular area of construction.

Job prospects.   Because there are no formal bachelor's degree programs in cost estimating, some employers have difficulty recruiting qualified cost estimators, resulting in good employment opportunities. Job prospects in construction should be best for those who have a degree in construction science, construction management, or building science or have years of practical experience in the various phases of construction or in a specialty craft area. Knowledge of Building Information Modeling software would also be helpful. For cost estimating jobs in manufacturing, those who have degrees in mathematics, statistics, engineering, accounting, business administration, or

Projections data from the National Employment Matrix

Occupational Title	SOC Code	Employment, 2008	Projected Employment, 2018	Change, 2008-2018	
				Number	Percent
Cost estimators...	13-1051	217,800	272,900	55,200	25

(NOTE) Data in this table are rounded. See the discussion of the employment projections table in the *Handbook* introductory chapter on *Occupational Information Included in the Handbook.*

economics, and who are familiar with cost estimation software should have the best job prospects.

In addition to job openings arising from employment growth, many additional openings should result annually from the need to replace workers who transfer to other occupations due to the sometimes stressful nature of the work, or who retire or leave the occupation for other reasons.

Employment of cost estimators, like that of many other construction workers, is sensitive to the fluctuations of the economy. Workers in these trades may experience periods of unemployment when the overall level of construction falls. On the other hand, shortages of these workers may occur in some areas during peak periods of building activity.

Earnings

Salaries of cost estimators vary widely by experience, education, size of firm, and industry. Median annual wages of wage and salary cost estimators in May 2008 were $56,510. The middle 50 percent earned between $42,720 and $74,320. The lowest 10 percent earned less than $33,150, and the highest 10 percent earned more than $94,470. Median annual wages in the industries employing the largest numbers of cost estimators were:

Nonresidential building construction	$65,410
Building equipment contractors	60,510
Building finishing contractors	55,430
Residential building construction	55,390
Foundation, structure, and building exterior contractors	54,670

Related Occupations

Other workers who quantitatively analyze cost information include:

	Page
Accountants and auditors	86
Budget analysts	93
Claims adjusters, appraisers, examiners, and investigators	96
Construction managers	38
Economists	209
Financial analysts	103
Financial managers	52
Industrial production managers	67
Insurance underwriters	106
Loan officers	109
Market and survey researchers	212
Operations research analysts	145
Personal financial advisors	118

Sources of Additional Information

Information about career opportunities, certification, educational programs, and cost-estimating techniques may be obtained from:

➤ AACE International, 209 Prairie Ave., Suite 100, Morgantown, WV 26501. Internet: **http://www.aacei.org**

➤ American Society of Professional Estimators (ASPE), 2525 Perimeter Place Drive, Suite 103, Nashville, TN 37214. Internet: **http://www.aspenational.org**

➤ Society of Cost Estimating and Analysis, 527 Maple Ave. East, Suite 301, Vienna, VA 22180. Internet: **http://www.sceaonline.org**

The Occupational Information Network (O*NET) provides information on a wide range of occupational characteristics. Links to O*NET appear at the end of the Internet version of this occupational statement, accessible at **http://www.bls.gov/ooh/ocos006.htm**

Financial Analysts

Significant Points

- Financial analyst positions require a bachelor's or master's degree.

- Positions may also require professional licenses and certifications.

- Keen competition is anticipated for these highly paid positions.

- Financial analysts earn high wages.

Nature of the Work

Financial analysts provide guidance to businesses and individuals making investment decisions. Financial analysts assess the performance of stocks, bonds, commodities, and other types of investments. Also called *securities analysts* and *investment analysts*, they work for banks, insurance companies, mutual and pension funds, securities firms, the business media, and other businesses, making investment decisions or recommendations. Financial analysts study company financial statements and analyze commodity prices, sales, costs, expenses, and tax rates to determine a company's value by projecting its future earnings. They often meet with company officials to gain a better insight into the firms' prospects and management.

Financial analysts can be divided into two categories: *buy side analysts* and *sell side analysts*. Analysts on the buy side work for companies that have a great deal of money to invest. These companies, called institutional investors, include mutual funds, hedge funds, insurance companies, independent money managers, and nonprofit organizations with large endowments. Buy side financial analysts devise investment strategies. Conversely, sell side analysts help securities dealers, such as banks and other firms, sell stocks, bonds, and other investments. The business media hire financial advisors that are supposed to be impartial, and occupy a role somewhere in the middle.

Financial analysts generally focus on trends impacting a specific industry, region, or type of product. For example, an analyst will focus on a subject area such as the utilities industry, an area such as Latin America, or the options market. Firms with larger research departments assign analysts even narrower subject areas. They must understand how new regulations, policies, and political and economic trends may impact the investments they are watching. *Risk analysts* evaluate the risk in portfolio decisions, project potential losses, and determine how to limit potential losses and volatility using diversification, currency futures, derivatives, short selling, and other investment decisions.

Financial analysts research and analyze financial data, helping managers make sound decisions.

Some experienced analysts called *portfolio managers* supervise a team of analysts and select the mix of products, industries, and regions for their company's investment portfolio. Hedge fund and mutual *fund managers* are called fund managers. Fund and portfolio managers frequently make split-second buy or sell decisions in reaction to quickly changing market conditions. These managers are not only responsible for the overall portfolio, but are also expected to explain investment decisions and strategies in meetings with investors.

Ratings analysts evaluate the ability of companies or governments to pay their debts, including bonds. On the basis of their evaluation, a management team rates the risk of a company or government defaulting on its bonds. Other financial analysts perform budget, cost, and credit analysis as part of their responsibilities.

Financial analysts use spreadsheet and statistical software packages to analyze financial data, spot trends, create portfolios, and develop forecasts. Analysts also use the data they find to measure the financial risks associated with making a particular investment decision. On the basis of their results, they recommend whether to buy, hold, or sell particular investments.

Work environment. Financial analysts usually work in offices. They may work long hours, travel frequently to visit companies or potential investors, and face the pressure of deadlines. Much of their research must be done after office hours because their days are filled with telephone calls and meetings.

Training, Other Qualifications, and Advancement

Financial analysts must have a bachelor's degree. Many positions require a master's degree in finance or a Master of Business Administration (MBA). Positions may also require professional licenses and certifications. However, licenses and certifications are generally only earned after someone is hired.

Education and training. A bachelor's or graduate degree is required for financial analysts. Most companies require a bachelor's degree in a related field, such as finance, business, accounting, statistics, or economics. An understanding of statistics, economics, and business is essential, and knowledge of accounting policies and procedures, corporate budgeting, and financial analysis methods is recommended. An MBA or a master's degree in finance is often required. Advanced courses or knowledge of options pricing, bond valuation, and risk management are important.

Licensure. The Financial Industry Regulatory Authority (FINRA) is the main licensing organization for the securities industry. Depending on an individual's work, different licenses may be required, although buy side analysts are less likely to need licenses. The majority of these licenses require sponsorship by an employer, so companies do not expect individuals to have these licenses before starting a job. Experienced workers who change jobs will need to have their licenses renewed with the new company.

Other qualifications. Strong math, analytical, and problem-solving skills are essential qualifications for financial analysts. Good communication skills are necessary because these workers must present complex financial concepts and strategies. Self-confidence, maturity, and the ability to work independently are important. Financial analysts must be detail-oriented, motivated to seek out obscure information, and familiar with the workings of the economy, tax laws, and money markets. Although much of the software they use is proprietary, financial analysts must be comfortable working with spreadsheets and statistical packages.

With the increasing global diversification of investments, companies are assigning more financial analysts to cover foreign markets. These analysts normally specialize in one country, such as Brazil, or one region, such as Latin America. Companies prefer financial analysts to have the international experience necessary to understand the language, culture, business environment, and political conditions in the country or region that they cover.

Certification and advancement. Although not always required, certifications enhance professional standing and are recommended by employers. Certifications are becoming increasingly common. Financial analysts can earn the Chartered Financial Analyst (CFA) designation, sponsored by the CFA Institute. To qualify for this designation, applicants need a bachelor's degree, four years of related work experience, and must pass three exams. Applicants can take the exams while they are obtaining the required work experience. Passing the exams requires several hundred hours of self-study. These exams cover subjects such as accounting, economics, securities analysis, financial markets and instruments, corporate finance, asset valuation, and portfolio management. Additional certifications are helpful for financial analysts who specialize in specific areas, such as risk management.

Financial analysts advance by moving into positions where they are responsible for larger or more important products. They may supervise teams of financial analysts. They may become portfolio managers or fund managers, directing the investment portfolios of their companies or funds.

Employment

Financial analysts held 250,600 jobs in 2008. Many financial analysts work at large financial institutions based in New York City or other major financial centers. About 47 percent of financial analysts worked in the finance and insurance industries, including securities and commodity brokers, banks and credit institutions, and insurance carriers. Others worked throughout private industry and government.

Job Outlook

Employment of financial analysts is expected to grow much faster than the average for all occupations. However, keen competition will continue for these well-paid jobs, especially for new entrants.

Employment change. As the level of investment increases, overall employment of financial analysts is expected to increase by 20 percent during the 2008–18 decade, which is much faster than the average for all occupations. Primary factors for this growth are increasing complexity and global diversification of investments and growth in the overall amount of assets under management. As the number and type of mutual and hedge funds and the amount of assets invested in these funds increase, companies will need more financial analysts to research and recommend investments. As the international investment increases, companies will need more analysts to cover the global range of investment options.

Job prospects. Despite employment growth, keen competition is expected for these high-paying jobs. Growth in financial services will create new positions, but there are still far more people who would like to enter the occupation. For those aspiring to financial analyst jobs, a strong academic background, including courses such as finance, accounting, and economics, is essential. Certifications and graduate degrees, such as a CFA certification or a master's degree in business or finance, significantly improve an applicant's prospects.

Earnings

Median annual wages, excluding bonuses, of wage and salary financial analysts were $73,150 in May 2008, which is more than double the national median wage. The middle 50 percent earned between $54,930 and $99,100. The lowest 10 percent earned less than $43,440, and the highest 10 percent earned more than $141,070. Annual performance bonuses are quite common and can be a significant part of their total earnings.

Related Occupations

Other jobs requiring expertise in finance and investment include:

Sources of Additional Information

For general information on securities industry employment, contact:

➤ Financial Industry Regulatory Authority (FINRA), 1735 K St. NW. Washington, DC 20006. Internet: **http://www.finra.org**

➤ Securities Industry and Financial Markets Association, 120 Broadway, 35th Floor, New York, NY 10271. Internet: **http://www.sifma.org**

For information on financial analyst careers and training, contact:

➤ American Academy of Financial Management, 200 L&A Rd., Suite B, Metairie, LA 70001. Internet: **http://www.aafm.us**

For information on financial analyst careers and CFA certification, contact:

➤ CFA Institute, 560 Ray C. Hunt Dr., Charlottesville, VA 22903. Internet: **http://www.cfainstitute.org**

For additional career information, see the *Occupational Outlook Quarterly* article "Financial analysts and personal financial advisors" online at **http://www.bls.gov/opub/ooq/2000/summer/art03.pdf** and in print at many libraries and career centers.

The Occupational Information Network (O*NET) provides information on a wide range of occupational characteristics. Links to O*NET appear at the end of the Internet version of this occupational statement, accessible at **http://www.bls.gov/ooh/ocos301.htm**

Projections data from the National Employment Matrix

Occupational Title	SOC Code	Employment, 2008	Projected Employment, 2018	Change, 2008-2018	
				Number	Percent
Financial analysts	13-2051	250,600	300,300	49,600	20

(NOTE) Data in this table are rounded. See the discussion of the employment projections table in the *Handbook* introductory chapter on *Occupational Information Included in the Handbook.*

Insurance Underwriters

Significant Points

- Most large insurance companies prefer to hire candidates who have a bachelor's degree or some insurance-related experience.

- Continuing education is necessary for advancement.

- Employment is expected to decline slowly as the spread of automated underwriting software increases worker productivity

- Job opportunities should be best for those with strong computer skills and a background in finance.

Nature of the Work

Insurance companies protect individuals and organizations from financial loss by assuming billions of dollars in risk each year—risks of car accident, property damage, illness, and other occurrences. *Underwriters* decide whether insurance is provided and, if so, under what terms. They identify and calculate the risk of loss from policyholders, establish who receives a policy, determine the appropriate premium, and write policies that cover this risk. An insurance company may lose business to competitors if risk underwriting is too conservative, or it may have to pay excessive claims if the underwriting actions are too liberal.

Using sophisticated computer software, underwriters analyze information in insurance applications to determine whether a risk is acceptable and will not result in a loss. Insurance applications often are supplemented with reports from loss-control representatives, medical reports, reports from data vendors, and actuarial studies. Underwriters then must decide whether to issue the policy and, if so, determine the appropriate premium. In making this determination, underwriters consider a wide variety of factors about the applicant. For example, an underwriter working in health insurance will consider age, family history, lifestyle, and current health, whereas an underwriter working for a property-casualty insurance company is concerned with the causes of loss to which property is exposed, such as hurricanes or earthquakes, and the safeguards taken by the applicant. Therefore, underwriters serve as the main link between the insurance carrier and the insurance agent.

Technology plays an important role in an underwriter's job. Underwriters use computer applications called "smart" systems to calculate risks more efficiently and accurately. Such systems—also known as "automated underwriting systems"—analyze and rate insurance applications, recommend acceptance or denial of the risk, and adjust the premium rate according to the risk. To start the process, underwriters create software rules to screen applicants based on certain criteria, such as income and credit score for mortgage applicants or age and family medical history for life insurance applicants. After the software completes its assessment, underwriters can either approve or refute the decision, or, if it is questionable, request additional information from the applicant. These automated systems allow underwriters to quickly make decisions and, in most cases, effectively make sound judgments and minimize losses.

The Internet also has aided underwriters in their work. Many insurance carriers' computer systems are linked to various databases on the Internet that allow immediate access to information—such as driving records and credit scores—necessary in determining a potential client's risk. This kind of access reduces the time and paperwork needed for an underwriter to complete a risk assessment.

Although there are many lines of insurance work, most underwriters specialize in one of four broad categories: life, health, mortgage, and property and casualty. Life and health insurance underwriters may further specialize in individual or group policies.

An increasing proportion of insurance sales, particularly in life and health insurance, are being made through group contracts. A standard group policy insures everyone in a specified group through a single contract at a standard premium. The group underwriter analyzes the overall composition of the group to ensure that the total risk is not excessive. Another type of group policy provides members of a group—senior citizens, for example—with individual policies that reflect their particular needs. These usually are casualty policies, such as those covering automobiles. The casualty underwriter analyzes the application of each group member and makes individual appraisals. Some group underwriters meet with union or employer representatives to discuss the types of policies available to their group.

Property and casualty underwriters specialize in either commercial or personal insurance and then by type of risk insured, such as fire, homeowners', automobile, or marine. In cases where property-casualty companies provide insurance through a single "package" policy covering various types of risks, the underwriter must be familiar with different types of insurance. For business insurance, the underwriter should be able to evaluate the firm's entire operation in appraising its application for insurance.

Work environment. Underwriters mainly have sedentary desk jobs that do not require strenuous physical activity. Most underwriters are based in a company headquarters or regional branch office, but they occasionally attend meetings away from home. Construction and marine underwriters frequently travel to inspect worksites and assess risks.

Although some overtime may be required, underwriters typically work a standard 40-hour week. Those in managerial positions often work more than 40 hours per week.

Training, Other Qualifications, and Advancement

Although there are no formal education requirements for becoming an underwriter, employers prefer candidates who have either a bachelor's degree or insurance-related experience and strong computer skills. Much of what an underwriter does may be learned through on-the-job training, so the majority of underwriters start their careers as trainees.

Education and training. For entry-level underwriting jobs, most large insurance companies prefer college graduates who have a degree in business administration or finance. However, a bachelor's degree in almost any field—plus courses in busi-

Insurance underwriters review insurance applications and determine the appropriate premium to charge a customer.

ness law and accounting—provides a good general background and may be sufficient to qualify entry-level jobseekers. Because computers are an integral part of most underwriters' jobs, some coursework with computers is also beneficial. Still, many employers prefer to hire candidates who have several years of related experience in underwriting or insurance.

New employees usually start as underwriter trainees or assistant underwriters. Under the supervision of an experienced risk analyst, beginning underwriters may help collect information on applicants and evaluate routine applications. Property and casualty trainees study claims files to become familiar with factors associated with certain types of losses. Many larger insurers offer work-study training programs, which generally last from a few months to a year. As trainees gain experience, they are assigned policy applications that are more complex and cover greater risks.

The computer programs many underwriters use to assess risk are continually being updated, so on-the-job computer training may continue throughout an underwriter's career.

Other qualifications. Underwriters must pay attention to detail and possess good judgment to make sound decisions. Additionally, good communication and interpersonal skills are beneficial because much of the underwriter's work involves dealing with agents and other professionals.

Certification and advancement. Continuing education is necessary for advancement, because changes in tax laws, government benefits programs, and other State and Federal regulations can affect the insurance needs of clients and businesses. Independent-study programs for experienced underwriters are also available. The Insurance Institute of America offers a training program for beginning underwriters. The Institute also offers the designation of Associate in Commercial Underwriting (ACU) for those starting a career in underwriting business insurance policies, or an Associate in Personal Insurance (API) for those interested in underwriting personal insurance policies. To earn either the ACU or API designation, underwriters complete a series of courses and examinations that generally last 1 to 2 years.

The American Institute for Chartered Property Casualty Underwriters awards the Chartered Property and Casualty Underwriter (CPCU) designation to experienced underwriters. Earning the CPCU designation requires passing eight exams, having at least 3 years of insurance experience, and abiding by the Institute's and CPCU Society's code of professional ethics.

The American College offers the equivalent Chartered Life Underwriter (CLU) designation and the Registered Health Underwriter (RHU) designation for life and health insurance professionals. For those new to the industry, the American College also offers the Life Underwriter Training Council Fellow (FUTCF), an introductory course that teaches basic insurance concepts.

Experienced underwriters who complete courses of study may advance to senior underwriter or underwriting manager positions. Some underwriting managers are promoted to senior managerial jobs, but these managers often need a master's degree. Other underwriters are attracted to the earnings potential of sales and, therefore, obtain State licenses to sell insurance and related financial products as agents or brokers.

Employment

Insurance underwriters held about 102,900 jobs in 2008. Insurance carriers employed 67 percent of all underwriters. Most of the remaining underwriters work in insurance agencies and brokerages.

Most underwriters are based in the insurance company's home office. But some, mainly in the property and casualty area, work out of regional branch offices of the insurance company. These underwriters usually have the authority to underwrite most risks and determine an appropriate rating without consulting the home office.

Job Outlook

Although employment is expected to decline slowly, job prospects will remain good because of high turnover.

Employment change. Employment of underwriters is expected to decline 4 percent during the 2008-18 decade. Demand for underwriters will continue to be offset by automation and technological advancement—factors that have resulted, in large part, to stagnant employment levels over the past two decades. For example, upgrades to underwriting software have helped

Projections data from the National Employment Matrix

Occupational Title	SOC Code	Employment, 2008	Projected Employment, 2018	Change, 2008-2018	
				Number	Percent
Insurance underwriters..	13-2053	102,900	98,700	-4,300	-4

(NOTE) Data in this table are rounded. See the discussion of the employment projections table in the *Handbook* introductory chapter on *Occupational Information Included in the Handbook.*

increase underwriter productivity. Automated underwriting quickly rates and analyzes insurance applications, reducing the need for underwriters. In addition, adoption of this technology into other segments of insurance, such as life and health and long-term care, will continue to impede employment growth through the projection period, although at a slower rate than in the past. Nonetheless, even as automated underwriting continues to be adopted and upgrades to underwriting software makes workers more productive, the need for humans to verify information will continue.

Additionally, some demand for underwriters may arise as insurance carriers try to restore profitability. As the carriers' returns on their investments have declined, insurers may place more emphasis on underwriting to generate revenues. An expected increase in sales of health insurance and long-term care insurance, designed specifically for the elderly, also may result in some new jobs. As members of the baby-boom generation grow older and a growing share of the Nation's population moves into the older age groups, more people are expected to purchase these kinds of insurance products.

Job prospects. Job opportunities should be best for those with experience in related insurance jobs, a background in finance, and strong computer and communication skills. The need to replace workers who retire or transfer to another occupation will create many job openings. In fact, high turnover will account for most job openings. High turnover among underwriters results, in part, from the limited upward mobility of workers in the occupation—a scenario that is likely to continue through the projections decade (2008-18).

New and emerging fields of insurance may also be a source of job opportunities for underwriters. Insurance carriers are always assessing new risks and offering new types of policies to meet changing circumstances. Underwriters are needed particularly in product development, where they assess risks and set the premiums for new lines of insurance. Growing demand for long-term care insurance—a relatively new product offered by insurance carriers—may also provide some job opportunities for underwriters.

Earnings

Median annual wages of wage and salary insurance underwriters were $56,790 in May 2008. The middle 50 percent earned between $43,490 and $76,700 a year. The lowest 10 percent earned less than $35,010, and the highest 10 percent earned more than $99,940. Median annual wages of underwriters working with insurance carriers were $57,480, while underwriters' median annual wages in agencies, brokerages, and other insurance-related activities were $54,410.

Insurance companies usually provide better-than-average benefits, including retirement plans and employer-financed

group life and health insurance. Insurance companies usually pay tuition for underwriting courses that their trainees complete, and some also offer salary incentives.

Related Occupations

Underwriters make decisions based on financial and statistical data. Other occupations with similar responsibilities include the following:

	Page
Accountants and auditors	86
Actuaries	125
Budget analysts	93
Cost estimators	100
Credit analysts	823
Financial managers	52
Loan officers	109

Other related jobs in the insurance industry include

Claims adjusters, appraisers, examiners, and investigators	96
Insurance sales agents	534

Sources of Additional Information

Information about a career as an insurance underwriter is available from the home offices of many insurance companies.

Information about the property-casualty insurance field can be obtained by contacting
➤ Insurance Information Institute, 110 William St., New York, NY 10038. Internet: **http://www.iii.org**

Information on the underwriting function and the CPCU and AU designations can be obtained from
➤ American Institute for Chartered Property and Casualty Underwriters and Insurance Institute of America, 720 Providence Rd., Suite 100, Malvern, PA 19355. Internet: **http://www.aicpcu.org**

➤ CPCU Society, 720 Providence Rd., Malvern, PA 19355. Internet: **http://www.cpcusociety.org**

Information on the CLU and RHU designations can be obtained from
➤ The American College, 270 S. Bryn Mawr Ave., Bryn Mawr, PA 19010. Internet: **http://www.theamericancollege.edu**

The Occupational Information Network (O*NET) provides information on a wide range of occupational characteristics. Links to O*NET appear at the end of the Internet version of this occupational statement, accessible at **http://www.bls.gov/ooh/ocos026.htm**

Loan Officers

Significant Points

- Nearly 9 out of 10 loan officers work for commercial banks, savings institutions, credit unions, and related financial institutions.

- Educational requirements range from a high school diploma for many loan officers to a bachelor's degree for commercial loan officers; previous banking, lending, or sales experience is highly valued.

- Good job opportunities are expected for mortgage and consumer loan officers and excellent opportunities are expected for commercial loan officers.

- Earnings often fluctuate with the number of loans generated, rising substantially when the economy is strong and interest rates are low.

Loan officers guide clients through the loan application process.

Nature of the Work

Many individuals take out loans to buy a house, car, or pay for a college education. Businesses use loans to start companies, purchase inventory, or invest in capital equipment. *Loan officers* facilitate this lending by finding potential clients and helping them to apply for loans. Loan officers gather information to determine the likelihood that individuals and businesses will repay the loan. Loan officers may also provide guidance to prospective borrowers who have problems qualifying for traditional loans. For example, loan officers might determine the most appropriate type of loan for a particular customer and explain specific requirements and restrictions associated with the loan.

Loan officers usually specialize in commercial, consumer, or mortgage loans. Commercial or business loans help companies pay for new equipment or expand operations. Consumer loans include home equity, automobile, and personal loans. Mortgage loans are loans made to purchase real estate or to refinance an existing mortgage.

Loan officers guide clients through the process of applying for a loan. The process begins with the client contacting the bank through a phone call, visiting a branch, or filling out a Web-based loan application. The loan officer obtains basic information from the client about the purpose of the loan and the applicant's ability to pay the loan. The loan officer may need to explain the different types of loans and credit terms available to the applicant. Loan officers answer questions about the process and sometimes assist clients in filling out the application.

After a client completes an application, the loan officer begins the process of analyzing and verifying the information on the application to determine the client's creditworthiness. Often, loan officers can quickly access the client's credit history by using underwriting software that determines if a client is eligible for the loan. When a credit history is not available or when unusual financial circumstances are present, the loan officer may request additional financial information from the client or, in the case of commercial loans, copies of the company's financial statements. Commercial loans are often too complex for a loan officer to rely solely on underwriting software. The variety in companies' financial statements and varying types of collateral require human judgment. Collateral is any asset, such as a factory, house, or car, owned by the borrower that becomes the property of the bank if the loan is not repaid. Loan officers comment on, and verify, the information of a loan application in a loan file, which is used to analyze whether the prospective loan meets the lending institution's requirements. Loan officers then decide, in consultation with their managers, whether to grant the loan.

Commercial loans are sometimes so large—for example, the loan needed to build a new shopping mall—that a single bank will not lend all of the money. In this case, a commercial loan officer may work with other banks or investment bankers to put together a package of loans from multiple sources to finance the project.

In many instances, loan officers act as salespeople. Commercial loan officers, for example, contact firms to determine their needs for loans. If a firm is seeking new funds, the loan officer will try to persuade the company to obtain the loan from his or her institution. Similarly, mortgage loan officers develop relationships with commercial and residential real estate agencies, so that when an individual or firm buys a property, the real estate agent might recommend contacting a specific loan officer for financing.

Some loan officers, called *loan underwriters*, specialize in evaluating a client's creditworthiness and may conduct a financial analysis or other risk assessment.

Other loan officers, referred to as *loan collection officers*, contact borrowers with delinquent loan accounts to help them find a method of repayment to avoid their defaulting on the loan. If a repayment plan cannot be developed, the loan collection officer initiates collateral liquidation, in which the lender seizes the collateral used to secure the loan—a home or car, for example—and sells it to repay the loan.

Work environment. Working as a loan officer usually involves considerable work outside the office. For example, commercial and mortgage loan officers frequently work away from their offices and rely on laptop computers and cellular telephones to keep in contact with their employers and clients. Mortgage loan officers often work out of their home or car, visiting offices or homes of clients to complete loan applications. Commercial loan officers sometimes travel to other cities to prepare complex loan agreements. Consumer loan officers, however, are likely to spend most of their time in an office.

Most loan officers work a standard 40-hour week, but many work longer, depending on the number of clients and the demand for loans. Mortgage loan officers can work especially long hours because they are free to take on as many customers as they choose. Loan officers are especially busy when interest rates are low, causing a surge in loan applications.

Training, Other Qualifications, and Advancement

Loan officers need a high school diploma and receive on-the-job training. Commercial loan officer positions often require a bachelor's degree in finance, economics, or a related field. Previous banking, lending, or sales experience is also highly valued by employers.

Education and training. Loan officer positions generally require a high school degree. Loan officers receive on-the-job training consisting of some formal company-sponsored training and informal training on the job over their first few months of employment. Commercial loan officer positions often require a bachelor's degree in finance, economics, or a related field. Because commercial loan officers analyze the finances of businesses applying for credit, they need to understand business accounting, financial statements, and cash flow analysis. Loan officers often advance to their positions after gaining experience in various other related occupations, such as teller or customer service representative.

Licensure. Recent federal legislation requires that all mortgage loan officers be licensed. Licensing requirements include at least 20 hours of coursework, passing a written exam, passing a background check, and having no felony convictions. There are also continuing education requirements for mortgage loan officers to maintain their licenses. There are currently no specific licensing requirements for other loan officers.

Other qualifications. People planning a career as a loan officer should be good at working with others, confident, and highly motivated. Loan officers must be willing to attend community events as representatives of their employer. Sales ability, good interpersonal and communication skills, and a strong desire to succeed also are important qualities for loan officers. Banks generally require their employees to pass a background check. Most employers also prefer applicants who are familiar with computers and banking and financial software.

Certification and advancement. Capable loan officers may advance to larger branches of their firms or to managerial positions. Some loan officers advance to supervise other loan officers and clerical staff.

Various banking associations and private schools offer courses and programs for students interested in lending and for experienced loan officers who want to keep their skills current. For example, the Bank Administration Institute, an affiliate of the American Banker's Association, offers the Loan Review Certificate Program for people who review and approve loans.

The Mortgage Bankers Association offers the Certified Mortgage Banker (CMB) designation to loan officers in real estate finance. The association offers three CMB designations: residential, commerce, and master to candidates who have 3 years of experience, earn educational credits, and pass an exam. Completion of these courses and programs generally enhances employment and advancement opportunities.

Employment

Loan officers held about 327,800 jobs in 2008. Nearly 9 out of 10 loan officers were employed by commercial banks, savings institutions, credit unions, and related financial institutions. Loan officers are employed throughout the Nation, but most work in urban and suburban areas. At some banks, particularly in rural areas, the branch or assistant manager often handles the loan application process.

Job Outlook

Loan officers can expect average employment growth. Good job opportunities should exist for loan officers.

Employment change. Employment of loan officers is projected to grow 10 percent between 2008 and 2018, which is about as fast as the average for all occupations. Employment growth will be driven by economic expansion and population increases—factors that generate demand for loans. Growth will be partially offset by increased automation that speeds the lending process and by the growing use of the Internet to apply for and obtain loans. However, these changes have also reduced the cost and complexity associated with refinancing loans, which could increase the number of loans originated.

The use of automated underwriting software has made the loan evaluation process much simpler than in the past. Underwriting software allows loan officers—particularly loan underwriters—to evaluate many more loans in less time. In addition, the mortgage application process has become highly automated and standardized, a simplification that has enabled mortgage loan vendors to offer their services over the Internet. Online vendors accept loan applications from customers over the Internet and determine which lenders have the best interest rates

Projections data from the National Employment Matrix

Occupational Title	SOC Code	Employment, 2008	Projected Employment, 2018	Change, 2008-2018	
				Number	Percent
Loan officers	13-2072	327,800	360,900	33,000	10

(NOTE) Data in this table are rounded. See the discussion of the employment projections table in the *Handbook* introductory chapter on *Occupational Information Included in the Handbook.*

for particular loans. With this knowledge, customers can go directly to the lending institution, thereby bypassing mortgage loan brokers. Shopping for loans on the Internet is expected to become more common in the future and to slow job growth for loan officers.

Job prospects. Most job openings will result from the need to replace workers who retire or otherwise leave the occupation permanently. Good job opportunities should exist for mortgage and consumer loan officers. College graduates and those with banking, lending, or sales experience should have the best job prospects. Excellent opportunities should exist for commercial loan officers as banks report having a hard time finding qualified candidates.

Job opportunities for loan officers are influenced by the volume of applications, which is determined largely by interest rates and by the overall level of economic activity. Although loans remain a major source of revenue for banks, demand for new loans fluctuates and affects the income and employment opportunities of loan officers. An upswing in the economy or a decline in interest rates often results in a surge in real estate buying and mortgage refinancing, requiring loan officers to work long hours processing applications and inducing lenders to hire additional loan officers. Loan officers often are paid by commission on the value of the loans they place, and when the real estate market slows they often suffer a decline in earnings and may even be subject to layoffs. The same applies to commercial loan officers, whose workloads increase during good economic times as companies seek to invest more in their businesses. In difficult economic conditions, an increase in the number of delinquent loans results in more demand for loan collection officers.

Earnings

Median annual wages of wage and salary loan officers were $54,700 in May 2008. The middle 50 percent earned between $39,710 and $76,860. The lowest 10 percent earned less than $30,850, while the top 10 percent earned more than $106,360. Median annual wages in the industries employing the largest numbers of loan officers were as follows:

Federal Executive Branch	$69,070
Management of companies and enterprises	58,100
Nondepository credit intermediation	54,240
Activities related to credit intermediation	54,140
Depository credit intermediation	53,490

The form of compensation for loan officers varies. Most are paid a commission based on the number of loans they originate. Some institutions pay only salaries, while others pay their loan officers a salary plus a commission or bonus based on the number of loans or the performance of the loans that they originated. Loan officers who are paid on commission usually earn more than those who earn only a salary, and those who work for smaller banks generally earn less than those employed by larger institutions.

Earnings often fluctuate with the number of loans generated, rising substantially when the economy is strong and interest rates are low.

Related Occupations

Loan officers help people manage financial assets and secure loans. Occupations that involve similar functions include:

Sources of Additional Information

Information about a career as a mortgage loan officer can be obtained from:
➤ Mortgage Bankers Association, 1331 L St. NW., Washington, DC 20005. Internet: **http://www.mortgagebankers.org**

State bankers' associations can furnish specific information about job opportunities in their State. Also, individual banks can supply information about job openings and the activities, responsibilities, and preferred qualifications of their loan officers.

The Occupational Information Network (O*NET) provides information on a wide range of occupational characteristics. Links to O*NET appear at the end of the Internet version of this occupational statement, accessible at **http://www.bls.gov/ooh/ocos018.htm**

Management Analysts

Significant Points

- Despite 24 percent employment growth, keen competition is expected for jobs; opportunities should be best for those with a graduate degree, specialized expertise, and a talent for salesmanship and public relations.

- About 26 percent, three times the average for all occupations, are self-employed.

- A bachelor's degree is sufficient for many entry-level government jobs; many positions in private industry require a master's degree, specialized expertise, or both.

Nature of the Work

As business becomes more complex, firms are continually faced with new challenges. They increasingly rely on *management analysts* to help them remain competitive amidst these changes. Management analysts, often referred to as *management consultants* in private industry, analyze and propose ways to improve an organization's structure, efficiency, or profits.

For example, a small but rapidly growing company might employ a consultant who is an expert in just-in-time invento-

Management analysts collect and analyze information in order to make recommendations to managers.

ry management to help improve its inventory-control system. In another case, a large company that has recently acquired a new division may hire management analysts to help reorganize the corporate structure and eliminate duplicate or nonessential jobs. In recent years, information technology and electronic commerce have provided new opportunities for management analysts. Companies hire consultants to develop strategies for entering and remaining competitive in the new electronic marketplace. (For information on computer specialists working in consulting, see the following statements elsewhere in the *Handbook*: computer software engineers; computer systems analysts; computer scientists; and computer programmers.)

Management analysts might be single practitioners or part of large international organizations employing thousands of other consultants. Some analysts and consultants specialize in a specific industry, such as healthcare or telecommunications, while others specialize by type of business function, such as human resources, marketing, logistics, or information systems. In government, management analysts tend to specialize by type of agency. The work of management analysts and consultants varies with each client or employer and from project to project. Some projects require a team of consultants, each specializing in one area. In other projects, consultants work independently with the organization's managers. In all cases, analysts and consultants collect, review, and analyze information in order to make recommendations to managers.

Both public and private organizations use consultants for a variety of reasons. Some lack the internal resources needed to handle a project, while others need a consultant's expertise to determine what resources will be required and what problems may be encountered if they pursue a particular opportunity. To retain a consultant, a company first solicits proposals from a number of consulting firms specializing in the area in which it needs assistance. These proposals include the estimated cost and scope of the project, staffing requirements, references from previous clients, and a completion deadline. The company then selects the proposal that best suits its needs. Some firms, however, employ internal management consulting groups rather than hiring outside consultants.

After obtaining an assignment or contract, management analysts first define the nature and extent of the problem that

they have been asked to solve. During this phase, they analyze relevant data—which may include annual revenues, employment, or expenditures—and interview managers and employees while observing their operations. The analysts or consultants then develop solutions to the problem. While preparing their recommendations, they take into account the nature of the organization, the relationship it has with others in the industry, and its internal organization and culture. Insight into the problem often is gained by building and solving mathematical models, such as one that shows how inventory levels affect costs and product delivery times.

Once they have decided on a course of action, consultants report their findings and recommendations to the client. Their suggestions usually are submitted in writing, but oral presentations regarding findings are also common. For some projects, management analysts are retained to help implement their suggestions.

Like their private-sector colleagues, management analysts in government agencies try to increase efficiency and worker productivity and to control costs. For example, if an agency is planning to purchase personal computers, it must first determine which type to buy, given its budget and data-processing needs. In this case, management analysts would assess the prices and characteristics of various machines and determine which ones best meet the agency's needs. Analysts may manage contracts for a wide range of goods and services to ensure quality performance and to prevent cost overruns.

Work environment. Management analysts usually divide their time between their offices and the client's site. In either situation, much of an analyst's time is spent indoors in clean, well-lit offices. Because they must spend a significant portion of their time with clients, analysts travel frequently.

Analysts and consultants generally work at least 40 hours a week. Uncompensated overtime is common, especially when project deadlines are approaching. Analysts may experience a great deal of stress when trying to meet a client's demands, often on a tight schedule.

Self-employed consultants can set their workload and hours and work at home. On the other hand, their livelihood depends on their ability to maintain and expand their client base. Salaried consultants also must impress potential clients to get and keep clients for their company.

Training, Other Qualifications, and Advancement
Entry requirements for management analysts vary. For some entry-level positions, a bachelor's degree is sufficient. For others, a master's degree or specialized expertise is required.

Education and training. Educational requirements for entry-level jobs in this field vary between private industry and government. Many employers in private industry generally seek individuals with a master's degree in business administration or a related discipline. Some employers also require additional years of experience in the field or industry in which the worker plans to consult. Other firms hire workers with a bachelor's degree as research analysts or associates and promote them to consultants after several years. Some government agencies require experience, graduate education, or both, but many also hire people with a bachelor's degree and little work experience for entry-level management analyst positions.

Few universities or colleges offer formal programs in management consulting; however, many fields of study provide a suitable educational background for this occupation because of the wide range of areas addressed by management analysts. Common fields of study include business, management, accounting, marketing, economics, statistics, computer and information science, or engineering. Most analysts also have years of experience in management, human resources, information technology, or other specialties. Analysts also routinely attend conferences to keep abreast of current developments in their field.

Other qualifications. Management analysts often work with minimal supervision, so they need to be self-motivated and disciplined. Analytical skills, the ability to get along with a wide range of people, strong oral and written communication skills, good judgment, time-management skills, and creativity are other desirable qualities. The ability to work in teams also is an important attribute as consulting teams become more common.

Certification and advancement. As consultants gain experience, they often become solely responsible for specific projects, taking on more responsibility and managing their own hours. At the senior level, consultants may supervise teams working on more complex projects and become more involved in seeking out new business. Those with exceptional skills may eventually become partners in the firm and focus on attracting new clients and bringing in revenue. Senior consultants who leave their consulting firms often move to senior management positions at non-consulting firms. Others with entrepreneurial ambition may open their own firms.

A high percentage of management consultants are self-employed, in part because business startup and overhead costs are low. Since many small consulting firms fail each year because of lack of managerial expertise and clients, persons interested in opening their own firm must have good organizational and marketing skills. Several years of consulting experience are also helpful.

The Institute of Management Consultants USA, Inc. offers the Certified Management Consultant (CMC) designation to those who meet minimum levels of education and experience, submit client reviews, and pass an interview and exam covering the IMC USA's Code of Ethics. Management consultants with a CMC designation must be recertified every 3 years. Certification is not mandatory for management consultants, but it may give a jobseeker a competitive advantage.

Employment

Management analysts held about 746,900 jobs in 2008. About 26 percent of these workers, three times the average for all occupations, were self-employed. Management analysts are found throughout the country, but employment is concentrated in large metropolitan areas. Management analysts work in a range of industries, including management, scientific, and technical consulting firms; computer systems design and related services firms; and Federal, State, and local governments.

Job Outlook

Employment of management analysts is expected to grow 24 percent, much faster than the average for all occupations. Despite projected rapid employment growth, keen competition is expected for jobs as management analysts because the independent and challenging nature of the work and the high earnings potential make this occupation attractive to many.

Employment change. Employment of management analysts is expected to grow by 24 percent, much faster than the average, over the 2008–18 decade, as industry and government increasingly rely on outside expertise to improve the performance of their organizations. Job growth is projected in very large consulting firms with international expertise and in smaller consulting firms that specialize in specific areas, such as biotechnology, healthcare, information technology, human resources, engineering, and marketing. Growth in the number of individual practitioners may be hindered by increasing use of consulting teams that are often more versatile.

Job growth for management analysts will be driven by a number of changes in the business environment that have forced firms to take a closer look at their operations. These changes include regulatory changes, developments in information technology, and the growth of electronic commerce. In addition, as firms try to solve regulatory changes due to the current economic credit and housing crisis, consultants will be hired to render advice on the recovery process. Firms will also hire information technology consultants who specialize in "green" or environmentally safe use of technology management consulting to help lower energy consumption and implement "green" initiatives. Traditional companies hire analysts to help design intranets, company Web sites, or to establish online businesses. New Internet startup companies hire analysts not only to design Web sites but also to advise them in traditional business practices, such as pricing strategies, marketing, and inventory and human resource management.

To offer clients better quality and a wider variety of services, consulting firms are partnering with traditional computer software and technology firms. Also, many computer firms are developing consulting practices of their own to take advantage of this expanding market. Although information technology consulting should remain one of the fastest growing consulting areas, employment in the computer services industry can be volatile, and so the most successful management analysts may also consult in other business areas.

Projections data from the National Employment Matrix

Occupational Title	SOC Code	Employment, 2008	Projected Employment, 2018	Change, 2008-2018	
				Number	Percent
Management analysts...	13-1111	746,900	925,200	178,300	24

(NOTE) Data in this table are rounded. See the discussion of the employment projections table in the *Handbook* introductory chapter on *Occupational Information Included in the Handbook.*

The growth of international business will also contribute to an increase in demand for management analysts. As U.S. firms expand their business abroad, many will hire management analysts to help them form the right strategy for entering the market; to advise them on legal matters pertaining to specific countries; or to help them with organizational, administrative, and other issues, especially if the U.S. company is involved in a partnership or merger with a local firm. These trends provide management analysts with more opportunities to travel or work abroad but also require them to have a more comprehensive knowledge of international business and foreign cultures and languages. Just as globalization creates new opportunities for management analysts, it also allows U.S. firms to hire management analysts in other countries; however, because international work is expected to increase the total amount of work, this development is not expected to adversely affect employment in this occupation.

Furthermore, as international and domestic markets become more competitive, firms will need to use resources more efficiently. Management analysts will be increasingly sought to help reduce costs, streamline operations, and develop marketing strategies. As this process expands and as businesses downsize, even more opportunities will be created for analysts to perform duties that were previously handled internally. Finally, more management analysts will also be needed in the public sector, as Federal, State, and local government agencies seek to improve efficiency.

Job prospects. Despite rapid employment growth, keen competition is expected. The pool of applicants from which employers can draw is quite large, since analysts can have very diverse educational backgrounds and work experience. Furthermore, the independent and challenging nature of the work, combined with high earnings potential, makes this occupation attractive to many. Job opportunities are expected to be best for those with a graduate degree, specialized expertise, and a talent for salesmanship and public relations.

Economic downturns can also have adverse effects on employment for some management consultants. In these times, businesses look to cut costs, and consultants may be considered an excess expense. On the other hand, some consultants might experience an increase in work during recessions because they advise businesses on how to cut costs and remain profitable.

Earnings

Salaries for management analysts vary widely by years of experience and education, geographic location, specific expertise, and size of employer. Generally, management analysts employed in large firms or in metropolitan areas have the highest salaries. Median annual wages of wage and salary management analysts in May 2008 were $73,570. The middle 50 percent earned between $54,890 and $99,700. The lowest 10 percent earned less than $41,910 and the highest 10 percent earned more than $133,850. Median annual wages in the industries employing the largest numbers of management analysts were:

Computer systems and design related services $82,090
Management, scientific, and technical
    consulting services 81,670
Federal Executive Branch 79,830
Management of companies and enterprises 73,760
State government...55,590

Salaried management analysts usually receive common benefits, such as health and life insurance, a retirement plan, vacation, and sick leave, as well as less common benefits, such as profit sharing and bonuses for outstanding work. In addition, all travel expenses usually are reimbursed by the employer. Self-employed consultants have to maintain their own office and provide their own benefits.

Related Occupations

Management analysts collect, review, and analyze data; make recommendations; and implement their ideas. Occupations with similar duties include:

	Page
Accountants and auditors	86
Budget analysts	93
Cost estimators	100
Economists	209
Financial analysts	103
Market and survey researchers	212
Operations research analysts	145
Personal financial advisors	118

Some management analysts specialize in information technology and work with computers, similar to:

Computer scientists	132
Computer systems analysts	140

Most management analysts also have managerial experience similar to that of:

Administrative services managers	29
Advertising, marketing, promotions, public relations, and sales managers	32
Financial managers	52
Human resources, training, and labor relations managers and specialists	61
Industrial production managers	67
Top executives	83

Sources of Additional Information

Information about career opportunities in management consulting is available from:

➤ Association of Management Consulting Firms, 370 Lexington Ave., Suite 2209, New York, NY 10017. Internet: **http://www.amcf.org**

Information about the Certified Management Consultant designation can be obtained from:

➤ Institute of Management Consultants USA, Inc., 2025 M St. NW., Suite 800, Washington, DC 20036. Internet: **http://www.imcusa.org**

Information on obtaining a management analyst position with the Federal Government is available from the Office of Personnel Management (OPM) through USAJOBS, the Federal Government's official employment information system. This resource for locating and applying for job opportunities can be accessed through the Internet at **http://www.usajobs.opm.gov** or through an interactive voice response telephone system at (703) 724-1850 or TDD (978) 461-8404. These numbers are not toll free, and charges may result. For advice on how to find and apply for Federal jobs, see the *Occupational Outlook Quarterly* article "How to get a job in the Federal Government," online at http://www.bls.gov/opub/ooq/2004/summer/art01.pdf.

The Occupational Information Network (O*NET) provides information on a wide range of occupational characteristics. Links to O*NET appear at the end of the Internet version of this occupational statement, accessible at http://www.bls.gov/ooh/ocos019.htm

Meeting and Convention Planners

Significant Points

- People with a variety of educational or work backgrounds can become meeting and convention planners.

- Planners often work long hours in the period prior to and during a meeting or convention, and extensive travel may be required.

- Employment is expected to grow faster than the average for all occupations.

- Opportunities will be best for individuals with a bachelor's degree and some experience as a meeting planner.

Nature of the Work

Meetings and conventions bring people together for a common purpose, and *meeting* and *convention planners* work to ensure that this purpose is achieved seamlessly. *Planners* coordinate every detail of meetings and conventions, from the speakers and meeting location to arranging for printed materials and audio-visual equipment.

The first step in planning a meeting or convention is determining the purpose, message, or impression that the sponsoring organization wants to communicate. Planners increasingly focus on how meetings affect the goals of their organizations; for example, they may survey prospective attendees to find out what motivates them and how they learn best. A more recent option for planners is to decide whether the meeting or convention can achieve goals in a virtual format versus the traditional meeting format. Virtual conferences are offered over the Internet where attendees view speakers and exhibits online. After this decision is made, planners then choose speakers, entertainment, and content, and arrange the program to present the organization's information in the most effective way.

Meeting and convention planners search for prospective meeting sites, primarily hotels and convention or conference centers. When choosing a site, the planner considers who the prospective attendees are and how they will get to the meeting. Being close to a major airport is important for organizations that have attendees traveling long distances who are pressed for time. The planner may also select a site based on its attractiveness to increase the number of attendees.

Once they have narrowed down possible locations for the meeting, planners issue requests for proposals to all possible meeting sites in which they are interested. These requests state the meeting dates and outline the planner's needs for the meeting or convention, including meeting and exhibit space, lodging, food and beverages, telecommunications, audio-visual requirements, transportation, and any other necessities. The establishments respond with proposals describing what space and services they can supply, and at what price. Meeting and convention planners review these proposals and either make recommendations to the clients or management or choose the site themselves.

Once the location is selected, meeting and convention planners arrange support services, coordinate with the facility, prepare the site staff for the meeting, and set up all forms of electronic communication needed for the meeting or convention, such as e-mail, voice mail, video, and online communication.

Meeting logistics, the management of the details of meetings and conventions, such as labor and materials, is another major component of the job. Planners register attendees and issue name badges, coordinate lodging reservations, and arrange transportation. They make sure that all necessary supplies are ordered and transported to the meeting site on time, that meeting rooms are equipped with sufficient seating and audio-visual equipment, that all exhibits and booths are set up properly, and that all materials are printed. They also make sure that the meeting adheres to fire and labor regulations and oversee food and beverage distribution.

There also is a financial management component of the work. Planners negotiate contracts with facilities and suppliers. These contracts, which have become increasingly complex, are often drawn up more than a year in advance of the meeting or convention. Contracts often include clauses requiring the planner to book a certain number of rooms for meetings in order to qualify for space discounts and imposing penalties if the rooms are not filled. Therefore, it is important that the planner closely estimates how many people will attend the meeting based on previous meeting attendance and current circumstances. Planners must also oversee the finances of meetings and conventions. They are given overall budgets by their organizations and must create a detailed budget, forecasting what each aspect of the event will cost. Additionally, some planners oversee meetings that contribute significantly to their organization's operating budget and must ensure that the event meets income goals.

An important part of the work is measuring how well the meeting's purpose was achieved. After determining what the objectives are, planners try to measure if objectives were met and if the meeting or conference was a success. The most common way to gauge their success is to have attendees fill out surveys about their experiences at the event. Planners can ask specific questions about what sessions were attended, how well organized the event appeared, how they felt about the overall experience, and ask for suggestions on how to improve the next event. If the purpose of a meeting or convention is publicity, a good measure of success would be how much press coverage the event received. A more precise measurement of meeting success, and one that is gaining importance, is return on investment. Planners compare the costs and benefits of an event and show whether it was worthwhile to the organization. For example, if a company holds a meeting to motivate its employees and improve company morale, the planner might track employee turnover before and after the meeting.

Some aspects of the work vary by the type of organization for which planners work. Those who work for associations must market their meetings to association members, convincing members that attending the meeting is worth their time and expense. Marketing is usually less important for corporate meeting planners because employees are generally required to attend company meetings. *Corporate planners* usually have shorter time frames in which to prepare their meetings. Planners who work in Federal, State, and local governments must learn how to operate within established government procedures, such as procedures and rules for procuring materials and booking lodging for government employees. *Government meeting planners* also need to be aware of any potential ethics violations.

Convention service managers, meeting professionals who work in hotels, convention centers, and similar establishments, act as liaisons between the meeting facility and planners who work for associations, businesses, or governments. They present food service options to outside planners, coordinate special requests, suggest hotel services based on the planner's budget, and otherwise help outside planners present effective meetings and conventions in their facilities.

In large organizations or those that sponsor large meetings or conventions, meeting professionals are more likely to specialize in a particular aspect of meeting planning. Some specialties are *conference coordinators*, who handle most of the meeting logistics; *registrars*, who handle advance registration and payment, name badges, and the set-up of on-site registration; and *education planners*, who coordinate the meeting content, including speakers and topics. In organizations that hold very large or complex meetings, there may be several senior positions, such as *manager of registration, education seminar coordinator*, or *conference services director*, with the entire meeting planning department headed by a department director.

Work environment. The work of meeting and convention planners may be considered either stressful or energizing, but there is no question that it is fast-paced and demanding. Planners oversee multiple operations at one time, face numerous deadlines, and orchestrate the activities of several different groups of people. Meeting and convention planners spend the majority of their time in offices, but during meetings, they work on-site at the hotel, convention center, or other meeting location. They travel regularly to attend meetings and to visit prospective meeting sites. The extent of travel depends upon the type of organization for which the planner works. Local and regional organizations require mostly regional travel, while national and international organizations require travel to more distant locales, including travel abroad.

Work hours can be long and irregular, with planners working more than 40 hours per week in the time leading up to a meeting and fewer hours after finishing a meeting. During meetings or conventions, planners may work very long days, starting as early as 5:00 a.m. and working until midnight. They are sometimes required to work on weekends.

Some physical activity is required, including long hours of standing and walking and some lifting and carrying of boxes of materials, exhibits, or supplies. Planners work with the public

Meeting and convention planners search for prospective meeting sites, primarily hotels and convention or conference centers.

and with workers from diverse backgrounds. They may get to travel to luxurious hotels and interesting places and meet speakers and meeting attendees from around the world, while enjoying a high level of autonomy.

Training, Other Qualifications, and Advancement

People with a variety of educational or work backgrounds become meeting and convention planners. Many migrate into the occupation after gaining planning experience. For example, an administrative assistant may begin planning small meetings and gradually move into a full-time position as a meeting and convention planner. Although there are some certification programs and college courses in meeting and convention planning available, most needed skills are learned through experience.

Education and training. Many employers prefer applicants who have a bachelor's degree, but this is not always required. The proportion of planners with a bachelor's degree is increasing because the work and responsibilities are becoming more complex.

Other planners enter the profession by gaining planning experience while working in another position, such as administrative assistant. Others enter the occupation after working in hotel sales or as marketing or catering coordinators. These are effective ways to learn about meeting and convention planning because these hotel personnel work with numerous meeting planners, participate in negotiations for hotel services, and witness many different meetings. Workers who enter the occupation in these ways often start at a higher level than those with bachelor's degrees and no experience.

Planners with college degrees have backgrounds in a variety of disciplines, but some useful undergraduate majors are marketing, public relations, communications, business, and hotel or hospitality management. Individuals who have studied hospitality management may start out with greater responsibilities than those with other academic backgrounds. College students may also gain experience by planning meetings for a university organization or club.

Several universities offer bachelor's or master's degrees with majors in meetings management. Additionally, meeting and convention planning continuing education programs are offered by a few universities and colleges. These programs are designed for career development of meeting professionals as well as for people wishing to enter the occupation. Some programs may require 40 to more than 100 classroom hours and may last anywhere from 1 semester to 2 years.

Once hired, most of the training is done informally on the job. Entry-level planners generally begin by performing small tasks under the supervision of senior meeting professionals. For example, they may issue requests for proposals and discuss the resulting proposals with higher level planners. They also may assist in registration, review of contracts, or the creation of meeting timelines, schedules, or objectives. They may start by planning small meetings, such as committee meetings. Those who start at small organizations have the opportunity to learn more quickly since they will be required to take on a larger number of tasks.

Other qualifications. Because meeting and convention planners communicate with a wide range of people, they must have excellent written and verbal communications skills and interpersonal skills in order to convey the needs of the organization effectively. In addition, they must be good at establishing and maintaining relationships with clients and suppliers.

Meeting and convention planners must be detail-oriented with excellent organizational skills, and they must be able to multi-task, meet tight deadlines, and maintain composure under pressure in a fast-paced environment. Quantitative and analytic skills are needed to formulate and follow budgets and to understand and negotiate contracts. The ability to speak multiple languages is a plus, since some planners must communicate with meeting attendees and speakers from around the world. Planners also need computer skills, such as the ability to use financial and registration software and the Internet.

Certification and advancement. To advance in this occupation, planners must volunteer to take on more responsibility and find new and better ways of doing things in their organizations. The most important factors are demonstrated skill on the job, determination, and gaining the respect of others within the organization. Because formal education is increasingly important, those who enter the occupation may enhance their professional standing by enrolling in meeting planning courses offered by professional meeting and convention planning organizations, colleges, or universities.

As meeting and convention planners prove themselves, they are given greater responsibilities. This may mean taking on a wider range of duties or moving to another planning specialty to gain experience in that area before moving to a higher level. For example, a planner may be promoted from conference coordinator, with responsibility for meeting logistics, to program coordinator, with responsibility for booking speakers and formatting the meeting's program. The next step up may be meeting manager, who supervises all parts of the meeting, and then

director of meetings, and then possibly department director of meetings and education. Another path for promotion is to move from a small organization to a larger one, taking on responsibility for larger meetings and conventions.

The Convention Industry Council offers the Certified Meeting Professional (CMP) credential, a voluntary certification for meeting and convention planners. Although the CMP is not required, it is widely recognized in the industry and may help in career advancement. To qualify, candidates must have a minimum of 3 years of meeting management experience, full-time employment in a meeting management capacity, and proof of accountability for successfully completed meetings. Those who qualify must then pass an examination that covers topics such as adult learning, financial management, facilities and services, logistics, and meeting programs.

The Society of Government Meeting Professionals (SGMP) offers the Certified Government Meeting Professional credential. This certification is not required to work as a government meeting planner. It may, however, be helpful to those who want to demonstrate knowledge of issues specific to planning government meetings, such as regulations and policies governing procurement and travel. To qualify for certification, candidates must have at least 1 year of membership in SGMP. Membership requires employment as a meeting planner within Federal, State, or local government or for a firm that works on government contracts. To become certified, members must take a 3-day course and pass an exam.

With significant experience, meeting planners may become independent meeting consultants, advance to vice president or executive director of an association, or start their own meeting planning firms.

Employment

Meeting and convention planners held about 56,600 jobs in 2008. About 27 percent worked for religious, grantmaking, civic, professional, and similar organizations and 14 percent worked for accommodation, including hotels and motels. The remaining worked for educational services, public and private, and in other industries that host meetings. About 6 percent of meeting planners were self-employed.

Job Outlook

Employment of meeting and convention planners is expected to grow faster than the average for all occupations. Opportunities will be best for individuals with a bachelor's degree and some meeting planning experience.

Employment change. Employment of meeting and convention planners is expected to grow 16 percent over the 2008-18 decade, which is faster than the average for all occupations. As businesses and organizations become increasingly international, meetings and conventions become even more important. In

Projections data from the National Employment Matrix

Occupational Title	SOC Code	Employment, 2008	Projected Employment, 2018	Change, 2008-2018	
				Number	Percent
Meeting and convention planners	13-1121	56,600	65,400	8,800	16

(NOTE) Data in this table are rounded. See the discussion of the employment projections table in the *Handbook* introductory chapter on *Occupational Information Included in the Handbook.*

organizations that span the country or the globe, the periodic meeting is increasingly the only time the organization can bring all of its members together. Despite the proliferation of alternative forms of communication, such as e-mail, videoconferencing, and the Internet, face-to-face interaction is still irreplaceable. In fact, these new forms of communication which foster interaction and connect individuals and groups that previously would not have collaborated actually increase the demand for meetings by these new groups and individuals. Industries that are experiencing high growth tend to experience corresponding growth in meetings and conferences.

Job prospects. In addition to openings from employment growth, there will be some job openings that arise due to the need to replace workers who leave this occupation. Opportunities will be best for individuals with a bachelor's degree and some meeting planning experience. A CMP is also viewed favorably by potential employers.

The skills that meeting planners develop are useful in whichever industry they work. They often do not need industry-specific knowledge, which allows them to change industries relatively easily. There will also be opportunities for freelance meeting planners to contract with organizations that do not maintain meeting planners on staff.

Demand for corporate meeting planners is susceptible to business cycle fluctuations because meetings are usually among the first expenses cut when budgets are tight. For associations, fluctuations are less pronounced because meetings are generally a source of revenue rather than an expense. However, since fewer people are able to attend association meetings during recessions, associations often reduce their meeting staff as well. Associations for industries such as healthcare, in which meeting attendance is required for professionals to maintain their licensure, are the least likely to experience cutbacks during downturns in the economy.

Earnings

Median annual wages of meeting and convention planners in May 2008 were $44,260. The middle 50 percent earned between $34,480 and $57,820. The lowest 10 percent earned less than $27,450, and the highest 10 percent earned more than $74,610. In May 2008, median annual wages in the industries employing the largest numbers of meeting and convention planners were as follows:

Management, scientific, and technical consulting services	$49,600
Business, professional, labor, political, and similar organizations	47,670
Other support services	44,290
Colleges, universities, and professional schools	41,860
Traveler accommodation	41,470

Related Occupations

Other occupations that have similar planning and organizing responsibilities include:

Sources of Additional Information

For information about meeting planner certification, contact:
➤ Convention Industry Council, 700 N. Fairfax St., Suite 510, Alexandria, VA 22314. Internet: **http://www.conventionindustry.org**

For information about the Certified Government Meeting Professional designation, contact:
➤ Society of Government Meeting Professionals, 908 King St., Lower Level, Alexandria, VA 22314. Internet: **http://www.sgmp.org**

For information about internships and on-campus student meeting planning organizations, contact:
➤ Professional Convention Management Association, 2301 S. Lake Shore Dr., Suite 1001, Chicago, IL 60616-1419. Internet: **http://www.pcma.org**

For information about meeting planning education, entering the profession, and career paths, contact:
➤ Meeting Professionals International, 3030 Lyndon B Johnson Fwy., Suite 1700, Dallas, TX 75234-2759. Internet: **http://www.mpiweb.org**

For additional career information about meeting and convention planners, see the *Occupational Outlook Quarterly* article "Meeting and convention planners," online at **http://www.bls.gov/opub/ooq/2005/fall/art03.pdf.**

The Occupational Information Network (O*NET) provides information on a wide range of occupational characteristics. Links to O*NET appear at the end of the Internet version of this occupational statement, accessible at **http://www.bls.gov/ooh/ocos298.htm**

Personal Financial Advisors

Significant Points

- Most personal financial advisors have a bachelor's degree.

- Math, analytical, and interpersonal skills are important.

- Keen competition is anticipated for these highly paid positions, despite much faster than average job growth.

- About 29 percent of personal financial advisors are self-employed.

Nature of the Work

Personal financial advisors assess the financial needs of individuals and assist them with investments, tax laws, and insurance decisions. Advisors help their clients identify and plan for short-term and long-term goals. Advisors help clients plan for retirement, education expenses, and general investment choices. Many also provide tax advice or sell insurance. Although most planners offer advice on a wide range of topics, some specialize in areas such as retirement and estate planning or risk management.

Personal financial advisors usually work with many clients and often must find their own customers.

Personal financial advisors usually work with many clients and often must find their own customers. Many personal financial advisors spend a great deal of their time marketing their services. Many advisors meet potential clients by giving seminars or through business and social networking. Finding clients and building a customer base is one of the most important aspects of becoming a successful financial advisor.

Financial advisors begin work with a client by setting up a consultation. This is usually an in-person meeting where the advisor obtains as much information as possible about the client's finances and goals. The advisor creates a comprehensive financial plan that identifies problem areas, makes recommendations for improvement, and selects appropriate investments compatible with the client's goals, attitude toward risk, and expectation or need for investment returns. Advisors sometimes seek advice from financial analysts, accountants, or lawyers.

Financial advisors usually meet with established clients at least once a year to update them on potential investments and adjust their financial plan to any life changes—such as marriage, disability, or retirement. Financial advisors also answer clients' questions regarding changes in benefit plans or the consequences of changing their job. Financial planners must educate their clients about risks and possible scenarios so that the clients don't harbor unrealistic expectations.

Many personal financial advisors are licensed to directly buy and sell financial products, such as stocks, bonds, derivatives, annuities, and insurance products. Depending upon the agreement they have with their clients, personal financial advisors may have their clients' permission to make decisions regarding the buying and selling of stocks and bonds.

Private bankers or *wealth managers* are personal financial advisors who work for people who have a lot of money to invest. Because they have so much capital, these clients resemble institutional investors and approach investing differently from the general public. Private bankers manage portfolios for these individuals using the resources of the bank, including teams of financial analysts, accountants, lawyers, and other professionals. Private bankers sell these services to wealthy individuals, generally spending most of their time working with a small number of clients. Private bankers normally directly manage their customers' finances.

Work environment. Personal financial advisors usually work in offices or their own homes. Personal financial advisors usually work standard business hours, but they also schedule meetings with clients in the evenings or on weekends. Many also teach evening classes or hold seminars to bring in more clients. Some personal financial advisors spend a fair amount of their time traveling, to attend conferences or training sessions or to visit clients.

Private bankers also generally work during standard business hours, but because they work so closely with their clients, they may have to be available outside normal hours upon request.

Training, Other Qualifications, and Advancement

Personal financial advisors must have a bachelor's degree. Many also earn a master's degree in finance or business administration or get professional designations. Math, analytical, and interpersonal skills are important.

Education and training. A bachelor's or graduate degree is strongly preferred for personal financial advisors. Employers usually do not require a specific field of study for personal financial advisors, but a bachelor's degree in accounting, finance, economics, business, mathematics, or law provides good preparation for the occupation. Courses in investments, taxes, estate planning, and risk management are also helpful. Programs in financial planning are becoming more available in colleges and universities.

Licensure. Personal financial advisors who directly buy or sell stocks, bonds, insurance policies, or specific investment advice need a combination of licenses that varies based upon the products they sell. In addition to those licenses, smaller firms that manage clients' investments must be registered with state regulators, and larger firms must be registered with the Securities and Exchange Commission. Personal financial advisors who choose to sell insurance need licenses issued by State boards. State licensing board information and requirements for registered investment advisors are available from the North American Securities Administrator Association.

Other qualifications. Personal financial advisors need strong math, analytical, and interpersonal skills. They need strong sales ability, including the ability to make a wide-range of customers feel comfortable. Personal financial advisor training emphasizes the different types of investors, and how to tailor advice to the investor's personality. They need the ability to present financial concepts to clients in easy-to-understand language. Some advisors have experience in a related occupation, such as accountant, auditor, insurance sales agent, or broker.

Private bankers may have previously worked as a financial analyst and need to understand and explain highly technical investment strategies and products.

Certification and advancement. Although not always required, certifications enhance professional standing and are

Projections data from the National Employment Matrix

Occupational Title	SOC Code	Employment, 2008	Projected Employment, 2018	Change, 2008-2018	
				Number	Percent
Personal financial advisors...	13-2052	208,400	271,200	62,800	30

(NOTE) Data in this table are rounded. See the discussion of the employment projections table in the *Handbook* introductory chapter on *Occupational Information Included in the Handbook.*

recommended by employers. Personal financial advisors may obtain the Certified Financial Planner (CFP) credential. This certification, issued by the Certified Financial Planner Board of Standards, requires 3 years of relevant experience; the completion of education requirements, including a bachelor's degree; passing a comprehensive examination, and adherence to a code of ethics. The exam tests the candidate's knowledge of the financial planning process, insurance and risk management, employee benefits planning, taxes and retirement planning, and investment and estate planning. Candidates are also required to have a working knowledge of debt management, planning liability, emergency fund reserves, and statistical modeling.

Personal financial advisors have several different paths to advancement. Those who work in firms may move into managerial positions. Others may choose to open their own branch offices for securities firms and serve as independent registered representatives of those firms.

Employment

Personal financial advisors held 208,400 jobs in May 2008. Jobs were spread throughout the country, although a significant number are located in New York, California, and Florida. About 63 percent worked in finance and insurance industries, including securities and commodity brokers, banks, insurance carriers, and financial investment firms. About 29 percent of personal financial advisors were self-employed, operating small investment advisory firms.

Job Outlook

Employment of personal financial advisors is expected to grow much faster than the average for all occupations. Despite strong job growth, keen competition will continue for these well paid jobs, especially for new entrants.

Employment change. Personal financial advisors are projected to grow by 30 percent over the 2008–18 period, which is much faster than the average for all occupations. Growing numbers of advisors will be needed to assist the millions of workers expected to retire in the next 10 years. As more members of the large baby boom generation reach their peak years of retirement savings, personal investments are expected to increase and more people will seek the help of experts. Many companies also have replaced traditional pension plans with retirement savings programs, so more individuals are managing their own retirements than in the past, creating jobs for advisors. In addition, as people are living longer, they should plan to finance longer retirements.

The growing number and assets of very wealthy individuals will help drive growth of private bankers and wealth managers. The need for private bankers to explain and manage increasing complexity of financial and investment products will continue to drive growth.

Job prospects. Personal financial advisors will face keen competition, as relatively low barriers to entry and high wages attract many new entrants. Many individuals enter the field by working for a bank or full-service brokerage. Because the occupation requires sales, people who have strong selling skills will ultimately be most successful. A college degree and certification can lend credibility.

Earnings

Median annual wages of wage and salary personal financial advisors were $69,050 in May 2008. The middle 50 percent earned between $46,390 and $119,290. Personal financial advisors who work for financial services firms are often paid a salary plus bonus. Bonuses are not included in the wage data listed here. Advisors who work for financial investment or planning firms or who are self-employed typically earn their money by charging a percentage of the clients' assets under management. They may also earn money by charging hourly fees for their services or through fees on stock and insurance purchases. Advisors generally receive commissions for financial products they sell, in addition to charging a fee. Wages of self-employed workers are not included in the earnings given here.

Related Occupations

Other jobs requiring expertise in finance and investment or in the sale of financial products include:

Sources of Additional Information

For general information on securities industry employment, contact:

➤ Financial Industry Regulatory Authority (FINRA), 1735 K St. NW., Washington, DC 20006. Internet: **http://www.finra.org**

➤ Securities Industry and Financial Markets Association, 120 Broadway, 35th Floor, New York, NY 10271. Internet: **http://www.sifma.org**

For information on state and federal investment advisor registration, contact:

➤ North American Securities Administrator Association, 750 First St. NE., Suite 1140, Washington, DC 20002. Internet: **http://www.nasaa.org**

➤ Securities and Exchange Commission (SEC), 100 F St. NE., Washington, DC 20549. Internet: **http://www.sec.gov**

For information on personal financial advisor careers, contact:
➤ Certified Financial Planner Board of Standards, Inc., 1425 K St. NW., Suite 500, Washington, DC 20005. Internet: **http://www.cfp.net**
➤ Financial Planning Association, 4100 E. Mississippi Ave., Suite 400, Denver, CO 80246-3053. Internet: **http://www.fpanet.org**

For additional career information, see the *Occupational Outlook Quarterly* article "Financial analysts and personal financial advisors" online at **http://www.bls.gov/opub/ooq/2000/summer/art03.pdf** and in print at many libraries and career centers.

The Occupational Information Network (O*NET) provides information on a wide range of occupational characteristics. Links to O*NET appear at the end of the Internet version of this occupational statement, accessible at **http://www.bls.gov/ooh/ocos302.htm**

Tax Examiners, Collectors, and Revenue Agents

Significant Points

- Tax examiners, collectors, and revenue agents work for Federal, State, and local governments.

- Many workers have a bachelor's degree, but relevant experience is important for many jobs.

- Employment is expected to grow as fast as the average, while retirements should create additional job openings.

- Competition will be greatest for positions with the Internal Revenue Service.

Nature of the Work

Taxes are one of the certainties of life, and as long as governments collect taxes, there will be jobs for tax examiners, collectors, and revenue agents. By reviewing tax returns, conducting audits, identifying taxes payable, and collecting overdue tax dollars, these workers ensure that governments obtain revenues from businesses and citizens.

Tax examiners do similar work, whether they are employed at the Federal, State, or local government level. They review filed tax returns for accuracy and determine whether tax credits and deductions are allowed by law. Because many States assess individual income taxes based on the taxpayer's reported Federal adjusted gross income, tax examiners working for the Federal Government report any adjustments or corrections they make to the States. State tax examiners then determine whether the adjustments affect the taxpayer's State tax liability. At the local level, tax examiners often have additional duties, but an integral part of the work still includes the need to determine the factual basis for claims for refunds.

Tax examiners usually deal with the simplest tax returns—those filed by individual taxpayers with few deductions or those filed by small businesses. At the entry level, many tax examiners perform clerical duties, such as reviewing tax returns and entering them into a computer system for processing. If there is a problem, tax examiners may contact the taxpayer to resolve it.

Tax examiners also review returns for accuracy, checking taxpayers' math and making sure that the amounts that they report match those reported from other sources, such as employers and banks. In addition, examiners verify that Social Security numbers match names and that taxpayers have correctly interpreted the instructions on tax forms.

Much of a tax examiner's job involves making sure that tax credits and deductions claimed by taxpayers are legitimate. Tax examiners contact taxpayers by mail or telephone to address discrepancies and request supporting documentation. They may notify taxpayers of any overpayment or underpayment and either issue a refund or request further payment. If a taxpayer owes additional taxes, tax examiners adjust the total amount by assessing fees, interest, and penalties and notify the taxpayer of the total liability. Although most tax examiners deal with uncomplicated returns, some may work with more complex tax issues, such as pensions or business net operating losses.

Revenue agents specialize in tax-related accounting work for the U.S. Internal Revenue Service (IRS) and for equivalent agencies in State and local governments. Like tax examiners, they audit returns for accuracy. However, revenue agents handle complicated income, sales, and excise tax returns of businesses and large corporations. As a result, their work differs in a number of ways from that of tax examiners.

Entry-level Federal revenue agents usually audit tax returns of small businesses whose market specializations are similar. As they develop expertise in an industry, such as construction, retail sales, or finance, insurance, and real estate, revenue agents work with tax returns of large corporations.

Many experienced revenue agents specialize; for example, they may focus exclusively on multinational businesses. But all revenue agents working for the Federal Government must keep abreast of the lengthy, complex, and frequently changing tax code. Computer technology has simplified the research process, allowing revenue agents Internet access to relevant legal bulletins, IRS notices, and tax-related court decisions. Revenue agents also use computers to analyze data and identify trends that help pinpoint tax offenders.

At the State level, revenue agents have duties similar to those of their counterparts in the Federal Government. State revenue agents use revenue adjustment reports forwarded by the IRS to determine whether adjustments made by Federal revenue agents affect a taxpayer's taxable income in the eyes of the States. In addition, State agents consider the sales and income taxes for their own States.

At the local level, revenue agents have varying titles and duties, but they still perform field audits or office audits of financial records for business firms. In some cases, local revenue agents also examine financial records of individuals. These local agents, like their State counterparts, rely on the information contained in Federal tax returns. However, local agents also

Many tax examiners, collectors, and revenue agents have a bachelor's degree, but relevant experience is important for many jobs.

must be knowledgeable enough to apply local tax laws regarding income, utility fees, or school taxes.

Collectors, also called *revenue officers* in the IRS, deal with delinquent accounts. The process of collecting a delinquent account starts with the revenue agent or tax examiner sending a report to the taxpayer. If the taxpayer makes no effort to resolve the delinquent account, the case is assigned to a collector. When a collector takes a case, he or she first sends the taxpayer a notice. The collector then works with the taxpayer on how to settle the debt.

In cases in which taxpayers fail to file a tax return, Federal collectors may request that the IRS prepare the return on a taxpayer's behalf. In other instances, collectors are responsible for verifying claims that delinquent taxpayers cannot pay their taxes. They investigate these claims by researching court information on the status of liens, mortgages, or financial statements; locating assets through third parties, such as neighbors or local departments of motor vehicles; and requesting legal summonses for other records. Ultimately, collectors must decide whether the IRS should take a lien—a claim on an asset such as a bank account, real estate, or an automobile—to settle a debt. Collectors also have the discretion to garnish wages—that is, take a portion of earned wages—to collect taxes owed.

A big part of a collector's job at the Federal level is imposing and following up on delinquent taxpayers' payment deadlines. For each case file, collectors must maintain records, including contacts, telephone numbers, and actions taken.

Like tax examiners and revenue agents, collectors use computers to maintain files. Computer technology also gives collectors access to data to help them identify high-risk debtors—those who are unlikely to pay or are likely to flee. Collectors at the IRS usually work independently. However, they call on experts when tax examiners or revenue agents find fraudulent returns,

or when the seizure of a property will involve complex legal steps.

At the State level, collectors decide whether to take action by reviewing tax returns filed in the State where they work. Collection work may be handled over the telephone or turned over to a collector who specializes in obtaining settlements. These collectors contact people directly and have the authority to issue subpoenas and request seizures of property. At the local levels, collectors have less power than their State and Federal counterparts. Although they can start the processes leading to the seizure of property and garnishment of wages, they must go through the local court system.

Work environment. Tax examiners, collectors, and revenue agents work in clean, pleasant, and comfortable office settings. Depending upon work assignment, travel may be necessary. Revenue agents at both the Federal and State levels spend a significant portion of their time in the offices of private firms, accessing tax-related records. Some agents may be permanently stationed in the offices of large corporations with complicated tax structures. Agents at the local level usually work in city halls or municipal buildings. Collectors travel to local courthouses, county and municipal seats of government, businesses, and taxpayers' homes to look up records, search for assets, and settle delinquent accounts.

Stress can result from the need to work under a deadline. Collectors also must face the unpleasant task of confronting delinquent taxpayers.

Tax examiners, collectors, and revenue agents generally work a 40-hour week, although some overtime might be needed during the tax season. State and local tax examiners, who may review sales, gasoline, and cigarette taxes instead of handling tax returns, may have a steadier workload year-round.

Training, Other Qualifications, and Advancement

Many tax examiners, collectors, and revenue agents have a bachelor's degree. But relevant experience, or a combination of postsecondary education and experience, is sufficient qualification for many jobs. Specialized experience is sufficient to qualify for many jobs in State and local government.

Education and training. In the Federal Government, workers must have a bachelor's degree or a combination of some college education and related experience. After being hired by the IRS, employees can expect to attend several multiweek training seminars. In State and local governments, workers often have an associate degree, some college-level business classes and specialized experience, or a high school diploma and specialized experience.

For more advanced entry-level positions, applicants often must have a bachelor's degree. Candidates may sometimes qualify without a bachelor's degree, however, if they can demonstrate experience working with tax records, tax laws and regulations, documents, financial accounts, or similar records.

Specific education and training requirements vary by occupational specialty.

Tax examiners usually must have a bachelor's degree in accounting or a related discipline or a combination of education and full-time accounting, auditing, or tax compliance work. Tax examiner candidates at the IRS must have a bachelor's degree or one year of full-time specialized experience, which could include full-time work in accounting, bookkeeping, or tax analysis. After they are hired, tax examiners receive some formal training. In addition, annual employer-provided updates keep tax examiners current with changes in procedures and regulations.

Collectors usually must have some combination of college education and experience in collections, management, customer service, or tax compliance, or as a loan officer or credit manager. A bachelor's degree is required for employment as a collector with the IRS. No additional experience is required, and experience may not be substituted for the degree. Degrees in business, finance, accounting, and criminal justice are good backgrounds.

Entry-level collectors receive formal and on-the-job training under an instructor's guidance before working independently. Collectors usually complete initial training by the end of their second year of service, but may receive advanced technical instruction as they gain seniority and take on more difficult cases. Also, collectors are encouraged to continue their professional education by attending meetings to exchange information about how changes in tax laws affect collection methods.

Revenue agents usually must have a bachelor's degree in accounting, business administration, economics, or a related discipline or a combination of education and full-time business administration, accounting, or auditing work. Revenue agents with the IRS must have either a bachelor's degree or 30 semester hours of accounting coursework along with specialized experience. Specialized experience includes full-time work in accounting, bookkeeping, or tax analysis.

Other qualifications. Tax examiners, collectors, and revenue agents work with confidential financial and personal information; therefore, trustworthiness is crucial for maintaining the confidentiality of individuals and businesses. Applicants for Federal Government jobs must submit to a background investigation.

Collectors need good interpersonal and communication skills because they deal directly with the public and because their reports are scrutinized when the tax agency must legally justify attempts to seize assets. They must be able to negotiate well and deal effectively with others in potentially confrontational situations.

Revenue agents need strong analytical, organizational, and time management skills. They also must be able to work independently, because they spend so much time away from their home office, and they must keep current with changes in the tax code and laws. Revenue agents that travel need a valid driver's license to perform their duties.

Advancement. Advancement potential within Federal, State, and local agencies varies for tax examiners, revenue agents, and collectors. For related jobs outside government, experienced workers can take a licensing exam administered by the Federal Government to become enrolled agents—nongovernment tax professionals authorized to represent taxpayers before the IRS.

Collectors who demonstrate leadership skills and a thorough knowledge of collection activities may advance to supervisory or managerial collector positions, in which they oversee the activities of other collectors. It is only these higher level supervisors and managers who may authorize the more serious actions against individuals and businesses. The more complex collection attempts which usually are directed at larger businesses are reserved for collectors at these higher levels.

Newly hired revenue agents expand their accounting knowledge and remain up to date by consulting auditing manuals and other sources for detailed information about individual industries. Employers also continually offer training in new auditing techniques and tax-related issues and court decisions. As revenue agents gain knowledge and experience, they may specialize in an industry, work with large corporations, and cover increasingly complex tax returns. Some revenue agent advancement specialties involve assisting in criminal investigations, auditing the books of suspected criminals, working with grand juries to help secure indictments, or becoming an international agent.

Employment

In 2008, tax examiners, revenue agents, and collectors held about 72,700 jobs. About 98 percent worked for government. About 2 percent were self employed. In the IRS, tax examiners and revenue agents predominate because of the role of the agency. Collectors make up a smaller proportion, because most disputed tax liabilities do not require enforced collection.

Job Outlook

Employment is expected to grow as fast as the average, while retirements over the next 10 years should create additional job openings at all levels of government.

Employment change. Employment of tax examiners, collectors, and revenue agents is projected to grow 13 percent during the 2008-18 decade, which is considered as fast as the average. Demand for tax examiners, revenue agents, and tax collectors will stem from changes in government policy toward tax enforcement and from growth in the number of businesses.

Two factors should increase the demand for revenue agents and tax collectors—the Federal Government is expected to increase its tax enforcement efforts, and new technology and information sharing among tax agencies make it easier for agencies to pinpoint potential offenders, increasing the number of cases for audit and collection.

The work of tax examiners is especially well suited to automation, adversely affecting demand for these workers in particular. In addition, more than 40 States and many local tax agencies contract out part of their tax collection functions to

Projections data from the National Employment Matrix

Occupational Title	SOC Code	Employment, 2008	Projected Employment, 2018	Change, 2008-2018	
				Number	Percent
Tax examiners, collectors, and revenue agents	13-2081	72,700	82,200	9,500	13

(NOTE) Data in this table are rounded. See the discussion of the employment projections table in the *Handbook* introductory chapter on *Occupational Information Included in the Handbook.*

private-sector collection agencies in order to reduce costs, and this trend is likely to continue. The IRS outsourced some tax collection activities, but the agency is ending this practice.

Job prospects. The large number of retirements expected over the next 10 years is expected to create many job openings at all levels of government. Both State and Federal tax agencies are continuing to focus enforcement on higher income taxpayers and businesses, which file more complicated tax returns. Because of this, workers with knowledge of accounting, tax laws, and experience working with complex tax issues will have the best opportunities.

Competition will be greatest for positions with the IRS. Opportunities at the Federal level will reflect the tightening or relaxation of budget constraints imposed on the IRS, the primary employer of these workers.

Employment at the State and local levels may fluctuate with the overall state of the economy. When the economy is contracting, State and local governments are likely to freeze hiring and lay off workers in response to budgetary constraints.

Earnings

In May 2008, median annual wages for all tax examiners, collectors, and revenue agents were $48,100. The middle 50 percent earned between $36,590 and $66,730. The bottom 10 percent earned less than $28,390, and the top 10 percent earned more than $89,630. However, wages vary considerably, depending on the level of government and occupational specialty. For example, in March 2009, the Federal Government's average annual salary was $42,035 for tax examiners, $91,507 for internal revenue agents, and $63,547 for tax specialists.

IRS employees receive family, vacation, and sick leave. Full-time permanent IRS employees are offered tax-deferred retirement savings and investment plans with employer matching contributions, health insurance, and life insurance.

Related Occupations

Other occupations that analyze and interpret financial data include:

Sources of Additional Information

Information on obtaining positions as tax examiners, collectors, or revenue agents with the Federal Government is available from the Office of Personnel Management through USAJOBS, the Federal Government's official employment information system. This resource for locating and applying for job opportunities can be accessed through the Internet at **http://www.usajobs.opm.gov** or through an interactive voice response telephone system at (703) 724-1850 or TDD (978) 461-8404. These numbers are not toll free, and charges may result.

State or local government personnel offices can provide information about tax examiner, collector, or revenue agent jobs at those levels of government.

For information about careers at the Internal Revenue Service, contact:

➤ Internal Revenue Service, 1111 Constitution Ave. NW., Washington, D.C. 20224. Internet: **http://www.jobs.irs.gov**

The Occupational Information Network (O*NET) provides information on a wide range of occupational characteristics. Links to O*NET appear at the end of the Internet version of this occupational statement, accessible at **http://www.bls.gov/ooh/ocos260.htm**

Professional and Related Occupations

Computer and Mathematical Occupations

Actuaries

Significant Points

- A strong background in mathematics is essential.

- Actuaries generally have a bachelor's degree and must pass a series of examinations—often taking 4 to 8 years—to gain full professional status.

- Competition for jobs will be keen as the number of qualified candidates is expected to exceed the number of positions available.

- About 55 percent of actuaries are employed by insurance carriers.

Nature of the Work

Through their knowledge of statistics, finance, and business, *actuaries* assess the risk of events occurring and help create policies for businesses and clients that minimize the cost of that risk. For this reason, actuaries are essential to the insurance industry.

Actuaries analyze data to estimate the probability and likely cost to the company of an event such as death, sickness, injury, disability, or loss of property. Actuaries also address financial matters, such as how a company should invest resources to maximize return on investments, or how an individual should invest in order to attain a certain retirement income level. Using their expertise in evaluating various types of risk, actuaries help design insurance policies, pension plans, and other financial strategies in a manner which will help ensure that the plans are maintained on a sound financial basis.

Most actuaries are employed in the insurance industry, specializing in either property and casualty insurance or life and health insurance. They use sophisticated modeling techniques to forecast the likelihood of certain events occurring, and the impact these events will have on claims and potential losses for the company. For example, property and casualty actuaries calculate the expected number of claims resulting from automobile accidents, which varies depending on the insured person's age, sex, driving history, type of car, and other factors. Actuaries ensure that the premium charged for such insurance will enable the company to cover potential claims and other expenses. This premium must be profitable, yet competitive with other insurance companies.

Within the life and health insurance fields, actuaries help companies develop health and long-term-care insurance policies by predicting the likelihood of occurrence of heart disease, diabetes, stroke, cancer, and other chronic ailments among a particular group of people who have something in common, such as living in a certain area or having a family history of illness. Such work of actuaries can be beneficial to both the consumer and the company because the ability to accurately predict the likelihood of a particular health event among a certain group ensures that premiums are assessed fairly based on the risk to the company. Additionally, life insurance actuaries help companies develop annuity and life insurance policies for individuals by estimating how long someone is expected to live.

Actuaries in other financial service industries manage credit and help set a price for corporate security offerings. They also devise new investment tools to help their firms compete with other companies. Pension actuaries work under the provisions of the Employee Retirement Income Security Act (ERISA) of 1974 which sets minimum standards for pension and health plans in private industry. Actuaries working for the government help manage social programs such as Social Security and Medicare.

Actuaries help determine corporate policy on risk, for example, and also help explain complex technical matters to company executives, government officials, shareholders, policyholders, or the general public. They may testify before public agencies on proposed legislation that affects their businesses or explain changes in contract provisions to customers. They also may help companies develop plans to enter new lines of business or new geographic markets by forecasting demand in competitive settings.

Consulting actuaries provide advice to clients on a contract basis. The duties of most consulting actuaries are similar to those of other actuaries. For example, some may evaluate company pension plans by calculating the future value of employee and employer contributions and determining whether the amounts are sufficient to meet the future needs of retirees. Others help companies reduce their insurance costs by offering them advice on how to lessen the risk of injury on the job. Consulting actuaries sometimes testify in court regarding the value of potential lifetime earnings of a person who is disabled or killed in an accident, the current value of future pension benefits (in divorce cases), or other values arrived at by complex calculations. Some actuaries work in reinsurance, a field in which one insurance company arranges to share a large prospective liability policy with another insurance company in exchange for a percentage of the premium.

Work environment. Actuaries have desk jobs, and their offices usually are comfortable and pleasant. While most actuaries work at least 40 hours a week, those in consulting type jobs may be required to travel and thus work more than 40 hours per week.

Training, Other Qualifications, and Advancement

Actuaries need a strong background in mathematics, statistics, and general business. They generally have a bachelor's degree and are required to pass a series of exams in order to become certified professionals.

Education and training. Actuaries need a strong foundation in mathematics and general business. Usually, actuaries earn an undergraduate degree in mathematics, statistics, or actuarial science, or a business-related field such as finance, economics, or business. While in college, students should complete coursework in economics, applied statistics, and corporate finance, which is a requirement for professional certification. Furthermore, many students obtain internships to gain experience in the profession prior to graduation. More than 100 colleges and universities offer an actuarial science program, and most offer a degree in mathematics, statistics, economics, or finance.

Increasingly, companies are requiring potential employees to have passed the initial actuarial exam described in the next section, which tests an individual's proficiency in mathematics—including calculus, probability, and statistics before being hired.

Beginning actuaries often rotate among different jobs in an organization, such as marketing, underwriting, financial reporting and product development, to learn various actuarial operations and phases of insurance work. At first, they prepare data for actuarial projects or perform other simple tasks. As they gain experience, actuaries may supervise clerks, prepare correspondence, draft reports, and conduct research. They may move from one company to another early in their careers as they advance to higher positions.

Licensure. Two professional societies sponsor programs leading to full professional status in their specialty: the Society of Actuaries (SOA) and the Casualty Actuarial Society (CAS). The SOA certifies actuaries in the fields of life insurance, health benefits systems, retirement systems, and finance and investment. The CAS gives a series of examinations in the property and casualty field, which includes automobile, homeowners, medical malpractice, workers compensation, and personal injury liability.

Four of the first seven exams in the SOA and CAS examination series are jointly sponsored by the two societies and

Actuaries need a strong background in mathematics.

cover the same material. For this reason, students do not need to commit themselves to a specialty until they have taken the initial examination, which tests an individual's competence in mathematics and helps evaluate their potential as actuaries. If candidates pass the initial exam, prospects can begin taking the next series of exams with the help of self-study guides and courses. Those who pass two or more examinations have better opportunities for employment at higher starting salaries than those who do not. These initial exams can be taken while the candidate is still in college.

Many candidates find work as an actuary immediately after graduation and work through the certification process while gaining some experience in the field. In fact, many employers pay the examination fees and provide their employees time to study. As actuaries pass exams, they are often rewarded with a pay increase. Despite the fact that employers are supportive during the exam process, home study is necessary and many actuaries study for months to prepare for each exam.

The process for gaining certification in the Casualty Actuarial Society is predominantly exam-based. To reach the first level of certification, the Associate or ACAS level, a candidate must complete seven exams, attend one course on professionalism and complete the coursework in applied statistics, corporate finance, and economics required by both the SOA and CAS. This process generally takes from 4 to 8 years. The next level, the Fellowship, or FCAS level, requires passing two additional exams in advanced topics, including investment and assets and dynamic financial analysis and the valuation of insurance. Most actuaries reach the fellowship level 2 to 3 years after attaining Associate status.

The certification process of the Society of Actuaries blends exams with computer learning modules and coursework. After taking the initial exams, candidates must choose a specialty—group and health benefits, individual life and annuities, retirement benefits, investments or finance/enterprise risk management. To reach the Associate or ASA level, a candidate must complete the initial five exams, the coursework in applied statistics, corporate finance, and economics required by the SOA and CAS, eight computer modules with two subsequent essays, and a seminar in professionalism. This process generally takes from 4 to 8 years. To attain the Fellowship or FSA level, a candidate must pass two additional exams within a chosen specialty and must complete three computer modules, a seminar in professionalism, and a course in fellowship admissions. Attaining Fellowship status usually takes an additional 2 to 3 years after becoming an Associate.

Specific requirements apply to pension actuaries, who verify the financial status of defined benefit pension plans for the Federal Government. These actuaries must be enrolled by the Joint Board of the U.S. Treasury Department and the U.S. Department of Labor for the Enrollment of Actuaries. To qualify for enrollment, applicants must meet certain experience requirements and pass two exams administered by the SOA, as stipulated by the Board.

Other qualifications. Actuaries should have strong computer skills and be able to develop and use spreadsheets and databases, as well as standard statistical analysis software. Knowledge of programming languages, such as Visual Basic for Applications, SAS, or SQL, is also useful. Companies also increasingly prefer well-rounded individuals who, in addition to having acquired a strong technical background, have some training in business and possess strong communication skills. Good interpersonal skills also are important, particularly for consulting actuaries.

To perform their duties effectively, actuaries must keep up with current economic and social trends and legislation, as well as developments in health, business, and finance that could affect insurance or investment practices.

Advancement. Advancement depends largely on job performance and the number of actuarial examinations passed. Actuaries with a broad knowledge of the insurance, pension, investment, or employee benefits fields can rise to executive positions in their companies, such as Chief Risk Officer or Chief Financial Officer. These generally require that actuaries use their abilities for assessing risk and apply it to the entire company as a whole. Actuaries with supervisory ability may advance to management positions in other areas, such as underwriting, accounting, data processing, marketing, and advertising. Some experienced actuaries move into consulting, often by opening their own consulting firm. A few actuaries transfer to college and university faculty positions. (See the section on teachers—postsecondary elsewhere in the *Handbook.*)

Employment

Actuaries held about 19,700 jobs in 2008. About 55 percent of all actuaries were employed by insurance carriers. Approximately 16 percent work for management, scientific and technical consulting services. Others worked for insurance agents and brokers and in the management of companies and enterprises industry. A relatively small number of actuaries are employed by government agencies.

Job Outlook

Employment is expected to grow much faster than the average for all occupations. Competition for jobs will be keen as the number of qualified candidates is expected to exceed the number of positions available.

Employment change. Employment of actuaries is expected to increase by 21 percent over the 2008–18 period, which is much faster than the average for all occupations. While employment in the insurance industry—the largest employer of actuaries—will experience some growth, greater job growth will occur in other industries, such as financial services and consulting.

Despite slower than average growth of the insurance industry, employment in this key sector is expected to increase during the projection period as actuaries will be needed to develop, price, and evaluate a variety of insurance products and calculate the costs of new risks. Natural disasters should continue to require the work of actuaries in property and casualty insurance while the growing popularity of annuities, a financial product offered primarily by life insurance companies, will also spur demand. Penetration among actuaries into non-traditional areas, such as the financial services sector, to help price corporate security offerings, for example, will also contribute to some employment growth.

Consulting firms should experience strong employment demand as an increasing number of industries utilize actuaries to assess risk. Increased regulation of managed healthcare companies and drafting healthcare legislation will also spur employment growth.

Nonetheless, growth may be, to a degree, offset by corporate downsizing and consolidation of the insurance industry—the largest employer of actuaries. Life insurance companies, for example, are expected to increasingly shed high level actuarial positions as companies merge and streamline operations. Pension actuaries will also experience declining demand. This is largely due to the decline of defined benefit plans, which required review by an actuary, in favor of investment-based retirement funds, such as 401ks.

Job prospects. Job seekers are likely to face competition because the number of job openings is expected to be less than the number of qualified applicants. College graduates who have passed two of the initial exams and completed an internship should enjoy the best prospects. A solid foundation in mathematics, including the ability to compute complex probability and statistics, is essential. Experience or skills in computer programming can also be important. In addition to job growth, a small number of jobs will open up each year to replace actuaries who retire or transfer to new jobs.

The best employment opportunities should be in consulting firms. Companies that may not find it cost-effective to employ their own actuaries are increasingly hiring consulting actuaries to analyze various risks. Openings should also be available in the healthcare field if changes take place in managed healthcare. The desire to contain healthcare costs will provide job opportunities for actuaries who will be needed to evaluate the risks associated with new medical issues, such as the impact of new diseases.

Because actuarial skills are increasingly seen as useful to other industries that deal with risk, such as the airline and the banking industries, additional job openings may be created in these industries.

Earnings

Median annual wages of actuaries were $84,810 in May 2008. The middle 50 percent earned between $62,020 and $119,110.

Projections data from the National Employment Matrix

Occupational Title	SOC Code	Employment, 2008	Projected Employment, 2018	Change, 2008-2018	
				Number	Percent
Actuaries	15-2011	19,700	23,900	4,200	21

(NOTE) Data in this table are rounded. See the discussion of the employment projections table in the *Handbook* introductory chapter on *Occupational Information Included in the Handbook.*

The lowest 10 percent had wages less than $49,150, while the top 10 percent earned more than $160,780.

According to the National Association of Colleges and Employers, annual starting salaries for graduates with a bachelor's degree in actuarial science averaged $56,320 in July 2009.

Related Occupations

Other workers whose jobs require mathematical and statistical skills include:

	Page
Accountants and auditors	86
Budget analysts	93
Economists	209
Financial analysts	103
Insurance underwriters	106
Market and survey researchers	212
Mathematicians	143
Personal financial advisors	118
Statisticians	148

Sources of Additional Information

Career information on actuaries specializing in pensions is available from:

➤ American Society of Pension Professionals & Actuaries, 4245 N. Fairfax Dr., Suite 750, Arlington, VA 22203. Internet: **http://www.aspa.org**

For information about actuarial careers in life and health insurance, employee benefits and pensions, and finance and investments, contact:

➤ Society of Actuaries (SOA), 475 N. Martingale Rd., Suite 600, Schaumburg, IL 60173-2226. Internet: **http://www.soa.org**

For information about actuarial careers in property and casualty insurance, contact:

➤ Casualty Actuarial Society (CAS), 4350 N. Fairfax Dr., Suite 250 Arlington, VA 22203. Internet: **http://www.casact.org**

➤ The SOA and CAS jointly sponsor a Web site for those interested in pursuing an actuarial career. Internet: **http://www.beanactuary.org**

For general information on a career as an actuary, contact:

➤ American Academy of Actuaries, 1850 M St. NW., Suite 300, Washington, DC 20036. Internet: **http://www.actuary.org**

The Occupational Information Network (O*NET) provides information on a wide range of occupational characteristics. Links to O*NET appear at the end of the Internet version of this occupational statement, accessible at

http://www.bls.gov/ooh/ocos041.htm

Computer Network, Systems, and Database Administrators

Significant Points

- Employment is projected to grow much faster than the average for all occupations and add 286,600 new jobs over the 2008–18 decade.

- Excellent job prospects are expected.

- Workers can enter this field with many different levels of formal education, but relevant computer skills are always needed.

Nature of the Work

Information Technology (IT) has become an integral part of modern life. Among its most important functions are the efficient transmission of information and the storage and analysis of information. The workers described below all help individuals and organizations share and store information through computer networks and systems, the Internet, and computer databases.

Network architects or *network engineers* are the designers of computer networks. They set up, test, and evaluate systems such as local area networks (LANs), wide area networks (WANs), the Internet, intranets, and other data communications systems. Systems are configured in many ways and can range from a connection between two offices in the same building to globally distributed networks, voice mail, and e-mail systems of a multinational organization. Network architects and engineers perform network modeling, analysis, and planning, which often require both hardware and software solutions. For example, setting up a network may involve the installation of several pieces of hardware, such as routers and hubs, wireless adaptors, and cables, as well as the installation and configuration of software, such as network drivers. These workers may also research related products and make necessary hardware and software recommendations, as well as address information security issues.

Network and computer systems administrators design, install, and support an organization's computer systems. They are responsible for LANs, WANs, network segments, and Internet and intranet systems. They work in a variety of environments, including large corporations, small businesses, and government organizations. They install and maintain network hardware and software, analyze problems, and monitor networks to ensure their availability to users. These workers gather data to evaluate a system's performance, identify user needs, and determine system and network requirements.

Systems administrators are responsible for maintaining system efficiency. They ensure that the design of an organization's computer system allows all of the components, including computers, the network, and software, to work properly together. Administrators also troubleshoot problems reported by users and by automated network monitoring systems and make recommendations for future system upgrades. Many of these workers are also responsible for maintaining network and system security.

Computer network, systems, and database administrators help organizations share and store information.

Database administrators work with database management software and determine ways to store, organize, analyze, use, and present data. They identify user needs and set up new computer databases. In many cases, database administrators must integrate data from old systems into a new system. They also test and coordinate modifications to the system when needed, and troubleshoot problems when they occur. An organization's database administrator ensures the performance of the system, understands the platform on which the database runs, and adds new users to the system. Because many databases are connected to the Internet, database administrators also must plan and coordinate security measures with network administrators. Some database administrators may also be responsible for database design, but this task is usually performed by *database designers* or *database analysts*. (Database designers are covered in the *Handbook* section on computer software engineers and computer programmers.)

Computer security specialists plan, coordinate, and maintain an organization's information security. These workers educate users about computer security, install security software, monitor networks for security breaches, respond to cyber attacks, and, in some cases, gather data and evidence to be used in prosecuting cyber crime. The responsibilities of computer security specialists have increased in recent years as cyber attacks have become more sophisticated.

Telecommunications specialists focus on the interaction between computer and communications equipment. These workers design voice, video, and data-communication systems, supervise the installation of the systems, and provide main-tenance and other services to clients after the systems are installed. They also test lines, oversee equipment repair, and may compile and maintain system records.

Web developers are responsible for the technical aspects of Web site creation. Using software languages and tools, they create applications for the Web. They identify a site's users and oversee its production and implementation. They determine the information that the site will contain and how it will be organized, and may use Web development software to integrate databases and other information systems. Some of these workers may be responsible for the visual appearance of Web sites. Using design software, they create pages that appeal to the tastes of the site's users.

Webmasters or *Web administrators* are responsible for maintaining Web sites. They oversee issues such as availability to users and speed of access, and are responsible for approving the content of the site. Webmasters also collect and analyze data on Web activity, traffic patterns, and other metrics, as well as monitor and respond to user feedback.

Work environment. Network and computer systems administrators, network architects, database administrators, computer security specialists, Web administrators, and Web developers normally work in well-lighted, comfortable offices or computer laboratories. Most work about 40 hours a week. However, about 15 percent of network and systems administrators; 14 percent of database administrators; and about 16 percent of network systems and data communications analysts (which includes network architects, telecommunications specialists, Web administrators, and Web developers) worked more than 50 hours per week in 2008. In addition, some of these workers may be required to be "on call" outside of normal business hours in order to resolve system failures or other problems.

As computer networks expand, more of these workers may be able to perform their duties from remote locations, reducing or eliminating the need to travel to the customer's workplace.

Injuries in these occupations are uncommon, but like other workers who spend long periods in front of a computer terminal typing on a keyboard, these workers are susceptible to eyestrain, back discomfort, and hand and wrist problems such as carpal tunnel syndrome.

Training, Other Qualifications, and Advancement

Training requirements vary by occupation. Workers can enter this field with many different levels of formal education, but relevant computer skills are always needed. Certification may improve an applicant's chances for employment and can help workers maintain adequate skill levels throughout their careers.

Education and training. Network and computer systems administrators often are required to have a bachelor's degree, although an associate degree or professional certification, along with related work experience, may be adequate for some positions. Most of these workers begin as computer support specialists before advancing into network or systems administration positions. (Computer support specialists are covered elsewhere in the *Handbook*.) Common majors for network and systems administrators are computer science, information science, and management information systems (MIS), but a degree in any field, supplemented with computer courses and experience, may be adequate. A bachelor's degree in a computer-related field generally takes 4 years to complete and includes courses in computer science, computer programming, computer engineering, mathematics, and statistics. Most programs also include general education courses such as English and communications. MIS programs usually are part of the business school or college and contain courses such as finance, marketing, accounting, and management, as well as systems design, networking, database management, and systems security.

For network architect and database administrator positions, a bachelor's degree in a computer-related field generally is required, although some employers prefer applicants with a master's degree in business administration (MBA) with a concentration in information systems. MBA programs usually require 2 years of study beyond the undergraduate degree, and, like undergraduate business programs, include courses on finance, marketing, accounting, and management, as well as database management, electronic business, and systems management and design. In addition to formal education, network architects may be required to have several years of relevant work experience.

For Webmasters, an associate degree or certification is sufficient although more advanced positions might require a computer-related bachelor's degree. For telecommunications specialists, employers prefer applicants with an associate degree in electronics or a related field, but for some positions, experience may substitute for formal education. Applicants for security specialist and Web developer positions generally need a bachelor's degree in a computer-related field, but for some positions, related experience and certification may be adequate.

Certification and other qualifications. Workers in these occupations must have strong problem-solving, analytical, and communication skills. Because they often deal with a number of tasks simultaneously, the ability to concentrate and pay close attention to detail also is important. Although these workers sometimes work independently, they frequently work in teams on large projects. As a result, they must be able to communicate effectively with other computer workers, such as programmers and managers, as well as with users or other staff who may have no computer background.

Jobseekers can enhance their employment opportunities by earning certifications, which are offered through product vendors, computer associations, and other training institutions. Many employers regard these certifications as the industry standard, and some require their employees to be certified. In some cases, applicants without formal education may use certification and experience to qualify for some positions.

Because technology changes rapidly, computer specialists must continue to acquire the latest skills. Many organizations offer intermediate and advanced certification programs that pertain to the most recent technological advancements.

Advancement. Entry-level network and computer systems administrators are involved in routine maintenance and monitoring of computer systems. After gaining experience and expertise, they are often able to advance to more senior-level positions. They may also advance to supervisory positions.

Database administrators and network architects may advance into managerial positions, such as chief technology officer, on the basis of their experience. Computer specialists with work experience and considerable expertise in a particular area may find opportunities as independent consultants.

Computer security specialists can advance into supervisory positions, or may move into other occupations, such as computer systems analysts.

Employment

Computer network, systems, and database administrators held about 961,200 jobs in 2008. Of these, 339,500 were network and computer systems administrators, 120,400 were database administrators, and 292,000 were network and data communications analysts. In addition, about 209,300 were classified as "computer specialists, all other," a residual category.

These workers were employed in a wide range of industries. About 14 percent of all computer network, systems, and database administrators were in computer systems design and related services. Substantial numbers of these workers were also employed in telecommunications companies, financial firms and insurance providers, business management organizations, schools, and government agencies. About 7 percent were self-employed.

Job Outlook

Employment is expected to grow much faster than the average, and job prospects should be excellent.

Employment change. Overall employment of computer network, systems, and database administrators is projected to increase by 30 percent from 2008 to 2018, much faster than the average for all occupations. In addition, this occupation will add 286,600 new jobs over that period. Growth, however, will vary by specialty.

Employment of network and computer systems administrators is expected to increase by 23 percent from 2008 to 2018. Computer networks are an integral part of business, and demand for these workers will increase as firms continue to invest in new technologies. The increasing adoption of mobile technologies means that more establishments will use the Internet to conduct business online. This growth translates into a need for systems administrators who can help organizations use technology to communicate with employees, clients, and consumers. Growth will also be driven by the increasing need for information security. As cyber attacks become more sophisticated, demand will increase for workers with security skills.

Employment of database administrators is expected to grow by 20 percent from 2008 to 2018. Demand for these workers is expected to increase as organizations need to store, organize, and analyze increasing amounts of data. In addition, as more databases are connected to the Internet, and as data security becomes increasingly important, a growing number of these workers will be needed to protect databases from attack.

Employment of network systems and data communications analysts is projected to increase by 53 percent from 2008 to 2018, placing it among the fastest growing of all occupations. This occupational category includes network architects and engineers, as well as Web administrators and developers. Demand for network architects and engineers will increase as organizations continue to upgrade their IT capacity and incorporate the newest technologies. The growing reliance on wireless networks will result in a need for many more of these workers.

Projections data from the National Employment Matrix

Occupational Title	SOC Code	Employment, 2008	Projected Employment, 2018	Change, 2008-2018	
				Number	Percent
Computer network, systems, and database administrators	–	961,200	1,247,800	286,600	30
Database administrators..	15-1061	120,400	144,700	24,400	20
Network and computer systems administrators	15-1071	339,500	418,400	78,900	23
Network systems and data communications analysts	15-1081	292,000	447,800	155,800	53
All other computer specialists...	15-1099	209,300	236,800	27,500	13

(NOTE) Data in this table are rounded. See the discussion of the employment projections table in the *Handbook* introductory chapter on *Occupational Information Included in the Handbook.*

Workers with knowledge of information security also will be in demand, as computer networks transmit an increasing amount of sensitive data.

Demand for Web administrators and Web developers will also be strong. More of these workers will be needed to accommodate the increasing amount of data sent over the Internet, as well as the growing number of Internet users. In addition, as the number of services provided over the Internet expands, Web administrators and developers will continue to see employment increases.

Growth in computer network, systems, and database administrators will be rapid in the computer systems design, data processing and hosting, software publishing, and technical consulting industries, as these types of establishments utilize or provide an increasing array of IT services. Growth will also be rapid in healthcare, as these organizations look to increase their efficiency and improve patient care through the use of information systems and other technology.

Growth in this occupation may be tempered somewhat by offshore outsourcing, as firms transfer work to countries with lower-prevailing wages and highly skilled work forces. In addition, the consolidation of IT services may increase efficiency, reducing the demand for workers.

Job prospects. Computer network, systems, and database administrators should continue to enjoy excellent job prospects. In general, applicants with a college degree and certification will have the best opportunities. However, for some of these occupations, opportunities will be available for applicants with related work experience. Job openings in these occupations will be the result of strong employment growth, as well as the need to replace workers who transfer to other occupations or leave the labor force.

Earnings

Median annual wages of network and computer systems administrators were $66,310 in May 2008. The middle 50 percent earned between $51,690 and $84,110. The lowest 10 percent earned less than $41,000, and the highest 10 percent earned more than $104,070. Median annual wages in the industries employing the largest numbers of network and computer systems administrators in May 2008 were as follows:

Management of companies and enterprises $70,680
Computer systems design and related services 70,490
Wired telecommunications carriers..............................66,950
Colleges, universities, and professional schools 57,380
Elementary and secondary schools 56,320

Median annual wages of database administrators were $69,740 in May 2008. The middle 50 percent earned between $52,340 and $91,850. The lowest 10 percent earned less than $39,900, and the highest 10 percent earned more than $111,950. In May 2008, median annual wages of database administrators employed in computer systems design and related services were $78,510, and for those in management of companies and enterprises, wages were $74,730.

Median annual wages of network systems and data communication analysts were $71,100 in May 2008. The middle 50 percent earned between $54,330 and $90,740. The lowest 10 percent earned less than $41,660, and the highest 10 percent earned more than $110,920. These wages encompass network architects, telecommunications specialists, Webmasters, and Web developers. Median annual wages in the industries employing the largest numbers of network systems and data communications analysts in May 2008 were as follows:

Wired telecommunications carriers............................$75,930
Insurance carriers 74,910
Management of companies and enterprises 73,720
Computer systems design and related services 72,410
Local government..64,230

Related Occupations

Other occupations that work with information technology include:

	Page
Computer and information systems managers 35
Computer scientists 132
Computer software engineers and computer programmers.......134
Computer support specialists 138
Computer systems analysts 140

Sources of Additional Information

For additional information about a career as a computer network, systems, or database administrator, contact:

➤ The League of Professional System Administrators, 15000 Commerce Pkwy., Suite C, Mount Laurel, NJ 08054. Internet: **http://www.lopsa.org**

➤ Data Management International, 19239 N. Dale Mabry Hwy. #132, Lutz, FL 33548. Internet: **http://www.dama.org**

Additional information on a career in information technology is available from the following organizations:

➤ Association for Computing Machinery (ACM), 2 Penn Plaza, Suite 701, New York, NY 10121-0701. Internet: **http://computingcareers.acm.org**

➤ Institute of Electrical and Electronics Engineers Computer Society, Headquarters Office, 2001 L St. NW., Suite 700 Washington, DC 20036-4910. Internet: **http://www.computer.org**

➤ National Workforce Center for Emerging Technologies, 3000 Landerholm Circle SE., Bellevue, WA 98007. Internet: **http://www.nwcet.org**

➤ University of Washington Computer Science and Engineering Department, AC101 Paul G. Allen Center, Box 352350, 185 Stevens Way, Seattle, WA 98195-2350. Internet: **http://www.cs.washington.edu/WhyCSE**

➤ National Center for Women and Information Technology, University of Colorado, Campus Box 322 UCB, Boulder, CO 80309-0322. Internet: **http://www.ncwit.org**

The Occupational Information Network (O*NET) provides information on a wide range of occupational characteristics. Links to O*NET appear at the end of the Internet version of this occupational statement, accessible at **http://www.bls.gov/ooh/ocos305.htm**

Computer Scientists

Significant Points

- Most computer scientists are required to possess a Ph.D.

- Employment is projected to increase much faster than the average for all occupations.

- Job prospects are expected to be excellent.

Nature of the Work
The widespread and increasing use of computers and information technology has generated a need for highly trained, innovative workers with extensive theoretical expertise. These workers, called *computer scientists*, are the designers, creators, and inventors of new technology. By creating new technology, or finding alternative uses for existing resources, they solve complex business, scientific, and general computing problems. Some computer scientists work on multidisciplinary projects, collaborating with electrical engineers, mechanical engineers, and other specialists.

Computer scientists conduct research on a wide array of topics. Examples include computer hardware architecture, virtual reality, and robotics. Scientists who research hardware architecture discover new ways for computers to process and transmit information. They design computer chips and processors, using new materials and techniques to make them work faster and give them more computing power. When working with virtual reality, scientists use technology to create life-like situations. For example, scientists may invent video games that make users feel like they are actually in the game. Computer scientists working with robotics try to create machines that can perform tasks on their own—

without people controlling them. Robots perform many tasks, such as sweeping floors in peoples' homes, assembling cars on factory production lines, and "auto-piloting" airplanes.

Computer science researchers employed by academic institutions (covered in the section on teachers—postsecondary, elsewhere in the *Handbook*) have job functions that are similar in many ways to those employed by other organizations. In general, researchers in academic settings have more flexibility to focus on pure theory, while those working in business or scientific organizations, covered here, usually focus on projects that have the possibility of producing patents and profits. Some researchers in non-academic settings, however, have considerable latitude in determining the direction of their research.

Work environment. Computer scientists normally work in offices or laboratories in comfortable surroundings. Like other workers who spend long periods in front of a computer terminal typing on a keyboard, computer scientists are susceptible to eyestrain, back discomfort, and hand and wrist problems such as carpal tunnel syndrome.

Training, Other Qualifications, and Advancement
A Ph.D. is required for most jobs, and an aptitude for math is important.

Computer scientists develop theories that lead to technological innovation.

Professional and Related Occupations 133

Education and training. Most computer scientists are required to possess a Ph.D. in computer science, computer engineering, or a closely related discipline. For some positions in the Federal Government, a bachelor's degree in a computer-related field may be adequate.

In order to be admitted to a Ph.D. program, applicants generally are required to obtain a bachelor's degree with a strong computer science or computer engineering component. Popular undergraduate majors for Ph.D. program applicants include computer science, computer engineering, software engineering, information systems, and information technology. A bachelor's degree generally takes 4 years to complete. A Ph.D. generally requires at least 5 years of study beyond the bachelor's degree. Ph.D. students usually spend the first two years taking classes on advanced topics, including computer and software systems, artificial intelligence, digital communication, and microprocessors. Students spend the remaining years conducting research on topics in computer science or computer engineering.

Other qualifications. Computer scientists must be able to think logically and creatively. They must possess a strong aptitude for math and other technical topics, as these are critical to the computing field. Because they often deal with a number of tasks simultaneously, the ability to concentrate and pay close attention to detail also is important. Although computer scientists sometimes work independently, they frequently work in teams on large projects. As a result, they must be able to communicate effectively with computer personnel, such as programmers and managers, as well as with users or other staff who may have no technical computer background.

Advancement. After they gain experience with an organization, computer scientists may advance into managerial or project leadership positions. Some choose to leave private industry for academic positions.

Employment

Computer scientists held about 28,900 jobs in 2008. Although they are increasingly employed in every sector of the economy, the greatest concentration of these workers, about 23 percent, was in the computer systems design and related services industry. Many computer scientists were also employed by software publishing firms, scientific research and development organizations, and in education.

Job Outlook

Employment growth is expected to be much faster than the average, and job prospects should be excellent.

Employment change. Employment of computer scientists is expected to grow by 24 percent from 2008 to 2018, which is much faster than the average for all occupations. Employment of these computer specialists is expected to grow as individuals and organizations continue to demand increasingly sophisticated technologies. Job increases will be driven, in part, by very rapid growth in computer systems design and related services industry, as well as the software publishing industry, which are projected to be among the fastest growing industries in the U.S. economy.

Computer scientists develop the theories that allow many new technologies to be developed. The demand for increasing efficiency in areas such as networking technology, computing speeds, software performance, and embedded systems will lead to employment growth. In addition, the growing emphasis on information security will lead to new jobs.

Job prospects. Computer scientists should enjoy excellent job prospects. Graduates from Ph.D. programs in computer science and engineering are in high demand, and many companies report difficulties finding sufficient numbers of these highly skilled workers. In addition to openings resulting from rapid growth in the occupation, some additional job openings will arise from the need to replace workers who move into other occupations or who leave the labor force.

Earnings

Median annual wages of computer and information scientists were $97,970 in May 2008. The middle 50 percent earned between $75,340 and $124,370. The lowest 10 percent earned less than $57,480, and the highest 10 percent earned more than $151,250. Median annual wages of computer and information scientists employed in computer systems design and related services in May 2008 were $99,900.

Related Occupations

Others who work with information technology, or who engage in research and development include:

Computer and information systems managers 35
Computer network, systems, and database administrators 128
Computer software engineers 161
    and computer programmers 134
Computer support specialists 138
Engineers
Teachers—postsecondary 282

Sources of Additional Information

Further information about computer careers is available from:
➤ Association for Computing Machinery (ACM), 2 Penn Plaza, Suite 701, New York, NY 10121-0701. Internet: **http://computingcareers.acm.org**

➤ Institute of Electrical and Electronics Engineers Computer Society, Headquarters Office, 2001 L St. NW., Suite 700 Washington, DC 20036-4910. Internet: **http://www.computer.org**

Projections data from the National Employment Matrix

Occupational Title	SOC Code	Employment, 2008	Projected Employment, 2018	Change, 2008-2018	
				Number	Percent
Computer and information scientists, research	15-1011	28,900	35,900	7,000	24

(NOTE) Data in this table are rounded. See the discussion of the employment projections table in the *Handbook* introductory chapter on *Occupational Information Included in the Handbook.*

➤ National Center for Women and Information Technology, University of Colorado, Campus Box 322 UCB, Boulder, CO 80309-0322. Internet: **http://www.ncwit.org**

➤ National Workforce Center for Emerging Technologies, 3000 Landerholm Circle SE., Bellevue, WA 98007. Internet: **http://www.nwcet.org**

➤ University of Washington Computer Science and Engineering Department, AC101 Paul G. Allen Center, Box 352350, 185 Stevens Way, Seattle, WA 98195-2350. Internet: **http://www.cs.washington.edu/WhyCSE**

The Occupational Information Network (O*NET) provides information on a wide range of occupational characteristics. Links to O*NET appear at the end of the Internet version of this occupational statement, accessible at **http://www.bls.gov/ooh/ocos304.htm**

Computer Software Engineers and Computer Programmers

Significant Points

- Computer software engineers are among the occupations projected to grow the fastest and add the most new jobs over the 2008–18 decade, resulting in excellent job prospects.

- Employment of computer programmers is expected to decline by 3 percent through 2018.

- Job prospects will be best for applicants with a bachelor's or higher degree and relevant experience.

Nature of the Work

Computer software engineers design and develop software. They apply the theories and principles of computer science and mathematical analysis to create, test, and evaluate the software applications and systems that make computers work. The tasks performed by these workers evolve quickly, reflecting changes in technology and new areas of specialization, as well as the changing practices of employers. (A separate section on computer hardware engineers appears in the engineers section of the *Handbook*.)

Software engineers design and develop many types of software, including computer games, business applications, operating systems, network control systems, and middleware. They must be experts in the theory of computing systems, the structure of software, and the nature and limitations of hardware to ensure that the underlying systems will work properly.

Computer software engineers begin by analyzing users' needs, and then design, test, and develop software to meet those needs. During this process they create flowcharts, diagrams, and other documentation, and may also create the detailed sets of instructions, called algorithms, that actually tell the computer what to do. They also may be responsible for converting these instructions into a computer language, a process called programming or coding, but this usually is the responsibility of *computer programmers.*

Computer software engineers can generally be divided into two categories: applications engineers and systems engineers. *Computer applications software engineers* analyze end users' needs and design, construct, deploy, and maintain general computer applications software or specialized utility programs. These workers use different programming languages, depending on the purpose of the program and the environment in which the program runs. The programming languages most often used are C, C++, Java, and Python. Some software engineers develop packaged computer applications, but most create or adapt customized applications for business and other organizations. Some of these workers also develop databases.

Computer systems software engineers coordinate the construction, maintenance, and expansion of an organization's computer systems. Working with the organization, they coordinate each department's computer needs—ordering, inventory, billing, and payroll recordkeeping, for example—and make suggestions about its technical direction. They also might set up the organization's intranets—networks that link computers within the organization and ease communication among various departments. Often, they are also responsible for the design and implementation of system security and data assurance.

Systems software engineers also work for companies that configure, implement, and install the computer systems of other organizations. These workers may be members of the marketing or sales staff, serving as the primary technical resource for sales workers, or providing logistical and technical support. Since the selling of complex computer systems often requires substantial customization to meet the needs of the purchaser, software engineers help to identify and explain needed changes. In addition, systems software engineers are responsible for ensuring security across the systems they are configuring.

Computer programmers write programs. After computer software engineers and systems analysts design software programs, the programmer converts that design into a logical series of instructions that the computer can follow (A section on computer systems analysts appears elsewhere in the *Handbook*.). The programmer codes these instructions in any of a number of programming languages, depending on the need. The most common languages are C++ and Python.

Computer programmers also update, repair, modify, and expand existing programs. Some, especially those working on large projects that involve many programmers, use computer-assisted software engineering (CASE) tools to automate much of the coding process. These tools enable a programmer to concentrate on writing the unique parts of a program. Programmers working on smaller projects often use "programmer environments," applications that increase productivity by combining compiling, code walk-through, code generation, test data generation, and debugging functions. Programmers also use libraries of basic code that can be modified or customized for a specific application. This approach yields more reliable and consistent programs and increases programmers' productivity by eliminating some routine steps.

As software design has continued to advance, and some programming functions have become automated, programmers have begun to assume some of the responsibilities that were once performed only by software engineers. As a result, some

Employment of computer software engineers and computer programmers is expected to grow much faster than the average.

computer programmers now assist software engineers in identifying user needs and designing certain parts of computer programs, as well as other functions.

Work environment. Computer software engineers and programmers normally work in clean, comfortable offices or in laboratories in which computer equipment is located. Software engineers who work for software vendors and consulting firms frequently travel to meet with customers. Telecommuting is becoming more common as technological advances allow more work to be done from remote locations.

Most software engineers and programmers work 40 hours a week, but about 15 percent of software engineers and 11 percent of programmers worked more than 50 hours a week in 2008. Injuries in these occupations are rare. However, like other workers who spend long periods in front of a computer terminal typing at a keyboard, engineers and programmers are susceptible to eyestrain, back discomfort, and hand and wrist problems such as carpal tunnel syndrome.

Training, Other Qualifications, and Advancement

A bachelor's degree commonly is required for software engineering jobs, although a master's degree is preferred for some positions. A bachelor's degree also is required for many computer programming jobs, although a 2-year degree or certificate may be adequate in some cases. Employers favor applicants who already have relevant skills and experience. Workers who keep up to date with the latest technology usually have good opportunities for advancement.

Education and training. For software engineering positions, most employers prefer applicants who have at least a bachelor's degree and broad knowledge of, and experience with, a variety of computer systems and technologies. The usual college majors for applications software engineers are computer science, software engineering, or mathematics. Systems software engineers often study computer science or computer information systems. Graduate degrees are preferred for some of the more complex jobs.

Many programmers require a bachelor's degree, but a 2-year degree or certificate may be adequate for some positions. Some computer programmers hold a college degree in computer science, mathematics, or information systems, whereas others have taken special courses in computer programming to supplement their degree in a field such as accounting, finance, or another area of business.

Employers who use computers for scientific or engineering applications usually prefer college graduates who have a degree in computer or information science, mathematics, engineering, or the physical sciences. Employers who use computers for business applications prefer to hire people who have had college courses in management information systems and business, and who possess strong programming skills. A graduate degree in a related field is required for some jobs.

In addition to educational attainment, employers highly value relevant programming skills and experience. Students seeking software engineering or programming jobs can enhance their employment opportunities by participating in internships. Some employers, such as large computer and consulting firms, train new employees in intensive, company-based programs.

As technology advances, employers will need workers with the latest skills. To help keep up with changing technology, workers may take continuing education and professional development seminars offered by employers, software vendors, colleges and universities, private training institutions, and professional computing societies. Computer software engineers also need skills related to the industry in which they work. Engineers working for a bank, for example, should have some expertise in finance so that they understand banks' computing needs.

Certification and other qualifications. Certification is a way to demonstrate a level of competence and may provide a jobseeker with a competitive advantage. Certification programs are generally offered by product vendors or software firms, which may require professionals who work with their products to be certified. Voluntary certification also is available through various other organizations, such as professional computing societies.

Computer software engineers and programmers must have strong problem-solving and analytical skills. Ingenuity and creativity are particularly important in order to design new, functional software programs. The ability to work with abstract concepts and to do technical analysis is especially important for systems engineers because they work with the software that controls the computer's operation. Engineers and programmers also must be able to communicate effectively with team members, other staff, and end users. Because they often deal with a number of tasks simultaneously, they must be able to concentrate and pay close attention to detail. Business skills are also important, especially for those wishing to advance to managerial positions.

Advancement. For skilled workers who keep up to date with the latest technology, prospects for advancement are good. Advancement opportunities for computer software engineers increase with experience. Eventually, they may become a project manager, manager of information systems, or chief information officer, especially if they have business skills and training. Some computer software engineers with several years of experience or expertise can find lucrative opportunities working as systems designers or independent consultants, particularly in

Projections data from the National Employment Matrix

Occupational Title	SOC Code	Employment, 2008	Projected Employment, 2018	Change, 2008-2018	
				Number	Percent
Computer software engineers and computer programmers	–	1,336,300	1,619,300	283,000	21
Computer programmers	15-1021	426,700	414,400	-12,300	-3
Computer software engineers	15-1030	909,600	1,204,800	295,200	32
Computer software engineers, applications	15-1031	514,800	689,900	175,100	34
Computer software engineers, systems software	15-1032	394,800	515,000	120,200	30

(NOTE) Data in this table are rounded. See the discussion of the employment projections table in the *Handbook* introductory chapter on *Occupational Information Included in the Handbook.*

specialized fields such as business-to-business transactions or security and data assurance.

In large organizations, programmers may be promoted to lead programmer and be given supervisory responsibilities. Some applications programmers may move into systems programming after they gain experience and take courses in systems software. With general business experience, programmers may become programmer-analysts or systems analysts, or may be promoted to managerial positions. Programmers with specialized knowledge and experience with a language or operating system may become computer software engineers. As employers increasingly contract with outside firms to do programming jobs, more opportunities should arise for experienced programmers with expertise in a specific area to work as consultants.

Employment

Computer software engineers and computer programmers held about 1.3 million jobs in 2008. Approximately 514,800 were computer applications software engineers, about 394,800 were computer systems software engineers, and about 426,700 were computer programmers. Although computer software engineers and computer programmers can be found in a wide range of industries about 32 percent were employed in computer systems design and related services. Many also worked for software publishers, manufacturers of computers and related electronic equipment, financial institutions, and insurance providers. About 48,200 computer software engineers and computer programmers were self-employed in 2008.

Job Outlook

Overall, employment of computer software engineers and computer programmers is projected to increase much faster than the average for all occupations. Job prospects should be best for those with a bachelor's degree and relevant experience.

Employment change. Overall, employment of computer software engineers and computer programmers is projected to increase by 21 percent from 2008 to 2018, much faster than the average for all occupations. This will be the result of rapid growth among computer software engineers, as employment of computer programmers is expected to decline.

Employment of computer software engineers is expected to increase by 32 percent from 2008–2018, which is much faster than the average for all occupations. In addition, this occupation will see a large number of new jobs, with more than 295,000 created between 2008 and 2018. Demand for computer software engineers will increase as computer networking continues to grow.

For example, expanding Internet technologies have spurred demand for computer software engineers who can develop Internet, intranet, and World Wide Web applications. Likewise, electronic data-processing systems in business, telecommunications, healthcare, government, and other settings continue to become more sophisticated and complex. Implementing, safeguarding, and updating computer systems and resolving problems will fuel the demand for growing numbers of systems software engineers.

New growth areas will also continue to arise from rapidly evolving technologies. The increasing uses of the Internet, the proliferation of Web sites, and mobile technology such the as wireless Internet have created a demand for a wide variety of new products. As more software is offered over the Internet, and as businesses demand customized software to meet their specific needs, applications and systems software engineers will be needed in greater numbers. In addition, the growing use of handheld computers will create demand for new mobile applications and software systems. As these devices become a larger part of the business environment, it will be necessary to integrate current computer systems with this new, more mobile technology.

In addition, information security concerns have given rise to new software needs. Concerns over "cyber security" should result in the continued investment in software that protects computer networks and electronic infrastructure. The expansion of this technology over the next 10 years will lead to an increased need for software engineers to design and develop secure applications and systems, and to integrate them into older systems.

As with other information technology jobs, offshore outsourcing may temper employment growth of computer software engineers. Firms may look to cut costs by shifting operations to foreign countries with lower prevailing wages and highly educated workers. Jobs in software engineering are less prone to being offshored than are jobs in computer programming, however, because software engineering requires innovation and intense research and development.

Employment of computer programmers is expected to decline slowly, decreasing by 3 percent from 2008 to 2018. Advances in programming languages and tools, the growing ability of users to write and implement their own programs, and the offshore outsourcing of programming jobs will contribute to this decline.

Because they can transmit their programs digitally, computer programmers can perform their job function from anywhere in the world, allowing companies to employ workers in countries that have lower prevailing wages. Computer programmers are at a much higher risk of having their jobs offshored than are workers involved in more complex and sophisticated information technology functions, such as software engineering. Much of the work of computer programmers requires little localized or specialized knowledge and can be made routine once knowledge of a particular programming language is mastered.

Nevertheless, employers will continue to need some local programmers, especially those who have strong technical skills and who understand an employer's business and its programming requirements. This means that programmers will have to keep abreast of changing programming languages and techniques. Furthermore, a recent trend of domestic sourcing may help to keep a number of programming jobs onshore. Instead of hiring workers in foreign locations, some organizations have begun to contract with programmers in low-cost areas of the United States. This allows them to reduce payroll expenses, while eliminating some of the logistical issues that arise with offshore outsourcing.

Job prospects. As a result of rapid employment growth over the 2008 to 2018 decade, job prospects for computer software engineers should be excellent. Those with practical experience and at least a bachelor's degree in a computer-related field should have the best opportunities. Employers will continue to seek computer professionals with strong programming, systems analysis, interpersonal, and business skills. In addition to jobs created through employment growth, many job openings will result from the need to replace workers who move into managerial positions, transfer to other occupations, or leave the labor force. Consulting opportunities for computer software engineers also should continue to grow as businesses seek help to manage, upgrade, and customize their increasingly complicated computer systems.

Although employment of computer programmers is projected to decline, numerous job openings will result from the need to replace workers who leave the labor force or transfer to other occupations. Prospects for these openings should be best for applicants with a bachelor's degree and experience with a variety of programming languages and tools. As technology evolves, however, and newer, more sophisticated tools emerge, programmers will need to update their skills in order to remain competitive. Obtaining vendor-specific or language-specific certification also can provide a competitive edge.

Earnings

In May 2008, median annual wages of wage-and-salary computer applications software engineers were $85,430. The middle 50 percent earned between $67,790 and $104,870. The lowest 10 percent earned less than $53,720, and the highest 10 percent earned more than $128,870. Median annual wages in the industries employing the largest numbers of computer applications software engineers in May 2008 were as follows:

Professional and commercial equipment and supplies merchant wholesalers	$93,740
Software publishers	87,710
Management of companies and enterprises	85,990
Computer systems design and related services	84,610
Insurance carriers	80,370

In May 2008, median annual wages of wage-and-salary computer systems software engineers were $92,430. The middle

50 percent earned between $73,200 and $113,960. The lowest 10 percent earned less than $57,810, and the highest 10 percent earned more than $135,780. Median annual wages in the industries employing the largest numbers of computer systems software engineers in May 2008 were as follows:

Scientific research and development services	$102,090
Computer and peripheral equipment manufacturing	101,270
Software publishers	93,590
Navigational measuring electromedical and control instruments manufacturing	91,720
Computer systems design and related services	91,610

Median annual wages of wage-and-salary computer programmers were $69,620 in May 2008. The middle 50 percent earned between $52,640 and $89,720 a year. The lowest 10 percent earned less than $40,080, and the highest 10 percent earned more than $111,450. Median annual wages in the industries employing the largest numbers of computer programmers in May 2008 are shown below:

Software publishers	$81,780
Management of companies and enterprises	71,040
Computer systems design and related services	70,270
Employment services	70,070
Insurance carriers	69,790

According to the National Association of Colleges and Employers, starting salary offers for graduates with a bachelor's degree in computer science averaged $61,407 in July 2009.

Related Occupations

Other professional workers who deal extensively with computer technology or data include:

Sources of Additional Information

State employment service offices can provide information about job openings for computer programmers. Municipal chambers of commerce are an additional source of information on an area's largest employers.

Further information about computer careers is available from:

➤ Association for Computing Machinery, 2 Penn Plaza, Suite 701, New York, NY 10121-0701. Internet: **http://computingcareers.acm.org**

➤ Institute of Electrical and Electronics Engineers Computer Society, Headquarters Office, 2001 L St. NW., Suite 700 Washington, DC 20036-4910. Internet: **http://www.computer.org**

➤ National Workforce Center for Emerging Technologies, 3000 Landerholm Circle SE., Bellevue, WA 98007. Internet: **http://www.nwcet.org**

➤ University of Washington Computer Science and Engineering Department, AC101 Paul G. Allen Center, Box 352350, 185 Stevens Way, Seattle, WA 98195-2350. Internet: **http://www.cs.washington.edu/WhyCSE**

➤ National Center for Women and Information Technology, University of Colorado, Campus Box 322 UCB, Boulder, CO 80309-0322. Internet: **http://www.ncwit.org**

The Occupational Information Network (O*NET) provides information on a wide range of occupational characteristics. Links to O*NET appear at the end of the Internet version of this occupational statement, accessible at **http://www.bls.gov/ooh/ocos303.htm**

Computer Support Specialists

Significant Points

- Job growth is projected to be faster than the average for all occupations.

- A bachelor's degree is required for some jobs, while an associate degree or certification is adequate for others.

- Job prospects should be good, especially for college graduates with relevant skills and experience.

Nature of the Work

Computer support specialists provide technical assistance, support, and advice to individuals and organizations that depend on information technology. They work within organizations that use computer systems, for computer hardware or software vendors, or for third-party organizations that provide support services on a contract basis, such as help-desk service firms. Support specialists are usually differentiated between technical support specialists and help-desk technicians.

Technical support specialists respond to inquiries from their organizations' computer users and may run automatic diagnostics programs to resolve problems. In addition, they may write training manuals and train computer users in the use of new computer hardware and software. These workers also oversee the daily performance of their company's computer systems, resolving technical problems with Local Area Networks (LAN), Wide Area Networks (WAN), and other systems.

Help-desk technicians respond to telephone calls and e-mail messages from customers looking for help with computer problems. In responding to these inquiries, help-desk technicians must listen carefully to the customer, ask questions to diagnose the nature of the problem, and then patiently walk the customer through the problem-solving steps. They also install, modify, clean, and repair computer hardware and software. Many computer support specialists start out at the help desk.

Help-desk technicians deal directly with customer issues, and their employers value them as a source of feedback on their products and services. They are consulted for information about what gives customers the most trouble, as well as other customer concerns.

Work environment. Computer support specialists normally work in well-lighted, comfortable offices or computer laboratories. Most work about 40 hours a week. Those who work for third-party support firms often are away from their offices, spending considerable time working at a client's location. As computer networks expand, more computer support specialists may be able to provide technical support from remote locations. This capability would reduce or eliminate travel to the customer's workplace, and may allow some support specialists to work from home.

Injuries in this occupation are uncommon, but like other workers who type on a keyboard for long periods, computer support specialists are susceptible to eyestrain, back discomfort, and hand and wrist problems such as carpal tunnel syndrome.

Training, Other Qualifications, and Advancement

A college degree is required for some computer support specialist positions, but an associate degree or certification may be sufficient for others. Strong problem-solving and communication skills are essential.

Education and training. Due to the wide range of skills required, there are many paths of entry to a job as a computer support specialist. Training requirements for computer support specialist positions vary, but many employers prefer to hire applicants with some formal college education. A bachelor's degree in computer science, computer engineering, or information systems is a prerequisite for some jobs; other jobs, however, may require only a computer-related associate degree. Some employers will hire applicants with a college degree in any field, as long as the applicant has the necessary technical skills. For some jobs, relevant computer experience and certifications may substitute for formal education.

Employment of computer support specialists is expected to increase faster than the average.

Projections data from the National Employment Matrix

Occupational Title	SOC Code	Employment, 2008	Projected Employment, 2018	Change, 2008-2018	
				Number	Percent
Computer support specialists	15-1041	565,700	643,700	78,000	14

(NOTE) Data in this table are rounded. See the discussion of the employment projections table in the *Handbook* introductory chapter on *Occupational Information Included in the Handbook.*

Most support specialists receive on-the-job training after being hired. This training can last anywhere from 1 week to 1 year, but a common length is about 3 months. Many computer support specialists, in order to keep up with changes in technology, continue to receive training throughout their careers by attending professional training programs offered by employers, hardware and software vendors, colleges and universities, and private training institutions.

Certification and other qualifications. For some jobs, professional certification may qualify an applicant for employment. Certification can demonstrate proficiency in a product or process, and help applicants obtain some entry-level positions. Some hardware and software vendors require their computer support specialists to be certified, and many of these will fund this training after an applicant is hired. Voluntary certification programs are offered by a wide variety of organizations, including product vendors and training institutions, and are available across the Nation.

People interested in becoming a computer support specialist must have strong problem-solving, analytical, and communication skills because troubleshooting and helping others are vital parts of the job. The constant interaction with other computer personnel, customers, and employees requires computer support specialists to communicate effectively via e-mail, over the phone, or in person. Strong writing skills are useful in writing e-mail responses and preparing manuals for employees and customers.

Advancement. Entry-level computer support specialists generally work directly with customers or in-house users. They may advance into positions that handle products or problems with higher levels of technical complexity. Some may advance into management roles. Some computer support specialists may find opportunities in other occupations, such as computer programmers or software engineers, designing products rather than assisting users. Promotions depend heavily on job performance, but formal education and professional certification can improve advancement opportunities. Advancement opportunities in hardware and software companies can occur quickly, sometimes within months.

Employment

Computer support specialists held about 565,700 jobs in 2008. Although they worked in a wide range of industries, about 18 percent were employed in the computer systems design and related services industry. Substantial numbers of these workers were also employed in administrative and support services companies, financial institutions, insurance companies, government agencies, educational institutions, software publishers, telecommunications organizations, and healthcare organizations.

Job Outlook

Employment is expected to increase faster than the average. Job prospects should be good, especially for those with a college degree and relevant skills.

Employment change. Employment of computer support specialists is expected to increase by 14 percent from 2008 to 2018, which is faster than the average for all occupations. Demand for these workers will result as organizations and individuals continue to adopt the newest forms of technology. As technology becomes more complex and widespread, support specialists will be needed in greater numbers to resolve the technical problems that arise. Businesses, especially, will demand greater levels of support, as information technology has become essential in the business environment.

Job growth will be fastest in several industries that rely heavily on technology. These include the computer systems design and related services industry; the data processing, hosting and related services industry; the software publishing industry; and the management, scientific, and technical consulting industry. These industries will employ a growing number of support specialists as they utilize and provide an increasing array of IT services. Healthcare and related establishments, in addition, may see substantial growth as these organizations look to improve their efficiency and patient care through the use of information systems and other technology.

Overall growth may be dampened, to a certain extent, as some jobs are outsourced to offshore locations. Advances in technology increasingly allow computer support specialists to provide assistance remotely. Some employers may seek to reduce expenses by hiring workers in areas that have lower prevailing wages.

Job prospects. Job prospects are expected to be good; those who possess a bachelor's degree, relevant technical and communication skills, and previous work experience should have even better opportunities than applicants with an associate degree or professional certification.

Earnings

Median annual wages of wage-and-salary computer support specialists were $43,450 in May 2008. The middle 50 percent earned between $33,680 and $55,990. The lowest 10 percent earned less than $26,580, and the highest 10 percent earned more than $70,750. Median annual wages in the industries employing the largest numbers of computer support specialists in May 2008 were as follows:

Professional and commercial equipment
and supplies merchant wholesalers $48,580
Management of companies and enterprises 45,200
Colleges, universities, and professional schools 43,130
Computer systems design and related services 43,080
Elementary and secondary schools 40,550

Related Occupations

Other occupations that deal with technology or respond to customer inquiries include:

Sources of Additional Information

For additional information about a career as a computer support specialist, contact:

➤ Association of Support Professionals, 122 Barnard Ave., Watertown, MA 02472. Internet: **http://asponline.com**

➤ HDI, 102 South Tejon, Suite 1200, Colorado Springs, CO, 80903. Internet: **http://www.thinkhdi.com**

For additional information about computer careers, contact:

➤ Association for Computing Machinery, 2 Penn Plaza, Suite 701, New York, NY 10121-0701. Internet: **http://computingcareers.acm.org**

➤ Institute of Electrical and Electronics Engineers Computer Society, Headquarters Office, 2001 L St. NW., Suite 700 Washington, DC 20036-4910. Internet: **http://www.computer.org**

➤ National Workforce Center for Emerging Technologies, 3000 Landerholm Circle SE., Bellevue, WA 98007. Internet: **http://www.nwcet.org**

➤ University of Washington Computer Science and Engineering Department, AC101 Paul G. Allen Center, Box 352350, 185 Stevens Way, Seattle, WA 98195-2350. Internet: **http://www.cs.washington.edu/WhyCSE**

➤ National Center for Women and Information Technology, University of Colorado, Campus Box 322 UCB, Boulder, CO 80309-0322. Internet: **http://www.ncwit.org**

The Occupational Information Network (O*NET) provides information on a wide range of occupational characteristics. Links to O*NET appear at the end of the Internet version of this occupational statement, accessible at **http://www.bls.gov/ooh/ocos306.htm**

Computer Systems Analysts

Significant Points

- Employment is expected to increase much faster than average.

- Excellent job prospects are expected as organizations continue to adopt increasingly sophisticated technologies.

- Employers generally prefer applicants who have at least a bachelor's degree; relevant work experience also is very important.

Nature of the Work

Nearly all organizations rely on computer and information technology (IT) to conduct business and operate efficiently. *Computer systems analysts* use IT tools to help enterprises of all sizes achieve their goals. They may design and develop new computer systems by choosing and configuring hardware and software, or they may devise ways to apply existing systems' resources to additional tasks.

Most systems analysts work with specific types of computer systems—for example, business, accounting, and financial systems or scientific and engineering systems—that vary with the kind of organization. Analysts who specialize in helping an organization select the proper system hardware and software are often called *system architects* or *system designers*. Analysts who specialize in developing and fine-tuning systems often have the more general title of *systems analysts*.

To begin an assignment, systems analysts consult with an organization's managers and users to define the goals of the system and then design a system to meet those goals. They specify the inputs that the system will access, decide how the inputs will be processed, and format the output to meet users' needs. Analysts use techniques such as structured analysis, data modeling, information engineering, mathematical model building, sampling, and a variety of accounting principles to ensure their plans are efficient and complete. They also may prepare cost-benefit and return-on-investment analyses to help management decide whether implementing the proposed technology would be financially feasible.

When a system is approved, systems analysts oversee the implementation of the required hardware and software components. They coordinate tests and observe the initial use of the system to ensure that it performs as planned. They prepare specifications, flow charts, and process diagrams for computer programmers to follow; then they work with programmers to "debug," or eliminate errors, from the system. Systems analysts who do more in-depth testing may be called *software quality assurance analysts*. In addition to running tests, these workers diagnose problems, recommend solutions, and determine whether program requirements have been met. After the system has been implemented, tested, and debugged, computer systems analysts may train its users and write instruction manuals.

In some organizations, *programmer-analysts* design and update the software that runs a computer. They also create custom applications tailored to their organization's tasks. Because they are responsible for both programming and systems analysis, these workers must be proficient in both areas. (A separate section on computer software engineers and computer programmers appears elsewhere in the *Handbook*.) As this dual proficiency becomes more common, analysts are increasingly working with databases, object-oriented programming languages, client–server applications, and multimedia and Internet technology.

One challenge created by expanding computer use is the need for different computer systems to communicate with each other. Many systems analysts are involved with "networking," connecting all the computers within an organization or across organizations, as when setting up e-commerce networks to facilitate business between companies.

Computer systems analysts use information technology to help organizations operate more effectively.

Work environment. Computer systems analysts work in offices or laboratories in comfortable surroundings. Many work about 40 hours a week, but some work more than 50 hours a week. Some analysts telecommute, using computers to work from remote locations.

Injuries in this occupation are uncommon, but computer systems analysts, like other workers who spend long periods typing on a computer, are susceptible to eyestrain, back discomfort, and hand and wrist problems such as carpal tunnel syndrome.

Training, Other Qualifications, and Advancement

Training requirements for computer systems analysts vary depending on the job, but many employers prefer applicants who have a bachelor's degree. Relevant work experience also is very important. Advancement opportunities are good for those with the necessary skills and experience.

Education and training. When hiring computer systems analysts, employers usually prefer applicants who have at least a bachelor's degree. For more technically complex jobs, people with graduate degrees are preferred. For jobs in a technical or scientific environment, employers often seek applicants who have at least a bachelor's degree in a technical field, such as computer science, information science, applied mathematics, engineering, or the physical sciences. For jobs in a business environment, employers often seek applicants with at least a bachelor's degree in a business-related field such as management information systems (MIS). Increasingly, employers are seeking individuals who have a master's degree in business administration (MBA) with a concentration in information systems.

Despite the preference for technical degrees, however, people who have degrees in other areas may find employment as systems analysts if they also have technical skills. Courses in computer science or related subjects combined with practical experience can qualify people for some jobs in the occupation.

Employers generally look for people with expertise relevant to the job. For example, systems analysts who wish to work for a bank may need some expertise in finance, and systems analysts who wish to work for a hospital may need some knowledge of health management. Furthermore, business enterprises generally prefer individuals with information technology, business, and accounting skills and frequently assist employees in obtaining these skills.

Technological advances come so rapidly in the computer field that continuous study is necessary to remain competitive. Employers, hardware and software vendors, colleges and universities, and private training institutions offer continuing education to help workers attain the latest skills. Additional training may come from professional development seminars offered by professional computing societies.

Other qualifications. Employers usually look for people who have broad knowledge and experience related to computer systems and technologies, strong problem-solving and analytical skills, and the ability to think logically. In addition, the ability to concentrate and pay close attention to detail is important because computer systems analysts often deal with many tasks simultaneously. Although these workers sometimes work independently, they frequently work in teams on large projects. Therefore, they must have good interpersonal skills and be able to communicate effectively with computer personnel, users, and other staff who may have no technical background.

Projections data from the National Employment Matrix

Occupational Title	SOC Code	Employment, 2008	Projected Employment, 2018	Change, 2008-2018	
				Number	Percent
Computer systems analysts..	15-1051	532,200	640,300	108,100	20

(NOTE) Data in this table are rounded. See the discussion of the employment projections table in the *Handbook* introductory chapter on *Occupational Information Included in the Handbook.*

Advancement. With experience, systems analysts may be promoted to senior or lead analyst. Those who possess leadership ability and good business skills also can become computer and information systems managers or can advance into executive positions such as chief information officer. Those with work experience and considerable expertise in a particular subject or application may find lucrative opportunities as independent consultants, or they may choose to start their own computer consulting firms.

Employment

Computer systems analysts held about 532,200 jobs in 2008. Although they are employed in many industries, 24 percent of these workers were in the computer systems design and related services industry. Computer systems analysts also were employed by governments; insurance companies; financial institutions; and business management firms. About 30,300 computer systems analysts were self-employed in 2008.

Job Outlook

Employment is expected to grow much faster than the average for all occupations, and job prospects should be excellent.

Employment change. Employment of computer systems analysts is expected to grow by 20 percent from 2008 to 2018, which is much faster than the average for all occupations. Demand for these workers will increase as organizations continue to adopt and integrate increasingly sophisticated technologies and as the need for information security grows.

As information technology becomes an increasingly important aspect of the business environment, the demand for computer networking, Internet, and intranet functions will drive demand for computer systems analysts. The increasing adoption of the wireless Internet, known as WiFi, and of personal mobile computers has created a need for new systems that can integrate these technologies into existing networks. Explosive growth in these areas is expected to fuel demand for analysts who are knowledgeable about systems development and integration. In addition, as sensitive data continues to be transmitted and stored electronically, the need for information security specialists is expected to grow rapidly. Furthermore, the healthcare industry is expected to increase its use of information technology and will demand the services of this occupation. The adoption of e-prescribing, electronic health records, and other IT platforms will drive this trend, creating a large number of new jobs.

As with other information technology jobs, employment growth may be tempered somewhat by offshoring. Firms may look to cut costs by shifting operations to foreign countries with lower prevailing wages and highly skilled workers. However, due to the high level of expertise that is required, as well as the frequent need to be near the job site, systems analysts are less likely to be offshored than other IT occupations.

Job prospects. Job prospects should be excellent. Job openings will occur as a result of strong job growth and from the need to replace workers who move into other occupations or who leave the labor force.

Earnings

Median annual wages of wage and salary computer systems analysts were $75,500 in May 2008. The middle 50 percent earned between $58,460 and $95,810 a year. The lowest 10 percent earned less than $45,390, and the highest 10 percent earned more than $118,440. Median annual wages in the industries employing the largest numbers of computer systems analysts in May 2008 were:

Professional and commercial equipment and supplies merchant wholesalers	$89,670
Computer systems design and related services	78,680
Data processing, hosting, and related services	78,010
Management of companies and enterprises	76,070
Insurance carriers	74,610

Related Occupations

Other workers who use computers extensively and who use logic and creativity to solve business and technical problems include:

	Page
Actuaries	125
Computer and information systems managers	35
Computer network, systems, and database administrators	128
Computer software engineers and computer programmers	134
Engineers	161
Management analysts	111
Mathematicians	143
Operations research analysts	145
Statisticians	148

Sources of Additional Information

Further information about computer careers is available from:
➤ Association for Computing Machinery (ACM), 2 Penn Plaza, Suite 701, New York, NY 10121-0701. Internet: **http://computingcareers.acm.org/**

➤ Institute of Electrical and Electronics Engineers Computer Society, Headquarters Office, 2001 L St. NW, Suite 700 Washington, DC 20036-4910. Internet: **http://www.computer.org**

➤ National Workforce Center for Emerging Technologies, 3000 Landerholm Circle SE, Bellevue, WA 98007. Internet: **http://www.nwcet.org**

➤ University of Washington Computer Science and Engineering Department, AC101 Paul G. Allen Center, Box 352350, 185 Stevens Way, Seattle, WA 98195-2350. Internet: **http://www.cs.washington.edu/WhyCSE**

➤ National Center for Women and Information Technology, University of Colorado, Campus Box 322 UCB, Boulder, CO 80309-0322. Internet: **http://www.ncwit.org**

The Occupational Information Network (O*NET) provides information on a wide range of occupational characteristics. Links to O*NET appear at the end of the Internet version of this occupational statement, accessible at **http://www.bls.gov/ooh/ocos287.htm**

Mathematicians

Significant Points

- A Ph.D. in mathematics usually is the minimum educational requirement, except in the Federal Government.

- Much faster than average employment growth is expected for mathematicians.

- Keen competition for jobs is expected.

- Ph.D. holders with a strong background in mathematics and a related field, such as computer science or engineering, should have better employment opportunities in related occupations.

Nature of the Work

Mathematics is one of the oldest and most fundamental sciences. *Mathematicians* use mathematical theory, computational techniques, algorithms, and the latest computer technology to solve economic, scientific, engineering, and business problems. The work of mathematicians falls into two broad classes: theoretical (pure) mathematics and applied mathematics. These classes, however, are not sharply defined and often overlap.

Theoretical mathematicians advance mathematical knowledge by developing new principles and recognizing previously unknown relationships between existing principles of mathematics. Although these workers seek to increase basic knowledge without necessarily considering its practical use, such pure and abstract knowledge has been instrumental in producing or furthering many scientific and engineering achievements. Many theoretical mathematicians are employed as university faculty, dividing their time between teaching and conducting research. (See the statement on teachers—postsecondary elsewhere in the *Handbook*.)

Applied mathematicians use theories and techniques, such as mathematical modeling and computational methods, to formulate and solve practical problems in business, government, engineering, and the physical, life, and social sciences. For example, they may analyze the most efficient way to schedule airline routes between cities, the effects and safety of new drugs, the aerodynamic characteristics of an experimental automobile, or the cost-effectiveness of alternative manufacturing processes.

Applied mathematicians working in industrial research and development may develop or enhance mathematical methods when solving a difficult problem. Some mathematicians, called cryptanalysts, analyze and decipher encryption systems—codes—designed to transmit military, political, financial, or law-enforcement-related information.

Applied mathematicians start with a practical problem, envision its separate elements, and then reduce the elements to mathematical variables. They often use computers to analyze relationships among the variables, and they solve complex problems by developing models with alternative solutions.

Individuals with titles other than mathematician also do work in applied mathematics. In fact, because mathematics is the foundation on which so many other academic disciplines are built, the number of workers using mathematical techniques is much greater than the number formally called mathematicians. For example, engineers, computer scientists, physicists, and economists are among those who use mathematics extensively. Some professionals, including statisticians, actuaries, and operations research analysts, are actually specialists in a particular branch of mathematics. (For more information, see the statements on actuaries, operations research analysts, and statisticians elsewhere in the *Handbook*.) Applied mathematicians frequently are required to collaborate with other workers in their organizations to find common solutions to problems.

Work environment. Mathematicians usually work in comfortable offices. They often are part of interdisciplinary teams that may include economists, engineers, computer scientists, physicists, technicians, and others. Deadlines, overtime work, special requests for information or analysis, and prolonged travel to attend seminars or conferences may be part of their jobs.

Mathematicians who work in academia usually have a mix of teaching and research responsibilities. These mathematicians may conduct research by themselves or in close collaboration with other mathematicians. Collaborators may work together at the same institution or from different locations, using technology such as e-mail to communicate. Mathematicians in academia also may be aided by graduate students.

Training, Other Qualifications, and Advancement

A Ph.D. degree in mathematics usually is the minimum educational requirement for prospective mathematicians, except in the Federal Government.

Education and training. In private industry, candidates for mathematician jobs typically need a Ph.D., although there may be opportunities for those with a master's degree. Most of the positions designated for mathematicians are in research-and-development laboratories, as part of technical teams.

In the Federal Government, entry-level job candidates usually must have at least a bachelor's degree with a major in mathematics or 24 semester hours of mathematics courses. Outside the Federal Government, bachelor's degree holders in mathematics usually are not qualified for most jobs, and many seek advanced degrees in mathematics or a related discipline. However, bachelor's degree holders who meet State certification

Applied mathematicians use math to solve practical problems.

requirements may become primary or secondary school mathematics teachers. (For additional information, see the statement on teachers- kindergarten, elementary, middle, and secondary elsewhere in the *Handbook*.)

Most colleges and universities offer a bachelor's degree in mathematics, and many universities offer master's and doctoral degrees in pure or applied mathematics. Courses usually required for these programs include calculus, differential equations, and linear and abstract algebra. Additional courses might include probability theory and statistics, mathematical analysis, numerical analysis, topology, discrete mathematics, and mathematical logic. In graduate programs, students also conduct research and take advanced courses, usually specializing in a subfield of mathematics.

Many colleges and universities advise or require students majoring in mathematics to take courses in a closely related field, such as computer science, engineering, life science, physical science, or economics. A double major in mathematics and another related discipline is particularly desirable to many employers. High school students who are prospective college mathematics majors should take as many mathematics courses as possible while in high school.

Other qualifications.   For jobs in applied mathematics, training in the field in which mathematics will be used is very important. Mathematics is used extensively in physics, actuarial science, statistics, engineering, and operations research. Computer science, business and industrial management, economics, finance, chemistry, geology, life sciences, and behavioral sciences are likewise dependent on applied mathematics. Mathematicians also should have substantial knowledge of computer programming, because most complex mathematical computation and much mathematical modeling are done on a computer.

Mathematicians need to have good reasoning to identify, analyze, and apply basic principles to technical problems. Communication skills also are important because mathematicians must be able to interact and discuss proposed solutions with people who may not have extensive knowledge of mathematics.

Advancement.   The majority of those with a master's degree in mathematics who work in private industry do so not as mathematicians but in related fields, such as computer science, where they have titles such as computer programmer, systems analyst, or systems engineer. In these occupations, workers can advance to management positions.

Employment

Mathematicians held about 2,900 jobs in 2008. Many people with mathematical backgrounds also worked in other occupations. For example, there were about 54,800 jobs for postsecondary mathematical science teachers in 2008.

Many mathematicians work for the Federal Government, primarily in the U.S. Department of Defense which accounts for about 81 percent of the mathematicians employed by the Federal Government. Many of the other mathematicians employed by the Federal Government work for the National Institute of Standards and Technology (NIST) or the National Aeronautics and Space Administration (NASA).

In the private sector, major employers include scientific research and development services and management, scientific, and technical consulting services. Some mathematicians also work for insurance carriers.

Job Outlook

Employment of mathematicians is expected to grow much faster than average. However, keen competition for jobs is expected.

Employment change.   Employment of mathematicians is expected to increase by 22 percent during the 2008–18 decade, which is much faster than average for all occupations. Advancements in technology usually lead to expanding applications of mathematics, and more workers with knowledge of mathematics will be required in the future. However, jobs in industry and government often require advanced knowledge of related scientific disciplines in addition to mathematics. The most common fields in which mathematicians study and find work are computer science and software development, physics, engineering, and operations research. Many mathematicians also are involved in financial analysis and in life sciences research.

Job prospects.   Job competition will remain keen because employment in this occupation is relatively small and few new jobs are expected. Ph.D. holders with a strong background in mathematics and a related discipline, such as engineering or computer science, and who apply mathematical theory to real-world problems will have the best job prospects in related occupations. In addition, mathematicians with experience in computer programming will better their job prospects in many occupations.

Holders of a master's degree in mathematics will face very strong competition for jobs in theoretical research. Because the number of Ph.D. degrees awarded in mathematics continues to exceed the number of available university positions—especially tenure-track positions—many graduates will need to find employment in industry and government.

Employment in theoretical mathematical research is sensitive to general economic fluctuations and to changes in government spending. Job prospects will be greatly influenced by changes in public and private funding for research and development.

Earnings

Median annual wages of mathematicians were $95,150 in May 2008. The middle 50 percent earned between $71,430

Projections data from the National Employment Matrix

Occupational Title	SOC Code	Employment, 2008	Projected Employment, 2018	Change, 2008-2018	
				Number	Percent
Mathematicians	15-2021	2,900	3,600	700	22

(NOTE) Data in this table are rounded. See the discussion of the employment projections table in the *Handbook* introductory chapter on *Occupational Information Included in the Handbook.*

and $119,480. The lowest 10 percent had earnings of less than $53,570, while the highest 10 percent earned more than $140,500.

In March 2009, the average annual salary in the Federal Government was $107,051 for mathematicians; $107,015 for mathematical statisticians; and $101,645 for cryptanalysts.

Related Occupations

Other occupations that require extensive knowledge of mathematics or, in some cases, a degree in mathematics include the following:

A strong background in mathematics also facilitates employment for the following workers:

Sources of Additional Information

For more information about careers and training in mathematics, especially for doctoral-level employment, contact
➤ American Mathematical Society, 201 Charles St., Providence, RI 02904-2294. Internet: http://www.ams.org

For specific information on careers in applied mathematics, contact
➤ Society for Industrial and Applied Mathematics, 3600 Market St. 6th Floor, Philadelphia, PA 19104-2688. Internet: http://www.siam.org

Information on obtaining positions as mathematicians with the Federal Government is available from the Office of Personnel Management through USAJOBS, the Federal Government's official employment information system. This resource for locating and applying for job opportunities can be accessed through the Internet at http://www.usajobs.gov or through an interactive voice response telephone system at (703) 724-1850 or TDD (978) 461-8404. These numbers are not toll free, and charges may result.

For advice on how to find and apply for Federal jobs, see the *Occupational Outlook Quarterly* article "How to get a job in the Federal Government," online at http://www.bls.gov/opub/ooq/2004/summer/art01.pdf.

The Occupational Information Network (O*NET) provides information on a wide range of occupational characteristics. Links to O*NET appear at the end of the Internet version of this occupational statement, accessible at http://www.bls.gov/ooh/ocos043.htm

Operations Research Analysts

Significant Points

- Candidates should have strong quantitative and computer skills; employers prefer workers who have completed advanced math courses.

- Employment is projected to grow much faster than average.

- Individuals with a master's or Ph.D. degree in operations research or management science should have excellent employment prospects; some entry-level positions are available to those with a bachelor's degree.

Nature of the Work

Operations research analysts formulate and apply mathematical modeling methods to develop and interpret information that assists management with policy formulation and other managerial functions. Using analytical techniques, operations research analysts help managers to make better decisions and solve problems. The procedures of operations research were first formalized by the military. They have been used in wartime to effectively deploy radar, search for enemy submarines, and get supplies to where they are most needed. In peacetime and in private enterprises, operations research is used in planning business ventures and analyzing options by using statistical analysis, data mining, simulation, computer modeling, linear programming, and other mathematical techniques.

In addition to the military, operations research analysts today are employed in almost every industry, as companies and organizations must effectively manage money, materials, equipment, people, and time. Operations research analysts reduce the complexity of these elements by applying analytical methods from mathematics, science, and engineering, to help companies make better decisions and improve efficiency. Using sophisticated software tools, operations research analysts are largely responsible for solving complex problems, such as setting up schedules for sports leagues or determining how to organize products in supermarkets. Presenting the pros and cons of each possible scenario, analysts present solutions to managers, who use the information to make decisions.

Analysts are often involved in top-level strategizing, planning, and forecasting. They help to allocate resources, measure performance, schedule, design production facilities and systems, manage the supply chain, set prices, coordinate transportation and distribution, or analyze large databases.

The duties of operations research analysts vary according to the structure and management of the organizations they are assisting. Some firms centralize operations research in one department; others use operations research in each division. Many analysts work with management consulting companies that perform contract work for other firms. Analysts working in these positions often have areas of specialization, such as transportation or finance. Because problems are very complex and often require expertise from many disciplines, most analysts work in teams.

Teams of analysts usually start projects by listening to managers describe problems. Analysts ask questions and search for data that may help to formally define a problem. For example, an operations research team for an auto manufacturer may be asked to determine the best inventory level for each of the parts needed on a production line and to determine the optimal number of windshields to be kept in stock. Too many windshields would be wasteful and expensive, whereas too few could halt production.

Analysts study the problem, breaking it into its components. Then they gather information from a variety of sources. To determine the optimal inventory, operations research analysts might talk with engineers about production levels, discuss purchasing arrangements with buyers, and examine storage-cost data provided by the accounting department. They might also find data on past inventory levels or other statistics that may help them to project their needs.

Relevant information in hand, the team determines the most appropriate analytical technique. Techniques used may include Monte Carlo simulations, linear and nonlinear programming, dynamic programming, queuing and other stochastic-process models, Markov decision processes, econometric methods, data envelopment analysis, neural networks, expert systems, decision analysis, and the analytic hierarchy process. Nearly all of these techniques involve the construction of mathematical models that attempt to describe the system. The problem of the windshields, for example, would be described as a set of equations that represent real-world conditions.

Using these models, the team can explicitly describe the different components and clarify the relationships among them. The model's inputs can then be altered to examine what might happen to the system under different circumstances. In most cases, a computer program is used to numerically evaluate the model.

A team will often run the model with a variety of different inputs to determine the results of each change. A model for airline flight scheduling, for example, might stipulate such things as connecting cities, the amount of fuel required to fly the routes, projected levels of passenger demand, varying ticket and fuel prices, pilot scheduling, and maintenance costs. Analysts may also use optimization techniques to determine the most cost effective or profit-maximizing solution for the airline.

Based on the results of the analysis, the operations research team presents recommendations to managers. Managers may ask analysts to modify and rerun the model with different inputs or change some aspect of the model before making their deci-

Operations research analysts can advance by becoming technical specialists or supervisors on more complicated projects.

sions. Once a manager reaches a final decision, the team usually works with others in the organization to ensure the plan's successful implementation.

Work environment. Operations research analysts generally work 40 hours a week; some, however, work longer. While most of their work is done in an office environment, they may spend time in the field, analyzing processes through direct observation. Because they work on projects that are of immediate interest to top managers, operations research analysts often are under pressure to meet deadlines.

Training, Other Qualifications, and Advancement

Some entry-level positions are available to those with a bachelor's degree in operations research, management science, or a related field, but higher degrees are required for many positions. Strong quantitative and computer skills are essential. Employers prefer workers who have completed advanced math courses.

Education and training. A bachelor's degree coupled with extensive coursework in mathematics and other quantitative subjects usually is the minimum education requirement. Many employers, however, prefer applicants with a master's degree in operations research, management science, or a closely related field—such as computer science, engineering, business, applied mathematics, or information systems. Dual graduate degrees in operations research and computer science are especially attractive to employers. There are numerous degree programs in operations research and closely related fields in colleges and universities across the United States.

Continuing education is important for operations research analysts. Keeping up to date with technological advances, software tools, and improvements in analytical methods is vital for maintaining their problem-solving skills.

Projections data from the National Employment Matrix

Occupational Title	SOC Code	Employment, 2008	Projected Employment, 2018	Change, 2008-2018	
				Number	Percent
Operations research analysts...	15-2031	63,000	76,900	13,900	22

(NOTE) Data in this table are rounded. See the discussion of the employment projections table in the *Handbook* introductory chapter on *Occupational Information Included in the Handbook.*

Other qualifications. Those considering careers as operations research analysts should be able to pay attention to detail because much time is spent on data analysis. Candidates should also have strong computer and quantitative skills and be able to perform complex research. Employers prefer analysts who understand how to use advanced operations research software and statistical packages. Although not always required, having programming skills can be very helpful.

Since operations research is a multi-disciplinary field, a background in political science, economics, statistics, engineering, accounting, and management can also be useful. Operations research analysts must be able to think logically, work well with people, and write and speak well.

Advancement. Beginning analysts usually perform routine computational work under the supervision of more experienced analysts. As novices gain knowledge and experience, they are assigned more complex tasks and are given greater autonomy to design models and solve problems.

Operations research analysts can advance by becoming technical specialists or project team leaders. Analysts also gain valuable insights into the industry where they work and may assume higher level managerial or administrative positions. Operations research analysts with significant experience or expertise may become independent consultants. Others may move into corporate management, where they eventually may become chief operating officers.

Employment

Operations research analysts held about 63,000 jobs in 2008. Major employers include computer systems design firms; insurance carriers and other financial institutions; management; telecommunications companies; and scientific, and technical consulting services firms. Most operations research analysts in the Federal Government work for the Department of Defense.

Job Outlook

Employment is projected to grow much faster than average. Individuals with a master's or Ph.D. degree in operations research or management science should have excellent job opportunities; some entry-level positions are available to those with a bachelor's degree.

Employment change. Employment of operations research analysts is expected to grow 22 percent over the 2008–18 period, much faster than the average for all occupations. As technology advances and companies further emphasize efficiency, demand for operations research analysis should continue to grow. Technological advancements have extended the availability of data access and storage, making information more readily available. Advancements in computing capabilities and analytical software have made it cheaper and faster for analysts to solve problems. As problem solving becomes cheaper and faster with technological advances, more firms will have the ability to employ or consult with analysts.

Additionally, organizations increasingly will be faced with the pressure of growing domestic and international competition and must work to maximize organizational efficiency. As a result, businesses increasingly will rely on operations research analysts to optimize profits by improving productivity

and reducing costs. As new technologies are introduced into the marketplace, operations research analysts will be needed to determine how to best use those new technologies.

Job prospects. Jobs for operations research analysts exist in almost every industry because of the diversity of applications for their work. As businesses and government agencies continue to contract out jobs to cut costs, opportunities for operations research analysts will be best in management, scientific, and technical consulting firms. The relatively small pool of qualified candidates will result in excellent opportunities for those with a master's or Ph.D. degree in operations research or management science. Operations research is not a particularly well-known field, which means there are fewer applicants competing for each job.

In addition to job growth, some openings will result from the need to replace analysts retiring or leaving the occupation for other reasons.

Earnings

Median annual wages of operations research analysts were $69,000 in May 2008. The middle 50 percent earned between $51,780 and $92,920. The lowest 10 percent had wages of less than $40,000, while the highest 10 percent earned more than $118,130. Median annual wages of operations research analysts working in management, scientific, and technical consulting services were $80,290 in May 2008. The average annual salary for operations research analysts in the Federal Government was $107,198 in March 2009.

Operations research analysts generally are paid fixed annual salaries with the possibility of bonuses. They also receive benefits typical of professional employees, such as medical and life insurance and 401(k) programs. Many employers offer training programs, including tuition reimbursement programs that allow analysts to attend advanced university classes.

Related Occupations

Operations research analysts apply advanced analytical methods to large, complicated problems, similar to:

Sources of Additional Information

For information on career opportunities and a list of degree programs for operations research analysts, contact:

➤ Institute for Operations Research and the Management Sciences, 7240 Parkway Dr., Suite 300, Hanover, MD 21076. Internet: **http://www.informs.org**

For information on operations research careers and degree programs in the Armed Forces, contact:

➤ Military Operations Research Society, 1703 N. Beauregard St., Suite 450, Alexandria, VA 22311. Internet: **http://www.mors.org**

Information on obtaining positions as operations research analysts with the Federal Government is available from the Office of Personnel Management through USA-JOBS, the Federal Government's official employment information system. This resource for locating and applying for job opportunities can be accessed through the Internet at **http://www.usajobs.opm.gov** or through an interactive voice response telephone system at (703) 724-1850 or TDD (978) 461-8404. These numbers are not toll free, and charges may result. For advice on how to find and apply for Federal jobs, see the *Occupational Outlook Quarterly* article "How to get a job in the Federal Government," online at **http://www.bls.gov/opub/ooq/2004/summer/art01.pdf.**

The Occupational Information Network (O*NET) provides information on a wide range of occupational characteristics. Links to O*NET appear at the end of the Internet version of this occupational statement, accessible at **http://www.bls.gov/ooh/ocos044.htm**

Statisticians

Significant Points

- About 30 percent of statisticians work for Federal, State, and local governments; private-industry employers include scientific research and development services, insurance carriers, and pharmaceutical and medicine manufacturing.

- A master's degree in statistics or mathematics is the minimum educational requirement for most jobs. Individuals with a degree in statistics are likely to have opportunities in a variety of fields.

Nature of the Work

Statistics is the scientific application of mathematical principles to the collection, analysis, and presentation of numerical data. *Statisticians* apply their mathematical and statistical knowledge to the design of surveys and experiments; the collection, processing, and analysis of data; and the interpretation of experiments and survey results. Opinion polls, statements about the accuracy of scales and other measuring devices, and information about average earnings in an occupation are all usually the work of statisticians.

Statisticians may apply their knowledge of statistical methods to a variety of subject areas, such as biology, economics, engineering, medicine, public health, psychology, marketing, education, and sports. Many economic, social, political, and military decisions cannot be made without statistical techniques, such as the design of experiments to gain Federal approval of a newly manufactured drug. Statistics might be needed to show whether the seemingly good results of a drug were likely because of the drug rather than just the effect of random variation in patient outcomes.

One technique that is especially useful to statisticians is sampling—obtaining information about a population of people or of a group of things by surveying a small portion of the total. For example, to determine the size of the audience for particular programs, television-rating services survey only a few thousand families, rather than all viewers. Statisticians decide where and how to gather the data, determine the type and size of the sample group, and develop the survey questionnaire or reporting form. They also prepare instructions for workers who will collect and tabulate the data. Finally, statisticians analyze, interpret, and summarize the data with the use of computer software.

In business and industry, statisticians play an important role in quality control and in product development and improvement. In an automobile company, for example, statisticians might design experiments in which engines are run until failure and breakdown in order to determine the failure time of engines exposed to extreme weather conditions. Working for a pharmaceutical company, statisticians might develop and evaluate the results of clinical trials to determine the safety and effectiveness of new medications. At a computer software firm, statisticians might help construct new statistical software packages to analyze data more accurately and efficiently. In addition to designing experiments for product development and testing, some statisticians are involved in deciding what products to manufacture, how much to charge for them, and to whom the products should be

Advanced computer programs have led to jobs for statisticians in many industries.

marketed. Statisticians also may manage assets and liabilities, determining the risks and returns of certain investments.

Nearly every government agency employs statisticians. Some government statisticians develop surveys that measure population growth, consumer prices, or unemployment. Other statisticians work for scientific, environmental, and agricultural agencies and may help figure out the average level of pesticides in drinking water, the number of endangered species living in a particular area, or the number of people afflicted with a certain disease. Statisticians also are employed in national defense agencies, determining the accuracy of new weapons and the likely effectiveness of defense strategies.

Because statistical specialists are employed in so many different kinds of work, specialists who use statistics often have different professional designations. For example, a person using statistical methods to analyze economic data may be called an *econometrician*, while statisticians in public health and medicine may hold titles such as *biostatistician* or *biometrician*.

Work environment. Statisticians generally work regular hours in an office environment. Sometimes, they may work more hours to meet deadlines.

Some statisticians travel to provide advice on research projects, supervise and set up surveys, or gather statistical data. Although e-mail and teleconferencing make it easier for statisticians to work with clients in different areas, there still are situations that require the statistician to be present, such as during meetings or while gathering data.

Training, Other Qualifications, and Advancement

A master's degree in statistics or mathematics is the minimum educational requirement, but research and academic jobs generally require a Ph.D., while Federal Government jobs require at least a bachelor's degree.

Education and training. A master's degree in statistics or mathematics usually is the minimum educational requirement for most statistician jobs. Research and academic positions usually require a Ph.D. in statistics. Beginning positions in industrial research often require a master's degree combined with several years of experience.

Jobs with the Federal Government require at least a bachelor's degree. The training required for employment as an entry-level statistician in the Federal Government is a bachelor's degree, including at least 15 semester hours of statistics or a combination of 15 hours of mathematics and statistics with at least 6 semester hours in statistics. Qualifying as a mathematical statistician in the Federal Government requires 24 semester hours of mathematics and statistics, with a minimum of 6 semester hours in statistics and 12 semester hours in an area of advanced mathematics, such as calculus, differential equations, or vector analysis.

Many colleges and universities offer degree programs in statistics, biostatistics, or mathematics, while other schools also offer graduate-level courses in applied statistics for students majoring in biology, business, economics, education, engineering, psychology, and other fields. Acceptance into graduate statistics programs does not require an undergraduate degree in statistics, although good training in mathematics is essential. Many schools also offer degrees in fields that include a sufficient number of courses in statistics to qualify graduates for some entry-level positions with the Federal Government. Required subjects for statistics majors include differential and integral calculus, statistical methods, mathematical modeling, and probability theory. Additional recommended courses for undergraduates include linear algebra, design and analysis of experiments, applied multivariate analysis, and mathematical statistics.

Because computers are used extensively for statistical applications, a strong background in computer science is highly recommended. For positions involving quality and improvement in productivity, training in engineering or physical science is useful. A background in biological, chemical, or health science is important for positions involving the preparation and testing of pharmaceutical or agricultural products. Courses in economics and business administration are valuable for many jobs in market research, business analysis, and forecasting.

Advancements in technology have made a great impact on statistics. Statistical modeling continues to become quicker and easier because of increased computational power and new analytical methods or software. Continuing education is important for statisticians, who need to stay abreast of emerging technologies to perform well.

Other qualifications. Good communication skills are important for statisticians who seek a job in private industry, because these statisticians often need to explain technical matters to persons without statistical expertise. An understanding of business and the economy also is valuable for those who plan to work in private industry.

Advancement. Beginning statisticians generally are supervised by an experienced statistician. With experience, they may advance to positions with more technical responsibility and, in some cases, supervisory duties. Opportunities for promotion are greater for people with advanced degrees. Master's and Ph.D. degree holders usually enjoy independence in their work and may engage in research, develop statistical methods, or, after a number of years of experience in a particular area, become statistical consultants.

Employment

Statisticians held about 22,600 jobs in 2008. About 20 percent of these jobs were in the Federal Government, where statisticians were concentrated in the Departments of Commerce, Agriculture, and Health and Human Services. Another 10 percent were found in State and local governments. Most of the remaining jobs were in private industry, especially in scientific research and development services, insurance carriers, and pharmaceutical and medicine manufacturing.

Projections data from the National Employment Matrix

Occupational Title	SOC Code	Employment, 2008	Projected Employment, 2018	Change, 2008-2018	
				Number	Percent
Statisticians	15-2041	22,600	25,500	2,900	13

(NOTE) Data in this table are rounded. See the discussion of the employment projections table in the *Handbook* introductory chapter on *Occupational Information Included in the Handbook.*

Job Outlook

Average employment growth is projected. Individuals with a degree in statistics should have opportunities in a variety of fields.

Employment change. Employment of statisticians is projected to grow 13 percent from 2008 to 2018, about as fast as the average for all occupations. The demand for individuals with a background is statistics is projected to grow, although some jobs will be in occupations with titles other than statistician.

The use of statistics is widespread and growing. Statistical models aid in decision making in both private industry and government. There will always be a demand for the skills statisticians provide. Technological advances are expected to spur demand for statisticians. Ever-faster computer processing allows statisticians to analyze greater amounts of data much more quickly and to gather and sort through large amounts of data that would not have been analyzed in the past. As data processing continues to become more efficient and less expensive, an increasing number of employers will want to employ statisticians to take advantage of the new information available.

Biostatisticians should experience employment growth, primarily because of the growing pharmaceuticals business. As pharmaceutical companies develop new treatments and medical technologies, biostatisticians will be needed to do research and clinical trials.

Job prospects. Individuals with a degree in statistics have opportunities in a variety of fields. For example, many jobs involve the analysis and interpretation of data from economics, biological science, psychology, computer software engineering, education, and other disciplines. Additional job openings will become available as currently employed statisticians transfer to other occupations, retire, or leave the workforce for other reasons.

Among graduates with a master's degree in statistics, those with a strong background in an allied field, such as finance, biology, engineering, or computer science, should have the best prospects of finding jobs related to their field of study.

Earnings

Median annual wage-and-salary wages of statisticians were $72,610 in May 2008. The middle 50 percent earned between $52,730 and $95,170. The lowest 10 percent earned less than $39,740, while the highest 10 percent earned more than $117,190.

The average annual salary for statisticians in the Federal Government was $92,322 in March 2009, while mathematical statisticians averaged $107,015.

Related Occupations

Among the people who work with statistics are those in such diverse occupations as the following:

Sources of Additional Information

For information about career opportunities in statistics, contact
➤ American Statistical Association, 732 North Washington St., Alexandria, VA 22314. Internet: **http://www.amstat.org**

For more information on doctoral-level careers and training in mathematics, a field closely related to statistics, contact
➤ American Mathematical Society, 201 Charles St., Providence, RI 02904. Internet: **http://www.ams.org**

Information on obtaining positions as statisticians with the Federal Government is available from the Office of Personnel Management through USAJOBS, the Federal Government's official employment information system. This resource for locating and applying for job opportunities can be accessed through the Internet at **http://www.usajobs.opm.gov** or through an interactive voice response telephone system at (703) 724-1850 or TDD (978) 461-8404. These numbers are not toll free, and charges may result.

For advice on how to find and apply for Federal jobs, see the *Occupational Outlook Quarterly* article "How to get a job in the Federal Government," online at **http://www.bls.gov/opub/ooq/2004/summer/art01.pdf.**

The Occupational Information Network (O*NET) provides information on a wide range of occupational characteristics. Links to O*NET appear at the end of the Internet version of this occupational statement, accessible at **http://www.bls.gov/ooh/ocos045.htm**

Architects, Surveyors, and Cartographers

Architects, Except Landscape and Naval

Significant Points

- About 21 percent of architects are self-employed—almost 3 times the proportion for all occupations.

- Licensing requirements include a professional degree in architecture, at least 3 years of practical work, training, and passing all divisions of the Architect Registration Examination.

- Architecture graduates may face competition, especially for jobs in the most prestigious firms.

Nature of the Work

People need places in which to live, work, play, learn, worship, meet, govern, shop, and eat. *Architects* are responsible for designing these places, whether they are private or public; indoors or out; rooms, buildings, or complexes. Architects are licensed professionals trained in the art and science of building design who develop the concepts for structures and turn those concepts into images and plans.

Architects create the overall look of buildings and other structures, but the design of a building involves far more than its appearance. Buildings also must be functional, safe, and economical and must suit the needs of the people who use them. Architects consider all these factors when they design buildings and other structures.

Architects may be involved in all phases of a construction project, from the initial discussion with the client through the final delivery of the completed structure. Their duties require specific skills—designing, engineering, managing, supervising, and communicating with clients and builders. Architects spend a great deal of time explaining their ideas to clients, construction contractors, and others. Successful architects must be able to communicate their unique vision persuasively.

It takes many years of education and experience to become a licensed architect.

The architect and client discuss the objectives, requirements, and budget of a project. In some cases, architects provide various predesign services: conducting feasibility and environmental impact studies, selecting a site, preparing cost analysis and land-use studies, or specifying the requirements the design must meet. For example, they may determine space requirements by researching the numbers and types of potential users of a building. The architect then prepares drawings and a report presenting ideas for the client to review.

After discussing and agreeing on the initial proposal, architects develop final construction plans that show the building's appearance and details for its construction. Accompanying these plans are drawings of the structural system; air-conditioning, heating, and ventilating systems; electrical systems; communications systems; plumbing; and, possibly, site and landscape plans. The plans also specify the building materials and, in some cases, the interior furnishings. In developing designs, architects follow building codes, zoning laws, fire regulations, and other ordinances, such as those requiring easy access by people who are disabled. Computer-aided design and drafting (CADD) and building information modeling (BIM) technology has replaced traditional paper and pencil as the most common method for creating design and construction drawings. Continual revision of plans on the basis of client needs and budget constraints is often necessary.

Architects may also assist clients in obtaining construction bids, selecting contractors, and negotiating construction contracts. As construction proceeds, they may visit building sites to make sure that contractors follow the design, adhere to the schedule, use the specified materials, and meet work quality standards. The job is not complete until all construction is finished, required tests are conducted, and construction costs are paid. Sometimes, architects also provide postconstruction services, such as facilities management. They advise on energy efficiency measures, evaluate how well the building design adapts to the needs of occupants, and make necessary improvements.

Often working with engineers, urban planners, interior designers, landscape architects, and other professionals, architects in fact spend a great deal of their time coordinating information from, and the work of, other professionals engaged in the same project.

They design a wide variety of buildings, such as office and apartment buildings, schools, churches, factories, hospitals, houses, and airport terminals. They also design complexes such as urban centers, college campuses, industrial parks, and entire communities.

Architects sometimes specialize in one phase of work. Some specialize in the design of one type of building—for example, hospitals, schools, or housing. Others focus on planning and predesign services or construction management and do minimal design work.

Work environment. Usually working in a comfortable environment, architects spend most of their time in offices consulting with clients, developing reports and drawings, and working with other architects and engineers. However, they often visit construction sites to review the progress of projects. In 2008, approximately 1 in 5 architects worked more than 50 hours per week, as long hours and work during nights and weekends is often necessary to meet deadlines.

Training, Other Qualifications, and Advancement

There are three main steps in becoming an architect: completing a professional degree in architecture; gaining work experience through an internship; and attaining licensure by passing the Architect Registration Exam.

Education and training. In most States, architects must hold a professional degree in architecture from one of the 117 schools of architecture that have degree programs accredited by the National Architectural Accrediting Board (NAAB). However, State architectural registration boards set their own standards, so graduation from a non-accredited program may meet the educational requirement for licensing in a few States.

Most architects earn their professional degree through a 5-year Bachelor of Architecture degree program, which is intended for students with no previous architectural training. Others earn a master's degree after completing a bachelor's degree in another field or after completing a preprofessional architecture program. A master's degree in architecture can take 1 to 5 years to complete depending on the extent of previous training in architecture.

The choice of degree depends on preference and educational background. Prospective architecture students should consider the options before committing to a program. For example, although the 5-year bachelor of architecture offers the most direct route to the professional degree, courses are specialized, and if the student does not complete the program, transferring to a program in another discipline may be difficult. A typical program includes courses in architectural history and theory, building design with an emphasis on CADD, structures, technology, construction methods, professional practice, math, physical sciences, and liberal arts. Central to most architectural programs is the design studio, where students apply the skills and concepts learned in the classroom and create drawings and three-dimensional models of their designs.

Many schools of architecture also offer postprofessional degrees for those who already have a bachelor's or master's degree in architecture or other areas. Although graduate education beyond the professional degree is not required for practicing architects, it may be useful for research, teaching, and certain specialties.

All State architectural registration boards require architecture graduates to complete a training period—usually at least 3 years—before they may sit for the licensing exam. Every State follows the training standards established by the Intern Development Program, a program of the American Institute of Architects and the National Council of Architectural Registration Boards (NCARB). These standards stipulate broad training under the supervision of a licensed architect. Most new graduates complete their training period by working as interns at architectural firms. Some States allow a portion of the training to occur in the offices of related professionals, such as engineers or general contractors. Architecture students who complete internships while still in school can count some of that time toward the 3-year training period.

Interns in architectural firms may assist in the design of one part of a project, help prepare architectural documents or drawings, build models, or prepare construction drawings on CADD. Interns also may research building codes and materials or write specifications for building materials, installation criteria, the quality of finishes, and other related details.

Licensure. All States and the District of Columbia require individuals to be licensed (registered) before they may call themselves architects and contract to provide architectural services. During the time between graduation and becoming licensed, architecture school graduates generally work in the field under the supervision of a licensed architect who takes legal responsibility for all work. Licensing requirements include a professional degree in architecture, a period of practical training or internship, and a passing score on all divisions of the Architect Registration Examination. The examination is broken into nine divisions consisting of either multiple choice or graphical questions. The eligibility period for completion of all divisions of the exam varies by State.

Most States also require some form of continuing education to maintain a license, and many others are expected to adopt mandatory continuing education. Requirements vary by State but usually involve the completion of a certain number of credits annually or biennially through workshops, formal university classes, conferences, self-study courses, or other sources.

Other qualifications. Architects must be able to communicate their ideas visually to their clients. Artistic and drawing ability is helpful, but not essential, to such communication. More important are a visual orientation and the ability to understand spatial relationships. Other important qualities for anyone interested in becoming an architect are creativity and the ability to work independently and as part of a team. Computer skills are also required for writing specifications, for 2-dimensional and 3- dimensional drafting using CADD programs, and for financial management.

Certification and advancement. A growing number of architects voluntarily seek certification by the National Council of Architectural Registration Boards. Certification is awarded after independent verification of the candidate's educational transcripts, employment record, and professional references. Certification can make it easier to become licensed across States. In fact, it is the primary requirement for reciprocity of licensing among State Boards that are NCARB members. In 2009, approximately one-third of all licensed architects had this certification.

After becoming licensed and gaining experience, architects take on increasingly complex assignments, eventually managing entire projects. In large firms, architects may advance to supervisory or managerial positions. Some architects become partners in established firms, while others set up their own practices. Some graduates with degrees in architecture also enter related fields, such as graphic, interior, or industrial design; urban planning; real estate development; civil engineering; and construction management.

Projections data from the National Employment Matrix

Occupational Title	SOC Code	Employment, 2008	Projected Employment, 2018	Change, 2008-2018	
				Number	Percent
Architects, except landscape and naval...	17-1011	141,200	164,200	22,900	16

(NOTE) Data in this table are rounded. See the discussion of the employment projections table in the *Handbook* introductory chapter on *Occupational Information Included in the Handbook.*

Employment

Architects held about 141,200 jobs in 2008. Approximately 68 percent of jobs were in the architectural, engineering, and related services industry. A small number worked for residential and nonresidential building construction firms and for government agencies responsible for housing, community planning, or construction of government buildings, such as the U.S. Departments of Defense and Interior and the General Services Administration. About 21 percent of architects are self-employed.

Job Outlook

Employment is expected to grow faster than the average for all occupations. Competition is expected, especially for positions at the most prestigious firms, and opportunities will be best for those architects who are able to distinguish themselves with their creativity.

Employment change. Employment of architects is expected to increase by 16 percent between 2008 and 2018, which is faster than the average for all occupations. Current demographic trends will lead to an increase in demand for architects. As the population of Sunbelt States continues to grow, the people living there will need new places to live and work. As the population continues to live longer and baby boomers retire, there will be a need for more healthcare facilities, nursing homes, and retirement communities. In education, buildings at all levels are getting older and enrollments continue to increase, which will require many school districts and universities to build new facilities and renovate existing ones.

In recent years, some architecture firms have outsourced the drafting of construction documents and basic design for large-scale commercial and residential projects to architecture firms overseas. This trend is expected to continue and may have a negative impact on employment growth for lower-level architects and interns who would normally gain experience by producing these drawings.

Job prospects. Besides employment growth, additional job openings will arise from the need to replace architects who transfer to other occupations or stop working for other reasons. A growing number of students are graduating with architectural degrees and some competition for entry-level jobs can be anticipated. Competition will be especially keen for jobs at the most prestigious architectural firms as prospective architects try to build their reputation. Prospective architects who have had internships while in school will have an advantage in obtaining positions after graduation. Opportunities will be best for those architects who are able to distinguish themselves from others with their creativity.

There should be demand for architects with knowledge of "green" design. Green design, also known as sustainable design, emphasizes the efficient use of resources such as energy and water, waste and pollution reduction, conservation, and environmentally friendly design, specifications, and materials. Rising energy costs and increased concern about the environment has led to many new buildings being built green.

Employment of architects is strongly tied to the activity of the construction industry and some types of construction are sensitive to cyclical changes in the economy. For example, during recessions nonresidential construction of office and retail space tends to fall as funding for these projects becomes harder to obtain and the demand for these spaces falls. Firms involved in the design of institutional buildings, such as schools, hospitals, nursing homes, and correctional facilities, will be less affected by fluctuations in the economy. Residential construction makes up a small portion of work for architects, so major changes in the housing market would not be as significant as fluctuations in the nonresidential market.

Opportunities are also geographically sensitive, and some parts of the Nation may have fewer new building projects. Also, many firms specialize in specific buildings, such as hospitals or office towers, and demand for these buildings may vary by region. Architects may find it increasingly necessary to gain reciprocity in order to compete for the best jobs and projects in other States.

Earnings

Median annual wages of wage-and-salary architects were $70,320 in May 2008. The middle 50 percent earned between $53,480 and $91,870. The lowest 10 percent earned less than $41,320, and the highest 10 percent earned more than $119,220. Those just starting their internships can expect to earn considerably less.

Earnings of partners in established architectural firms may fluctuate because of changing business conditions. Some architects may have difficulty establishing their own practices and may go through a period when their expenses are greater than their income, requiring substantial financial resources.

Many firms pay tuition and fees toward continuing education requirements for their employees.

Related Occupations

Others workers involved in the construction and maintenance of buildings include:

Architects design buildings and related structures. Other occupations with design responsibilities include:

Sources of Additional Information

Information about education and careers in architecture can be obtained from:

➤ The American Institute of Architects, 1735 New York Ave. NW, Washington, DC 20006. Internet: **http://www.aia.org**

➤ The National Architectural Accrediting Board, 1735 New York Ave. NW, Washington, DC 20006. Internet: **http://www.naab.org**

➤ The National Council of Architectural Registration Boards, Suite 700K, 1801 K St. NW, Washington, D.C. 20006. Internet: **http://www.ncarb.org**

➤ The American Institute of Architects and the American Institute of Architecture Students jointly sponsor a Web site: **http://www.archcareers.org**

The Occupational Information Network (O*NET) provides information on a wide range of occupational characteristics. Links to O*NET appear at the end of the Internet version of this occupational statement, accessible at **http://www.bls.gov/ooh/ocos038.htm**

Landscape Architects

Significant Points

● About 21 percent of landscape architects are self-employed—almost 3 times the proportion for all occupations.

● Almost all States require landscape architects to be licensed, which generally requires a degree in landscape architecture from an accredited school, work experience, and a passing score on the Landscape Architect Registration Exam.

● Good job opportunities are expected, but new graduates may face competition for jobs in the largest and most prestigious firms.

Nature of the Work

People enjoy attractively designed gardens, public parks and playgrounds, residential areas, college campuses, shopping centers, golf courses, and parkways. *Landscape architects* design these areas so they are not only functional but also beautiful and harmonious with the natural environment. They plan the location of buildings, roads, and walkways, and the arrangement of flowers, shrubs, and trees. They also design and plan the restoration of natural places disturbed by humans, such as wetlands, stream corridors, mined areas, and forested land.

Working with building architects, surveyors, and engineers, landscape architects help determine the best arrangement of roads and buildings. They also collaborate with environmental scientists, foresters, and other professionals to find the best way to conserve or restore natural resources. Once these decisions are made, landscape architects create detailed plans indicating new topography, vegetation, walkways, and other landscaping details, such as fountains and decorative features.

In planning a site, landscape architects first consider the purpose of the project and the funds available. They then analyze the natural elements of the site, such as the climate, soil, slope of the land, drainage, and vegetation. They also assess existing buildings, roads, walkways, and utilities to determine what improvements are necessary. At all stages, they evaluate the project's impact on the local ecosystem.

After studying and analyzing the site, landscape architects prepare a preliminary design. To address the needs of the client, as well as the conditions at the site, they frequently make changes before a final design is approved. They also take into account any local, State, or Federal regulations, such as those protecting wetlands or historic resources. In preparing designs, computer-aided design (CAD) has become an essential tool for most landscape architects. Many landscape architects also use video simulation to help clients envision the proposed ideas and plans. For larger scale site planning, landscape architects also use geographic information systems (GIS) technology, a computer mapping system.

Throughout all phases of planning and design, landscape architects consult with other professionals, such as civil engineers, hydrologists, or building architects, involved in the project. Once the design is complete, they prepare a proposal for the client. They produce detailed plans of the site, including written reports, sketches, models, photographs, land-use studies, and cost estimates and submit them for approval by the client and by regulatory agencies. When the plans are approved, landscape architects prepare working drawings showing all existing and proposed features. They also outline in detail the methods of construction and draw up a list of necessary materials. Landscape architects then monitor the implementation of their design, while general contractors or landscape contractors usually direct the actual construction of the site and installation of plantings.

Landscape architects are involved in a wide variety of construction projects.

Some landscape architects work on a variety of types of projects. Others specialize in a particular area, such as street and highway beautification, waterfront improvement projects, parks and playgrounds, or shopping centers. Still others work in regional planning and resource management; feasibility, environmental impact, and cost studies; or site construction. Increasingly, landscape architects work in environmental remediation, such as preservation and restoration of wetlands or abatement of stormwater run-off in new developments. Historic landscape preservation and restoration is another area where landscape architects increasingly play a role.

Landscape architects who work for government agencies do site and landscape design for government buildings, parks, and other public lands, as well as park and recreation planning in national parks and forests. In addition, they may prepare environmental impact statements and studies on environmental issues such as public land-use planning.

Work environment. Landscape architects spend most of their time in offices creating plans and designs, preparing models and cost estimates, doing research, or attending meetings with clients and other professionals involved in a design or planning project. The remainder of their time is spent at the site. During the design and planning stage, landscape architects visit and analyze the site to verify that the design can be incorporated into the landscape. After the plans and specifications are completed, they may spend additional time at the site observing or supervising the construction. Those who work in large national or regional firms can spend considerably more time out of the office traveling to sites.

Although many landscape architects work approximately 40 hours per week, about 1 in 5 worked more than 50 hours per week in 2008, as long hours and work during nights and weekends is often necessary to meet deadlines.

Training, Other Qualifications, and Advancement

Almost every State requires landscape architects to be licensed. While requirements vary among the States, they usually include a degree in landscape architecture from an accredited school; work experience; and a passing score on the Landscape Architect Registration Exam.

Education and training. A bachelor's or master's degree in landscape architecture usually is necessary for entry into the profession. Sixty-seven colleges and universities offered undergraduate or graduate programs in landscape architecture that were accredited by the Landscape Architecture Accreditation Board of the American Society of Landscape Architects in 2009. There are two undergraduate professional degrees: a Bachelor of Landscape Architecture (BLA) and a Bachelor of Science in Landscape Architecture (BSLA). These programs usually require 4 or 5 years of study for completion. Those who hold an undergraduate degree in a field other than landscape architecture can enroll in a Master of Landscape Architecture (MLA) graduate degree program, which typically takes 3 years of full-time study to complete. Those who hold undergraduate degrees in landscape architecture can earn their MLA in 2 years.

Courses required in these programs usually include subjects such as surveying, landscape design and construction, landscape ecology, site design, and urban and regional planning. Other courses include history of landscape architecture, plant and soil science, geology, professional practice, and general management. The design studio is a key component of any curriculum. Whenever possible, students are assigned real projects, providing them with valuable hands-on experience. While working on these projects, students become proficient in the use of computer-aided design, model building, geographic information systems, and video simulation.

Many employers recommend that prospective landscape architects complete a summer internship with a landscape architecture firm during their formal educational studies. Interns are able to hone their technical skills and gain an understanding of the day-to-day operations of the business, including how to win clients, generate fees, and work within a budget.

Licensure and certification. As of 2009, there were 49 States that required landscape architects to be licensed. Licensing is based on the Landscape Architect Registration Examination (L.A.R.E.), sponsored by the Council of Landscape Architectural Registration Boards, and administered in two portions, a graphic portion and a multiple-choice portion. Applicants wishing to take the exam usually need a degree from an accredited school plus 1 to 4 years of work experience under the supervision of a licensed landscape architect, although standards vary by State. For those without an accredited landscape architecture degree, most states provide alternative paths to qualify to take the L.A.R.E., usually requiring more work experience. Currently, 13 States require that a State examination be passed in addition to the L.A.R.E. to satisfy registration requirements. State examinations focus on laws, environmental regulations, plants, soils, climate, and any other characteristics unique to the State.

Because requirements for licensure are not uniform, landscape architects may find it difficult to transfer their registration from one State to another. National standards include graduating from an accredited program, serving 3 years of internship under the supervision of a registered landscape architect, and passing the L.A.R.E. can satisfy requirements in most States. By meeting national requirements, a landscape architect can also obtain certification from the Council of Landscape Architectural Registration Boards which can be useful in obtaining reciprocal licensure in other States.

In States where licensure is required, new hires may be called "apprentices" or "intern landscape architects" until they be-

Projections data from the National Employment Matrix

Occupational Title	SOC Code	Employment, 2008	Projected Employment, 2018	Change, 2008-2018	
				Number	Percent
Landscape architects	17-1012	26,700	32,000	5,300	20

(NOTE) Data in this table are rounded. See the discussion of the employment projections table in the *Handbook* introductory chapter on *Occupational Information Included in the Handbook.*

come licensed. Their duties vary depending on the type and size of the employing firm. They may do project research or prepare working drawings, construction documents, or base maps of the area to be designed. Some are allowed to participate in the actual design of a project. However, interns must perform all work under the supervision of a licensed landscape architect. Additionally, all drawings and specifications must be signed and sealed by the licensed landscape architect, who takes legal responsibility for the work. After gaining experience and becoming licensed, landscape architects usually can carry a design through all stages of development.

A majority of States require some form of continuing education to maintain a license. Requirements usually involve the completion of workshops, seminars, formal university classes, conferences, self-study courses, or other classes.

The Federal Government does not require its landscape architects to be licensed. Candidates for entry positions with the Federal Government should have a bachelor's or master's degree in landscape architecture.

Other qualifications.   People planning a career in landscape architecture should appreciate nature, enjoy working with their hands, and possess strong analytical skills. Creative vision and artistic talent also are desirable qualities. Good oral and written communication skills are essential. Landscape architects must be able to convey their ideas to other professionals and clients and to make presentations before large groups. Landscape architects must also be able to draft and design using CAD software. Knowledge of computer applications of all kinds, including word processing, desktop publishing, and spreadsheets is also important. Landscape architects use these tools to develop presentations, proposals, reports, and land impact studies for clients, colleagues, and superiors.

Many landscape architects are self-employed. Self-discipline, business acumen, and good marketing skills are important qualities for those who choose to open their own business. Even with these qualities, however, some may struggle while building a client base.

Advancement.   After several years, landscape architects may become project managers, taking on the responsibility for meeting schedules and budgets, in addition to overseeing the project design. Later, they may become associates or partners of a firm, with a proprietary interest in the business.

Those with landscape architecture training also qualify for jobs closely related to landscape architecture, and may, after gaining some experience, become construction supervisors, land or environmental planners, or landscape consultants.

Employment

Landscape architects held about 26,700 jobs in 2008. About 51 percent of landscape architects were employed in architectural, engineering, and related services. State and local governments employed approximately 6 percent. About 21 percent of landscape architects were self-employed.

Employment of landscape architects is concentrated in urban and suburban areas throughout the country; some landscape architects work in rural areas, particularly those employed by the Federal Government to plan and design parks and recreation areas.

Job Outlook

Employment is expected to grow much faster than the average for all occupations. There should be good job prospects overall, but new graduates may face competition for jobs in the largest and most prestigious landscape architecture firms.

Employment change.   Employment of landscape architects is expected to increase by 20 percent during the 2008–18 decade, which is much faster than the average for all occupations. Employment will grow as the planning and development of new construction, together with the continued redevelopment of existing buildings, creates more opportunities for landscape architects. With land costs rising and the public desiring more beautiful spaces, the importance of good site planning and landscape design is growing.

Additionally, environmental concerns and increased demand for sustainably designed construction projects will spur demand for the services of landscape architects. For example, landscape architects are involved in designing green roofs that are covered with some form of vegetation, and that can significantly reduce costs associated with heating and cooling a building, as well as reduce air and water pollution. Landscape architects will also be needed to design plans to manage storm water run-off in a way that avoids pollution of waterways and conserves water resources.

Job prospects.   There should be good job opportunities overall as demand for landscape architecture services increases, but new graduates can expect to face competition for jobs in the largest and most prestigious landscape architecture firms. Many employers prefer to hire entry-level landscape architects who have internship experience, which significantly reduces the amount of on-the-job training required. Opportunities will be best for landscape architects who develop strong technical skills—such as computer design—communication skills, and knowledge of environmental codes and regulations. Those with additional training or experience in urban planning increase their opportunities for employment in landscape architecture firms that specialize in site planning as well as landscape design.

Opportunities will vary by year and geographic region, depending on local economic conditions. During a recession, when real estate sales and construction slow down, landscape architects may face greater competition for jobs and sometimes layoffs. But because landscape architects can work on many different types of projects, they may have steadier work than other design professionals when traditional construction slows.

In addition to growth, the need to replace landscape architects who retire or leave the labor force will produce some job openings.

Earnings

In May 2008, median annual wages for landscape architects were $58,960. The middle 50 percent earned between $45,840 and $77,610. The lowest 10 percent earned less than $36,520 and the highest 10 percent earned over $97,370. Architectural, engineering, and related services employed more landscape architects than any other group of industries, and there the median annual wages were $59,610 in May 2008.

Related Occupations

Landscape architects use their knowledge of design, construction, land-use planning, and environmental issues to develop a landscape project. Others whose work requires similar skills are:

Sources of Additional Information

Additional information, including a list of colleges and universities offering accredited programs in landscape architecture, is available from:

➤ American Society of Landscape Architects, Career Information, 636 Eye St. NW., Washington, DC 20001-3736. Internet: **http://www.asla.org**

General information on registration or licensing requirements is available from:

➤ Council of Landscape Architectural Registration Boards, 3949 Pender Dr., Suite 120, Vienna, VA 22030. Internet: **http://www.clarb.org**

The Occupational Information Network (O*NET) provides information on a wide range of occupational characteristics. Links to O*NET appear at the end of the Internet version of this occupational statement, accessible at **http://www.bls.gov/ooh/ocos039.htm**

Surveyors, Cartographers, Photogrammetrists, and Surveying and Mapping Technicians

Significant Points

- About 7 out of 10 jobs were in architectural, engineering, and related services.

- Employment is expected to grow faster than the average for all occupations.

- Surveyors, cartographers, and photogrammetrists who have a bachelor's degree and strong technical skills should have favorable job prospects.

Nature of the Work

Surveyors, cartographers, photogrammetrists, and surveying and mapping technicians are responsible for measuring and mapping the Earth's surface. *Surveyors* establish official land, airspace, and water boundaries. They write descriptions of land for deeds, leases, and other legal documents; define airspace for airports; and take measurements of construction and mineral sites. Other surveyors provide data about the shape, contour, location, elevation, or dimension of land or land features. *Cartographers and photogrammetrists* collect, analyze, interpret, and map geographic information using data from surveys and photographs. *Surveying and mapping technicians* assist these professionals by collecting data in the field, making calculations, and helping with computer-aided drafting. Collectively, these occupations play key roles in the field of geospatial information.

Surveyors measure distances, directions, and angles between points on, above, and below the Earth's surface. In the field, they select known survey reference points and determine the precise location of important features in the survey area using specialized equipment. Surveyors also research legal records, look for evidence of previous boundaries, and analyze data to determine the location of boundary lines. They are sometimes called to provide expert testimony in court regarding their work or the work of other surveyors. Surveyors also record their results, verify the accuracy of data, and prepare plots, maps, and reports.

Some surveyors perform specialized functions that support the work of other surveyors, cartographers, and photogrammetrists. For example, *geodetic surveyors* use high-accuracy techniques, including satellite observations, to measure large areas of the earth's surface. *Geophysical prospecting surveyors* mark sites for subsurface exploration, usually to look for petroleum. *Marine or hydrographic surveyors* survey harbors, rivers, and other bodies of water to determine shorelines, the topography of the bottom, water depth, and other features.

Surveyors use the Global Positioning System (GPS) to locate reference points with a high degree of precision. To use this system, a surveyor places a satellite signal receiver—a small instrument mounted on a tripod—on a desired point, and another receiver on a point for which the geographic position is known. The receiver simultaneously collects information from several satellites and the known reference point to establish a precise position. The receiver also can be placed in a vehicle for tracing out road systems. Because receivers now come in different sizes and shapes, and because the cost of receivers has fallen, much more surveying work can be done with GPS. Surveyors then interpret and check the results produced by GPS.

Field measurements are often taken by a survey party that gathers the information needed by the surveyor. A typical survey party consists of a *party chief* and one or more surveying technicians and helpers. The party chief, who may be either a surveyor or a senior surveying technician, leads day-to-day work activities. Surveying technicians assist the party chief by adjusting and operating surveying instruments, such as the total station, which measures and records angles and distances simultaneously. Surveying technicians compile notes, make sketches, and enter the data obtained from surveying instruments into computers either in the field or at the office.

Photogrammetrists and cartographers measure, map, and chart the Earth's surface. Their work involves everything from performing geographical research and compiling data to producing maps. They collect, analyze, and interpret both spatial data—such as latitude, longitude, elevation, and distance—and nonspatial data—such as population density, land-use patterns, annual precipitation levels, and demographic characteristics. Their maps may give both physical and social characteristics of the land. They prepare maps in either digital or graphic form, using information provided by geodetic surveys and remote sensing systems including aerial cameras, satellites, light-imaging detection and ranging (LIDAR), or other technologies.

LIDAR uses lasers attached to planes and other equipment to digitally map the topography of the Earth. It is often more accurate than traditional surveying methods and also can be used to collect other forms of data, such as the location and density of forests. Data developed by LIDAR can be used by surveyors, cartographers, and photogrammetrists to provide spatial information to specialists in geology, seismology, forestry, construction, and other fields.

Geographic Information Systems (GIS) have become an integral tool for surveyors, cartographers, photogrammetrists, and surveying and mapping technicians. Workers use GIS to assemble, integrate, analyze, and display data about location in a digital format. They also use GIS to compile information from a variety of sources. GIS typically are used to make maps which combine information useful for environmental studies, geology, engineering, planning, business marketing, and other disciplines. As more of these systems are developed, many mapping specialists are being called *geographic information specialists*.

Work environment. Surveyors and surveying technicians usually work an 8-hour day, 5 days a week and may spend a lot of time outdoors. Sometimes, they work longer hours during the summer, when weather and light conditions are most suitable for fieldwork. Construction-related work may be limited during times of inclement weather.

Surveyors and technicians engage in active, sometimes strenuous, work. They often stand for long periods, walk considerable distances, and climb hills with heavy packs of instruments and other equipment. They also can be exposed to all types of weather. Traveling is sometimes part of the job, and surveyors and technicians may commute long distances, stay away from home overnight, or temporarily relocate near a survey site. Surveyors also work indoors while planning surveys, searching court records for deed information, analyzing data, and preparing reports and maps.

Cartographers and photogrammetrists spend most of their time in offices using computers. However, certain jobs may require extensive field work to verify results and acquire data.

Training, Other Qualifications, and Advancement

Most surveyors, cartographers, and photogrammetrists have a bachelor's degree in surveying or a related field. Every State requires that surveyors be licensed.

Education and training. In the past, many people with little formal training started as members of survey crews and worked their way up to become licensed surveyors, but this has become increasingly difficult. Now, most surveyors need a bachelor's degree. A number of universities offer bachelor's degree programs in surveying, and many community colleges, technical institutes, and vocational schools offer 1-year, 2-year, and 3-year programs in surveying or surveying technology.

Cartographers and photogrammetrists usually have a bachelor's degree in cartography, geography, surveying, engineering, forestry, computer science, or a physical science, although a few enter these positions after working as technicians. With the development of GIS, cartographers and photogrammetrists need more education and stronger technical skills—including more experience with computers—than in the past.

Most cartographic and photogrammetric technicians also have specialized postsecondary education. High school students interested in surveying and cartography should take courses in algebra, geometry, trigonometry, drafting, mechanical drawing, and computer science.

Licensure. All 50 States and all U.S. territories license surveyors. For licensure, most State licensing boards require that individuals pass a series of written examinations given by the National Council of Examiners for Engineering and Surveying (NCEES). After passing a first exam, the Fundamentals of Surveying, most candidates work under the supervision of an experienced surveyor for 4 years before taking a second exam,

Land surveyors frequently take measurements in the field.

Projections data from the National Employment Matrix

Occupational Title	SOC Code	Employment, 2008	Projected Employment, 2018	Change, 2008-2018	
				Number	Percent
Surveyors, cartographers, photogrammetrists, and surveying and mapping technicians......	–	147,000	174,500	27,600	19
Surveyors, cartographers, and photogrammetrists........	17-1020	70,000	81,800	11,900	17
Cartographers and photogrammetrists.....................	17-1021	12,300	15,600	3,300	27
Surveyors	17-1022	57,600	66,200	8,600	15
Surveying and mapping technicians	17-3031	77,000	92,700	15,700	20

(NOTE) Data in this table are rounded. See the discussion of the employment projections table in the *Handbook* introductory chapter on *Occupational Information Included in the Handbook.*

the Principles and Practice of Surveying. Additionally, most States also require surveyors to pass a written examination prepared by the State licensing board.

Specific requirements for training and education vary among the States. An increasing number of States require a bachelor's degree in surveying or in a closely related field, such as civil engineering or forestry, regardless of the number of years of experience. Some States require the degree to be from a school accredited by the Accreditation Board for Engineering and Technology (ABET). Most States also have a continuing education requirement.

Additionally, a number of States require cartographers and photogrammetrists to be licensed as surveyors, and some States have specific licenses for photogrammetrists.

Other qualifications. Surveyors, cartographers, and photogrammetrists should be able to visualize objects, distances, sizes, and abstract forms. They must work with precision and accuracy because mistakes can be costly. Surveying and mapping is a cooperative operation, so good interpersonal skills and the ability to work as part of a team is important.

Certification and advancement. High school graduates with no formal training in surveying usually start as apprentices. Beginners with postsecondary school training in surveying usually can start as technicians or assistants. With on-the-job experience and formal training in surveying—either in an institutional program or from a correspondence school—workers may advance to senior survey technician, then to party chief. Depending on State licensing requirements, they may advance to licensed surveyor in some cases.

The National Society of Professional Surveyors, a member organization of the American Congress on Surveying and Mapping, has a voluntary certification program for surveying technicians. Technicians are certified at four levels requiring progressive amounts of experience and the passing of written examinations. Although not required for State licensure, many employers require certification for promotion to positions with greater responsibilities.

The American Society for Photogrammetry and Remote Sensing (ASPRS) has voluntary certification programs for technicians and professionals in photogrammetry, remote sensing, and GIS. To qualify for these professional distinctions, individuals must meet work experience and training standards and pass a written examination. The professional recognition these certifications bestow can help workers gain promotions.

Employment

Surveyors, cartographers, photogrammetrists, and surveying technicians held about 147,000 jobs in 2008. Employment was distributed by occupational specialty as follows:

Surveying and mapping technicians............................77,000
Surveyors..57,600
Cartographers and photogrammetrists 12,300

The architectural, engineering, and related services industry—including firms that provided surveying and mapping services to other industries on a contract basis—provided 7 out of 10 jobs for these workers. Federal, State, and local governmental agencies provided about 15 percent of these jobs. Major Federal Government employers are the U.S. Geological Survey (USGS), the Bureau of Land Management (BLM), the National Oceanic and Atmospheric Administration, the U.S. Forest Service, and the Army Corps of Engineers. Most surveyors in State and local government work for highway departments or urban planning and redevelopment agencies. Utility companies also employ surveyors, cartographers, photogrammetrists, and surveying technicians.

Job Outlook

These occupations should experience faster than average employment growth. Surveyors, cartographers, and photogrammetrists who have a bachelor's degree and strong technical skills should have favorable job prospects.

Employment change. Employment of surveyors, cartographers, photogrammetrists, and surveying and mapping technicians is expected to grow 19 percent from 2008 to 2018, which is faster than the average for all occupations. Increasing demand for fast, accurate, and complete geographic information will be the main source of job growth.

An increasing number of firms are interested in geographic information and its applications. For example, GIS can be used to create maps and information used in emergency planning, security, marketing, urban planning, natural resource exploration, construction, and other applications. Also, the increased popularity of online interactive mapping systems and GPS devices have created a higher demand for and awareness of current and accurate digital geographic information among consumers.

Growth in construction stemming from increases in the population and the related need to upgrade the Nation's infrastructure will cause growth for surveyors and surveying technicians who ensure that projects are completed with precision and in line with original plans. These workers are usually the first on the job for any major construction project, and they provide information and recommendations to engineers, architects, contractors, and other professionals during all phases of a construction project.

Job prospects. In addition to openings from growth, job openings will continue to arise from the need to replace workers who transfer to other occupations or who leave the labor force altogether. Many cartographers and surveyors are approaching retirement age. Surveyors, cartographers, and photogrammetrists who have a bachelor's degree and strong technical skills should have favorable job prospects.

Opportunities for surveyors, cartographers, photogrammetrists, and technicians should remain concentrated in engineering, surveying, mapping, building inspection, and drafting services firms. Increasing demand for geographic data, as opposed to traditional surveying services, will mean better opportunities for mapping technicians and professionals who are involved in the development and use of GIS and digital mapmaking.

The demand for traditional surveying services is strongly tied to construction activity and opportunities will vary by year and geographic region, depending on local economic conditions. During a recession, when real estate sales and construction slow down, surveyors and surveying technicians may face greater competition for jobs and sometimes layoffs. However, because these workers can work on many different types of projects, they may have steadier work than other workers when construction slows.

Earnings

Median annual wages of cartographers and photogrammetrists were $51,180 in May 2008. The middle 50 percent earned between $39,510 and $69,220. The lowest 10 percent earned less than $31,440 and the highest 10 percent earned more than $87,620.

Median annual wages of surveyors were $52,980 in May 2008. The middle 50 percent earned between $38,800 and $70,010. The lowest 10 percent earned less than $29,600 and the highest 10 percent earned more than $85,620. Median annual wages of surveyors employed in architectural, engineering, and related services were $51,870 in May 2008.

Median annual wages of surveying and mapping technicians were $35,120 in May 2008. The middle 50 percent earned between $27,370 and $45,860. The lowest 10 percent earned less than $21,680, and the highest 10 percent earned more than $58,030. Median annual wages of surveying and mapping technicians employed in architectural, engineering, and related services were $33,220 in May 2008, while those

employed by local governments had median annual wages of $40,510.

Related Occupations

Workers who use surveying data in land development and construction include:

	Page
Architects, except landscape and naval	151
Engineers	161
Landscape architects	154

Cartography is related to the work of:

Environmental scientists and specialists	199
Social scientists, other	226
Urban and regional planners	220

Sources of Additional Information

For career information on surveyors, cartographers, photogrammetrists, and surveying technicians, contact:
➤ American Congress on Surveying and Mapping, 6 Montgomery Village Ave., Suite 403, Gaithersburg, MD 20879. Internet: **http://www.acsm.net**

Information about career opportunities, licensure requirements, and the surveying technician certification program is available from:
➤ National Society of Professional Surveyors, 6 Montgomery Village Ave., Suite 403, Gaithersburg, MD 20879. Internet: **http://www.nspsmo.org**

For information on a career as a geodetic surveyor, contact:
➤ American Association of Geodetic Surveying (AAGS), 6 Montgomery Village Ave., Suite 403, Gaithersburg, MD 20879. Internet: **http://www.aagsmo.org**

For career information on photogrammetrists, photogrammetric technicians, remote sensing scientists, and image-based cartographers or geographic information system specialists, contact:
➤ ASPRS: Imaging and Geospatial Information Society, 5410 Grosvenor Lane, Suite 210, Bethesda, MD 20814-2160. Internet: **http://www.asprs.org**

Information on careers in remote sensing, photogrammetry, surveying, GIS, and other geography-related disciplines also is available from the Spring 2005 *Occupational Outlook Quarterly* article, "Geography Jobs", available online at **http://www.bls.gov/opub/ooq/2005/spring/art01.pdf.**

The Occupational Information Network (O*NET) provides information on a wide range of occupational characteristics. Links to O*NET appear at the end of the Internet version of this occupational statement, accessible at **http://www.bls.gov/ooh/ocos040.htm**

Engineers

Significant Points

- Employment is projected to grow about as fast as the average for all occupations, although growth will vary by specialty; overall job opportunities for engineers are expected to be good.

- A bachelor's degree in engineering is required for most entry-level jobs, but some research positions may require a graduate degree.

- Starting salaries are among the highest of all college graduates.

- Continuing education is critical for engineers in order to keep up with improvements in technology.

Nature of the Work

Engineers apply the principles of science and mathematics to develop economical solutions to technical problems. Their work is the link between scientific discoveries and the commercial applications that meet societal and consumer needs.

Many engineers develop new products. During the process, they consider several factors. For example, in developing an industrial robot, engineers specify the functional requirements precisely; design and test the robot's components; integrate the components to produce the final design; and evaluate the design's overall effectiveness, cost, reliability, and safety. This process applies to the development of many different products, such as chemicals, computers, powerplants, helicopters, and toys.

In addition to their involvement in design and development, many engineers work in testing, production, or maintenance. These engineers supervise production in factories, determine the causes of a component's failure, and test manufactured products to maintain quality. They also estimate the time and cost required to complete projects. Supervisory engineers are responsible for major components or entire projects. (See the statement on engineering and natural sciences managers elsewhere in the *Handbook*.)

Engineers use computers extensively to produce and analyze designs; to simulate and test how a machine, structure, or system operates; to generate specifications for parts; to monitor the quality of products; and to control the efficiency of processes. Nanotechnology, which involves the creation of high-performance materials and components by integrating atoms and molecules, also is introducing entirely new principles to the design process.

Most engineers specialize. Following are details on the 17 engineering specialties covered in the Federal Government's Standard Occupational Classification (SOC) system. Numerous other specialties are recognized by professional societies, and each of the major branches of engineering has numerous subdivisions. Civil engineering, for example, includes structural and transportation engineering, and materials engineering includes ceramic, metallurgical, and polymer engineering. Engineers also may specialize in one industry, such as motor vehicles, or in one type of technology, such as turbines or semiconductor materials.

Aerospace engineers design, test, and supervise the manufacture of aircraft, spacecraft, and missiles. Those who work with aircraft are called *aeronautical engineers*, and those working specifically with spacecraft are *astronautical engineers*. Aerospace engineers develop new technologies for use in aviation, defense systems, and space exploration, often specializing in areas such as structural design, guidance, navigation and control, instrumentation and communication, and production methods. They also may specialize in a particular type of aerospace product, such as commercial aircraft, military fighter jets, helicopters, spacecraft, or missiles and rockets, and may become experts in aerodynamics, thermodynamics, celestial mechanics, propulsion, acoustics, or guidance and control systems.

Agricultural engineers apply their knowledge of engineering technology and science to agriculture and the efficient use of biological resources. Accordingly, they also are referred to as *biological and agricultural engineers*. They design agricultural machinery, equipment, sensors, processes, and structures, such as those used for crop storage. Some engineers specialize in areas such as power systems and machinery design, structural and environmental engineering, and food and bioprocess engineering. They develop ways to conserve soil and water and to improve the processing of agricultural products. Agricultural engineers often work in research and development, production, sales, or management.

Biomedical engineers develop devices and procedures that solve medical and health-related problems by combining their knowledge of biology and medicine with engineering principles and practices. Many do research, along with medical scientists, to develop and evaluate systems and products such as artificial organs, prostheses (artificial devices that replace missing body parts), instrumentation, medical information systems, and health management and care delivery systems. Biomedical engineers also may design devices used in various medical procedures, imaging systems such as magnetic resonance

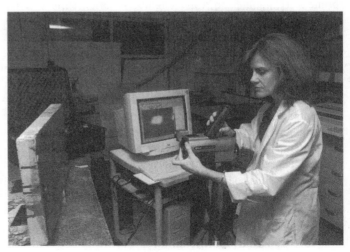

Engineers design tests for new products.

imaging (MRI), and devices for automating insulin injections or controlling body functions. Most engineers in this specialty need a sound background in another engineering specialty, such as mechanical or electronics engineering, in addition to specialized biomedical training. Some specialties within biomedical engineering are biomaterials, biomechanics, medical imaging, rehabilitation engineering, and orthopedic engineering.

Chemical engineers apply the principles of chemistry to solve problems involving the production or use of chemicals and other products. They design equipment and processes for large-scale chemical manufacturing, plan and test methods of manufacturing products and treating byproducts, and supervise production. Chemical engineers also work in a variety of manufacturing industries other than chemical manufacturing, such as those producing energy, electronics, food, clothing, and paper. In addition, they work in healthcare, biotechnology, and business services. Chemical engineers apply principles of physics, mathematics, and mechanical and electrical engineering, as well as chemistry. Some may specialize in a particular chemical process, such as oxidation or polymerization. Others specialize in a particular field, such as nanomaterials, or in the development of specific products. They must be aware of all aspects of chemical manufacturing and how the manufacturing process affects the environment and the safety of workers and consumers.

Civil engineers design and supervise the construction of roads, buildings, airports, tunnels, dams, bridges, and water supply and sewage systems. They must consider many factors in the design process from the construction costs and expected lifetime of a project to government regulations and potential environmental hazards such as earthquakes and hurricanes. Civil engineering, considered one of the oldest engineering disciplines, encompasses many specialties. The major ones are structural, water resources, construction, transportation, and geotechnical engineering. Many civil engineers hold supervisory or administrative positions, from supervisor of a construction site to city engineer. Others may work in design, construction, research, and teaching.

Computer hardware engineers research, design, develop, test, and oversee the manufacture and installation of computer hardware, including computer chips, circuit boards, computer systems, and related equipment such as keyboards, routers, and printers. (Computer software engineers—often simply called computer engineers—design and develop the software systems that control computers. These workers are covered elsewhere in the *Handbook*.) The work of computer hardware engineers is similar to that of electronics engineers in that they may design and test circuits and other electronic components; however, computer hardware engineers do that work only as it relates to computers and computer-related equipment. The rapid advances in computer technology are largely a result of the research, development, and design efforts of these engineers.

Electrical engineers design, develop, test, and supervise the manufacture of electrical equipment. Some of this equipment includes electric motors; machinery controls, lighting, and wiring in buildings; radar and navigation systems; communications systems; and power generation, control, and transmission devices used by electric utilities. Electrical engineers also design the electrical systems of automobiles and aircraft. Al-

though the terms *electrical* and *electronics engineering* often are used interchangeably in academia and industry, electrical engineers traditionally have focused on the generation and supply of power, whereas electronics engineers have worked on applications of electricity to control systems or signal processing. Electrical engineers specialize in areas such as power systems engineering or electrical equipment manufacturing.

Electronics engineers, except computer, are responsible for a wide range of technologies, from portable music players to global positioning systems (GPS), which can continuously provide the location of, for example, a vehicle. Electronics engineers design, develop, test, and supervise the manufacture of electronic equipment such as broadcast and communications systems. Many electronics engineers also work in areas closely related to computers. However, engineers whose work is related exclusively to computer hardware are considered computer hardware engineers. Electronics engineers specialize in areas such as communications, signal processing, and control systems or have a specialty within one of these areas—control systems or aviation electronics, for example.

Environmental engineers use the principles of biology and chemistry to develop solutions to environmental problems. They are involved in water and air pollution control, recycling, waste disposal, and public health issues. Environmental engineers conduct hazardous-waste management studies in which they evaluate the significance of the hazard, advise on its treatment and containment, and develop regulations to prevent mishaps. They design municipal water supply and industrial wastewater treatment systems, conduct research on the environmental impact of proposed construction projects, analyze scientific data, and perform quality-control checks. Environmental engineers are concerned with local and worldwide environmental issues. Some may study and attempt to minimize the effects of acid rain, global warming, automobile emissions, and ozone depletion. They also may be involved in the protection of wildlife. Many environmental engineers work as consultants, helping their clients to comply with regulations, prevent environmental damage, and clean up hazardous sites.

Health and safety engineers, except mining safety engineers and inspectors, prevent harm to people and property by applying their knowledge of systems engineering and me-

Some engineers, like mining and civil engineers, work outside.

chanical, chemical, and human performance principles. Using this specialized knowledge, they identify and measure potential hazards, such as the risk of fires or the dangers involved in handling toxic chemicals. They recommend appropriate loss prevention measures according to their probability of harm and potential damage. Health and safety engineers develop procedures and designs to reduce the risk of illness, injury, or damage. Some work in manufacturing industries to ensure that the designs of new products do not create unnecessary hazards. They must be able to anticipate, recognize, and evaluate hazardous conditions, as well as develop hazard control methods.

Industrial engineers determine the most effective ways to use the basic factors of production—people, machines, materials, information, and energy—to make a product or provide a service. They are concerned primarily with increasing productivity through the management of people, methods of business organization, and technology. To maximize efficiency, industrial engineers study product requirements carefully and then design manufacturing and information systems to meet those requirements with the help of mathematical methods and models. They develop management control systems to aid in financial planning and cost analysis, and they design production planning and control systems to coordinate activities and ensure product quality. They also design or improve systems for the physical distribution of goods and services and determine the most efficient plant locations. Industrial engineers develop wage and salary administration systems and job evaluation programs. Many industrial engineers move into management positions because the work is closely related to the work of managers.

Marine engineers and naval architects are involved in the design, construction, and maintenance of ships, boats, and related equipment. They design and supervise the construction of everything from aircraft carriers to submarines and from sailboats to tankers. Naval architects work on the basic design of ships, including the form and stability of hulls. Marine engineers work on the propulsion, steering, and other systems of ships. Marine engineers and naval architects apply knowledge from a range of fields to the entire process by which water vehicles are designed and produced. Other workers who operate or supervise the operation of marine machinery on ships and other vessels sometimes may be called marine engineers or, more frequently, ship engineers, but they do different work and are covered under water transportation occupations elsewhere in the *Handbook*.

Materials engineers are involved in the development, processing, and testing of the materials used to create a range of products, from computer chips and aircraft wings to golf clubs and snow skis. They work with metals, ceramics, plastics, semiconductors, and composites to create new materials that meet certain mechanical, electrical, and chemical requirements. They also are involved in selecting materials for new applications. Materials engineers have developed the ability to create and then study materials at an atomic level, using advanced processes to replicate the characteristics of those materials and their components with computers. Most materials engineers specialize in a particular material. For example,

metallurgical engineers specialize in metals such as steel, and ceramic engineers develop ceramic materials and the processes for making them into useful products such as glassware or fiber-optic communication lines.

Mechanical engineers research, design, develop, manufacture, and test tools, engines, machines, and other mechanical devices. Mechanical engineering is one of the broadest engineering disciplines. Engineers in this discipline work on power-producing machines such as electric generators, internal combustion engines, and steam and gas turbines. They also work on power-using machines such as refrigeration and air-conditioning equipment, machine tools, material-handling systems, elevators and escalators, industrial production equipment, and robots used in manufacturing. Some mechanical engineers design tools that other engineers need for their work. In addition, mechanical engineers work in manufacturing or agriculture production, maintenance, or technical sales; many become administrators or managers.

Mining and geological engineers, including mining safety engineers, find, extract, and prepare coal, metals, and minerals for use by manufacturing industries and utilities. They design open-pit and underground mines, supervise the construction of mine shafts and tunnels in underground operations, and devise methods for transporting minerals to processing plants. Mining engineers are responsible for the safe, economical, and environmentally sound operation of mines. Some mining engineers work with geologists and metallurgical engineers to locate and appraise new ore deposits. Others develop new mining equipment or direct mineral-processing operations that separate minerals from the dirt, rock, and other materials with which they are mixed. Mining engineers frequently specialize in the mining of one mineral or metal, such as coal or gold. With increased emphasis on protecting the environment, many mining engineers are working to solve problems related to land reclamation and to water and air pollution. Mining safety engineers use their knowledge of mine design and practices to ensure the safety of workers and to comply with State and Federal safety regulations. They inspect the surfaces of walls and roofs, monitor air quality, and examine mining equipment for compliance with safety practices.

Engineers typically need a bachelor's degree.

Nuclear engineers research and develop the processes, instruments, and systems used to derive benefits from nuclear energy and radiation. They design, develop, monitor, and operate nuclear plants to generate power. They may work on the nuclear fuel cycle—the production, handling, and use of nuclear fuel and the safe disposal of waste produced by the generation of nuclear energy—or on the development of fusion energy. Some specialize in the development of nuclear power sources for naval vessels or spacecraft; others find industrial and medical uses for radioactive materials—for example, in equipment used to diagnose and treat medical problems.

Petroleum engineers design methods for extracting oil and gas from deposits below the earth. Once these resources have been discovered, petroleum engineers work with geologists and other specialists to understand the geologic formation and properties of the rock containing the reservoir, to determine the drilling methods to be used, and to monitor drilling and production operations. They design equipment and processes to achieve the maximum profitable recovery of oil and gas. Because only a small proportion of oil and gas in a reservoir flows out under natural forces, petroleum engineers develop and use various enhanced recovery methods, including injecting water, chemicals, gases, or steam into an oil reservoir to force out more of the oil and doing computer-controlled drilling or fracturing to connect a larger area of a reservoir to a single well. Because even the best techniques in use today recover only a portion of the oil and gas in a reservoir, petroleum engineers research and develop technology and methods for increasing the recovery of these resources and lowering the cost of drilling and production operations.

Work environment.　Most engineers work in office buildings, laboratories, or industrial plants. Others may spend time outdoors at construction sites and oil and gas exploration and production sites, where they monitor or direct operations or solve onsite problems. Some engineers travel extensively to plants or worksites here and abroad.

Many engineers work a standard 40-hour week. At times, deadlines or design standards may bring extra pressure to a job, requiring engineers to work longer hours.

Training, Other Qualifications, and Advancement

Engineers typically enter the occupation with a bachelor's degree in an engineering specialty, but some basic research positions may require a graduate degree. Engineers offering their services directly to the public must be licensed. Continuing education to keep current with rapidly changing technology is important for engineers.

Education and training.　A bachelor's degree in engineering is required for almost all entry-level engineering jobs. College graduates with a degree in a natural science or mathematics occasionally may qualify for some engineering jobs, especially in specialties that are in high demand. Most engineering degrees are granted in electrical and electronics engineering, mechanical engineering, and civil engineering. However, engineers trained in one branch may work in related branches. For example, many aerospace engineers have training in mechanical engineering. This flexibility allows employers to meet staffing needs in new technologies and specialties in which engineers

may be in short supply. It also allows engineers to shift to fields with better employment prospects or to those which more closely match their interests.

Most engineering programs involve a concentration of study in an engineering specialty, along with courses in both mathematics and the physical and life sciences. Many programs also include courses in general engineering. A design course, sometimes accompanied by a computer or laboratory class or both, is part of the curriculum of most programs. Often, general courses not directly related to engineering, such as those in the social sciences or humanities, also are required.

In addition to the standard engineering degree, many colleges offer 2-year or 4-year degree programs in engineering technology. These programs, which usually include various hands-on laboratory classes that focus on current issues in the application of engineering principles, prepare students for practical design and production work, rather than for jobs that require more theoretical and scientific knowledge. Graduates of 4-year technology programs may get jobs similar to those obtained by graduates with a bachelor's degree in engineering. Engineering technology graduates, however, are not qualified to register as professional engineers under the same terms as graduates with degrees in engineering. Some employers regard technology program graduates as having skills between those of a technician and an engineer.

Graduate training is essential for engineering faculty positions and some research and development programs, but is not required for the majority of entry-level engineering jobs. Many experienced engineers obtain graduate degrees in engineering or business administration to learn new technology and broaden their education. Numerous high-level executives in government and industry began their careers as engineers.

The Accreditation Board for Engineering and Technology (ABET) accredits college and university programs in engineering and engineering technology. ABET accreditation is based on a program's faculty, curriculum, and facilities; the achievement of a program's students; program improvements; and institutional commitment to specific principles of quality and ethics. Graduation from an ABET-accredited program may be required for engineers who need to be licensed.

Although most institutions offer programs in the major branches of engineering, only a few offer programs in the smaller specialties. Also, programs with the same title may vary in content. For example, some programs emphasize industrial practices, preparing students for a job in industry, whereas others are more theoretical and are designed to prepare students for graduate work. Therefore, students should investigate curricula and check accreditations carefully before selecting a college.

Admissions requirements for undergraduate engineering schools include a solid background in mathematics (algebra, geometry, trigonometry, and calculus) and science (biology, chemistry, and physics), in addition to courses in English, social studies, and humanities. Bachelor's degree programs in engineering typically are designed to last 4 years, but many students find that it takes between 4 and 5 years to complete their studies. In a typical 4-year college curriculum, the first 2 years are spent studying mathematics, basic sciences, introductory engineering, humanities, and social sciences. In the last 2 years, most courses are in engineering, usually with a concentration in one specialty. Some programs offer a general engineering curriculum; students then specialize on the job or in graduate school.

Some engineering schools have agreements with 2-year colleges whereby the college provides the initial engineering education and the engineering school automatically admits students for their last 2 years. In addition, a few engineering schools have arrangements that allow students who spend 3 years in a liberal arts college studying preengineering subjects and 2 years in an engineering school studying core subjects to receive a bachelor's degree from each school. Some colleges and universities offer 5-year master's degree programs. Some 5-year or even 6-year cooperative plans combine classroom study with practical work, permitting students to gain valuable experience and to finance part of their education.

Licensure. All 50 States and the District of Columbia require licensure for engineers who offer their services directly to the public. Engineers who are licensed are called professional engineers (PEs). This licensure generally requires a degree from an ABET-accredited engineering program, 4 years of relevant work experience, and completion of a State examination. Recent graduates can start the licensing process by taking the examination in two stages. The initial Fundamentals of Engineering (FE) examination can be taken upon graduation. Engineers who pass this examination commonly are called engineers in training (EITs) or engineer interns (EIs). After acquiring suitable work experience, EITs can take the second examination, called the Principles and Practice of Engineering exam. Several States have imposed mandatory continuing education requirements for relicensure. Most States recognize licensure from other States, provided that the manner in which the initial license was obtained meets or exceeds their own licensure requirements. Many civil, mechanical, and chemical engineers are licensed PEs. Independently of licensure, various certification programs are offered by professional organizations to demonstrate competency in specific fields of engineering.

Other qualifications. Engineers should be creative, inquisitive, analytical, and detail oriented. They should be able to work as part of a team and to communicate well, both orally and in writing. Communication abilities are becoming increasingly important as engineers interact more frequently with specialists in a wide range of fields outside engineering.

Engineers who work for the Federal Government usually must be U.S. citizens. Some engineers, particularly nuclear engineers and aerospace and other engineers working for defense contractors, may need to hold a security clearance.

Certification and advancement. Beginning engineering graduates usually work under the supervision of experienced engineers and, in large companies, also may receive formal classroom or seminar-type training. As new engineers gain knowledge and experience, they are assigned more difficult projects with greater independence to develop designs, solve problems, and make decisions. Engineers may advance to become technical specialists or to supervise a staff or team of engineers and technicians. Some eventually may become engineering managers or enter other managerial or sales jobs. In sales, an engineering background enables them to discuss a product's technical aspects and assist in product planning, installation, and use. (See the statements under management and business and financial operations occupations, and the statement on sales engineers elsewhere in the *Handbook.*)

Projections data from the National Employment Matrix

Occupational Title	SOC Code	Employment, 2008	Projected Employment, 2018	Change, 2008-2018	
				Number	Percent
Engineers...	17-2000	1,571,900	1,750,300	178,300	11
Aerospace engineers	17-2011	71,600	79,100	7,400	10
Agricultural engineers....................................	17-2021	2,700	3,000	300	12
Biomedical engineers......................................	17-2031	16,000	27,600	11,600	72
Chemical engineers...	17-2041	31,700	31,000	-600	-2
Civil engineers	17-2051	278,400	345,900	67,600	24
Computer hardware engineers	17-2061	74,700	77,500	2,800	4
Electrical and electronics engineers................	17-2070	301,500	304,600	3,100	1
Electrical engineers....................................	17-2071	157,800	160,500	2,700	2
Electronics engineers, except computer......	17-2072	143,700	144,100	400	0
Environmental engineers.................................	17-2081	54,300	70,900	16,600	31
Industrial engineers, including health and safety........................	17-2110	240,400	273,700	33,200	14
Health and safety engineers, except mining safety engineers and inspectors..	17-2111	25,700	28,300	2,600	10
Industrial engineers....................................	17-2112	214,800	245,300	30,600	14
Marine engineers and naval architects	17-2121	8,500	9,000	500	6
Materials engineers	17-2131	24,400	26,600	2,300	9
Mechanical engineers......................................	17-2141	238,700	253,100	14,400	6
Mining and geological engineers, including mining safety engineers	17-2151	7,100	8,200	1,100	15
Nuclear engineers...	17-2161	16,900	18,800	1,900	11
Petroleum engineers..	17-2171	21,900	25,900	4,000	18
All other engineers...	17-2199	183,200	195,400	12,200	7

(NOTE) Data in this table are rounded. See the discussion of the employment projections table in the *Handbook* introductory chapter on *Occupational Information Included in the Handbook.*

Numerous professional certifications for engineers exist and may be beneficial for advancement to senior technical or managerial positions. Many certification programs are offered by the professional societies listed as sources of additional information for engineering specialties at the end of this statement.

Employment

In 2008, engineers held about 1.6 million jobs. Following is the distribution of employment by engineering specialty:

Civil engineers..278,400
Mechanical engineers..238,700
Industrial engineers 214,800
Electrical engineers 157,800
Electronics engineers, except computer....................143,700
Computer hardware engineers.....................................74,700
Aerospace engineers..71,600
Environmental engineers...54,300
Chemical engineers..31,700
Health and safety engineers, except mining safety
    engineers and inspectors...25,700
Materials engineers 24,400
Petroleum engineers...21,900
Nuclear engineers..16,900
Biomedical engineers...16,000
Marine engineers and naval architects 8,500
Mining and geological engineers, including mining
    safety engineers 7,100
Agricultural engineers...2,700
All other engineers 183,200

About 36 percent of engineering jobs were found in manufacturing industries, and another 30 percent were in the professional, scientific, and technical services industries, primarily in architectural, engineering, and related services. Many engineers also worked in the construction, telecommunications, and wholesale trade industries.

Federal, State, and local governments employed about 12 percent of engineers in 2008. About 6 percent were in the Federal Government, mainly in the U.S. Departments of Defense, Transportation, Agriculture, Interior, and Energy, and in the National Aeronautics and Space Administration. Many engineers in State and local government agencies worked in highway and public works departments. In 2008, about 3 percent of engineers were self-employed, many as consultants.

Engineers are employed in every State, in small and large cities and in rural areas. Some branches of engineering are concentrated in particular industries and geographic areas; for example, petroleum engineering jobs tend to be located in States with sizable petroleum deposits, such as Texas, Louisiana, Oklahoma, Alaska, and California. Other branches, such as civil engineering, are widely dispersed, and engineers in these fields often move from place to place to work on different projects.

Job Outlook

Employment of engineers is expected to grow about as fast as the average for all occupations over the next decade, but growth will vary by specialty. Biomedical engineers should experience the fastest growth, while civil engineers should see the largest employment increase. Overall job opportunities in engineering are expected to be good.

Overall employment change. Overall engineering employment is expected to grow by 11 percent over the 2008–18 decade, about as fast as the average for all occupations. Engineers traditionally have been concentrated in slower growing or declining manufacturing industries, in which they will continue to be needed to design, build, test, and improve manufactured products. However, increasing employment of engineers in engineering, research and development, and consulting services industries should generate most of the employment growth. The job outlook varies by engineering specialty, as discussed later.

Competitive pressures and advancing technology will force companies to improve and update product designs and to optimize their manufacturing processes. Employers will rely on engineers to increase productivity and expand output of goods and services. New technologies continue to improve the design process, enabling engineers to produce and analyze various product designs much more rapidly than in the past. Unlike the situation in some other occupations, however, technological advances are not expected to substantially limit employment opportunities in engineering, because engineers are needed to provide the ideas that lead to improved products and more productive processes.

The continued globalization of engineering work will likely dampen domestic employment growth to some degree. There are many well-trained, often English-speaking engineers available around the world who are willing to work at much lower salaries than U.S. engineers. The rise of the Internet has made it relatively easy for part of the engineering work previously done by engineers in this country to be done by engineers in other countries, a factor that will tend to hold down employment growth. Even so, there will always be a need for onsite engineers to interact with other employees and clients.

Overall job prospects. Overall job opportunities in engineering are expected to be good, and, indeed, prospects will be excellent in certain specialties. In addition to openings from job growth, many openings will be created by the need to replace current engineers who retire; transfer to management, sales, or other occupations; or leave engineering for other reasons.

Many engineers work on long-term research and development projects or in other activities that continue even during economic slowdowns. In industries such as electronics and aerospace, however, large cutbacks in defense expenditures and in government funding for research and development have resulted in significant layoffs of engineers in the past. The trend toward contracting for engineering work with engineering services firms, both domestic and foreign, also has made engineers more vulnerable to layoffs during periods of lower demand.

It is important for engineers, as it is for workers in other technical and scientific occupations, to continue their education throughout their careers, because much of their value to their employer depends on their knowledge of the latest technology. Engineers in high-technology areas, such as biotechnology or information technology, may find that their technical knowledge will become outdated rapidly. By keeping current in their field, engineers will be able to deliver the best solutions and greatest value to their employers. Engineers who have not

Job opportunities should be favorable for graduates of engineering programs.

kept current in their field may find themselves at a disadvantage when seeking promotions or during layoffs.

Employment change and job outlook by engineering specialty.

Aerospace engineers are expected to have 10 percent growth in employment over the projections decade, about as fast as the average for all occupations. New technologies and new designs for commercial and military aircraft and spacecraft produced during the next decade should spur demand for aerospace engineers. The employment outlook for aerospace engineers appears favorable. Although the number of degrees granted in aerospace engineering has begun to increase after many years of declines, new graduates continue to be needed to replace aerospace engineers who retire or leave the occupation for other reasons.

Agricultural engineers are expected to have employment growth of 12 percent over the projections decade, about as fast as the average for all occupations. Employment growth should result from the need to increase crop yields to feed an expanding population and to produce crops used as renewable energy sources. Moreover, engineers will be needed to develop more efficient agricultural production and to conserve resources. In addition, engineers will be needed to meet the increasing demand for biosensors, used to determine the optimal treatment of crops.

Biomedical engineers are expected to have employment growth of 72 percent over the projections decade, much faster than the average for all occupations. The aging of the population and a growing focus on health issues will drive demand for better medical devices and equipment designed by biomedical engineers. Along with the demand for more sophisticated medical equipment and procedures, an increased concern for cost-effectiveness will boost demand for biomedical engineers, particularly in pharmaceutical manufacturing and related industries. Because of the growing interest in this field, the number of degrees granted in biomedical engineering has increased greatly. Many biomedical engineers, particularly those employed in research laboratories, need a graduate degree.

Chemical engineers are expected to have an employment decline of 2 percent over the projections decade. Overall employment in the chemical manufacturing industry is expected to continue to decline, although chemical companies will continue to employ chemical engineers to research and develop new chemicals and more efficient processes to increase output of existing chemicals. However, there will be employment growth for chemical engineers in service-providing industries, such as professional, scientific, and technical services, particularly for research in energy and the developing fields of biotechnology and nanotechnology.

Civil engineers are expected to have employment growth of 24 percent over the projections decade, much faster than the average for all occupations. Spurred by general population growth and the related need to improve the Nation's infrastructure, more civil engineers will be needed to design and construct or expand transportation, water supply, and pollution control systems, and buildings and building complexes. They also will be needed to repair or replace existing roads, bridges, and other public structures. Because construction industries and architectural, engineering, and related services employ many civil engineers, employment opportunities will vary by geographic area and may decrease during economic slowdowns, when construction is often curtailed.

Computer hardware engineers are expected to have employment growth of 4 percent over the projections decade, slower than the average for all occupations. Although the use of information technology continues to expand rapidly, the manufacture of computer hardware is expected to be adversely affected by intense foreign competition. As computer and semiconductor manufacturers contract out more of their engineering needs to both domestic and foreign design firms, much of the growth in employment of hardware engineers is expected to take place in the computer systems design and related services industry.

Electrical engineers are expected to have employment growth of 2 percent over the projections decade. Although strong demand for electrical devices—including electric power generators, wireless phone transmitters, high-density batteries, and navigation systems—should spur job growth, international competition and the use of engineering services performed in other countries will limit employment growth. Electrical engineers working in firms providing engineering expertise and design services to manufacturers should have better job prospects.

Electronics engineers, except computer, are expected to experience little to no employment change over the projections decade. Although rising demand for electronic goods—including communications equipment, defense-related equipment, medical electronics, and consumer products—should continue to increase demand for electronics engineers, foreign competition in electronic products development and the use of engineering services performed in other countries will limit employment growth. Growth is expected to be fastest in service-providing industries—particularly in firms that provide engineering and design services.

Environmental engineers are expected to have employment growth of 31 percent over the projections decade, much faster than the average for all occupations. More environmental engineers will be needed to help companies comply with environmental regulations and to develop methods of cleaning up environmental hazards. A shift in emphasis toward preventing problems rather than controlling those which already exist, as well as increasing public health concerns resulting from population growth, also are expected to spur demand for environmental engineers. Because of this employment growth, job opportunities should be favorable.

Health and safety engineers, except mining safety engineers and inspectors, are expected to have employment growth of 10 percent over the projections decade, about as fast as the average for all occupations. Because health and safety engineers make production processes and products as safe as possible, their services should be in demand as concern increases for health and safety within work environments. As new technologies for production or processing are developed, health and safety engineers will be needed to ensure that they are safe.

Industrial engineers are expected to have employment growth of 14 percent over the projections decade, faster than the average for all occupations. As firms look for new ways to reduce costs and raise productivity, they increasingly will turn to industrial engineers to develop more efficient processes and reduce costs, delays, and waste. This focus should lead to job growth for these engineers, even in some manufacturing industries with declining employment overall. Because their work is similar to that done in management occupations, many industrial engineers leave the occupation to become managers. Numerous openings will be created by the need to replace industrial engineers who transfer to other occupations or leave the labor force.

Marine engineers and naval architects are expected to have employment growth of 6 percent over the projections decade, slower than the average for all occupations. Continued demand for naval vessels and recreational small craft should more than offset the long-term decline in the domestic design and construction of large oceangoing vessels. Good prospects are expected for marine engineers and naval architects because of growth in employment, the need to replace workers who retire

or take other jobs, and the limited number of students pursuing careers in this occupation.

Materials engineers are expected to have employment growth of 9 percent over the projections decade, about as fast as the average for all occupations. Growth should result from increased use of composite and other nontraditional materials developed through biotechnology and nanotechnology research. As manufacturing firms contract for their materials engineering needs, most employment growth is expected in professional, scientific, and technical services industries.

Mechanical engineers are expected to have employment growth of 6 percent over the projections decade, slower than the average for all occupations. Mechanical engineers are involved in the production of a wide range of products, and continued efforts to improve those products will create continued demand for their services. In addition, some new job opportunities will be created through the effects of emerging technologies in biotechnology, materials science, and nanotechnology. Additional opportunities outside of mechanical engineering will exist because the skills acquired through earning a degree in mechanical engineering often can be applied in other engineering specialties.

Mining and geological engineers, including mining safety engineers, are expected to have employment growth of 15 percent over the projections decade, faster than the average for all occupations. Following a lengthy period of decline, strong growth in demand for minerals is expected to create some employment growth over the 2008–18 period. Moreover, many currently employed mining engineers are approaching retirement age, a factor that should create additional job openings. Furthermore, relatively few schools offer mining engineering programs, resulting in good job opportunities for graduates. The best opportunities may require frequent travel or even living overseas for extended periods as mining operations around the world recruit graduates of U.S. mining engineering programs.

Nuclear engineers are expected to have employment growth of 11 percent over the projections decade, about as fast as the

Table 1. Earnings distribution by engineering specialty, May 2008.

Specialty	Lowest 10%	Lowest 25%	Median	Highest 25%	Highest 10%
Aerospace engineers	$58,130	$72,390	$92,520	$114,530	$134,570
Agricultural engineers	43,150	55,430	68,730	86,400	108,470
Biomedical engineers	47,640	59,420	77,400	98,830	121,970
Chemical engineers	53,730	67,420	84,680	105,000	130,240
Civil engineers	48,140	58,960	74,600	94,470	115,630
Computer hardware engineers	59,170	76,250	97,400	122,750	148,590
Electrical engineers	52,990	64,910	82,160	102,520	125,810
Electronics engineers, except computer	55,330	68,400	86,370	106,870	129,920
Environmental engineers	45,310	56,980	74,020	94,280	115,430
Health and safety engineers, except mining safety engineers and inspectors	43,540	56,190	72,490	90,740	106,220
Industrial engineers	47,720	59,120	73,820	91,020	107,270
Marine engineers and naval architects	43,070	57,060	74,140	94,840	118,630
Materials engineers	51,420	63,830	81,820	102,040	124,470
Mechanical engineers	47,900	59,230	74,920	94,400	114,740
Mining and geological engineers, including mining safety engineers	45,020	57,970	75,960	96,030	122,750
Nuclear engineers	68,300	82,540	97,080	115,170	136,880
Petroleum engineers	57,820	80,040	108,020	148,700	>166,400
Engineers, all other	49,270	67,360	88,570	110,310	132,070

average for all occupations. Most job growth will be in research and development and engineering services. Although no commercial nuclear power plants have been built in the United States for many years, increased interest in nuclear power as an energy source will spur demand for nuclear engineers to research and develop new designs for reactors. They also will be needed to work in defense-related areas, to develop nuclear medical technology, and to improve and enforce waste management and safety standards. Nuclear engineers are expected to have good employment opportunities because the small number of nuclear engineering graduates is likely to be in rough balance with the number of job openings.

Petroleum engineers are expected to have employment growth of 18 percent over the projections decade, faster than the average for all occupations. Petroleum engineers increasingly will be needed to develop new resources, as well as new methods of extracting more from existing sources. Excellent opportunities are expected for petroleum engineers because the number of job openings is likely to exceed the relatively small number of graduates. Petroleum engineers work around the world, and in fact, the best employment opportunities may include some work in other countries.

Earnings

Earnings for engineers vary significantly by specialty, industry, and education. Variation in median earnings and in the earnings distributions for engineers in a number of specialties is especially significant. Table 1 shows wage distributions in May 2008 for engineers in specialties covered in this statement.

In the Federal Government, mean annual salaries for engineers ranged from $81,085 in agricultural engineering to $126,788 in ceramic engineering in March 2009.

As a group, engineers earn some of the highest average starting salaries among those holding bachelor's degrees. Average starting salary offers for graduates of bachelor's degree programs in engineering, according to a July 2009 survey by the National Association of Colleges and Employers, were as follows:

Petroleum	$83,121
Chemical	64,902
Mining and Mineral	64,404
Computer	61,738
Nuclear	61,610
Electrical/electronics and communications	60,125
Mechanical	58,766
Industrial/manufacturing	58,358
Materials	57,349
Aerospace/aeronautical/astronautical	56,311
Agricultural	54,352
Bioengineering and biomedical	54,158
Civil	52,048

Related Occupations

Engineers apply the principles of natural science and mathematics in their work. Other workers who use scientific and mathematical principles include the following:

Sources of Additional Information

Information about careers in engineering is available from:
➤ JETS, 1420 King St., Suite 405, Alexandria, VA 22314. Internet: **http://www.jets.org**

Information on ABET-accredited engineering programs is available from:
➤ ABET, Inc., 111 Market Place, Suite 1050, Baltimore, MD 21202. Internet: **http://www.abet.org**

Those interested in information on the Professional Engineer licensure should contact:
➤ National Council of Examiners for Engineering and Surveying, P.O. Box 1686, Clemson, SC 29633. Internet: **http://www.ncees.org**

➤ National Society of Professional Engineers, 1420 **King** St., **Alexandria, VA 22314.** Internet: **http://www.nspe.org**

Information on general engineering education and career resources is available from:
➤ American Society for Engineering Education, 1818 N St. NW., Suite 600, Washington, DC 20036. Internet: **http://www.asee.org**

Information on obtaining engineering positions with the Federal Government is available from the Office of Personnel Management through USAJOBS, the Federal Government's official employment information system. This resource for locating and applying for job opportunities can be accessed through the Internet at **http://www.usajobs.opm.gov** or through an interactive voice response telephone system at (703) 724–1850 or TDD (978) 461–8404. These numbers are not toll free, and charges may result. For advice on how to find and apply for Federal jobs, see the *Occupational Outlook Quarterly* article "How to get a job in the Federal Government," online at **http://www.bls.gov/opub/ooq/2004/summer/art01.pdf.**

For more detailed information on an engineering specialty, contact societies representing the individual branches of engineering. Each can provide information about careers in the particular branch.

Aerospace engineers
➤ American Institute of Aeronautics and Astronautics, Inc., 1801 Alexander Bell Dr., Suite 500, Reston, VA 20191. Internet: **http://www.aiaa.org**

Agricultural engineers
➤ American Society of Agricultural and Biological Engineers, 2950 Niles Rd., St. Joseph, MI 49085. Internet: **http://www.asabe.org**

Biomedical engineers
➤ Biomedical Engineering Society, 8401 Corporate Dr., Suite 140, Landover, MD 20785. Internet: **http://www.bmes.org**

Chemical engineers
➤ American Chemical Society, Department of Career Services, 1155 16th St. NW., Washington, DC 20036. Internet: **http://www.chemistry.org**

➤ American Institute of Chemical Engineers, 3 Park Ave., New York, NY 10016. Internet: **http://www.aiche.org**

Civil engineers
➤ American Society of Civil Engineers, 1801 Alexander Bell Dr., Reston, VA 20191. Internet: **http://www.asce.org**

Computer hardware engineers
➤ IEEE Computer Society, 2001 L St. NW., Suite 700., Washington, DC 20036. Internet: **http://www.computer.org**

Electrical and electronics engineers
➤ IEEE–USA, 2001 L St. NW., Suite 700, Washington, DC 20036. Internet: **http://www.ieeeusa.org**

Environmental engineers
➤ American Academy of Environmental Engineers, 130 Holiday Court, Suite 100, Annapolis, MD 21401. Internet: **http://www.aaee.net**

Health and safety engineers
➤ American Society of Safety Engineers, 1800 E Oakton St., Des Plaines, IL 60018. Internet: **http://www.asse.org**

Industrial engineers
➤ Institute of Industrial Engineers, 3577 Parkway Lane, Suite 200, Norcross, GA 30092. Internet: **http://www.iienet.org**

Marine engineers and naval architects
➤ Society of Naval Architects and Marine Engineers, 601 Pavonia Ave., Jersey City, NJ 07306. Internet: **http://www.sname.org**

Materials engineers
➤ ASM International, 9639 Kinsman Rd., Materials Park, OH 44073. Internet: **http://www.asminternational.org**

➤ Minerals, Metals, and Materials Society, 184 Thorn Hill Rd., Warrendale, PA 15086. Internet: **http://www.tms.org**

Mechanical engineers
➤ American Society of Mechanical Engineers, 3 Park Ave., New York, NY 10016. Internet: **http://www.asme.org**

➤ SAE International, 400 Commonwealth Dr., Warrendale, PA 15096. Internet: **http://www.sae.org**

Mining and geological engineers, including mining safety engineers
➤ Society for Mining, Metallurgy, and Exploration, Inc., 8307 Shaffer Parkway, Littleton, CO 80127. Internet: **http://www.smenet.org**

Nuclear engineers
➤ American Nuclear Society, 555 North Kensington Ave., La Grange Park, IL 60526. Internet: **http://www.ans.org**

Petroleum engineers
➤ Society of Petroleum Engineers, 222 Palisades Creek Dr., Richardson, TX 75080. Internet: **http://www.spe.org**

The Occupational Information Network (O*NET) provides information on a wide range of occupational characteristics. Links to O*NET appear at the end of the Internet version of this occupational statement, accessible at **http://www.bls.gov/ooh/ocos027.htm**

Drafters and Engineering Technicians

Drafters

Significant Points

- Opportunities should be best for individuals with at least 2 years of postsecondary training in drafting.

- Overall employment is projected to grow more slowly than average, but growth will vary by specialty.

- Demand for various types of drafters depends on the needs of local industry.

Nature of the Work

Drafters prepare technical drawings and plans, which are used by production and construction workers to build everything from microchips to skyscrapers.

Drafters' drawings provide visual guidelines and show how to construct a product or structure. Drawings include technical details and specify dimensions, materials, and procedures. Drafters fill in technical details using drawings, rough sketches, specifications, and calculations made by engineers, surveyors, architects, or scientists. For example, many drafters use their knowledge of standardized building techniques to draw in the details of structures. Some use their understanding of engineering and manufacturing theory and standards to draw the parts of a machine; they determine design elements, such as the numbers and kinds of fasteners needed to assemble the machine. Drafters use technical handbooks, tables, calculators, and computers to complete their work.

Most drafters use Computer Aided Design and Drafting (CADD) systems to prepare drawings. Consequently, some drafters may be referred to as CADD operators. With CADD systems, drafters can create and store drawings electronically so that they can be viewed, printed, or programmed directly into automated manufacturing systems. CADD systems also permit drafters to quickly prepare variations of a design. Although drafters use CADD extensively, they still need knowledge of traditional drafting techniques in order to fully understand and explain concepts.

Drafting work has many specialties; the most common types of drafters are the following:

Aeronautical drafters prepare engineering drawings that detail plans and specifications used in the manufacture of aircraft, missiles, and related parts.

Architectural drafters draw architectural and structural features of buildings for new construction projects. These workers may specialize in a type of building, such as residential or commercial, or in a kind of material used, such as reinforced concrete, masonry, steel, or timber.

Civil drafters prepare drawings and topographical and relief maps used in major construction or civil engineering projects, such as highways, bridges, pipelines, flood-control projects, and water and sewage systems.

Electrical drafters prepare wiring and layout diagrams used by workers who erect, install, and repair electrical equipment and wiring in communication centers, power plants, electrical distribution systems, and buildings.

Electronics drafters draw wiring diagrams, circuit board assembly diagrams, schematics, and layout drawings used in the manufacture, installation, and repair of electronic devices and components.

Mechanical drafters prepare drawings showing the detail and method of assembly of a wide variety of machinery and mechanical devices, indicating dimensions, fastening methods, and other requirements.

Process piping or pipeline drafters prepare drawings used in the layout, construction, and operation of oil and gas fields, refineries, chemical plants, and process piping systems.

Work environment. Drafters usually work in comfortable offices. Because they spend long periods in front of computers doing detailed work, drafters may be susceptible to eyestrain, back discomfort, and hand and wrist problems. Most drafters work a standard 40-hour week; only a small number work part time.

Training, Other Qualifications, and Advancement

Employers prefer applicants who have completed postsecondary school training in drafting, which is offered by technical institutes, community colleges, and some 4-year colleges and universities. Employers are most interested in applicants with well-developed drafting and mechanical drawing skills; knowledge of drafting standards, mathematics, science, and engineering technology; and a solid background in CADD techniques.

Most drafters use computer-aided design and drafting software.

Education and training. High school courses in mathematics, science, computer technology, design, computer graphics, and, where available, drafting are useful for people considering a drafting career. Employers prefer applicants who have also completed training after high school at a technical institute, community college, or 4-year college or university. Prospective students should contact prospective employers to ask which schools they prefer and contact schools to ask for information about the kinds of jobs their graduates have, the type and condition of instructional facilities and equipment, and teacher qualifications.

Technical institutes offer intensive technical training, but they provide a less general education than do community colleges. Either certificates or diplomas may be awarded, and programs can vary considerably in length and in the types of courses offered. Many technical institutes offer 2-year associate degree programs.

Community colleges offer programs similar to those in technical institutes but include more classes in drafting theory and also often require general education classes. Courses taken at community colleges are more likely to be accepted for credit at 4-year colleges. After completing a 2-year associate degree program, graduates may obtain jobs as drafters or continue their education in a related field at a 4-year college. Most 4-year colleges do not offer training in drafting, but they do offer classes

Projections data from the National Employment Matrix

Occupational Title	SOC Code	Employment, 2008	Projected Employment, 2018	Change, 2008-2018	
				Number	Percent
Drafters	17-3010	251,900	262,500	10,700	4
Architectural and civil drafters	17-3011	118,400	129,100	10,800	9
Electrical and electronics drafters...	17-3012	33,600	33,900	300	1
Mechanical drafters..	17-3013	78,700	77,800	-900	-1
Drafters, all other	17-3019	21,200	21,700	500	2

(NOTE) Data in this table are rounded. See the discussion of the employment projections table in the *Handbook* introductory chapter on *Occupational Information Included in the Handbook*.

in engineering, architecture, and mathematics that are useful for obtaining a job as a drafter.

Technical training obtained in the Armed Forces also can be applied in civilian drafting jobs. Some additional training may be necessary, depending on the technical area or military specialty.

Training differs somewhat within the drafting specialties, although the basics, such as mathematics, are similar. In an electronics drafting program, for example, students learn how to depict electronic components and circuits in drawings. In architectural drafting, they learn the technical specifications of buildings.

Certification and other qualifications. Mechanical ability and visual aptitude are important for drafters. Prospective drafters should be able to draw well and perform detailed work accurately. Artistic ability is helpful in some specialized fields, as is knowledge of manufacturing and construction methods. In addition, prospective drafters should have good interpersonal skills because they work closely with engineers, surveyors, architects, and other professionals and, sometimes, with customers.

The American Design Drafting Association (ADDA) has established a certification program for drafters. Although employers usually do not require drafters to be certified, certification demonstrates knowledge and an understanding of nationally recognized practices. Individuals who wish to become certified must pass the Drafter Certification Test, which is administered periodically at ADDA-authorized sites. Applicants are tested on basic drafting concepts, such as geometric construction, working drawings, and architectural terms and standards.

Advancement. Entry-level or junior drafters usually do routine work under close supervision. After gaining experience, they may become intermediate drafters and progress to more difficult work with less supervision. At the intermediate level, they may need to exercise more judgment and perform calculations when preparing and modifying drawings. Drafters may eventually advance to senior drafter, designer, or supervisor. Many employers pay for continuing education; with appropriate college degrees, drafters may go on to become engineering technicians, engineers, or architects.

Employment

Drafters held about 251,900 jobs in 2008. Architectural and civil drafters held 47 percent of these jobs, mechanical drafters held about 31 percent, and electrical and electronics drafters held about 13 percent.

About 52 percent of all jobs for drafters were in architectural, engineering, and related services firms that design construction projects or do other engineering work on a contract basis for other industries. Another 24 percent of jobs were in manufacturing industries such as machinery, fabricated metal products, computer and electronic products, and transportation-equipment manufacturing. Approximately 3 percent of drafters were self-employed in 2008.

Job Outlook

Drafters can expect slower than average employment growth, with the best opportunities expected for those with at least 2 years of postsecondary training.

Employment change. Employment of drafters is expected to grow by 4 percent between 2008 and 2018, which is slower than the average for all occupations. However, growth will vary by specialty.

Architectural and civil drafting is expected to be the fastest growing specialty, increasing by 9 percent, which is about as fast as the average. Increases in overall construction activity stemming from U.S. population growth and the related need to improve the Nation's infrastructure should spur demand for drafters trained in architectural and civil design.

In contrast to employment of architectural and civil drafters, little or no change in employment is expected of mechanical drafters and of electronic and electrical drafters. Many of these workers are concentrated in slow-growing or declining manufacturing industries that offer few opportunities for growth related to expansion. However, increasingly complex design problems associated with new products and manufacturing processes will increase the demand for mechanical drafters and electronic and electrical drafters employed in engineering and drafting services firms that will be charged with finding solutions to these problems.

Across all specialties, CADD systems that are more powerful and easier to use will allow many tasks to be done by other technical professionals, thus curbing demand for drafters. Job growth also should be slowed as some drafting work, which can be done by sending CADD files over the Internet, is outsourced offshore to countries that pay lower wages.

Job prospects. Opportunities should be best for individuals with at least 2 years of postsecondary training in a drafting program that provides strong technical skills and considerable experience with CADD systems. CADD has increased the complexity of drafting applications while enhancing the productivity of drafters. It also has enhanced the nature of drafting by creating more possibilities for design and drafting. As technology continues to advance, employers will look for drafters with a strong background in fundamental drafting principles, a high level of technical sophistication, and the ability to apply their knowledge to a broader range of responsibilities. Most job openings are expected to arise from the need to replace drafters who transfer to other occupations or leave the labor force completely.

Employment of drafters remains tied to industries that are sensitive to cyclical changes in the economy, primarily construction and manufacturing. During recessions, drafters may be laid off. However, a growing number of drafters should continue to find employment on a temporary or contract basis as more companies turn to the employment services industry to meet their changing needs.

Demand for particular drafting specialties varies throughout the country because employment usually is contingent on the needs of local industry.

Earnings

Drafters' earnings vary by specialty, location, and level of responsibility. Median annual wages of architectural and civil drafters were $44,490 in May 2008. The middle 50 percent earned between $35,290 and $55,740. The lowest 10 percent earned less than $28,220, and the highest 10 percent earned more than $67,110. Median annual wages for architectural and civil drafters in architectural, engineering, and related services were $44,390.

Median annual wages of mechanical drafters were $46,640 in May 2008. The middle 50 percent earned between $36,490 and $59,010. The lowest 10 percent earned less than $29,390, and the highest 10 percent earned more than $71,340. Median annual wages for mechanical drafters in architectural, engineering, and related services were $47,630.

Median annual wages of electrical and electronics drafters were $51,320 in May 2008. The middle 50 percent earned between $40,210 and $65,400. The lowest 10 percent earned less than $32,050, and the highest 10 percent earned more than $79,790. In architectural, engineering, and related services, median annual wages for electrical and electronics drafters were $47,910.

Related Occupations

Other workers who prepare or analyze detailed drawings and make precise calculations and measurements include:

Sources of Additional Information

Information on schools offering programs in drafting and related fields is available from:

➤ Accrediting Commission of Career Schools and Colleges, 2101 Wilson Blvd., Suite 302, Arlington, VA 22201. Internet: **http://www.accsc.org**

Information about certification is available from:
➤ American Design Drafting Association, 105 E. Main St., Newbern, TN 38059. Internet: **http://www.adda.org**

The Occupational Information Network (O*NET) provides information on a wide range of occupational characteristics. Links to O*NET appear at the end of the Internet version of this occupational statement, accessible at **http://www.bls.gov/ooh/ocos111.htm**

Engineering Technicians

Significant Points

- Electrical and electronic engineering technicians make up 33 percent of all engineering technicians.

- Employment of engineering technicians is influenced by economic conditions similar to those which affect engineers; as a result, job outlook varies by specialty.

- Opportunities will be best for individuals with an associate degree or other postsecondary training in engineering technology.

Nature of the Work

Engineering technicians use the principles and theories of science, engineering, and mathematics to solve technical problems in research and development, manufacturing, sales, construction, inspection, and maintenance. Their work is more narrowly focused and application-oriented than that of scientists and engineers. Many engineering technicians assist engineers and scientists, especially in research and development. Others work in quality control, inspecting products and processes, conducting tests, or collecting data. In manufacturing, they may assist in product design, development, or production. Although many workers who repair or maintain various types of electrical, electronic, or mechanical equipment are called technicians, those workers are covered in the *Handbook* section on installation, maintenance, and repair occupations.

Engineering technicians who work in research and development build or set up equipment, prepare and conduct experiments, collect data, calculate or record results, and help engineers or scientists in other ways, such as making prototype versions of newly designed equipment. They also assist in design work, often using computer-aided design and drafting (CADD) equipment.

Most engineering technicians specialize, learning skills and working in the same disciplines as engineers. Occupational titles, therefore, tend to reflect this similarity. The Handbook does not cover in detail some branches of engineering technology, such as chemical engineering technology (the development of new chemical products and processes) and bioengineering technology (the development and implementation of biomedical equipment), for which there are accredited programs of study.

Engineering technicians assist engineers in designing and testing new products.

Aerospace engineering and operations technicians operate and maintain equipment used to test aircraft and spacecraft. New aircraft designs are subjected to years of testing before they are put into service, since failure of key components during flight can be fatal. Technicians may calibrate test equipment, such as wind tunnels, and determine causes of equipment malfunctions. They may also program and run computer simulations that test new designs virtually. Using computer and communications systems, aerospace engineering and operations technicians often record and interpret test data.

Civil engineering technicians help civil engineers plan and oversee the construction of highways, buildings, bridges, dams, wastewater treatment systems, and other structures. Some estimate construction costs and specify materials to be used, and some may even prepare drawings or perform land-surveying duties. Others may set up and monitor instruments used to study traffic conditions. (Cost estimators; construction and building inspectors; drafters; and surveyors, cartographers, photogrammetrists, and surveying and mapping technicians are covered elsewhere in the Handbook.)

Electrical and electronic engineering technicians help design, develop, test, and manufacture electrical and electronic equipment such as communication equipment, medical monitoring devices, navigational equipment, and computers. They may work in product evaluation and testing, using measuring and diagnostic devices to adjust, test, and repair equipment. (Workers whose jobs primarily involve repairing electrical and electronic equipment are often are referred to as electronics technicians, but they are included with electrical and electronics installers and repairers elsewhere in the Handbook.)

Electro-mechanical engineering technicians combine knowledge of mechanical engineering technology with knowledge of electrical and electronic circuits to design, develop, test, and manufacture electronic and computer-controlled mechanical systems, such as robotic assembly machines. They also operate these machines in factories and other worksites. Their work often overlaps that of both electrical and electronic engineering technicians and mechanical engineering technicians.

Environmental engineering technicians work closely with environmental engineers and scientists in developing methods and devices used in the prevention, control, or remediation of environmental hazards. They inspect and maintain equipment related to air pollution and recycling. Some inspect water and wastewater treatment systems to ensure that pollution control requirements are met.

Industrial engineering technicians study the efficient use of personnel, materials, and machines in factories, stores, repair shops, and offices. Working under the direction of industrial engineers, they prepare layouts of machinery and equipment, plan the flow of work, conduct statistical studies of production time or quality, and analyze production costs.

Mechanical engineering technicians help engineers design, develop, test, and manufacture industrial machinery, consumer products, and other equipment. They may assist in product tests by, for example, setting up instrumentation for auto crash tests. They may make sketches and rough layouts, record and analyze data, make calculations and estimates, and report on their findings. When planning production, mechanical engineering technicians prepare layouts and drawings of the assembly process and of parts to be manufactured. They estimate labor costs, equipment life, and plant space. Some test and inspect machines and equipment or work with engineers to eliminate production problems.

Work environment. Most engineering technicians work 40 hours a week in laboratories, in offices, in manufacturing or industrial plants, or on construction sites. Some may be exposed to hazards from equipment, chemicals, or toxic materials, but incidents are rare as long as proper procedures are followed.

Training, Other Qualifications, and Advancement

Most employers prefer to hire engineering technicians with an associate degree or other postsecondary training in engineering technology. Training is available at technical institutes, at community colleges, at extension divisions of colleges and universities, at public and private vocational-technical schools, and in the Armed Forces.

Education and training. Although it may be possible to qualify for certain engineering technician jobs without formal training, most employers prefer to hire someone with a 2-year associate degree or other postsecondary training in engineering technology. Workers with less formal engineering technology training need more time to learn skills while on the job. Prospective engineering technicians should take as many high school science and math courses as possible to prepare for programs in engineering technology after high school.

Most 2-year associate degree programs accredited by the Technology Accreditation Commission of the Accreditation Board for Engineering and Technology (ABET) include at least college algebra and trigonometry and one or two basic science courses. Depending on the specialty, more math or science may be required. About 700 ABET-accredited programs are offered in engineering technology specialties.

The type of technical courses required depends on the specialty. For example, prospective mechanical engineering technicians may take courses in fluid mechanics, thermodynamics, and mechanical design; prospective electrical engineering technicians may need classes in electrical circuits, microprocessors, and digital electronics; and those preparing to work in environmental engineering technology need courses

Projections data from the National Employment Matrix

Occupational Title	SOC Code	Employment, 2008	Projected Employment, 2018	Change, 2008-2018	
				Number	Percent
Engineering technicians, except drafters	17-3020	497,300	523,100	25,800	5
Aerospace engineering and operations technicians	17-3021	8,700	8,900	200	2
Civil engineering technicians..	17-3022	91,700	107,200	15,500	17
Electrical and electronic engineering technicians........................	17-3023	164,000	160,400	-3,600	-2
Electro-mechanical technicians	17-3024	16,400	15,600	-800	-5
Environmental engineering technicians......................................	17-3025	21,200	27,500	6,400	30
Industrial engineering technicians	17-3026	72,600	77,400	4,800	7
Mechanical engineering technicians..	17-3027	46,100	45,500	-700	-1
Engineering technicians, except drafters, all other	17-3029	76,600	80,600	4,000	5

(NOTE) Data in this table are rounded. See the discussion of the employment projections table in the *Handbook* introductory chapter on *Occupational Information Included in the Handbook.*

in environmental regulations and safe handling of hazardous materials.

Technical institutes offer intensive technical training through application and practice, but they provide less theory and general education than do community colleges. Many technical institutes offer 2-year associate degree programs and are similar to or part of a community college or State university system. Other technical institutes are run by private organizations, with programs that vary considerably in length and types of courses offered.

Community colleges offer curriculums that are similar to those in technical institutes but include more theory and liberal arts. There may be little or no difference between programs at technical institutes and community colleges, as both offer associate degrees. After completing the 2-year program, some graduates get jobs as engineering technicians, whereas others continue their education at 4-year colleges. However, an associate degree in pre-engineering is different from one in engineering technology. Students who enroll in a 2-year pre-engineering program may find it difficult to find work as an engineering technician if they decide not to enter a 4-year engineering program because pre-engineering programs usually focus less on hands-on applications and more on academic preparatory work. Conversely, graduates of 2-year engineering technology programs may not receive credit for some of the courses they have taken if they choose to transfer to a 4-year engineering program. Colleges having 4-year programs usually do not offer engineering technician training, but college courses in science, engineering, and mathematics are useful for obtaining a job as an engineering technician. Many 4-year colleges offer bachelor's degrees in engineering technology, but graduates of these programs often are hired to work as technologists or applied engineers, not technicians.

Vocational-technical schools, another source of technical training, include postsecondary public institutions that serve local students and emphasize training needed by local employers. Most schools that offer training to become an engineering technician require a high school diploma or its equivalent for admission.

Other training in technical areas may be obtained in the Armed Forces. Many military technical training programs are highly regarded by employers. However, skills acquired in military programs are often narrowly focused and may be less applicable in civilian industry, which often requires broader

training. Therefore, some additional training may be needed, depending on the acquired skills and the kind of job.

Other qualifications. Because many engineering technicians assist in design work, creativity is desirable. Good communication skills and the ability to work well with others also are important because engineering technicians are typically part of a team of engineers and other technicians.

Certification and advancement. Engineering technicians usually begin by performing routine duties under the close supervision of an experienced technician, technologist, engineer, or scientist. As they gain experience, they are given more difficult assignments with only general supervision. Some engineering technicians eventually become supervisors.

Employment

Engineering technicians held 497,300 jobs in 2008. Approximately 33 percent were electrical and electronic engineering technicians, as indicated by the following tabulation.

Electrical and electronic engineering technicians	164,000
Civil engineering technicians	91,700
Industrial engineering technicians	72,600
Mechanical engineering technicians	46,100
Environmental engineering technicians	21,200
Electro-mechanical technicians	16,400
Aerospace engineering and operations technicians	8,700
Engineering technicians, except drafters, all other	76,600

About 34 percent of all engineering technicians worked in manufacturing. Another 25 percent worked in professional, scientific, and technical service industries, mostly in engineering or business services companies that do engineering work on contract for government, manufacturing firms, or other organizations.

In 2008, the Federal Government employed 35,300 engineering technicians. State governments employed 31,300, and local governments employed 25,100.

Job Outlook

Overall employment of engineering technicians is expected to grow slower than the average for all occupations, but projected growth and job prospects vary by specialty. Opportunities will be best for individuals with an associate degree or other postsecondary training in engineering technology.

Employment change. Overall employment of engineering technicians is expected to grow by 5 percent between 2008 and 2018, slower than the average for all occupations. Competitive pressures will force companies to improve and update manufacturing facilities and product designs, although increased efficiencies and automation of many support activities will curtail job growth for engineering technicians.

Employment of engineering technicians in some design functions may also be affected by increasing globalization of the development process. To reduce costs and speed project completion, some companies may relocate part of their development operations to facilities overseas, affecting both engineers and engineering technicians—particularly in electronics and computer-related specialties. However, some aspects of the work of engineering technicians require on-site presence, particularly in the environmental, civil, and industrial specialties, so demand for these engineering technicians within the United States should continue to grow.

Because engineering technicians work closely with engineers, employment of engineering technicians is often influenced by the same local and national economic conditions that affect engineers. As a result, the employment outlook varies with industry and specialization.

Aerospace engineering and operations technicians are expected to have 2 percent employment growth between 2008 and 2018, signifying little or no change. Although demand for aerospace products will continue to grow, increased use of computer simulations for designing and testing new products will diminish the need for new aerospace engineering technicians.

Civil engineering technicians are expected to have 17 percent employment growth between 2008 and 2018, faster than the average for all occupations. Spurred by population growth and the related need to improve the Nation's infrastructure, more civil engineering technicians will be needed to expand transportation, water supply, and pollution control systems, as well as large buildings and building complexes. They also will be needed to repair or replace existing roads, bridges, and other public structures.

The number of electrical and electronic engineering technician jobs is expected to decline by 2 percent between 2008 and 2018, signifying little or no change. Despite rising demand for electronic goods—including communications equipment, defense-related equipment, medical electronics, and consumer products—foreign competition in design and manufacturing, together with increased efficiencies in the design process, will reduce demand for these workers.

The number of electro-mechanical technician jobs is expected to decline moderately by 5 percent between 2008 and 2018. As with the closely related electrical and electronic engineering technicians and mechanical engineering technicians, job losses will be caused by increased productivity in the design and manufacture of electro-mechanical products such as unmanned aircraft and robotic equipment.

Environmental engineering technicians are expected to have 30 percent employment growth between 2008 and 2018, much faster than the average for all occupations. More environmental engineering technicians will be needed to comply with en-

vironmental regulations and to develop methods of cleaning up existing hazards. A shift in emphasis toward preventing problems rather than controlling those which already exist, as well as increasing public health concerns resulting from population growth, also will spur demand.

Industrial engineering technicians are expected to have 7 percent employment growth between 2008 and 2018, about as fast as average. As firms continue to seek new means of reducing costs and increasing productivity, demand for industrial engineering technicians to analyze and improve production processes should increase. This should lead to some job growth even in manufacturing industries with slowly growing or declining employment.

Mechanical engineering technicians are expected to decline by 1 percent between 2008 and 2018, which represents little or no change. Increased foreign competition in both design services and manufacturing, together with improved efficiencies in design and testing, will reduce the need for mechanical engineering technicians.

Job prospects. Job prospects will vary by specialty and location, as employment is influenced by economic conditions similar to those which affect engineers. In general, opportunities will be best for individuals with an associate degree or other postsecondary training in engineering technology. As technology becomes more sophisticated, employers will continue to look for technicians who are skilled in new technology and who require little additional training. Even in specialties that are expected to experience job declines, there will still be job openings resulting from the need to replace technicians who retire or leave the labor force for any other reason.

Earnings

Median annual wages in May 2008 of engineering technicians by specialty are shown in the following tabulation.

Aerospace engineering and operations technicians	$55,040
Electrical and electronic engineering technicians	53,240
Mechanical engineering technicians	48,130
Industrial engineering technicians	47,180
Electro-mechanical technicians	46,310
Civil engineering technicians	44,290
Environmental engineering technicians	41,100

Median annual wages of wage and salary electrical and electronic engineering technicians were $53,240 in May 2008. The middle 50 percent earned between $41,550 and $64,120. The lowest 10 percent earned less than $32,490, and the highest 10 percent earned more than $78,560. Median annual earnings in the industries employing the largest numbers of electrical and electronic engineering technicians were:

Wired telecommunications carriers	$56,080
Architectural, engineering, and related services	51,650
Semiconductor and other electronic component manufacturing	48,960
Navigational, measuring, electromedical, and control instruments manufacturing	48,200
Employment services	42,960

In May 2008, median annual wages for aerospace engineering and operations technicians in the aerospace products and parts manufacturing industry were $52,150, and the median annual salary for environmental engineering technicians in the architectural, engineering, and related services industry was $39,510. Median annual wages for civil engineering technicians in the architectural, engineering, and related services industry were $43,880. The median annual wage for industrial engineering technicians in the semiconductor and other electronic component manufacturing industry was $43,760. In the architectural, engineering, and related services industry, the median annual wage for mechanical engineering technicians was $47,130. Electro-mechanical technicians earned a median annual wage of $44,580 in the semiconductor and other electronic component manufacturing industry.

Related Occupations

Engineering technicians apply scientific and engineering skills that are usually gained in postsecondary programs below the bachelor's degree level. Similar occupations include:

Sources of Additional Information

Information about careers in engineering technology is available from:
➤ JETS (Junior Engineering Technical Society), 1420 King St., Suite 405, Alexandria, VA 22314. Internet: **http://www.jets.org**

➤ Pathways to Technology. Internet: **http://www.pathwaystotechnology.org**

Information on engineering technology programs accredited by the Accreditation Board for Engineering and Technology is available from:
➤ ABET, Inc., 111 Market Place, Suite 1050, Baltimore, MD 21202. Internet: **http://www.abet.org**

The Occupational Information Network (O*NET) provides information on a wide range of occupational characteristics. Links to O*NET appear at the end of the Internet version of this occupational statement, accessible at **http://www.bls.gov/ooh/ocos112.htm**

Life Scientists

Agricultural and Food Scientists

Significant Points

- Faster than average growth is expected as agricultural and food scientists develop new products using biotechnology and work to limit the negative environmental impact of agriculture.

- A bachelor's degree in agricultural science is sufficient for most jobs in product development; a master's or Ph.D. degree is generally required for research positions.

- Opportunities are expected to be good.

Nature of the Work

The work of agricultural and food scientists plays an important role in maintaining the Nation's food supply by ensuring agricultural productivity and food safety. *Agricultural scientists* study farm crops and animals and develop ways of improving their quantity and quality. They look for ways to improve crop yield, control pests and weeds more safely and effectively, and conserve soil and water. They research methods of converting raw agricultural commodities into attractive and healthy food products for consumers. Some agricultural scientists look for ways to use agricultural products for fuels.

In recent years, advances in the study of genetics have spurred the growth of biotechnology. Some agricultural and food scientists use biotechnology to manipulate the genetic material of plants and crops, attempting to make these organisms more productive or resistant to disease. Advances in biotechnology have opened up research opportunities in many areas of agricultural and food science, including commercial applications in agriculture, environmental remediation, and the food industry. Interest in the production of biofuels, or fuels manufactured from agricultural derivatives, has also increased. Some agricultural scientists work with biologists and chemists to develop more efficient processes for turning crops into energy sources, such as ethanol produced from corn.

Another emerging technology expected to affect agriculture is nanotechnology—a molecular manufacturing technology which promises to revolutionize methods of testing agricultural and food products for contamination or spoilage. Some food scientists are using nanotechnology to develop sensors that can quickly and accurately detect contaminant molecules in food.

Many agricultural scientists work in basic or applied research and development. Basic research seeks to understand the biological and chemical processes by which crops and livestock grow, such as determining the role of a particular gene in plant growth. Applied research uses this knowledge to discover mechanisms to improve the quality, quantity, and safety of agricultural products. Other agricultural scientists manage or administer research and development programs, or manage marketing or production operations in companies that produce food products or agricultural chemicals, supplies, and machinery. Some agricultural scientists are consultants to business firms, private clients, or government.

Some agricultural and food scientists conduct experiments on new varieties of crops.

Depending on the agricultural or food scientist's area of specialization, the nature of the work performed varies.

Food scientists and technologists usually work in the food processing industry, universities, or the Federal Government to create and improve food products. They use their knowledge of chemistry, physics, engineering, microbiology, biotechnology, and other sciences to develop new or better ways of preserving, processing, packaging, storing, and delivering foods. Some food scientists engage in basic research, discovering new food sources; analyzing food content to determine levels of vitamins, fat, sugar, or protein; or searching for substitutes for harmful or undesirable additives, such as nitrites. Others engage in applied research, finding ways to improve the content of food or to remove harmful additives. They also develop ways to process, preserve, package, or store food according to industry and government regulations. Some continue to research improvements in traditional food processing techniques, such as baking, blanching, canning, drying, evaporation, and pasteurization. Other food scientists enforce government regulations, inspecting food processing areas and ensuring that sanitation, safety, quality, and waste management standards are met.

Food technologists generally work in product development, applying the findings from food science research to improve the selection, preservation, processing, packaging, and distribution of food.

Plant scientists study plants, helping producers of food, feed, and fiber crops to feed a growing population and to conserve natural resources. *Agronomists* and *crop scientists* not only help increase productivity, but also study ways to improve the nutritional value of crops and the quality of seed, often through biotechnology. Some crop scientists study the breeding, physiology, and management of crops and use genetic engineering to develop crops resistant to pests and drought. Some plant scientists develop new technologies to control or eliminate pests and to prevent their spread in ways appropriate to the specific environment. They also conduct research or oversee activities to halt the spread of insect-borne disease.

Soil scientists study the chemical, physical, biological, and mineralogical composition of soils as it relates to plant growth. They also study the responses of various soil types to fertilizers, tillage practices, and crop rotation. Many soil scientists who work for the Federal Government conduct soil surveys, classifying and mapping soils. They provide information and recommendations to farmers and other landowners regarding the best use of land and plants to avoid or correct problems, such as erosion. They may also consult with engineers and other technical personnel working on construction projects about the effects of, and solutions to, soil problems. Because soil science is closely related to environmental science, persons trained in soil science also work to ensure environmental quality and effective land use.

Animal scientists work to develop better, more efficient ways of producing and processing meat, poultry, eggs, and milk. Dairy scientists, poultry scientists, animal breeders, and other scientists in related fields study the genetics, nutrition, reproduction, and growth of domestic farm animals. Some animal scientists inspect and grade livestock food products, purchase livestock, or work in technical sales or marketing. As extension agents or consultants, animal scientists advise agricultural producers on how to upgrade animal housing facilities properly, lower animal mortality rates, handle waste matter, or increase production of animal products, such as milk or eggs.

Work environment. Agricultural scientists involved in management or basic research tend to work regular hours in offices and laboratories. The work environment for those engaged in applied research or product development varies, depending on specialty and type of employer. For example, food scientists in private industry may work in test kitchens while investigating new processing techniques. Animal scientists working for Federal, State, or university research stations may spend part of their time at dairies, farrowing houses, feedlots, farm animal facilities, or outdoors conducting research. Soil and crop scientists also spend time outdoors conducting research on farms and agricultural research stations.

Training, Other Qualifications, and Advancement
A bachelor's degree in agricultural science is sufficient for private industry jobs in product development or applied re-

Projections data from the National Employment Matrix

Occupational Title	SOC Code	Employment, 2008	Projected Employment, 2018	Change, 2008-2018	
				Number	Percent
Agricultural and food scientists	19-1010	31,000	35,900	4,800	16
Animal scientists...	19-1011	3,700	4,200	500	13
Food scientists and technologists...	19-1012	13,400	15,600	2,200	16
Soil and plant Scientists...	19-1013	13,900	16,100	2,200	15

(NOTE) Data in this table are rounded. See the discussion of the employment projections table in the *Handbook* introductory chapter on *Occupational Information Included in the Handbook.*

search, but a master's or doctoral degree is generally required for research jobs at universities.

Education and training. Training requirements for agricultural scientists depend on the type of work they perform. Most jobs in the farming and food processing industry require a bachelor's degree, but a master's or doctoral degree is usually required for research positions at universities. A Ph.D. in agricultural science is also needed for college teaching and for advancement to senior research positions. Degrees in related sciences such as biology, chemistry, or physics or in related engineering specialties also may qualify people for many agricultural science jobs.

All States have a land-grant college that offers agricultural science degrees. Many other colleges and universities also offer agricultural science degrees or agricultural science courses. However, not every school offers all specialties. A typical undergraduate agricultural science curriculum includes communications, mathematics, economics, business, and physical and life sciences courses, in addition to a wide variety of technical agricultural science courses. For example, degrees in animal sciences may include courses on animal breeding, reproductive physiology, nutrition, and meat and muscle biology. Graduate students usually specialize in a subfield of agricultural science, such as animal breeding and genetics, crop science, or horticulture science, depending on their interests. For example, those interested in doing genetic and biotechnological research in the food industry need a strong background in life and physical sciences, such as cell and molecular biology, microbiology, and inorganic and organic chemistry. Undergraduate students, however, need not specialize. In fact, undergraduates who are broadly trained often have greater career flexibility.

Students preparing to be food scientists take courses such as food chemistry, food analysis, food microbiology, food engineering, and food processing operations. Those preparing to be soil and plant scientists take courses in plant pathology, soil chemistry, entomology, plant physiology, and biochemistry, among others. Advanced degree programs include classroom and fieldwork, laboratory research, and a thesis or dissertation based on independent research.

Licensure. Some States require soil scientists to be licensed to practice. Licensing requirements vary by State, but generally include holding a bachelor's degree with a certain number of credit hours in soil science, a certain number of years working under a licensed scientist, and passage of an examination.

Other qualifications. Agricultural and food scientists should be able to work independently or as part of a team and be able to communicate clearly and concisely, both orally and in writing. Most of these scientists also need an understanding of basic business principles, the ability to apply statistical techniques, and the ability to use computers to analyze data and to control biological and chemical processing.

Certification and advancement. Agricultural scientists who have advanced degrees usually begin in research or teaching. With experience, they may advance to jobs as supervisors of research programs or managers of other agriculture-related activities.

The American Society of Agronomy certifies agronomists and crop advisors, and the Soil Science Society of America certifies soil scientists and soil classifiers. Certification is not necessary to work in these occupations, but it may improve opportunities by providing proof of a worker's qualifications. Certification in agronomy requires a bachelor's degree in agronomy or a related field and 5 years of experience, a master's degree and 3 years, or a doctoral degree and 1 year. Crop advising certification requires either 4 years of experience or a bachelor's degree in agriculture and 2 years of experience. To become certified in soil science or soil classification, applicants must have a bachelor's degree in soil science and 5 years of experience or a graduate degree and 3 years of experience. To receive any of these certifications, applicants must also pass designated examinations and agree to adhere to a code of ethics. Each certification is maintained through continuing education.

Employment

Agricultural and food scientists held about 31,000 jobs in 2008. Soil and plant scientists accounted for 13,900, food scientists and technologist for 13,400, while the remaining 3,700 were animal scientists. In addition, many people trained in these sciences held faculty positions in colleges and universities. (See the statement on teachers—postsecondary elsewhere in the *Handbook.*)

About 20 percent worked for manufacturing companies, mainly in food and pharmaceutical manufacturing, and another 15 percent worked in educational institutions. The Federal Government employed about 7 percent, mostly in the U.S. Department of Agriculture. Other agricultural and food scientists worked for research and development laboratories and wholesale distributors. About 12 percent of agricultural scientists were self-employed in 2008, mainly as consultants.

Job Outlook

Job growth among agricultural and food scientists should be faster than the average for all occupations. Opportunities are expected to be good over the next decade, particularly in food science and technology and in agronomy.

Employment change. Employment of agricultural and food scientists is expected to grow by 16 percent between 2008 and 2018, faster than the average for all occupations. Job growth will stem primarily from efforts to increase the quantity and quality of food produced for a growing population. Additionally, an increasing awareness about the health effects of certain types of foods and the effects of food production on the environment, will give rise to research into the best methods of food production.

Emerging biotechnologies will continue to play a large role in agricultural research, and applying these advances will provide many employment opportunities for scientists. For example, they may use findings from genomics to create agricultural products with higher yields and resistance to pests and pathogens. New developments will also be used to improve the quality and safety of prepared food products bought by consumers.

Agricultural scientists will also be needed to balance increased agricultural output with protection and preservation of soil, water, and ecosystems. They increasingly will help develop sustainable agricultural practices by creating and implementing plans to manage pests, crops, soil fertility and erosion, and animal waste in ways that reduce the use of harmful chemicals and minimize damage to the natural environment. In addition, demand for biofuels—renewable energy sources derived from plants—is expected to increase. Agricultural scientists will be needed both to find new techniques for converting organic material into usable energy sources and to find ways to increase the output of crops used in these products.

Job growth for food scientists and technologists will be driven by the demand for new food products and food safety measures. Food research is expected to increase because of heightened public awareness of diet, health, food safety, and biosecurity—preventing the introduction of infectious agents into herds of animals. Advances in biotechnology and nanotechnology should also spur demand, as food scientists and technologists apply these technologies to testing and monitoring food safety.

Job prospects. Opportunities should be good for agricultural and food scientists in almost all fields. Those with a bachelor's degree should experience very good opportunities in food science and technology and in agronomy. Those with a master's or Ph.D. degree in agricultural and food science will also experience good opportunities, although positions in basic research and teaching at colleges and universities are limited.

Many people with bachelor's degrees in agricultural sciences also find work in positions related to agricultural or food science, rather than in jobs as agricultural or food scientists. A bachelor's degree in agricultural science is useful for managerial jobs in farm-related or ranch-related businesses, such as farm credit institutions or companies that manufacture or sell feed, fertilizer, seed, and farm equipment. In some cases, people with a bachelor's degree can provide consulting services or work in sales and marketing—promoting high-demand products such as organic foods. Bachelor's degrees

in agricultural science also may help people become farmers, ranchers, and agricultural managers; agricultural inspectors; or purchasing agents for agricultural commodity or farm supply companies.

Employment of agricultural and food scientists is relatively stable during periods of economic recession. Layoffs are less likely among agricultural and food scientists than in some other occupations, because food is a staple item and its demand fluctuates very little with economic activity.

Earnings

Median annual wages of food scientists and technologists were $59,520 in May 2008. The middle 50 percent earned between $43,600 and $81,340. The lowest 10 percent earned less than $33,790, and the highest 10 percent earned more than $104,520. Median annual wages of soil and plant scientists were $58,390 in May 2008. The middle 50 percent earned between $44,150 and $78,080. The lowest 10 percent earned less than $34,260, and the highest 10 percent earned more than $105,340. In May 2008, median annual wages of animal scientists were $56,030.

The average Federal salary in 2009 was $104,184 in animal science and $79,158 in soil science.

According to the National Association of Colleges and Employers, beginning salary offers in July 2009 for graduates with a bachelor's degree in animal sciences averaged $33,732 a year; plant sciences, $33,456 a year; and in other agricultural sciences, $34,699 a year.

Related Occupations

The work of agricultural scientists is closely related to that of other scientists, including:

	Page
Biological scientists	181
Chemists and materials scientists	195
Conservation scientists and foresters	185
Medical scientists	189

Other occupations that relate to agricultural production include:
Farmers, ranchers, and agricultural managers	48

Another occupation that works closely with animals:
Veterinarians	402

Sources of Additional Information

Information on careers in agricultural science is available from Purdue University and the U.S. Department of Agriculture at: **http://www.agriculture.purdue.edu/USDA/careers**

Information on careers in food science and technology is available from:
➤ Institute of Food Technologists, 525 W. Van Buren, Suite 1000, Chicago, IL 60607. Internet: **http://www.ift.org**

Information on careers in plant and soil sciences is available from:
➤ American Society of Agronomy, 677 S. Segoe Rd., Madison, WI 53711-1086. Internet: **http://www.agronomy.org**

➤ Crop Science Society of America, 677 S. Segoe Rd., Madison, WI 53711-1086. Internet: **http://www.crops.org**

➤ Soil Science Society of America, 677 S. Segoe Rd., Madison, WI 53711-1086. Internet: **http://www.soils.org**

Information on getting a job as an agricultural scientist with the Federal Government is available from the Office of Personnel Management through USAJOBS, the Federal Government's official employment information system. This resource for locating and applying for job opportunities can be accessed through the Internet at **http://www.usajobs.opm.gov** or through an interactive voice response telephone system at (703) 724-1850 or TDD (978) 461-8404. These numbers are not toll free, so charges may result.

The Occupational Information Network (O*NET) provides information on a wide range of occupational characteristics. Links to O*NET appear at the end of the Internet version of this occupational statement, accessible at **http://www.bls.gov/ooh/ocos046.htm**

Biological Scientists

Significant Points

- Biotechnological research and development should continue to drive much faster than average employment growth.

- A Ph.D. is usually required for independent research, but a bachelor's degree is sufficient for some jobs in applied research or product development; temporary postdoctoral research positions are common.

- Competition for independent research positions in academia is expected.

Nature of the Work

Biological scientists study living organisms and their relationship to the environment. They perform research to gain a better understanding of fundamental life processes and apply that understanding to developing new products or processes. Research can be broken down into two categories: basic and applied. Basic research is conducted without any intended aim; the goal is simply to expand on human knowledge. Applied research is directed towards solving a particular problem. Most biological scientists specialize in one area of biology, such as zoology (the study of animals) or microbiology (the study of microscopic organisms). (Medical scientists, whose work is closely related to that of biological scientists, are discussed elsewhere in the *Handbook*.)

Basic research in biological sciences advances our knowledge of living organisms so that we can develop solutions to human health problems and improve the natural environment. These biological scientists mostly work in government, university, or private industry laboratories, often exploring new areas of research. Many expand on specialized research they started in graduate school.

Many biological scientists involved in basic research must submit grant proposals to obtain funding for their projects. Colleges and universities, private foundations, and Federal Government agencies, such as the National Institutes of Health and the National Science Foundation, contribute to the support of scientists whose research proposals are determined to be financially feasible and to have the potential to advance new ideas or processes.

Biological scientists who work in applied research or product development apply knowledge gained through basic research to develop new drugs, treatments, and medical diagnostic tests; increase crop yields; and develop new biofuels. They usually have less freedom than basic researchers do to choose the emphasis of their research, and they spend more time working on marketable treatments to meet the business goals of their employers. Biological scientists doing applied research and product development often work in teams, interacting with engineers, scientists of other disciplines, business managers, and technicians. Those working in private industry may be required to describe their research plans or results to nonscientists who are in a position to veto or approve their ideas. These scientists must consider the business effects of their work. Some biological scientists also work with customers or suppliers and manage budgets.

Scientists usually conduct research in laboratories using a wide variety of other equipment. Some conduct experiments involving animals or plants. This is particularly true of botanists, physiologists, and zoologists. Some biological research also takes place outside the laboratory. For example, a botanist might do field research in tropical rain forests to see which plants grow there, or an ecologist might study how a forest area recovers after a fire. Some marine biologists also work outdoors, often on research vessels from which they study fish, plankton, or other marine organisms.

Swift advances in knowledge of genetics and organic molecules spurred growth in the field of biotechnology, transforming the industries in which biological scientists work. Biological scientists can now manipulate the genetic material of animals and plants, attempting to make organisms more productive or resistant to disease. Those working on various genome (chromosomes with their associated genes) projects isolate genes and determine their function. This work continues to lead to the discovery of genes associated with specific diseases and inherited health risks, such as sickle cell anemia. Advances in biotechnology have created research opportunities in almost all areas of biology, with commercial applications in areas such as medicine, agriculture, and environmental remediation.

Most biological scientists specialize in the study of a certain type of organism or in a specific activity, although recent advances have blurred some traditional classifications.

Aquatic biologists study micro-organisms, plants, and animals living in water. *Marine biologists* study salt water organisms, and *limnologists* study fresh water organisms. Much of the work of marine biology centers on molecular biology, the study of the biochemical processes that take place inside living cells. Marine biologists are sometimes called oceanographers, a broader field that also includes the study of the physical characteristics of oceans and the ocean floor. (See the *Handbook* statement on geoscientists and hydrologists.)

Biochemists study the chemical composition of living things. They analyze the complex chemical combinations and reactions involved in metabolism, reproduction, and growth. Biochem-

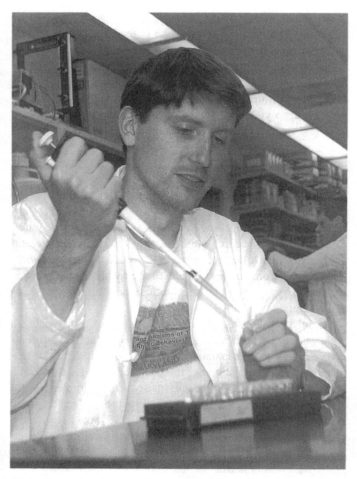

Biological scientists conduct research in college or university, private industry, and government laboratories.

ists do most of their work in biotechnology, which involves understanding the complex chemistry of life.

Biophysicists study how physics, such as electrical and mechanical energy, relates to living cells and organisms. They perform research in fields such as neuroscience or bioinformatics (the use of computers to process biological information, usually at the molecular level).

Microbiologists investigate the growth and characteristics of microscopic organisms such as bacteria, algae, or fungi. Most microbiologists specialize in environmental, food, agricultural, or industrial microbiology; virology (the study of viruses); immunology (the study of mechanisms that fight infections); or bioinformatics. Many microbiologists use biotechnology to advance knowledge of cell reproduction and human disease.

Physiologists study life functions of plants and animals, both in the whole organism and at the cellular or molecular level, under normal and abnormal conditions. Physiologists often specialize in functions such as growth, reproduction, photosynthesis, respiration, or movement, or in the physiology of a certain area or system of the organism.

Botanists study plants and their environments. Some study all aspects of plant life, including algae, fungi, lichens, mosses, ferns, conifers, and flowering plants; others specialize in areas such as identification and classification of plants, the structure and function of plant parts, the biochemistry of plant processes, the causes and cures of plant diseases, the interaction of plants

with other organisms and the environment, and the geological record of plants.

Zoologists and wildlife biologists study animals and wildlife—their origin, behavior, diseases, and life processes. Some experiment with live animals in controlled or natural surroundings, while others dissect dead animals to study their structure. Zoologists and wildlife biologists also may collect and analyze biological data to determine the environmental effects of current and potential uses of land and water areas. Zoologists are usually identified by the animal group they study—ornithologists study birds, for example, mammalogists study mammals, herpetologists study reptiles, and ichthyologists study fish.

Ecologists investigate the relationships among organisms and between organisms and their environments. They examine the effects of population size, pollutants, rainfall, temperature, and altitude. Using knowledge of various scientific disciplines, ecologists may collect, study, and report data on the quality of air, food, soil, and water.

(Two other occupations closely related to biological scientists are covered in more detail elsewhere in the *Handbook*: agricultural and food scientists, who study domesticated plants and animals consumed as food, and medical scientists, who study human diseases and human health.)

Work environment. Most biologists spend their time in laboratories conducting research and in offices writing up results and keeping up with the latest research discoveries. Some biological scientists, particularly botanists, ecologists, and zoologists, do field studies that involve strenuous physical activity and primitive living conditions for extended periods of time. Biological scientists in the field may work in warm or cold climates, in all kinds of weather. Biological scientists usually are not exposed to unsafe or unhealthy conditions. Those who work with dangerous organisms or toxic substances in the laboratory must follow strict safety procedures to avoid contamination.

Many biological scientists, particularly those employed in academic settings, depend on grant money to support their research. They may be under pressure to meet deadlines and to conform to rigid grant-writing specifications when preparing proposals to seek new or extended funding.

Biological scientists typically work regular hours. While the 40-hour workweek is common, some biological scientists work longer hours. Some researchers may be required to work odd hours in laboratories or other locations (especially while in the field), depending on the nature of their research.

Training, Other Qualifications, and Advancement

Most biological scientists need a Ph.D. in biology or one of its subfields to work in independent research or development positions. Other positions are available to those with a master's or bachelor's degree in the field.

Education and training. A Ph.D. is usually necessary for independent research, particularly in academia, as well as for advancement to administrative positions. A bachelor's or master's degree is sufficient for some jobs in applied research, product development, management, or inspection; it also may be sufficient to work as a research technician or a teacher. Many with a bachelor's degree in biology enter medical, dental, veterinary,

Projections data from the National Employment Matrix

Occupational Title	SOC Code	Employment, 2008	Projected Employment, 2018	Change, 2008-2018	
				Number	Percent
Biological scientists	19-1020	91,300	110,500	19,200	21
Biochemists and biophysicists	19-1021	23,200	31,900	8,700	37
Microbiologists	19-1022	16,900	18,900	2,100	12
Zoologists and wildlife biologists	19-1023	19,500	22,000	2,500	13
Biological scientists, all other	19-1029	31,700	37,600	5,900	19

(NOTE) Data in this table are rounded. See the discussion of the employment projections table in the *Handbook* introductory chapter on *Occupational Information Included in the Handbook.*

or other health profession schools, or find jobs as high school science teachers. (See the statement on teachers—kindergarten, elementary, middle, and secondary.)

In addition to required courses in chemistry and biology, undergraduate biological science majors usually study allied disciplines such as mathematics, physics, engineering, and computer science. Computer courses are beneficial for modeling and simulating biological processes, operating some laboratory equipment, and performing research in the emerging field of bioinformatics. Those interested in studying the environment also should take courses in environmental studies and become familiar with applicable legislation and regulations.

Most colleges and universities offer bachelor's degrees in biological science, and many offer advanced degrees. Advanced degree programs often emphasize a subfield, such as microbiology or botany, but not all universities offer curricula in all subfields. Larger universities frequently have separate departments specializing in different areas of biological science. For example, a program in botany might cover agronomy, horticulture, or plant pathology. Advanced degree programs typically include classroom and fieldwork, laboratory research, and a thesis or dissertation. A master's degree generally takes 2 years, and a doctoral degree 5-6 years of full-time study.

Biological scientists with a Ph.D. often take temporary postdoctoral positions that provide specialized research experience. Postdoctoral positions may offer the opportunity to publish research findings. A solid record of published research is essential in obtaining a permanent position performing basic research, especially for those seeking a permanent college or university faculty position.

Other qualifications. Biological scientists should be able to work independently or as part of a team and be able to communicate clearly and concisely, both orally and in writing. Those in private industry, especially those who aspire to management or administrative positions, should possess strong business and communication skills and be familiar with regulatory issues and marketing and management techniques. Those doing field research in remote areas must have physical stamina. Biological scientists also must have patience and self-discipline to conduct long and detailed research projects.

Advancement. As they gain experience, biological scientists typically gain greater control over their research and may advance to become lead researchers directing a team of scientists and technicians. Some work as consultants to businesses or to government agencies. However, those dependent on research grants are still constrained by funding agencies, and may spend much of their time writing grant proposals. Others

choose to move into managerial positions and become natural science managers (see engineering and natural sciences managers elsewhere in the *Handbook*). They may plan and administer programs for testing foods and drugs, for example, or direct activities at zoos or botanical gardens. Those who pursue management careers spend much of their time preparing budgets and schedules. Some leave biology for nontechnical managerial, administrative, or sales jobs.

Employment

Biological scientists held about 91,300 jobs in 2008. In addition, many biological scientists held biology faculty positions in colleges and universities but are not included in these numbers. Those whose primary work involves teaching and research are considered postsecondary teachers. (See the statement on teachers—postsecondary elsewhere in the *Handbook*.)

About 40 percent of all biological scientists were employed by Federal, State, and local governments. Federal biological scientists worked mainly for the U.S. Departments of Agriculture, Interior, and Defense and for the National Institutes of Health. Most of the rest worked in scientific research and testing laboratories, the pharmaceutical and medicine manufacturing industry, or educational institutions.

Job Outlook

Employment of biological scientists is expected to increase much faster than the average for all occupations although there will continue to be competition for some basic research positions.

Employment change. Employment of biological scientists is projected to grow 21 percent over the 2008–18 decade, much faster than the average for all occupations, as biotechnological research and development continues to drive job growth. Biological scientists enjoyed very rapid employment gains over the past few decades—reflecting, in part, the growth of the biotechnology industry. Employment growth will moderate somewhat as the biotechnology industry matures, with fewer new firms being founded and existing firms merging or being absorbed by larger biotechnology or pharmaceutical firms. However, much of the basic biological research done in recent years has resulted in new knowledge, including the isolation and identification of genes. Biological scientists will be needed to take this knowledge to the next stage, understanding how certain genes function within an entire organism, so that medical treatments can be developed to treat various diseases. Even pharmaceutical and other firms not solely engaged in biotechnology use biotechnology techniques extensively, spurring employment for biological scientists. For example, biological scientists are continuing to help farmers increase crop yields by pinpointing genes that can help crops, such as wheat, grow in more extreme climate conditions.

In addition, efforts to discover new and improved ways to clean up and preserve the environment will continue to add to job growth. More biological scientists will be needed to determine the environmental impact of industry and government actions and to prevent or correct environmental problems, such as the negative effects of pesticide use. Some biological scientists will find opportunities in environmental regulatory agencies, while others will use their expertise to advise lawmakers on legislation to save environmentally sensitive areas. New industrial applications of biotechnology, such as new methods for producing biofuels, also will spur demand for biological scientists.

The Federal Government is a major source of funding for basic research and development, including many areas of medical research that relate to biological science. Large budget increases at the National Institutes of Health in the early part of the decade led to increases in Federal basic research and development expenditures, with research grants growing both in number and dollar amount. However, the increase in expenditures slowed substantially in recent years. Going forward, the level of Federal funding will continue to impact competition for winning and renewing research grants.

There will continue to be demand for biological scientists specializing in botany, zoology, and marine biology, but opportunities will be limited because of the small size of these fields. Marine biology, despite its attractiveness as a career, is a very small specialty within biological science.

Job prospects. Doctoral degree holders are expected to face competition for basic research positions in academia. Furthermore, should the number of advanced degrees awarded continue to grow, applicants for research grants are likely to face even more competition. Currently, about 1 in 4 grant proposals are approved for long-term research projects. In general, applied research positions in private industry are somewhat easier to obtain, but may become more competitive if increasing numbers of scientists seek jobs in private industry because of the difficulty finding positions in colleges and universities.

Prospective marine biology students should be aware that those who would like to enter this specialty far outnumber the very few openings that occur each year for the type of glamorous research jobs that many would like to obtain. Almost all marine biologists who do basic research have a Ph.D.

People with bachelor's and master's degrees are expected to have more opportunities in nonscientist jobs related to biology, in fields like sales, marketing, publishing, and research management. Non-Ph.D.s also may fill positions as science or engineering technicians or as medical health technologists and technicians. Some become high school biology teachers.

Biological scientists are less likely to lose their jobs during recessions than those in other occupations, because many are employed on long-term research projects. However, an economic downturn could influence the amount of money allocated to new research and development efforts, particularly in areas of risky or innovative research. An economic downturn also could limit the possibility of extension or renewal of existing projects.

Earnings

Median annual wages of biochemists and biophysicists were $82,840 in May 2008. The middle 50 percent earned between $59,260 and $108,950. The lowest 10 percent earned less than $44,320, and the highest 10 percent earned more than $139,440. Median annual wages of biochemists and biophysicists employed in scientific research and development services were $85,870 in May 2008.

Median annual wages of microbiologists were $64,350 in May 2008. The middle 50 percent earned between $48,330 and $87,040. The lowest 10 percent earned less than $38,240, and the highest 10 percent earned more than $111,300.

Median annual wages of zoologists and wildlife biologists were $55,290 in May 2008. The middle 50 percent earned between $43,060 and $70,500. The lowest 10 percent earned less than $33,550, and the highest 10 percent earned more than $90,850.

According to the National Association of Colleges and Employers, beginning salary offers in July 2009 averaged $33,254 a year for bachelor's degree recipients in biological and life sciences.

In the Federal Government in March 2009, microbiologists earned an average annual salary of $97,264; ecologists, $84,283; physiologists, $109,323; geneticists, $99,752; zoologists, $116,908; and botanists, $72,792.

Related Occupations

Other life science research occupations include:

	Page
Agricultural and food scientists	177
Conservation scientists and foresters	185
Engineering and natural sciences managers	46
Epidemiologists	446
Medical scientists	189
Teachers—postsecondary	282

Other health-related specialists with similar levels of education include:

Dentists	363
Physicians and surgeons	381
Veterinarians	402

Sources of Additional Information

For information on careers in the biological sciences, contact:
➤ American Institute of Biological Sciences, 1444 I St. NW., Suite 200, Washington, DC 20005. Internet: **http://www.aibs.org**

➤ Federation of American Societies for Experimental Biology, 9650 Rockville Pike, Bethesda, MD 20814. Internet: **http://www.faseb.org**

For information on careers in biochemistry or molecular biology, contact:
➤ American Society for Biochemistry and Molecular Biology, 9650 Rockville Pike, Bethesda, MD 20814. Internet: **http://www.asbmb.org**

For information on careers in botany, contact:
➤ The Botanical Society of America, P.O. Box 299, St. Louis, MO 63166. Internet: **http://www.botany.org**

For information on careers in cell biology, contact:
➤ American Society for Cell Biology, 8120 Woodmont Ave, Suite 750, Bethesda, MD 20814. Internet: **http://www.ascb.org**

For information on careers in ecology, contact:
➤ Ecological Society of America, 1990 M St. NW, Suite 700, Washington, DC 20036. Internet: **http://www.esa.org**

For information on careers in microbiology, contact:
➤ American Society for Microbiology, Career Information—Education Department, 1752 N St. NW., Washington, DC 20036. Internet: **http://www.asm.org**

For information on careers in physiology, contact:
➤ American Physiology Society, 9650 Rockville Pike, Bethesda, MD 20814. Internet: **http://www.the-aps.org**

Information on obtaining a biological scientist position with the Federal Government is available from the Office of Personnel Management through USAJOBS, the Federal Government's official employment information system. This resource for locating and applying for job opportunities can be accessed through the Internet at **http://www.usajobs.opm.gov** or through an interactive voice response telephone system at (703) 724-1850 or TDD (978) 461-8404. These numbers are not toll free, so charges may result.

The Occupational Information Network (O*NET) provides information on a wide range of occupational characteristics. Links to O*NET appear at the end of the Internet version of this occupational statement, accessible at **http://www.bls.gov/ooh/ocos047.htm**

Conservation Scientists and Foresters

Significant Points

- About 68 percent of conservation scientists and foresters work for Federal, State, or local governments.

- Most jobs require a bachelor's degree; research and teaching positions usually require a graduate degree.

- Foresters and conservation scientists should enjoy working outdoors, be able to tolerate extensive walking and other types of physical exertion, and be willing to relocate to find work.

- In addition to job openings from growth, many openings are expected as today's conservation scientists and foresters retire.

Nature of the Work

Conservation scientists and foresters manage the use and development of forests, rangelands, and other natural resources. These lands supply wood products, livestock forage, minerals, and water. They serve as sites for recreational activities

Conservation scientists and foresters often work outdoors.

and provide habitats for wildlife. Some workers advise private landowners on the use and management of their land and may design and implement programs that make the land healthier and more productive. Others work to conserve or restore public or private lands. Conservation scientists and foresters often specialize in one of several areas, such as soil conservation, urban forestry, pest management, native species, or forest economics.

Foresters oversee our Nation's forests and direct activities on them for economic, recreational, conservational, and environmental purposes. Individual landowners, the public, and industry own most of the forested land in this country, and they require the expertise of foresters to keep the forests healthy and sustainable. Often, this means coming up with a plan to keep the forests free from disease, harmful insects, and damaging wildfires by planning, for example, when and where to plant trees and vegetation and when to cut timber. It also may mean coming up with ways to make the land profitable but still protected for future generations.

Foresters have a wide range of duties, depending on whom they are working for. Some primary duties of foresters include drawing up plans to regenerate forested lands, monitoring the progress of those lands, and supervising harvests. Land management foresters choose and direct the preparation of sites on which trees will be planted. They oversee controlled burning and the use of bulldozers or herbicides to clear weeds, brush, and logging debris. They advise on the type, number, and placement of trees to be planted. Foresters then monitor the seedlings to ensure healthy growth and to determine the best time for harvesting. If they detect signs of disease or harmful insects, they consult with specialists in forest pest management to decide on the best treatment. When the trees reach a certain size, foresters decide which trees should be harvested and sold to sawmills.

Procurement foresters make up a large share of foresters. Their job is to buy timber, typically for a sawmill or wood products manufacturer, by contacting local forest owners and negotiating a sale. This activity typically involves taking inventory of the type, amount, and location of all standing timber on the property, a process known as timber cruising. They then appraise the timber's worth, negotiate its purchase, and draw up a contract for purchase. Next, the forester subcontracts with loggers or pulpwood cutters for tree removal and to aid in laying out roads to access the timber. Throughout the process, foresters maintain close contact with the subcontractor and the landowner to ensure that the work meets the landowner's requirements and Federal, State, and local environmental regulations.

Throughout the forest management and procurement processes, foresters often are responsible for conserving wildlife habitats and creek beds within forests, maintaining water quality and soil stability, and complying with environmental regulations. Foresters must balance the desire to conserve forested ecosystems with the need to use forest resources for recreational or economic purposes. For example, foresters increasingly are working with landowners to find ways to generate money from forested lands, such as using them for hunting or other recreational activity, without cutting down trees. A major concern of foresters is the prevention of devastating wildfires. Using a variety of techniques, including the thinning of forests and controlled burns (to clear brush), foresters work with governments and private landowners to minimize the impact of fire on the forest. During a fire, they work with or supervise firefighters and plan ways to contain the fire.

Some foresters, mostly in the Federal Government, perform research on issues facing forests and related natural resources. They may study tree improvement and harvesting techniques; global climate change; protection of forests from pests, diseases, and fire; improving wildlife habitats; forest recreation; and other topics. State foresters may perform some research, but more often work with private landowners in developing forest management plans. Both Federal and State foresters enforce relevant environmental laws, including laws on water quality and fire suppression.

Relatively new fields in forestry are urban forestry and conservation education. Urban foresters live and work in larger cities and manage urban trees. They are concerned with quality-of-life issues, such as air quality, shade, beautification, storm water runoff, and property values. Conservation education foresters train teachers and students about sound forest stewardship.

Conservation scientists manage, improve, and protect the country's natural resources. They work with landowners and Federal, State, and local governments to devise ways to use and improve the land while safeguarding the environment. Conservation scientists advise farmers, farm managers, and ranchers on how they can improve their land for agricultural purposes and to control erosion. A growing number of conservation scientists also are advising landowners and governments on recreational uses for the land.

Two of the more common conservation scientists are *range managers* and *soil conservationists*. Range managers, also called range conservationists, range ecologists, or range scientists, study, manage, improve, and protect rangelands to maximize their use without damaging the environment. Rangelands cover hundreds of millions of acres of the United States, mostly in western States and Alaska. They contain many natural resources, including grass and shrubs for animal grazing, wildlife habitats, water from vast watersheds, recreation facilities, and valuable mineral and energy resources.

Range managers may inventory soils, plants, and animals; develop resource management plans; help to restore degraded ecosystems; or assist in managing a ranch. For example, they may help ranchers attain optimum livestock production by determining the number and kind of animals to graze, the grazing system to use, and the best season for grazing. At the same time, however, range managers maintain soil stability and vegetation for other uses, such as wildlife habitats and outdoor recreation. Like foresters, range managers work to prevent and mitigate wildfires and invasive animal species. They also plan and implement revegetation of disturbed sites.

Soil and *water conservationists* provide technical assistance to farmers, ranchers, forest managers, State and local agencies, and others concerned with the conservation of soil, water, and related natural resources. For private landowners, they develop programs designed to make the most productive use of land without damaging it. Soil conservationists also assist landowners by visiting areas with erosion problems, finding the source of the problem, and helping landowners and managers develop management practices to combat it. Water conservationists also assist private landowners and Federal, State, and local governments by advising on water quality, preserving water supplies, preventing groundwater contamination, and management and conservation of water resources.

Conservation scientists and foresters use a number of tools to perform their jobs. Clinometers measure the heights of trees, diameter tapes measure tree diameters, and increment borers and bark gauges measure the growth of trees so that timber volumes can be computed and growth rates estimated. Remote sensing (aerial photographs and other imagery taken from airplanes and satellites) and geographic information systems (GIS) data often are used for mapping large forest or range areas and for detecting widespread trends of forest and land use. Once a map is generated, data are digitized to create a computerized inventory of information required to manage the land and its resources. Hand-held computers, global positioning systems (GPS), and Internet-based applications are used extensively.

Work environment. Working conditions vary considerably. Some foresters and conservation scientists work regular hours in offices or laboratories, but others may split their time between fieldwork and office work. Independent consultants and new, less experienced workers spend the majority of their time outdoors overseeing or participating in hands-on work. Fieldwork can involve long hours alone.

The work can be physically demanding. Some conservation scientists and foresters work outdoors in all types of weather, sometimes in isolated areas, and consequently may need to walk long distances through densely wooded land to carry out their work. Natural disasters may cause foresters and conservation scientists to work long hours during emergencies. For example, foresters often have to work long hours during fire season, and conservation scientists frequently are called to prevent erosion after a forest fire and to provide emergency help after floods, mud slides, and tropical storms.

Foresters employed by Federal and State governments usually work 40 hours a week, but not always on a standard schedule. In field positions, foresters often work for long blocks of time—10 days straight, followed by 4 days off, for example. Overtime may be necessary when working in firefighting, law enforcement, or natural-disaster response.

Training, Other Qualifications, and Advancement

Most forester and conservation scientist jobs require a bachelor's degree. Research and teaching positions usually require a graduate degree.

Education and training. A bachelor's degree in forestry, biology, natural resource management, environmental sciences, or a related discipline is the minimum educational requirement for careers in forestry. In the Federal Government, a combination of experience and appropriate education may substitute for a bachelor's degree, but competition for jobs makes this route to a career in the occupation less common. Foresters who wish to do research or to teach usually need an advanced degree, preferably a Ph.D.

Conservation scientists generally have at least a bachelor's degree in a field such as natural resource management, rangeland management, agricultural science, or environmental science. A master's degree or Ph.D. usually is required for teaching and research positions.

Most land-grant colleges and universities offer degrees in forestry. The Society of American Foresters accredits about 50 degree programs throughout the country. Curricula focus on four areas: forest ecology and biology, measurement of forest resources, management of forest resources, and public policy. Students should balance general science courses such as ecology, biology, tree physiology, taxonomy, and soil formation with technical forestry courses such as forest inventory, wildlife habitat assessment, remote sensing, land surveying, GPS technology, integrated forest resource management, forest protection, and silviculture (the care and cultivation of forest trees). In addition, mathematics, statistics, and computer science courses are recommended. Courses in resource policy and administration—specifically, forest economics and business administration—also are helpful. Forestry curricula increasingly are including courses on wetlands analysis and sustainability and regulatory issues because prospective foresters need a strong grasp of Federal, State, and local policy issues and an understanding of complex environmental regulations.

Many colleges require students to complete a field session either in a camp operated by the college or in a cooperative work-study program with a Federal or State agency or in private industry. All schools encourage students to take summer jobs that provide experience in forestry or conservation work.

Range managers usually have a degree in range management or range science. Nine colleges and universities that are accredited by the Society of Range Management offer degrees in the subject. More than 40 other schools offer coursework in range science or in a closely related discipline. Range management courses combine plant, animal, and soil sciences with principles of ecology and resource management. Desirable electives include statistics, forestry, hydrology, agronomy, wildlife, animal husbandry, computer science, and recreation. Selection of a minor in range management, such as wildlife ecology, watershed management, animal science, or agricultural economics, can often enhance one's qualifications for certain types of employment.

Very few colleges and universities offer degrees in soil conservation. Most soil conservationists have degrees in environmental studies, agronomy, general agriculture, hydrology, or crop or soil science; some have degrees in related fields such as wildlife biology, forestry, and range management. Programs of study usually include 30 semester hours in natural resources or agriculture, with at least 3 hours in soil science.

Licensure. Sixteen States sponsor some type of credentialing process for foresters. Alabama, California, Connecticut, Maine, Maryland, Massachusetts, and New Hampshire have licensing statutes. Arkansas, Georgia, Mississippi, North Carolina, and South Carolina have mandatory registration statutes, and Michigan, New Jersey, Oklahoma, and West Virginia have voluntary registration statutes. Both licensing and registration requirements usually entail completing a 4-year degree in forestry and several years of forestry work experience. Candidates pursuing licensing also may be required to pass a comprehensive written exam.

Other qualifications. Foresters and conservation scientists should enjoy working outdoors, be able to tolerate extensive walking and other types of physical exertion, and be willing to relocate to find work. The ability to use technology and quantitative tools also is important. Foresters and conservation scientists must work well with people and have good communication skills.

Certification and advancement. Over time, many conservation scientists and foresters advance to take on managerial duties. They also may conduct research or work on policy issues, often after gaining an advanced degree.

One option for advancement in these occupations is to become certified. The Society of American Foresters certifies foresters who have at least a bachelor's degree from one of the 50 forestry programs accredited by the Society or from a forestry program that, though not accredited by the Society, is substantially equivalent. In addition, the candidate must have 5 years of qualifying professional experience and pass an examination.

The Society for Range Management offers two types of certification: one as a certified professional in rangeland management and another as a certified range management consultant. Candidates seeking certification must have at least a bachelor's degree in range science or a closely related field, a minimum of 6 years of full-time work experience, and a passing score on an exam.

Recent forestry and conservation scientist graduates usually work under the supervision of experienced foresters or scientists. After gaining experience, they may advance to positions with more responsibilities. In the Federal Government, most entry-level foresters work in forest resource management. Experienced Federal foresters may supervise a ranger district and may advance to forest supervisor, regional forester, or a top administrative position in the national headquarters, where they may work on issues related to forest policy.

In private industry, foresters start by learning the practical and administrative aspects of the business and by acquiring

Projections data from the National Employment Matrix

Occupational Title	SOC Code	Employment, 2008	Projected Employment, 2018	Change, 2008-2018	
				Number	Percent
Conservation scientists and foresters..	19-1030	29,800	33,400	3,600	12
Conservation scientists...	19-1031	18,300	20,500	2,200	12
Foresters..	19-1032	11,500	12,900	1,400	12

(NOTE) Data in this table are rounded. See the discussion of the employment projections table in the *Handbook* introductory chapter on *Occupational Information Included in the Handbook.*

comprehensive technical training. Then they are introduced to contract writing, timber harvesting, and decisionmaking. Some foresters work their way up to top managerial positions. Foresters in management usually leave fieldwork behind, spending more of their time in an office, working with teams to develop management plans and supervising others. After gaining several years of experience, some foresters may become consultants, working alone or with one or several partners. They contract with State or local governments, private landowners, private industry, or other forestry consulting groups.

Soil conservationists usually begin working within one county or conservation district and, with experience, may advance to the area, State, regional, or national level. Also, soil conservationists can transfer to related occupations, such as farm or ranch management advisor or land appraiser.

Employment

Conservation scientists and foresters held about 29,800 jobs in 2008. Conservation scientist jobs are heavily concentrated in government, where 74 percent are employed. At the Federal level, soil conservationists are employed primarily in the U.S. Department of Agriculture's (USDA) Natural Resource Conservation Service. Most range managers work in the USDA's Forest Service, the U.S. Department of the Interior's Bureau of Land Management, or the Natural Resource Conservation Service. A small number are self-employed and others work for nonprofit organizations or in consulting firms.

About 60 percent of all foresters work for Federal, State and local governments. Federal Government foresters are concentrated in the USDA's Forest Service. A few foresters are self-employed, generally working as consultants or procurement foresters. Others work for sawmills, wood products manufacturers, logging companies, and the forestry industry.

Although conservation scientists and foresters work in every State, employment of foresters is concentrated in the western and southeastern States, where many national and private forests and parks, and most of the lumber and pulpwood-producing forests, are located. Range managers work almost entirely in the western States, where most of the rangeland is located. Soil conservationists, are employed in almost every county in the country. Some foresters and conservation scientists hold positions in colleges and universities.

Job Outlook

Employment is expected to grow about as fast as average. In addition to job openings from growth, many openings are expected as today's conservation scientists and foresters retire.

Employment change. Employment of conservation scientists and foresters is expected to grow by 12 percent during the 2008–18 decade, about as fast as the average for all occupations. A majority of conservation scientists and foresters are employed by Federal, State, and local governments, and a large percentage of new jobs will be found in these areas. In recent years, the prevention and mitigation of wildfires has become the primary concern for government agencies managing forests and rangelands. The development of previously unused lands, in addition to changing weather conditions, has contributed to increasingly devastating and costly fires. Increases in funding and new programs will create new opportunities for foresters and range managers. Workers will be needed to manage lands in order to minimize the risk of fires and mitigate their impact should they occur. Restoring lands affected by fires also will be a major task, particularly in the southwestern and western States, where such fires are most common.

Beyond wildfire management, several other factors will influence demand on the part of governments for conservation scientists and foresters. New city-planning and urban revitalization initiatives will increase the need for workers with expertise in urban forestry. Demand for soil and water scientists, whose main function is providing technical expertise to farmers and ranchers, will increase as the safety and sustainability of the food supply becomes more of a concern.

In addition, increased investments in conservation programs will contribute to job growth for conservation scientists and foresters. The use of forests to sequester carbon emissions will create a need for foresters with expertise in this area. The desire to develop renewable forms of energy will increase the need for wood and other biomass products; consequently, more workers will be needed to manage those resources. Many of these jobs will be in the private-sector consulting industry, although government workers will be needed as well to manage these activities on Federal and State lands.

Growth in other private-sector jobs is expected to vary among different types of employers and specific occupations. Companies involved in natural-resource exploration and land development need to manage the use of soil and water systems while complying with environmental regulations. Growth in these companies will create new opportunities for consultant range managers and soil and water scientists. Procurement foresters will see the fewest new jobs, as a result of overall slow growth in the timber and logging industry. Recent large-scale sales of forestlands by industry has resulted in a loss of jobs within the traditional forest industry while creating limited opportunities with timber investment management organizations and real estate investment trusts. Self-employed foresters, who advise private landowners on a contract basis, will see modest growth.

Job prospects. The Federal Government and some State governments expect a large number of their workers to retire over the next decade. As a result, there is likely to be a large number of job openings for foresters and conservation scientists in government. In general, workers with a 4-year degree from an accredited university program, along with good technical and communication skills, should have the best opportunities for entry-level work.

Earnings

Median annual wages of conservation scientists in May 2008 were $58,720. The middle 50 percent earned between $45,320 and $73,280. The lowest 10 percent earned less than $35,190, and the highest 10 percent earned more than $86,910.

Median annual wages of foresters in 2008 were $53,750. The middle 50 percent earned between $42,980 and $65,000. The lowest 10 percent earned less than $34,710, and the highest 10 percent earned more than $78,350.

For Federal Government workers in forestry, the average annual salary was $71,558 in March 2009. For Federal workers in rangeland management, it was $64,564, and for soil conservation workers it was $69,483.

Conservation scientists and foresters who work for Federal, State, and local governments, and those who work for large private firms, generally receive more generous benefits than do those working for smaller firms. Governments usually have good pension, health, and leave plans as well.

Related Occupations

Conservation scientists and foresters manage, develop, and protect natural resources. Other workers with similar responsibilities include:

Sources of Additional Information

For information about forestry careers and schools offering education in forestry, visit the Society of American Foresters' Web site or send a self-addressed, stamped business envelope to:
➤ Society of American Foresters, 5400 Grosvenor Ln., Bethesda, MD 20814-2198. Internet: **http://www.safnet.org**

Information about careers in forestry—particularly conservation forestry and land management—can be found through the Forest Guild:
➤ Forest Guild, P.O. Box 519, Santa Fe, NM 87504. Internet: **http://www.forestguild.org**

Information about a career as a range manager, as well as a list of schools offering training, is available from:
➤ Society for Range Management, 10030 West 27th Ave., Wheat Ridge, CO 80215-6601. Internet: **http://www.rangelands.org**

Information on getting a job as a conservation scientist or forester with the Federal Government is available from the Office of Personnel Management (OPM) through USAJOBS, the Federal Government's official employment information system. This resource for locating and applying for job opportunities can be accessed through the Internet at **http://www.usajobs.opm.gov** or through an interactive voice response telephone system at (703) 724-1850 or TDD (978) 461-8404. These numbers are not toll free, and charges may result. For advice on how to find and apply for jobs, see the *Occupational Outlook Quarterly* article "How to get a job in the Federal Government," online at **http://www.bls.gov/opub/ooq/2004/summer/art01.pdf.**

The Occupational Information Network (O*NET) provides information on a wide range of occupational characteristics. Links to O*NET appear at the end of the Internet version of this occupational statement, accessible at **http://www.bls.gov/ooh/ocos048.htm**

Medical Scientists

Significant Points

- Most medical scientists need a Ph.D. in a biological science; some also hold a medical degree.

- Some medical scientists work in research laboratories at universities and hospitals; others work for pharmaceutical or biotechnology companies.

- Medical scientists with both a Ph.D. and M.D. are likely to have the best opportunities.

Nature of the Work

Medical scientists research human diseases and conditions with the goal of improving human health. Most medical scientists conduct biomedical research and development to advance knowledge of life processes and of other living organisms that affect human health, including viruses, bacteria, and other infectious agents. Past research has resulted in advances in diagnosis, treatment, and prevention of many diseases. Basic medical research continues to build the foundation for new vaccines, drugs, and treatment procedures. Medical scientists engage in laboratory research, clinical investigation, technical writing, drug development, regulatory review, and related activities.

Medical scientists study biological systems to understand the causes of disease and other health problems. For example, some try to identify changes in cells or in chromosomes that signal the development of medical problems. They use this knowledge to develop treatments and design research tools and techniques that have medical applications. Medical scientists involved in cancer research may formulate a combination of drugs that will lessen the effects of the disease. They can then work with physicians to administer these drugs to patients in clinical trials, monitor their reactions, and observe the results. They may draw blood, excise tissue, or perform other invasive procedures. Medical scientists examine the results of clinical trials and adjust the dosage levels to reduce negative side effects or to induce better results. In addition to developing treatments for

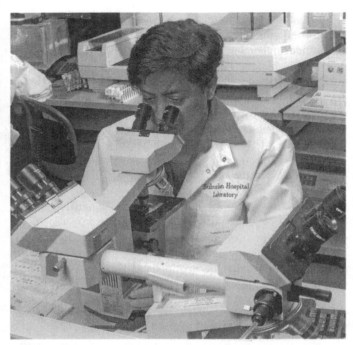

Research conducted by medical scientists has resulted in advanced treatments for many diseases.

medical conditions, medical scientists attempt to discover ways to prevent health problems. For example, they may study the link between smoking and lung cancer or between alcoholism and liver disease.

Many medical scientists conduct independent research in university, hospital, or government laboratories, exploring new areas of research or expanding on specialized research that they began in graduate school. Medical scientists working in colleges and universities, hospitals, and nonprofit medical research organizations typically submit grant proposals to obtain funding for their projects. The Federal Government's National Institutes of Health (NIH) provides funding support for researchers whose proposals are determined to be financially feasible and to have the potential to advance new ideas or processes that benefit human health. Medical scientists who rely on grant money may be under pressure to meet deadlines and to conform to rigid grant-writing specifications when preparing proposals to seek new or extended funding.

Most medical scientists who work in private industry conduct applied research or support product development, using knowledge discovered through research to develop new drugs and medical treatments. They usually have less autonomy than do medical researchers in academia to choose the emphasis of their research. Medical scientists spend more time working on marketable treatments to meet the business goals of their employers. Medical scientists in private industry may also be required to explain their research plans or results to nonscientists who are in a position to reject or approve their ideas, potentially for business reasons rather than scientific merit. Medical scientists increasingly work as part of teams, interacting with engineers, scientists of other disciplines, business managers, and technicians.

Swift advances in basic medical knowledge related to genetics and organic molecules have spurred growth in the field of biotechnology. Discovery of important drugs, including human insulin and growth hormone, is the result of research using biotechnology techniques, such as recombining DNA. Many other substances not previously available in large quantities are now produced by biotechnological means; some may one day be useful in treating diseases such as Parkinson's or Alzheimer's. Today, many medical scientists are involved in the science of genetic engineering—isolating, identifying, and sequencing human genes to determine their functions. This work continues to lead to the discovery of genes associated with specific diseases and inherited health risks, such as sickle cell anemia. These advances in biotechnology have opened up research opportunities in almost all areas of medical science.

Work environment. Medical scientists who conduct research usually work in laboratories and use a wide variety of equipment. Some may work directly with individual patients or larger groups as they administer drugs and monitor patients during clinical trials. Often, these medical scientists also spend time working in clinics and hospitals. Medical scientists are not usually exposed to unsafe or unhealthy conditions; however, those scientists who work with dangerous organisms or toxic substances must follow strict safety procedures to avoid contamination.

Medical scientists typically work regular hours in offices or laboratories, but longer hours are not uncommon. Researchers may be required to work odd hours in laboratories or other locations, depending on the nature of their research.

Training, Other Qualifications, and Advancement
A Ph.D. in a biological science is the minimum education required for most prospective medical scientists. However, some medical scientists also earn medical degrees in order to perform clinical work. A period of postdoctoral work in the laboratory of a senior researcher is becoming increasingly common for medical scientists.

Education and training. A Ph.D. in the biological sciences typically qualifies people to research basic life processes or particular medical problems and to analyze the results of experiments. Some medical scientists obtain a medical degree, instead of a Ph.D., but do not become licensed physicians, because they prefer research to clinical practice. It is particularly helpful for medical scientists to earn both a Ph.D. and a medical degree.

Students planning careers as medical scientists should pursue a bachelor's degree in a biological science. In addition to required courses in chemistry and biology, undergraduates should study allied disciplines, such as mathematics, engineering, physics, and computer science. General humanities courses are also beneficial, as writing and communication skills are necessary for drafting grant proposals and publishing research results.

Once students have completed undergraduate studies, there are two main paths for prospective medical scientists. They can enroll in a university Ph.D. program in the biological sciences; these programs typically take about 6 years of study, and students specialize in one particular field, such as genetics, pathology, or bioinformatics. They can also enroll in a joint M.D./Ph.D. program at a medical college; these programs typically take 7 to 8 years of study, where students learn both the clinical

Projections data from the National Employment Matrix

Occupational Title	SOC Code	Employment, 2008	Projected Employment, 2018	Change, 2008-2018	
				Number	Percent
Medical scientists, except epidemiologists..	19-1042	109,400	153,600	44,200	40

(NOTE) Data in this table are rounded. See the discussion of the employment projections table in the *Handbook* introductory chapter on *Occupational Information Included in the Handbook.*

skills needed to be a physician and the research skills needed to be a scientist.

In addition to formal education, medical scientists usually spend some time in a postdoctoral position before they apply for permanent jobs. Postdoctoral work provides valuable laboratory experience, including experience in specific processes and techniques such as gene splicing, which is transferable to other research projects. In some institutions, the postdoctoral position can lead to a permanent job.

Licensure. Medical scientists who administer drug or gene therapy to human patients, or who otherwise interact medically with patients—drawing blood, excising tissue, or performing other invasive procedures—must be licensed physicians. To be licensed, physicians must graduate from an accredited medical school, pass a licensing examination, and complete 1 to 7 years of graduate medical education. (See the statement on physicians and surgeons elsewhere in the *Handbook.*)

Other qualifications. Medical scientists should be able to work independently or as part of a team and be able to communicate clearly and concisely, both orally and in writing. Those in private industry, especially those who aspire to consulting and administrative positions, should possess strong communication skills so that they can provide instruction and advice to physicians and other healthcare professionals.

Advancement. Advancement among medical scientists usually takes the form of greater independence in their work, larger budgets, or tenure in university positions. Others choose to move into managerial positions and become natural science managers (see engineering and natural sciences managers elsewhere in the *Handbook*). Those who pursue management careers spend more time preparing budgets and schedules.

Employment

Medical scientists held about 109,400 jobs in 2008. About 31 percent of medical scientists were employed in scientific research and development services firms. Another 27 percent were employed in educational services; 13 percent were employed in pharmaceutical and medicine manufacturing; and 10 percent were employed in hospitals.

Job Outlook

Medical scientists are expected to grow much faster than average over the coming decade. Those with both a Ph.D. and M.D. are likely to experience the best opportunities.

Employment change. Employment of medical scientists is expected to increase 40 percent over the 2008-18 decade, much faster than the average for all occupations. Medical scientists have enjoyed rapid gains in employment since the 1980s—reflecting, in part, the growth of biotechnology as an industry. Much of the basic biological and medical research done in recent years has resulted in new knowledge, including the isolation and identification of genes. Medical scientists will be needed to take this knowledge to the next stage—understanding how certain genes function within an entire organism—so that medical treatments can be developed for various diseases. Even pharmaceutical and other firms not solely engaged in biotechnology have adopted biotechnology techniques, thus creating employment for medical scientists. However, job growth will moderate from its previous heights as the biotechnology industry matures and begins to grow at a slower rate. Some companies may also conduct more of their research and development in lower-wage countries, further limiting employment growth.

Employment growth should also occur as a result of the expected expansion in research related to illnesses such as AIDS, cancer, and avian flu, along with growing treatment problems, such as antibiotic resistance. Moreover, environmental conditions such as overcrowding and the increasing frequency of international travel will tend to spread existing diseases and give rise to new ones. Medical scientists will continue to be needed because they greatly contribute to the development of treatments and medicines that improve human health.

The Federal Government is a major source of funding for medical research. Large budget increases at the National Institutes of Health in the early part of the decade led to increases in Federal basic research and development expenditures, with research grants growing both in number and dollar amount. However, the increase in expenditures slowed substantially in recent years. Going forward, the level of Federal funding will continue to impact competition for winning and renewing research grants.

Job prospects. Medical scientists with both doctoral and medical degrees are likely to experience the best opportunities. Workers with both a biological and professional medical background will have a distinct advantage in competing for research funding, as certain opportunities are only open to those with both qualifications.

Medical scientists are less likely to lose their jobs during recessions than workers in many other occupations because they are employed on long-term research projects. However, a recession could influence the amount of money allocated to new research and development, particularly in areas of risky or innovative medical research. A recession also could limit extensions or renewals of existing projects.

Earnings

Median annual wages of medical scientists, except epidemiologists, were $72,590 in May 2008. The middle 50 percent of these workers earned between $51,640 and $101,290. The lowest 10 percent earned less than $39,870, and the highest 10 percent earned more than $134,770. Median annual wages in the industries employing the largest numbers of medical scientists were:

Drugs and druggists' sundries
merchant wholesalers $90,640
Pharmaceutical and medicine manufacturing 87,500
Scientific research and development services 79,210
General medical and surgical hospitals........................74,230
Colleges, universities, and professional schools 52,880

Earnings are lower and benefits limited for medical scientists in postdoctoral placements; workers in permanent positions typically receive higher wages and excellent benefits, in addition to job security.

Related Occupations

Other life science research occupations include:

Sources of Additional Information

For general information on medical scientists, contact:
➤ Federation of American Societies for Experimental Biology, 9650 Rockville Pike, Bethesda, MD 20814. Internet: http://www.faseb.org

For information on and a listing of M.D./Ph.D. programs, contact:
➤ National Association of M.D./Ph.D. Programs. Internet: http://www.aamc.org/students/considering/research/mdphd/

For information on pharmaceutical scientists, contact:
➤ American Association of Pharmaceutical Scientists (AAPS), 2107 Wilson Blvd., Suite 700, Arlington, VA 22201. Internet: http://www.aapspharmaceutica.org

For information on careers in pharmacology, contact:
➤ American Society for Pharmacology and Experimental Therapeutics, 9650 Rockville Pike, Bethesda, MD 20814. Internet: http://www.aspet.org

Information on obtaining a medical scientist position with the Federal Government is available from the Office of Personnel Management through USAJOBS, the Federal Government's official employment information system. This resource for locating and applying for job opportunities can be accessed through the Internet at http://www.usajobs.opm.gov or through an interactive voice response telephone system at (703) 724-1850 or TDD (978) 461-8404. These numbers are not toll free, and charges may result. For advice on how to find and apply for Federal jobs, see the *Occupational Outlook Quarterly* article "How to get a job in the Federal Government," online at http://www.bls.gov/opub/ooq/2004/summer/art01.pdf.

The Occupational Information Network (O*NET) provides information on a wide range of occupational characteristics. Links to O*NET appear at the end of the Internet version of this occupational statement, accessible at http://www.bls.gov/ooh/ocos309.htm

Physical Scientists

Atmospheric Scientists

Significant Points

- About 34 percent of atmospheric scientists are employed by the Federal Government; most of these work in the National Weather Service.

- A bachelor's degree in meteorology, or in a closely related field with courses in meteorology, is the minimum educational requirement; a master's degree is necessary for some positions, and a Ph.D. degree is required for most basic research positions.

- Keen competition is expected for jobs; those with graduate degrees should enjoy better prospects than those with only a bachelor's degree.

Nature of the Work

Atmospheric science is the study of the atmosphere—the blanket of air covering the Earth. Atmospheric scientists study the atmosphere's physical characteristics, motions, and processes, and the way in which these factors affect the rest of our environment. The best-known application of this knowledge is forecasting the weather. In addition to predicting the weather, atmospheric scientists attempt to identify and interpret climate trends, understand past weather, and analyze current weather. Weather information and atmospheric research are also applied in air-pollution control, agriculture, forestry, air and sea transportation, defense, and the study of possible trends in the Earth's climate, such as global warming, droughts, and ozone depletion.

Atmospheric scientists who forecast the weather are known as *operational meteorologists*; they are the largest group of specialists. These scientists study the Earth's air pressure, temperature, humidity, and wind velocity, and they apply physical and mathematical relationships to make short-range and long-range weather forecasts. Their data come from weather satellites, radars, sensors, and stations in many parts of the world. Meteorologists use sophisticated computer models of the world's atmosphere to make long-term, short-term, and local-area forecasts. More accurate instruments for measuring and observing weather conditions, as well as high-speed computers to process and analyze weather data, have revolutionized weather forecasting. Using satellite data, climate theory, and sophisticated computer models of the world's atmosphere, meteorologists can more effectively interpret the results of these models to make local-area weather predictions. These forecasts inform not only the general public, but also those who need accurate weather information for economic and safety reasons, such as the shipping, air transportation, agriculture, fishing, forestry, and utilities industries.

Meteorologists use data collected from sophisticated technologies like atmospheric satellite monitoring equipment and ground-based radar systems. Doppler radar, for example, can detect airflow patterns in violent storm systems, allowing forecasters to better predict thunderstorms, flash floods, tornadoes, and other hazardous winds, and to monitor the direction and intensity of storms. They also monitor surface weather stations and launch weather balloons, which carry equipment that measures wind, temperature, and humidity in the upper atmosphere.

While meteorologists study and forecast weather patterns in the short term, *climatologists* study seasonal variations in weather over months, years, or even centuries. They may collect, analyze, and interpret past records of wind, rainfall, sunshine, and temperature in specific areas or regions. Some look at patterns in weather over past years to determine, for example, whether a coming season will be colder or warmer than usual. Their studies are used to design buildings, plan heating and cooling systems, and aid in effective land use and agricultural production.

Some atmospheric scientists work exclusively in research. *Physical meteorologists*, for example, study the atmosphere's chemical and physical properties; the transmission of light, sound, and radio waves; and the transfer of energy in the atmosphere. They also study other atmospheric phenomena, such as the factors affecting the formation of clouds, rain, and snow; the dispersal of air pollutants over urban areas; and the mechanics of severe storms. Environmental problems, such as pollution and shortages of fresh water, have widened the scope of the meteorological profession. *Environmental meteorologists* study these problems and may evaluate and report on air quality for environmental impact statements. Other research meteorologists examine the most effective ways to control or diminish air pollution.

Work environment. Weather stations are found everywhere—at airports, in or near cities, and in isolated and remote areas. In addition to analyzing information in offices, some atmospheric scientists also spend time observing weather conditions on the ground or from aircraft. Weather forecasters who work for radio or television stations broadcast their reports from station studios, and may work evenings and weekends. Meteorologists in smaller weather offices often work alone; in larger ones, they work as part of a team. Those who

Atmospheric scientists monitor current weather conditions and make weather forecasts.

work for private consulting firms or for companies analyzing and monitoring emissions to improve air quality usually work with other scientists or engineers; fieldwork and travel may be common for these workers.

Most weather stations operate around the clock, 7 days a week, as weather conditions can change rapidly and timely information is essential, particularly during periods of severe weather. As a result, jobs in such facilities involve night, weekend, and holiday work, often with rotating shifts. During weather emergencies, such as hurricanes, meteorologists may work extended hours. Operational meteorologists also are often under pressure to meet forecast deadlines. Meteorologists and research scientists who are not involved in forecasting tasks work regular hours, usually in offices.

Training, Other Qualifications, and Advancement
A bachelor's degree in meteorology or atmospheric science, or in a closely related field with courses in meteorology, usually is the minimum educational requirement for an entry-level position. A master's degree is necessary for some positions, and a Ph.D. degree is required for most basic research positions.

Education and training. The preferred educational requirement for entry-level meteorologists in the Federal Government is a bachelor's degree—not necessarily in meteorology—with at least 24 semester hours of meteorology/atmospheric science courses, including 6 hours in the analysis and prediction of weather systems, 6 hours of atmospheric dynamics and thermodynamics, 3 hours of physical meteorology, and 2 hours of remote sensing of the atmosphere or instrumentation. Other required courses include 3 semester hours of ordinary differential equations, 6 hours of college physics, and at least 9 hours of courses appropriate for a physical science major—such as statistics, chemistry, physical oceanography, physical climatology, physical hydrology, radiative transfer, aeronomy (the study of the upper atmosphere), advanced thermodynamics, advanced electricity and magnetism, light and optics, and computer science.

Although positions in operational meteorology are available for those with only a bachelor's degree, obtaining a second bachelor's degree in a related technical field or a master's degree enhances employment opportunities, pay, and advance-

Projections data from the National Employment Matrix

Occupational Title	SOC Code	Employment, 2008	Projected Employment, 2018	Change, 2008-2018	
				Number	Percent
Atmospheric and space scientists..	19-2021	9,400	10,800	1,400	15

(NOTE) Data in this table are rounded. See the discussion of the employment projections table in the *Handbook* introductory chapter on *Occupational Information Included in the Handbook.*

ment potential. A Ph.D. typically is required only for research positions at universities. Students planning on a career in research and development do not necessarily need to major in atmospheric science or meteorology as an undergraduate. In fact, a bachelor's degree in mathematics, physics, or engineering provides excellent preparation for graduate study in atmospheric science.

Because atmospheric science is a small field, relatively few colleges and universities offer degrees in meteorology or atmospheric science, although many departments of physics, earth science, geography, and geophysics offer atmospheric science and related courses. In 2009, the American Meteorological Society listed approximately 100 undergraduate and graduate atmospheric science programs. Many of these programs combine the study of meteorology with another field, such as agriculture, hydrology, oceanography, engineering, or physics. For example, hydrometeorology is the blending of hydrology (the science of Earth's water) and meteorology, and is the field concerned with the effect of precipitation on the hydrologic cycle and the environment.

Prospective students should make certain that courses required by the National Weather Service and other employers are offered at the college they are considering. Computer science courses, additional meteorology courses, a strong background in mathematics and physics, and good communication skills are important to prospective employers.

Students also should take courses in subjects that are most relevant to their desired area of specialization. For example, those who wish to become broadcast meteorologists for radio or television stations should develop excellent communication skills through courses in speech, journalism, and related fields. Students interested in air quality work should take courses in chemistry and supplement their technical training with coursework in policy or government affairs. Prospective meteorologists seeking opportunities at weather consulting firms should possess knowledge of business, statistics, and economics, as an increasing emphasis is being placed on long-range seasonal forecasting to assist businesses.

Beginning atmospheric scientists often do routine data collection, computation, or analysis, and some basic forecasting. Entry-level operational meteorologists in the Federal Government usually are placed in intern positions for training and experience. During this period, they learn about the Weather Service's forecasting equipment and procedures, and rotate to different offices to learn about various weather systems. After completing the training period, they are assigned to a permanent duty station.

Certification and advancement. The American Meteorological Society (AMS) offers the Certified Consulting Meteo-

rologist professional certification for consulting meteorologists. Applicants must meet formal education requirements, pass an examination to demonstrate thorough meteorological knowledge, have a minimum of 5 years of experience or a combination of experience plus an advanced degree, and provide character references from fellow professionals. In addition, AMS also offers the Certified Broadcast Meteorologist designation for meteorologists in television and radio. Applicants must hold a bachelor's degree in atmospheric science or meteorology, complete an examination, and submit examples of their weather broadcasts for review. Both certifications also require periodic continuing education.

Experienced meteorologists may advance to supervisory or administrative jobs, or may handle more complex forecasting jobs. After several years of experience, some meteorologists establish their own weather consulting services.

Employment

Atmospheric scientists held about 9,400 jobs in 2008. This does not include individuals employed in college and university departments of meteorology or atmospheric science, physics, earth science, or geophysics; these individuals are classified as college or university faculty, rather than atmospheric scientists. (See the statement on teachers—postsecondary elsewhere in the *Handbook*.)

The Federal Government was the largest single employer of atmospheric scientists, accounting for about 34 percent of employment. The National Oceanic and Atmospheric Administration (NOAA) employed most Federal meteorologists in National Weather Service stations throughout the Nation; the remainder of NOAA's meteorologists worked mainly in research and development or management. The U.S. Department of Defense employed several hundred civilian meteorologists. In addition to civilian meteorologists, hundreds of Armed Forces members are involved in forecasting and other meteorological work. (See the statement on job opportunities in the Armed Forces elsewhere in the *Handbook*.) Others worked for professional, scientific, and technical services firms, including private weather consulting services, and in radio and television broadcasting.

Job Outlook

Employment is expected to increase faster than average. Applicants face keen competition; those with graduate degrees should enjoy better prospects than those with only a bachelor's degree.

Employment change. Employment of atmospheric scientists is projected to grow 15 percent over the 2008-18 decade, faster than the average for all occupations. Most new jobs are expected to arise in private industry. As research leads to continuing improvements in weather forecasting, demand should grow for private weather consulting firms to provide more detailed information than has formerly been available, especially to climate-sensitive industries. Farmers, commodity investors, insurance companies, utilities, and transportation and construction firms can greatly benefit from additional weather information more closely targeted to their needs than the general information provided by the National Weather Service. Additionally, research on seasonal and other long-range forecasting is yielding positive results, which should spur demand for more atmospheric scientists to interpret these forecasts and advise climate-sensitive industries. However, because many customers for private weather services are in industries sensitive to fluctuations in the economy, the sales and growth of private weather services depend on the health of the economy.

There will continue to be demand for atmospheric scientists to analyze and monitor the dispersion of pollutants into the air to ensure compliance with Federal environmental regulations, but related employment increases are expected to be small. Efforts toward making and improving global weather observations also could have a positive impact on employment.

Job prospects. Atmospheric scientists will face keen competition, as the number of graduates from college and university atmospheric sciences programs is expected to exceed the number of openings in the field. Although overall opportunities will be limited, the best prospects will be in private industry. Few opportunities are expected in government as atmospheric scientists will only need to be hired to replace workers who retire or leave the field. Openings for academic researchers will be limited due to the small number of positions. Workers with graduate degrees should enjoy better prospects than those with only a bachelor's degree.

Earnings

Median annual wages of atmospheric scientists in May 2008 were $81,290. The middle 50 percent earned between $55,140 and $101,340. The lowest 10 percent earned less than $38,990, and the highest 10 percent earned more than $127,100.

The average salary for meteorologists employed by the Federal Government was $93,661 in March 2009.

Related Occupations

Workers in other occupations concerned with the physical environment include:

Sources of Additional Information

General information about careers in atmospheric sciences is provided by the University Corporation for Atmospheric Research at: **http://www.ucar.edu/student_recruiting**

Information about careers in meteorology and a listing of colleges and universities offering meteorology programs is provided by the American Meteorological Society at: **http://www.ametsoc.org**

Information about meteorology careers in the Federal Government can be obtained from the National Oceanic and Atmospheric Administration at: **http://www.careers.noaa.gov**

Information on obtaining a position as a meteorologist with the Federal Government is available from the Office of Personnel Management through USAJOBS, the Federal Government's official employment information system. This resource for locating and applying for job opportunities can be accessed at **http://www.usajobs.opm.gov** or through an interactive voice response telephone system at (703) 724-1850 or TDD (978) 461-8404. These numbers are not toll free, so charges may result.

The Occupational Information Network (O*NET) provides information on a wide range of occupational characteristics. Links to O*NET appear at the end of the Internet version of this occupational statement, accessible at **http://www.bls.gov/ooh/ocos051.htm**

Chemists and Materials Scientists

Significant Points

- A bachelor's degree in chemistry or a related discipline is the minimum educational requirement; however, many research jobs require a master's degree or a Ph.D.

- Job growth will occur in professional, scientific, and technical services firms as manufacturing companies continue to outsource their research and development and testing operations to these smaller, specialized firms.

- New chemists at all levels may experience competition for jobs, particularly in declining chemical manufacturing industries; graduates with a master's degree, and particularly those with a Ph.D., will enjoy better opportunities at larger pharmaceutical and biotechnology firms.

Nature of the Work

Everything in the environment, whether naturally occurring or of human design, is composed of chemicals. Chemists and materials scientists search for new knowledge about chemicals and use it to improve life. Chemical research has led to the discovery and development of new and improved synthetic fibers, paints, adhesives, drugs, cosmetics, electronic components, lubricants, and thousands of other products. Chemists and materials scientists also develop processes such as improved oil refining and petrochemical processing that save energy and reduce pollution. Applications of materials science include studies of superconducting materials, graphite materials, integrated-circuit chips, and fuel cells. Research on the chemistry of living things spurs advances in medicine, agriculture, food processing, and other fields.

Chemists and materials scientists develop new uses for substances and materials.

Many chemists and materials scientists work in research and development (R&D). In basic research, they investigate the properties, composition, and structure of matter and the laws that govern the combination of elements and reactions of substances to each other. In applied R&D, these scientists create new products and processes or improve existing ones, often using knowledge gained from basic research. For example, the development of synthetic rubber and plastics resulted from research on small molecules uniting to form large ones, a process called polymerization. R&D chemists and materials scientists use computers and a wide variety of sophisticated laboratory instrumentation for modeling, simulation, and experimental analysis.

Developments in technology and the use of computers have allowed chemists and materials scientists to practice new, more efficient techniques, such as combinatorial chemistry. This technique makes and tests large quantities of chemical compounds simultaneously to find those with certain desired properties. Combinatorial chemistry allows chemists to produce thousands of compounds more quickly and less expensively than was formerly possible. In some cases, chemists use virtual libraries of millions of chemicals to find compounds with certain characteristics, allowing them to synthesize only the most promising candidates.

Scientific R&D in general has become more interdisciplinary in recent years; as a result, many chemists no longer work individually. Instead they will often be part of research teams that include other scientists, such as biologists and physicists; computer specialists; and engineers. (*Biochemists*, whose work encompasses both biology and chemistry, are discussed in the *Handbook* statement on biological scientists.)

Chemists also work in production and quality control in chemical manufacturing plants. They prepare instructions for plant workers that specify ingredients, mixing times, and temperatures for each stage in the process. They also monitor automated processes to ensure proper product yield and test samples of raw materials or finished products to ensure that these samples meet industry and government standards, including regulations governing pollution. Chemists report and document test results and analyze those results in hopes of improving existing theories or developing new test methods.

Chemists often specialize in a particular branch of the field. *Analytical chemists* determine the structure, composition, and nature of substances by examining and identifying their various elements or compounds. These chemists are crucial to the pharmaceutical industry because pharmaceutical companies need to know the identity of compounds that they hope to turn into drugs. Furthermore, analytical chemists develop techniques and study the relationships and interactions among the parts of compounds. They also identify the presence and concentration of chemical pollutants in water, soil, and the air.

Organic chemists study the chemistry of the vast number of carbon compounds that make up all living things. They synthesize elements or simple compounds to create new compounds or substances that have different properties and applications. These compounds have in turn been used to develop many commercial products, such as drugs, plastics, and elastomers (elastic substances similar to rubber). *Inorganic chemists* study compounds consisting mainly of elements other than carbon, such as those in electronic components.

Physical and *theoretical chemists* study the physical characteristics of atoms and molecules and the theoretical properties of matter; and they investigate how chemical reactions work. Their research may result in new and better energy sources. *Macromolecular chemists* study the behavior of atoms and molecules. *Medicinal chemists* study the structural properties of compounds intended for applications to human medicine.

Materials chemists study and develop new materials to improve existing products or make new ones. In fact, virtually all chemists are involved in this quest in one way or another.

The work of materials chemists is similar to, but separate from, the work of *materials scientists*. Materials scientists tend to have a more interdisciplinary background, as they apply the principles of physics and engineering as well as chemistry to study all aspects of materials. Chemistry, however, plays the primary role in materials science because it provides information about the structure and composition of materials.

Materials scientists study the structures and chemical properties of various materials to develop new products or enhance existing ones. They also determine ways to strengthen or combine materials or develop new materials for use in a variety of products. Materials science encompasses the natural and synthetic materials used in a wide range of products and structures, from airplanes, cars, and bridges to clothing and household goods.

Materials scientists often specialize in a specific type of material, such as ceramics or metals.

Work environment. Chemists and materials scientists usually work regular hours in offices and laboratories. R&D chemists and materials scientists spend much time in laboratories but also work in offices when they do theoretical research or plan, record, and report on their lab research. Although some laboratories are small, others are large enough to incorporate prototype chemical manufacturing facilities and advanced testing equipment. In addition to working in a laboratory, materials scientists also work with engineers and processing specialists in industrial manufacturing facilities. Chemists do some of their work in a chemical plant or outdoors—gathering water samples to test for pollutants, for example. Some chemists are exposed to health or safety hazards when handling certain chemicals, but there is little risk if proper procedures are followed.

Chemists and materials scientists typically work regular hours. A 40-hour workweek is usual, but longer hours are not uncommon. Researchers may be required to work odd hours in laboratories or other locations, depending on the nature of their research.

Training, Other Qualifications, and Advancement

A bachelor's degree in chemistry or a related discipline is the minimum educational requirement; however, many research jobs require a master's degree or, more often, a Ph.D.

Education and training. A bachelor's degree in chemistry, or in a related discipline together with a significant background in chemistry, usually is required for entry-level chemist jobs. Although some materials scientists hold a degree in materials science, these scientists also commonly have a degree in chemistry, physics, or electrical engineering. Most research jobs in chemistry and materials science require a master's degree or, more frequently, a Ph.D.

Many colleges and universities offer degree programs in chemistry. In 2009, the American Chemical Society (ACS) had approved about 650 bachelors, 310 masters, and 200 doctoral degree programs. In addition to these programs, other advanced degree programs in chemistry were offered at several hundred colleges and universities. The number of colleges that offer a degree program in materials science is small but gradually increasing; many engineering schools offer degrees in the joint field of materials science and engineering.

Students planning careers as chemists or materials scientists should take courses in science and mathematics, should like working with their hands to build scientific apparatus and perform laboratory experiments, and should like computer modeling.

In addition to taking required courses in analytical, inorganic, organic, and physical chemistry, undergraduate chemistry majors usually study biological sciences; mathematics; physics; and, increasingly, computer science. Computer courses are essential because employers prefer to hire job applicants who are able to apply computer skills to modeling and simulation tasks and are able to operate computerized laboratory equipment. These abilities are increasingly important as combinatorial chemistry and advanced screening techniques are more widely applied. Courses in statistics are useful because both chemists and materials scientists need the ability to apply basic statistical techniques.

People interested in environmental specialties also should take courses in environmental studies and become familiar with current legislation and regulations. Specific courses should include atmospheric, water, and soil chemistry and energy.

Graduate students studying chemistry commonly specialize in a subfield, such as analytical chemistry or polymer chemistry, depending on their interests and the kind of work they wish to do. For example, those interested in doing drug research in the pharmaceutical industry usually develop a strong background in medicinal or synthetic organic chemistry. However, students normally need not specialize at the undergraduate level. In fact, undergraduates who are broadly trained have more flexibility when searching for jobs than if they have narrowly defined their interests. Most employers provide new graduates with additional training or education.

In government or industry, beginning chemists with a bachelor's degree work in quality control, perform analytical testing, or assist senior chemists in R&D laboratories. Many employers prefer to hire chemists and materials scientists with a Ph.D., or at least a master's degree, to lead basic and applied research. Within materials science, a broad background in various sciences is preferred. This broad base may be obtained through degrees in physics, engineering, or chemistry. Although many companies prefer hiring Ph.D.s, some may employ materials scientists with a bachelor's or master's degree.

Other qualifications. Because R&D chemists and materials scientists are increasingly expected to work on interdisciplinary teams, some understanding of other disciplines, including business and marketing or economics, is desirable, along with leadership ability and good oral and written communication skills. Interaction among specialists in this field is increasing, especially for specialty chemists in drug development. One type of chemist often relies on the findings of another type of chemist. For example, an organic chemist must understand findings on the identity of compounds prepared by an analytical chemist.

Experience, either in academic laboratories or through internships, fellowships, or work-study programs in industry, also is useful. Some employers of research chemists, particularly in the pharmaceutical industry, prefer to hire individuals with several years of postdoctoral experience.

Perseverance, curiosity, and the ability to concentrate on detail and to work independently are essential.

Advancement. Advancement among chemists and materials scientists usually takes the form of greater independence in their work or larger budgets. Others choose to move into managerial positions and become natural sciences managers (covered in the *Handbook* statement on engineering and natural sciences managers). Those who pursue management careers spend more time preparing budgets and schedules and setting research strategy. Chemists or materials scientists who develop new products or processes sometimes form their own companies or join new firms to develop these ideas.

Employment

Chemists and materials scientists held about 94,100 jobs in 2008. Chemists accounted for about 84,300 of these, and ma-

Projections data from the National Employment Matrix

Occupational Title	SOC Code	Employment, 2008	Projected Employment, 2018	Change, 2008-2018	
				Number	Percent
Chemists and materials scientists....................................	19-2030	94,100	97,300	3,300	3
Chemists...	19-2031	84,300	86,400	2,100	2
Materials scientists..	19-2032	9,700	10,900	1,200	12

(NOTE) Data in this table are rounded. See the discussion of the employment projections table in the *Handbook* introductory chapter on *Occupational Information Included in the Handbook.*

terials scientists accounted for about 9,700 jobs. In addition, 24,800 chemists held faculty positions; these workers are covered in the statement on teachers—postsecondary, elsewhere in the *Handbook.*

About 42 percent of all chemists and material scientists were employed in manufacturing firms—mostly in the chemical manufacturing industry. Firms in this industry produce plastics and synthetic materials, drugs, soaps and cleaners, pesticides and fertilizers, paint, industrial organic chemicals, and other chemical products. About 18 percent of chemists and material scientists worked in scientific research and development services; 9 percent worked in testing labs. Companies whose products are made of metals, ceramics, plastics, and rubber employ most materials scientists.

Chemists and materials scientists are employed in all parts of the country, but they are mainly concentrated in large industrial areas.

Job Outlook

Job growth is expected to be slower than the average for all occupations. New chemists at all levels may experience competition for jobs, particularly in declining chemical manufacturing industries. Graduates with a master's degree or a Ph.D. will enjoy better opportunities, especially at larger pharmaceutical and biotechnology firms.

Employment change. Employment of chemists and materials scientists is expected to grow by 3 percent over the 2008-18 decade, slower than the average for all occupations. Job growth will occur in professional, scientific, and technical services firms as manufacturing companies continue to outsource their R&D and testing operations to these smaller, specialized firms. Chemists will see 2 percent growth as increases in biotechnology-related fields will be tempered by declines in other chemical manufacturing. Employment of materials scientists is projected to grow by 12 percent as manufacturers seek to improve the quality of their products by using new materials and manufacturing processes.

Demand for chemists is expected to be driven by biotechnology firms. Biotechnological research, including studies of human genes, continues to offer possibilities for the development of new drugs and products to combat illnesses and diseases that have previously been unresponsive to treatments derived by traditional chemical processes.

The chemical manufacturing industry is expected to employ fewer chemists as companies divest their R&D operations. To control costs, most chemical companies, including many large pharmaceutical and biotechnology companies, will increasingly turn to scientific R&D services firms to perform specialized research and other work formerly done by in-house chem-

ists. As a result, these firms will experience healthy job growth. Also, companies are expected to conduct an increasing amount of manufacturing and research in lower-wage countries, further limiting domestic employment growth. Quality control will continue to be an important issue in chemical manufacturing and other industries that use chemicals in their manufacturing processes.

Chemists also will be employed to develop and improve the technologies and processes used to produce chemicals for all purposes and to monitor and measure air and water pollutants to ensure compliance with local, State, and Federal environmental regulations. Environmental research will offer many new opportunities for chemists and materials scientists. To satisfy public concerns and to comply with government regulations, chemical manufacturing industries will continue to invest billions of dollars each year in technology that reduces pollution and cleans up existing waste sites. Research into traditional and alternative energy sources should also lead to employment growth among chemists.

Job prospects. New chemists at all levels may experience competition for jobs, particularly in declining chemical manufacturing industries. Pharmaceutical and biotechnology firms will continue to be a primary source of chemistry jobs, but graduates with a bachelor's degree in chemistry may also find science-related jobs in sales, marketing, and management. Some bachelor's degree holders become chemical technicians or technologists or high school chemistry teachers. In addition, they may qualify for assistant research positions at smaller research organizations.

Graduates with an advanced degree, particularly those with a Ph.D., are expected to enjoy somewhat better opportunities. Larger pharmaceutical and biotechnology firms provide openings for these workers at research laboratories, and many others work in colleges and universities. Furthermore, chemists with an advanced degree will continue to fill most senior research and upper management positions; however, similar to applicants in other occupations, chemist applicants face strong competition for the limited number of upper management jobs.

In addition to job openings resulting from employment growth, some job openings will result from the need to replace chemists and materials scientists who retire or otherwise leave the labor force.

During periods of economic recession, layoffs of chemists may occur—especially in the industrial chemicals industry. Layoffs are less likely in the pharmaceutical industry, where long development cycles generally overshadow short-term economic conditions. The traditional chemical industries, however, provide many raw materials to the automotive manufacturing and construction industries, both of which are vulnerable to temporary slowdowns during recessions.

Earnings

Median annual wages of chemists in May 2008 were $66,230. The middle 50 percent earned between $48,630 and $89,660. The lowest 10 percent earned less than $37,840, and the highest 10 percent earned more than $113,080. Median annual wages in the industries employing the largest numbers of chemists in 2008 are shown below:

Federal Executive Branch	$95,690
Scientific research and development services	76,450
Pharmaceutical and medicine manufacturing	66,520
Basic chemical manufacturing	63,630
Architectural, engineering, and related services	51,180

Median annual wages of materials scientists in May 2008 were $80,230. The middle 50 percent earned between $59,180 and $102,180. The lowest 10 percent earned less than $43,670, and the highest 10 percent earned more than $124,010.

According to the National Association of Colleges and Employers, beginning salary offers in July 2009 for graduates with a bachelor's degree in chemistry averaged $39,897 a year.

In March 2009, annual earnings of chemists in nonsupervisory, supervisory, and managerial positions in the Federal Government averaged $101,687.

Related Occupations

The research and analysis conducted by chemists and materials scientists is closely related to work done by:

Sources of Additional Information

General information on career opportunities and earnings for chemists is available from:
➤ American Chemical Society, Education Division, 1155 16th St. NW., Washington, DC 20036. Internet: http://www.acs.org

Information on obtaining a position as a chemist with the Federal Government is available from the Office of Personnel Management through USAJOBS, the Federal Government's official employment information system. This resource for locating and applying for job opportunities can be accessed through the Internet at http://www.usajobs.opm.gov or through an interactive voice response telephone system at (703) 724-1850 or TDD (978) 461-8404. These numbers are not toll free, and charges may result.

The Occupational Information Network (O*NET) provides information on a wide range of occupational characteristics. Links to O*NET appear at the end of the In-ternet version of this occupational statement, accessible at http://www.bls.gov/ooh/ocos049.htm

Environmental Scientists and Specialists

Significant Points

- Federal, State, and local governments employ 44 percent of all environmental scientists and specialists.
- A bachelor's degree in any life or physical science is generally sufficient for most entry-level positions, although many employers prefer a master's degree.
- Job prospects are expected to be favorable, particularly for environmental health workers in State and local government.

Nature of the Work

Environmental scientists and specialists use their knowledge of the natural sciences to protect the environment by identifying problems and finding solutions that minimize hazards to the health of the environment and the population. They analyze measurements or observations of air, food, water, and soil to determine the way to clean and preserve the environment. Understanding the issues involved in protecting the environment—degradation, conservation, recycling, and replenishment—is central to the work of environmental scientists. They often use this understanding to design and monitor waste disposal sites, preserve water supplies, and reclaim contaminated land and water. They also write risk assessments, describing the likely affect of construction and other environmental changes; write technical proposals; and give presentations to managers and regulators.

The Federal Government and most State and local governments enact regulations to ensure that there is clean air to breathe, safe water to drink, and no hazardous materials in the soil. The regulations also place limits on development, particularly near sensitive parts of the ecosystem, such as wetlands. Many environmental scientists and specialists work for the government, ensuring that these regulations are followed and limiting the impact of human activity on the environment. Others monitor environmental impacts on the health of the population, checking for risks of disease and providing information about health hazards.

Environmental scientists also work with private companies to help them comply with environmental regulations and policies. They are usually hired by consulting firms to solve problems. Most consulting firms fall into two categories—large multidisciplinary engineering companies, the largest of which may employ thousands of workers, and small niche firms that may employ only a few workers. When looking for jobs, environmental scientists should consider the type of firm and the scope of the projects it undertakes. In larger firms, environmental scientists are more likely to engage in large, long-term projects in which they will work with people in other scientific disciplines. In smaller specialty firms, however, they work more often with

Environmental scientists research methods to reduce hazards that affect the environment or public health.

business professionals and clients in government and the private sector.

Environmental scientists who work on policy formation may help identify ways that human behavior can be modified in the future to avoid such problems as ground-water contamination and depletion of the ozone layer. Some environmental scientists work in managerial positions, usually after spending some time performing research or learning about environmental laws and regulations.

Many environmental scientists do work and have training that is similar to other physical or life scientists, but they focus on environmental issues. Many specialize in subfields such as environmental ecology and conservation, environmental chemistry, environmental biology, or fisheries science. Specialties affect the specific activities that environmental scientists perform, although recent understandings of the interconnectedness of life processes have blurred some traditional classifications. For example, *environmental ecologists* study the relationships between organisms and their environments and the effects of factors such as population size, pollutants, rainfall, temperature, and altitude, on both. They may collect, study, and report data on air, soil, and water using their knowledge of various scientific disciplines. *Ecological modelers* study ecosystems, pollution control, and resource management using mathematical modeling, systems analysis, thermodynamics, and computer techniques. *Environmental chemists* study the toxicity of various chemicals, that is, how those chemicals affect plants, animals, and people. (Information on geoscientists and hydrologists, who also study the Earth, is located elsewhere in the *Handbook*.)

Environmental scientists in research positions with the Federal Government or in colleges and universities often have to find funding for their work by writing grant proposals. Consultants face similar pressures to market their skills and write proposals so that they will have steady work.

Work environment. Many entry-level environmental scientists and specialists spend a significant amount of time in the field, while more experienced workers generally devote more time to office or laboratory work. Some environmental scientists, such as environmental ecologists and environmental chemists, often take field trips that involve physical activity. Environmental scientists in the field may work in warm or cold climates, in all kinds of weather. Travel often is required to meet with prospective clients.

Researchers and consultants might face stress when looking for funding. Occasionally, those who write technical reports to business clients and regulators may be under pressure to meet deadlines and thus have to work long hours.

Training, Other Qualifications, and Advancement
A bachelor's degree is sufficient for most jobs in government and private sector companies, although a master's degree is often preferred. A Ph.D. is usually only necessary for jobs in college teaching or research.

Education and training. A bachelor's degree in an earth science is adequate for entry-level positions, although many companies prefer to hire environmental scientists with a master's degree in environmental science or a related natural science. A doctoral degree generally is necessary only for college teaching and some research positions. Some environmental scientists and specialists have a degree in environmental science, but many earn degrees in biology, chemistry, physics, or the geosciences and then apply their education to the environment. They often need research or work experience related to environmental science.

A bachelor's degree in environmental science offers an interdisciplinary approach to the natural sciences, with an emphasis on biology, chemistry, and geology. Undergraduate environmental science majors typically focus on data analysis and physical geography, which are particularly useful in studying pollution abatement, water resources, or ecosystem protection, restoration, and management. Understanding the geochemistry of inorganic compounds is becoming increasingly important in developing remediation goals. Students interested in working in the environmental or regulatory fields, either in environmental consulting firms or for Federal or State governments, should take courses in hydrology, hazardous-waste management, environmental legislation, chemistry, fluid mechanics, and geologic logging, which is the gathering of geologic data. An understanding of environmental regulations and government permit issues also is valuable.

For environmental scientists and specialists who consult, courses in business, finance, marketing, or economics may be useful. In addition, combining environmental science training with other disciplines such as engineering or business, qualifies these scientists for the widest range of jobs.

Other qualifications. Computer skills are essential for prospective environmental scientists. Students who have some experience with computer modeling, data analysis and integration, digital mapping, remote sensing, and Geographic Information Systems (GIS) will be the most prepared to enter the job market.

Environmental scientists and specialists usually work as part of a team with other scientists, engineers, and technicians, and they must often write technical reports and research proposals

Projections data from the National Employment Matrix

Occupational Title	SOC Code	Employment, 2008	Projected Employment, 2018	Change, 2008-2018	
				Number	Percent
Environmental scientists and specialists, including health	19-2041	85,900	109,800	23,900	28

(NOTE) Data in this table are rounded. See the discussion of the employment projections table in the *Handbook* introductory chapter on *Occupational Information Included in the Handbook.*

that communicate their research results or ideas to company managers, regulators, and the public. Environmental health specialists also work closely with the public, providing and collecting information on public health risks. As a result, strong oral and written communication skills are essential.

Advancement. Environmental scientists and specialists often begin their careers as field analysts or as research assistants or technicians in laboratories or offices. They are given more difficult assignments and more autonomy as they gain experience. Eventually, they may be promoted to project leader, program manager, or some other management and research position. (Information on engineering and natural sciences managers is located elsewhere in the *Handbook.*)

Employment

Environmental scientists and specialists held about 85,900 jobs in 2008. An additional 6,200 jobs were held by environmental science faculty; these workers are covered in the statement on teachers—postsecondary elsewhere in the *Handbook.*

About 37 percent of environmental scientists were employed in State and local governments; 21 percent in management, scientific, and technical consulting services; 15 percent in architectural, engineering and related services; and 7 percent in the Federal Government, primarily in the Environmental Protection Agency (EPA) and the Department of Defense.

Job Outlook

Employment is expected to grow much faster than the average for all occupations. Job prospects are expected to be favorable, particularly in State and local government.

Employment change. Employment of environmental scientists and specialists is expected to increase by 28 percent between 2008 and 2018, much faster than the average for all occupations. Job growth should be strongest in private-sector consulting firms. Growth in employment will be spurred largely by the increasing demands placed on the environment by population growth and increasing awareness of the problems caused by environmental degradation. Further demand should result from the need to comply with complex environmental laws and regulations, particularly those regarding ground-water decontamination and clean air.

Much job growth will result from a continued need to monitor the quality of the environment, to interpret the impact of human actions on terrestrial and aquatic ecosystems, and to develop strategies for restoring ecosystems. In addition, environmental scientists will be needed to help planners develop and construct buildings, transportation corridors, and utilities that protect water resources and reflect efficient and beneficial land use.

Many environmental scientists and specialists work in consulting. Consulting firms have hired these scientists to help businesses and government address issues related to underground tanks, land disposal areas, and other hazardous-waste-manage-

ment facilities. Currently, environmental consulting is evolving from investigations to creating remediation and engineering solutions. At the same time, the regulatory climate is moving from a rigid structure to a more flexible risk-based approach. These factors, coupled with new Federal and State initiatives that integrate environmental activities into the business process itself, will result in a greater focus on waste minimization, resource recovery, pollution prevention, and the consideration of environmental effects during product development. This shift in focus to preventive management will provide many new opportunities for environmental scientists in consulting roles.

Job prospects. In addition to job openings due to growth, there will be additional demand for new environmental scientists to replace those who retire, advance to management positions, or change careers. Job prospects for environmental scientists will be good, particularly for jobs in State and local government.

During periods of economic recession, layoffs of environmental scientists and specialists may occur in consulting firms, particularly when there is a slowdown in new construction; layoffs are much less likely in government.

Earnings

Median annual wages of environmental scientists and specialists were $59,750 in May 2008. The middle 50 percent earned between $45,340 and $78,980. The lowest 10 percent earned less than $36,310, and the highest 10 percent earned more than $102,610.

According to the National Association of Colleges and Employers, beginning salary offers in July 2009 for graduates with bachelor's degrees in an environmental science averaged $39,160 a year.

Related Occupations

Other occupations that deal with preserving or researching the natural environment include:

Sources of Additional Information

Information on training and career opportunities for environmental scientists and specialists is available from:

➤ American Geological Institute, 4220 King St., Alexandria, VA 22302. Internet: **http://www.agiweb.org**

Information on obtaining a position as an environmental protection specialist with the Federal Government is available from the Office of Personnel Management through USAJOBS, the Federal Government's official employment information system. This resource for locating and applying for job opportunities can be accessed through the Internet at **http://www.usajobs.opm.gov** or through an interactive voice response telephone system at (703) 724-1850 or TDD (978) 461-8404. These numbers are not toll free, and charges may result.

The Occupational Information Network (O*NET) provides information on a wide range of occupational characteristics. Links to O*NET appear at the end of the Internet version of this occupational statement, accessible at **http://www.bls.gov/ooh/ocos311.htm**

Geoscientists and Hydrologists

Significant Points

- Work at remote field sites is common.

- Twenty-three percent of all geoscientists and hydrologists are employed in government.

- Employers prefer applicants with a master's degree for most positions; a Ph.D. degree is required for most research and college teaching positions.

- Excellent job opportunities are expected for geoscientists with a master's degree.

Nature of the Work

Geoscientists and *hydrologists* study the composition, structure, and other physical aspects of the Earth, and the Earth's geologic past and present by using sophisticated instruments to analyze the composition of earth, rock, and water. Many geoscientists and hydrologists help to search for natural resources such as groundwater, minerals, metals, and petroleum. Others work closely with environmental and other scientists to preserve and clean up the environment.

Geoscientists usually study and work in one of several closely related geosciences fields, including geology, geophysics, and hydrology. *Geologists* study the composition, processes, and history of the Earth. They try to find out how rocks were formed and what has happened to them since their formation. They also study the evolution of life by analyzing plant and animal fossils. *Geophysicists* use the principles of physics, mathematics, and chemistry to study not only the Earth's surface, but also its internal composition, ground and surface waters, atmosphere, oceans, and magnetic, electrical, and gravitational forces. Hydrologists study the quantity, distribution, circulation, and physical properties of water and the water cycle.

Within these major geoscience fields, there are numerous subspecialties. For example, *petroleum geologists* map the subsurface of the ocean or land as they explore the terrain for oil and gas deposits. They use sophisticated instrumentation and computers to interpret geological information. *Engineering geologists* apply geologic principles to the fields of civil and environmental engineering, offering advice on major construction projects and assisting in environmental remediation and natural hazard-reduction projects. *Mineralogists* analyze and classify minerals and precious stones according to their composition and structure, and study the environment surrounding rocks in order to find new mineral resources. *Sedimentologists* study the nature, origin, distribution, and alteration of sediments, such as sand, silt, and mud. These sediments may contain oil, gas, coal, and many other mineral deposits. *Paleontologists* study fossils found in geological formations to trace the evolution of plant and animal life and the geologic history of the Earth. *Stratigraphers* examine the formation and layering of rocks to understand the environment which formed them. *Volcanologists* investigate volcanoes and volcanic phenomena to try to predict the potential for future eruptions and hazards to human health and welfare. *Glacial geologists* study the physical properties and movement of glaciers and ice sheets. *Geochemists* study the nature and distribution of chemical elements in groundwater and earth materials.

Geoscientists study the earth, often looking for natural resources.

Geophysicists specialize in areas such as geodesy, seismology, and magnetic geophysics. *Geodesists* study the Earth's size, shape, gravitational field, tides, polar motion, and rotation. *Seismologists* interpret data from seismographs and other geophysical instruments to detect earthquakes and locate earthquake-related faults. *Geomagnetists* measure the Earth's magnetic field and use measurements taken over the past few centuries to devise theoretical models that explain the Earth's origin. *Paleomagnetists* interpret fossil magnetization in rocks and sediments from the continents and oceans to record the spreading of the sea floor, the wandering of the continents, and the many reversals of polarity that the Earth's magnetic field has undergone through time. Other geophysicists study atmospheric sciences and space physics. (See the statements on atmospheric scientists or on physicists and astronomers, both elsewhere in the *Handbook*.)

Hydrologists often specialize in either underground water or surface water. They examine the form and intensity of precipitation, its rate of infiltration into the soil, its movement through the Earth, and its return to the ocean and atmosphere. Hydrologists use sophisticated techniques and instruments. For example, they may use remote sensing technology, data assimilation, and numerical modeling to monitor the change in regional and global water cycles. Some surface-water hydrologists use sensitive stream-measuring devices to assess flow rates and water quality.

Oceanographers use their knowledge of geosciences, in addition to biology and chemistry, to study the world's oceans and coastal waters. They study the motion and circulation of ocean waters; the physical and chemical properties of the oceans; and how these properties affect coastal areas, climate, and weather. (*Biological oceanographers*, often called marine biologists, study the distribution and migration patterns of the many diverse forms of sea life in the ocean; the statement on biological scientists discusses this occupation elsewhere in the *Handbook*.)

Geoscientists in research positions with the Federal Government or in colleges and universities frequently are required to design programs and write grant proposals in order to fund their research. Geoscientists in consulting jobs face similar pressures to market their skills and write proposals so that they will have steady work.

Work environment. Geoscientists and hydrologists can spend a large part of their time in the field, identifying and examining geological formation, studying data collected by remote sensing instruments, conducting geological surveys, constructing field maps, and using instruments to measure the Earth's gravity and magnetic field. They often perform seismic studies, for example, which involve bouncing energy waves off buried layers of rock, to search for oil and gas or to understand the structure of the subsurface layers. Similarly, they use seismic signals generated by an earthquake to determine the earthquake's location and intensity. In laboratories, they examine the chemical and physical properties of specimens. They study fossil remains of animal and plant life or experiment with the flow of water and oil through rocks.

Some geoscientists and hydrologists spend the majority of their time in an office, but many others divide their time between fieldwork and office or laboratory work. Work at remote field sites is common. Some specialists, such as volcanologists, often take field trips that involve significant physical activity and some risk. In the field they work in warm or cold climates and in all kinds of weather. In their research, they may dig or chip with a hammer, scoop with a net, and carry equipment in a backpack. Oceanographers may spend considerable time at sea on academic research ships. Geologists frequently travel to remote field sites by helicopter or 4-wheel-drive vehicles and cover large areas on foot. Many exploration geologists and geophysicists work in foreign countries, sometimes in remote areas and under difficult conditions. Travel often is required to meet with prospective clients or investors. Fieldwork often requires working long and irregular hours.

Training, Other Qualifications, and Advancement

A master's degree is the primary educational requirement for most positions. A Ph.D. is necessary for most research and college teaching positions.

Education and training. A bachelor's degree is adequate for a few entry-level positions, but most geoscientists and hydrologists need a master's degree, which is the preferred educational requirement for most research positions in private industry, Federal agencies, and State geological surveys. A Ph.D. is necessary for most high-level research and college teaching positions, but is generally not required for other jobs.

Many colleges and universities offer bachelor's and graduate degrees in the geosciences. Traditional geoscience courses emphasizing classical geologic methods and topics (such as mineralogy, petrology, paleontology, stratigraphy, and structural geology) are important for all geoscientists. People who study physics, chemistry, biology, mathematics, engineering, or computer science may also qualify for some geoscience positions if their course work includes geology.

Most universities do not offer degrees in hydrology, but instead offer concentrations in hydrology or water studies in their geoscience, environmental science, or engineering departments. Students interested in hydrology should take courses in the physical sciences, geophysics, chemistry, engineering science, soil science, mathematics, aquatic biology, atmospheric science, geology, oceanography, hydrogeology, and the management or conservation of water resources.

Licensure and certification. A number of States require geoscientists and hydrologists who offer their services directly to the public to obtain a license from a State licensing board. Licensing requirements vary by State but typically include education and experience requirements and a passing score on an examination. In States that do not require a license, workers can obtain voluntary certifications. For example, the American Institute of Hydrology offers certification programs in professional hydrology that have similar requirements to State licensure programs.

Other qualifications. Computer skills are essential for prospective geoscientists and hydrologists; students who have experience with computer modeling, data analysis and integration, digital mapping, remote sensing, and Geographic Information Systems (GIS) will be the most prepared entering the job market. Knowledge of the Global Positioning System (GPS)—a

Projections data from the National Employment Matrix

Occupational Title	SOC Code	Employment, 2008	Projected Employment, 2018	Change, 2008-2018	
				Number	Percent
Geoscientists and hydrologists...	–	41,700	49,100	7,400	18
Geoscientists, except hydrologists and geographers....................	19-2042	33,600	39,400	5,900	18
Hydrologists..	19-2043	8,100	9,600	1,500	18

(NOTE) Data in this table are rounded. See the discussion of the employment projections table in the *Handbook* introductory chapter on *Occupational Information Included in the Handbook.*

locator system that uses satellites—has also become essential. Some employers seek applicants with field experience, so a summer internship is often helpful.

Because geoscientists and hydrologists usually work as part of a team with other geoscientists and with environmental scientists, engineers, and technicians, they must have good interpersonal skills. Strong oral and written communication skills also are important because writing technical reports and research proposals and explaining research results in person are important aspects of the work. Some jobs, particularly for petroleum geologists, require foreign travel, and for these positions knowledge of a second language is beneficial.

These workers must be inquisitive, able to think logically, and capable of complex analytical thinking, including spatial visualization and the ability to infer conclusions from sparse data. Geoscientists and hydrologists involved in fieldwork must have physical stamina.

Advancement. Geoscientists and hydrologists often begin their careers in field exploration or as research assistants or technicians in laboratories or offices. As they gain experience, they take on more complex and difficult assignments. Eventually, some are promoted to project leader, program manager, or to a senior research position. Those who choose to work in management will spend more time scheduling, budgeting, and reporting to top executives or clients. (See the statement on engineering and natural sciences managers elsewhere in the *Handbook.*)

Employment

Geoscientists held about 33,600 jobs in 2008, while another 8,100 were employed as hydrologists. Many more individuals held geoscience faculty positions in colleges and universities, but they are classified as college and university faculty. (See the statement on teachers—postsecondary elsewhere in the *Handbook.*)

About 23 percent of geoscientists were employed in architectural, engineering, and related services and 19 percent worked for oil and gas extraction companies. State agencies such as State geological surveys and State departments of conservation employed another 9 percent of geoscientists. Eight percent worked for the Federal Government, including geologists, geophysicists, and oceanographers, mostly within the U.S. Department of the Interior for the U.S. Geological Survey (USGS) and within the U.S. Department of Defense.

Among hydrologists, 26 percent were employed in architectural, engineering, and related services, and 19 percent worked for management, scientific, and technical consulting services. The Federal Government employed about 27 percent of hydrologists, mostly within the U.S. Department of the Interior for the

U.S. Geological Survey (USGS) and within the U.S. Department of Defense.

Job Outlook

Employment of geoscientists and hydrologists is expected to grow faster than the average for all occupations. Graduates with a master's degree in geoscience can expect excellent job opportunities, but Ph.D.s may face competition for research and college teaching jobs.

Employment change. Employment growth of 18 percent is expected for geoscientists and hydrologists between 2008 and 2018, which is faster than the average for all occupations. The need for energy, environmental protection, and responsible land and water management will spur employment demand. Employment in management, scientific, and technical consulting services should continue to grow as more geoscientists work as consultants. These services have increased their hiring of geoscientists in recent years because of increased government contracting and private corporations' need for technical assistance and environmental management plans. Moreover, many geoscientists and hydrologists monitor the quality of the environment, checking for problems such as deteriorating coastal environments and soil and water contamination—all of which will create employment growth for them. An expected increase in highway building and other infrastructure projects will also be a source of jobs for engineering geologists.

Many geoscientists work in the exploration and production of oil and gas. Historically, employment of petroleum geoscientists has been cyclical and affected considerably by the price of oil and gas. When prices are low, oil and gas producers curtail exploration activities and may lay off geologists. When prices are high, companies have the funds and incentive to renew exploration efforts and to hire geoscientists in larger numbers. In the long term, continued high oil prices are expected to maintain demand for workers who can find new resource deposits. Geoscientists who speak a foreign language and who are willing to work abroad should enjoy the best opportunities, as the need for energy, construction materials, and a broad range of geoscience expertise grows in developing nations.

Demand for hydrologists should also be strong as the population increases and moves to more environmentally sensitive locations. As people increasingly migrate toward coastal regions, for example, hydrologists will be needed to assess building sites for potential geologic hazards and to mitigate the effects of natural hazards such as floods, landslides, and hurricanes. Hydrologists also will be needed to study hazardous-waste sites and determine the effect of pollutants on soil and ground water so that engineers can design remediation systems. Increased government regulations, such as those regarding the management of storm water, and issues related to water conservation, deteriorating coastal environments, and rising sea levels also will stimulate employment growth for these workers.

Job prospects. Graduates with a master's degree in geoscience should have excellent opportunities, especially in consulting firms and in the oil and gas industry. In addition to demand resulting from job growth, replacing those who leave the occupation for retirement, managerial positions, or other careers will generate a number of jobs. A significant number of geoscientists are approaching retirement age, and without increases in the number of students earning master's degrees in the geosciences, job openings may exceed the number of qualified job-seekers over the 2008–18 projection period. However, geoscientists with doctoral degrees, who primarily work as college and university faculty or do research, may face competition. There are few openings for new graduates with only a bachelor's degree in geoscience, but these graduates may have favorable opportunities in related occupations, such as high school science teacher or science technician.

Job prospects for hydrologists should be favorable, particularly for those with field experience. Demand for hydrologists who understand both the scientific and engineering aspects of waste remediation should be strong.

There will be fewer opportunities for geoscientists and hydrologists in Federal and State government, mostly because of budget constraints at key agencies, such as the U.S. Geological Service, and the trend among governments toward contracting out to consulting firms instead of hiring new government employees. However, departures of geoscientists who retire or leave the government for other reasons will result in some job openings over the next decade.

Geoscientists may face layoffs during periods of economic recession, but the prices of commodities are a much more important source of volatility; for those working in the oil and gas or mining industries, the cyclical nature of commodity prices determines demand. When prices are high, jobs are plentiful, but when prices fall, positions become scarce.

Earnings

Median annual wages of geoscientists were $79,160 in May 2008. The middle 50 percent earned between $54,470 and $113,390; the lowest 10 percent earned less than $41,700, and the highest 10 percent more than $155,430.

The petroleum, mineral, and mining industries offer higher salaries, but less job security, than other industries because economic downturns sometimes cause layoffs. Median annual wages for the industries employing the largest number of geoscientists in May 2008 were as follows:

Oil and gas extraction	$127,560
Federal Executive Branch	90,220
Architectural, engineering, and related services	66,770
Management, scientific, and technical consulting services	62,070
State government	57,700

Median annual wages of hydrologists were $71,450 in May 2008. The middle 50 percent earned between $54,910 and $89,200; the lowest 10 percent earned less than $44,410, and the highest 10 percent more than $105,010.

In March 2009, the Federal Government's average salary was $94,085 for geologists, $108,118 for geophysicists, $89,404 for hydrologists, and $105,671 for oceanographers.

Related Occupations

Other occupations related to the physical environment include:

Many geoscientists work in the petroleum and natural gas industry, an industry that also employs numerous other workers whose jobs deal with the scientific and technical aspects of the exploration and extraction of petroleum and natural gas, including:

Sources of Additional Information

Information on training and career opportunities for geoscientists and hydrologists is available from:
➤ American Geological Institute, 4220 King St., Alexandria, VA 22302-1502. Internet: **http://www.agiweb.org**

Information on careers in petroleum geology is available from:
➤ American Association of Petroleum Geologists, P.O. Box 979, Tulsa, OK 74101. Internet: **http://www.aapg.org**

Information on careers and certification in hydrology is available from:
➤ American Institute of Hydrology, Engineering D–Mail Code 6603, Southern Illinois University Carbondale, 1230 Lincoln Dr., Carbondale, IL 62901. Internet: **http://www.aihydrology.org**

Information on obtaining a position as a geologist, geophysicist, hydrologist, or oceanographer with the Federal Government is available from the Office of Personnel Management through USAJOBS, the Federal Government's official employment information system. This resource for locating and applying for job opportunities can be accessed through the Internet at **http://www.usajobs.opm.gov** or through an interactive voice response telephone system at (703) 724-1850 or TDD (978) 461-8404. These numbers are not toll free, and charges may result.

The Occupational Information Network (O*NET) provides information on a wide range of occupational characteristics. Links to O*NET appear at the end of the Internet version of this occupational statement, accessible at **http://www.bls.gov/ooh/ocos312.htm**

Physicists and Astronomers

Significant Points

- Scientific research and development services firms and the Federal Government employ over half of all physicists and astronomers.

- Most jobs in basic research usually require a doctoral degree; master's degree holders qualify for some jobs in applied research and development; bachelor's degree holders often qualify as research assistants or for other physics-related occupations, such as technicians.

- Applicants may face competition for basic research positions due to limited funding; however, those with a background in physics or astronomy may have good opportunities in related fields, such as engineering and technology.

Nature of the Work

Physicists and astronomers conduct research to understand the nature of the universe and everything in it. These scientists observe, measure, interpret, and develop theories to explain celestial and physical phenomena using mathematics. From the vastness of space to the infinitesimal scale of subatomic particles, they study the fundamental properties of the natural world and apply the knowledge gained to design new technologies.

Physicists explore and identify basic principles and laws governing the motion, energy, structure, and interactions of matter. Some physicists study theoretical areas, such as the nature of time and the origin of the universe; others apply their knowledge of physics to practical areas, such as the development of advanced materials, electronic and optical devices, and medical equipment.

Physicists design and perform experiments with sophisticated equipment such as lasers, particle accelerators, electron microscopes, and mass spectrometers. On the basis of their observations and analysis, they attempt to discover and explain laws describing the forces of nature, such as gravity, electromagnetism, and nuclear interactions. Experiments also help physicists find ways to apply physical laws and theories to problems in nuclear energy, electronics, optics, materials, communications, aerospace technology, and medical instrumentation.

Astronomers use the principles of physics and mathematics to learn about the fundamental nature of the universe and its components, including the sun, moon, planets, stars, and galaxies. As such, astronomy is sometimes considered a subfield of physics. They also apply their knowledge to solve problems in navigation, space flight, and satellite communications and to develop the instrumentation and techniques used to observe and collect astronomical data.

Most physicists and astronomers work in research and development. Some conduct basic research with the sole aim of increasing scientific knowledge. Others conduct applied research and development, which builds upon the discoveries made through basic research to develop practical applications of this knowledge, such as new devices, products, and processes. For example, knowledge gained through basic research in solid-state physics led to the development of transistors and, then, integrated circuits used in computers.

Physicists also design research equipment, which often has additional unanticipated uses. For example, lasers are used in surgery, microwave devices function in ovens, and measuring instruments can analyze blood or the chemical content of foods.

A small number of physicists work in inspection, testing, quality control, and other production-related jobs in industry.

Much physics research is done in small or medium-sized laboratories. However, experiments in plasma, nuclear, and high-energy physics, as well as in some other areas of physics, require extremely large and expensive equipment, such as particle accelerators and nuclear reactors. Physicists in these subfields often work in large teams. Although physics research may require extensive experimentation in laboratories, research physicists still spend much time in offices planning, recording, analyzing, and reporting on research.

Physicists generally specialize in one of many subfields, such as elementary particle physics, nuclear physics, atomic and molecular physics, condensed matter physics, optics, acoustics, space physics, or plasma physics. Some specialize in a subdivision of one of these subfields. For example, within condensed-matter physics, specialties include superconductivity, crystallography, and semiconductors. However, all physics involves the same fundamental principles, so specialties may overlap, and physicists may switch from one subfield to another. Also, growing numbers of physicists work in interdisciplinary fields, such as biophysics, chemical physics, and geophysics. (Biophysicists are covered in the statement on biological scientists elsewhere in the *Handbook*).

Almost all astronomers do research. Some are theoreticians, working on the laws governing the structure and evolution of astronomical objects. Others analyze large quantities of data gathered by observatories and satellites and write scientific papers or reports on their findings. Some astronomers actually operate large space-based or ground-based telescopes, usually as part of a team. However, astronomers may spend only a few weeks each year making observations with optical telescopes, radio telescopes, and other instruments.

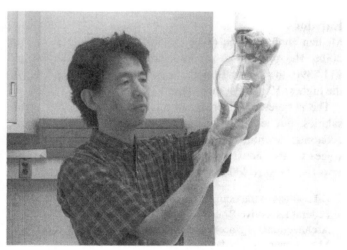

Research jobs for physicists and astronomers usually require a Ph.D.

Projections data from the National Employment Matrix

Occupational Title	SOC Code	Employment, 2008	Projected Employment, 2018	Change, 2008-2018	
				Number	Percent
Astronomers and physicists	19-2010	17,100	19,800	2,700	16
Astronomers...	19-2011	1,500	1,700	200	16
Physicists...	19-2012	15,600	18,100	2,500	16

(NOTE) Data in this table are rounded. See the discussion of the employment projections table in the *Handbook* introductory chapter on *Occupational Information Included in the Handbook.*

For many years, satellites and other space-based instruments, such as the Hubble space telescope, have provided prodigious amounts of astronomical data. New technology has lead to improvements in analytical techniques and instruments, such as computers and optical telescopes and mounts, and is creating a resurgence in ground-based research.

A small number of astronomers work in museums housing planetariums. These astronomers develop and revise programs presented to the public and may direct planetarium operations.

Work environment. Most physicists and astronomers do not encounter unusual hazards in their work. Some physicists temporarily work away from home at national or international facilities with unique equipment, such as particle accelerators. Astronomers who make observations with ground-based telescopes may spend many hours working in observatories; this work usually involves travel to remote locations and may require working at night. Physicists and astronomers whose work depends on grant money often are under pressure to write grant proposals to keep their work funded.

Physicists often work regular hours in laboratories and offices. At times, however, those who are deeply involved in research may work long or irregular hours. Astronomers may need to work at odd hours to observe celestial phenomena, particularly those working with ground-based telescopes.

Training, Other Qualifications, and Advancement
Because most jobs are in basic research and development, a doctoral degree is the usual educational requirement for physicists and astronomers. Master's degree holders qualify for some jobs in applied research and development, whereas bachelor's degree holders often qualify as research assistants or for jobs in other fields where a physics background is good preparation, such as engineering and technology.

Education and training. A Ph.D. degree in physics or closely related fields is typically required for basic research positions, independent research in industry, faculty positions, and advancement to managerial positions. Graduate study in physics prepares students for a career in research through rigorous training in theory, methodology, and mathematics. Most physicists specialize in a subfield during graduate school and continue working in that area afterwards.

Additional experience and training in a postdoctoral research appointment, although not required, is important for physicists and astronomers aspiring to permanent positions in basic research in universities and government laboratories. Many physics and astronomy Ph.D. holders ultimately teach at the college or university level.

Master's degree holders usually do not qualify for basic research positions, but may qualify for many kinds of jobs requiring a physics background, including positions in manufacturing and applied research and development. Increasingly, many master's degree programs are specifically preparing students for physics-related research and development that does not require a Ph.D. degree. These programs teach students specific research skills that can be used in private-industry jobs. In addition, a master's degree coupled with State certification usually qualifies one for teaching jobs in high schools or at 2-year colleges.

Those with bachelor's degrees in physics are rarely qualified to fill positions in research or in teaching at the college level. They are, however, usually qualified to work as technicians or research assistants in engineering-related areas, in software development and other scientific fields, or in setting up computer networks and sophisticated laboratory equipment. Increasingly, some may qualify for applied research jobs in private industry or take on nontraditional physics roles, often in computer science, such as systems analysts or database administrators. Some become science teachers in secondary schools.

Holders of a bachelor's or master's degree in astronomy often enter an unrelated field where their strong analytical background provides good preparation. However, they are also qualified to work in planetariums running science shows, to assist astronomers doing research, and to operate space-based and ground-based telescopes and other astronomical instrumentation. (See the statements on engineers, geoscientists, computer scientists, computer software engineers and computer programmers, and computer systems analysts elsewhere in the *Handbook*.)

Many colleges and universities offer a bachelor's degree in physics. Undergraduate programs provide a broad background in the natural sciences and mathematics. Typical physics courses include electromagnetism, optics, thermodynamics, atomic physics, and quantum mechanics.

Approximately 190 universities offer Ph.D. degrees in physics; more than 60 additional colleges offer a master's as their highest degree in physics. Graduate students usually concentrate in a subfield of physics, such as elementary particles or condensed matter. Many begin studying for their doctorate immediately after receiving their bachelor's degree; a typical Ph.D. program takes about 6 years to complete.

About 75 universities grant degrees in astronomy, either through an astronomy, physics, or combined physics-astronomy department. About half of all astronomy departments are combined with physics departments, while the remainder are administered separately. With about 40 doctoral programs in astronomy, applicants face considerable competition for available slots. Those planning a career in the subject should have a strong physics background. In fact, an undergraduate degree in either physics or astronomy is excellent preparation, followed by a Ph.D. in astronomy.

Many physics and astronomy Ph.D. holders begin their careers in a postdoctoral research position, in which they may work with experienced physicists as they continue to learn about their specialties or develop a broader understanding of related areas of research. Initial work may be under the close supervision of senior scientists. As they gain experience, physicists perform increasingly complex tasks and achieve greater independence in their work. Experience, either in academic laboratories or through internships, fellowships, or work-study programs in industry, also is useful. Some employers of research physicists, particularly in the information technology industry, prefer to hire individuals with several years of postdoctoral experience.

Other qualifications. Mathematical ability, problem-solving and analytical skills, an inquisitive mind, imagination, and initiative are important traits for anyone planning a career in physics or astronomy. Prospective physicists who hope to work in industrial laboratories applying physics knowledge to practical problems should broaden their educational background to include courses outside of physics, such as economics, information technology, and business management. Good oral and written communication skills also are important because many physicists work as part of a team, write research papers or proposals, or have contact with clients or customers who do not have a physics background.

Certain sensitive research positions with the Federal Government and in fields such as nuclear energy may require applicants to be U.S. citizens and to hold a security clearance.

Advancement. Advancement among physicists and astronomers usually takes the form of greater independence in their work, larger budgets, or tenure in university positions. Others choose to move into managerial positions and become natural science managers (engineering and natural sciences managers are discussed elsewhere in the *Handbook*). Those who pursue management careers spend more time preparing budgets and schedules. Those who develop new products or processes sometimes form their own companies or join new firms to develop these ideas.

Employment

Physicists and astronomers held about 17,100 jobs in 2008. Physicists accounted for about 15,600 of these, while astronomers accounted for only about 1,500 jobs. In addition, there were about 15,500 physicists employed in faculty positions; these workers are covered in more detail in the statement on teachers—postsecondary elsewhere in the *Handbook*.

About 39 percent of physicists and astronomers worked for the scientific research and development services industry, which includes employees of the 36 Federally Funded Research and Development Centers. These centers, sometimes referred to as national laboratories, perform a significant amount of basic research in the physical sciences. They are funded by government agencies such as the Department of Energy and the Department of Defense, but are administered by universities or private corporations. The Federal Government directly employed another 22 percent, mostly in the U.S. Department of Defense, but also in the National Aeronautics and Space Administration (NASA) and in the U.S. Departments of Commerce, Health and Human Services, and Energy. Other physicists and astronomers worked in nonfaculty research positions at educational institutions and hospitals.

Although physicists and astronomers are employed in all parts of the country, most work in areas in which universities, large research laboratories, or observatories are located.

Job Outlook

Physicists and astronomers should experience faster than average job growth, but may face competition for basic research positions due to limited funding. However, those with a background in physics or astronomy may have good opportunities in related occupations.

Employment change. Employment of physicists and astronomers is expected to grow 16 percent, faster than the average for all occupations during the 2008-18 decade.

Federal research expenditures are the major source of physics-related and astronomy-related research funds, especially for basic research. For most of the past decade there has been limited growth in Federal funding for physics and astronomy research as most of the growth in Federal research funding has been devoted to the life sciences. However, the America COMPETES Act, passed by Congress in 2007, sets a goal to double funding for the physical sciences through the National Science Foundation and the Department of Energy's Office of Science by the year 2016, and recent budgets for these agencies have seen large increases. If these increases continue, it will result in more opportunities in basic research for Ph.D. physicists and astronomers.

Although research and development expenditures in private industry will continue to grow, many research laboratories in private industry are expected to continue to reduce basic research, which includes much physics research, in favor of applied or manufacturing research and product and software development. Nevertheless, people with a physics background continue to be in demand in information technology, semiconductor technology, and other applied sciences. This trend is expected to continue; however, many of the new workers will have job titles such as computer software engineer, computer programmer, or systems analyst or developer, rather than physicist.

Job prospects. In addition to job growth, the need to replace physicists and astronomers who retire or otherwise leave the occupation permanently will account for many job openings. In recent years the number of doctorates granted in physics has been somewhat greater than the number of job openings for traditional physics research positions in colleges and universities and in research centers. Recent increases in undergraduate physics enrollments may also lead to growth in enrollments in graduate physics programs, so that there may be an increase in the number of doctoral degrees granted that could intensify the competition for basic research positions. However, demand has grown in other related occupations for those with advanced training in physics. Prospects should be favorable for physicists in applied research, development, and related technical fields.

Opportunities should also be numerous for those with a master's degree, particularly graduates from programs preparing students for related work in applied research and development, product design, and manufacturing positions in private industry. Many of these positions, however, will have titles other than physicist, such as engineer or computer scientist.

People with only a bachelor's degree in physics or astronomy are usually not qualified for physics or astronomy research jobs, but they may qualify for a wide range of positions related to engineering, mathematics, computer science, environmental science, and some nonscience fields, such as finance. Those who meet State certification requirements can become high school physics teachers, an occupation in strong demand in many school districts. Some States require new teachers to obtain a master's degree in education within a certain time. (See the statement on teachers—kindergarten, elementary, middle, and secondary elsewhere in the *Handbook*.) Despite competition for traditional physics and astronomy research jobs, graduates with a physics or astronomy degree at any level will find their knowledge of science and mathematics useful for entry into many other occupations.

Despite their small numbers, astronomers can expect good job prospects in government and academia over the projection period. Since astronomers are particularly dependent upon government funding, Federal budgetary decisions will have a sizable influence on job prospects for astronomers.

Earnings

Median annual wages of physicists were $102,890 in May 2008. The middle 50 percent earned between $80,040 and $130,980. The lowest 10 percent earned less than $57,160, and the highest 10 percent earned more than 159,400.

Median annual wages of astronomers were $101,300 in May 2008. The middle 50 percent earned between $63,610 and $133,630, the lowest 10 percent less than $45,330, and the highest 10 percent more than $156,720.

The average annual salary for physicists employed by the Federal Government was $118,971 in March 2009; for astronomy and space scientists, it was $130,833.

Related Occupations

The work of physicists and astronomers relates closely to that of other physical scientists and engineers, such as:

Physicists and astronomers also work extensively with computers and data, similar to the work of:

Sources of Additional Information

Further information on career opportunities in physics is available from the following organizations:

➤ American Institute of Physics, Career Services Division and Education and Employment Division, One Physics Ellipse, College Park, MD 20740-3843. Internet: **http://www.aip.org**

➤ American Physical Society, One Physics Ellipse, College Park, MD 20740-3844. Internet: **http://www.aps.org**

The Occupational Information Network (O*NET) provides information on a wide range of occupational characteristics. Links to O*NET appear at the end of the Internet version of this occupational statement, accessible at **http://www.bls.gov/ooh/ocos052.htm**

Social Scientists and Related Occupations

Economists

Significant Points

- Slower than average job growth is expected, as the vast majority of bachelor's degree holders in economics find employment in closely related fields, such as business, finance, or insurance.

- Candidates who hold a master's or Ph.D. degree in economics will have the best employment prospects and advancement opportunities; some entry-level positions are available to those with a bachelor's degree.

- Quantitative skills are important in all economics specialties.

Nature of the Work

Economists study how society distributes resources, such as land, labor, raw materials, and machinery, to produce goods and services. They conduct research, collect and analyze data, monitor economic trends, and develop forecasts on a wide variety of issues, including energy costs, inflation, interest rates, exchange rates, business cycles, taxes, and employment levels, among others.

Economists develop methods for obtaining the data they need. For example, sampling techniques may be used to conduct a survey, and various mathematical modeling techniques may be used to develop forecasts. Preparing reports, including tables and charts, on research results also is an important part of an economist's job, as is presenting economic and statistical concepts in a clear and meaningful way for those who do not have a background in economics. Some economists also perform economic analysis for the media.

Many economists specialize in a particular area of economics, although general knowledge of basic economic principles is essential. *Microeconomists* study the supply and demand decisions of individuals and firms, such as how profits can be maximized and the quantity of a good or service that consumers will demand at a certain price. *Industrial economists* and *organizational economists* study the market structure of particular industries in terms of the number of competitors within those industries and examine the market decisions of competitive firms and monopolies. These economists also may be concerned with antitrust policy and its impact on market structure. *Macroeconomists* study historical trends in the whole economy and forecast future trends in areas such as unemployment, inflation, economic growth, productivity, and investment. *Monetary economists* and *financial economists* do work that is similar to that done by macroeconomists. These workers study the money and banking system and the effects of changing interest rates. *International economists* study global financial markets, currencies and exchange rates, and the effects of various trade policies such as tariffs. *Labor economists* and *demographic economists* study the supply and demand for labor and the determination of wages. These economists also try to explain the reasons for unemployment and the effects of changing demographic trends, such as an aging population and increasing immigration, on labor markets. *Public finance economists* are involved primarily in studying the role of the government in the economy and the effects of tax cuts, budget deficits, and welfare policies. *Econometricians* investigate all areas of economics and apply mathematical techniques such as calculus, game theory, and regression analysis to their research. With these techniques, they formulate economic models that help explain economic relationships that can be used to develop forecasts about business cycles, the effects of a specific rate of inflation on the economy, the effects of tax legislation on unemployment levels, and other economic phenomena.

Many economists apply these areas of economics to health, education, agriculture, urban and regional economics, law, history, energy, the environment, and other issues. Economists working for corporations are involved primarily in microeconomic issues, such as forecasting consumer demand and sales of the firm's products. Some analyze their competitors' market share and advise their company on how to handle the competition. Others monitor legislation passed by Congress, such as environmental and worker safety regulations, and assess how new laws will affect the corporation. Corporations with many international branches or subsidiaries might employ economists to monitor the economic situations in countries where they do business or to provide a risk assessment of a country into which the company is considering expanding.

Economists working in economic consulting or research firms sometimes perform the same tasks as economists working for corporations. However, economists in consulting firms also perform much of the macroeconomic analysis and forecasting conducted in the United States. Their analyses and forecasts are frequently published in newspapers and journal articles.

Another large employer of economists is government. Economists in the Federal Government administer most of the surveys and collect the majority of the economic data about the United States. For example, economists in the U.S. Department of Commerce collect and analyze data on the production, distribution, and consumption of commodities produced in the United States, and economists employed by the U.S. Department of Labor collect and analyze data on the domestic economy, including data on prices, wages, employment, productivity, and safety and health.

Economists who work for government agencies also assess economic conditions in the United States and abroad to estimate the effects of specific changes in legislation and public policy. Government economists advise policy makers in areas such as the deregulation of industries, the effects of changes to Social Security, the effects of tax cuts on the budget deficit, and the effectiveness of imposing tariffs on imported goods. An economist working in State or local government might analyze data on the growth of school-age or prison populations and on employment and unemployment rates to project future spending needs.

Work environment. Economists have structured work schedules. They often work alone, writing reports, preparing statistical charts, and using computers, but they also may be an integral part of a research team. Many work under pressure of deadlines and tight schedules, which may require overtime. Their routine may be interrupted by special requests for data and by the need to attend meetings or conferences. Some travel may be necessary.

Training, Other Qualifications, and Advancement

Some entry-level positions for economists are available to those with a bachelor's degree, but higher degrees are required for many positions. Prospective economists need good quantitative skills.

Education and training. A master's or Ph.D. degree in economics is required for many private sector economist jobs and for advancement to higher-level positions. In the Federal Government, candidates for entry-level economist positions must have a bachelor's degree with a minimum of 21 semester hours

Preparing reports on the results of economic research is an important part of an economist's job.

Projections data from the National Employment Matrix

Occupational Title	SOC Code	Employment, 2008	Projected Employment, 2018	Change, 2008-2018	
				Number	Percent
Economists...	19-3011	14,600	15,500	900	6

(NOTE) Data in this table are rounded. See the discussion of the employment projections table in the *Handbook* introductory chapter on *Occupational Information Included in the Handbook.*

of economics and 3 hours of statistics, accounting, or calculus, or a combination of education and experience.

Economics includes numerous specialties at the graduate level, such as econometrics, international economics, and labor economics. Students should select graduate schools that are strong in the specialties that interest them. Some schools help graduate students find internships or part-time employment in government agencies, economic consulting or research firms, or financial institutions before graduation.

Undergraduate economics majors can choose from a variety of courses, ranging from microeconomics, macroeconomics, and econometrics to more philosophical courses, such as the history of economic thought. Because of the importance of quantitative skills to economists, courses in mathematics, statistics, econometrics, sampling theory and survey design, and computer science are extremely helpful.

Whether working in government, industry, research organizations, or consulting firms, economists with a bachelor's degree usually qualify for entry-level positions as a research assistant, for marketing or finance positions, or for various sales jobs. A master's degree usually is required to qualify for more responsible research and administrative positions. A Ph.D. is necessary for top economist positions in many organizations.

Aspiring economists should gain experience gathering and analyzing data, conducting interviews or surveys, and writing reports on their findings while in college. This experience can prove invaluable later in obtaining a full-time position in the field because much of the economist's work, especially in the beginning, may center on these duties. With experience, economists eventually are assigned their own research projects. Related job experience, such as work as a stock or bond trader, might be advantageous.

Other qualifications. Those considering careers as economists should be able to pay attention to details because much time is spent on precise data analysis. Candidates also should have strong computer and quantitative skills and be able to perform complex research. Patience and persistence are necessary qualities, given that economists must spend long hours on independent study and problem solving. Good communication skills also are useful, as economists must be able to present their findings, both orally and in writing, in a clear, concise manner.

Advancement.   With experience or an advanced degree, economists may advance to positions of greater responsibility, including administration and independent research.

Many people with an economics background become teachers. (See the statement on teachers—postsecondary elsewhere in the *Handbook.*) A master's degree usually is the minimum requirement for a job as an instructor in a community college. In most colleges and universities, however, a Ph.D. is necessary for appointment as an instructor. A Ph.D. and publications in

academic journals are required for a professorship, tenure, and promotion.

Employment

Economists held about 14,600 jobs in 2008. Government employed 53 percent of economists, in a wide range of agencies, with 31 percent in Federal Government and 22 percent in State and local government. The remaining jobs were spread throughout private industry, particularly in scientific research and development services and management, scientific, and technical consulting services. A number of economists combine a full-time job in government, academia, or business with part-time or consulting work in another setting.

Employment of economists is concentrated in large cities. Some work abroad for companies with major international operations, for U.S. Government agencies, and for international organizations, such as the World Bank, International Monetary Fund, and United Nations.

In addition to the previously mentioned jobs, economists who hold faculty positions in colleges and universities are counted as postsecondary teachers.

Job Outlook

Employment of economists is expected to grow more slowly than the average for all occupations. The demand for workers who have knowledge of economics is projected to grow faster, but these workers will commonly find employment in fields outside of economics, such as business, finance, or insurance. Job prospects for economists will be best for those with graduate degrees in economics.

Employment change.   Employment of economists is expected to grow 6 percent from 2008 to 2018, which is slower than the average for all occupations. Demand for economic analysis should grow, but the increase in the number of economist jobs will be tempered as firms hire workers for niche areas with specialized titles. Many workers with economic backgrounds will work in related fields with more specific job titles, such as financial analyst, market analyst, public policy consultant, researcher or research assistant, purchasing manager, or a variety of positions in business and the insurance industry. Overall employment growth also will be slowed because of the relatively high number of economists—about 53 percent—employed in declining government sectors.

Employment growth should be fastest in private industry, especially in management, scientific, and technical consulting services. Rising demand for economic analysis in virtually every industry should stem from the growing complexity of the global economy, the effects of competition on businesses, and increased reliance on quantitative methods for analyzing and forecasting business, sales, and other economic trends. Some corporations choose to hire economic consultants to fill these needs, rather than keeping an economist on staff. This practice should result in more economists being employed in consulting services.

Job prospects. In addition to job openings from growth, the need to replace experienced workers who retire or leave the labor force for other reasons will create openings for economists.

Individuals with a background in economics should have opportunities in various occupations. Some examples of job titles often held by those with an economics background are financial analyst, market analyst, public policy consultant, researcher or research assistant, and purchasing manager.

People who have a master's or Ph.D. degree in economics, who are skilled in quantitative techniques and their application to economic modeling and forecasting, and who also have good communications skills, should have the best job opportunities. Like those in many other disciplines, some economists leave the occupation to become professors, but competition for tenured teaching positions will remain keen.

Bachelor's degree holders will face competition for the limited number of economist positions for which they qualify. However, they will qualify for a number of other positions that can use their broad-based economics knowledge. Many graduates with bachelor's degrees will find jobs in business, finance, insurance, or related fields. Numerous positions in sales should also be available. Bachelor's degree holders with good quantitative skills and a strong background in mathematics, statistics, survey design, and computer science also may be hired as researchers. Some will find jobs in government.

Candidates who meet State certification requirements may become high school economics teachers. The demand for secondary school economics teachers is expected to grow, as economics becomes an increasingly important and popular course. (See the statement on teachers—kindergarten, elementary, middle, and secondary elsewhere in the *Handbook*.)

Earnings
Median annual wage and salary wages of economists were $83,590 in May 2008. The middle 50 percent earned between $59,390 and $113,590. The lowest 10 percent earned less than $44,050, and the highest 10 percent earned more than $149,110.

In March 2009, the average annual salary for economists employed by the Federal Government was $108,010. Starting salaries were higher in selected geographical areas where the prevailing local pay was higher.

Related Occupations
Other workers who are concerned with understanding and interpreting financial matters include:

Sources of Additional Information
For information on careers in business economics, contact:
➤ National Association for Business Economics, 1233 20th St. NW., Suite 505, Washington, DC 20036. Internet: **http://www.nabe.com**

Information on obtaining positions as economists with the Federal Government is available from the Office of Personnel Management through USAJOBS, the Federal Government's official employment information system. This resource for locating and applying for job opportunities can be accessed through the Internet at **http://www.usajobs.gov** or through an interactive voice response telephone system at (703) 724-1850. The number is not toll free, and charges may result. For advice on how to find and apply for Federal jobs, see the *Occupational Outlook Quarterly* article "How to get a job in the Federal Government," online at **http://www.bls.gov/opub/ooq/2004/summer/art01.pdf.**

The Occupational Information Network (O*NET) provides information on a wide range of occupational characteristics. Links to O*NET appear at the end of the Internet version of this occupational statement, accessible at **http://www.bls.gov/ooh/ocos055.htm**

Market and Survey Researchers

Significant Points

- Market and survey researchers can enter the occupation with a bachelor's degree, but those with a master's or Ph.D. in marketing or a social science should enjoy the best opportunities.

- Researchers need strong quantitative skills and, increasingly, knowledge of conducting web-based surveys.

- Employment is expected to grow much faster than average.

Nature of the Work
Market and survey researchers gather information about what people think. Market research analysts help companies understand what types of products people want, determine who will buy them and at what price. Gathering statistical data on competitors and examining prices, sales, and methods of marketing and distribution, they analyze data on past sales to predict future sales.

Market and survey researchers often use surveys to assess consumer preferences.

Market research analysts devise methods and procedures for obtaining the data they need by designing surveys to assess consumer preferences. While a majority of surveys are conducted through the Internet and telephone, other methods may include focus group discussions, mail responses, or setting up booths in public places, such as shopping malls, for example. Trained interviewers usually conduct the surveys under a market research analyst's direction.

Market opinion research has contributed greatly to a higher standard of living as most products and services consumers purchase are available with the aid of market research. By making recommendations to their client or employer, market research analysts provide companies with vital information to help them make decisions on the promotion, distribution, and design of products or services. For example, child proof closures on medicine bottles exist because research helped define the most workable design; and the growing variety of ready to cook meals, such as microwaveable soups and prepackaged meat products, exist because of increasing public demand for fast and convenient meals. The information also may be used to determine whether the company should add new lines of merchandise, open new branches, or otherwise diversify the company's operations. Market research analysts also help develop advertising brochures and commercials, sales plans, and product promotions such as rebates and giveaways based on their knowledge of the consumer being targeted.

Survey researchers also gather information about people and their opinions, but these workers focus exclusively on designing and conducting surveys. They work for a variety of clients—such as corporations, government agencies, political candidates—gathering information to help make fiscal or policy decisions, measure the effectiveness of those decisions, and improve customer satisfaction. Survey researchers may conduct opinion research to determine public attitudes on various issues; the research results may help political or business leaders measure public support for their electoral prospects or social policies. Like market research analysts, survey researchers may use a variety of mediums to conduct surveys, such as the Internet, telephone interviews, or questionnaires sent through the mail. They also may supervise interviewers who conduct surveys in person or over the telephone.

Survey researchers design surveys in many different formats, depending upon the scope of their research and the method of collection. Interview surveys, for example, are common because they can increase participation rates. Survey researchers may consult with economists, statisticians, market research analysts, or other data users in order to design surveys. They also may present survey results to clients.

Work environment. Market and survey researchers generally have structured work schedules. They often work alone, writing reports and preparing statistical charts on computers, but they sometimes may be part of a research team. Market researchers who conduct personal interviews have frequent contact with the public. Most work under pressure of deadlines and tight schedules, which may require overtime. Travel may be necessary.

Training, Other Qualifications, and Advancement
While a bachelor's degree is often sufficient for entry-level market and survey research jobs, higher degrees are usually required for advancement and more technical positions. Strong quantitative skills and keeping current with the latest methods of developing, conducting, and analyzing surveys and other data also are important for advancement.

Education and training. A bachelor's degree is the minimum educational requirement for many market and survey research jobs. However, a master's degree is usually required for more technical positions.

In addition to completing courses in business, marketing, and consumer behavior, prospective market and survey researchers should take social science courses, including economics, psychology and sociology. Because of the importance of quantitative skills to market and survey researchers, courses in mathematics, statistics, sampling theory and survey design, and computer science are extremely helpful. Market and survey researchers often earn advanced degrees in business administration, marketing, statistics, communications, or other closely related disciplines.

While in college, aspiring market and survey researchers should gain experience gathering and analyzing data, conducting interviews or surveys, and writing reports on their findings. This experience can prove invaluable toward obtaining a full-time position in the field, because much of the work may center on these duties. Some schools help graduate students find internships or part-time employment in government agencies, consulting firms, financial institutions, or marketing research firms prior to graduation.

Other qualifications. Market and survey researchers spend a lot of time performing precise data analysis, so being detail-oriented is critical. Patience and persistence are also necessary qualities because these workers devote long hours to independent study and problem solving. At the same time, they must work well with others as market and survey researchers sometimes oversee the interviewing of individuals. Communication skills are important, too, because the wording of surveys is critical, and researchers must be able to present their findings both orally and in writing.

Certification and advancement. Market research analysts often begin their careers by assisting others prior to being assigned independent research projects. With experience, con-

Projections data from the National Employment Matrix

Occupational Title	SOC Code	Employment, 2008	Projected Employment, 2018	Change, 2008-2018	
				Number	Percent
Market and survey researchers...	19-3020	273,200	350,500	77,200	28
Market research analysts...	19-3021	249,800	319,900	70,100	28
Survey researchers	19-3022	23,400	30,500	7,100	30

(NOTE) Data in this table are rounded. See the discussion of the employment projections table in the *Handbook* introductory chapter on *Occupational Information Included in the Handbook.*

tinuing education, and advanced degrees, they may advance to more responsible positions in this occupation. Those with expertise in marketing or survey research may choose to teach. (See the statement on teachers—postsecondary elsewhere in the *Handbook.*) While a master's degree is often sufficient to teach as a marketing or survey research instructor in junior and community colleges, most colleges and universities require instructors to hold a Ph.D. A Ph.D. and extensive publications in academic journals are needed for professorship, tenure, and promotion. Others advance to supervisory or managerial positions. Many corporation and government executives have a strong background in marketing.

Advancement in this occupation may be helped by obtaining certification. The Marketing Research Association (MRA) offers a certification program for professional researchers who wish to demonstrate their expertise. The Professional Researcher Certification (PRC) is awarded for two levels of knowledge: practitioner and expert. Prior to gaining certification, each level of knowledge requires certain criteria to be met, consisting largely of education and experience, and also previous membership to at least one professional marketing research organization. Those who have been granted the PRC designation require continuing education within their particular discipline, and individuals must apply to renew their certification every 2 years.

Employment

Market and survey researchers held about 273,200 jobs in 2008, most of which—249,800—were held by market research analysts. Because of the applicability of market research to many industries, market research analysts are employed throughout the economy. The industries that employed the largest number of market research analysts in 2008 were management, scientific, and technical consulting services; management of companies and enterprises; computer systems design and related services; insurance carriers; and other professional, scientific, and technical services—which includes marketing research and public opinion polling.

Survey researchers held about 23,400 jobs in 2008. Most were employed primarily by firms in other professional, scientific, and technical services—which include market research and public opinion polling; scientific research and development services; and management, scientific, and technical consulting services. About 9 percent of survey researchers worked in educational services—which includes colleges, universities, and professional schools.

A number of market and survey researchers combine a full-time job in government, academia, or business with part-time consulting work in another setting. About 7 percent of market and survey researchers are self-employed.

Besides holding the previously mentioned jobs, many people who perform market and survey research held faculty positions in colleges and universities. These workers are counted as postsecondary teachers rather than market and survey researchers.

Job Outlook

Employment growth of market and survey researchers is projected to be much faster than average. Job opportunities should be best for jobseekers with a master's or Ph.D. degree in marketing or a social science and with strong quantitative skills.

Employment change. Overall employment of market and survey researchers is projected to grow 28 percent from 2008 to 2018, much faster than the average for all occupations. Market research analysts, the larger specialty, will experience much faster than average job growth because competition between companies seeking to expand their market and sales of their products will generate a growing need for marketing professionals. Marketing research provides organizations valuable feedback from purchasers, allowing companies to evaluate consumer satisfaction and adjust their marketing strategies and plan more effectively for the future. Future locations of stores and shopping centers, for example, will be determined by marketing research, as will consumer preference of virtually all products and services. In addition, globalization of the marketplace creates a need for more market researchers to analyze foreign markets and competition.

Survey researchers, a much smaller specialty, will also increase much faster than average as public policy groups and all levels of governments increasingly use public opinion research to help determine a variety of issues, such as the best mass transit systems, social programs, and special services for school children and senior citizens that will be needed. Survey researchers will also be needed to meet the growing demand for market and opinion research as an increasingly competitive economy requires businesses and organizations to allocate advertising funds and other expenditures more effectively and efficiently.

Job prospects. Bachelor's degree holders may face competition for market research jobs, as many positions, especially technical ones, require a master's or doctoral degree. Among bachelor's degree holders, those with good quantitative skills, including a strong background in mathematics, statistics, survey design, and computer science, will have the best opportunities. Those with a background in consumer behavior or an undergraduate degree in a social science—psychology, sociology, or economics—may qualify for less technical positions, such as a public opinion researcher. Obtaining the Professional Researcher Certification also can be important as it demonstrates competence and professionalism among potential candidates. Overall, job opportunities should be best for jobseekers with a master's or Ph.D. degree in marketing or a related field and with strong quantitative skills. Market research analysts should have the best opportunities in consulting firms and marketing research firms as companies find it more profitable to contract for market research services rather than support their own marketing department. However, other organizations, including computer systems design companies, software publishers, financial services organizations, healthcare institutions, advertising firms, and insurance companies, may also offer job opportunities for market research analysts. Increasingly, market research analysts not only collect and analyze information, but also help clients implement ideas and recommendations.

There will be fewer job opportunities for survey researchers since it is a relatively smaller occupation and a greater number of candidates qualify for these positions. The best prospects will come from growth in the market research and public opinion polling industry, which employs many survey researchers.

Earnings

Median annual wages of market research analysts in May 2008 were $61,070. The middle 50 percent earned between $43,990 and $85,510. The lowest 10 percent earned less than $33,770, and the highest 10 percent earned more than $112,410. Median annual wages in the industries employing the largest numbers of market research analysts in May 2008 were:

Computer systems design and related services	$77,170
Management of companies and enterprises	65,880
Other professional, scientific, and technical services	58,480
Advertising, public relations, and related services	56,730
Management, scientific, and technical consulting services	55,570

Median annual wages of survey researchers in May 2008 were $36,220. The middle 50 percent earned between $22,290 and $54,480. The lowest 10 percent earned less than $17,650, and the highest 10 percent earned more than $75,940. Median annual wages of survey researchers in other professional, scientific, and technical services were $26,440.

Related Occupations

Market and survey researchers perform research to find out how well the market will receive products, services, and ideas. This research may include planning, implementing, and analyzing surveys to determine the needs and preferences of people. Other jobs using these skills include:

When analyzing data, market and survey researchers must use quantitative skills similar to those of:

Market and survey researchers often are concerned with public opinion, as are:

Sources of Additional Information

For information about careers and certification in market research, contact:

➤ Marketing Research Association, 110 National Dr., 2nd Floor, Glastonbury, CT 06033. Internet: **http://www.mra-net.org**

For information about careers in survey research, contact:
➤ Council of American Survey Research Organizations, 170 North Country Rd., Suite 4, Port Jefferson, NY 11777. Internet: **http://www.casro.org**

The Occupational Information Network (O*NET) provides information on a wide range of occupational characteristics. Links to O*NET appear at the end of the Internet version of this occupational statement, accessible at **http://www.bls.gov/ooh/ocos013.htm**

Psychologists

Significant Points

- About 34 percent of psychologists are self-employed, mainly as private practitioners and independent consultants.

- Employment growth will vary by specialty; for example, clinical, counseling, and school psychologists will have 11 percent growth; industrial-organizational psychologists, 26 percent growth; and 14 percent growth is expected for all other psychologists.

- Acceptance to graduate psychology programs is highly competitive.

- Job opportunities should be the best for those with a doctoral degree in a subfield, such as health; those with a master's degree will have good prospects in industrial-organization; bachelor's degree holders will have limited prospects.

Nature of the Work

Psychologists study mental processes and human behavior by observing, interpreting, and recording how people and other animals relate to one another and the environment. To do this, psychologists often look for patterns that will help them understand and predict behavior using scientific methods, principles, or procedures to test their ideas. Through such research studies, psychologists have learned much that can help increase understanding between individuals, groups, organizations, institutions, nations, and cultures.

Psychologists who deal directly with patients must be emotionally stable, mature, sensitive, and have strong communication skills.

Like other social scientists, psychologists formulate theories, or hypotheses, which are possible explanations for what they observe. But unlike other social science disciplines, psychologists often concentrate on individual behavior and, specifically, in the beliefs and feelings that influence a person's actions.

Research methods vary with the topic which they study, but by and large, the chief techniques used are observation, assessment, and experimentation. Psychologists sometimes gather information and evaluate behavior through controlled laboratory experiments, hypnosis, biofeedback, psychoanalysis, or psychotherapy, or by administering personality, performance, aptitude, or intelligence tests. Other methods include interviews, questionnaires, clinical studies, surveys, and observation—looking for cause-and-effect relationships between events and for broad patterns of behavior.

Research in psychology seeks to understand and explain thought, emotion, feelings, or behavior. The research findings of psychologists have greatly increased our understanding of why people and animals behave as they do. For example, psychologists have discovered how personality develops and how to promote healthy development. They have gained knowledge of how to diagnose and treat alcoholism and substance abuse, how to help people change bad habits and conduct, and how to help students learn. They understand the conditions that can make workers more productive. Insights provided by psychologists can help people function better as individuals, friends, family members, and workers.

Psychologists may perform a variety of duties in a vast number of industries. For example, those working in health service fields may provide mental health care in hospitals, clinics, schools, or private settings. Psychologists employed in applied settings, such as business, industry, government, or nonprofit organizations, may provide training, conduct research, design organizational systems, and act as advocates for psychology.

Psychologists apply their knowledge to a wide range of endeavors, including health and human services, management, education, law, and sports. They usually specialize in one of many different areas.

Clinical psychologists—who constitute the largest specialty—are concerned with the assessment, diagnosis, treatment, and prevention of mental disorders. While some clinical psychologists specialize in treating severe psychological disorders, such as schizophrenia and depression, many others may help people deal with personal issues, such as divorce or the death of a loved one. Often times, clinical psychologists provide an opportunity to talk and think about things that are confusing or worrying, offering different ways of interpreting and understanding problems and situations. They are trained to use a variety of approaches aimed at helping individuals, and the strategies used are generally determined by the specialty they work in.

Clinical psychologists often interview patients and give diagnostic tests in their own private offices. They may provide individual, family, or group psychotherapy and may design and implement behavior modification programs. Some clinical psychologists work in hospitals where they collaborate with physicians and other specialists to develop and implement treatment and intervention programs that patients can understand and comply with. Other clinical psychologists work in universities and medical schools, where they train graduate students in the delivery of mental health and behavioral medicine services. A few work in physical rehabilitation settings, treating patients with spinal cord injuries, chronic pain or illness, stroke, arthritis, or neurological conditions. Others may work in community mental health centers, crisis counseling services, or drug rehabilitation centers, offering evaluation, therapy, remediation, and consultation.

Areas of specialization within clinical psychology include health psychology, neuropsychology, geropsychology, and child psychology. *Health psychologists* study how biological, psychological, and social factors affect health and illness. They promote healthy living and disease prevention through counseling, and they focus on how patients adjust to illnesses and treatments and view their quality of life. *Neuropsychologists* study the relation between the brain and behavior. They often work in stroke and head injury programs. *Geropsychologists* deal with the special problems faced by the elderly. Work may include helping older persons cope with stresses that are common in late life, such as loss of loved ones, relocation, medical conditions, and increased care-giving demands. Clinical psychologists may further specialize in these fields by focusing their work in a number of niche areas including mental health, learning disabilities, emotional disturbances, or substance abuse. The emergence and growth of these, and other, specialties reflects the increasing participation of psychologists in direct services to special patient populations.

Often, clinical psychologists consult with other medical personnel regarding the best treatment for patients, especially treatment that includes medication. Clinical psychologists generally are not permitted to prescribe medication to treat patients; only psychiatrists and other medical doctors may prescribe most medications. (See the statement on physicians and surgeons elsewhere in the *Handbook*.) However, two States—Louisiana and New Mexico—currently allow appropriately trained clinical psychologists to prescribe medication with some limitations.

Counseling psychologists advise people on how to deal with problems of everyday living, including problems in the home, place of work, or community, to help improve their quality of life. They foster well-being by promoting good mental health and preventing mental, physical, and social disorders. They work in settings such as university or crisis counseling centers, hospitals, rehabilitation centers, and individual or group practices. (See also the statements on counselors and social workers elsewhere in the *Handbook*.)

School psychologists work with students in early childhood and elementary and secondary schools. They collaborate with teachers, parents, and school personnel to create safe, healthy, and supportive learning environments for all students. School psychologists address students' learning and behavioral problems, suggest improvements to classroom management strategies or parenting techniques, and evaluate students with disabilities and gifted and talented students to help determine the best way to educate them.

They improve teaching, learning, and socialization strategies based on their understanding of the psychology of learning environments. They also may evaluate the effectiveness of academic programs, prevention programs, behavior management procedures, and other services provided in the school setting.

Industrial-organizational psychologists apply psychological principles and research methods to the workplace in the interest of improving the quality of worklife. They also are involved in research on management and marketing problems. They screen, train, and counsel applicants for jobs, as well as perform organizational development and analysis. An industrial psychologist might work with management to reorganize the work setting in order to enhance productivity. Industrial psychologists frequently act as consultants, brought in by management to solve a particular problem.

Developmental psychologists study the physiological, cognitive, and social development that takes place throughout life. Some specialize in behavior during infancy, childhood, and adolescence, or changes that occur during maturity or old age. Developmental psychologists also may study developmental disabilities and their effects. Increasingly, research is developing ways to help elderly people remain independent as long as possible.

Social psychologists examine people's interactions with others and with the social environment. They work in organizational consultation, marketing research, systems design, or other applied psychology fields. Many social psychologists specialize in a niche area, such as group behavior, leadership, attitudes, and perception.

Experimental or *research psychologists* work in university and private research centers and in business, nonprofit, and governmental organizations. They study the behavior of both human beings and animals, such as rats, monkeys, and pigeons. Prominent areas of study in experimental research include mo-tivation, thought, attention, learning and memory, sensory and perceptual processes, effects of substance abuse, and genetic and neurological factors affecting behavior.

Forensic psychologists use psychological principles in the legal and criminal justice system to help judges, attorneys, and other legal professionals understand the psychological findings of a particular case. They are usually designated as an expert witness and typically specialize in one of three areas: family court, civil court, and criminal court. Forensic psychologists who work in family court may offer psychotherapy services, perform child custody evaluations, or investigate reports of child abuse. Those working in civil courts may assess competency, provide second opinions, and provide psychotherapy to crime victims. Criminal court forensic psychologists often conduct evaluations of mental competency, work with child witnesses, and provide assessment of juvenile or adult offenders.

Work environment. Psychologists' work environments vary by subfield and place of employment. For example, clinical, school, and counseling psychologists in private practice frequently have their own offices and set their own hours. However, they usually offer evening and weekend hours to accommodate their clients. Those employed in hospitals, nursing homes, and other health care facilities may work shifts that include evenings and weekends, and those who work in schools and clinics generally work regular daytime hours. Most psychologists in government and industry have structured schedules.

Psychologists employed as faculty by colleges and universities divide their time between teaching and research and also may have administrative responsibilities; many have part-time consulting practices.

Increasingly, a good number of psychologists work as part of a team, consulting with other psychologists and medical professionals. Many experience pressures because of deadlines, tight schedules, and overtime.

Training, Other Qualifications, and Advancement

A master's or doctoral degree, and a license, are required for most psychologists.

Education and training. A doctoral degree usually is required for independent practice as a psychologist. Psychologists with a Ph.D. or Doctor of Psychology (Psy.D.) qualify for a wide range of teaching, research, clinical, and counseling positions in universities, health care services, elementary and secondary schools, private industry, and government. Psychologists with a doctoral degree often work in clinical positions or in private practices, but they also sometimes teach, conduct research, or carry out administrative responsibilities.

A doctoral degree generally requires about 5 years of full-time graduate study, culminating in a dissertation based on original research. Courses in quantitative experimental methods and research design, which include the use of computer-based analysis, are an integral part of graduate study and are necessary to complete the dissertation. The Psy.D. degree may be based on practical work and examinations rather than a dissertation. In clinical, counseling, and school psychology, the requirements for the doctoral degree usually include an additional year of post-doctoral supervised experience.

A specialist degree or its equivalent is required in most States for an individual to work as a school psychologist, although some States credential school psychologists with master's degrees. A specialist (Ed.S.) degree in school psychology requires a minimum of 2 years of full-time graduate study (at least 60 graduate semester hours) and a 1-year full-time internship during the third year. Because their professional practice addresses educational and mental health components of students' development, school psychologists' training includes coursework in both education and psychology.

People with a master's degree in psychology may work as industrial-organizational psychologists. They also may work as psychological assistants conducting research under the direct supervision of doctoral-level psychologists. A master's degree in psychology requires at least 2 years of full-time graduate study. Requirements usually include practical experience in an applied setting and a master's thesis based on an original research project.

Competition for admission to graduate psychology programs is keen. Some universities require applicants to have an undergraduate major in psychology. Others prefer only coursework in basic psychology with additional courses in the biological, physical, and social sciences, and in statistics and mathematics.

A bachelor's degree in psychology qualifies a person to assist psychologists and other professionals in community mental health centers, vocational rehabilitation offices, and correctional programs. Bachelor's degree holders may also work as administrative assistants for psychologists. Many, however, find employment in other areas, such as sales, service, or business management.

In the Federal Government, candidates must have a bachelor's degree with a minimum of 24 semester hours in psychology, or a combination of education and experience to qualify for entry-level positions. However, competition for these jobs is keen because this is one of the few ways in which one can work as a psychologist without an advanced degree.

The American Psychological Association (APA) presently accredits doctoral training programs in clinical, counseling, and school psychology, as well as institutions that provide internships for doctoral students in school, clinical, and counseling psychology. The National Association of School Psychologists, with the assistance of the National Council for Accreditation of Teacher Education, helps to approve advanced degree programs in school psychology.

Clinical psychologists in Louisiana and New Mexico who prescribe medication are required to complete a post-doctoral master's degree in clinical psychopharmacology and pass a National exam approved by the State Board of Examiners of psychologists.

Licensure. Psychologists in a solo or group practice or those who offer any type of patient care—including clinical, counseling, and school psychologists—must meet certification or licensing requirements in all States and the District of Columbia. Licensing laws vary by State and by type of position and require licensed or certified psychologists to limit their practice to areas in which they have developed professional competence through training and experience. Clinical and counseling psychologists usually need a doctorate in psychology, an approved

internship, and 1 to 2 years of professional experience. In addition, all States require that applicants pass an examination. Most State licensing boards administer a standardized test, and many supplement that with additional oral or essay questions. Some States require continuing education for renewal of the license.

The National Association of School Psychologists (NASP) awards the Nationally Certified School Psychologist (NCSP) designation, which recognizes professional competency in school psychology at a national, rather than State, level. Currently, 31 States recognize the NCSP and allow those with the certification to transfer credentials from one State to another without taking a new certification exam. In States that recognize the NCSP, the requirements for certification or licensure and those for the NCSP often are the same or similar. Requirements for the NCSP include the completion of 60 graduate semester hours in school psychology; a 1,200-hour internship, 600 hours of which must be completed in a school setting; and a passing score on the National School Psychology Examination.

Other qualifications. Aspiring psychologists who are interested in direct patient care must be emotionally stable, mature, and able to deal effectively with people. Sensitivity, compassion, good communication skills, and the ability to lead and inspire others are particularly important qualities for people wishing to do clinical work and counseling. Research psychologists should be capable of detailed work both independently and as part of a team. Patience and perseverance are vital qualities, because achieving results in the psychological treatment of patients or in research may take a long time.

Certification and advancement. The American Board of Professional Psychology (ABPP) recognizes professional achievement by awarding specialty certification in 13 different areas, such as psychoanalysis, rehabilitation, forensic, group, school, clinical health, and couple and family. To obtain board certification in a specialty, candidates must meet general criteria which consist of having a doctorate in psychology, as well as State licensure. Each candidate must then meet additional criteria of the specialty field, which is usually a combination of postdoctoral training in their specialty, several years of experience, and professional endorsements, as determined by the ABPP. Applicants are then required to pass the specialty board examination.

Psychologists can improve their advancement opportunities by earning an advanced degree and by participation in continuing education. Many psychologists opt to start their own private practice after gaining experience working in the field.

Employment

Psychologists held about 170,200 jobs in 2008. Educational institutions employed about 29 percent of psychologists in positions other than teaching, such as counseling, testing, research, and administration. About 21 percent were employed in health care, primarily in offices of mental health practitioners, hospitals, physicians' offices, and outpatient mental health and substance abuse centers. Government agencies at the State and local levels employed psychologists in correctional facilities, law enforcement, and other settings.

Projections data from the National Employment Matrix

Occupational Title	SOC Code	Employment, 2008	Projected Employment, 2018	Change, 2008-2018	
				Number	Percent
Psychologists..	19-3030	170,200	190,000	19,700	12
Clinical, counseling, and school psychologists............................	19-3031	152,000	168,800	16,800	11
Industrial-organizational psychologists	19-3032	2,300	2,900	600	26
Psychologists, all other	19-3039	15,900	18,300	2,300	14

(NOTE) Data in this table are rounded. See the discussion of the employment projections table in the *Handbook* introductory chapter on *Occupational Information Included in the Handbook.*

After several years of experience, some psychologists—usually those with doctoral degrees—enter private practice or set up private research or consulting firms. About 34 percent of psychologists were self-employed in 2008—mainly as private practitioners.

In addition to the previously mentioned jobs, many psychologists held faculty positions at colleges and universities and as high school psychology teachers. (See the statements on teachers—postsecondary and teachers—kindergarten, elementary, middle, and secondary elsewhere in the *Handbook*.)

Job Outlook

Employment of psychologists is expected to grow as fast as average. Job prospects should be the best for people who have a doctoral degree from a leading university in an applied specialty, such as counseling or health, and those with a specialist or doctoral degree in school psychology. Master's degree holders in fields other than industrial-organizational psychology will face keen competition. Opportunities will be limited for bachelor's degree holders.

Employment change. Employment of psychologists is expected to grow 12 percent from 2008 to 2018, about as fast as the average for all occupations. Employment will grow because of increased demand for psychological services in schools, hospitals, social service agencies, mental health centers, substance abuse treatment clinics, consulting firms, and private companies.

Demand for school psychologists will be driven by a growing awareness of how students' mental health and behavioral problems, such as bullying, affect learning. School psychologists will also be needed for general student counseling on a variety of other issues, including working with students with disabilities or with special needs, tackling drug abuse, and consulting and managing personal crisis.

Spurring demand for clinical psychologists will continue to be the rising healthcare costs associated with unhealthy lifestyles, such as smoking, alcoholism, and obesity, which have made prevention and treatment more critical. An increase in the number of employee assistance programs, which help workers deal with personal problems, also should lead to employment growth for clinical and counseling specialties. More clinical and counseling psychologists will be needed to help people deal with depression and other mental disorders, marriage and family problems, job stress, and addiction. The growing number of elderly will increase the demand for psychologists trained in geropsychology to help people deal with the mental and physical changes that occur as individuals grow older. There also will

be increased need for psychologists to work with returning veterans.

Industrial-organizational psychologists also will be in demand to help to boost worker productivity and retention rates in a wide range of businesses. Industrial-organizational psychologists will help companies deal with issues such as workplace diversity and antidiscrimination policies. Companies also will use psychologists' expertise in survey design, analysis, and research to develop tools for marketing evaluation and statistical analysis.

Job prospects. Job prospects should be best for people who have a doctoral degree from a leading university in an applied specialty, such as counseling or health, and those with a specialist or doctoral degree in school psychology. Psychologists with extensive training in quantitative research methods and computer science may have a competitive edge over applicants without such background.

Master's degree holders in fields other than industrial-organizational psychology will face keen competition for jobs because of the limited number of positions that require only a master's degree. Master's degree holders may find jobs as psychological assistants or counselors, providing mental health services under the direct supervision of a licensed psychologist. Still, others may find jobs involving research and data collection and analysis in universities, government, or private companies.

Opportunities directly related to psychology will be limited for bachelor's degree holders. Some may find jobs as assistants in rehabilitation centers or in other jobs involving data collection and analysis. Those who meet State certification requirements may become high school psychology teachers.

Earnings

Median annual wages of wage and salary clinical, counseling, and school psychologists were $64,140 in May 2008. The middle 50 percent earned between $48,700 and $82,800. The lowest 10 percent earned less than $37,900, and the highest 10 percent earned more than $106,840. Median annual wages in the industries employing the largest numbers of clinical, counseling, and school psychologists were:

Offices of other health practitioners	$68,400
Elementary and secondary schools	65,710
State government	63,710
Outpatient care centers	59,130
Individual and family services	57,440

Median annual wages of wage and salary industrial-organizational psychologists were $77,010 in May 2008. The middle 50 percent earned between $54,100 and $115,720. The lowest

10 percent earned less than $38,690, and the highest 10 percent earned more than $149,120.

In 2008, about 31 percent of all psychologists were members of a union.

Related Occupations
Psychologists work with people, developing relationships and comforting them. Other occupations with similar duties include:

Psychologists also sometimes diagnose and treat problems and help patients recover. These duties are similar to those for:

Sources of Additional Information
For information on careers, educational requirements, financial assistance, and licensing in all fields of psychology, contact:
➤ American Psychological Association, Center for Psychology Workforce Analysis and Research and Education Directorate, 750 First St. NE., Washington, DC 20002. Internet: **http://www.apa.org/students**

For information on careers, educational requirements, certification, and licensing of school psychologists, contact:
➤ National Association of School Psychologists, 4340 East West Hwy., Suite 402, Bethesda, MD 20814. Internet: **http://www.nasponline.org**

Information about State licensing requirements is available from:
➤ Association of State and Provincial Psychology Boards, P.O. Box 241245, Montgomery, AL 36124. Internet: **http://www.asppb.org**

Information about psychology specialty certifications is available from:
➤ American Board of Professional Psychology, 600 Market St., Suite 300, Chapel Hill, NC 27516. Internet: **http://www.abpp.org**

The Occupational Information Network (O*NET) provides information on a wide range of occupational characteristics. Links to O*NET appear at the end of the Internet version of this occupational statement, accessible at **http://www.bls.gov/ooh/ocos056.htm**

Urban and Regional Planners

Significant Points

- Local governments employ about 66 percent of urban and regional planners.

- Employment is projected to grow 19 percent, which is faster than the average.

- Most new jobs will be in affluent, rapidly growing communities.

- Job prospects will be best for those with a master's degree; bachelor's degree holders with additional skills in GIS or mapping may find entry-level positions, but advancement opportunities are limited.

Nature of the Work
Urban and *regional planners* develop long- and short-term plans for the use of land and the growth and revitalization of urban, suburban, and rural communities and the region in which they are located. They help local officials alleviate social, economic, and environmental problems by recommending locations for roads, schools, and other infrastructure and suggesting zoning regulations for private property—work that requires forecasting the future needs of the population. Because local governments employ the majority of urban and regional planners, they often are referred to as community or city planners.

Planners promote the best use of a community's land and resources for residential, commercial, institutional, and recreational purposes. They address environmental, economic, and social health issues of a community as it grows and changes. They may formulate plans relating to the construction of new school buildings, public housing, or other kinds of infrastructure. Planners also may help to make decisions about developing resources and protecting ecologically sensitive regions. Some planners are involved in environmental issues including pollution control, wetland preservation, forest conservation, and the location of new landfills. Planners also may help to draft legislation on environmental, social, and economic issues, such as planning a new park, sheltering the homeless, or making the region more attractive to businesses.

Before preparing plans for community development, planners study and report on the current use of land for residential, business, and community purposes. Their reports include information on the location and capacity of streets, highways, airports, water and sewer lines, schools, libraries, and cultural and recreational sites. They also provide data on the types of industries in the community, the characteristics of the population, and employment and economic trends. Using this information, along with input from citizens, planners try to optimize land use for buildings and other public facilities. Planners prepare reports showing how their programs can be carried out and what they will cost.

Planners examine proposed community facilities, such as schools, to ensure that these facilities will meet the needs of a growing or changing population. They keep abreast of economic and legal issues related to zoning codes, building codes,

Urban and regional planners develop plans to use land for the growth and revitalization of communities.

and environmental regulations. Planners also deal with land-use issues created by population movements. For example, as suburban growth and economic development create more jobs outside cities, the need for public transportation that gets workers to those jobs increases. In response, planners develop and model possible transportation systems and explain them to planning boards and the general public.

Planners use computers to record and analyze information and to prepare reports and recommendations for government executives, developers and builders. Computer databases, spreadsheets, and analytical techniques are used to project program costs and forecast future trends in employment, housing, transportation, or population. Widespread use of computerized geographic information systems (GIS) enable planners to map land areas, to overlay maps with geographic variables such as population density, and to combine or manipulate geographic information to produce alternative plans for land use or development.

Urban and regional planners often work with land developers, civic leaders, and public officials and may function as mediators in community disputes, presenting alternatives that are acceptable to opposing parties. Planners may prepare material for community relations programs, speak at civic meetings, and

appear before legislative committees to explain and defend their proposals.

Most urban and regional planners focus on one or more areas of specialization, such as transportation planning, urban design, community development and redevelopment, and land-use or code enforcement. While planners may specialize in these, and other, areas, they are also required to keep the bigger picture in mind and do what's best for the community as a whole.

Work environment. Urban and regional planners often travel to sites intended for development or regulation to inspect the features of the land. Those involved in site development inspections may spend most of their time in the field. Although most planners have a scheduled 40-hour workweek, they frequently attend evening or weekend meetings or public hearings with citizens' groups. Planners may experience the pressure of deadlines and tight work schedules, as well as political pressure generated by interest groups affected by proposals related to urban development and land use.

Training, Other Qualifications, and Advancement

A master's degree from an accredited planning program provides the best training for a wide range of planning positions. Experience and acquiring certification lead to the best opportunities for advancement.

Education and training. Most entry-level jobs in Federal, State, and local governments require a master's degree from an accredited program in urban or regional planning or a related field, such as urban design, environmental planning, or geography. Students are admitted to master's degree programs in planning with a wide range of undergraduate backgrounds, such as a bachelor's degree in economics, geography, political science, or environmental design. Several schools offer a bachelor's degree in urban planning, and graduates from these programs qualify for some entry-level positions, but their advancement opportunities are often limited unless they acquire an advanced degree.

In 2009, 67 colleges and universities offered an accredited master's degree program, and 15 offered an accredited bachelor's degree program, in planning. Accreditation for these programs is from the Planning Accreditation Board, which consists of three sponsoring organizations: the American Institute of Certified Planners, the American Planning Association, and the Association of Collegiate Schools of Planning.

Most college and university planning departments offer specialization in areas such as community development and redevelopment, land-use or code enforcement, transportation planning, environmental and natural resources planning, urban design, and economic planning and development.

Highly recommended also are courses in related disciplines, such as architecture, law, earth sciences, demography, geography, economics, finance, health administration, and management. Because familiarity with computer models and statistical techniques is important, courses in statistics, computer science, and GIS also are recommended or required.

Graduate students spend considerable time in seminars, workshops, and laboratory courses, learning to analyze and solve planning problems. They are often required to work in a planning office part time or during the summer. Local government planning offices frequently offer students internships,

Projections data from the National Employment Matrix

Occupational Title	SOC Code	Employment, 2008	Projected Employment, 2018	Change, 2008-2018	
				Number	Percent
Urban and regional planners	19-3051	38,400	45,700	7,300	19

(NOTE) Data in this table are rounded. See the discussion of the employment projections table in the *Handbook* introductory chapter on *Occupational Information Included in the Handbook.*

providing experience that proves invaluable in obtaining a full-time planning position after graduation.

Licensure. As of 2009, New Jersey was the only State that required planners to be licensed, although Michigan required registration to use the title "community planner." Licensure in New Jersey is based on two examinations—one testing general knowledge of planning and another testing specific New Jersey planning laws. Registration as a community planner in Michigan is based on professional experience and national and State examinations.

Other qualifications. Planners must be able to think in terms of spatial relationships and visualize the effects of their plans and designs. They should be flexible and be able to reconcile different viewpoints and make constructive policy recommendations. The ability to communicate effectively, both orally and in writing, is necessary for anyone interested in this field.

Certification and advancement. The American Institute of Certified Planners (AICP), a professional institute within the American Planning Association, grants certification to individuals who have the appropriate combination of education and professional experience and pass an examination. Professional development activities are required to maintain certification, which can be very helpful for promotion.

After a few years of experience, planners may advance to assignments requiring a high degree of independent judgment, such as designing the physical layout of a large development or recommending policy and budget options. Some public sector planners are promoted to community planning director and spend a great deal of time meeting with officials, speaking to civic groups, and supervising a staff. Further advancement occurs through a transfer to a larger jurisdiction with more complex problems and greater responsibilities or into related occupations, such as director of community or economic development.

Employment

Urban and regional planners held about 38,400 jobs in 2008. About 66 percent were employed by local governments. Companies involved with architectural, engineering, and related services, as well as management, scientific, and technical consulting services, employ an increasing proportion of planners in the private sector.

Job Outlook

Faster than average employment growth is projected for urban and regional planners. Most new jobs will be in affluent, rapidly expanding communities. Job prospects will be best for those with a master's degree; bachelor's degree holders with additional skills in GIS or mapping may find entry level positions, but advancement opportunities are limited.

Employment change. Employment of urban and regional planners is expected to grow 19 percent from 2008 to 2018, faster than the average for all occupations. Employment growth will be driven by the need for State and local governments to provide public services such as regulation of commercial development, the environment, transportation, housing, and land use and development for an expanding population. Nongovernmental initiatives dealing with historic preservation and redevelopment will also create employment growth.

The fastest job growth for urban and regional planners will occur in the private sector, primarily in the professional, scientific, and technical services industries. Specifically, planners will be employed by architecture and engineering firms to assist private developers and builders with broader issues, such as those related to storm water management, permits, and environmental regulation, to more specific ones, such as helping to design security measures for a building that are effective but also subtle and able to blend in with the surrounding area.

Many additional jobs for urban and regional planners will be in local government, as planners will be needed to address an array of problems associated with population growth, especially in affluent, rapidly expanding communities. For example, new housing developments require roads, sewer systems, fire stations, schools, libraries, and recreation facilities that must be planned for within budgetary constraints.

Job prospects. Besides opportunities from employment growth, job openings will arise from the need to replace experienced planners who transfer to other occupations, retire, or leave the labor force for other reasons. Graduates with a master's degree from an accredited program should have much better job opportunities than those with only a bachelor's degree. Additionally, AICP certified planners should have the best opportunities for advancement. Computers and software—especially GIS software—are increasingly being used in planning; therefore, candidates with strong computer skills and GIS experience will have an advantage in the job market.

Earnings

Median annual wages of urban and regional planners were $59,810 in May 2008. The middle 50 percent earned between $47,050 and $75,630. The lowest 10 percent earned less than $37,960, and the highest 10 percent earned more than $91,520. Median annual wages in the industries employing the largest numbers of urban and regional planners in May 2008 were:

Architectural, engineering, and related services $63,770
Scientific research and development services 60,750
Management, scientific, and technical
   consulting services 59,160
Local government...58,260
Colleges, universities, and professional schools 57,520

Related Occupations

Urban and regional planners develop plans for the growth of urban, suburban, and rural communities. Others whose work is similar include:

Sources of Additional Information

Information on careers, salaries, and certification in urban and regional planning is available from:

➤ American Planning Association, 1776 Massachusetts Ave. NW., Suite 400, Washington, DC 20036. Internet: **http://www.planning.org**

Information on accredited urban and regional planning programs is available from:

➤ Association of Collegiate Schools of Planning, 6311 Mallard Trace, Tallahassee, FL 32312. Internet: **http://www.acsp.org**

For additional information on urban and regional planning and on related occupations, see "Geography jobs" in the Spring 2005 *Occupational Outlook Quarterly*. The article is online at **http://www.bls.gov/opub/ooq/2005/spring/art01.pdf**

The Occupational Information Network (O*NET) provides information on a wide range of occupational characteristics. Links to O*NET appear at the end of the Internet version of this occupational statement, accessible at **http://www.bls.gov/ooh/ocos057.htm**

Sociologists and Political Scientists

Significant Points

- The vast majority of bachelor's degree holders in sociology and political science find employment in niche areas with specialized titles, such as market analyst, research assistant, writer, or policy analyst.

- Employment growth of sociologists is projected to grow much faster than average; political scientists, faster than the average.

- Candidates who hold a master's or Ph.D. degree will have the best employment prospects and advancement opportunities; competition for teaching positions, while keen, should ease as the expected number of retirements increases.

- Quantitative and qualitative skills are important for all workers.

Nature of the Work

Sociologists and *political scientists* study all aspects of human society and political systems—from social behavior and the origin of social groups to the origin, development, and operation of political systems. Their research provides insights into different ways individuals, groups, and governments make decisions, exercise power, and respond to change. Through their studies and analyses, sociologists and political scientists suggest solutions to social, business, personal, and governmental problems. In fact, many work as public *policy analysts* for government or private organizations. (Archaeologists, anthropologists, geographers, and historians, whose work is closely related to that of sociologists and political scientists, are discussed elsewhere in the *Handbook*.)

Sociologists study society and social behavior by examining the groups, cultures, organizations, and social institutions people form. They also study the activities in which people participate, including activities conducted in social, religious, political, economic, and business organizations. They study the behavior of, and interaction among, groups, organizations, institutions, and nations, and how they react to phenomena such as the spread of technology, crime, social movements, and epidemics of illness. They also trace the origin and growth of these groups and interactions. Sociologists analyze how social influences affect different individuals and groups, and the ways organizations and institutions affect the daily lives of those same people. To analyze these social patterns, sociologists usually begin by designing research projects that incorporate a variety of methods, including historical analysis, comparative analysis, and quantitative and qualitative techniques. Through this process of applied research, they construct theories and produce information that attempts to explain certain social trends or that will enable people to make better decisions or manage their affairs more effectively. The results of sociological research aid educators, lawmakers, administrators, and others who are interested in resolving social problems and formulating public policy. Most sociologists work in one or more specialties, such as social organization, stratification, and mobility; racial and ethnic relations; education; the family; social psychology;

Sociologists study the behavior of groups, organizations, institutions, and nations, and how they react to phenomena such as the spread of technology, crime, social movements, and epidemics of illness.

Projections data from the National Employment Matrix

Occupational Title	SOC Code	Employment, 2008	Projected Employment, 2018	Change, 2008-2018	
				Number	Percent
Sociologists and political scientists	–	9,000	10,900	1,900	21
Sociologists...	19-3041	4,900	6,000	1,100	22
Political scientists...	19-3094	4,100	4,900	800	19

(NOTE) Data in this table are rounded. See the discussion of the employment projections table in the *Handbook* introductory chapter on *Occupational Information Included in the Handbook.*

urban, rural, political, and comparative sociology; gender relations; demography; gerontology; criminology; and sociological practice.

Political scientists conduct research on a wide range of subjects, such as relations between the United States and other countries, the institutions and political life of nations, the politics of small towns or major metropolises, and the decisions of the U.S. Supreme Court. Studying and evaluating topics such as public opinion, political decisionmaking, ideology, and public policy, they analyze the structure and operation of governments, as well as various other entities. Depending on the topic, a political scientist might analyze a public-opinion survey, study election results or public documents, or interview public officials. Occasionally, they may collaborate with government economists to assess the effects of specific changes in legislation or public policy, such as the effects of the deregulation of industries or of changes in Social Security. Through academic publications, written reports, or public presentations, political scientists present their research reports and often identify new issues for research and analysis. Many political scientists forecast political, social, and economic trends.

Political scientists frequently work as policy analysts for government or in labor, political, or professional organizations, some of which are nonprofit. These workers gather and analyze information to assist in the planning, development, review, and interpretation of government or industrial policies. They use the results of their research to raise public awareness of social issues, such as crime prevention, access to healthcare, and protection of the environment, hoping to influence government action. Most political scientists—about 63 percent—work for the Federal Government. Some find work in research and development firms performing work for the Federal Government on a contract basis. The relatively few who work in the Foreign Service may help formulate and implement foreign policy.

Work environment. Most sociologists and political scientists have regular hours. Generally working behind a desk, either alone or in collaboration with other social scientists, they read and write research articles or reports. Many experience the pressures of writing and publishing, as well as those associated with deadlines and tight schedules. Some sociologists may be required to attend meetings. Political scientists on foreign assignment must adjust to unfamiliar cultures, climates, and languages.

Sociologists and political scientists employed by colleges and universities usually have flexible work schedules, often dividing their time among teaching, research, writing, consulting, and administrative responsibilities. Those who teach in these settings are classified as postsecondary teachers. (See the statement on teachers—postsecondary elsewhere in the *Handbook*.)

Training, Other Qualifications, and Advancement

Some entry-level positions for sociologists and political scientists are available to those with a bachelor's degree, but higher degrees are required for the majority of positions. Prospects need good quantitative and qualitative skills.

Education and training. Whether working in government, industry, research organizations, or consulting firms, sociologists and political scientists with a bachelor's degree usually qualify for entry-level positions as a market analyst, research assistant, writer, or policy analyst. Graduates with master's degrees in applied specialties usually qualify for most administrative and research positions, while a Ph.D. degree is typically required for college and university teaching positions.

Training in statistics and mathematics is essential for many political scientists, who increasingly are using mathematical and quantitative research methods. The ability to use computers for research purposes is mandatory in most disciplines.

Many sociology and political science students can benefit greatly from internships. Numerous government agencies, as well as nonprofit and other organizations, offer internships or volunteer research opportunities. Also, the vast majority of colleges and universities have student organizations devoted to specific public policy issues, and many provide opportunities for debates, often hosted by the political science department.

While in college, aspiring sociologists and political scientists should gain experience gathering and analyzing data, conducting interviews or surveys, and writing reports on their findings. This experience can prove invaluable later in obtaining a full-time position in the field, because much of the work, especially in the beginning, may center on these duties.

Other qualifications. Sociologists and political scientists need excellent written and oral communication skills to report research findings and to collaborate on research. Successful workers also need intellectual curiosity and creativity because they constantly are seeking new information about people, things, and ideas. The ability to think logically and methodically also is essential in analyzing complicated issues, such as the relative merits of various forms of government.

Advancement. Many sociologists and political scientists choose to teach in their field, often while pursuing their own research. These workers are usually classified as postsecondary teachers. The minimum requirement for most positions in colleges and universities is a Ph.D. degree. Graduates with a master's degree in sociology or political science may qualify for teaching positions in community colleges.

Employment

Sociologists and political scientists held about 9,000 jobs in 2008, of which 4,900 were held by sociologists. Most sociologists worked as researchers, administrators, and counselors for a wide range of employers. The industries that employed the largest number of sociologists in 2008 were scientific research and development services, social advocacy organizations, and State and local government, excluding education and hospitals.

Many sociologists—about 37 percent—teach in colleges and universities and in secondary and elementary schools. (For more information, see teachers—postsecondary and teachers—kindergarten, elementary, middle, and secondary elsewhere in the *Handbook*.)

Political scientists held about 4,100 jobs in 2008. About 63 percent worked for the Federal Government. Most of the remainder worked in scientific research and development services and religious, grantmaking, civic, professional, and similar organizations.

Job Outlook

Employment growth of sociologists and political scientists is projected to grow much faster than the average. Job opportunities should be best for jobseekers with a master's or PhD degree in a social science and with strong quantitative skills.

Employment change. Overall employment of sociologists and political scientists is expected to grow 21 percent from 2008 to 2018, much faster than the average for all occupations. Sociologists will experience much faster than average job growth because the incorporation of sociology into research in other fields continues to increase. Sociologists possess broad training and education in analytical, methodological, conceptual, and quantitative and qualitative analysis and research, so their skills can be applied to many different occupations. As a result, many workers with sociology backgrounds will find work in niche areas with specialized titles, such as market analyst, research assistant, writer, and policy analyst. Some sociologists may find work conducting policy research for consulting firms, and their knowledge of society and social behavior may be used as well by a variety of companies in product development, marketing, and advertising. Demand for sociologists also will stem from growth in the number of social, political, and business associations and organizations, including many nonprofit organizations, to conduct various evaluations and statistical work.

Employment of political scientists is projected to grow faster than average, reflecting the growing importance of public policy and research. Demand for political science research is growing because of increasing interest in politics, foreign affairs, and public policy, including social and environmental policy issues, healthcare, and immigration. Political scientists will use their knowledge of political institutions to further the interests of nonprofit, political lobbying, and social and civic organizations. Job growth also may be driven by the budget constraints of public resources. As a growing population exerts excess demand on certain public services, political scientists will be needed to analyze the effects and efficiencies of those services, as well as to offer solutions.

Job prospects. In addition to opportunities arising from employment growth, a growing number of job openings will come from the need to replace those who retire, enter teaching or other occupations, or leave their social science occupation for other reasons.

People seeking sociologist and political scientist positions may face competition for jobs, and those with higher educational attainment will have the best prospects. Many jobs in policy, research, or marketing, for which bachelor's degree holders qualify, are not advertised exclusively as sociologist or political scientist positions. Because of the wide range of skills and knowledge possessed by these workers, many compete for jobs with other workers, such as anthropologists and archaeologists, geographers, historians, market and survey researchers, psychologists, engineers, and statisticians.

Some people with a Ph.D. degree in sociology will find opportunities as university faculty rather than as applied sociologists. Although there will be competition for tenured positions, the number of faculty expected to retire over the decade and the increasing number of part-time or short-term faculty positions will lead to better opportunities in colleges and universities than in the past. The growing importance and popularity of social science subjects in secondary schools also is strengthening the demand for social science teachers at that level.

People who have a master's or Ph.D. degree in political science, who are skilled in quantitative and qualitative techniques, and who also have specialized skills should have the best opportunities. Some will find jobs in the Federal Government as the expected number of retirements increases.

Earnings

Median annual wages of sociologists in May 2008 were $68,570. The middle 50 percent earned between $51,110 and $92,220. The lowest 10 percent earned less than $40,720, and the highest 10 percent earned more than $122,130. Median annual wages of sociologists in scientific research and development services were $72,170.

Median annual wages of political scientists in May 2008 were $104,130. The middle 50 percent earned between $74,040 and $124,490. The lowest 10 percent earned less than $47,220, and the highest 10 percent earned more than $146,880.

In March 2009, the Federal Government's average salary was $100,824 for sociologists. Beginning salaries were higher in selected areas of the country where the prevailing local pay level was higher.

Related Occupations

The duties and training of sociologists are similar to those of other social scientists, including the following:

Many sociologists conduct surveys, study social problems, teach, and work in museums, performing tasks similar to those of the following professionals:

Political scientists often research the legal system and analyze current events, as do the following workers:

Sources of Additional Information

Information about careers in sociology is available from:

➤ American Sociological Association, 1430 K St. NW., Suite 600, Washington, DC 20005. Internet: **http://www.asanet.org**

For information about careers in political science, contact:

➤ American Political Science Association, 1527 New Hampshire Ave. NW., Washington, DC 20036. Internet: **http://www.apsanet.org**

For information about careers in public policy, contact:

➤ National Association of Schools of Public Affairs and Administration, 1029 Vermont Ave. NW., Suite 1100, Washington, DC 20005. Internet: **http://www.naspaa.org**

For information about careers in policy analysis, an important task for some social scientists, see "Policy analysts: Shaping society through research and problem-solving," online at **http://www.bls.gov/opub/ooq/2007/spring/art03.pdf** and in the spring 2007 issue of the *Occupational Outlook Quarterly*.

The Occupational Information Network (O*NET) provides information on a wide range of occupational characteristics. Links to O*NET appear at the end of the Internet version of this occupational statement, accessible at **http://www.bls.gov/ooh/ocos314.htm**

Social Scientists, Other

Significant Points

- Projected job growth varies by specialty; for example, anthropologists and archaeologists can expect 28 percent employment growth; geographers, 26 percent; and historians, 11 percent.

- Candidates who hold a master's or Ph.D. degree in a social science will have the best employment prospects and advancement opportunities; some entry-level positions are available to those with a bachelor's degree.

- Despite much faster than average job growth overall, applicants are likely to face competition because the number of qualified candidates is expected to exceed the number of positions available.

Nature of the Work

The major social science occupations covered in this statement are anthropologists, archaeologists, geographers, and historians. (Sociologists, political scientists, economists, market and survey researchers, psychologists, and urban and regional planners are covered elsewhere in the *Handbook*.)

Social scientists study all aspects of society—from past events and achievements to human behavior and relationships among groups. Their research provides insights into the different ways individuals, groups, and institutions make decisions, exercise power, and respond to change. They look at data in detail, such as studying the data they've collected, reanalyzing already existing data, analyzing historical records and documents, and interpreting the effect of location on culture and other aspects of society. Through their studies and analyses, social scientists offer insight into the physical, social, and cultural development of humans, as well as the links between human activity and the environment. Following are brief discussions of several major types of social scientists. Specialists in one field may find that their research overlaps work being conducted in another discipline.

Anthropologists study the origin, development, and behavior of humans. They examine the ways of life, languages, archaeological remains, and physical characteristics of people in various parts of the world. They also examine the customs, values, and social patterns of different cultures, often through comparative analyses. Some anthropologists study current human concerns, such as overpopulation, warfare, and poverty, while others study the prehistory of *Homo sapiens*, including the evolution of the human brain. Anthropologists usually concentrate on one of four subfields: sociocultural, linguistics, biological, and physical anthropology. *Sociocultural anthropologists* study the customs, cultures, and social lives of groups in settings that range from unindustrialized societies to modern urban centers. They often do this through observation or face-to-face interviews with a particular group, comparing findings of one particular group with that of another. For example, they may seek to learn the reasons behind face painting or scarification of individuals within a society to better understand the overall culture of that society. Such an analysis usually takes form of a specific focus—for example, economics, politics, religion, or art. *Linguistic anthropologists* investigate the history of, role of, and changes to, language over time in various cultures. *Biological anthropologists* research the evolution of the human body, look for the earliest evidences of human life, and analyze how culture and biology influence one another. *Physical anthropologists* examine human remains found at archaeological sites in order to understand population demographics and factors, such as nutrition and disease, that affected these populations.

Archaeologists examine and recover material evidence, including tools, pottery, cave paintings, the ruins of buildings, and other objects remaining from past human cultures in order to learn about the history, customs, and living habits of earlier civilizations. With continued technological advances making it increasingly possible to detect the presence of underground anomalies without digging, archaeologists can now target excavation sites better than they previously could.

Most archaeologists work at consulting and research firms—specifically, at cultural resource management (CRM) firms whose services often are contracted by developers, construction companies, and, sometimes, the Federal Government. CRM workers are responsible mainly for identifying, assessing, and preserving archaeological and historical sites on private and public land, such as National parks, to ensure that the builder is complying with legislation pertaining to preservation. Archaeologists in museums and historic sites often handle the locale's artifacts collection, educate the public through interactive programs and presentations, or become administrators who supervise programs related to research, collections, and exhibitions. Another large employer of archaeologists is the government. Many archaeologists in the Federal Government conduct research for the U.S. Department of Interior's National Park Service. Some also work as administrators.

Geographers study the earth and its land, features, inhabitants, and phenomena. Most geographers work in one of two main branches of geography: physical and cultural. *Physical geographers* examine the physical aspects of a region, including its land forms, climates, soils, vegetation, water, plants, and animals. *Cultural geographers* analyze the spatial implications of human activities within a given area, including its economic activities, social characteristics, and political organization, and are further classified on the basis of their specific focus. For example, *economic geographers* study the distribution of resources and economic activities. *Political geographers* are concerned with the relationship of geography to political phenomena. *Urban* and *transportation geographers* study cities and metropolitan areas. *Regional geographers* study the physical, economic, political, and cultural characteristics of regions ranging in size from a congressional district to entire continents. *Medical geographers* investigate health care delivery systems, epidemiology (the study of the causes and control of epidemics), and the effect of the environment on health.

Geographers incorporate many different technologies into their work, such as geographic information systems (GISs), global positioning systems (GPSs), and remote sensing. For example, a geographer may use GIS and GPS to track information on population growth, traffic patterns, environmental hazards, natural resources, and weather patterns, all in digital format. By overlaying remotely sensed aerial or satellite images with GIS data, such as population density, they create computerized maps that can advise governments, businesses, and the general public

Social scientists often read and write research articles or reports.

on a variety of issues, including the impact of natural disasters and the development of houses, roads, and landfills. As more of these systems are created and refined, a good number of mapping specialists are being called *geographic information specialists*. In addition, many of the people who study geography and work with GIS technology are classified into other occupations, such as surveyors, cartographers, photogrammetrists, and survey and mapping technicians (who develop maps and other location-based information), urban and regional planners (who help to decide on and evaluate the locations of building and roads and other aspects of physical society), and geoscientists (who study earthquakes and other physical aspects of the Earth). (These occupations are described elsewhere in the *Handbook.*)

Historians research, analyze, and interpret the past. They use many sources of information in their research, including government and institutional records, newspapers and other periodicals, photographs, interviews, films, and unpublished manuscripts such as personal diaries and letters. Historians usually specialize in a country or region, a particular period, or a particular field, such as social, intellectual, cultural, political, or diplomatic history. Many communicate their research and findings through books, articles, or essays.

The majority of historians conduct some form of research and analysis for State and local government. Others help study and preserve archival materials and artifacts in museums, visitor centers, and historic buildings and sites. Those with a bachelor's degree in history may work as high school history teachers. (See the statement on teachers—kindergarten, elementary, middle, and secondary elsewhere in the *Handbook.*)

Work environment. Most social scientists have regular hours. Although they work most often as an integral part of a research team, they sometimes work alone, writing reports of their findings. Travel may be necessary to collect information or attend meetings, and those on foreign assignment must adjust to unfamiliar cultures, climates, and languages.

Some social scientists do fieldwork. For example, anthropologists, archaeologists, and geographers may travel to remote areas, live among the people they study, learn their languages, and stay for long periods at the site of their investigations. They may work under rugged conditions, and their work may involve strenuous physical exertion.

Social scientists employed by colleges and universities usually have flexible work schedules, often dividing their time among teaching, research, writing, consulting, and administrative responsibilities. Those who teach in these settings are classified as postsecondary teachers. (See the statement on teachers—postsecondary elsewhere in the *Handbook.*)

Training, Other Qualifications, and Advancement

The educational attainment of social scientists is among the highest of all occupations, with most positions requiring a master's or Ph.D. degree. Some entry-level positions are available to those with a bachelor's degree. All social scientists need good analytical skills.

Education and training. Graduates with master's degrees in applied specialties usually are qualified for positions outside of colleges and universities, although requirements vary by field. A Ph.D. degree may be required for higher level teaching positions. Bachelor's degree holders have limited opportunities;

Projections data from the National Employment Matrix

Occupational Title	SOC Code	Employment, 2008	Projected Employment, 2018	Change, 2008-2018	
				Number	Percent
Social scientists, other...	–	11,100	13,500	2,400	22
Anthropologists and archeologists...	19-3091	5,800	7,400	1,600	28
Geographers	19-3092	1,300	1,600	300	26
Historians...	19-3093	4,100	4,500	500	11

(NOTE) Data in this table are rounded. See the discussion of the employment projections table in the *Handbook* introductory chapter on *Occupational Information Included in the Handbook.*

however, a bachelor's degree does provide a suitable background for many different kinds of entry-level jobs in related occupations, such as research assistant, writer, management trainee, and market analyst. In addition, bachelor's degree holders in history often qualify for elementary, middle, and high school teaching positions.

Training in statistics and mathematics is essential for many social scientists, most of whom increasingly are using mathematical and quantitative research methods. The ability to use computers for research purposes is mandatory in most disciplines. Social scientists also must keep up to date on the latest technological advances that affect their discipline and research. For example, most geographers use GIS technology extensively, and a growing number of archaeologists are beginning to incorporate the technology into their work.

Many social science students also benefit from internships or field experience. Numerous local museums, historical societies, government agencies, and nonprofit and other organizations offer internships or volunteer research opportunities. Archaeological field schools instruct future anthropologists, archaeologists, and historians in how to excavate, record, and interpret historical sites.

Other qualifications. Social scientists need excellent written and oral communication skills to report research findings and to collaborate on research. The ability to think logically and methodically also is essential in analyzing complicated issues. Objectivity, an open mind, and systematic work habits are important in all kinds of social science research. Perseverance, too, often is necessary, as when an anthropologist spends years studying artifacts from an ancient civilization before making a final analysis and interpretation.

Certification and advancement. The GIS Certification Institute (GISCI) has voluntary certification programs for geography professionals in GIS. To qualify for professional distinction, individuals must meet education and experience requirements and pass a written examination. The professional recognition these certifications bestow can often help geographers find employment—especially those who do not have a master's or Ph.D. degree. Workers in these jobs, however, may not be called "geographers," but instead may be referred to by a different title, such as "GIS analyst" or "GIS specialist."

Some social scientists advance to top-level research and administrative positions. Advancement often depends on the number and quality of reports that social scientists publish or their ability to design studies.

Employment

Anthropologists and archaeologists, geographers, and historians held about 11,100 jobs in 2008. Professional, scientific, and

technical services employed 37 percent of all workers. A small amount—about 2 percent—was self-employed.

Job Outlook

Overall employment is projected to grow much faster than average, but varies by detailed occupation. For anthropologists and archaeologists, opportunities will be best with management, scientific, and technical consulting services companies. For geographers, opportunities will be best for those who have GIS experience or knowledge. Keen competition is expected for historian jobs because the number of applicants typically outnumbers the number of positions available.

Employment change. Overall employment of anthropologists and archaeologists, geographers, and historians is expected to grow by 22 percent from 2008 to 2018, which is much faster than the average for all occupations. Anthropologists and archaeologists, the largest specialty, is expected to grow by 28 percent, driven by growth in the management, scientific, and technical consulting services industry. Anthropologists who work as consultants will be needed to apply their analytical skills and knowledge to problems ranging from economic development to forensics. A growing number of anthropologists also will be needed in specific segments of the Federal Government, such as the U.S. Department of Defense, to assess the regional customs and values—or "cultural terrain"—of a particular society in specific parts of the world. Employment growth of archaeologists will be driven by higher levels of overall construction, including large-scale transportation projects and upgrades to the Nation's infrastructure. As construction projects increase, more archaeologists will be needed to ensure that Federal laws related to the preservation of archaeological and historical sites and artifacts are met.

Employment of geographers is expected to increase by 26 percent because the Federal Government—the largest employer—is projected to grow faster than in the past. Outside of the Federal Government, geographers will be needed to advise businesses, local municipalities, real estate developers, utilities, and telecommunications firms regarding where to build new roads, buildings, powerplants, and cable lines. Geographers also will be needed to advise about environmental matters, such as where to build a landfill and where to preserve wetland habitats.

Employment of historians is expected to grow by 11 percent, reflecting the relatively few jobs outside of Federal, State, and local Government. Nonetheless, historians possess broad training and education in writing, analytical research, and coherent thinking, so their skills can be applied to many different occupations. As a result, many workers with a history background will find work in niche areas with specialized titles, such as researcher, writer, or policy analyst.

Job prospects. In addition to opportunities arising from employment growth, some job openings for social scientists will come from the need to replace those who retire or who leave the occupation for other reasons. Some social scientists leave the occupation to become professors, but competition for tenured teaching positions will be keen.

Overall, people seeking social science positions are likely to face competition for jobs. Candidates who have a master's or Ph.D. degree in a social science, who are skilled in quantitative research methods, and who also have good written and communications skills are likely to have the best job opportunities. In addition, many jobs in policy, research, or marketing, for which social scientists qualify, are not advertised exclusively as social scientist positions.

Anthropologists and archaeologists will experience the best job prospects at management, scientific, and technical consulting firms. Those with a bachelor's degree in archaeology usually qualify to be a field technician.

Geographers with a background in GIS will find numerous job opportunities applying GIS technology in nontraditional areas, such as emergency assistance, where GISs can track the locations of ambulances, police, and fire rescue units and their proximity to the emergency. Workers in these jobs may not be called "geographers," but instead may be referred to by a different title, such as "GIS analyst" or "GIS specialist."

Historians will find jobs mainly in policy or research. Historians may find opportunities with historic preservation societies or by working as a consultant as public interest in preserving and restoring historical sites increases. Many workers with a history background also choose to teach in elementary, middle, and secondary schools.

Earnings

Wages of anthropologists and archaeologists, geographers, and historians vary. Median annual wages for anthropologists and archaeologists were $53,910 in May 2008. The middle 50 percent earned between $39,200 and $70,980. The lowest 10 percent earned less than $32,150, and the highest 10 percent earned more than $89,490.

Median annual wages of geographers were $66,600 in May 2008. The middle 50 percent earned between $51,390 and $82,590. The lowest 10 percent earned less than $38,780, and the highest 10 percent earned more than $97,540.

For historians, median annual wages were $54,530 in May 2008. The middle 50 percent earned between $33,570 and $77,290. The lowest 10 percent earned less than $25,670, and the highest 10 percent earned more than $96,530.

In March 2009, the Federal Government's average annual salary for anthropologists was $88,302; for archaeologists, $70,606; for geographers, $79,223; and for historians, $87,730. Beginning salaries were higher in selected areas of the country where the prevailing local pay level was higher.

Related Occupations

The duties and training of anthropologists and archaeologists, geographers, and historians are similar to those of other social scientists, including the following:

Many social scientists conduct surveys, study social problems, teach, and work in museums, performing tasks similar to those of the following professionals:

Geographers often study the Earth's environment and natural resources, as do:

Geographers also use GIS computer technology to make maps. Other workers in occupations with similar duties include the following:

Sources of Additional Information

For information about careers in anthropology, contact:
➤ American Anthropological Association, 2200 Wilson Blvd., Suite 600, Arlington, VA 22201. Internet: **http://www.aaanet.org**

For information about careers in archaeology, contact:
➤ Archaeological Institute of America, 656 Beacon St., 6th Floor, Boston, MA 02215. Internet: **http://www.archaeological.org**

➤ Society for American Archaeology, 900 2nd St. NE., Suite 12, Washington, DC 20002. Internet: **http://www.saa.org**

For information about careers in geography, contact:
➤ Association of American Geographers, 1710 16th St. NW., Washington, DC 20009. Internet: **http://www.aag.org**

See also "Geography jobs," online at **http://www.bls.gov/opub/ooq/2005/spring/art01.pdf** and in the spring 2005 issue of the *Occupational Outlook Quarterly*.

Information on careers for historians is available from:
➤ American Historical Association, 400 A St. SE., Washington, DC 20003. Internet: **http://www.historians.org**

The Occupational Information Network (O*NET) provides information on a wide range of occupational characteristics. Links to O*NET appear at the end of the Internet version of this occupational statement, accessible at **http://www.bls.gov/ooh/ocos315.htm**

Science Technicians

Significant Points

- Many science technicians work indoors in laboratory settings, but certain technicians work outdoors, sometimes in remote locations.

- Most science technicians need some postsecondary training, such as an associate degree or a certificate in applied science or science-related technology; biological and forensic science technicians usually need a bachelor's degree.

- Overall growth is expected to be about as fast as average, although growth will vary by specialty.

- Job opportunities are expected to be best for graduates of applied science technology programs who are well trained on equipment used in laboratories or production facilities.

Nature of the Work

Science technicians use the principles and theories of science and mathematics to assist in research and development and to help invent and improve products and processes. However, their jobs are more practically oriented than those of scientists. Technicians set up, operate, and maintain laboratory instruments, monitor experiments, make observations, calculate and record results, and often develop conclusions. They must keep detailed logs of all of their work. Those who perform production work monitor manufacturing processes and may ensure quality by testing products for proper proportions of ingredients, for purity, or for strength and durability.

As laboratory instrumentation and procedures have become more complex, the role of science technicians in research and development has expanded. In addition to performing routine tasks, many technicians, under the direction of scientists, now develop and adapt laboratory procedures to achieve the best results, interpret data, and devise solutions to problems. Technicians must develop expert knowledge of laboratory equipment so that they can adjust settings when necessary and recognize when equipment is malfunctioning.

Most science technicians specialize, learning their skills and working in the same disciplines in which scientists work. Occupational titles, therefore, tend to follow the same structure as those for scientists.

Agricultural and food science technicians work with related scientists to conduct research, development, and testing on food and other agricultural products. Agricultural technicians are involved in food, fiber, and animal research, production, and processing. Some conduct tests and experiments to improve the yield and quality of crops or to increase the resistance of plants and animals to disease, insects, or other hazards. Other agricultural technicians breed animals for the purpose of investigating nutrition. Food science technicians assist food scientists and technologists in research and development, production technology, and quality control. For example, food science technicians

may conduct tests on food additives and preservatives to ensure compliance with Food and Drug Administration regulations regarding color, texture, and nutrients. These technicians analyze, record, and compile test results; order supplies to maintain laboratory inventory; and clean and sterilize laboratory equipment.

Biological technicians work with biologists studying living organisms. Many assist scientists who conduct medical research—helping to find a cure for cancer or AIDS, for example. Those who work in pharmaceutical companies help develop and manufacture medicines. Those working in the field of microbiology generally work as laboratory assistants, studying living organisms and infectious agents. Biological technicians also analyze organic substances, such as blood, food, and drugs. Biological technicians working in biotechnology apply knowledge and techniques gained from basic research, including gene splicing and recombinant DNA, and apply them to product development.

Chemical technicians work with chemists and chemical engineers, developing and using chemicals and related products and equipment. Generally, there are two types of chemical technicians: research technicians who work in experimental laboratories and process control technicians who work in manufacturing or other industrial plants. Many chemical technicians working in research and development conduct a variety of laboratory procedures, from routine process control to complex research projects. For example, they may collect and analyze samples of air and water to monitor pollution levels, or they may produce compounds through complex organic synthesis. Most process technicians work in manufacturing, testing packaging for design, integrity of materials, and environmental acceptability. Often, process technicians who work in plants focus on quality assurance, monitoring product quality or production processes and developing new production techniques. A few work in shipping to provide technical support and expertise.

Environmental science and protection technicians perform laboratory and field tests to monitor environmental resources and determine the contaminants and sources of pollution in the environment. They may collect samples for testing or be involved in abating and controlling sources of environmental pollution. Some are responsible for waste management operations, control and management of hazardous materials inventory, or general activities involving regulatory compliance. Many environmental science technicians employed at private consulting firms work directly under the supervision of an environmental scientist.

Forensic science technicians investigate crimes by collecting and analyzing physical evidence. Often, they specialize in areas such as DNA analysis or firearm examination, performing tests on weapons or on substances such as fiber, glass, hair, tissue, and body fluids to determine their significance to the investigation. Proper collection and storage methods are important to protect the evidence. Forensic science technicians also prepare reports to document their findings and the laboratory techniques used, and they may provide information and expert opinions to

Science technicians monitor experiments and record the results.

investigators. When criminal cases come to trial, forensic science technicians often give testimony as expert witnesses on laboratory findings by identifying and classifying substances, materials, and other evidence collected at the scene of a crime. Some forensic science technicians work closely with other experts or technicians. For example, a forensic science technician may consult either a medical expert about the exact time and cause of a death or another technician who specializes in DNA typing in hopes of matching a DNA type to a suspect.

Forest and conservation technicians compile data on the size, content, and condition of natural lands, such as rangeland and forests. These workers usually work under the supervision of a conservation scientist or forester, doing specific tasks such as measuring timber, tracking wildlife movement, assisting in road building operations, and locating property lines and features. They may gather basic information, such as data on water and soil quality, disease and insect damage to trees and other plants, and conditions that may pose a fire hazard. In addition, forest and conservation technicians train and lead forest and conservation workers in seasonal activities, such as planting tree seedlings and maintaining recreational facilities. Increasing numbers of forest and conservation technicians work in urban forestry—the study of individual trees in cities—and other nontraditional specialties, rather than in forests or rural areas.

Geological and petroleum technicians assist in oil and gas exploration operations, collecting and examining geological data or testing geological samples to determine their petroleum content and their mineral and element composition. Some petroleum technicians, called scouts, collect information about oil well and gas well drilling operations, geological and geophysical prospecting, and land or lease contracts.

Nuclear technicians operate nuclear test and research equipment, monitor radiation, and assist nuclear engineers and physicists in research. Some also operate remote-controlled equipment to manipulate radioactive materials or materials exposed to radioactivity. Workers who control nuclear reactors are classified as *nuclear power reactor operators*, and are not included in this statement. (See the statement on power plant operators, distributors, and dispatchers elsewhere in the *Handbook*.)

Other science technicians perform a wide range of activities. Some collect weather information or assist oceanographers; others work as laser technicians or radiographers.

Work environment. Science technicians work under a wide variety of conditions. Most work indoors, usually in laboratories, and have regular hours. Some occasionally work irregular hours to monitor experiments that cannot be completed during regular working hours. Production technicians often work in 8-hour shifts around the clock. Others, such as agricultural, forest and conservation, geological and petroleum, and environmental science and protection technicians, perform much of their work outdoors, sometimes in remote locations.

Advances in automation and information technology require technicians to operate more sophisticated laboratory equipment. Science technicians make extensive use of computers, electronic measuring equipment, and traditional experimental apparatus.

Some science technicians may be exposed to hazards from equipment, chemicals, or toxic materials. Chemical technicians sometimes work with toxic chemicals or radioactive isotopes; nuclear technicians may be exposed to radiation, and biological technicians sometimes work with disease-causing organisms or radioactive agents. Forensic science technicians often are exposed to human body fluids and firearms. However, these working conditions pose little risk if proper safety procedures are followed. For forensic science technicians, collecting evidence from crime scenes can be distressing and unpleasant.

Training, Other Qualifications, and Advancement

Most science technicians need some formal postsecondary training, such as an associate degree or a certificate in applied science or science-related technology. Biological and forensic science technicians usually need a bachelor's degree. Science technicians with a high school diploma and no college degree typically begin work as trainees under the direct supervision of a more experienced technician, and they eventually earn a 2-year degree in science technology.

Education and training. There are many ways to qualify for a job as a science technician. Most employers prefer applicants who have at least 2 years of specialized postsecondary training or an associate degree in applied science or science-related technology. Some science technicians have a bachelor's degree in the natural sciences, while others have no formal postsecondary education and learn their skills on the job.

Some science technician specialties have higher education requirements. For example, biological technicians often need a bachelor's degree in biology or a closely related field. Forensic science positions also typically require a bachelor's degree, either in forensic science or another natural science. Knowledge and understanding of legal procedures also can be helpful. Chemical technician positions in research and development also often require a bachelor's degree, but most chemical process technicians have a 2-year degree instead, usually an associate degree in process technology.

Many technical and community colleges offer programs in a specific technology or more general education in science and mathematics. A number of associate degree programs are designed to provide easy transfer to bachelor's degree programs at colleges or universities. Technical institutes usually offer technician training, but they provide less theory and general education than community colleges. The length of programs at technical institutes varies, although 1-year certificate programs and 2-year associate degree programs are common. Some schools offer cooperative-education or internship programs, allowing students the opportunity to work at a local company or some other workplace while attending classes during alternate terms. Participation in such programs can significantly enhance a student's employment prospects.

Whatever their formal education, science technicians usually need hands-on training, which they can receive either in school or on the job. Job candidates with extensive hands-on experience using a variety of laboratory equipment, including computers and related equipment, usually require only a short period of on-the-job training. Those with a high school diploma and no college degree typically have a more extensive training program where they work as trainees under the direct supervision of a more experienced technician.

People interested in careers as science technicians should take as many high school science and math courses as possible. Science courses taken beyond high school, in an associate or bachelor's degree program, should be laboratory oriented, with an emphasis on bench skills. A solid background in applied chemistry, physics, and math is vital.

Other qualifications. Communication skills are important because technicians are often required to report their findings both orally and in writing. In addition, technicians should be able to work well with others. Because computers often are used in research and development laboratories, technicians should also have strong computer skills, especially in computer modeling. Organizational ability and skill in interpreting scientific results are important as well, as are high mechanical aptitude, attention to detail, and analytical thinking.

Advancement. Technicians usually begin work as trainees in routine positions under the direct supervision of a scientist or a more experienced technician. As they gain experience, technicians take on more responsibility and carry out assignments under only general supervision, and some eventually become supervisors. Technicians who have a bachelor's degree often are able to advance to scientist positions in their field after a few years of experience working as a technician or after earning a graduate degree.

Employment

Science technicians held about 270,800 jobs in 2008. As indicated by the following tabulation, chemical and biological technicians accounted for 54 percent of all jobs:

Biological technicians	79,500
Chemical technicians	66,100
Environmental science and protection technicians, including health	35,000
Forest and conservation technicians	34,000
Agricultural and food science technicians	21,900
Geological and petroleum technicians	15,200
Forensic science technicians	12,800
Nuclear technicians	6,400

About 30 percent of biological technicians worked in professional, scientific, or technical services firms; most other biological technicians worked in educational services, government, or pharmaceutical and medicine manufacturing. Chemical technicians primarily worked in chemical manufacturing and professional, scientific, or technical services firms. Most environmental science and protection technicians worked for professional, scientific, and technical services firms and for State and local governments. About 75 percent of forest and conservation technicians held jobs in the Federal Government, mostly in the Forest Service. Around 34 percent of agricultural and food science technicians worked in educational institutions and 25 percent worked for food manufacturing companies. Forensic science technicians worked primarily for State and local governments. Approximately 56 percent of all geological and petroleum technicians worked in the mining and oil and gas industries, while 51 percent of nuclear technicians worked for utilities.

Job Outlook

Employment of science technicians is projected to grow about as fast as the average for all occupations, although employment change will vary by specialty. Job opportunities are expected to be best for graduates of applied science technology programs who are well trained on equipment used in laboratories or production facilities.

Employment change. Overall employment of science technicians is expected to grow by 12 percent during the 2008–18 decade, about as fast as the average for all occupations. The continued growth of scientific and medical research—particu-

Projections data from the National Employment Matrix

Occupational Title	SOC Code	Employment, 2008	Projected Employment, 2018	Change, 2008-2018 Number	Change, 2008-2018 Percent
Science technicians	–	270,800	302,600	31,800	12
Agricultural and food science technicians	19-4011	21,900	23,800	1,900	9
Biological technicians	19-4021	79,500	93,500	14,000	18
Chemical technicians	19-4031	66,100	65,500	-500	-1
Geological and petroleum technicians	19-4041	15,200	15,400	200	2
Nuclear technicians	19-4051	6,400	7,000	600	9
Environmental science and protection technicians, including health	19-4091	35,000	45,200	10,100	29
Forensic science technicians	19-4092	12,800	15,300	2,500	20
Forest and conservation technicians	19-4093	34,000	36,900	2,900	9

(NOTE) Data in this table are rounded. See the discussion of the employment projections table in the *Handbook* introductory chapter on *Occupational Information Included in the Handbook.*

larly research related to biotechnology—will be the primary driver of employment growth, but the development and production of technical products should also stimulate demand for science technicians in many industries.

Employment of biological technicians should increase by 18 percent, faster than average, as the growing number of agricultural and medicinal products developed from the results of biotechnology research boosts demand for these workers. Also, an aging population and continued competition among pharmaceutical companies are expected to contribute to the need for innovative and improved drugs, further spurring demand. Most growth in employment will be in professional, scientific, and technical services and in educational services.

Job growth for chemical technicians is projected to decline by 1 percent, signifying little or no change. The chemical manufacturing industry, except pharmaceutical and medicine manufacturing, is anticipated to experience a decline in overall employment as companies downsize and turn to outside contractors and overseas production. However, there will still be a need for chemical technicians, particularly in pharmaceutical research.

Employment of environmental science and protection technicians is expected to grow much faster than average, at a rate of 29 percent; these workers will be needed to help regulate waste products; to collect air, water, and soil samples for measuring levels of pollutants; to monitor compliance with environmental regulations; and to clean up contaminated sites. Most of this growth is expected to be in firms that assist other companies in environmental monitoring, management, and regulatory compliance.

Employment of forest and conservation technicians is expected to grow by 9 percent, about as fast as average. Opportunities at State and local governments within specialties such as urban forestry may provide some new jobs. In addition, an increased emphasis on specific conservation issues, such as environmental protection, preservation of water resources, and control of exotic and invasive pests, will spur demand.

Employment of agricultural and food science technicians is projected to grow by 9 percent, about as fast as average. Research in biotechnology and other areas of agricultural science will increase as it becomes more important to balance greater agricultural output with protection and preservation of soil, water, and the ecosystem. In addition, there will be increased research into the use of agricultural products as energy sources, also known as biofuels.

Jobs for forensic science technicians are expected to increase by 20 percent, much faster than average. Employment growth in State and local government should be driven by the increasing application of forensic science techniques, such as DNA analysis, to examine, solve, and prevent crime.

Employment growth of about 2 percent, representing little or no change, is expected for geological and petroleum technicians as oil companies continue to search for new resource deposits to meet world demand for petroleum products and natural gas. The outlook for these workers is strongly tied to the price of oil; historically, when prices are low, companies limit exploration and curtail hiring of technicians, but when prices are high, they expand exploration activities. In the long run, continued high oil prices will maintain demand for these workers.

Nuclear technicians should grow by 9 percent, about as fast as average, as more are needed to monitor the Nation's aging fleet of nuclear reactors and research future advances in nuclear power. Although no new nuclear power plants have been built for decades in the United States, energy demand has recently renewed interest in this form of electricity generation and may lead to future construction. Technicians also will be needed to work in defense-related areas, to develop nuclear medical technology, and to improve and enforce waste management and safety standards.

Job prospects. In addition to job openings created by growth, many openings should arise from the need to replace technicians who retire or leave the labor force for other reasons. Job opportunities are expected to be best for graduates of applied science technology programs who are well trained on equipment used in laboratories or production facilities. As the instrumentation and techniques used in industrial research, development, and production become increasingly more complex, employers will seek individuals with highly developed technical skills.

Earnings

Median hourly wages of science technicians in May 2008 were as follows:

Nuclear technicians $32.64
Geological and petroleum technicians 25.65
Forensic science technicians 23.97
Chemical technicians 20.25
Environmental science and protection technicians,
    including health 19.34
Biological technicians 18.46
Agricultural and food science technicians 16.34
Forest and conservation technicians..............................15.39

In March 2009, the average annual salary in the Federal Government was $39,538 for biological science technicians, $55,527 for physical science technicians, and $42,733 for forestry technicians.

Related Occupations

Other technicians who apply scientific principles and who usually have some postsecondary education include

Sources of Additional Information

General information on a variety of technology fields is available from the Pathways to Technology Web site: **http://www.pathwaystotechnology.org**

For information about a career as a biological technician, contact:

➤ Bio-Link, 1855 Folsom St., Ste 643, San Francisco, CA 94103. Internet: **http://www.bio-link.org**

For information about a career as a chemical technician, contact:

➤ American Chemical Society, Education Division, Career Publications, 1155 16th St. NW., Washington, DC 20036. Internet: **http://www.acs.org**

For career information and a list of undergraduate, graduate, and doctoral programs in forensic sciences, contact:

➤ American Academy of Forensic Sciences, 410 North 21st St., Colorado Springs, CO, 80904. Internet: **http://www.aafs.org**

For general information on forestry technicians and a list of schools offering education in forestry, contact:

➤ Society of American Foresters, 5400 Grosvenor Ln., Bethesda, MD 20814. Internet: **http://www.safnet.org**

The Occupational Information Network (O*NET) provides information on a wide range of occupational characteristics. Links to O*NET appear at the end of the Internet version of this occupational statement, accessible at **http://www.bls.gov/ooh/ocos115.htm**

Community and Social Services Occupations

Counselors

Significant Points

- People interested in counseling should have a strong desire to help others and should be able to inspire respect, trust, and confidence.

- Education and training requirements vary by State and specialty, but a master's degree is required to become a licensed counselor.

- Projected job growth varies by specialty, but job opportunities should be favorable as job openings are expected to exceed the number of graduates from counseling programs.

Nature of the Work

Counselors work in diverse community settings designed to provide a variety of counseling, rehabilitation, and support services. Their duties vary greatly, depending on their specialty, which is determined by the setting in which they work and the population they serve. Although the specific setting may have an implied scope of practice, counselors frequently are challenged with children, adolescents, adults, or families that have multiple issues, such as mental health disorders and addiction, disability and employment needs, school problems or career counseling needs, and trauma. Counselors must recognize these issues in order to provide their clients with appropriate counseling and support.

Educational, vocational, and school counselors provide individuals and groups with career, personal, social and educational counseling. School counselors assist students of all levels, from elementary school to postsecondary education. They advocate for students and work with other individuals and organizations to promote the academic, career, personal, and social development of children and youth. School counselors help students evaluate their abilities, interests, talents, and personalities to develop realistic academic and career goals. Counselors use interviews, counseling sessions, interest and aptitude assessment tests, and other methods to evaluate and advise students. They also operate career information centers and career education programs. Often, counselors work with students who have academic and social development problems or other special needs.

Elementary school counselors provide individual, small-group, and classroom guidance services to students. Counselors observe children during classroom and play activities and confer with their teachers and parents to evaluate the children's strengths, problems, or special needs. In conjunction with teachers and administrators, they make sure that the curriculum addresses both the academic and the developmental needs of students. Elementary school counselors do less vocational and academic counseling than high school counselors do.

High school counselors advise students regarding college majors, admission requirements, entrance exams, financial aid, trade or technical schools, and apprenticeship programs. They help students develop job search skills, such as resume writing and interviewing techniques. College career planning and placement counselors assist alumni or students with career development and job-hunting techniques.

School counselors at all levels help students to understand and deal with social, behavioral, and personal problems. These counselors emphasize preventive and developmental counseling to enhance students' personal, social, and academic growth and to provide students with the life skills needed to deal with problems before they worsen. Counselors provide special services, including alcohol and drug prevention programs and conflict resolution classes. They also try to identify cases of domestic abuse and other family problems that can affect a student's development.

Counselors interact with students individually, in small groups, or as an entire class. They consult and collaborate with parents, teachers, school administrators, school psychologists, medical professionals, and social workers to develop and implement strategies to help students succeed.

Vocational counselors, also called *employment counselors* or *career counselors*, usually provide career counseling outside the school setting. Their chief focus is helping individuals with career decisions. Vocational counselors explore and evaluate the client's education, training, work history, interests, skills, and personality traits. They may arrange for aptitude and achievement tests to help the client make career decisions. They also work with individuals to develop their job-search skills and assist clients in locating and applying for jobs. In addition, career counselors provide support to people experiencing job loss, job stress, or other career transition issues.

Rehabilitation counselors help people deal with the personal, social, and vocational effects of disabilities. They counsel people with both physical and emotional disabilities resulting from birth defects, illness or disease, accidents, or other causes. They evaluate the strengths and limitations of individuals, provide personal and vocational counseling, offer case management support, and arrange for medical care, vocational training, and job placement. Rehabilitation counselors interview both individuals with disabilities and their families, evaluate school and medical reports, and confer with physicians, psychologists, employers, and physical, occupational, and speech therapists to determine the capabilities and skills of the individual. They develop individual rehabilitation programs by conferring with the client. These programs often include training to help individuals develop job skills, become employed, and provide opportunities for community integration. Rehabilitation counselors are trained to recognize and to help lessen environmental and attitudinal barriers. Such help may include providing education, and advocacy services to individuals, families, employers, and others in the community. Rehabilitation counselors work toward increasing the person's capacity to live independently by facilitating and coordinating with other service providers.

Mental health counselors work with individuals, families, and groups to address and treat mental and emotional disorders and to promote mental health. They are trained in a variety of therapeutic techniques used to address issues such as depression, anxiety, addiction and substance abuse, suicidal impulses, stress, trauma, low self-esteem, and grief. They also help with job and career concerns, educational decisions, mental and emotional health issues, and relationship problems. In addition, they may be involved in community outreach, advocacy, and mediation activities. Some specialize in delivering mental health services for the elderly. Mental health counselors often work closely with other mental health specialists, such as psychiatrists, psychologists, clinical social workers, psychiatric nurses, and school counselors. (Information on psychologists, registered nurses, social workers, and physicians and surgeons, which includes psychiatrists, appears elsewhere in the *Handbook*.)

Substance abuse and behavioral disorder counselors help people who have problems with alcohol, drugs, gambling, and eating disorders. They counsel individuals to help them to identify behaviors and problems related to their addiction. Counseling can be done on an individual basis, but is frequently done in a group setting and can include crisis counseling, daily or weekly counseling, or drop-in counseling supports. Counselors are trained to assist in developing personalized recovery programs that help to establish healthy behaviors and provide coping strategies. Often, these counselors also will work with family members who are affected by the addictions of their loved ones. Some counselors conduct programs and community outreach aimed at preventing addiction and educating the pub-

Counselors work in diverse community settings designed to provide a variety of counseling, rehabilitation, and support services.

lic. Counselors must be able to recognize how addiction affects the entire person and those around him or her.

Marriage and family therapists apply family systems theory, principles, and techniques to address and treat mental and emotional disorders. In doing so, they modify people's perceptions and behaviors, enhance communication and understanding among family members, and help to prevent family and individual crises. They may work with individuals, families, couples, and groups. Marriage and family therapy differs from traditional therapy because less emphasis is placed on an identified client or internal psychological conflict. The focus is on viewing and understanding their clients' symptoms and interactions within their existing environment. Marriage and family therapists also may make appropriate referrals to psychiatric resources, perform research, and teach courses in human development and interpersonal relationships.

Work environment. The work environment can vary greatly, depending on the occupational specialty. School counselors work predominantly in schools, where they usually have an office but also may work in classrooms. Other counselors may work in a private practice, community health organizations, day treatment programs, or hospitals. Many counselors work in an office where they see clients throughout the day, although counselors may frequently be required to provide services out in the community.

Training, Other Qualifications, and Advancement

Education and training requirements for counselors are often very detailed and vary by State and specialty, but a master's degree usually is required to become a licensed counselor. Prospective counselors should check with State and local governments, prospective employers, and national voluntary certification organizations to determine which requirements apply.

Education and training. Education requirements vary with the occupational specialty and State licensure and certification requirements. A master's degree usually is required to be licensed or certified as a counselor. Counselor education programs in colleges and universities often are found in departments of education, psychology, or human services. Fields of study may include college student affairs, elementary or secondary school counseling, education, gerontological counseling, marriage and family therapy, substance abuse or addictions counseling, rehabilitation counseling, agency or community counseling, clinical mental health counseling, career counseling, and related fields. Courses frequently are grouped into core areas, including human growth and development, social and cultural diversity, relationships, group work, career development, counseling techniques, assessment, research and program evaluation, and professional ethics and identity. In an accredited master's degree program, 48 to 60 semester hours of graduate study, including a period of supervised clinical experience in counseling, typically are required.

Some employers provide training for newly hired counselors. Others may offer time off or tuition assistance to complete a graduate degree. Often, counselors must participate in graduate studies, workshops, and personal studies to maintain their certificates and licenses.

Licensure. Licensure requirements differ greatly by State, occupational specialty, and work setting. Some States require school counselors to hold a State school counseling certification and to have completed at least some graduate coursework; most require the completion of a master's degree. Some States require school counselors to be licensed, which generally entails completing continuing education credits. Some States require public school counselors to have both counseling and teaching certificates and to have had some teaching experience.

For counselors based outside of schools, 49 States and the District of Columbia have some form of counselor licensure that governs the practice of counseling. In addition, all 50 States and the District of Columbia have some licensure requirement for marriage and family therapists. Requirements for both counselors and marriage and family therapists typically include the completion of a master's degree in counseling or marriage and family therapy, the accumulation of 2 years or 3,000 hours of supervised clinical experience beyond the master's degree level, the passage of a State-recognized exam, adherence to ethical codes and standards, and the completion of annual continuing education credits. However, counselors working in certain settings or in a particular specialty may face different licensure requirements. For example, a career counselor working in private practice may need a license, but a counselor working for a college career center may not. In addition, substance abuse and behavior disorder counselors generally are governed by a different State agency or board than are other counselors. The criteria for their licensure can vary greatly, and in some cases these counselors may need only a high school diploma and certification. Those interested in entering the field must research State and specialty requirements to determine what qualifications are necessary.

Other qualifications. People interested in counseling should have a strong desire to help others and should be able to inspire respect, trust, and confidence. They should be able to work independently or as part of a team. Counselors must follow the code of ethics associated with their respective certifications and licenses.

Counselors must possess high physical and emotional energy to handle the array of problems that they address. Dealing daily with these problems can cause stress.

Certification and advancement. Some counselors elect to be certified by the National Board for Certified Counselors, which grants a general practice credential of National Certified Counselor. This national certification is voluntary and is distinct from State licensing. However, in some States, those who pass the national exam are exempt from taking a State certification exam. The board also offers specialty certifications in school, clinical mental health, and addiction counseling.

The Commission on Rehabilitation Counselor Certification offers voluntary national certification for rehabilitation counselors. Many State and local governments and other employers require rehabilitation counselors to have this certification. To become certified, rehabilitation counselors usually must graduate from an accredited educational program, complete an internship, and pass a written examination. Certification requirements vary, however, according to an applicant's educational history. Employment experience, for example, is required for those with a counseling degree in a specialty other than rehabilitation. To maintain their certification, counselors must successfully retake the certification exam or complete 100 credit hours of acceptable continuing education every 5 years.

Other counseling organizations also offer certification in particular counseling specialties. Usually, becoming certified is voluntary, but having certification may enhance one's job prospects.

Prospects for advancement vary by counseling field. School counselors can become directors or supervisors of counseling, guidance, or pupil personnel services; or, usually with further graduate education, they may become counselor educators, counseling psychologists, or school administrators. (Psychologists and education administrators are covered elsewhere in the *Handbook.*) Some counselors choose to work for a State's department of education.

Some marriage and family therapists, especially those with doctorates in family therapy, become supervisors, teachers, researchers, or advanced clinicians in the discipline. Counselors also may become supervisors or administrators in their agencies. Some counselors move into research, consulting, or college teaching or go into private or group practice. Some may choose to pursue a doctoral degree to improve their chances for advancement.

Employment

Counselors held about 665,500 jobs in 2008. Employment was distributed among the counseling specialties as follows:

Educational, vocational, and school counselors.........275,800
Rehabilitation counselors...129,500
Mental health counselors..113,300
Substance abuse and behavioral disorder counselors...86,100
Marriage and family therapists.....................................27,300
Counselors, all other...33,400

A growing number of counselors are self-employed and work in group practices or private practice, due in part to laws allowing counselors to be paid for their services by insurance

Projections data from the National Employment Matrix

Occupational Title	SOC Code	Employment, 2008	Projected Employment, 2018	Change, 2008-2018	
				Number	Percent
Counselors..	21-1010	665,500	782,200	116,800	18
Substance abuse and behavioral disorder counselors...................	21-1011	86,100	104,200	18,100	21
Educational, vocational, and school counselors...........................	21-1012	275,800	314,400	38,600	14
Marriage and family therapists	21-1013	27,300	31,300	3,900	14
Mental health counselors	21-1014	113,300	140,400	27,200	24
Rehabilitation counselors..	21-1015	129,500	154,100	24,500	19
Counselors, all other	21-1019	33,400	37,800	4,400	13

(NOTE) Data in this table are rounded. See the discussion of the employment projections table in the *Handbook* introductory chapter on *Occupational Information Included in the Handbook.*

companies and to the growing recognition that counselors are well-trained, effective professionals.

Job Outlook

Employment is expected to grow faster than the average for all occupations. Projected job growth varies by specialty, but job opportunities should be favorable because job openings are expected to exceed the number of graduates from counseling programs, especially in rural areas.

Employment change. Overall employment of counselors is expected to increase by 18 percent between 2008 and 2018, which is faster than the average for all occupations. However, growth is expected to vary by specialty.

Employment of substance abuse and behavioral disorder counselors is expected to grow by 21 percent, which is much faster than the average for all occupations. As society becomes more knowledgeable about addiction, more people are seeking treatment. Furthermore, drug offenders are increasingly being sent to treatment programs rather than to jail.

Employment for educational, vocational, and school counselors is expected to grow by 14 percent, which is faster than the average for all occupations. Demand for vocational or career counselors should grow as multiple job and career changes become common and as workers become increasingly aware of counseling services. States require elementary schools to employ counselors. Expansion of the responsibilities of school counselors also is likely to lead to increases in their employment. For example, counselors are becoming more involved in crisis and preventive counseling, helping students deal with issues ranging from drug and alcohol abuse to death and suicide. Although schools and governments realize the value of counselors in helping their students to achieve academic success, budget constraints at every school level will dampen the job growth of school counselors. Federal grants and subsidies may help to offset tight budgets and allow the reduction in student-to-counselor ratios to continue.

Employment of mental health counselors is expected to grow by 24 percent, which is much faster than the average for all occupations. Under managed care systems, insurance companies increasingly are providing for reimbursement of counselors as a less costly alternative to psychiatrists and psychologists. In addition, there has been increased demand for mental health services as individuals become more willing to seek help.

Jobs for rehabilitation counselors are expected to grow by 19 percent, which is faster than the average for all occupations.

The number of people who will need rehabilitation counseling will increase as the size of the elderly population, whose members become injured or disabled at a higher rate than other age groups, increases and as treatment for mental health related disabilities increases.

Marriage and family therapists will experience growth of 14 percent, which is faster than the average for all occupations, in part because of an increased recognition of the field. It is becoming more common for people to seek help for their marital and family problems than it was in the past.

Job prospects. Job opportunities should be favorable because job openings are expected to exceed the number of graduates from counseling programs, particularly in rural areas. Substance abuse counselors should enjoy particularly good job prospects.

Earnings

Median annual wages of educational, vocational, and school counselors in May 2008 were $51,050. The middle 50 percent earned between $38,740 and $65,360. The lowest 10 percent earned less than $29,360, and the highest 10 percent earned more than $82,330. School counselors can earn additional income by working summers in the school system or in other jobs. Median annual wages in the industries employing the largest numbers of educational, vocational, and school counselors were as follows:

```
Elementary and secondary schools ...........................$57,800
Junior colleges................................................................50,440
Colleges, universities, and professional schools ..........43,980
Vocational rehabilitation services................................35,220
Individual and family services ....................................33,780
```

Median annual wages of substance abuse and behavioral disorder counselors in May 2008 were $37,030. The middle 50 percent earned between $29,410 and $47,290. The lowest 10 percent earned less than $24,240, and the highest 10 percent earned more than $59,460. Median annual wages in the industries employing the largest numbers of substance abuse and behavioral disorder counselors were as follows:

```
General medical and surgical hospitals......................$44,130
Local government........................................................41,660
Outpatient care centers...............................................36,650
Individual and family services ....................................35,210
Residential mental retardation, mental health and
    substance facilities.................................................31,300
```

Median annual wages of mental health counselors in May 2008 were $36,810. The middle 50 percent earned between $28,930 and $48,580. The lowest 10 percent earned less than $23,580, and the highest 10 percent earned more than $63,100. Median annual wages in the industries employing the largest numbers of mental health counselors were as follows:

Local government	$45,510
Offices of other health practitioners	40,880
Outpatient care centers	37,590
Individual and family services	36,130
Residential mental retardation, mental health and substance abuse facilities	29,950

Median annual wages of rehabilitation counselors in May 2008 were $30,930. The middle 50 percent earned between $24,110 and $41,240. The lowest 10 percent earned less than $20,150, and the highest 10 percent earned more than $56,550. Median annual wages in the industries employing the largest numbers of rehabilitation counselors were as follows:

State government	$45,350
Local government	38,800
Vocational rehabilitation services	29,060
Individual and family services	28,290
Residential mental retardation, mental health and substance facilities	25,950

Median annual wages of marriage and family therapists in May 2008 were $44,590. The middle 50 percent earned between $34,840 and $56,320. The lowest 10 percent earned less than $27,810, and the highest 10 percent earned more than $70,830. Median annual wages in the industries employing the largest numbers of marriage and family therapists were as follows:

State government	$50,770
Local government	48,220
Outpatient care centers	46,830
Offices of other health practitioners	41,220
Individual and family services	39,690

Self-employed counselors who have well-established practices, as well as counselors employed in group practices, usually have the highest earnings.

Related Occupations

Counselors help people evaluate their interests, abilities, and disabilities and deal with personal, social, academic, and career problems. Others who help people in similar ways include:

Sources of Additional Information

For general information about counseling, as well as information on specialties such as school, college, mental health, rehabilitation, multicultural, career, marriage and family, and gerontological counseling, contact:

➤ American Counseling Association, 5999 Stevenson Ave., Alexandria, VA 22304. Internet: **http://www.counseling.org**

For information on school counselors, contact:
➤ American School Counselors Association, 1101 King St., Suite 625, Alexandria, VA 22314. Internet: **http://www.schoolcounselor.org**

For information on mental health counselors, contact:
➤ American Mental Health Counselors Association, 801 N. Fairfax St., Suite 304, Alexandria, VA 22314. Internet: **http://www.amhca.org**

For information on marriage and family therapists, contact:
➤ American Association for Marriage and Family Therapy, 112 South Alfred St., Alexandria, VA 22314. Internet: **http://www.aamft.org**

For information on accredited counseling and related training programs, contact:
➤ Council for Accreditation of Counseling and Related Educational Programs, American Counseling Association, 1001 N. Fairfax St., Suite 510, Alexandria, VA 22314. Internet: **http://www.cacrep.org**

For information on national certification requirements for counselors, contact:
➤ National Board for Certified Counselors, Inc, 3 Terrace Way, Greensboro, NC 27403. Internet: **http://www.nbcc.org**

State departments of education can supply information on colleges and universities offering guidance and counseling training that meets State certification and licensure requirements.

State employment service offices have information about job opportunities and entrance requirements for counselors.

The Occupational Information Network (O*NET) provides information on a wide range of occupational characteristics. Links to O*NET appear at the end of the Internet version of this occupational statement, accessible at **http://www.bls.gov/ooh/ocos067.htm**

Health Educators

Significant Points

- 51 percent of health educators work in health care and social assistance, and an additional 23 percent work in government.

- A bachelor's degree is the minimum requirement for entry-level jobs, but a master's degree may be required for certain positions or for advancement.

- Faster than average job growth is expected.

Nature of the Work

Health educators work to encourage healthy lifestyles and wellness through educating individuals and communities about behaviors that can prevent diseases, injuries, and other health problems.

Health educators attempt to prevent illnesses by informing and educating individuals and communities about health-related topics, such as proper nutrition, the importance of exercise, how to avoid sexually transmitted diseases, and the habits and behaviors necessary to avoid illness. They begin by assessing the needs of their audience, which includes determining the appropriate topics to cover. For example, they may hold programs on self-examination for breast cancer to women or may teach classes on the effects of binge drinking to college students. Health educators must take the cultural norms of their audience into account. For example, programs targeted at the elderly need to be different from those aimed at a college-aged population.

After assessing their audiences' needs, health educators must decide how to meet those needs. Health educators have a lot of options in putting together programs. They may organize an event, such as a lecture, class, demonstration or health screening, or they may develop educational material, such as a video, pamphlet or brochure. Often, these tasks require working with other people in a team or on a committee. Health educators must plan programs that are consistent with the goals and objectives of their employers. For example, many nonprofit organizations educate the public about one disease or health topic, and, therefore, limit the programs they issue.

Next, health educators need to implement their proposed plan. This may require locating funding by applying for grants, writing curriculums for classes, or creating materials that would be made available to the public. Also, programs may require dealing with logistical tasks, such as finding speakers or locations for the event.

Generally, after a program is presented, health educators evaluate its success. Methods of evaluation vary based on the program in question. For example, they may ask participants to provide feedback using a survey about the program. Through evaluation, health educators can improve plans for the future by learning from mistakes and capitalizing on strengths.

Although programming is a large part of their job, health educators also serve as a resource on health topics. This may include locating services, reference material, and other resources and referring individuals or groups to organizations or medical professionals.

Even though all health educators share the same overarching goal, their duties can vary depending on where they work. Most health educators work in medical care settings, colleges and universities, schools, public health departments, nonprofit organizations, and private business.

Within medical care facilities, health educators tend to work one-on-one with patients and their families. In this setting, a health educator's goal is to educate individual patients on their diagnosis and how that may change or affect their lifestyle. To this end, they may explain the necessary procedures or surgeries as well as how patients will need to alter their lifestyles to manage their illness or return to full health. They may also direct patients to outside resources, such as support groups, home health agencies, or social services. Often, health educators work closely with physicians, nurses, and other staff to cre-

ate educational programs or materials, such as brochures, Web sites, and classes. In some cases, health educators train hospital staff about how to better interact with patients.

Health educators in colleges and universities work primarily with students. Generally, these educators create programs on topics that affect young adults, such as sexual activity, smoking, and alcohol. They may need to alter their teaching methods to attract audiences to their events. For example, health educators might show a popular movie followed by a discussion or hold programs in dormitories or cafeterias. They may teach courses for credit or give lectures on health-related topics. Often, they train students as peer educators to lead their own programs.

Health educators in schools are typically employed in secondary schools, where they may teach health class. They develop lesson plans that are relevant and age appropriate to their students. Educators may need to cover sensitive topics, such as sexually transmitted diseases or alcohol and drug abuse and may also teach another subject concurrently, such as science or physical education. Sometimes, they may develop the health education curriculum for the school or for the entire school district. (For more information, see the statement on secondary school teachers elsewhere in the *Handbook*.)

Heath educators in public health are employed primarily by State and local departments of public health and administer State-mandated programs. They also develop educational materials for use by other public health officials. During an emergency, health educators may be responsible for disseminating information to both the media and the public. They work closely with nonprofit organizations to help them get the resources they need, such as funding. Educators often serve as members of statewide councils or national committees on topics such as aging. As part of this work, they inform other professionals in changes to health policy.

In nonprofits, which may be referred to community health organizations, health educators provide the public with information related to health and educate people about the resources available to help people in the community. While some organizations target a particular audience, others educate the community regarding one disease or health issue. Therefore, health educators may be limited in either the topics they cover, the populations they serve, or both. Work in this setting may include creating print-based material for distribution to the community, often in conjunction with organizing lectures, health screenings, and activities related to increasing health awareness. Health educators may also form and lead community coalitions to address public health issues ranging from water quality to healthy food availability or access to safe exercise areas. They can work to set policy that will improve public health. Examples include working to advance legislation for prohibition of smoking in public areas and limitation of junk food in vending machines in schools.

When working in private businesses, health educators create programs to inform its employees and that fit into workers' schedules by arranging lunchtime speakers or daylong health screenings so that workers may come when attendance is convenient. Educators in these business settings must align their work with the overall goals of their employers.

Work environment.   Health educators work in various environments based on the industry in which they are employed. In public health, nonprofit organizations, corporations and businesses, colleges and universities, and medical care settings, they primarily work in offices. However, they may spend a lot of time away from the office implementing and attending programs, meeting with community organizers, speaking with patients, or teaching classes. Health educators in schools spend the majority of their day in classrooms.

Health educators generally work 40-hour weeks. When programs, events, or meetings are scheduled, however, they may need to work evenings or weekends.

Training, Other Qualifications, and Advancement

A bachelor's degree is generally required for entry-level health educator positions, but some employers prefer a bachelor's degree and some related experience gained through an internship or volunteer work. A master's degree may be required for some positions and is usually required for advancement.

Education and training.   Entry-level health educator positions generally require a bachelor's degree from a health education program. These programs teach students the theories and methods of health education and develop the skills necessary to implement health education programs. Courses in psychology, human development, and a foreign language are helpful, and experience gained through an internship or other volunteer opportunities can make applicants more appealing to employers.

Graduate programs in health education are often offered under titles such as community health education, school health education, public health education, or health promotion. These programs lead to a Master of Arts, Master of Science, Master of Education, or a Master of Public Health degree. Many students pursue a master's in health education after majoring in or working in a related field, such as nursing or psychology. A master's degree is required for most health educator positions in public health.

Some employers may require and pay for educators to take continuing education courses to keep their skills up to date.

Other qualifications.   Health educators spend much of their time working with people and must be comfortable working with both individuals and groups. They need to be good communicators and comfortable speaking in public as they may need to teach classes or give presentations. Health educators often work with diverse populations, so they must be sensitive to cultural differences and open to working with people of varied backgrounds. Health educators often create new programs or materials, so they should be creative and skilled writers.

Certification and advancement.   Health educators may choose to become a Certified Health Education Specialist (CHES), a credential offered by the National Commission of Health Education Credentialing, Inc. The certification is awarded after candidates pass an examination on the basic areas of responsibility for a health educator. The exam is aimed at entry-level educators who have already completed at least a bachelor's degree in health education or are within 3 months of completion. In addition, to maintain certification, health educators must complete 75 hours of approved continuing education courses or seminars over a 5-year period. Some employers pre-

Health educators attempt to prevent illnesses by informing and educating individuals and communities about health-related topics.

fer to hire applicants who are certified, and some States may require health educator certification to work in a public health department. However, many employers do not require their workers to have the certification.

A graduate degree is usually required to advance past an entry-level position to jobs such as executive director, supervisor, or senior health educator. Workers in these positions may spend more time on planning and evaluating programs than on their implementation but may need to supervise other health educators who implement the programs. Some health educators pursue a doctoral degree in health education and may transfer to research positions or become professors of health education. (See the statement on postsecondary teachers elsewhere in the *Handbook.*)

Employment

Health educators held about 66,200 jobs in 2008. They work primarily in two industries, with 51 percent working in health care and social assistance and 23 percent working in government. In addition, a small percent of health educators work in grant-making services and social advocacy organizations.

Job Outlook

Employment of health educators is expected to grow faster than the average for all occupations, and job prospects are expected to be favorable.

Employment change.   Employment of health educators is expected to grow by 18 percent, which is faster than the average for all occupations through 2018. Growth will result from the rising cost of healthcare.

The rising cost of healthcare has increased the need for health educators. As healthcare costs continue to rise, insurance companies, employers, and governments are attempting to find ways to curb costs. One of the more cost-effective ways is to employ health educators to teach people how to live healthy lives and avoid costly treatments for illnesses. There are a number of illnesses, such as lung cancer, HIV, heart disease and skin cancer, that may be avoided with lifestyle changes. Health educators are necessary to help the public better understand the effects of their behavior on their health. Other illnesses, such as breast

Projections data from the National Employment Matrix

Occupational Title	SOC Code	Employment, 2008	Projected Employment, 2018	Change, 2008-2018	
				Number	Percent
Health educators..	21-1091	66,200	78,200	12,000	18

(NOTE) Data in this table are rounded. See the discussion of the employment projections table in the *Handbook* introductory chapter on *Occupational Information Included in the Handbook.*

and testicular cancer, are best treated with early detection, so it is important for people to understand how to detect possible problems on their own. The need to provide the public with this kind of information will result in State and local governments, hospitals, and businesses employing a growing number of health educators.

Demand for health educators is expected to increase in most industries, but their employment may decrease in secondary schools. Many schools, facing budget cuts, ask teachers trained in other fields, such as science or physical education, to teach the subject of health education.

Job prospects. Job prospects for health educators are expected to be favorable, but those who have acquired experience through internships or volunteer jobs will have better prospects. A graduate degree is preferred by employers in public health and for non-entry-level positions.

Earnings

Median annual wages of health educators were $44,000 in May 2008; the middle 50 percent earned between $33,170 and $60,810. The lowest 10 percent earned less than $26,210, and the highest 10 percent earned more than $78,260.

Median annual wages in the industries employing the largest numbers of health educators in May 2008 were as follows:

General medical and surgical hospitals......................$56,390
Colleges, universities and professional schools 49,050
Local government..43,040
Outpatient care centers..36,830
Individual and family services 36,050

Related Occupations

Health educators work closely with people to alter their behavior. Other occupations with similar skills include:

	Page
Counselors..	234
Psychologists...	215
Registered nurses	392
Social and human service assistants......................	244
Social workers...	246
Teachers- kindergarten, elementary, middle, and secondary...	288

Sources of Additional Information

For further information about health educators, contact:
➤ American Association for Health Education, 1900 Association Drive, Reston, VA 20191-1598. Internet: **http://www.aahperd.org/aahe/**

➤ Society for Public Health Education, 10 G Street, NE, Suite 605, Washington, DC 20002-4242. Internet: **http://www.sophe.org**

For information on voluntary credentialing and job opportunities, contact:
➤ The National Commission for Health Education Credentialing, Inc. 1541 Alta Drive, Suite 303, Whitehall, PA 18052-5642. Internet: **http://www.nchec.org**

The Occupational Information Network (O*NET) provides information on a wide range of occupational characteristics. Links to O*NET appear at the end of the Internet version of this occupational statement, accessible at **http://www.bls.gov/ooh/ocos063.htm**

Probation Officers and Correctional Treatment Specialists

Significant Points

- State and local governments employ most of these workers.

- A bachelor's degree in social work, criminal justice, psychology, or a related field is usually required.

- Employment growth, which is projected to be faster than the average, is dependent on government funding.

- Job opportunities are expected to be excellent.

Nature of the Work

Many people who are convicted of crimes are placed on probation, instead of being sent to prison. People who have served time in prison are often released on parole. During probation and parole, offenders must stay out of trouble and meet various other requirements. Probation officers, parole officers, and correctional treatment specialists work with and monitor offenders to prevent them from committing new crimes.

Probation officers, who are called *community supervision officers* in some States, supervise people who have been placed on probation. *Correctional treatment specialists*, who may also be known as *case managers* or *correctional counselors*, counsel offenders and create rehabilitation plans for them to follow when they are no longer in prison or on parole. *Parole officers* perform many of the same duties that probation officers perform. The difference is that parole officers supervise offenders who have been released from prison, whereas probation officers work with those who are sentenced to probation instead of prison. *Pretrial services officers* conduct pretrial investigations, the findings of which help determine whether suspects should be released before their trial. In most jurisdictions, probation is a county function and parole is a State function.

Probation and parole officers supervise offenders on probation or parole through personal contact with the offenders and their families. Instead of requiring offenders to come to them, many officers meet offenders in their homes and at their places of employment or therapy. Probation and parole agencies also seek the assistance of community organizations, such as religious institutions, neighborhood groups, and local residents, to monitor the behavior of many offenders. Some offenders are required to wear an electronic device so officers can monitor their location and movements. Probation and parole officers may arrange for offenders to get substance abuse rehabilitation or job training. Probation officers usually work with either adults or juveniles exclusively. Juvenile probation is also called aftercare. Only in small, usually rural, jurisdictions do probation officers counsel both adults and juveniles. In some States, the jobs of parole and probation officers are combined.

Probation officers also spend much of their time working for the courts. They investigate the backgrounds of the accused, write presentence reports, and recommend sentences. They review sentencing recommendations with offenders and their families before submitting them to the court. Probation officers may be required to testify in court as to their findings and recommendations. They also attend hearings to update the court on offenders' efforts at rehabilitation and compliance with the terms of their sentences.

Correctional treatment specialists work in jails, prisons, or parole or probation agencies. In jails and prisons, they monitor the progress of inmates. They may evaluate inmates using questionnaires and psychological tests. They also work with inmates, probation officers, and other agencies to develop parole and release plans. Their case reports, which discuss the inmate's history and likelihood of committing another crime, are provided to the appropriate parole board when their clients are eligible for release. In addition, correctional treatment specialists plan education and training programs to improve offenders' job skills and provide them with coping, anger management, and drug and sexual abuse counseling either individually or in groups. They usually write treatment plans and summaries for each client. Correctional treatment specialists working in parole and probation agencies perform many of the same duties as their counterparts who work in correctional institutions.

The number of cases a probation officer or correctional treatment specialist handles at one time depends on the needs of offenders and the risks they pose. Higher risk offenders and those who need more counseling usually command more of the officer's time and resources. Caseload size also varies by agency jurisdiction. Consequently, officers may handle from 20 to more than 100 active cases at a time.

Computers, telephones, and fax machines enable the officers to handle the caseload. Probation officers may telecommute from their homes. Other technological advancements, such as electronic monitoring devices, reporting kiosks, and drug screening, also assist probation officers and correctional treatment specialists in supervising and counseling offenders.

Pretrial services officers conduct pretrial investigations, the findings of which help determine whether suspects should be released before their trial. When suspects are released before their trial, pretrial services officers supervise them to make sure they adhere to the terms of their release and that they show up for trial. In most jurisdictions, including the Federal courts system, probation officers perform the functions of pretrial services officers.

Work environment. Probation officers and correctional treatment specialists work with criminal offenders, some of whom may be dangerous. While supervising offenders, they usually interact with many other individuals, such as family members and friends of their clients, who may be angry, upset, or difficult to work with. Workers may be assigned to fieldwork in high-crime areas or in institutions where there is a risk of violence or communicable disease.

Probation officers and correctional treatment specialists are required to meet many court-imposed deadlines, which contribute to heavy workloads. In addition, extensive travel and fieldwork may be required to meet with offenders who are on probation or parole. Workers may be required to carry a firearm or other weapon for protection. They also may be required to collect and transport urine samples of offenders for drug testing. All of these factors make for a stressful work environment. Although the high stress levels can make these jobs very difficult at times, this work also can be very rewarding. Many workers obtain personal satisfaction from counseling members of their community and helping them become productive citizens.

Probation officers and correctional treatment specialists generally work a 40-hour week, but some may work longer. They may be on call 24 hours a day to supervise and assist offenders at any time.

Training, Other Qualifications, and Advancement
Qualifications vary by agency, but a bachelor's degree is usually required. Most employers require candidates to pass oral, written, and psychological examinations.

Education and training. A bachelor's degree in social work, criminal justice, psychology, or a related field is usually required. Some employers require a master's degree in criminal justice, social work, psychology, or a related field for can-

Probation and parole officers supervise offenders on probation or parole through personal contact with the offenders and their families.

Projections data from the National Employment Matrix

Occupational Title	SOC Code	Employment, 2008	Projected Employment, 2018	Change, 2008-2018	
				Number	Percent
Probation officers and correctional treatment specialists..................	21-1092	103,400	123,300	19,900	19

(NOTE) Data in this table are rounded. See the discussion of the employment projections table in the *Handbook* introductory chapter on *Occupational Information Included in the Handbook*.

didates who do not have previous related experience. Different employers have different requirements for what counts as related experience. It may include work in probation, pretrial services, parole, corrections, criminal investigations, substance abuse treatment, social work, or counseling.

Most probation officers and some correctional treatment specialists are required to complete a training program sponsored by their State government or the Federal Government, after which a certification test may be required. Most probation officers and correctional treatment specialists work as trainees or on a probationary period for up to a year before being offered a permanent position.

Other qualifications. Applicants usually take written, oral, psychological, and physical examinations. Prospective probation officers or correctional treatment specialists should be in good physical and emotional condition. Most agencies require applicants to be at least 21 years old and, for Federal employment, not older than 37. Those convicted of felonies may not be eligible for employment in this occupation. A valid driver's license is often required.

Familiarity with the use of computers is often required, due to the use of computer technology in probation and parole work. Candidates also should be knowledgeable about laws and regulations pertaining to corrections. Probation officers and correctional treatment specialists should have strong writing skills because they are required to prepare many reports. They should also have excellent listening and interpersonal skills to work effectively with offenders.

Advancement. A typical agency has probation and parole officers and correctional treatment specialists with varying amounts of experience, as well as supervisors. Advancement is primarily based on experience and performance. A graduate degree, such as a master's degree in criminal justice, social work, or psychology, may be helpful or required for advancement.

Employment

Probation officers and correctional treatment specialists held about 103,400 jobs in 2008. Most jobs are in State or local governments. Depending on the State, probation officers and correctional treatment specialists may be employed solely by State or local government, or they are employed at both levels. Jobs are more plentiful in urban areas than in rural ones. In the Federal Government, probation officers are employed by the U.S. courts, and correctional treatment specialists are employed by the U.S. Department of Justice's Bureau of Prisons.

Job Outlook

Employment of probation officers and correctional treatment specialists is projected to grow faster than the average for all occupations through 2018. Job opportunities are expected to be excellent.

Employment change. Employment of probation officers and correctional treatment specialists is projected to grow about 19 percent between 2008 and 2018, faster than the average for all occupations. Mandatory sentencing guidelines calling for longer sentences and reduced parole for inmates have resulted in a large increase in the prison population. However, mandatory sentencing guidelines are being reconsidered in many States because of budgetary constraints, court decisions, and doubts about the guidelines' effectiveness. Instead, there may be more emphasis in many States on rehabilitation and alternate forms of punishment, such as probation, that will spur demand for probation and parole officers and correctional treatment specialists. Additionally, there will be a need for parole officers to supervise the large number of currently incarcerated people when they are released from prison.

However, employment growth depends primarily on the amount of government funding that is allocated to corrections, and especially to probation and parole systems. Although community supervision is far less expensive than keeping offenders in prison, a change in political trends toward more imprisonment and away from community supervision could result in reduced employment opportunities.

Job prospects. In addition to openings due to growth, many openings will be created by replacement needs, especially openings due to the large number of these workers who are expected to retire. This occupation is not attractive to some potential entrants due to relatively low earnings, heavy workloads, and high stress. For these reasons, job opportunities are expected to be excellent.

Earnings

Median annual wages of probation officers and correctional treatment specialists in May 2008 were $45,910. The middle 50 percent earned between $35,990 and $60,430. The lowest 10 percent earned less than $29,490, and the highest 10 percent earned more than $78,210. In May 2008, median annual wages for probation officers and correctional treatment specialists employed in State government were $46,580; those employed in local government earned $46,420. Higher wages tend to be found in urban areas.

Related Occupations

Other workers who help treat and care of people include:

Sources of Additional Information

For information about criminal justice job opportunities in your area, contact your State's department of corrections, criminal justice, or probation.

Further information about probation officers and correctional treatment specialists is available from:

➤ American Probation and Parole Association, P.O. Box 11910, Lexington, KY 40578. Internet: **http://www.appa-net.org**

The Occupational Information Network (O*NET) provides information on a wide range of occupational characteristics. Links to O*NET appear at the end of the Internet version of this occupational statement, accessible at **http://www.bls.gov/ooh/ocos265.htm**

Social and Human Service Assistants

Significant Points

- A high school diploma is the minimum educational requirement, but employers often seek individuals with relevant work experience or education beyond high school.

- Employment is projected to grow much faster than the average for all occupations.

- Job opportunities should be excellent, particularly for applicants with appropriate postsecondary education; but wages remain low.

Nature of the Work

Social and human service assistants help social workers, healthcare workers, and other professionals to provide services to people. Social and human service assistant is a generic term for workers with a wide array of job titles, including *human service worker, case management aide, social work assistant, community support worker, mental health aide, community outreach worker, life skills counselor, social services aide, youth worker, psychological aide, client advocate,* or *gerontology aide.* They usually work under the direction of workers from a variety of fields, such as nursing, psychiatry, psychology, or social work. The amount of responsibility and supervision they are given varies a great deal. Some have little direct supervision. For example, they may run a group home. Others work under close direction.

Social and human service assistants provide services to clients to help them improve their quality of life. They assess clients' needs, investigate their eligibility for benefits and services such as food stamps, Medicaid and welfare, and help clients obtain them. They also arrange for transportation, if necessary, and provide emotional support. They monitor and keep case records on clients and report progress to supervisors and case managers.

Social and human service assistants play a variety of roles in the community. For example, they may organize and lead group activities, assist clients in need of counseling or crisis intervention, or administer food banks or emergency fuel programs.

In halfway houses, group homes, and government-supported housing programs, they assist adults who need supervision with personal hygiene and daily living tasks. They review clients' records, ensure that they take prescribed medication, talk with family members, and confer with medical personnel and other caregivers to provide insight into clients' needs. Assistants also give emotional support and help clients become involved in community recreation programs and other activities.

In psychiatric hospitals, rehabilitation programs, and out-patient clinics, social and human service assistants work with psychiatrists, psychologists, social workers, and others to help clients master everyday living skills, communicate more effectively, and live well with others. They support the client's participation in a treatment plan, such as individual or group counseling or occupational therapy.

The work, while satisfying, can be emotionally draining. Understaffing and relatively low pay can add to the pressure.

Work environment. Working conditions of social and human service assistants vary. Some work in offices, clinics, and hospitals, while others work in group homes, shelters, and day programs. Traveling to see clients is required for some jobs. Sometimes working with clients can be dangerous, even though most agencies do everything they can to ensure their workers' safety. Some work in the evening and on weekends.

Training, Other Qualifications, and Advancement

A high school diploma is the minimum education requirement, but employers often seek individuals with relevant work experience or education beyond high school.

Education and training. Many employers prefer to hire people with some education beyond high school. Certificates or associate degrees in subjects such as human services, gerontology or one of the social or behavioral sciences meet many employers' requirements. Some jobs may require a bachelor's or master's degree in human services or a related field, such as counseling, rehabilitation, or social work.

Human services degree programs have a core curriculum that trains students to observe patients and record information, conduct patient interviews, implement treatment plans, employ

Social and human service assistants help social workers, healthcare workers, and other professionals to provide services to people.

Projections data from the National Employment Matrix

Occupational Title	SOC Code	Employment, 2008	Projected Employment, 2018	Change, 2008-2018	
				Number	Percent
Social and human service assistants	21-1093	352,000	431,500	79,400	23

(NOTE) Data in this table are rounded. See the discussion of the employment projections table in the *Handbook* introductory chapter on *Occupational Information Included in the Handbook.*

problem-solving techniques, handle crisis intervention matters, and use proper case management and referral procedures. Many programs utilize field work to give students hands-on experience. General education courses in liberal arts, sciences, and the humanities also are part of most curriculums. Most programs also offer specialized courses related to addictions, gerontology, child protection, and other areas. Many degree programs require completion of a supervised internship.

Workers level of education often determines the kind of work they are assigned and the degree of responsibility that is given to them. For example, workers with no more than a high school education are likely to work in direct-care services and helping clients to fill out paperwork. They may receive extensive on-the-job training on how to perform these tasks. Workers with a college degree, however, might do supportive counseling, coordinate program activities, or manage a group home. Social and human service assistants with proven leadership ability, especially acquired from paid or volunteer experience in social services, often have greater autonomy in their work. Regardless of the academic or work background of employees, most employers provide some form of in-service training, such as seminars and workshops, to their employees.

Other qualifications. These workers should have a strong desire to help others, effective communication skills, a sense of responsibility, and the ability to manage time effectively. Many human services jobs involve direct contact with people who are vulnerable to exploitation or mistreatment; so patience and understanding are also highly valued characteristics.

It is becoming more common for employers to require a criminal background check, and in some settings, workers may be required to have a valid driver's license.

Advancement. Formal education is almost always necessary for advancement. In general, advancement to case management, or social work jobs requires a bachelor's or master's degree in human services, counseling, rehabilitation, social work, or a related field.

Employment

Social and human service assistants held about 352,000 jobs in 2008. More than 65 percent were employed in the health care and social assistance industries and almost 24 percent were employed by State and local governments.

Job Outlook

Employment of social and human service assistants is expected to grow much faster than the average for all occupations. Job prospects are expected to be excellent, particularly for applicants with relevant postsecondary education.

Employment change. The number of social and human service assistants is expected to grow by nearly 23 percent between 2008 and 2018, which is much faster than the average for

all occupations. This is due in large part to the aging population and increased demand for mental health and substance abuse treatment.

As the elderly population continues to grow, the demand for social and human service assistants will expand. This is due in large part to the increased need for social services demanded by this population, such as adult day care, meal delivery programs and support during medical crises. Social and human service assistants, who assist in locating and providing these services, will be needed to meet this increased demand.

Opportunities are expected to be good in private social service agencies. Employment in private agencies will grow, as State and local governments continue to contract out services to the private sector in an effort to cut costs.

The number of jobs for social and human service assistants in State and local governments will grow, but not as fast as employment for social and human service assistants in other industries. Employment in the public sector may fluctuate with the level of funding provided by State and local governments and with the number of services contracted out to private organizations.

Job prospects. Job prospects for social and human service assistants are expected to be excellent, particularly for individuals with appropriate education after high school. Job openings will come from job growth, but also from the need to replace workers, who advance into new positions, retire, or leave the workforce for other reasons. There will be more competition for jobs in urban areas than in rural ones, but qualified applicants should have little difficulty finding employment.

Earnings

Median annual wages of social and human service assistants were $27,280 in May 2008. The middle 50 percent earned between $21,860 and $34,590. The top 10 percent earned more than $43,510, while the lowest 10 percent earned less than $17,900.

Median annual wages in the industries employing the largest numbers of social and human service assistants in May 2008 were:

State government...	$35,510
Local government...	32,560
Individual and family services	26,250
Vocational rehabilitation services.................................	23,910
Residential mental retardation, mental health and substance abuse facilities...	23,580

Related Occupations

Workers in other occupations that require skills similar to those of social and human service assistants include:

Sources of Additional Information

For information on programs and careers in human services, contact:

➤ Council for Standards in Human Services Education, 1935 S. Plum Grove Road, PMB 297, Palatine, IL 60067. Internet: **http://www.cshse.org**

➤ National Organization for Human Services, 5341 Old Highway 5, Suite 206, #214, Woodstock, GA 30188. Internet: **http://www.nationalhumanservices.org**

Information on job openings may be available from State employment service offices or directly from city, county, or State departments of health, mental health and mental retardation, and human resources.

The Occupational Information Network (O*NET) provides information on a wide range of occupational characteristics. Links to O*NET appear at the end of the Internet version of this occupational statement, accessible at **http://www.bls.gov/ooh/ocos059.htm**

Social Workers

Significant Points

- Employment is projected to grow faster than the average for all occupations.

- About 54 percent of jobs were in health care and social assistance industries, and 31 percent work for government.

- While a bachelor's degree is necessary for entry-level positions, a master's degree in social work or a related field is necessary for some positions.

- Job prospects are expected to be favorable, particularly for social workers who specialize in the aging population or work in rural areas.

Nature of the Work

Social work is a profession for those with a strong desire to help improve people's lives. *Social workers* assist people by helping them cope with and solve issues in their everyday lives, such as family and personal problems and dealing with relationships. Some social workers help clients who face a disability, life-threatening disease, social problem, such as inadequate housing, unemployment, or substance abuse. Social workers also assist families that have serious domestic conflicts, sometimes involving child or spousal abuse. Additionally, they may conduct research, advocate for improved services, or become involved in planning or policy development. Many social workers specialize in serving a particular population or working in a specific setting. In all settings, these workers may also be called *licensed clinical social workers*, if they hold the appropriate State mandated license.

Child, family, and school social workers provide social services and assistance to improve the social and psychological functioning of children and their families. Workers in this field assess their client's needs and offer assistance to improve their situation. This often includes coordinating available services to assist a child or family. They may assist single parents in finding day care, arrange adoptions, or help find foster homes for neglected, abandoned, or abused children. These workers may specialize in working with a particular problem, population or setting, such as child protective services, adoption, homelessness, domestic violence, or foster care.

In schools, social workers often serve as the link between students' families and the school, working with parents, guardians, teachers, and other school officials to ensure that students reach their academic and personal potential. They also assist students in dealing with stress or emotional problems. Many school social workers work directly with children with disabilities and their families. In addition, they address problems such as misbehavior, truancy, teenage pregnancy, and drug and alcohol problems and advise teachers on how to cope with difficult students. School social workers may teach workshops to entire classes on topics like conflict resolution.

Child, family, and school social workers may be known as child welfare social workers, family services social workers, or child protective services social workers. These workers often work for individual and family services agencies, schools, or State or local governments.

Medical and public health social workers provide psychosocial support to individuals, families, or vulnerable populations so they can cope with chronic, acute, or terminal illnesses, such as Alzheimer's disease, cancer, or AIDS. They also advise family caregivers, counsel patients, and help plan for patients' needs after discharge from hospitals. They may arrange for at-home services, such as meals-on-wheels or home care. Some work on interdisciplinary teams that evaluate certain kinds of patients, such as geriatric or organ transplant patients.

Some specialize in services for senior citizens and their families. These social workers may run support groups for the adult children of aging parents. Also, they may assess, coordinate, and monitor services such as housing, transportation, and long-term care. These workers may be known as gerontological social workers.

Medical and public health social workers may work for hospitals, nursing and personal care facilities, individual and family services agencies, or local governments.

Mental health and substance abuse social workers assess and treat individuals with mental illness or substance abuse problems. Such services include individual and group therapy, outreach, crisis intervention, social rehabilitation, and teaching skills needed for everyday living. They also may help plan for supportive services to ease clients' return to the community when leaving in-patient facilities. They may provide services to assist family members of those who suffer from addiction or other mental health issues. These workers may work in out-patient facilities, where clients come in for treatment and then leave, or in inpatient programs, where patients reside at the facility. Some mental health and substance social workers may work in employee-assistance programs. In this setting, they may help people cope with job-related pressures or with personal problems that affect the quality of their work. Other social workers work in private practice, where they are employed directly by the client. These social workers may be known as *clinical social workers*, *occupational social workers*, or *substance abuse social workers*. (Counselors and psychologists, who may provide similar services, are discussed elsewhere in the *Handbook*.)

Other types of social workers include *social work administrators*, *researchers*, *planners* and *policymakers*, who develop and implement programs to address issues such as child abuse, homelessness, substance abuse, poverty, and violence. These workers research and analyze policies, programs, and regulations. They identify social problems and suggest legislative and other solutions. They may help raise funds or write grants to support these programs.

Work environment. Social workers usually spend most of their time in an office or residential facility, but they also may travel locally to visit clients, meet with service providers, or attend meetings. Some may meet with clients in one of several offices within a local area. Social work, while satisfying, can be challenging. Understaffing and large caseloads add to the pressure in some agencies. Full-time social workers usually work a standard 40-hour week, but some occasionally work evenings and weekends to meet with clients, attend community meetings, and handle emergencies. Some work part time, particularly in voluntary nonprofit agencies.

Training, Other Qualifications, and Advancement
A bachelor's degree is the minimum requirement for entry into the occupation, but some positions require an advanced degree. All States and the District of Columbia have some licensure, certification, or registration requirement; but these regulations vary.

Education and training. A bachelor's degree in social work (BSW) is the most common minimum requirement to qualify for a job as a social worker; however, majors in psychology, sociology, and related fields may qualify for some entry-level jobs, especially in small community agencies. Although a bachelor's degree is sufficient for entry into the field, an advanced degree is required for some positions. A master's degree in social work (MSW) is typically required for positions in health and school settings and is required for clinical work, as well. Some jobs in public and private agencies may require an advanced degree, such as an MSW with a concentration in

Social workers help people resolve issues in their lives.

social services policy or administration. Supervisory, administrative, and staff training positions usually require an advanced degree. College and university teaching positions and most research appointments normally require a doctorate in social work (DSW or Ph.D.).

As of June 2009, the Council on Social Work Education accredited 468 bachelor's programs and 196 master's programs. The Group for the Advancement of Doctoral Education listed 74 doctoral programs in social work (DSW or Ph.D.) in the United States. Bachelor degree programs prepare graduates for direct service positions, such as caseworker, mental health assistant, group home worker and residential counselor. These programs include courses in social work values and ethics, dealing with a culturally diverse clientele and at-risk populations, promotion of social and economic justice, human behavior and the social environment, social welfare policy and services, social work practice, social research methods, and field education. Accredited programs require a minimum of 400 hours of supervised field experience.

Master's degree programs prepare graduates for work in their chosen field of concentration and continue to develop the skills required to perform clinical assessments, manage large caseloads, take on supervisory roles, and explore new ways of drawing upon social services to meet the needs of clients. Master's programs usually last 2 years and include a minimum of 900 hours of supervised field instruction or internship. A part-time program may take 4 years. Entry into a master's program does not require a bachelor's degree in social work, but courses in psychology, biology, sociology, economics, political science, and social work are recommended. In addition, a second language can be very helpful. Most master's programs offer advanced standing for those with a bachelor's degree from an accredited social work program.

Licensure. All States and the District of Columbia have licensing, certification, or registration requirements regarding social work practice and the use of professional titles. Most States require 2 years or 3,000 hours of supervised clinical experience for licensure of clinical social workers. Due to some limitations on what settings unlicensed social workers may work and some variation in the requirements to obtain a license, those

Projections data from the National Employment Matrix

Occupational Title	SOC Code	Employment, 2008	Projected Employment, 2018	Change, 2008-2018	
				Number	Percent
Social workers..	21-1020	642,000	745,400	103,400	16
Child, family, and school social workers.....................................	21-1021	292,600	328,700	36,100	12
Medical and public health social workers....................................	21-1022	138,700	169,800	31,100	22
Mental health and substance abuse social workers......................	21-1023	137,300	164,100	26,800	20
Social workers, all other..	21-1029	73,400	82,800	9,400	13

(NOTE) Data in this table are rounded. See the discussion of the employment projections table in the *Handbook* introductory chapter on *Occupational Information Included in the Handbook.*

interested in becoming a social worker should research requirements in their State.

Other qualifications. Social workers should be emotionally mature, objective, and sensitive to people and their problems. They must be able to handle responsibility, work independently, and maintain good working relationships with clients and coworkers. Volunteer or paid jobs as a social work aide can help people test their interest in this field.

Certification and advancement. Advancement to supervisor, program manager, assistant director, or executive director of a social service agency or department usually requires an advanced degree and related work experience. Other career options for social workers include teaching, research, and consulting. Some of these workers help formulate government policies, by analyzing and advocating policy positions in government agencies, in research institutions, and on legislators' staffs.

Some social workers go into private practice. Most private practitioners are clinical social workers who provide psychotherapy, usually paid for through health insurance or by the client themselves. Private practitioners must have at least a master's degree and a period of supervised work experience. A network of contacts for referrals also is essential.

Employment

Social workers held about 642,000 jobs, in 2008. About 54 percent jobs were in health care and social assistance industries, and 31 percent were employed by government agencies. Although most social workers are employed in cities or suburbs, some work in rural areas. Employment by type of social worker, in 2008, follows:

Child, family and school social workers....................292,600
Medical and public health social workers.................138,700
Mental health and substance abuse social workers....137,300
Social workers, all other...73,400

Job Outlook

Employment for social workers is expected to grow faster than the average for all occupations through 2018. Job prospects are expected to be favorable, particularly for social workers who specialize in the aging population or work in rural areas.

Employment change. Employment of social workers is expected to increase by 16 percent during the 2008–18 decade, which is faster than the average for all occupations. The growing elderly population and the aging baby boom generation will create greater demand for health and social services, resulting in rapid job growth among gerontological social workers. Em-

ployment of social workers in private social service agencies also will increase.

Employment of child, family, and school social workers is expected to grow by about 12 percent, which is as fast as the average for all occupations. Demand for child and family social workers should continue, as these workers are needed to investigate child abuse cases, place children in foster care and with adoptive families. However, growth for these workers may be hampered by the budget constraints of state and local governments, who are amongst the largest employers of these workers. Furthermore, demand for school social workers will continue and lead to more jobs as efforts are expanded to respond to rising student enrollments, as well as the continued emphasis on integrating children with disabilities into the general school population. There could be competition for school social work jobs in some areas because of the limited number of openings. The availability of Federal, State, and local funding will be a major factor in determining the actual job growth in schools.

Mental health and substance abuse social workers will grow by almost 20 percent over the 2008–18 decade, which is much faster than the average. In particular, social workers specializing in substance abuse will experience strong demand. Substance abusers are increasingly being placed into treatment programs instead of being sentenced to prison. Also, growing numbers of the substance abusers sentenced to prison or probation are, increasingly being required by correctional systems to have substance abuse treatment added as a condition to their sentence or probation. As this trend grows, demand will strengthen for treatment programs and social workers to assist abusers on the road to recovery. Opportunities for social workers in private practice will expand, as they are preferred over more costly psychologists. Furthermore, the passage of legislation that requires insurance plans offered by employers to cover mental health treatment in a manner that is equal to treatment of physical health may increase the demand for mental health treatment.

Growth of medical and public health social workers is expected to be about 22 percent, which is much faster than the average for all occupations. One of the major contributing factors is the rise in the elderly population. These social workers will be needed to assist in finding the best care and assistance for the aging, as well as to support their families. Employment opportunities for social workers with backgrounds in gerontology should be excellent, particularly in the growing numbers of assisted-living and senior-living communities. The expanding senior population also will spur demand for social workers in nursing homes, long-term care facilities, home care agencies, and hospices.

Job prospects. Job prospects are expected to be favorable. Many job openings will stem from growth and the need to replace social workers who leave the occupation. However, competition for social worker jobs is expected in cities where training programs for social workers are prevalent. Opportunities should be good in rural areas, which often find it difficult to attract and retain qualified staff. By specialty, job prospects may be best for those social workers with a background in gerontology and substance abuse treatment.

Earnings

Median annual wages of child, family, and school social workers were $39,530 in May 2008. The middle 50 percent earned between $31,040 and $52,080. The lowest 10 percent earned less than $25,870, and the top 10 percent earned more than $66,430. Median annual wages in the industries employing the largest numbers of child, family, and school social workers in May 2008 were:

Elementary and secondary schools	$53,860
Local government	46,650
State government	39,600
Individual and family services	34,450
Other residential care facilities	34,270

Median annual wages of medical and public health social workers were $46,650 in May 2008. The middle 50 percent earned between $35,550 and $57,690. The lowest 10 percent earned less than $28,100, and the top 10 percent earned more than $69,090. Median annual wages in the industries employing the largest numbers of medical and public health social workers in May 2008 were:

General medical and surgical hospitals	$51,470
Home health care services	46,930
Local government	44,140
Nursing care facilities	41,080
Individual and family services	38,370

Median annual wages of mental health and substance abuse social workers were $37,210 in May 2008. The middle 50 percent earned between $28,910 and $48,560. The lowest 10 percent earned less than $21,770, and the top 10 percent earned more than $61,430. Median annual wages in the industries employing the largest numbers of mental health and substance abuse social workers in May 2008 were:

Outpatient care centers	$36,660
Individual and family services	35,900
Residential mental retardation, mental health and substance abuse facilities	33,950

Median annual wages of social workers, all other were $46,220 in May 2008. The middle 50 percent earned between $34,420 and $60,850. The lowest 10 percent earned less than $27,400, and the top 10 percent earned more than $74,040. Median annual wages in the industries employing the largest numbers of social workers, all other in May 2008 were:

General medical and surgical hospitals	$55,940
Local government	51,700
Individual and family services	36,660
Residential mental retardation, mental health and substance abuse facilities	36,460
Community food and housing, and emergency and other relief services	31,890

About 24 percent of social workers are members of a union or covered by a union contract.

Related Occupations

Through direct counseling or referral to other services, social workers help people solve a range of personal problems. Workers in occupations with similar duties include:

Sources of Additional Information

For information about career opportunities in social work and voluntary credentials for social workers, contact:

➤ National Association of Social Workers, 750 First St. NE., Suite 700, Washington, DC 20002-4241. Internet: **http://www.socialworkers.org**

➤ Center for Clinical Social Work, 27 Congress St., Suite 501, Salem, MA 01970. Internet: **http://www.centercsw.org**

For a listing of accredited social work programs, contact:

➤ Council on Social Work Education, 1725 Duke St., Suite 500, Alexandria, VA 22314-3457. Internet: **http://www.cswe.org**

Information on licensing requirements and testing procedures for each State may be obtained from State licensing authorities, or from:

➤ Association of Social Work Boards, 400 South Ridge Pkwy., Suite B, Culpeper, VA 22701. Internet: **http://www.aswb.org**

The Occupational Information Network (O*NET) provides information on a wide range of occupational characteristics. Links to O*NET appear at the end of the Internet version of this occupational statement, accessible at **http://www.bls.gov/ooh/ocos060.htm**

Legal Occupations

Court Reporters

Significant Points

- Job prospects are expected to be excellent, especially for those with certification.

- Demand for real-time broadcast captioning and translating will spur employment growth.

- The amount of training required to become a court reporter varies by specialization; licensure requirements vary by State.

Nature of the Work

Court reporters usually create verbatim transcripts of speeches, conversations, legal proceedings, meetings, and other events. Written accounts of spoken words are sometimes necessary for correspondence, records, or legal proof, and court reporters provide those accounts. Court reporters play a critical role not only in judicial proceedings, but also at every meeting where the spoken word must be preserved as a written transcript. They are responsible for ensuring a complete, accurate, and secure legal record. In addition to preparing and protecting the legal record, many court reporters assist judges and trial attorneys in a variety of ways, such as organizing and searching for information in the official record or making suggestions to judges and attorneys regarding courtroom administration and procedure. Increasingly, court reporters provide closed-captioning and real-time translating services to the deaf and hard-of-hearing community.

There are several methods of court reporting; the most common is called stenographic. Using a stenotype machine, stenotypists document all statements made in official proceedings. The machine allows them to press multiple keys at once to record combinations of letters representing sounds, words, or phrases. These symbols are electronically recorded and then translated and displayed as text in a process called computer-aided transcription (CAT). In real-time court reporting, the stenotype machine is linked to computers for real-time captioning, often of television programs. As the reporter keys in the symbols, the spoken words instantly appear as text on the screen.

Another method of court reporting is electronic reporting. This method uses audio equipment to record court proceedings. The court reporter monitors the process, takes notes to identify speakers, and listens to the recording to ensure its clarity and quality. The equipment used may include analog tape recorders or digital equipment. Electronic reporters and transcribers often are responsible for producing a written transcript of the recorded proceeding.

Voice writing is yet another method of court reporting. Using the voice-writing method, a court reporter speaks directly into a voice silencer—a hand-held mask containing a microphone. As the reporter repeats the testimony into the recorder, the mask prevents the reporter from being heard during testimony. Voice writers record everything that is said by judges, witnesses, attorneys, and other parties to a proceeding, including gestures and emotional reactions. Written transcripts are prepared afterwards from the recordings.

Court reporters are responsible for a number of duties both before and after transcribing events. Stenographic or voice-writing reporters must create and maintain the computer dictionary that they use to translate their keystroke codes or voice files into written text. They may customize the dictionary with parts of words, entire words, or terminology specific to the proceeding, program, or event—such as a religious service—they plan to transcribe. After documenting proceedings, stenographic reporters must edit the computer-generated translation for correct grammar. All reporters are responsible for accurate identification of proper names and places. Electronic reporters ensure that the record or testimony is discernible. Reporters usually prepare written transcripts, make copies, and provide information from the transcript to courts, counsels, parties, and the public on request. Court reporters also develop procedures for easy storage and retrieval of all stenographic notes, voice files, (commonly referred to as "stenograms"), or audio recordings in paper or digital format.

Although many court reporters record official proceedings in the courtroom, others work outside the courts. For example, court reporters, called webcasters or Internet information reporters, capture sales meetings, press conferences, product introductions, and technical training seminars and instantly transmit them to all parties involved via computers. As participants speak into telephones or microphones, the words appear on all of the participants' computer monitors simultaneously. Still other court reporters capture the proceedings taking place in government agencies at all levels, from the U.S. Congress to State and local governing bodies. Court reporters who specialize in captioning live television programming for people with hearing loss are commonly known as broadcast captioners. They work for television networks or cable stations, captioning news, emergency broadcasts, sporting events, and other programming.

A version of the captioning process that allows reporters to provide more personalized services for deaf and hard-of-hearing people is Communication Access Real-time Translation (CART). CART reporters often work with hard-of-hearing students and people who are learning English as a second language, captioning high school and college classes and providing transcripts at the end of the sessions. CART reporters also accompany deaf clients to events, including conventions, doctor's appointments, or wherever communication access is needed. CART providers are increasingly furnishing this service remotely, because an Internet or phone connection allows for immediate communication access regardless of location. With CART and broadcast captioning, the level of understanding gained by a person with hearing loss depends entirely on the skill of the court reporter. In an emergency, such as a tornado or a hurricane, people's safety may depend on the accuracy of information provided in the form of captioning.

Some voice writers produce a transcript in real time, using computer speech recognition technology. Other voice writers prefer to translate their voice files after the proceeding is over, or they transcribe the files manually, without using speech recognition at all. In any event, speech recognition-enabled voice writers pursue not only court reporting careers, but also careers as closed captioners, CART reporters for hearing-impaired individuals, and Internet streaming text providers or caption providers.

Work environment. The majority of court reporters work in comfortable settings, such as offices of attorneys, courtrooms, legislatures, and conventions. An increasing number of court reporters are working from home-based offices as independent contractors or freelancers.

Work in this occupation presents few hazards, although sitting in the same position for long periods can be tiring and workers can suffer wrist, back, neck, or eye strain. Workers also risk repetitive stress injuries such as carpal tunnel syndrome. In addition, the pressure to be accurate and fast can be stressful.

Many official court reporters work a standard 40-hour week, and they often work additional hours at home preparing transcripts. Self-employed court reporters, or freelancers, usually work flexible hours, including part time, evenings, and weekends, or they may be on call.

Training, Other Qualifications, and Advancement
The amount of training required to become a court reporter varies by specialization. Licensure requirements vary by State.

Education and training. The amount of training required to become a court reporter varies with the type of reporting chosen. It usually takes less than a year to become a novice voice writer, although it takes at least 2 years to become proficient

Voice writers record everything that is said by judges, witnesses, attorneys, and others in a court proceeding, and prepare written transcripts.

at real-time voice writing. Electronic reporters and transcribers learn their skills on the job. The average length of time it takes to become a real-time stenographic court reporter is 33 months. Training is offered by about 100 postsecondary vocational and technical schools and colleges. The National Court Reporters Association (NCRA) has certified more than 60 programs, all of which offer courses in stenotype computer-aided transcription and real-time reporting. NCRA-certified programs require students to capture a minimum of 225 words per minute, a requirement for Federal Government employment as well.

Electronic court reporters use audio-capture technology and, therefore, usually learn their skills on the job. Students read manuals, review them with their trainers, and observe skilled electronic transcribers perform procedures. Court electronic transcribers generally obtain initial technical training from a vendor when the audio-capture technology is placed in service, with further court-specific training provided on the job. In a private company or organization, hands-on training occurs under direct supervision of an established practitioner or firm.

Licensure. Some States require voice writers to pass a test and to earn State licensure. As a substitute for State licensure, the National Verbatim Reporters Association offers three national certifications to voice writers: Certified Verbatim Reporter (CVR), Certificate of Merit (CM), and Real-Time Verbatim Reporter (RVR). Earning these certifications is sufficient for licensure in States where the voice method of court reporting is permitted. Candidates for the CVR must pass a written test involving spelling, punctuation, and vocabulary, legal and medical terminology, as well as three 5-minute dictation and transcription examinations that test for speed, accuracy, and silence. The CM requires additional levels of speed, knowledge, and accuracy. The RVR certification measures the candidate's skill at real-time transcription, judicial reporting, CART reporting, and captioning, including webcasting. To retain these certifications, the voice writer must obtain continuing education credits. Credits are given for voice writer education courses, continuing legal education courses, and college courses.

Some States require court reporters to be notary publics. Others require the Certified Court Reporter (CCR) designation, for which a reporter must pass a State test administered by a board of examiners.

Other qualifications. In addition to possessing speed and accuracy, court reporters must have excellent listening skills and hearing, good English grammar and vocabulary, and punctuation skills. Court reporters also must work well under time and deadline pressures and be able to concentrate for long periods. They must be aware of business practices and current events, as well as the correct spelling of names of people, places, and events that may be mentioned in a broadcast or in court proceedings. For those who work in courtrooms, an expert knowledge of legal terminology and criminal and appellate procedure is essential. Because capturing proceedings requires the use of computerized stenography or speech recognition equipment, court reporters must be knowledgeable about computer hardware and software applications. Voice writers must learn to listen and speak simultaneously and very quickly and quietly, while also identifying speakers and describing peripheral activities in the courtroom or deposition room.

Projections data from the National Employment Matrix

Occupational Title	SOC Code	Employment, 2008	Projected Employment, 2018	Change, 2008-2018	
				Number	Percent
Court reporters	23-2091	21,500	25,400	3,900	18

(NOTE) Data in this table are rounded. See the discussion of the employment projections table in the *Handbook* introductory chapter on *Occupational Information Included in the Handbook*.

Certification and advancement. Certifications can help court reporters get jobs and advance in their careers. Several associations offer certifications for different types of reporters.

The National Court Reporters Association confers the entry-level designation Registered Professional Reporter (RPR) upon those who pass a four-part examination and participate in mandatory continuing education programs. Although voluntary, the designation is recognized as a mark of distinction in the field.

A court reporter may obtain additional certifications that demonstrate higher levels of experience and competency, such as Registered Merit Reporter (RMR) and Registered Diplomate Reporter (RDR). The NCRA also offers the designations Certified Realtime Reporter (CRR), Certified Broadcast Captioner (CBC), and Certified CART Provider (CCP), designed primarily for those who caption media programs or assist people who are deaf.

With experience and education, court reporters also can receive certification in administrative and management, consulting, or teaching positions.

The United States Court Reporters Association offers another voluntary certification designation, the Federal Certified Realtime Reporter (FCRR), for court reporters working in Federal courts. The exam is designed to test the basic real-time skills of Federal court reporters and is recognized by the Administrative Office for the United States District Courts for purposes of real-time certification.

The American Association of Electronic Reporters and Transcribers (AAERT) certifies electronic court reporters. Certification is voluntary and includes a written and a practical examination. To be eligible to take the exams, candidates must have at least 2 years of court reporting or transcribing experience, must be eligible for notary public commissions in their States, and must have completed high school. AAERT offers three types of certificates: Certified Electronic Court Reporter (CER), Certified Electronic Court Transcriber (CET), and Certified Electronic Court Reporter and Transcriber (CERT). Some employers may require electronic court reporters and transcribers to obtain certificates once they are eligible.

Employment

Court reporters held about 21,500 jobs in 2008. A little more than half worked for State and local governments, a reflection of the large number of court reporters working in courts, legislatures, and various agencies. Most of the remaining wage and salary workers were employed by court reporting agencies.

Job Outlook

Employment is projected to grow by 18 percent, reflecting the demand for real-time broadcast captioning and translating. Job opportunities should be excellent, especially for those with certification.

Employment change. Employment of court reporters is projected to grow 18 percent, faster than the average for all occupations between 2008 and 2018. Demand for court reporter services will be spurred by the continuing need for accurate transcription of proceedings in courts and in pretrial depositions, by the growing need to create captions for live television, and by the need to provide other real-time broadcast captioning and translating services for the deaf and the hard of hearing.

Increasing numbers of civil and criminal cases are expected to create new jobs for court reporters, but budget constraints are expected to limit the ability of Federal, State, and local courts to expand, thereby also limiting the demand for traditional court reporting services in courtrooms and other legal venues. Further, because of the difficulty in attracting court reporters and in controlling costs, some courtrooms have installed tape recorders that are maintained by electronic court reporters and transcribers to record court proceedings. However, because courts use electronic reporters and transcribers only in a limited capacity, traditional stenographic court reporters will continue to be used in felony trials and other proceedings. Despite the use of audiotape and videotape technology, court reporters can quickly turn spoken words into readable, searchable, permanent text, and they will continue to be needed to produce written legal transcripts and proceedings for publication.

Voice writers have become more widely accepted as the accuracy of speech recognition technology improves. Still, many courts allow only stenotypists to perform court reporting duties.

Increasingly, court reporters will be needed for captioning outside of legal proceedings. Not only is there Federal legislation mandating that all new television programming be captioned for the deaf and the hard of hearing, but all new Spanish-language programming likewise must be captioned by 2010. In addition, the Americans with Disabilities Act gives deaf and hard-of-hearing students in colleges and universities the right to request access to real-time translation in their classes. These factors are expected to continue to increase the demand for court reporters who provide CART services. Although such services forgo transcripts and differ from traditional court reporting, they require the same skills that court reporters learn in their training.

Job prospects. Job opportunities for court reporters are expected to be excellent as job openings continue to outnumber jobseekers in some areas. Court reporters with certification and those who choose to specialize in providing CART, broadcast captioning, or webcasting services should have the best job opportunities. Court reporters who are willing to relocate to rural areas or large cities, where demand for court reporters' services is very high, should have good job opportunities. The favorable job market also reflects the fact that fewer people are entering this profession, particularly as stenographic typists.

Earnings

Court reporters had median annual wages of $49,710 in May 2008. The middle 50 percent earned between $35,390 and $67,430. The lowest paid 10 percent earned less than $25,360, and the highest paid 10 percent earned more than $83,500. Median annual wages in May 2008 were $51,150 for court reporters working in local government and $44,670 for those working in business support services.

Compensation and compensation methods for court reporters vary with the type of reporting job, the experience of the individual reporter, the level of certification achieved, and the region of the country. Official court reporters earn a salary and a per-page fee for transcripts. Many salaried court reporters supplement their income by doing freelance work. Freelance court reporters are paid per job and receive a per-page fee for transcripts. CART providers are paid by the hour. Captioners receive a salary and benefits if they work as employees of a captioning company. Captioners working as independent contractors are paid by the hour.

Related Occupations

Other workers who type, record information, and process paperwork include:

Sources of Additional Information

State employment service offices can provide information about job openings for court reporters. For information about careers, training, and certification in court reporting, contact:

➤ American Association of Electronic Reporters and Transcribers, 2900 Fairhope Road, Wilmington, DE 19810. Internet: **http://www.aaert.org**

➤ National Court Reporters Association, 8224 Old Courthouse Rd., Vienna, VA 22182. Internet: **http://www.ncraonline.org**

➤ National Verbatim Reporters Association, 629 North Main St., Hattiesburg, MS 39401. Internet: **http://www.nvra.org**

➤ United States Court Reporters Association, 4725 N. Western Ave., Suite 240, Chicago, IL 60625-2012. Internet: **http://www.uscra.org**

The Occupational Information Network (O*NET) provides information on a wide range of occupational characteristics. Links to O*NET appear at the end of the Internet version of this occupational statement, accessible at **http://www.bls.gov/ooh/ocos152.htm**

Judges, Magistrates, and Other Judicial Workers

Significant Points

- A bachelor's degree and work experience are the minimum requirements for a judgeship or magistrate position, but most workers have law degrees and some are elected; training requirements for arbitrators, mediators, and conciliators vary.
- Overall employment is projected to grow more slowly than average, but this varies by occupational specialty.
- Competition is expected for judge or magistrate jobs because of the prestige associated with serving on the bench.

Nature of the Work

Judges, magistrates, and other judicial workers apply the law and oversee the legal process in courts. They preside over cases concerning every aspect of society, from traffic offenses, to disputes over the management of professional sports, to issues concerning the rights of huge corporations. All judicial workers must ensure that trials and hearings are conducted fairly and that the court safeguards the legal rights of all parties involved.

The most visible responsibility of judges is presiding over trials or hearings and listening as attorneys represent their clients. Judges rule on the admissibility of evidence and the methods of conducting testimony, and they may be called on to settle disputes between opposing attorneys. Also, they ensure that rules and procedures are followed, and if unusual circumstances arise for which standard procedures have not been established, judges interpret the law to determine how the trial will proceed.

Judges often hold pretrial hearings for cases. They listen to allegations and determine whether the evidence presented merits a trial. In criminal cases, judges may decide that people charged with crimes should be held in jail pending trial, or they may set conditions for their release. In civil cases, judges and magistrates occasionally impose restrictions on the parties until a trial is held.

In many trials, juries are selected to decide guilt or innocence in criminal cases, or liability and compensation in civil cases. Judges instruct juries on applicable laws, direct them to deduce the facts from the evidence presented, and hear their verdict. When the law does not require a jury trial or when the parties waive their right to a jury, judges decide cases. In such instances, the judge determines guilt in criminal cases and imposes sentences on the guilty; in civil cases, the judge awards relief—such as compensation for damages—to the winning parties to the lawsuit.

Judges also work outside the courtroom, in their chambers or private offices. There, judges read documents on pleadings and motions, research legal issues, write opinions, and oversee the court's operations. In some jurisdictions, judges also manage the court's administrative and clerical staff.

Judges' duties vary according to the extent of their jurisdictions and powers. *General trial court judges* of the Federal and

State court systems have jurisdiction over any case in their system. They usually try civil cases that transcend the jurisdiction of lower courts and all cases involving felony offenses. Federal and State *appellate court judges*, although few in number, have the power to overrule decisions made by trial court judges or *administrative law judges*. Appellate court judges overrule decisions if they determine that legal errors were made in a case or if legal precedent does not support the judgment of the lower court. Appellate court judges rule on a small number of cases and rarely have direct contact with litigants—the people who bring the case or who are on trial. Instead, they usually base their decisions on the lower court's records and on lawyers' written and oral arguments.

Many State court judges hear only certain types of cases. A variety of titles are assigned to these judges; among the most common are *municipal court judge*, *county court judge*, *magistrate*, and *justice of the peace*. Traffic violations, misdemeanors, small-claims cases, and pretrial hearings constitute the bulk of the work of these judges, but some States allow them to handle cases involving domestic relations, probate, contracts, and other selected areas of the law.

Administrative law judges, sometimes called *hearing officers* or *adjudicators*, are employed by government agencies to make determinations for administrative agencies. These judges make decisions on, for example, (1) a person's eligibility for various Social Security or workers' compensation benefits, (2) protection of the environment, (3) the enforcement of health and safety regulations, (4) employment discrimination, and (5) compliance with economic regulatory requirements.

Some people work as *arbitrators*, *mediators*, or *conciliators* instead of as judges or magistrates. They assist with alternative dispute resolution—a collection of processes used to settle disputes outside of court. All hearings are private and confidential, and the processes are less formal than a court trial. If no settlement is reached, no statements made during the proceedings are admissible as evidence in any subsequent litigation.

There are two main types of arbitration: compulsory and voluntary. During compulsory arbitration, opposing parties submit their dispute to one or more impartial persons, called arbitrators, for a final and nonbinding decision. Either party may reject the ruling and request a trial in court. Voluntary arbitration is a process in which opposing parties choose one or more arbitrators to hear their dispute and submit a final, binding decision.

Arbitrators usually are attorneys or businesspeople with expertise in a particular field. In arbitration, parties identify, in advance, the issues to be resolved, the scope of the relief to be awarded, and many of the procedural aspects of the process.

Mediators are neutral parties who help people to resolve their disputes outside of court. Parties to a dispute often use mediators when they wish to preserve their relationship. A mediator may offer suggestions, but resolution of the dispute rests with the parties themselves. Mediation proceedings also are confidential and private. If the parties are unable to reach a settlement, they are free to pursue other options. The parties usually decide in advance how they will share the cost of mediation. However, many mediators volunteer their services, or they may be court staff. Courts ask that mediators provide their services at the lowest possible rate and that the parties split the cost.

Judges decide cases when the law does not require a jury trial or when the parties waive their right to a jury.

Conciliation, or facilitation, is similar to mediation. The conciliator's role is to guide the parties to a settlement. The parties must decide in advance whether they will be bound by the conciliator's recommendations.

Arbitrators, mediators, or conciliators also use other forms of dispute resolution, including executive minitrials, early neutral evaluations, and summary jury trials. An executive minitrial is a process that involves negotiation including senior executives who have no involvement with the issues that led to the disagreement. Senior executives from each side listen to a summary of key elements of the dispute presented by each of the parties. The presentations may be made to the executives on their own, or by agreement of the parties, a neutral third party may be present. In early neutral evaluation, a person experienced in the subject matter of a litigated dispute will hold a brief, nonbinding meeting to hear the parties outline the key elements of their cases. The evaluator will identify the main issues and explore the possibility of settlement. If a settlement can't be reached, the evaluator may assist the parties by indicating procedural recommendations. A summary jury trial is a form of alternative dispute resolution in which jurors are asked to render a nonbinding verdict after an expedited hearing. The verdict may be binding if the parties consent.

Work environment. Judges, magistrates, and other judicial workers do most of their work in offices, law libraries, and courtrooms. Work in these occupations presents few hazards, although sitting in the same position in the courtroom for long periods can be tiring. Most judges wear robes when they are in a courtroom. Judges typically work a standard 40-hour week, but many work more than 50 hours per week. Some judges with limited jurisdiction are employed part time and divide their time between their judicial responsibilities and other careers.

Arbitrators, mediators, and conciliators usually work in private offices or meeting rooms; no public record of the proceedings is kept. Arbitrators, mediators, and conciliators often travel to a site chosen for negotiations, but some work from home. Arbitrators, mediators, and conciliators usually work a standard 35- to 40-hour week. However, longer hours might be necessary when contract agreements are being prepared and negotiated.

Training, Other Qualifications, and Advancement
A bachelor's degree and work experience usually constitute the minimum requirements for judges and magistrates, but most workers have law degrees and some are elected. Training requirements for arbitrators, mediators, and conciliators vary.

Education and training. Most judges have been lawyers. In fact, Federal and State judges usually are required to be lawyers, which means that they have attended law school and passed an examination. About 40 States allow nonlawyers to hold limited-jurisdiction judgeships, but opportunities are better for those with law experience.

Federal administrative law judges must be lawyers and pass a competitive examination administered by the U.S. Office of Personnel Management. Some State administrative law judges and other hearing officials are not required to be lawyers.

All States have some type of orientation for newly elected or appointed judges. The Federal Judicial Center, American Bar Association, National Judicial College, and National Center for State Courts provide judicial education and training for judges and other judicial-branch personnel. General and continuing education courses usually last from a few days to 3 weeks. More than half of all States, as well as Puerto Rico, require judges to take continuing education courses while serving on the bench.

Training for arbitrators, mediators, and conciliators is available through independent mediation programs, national and local mediation membership organizations, and postsecondary schools. To practice in State-funded or court-funded mediation programs, mediators usually must meet specific training or experience standards, which vary by State and court. Most mediators complete a 40-hour basic course and a 20-hour advanced training course. Some people receive training by volunteering at a community mediation center or by co-mediating cases with an experienced mediator. Others go on to complete an advanced degree that consists of a 2-year master's program in dispute resolution or conflict management, a 4-year to 5-year doctoral program, or a certificate program in conflict resolution at a college or university. Many mediators have a law (JD) degree, but master's degrees in public policy, law, and related fields also provide good background for prospective arbitrators, mediators, and conciliators.

Licensure. There are no national credentials or licensure requirements for arbitrators, mediators, and conciliators. In fact, State regulatory requirements vary widely. Some States require arbitrators to be experienced lawyers. Some States license mediators while other States register or certify them.

Currently, only five States—Florida, New Hampshire, North Carolina, South Carolina, and Virginia—have certification programs. In addition, at the Federal level, the U.S. Department of the Navy certifies mediators who have met the Department's requirements.

Increasingly, credentialing programs are being offered through professional organizations. For example, the American Arbitration Association requires mediators listed on its mediation panel to complete their training course, receive recommendations from the trainers, and complete an apprenticeship.

Other qualifications. Judges and magistrates must be appointed or elected a procedure that often takes political support. Federal administrative law judges are appointed by various Federal agencies, with virtually lifetime tenure. Federal magistrate judges are appointed by district judges—the life-tenured Federal judges of district courts—to serve in a U.S. district court for 8 years. A part-time Federal magistrate judge's term of office is 4 years. Some State judges are appointed, but the remainder are elected in partisan or nonpartisan State elections. Many State and local judges serve fixed renewable terms ranging from 4 to 6 years for some trial court judgeships to as long as 14 years or even life for other trial or appellate court judgeships. Judicial nominating commissions, composed of members of the bar and the public, are used to screen candidates for judgeships in many States and for some Federal judgeships.

Arbitrators, mediators, and conciliators must have knowledge of different mediation techniques and processes as well as knowledge of dispute resolution methods in order to be able to do their jobs successfully. They also must have good communication and listening skills and the ability to run successful meetings and negotiate a solution to a dispute. The ability to evaluate large amounts of information that are sometimes complex is essential. Good writing skills and technical problem-solving skills also is a must. Arbitrators, mediators, and conciliators who specialize in a particular area, such as construction or insurance, may need to have knowledge of that industry and must be able to relate well to people from different cultures and backgrounds.

Advancement. Some judicial workers move to higher courts or to courts with broader jurisdiction. Advancement for alternative-dispute workers includes taking on more complex cases, starting a business, practicing law, or becoming district court judges.

Employment
Judges, magistrates, and other judicial workers held 51,200 jobs in 2008. Judges, magistrate judges, and magistrates held 26,900 jobs, all in State and local governments. Administrative law judges, adjudicators, and hearing officers held 14,400 jobs, with 24 percent in the Federal Government. Arbitrators, mediators, and conciliators held another 9,900 jobs. Approximately 26 percent worked for State and local governments. The remainder worked for labor organizations, law offices, insurance carriers, and other private companies and organizations that specialize in providing dispute resolution services.

Job Outlook
Overall employment is projected to grow more slowly than average, but varies by specialty. Judges and magistrates are ex-

Projections data from the National Employment Matrix

Occupational Title	SOC Code	Employment, 2008	Projected Employment, 2018	Change, 2008-2018	
				Number	Percent
Judges, magistrates, and other judicial workers.............................	23-1020	51,200	53,100	1,800	4
Administrative law judges, adjudicators, and hearing officers	23-1021	14,400	15,500	1,200	8
Arbitrators, mediators, and conciliators..	23-1022	9,900	11,300	1,400	14
Judges, magistrate judges, and magistrates...................................	23-1023	26,900	26,200	-700	-3

(NOTE) Data in this table are rounded. See the discussion of the employment projections table in the *Handbook* introductory chapter on *Occupational Information Included in the Handbook*.

pected to encounter competition for jobs because of the prestige associated with serving on the bench.

Employment change. Overall employment of judges, magistrates, and other judicial workers is expected to grow 4 percent over the 2008–18 projection period, slower than the average for all occupations. Budgetary pressures at all levels of government are expected to hold down the hiring of judges despite rising caseloads, particularly in Federal courts. However, the continued need to cope with crime and settle disputes, as well as the public's willingness to go to court to settle disputes, should spur demand for judges.

Demographic shifts in the population also will spur demand for judges. For instance, the number of immigrants migrating to the United States will continue to rise, thereby increasing the demand for judges to handle the complex issues associated with immigrants. In addition, demand for judges will increase because, as the U.S. population ages, the courts are expected to reform guardianship policies and practices and develop new strategies to address elder abuse. Both the quantity and the complexity of judges' work have increased because of developments in information technology, medical science, electronic commerce, and globalization.

Employment of arbitrators, mediators, and conciliators is expected to grow faster than the average for all occupations through 2018. Many individuals and businesses try to avoid litigation, which can involve lengthy delays, high costs, unwanted publicity, and ill will. Arbitration and other alternatives to litigation usually are faster, less expensive, and more conclusive, spurring demand for the services of arbitrators, mediators, and conciliators. Demand also will continue to increase for arbitrators, mediators, and conciliators because all jurisdictions now have some type of alternative dispute resolution program. Some jurisdictions have programs requiring disputants to meet with a mediator in certain circumstances, such as when attempting to resolve child custody issues.

Job prospects. The prestige associated with serving on the bench will ensure continued competition for judge and magistrate positions. However, a growing number of candidates are choosing to forgo the bench and work in the private sector, where pay may be significantly higher. This trend may lessen the competition somewhat. Turnover is low among judges, and most job openings will arise as they retire. Additional openings will occur when new judgeships are authorized by law or when judges are elevated to higher judicial offices.

Jobs should be available for arbitrators, mediators, and conciliators, but opportunities may be limited because, as with judges, turnover is low. Once these workers have the appropriate qualifications and skills, they tend to remain in the occupa-

tion for many years. Those with certification and specialization in one or more areas of arbitration, mediation, or conciliation should have the best job opportunities.

Earnings

Judges, magistrate judges, and magistrates had median annual wages of $110,220 in May 2008. The middle 50 percent earned between $51,760 and $141,190. The top 10 percent earned more than $162,140, while the bottom 10 percent earned less than $32,290. Median annual wages in the industries employing the largest numbers of judges, magistrate judges, and magistrates in May 2008 were $126,080 in State government and $77,390 in local government. Administrative law judges, adjudicators, and hearing officers earned annual median wages of $76,940, and arbitrators, mediators, and conciliators earned an annual median of $50,660.

In the Federal court system, the Chief Justice of the U.S. Supreme Court earned $217,400 in January 2008, and the Associate Justices averaged $208,100. Federal court-of-appeals judges earned an average of $179,500 a year, while district court judges had average salaries of $169,300, as did judges in the Court of Federal Claims and the Court of International Trade. Federal judges with limited jurisdiction, such as magistrates and bankruptcy judges, had average salaries of $155,756.

According to a 2008 survey by the National Center for State Courts, salaries of chief justices of State highest courts averaged $150,850 and ranged from $107,404 to $228,856. Annual salaries of associate justices of the State highest courts averaged $145,194 and ranged from $106,185 to $218,237. Salaries of State intermediate appellate court judges averaged $141,263 and ranged from $105,050 to $204,599. Salaries of State judges of general jurisdiction trial courts averaged $130,533 and ranged from $99,234 to $178,789.

Most salaried judges are provided health, life, and dental insurance; pension plans; judicial immunity protection; expense accounts; vacation, holiday, and sick leave; and contributions to retirement plans made on their behalf. In many States, judicial compensation committees, which make recommendations on the amount of salary increases, determine judicial salaries. States without commissions have statutes that regulate judicial salaries, link judicial salaries to increases in pay for Federal judges, or adjust annual pay according to the change in the Consumer Price Index, calculated by the U.S. Bureau of Labor Statistics.

Related Occupations

Other occupations that require legal training and mediation skills include:

Sources of Additional Information

Information on judges, magistrates, and other judicial workers may be obtained from:

➤ National Center for State Courts, 300 Newport Ave., Williamsburg, VA 23185-4147. Internet: **http://www.ncsc.org**

Information on arbitrators, mediators, and conciliators may be obtained from:

➤ American Arbitration Association, 1633 Broadway, Floor 10, New York, NY 10019. Internet: **http://www.adr.org**

Information on Federal judges is available from:

➤ Administrative Office of the United States Courts, One Columbus Circle, NE., Washington, DC 20544. Internet: **http://www.uscourts.gov**

The Occupational Information Network (O*NET) provides information on a wide range of occupational characteristics. Links to O*NET appear at the end of the Internet version of this occupational statement, accessible at **http://www.bls.gov/ooh/ocos272.htm**

Lawyers

Significant Points

- About 26 percent of lawyers are self-employed, either as partners in law firms or in solo practices.

- Formal requirements to become a lawyer usually include a 4-year college degree, 3 years of law school, and passing a written bar examination; however, some requirements may vary by State.

- Competition for admission to most law schools is intense.

- Competition for job openings should be keen because of the large number of students graduating from law school each year.

Nature of the Work

The legal system affects nearly every aspect of our society, from buying a home to crossing the street. *Lawyers* form the backbone of this system, linking it to society in numerous ways. They hold positions of great responsibility and are obligated to adhere to a strict code of ethics.

Lawyers, also called *attorneys*, act as both advocates and advisors in our society. As advocates, they represent one of the parties in criminal and civil trials by presenting evidence and arguing in court to support their client. As advisors, lawyers counsel their clients about their legal rights and obligations and suggest particular courses of action in business and personal matters. Whether acting as an advocate or an advisor, all attorneys research the intent of laws and judicial decisions and apply the law to the specific circumstances faced by their clients.

The more detailed aspects of a lawyer's job depend upon his or her field of specialization and position. Although all lawyers are licensed to represent parties in court, some appear in court more frequently than others. Trial lawyers spend the majority of their time outside the courtroom, conducting research, interviewing clients and witnesses, and handling other details in preparation for a trial.

Lawyers may specialize in a number of areas, such as bankruptcy, probate, international, elder, or environmental law. Those specializing in, for example, environmental law may represent interest groups, waste disposal companies, or construction firms in their dealings with the U.S. Environmental Protection Agency and other Federal and State agencies. These lawyers help clients prepare and file for licenses and applications for approval before certain activities are permitted to occur. Some lawyers specialize in the growing field of intellectual property, helping to protect clients' claims to copyrights, artwork under contract, product designs, and computer programs. Other lawyers advise insurance companies about the legality of insurance transactions, guiding the company in writing insurance policies to conform to the law and to protect the companies from unwarranted claims. When claims are filed against insurance companies, these attorneys review the claims and represent the companies in court.

Most lawyers are in private practice, concentrating on criminal or civil law. In criminal law, lawyers represent individuals who have been charged with crimes and argue their cases in courts of law. Attorneys dealing with civil law assist clients with litigation, wills, trusts, contracts, mortgages, titles, and leases. Other lawyers handle only public-interest cases—civil or criminal—concentrating on particular causes and choosing cases that might have an impact on the way law is applied. Lawyers sometimes are employed full time by a single client. If the client is a corporation, the lawyer is known as "house counsel" and usually advises the company concerning legal issues related to its business activities. These issues might involve patents, government regulations, contracts with other companies, property interests, or collective-bargaining agreements with unions.

A significant number of attorneys are employed at the various levels of government. Some work for State attorneys general, prosecutors, and public defenders in criminal courts. At the Federal level, attorneys investigate cases for the U.S. Department of Justice and other agencies. Government lawyers also help develop programs, draft and interpret laws and legislation, establish enforcement procedures, and argue civil and criminal cases on behalf of the government.

Other lawyers work for legal aid societies—private, nonprofit organizations established to serve disadvantaged people. These lawyers generally handle civil, rather than criminal, cases.

Lawyers are increasingly using various forms of technology to perform more efficiently. Although all lawyers continue to use law libraries to prepare cases, most supplement conventional printed sources with computer sources, such as the Internet and legal databases. Software is used to search this legal literature automatically and to identify legal texts relevant to a specific case. In litigation involving many supporting documents, lawyers may use computers to organize and index materials. Lawyers must be geographically mobile and able to reach their clients in a timely matter, so they might use electronic filing, Web and videoconferencing, mobile electronic devices, and voice-recognition technology to share information more effectively.

Work environment. Lawyers do most of their work in offices, law libraries, and courtrooms. They sometimes meet in clients' homes or places of business and, when necessary, in hospitals or prisons. They may travel to attend meetings, gather evidence, and appear before courts, legislative bodies, and other authorities. They also may face particularly heavy pressure when a case is being tried. Preparation for court includes understanding the latest laws and judicial decisions.

Salaried lawyers usually have structured work schedules. Lawyers who are in private practice or those who work for large firms may work irregular hours, including weekends, while conducting research, conferring with clients, or preparing briefs during nonoffice hours. Lawyers often work long hours; of those who work full time, about 33 percent work 50 or more hours per week.

Training, Other Qualifications, and Advancement

Formal requirements to become a lawyer usually include a 4-year college degree, 3 years of law school, and passing a written bar examination; however, some requirements vary by State. Competition for admission to most law schools is intense. Federal courts and agencies set their own qualifications for those practicing before or in them.

Education and training. Becoming a lawyer usually takes 7 years of full-time study after high school—4 years of undergraduate study, followed by 3 years of law school. Law school applicants must have a bachelor's degree to qualify for admission. To meet the needs of students who can attend only part time, a number of law schools have night or part-time divisions.

Although there is no recommended "prelaw" undergraduate major, prospective lawyers should develop proficiency in writing and speaking, reading, researching, analyzing, and thinking logically—skills needed to succeed both in law school and in the law. Regardless of major, a multidisciplinary background is recommended. Courses in English, foreign languages, public speaking, government, philosophy, history, economics, mathematics, and computer science, among others, are useful. Students interested in a particular aspect of law may find related courses helpful. For example, prospective patent lawyers need a strong background in engineering or science, and future tax lawyers must have extensive knowledge of accounting.

Acceptance by most law schools depends on the applicant's ability to demonstrate an aptitude for the study of law, usually through undergraduate grades, the Law School Admission Test (LSAT), the quality of the applicant's undergraduate school, any prior work experience, and sometimes, a personal interview. However, law schools vary in the weight they place on each of these and other factors.

Trial lawyers spend most of their time outside the courtroom conducting research, interviewing clients and witnesses, and handling other details in preparation for a trial.

All law schools approved by the American Bar Association (ABA) require applicants to take the LSAT. As of June 2008, there were 200 ABA-accredited law schools; others were approved by State authorities only. Nearly all law schools require applicants to have certified transcripts sent to the Law School Data Assembly Service, which then submits the applicants' LSAT scores and their standardized records of college grades to the law schools of their choice. The Law School Admission Council administers both this service and the LSAT. Competition for admission to many law schools—especially the most prestigious ones—is usually intense, with the number of applicants greatly exceeding the number that can be admitted.

During the first year or year and a half of law school, students usually study core courses, such as constitutional law, contracts, property law, torts, civil procedure, and legal writing. In the remaining time, they may choose specialized courses in fields such as tax, labor, or corporate law. Law students often gain practical experience by participating in school-sponsored legal clinics; in the school's moot court competitions, in which students conduct appellate arguments; in practice trials under the supervision of experienced lawyers and judges; and through research and writing on legal issues for the school's law journals.

Projections data from the National Employment Matrix

Occupational Title	SOC Code	Employment, 2008	Projected Employment, 2018	Change, 2008-2018	
				Number	Percent
Lawyers..	23-1011	759,200	857,700	98,500	13

(NOTE) Data in this table are rounded. See the discussion of the employment projections table in the *Handbook* introductory chapter on *Occupational Information Included in the Handbook.*

A number of law schools have clinical programs in which students gain legal experience through practice trials and projects under the supervision of lawyers and law school faculty. Law school clinical programs might include work in, for example, legal-aid offices or on legislative committees. Part-time or summer clerkships in law firms, government agencies, and corporate legal departments also provide valuable experience. Such training can lead directly to a job after graduation and can help students decide what kind of practice best suits them. Law school graduates receive the degree of *juris doctor* (J.D.), a first professional degree.

Advanced law degrees may be desirable for those planning to specialize, perform research, or teach. Some law students pursue joint degree programs, which usually require an additional semester or year of study. Joint degree programs are offered in a number of areas, including business administration or public administration.

After graduation, lawyers must keep informed about legal and nonlegal developments that affect their practices. In 2008, 46 States and jurisdictions required lawyers to participate in mandatory continuing legal education. Many law schools and State and local bar associations provide continuing education courses that help lawyers stay abreast of recent developments. Some States allow continuing education credits to be obtained through participation in seminars on the Internet.

Licensure. To practice law in the courts of any State or other jurisdiction, a person must be licensed, or admitted to its bar, under rules established by the jurisdiction's highest court. All States require that applicants for admission to the bar pass a written bar examination; most States also require applicants to pass a separate written ethics examination. Lawyers who have been admitted to the bar in one State occasionally may be admitted to the bar in another without taking another examination if they meet the latter jurisdiction's standards of good moral character and a specified period of legal experience. In most cases, however, lawyers must pass the bar examination in each State in which they plan to practice. Federal courts and agencies set their own qualifications for those practicing before or in them.

To qualify for the bar examination in most States, an applicant must earn a college degree and graduate from a law school accredited by the ABA or the proper State authorities. ABA accreditation signifies that the law school—particularly its library and faculty—meets certain standards. With certain exceptions, graduates of schools not approved by the ABA are restricted to taking the bar examination and practicing in the State or other jurisdiction in which the school is located; most of these schools are in California.

Although there is no nationwide bar examination, 48 States, the District of Columbia, Guam, the Northern Mariana Islands, Puerto Rico, and the Virgin Islands require the 6-hour Multistate Bar Examination (MBE) as part of their overall bar examination; the MBE is not required in Louisiana or Washington. The MBE covers a broad range of issues, and sometimes a locally prepared State bar examination is given in addition to it. The 3-hour Multistate Essay Examination (MEE) is used as part of the bar examination in several States. States vary in their use of MBE and MEE scores.

Many States also require the Multistate Performance Test to test the practical skills of beginning lawyers. Requirements vary by State, although the test usually is taken at the same time as the bar exam and is a one-time requirement.

In 2008, law school graduates in 52 jurisdictions were required to pass the Multistate Professional Responsibility Examination (MPRE), which tests their knowledge of the ABA codes on professional responsibility and judicial conduct. In some States, the MPRE may be taken during law school, usually after completing a course on legal ethics.

Other qualifications. The practice of law involves a great deal of responsibility. Individuals planning careers in law should like to work with people and be able to win the respect and confidence of their clients, associates, and the public. Perseverance, creativity, and reasoning ability also are essential to lawyers, who often analyze complex cases and handle new and unique legal problems.

Trial lawyers, who specialize in trial work, must be able to think quickly and speak with ease and authority. In addition, familiarity with courtroom rules and strategy is particularly important in trial work.

Advancement. Most beginning lawyers start in salaried positions. Newly hired attorneys usually start as associates and work with more experienced lawyers or judges. After several years, some lawyers are admitted to partnership in their firm, which means that they are partial owners of the firm, or go into practice for themselves. Some experienced lawyers are nominated or elected to judgeships. (See the section on judges, magistrates, and other judicial workers elsewhere in the *Handbook.*) Others become full-time law school faculty or administrators; a growing number of these lawyers have advanced degrees in other fields as well.

Some attorneys use their legal training in administrative or managerial positions in various departments of large corporations. A transfer from a corporation's legal department to another department is often viewed as a way to gain administrative experience and rise in the ranks of management.

Employment

Lawyers held about 759,200 jobs in 2008. Approximately 26 percent of lawyers were self-employed, practicing either as partners in law firms or in solo practices. Most salaried lawyers held positions in government, in law firms or other corporations, or in nonprofit organizations. Most government-employed lawyers worked at the local level. In the Federal Government, lawyers

Projections data from the National Employment Matrix

Occupational Title	SOC Code	Employment, 2008	Projected Employment, 2018	Change, 2008-2018	
				Number	Percent
Paralegals and legal assistants...	23-2011	263,800	337,900	74,100	28

(NOTE) Data in this table are rounded. See the discussion of the employment projections table in the *Handbook* introductory chapter on *Occupational Information Included in the Handbook*.

worked for many different agencies, but were concentrated in the Departments of Justice, Treasury, and Defense. Many salaried lawyers working outside of government were employed as house counsel by public utilities, banks, insurance companies, real-estate agencies, manufacturing firms, and other business firms and nonprofit organizations. Some also had part-time independent practices, while others worked part time as lawyers and full time in another occupation.

A relatively small number of trained attorneys work in law schools and are not included in the employment estimate for lawyers. Most are faculty members who specialize in one or more subjects; however, some serve as administrators. Others work full time in nonacademic settings and teach part time. (For additional information, see the *Handbook* section on teachers—postsecondary.)

Job Outlook

About as fast as the average employment growth is projected, but job competition is expected to be keen.

Employment change. Employment of lawyers is expected to grow 13 percent during the 2008-18 decade, about as fast as the average for all occupations. Growth in the population and in the level of business activity is expected to create more legal transactions, civil disputes, and criminal cases. Job growth among lawyers also will result from increasing demand for legal services in such areas as health care, intellectual property, bankruptcy, corporate and security litigation, antitrust law, and environmental law. In addition, the wider availability and affordability of legal clinics should result in increased use of legal services by middle-income people. However, growth in demand for lawyers will be constrained as businesses increasingly use large accounting firms and paralegals to perform some of the same functions that lawyers do. For example, accounting firms may provide employee-benefit counseling, process documents, or handle various other services previously performed by a law firm. Also, mediation and dispute resolution are increasingly being used as alternatives to litigation.

Job growth for lawyers will continue to be concentrated in salaried jobs as businesses and all levels of government employ a growing number of staff attorneys. Most salaried positions are in urban areas where government agencies, law firms, and big corporations are concentrated. The number of self-employed lawyers is expected to grow slowly, reflecting the difficulty of establishing a profitable new practice in the face of competition from larger, established law firms. Moreover, the growing complexity of the law, which encourages specialization, along with the cost of maintaining up-to-date legal research materials, favors larger firms.

Job prospects. Competition for job openings should continue to be keen because of the large number of students graduating from law school each year. Graduates with superior academic records from highly regarded law schools will have the best job opportunities. Perhaps as a result of competition for attorney positions, lawyers are increasingly finding work in less traditional areas for which legal training is an asset, but not normally a requirement—for example, administrative, managerial, and business positions in banks, insurance firms, real estate companies, government agencies, and other organizations. Employment opportunities are expected to continue to arise in these organizations at a growing rate.

As in the past, some graduates may have to accept positions outside of their field of interest or for which they feel overqualified. Some recent law school graduates who have been unable to find permanent positions are turning to the growing number of temporary staffing firms that place attorneys in short-term jobs. This service allows companies to hire lawyers on an "as-needed" basis and permits beginning lawyers to develop practical skills.

Because of the keen competition for jobs, a law graduate's geographic mobility and work experience are assuming greater importance. Willingness to relocate may be an advantage in getting a job, but to be licensed in another State, a lawyer may have to take an additional State bar examination. In addition, employers increasingly are seeking graduates who have advanced law degrees and experience in a specialty, such as tax, patent, or admiralty law.

Job opportunities often are adversely affected by cyclical swings in the economy. During recessions, demand declines for some discretionary legal services, such as planning estates, drafting wills, and handling real estate transactions. Also, corporations are less likely to litigate cases when declining sales and profits restrict their budgets. Some corporations and law firms will not hire new attorneys until business improves, and these establishments may even cut staff to contain costs. Several factors, however, mitigate the overall impact of recessions on lawyers; during recessions, for example, individuals and corporations face other legal problems, such as bankruptcies, foreclosures, and divorces—all requiring legal action.

For lawyers who wish to work independently, establishing a new practice will probably be easiest in small towns and expanding suburban areas. In such communities, competition from larger, established law firms is likely to be less than in big cities, and new lawyers may find it easier to establish a reputation among potential clients.

Earnings

In May 2008, the median annual wages of all wage-and-salaried lawyers were $110,590. The middle half of the occupation earned between $74,980 and $163,320. Median annual wages in the industries employing the largest numbers of lawyers in May 2008 were:

Management of companies and enterprises	$145,770
Federal Executive Branch	126,080
Legal services	116,550
Local government	82,590
State government	78,540

Salaries of experienced attorneys vary widely according to the type, size, and location of their employer. Lawyers who own their own practices usually earn less than those who are partners in law firms. Lawyers starting their own practice may need to work part time in other occupations to supplement their income until their practice is well established.

Median salaries of lawyers 9 months after graduation from law school in 2007 varied by type of work, as indicated in table 1.

Table 1. Median salaries, 9 months after graduation

Employer	Salary
All graduates	$68,500
Private practice	108,500
Business	69,100
Government	50,000
Academic/judicial clerkships	48,000
SOURCE: National Association of Law Placement	

Most salaried lawyers are provided health and life insurance, and contributions are made to retirement plans on their behalf. Lawyers who practice independently are covered only if they arrange and pay for such benefits themselves.

Related Occupations

Legal training is necessary in many other occupations, including:

Sources of Additional Information

Information on law schools and a career in law may be obtained from the following organizations:

➤ American Bar Association, 321 North Clark St., Chicago, IL 60654. Internet: **http://www.abanet.org**

➤ National Association for Law Placement, 1025 Connecticut Ave. NW., Suite 1110, Washington, DC 20036. Internet: **http://www.nalp.org**

Information on the LSAT, the Law School Data Assembly Service, the law school application process, and financial aid available to law students may be obtained from:

➤ Law School Admission Council, 662 Penn St., Newtown, PA 18940. Internet: **http://www.lsac.org**

Information on obtaining positions as lawyers with the Federal Government is available from the Office of Personnel Management through USAJOBS, the Federal Government's official

employment information system. This resource for locating and applying for job opportunities can be accessed through the Internet at **http://www.usajobs.opm.gov** or through an interactive voice response telephone system at (703) 724-1850 or TDD (978) 461-8404. These numbers are not toll free, and charges may result. For advice on how to find and apply for Federal jobs, see the *Occupational Outlook Quarterly* article "How to get a job in the Federal Government," online at **http://www.bls.gov/opub/ooq/2004/summer/art01.pdf.**

The requirements for admission to the bar in a particular State or other jurisdiction may be obtained at the State capital, from the clerk of the Supreme Court, or from the administrator of the State Board of Bar Examiners.

The Occupational Information Network (O*NET) provides information on a wide range of occupational characteristics. Links to O*NET appear at the end of the Internet version of this occupational statement, accessible at **http://www.bls.gov/ooh/ocos053.htm**

Paralegals and Legal Assistants

Significant Points

- Despite projected much faster-than-average employment growth, competition for jobs is expected.

- Formally trained, experienced paralegals should have the best employment opportunities.

- Most entrants have an associate's degree in paralegal studies, or a bachelor's degree in another field and a certificate in paralegal studies.

- About 71 percent work for law firms.

Nature of the Work

Although lawyers assume ultimate responsibility for legal work, they often delegate many of their tasks to paralegals. In fact, *paralegals*—also called *legal assistants*—are continuing to assume new responsibilities in legal offices and perform many of the same tasks as lawyers. Nevertheless, they are explicitly prohibited from carrying out duties considered to be within the scope of practice of law, such as setting legal fees, giving legal advice, and presenting cases in court.

One of a paralegal's most important tasks is helping lawyers prepare for closings, hearings, trials, and corporate meetings. Paralegals might investigate the facts of cases and ensure that all relevant information is considered. They also identify appropriate laws, judicial decisions, legal articles, and other materials that are relevant to assigned cases. After they analyze and organize the information, paralegals may prepare written reports that attorneys use in determining how cases should be handled. If attorneys decide to file lawsuits on behalf of clients, paralegals may help prepare the legal arguments, draft pleadings and motions to be filed with the court, obtain affidavits, and assist attorneys during trials. Paralegals also organize and track files of all important case documents and make them available and easily accessible to attorneys.

In addition to this preparatory work, paralegals perform a number of other functions. For example, they help draft contracts, mortgages, and separation agreements. They also may assist in preparing tax returns, establishing trust funds, and planning estates. Some paralegals coordinate the activities of other law office employees and maintain financial office records.

Computer software packages and the Internet are used to search legal literature stored in computer databases and on CD-ROM. In litigation involving many supporting documents, paralegals usually use computer databases to retrieve, organize, and index various materials. Imaging software allows paralegals to scan documents directly into a database, while billing programs help them to track hours billed to clients. Computer software packages also are used to perform tax computations and explore the consequences of various tax strategies for clients.

Paralegals are found in all types of organizations, but most are employed by law firms, corporate legal departments, and various government offices. In these organizations, they can work in many different areas of the law, including litigation, personal injury, corporate law, criminal law, employee benefits, intellectual property, labor law, bankruptcy, immigration, family law, and real estate. As the law becomes more complex, paralegals become more specialized. Within specialties, functions are often broken down further. For example, paralegals specializing in labor law may concentrate exclusively on employee benefits. In small and medium-size law firms, duties are often more general.

The tasks of paralegals differ widely according to the type of organization for which they work. *Corporate paralegals* often assist attorneys with employee contracts, shareholder agreements, stock-option plans, and employee benefit plans. They also may help prepare and file annual financial reports, maintain corporate minutes' record resolutions, and prepare forms to secure loans for the corporation. Corporate paralegals often monitor and review government regulations to ensure that the corporation is aware of new requirements and is operating within the law. Increasingly, experienced corporate paralegals or paralegal managers are assuming additional supervisory responsibilities, such as overseeing team projects.

The duties of paralegals who work in the public sector usually vary by agency. In general, *litigation paralegals* analyze legal material for internal use, maintain reference files, conduct research for attorneys, and collect and analyze evidence for agency hearings. They may prepare informative or explanatory material on laws, agency regulations, and agency policy for general use by the agency and the public. Paralegals employed in community legal-service projects help the poor, the aged, and others who are in need of legal assistance. They file forms, conduct research, prepare documents, and, when authorized by law, may represent clients at administrative hearings.

Work environment. Paralegals handle many routine assignments, particularly when they are inexperienced. As they gain experience, paralegals usually assume more varied tasks with additional responsibility. Paralegals do most of their work in offices and law libraries. Occasionally, they travel to gather information and perform other duties.

Paralegals employed by corporations and government usually work a standard 40-hour week. Although most paralegals work year round, some are temporarily employed during busy times of the year. Paralegals who work for law firms sometimes work very long hours when they are under pressure to meet deadlines.

Training, Other Qualifications, and Advancement

Most entrants have an associate's degree in paralegal studies, or a bachelor's degree in another field and a certificate in paralegal studies. Some employers train paralegals on the job.

Education and training. There are several ways to become a paralegal. The most common is through a community college paralegal program that leads to an associate degree. Another common method of entry, mainly for those who already have a college degree, is earning a certificate in paralegal studies. A small number of schools offer bachelor's and master's degrees in paralegal studies. Finally, some employers train paralegals on the job.

Associate's and bachelor's degree programs usually combine paralegal training with courses in other academic subjects. Certificate programs vary significantly, with some taking only a few months to complete. Most certificate programs provide intensive paralegal training for individuals who already hold college degrees.

More than 1,000 colleges and universities, law schools, and proprietary schools offer formal paralegal training programs. Approximately 260 paralegal programs are approved by the American Bar Association (ABA). Although not required by many employers, graduation from an ABA-approved program can enhance employment opportunities. Admission requirements vary. Some schools require certain college courses or a bachelor's degree, while others accept high school graduates or those with legal experience. A few schools require standardized tests and personal interviews.

The quality of paralegal training programs varies; some programs may include job placement services. If possible, prospective students should examine the experiences of recent graduates before enrolling in a paralegal program. Training programs usually include courses in legal research and the legal applications of computers. Many paralegal training programs also offer an internship, in which students gain practical experience by working for several months in a private law firm, the

In litigation involving many supporting documents, paralegals usually use computer databases to retrieve, organize, and index various materials.

office of a public defender or attorney general, a corporate legal department, a legal aid organization, a bank, or a government agency. Internship experience is a valuable asset in seeking a job after graduation.

Some employers train paralegals on the job, hiring college graduates with no legal experience or promoting experienced legal secretaries. Some entrants have experience in a technical field that is useful to law firms, such as a background in tax preparation or criminal justice. Nursing or health administration experience is valuable in personal-injury law practices.

Certification and other qualifications. Although most employers do not require certification, earning voluntary certification from a professional national or local paralegal organization may offer advantages in the labor market. Many national and local paralegal organizations offer voluntary paralegal certifications by requiring students to pass an exam. Other organizations offer voluntary paralegal certifications by meeting certain criteria such as experience and education.

The National Association of Legal Assistants (NALA), for example, has established standards for certification that require various combinations of education and experience. Paralegals who meet these standards are eligible to take a 2-day examination. Those who pass the exam may use the Certified Legal Assistant (CLA) or Certified Paralegal (CP) credential. NALA certification is for a period of five years and 50 hours of continuing education is required for recertification. According to the NALA, as of September 4, 2009, there were 15,652 Certified Paralegals in the United States. NALA also offers the Advanced Paralegal Certification for experienced paralegals who want to specialize. The Advanced Paralegal Certification program is a curriculum-based program offered on the Internet.

The American Alliance of Paralegals, Inc., offers the American Alliance Certified Paralegal (AACP) credential, a voluntary certification program. Paralegals seeking the AACP certification must possess at least 5 years of paralegal experience and meet one of three educational criteria. Certification must be renewed every 2 years, including the completion of 18 hours of continuing education.

In addition, the National Federation of Paralegal Associations (NFPA) offers the Registered Paralegal (RP) designation to paralegals with a bachelor's degree and at least 2 years of experience who pass an exam. To maintain the credential, workers must complete 12 hours of continuing education every 2 years. The National Association of Legal Secretaries (NALS) offers the Professional Paralegal (PP) certification to those who pass a four-part exam. Recertification requires 75 hours of continuing education.

Paralegals must be able to document and present their findings and opinions to their supervising attorney. They need to understand legal terminology and have good research and investigative skills. Familiarity with the operation and applications of computers in legal research and litigation support also is important. Paralegals should stay informed of new developments in the laws that affect their area of practice. Participation in continuing legal education seminars allows paralegals to maintain and expand their knowledge of the law. In fact, all paralegals in California must complete 4 hours of mandatory continuing education in either general law or a specialized area of law.

Because paralegals frequently deal with the public, they should be courteous and uphold the ethical standards of the legal profession. The NALA, the NFPA, and a few States have established ethical guidelines for paralegals to follow.

Advancement. Paralegals usually are given more responsibilities and require less supervision as they gain work experience. Experienced paralegals who work in large law firms, corporate legal departments, or government agencies may supervise and delegate assignments to other paralegals and clerical staff. Advancement opportunities also include promotion to managerial and other law-related positions within the firm or corporate legal department. However, some paralegals find it easier to move to another law firm when seeking increased responsibility or advancement.

Employment

Paralegals and legal assistants held about 263,800 jobs in 2008. Private law firms employed 71 percent; most of the remainder worked for corporate legal departments and various levels of government. Within the Federal Government, the U.S. Department of Justice is the largest employer, followed by the Social Security Administration and the U.S. Department of the Treasury. A small number of paralegals own their own businesses and work as freelance legal assistants, contracting their services to attorneys or corporate legal departments.

Job Outlook

Despite projected much faster-than-average employment growth, competition for jobs is expected to continue as many people seek to go into this profession; experienced, formally trained paralegals should have the best employment opportunities.

Employment change. Employment of paralegals and legal assistants is projected to grow 28 percent between 2008 and 2018, much faster than the average for all occupations. Employers are trying to reduce costs and increase the availability and efficiency of legal services by hiring paralegals to perform tasks once done by lawyers. Paralegals are performing a wider variety of duties, making them more useful to businesses.

Demand for paralegals also is expected to grow as an expanding population increasingly requires legal services, especially in areas such as intellectual property, health care, international law, elder issues, criminal law, and environmental law. The growth of prepaid legal plans also should contribute to the demand for legal services.

Private law firms will continue to be the largest employers of paralegals, but a growing array of other organizations, such as corporate legal departments, insurance companies, real-estate and title insurance firms, and banks also hire paralegals. Corporations in particular are expected to increase their in-house legal departments to cut costs. The wide range of tasks paralegals can perform has helped to increase their employment in small and medium-size establishments of all types.

Job prospects. In addition to new jobs created by employment growth, more job openings will arise as people leave the occupation. There will be demand for paralegals who specialize in areas such as real estate, bankruptcy, medical malpractice, and product liability. Community legal service programs, which provide assistance to the poor, elderly, minorities, and middle-income families, will employ additional paralegals to minimize expenses and serve the most people. Job opportunities also are expected in Federal, State, and local government agencies, consumer organizations, and the courts. However, this occupation attracts many applicants, creating competition for jobs. Experienced, formally trained paralegals should have the best job prospects.

To a limited extent, paralegal jobs are affected by the business cycle. During recessions, demand declines for some discretionary legal services, such as planning estates, drafting wills, and handling real estate transactions. Corporations are less inclined to initiate certain types of litigation when falling sales and profits lead to fiscal belt tightening. As a result, full-time paralegals employed in offices adversely affected by a recession may be laid off or have their work hours reduced. However, during recessions, corporations and individuals are more likely to face problems that require legal assistance, such as bankruptcies, foreclosures, and divorces. Paralegals, who provide many of the same legal services as lawyers at a lower cost, tend to fare relatively better in difficult economic conditions.

Earnings

Wages of paralegals and legal assistants vary greatly. Salaries depend on education, training, experience, the type and size of employer, and the geographic location of the job. In general, paralegals who work for large law firms or in large metropolitan areas earn more than those who work for smaller firms or in less populated regions. In May 2008, full-time wage-and-salary paralegals and legal assistants earned $46,120. The middle 50 percent earned between $36,080 and $59,310. The top 10 percent earned more than $73,450, and the bottom 10 percent earned less than $29,260. Median annual wages in the industries employing the largest numbers of paralegals were:

Federal Executive Branch	$58,540
Management of companies and enterprises	55,910
Insurance carriers	52,200
Employment services	50,050
Legal services	44,480

In addition to earning a salary, many paralegals receive bonuses, in part to compensate them for sometimes having to work long hours. Paralegals also receive vacation, paid sick leave, a savings plan, life insurance, personal paid time off, dental insurance, and reimbursement for continuing legal education.

Related Occupations

Among the other occupations that call for a specialized understanding of the law, but that do not require the extensive training of a lawyer are:

	Page
Claims adjusters, examiners, and investigators	96
Law clerks	824
Occupational health and safety specialists	428
Occupational health and safety technicians	431
Title examiners, abstractors, and searchers	825

Sources of Additional Information

General information on a career as a paralegal can be obtained from:

➤ Standing Committee on Paralegals, American Bar Association, 321 North Clark St., Chicago, IL 60654. Internet: **http://www.abanet.org/legalservices/paralegals**

For information on the Certified Legal Assistant exam, schools that offer training programs in a specific State, and standards and guidelines for paralegals, contact:

➤ National Association of Legal Assistants, Inc., 1516 South Boston St., Suite 200, Tulsa, OK 74119. Internet: **http://www.nala.org**

Information on the Paralegal Advanced Competency Exam, paralegal careers, paralegal training programs, job postings, and local associations is available from:

➤ National Federation of Paralegal Associations, P.O. Box 2016, Edmonds, WA 98020. Internet: **http://www.paralegals.org**

Information on paralegal training programs, including the pamphlet *How to Choose a Paralegal Education Program*, may be obtained from:

➤ American Association for Paralegal Education, 19 Mantua Rd., Mt. Royal, NJ 08061. Internet: **http://www.aafpe.org**

Information on paralegal careers, certification, and job postings is available from:

➤ American Alliance of Paralegals, Inc., Suite 134-146, 4001 Kennett Pike, Wilmington, DE, 19807. Internet: **http://www.aapipara.org**

For information on the Professional Paralegal exam, schools that offer training programs in a specific State, and standards and guidelines for paralegals, contact:

➤ National Association of Legal Secretaries, 8159 E. 41st St., Tulsa, OK 74145. Internet: **http://www.nals.org**

Information on obtaining positions as a paralegal or legal assistant with the Federal Government is available from the Office of Personnel Management through USAJOBS, the Federal Government's official employment information system. This resource for locating and applying for job opportunities can be accessed through the Internet at **http://www.usajobs.opm.gov** or through an interactive voice response telephone system at (703) 724-1850 or TDD (978) 461-8404. These numbers are not toll free, and charges may result. For advice on how to find and apply for Federal jobs, see the *Occupational Outlook Quarterly* article "How to get a job in the Federal Government," online at **http://www.bls.gov/opub/ooq/2004/summer/art01.pdf**.

The Occupational Information Network (O*NET) provides information on a wide range of occupational characteristics. Links to O*NET appear at the end of the Internet version of this occupational statement, accessible at **http://www.bls.gov/ooh/ocos114.htm**

Education, Training, Library, and Museum Occupations

Archivists, Curators, and Museum Technicians

Significant Points

- Most worked in museums, historical sites, and similar venues; in educational institutions; or in Federal, State, or local government.

- A graduate degree and related work experience are required for most positions; museum technicians may enter with a bachelor's degree.

- Keen competition is expected for most jobs because qualified applicants generally outnumber job openings.

Nature of the Work

Archivists, curators, and museum technicians work for museums, governments, zoos, colleges and universities, corporations, and other institutions that require experts to preserve important records and artifacts. These workers preserve important objects and documents, including works of art, transcripts of meetings, photographs, coins and stamps, and historic objects.

Archivists and curators plan and oversee the arrangement, cataloguing, and exhibition of collections. They also maintain collections with technicians and conservators. They acquire and preserve important documents and other valuable items for permanent storage or display. They also describe, catalogue, and analyze, valuable objects for the benefit of researchers and the public.

Archivists and curators may coordinate educational and public outreach programs, such as tours, workshops, lectures, and classes, and may work with the boards of institutions to administer plans and policies. They also may research topics or items relevant to their collections.

Although some duties of archivists and curators are similar, the types of items they deal with differ: archivists mainly handle records and documents that are retained because of their importance and potential value, while curators usually handle objects with cultural, biological, or historical significance, such as sculptures, textiles, and paintings.

Archivists collect, organize, and maintain control over a wide range of information deemed important enough for permanent safekeeping. This information takes many forms: photographs, films, video and sound recordings, and electronic data files in a wide variety of formats, as well as more traditional paper records, letters, and documents.

In accordance with accepted standards and practices, archivists maintain records to ensure the long-term preservation and easy retrieval of documents and information. Records may be saved on any medium, including paper, film, videotape, audiotape, computer disk, or DVD. They also may be copied onto some other format to protect the original and to make the records more user accessible. As various storage media evolve, archivists must keep abreast of technological advances in electronic information storage.

Generally, computers are used to generate and maintain archival records. Professional standards for the use of computers in handling archival records, especially electronic, are still evolving. However, computer capabilities will continue to expand and more records will be stored and exhibited electronically, providing both increased access and better protection for archived documents.

Archivists often specialize in an area of history so they can more accurately determine which records in that area qualify for retention and should become part of the archives. Archivists also may work with specialized forms of records, such as manuscripts, electronic records, web sites, photographs, cartographic records, motion pictures, or sound recordings.

Curators administer museums, zoos, aquariums, botanical gardens, nature centers, and historic sites. The museum director often is a curator. Curators direct the acquisition, storage, and exhibition of collections, including negotiating and authorizing the purchase, sale, exchange, or loan of collections. They are also responsible for authenticating, evaluating, and categorizing the specimens in a collection. Curators often oversee and help conduct the institution's research projects and related educational programs. Today, an increasing part of a curator's duties involves fundraising and promotion, which may include the writing and reviewing of grant proposals, journal articles, and publicity materials, as well as attendance at meetings, conventions, and civic events.

Most curators specialize in a particular field, such as botany, art, paleontology, or history. Those working in large institutions may be highly specialized. A large natural history museum, for example, would employ separate curators for its collections of birds, fishes, insects, and mammals. Some curators maintain their collections, others do research, and others perform administrative tasks. In small institutions with only one or a few curators, one curator may be responsible for a number of tasks, from maintaining collections to directing the affairs of the museum.

Conservators manage, care for, preserve, treat, and document works of art, artifacts, and specimens—work that may require substantial historical, scientific, and archaeological research. They use x rays, chemical testing, microscopes, special lights, and other laboratory equipment and techniques to examine objects and determine their condition and the appropriate method for preserving them. Conservators document their findings and treat items to minimize their deterioration or to restore them to their original state. Conservators usually specialize in a particular material or group of objects, such as documents and books, paintings, decorative arts, textiles, metals, or architectural material. In addition to their conservation work, conservators participate in outreach programs, research topics in their area of specialty, and write articles for scholarly journals. They may be employed by museums or work on a freelance basis.

Museum technicians, commonly known as registrars, assist curators by performing various preparatory and maintenance tasks on museum items. Registrars may also answer public inquiries and assist curators and outside scholars in using collections. Archives technicians help archivists organize, maintain, and provide access to historical documentary materials.

Work environment. The working conditions of archivists and curators vary. Some spend most of their time working with the public, providing reference assistance and educational services. Others perform research or process records, which reduces the opportunity to work with others. Those who restore and install exhibits or work with bulky, heavy record containers may lift objects, climb, or stretch. Those in zoos, botanical gardens, and other outdoor museums and historic sites frequently walk great distances. Conservators work in conservation laboratories. The size of the objects in the collection they are working with determines the amount of effort involved in lifting, reaching, and moving objects.

Curators who work in large institutions may travel extensively to evaluate potential additions to the collection, organize exhibitions, and conduct research in their area of expertise. However, travel is rare for curators employed in small institutions.

Training, Other Qualifications, and Advancement

Employment as an archivist, conservator, or curator usually requires graduate education and related work experience. While completing their formal education, many archivists and curators work in archives or museums to gain "hands-on" experience. Registrars often start work with a bachelor's degree.

Education and training. Although archivists earn a variety of undergraduate degrees, a graduate degree in history or library science with courses in archival science is preferred by most employers. Many colleges and universities offer courses or practical training in archival techniques as part of their history, library science, or other curriculum. A few institutions offer master's degrees in archival studies. Some positions may require knowledge of the discipline related to the collection, such as computer science, business, or medicine. There are many archives that offer volunteer opportunities where students can gain experience.

For employment as a curator, most museums require a master's degree in an appropriate discipline of the museum's specialty—art, history, or archaeology—or in museum studies. Some employers prefer a doctoral degree, particularly for curators in natural history or science museums. Earning two graduate degrees—in museum studies (museology) and a specialized subject—may give a candidate a distinct advantage in a competitive job market. In small museums, curatorial positions may be available to individuals with a bachelor's degree. Because curators, particularly those in small museums, may have administrative and managerial responsibilities, courses in business administration, public relations, marketing, and fundraising also are recommended. For some positions, an internship of full-time museum work supplemented by courses in museum practices is needed.

When hiring conservators, employers look for a master's degree in conservation or in a closely related field, together with substantial experience. There are only a few graduate programs in museum conservation techniques in the United States. Competition for entry to these programs is keen; to qualify, a student must have a background in chemistry, archaeology or studio art,

Archivists and curators plan and oversee the arrangement, cataloguing, and exhibition of collections.

and art history, as well as work experience. For some programs, knowledge of a foreign language also is helpful. Conservation apprenticeships or internships as an undergraduate can enhance one's admission prospects. Graduate programs last 2 to 4 years, the latter years of which include internship training. A few individuals enter conservation through apprenticeships with museums, nonprofit organizations, and conservators in private practice. Apprenticeships should be supplemented with courses in chemistry, studio art, and history. Apprenticeship training, although accepted, is a more difficult and increasingly scarce route into the conservation profession.

Museum technicians usually need a bachelor's degree in an appropriate discipline of the museum's specialty, training in museum studies, or previous experience working in museums, particularly in the design of exhibits. Similarly, archives technicians usually need a bachelor's degree in library science or history, or relevant work experience. Relatively few schools grant a bachelor's degree in museum studies. More common are undergraduate minors or tracks of study that are part of an undergraduate degree in a related field, such as art history, history, or archaeology. Students interested in further study may obtain a master's degree in museum studies, offered in colleges and universities throughout the country. However, many employers feel that, while museum studies are helpful, a thorough knowledge of the museum's specialty and museum work experience are more important.

Certification and other qualifications. The Academy of Certified Archivists offers voluntary certification for archivists. The designation "Certified Archivist" can be obtained by those with at least a master's degree and a year of appropriate archival experience. The certification process requires candidates to pass a written examination, and they must renew their certification periodically.

Archivists need research skills and analytical ability to understand the content of documents and the context in which they were created. They must also be able to decipher deteriorated or poor-quality printed matter, handwritten manuscripts, photographs, or films. A background in preservation management is often required of archivists because they are responsible for taking proper care of their records. Archivists also must be able

Projections data from the National Employment Matrix

Occupational Title	SOC Code	Employment, 2008	Projected Employment, 2018	Change, 2008-2018	
				Number	Percent
Archivists, curators, and museum technicians...................................	25-4010	29,100	35,000	5,900	20
Archivists	25-4011	6,300	6,700	400	7
Curators..	25-4012	11,700	14,400	2,700	23
Museum Technicians and Conservators..	25-4013	11,100	13,900	2,800	26

(NOTE) Data in this table are rounded. See the discussion of the employment projections table in the *Handbook* introductory chapter on *Occupational Information Included in the Handbook.*

to organize large amounts of information and write clear instructions for its retrieval and use. In addition, computer skills and the ability to work with electronic records and databases are very important. Because electronic records are becoming the prevalent form of recordkeeping, and archivists must create searchable databases, knowledge of Web technology may be required.

Curatorial positions often require knowledge in a number of fields. For historic and artistic conservation, courses in chemistry, physics, and art are desirable. Like archivists, curators need computer skills and the ability to work with electronic databases. Many curators are responsible for posting information on the Internet, so they also need to be familiar with digital imaging, scanning technology, and copyright law.

Curators must be flexible because of their wide variety of duties, including the design and presentation of exhibits. In small museums, curators need manual dexterity to build exhibits or restore objects. Leadership ability and business skills are important for museum directors, while marketing skills are valuable in increasing museum attendance and fundraising.

Advancement. Continuing education is available through meetings, conferences, and workshops sponsored by archival, historical, and museum associations. Some larger organizations, such as the National Archives in Washington, D.C., offer such training in-house.

Many archives, including one-person shops, are very small and have limited opportunities for promotion. Archivists typically advance by transferring to a larger unit that has supervisory positions. A doctorate in history, library science, or a related field may be needed for some advanced positions, such as director of a State archive.

In large museums, curators may advance through several levels of responsibility, eventually becoming the museum director. Curators in smaller museums often advance to larger ones. Individual research and publications are important for advancement in larger institutions.

Technician positions often serve as a steppingstone for individuals interested in archival and curatorial work. Except in small museums, a master's degree is needed for advancement.

Employment

Archivists, curators, and museum technicians held about 29,100 jobs in 2008. About 39 percent were employed in museums, historical sites, and similar institutions and 18 percent worked for public and private educational services. Around 30 percent of archivists, curators, and museum technicians worked in Federal, State, and local government, excluding educational institutions. Most Federal archivists work for the National Archives

and Records Administration; others manage military archives in the U.S. Department of Defense. Most Federal Government curators work at the Smithsonian Institution, in the military museums of the U.S. Department of Defense, and in archaeological and other museums and historic sites managed by the U.S. Department of the Interior. All State governments have archival or historical record sections employing archivists. State and local governments also have numerous historical museums, parks, libraries, and zoos employing curators.

Some large corporations that have archives or record centers employ archivists to manage the growing volume of records created or maintained as required by law or necessary to the firm's operations. Religious and fraternal organizations, professional associations, conservation organizations, major private collectors, and research firms also employ archivists and curators.

Conservators may work under contract to treat particular items, rather than as regular employees of a museum or other institution. These conservators may work on their own as private contractors, or they may work as an employee of a conservation laboratory or regional conservation center that contracts their services to museums. Most Federal conservators work for the Smithsonian Institution, Library of Congress, and National Archives and Records Administration.

Job Outlook

Much faster than average employment growth is projected. Keen competition is expected for most jobs as archivists, curators, and museum technicians because qualified applicants generally outnumber job openings.

Employment change. Employment of archivists, curators, and museum technicians is expected to increase 20 percent over the 2008-18 decade, which is much faster than the average for all occupations. Jobs for archivists are expected to increase as public and private organizations require organization of and access to increasing volumes of records and information. Public interest in science, art, history, and technology will continue, creating opportunities for curators, conservators, and museum technicians. Museum attendance is expected to continue to be good. Many museums remain financially healthy and will schedule building and renovation projects as money is available.

Demand for archivists who specialize in electronic records and records management will grow more rapidly than the demand for archivists who specialize in older media formats.

Job prospects. Keen competition is expected for most jobs as archivists, curators, and museum technicians because qualified applicants generally outnumber job openings. Graduates with highly specialized training, such as master's degrees in both library science and history, with a concentration in archives or records management and extensive computer skills, should have the best opportunities for jobs as archivists. Opportunities for those who manage electronic records are expected to be better than for those who specialize in older media formats.

Curator jobs, in particular, are attractive to many people, and many applicants have the necessary training and knowledge of the subject. But because there are relatively few openings, candidates may have to work part time, as an intern, or even as a volunteer assistant curator or research associate after completing their formal education. Substantial work experience in collection management, research, exhibit design, or restoration, as well as database management skills, will be necessary for permanent status.

Conservators also can expect competition for jobs. Competition is stiff for the limited number of openings in conservation graduate programs, and applicants need a technical background. Conservator program graduates with knowledge of a foreign language and a willingness to relocate will have better job opportunities.

Museums and other cultural institutions can be subject to cuts in funding during recessions or periods of budget tightening, reducing demand for these workers. Although the number of archivists and curators who move to other occupations is relatively low, the need to replace workers who retire or leave the occupation will create some job openings. However, workers in these occupations tend to work beyond the typical retirement age of workers in other occupations.

Earnings

Median annual wages of archivists in May 2008 were $45,020. The middle 50 percent earned between $34,050 and $60,150. The lowest 10 percent earned less than $26,600, and the highest 10 percent earned more than $76,790. Median annual wages of curators in May 2008 were $47,220. The middle 50 percent earned between $34,910 and $63,940. The lowest 10 percent earned less than $26,850, and the highest 10 percent earned more than $83,290. Median annual wages of museum technicians and conservators in May 2008 were $36,660. The middle 50 percent earned between $28,030 and $49,170. The lowest 10 percent earned less than $22,320, and the highest 10 percent earned more than $66,060.

In March 2009, the average annual salary for archivists in the Federal Government was $83,758; for museum curators, $90,205; for museum specialists and technicians, $62,520; and for archives technicians, $43,662.

Related Occupations

Other occupations that preserve, organize, and display objects or information of interest include:

	Page
Artists and related workers	301
Librarians	270

Social scientists, other (such as anthropologists, archeologists, or historians)

Sources of Additional Information

For information on archivists and on schools offering courses in archival studies, contact:

➤ Society of American Archivists, 17 North State St., Suite 1425, Chicago, IL 60602-3315. Internet: **http://www.archivists.org**

For general information about careers as a curator and schools offering courses in museum studies, contact:
➤ American Association of Museums, 1575 Eye St. NW., Suite 400, Washington, DC 20005. Internet: **http://www.aam-us.org**

For information about careers and education programs in conservation and preservation, contact:
➤ American Institute for Conservation of Historic and Artistic Works, 1156 15th St. NW., Suite 320, Washington, DC 20005-1714. Internet: **http://www.conservation-us.org**

For information about archivists and archivist certification, contact:
➤ Academy of Certified Archivists, 1450 Western Ave. Suite 101, Albany, NY 12203. Internet: **http://www.certifiedarchivists.org**

For information about government archivists, contact:
➤ National Association of Government Archivists and Records Administrators, 1450 Western Ave. Suite 101, Albany, NY 12203. Internet: **http://www.nagara.org**

Information on obtaining positions as archivists, curators, and museum technicians with the Federal Government is available from the Office of Personnel Management through USAJOBS, the Federal Government's official employment information system. This resource for locating and applying for job opportunities can be accessed through the Internet at **http://www.usajobs.opm.gov** or through an interactive voice response telephone system at (703) 724-1850 or TDD (978) 461-8404. These numbers are not toll free, and charges may result.

The Occupational Information Network (O*NET) provides information on a wide range of occupational characteristics. Links to O*NET appear at the end of the Internet version of this occupational statement, accessible at **http://www.bls.gov/ooh/ocos065.htm**

Instructional Coordinators

Significant Points

- Many instructional coordinators have experience as teachers or education administrators.

- A master's degree is required for positions in public schools and preferred for jobs in other settings.

- Employment is projected to grow much faster than average, reflecting the need to meet new educational standards, train teachers, and develop new materials.

- Favorable job prospects are expected.

Nature of the Work

Instructional coordinators—also known as *curriculum specialists*, *personnel development specialists*, *instructional coaches*, or *directors of instructional material*—play a large role in improving the quality of education in the classroom. They develop curricula, select textbooks and other materials, train teachers, and assess educational programs for quality and adherence to regulations and standards. They also assist in implementing new technology in the classroom. At the primary and secondary school levels, instructional coordinators often specialize in a specific subject, such as reading, language arts, mathematics, or science.

Instructional coordinators evaluate how well a school or training program's curriculum, or plan of study, meets students' needs. Based on their research and observations of instructional practice, they recommend improvements. They research teaching methods and techniques and develop procedures to ensure that instructors are implementing the curriculum successfully and meeting program goals. To aid in their evaluation, they may meet with members of educational committees and advisory groups to explore how curriculum materials relate to occupations and meet students' needs. Coordinators also may develop questionnaires and interview school staff about the curriculum.

Some instructional coordinators review textbooks, software, and other educational materials to make recommendations. They monitor the ways in which teachers use materials in the classroom and supervise workers who catalogue, distribute, and maintain a school's educational materials and equipment.

Some instructional coordinators find ways to use technology to enhance student learning and monitor the introduction of new technology into a school's curriculum. In addition, instructional coordinators might recommend educational software, such as interactive books and exercises designed to enhance student literacy and develop math skills. Instructional coordinators may invite experts to help integrate technological materials into the curriculum.

Besides developing curriculum and instructional materials, many of these workers plan and provide onsite education for teachers and administrators. Instructional coordinators mentor new teachers and train experienced ones in the latest instructional methods. This role becomes especially important when a school district introduces new content, programs, or a different organizational structure. For example, when a State or school district introduces standards or tests that students must pass, instructional coordinators often advise teachers on the content of those standards and provide instruction on how to implement them in the classroom.

Work environment.   Many instructional coordinators work long hours. They often work year round. Some spend much of their time traveling between schools and meeting with teachers and administrators. The opportunity to shape and improve instructional curricula and work in an academic environment can be satisfying. However, some instructional coordinators find the work stressful because they are continually accountable to school administrators.

Training, Other Qualifications, and Advancement

The minimum educational requirement for most instructional coordinator positions in public schools is a master's degree or higher—usually in education—plus a State teacher or administrator license. A master's degree also is preferred for positions in other settings.

Instructional coordinators evaluate how well a school or training program's curriculum meets students' needs.

Education and training.   Instructional coordinators should have training in curriculum development and instruction or in the specific field for which they are responsible, such as mathematics or history. Courses in research design teach how to create and implement research studies to determine the effectiveness of a given method of instruction or curriculum and how to measure and improve student performance.

Instructional coordinators are usually required to take continuing education courses to keep their skills current. Topics may include teacher evaluation techniques, curriculum training, new teacher orientation, consulting and teacher support, and observation and analysis of teaching.

Licensure.   Instructional coordinators must be licensed to work in public schools. Some States require a teaching license, whereas others require an education administrator license.

Other qualifications.   Instructional coordinators must have a good understanding of how to teach specific groups of students and expertise in developing educational materials. As a result, many people become instructional coordinators after working for several years as teachers. Also beneficial is work experience in an education administrator position, such as a principal or assistant principal, or in another advisory role, such as a master teacher, department chair or lead teacher.

Instructional coordinators must be able to make sound decisions about curriculum options and to organize and coordinate work efficiently. They should have strong interpersonal and communication skills. Familiarity with computer technology also is important for instructional coordinators, who are increasingly involved in gathering technical information for students and teachers.

Advancement.   Depending on experience and educational attainment, instructional coordinators may advance to higher administrative positions in a school system or to management or executive positions in private industry.

Employment

Instructional coordinators held about 133,900 jobs in 2008. About 70 percent worked in public or private educational institutions. Other employing industries included State and local

Projections data from the National Employment Matrix

Occupational Title	SOC Code	Employment, 2008	Projected Employment, 2018	Change, 2008-2018	
				Number	Percent
Instructional coordinators	25-9031	133,900	165,000	31,100	23

(NOTE) Data in this table are rounded. See the discussion of the employment projections table in the *Handbook* introductory chapter on *Occupational Information Included in the Handbook.*

government, individual and family services, and child day care services.

Job Outlook

Much faster than average job growth is projected. Job opportunities should be favorable, particularly for those with experience in math and reading curriculum development.

Employment change. The number of instructional coordinators is expected to grow by 23 percent over the 2008–18 decade, which is much faster than the average for all occupations. These workers will be instrumental in developing new curricula to meet the demands of a changing society and in training teachers. Although budget constraints may limit employment growth to some extent, a continuing emphasis on improving the quality of education should result in an increasing demand for these workers. The emphasis on accountability also should increase at all levels of government and cause more schools to focus on improving standards of educational quality and student performance. Growing numbers of coordinators will be needed to incorporate the new standards into existing curricula and ensure that teachers and administrators are informed of changes.

Additional job growth for instructional coordinators will stem from an increasing emphasis on lifelong learning and on programs for students with special needs, including those for whom English is a second language. These students often require more educational resources and consolidated planning and management within the educational system.

Job prospects. Favorable job prospects are expected. Opportunities should be best for those who specialize in subjects targeted for improvement by the No Child Left Behind Act—reading, math, and science. There also will be a need for more instructional coordinators to show teachers how to use technology in the classroom.

Earnings

Median annual wages of instructional coordinators in May 2008 were $56,880. The middle 50 percent earned between $42,070 and $75,000. The lowest 10 percent earned less than $31,800, and the highest 10 percent earned more than $93,250.

Related Occupations

Instructional coordinators are professionals involved in education, training, and development. Occupations with similar characteristics include:

Sources of Additional Information

Information on requirements and job opportunities for instructional coordinators is available from local school systems and State departments of education.

The Occupational Information Network (O*NET) provides information on a wide range of occupational characteristics. Links to O*NET appear at the end of the Internet version of this occupational statement, accessible at **http://www.bls.gov/ooh/ocos269.htm**

Librarians

Significant Points

- Librarians use the latest information technology to perform research, classify materials, and help students and library patrons seek information.

- A master's degree in library science is required for most librarian positions, although school librarians also often need to meet State teaching license requirements.

- Growth is expected to be as fast as the average and job opportunities are expected to be favorable, as a large number of librarians are likely to retire in the coming decade.

Nature of the Work

The traditional concept of a library is being redefined from a place to access paper records or books to one that also houses the most advanced electronic resources, including the Internet, digital libraries, and remote access to a wide range of information sources. Consequently, *librarians*, often called information professionals, combine traditional duties with tasks involving quickly changing technology. Librarians help people find information and use it effectively for personal and professional purposes. They must have knowledge of a wide variety of scholarly and public information sources and must follow trends related to publishing, computers, and the media to oversee the selection and organization of library materials. Librarians manage staff and develop and direct information programs and systems for the public and ensure that information is organized in a manner that meets users' needs.

Librarian positions focus on one of three aspects of library work: user services, technical services, and administrative services. Librarians in user services, such as reference and children's librarians, work with patrons to help them find the information they need. The job involves analyzing users' needs to determine what information is appropriate and searching for, acquiring, and providing the information. The job also includes an instructional role, such as showing users how to find and evaluate information. For example, librarians commonly help users navigate the Internet so they can search for and evaluate information efficiently. Librarians in technical services, such as acquisitions and cataloguing, acquire, prepare, and classify materials so patrons can find it easily. Some write abstracts and summaries. Often, these librarians do not deal directly with the public. Librarians in administrative services oversee the management and planning of libraries: they negotiate contracts for services, materials, and equipment; supervise library employees; perform public-relations and fundraising duties; prepare budgets; and direct activities to ensure that everything functions properly.

In small libraries or information centers, librarians usually handle all aspects of library operations. They read book reviews, publishers' announcements, and catalogues to keep up with current literature and other available resources, and they select and purchase materials from publishers, wholesalers, and distributors. Librarians prepare new materials, classifying them by subject matter and describing books and other library materials to make them easy to find. Librarians supervise assistants, who enter classification information and descriptions of materials into electronic catalogs. In large libraries, librarians often specialize in a single area, such as acquisitions, cataloguing, bibliography, reference, special collections, or administration. Therefore, good teamwork is important.

Librarians also recommend materials. Many analyze collections and compile lists of books, periodicals, articles, audiovisual materials, and electronic resources on particular subjects. They collect and organize books, pamphlets, manuscripts, and other materials in a specific field, such as rare books, genealogy, or music. In addition, they coordinate programs such as storytelling for children and literacy skills and book talks for adults. Some conduct classes, publicize services, write grants, and oversee other administrative matters.

Many libraries have access to remote databases and maintain their own computerized databases. The widespread use of electronic resources makes database-searching skills important for librarians. Librarians develop and index databases and help train users to develop searching skills. Some libraries are forming consortiums with other libraries to allow patrons to access a wider range of databases and to submit information requests to several libraries simultaneously. The Internet also has greatly expanded the amount of available reference information. Librarians must know how to use these resources and inform the public about the wealth of information they contain.

Librarians are classified according to the type of library in which they work: a public library; school library media center; college, university, or other academic library; or special library. Librarians in special libraries work in information centers or libraries maintained by government agencies or corporations, law firms, advertising agencies, museums, professional associations, unions, medical centers, hospitals, religious organizations, or research laboratories. They acquire and arrange an

Librarians help people find information and use it effectively for personal and professional purposes.

organization's information resources, which usually are limited to subjects of special interest to the organization. They can provide vital information services by preparing abstracts and indexes of current periodicals, organizing bibliographies, or analyzing background information and preparing reports on areas of particular interest. For example, a *special librarian* working for a corporation could provide the sales department with information on competitors or new developments affecting the field. A *medical librarian* may provide information about new medical treatments, clinical trials, and standard procedures to health professionals, patients, consumers, and corporations. *Government document librarians,* who work in a variety of depository libraries in each of the States, preserve and disseminate government publications, records, and other documents that make up a historical record of government actions.

Some librarians work with specific groups, such as children, young adults, adults, or the disadvantaged. In school library media centers, librarians—often called *school media specialists*—help teachers develop curricula and acquire materials for classroom instruction. They also conduct classes for students on how to use library resources for research projects.

Librarians with computer and information systems skills can work as *automated-systems librarians*, planning and operating computer systems, and as information architects, designing information storage and retrieval systems and developing procedures for collecting, organizing, interpreting, and classifying information. These librarians analyze and plan for future information needs. (See the section on computer scientists elsewhere in the *Handbook.*) Automated information systems enable librarians to focus on administrative and budgeting responsibilities, grant writing, and specialized research requests, while delegating more routine services responsibilities to technicians. (See the section on library technicians and library assistants elsewhere in the *Handbook.*)

More and more, librarians apply their information management and research skills to arenas outside of libraries—for example, database development, reference tool development, information systems, publishing, Internet coordination, marketing, Web content management and design, and training of database users. Entrepreneurial librarians sometimes start their own consulting practices, acting as freelance librarians or information brokers and providing services to other libraries, businesses, or government agencies.

Work environment. Librarians spend a significant portion of time at their desks or in front of computer terminals; extended work at video display terminals can cause eyestrain and headaches. Assisting users in obtaining information or books for their jobs, homework, or recreational reading can be challenging and satisfying, but working with users under deadlines can be demanding and stressful. Some librarians lift and carry books, and some climb ladders to reach high stacks, although most modern libraries have readily accessible stacks. Librarians in small settings without support staff sometimes shelve books themselves.

Twenty-five percent of librarians work part time. Public and college librarians often work weekends, evenings, and some holidays. School librarians usually have the same workday and vacation schedules as classroom teachers. Special librarians usually work normal business hours, but in fast-paced industries—such as advertising or legal services—they can work longer hours, when needed.

Training, Other Qualifications, and Advancement

A master's degree in library science (MLS) is necessary for librarian positions in most public, academic, and special libraries. School librarians may not need an MLS but must meet State teaching license requirements.

Education and training. Entry into a library science graduate program requires a bachelor's degree, but any undergraduate major is acceptable. Many colleges and universities offer library science programs, but employers often prefer graduates of the 49 schools in the United States accredited by the American Library Association. Most programs take 1 year to complete; some take 2. A typical graduate program includes courses in the foundations of library and information science, such as the history of books and printing, intellectual freedom and censorship, and the role of libraries and information in society. Other basic courses cover the selection and processing of materials, the organization of information, research methods and strategies, and user services. Prospective librarians also study online reference systems, Internet search methods, and automated circulation systems. Elective course options include resources for children or young adults; classification, cataloguing, indexing, and abstracting; and library administration. Computer-related course work is an increasingly important part of an MLS degree. Some programs offer interdisciplinary degrees combining technical courses in information science with traditional training in library science.

The MLS degree provides general preparation for library work, but some individuals specialize in a particular area, such as reference, technical services, or children's services. A Ph.D. in library and information science is advantageous for a college

teaching position or a top administrative job in a college or university library or large public library system.

Licensure. States generally have certification requirements for librarians in public schools and local libraries, though there are wide variations among States. School librarians in 20 States need a master's degree, either an MLS or a master's in education with a specialization in library media. In addition, over half of all States require that school librarians hold teacher certifications, although not all require teaching experience. Some States may also require librarians to pass a comprehensive assessment. Most States also have developed certification standards for local public libraries, although in some States these guidelines are voluntary.

Other qualifications. In addition to an MLS degree, librarians in a special library, such as a law or corporate library, usually supplement their education with knowledge of the field in which they are specializing, sometimes earning a master's, doctoral, or professional degree in the subject. Areas of specialization include medicine, law, business, engineering, and the natural and social sciences. For example, a librarian working for a law firm may hold both library science and law degrees, while medical librarians should have a strong background in the sciences. In some jobs, knowledge of a foreign language is needed.

Librarians participate in continuing education and training to stay up to date with new information systems and technology.

Advancement. Experienced librarians can advance to administrative positions, such as department head, library director, or chief information officer.

Employment

Librarians held about 159,900 jobs in 2008. About 59 percent were employed by public and private educational institutions and 27 percent were employed by local government.

Job Outlook

Job growth is expected to be as fast as the average and job opportunities are expected to be favorable, as a large number of librarians are likely to retire in the coming decade.

Employment change. Employment of librarians is expected to grow by 8 percent between 2008 and 2018, which is as fast as the average for all occupations. Growth in the number of librarians will be limited by government budget constraints and the increasing use of electronic resources. Both will result in the hiring of fewer librarians and the replacement of librarians with less costly library technicians and assistants. As electronic resources become more common and patrons and support staff become more familiar with their use, fewer librarians are needed to maintain and assist users with these resources. In addition, many libraries are equipped for users to access library resources directly from their homes or offices through library Web sites. Some users bypass librarians altogether and conduct research on their own. However, librarians continue to be in

Projections data from the National Employment Matrix

Occupational Title	SOC Code	Employment, 2008	Projected Employment, 2018	Change, 2008-2018	
				Number	Percent
Librarians	25-4021	159,900	172,400	12,500	8

(NOTE) Data in this table are rounded. See the discussion of the employment projections table in the *Handbook* introductory chapter on *Occupational Information Included in the Handbook.*

demand to manage staff, help users develop database-searching techniques, address complicated reference requests, choose materials, and help users to define their needs.

Jobs for librarians outside traditional settings will grow the fastest over the decade. Nontraditional librarian jobs include working as information brokers and working for private corporations, nonprofit organizations, and consulting firms. Many companies are turning to librarians because of their research and organizational skills and their knowledge of computer databases and library automation systems. Librarians can review vast amounts of information and analyze, evaluate, and organize it according to a company's specific needs. Librarians also are hired by organizations to set up information on the Internet. Librarians working in these settings may be classified as systems analysts, database specialists and trainers, webmasters or Web developers, or local area network (LAN) coordinators.

Job prospects. Job prospects are expected to be favorable. On average, workers in this occupation tend to be older than workers in the rest of the economy. As a result, there may be more workers retiring from this occupation than other occupations. However, relatively large numbers of graduates from MLS programs may cause competition in some areas and for some jobs.

Earnings

Salaries of librarians vary according to the individual's qualifications and the type, size, and location of the library. Librarians with primarily administrative duties often have greater earnings. Median annual wages of librarians in May 2008 were $52,530. The middle 50 percent earned between $42,240 and $65,300. The lowest 10 percent earned less than $33,190, and the highest 10 percent earned more than $81,130. Median annual wages in the industries employing the largest numbers of librarians in May 2008 were as follows:

Junior colleges	$55,250
Colleges, universities, and professional schools	55,180
Elementary and secondary schools	54,650
Other information services	48,060
Local government	47,940

The average annual salary for all librarians in the Federal Government in nonsupervisory, supervisory, and managerial positions was $84,796 in March 2009.

About 30 percent librarians were members of a union in 2008 or were covered under a union contract.

Related Occupations

Librarians play an important role in the transfer of knowledge and ideas by providing people with information. Jobs requiring similar analytical, organizational and communication skills include:

Sources of Additional Information

For information on a career as a librarian and information on accredited library education programs and scholarships, contact:
➤ American Library Association, Office for Human Resource Development and Recruitment, 50 East Huron St., Chicago, IL 60611. Internet: **http://www.ala.org/ala/educationcareers/index.cfm**

For information on a career as a special librarian, contact:
➤ Special Libraries Association, 331 South Patrick St., Alexandria, VA 22314-3501. Internet: **http://www.sla.org**

For information on a career as a law librarian, scholarship information, and a list of ALA-accredited schools offering programs in law librarianship, contact:
➤ American Association of Law Libraries, 105 W. Adams Street, Suite 3300, Chicago, IL 60603. Internet: **http://www.aallnet.org**

For information on employment opportunities for health sciences librarians and for scholarship information, credentialing information, and a list of MLA-accredited schools offering programs in health sciences librarianship, contact:
➤ Medical Library Association, 65 East Wacker Place, Suite 1900, Chicago, IL 60601-7246. Internet: **http://www.mlanet.org**

Information concerning requirements and application procedures for positions in the Library of Congress can be obtained directly from:
➤ Human Resources Office, Library of Congress, 101 Independence Ave. SE., Washington, DC 20540-2231. Internet: **http://www.loc.gov/hr**

State library agencies can furnish information on scholarships available through their offices, requirements for certification, and general information about career prospects in the particular State of interest. Several of these agencies maintain job hot lines reporting openings for librarians.

State departments of education can furnish information on certification requirements and job opportunities for school librarians.

The Occupational Information Network (O*NET) provides information on a wide range of occupational characteristics. Links to O*NET appear at the end of the Internet version of this occupational statement, accessible at **http://www.bls.gov/ooh/ocos068.htm**

Library Technicians and Library Assistants

Significant Points

- Improved technology enables library technicians to perform tasks once done by librarians.

- Training requirements range from a high school diploma to an associate degree, but computer skills are necessary for all workers.

- Job prospects should be good.

Nature of the Work

Library technicians and assistants help librarians acquire, prepare, and organize materials and assist users in locating the appropriate resources. These workers usually work under the supervision of a librarian, although they sometimes work independently. In small libraries, they handle a range of duties, while those in large libraries usually specialize. The duties of technicians and assistants are expanding and evolving as libraries increasingly use the Internet and other technologies to share information. They are increasingly responsible for daily library operations. Depending on where they work, these workers can have other titles, such as library technical assistant, media aide, library media assistant, library aide, or circulation assistant.

In some libraries, library technicians may have more responsibilities than library assistants. Technicians may be responsible for administering library programs, working with librarians to acquire new materials, and overseeing lower level staff. Assistants may be assigned more clerical duties, like shelving books, checking in returned material and assisting patrons with basic questions and requests.

Library technicians and assistants direct library users to standard references, organize and maintain periodicals, prepare volumes for binding, handle interlibrary loan requests, prepare invoices, perform routine cataloguing and coding of library materials and, retrieve information from computer databases. Some of these workers may supervise other support staff.

At the circulation desk, library technicians and assistants loan and collect books, periodicals, videotapes, and other materials. When an item is borrowed, assistants scan it and the patron's library card to record the transaction in the library database; they then stamp the due date on the item or print a receipt with the due date. When an item is returned, assistants inspect it for damage and scan it to record its return. Electronic circulation systems automatically generate notices reminding patrons that their materials are overdue, but library assistants may review the record for accuracy before sending out the notice. Library assistants also register new patrons and issue them library cards. They answer patrons' questions or refer them to a librarian.

The automation of recordkeeping has reduced the amount of clerical work performed by library technicians and assistants. Many libraries now offer self-service registration and circulation areas, where patrons can register for library cards and check out materials themselves. These technologies decrease the time library technicians spend recording and inputting records. At the same time, these systems require more of the technicians' time to ensure they continue to operate smoothly.

Throughout the library, assistants and technicians sort returned books, periodicals, and other items and put them on their designated shelves, in the appropriate files, or in storage areas. Before reshelving returned materials, they look for any damage and try to make repairs. For example, they may use tape or paste to repair torn pages or book covers and use other specialized processes to repair more valuable materials.

These workers may also locate materials being loaned to a patron or another library. Because nearly all library catalogs are computerized, they must be familiar with computers. They sometimes help patrons with computer searches.

Library technicians and assistants help librarians acquire, prepare, and organize materials and assist users in locating the appropriate resources.

Some library technicians and assistants specialize in helping patrons who have vision problems. Sometimes referred to as braille-and-talking-books clerks, these assistants review the borrower's list of desired reading materials, and locate those materials or close substitutes from the library collection of large-type or braille volumes and books on tape. They then give or mail the materials to the borrower.

Technicians and assistants also market library services. They participate in and help plan reader advisory programs, used-book sales, and outreach programs. They may also design posters, bulletin boards, or displays to inform patrons of library events and services.

As libraries increasingly use the Internet, virtual libraries, and other electronic resources, the duties of library technicians and assistants are changing. In fact, new technologies allow some of these workers to assume responsibilities which were previously performed only by librarians. They now catalog most new acquisitions and oversee the circulation of all library materials. They often maintain, update, and help customize electronic databases. They also may help to maintain the library's Web site and instruct patrons how to use the library's computers.

Some of these workers operate and maintain audiovisual equipment, such as projectors, tape and CD players, and DVD and videocassette players. They also assist users with microfilm or microfiche readers.

In school libraries, technicians and assistants encourage and teach students to use the library and media center. They also help teachers obtain instructional materials, and they assist students with assignments.

Some work in special libraries maintained by government agencies, corporations, law firms, advertising agencies, museums, professional societies, medical centers, or research laboratories. These technicians conduct literature searches, compile bibliographies, and prepare abstracts, usually on subjects of particular interest to the organization.

To extend library services to more patrons, many libraries operate bookmobiles that are often run by library technicians and assistants. They take bookmobiles—trucks stocked with books—to shopping centers, apartment complexes, schools, nursing homes, and other places. They may operate a bookmobile alone or with other library employees. Those who drive bookmobiles are responsible for answering patrons' questions, receiving and checking out books, collecting fines, maintaining the book collection, shelving materials, and occasionally operating audiovisual equipment to show slides or movies. They keep track of mileage and sometimes are responsible for maintenance of the vehicle and any equipment, such as photocopiers, in it. Many bookmobiles are equipped with personal computers linked to the main library Internet system, allowing patrons access to electronic resources.

Work environment. Library technicians and assistants who prepare library materials sit at desks or computer terminals for long periods and can develop headaches or eyestrain. They may lift and carry books, climb ladders to reach high stacks, and bend low to shelve books on bottom shelves. Workers who work in bookmobiles may assist handicapped or elderly patrons to the bookmobile or shovel snow to ensure their safety. They may enter hospitals or nursing homes to deliver books.

Workers in school libraries work regular school hours. Those in public libraries and college and university libraries may work weekends, evenings, and some holidays. In corporate libraries, workers usually work normal business hours, although they often work overtime as well. The schedules of workers who drive bookmobiles often depend on the size of the area being served. About 61 percent of library assistants work part time, making the job appealing to retirees, students, and others interested in flexible schedules.

Training, Other Qualifications, and Advancement
Training requirements for library technicians vary widely, ranging from a high school diploma to specialized postsecondary training. Some employers only hire individuals who have library work experience or college training related to libraries; others train inexperienced workers on the job.

Library assistants receive most of their training on the job. No formal education is required, although familiarity with computers is helpful.

Education and training. Most libraries prefer to hire technicians who have earned a certificate or associate degree, but some smaller libraries may hire individuals with only a high school diploma.

Many library technicians in public schools must meet the same requirements as teacher assistants. Those in Title 1 schools—schools that receive special funding because of the high percentage of low income students enrolled—must hold an associate or higher degree, have a minimum of 2 years of college, or pass a rigorous State or local exam.

Associate degree and certificate programs for library technicians include courses in liberal arts and subjects related to libraries. Students learn about library organization and operation and how to order, process, catalogue, locate, and circulate library materials and media. They often learn to use library automation systems. Libraries and associations offer continuing education courses to inform technicians of new developments in the field.

Training requirements for library assistants are generally minimal; most libraries prefer to hire workers with a high school diploma or GED, although libraries also hire high school students for these positions. No formal postsecondary training is expected. Some employers hire individuals with experience in other clerical jobs; others train inexperienced workers on the job.

Other qualifications. Given the rapid spread of automation in libraries, computer skills are a necessity. Knowledge of databases, library automation systems, online library systems, online public access systems, and circulation systems is particularly valuable. Many bookmobile drivers must have a commercial driver's license. Knowledge of databases and other library automation systems is especially useful. These workers should be able to pay close attention to detail, as the proper shelving or storage of materials is essential.

Advancement. Library technicians and assistants usually advance by assuming added responsibilities. For example, they often start at the circulation desk, checking books in and out. After gaining experience, they may become responsible for storing and verifying information. As they advance, they may become involved in budget and personnel matters. Some advance to supervisory positions and are in charge of the day-to-day operation of their departments or, sometimes, a small library. Those who earn a graduate degree in library sciences can become librarians.

Employment
Library technicians held about 120,600 jobs in 2008; about 51 percent were employed by local governments. The Federal Government employs library technicians primarily at the U.S. Department of Defense.

Library assistants held about 122,000 jobs in 2008. About 52 percent of these workers were employed by local governments.

Job Outlook
Employment of library technicians and assistants is expected to grow about 10 percent, which is about as fast as the average for all occupations. Opportunities will be best for those with specialized postsecondary library training. Prospects should be good, because many workers leave these jobs and need to be replaced.

Employment change. Between 2008 and 2018, the number of library technicians is expected to grow about 9 percent, which is about as fast as the average for all occupations and the number of library assistants is expected to grow by about 11 percent, which is about as fast as the average for all occupations. Increasing use of library automation creates more opportunities for these workers. Electronic information systems have simplified some tasks, enabling them to be performed by technicians, rather than librarians, and spurring demand for technicians. However, job growth in educational institutions will be limited by slowing enrollment growth. In addition, public libraries often face budget pressures, which hold down overall growth in library services. However, this may result in the hiring of more of these workers, because they are paid less than librarians and, thus, represent a lower-cost way to offer some library services. Employment should grow more rapidly in special libraries because increasing numbers of professionals and other workers use those libraries. Because these workers are largely employed by public institutions, they are not directly affected by the ups

Projections data from the National Employment Matrix

Occupational Title	SOC Code	Employment, 2008	Projected Employment, 2018	Change, 2008-2018	
				Number	Percent
Library technicians and library assistants...	–	242,500	266,700	24,200	10
Library technicians...	25-4031	120,600	131,200	10,600	9
Library assistants, clerical...	43-4121	122,000	135,500	13,500	11

(NOTE) Data in this table are rounded. See the discussion of the employment projections table in the *Handbook* introductory chapter on *Occupational Information Included in the Handbook.*

and downs of the business cycle, but they may be affected by changes in the level of government funding for libraries.

Job prospects. Job prospects should be favorable. In addition to job openings from employment growth, some openings will result from the need to replace library technicians who transfer to other occupations or leave the labor force. Opportunities will be best for library technicians with specialized postsecondary library training. Each year, many people leave this relatively low-paying occupation for other occupations that offer higher pay or full-time work. This creates good job opportunities for those who want to become library assistants.

Earnings

Median hourly wages of library technicians in May 2008 were $13.86. The middle 50 percent earned between $10.55 and $17.77. The lowest 10 percent earned less than $8.23, and the highest 10 percent earned more than $22.01. Median hourly wages in the industries employing the largest numbers of library technicians in May 2008 were as follows:

Colleges, universities, and professional schools	$15.91
Junior colleges...	15.15
Other information services....................................	13.59
Local government..	13.22
Elementary and secondary schools	13.03

Salaries of library technicians in the Federal Government averaged $44,265 in March 2009.

Median hourly wages of library assistants were $10.88 in May 2008. The middle 50 percent earned between $8.52 and $14.18. The lowest 10 percent earned less than $7.47, and the highest 10 percent earned more than $17.61.

Median hourly wages in the industries employing the largest numbers of library assistants in May 2008 were as follows:

Colleges, universities and professional schools	$12.92
Junior colleges...	12.07
Elementary and secondary schools	11.79
Local government..	10.21
Other information services....................................	9.61

Related Occupations

Library technicians and assistants perform organizational and administrative duties. Workers in other occupations with similar duties include:

Sources of Additional Information

For general career information on library technicians, including information on training programs, contact:

➤ American Library Association, Office for Human Resource Development and Recruitment, 50 East Huron St., Chicago, IL 60611. Internet: **http://www.ala.org/ala/educationcareers/index.cfm**

Information concerning requirements and application procedures for positions in the Library of Congress can be obtained directly from:

➤ Human Resources Office, Library of Congress, 101 Independence Ave. SE., Washington, DC 20540-2231. Internet: **http://www.loc.gov/hr**

State library agencies can furnish information on requirements for technicians and general information about career prospects in the State. Several of these agencies maintain job hot lines that report openings for library technicians.

State departments of education can furnish information on requirements and job opportunities for school library technicians.

The Occupational Information Network (O*NET) provides information on a wide range of occupational characteristics. Links to O*NET appear at the end of the Internet version of this occupational statement, accessible at **http://www.bls.gov/ooh/ocos316.htm**

Teacher Assistants

Significant Points

- Almost 40 percent of teacher assistants work part time.

- Educational requirements range from a high school diploma to some college training.

- Favorable job prospects are expected.

- Opportunities should be best for those with at least 2 years of formal postsecondary education, those with experience in helping special education students, or those who can speak a foreign language.

Nature of the Work

Teacher assistants provide instructional and clerical support for classroom teachers, allowing teachers more time for lesson planning and teaching. They support and assist children in learning class material using the teacher's lesson plans, providing students with individualized attention. Teacher assistants also supervise students in the cafeteria, schoolyard, and hallways, or on field trips; they record grades, set up equipment, and help prepare materials for instruction. Teacher assistants also are called teacher aides or instructional aides. Some assistants refer to themselves as paraprofessionals or paraeducators.

Some teacher assistants perform exclusively non-instructional or clerical tasks, such as monitoring nonacademic settings. Playground and lunchroom attendants are examples of such assistants. Most teacher assistants, however, perform a combination of instructional and clerical duties. They generally provide instructional reinforcement to children, under the direction and guidance of teachers. They work with students individually or in small groups—listening while students read, reviewing or reinforcing class lessons, or helping them find information for reports. At the secondary school level, teacher assistants often specialize in a certain subject, such as math or science. Teacher assistants often take charge of special projects and prepare equipment or exhibits, such as for a science demonstration. Some assistants work in computer laboratories, helping students to use computers and educational software programs.

In addition to instructing, assisting, and supervising students, teacher assistants may grade tests and papers, check homework, keep health and attendance records, do typing and filing, and duplicate materials. They also stock supplies, operate audiovisual equipment, and keep classroom equipment in order.

Teacher assistants support and assist children in learning class material, using the teacher's lesson plans.

Many teacher assistants work extensively with special education students. As schools become more inclusive and integrate special education students into general education classrooms, teacher assistants in both general education and special education classrooms increasingly assist students with disabilities. They attend to the physical needs of students with disabilities, including feeding, teaching grooming habits, and assisting students riding the school bus. They also provide personal attention to students with other special needs, such as those who speak English as a second language and those who need remedial education. Some work with young adults to help them obtain a job or to help them apply for community services that will support them after their schooling ends. Teacher assistants help assess a student's progress by observing the student's performance and recording relevant data.

Although the majority of teacher assistants work in primary and secondary educational settings, others work in preschools and other child care centers. Often, one or two assistants will work with a lead teacher in order to better provide the individual attention that young children require. In addition to assisting in educational instruction, teacher assistants supervise the children at play and assist in feeding and other basic care activities.

Teacher assistants also work with infants and toddlers who have developmental delays or other disabilities. Under the guidance of a teacher or therapist, teacher assistants perform exercises or play games to help the child develop physically and behaviorally.

Work environment. Teacher assistants work in a variety of settings—including preschools, child care centers, and religious and community centers, where they work with young adults—but most work in classrooms in elementary, middle, and secondary schools. They also may work outdoors, supervising recess when weather allows, and they may spend time standing, walking, or kneeling. However, many spend much of the day sitting while working with students.

Approximately 40 percent of teacher assistants work part time. Most assistants who provide educational instruction work the traditional 9-month to 10-month school year.

Seeing students develop and learn can be very rewarding. However, working closely with students can be both physically and emotionally tiring. Teacher assistants who work with special education students often perform more strenuous tasks, including lifting, as they help students with their daily routine. Those who perform clerical work may tire of administrative duties, such as copying materials or entering data.

Training, Other Qualifications, and Advancement

Training requirements for teacher assistants vary by State or school district and range from a high school diploma to some college training. Increasingly, employers are preferring applicants with some related college coursework.

Education and training. Many teacher assistants need only a high school diploma and on-the-job training. However, a college degree or related coursework in child development improves job opportunities. In fact, teacher assistants who work in Title 1 schools—those with a large proportion of students from low-income households—must have college train-

Projections data from the National Employment Matrix

Occupational Title	SOC Code	Employment, 2008	Projected Employment, 2018	Change, 2008-2018	
				Number	Percent
Teacher assistants...	25-9041	1,312,700	1,447,600	134,900	10

(NOTE) Data in this table are rounded. See the discussion of the employment projections table in the *Handbook* introductory chapter on *Occupational Information Included in the Handbook.*

ing or proven academic skills. They face Federal mandates that require assistants to hold a 2-year or higher degree, have a minimum of 2 years of college, or pass a rigorous State or local assessment.

A number of colleges offer associate degrees or certificate programs that either prepare graduates to work as teacher assistants or provide additional training for current teacher assistants.

All teacher assistants receive some on-the-job training. Teacher assistants need to become familiar with the school system and with the operation and rules of the school they work in. Those who tutor and review lessons must learn and understand the class materials and instructional methods used by the teacher. Teacher assistants also must know how to operate audiovisual equipment, keep records, and prepare instructional materials, as well as have adequate computer skills.

Other qualifications. Many schools require previous experience in working with children and a valid driver's license. Most require the applicant to pass a background check. Teacher assistants should enjoy working with children from a wide range of cultural backgrounds and be able to handle classroom situations with fairness and patience. Teacher assistants also must demonstrate initiative and a willingness to follow a teacher's directions. They must have good writing skills and be able to communicate effectively with students and teachers. Teacher assistants who speak a second language, especially Spanish, are in great demand for communicating with growing numbers of students and parents whose primary language is not English.

Advancement. Advancement for teacher assistants—usually in the form of higher earnings or increased responsibility—comes primarily with experience or additional education. Some school districts provide time away from the job or tuition reimbursement so that teacher assistants can earn their bachelor's degrees and pursue licensed teaching positions. In return for tuition reimbursement, assistants are often required to teach for a certain length of time in the school district.

Employment

Teacher assistants held about 1.3 million jobs in 2008. Many worked for public and private educational institutions. Child care centers and religious organizations employed most of the rest.

Job Outlook

Many job openings are expected for teacher assistants due to turnover and about as fast as the average employment growth in this large occupation, resulting in favorable job prospects.

Employment change. Employment of teacher assistants is expected to grow by 10 percent between 2008 and 2018, which is about as fast as the average for all occupations. School enroll-

ments are projected to increase slowly over the next decade, but faster growth is expected among special education students and students for whom English is a second language, and those students will increase as a share of the total school-age population. Teacher assistants often are necessary to provide these students with the attention they require.

Legislation that requires both students with disabilities and nonnative English speakers to receive an education equal to that of other students will continue to generate jobs for teacher assistants, who help to accommodate these students' special needs. Children with special needs require more personal attention, and teachers rely heavily on teacher assistants to provide much of that attention. An increasing number of afterschool programs and summer programs also will create new opportunities for teacher assistants.

The greater focus on school quality and accountability that has prevailed in recent years is likely to lead to an increased demand for teacher assistants as well. Growing numbers of teacher assistants may be needed to help teachers prepare students for standardized testing and to provide extra assistance to students who perform poorly on the tests. Job growth of assistants may be moderated, however, if schools are encouraged to hire more teachers for instructional purposes.

Job prospects. Favorable job prospects are expected. Opportunities for teacher assistant jobs should be best for those with at least 2 years of formal postsecondary education, those with experience in helping special education students, and those who can speak a foreign language. Demand is expected to vary by region of the country. Regions in which the population and school enrollments are expected to grow faster, such as many communities in the South and West, should have rapid growth in the demand for teacher assistants.

In addition to job openings stemming from employment growth, numerous openings will arise as assistants leave their jobs and must be replaced. Many assistant jobs require limited formal education and offer relatively low pay, so many workers transfer to other occupations or leave the labor force to assume family responsibilities, return to school, or for other reasons.

Although opportunities will be favorable, there may be a limited number of full-time positions because many school districts prefer to hire these workers part time.

Earnings

Median annual wages of teacher assistants in May 2008 were $22,200. The middle 50 percent earned between $17,610 and $28,180. The lowest 10 percent earned less than $15,340, and the highest 10 percent earned more than $33,980.

Full-time workers usually receive health coverage and other benefits. Teacher assistants who work part time ordinarily do not receive benefits. In 2008, about 37 percent of teacher assistants belonged to unions or were covered by a union contract—

mainly the American Federation of Teachers and the National Education Association—which bargain with school systems over wages, hours, and the terms and conditions of employment.

Related Occupations

Teacher assistants who instruct children have duties similar to those of

Sources of Additional Information

For information on teacher assistants, including training and certification, contact:

➤ American Federation of Teachers, Paraprofessional and School Related Personnel Division, 555 New Jersey Ave. NW., Washington, DC 20001. Internet: **http://www.aft.org/psrp/index.html**

➤ National Education Association, Educational Support Personnel Division, 1201 16th Street, NW., Washington, DC 20036. Internet: **http://www.nea.org/esphome**

➤ National Resource Center for Paraprofessionals, 6526 Old Main Hill, Utah State University, Logan, UT 84322. Internet: **http://www.nrcpara.org**

Human resource departments in school systems, school administrators, and State departments of education also can provide details about employment opportunities and required qualifications for teacher assistant jobs.

The Occupational Information Network (O*NET) provides information on a wide range of occupational characteristics. Links to O*NET appear at the end of the Internet version of this occupational statement, accessible at **http://www.bls.gov/ooh/ocos153.htm**

Teachers—Adult Literacy and Remedial Education

Significant Points

- Many adult literacy and remedial education teachers work part time and receive no benefits.

- Many programs require teachers to have at least a bachelor's degree; a public school teaching license may be required for publicly run programs in most States.

- Job opportunities are expected to be favorable, particularly for teachers of English to speakers of other languages.

Nature of the Work

Adult literacy and remedial education teachers instruct adults and out-of-school youths in reading, writing, speaking English, and math—skills to equip them to solve problems, improve their job opportunities, and further their education. The instruction provided by these teachers can be divided into three principal categories: adult basic education (ABE), which is geared toward adults whose skills are either at or below an eighth-grade level; adult secondary education (ASE), which is geared towards students who wish to obtain their General Educational Development (GED) certificate or other high school equivalency credential; and English literacy instruction for adults with limited proficiency in English. Many students in these adult education classes traditionally have been those who did not graduate from high school or who passed through school without acquiring the knowledge needed to meet their educational or career goals. Increasingly, students in these classes are immigrants or other people whose native language is not English. Educators who work with adult English-language learners are usually called teachers of English as a second language (ESL) or teachers of English to speakers of other languages (ESOL).

Adult basic education teachers teach basic academic courses in mathematics, languages, history, reading, writing, science, and other areas, using instructional methods geared toward adult learning. They teach these subjects to students 16 years of age and older who demonstrate the need to increase their skills in one or more of these subjects. Classes are taught to appeal to a variety of learning styles and usually include large-group, small-group, and one-on-one instruction. Because the students often are at different proficiency levels for different subjects, students' skills must be assessed beforehand. This assessment may be performed by the teacher, but is often performed by another member of the program staff. In many programs, the assessment is used to develop an individualized education plan for each student. Teachers are required to formally evaluate students periodically to determine their progress and potential for advancement to the next level. However, they informally evaluate their progress continuously.

Teachers in adult basic education may assist students in acquiring effective study skills and the self-confidence they need to reenter an academic environment. They also may encounter students with learning or physical disabilities that require additional expertise. These workers should possess an understanding of how to help these students achieve their goals, but they also may need to have the knowledge to detect challenges their students may face and provide them with access to a broader system of additional services to address these challenges.

Adult secondary education or GED teachers provide help in acquiring the necessary knowledge and skills to pass the test required to earn a GED. Earning a GED requires passing a series of five tests in reading, writing, mathematics, science, and social studies; most teachers instruct students in all subject areas. To help students pass the tests and succeed later in life, teachers not only provide subject matter instruction but also focus on improving the communication, information-processing, problem-solving, and critical-thinking skills necessary for further education and successful careers.

ESOL teachers or English Language Learners Teachers help adults to speak, listen, read, and write in English, often in the context of real-life situations to promote learning. Students learn writing and conversational skills or may focus on learning more academic or job-related communication skills depending on their skill level. ESOL teachers work with adults from a wide range of backgrounds. They need to be prepared to work with learners of all ages and from many different language backgrounds. Some students may have extensive educational experiences in their native countries, while others may have very little. As a result, some students may progress faster than others, so teachers must be able to tailor their instruction to the needs and abilities of their students. Because the teacher and students often do not share a common native language, creativity is an important part of fostering communication in the classroom and achieving learning goals. These workers teach students from a variety of cultural backgrounds and, therefore, they must be sensitive to differences in culture and backgrounds.

Teachers at all levels assist their students with finding additional resources in the community. This may include helping them find community resources such as healthcare, job placement agencies or other educational institutions for additional education, like community colleges or other postsecondary institutions.

All adult literacy and remedial teachers must prepare lessons beforehand, do any related paperwork, and stay current in their fields. Attendance for students is mostly voluntary and coursework is rarely graded. Because computers are increasingly being used to supplement instruction in basic skills and in teaching ESOL, many teachers also must learn the latest applications for computers in the classroom.

Work environment. Because many adult literacy and remedial education teachers work with adult students, they do not encounter some of the behavioral or social problems sometimes found with younger students. Adults attend by choice, are highly motivated, and may bring years of experience to the classroom—attributes that can make teaching these students rewarding and satisfying. However, some students may have had difficult experiences learning particular subjects or material in the past that creates roadblocks to learning that teachers must work to overcome. Also, many adult education programs are located in cramped facilities that lack modern amenities, which can be frustrating for teachers.

A large number of these teachers work part time. Some have several part-time teaching assignments or work full time in addition to their part-time teaching job. Classes for adults are held on days and at times that best accommodate students who may have job or family responsibilities, so evening and weekend work is common.

Training, Other Qualifications, and Advancement
Nearly all programs require teachers to have at least a bachelor's degree, but some require a master's degree in adult education or ESOL instruction. Some States require teachers to have a public school teacher license or a license specifically for adult education teachers.

Education and training. In most States, adult education teachers need at least a bachelor's degree, although some pro-

Adult literacy and remedial education teachers instruct adults in reading, writing, speaking English, and math.

grams prefer or require a master's degree. Programs may also prefer to hire those with teaching experience, especially with adults. Many colleges and universities offer master's degrees or graduate certificates in teaching adult education or ESOL, although some adult education programs offer classes or workshops on related topics relevant for their teachers. These include classes on teaching adults, using technology to teach, working with learners from a variety of cultures, and teaching adults with learning disabilities. ESOL teachers also should have courses or training in second-language acquisition theory and linguistics. In addition, knowledge of the citizenship and naturalization process may be useful. Knowledge of a second language is not necessary to teach ESOL students, but can be helpful in understanding the students' perspectives. GED teachers should know what is required to pass the GED and be able to instruct students in the subject matter.

Professional development among adult education and literacy teachers varies widely. Both part-time and full-time teachers are expected to participate in ongoing professional development activities in order to keep current on new developments in the field and to enhance skills already acquired. Each State's professional development system reflects the unique needs and organizational structure of that State. Attendance by teachers at professional development workshops and other activities is

Projections data from the National Employment Matrix

Occupational Title	SOC Code	Employment, 2008	Projected Employment, 2018	Change, 2008-2018	
				Number	Percent
Adult literacy, remedial education, and GED teachers and instructors..	25-3011	96,000	110,400	14,500	15

(NOTE) Data in this table are rounded. See the discussion of the employment projections table in the *Handbook* introductory chapter on *Occupational Information Included in the Handbook.*

often outlined in State or local policy. Some teachers are able to access professional development activities through alternative delivery systems such as the Internet or distance learning.

Licensure. Many States require teachers in these programs to have some form of license if they are employed in a State or local government-run program. Some States have specific licenses for adult education teachers, while others require a public school teacher license. Requirements for a license typically consist of a bachelor's degree and completion of an approved teacher training program.

Other qualifications. Adult education and literacy teachers must have the ability to work with students who come from a variety of cultural, educational, and economic backgrounds. They must be understanding and respectful of their students' circumstances and be familiar with their concerns. All teachers, both paid and volunteer, should be able to communicate well and motivate their students.

Advancement. Opportunities for advancement for adult education and literacy teachers vary from State to State and program to program. Some part-time teachers are able to move into full-time teaching positions or program administrator positions, such as coordinator or director, when such vacancies occur. Others may decide to use their classroom experience to move into policy work at a nonprofit organization or with the local, State, or Federal Government to perform research or to write teaching materials.

Employment

Teachers of adult literacy and remedial education held about 96,000 jobs in 2008. Additional teachers worked as unpaid volunteers. Many of the jobs are Federally funded, with additional funds coming from State and local governments. The majority of these teachers are employed by the educational services industry.

Job Outlook

Employment is expected to grow faster than average, and many job openings are expected due to the need to replace people who leave the occupation or retire. Job opportunities are expected to be favorable, particularly for teachers of English to speakers of other languages.

Employment change. Employment of adult literacy and remedial education teachers is expected to grow by 15 percent through 2018, which is faster than the average for all occupations. As employers increasingly require a more literate workforce, workers' demand for adult literacy, basic education, and secondary education classes is expected to grow. Significant employment growth is anticipated especially for ESOL teachers, who will be needed by the increasing number of immigrants and other residents living in this country who need to learn or improve their English skills. In addition, greater proportions of these groups are expected to take ESOL classes.

The demand for adult literacy and basic and secondary education often fluctuates with the economy. When the economy is good and workers are hard to find, employers may relax their standards and hire workers without a degree or GED or good proficiency in English. As the economy softens, employers can be more selective, and more students may find that they need additional education to get a job. In addition, adult education classes often are subject to changes in funding levels, which can cause the number of teaching jobs to fluctuate from year to year. In particular, budget pressures may limit Federal funding of adult education, which may cause programs to rely more on volunteers if other organizations and governments do not make up the difference. Other factors such as immigration policies and the relative prosperity of the United States compared with other countries also may have an impact on the number of immigrants entering this country and, consequently, on the demand for ESOL teachers.

Job prospects. Job prospects should be favorable as high turnover among part-time workers creates many openings. Opportunities will be best for ESOL teachers, particularly in States that have large populations of residents who have limited English skills—such as California, Florida, Texas, and New York. However, many other parts of the country have begun to attract large numbers of immigrants, making good opportunities in this field widely available.

Earnings

Median hourly wages of adult literacy and remedial education teachers were $22.26 in May 2008. The middle 50 percent earned between $16.65 and $29.78. The lowest 10 percent earned less than $12.48, and the highest 10 percent earned more than $38.95. Part-time adult literacy and remedial education instructors are usually paid by the hour or for each class that they teach, and receive few or no benefits. Full-time teachers are generally paid a salary and receive health insurance and other benefits if they work for a school system or government.

Related Occupations

Adult literacy and basic and secondary education teachers require a wide variety of skills and aptitudes. Not only must they be able to teach and motivate students (including, at times, those with learning disabilities), but they also must often take on roles as advisers and mentors. They may also work with people who speak different languages. Workers in other occupations that require these aptitudes include:

Sources of Additional Information

Information on adult literacy, basic and secondary education programs, and teacher certification requirements is available from State departments of education, local school districts, and literacy resource centers. Information also may be obtained through local religious and charitable organizations.

For information on adult education and family literacy programs, contact:

➤ The U.S. Department of Education, Office of Vocational and Adult Education, Potomac Center Plaza, 400 Maryland Ave. SW., Washington, DC 20202. Internet: **http://www.ed.gov/about/offices/list/ovae/index.html**

For information on teaching English as a second language, contact:

➤ The Center for Adult English Language Acquisition, 4646 40th St. NW., Suite 200, Washington, DC 20016. Internet: **http://www.cal.org/caela**

The Occupational Information Network (O*NET) provides information on a wide range of occupational characteristics. Links to O*NET appear at the end of the Internet version of this occupational statement, accessible at **http://www.bls.gov/ooh/ocos289.htm**

Teachers—Postsecondary

Significant Points

- Many postsecondary teachers find the environment intellectually stimulating and rewarding because they are surrounded by others who enjoy the subject.

- Educational qualifications range from expertise in a particular field to a Ph.D., depending on the subject taught and the type of educational institution.

- Competition is expected for tenure-track positions; better opportunities are expected for part-time or non-tenure-track positions.

- Ph.D. recipients should experience the best job prospects.

Nature of the Work

Postsecondary teachers instruct students in a wide variety of academic and vocational subjects beyond the high school level.

Most of these students are working toward a degree, but many others are studying for a certificate or certification to improve their knowledge or career skills. Postsecondary teachers include college and university faculty, postsecondary career and technical education teachers, and graduate teaching assistants. Teaching in any venue involves forming a lesson plan, presenting material to students, responding to students learning needs, and evaluating students' progress. In addition to teaching, postsecondary teachers, particularly those at 4-year colleges and universities, perform a significant amount of research in the subject they teach. They also must keep up with new developments in their field and may consult with government, business, nonprofit, and community organizations.

College and university faculty make up the majority of postsecondary teachers. Faculty usually are organized into departments or divisions based on academic subject or field. They typically teach several related courses in their subject—algebra, calculus, and statistics, for example. They may instruct undergraduate or graduate students or both. College and university faculty may give lectures to several hundred students in large halls, lead small seminars, or supervise students in laboratories. They prepare lectures, exercises, and laboratory experiments; grade exams and papers; and advise and work with students individually. In universities, they also supervise graduate students' teaching and research. College faculty work with an increasingly varied student population made up of growing shares of part-time, older, and culturally and racially diverse students.

Faculty keep up with developments in their field by reading current literature, talking with colleagues, and participating in professional conferences. They also are encouraged to do their own research to expand knowledge in their field by performing experiments, collecting and analyzing data, or examining original documents, literature, and other source material. They publish their findings in scholarly journals, books, and electronic media.

Most postsecondary teachers use computer technology extensively, including the Internet, e-mail, and software programs. They may use computers in the classroom as teaching aids and may post course content, class notes, class schedules, and other information on the Internet. The use of e-mail, instant messages, and other computer utilities has improved communications greatly between students and teachers.

Some instructors use the Internet to teach courses to students at remote sites. These distance-learning courses are becoming an increasingly popular option for students who work while attending school. Faculty who teach these courses must be able to adapt existing courses to make them successful online or design a new course that takes advantage of the online format.

Most full-time faculty members serve on academic or administrative committees that deal with the policies of their institution, departmental matters, academic issues, curricula, budgets, purchases of equipment, and hiring. Some work with student and community organizations. Department chairpersons are faculty members who usually teach some courses but have heavier administrative responsibilities.

The proportion of time spent on research, teaching, administrative, and other duties varies by individual circumstance and type of institution. The teaching load often is heavier in 2-year

Postsecondary teachers instruct students in a wide variety of academic and vocational subjects beyond the high school level.

colleges and somewhat lighter at 4-year institutions. At all types of institutions, full professors—those who have reached the highest level in their field—usually spend a larger portion of their time conducting research than do assistant professors, instructors, and lecturers.

An increasing number of postsecondary educators are working in alternative schools or in programs aimed at providing career-related education for working adults. Courses usually are offered online or on nights and weekends. Instructors at these programs generally work part time and are responsible only for teaching, with little to no administrative and research responsibilities.

Graduate teaching assistants, often referred to as graduate TAs, assist faculty, department chairs, or other professional staff at colleges and universities by teaching or performing teaching-related duties. In addition, assistants have their own school commitments as students working toward earning a graduate degree, such as a Ph.D. Some teaching assistants have full responsibility for teaching a course, usually one that is introductory. Such teaching can include preparing lectures and exams, as well as assigning final grades to students. Others help faculty members by doing a variety of tasks such as grading papers, monitoring exams, holding office hours or help sessions for students, conducting laboratory sessions, and administering

quizzes to the class. Because each faculty member has his or her own needs, teaching assistants generally meet initially with the faculty member whom they are going to assist in order to determine exactly what is expected of them. For example, some faculty members prefer assistants to sit in on classes, whereas others assign them other tasks to do during class time. Graduate teaching assistants may work one-on-one with a faculty member, or, in large classes, they may be one of several assistants.

Work environment. Many postsecondary teachers find the environment intellectually stimulating and rewarding because they are surrounded by others who enjoy the subject. The ability to share their expertise with others also is appealing to many.

Most postsecondary teachers have flexible schedules. They must be present for classes, usually 12 to 16 hours per week, and for faculty and committee meetings. Most establish regular office hours for student consultations, usually 3 to 6 hours per week. Otherwise, teachers are free to decide when and where they will work and how much time to devote to course preparation, grading, study, research, graduate student supervision, and other activities.

Classes typically are scheduled to take place during weekdays, although some occur at night or on the weekend. For teachers at 2-year community colleges or institutions with large enrollments of older students who have full-time jobs or family responsibilities, night and weekend classes are common. Most colleges and universities require teachers to work 9 months of the year, which allows them time to teach additional courses, do research, travel, or pursue nonacademic interests during the summer and on school holidays.

About 29 percent of postsecondary teachers worked part time in 2008. Some part-timers, known as adjunct faculty, have primary jobs outside of academia—in government, private-industry, or nonprofit research organizations—and teach on the side. Others have multiple part-time teaching positions at different institutions. Most graduate teaching assistants work part time while pursuing their graduate studies. The number of hours that they work may vary with their assignments.

University faculty may experience a conflict between their responsibility to teach students and the pressure to do research and publish their findings. This may be a particular problem for young faculty seeking advancement in 4-year research universities. Also, recent cutbacks in support workers and the hiring of more part-time faculty have put a greater administrative burden on full-time faculty. In addition, requirements to teach online classes have added greatly to the workloads of postsecondary teachers. Many find that developing the courses to put online is very time consuming, especially when they have to familiarize themselves with the format and answer large amounts of e-mail.

Like college and university faculty, graduate TAs usually have flexibility in their work schedules, but they also must spend a considerable amount of time pursuing their own academic coursework and studies. Work may be stressful, particularly when assistants are given full responsibility for teaching a class. However, these types of positions allow graduate students the opportunity to gain valuable teaching experience, which is especially helpful for those who seek to become college faculty members after completing their degree.

Training, Other Qualifications, and Advancement

The education and training required of postsecondary teachers varies widely, depending on the subject taught and the educational institution employing them. Educational requirements for teachers generally are highest at research universities, where a Ph.D. is the most commonly held degree.

Education and training. Four-year colleges and universities usually require candidates for full-time, tenure-track positions to hold a doctoral degree. However, they may hire master's degree holders or doctoral candidates for certain disciplines, such as the arts, or for part-time and temporary jobs.

Doctoral programs take an average of 6 years of full-time study beyond the bachelor's degree, including time spent completing a master's degree and a dissertation. Some programs, such as those in the humanities, may take longer to complete; others, such as those in engineering, usually are shorter. Candidates specialize in a subfield of a discipline—for example, organic chemistry, counseling psychology, or European history—and also take courses covering the entire discipline. Programs typically include 20 or more increasingly specialized courses and seminars, plus comprehensive examinations in all major areas of the field. Candidates also must complete a dissertation—a paper on original research in the candidate's major field of study. The dissertation sets forth an original hypothesis or proposes a model and tests it. Students in the natural sciences and engineering often do theoretical or laboratory work; in the humanities, they study original documents and other published material. The dissertation is done under the guidance of one or more faculty advisors and usually takes 1 or 2 years of full-time work.

In 2-year colleges, master's degree holders fill most full-time teaching positions. However, in certain fields where there may be more applicants than available jobs, institutions can be more selective in their hiring practices. In these fields, master's degree holders may be passed over in favor of candidates holding Ph.D.s. Many 2-year institutions increasingly prefer job applicants to have some teaching experience or experience with distance learning. Preference also may be given to those holding dual master's degrees, especially at smaller institutions, because those with dual degrees can teach more subjects.

Other qualifications. Postsecondary teachers should communicate and relate well with students, enjoy working with them, and be able to motivate them. They should have inquiring and analytical minds and a strong desire to pursue and disseminate knowledge. In addition, they must be self-motivated and able to work in an environment in which they receive little direct supervision.

Obtaining a position as a graduate teaching assistant is a good way to gain college teaching experience. To qualify, candidates must be enrolled in a graduate school program. In addition, some colleges and universities require teaching assistants to attend classes or take some training prior to being given responsibility for a course.

Although graduate teaching assistants usually work at the institution and in the department where they are earning their degree, teaching or internship positions for graduate students at institutions that do not grant a graduate degree have become more common in recent years. For example, a program called Preparing Future Faculty, administered by the Association of American Colleges and Universities and the Council of Graduate Schools, has led to the creation of many programs that are now independent. These programs offer graduate students at research universities the opportunity to work as teaching assistants at other types of institutions, such as liberal arts or community colleges. Working with a mentor, graduate students teach classes and learn how to improve their teaching techniques. They may attend faculty and committee meetings, develop a curriculum, and learn how to balance the teaching, research, and administrative roles of faculty. These programs provide valuable learning opportunities for graduate students interested in teaching at the postsecondary level and also help to make these students aware of the differences among the various types of institutions at which they may someday work.

Some degree holders, particularly those with degrees in the natural sciences, do postdoctoral research before taking a faculty position. Some Ph.D.s are able to extend postdoctoral appointments or take new ones if they are unable to find a faculty job. Most of these appointments offer a nominal salary.

Advancement. For faculty a major goal in the traditional academic career is attaining tenure, which can take approximately 7 years, with faculty moving up the ranks in tenure-track positions as they meet specific criteria. The ranks are instructor, assistant professor, associate professor, and professor. Colleges and universities usually hire new tenure-track faculty as instructors or assistant professors under term contracts. At the end of the period, their record of teaching, research, and overall contribution to the institution is reviewed, and tenure may be granted if the review is favorable. Those denied tenure usually must leave the institution. Tenured professors cannot be fired without just cause and due process. Tenure protects the faculty member's academic freedom—the ability to advocate controversial or unpopular ideas through teaching and conducting research without fear of being fired. Tenure also gives both faculty and institutions the stability needed for effective research and teaching, and it provides financial security for faculty. Some institutions have adopted post-tenure review policies to encourage ongoing evaluation of tenured faculty.

The number of tenure-track positions is declining as institutions seek flexibility in dealing with financial matters and changing student interests. Institutions are relying more heavily on limited-term contracts and part-time, or adjunct, faculty, thus shrinking the total pool of tenured faculty. Limited-term

Projections data from the National Employment Matrix

Occupational Title	SOC Code	Employment, 2008	Projected Employment, 2018	Change, 2008-2018	
				Number	Percent
Postsecondary teachers	25-1000	1,699,200	1,956,100	256,900	15

(NOTE) Data in this table are rounded. See the discussion of the employment projections table in the *Handbook* introductory chapter on *Occupational Information Included in the Handbook.*

contracts, typically for 2 to 5 years, may be terminated or extended when they expire and generally do not lead to the granting of tenure. In addition, some institutions have limited the percentage of the faculty that can be tenured.

For tenured postsecondary teachers, further advancement involves a move into an administrative or managerial position, such as departmental chairperson, dean, or president. At 4-year institutions, such advancement requires a doctoral degree. At 2-year colleges, a doctorate is helpful but not usually required for advancement, except for advancement to some top administrative positions, which generally required a doctorate. (Deans and departmental chairpersons are covered in the *Handbook* statement on education administrators, while college presidents are included in the Handbook statement on top executives.)

Employment

Postsecondary teachers held nearly 1.7 million jobs in 2008. The following tabulation shows postsecondary teaching jobs in specialties having 20,000 or more jobs in 2008:

Graduate teaching assistants	159,700
Health specialties teachers	155,300
Vocational education teachers	120,200
Art, drama, and music teachers	93,800
Business teachers	85,400
English language and literature teachers	74,800
Education teachers	70,200
Biological science teachers	64,700
Nursing instructors and teachers	55,100
Mathematical science teachers	54,800
Engineering teachers	40,600
Psychology teachers	38,900
Computer science teachers	38,800
Foreign language and literature teachers	32,100
Communications teachers	29,900
History teachers	26,000
Philosophy and religion teachers	25,100
Chemistry teachers	24,800
Recreation and fitness studies teachers	21,000
Sociology teachers	20,300
Postsecondary teachers, all other	298,000

Job Outlook

Job openings will stem from faster than the average employment growth and many expected retirements. Competition is expected for tenure-track positions; better opportunities are expected for part-time or non-tenure-track positions. Ph.D. recipients should experience the best job prospects.

Employment change. Postsecondary teachers are expected to grow by 15 percent between 2008 and 2018, which is faster than the average for all occupations. Projected growth in the occupation will be due primarily to increases in college and university enrollment over the next decade. This enrollment growth stems mainly from the expected increase in the population of 18- to 24-year-olds, who constitute the majority of students at postsecondary institutions, and from the increasing number of high school graduates who choose to attend these institutions. Adults returning to college to enhance their career prospects or to update their skills also will continue to create new opportunities for postsecondary teachers, par-

ticularly at community colleges and for-profit institutions that cater to working adults. However, many postsecondary educational institutions receive a significant portion of their funding from State and local governments, so expansion of public higher education will be limited by State and local budgets.

Job prospects. Competition is expected for tenure-track positions; better opportunities are expected for part-time or non-tenure-track positions. A significant number of openings in this occupation will be created by growth in enrollments and the need to replace the large numbers of postsecondary teachers who are likely to retire over the next decade. Many postsecondary teachers were hired in the late 1960s and the 1970s to teach members of the baby-boom generation, and they are expected to retire in growing numbers in the years ahead. Ph.D. recipients should experience the best job prospects.

Although competition will remain tight for tenure-track positions at 4-year colleges and universities, there will be available a considerable number of part-time and renewable term appointments at these institutions and at community colleges. Opportunities will be available for master's degree holders because there will be considerable growth at community colleges, career education programs, and other institutions that employ them.

Opportunities for graduate teaching assistants are expected to be good, reflecting expectations of higher undergraduate enrollments. Graduate teaching assistants play an integral role in the postsecondary education system, and they are expected to continue to do so in the future.

One of the main reasons students attend postsecondary institutions is to prepare themselves for careers, so the best job prospects for postsecondary teachers are likely to be in rapidly growing fields that offer many nonacademic career options, such as business, nursing and other health specialties, and biological sciences.

Earnings

Median annual earnings of all postsecondary teachers in May 2008 were $58,830. The middle 50 percent earned between $41,600 and $83,960. The lowest 10 percent earned less than $28,870, and the highest 10 percent earned more than $121,850.

Earnings for college faculty vary with the rank and type of institution, geographic area, and field. According to a 2008–09 survey by the American Association of University Professors, salaries for full-time faculty averaged $79,439. By rank, the average was $108,749 for professors, $76,147 for associate professors, $63,827 for assistant professors, $45,977 for instructors, and $52,436 for lecturers. In 2008–09, full-time faculty salaries averaged $92,257 in private independent institutions, $77,009 in public institutions, and $71,857 in religiously affiliated private colleges and universities. Faculty in 4-year institutions earn higher salaries, on average, than do those in 2-year schools. In fields with high-paying nonacademic alternatives—medicine, law, engineering, and business, among others—earnings exceed these averages. In others fields, such as the humanities and education, earnings are lower. Earnings for postsecondary career and technical education teachers vary widely by subject, academic credentials, experience, and region of the country.

Many faculty members have significant earnings from consulting, teaching additional courses, research, writing for publication, or other employment, in addition to their base salary. Many college and university faculty enjoy unique benefits, including access to campus facilities, tuition waivers for dependents, housing and travel allowances, and paid leave for sabbaticals. Part-time faculty and instructors usually have fewer benefits than full-time faculty have.

Related Occupations

Postsecondary teaching requires the ability to communicate ideas well, motivate students, and be creative. Workers in other occupations that require these skills are:

Sources of Additional Information

Professional societies related to a field of study often provide information on academic and nonacademic employment opportunities. Names and addresses of many of these societies appear in statements elsewhere in the *Handbook*.

Special publications on higher education, such as The Chronicle of Higher Education, list specific employment opportunities for faculty. These publications are available in libraries.

For information on the Preparing Future Faculty program, contact:

➤ Council of Graduate Schools, One Dupont Circle NW., Suite 230, Washington, DC 20036-1173. Internet: **http://www.preparing-faculty.org**

The Occupational Information Network (O*NET) provides information on a wide range of occupational characteristics. Links to O*NET appear at the end of the Internet version of this occupational statement, accessible at **http://www.bls.gov/ooh/ocos066.htm**

Teachers—Preschool, Except Special Education

Significant Points

- Training requirements are set by each State and range from a high school diploma to a college degree, although a high school diploma and a little experience is adequate for many preschool teaching jobs.

- Employment of preschool teachers is projected to grow faster than the average through 2018. Job prospects are expected to be excellent due to high turnover.

Nature of the Work

Preschool teachers nurture, teach, and care for children who have not yet entered kindergarten. They provide early childhood care and education through a variety of teaching strategies. They teach children, usually aged 3 to 5, both in groups and one on one. They do so by planning and implementing a curriculum that covers various areas of a child's development, such as motor skills, social and emotional development, and language development.

Preschool teachers play a vital role in the development of children. They introduce children to reading and writing, expanded vocabulary, creative arts, science, and social studies. They use games, music, artwork, films, books, computers, and other tools to teach concepts and skills.

Preschool children learn mainly through investigation, play, and formal teaching. Preschool teachers capitalize on children's play to further language and vocabulary development (using storytelling, rhyming games, and acting games), improve social skills (having the children work together to build a neighborhood in a sandbox), and introduce scientific and mathematical concepts (showing the children how to balance and count blocks when building a bridge or how to mix colors when painting). Thus, an approach that includes small and large group activities, one-on-one instruction, and learning through

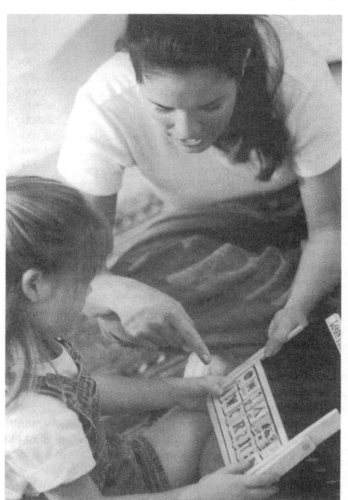

Preschool teachers nurture, teach, and care for children who have not yet entered kindergarten.

Projections data from the National Employment Matrix

Occupational Title	SOC Code	Employment, 2008	Projected Employment, 2018	Change, 2008-2018	
				Number	Percent
Preschool teachers, except special education....................................	25-2011	457,200	543,900	86,700	19

(NOTE) Data in this table are rounded. See the discussion of the employment projections table in the *Handbook* introductory chapter on *Occupational Information Included in the Handbook.*

creative activities such as art, dance, and music, is adopted to teach preschool children. Letter recognition, phonics, numbers, and awareness of nature and science are introduced at the preschool level to prepare students for kindergarten.

Preschool teachers often work with students from varied ethnic, racial, and religious backgrounds. With growing minority populations in most parts of the country, it is important for teachers to be able to work effectively with a diverse student population. Accordingly, some schools offer training to help teachers enhance their awareness and understanding of different cultures. Teachers may also include multicultural programming in their lesson plans, to address the needs of all students, regardless of their cultural background.

Work environment. Seeing students develop new skills and gain an appreciation of knowledge and learning can be very rewarding. Preschool teachers in private programs and schools generally enjoy smaller class sizes and more control over establishing the curriculum and setting standards for performance and discipline.

Part-time schedules are common among preschool teachers. Many teachers work the traditional 10-month school year with a 2-month vacation during the summer. During the vacation break, those on the 10-month schedule may teach in summer sessions, take other jobs, travel, or pursue personal interests. Many enroll in college courses or workshops to continue their education. Teachers in districts with a year-round schedule typically work 8 weeks, are on vacation for 1 week, and have a 5-week midwinter break. Preschool teachers working in day care settings often work year round.

Training, Other Qualifications, and Advancement
Education requirements vary greatly from State to State and range from a high school diploma to a college degree. The requirements also vary based on employer requirements and the source of the funding of the preschool program.

Education and training. The training and qualifications required of preschool teachers vary widely. Each State has its own licensing requirements that regulate caregiver training. These requirements range from a high school diploma and a national Child Development Associate (CDA) credential to community college courses or a college degree in child development or early childhood education.

Different public funding streams may set other education and professional development requirements. For example, many States have separate funding for prekindergarten programs for 4-year-old children and typically set higher education degree requirements for those teachers, including those providing prekindergarten in a child care center. Head Start programs must meet Federal standards for teacher requirements. For example, by 2011 all Head Start teachers must have at least an associate degree.

Some employers may prefer workers who have taken secondary or postsecondary courses in child development and early childhood education or who have work experience in a child care setting. Other employers require their own specialized training. An increasing number of employers require at least an associate degree in early childhood education

Other qualifications. In addition to being knowledgeable about the subjects they teach, preschool teachers must have the ability to communicate, inspire trust and confidence, and motivate students, as well as an understanding of the students' educational and emotional needs. Preschool teachers must be able to recognize and respond to individual and cultural differences in students and employ different teaching methods that will result in higher student achievement. They should be organized, dependable, patient, and creative. Teachers also must be able to work cooperatively and communicate effectively with other teachers, support staff, parents, and members of the community. Private schools associated with religious institutions also desire candidates who share the values that are important to the institution.

Advancement. Preschool teachers usually work their way up from assistant teacher, to teacher, to lead teacher—who may be responsible for the instruction of several classes—and, finally, to director of the center. Those with a bachelor's degree frequently are qualified to teach kindergarten through grade 3 as well. Teaching at these higher grades often results in higher pay.

Employment
Preschool teachers, except special education, held 457,200 jobs in 2008. They are most often employed in child day care services (65 percent), and public and private educational services (15 percent). Employment of teachers is geographically distributed much the same as the population.

Job Outlook
Employment of preschool teachers is projected to grow faster than the average through 2018. Job prospects are expected to be excellent due to high turnover.

Employment change. Employment of preschool teachers is expected to grow by 19 percent from 2008 to 2018, which is faster than the average for all occupations. Continued emphasis on early childhood education is increasing the demand for preschool teachers. Some States are instituting programs to improve early childhood education, such as offering full day and universal preschool. These programs, along with projected higher enrollment growth for preschool age children, will create new jobs for preschool teachers.

However, this growth will be moderated by slower growth in the number of children aged 3 to 5, the age group most often enrolled in preschool programs. In addition, these workers are often assisted by child care workers and teachers assistants and higher demand for these workers may temper growth for preschool teachers.

Job prospects. High replacement needs should create good job opportunities for preschool teachers. Qualified persons who are interested in this work should have little trouble finding and keeping a job. Many preschool teachers must be replaced each year as they leave the occupation to fulfill family responsibilities, to study, or for other reasons. Others leave because they are interested in pursuing other occupations or because of low wages.

Earnings
Median annual wages of preschool teachers were $23,870 in May 2008; the middle 50 percent earned $18,840 to $31,430; the bottom 10 percent earned less than $16,030 and the top 10 percent earned more than $41,660.

Related Occupations
Preschool teaching requires a talent for working with young children; related occupations include the following:

Sources of Additional Information
Information on licensure or certification requirements and approved teacher training institutions is available from local school systems and State departments of education.

For information on careers in educating children and issues affecting preschool teachers, contact either of the following organizations:

➤ National Association for the Education of Young Children, 1313 L St. NW., Suite 500, Washington, DC 20005. Internet: **http://www.naeyc.org**

➤ Council for Professional Recognition, 2460 16th St. NW., Washington, DC 20009-3575. Internet: **http://www.cdacouncil.org**

The Occupational Information Network (O*NET) provides information on a wide range of occupational characteristics. Links to O*NET appear at the end of the Internet version of this occupational statement, accessible at **http://www.bls.gov/ooh/ocos317.htm**

Teachers—Kindergarten, Elementary, Middle, and Secondary

Significant Points

- Public school teachers must be licensed, which typically requires a bachelor's degree and the completion of an approved teacher education program; private school teachers do not have to be licensed but may still need a bachelor's degree.

- Many States offer alternative licensing programs to attract people into teaching, especially for hard-to-fill positions.

- Teachers must have the ability to communicate, inspire trust and confidence, and motivate students, as well as understand students' educational and emotional needs.

- Job prospects are best for teachers in high-demand fields, such as mathematics, science, and bilingual education, and in less desirable urban or rural school districts.

Nature of the Work
Teachers play an important role in fostering the intellectual and social development of children during their formative years. The education that students acquire is key to determining the future of those students. Whether in elementary or high schools or in private or public schools, teachers provide the tools and the environment for their students to develop into responsible adults.

Teachers act as facilitators or coaches, using classroom presentations or individual instruction to help students learn and apply concepts in subjects such as science, mathematics, and English. They plan, evaluate, and assign lessons; prepare, administer, and grade tests; listen to oral presentations; and maintain classroom discipline. Teachers observe and evaluate a student's performance and potential. They are increasingly asked to use new assessment methods. For example, teachers may examine a portfolio of a student's artwork or writing in order to judge the student's overall progress. They then can provide additional assistance in areas in which the student needs help. Teachers also grade papers, prepare report cards, and meet with parents and school staff to discuss a student's academic progress or personal problems.

Many teachers use a hands-on approach that utilizes props to help children understand abstract concepts, solve problems, and develop critical thinking skills. For example, they may teach the concepts of numbers or of addition and subtraction by playing board games. As the children get older, teachers use more sophisticated approaches, such as demonstrating science experiments or working with computers. They also encourage collaboration in solving problems by having students work in groups to discuss and solve the problems together. To be prepared for success later in life, students must be able to interact with others, adapt to new technology, and think through problems logically.

Kindergarten and elementary school teachers play a vital role in the development of children. What children learn and experience during their early years can shape their views of themselves and the world and can affect their later success or failure in school, work, and their personal lives. Kindergarten and elementary school teachers introduce children to mathematics, language, science, and social studies. They use games, music, artwork, films, books, computers, and other tools to teach basic skills.

Kindergarten teachers use play and hands-on teaching, but academics begin to take priority in kindergarten classrooms. Letter recognition, phonics, numbers, and awareness of nature and science, introduced at the preschool level, are taught primarily in kindergarten.

Most elementary school teachers instruct one class of children in several subjects. In some schools, two or more teachers work as a team and are jointly responsible for a group of students in at least one subject. In other schools, a teacher may teach one special subject—usually music, art, reading, science, arithmetic, or physical education—to a number of classes. A small but growing number of teachers instruct multilevel classrooms, with students at several different learning levels.

Middle school teachers and secondary school teachers help students delve more deeply into subjects introduced in elementary school and expose them to more information about the world. Middle and secondary school teachers specialize in a specific subject, such as English, Spanish, mathematics, history, or biology. They also may teach subjects that are career oriented. Additional responsibilities of middle and secondary school teachers may include career guidance and job placement, as well as following up with students after graduation. (Special education teachers, who instruct elementary and secondary school students with a variety of disabilities, and vocational teachers, who provide career and technical education, are elsewhere in the Handbook.)

In addition to conducting classroom activities, teachers oversee study halls and homerooms, supervise extracurricular activities, and accompany students on field trips. They may identify students who have physical or mental problems and refer the students to the proper authorities. Secondary school teachers occasionally assist students in choosing courses, colleges, and careers. Teachers also participate in education conferences and workshops.

Computers play an integral role in the education teachers provide. Resources such as educational software and the Internet expose students to a vast range of experiences and promote interactive learning. Through the Internet, students can communicate with other students anywhere in the world, allowing them to share experiences and viewpoints. Students also use the Internet for individual research projects and to gather information. Computers play a role in other classroom activities as well, from solving math problems to learning English as a second language. Teachers also may use computers to record grades and perform other administrative and clerical duties. They must continually update their skills so that they can instruct and use the latest technology in the classroom.

Teachers play an important role in fostering the intellectual and social development of children.

Teachers often work with students from varied ethnic, racial, and religious backgrounds. With growing minority populations in most parts of the country, it is important for teachers to work effectively with a diverse student population. Accordingly, some schools offer training to help teachers enhance their awareness and understanding of different cultures. Teachers may include multicultural programming in their lesson plans, to address the needs of all students, regardless of their cultural background.

In recent years, site-based management, which allows teachers and parents to participate actively in management decisions regarding school operations, has gained popularity. In many schools, teachers are increasingly becoming involved in making decisions regarding the budget, personnel, textbooks, curriculum design, and teaching methods.

Work environment. Seeing students develop new skills and gain an appreciation of knowledge and learning can be very rewarding. However, teaching may be frustrating when one is dealing with unmotivated or disrespectful students. Occasionally, teachers must cope with unruly behavior and violence in the schools. Teachers may experience stress in dealing with large classes, heavy workloads, or old schools that are run down and lack modern amenities. Accountability standards also may increase stress levels, with teachers expected to produce students who are able to exhibit a satisfactory performance on standardized tests in core subjects. Many teachers, particularly in public schools, also are frustrated by the lack of control they have over what they are required to teach.

Teachers in private schools generally enjoy smaller class sizes and more control over establishing the curriculum and setting standards for performance and discipline. Their students also tend to be more motivated, since private schools can be selective in their admissions processes.

Teachers are sometimes isolated from their colleagues because they work alone in a classroom of students. However, some schools allow teachers to work in teams and with mentors, to enhance their professional development.

Many teachers work more than 40 hours a week, including school duties performed outside the classroom. Part-time schedules are more common among kindergarten teachers. Although most school districts have gone to all-day kindergartens, some kindergarten teachers still teach two kindergarten classes a day. Most teachers work the traditional 10-month school year, with a 2-month vacation during the summer. During the vacation break, those on the 10-month schedule may teach in summer sessions, take other jobs, travel, or pursue personal interests. Many enroll in college courses or workshops to continue their education. Teachers in districts with a year-round schedule typically work 8 weeks, are on vacation for 1 week, and have a 5-week midwinter break.

Most States have tenure laws that prevent public school teachers from being fired without just cause and due process. Teachers may obtain tenure after they have satisfactorily completed a probationary period of teaching, normally 3 years. Tenure does not absolutely guarantee a job, but it does provide some security.

Training, Other Qualifications, and Advancement

The traditional route to becoming a public school teacher involves completing a bachelor's degree from a teacher education program and then obtaining a license. However, most States now offer alternative routes to licensure for those who have a college degree in other fields. Private school teachers do not have to be licensed but may still need a bachelor's degree.

Education and training. Traditional education programs for kindergarten and elementary school teachers include courses designed specifically for those preparing to teach. Among these courses are mathematics, physical science, social science, music, art, and literature, as well as prescribed professional education courses, such as philosophy of education, psychology of learning, and teaching methods. Aspiring secondary school teachers most often major in the subject they plan to teach, while also taking a program of study in teacher preparation. Many 4-year colleges require students to wait until their sophomore year before applying for admission to teacher education programs. To maintain their accreditation, teacher education programs are now required to include classes in the use of computers and other technologies. Most programs require students to perform a student-teaching internship. Teacher education programs are accredited by the National Council for Accreditation of Teacher Education and the Teacher Education Accreditation Council. Graduation from an accredited program is not necessary to become a teacher, but it may make fulfilling licensure requirements easier.

Many States now offer professional development schools, which are partnerships between universities and elementary or secondary schools. Professional development schools merge theory with practice and allow the student to experience a year of teaching firsthand, under professional guidance. Students enter these 1-year programs after the completion of their bachelor's degree.

Licensure and certification. All 50 States and the District of Columbia require public school teachers to be licensed.

Licensure is not required for teachers in most private schools. Usually licensure is granted by the State Board of Education or a licensure advisory committee. Teachers may be licensed to teach the early childhood grades (usually preschool through grade 3); the elementary grades (grades 1 through 6 or 8); the middle grades (grades 5 through 8); a secondary-education subject area (usually grades 7 through 12); or a special subject, such as reading or music (usually grades kindergarten through 12).

Requirements for regular licenses to teach kindergarten through grade 12 vary by State. However, all States require general education teachers to have a bachelor's degree and to have completed an approved teacher training program with a prescribed number of subject and education credits, as well as supervised practice teaching. Some States also require technology training and the attainment of a minimum grade point average. A number of States require that teachers obtain a master's degree in education within a specified period after they begin teaching.

Almost all States require applicants for a teacher's license to be tested for competency in basic skills, such as reading and writing, and in teaching and require teachers to exhibit proficiency in their subject. Many school systems are moving toward implementing performance-based systems for licensure, which usually require teachers to demonstrate satisfactory teaching performance over an extended period in order to obtain a provisional license, in addition to passing an examination in their subject. Most States require teachers to complete a minimum number of hours of continuing education to renew their license. Many States have reciprocity agreements that make it easier for teachers licensed in one State to become licensed in another.

All States now also offer alternative licensure programs for teachers who have a bachelor's degree in the subject they will teach, but who lack the necessary education courses required for a regular license. Many of these alternative licensure programs are designed to ease shortages of teachers of certain subjects, such as mathematics and science. Other programs provide teachers for urban and rural schools that have difficulty filling positions with teachers from traditional licensure programs. Alternative licensure programs are intended to attract people into teaching who do not fulfill traditional licensing standards, including recent college graduates who did not complete education programs and those changing from another career to teaching. In some programs, individuals begin teaching quickly under provisional licensure under the close supervision of experienced educators while taking education courses outside school hours. If they progress satisfactorily, they receive regular licensure after working for 1 or 2 years. In other programs, college graduates who do not meet licensure requirements take only those courses that they lack and then become licensed. This approach may take 1 or 2 semesters of full-time study. The coursework for alternative certification programs may leads to a master's degree. In extreme circumstances, when schools cannot attract enough qualified teachers to fill positions, States may issue emergency licenses that let individuals who do not meet the requirements for a regular license begin teaching immediately.

Projections data from the National Employment Matrix

Occupational Title	SOC Code	Employment, 2008	Projected Employment, 2018	Change, 2008-2018	
				Number	Percent
Teachers—kindergarten, elementary, middle, and secondary...........	–	3,476,200	3,944,900	468,600	13
Kindergarten teachers, except special education	25-2012	179,500	206,500	27,000	15
Elementary school teachers, except special education..................	25-2021	1,549,500	1,793,700	244,200	16
Middle school teachers, except special and vocational education	25-2022	659,500	760,600	101,200	15
Secondary school teachers, except special and vocational education..	25-2031	1,087,700	1,184,100	96,300	9

(NOTE) Data in this table are rounded. See the discussion of the employment projections table in the *Handbook* introductory chapter on *Occupational Information Included in the Handbook*.

Private schools are generally exempt from meeting State licensing standards. For secondary school teacher jobs, they prefer candidates who have a bachelor's degree in the subject they intend to teach, or in childhood education for elementary school teachers. They seek candidates from among recent college graduates, as well as from those who have established careers in other fields.

Other qualifications. In addition to being knowledgeable about the subjects they teach, teachers must have the ability to communicate, inspire trust and confidence, and motivate students, as well as understand the students' educational and emotional needs. Teachers must be able to recognize and respond to individual and cultural differences in students and employ different teaching methods that will result in higher student achievement. They should be organized, dependable, patient, and creative. Teachers also must be able to work cooperatively and communicate effectively with other teachers, support staff, parents, and members of the community. Private schools associated with religious institutions desire candidates who share the values that are important to the institution.

Certification and advancement. In some cases, teachers of kindergarten through high school may attain professional certification in order to demonstrate competency beyond that required for a license. The National Board for Professional Teaching Standards offers a voluntary national certification. All States recognize national certification, and many States and school districts provide special benefits to teachers who earn certification. Benefits typically include higher salaries and reimbursement for continuing education and certification fees. In addition, many States allow nationally certified teachers to carry a license from one State to another.

With further preparation, teachers may move into such positions as school librarians, reading specialists, instructional coordinators, and guidance counselors. Teachers may become administrators or supervisors. In some systems, highly qualified experienced teachers can become senior or mentor teachers, with higher pay and additional responsibilities. They guide and assist less experienced teachers while keeping most of their own teaching responsibilities.

Employment

Kindergarten, elementary school, middle school, and secondary school teachers, held about 3.5 million jobs in 2008. Of the teachers in those jobs, about 179,500 were kindergarten teachers, 1.5 million were elementary school teachers, 659,500 were middle school teachers, and 1.1 million were secondary school

teachers. Employment of teachers is geographically distributed much the same as the population.

Job Outlook

Employment is projected to grow about as fast as the average for all occupations. Job prospects are best for teachers in high-demand fields, such as mathematics, science, and bilingual education, and in less desirable urban or rural school districts.

Employment change. Employment of kindergarten, elementary, middle, and secondary school teachers is expected to grow by 13 percent between 2008 and 2018, which is about as fast as the average for all occupations.

Through 2018, overall student enrollments in elementary, middle, and secondary schools—a key factor in the demand for teachers—are expected to rise more slowly than in the past as children of the baby-boom generation leave the school system. Projected enrollments will vary by region. Rapidly growing States in the South and West will experience the largest enrollment increases. Enrollments in the Midwest are expected to hold relatively steady, while those in the Northeast are expected to decline. Teachers who are geographically mobile and who obtain licensure in more than one subject are likely to have a distinct advantage in finding a job.

The number of teachers employed is dependent on State and local expenditures for education and on the enactment of legislation to increase the quality and scope of public education. At the Federal level, there has been a large increase in funding for education, particularly for the hiring of qualified teachers in lower income areas.

Job prospects. Job opportunities for teachers will vary with the locality, grade level, and subject taught. Most job openings will result from the need to replace the large number of teachers who are expected to retire over the 2008–18 period. Also, many beginning teachers—especially those employed in poor, urban schools—decide to leave teaching for other careers after a year or two, creating additional job openings for teachers.

Job prospects should be better in inner cities and rural areas than in suburban districts. Many inner cities—often characterized by overcrowded, ill-equipped schools and higher-than-average poverty rates—and rural areas—characterized by their remote location and relatively low salaries—have difficulty attracting and retaining enough teachers. Currently, many school districts have difficulty hiring qualified teachers in some subject areas—most often mathematics, science (especially chemistry and physics), bilingual education, and foreign languages. Increasing enrollments of minorities, coupled with a shortage of minority teachers, should cause efforts to recruit minority teachers to intensify. Also, the number of non-English-speaking students will continue to grow, creating demand for bilingual teachers and for those who teach English as a second language. Specialties that have an adequate number of qualified teachers include general elementary education, physical education, and social studies.

The supply of teachers is expected to increase in response to reports of improved job prospects, better pay, more teacher involvement in school policy, and greater public interest in education. In addition, more teachers may be drawn from a reserve pool of career changers, substitute teachers, and teachers completing alternative certification programs. In recent years, the total number of bachelor's and master's degrees granted in education has been increasing slowly. But many States have implemented policies that will encourage even more students to become teachers because of a shortage of teachers in certain locations and in anticipation of the loss of a number of teachers to retirement.

Earnings
Median annual wages of kindergarten, elementary, middle, and secondary school teachers ranged from $47,100 to $51,180 in May 2008; the lowest 10 percent earned $30,970 to $34,280; the top 10 percent earned $75,190 to $80,970.

According to the American Federation of Teachers, beginning teachers with a bachelor's degree earned an average of $33,227 in the 2005–2006 school year.

In 2008, of the majority of all elementary, middle, and secondary school teachers belonged to unions—mainly the American Federation of Teachers and the National Education Association—that bargain with school systems over salaries, hours, and other terms and conditions of employment.

Teachers can boost their earnings in a number of ways. In some schools, teachers receive extra pay for coaching sports and working with students in extracurricular activities. Getting a master's degree or national certification often results in a raise in pay, as does acting as a mentor. Some teachers earn extra income during the summer by teaching summer school or performing other jobs in the school system. Although private school teachers generally earn less than public school teachers, they may be given other benefits, such as free or subsidized housing.

Related Occupations
Kindergarten, elementary school, middle school, and secondary school teaching requires a variety of skills and aptitudes, including a talent for working with children; organizational, administrative, and recordkeeping abilities; research and communication skills; the power to influence, motivate, and train others; patience; and creativity. Workers in other occupations requiring some of these aptitudes include:

Sources of Additional Information
Information on licensure or certification requirements and approved teacher training institutions is available from local school systems and State departments of education.

Information on teachers' unions and education-related issues may be obtained from:
➤ American Federation of Teachers, 555 New Jersey Ave. NW., Washington, DC 20001. Internet: **http://www.aft.org**

➤ National Education Association, 1201 16th St. NW., Washington, DC 20036. Internet: **http://www.nea.org**

A list of institutions with accredited teacher education programs can be obtained from:
➤ National Council for Accreditation of Teacher Education, 2010 Massachusetts Ave. NW., Suite 500, Washington, DC 20036-1023. Internet: **http://www.ncate.org**

➤ Teacher Education Accreditation Council, Suite 300, One Dupont Circle, Suite 320 Washington, DC 20036. Internet: **http://www.teac.org**

Information on alternative certification programs can be obtained from:
➤ National Center for Alternative Certification, 4401A Connecticut Ave., NW., Suite 212, Washington, DC 20008. Internet: **http://www.teach-now.org**

Information on National Board Certification can be obtained from:
➤ National Board for Professional Teaching Standards, 1525 Wilson Blvd., Suite 500, Arlington, VA 22209. Internet: **http://www.nbpts.org**

The Occupational Information Network (O*NET) provides information on a wide range of occupational characteristics. Links to O*NET appear at the end of the Internet version of this occupational statement, accessible at **http://www.bls.gov/ooh/ocos318.htm**

Teachers—Self-Enrichment Education

Significant Points

- Many self-enrichment teachers are self-employed or work part time.

- Teachers should have knowledge and enthusiasm for their subject, but little formal training is required.

- Employment is projected to grow much faster than the average for all occupations, and job prospects should be favorable; opportunities may vary by subject taught.

Nature of the Work

Self-enrichment teachers provide instruction on a wide variety of subjects that students take for fun or self-improvement. Some teach classes that provide students with useful life skills, such as cooking, personal finance, and time management. Others provide group instruction intended solely for recreation, such as photography, pottery, and painting. Many others provide one-on-one instruction in a variety of subjects, including singing, or playing a musical instrument. Some teachers conduct courses on academic subjects, such as literature, foreign languages, and history, in a nonacademic setting. The classes taught by self-enrichment teachers seldom lead to a degree and attendance is voluntary. At the same time, these courses can provide students with useful skills, such as knowledge of computers or foreign languages, which make them more attractive to employers.

Among self-enrichment teachers, their styles and methods of instruction can differ greatly. Most self-enrichment classes are relatively informal. Some classes, such as pottery or sewing, may be largely hands-on, with the instructor demonstrating methods or techniques for the class, observing students as they attempt to do it themselves, and pointing out mistakes to students and offering suggestions for improving their techniques. Other classes, such as those involving financial planning or religion and spirituality, might center on lectures or rely more heavily on group discussions. Self-enrichment teachers may also teach classes offered through religious institutions, such as marriage preparation or classes in religion for children.

Many of the classes that self-enrichment educators teach are shorter in duration than classes taken for academic credit; some finish in 1 or 2 days or several weeks. These brief classes tend to be introductory in nature and generally focus on only one topic—for example, a cooking class that teaches students how to make bread. Some self-enrichment classes introduce children and youth to activities such as piano or drama, and they may be designed to last from 1 week to several months.

Many self-enrichment teachers provide one-on-one lessons to students. The instructor might only work with the student for 1 or 2 hours per week and then provide the student with instructions on what to practice in the interim until the next lesson. Many instructors work with the same students on a weekly basis for years and derive satisfaction from observing them mature and gain expertise.

All self-enrichment teachers must prepare lessons beforehand and stay current in their fields. The amount of time required for preparation can vary greatly, depending on the subject being taught and the length of the course. Many self-enrichment teachers are self employed and provide instruction as part of a personal business. As such, they must collect any fees or tuition and keep records of their students' accounts. Although not a requirement for most self-enrichment classes, teachers often use computers and other modern technologies in their instruction or to maintain their business records.

Work environment. Few self-enrichment education teachers are full-time salaried workers. Most either work part time or are self-employed. Some have several part-time teaching assignments, but it is most common for teachers to have a full-time job in another occupation, often related to the subject that they teach. Although jobs in this occupation are primarily part time and pay is relatively low, most teachers enjoy their work because it gives them the opportunity to share with others a subject that they enjoy.

Many classes for adults are held in the evenings and on weekends to accommodate students who have a job or family responsibilities. Similarly, self-enrichment classes for children are usually held after school, on weekends, or during school vacations.

Because students in self-enrichment programs attend classes by choice, they tend to be highly motivated and eager to learn. Students bring their own unique experiences to class, and many teachers find this aspect of the work especially rewarding and satisfying. Self-enrichment teachers must have a great deal of patience, however, particularly when working with young children.

Training, Other Qualifications, and Advancement

The main qualification for self-enrichment teachers is expertise in their subject area, but requirements vary greatly with the type of class taught and the place of employment.

Education and training. In general, there are few educational or training requirements for a job as a self-enrichment teacher beyond being an expert in the subject taught. To demonstrate expertise, however, self enrichment teachers may be required to have formal training in disciplines such as art or music, where specific teacher training programs are available. Prospective dance teachers, for example, may complete programs that prepare them to teach many types of dance—from ballroom to ballet. Other employers may require a portfolio of a teacher's work. For example, to secure a job teaching a photography course, an applicant often needs to show examples of previous work. Some self-enrichment teachers are trained educators or other professionals who teach enrichment classes in their spare time. In many self-enrichment fields, however, instructors are simply experienced in the field, and want to share that experience with others.

Other qualifications. Self-enrichment teachers should have good speaking skills and a talent for making the subject interesting. Patience and the ability to explain and instruct students

Self-enrichment teachers provide instruction on a wide variety of subjects that students take for pleasure or self-improvement.

Projections data from the National Employment Matrix

Occupational Title	SOC Code	Employment, 2008	Projected Employment, 2018	Change, 2008-2018	
				Number	Percent
Self-enrichment education teachers	25-3021	253,600	334,900	81,300	32

(NOTE) Data in this table are rounded. See the discussion of the employment projections table in the *Handbook* introductory chapter on *Occupational Information Included in the Handbook.*

at a basic level are important as well, particularly for teachers who work with children.

Advancement. Opportunities for advancement in this profession are limited. Some part-time teachers are able to move into full-time teaching positions or program administrator positions, such as coordinator or director. Experienced teachers may mentor new instructors.

Employment

Teachers of self-enrichment education held about 253,600 jobs in 2008. The largest numbers of teachers were employed by public and private educational institutions and providers of social assistance.

Job Outlook

Employment of self-enrichment education teachers is expected to grow much faster than the average for all occupations, and job prospects should be favorable. New opportunities arise constantly because many of these kinds of jobs are short term and they are often held as a second job.

Employment change. Employment of self-enrichment education teachers is expected to increase over the 2008–18 period by 32 percent, which is much faster than the average for all occupations. The need for self-enrichment teachers is expected to grow as more people embrace lifelong learning and course offerings expand. Demand for self-enrichment education will also increase, as more people seek to gain or improve skills that will make them more attractive to prospective employers. Some self-enrichment teachers offer instruction in foreign languages, computer programming or applications, public speaking, and many other subjects that help students gain marketable skills. People increasingly take courses to improve their job skills, which creates more demand for self-enrichment teachers.

Job prospects. Job prospects should be generally favorable in the coming decade, as increasing demand and high turnover create many opportunities. These opportunities may vary, however, because some fields have more prospective teachers than others. Opportunities should be best for teachers of subjects that are not easily researched on the Internet and those that benefit from hands-on experiences, such as cooking, crafts, and the arts. Classes on self-improvement, personal finance, and computer and Internet-related subjects are also expected to be popular.

Earnings

Median hourly wages of self-enrichment teachers were $17.17 in May 2008. The middle 50 percent earned between $12.50 and $24.98. The lowest 10 percent earned less than $9.15, and the highest 10 percent earned more than $32.68. Self-enrichment teachers are generally paid by the hour or for each class that

they teach. Earnings may also be tied to the number of students enrolled in the class.

Part-time instructors are usually paid for each class that they teach, and receive few benefits. Full-time teachers are generally paid a salary and may receive health insurance and other benefits.

Related Occupations

The work of self-enrichment teachers is closely related to:

Sources of Additional Information

For information on employment of self-enrichment teachers, contact local schools, colleges, or companies that offer self-enrichment programs.

The Occupational Information Network (O*NET) provides information on a wide range of occupational characteristics. Links to O*NET appear at the end of the Internet version of this occupational statement, accessible at **http://www.bls.gov/ooh/ocos064.htm**

Teachers—Special Education

Significant Points

- Special education teachers must be organized, patient, able to motivate students, understanding of their students' special needs, and accepting of differences in others.

- All States require teachers to be licensed; traditional licensing requires the completion of a special education teacher training program and at least a bachelor's degree, although some States require a master's degree.

- Many States offer alternative licensure programs to attract college graduates who do not have training in education.

- Excellent job prospects are expected due to rising enrollments of special education students and reported shortages of qualified teachers.

Nature of the Work

Special education teachers work with children and youths who have a variety of disabilities. A small number of special education teachers work with students with severe cognitive, emotional, or physical disabilities, primarily teaching them life skills and basic literacy. However, the majority of special education teachers work with children with mild to moderate disabilities, using or modifying the general education curriculum to meet the child's individual needs and providing required remedial instruction. Most special education teachers instruct students at the preschool, elementary, middle, and secondary school level, although some work with infants and toddlers.

The various types of disabilities that may qualify individuals for special education programs are as follows: specific learning disabilities, speech or language impairments, mental retardation, emotional disturbance, multiple disabilities, hearing impairments, orthopedic impairments, visual impairments, autism, combined deafness and blindness, traumatic brain injury, and other health impairments. Students are identified under one or more of these categories. Early identification of a child with special needs is an important part of a special education teacher's job, because early intervention is essential in educating children with disabilities.

Special education teachers use various techniques to promote learning. Depending on the student, teaching methods can include intensive individualized instruction, problem-solving assignments, and small-group work. When students need special accommodations to learn the general curriculum or to take a test, special education teachers ensure that appropriate accommodations are provided, such as having material read orally or lengthening the time allowed to take the test.

Special education teachers help to develop an Individualized Education Program (IEP) for each student receiving special education. The IEP sets personalized goals for the student and is tailored to that student's individual needs and abilities. When appropriate, the program includes a transition plan outlining specific steps to prepare students for middle school or high school or, in the case of older students, a job or postsecondary study. Teachers review the IEP with the student's parents, school administrators, and the student's general education teachers. Teachers work closely with parents to inform them of their children's progress and suggest techniques to promote learning outside of school.

Special education teachers design and teach appropriate curricula, assign work geared toward each student's needs and abilities, and grade papers and homework assignments. They are involved in the student's behavioral, social, and academic development, helping them develop emotionally and interact effectively in social situations. Preparing special education students for daily life after graduation also is an important aspect of the job. Teachers provide students with career counseling or help them learn life skills, such as balancing a checkbook.

As schools become more inclusive, special education teachers and general education teachers increasingly work together in general education classrooms. Special education teachers help general educators adapt curriculum materials and teaching techniques to meet the needs of students with disabilities. They coordinate the work of teachers, teacher assistants, and related personnel, such as therapists and social workers, to meet the individualized needs of the student within inclusive special education programs. A large part of a special education teacher's job involves communicating and coordinating with others involved in the child's well-being, including parents, social workers, school psychologists, occupational and physical therapists, school administrators, and other teachers.

Special education teachers work in a variety of settings. Some have their own classrooms and teach only special education students; others work as special education resource teachers and offer individualized help to students in general education classrooms; still others teach together with general education teachers in classes including both general and special education students. Some teachers work with special education students for several hours a day in a resource room, separate from their general education classroom. Considerably fewer special education teachers work in residential facilities or tutor students in homebound or hospital environments.

Some special education teachers work with infants and toddlers in the child's home with his or her parents. Many of these infants have challenges that slow or preclude normal development. Special education teachers help parents learn techniques and activities designed to stimulate the infant and encourage the growth and development of the child's skills. Toddlers usually receive their services at a preschool where special education

Special education teachers work with young people who have a variety of disabilities.

Projections data from the National Employment Matrix

Occupational Title	SOC Code	Employment, 2008	Projected Employment, 2018	Change, 2008-2018	
				Number	Percent
Special education teachers	25-2040	473,000	554,900	81,900	17
Special education teachers, preschool, kindergarten, and elementary school	25-2041	226,000	270,300	44,300	20
Special education teachers, middle school..................................	25-2042	100,300	118,400	18,100	18
Special education teachers, secondary school	25-2043	146,700	166,200	19,500	13

(NOTE) Data in this table are rounded. See the discussion of the employment projections table in the *Handbook* introductory chapter on *Occupational Information Included in the Handbook.*

teachers help them develop social, self-help, motor, language, and cognitive skills, often through the use of play.

Technology is becoming increasingly important in special education. Teachers use specialized equipment such as computers with synthesized speech, interactive educational software programs, and audiotapes to assist children.

Work environment. Special education teachers enjoy the challenge of working with students with disabilities and the opportunity to establish meaningful relationships with them. Although helping these students can be highly rewarding, the work also can be emotionally demanding and physically draining. Many special education teachers are under considerable stress due to heavy workloads and administrative tasks. They must produce a substantial amount of paperwork documenting each student's progress and work under the threat of litigation against the school or district by parents if correct procedures are not followed or if the parents feel that their child is not receiving an adequate education. Recently passed legislation, however, is intended to reduce the burden of paperwork and the threat of litigation. The physical and emotional demands of the job cause some special education teachers to leave the occupation.

Some schools offer year-round education for special education students, but most special education teachers work only the traditional 10-month school year.

Training, Other Qualifications, and Advancement

All States require special education teachers to be licensed, which typically requires at least a bachelor's degree and the completion of an approved training program in special education teaching. Some States require a master's degree. Most States have alternative methods for entry for bachelor's degree holders who do not have training in education.

Education and training. Many colleges and universities across the United States offer programs in special education at the undergraduate, master's, and doctoral degree levels. Special education teachers often undergo longer periods of training than do general education teachers. Most bachelor's degree programs last four years and include general and specialized courses in special education. However, an increasing number of institutions are requiring a fifth year or other graduate-level preparation. Some programs require specialization, while others offer generalized special education degrees. The last year of the program usually is spent student teaching in a classroom supervised by a certified special education teacher.

Licensure. All 50 States and the District of Columbia require special education teachers to be licensed. The State board of education or a licensure advisory committee usually grants

licenses, and licensure varies by State. In some States, special education teachers receive a general education credential to teach kindergarten through grade 12. These teachers then train in a specialty, such as learning disabilities or behavioral disorders. Many States offer general special education licenses across a variety of disability categories, while others license several different specialties within special education.

For traditional licensing, all States require a bachelor's degree and the completion of an approved teacher preparation program with a prescribed number of subject and education credits and supervised practice teaching. However, some States also require a master's degree in special education, which involves at least 1 year of additional coursework, including a specialization, beyond the bachelor's degree. Most States require a prospective teacher to pass a professional assessment test as well. Some States have reciprocity agreements allowing special education teachers to transfer their licenses from one State to another, but many others still require that experienced teachers reapply and pass licensing requirements to work in the State.

Most States also offer alternative routes to licensing that are intended to attract people into teaching who do not fulfill traditional licensing standards. Most alternative licensure programs are open to anyone with a bachelor's degree, although some are designed for recent college graduates or professionals in other education occupations. Programs typically require the completion of a period of supervised preparation and instruction through a partnering college or university and passing an assessment test while teaching under supervision for a period of 1 to 2 years.

Other qualifications. Special education teachers must be organized, patient, able to motivate students, understanding of their students' special needs, and accepting of differences in others. Teachers must be creative and apply different types of teaching methods to reach students who are having difficulty learning. Communication and cooperation are essential skills because special education teachers spend a great deal of time interacting with others, including students, parents, and school faculty and administrators.

Advancement. Special education teachers can advance to become supervisors or administrators. They also may earn advanced degrees and become instructors in colleges that prepare others to teach special education. In some school systems, highly experienced teachers can become mentors to less experienced teachers.

Employment

Special education teachers held a total of about 473,000 jobs in 2008. Nearly all worked in public and private educational institutions. A few worked for individual and social assistance agencies or residential facilities, or in homebound or hospital environments.

Job Outlook

Employment is expected to increase faster than the average for all occupations. Job prospects should be excellent because many districts report problems finding adequate numbers of licensed special education teachers.

Employment change. The number of special education teachers is expected to increase by 17 percent from 2008 to 2018, which is faster than the average for all occupations. Although student enrollments in general are expected to grow more slowly than in the past, continued increases in the number of special education students needing services will generate a greater need for special education teachers.

The number of students requiring special education services has grown steadily in recent years because of improvements that have allowed learning disabilities to be diagnosed at earlier ages. In addition, legislation emphasizing training and employment for individuals with disabilities and educational reforms requiring higher standards for graduation have increased demand for special education services. Also, the percentage of foreign-born special education students is expected to grow as teachers become more adept in recognizing disabilities in that population. Finally, more parents are expected to seek special services for children who have difficulty meeting the new, higher standards required of students.

Job prospects. In addition to job openings resulting from growth, a large number of openings will result from the need to replace special education teachers who switch to teaching general education, change careers altogether, or retire. At the same time, many school districts report difficulty finding sufficient numbers of qualified teachers. As a result, special education teachers should have excellent job prospects.

The job outlook does vary by geographic area and specialty. Although most areas of the country report difficulty finding qualified applicants, positions in inner cities and rural areas usually are more plentiful than job openings in suburban or wealthy urban areas. Student populations also are expected to increase more rapidly in certain parts of the country, such as the South and West, resulting in increased demand for special education teachers in those regions. In addition, job opportunities may be better in certain specialties—for example, teachers who work with children with multiple disabilities or those who work with children with severe disabilities such as autism—because of large increases in the enrollment of special education students classified into those categories. Legislation encouraging early intervention and special education for infants, toddlers, and preschoolers has created a need for early childhood special education teachers. Bilingual special education teachers and those with multicultural experience also are needed, to work with an increasingly diverse student population.

Earnings

Median annual wages in May 2008 of special education teachers who worked primarily in preschools, kindergartens, and elementary schools were $50,020. The middle 50 percent earned between $40,480 and $63,500. The lowest 10 percent earned less than $33,770, and the highest 10 percent earned more than $78,980

Median annual wages of middle school special education teachers were $50,810. The middle 50 percent earned between $41,720 and $63,480. The lowest 10 percent earned less than $35,180, and the highest 10 percent earned more than $78,200.

Median annual wages of special education teachers who worked primarily in secondary schools were $51,340. The middle 50 percent earned between $41,810 and $65,680. The lowest 10 percent earned less than $35,150, and the highest 10 percent earned more than $82,000.

In 2008, about 64 percent of special education teachers belonged to unions or were covered by union contracts.

In most schools, teachers receive extra pay for coaching sports and working with students in extracurricular activities. Some teachers earn extra income during the summer, working in the school system or in other jobs.

Related Occupations

Special education teachers work with students who have disabilities and special needs. Other occupations involved with the identification, evaluation, and development of students with disabilities include:

Sources of Additional Information

For information on professions related to early intervention and education for children with disabilities, listings of schools with special education training programs, information on teacher certification, and general information on related personnel issues, contact:

➤ The Council for Exceptional Children, 1110 N. Glebe Rd., Suite 300, Arlington, VA 22201. Internet: **http://www.cec.sped.org**

➤ National Center for Special Education Personnel and Related Service Providers, National Association of State Directors of Special Education, 1800 Diagonal Rd., Suite 320, Alexandria, VA 22314. Internet: **http://www.personnelcenter.org**

To learn more about the special education teacher certification and licensing requirements in individual States, contact the State's department of education.

The Occupational Information Network (O*NET) provides information on a wide range of occupational characteristics. Links to O*NET appear at the end of the Internet version of this occupational statement, accessible at **http://www.bls.gov/ooh/ocos070.htm**

Teachers—Vocational

Significant Points

- Traditionally, becoming a vocational education teacher requires a bachelor's degree from a teacher education program and a teacher's license for which requirements vary from State to State.

- Most States now offer alternative routes to licensure for those who have work experience in their field.

- Employment growth is expected to be as fast as the average for all occupations, with favorable job prospects.

Nature of the Work

Vocational education teachers, commonly called career and technical education (CTE) teachers or career-technology teachers, instruct and train students to work in a wide variety of fields. Career and technical education courses train students to enter a particular career and prepare them for the world of work.

Career and technical teachers in middle and secondary schools may be introducing students to a trade or skill for the first time. They often teach courses that are in high demand by area employers, who often provide input into the curriculum and offer internships or apprenticeships to students at the secondary school level. Many vocational teachers play an active role in building and overseeing these partnerships. Additional responsibilities of middle and secondary school teachers may include providing career guidance, helping with job placement, and following up with students after graduation. Secondary

Vocational education teachers in middle and secondary schools may introduce students to a trade or skill for the first time.

CTE teachers are also responsible for coordinating their curriculum offerings with community, technical and 4-year colleges under current Federal law.

CTE teachers may teach in traditional comprehensive schools. Within comprehensive secondary schools, CTE teachers may be part of a career academy where they work closely with academic colleagues to create a career-themed, school-within-a-school. They may teach in a regional CTE centers that serve students from many districts who come for half-days. Other CTE teachers may teach in a CTE secondary school where students are in shops and labs for most of the school day.

At the secondary school level, the focus is on preparing students to enter the workforce or to continue on to additional training at the postsecondary level. In addition, CTE teachers aim to reinforce and strengthen material learned by their students in academic classes. To achieve these ends, teachers use a variety of techniques and methods to ensure that students understand the material, such as classroom lectures, hands-on activities done in a laboratory, experiential or work-based learning, and involvement in co-curricular organizations. In the classroom, CTE teachers lecture students on the theories and techniques used in the field. They may discuss the history of the profession or laws and regulations that govern the industry. In addition, teachers may provide demonstrations of tasks, techniques, or tools used in the field. In the lab, teachers assign the students tasks, oversee their progress, and assist students as they encounter problems or need additional instruction or direction. Experiential or work-based learning allows students the opportunity to apply what they have learned in the classroom in real world settings. Students may use class time to work in the field at a business willing to let them learn on the job, and the business provides feedback about the student's performance to the teacher. In some schools, students may run businesses that are owned by the school, such as the school store, to apply their knowledge and skills in a non-classroom setting. Finally, CTE teachers may serve as the advisor for co-curricular student organizations that provide students with additional opportunities to reinforce what they have learned in the classroom.

How teachers use these different settings and techniques varies with their specialized field. These fields include agricultural science, family and consumer science, health occupations, business and marketing, trade and industry, and technology education.

In agricultural science, students learn a wide variety of subjects related to the science and business of agriculture. Classes may cover topics like agricultural production; agricultural-related business; horticulture; agri-science; small animal care; veterinary science; and plant, animal, and food systems. Teachers in this subject may have students plant and care for crops or tend to animals to apply what they have learned in the classroom.

CTE teachers in family and consumer science teach students about culinary arts; sewing; child development; family and consumer services; and food science, dietetics, and nutrition. Students in these settings may run early childhood education classes with teacher supervision, manufacture and market clothing, or create menus and cook for a school function.

Projections data from the National Employment Matrix

Occupational Title	SOC Code	Employment, 2008	Projected Employment, 2018	Change, 2008-2018	
				Number	Percent
Teachers—vocational..	–	115,100	125,100	10,100	9
Vocational education teachers, middle school	25-2023	15,600	16,100	500	3
Vocational education teachers, secondary school	25-2032	99,400	109,000	9,600	10

(NOTE) Data in this table are rounded. See the discussion of the employment projections table in the *Handbook* introductory chapter on *Occupational Information Included in the Handbook.*

In health-related occupations, students learn the skills necessary to work as technicians or assistants in the medical field. This may include learning the skills necessary to become a nurse or dental assistant. Teachers in this field may have students practice their skills by measuring blood pressure or practicing fundamental tasks like administering blood sugar and blood type tests on other staff in the school. Some programs allow students to receive the certifications necessary to enter the field.

Business and marketing students learn the skills necessary to run a business or make sales. They may learn computer programs or how to market a product. They may also learn the basics of financial management for a business. CTE teachers specializing in business and marketing may spend time with students in computer labs to teach them computer skills, or they may guide students as they develop and establish a business. Many programs operate school-based enterprises where students operate real businesses open to the public.

CTE teachers in trade and industry may cover a wide range of topics, such as auto mechanics, cosmetology, heating and air conditioning, electrical wiring, television production, computer networking and computer repair, or auto body repair. These teachers specialize in one of these areas and teach classes in their area of expertise. Many teachers in this field use lab work extensively to allow students to learn with a hands-on approach.

Teachers in technology aim to teach the same subjects that are taught in general education classes, such as math and science, through technology. This may include supervising students as they build a robot to learn about physics, computer science, and math. This type of program is often seen as a precursor to engineering programs.

Work environment. Helping students develop new skills and gain an appreciation of knowledge and learning can be very rewarding. However, teachers may get frustrated when dealing with unmotivated or disrespectful students. Occasionally, teachers must cope with unruly behavior and violence at school. Teachers may experience stress from dealing with large classes, heavy workloads, or schools that are run down and lack many modern amenities.

Teachers are sometimes isolated from their colleagues because they work alone in a classroom of students. However, some schools allow teachers to work in teams and with mentors to enhance their professional development. However, CTE teachers often have specific responsibilities that have them in the community during part of the school day working with their business and industry partners.

Including school duties performed outside the classroom, many teachers work more than 40 hours a week. Most middle and secondary school CTE teachers work the traditional ten

month school year with a 2-month vacation during the summer. During the vacation break, those on the ten month schedule may teach in summer sessions, take other jobs, travel, or pursue personal interest s. Some enroll in college courses or workshops to continue their education. Teachers in districts with a year-round schedule typically work eight weeks and then have one week of vacation, as well as a five week midwinter break. CTE teachers with active work-based learning programs may be on twelve month contracts to provide time for them to engage in job development for current and future students.

Most States have tenure laws that prevent public school teachers from being fired without just cause and due process. Teachers may obtain tenure after they have satisfactorily completed a probationary period of teaching, normally three years. Tenure does not absolutely guarantee a job, but it does provide some security.

Training, Other Qualifications, and Advancement

The traditional route to becoming a career and technical education teacher at the middle or secondary school level requires completing a bachelor's degree from a teacher education program and then obtaining a license. However, most States now offer alternative routes to licensure for those who have work experience in their field.

Education and training. Traditionally, most aspiring CTE teachers obtain a bachelor's degree and often major in the subject they plan to teach while also completing a program of study in teacher preparation. However, with the proper amount of work experience in the chosen teaching field, many states allow CTE teachers to enter the occupation with a bachelor's degree minus the teacher preparation program or with only a high school diploma.

Licensure and certification. All 50 States and the District of Columbia require public school CTE teachers in middle and secondary schools to be licensed. Usually licensure is granted by the State Board of Education or a licensure advisory committee. All States require teachers to have a bachelor's degree and to have completed an approved teacher training program with a prescribed number of subject and education credits, as well as supervised practice teaching. Some States also require technology training and the attainment of a minimum grade point average. A number of States require teachers to obtain a master's degree in education within a specified period after they begin teaching. Almost all States require an applicant for a teacher's license to take a competency test. Most States require teachers to complete a minimum number of hours of continuing education to renew their license. Many States have reciprocity agreements that make it easier for teachers licensed in one State to become licensed in another.

However, there are alternative routes to licensure which allow those who did not go through traditional teacher preparation program to become licensed CTE teachers. Often this requires work experience in additional to a high school diploma or a bachelors degree without teacher preparation. The educational requirement varies depending on the State and the amount of experience the applicant has.

Other qualifications.   In addition to being knowledgeable about the subjects they teach, teachers must be good communicators and inspire trust and confidence. They should motivate students and understand the students' educational and emotional needs. Teachers must recognize and respond to individual and cultural differences in students and employ different teaching methods that will result in higher student achievement. They should be organized, dependable, patient, and creative. Teachers also must be able to work cooperatively and communicate effectively with other teachers, support staff, parents, and members of the community.

Advancement.   Teachers may become administrators or supervisors, although the number of these positions is limited and competition for them can be intense. In some systems, highly qualified, experienced teachers can become senior or mentor teachers, with higher pay and additional responsibilities. They guide and assist less experienced teachers while keeping most of their own teaching responsibilities. CTE teachers may also move to teaching classes at the postsecondary level.

Employment

Vocational education teachers held 115,100 jobs in 2008. Of these jobs, vocational education teachers in middle schools held 15,600 jobs and vocational education teachers in secondary schools held 99,400 jobs. Most were employed in public and private educational institutions.

Job Outlook

Employment of vocational teachers is expected to grow as fast as the average as student enrollments continue to increase.

Employment change.   Employment of vocational education teachers is expected to grow by 9 percent from 2008 to 2018, which as fast as the average than all occupations. Employment of middle school vocational education teachers is expected to grow by 3 percent, which is more slowly than the average for all occupations and employment of secondary school vocational education teachers is expected to grow by 10 percent, which about as fast as the average for all occupations. This growth is due in large part to continued growth in school enrollments, which increases demand for these workers. However, growth will be limited by an increased focused on traditional academic subjects.

Through 2018, overall student enrollments in middle, and secondary schools—a key factor in the demand for teachers—are expected to rise more slowly than in the past as children of the baby-boom generation leave the school system. Projected enrollments will vary by region. Rapidly growing States in the South and West will experience the largest enrollment increases. Enrollments in the Midwest are expected to hold relatively steady, while those in the Northeast are expected to decline. Teachers who are geographically mobile and who obtain licensure in more than one subject are likely to have a distinct advantage in finding a job.

Growth in this occupation will be slowed somewhat by an increased focus on traditional academics subjects, like reading and math, and away from career specific training at the middle and secondary school levels. As a result, growth in the employment of vocational education teachers may be limited.

Job prospects.   Opportunities in this occupation are expected to be favorable as workers currently employed in this occupation leave the field to retire or for other opportunities.

Earnings

Median annual wages of vocational education teachers in middle schools in May 2008 were $47,870. The middle 50 percent earned between $39,460 and $59,470. The lowest 10 percent earned less than $34,020, and the highest 10 percent earned more than $72,720.

Median annual wages of vocational education teachers in secondary schools in May 2008 were $51,580. The middle 50 percent earned between $42,110 and $64,120. The lowest 10 percent earned less than $34,980, and the highest 10 percent earned more than $77,950.

Related Occupations

Teaching requires the ability to communicate ideas well, motivate students, and be creative. Workers in other occupations that require these skills are

Sources of Additional Information

For information on career and technical education teaching positions, contact State departments of career and technical education. General information on adult and career and technical education is available from:

➤ Association for Career and Technical Education, 1410 King St., Alexandria, VA 22314. Internet: **http://www.acteonline.org**

The Occupational Information Network (O*NET) provides information on a wide range of occupational characteristics. Links to O*NET appear at the end of the Internet version of this occupational statement, accessible at **http://www.bls.gov/ooh/ocos358.htm**

Art and Design Occupations

Artists and Related Workers

Significant Points

- About 60 percent of artists and related workers are self-employed.

- Keen competition is expected for both salaried jobs and freelance work because the arts attract many talented people with creative ability.

- Artists usually develop their skills through a bachelor's degree program or other postsecondary training in art or design.

- Earnings for self-employed artists vary widely; some well-established artists earn more than salaried artists, while others find it difficult to rely solely on income earned from selling art.

Nature of the Work

Artists create art to communicate ideas, thoughts, or feelings. They use a variety of methods—painting, sculpting, or illustration—and an assortment of materials, including oils, watercolors, acrylics, pastels, pencils, pen and ink, plaster, clay, and computers. Artists' works may be realistic, stylized, or abstract and may depict objects, people, nature, or events.

Artists generally fall into one of four categories. *Art directors* formulate design concepts and presentation approaches for visual communications. Craft artists create or reproduce handmade objects for sale or exhibition. Fine artists, including painters, sculptors, and illustrators, create original artwork, using a variety of media and techniques. Multimedia artists and animators create special effects, animation, or other visual images on film, on video, or with computers or other electronic media. (Designers, including graphic designers, are discussed elsewhere in the Handbook.)

Art directors develop design concepts and review material that is to appear in periodicals, newspapers, and other printed or digital media. They control the overall visual direction of a project in fields such as advertising and publishing. They decide how best to present a concept visually, so that it is organized, eye catching, and appealing. Art directors decide which photographs or artwork to use and oversee the design, layout, and production of material to be produced. They may direct workers engaged in artwork, design, layout, and copywriting.

Craft artists make a wide variety of objects, mostly by hand, that are sold in their own studios, in retail outlets, or at arts-and-crafts shows. Some craft artists display their works in galleries and museums. Craft artists work with many different materials, including ceramics, glass, textiles, wood, metal, and paper, to create unique pieces of art such as pottery, stained glass, quilts, tapestries, lace, candles, and clothing. Many craft artists also use fine-art techniques—for example, painting, sketching, and printing—to add finishing touches to their art.

Fine artists typically display their work in museums, commercial art galleries, corporate collections, and private homes. Some of their artwork may be commissioned (done on request from clients), but most is sold by the artist or through private art galleries or dealers. The gallery and the artist predetermine how much each will earn from the sale. Only the most successful fine artists are able to support themselves solely through the sale of their works. Most fine artists have at least one other job to support their art careers. Some work in museums or art galleries as fine-arts directors or as curators, planning and setting up art exhibits. A few artists work as art critics for newspapers or magazines or as consultants to foundations or institutional collectors. Other artists teach art classes or conduct workshops in schools or in their own studios. Some artists also hold full-time or part-time jobs unrelated to art and pursue fine art as a hobby or second career.

Usually, fine artists specialize in one or two art forms, such as painting, illustrating, sketching, sculpting, printmaking, and restoring. Painters, illustrators, cartoonists, and sketch artists work with two-dimensional art forms, using shading, perspective, and color to produce realistic scenes or abstractions.

Illustrators usually create pictures for books, magazines, and other publications and for commercial products such as textiles, wrapping paper, stationery, greeting cards, and calendars. Increasingly, illustrators are working in digital format—for example, creating scenery or objects for a video game. This has created new opportunities for illustrators to work with animators and in broadcast media.

Medical and scientific illustrators combine drawing skills with knowledge of biology or other sciences. Medical illustrators work digitally or traditionally to create images of human anatomy and surgical procedures as well as three-dimensional models and animations. Scientific illustrators draw animal and plant life, atomic and molecular structures, and geologic and planetary formations. These illustrations are used in medical and scientific publications and in audiovisual presentations for teaching purposes. Illustrators also work for lawyers, producing exhibits for court cases.

Cartoonists draw political, advertising, social, and sports cartoons. Some cartoonists work with others who create the idea or story and write captions. Some cartoonists write captions themselves. Most cartoonists have comic, critical, or dramatic talents in addition to drawing skills.

Sketch artists create likenesses of subjects with pencil, charcoal, or pastels. Sketches are used by law enforcement agencies to assist in identifying suspects, by the news media to depict courtroom scenes, and by individual patrons for their own enjoyment.

Sculptors design three-dimensional artworks, either by molding and joining materials such as clay, glass, wire, plastic, fabric, or metal, or by cutting and carving forms from a block of plaster, wood, or stone. Some sculptors combine various materials to create mixed-media installations. Some incorporate light, sound, and motion into their works.

Many artists receive formal training in their specialty.

Printmakers create printed images from designs cut or etched into wood, stone, or metal. After creating the design, the artist uses a printing press to roll the image onto paper or fabric. Some make prints by pressing the inked surface onto paper by hand or by graphically encoding and processing data, using a computer. The digitized images can then be printed onto paper.

Painting restorers preserve and restore damaged and faded paintings. They apply solvents and cleaning agents to clean the surfaces of the paintings, they reconstruct or retouch damaged areas, and they apply preservatives to protect the paintings. Restoration is highly detailed work and usually is reserved for experts in the field.

Multimedia artists and animators work primarily in motion picture and video industries, advertising, and computer systems design services. They draw by hand and use computers to create the series of pictures that form the animated images or special effects seen in movies, television programs, and computer games. Some draw storyboards for television commercials, movies, and animated features. Storyboards present television commercials in a series of scenes similar to a comic strip and allow an advertising agency to evaluate commercials proposed by advertising companies. Storyboards also serve as guides to placing actors and cameras on the television or motion picture set and to other production details. Many multimedia artists

model objects in three dimensions by computer and work with programmers to make the images move.

Work environment. Many artists work in fine art or commercial art studios located in office buildings, warehouses, or lofts. Others work in private studios in their homes. Some fine artists share studio space, where they also may exhibit their work. Studio surroundings usually are well lighted and ventilated; however, fine artists may be exposed to fumes from glue, paint, ink, and other materials and to dust or other residue from filings, splattered paint, or spilled cleaners and other fluids. Artists who sit at drafting tables or who use computers for extended periods may experience back pain, eyestrain, or fatigue.

Artists employed by publishing companies, advertising agencies, and design firms generally work a standard workweek. During busy periods, they may work overtime to meet deadlines. Self-employed artists can set their own hours. They may spend much time and effort selling their artwork to potential customers or clients and building a reputation.

Training, Other Qualifications, and Advancement

Art directors usually have years of work experience and generally need at least a bachelor's degree. Because of the level of technical expertise demanded, multimedia artists and animators also need a bachelor's degree. Although formal schooling is not strictly required for craft and fine artists, it is very difficult to become skilled enough to make a living without some training.

Education and training. Many colleges and universities offer programs leading to a bachelor's or master's degree in fine arts. Courses usually include core subjects such as English, social science, and natural science, in addition to art history and studio art. Independent schools of art and design also offer postsecondary studio training in the craft, fine, and multimedia arts leading to certificates in the specialties or to an associate or bachelor's degree in fine arts. Typically, these programs focus more intensively on studio work than do the academic programs in a university setting. In 2009 the National Association of Schools of Art and Design accredited approximately 300 postsecondary institutions with programs in art and design; most of these schools award a degree in art.

Art directors usually begin as entry-level artists or designers in advertising, publishing, design, or motion picture production firms. An artist is promoted to art director after having demonstrated artistic and leadership abilities. Depending on the scope of their responsibilities, some art directors may pursue a degree in art administration or management, which teaches business skills such as project management and finance.

Many educational programs in art also provide training in computer techniques. Computers are used widely in the visual arts, and knowledge and training in computer graphics and other visual display software are critical elements of many jobs in these fields.

Medical illustrators must have both a demonstrated artistic ability and a detailed knowledge of living organisms, surgical and medical procedures, and human and animal anatomy. A bachelor's degree combining art and premedical courses usually is required. However, most medical illustrators also choose to pursue a master's degree in medical illustration. This degree is offered in four accredited schools in the United States.

Projections data from the National Employment Matrix

Occupational Title	SOC Code	Employment, 2008	Projected Employment, 2018	Change, 2008-2018	
				Number	Percent
Artists and related workers	27-1010	221,900	247,700	25,800	12
Art directors	27-1011	84,200	94,000	9,800	12
Craft artists..	27-1012	13,600	14,600	1,000	7
Fine artists, including painters, sculptors, and illustrators............	27-1013	23,600	25,700	2,100	9
Multi-media artists and animators	27-1014	79,000	90,200	11,200	14
Artists and related workers, all other	27-1019	21,500	23,200	1,700	8

(NOTE) Data in this table are rounded. See the discussion of the employment projections table in the *Handbook* introductory chapter on *Occupational Information Included in the Handbook.*

Those who want to teach fine arts at public elementary or secondary schools usually must have a teaching certificate in addition to a bachelor's degree. An advanced degree in fine arts or arts administration is usually necessary for management or administrative positions in government or in foundations or for teaching in colleges and universities. (See the statements titled "teachers—postsecondary" and "teachers—kindergarten, elementary, middle, and secondary school" elsewhere in the *Handbook.*)

Other qualifications. Evidence of appropriate talent and skill, displayed in an artist's portfolio, is an important factor used by art directors, clients, and others in deciding whether to hire an individual or contract for his or her work. A portfolio is a collection of samples of the artist's best work. Assembling a successful portfolio requires skills usually developed through postsecondary training in art or visual communications. Internships also provide excellent opportunities for artists to develop and enhance their portfolios.

Advancement. Artists hired by firms often start with relatively routine work. While doing this work, however, they may observe other artists and practice their own skills.

Craft and fine artists advance professionally as their work circulates and as they establish a reputation for a particular style. Many of the most successful artists continually develop new ideas, and their work often evolves over time.

Many artists do freelance work while continuing to hold a full-time job until they are established. Others freelance part time while still in school to develop experience and to build a portfolio of published work.

Freelance artists try to develop a set of clients who regularly contract for work. Some freelance artists are widely recognized for their skill in specialties such as cartooning or children's book illustration. These artists may earn high incomes and can choose the type of work they do.

Employment

Artists held about 221,900 jobs in 2008. About 60 percent were self-employed. Employment was distributed as follows:

Art directors	84,200
Multimedia artists and animators	79,000
Fine artists, including painters, sculpters and illustrators	23,600
Craft artists..	13,600
Artists and related workers, all other	21,500

Of the artists who were not self-employed, many worked for advertising and related services; newspaper, periodical, book, and software publishers; motion picture and video industries; specialized design services; and computer systems design and related services. Some self-employed artists offered their services to advertising agencies, design firms, publishing houses, and other businesses.

Job Outlook

Employment is projected to grow about as fast as the average. Competition for jobs is expected to be keen for both salaried and freelance jobs in all specialties because the number of people with creative ability and an interest in this career is expected to continue to exceed the number of available openings. Despite the competition, employers and individual clients are always on the lookout for talented and creative artists.

Employment change. Employment of artists and related workers is expected to grow 12 percent through 2018, about as fast as the average for all occupations. An increasing reliance on artists to create digital or multimedia artwork will drive growth.

Art directors will see an increase in jobs in advertising due to demand for the overall vision they bring to a project. However, declining opportunities in publishing will hold down job growth. With many magazines moving to an online-only format, art directors are used less in this field.

Demand for illustrators who work on a computer will increase as media companies use more detailed images and backgrounds in their designs. However, illustrators and cartoonists who work in publishing may see job opportunities decline as newspapers continue to cut staffs. Many are instead opting to post their work on political Web sites and online publications. The small number of medical illustrators will also be in greater demand as medical research continues to grow.

Demand for multimedia artists and animators will increase as consumers continue to demand more realistic video games, movie and television special effects, and 3D animated movies. Additional job openings will arise from an increasing need for computer graphics in the growing number of mobile technologies. The demand for animators is also increasing in alternative areas such as scientific research and design services. Some lower priority animation has been offshored, negatively affecting employment of animators.

Job prospects. Competition for jobs as artists and related workers will be keen because there are more qualified candidates than available jobs. Employers in all industries should be able to choose from among the most qualified candidates.

Despite the competition, studios, galleries, and individual clients are always on the lookout for artists who display outstanding talent, creativity, and style. Among craft and fine artists, talented individuals who have developed a mastery of artistic techniques and skills will have the best job prospects. Multimedia artists and animators should have better job opportunities than other artists but still will experience competition. Despite an expanding number of opportunities, art directors should experience keen competition for the available openings. Craft and fine artists work mostly on a freelance or commission basis and may find it difficult to earn a living solely by selling their artwork. Only the most successful craft and fine artists receive major commissions for their work. Competition among artists for the privilege of being shown in galleries is expected to remain intense, as will competition for grants from sponsors such as private foundations, State and local arts councils, and the National Endowment for the Arts. Because of their reliance on grants, and because the demand for artwork is dependent on consumers having disposable income, many of these artists will find that their income fluctuates with the overall economy.

Earnings

Median annual wages of salaried art directors were $76,980 in May 2008. The middle 50 percent earned between $54,490 and $108,090. The lowest 10 percent earned less than $40,730, and the highest 10 percent earned more than $154,840. Median annual wages were $80,170 in advertising, public relations and related services.

Median annual wages of salaried craft artists were $29,080. The middle 50 percent earned between $20,730 and $39,120. The lowest 10 percent earned less than $16,290, and the highest 10 percent earned more than $54,550.

Median annual wages of salaried fine artists, including painters, sculptors, and illustrators, were $42,650. The middle 50 percent earned between $29,230 and $60,650. The lowest 10 percent earned less than $20,780, and the highest 10 percent earned more than $83,410.

Median annual wages of salaried multimedia artists and animators were $56,330. The middle 50 percent earned between $41,710 and $77,010. The lowest 10 percent earned less than $31,570, and the highest 10 percent earned more than $100,390. Median annual wages were $65,600 in motion picture and video industries, and $52,530 in advertising and related services.

Earnings for self-employed artists vary widely. Some charge only a nominal fee while they gain experience and build a reputation for their work. Others, such as well-established freelance fine artists and illustrators, can earn more than salaried artists. Many, however, find it difficult to rely solely on income earned from selling paintings or other works of art. Like other self-employed workers, freelance artists must provide their own benefits.

Related Occupations

Other workers who apply artistic skills include:

Some workers who use computers extensively and may require art skills are:

Sources of Additional Information

For general information about art and design and a list of accredited college-level programs, contact:
➤ National Association of Schools of Art and Design, 11250 Roger Bacon Dr., Suite 21, Reston, VA 20190. Internet: **http://nasad.arts-accredit.org**

For information on careers in the craft arts and for a list of schools and workshops, contact:
➤ American Craft Council Library, 72 Spring St., 6th Floor, New York, NY 10012. Internet: **http://www.craftcouncil.org**

For information on careers in illustration, contact:
➤ Society of Illustrators, 128 E. 63rd St., New York, NY 10065. Internet: **http://www.societyillustrators.org**

For information on careers in medical illustration, contact:
➤ Association of Medical Illustrators, P.O. Box 1897 Lawrence, KS 66044. Internet: **http://www.ami.org**

For information on workshops, scholarships, internships, and competitions for art students interested in advertising careers, contact:
➤ Art Directors Club, 106 W. 29th St., New York, NY 10001. Internet: **http://www.adcglobal.org**

The Occupational Information Network (O*NET) provides information on a wide range of occupational characteristics. Links to O*NET appear at the end of the Internet version of this occupational statement, accessible at **http://www.bls.gov/ooh/ocos092.htm**

Commercial and Industrial Designers

Significant Points

- Commercial and industrial designers usually work closely with a range of specialists including engineers, materials scientists, marketing and corporate strategy staff, cost estimators, and accountants.

- A bachelor's degree is usually required for entry.

- Keen competition for jobs is expected.

Nature of the Work

Commercial and industrial designers combine the fields of art, business, and engineering to design the products people use every day. In fact, these designers are responsible for the style, function, quality, and safety of almost every manufactured good. Usually designers specialize in one particular product category, such as automobiles and other transportation vehicles, appli-

Many commercial and industrial designers use computer-aided design software to create new products.

ances, technology goods, medical equipment, furniture, toys, tools and construction equipment, or housewares.

The first steps in developing a new design, or altering an existing one, are to determine the requirements of the client, the purpose of the product, and the tastes of customers or users. When creating a new design, designers often begin by researching the product user or the context in which the product will be used. They ascertain desired product characteristics, such as size, shape, weight, color, materials used, cost, ease of use, fit, and safety. To gather this information, designers meet with clients, conduct market research, read design and consumer publications, attend trade shows, and visit potential users, suppliers and manufacturers.

Next, designers prepare conceptual sketches or diagrams— by hand or with the aid of a computer—to illustrate their vision of the product. After conducting research and consulting with a creative director or other members of the product development team, designers then create detailed sketches or renderings using computer-aided design (CAD) tools. Computer models make it easier to adjust designs and to experiment with a greater number of alternatives, speeding and improving the design process. Industrial designers who work for manufacturing firms also use computer-aided industrial design (CAID) tools to create designs and machine-readable instructions that can direct automated production tools to build the designed product to exact specifications.

Designers present the designs and prototypes to their client or managers and incorporate any changes and suggestions. Designers often work with engineers, accountants, and cost estimators to determine if a product can be made safer, easier to assemble or use, or cheaper to manufacture. Before a product is completed and manufactured, designers may participate in usability and safety tests, watching consumers use prototypes and then making adjustments based on those observations.

Increasingly, designers are working with corporate strategy staff to ensure that their designs fit into the company's business plan and strategic vision. They work with marketing staff to develop plans to best market new product designs to consumers. They work to design products that accurately reflect the company's image and values. And although designers have always tried to identify and design products that fit consumers' needs, more designers are now focused on creating that product before a competitor does. More of today's designers must also focus on creating innovative products as well as considering the style and technical aspects of the product.

Work environment. Designers employed by manufacturing establishments, large corporations, or design firms generally work regular hours in well-lighted and comfortable settings. Designers in smaller design consulting firms, or those who freelance, may work under a contract to do specific tasks or designs. They frequently adjust their workday to suit their clients' schedules and deadlines, meeting with the clients evenings or weekends when necessary. Consultants and self-employed designers tend to work longer hours and in smaller, more congested, environments. Additional hours may be required to meet deadlines.

Designers may work in their own offices or studios or in clients' homes or offices. They also may travel to other locations, such as testing facilities, design centers, clients' exhibit sites, users' homes or workplaces, and manufacturing facilities. With the increased speed and sophistication of computers and advanced communications networks, designers may form international design teams and serve a more geographically dispersed clientele.

Training, Other Qualifications, and Advancement

A bachelor's degree is required for most entry-level commercial and industrial design positions. Experience through internships and a good portfolio of work are also important for jobseekers to have.

Education and training. A bachelor's degree in industrial design, architecture, or engineering is required for most entry-level commercial and industrial design jobs. Coursework includes principles of design, sketching, computer-aided design, industrial materials and processes, manufacturing methods, and some classes in engineering, physical science, mathematics, psychology, and anthropology. Many programs also include internships at design or manufacturing firms.

Because of the growing emphasis on strategic design and how products fit into a firm's overall business plan, an increasing number of designers are pursing a master's degree in business administration to gain business skills.

The National Association of Schools of Art and Design accredits approximately 300 postsecondary colleges, universities, and private institutes with programs in art and design. About 40

Projections data from the National Employment Matrix

Occupational Title	SOC Code	Employment, 2008	Projected Employment, 2018	Change, 2008-2018	
				Number	Percent
Commercial and industrial designers..	27-1021	44,300	48,300	4,000	9

(NOTE) Data in this table are rounded. See the discussion of the employment projections table in the *Handbook* introductory chapter on *Occupational Information Included in the Handbook.*

of these schools award a bachelor's degree in industrial design. Many schools require the successful completion of 1 year of basic art and design courses before entry into a bachelor's degree program. Applicants also may be required to submit sketches and other examples of their artistic ability.

Other qualifications. Creativity and technical knowledge are crucial in this occupation. People in this field must have a strong sense of the esthetic—an eye for color and detail and a sense of balance and proportion. Employers expect new designers to know computer-aided design software, but despite the advancement of this software, sketching ability remains important. Designers must also understand the technical aspects of how products function. The deciding factor in getting a job often is a good portfolio—examples of a person's best work.

Designers must be imaginative and persistent and must be able to communicate their ideas visually, verbally, and in writing. Because tastes and styles can change quickly, designers need to be well read, open to new ideas and influences, and quick to react to changing trends. Problem-solving skills and the ability to work independently and under pressure also are important traits. People in this field need self-discipline to start projects on their own, to budget their time, and to meet deadlines and production schedules.

As strategic design becomes more important, employers will seek designers with project management skills and knowledge of accounting, marketing, quality assurance, purchasing, and strategic planning. Good business sense and sales ability are important, especially for those who freelance or run their own business.

Advancement. Beginning commercial and industrial designers usually receive on-the-job training and normally need a few years of training before they can advance to higher level positions. Experienced designers in large firms may advance to chief designer, design department head, or other supervisory positions. Some designers leave the occupation to become teachers in design schools or in colleges and universities. Many faculty members continue to consult privately or operate small design studios to complement their classroom activities. Some experienced designers open their own design firms.

Employment
Commercial and industrial designers held about 44,300 jobs in 2008. About 30 percent of designers were employed by manufacturing firms, 9 percent worked in architectural, engineering and related services and another 8 percent worked for specialized design services firms.

Job Outlook
Employment is expected to grow about as fast as the average. Keen competition for jobs is expected; those with strong back-

grounds in engineering and computer-aided design and business knowledge will have the best prospects.

Employment change. Employment of commercial and industrial designers is expected to grow 9 percent between 2008 and 2018, as fast as the average for all occupations. Employment growth will arise from an increase in consumer and business demand for new or upgraded products. The continued emphasis on the quality and safety of products, the increasing demand for new products that are easy and comfortable to use, and the development of high-technology products in consumer electronics, medicine, transportation, and other fields will increase the demand for commercial and industrial designers.

However, some companies use design firms overseas, especially for the design of high-technology products. These overseas design firms are located closer to their suppliers, which reduces the time it takes to design and sell a product—an important consideration when technology is changing quickly. This offshoring of design work could continue to slow employment growth of U.S. commercial and industrial designers.

Despite the increase in design work performed overseas, most design jobs, particularly jobs not related to high-technology product design, will still remain in the U.S. Design is essential to a firm's success, and firms will want to retain control over the design process.

Job prospects. Competition for jobs will be keen because many talented individuals are attracted to the design field. The best job opportunities will be in specialized design firms which are used by manufacturers to design products or parts of products. Increasingly, manufacturers have been outsourcing design work to these design services firms to cut costs and to find the most qualified design talent, creating more opportunities in these firms.

As the demand for design work becomes more consumer-driven, designers who can closely monitor, and react to, changing customer demands—and who can work with marking and strategic planning staffs to come up with new products—will also improve their job prospects.

Employment of designers can be affected by fluctuations in the economy. For example, during periods of economic downturns, companies may cut research and development spending, including new product development.

Earnings
Median annual wage-and-salary wages for commercial and industrial designers were $57,350 in May 2008. The middle 50 percent earned between $41,550 and $76,700. The lowest 10 percent earned less than $31,400, and the highest 10 percent earned more than $97,770. Median annual wages of salaried

commercial and industrial designers in the largest industries that employed them in May 2008 were:

Management of companies and enterprises $63,940
Architectural, engineering, and related services 61,450
Specialized design services..59,150
Other miscellaneous manufacturing.............................50,990

Related Occupations

Workers in other art and design occupations include:

Some other occupations that require computer-aided design skills are:

Sources of Additional Information

For general career information on commercial and industrial design, contact:

➤ Industrial Designers Society of America, 45195 Business Court, Suite 250, Dulles, VA 20166. Internet: **http://www.idsa.org**

For general information about art and design and a list of accredited college-level programs, contact:

➤ National Association of Schools of Art and Design, 11250 Roger Bacon Dr., Suite 21, Reston, VA 20190. Internet: **http://nasad.arts-accredit.org**

The Occupational Information Network (O*NET) provides information on a wide range of occupational characteristics. Links to O*NET appear at the end of the Internet version of this occupational statement, accessible at **http://www.bls.gov/ooh/ocos290.htm**

Fashion Designers

Significant Points

- The highest numbers of fashion designers were employed in New York and California.

- Employers usually seek designers with a 2-year or 4-year degree who are knowledgeable about textiles, fabrics, ornamentation, and fashion trends.

- Keen competition for jobs is expected as many applicants are attracted to the creativity and glamour associated with the occupation.

Nature of the Work

Fashion designers help create the billions of dresses, suits, shoes, and other clothing and accessories purchased every year by consumers. Designers study fashion trends, sketch designs of clothing and accessories, select colors and fabrics, and oversee the final production of their designs. *Clothing designers* create and help produce men's, women's, and children's apparel, including casual wear, suits, sportswear, formalwear, outerwear, maternity, and intimate apparel. Footwear designers help create and produce different styles of shoes and boots. Accessory designers help create and produce items such as handbags, belts, scarves, hats, hosiery, and eyewear, which add the finishing touches to an outfit. (The work of jewelers and precious stone and metal workers is described elsewhere in the Handbook.) Some fashion designers specialize in clothing, footwear, or accessory design, but others create designs in all three fashion categories.

The design process from initial design concept to final production takes between 18 and 24 months. The first step in creating a design is researching current fashion and making predictions of future trends. Some designers conduct their own research, while others rely on trend reports published by fashion industry trade groups. Trend reports indicate what styles, colors, and fabrics will be popular for a particular season in the future. Textile manufacturers use these trend reports to begin designing fabrics and patterns while fashion designers begin to sketch preliminary designs. Designers then visit manufacturers or trade shows to procure samples of fabrics and decide which fabrics to use with which designs.

Once designs and fabrics are chosen, a prototype of the article using cheaper materials is created and then tried on a model to see what adjustments to the design need to be made. This also helps designers to narrow their choices of designs to offer for sale. After the final adjustments and selections have been made, samples of the article using the actual materials are sewn and then marketed to clothing retailers. Many designs are shown at fashion and trade shows a few times a year. Retailers at the shows place orders for certain items, which are then manufactured and distributed to stores.

Computer-aided design (CAD) is increasingly being used in the fashion design industry. Although most designers initially sketch designs by hand, a growing number also translate these hand sketches to the computer. CAD allows designers to view designs of clothing on virtual models and in various colors and shapes, thus saving time by requiring fewer adjustments of prototypes and samples later.

Depending on the size of their design firm and their experience, fashion designers may have varying levels of involvement in different aspects of design and production. In large design firms, fashion designers often are the lead designers who are responsible for creating the designs, choosing the colors and fabrics, and overseeing technical designers who turn the designs into a final product. They are responsible for creating the prototypes and patterns and work with the manufacturers and suppliers during the production stages. Large design houses also employ their own patternmakers, tailors, and sewers who create the master patterns for the design and sew the prototypes and samples. Designers working in small firms,

Fashion designers study trends and design clothing and accessories for consumers.

or those new to the job, usually perform most of the technical, patternmaking, and sewing tasks, in addition to designing the clothing. (The work of pattern makers, hand sewers, and tailors is covered in the statement on textile, apparel, and furnishings occupations elsewhere in the *Handbook*.)

Fashion designers working for apparel wholesalers or manufacturers create designs for the mass market. These designs are manufactured in various sizes and colors. A small number of high-fashion (haute couture) designers are self-employed and create custom designs for individual clients, usually at very high prices. Other high-fashion designers sell their designs in their own retail stores or cater to specialty stores or high-fashion department stores. These designers create a mixture of original garments and those that follow established fashion trends.

Some fashion designers specialize in costume design for performing arts, motion picture, and television productions. The work of costume designers is similar to other fashion designers. Costume designers, however, perform extensive research on the styles worn during the period in which the performance takes place, or they work with directors to select and create appropriate attire. They make sketches of designs, select fabric and other materials, and oversee the production of the costumes. They also must stay within the costume budget for the particular production item.

Work environment. Fashion designers employed by manufacturing establishments, wholesalers, or design firms generally work regular hours in well-lighted and comfortable settings. Designers who freelance generally work on a contract, or by the job. They frequently adjust their workday to suit their clients' schedules and deadlines, meeting with the clients during evenings or weekends when necessary. Freelance designers tend to work longer hours and in smaller, more congested, environments, and are under pressure to please clients and to find new ones in order to maintain a steady income. Regardless of their work setting, all fashion designers occasionally work long hours to meet production deadlines or prepare for fashion shows.

The global nature of the fashion business requires constant communication with suppliers, manufacturers, and customers all over the United States and the world. Most fashion designers travel several times a year to trade and fashion shows to learn about the latest fashion trends. Designers also may travel frequently to meet with fabric and materials suppliers and with manufacturers who produce the final apparel products.

Training, Other Qualifications, and Advancement
In fashion design, employers usually seek individuals with a 2-year or 4-year degree who are knowledgeable about textiles, fabrics, ornamentation, and fashion trends.

Education and training. Fashion designers typically need an associate or a bachelor's degree in fashion design. Some fashion designers also combine a fashion design degree with a business, marketing, or fashion merchandising degree, especially those who want to run their own business or retail store. Basic coursework includes color, textiles, sewing and tailoring, pattern making, fashion history, computer-aided design (CAD), and design of different types of clothing such as menswear or footwear. Coursework in human anatomy, mathematics, and psychology also is useful.

The National Association of Schools of Art and Design accredits approximately 300 postsecondary institutions with programs in art and design. Most of these schools award degrees in fashion design. Many schools do not allow formal entry into a program until a student has successfully completed basic art and design courses. Applicants usually have to submit sketches and other examples of their artistic ability.

Aspiring fashion designers can learn these necessary skills through internships with design or manufacturing firms. Some designers also gain valuable experience working in retail stores, as personal stylists, or as custom tailors. Such experience can help designers gain sales and marketing skills while learning what styles and fabrics look good on different people.

Designers also can gain exposure to potential employers by entering their designs in student or amateur contests. Because of the global nature of the fashion industry, experience in one of the international fashion centers, such as Milan or Paris, can be useful.

Other qualifications. Designers must have a strong sense of the esthetic—an eye for color and detail, a sense of balance and proportion, and an appreciation for beauty. Fashion designers also need excellent communication and problem-solving skills. Despite the advancement of computer-aided design, sketching ability remains an important advantage in fashion design. A good portfolio—a collection of a person's best work—often is the deciding factor in getting a job.

In addition to creativity, fashion designers also need to have sewing and patternmaking skills, even if they do not perform these tasks themselves. Designers need to be able to understand these skills so they can give proper instruction in how the garment should be constructed. Fashion designers also need strong sales and presentation skills to persuade clients to purchase their designs. Good teamwork and communication skills also are necessary because increasingly the business requires constant contact with suppliers, manufacturers, and buyers around the world.

Projections data from the National Employment Matrix

Occupational Title	SOC Code	Employment, 2008	Projected Employment, 2018	Change, 2008-2018	
				Number	Percent
Fashion designers..	27-1022	22,700	22,900	200	1

(NOTE) Data in this table are rounded. See the discussion of the employment projections table in the *Handbook* introductory chapter on *Occupational Information Included in the Handbook.*

Advancement. Beginning fashion designers usually start out as pattern makers or sketching assistants for more experienced designers before advancing to higher level positions. Experienced designers may advance to chief designer, design department head, or another supervisory position. Some designers may start their own design company, or sell their designs in their own retail stores. A few of the most successful designers can work for high-fashion design houses that offer personalized design services to wealthy clients.

Employment

Fashion designers held about 22,700 jobs in 2008. About 31 percent of fashion designers worked for apparel, piece goods, and notions merchant wholesalers; and 13 percent worked for apparel manufacturers. Many others were self employed.

Employment of fashion designers tends to be concentrated in regional fashion centers. In 2008, the highest numbers of fashion designers were employed in New York and California.

Job Outlook

Little or no change in employment is projected. Competition for jobs is expected to be keen as many applicants are attracted to the creativity and glamour associated with the occupation.

Employment change. Employment of fashion designers is projected to grow by 1 percent between 2008 and 2018. Some new jobs will arise from an increasing population demanding more clothing, footwear, and accessories. Demand is increasing for stylish clothing that is affordable, especially among middle-income consumers which will increase the need for fashion designers among apparel wholesalers. However, job opportunities in cut and sew manufacturing will continue to decline as apparel is increasingly manufactured overseas. Employment of fashion designers in this industry will not decline as fast as other occupations because firms are more likely to keep design work in house.

Job prospects. Job competition is expected be keen as many applicants are attracted to the creativity and glamour associated with the occupation. The best job opportunities will be in design firms that design mass-market clothing sold in department stores and retail chain stores, such as apparel wholesale firms. Few employment opportunities are expected in design firms that cater to high-end department stores and specialty boutiques as demand for expensive, high-fashion design declines relative to other luxury goods and services.

Earnings

Median annual wages for salaried fashion designers were $61,160 in May 2008. The middle 50 percent earned between $42,150 and $87,120. The lowest 10 percent earned less than $32,150, and the highest 10 percent earned more than $124,780. Median annual wages of salaried fashion designers in the largest industries that employed them in May 2008 were:

Management of companies and enterprises	$72,560
Cut and sew apparel manufacturing	66,000
Apparel, piece goods, and notions merchant wholesalers	61,600
Specialized design services	59,560

Earnings in fashion design can vary widely based on the employer and years of experience. Starting salaries in fashion design tend to be very low until designers are established in this occupation. Salaried fashion designers usually earn higher and more stable incomes than self-employed or freelance designers. However, a few of the most successful self-employed fashion designers may earn many times the salary of the highest paid salaried designers. Self-employed fashion designers must provide their own benefits and retirement.

Related Occupations

Workers in other art and design occupations include:

Sources of Additional Information

For general information about art and design and a list of accredited college-level programs, contact:

➤ National Association of Schools of Art and Design, 11250 Roger Bacon Dr., Suite 21, Reston, VA 20190. Internet: **http://nasad.arts-accredit.org**

For general information about careers in fashion design, contact:

➤ Fashion Group International, 8 West 40th St., 7th Floor, New York, NY 10018. Internet: **http://www.fgi.org**

The Occupational Information Network (O*NET) provides information on a wide range of occupational characteristics. Links to O*NET appear at the end of the Internet version of this occupational statement, accessible at

http://www.bls.gov/ooh/ocos291.htm

Floral Designers

Significant Points

- Despite the projected decline in employment, job opportunities should be good as many people leave this occupation, due to relatively low wages and limited advancement opportunities.

- Floral design is the only design specialty that does not require formal postsecondary training.

- Many floral designers work long hours on weekends and holidays, filling orders and setting up decorations for weddings and other events.

Nature of the Work

Floral designers, or *florists*, cut live, dried, or silk flowers and other greenery and arrange them into displays of various sizes and shapes. These workers design displays by selecting flowers, containers, and ribbons and arranging them into bouquets, corsages, centerpieces of tables, wreaths, etc. for weddings, funerals, holidays, and other special occasions. Some floral designers also use accessories such as balloons, candles, toys, candy, and gift baskets as part of their displays.

Job duties often vary by employment setting. Most floral designers work in small independent floral shops that specialize in custom orders and also handle large orders for weddings, caterers, or interior designers. Floral designers may meet with customers to discuss the arrangement or work from a written order. They note the occasion, the customer's preferences, the price of the order, the time the floral display or plant is to be ready, and the place to which it is to be delivered. For special occasions, floral designers usually will help set up floral decorations. Floral designers also will prearrange a few displays to have available for walk-in customers or last-minute orders. Some floral designers also assist interior designers in creating live or silk displays for hotels, restaurants, and private residences.

A number of floral designers work in the floral departments of grocery stores or for Internet florists, which specialize in creating prearranged floral decorations and bouquets. These floral retailers also may fill small custom orders for special occasions and funerals, but most grocery store florists do not deliver to clients or handle large custom orders.

Florists who work for wholesale flower distributors assist in the selection of different types of flowers and greenery to purchase and sell to retail florists. Wholesale floral designers also select flowers for displays that they use as examples for retail florists.

Self-employed floral designers must handle the various aspects of running their own businesses, such as selecting and purchasing flowers, hiring and supervising staff, and maintaining financial records. Self-employed designers also may run gift shops or wedding consultation businesses in addition to providing floral design services. Some conduct design workshops for amateur gardeners or others with an interest in floral design.

Work environment. Most floral designers work in comfortable and well-lit spaces in retail outlets or at home, although working outdoors sometimes is required. Designers also may make frequent short trips delivering flowers, setting up arrangements for special events, and procuring flowers and other supplies.

Floral designers have frequent contact with customers and must work to satisfy their demands, including last-minute holiday and funeral orders. Because many flowers are perishable, most orders cannot be completed too far in advance. Consequently, some designers work long hours before and during holidays. Some also work nights and weekends to complete large orders for weddings and other special events.

Floral designers may suffer back strain from lifting and carrying heavy flower arrangements. Designers also may suffer allergic reactions to certain types of pollen when working with flowers. In addition, they frequently use sharp objects—scissors, knives, and metal wire—that can cause injuries if handled improperly. However, injuries can be mitigated by following proper procedures.

Training, Other Qualifications, and Advancement

Floral design is the only design occupation that does not require formal postsecondary training; most floral designers learn their skills on the job. Employers generally look for high school graduates who have creativity, a flair for arranging flowers, and a desire to learn.

Education and training. Most floral designers have a high school diploma or equivalent and learn their skills on the job over the course of a few months. Although typically not required, some private floral schools, vocational schools, and community colleges award certificates in floral design. These programs generally require a high school diploma for admission and last from several weeks to 1 year. Floral design courses teach the basics of arranging flowers, including the different types of flowers, their color and texture, cutting and taping techniques, tying bows and ribbons, proper handling and care of flowers, floral trends, and pricing.

Some floral designers also can earn an associate or bachelor's degree at a community college or university. Some programs offer formal degrees in floral design, while others offer degrees in floriculture, horticulture, or ornamental horticulture. In addition to floral design courses, these programs teach courses in

Most floral designers work in small independent floral shops.

Projections data from the National Employment Matrix

Occupational Title	SOC Code	Employment, 2008	Projected Employment, 2018	Change, 2008-2018	
				Number	Percent
Floral designers..	27-1023	76,100	74,200	-1,900	-3

(NOTE) Data in this table are rounded. See the discussion of the employment projections table in the *Handbook* introductory chapter on *Occupational Information Included in the Handbook*.

botany, chemistry, hydrology, microbiology, pesticides, and soil management.

Since many floral designers manage their own business, additional courses in business, accounting, marketing, and computer technology are helpful.

Certification and other qualifications. The American Institute of Floral Designers offers an accreditation examination as an indication of professional achievement in floral design. The exam consists of a written part covering floral terminology and an onsite floral-arranging part in which candidates have 4 hours to complete five floral designs: funeral tributes, table arrangements, wedding arrangements, wearable flowers, and a category of the candidate's choosing.

Floral designers must be creative, service oriented, and able to communicate their ideas visually and verbally. Because trends in floral design change fairly quickly, designers must be open to new ideas and react quickly to changing trends. Problem-solving skills and the ability to work independently and under pressure also are important traits. Individuals in this field need self-discipline to budget their time and meet deadlines.

Advancement. Many florists gain their initial experience working as cashiers or delivery people in retail floral stores. The completion of formal design training, however, is an asset for floral designers, particularly those interested in advancing to chief floral designer or in opening their own businesses.

Advancement in the floral field is limited. After a few years of on-the-job training, designers can either advance to a supervisory position or open their own floral shop.

Employment

Floral designers held about 76,100 jobs in 2008. About 50 percent of all floral designers worked in florist shops. Another 12 percent worked in the floral departments of grocery stores.

Job Outlook

Despite the decline in employment, job opportunities are expected to be good as many people leave this occupation because of relatively low wages and limited advancement opportunities.

Employment change. Employment of floral designers is expected to decline slowly, by 3 percent, between 2008 and 2018. The need for floral designers will decline as people purchase fewer elaborate floral decorations for their everyday lives. Even though more people will demand fresh flowers in their homes and offices, as competition from grocery stores lowers the cost of flowers and increases the convenience of buying them, these flower arrangements tend to be simpler than those from traditional retail florists and, therefore, require fewer designers. On the other hand, this decline may be moderated by the continued demand for floral decorations, due to increases in the number and lavishness of weddings and other special events.

Mass merchandisers like grocery stores offer cheaper and simper flower arrangements, at much greater convenience, than small retail florists do. They have become more appealing when it comes to consumer's daily needs. Specialty floral retailers will continue to be needed for custom orders but are being steadily replaced when it comes to everyday sales.

Job prospects. Job opportunities should be good, because many people leave their jobs, particularly in retail florists, due to comparatively low wages and limited opportunities for advancement. Opportunities should be good in grocery store and Internet floral shops, as sales of floral arrangements from these outlets grow. Prearranged displays and gifts available in these stores appeal to consumers because of the convenience and because of prices that are lower than can be found in independent floral shops.

As mass marketers capture more of the small flower orders, independent floral shops are increasingly finding themselves under pressure to remain profitable. Many independent shops have added online ordering systems to compete with Internet florists. Others are trying to distinguish their services by specializing in certain areas of floral design or by combining floral design with event planning and interior design services. Some florists also are adding holiday decorating services in which they will set up decorations for businesses and residences.

Discretionary spending on flowers and floral products is highly sensitive to the state of the economy, and during economic downturns employment may fall off as floral expenditures decline.

Earnings

Median annual wages for wage and salary floral designers were $23,230 in May 2008. The middle 50 percent earned between $18,690 and $29,330. The lowest 10 percent earned less than $16,210, and the highest 10 percent earned more than $35,010. Median annual wages were $25,160 in grocery stores and $22,710 in florists.

Related Occupations

Other art and design occupations include:

Other occupations involved directly with plants and flowers include:

Sources of Additional Information

For information about careers in floral design, contact:

➤ American Institute of Floral Designers, 720 Light St., Baltimore, MD 21230. Internet: **http://www.aifd.org**

➤ Society of American Florists, 1601 Duke St., Alexandria, VA 22314. Internet: **http://www.safnow.org**

To learn more about designing flowers for weddings and funerals, see "Jobs in weddings and funerals: Working with the betrothed and the bereaved," in the winter 2006 *Occupational Outlook Quarterly* and online at **http://www.bls.gov/opub/ooq/2006/winter/art03.pdf.**

The Occupational Information Network (O*NET) provides information on a wide range of occupational characteristics. Links to O*NET appear at the end of the Internet version of this occupational statement, accessible at **http://www.bls.gov/ooh/ocos292.htm**

Graphic Designers

Significant Points

- Employment is expected to grow about as fast as the average, with many new jobs associated with interactive media.

- A bachelor's degree in graphic design is usually required.

- Jobseekers are expected to face keen competition; individuals with Web site design and animation experience will have the best opportunities.

Nature of the Work

Graphic designers—or *graphic artists*—plan, analyze, and create visual solutions to communications problems. They find the most effective way to get messages across in print and electronic media using color, type, illustration, photography, animation, and various print and layout techniques. Graphic designers develop the overall layout and production design of magazines, newspapers, journals, corporate reports, and other publications. They also produce promotional displays, packaging, and marketing brochures for products and services, design distinctive logos for products and businesses, and develop signs and signage systems—called environmental graphics—for business and government. An increasing number of graphic designers also develop material for Internet Web pages, interactive media, and multimedia projects. Graphic designers also may produce the credits that appear before and after television programs and movies.

The first step in developing a new design is to determine the needs of the client, the message the design should portray, and its appeal to customers or users. Graphic designers consider cognitive, cultural, physical, and social factors in planning and executing designs for the target audience. Designers gather relevant information by meeting with clients, creative or art directors, and by performing their own research. Identifying the needs of consumers is becoming increasingly important for graphic designers as they continue to develop corporate communication strategies in addition to creating designs and layouts.

Graphic designers prepare sketches or layouts—by hand or with the aid of a computer—to illustrate their vision for the design. They select colors, sound, artwork, photography, animation, style of type, and other visual elements for the design. Designers also select the size and arrangement of the different elements on the page or screen. They may create graphs and charts from data for use in publications, and they often consult with copywriters on any text that accompanies the design. Designers then present the completed design to their clients or art or creative director for approval. In printing and publishing firms, graphic designers also may assist the printers by selecting the type of paper and ink for the publication and reviewing the mock-up design for errors before final publication.

Graphic designers use specialized computer software packages to help them create layouts and design elements and to program animated graphics.

Graphic designers sometimes supervise assistants who follow instructions to complete parts of the design process. Designers who run their own businesses also may devote a considerable time to developing new business contacts, choosing equipment, and performing administrative tasks, such as reviewing catalogues and ordering samples. The need for up-to-date computer and communications equipment is an ongoing consideration for graphic designers.

Work environment. Working conditions and places of employment vary. Graphic designers employed by large advertising, publishing, or design firms generally work regular hours in well-lighted and comfortable settings. Designers in smaller design consulting firms and those who freelance generally work on a contract, or job, basis. They frequently adjust their workday to suit their clients' schedules and deadlines. Consultants and self-employed designers tend to work longer hours and in smaller, more congested, environments.

Designers may work in their own offices or studios or in clients' offices. Designers who are paid by the assignment are under pressure to please existing clients and to find new ones to maintain a steady income. All designers sometimes face frustration when their designs are rejected or when their

Graphic designers must be familiar with computer graphics and design software.

Projections data from the National Employment Matrix

Occupational Title	SOC Code	Employment, 2008	Projected Employment, 2018	Change, 2008-2018	
				Number	Percent
Graphic designers..	27-1024	286,100	323,100	36,900	13

(NOTE) Data in this table are rounded. See the discussion of the employment projections table in the *Handbook* introductory chapter on *Occupational Information Included in the Handbook.*

work is not as creative as they wish. Graphic designers may work evenings or weekends to meet production schedules, especially in the printing and publishing industries where deadlines are shorter and more frequent.

Training, Other Qualifications, and Advancement
A bachelor's degree in graphic design is usually required. Creativity, communication, and problem-solving skills are important, as are a familiarity with computer graphics and design software.

Education and training. A bachelor's degree in graphic design is usually required for most entry-level and advanced graphic design positions. Bachelor's degree programs in fine arts or graphic design are offered at many colleges, universities, and private design schools. Most curriculums include studio art, principles of design, computerized design, commercial graphics production, printing techniques, and Web site design. In addition to design courses, a liberal arts education that includes courses in art history, writing, psychology, sociology, foreign languages and cultural studies, marketing, and business are useful in helping designers work effectively.

Associate degrees and certificates in graphic design also are available from 2-year and 3-year professional schools, and graduates of these programs normally qualify as assistants to graphic designers or for positions requiring technical skills only. Creative individuals who wish to pursue a career in graphic design—and who already possess a bachelor's degree in another field—can complete a 2-year or 3-year program in graphic design to learn the technical requirements.

The National Association of Schools of Art and Design accredits about 300 postsecondary institutions with programs in art and design. Most of these schools award a degree in graphic design. Many schools do not allow formal entry into a bachelor's degree program until a student has successfully finished a year of basic art and design courses, which can be completed in high school. Applicants may be required to submit sketches and other examples of their artistic ability.

Graphic designers must keep up with new and updated computer graphics and design software, either on their own or through formal software training programs.

Other qualifications. In addition to postsecondary training in graphic design, creativity, communication, and problem-solving skills are crucial. Graphic designers must be creative and able to communicate their ideas visually, verbally, and in writing. They also must have an eye for details. Designers show employers these traits by putting together a portfolio—a collection of examples of a person's best work. A good portfolio often is the deciding factor in getting a job.

Because consumer tastes can change fairly quickly, designers also need to be well read, open to new ideas and influ-

ences, and quick to react to changing trends. The ability to work independently and under pressure are equally important traits. People in this field need self-discipline to start projects on their own, to budget their time, and to meet deadlines and production schedules. Good business sense and sales ability also are important, especially for those who freelance or run their own firms.

Advancement. Beginning graphic designers usually need 1 to 3 years of working experience before they can advance to higher positions. Experienced graphic designers in large firms may advance to chief designer, art or creative director, or other supervisory positions. Some designers leave the occupation to become teachers in design schools or in colleges and universities. Many faculty members continue to consult privately or operate small design studios to complement their classroom activities. Some experienced designers open their own firms or choose to specialize in one area of graphic design.

Employment
Graphic designers held about 286,100 jobs in 2008. Most graphic designers worked in specialized design services; advertising and related services; printing and related support activities; or newspaper, periodical, book, and directory publishers. A small number of designers produced computer graphics for computer systems design firms.

Some designers do freelance work—full time or part time—in addition to holding a salaried job in design or in another occupation.

Job Outlook
Employment is expected grow about as fast as average. Keen competition for jobs is expected; individuals with Web site design and animation experience will have the best opportunities.

Employment change. Employment of graphic designers is expected to grow 13 percent, as fast as the average for all occupations from 2008 to 2018, as demand for graphic design continues to increase from advertisers and computer design firms.

Moreover, graphic designers with Web site design and animation experience will especially be needed as demand increases for design projects for interactive media—Web sites, mobile phones, and other technology. Demand for graphic designers also will increase as advertising firms create print and Web marketing and promotional materials for a growing number of products and services. Growth in Internet advertising, in particular, is expected to increase the number of designers. However, growth may be tempered by reduced demand in the print publishing, where many graphic designers are employed.

Job prospects. Graphic designers are expected to face keen competition for available positions. Many talented individuals are attracted to careers as graphic designers. Individuals with Web site design and animation experience will have the best opportunities.

Graphic designers with a broad liberal arts education and experience in marketing and business management will be best suited for positions developing communication strategies.

Earnings

Median annual wages for graphic designers were $42,400 in May 2008. The middle 50 percent earned between $32,600 and $56,620. The lowest 10 percent earned less than $26,110, and the highest 10 percent earned more than $74,660. May 2008 median annual wages in the industries employing the largest numbers of graphic designers were:

Computer systems design and related services $47,860
Specialized design services..45,870
Advertising, public relations and related services.....43,540
Newspaper, periodical, book, and
    directory publishers..36,910
Printing and related support activities........................36,100

According to the American Institute of Graphic Arts, median annual cash compensation for entry-level designers was $35,000 in 2008. Staff-level graphic designers earned a median of $45,000. Senior designers, who may supervise junior staff or have some decision-making authority that reflects their knowledge of graphic design, earned a median of $60,000. Solo designers who freelanced or worked under contract to another company reported median earnings of $57,000. Design directors, the creative heads of design firms or in-house corporate design departments, earned $95,000. Graphic designers with ownership or partnership interests in a firm or who were principals of the firm in some other capacity earned $95,000.

Related Occupations

Workers in other occupations in the art and design field include:

Other occupations that require computer-aided design skills include:

Other occupations involved in the design, layout, and copy of publications include:

Sources of Additional Information

For general information about art and design and a list of accredited college-level programs, contact:
➤ National Association of Schools of Art and Design, 11250 Roger Bacon Dr., Suite 21, Reston, VA 20190-5248. Internet: **http://nasad.arts-accredit.org**

For information about various design careers, contact:
➤ American Institute of Graphic Arts, 164 Fifth Ave., New York, NY 10010. Internet: **http://www.aiga.org**

For information on workshops, scholarships, internships, and competitions for graphic design students interested in advertising careers, contact:
➤ Art Directors Club, 106 West 29th St., New York, NY 10001. Internet: **http://www.adcglobal.org**

The Occupational Information Network (O*NET) provides information on a wide range of occupational characteristics. Links to O*NET appear at the end of the Internet version of this occupational statement, accessible at **http://www.bls.gov/ooh/ocos090.htm**

Interior Designers

Significant Points

- Keen competition is expected for jobs because many talented individuals are attracted to this occupation.

- Self employment is common; many interior designers work in small firms or on a contract basis.

- Postsecondary education—either an associate or a bachelor's degree—is necessary for entry-level positions; some States license interior designers.

Nature of the Work

Interior designers draw upon many disciplines to enhance the function, safety, and aesthetics of interior spaces. Their main concerns are with how different colors, textures, furniture, lighting, and space work together to meet the needs of a building's occupants. Designers plan interior spaces of almost every type of building, including offices, airport terminals, theaters, shopping malls, restaurants, hotels, schools, hospitals, and private residences. Good design can boost office productivity, increase sales, attract a more affluent clientele, provide a more relaxing hospital stay, or increase a building's market value.

Traditionally, most interior designers focused on decorating—choosing a style and color palette and then selecting appropriate furniture, floor and window coverings, artwork, and lighting. However, an increasing number of designers are becoming involved in architectural detailing, such as crown molding and built-in bookshelves, and in planning layouts of buildings undergoing renovation, including helping to determine the location of windows, stairways, escalators, and walkways.

Interior designers must be able to read blueprints, understand building and fire codes, and know how to make space accessible to people who are disabled. Designers frequently collaborate with architects, electricians, and building contractors to ensure that designs are safe and meet construction requirements.

An increasing number of interior designers are involved with architectural detailing.

Whatever space they are working on, almost all designers follow the same process. The first step, known as programming, is to determine the client's needs and wishes. The designer usually meets face-to-face with the client to find out how the space will be used and to get an idea of the client's preferences and budget. For example, the designer might inquire about a family's cooking habits if the family is remodeling a kitchen or ask about a store or restaurant's target customer to pick an appropriate motif. The designer also will visit the space to take inventory of existing furniture and equipment and identify positive attributes of the space and potential problems.

After collecting this information, the designer formulates a design plan and estimates costs. Today, designs often are created with the use of computer-aided design (CAD) software, which provides more detail and easier corrections than sketches made by hand. Upon completing the design plan, the designer will present it to the client and make revisions based on the client's input.

When the design concept is finalized, the designer will begin specifying the materials, finishes, and furnishings required, such as furniture, lighting, flooring, wall covering, and artwork. Depending on the complexity of the project, the designer also might submit drawings for approval by a construction inspector to ensure that the design meets building codes. If a project requires structural work, the designer works with an architect or engineer for that part of the project. Most designs also require the hiring of contractors to do technical work, such as lighting, plumbing, and electrical wiring. Often designers choose contractors and write work contracts.

Finally, the designer develops a timeline for the project, coordinates contractor work schedules, and makes sure work is completed on time. The designer oversees the installation of the design elements, and after the project is complete, the designer, together with the client, pay follow-up visits to the building site to ensure that the client is satisfied. If the client is not satisfied, the designer makes corrections.

Designers who work for furniture or home and garden stores sell merchandise in addition to offering design services. In-store designers provide services, such as selecting a style and color scheme that fits the client's needs or finding suitable accessories and lighting, similar to those offered by other interior designers.

However, in-store designers rarely visit clients' spaces and use only a particular store's products or catalogs.

Interior designers sometimes supervise assistants who carry out their plans and perform administrative tasks, such as reviewing catalogues and ordering samples. Designers who run their own businesses also may devote considerable time to developing new business contacts, examining equipment and space needs, and attending to business matters.

Although most interior designers do many kinds of projects, some specialize in one area of interior design. Some specialize in the type of building space—usually residential or commercial—while others specialize in a certain design element or type of client, such as healthcare facilities. The most common specialties of this kind are lighting, kitchen and bath, and closet designs. However, designers can specialize in almost any area of design, including acoustics and noise abatement, security, electronics and home theaters, home spas, and indoor gardens.

Three areas of design that are becoming increasingly popular are ergonomic design, elder design, and environmental—or green—design. Ergonomic design involves designing work spaces and furniture that emphasize good posture and minimize muscle strain on the body. Elder design involves planning interior space to aid in the movement of people who are elderly and disabled. Green design involves selecting furniture and carpets that are free of chemicals and hypoallergenic and selecting construction materials that are energy-efficient or are made from renewable resources.

Work environment. Working conditions and places of employment vary. Interior designers employed by large corporations or design firms generally work regular hours in well-lighted and comfortable settings. Designers in smaller design consulting firms or those who freelance generally work on a contract, or job, basis. They frequently adjust their workday to suit their clients' schedules and deadlines, meeting with clients during evening or weekend hours when necessary. Consultants and self-employed designers tend to work longer hours and in smaller, more congested environments.

Interior designers may work under stress to meet deadlines, stay on budget, and please clients. Self-employed designers also are under pressure to find new clients to maintain a steady income.

Designers may work in their own offices or studios or in clients' homes or offices. They also may travel to other locations, such as showrooms, design centers, clients' exhibit sites, and manufacturing facilities. With the increased speed and sophistication of computers and advanced communications networks, designers may form international design teams, serve a more geographically dispersed clientele, research design alternatives by using information on the Internet, and purchase supplies electronically.

Training, Other Qualifications, and Advancement
An associate or bachelor's degree is needed for entry-level positions in interior design. Some States license interior designers.

Education and training. Postsecondary education is necessary for entry-level positions in interior design. Training programs are available from professional design schools or from colleges and universities and usually take 2 to 4 years to complete. Graduates of 2-year or 3-year programs are awarded certificates or associate degrees in interior design and normally qualify as assistants to interior designers upon graduation. Graduates with a bachelor's degree usually qualify for a formal design apprenticeship program.

The National Association of Schools of Art and Design accredits approximately 300 postsecondary institutions with programs in art and design. Most of these schools award a degree in interior design. Applicants may be required to submit sketches and other examples of their artistic ability. Basic coursework includes CAD, drawing, perspective, spatial planning, color and fabrics, furniture design, architecture, ergonomics, ethics, and psychology.

The Council for Interior Design Accreditation also accredits interior design programs that lead to a bachelor's or master's degree. In 2008, there were over 150 accredited programs in interior design in the United States; most are part of schools or departments of art, architecture, and home economics.

After the completion of formal training, interior designers can enter a 1-year to 3-year apprenticeship to gain experience before working on their own. Most apprentices work in design or architecture firms under the supervision of an experienced designer. Apprentices also may choose to gain experience working as an in-store designer in furniture stores. The National Council for Interior Design Qualification offers the Interior Design Experience Program, which helps entry-level interior designers gain valuable work experience by supervising their work and offering mentoring services to new designers.

Licensure.   A number of States register or license interior designers. The National Council for Interior Design Qualification administers the licensing exam for interior design qualification. To be eligible to take the exam, applicants must have at least 6 years of combined education and experience in interior design, of which at least 2 years must be postsecondary education.

Once candidates have passed the qualifying exam, they are granted the title of Certified, Registered, or Licensed Interior Designer, depending on the State. Continuing education is often required to maintain licensure.

Other qualifications.   Employers increasingly prefer interior designers who are familiar with computer-aided design software and the basics of architecture and engineering to ensure that their designs meet building safety codes.

In addition to possessing technical knowledge, interior designers must be creative, imaginative, and persistent and must be able to communicate their ideas visually, verbally, and in writing. Because tastes in style can change fairly quickly, designers need to be well read, open to new ideas and influences, and quick to react to changing trends. Problem-solving skills and the ability to work independently and under pressure are additional important traits. People in this field need self-discipline to start projects on their own, to budget their time,

and to meet deadlines and production schedules. Good business sense and sales ability also are important, especially for those who freelance or run their own business.

Certification and advancement.   Optional certifications in residential kitchen and bath design are available from the National Kitchen and Bath Association. The association offers several different levels of certification for kitchen and bath designers, each achieved through training seminars and certification exams.

Beginning interior designers receive on-the-job training and normally need 1 to 3 years of training before they can advance to higher level positions. Experienced designers in large firms may advance to chief designer, design department head, or some other supervisory position. Some experienced designers open their own firms or decide to specialize in one aspect of interior design. Other designers leave the occupation to become teachers in schools of design or in colleges and universities. Many faculty members continue to consult privately or operate small design studios to complement their classroom activities.

Employment

Interior designers held about 71,700 jobs in 2008. About 30 percent of interior designers worked in specialized design services. Additionally, 14 percent of interior designers provided design services in architectural and landscape architectural services and 9 percent worked in furniture and home-furnishing stores. Many interior designers also performed freelance work in addition to holding a salaried job in interior design or another occupation.

Job Outlook

Employment is expected to grow faster than average; however, keen competition for jobs is expected.

Employment change.   Employment of interior designers is expected to grow 19 percent from 2008 to 2018, faster than the average for all occupations. An increasing interest in interior design and awareness of its benefits will increase demand for designers. As businesses realize the improvements that can be made to worker and customer satisfaction through good design, they will use interior designers to redesign their offices and stores.

Homeowners are increasingly using the services of interior designers when they plan new additions, remodel aging kitchens and bathrooms, and update the general décor of their home. Many homeowners also have requested design help in creating year-round outdoor living spaces and home theater systems.

Demand for interior design services from the healthcare industry is expected to be high because of an anticipated increase in demand for facilities that will accommodate the aging population. Designers will be needed to make these facilities as comfortable and homelike as possible for patients. There will also

Projections data from the National Employment Matrix

Occupational Title	SOC Code	Employment, 2008	Projected Employment, 2018	Change, 2008-2018	
				Number	Percent
Interior designers	27-1025	71,700	85,600	13,900	19

(NOTE) Data in this table are rounded. See the discussion of the employment projections table in the *Handbook* introductory chapter on *Occupational Information Included in the Handbook.*

be demand from businesses in the hospitality industry—hotels, resorts, and restaurants—where good design work can help attract more business.

Some interior designers choose to specialize in one design element to create a niche for themselves in an increasingly competitive market. The demand for kitchen and bath design is growing in response to the growing demand for home remodeling. Designs using the latest technology in, for example, home theaters, state-of-the-art conference facilities, and security systems are expected to be especially popular. In addition, demand for home spas, indoor gardens, and outdoor living space should continue to increase.

Extensive knowledge of ergonomics and green design are expected to be in demand. Ergonomic design has gained in popularity with the growth in the elderly population and workplace safety requirements. The public's growing awareness of environmental quality and the growing number of individuals with allergies and asthma are expected to increase the demand for green design.

Job prospects. Interior designers are expected to face keen competition for available positions because many talented individuals are attracted to this profession. Individuals with little or no formal training in interior design, as well as those lacking creativity and perseverance, will find it very difficult to establish and maintain a career in this occupation. Designers with formal training or experience in green or energy efficient-design in particular are expected to have better job prospects due to increased interest in this area.

As the economy grows, more private businesses and consumers will request the services of interior designers. However, design services are considered a luxury expense and may be subject to fluctuations in the economy. For example, decreases in consumer and business income and spending caused by a slow economy can have a detrimental effect on employment of interior designers.

Earnings

Median annual wages for interior designers were $44,950 in May 2008. The middle 50 percent earned between $34,620 and $61,880. The lowest 10 percent earned less than $27,230, and the highest 10 percent earned more than $82,750. Median annual wages in the industries employing the largest numbers of interior designers in May 2008 were:

Architectural, engineering, and related services $49,290
Specialized design services..45,470
Furniture stores...41,080
Building material and supplies dealers 40,040

Interior design salaries vary widely with the specialty, type of employer, number of years of experience, and reputation of the individuals. Among salaried interior designers, those in large specialized design and architectural firms tend to earn higher and more stable salaries. Interior designers working in retail stores usually earn a commission, which can be irregular.

For residential design projects, self-employed interior designers and those working in smaller firms usually earn a per-hour consulting fee, plus a percentage of the total cost of furniture, lighting, artwork, and other design elements. For commercial projects, they might charge a per-hour consulting fee, charge by the square footage, or charge a flat fee for the whole project. Also, designers who use specialty contractors usually earn a percentage of the contractor's earnings on the project in return for hiring the contractor. Self-employed designers must provide their own benefits.

Related Occupations

Workers in other occupations who design or arrange objects to enhance their appearance and function include:

Sources of Additional Information

For information on degrees, continuing education, and licensure programs in interior design and interior design research, contact:
➤ American Society of Interior Designers, 608 Massachusetts Ave. NE., Washington, DC 20002. Internet: **http://www.asid.org**

For a list of schools with accredited bachelor's degree programs in interior design, contact:
➤ Council for Interior Design Accreditation, 206 Granville Ave, Suite 350, Grand Rapids, MI 49503. Internet: **http://www.accredit-id.org**

For general information about art and design and a list of accredited college-level programs, contact:
➤ National Association of Schools of Art and Design, 11250 Roger Bacon Dr., Suite 21, Reston, VA 20190. Internet: **http://nasad.arts-accredit.org**

For information on State licensing requirements and exams, and the Interior Design Experience Program, contact:
➤ National Council for Interior Design Qualification, 1602 L St. NW., Suite 200, Washington, DC 20036. Internet: **http://www.ncidq.org**

For information on careers, continuing education, and certification programs in the interior design specialty of residential kitchen and bath design, contact:
➤ National Kitchen and Bath Association, 687 Willow Grove St., Hackettstown, NJ 07840. Internet: **http://www.nkba.org/student**

The Occupational Information Network (O*NET) provides information on a wide range of occupational characteristics. Links to O*NET appear at the end of the Internet version of this occupational statement, accessible at **http://www.bls.gov/ooh/ocos293.htm**

Entertainers and Performers, Sports and Related Occupations

Actors, Producers, and Directors

Significant Points

- Actors endure long periods of unemployment, intense competition for roles, and frequent rejections in auditions.

- Formal training through a university or acting conservatory is typical; however, many actors, producers, and directors find work on the basis of their experience and talent alone.

- Because earnings may be erratic, many actors, producers, and directors supplement their incomes by holding jobs in other fields.

Nature of the Work

Actors, producers, and directors express ideas and create images in theater, film, radio, television, and other performing arts media. They interpret a writer's script to entertain, inform, or instruct an audience. Although many actors, producers, and directors work in New York or Los Angeles, far more work in other places. They perform, direct, and produce in local or regional television studios, theaters, or film production companies, often creating advertising or training films or small-scale independent movies.

Actors perform in stage, radio, television, video, or motion picture productions. They also work in cabarets, nightclubs, and theme parks. Actors portray characters, and, for more complex roles, they research their character's traits and circumstances so that they can better understand a script.

Most actors struggle to find steady work and only a few achieve recognition as stars. Others work as "*extras*," with no lines to deliver. Some actors do voiceover and narration work for advertisements, animated features, books on tape, and other electronic media. They also teach in high school or university drama departments, acting conservatories, or public programs.

Producers are entrepreneurs who make the business and financial decisions involving a motion picture, television show, or stage production. They select scripts, approve the development of ideas, arrange financing, and determine the size and cost of the endeavor. Producers hire or approve directors, principal cast members, and key production staff members.

Large productions often have associate, assistant, or line producers who share responsibilities. The number of producers and their specific job duties vary with the size and budget of each production; however, all work is done under the overall direction of an executive producer. Together the producers coordinate the activities of writers, directors, managers, and agents to ensure that each project stays on schedule and within budget.

Directors are responsible for the overall creative decisions of a production. They interpret scripts, audition and select cast members, conduct rehearsals, and direct the work of cast and crew. They approve the design elements of a production, including the sets, costumes, choreography, and music. As with producers, large productions often have many levels of directors working on them. Assistant directors cue the performers and technicians, telling them when to make entrances or light, sound, or set changes. All directors must ultimately answer to the executive producer, who has the final say on all factors related to the production.

Work environment. Actors, producers, and directors work under constant pressure. Many face stress from the continual need to find their next job. To succeed, actors, producers, and directors need patience and commitment to their craft. Actors strive to deliver flawless performances, often while working under undesirable and unpleasant conditions. Producers and directors organize rehearsals and meet with writers, designers, financial backers, and production technicians. They experience stress not only from these activities, but also from the need to adhere to budgets, union work rules, and production schedules.

Work assignments typically are short term—ranging from 1 day to a few months—which means that workers frequently experience long periods of unemployment between jobs. The uncertain nature of the work results in unpredictable earnings and intense competition for jobs. Often, actors, producers, and directors must hold other jobs in order to sustain a living.

Work hours are often long and irregular—evening and weekend work is a regular part of life in the performing arts. Actors, producers, and directors who work in theater may travel with a touring show across the country, whereas those who work in film may work on location, sometimes under adverse weather conditions. Actors who perform in a television series often appear on camera with little preparation time, because scripts tend to be revised frequently or even written moments before taping. Those who appear live or before a studio audience must be able to handle impromptu situations and calmly ad lib, or substitute, lines when necessary.

Actors, producers, and directors often work long, irregular hours.

Actors should be in good physical condition and have the necessary stamina and coordination to move about theater stages and large movie and television studio lots. They also need to maneuver about complex technical sets while staying in character and projecting their voices audibly. Actors must be fit to endure heat from stage or studio lights and the weight of heavy costumes. Producers and directors ensure the safety of actors by conducting extra rehearsals on the set so that the actors can learn the layout of set pieces and props, by allowing time for warm-ups and stretching exercises to guard against physical and vocal injuries, and by providing an adequate number of breaks to prevent heat exhaustion and dehydration.

Training, Other Qualifications, and Advancement

People who become actors, producers, and directors follow many paths to employment. The most important qualities employers look for are creative instincts, innate talent, and the intellectual capacity to perform. The best way to prepare for a career as an actor, especially in the theater, is through formal dramatic training, preferably obtained as part of a bachelor's degree program. Producers and especially directors need experience in the field, either as actors or in other related jobs.

Education and training. Formal dramatic training, either through an acting conservatory or a university program, generally is necessary for these jobs, but some people successfully enter the field without it. Most people studying for a bachelor's degree take courses in radio and television broadcasting, communications, film, theater, drama, or dramatic literature. Many stage actors continue their academic training and receive a Master of Fine Arts (MFA) degree. Advanced curricula may include courses in stage speech and movement, directing, playwriting, and design, as well as intensive acting workshops. The National Association of Schools of Theatre accredits over 150 programs in theater arts.

Most aspiring actors participate in high school and college plays, work at college radio or television stations, or perform with local community theater groups. Local and regional theater experience may also help many young actors hone their skills. In television and film, actors and directors typically start in smaller roles or independent movie production companies and then work their way up to larger productions. Actors, regardless of their level of experience, may pursue workshop training through acting conservatories or mentoring by a drama coach.

There are no specific training requirements for producers. They come from many different backgrounds. Actors, writers, film editors, and business managers commonly enter the field. Producers often start in a theatrical management office, working for a press agent, managing director, or business manager. Some start in a performing arts union or service organization. Others work behind the scenes with successful directors, serve on the boards of art companies, or promote their own projects. Although there are no formal training programs for producers, a number of colleges and universities offer degree programs in arts management and in managing nonprofit organizations.

Some directors have experience as actors or writers, while others gain experience in the field by assisting established directors. Many also have formal training in directing.

Other qualifications. Actors need talent and creativity that will enable them to portray different characters. Because competition for parts is fierce, versatility and a wide range of related performance skills, such as singing, dancing, skating, juggling, acrobatics, or miming are especially useful. Actors must have poise, stage presence, the ability to affect an audience, and the ability to follow direction. Modeling experience also may be helpful. Physical appearance, such as having certain features and being the specified size and weight, often is a deciding factor in who gets a particular role.

Some actors begin as movie extras. To become an extra, one usually must be listed by casting agencies that supply extras to the major movie studios in Hollywood. Applicants are accepted only when the number of people of a particular type on the list—for example, athletic young women, old men, or small children—falls below what is needed. In recent years, only a very small proportion of applicants have succeeded in being listed.

Like actors, directors and producers need talent and creativity. Directors need management ability because they are often in charge of a large number of people in a production. Producers need business acumen.

Advancement. As the reputations and box-office draw of actors, producers, and directors grow, some of them work on bigger budget productions, on network or syndicated broadcasts, in more prestigious theaters, or in larger markets. Actors may advance to lead roles and receive star billing. A few actors move into acting-related jobs, becoming drama coaches, directors, or producers. Some actors teach drama privately or in colleges and universities.

Employment

In May 2008, actors, producers, and directors held about 155,100 jobs, primarily in the motion picture and video, performing arts, and broadcast industries. This statistic does not capture large number of actors, producers, and directors who were available for work but were between jobs during the month in which data were collected. About 21 percent of actors, producers, and directors were self-employed.

Employment in motion pictures and in films for television is centered in New York and Los Angeles. However, small studios exist throughout the country. Many films are shot on location and may employ local professional and nonprofessional actors. In television, opportunities are concentrated in the network centers of New York and Los Angeles, but cable television services and local television stations around the country also employ many actors, producers, and directors.

Employment in the theater, and in other performing arts companies, is cyclical—higher in the fall and spring seasons—and concentrated in New York and other major cities with large commercial houses for musicals and touring productions. Also, many cities support established professional regional theaters that operate on a seasonal or year-round basis.

Projections data from the National Employment Matrix

Occupational Title	SOC Code	Employment, 2008	Projected Employment, 2018	Change, 2008-2018	
				Number	Percent
Actors, producers, and directors	27-2010	155,100	172,000	16,900	11
Actors..	27-2011	56,500	63,700	7,200	13
Producers and directors..	27-2012	98,600	108,300	9,700	10

(NOTE) Data in this table are rounded. See the discussion of the employment projections table in the *Handbook* introductory chapter on *Occupational Information Included in the Handbook*.

Actors, producers, and directors may find work in summer festivals, on cruise lines, and in theme parks. Many smaller, nonprofit professional companies, such as repertory companies, dinner theaters, and theaters affiliated with drama schools, acting conservatories, and universities, provide employment opportunities for local amateur talent and professional entertainers. Auditions typically are held in New York for many productions across the country and for shows that go on the road.

Job Outlook

Employment is expected to grow as fast as the average for all occupations. Competition for jobs will be keen. Although a growing number of people aspire to enter these professions, many will leave the field early because the work—when it is available—is hard, the hours are long, and the pay is often low.

Employment change. Employment in these occupations is expected to grow 11 percent during the 2008–18 decade, about as fast as the average for all occupations. Expanding cable and satellite television operations and increasing box-office receipts of major studio and independent films will increase the need for workers. Additionally, a rising demand for U.S. films in other countries should create more employment opportunities for actors, producers, and directors. Also fueling job growth is the continued development of interactive media, online movies, and mobile content produced for cell phones or other portable electronic devices. Attendance at live theater performances should continue to be steady, and drive employment of stage actors, producers and directors. However, station consolidation may restrict employment opportunities in the broadcasting industry for producers and directors.

Job prospects. Competition for acting jobs is intense, as the number of actors auditioning for roles greatly exceeds the number of parts that become available. Only performers with the most stamina and talent will find regular employment.

Venues for live entertainment, such as theaters, touring productions, and repertory theaters in many major metropolitan areas, as well as theme parks and resorts, are expected to offer many job opportunities. However, prospects in these venues are variable because they fluctuate with economic conditions.

Earnings

Many of the most successful actors, producers, and directors have extraordinarily high earnings, but many more of these professionals, faced with erratic earnings, supplement their income by holding jobs in other fields.

Median hourly wages of actors were $16.59 in May 2008. The middle 50 percent earned between $9.81 and $29.57.

Median hourly wages were $14.48 in performing arts companies and $28.72 in the motion picture and video industry. Annual wage data for actors were not available because of the wide variation in the number of hours worked by actors and the short-term nature of many jobs, which may last for 1 day or 1 week; it is extremely rare for actors to have guaranteed employment that exceeds 3 to 6 months.

Median annual wages of producers and directors were $64,430 in 2008. The middle 50 percent earned between $41,890 and $105,070. Median annual wages were $85,940 in the motion picture and video industry and $55,380 in radio and television broadcasting.

Minimum salaries, hours of work, and other conditions of employment are often covered in collective bargaining agreements between the producers and the unions representing workers. While these unions generally determine minimum salaries, any actor or director may negotiate for a salary higher than the minimum.

A joint agreement between the Screen Actors Guild (SAG) and the American Federation of Television and Radio Artists (AFTRA) guarantees all unionized motion picture and television actors with speaking parts a minimum daily rate of $782 or $2,713 for a 5-day week as of June 2009. Actors also receive contributions to their health and pension plans and additional compensation for reruns and foreign telecasts of the productions in which they appear.

Some well-known actors earn well above the minimum; their salaries are many times the figures cited here, creating the false impression that all actors are highly paid. For example, of the nearly 100,000 SAG members, only about 50 might fall into this category. The average income that SAG members earn from acting is low because employment is sporadic and most actors must supplement their incomes by holding jobs in other occupations.

Actors Equity Association (AEA), which represents stage actors, has negotiated minimum weekly salary requirements for their members. Salaries vary depending on the theater or venue the actor is employed in. Many stage directors belong to the Society of Stage Directors and Choreographers (SSDC), and most film and television directors belong to the Directors Guild of America. Earnings of stage directors vary greatly. The SSDC usually negotiates salary contracts which include royalties (additional income based on the number of performances) with smaller theaters. Regional theaters may hire directors for longer periods, increasing compensation accordingly. The highest paid directors work on Broadway; in addition to their contract fee, they also receive payment in the form of royalties—a negotiated percentage of gross box-office receipts—that can exceed the contract fee for long-running box-office successes.

Stage producers seldom receive a set fee; instead, they get a percentage of a show's earnings or ticket sales.

Related Occupations

Other performing artists who may need acting skills include:

Sources of Additional Information

For general information about theater arts and a list of accredited college-level programs, contact:

➤ National Association of Schools of Theater, 11250 Roger Bacon Dr., Suite 21, Reston, VA 20190. Internet: **http://nast.arts-accredit.org**

For general information on actors, producers, and directors, contact the following organizations:

➤ Actors' Equity Association, 165 West 46th St., New York, NY 10036. Internet: **http://www.actorsequity.org**

➤ Screen Actors Guild, 5757 Wilshire Blvd. 7th floor, Los Angeles, CA 90036-3600. Internet: **http://www.sag.org**

➤ Producers Guild of America. Internet: **http://www.producersguild.org**

The Occupational Information Network (O*NET) provides information on a wide range of occupational characteristics. Links to O*NET appear at the end of the Internet version of this occupational statement, accessible at **http://www.bls.gov/ooh/ocos093.htm**

Athletes, Coaches, Umpires, and Related Workers

Significant Points

- These jobs require immense overall knowledge of the game, usually acquired through years of experience at lower levels.

- Career-ending injuries are always a risk for athletes.

- Job opportunities will be best for part-time coaches, sports instructors, umpires, referees, and sports officials in high schools, sports clubs, and other settings.

- Aspiring professional athletes will continue to face extremely keen competition.

Nature of the Work

Few people who dream of becoming paid professional *athletes*, *coaches*, or *sports officials* beat the odds and make a full-time living from professional athletics. Professional athletes often have short careers with little job security. Even though the chances of employment as a professional athlete are slim, there are many opportunities for at least a part-time job as a coach, instructor, referee, or umpire in amateur athletics or in high school, college, or university sports.

Athletes and *sports competitors* compete in organized, officiated sports events to entertain spectators. When playing a game, athletes are required to understand the strategies of their game while obeying the rules and regulations of the sport. The events in which they compete include both team sports, such as baseball, basketball, football, hockey, and soccer, and individual sports, such as golf, tennis, and bowling. The level of play varies from unpaid high school athletics to professional sports, in which the best from around the world compete in events broadcast on international television.

Being an athlete involves more than competing in athletic events. Athletes spend many hours each day practicing skills and improving teamwork under the guidance of a coach or a sports instructor. They view videotapes to critique their own performances and techniques and to learn their opponents' tendencies and weaknesses to gain a competitive advantage. Some athletes work regularly with strength trainers to gain muscle and stamina and to prevent injury. Many athletes push their bodies to the limit during both practice and play, so career-ending injury always is a risk; even minor injuries may put a player at risk of replacement. Because competition at all levels is extremely intense and job security is always precarious, many athletes train year round to maintain excellent form and technique and peak physical condition. Very little downtime from the sport exists at the professional level. Some athletes must conform to regimented diets to supplement any physical training program.

Coaches organize amateur and professional athletes and teach them the fundamental skills of individual and team sports. (In individual sports, *instructors* sometimes may fill this role.) Coaches train athletes for competition by holding practice sessions to perform drills that improve the athletes' form, technique, skills, and stamina. Along with refining athletes' individual skills, coaches are responsible for instilling good sportsmanship, a competitive spirit, and teamwork and for managing their teams during both practice sessions and competitions. Before competition, coaches evaluate or scout the opposing team to determine game strategies and practice specific plays. During competition, coaches may call specific plays intended to surprise or overpower the opponent, and they may substitute players for optimum team chemistry and success. Coaches' additional tasks may include selecting, storing, issuing, and taking inventory of equipment, materials, and supplies.

Many coaches in high schools are primarily teachers of academic subjects who supplement their income by coaching part time. (For more information on high school teachers, see the statement on teachers—kindergarten, elementary, middle, and secondary, elsewhere in the *Handbook*.) College coaches consider coaching a full-time discipline and may be away from

Coaches organize amateur and professional athletes and teach them the fundamental skills of individual and team sports.

home frequently as they travel to competitions and to scout and recruit prospective players.

Sports instructors teach professional and nonprofessional athletes individually. They organize, instruct, train, and lead athletes in indoor and outdoor sports such as bowling, tennis, golf, and swimming. Because activities are as diverse as weight lifting, gymnastics, scuba diving, and karate, instructors tend to specialize in one or a few activities. Like coaches, sports instructors also may hold daily practice sessions and be responsible for any needed equipment and supplies. Using their knowledge of their sport and of physiology, they determine the type and level of difficulty of exercises, prescribe specific drills, and correct athletes' techniques. Some instructors also teach and demonstrate the use of training apparatus, such as trampolines or weights, for correcting athletes' weaknesses and enhancing their conditioning. Like coaches, sports instructors evaluate the athlete and the athlete's opponents to devise a competitive game strategy.

Coaches and sports instructors sometimes differ in their approaches to athletes because of the focus of their work. For example, while coaches manage the team during a game to optimize its chance for victory, sports instructors—such as those who work for professional tennis players—often are not permitted to instruct their athletes during competition. Sports instructors spend more of their time with athletes working one-on-one, which permits them to design customized training programs for each individual. Motivating athletes to play hard challenges most coaches and sports instructors but is vital for the athlete's success. Many coaches and instructors derive great satisfaction working with children or young adults, helping them to learn new physical and social skills, improve their physical condition, and achieve success in their sport.

Umpires, *referees*, and *other sports officials* officiate at competitive athletic and sporting events. They observe the play and impose penalties for infractions as established by the rules and regulations of the various sports. Umpires, referees, and sports officials anticipate play and position themselves to best see the action, assess the situation, and determine any violations. Some sports officials, such as boxing referees, may work independently, while others such as umpires work in groups. Regard-less of the sport, the job is highly stressful because officials are often required to make a decision in a split second, sometimes resulting in strong disagreement among competitors, coaches, and spectators.

Professional *scouts* evaluate the skills of both amateur and professional athletes to determine talent and potential. As a sports intelligence agent, the scout's primary duty is to seek out top athletic candidates for the team he or she represents. At the professional level, scouts typically work for scouting organizations or as freelance scouts. In locating new talent, scouts perform their work in secrecy so as not to "tip off" their opponents about their interest in certain players. At the college level, the head scout often is an assistant coach, although freelance scouts may aid colleges by reporting to coaches about exceptional players. Scouts at this level seek talented high school athletes by reading newspapers, contacting high school coaches and alumni, attending high school games, and studying videotapes of prospects' performances. They also evaluate potential players' background and personal characteristics, such as motivation and discipline, by talking to the players' coaches, parents, and teachers.

Work environment. Irregular work hours are common for athletes, coaches, umpires, referees, and other sports officials. They often work Saturdays, Sundays, evenings, and holidays. Athletes and full-time coaches usually work more than 40 hours a week for several months during the sports season, if not most of the year. High school coaches in educational institutions often coach more than one sport.

Athletes, coaches, and sports officials who participate in competitions that are held outdoors may be exposed to all weather conditions of the season. Athletes, coaches, and some sports officials frequently travel to sporting events. Scouts also travel extensively in locating talent. Athletes, coaches, and sports officials regularly encounter verbal abuse. Officials also face possible physical assault and, increasingly, lawsuits from injured athletes based on their officiating decisions.

Athletes and sports competitors had one of the highest rates of nonfatal on-the-job injuries. Coaches and sports' officials also face the risk of injury, but the risk is not as great as that faced by athletes and sports competitors.

Training, Other Qualifications, and Advancement

Education and training requirements for athletes, coaches, umpires, and related workers vary greatly by the level and type of sport. Regardless of the sport or occupation, these jobs require immense overall knowledge of the game, usually acquired through years of experience at lower levels.

Education and training. Most athletes, coaches, umpires, and related workers get their training from having played in the sport at some level. All of these sports-related workers need to have an extensive knowledge of the way the sport is played, its rules and regulations, and strategies, which is often acquired by playing the sport in school or recreation center, but also with the help of instructors or coaches, or in a camp that teaches the fundamentals of the sport.

Athletes get their training in several ways. For most team sports, athletes gain experience by competing in high school and collegiate athletics or on club teams. Although a high school or college degree may not be required to enter the sport, most athletes who get their training this way are often required to maintain specific academic standards to remain eligible to play, which often results in earning a degree. Other athletes, in gymnastics or tennis for example, learn their sport by taking private or group lessons.

Although there may not be a specific education requirement, head coaches at public secondary schools and sports instructors at all levels usually must have a bachelor's degree. For high school coaching and sports instructor jobs, schools usually prefer, and may have to hire teachers willing to take on these part time jobs. If no suitable teacher is found, schools hire someone from outside. College coaches also usually are required to have a bachelor's degree. Degree programs specifically related to coaching include exercise and sports science, physiology, kinesiology, nutrition and fitness, physical education, and sports medicine. Some entry-level positions for coaches or instructors require only experience derived as a participant in the sport or activity.

Each sport has specific requirements for umpires, referees, and other sports officials; some require these officials to pass a test of their knowledge of the sport. Umpires, referees, and other sports officials often begin their careers and gain needed experience by volunteering for intramural, community, and recreational league competitions. They are often required to attend some form of training course or academy.

Scouting jobs often requires experience playing a sport at the college or professional level that makes it possible to spot young players who possess athletic ability and skills. Most beginning scouting jobs are as part-time talent spotters in a particular area or region.

Licensure and certification. The need for athletes, coaches, umpires, and related workers to be licensed or certified to practice varies by sport and by locality. For example, in drag racing, drivers need to graduate from approved schools in order to be licensed to compete in the various drag racing series. The governing body of the sport may revoke licenses and suspend players who do not meet the required performance, education, or training. In addition, athletes may have their licenses or certification suspended for inappropriate activity.

Most public high school coaches need to meet State requirements for certification to become a head coach. Certification, however, may not be required for coaching and sports instructor jobs in private schools. College coaches may be required to be certified. For those interested in becoming scuba, tennis, golf, karate, or other kind of instructor, certification is highly desirable and may be required. There are many certifying organizations specific to the various sports, and their requirements vary. Coaches' certification often requires that one must be at least 18 years old and certified in cardiopulmonary resuscitation (CPR). Participation in a clinic, camp, or school also usually is required for certification. Part-time workers and those in smaller facilities are less likely to need formal education or training and may not need certification.

To officiate at high school athletic events, umpires, referees, and other officials must register with the State agency that oversees high school athletics and pass an exam on the rules of the particular game. For college refereeing, candidates must be certified by an officiating school and be evaluated during a probationary period. Some larger college sports conferences require officials to have certification and other qualifications, such as residence in or near the conference boundaries, along with several years of experience officiating at high school, community college, or other college conference games.

Other qualifications. Athletes, coaches, umpires, and related workers often direct teams or compete on them. Thus these workers must relate well to others and possess good communication and leadership skills. They may need to pass a background check and applicable drug tests. Athletes who seek to compete professionally must have extraordinary talent, desire, and dedication to training. Coaches must be resourceful and flexible to successfully instruct and motivate individuals and groups of athletes. Officials need good vision, reflexes, and the ability to make decisions quickly.

Advancement. For most athletes, turning professional is the biggest advancement. They often begin to compete immediately, although some may spend more time "on the bench", as a reserve, to gain experience. In some sports, such as baseball, athletes may begin their professional career on a minor league team before moving up to the major leagues. Professional athletes generally advance in their sport by winning and achieving accolades and earning a higher salary.

Many coaches begin their careers as assistant coaches to gain the knowledge and experience needed to become a head coach. Head coaches at large schools and colleges that strive to compete at the highest levels of a sport require substantial experience as a head coach at another school or as an assistant coach. To reach the ranks of professional coaching, a person usually needs years of coaching experience and a winning record in the lower ranks or experience as an athlete in that sport.

Standards for umpires and other officials become more stringent as the level of competition advances. A local or State academy may be required to referee a school baseball game. Those seeking to officiate at minor or major league games must attend a professional umpire training school. To advance to umpiring in Major League Baseball, umpires usually need 7 to 10 years of experience in various minor leagues before being considered for major league jobs.

Finding talented players is essential for scouts to advance. Hard work and a record of success often lead to full-time jobs and responsibility for scouting in more areas. Some scouts advance to scouting director jobs or various administrative positions in sports.

Employment

Athletes, coaches, umpires, and related workers held about 258,100 jobs in 2008. Coaches and scouts held 225,700 jobs; athletes and sports competitors, 16,500; and umpires, referees, and other sports officials, 15,900. About half of all athletes, coaches, umpires, and related workers worked part time or maintained variable schedules. Many sports officials and coaches receive such small and irregular payments for their services—occasional officiating at club games, for example—that they may not consider themselves employed in these occupations, even part time.

Among those employed in wage and salary jobs, 52 percent held jobs in public and private educational services. About 13 percent worked in amusement, gambling, and recreation in-

Projections data from the National Employment Matrix

Occupational Title	SOC Code	Employment, 2008	Projected Employment, 2018	Change, 2008-2018	
				Number	Percent
Athletes, coaches, umpires, and related workers	27-2020	258,100	317,700	59,600	23
Athletes and sports competitors..	27-2021	16,500	18,400	1,900	12
Coaches and scouts	27-2022	225,700	281,700	56,000	25
Umpires, referees, and other sports officials................................	27-2023	15,900	17,600	1,700	10

(NOTE) Data in this table are rounded. See the discussion of the employment projections table in the *Handbook* introductory chapter on *Occupational Information Included in the Handbook.*

dustries, including golf and tennis clubs, gymnasiums, health clubs, judo and karate schools, riding stables, swim clubs, and other sports and recreation facilities. Another 6 percent worked in the spectator sports industry.

About 16 percent of workers in this occupation were self-employed, earning prize money or fees for lessons, scouting, or officiating assignments. Many other coaches and sports officials, although technically not self-employed, have such irregular or tenuous working arrangements that their working conditions resemble those of self-employment.

Job Outlook

Employment of athletes, coaches, umpires, and related workers is expected to grow much faster than the average for all occupations through 2018. Very keen competition is expected for jobs at the highest levels of sports with progressively more favorable opportunities in lower levels of competition.

Employment change. Employment of athletes, coaches, umpires, and related workers is expected to increase by 23 percent from 2008 to 2018, which is much faster than the average for all occupations. A larger population overall that will continue to participate in organized sports for entertainment, recreation, and physical conditioning will boost demand for these workers, particularly for coaches, umpires, sports instructors, and other related workers. Job growth also will be driven by the increasing number of retirees who are expected to participate more in leisure activities such as golf and tennis, which require instruction. Additionally, the demand for private sports instruction is expected to grow among young athletes as parents try to help their children reach their full potential. Future expansion of new professional teams and leagues may create additional openings for all of these workers.

Additional coaches and instructors are expected to be needed as school and college athletic programs expand. Population growth is expected to cause the construction of additional schools, but funding for athletic programs often is cut first when budgets become tight. Still, the popularity of team sports often enables shortfalls to be offset with the assistance from fundraisers, booster clubs, and parents. In colleges, most of the expansion is expected to be in women's sports.

Job prospects. Persons who are State-certified to teach academic subjects are likely to have the best prospects for obtaining coaching and instructor jobs in schools. The need to replace the many high school coaches will provide most coaching opportunities.

Competition for professional athlete jobs will continue to be extremely keen. In major sports, such as basketball and football, only about 1 in 5,000 high school athletes becomes professional

in these sports. The expansion of nontraditional sports may create some additional opportunities. Because most professional athletes' careers last only a few years due to debilitating injuries and age, annual replacement needs for these jobs is high, creating some job opportunities. However, the talented young men and women who dream of becoming sports superstars greatly outnumber the number of openings.

Opportunities should be best for persons seeking part-time umpire, referee, and other sports official jobs at the high school level. Coaches in girls' and women's sports may have better opportunities and face less competition for positions. Competition is expected for higher paying jobs at the college level and will be even greater for jobs in professional sports. Competition should be keen for paying jobs as scouts, particularly for professional teams, because the number of available positions is limited.

Earnings

Median annual wages of athletes and sports competitors were $40,480 in May 2008. The middle 50 percent earned between $21,760 and $93,710. The highest paid professional athletes earn much more.

Median annual wages of umpires and related workers were $23,730 in May 2008. The middle 50 percent earned between $17,410 and $33,150. The lowest paid 10 percent earned less than $15,450, and the highest paid 10 percent earned more than $48,310.

In May 2008, median annual wages of coaches and scouts were $28,340. The middle 50 percent earned between $18,220 and $43,440. The lowest paid 10 percent earned less than $15,530, and the highest paid 10 percent earned more than $62,660. However, the highest paid professional coaches earn much more. Median annual wages in the industries employing the largest numbers of coaches and scouts in May 2008 are shown below:

Colleges, universities, and professional schools $39,550
Other amusement and recreation industries.................28,720
Other schools and instruction.......................................25,740
Elementary and secondary schools 22,390

Wages vary by level of education, certification, and geographic region. Some instructors and coaches are paid a salary, while others may be paid by the hour, per session, or based on the number of participants.

Related Occupations

Other occupations involved with athletes or sports include:

Sources of Additional Information

For information about sports officiating for team and individual sports, contact:

➤ National Association of Sports Officials, 2017 Lathrop Ave., Racine, WI 53405. Internet: **http://www.naso.org**

For additional information related to individual sports, refer to the organization that represents the sport.

The Occupational Information Network (O*NET) provides information on a wide range of occupational characteristics. Links to O*NET appear at the end of the Internet version of this occupational statement, accessible at **http://www.bls.gov/ooh/ocos251.htm**

Dancers and Choreographers

Significant Points

- Many dancers stop performing by their late thirties, but some remain in the field as choreographers, dance teachers, or artistic directors.

- Most dancers begin formal training at an early age—between 5 and 15—and many have their first professional audition by age 17 or 18; becoming a choreographer usually requires years of experience.

- Dancers and choreographers face intense competition; only the most talented find regular work.

- Earnings from dancing are usually low because employment is irregular; dancers often supplement their income.

Nature of the Work

Complex movements and dances on stage and screen do not happen without a lot of hard work. *Dancers* spend years learning dances and honing skills, as do most *choreographers*. Together, they then translate those skills into movement that expresses ideas and stories.

Dancers perform in a variety of settings, including opera, musical theater, and other musical productions, and may present folk, ethnic, tap, jazz, or other popular kinds of dance. They also perform in television, movies, music videos, and commercials, in which they may sing and act. Dancers most often perform as part of a group, although a few top artists perform solo.

Choreographers create original dances and develop new interpretations of existing dances. They work in theaters, dance schools, dance and movie studios, and at fashion shows, and are involved in auditioning performers for dance parts. Because few dance routines are written down, choreographers instruct performers at rehearsals to achieve the desired effect, often by demonstrating the exact technique. Choreographers also work with performers other than dancers. For example, the complex martial arts scenes in movies are arranged by choreographers who specialize in the martial arts. Choreographers also may help coordinate costume design and lighting, as well as choose the music and sound effects that convey the intended message.

Work environment. Dance is strenuous. In fact, dancers have one of the highest rates of nonfatal on-the-job injury. Many dancers, as a result, stop performing by their late thirties because of the physical demands on the body. Nonetheless, some continue to work in the field as choreographers, artistic directors, and dance teachers and coaches, while a small number may move into administrative positions, such as company managers. A few celebrated dancers, however, continue performing most of their lives.

Many dance companies tour for part of the year to supplement a limited performance schedule at home. Dancers who perform in musical productions and other family entertainment spend much of their time on the road; others work in nightclubs or on cruise ships. Most dance performances are in the evening, whereas rehearsals and practice usually take place during the day. As a result, dancers often work very long and late hours. Generally, dancers and choreographers work in modern and temperature-controlled facilities; however, some studios may be older and less comfortable.

Training, Other Qualifications, and Advancement

Dancers generally need long-term on-the-job training to be successful. Most dancers begin formal training at an early age—between 5 and 15—and many have their first professional audition by age 17 or 18. Some earn a bachelor's degree or attend dance school, although neither is required. Becoming a choreographer usually requires years of experience.

Most dancers begin formal training at an early age and many have their first professional audition by age 17 or 18.

Education and training. Training varies with the type of dance and is a continuous part of all dancers' careers. Many believe that dancers should start with a good foundation in classical technique before selecting a particular style. Ballet training for girls usually begins between the ages of 5 to 8 with a private teacher or through an independent ballet school, with more serious training beginning between the ages of 10 and 12. Boys often begin their ballet training between the ages of 10 and 15. Students who demonstrate potential in their early teens may seek out more intensive and advanced professional training. At about this time, students should begin to focus their training on a particular style and decide whether to pursue additional training through a dance company's school or a college dance program. Leading dance school companies often have summer training programs from which they select candidates for admission to their regular full-time training programs. Formal training for modern and culturally specific dances often begins later than training in ballet; however, many folk dance forms are taught to very young children. As a result, a good number of dancers have their first professional auditions by age 17 or 18.

Training is an important component of professional dancers' careers. Dancers normally spend 8 hours a day in class and rehearsal, keeping their bodies in shape and preparing for performances. Their daily training period usually includes time to warm up and cool down before and after classes and rehearsals.

Because of the strenuous and time-consuming training required, some dancers view formal education as secondary. However, a broad, general education including music, literature, history, and the visual arts is helpful in the interpretation of dramatic episodes, ideas, and feelings. Dancers sometimes conduct research to learn more about the part they are playing.

Many colleges and universities award bachelor's or master's degrees in dance, typically through departments of dance, theater, or fine arts. The National Association of Schools of Dance is made up of 74 accredited dance programs. Many programs concentrate on modern dance, but some also offer courses in jazz, culturally specific dance, ballet, or classical techniques. Courses in dance composition, history and criticism, and movement analysis are also available.

A college education is not essential for employment as a professional dancer; however, many dancers obtain degrees in unrelated fields to prepare themselves for careers after dance. The completion of a college program in dance and education is usually essential to qualify to teach dance in college, high school, or elementary school. (See the statement on teachers—postsecondary and teachers—kindergarten, elementary, middle, and secondary elsewhere in the *Handbook.*) Colleges and conservatories sometimes require graduate degrees but may accept performance experience. A college background is not necessary for teaching dance or choreography in local recreational programs. Studio schools prefer teachers to have experience as performers.

Choreographers should have a thorough understanding of the dance style that they arrange. This often is gained through years of performing and practicing. Some dance conservatories offer choreography courses.

Other qualifications. Because of the rigorous practice schedules of most dancers and choreographers, self-discipline, patience, perseverance, and a devotion to dance are essential for success in the field. Dancers and choreographers also must possess good problem-solving skills and an ability to work with people. Dancers, above all, must have good health and physical stamina, along with flexibility, agility, coordination, and grace, a sense of rhythm, a feeling for music, and a creative ability to express themselves through movement. Choreographers should possess many of the same attributes while also being able to plan and coordinate activities.

Because dancers and choreographers are typically members of an ensemble made up of other dancers, musicians, and directors or choreographers, they must be able to function as part of a team. They also should be highly motivated and prepared to face the anxiety of intermittent employment and rejections when looking for work.

Advancement. For dancers, advancement takes the form of a growing reputation, more frequent work, bigger and better roles, and higher pay. Some dancers may take on added responsibilities, such as by becoming a dance captain in musical theater or ballet master/ballet mistress in concert dance companies, by leading rehearsals, or by working with less experienced dancers in the absence of a choreographer.

Choreographers typically are experienced dancers with years of practice working in the theater. Through their performance as dancers, they develop reputations that often lead to opportunities to choreograph productions.

Employment

Professional dancers and choreographers held about 29,200 jobs in 2008. Many others were between engagements; as a result, the total number of people available for work as dancers over the course of the year was greater. Dancers and choreographers worked in a variety of industries, such as public and private educational services, which includes dance studios and schools, as well as colleges and universities; food services and drinking establishments; performing arts companies, which include dance, theater, and opera companies; and amusement and recreation venues, such as casinos and theme parks. About 14 percent of dancers and choreographers were self-employed.

Most major cities serve as home to major dance companies; however, many smaller communities across the Nation also support home-grown, full-time professional dance companies.

Job Outlook

Employment is expected to grow more slowly than the average. Dancers and choreographers face intense competition for jobs. Only the most talented find regular employment.

Employment change. Employment of dancers and choreographers is expected to grow 6 percent during the 2008–18 decade, more slowly than the average for all occupations. The public's interest in dance will sustain large and mid-size dance companies, but limited funding from public and private organizations is not expected to allow for additional dance com-

Projections data from the National Employment Matrix

Occupational Title	SOC Code	Employment, 2008	Projected Employment, 2018	Change, 2008-2018	
				Number	Percent
Dancers and choreographers	27-2030	29,200	30,900	1,700	6
Dancers	27-2031	13,000	13,900	900	7
Choreographers	27-2032	16,200	17,000	900	5

(NOTE) Data in this table are rounded. See the discussion of the employment projections table in the *Handbook* introductory chapter on *Occupational Information Included in the Handbook.*

panies. For many small organizations, the result will be fewer performances and more limited employment opportunities.

Job prospects. Because many people enjoy dance and would like to make their careers in dance, dancers and choreographers face intense competition for jobs. Only the most talented find regular employment.

Although job openings will arise each year because dancers and choreographers retire or leave the occupation for other reasons, the number of applicants will continue to vastly exceed the number of job openings.

National dance companies likely will continue to provide jobs in this field. Opera companies and dance groups affiliated with television and motion pictures also will offer some opportunities. Moreover, the growing popularity of dance for recreational and fitness purposes has resulted in increased opportunities to teach dance, especially for older dancers who may be transitioning to another field. Musicians will provide a small number of openings for both dancers and choreographers, and candidates are expected to face keen competition. Amusement parks and cruise ships should also provide some opportunities for dancers and choreographers.

Earnings

Median hourly wages of dancers were $12.22 in May 2008. The middle 50 percent earned between $8.03 and $18.82. The lowest 10 percent earned less than $7.28, and the highest 10 percent earned more than $27.26. Annual wage data for dancers were not available, because the wide variation in the number of hours worked by dancers and the short-term nature of many jobs—which may last for 1 day or 1 week—make it rare for dancers to have guaranteed employment that exceeds a few months. Median hourly wages in the industries employing the largest number of dancers were as follows:

Performing arts companies..$15.30	
Other amusement and recreation industries 11.56	
Other schools and instruction.......................................10.00	
Drinking places (alcoholic beverages) 8.01	

Median annual wages of salaried choreographers were $38,520 in May 2008. The middle 50 percent earned between $25,320 and $55,360. The lowest 10 percent earned less than $17,880, and the highest 10 percent earned more than $67,160. Median annual wages were $37,570 in "other schools and instruction," the North American Industry Classification System category that includes dance studios and schools.

Dancers who were on tour usually received an additional allowance for room and board, as well as extra compensation

for overtime. Earnings from dancing are usually low because employment is irregular. Dancers often supplement their income by working as guest artists with other dance companies, teaching dance, or taking jobs unrelated to the field.

Earnings of dancers at some of the largest companies and in commercial settings are governed by union contracts. Some dancers in major opera ballet, classical ballet, and modern dance corps belong to the American Guild of Musical Artists, Inc. of the AFL-CIO; those who appear on live or videotaped television programs belong to the American Federation of Television and Radio Artists; those who perform in films and on television belong to the Screen Actors Guild; and those in musical theater are members of the Actors' Equity Association. The unions and producers sign basic agreements specifying minimum salary rates, hours of work, benefits, and other conditions of employment. However, the contract each dancer signs with the producer of the show may be more favorable than the basic agreement.

Most salaried dancers and choreographers covered by union contracts receive some paid sick leave and various health and pension benefits, including extended sick pay and family-leave benefits provided by their unions. Employers contribute toward these benefits. Dancers and choreographers not covered by union contracts usually do not enjoy such benefits.

Related Occupations

Other occupations that perform before audiences include:

	Page
Actors, producers, and directors 318	
Athletes, coaches, umpires, and related workers 321	
Musicians, singers, and related workers 328	

Occupations directly involved in the production of dance programs include:

Barbers, cosmetologists, and other personal appearance workers 507	
Fashion designers 307	
Set and exhibit designers... 825	

Sources of Additional Information

For general information about dance and a list of accredited college-level programs, contact:
➤ National Association of Schools of Dance, 11250 Roger Bacon Dr., Suite 21, Reston, VA 20190. Internet: **http://nasd.arts-accredit.org**

For information about dance and dance companies, contact:
➤ Dance/USA, 1111 16th St. NW., Suite 300, Washington, DC 20036. Internet: **http://www.danceusa.org**

The Occupational Information Network (O*NET) provides information on a wide range of occupational characteristics. Links to O*NET appear at the end of the Internet version of this occupational statement, accessible at **http://www.bls.gov/ooh/ocos094.htm**

Musicians, Singers, and Related Workers

Significant Points

- Part-time schedules—typically at night and on weekends—intermittent unemployment, and rejection when auditioning for work are common; many musicians and singers supplement their income with earnings from other sources.

- Aspiring musicians and singers begin studying an instrument or training their voice at an early age.

- Competition for jobs, especially full-time jobs, is keen; talented individuals who can play several instruments and perform a wide range of musical styles should enjoy the best job prospects.

Nature of the Work

Musicians, singers, and related workers play musical instruments, sing, compose or arrange music, or conduct groups in instrumental or vocal performances. They perform solo or as part of a group, mostly in front of live audiences in nightclubs, concert halls, and theaters. They also perform in recording or production studios for radio, TV, film, or video games. Regardless of the setting, they spend considerable time practicing alone and with their bands, orchestras, or other musical ensembles.

Musicians play one or more musical instruments. Many musicians learn to play several related instruments and can perform equally well in several musical styles. Instrumental musicians, for example, may play in a symphony orchestra, rock group, or jazz combo one night, appear in another ensemble the next, and work in a studio band the following day. Some play a variety of string, brass, woodwind, or percussion instruments or electronic synthesizers.

Singers use their knowledge of voice production, melody, and harmony to interpret music and text. They sing character parts or perform in their own individual styles. Singers often are classified according to their voice range—soprano, contralto, tenor, baritone, or bass—or by the type of music they sing, such as rock, pop, folk, opera, rap, or country.

Music directors and *conductors* conduct, direct, plan, and lead instrumental or vocal performances by musical groups such as orchestras, choirs, and glee clubs. These leaders audition and select musicians, choose the music most appropriate for their talents and abilities, and direct rehearsals and performances. *Choral directors* lead choirs and glee clubs, sometimes working with a band or an orchestra conductor. Directors audition and select singers and lead them at rehearsals and performances to achieve harmony, rhythm, tempo, shading, and other desired musical effects.

Composers create original music such as symphonies, operas, sonatas, radio and television jingles, film scores, and popular songs. They transcribe ideas into musical notation, using harmony, rhythm, melody, and tonal structure. Although most composers and songwriters practice their craft on instruments and transcribe the notes with pen and paper, some use computer software to compose and edit their music.

Arrangers transcribe and adapt musical compositions to a particular style for orchestras, bands, choral groups, or individuals. Components of music—including tempo, volume, and the mix of instruments needed—are arranged to express the composer's message. Although some arrangers write directly into a musical composition, others use computer software to make changes.

Work environment. Musicians typically perform at night and on weekends. They spend much additional time practicing or in rehearsal. Full-time musicians with long-term employment contracts, such as those with symphony orchestras or television and film production companies, enjoy steady work and less travel. Nightclub, solo, or recital musicians frequently travel to perform in a variety of local settings and may tour nationally or internationally. Because many musicians find only part-time or intermittent work and experience unemployment between engagements, they often supplement their income with other types of jobs. The stress of constantly looking for work leads many musicians to accept permanent full-time jobs in other occupations while working part time as musicians.

Most instrumental musicians work closely with a variety of other people, including colleagues, agents, employers, sponsors, and audiences. Although they usually work indoors, some perform outdoors for parades, concerts, and festivals. In some nightclubs and restaurants, smoke and odors may be present and lighting and ventilation may be poor.

Training, Other Qualifications, and Advancement

Long-term on-the-job training is the most common way people learn to become musicians or singers. Aspiring musicians begin studying an instrument at an early age. They may gain valuable experience playing in a school or community band or orchestra or with a group of friends. Singers usually start training when their voices mature. Participation in school musicals or choirs often provides good early training and experience. Compos-

Musicians face keen competition, especially for full-time jobs.

Projections data from the National Employment Matrix

Occupational Title	SOC Code	Employment, 2008	Projected Employment, 2018	Change, 2008-2018	
				Number	Percent
Musicians, singers, and related workers	27-2040	240,000	259,600	19,600	8
Music directors and composers..	27-2041	53,600	59,000	5,300	10
Musicians and singers..	27-2042	186,400	200,600	14,200	8

(NOTE) Data in this table are rounded. See the discussion of the employment projections table in the *Handbook* introductory chapter on *Occupational Information Included in the Handbook.*

ers and music directors usually require a bachelor's degree in a related field.

Education and training. Musicians need extensive and prolonged training and practice to acquire the skills and knowledge necessary to interpret music at a professional level. Like other artists, musicians and singers continually strive to improve their abilities. Formal training may be obtained through private study with an accomplished musician, in a college or university music program, or in a music conservatory. An audition generally is necessary to qualify for university or conservatory study. The National Association of Schools of Music is made up of 615 accredited college-level programs in music. Courses typically include music theory, music interpretation, composition, conducting, and performance, either with a particular instrument or a voice performance. Music directors, composers, conductors, and arrangers need considerable related work experience or advanced training in these subjects.

A master's or doctoral degree usually is required to teach advanced music courses in colleges and universities; a bachelor's degree may be sufficient to teach basic courses. A degree in music education qualifies graduates for a State certificate to teach music in public elementary or secondary schools. (Information related to teachers—postsecondary and teachers—kindergarten, elementary, middle, and secondary can be found elsewhere in the *Handbook.*) Musicians who do not meet public school music education requirements may teach in private schools and recreation associations or instruct individual students in private sessions.

Other qualifications. Musicians must be knowledgeable about a broad range of musical styles. Having a broader range of interest, knowledge, and training can help expand employment opportunities and musical abilities. Voice training and private instrumental lessons, especially when taken at a young age, also help develop technique and enhance one's performance.

Young persons considering careers in music should have musical talent, versatility, creativity, poise, and good stage presence. Self-discipline is vital because producing a quality performance on a consistent basis requires constant study and practice. Musicians who play in concerts or in nightclubs and those who tour must have physical stamina to endure frequent travel and an irregular performance schedule. Musicians and singers also must be prepared to face the anxiety of intermittent employment and of rejection when auditioning for work.

Advancement. Advancement for musicians usually means becoming better known, finding work more easily, and performing for higher earnings. Successful musicians often rely on agents or managers to find them performing engagements, negotiate contracts, and develop their careers.

Employment

Musicians, singers, and related workers held about 240,000 jobs in 2008, of which 186,400 were held by musicians and singers; 53,600 were music directors and composers. Around 43 percent worked part time; 50 percent were self-employed. Many found jobs in cities in which entertainment and recording activities are concentrated, such as New York, Los Angeles, Las Vegas, Chicago, and Nashville.

Musicians, singers, and related workers are employed in a variety of settings. Of those who earn a wage or salary, 33 percent were employed by religious, grantmaking, civic, professional, and similar organizations and 12 percent by performing arts companies, such as professional orchestras, small chamber music groups, opera companies, musical theater companies, and ballet troupes. Musicians and singers also perform in nightclubs and restaurants and for weddings and other events. Well-known musicians and groups may perform in concerts, appear on radio and television broadcasts, and make recordings and music videos. The U.S. Armed Forces also offer careers in their bands and smaller musical groups. (Information related to job opportunities in the armed forces can be found elsewhere in the *Handbook.*)

Job Outlook

Employment is expected to grow as fast as average. Keen competition for jobs, especially full-time jobs, is expected to continue. Talented individuals who are skilled in multiple instruments and musical styles will have the best job prospects.

Employment change. Employment of musicians, singers, and related workers is expected to grow 8 percent during the 2008–18 decade, as fast as the average for all occupations. Most new wage-and-salary jobs for musicians will arise in religious organizations. Slower than average employment growth is expected for self-employed musicians, who generally perform in nightclubs, concert tours, and other venues. The Internet and other new forms of media may provide independent musicians and singers alternative methods for distributing music.

Job prospects. Growth in demand for musicians will generate a number of job opportunities, and many openings also will arise from the need to replace those who leave the field each year because they are unable to make a living solely as musicians or singers, as well as those who leave for other reasons.

Competition for jobs as musicians, singers, and related workers—especially full-time jobs—is expected to be keen. The vast number of people with the desire to perform will continue to greatly exceed the number of openings. New musicians or singers will have their best chance of landing a job with smaller, community-based performing arts groups or as freelance artists. Instrumentalists should have better opportunities than singers because of a larger pool of work. Talented individuals who are skilled in multiple instruments or musical styles will have the best job prospects. However, talent alone is no guarantee of success: many people start out to become musicians or singers but leave the profession because they find the work difficult, the discipline demanding, and the long periods of intermittent unemployment a hardship.

Earnings

Median hourly wages of wage-and-salary musicians and singers were $21.24 in May 2008. The middle 50 percent earned between $11.49 and $36.36. The lowest 10 percent earned less than $7.64, and the highest 10 percent earned more than $59.92. Median hourly wages were $23.68 in performing arts companies and $12.50 in religious organizations. Annual wage data for musicians and singers were not available because of the wide variation in the number of hours worked by musicians and singers and the short-term nature of many jobs. It is rare for musicians and singers to have guaranteed employment that exceeds 3 to 6 months.

Median annual wages of salaried music directors and composers were $41,270 in May 2008. The middle 50 percent earned between $26,480 and $63,200. The lowest 10 percent earned less than $16,750, and the highest 10 percent earned more than $107,280.

For self-employed musicians and singers, earnings typically reflect the number of jobs a freelance musician or singer played or the number of hours and weeks of contract work, in addition to a performer's professional reputation and setting. Performers who can fill large concert halls, arenas, or outdoor stadiums generally command higher pay than those who perform in local clubs. Soloists or headliners usually receive higher earnings than band members or opening acts. The most successful musicians earn performance or recording fees that far exceed the median earnings.

The American Federation of Musicians negotiates minimum contracts for major orchestras during the performing season. Each orchestra works out a separate contract with its local union, but individual musicians may negotiate higher salaries. In regional orchestras, minimum salaries often are less because fewer performances are scheduled. Regional orchestra musicians frequently are paid for their services without any guarantee of future employment. Community orchestras often have limited funding and offer salaries that are much lower for seasons of shorter duration.

Although musicians employed by some symphony orchestras work under master wage agreements, which guarantee a season's work up to 52 weeks, many other musicians face relatively long periods of unemployment between jobs. Even when employed, many musicians and singers work part time in unrelated occupations. Thus, their earnings for music usually are lower than earnings in many other occupations. Moreover, because they may not work steadily for one employer, some performers cannot qualify for unemployment compensation and few have typical benefits such as sick leave or paid vacations. For these reasons, many musicians give private lessons or take jobs unrelated to music to supplement their earnings as performers.

Many musicians belong to a local of the American Federation of Musicians. Professional singers who perform live often belong to a branch of the American Guild of Musical Artists; those who record for the broadcast industries may belong to the American Federation of Television and Radio Artists.

Related Occupations

Other occupations that require a technical knowledge of musical instruments include the following:

Musical instrument repairers and tuners 721

Musicians, singers, and related workers are involved in the performing arts, as are the following workers:

Actors, producers, and directors 318
Announcers 331
Dancers and choreographers 325

Sources of Additional Information

For general information about music and music teacher education and a list of accredited college-level programs, contact:

➤ National Association of Schools of Music, 11250 Roger Bacon Dr., Suite 21, Reston, VA 20190. Internet: **http://nasm.arts-accredit.org**

The Occupational Information Network (O*NET) provides information on a wide range of occupational characteristics. Links to O*NET appear at the end of the Internet version of this occupational statement, accessible at **http://www.bls.gov/ooh/ocos095.htm**

Media and Communication-Related Occupations

Announcers

Significant Points

- Competition for announcer jobs will continue to be keen.
- Jobs at small stations usually have low pay, but offer the best opportunities for inexperienced announcers.
- Applicants who have completed internships or have related work experience, and those with more advanced computer skills, may have an advantage in the job market.
- Employment is projected to decline slowly.

Nature of the Work

Radio and television announcers perform a variety of tasks on and off the air. They announce station program information, such as program schedules and station breaks for commercials, or public-service information, and they introduce and close programs. Announcers read prepared scripts or make ad-lib commentary on the air as they present news, sports, the weather, the time, and commercials. If a written script is required, they may do the research and writing. Announcers also interview guests and moderate panels or discussions. Some provide commentary for the audience during sporting events, at parades, and on other occasions. Announcers often are well known to radio and television audiences and may make promotional appearances and do remote broadcasts for their stations.

Announcers at smaller stations may have more off-air duties as well. They may operate the control board, monitor the transmitter, sell commercial time to advertisers, keep a log of the station's daily programming, and produce advertisements and other recorded material. At many radio stations, announcers do much of the work previously performed by editors and broadcast technicians, such as operating the control board, which is used to broadcast programming, commercials, and public-service announcements according to the station's schedule. (See the statement on broadcast and sound engineering technicians and radio operators elsewhere in the *Handbook*.) Public radio and television announcers also are involved in station fundraising efforts.

Announcers frequently participate in community activities. Sports announcers, for example, may serve as masters of ceremony at sports club banquets or may greet customers at openings of sporting-goods stores.

Radio announcers who broadcast music often are called *disc jockeys* (*DJs*). Some DJs specialize in one kind of music, announcing selections as they air them. Most DJs do not select much of the music they play (although they often did so in the past); instead, they follow schedules of commercials, talk, and music provided to them by management. While on the air, DJs comment on the music, weather, and traffic. They may take requests from listeners, interview guests, and manage listener contests. Many radio stations now require DJs to update their station Web site.

Some DJs announce and play music at clubs, dances, restaurants, and weddings. They often have their own equipment with which to play the music. Many are self-employed and rent their services out on a job-by-job basis.

Show hosts may specialize in a certain area of interest, such as politics, personal finance, sports, or health. They contribute to the preparation of the program's content, interview guests, and discuss issues with viewers, listeners, or the studio audience.

Public-address system announcers provide information to the audience at sporting, performing arts, and other events.

Work environment. Announcers usually work in well-lighted, air-conditioned, soundproof studios. Announcers often work within tight schedules, which can be physically and mentally stressful. For many announcers, the intangible rewards—creative work, many personal contacts, and the satisfaction of becoming widely known—far outweigh the disadvantages of irregular and often unpredictable hours, work pressures, and disrupted personal lives.

The broadcast day is long for radio and TV stations—many are on the air 24 hours a day—so announcers can expect to work unusual hours. Many present early-morning shows, when most people are getting ready for work or commuting, while others do late-night programs. The shifts, however, are not as varied as in the past, because new technology has allowed stations to eliminate most of the overnight hours. Many announcers work part time.

Radio announcers who broadcast music often are called disc jockeys, or DJs.

Projections data from the National Employment Matrix

Occupational Title	SOC Code	Employment, 2008	Projected Employment, 2018	Change, 2008-2018	
				Number	Percent
Announcers	27-3010	67,400	65,000	-2,400	-4
Radio and television announcers..	27-3011	55,100	51,700	-3,400	-6
Public address system and other announcers..............................	27-3012	12,300	13,300	1,000	8

(NOTE) Data in this table are rounded. See the discussion of the employment projections table in the *Handbook* introductory chapter on *Occupational Information Included in the Handbook.*

Training, Other Qualifications, and Advancement

Entry into this occupation is highly competitive, and postsecondary education or long-term on-the-job training is common. Trainees usually must have several years of experience in the industry before receiving an opportunity to work on the air. An applicant's delivery and—in television—appearance and style are important.

Education and training. Formal training in broadcasting from college or a technical school is valuable. These programs prepare students to work with the computer equipment and software to which they might otherwise not have access. In radio, many announcers will also need Web site editing skills. It is common for announcers to have a bachelor's degree in a subject such as communications, broadcasting, or journalism. High school and college courses in English, public speaking, drama, foreign languages, and computer science are valuable, and hobbies such as sports and music are additional assets.

There are many broadcast programs available and they have varying reputations. Individuals considering enrolling in a broadcasting school should contact personnel managers of radio and television stations, as well as broadcasting trade organizations, to determine the school's reputation for producing suitably trained candidates.

Announcers are often required to complete long-term on-the-job training. This can be accomplished at campus radio or TV facilities and at commercial stations while students serve as interns. Work experience at college or high school radio or TV stations is very valuable. Oftentimes, even for entry-level positions, employees need to have experience, which students can acquire at these stations. Paid or unpaid internships also provide students with hands-on training and the chance to establish contacts in the industry. Unpaid interns frequently receive college credit and are allowed to observe and assist station employees. This experience sometimes leads to paid internships which are valuable because interns may do work ordinarily performed by regular employees.

Once hired by a television station, an employee usually starts out as a production assistant, researcher, or reporter and is given a chance to move into announcing if he or she shows an aptitude for "on-air" work. A beginner's chance of landing an on-air job is remote. The best chances for an on-air job for inexperienced announcers may be as a substitute for a familiar announcer at a small radio station. In radio, newcomers usually start out taping interviews and operating equipment.

Other qualifications. Announcers must have a pleasant and well-controlled voice, good timing, excellent pronunciation, and correct grammar. College broadcasting programs offer courses, such as voice and diction, to help students improve their vocal qualities. Television announcers need a neat, pleasing appearance as well. Knowledge of theater, sports, music, business, politics, and other subjects likely to be covered in broadcasts improves one's chances for success. Announcers, especially those seeking radio careers, should have good information technology skills and be capable of using computers, editing equipment, and other broadcast-related devices because new advances in technology have made these abilities important. Announcers also need strong writing skills, because they normally write their own material. In addition, they should be able to ad lib all or part of a show and to work under tight deadlines. The most successful announcers attract a large audience by combining a pleasing personality and voice with an appealing style.

Advancement. Announcers usually begin at a station in a small community and, if they are qualified, may move to a better paying job in a large city. They also may advance by hosting a regular program as a disc jockey, sportscaster, or other specialist. Competition for employment by networks is particularly intense, and employees will need a college degree with at least several years of successful announcing experience if they wish to advance.

Employment

Announcers held about 67,400 jobs in 2008. About 51 percent were employed in radio and television broadcasting. Many other announcers were self-employed freelance announcers, who sold their services to networks and stations, advertising agencies, other independent producers, or to sponsors of local events.

Job Outlook

Competition for jobs as announcers will be keen because the broadcasting field attracts many more jobseekers than there are jobs. Furthermore, employment of announcers is projected to decline slowly. In some cases, announcers leave the field because they cannot advance to better paying jobs. Changes in station ownership, format, and ratings frequently cause periods of unemployment for many announcers.

Employment change. Employment of announcers is expected to decline by 4 percent from 2008 to 2018. Improving technology continues to increase the productivity of announcers, reducing the time required to edit material or perform other off-air technical and production work. The ability of radio announcers to broadcast a program live and record a show for another time has eliminated most late-night shifts and allowed multiple stations to use material from the same announcer. Increasing consolidation among broadcasting companies also may contribute to the increased use of syndicated programming and programs originating outside a station's viewing or listening area. The growth of alternative media sources, such as satellite radio, may contribute to the expected decline.

A possible positive area for radio announcers is hybrid digital (HD) radio, which broadcasters hope will increase in the coming years. HD radio offers more channels and could result in higher demand for on-air personalities. There will always be some demand for this occupation, because the public continues to desire local radio and television broadcasting and announcers play a necessary role in bringing it to them.

Job prospects.   Some job openings will arise from the need to replace those who transfer to other kinds of work or leave the labor force. Nevertheless, competition for jobs as announcers will be keen because the broadcasting field attracts many more jobseekers than there are jobs. Small radio stations are more inclined to hire beginners, but the pay is low. Applicants who have completed internships and those with related work experience usually receive preference for available positions. Jobseekers with good computer and technical skills also will have an advantage. Large stations will seek announcers who have proven that they can attract and retain a sizable audience, because competition for ratings is so intense in major metropolitan areas. Announcers who are knowledgeable about business, consumer, and health news also may have an advantage over others. Although subject-matter specialization is more common at large stations and the networks, many small stations also encourage it. There will be some opportunities for self-employed DJs who provide music at clubs and special events, but most of these jobs will be part time.

Earnings

Salaries in broadcasting vary widely, but generally are relatively low, except for announcers who work for large stations in major markets or for networks. Earnings are higher in television than in radio and higher in commercial broadcasting than in public broadcasting.

Median hourly wages of radio and television announcers in May 2008 were $12.95. The middle 50 percent earned between $9.05 and $20.31. The lowest 10 percent earned less than $7.45, and the highest 10 percent earned more than $36.42. Median hourly wages of announcers in the radio and television broadcasting industry were $12.61.

Median hourly wages of public address and other system announcers in May 2008 were $13.18. The middle 50 percent earned between $8.82 and $21.04. The lowest 10 percent earned less than $7.51 and the highest 10 percent earned more than $33.58.

Related Occupations

The success of announcers depends upon how well they communicate. Others who must be skilled at oral communication include:

Many announcers also must entertain their audience, so their work is similar to that of other entertainment-related occupations, such as:

Some announcers write their own material, as do:

Announcers perform a variety of duties, including some technical operations similar to those performed by:

Sources of Additional Information

General information on the broadcasting industry, in which many announcers are employed, is available from:

➤ National Association of Broadcasters, 1771 N St. NW., Washington, DC 20036. Internet: **http://www.nab.org**

The Occupational Information Network (O*NET) provides information on a wide range of occupational characteristics.   Links to O*NET appear at the end of the Internet version of this occupational statement, accessible at **http://www.bls.gov/ooh/ocos087.htm**

Authors, Writers, and Editors

Significant Points

- Most jobs require a college degree, preferably in communications, journalism, or English.

- Keen competition is expected for writing and editing jobs as many people are attracted to this occupation.

- Online publications and services are growing in number and sophistication, spurring the demand for writers and editors with Web or multimedia experience.

Nature of the Work

Authors, writers and editors produce a wide variety of written materials in an increasing number of ways. They develop content using any number of multimedia formats that can be read, listened to, or viewed onscreen. Although many people write as part of their primary job, or on online chats or blogs, only writers and editors who are paid to primarily write or edit are included in this occupation. (News analysts, reporters and correspondents, who gather information and prepare stories about newsworthy events, and technical writers, who help explain highly technical information to less technical audiences, are described elsewhere in the *Handbook*.)

Writers and authors develop original written materials for books, magazines, trade journals, online publications, company newsletters, and advertisements. Their works are classified broadly as either fiction or nonfiction and writers often are identified by the type of writing they do—for example, *novelists*, *playwrights*, *biographers*, and *textbook writers*. Writers such as *songwriters*, *screenwriters*, or *scriptwriters*, produce content for radio and television broadcasts, motion pictures, and other types of performance. An increasing number of writers are producing scripted material directly for the Web and other communication devices.

Copy writers prepare advertising copy for use in publications or for broadcasting and they write other materials to promote the sale of a good or service. They often must work with the client to produce advertising themes or slogans and may be involved in the marketing of the product or service.

All writers conduct research on their topics, which they gather through personal observation, library and Internet research, and interviews. Some staff writers who work in the newspaper or magazine publishing industry are news analysts, reporters, and correspondents and like most writers are typically assigned articles to write by editors and publishers, and may propose their own story ideas. Writers, especially of nonfiction, are expected to establish their credibility with editors and readers through strong research and the use of appropriate sources and citations. Writers and authors then select the material they want to use, organize it, and use the written word to express story lines, ideas, or to convey information. With help from editors, they may revise or rewrite sections, searching for the best organization or the right phrasing.

Most writers and editors use desktop or electronic publishing software, scanners, and other electronic communications equipment in the production of their material. In addition, because many writers today prepare material directly for the Internet, such as online newspapers and text for video games, they should be knowledgeable about graphic design, page layout, and multimedia software. In addition, they should be familiar with interactive technologies of the Web so that they can blend text, graphics, and sound together. Some writers maintain blogs or issue text messages as a way of keeping in touch with readers or providing information to them quickly, but only those who are paid to write their blogs or send text messages may be considered writers.

An increasing number of writers today are *freelance writers*—that is, they are self-employed and make their living by selling their written content to book and magazine publishers, news organizations, advertising agencies, or movie, theater, or television producers or by working under contract with an organization. Some writers may be commissioned by a sponsor to write a script; others to write a book on the basis of a proposal in the form of a draft or an outline. Many freelance writers are hired to complete specific short-term or recurring assignments, such as contributing a column or a series of articles on a specific topic to a news agency or for an organization's newsletter.

Editors review, rewrite, and edit the work of writers. They also may do original writing. An editor's responsibilities vary with the employer and type and level of editorial position held. Editorial duties may include planning the content of books, journals, magazines, and other general-interest publications. Editors also review story ideas proposed by staff and freelance writers then decide what material will appeal to readers. They review and edit drafts of books and articles, offer comments to improve the work, and suggest possible titles. In addition, they may oversee the production of publications. In the book-publishing industry, an editor's primary responsibility is

Authors, writers, and editors check their sources and facts for accuracy.

to review proposals for books and decide whether to buy the publication rights from the author.

Most editors begin work as writers. Those who are particularly adept at identifying stories, recognizing writing talent, and interacting with writers, may be interested in editing jobs.

Major newspapers and newsmagazines usually employ several types of editors. The *executive editor* oversees *assistant editors*, and generally has the final say about what stories are published and how they are covered. Assistant editors have responsibility for particular subjects, such as local news, international news, feature stories, or sports. The *managing editor* usually is responsible for the daily operation of the news department. *Assignment editors* determine which reporters will cover a given story.

In smaller organizations—such as small daily or weekly newspapers—a single editor may do everything or share responsibility with only a few other people. Executive and managing editors typically hire writers, reporters, and other employees. They also plan budgets and negotiate contracts with freelance writers, sometimes called "stringers" in the news industry. *Copy editors*, review copy for errors in grammar, punctuation, and spelling and check the copy for readability, style, and agreement with editorial policy. They suggest revisions, such as changing words and rearranging sentences and paragraphs, to improve clarity or accuracy. They may also carry out research and confirm sources for writers and verify facts, dates, and statistics. In addition, they may arrange page layouts of articles, photographs, and advertising; compose headlines; and prepare copy for printing.

Editors often employ others, such as interns, fact checkers, or editorial assistants, for some entry-level positions. While gaining practical experience in a newsroom, they may carry out research and verify facts, dates, and statistics for other writers. In addition, they may arrange page layouts of articles, photographs, and advertising; compose headlines; and prepare copy for printing. *Publication assistants* who work for book publishing houses may read and evaluate manuscripts submitted by freelance writers, proofread printers' galleys, and answer inquiries about published material. Assistants on small newspapers or in smaller media markets may compile articles available from wire services or the Internet, answer phones, and proofread articles.

Work environment. Advances in electronic communications have changed the work environment for many writers. Laptop computers and wireless communications technologies allow growing numbers of writers and authors to work from home and on the road. The ability to send e-mail or text messages, transmit and download stories, perform research, or review materials using the Internet allows writers and editors greater flexibility in where and how they complete assignments. Still, some writers and authors work in offices and many travel to conduct on-site research on their topic.

Some writers keep regular office hours, either to maintain contact with sources and editors or to establish a writing routine, but most writers set their own hours. Many writers—especially freelance writers—are paid per assignment; therefore, they work any number of hours necessary to meet a deadline. As a result, writers must be willing to work evenings, nights, or weekends to produce a piece acceptable to an editor or client by the deadline.

While many freelance writers enjoy running their own businesses and the advantages of working flexible hours, most routinely face the pressures of juggling multiple projects with competing demands and the continual need to find new work. Deadline pressures and long, erratic work hours—often part of the daily routine in these jobs—may cause stress, fatigue, or burnout. In addition, the use of computers for extended periods may cause some individuals to experience back pain, eyestrain, or fatigue.

Editors' schedules generally are determined by the production schedule and the type of editorial position. Most salaried editors work in busy offices much of the time and have to deal with production deadline pressures and the stresses of ensuring that the information they publish is accurate. As a result, editors often work long hours, especially at those times leading up to a publication deadline, which can be daily or even more frequently when editing material for the Internet or for a live broadcast. Overseeing and coordinating multiple writing projects simultaneously is common in these jobs, which may lead to stress, fatigue, or other chronic problems. Freelance editors face the added pressures of finding work on an ongoing basis and continually adjusting to new work environments.

Training, Other Qualifications, and Advancement

A college degree generally is required for a position as an author, writer, or editor. Good facility with computers and communications equipment is necessary in order to stay in touch with sources, editors, and other writers while working on assignments, whether from home, an office, or while traveling.

Education and training. A bachelor's degree or higher is typically needed for a job as an author, writer, or editor. Be-

cause writing skills are essential in this occupation, many employers like to hire people with degrees in communications, journalism, or English, but those with other backgrounds and who can demonstrate good writing skills may also find jobs as writers. Writers who want to focus on writing about a particular topic may need formal training or experience related to that topic. For example, textbook writers and fashion editors may need expertise in their subject areas that they acquired either through formal academic training or work experience. The Internet and other media allow some people to gain writing experience through blog posts, text messages, or self-publishing software. Some of this writing may lead to paid assignments based upon the quality of the writing, unique perspective, or the size of the potential audience, without regard to the absence of a degree.

Training and experience for author, writer, and editor jobs can be obtained by working on high school and college newspapers, community newspapers, and radio and television stations and submissions to literary magazines. College theater and music programs offer playwrights and songwriters an opportunity for them to have their work performed. Many magazines, newspapers, and broadcast stations also have internships for students. Interns may write stories, conduct research and interviews, and learn about the publishing or broadcasting business.

Other qualifications. Authors, writers and editors must be able to express ideas clearly and logically and should enjoy writing. Creativity, curiosity, a broad range of knowledge, self-motivation, and perseverance are also valuable. Authors, writers, and editors must demonstrate good judgment and a strong sense of ethics in deciding what material to publish. In addition, the ability to concentrate and to work under pressure is essential. Editors also need tact and the ability to guide and encourage others in their work.

Familiarity with electronic publishing, graphics, Web design, and multimedia production increasingly is needed. Use of electronic and wireless communications equipment to send e-mail, transmit work, and review copy often is necessary. Online publications require knowledge of computer software and editing tools used to combine text with graphics, audio, video, and animation.

Advancement. Writers and authors generally advance by building a reputation, taking on more complex writing assignments, and getting published in more prestigious markets and publications. Examples of previously published work form the best route to advancement. Establishing a track record for meeting deadlines also makes it easier to get future assignments. Writing for smaller businesses, local newspapers, advertising agencies, or not-for-profit organizations either as a staff writer or on a freelance basis, allows beginning writers and authors to begin writing right away and take credit for their work. Opportunities for advancement within these organizations may be limited, because they either do not have enough regular work or do not need more advanced writing.

In larger businesses, jobs and promotions usually are more formally structured. Beginners often read submissions, do research, fact check articles, or copy edit drafts, and advance to writing and editing more substantive stories and articles.

Projections data from the National Employment Matrix

Occupational Title	SOC Code	Employment, 2008	Projected Employment, 2018	Change, 2008-2018	
				Number	Percent
Authors, writers, and editors...	–	281,300	303,300	22,100	8
Editors..	27-3041	129,600	129,200	-400	0
Writers and authors..	27-3043	151,700	174,100	22,500	15

(NOTE) Data in this table are rounded. See the discussion of the employment projections table in the *Handbook* introductory chapter on *Occupational Information Included in the Handbook.*

Most editors begin work as writers. Those who are particularly adept at identifying stories, recognizing writing talent, and interacting with writers, may be interested in editing jobs. Except for copy editors, most editors hold management positions and must also enjoy making decisions related to running a business. For them, advancement generally means moving up the corporate ladder or to publications with larger circulation or greater prestige. Copy editors may move into original writing or substantive editing positions or become freelancers.

Employment

Authors, writers and editors held about 281,300 jobs in 2008. Writers and authors held about 151,700 jobs and editors held about 129,600 jobs. About 70 percent of writers and authors were self-employed, while 12 percent of editors were self-employed.

Among the 30 percent of salaried writers and authors, about half work in the professional, scientific, and technical services and in publishing (except Internet) industries. These industries include advertising, public relations and related services and newspaper, periodical, book, and directory publishers, respectively. Other salaried writers and authors work in broadcasting, professional and social organizations, and the motion picture and video industries.

While 51 percent of salaried editors worked in the publishing, except Internet industry (half of those for newspapers), a large number of editors were also employed in other industries. Business, professional and social organizations, information services, and educational institutions employed editors to work on their publications or Web content.

Jobs are somewhat concentrated in major media and entertainment markets—Boston, Chicago, Los Angeles, New York, and Washington, DC—but improved communications and Internet capabilities allow writers to work from almost anywhere. Many prefer to work outside these cities and travel regularly to meet with publishers and clients and to do research or conduct interviews in person. As a result, job location is less of a requirement for many writing or editing positions than it once was.

Job Outlook

Employment is expected to grow about as fast as average. Keen competition is expected for writing and editing jobs as many people are attracted to this occupation. At the same time, many employers are downsizing.

Employment change. Employment of authors, writers, and editors is expected to grow 8 percent, about as fast as the average for all occupations, from 2008 to 2018. Employment in salaried writing and editing positions is expected to increase slightly as jobs become more prevalent throughout the economy. Companies in a wide array of industries are using newer multimedia technologies and online media to reach a more technology friendly consumer and meet the growing demand for Web-based information. Online publications and services are growing in number and sophistication, spurring the demand for authors, writers, and editors, especially those with Web or multimedia experience. Businesses and organizations are adding text messaging services to expanded newsletters and Web sites as a way of attracting new customers. They may hire writers or editors on either a salaried or freelance basis to contribute additional content. Some publishing companies however, especially those that rely on advertising revenues and sales receipts to support large staffs of writers, will employ fewer writers and editors. But many experienced writers and editors will find work with nonprofit organizations and associations in their public relations offices, or in the public affairs departments of large companies or agencies. Others will find freelance work for newspaper, magazine, or journal publishers; some will write books.

Job prospects. Competition is expected for writing and editing jobs as many people are attracted to this occupation. Competition for jobs with established newspaper and magazines will be particularly keen as many organizations move their publication focus from a print to an online presence and as the publishing industry continues to contract. Writers and editors who have adapted to the new media and are comfortable writing for and working with a variety of electronic and digital tools will have an advantage in finding new work. The declining costs of self-publishing and the growing popularity of electronic books and book readers will allow many freelancers to get their work published. Some job openings will arise as experienced workers retire, transfer to other occupations, or leave the labor force.

Earnings

Median annual wages for salaried writers and authors were $53,070 in May 2008. The middle 50 percent earned between $38,150 and $75,060. The lowest 10 percent earned less than $28,020, and the highest 10 percent earned more than $106,630. Median annual wages were $58,740 for those working in advertising, public relations, and related services and $43,450 for those working for in newspaper, periodical, book and directory publishers.

Median annual wages for salaried editors were $49,990 in May 2008. The middle 50 percent earned between $36,690 and $69,140. The lowest 10 percent earned less than $28,090, and the highest 10 percent earned more than $95,490. Median annual wages of those working for newspaper, periodical, book, and directory publishers were $49,280.

Freelance writers earn income from their articles, books, and less commonly, television and movie scripts. While most work on an individual project basis for multiple publishers, many support themselves with income derived from other sources. Unless gotten from another job, freelancers generally have to provide for their own health insurance and pension.

Related Occupations

Writers and editors communicate ideas and information. Other communications occupations include:

Sources of Additional Information

For information about freelance writing careers, contact:
➤ American Society of Journalists and Authors, 1501 Broadway, Suite 302, New York, NY 10036. Internet: **http://www.asja.org**

For information about accredited creative writing programs and creative writing conferences, contact:
➤ The Association of Writers and Writing Programs, George Mason University; MS 1E3, Fairfax, VA 22030-4444. Internet: **http://www.awpwriter.org**

The Occupational Information Network (O*NET) provides information on a wide range of occupational characteristics. Links to O*NET appear at the end of the Internet version of this occupational statement, accessible at **http://www.bls.gov/ooh/ocos320.htm**

Broadcast and Sound Engineering Technicians and Radio Operators

Significant Points

- Job applicants will face keen competition for jobs in major metropolitan areas, where pay generally is higher; prospects are expected to be better in small cities and towns.

- Technical school, community college, or college training in broadcast technology, electronics, or computer networking provides the best preparation.

- About 29 percent of these workers are in broadcasting, mainly in radio and television stations, and 15 percent work in the motion picture, video, and sound recording industries.

- Evening, weekend, and holiday work is common.

Nature of the Work

Broadcast and sound engineering technicians and radio operators perform a wide variety of tasks. Their duties include setting up and maintaining the electrical equipment used in nearly all radio and television broadcasts, concerts, plays, sound recordings, and movies. There are many specialized occupations in this field.

Audio and video equipment technicians set up and operate audio and video equipment, including microphones, speakers, video screens, projectors, video monitors, and recording equipment. They also connect wires and cables and set up and operate sound and mixing boards and related electronic equipment for concerts, sports events, meetings and conventions, presentations, and news conferences. They may set up and operate associated spotlights and other custom lighting systems. They also are needed to install and maintain equipment in many large businesses and universities that are upgrading their facilities with audio and video equipment.

Broadcast technicians set up, operate, and maintain equipment that regulates the signal strength, the clarity, and the ranges of sounds and colors of radio or television broadcasts. These technicians also operate control panels to select the source of the material. Technicians may switch from one camera or studio to another, from film to live programming, or from network to local programming.

Sound engineering technicians operate machines and equipment to record, synchronize, mix, or reproduce music, voices, or sound effects in recording studios, sporting arenas, theater productions, or movie and video productions.

Broadcast and sound engineering technicians and radio operators perform a variety of duties at small stations. At large stations and at the networks, technicians are more specialized, although job assignments may change from day to day. The terms "operator," "engineer," and "technician" often are used interchangeably to describe these workers. They may monitor and log outgoing signals and operate transmitters; set up, adjust, service, and repair electronic broadcasting equipment; and regulate fidelity, brightness, contrast, volume, and sound quality of television broadcasts.

Technicians also work in program production. *Recording engineers* operate and maintain video and sound recording equipment. They may operate equipment designed to produce special effects, such as the illusion of a bolt of lightning or a police siren. *Sound mixers* or *re-recording mixers* produce soundtracks for movies or television programs. After filming or recording is complete, these workers may use a process called "dubbing" to insert sounds. *Field technicians* set up and operate portable transmission equipment outside the studio. Because television news coverage requires so much electronic equipment and the technology is changing so rapidly, many stations assign technicians exclusively to news. *Chief engineers*, *transmission engineers*, and *broadcast field supervisors* oversee other technicians and maintain broadcasting equipment.

Radio operators mainly receive and transmit communications using a variety of tools. These workers also repair equipment, using such devices as electronic testing equipment, hand tools, and power tools. One of their major duties is to help ensure communication systems remain in good condition.

Work environment. Broadcast and sound engineering technicians and radio operators generally work indoors in pleasant surroundings. However, those who broadcast news and other programs from locations outside the studio may work outdoors in all types of weather or in other dangerous conditions. Technicians doing maintenance may climb poles or antenna towers, and those setting up equipment do heavy lifting.

Technicians at large stations and the networks usually work a 40-hour week under great pressure to meet broadcast deadlines, and may occasionally work overtime. Technicians at small stations routinely work more than 40 hours a week. Evening, weekend, and holiday work is usual because most stations are on the air 18 to 24 hours a day, 7 days a week. Some technicians need to be available on call whenever the station is broadcasting; technicians must handle any problems that occur during this time.

Technicians who work on motion pictures may be on a tight schedule and may work long hours to meet contractual deadlines.

Training, Other Qualifications, and Advancement

Broadcast and sound engineering technicians, as well as audio and video equipment technicians, should have some kind of formal training related to their field. Radio operators do not need an education beyond high school and can usually learn their jobs through several months of on-the-job training.

Education and training. Audio and video equipment technicians should complete a technical-training program related to the field, which may take several months to a year to complete. Many recent entrants to the field have also received an associate degree or bachelor's degree, although it is generally not required for entry-level positions. In addition to coursework, experience in high school or college audiovisual clubs can provide a student with good training for this occupation. Working as an assistant is a useful way to gain experience and knowledge for an entry-level employee.

For broadcast technicians an associate degree in broadcast technology, electronics, computer networking, or a related field is generally recommended. Because of the competitiveness of the broadcast industry, many jobs require a bachelor's degree. A four-year degree also gives employees much better prospects for advancement in the field.

Most entry-level employees find jobs in small markets or with small stations in big markets and can transfer to larger, better paying stations after gaining experience and learning the necessary skills. Small stations usually value more general skills since they have fewer employees doing less specialized work. Large stations almost never hire someone without previous experience, and they value more specialized skills. Working at a college radio or television station can be very advantageous for prospective employees.

Sound engineering technicians usually complete a vocational program, which can take about a year, although there are shorter programs. Prospective technicians should take high school courses in math, physics, and electronics. Technicians need to have excellent computer training to be successful in this field.

Radio operators are not usually required to complete any formal training. This is an entry-level position that generally requires on-the-job training.

In the motion picture industry, people are hired as apprentice editorial assistants and work their way up to jobs requiring higher level skills. Employers in the motion picture industry

Broadcast technicians set up, operate, and maintain electrical equipment.

usually hire experienced freelance technicians on a picture-by-picture basis. Reputation and perseverance are important in getting jobs.

Continuing education to become familiar with emerging technologies is recommended for all broadcast and sound engineering technicians and radio operators.

Other qualifications. Broadcast and sound engineering technicians and radio operators need skills in information technology and electronics since most recording, editing, and broadcasting are done on computers. Prospective technicians must have manual dexterity and an aptitude for working with electrical, electronic, and mechanical systems and equipment.

Certification and advancement. Licensing is not required for broadcast technicians. However, certification by the Society of Broadcast Engineers is issued to experienced technicians who pass an examination, and the certification may help with advancement.

Experienced technicians can become supervisory technicians or chief engineers. A college degree in engineering is needed to become chief engineer at large television stations.

Employment

Broadcast and sound engineering technicians and radio operators held about 114,600 jobs in 2008. Their employment was distributed among the following detailed occupations:

Audio and video equipment technicians 55,400
Broadcast technicians..38,800
Sound engineering technicians.....................................19,500
Radio operators 1,000

About 29 percent of broadcast and sound engineering technicians and radio operators worked in broadcasting (except Internet broadcasting), and 15 percent worked in the motion picture, video, and sound recording industries. About 13 percent were

Projections data from the National Employment Matrix

Occupational Title	SOC Code	Employment, 2008	Projected Employment, 2018	Change, 2008-2018	
				Number	Percent
Broadcast and sound engineering technicians and radio operators ..	27-4010	114,600	123,600	9,000	8
Audio and video equipment technicians	27-4011	55,400	62,400	7,000	13
Broadcast technicians...	27-4012	38,800	39,400	700	2
Radio operators	27-4013	1,000	1,100	100	9
Sound engineering technicians	27-4014	19,500	20,700	1,200	6

(NOTE) Data in this table are rounded. See the discussion of the employment projections table in the *Handbook* introductory chapter on *Occupational Information Included in the Handbook.*

self-employed. Television stations employ, on average, many more technicians than radio stations. Some technicians are employed in other industries, producing employee communications, sales, and training programs. Technician jobs in television and radio are located in virtually all U.S. cities; jobs in radio also are found in many small towns. The highest paying and most specialized jobs are concentrated in New York City, Los Angeles, Chicago, and Washington, DC—the headquarters of most network and news programs. Motion picture production jobs are concentrated in Los Angeles and New York City.

Job Outlook

Employment is expected to grow about as fast as the average through 2018. But people seeking entry-level jobs as technicians in broadcasting are expected to face keen competition in major metropolitan areas. Prospects are expected to be better in small cities and towns.

Employment change. Overall employment of broadcast and sound engineering technicians and radio operators is expected to grow by 8 percent over the 2008–18 decade, which is about as fast as the average of all occupations. Projected job growth varies among detailed occupations in this field. Employment of audio and video equipment technicians is expected to grow 13 percent, about as fast as average. Audio and video equipment is in heavy demand in many new buildings, especially new schools, and in existing schools as well. Many new technicians will be needed, not only to install, but to maintain and repair the equipment as well. A growing number of companies will plan permanent departments employing audio and video technicians. An increase in the use of digital signage will also lead to higher demand for audio and video equipment technicians. In the motion picture industry, employment for these workers will grow because they are needed to install digital movie screens.

Employment of broadcast technicians is expected to grow by 2 percent, signifying little or no change, and employment of sound engineering technicians is expected to grow by 6 percent, which is slower than average. Advancements in technology will enhance the capabilities of technicians to produce higher quality radio and television programming; however, this improved technology will also increase the productivity of technicians, which may hold down employment growth. Jobs in radio and television broadcasting will also be limited by further consolidation of stations and by labor-saving advances, such as computer-controlled programming. In the cable and pay portion of the broadcasting industry, employment is expected to grow as the range of products and services expands, including cable Internet access and video-on-demand.

An area in which technicians will be in increasing demand over the next several years is mobile broadcasting.

Job prospects. People seeking entry-level jobs as broadcast technicians are expected to face keen competition because of the large number of people attracted by the glamour of working in television or radio. Competition will be stronger in large metropolitan areas where pay is generally higher and the number of job seekers usually exceeds the number of openings. Prospects for entry-level positions are expected to be better in small cities and towns, provided that the jobseeker has appropriate training.

Earnings

Television stations usually pay higher salaries than radio stations, commercial broadcasting usually pays more than noncommercial broadcasting, and stations in large markets pay more than those in small markets.

Median annual wages of audio and video equipment technicians in May 2008 were $38,050. The middle 50 percent earned between $28,130 and $51,780. The lowest 10 percent earned less than $21,500, and the highest 10 percent earned more than $66,030. Median annual wages in motion picture and video industries, which employed the largest number of audio and video equipment technicians, were $39,410.

Median annual wages of broadcast technicians in May 2008 were $32,900. The middle 50 percent earned between $22,900 and $49,340. The lowest 10 percent earned less than $17,510, and the highest 10 percent earned more than $66,550. Median annual wages in radio and television broadcasting, which employed the largest number of broadcast technicians, were $29,220.

Median annual wages of sound engineering technicians in May 2008 were $47,490. The middle 50 percent earned between $32,770 and $69,700. The lowest 10 percent earned less than $23,790, and the highest 10 percent earned more than $92,700.

Median annual wages of radio operators in May 2008 were $37,120. The middle 50 percent earned between $27,890 and $48,200. The lowest 10 percent earned less than $19,240, and the highest 10 percent earned more than $61,290.

Related Occupations

Other occupations that need the electronics training necessary to operate technical equipment include:

Broadcast and sound engineering technicians also may operate computer networks, as do:

Other occupations that screen incoming calls on some live radio and television programs are:

Sources of Additional Information

For career information and links to employment resources, contact:

➤ National Association of Broadcasters, 1771 N St. NW., Washington, DC 20036. Internet: **http://www.nab.org**

For information on certification and links to employment information, contact:

➤ Society of Broadcast Engineers, 9102 North Meridian St., Suite 150, Indianapolis, IN 46260. Internet: **http://www.sbe.org**

For information on audio and video equipment technicians, contact:

➤ InfoComm International, 11242 Waples Mill Rd., Suite 200, Fairfax, VA 22030. Internet: **http://www.infocomm.org**

The Occupational Information Network (O*NET) provides information on a wide range of occupational characteristics. Links to O*NET appear at the end of the Internet version of this occupational statement, accessible at **http://www.bls.gov/ooh/ocos109.htm**

Interpreters and Translators

Significant Points

- About 26 percent of interpreters and translators are self-employed; many freelance and work in this occupation only sporadically.

- In addition to needing fluency in at least two languages, many interpreters and translators need a bachelor's degree.

- Employment is expected to grow much faster than average.

- Job prospects vary by specialty and language.

Nature of the Work

Interpreters and translators facilitate the cross-cultural communication necessary in today's society by converting one language into another. However, these language specialists do more than simply translate words—they relay concepts and ideas between languages. They must thoroughly understand the subject matter in which they work in order to accurately convey information from one language into another. In addition, they must be sensitive to the cultures associated with their languages of expertise.

Although some people do both, interpreting and translation are different professions. Interpreters deal with spoken words, translators with written words. Each task requires a distinct set of skills and aptitudes, and most people are better suited for one or the other. While interpreters often interpret into and from both languages, translators generally translate only into their native language.

Interpreters convert one spoken language into another—or, in the case of sign-language interpreters, between spoken communication and sign language. Interpreting requires that one pay attention carefully, understand what is communicated in both languages, and express thoughts and ideas clearly. Strong research and analytical skills, mental dexterity, and an exceptional memory also are important.

There are two modes of interpreting: simultaneous, and consecutive. Simultaneous interpreting requires interpreters to listen and speak (or sign) at the same time someone is speaking or signing. Ideally, simultaneous interpreters should be so familiar with a subject that they are able to anticipate the end of the speaker's sentence. Because they need a high degree of concentration, simultaneous interpreters work in pairs, with each interpreting for 20-minute to 30-minute periods. This type of interpreting is required at international conferences and is sometimes used in the courts.

In contrast to the immediacy of simultaneous interpreting, consecutive interpreting begins only after the speaker has verbalized a group of words or sentences. Consecutive interpreters often take notes while listening to the speakers, so they must develop some type of note-taking or shorthand system. This form of interpreting is used most often for person-to-person communication, during which the interpreter is positioned near both parties.

Translators convert written materials from one language into another. They must have excellent writing and analytical ability, and because the translations that they produce must be accurate, they also need good editing skills.

Translating involves more than replacing a word with its equivalent in another language; sentences and ideas must be manipulated to flow with the same coherence as those in the source document so that the translation reads as though it originated in the target language. Translators also must bear in mind any cultural references that may need to be explained to the intended audience, such as colloquialisms, slang, and other expressions that do not translate literally. Some subjects may be more difficult than others to translate because words or passages may have multiple meanings that make several translations possible. Not surprisingly, translated work often goes through multiple revisions before final text is submitted.

Nearly all translation work is done on a computer, and most assignments are received and submitted electronically. This enables translators to work from almost anywhere, and a large percentage of them work from home. The Internet provides advanced research capabilities and valuable language resources, such as specialized dictionaries and glossaries. In some cases, use of computer-assisted translation—including memory tools that provide comparisons of previous translations with current work—helps save time and reduce repetition.

The services of interpreters and translators are needed in a number of subject areas. While these workers may not completely specialize in a particular field or industry, many do fo-

Interpreters and translators must have a thorough understanding of various languages.

cus on one area of expertise. Some of the most common areas are described below; however, interpreters and translators may work in a variety of other areas also, including business, education, social services, and entertainment.

Judiciary interpreters and translators facilitate communication for people with limited English proficiency who find it challenging to communicate in a legal setting. Legal translators must be thoroughly familiar with the language and functions of the U.S. judicial system, as well as other countries' legal systems. Court interpreters work in a variety of legal settings, such as attorney-client meetings, preliminary hearings, arraignments, depositions, and trials. Success as a court interpreter requires an understanding of both legal terminology and colloquial language. In addition to interpreting what is said, court interpreters also may be required to read written documents aloud in a language other than that in which they were written, a task known as sight translation.

Medical interpreters and translator, sometimes referred to as *healthcare interpreters and translators*, provide language services to healthcare patients with limited English proficiency. Medical interpreters help patients to communicate with doctors, nurses, and other medical staff. Translators working in this specialty primarily convert patient materials and informational brochures issued by hospitals and medical facilities into the desired language. Interpreters in this field need a strong grasp of medical and colloquial terminology in both languages, along with cultural sensitivity to help the patient receive the information.

Sign-language interpreters facilitate communication between people who are deaf or hard of hearing and people who can hear. Sign-language interpreters must be fluent in English and in American Sign Language (ASL), which combines signing, finger spelling, and specific body language. Most sign-language interpreters either interpret, aiding communication between English and ASL, or transliterate, facilitating communication between English and contact signing—a form of signing that uses a more English language-based word order. Some interpreters specialize in oral interpreting for people who are deaf or hard of hearing and lip-read instead of sign. Other specialties include tactile signing, which is interpreting for people who are blind as well as deaf by making manual signs into their hands, using cued speech, and signing exact English.

Conference interpreters work at conferences that have non-English-speaking attendees. The work is often in the field of international business or diplomacy, although conference interpreters can interpret for any organization that works with speakers of foreign languages. Employers prefer high-level interpreters who have the ability to translate from at least two languages into one native language—for example, the ability to interpret from Spanish and French into English. For some positions, such as those with the United Nations, this qualification is mandatory.

Guide or escort interpreters accompany either U.S. visitors abroad or foreign visitors in the United States to ensure that they are able to communicate during their stay. These specialists interpret on a variety of subjects, both on an informal basis and on a professional level. Most of their interpreting is consecutive, and work is generally shared by two interpreters when the assignment requires more than an 8-hour day. Frequent travel, often for days or weeks at a time, is common, and it is an aspect of the job that some find particularly appealing.

Literary translators adapt written literature from one language into another. They may translate any number of documents, including journal articles, books, poetry, and short stories. Literary translation is related to creative writing; literary translators must create a new text in the target language that reproduces the content and style of the original. Whenever possible, literary translators work closely with authors to best capture their intended meanings and literary characteristics.

Localization translators completely adapt a product or service for use in a different language and culture. The goal of these specialists is to make it appear as though a product originated in the country where it will be sold and supported. At its earlier stages, this work dealt primarily with software localization, but the specialty has expanded to include the adaptation of Internet sites, marketing, publications, and products and services in manufacturing and other business sectors.

Work environment. Interpreters work in a wide variety of settings, such as schools, hospitals, courtrooms, and conference centers. Translators usually work alone, and they must frequently perform under pressure of deadlines and tight schedules. Technology allows translators to work from almost anywhere, and many choose to work from home.

Because many interpreters and translators freelance, their schedules often vary, with periods of limited work interspersed with periods requiring long, irregular hours. For those who freelance, a significant amount of time must be dedicated to looking for jobs. Interpreters who work over the telephone or through videoconferencing generally work in call centers in urban areas and keep to a standard 5-day, 40-hour workweek.

Training, Other Qualifications, and Advancement
Interpreters and translators must be fluent in at least two languages. Their educational backgrounds may vary widely, but many need a bachelor's degree. Many also complete job-specific training programs.

Education and training. The educational backgrounds of interpreters and translators vary. Knowing at least two languages is essential. Although it is not necessary to have been raised bilingual to succeed, many interpreters and translators grew up speaking two languages.

In high school, students can prepare for these careers by taking a broad range of courses that include English writing and comprehension, foreign languages, and basic computer proficiency. Other helpful pursuits include spending time abroad, engaging in direct contact with foreign cultures, and reading extensively on a variety of subjects in English and at least one other language.

Beyond high school, there are many educational options. Although a bachelor's degree is often required for jobs, majoring in a language is not always necessary. An educational background in a particular field of study can provide a natural area of subject-matter expertise. However, specialized training in how to do the work is generally required. Formal programs in interpreting and translation are available at colleges nationwide and through nonuniversity training programs, conferences, and courses. Many people who work as conference interpreters or in more technical areas—such as localization, engineering, or finance—have master's degrees, while those working in the community as court or medical interpreters or translators are more likely to complete job-specific training programs.

Other qualifications. Experience is an essential part of a successful career in either interpreting or translation. In fact, many agencies or companies use only the services of people who have worked in the field for 3 to 5 years or who have a degree in translation studies, or both.

A good way for translators to learn firsthand about the profession is to start out working in-house for a translation company; however, such jobs are not very numerous. People seeking to enter interpreter or translator jobs should begin by getting experience whatever way possible—even if it means doing informal or volunteer work.

Volunteer opportunities are available through community organizations, hospitals, and sporting events, such as marathons, that involve international competitors. The American Translators Association works with the Red Cross to provide volunteer interpreters in crisis situations. Any translation can be used as an example for potential clients, even translation done as practice.

Paid or unpaid internships and apprenticeships are other ways for interpreters and translators to get started. Escort interpreting may offer an opportunity for inexperienced candidates to work alongside a more seasoned interpreter. Interpreters might also find it easier to break into areas with particularly high demand for language services, such as court or medical interpreting.

Whatever path of entry they pursue, new interpreters and translators should establish mentoring relationships to build their skills, confidence, and professional network. Mentoring

may be formal, such as through a professional association, or informal with a coworker or an acquaintance who has experience as an interpreter or translator. Both the American Translators Association and the Registry of Interpreters for the Deaf offer formal mentoring programs.

Translators working in localization need a solid grasp of the languages to be translated, a thorough understanding of technical concepts and vocabulary, and a high degree of knowledge about the intended target audience or users of the product. Because software often is involved, it is not uncommon for people who work in this area of translation to have a strong background in computer science or to have computer-related work experience.

Self-employed and freelance interpreters and translators need general business skills to successfully manage their finances and careers. They must set prices for their work, bill customers, keep financial records, and market their services to attract new business and build their client base.

Certification and advancement. There is currently no universal form of certification required of interpreters and translators in the United States. However there are a variety of different tests that workers can take to demonstrate proficiency, which may be helpful in gaining employment. For example, the American Translators Association provides certification in 24 language combinations involving English for its members.

Federal courts have certification for Spanish, Navajo, and Haitian Creole interpreters, and many State and municipal courts offer their own forms of certification. The National Association of Judiciary Interpreters and Translators also offers certification for court interpreting.

The U.S. Department of State has a three-test series for prospective interpreters—one test in simple consecutive interpreting (for escort work), another in simultaneous interpreting (for court or seminar work), and a third in conference-level interpreting (for international conferences)—as well as a test for prospective translators. These tests are not considered a credential, but successful completion indicates that a person has a significant level of skill in the field. Additionally, the International Association of Conference Interpreters offers certification for conference interpreters

The National Association of the Deaf and the Registry of Interpreters for the Deaf (RID) jointly offer certification for general sign interpreters. In addition, the registry offers specialty tests in legal interpreting, speech reading, and deaf-to-deaf interpreting—which includes interpreting among deaf speakers with different native languages and from ASL to tactile signing.

Once interpreters and translators have gained sufficient experience, they may then move up to more difficult or prestigious assignments, may seek certification, may be given editorial responsibility, or may eventually manage or start a translation agency.

Projections data from the National Employment Matrix

Occupational Title	SOC Code	Employment, 2008	Projected Employment, 2018	Change, 2008-2018	
				Number	Percent
Interpreters and translators...	27-3091	50,900	62,200	11,300	22

(NOTE) Data in this table are rounded. See the discussion of the employment projections table in the *Handbook* introductory chapter on *Occupational Information Included in the Handbook.*

Many self-employed interpreters and translators start businesses by submitting resumes and samples to many different translation and interpreting agencies and then wait to be contacted when an agency matches their skills with a job. Work is often acquired by word of mouth or through referrals from existing clients.

Employment

Interpreters and translators held about 50,900 jobs in 2008. However, the actual number of interpreters and translators is probably significantly higher because many work in the occupation only sporadically. Interpreters and translators are employed in a variety of industries, reflecting the diversity of employment options in the field. About 28 percent worked in public and private educational institutions, such as schools, colleges, and universities. About 13 percent worked in health care and social assistance, many of whom worked for hospitals. Another 9 percent worked in other areas of government, such as Federal, State, and local courts. Other employers of interpreters and translators include interpreting and translation agencies, publishing companies, telephone companies, and airlines.

About 26 percent of interpreters and translators are self-employed. Many who freelance in the occupation work only part time, relying on other sources of income to supplement earnings from interpreting or translation.

Job Outlook

Interpreters and translators can expect much faster than average employment growth. Job prospects vary by specialty and language.

Employment change. Employment of interpreters and translators is projected to increase 22 percent over the 2008–18 decade, which is much faster than the average for all occupations. Higher demand for interpreters and translators results directly from the broadening of international ties and the large increases in the number of non-English speaking people in the United States. Both of these trends are expected to continue throughout the projections period, contributing to relatively rapid growth in the number of jobs for interpreters and translators across all industries in the economy.

Demand will remain strong for translators of frequently translated languages, such as Portuguese, French, Italian, German, and Spanish. Demand should also be strong for translators of Arabic and other Middle Eastern languages and for the principal East Asian languages—Chinese, Japanese, and Korean. Demand for American Sign Language interpreters will grow rapidly, driven by the increasing use of video relay services, which allow individuals to conduct video calls using a sign language interpreter over an Internet connection.

Technology has made the work of interpreters and translators easier. However, technology is not likely to have a negative impact on employment of interpreters and translators because such innovations are incapable of producing work comparable with work produced by these professionals.

Job prospects. Urban areas, especially Washington, DC, New York, and cities in California, provide the largest numbers of employment possibilities, especially for interpreters; however, as the immigrant population spreads into more rural areas, jobs in smaller communities will become more widely available.

Job prospects for interpreters and translators vary by specialty and language. For example, interpreters and translators of Spanish should have good job opportunities because of expected increases in the Hispanic population in the United States. Demand is expected to be strong for interpreters and translators specializing in healthcare and law because it is critical that information be fully understood among all parties in these areas. Additionally, there should be demand for specialists in localization, driven by the globalization of business and the expansion of the Internet; however, demand may be dampened somewhat by outsourcing of localization work to other countries. Given the shortage of interpreters and translators meeting the desired skill level of employers, interpreters for the deaf will continue to have favorable employment prospects. On the other hand, competition can be expected for both conference interpreter and literary translator positions because of the small number of job opportunities in these specialties.

Earnings

Wage and salary interpreters and translators had median hourly wages of $38,850 in May 2008. The middle 50 percent earned between $28,940 and $52,240. The lowest 10 percent earned less than $22,170, and the highest 10 percent earned more than $69,190. Individuals classified as language specialists in the Federal Government earned an average of $79,865 annually in March 2009.

Earnings depend on language, subject matter, skill, experience, education, certification, and type of employer, and salaries of interpreters and translators can vary widely. Interpreters and translators who know languages for which there is a greater demand, or which relatively few people can translate, often have higher earnings, as do those who perform services requiring a high level of skill, such as conference interpreters.

For those who are not salaried, earnings typically fluctuate, depending on the availability of work. Freelance interpreters usually earn an hourly rate, whereas translators who freelance typically earn a rate per word or per hour.

Related Occupations

Interpreters and translators use their multilingual skills, as do teachers of languages. These include:

Translators prepare texts for publication or dissemination; other workers involved in this process include:

Interpreters or translators working in a legal or healthcare environment are required to have a knowledge of terms and concepts that is similar to that of other workers in these fields, such as:

Sources of Additional Information

Organizations dedicated to these professions can provide valuable advice and guidance to people interested in learning more about interpreting and translation. The language services division of local hospitals or courthouses also may have information about available opportunities.

For general career information, contact:

➤ American Translators Association, 225 Reinekers Ln., Suite 590, Alexandria, VA 22314. Internet: **http://www.atanet.org**

For more detailed information by specialty, contact the association affiliated with the subject area in question. See, for example, the following:

➤ American Literary Translators Association, University of Texas at Dallas, 800 W. Campbell Rd., Mail Station JO51, Richardson, TX 75080-3021. Internet: **http://www.utdallas.edu/alta**

➤ International Medical Interpreters Association, 800 Washington Street, Box 271, Boston, MA 02111-1845. Internet: **http://www.imiaweb.org**

➤ Localization Industry Standards Association, Domaine en Prael, CH-1323 RomainmÙtier, Switzerland. Internet: **http://www.lisa.org**

➤ National Association of Judiciary Interpreters and Translators, 1707 L St. NW., Suite 570, Washington, DC 20036. Internet: **http://www.najit.org**

➤ National Council on Interpreting in Health Care, 5505 Connecticut Ave. NW., Suite 119, Washington, DC 20015. Internet: **http://www.ncihc.org**

➤ Registry of Interpreters for the Deaf, 333 Commerce St., Alexandria, VA 22314. Internet: **http://www.rid.org**

For information about testing to become a contract interpreter or translator with the U.S. State Department, contact:

➤ U.S. Department of State, Office of Language Services, 2401 E St. NW., SA-1, Room H1400, Washington, DC 20522. Internet: **http://languageservices.state.gov**

Information on obtaining a position as an interpreter and translator with the Federal Government is available from the Office of Personnel Management through USAJOBS, the Federal Government's official employment information system. This resource for locating and applying for job opportunities can be accessed through the Internet at **http://www.usajobs.opm.gov** or through an interactive voice response telephone system at (703) 724-1850 or TDD (978) 461-8404. These numbers are not toll free, and charges may result. For advice on how to find and apply for Federal jobs, see the *Occupational Outlook Quarterly* article "How to get a job in the Federal Government," online at **http://www.bls.gov/opub/ooq/2004/summer/art01.pdf.**
The Occupational Information Network (O*NET) provides information on a wide range of occupational characteristics. Links to O*NET appear at the end of the Internet version of this occupational statement, accessible at **http://www.bls.gov/ooh/ocos175.htm**

News Analysts, Reporters, and Correspondents

Significant Points

- Competition will be keen for jobs at large metropolitan and national newspapers, broadcast stations, and magazines; small publications and broadcast stations and online newspapers and magazines should provide the best opportunities.

- Most employers prefer individuals with a bachelor's degree in journalism or mass communications and experience gained at school newspapers or broadcasting stations or through internships with news organizations.

- Jobs often involve long, irregular hours and pressure to meet deadlines.

Nature of the Work

News analysts, reporters, and correspondents gather information, prepare stories, and make broadcasts that inform the public about local, State, national, and international events; present points of view on current issues; and report on the actions of public officials, corporate executives, interest groups, and others who exercise power.

News analysts—also called *newscasters* or *news anchors*—examine, interpret, and broadcast news received from various sources. News anchors present news stories and introduce videotaped news or live transmissions from on-the-scene reporters. *News correspondents* report on news occurring in the large U.S. and foreign cities where they are stationed.

In covering a story, *reporters*, sometimes referred to as *journalists*, investigate leads and news tips, look at documents, observe events at the scene, and interview people. Reporters take notes and also may take photographs or shoot videos. At their office, they organize the material, determine the focus or emphasis, write their stories, and edit accompanying video material. Many reporters enter information or write stories on laptop computers and electronically submit the material to their offices from remote locations. Increasingly, reporters are asked to maintain and produce material for a newspaper's Web site. In some cases, *newswriters* write a story from information collected and submitted by reporters. Radio and television reporters often compose stories and report "live" from the scene. At times, they later tape an introduction to or commentary on their story in the studio. Some journalists also interpret the news or offer opinions to readers, viewers, or listeners. In this role, they are called *commentators* or *columnists*.

Newscasters at large stations and networks usually specialize in a particular type of news, such as sports or weather. *Weathercasters*, also called weather reporters, report current and forecasted weather conditions. They gather information from national satellite weather services, wire services, and local and regional weather bureaus. Some weathercasters are trained meteorologists and can develop their own weather forecasts. (See the statement on atmospheric scientists elsewhere in

Television reporters often compose stories and report "live" from the scene.

the *Handbook.*) *Sportscasters* select, write, and deliver sports news, which may include interviews with sports personalities and coverage of games and other sporting events.

General-assignment reporters write about newsworthy occurrences—such as accidents, political rallies, visits of celebrities, or business closings—as assigned. Large newspapers and radio and television stations assign reporters to gather news about specific topics—for example, crime or education. Some reporters specialize in fields such as health, politics, foreign affairs, sports, theater, consumer affairs, social events, science, business, or religion. Investigative reporters cover stories that may take many days or weeks of information gathering.

Some publications use teams of reporters instead of assigning each reporter one specific topic. As a member of a team, a reporter can cover a greater variety of stories. News teams may include reporters, editors, graphic artists, and photographers working together to complete a story.

Reporters on small publications cover all aspects of the news. They take photographs, write headlines, lay out pages, edit wire-service stories, and write editorials. Some also solicit advertisements, sell subscriptions, and perform general office work.

Work environment. The work of news analysts, reporters, and correspondents is usually hectic. They are under great pressure to meet deadlines. Broadcasts sometimes are aired with little or no time for preparation. Some news analysts, reporters, and correspondents work in comfortable, private offices; oth-

ers work in large rooms filled with the sound of keyboards and computer printers, as well as the voices of other reporters. Curious onlookers, police, or other emergency workers can distract those reporting from the scene for radio and television. Covering wars, political uprisings, fires, floods, and similar events can be dangerous; however, the rate of injuries for reporters and correspondents is relatively low.

Work hours vary. Reporters on morning papers often work from late afternoon until midnight. Radio and television reporters usually are assigned to a day or evening shift. Magazine reporters usually work during the day.

Reporters sometimes have to change their work hours to meet a deadline or to follow late-breaking developments. Their work may require long hours, irregular schedules, and some travel. Because many stations and networks are on the air 24 hours a day, newscasters can expect to work unusual hours.

Training, Other Qualifications, and Advancement

Most employers prefer individuals with a bachelor's degree in journalism or mass communications, but some hire graduates with other majors. They look for experience at school newspapers or broadcasting stations, and internships with news organizations. Large-city newspapers and stations also may prefer candidates with a degree in a subject-matter specialty such as economics, political science, or business. Some large newspapers and broadcasters may hire only experienced reporters.

Education and training. More than 1,500 institutions offer programs in communications, journalism, and related programs. In 2008, more than 100 of these were accredited by the Accrediting Council on Education in Journalism and Mass Communications. Most of the courses in a typical curriculum are in liberal arts; the remaining courses are in journalism. The most important skills for journalism students to learn are writing and communication. Students planning a career in broadcasting take courses in radio and television news and production. Those planning newspaper or magazine careers usually specialize in more specific forms of writing. To create stories for online media, they need to learn to use computer software to combine online story text with audio and video elements and graphics.

Some schools also offer a master's or Ph.D. degree in journalism. Some graduate programs are intended primarily as preparation for news careers, while others prepare journalism teachers, researchers and theorists, and advertising and public-relations workers.

High school courses in English, journalism, and social studies provide a good foundation for college programs. Useful college liberal arts courses include English, with an emphasis on writing; sociology; political science; economics; history; and psychology. Courses in computer science, business, and speech are useful as well. Fluency in a foreign language is necessary in some jobs.

Employers report that practical experience is the most important part of education and training. Upon graduation, many students already have gained much practical experience through part-time or summer jobs or through internships with news organizations. Most newspapers, magazines, and broadcast news organizations offer reporting and editing internships. Work on high school and college newspapers, at broadcast-

Projections data from the National Employment Matrix

Occupational Title	SOC Code	Employment, 2008	Projected Employment, 2018	Change, 2008-2018	
				Number	Percent
News analysts, reporters and correspondents	27-3020	69,300	64,900	-4,400	-6
Broadcast news analysts..	27-3021	7,700	8,000	300	4
Reporters and correspondents...	27-3022	61,600	56,900	-4,700	-8

(NOTE) Data in this table are rounded. See the discussion of the employment projections table in the *Handbook* introductory chapter on *Occupational Information Included in the Handbook.*

ing stations, or on community papers also provides practical training. In addition, journalism scholarships, fellowships, and assistantships awarded to college journalism students by universities, newspapers, foundations, and professional organizations are helpful. Experience as a freelancer or stringer—a part-time reporter who is paid only for stories printed—is advantageous.

Other qualifications. Reporters typically need more than good word-processing skills. Computer graphics and desktop-publishing skills are essential as well. Students should be completely proficient in all forms of multimedia. Computer-assisted reporting involves the use of computers to analyze data in search of a story. This technique and the interpretation of the results require computer skills and familiarity with databases. Knowledge of news photography also is valuable for entry-level positions, which sometimes combine the responsibilities of a reporter with those of a camera operator or photographer.

Reporters should be dedicated to providing accurate and impartial news. Accuracy is important both to serve the public and because untrue or libelous statements can lead to lawsuits. A nose for news, persistence, initiative, poise, resourcefulness, a good memory, and physical stamina are important, as is the emotional stability to deal with pressing deadlines, irregular hours, and dangerous assignments. Broadcast reporters and news analysts must be comfortable on camera. All reporters must be at ease in unfamiliar places and with a variety of people. Positions involving on-air work require a pleasant voice and appearance.

Advancement. Most reporters start at small publications or broadcast stations as general assignment reporters or copy editors. They are usually assigned to cover court proceedings and civic and club meetings, summarize speeches, and write obituaries. With experience, they report more difficult assignments or specialize in a particular field. Large publications and stations generally require new reporters to have several years of experience.

Some news analysts and reporters can advance by moving to larger newspapers or stations. A few experienced reporters become columnists, correspondents, writers, announcers, or public-relations specialists. Others become editors in print journalism or program managers in broadcast journalism, supervising reporters. Some eventually become broadcasting or publishing industry managers.

Employment

News analysts, reporters, and correspondents held about 69,300 jobs in 2008. About 53 percent worked for newspaper, periodical, book, and directory publishers. Another 21 percent worked in radio and television broadcasting. About 19 percent

of news analysts, reporters, and correspondents were self-employed (freelancers or stringers).

Job Outlook

Employment is expected to decline moderately through 2018. Competition will continue to be keen for jobs on large metropolitan and national newspapers, broadcast stations and networks, and magazines. Small broadcast stations and publications and online newspapers and magazines should provide the best opportunities. Talented writers who can handle highly specialized scientific or technical subjects will have an advantage.

Employment change. Employment of news analysts, reporters, and correspondents is expected to decline 6 percent between 2008 and 2018. Many factors will contribute to the decline in this occupation. Consolidation and convergence should continue in the publishing and broadcasting industries. As a result, companies will be better able to allocate their news analysts, reporters, and correspondents to cover news stories. Since broadcasting and newspapers—the two industries employing most of these workers—are dependent on advertising revenue, employment growth will suffer during an economic downturn. Improving technology may eventually lead to more employment growth in this occupation by opening up new areas of work, such as online or mobile news divisions. The continued demand for news will create some job opportunities. Job openings also will result from the need to replace workers who leave their occupations permanently; some news analysts, reporters, and correspondents find the work too stressful and hectic or do not like the lifestyle, and transfer to other occupations.

Job prospects. Competition will continue to be keen for jobs at large metropolitan and national newspapers, broadcast stations and networks, and magazines. Job opportunities will be best for applicants in the expanding world of new media, such as online newspapers or magazines. Small local papers and news stations also will provide greater job prospects for potential reporters and news analysts. For beginning newspaper reporters, freelancing will supply more opportunities for employment as well. Students with a background in journalism as well as another subject, such as politics, economics, or biology, will have an advantage over those without additional background knowledge in moving beyond an entry-level position.

Journalism graduates have the background for work in closely related fields such as advertising and public relations or communications, and many take jobs in these fields. Other graduates accept sales, managerial, or other nonmedia positions.

Earnings

Salaries for news analysts, reporters, and correspondents vary widely. Median annual wages of reporters and correspondents were $34,850 in May 2008. The middle 50 percent earned between $25,760 and $52,160. The lowest 10 percent earned less than $20,180, and the highest 10 percent earned more than $77,480. Median annual wages of reporters and correspondents were $33,430 in newspaper, periodical, book, and directory publishing, and $37,710 in radio and television broadcasting.

Median annual wages of broadcast news analysts were $51,260 in May 2008. The middle 50 percent earned between $32,000 and $88,630. The lowest 10 percent earned less than $23,470, and the highest 10 percent earned more than $156,200. Median annual wages of broadcast news analysts were $51,890 in radio and television broadcasting.

Related Occupations

News analysts, reporters, and correspondents must write clearly and effectively to succeed in their profession. Others for whom good writing ability is essential include:

Many news analysts, reporters, and correspondents also must communicate information orally. Others for whom oral communication skills are important are:

Sources of Additional Information

For information on broadcasting education and scholarship resources, contact:

➤ National Association of Broadcasters, 1771 N St. NW, Washington, DC 20036. Internet: **http://www.nab.org**

Information on careers in journalism, colleges and universities offering degree programs in journalism or communications, and journalism scholarships and internships may be obtained from:

➤ Dow Jones Newspaper Fund, Inc., P.O. Box 300, Princeton, NJ 08543-0300. Internet: **https://www.newspaperfund.org**

For a list of schools with accredited programs in journalism and mass communications, send a stamped, self-addressed envelope to:

➤ Accrediting Council on Education in Journalism and Mass Communications, University of Kansas School of Journalism and Mass Communications, Stauffer-Flint Hall, 1435 Jayhawk Blvd., Lawrence, KS 66045. Internet: **http://www.ku.edu/~acejmc/STUDENT/STUDENT.SHTML**

Names and locations of newspapers and a list of schools and departments of journalism are published in the *Editor and Publisher International Year Book*, available in most public libraries and newspaper offices.

The Occupational Information Network (O*NET) provides information on a wide range of occupational characteristics. Links to O*NET appear at the end of the Internet version of this occupational statement, accessible at **http://www.bls.gov/ooh/ocos088.htm**

Photographers

Significant Points

- Competition for jobs is expected to be keen because the work is attractive to many people.

- Technical expertise, a "good eye," and creativity, are essential, and some photographers need a college degree.

- More than half of all photographers are self-employed, a much higher proportion than for most occupations.

Nature of the Work

Photographers produce and preserve images that paint a picture, tell a story, or record an event. To create commercial-quality photographs, photographers need technical expertise, creativity, and the appropriate professional equipment. Producing a successful picture requires choosing and presenting a subject to achieve a particular effect, and selecting the right cameras and other photographic enhancing tools. For example, photographers may enhance the subject's appearance with natural or artificial light, shoot the subject from an interesting angle, draw attention to a particular aspect of the subject by blurring the background, or use various lenses to produce desired levels of detail at various distances from the subject.

Today, most photographers use digital cameras instead of traditional silver-halide film cameras, although some photographers use both types, depending on their own preference and the nature of the assignment. Regardless of the camera they use, photographers also employ an array of other equipment—from lenses, filters, and tripods to flash attachments and specially constructed lighting equipment—to improve the quality of their work.

Digital cameras capture images electronically, allowing them to be edited on a computer. Images can be stored on portable memory devices such as compact disks, memory cards, and flash drives. Once the raw image has been transferred to a computer, photographers can use processing software to crop or modify the image and enhance it through color correction and other specialized effects. As soon as a photographer has finished editing the image, it can be sent anywhere in the world over the Internet.

Photographers also can create electronic portfolios of their work and display them on their own webpage, allowing them to reach prospective customers directly. Digital technology also allows the production of larger, more colorful, and more accurate prints or images for use in advertising, photographic art, and scientific research. Photographers who process their own digital images need to be proficient in the use of computers, high-quality printers, and editing software.

Photographers who use cameras with silver-halide film often send their film to laboratories for processing. Color film requires expensive equipment and exacting conditions for correct processing and printing. (See the statement on photographic process workers and processing machine operators elsewhere in the *Handbook*.) Other photographers, especially those using black and white film or creating special effects, develop and print their own photographs using their own fully equipped darkrooms,. Photographers who develop their own film must invest in additional developing and printing equipment and acquire the technical skills to operate it.

Some photographers specialize in areas such as portrait, commercial and industrial, scientific, news, or fine arts photography. *Portrait photographers* take pictures of individuals or groups of people and usually work in their own studios. Some specialize in weddings, religious ceremonies, or school photographs and they may work on location. Portrait photographers who own and operate their own business have many responsibilities in addition to taking pictures. They must arrange for advertising, schedule appointments, set and adjust equipment, purchase supplies, keep records, bill customers, pay bills, and—if they have employees—hire, train, and direct their workers. Many also process their own images, design albums, and mount and frame the finished photographs.

Commercial and industrial photographers take pictures of various subjects, such as buildings, models, merchandise, artifacts, and landscapes. These photographs are used in a variety of media, including books, reports, advertisements, and catalogs. Industrial photographers often take pictures of equipment, machinery, products, workers, and company officials. The pictures are used for various purposes—for example, analysis of engineering projects, publicity, or records of equipment development or deployment. This photography frequently is done on location.

Scientific photographers take images of a variety of subjects to record scientific or medical data or phenomena, using knowledge of scientific procedures. They typically possess additional knowledge in areas such as engineering, medicine, biology, or chemistry.

News photographers, also called *photojournalists*, photograph newsworthy people, places, and sporting, political, and community events for newspapers, journals, magazines, or television.

Fine arts photographers sell their photographs as fine artwork. In addition to technical proficiency, fine arts photographers need artistic talent and creativity.

Self-employed, or freelance, photographers usually specialize in one of the above fields. In addition to carrying out assignments under direct contract with clients, they may license the use of their photographs through stock-photo agencies or market their work directly to the public. Stock-photo agencies sell magazines and other customers the right to use photographs, and pay the photographer a commission. These agencies require an application from the photographer and a sizable portfolio of pictures. Once accepted, photographers usually are required to submit a large number of new photographs each year. Self-employed photographers must also

have a thorough understanding of copyright laws in order to protect their work.

Most photographers spend only a small portion of their work schedule actually taking photographs. Their most common activities are editing images on a computer—if they use a digital camera—and looking for new business—if they are self-employed.

Work environment. Working conditions for photographers vary considerably. Some photographers may work a 5-day, 40-hour week. News photographers, however, often work long, irregular hours and must be available to work on short notice. Many photographers work part time or on variable schedules.

Portrait photographers usually work in their own studios but also may travel to take photographs at the client's location, such as a school, a company office, or a private home. News and commercial photographers frequently travel locally, stay overnight on assignments, or travel to distant places for long periods.

Some photographers work in uncomfortable or even dangerous surroundings, especially news photographers covering accidents, natural disasters, civil unrest, or military conflicts. Many photographers must wait long hours in all kinds of weather for an event to take place and stand or walk for long

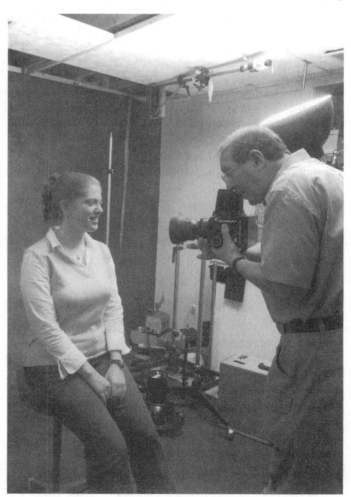

Portrait photographers take pictures of individuals or groups of people and often work out of their own studios.

periods while carrying heavy equipment. News photographers often work under strict deadlines.

Self-employment allows for greater autonomy, freedom of expression, and flexible scheduling. However, income can be uncertain and the continuous, time-consuming search for new clients can be stressful. Some self-employed photographers hire assistants who help seek out new business.

Training, Other Qualifications, and Advancement

Employers usually seek applicants with a "good eye," imagination, and creativity, as well as a good technical understanding of photography. Photojournalists or industrial or scientific photographers generally need a college degree. Freelance and portrait photographers need technical proficiency, gained through a degree, training program, or experience.

Education and training. Entry-level positions in photojournalism or in industrial or scientific photography generally require a college degree in photography or in a field related to the industry in which the photographer seeks employment. Entry-level freelance or portrait photographers need technical proficiency. Some complete a college degree or vocational training programs.

Photography courses are offered by many universities, community and junior colleges, vocational-technical institutes, and private trade and technical schools. Basic courses in photography cover equipment, processes, and techniques. Learning good business and marketing skills is important and some bachelor's degree programs offer courses focusing on them. Art schools offer useful training in photographic design and composition.

Photographers may start out as assistants to experienced photographers. Assistants acquire the technical knowledge needed to be a successful photographer and also learn other skills necessary to run a portrait or commercial photography business.

Individuals interested in a career in photography should try to develop contacts in the field by subscribing to photographic newsletters and magazines, joining camera clubs, and seeking summer or part-time employment in camera stores, newspapers, or photo studios.

Other qualifications. Photographers need good eyesight, artistic ability, and good hand-eye coordination. They should be patient, accurate, and detail-oriented and should be able to work well with others, as they frequently deal with clients, graphic designers, and advertising and publishing specialists. Photographers need to know how to use computer software programs and applications that allow them to prepare and edit images, and those who market directly to clients should know how to use the Internet to display their work.

Portrait photographers need the ability to help people relax in front of the camera. Commercial and fine arts photographers must be imaginative and original. News photographers must not only be good with a camera, but also understand the story be-

hind an event so that their pictures match the story. They must be decisive in recognizing a potentially good photograph and act quickly to capture it.

Many photographers have websites which highlight an online portfolio that they use to attract work from magazines or advertising agencies. For freelance photographers, maintaining their website is essential.

Photographers who operate their own business, or freelance, need business skills as well as talent. These individuals must know how to prepare a business plan; submit bids; write contracts; keep financial records; market their work; hire models, if needed; get permission to shoot on locations that normally are not open to the public; obtain releases to use photographs of people; license and price photographs; and secure copyright protection for their work. To protect their rights and their work, self-employed photographers require basic knowledge of licensing and copyright laws, as well as knowledge of contracts and negotiation procedures.

Freelance photographers also should develop an individual style of photography to differentiate themselves from the competition.

Advancement. After several years of experience, magazine and news photographers may advance to photography or picture editor positions. Some photographers teach at technical schools, film schools, or universities.

Employment

Photographers held about 152,000 jobs in 2008. More than half were self-employed, a much higher proportion than for most occupations. Some self-employed photographers have contracts with advertising agencies, magazine publishers, or other businesses to do individual projects for a set fee, while others operate portrait studios or provide photographs to stock-photo agencies.

Most salaried photographers work in portrait or commercial photography studios; most of the others work for newspapers, magazines, and advertising agencies. Photographers work in all areas of the country, but most are employed in metropolitan areas.

Job Outlook

Employment is expected to grow as fast as the average for all occupations. Photographers can expect keen competition for job openings because the work is attractive to many people.

Employment change. Employment of photographers is expected to grow 12 percent over the 2008-18 period, about as fast as the average for all occupations. Demand for portrait photographers should increase as the population grows. Moreover, growth of Internet versions of magazines, journals, and newspapers will require increasing numbers of commercial photographers to provide digital images. The Internet and im-

Projections data from the National Employment Matrix

Occupational Title	SOC Code	Employment, 2008	Projected Employment, 2018	Change, 2008-2018	
				Number	Percent
Photographers	27-4021	152,000	169,500	17,500	12

(NOTE) Data in this table are rounded. See the discussion of the employment projections table in the *Handbook* introductory chapter on *Occupational Information Included in the Handbook.*

proved data management programs also should make it easier for freelancers to market directly to their customers, increasing opportunities for self-employment and decreasing reliance on stock photo agencies.

Job growth, however, will be constrained somewhat by the widespread use of digital photography and the falling price of digital equipment. Improvements in digital technology reduce barriers of entry into this profession and allow more individual consumers and businesses to produce, store, and access photographic images on their own. News and commercial photographers may be the most adversely affected by this increase in amateur photographers and non-copyrighted photos. Declines in the newspaper industry also will reduce demand for news photographers to provide still images for print.

Job prospects. Photographers can expect keen competition for job openings because the work is attractive to many people. The number of individuals interested in positions as commercial and news photographers is usually much greater than the number of openings. Salaried jobs in particular may be difficult to find as more companies contract with freelancers rather than hire their own photographers. Those who succeed in landing a salaried job or attracting enough work to earn a living by freelancing are likely to be adept at operating a business and to be among the most creative. They will be able to find and exploit the new opportunities available from rapidly changing technologies. Related work experience, job-related training, or some unique skill or talent—such as a background in computers or electronics or knowledge of a second language—also improve a photographer's job prospects.

Earnings
Median annual wages of salaried photographers were $29,440 in May 2008. The middle 50 percent earned between $20,620 and $43,530. The lowest 10 percent earned less than $16,920, and the highest 10 percent earned more than $62,430. Median annual wages in the photographic services industry, which employed the largest numbers of salaried photographers, were $26,160.

Salaried photographers—most of whom work full time—tend to earn more than those who are self-employed. Because most freelance and portrait photographers purchase their own equipment, they incur considerable expense acquiring and maintaining cameras and accessories. Unlike news and commercial photographers, few fine arts photographers are successful enough to support themselves solely through their art.

Related Occupations
Other occupations requiring artistic talent and creativity include:

Photojournalists are often required to cover news stories much the same as:

The processing work that photographers do on computers is similar to the work of:

Sources of Additional Information
Career information on photography is available from:

➤ Professional Photographers of America, Inc., 229 Peachtree St. NE, Suite 2200, Atlanta, GA 30303. Internet: **http://www.ppa.com**

➤ National Press Photographers Association, Inc., 3200 Croasdaile Dr., Suite 306, Durham, NC 27705. Internet: **http://www.nppa.org**

➤ American Society of Media Photographers, Inc., 150 North Second St., Philadelphia, PA 19106. Internet: **http://www.asmp.org**

The Occupational Information Network (O*NET) provides information on a wide range of occupational characteristics. Links to O*NET appear at the end of the Internet version of this occupational statement, accessible at **http://www.bls.gov/ooh/ocos264.htm**

Public Relations Specialists

Significant Points

* Although employment is projected to grow much faster than average, keen competition is expected for entry-level jobs.

* Opportunities should be best for college graduates who combine a degree in public relations, journalism, or another communications-related field with a public relations internship or other related work experience.

* Strong communication skills are essential.

Nature of the Work
An organization's reputation, profitability, and its continued existence can depend on the degree to which its targeted public supports its goals and policies. Public relations specialists—also referred to as *communications specialists* and *media specialists*, among other titles—serve as advocates for clients seeking to build and maintain positive relationships with the public. Their clients include businesses, nonprofit associations, universities, hospitals, and other organizations, and build and maintain positive relationships with the public. As managers recognize the link between good public relations and the success of their organizations, they increasingly rely on public relations specialists for advice on the strategy and policy of their communications.

Public relations specialists handle organizational functions, such as media, community, consumer, industry, and governmental relations; political campaigns; interest-group representation; conflict mediation; and employee and investor relations. Public relations specialists must understand the attitudes and concerns of community, consumer, employee, and public interest groups to establish and maintain cooperative relationships between them and representatives from print and broadcast journalism.

Public relations specialists draft press releases and contact people in the media who might print or broadcast their material. Many radio or television special reports, newspaper stories, and magazine articles start at the desks of public relations specialists. Sometimes, the subject of a press release is an organization and its policies toward employees or its role in the community. For example, a press release might describe a public issue, such as health, energy, or the environment, and what an organization does to advance that issue.

Public relations specialists also arrange and conduct programs to maintain contact between organization representatives and the public. For example, public relations specialists set up speaking engagements and prepare speeches for officials. These media specialists represent employers at community projects; make film, slide, and other visual presentations for meetings and school assemblies; and plan conventions.

In government, public relations specialists may be called *press secretaries*. They keep the public informed about the activities of agencies and officials. For example, *public affairs specialists* in the U.S. Department of State alert the public of travel advisories and of U.S. positions on foreign issues. A press secretary for a member of Congress informs constituents of the representative's accomplishments.

In large organizations, the key public relations executive, who often is a vice president, may develop overall plans and policies with other executives. In addition, public relations departments employ public relations specialists to write, research, prepare materials, maintain contacts, and respond to inquiries.

People who handle publicity for an individual or who direct public relations for a small organization may deal with all aspects of the job. These public relations specialists contact people, plan and research, and prepare materials for distribution. They also may handle advertising or sales promotion work to support marketing efforts.

Work environment. Public relations specialists work in busy offices. The pressures of deadlines and tight work schedules can be stressful.

Some public relations specialists work a standard 35- to 40-hour week, but overtime is common, and work schedules can be irregular and are frequently interrupted. Occasionally, they must be at the job or on call around the clock, especially if there is an emergency or crisis. Schedules often have to be rearranged so workers can meet deadlines, deliver speeches, attend meetings and community activities, and travel.

Training, Other Qualifications, and Advancement

A bachelor's degree in a communications-related field combined with public relations experience is excellent preparation for a person interested in public relations work.

Education and training. Many entry-level public relations specialists have a college degree in public relations, journalism, marketing, or communications. Some firms seek college gradu-

As managers recognize the importance of good public relations, they increasingly rely on the advice of public relations specialists.

ates who have worked in electronic or print journalism. Other employers seek applicants with demonstrated communication skills and training or experience in a field related to the firm's business—information technology, health care, science, engineering, sales, or finance, for example.

Many colleges and universities offer bachelor's and postsecondary programs leading to a degree in public relations, usually in a journalism or communications department. In addition, many other colleges offer courses in this field. Courses in advertising, business administration, finance, political science, psychology, sociology, and creative writing also are helpful. Specialties may be offered in public relations for business, government, and nonprofit organizations.

Internships in public relations provide students with valuable experience and training and are the best route to finding entry-level employment. Membership in local chapters of the Public Relations Student Society of America (affiliated with the Public Relations Society of America) or in student chapters of the International Association of Business Communicators provides an opportunity for students to exchange views with public relations specialists and to make professional contacts that may help them to find a full-time job after graduation.

Some organizations, particularly those with large public relations staffs, have formal training programs for new employees. In smaller organizations, new employees work under the guidance of experienced staff members. Entry-level workers often maintain files of material about company activities, skim newspapers and magazines for appropriate articles to clip, and assemble information for speeches and pamphlets. New workers also may answer calls from the press and the public, prepare invitation lists and details for press conferences, or escort visitors and clients. After gaining experience, they write news releases, speeches, and articles for publication or plan and carry out public relations programs. Public relations specialists in smaller firms usually get well-rounded experience, whereas those in larger firms become more specialized.

Other qualifications. In addition to the ability to communicate thoughts clearly and simply, public relations specialists must show creativity, initiative, and good judgment. Decision-making, problem-solving, and research skills also are important. People who choose public relations as a career should have an outgoing personality, self-confidence, an understanding of human psychology, and an enthusiasm for motivating people. They should be assertive but able to participate as part of a team and be open to new ideas.

Certification and advancement. The Universal Accreditation Board accredits public relations specialists who are members of the Public Relations Society of America and who participate in the Examination for Accreditation in Public Relations process. This process includes both a readiness review and an examination, which are designed for candidates who have at least 5 years of full-time work or teaching experience in public relations and who have earned a bachelor's degree in a communications-related field. The readiness review includes a written submission by each candidate, a portfolio review, and dialogue between the candidate and a three-member panel. Candidates who successfully advance through readiness review and pass the computer-based examination earn the Accredited in Public Relations (APR) designation.

The International Association of Business Communicators (IABC) also has an accreditation program for professionals in the communications field, including public relations specialists. Those who meet all the requirements of the program earn the Accredited Business Communicator (ABC) designation. Candidates must have at least 5 years of experience and a bachelor's degree in a communications field and must pass written and oral examinations. They also must submit a portfolio of work samples that demonstrate involvement in a range of communications projects and a thorough understanding of communications planning.

Employers may consider professional recognition through accreditation as a sign of competence in this field, and such designations could be especially helpful in a competitive job market.

Public relations specialists who show that they can handle more demanding assignments are more likely to be promoted to supervisory jobs than those who are unable to do so. In public relations firms, an entry-level worker might be hired as a junior account executive and be promoted over the course of a career to account executive, senior account executive, account manager, and, eventually, vice president. Specialists in corporate public relations follow a similar career path, although the job titles may differ.

Some experienced public relations specialists start their own consulting firms. (For more information on public relations managers, see the *Handbook* statement on advertising, marketing, promotions, public relations, and sales managers.)

Employment

Public relations specialists held about 275,200 jobs in 2008. They are concentrated in service-providing industries, such as advertising and related services; health care and social assistance; educational services; and government. Others work for communications firms, financial institutions, and government agencies.

Public relations specialists are concentrated in large cities, where press services and other communications facilities are readily available and where many businesses and trade associations have their headquarters. Many public relations consulting firms, for example, are in New York, Los Angeles, San Francisco, Chicago, and Washington, D.C. There is a trend, however, toward public relations jobs to be dispersed throughout the Nation, closer to clients.

Job Outlook

Employment is projected to grow much faster than average; however, keen competition is expected for entry-level jobs.

Employment change. Employment of public relations specialists is expected to grow 24 percent from 2008 to 2018, much faster than the average for all occupations. The need for good public relations in an increasingly competitive and global business environment should spur demand for these workers, especially those with specialized knowledge or international experience. Employees who possess additional language capabilities also are in great demand.

The recent emergence of social media in the public relations is expected to increase job growth as well. Many public relations firms are expanding their use of these tools, and specialists with skills in them will be needed.

Employment in public relations firms is expected to grow as firms hire contractors to provide public relations services, rather than support more full-time staff when additional work is needed.

Among detailed industries, the largest job growth will continue to be in advertising and related services.

Job prospects. Keen competition likely will continue for entry-level public relations jobs, as the number of qualified applicants is expected to exceed the number of job openings. Many people are attracted to this profession because of the high-profile nature of the work. Opportunities should be best for college graduates who combine a degree in journalism, public relations, or another communications-related field with a public relations internship or other related work experience. Applicants who do

Projections data from the National Employment Matrix

Occupational Title	SOC Code	Employment, 2008	Projected Employment, 2018	Change, 2008-2018	
				Number	Percent
Public relations specialists	27-3031	275,200	341,300	66,200	24

(NOTE) Data in this table are rounded. See the discussion of the employment projections table in the *Handbook* introductory chapter on *Occupational Information Included in the Handbook.*

not have the appropriate educational background or work experience will face the toughest obstacles.

Additional job opportunities should result from the need to replace public relations specialists who retire or leave the occupation for other reasons.

Earnings

Median annual wages for salaried public relations specialists were $51,280 in May 2008. The middle 50 percent earned between $38,400 and $71,670; the lowest 10 percent earned less than $30,140, and the top 10 percent earned more than $97,910. Median annual wages in the industries employing the largest numbers of public relations specialists in May 2008 were:

Management of companies and enterprises	$55,530
Business, professional, labor, political, and similar organizations	55,460
Advertising, public relations and related services	55,290
Local government	51,340
Colleges, universities, and professional schools	46,660

Related Occupations

Public relations specialists create favorable attitudes among various organizations, interest groups, and the public through effective communication. Other workers with similar jobs include:

	Page
Advertising, marketing, promotions, public relations, and sales managers	32
Demonstrators and product promoters	532
Lawyers	257
Market and survey researchers	212
News analysts, reporters, and correspondents	344
Sales representatives, wholesale and manufacturing	547

Sources of Additional Information

A comprehensive directory of schools offering degree programs, a sequence of study in public relations, a brochure on careers in public relations, and an online brochure entitled *Where Shall I Go to Study Advertising and Public Relations?* are available from:

➤ Public Relations Society of America, Inc., 33 Maiden Lane, New York, NY 10038-5150. Internet: **http://www.prsa.org**

For information on accreditation for public relations professionals and the IABC Student Web site, contact:

➤ International Association of Business Communicators, 601 Montgomery St. Suite 1900, San Francisco, CA 94111.

The Occupational Information Network (O*NET) provides information on a wide range of occupational characteristics. Links to O*NET appear at the end of the Internet version of this occupational statement, accessible at

http://www.bls.gov/ooh/ocos086.htm

Technical Writers

Significant Points

- Most jobs in this occupation require a college degree—preferably in communications, journalism, or English—but a degree in a technical subject may be useful.

- Job prospects for most technical writing jobs are expected to be good, particularly for those with Web or multimedia experience.

- Excellent communications skills, curiosity, and attention to detail are highly desired traits.

Nature of the Work

Technical writers, also called *technical communicators*, put technical information into easily understandable language. They work primarily in information-technology-related industries, coordinating the development and dissemination of technical content for a variety of users; however, a growing number of technical communicators are using technical content to resolve business communications problems in a diversifying number of industries. Included in their products are operating instructions, how-to manuals, assembly instructions, and other documentation needed for online help and by technical support staff, consumers, and other users within the company or industry. Technical writers also develop documentation for computer programs and set up communications systems with consumers to assess customer satisfaction and quality control matters. In addition, they commonly work in engineering, scientific, healthcare, and other areas in which highly specialized material needs to be explained to a diverse audience, often of laypersons.

Technical writers often work with engineers, scientists, computer specialists, and software developers to manage the flow of information among project workgroups during development and testing. They also may work with product liability specialists and customer service or call center managers to improve the quality of product support and end-user assistance. Technical writers also oversee the preparation of illustrations, photographs, diagrams, and charts. Technical writers increasingly are using a variety of multimedia formats to convey information in such a way that complex concepts can be understood easily by users of the information.

Applying their knowledge of the user of the product, technical writers may serve as part of a team conducting usability studies to help improve the design of a product that is in the prototype stage. Technical writers may conduct research on their topics through personal observation, library and Internet research, and discussions with technical specialists. They also are expected to demonstrate their understanding of the subject matter and establish their credibility with their colleagues.

Technical writers use computers and other electronic communications equipment extensively in performing their work. They also work regularly with desktop and other electronic publishing software and prepare material directly for the Internet. Technical writers may work with graphic design, page layout, and multimedia software; increasingly, they are preparing documents by using the interactive technologies of the Web to blend text, graphics, multidimensional images, and sound.

Some technical writers work on a freelance or contract basis. They either are self-employed or work for a technical consulting firm and may be hired to complete specific short-term or recurring assignments, such as writing about a new product or coordinating the work and communications of different units to keep a project on track. Whether a project is to be coordinated among an organization's departments or among autonomous companies, technical writers ensure that the different entities share information and mediate differences in favor of the end user in order to bring a product to market sooner.

Work environment. Advances in computer and communications technologies make it possible for technical writers to work from almost anywhere. Laptop computers and wireless communications permit technical writers to work from home, an office, or on the road. The ability to use the Internet to e-mail, transmit, and download information and assignments, conduct research, or review materials allows them greater flexibility in where and how they complete assignments.

Many technical writers work with people located around the world and with specialists in highly technical fields, such as science and engineering. As a result, they must be able to assimilate complex information quickly and be comfortable working with people from diverse professional and cultural backgrounds. Although most technical writers are employed directly by the companies that use their services, many freelance writers are paid on a project basis and routinely face the pressures of juggling multiple projects and the continual need to find new work. Technical writers may be expected to work evenings, nights, or weekends to coordinate with those in other time zones, meet deadlines, or produce information that complies with project requirements and is acceptable to the client.

Training, Other Qualifications, and Advancement

A college degree is required for a position as a technical writer. In addition, knowledge in a technical subject, as well as experience in Web design and computer graphics, is important.

Education and training. Employers look for candidates with a bachelor's degree, often preferring those with a major in

Technical writers use computer and communications technologies extensively, which allows them to work from home or wherever their work takes them.

communications, journalism, or English. Some technical writing jobs may require both experience and either a degree or knowledge in a specialized field—for example, engineering, medicine, or one of the sciences; others have broader requirements, such as a background in liberal arts. Knowledge of a second language is helpful for some positions. Experience in Web design and computer graphics also is helpful, because of the growing use of online technical documentation.

Other qualifications. Technical writers must have excellent writing and communication skills and be able to express ideas clearly and logically in a variety of media. Increasingly, technical writers need familiarity with electronic publishing, graphics, and sound and video production. Also needed is knowledge of computer software for combining online text with graphics, audio, video, and animation, as well as the ability to manage large, complex, and interconnected files.

Technical writers must be detail oriented, curious, persistent in solving problems, self-motivated, and able to understand complex material and explain it clearly. Technical writers also must demonstrate good working relationships and sensitivity toward others, especially those from different backgrounds. In addition, the ability to work under pressure and in a variety of work settings is essential.

Advancement. Some technical writers begin their careers not as writers, but as specialists in a technical field or as research assistants or trainees in a technical information department. By transferring or developing technical communication skills, they eventually assume primary responsibilities for technical writing. In small firms, beginning technical writers may work on projects right away; in larger companies with more standard procedures, beginners may observe experienced technical writers and interact with specialists before being assigned projects. Prospects for advancement generally include working on more complex projects, leading or training junior staff, and getting enough work to make it as a freelancer.

Many firms and freelancers provide technical writing services on a contract basis, often to small or not-for-profit organizations that do not have enough regular work to employ technical writers full time. Building a reputation and establishing a record for meeting deadlines also makes it easier to get future assignments. An experienced, credible, and reliable freelance technical writer or editor often is able to establish long-term dealings with the same companies.

Employment

Technical writers held about 48,900 jobs in 2008. There are technical writers in almost every industry, but they are concentrated in industries related to computer systems and software, publishing (except Internet), science, and engineering. The industry that employed the most technical writers in 2008 was the computer systems design industry, which had 18 percent of these workers. The second-largest employer was the computer and electronic manufacturing industry, with 8 percent of workers. Software publishers; architectural, engineering, and related services; management, scientific, and technical consulting services; and scientific research and development services industries also employed a sizeable number of technical writers. Two percent of technical writers were self-employed in 2008.

Projections data from the National Employment Matrix

Occupational Title	SOC Code	Employment, 2008	Projected Employment, 2018	Change, 2008-2018	
				Number	Percent
Technical writers	27-3042	48,900	57,800	8,900	18

(NOTE) Data in this table are rounded. See the discussion of the employment projections table in the *Handbook* introductory chapter on *Occupational Information Included in the Handbook.*

Jobs usually are concentrated in areas with high information technology or scientific and technical research industry employment, such as San Francisco and San Jose, CA; Boston, MA; and Washington, DC. However, technology permits technical writers to work in one location while communicating with clients and colleagues in another. As a result, geographic concentration is less of a requirement than it once was.

Job Outlook

Employment of technical writers is expected to grow faster than the average for all occupations as the need to explain a growing number of electronic and scientific products increases. Job prospects are expected to be good for those with solid writing and communications skills and a technical background.

Employment change. Employment of technical writers is expected to grow 18 percent, or faster than the average for all occupations, from 2008 to 2018. Demand over this decade is expected to increase because of the continuing expansion of scientific and technical information and the growing presence of customer service and Web-based product support networks. Legal, scientific, and technological developments and discoveries will generate demand for people who can interpret technical information for a general audience. Rapid growth and change in the high-technology and electronics industries will result in a greater need for people who can write users' guides, instruction manuals, and training materials in a variety of formats and communicate information clearly to others. This occupation requires workers who are both skilled writers and effective communicators and familiar with a specialized subject area.

Increasing acceptance of interactive media to provide nearly real-time information will create employment opportunities for technical writers because of the need to revise online information. Businesses and organizations are making more material available online often in formats that permit greater scrutiny and comparison of detailed information. The growing amount and complexity of information available on the Web will spur demand for technical writers. Professional, scientific, and technical services firms will continue to grow and should be a good source of new jobs even as the occupation finds acceptance in a broader range of industries, including data processing, hosting, and related services and educational services.

Job prospects. Job prospects, especially for applicants with solid communication and technical skills, are expected to be good. The growing reliance on technologically sophisticated products in the home and the workplace and the increasing complexity of medical or scientific information needed for daily living will create many new job opportunities for technical writers. However, competition will exist for technical writ-

ing positions with more desirable companies and for workers who are new to the occupation.

In addition to job openings created by employment growth, some openings will arise as experienced workers retire, transfer to other occupations, or leave the labor force. Also, many freelancers may not earn enough money by freelancing to remain in the occupation, thus generating additional job openings.

Earnings

Median annual wages for salaried technical writers were $61,620 in May 2008. The middle 50 percent earned between $47,100 and $78,910. The lowest 10 percent earned less than $36,500, and the highest 10 percent earned more than $97,460. Median annual wages in the industries employing the largest number of technical writers were:

Software publishers	$71,640
Computer systems design and related services	64,380
Management, scientific, and technical consulting services	62,920
Employment services	61,810
Architectural, engineering, and related services	60,140

Related Occupations

Technical writers communicate ideas and information. Other occupations requiring good communications skills include the following:

	Page
Announcers	331
Authors, writers, and editors	333
Interpreters and translators...	340
Public relations specialists	350

Sources of Additional Information

For information on careers in technical writing, contact:
➤ Society for Technical Communication, Inc., 9401 Lee Highway, Suite 300, Fairfax, VA 22031. Internet: **http://www.stc.org**

The Occupational Information Network (O*NET) provides information on a wide range of occupational characteristics. Links to O*NET appear at the end of the Internet version of this occupational statement, accessible at

http://www.bls.gov/ooh/ocos319.htm

Television, Video, and Motion Picture Camera Operators and Editors

Significant Points

- Keen competition for jobs is expected due to the large number of people who wish to enter the broadcasting and motion picture industries.

- Opportunities will be best for those with a bachelor's degree or postsecondary training.

Nature of the Work

Television, video, and motion picture camera operators produce images that tell a story, inform or entertain an audience, or record an event. Film and video editors edit soundtracks, film, and video for the motion picture, cable, and broadcast television industries. Some camera operators do their own editing.

Camera operators use television, video, or motion picture cameras to shoot a wide range of material, including television series, studio programs, news and sporting events, music videos, motion pictures, documentaries, and training sessions. This material is constructed from many different shots by film and video editors. With the increase in digital technology, the editing work is now done on a computer. Many camera operators and editors are employed by independent television stations; local affiliate stations of television networks; large cable and television networks; or smaller, independent production companies.

Making commercial-quality movies and video programs requires technical expertise and creativity. Producing successful images requires choosing and presenting interesting material, selecting appropriate equipment, and applying a steady hand to ensure smooth, natural movement of the camera.

Videographers film or videotape private ceremonies and special events, such as weddings. Some record and post short videos on Web sites for businesses. *Studio camera operators* work in a broadcast studio and usually videotape their subjects from a fixed position. *News camera operators*, also called *electronic news-gathering (ENG) operators*, work as part of a reporting team, following newsworthy events as they unfold. To capture live events, they must anticipate the action and act quickly. ENG operators sometimes edit raw footage on the spot for relay to a television affiliate for broadcast.

Camera operators employed in the entertainment field use motion picture cameras to film movies, television programs, and commercials. Those who film motion pictures also are known as cinematographers. Some specialize in filming cartoons or special effects. Cinematographers may be an integral part of the action, using cameras in any of several different mounts. For example, the camera can be stationary and shoot whatever passes in front of the lens, or it can be mounted on a track, with the camera operator responsible for shooting the scene from different angles or directions. Wider use of digital cameras has enhanced the number of angles and the clarity that a camera operator can provide. Other camera operators sit on cranes and follow the action while crane operators move them into position. *Steadicam operators* mount a harness and carry the camera on their shoulders to provide a clear picture while they move about the action. Camera operators who work in the entertainment field often meet with a director of photography to discuss ways of filming, editing, and improving scenes.

Work environment. ENG operators and those who cover major events, such as conventions or sporting events, frequently travel locally and stay overnight or travel to distant places for longer periods. Camera operators filming television programs or motion pictures may travel to film on location.

Some camera operators—especially ENG operators covering accidents, natural disasters, civil unrest, or military conflicts—work in uncomfortable or even dangerous surroundings; however the occupation as a whole does not tend to suffer more work related injuries than other occupations. Many camera operators must wait long hours in all kinds of weather for an event to take place and must stand or walk for long periods while carrying heavy equipment. ENG operators often work under strict deadlines.

Hours of work and working schedules for camera operators and editors vary considerably. Those employed by television and cable networks or advertising agencies may work long hours to meet production schedules. ENG operators often work long, irregular hours and must be available to work on short notice. Camera operators and editors working in motion picture production also may work long, irregular hours.

Training, Other Qualifications, and Advancement

Television, video, and motion picture camera operators and editors usually acquire their skills through formal postsecondary training at film schools, colleges, universities, or photographic institutes. A bachelor's degree is required for most positions. Employers usually seek applicants with a good eye, imagination, and creativity, as well as a good technical understanding of how the camera operates.

Education and training. Many universities, community and junior colleges, and private trade and technical schools offer courses in camera operation and videography. Basic courses cover equipment, processes, and techniques. It is very important for camera operators to have a good understanding of computer technology and knowledge of digital cameras. Bachelor's degree programs, especially those including business courses,

Film and video editors edit soundtracks, film, and video for the motion picture and cable and broadcast television industries.

Projections data from the National Employment Matrix

Occupational Title	SOC Code	Employment, 2008	Projected Employment, 2018	Change, 2008-2018	
				Number	Percent
Television, video, and motion picture camera operators and editors	27-4030	51,900	57,300	5,400	11
Camera operators, television, video, and motion picture..............	27-4031	26,300	28,800	2,400	9
Film and video editors	27-4032	25,500	28,600	3,000	12

(NOTE) Data in this table are rounded. See the discussion of the employment projections table in the *Handbook* introductory chapter on *Occupational Information Included in the Handbook.*

provide a well-rounded education. Film schools also may provide training on the artistic aspects of filmmaking.

Individuals interested in camera operations should subscribe to videographic newsletters and magazines, join audio-video clubs, and seek summer or part-time employment in cable and television networks, motion picture studios, or camera and video stores.

To enter the occupation, many camera operators first become production assistants, to learn how film and video production works. In entry-level jobs they learn to set up lights, cameras, and other equipment. They also may receive routine assignments requiring adjustments to their cameras or decisions on what subject matter to capture. Camera operators in the film and television industries usually are hired for a project on the basis of recommendations from individuals such as producers, directors of photography, and camera assistants from previous projects or through interviews with the producer. A good professional reputation is important in finding employment. ENG and studio camera operators who work for television affiliates usually start in small markets to gain experience.

Other qualifications. Camera operators need good eyesight, artistic ability, and hand-eye coordination. They should be patient, accurate, and detail oriented. Camera operators also should have good communication skills and, if needed, the ability to hold a camera by hand for extended periods.

Camera operators who run their own businesses or do freelance work need business skills as well as talent. These individuals must know how to submit bids, write contracts, get permission to shoot on locations that normally are not open to the public, obtain legal permission to use film or tape of people, price their services, secure copyright protection for their work, and keep financial records.

Advancement. With experience, operators may advance to more demanding assignments or to positions with larger or network television stations. Advancement for ENG operators may mean moving to larger media markets. Other camera operators and editors may become directors of photography for movie studios, advertising agencies, or television programs. Some teach at technical schools, film schools, or universities.

Employment

Television, video, and motion picture camera operators and editors held about 51,900 jobs in 2008. About 26,300 were camera operators, and film and video editors held about 25,500 jobs.

Many are employed by independent television stations, local affiliate stations of television networks or broadcast groups, large cable and television networks, or smaller, independent production companies. There also are a large number of self employed camera operators and film editors. Some self-employed

camera operators contract with television networks, documentary or independent filmmakers, advertising agencies, or trade show or convention sponsors to work on individual projects for a set fee, often at a daily rate.

Most of the salaried camera operators and editors were employed by television broadcasting stations or motion picture studios. 37 percent of the salaried camera operators and editors worked for motion picture and video industry while 18 percent worked in television broadcasting. Most camera operators and editors worked in large metropolitan areas.

Job Outlook

Keen competition for jobs is expected due to the large number of people who wish to enter the broadcasting and motion picture industries, in which many camera operators and editors are employed. Those with the most experience and the most advanced computer skills will have the best job opportunities. Employment is expected to grow about as fast as the average for all occupations.

Employment change. Employment of camera operators and editors is expected to grow 11 percent over the 2008–18 decade, which is as fast as the average for all occupations through 2018. As the motion picture industry expands, demand for camera operators and editors will expand also. Camera operators will be needed to film made-for-Internet broadcasts, such as music videos, digital movies, sports features, and general entertainment programming. As the market for professional Internet video grows, camera operators may see increases in employment. Growth will be tempered, however, by the increased offshore production of motion pictures. Job growth for studio camera operators in television broadcasting will be slowed by the use of automated cameras under the control of a single person working either on the studio floor or in a director's booth. For ENG camera operators and editors, growth may be tempered by the combination of roles and other cost-cutting measures at broadcast stations. For videographers, computer and Internet services will provide new outlets for interactive productions.

Job prospects. Television, video, and motion picture camera operators and editors can expect keen competition for job openings because of the large number of people who wish to enter the broadcasting and motion picture industries, in which many of these workers are employed. The number of individuals interested in positions as videographers and movie camera operators usually is much greater than the number of openings. Those who succeed in landing a salaried job or attracting enough work to earn a living by freelancing are likely to be the most creative and highly motivated people, able to adapt to rapidly changing technologies and adept at operating a business. The change to digital cameras has increased the importance of strong computer skills. Those with the most experience and the most advanced computer skills will have the best job opportunities.

Earnings

Median annual wages for television, video, and motion picture camera operators were $41,670 in May 2008. The middle 50 percent earned between $29,020 and $59,970. The lowest 10 percent earned less than $21,710, and the highest 10 percent earned more than $79,440. Median annual wages were $40,910 in the motion picture and video industries and $36,250 in radio and television broadcasting.

Median annual wages for film and video editors were $50,560 in May 2008. The middle 50 percent earned between $33,060 and $77,700. The lowest 10 percent earned less than $24,640, and the highest 10 percent earned more than $112,410. Median annual wages were $56,170 in the motion picture and video industries, which employed the largest numbers of film and video editors.

Freelance camera operators' earnings tend to fluctuate each year. Because most freelance camera operators purchase their own equipment, they incur considerable expense acquiring and maintaining cameras and accessories. Some camera operators belong to unions, including the International Alliance of Theatrical Stage Employees and the National Association of Broadcast Employees and Technicians.

Related Occupations

Related arts and media occupations include:

Sources of Additional Information

For information about careers as a camera operator, contact:
➤ International Cinematographer's Guild, 80 Eighth Ave., 14th Floor, New York, NY 10011.

➤ National Association of Broadcast Employees and Technicians, 501 Third St. NW., 6th floor, Washington, DC 20001. Internet: **http://www.nabetcwa.org**

Information about career and employment opportunities for camera operators and film and video editors also is available from local offices of State employment service agencies, local offices of the relevant trade unions, and local television and film production companies that employ these workers.

The Occupational Information Network (O*NET) provides information on a wide range of occupational characteristics. Links to O*NET appear at the end of the Internet version of this occupational statement, accessible at **http://www.bls.gov/ooh/ocos091.htm**

Health Diagnosing and Treating Practitioners

Audiologists

Significant Points

- About 64 percent worked in health care facilities; many others were employed by educational services.

- All States regulate licensure of audiologists; requirements vary by State.

- A master's degree in audiology (hearing) is the standard level of education required; however, a doctoral degree is becoming more common for new entrants.

- Job prospects will be favorable for those possessing the doctoral (Au.D.) degree.

Nature of the Work

Audiologists work with people who have hearing, balance, and related ear problems. They examine individuals of all ages and identify those with the symptoms of hearing loss and other auditory, balance, and related sensory and neural problems. They then assess the nature and extent of the problems and help the individuals manage them. Using audiometers, computers, and other testing devices, they measure the loudness at which a person begins to hear sounds, the ability to distinguish between sounds, and the impact of hearing loss on an individual's daily life. In addition, audiologists use computer equipment to evaluate and diagnose balance disorders. Audiologists interpret these results and may coordinate them with medical, educational, and psychological information to make a diagnosis and determine a course of treatment.

Hearing disorders can result from a variety of causes including trauma at birth, viral infections, genetic disorders, exposure to loud noise, certain medications, or aging. Treatment may include examining and cleaning the ear canal, fitting and dispensing hearing aids, and fitting and programming cochlear implants. Audiologic treatment also includes counseling on adjusting to hearing loss, training on the use of hearing instruments, and teaching communication strategies for use in a variety of environments. For example, they may provide instruction in listening strategies. Audiologists also may recommend, fit, and dispense personal or large-area amplification systems and alerting devices.

In audiology clinics, audiologists may independently develop and carry out treatment programs. They keep records on the initial evaluation, progress, and discharge of patients. In other settings, audiologists may work with other health and education providers as part of a team in planning and implementing services for children and adults. Audiologists who diagnose and treat balance disorders often work in collaboration with physicians, and physical and occupational therapists.

Some audiologists specialize in work with the elderly, children, or hearing-impaired individuals who need special treatment programs. Others develop and implement ways to protect workers' hearing from on-the-job injuries. They measure noise levels in workplaces and conduct hearing protection programs in factories and in schools and communities.

Audiologists who work in private practice also manage the business aspects of running an office, such as developing a patient base, hiring employees, keeping records, and ordering equipment and supplies.

Some audiologists conduct research on types of, and treatment for, hearing, balance, and related disorders. Others design and develop equipment or techniques for diagnosing and treating these disorders.

Work environment. Audiologists usually work at a desk or table in clean, comfortable surroundings. The job is not physically demanding but does require attention to detail and intense concentration. The emotional needs of patients and their families may be demanding. Most full-time audiologists work about 40 hours per week, which may include weekends and evenings to meet the needs of patients. Those who work on a contract basis may spend a substantial amount of time traveling between facilities.

Training, Other Qualifications, and Advancement

All States regulate licensure of audiologists; requirements vary by State. At least a master's degree in audiology is required, but a doctoral degree is increasingly necessary.

Education and training. Individuals pursuing a career will need to earn a doctoral degree. In 2009, 18 States required a doctoral degree or its equivalent for new applicants to practice audiology. The doctoral degree in audiology is a graduate program typically lasting 4 years and resulting in the Au.D. designation.

The Council on Academic Accreditation (CAA) is an entity of the American Speech-Language-Hearing Association (ASHA) that accredits education programs in audiology. In 2009, the CAA accredited 70 doctoral programs in audiology. Graduation

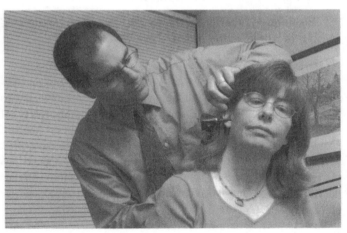

Audiologists examine individuals and identify symptoms of hearing loss and other auditory, balance, and related sensory and neural problems.

from an accredited program may be required to obtain a license in some States and professional credentialing.

Requirements for admission to programs in audiology include courses in English, mathematics, physics, chemistry, biology, psychology, and communication. Graduate coursework in audiology includes anatomy; physiology; physics; genetics; normal and abnormal communication development; auditory, balance, and neural systems assessment and treatment; diagnosis and treatment; pharmacology; and ethics. Graduate curriculums also include supervised clinical practicum and externships.

Licensure and certification. Audiologists are regulated by licensure in all 50 States. Eighteen of those States require a doctoral degree for licensure. Some States regulate the practice of audiology and the dispensing of hearing aids separately, meaning some States will require an additional license called a Hearing Aid Dispenser license. Many States require that audiologists complete continuing education for license renewal. Eligibility requirements, hearing aid dispensing requirements, and continuing education requirements vary from State to State. For specific requirements, contact your State's medical or health board.

Audiologists can earn the Certificate of Clinical Competence in Audiology (CCC-A) offered by the American Speech-Language-Hearing Association; they may also be credentialed through the American Board of Audiology. Professional credentialing may satisfy some or all of the requirements for State licensure.

Other qualifications. Audiologists should be able to effectively communicate diagnostic test results, diagnoses, and proposed treatments in a manner easily understood by their patients. They must be able to approach problems objectively and provide support to patients and their families. Because a patient's progress may be slow, patience, compassion, and good listening skills are necessary.

It is important for audiologists to be aware of new diagnostic and treatment technologies. Most audiologists participate in continuing education courses to learn new methods and technologies.

Advancement. With experience, audiologists can advance to open their own private practice. Audiologists working in hospitals and clinics can advance to management or supervisory positions.

Employment

Audiologists held about 12,800 jobs in 2008. About 64 percent of all jobs were in healthcare facilities—offices of physicians or other health practitioners, including audiologists; hospitals; and outpatient care centers. About 14 percent of jobs were in educational services. Other jobs for audiologists were in health and personal care stores and in State and local governments.

Job Outlook

Much faster than average employment growth is projected. However, because of the small size of the occupation, few job openings are expected. Job prospects will be favorable for those possessing the Au.D. degree.

Employment change. Employment of audiologists is expected to grow 25 percent from 2008 to 2018, much faster than

Projections data from the National Employment Matrix

Occupational Title	SOC Code	Employment, 2008	Projected Employment, 2018	Change, 2008-2018	
				Number	Percent
Audiologists	29-1121	12,800	16,000	3,200	25

(NOTE) Data in this table are rounded. See the discussion of the employment projections table in the *Handbook* introductory chapter on *Occupational Information Included in the Handbook*.

average for all occupations. Hearing loss is strongly associated with aging, so increased growth in older population groups will cause the number of people with hearing and balance impairments to increase markedly.

Medical advances also are improving the survival rate of premature infants and trauma victims, who then need assessment and sometimes treatment. Greater awareness of the importance of early identification and diagnosis of hearing disorders in infants also will increase employment. In addition to medical advances, technological advances in hearing aids may drive demand. Digital hearing aids have become smaller in size and also have quality improving technologies like reducing feedback. Demand may be spurred by those who switch from analog to digital hearing aids, as well as those who will desire new or first-time hearing aids because they are becoming less visible.

Employment in educational services will increase along with growth in elementary and secondary school enrollments, including enrollment of special education students.

Growth in employment of audiologists will be moderated by limitations on reimbursements made by third-party payers for the tests and services they provide.

Job prospects. Job prospects will be favorable for those possessing the Au.D. degree. Only a few job openings for audiologists will arise from the need to replace those who leave the occupation, because the occupation is relatively small and workers tend to stay in this occupation until they retire. Demand may be greater in areas with large numbers of retirees, so audiologists who are willing to relocate may have the best job prospects.

Earnings

Median annual wages of audiologists were $62,030 in May 2008. The middle 50 percent earned between $50,470 and $78,380. The lowest 10 percent earned less than $40,360, and the highest 10 percent earned more than $98,880. Some employers may pay for continuing education courses. About 15 percent of audiologists were union members or covered under union contracts in 2008.

Related Occupations

Audiologists specialize in the prevention, diagnosis, and treatment of hearing problems. Workers who treat other problems related to physical or mental health include:

Sources of Additional Information

State licensing boards can provide information on licensure requirements. State departments of education can supply information on certification requirements for those who wish to work in public schools.

For information on the specific requirements of your State, contact that State's licensing board. Career information, a description of the CCC-A credential, and information on State licensure is available from:
➤ American Speech-Language-Hearing Association, 2200 Research Blvd., Rockville, MD 20850. Internet: **http://www.asha.org**

For information on the Au.D. degree, contact:
➤ Audiology Foundation of America, 8 N. 3rd St., Suite 301, Lafayette, IN 47901. Internet: **http://www.audfound.org**

The Occupational Information Network (O*NET) provides information on a wide range of occupational characteristics. Links to O*NET appear at the end of the Internet version of this occupational statement, accessible at **http://www.bls.gov/ooh/ocos085.htm**

Chiropractors

Significant Points

- Job prospects should be good.

- Chiropractors must be licensed, requiring 2 to 4 years of undergraduate education, the completion of a 4-year chiropractic college course, and passing scores on national and State examinations.

- About 44 percent of chiropractors are self-employed.

- Earnings typically are relatively low in the beginning but increase as the practice grows.

Nature of the Work

Chiropractors, also known as *doctors of chiropractic* or *chiropractic physicians*, diagnose and treat patients with health problems of the musculoskeletal system and treat the effects of those problems on the nervous system and on general health. Many chiropractic treatments deal specifically with the spine and the manipulation of the spine. Chiropractic is based on the principle that spinal joint misalignments interfere with the nervous system and can result in lower resistance to disease and many different conditions of diminished health.

The chiropractic approach to healthcare focuses on the patient's overall health. Chiropractors provide natural, drugless, nonsurgical health treatments, relying on the body's inherent recuperative abilities. They also recognize that many factors

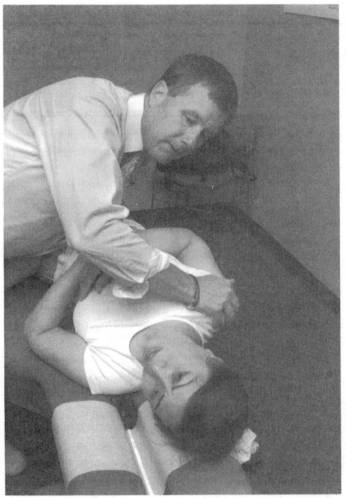

Chiropractors analyze the patient's posture and spine and may manually adjust the spinal column.

affect health, including exercise, diet, rest, environment, and heredity. Chiropractors recommend changes in lifestyle that affect those factors. In some situations, chiropractors refer patients to or consult with other health practitioners.

Like other health practitioners, chiropractors follow a standard routine to get information needed to diagnose and treat patients. They take the patient's health history; conduct physical, neurological, and orthopedic examinations; and may order laboratory tests. X rays and other diagnostic images are important tools because of the chiropractor's emphasis on the spine and its proper function. Chiropractors also analyze the patient's posture and spine using a specialized technique. For patients whose health problems can be traced to the musculoskeletal system, chiropractors manually adjust the spinal column.

Some chiropractors use additional procedures in their practices, including therapies using heat, water, light, massage, ultrasound, electric currents, and acupuncture . They may apply supports such as straps, tape, braces, or shoe inserts. Chiropractors often counsel patients about health concepts such as nutrition, exercise, changes in lifestyle, and stress management, but chiropractors do not prescribe drugs or perform surgery.

In addition to general chiropractic practice, some chiropractors specialize in sports injuries, neurology, orthopedics, pediatrics, nutrition, internal disorders, or diagnostic imaging.

Many chiropractors are solo or group practitioners who also have the administrative responsibilities of running a practice. In larger offices, chiropractors delegate these tasks to office managers and chiropractic assistants. Chiropractors in private practice are responsible for developing a patient base, hiring employees, and keeping records.

Work environment. Chiropractors work in clean, comfortable offices. Like other health practitioners, chiropractors are sometimes on their feet for long periods. Chiropractors who take X rays must employ appropriate precautions against the dangers of repeated exposure to radiation.

Chiropractors work, on average, about 40 hours per week, although longer hours are not uncommon. Solo practitioners set their own hours but may work evenings or weekends to accommodate patients. Like other healthcare practitioners, chiropractors in a group practice will sometimes be on call or treat patients of other chiropractors in the group.

Training, Other Qualifications, and Advancement

Chiropractors must be licensed, which requires 2 to 4 years of undergraduate education, the completion of a 4-year chiropractic college course, and passing scores on national and State examinations.

Education and training. In 2009, 16 chiropractic programs in the United States were accredited by the Council on Chiropractic Education. Applicants must have at least 90 semester hours of undergraduate study leading toward a bachelor's degree, including courses in English, the social sciences or humanities, organic and inorganic chemistry, biology, physics, and psychology. Many applicants have a bachelor's degree, which may eventually become the minimum entry requirement. Several chiropractic colleges offer prechiropractic study, as well as a bachelor's degree program. Recognition of prechiropractic education offered by chiropractic colleges varies among the States.

Chiropractic programs require a minimum of 4,200 hours of combined classroom, laboratory, and clinical experience. During the first 2 years, most chiropractic programs emphasize classroom and laboratory work in sciences such as anatomy, physiology, public health, microbiology, pathology, and biochemistry. The last 2 years focus on courses in manipulation and spinal adjustment and provide clinical experience in physical and laboratory diagnosis, neurology, orthopedics, geriatrics, physiotherapy, and nutrition. Chiropractic programs and institutions grant the degree of Doctor of Chiropractic (D.C.).

Chiropractic colleges also offer postdoctoral training in orthopedics, neurology, sports injuries, nutrition, rehabilitation, radiology, industrial consulting, family practice, pediatrics, and applied chiropractic sciences. Once such training is complete, chiropractors may take specialty exams leading to "diplomate" status in a given specialty. Exams are administered by chiropractic specialty boards.

Licensure. All States and the District of Columbia regulate the practice of chiropractic and grant licenses to chiropractors who meet the educational and examination requirements estab-

Projections data from the National Employment Matrix

Occupational Title	SOC Code	Employment, 2008	Projected Employment, 2018	Change, 2008-2018	
				Number	Percent
Chiropractors..	29-1011	49,100	58,700	9,600	20

(NOTE) Data in this table are rounded. See the discussion of the employment projections table in the *Handbook* introductory chapter on *Occupational Information Included in the Handbook*.

lished by the State. Chiropractors can practice only in States where they are licensed. Some States have agreements permitting chiropractors licensed in one State to obtain a license in another without further examination, provided that their educational, examination, and practice credentials meet State specifications.

Most State licensing boards require at least 2 years of undergraduate education, but an increasing number are requiring a 4-year bachelor's degree. All boards require the completion of a 4-year program at an accredited chiropractic college leading to the Doctor of Chiropractic degree.

For licensure, most State boards recognize either all or part of the four-part test administered by the National Board of Chiropractic Examiners. State examinations may supplement the National Board tests, depending on State requirements. All States except New Jersey require the completion of a specified number of hours of continuing education each year in order to maintain licensure. Chiropractic associations and accredited chiropractic programs and institutions offer continuing education programs.

Other qualifications. Chiropractic requires keen observation to detect physical abnormalities. It also takes considerable manual dexterity, but not unusual strength or endurance, to perform adjustments. Chiropractors should be able to work independently and handle responsibility. As in other health-related occupations, empathy, understanding, and the desire to help others are good qualities for dealing effectively with patients.

Advancement. Newly licensed chiropractors can set up a new practice, purchase an established one, or enter into partnership with an established practitioner. They also may take a salaried position with an established chiropractor, a group practice, or a healthcare facility.

Employment

Chiropractors held about 49,100 jobs in 2008. Most chiropractors work in a solo practice, although some are in group practice or work for other chiropractors. A small number teach, conduct research at chiropractic institutions, or work in hospitals and clinics. Approximately 44 percent of chiropractors were self-employed.

Many chiropractors are located in small communities. However, the distribution of chiropractors is not geographically uniform. This occurs primarily because new chiropractors frequently establish their practices in close proximity to one of the few chiropractic educational institutions.

Job Outlook

Employment is projected to grow much faster than average. Job prospects should be good.

Employment change. Employment of chiropractors is expected to increase 20 percent between 2008 and 2018, much faster than the average for all occupations. Projected job growth

stems from increasing consumer demand for alternative health care. Because chiropractors emphasize the importance of healthy lifestyles and do not prescribe drugs or perform surgery, chiropractic care is appealing to many health-conscious Americans. Chiropractic treatment of the back, neck, extremities, and joints has become more accepted as a result of research and changing attitudes about alternative, noninvasive healthcare practices. Chiropractors who specialize in pediatric care will be in demand as chiropractic spinal treatment is very gentle and children enjoy subsequent visits. The rapidly expanding older population, with its increased likelihood of mechanical and structural problems, also will increase demand for chiropractors.

Demand for chiropractic treatment, however, is related to the ability of patients to pay, either directly or through health insurance. Although more insurance plans now cover chiropractic services, the extent of such coverage varies among plans. Chiropractors must educate communities about the benefits of chiropractic care in order to establish a successful practice.

Job prospects. Job prospects for new chiropractors are expected to be good, especially for those who enter a multi-disciplined practice, consisting of, for example, a chiropractor, physical therapist, and medical doctor. Multi-disciplined practices are cost effective and allow patients to remain in-house. Should a patient be referred to a medical doctor, they may use the "in-house" doctor or one of their own choosing. Chiropractors usually remain in the occupation until they retire and few transfer to other occupations, so replacement needs arise almost entirely from retirements. Establishing a new practice will be easiest in areas with a low concentration of chiropractors.

Earnings

Median annual wages of salaried chiropractors were $66,490 in May 2008. The middle 50 percent earned between $45,540 and $96,700 a year.

In 2009, the mean salary for chiropractors was $94,454 according to a survey conducted by *Chiropractic Economics* magazine.

In chiropractic, as in other types of independent practice, earnings are relatively low in the beginning and increase as the practice grows. Geographic location and the characteristics and qualifications of the practitioner also may influence earnings.

Salaried chiropractors typically receive heath insurance and retirement benefits from their employers, whereas self-employed chiropractors must provide for their own health insurance and retirement.

Related Occupations

Chiropractors treat patients and work to prevent bodily disorders and injuries. So do:

Sources of Additional Information

General information on a career as a chiropractor is available from the following organizations:

➤ American Chiropractic Association, 1701 Clarendon Blvd., Arlington, VA 22209. Internet: **http://www.acatoday.org**

➤ International Chiropractors Association, 1110 North Glebe Rd., Suite 650, Arlington, VA 22201. Internet: **http://www.chiropractic.org**

➤ World Chiropractic Alliance, 2950 N. Dobson Rd., Suite 3, Chandler, AZ 85224.

For a list of chiropractic programs and institutions, as well as general information on chiropractic education, contact:

➤ Council on Chiropractic Education, 8049 North 85th Way, Scottsdale, AZ 85258-4321. Internet: **http://www.cce-usa.org**

For information on State education and licensure requirements, contact:

➤ Federation of Chiropractic Licensing Boards, 5401 W. 10th St., Suite 101, Greeley, CO 80634-4400. Internet: **http://www.fclb.org**

For more information on the national chiropractic licensing exam, contact:

➤ National Board of Chiropractic Examiners, 901 54th Ave., Greeley, CO 80634. Internet: **http://www.nbce.org**

For information on admission requirements to a specific chiropractic college, as well as scholarship and loan information, contact the college's admissions office.

The Occupational Information Network (O*NET) provides information on a wide range of occupational characteristics. Links to O*NET appear at the end of the Internet version of this occupational statement, accessible at **http://www.bls.gov/ooh/ocos071.htm**

Dentists

Significant Points

- About 3 out of 4 dentists are solo practitioners.

- Dentists must graduate from an accredited dental school and pass written and practical examinations; competition for admission to dental school is keen.

- Faster than average employment growth is projected.

- Job prospects should be good, reflecting the need to replace the large number of dentists expected to retire.

Nature of the Work

Dentists diagnose and treat problems with teeth and tissues in the mouth, along with giving advice and administering care to help prevent future problems. They provide instruction on diet, brushing, flossing, the use of fluorides, and other aspects of dental care. They remove tooth decay, fill cavities, examine x rays, place protective plastic sealants on children's teeth, straighten teeth, and repair fractured teeth. They also perform corrective surgery on gums and supporting bones to treat gum diseases. Dentists extract teeth and make models and measurements for dentures to replace missing teeth. They also administer anesthetics and write prescriptions for antibiotics and other medications.

Dentists use a variety of equipment, including x-ray machines, drills, mouth mirrors, probes, forceps, brushes, and scalpels. Lasers, digital scanners, and other computer technologies also may be used. Dentists wear masks, gloves, and safety glasses to protect themselves and their patients from infectious diseases.

Dentists in private practice oversee a variety of administrative tasks, including bookkeeping and the buying of equipment and supplies. They may employ and supervise dental hygienists, dental assistants, dental laboratory technicians, and reception-

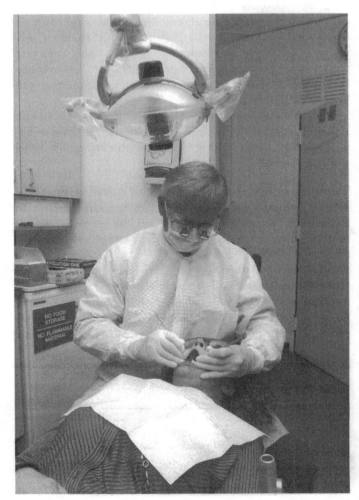

Dentists remove tooth decay, fill cavities, and repair fractured teeth.

ists. (These occupations are described elsewhere in the *Handbook*.)

Most dentists are general practitioners, handling a variety of dental needs. Other dentists practice in any of nine specialty areas. *Orthodontists*, the largest group of specialists, straighten teeth by applying pressure to the teeth with braces or other appliances. The next largest group, *oral* and *maxillofacial surgeons*, operates on the mouth, jaws, teeth, gums, neck, and head. The remainder may specialize as *pediatric dentists* (focusing on dentistry for children and special-needs patients); *periodontists* (treating gums and bone supporting the teeth); *prosthodontists* (replacing missing teeth with permanent fixtures, such as crowns and bridges, or with removable fixtures such as dentures); *endodontists* (performing root-canal therapy); *oral pathologists* (diagnosing oral diseases); *oral* and *maxillofacial radiologists* (diagnosing diseases in the head and neck through the use of imaging technologies); or *dental public health specialists* (promoting good dental health and preventing dental diseases within the community).

Work environment.   Most dentists are solo practitioners, meaning that they own their own businesses and work alone or with a small staff. Some dentists have partners, and a few work for other dentists as associate dentists.

Most dentists work 4 or 5 days a week. Some work evenings and weekends to meet their patients' needs. The number of hours worked varies greatly among dentists. Most full-time dentists work between 35 and 40 hours a week. However, others, especially those who are trying to establish a new practice, work more. Also, experienced dentists often work fewer hours. It is common for dentists to continue in part-time practice well beyond the usual retirement age.

Dentists usually work in the safety of an office environment. However, work-related injuries can occur, such as those resulting from the use of hand-held tools when performing dental work on patients.

Training, Other Qualifications, and Advancement

All 50 States and the District of Columbia require dentists to be licensed. To qualify for a license in most States, candidates must graduate from an accredited dental school and pass written and practical examinations.

Education and training.   In 2008, there were 57 dental schools in the United States accredited by the American Dental Association's (ADA's) Commission on Dental Accreditation. Dental schools require a minimum of 2 years of college-level predental education prior to admittance. Most dental students have at least a bachelor's degree before entering dental school, although a few applicants are accepted to dental school after 2 or 3 years of college and complete their bachelor's degree while attending dental school. According to the ADA, 85 percent of dental students had a bachelor's degree prior to beginning their dental program in the 2006-07 academic year.

High school and college students who want to become dentists should take courses in biology, chemistry, physics, health, and mathematics. College undergraduates planning on applying to dental school are required to take many science courses. Because of this, some choose a major in a science, such as biology or chemistry, whereas others take the required science coursework while pursuing a major in another subject.

All dental schools require applicants to take the Dental Admissions Test (DAT). When selecting students, schools consider scores earned on the DAT, applicants' grade point averages, and information gathered through recommendations and interviews. Competition for admission to dental school is keen.

Dental school usually lasts 4 academic years. Studies begin with classroom instruction and laboratory work in science, including anatomy, microbiology, biochemistry, and physiology. Beginning courses in clinical sciences, including laboratory techniques, are also completed. During the last 2 years, students treat patients, usually in dental clinics, under the supervision of licensed dentists. Most dental schools award the degree of Doctor of Dental Surgery (DDS). Others award an equivalent degree, Doctor of Dental Medicine (DMD).

Licensure.   Licensing is required to practice as a dentist. In most States, licensure requires passing written and practical examinations in addition to having a degree from an accredited dental school. Candidates may fulfill the written part of the State licensing requirements by passing the National Board Dental Examinations. Individual States or regional testing agencies administer the written or practical examinations.

Individuals can be licensed to practice any of the 9 recognized specialties in all 50 States and the District of Columbia. Requirements include 2 to 4 years of postgraduate education and, in some cases, the completion of a special State examination. A postgraduate residency term also may be required, usually lasting up to 2 years. Most State licenses permit dentists to engage in both general and specialized practice.

Other qualifications.   Dentistry requires diagnostic ability and manual skills. Dentists should have good visual memory; excellent judgment regarding space, shape, and color; a high degree of manual dexterity; and scientific ability. Good busi-

Projections data from the National Employment Matrix

Occupational Title	SOC Code	Employment, 2008	Projected Employment, 2018	Change, 2008-2018	
				Number	Percent
Dentists	29-1020	141,900	164,000	22,100	16
Dentists, general...............................	29-1021	120,200	138,600	18,400	15
Oral and maxillofacial surgeons	29-1022	6,700	7,700	1,000	15
Orthodontists......................................	29-1023	7,700	9,200	1,500	20
Prosthodontists...................................	29-1024	500	700	100	28
Dentists, all other specialists..............	29-1029	6,900	7,900	1,000	15

(NOTE) Data in this table are rounded. See the discussion of the employment projections table in the *Handbook* introductory chapter on *Occupational Information Included in the Handbook.*

ness sense, self-discipline, and good communication skills are helpful for success in private practice.

Advancement. Dentists and aspiring dentists who want to teach or conduct research full time usually spend an additional 2 to 5 years in advanced dental training, in programs operated by dental schools or hospitals. Many private practitioners also teach part time, including supervising students in dental school clinics. (See the statement on teachers—postsecondary elsewhere in the *Handbook*.)

Some dental school graduates work for established dentists as associates for 1 to 2 years to gain experience and save money to equip an office of their own. Most dental school graduates, however, purchase an established practice or open a new one immediately after graduation.

Employment

Dentists held about 141,900 jobs in 2008. Employment was distributed among general practitioners and specialists as follows:

Dentists, general...120,200
Orthodontists...7,700
Oral and maxillofacial surgeons.....................................6,700
Prosthodontists..500
Dentists, all other specialists..6,900

Approximately 15 percent of all dentists were specialists. About 28 percent of dentists were self-employed and not incorporated. Very few salaried dentists worked in hospitals and offices of physicians. Almost all dentists work in private practice. According to the American Dental Association, about 3 out of 4 dentists in private practice are solo proprietors, and almost 15 percent belonged to a partnership.

Job Outlook

Employment is projected to grow faster than the average. Job prospects should be good, reflecting the need to replace the large number of dentists expected to retire.

Employment change. Employment of dentists is projected to grow by 16 percent through 2018, which is faster than the average for all occupations. The demand for dental services is expected to continue to increase. The overall U.S. population is growing, and the elderly segment of the population is growing even faster; these phenomena will increase the demand for dental care. Many members of the baby-boom generation will need complicated dental work. In addition, elderly people are more likely to retain their teeth than were their predecessors, so they will require much more care than in the past. The younger generation will continue to need preventive checkups despite an overall increase in the dental health of the public over the last few decades. Recently, some private insurance providers have increased their dental coverage. If this trend continues, people with new or expanded dental insurance will be more likely to visit a dentist than in the past. Also, although they are currently a small proportion of dental expenditures, cosmetic dental services, such as providing teeth-whitening treatments, will become increasingly popular. This trend is expected to continue as new technologies allow these procedures to take less time and be much less invasive.

However, employment of dentists is not expected to keep pace with the increased demand for dental services. Productivity increases from new technology, as well as the tendency to assign more tasks to dental hygienists and assistants, will allow dentists to perform more work than they have in the past. As their practices expand, dentists are likely to hire more hygienists and dental assistants to handle routine services.

Dentists will increasingly provide care and instruction aimed at preventing the loss of teeth, rather than simply providing treatments such as fillings. Improvements in dental technology also will allow dentists to offer more effective and less painful treatment to their patients.

Job prospects. As an increasing number of dentists from the baby-boom generation reach retirement age, many of them will retire or work fewer hours and stop taking on new patients. Furthermore, the number of applicants to, and graduates from, dental schools has increased in recent years. Job prospects should be good, because younger dentists will be able to take over the work of older dentists who retire or cut back on hours, as well as provide dental services to accommodate the growing demand.

Demand for dental services tends to follow the business cycle, primarily because these services usually are paid for either by the patient or by private insurance companies. As a result, during slow times in the economy, demand for dental services can decrease; consequently, dentists may have difficulty finding employment, or if already in an established practice, they may work fewer hours because of reduced demand.

Earnings

Median annual wages of salaried general dentists were $142,870 in May 2008. Earnings vary according to number of years in practice, location, hours worked, and specialty. Self-employed dentists in private practice tend to earn more than salaried dentists.

Dentists who are salaried often receive benefits paid by their employer, with health insurance and malpractice insurance being among the most common. However, like other business owners, self-employed dentists must provide their own health insurance, life insurance, retirement plans, and other benefits.

Related Occupations

Dentists examine, diagnose, prevent, and treat diseases and abnormalities. Other workers who perform similar tasks include:

Sources of Additional Information

For information on dentistry as a career, a list of accredited dental schools, and a list of State boards of dental examiners, contact:

➤ American Dental Association, Commission on Dental Accreditation, 211 E. Chicago Ave., Chicago, IL 60611. Internet: **http://www.ada.org**

For information on admission to dental schools, contact:

➤ American Dental Education Association, 1400 K St. NW., Suite 1100, Washington, DC 20005. Internet: **http://www.adea.org**

For more information on general dentistry or on a specific dental specialty, contact:

➤ Academy of General Dentistry, 211 East Chicago Ave., Suite 900, Chicago, IL 60611. Internet: **http://www.agd.org**

➤ American Association of Orthodontists, 401 North Lindbergh Blvd., St. Louis, MO 63141. Internet: **http://www.braces.org**

➤ American Association of Oral and Maxillofacial Surgeons, 9700 West Bryn Mawr Ave., Rosemont, IL 60018. Internet: **http://www.aaoms.org**

➤ American Academy of Pediatric Dentistry, 211 East Chicago Ave., Suite 1700, Chicago, IL 60611. Internet: **http://www.aapd.org**

➤ American Academy of Periodontology, 737 North Michigan Ave., Suite 800, Chicago, IL 60611. Internet: **http://www.perio.org**

➤ American Academy of Prosthodontists, 211 East Chicago Ave., Suite 1000, Chicago, IL 60611. Internet: **http://www.prosthodontics.org**

➤ American Association of Endodontists, 211 East Chicago Ave., Suite 1100, Chicago, IL 60611. Internet: **http://www.aae.org**

➤ American Academy of Oral and Maxillofacial Radiology, P.O. Box 1010, Evans, GA 30809. Internet: **http://www.aaomr.org**

➤ American Association of Public Health Dentistry, 3085 Stevenson Dr., Suite 200, Springfield, IL 62703. Internet: **http://www.aaphd.org**

People interested in practicing dentistry should obtain the requirements for licensure from the board of dental examiners of the State in which they plan to work.

To obtain information on scholarships, grants, and loans, including Federal financial aid, prospective dental students should contact the office of student financial aid at the schools to which they apply.

The Occupational Information Network (O*NET) provides information on a wide range of occupational characteristics. Links to O*NET appear at the end of the Internet version of this occupational statement, accessible at

http://www.bls.gov/ooh/ocos072.htm

Dietitians and Nutritionists

Significant Points

- Most jobs are in hospitals, nursing care facilities, outpatient care centers, and offices of physicians or other health practitioners.

- Dietitians and nutritionists need at least a bachelor's degree; licensure, certification, or registration requirements vary by State.

- Applicants with specialized training, an advanced degree, or certifications beyond the particular State's minimum requirement should enjoy the best job opportunities.

Nature of the Work

Dietitians and nutritionists plan food and nutrition programs, supervise meal preparation, and oversee the serving of meals. They prevent and treat illnesses by promoting healthy eating habits and recommending dietary modifications. For example, dietitians might teach a patient with high blood pressure how to use less salt when preparing meals, or create a diet reduced in fat and sugar for an overweight patient.

Dietitians manage food service systems for institutions such as hospitals and schools, promote sound eating habits through education, and conduct research. Many dietitians specialize, becoming a clinical dietitian, community dietitian, management dietitian, or consultant.

Clinical dietitians provide nutritional services to patients in hospitals, nursing care facilities, and other institutions. They assess patients' nutritional needs, develop and implement nutrition programs, and evaluate and report the results. They also

Dietitians counsel individuals and groups on nutritional practices designed to prevent disease and promote health.

confer with doctors and other healthcare professionals to coordinate medical and nutritional needs. Some clinical dietitians specialize in managing the weight of overweight patients or in the care of renal (kidney), diabetic, or critically ill patients. In addition, clinical dietitians in nursing care facilities, small hospitals, or correctional facilities may manage the food service department.

Community dietitians counsel individuals and groups on nutritional practices designed to prevent disease and promote health. Working in places such as public health clinics, home health agencies, and health maintenance organizations, community dietitians evaluate individual needs, develop nutritional care plans, and instruct individuals and their families. Dietitians working in home health agencies provide instruction on grocery shopping and food preparation to the elderly, children, and individuals with special needs.

Increased public interest in nutrition has led to job opportunities in food manufacturing, advertising, and marketing. In these areas, dietitians analyze foods, prepare literature for distribution, or report on issues such as dietary fiber, vitamin supplements, or the nutritional content of recipes.

Management dietitians oversee large-scale meal planning and preparation in healthcare facilities, company cafeterias, prisons, and schools. They hire, train, and direct other dietitians and food service workers; budget for and purchase food, equipment, and supplies; enforce sanitary and safety regulations; and prepare records and reports.

Consultant dietitians work under contract with healthcare facilities or in their own private practice. They perform nutrition screenings for their clients and offer advice on diet-related concerns such as weight loss and cholesterol reduction. Some work for wellness programs, sports teams, supermarkets, and other nutrition-related businesses. They may consult with food service managers, providing expertise in sanitation, safety procedures, menu development, budgeting, and planning.

Work environment. Dietitians and nutritionists usually work in clean, well-lighted, and well-ventilated areas. However, some work in hot, congested kitchens. Many dietitians and nutritionists are on their feet for much of the workday.

Most full-time dietitians and nutritionists work a standard 40-hour week, although some work weekends. About 19 percent worked part time in 2008.

Training, Other Qualifications, and Advancement

Dietitians and nutritionists need at least a bachelor's degree. Licensure, certification, or registration requirements vary by State.

Education and training. Becoming a dietitian or nutritionist usually requires at least a bachelor's degree in dietetics, foods and nutrition, food service systems management, or a related area. Graduate degrees also are available. College students in these majors take courses in foods, nutrition, institution management, chemistry, biochemistry, biology, microbiology, and physiology. Other suggested courses include business, mathematics, statistics, computer science, psychology, sociology, and economics. High school students interested in becoming a dietitian or nutritionist should take courses in biology, chemistry, mathematics, health, and communications.

As of 2008, there were 279 bachelor's degree programs and 18 master's degree programs approved by the American Dietetic Association's Commission on Accreditation for Dietetics Education.

Licensure. Of the 48 States and jurisdictions with laws governing dietetics, 35 require licensure, 12 require statutory certification, and 1 require registration. Specific requirements vary by State. As a result, interested candidates should determine the requirements of the State in which they want to work before sitting for any exam.

In States that require licensure, only people who are licensed can work as dietitians and nutritionists. States that require statutory certification limit the use of occupational titles to people who meet certain requirements; individuals without certification can still practice as a dietitian or nutritionist but without using certain titles. Registration is the least restrictive form of State regulation of dietitians and nutritionists. Unregistered people are permitted to practice as a dietitian or nutritionist.

Certification and other qualifications. Although not required, the Commission on Dietetic Registration of the American Dietetic Association awards the Registered Dietitian credential to those who pass an exam after completing academic coursework and a supervised internship. This certification is different from the statutory certification regulated by some States and discussed in the previous section. To maintain a Registered Dietitian status, workers must complete at least 75 credit hours in approved continuing education classes every 5 years.

A supervised internship, required for certification, can be completed in one of two ways. The first requires the completion of a program accredited by the Commission on Dietetic Registration. As of September 2009, there were 51 accredited programs that combined academic and supervised practice experience and generally lasted 4 to 5 years. The second option requires the completion of 900 hours of supervised practice experience in any of the 243 accredited internships. These internships may be full-time programs lasting 6 to 12 months or part-time programs lasting 2 years.

Advancement. Experienced dietitians may advance to management positions, such as assistant director, associate director, or director of a dietetic department, or may become self-employed. Some dietitians specialize in areas such as renal, diabetic, cardiovascular, or pediatric dietetics. Others leave the occupation to become sales representatives for equipment, pharmaceutical, or food manufacturers. A master's degree can help some workers to advance their careers, particularly in career paths related to research, advanced clinical positions, or public health.

Employment

Dietitians and nutritionists held about 60,300 jobs in 2008. More than half of all jobs were in hospitals, nursing care facilities, outpatient care centers, or offices of physicians and other health practitioners. State and local government agencies provided additional jobs—mostly in correctional facilities, health departments, and other public-health-related areas. Some dietitians and nutritionists were employed in special food services, an industry made up of firms providing food services on con-

Projections data from the National Employment Matrix

Occupational Title	SOC Code	Employment, 2008	Projected Employment, 2018	Change, 2008-2018	
				Number	Percent
Dietitians and nutritionists	29-1031	60,300	65,800	5,600	9

(NOTE) Data in this table are rounded. See the discussion of the employment projections table in the *Handbook* introductory chapter on *Occupational Information Included in the Handbook.*

tract to facilities such as colleges and universities, airlines, correctional facilities, and company cafeterias.

Other jobs were in public and private educational services, community care facilities for the elderly (which includes assisted-living facilities), individual and family services, home healthcare services, and the Federal Government—mostly in the U.S. Department of Veterans Affairs. Some dietitians were self-employed, working as consultants to facilities such as hospitals and nursing care facilities or providing dietary counseling to individuals.

Job Outlook

Average employment growth is projected. Applicants with specialized training, an advanced degree, or certifications beyond the particular State's minimum requirement should enjoy the best job opportunities.

Employment change. Employment of dietitians and nutritionists is expected to increase 9 percent during the 2008–18 projection decade, about as fast as the average for all occupations. Job growth will result from an increasing emphasis on disease prevention through improved dietary habits. A growing and aging population will boost demand for nutritional counseling and treatment in hospitals, residential care facilities, schools, prisons, community health programs, and home healthcare agencies. Public interest in nutrition and increased emphasis on health education and prudent lifestyles also will spur demand, especially in food service management.

Also, with increased public awareness of obesity and diabetes, Medicare coverage has been expanded to include medical nutrition therapy for renal and diabetic patients, creating job growth for dietitians and nutritionists specializing in those diseases.

Employment growth, however, may be constrained if some employers substitute other workers, such as health educators, food service managers, and dietetic technicians, to do work related to nutrition. Also, demand for nutritional therapy services is related to the ability of patients to pay, either out-of-pocket or through health insurance, and although more insurance plans now cover nutritional therapy services, the extent of such coverage varies among plans. Growth may be curbed by limitations on insurance reimbursement for dietetic services.

Hospitals will continue to employ a large number of dietitians and nutritionists to provide medical nutritional therapy and plan meals. But hospitals also will continue to contract with outside agencies for food service and move medical nutritional therapy to outpatient care facilities, slowing job growth in hospitals relative to food service, outpatient facilities, and other employers.

Finally, the number of dietitian positions in nursing care facilities is expected to decline, as these establishments continue to contract with outside agencies for food services. However, employment is expected to grow rapidly in contract providers

of food services, in outpatient care centers, and in offices of physicians and other health practitioners.

Job prospects. In addition to employment growth, job openings will result from the need to replace experienced workers who retire or leave the occupation for other reasons. Applicants with specialized training, an advanced degree, or certifications beyond the particular State's minimum requirement should enjoy the best job opportunities. Demand for dietitians should be particularly strong in outpatient care facilities, offices of physicians, and food service management. Applicants without a bachelor's degree will face keen competition for jobs.

Dietitians with specialized training, an advanced degree, or certifications beyond the particular State's minimum requirement will experience the best job opportunities. Those specializing in renal and diabetic nutrition or gerontological nutrition will benefit from the growing number of diabetics and the aging of the population.

Earnings

Median annual wages of dietitians and nutritionists were $50,590 in May 2008. The middle 50 percent earned between $41,060 and $61,790. The lowest 10 percent earned less than $31,460, and the highest 10 percent earned more than $73,410. Median annual wages in the industries employing the largest numbers of dietitians and nutritionists in May 2008 were:

Outpatient care centers..	$52,120
General medical and surgical hospitals........................	51,390
Nursing care facilities	51,110
Local government..	47,390
Special food services..	45,410

According to the American Dietetic Association, median annual wages for registered dietitians in 2007 varied by practice area as follows: $60,008 in consultation and business; $64,002 in food and nutrition management; $66,061 in education and research; $52,000 in clinical nutrition/ambulatory care; $53,997 in clinical nutrition/long-term care; $48,006 in community nutrition; and $48,984 in clinical nutrition/acute care. Salaries also vary by years in practice, education level, and geographic region.

Related Occupations

Other workers who may apply the principles of dietetics include:

	Page
Dietetic technicians...	824
Food service managers..	55
Health educators..	238
Registered nurses	392

Sources of Additional Information

For a list of academic programs, scholarships, and other information about dietitians, contact:

➤ The American Dietetic Association, 120 South Riverside Plaza, Suite 2000, Chicago, IL 60606-6995. Internet: **http://www.eatright.org**

For information on the Registered Dietitian exam and other specialty credentials, contact:

➤ The Commission on Dietetic Registration, 120 South Riverside Plaza, Suite 2000, Chicago, IL 60606-6995. Internet: **http://www.cdrnet.org**

The Occupational Information Network (O*NET) provides information on a wide range of occupational characteristics. Links to O*NET appear at the end of the Internet version of this occupational statement, accessible at **http://www.bls.gov/ooh/ocos077.htm**

Occupational Therapists

Significant Points

- Employment is expected to grow much faster than average, and job opportunities should be good, especially for therapists treating the elderly.

- Occupational therapists are regulated in all 50 States; requirements vary by State.

- Occupational therapists are increasingly taking on supervisory roles, allowing assistants and aides to work more closely with clients under the guidance of a therapist.

Nature of the Work

Occupational therapists help patients improve their ability to perform tasks in living and working environments. They work with individuals who suffer from a mentally, physically, developmentally, or emotionally disabling condition. Occupational therapists use treatments to develop, recover, or maintain the daily living and work skills of their patients. The therapist helps clients not only to improve their basic motor functions and reasoning abilities, but also to compensate for permanent loss of function. The goal is to help clients have independent, productive, and satisfying lives.

Occupational therapists help clients to perform all types of activities, from using a computer to caring for daily needs such as dressing, cooking, and eating. Physical exercises may be used to increase strength and dexterity, while other activities may be chosen to improve visual acuity or the ability to discern patterns. For example, a client with short-term memory loss might be encouraged to make lists to aid recall, and a person with coordination problems might be assigned exercises to improve hand-eye coordination. Occupational therapists also use computer programs to help clients improve decision-making, abstract-reasoning, problem-solving, and perceptual skills, as well as memory, sequencing, and coordination—all of which are important for independent living.

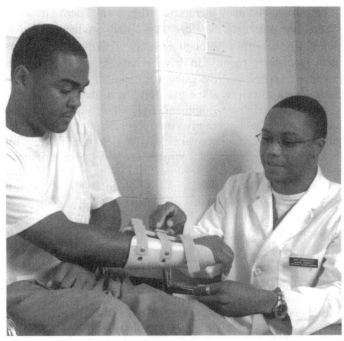

Occupational therapists help patients learn to perform all types of activities, from using a computer to caring for daily needs such as dressing, cooking, and eating.

Patients with permanent disabilities, such as spinal cord injuries, cerebral palsy, or muscular dystrophy, often need special instruction to master certain daily tasks. For these individuals, therapists demonstrate the use of adaptive equipment, including wheelchairs, orthoses, eating aids, and dressing aids. They also design or build special equipment needed at home or at work, including computer-aided adaptive equipment. They teach clients how to use the equipment to improve communication and control various situations in their environment.

Some occupational therapists treat individuals whose ability to function in a work environment has been impaired. These practitioners might arrange employment, evaluate the work space, plan work activities, and assess the client's progress. Therapists also may collaborate with the client and the employer to modify the work environment so that the client can succeed at work.

Assessing and recording a client's activities and progress is an important part of an occupational therapist's job. Accurate records are essential for evaluating clients, for billing, and for reporting to physicians and other healthcare providers.

Occupational therapists may work exclusively with individuals in a particular age group or with a particular disability. In schools, for example, they evaluate children's capabilities, recommend and provide therapy, modify classroom equipment, and help children participate in school activities. A therapist may work with children individually, lead small groups in the classroom, consult with a teacher, or serve on an administrative committee. Some therapists provide early intervention therapy to infants and toddlers who have, or are at risk of having, developmental delays. Therapies may include facilitating the use of the hands and promoting skills for listening, following directions, social play, dressing, or grooming.

Other occupational therapists work with elderly patients. These therapists help the elderly lead more productive, active, and independent lives through a variety of methods. Therapists with specialized training in driver rehabilitation assess an individual's ability to drive using both clinical and on-the-road tests. The evaluations allow the therapist to make recommendations for adaptive equipment, training to prolong driving independence, and alternative transportation options. Occupational therapists also work with clients to assess their homes for hazards and to identify environmental factors that contribute to falls.

Occupational therapists in mental health settings treat individuals who are mentally ill, developmentally challenged, or emotionally disturbed. To treat these problems, therapists choose activities that help people learn to engage in and cope with daily life. Activities might include time management skills, budgeting, shopping, homemaking, and the use of public transportation. Occupational therapists also work with individuals who are dealing with alcoholism, drug abuse, depression, eating disorders, or stress-related disorders.

Work environment. In large rehabilitation centers, therapists may work in spacious rooms equipped with machines, tools, and other devices generating noise. The work can be tiring because therapists are on their feet much of the time. Therapists also face hazards such as back strain from lifting and moving clients and equipment.

Occupational therapists working for one employer full-time usually work a 40-hour week. Around 31 percent of occupational therapists worked part-time. It is not uncommon for occupational therapists to work for more than one employer at multiple facilities, which may involve significant travel time. Those in schools may participate in meetings and other activities during and after the school day.

Training, Other Qualifications, and Advancement

Occupational therapists are regulated in all 50 States. Individuals pursuing a career as an occupational therapist usually need to earn a post-baccalaureate degree from an accredited college or university or education deemed equivalent.

Education and training. A master's degree or higher in occupational therapy is the typical minimum requirement for entry into the field. In addition, occupational therapists must attend an academic program accredited by the Accreditation Council for Occupational Therapy Education (ACOTE) in order to sit for the national certifying exam. In 2009, 150 master's degree programs or combined bachelor's and master's degree programs were accredited, and 4 doctoral degree programs were accredited. Most schools have full-time programs, although a growing number are offering weekend or part-time programs as well. Coursework in occupational therapy programs include the physical, biological, and behavioral sciences as well as the ap-

plication of occupational therapy theory and skills. All accredited programs require at least 24 weeks of supervised fieldwork as part of the academic curriculum.

People considering this profession should take high school courses in biology, chemistry, physics, health, art, and the social sciences. College admissions offices also look favorably on paid or volunteer experience in the healthcare field. Relevant undergraduate majors include biology, psychology, sociology, anthropology, liberal arts, and anatomy.

Licensure. All States regulate the practice of occupational therapy. To obtain a license, applicants must graduate from an accredited educational program and pass a national certification examination. Those who pass the exam are awarded the title "Occupational Therapist Registered (OTR)." Specific eligibility requirements for licensure vary by State; contact your State's licensing board for details.

Some States have additional requirements for therapists who work in schools or early intervention programs. These requirements may include education-related classes, an education practice certificate, or early intervention certification.

Certification and other qualifications. Certification is voluntary. The National Board for Certifying Occupational Therapy certifies occupational therapists through a national certifying exam. Those who pass the test are awarded the title Occupational Therapist Registered (OTR). In some States, the national certifying exam meets requirements for regulation while other States have their own licensing exam.

Occupational therapists are expected to continue their professional development by participating in continuing education courses and workshops. In fact, a number of States require continuing education as a condition of maintaining licensure.

Occupational therapists need patience and strong interpersonal skills to inspire trust and respect in their clients. Patience is necessary because many clients may not show immediate improvement. Ingenuity and imagination in adapting activities to individual needs are assets. Those working in home healthcare services also must be able to adapt to a variety of settings.

Advancement. Therapists are increasingly taking on supervisory roles in addition to their supervision of occupational therapy assistants and aides. Occupational therapists may advance their careers by taking on administrative duties at hospitals or rehabilitation centers.

Occupational therapists also can advance by specializing in a clinical area and gaining expertise in treating a certain type of patient or ailment. Therapists may specialize in gerontology, mental health, pediatrics, and physical rehabilitation. In addition, some occupational therapists choose to teach classes in accredited occupational therapy educational programs.

Projections data from the National Employment Matrix

Occupational Title	SOC Code	Employment, 2008	Projected Employment, 2018	Change, 2008-2018	
				Number	Percent
Occupational therapists...	29-1122	104,500	131,300	26,800	26

(NOTE) Data in this table are rounded. See the discussion of the employment projections table in the *Handbook* introductory chapter on *Occupational Information Included in the Handbook.*

Employment

Occupational therapists held about 104,500 jobs in 2008. The largest number of occupational therapist jobs was in ambulatory health care services, which employed about 29 percent of occupational therapists. Other major employers were hospitals, offices of other health practitioners (including offices of occupational therapists), public and private educational services, and nursing care facilities. Some occupational therapists were employed by home health care services, outpatient care centers, offices of physicians, individual and family services, community care facilities for the elderly, and government agencies.

A small number of occupational therapists were self-employed in private practice. These practitioners treated clients referred by other health professionals. They also provided contract or consulting services to nursing care facilities, schools, adult day care programs, and home healthcare agencies.

Job Outlook

Employment is expected to grow much faster than average. Job opportunities should be good, especially for occupational therapists treating the elderly.

Employment change. Employment of occupational therapists is expected to increase by 26 percent between 2008 and 2018, much faster than the average for all occupations. The increasing elderly population will drive growth in the demand for occupational therapy services. The demand for occupational therapists should continue to rise as a result of the increasing number of individuals with disabilities or limited function who require therapy services. Older persons have an increased incidence of heart attack and stroke, which will spur demand for therapeutic services. Growth in the population 75 years and older—an age group that suffers from high incidences of disabling conditions—also will increase demand for therapeutic services. In addition, medical advances now enable more patients with critical problems to survive—patients who ultimately may need extensive therapy. However, growth may be dampened by the impact of Federal legislation imposing limits on reimbursement for therapy services.

Hospitals will continue to employ a large number of occupational therapists to provide therapy services to acutely ill inpatients. Hospitals also will need occupational therapists to staff their outpatient rehabilitation programs.

Employment growth in schools will result from the expansion of the school-age population and the federally funded extension of services for disabled students. Therapists will be needed to help children with disabilities prepare to enter special education programs.

Job prospects. Job opportunities should be good for licensed occupational therapists in all settings, particularly in acute hospital, rehabilitation, and orthopedic settings because the elderly receive most of their treatment in these settings. Occupational therapists with specialized knowledge in a treatment area also will have increased job prospects. Driver rehabilitation, training for the elderly, and ergonomic consulting are emerging practice areas for occupational therapy.

Earnings

Median annual wages of occupational therapists were $66,780 in May 2008. The middle 50 percent earned between $55,090 and $81,290. The lowest 10 percent earned less than $42,820, and the highest 10 percent earned more than $98,310. Median annual wages in the industries employing the largest numbers of occupational therapists in May 2008 were:

Home health care services	$74,510
Nursing care facilities	72,790
Offices of other health care practitioners	69,360
General medical and surgical hospitals	68,100
Elementary and secondary schools	60,020

Related Occupations

Occupational therapists use specialized knowledge to help individuals perform daily living skills and achieve maximum independence. Other occupations performing similar duties include:

	Page
Athletic trainers	405
Physical therapists	377
Recreational therapists	389
Respiratory therapists	397
Speech-language pathologists	399

Sources of Additional Information

For more information on occupational therapy as a career, contact:

➤ American Occupational Therapy Association, 4720 Montgomery Lane, PO Box 31220, Bethesda, MD 20824-1220. Internet: **http://www.aota.org**

For information regarding the requirements to practice as an occupational therapist in schools, contact the appropriate occupational therapy regulatory agency for your State.

The Occupational Information Network (O*NET) provides information on a wide range of occupational characteristics. Links to O*NET appear at the end of the Internet version of this occupational statement, accessible at **http://www.bls.gov/ooh/ocos078.htm**

Optometrists

Significant Points

- Admission to optometry school is competitive; only about 1 in 3 applicants was accepted in 2007.

- Graduation from an accredited college of Optometry and a State license administered by the National Board of Examiners in Optometry are required.

- Employment is expected to grow much faster than the average in response to the vision care needs of a growing and aging population.

- Job opportunities are likely to be excellent.

Nature of the Work

Optometrists, also known as *doctors of optometry*, or ODs, are the main providers of vision care. They examine people's eyes to diagnose vision problems, such as nearsightedness and farsightedness, and they test patients' depth and color percep-

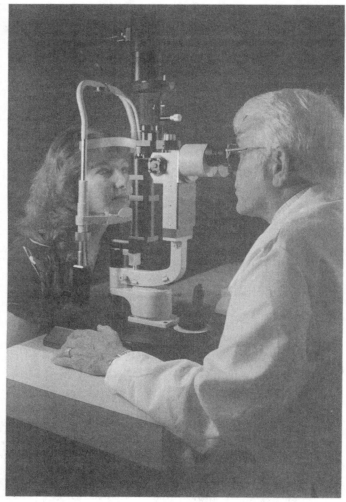

The Doctor of Optometry degree requires the completion of a 4-year program at an accredited optometry school.

tion and ability to focus and coordinate the eyes. Optometrists may prescribe eyeglasses or contact lenses, or they may provide other treatments, such as vision therapy or low-vision rehabilitation.

Optometrists also test for glaucoma and other eye diseases and diagnose conditions caused by systemic diseases such as diabetes and high blood pressure, referring patients to other health practitioners as needed. They prescribe medication to treat vision problems or eye diseases, and some provide preoperative and postoperative care to cataract patients, as well as to patients who have had corrective laser surgery. Like other physicians, optometrists encourage preventative measures by promoting nutrition and hygiene education to their patients to minimize the risk of eye disease.

Although most work in a general practice as a primary care optometrist, some optometrists prefer to specialize in a particular field, such as contact lenses, geriatrics, pediatrics, or vision therapy. As a result, an increasing number of optometrists are forming group practices in which each group member specializes in a specific area while still remaining a full scope practitioner. For example, an expert in low-vision rehabilitation may help legally blind patients by custom fitting them with a magnifying device that will enable them to read.

Some may specialize in occupational vision, developing ways to protect workers' eyes from on-the-job strain or injury. Others may focus on sports vision, head trauma, or ocular disease and special testing. A few optometrists teach optometry, perform research, or consult.

Most optometrists are private practitioners who also handle the business aspects of running an office, such as developing a patient base, hiring employees, keeping paper and electronic records, and ordering equipment and supplies. Optometrists who operate franchise optical stores also may have some of these duties.

Optometrists should not be confused with ophthalmologists or dispensing opticians. Ophthalmologists are physicians who perform eye surgery, as well as diagnose and treat eye diseases and injuries. Like optometrists, they also examine eyes and prescribe eyeglasses and contact lenses. Dispensing opticians fit and adjust eyeglasses and, in some States, may fit contact lenses according to prescriptions written by ophthalmologists or optometrists. (See the sections on physicians and surgeons; and opticians, dispensing, elsewhere in the *Handbook*.)

Work environment. Optometrists usually work in their own offices that are clean, well lighted, and comfortable. Although most full-time optometrists work standard business hours, some work weekends and evenings to suit the needs of patients. Emergency calls, once uncommon, have increased with the passage of therapeutic-drug laws expanding optometrists' ability to prescribe medications.

Training, Other Qualifications, and Advancement

The Doctor of Optometry degree requires the completion of a 4-year program at an accredited school of optometry, preceded by at least 3 years of preoptometric study at an accredited college or university. All States require optometrists to be licensed.

Education and training. Optometrists need a Doctor of Optometry degree, which requires the completion of a 4-year program at an accredited school of optometry. In 2009, there were 19 colleges of optometry in the U.S. and 1 in Puerto Rico that offered programs accredited by the Accreditation Council on Optometric Education of the American Optometric Association. Requirements for admission to optometry schools include college courses in English, mathematics, physics, chemistry, and biology. Because a strong background in science is important, many applicants to optometry school major in a science, such as biology or chemistry, as undergraduates. Other applicants major in another subject and take many science courses offering laboratory experience.

Admission to optometry school is competitive; about 1 in 3 applicants was accepted in 2007. All applicants must take the Optometry Admissions Test (OAT), a standardized exam which measures academic ability and scientific comprehension. The OAT consists of four tests: survey of the natural sciences, such as biology, general chemistry, and organic chemistry; reading comprehension; physics; and quantitative reasoning. As a result, most applicants take the test after their sophomore or junior year in college, allowing them an opportunity to take the test again and raise their score. A few applicants are accepted to optometry school after 3 years of

Projections data from the National Employment Matrix

Occupational Title	SOC Code	Employment, 2008	Projected Employment, 2018	Change, 2008-2018	
				Number	Percent
Optometrists...	29-1041	34,800	43,200	8,500	24

(NOTE) Data in this table are rounded. See the discussion of the employment projections table in the *Handbook* introductory chapter on *Occupational Information Included in the Handbook.*

college and complete their bachelor's degree while attending optometry school. However, most students accepted by a school or college of optometry have completed an undergraduate degree. Each institution has its own undergraduate prerequisites, so applicants should contact the school or college of their choice for specific requirements.

Optometry programs include classroom and laboratory study of health and visual sciences and clinical training in the diagnosis and treatment of eye disorders. Courses in pharmacology, optics, vision science, biochemistry, and systemic diseases are included.

One-year postgraduate clinical residency programs are available for optometrists who wish to obtain advanced clinical competence within a particular area of optometry. Specialty areas for residency programs include family practice optometry, pediatric optometry, geriatric optometry, vision therapy and rehabilitation, low-vision rehabilitation, cornea and contact lenses, refractive and ocular surgery, primary eye care optometry, and ocular disease.

Licensure. All States and the District of Columbia require that optometrists be licensed. Applicants for a license must have a Doctor of Optometry degree from an accredited optometry school and must pass both a written National Board examination and a National, regional, or State clinical examination. The written and clinical examinations of the National Board of Examiners in Optometry usually are taken during the student's academic career. Many States also require applicants to pass an examination on relevant State laws. Licenses must be renewed every 1 to 3 years and, in all States, continuing education credits are needed for renewal.

Other qualifications. Business acumen, self-discipline, and the ability to deal tactfully with patients are important for success. The work of optometrists also requires attention to detail and manual dexterity.

Advancement. Optometrists who wish to teach or conduct research may study for a master's degree or Ph.D. in visual science, physiological optics, neurophysiology, public health, health administration, health information and communication, or health education.

Employment

Optometrists held about 34,800 jobs in 2008. Salaried jobs for optometrists were primarily in offices of optometrists; offices of physicians, including ophthalmologists; and health and personal care stores, including optical goods stores. A few salaried jobs for optometrists were in hospitals, the Federal Government, or outpatient care centers, including health maintenance organizations. About 25 percent of optometrists are self-employed. According to a 2008 survey by the American Optometric Association, most self-employed optometrists worked in private practice or in partnership with other health

care professionals. A small number worked for optical chains or franchises or as independent contractors.

Job Outlook

Employment of optometrists is expected to grow much faster than the average for all occupations through 2018, in response to the vision care needs of a growing and aging population. Excellent job opportunities are expected.

Employment change. Employment of optometrists is projected to grow 24 percent between 2008 and 2018. A growing population that recognizes the importance of good eye care will increase demand for optometrists. Also, an increasing number of health insurance plans that include vision care should generate more job growth.

As the population ages, there will likely be more visits to optometrists and ophthalmologists because of the onset of vision problems that occur at older ages, such as cataracts, glaucoma, and macular degeneration. In addition, increased incidences of diabetes and hypertension in the general population as well as in the elderly will generate greater demand for optometric services as these diseases often affect eyesight.

Employment of optometrists would grow more rapidly if not for productivity gains expected to allow each optometrist to see more patients. These expected gains stem from greater use of optometric assistants and other support personnel, who can reduce the amount of time optometrists need with each patient.

The increasing popularity of laser surgery to correct some vision problems was previously thought to have an adverse effect on the demand for optometrists as patients often do not require eyeglasses afterward. However, optometrists will still be needed to provide preoperative and postoperative care for laser surgery patients, therefore laser eye surgery will likely have little to no impact on the employment of optometrists.

Job prospects. Excellent job opportunities are expected over the next decade because there are only 19 schools of optometry in the United States, resulting in a limited number of graduates—about 1,200—each year. This number is not expected to keep pace with demand. However, admission to optometry school is competitive.

In addition to job growth, the need to replace optometrists who retire will also create many employment opportunities. According to the American Optometric Association, nearly one-quarter of practicing optometrists are approaching retirement age. As they begin to retire, many opportunities will arise, particularly in individual and group practices.

Earnings

Median annual wages of salaried optometrists were $96,320 in May 2008. The middle 50 percent earned between $70,140 and $125,460. Median annual wages of salaried optometrists in offices of optometrists were $92,670. Salaried optometrists tend to earn more initially than do optometrists who set up their own practices. In the long run, however, those in private practice usually earn more.

According to the American Optometric Association, average annual income for self-employed optometrists was $175,329 in 2007.

Self-employed optometrists, including those in individual, partnerships, and group practice, continue to earn higher income than those in other settings. Earnings also vary by group size. For example, practitioners in large groups—six or more—earn $159,300; practitioners in mid-sized groups—three to five people—earn $179,205; those in small practices—two people—earn $176,944; and individual practitioners earn an average of $134,094. Self-employed optometrists must also provide their own benefits. Practitioners associated with optical chains earn $100,704 on average. However, they typically enjoy paid vacation, sick leave, and pension contributions.

Related Occupations

Other workers who apply scientific knowledge to prevent, diagnose, and treat disorders and injuries include the following:

Sources of Additional Information

For information on optometry as a career and a list of accredited optometric institutions of education, contact:
➤ Association of Schools and Colleges of Optometry, 6110 Executive Blvd., Suite 420, Rockville, MD 20852. Internet: **http://www.opted.org**

Additional career information is available from:
➤ American Optometric Association, Educational Services, 243 N. Lindbergh Blvd., St. Louis, MO 63141. Internet: **http://www.aoa.org**

The board of optometry in each State can supply information on licensing requirements.

For information on specific admission requirements and sources of financial aid, contact the admissions officers of individual optometry schools.

The Occupational Information Network (O*NET) provides information on a wide range of occupational characteristics. Links to O*NET appear at the end of the Internet version of this occupational statement, accessible at

http://www.bls.gov/ooh/ocos073.htm

Pharmacists

Significant Points

- Excellent job opportunities are expected.
- Earnings are relatively high, but some pharmacists are required to work nights, weekends, and holidays.
- Pharmacists are becoming more involved in counseling patients and planning drug therapy programs.
- Pharmacists must graduate from an accredited college of pharmacy and pass a series of examinations to be licensed.

Nature of the Work

Pharmacists distribute prescription drugs to individuals. They also advise their patients, physicians, and other health practitioners on the selection, dosages, interactions, and side effects of medications, as well as monitor the health and progress of those patients to ensure that they are using their medications safely and effectively. Compounding—the actual mixing of ingredients to form medications—is a small part of a pharmacist's practice, because most medicines are produced by pharmaceutical companies in standard dosages and drug delivery forms. Most pharmacists work in a community setting, such as a retail drugstore, or in a healthcare facility, such as a hospital.

Pharmacists in community pharmacies dispense medications, counsel patients on the use of prescription and over-the-counter medications, and advise physicians about medication therapy. They also advise patients about general health topics, such as diet, exercise, and stress management, and provide information on products, such as durable medical equipment or home healthcare supplies. In addition, they often complete third-party insurance forms and other paperwork. Those who own or manage community pharmacies may sell non-health-related merchandise, hire and supervise personnel, and oversee the general operation of the pharmacy. Some community pharmacists provide specialized services to help patients with conditions such as diabetes, asthma, smoking cessation, or high

Pharmacists provide prescription medications to patients in hospitals, grocery stores, and a variety of other settings.

blood pressure. Some pharmacists are trained to administer vaccinations.

Pharmacists in healthcare facilities dispense medications and advise the medical staff on the selection and effects of drugs. They may make sterile solutions to be administered intravenously. They also plan, monitor, and evaluate drug programs or regimens. They may counsel hospitalized patients on the use of drugs before the patients are discharged.

Some pharmacists specialize in specific drug therapy areas, such as intravenous nutrition support, oncology (cancer), nuclear pharmacy (used for chemotherapy), geriatric pharmacy, and psychiatric pharmacy (the use of drugs to treat mental disorders).

Most pharmacists keep confidential computerized records of patients' drug therapies to prevent harmful drug interactions. Pharmacists are responsible for the accuracy of every prescription that is filled, but they often rely upon pharmacy technicians to assist them in the dispensing medications. (Pharmacy technicians are covered elsewhere in the *Handbook*.) Thus, the pharmacist may delegate prescription-filling and administrative tasks and supervise their completion. Pharmacists also frequently oversee pharmacy students serving as interns.

Some pharmacists are involved in research for pharmaceutical manufacturers, developing new drugs and testing their effects. Others work in marketing or sales, providing clients with expertise on the use, effectiveness, and possible side effects of drugs. Some pharmacists work for health insurance companies, developing pharmacy benefit packages and carrying out cost-benefit analyses on certain drugs. Other pharmacists work for the government, managed care organizations, public healthcare services, or the armed services. Finally, some pharmacists are employed full time or part time as college faculty, teaching classes and performing research in a wide range of areas.

Work environment. Pharmacists work in clean, well-lighted, and well-ventilated areas. Many pharmacists spend most of their workday on their feet. When working with sterile or dangerous pharmaceutical products, pharmacists wear gloves, masks, and other protective equipment.

Most pharmacists work about 40 hours a week, but about 12 percent worked more than 50 hours per week in 2008. In addition, about 19 percent of pharmacists worked part-time. Many community and hospital pharmacies are open for extended hours, so pharmacists may be required to work nights, weekends, and holidays. Consultant pharmacists may travel to healthcare facilities to monitor patients' drug therapies.

Training, Other Qualifications, and Advancement

A license is required in all States and the District of Columbia, as well as in Guam, Puerto Rico, and the U.S. Virgin Islands. In order to obtain a license, pharmacists generally must earn a

Doctor of Pharmacy (Pharm.D.) degree from a college of pharmacy and pass several examinations.

Education and training. Pharmacists who are trained in the United States must earn a Pharm.D. degree from an accredited college or school of pharmacy. The Pharm.D. degree has replaced the Bachelor of Pharmacy degree, which is no longer being awarded. To be admitted to a Pharm.D. program, an applicant must have completed at least 2 years of specific professional study. This requirement generally includes courses in mathematics and natural sciences, such as chemistry, biology, and physics, as well as courses in the humanities and social sciences. In addition, most applicants have completed 3 or more years at a college or university before moving on to a Pharm.D. program, although this is not specifically required.

Pharm.D. programs generally take 4 years to complete. The courses offered are designed to teach students about all aspects of drug therapy. In addition, students learn how to communicate with patients and other healthcare providers about drug information and patient care. Students also learn professional ethics, concepts of public health, and business management. In addition to receiving classroom instruction, students in Pharm.D. programs spend time working with licensed pharmacists in a variety of practice settings.

Some Pharm.D. graduates obtain further training through 1-year or 2-year residency programs or fellowships. Pharmacy residencies are postgraduate training programs in pharmacy practice and usually require the completion of a research project. The programs are often mandatory for pharmacists who wish to work in a clinical setting. Pharmacy fellowships are highly individualized programs that are designed to prepare participants to work in a specialized area of pharmacy, such clinical practice or research laboratories. Some pharmacists who own their own pharmacy obtain a master's degree in business administration (MBA). Others may obtain a degree in public administration or public health.

Licensure. A license to practice pharmacy is required in all States and the District of Columbia, as well as in Guam, Puerto Rico, and the U.S. Virgin Islands. To obtain a license, a prospective pharmacist generally must obtain a Pharm.D. degree from a college of pharmacy that has been approved by the Accreditation Council for Pharmacy Education. After obtaining the Pharm.D. degree, the individual must pass a series of examinations. All States, U.S. territories, and the District of Columbia require the North American Pharmacist Licensure Exam (NAPLEX), which tests pharmacy skills and knowledge. Forty-four States and the District of Columbia also require the Multistate Pharmacy Jurisprudence Exam (MPJE), which tests pharmacy law. Both exams are administered by the National Association of Boards of Pharmacy (NABP). Each of the eight States and territories that do not require the MJPE has its own pharmacy law exam. Besides requiring the NAPLEX and law examina-

Projections data from the National Employment Matrix

Occupational Title	SOC Code	Employment, 2008	Projected Employment, 2018	Change, 2008-2018	
				Number	Percent
Pharmacists	29-1051	269,900	315,800	45,900	17

(NOTE) Data in this table are rounded. See the discussion of the employment projections table in the *Handbook* introductory chapter on *Occupational Information Included in the Handbook.*

tion, some States and territories require additional exams that are unique to their jurisdictions. All jurisdictions also require a specified number of hours of experience in a practice setting before a license is awarded. In most jurisdictions, this requirement can be met while obtaining the Pharm.D. In many States, applicants must meet an age requirement before a license can be obtained, and some States require a criminal background check.

All States and U.S. territories except Puerto Rico permit licensure for graduates of foreign pharmacy schools. These individuals must apply for certification from the Foreign Pharmacy Graduate Examination Committee (FPGEC). Once certified, they must pass the Foreign Pharmacy Graduate Equivalency Examination (FPGEE), Test of English as a Foreign Language (TOEFL) exam, and Test of Spoken English (TSE) exam. Then they must pass all of the exams required by the licensing jurisdiction, such as the NAPLEX and MJPE, and meet the requirements for practical experience. In some States, applicants who graduated from programs accredited by the Canadian Council for Accreditation of Pharmacy Programs (CCAPP) between 1993 and 2004 are exempt from FPGEC certification and examination requirements.

Other qualifications. Prospective pharmacists should have scientific aptitude, good interpersonal skills, and a desire to help others. They also must be conscientious and pay close attention to detail, because the decisions they make affect human lives.

Advancement. In community pharmacies, pharmacists usually begin at the staff level. Pharmacists in chain drugstores may be promoted to pharmacy supervisor or store manager. Some pharmacists may be promoted to manager at the district or regional level and, later, to an executive position within the chain's headquarters. Hospital pharmacists may advance to supervisory or administrative positions. Some pharmacists become owners or part owners of independent pharmacies. Pharmacists in the pharmaceutical industry may advance in marketing, sales, research, quality control, production, or other areas.

Employment

Pharmacists held about 269,900 jobs in 2008. About 65 percent worked in retail settings. Most of these were salaried employees, but a small number were self-employed owners. About 22 percent of pharmacists worked in hospitals. A small proportion worked in mail-order and Internet pharmacies, pharmaceutical wholesalers, offices of physicians, and the Federal Government.

Job Outlook

Employment is expected to increase faster than the average. As a result of job growth, the need to replace workers who leave the occupation, and the limited capacity of training programs, job prospects should be excellent.

Employment change. Employment of pharmacists is expected to grow by 17 percent between 2008 and 2018, which is faster than the average for all occupations. The increasing numbers of middle-aged and elderly people—who use more prescription drugs than younger people—will continue to spur demand for pharmacists throughout the projection period. In addition, as scientific advances lead to new drug products, and as an increasing number of people obtain prescription drug coverage, the need for these workers will continue to expand.

Pharmacists also are becoming more involved in patient care. As prescription drugs become more complex, and as the number of people taking multiple medications increases, the potential for dangerous drug interactions will grow. Pharmacists will be needed to counsel patients on the proper use of medication, assist in drug selection and dosage, and monitor complex drug regimens. This need will lead to rapid growth for pharmacists in medical care establishments, such as doctors' offices, outpatient care centers, and nursing care facilities.

Demand also will increase in mail-order pharmacies, which often are more efficient than pharmacies in other practice settings. Employment also will continue to grow in hospitals, drugstores, grocery stores, and mass retailers, because pharmacies in these settings will continue to process the majority of all prescriptions and increasingly will offer patient care services, such as the administration of vaccines.

Job prospects. Job prospects are expected to be excellent over the 2008–18 period. Employers in many parts of the country report difficulty in attracting and retaining adequate numbers of pharmacists—primarily the result of the limited training capacity of Pharm.D. programs. In addition, as a larger percentage of pharmacists elects to work part time, more individuals will be needed to fill the same number of prescriptions. Job openings also will result from faster than average employment growth and from the need to replace workers who retire or leave the occupation for other reasons.

Earnings

Median annual wages of wage and salary pharmacists in May 2008 were $106,410. The middle 50 percent earned between $92,670 and $121,310 a year. The lowest 10 percent earned less than $77,390, and the highest 10 percent earned more than $131,440 a year.

Related Occupations

Other workers who are employed in pharmacies, work with pharmaceutical compounds, or are involved in patient care include:

	Page
Biological scientists	181
Medical scientists	189
Pharmacy technicians and aides	436
Physicians and surgeons	381
Registered nurses	392

Sources of Additional Information

For information on pharmacy as a career, preprofessional and professional requirements, programs offered by colleges of pharmacy, and student financial aid, contact:

➤ American Association of Colleges of Pharmacy, 1727 King St., Alexandria, VA 22314. Internet: **http://www.aacp.org**

General information on careers in pharmacy is available from:

➤ American Society of Health-System Pharmacists, 7272 Wisconsin Ave., Bethesda, MD 20814. Internet: **http://www.ashp.org**

➤ National Association of Chain Drug Stores, 413 N. Lee St., Alexandria, VA 22313. Internet: **http://www.nacds.org**

➤ Academy of Managed Care Pharmacy, 100 North Pitt St., Suite 400, Alexandria, VA 22314. Internet: **http://www.amcp.org**

➤ American Pharmacists Association, 2215 Constitution Ave. NW., Washington, DC 20037. Internet: **http://www.pharmacist.com**

Information on the North American Pharmacist Licensure Exam (NAPLEX) and the Multistate Pharmacy Jurisprudence Exam (MPJE) is available from:

➤ National Association of Boards of Pharmacy, 1600 Feehanville Dr., Mount Prospect, IL 60056. Internet: **http://www.nabp.net**

State licensure requirements are available from each State's board of pharmacy. Information on specific college entrance requirements, curricula, and financial aid is available from any college of pharmacy.

The Occupational Information Network (O*NET) provides information on a wide range of occupational characteristics. Links to O*NET appear at the end of the Internet version of this occupational statement, accessible at **http://www.bls.gov/ooh/ocos079.htm**

Physical Therapists

Significant Points

- Employment is expected to grow much faster than average.

- Job opportunities should be good.

- Today's entrants to this profession need a post-baccalaureate degree from an accredited physical therapist program.

- About 60 percent of physical therapists work in hospitals or in offices of other health practitioners.

Nature of the Work

Physical therapists, sometimes referred to as simply *PTs*, are healthcare professionals who diagnose and treat individuals of all ages, from newborns to the very oldest, who have medical problems or other health-related conditions, illnesses, or injuries that limits their abilities to move and perform functional activities as well as they would like in their daily lives. Physical therapists examine each individual and develop a plan using treatment techniques to promote the ability to move, reduce pain, restore function, and prevent disability. In addition, PTs work with individuals to prevent the loss of mobility before it occurs by developing fitness and wellness-oriented programs for healthier and more active lifestyles.

Physical therapists provide care to people of all ages who have functional problems resulting from, for example, back and neck injuries, sprains/strains and fractures, arthritis, burns, amputations, stroke, multiple sclerosis, conditions such as cerebral palsy and spina bifida, and injuries related to work and sports. Physical therapy care and services are provided by physical therapists and physical therapist assistants who work under the direction and supervision of a physical therapist. Physical therapists evaluate and diagnose movement dysfunction and use interventions to treat patient/clients. Interventions may include therapeutic exercise, functional training, manual therapy techniques, assistive and adaptive devices and equipment, and physical agents and electrotherapeutic modalities.

Physical therapists often consult and practice with a variety of other professionals, such as physicians, dentists, nurses, educators, social workers, occupational therapists, speech-language pathologists, and audiologists.

Work environment. Physical therapists practice in hospitals, outpatient clinics, and private offices that have specially equipped facilities. These jobs can be physically demanding, because therapists may have to stoop, kneel, crouch, lift, and stand for long periods. In addition, physical therapists move heavy equipment and lift patients or help them turn, stand, or walk.

In 2008, most full-time physical therapists worked a 40-hour week; some worked evenings and weekends to fit their patients' schedules. About 27 percent of physical therapists worked part-time.

Training, Other Qualifications, and Advancement

Today's entrants to this profession need a post-baccalaureate degree from an accredited physical therapy program. All States regulate the practice of physical therapy, which usually requires passing scores on national and State examinations.

Education and training. The American Physical Therapy Association's accrediting body, called the Commission on Accreditation of Physical Therapy Education (CAPTE), accredits entry-level academic programs in physical therapy. In 2009, there were 212 physical therapist education programs. Of these accredited programs, 12 awarded master's degrees; and 200 awarded doctoral degrees. Currently, only graduate degree physical therapist programs are accredited. Master's degree programs typically are

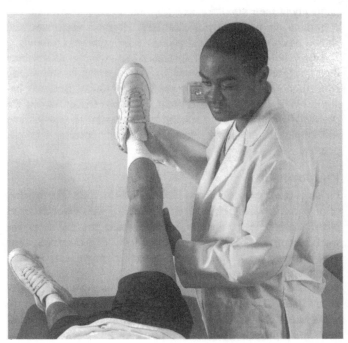

Physical therapists may practice in hospitals, clinics, private offices, private homes, or schools.

Projections data from the National Employment Matrix

Occupational Title	SOC Code	Employment, 2008	Projected Employment, 2018	Change, 2008-2018	
				Number	Percent
Physical therapists..	29-1123	185,500	241,700	56,200	30

(NOTE) Data in this table are rounded. See the discussion of the employment projections table in the *Handbook* introductory chapter on *Occupational Information Included in the Handbook.*

2 to 2.5 years in length, while doctoral degree programs last 3 years.

Physical therapist education programs include foundational science courses, such as biology, anatomy, physiology, cellular histology, exercise physiology, neuroscience, biomechanics, pharmacology, pathology, and radiology/imaging, as well as behavioral science courses, such as evidence-based practice and clinical reasoning. Some of the clinically-based courses include medical screening, examination tests and measures, diagnostic process, therapeutic interventions, outcomes assessment, and practice management. In addition to classroom and laboratory instruction, students receive supervised clinical experience.

Among the undergraduate courses that are useful when one applies to a physical therapist education program are anatomy, biology, chemistry, physics, social science, mathematics, and statistics. Before granting admission, many programs require volunteer experience in the physical therapy department of a hospital or clinic.

Licensure. All States regulate the practice of physical therapy. Eligibility requirements vary by State. Typical requirements for physical therapists include graduation from an accredited physical therapy education program; passing the National Physical Therapy Examination; and fulfilling State requirements such as jurisprudence exams. A number of States require continuing education as a condition of maintaining licensure.

Other qualifications. Physical therapists should have strong interpersonal and communication skills, so they can educate patients about their condition and physical therapy treatments and communicate with patients' families. Physical therapists also should be compassionate and possess a desire to help patients.

Advancement. Physical therapists are expected to continue their professional development by participating in continuing education courses and workshops. Some physical therapists become board certified in a clinical specialty. Opportunities for physical therapists exist in academia and research. Some become self-employed, providing contract services or opening a private practice.

Employment

Physical therapists held about 185,500 jobs in 2008. The number of physical therapist jobs is probably greater than the number of practicing physical therapists, because some physical therapists work part time, holding two or more jobs. For example, some may work in a private practice, but also work part time in another healthcare facility.

About 60 percent of physical therapists worked in hospitals or in offices of other health practitioners. Other jobs were in the home health care services industry, nursing care facilities, outpatient care centers, and offices of physicians. Some physical therapists were self-employed in private practices, seeing individual patients and contracting to provide services in hospitals, rehabili-

tation centers, nursing care facilities, home healthcare agencies, adult day care programs, and schools. Physical therapists also teach in academic institutions and conduct research.

Job Outlook

Employment is expected to grow much faster than average. Job opportunities should be good.

Employment change. Employment of physical therapists is expected to grow by 30 percent from 2008 to 2018, much faster than the average for all occupations. Changes to restrictions on reimbursement for physical therapy services by third-party payers will increase patient access to services and, thus, increase demand. The increasing elderly population will drive growth in the demand for physical therapy services. The elderly population is particularly vulnerable to chronic and debilitating conditions that require therapeutic services. Also, the baby-boom generation is entering the prime age for heart attacks and strokes, increasing the demand for cardiac and physical rehabilitation. Medical and technological developments will permit a greater percentage of trauma victims and newborns with birth defects to survive, creating additional demand for rehabilitative care. In addition, growth may result from advances in medical technology and the use of evidence-base practices, which could permit the treatment of an increasing number of disabling conditions that were untreatable in the past.

In addition, the federally mandated Individuals with Disabilities Education Act guarantees that students have access to services from physical therapists and other therapeutic and rehabilitative services. Demand for physical therapists will continue in schools.

Job prospects. Job opportunities will be good for licensed physical therapists in all settings. Job opportunities should be particularly good in acute hospital, skilled nursing, and orthopedic settings, where the elderly are most often treated. Job prospects should be especially favorable in rural areas as many physical therapists tend to cluster in highly populated urban and suburban areas.

Earnings

Median annual wages of physical therapists were $72,790 in May 2008. The middle 50 percent earned between $60,300 and $85,540. The lowest 10 percent earned less than $50,350, and the highest 10 percent earned more than $104,350. Median annual wages in the industries employing the largest numbers of physical therapists in May 2008 were:

Home health care services...$77,630
Nursing care facilities 76,680
General medical and surgical hospitals.......................73,270
Offices of physicians...72,790
Offices of other health practitioners...........................71,400

Related Occupations

Physical therapists rehabilitate people with physical disabilities and provide wellness and prevention programs. Others who work in the rehabilitation field include:

Sources of Additional Information

Additional career information and a list of accredited educational programs in physical therapy are available from:

➤ American Physical Therapy Association, 1111 North Fairfax St., Alexandria, VA 22314-1488. Internet: **http://www.apta.org**

➤ In addition, the American Physical Therapy Association has developed the PT Centralized Application Service (PTCAS) that allows one to apply to some of the accredited physical therapist programs. Internet: **http://www.ptcas.org**

The Occupational Information Network (O*NET) provides information on a wide range of occupational characteristics. Links to O*NET appear at the end of the Internet version of this occupational statement, accessible at **http://www.bls.gov/ooh/ocos080.htm**

Physician Assistants

Significant Points

- Requirements for admission to training programs vary; most applicants have a college degree and some health-related work experience.

- Physician assistants must complete an accredited education program and pass a national exam in order to obtain a license.

- Employment is projected to grow much faster than the average.

- Job opportunities should be good, particularly in rural and inner-city healthcare facilities.

Nature of the Work

Physician assistants (PAs) practice medicine under the supervision of physicians and surgeons. They should not be confused with medical assistants, who perform routine clinical and clerical tasks. (Medical assistants are discussed elsewhere in the *Handbook*.) PAs are formally trained to provide diagnostic, therapeutic, and preventive healthcare services, as delegated by a physician. Working as members of a healthcare team, they take medical histories, examine and treat patients, order and interpret laboratory tests and x rays, and make diagnoses. They also treat minor injuries by suturing, splinting, and casting. PAs record progress notes, instruct and counsel patients, and order or carry out therapy. Physician assistants also may prescribe certain medications. In some establishments, a PA is responsible for managerial duties, such as ordering medical supplies or equipment and supervising medical technicians and assistants.

Physician assistants work under the supervision of a physician. However, PAs may be the principal care providers in rural or inner-city clinics where a physician is present for only 1 or 2 days each week. In such cases, the PA confers with the supervising physician and other medical professionals as needed and as required by law. PAs also may make house calls or go to hospitals and nursing care facilities to check on patients, after which they report back to the physician.

The duties of physician assistants are determined by the supervising physician and by State law. Aspiring PAs should investigate the laws and regulations in the States in which they wish to practice.

Many PAs work in primary care specialties, such as general internal medicine, pediatrics, and family medicine. Other specialty areas include general and thoracic surgery, emergency medicine, orthopedics, and geriatrics. PAs specializing in surgery provide preoperative and postoperative care and may work as first or second assistants during major surgery.

Work environment. Although PAs usually work in a comfortable, well-lighted environment, those in surgery often stand for long periods. At times, the job requires a considerable amount of walking.

PA's work schedules may vary according to the practice setting and often depend on the hours of the supervising physician. The workweek of hospital-based PAs may include weekends, nights, or early morning hospital rounds to visit patients. These workers also may be on call. PAs in clinics usually work about a 40-hour week.

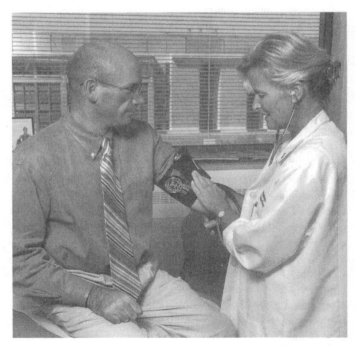

Physician assistants are formally trained to provide diagnostic, therapeutic, and preventive healthcare services, under the supervision of a physician.

Projections data from the National Employment Matrix

Occupational Title	SOC Code	Employment, 2008	Projected Employment, 2018	Change, 2008-2018	
				Number	Percent
Physician assistants..	29-1071	74,800	103,900	29,200	39

(NOTE) Data in this table are rounded. See the discussion of the employment projections table in the *Handbook* introductory chapter on *Occupational Information Included in the Handbook.*

Training, Other Qualifications, and Advancement

Requirements for admission to training programs vary; most applicants have a college degree and some health-related work experience. All States require physician assistants to complete an accredited, formal education program and pass a national exam to obtain a license.

Education and training. Physician assistant educational programs usually take at least 2 years to complete for full-time students. Most programs are at schools of allied health, academic health centers, medical schools, or 4-year colleges; a few are at community colleges, are part of the military, or are at hospitals. Many accredited PA programs have clinical teaching affiliations with medical schools.

In 2008, 142 education programs for physician assistants were accredited or provisionally accredited by the Accreditation Review Commission on Education for the Physician Assistant. Eighty percent, or 113, of these programs offered the option of a master's degree, 21 of them offered a bachelor's degree, 3 awarded associate degrees, and 5 awarded a certificate.

Most applicants to PA educational programs already have a college degree and some health-related work experience; however, admissions requirements vary from program to program. Many PAs have prior experience as registered nurses, emergency medical technicians, and paramedics.

PA education includes classroom and laboratory instruction in subjects like biochemistry, pathology, human anatomy, physiology, clinical pharmacology, clinical medicine, physical diagnosis, and medical ethics. PA programs also include supervised clinical training in several areas, including family medicine, internal medicine, surgery, prenatal care and gynecology, geriatrics, emergency medicine, and pediatrics. Sometimes, PA students serve in one or more of these areas under the supervision of a physician who is seeking to hire a PA. The rotation may lead to permanent employment in one of the areas where the student works.

Licensure. All States and the District of Columbia have legislation governing the practice of physician assistants. All jurisdictions require physician assistants to pass the Physician Assistant National Certifying Examination, administered by the National Commission on Certification of Physician Assistants (NCCPA) and open only to graduates of accredited PA education programs. Only those who have successfully completed the examination may use the credential "Physician Assistant-Certified." To remain certified, PAs must complete 100 hours of continuing medical education every 2 years. Every 6 years, they must pass a recertification examination or complete an alternative program combining learning experiences and a take-home examination.

Other qualifications. Physician assistants must have a desire to serve patients and be self-motivated. PAs also must have a good bedside manner, emotional stability, and the ability to make decisions in emergencies. Physician assistants should have an enthusiasm for lifelong learning, because their eligibility to practice depends on continuing education.

Advancement. Some PAs pursue additional education in a specialty. PA postgraduate educational programs are available in areas such as internal medicine, rural primary care, emergency medicine, surgery, pediatrics, neonatology, and occupational medicine. Candidates must be graduates of an accredited program and be certified by the NCCPA.

As they attain greater clinical knowledge and experience, PAs can earn new responsibilities and higher wages. However, by the very nature of the profession, clinically practicing PAs always are supervised by physicians.

Employment

Physician assistants held about 74,800 jobs in 2008. The number of jobs is greater than the number of practicing PAs because some hold two or more jobs. For example, some PAs work with a supervising physician but also work in another healthcare facility. According to the American Academy of Physician Assistants, about 15 percent of actively practicing PAs worked in more than one clinical job concurrently in 2008.

More than 53 percent of jobs for PAs were in the offices of physicians. About 24 percent were in general medical and surgical hospitals, public or private. The rest were mostly in outpatient care centers, including health maintenance organizations; the Federal Government; and public or private colleges, universities, and professional schools. Very few were self-employed.

Job Outlook

Employment is expected to grow much faster than the average for all occupations. Job opportunities for PAs should be good, particularly in rural and inner-city healthcare facilities.

Employment change. Employment of physician assistants is expected to grow by 39 percent from 2008 to 2018, much faster than the average for all occupations. Projected rapid job growth reflects the expansion of healthcare industries and an emphasis on cost containment, which results in increasing use of PAs by healthcare establishments.

Physicians and institutions are expected to employ more PAs to provide primary care and to assist with medical and surgical procedures because PAs are cost-effective and productive members of the healthcare team. Physician assistants can relieve physicians of routine duties and procedures. Healthcare providers will use more physician assistants as States continue to expand PAs' scope of practice by allowing them to perform more procedures.

Besides working in traditional office-based settings, PAs should find a growing number of jobs in institutional settings such as hospitals, academic medical centers, public clinics, and prisons.

Job prospects. Job opportunities for PAs should be good, particularly in rural and inner-city clinics because those settings have difficulty attracting physicians. Job openings will result both from employment growth and from the need to replace physician assistants who retire or leave the occupation permanently. Opportunities will be best in States that allow PAs a wider scope of practice.

Earnings
The median annual wage of physician assistants was $81,230 in May 2008. The middle 50 percent of physician assistants earned between $68,210 and $97,070. The lowest 10 percent earned less than $51,360, and the highest 10 percent earned more than $110,240. Median annual wages in the industries employing the largest numbers of physician assistants in May 2008 were:

General medical and surgical hospitals	$84,550
Outpatient care centers	84,390
Offices of physicians	80,440
Federal Executive Branch	78,200
Colleges, universities, and professional schools	74,200

According to the American Academy of Physician Assistants' 2008 Census Report, median income for physician assistants in full-time clinical practice was $85,710 in 2008; median income for first-year graduates was $74,470. Income varies by specialty, practice setting, geographical location, and years of experience. Employers often pay for their employees' professional liability insurance, registration fees with the Drug Enforcement Administration, State licensing fees, and credentialing fees.

Related Occupations
Occupations with similar educational backgrounds, healthcare experience, and/or responsibilities include:

Sources of Additional Information
For information on a career as a physician assistant, including a list of accredited programs, contact:
➤ American Academy of Physician Assistants Information Center, 950 North Washington St., Alexandria, VA 22314. Internet: **http://www.aapa.org**

For a list of accredited physician assistant programs, contact:
➤ Accreditation Review Commission on Education for the Physician Assistants, 12000 Findley Road, Suite 240, Johns Creek, Georgia 30097. Internet: **http://www.arc-pa.org**

For eligibility requirements and a description of the Physician Assistant National Certifying Examination, contact:
➤ National Commission on Certification of Physician Assistants, Inc., 12000 Findley Rd., Suite 200, Duluth, GA 30097. Internet: **http://www.nccpa.net**

The Occupational Information Network (O*NET) provides information on a wide range of occupational char-

acteristics. Links to O*NET appear at the end of the Internet version of this occupational statement, accessible at **http://www.bls.gov/ooh/ocos081.htm**

Physicians and Surgeons

Significant Points
- Many physicians and surgeons work long, irregular hours.
- Acceptance to medical school is highly competitive.
- Formal education and training requirements—typically 4 years of undergraduate school, 4 years of medical school, and 3 to 8 years of internship and residency—are among the most demanding of any occupation, but earnings are among the highest.
- Job opportunities should be very good, particularly in rural and low-income areas.

Nature of the Work
Physicians and surgeons diagnose illnesses and prescribe and administer treatment for people suffering from injury or disease. Physicians examine patients, obtain medical histories, and order, perform, and interpret diagnostic tests. They counsel patients on diet, hygiene, and preventive health care.

There are two types of physicians: *M.D.* (*Medical Doctor*) and D.O. (*Doctor of Osteopathic Medicine*). M.D.s also are known as *allopathic physicians*. While both M.D.s and D.O.s may use all accepted methods of treatment, including drugs and surgery, D.O.s place special emphasis on the body's musculoskeletal system, preventive medicine, and holistic patient care. D.O.s are most likely to be primary care specialists although they can be found in all specialties. About half of D.O.s practice general or family medicine, general internal medicine, or general pediatrics.

Physicians work in one or more of several specialties, including, but not limited to, anesthesiology, family and general medicine, general internal medicine, general pediatrics, obstetrics and gynecology, psychiatry, and surgery.

Anesthesiologists focus on the care of surgical patients and pain relief. Like other physicians, they evaluate and treat patients and direct the efforts of their staffs. Through continual monitoring and assessment, these critical care specialists are responsible for maintenance of the patient's vital life functions—heart rate, body temperature, blood pressure, breathing—during surgery. They also work outside of the operating room, providing pain relief in the intensive care unit, during labor and delivery, and for those who suffer from chronic pain. Anesthesiologists confer with other physicians and surgeons about appropriate treatments and procedures before, during, and after operations.

Family and general physicians often provide the first point of contact for people seeking health care, by acting as the traditional family physician. They assess and treat a wide range of conditions, from sinus and respiratory infections to broken bones. Family and general physician typically have a base of

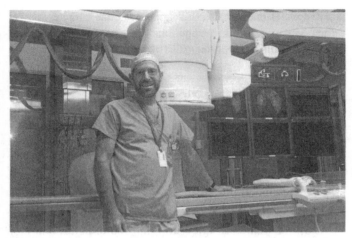

Physicians examine patients, obtain medical histories, and order, perform, and interpret diagnostic tests.

regular, long-term patients. These doctors refer patients with more serious conditions to specialists or other health care facilities for more intensive care.

General internists diagnose and provide nonsurgical treatment for a wide range of problems that affect internal organ systems, such as the stomach, kidneys, liver, and digestive tract. Internists use a variety of diagnostic techniques to treat patients through medication or hospitalization. Like general practitioners, general internists commonly act as primary care specialists. They treat patients referred from other specialists and, in turn, they refer patients to other specialists when more complex care is required.

General pediatricians care for the health of infants, children, teenagers, and young adults. They specialize in the diagnosis and treatment of a variety of ailments specific to young people and track patients' growth to adulthood. Like most physicians, pediatricians work with different health care workers, such as nurses and other physicians, to assess and treat children with various ailments. Most of the work of pediatricians involves treating day-to-day illnesses—minor injuries, infectious diseases, and immunizations—that are common to children, much as a general practitioner treats adults. Some pediatricians specialize in pediatric surgery or serious medical conditions, such as autoimmune disorders or serious chronic ailments.

Obstetricians and gynecologists (OB/GYNs) specialize in women's health. They are responsible for women's general medical care, and they also provide care related to pregnancy and the reproductive system. Like general practitioners, OB/GYNs attempt to prevent, diagnose, and treat general health problems, but they focus on ailments specific to the female anatomy, such as cancers of the breast or cervix, urinary tract and pelvic disorders, and hormonal disorders. OB/GYNs also specialize in childbirth, which includes treating and counseling women throughout their pregnancy, from giving prenatal diagnoses to assisting with delivery and providing postpartum care.

Psychiatrists are the primary mental health caregivers. They assess and treat mental illnesses through a combination of psychotherapy, psychoanalysis, hospitalization, and medication. Psychotherapy involves regular discussions with patients about their problems; the psychiatrist helps them find solutions through changes in their behavioral patterns, the exploration of their past experiences, or group and family therapy sessions. Psychoanalysis involves long-term psychotherapy and counseling for patients. In many cases, medications are administered to correct chemical imbalances that cause emotional problems.

Surgeons specialize in the treatment of injury, disease, and deformity through operations. Using a variety of instruments, and with patients under anesthesia, a surgeon corrects physical deformities, repairs bone and tissue after injuries, or performs preventive surgeries on patients with debilitating diseases or disorders. Although a large number perform general surgery, many surgeons choose to specialize in a specific area. One of the most prevalent specialties is orthopedic surgery: the treatment of the musculoskeletal system. Others include neurological surgery (treatment of the brain and nervous system), cardiovascular surgery, otolaryngology (treatment of the ear, nose, and throat), and plastic or reconstructive surgery. Like other physicians, surgeons also examine patients, perform and interpret diagnostic tests, and counsel patients on preventive health care.

Other physicians and surgeons work in a number of other medical and surgical specialists, including allergists, cardiologists, dermatologists, emergency physicians, gastroenterologists, ophthalmologists, pathologists, and radiologists.

Work environment. Many physicians—primarily general and family practitioners, general internists, pediatricians, OB/GYNs, and psychiatrists—work in small private offices or clinics, often assisted by a small staff of nurses and other administrative personnel. Increasingly, physicians are practicing in groups or health care organizations that provide backup coverage and allow for more time off. Physicians in a group practice or health care organization often work as part of a team that coordinates care for a number of patients; they are less independent than the solo practitioners of the past. Surgeons and anesthesiologists usually work in well-lighted, sterile environments while performing surgery and often stand for long periods. Most work in hospitals or in surgical outpatient centers.

Many physicians and surgeons work long, irregular hours. In 2008, 43 percent of all physicians and surgeons worked 50 or more hours a week. Nine percent of all physicians and surgeons worked part-time. Physicians and surgeons travel between office and hospital to care for their patients. While on call, a physician will deal with many patients' concerns over the phone and make emergency visits to hospitals or nursing homes.

Training, Other Qualifications, and Advancement
The common path to practicing as a physician requires 8 years of education beyond high school and 3 to 8 additional years of internship and residency. All States, the District of Columbia, and U.S. territories license physicians.

Education and training. Formal education and training requirements for physicians are among the most demanding of any occupation—4 years of undergraduate school, 4 years of medical school, and 3 to 8 years of internship and residency, depending on the specialty selected. A few medical schools offer combined undergraduate and medical school programs that last 6 or 7 years rather than the customary 8 years.

Premedical students must complete undergraduate work in physics, biology, mathematics, English, and inorganic and organic chemistry. Students also take courses in the humanities and the social sciences. Some students volunteer at local hospitals or clinics to gain practical experience in the health professions.

The minimum educational requirement for entry into medical school is 3 years of college; most applicants, however, have at least a bachelor's degree, and many have advanced degrees. In 2008, there were 129 medical schools accredited by the Liaison Committee on Medical Education (LCME). The LCME is the national accrediting body for M.D. medical education programs. The American Osteopathic Association accredits schools that award a D.O. degree; there were 25 schools accredited in 31 locations in 2008.

Acceptance to medical school is highly competitive. Most applicants must submit transcripts, scores from the Medical College Admission Test, and letters of recommendation. Schools also consider an applicant's character, personality, leadership qualities, and participation in extracurricular activities. Most schools require an interview with members of the admissions committee.

Students spend most of the first 2 years of medical school in laboratories and classrooms, taking courses such as anatomy, biochemistry, physiology, pharmacology, psychology, microbiology, pathology, medical ethics, and laws governing medicine. They also learn to take medical histories, examine patients, and diagnose illnesses. During their last 2 years, students work with patients under the supervision of experienced physicians in hospitals and clinics, learning acute, chronic, preventive, and rehabilitative care. Through rotations in internal medicine, family practice, obstetrics and gynecology, pediatrics, psychiatry, and surgery, they gain experience in the diagnosis and treatment of illness.

Following medical school, almost all M.D.s enter a residency—graduate medical education in a specialty that takes the form of paid on-the-job training, usually in a hospital. Most D.O.s serve a 12-month rotating internship after graduation and before entering a residency, which may last 2 to 6 years.

A physician's training is costly. According to the Association of American Medical Colleges, in 2007 85 percent of public medical school graduates and 86 percent of private medical school graduates were in debt for educational expenses.

Licensure and certification. To practice medicine as a physician, all States, the District of Columbia, and U.S. territories require licensing. All physicians and surgeons practicing in the United States must pass the United States Medical Licensing Examination (USMLE). To be eligible to take the USMLE in its entirety, physicians must graduate from an accredited medical school. Although physicians licensed in one State usually can get a license to practice in another without further examination, some States limit reciprocity. Graduates of foreign medical schools generally can qualify for licensure after passing an examination and completing a U.S. residency. For specific information on licensing in a given State, contact that State's medical board.

M.D.s and D.O.s seeking board certification in a specialty may spend up to 7 years in residency training, depending on the specialty. A final examination immediately after residency or after 1 or 2 years of practice is also necessary for certification by a member board of the American Board of Medical Special-

ists (ABMS) or the American Osteopathic Association (AOA). The ABMS represents 24 boards related to medical specialties ranging from allergy and immunology to urology. The AOA has approved 18 specialty boards, ranging from anesthesiology to surgery. For certification in a subspecialty, physicians usually need another 1 to 2 years of residency.

Other qualifications. People who wish to become physicians must have a desire to serve patients, be self-motivated, and be able to survive the pressures and long hours of medical education and practice. Physicians also must have a good bedside manner, emotional stability, and the ability to make decisions in emergencies. Prospective physicians must be willing to study throughout their career to keep up with medical advances.

Advancement. Some physicians and surgeons advance by gaining expertise in specialties and subspecialties and by developing a reputation for excellence among their peers and patients. Physicians and surgeons may also start their own practice or join a group practice. Others teach residents and other new doctors, and some advance to supervisory and managerial roles in hospitals, clinics, and other settings.

Employment

Physicians and surgeons held about 661,400 jobs in 2008; approximately 12 percent were self-employed. About 53 percent of wage-and-salary physicians and surgeons worked in offices of physicians, and 19 percent were employed by hospitals. Others practiced in Federal, State, and local governments, educational services, and outpatient care centers.

According to 2007 data from the American Medical Association (AMA), 32 percent of physicians in patient care were in primary care, but not in a subspecialty of primary care. (See table 1.)

Table 1. Percent distribution of active physicians in patient care by specialty, 2007

Specialty	Percent
Internal medicine	20
Family medicine/general practice	12
Pediatrics	10
Obstetrics and gynecology	6
Anesthesiology	6
Psychiatry	5
General Surgery	5
Emergency Medicine	4
SOURCE: American Medical Association, 2009 Physican Characteristic and Distribution in the US.	

A growing number of physicians are partners or wage-and-salary employees of group practices. Organized as clinics or as associations of physicians, medical groups can more easily afford expensive medical equipment, share support staff, and benefit from other business advantages.

According to the AMA, the New England and Middle Atlantic States have the highest ratios of physicians to population; the South Central and Mountain States have the lowest. Physicians tend to locate in urban areas, close to hospitals and education centers. AMA data showed that in 2007, about 75 percent of physicians in patient care were located in metropolitan areas while the remaining 25 percent were located in rural areas.

Projections data from the National Employment Matrix

Occupational Title	SOC Code	Employment, 2008	Projected Employment, 2018	Change, 2008-2018	
				Number	Percent
Physicians and surgeons..	29-1060	661,400	805,500	144,100	22

(NOTE) Data in this table are rounded. See the discussion of the employment projections table in the *Handbook* introductory chapter on *Occupational Information Included in the Handbook.*

Job Outlook

Employment is expected to grow much faster than the average for all occupations. Job opportunities should be very good, particularly in rural and low-income areas.

Employment change. Employment of physicians and surgeons is projected to grow 22 percent from 2008 to 2018, much faster than the average for all occupations. Job growth will occur because of continued expansion of health care-related industries. The growing and aging population will drive overall growth in the demand for physician services, as consumers continue to demand high levels of care using the latest technologies, diagnostic tests, and therapies. Many medical schools are increasing their enrollments based on perceived new demand for physicians.

Despite growing demand for physicians and surgeons, some factors will temper growth. For example, new technologies allow physicians to be more productive. This means physicians can diagnose and treat more patients in the same amount of time. The rising cost of health care can dramatically affect demand for physicians' services. Physician assistants and nurse practitioners, who can perform many of the routine duties of physicians at a fraction of the cost, may be increasingly used. Furthermore, demand for physicians' services is highly sensitive to changes in health care reimbursement policies. If changes to health coverage result in higher out-of-pocket costs for consumers, they may demand fewer physician services.

Job prospects. Opportunities for individuals interested in becoming physicians and surgeons are expected to be very good. In addition to job openings from employment growth, openings will result from the need to replace the relatively high number of physicians and surgeons expected to retire over the 2008–18 decade.

Job prospects should be particularly good for physicians willing to practice in rural and low-income areas because these medically underserved areas typically have difficulty attracting these workers. Job prospects will also be especially good for physicians in specialties that afflict the rapidly growing elderly population. Examples of such specialties are cardiology and radiology because the risks for heart disease and cancer increase as people age.

Earnings

Earnings of physicians and surgeons are among the highest of any occupation. According to the Medical Group Management Association's Physician Compensation and Production Survey, median total compensation for physicians varied by their type of practice. In 2008, physicians practicing primary care had total median annual compensation of $186,044, and physicians practicing in medical specialties earned total median annual compensation of $339,738.

Self-employed physicians—those who own or are part owners of their medical practice—generally have higher median incomes than salaried physicians. Earnings vary according to number of years in practice, geographic region, hours worked, skill, personality, and professional reputation. Self-employed physicians and surgeons must provide for their own health insurance and retirement.

Related Occupations

Physicians work to prevent, diagnose, and treat diseases, disorders, and injuries. Other health care practitioners who need similar skills and who exercise critical judgment include:

	Page
Chiropractors...	360
Dentists...	363
Optometrists	371
Physician assistants	379
Podiatrists...	385
Registered nurses	392
Veterinarians..	402

Sources of Additional Information

For a list of medical schools and residency programs, as well as general information on premedical education, financial aid, and medicine as a career contact:

➤ Association of American Medical Colleges, Section for Student Services, 2450 N St. NW., Washington, DC 20037. Internet: **http://www.aamc.org/students**

For information on licensing, contact:
➤ Federation of State Medical Boards, P.O. Box 619850 Dallas, TX 75261-9850. Internet: **http://www.fsmb.org**

For general information on physicians, contact:
➤ American Medical Association, 515 N. State St., Chicago, IL 60654. Internet:
http://www.ama-assn.org/go/becominganmd

➤ American Osteopathic Association, Department of Communications, 142 East Ontario St., Chicago, IL 60611. Internet: **http://www.osteopathic.org**

For information about various medical specialties, contact:
➤ American Academy of Family Physicians, Resident Student Activities Department, P.O. Box 11210, Shawnee Mission, KS 66207-1210. Internet: **http://fmignet.aafp.org**

➤ American Board of Medical Specialties, 222 N. LaSalle St., Suite 1500, Chicago, IL 60601. Internet: **http://www.abms.org**

➤ American College of Obstetricians and Gynecologists, P.O. Box 96920, Washington, DC 20090. Internet: **http://www.acog.org**

➤ American College of Surgeons, Division of Education, 633 North Saint Clair St., Chicago, IL 60611. Internet: **http://www.facs.org**

➤ American Psychiatric Association, 1000 Wilson Blvd., Suite 1825, Arlington, VA 22209. Internet: **http://www.psych.org**

➤ American Society of Anesthesiologists, 520 N. Northwest Hwy., Park Ridge, IL 60068. Internet: **http://www.asahq.org/career/homepage.htm**

Information on Federal scholarships and loans is available from the directors of student financial aid at schools of medicine. Information on licensing is available from State boards of examiners.

The Occupational Information Network (O*NET) provides information on a wide range of occupational characteristics. Links to O*NET appear at the end of the Internet version of this occupational statement, accessible at **http://www.bls.gov/ooh/ocos074.htm**

Podiatrists

Significant Points

- Podiatrists must be licensed, requiring 3 to 4 years of undergraduate education, the completion of a 4-year podiatric college program, and passing scores on national and State examinations.

- Job opportunities should be good for entry-level graduates of accredited podiatric medicine programs.

- Opportunities will be better in group medical practices, clinics, and health networks than in traditional, solo practices.

- Podiatrists enjoy very high earnings.

Nature of the Work

Americans spend a great deal of time on their feet. As the Nation becomes more active across all age groups, the need for foot care will become increasingly important. *Podiatrists*, also known as *doctors of podiatric medicine* (DPMs), diagnose and treat disorders, diseases, and injuries of the foot and lower leg.

Podiatrists treat corns, calluses, ingrown toenails, bunions, heel spurs, and arch problems; ankle and foot injuries, deformities, and infections; and foot complaints associated with diabetes and other diseases. To treat these problems, podiatrists prescribe drugs and physical therapy, set fractures, and perform surgery. They also fit corrective shoe inserts called orthotics, design plaster casts and strappings to correct deformities, and design custom-made shoes. Podiatrists may use a force plate or scanner to help design the orthotics: patients walk across a plate connected to a computer that "reads" their feet, picking up pressure points and weight distribution. From the computer readout, podiatrists order the correct design or recommend another kind of treatment.

To diagnose a foot problem, podiatrists also may order X rays and laboratory tests. The foot may be the first area to show signs

Podiatrists diagnose and treat disorders, diseases, and injuries of the foot and lower leg.

of serious conditions such as arthritis, diabetes, and heart disease. For example, patients with diabetes are prone to foot ulcers and infections because of poor circulation. Podiatrists consult with and refer patients to other health practitioners when they detect symptoms of these disorders.

Most podiatrists have a solo practice, although more are forming group practices with other podiatrists or health practitioners. Some specialize in surgery, orthopedics, primary care, or public health. Besides these board-certified specialties, podiatrists may practice other specialties, such as sports medicine, pediatrics, dermatology, radiology, geriatrics, or diabetic foot care.

Podiatrists who are in private practice are responsible for running a small business. They may hire employees, order supplies, and keep records, among other tasks. In addition, some educate the community on the benefits of foot care through speaking engagements and advertising.

Work environment. Podiatrists usually work in small private offices or clinics, sometimes supported by a small staff of assistants and other administrative personnel. They also may spend time visiting patients in nursing homes or performing surgery at hospitals or ambulatory surgical centers. Work hours vary from 30-60 hours per week. Podiatrists with private practices may set their own hours but may work evenings and weekends to accommodate their patients. Podiatrists usually treat fewer emergencies than other doctors.

Training, Other Qualifications, and Advancement

Podiatrists must be licensed, requiring 3 to 4 years of undergraduate education, the completion of a 4-year podiatric college program, and passing scores on national and State examinations.

Education and training. Prerequisites for admission to a college of podiatric medicine include the completion of at least 90 semester hours of undergraduate study, an acceptable grade point average, and suitable scores on the Medical College Admission Test. (Some colleges also may accept the Dental Admission Test or the Graduate Record Exam.)

Admission to podiatric colleges usually requires at least 8 semester hours each of biology, inorganic chemistry, organic chemistry, and physics and at least 6 hours of English. The science courses should be those designed for premedical students. Extracurricular and community activities, personal interviews, and letters of recommendation are also important. About 95 percent of podiatric students have at least a bachelor's degree.

In 2008, there were eight colleges of podiatric medicine fully accredited by the Council on Podiatric Medical Education. Colleges of podiatric medicine offer a 4-year program whose core curriculum is similar to that in other schools of medicine. During the first 2 years, students receive classroom instruction in basic sciences, including anatomy, chemistry, pathology, and pharmacology. Third-year and fourth-year students have clinical rotations in private practices, hospitals, and clinics. During these rotations, they learn how to take general and podiatric histories, perform routine physical examinations, interpret tests and findings, make diagnoses, and perform therapeutic procedures. Graduates receive the degree of Doctor of Podiatric Medicine (DPM).

Most graduates complete a hospital-based residency program after receiving a DPM. Residency programs last from 2 to 4 years. Residents receive advanced training in podiatric medicine and surgery and serve clinical rotations in anesthesiology, internal medicine, infectious disease, pediatrics, emergency medicine, and orthopedic and general surgery. Residencies lasting more than 1 year provide more extensive training in specialty areas.

Licensure. All States and the District of Columbia require a license for the practice of podiatric medicine. Each State defines its own licensing requirements, although many States grant reciprocity to podiatrists who are licensed in another State. Applicants for licensure must be graduates of an accredited college of podiatric medicine and must pass written and oral examinations. Some States permit applicants to substitute the examination of the National Board of Podiatric Medical Examiners, given in the second and fourth years of podiatric medical college, for part or all of the written State examination. In general, States require a minimum of 2 years of postgraduate residency training in an approved healthcare institution. For licensure renewal, most States require continuing education.

Other qualifications. People planning a career in podiatry should have scientific aptitude, manual dexterity, interpersonal skills, and a friendly bedside manner. In private practice, podiatrists also should have good business sense.

Certification and advancement. There are a number of certifying boards for the podiatric specialties of orthopedics, primary medicine, and surgery. Certification has requirements beyond licensure. Each board requires advanced training, the completion of written and oral examinations, and experience as a practicing podiatrist. Most managed-care organizations prefer board-certified podiatrists.

Podiatrists may advance to become professors at colleges of podiatric medicine, department chiefs in hospitals, or general health administrators.

Employment

Podiatrists held about 12,200 jobs in 2008. About 19 percent of podiatrists were self-employed. Most podiatrists were solo practitioners, although more are entering group practices with other podiatrists or other health practitioners. Solo practitioners were either unincorporated self-employed workers or incorporated wage and salary workers in offices of other health practitioners. Other podiatrists were employed by hospitals and the Federal Government.

Job Outlook

Employment is expected to increase about as fast as average. Job prospects should be good.

Employment change. Employment of podiatrists is expected to increase by 9 percent from 2008 to 2018, about as fast as the average for all occupations. More people will turn to podiatrists for foot care because of the rising number of injuries sustained by a more active and increasingly older population. Also, demand for podiatrists will increase because of the rising number of Americans who are diagnosed with diabetes and who are severely overweight. People with diabetes have circulatory problems that create the need for them to seek the aid of podiatrists; persons who experience rapid weight gain may have intense pressure on the foot and ankle, and therefore need the services of podiatrists.

Medicare and most private health insurance programs cover acute medical and surgical foot services, as well as diagnostic X rays and leg braces. Details of such coverage vary among plans. However, routine foot care, including the removal of corns and calluses, is not usually covered unless the patient has a systemic condition that has resulted in severe circulatory problems or areas of desensitization in the legs or feet. Like dental services, podiatric care is often discretionary and, therefore, more dependent on disposable income than some other medical services.

Employment of podiatrists would grow even faster were it not for continued emphasis on controlling the costs of specialty

Projections data from the National Employment Matrix

Occupational Title	SOC Code	Employment, 2008	Projected Employment, 2018	Change, 2008-2018	
				Number	Percent
Podiatrists..	29-1081	12,200	13,300	1,100	9

(NOTE) Data in this table are rounded. See the discussion of the employment projections table in the *Handbook* introductory chapter on *Occupational Information Included in the Handbook.*

healthcare. Insurers will balance the cost of sending patients to podiatrists against the cost and availability of substitute practitioners, such as physicians, chiropractors, and physical therapists.

Job prospects. Although the occupation is small and most podiatrists continue to practice until retirement, job opportunities should be good for entry-level graduates of accredited podiatric medicine programs. Job growth, coupled with the need to replace podiatrists who stop practicing, should create enough job openings for the supply of new podiatric medicine graduates. Opportunities will be better for board-certified podiatrists because many managed-care organizations require board certification. Newly trained podiatrists will find more opportunities in group medical practices, clinics, and health networks than in traditional solo practices. Establishing a practice will be most difficult in the areas surrounding colleges of podiatric medicine, where podiatrists concentrate.

Earnings

Podiatrists enjoy very high earnings. Median annual wages of salaried podiatrists were $113,560 in May 2008. Additionally, a survey by *Podiatry Management Magazine* reported median net income of $114,768 in 2008. Podiatrists in partnerships tended to earn higher net incomes than those in solo practice. Salaried podiatrists typically receive heath insurance and retirement benefits from their employer, whereas self-employed podiatrists must provide for their own health insurance and retirement. Also, solo practitioners must absorb the costs of running their own offices.

Related Occupations

Other workers who apply medical knowledge to prevent, diagnose, and treat muscle and bone disorders and injuries include:

Workers who specialize in developing orthopedic shoe inserts, braces, and prosthetic limbs are:

Sources of Additional Information

For information on a career in podiatric medicine, contact:
➤ American Podiatric Medical Association, 9312 Old Georgetown Rd., Bethesda, MD 20814-1621. Internet: **http://www.apma.org**

Information on colleges of podiatric medicine and their entrance requirements, curricula, and student financial aid is available from:
➤ American Association of Colleges of Podiatric Medicine, 15850 Crabbs Branch Way, Suite 320, Rockville, MD 20855. Internet: **http://www.aacpm.org**

The Occupational Information Network (O*NET) provides information on a wide range of occupational char-

acteristics. Links to O*NET appear at the end of the Internet version of this occupational statement, accessible at **http://www.bls.gov/ooh/ocos075.htm**

Radiation Therapists

Significant Points

- A bachelor's degree, associate degree, or certificate in radiation therapy is generally required.
- Employment is projected to grow much faster than the average for all occupations.
- Good job opportunities are expected.
- Earnings are relatively high.

Nature of the Work

Radiation therapy is used to treat cancer in the human body. As part of a medical radiation oncology team, radiation therapists use machines called linear accelerators to administer radiation treatment to patients. Linear accelerators are most commonly used in a procedure called external beam therapy, which projects high-energy x-rays at targeted cancer cells. As the X-rays collide with human tissue, they produce highly energized ions that can shrink and eliminate cancerous tumors. Radiation therapy is sometimes used as the sole treatment for cancer, but it is usually used in conjunction with chemotherapy or surgery.

Before treatment can begin, the oncology team has to develop a treatment plan. To create this plan, the radiation therapist must first use an X-ray imaging machine or computer tomography (CT) scan to pinpoint the location of the tumor. Then, a radiation oncologist (a physician who specializes in therapeutic radiology) and a radiation physicist (a worker who calibrates the linear accelerator) determine the best way to administer treatment. The therapist completes the plan by positioning the patient and adjusting the linear accelerator to the specifications developed by the team, recording the details so that these conditions can be replicated during treatment. The

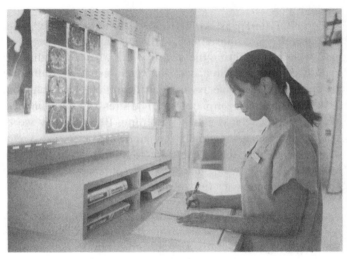

Radiation therapists have good job prospects.

Projections data from the National Employment Matrix

Occupational Title	SOC Code	Employment, 2008	Projected Employment, 2018	Change, 2008-2018	
				Number	Percent
Radiation therapists..	29-1124	15,200	19,400	4,100	27

(NOTE) Data in this table are rounded. See the discussion of the employment projections table in the *Handbook* introductory chapter on *Occupational Information Included in the Handbook*.

therapist later explains the treatment plan to the patient and answers any questions that the patient may have.

The next step in the process is treatment. To begin each treatment session, the radiation therapist uses the guidelines developed during the planning phase to position the patient and adjust the linear accelerator. Then, from a separate room that is protected from the X-ray radiation, the therapist operates the linear accelerator and monitors the patient's condition through a TV monitor and an intercom system. Treatment can take anywhere from 10 to 30 minutes.

During the treatment phase, the radiation therapist monitors the patient's physical condition to determine whether the patient is having any adverse reactions to the treatment. The therapist must also be aware of the patient's emotional well-being. Because many patients are under stress and are emotionally fragile, it is important for the therapist to maintain a positive attitude and provide emotional support.

Radiation therapists keep detailed records of their patients' treatments. These records include information such as the dose of radiation used for each treatment, the total amount of radiation used to date, the area treated, and the patient's reactions. Radiation oncologists and dosimetrists (technicians who calculate the dose of radiation that will be used for treatment) review these records to ensure that the treatment plan is working, to monitor the amount of radiation exposure that the patient has received, and to keep side effects to a minimum. Therapists also may assist dosimetrists with routine aspects of dosimetry, the process used to calculate radiation dosages.

Work environment. Radiation therapists work in hospitals or in cancer treatment centers. These places are clean, well lighted, and well ventilated. Therapists do a considerable amount of lifting and must be able to help disabled patients get on and off treatment tables. They spend most of their time on their feet.

Radiation therapists generally work 40 hours a week, and unlike workers in some other healthcare occupations, they normally work only during the day. However, because radiation therapy emergencies do occur, some therapists are required to be on call and may have to work outside of their normal hours.

Working with cancer patients can be stressful, but many radiation therapists also find it rewarding. Because they work around radioactive materials, radiation therapists take great care to ensure that they are not exposed to dangerous levels of radiation. By following standard safety procedures, radiation therapists can prevent overexposure.

Training, Other Qualifications, and Advancement

A bachelor's degree, associate degree, or certificate in radiation therapy generally is required. Many States require radiation therapists to be licensed, and most employers require certification. With experience, therapists can advance to managerial positions.

Education and training. Employers usually require applicants to complete an associate or a bachelor's degree program in radiation therapy. Individuals also may become qualified by completing an associate or a bachelor's degree program in radiography, which is the study of radiological imaging, and then by completing a 12-month certificate program in radiation therapy. Radiation therapy programs include core courses on radiation therapy procedures and the scientific theories behind them. In addition, such programs often include courses on human anatomy and physiology, physics, algebra, precalculus, writing, public speaking, computer science, and research methodology. In 2009, there were 102 radiation therapy programs in the U.S. that were accredited by the American Registry of Radiologic Technologists (ARRT).

Licensure. In 2009, 33 States required radiation therapists to be licensed by a State accrediting board. Licensing requirements vary by State, but many States require applicants to pass the ARRT certification examination. Further information is available from individual State licensing offices.

Certification and other qualifications. Some States, as well as many employers, require radiation therapists to be certified by ARRT. To become ARRT-certified, an applicant must complete an accredited radiation therapy program, adhere to ARRT ethical standards, and pass the ARRT certification examination. The examination covers radiation protection and quality assurance, clinical concepts in radiation oncology, treatment planning, treatment delivery, and patient care and education. Candidates also must demonstrate competency in several clinical practices including patient care activities; simulation procedures; dosimetry calculations; fabrication of beam modification devices; low-volume, high-risk procedures; and the application of radiation.

ARRT certification is valid for 1 year, after which therapists must renew their certification. Requirements for renewal include abiding by the ARRT ethical standards, paying annual dues, and satisfying continuing education requirements. Continuing education requirements must be met every 2 years and include either the completion of 24 course credits related to radiation therapy or the attainment of ARRT certification in a discipline other than radiation therapy. Certification renewal, however, may not be required by all States or employers that require initial certification.

All radiation therapists need good communication skills because their work involves a great deal of interaction with patients. Individuals interested in becoming radiation therapists should be psychologically capable of working with cancer patients. They should be caring and empathetic because they work with patients who are ill and under stress. They should be able to keep accurate, detailed records. They also should be physically fit because they work on their feet for long periods and lift and move disabled patients.

Advancement. Experienced radiation therapists may advance to manage radiation therapy programs in treatment centers or other health care facilities. Managers generally continue to treat patients while taking on management responsibilities. Other advancement opportunities include teaching, technical sales, and research. With additional training and certification, therapists also can become dosimetrists, who use complex mathematical formulas to calculate proper radiation doses.

Employment

Radiation therapists held about 15,200 jobs in 2008. About 70 percent worked in hospitals, and about 18 percent worked in the offices of physicians. A small proportion worked in outpatient care centers and medical and diagnostic laboratories.

Job Outlook

Employment is expected to increase much faster than the average, and job prospects should be good.

Employment change. Employment of radiation therapists is projected to grow by 27 percent between 2008 and 2018, which is much faster than the average for all occupations. The growing elderly population is expected to cause an increase in the number of people needing treatment. In addition, as radiation technology becomes safer and more effective, it will be prescribed more often, leading to an increased demand for radiation therapists. Growth is likely to be rapid across all practice settings, including hospitals, physicians' offices, and outpatient centers.

Job prospects. Job prospects are expected to be good. Job openings will result from employment growth and from the need to replace workers who retire or leave the occupation for other reasons. Applicants with a bachelor's degree and related work experience may have the best opportunities.

Earnings

Median annual wages of radiation therapists were $72,910 in May 2008. The middle 50 percent earned between $59,050 and $87,910. The lowest 10 percent earned less than $47,910, and the highest 10 percent earned more than $104,350. Some employers also reimburse their employees for the cost of continuing education.

Related Occupations

Other occupations that administer medical treatment to patients include

Sources of Additional Information

Information on certification by the American Registry of Radiologic Technologists and on accredited radiation therapy programs may be obtained from:

➤ American Registry of Radiologic Technologists, 1255 Northland Dr., St. Paul, MN 55120. Internet: **http://www.arrt.org**

Information on careers in radiation therapy may be obtained from:

➤ American Society of Radiologic Technologists, 15000 Central Ave. SE., Albuquerque, NM 87123. Internet: **http://www.asrt.org**

The Occupational Information Network (O*NET) provides information on a wide range of occupational characteristics. Links to O*NET appear at the end of the Internet version of this occupational statement, accessible at **http://www.bls.gov/ooh/ocos299.htm**

Recreational Therapists

Significant Points

- Applicants for recreational therapist jobs will experience competition.

- A bachelor's degree in therapeutic recreation is the usual educational requirement.

- Some States regulate recreational therapists through licensure, registration, or regulation of titles, but requirements vary.

- Recreational therapists should be comfortable working with persons who are ill or who have disabilities.

Nature of the Work

Recreational therapists, also referred to as *therapeutic recreation specialists*, provide treatment services and recreation activities for individuals with disabilities or illnesses. Using a variety of techniques, including arts and crafts, animals, sports, games, dance and movement, drama, music, and community outings, therapists improve and maintain the physical, mental, and emotional well-being of their clients. Therapists help individuals reduce depression, stress, and anxiety; recover basic motor functioning and reasoning abilities; build confidence; and socialize effectively so that they can enjoy greater independence and reduce or eliminate the effects of their illness or disability. In addition, therapists help people with disabilities integrate into the community by teaching them how to use community resources and recreational activities. Recreational therapists are different from *recreation workers*, who organize recreational activities primarily for enjoyment. (Recreation workers are discussed elsewhere in the *Handbook*.)

In acute healthcare settings, such as hospitals and rehabilitation centers, recreational therapists treat and rehabilitate individuals with specific health conditions, usually in conjunction or collaboration with physicians, nurses, psychologists, social workers, and physical and occupational therapists. In long-term and residential care facilities, recreational therapists use leisure activities—especially structured group programs—to improve and maintain their clients' general health and well-being. They also may provide interventions to prevent the client from suffering further medical problems and complications.

Recreational therapists assess clients using information from observations, medical records, standardized assessments, the medical staff, the clients' families, and the clients themselves. They then develop and carry out therapeutic interventions consistent with the clients' needs and interests. For example, they may encourage clients who are isolated from others or who have limited social skills to play games with others, and they may teach right-handed people with right-side paralysis how to use their unaffected left side to throw a ball or swing a racket. Recreational therapists may instruct patients in relaxation techniques to reduce stress and tension, stretching and limbering exercises, proper body mechanics for participation in recreational activities, pacing and energy conservation techniques, and team activities. As they work, therapists observe and document a patient's participation, reactions, and progress.

Community-based recreational therapists may work in park and recreation departments, special education programs for school districts, or assisted living, adult day care, and substance abuse rehabilitation centers. In these programs, therapists use interventions to develop specific skills, while providing opportunities for exercise, mental stimulation, creativity, and fun. Those few who work in schools help counselors, teachers, and parents address the special needs of students, including easing disabled students' transition into adult life.

Work environment. Recreational therapists provide services in special activity rooms but also plan activities and prepare documentation in offices. When working with clients during community integration programs, they may travel locally to teach clients how to use public transportation and other pub-

lic areas, such as parks, playgrounds, swimming pools, restaurants, and theaters. Therapists often lift and carry equipment.

Recreational therapists generally work a 40-hour week. Work hours may include some evenings, weekends, and holidays. Some therapists may work part time and for more than one employer, requiring travel.

Training, Other Qualifications, and Advancement
A bachelor's degree with a major or concentration in therapeutic recreation is the usual requirement. Some States regulate recreational therapists, but requirements vary.

Education and training. Most entry-level recreational therapists need a bachelor's degree in therapeutic recreation, or in recreation with a concentration in therapeutic recreation. A few may qualify with some combination of education, training, and work experience that would be equivalent to what is considered competent in the field. There are more than 100 academic programs that prepare students to become recreational therapists. Most offer bachelor's degrees, although some offer associate's, master's, or doctoral degrees. Therapeutic recreation programs include courses in assessment, treatment and program planning, intervention design, and evaluation. Students also study human anatomy, physiology, abnormal psychology, medical and psychiatric terminology, characteristics of illnesses and disabilities, professional ethics, and the use of assistive devices and technology. Bachelor's degree programs include an internship in the field as part of their curriculum.

Licensure. Some States regulate recreational therapists through licensure, registration, or regulation of titles. Requirements vary by State. In 2009, Oklahoma, North Carolina, Utah, and New Hampshire required licensure to practice as a recreational therapist. For specifics on regulations and requirements, contact the State's medical board.

Certification and other qualifications. Although certification is voluntary, most employers prefer to hire candidates who are certified therapeutic recreation specialists. Work in clinical settings often requires certification by the National Council for Therapeutic Recreation Certification. The council offers the Certified Therapeutic Recreation Specialist credential to candidates who pass a written certification examination and complete a supervised internship of at least 480 hours. A minimum of a bachelor's degree in recreational therapy from an accredited institution is required for credentialing, but some may qualify with equivalent education, training, and experience. Therapists must meet additional requirements to maintain certification. For specific details on credentialing, contact the National Council for Therapeutic Recreation Certification. (See Sources of Additional Information below for address.)

Recreational therapists may dedicate themselves to a certain type of therapy. Therapists wanting to practice a concentration can also earn certifications in specific therapies, such as art therapy and aquatic therapy.

Recreational therapists must be comfortable working with people who are ill or disabled. Therapists must be patient, tactful, and persuasive when working with people who have a variety of special needs. Ingenuity, a sense of humor, and imagination are needed to adapt activities to individual needs, and good

Recreational therapists observe and document a patient's participation, reaction, and progress.

Projections data from the National Employment Matrix

Occupational Title	SOC Code	Employment, 2008	Projected Employment, 2018	Change, 2008-2018	
				Number	Percent
Recreational therapists..	29-1125	23,300	26,700	3,400	15

(NOTE) Data in this table are rounded. See the discussion of the employment projections table in the *Handbook* introductory chapter on *Occupational Information Included in the Handbook.*

physical coordination is necessary to demonstrate or participate in recreational activities.

Advancement. Therapists may advance to supervisory or administrative positions. Some teach, conduct research, or consult for health or social services agencies.

Employment

Recreational therapists held about 23,300 jobs in 2008. About 24 percent were in nursing care facilities. Others worked primarily in hospitals, residential care facilities, and State and local government agencies.

Job Outlook

Employment is projected to grow faster than the average. Applicants will face competition for jobs.

Employment change. Employment of recreational therapists is expected to increase 15 percent from 2008 to 2018, faster than the average for all occupations. Job growth will stem from the therapy needs of the aging population. With age comes an inevitable decrease in physical ability and, in some cases, mental ability, which can be limited or managed with recreation therapy. In nursing care facilities—the largest industry employing recreational therapists—employment will grow faster than the occupation as a whole as the number of older adults continues to grow.

Employment growth in schools will result from the expansion of the school-age population and the federally funded extension of services for disabled students.

Reimbursement for recreational therapy services will continue to affect how and where therapeutic recreation is provided. As payers and employers try to contain costs, recreation therapy services will shift to outpatient settings and away from hospitals.

Job prospects. Recreational therapists will experience competition for jobs. Lower paid recreational therapy aides may be increasingly used in an effort to contain costs. Job opportunities should be best for people with a bachelor's degree in therapeutic recreation and the Certified Therapeutic Recreation Specialist credential. Recreational therapists might experience more competition for jobs in certain regions of the country as jobs in therapeutic recreation tend to cluster in more densely populated areas.

Earnings

Median annual wages of recreational therapists were $38,370 in May 2008. The middle 50 percent earned between $29,660 and $49,140. The lowest 10 percent earned less than $23,150,

and the highest 10 percent earned more than $60,280. Median annual wages in the industries employing the largest numbers of recreational therapists in May 2008 were:

General medical and surgical hospitals	$42,210
State government	40,310
Psychiatric and substance abuse hospitals	40,150
Nursing care facilities	33,920
Community care facilities for the elderly	33,490

Related Occupations

Recreational therapists primarily design activities to help people with disabilities lead more fulfilling and independent lives. Other occupations in therapy and rehabilitation include:

Sources of Additional Information

For information and materials on careers and academic programs in recreational therapy, contact:

➤ American Therapeutic Recreation Association, 629 N. Main St., Hattiesburg, MS 39401. Internet: **http://atra-online.com/**

➤ National Therapeutic Recreation Society, 22377 Belmont Ridge Rd., Ashburn, VA 20148-4501. Internet: **http://www.nrpa.org/**

Information on certification may be obtained from:

➤ National Council for Therapeutic Recreation Certification, 7 Elmwood Dr., New City, NY 10956. Internet: **http://www.nctrc.org**

For information on licensure requirements, contact the appropriate recreational therapy regulatory agency for your State.

The Occupational Information Network (O*NET) provides information on a wide range of occupational characteristics. Links to O*NET appear at the end of the Internet version of this occupational statement, accessible at

http://www.bls.gov/ooh/ocos082.htm

Registered Nurses

Significant Points

- Registered nurses (RNs) constitute the largest health-care occupation, with 2.6 million jobs.

- About 60 percent of RN jobs are in hospitals.

- The three typical educational paths to registered nursing are a bachelor's degree, an associate degree, and a diploma from an approved nursing program; advanced practice nurses—clinical nurse specialists, nurse anesthetists, nurse-midwives, and nurse practitioners—need a master's degree.

- Overall job opportunities are expected to be excellent, but may vary by employment and geographic setting; some employers report difficulty in attracting and retaining an adequate number of RNs.

Nature of the Work

Registered nurses (RNs), regardless of specialty or work setting, treat patients, educate patients and the public about various medical conditions, and provide advice and emotional support to patients' family members. RNs record patients' medical histories and symptoms, help perform diagnostic tests and analyze results, operate medical machinery, administer treatment and medications, and help with patient follow-up and rehabilitation.

RNs teach patients and their families how to manage their illnesses or injuries, explaining post-treatment home care needs; diet, nutrition, and exercise programs; and self-administration of medication and physical therapy. Some RNs may work to promote general health by educating the public on warning signs and symptoms of disease. RNs also might run general health screening or immunization clinics, blood drives, and public seminars on various conditions.

When caring for patients, RNs establish a care plan or contribute to an existing plan. Plans may include numerous activities, such as administering medication, including careful checking of dosages and avoiding interactions; starting, maintaining, and discontinuing intravenous (IV) lines for fluid, medication, blood, and blood products; administering therapies and treatments; observing the patient and recording those observations; and consulting with physicians and other healthcare clinicians. Some RNs provide direction to licensed practical nurses and nursing aides regarding patient care. (See the statements on licensed practical and licensed vocational nurses; nursing and psychiatric aides; and home health aides elsewhere in the Handbook). RNs with advanced educational preparation and training may perform diagnostic and therapeutic procedures and may have prescriptive authority.

Specific work responsibilities will vary from one RN to the next. An RN's duties and title are often determined by their work setting or patient population served. RNs can specialize in one or more areas of patient care. There generally are four ways to specialize. RNs may work a particular setting or type of treatment, such as *perioperative nurses*, who work in operating rooms and assist surgeons. RNs may specialize in specific health conditions, as do *diabetes management nurses*, who assist patients to manage diabetes. Other RNs specialize in working with one or more organs or body system types, such as *dermatology nurses*, who work with patients who have skin disorders. RNs may also specialize with a well-defined population, such as *geriatric nurses*, who work with the elderly. Some RNs may combine specialties. For example, *pediatric oncology nurses* deal with children and adolescents who have cancer. The opportunities for specialization in registered nursing are extensive and are often determined on the job.

There are many options for RNs who specialize in a work setting or type of treatment. *Ambulatory care nurses* provide preventive care and treat patients with a variety of illnesses and injuries in physicians' offices or in clinics. Some ambulatory care nurses are involved in telehealth, providing care and advice through electronic communications media such as videoconferencing, the Internet, or by telephone. *Critical care nurses* provide care to patients with serious, complex, and acute illnesses or injuries that require very close monitoring and extensive medication protocols and therapies. Critical care nurses often work in critical or intensive care hospital units. *Emergency*, or *trauma*, *nurses* work in hospital or stand-alone emergency departments, providing initial assessments and care for patients with life-threatening conditions. Some emergency nurses may become qualified to serve as *transport nurses*, who provide medical care to patients who are transported by helicopter or airplane to the nearest medical facility. *Holistic nurses* provide care such as acupuncture, massage and aroma therapy, and biofeedback, which are meant to treat patients' mental and spiritual health in addition to their physical health. *Home health care nurses* provide at-home nursing care for patients, often as follow-up care after discharge from a hospital or from a rehabilitation, long-term care, or skilled nursing facility. *Hospice and palliative care nurses* provide care, most often in home or hospice settings, focused on maintaining quality of life for terminally ill patients. *Infusion nurses* administer medications, fluids, and blood to patients through injections into patients' veins. *Long-term care nurses* provide healthcare services on a recurring basis to patients with chronic physical or mental disorders, often in long-term care or skilled nursing facilities. *Medical-surgical nurses* provide health promotion and basic medical care to patients with various medical and surgical diagnoses. *Occupational health nurses* seek to prevent job-related injuries and illnesses, provide monitoring and emergency care services, and help employers implement health and safety standards. *Perianesthesia nurses* provide preoperative and postoperative care to patients undergoing anesthesia during surgery or other procedure. Perioperative nurses assist surgeons by selecting and handling instruments, controlling bleeding, and suturing incisions. Some of these nurses also can specialize in plastic and reconstructive surgery. *Psychiatric-mental health nurses* treat patients with personality and mood disorders. *Radiology nurses* provide care to patients undergoing diagnostic radiation procedures such as ultrasounds, magnetic resonance imaging, and radiation therapy for oncology diagnoses. *Rehabilitation nurses* care for patients with temporary and permanent disabilities. *Transplant nurses* care for both transplant recipients and living donors and monitor signs of organ rejection.

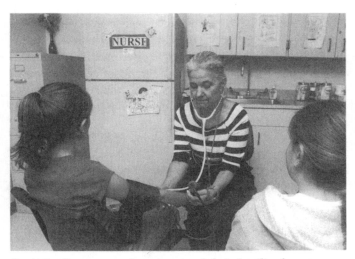

Registered nurses teach patients and their families how to manage their illness or injury.

RNs specializing in a particular disease, ailment, or healthcare condition are employed in virtually all work settings, including physicians' offices, outpatient treatment facilities, home healthcare agencies, and hospitals. *Addictions nurses* care for patients seeking help with alcohol, drug, tobacco, and other addictions. *Intellectual and developmental disabilities nurses* provide care for patients with physical, mental, or behavioral disabilities; care may include help with feeding, controlling bodily functions, sitting or standing independently, and speaking or other communication. *Diabetes management nurses* help diabetics to manage their disease by teaching them proper nutrition and showing them how to test blood sugar levels and administer insulin injections. *Genetics nurses* provide early detection screenings, counseling, and treatment of patients with genetic disorders, including cystic fibrosis and Huntington's disease. *HIV/AIDS nurses* care for patients diagnosed with HIV and AIDS. *Oncology nurses* care for patients with various types of cancer and may assist in the administration of radiation and chemotherapies and follow-up monitoring. *Wound, ostomy, and continence nurses* treat patients with wounds caused by traumatic injury, ulcers, or arterial disease; provide postoperative care for patients with openings that allow for alternative methods of bodily waste elimination; and treat patients with urinary and fecal incontinence.

RNs specializing in treatment of a particular organ or body system usually are employed in hospital specialty or critical care units, specialty clinics, and outpatient care facilities. *Cardiovascular nurses* treat patients with coronary heart disease and those who have had heart surgery, providing services such as postoperative rehabilitation. *Dermatology nurses* treat patients with disorders of the skin, such as skin cancer and psoriasis. *Gastroenterology nurses* treat patients with digestive and intestinal disorders, including ulcers, acid reflux disease, and abdominal bleeding. Some nurses in this field also assist in specialized procedures such as endoscopies, which look inside the gastrointestinal tract using a tube equipped with a light and a camera that can capture images of diseased tissue. *Gynecology nurses* provide care to women with disorders of the reproductive system, including endometriosis, cancer, and sexually transmitted diseases. *Nephrology nurses* care for patients with

kidney disease caused by diabetes, hypertension, or substance abuse. *Neuroscience nurses* care for patients with dysfunctions of the nervous system, including brain and spinal cord injuries and seizures. *Ophthalmic nurses* provide care to patients with disorders of the eyes, including blindness and glaucoma, and to patients undergoing eye surgery. *Orthopedic nurses* care for patients with muscular and skeletal problems, including arthritis, bone fractures, and muscular dystrophy. *Otorhinolaryngology nurses* care for patients with ear, nose, and throat disorders, such as cleft palates, allergies, and sinus disorders. *Respiratory nurses* provide care to patients with respiratory disorders such as asthma, tuberculosis, and cystic fibrosis. *Urology nurses* care for patients with disorders of the kidneys, urinary tract, and male reproductive organs, including infections, kidney and bladder stones, and cancers.

RNs who specialize by population provide preventive and acute care in all healthcare settings to the segment of the population in which they specialize, including newborns (neonatology), children and adolescents (pediatrics), adults, and the elderly (gerontology or geriatrics). RNs also may provide basic healthcare to patients outside of healthcare settings in such venues as including correctional facilities, schools, summer camps, and the military. Some RNs travel around the United States and throughout the world providing care to patients in areas with shortages of healthcare workers.

Most RNs work as staff nurses as members of a team providing critical healthcare. However, some RNs choose to become advanced practice nurses, who work independently or in collaboration with physicians, and may focus on the provision of primary care services. *Clinical nurse specialists* provide direct patient care and expert consultations in one of many nursing specialties, such as psychiatric-mental health. *Nurse anesthetists* provide anesthesia and related care before and after surgical, therapeutic, diagnostic and obstetrical procedures. They also provide pain management and emergency services, such as airway management. *Nurse-midwives* provide primary care to women, including gynecological exams, family planning advice, prenatal care, assistance in labor and delivery, and neonatal care. *Nurse practitioners* serve as primary and specialty care providers, providing a blend of nursing and healthcare services to patients and families. The most common specialty areas for nurse practitioners are family practice, adult practice, women's health, pediatrics, acute care, and geriatrics. However, there are a variety of other specialties that nurse practitioners can choose, including neonatology and mental health. Advanced practice nurses can prescribe medications in all States and in the District of Columbia.

Some nurses have jobs that require little or no direct patient care, but still require an active RN license. *Forensics nurses* participate in the scientific investigation and treatment of abuse victims, violence, criminal activity, and traumatic accident. *Infection control nurses* identify, track, and control infectious outbreaks in healthcare facilities and develop programs for outbreak prevention and response to biological terrorism. *Nurse educators* plan, develop, implement, and evaluate educational programs and curricula for the professional development of student nurses and RNs. *Nurse informaticists* manage and communicate nursing data and information to improve decision making by consumers, patients, nurses, and other healthcare providers. RNs also may work as healthcare consultants, public policy advisors, pharmaceutical and medical supply researchers and salespersons, and medical writers and editors.

Work environment. Most RNs work in well-lit, comfortable healthcare facilities. Home health and public health nurses travel to patients' homes, schools, community centers, and other sites. RNs may spend considerable time walking, bending, stretching, and standing. Patients in hospitals and nursing care facilities require 24-hour care; consequently, nurses in these institutions may work nights, weekends, and holidays. RNs also may be on call—available to work on short notice. Nurses who work in offices, schools, and other settings that do not provide 24-hour care are more likely to work regular business hours. About 20 percent of RNs worked part time in 2008.

RNs may be in close contact with individuals who have infectious diseases and with toxic, harmful, or potentially hazardous compounds, solutions, and medications. RNs must observe rigid, standardized guidelines to guard against disease and other dangers, such as those posed by radiation, accidental needle sticks, chemicals used to sterilize instruments, and anesthetics. In addition, they are vulnerable to back injury when moving patients.

Training, Other Qualifications, and Advancement

The three typical educational paths to registered nursing are a bachelor's degree, an associate degree, and a diploma from an approved nursing program. Nurses most commonly enter the occupation by completing an associate degree or bachelor's degree program. Individuals then must complete a national licensing examination in order to obtain a nursing license. Advanced practice nurses—clinical nurse specialists, nurse anesthetists, nurse-midwives, and nurse practitioners—need a master's degree.

Education and training. There are three typical educational paths to registered nursing—a bachelor's of science degree in nursing (BSN), an associate degree in nursing (ADN), and a diploma. BSN programs, offered by colleges and universities, take about 4 years to complete. ADN programs, offered by community and junior colleges, take about 2 to 3 years to complete. Diploma programs, administered in hospitals, last about 3 years. Generally, licensed graduates of any of the three types of educational programs qualify for entry-level positions as a staff nurse. There are hundreds of registered nursing programs that result in an ADN or BSN; however, there are relatively few diploma programs.

Individuals considering a career in nursing should carefully weigh the advantages and disadvantages of enrolling in each type of education program. Advancement opportunities may be more limited for ADN and diploma holders compared to RNs who obtain a BSN or higher. Individuals who complete a bach-

elor's degree receive more training in areas such as communication, leadership, and critical thinking, all of which are becoming more important as nursing practice becomes more complex. Additionally, bachelor's degree programs offer more clinical experience in nonhospital settings. A bachelor's or higher degree is often necessary for administrative positions, research, consulting, and teaching

Many RNs with an ADN or diploma later enter bachelor's degree programs to prepare for a broader scope of nursing practice. Often, they can find an entry-level position and then take advantage of tuition reimbursement benefits to work toward a BSN by completing an RN-to-BSN program. Accelerated master's degree in nursing (MSN) programs also are available. They typically take 3-4 years to complete full time and result in the award of both the BSN and MSN.

There are education programs available for people interested in switching to a career in nursing as well. Individuals who already hold a bachelor's degree in another field may enroll in an accelerated BSN program. Accelerated BSN programs last 12 to 18 months and provide the fastest route to a BSN for individuals who already hold a degree. MSN programs also are available for individuals who hold a bachelor's or higher degree in another field; master's degree programs usually last 2 years.

All nursing education programs include classroom instruction and supervised clinical experience in hospitals and other healthcare facilities. Students take courses in anatomy, physiology, microbiology, chemistry, nutrition, psychology and other behavioral sciences, and nursing. Coursework also includes the liberal arts for ADN and BSN students.

Supervised clinical experience is provided in hospital departments such as pediatrics, psychiatry, maternity, and surgery. A number of programs include clinical experience in nursing care facilities, public health departments, home health agencies, and ambulatory clinics.

Licensure and certification. In all States, the District of Columbia, and U.S. territories, students must graduate from an approved nursing program and pass a national licensing examination, known as the National Council Licensure Examination, or NCLEX-RN, in order to obtain a nursing license. Other eligibility requirements for licensure vary by State. Contact your State's board of nursing for details.

Other qualifications. Nurses should be caring, sympathetic, responsible, and detail oriented. They must be able to direct or supervise others, correctly assess patients' conditions, and determine when consultation is required. They need emotional stability to cope with human suffering, emergencies, and other stresses.

RNs should enjoy learning because continuing education credits are required by some States and/or employers at regular intervals. Career-long learning is a distinct reality for RNs.

Projections data from the National Employment Matrix

Occupational Title	SOC Code	Employment, 2008	Projected Employment, 2018	Change, 2008-2018	
				Number	Percent
Registered nurses	29-1111	2,618,700	3,200,200	581,500	22

(NOTE) Data in this table are rounded. See the discussion of the employment projections table in the *Handbook* introductory chapter on *Occupational Information Included in the Handbook.*

Some nurses may become credentialed in specialties such as ambulatory care, gerontology, informatics, pediatrics, and many others. Credentialing for RNs is available from the American Nursing Credentialing Center, the National League for Nursing, and many others. Although credentialing is usually voluntary, it demonstrates adherence to a higher standard and some employers may require it.

Advancement. Most RNs begin as staff nurses in hospitals and, with experience and good performance, often move to other settings or are promoted to positions with more responsibility. In management, nurses can advance from assistant unit manager or head nurse to more senior-level administrative roles of assistant director, director, vice president, or chief of nursing. Increasingly, management-level nursing positions require a graduate or an advanced degree in nursing or health services administration. Administrative positions require leadership, communication and negotiation skills, and good judgment.

Some RNs choose to become advanced practice nurses, who work independently or in collaboration with physicians, and may focus on providing primary care services. There are four types of advanced practice nurses: clinical nurse specialists, nurse anesthetists, nurse-midwives, and nurse practitioners. Clinical nurse specialists provide direct patient care and expert consultations in one of many nursing specialties, such as psychiatric-mental health. Nurse anesthetists provide anesthesia and related care before and after surgical, therapeutic, diagnostic, and obstetrical procedures. They also provide pain management and emergency services, such as airway management. Nurse-midwives provide primary care to women, including gynecological exams, family planning advice, prenatal care, assistance in labor and delivery, and neonatal care. Nurse practitioners serve as primary and specialty care providers, providing a blend of nursing and healthcare services to patients and families.

All four types of advanced practice nurses require at least a master's degree. In addition, all States specifically define requirements for registered nurses in advanced practice roles. Advanced practice nurses may prescribe medicine, but the authority to prescribe varies by State. Contact your State's board of nursing for specific regulations regarding advanced practice nurses.

Some nurses move into the business side of healthcare. Their nursing expertise and experience on a healthcare team equip them to manage ambulatory, acute, home-based, and chronic care businesses. Employers—including hospitals, insurance companies, pharmaceutical manufacturers, and managed care organizations, among others—need RNs for health planning and development, marketing, consulting, policy development, and quality assurance. Other nurses work as college and university faculty or conduct research.

Employment

As the largest healthcare occupation, registered nurses held about 2.6 million jobs in 2008. Hospitals employed the majority of RNs, with 60 percent of such jobs. About 8 percent of jobs were in offices of physicians, 5 percent in home health care services, 5 percent in nursing care facilities, and 3 percent in employment services. The remainder worked mostly in government agencies, social assistance agencies, and educational services.

Job Outlook

Overall job opportunities for registered nurses are expected to be excellent, but may vary by employment and geographic setting. Some employers report difficulty in attracting and retaining an adequate number of RNs. Employment of RNs is expected to grow much faster than the average and, because the occupation is very large, 581,500 new jobs will result, among the largest number of new jobs for any occupation. Additionally, hundreds of thousands of job openings will result from the need to replace experienced nurses who leave the occupation.

Employment change. Employment of registered nurses is expected to grow by 22 percent from 2008 to 2018, much faster than the average for all occupations. Growth will be driven by technological advances in patient care, which permit a greater number of health problems to be treated, and by an increasing emphasis on preventive care. In addition, the number of older people, who are much more likely than younger people to need nursing care, is projected to grow rapidly.

However, employment of RNs will not grow at the same rate in every industry. The projected growth rates for RNs in the industries with the highest employment of these workers are:

Offices of physicians	48%
Home health care services	33
Nursing care facilities	25
Employment services	24
Hospitals, public and private	17

Employment is expected to grow more slowly in hospitals—healthcare's largest industry—than in most other healthcare industries. While the intensity of nursing care is likely to increase, requiring more nurses per patient, the number of inpatients (those who remain in the hospital for more than 24 hours) is not likely to grow by much. Patients are being discharged earlier, and more procedures are being done on an outpatient basis, both inside and outside hospitals. Rapid growth is expected in hospital outpatient facilities, such as those providing same-day surgery, rehabilitation, and chemotherapy.

More and more sophisticated procedures, once performed only in hospitals, are being performed in physicians' offices and in outpatient care centers, such as freestanding ambulatory surgical and emergency centers. Accordingly, employment is expected to grow fast in these places as healthcare in general expands.

Employment in nursing care facilities is expected to grow because of increases in the number of older persons, many of whom require long-term care. Many elderly patients want to be treated at home or in residential care facilities, which will drive demand for RNs in those settings. The financial pressure on hospitals to discharge patients as soon as possible should produce more admissions to nursing and residential care facilities and referrals to home healthcare. Job growth also is expected in units that provide specialized long-term rehabilitation for stroke and head injury patients, as well as units that treat Alzheimer's victims.

Employment in home healthcare is expected to increase in response to the growing number of older persons with functional disabilities, consumer preference for care in the home, and technological advances that make it possible to bring increasingly complex treatments into the home. The type of care demanded will require nurses who are able to perform complex procedures.

Job prospects. Overall job opportunities are expected to be excellent for registered nurses. Employers in some parts of the country and in certain employment settings report difficulty in attracting and retaining an adequate number of RNs, primarily because of an aging RN workforce and a lack of younger workers to fill positions. Qualified applicants to nursing schools are being turned away because of a shortage of nursing faculty. The need for nursing faculty will only increase as many instructors near retirement. Despite the slower employment growth in hospitals, job opportunities should still be excellent because of the relatively high turnover of hospital nurses. To attract and retain qualified nurses, hospitals may offer signing bonuses, family-friendly work schedules, or subsidized training. Although faster employment growth is projected in physicians' offices and outpatient care centers, RNs may face greater competition for these positions because they generally offer regular working hours and more comfortable working environments. Generally, RNs with at least a bachelor's degree will have better job prospects than those without a bachelor's. In addition, all four advanced practice specialties—clinical nurse specialists, nurse practitioners, nurse-midwives, and nurse anesthetists—will be in high demand, particularly in medically underserved areas such as inner cities and rural areas. Relative to physicians, these RNs increasingly serve as lower-cost primary care providers.

Earnings

Median annual wages of registered nurses were $62,450 in May 2008. The middle 50 percent earned between $51,640 and $76,570. The lowest 10 percent earned less than $43,410, and the highest 10 percent earned more than $92,240. Median annual wages in the industries employing the largest numbers of registered nurses in May 2008 were:

Employment services	$68,160
General medical and surgical hospitals	63,880
Offices of physicians	59,210
Home health care services	58,740
Nursing care facilities	57,060

Many employers offer flexible work schedules, child care, educational benefits, and bonuses. About 21 percent of registered nurses are union members or covered by union contract.

Related Occupations

Because of the number of specialties for registered nurses, and the variety of responsibilities and duties, many other healthcare occupations are similar in some aspects of their job. Some healthcare occupations with similar levels of responsibility that work under the direction of physicians or dentists are:

Sources of Additional Information

For information on a career as a registered nurse and nursing education, contact:

➤ National League for Nursing, 61 Broadway, 33rd Floor, New York, NY 10006. Internet: **http://www.nln.org**

For information on baccalaureate and graduate nursing education, nursing career options, and financial aid, contact:

➤ American Association of Colleges of Nursing, 1 Dupont Circle NW., Suite 530, Washington, DC 20036. Internet: **http://www.aacn.nche.edu**

For additional information on registered nurses, including credentialing, contact:

➤ American Nurses Association, 8515 Georgia Ave., Suite 400, Silver Spring, MD 20910. Internet: **http://nursingworld.org**

For information on the National Council Licensure Examination (NCLEX-RN) and a list of individual State boards of nursing, contact:

➤ National Council of State Boards of Nursing, 111 E. Wacker Dr., Suite 2900, Chicago, IL 60601. Internet: **http://www.ncsbn.org**

For a list of accredited clinical nurse specialist programs, contact:

➤ National Association of Clinical Nurse Specialists, 2090 Linglestown Rd., Suite 107, Harrisburg, PA 17110. Internet: **http://www.nacns.org**

For information on nurse anesthetists, including a list of accredited programs, contact:

➤ American Association of Nurse Anesthetists, 222 S. Prospect Ave., Park Ridge, IL 60068. Internet: **http://www.aana.com/**

For information on nurse-midwives, including a list of accredited programs, contact:

➤ American College of Nurse-Midwives, 8403 Colesville Rd., Suite 1550, Silver Spring, MD 20910. Internet: **http://www.midwife.org**

For information on nurse practitioners, including a list of accredited programs, contact:

➤ American Academy of Nurse Practitioners, P.O. Box 12846, Austin, TX 78711. Internet: **http://www.aanp.org**

For additional information on registered nurses in all fields and specialties, contact:

➤ American Society of Registered Nurses, 1001 Bridgeway, Suite 233, Sausalito, CA 94965. Internet: **http://www.asrn.org**

The Occupational Information Network (O*NET) provides information on a wide range of occupational characteristics. Links to O*NET appear at the end of the Internet version of this occupational statement, accessible at **http://www.bls.gov/ooh/ocos083.htm**

Respiratory Therapists

Significant Points

- Job opportunities should be very good.

- Hospitals will account for the vast majority of job openings, but a growing number of openings will arise in other settings.

- An associate degree is the minimum educational requirement, but a bachelor's or master's degree may be important for advancement.

- All States, except Alaska and Hawaii, require respiratory therapists to be licensed.

Nature of the Work

Respiratory therapists—also known as r*espiratory care practitioners*—evaluate, treat, and care for patients with breathing or other cardiopulmonary disorders. Practicing under the direction of a physician, respiratory therapists assume primary responsibility for all respiratory care therapeutic treatments and diagnostic procedures, including the supervision of respiratory therapy technicians. They consult with physicians and other healthcare staff to help develop and modify patient care plans. Therapists also provide complex therapy requiring considerable independent judgment, such as caring for patients on life support in intensive-care units of hospitals.

Respiratory therapists evaluate and treat all types of patients, ranging from premature infants whose lungs are not fully developed to elderly people whose lungs are diseased. They provide temporary relief to patients with chronic asthma or emphysema and give emergency care to patients who are victims of a heart attack, stroke, drowning, or shock.

Respiratory therapists interview patients, perform limited physical examinations, and conduct diagnostic tests. For ex-

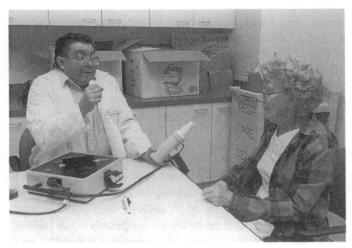

Respiratory therapists interview patients, perform limited physical examinations, and conduct diagnostic tests.

ample, respiratory therapists test a patient's breathing capacity and determine the concentration of oxygen and other gases in a patient's blood. They also measure a patient's pH, which indicates the acidity or alkalinity of the blood. To evaluate a patient's lung capacity, respiratory therapists have the patient breathe into an instrument that measures the volume and flow of oxygen during inhalation and exhalation. By comparing the reading with the norm for the patient's age, height, weight, and sex, respiratory therapists can provide information that helps determine whether the patient has any lung deficiencies. To analyze oxygen, carbon dioxide, and blood pH levels, therapists draw an arterial blood sample, place it in a blood gas analyzer, and relay the results to a physician, who then makes treatment decisions.

To treat patients, respiratory therapists use oxygen or oxygen mixtures, chest physiotherapy, and aerosol medications— liquid medications suspended in a gas that forms a mist which is inhaled. They teach patients how to inhale the aerosol properly to ensure its effectiveness. When a patient has difficulty getting enough oxygen into his or her blood, therapists increase the patient's concentration of oxygen by placing an oxygen mask or nasal cannula on the patient and setting the oxygen flow at the level prescribed by a physician. Therapists also connect patients who cannot breathe on their own to ventilators that deliver pressurized oxygen into the lungs. The therapists insert a tube into the patient's trachea, or windpipe; connect the tube to the ventilator; and set the rate, volume, and oxygen concentration of the oxygen mixture entering the patient's lungs.

Therapists perform regular assessments of patients and equipment. If a patient appears to be having difficulty breathing or if the oxygen, carbon dioxide, or pH level of the blood is abnormal, therapists change the ventilator setting according to the doctor's orders or check the equipment for mechanical problems.

Respiratory therapists perform chest physiotherapy on patients to remove mucus from their lungs and make it easier for them to breathe. Therapists place patients in positions that help drain mucus, and then vibrate the patients' rib cages, often by tapping on the chest, and tell the patients to cough. Chest physiotherapy may be needed after surgery, for example, because anesthesia depresses respiration. As a result, physiotherapy may be prescribed to help get the patient's lungs back to normal and to prevent congestion. Chest physiotherapy also helps patients suffering from lung diseases, such as cystic fibrosis, that cause mucus to collect in the lungs.

Therapists who work in home care teach patients and their families to use ventilators and other life-support systems. In addition, these therapists visit patients in their homes to inspect and clean equipment, evaluate the home environment, and ensure that patients have sufficient knowledge of their diseases and the proper use of their medications and equipment. Therapists also make emergency visits if equipment problems arise.

In some hospitals, therapists perform tasks that fall outside their traditional role. Therapists are becoming involved in areas such as pulmonary rehabilitation, smoking-cessation counseling, disease prevention, case management, and poly-

Projections data from the National Employment Matrix

Occupational Title	SOC Code	Employment, 2008	Projected Employment, 2018	Change, 2008-2018	
				Number	Percent
Respiratory therapists..	29-1126	105,900	128,100	22,100	21

(NOTE) Data in this table are rounded. See the discussion of the employment projections table in the *Handbook* introductory chapter on *Occupational Information Included in the Handbook.*

somnography—the diagnosis of breathing disorders during sleep, such as apnea. Respiratory therapists also increasingly treat critical-care patients, either as part of surface and air transport teams or as part of rapid-response teams in hospitals.

Work environment. Respiratory therapists generally work between 35 and 40 hours a week. Because hospitals operate around the clock, therapists can work evenings, nights, or weekends. They spend long periods standing and walking between patients' rooms. In an emergency, therapists work under the stress of the situation. Respiratory therapists employed in home healthcare must travel frequently to patients' homes.

Respiratory therapists are trained to work with gases stored under pressure. Adherence to safety precautions and regular maintenance and testing of equipment minimize the risk of injury. As in many other health occupations, respiratory therapists are exposed to infectious diseases, but by carefully following proper procedures, they can minimize these risks.

Training, Other Qualifications, and Advancement
An associate degree is the minimum educational requirement, but a bachelor's or master's degree may be important for advancement. All States, except Alaska and Hawaii, require respiratory therapists to be licensed.

Education and training. An associate degree is required to become a respiratory therapist. Training is offered at the post-secondary level by colleges and universities, medical schools, vocational-technical institutes, and the Armed Forces. Most programs award associate or bachelor's degree and prepare graduates for jobs as advanced respiratory therapists. A limited number of associate degree programs lead to jobs as entry-level respiratory therapists. According to the Commission on Accreditation of Allied Health Education Programs (CAA-HEP), 31 entry-level and 346 advanced respiratory therapy programs were accredited in the United States in 2008.

Among the areas of study in respiratory therapy programs are human anatomy and physiology, pathophysiology, chemistry, physics, microbiology, pharmacology, and mathematics. Other courses deal with therapeutic and diagnostic procedures and tests, equipment, patient assessment, cardiopulmonary resuscitation, the application of clinical practice guidelines, patient care outside of hospitals, cardiac and pulmonary rehabilitation, respiratory health promotion and disease prevention, and medical recordkeeping and reimbursement.

High school students interested in applying to respiratory therapy programs should take courses in health, biology, mathematics, chemistry, and physics. Respiratory care involves basic mathematical problem solving and an understanding of chemical and physical principles. For example, respiratory care workers must be able to compute dosages of medication and calculate gas concentrations.

Licensure and certification. A license is required to practice as a respiratory therapist, except in Alaska and Hawaii. Also, most employers require respiratory therapists to maintain a cardiopulmonary resuscitation (CPR) certification.

Licensure is usually based, in large part, on meeting the requirements for certification from the National Board for Respiratory Care (NBRC). The board offers the Certified Respiratory Therapist (CRT) credential to those who graduate from entry-level or advanced programs accredited by CAA-HEP or the Committee on Accreditation for Respiratory Care (CoARC) and who also pass an exam.

The board also awards the Registered Respiratory Therapist (RRT) to CRTs who have graduated from advanced programs and pass two separate examinations. Supervisory positions and intensive-care specialties usually require the RRT.

Other qualifications. Therapists should be sensitive to a patient's physical and psychological needs. Respiratory care practitioners must pay attention to detail, follow instructions, and work as part of a team. In addition, operating advanced equipment requires proficiency with computers.

Advancement. Respiratory therapists advance in clinical practice by moving from general care to the care of critically ill patients who have significant problems in other organ systems, such as the heart or kidneys. Respiratory therapists, especially those with a bachelor's or master's degree, also may advance to supervisory or managerial positions in a respiratory therapy department. Respiratory therapists in home healthcare and equipment rental firms may become branch managers. Some respiratory therapists advance by moving into teaching positions. Some others use the knowledge gained as a respiratory therapist to work in another industry, such as developing, marketing, or selling pharmaceuticals and medical devices.

Employment
Respiratory therapists held about 105,900 jobs in 2008. About 81 percent of jobs were in hospitals, mainly in departments of respiratory care, anesthesiology, or pulmonary medicine. Most of the remaining jobs were in offices of physicians or other health practitioners, consumer-goods rental firms that supply respiratory equipment for home use, nursing care facilities, employment services, and home healthcare services.

Job Outlook
Much faster than average growth is projected for respiratory therapists. Job opportunities should be very good.

Employment change. Employment of respiratory therapists is expected to grow by 21 percent from 2008 to 2018, much faster than the average for all occupations. The increasing demand will come from substantial growth in the middle-aged and elderly population—a development that will heighten the incidence of cardiopulmonary disease. Growth in demand also will result from the expanding role of respiratory therapists in case management, disease prevention, emergency care, and the early detection of pulmonary disorders.

Older Americans suffer most from respiratory ailments and cardiopulmonary diseases, such as pneumonia, chronic bronchitis, emphysema, and heart disease. As the number of older persons increases, the need for respiratory therapists is expected to increase as well. In addition, advances in inhalable medications and in the treatment of lung transplant patients, heart attack and accident victims, and premature infants—many of whom depend on a ventilator during part of their treatment—will increase the demand for the services of respiratory care practitioners.

Job prospects. Job opportunities are expected to be very good, especially for those with a bachelor's degree and certification, and those with cardiopulmonary care skills or experience working with infants. The vast majority of job openings will continue to be in hospitals. However, a growing number of openings are expected to be outside of hospitals, especially in home health care services, offices of physicians or other health practitioners, consumer-goods rental firms, or in the employment services industry as a temporary worker in various settings.

Earnings

Median annual wages of wage-and-salary respiratory therapists were $52,200 in May 2008. The middle 50 percent earned between $44,490 and $61,720. The lowest 10 percent earned less than $37,920 and the highest 10 percent earned more than $69,800.

Related Occupations

Under the supervision of a physician, respiratory therapists administer respiratory care and life support to patients with heart and lung difficulties. Other workers who care for, treat, or train people to improve their physical condition include:

Respiratory care practitioners work with advanced medical technology, as do other healthcare technicians including:

Sources of Additional Information

Information concerning a career in respiratory care is available from:

➤ American Association for Respiratory Care, 9425 N. MacArthur Blvd., Suite 100, Irving, TX 75063. Internet: **http://www.aarc.org**

For a list of accredited educational programs for respiratory care practitioners, contact either of the following organizations:

➤ Commission on Accreditation for Allied Health Education Programs, 1361 Park St., Clearwater, FL 33756. Internet: **http://www.caahep.org**

➤ Committee on Accreditation for Respiratory Care, 1248 Harwood Rd., Bedford, TX 76021.

Information on gaining credentials in respiratory care and a list of State licensing agencies can be obtained from:
➤ National Board for Respiratory Care, Inc., 18000 W. 105th St., Olathe, KS 66061. Internet: **http://www.nbrc.org**

The Occupational Information Network (O*NET) provides information on a wide range of occupational characteristics. Links to O*NET appear at the end of the Internet version of this occupational statement, accessible at **http://www.bls.gov/ooh/ocos321.htm**

Speech-Language Pathologists

Significant Points

- About 48 percent worked in educational services; most others were employed by health care and social assistance facilities.

- A master's degree in speech-language pathology is the standard educational requirement; almost all States regulate these workers, and licensing requirements vary.

- Favorable job opportunities are expected.

Nature of the Work

Speech-language pathologists, sometimes called *speech therapists*, assess, diagnose, treat, and help to prevent disorders related to speech, language, cognitive-communication, voice, swallowing, and fluency.

Speech-language pathologists work with people who cannot produce speech sounds or cannot produce them clearly; those with speech rhythm and fluency problems, such as stuttering; people with voice disorders, such as inappropriate pitch or harsh voice; those with problems understanding and producing language; those who wish to improve their communication skills by modifying an accent; and those with cognitive communication impairments, such as attention, memory, and problem-solving disorders. They also work with people who have swallowing difficulties.

Speech, language, and swallowing difficulties can result from a variety of causes including stroke, brain injury or deterioration, developmental delays or disorders, learning disabilities, cerebral palsy, cleft palate, voice pathology, mental retardation, hearing loss, or emotional problems. Problems can be congenital, developmental, or acquired. Speech-language pathologists use special instruments and qualitative and quantitative assessment methods, including standardized tests, to analyze and diagnose the nature and extent of impairments.

Speech-language pathologists develop an individualized plan of care, tailored to each patient's needs. For individuals with little or no speech capability, speech-language pathologists may select augmentative or alternative communication methods, in-

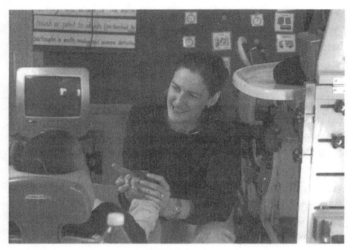

Speech-language pathologists usually work at desks or tables in clean comfortable surroundings.

cluding automated devices and sign language, and teach their use. They teach patients how to make sounds, improve their voices, or increase their oral or written language skills to communicate more effectively. They also teach individuals how to strengthen muscles or use compensatory strategies to swallow without choking or inhaling food or liquid. Speech-language pathologists help patients develop, or recover, reliable communication and swallowing skills so patients can fulfill their educational, vocational, and social roles.

Speech-language pathologists keep records on the initial evaluation, progress, and discharge of clients. This helps pinpoint problems, tracks client progress, and justifies the cost of treatment when applying for reimbursement. They counsel individuals and their families concerning communication disorders and how to cope with the stress and misunderstanding that often accompany them. They also work with family members to recognize and change behavior patterns that impede communication and treatment and show them communication-enhancing techniques to use at home.

Most speech-language pathologists provide direct clinical services to individuals with communication or swallowing disorders. In medical facilities, they may perform their job in conjunction with physicians, social workers, psychologists, and other therapists. Speech-language pathologists in schools collaborate with teachers, special educators, interpreters, other school personnel, and parents to develop and implement individual or group programs, provide counseling, and support classroom activities.

Some speech-language pathologists conduct research on how people communicate. Others design and develop equipment or techniques for diagnosing and treating speech problems.

Work environment. Speech-language pathologists usually work at a desk or table in clean comfortable surroundings. In medical settings, they may work at the patient's bedside and assist in positioning the patient. In schools, they may work with students in an office or classroom. Some work in the client's home.

Although the work is not physically demanding, it requires attention to detail and intense concentration. The emotional needs of clients and their families may be demanding. Most full-time speech-language pathologists work 40 hours per week. About 20 percent of speech-language pathologists worked part-time in 2008. Those who work on a contract basis may spend a substantial amount of time traveling between facilities.

Training, Other Qualifications, and Advancement

A master's degree is the most common level of education among speech-language pathologists. Licensure or certification requirements also exist, but vary by State.

Education and training. Most speech-language pathologist jobs require a master's degree. The Council on Academic Accreditation is an entity of the American Speech-Language-Hearing Association; it accredits postsecondary academic programs in speech-language pathology. While graduation from an accredited program is not always required, it is required by some States for licensure and is mandatory for professional credentialing from the American Speech-Language-Hearing Association. In 2009, about 240 colleges and universities offered graduate programs, at both the master's and doctoral levels, in speech-language pathology accredited by the Council on Academic Accreditation. Speech-language pathology courses cover anatomy, physiology, and the development of the areas of the body involved in speech, language, and swallowing; the nature of disorders; principles of acoustics; and psychological aspects of communication. Graduate students may also learn to evaluate and treat speech, language, and swallowing disorders as part of curriculum in supervised clinical practicum.

Licensure and certification. In 2009, 47 States regulated speech-language pathologists. Typical licensing requirements are a master's degree from an accredited college or university; a passing score on the national examination on speech-language pathology, offered through the Praxis Series of the Educational Testing Service; 300 to 375 hours of supervised clinical experience; and 9 months of postgraduate professional clinical experience. Most States have continuing education requirements for licensure renewal. Medicaid, Medicare, and private health insurers generally require a practitioner to be licensed to qualify for reimbursement. For specific regulation and eligibility requirements contact your State's regulatory board.

State regulation of speech-language pathologists may differ for pathologists practicing in schools. For information on State regulation of speech-language pathologists in public schools contact your State's Department of Education. The Certificate of Clinical Competence in Speech-Language Pathology (CCC-

Projections data from the National Employment Matrix

Occupational Title	SOC Code	Employment, 2008	Projected Employment, 2018	Change, 2008-2018	
				Number	Percent
Speech-language pathologists...	29-1127	119,300	141,400	22,100	19

(NOTE) Data in this table are rounded. See the discussion of the employment projections table in the *Handbook* introductory chapter on *Occupational Information Included in the Handbook.*

SLP) credential offered by the American Speech-Language-Hearing Association is a voluntary credential; however, the CCC-SLP meets some or all of the requirements for licensure in some States. To earn a CCC, a person must have a graduate degree from an accredited university, which typically includes a 400-hour supervised clinical practicum, complete a 36-week full-time postgraduate clinical fellowship, and pass the Praxis Series examination in speech-language pathology administered by the Educational Testing Service.

Other qualifications. Speech-language pathologists should be able to effectively communicate diagnostic test results, diagnoses, and proposed treatment in a manner easily understood by their patients and their families. They must be able to approach problems objectively and be supportive. Because a patient's progress may be slow, patience, compassion, and good listening skills are necessary.

Advancement. As speech-language pathologists gain clinical experience and engage in continuing professional education, many develop expertise with certain populations, such as preschoolers and adolescents, or disorders, such as aphasia and learning disabilities. Some may obtain board recognition in a specialty area, such as child language, fluency, or feeding and swallowing. Experienced clinicians may become mentors or supervisors of other therapists or be promoted to administrative positions.

Employment

Speech-language pathologists held about 119,300 jobs in 2008. About 48 percent were employed in educational services. Others were employed in hospitals; offices of other health practitioners, including speech-language pathologists; nursing care facilities; home health care services; individual and family services; outpatient care centers; and child day care centers.

Nine percent of speech-language pathologists were self-employed in 2008. They contract to provide services in schools, offices of physicians, hospitals, or nursing care facilities, or work as consultants to industry.

Job Outlook

Faster than average employment growth is projected. Job opportunities are expected to be favorable.

Employment change. Employment of speech-language pathologists is expected to grow by 19 percent from 2008 to 2018, faster than the average for all occupations. As the members of the baby-boom generation continue to age, the possibility of neurological disorders and associated speech, language, and swallowing impairments increases. Medical advances also are improving the survival rate of premature infants and trauma and stroke victims, who then need assessment and sometimes treatment.

Employment in educational services will increase with the growth in elementary and secondary school enrollments, including enrollment of special education students. The 2004 Individuals with Disabilities Education Act is a Federal law that guarantees special education and related services to all eligible children with disabilities. Greater awareness of the importance of early identification and diagnosis of speech and language disorders in young children will also increase employment.

In healthcare facilities, restrictions on reimbursement for therapy services may limit the growth of speech-language pathologist jobs in the near term. However, the long-run demand for therapists should continue to rise as growth in the number of individuals with disabilities or limited function spurs demand for therapy services.

The number of speech-language pathologists in private practice should increase because hospitals, schools, and nursing care facilities will contain costs by increasingly contracting out for these services.

Job prospects. In addition to job growth, a number of job openings in speech-language pathology will be due to retirements. Opportunities should be favorable, particularly for those with the ability to speak a second language, such as Spanish. Demand for speech-language pathologists can be regional so job prospects are expected to be favorable for those who are willing to relocate, particularly to areas experiencing difficulty in attracting and hiring speech-language pathologists.

Earnings

Median annual wages of speech-language pathologists were $62,930 in May 2008. The middle 50 percent earned between $50,330 and $79,620. The lowest 10 percent earned less than $41,240, and the highest 10 percent earned more than $99,220. Median annual wages in the industries employing the largest numbers of speech-language pathologists were:

Nursing care facilities	$79,120
Home health care services	77,030
General medical and surgical hospitals	68,430
Offices of other health practitioners	67,910
Elementary and secondary schools	58,140

Some employers may reimburse speech-language pathologists for their required continuing education credits. About 40 percent of speech-language pathologists were union members or covered by union contract in 2008.

Related Occupations

Speech-language pathologists specialize in the prevention, diagnosis, and treatment of speech and language problems. Workers who treat other physical and mental health problems include:

	Page
Audiologists	358
Occupational therapists	369
Physical therapists	377
Psychologists	215
Recreational therapists	389

Sources of Additional Information

State licensing boards can provide information on licensure requirements. State departments of education can supply information on certification requirements for those who wish to work in public schools.

For information on careers in speech-language pathology, a description of the CCC-SLP credential, and a listing of accredited graduate programs in speech-language pathology, contact:

➤ American Speech-Language-Hearing Association, 2200 Research Blvd., Rockville, MD 20850. Internet: **http://www.asha.org**

The Occupational Information Network (O*NET) provides information on a wide range of occupational characteristics. Links to O*NET appear at the end of the Internet version of this occupational statement, accessible at **http://www.bls.gov/ooh/ocos099.htm**

Veterinarians

Significant Points

- Veterinarians should love animals and be able to get along with their owners.

- Graduation from an accredited college of veterinary medicine and a State license are required; admission to veterinary school is competitive.

- Job opportunities should be excellent.

- About 80 percent of veterinarians work in private practice.

Nature of the Work

Veterinarians diagnose and treat diseases and dysfunctions of animals. Specifically, they care for the health of pets, livestock, and animals in zoos, racetracks, and laboratories. Some veterinarians use their skills to protect humans against diseases carried by animals and conduct clinical research on human and animal health problems. Others work in basic research, broadening our knowledge of animals and medical science, and in applied research, developing new ways to use knowledge.

Most veterinarians diagnose animal health problems, vaccinate against diseases, medicate animals suffering from infections or illnesses, treat and dress wounds, set fractures, perform surgery, and advise owners about animal feeding, behavior, and breeding.

According to the American Medical Veterinary Association, 77 percent of veterinarians who work in private medical practices treat pets. These practitioners usually care for dogs and cats but also treat birds, reptiles, rabbits, ferrets, and other animals that can be kept as pets. About 16 percent of veterinarians work in private mixed and food animal practices, where they see pigs, goats, cattle, sheep, and some wild animals in addition to farm animals. A small proportion of private-practice veterinarians, about 6 percent, work exclusively with horses.

Veterinarians who work with food animals or horses usually drive to farms or ranches to provide veterinary services for herds or individual animals. These veterinarians test for and vaccinate against diseases and consult with farm or ranch owners and managers regarding animal production, feeding, and housing issues. They also treat and dress wounds, set fractures, and perform surgery, including cesarean sections on birthing animals. Other veterinarians care for zoo, aquarium, or laboratory animals. Veterinarians of all types euthanize animals when necessary.

Veterinarians who treat animals use medical equipment such as stethoscopes, surgical instruments, and diagnostic equipment, including radiographic and ultrasound equipment. Veterinarians working in research use a full range of sophisticated laboratory equipment.

Some veterinarians contribute to human as well as animal health. A number of veterinarians work with physicians and scientists as they research ways to prevent and treat various human health problems. For example, veterinarians contributed greatly to conquering malaria and yellow fever, solved the mystery of botulism, produced an anticoagulant used to treat some people with heart disease, and defined and developed surgical techniques for humans, such as hip and knee joint replacements and limb and organ transplants. Today, some determine the effects of drug therapies, antibiotics, or new surgical techniques by testing them on animals.

Some veterinarians are involved in food safety and inspection. Veterinarians who are livestock inspectors, for example, check animals for transmissible diseases such as E. coli, advise owners on the treatment of their animals, and may quarantine animals. Veterinarians who are meat, poultry, or egg product inspectors examine slaughtering and processing plants, check live animals and carcasses for disease, and enforce government regulations regarding food purity and sanitation. More veterinarians are finding opportunities in food security as they ensure that the Nation has abundant and safe food supplies. Veterinarians involved in food security often work along the country's borders as animal and plant health inspectors, where they examine imports and exports of animal products to prevent disease here and in foreign countries. Many of these workers are employed by the Department of Agriculture's Animal and Plant Health Inspection Service division, or the U.S. Food and Drug Administration's Center for Veterinary Medicine.

Work environment. Veterinarians in private or clinical practice often work long hours in a noisy indoor environment. Sometimes they have to deal with emotional or demanding pet owners. When working with animals that are frightened or in pain, veterinarians risk being bitten, kicked, or scratched.

Veterinarians who work with food animals or horses spend time driving between their offices and farms or ranches. They

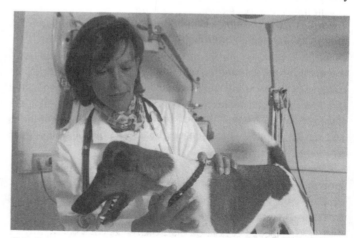

Employment opportunities for veterinarians are expected to be very good, but competition for admission to veterinary school is keen.

work outdoors in all kinds of weather and may have to treat animals or perform surgery, often under unsanitary conditions.

Veterinarians working in nonclinical areas, such as public health and research, work in clean, well-lit offices or laboratories and have working conditions similar to those of other professionals who work in these environments. Veterinarians in nonclinical areas spend much of their time dealing with people rather than animals.

Veterinarians often work long hours. Those in group practices may take turns being on call for evening, night, or weekend work; solo practitioners may work extended hours (including weekend hours), responding to emergencies or squeezing in unexpected appointments.

Training, Other Qualifications, and Advancement

Veterinarians must obtain a Doctor of Veterinary Medicine degree and a State license. Admission to veterinary school is competitive.

Education and training. Prospective veterinarians must graduate with a Doctor of Veterinary Medicine (D.V.M. or V.M.D.) degree from a 4-year program at an accredited college of veterinary medicine. There are 28 colleges in 26 States that meet accreditation standards set by the Council on Education of the American Veterinary Medical Association (AVMA).

The prerequisites for admission to veterinary programs vary. Many programs do not require a bachelor's degree for entrance, but all require a significant number of credit hours—ranging from 45 to 90 semester hours—at the undergraduate level. However, most of the students admitted have completed an undergraduate program and earned a bachelor's degree. Applicants without a degree face a difficult task in gaining admittance.

Preveterinary courses should emphasize the sciences. Veterinary medical colleges typically require applicants to have taken classes in organic and inorganic chemistry, physics, biochemistry, general biology, animal biology, animal nutrition, genetics, vertebrate embryology, cellular biology, microbiology, zoology, and systemic physiology. Some programs require calculus; some require only statistics, college algebra and trigonometry, or pre-calculus. Most veterinary medical colleges also require some courses in English or literature, other humanities, and the social sciences. Increasingly, courses in general business management and career development have become a standard part of the curriculum to teach new graduates how to effectively run a practice.

In addition to satisfying preveterinary course requirements, applicants must submit test scores from the Graduate Record Examination (GRE), the Veterinary College Admission Test (VCAT), or the Medical College Admission Test (MCAT), depending on the preference of the college to which they are applying. Currently, 22 schools require the GRE, 4 require the VCAT, and 2 accept the MCAT.

Admission to veterinary school is competitive. The number of accredited veterinary colleges has remained largely the same since 1983, but the number of applicants has risen significantly. Only about 1 in 3 applicants was accepted in 2007.

New graduates with a Doctor of Veterinary Medicine degree may begin to practice veterinary medicine once they receive their license, but many new graduates choose to enter a 1-year internship. Interns receive a small salary but often find that their internship experience leads to better paying opportunities later, relative to those of other veterinarians. Veterinarians who then seek board certification also must complete a 3-year to 4-year residency program that provides intensive training in one of the 39 AVMA-recognized veterinary specialties including internal medicine, oncology, pathology, dentistry, nutrition, radiology, surgery, dermatology, anesthesiology, neurology, cardiology, ophthalmology, preventive medicine, and exotic-small-animal medicine.

Licensure. All States and the District of Columbia require that veterinarians be licensed before they can practice. The only exemptions are for veterinarians working for some Federal agencies and some State governments. Licensing is controlled by the States and is not uniform, although all States require the successful completion of the D.V.M. degree—or equivalent education—and a passing grade on a national board examination, the North American Veterinary Licensing Exam. This 8-hour examination consists of 360 multiple-choice questions covering all aspects of veterinary medicine as well as visual materials designed to test diagnostic skills.

The Educational Commission for Foreign Veterinary Graduates grants certification to individuals trained outside the United States who demonstrate that they meet specified requirements for English language and clinical proficiency. This certification fulfills the educational requirement for licensure in all States.

Most States also require candidates to pass a State jurisprudence examination covering State laws and regulations. Some States do additional testing on clinical competency as well. There are few reciprocal agreements between States, so veterinarians who wish to practice in a different State usually must first pass that State's examinations.

Other qualifications. When deciding whom to admit, some veterinary medical colleges place heavy consideration on candidates' veterinary and animal experience. Formal experience, such as work with veterinarians or scientists in clinics, agribusiness, research, or some area of health science, is particularly advantageous. Less formal experience, such as working with animals on a farm, or at a stable or animal shelter, also can be helpful. Students must demonstrate ambition and an eagerness to work with animals.

Prospective veterinarians should love animals and have the ability to get along with their owners, especially pet owners,

Projections data from the National Employment Matrix

Occupational Title	SOC Code	Employment, 2008	Projected Employment, 2018	Change, 2008-2018	
				Number	Percent
Veterinarians	29-1131	59,700	79,400	19,700	33

(NOTE) Data in this table are rounded. See the discussion of the employment projections table in the *Handbook* introductory chapter on *Occupational Information Included in the Handbook.*

who usually have strong bonds with their pets. They need good manual dexterity. Veterinarians who intend to go into private practice should possess excellent communication and business skills, because they will need to successfully manage their practice and employees and promote, market, and sell their services.

Advancement. Most veterinarians begin as employees in established group practices. Despite the substantial financial investment in equipment, office space, and staff, many veterinarians with experience eventually set up their own practice or purchase an established one.

Newly trained veterinarians can become U.S. Government meat and poultry inspectors, disease-control workers, animal welfare and safety workers, epidemiologists, research assistants, or commissioned officers in the U.S. Public Health Service or various branches of the U.S. Armed Forces. A State license may be required.

Nearly all States have continuing education requirements for licensed veterinarians. Requirements differ by State and may involve attending a class or otherwise demonstrating knowledge of recent medical and veterinary advances.

Employment

Veterinarians held about 59,700 jobs in 2008. According to the American Veterinary Medical Association, 80 percent of veterinarians were employed in a solo or group practice. Most others were salaried employees of colleges or universities; medical schools; private industry, such as research laboratories and pharmaceutical companies; and Federal, State, or local government.

The Federal Government employed about 1,300 civilian veterinarians, chiefly in the U.S. Department of Agriculture and the U.S. Food and Drug Administration's Center for Veterinary Medicine. A few veterinarians work for zoos, but most veterinarians caring for zoo animals are private practitioners who contract with the zoos to provide services, usually on a part-time basis.

In addition, many veterinarians hold veterinary faculty positions in colleges and universities and are classified as teachers. (See the statement on teachers—postsecondary elsewhere in the *Handbook.*)

Job Outlook

Employment is expected to increase much faster than average. Excellent job opportunities are expected.

Employment change. Employment of veterinarians is expected to increase 33 percent over the 2008–18 decade, much faster than the average for all occupations. Veterinarians usually practice in animal hospitals or clinics and care primarily for small pets. Recent trends indicate particularly strong interest in cats as pets. Faster growth of the cat population is expected to increase the demand for feline medicine and veterinary services, while demand for veterinary care for dogs should continue to grow at a more modest pace.

Many pet owners consider their pets as members of the family, which serves as evidence that people are placing a higher value on their pets and is an example of the *human-animal bond.* These pet owners are becoming more aware of the availability of advanced care and are more willing to pay for intensive veterinary care than owners in the past. Furthermore,

the number of pet owners purchasing pet insurance is rising, increasing the likelihood that considerable money will be spent on veterinary care.

More pet owners also will take advantage of nontraditional veterinary services, such as cancer treatment and preventive dental care. Modern veterinary services have caught up to human medicine; certain procedures, such as hip replacement, kidney transplants, and blood transfusions, which were once only available for humans, are now available for animals.

Continued support for public health and food and animal safety, national disease control programs, and biomedical research on human health problems will contribute to the demand for veterinarians, although the number of positions in these areas is smaller than the number in private practice. Homeland security also may provide opportunities for veterinarians involved in efforts to maintain abundant food supplies and minimize animal diseases in the United States and in foreign countries.

Job prospects. Excellent job opportunities are expected because there are only 28 accredited schools of veterinary medicine in the United States, resulting in a limited number of graduates—about 2,500—each year. However, admission to veterinary school is competitive.

New graduates continue to be attracted to companion-animal medicine because they usually prefer to deal with pets and to live and work near heavily populated areas, where most pet owners live. Employment opportunities are very good in cities and suburbs but even better in rural areas because fewer veterinarians compete to work there.

Beginning veterinarians may take positions requiring evening or weekend work to accommodate the extended hours of operation that many practices are offering. Some veterinarians take salaried positions in retail stores offering veterinary services. Self-employed veterinarians usually have to work hard and long to build a sufficient client base.

The number of jobs for farm-animal veterinarians is likely to grow more slowly than the number of jobs for companion-animal veterinarians. Nevertheless, job prospects should be excellent for farm-animal veterinarians because of their lower earnings and because many veterinarians do not want to work outside or in rural or isolated areas.

Veterinarians with training in food safety and security, animal health and welfare, and public health and epidemiology should have the best opportunities for a career in the Federal Government.

Earnings

Median annual wages of veterinarians were $79,050 in May 2008. The middle 50 percent earned between $61,370 and $104,110. The lowest 10 percent earned less than $46,610, and the highest 10 percent earned more than $143,660.

The average annual salary for veterinarians in the Federal Government was $93,398 in March 2009.

According to a survey by the American Veterinary Medical Association, average starting salaries of veterinary medical college graduates in 2008 varied by type of practice as follows:

Small animals, exclusively $64,744
Large animals, exclusively 62,424
Small animals, predominantly 61,753

Mixed animals 58,522
Large animals, predominantly 57,745
Equine (horses) 41,636

Related Occupations

Sources of Additional Information

For additional information on careers in veterinary medicine, a list of U.S. schools and colleges of veterinary medicine, and accreditation policies, send a letter-size, self-addressed, stamped envelope to:

➤ American Veterinary Medical Association, 1931 N. Meacham Rd., Suite 100, Schaumburg, IL 60173. Internet: **http://www.avma.org**

For information on veterinary education, contact:

➤ Association of American Veterinary Medical Colleges, 1101 Vermont Ave. NW., Suite 301, Washington, DC 20005. Internet: **http://www.aavmc.org**

For information on scholarships, grants, and loans, contact the financial aid officer at the veterinary schools to which you wish to apply.

For information on veterinarians working in zoos, see the *Occupational Outlook Quarterly* article "Wild jobs with wildlife," online at **http://www.bls.gov/opub/ooq/2001/spring/art01.pdf.**

Information on obtaining a veterinary position with the Federal Government is available from the Office of Personnel Management through USAJOBS, the Federal Government's official employment information system. This resource for locating and applying for job opportunities can be accessed through the Internet at **http://www.usajobs.opm.gov** or through an interactive voice response telephone system at (703) 724-1850 or TDD (978) 461-8404. These numbers are not toll free, so charges may result. For advice on how to find and apply for Federal jobs, see the *Occupational Outlook Quarterly* article "How to get a job in the Federal Government," available online at **http://www.bls.gov/opub/ooq/2004/summer/art01.pdf.**

The Occupational Information Network (O*NET) provides information on a wide range of occupational characteristics. Links to O*NET appear at the end of the Internet version of this occupational statement, accessible at **http://www.bls.gov/ooh/ocos076.htm**

Health Technologists and Technicians

Athletic Trainers

Significant Points

- A bachelor's degree is usually the minimum requirement, but many athletic trainers hold a master's or doctoral degree.

- Long hours, sometimes including nights and weekends, are common.

- Job prospects should be good in the healthcare industry and in high schools, but competition is expected for positions with professional and college sports teams.

Nature of the Work

Athletic trainers help prevent and treat injuries for people of all ages. Their patients and clients include everyone from professional athletes to industrial workers. Recognized by the American Medical Association as allied health professionals, athletic trainers specialize in the prevention, diagnosis, assessment, treatment, and rehabilitation of muscle and bone injuries and illnesses. Athletic trainers, as one of the first healthcare providers on the scene when injuries occur, must be able to recognize, evaluate, and assess injuries and provide immediate care when needed. Athletic trainers should not be confused with fitness trainers or personal trainers, who are not healthcare workers, but rather train people

to become physically fit. (Fitness workers are discussed elsewhere in the *Handbook.*)

Athletic trainers try to prevent injuries by educating people on how to reduce their risk for injuries and by advising them on the proper use of equipment, exercises to improve balance and strength, and home exercises and therapy programs. They also help apply protective or injury-preventive devices such as tape, bandages, and braces.

Athletic trainers may work under the direction of a licensed physician, and in cooperation with other healthcare providers. The extent of the direction ranges from discussing specific injuries and treatment options with a physician to performing evaluations and treatments as directed by a physician. Some athletic trainers meet with the team physician or consulting physician once or twice a week; others interact with a physician every day. Athletic trainers often have administrative responsibilities. These may include regular meetings with an athletic director, physician practice manager, or other administrative officer to deal with budgets, purchasing, policy implementation, and other business-related issues.

Work environment. The industry and individual employer are significant in determining the work environment of athletic trainers. Many athletic trainers work indoors most of the time; others, especially those in some sports-related jobs, spend much of their time working outdoors. The job also might require standing for long periods, working with medi-

Athletic trainers apply protective devices such as tape, bandages, and braces.

cal equipment or machinery, and being able to walk, run, kneel, stoop, or crawl. Travel may be required.

Schedules vary by work setting. Athletic trainers in nonsports settings generally have an established schedule—usually about 40 to 50 hours per week—with nights and weekends off. Athletic trainers working in hospitals and clinics may spend part of their time working at other locations doing outreach services. The most common outreach programs include conducting athletic training services and speaking at high schools, colleges, and commercial businesses.

Athletic trainers in sports settings have schedules that are longer and more variable. These athletic trainers must be present for team practices and competitions, which often are on evenings and weekends, and their schedules can change on short notice when games and practices have to be rescheduled. In high schools, athletic trainers who also teach may work 60 to 70 hours a week, or more. In National Collegiate Athletic Association Division I colleges and universities, athletic trainers generally work with one team; when that team's sport is in season, working at least 50 to 60 hours a week is common. Athletic trainers in smaller colleges and universities often work with several teams and have teaching responsibilities. During the off-season, a 40-hour to 50-hour work week may be normal in most settings. Athletic trainers for professional sports teams generally work the most hours per week. During training camps, practices, and competitions, they may be required to work up to 12 hours a day.

There is some stress involved with being an athletic trainer. The work of athletic trainers requires frequent interaction with others. They consult with physicians as well as have frequent contact with athletes and patients to discuss and administer treatments, rehabilitation programs, injury-preventive practices, and other health-related issues.

Athletic trainers are responsible for their clients' health, and sometimes have to make quick decisions that could affect the health or career of their clients. Athletics trainers also can be affected by the pressure to win that is typical of competitive sports teams.

Training, Other Qualifications, and Advancement

A bachelor's degree is usually the minimum requirement, but many athletic trainers hold a master's or doctoral degree. In 2009, 47 States required athletic trainers to be licensed or hold some form of registration.

Education and training. A bachelor's degree from an accredited college or university is required for almost all jobs as an athletic trainer. In 2009, there were about 350 accredited undergraduate programs nationwide. Students in these programs are educated both in the classroom and in clinical settings. Formal education includes many science and health-related courses, such as human anatomy, physiology, nutrition, and biomechanics.

According to the National Athletic Trainers' Association, almost 70 percent of athletic trainers have a master's degree or higher. Athletic trainers may need a master's or higher degree to be eligible for some positions, especially those in colleges and universities, and to increase their advancement opportunities. Because some positions in high schools involve teaching along with athletic trainer responsibilities, a teaching certificate or license could be required.

Licensure and certification. In 2009, 47 States required athletic trainers to be licensed or registered; this requires certification from the Board of Certification, Inc. (BOC). For BOC certification, athletic trainers need a bachelor's or master's degree from an accredited athletic training program and must pass a rigorous examination. To retain certification, credential holders must continue taking medical-related courses and adhere to the BOC standards of practice. In Alaska, California, West Virginia, and the District of Columbia where licensure is not required, certification is voluntary but may be helpful for those seeking jobs and advancement.

Other qualifications. Because all athletic trainers deal directly with a variety of people, they need good social and communication skills. They should be able to manage difficult situations and the stress associated with them, such as when disagreements arise with coaches, patients, clients, or parents regarding suggested treatment. Athletic trainers also should be organized, be able to manage time wisely, be inquisitive, and have a strong desire to help people.

Advancement. There are a few ways for athletic trainers to advance. Some athletic trainers advance by switching teams or sports to gain additional responsibility or pay. Assistant athletic trainers may become head athletic trainers and, eventually, athletic directors or physician, hospital or clinic practice

Projections data from the National Employment Matrix

Occupational Title	SOC Code	Employment, 2008	Projected Employment, 2018	Change, 2008-2018	
				Number	Percent
Athletic trainers..	29-9091	16,300	22,400	6,000	37

(NOTE) Data in this table are rounded. See the discussion of the employment projections table in the *Handbook* introductory chapter on *Occupational Information Included in the Handbook.*

administrators where they assume a management role. Some athletic trainers move into sales and marketing positions, using their expertise to sell medical and athletic equipment.

Employment

Athletic trainers held about 16,300 jobs in 2008 and are found in every part of the country. Most athletic trainer jobs are related to sports, although an increasing number also work in nonsports settings. About 39 percent were found in public and private educational services, primarily in colleges, universities, and high schools. Another 38 percent of athletic trainers worked in healthcare, including jobs in hospitals, offices of physicians, and offices of other health practitioners. About 13 percent worked in fitness and recreational sports centers. Around 5 percent work in spectator sports.

Job Outlook

Employment is projected to grow much faster than average. Job prospects should be good in the healthcare industry and in high schools, but competition is expected for positions with professional and college sports teams.

Employment change. Employment of athletic trainers is projected to grow 37 percent from 2008 to 2018, much faster than the average for all occupations, because of their role in preventing injuries and reducing healthcare costs. Job growth will be concentrated in the healthcare industry, including hospitals and offices of health practitioners. Fitness and recreation sports centers also will provide new jobs, as these establishments grow and continue to need additional athletic trainers to provide support for their clients. Growth in positions with sports teams will be somewhat slower, however, as most professional sports clubs and colleges and universities already have complete athletic training staffs.

The demand for healthcare, with an emphasis on preventive care, should grow as the population ages and as a way to reduce healthcare costs. Increased licensure requirements and regulation has led to a greater acceptance of athletic trainers as qualified healthcare providers. As a result, third-party reimbursement is expected to continue to grow for athletic training services. Athletic trainers will benefit from this expansion because they provide a cost-effective way to increase the number of health professionals in an office or other setting.

In some States, there are efforts underway to have an athletic trainer in every high school to work with student-athletes, which may lead to growth in the number of athletic trainers employed in high schools. In addition, as more young athletes specialize in certain sports, there is increasing demand for athletic trainers to deal with repetitive stress injuries.

As athletic trainers continue to expand their services, more employers are expected to use these workers to reduce healthcare costs by preventing work-related injuries. Athletic trainers can help prevent injuries and provide immediate treatment for many injuries that occur. For example, some athletic trainers may be hired to increase the fitness and performance of police and firefighters.

Job prospects. Job prospects should be good for athletic trainers in the healthcare industry and in high schools. Those looking for a position with a professional or college sports team may face competition.

Because of relatively low turnover, the settings with the best job prospects will be the ones that are expected to have the most job growth, primarily positions in the healthcare and fitness and recreational sports centers industries. Additional job opportunities may arise in elementary and secondary schools as more positions are created. Some of these positions also will require teaching responsibilities.

There are relatively few positions for professional and collegiate sports teams in comparison to the number of applicants. Turnover among professional sports team athletic trainers is also limited. Many athletic trainers prefer to continue to work with the same coaches, administrators, and players when a good working relationship already exists.

There also are opportunities for athletic trainers to join the military, although they would not be classified as an athletic trainer. Enlisted soldiers and officers who are athletic trainers are usually placed in another program, such as health educator or training specialist, in which their skills are useful. (For information on military careers, see the *Handbook* statement on job opportunities in the Armed Forces.)

This occupation is expected to continue to change over the next decade, including more administrative responsibilities, adapting to new technology, and working with larger populations, and jobseekers must be prepared to adapt to these changes.

Earnings

Most athletic trainers work in full-time positions, and typically receive benefits. The salary of an athletic trainer depends on experience and job responsibilities, and varies by job setting. Median annual wages for athletic trainers were $39,640 in May 2008. The middle 50 percent earned between $32,070 and $49,250. The lowest 10 percent earned less than $23,450, while the top 10 percent earned more than $60,960.

Many employers pay for some of the continuing education required for athletic trainers to remain certified, although the amount covered varies from employer to employer.

Related Occupations

Other American Medical Association allied health professionals include:

Sources of Additional Information

For further information on careers in athletic training, contact:
➤ National Athletic Trainers' Association, 2952 Stemmons Freeway, Suite 200, Dallas, TX 75247. Internet: **http://www.nata.org**

For further information on certification, contact:
➤ Board of Certification, Inc., 1415 Harney St., Suite 200, Omaha, NE 68102. Internet: **http://www.bocatc.org**

The Occupational Information Network (O*NET) provides information on a wide range of occupational characteristics. Links to O*NET appear at the end of the Internet version of this occupational statement, accessible at **http://www.bls.gov/ooh/ocos294.htm**

Cardiovascular Technologists and Technicians

Significant Points

- Employment is expected to grow much faster than average.

- Technologists and technicians with multiple professional credentials, trained to perform a wide range of procedures, will have the best prospects.

- About 77 percent of jobs are in hospitals.

- Workers typically need a 2-year associate degree at a junior or community college; most employers also require a professional credential.

Nature of the Work

Cardiovascular technologists and technicians assist physicians in diagnosing and treating cardiac (heart) and peripheral vascular (blood vessel) ailments.

Cardiovascular technologists and technicians schedule appointments, review physicians' interpretations and patient files, and monitor patients' heart rates. They also operate and care for testing equipment, explain test procedures, and compare findings to a standard to identify problems. Other day-to-day activities vary significantly between specialties.

Technologists may specialize in different areas of practice: invasive cardiology, non-invasive—which includes echocardiography—or vascular technology. Technicians specialize in electrocardiograms and stress testing.

Invasive cardiology. Cardiovascular technologists specializing in invasive procedures are called *cardiology technologists.* They assist physicians with cardiac catheterization procedures in which a small tube, or catheter, is threaded through a patient's artery from a spot on the patient's groin to the heart. The procedure can determine whether a blockage exists in the blood vessels that supply the heart muscle or help to diagnose other problems. Some of these procedures may involve balloon angioplasty, which can be used to treat blockages of blood vessels or heart valves without the need for heart surgery. Cardiology technologists assist physicians as they insert a catheter with a balloon on the end to the point of the obstruction. Catheters are also used in electrophysiology tests, which help locate the specific areas of heart tissue that give rise to the abnormal electrical impulses that cause arrhythmias.

Technologists prepare patients for cardiac catheterization by first positioning them on an examining table and then shaving, cleaning, and administering anesthesia to the top of their leg near the groin. During the procedures, they monitor patients' blood pressure and heart rate with EKG equipment and notify the physician if something appears to be wrong. Some cardiology technologists also prepare and monitor patients during open-heart surgery and during the insertion of pacemakers and stents that open up blockages in arteries to the heart and major blood vessels.

Noninvasive technology. Technologists who specialize in echocardiography or vascular technology perform noninvasive tests. Tests are called "noninvasive" if they do not require the insertion of probes or other instruments into the patient's body. For example, procedures such as Doppler ultrasound transmit high-frequency sound waves into areas of the patient's body and then processes reflected echoes of the sound waves to form an image. Technologists view the ultrasound image on a screen and may record the image on videotape or photograph it for interpretation and diagnosis by a physician. (See the statement on diagnostic medical sonographers elsewhere in the *Handbook* to learn more about other sonographers.)

Echocardiographers. Technologists who use ultrasound to examine the heart chambers, valves, and vessels are referred to as *cardiac sonographers*, or *echocardiographers*. They use ultrasound instrumentation to create images called echocardiograms. An echocardiogram may be performed while the patient is either resting or physically active. Technologists may administer medication to physically active patients to assess their heart function. Cardiac sonographers also may assist physicians who perform other procedures.

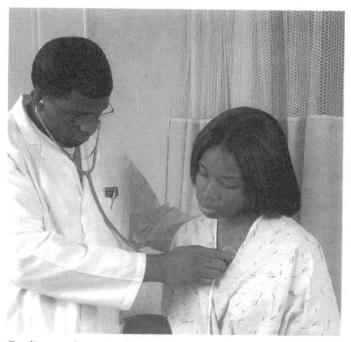

Cardiovascular technologists may specialize in invasive cardiology, echocardiography, and vascular technology.

Vascular technologists. Technologists who assist physicians in the diagnosis of disorders affecting the circulation are known as *vascular technologists* or *vascular sonographers.* Vascular technologists complete patients' medical history, evaluate pulses and assess blood flow in arteries and veins by listening to the vascular flow sounds for abnormalities, and assure the appropriate vascular test has been ordered. Then they perform a noninvasive procedure using ultrasound instruments to record vascular information such as vascular blood flow, blood pressure, oxygen saturation, cerebral circulation, peripheral circulation, and abdominal circulation. Many of these tests are performed during or immediately after surgery. Vascular technologists then provide a summary of findings to the physician to aid in patient diagnosis and management.

Cardiographic technicians. Technicians who specialize in electrocardiography, or EKG, stress testing, and perform Holter monitor procedures are known as *cardiographic* or *electrocardiograph* (or *EKG*) *technicians.*

Technicians take EKGs, which trace electrical impulses transmitted by the heart, attach electrodes to the patient's chest, arms, and legs, and then manipulate switches on an EKG machine to obtain a reading. An EKG is printed out for interpretation by the physician. This test is done before most kinds of surgery or as part of a routine physical examination.

EKG technicians with advanced training perform Holter monitor and stress testing. For Holter monitoring, technicians place electrodes on the patient's chest and attach a portable EKG monitor to the patient's belt. Following 24 or more hours of normal activity by the patient, the technician removes a tape from the monitor and places it in a scanner. After checking the quality of the recorded impulses on an electronic screen, the technician usually prints the information from the tape for analysis by a physician. Physicians use the output from the scanner to diagnose heart ailments, such as heart rhythm abnormalities or problems with pacemakers.

For a treadmill stress test, EKG technicians document the patient's medical history, explain the procedure, connect the patient to an EKG monitor, and obtain a baseline reading and resting blood pressure. Next, they monitor the heart's performance while the patient is walking on a treadmill, gradually increasing the treadmill's speed to observe the effect of increased exertion. Like vascular technologists and cardiac sonographers, cardiographic technicians who perform EKGs, Holter monitoring, and stress tests are known as "noninvasive" technicians.

Work environment. Cardiovascular technologists and technicians spend a lot of time walking and standing. Heavy lifting may be involved to move equipment or transfer patients. Those who work in catheterization laboratories may face stressful working conditions because they are in close contact with patients with serious heart ailments. For example, some patients may encounter complications that have life-or-death implications.

Some cardiovascular technologists and technicians may have the potential for radiation exposure. However, exposure is kept to a minimum by strict adherence to radiation safety guidelines, such as wearing heavy protective aprons while conducting certain procedures. In addition, those who use sonography can be at an increased risk for musculoskeletal disorders such as carpel tunnel syndrome, neck and back strain, and eye strain. However, greater use of ergonomic equipment and an increasing awareness will continue to minimize such risks.

Technologists and technicians generally work a 5-day, 40-hour week that may include weekends. Those in catheterization laboratories tend to work longer hours and may work evenings. They also may be on call during the night and on weekends. About 18 percent worked part-time in 2008.

Training, Other Qualifications, and Advancement

Cardiovascular technologists typically need an associate degree for entry-level employment. Most employers also require a professional credential. Technicians also receive on-the-job training.

Education and training. The majority of cardiovascular technologists, vascular technologists, and cardiac sonographers complete a 2-year junior or community college program resulting in an associate degree. However, 4-year programs are increasingly available. The first year is dedicated to core courses and is followed by a year of specialized instruction in either invasive cardiovascular, noninvasive cardiovascular, or noninvasive vascular technology. Those who are qualified in an allied health profession need to complete only the year of specialized instruction.

The Commission on Accreditation of Allied Health Professionals (CAAHEP) accredits cardiovascular technology education programs. In January 2009, there were 34 accredited programs. Similarly, those who want to study echocardiography or vascular sonography may also attend CAAHEP-accredited programs in diagnostic medical sonography. In 2009, there were 168 such accredited programs. Those who attend these accredited programs are eligible to obtain professional certification.

Unlike most other cardiovascular technologists and technicians, most EKG technicians are trained on the job by an EKG supervisor or a cardiologist. On-the-job training for EKG technicians usually takes about 4 to 6 weeks. Most employers prefer to train people already in the healthcare field—nursing aides, for example. Some EKG technicians are students enrolled in 2-year programs to become technologists, working part time to gain experience and make contact with employers. For technicians who perform Holter monitoring on-the-job training may last around 18 to 24 months. One-year certification programs also exist for basic EKGs, Holter monitoring, and stress testing and can be an alternative to on-the-job training.

Licensure and certification. Credentialing is voluntary. However, it is the professional standard and most employ-

Projections data from the National Employment Matrix

Occupational Title	SOC Code	Employment, 2008	Projected Employment, 2018	Change, 2008-2018	
				Number	Percent
Cardiovascular technologists and technicians..................................	29-2031	49,500	61,400	11,900	24

(NOTE) Data in this table are rounded. See the discussion of the employment projections table in the *Handbook* introductory chapter on *Occupational Information Included in the Handbook.*

ers require credentialing. Credentialing for cardiovascular technologists is available from Cardiovascular Credentialing International (CCI) and the American Registry of Diagnostic Medical Sonographers (ARDMS). Most credentials require that technologists complete an accredited education program to qualify to sit for credentialing examination. Continuing education is required in most cases to maintain certification. For specific requirements, contact the credentialing body.

Other qualifications. Cardiovascular technologists and technicians must be reliable, have mechanical aptitude, and be able to follow detailed instructions. A pleasant, relaxed manner for putting patients at ease is an asset. They must be articulate as they must communicate technically with physicians and also explain procedures simply to patients.

Advancement. Technicians may advance to the technologist level of practice with supplemental formal education and credentialing.

Technologists can advance to higher levels of the profession as many institutions structure the occupation with multiple levels, each having an increasing amount of responsibility. Advancement may occur through multiple credentialing in more than one cardiovascular specialty or through work experience. Technologists may also advance into supervisory or management positions. Other possibilities include working in an educational setting or conducting laboratory work.

Employment

Cardiovascular technologists and technicians held about 49,500 jobs in 2008. About 77 percent of jobs were in hospitals (public and private), primarily in cardiology departments. The remaining jobs were mostly in offices of physicians, including cardiologists, or in medical and diagnostic laboratories, including diagnostic imaging centers.

Job Outlook

Employment is expected to grow much faster than the average; technologists and technicians with multiple professional credentials, trained to perform a wide range of procedures, will have the best prospects.

Employment change. Employment of cardiovascular technologists and technicians is expected to increase 24 percent through the year 2018, much faster than the average for all occupations. Demand will stem from the prevalence of heart disease and the aging population, because older people have a higher incidence of heart disease and other complications of the heart and vascular system. Procedures such as ultrasound imaging and radiology are being performed more often as a replacement for more expensive and more invasive procedures. Due to advances in medicine and greater public awareness, signs of vascular disease can be detected earlier, creating demand for cardiovascular technologists and technicians to perform various procedures.

Employment of vascular technologists and echocardiographers will grow as advances in vascular technology and sonography reduce the need for more costly and invasive procedures. However, fewer EKG technicians will be needed, as hospitals train nursing aides and others to perform basic EKG procedures. Individuals trained in Holter monitoring and stress testing are expected to have more favorable job prospects than those who can perform only a basic EKG.

The rules governing reimbursement by Medicare and Medicaid for medical procedures will affect the frequency of their use and demand for imaging technologists.

Job prospects. In addition to job growth, job openings for cardiovascular technologists and technicians will arise from replacement needs as individuals transfer to other jobs or leave the labor force. Job prospects will be best for those with multiple professional credentials, trained to perform a wide range of procedures. Those willing to relocate or work irregular hours also will have better job opportunities.

It is not uncommon for cardiovascular technologists and technicians to move between the specialties within the occupation by obtaining certification in more than one specialty. Technologists with multiple credentials will be the most marketable to employers.

Earnings

Median annual wages of cardiovascular technologists and technicians were $47,010 in May 2008. The middle 50 percent earned between $32,800 and $61,580. The lowest 10 percent earned less than $25,510, and the highest 10 percent earned more than $74,760. Median annual wages of cardiovascular technologists and technicians in 2008 were $48,590 in offices of physicians and $46,670 in general medical and surgical hospitals.

Related Occupations

Cardiovascular technologists and technicians operate sophisticated equipment that helps physicians and other health practitioners to diagnose and treat patients. Similar occupations include:

	Page
Diagnostic medical sonographers	416
Nuclear medicine technologists	426
Radiation therapists	387
Radiologic technologists and technicians	438
Respiratory therapy technicians	446

Sources of Additional Information

For general information about a career in cardiovascular technology, contact:

➤ Alliance of Cardiovascular Professionals, P.O. Box 2007 Midlothian, VA†23113. Internet: **http://www.acp-online.org**

For a list of accredited programs in cardiovascular technology, contact:

➤ Committee on Accreditation for Allied Health Education Programs, 1361 Park St., Clearwater, FL 33756. Internet: **http://www.caahep.org**

➤ Society for Vascular Ultrasound, 4601 Presidents Dr., Suite 260, Lanham, MD 20706. Internet: **http://www.svunet.org**

For information regarding registration and certification, contact:

➤ Cardiovascular Credentialing International, 1500 Sunday Dr., Suite 102, Raleigh, NC 27607. Internet: **http://www.cci-online.org**

> American Registry of Diagnostic Medical Sonographers, 51 Monroe St., Plaza East One, Rockville, MD 20850-2400. Internet: **http://www.ardms.org**

The Occupational Information Network (O*NET) provides information on a wide range of occupational characteristics. Links to O*NET appear at the end of the Internet version of this occupational statement, accessible at **http://www.bls.gov/ooh/ocos100.htm**

Clinical Laboratory Technologists and Technicians

Significant Points

- Excellent job opportunities are expected.

- Clinical laboratory technologists usually have a bachelor's degree with a major in medical technology or in one of the life sciences; clinical laboratory technicians generally need either an associate degree or a certificate.

- Most jobs will continue to be in hospitals, but employment will grow rapidly in other settings, as well.

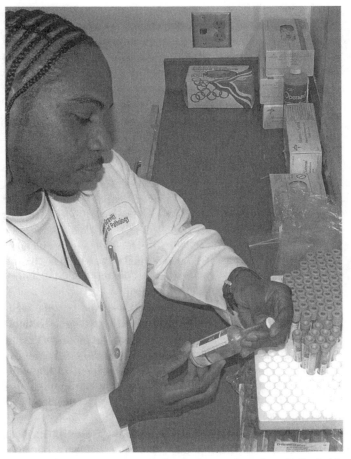

Clinical laboratory personnel examine and analyze body fluids and cells.

Nature of the Work

Clinical laboratory testing plays a crucial role in the detection, diagnosis, and treatment of disease. *Clinical laboratory technologists*, also referred to as clinical laboratory scientists or medical technologists, and clinical laboratory technicians, also known as medical technicians or medical laboratory technicians, perform most of these tests.

Clinical laboratory personnel examine and analyze body fluids, and cells. They look for bacteria, parasites, and other microorganisms; analyze the chemical content of fluids; match blood for transfusions; and test for drug levels in the blood that show how a patient is responding to treatment. Technologists also prepare specimens for examination, count cells, and look for abnormal cells in blood and body fluids. They use microscopes, cell counters, and other sophisticated laboratory equipment. They also use automated equipment and computerized instruments capable of performing a number of tests simultaneously. After testing and examining a specimen, they analyze the results and relay them to physicians.

With increasing automation and the use of computer technology, the work of technologists and technicians has become less hands-on and more analytical. The complexity of tests performed, the level of judgment needed, and the amount of responsibility workers assume depend largely on the amount of education and experience they have. Clinical laboratory technologists usually do more complex tasks than clinical laboratory technicians do.

Clinical laboratory technologists perform complex chemical, biological, hematological, immunologic, microscopic, and bacteriological tests. Technologists microscopically examine blood and other body fluids. They make cultures of body fluid and tissue samples, to determine the presence of bacteria, fungi, parasites, or other microorganisms. Technologists analyze samples for chemical content or a chemical reaction and determine concentrations of compounds such as blood glucose and cholesterol levels. They also type and cross match blood samples for transfusions.

Clinical laboratory technologists evaluate test results, develop and modify procedures, and establish and monitor programs, to ensure the accuracy of tests. Some technologists supervise clinical laboratory technicians.

Technologists in small laboratories perform many types of tests, whereas those in large laboratories generally specialize. Clinical chemistry technologists, for example, prepare specimens and analyze the chemical and hormonal contents of body fluids. Microbiology technologists examine and identify bacteria and other microorganisms. Blood bank technologists, or immunohematology technologists, collect, type, and prepare blood and its components for transfusions. Immunology technologists examine elements of the human immune system and its response to foreign bodies. Cytotechnologists prepare slides of body cells and examine these cells microscopically for abnormalities that may signal the beginning of a cancerous growth. Molecular biology technologists perform complex protein and nucleic acid testing on cell samples.

Clinical laboratory technicians perform less complex tests and laboratory procedures than technologists do. Technicians may prepare specimens and operate automated analyzers, for example, or they may perform manual tests in accordance with

Projections data from the National Employment Matrix

Occupational Title	SOC Code	Employment, 2008	Projected Employment, 2018	Change, 2008-2018	
				Number	Percent
Clinical laboratory technologists and technicians............................	29-2010	328,100	373,600	45,600	14
Medical and clinical laboratory technologists	29-2011	172,400	193,000	20,500	12
Medical and clinical laboratory technicians	29-2012	155,600	180,700	25,000	16

(NOTE) Data in this table are rounded. See the discussion of the employment projections table in the *Handbook* introductory chapter on *Occupational Information Included in the Handbook.*

detailed instructions. They usually work under the supervision of medical and clinical laboratory technologists or laboratory managers. Like technologists, clinical laboratory technicians may work in several areas of the clinical laboratory or specialize in just one. Phlebotomists collect blood samples, for example, and *histotechnicians* cut and stain tissue specimens for microscopic examination by pathologists.

Work environment. Clinical laboratory personnel are trained to work with infectious specimens. When proper methods of infection control and sterilization are followed, few hazards exist. Protective masks, gloves, and goggles often are necessary to ensure the safety of laboratory personnel.

Working conditions vary with the size and type of employment setting. Laboratories usually are well lighted and clean; however, specimens, solutions, and reagents used in the laboratory sometimes produce fumes. Laboratory workers may spend a great deal of time on their feet.

Hours of clinical laboratory technologists and technicians vary with the size and type of employment setting. In large hospitals or in independent laboratories that operate continuously, personnel usually work the day, evening, or night shift and may work weekends and holidays. Laboratory personnel in small facilities may work on rotating shifts, rather than on a regular shift. In some facilities, laboratory personnel are on call several nights a week or on weekends, in case of an emergency.

Training, Other Qualifications, and Advancement

Clinical laboratory technologists generally require a bachelor's degree in medical technology or in one of the life sciences; clinical laboratory technicians usually need an associate degree or a certificate.

Education and training. The usual requirement for an entry-level position as a clinical laboratory technologist is a bachelor's degree with a major in medical technology or one of the life sciences; however, it is possible to qualify for some jobs with a combination of education and on-the-job and specialized training. Universities and hospitals offer medical technology programs.

Bachelor's degree programs in medical technology include courses in chemistry, biological sciences, microbiology, mathematics, and statistics, as well as specialized courses devoted to knowledge and skills used in the clinical laboratory. Many programs also offer or require courses in management, business, and computer applications. The Clinical Laboratory Improvement Act requires technologists who perform highly complex tests to have at least an associate degree.

Medical and clinical laboratory technicians generally have either an associate degree from a community or junior college or

a certificate from a hospital, a vocational or technical school, or the Armed Forces. A few technicians learn their skills on the job.

The National Accrediting Agency for Clinical Laboratory Sciences (NAACLS) fully accredits about 479 programs for medical and clinical laboratory technologists, medical and clinical laboratory technicians, histotechnologists and histotechnicians, cytogenetic technologists, and diagnostic molecular scientists. NAACLS also approves about 60 programs in phlebotomy and clinical assisting. Other nationally recognized agencies that accredit specific areas for clinical laboratory workers include the Commission on Accreditation of Allied Health Education Programs and the Accrediting Bureau of Health Education Schools.

Licensure. Some States require laboratory personnel to be licensed or registered. Licensure of technologists often requires a bachelor's degree and the passing of an exam, but requirements vary by State and specialty. Information on licensure is available from State departments of health or boards of occupational licensing.

Certification and other qualifications. Many employers prefer applicants who are certified by a recognized professional association. Associations offering certification include the Board of Registry of the American Society for Clinical Pathology, the American Medical Technologists, the National Credentialing Agency for Laboratory Personnel, and the Board of Registry of the American Association of Bioanalysts. These agencies have different requirements for certification and different organizational sponsors.

In addition to certification, employers seek clinical laboratory personnel with good analytical judgment and the ability to work under pressure. Technologists in particular are expected to be good at problem solving. Close attention to detail is also essential for laboratory personnel because small differences or changes in test substances or numerical readouts can be crucial to a diagnosis. Manual dexterity and normal color vision are highly desirable, and with the widespread use of automated laboratory equipment, computer skills are important.

Advancement. Technicians can advance and become technologists through additional education and experience. Technologists may advance to supervisory positions in laboratory work or may become chief medical or clinical laboratory technologists or laboratory managers in hospitals. Manufacturers of home diagnostic testing kits and laboratory equipment and supplies also seek experienced technologists to work in product development, marketing, and sales.

Professional certification and a graduate degree in medical technology, one of the biological sciences, chemistry, management, or education usually speeds advancement. A doctorate usually is needed to become a laboratory director. Federal regulation requires directors of moderately complex laboratories to have either a master's degree or a bachelor's degree, combined with the appropriate amount of training and experience.

Employment

Clinical laboratory technologists and technicians held about 328,100 jobs in 2008. More than half of jobs were in hospitals. Most of the remaining jobs were in offices of physicians and in medical and diagnostic laboratories. A small proportion was in educational services and in all other ambulatory health care services.

Job Outlook

Rapid job growth and excellent job opportunities are expected. Most jobs will continue to be in hospitals, but employment will grow rapidly in other settings, as well.

Employment change. Employment of clinical laboratory workers is expected to grow by 14 percent between 2008 and 2018, faster than the average for all occupations. The volume of laboratory tests continues to increase with both population growth and the development of new types of tests.

Technological advances will continue to have opposing effects on employment. On the one hand, new, increasingly powerful diagnostic tests and advances in genomics—the study of the genetic information of a cell or organism—will encourage additional testing and spur employment. On the other hand, research and development efforts targeted at simplifying and automating routine testing procedures may enhance the ability of nonlaboratory personnel—physicians and patients in particular—to perform tests now conducted in laboratories.

Although hospitals are expected to continue to be the major employer of clinical laboratory workers, employment is expected also to grow rapidly in medical and diagnostic laboratories, offices of physicians, and all other ambulatory health care services.

Job prospects. Job opportunities are expected to be excellent because the number of job openings is expected to continue to exceed the number of jobseekers. Although significant, job growth will not be the only source of opportunities. As in most occupations, many additional openings will result from the need to replace workers who transfer to other occupations, retire, or stop working for some other reason. Willingness to relocate will further enhance one's job prospects.

Earnings

Median annual wages of medical and clinical laboratory technologists were $53,500 in May 2008. The middle 50 percent earned between $44,560 and $63,420. The lowest 10 percent earned less than $36,180, and the highest 10 percent earned more than $74,680. Median annual wages in the industries employing the largest numbers of medical and clinical laboratory technologists were:

Federal Executive Branch	$59,800
General medical and surgical hospitals	54,220
Medical and diagnostic laboratories	53,360
Offices of physicians	49,080
Colleges, universities, and professional schools	47,890

Median annual wages of medical and clinical laboratory technicians were $35,380 in May 2008. The middle 50 percent

earned between $28,420 and $44,310. The lowest 10 percent earned less than $23,480, and the highest 10 percent earned more than $53,520. Median annual wages in the industries employing the largest numbers of medical and clinical laboratory technicians were:

General medical and surgical hospitals	$36,840
Colleges, universities, and professional schools	36,290
Offices of physicians	33,980
Medical and diagnostic laboratories	32,630
Other ambulatory health care services	31,320

According to the American Society for Clinical Pathology, median hourly wages of staff clinical laboratory technologists and technicians, in various specialties and laboratory types, in 2007 were:

Table 1. Median hourly wages by specialties and laboratory type, 2007.

Occupation	Hospital	Private clinic	Physician office laboratory
Cytotechnologist	$27.55	$28.75	$26.24
Histotechnologist	22.93	23.35	25.00
Medical technologist	23.45	23.00	20.00
Histotechnician	20.00	20.00	21.00
Medical laboratory technician	18.54	17.00	16.96
Phlebotomist	12.50	12.50	13.00
SOURCE: American Society for Clinical Pathology			

Related Occupations

Clinical laboratory technologists and technicians analyze body fluids, tissue, and other substances, using a variety of tests. Similar or related procedures are performed by:

	Page
Chemists and materials scientists	195
Science technicians	230
Veterinary technologists and technicians	443

Sources of Additional Information

For a list of accredited and approved educational programs for clinical laboratory personnel, contact:
➤ National Accrediting Agency for Clinical Laboratory Sciences, 5600 N. River Rd., Suite 720, Rosemont, IL 60018. Internet: **http://www.naacls.org**

Information on certification is available from:
➤ American Association of Bioanalysts, Board of Registry, 906 Olive St., Suite 1200, St. Louis, MO 63101. Internet: **http://www.aab.org**

➤ American Medical Technologists, 10700 W. Higgins Rd., Suite 150, Rosemont, IL 60018. Internet: **http://www.amt1.com**

➤ American Society for Clinical Pathology, 33 West Monroe St., Suite 1600, Chicago, IL 60603. Internet: **http://www.ascp.org**

➤ National Credentialing Agency for Laboratory Personnel, P.O. Box 15945-289, Lenexa, KS 66285. Internet: **http://www.nca-info.org**

Additional career information is available from:

➤ American Association of Blood Banks, 8101 Glenbrook Rd., Bethesda, MD 20814. Internet: **http://www.aabb.org**

➤ American Society for Clinical Laboratory Science, 6701 Democracy Blvd., Suite 300, Bethesda, MD 20817. Internet: **http://www.ascls.org**

➤ American Society for Cytopathology, 100 West 10th St., Suite 605, Wilmington, DE 19801. Internet: **http://www.cytopathology.org**

➤ Clinical Laboratory Management Association, 993 Old Eagle School Rd., Suite 405, Wayne, PA 19087. Internet: **http://www.clma.org**

The Occupational Information Network (O*NET) provides information on a wide range of occupational characteristics. Links to O*NET appear at the end of the Internet version of this occupational statement, accessible at **http://www.bls.gov/ooh/ocos096.htm**

Dental Hygienists

Significant Points

- A degree from an accredited dental hygiene school and a State license are required for this job.

- Dental hygienists rank among the fastest growing occupations.

- Job prospects are expected to be favorable in most areas, but strong competition for jobs is likely in some areas.

- About half of all dental hygienists work part time, and flexible scheduling is a distinctive feature of this job.

Nature of the Work

Dental hygienists remove soft and hard deposits from teeth, teach patients how to practice good oral hygiene, and provide other preventive dental care. They examine patients' teeth and gums, recording the presence of diseases or abnormalities.

Dental hygienists use an assortment of tools to complete their tasks. Hand and rotary instruments and ultrasonic devices are used to clean and polish teeth, which includes removing tartar, stains, and plaque. Hygienists use x-ray machines to take dental pictures, and sometimes develop the film. They may use models of teeth to explain oral hygiene, perform root planning as a periodontal therapy, or apply cavity-preventative agents such as fluorides and pit and fissure sealants.

Other tasks hygienists may perform vary by State. In some States, hygienists are allowed to administer anesthetics, while in others they administer local anesthetics using syringes. Some States also allow hygienists to place and carve filling materials, temporary fillings, and periodontal dressings; remove sutures; and smooth and polish metal restorations.

Dental hygienists also help patients develop and maintain good oral health. For example, they may explain the relationship between diet and oral health or inform patients how to select toothbrushes and show them how to brush and floss their teeth.

Hygienists sometimes make a diagnosis and other times prepare clinical and laboratory diagnostic tests for the dentist to interpret. Hygienists sometimes work chair-side with the dentist during treatment.

Work environment. Dental hygienists work in clean, well-lighted offices. Important health safeguards include strict adherence to proper radiological procedures and the use of appropriate protective devices when administering anesthetic gas. Dental hygienists also wear safety glasses, surgical masks, and gloves to protect themselves and patients from infectious diseases. Dental hygienists also should be careful to avoid possible shoulder and neck injury from sitting for long periods of time while working with patients.

Flexible scheduling is a distinctive feature of this job. Full-time, part-time, evening, and weekend schedules are common. Dentists frequently hire hygienists to work only 2 or 3 days a week, so hygienists may hold jobs in more than one dental office. In 2008, about half of all dental hygienists worked part time—less than 35 hours a week.

Training, Other Qualifications, and Advancement

A degree from an accredited dental hygiene school and a State license are required for this job.

Education and training. A high school diploma and college entrance test scores are usually required for admission to a dental hygiene program. High school students interested in becoming dental hygienists should take courses in biology, chemistry, and mathematics. Some dental hygiene programs also require applicants to have completed at least one year of college. Specific entrance requirements typically vary from one school to another.

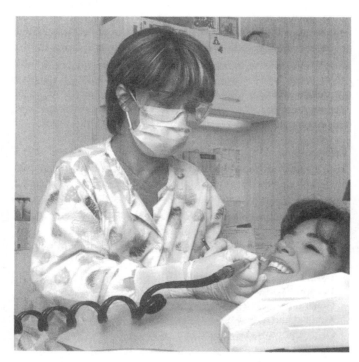

Dental hygienists remove soft and hard deposits from teeth and teach patients how to practice good oral hygiene.

Projections data from the National Employment Matrix

Occupational Title	SOC Code	Employment, 2008	Projected Employment, 2018	Change, 2008-2018	
				Number	Percent
Dental hygienists...	29-2021	174,100	237,000	62,900	36

(NOTE) Data in this table are rounded. See the discussion of the employment projections table in the *Handbook* introductory chapter on *Occupational Information Included in the Handbook.*

In 2008, there were 301 dental hygiene programs accredited by the Commission on Dental Accreditation. Most dental hygiene programs grant an associate degree, although some also offer a certificate, a bachelor's degree, or a master's degree. A minimum of an associate degree or certificate in dental hygiene is generally required for practice in a private dental office. A bachelor's or master's degree usually is required for research, teaching, or clinical practice in public or school health programs.

Schools offer laboratory, clinical, and classroom instruction in subjects such as anatomy, physiology, chemistry, microbiology, pharmacology, nutrition, radiography, histology (the study of tissue structure), periodontology (the study of gum diseases), pathology, dental materials, clinical dental hygiene, and social and behavioral sciences.

Licensure. Dental hygienists must be licensed by the State in which they practice. Nearly all States require candidates to graduate from an accredited dental hygiene school and pass both a written and clinical examination. The American Dental Association's (ADA) Joint Commission on National Dental Examinations administers the written examination, which is accepted by all States and the District of Columbia. State or regional testing agencies administer the clinical examination. In addition, most States require an examination on the legal aspects of dental hygiene practice. Alabama is the only State that does not require candidates to take the ADA written exam. Instead, they require that candidates meet the requirements of the Alabama Dental Hygiene Program, which mandates taking courses, completing on-the-job training at a dentist's office, and passing a separate State administered licensing examination.

Other qualifications. Dental hygienists should work well with others because they work closely with dentists and dental assistants, as well as dealing directly with patients. Hygienists also need good manual dexterity, because they use dental instruments within patients' mouths, with little room for error.

Advancement. Advancement opportunities usually come from working outside a typical dentist's office, and usually require a bachelor's or master's degree in dental hygiene. Some dental hygienists may choose to pursue a career teaching at a dental hygiene program, working in public health, or working in a corporate setting.

Employment

Dental hygienists held about 174,100 jobs in 2008. Because multiple job holding is common in this field, the number of jobs exceeds the number of hygienists. About 51 percent of dental hygienists worked part time. Almost all jobs for dental hygienists—about 96 percent—were in offices of dentists. A very small number worked for employment services, in physicians' offices, or in other industries.

Job Outlook

Dental hygienists rank among the fastest growing occupations. Job prospects are expected to be favorable in most areas, but competition for jobs is likely in some areas.

Employment change. Employment of dental hygienists is expected to grow 36 percent through 2018, which is much faster than the average for all occupations. This projected growth ranks dental hygienists among the fastest growing occupations, in response to increasing demand for dental care and more use of hygienists.

The demand for dental services will grow because of population growth, older people increasingly retaining more teeth, and a growing emphasis on preventative dental care. To help meet this demand, facilities that provide dental care, particularly dentists' offices, will increasingly employ dental hygienists, often to perform services that have been performed by dentists in the past. Ongoing research indicating a link between oral health and general health also will spur the demand for preventative dental services, which are typically provided by dental hygienists.

Job prospects. Job prospects are expected to be favorable in most areas, but will vary by geographical location. Because graduates are permitted to practice only in the State in which they are licensed, hygienists wishing to practice in areas that have an abundance of dental hygiene programs may experience strong competition for jobs.

Older dentists, who have been less likely to employ dental hygienists, are leaving the occupation and will be replaced by recent graduates, who are more likely to employ one or more hygienists. In addition, as dentists' workloads increase, they are expected to hire more hygienists to perform preventive dental care, such as cleaning, so that they may devote their own time to more complex procedures.

Earnings

Median annual wages of dental hygienists were $66,570 in May 2008. The middle 50 percent earned between $55,220 and $78,990. The lowest 10 percent earned less than $44,180, and the highest 10 percent earned more than $91,470.

Earnings vary by geographic location, employment setting, and years of experience. Dental hygienists may be paid on an hourly, daily, salary, or commission basis.

Benefits vary substantially by practice setting and may be contingent upon full-time employment. According to a 2009 survey conducted by the American Dental Hygienist Association, about half of all hygienists reported receiving some form of employment benefits. Of those receiving benefits, paid vacation, sick leave, and retirement plans were the most common.

Related Occupations

Other workers supporting health practitioners in an office setting include:

Sources of Additional Information

For information on a career in dental hygiene, including educational requirements, and on available accredited programs, contact:

➤ American Dental Hygienists Association, 444 N. Michigan Ave., Suite 3400, Chicago, IL 60611. Internet: **http://www.adha.org**

For information about accredited programs and educational requirements, contact:

➤ Commission on Dental Accreditation, American Dental Association, 211 E. Chicago Ave., Chicago, IL 60611. Internet: **http://www.ada.org/prof/ed/accred/commission/index.asp**

The State Board of Dental Examiners in each State can supply information on licensing requirements.

The Occupational Information Network (O*NET) provides information on a wide range of occupational characteristics. Links to O*NET appear at the end of the Internet version of this occupational statement, accessible at **http://www.bls.gov/ooh/ocos097.htm**

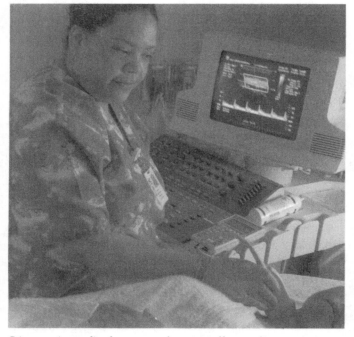

Diagnostic medical sonographers usually use diagnostic imaging machines in dark rooms, but may also perform procedures at a patient's bedside.

Diagnostic Medical Sonographers

Significant Points

- Job opportunities should be favorable.
- Employment will grow as sonography becomes an increasingly attractive alternative to radiological procedures.
- Hospitals employed about 59 percent of all sonographers.
- Sonographers may receive education and training in hospitals, vocational-technical institutions, colleges or universities, or the Armed Forces.

Nature of the Work

Diagnostic imaging embraces several procedures that aid in diagnosing ailments. The most familiar procedures are the x ray and magnetic resonance imaging; however, not all imaging technologies use ionizing, radiation, or radio waves. Sonography, or ultrasonography, is the use of sound waves to generate an image for the assessment and diagnosis of various medical conditions. Sonography is commonly associated with obstetrics and the use of ultrasound imaging during pregnancy, but this technology has many other applications in the diagnosis and treatment of medical conditions throughout the body.

Diagnostic medical sonographers use special equipment to direct high frequency sound waves into areas of the patient's body. Sonographers operate the equipment, which collects reflected echoes and forms an image that may be videotaped, transmitted, or photographed for interpretation and diagnosis by a physician.

Sonographers begin by explaining the procedure to the patient and recording any medical history that may be relevant to the condition being viewed. They then select appropriate equipment settings and direct the patient to move into positions that will provide the best view. To perform the exam, sonographers use a transducer, which transmits sound waves in a cone-shaped or rectangle-shaped beam. Although techniques vary by the area being examined, sonographers usually spread a special gel on the skin to aid the transmission of sound waves.

Viewing the screen during the scan, sonographers look for subtle visual cues that contrast healthy areas with unhealthy ones. They decide whether the images are satisfactory for diagnostic purposes and select which ones to store and show to the physician. Sonographers take measurements, calculate values, and analyze the results in preliminary findings for the physicians.

In addition to working directly with patients, diagnostic medical sonographers keep patient records and adjust and maintain equipment. They also may prepare work schedules, evaluate equipment purchases, or manage a sonography or diagnostic imaging department.

Diagnostic medical sonographers may specialize in obstetric and gynecologic sonography (images of the female reproductive system), abdominal sonography (images of the liver, kidneys, gallbladder, spleen, and pancreas), neurosonography (images of the brain and other parts of the nervous system), or breast sonography. In addition, sonographers may specialize in vascular sonography or cardiac sonography. (Vascular sonographers and cardiac sonographers are covered in the Handbook statement on cardiovascular technologists and technicians.)

Obstetric and gynecologic sonographers specialize in the imaging of the female reproductive system. Included in the discipline is one of the more well-known uses of sonography: examining the fetus of a pregnant woman to track the baby's growth and health.

Abdominal sonographers inspect a patient's abdominal cavity to help diagnose and treat conditions primarily involving the gallbladder, bile ducts, kidneys, liver, pancreas, spleen, and male reproductive system. Abdominal sonographers also are able to scan parts of the chest, although studies of the heart using sonography usually are done by echocardiographers.

Neurosonographers focus on the nervous system, including the brain. In neonatal care, neurosonographers study and diagnose neurological and nervous system disorders in premature infants. Like other sonographers, neurosonographers operate transducers to perform the sonogram, but they use frequencies and beam shapes different from those used by obstetric and abdominal sonographers.

Breast sonographers use sonography to study diseases of the breasts. Sonography aids mammography in the detection of breast cancer. Breast sonography also is used to track tumors, monitor blood supply conditions, and assist in the accurate biopsy of breast tissue. Breast sonographers use high-frequency transducers made exclusively to study breast tissue.

Work environment. Sonographers typically work in health-care facilities that are clean. They usually work at diagnostic imaging machines in darkened rooms, but they also may perform procedures at patients' bedsides. Sonographers may be on their feet for long periods of time and may have to lift or turn disabled patients.

Some sonographers work as contract employees and may travel to several healthcare facilities in an area. Similarly, some sonographers work with mobile imaging service providers and travel to patients and use mobile diagnostic imaging equipment to provide service in areas that otherwise would not have access to such services.

Most full-time sonographers work about 40 hours a week. Some sonographers work overtime. Also, sonographers may have evening and weekend hours when they are on call and must be ready to report to work on short notice.

Training, Other Qualifications, and Advancement

Diagnostic medical sonography is an occupation to which there are multiple paths of entry. Formal education in sonography, training, or a combination of these are accepted by employers. Employers do prefer sonographers who have received education from an accredited program or completed training in an accredited practice, and who are registered.

Education and training. There are several avenues for entry into the field of diagnostic medical sonography. Sonographers may train in hospitals, vocational-technical institutions, colleges or universities, or the Armed Forces. Some training programs prefer applicants with experience in other health care professions or high school graduates with courses in mathematics, health, and science.

Colleges and universities offer formal training in both 2-year and 4-year programs, resulting in either an associate or a bachelor's degree. Two-year programs are the most prevalent. Coursework includes classes in anatomy, physiology, instrumentation, basic physics, patient care, and medical ethics. In 2008, the Commission on Accreditation of Allied Health Education Programs (CAAHEP) accredited over 150 training programs. Accredited programs are offered by colleges and universities. Some hospital programs are accredited as well.

A few 1-year programs that typically result in a vocational certificate also are accepted as proper education by employers. These programs are useful usually only for workers already employed in a healthcare occupation who seek to increase their marketability by training in sonography. One-year vocational-certificate programs are not accredited by the CAAHEP.

Certification and other qualifications. No States require licensure in diagnostic medical sonography. However, sonographers may become credentialed by one of the professional certifying bodies. Most employers prefer to hire registered sonographers because registration provides an objective measure of an individual's professional standing. To become registered, one must first become eligible to take the examination by completing the proper education, training, or work experience. The exam typically includes a physics and instrumentation exam in a sonography specialty. Typically, sonographers must complete a required number of continuing-education hours to maintain registration. For specific details on credentialing, contact the certifying organization.

The American Registry for Diagnostic Medical Sonography (ARDMS) certifies each person who passes the exam as a Registered Diagnostic Medical Sonographer (RDMS). This credential can be obtained for several different specialty areas like the abdomen, breast, or nervous system. The ARDMS also credentials cardiac and vascular sonographers. The American Registry of Radiologic Technologist offers credentials in breast and vascular sonography. The Cardiovascular

Projections data from the National Employment Matrix

Occupational Title	SOC Code	Employment, 2008	Projected Employment, 2018	Change, 2008-2018	
				Number	Percent
Diagnostic medical sonographers	29-2032	50,300	59,500	9,200	18

(NOTE) Data in this table are rounded. See the discussion of the employment projections table in the *Handbook* introductory chapter on *Occupational Information Included in the Handbook.*

Credentialing International credentials cardiac sonographers. (Vascular sonographers and cardiac sonographers are covered in the *Handbook* statement on cardiovascular technologists and technicians.)

Sonographers should have good communication and interpersonal skills, because they must be able to explain technical procedures and results to their patients, some of whom may be nervous. Good hand-eye coordination is particularly important to obtaining quality images. It is very important that sonographers enjoy lifelong learning, because continuing education is crucial to workers in the ever-changing field of diagnostic medicine.

Advancement. Sonographers can seek advancement by obtaining competency in more than one specialty. For example, obstetric sonographers might seek training in abdominal sonography to broaden their opportunities and increase their marketability. Sonographers also may seek multiple credentials—for example, being both a registered diagnostic medical sonographer and a registered diagnostic cardiac sonographer.

Sonographers may advance by taking supervisory, managerial, or administrative positions.

Employment

Diagnostic medical sonographers held about 50,300 jobs in 2008. About 59 percent of all sonographer jobs were in public and private hospitals. The remaining jobs were typically in offices of physicians, medical and diagnostic laboratories, and outpatient care centers.

Job Outlook

Faster than average employment growth is expected. Job opportunities should be favorable.

Employment change. Employment of diagnostic medical sonographers is expected to increase by about 18 percent through 2018—faster than the average for all occupations. As the population continues to age, there will be an increasing demand for diagnostic imaging. Additional job growth is expected as healthcare providers increasingly utilize ultrasound imaging as a safer and more cost-effective alternative to radiological procedures. Ultrasound imaging technology is expected to evolve rapidly and spawn many new sonography procedures, enabling sonographers to scan and image areas of the body where ultrasound has not traditionally been used.

Hospitals will remain the principal employer of diagnostic medical sonographers. However, employment is expected to grow more rapidly in offices of physicians and in medical and diagnostic laboratories. Health care facilities such as these are expected to increase in number because of the strong shift toward outpatient care, encouraged by third-party payers and made possible by technological advances and less expensive ultrasound equipment that permit more procedures to be performed outside of hospitals.

Job prospects. Job opportunities should be favorable. In addition to job openings from growth, some openings will arise from the need to replace sonographers who retire or leave the occupation permanently. However, job opportunities will vary by geographic area. Sonographers willing to relocate will have the best job opportunities. Sonographers with mul-

tiple specialties or multiple credentials also will have good prospects.

Earnings

The median annual wage of diagnostic medical sonographers was $61,980 in May 2008. The middle 50 percent of sonographers earned wages between $52,570 and $73,680 a year. The lowest 10 percent earned less than $43,600, and the highest 10 percent earned more than $83,950. Median annual wages of diagnostic medical sonographers in May 2008 were $62,340 in offices of physicians and $61,870 in general medical and surgical hospitals.

Related Occupations

Health care occupations with similar diagnostic and treatment responsibilities include:

Sources of Additional Information

For information on a career as a diagnostic medical sonographer, contact:
➤ Society of Diagnostic Medical Sonography, 2745 Dallas Pkwy., Suite 350, Plano, TX 75093-8730. Internet: **http://www.sdms.org**

For information on becoming a registered diagnostic medical sonographer, contact:
➤ American Registry for Diagnostic Medical Sonography, 51 Monroe St., Plaza East One, Rockville, MD 20850-2400. Internet: **http://www.ardms.org**

For certification information, contact:
➤ American Registry of Radiologic Technologists, 1255 Northland Dr., St. Paul, MN 55120-1155. Internet: **http://www.arrt.org**

For more information on ultrasound in medicine and accredited practices, contact:
➤ American Institute of Ultrasound in Medicine, 14750 Sweitzer Lane, Suite 100, Laurel, MD 20707. Internet: **http://www.aium.org**

For a current list of accredited education programs in diagnostic medical sonography, contact:
➤ Joint Review Committee on Education in Diagnostic Medical Sonography, 2025 Woodlane Dr., St. Paul, MN 55125-2998. Internet: **http://www.jrcdms.org**

➤ Commission on Accreditation of Allied Health Education Programs, 1361 Park St., Clearwater, FL 33756. Internet: **http://www.caahep.org**

The Occupational Information Network (O*NET) provides information on a wide range of occupational characteristics. Links to O*NET appear at the end of the Internet version of this occupational statement, accessible at **http://www.bls.gov/ooh/ocos273.htm**

Emergency Medical Technicians and Paramedics

Significant Points

- Employment is projected to grow as fast as the average for all occupations.

- Emergency medical technicians and paramedics need formal training and certification or licensure, but requirements vary by State.

- Emergency services function 24 hours a day, so emergency medical technicians and paramedics have irregular working hours.

- Opportunities will be best for those who have earned advanced certifications.

Nature of the Work

People's lives often depend on the quick reaction and competent care of *emergency medical technicians (EMTs) and paramedics*. Incidents as varied as automobile accidents, heart attacks, slips and falls, childbirth, and gunshot wounds require immediate medical attention. EMTs and paramedics provide this vital service as they care for and transport the sick or injured to a medical facility.

In an emergency, EMTs and paramedics are typically dispatched by a 911 operator to the scene, where they often work with police and fire fighters. (Police and fire fighters are discussed elsewhere in the Handbook.) Once they arrive, EMTs and paramedics assess the nature of the patient's condition, while trying to determine whether the patient has any preexisting medical conditions. Following protocols and guidelines, they provide emergency care and transport the patient to a medical facility. EMTs and paramedics operate in emergency medical services systems where a physician provides medical direction and oversight.

EMTs and paramedics use special equipment, such as backboards, to immobilize patients before placing them on stretchers and securing them in the ambulance for transport to a medical facility. These workers generally work in teams. During the transport of a patient, one EMT or paramedic drives, while the other monitors the patient's vital signs and gives additional care, as needed. Some paramedics work as part of a helicopter's flight crew to quickly transport critically ill or injured patients to hospital trauma centers.

At the medical facility, EMTs and paramedics help transfer patients to the emergency department, report their observations and actions to emergency department staff, and may provide additional emergency treatment. After each run, EMTs and paramedics document the trip, replace used supplies and check equipment. If a transported patient has a contagious disease, EMTs and paramedics decontaminate the interior of the ambulance and report cases to the proper authorities.

EMTs and paramedics also provide transportation for patients from one medical facility to another, particularly if they work for private ambulance services. Patients often need to be transferred to a hospital that specializes in treating their injury or illness or to facility that provides long-term care, like nursing homes.

Beyond these general duties, the specific responsibilities of EMTs and paramedics depend on their level of qualification and training. The National Registry of Emergency Medical Technicians (NREMT) certifies emergency medical service providers at five levels: First Responder; EMT-Basic; EMT-Intermediate (which has two levels called 1985 and 1999) and Paramedic. Some States, however, have their own certification programs and use distinct names and titles.

The EMT-Basic represents the first response of the emergency medical system. An EMT trained at this level is prepared to care for patients at the scene of an accident and while transporting patients by ambulance to the hospital under the direction of more highly trained medical personnel. The EMT-Basic has the emergency skills to assess a patient's condition and manage respiratory, cardiac, and trauma emergencies.

The EMT-Intermediate has more advanced training. However, the specific tasks that those certified at this level are allowed to perform varies greatly from State to State.

Paramedics provide more extensive pre-hospital care than do EMTs. In addition to carrying out the procedures of the other levels, paramedics administer medications orally and intravenously, interpret electrocardiograms (EKGs), perform endotracheal intubations, and use monitors and other complex equipment. However, like the EMT-Intermediate level, what paramedics are permitted to do varies by State.

Work environment. EMTs and paramedics work both indoors and out, in all types of weather. They are required to do considerable kneeling, bending, and heavy lifting. These workers are at a higher risk for contracting illnesses or experiencing injuries on the job than workers in other occupations. They risk noise-induced hearing loss from sirens and back injuries from lifting patients. In addition, EMTs and paramedics may be exposed to communicable diseases, such as hepatitis-B and AIDS, as well as to violence from mentally unstable or combative patients. The work is not only physically strenuous but can be stressful, sometimes involving life-or-death situations and suffering patients. Nonetheless, many people find the

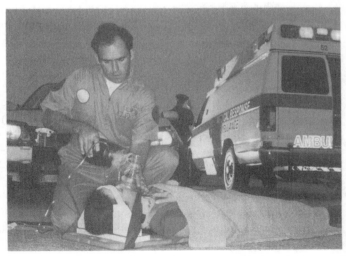

Lives often depend on the quick reaction and competent care of emergency medical technicians and paramedics.

Projections data from the National Employment Matrix

Occupational Title	SOC Code	Employment, 2008	Projected Employment, 2018	Change, 2008-2018	
				Number	Percent
Emergency medical technicians and paramedics............................	29-2041	210,700	229,700	19,000	9

(NOTE) Data in this table are rounded. See the discussion of the employment projections table in the *Handbook* introductory chapter on *Occupational Information Included in the Handbook*.

work exciting and challenging and enjoy the opportunity to help others. These workers experienced a larger than average number of work-related injuries or illnesses

Many EMTs and paramedics are required to work more than 40 hours a week. Because emergency services function 24 hours a day, EMTs and paramedics may have irregular working hours.

Training, Other Qualifications, and Advancement

Generally, a high school diploma is required to enter a training program to become an EMT or paramedic. Workers must complete a formal training and certification process.

Education and training. A high school diploma is usually required to enter a formal emergency medical technician training program. Training is offered at progressive levels: EMT-Basic, EMT-Intermediate, and Paramedic.

At the EMT-Basic level, coursework emphasizes emergency skills, such as managing respiratory, trauma, and cardiac emergencies, and patient assessment. Formal courses are often combined with time in an emergency department or ambulance. The program provides instruction and practice in dealing with bleeding, fractures, airway obstruction, cardiac arrest, and emergency childbirth. Students learn how to use and maintain common emergency equipment, such as backboards, suction devices, splints, oxygen delivery systems, and stretchers. Graduates of approved EMT-Basic training programs must pass a written and practical examination administered by the State licensing agency or the NREMT.

At the EMT-Intermediate level, training requirements vary by State. The nationally defined levels, EMT-Intermediate 1985 and EMT-Intermediate 1999, typically require 30 to 350 hours of training based on scope of practice. Students learn advanced skills such the use of advanced airway devices, intravenous fluids, and some medications.

The most advanced level of training for this occupation is Paramedic. At this level, the caregiver receives training in anatomy and physiology as well as advanced medical skills. Most commonly, the training is conducted in community colleges and technical schools and may result in an associate's degree. These programs may take up to one to two years. Such education prepares the graduate to take the NREMT examination to become certified as a Paramedic. Extensive related coursework and clinical and field experience is required. Refresher courses and continuing education are available for EMTs and paramedics at all levels.

Licensure. All 50 States require EMTs and Paramedics to be licensed, but the levels and titles vary from State to State. In most States and the District of Columbia certification by the NREMT is required at some or all levels. Some States administer their own certification examination or provide the option of taking either the NREMT or State examination. In most States, licensure renewal is required every two to

three years and generally, EMTs and Paramedics must take refresher training courses or complete continuing education requirements. Many States restrict licensure based on an individual's criminal history.

Other qualifications. EMTs and paramedics should be emotionally stable, have good dexterity, agility, and physical coordination, and be able to lift and carry heavy loads. They also need good eyesight (corrective lenses may be used) with accurate color vision. Many employers require a criminal background check.

Advancement. Paramedics can become supervisors, operations managers, administrative directors, or executive directors of emergency services. Some EMTs and paramedics become instructors, dispatchers, or physician assistants; others move into sales or marketing of emergency medical equipment. A number of people become EMTs and paramedics to test their interest in health care before training as registered nurses, physicians, or other health workers.

Employment

EMTs and paramedics held about 210,700 jobs in 2008. Most career EMTs and paramedics work in metropolitan areas. Volunteer EMTs and paramedics are more common in small cities, towns, and rural areas. These individuals volunteer for fire departments, emergency medical services, or hospitals and may respond to only a few calls per month.

Paid EMTs and paramedics were employed in a number of industries. About 45 percent worked as employees of ambulance services. About 29 percent worked in local government. Another 20 percent worked in hospitals.

Job Outlook

Employment for EMTs and paramedics is expected to grow about as fast as the average for all occupations through 2018. Job prospects should be good, particularly in cities and private ambulance services.

Employment change. Employment of emergency medical technicians and paramedics is expected to grow 9 percent between 2008 and 2018, which is about as fast as the average for all occupations. Growth in this occupation is due in large part to increasing call volume due to aging population. As a large segment of the population—aging members of the baby boom generation—becomes more likely to have medical emergencies, demand will increase for EMTs and paramedics. In addition, the time that EMTs and paramedics must spend with each patient is increasing as emergency departments across the country are experiencing overcrowding. As a result, when an ambulance arrives, it takes longer to transfer the patient from the care of the EMTs and paramedics to the staff of the emergency department. In addition, some emergency departments divert ambulances to other hospitals when they are too busy to take on new patients. As a result, ambulances may not be able to go to the nearest hospital, which increases the amount of time spent in transit. Both these factors result in EMTs and paramedics spending more time with each patient, which means more workers are needed to meet demand.

In addition, hospitals are increasingly specializing in treating a particular illness or injury. This results in more patients needing to be transferred to the hospital best able to treat them. Most patients must be transferred by ambulance, so their condition can be monitored en route. Therefore, more demand for transfers between hospitals increases the demand for the services of EMTs and paramedics.

There also still will be demand for part-time, volunteer EMTs and paramedics in rural areas and smaller metropolitan areas.

Job prospects. Job prospects should be favorable. Many job openings will arise from growth and from the need to replace workers who leave the occupation because of the limited potential for advancement, as well as the modest pay and benefits in private-sector jobs. In addition, full-time paid EMTs and paramedics will be needed to replace unpaid volunteers. Emergency medical service agencies find it increasingly difficult to recruit and retain unpaid volunteers because of the amount of training and the large time commitment these positions require. As a result, more paid EMTs and paramedics are needed.

Competition will be greater for jobs in local government, including fire, police, and independent third-service rescue squad departments that tend to have better salaries and benefits. EMTs and paramedics who have advanced education and certifications should enjoy the most favorable job prospects, as clients and patients demand higher levels of care before arriving at the hospital.

Earnings

Earnings of EMTs and paramedics depend on the employment setting and geographic location of their jobs, as well as their training and experience. Median hourly wages of EMTs and paramedics were $14.10 in May 2008. The middle 50 percent earned between $11.13 and $18.28. The lowest 10 percent earned less than $9.08, and the highest 10 percent earned more than $23.77. Median hourly wages in the industries employing the largest numbers of EMTs and paramedics in May 2008 were $12.99 in other ambulatory health care services and $15.45 in local government.

In 2008, about 27 percent of EMTs and paramedics belonged to a union or were covered by a union contract.

Related Occupations

Other workers in occupations that require quick and level-headed reactions to life-or-death situations are:

Licensed practical nurses may assist patients with bathing, dressing, standing, and walking.

Sources of Additional Information

General information about emergency medical technicians and paramedics is available from:

➤ National Association of Emergency Medical Technicians, P.O. Box 1400, Clinton, MS 39060-1400. Internet: **http://www.naemt.org**

➤ National Highway Traffic Safety Administration, Office of Emergency Medical Services, 1200 New Jersey Ave., SE, NTI-140, Washington, DC 20590. Internet: **http://www.ems.gov**

➤ National Registry of Emergency Medical Technicians, Rocco V. Morando Bldg., 6610 Busch Blvd., P.O. Box 29233, Columbus, OH 43229. Internet: **http://www.nremt.org**

The Occupational Information Network (O*NET) provides information on a wide range of occupational characteristics. Links to O*NET appear at the end of the Internet version of this occupational statement, accessible at **http://www.bls.gov/ooh/ocos101.htm**

Licensed Practical and Licensed Vocational Nurses

Significant Points

- Most training programs last about 1 year and are offered by vocational or technical schools or community or junior colleges.

- Overall job prospects are expected to be very good, but job outlook varies by industry.

- Replacement needs will be a major source of job openings, as many workers leave the occupation permanently.

Nature of the Work

Licensed practical nurses (LPNs), or *licensed vocational nurses (LVNs),* care for people who are sick, injured, convalescent, or disabled under the direction of physicians and registered nurses. (The work of physicians and surgeons and of registered nurses

Projections data from the National Employment Matrix

Occupational Title	SOC Code	Employment, 2008	Projected Employment, 2018	Change, 2008-2018	
				Number	Percent
Licensed practical and licensed vocational nurses............................	29-2061	753,600	909,200	155,600	21

(NOTE) Data in this table are rounded. See the discussion of the employment projections table in the *Handbook* introductory chapter on *Occupational Information Included in the Handbook.*

is described elsewhere in the Handbook.) The nature of the direction and supervision required varies by State and job setting.

LPNs care for patients in many ways. Often, they provide basic bedside care. Many LPNs measure and record patients' vital signs such as height, weight, temperature, blood pressure, pulse, and respiration. They also prepare and give injections and enemas, monitor catheters, dress wounds, and give alcohol rubs and massages. To help keep patients comfortable, they assist with bathing, dressing, and personal hygiene, moving in bed, standing, and walking. They might also feed patients who need help eating. Experienced LPNs may supervise nursing assistants and aides.

As part of their work, LPNs collect samples for testing, perform routine laboratory tests, and record food and fluid intake and output. They clean and monitor medical equipment. Sometimes, they help physicians and registered nurses perform tests and procedures. Some LPNs help to deliver, care for, and feed infants.

LPNs also monitor their patients and report adverse reactions to medications or treatments. LPNs gather information from patients, including their health history and how they are currently feeling. They may use this information to complete insurance forms, pre-authorizations, and referrals, and they share information with registered nurses and doctors to help determine the best course of care for a patient. LPNs often teach family members how to care for a relative or teach patients about good health habits.

Most LPNs are generalists and will work in any area of healthcare. However, some work in a specialized setting, such as a nursing home, a doctor's office, or in home health care. LPNs in nursing care facilities help to evaluate residents' needs, develop care plans, and supervise the care provided by nursing aides. In doctors' offices and clinics, they may be responsible for making appointments, keeping records, and performing other clerical duties. LPNs who work in home health care may prepare meals and teach family members simple nursing tasks.

In some States, LPNs are permitted to administer prescribed medicines, start intravenous fluids, and provide care to ventilator-dependent patients.

Work environment.   Most licensed practical nurses work a 40-hour week. In some work settings where patients need round-the-clock care, LPNs may have to work nights, weekends, and holidays. About 18 percent of LPNs and LVN's worked part-time in 2008. They often stand for long periods and help patients move in bed, stand, or walk.

LPNs may face hazards from caustic chemicals, radiation, and infectious diseases. They are subject to back injuries when moving patients. They often must deal with the stress of heavy workloads. In addition, the patients they care for may be confused, agitated, or uncooperative.

Training, Other Qualifications, and Advancement

Most practical nursing training programs last about 1 year, and are offered by vocational and technical schools or community or junior colleges. LPNs must be licensed to practice.

Education and training.   LPNs must complete a State-approved training program in practical nursing to be eligible for licensure. Contact your State's board of nursing for a list of approved programs. Most training programs are available from technical and vocational schools or community and junior colleges. Other programs are available through high schools, hospitals, and colleges and universities. A high school diploma or its equivalent usually is required for entry, although some programs accept candidates without a diploma, and some programs are part of a high school curriculum.

Most year-long practical nursing programs include both classroom study and supervised clinical practice (patient care). Classroom study covers basic nursing concepts and subjects related to patient care, including anatomy, physiology, medical-surgical nursing, pediatrics, obstetrics nursing, pharmacology, nutrition, and first aid. Clinical practice usually is in a hospital but sometimes includes other settings.

Licensure.   The National Council Licensure Examination, or NCLEX-PN, is required in order to obtain licensure as an LPN. The exam is developed and administered by the National Council of State Boards of Nursing. The NCLEX-PN is a computer-based exam and varies in length. The exam covers four major *Client Needs* categories: safe and effective care environment, health promotion and maintenance, psychosocial integrity, and physiological integrity. Eligibility for licensure may vary by State; for details, contact your State's board of nursing.

Other qualifications.   LPNs should have a caring, sympathetic nature. They should be emotionally stable because working with the sick and injured can be stressful. They also need to be observant, and to have good decision-making and communication skills. As part of a healthcare team, they must be able to follow orders and work under close supervision.

LPNs should enjoy learning because continuing education credits are required by some States and/or employers at regular intervals. Career-long learning is a distinct reality for LPNs.

Advancement.   In some employment settings, such as nursing homes, LPNs can advance to become charge nurses who oversee the work of other LPNs and nursing aides.

LPNs may become credentialed in specialties like IV therapy, gerontology, long-term care, and pharmacology.

Some LPNs also choose to become registered nurses through LPN-to-RN training programs.

Employment

Licensed practical and licensed vocational nurses held about 753,600 jobs in 2008. About 25 percent of LPNs worked in hospitals, 28 percent in nursing care facilities, and another 12 percent in offices of physicians. Others worked for home health care services; employment services; residential care facilities; community care facilities for the elderly; outpatient care centers; and Federal, State, and local government agencies.

Job Outlook

Employment of LPNs is projected to grow much faster than average. Overall job prospects are expected to be very good, but job outlook varies by industry. The best job opportunities will occur in nursing care facilities and home health care services.

Employment change. Employment of LPNs is expected to grow by 21 percent between 2008 and 2018, much faster than the average for all occupations, in response to the long-term care needs of an increasing elderly population and the general increase in demand for healthcare services.

Demand for LPNs will be driven by the increase in the share of the older population. Older persons have an increased incidence of injury and illness, which will increase their demand for healthcare services. In addition, with better medical technology, people are living longer, increasing the demand for long-term healthcare. Job growth will occur over all healthcare settings but especially those that service the geriatric population like nursing care facilities, community care facilities, and home health care services.

In order to contain healthcare costs, many procedures once performed only in hospitals are being performed in physicians' offices and in outpatient care centers, largely because of advances in technology. As a result, the number of LPNs should increase faster in these facilities than in hospitals. Nevertheless, hospitals will continue to demand the services of LPNs and will remain one of the largest employer of these workers.

Job prospects. In addition to projected job growth, job openings will result from replacement needs, as many workers leave the occupation permanently. Very good job opportunities are expected. Rapid employment growth is projected in most health care industries, with the best job opportunities occurring in nursing care facilities and in home health care services. There is a perceived inadequacy of available healthcare in many rural areas, so LPNs willing to locate in rural areas should have good job prospects.

Earnings

Median annual wages of licensed practical and licensed vocational nurses were $39,030 in May 2008. The middle 50 percent earned between $33,360 and $46,710. The lowest 10 percent earned less than $28,260, and the highest 10 percent earned more than $53,580. Median annual wages in the industries employing the largest numbers of licensed practical and licensed vocational nurses in May 2008 were:

Employment services	$44,690
Nursing care facilities	40,580
Home health care services	39,510
General medical and surgical hospitals	38,080
Offices of physicians	35,020

Related Occupations

LPNs work closely with people while helping them. Other healthcare occupations that work closely with patients include:

	Page
Athletic trainers	405
Emergency medical technicians and paramedics	419
Home health aides and personal and home care aides	449
Medical assistants	455
Nursing and psychiatric aides	460
Registered nurses	392

Sources of Additional Information

For information about practical nursing and specialty credentialing, contact the following organizations:
➤ National Association for Practical Nurse Education and Service, Inc., 1940 Duke St., Suite 200, Alexandria, VA 22314. Internet: **http://www.napnes.org**

➤ National Federation of Licensed Practical Nurses, Inc., 605 Poole Dr., Garner, NC 27529. Internet: **http://www.nflpn.org**

➤ National League for Nursing, 61 Broadway, 33rd floor, New York, NY 10006. Internet: **http://www.nln.org**

Information on the NCLEX-PN licensing exam is available from:
➤ National Council of State Boards of Nursing, 111 East Wacker Dr., Suite 2900, Chicago, IL 60601. Internet: **http://www.ncsbn.org**

Lists of State-approved LPN programs are available from individual State boards of nursing.

The Occupational Information Network (O*NET) provides information on a wide range of occupational characteristics. Links to O*NET appear at the end of the Internet version of this occupational statement, accessible at **http://www.bls.gov/ooh/ocos102.htm**

Medical Records and Health Information Technicians

Significant Points

- Employment is expected to grow much faster than the average.

- Job prospects should be very good, particularly for technicians with strong computer software skills.

- Entrants usually have an associate degree.

- This is one of the few health-related occupations in which there is no direct hands-on patient care.

Nature of the Work

Medical records and health information technicians assemble patients' health information including medical history, symptoms, examination results, diagnostic tests, treatment methods, and all other healthcare provider services. Technicians organize and manage health information data by ensuring its quality, accuracy, accessibility, and security. They regularly communicate with physicians and other healthcare professionals to clarify diagnoses or to obtain additional information.

The increasing use of electronic health records (EHR) will continue to broaden and alter the job responsibilities of health information technicians. For example, with the use of EHRs, technicians must be familiar with EHR computer software, maintaining EHR security, and analyzing electronic data to improve healthcare information. Health information technicians use EHR software to maintain data on patient safety, patterns of disease, and disease treatment and outcome. Technicians also may assist with improving EHR software usability and may contribute to the development and maintenance of health information networks.

Medical records and health information technicians' duties vary with the size of the facility where they work. Technicians can specialize in many aspects of health information.

Some medical records and health information technicians specialize in codifying patients' medical information for reimbursement purposes. Technicians who specialize in coding are called medical coders or coding specialists. Medical coders assign a code to each diagnosis and procedure by using classification systems software. The classification system determines the amount for which healthcare providers will be reimbursed if the patient is covered by Medicare, Medicaid, or other insurance programs using the system. Coders may use several coding systems, such as those required for ambulatory settings, physician offices, or long-term care.

Medical records and health information technicians also may specialize in cancer registry. Cancer (or tumor) registrars maintain facility, regional, and national databases of cancer patients. Registrars review patient records and pathology reports, and assign codes for the diagnosis and treatment of different cancers and selected benign tumors. Registrars conduct annual followups to track treatment, survival, and recovery. This information is used to calculate survivor rates and success rates of various types of treatment, to locate geographic areas with high incidences of certain cancers, and to identify potential participants for clinical drug trials.

Work environment. Medical records and health information technicians work in pleasant and comfortable offices.

Some medical records and health information technicians specialize in coding medical information for insurance purposes.

This is one of the few health-related occupations in which there is no direct hands-on patient care.

Medical records and health information technicians usually work a typical 40-hour week. Some overtime may be required. In health facilities that are open 24 hours a day, 7 days a week, technicians may work day, evening, and night shifts. About 14 percent of technicians worked part-time in 2008.

Training, Other Qualifications, and Advancement
Entry-level medical records and health information technicians usually have an associate degree. Many employers favor technicians who have a Registered Health Information Technicians (RHIT) credential.

Education and training. Medical records and health information technicians generally have an associate degree. Typical coursework in health information technology includes medical terminology, anatomy and physiology, health data requirements and standards, clinical classification and coding systems, data analysis, health care reimbursement methods, database security and management, and quality improvement methods. Applicants can improve their chances of admission into a postsecondary program by taking biology, math, chemistry, health, and computer science courses in high school.

Certification and other qualifications. Most employers prefer to hire credentialed medical record and health information technicians. A number of organizations offer credentials typically based on passing a credentialing exam. Most credentialing programs require regular recertification and continuing education to maintain the credential. Many coding credentials require an amount of time in coding experience in the work setting.

The American Health Information Management Association (AHIMA) offers credentialing as a Registered Health Information Technicians (RHIT). To obtain the RHIT credential, an individual must graduate from a 2-year associate degree program accredited by the Commission on Accreditation for Health Informatics and Information Management Education (CAHIIM) and pass an AHIMA-administered written examination. In 2008, there were more than 200 CAHIIM-accredited health information technology colleges and universities programs.

The American Academy of Professional Coders (AAPC) offers coding credentials. The Board of Medical Specialty Coding (BMSC) and Professional Association of Health care Coding Specialists (PAHCS) both offer credentialing in specialty coding. The National Cancer Registrars Association (NCRA) offers a credential as a Certified Tumor Registrar (CTR). To learn more about the credentials available and their specific requirements, contact the credentialing organization.

Health information technicians and coders should possess good oral and written communication skills as they often serve as liaisons between healthcare facilities, insurance companies, and other establishments. Candidates proficient with computer software and technology will be appealing to employers as healthcare facilities continue to adopt electronic health records. Medical records and health informa-

Projections data from the National Employment Matrix

Occupational Title	SOC Code	Employment, 2008	Projected Employment, 2018	Change, 2008-2018	
				Number	Percent
Medical records and health information technicians	29-2071	172,500	207,600	35,100	20

(NOTE) Data in this table are rounded. See the discussion of the employment projections table in the *Handbook* introductory chapter on *Occupational Information Included in the Handbook.*

tion technicians should enjoy learning, as continuing education is important in the occupation.

Advancement. Experienced medical records and health information technicians usually advance their careers by obtaining a bachelor's or master's degree or by seeking an advanced specialty certification. Technicians with a bachelor's or master's degree can advance and become a health information manager. (See the statement on medical and health services managers elsewhere in the *Hankdbook* for more information on health information managers.) Technicians can also obtain advanced specialty certification. Advanced specialty certification is typically experience-based, but may require additional formal education depending on the certifying organization.

Employment

Medical records and health information technicians held about 172,500 jobs in 2008. About 39 percent of jobs were in hospitals. Health information technicians work at a number of health care providers such as offices of physicians, nursing care facilities, outpatient care centers, and home health care services. Technicians also may be employed outside of health care facilities, such as in Federal Government agencies.

Job Outlook

Employment is expected to grow much faster than the average. Job prospects should be very good; technicians with a strong understanding of technology and computer software will be in particularly high demand.

Employment change. Employment of medical records and health information technicians is expected to increase by 20 percent, much faster than the average for all occupations through 2018. Employment growth will result from the increase in the number of medical tests, treatments, and procedures that will be performed. As the population continues to age, the occurrence of health-related problems will increase. Cancer registrars should experience job growth as the incidence of cancer increases from an aging population.

In addition, with the increasing use of electronic health records, more technicians will be needed to complete the new responsibilities associated with electronic data management.

Job prospects. Job prospects should be very good. In addition to job growth, numerous openings will result from the need to replace medical record and health information technicians who retire or leave the occupation permanently. Technicians that demonstrate a strong understanding of technology and computer software will be in particularly high demand.

Earnings

The median annual wage of medical records and health information technicians was $30,610 in May 2008. The middle 50 percent earned between $24,290 and $39,490. The lowest 10 percent earned less than $20,440, and the highest 10 percent earned more than $50,060. Median annual wages in the industries employing the largest numbers of medical records and health information technicians in May 2008 were:

Federal Executive Branch	$42,760
General medical and surgical hospitals	32,600
Nursing care facilities	30,660
Outpatient care centers	29,160
Offices of physicians	26,210

Related Occupations

Health care occupations with similar responsibilities include:

Sources of Additional Information

A list of accredited training programs is available from:
➤ The Commission on Accreditation for Health Informatics and Information Management Education, 233 N. Michigan Ave, 21st Floor, Chicago, IL 60601-5800. Internet: **http://www.cahiim.org**

For information careers and credentialing, contact:
➤ American Health Information Management Association, 233 N. Michigan Ave., 21st Floor, Chicago, IL 60601-5809. Internet: **http://www.ahima.org** or **http://himcareers.ahima.org**

➤ American Academy of Professional Coders, 2480 South 3850 West, Suite B, Salt Lake City, UT 84120. Internet: **http://www.aapc.com**

➤ Practice Management Institute, 9501 Console Dr., Suite 100, San Antonio, TX 78229. Internet: **http://www.pmimd.com**

➤ Professional Association of Healthcare Coding Specialists, 218 E. Bearss Ave., #354, Tampa, FL 33613. Internet: **http://www.pahcs.org**

➤ National Cancer Registrars Association, 1340 Braddock Place, Suite 203, Alexandria, VA 22314. Internet: **http://www.ncra-usa.org**

The Occupational Information Network (O*NET) provides information on a wide range of occupational characteristics. Links to O*NET appear at the end of the Internet version of this occupational statement, accessible at

http://www.bls.gov/ooh/ocos103.htm

Nuclear Medicine Technologists

Significant Points

- Keen competition is expected for most positions.

- Technologists with training in multiple diagnostic methods, or in nuclear cardiology, should have the best prospects.

- Nuclear medicine technology programs range in length from 1 to 4 years and lead to a certificate, an associate degree, or a bachelor's degree.

- About 66 percent of nuclear medicine technologists work in hospitals.

Nature of the Work

Diagnostic imaging embraces several procedures that aid in diagnosing ailments, the most familiar imaging being the x ray. In nuclear medicine, radionuclides—unstable atoms that emit radiation spontaneously—are used to diagnose and treat disease. Radionuclides are purified and compounded to form radiopharmaceuticals. *Nuclear medicine technologists* administer radiopharmaceuticals to patients and then monitor the characteristics and functions of tissues or organs in which the drugs localize. Abnormal areas show higher-than-expected or lower-than-expected concentrations of radioactivity. Nuclear medicine differs from other diagnostic imaging technologies because it determines the presence of disease on the basis of metabolic changes, rather than changes in organ structure.

Nuclear medicine technologists operate cameras that detect and map the radioactive drug in a patient's body to create diagnostic images. After explaining test procedures to patients, technologists prepare a dosage of the radiopharmaceutical and administer it by mouth, injection, inhalation, or other means. They position patients and start a gamma scintillation camera, or "scanner," which creates images of the distribution of a radiopharmaceutical as it localizes in and emits signals from the patient's body. The images are produced on a computer screen or on film for a physician to interpret.

When preparing radiopharmaceuticals, technologists adhere to safety standards that keep the chance of radiation exposure as low as possible to workers and patients. Technologists keep patient records and document the amount and type of radionuclides that they receive, use, and discard.

There are two areas of specialty for nuclear medicine technologists—nuclear cardiology and positron emission tomography (PET). Nuclear cardiology typically involves myocardial perfusion imaging, which, like most nuclear medicine, uses radiopharmaceuticals and cameras to image the body. Myocardial perfusion imaging, however, requires that patients perform exercise so the technologist can image the heart and blood flow. Technologists specializing in PET operate a special medical imaging device that produces a 3-D image of the body.

Work environment. Physical stamina is important because nuclear medicine technologists are on their feet much of the

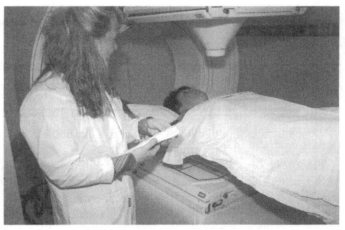

Nuclear medicine technologists operate complicated equipment that requires mechanical ability and manual dexterity.

day and may have to lift or turn disabled patients. In addition, technologists must operate complicated equipment that requires mechanical ability and manual dexterity.

Although the potential for radiation exposure exists in this field, it is minimized by the use of shielded syringes, gloves, and other protective devices and by adherence to strict radiation safety guidelines. The amount of radiation in a nuclear medicine procedure is comparable to that received during a diagnostic x ray procedure. Technologists also wear badges that measure radiation levels. Because of safety precautions, badge measurements rarely exceed established safety levels.

Nuclear medicine technologists generally work a 40-hour week. Some technologists also may have on-call hours, including evening or weekend hours, in departments that operate on an extended schedule. Opportunities for part-time and shift work also are available. Those employed by mobile imaging services may be required to travel to several locations.

Training, Other Qualifications, and Advancement

Nuclear medicine technology programs range in length from 1 to 4 years and lead to a certificate, an associate degree, or a bachelor's degree. Many employers and an increasing number of States require certification or licensure. Aspiring nuclear medicine technologists should check the requirements of the State in which they plan to work.

Education and training. Generally, certificate programs are offered in hospitals, associate degree programs in community colleges, and bachelor's degree programs in 4-year colleges and universities. Courses cover the physical sciences, biological effects of radiation exposure, radiation protection and procedures, the use of radiopharmaceuticals, imaging techniques, and computer applications.

One-year certificate programs are typically for health professionals who already possess an associate or bachelor's degree—especially radiologic technologists and diagnostic medical sonographers—but who wish to specialize in nuclear medicine. The programs also attract medical technologists, registered nurses, and others who wish to change fields or specialize.

The Joint Review Committee on Education Programs in Nuclear Medicine Technology accredits associate and bach-

Projections data from the National Employment Matrix

Occupational Title	SOC Code	Employment, 2008	Projected Employment, 2018	Change, 2008-2018	
				Number	Percent
Nuclear medicine technologists	29-2033	21,800	25,400	3,600	16

(NOTE) Data in this table are rounded. See the discussion of the employment projections table in the *Handbook* introductory chapter on *Occupational Information Included in the Handbook.*

elor's degree training programs in nuclear medicine technology. In 2008, there were more than 100 accredited programs available.

Licensure. Requirements for licensure of nuclear medicine technologists vary from State to State, so it is important that aspiring technologists check the requirements of the State in which they plan to work. In 2008, 25 States licensed nuclear medicine technologists. In addition, many third-party payers require nuclear medicine technologists to be certified in order for the healthcare facility to receive reimbursement for imaging procedures.

Certification and other qualifications. Certification is voluntary but it has become the generally accepted standard for nuclear medicine technologists and those who employ them. Certification is available from the American Registry of Radiologic Technologists (ARRT) and from the Nuclear Medicine Technology Certification Board (NMTCB). Some technologists receive certification from both agencies. ARRT and NMTCB have different eligibility requirements, but both require that workers pass a comprehensive exam to become certified.

In addition to the general certification requirements, certified technologists also must complete a certain number of continuing education hours to retain certification. Continuing education is required primarily because of the frequent technological and innovative changes in the field of nuclear medicine.

Technologists must have good communication skills to effectively interact with patients and their families and should be sensitive to patients' physical and psychological needs. Nuclear medicine technologists must be able to work independently as they may have little direct supervision. Technologists also need to be detailed-oriented and meticulous when performing procedures to assure that all regulations are being followed.

Advancement. Technologists may advance to supervisory positions or to chief technologist with significant work experience. With advanced education, it is possible for some technologists to become department administrators or directors.

Some technologists specialize in clinical areas, such as nuclear cardiology or PET scanning. Some become instructors in, or directors of, nuclear medicine technology programs, a step that usually requires a bachelor's or master's degree in the subject. Others may leave the occupation to work as sales or training representatives for medical equipment or radiopharmaceutical manufacturing firms; some become radiation safety officers in regulatory agencies or hospitals.

Employment

Nuclear medicine technologists held about 21,800 jobs in 2008. About 66 percent of all nuclear medicine technologist jobs were in hospitals—private and public. A majority of the rest were in offices of physicians or in medical and diagnostic laboratories, including diagnostic imaging centers.

Job Outlook

Faster than average job growth is projected. However, keen competition is expected for most positions.

Employment change. Employment of nuclear medicine technologists is expected to increase by 16 percent from 2008 to 2018, faster than the average for all occupations. Growth will arise from technological advancement, the development of new nuclear medicine treatments, and an increase in the number of middle-aged and elderly persons, who are the primary users of diagnostic and treatment procedures.

Technological innovations may increase the diagnostic uses of nuclear medicine. New nuclear medical imaging technologies, including PET and single photon emission computed tomography (SPECT), are expected to be used increasingly. Cost considerations will affect the speed with which these new applications of nuclear medicine grow. Healthcare facilities contemplating these procedures will have to consider equipment costs, reimbursement policies, and the number of potential users. Although these new imaging technologies will be used more often, they will likely replace older technologies, not supplement them. Thus, only a small amount of job growth will stem from the adoption of new technologies.

Job prospects. In spite of growth in nuclear medicine, the number of openings into the occupation each year will be relatively low. Job competition will be keen because the supply of properly trained nuclear medicine technologists is expected to exceed the number of job openings for technologists. Technologists who have training in multiple diagnostic methods, such as radiologic technology and diagnostic medical sonography, or in nuclear cardiology, should have the best prospects.

Earnings

The median annual wage of nuclear medicine technologists was $66,660 in May 2008. The middle 50 percent earned between $57,270 and $78,240. The lowest 10 percent earned less than $48,450, and the highest 10 percent earned more than $87,770. The median annual wage of nuclear medicine technologists in general medical and surgical hospitals was $66,320.

Related Occupations

Other healthcare occupations that use radiation or do diagnostic imaging are:

Sources of Additional Information

Additional information on a career as a nuclear medicine technologist is available from:

➤ Society of Nuclear Medicine Technologists, 1850 Samuel Morse Dr., Reston, VA 20190. Internet: **http://www.snm.org**

For a list of accredited programs in nuclear medicine technology, contact:

➤ Joint Review Committee on Educational Programs in Nuclear Medicine Technology, 2000 W. Danforth Rd., Suite 130 #203, Edmond, OK 73003. Internet: **http://www.jrcnmt.org**

Information on certification is available from:

➤ Nuclear Medicine Technology Certification Board, 3558 Habersham at Northlake, Building 1, Tucker, GA 30084. Internet: **http://www.nmtcb.org**

➤ American Registry of Radiologic Technologists, 1255 Northland Dr., St. Paul, MN 55120-1155. Internet: **http://www.arrt.org**

The Occupational Information Network (O*NET) provides information on a wide range of occupational characteristics. Links to O*NET appear at the end of the Internet version of this occupational statement, accessible at **http://www.bls.gov/ooh/ocos104.htm**

Occupational Health and Safety Specialists

Significant Points

- About 41 percent of occupational health and safety specialists work in Federal, State, and local government agencies that enforce rules on safety, health, and the environment.

- Most jobs require a bachelor's degree in occupational health, safety, or a related field; some require advanced degrees.

- Projected average employment growth reflects a balance of continuing public demand for a safe and healthy work environment against the desire for smaller government and fewer regulations.

- Individuals with a well-rounded breadth of knowledge in more than one health and safety specialty will have the best job prospects.

Nature of the Work

Occupational health and safety specialists, also known as safety and health professionals or *occupational health and safety inspectors*, help prevent harm to workers, property, the environment, and the general public. For example, they may design safe work spaces, inspect machines, or test air quality. In addition to making workers safer, specialists aim to increase worker productivity by reducing absenteeism and equipment downtime—and to save money by lowering insurance premiums and workers' compensation payments, and preventing government fines.

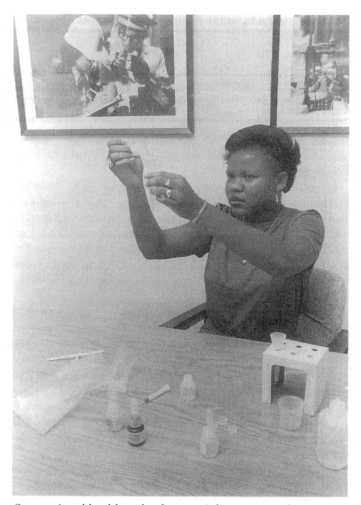

Occupational health and safety specialists may conduct inspections and inform an organization's managers of areas not in compliance with State and Federal laws and employer policies.

Specialists working for governments conduct safety inspections and impose fines. Specialists often work with occupational health and safety technicians to ensure work place safety. (See the statement on occupational health and safety technicians elsewhere in the Handbook.)

Occupational health and safety specialists analyze work environments and design programs to control, eliminate, and prevent disease or injury. They look for chemical, physical, radiological, and biological hazards. They also work to make more equipment ergonomic—designed to promote proper body positioning, increase worker comfort, and decrease fatigue. Specialists may conduct inspections and inform an organization's management of areas not in compliance with State and Federal laws or employer policies. They also advise management on the cost and effectiveness of safety and health programs. Some provide training on new regulations and policies or on how to recognize hazards.

Some specialists develop methods to predict hazards from historical data and other information sources. They use these methods and their own knowledge and experience to evaluate current equipment, products, facilities, or processes and those planned for future use. For example, they might uncover patterns in injury data that show that many injuries are caused by a specific type of system failure, human error, or weakness in procedures. They evaluate the probability and severity of accidents and identify where controls need to be implemented to reduce or eliminate risk. If a new program or practice is required, they propose it to management and monitor results if it is implemented. Specialists may also conduct safety training. Training sessions might show how to recognize hazards, for example, or explain new regulations, production processes, and safe work methods. If an injury or illness occurs, occupational health and safety specialists help investigate, studying its causes and recommending remedial action. Some occupational health and safety specialists help workers to return to work after accidents and injuries.

Some specialists, often called loss prevention specialists, work for insurance companies, inspecting the facilities that they insure and suggesting and helping to implement improvements.

Occupational health and safety specialists frequently communicate with management about the status of health and safety programs. They also might consult with engineers or physicians.

Specialists monitor safety measurements in order to advise management of safety performance to correct existing safety hazards and to avoid future hazards; they write reports, including accident reports, and enter information on Occupational Safety and Health Administration recordkeeping forms. They also may prepare documents used in legal proceedings and give testimony in court. Those who develop expertise in specific areas may develop occupational health and safety systems, including policies, procedures, and manuals. Some specialists plan budgets needed to implement programs that help achieve safe work practices.

The responsibilities of occupational health and safety specialists vary by industry, workplace, and types of hazards affecting employees. Environmental protection officers evaluate and coordinate the storage and handling of hazardous waste, the cleanup of contaminated soil or water, or other activities that affect the environment. Ergonomists consider the design of industrial, office, and other equipment to maximize worker comfort, safety, and productivity. Health physicists work in places that use radiation and radioactive material, helping to protect people and the environment from hazardous radiation exposure. Industrial hygienists examine the workplace for health hazards, such as exposure to lead, asbestos, noise, pesticides, or communicable diseases.

Work environment. Occupational health and safety specialists work in a variety of settings such as offices, factories, and mines. Their jobs often involve considerable fieldwork and travel.

Occupational health and safety specialists may be exposed to many of the same strenuous, dangerous, or stressful conditions faced by industrial employees. The majority of occupational health and safety specialist work the typical 40 hour week. Some specialists may work over-time, and often irregular, hours.

Training, Other Qualifications, and Advancement
Most jobs require a bachelor's degree in occupational health, safety, or a related field; some require advanced degrees. All spe-

cialists are trained in the applicable laws or inspection procedures through some combination of classroom and on-the-job training.

Education and training. Most employers require occupational health and safety specialists to have a bachelor's degree in occupational health, safety, or a related field, such as engineering, biology, or chemistry. For some positions, a master's degree in industrial hygiene, health physics, or a related subject is required. High school students interested in enrolling in a college program should complete courses in English, mathematics, chemistry, biology, and physics. College courses may include radiation science, hazardous material management and control, risk communications, principles of ergonomics, and respiratory protection. Course work will vary depending on the degree pursued. For example, course requirements for students seeking a degree in industrial hygiene will differ from course requirements for health physics degree seekers.

In order to become credentialed, most accrediting bodies require that specialists have attended either a regional or nationally accredited educational institution. Work experience is important in this occupation; it is typically beneficial for prospective students to select an education program that offers opportunities to complete internships.

All occupational health and safety specialists are trained in the applicable laws or inspection procedures through some combination of classroom and on-the-job training.

Certification and other qualifications. Credentialing is voluntary, although many employers encourage it. Credentialing is available through several organizations depending on the specialists' field of work. Organizations credentialing health and safety professionals include the American Board of Health Physicists; the American Indoor Air Quality Council; the American Board of Industrial Hygiene; and the Board of Certified Safety Professionals.

Requirements for credentials vary. Most require specific education and experience in order to be eligible to sit for the certification exam. Once certified, specialists are usually required to complete periodic continuing education for recertification. For information on credentials offered and requirements contact the credentialing organization.

People interested in this occupation should be responsible and enjoy detailed work. Occupational health and safety specialists also should be able to communicate well. Work experience as an occupational health and safety professional may also be a prerequisite for many positions.

Advancement. Occupational health and safety specialists who work for the Federal Government advance through their career ladder to a specified full-performance level if their work is satisfactory. For positions above this level, usually supervisory positions, advancement is competitive and based on agency needs and individual merit. Advancement opportunities in State

Projections data from the National Employment Matrix

Occupational Title	SOC Code	Employment, 2008	Projected Employment, 2018	Change, 2008-2018	
				Number	Percent
Occupational health and safety specialists......................................	29-9011	55,800	62,000	6,200	11

(NOTE) Data in this table are rounded. See the discussion of the employment projections table in the *Handbook* introductory chapter on *Occupational Information Included in the Handbook.*

and local governments and the private sector are often similar to those in the Federal Government.

Specialists with broad education and experience and those who are well versed in numerous business functions usually have the best advancement opportunities. One way to keep up with current professional developments is to join a professional membership society. These organizations offer journals, continuing education courses, and conferences, which provide learning and networking opportunities and can help workers and students to advance.

Typically an advanced degree and substantial work experience are needed to compete for leadership or senior roles

Employment

Occupational health and safety specialists held about 55,800 jobs in 2008. While the majority of jobs were spread throughout the private sector; about 41 percent of specialists worked for Federal, State, and local government agencies.

Within the Federal Government, most jobs are as Occupational Safety and Health Administration inspectors, who enforce U.S. Department of Labor regulations and impose fines. Within the U.S. Department of Health and Human Services, the National Institute of Occupational Safety and Health hires occupational health and safety specialists to offer companies help in evaluating safety without the risk of fines. Most large government agencies also employ occupational health and safety specialists who work to protect agency employees.

Most private companies either employ their own occupational health and safety workers or contract with them. Most contract work is done through consulting companies, but some specialists are self-employed.

In addition to working for governments, occupational health and safety specialists were employed in manufacturing firms; hospitals; educational services; scientific and technical consulting services; mining, quarrying, and oil and gas extraction, and construction.

Job Outlook

Average employment growth is expected; additional opportunities will arise from the need to replace workers who leave the occupation. Individuals with a well-rounded breadth of knowledge in more than one health and safety specialty will have the best job prospects.

Employment change. Employment of occupational health and safety specialists is expected to increase 11 percent during the 2008-18 decade, about as fast as the average for all occupations, reflecting a balance of continuing public demand for a safe and healthy work environment against the desire for fewer government regulations.

More specialists will be needed to cope with technological advances in safety equipment and threats, changing regulations, and increasing public expectations. In private industry, employment growth will reflect continuing self-enforcement of government and company regulations and policies.

Insurance and worker's compensation costs have become a financial concern for many employers and insurance companies. As a result, job growth should be good for those specializing in loss prevention, especially in construction safety and in ergonomics.

Growth for occupational health and safety specialists may be hampered by the number of manufacturing and other industry firms offshoring their operations. In addition, the number of

workers who telecommute is increasing. Since occupational health and safety specialists do not have access to home offices, their ability to ensure health and safety of workers in home offices is limited.

Job prospects. In addition to job openings from growth, job openings will arise from the need to replace workers who transfer to other occupations, retire, or leave for other reasons.

As the lines continue to blur between specific health and safety specialties like industrial hygiene, health physics, and loss prevention, individuals with a well-rounded breadth of knowledge in more than one health and safety specialty will have the best job prospects.

Employment of occupational health and safety specialists in the private sector is somewhat affected by general economic fluctuations. Federal, State, and local governments provide considerable job security; these workers are less likely to be affected by changes in the economy.

Earnings

Median annual wages of occupational health and safety specialists were $62,250 in May 2008. The middle 50 percent earned between $47,490 and $77,880. The lowest 10 percent earned less than $35,870, and the highest 10 percent earned more than $93,620. Median annual wages in the industries employing the largest numbers of occupational health and safety specialists in May 2008 were:

Federal Executive Branch	$73,180
General medical and surgical hospitals	63,910
Management, scientific, and technicial consulting services	57,600
Local government	56,300
State government	55,600

Most occupational health and safety specialists work in large private firms or for Federal, State, and local governments, most of which generally offer benefits more generous than those offered by smaller firms.

Related Occupations

Occupational health and safety specialists help to ensure that safety and health laws and regulations are obeyed. Other occupations that inspect and enforce laws and regulations include:

	Page
Agricultural inspectors	612
Construction and building inspectors	628
Fire inspectors and investigators	525
Occupational health and safety technicians	431

Sources of Additional Information

Information about jobs in Federal, State, and local governments and in private industry is available from State employment service offices.

For information on a career as an industrial hygienist, contact:

➤ American Industrial Hygiene Association, 2700 Prosperity Ave., Suite 250, Fairfax, VA 22031. Internet: **http://www.aiha.org**

For information on credentialing in industrial hygiene, contact:

➤ American Board of Industrial Hygiene, 6015 West St. Joseph Hwy., Suite 102, Lansing, MI 48917. Internet: **http://www.abih.org**

For more information on professions in safety, a list of safety and related academic programs, and credentialing, contact:
➤ Board of Certified Safety Professionals, 208 Burwash Ave., Savoy, IL 61874. Internet: **http://www.bcsp.org**

For information on a career as a health physicist, contact:
➤ Health Physics Society, 1313 Dolley Madison Blvd., Suite 402, McLean, VA 22101. Internet: **http://www.hps.org**

For additional career information, contact:
➤ U.S. Department of Health and Human Services, Center for Disease Control and Prevention, National Institute of Occupational Safety and Health, 395 E Street SW., Suite 9200, Patriots Plaza Building, Washington, DC 20201. Internet: **http://www.cdc.gov/niosh**

➤ U.S. Department of Labor, Occupational Safety and Health Administration, Office of Communication, 200 Constitution Ave. NW., Washington, DC 20210. Internet: **http://www.osha.gov**

Information on obtaining positions as occupational health and safety specialists with the Federal Government is available from the Office of Personnel Management through USAJOBS, the Federal Government's official employment information system. This resource for locating and applying for job opportunities can be accessed through the Internet at **http://www.usajobs.gov/or** through an interactive voice response telephone system at (703) 724-1850, (866) 204-2858 or TDD (978) 461-8404. These numbers are not all toll free, and charges may result.

The Occupational Information Network (O*NET) provides information on a wide range of occupational characteristics. Links to O*NET appear at the end of the Internet version of this occupational statement, accessible at **http://www.bls.gov/ooh/ocos323.htm**

Occupational Health and Safety Technicians

Significant Points

- About 22 percent of technicians worked in government agencies that enforce rules on safety, health, and the environment.

- Technicians attend postsecondary school or enter the occupation through work experience and training.

- Individuals with a well-rounded breadth of knowledge in more than one health and safety specialty will have the best job prospects.

Nature of the Work

Occupational health and safety technicians work with occupational health and safety specialists to help prevent harm to workers, property, the environment, and the general public. (See the statement on occupational health and safety

Occupational health and safety technicians prepare and calibrate scientific equipment.

specialists elsewhere in the Handbook.) For example, they might help design safe work spaces, inspect machines, or test air quality. In addition to making workers safer, technicians work with specialists to increase worker productivity by reducing absenteeism and equipment downtime, and to save money by lowering insurance premiums and workers' compensation payments, and preventing government fines. Some technicians work for governments conducting safety inspections and imposing fines.

Occupational health and safety technicians take measurements and collect workplace data either for routine inspection or as directed by a specialist. Technicians often focus on testing air, water, machines, and other elements of the work environment. They collect data that occupational health and safety specialists then analyze. Usually working under the supervision of specialists, they also help to implement and evaluate safety programs.

To measure hazards, such as noise or radiation, occupational health and safety technicians prepare and calibrate scientific equipment. They must properly collect and handle samples of dust, gases, vapors, and other potentially toxic materials to ensure personal safety and accurate test results.

To ensure that machinery and equipment complies with appropriate safety regulations, occupational health and safety technicians may examine and test machinery and equipment, such as lifting devices, machine guards, or scaffolding. They may check that personal protective equipment, such as masks, respirators, protective eyewear, or hardhats, is being used according to regulations. They also check that hazardous materials are stored correctly. They test and identify work areas for potential accident and health hazards, such as toxic vapors, mold, mildew, and explosive gas-air mixtures and help implement appropriate control measures, such as adjustments to ventilation systems. Their inspection of the workplace might involve talking with workers and observing their work, as well as inspecting elements in their work environment, such as lighting, tools, and equipment.

The responsibilities of occupational health and safety technicians vary by industry, workplace, and types of hazards affecting employees. Mine examiners, for example, are technicians who inspect mines for proper air flow and health hazards such as the buildup of methane or other noxious gases. Environmental protection technicians evaluate and coordinate the storage and handling of hazardous waste, the cleanup of contaminated soil or water, or other activities that affect the environment. Health physics technicians work in places that use radiation and radioactive material, helping to protect people and the environment from hazardous radiation exposure. Industrial hygiene technicians examine the workplace for health hazards, such as exposure to lead, asbestos, pesticides, or communicable diseases.

Work environment. Occupational health and safety technicians work in a variety of settings from offices and factories to mines. Their jobs often involve considerable fieldwork, and some require frequent travel.

Occupational health and safety technicians may be exposed to many of the same strenuous, dangerous, or stressful conditions faced by industrial employees. They may find themselves in an adversarial role if an organization disagrees with their recommendations. Most technicians work the typical 40 hour week. Some occupational health and safety technicians may be required to work overtime, and often irregular, hours.

Training, Other Qualifications, and Advancement

Technicians attend postsecondary school or enter the occupation through work experience and training. All occupational health and safety technicians are trained in the applicable laws or inspection procedures through some combination of classroom and on-the-job training.

Education and training. There are multiple paths to entry-level employment as an occupational health and safety technicians. Some technicians attend postsecondary school and typically earn an associate degree or certificate. Other technicians enter the occupation through work experience and training. In this case, an individual typically already works in the industry and may volunteer with their employer to take on health and safety responsibilities. These workers then usually receive on-the-job training coupled with some formal education. All occupational health and safety technicians are trained in the applicable laws or inspection procedures through some combination of classroom and on-the-job training.

Recommended high school courses include English, mathematics, chemistry, biology, and physics.

Certification and other qualifications. Although voluntary, many employers encourage credentialing. The Council on Certification of Health, Environmental, and Safety Technologists offers credentialing at the technician level. For specific requirements for each credential, contact the certifying body. Most certifications require completing periodic continuing education for recertification.

In general, people who want to enter this occupation should be responsible and like detailed work. Occupational health and safety technicians also should be able to communicate well.

Advancement. Occupational health and safety technicians who work for the Federal Government advance through their career ladder to a specified full-performance level if their work is satisfactory. For positions above this level, usually supervisory positions, advancement is competitive and based on agency needs and individual merit. Advancement opportunities in State and local governments and the private sector are often similar to those in the Federal Government.

Technicians with broad education and experience and those who are well versed in numerous business functions usually have the best advancement opportunities. One way to keep up with current professional developments is to join a professional society. These organizations offer journals, continuing education courses, and conferences that provide learning and networking opportunities and can help workers and students to advance.

With a bachelor's or advanced degree, technicians can become occupational health and safety specialists.

Employment

Occupational health and safety technicians held about 10,900 jobs in 2008. While the majority of jobs were spread throughout the private sector, about 22 percent of technicians worked for government agencies.

Most private companies either employ their own occupational health and safety workers or contract with them. Most contract work is done through consulting companies.

In addition to working for governments, occupational health and safety technicians were employed in manufacturing firms; public and private hospitals; educational services; scientific and technical consulting services; administrative and support services; and support activity for mining.

Job Outlook

Faster than average employment growth is expected; additional opportunities will arise from the need to replace workers who leave the occupation. Individuals with a well-

Projections data from the National Employment Matrix

Occupational Title	SOC Code	Employment, 2008	Projected Employment, 2018	Change, 2008-2018	
				Number	Percent
Occupational health and safety technicians	29-9012	10,900	12,500	1,600	14

(NOTE) Data in this table are rounded. See the discussion of the employment projections table in the *Handbook* introductory chapter on *Occupational Information Included in the Handbook.*

rounded breadth of knowledge in more than one health and safety specialty will have the best job prospects.

Employment change. Employment of occupational health and safety technicians is expected to increase 14 percent during the 2008-18 decade, faster than the average for all occupations, reflecting a balance of continuing public demand for a safe and healthy work environment against the desire for fewer government regulations.

More technicians will be needed to cope with technological advances in safety equipment and threats, changing regulations, and increasing public expectations. In private industry, employment growth will reflect overall business growth and continuing self-enforcement of government and company regulations and policies.

Although most occupational health and safety technicians work under supervision of specialists, technicians can complete many of the routine job tasks with little or no supervision. As a result in order to contain costs, some employers operate with more technicians and fewer specialists.

Growth for occupational health and safety technicians may be hampered by the number of manufacturing and other industry firms offshoring their operations. Also, the increasing popularity of telecommuting, or working at home, will result in less work space for technicians to inspect.

Job prospects. In addition to job openings from growth, job openings will arise from the need to replace workers who transfer to other occupations, retire, or leave for other reasons. Health and safety technicians with a wide breadth of knowledge in more than one area of health and safety along with general business functions will have the best prospects.

Employment of occupational health and safety technicians in the private sector is somewhat affected by general economic fluctuations. Federal, State, and local governments provide considerable job security; workers are less likely to be affected by changes in the economy.

Earnings

Median annual wages of occupational health and safety technicians were $45,360 in May 2008. The middle 50 percent earned between $35,160 and $57,110. The lowest 10 percent earned less than $26,540, and the highest 10 percent earned more than $73,050. Median annual wages in the industries employing the largest numbers of occupational health and safety specialists and technicians in May 2008 were:

Support activities for mining	$56,060
Local government	45,320
Colleges, universities, and professional schools	44,990
General medical and surgical hospitals	41,490
Management, scientific, and technical consulting	41,100

Most occupational health and safety technicians work in large private firms or for Federal, State, and local governments, most of which generally offer benefits more generous than those offered by smaller firms.

Related Occupations

Occupational health and safety technicians help to inspect and ensure that safety and health laws and regulations are obeyed. Others who enforce regulations include:

	Page
Agricultural inspectors	612
Construction and building inspectors	628
Fire inspectors and investigators	525
Occupational health and safety specialists	428

Sources of Additional Information

Information about jobs in Federal, State, and local governments and in private industry is available from State employment service offices.

For information on industrial hygiene, contact:
➤ American Industrial Hygiene Association, 2700 Prosperity Ave., Suite 250, Fairfax, VA 22031. Internet: **http://www.aiha.org**

For more information on careers in safety and a list of safety and related academic programs, contact:
➤ Board of Certified Safety Professionals, 208 Burwash Ave., Savoy, IL 61874. Internet: **http://www.bcsp.org**

For information on credentialing, contact:
➤ Council on Certification of Health, Environmental, and Safety Technologists, 208 Burwash Ave., Savoy, IL 61874. Internet: **http://www.cchest.org**

For information on health physics, contact:
➤ Health Physics Society, 1313 Dolley Madison Blvd., Suite 402, McLean, VA 22101. Internet: **http://www.hps.org**

For additional career information, contact:
➤ U.S. Department of Health and Human Services, Center for Disease Control and Prevention, National Institute of Occupational Safety and Health, 395 E Street SW., Suite 9200, Patriots Plaza Building, Washington, DC 20201. Internet: **http://www.cdc.gov/niosh**

➤ U.S. Department of Labor, Occupational Safety and Health Administration, Office of Communication, 200 Constitution Ave. NW., Washington, DC 20210. Internet: **http://www.osha.gov**

Information on obtaining positions as occupational health and safety specialists and technicians with the Federal Government is available from the Office of Personnel Management through USAJOBS, the Federal Government's official employment information system. This resource for locating and applying for job opportunities can be accessed through the Internet at **http://www.usajobs.gov/** or through an interactive voice response telephone system at (703) 724-1850, (866) 204-2858 or TDD (978) 461-8404. These numbers are not all toll free, and charges may result.

The Occupational Information Network (O*NET) provides information on a wide range of occupational characteristics. Links to O*NET appear at the end of the Internet version of this occupational statement, accessible at **http://www.bls.gov/ooh/ocos324.htm**

Opticians, Dispensing

Significant Points

- Employers increasingly prefer dispensing opticians to complete certification or graduate from an accredited 2-year associate's degree program in opticianry; some large employers may provide an apprenticeship.

- A license to practice is required by 22 States.

- Employment growth is projected to be average and reflect the steady demand for corrective lenses and fashionable eyeglass frames.

- Job opportunities are likely to be very good.

Nature of the Work

Helping people see better and look good at the same time is the job of a dispensing optician. *Dispensing opticians* help select and fit eyeglasses and contact lenses for people with eye problems, following prescriptions written by ophthalmologists or optometrists. (The work of optometrists is described elsewhere in the *Handbook*. See the section on physicians and surgeons for information about ophthalmologists.) Dispensing opticians recommend eyeglass frames, lenses, and lens coatings after considering the prescription and the customer's occupation, habits, and facial features. When fitting new eyeglasses, opticians use sophisticated diagnostic instruments to measure various characteristics of a client's eyes, including the thickness, width, curvature, and surface topography of the cornea. They also obtain a customer's prescription history to re-make eyeglasses or contact lenses, or they may verify a prescription with the examining optometrist or ophthalmologist.

Dispensing opticians prepare work orders that give ophthalmic laboratory technicians the information they need to grind and insert lenses into a frame. (See the section on ophthalmic laboratory technicians elsewhere in the Handbook.) The work order includes prescriptions for lenses and information on their size, material, color, and style. Some dispensing opticians grind and insert lenses themselves. They may also apply tint to lenses. After the glasses are made, dispensing opticians verify that the lenses meet the specifications, and then they may reshape or bend the frames with pliers for a custom fit.

Many opticians also spend time fixing and refitting broken frames, as well as instructing clients about wearing or caring for eyeglasses. Additionally, administrative duties have become a major part of their work, including keeping records on customers' prescriptions, work orders, and payments, and tracking inventory and sales.

Some dispensing opticians, after additional education and training, specialize in fitting contacts, artificial eyes, or cosmetic shells to cover blemished eyes. To fit contact lenses, dispensing opticians measure the shape and size of the eye, select the type of contact lens material, and prepare work orders specifying the prescription and lens size. Dispensing opticians observe customers' eyes, corneas, lids, and contact lenses with sophisticated instruments and microscopes. During several followup visits, opticians teach proper insertion, removal, and care of contact lenses.

Work environment. Dispensing opticians work indoors mainly in medical offices, optical stores, or in large department or club stores. Opticians spend a fair amount of time on their feet. If they prepare lenses, they need to take precautions against the hazards of glass cutting, chemicals, and machinery. Although most dispensing opticians work during regular business hours, those in retail stores may work evenings and weekends. Some work part time.

Training, Other Qualifications, and Advancement

Many employers increasingly prefer dispensing opticians to complete certification or graduate from an accredited 2-year associate's degree program in opticianry; some large employers may provide an apprenticeship that may last two years or longer.

Education and training. Although a high school diploma is all that is required to get into this occupation, most workers have completed at least some college courses or a degree. Classes in physics, basic anatomy, algebra, and trigonometry as well as experience with computers are particularly valuable. These classes prepare dispensing opticians to learn job skills, including optical mathematics, optical physics, and the use of precision measuring instruments and other machinery and tools.

Structured apprenticeship programs are more commonly available in States where licensing is not mandatory, and these programs are usually offered by large employers. Apprentices receive technical instruction along with training in office management and sales. Under the supervision of an experienced optician, optometrist, or ophthalmologist, apprentices work directly with patients, fitting eyeglasses and contact lenses.

Formal training in the field is offered in community colleges and in a few 4-year colleges and universities. As of 2008, the Commission on Opticianry Accreditation accredited 22 associate degree programs in 13 states. Graduation from an accredited program in opticianry can be advantageous as it provides a nationally recognized credential.

Licensure. As of 2009, twenty-two States require dispensing opticians to be licensed. States may require individuals to pass one or more of the following for licensure: a State practi-

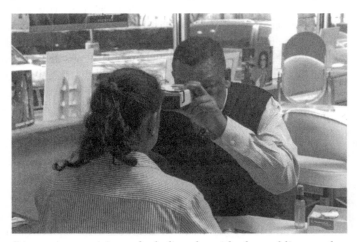

Dispensing opticians deal directly with the public, so they should be tactful, pleasant, and communicate well.

Projections data from the National Employment Matrix

Occupational Title	SOC Code	Employment, 2008	Projected Employment, 2018	Change, 2008-2018	
				Number	Percent
Opticians, dispensing	29-2081	59,800	67,800	8,000	13

(NOTE) Data in this table are rounded. See the discussion of the employment projections table in the *Handbook* introductory chapter on *Occupational Information Included in the Handbook.*

cal examination, a State written examination, and certification examinations offered by the American Board of Opticianry (ABO) and the National Contact Lens Examiners (NCLE). To qualify for the examinations, States often require applicants to complete postsecondary training or work as apprentices for 2 to 4 years.

Some States allow graduates of opticianry programs to take the licensure exam immediately upon graduation; others require a few months to a year of experience. Continuing education is commonly required for licensure renewal. Information about specific licensing requirements is available from the State board of occupational licensing.

Certification and other qualifications. Any optician can apply to the ABO and the NCLE for certification of their skills. Certification signifies to customers and employers that an optician has a certain level of expertise. Certification must be renewed every 3 years through continuing education. The State of Texas offers voluntary registration for the occupation.

Dispensing opticians deal directly with the public, so they should be tactful, pleasant, and able to communicate well. Fitting contact lenses requires considerable skill, care, and patience, so manual dexterity and the ability to do precision work are essential.

Advancement. A few experienced dispensing opticians open their own optical stores. Some become managers of optical stores or sales representatives for wholesalers or manufacturers of eyeglasses or lenses.

Employment

Dispensing opticians held about 59,800 jobs in 2008. About 40 percent worked in offices of optometrists. Another 33 percent worked in health and personal care stores, including optical goods stores. Many of these stores offer one-stop shopping where customers can have their eyes examined, choose frames, and have glasses made on the spot. Some opticians work in optical departments of department stores or other general merchandise stores, such as warehouse clubs and superstores. About 13 percent worked in offices of physicians, primarily ophthalmologists, who sell glasses directly to patients. One percent were self-employed and ran their own unincorporated businesses.

Job Outlook

Employment of dispensing opticians is expected to grow about as fast as average for all occupations through 2018, as the population ages and demand for corrective lenses increases. Very good job prospects are expected.

Employment change. Employment in this occupation is expected to rise 13 percent over the 2008–18 decade. Middle age is a time when many individuals use corrective lenses for the first time, and elderly persons generally require more vision care than others. As the share of the population in these older age groups increases and as people live longer, more opticians will be needed to provide service to them. In addition, awareness of the importance of regular eye exams is increasing across all age groups, especially children and those over the age of 65. Recent trends indicate a movement toward a "low vision" society, where a growing number of people view things that are closer in distance, such as computer monitors, over the course of an average day. This trend is expected to increase the need for eye care services. Fashion also influences demand. Frames come in a growing variety of styles, colors, and sizes, encouraging people to buy more than one pair.

Somewhat moderating the need for optician services is the increasing use of laser surgery to correct vision problems. Although the surgery remains relatively more expensive than eyewear, patients who successfully undergo this surgery may not require glasses or contact lenses for several years. Also, new technology is allowing workers to make the measurements needed to fit glasses and therefore allowing dispensing opticians to work faster, limiting the need for more workers.

Job prospects. Overall, the need to replace dispensing opticians who retire or leave the occupation will result in very good job prospects. Employment opportunities for opticians in offices of optometrists—the largest employer—will be particularly good as an increasing number of ophthalmologists are expected to utilize better trained opticians to handle more tasks, allowing ophthalmologists to see more patients.

Job opportunities also will be good at general merchandise stores because this segment is expected to experience much faster than average growth, as well as high turnover due to less favorable working conditions, such as long hours and mandatory weekend shifts.

Nonetheless, the number of job openings overall will be somewhat limited because the occupation is small. Also, dispensing opticians are vulnerable to changes in the business cycle because eyewear purchases often can be deferred for a time. Job prospects will be best for those who have certification and those who have completed a formal opticianry program. Job candidates with extensive knowledge of new technology, including new refraction systems, framing materials, and edging techniques, should also experience favorable conditions.

Earnings

Median annual wages of dispensing opticians were $32,810 in May 2008. The middle 50 percent earned between $26,170 and $41,930. The lowest 10 percent earned less than $21,250, and the highest 10 percent earned more than $50,580. Median annual wages in the industries employing the largest numbers of dispensing opticians in May 2008 were:

Other general merchandise stores $40,080
Health and personal care stores..................................34,700
Offices of physicians 34,090
Department stores..33,750
Offices of optometrists 30,460

Benefits for opticians are generally determined by the industries in which they are employed. In general, those who work part-time or in small retail shops have fewer benefits than those who may work for large optical chains or department stores. Self-employed opticians must provide their own benefits.

Related Occupations
Other workers who deal with customers and perform delicate work include the following:

	Page
Jewelers and precious stone and metal workers	770
Ophthalmic laboratory technicians	774
Orthotists and prosthetists	825

Sources of Additional Information
To learn about apprenticeship programs and State licensing requirements, contact:
➤ Opticians Association of America, 4064 E. Fir Hill Drive, Lakeland, TN 38002. Internet: **http://www.oaa.org**

To learn about voluntary certification for opticians who fit eyeglasses, as well as a list of State licensing boards for opticians, contact:
➤ American Board of Opticianry, 6506 Loisdale Rd., Suite 209, Springfield, VA 22150. Internet: **http://www.abo.org**

For information on voluntary certification for dispensing opticians who fit contact lenses, contact:
➤ National Contact Lens Examiners, 6506 Loisdale Rd., Suite 209, Springfield, VA 22150. Internet: **http://www.abo-ncle.org**

For a list of the 22 associate's degree programs accredited by the Commission on Opticianry Accreditation, contact:
➤ National Federation of Opticianry Schools, 2800 Springport Road, Jackson, MI 49202. Internet: **http://www.nfos.org**

The Occupational Information Network (O*NET) provides information on a wide range of occupational characteristics. Links to O*NET appear at the end of the Internet version of this occupational statement, accessible at **http://www.bls.gov/ooh/ocos098.htm**

Pharmacy Technicians and Aides

Significant Points

- Job opportunities are expected to be good, especially for those with certification or previous work experience.

- Many technicians and aides work evenings, weekends, and holidays.

- About 75 percent of jobs were in a retail setting.

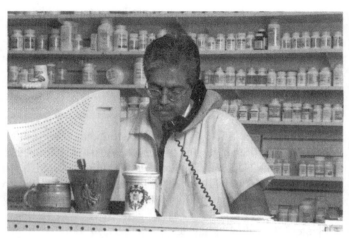

Pharmacy technicians and aides answer phones, operate cash registers, and prepare medications for patients.

Nature of the Work
Pharmacy technicians and aides help licensed pharmacists prepare prescription medications, provide customer service, and perform administrative duties within a pharmacy setting. Pharmacy technicians generally are responsible for receiving prescription requests, counting tablets, and labeling bottles, while pharmacy aides perform administrative functions such as answering phones, stocking shelves, and operating cash registers. In organizations that do not have aides, however, pharmacy technicians may be responsible for these clerical duties.

Pharmacy technicians who work in retail or mail-order pharmacies have various responsibilities, depending on State rules and regulations. Technicians receive written prescription requests from patients. They also may receive prescriptions sent electronically from doctors' offices, and in some States they are permitted to process requests by phone. They must verify that the information on the prescription is complete and accurate. To prepare the prescription, technicians retrieve, count, pour, weigh, measure, and sometimes mix the medication. Then they prepare the prescription labels, select the type of container, and affix the prescription and auxiliary labels to the container. Once the prescription is filled, technicians price and file the prescription, which must be checked by a pharmacist before it is given to the patient. Technicians may establish and maintain patient profiles, as well as prepare insurance claim forms. Technicians always refer any questions regarding prescriptions, drug information, or health matters to a pharmacist. (See the section on pharmacists elsewhere in the Handbook.)

In hospitals, nursing homes, and assisted-living facilities, technicians have added responsibilities, including preparing sterile solutions and delivering medications to nurses or physicians. Technician may also record the information about the prescribed medication onto the patient's profile.

Pharmacy aides work closely with pharmacy technicians. They primarily perform administrative duties such as answering telephones, stocking shelves, and operating cash registers. They also may prepare insurance forms and maintain patient profiles. Unlike pharmacy technicians, pharmacy aides do not prepare prescriptions or mix medications.

Work environment. Pharmacy technicians and aides work in clean, organized, well-lighted, and well-ventilated areas. Most of their workday is spent on their feet. They may be required to lift heavy boxes or to use stepladders to retrieve supplies from high shelves.

Technicians and aides often have varying schedules that include nights, weekends, and holidays. In facilities that are open 24 hours a day, such as hospital pharmacies, technicians and aides may be required to work nights. Many technicians and aides work part time.

Training, Other Qualifications, and Advancement

There is no national training standard for pharmacy technicians, but employers favor applicants who have formal training, certification, or previous experience. There also are no formal training requirements for pharmacy aides, but a high school diploma may increase an applicant's prospects for employment.

Education and training. There are no standard training requirements for pharmacy technicians, but some States require a high school diploma or its equivalent. Although most pharmacy technicians receive informal on-the-job training, employers favor those who have completed formal training and certification. On-the-job training generally ranges between 3 and 12 months.

Formal technician education programs are available through a variety of organizations, including community colleges, vocational schools, hospitals, and the military. These programs range from 6 months to 2 years and include classroom and laboratory work. They cover a variety of subject areas, such as medical and pharmaceutical terminology, pharmaceutical calculations, pharmacy recordkeeping, pharmaceutical techniques, and pharmacy law and ethics. Technicians also are required to learn the names, actions, uses, and doses of the medications they work with. Many training programs include internships, in which students gain hands-on experience in actual pharmacies. After completion, students receive a diploma, a certificate, or an associate's degree, depending on the program.

There are no formal education requirements for pharmacy aides, but employers may favor applicants with a high school diploma or its equivalent. Experience operating a cash register, interacting with customers, managing inventory, and using computers may be helpful. Pharmacy aides also receive informal on-the-job training that generally lasts less than 3 months.

Certification and other qualifications. In most States, pharmacy technicians must be registered with the State board of pharmacy. Eligibility requirements vary, but in some States applicants must possess a high school diploma or its equivalent and pay an application fee.

Most States do not require technicians to be certified, but voluntary certification is available through several private organizations. The Pharmacy Technician Certification Board (PTCB) and the Institute for the Certification of Pharmacy Technicians

(ICPT) administer national certification examinations. Certification through such programs may enhance an applicant's prospects for employment and is required by some States and employers. To be eligible for either exam, candidates must have a high school diploma or its equivalent and no felony convictions of any kind. In addition, applicants for the PTCB exam must not have had any drug-related or pharmacy-related convictions, including misdemeanors. Many employers will reimburse the cost of the exams.

Under these programs, technicians must be recertified every 2 years. Recertification requires 20 hours of continuing education within the 2-year certification period. Continuing education hours can be earned from several different sources, including colleges, pharmacy associations, and pharmacy technician training programs. Up to 10 hours of continuing education also can be earned on the job under the direct supervision and instruction of a pharmacist.

Good customer service and communication skills are needed because pharmacy technicians and aides interact with patients, coworkers, and healthcare professionals. Basic mathematics, spelling, and reading skills also are important, as technicians must interpret prescription orders and verify drug doses. Technicians also must be precise: details are sometimes a matter of life and death.

Advancement. Advancement opportunities generally are limited, but in large pharmacies and health systems pharmacy technicians and aides with significant training or experience can be promoted to supervisory positions. Some may advance into specialty positions such as chemotherapy technician or nuclear pharmacy technician. Others may move into sales. With a substantial amount of formal training, some technicians and aides go on to become pharmacists.

Employment

Pharmacy technicians and aides held about 381,200 jobs in 2008. Of these, about 326,300 were pharmacy technicians and about 54,900 were pharmacy aides. About 75 percent of jobs were in a retail setting, and about 16 percent were in hospitals.

Job Outlook

Employment is expected to increase much faster than the average, and job opportunities are expected to be good.

Employment change. Employment of pharmacy technicians and aides is expected to increase by 25 percent from 2008 to 2018, which is much faster than the average for all occupations. The increased number of middle-aged and elderly people—who use more prescription drugs than younger people—will spur demand for pharmacy workers throughout the projection period. In addition, as scientific advances lead to new drugs,

Projections data from the National Employment Matrix

Occupational Title	SOC Code	Employment, 2008	Projected Employment, 2018	Change, 2008-2018	
				Number	Percent
Pharmacy technicians and aides..	–	381,200	477,500	96,300	25
Pharmacy technicians...	29-2052	326,300	426,000	99,800	31
Pharmacy aides	31-9095	54,900	51,500	-3,500	-6

(NOTE) Data in this table are rounded. See the discussion of the employment projections table in the *Handbook* introductory chapter on *Occupational Information Included in the Handbook.*

and as more people obtain prescription drug coverage, pharmacy workers will be needed in growing numbers.

Employment of pharmacy technicians is expected to increase by 31 percent. As cost-conscious insurers begin to use pharmacies as patient-care centers and pharmacists become more involved in patient care, pharmacy technicians will continue to see an expansion of their role in the pharmacy. In addition, they will increasingly adopt some of the administrative duties that were previously performed by pharmacy aides, such as answering phones and stocking shelves. As a result of this development, demand for pharmacy aides should decrease, and employment is expected to decline moderately, decreasing by 6 percent over the projection period.

Job prospects. Job opportunities for pharmacy technicians are expected to be good, especially for those with previous experience, formal training, or certification. Job openings will result from employment growth, as well as the need to replace workers who transfer to other occupations or leave the labor force.

Despite declining employment, job prospects for pharmacy aides also are expected to be good. As people leave this occupation, new applicants will be needed to fill the positions that remain.

Earnings

Median hourly wages of wage and salary pharmacy technicians in May 2008 were $13.32. The middle 50 percent earned between $10.95 and $15.88. The lowest 10 percent earned less than $9.27, and the highest 10 percent earned more than $18.98.

Median hourly wages of wage and salary pharmacy aides were $9.66 in May 2008. The middle 50 percent earned between $8.47 and $11.62. The lowest 10 percent earned less than $7.69, and the highest 10 percent earned more than $14.26.

Certified technicians may earn more than non-certified technicians. Some technicians and aides belong to unions representing hospital or grocery store workers.

Related Occupations

Other occupations related to healthcare include the following:

Sources of Additional Information

For information on pharmacy technician certification programs, contact:

➤ Pharmacy Technician Certification Board, 2215 Constitution Ave. NW., Washington DC 20037-2985. Internet: **http://www.ptcb.org**

➤ Institute for the Certification of Pharmacy Technicians, 2536 S. Old Hwy. 94, Suite 224, St. Charles, MO 63303. Internet: **http://www.nationaltechexam.org**

For a list of accredited pharmacy technician training programs, contact:

➤ American Society of Health-System Pharmacists, 7272 Wisconsin Ave., Bethesda, MD 20814. Internet: **http://www.ashp.org**

For pharmacy technician career information, contact:
➤ National Pharmacy Technician Association, P.O. Box 683148, Houston, TX 77268. Internet: **http://www.pharmacytechnician.org**

The Occupational Information Network (O*NET) provides information on a wide range of occupational characteristics. Links to O*NET appear at the end of the Internet version of this occupational statement, accessible at **http://www.bls.gov/ooh/ocos325.htm**

Radiologic Technologists and Technicians

Significant Points

- Employment is projected to grow faster than average; those with knowledge of more than one diagnostic imaging procedure will have the best employment opportunities.

- Formal training programs in radiography are offered in hospitals or colleges and universities and lead to a certificate, an associate degree, or a bachelor's degree.

- Most States require licensure, and requirements vary.

- Although hospitals will remain the primary employer, a number of new jobs will be found in physicians' offices and diagnostic imaging centers.

Nature of the Work

Radiologic technologists and technicians perform diagnostic imaging examination. Radiologic technicians perform imaging examinations like x rays while technologists use other imaging modalities such as computed tomography, magnetic resonance imaging, and mammography.

Radiologic technicians, sometimes referred to as radiographers, produce x-ray films (radiographs) of parts of the human body for use in diagnosing medical problems. They prepare patients for radiologic examinations by explaining the procedure, removing jewelry and other articles through which x rays cannot pass, and positioning patients so that the parts of the body can be appropriately radiographed. To prevent unnecessary exposure to radiation, these workers surround the exposed area with radiation protection devices, such as lead shields, or limit the size of the x-ray beam. Radiographers position radiographic equipment at the correct angle and height over the appropriate area of a patient's body. Using instruments similar to a measuring tape they may measure the thickness of the section to be radiographed and set controls on the x-ray machine to produce radiographs of the appropriate density, detail, and contrast.

Radiologic technologists and technicians must follow physicians' orders precisely and conform to regulations concerning the use of radiation to protect themselves, their patients, and their coworkers from unnecessary exposure.

In addition to preparing patients and operating equipment, radiologic technologists and technicians keep patient records and adjust and maintain equipment. They also may prepare work schedules, evaluate purchases of equipment, or manage a radiology department.

Radiologic technologists perform more complex imaging procedures. When performing fluoroscopies, for example, radiologic technologists prepare a solution for the patient to drink, allowing the radiologist (a physician who interprets radiographs) to see soft tissues in the body.

Some radiologic technologists specialize in computed tomography (CT), as CT technologists. CT scans produce a substantial amount of cross-sectional x rays of an area of the body. From those cross-sectional x rays, a three-dimensional image is made. The CT uses ionizing radiation; therefore, it requires the same precautionary measures that are used with x rays.

Radiologic technologists also can specialize in Magnetic Resonance Imaging (MR) as *MR technologists*. MR, like CT, produces multiple cross-sectional images to create a 3-dimensional image. Unlike CT and x rays, MR uses non-ionizing radio frequency to generate image contrast.

Radiologic technologists might also specialize in mammography. Mammographers use low dose x-ray systems to produce images of the breast.

In addition to radiologic technologists, others who conduct diagnostic imaging procedures include cardiovascular technologists and technicians, diagnostic medical sonographers, and nuclear medicine technologists. (Each is discussed elsewhere in the Handbook.)

Work environment. Physical stamina is important in this occupation because technologists and technicians are on their feet for long periods and may lift or turn disabled patients. Technologists and technicians work at diagnostic machines but also may perform some procedures at patients' bedsides. Some travel to patients in large vans equipped with sophisticated diagnostic equipment.

Although radiation hazards exist in this occupation, they are minimized by the use of lead aprons, gloves, and other shielding devices, and by instruments monitoring exposure to radiation. Technologists and technicians wear badges measuring radiation levels in the radiation area, and detailed records are kept on their cumulative lifetime dose.

Most full-time radiologic technologists and technicians work about 40 hours a week. They may, however, have evening, weekend, or on-call hours. Some radiologic technologists and technicians work part time for more than one employer; for those, travel to and from facilities must be considered.

Training, Other Qualifications, and Advancement

There are multiple paths to entry into this profession offered in hospitals or colleges and universities. Most States require licensure, and requirements vary.

Education and training. Formal training programs in radiography lead to a certificate, an associate degree, or a bachelor's degree. An associate degree is the most prevalent form of educational attainment among radiologic technologists and tech-

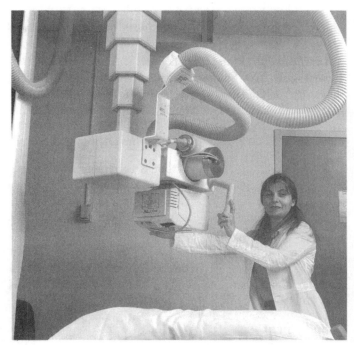

Radiologic technologists prepare patients for radiologic examinations by explaining the procedures, removing jewelry, and positioning patients.

nicians. Some may receive a certificate. Certificate programs typically last around 21-24 months.

The Joint Review Committee on Education in Radiologic Technology accredits formal training programs in radiography. The committee accredited 213 programs resulting in a certificate, 397 programs resulting in an associate degree, and 35 resulting in a bachelor's degree in 2009. The programs provide both classroom and clinical instruction in anatomy and physiology, patient care procedures, radiation physics, radiation protection, principles of imaging, medical terminology, positioning of patients, medical ethics, radiobiology, and pathology.

Students interested in radiologic technology should take high school courses in mathematics, physics, chemistry, and biology.

Licensure. Federal legislation protects the public from the hazards of unnecessary exposure to medical and dental radiation by ensuring that operators of radiologic equipment are properly trained. However, it is up to each State to require licensure of radiologic technologists. Most States require licensure for practicing radiologic technologists. Licensing requirements vary by State; for specific requirements contact your State's health board.

Certification and other qualifications. The American Registry of Radiologic Technologists (ARRT) offers voluntary certification for radiologic technologists. In addition, a number of States use ARRT-administered exams for State licensing purposes. To be eligible for certification, technologists must graduate from an ARRT-approved accredited program and pass an examination. Many employers prefer to hire certified radiologic technologists. In order to maintain an ARRT certification, 24 hours of continuing education must be completed every 2 years.

Radiologic technologists should be sensitive to patients' physical and psychological needs. They must pay attention to detail, follow instructions, and work as part of a team. In addition, operating complicated equipment requires mechanical ability and manual dexterity.

Advancement. With experience and additional training, staff technologists may become specialists, performing CT scanning, MR, mammography, or bone densitometry. Technologists also may advance, with additional education and certification, to become a radiologist assistant. The ARRT offers specialty certification in many radiologic specialties as well as a credentialing for radiologist assistants.

Experienced technologists also may be promoted to supervisor, chief radiologic technologist, and, ultimately, department administrator or director. Depending on the institution, courses or a master's degree in business or health administration may be necessary for the director's position.

Some technologists progress by specializing in the occupation to become instructors or directors in radiologic technology educational programs; others take jobs as sales representatives or instructors with equipment manufacturers.

Employment

Radiologic technologists held about 214,700 jobs in 2008. About 61 percent of all jobs were in hospitals. Most other jobs were in offices of physicians; medical and diagnostic laboratories, including diagnostic imaging centers; and outpatient care centers.

Job Outlook

Employment is projected to grow faster than average. Those with knowledge of more than one diagnostic imaging procedure—such as CT, MR, and mammography—will have the best employment opportunities.

Employment change. Employment of radiologic technologists is expected to increase by about 17 percent from 2008 to 2018, faster than the average for all occupations. As the population grows and ages, there will be an increasing demand for diagnostic imaging. With age comes increased incidence of illness and injury, which often requires diagnostic imaging for diagnosis. In addition to diagnosis, diagnostic imaging is used to monitor the progress of disease treatment. With the increasing success of medical technologies in treating disease, diagnostic imaging will increasingly be needed to monitor progress of treatment.

The extent to which diagnostic imaging procedures are performed depends largely on cost and reimbursement considerations. However, accurate early disease detection allows for lower cost of treatment in the long run, which many third-party payers find favorable.

Although hospitals will remain the principal employer of radiologic technologists, a number of new jobs will be found in offices of physicians and diagnostic imaging centers. As technology advances many imaging modalities are becoming less expensive and more feasible to have in a physician's office

Job prospects. In addition to job growth, job openings also will arise from the need to replace technologists who leave the occupation. Those with knowledge of more than one diagnostic imaging procedure—such as CT, MR, and mammography—will have the best employment opportunities as employers seek to control costs by using multi-credentialed employees.

Demand for radiologic technologists and technicians can tend to be regional with some areas having large demand, while other areas are saturated. Technologists and technicians willing to relocate may have better job prospects.

CT is continuing to become a frontline diagnosis tool. Instead of taking x rays to decide whether a CT is needed, as was the practice before, it is often the first choice for imaging because of its accuracy. MR also is increasingly used. Technologists with credentialing in either of these specialties will be very marketable to employers.

Earnings

The median annual wage of radiologic technologists was $52,210 in May 2008. The middle 50 percent earned between $42,710 and $63,010. The lowest 10 percent earned less than $35,100, and the highest 10 percent earned more than $74,970. Median annual wages in the industries employing the largest numbers of radiologic technologists in 2008 were:

Medical and diagnostic laboratories	$55,210
Federal Executive Branch	53,650
General medical and surgical hospitals	52,890
Outpatient care centers	50,840
Offices of physicians	48,530

Related Occupations

Radiologic technologists operate sophisticated equipment to help physicians, dentists, and other health practitioners diagnose and treat patients. Workers in related healthcare occupations include:

	Page
Cardiovascular technologists and technicians	408
Diagnostic medical sonographers	416
Nuclear medicine technologists	426
Radiation therapists	387

Sources of Additional Information

For information on careers in radiologic technology, contact:
➤ American Society of Radiologic Technologists, 15000 Central Ave. SE., Albuquerque, NM 87123. Internet: **http://www.asrt.org**

For the current list of accredited education programs in radiography, contact:

Projections data from the National Employment Matrix

Occupational Title	SOC Code	Employment, 2008	Projected Employment, 2018	Change, 2008-2018	
				Number	Percent
Radiologic technologists and technicians	29-2034	214,700	251,700	37,000	17

(NOTE) Data in this table are rounded. See the discussion of the employment projections table in the *Handbook* introductory chapter on *Occupational Information Included in the Handbook.*

> Joint Review Committee on Education in Radiologic Technology, 20 N. Wacker Dr., Suite 2850, Chicago, IL 60606-3182. Internet: **http://www.jrcert.org**

For certification information, contact:
> American Registry of Radiologic Technologists, 1255 Northland Dr., St. Paul, MN 55120-1155. Internet: **http://www.arrt.org**

The Occupational Information Network (O*NET) provides information on a wide range of occupational characteristics. Links to O*NET appear at the end of the Internet version of this occupational statement, accessible at **http://www.bls.gov/ooh/ocos105.htm**

Surgical Technologists

Significant Points

- Employment is expected to grow much faster than average.

- Job opportunities will be best for technologists who are certified and for those who are willing to relocate.

- Training programs last 9 to 24 months and lead to a certificate, diploma, or associate's degree.

- Hospitals will continue to be the primary employer, although much faster employment growth is expected in other healthcare industries.

Nature of the Work

Surgical technologists, also called scrubs and surgical or operating room technicians, assist in surgical operations under the supervision of surgeons, registered nurses, or other surgical personnel. Surgical technologists are members of operating room teams, which most commonly include surgeons, anesthesiologists, and circulating nurses.

Before an operation, surgical technologists help prepare the operating room by setting up surgical instruments and equipment, sterile drapes, and sterile solutions. They assemble both sterile and nonsterile equipment, as well as check and adjust it to ensure that it is working properly. Technologists also get patients ready for surgery by washing, shaving, and disinfecting incision sites. They transport patients to the operating room, help position them on the operating table, and cover them with sterile surgical drapes. Technologists also observe patients' vital signs, check charts, and help the surgical team put on sterile gowns and gloves.

During surgery, technologists pass instruments and other sterile supplies to surgeons and surgical assistants. They may hold retractors, cut sutures, and help count sponges, needles, supplies, and instruments. Surgical technologists help prepare, care for, and dispose of specimens taken for laboratory analysis and help apply dressings. Some operate sterilizers, lights, or suction machines and help operate diagnostic equipment.

After an operation, surgical technologists may help transfer patients to the recovery room and clean and restock the operating room.

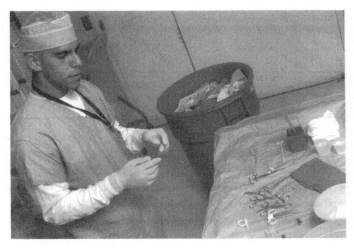

Before an operation, surgical technologists help prepare the operating room by setting up surgical instruments and equipment, sterile drapes, and sterile solutions.

Certified surgical technologists with additional specialized education or training also may act in the role of the surgical first assistant or circulator. Under the surgeon's direction, the surgical first assistant, as defined by the American College of Surgeons (ACS), provides aid in exposure, hemostasis (controlling blood flow and stopping or preventing hemorrhage), and other technical functions that help the surgeon carry out a safe operation. A circulating technologist is the "unsterile" member of the surgical team who interviews the patient before surgery, prepares the patient for surgery, helps with anesthesia, obtains and opens packages for the "sterile" people to remove the sterile contents during the procedure, keeps a written account of the surgical procedure, and answers the surgeon's questions about the patient during the surgery.

Work environment. Surgical technologists work in clean, well-lighted, cool environments. They must stand for long periods and remain alert during operations. At times, they may be exposed to communicable diseases and unpleasant sights, odors, and materials.

Most surgical technologists work a regular 40-hour week, although they may be on call or work nights, weekends, and holidays on a rotating basis.

Training, Other Qualifications, and Advancement

Training programs last 9 to 24 months and lead to a certificate, diploma, or associate's degree. Professional certification can help in getting jobs and promotions.

Education and training. Surgical technologists receive their training in formal programs offered by community and junior colleges, vocational schools, universities, hospitals, and the military. In 2008, the Commission on Accreditation of Allied Health Education Programs (CAAHEP) recognized more than 450 accredited training programs. Programs last from 9 to 24 months and lead to a certificate, diploma, or associate's degree. High school graduation normally is required for admission. Recommended high school courses include health, biology, chemistry, and mathematics.

Programs provide classroom education and supervised clinical experience. Students take courses in anatomy, physiology, microbiology, pharmacology, professional ethics, and medical

Projections data from the National Employment Matrix

Occupational Title	SOC Code	Employment, 2008	Projected Employment, 2018	Change, 2008-2018	
				Number	Percent
Surgical technologists	29-2055	91,500	114,700	23,200	25

(NOTE) Data in this table are rounded. See the discussion of the employment projections table in the *Handbook* introductory chapter on *Occupational Information Included in the Handbook.*

terminology. Other topics covered include the care and safety of patients during surgery, sterile techniques, and surgical procedures. Students also learn to sterilize instruments; prevent and control infection; and handle special drugs, solutions, supplies, and equipment.

Certification and other qualifications. Most employers prefer to hire certified technologists. Technologists may obtain voluntary professional certification from the Liaison Council on Certification for the Surgical Technologist by graduating from a CAAHEP-accredited program and passing a national certification examination. They may then use the Certified Surgical Technologist (CST) designation. In order to maintain certification, certified surgical technologists must earn 60 hours of approved continuing education over a 4-year period or retake and pass the certifying exam at the end of the 4-year period.

Certification also may be obtained from the National Center for Competency Testing (NCCT). To qualify to take the exam, candidates follow one of three paths: complete an accredited training program, undergo a 2-year hospital on-the-job training program, or acquire 7 years of experience working in the field. After passing the exam, individuals may use the designation Tech in Surgery-Certified, TS-C (NCCT). This certification must be renewed every 5 years through either continuing education or reexamination.

Surgical technologists need manual dexterity to handle instruments quickly. They also must be conscientious, orderly, and emotionally stable to handle the demands of the operating room environment. Technologists must respond quickly and must be familiar with operating procedures in order to have instruments ready for surgeons without having to be told to do so. They are expected to keep abreast of new developments in the field.

Advancement. Technologists advance by specializing in a particular area of surgery, such as neurosurgery or open-heart surgery. They also may work as circulating technologists. With additional training, some technologists advance to first assistant. Some surgical technologists manage central supply departments in hospitals or take positions with insurance companies, sterile supply services, and operating equipment firms.

Employment

Surgical technologists held about 91,500 jobs in 2008. About 71 percent of jobs for surgical technologists were in hospitals, mainly in operating and delivery rooms. Other jobs were in offices of physicians or dentists who perform outpatient surgery and in outpatient care centers, including ambulatory surgical centers. A few technologists, known as private scrubs, are employed directly by surgeons who have special surgical teams, such as those for liver transplants.

Job Outlook

Employment is expected to grow much faster than average. Job opportunities will be best for technologists who are certified and for those who are willing to relocate.

Employment change. Employment of surgical technologists is expected to grow 25 percent between 2008 and 2018, much faster than the average for all occupations, as the volume of surgeries increases. The number of surgical procedures is expected to continue to rise as the population grows and ages. Older people, including the baby-boom generation, which generally requires more surgical procedures, will continue to account for a larger portion of the U.S. population. In addition, technological advances, such as fiber optics and laser technology, have permitted an increasing number of new surgical procedures to be performed and also have allowed surgical technologists to assist with a greater number of procedures.

Hospitals will continue to be the primary employer of surgical technologists, as they try to reduce costs by replacing nurses in the operating room. However, because of better paying opportunities, much faster employment growth is expected in offices of physicians and in outpatient care centers, including ambulatory surgical centers.

Job prospects. Job opportunities will be best for technologists who are certified and for those who are willing to relocate.

Earnings

Median annual wages of wage-and-salary surgical technologists were $38,740 in May 2008. The middle 50 percent earned between $32,490 and $46,910. The lowest 10 percent earned less than $27,510, and the highest 10 percent earned more than $54,300. Median annual wages in the industries employing the largest numbers of surgical technologists were as follows:

Specialty (except psychiatric and substance abuse) hospitals	$40,880
Outpatient care centers	39,660
General medical and surgical hospitals	38,640
Offices of physicians	38,520
Offices of dentists	36,380

Wages of surgical technologists vary with their experience and education, the responsibilities of the position, the working hours, and the economy of a given region of the country. Benefits provided by most employers include paid vacation and sick leave; health, medical, vision, dental, and life insurance; and a retirement program. A few employers also provide tuition reimbursement and child care benefits.

Related Occupations

Other health occupations requiring approximately 1 year of training after high school include the following:

Sources of Additional Information

For additional information on a career as a surgical technologist, and for a list of CAAHEP-accredited programs, contact:
➤ Association of Surgical Technologists, 6 West Dry Creek Circle, Suite 200, Littleton, CO 80120. Internet: **http://www.ast.org**

For information on becoming a Certified Surgical Technologist, contact:
➤ Liaison Council on Certification for the Surgical Technologist, 6 West Dry Creek Circle, Suite 100, Littleton, CO 80120. Internet: **http://www.lcc-st.org**

For information on becoming a Tech in Surgery-Certified, contact:
➤ National Center for Competency Testing, 7007 College Blvd., Suite 705, Overland Park, KS 66211.

The Occupational Information Network (O*NET) provides information on a wide range of occupational characteristics. Links to O*NET appear at the end of the Internet version of this occupational statement, accessible at **http://www.bls.gov/ooh/ocos106.htm**

Veterinary Technologists and Technicians

Significant Points

- Animal lovers get satisfaction from this occupation, but aspects of the work can be unpleasant, physically and emotionally demanding, and sometimes dangerous.

- There are primarily two levels of education and training for entry to this occupation: a 2-year program for veterinary technicians and a 4-year program for veterinary technologists.

- Employment is expected to grow much faster than average.

- Overall job opportunities should be excellent; however, keen competition is expected for jobs in zoos and aquariums.

Nature of the Work

Owners of pets and other animals today expect superior veterinary care. To provide this service, veterinarians use the skills of *veterinary technologists* and technicians, who perform many of the same duties for a veterinarian that a nurse would for a

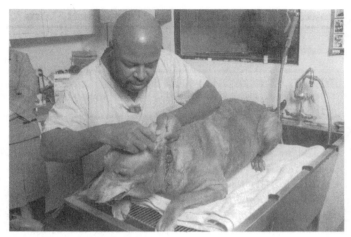

Veterinary technologists and technicians often assist veterinarians by conducting tests.

physician. Although specific job duties vary by employer, there is often little difference between the tasks carried out by technicians and technologists, despite differences in formal education and training. However, most technicians work in private clinical practice while many technologists have the option to work in more advanced research-related jobs.

Veterinary technologists and technicians typically conduct clinical work in a private practice under the supervision of a licensed veterinarian. Veterinary technologists and technicians often perform various medical tests and treat and diagnose medical conditions and diseases in animals. For example, they may perform laboratory tests such as urinalysis and blood counts, assist with dental care, prepare tissue samples, take blood samples, and assist veterinarians in a variety of other diagnostic tests. While most of these duties are performed in a laboratory setting, many are not. For example, some veterinary technicians record patients' case histories, expose and develop x rays and radiographs, and provide specialized nursing care. In addition, experienced veterinary technicians may discuss a pet's condition with its owners and train new clinic personnel. Veterinary technologists and technicians assisting small-animal practitioners usually care for small pets, such as cats and dogs, but can perform a variety of duties with mice, rats, sheep, pigs, cattle, monkeys, birds, fish, and frogs. Very few veterinary technologists work in mixed animal practices where they care for both small pets and large, nondomestic animals.

Besides working in private clinics and animal hospitals, some veterinary technologists and technicians work in research facilities under the guidance of veterinarians or physicians. In this role, they may administer medications, prepare samples for laboratory examinations, or record information on an animal's genealogy, diet, weight, medications, food intake, and clinical signs of pain and distress. Some may sterilize laboratory and surgical equipment and provide routine postoperative care. Occasionally, veterinary technologists vaccinate newly admitted animals and may have to euthanize seriously ill, severely injured, or unwanted animals.

While the goal of most veterinary technologists and technicians is to promote animal health, some contribute to human health, as well. Veterinary technologists occasionally assist veterinarians in implementing research projects as they work with

Projections data from the National Employment Matrix

Occupational Title	SOC Code	Employment, 2008	Projected Employment, 2018	Change, 2008-2018	
				Number	Percent
Veterinary technologists and technicians...	29-2056	79,600	108,100	28,500	36

(NOTE) Data in this table are rounded. See the discussion of the employment projections table in the *Handbook* introductory chapter on *Occupational Information Included in the Handbook.*

other scientists in medical-related fields such as gene therapy and cloning. Some find opportunities in biomedical research, wildlife medicine, livestock management, pharmaceutical sales, and increasingly, in biosecurity and disaster preparedness.

Work environment. While people who love animals get satisfaction from helping them, some of the work may be unpleasant, physically and emotionally demanding, and sometimes dangerous. Data from the U.S. Bureau of Labor Statistics show that full-time veterinary technologists and technicians experienced a work-related injury and illness rate that was much higher than the national average. At times, veterinary technicians must clean cages and lift, hold, or restrain animals, risking exposure to bites or scratches. These workers must take precautions when treating animals with germicides or insecticides. The work setting can be noisy.

Veterinary technologists and technicians who witness abused animals or who euthanize unwanted, aged, or hopelessly injured animals may experience emotional stress. Those working for humane societies and animal shelters often deal with the public, some of whom might react with hostility to any implication that the owners are neglecting or abusing their pets. Such workers must maintain a calm and professional demeanor while they enforce the laws regarding animal care.

In some animal hospitals, research facilities, and animal shelters, a veterinary technician is on duty 24 hours a day, which means that some work night shifts. Most full-time veterinary technologists and technicians work about 40 hours a week, although some work 50 or more hours a week.

Training, Other Qualifications, and Advancement
There are primarily two levels of education and training for entry to this occupation: a 2-year program for veterinary technicians and a 4-year program for veterinary technologists.

Education and training. Most entry-level veterinary technicians have a 2-year associate degree from an American Veterinary Medical Association (AVMA)-accredited community college program in veterinary technology in which courses are taught in clinical and laboratory settings using live animals. Currently, about 20 colleges offer veterinary technology programs that are longer and that culminate in a 4-year bachelor's degree in veterinary technology. These 4-year colleges, in addition to some vocational schools, also offer 2-year programs in laboratory animal science. About 10 schools offer distance learning.

In 2009, about 160 veterinary technology programs in 45 States were accredited by the American Veterinary Medical Association (AVMA). Graduation from an AVMA-accredited veterinary technology program allows students to take the credentialing exam in any State in the country.

Those interested in careers as veterinary technologists and technicians should take as many high school science, biology,

and math courses as possible. Science courses taken beyond high school, in an associate or bachelor's degree program, should emphasize practical skills in a clinical or laboratory setting.

Technologists and technicians usually begin work as trainees under the direct supervision of a veterinarian. Entry-level workers whose training or educational background encompasses extensive hands-on experience with diagnostic and medical equipment usually require a shorter period of on-the-job training.

Licensure and certification. Each State regulates veterinary technicians and technologists differently; however, all States require them to pass a credentialing exam following coursework. Passing the State exam assures the public that the technician or technologist has sufficient knowledge to work in a veterinary clinic or hospital. Candidates are tested for competency through an examination that includes oral, written, and practical portions and that is regulated by the State Board of Veterinary Examiners or the appropriate State agency. Depending on the State, candidates may become registered, licensed, or certified. Most States, however, use the National Veterinary Technician (NVT) exam. Prospects usually can have their passing scores transferred from one State to another, so long as both States use the same exam.

Employers recommend American Association for Laboratory Animal Science (AALAS) certification for those seeking employment in a research facility. AALAS offers certification for three levels of technician competence, with a focus on three principal areas—animal husbandry, facility management, and animal health and welfare. Those who wish to become certified must satisfy a combination of education and experience requirements prior to taking the AALAS examination. Work experience must be directly related to the maintenance, health, and well-being of laboratory animals and must be gained in a laboratory animal facility as defined by AALAS. Candidates who meet the necessary criteria can begin pursuing the desired certification on the basis of their qualifications. The lowest level of certification is Assistant Laboratory Animal Technician (ALAT), the second level is Laboratory Animal Technician (LAT), and the highest level of certification is Laboratory Animal Technologist (LATG). The AALAS examination consists of multiple-choice questions and is longer and more difficult for higher levels of certification, ranging from 2 hours and 120 multiple choice questions for the ALAT, to 3 hours and 180 multiple choice questions for the LATG.

Other qualifications. As veterinary technologists and technicians often deal with pet owners, communication skills are very important. In addition, technologists and technicians should be able to work well with others, because teamwork with veterinarians and other veterinary technicians is common.

Organizational ability and the ability to pay attention to detail also are important.

Advancement. As they gain experience, technologists and technicians take on more responsibility and carry out more assignments with little veterinary supervision. Some eventually may become supervisors.

Employment

Veterinary technologists and technicians held about 79,600 jobs in 2008. About 91 percent worked in veterinary services. The remainder worked in boarding kennels, animal shelters, rescue leagues, and zoos.

Job Outlook

Excellent job opportunities will stem from the need to replace veterinary technologists and technicians who leave the occupation and from the limited output of qualified veterinary technicians from 2-year programs, which are not expected to meet the demand over the 2008-18 period. Employment is expected to grow much faster than average.

Employment change. Employment of veterinary technologists and technicians is expected to grow 36 percent over the 2008–18 projection period, which is much faster than the average for all occupations. Pet owners are becoming more affluent and more willing to pay for advanced veterinary care because many of them consider their pet to be part of the family. This growing affluence and view of pets will continue to increase the demand for veterinary care. The vast majority of veterinary technicians work at private clinical practices under veterinarians. As the number of veterinarians grows to meet the demand for veterinary care, so will the number of veterinary technicians needed to assist them.

The number of pet owners who take advantage of veterinary services for their pets is expected to grow over the projection period, increasing employment opportunities. The availability of advanced veterinary services, such as preventive dental care and surgical procedures, also will provide opportunities for workers specializing in those areas as they will be needed to assist licensed veterinarians. The growing number of cats kept as companion pets is expected to boost the demand for feline medicine and services. Further demand for these workers will stem from the desire to replace veterinary assistants with more highly skilled technicians in animal clinics and hospitals, shelters, boarding kennels, animal control facilities, and humane societies.

Continued support for public health, food and animal safety, and national disease control programs, as well as biomedical research on human health problems, also will contribute to the demand for veterinary technologists, although the number of positions in these areas is fewer than in private practice

Job prospects. Excellent job opportunities are expected because of the relatively few veterinary technology graduates each year. The number of 2-year programs has recently grown to about 160, but due to small class sizes, fewer than 3,800 graduates are anticipated each year, a number that is not expected to meet demand. Additionally, many veterinary technicians remain in the field less than 10 years, so the need to replace workers who leave the occupation each year also will produce many job opportunities.

Veterinary technologists also will enjoy excellent job opportunities due to the relatively few graduates from 4- year programs—about 500 annually. However, unlike veterinary technicians who usually work in private clinical practice, veterinary technologists will have better opportunities for research jobs in a variety of settings, including biomedical facilities, diagnostic laboratories, wildlife facilities, drug and food manufacturing companies, and food safety inspection facilities.

Despite the relatively few number of graduates each year, keen competition is expected for veterinary technician jobs in zoos and aquariums, due to expected slow growth in facility capacity, low turnover among workers, the limited number of positions, and the fact that the work in zoos and aquariums attracts many candidates.

Employment of veterinary technicians and technologists is relatively stable during periods of economic recession. Layoffs are less likely to occur among veterinary technologists and technicians than in some other occupations because animals will continue to require medical care.

Earnings

Median annual wages of veterinary technologists and technicians were $28,900 in May 2008. The middle 50 percent earned between $23,580 and $34,960. The bottom 10 percent earned less than $19,770, and the top 10 percent earned more than $41,490. Veterinary technologists in research jobs may earn more than veterinary technicians in other types of jobs.

Related Occupations

Others who work extensively with animals include:

	Page
Animal care and service workers	504
Veterinarians	402
Veterinary assistants and laboratory animal caretakers	826

Sources of Additional Information

For information on certification as a laboratory animal technician or technologist, contact:

➤ American Association for Laboratory Animal Science, 9190 Crestwyn Hills Dr., Memphis, TN 38125. Internet: **http://www.aalas.org**

For information on careers in veterinary medicine and a listing of AVMA-accredited veterinary technology programs, contact:

➤ American Veterinary Medical Association, 1931 N. Meacham Rd., Suite 100, Schaumburg, IL 60173-4360. Internet: **http://www.avma.org**

The Occupational Information Network (O*NET) provides information on a wide range of occupational characteristics. Links to O*NET appear at the end of the Internet version of this occupational statement, accessible at **http://www.bls.gov/ooh/ocos183.htm**

Other Professional and Related Occupations

Epidemiologists

Nature of the Work
Epidemiologists investigate and describe the causes and spread of disease, and develop the means for prevention or control. *Applied epidemiologists*, who usually work for State health agencies, respond to disease outbreaks, determining their causes and helping to contain them. *Research epidemiologists* study diseases in laboratories and in the field to determine how to prevent future outbreaks.

Education and Training
Most applied epidemiologists are required to have a master's degree from a school of public health. Some research epidemiologists may need a Ph.D. or medical degree, depending on the work they perform.

Job Outlook
Current and projected employment:

2008 Employment 4,800
2018 Employment 5,500
Employment change...700
Growth rate.. 15%

Employment change. Faster than average employment growth is projected for epidemiologists. A heightened awareness of bioterrorism and rare but infectious diseases, such as West Nile Virus or Avian flu, should spur demand for these workers.

Job prospects. Epidemiologists can expect excellent opportunities. Many States report shortages of qualified workers for applied epidemiology positions. There is greater competition for jobs as research epidemiologists.

Earnings
Median annual wages for epidemiologists were $61,360 in May 2008.

Related Occupations

	Page
Biological scientists	181
Health educators	238
Medical scientists	189
Physicians and surgeons	381

Sources of Additional Information
➤ Centers for Disease Control and Prevention, 1600 Clifton Rd, Atlanta, GA 30333. Internet: **http://www.cdc.gov/phtrain/epidemiology.html**

The Occupational Information Network (O*NET) provides information on a wide range of occupational characteristics. Links to O*NET appear at the end of the Internet version of this occupational statement, accessible at **http://www.bls.gov/ooh/ocos310.htm**

Respiratory Therapy Technicians

Nature of the Work
Respiratory therapy technicians follow specific, well-defined respiratory care procedures under the direction of respiratory therapists and physicians. They help to evaluate, treat, and care for patients with breathing or other cardiopulmonary disorders.

Education and Training
An associate degree generally is required to work as a respiratory therapy technician. However, the entry-level requirement is a postsecondary certificate from an accredited school.

Job Outlook
Current and projected employment:

2008 Employment 16,500
2018 Employment 16,400
Employment change... -200
Growth rate... -1%

Employment change. Little or no change in employment growth is projected for respiratory therapy technicians. Most work in respiratory care is being done by respiratory therapists, resulting in limited demand for respiratory therapy technicians.

Job prospects. Respiratory therapy technicians can expect keen competition. Very few openings for respiratory therapy technicians are expected, as the work is increasingly performed by respiratory therapists.

Earnings
Median annual wages for respiratory therapy technicians were $42,430 in May 2008.

Related Occupations

	Page
Physicians and surgeons	381
Respiratory therapists	397

Sources of Additional Information
➤ American Association for Respiratory Care, 9425 N. MacArthur Blvd., Suite 100, Irving, TX 75063. Internet: **http://www.aarc.org**

The Occupational Information Network (O*NET) provides information on a wide range of occupational characteristics. Links to O*NET appear at the end of the Internet version of this occupational statement, accessible at **http://www.bls.gov/ooh/ocos322.htm**

Service Occupations

Healthcare Support Occupations

Dental Assistants

Significant Points

- Job prospects should be excellent.

- Dentists are expected to hire more assistants to perform routine tasks so dentists may devote their time to more complex procedures.

- Many assistants learn their skills on the job, although an increasing number are trained in dental-assisting programs; most programs take 1 year or less to complete.

- More than one-third of dental assistants worked part time in 2008.

Nature of the Work

Dental assistants perform a variety of patient care, office, and laboratory duties. They sterilize and disinfect instruments and equipment, prepare and lay out the instruments and materials required to treat each patient, and obtain and update patients' dental records. Assistants make patients comfortable in the dental chair and prepare them for treatment. During dental procedures, assistants work alongside the dentist to provide assistance. They hand instruments and materials to dentists and keep patients' mouths dry and clear by using suction hoses or other devices. They also instruct patients on postoperative and general oral health care.

Dental assistants may prepare materials for impressions and restorations, and process dental x rays as directed by a dentist. They also may remove sutures, apply topical anesthetics to gums or cavity-preventive agents to teeth, remove excess cement used in the filling process, and place dental dams to isolate teeth for treatment. Many States are expanding dental assistants' duties to include tasks such as coronal polishing and restorative dentistry functions for those assistants who meet specific training and experience requirements.

Dental assistants with laboratory duties make casts of the teeth and mouth from impressions, clean and polish removable appliances, and make temporary crowns. Those with office duties schedule and confirm appointments, receive patients, keep treatment records, send bills, receive payments, and order dental supplies and materials.

Dental assistants must work closely with, and under the supervision of, dentists. (See the statement on dentists elsewhere in the *Handbook*.) Additionally, dental assistants should not be confused with dental hygienists, who are licensed to perform a different set of clinical tasks. (See the statement on dental hygienists elsewhere in the *Handbook*.)

Work environment. Dental assistants work in a well-lighted, clean environment. Their work area is usually near the dental chair so that they can arrange instruments, materials, and medication and hand them to the dentist when needed. Dental assistants must wear gloves, masks, eyewear, and protective clothing to protect themselves and their patients from infectious diseases. Assistants also follow safety procedures to minimize the risks associated with the use of x-ray machines.

Almost half of dental assistants had a 35- to 40-hour workweek in 2008. More than one-third worked part time, or less than 35 hours per week, and many others have variable schedules. Depending on the hours of the dental office where they work, assistants may have to work on Saturdays or evenings. Some dental assistants hold multiple jobs by working at dental offices that are open on different days or by scheduling their work at a second office around the hours they work at their primary office.

Training, Other Qualifications, and Advancement

Many assistants learn their skills on the job, although an increasing number are trained in dental-assisting programs offered by community and junior colleges, trade schools, technical institutes, or the Armed Forces. Most programs take 1 year to complete. For assistants to perform more advanced functions, or to have the ability to complete radiological procedures, many States require assistants to obtain a license or certification.

Education and training. In most States, there are no formal education or training requirements to become an entry-level dental assistant. High school students interested in a career as a dental assistant should take courses in biology, chemistry, health, and office practices. For those wishing to pursue further education, the Commission on Dental Accreditation (CODA) approved 281 dental-assisting training programs in 2009. Programs include classroom, laboratory, and preclinical instruction in dental-assisting skills and related theory. Most programs take close to 1 year to complete and lead to a certificate or diploma. Two-year programs offered in community and junior colleges lead to an associate degree. All programs require a high school diploma or its equivalent, and some require science or computer-related courses for admission. A number of private vocational schools offer 4- to 6-month courses in dental assisting, but the Commission on Dental Accreditation does not accredit these programs.

A large number of dental assistants learn through on-the-job training. In these situations, the employing dentist or other dental assistants in the dental office teach the new assistant dental terminology, the names of the instruments, how to perform daily duties, how to interact with patients, and other things necessary to help keep the dental office running smoothly. While some things can be picked up easily, it may be a few months before new dental assistants are completely knowledgeable about their duties and comfortable doing all their tasks without assistance.

A period of on-the-job training is often required even for those who have completed a dental-assisting program or have some previous experience. Different dentists may have their own styles of doing things that need to be learned before an assistant can be comfortable working with them. Office-specific information, such

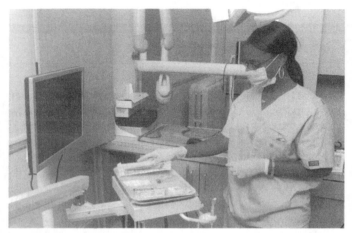

Dental assistants sterilize and disinfect instruments and equipment.

as where files and instruments are kept, will need to be learned at each new job. Also, as dental technology changes, dental assistants need to stay familiar with the instruments and procedures that they will be using or helping dentists to use. On-the-job training may be sufficient to keep assistants up-to-date on these matters.

Licensure and certification. Most States regulate the duties that dental assistants are allowed to perform. Some States require licensure or registration to perform expanded functions or to perform radiological procedures within a dentist's office. Licensure may include attending an accredited dental assisting program and passing a written or practical examination. Many States also require continuing education to maintain licensure or registration. However, a few States allow dental assistants to perform any function delegated to them by the dentist. Since requirements vary widely by State, it is recommended to contact the appropriate State board directly for specific requirements.

The Certified Dental Assistant (CDA) credential, administered by the Dental Assisting National Board (DANB), is recognized or required in more than 37 States toward meeting various requirements. Candidates may qualify to take the DANB certification examination by graduating from a CODA-accredited dental assisting education program or by having 2 years of full-time, or 4 years of part-time, experience as a dental assistant. In addition, applicants must have current certification in cardiopulmonary resuscitation. For annual recertification, individuals must earn continuing education credits. Other organizations offer registration, most often at the State level.

Individual States have also adopted different standards for dental assistants who perform certain advanced duties. In some States, dental assistants who perform radiological procedures must complete additional training distinct from that required to perform other expanded functions. Completion of the Radiation Health and Safety examination or the Certified Dental Assistant examination offered by Dental Assisting National Board (DANB) meets the standards in 30 States and the District of Columbia. Some States require completion of a State-approved course in radiology as well. Twelve States have no formal requirements to perform radiological procedures.

Other qualifications. Dental assistants must be a second pair of hands for a dentist; therefore, dentists look for people who are reliable, work well with others, and have good manual dexterity.

Certification and advancement. Without further education, advancement opportunities are limited. Some dental assistants become office managers, dental-assisting instructors, dental product sales representatives, or insurance claims processors for dental insurance companies. Others go back to school to become dental hygienists. For many, this entry-level occupation provides basic training and experience and serves as a steppingstone to more highly skilled and higher paying jobs. Assistants wishing to take on expanded functions or perform radiological procedures may choose to complete coursework in those functions allowed under State regulation or, if required, obtain a State-issued license.

Employment

Dental assistants held about 295,300 jobs in 2008. About 93 percent of all jobs for dental assistants were in offices of dentists. A small number of jobs were in the Federal, State, and local governments or in offices of physicians.

Job Outlook

Employment is expected to increase much faster than average; job prospects are expected to be excellent.

Employment change. Employment is expected to grow 36 percent from 2008 to 2018, which is much faster than the average for all occupations. In fact, dental assistants are expected to be among the fastest growing occupations over the 2008–18 projection period. Population growth, greater retention of natural teeth by middle-aged and older people, and an increased focus on preventative dental care for younger generations will fuel demand for dental services. Older dentists, who have been less likely to employ assistants or have employed fewer, are leaving the occupation and will be replaced by recent graduates, who are more likely to use one or more assistants. In addition, as dentists' workloads increase, they are expected to hire more assistants to perform routine tasks, so that they may devote their own time to more complex procedures.

Job prospects. Job prospects should be excellent, as dentists continue to need the aid of qualified dental assistants. There will be many opportunities for entry-level positions, but some dentists prefer to hire experienced assistants, those who have completed a dental-assisting program, or have met State requirements to take on expanded functions within the office.

Projections data from the National Employment Matrix

Occupational Title	SOC Code	Employment, 2008	Projected Employment, 2018	Change, 2008-2018	
				Number	Percent
Dental assistants..	31-9091	295,300	400,900	105,600	36

(NOTE) Data in this table are rounded. See the discussion of the employment projections table in the *Handbook* introductory chapter on *Occupational Information Included in the Handbook.*

In addition to job openings due to employment growth, some job openings will arise out of the need to replace assistants who transfer to other occupations, retire, or leave for other reasons.

Earnings

Median annual wages of dental assistants were $32,380 in May 2008. The middle 50 percent earned between $26,980 and $38,960. The lowest 10 percent earned less than $22,270, and the highest 10 percent earned more than $46,150.

Benefits vary substantially by practice setting and may be contingent upon full-time employment. According to a 2008 survey conducted by the Dental Assisting National Board (DANB), 86 percent of Certified Dental Assistants (CDA) reported receiving paid vacation from their employers, and more than half of CDAs received health benefits.

Related Occupations

Other workers support health practitioners, including:

	Page
Dental hygienists	414
Medical assistants	455
Occupational therapist assistants and aides	462
Pharmacy technicians and aides	436
Physical therapist assistants and aides	465
Surgical technologists	441

Sources of Additional Information

Information about career opportunities and accredited dental assistant programs is available from:

➤ Commission on Dental Accreditation,

American Dental Association, 211 East Chicago

Ave., Suite 1900, Chicago, IL 60611. Internet:

http://www.ada.org/prof/ed/accred/commission/index.asp

For information on becoming a Certified Dental Assistant and a list of State boards of dentistry, contact:

➤ Dental Assisting National Board, Inc., 444 N.

Michigan Ave., Suite 900, Chicago, IL 60611. Internet:

http://www.danb.org

For more information on a career as a dental assistant and general information about continuing education, contact:

➤ American Dental Assistants Association, 35 East

Wacker Dr., Suite 1730, Chicago, IL 60601. Internet:

http://www.dentalassistant.org

The Occupational Information Network (O*NET) provides information on a wide range of occupational characteristics. Links to O*NET appear at the end of the Internet version of this occupational statement, accessible at **http://www.bls.gov/ooh/ocos163.htm**

Home Health Aides and Personal and Home Care Aides

Significant Points

- Job opportunities are expected to be excellent because of rapid growth in home healthcare and high replacement needs.

- Training requirements vary from State to State, the type of home services agency, and funding source covering the costs of services.

- Many of these workers work part time and weekends or evenings to suit the needs of their clients.

Nature of the Work

Home health aides and personal and home care aides help people who are disabled, chronically ill, or cognitively impaired and older adults, who may need assistance, live in their own homes or in residential facilities instead of in health facilities or institutions. They also assist people in hospices and day programs and help individuals with disabilities go to work and remain engaged in their communities. Most aides work with elderly or physically or mentally disabled clients who need more care than family or friends can provide. Others help discharge hospital patients who have relatively short-term needs.

Aides provide light housekeeping and homemaking tasks such as laundry, change bed linens, shop for food, plan and prepare meals. Aides also may help clients get out of bed, bathe, dress, and groom. Some accompany clients to doctors' appointments or on other errands.

Home health aides and personal and home care aides provide instruction and psychological support to their clients. They may advise families and patients on nutrition, cleanliness, and household tasks.

Aides' daily routine may vary. They may go to the same home every day or week for months or even years, and often visit four or five clients on the same day. However, some aides may work solely with one client who is in need of more care and attention. In some situations, this may involve working with other aides in shifts so that the client has an aide throughout the day and night. Aides also work with clients, particularly younger adults at schools or at the client's work site.

In general, home health aides and personal and home care aides have similar job duties. However, there are some small differences.

Home health aides typically work for certified home health or hospice agencies that receive government funding and therefore must comply with regulations from to receive funding. This means that they must work under the direct supervision of a medical professional, usually a nurse. These aides keep records of services performed and of clients' condition and progress. They report changes in the client's condition to the supervisor or case manager. Aides also work with therapists and other medical staff.

Home health aides may provide some basic health-related services, such as checking patients' pulse rate, temperature, and

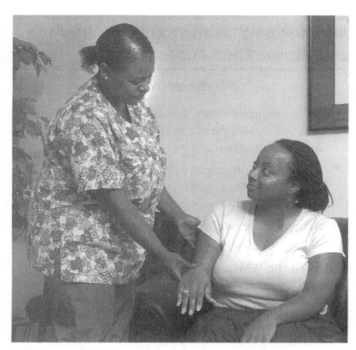

Home health aides and personal and home care aides help people in their own homes or in residential facilities.

respiration rate. They also may help with simple prescribed exercises and assist with medications administration. Occasionally, they change simple dressings, give massages, provide skin care, or assist with braces and artificial limbs. With special training, experienced home health aides also may assist with medical equipment such as ventilators, which help patients breathe.

Personal and home care aides—also called homemakers, caregivers, companions, and personal attendants—work for various public and private agencies that provide home care services. In these agencies, caregivers are likely supervised by a licensed nurse, social worker, or other non-medical managers. Aides receive detailed instructions explaining when to visit clients and what services to perform for them. However, personal and home care aides work independently, with only periodic visits by their supervisors. These caregivers may work with only one client each day or five or six clients once a day every week or every 2 weeks.

Some aides are hired directly by the patient or the patient's family. In these situations, personal and home care aides are supervised and assigned tasks directly by the patient or the patient's family.

Aides may also work with individuals who are developmentally or intellectually disabled. These workers are often called direct support professionals and they may assist in implementing a behavior plan, teaching self-care skills and providing employment support, as well as providing a range of other personal assistance services.

Work environment. Work as an aide can be physically demanding. Aides must guard against back injury because they may have to move patients into and out of bed or help them to stand or walk. Aides also may face hazards from minor infections and exposure to communicable diseases, such as hepatitis, but can avoid infections by following proper procedures. Because mechanical lifting devices available in institutional

settings are not as frequently available in patients' homes, home health aides must take extra care to avoid injuries resulting from overexertion when they assist patients. These workers experienced a larger than average number of work-related injuries or illnesses

Aides also perform tasks that some may consider unpleasant, such as emptying bedpans and changing soiled bed linens. The patients they care for may be disoriented, irritable, or uncooperative. Although their work can be emotionally demanding, many aides gain satisfaction from assisting those in need.

Most aides work with a number of different patients, each job lasting a few hours, days, or weeks. They often visit multiple patients on the same day. Surroundings differ by case. Some homes are neat and pleasant, whereas others are untidy and depressing. Some clients are pleasant and cooperative; others are angry, abusive, depressed, or otherwise difficult.

Home health aides and personal and home care aides generally work alone, with periodic visits from their supervisor. They receive detailed instructions explaining when to visit patients and what services to perform. Aides are responsible for getting to patients' homes, and they may spend a good portion of the work day traveling from one patient to another.

Many of these workers work part time and weekends or evenings to suit the needs of their clients.

Training, Other Qualifications, and Advancement
Home health aides must receive formal training and pass a competency test to work for certified home health or hospice agencies that receive reimbursement from Medicare or Medicaid. Personal and home care aides, however, face a wide range of requirements, which vary from State to State.

Education and training. Home health aides and personal and home care aides are generally not required to have a high school diploma. They usually are trained on the job by registered nurses, licensed practical nurses, experienced aides, or their supervisor. Aides are instructed on how to cook for a client, including on special diets. Furthermore, they may be trained in basic housekeeping tasks, such as making a bed and keeping the home sanitary and safe for the client. Generally, they are taught how to respond to an emergency, learning basic safety techniques. Employers also may train aides to conduct themselves in a professional and courteous manner while in a client's home. Some clients prefer that tasks are done a certain way and will teach the aide. A competency evaluation may be required to ensure that the aide can perform the required tasks.

Licensure. Home health aides who work for agencies that receive reimbursement from Medicare or Medicaid must receive a minimum level of training. They must complete both a training program consisting of a minimum of 75 hours and a competency evaluation or state certification program. Training includes information regarding personal hygiene, safe transfer techniques, reading and recording vital signs, infection control, and basic nutrition. Aides may take a competency exam to become certified without taking any of the training. At a minimum, 16 hours of supervised practical training are required before an aide has direct contact with a resident. These certification requirements represent the minimum, as outlined by the Federal Government. Some States may require additional hours of training to become certified.

Personal and home care aides are not required to be certified.

Other qualifications. Aides should have a desire to help people. They should be responsible, compassionate, patient, emotionally stable, and cheerful. In addition, aides should be tactful, honest, and discreet, because they work in private homes. Aides also must be in good health. A physical examination, including State-mandated tests for tuberculosis and other diseases, may be required. A criminal background check and a good driving record also may be required for employment.

Certification and advancement. The National Association for Home Care and Hospice (NAHC) offers national certification for aides. Certification is a voluntary demonstration that the individual has met industry standards. Certification requires the completion of 75 hours of training; observation and documentation of 17 skills for competency, assessed by a registered nurse; and the passing of a written exam developed by NAHC.

Advancement for home health aides and personal and home care aides is limited. In some agencies, workers start out performing homemaker duties, such as cleaning. With experience and training, they may take on more personal care duties. Some aides choose to receive additional training to become nursing aides, licensed practical nurses, or registered nurses. Some may start their own home care agency or work as a self-employed aide. Self-employed aides have no agency affiliation or supervision and accept clients, set fees, and arrange work schedules on their own.

Employment

Home health aides and personal and home care aides held about 1.7 million jobs in 2008. The majority of jobs were in home healthcare services, individual and family services, residential care facilities, and private households.

Job Outlook

Excellent job opportunities are expected for this occupation because rapid employment growth and high replacement needs are projected to produce a large number of job openings.

Employment change. Employment of home health aides is projected to grow by 50 percent between 2008 and 2018, which is much faster than the average for all occupations. Employment of personal and home care aides is expected to grow by 46 percent from 2008 to 2018, which is much faster than the average for all occupations. For both occupations, the expected growth is due, in large part, to the projected rise in the number of elderly people, an age group that often has mounting health problems and that needs some assistance with daily activities. The elderly and other clients, such as the mentally disabled, increasingly rely on home care.

This trend reflects several developments. Inpatient care in hospitals and nursing homes can be extremely expensive, so more patients return to their homes from these facilities as quickly as possible in order to contain costs. Patients, who need assistance with everyday tasks and household chores rather than medical care, can reduce medical expenses by returning to their homes. Furthermore, most patients—particularly the elderly—prefer care in their homes rather than in nursing homes or other in-patient facilities. This development is aided by the realization that treatment can be more effective in familiar surroundings.

Job prospects. In addition to job openings created by the increased demand for these workers, replacement needs are expected to lead to many openings. The relatively low skill requirements, low pay, and high emotional demands of the work result in high replacement needs. For these same reasons, many people are reluctant to seek jobs in the occupation. Therefore, persons who are interested in and suited for this work—particularly those with experience or training as personal care, home health, or nursing aides—should have excellent job prospects.

Earnings

Median hourly wages of wage-and-salary personal and home care aides were $9.22 in May 2008. The middle 50 percent earned between $7.81 and $10.98 an hour. The lowest 10 percent earned less than $6.84, and the highest 10 percent earned more than $12.33 an hour. Median hourly wages in the industries employing the largest numbers of personal and home care aides were as follows:

Individual and family services $9.77
Employment services 9.76
Residential mental retardation, mental health and
   substance abuse facilities..9.70
Vocational rehabilitation services...................................9.58
Home health care services..7.94

Median hourly wages of home health aides were $9.84 in May 2008. The middle 50 percent earned between $8.52 and $11.69 an hour. The lowest 10 percent earned less than $7.65, and the highest 10 percent earned more than $13.93 an hour. Median hourly wages in the industries employing the largest numbers of home health aides in May 2008 were:

Nursing care facilities $10.20
Residential mental retardation, mental health and
   substance abuse facilities..10.02
Home health care services...9.70
Individual and family services 9.48
Community care facilities for the elderly........................9.44

Projections data from the National Employment Matrix

Occupational Title	SOC Code	Employment, 2008	Projected Employment, 2018	Change, 2008-2018	
				Number	Percent
Home health aides and personal and home care aides......................	–	1,738,800	2,575,600	836,700	48
Home health aides...	31-1011	921,700	1,382,600	460,900	50
Personal and home care aides	39-9021	817,200	1,193,000	375,800	46

(NOTE) Data in this table are rounded. See the discussion of the employment projections table in the *Handbook* introductory chapter on *Occupational Information Included in the Handbook.*

Aides receive slight pay increases with experience and added responsibility. Usually, they are paid only for the time worked in the home, not for travel time between jobs, and must pay for their travel costs from their earnings. Most employers hire only on-call hourly workers.

Related Occupations

Home health aides and personal and home care aides combine the duties of caregivers and social service workers. Workers in related occupations that involve personal contact to help others include:

Sources of Additional Information

Information on licensing requirements for nursing and home health aides, as well as lists of State-approved nursing aide programs, are available from State departments of public health, departments of occupational licensing, boards of nursing, and home care associations.

For information about voluntary credentials for personal and home care aides, contact:

➤ National Association for Home Care and Hospice, 228 Seventh St. SE., Washington, DC 20003. Internet: **http://www.nahc.org**

The Occupational Information Network (O*NET) provides information on a wide range of occupational characteristics. Links to O*NET appear at the end of the Internet version of this occupational statement, accessible at **http://www.bls.gov/ooh/ocos326.htm**

Massage Therapists

Significant Points

- This occupation includes a large percentage of part-time and self-employed workers.

- Many States require formal training and licensure in order to practice massage therapy.

- Employment is expected to grow faster than average as more people learn about the benefits of massage therapy.

Nature of the Work

Massage therapy is the practice of using touch to manipulate the soft-tissue muscles of the body. It is performed for a variety of reasons, including treating painful ailments, decompressing tired and overworked muscles, reducing stress, rehabilitating sports injuries, and promoting general health. Clients often seek massage for its medical benefit and for relaxation purposes, and there is a wide range of massage treatments available.

Massage therapists can specialize in more than 80 different types of massage, called modalities. Swedish massage, deep-tissue massage, reflexology, acupressure, sports massage, and neuromuscular massage are just a few of the many approaches to massage therapy. Most massage therapists specialize in several modalities, which require different techniques. Some use exaggerated strokes ranging the length of a body part, while others use quick, percussion-like strokes with a cupped or closed hand. A massage can be as long as 2 hours or as short as 5 or 10 minutes. Usually, the type of massage given depends on the client's needs and physical condition. For example, therapists may use special techniques for elderly clients that they would not use for athletes, and they would use approaches for clients with injuries that would not be appropriate for clients seeking relaxation. Also, some forms of massage are given solely to one type of client; for example, prenatal massage and infant massage are given to pregnant women and new mothers, respectively.

Massage therapists work by appointment. Before beginning a massage therapy session, therapists conduct an informal interview with the client to learn the person's medical history and desired results from the massage. This interview gives therapists a chance to discuss which techniques could be beneficial to the client and which could be harmful. Because massage therapists tend to specialize in only a few areas of massage, customers will often be referred to or seek a therapist with a certain type of massage in mind. Based on the person's goals, ailments, medical history, and stress-related or pain-related problem areas, a massage therapist will conclude whether a massage would be harmful and if not, move forward with the session. While giving the massage, therapists alter their approach or concentrate on areas of particular discomfort as necessary.

Many modalities of massage therapy use massage oils, lotions, or creams to massage and rub the client's muscles. Most massage therapists, particularly those who are self-employed, supply their own table or chair, sheets, pillows, and body lotions or oils. Most modalities of massage require clients to be covered in a sheet or blanket and to be undressed or wear loose-

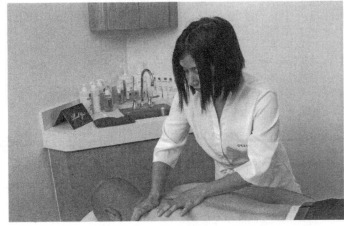

Massage therapists apply pressure to relieve stress and promote health.

fitting clothing. The therapist exposes only the body part being massaged. Some types of massage are done without oils or lotions and are performed with the client fully clothed.

Massage therapists must develop a rapport with their clients if repeat customers are to be secured. Because those who seek a therapist tend to make regular visits, developing a loyal clientele is an important part of becoming successful.

Work environment. Massage therapists work in an array of settings, both private and public: private offices, studios, hospitals, nursing homes, fitness centers, sports medicine facilities, airports, and shopping malls, for example. Some massage therapists also travel to clients' homes or offices to provide a massage. It is common for full-time massage therapists to divide their time among several different settings, depending on the clients and locations scheduled.

Most massage therapists give massages in dimly lit settings. Using candles and/or incense is not uncommon. Ambient or other calm, soothing music is often played. The dim lighting, smells, and background noise are meant to put clients at ease. However, when visiting a client's office, a massage therapist may not have those amenities. The working conditions depend heavily on a therapist's location and what the client wants.

Because massage is physically demanding, massage therapists can succumb to injury if the proper technique is not used. Repetitive-motion problems and fatigue from standing for extended lengths of time are most common. These risks can be limited by the use of good techniques, proper spacing between sessions, exercise, and, in many cases, by the therapists themselves receiving a massage on a regular basis.

Because of the physical nature of the work and the time needed in between sessions, massage therapists typically work less than 40 hours per week. Most therapists who work 15 to 30 hours per week consider themselves to be full-time workers, because when time for travel, for setting up equipment, and for completing business functions, such as billing, are added, a massage therapist's hours per week may very well be more than 40 hours. About 48 percent of all massage therapists worked part time and 19 percent had variable schedules in 2008.

Training, Other Qualifications, and Advancement

In 2009, 42 States and the District of Columbia had laws regulating massage therapy in some way. Most of the boards governing massage therapy in these States require practicing massage therapists to complete a formal education program and pass an examination. As of 2009, States without licensure requirements were Alaska, Idaho, Kansas, Minnesota, Montana, Oklahoma, Vermont, and Wyoming. In these States, massage therapy may be regulated at the local level. Because laws often change, it is best to check information on licensing, certification, and accreditation on a State-by-State basis.

Education and training. Training standards and requirements for massage therapists vary greatly by State and locality. Education programs are typically found in private or public postsecondary institutions and can require 500 hours of study or more to complete. A high school diploma or equivalent degree is usually required for admission. Massage therapy programs generally cover subjects such as anatomy; physiology, the study of organs and tissues; kinesiology, the study of motion and body mechanics; business management; ethics; and the hands-on practice of massage techniques. Training programs may concentrate on certain modalities of massage. Several programs also provide alumni services such as post-graduate job placement and continuing educational services. Both full-time and part-time programs are available.

Massage therapy programs vary in accreditation. Generally, they are approved by a State board, and they also may be accredited by an independent accrediting agency. In States that regulate massage therapy, graduation from an approved school or training program usually is required in order to practice. Some State regulations require that therapists keep up on their knowledge and technique through continuing education.

Licensure. In States with massage therapy regulations, workers must obtain a license after graduating from a training program and prior to practicing massage. Passage of an examination is usually required for licensure. The examination may be solely a State exam or one of two nationally recognized tests: the National Certification Examination for Therapeutic Massage and Bodywork (NCETMB) and the Massage and Bodywork Licensing Examination (MBLEx). Massage therapy licensure boards decide which certifications and tests to accept on a State-by-State basis. Therefore, those wishing to practice massage therapy should look into legal requirements for the State and locality in which they intend to practice. A fee and periodic renewal of licensure also may be required.

Other qualifications. Strong communication skills and a friendly, empathetic personality are extremely helpful qualities for fostering a trusting relationship with clients and, in turn, expanding one's client base. Massage can be a delicate issue for some clients, and because of this, making clients feel comfortable is one of the most important skills for massage therapists.

Advancement. Because of the nature of massage therapy, opportunities for advancement are limited. However, with increased experience and an expanding client base, there are opportunities for therapists to increase client fees and, therefore, income. Therapists also may become managers of the office in which they work and may teach in a training program. In addition, those who are well organized and have an entrepreneurial spirit may go into business for themselves. Self-employed massage therapists with a large client base have the highest earnings.

Employment

Massage therapists held about 122,400 jobs in 2008. About 57 percent were self-employed. Many more people practice massage therapy as a secondary source of income. Of those who were self-employed, most owned their own businesses or worked as independent contractors. Others found employment in personal care services establishments, the offices of physicians and chiropractors, fitness and recreational sports centers and hotels. Although massage therapists can find jobs throughout the country, employment is concentrated in metropolitan areas, as well as resort and destination locales.

Job Outlook

Employment of massage therapists is expected to grow faster than average. Opportunities should be available to those who complete formal training programs and pass a professionally recognized examination, but new massage therapists should ex-

Projections data from the National Employment Matrix

Occupational Title	SOC Code	Employment, 2008	Projected Employment, 2018	Change, 2008-2018	
				Number	Percent
Massage therapists	31-9011	122,400	145,600	23,200	19

(NOTE) Data in this table are rounded. See the discussion of the employment projections table in the *Handbook* introductory chapter on *Occupational Information Included in the Handbook.*

pect to work only part time until they can build a client base of their own.

Employment change. Employment of massage therapists is expected to increase by 19 percent from 2008 to 2018, faster than the average for all occupations. Employment will grow as more people learn about the benefits of massage therapy.

Continued growth in the demand for massage services will lead to new openings for massage therapists. The number of spas, which employ a large number of therapists, has increased in recent years and will continue to do so. At the same time, there are an increasing number of massage clinic franchises, many of which offer massages cheaper than at spas and resorts, making them available to a wider range of customers. In addition, as an increasing number of States adopt licensing requirements and standards for therapists, the practice of massage is likely to be respected and accepted by more and more people.

Massage also offers specific benefits to particular groups of people, whose continued demand for massage services will lead to overall growth for the occupation. For example, as workplaces try to distinguish themselves as employee-friendly, providing professional in-office, seated massages for employees is becoming a popular on-the-job benefit. Older citizens in nursing homes or assisted-living facilities also are finding benefits from massage, such as increased energy levels and reduced health problems. Demand for massage therapy should grow among older age groups because they increasingly are enjoying longer, more active lives and persons aged 55 years and older are projected to be the most rapidly growing segment of the U.S. population over the next decade. However, demand for massage therapy is presently greatest among young adults, who lack the concerns about massage that previous generations had.

Job prospects. In States that regulate massage therapy, opportunities should be available to those who complete formal training programs and pass a professionally recognized examination. However, new massage therapists should expect to work only part time in spas, hotels, hospitals, physical therapy centers, and other businesses until they can build a client base of their own. Because referrals are a very important source of work for massage therapists, networking will increase the number of job opportunities. Joining a professional association also can help build strong contacts and further increase the likelihood of steady work.

Earnings

Median hourly wages of massage therapists, including gratuities, were $16.78 in May 2008. The middle 50 percent earned between $11.36 and $25.14. The lowest 10 percent earned less than $8.01, and the highest 10 percent earned more than $33.47.

Because many therapists work part time, yearly earnings can vary considerably, depending on the therapist's schedule. Generally, massage therapists earn some portion of their income as gratuities. For those who work in a hospital or other clinical setting, however, tipping is not common.

As is typical for most workers who are self-employed and work part time, few benefits are provided.

Related Occupations

Massage therapists provide services that promote relaxation or physical well-being for clients. Other workers who provide similar services include:

	Page
Athletic trainers	405
Chiropractors	360
Physical therapist assistants and aides	465
Physical therapists	377

Sources of Additional Information

General information on becoming a massage therapist is available from State regulatory boards.

For more information on becoming a massage therapist, contact:
➤ Associated Bodywork & Massage Professionals, 25188 Genesee Trail Road, Suite 200 Golden, CO 80401. Internet: **http://www.massagetherapy.com/careers/index.php**

➤ American Massage Therapy Association, 500 Davis St., Suite 900, Evanston, IL 60201. Internet: **http://www.amtamassage.org**

For a directory of schools providing accredited massage therapy training programs, contact:
➤ Accrediting Commission of Career Schools and Colleges, 2101 Wilson Blvd., Suite 302, Arlington, VA 22201. Internet: **http://www.accsc.org**

➤ Commission on Massage Therapy Accreditation, 5335 Wisconsin Ave. NW., Suite 440, Washington, DC, 20015. Internet: **http://www.comta.org**

Information on national testing and national certification is available from:
➤ Federation of State Massage Therapy Boards, 7111 W 151st St., Suite 356, Overland Park, Kansas 66223. Internet: **http://www.fsmtb.org**

➤ National Certification Board for Therapeutic Massage and Bodywork, 1901 S. Meyers Rd., Suite 240, Oakbrook Terrace, IL 60181. Internet: **http://www.ncbtmb.org**

The Occupational Information Network (O*NET) provides information on a wide range of occupational characteristics. Links to O*NET appear at the end of the Internet version of this occupational statement, accessible at **http://www.bls.gov/ooh/ocos295.htm**

Medical Assistants

Significant Points

- Employment is projected to grow much faster than average, ranking medical assistants among the fastest growing occupations over the 2008–18 decade.

- Job prospects should be excellent.

- About 62 percent of medical assistants work in offices of physicians.

- Some medical assistants are trained on the job, but many complete 1-year or 2-year programs.

Nature of the Work

Medical assistants perform administrative and clinical tasks to keep the offices of physicians, podiatrists, chiropractors, and other health practitioners running smoothly. The duties of medical assistants vary from office to office, depending on the location and size of the practice and the practitioner's specialty. In small practices, medical assistants usually do many different kinds of tasks, handling both administrative and clinical duties and reporting directly to an office manager, physician, or other health practitioner. Those in large practices tend to specialize in a particular area, under the supervision of department administrators. Medical assistants should not be confused with physician assistants, who examine, diagnose, and treat patients under the direct supervision of a physician. (Physician assistants are discussed elsewhere in the *Handbook*.)

Administrative medical assistants update and file patients' medical records, fill out insurance forms, and arrange for hospital admissions and laboratory services. They also perform tasks less specific to medical settings, such as answering telephones, greeting patients, handling correspondence, scheduling appointments, and handling billing and bookkeeping.

Clinical medical assistants have various duties, depending on State law. Some common tasks include taking medical histories and recording vital signs, explaining treatment procedures to patients, preparing patients for examinations, and assisting physicians during examinations. Medical assistants collect and prepare

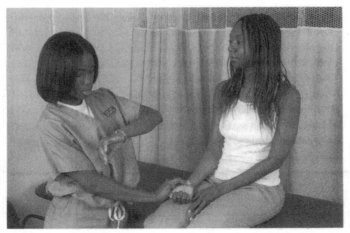

Medical assistants often take medical histories and record vital signs of patients.

laboratory specimens and sometimes perform basic laboratory tests, dispose of contaminated supplies, and sterilize medical instruments. As directed by a physician, they might instruct patients about medications and special diets, prepare and administer medications, authorize drug refills, telephone prescriptions to a pharmacy, draw blood, prepare patients for x rays, take electrocardiograms, remove sutures, and change dressings. Medical assistants also may arrange examining room instruments and equipment, purchase and maintain supplies and equipment, and keep waiting and examining rooms neat and clean.

Ophthalmic medical assistants, *optometric assistants*, and *podiatric medical assistants* are examples of specialized assistants who have additional duties. Ophthalmic medical assistants help ophthalmologists provide eye care. They conduct diagnostic tests, measure and record vision, and test eye muscle function. They apply eye dressings and also show patients how to insert, remove, and care for contact lenses. Under the direction of the physician, ophthalmic medical assistants may administer eye medications. They also maintain optical and surgical instruments and may assist the ophthalmologist in surgery. Optometric assistants also help provide eye care, working with optometrists. They provide chair-side assistance, instruct patients about contact lens use and care, conduct preliminary tests on patients, and otherwise provide assistance while working directly with an optometrist. Podiatric medical assistants make castings of feet, expose and develop x rays, and assist podiatrists in surgery.

Work environment. Medical assistants work in well-lighted, clean environments. They constantly interact with other people and may have to handle several responsibilities at once. Most full-time medical assistants work a regular 40-hour week. However, medical assistants may work part time, evenings, or weekends.

Training, Other Qualifications, and Advancement

Some medical assistants are trained on the job, but many complete 1- or 2-year programs. Almost all medical assistants have at least a high school diploma, although there are no formal education or training requirements.

Education and training. Medical assisting programs are offered in vocational-technical high schools, postsecondary vocational schools, and community and junior colleges. Postsecondary programs usually last either 1 year and result in a certificate or diploma, or 2 years and result in an associate degree. Courses cover anatomy, physiology, and medical terminology, as well as keyboarding, transcription, recordkeeping, accounting, and insurance processing. Students learn laboratory techniques, clinical and diagnostic procedures, pharmaceutical principles, the administration of medications, and first aid. They study office practices, patient relations, medical law, and ethics. There are two accrediting bodies that accredit medical assisting programs. Accredited programs often include an internship that provides practical experience in physicians' offices or other healthcare facilities.

Formal training in medical assisting, while generally preferred, is not required. Many medical assistants are trained on the job, and usually only need to have a high school diploma or the equivalent. Recommended high school courses include mathematics, health, biology, keyboarding, bookkeeping, computers, and office skills. Volunteer experience in the healthcare field also is helpful. Medical assistants who are trained on the job usually spend their first few months attending training sessions and working closely with more experienced workers.

Some States allow medical assistants to perform more advanced procedures, such as giving injections or taking x rays, after passing a test or taking a course.

Other qualifications. Medical assistants deal with the public; therefore, they must be neat and well groomed and have a courteous, pleasant manner and they must be able to put patients at ease and explain physicians' instructions. They must respect the confidential nature of medical information. Clinical duties require a reasonable level of manual dexterity and visual acuity.

Certification and advancement. Although not required, certification indicates that a medical assistant meets certain standards of knowledge. It may also help to distinguish an experienced or formally trained assistant from an entry-level assistant, which may lead to a higher salary or more employment opportunities. There are various associations—such as the American Association of Medical Assistants (AAMA) and Association of Medical Technologists (AMT)—that award certification credentials to medical assistants. The certification process varies by association. It is also possible to become certified in a specialty, such as podiatry, optometry, or ophthalmology.

Medical assistants may also advance to other occupations through experience or additional training. For example, some may go on to teach medical assisting, and others pursue additional education to become nurses or other healthcare workers. Administrative medical assistants may advance to office managers, or qualify for a variety of administrative support occupations.

Employment

Medical assistants held about 483,600 jobs in 2008. About 62 percent worked in offices of physicians; 13 percent worked in public and private hospitals, including inpatient and outpatient facilities; and 11 percent worked in offices of other health practitioners, such as chiropractors and optometrists. Most of the remainder worked in other health care industries, such as outpatient care centers and nursing and residential care facilities.

Job Outlook

Employment is projected to grow much faster than average, ranking medical assistants among the fastest growing occupations over the 2008–18 decade. Job opportunities should be excellent, particularly for those with formal training or experience, and certification.

Employment change. Employment of medical assistants is expected to grow 34 percent from 2008 to 2018, much faster than the average for all occupations. As the health care industry expands because of technological advances in medicine and the growth and aging of the population, there will be an increased need for all health care workers. The increasing prevalence of certain conditions, such as obesity and diabetes, also will increase demand for health care services and medical assistants.

Increasing use of medical assistants to allow doctors to care for more patients will further stimulate job growth.

Helping to drive job growth is the increasing number of group practices, clinics, and other health care facilities that need a high proportion of support personnel, particularly medical assistants who can handle both administrative and clinical duties. In addition, medical assistants work mostly in primary care, a consistently growing sector of the health care industry.

Job prospects. Jobseekers who want to work as a medical assistant should find excellent job prospects. Medical assistants are projected to account for a very large number of new jobs, and many other opportunities will come from the need to replace workers leaving the occupation. Medical assistants with formal training or experience—particularly those with certification—should have the best job opportunities, since employers generally prefer to hire these workers.

Earnings

The earnings of medical assistants vary, depending on their experience, skill level, and location. Median annual wages of wage-and-salary medical assistants were $28,300 in May 2008. The middle 50 percent earned between $23,700 and $33,050. The lowest 10 percent earned less than $20,600, and the highest 10 percent earned more than $39,570. Median annual wages in the industries employing the largest numbers of medical assistants in May 2008 were:

General medical and surgical hospitals......................$29,720
Colleges, universities, and professional schools..........28,820
Offices of physicians..28,710
Outpatient care centers...28,570
Offices of other health practitioners...........................25,240

Related Occupations

Medical assistants perform work similar to the tasks completed by other workers in medical support occupations. Administrative medical assistants do work similar to that of:

Projections data from the National Employment Matrix

Occupational Title	SOC Code	Employment, 2008	Projected Employment, 2018	Change, 2008-2018	
				Number	Percent
Medical assistants	31-9092	483,600	647,500	163,900	34

(NOTE) Data in this table are rounded. See the discussion of the employment projections table in the *Handbook* introductory chapter on *Occupational Information Included in the Handbook.*

Sources of Additional Information

Information about career opportunities and certification for medical assistants is available from:

➤ American Association of Medical Assistants, 20 North Wacker Dr., Suite 1575, Chicago, IL 60606. Internet: **http://www.aama-ntl.org**

➤ American Medical Technologists, 10700 West Higgins Rd., Suite 150, Rosemont, IL 60018. Internet: **http://www.amt1.com**

➤ National Healthcareer Association, 7 Ridgedale Ave., Suite 203, Cedar Knolls, NJ 07927. Internet: **http://www.nhanow.com**

For lists of accredited educational programs in medical assisting, contact:

➤ Accrediting Bureau of Health Education Schools, 7777 Leesburg Pike, Suite 314 N, Falls Church, VA 22043. Internet: **http://www.abhes.org**

➤ Commission on Accreditation of Allied Health Education Programs, 1361 Park St., Clearwater, FL 33756. Internet: **http://www.caahep.org**

Information about career opportunities, training programs, and certification for ophthalmic medical personnel is available from:

➤ Joint Commission on Allied Health Personnel in Ophthalmology, 2025 Woodlane Dr., St. Paul, MN 55125. Internet: **http://www.jcahpo.org**

Information about career opportunities, training programs, and certification for optometric assistants is available from:

➤ American Optometric Association, 243 N. Lindbergh Blvd., St. Louis, MO 63141. Internet: **http://www.aoa.org**

Information about certification for podiatric assistants is available from:

➤ American Society of Podiatric Medical Assistants, 2124 South Austin Blvd., Cicero, IL 60804. Internet: **http://www.aspma.org**

The Occupational Information Network (O*NET) provides information on a wide range of occupational characteristics. Links to O*NET appear at the end of the Internet version of this occupational statement, accessible at **http://www.bls.gov/ooh/ocos164.htm**

Medical Transcriptionists

Significant Points

- Job opportunities will be good, especially for those who are certified.

- Employers prefer medical transcriptionists who have completed a postsecondary training program.

- Many medical transcriptionists telecommute from home-based offices.

- About 36 percent worked in hospitals, and another 23 percent worked in offices of physicians.

Nature of the Work

Medical transcriptionists listen to dictated recordings made by physicians and other healthcare professionals and transcribe them into medical reports, correspondence, and other administrative material. They generally listen to recordings on a headset, using a foot pedal to pause the recording when necessary, and key the text into a personal computer or word processor, editing as necessary for grammar and clarity. The documents they produce include discharge summaries, medical history and physical examination reports, operative reports, consultation reports, autopsy reports, diagnostic-imaging studies, progress notes, and referral letters. Medical transcriptionists return transcribed documents to the physicians or other healthcare professionals who dictated them for review and signature or correction. These documents eventually become part of patients' permanent files.

To understand and accurately transcribe dictated reports, medical transcriptionists must understand medical terminology, anatomy and physiology, diagnostic procedures, pharmacology, and treatment assessments. They also must be able to translate medical jargon and abbreviations into their expanded forms. To help identify terms appropriately, transcriptionists refer to standard medical reference materials—both printed and electronic; some of these are available over the Internet. Medical transcriptionists must comply with specific standards that apply to the style of medical records and to the legal and ethical requirements for keeping patient information confidential.

Experienced transcriptionists spot mistakes or inconsistencies in a medical report and check to correct the information. Their ability to understand and correctly transcribe patient assessments and treatments reduces the chance of patients receiving ineffective or even harmful treatments and ensures high-quality patient care.

Currently, most healthcare providers use either digital or analog dictating equipment to transmit dictation to medical transcriptionists. The Internet has grown to be a popular mode for transmitting documentation. Many transcriptionists receive dictation over the Internet and are able to quickly return transcribed documents to clients for approval. Also, because of the popularity of using the Internet to transmit documentation, many medical transcription departments are beginning to work closely with programmers and information systems staff to stream in voice communication that provides seamless data transfers through network interfaces. This practice allows medical transcriptionists the convenience of having hand-held personal computers or personal data assistants (PDAs) that utilize software for dictation.

Another increasingly popular method uses speech recognition technology, which electronically translates sound into text and creates drafts of reports. Transcriptionists then format the reports; edit them for mistakes in translation, punctuation, or grammar; and check for consistency and any wording that doesn't make sense medically. Transcriptionists working in specialties such as radiology or pathology, which have standardized terminology, are more likely to use speech recognition technology, a medium that will become more widespread in all specialties as it becomes more sophisticated and is better

Transcriptionists receive dictation over the Internet and are able to quickly return transcribed documents to clients for approval.

able to recognize and more accurately transcribe diverse modes of speech.

Medical transcriptionists who work in physicians' offices may have other office duties, such as receiving patients, scheduling appointments, answering the telephone, and handling incoming and outgoing mail. Medical secretaries, discussed in the statement on *secretaries and administrative assistants* elsewhere in the *Handbook*, also may perform transcription as part of their jobs.

Work environment.   The majority of these workers are employed in comfortable settings, such as hospitals, physicians' offices, transcription service offices, clinics, laboratories, medical libraries, government medical facilities, or their own homes. Many medical transcriptionists telecommute from home-based offices.

Workers usually sit in the same position for long periods. They can suffer wrist, back, neck, or eye problems caused by strain and risk repetitive motion injuries such as carpal tunnel syndrome. The constant pressure to be accurate and productive also can be stressful.

Many medical transcriptionists work a standard 40-hour week. Self-employed medical transcriptionists are more likely to work irregular hours—including part time, evenings, and weekends. Some may be on call at any time.

Training, Other Qualifications, and Advancement
Postsecondary training in medical transcription is preferred by employers; writing and computer skills also are important.

Education and training.   Employers prefer to hire transcriptionists who have completed postsecondary training in medical transcription offered by many vocational schools, community colleges, and distance-learning programs.

Completion of a 2-year associate's degree or 1-year certificate program—including coursework in anatomy, medical terminology, legal issues relating to healthcare documentation, and English grammar and punctuation—is highly recommended, but not always required. Many of these programs include supervised on-the-job experience. Some transcriptionists, especially those already familiar with medical terminology from previous experience as a nurse or medical secretary, become proficient through refresher courses and training.

Formal accreditation is not required for medical transcription programs. However, the Approval Committee for Certificate Programs (AACP)—established by the Association for Healthcare Documentation Integrity (AHDI) and the American Health Information Management Association—offers voluntary accreditation for medical transcription programs. Although voluntary, the completion of an ACCP-approved program may be required for transcriptionists seeking certification.

Certification and other qualifications.   The AHDI awards two voluntary designations; Registered Medical Transcriptionist (RMT) and Certified Medical Transcriptionist (CMT). Medical transcriptionists who are recent graduates of medical transcription educational programs or who have fewer than 2 years' experience in acute care may become a registered RMT. The credential is awarded upon successfully passing the AHDI level-1 registered medical transcription exam. The CMT designation requires at least 2 years of acute care experience using different format, report, and dictation types in multiple-specialty surgery areas. Candidates also must earn a passing score on a certification examination. Because medicine is constantly evolving, medical transcriptionists are encouraged to update their skills regularly. In order to be recertified, RMTs and CMTs must pay a recertification fee. In addition to the fee, RMTs must earn a minimum of 30 continuing education credits in required categories during their 3-year cycle. CMTs must successfully complete an online course and final exam during the 3-year cycle. As in many other fields, certification is recognized as a sign of competence.

Graduates of an ACCP-approved program who earn the RMT credential are eligible to participate in the Registered Apprenticeship Program sponsored by the Medical Transcription Industry Association through the U.S. Department of Labor. The program offers structured on-the-job learning and related technical instruction for qualified medical transcriptionists entering the profession.

In addition to understanding medical terminology, transcriptionists must have good English grammar and punctuation skills and proficiency with personal computers and word-processing software. Normal hearing acuity and good listening skills also are necessary. Employers usually require applicants to take pre-employment tests.

Advancement.   With experience, medical transcriptionists can advance to supervisory positions, home-based work, editing, consulting, or teaching. Some become owners of medical transcription businesses. With additional education or training, some become medical records and health information technicians, medical coders, or medical records and health information administrators.

Employment

Medical transcriptionists held about 105,200 jobs in 2008. About 36 percent worked in hospitals and another 23 percent worked in offices of physicians. Others worked for business support services; medical and diagnostic laboratories; outpatient care centers; offices of physical, occupational, and speech therapists; and offices of audiologists.

Job Outlook

Employment of medical transcriptionists is projected to grow about as fast as the average; job opportunities should be good, especially for those who are certified.

Employment change.   Employment of medical transcriptionists is projected to grow by 11 percent from 2008 to 2018, about as fast as the average for all occupations. Demand for medical transcription services will continue to be spurred by a growing and aging population. Older age groups receive proportionally greater numbers of medical tests, treatments, and procedures that require documentation. A high level of demand for transcription services also will be sustained by the continued need for electronic documentation that can be shared easily among providers, third-party payers, regulators, consumers, and health information systems. Growing numbers of medical transcriptionists will be needed to amend patients' records, edit documents from speech recognition systems, and identify discrepancies in medical reports.

Contracting out transcription work overseas and advancements in speech recognition technology are not expected to significantly reduce the need for well-trained medical transcriptionists. Outsourcing transcription work abroad—to countries such as India, Pakistan, Philippines, Barbados, and Canada—has grown more popular as transmitting confidential health information over the Internet has become more secure; however, the demand for overseas transcription services is expected only to supplement the demand for well-trained domestic medical transcriptionists. In addition, reports transcribed by overseas medical transcription services usually require editing for accuracy by domestic medical transcriptionists before they meet U.S. quality standards.

Speech recognition technology allows physicians and other health professionals to dictate medical reports to a computer, which immediately creates an electronic document. In spite of the advances in this technology, the software has been slow to grasp and analyze the human voice, the English language, and the medical vernacular with all its diversity. As a result, there will continue to be a need for skilled medical transcriptionists to identify and appropriately edit the inevitable errors created by speech recognition systems and to create a final document.

Job prospects.   Job opportunities will be good, especially for those who are certified. Hospitals will continue to employ a large percentage of medical transcriptionists, but job growth will be in other industries. An increasing demand for standardized records should result in rapid employment growth in physicians' offices, especially in large group practices.

Earnings

Wage-and-salary medical transcriptionists had median hourly wages of $15.41 in May 2008. The middle 50 percent earned between $13.02 and $18.55. The lowest 10 percent earned less than $10.76, and the highest 10 percent earned more than $21.81. Median hourly wages in the industries employing the largest numbers of medical transcriptionists were as follows:

Medical and diagnostic laboratories	$17.26
General medical and surgical hospitals	15.88
Outpatient care centers	15.46
Offices of physicians	15.02
Business support services	14.52

Compensation arrangements for medical transcriptionists vary. Some are paid on the basis of the number of hours they work or the number of lines they transcribe. Others receive a base pay per hour, with incentives for extra production. Employees of transcription services and independent contractors almost always receive production-based pay. Independent contractors earn more than do transcriptionists who work for others, but independent contractors have higher expenses than their corporate counterparts, receive no benefits, and may face a higher risk of termination than do wage-and-salary transcriptionists.

Related Occupations

Workers in other occupations also type, record information, and process paperwork. Among these workers are the following:

Other workers who provide medical support include the following:

Projections data from the National Employment Matrix

Occupational Title	SOC Code	Employment, 2008	Projected Employment, 2018	Change, 2008-2018	
				Number	Percent
Medical transcriptionists	31-9094	105,200	116,900	11,700	11

(NOTE) Data in this table are rounded. See the discussion of the employment projections table in the *Handbook* introductory chapter on *Occupational Information Included in the Handbook.*

Sources of Additional Information

For information on a career as a medical transcriptionist, contact:

➤ Association for Healthcare Documentation Integrity, 4230 Kiernan Ave., Suite 130, Modesto, CA 95356. Internet: **http://www.ahdionline.org**

State employment service offices can provide information about job openings for medical transcriptionists.

The Occupational Information Network (O*NET) provides information on a wide range of occupational characteristics. Links to O*NET appear at the end of the Internet version of this occupational statement, accessible at **http://www.bls.gov/ooh/ocos271.htm**

Nursing and Psychiatric Aides

Significant Points

- Numerous job openings and excellent job opportunities are expected.

- Most jobs are in nursing and residential care facilities and in hospitals.

- A high school diploma is required for many jobs; specific qualifications vary by occupation, State laws, and work setting.

- This occupation is characterized by modest entry requirements, low pay, high physical and emotional demands, and limited advancement opportunities.

Nature of the Work

Nursing and psychiatric aides help care for physically or mentally ill, injured, disabled, or infirm individuals in hospitals, nursing care facilities, and mental health settings. Nursing aides and home health aides are among the occupations commonly referred to as direct care workers, due to their role in working with patients who need long-term care. The specific care they give depends on their specialty.

Nursing aides, also known as *nurse aides, nursing assistants, certified nursing assistants, geriatric aides, unlicensed assistive personnel, orderlies, or hospital attendants*, provide hands-on care and perform routine tasks under the supervision of nursing and medical staff. Specific tasks vary, with aides handling many aspects of a patient's care. They often help patients to eat, dress, and bathe. They also answer calls for help, deliver messages, serve meals, make beds, and tidy up rooms. Aides sometimes are responsible for taking a patient's temperature, pulse rate, respiration rate, or blood pressure. They also may help provide care to patients by helping them get out of bed and walk, escorting them to operating and examining rooms, or providing skin care. Some aides help other medical staff by setting up equipment, storing and moving supplies, and assisting with some procedures. Aides also observe patients' physical, mental, and emotional conditions and report any change to the nursing or medical staff.

Nursing aides employed in nursing care facilities often are the principal caregivers and have more contact with residents than do other members of the staff. Because some residents may stay in a nursing care facility for months or even years, aides develop positive, caring relationships with their patients.

Psychiatric aides, also known as mental health assistants or psychiatric nursing assistants, care for mentally impaired or emotionally disturbed individuals. They work under a team that may include psychiatrists, psychologists, psychiatric nurses, social workers, and therapists. In addition to helping patients to dress, bathe, groom themselves, and eat, psychiatric aides socialize with them and lead them in educational and recreational activities. Psychiatric aides may play card games or other games with patients, watch television with them, or participate in group activities, such as playing sports or going on field trips. They observe patients and report any physical or behavioral signs that might be important for the professional staff to know. They accompany patients to and from therapy and treatment. Because they have such close contact with patients, psychiatric aides can have a great deal of influence on their outlook and treatment.

Work environment. Work as an aide can be physically demanding. Aides spend many hours standing and walking, and they often face heavy workloads. Aides must guard against back injury, because they may have to move patients into and out of bed or help them stand or walk. It is important for aides to be trained in and to follow the proper procedures for lifting and moving patients. Aides also may face hazards from minor infections and major diseases, such as hepatitis, but can avoid infections by following proper procedures. Nursing aides, orderlies, and attendants and psychiatric aides have some of the highest non-fatal injuries and illness rates for all occupations, in the 98th and 99th percentiles in 2007.

Aides also perform tasks that some may consider unpleasant, such as emptying bedpans and changing soiled bed linens. The patients they care for may be disoriented, irritable, or uncooperative. Psychiatric aides must be prepared to care for patients whose illnesses may cause violent behavior. Although their work can be emotionally demanding, many aides gain satisfaction from assisting those in need.

Most full-time aides work about 40 hours per week, but because patients need care 24 hours a day, some aides work evenings, nights, weekends, and holidays. In 2008 about 24 percent

Nursing aides often help patients to eat, dress, and bathe.

of nursing aides, orderlies, and attendants and psychiatric aides worked part-time.

Training, Other Qualifications, and Advancement

In many cases, a high school diploma or equivalent is necessary for a job as a nursing or psychiatric aide. Specific qualifications vary by occupation, State laws, and work setting. Advancement opportunities are limited.

Education and training. Nursing and psychiatric aide training is offered in high schools, vocational-technical centers, some nursing care facilities, and some community colleges. Courses cover body mechanics, nutrition, anatomy and physiology, infection control, communication skills, and resident rights. Personal care skills, such as how to help patients bathe, eat, and groom themselves, also are taught. Hospitals may require previous experience as a nursing aide or home health aide. Some States also require psychiatric aides to complete a formal training program. However, most psychiatric aides learn their skills on the job from experienced workers.

Some employers provide classroom instruction for newly hired aides, while others rely exclusively on informal on-the-job instruction by a licensed nurse or an experienced aide. Such training may last from several days to a few months. Aides also may attend lectures, workshops, and in-service training.

Licensure and certification. Federal Government requirements exist for nursing aides who work in nursing care facilities. These aides must complete a minimum of 75 hours of State-approved training and pass a competency evaluation. Aides who complete the program are known as certified nurse assistants (CNAs) and are placed on the State registry of nurse aides. Additional requirements may exist, but vary by State. Therefore, individuals should contact their State board directly for applicable information.

Other qualifications. Aides must be in good health. A physical examination, including State-regulated disease tests, may be required. A criminal background check also is usually required for employment.

Applicants should be tactful, patient, understanding, emotionally stable, and dependable and should have a desire to help people. They also should be able to work as part of a team, have good communication skills, and be willing to perform repetitive, routine tasks.

Advancement. Opportunities for advancement within these occupations are limited. Aides generally need additional formal training or education to enter other health occupations. The most common healthcare occupations for former aides are licensed practical nurse, registered nurse, and medical assistant.

For some individuals, these occupations serve as entry-level jobs. For example, some high school and college students gain experience working in these occupations while attending school. And experience as an aide can help individuals decide whether to pursue a career in healthcare.

Employment

Nursing and psychiatric aides held about 1.5 million jobs in 2008. Nursing aides, orderlies, and attendants held the most jobs—approximately 1.5 million, and psychiatric aides held about 62,500 jobs. About 41 percent of nursing aides, orderlies, and attendants worked in nursing care facilities and another 29 percent worked in hospitals. About 50 percent of all psychiatric aides worked in hospitals. Others were employed in residential care facilities, government agencies, outpatient care centers, and individual and family services.

Job Outlook

Employment is projected to grow faster than the average. Excellent job opportunities are expected.

Employment change. Overall employment of nursing and psychiatric aides is projected to grow 18 percent between 2008 and 2018, faster than the average for all occupations. However, growth will vary for individual occupations. Employment for nursing aides, orderlies, and attendants will grow 19 percent, faster than the average for all occupations, predominantly in response to the long-term care needs of an increasing elderly population. Financial pressures on hospitals to discharge patients as soon as possible should boost admissions to nursing care facilities. As a result, new jobs will be more numerous in nursing and residential care facilities than in hospitals, and growth will be especially strong in community care facilities for the elderly. Modern medical technology will also drive demand for nursing aides, because as the technology saves and extends more lives, it increases the need for long-term care provided by aides. However, employment growth is not expected to be as fast as for other healthcare support occupations, largely because nursing aides are concentrated in the relatively slower growing nursing and residential care facilities industry sector. In addition, growth will be hindered by nursing facilities' reliance on government funding, which does not increase as fast as the cost of patient care. Government funding limits the number of nursing aides nursing facilities can afford to have on staff.

Psychiatric aides are expected to grow 6 percent, more slowly than average. Psychiatric aides are a small occupation compared to nursing aides, orderlies, and attendants. Most psychiatric aides currently work in hospitals, but the industries most likely to see growth will be residential facilities for people with developmental

Projections data from the National Employment Matrix

Occupational Title	SOC Code	Employment, 2008	Projected Employment, 2018	Change, 2008-2018	
				Number	Percent
Nursing and psychiatric aides	–	1,532,300	1,811,800	279,600	18
Nursing aides, orderlies, and attendants	31-1012	1,469,800	1,745,800	276,000	19
Psychiatric aides...	31-1013	62,500	66,100	3,600	6

(NOTE) Data in this table are rounded. See the discussion of the employment projections table in the *Handbook* introductory chapter on *Occupational Information Included in the Handbook.*

disabilities, mental illness, and substance abuse problems. There is a long-term trend toward treating psychiatric patients outside of hospitals, because it is more cost effective and allows patients greater independence. Demand for psychiatric aides in residential facilities will rise in response to increases in the number of older persons, many of whom will require mental health services. Demand for these workers will also grow as an increasing number of mentally disabled adults, formerly cared for by their elderly parents, will need care. Job growth also could be affected by changes in government funding of programs for the mentally ill.

Job prospects. High replacement needs for nursing and psychiatric aides reflect modest entry requirements, low pay, high physical and emotional demands, and limited opportunities for advancement within the occupation. For these same reasons, the number of people looking to enter the occupation will be limited. Many aides leave the occupation to attend training programs for other healthcare occupations. Therefore, people who are interested in, and suited for, this work should have excellent job opportunities.

Earnings

Median hourly wages of nursing aides, orderlies, and attendants were $11.46 in May 2008. The middle 50 percent earned between $9.71 and $13.76 an hour. The lowest 10 percent earned less than $8.34, and the highest 10 percent earned more than $15.97 an hour. Median hourly wages in the industries employing the largest numbers of nursing aides, orderlies, and attendants in May 2008 were:

Employment services	$12.10
General medical and surgical hospitals	12.05
Nursing care facilities	11.13
Community care facilities for the elderly	10.91
Home health care services	10.58

Median hourly wages of psychiatric aides were $12.77 in May 2008. The middle 50 percent earned between $10.00 and $15.63 an hour. The lowest 10 percent earned less than $8.35, and the highest 10 percent earned more than $18.77 an hour. Median hourly wages in the industries employing the largest numbers of psychiatric aides in May 2008 were:

Psychiatric and substance abuse hospitals	$13.43
General medical and surgical hospitals	13.29
Nursing care facilities	11.66
Individual and family services	10.78
Residential mental retardation, mental health and substance abuse facilities	9.89

Related Occupations

Other occupations that help people who need routine care or treatment include:

	Page
Child care workers	510
Home health aides and personal and home care aides	449
Licensed practical and licensed vocational nurses	421
Medical assistants	455
Occupational therapist assistants and aides	462
Registered nurses	392
Social and human service assistants	244

Sources of Additional Information

Information about employment opportunities may be obtained from local hospitals, nursing care facilities, home healthcare agencies, psychiatric facilities, State boards of nursing, and local offices of the State employment service.

Information on licensing requirements for nursing aides, and lists of State-approved nursing aide programs are available from State departments of public health, departments of occupational licensing, and boards of nursing.

For more information on nursing aides, orderlies, and attendants, contact:

➤ National Association of Health Care Assistants, 1201 L St. NW., Washington, DC 20005. Internet: **http://www.nahcacares.org**

➤ National Network of Career Nursing Assistants 3577 Easton Rd., Norton, OH 44203. Internet: **http://www.cna-network.org**

For more information on the assisted living, nursing facility, developmentally-disabled, and subacute care provider industry, contact:

➤ American Health Care Association, 1201 L St. NW., Washington, DC 20005. Internet: **http://www.ahca.org/**

The Occupational Information Network (O*NET) provides information on a wide range of occupational characteristics. Links to O*NET appear at the end of the Internet version of this occupational statement, accessible at **http://www.bls.gov/ooh/ocos327.htm**

Occupational Therapist Assistants and Aides

Significant Points

- Typical entry-level education for occupational therapist assistants is an associate degree; in contrast, occupational therapist aides usually receive their training on the job.

- Many States regulate the practice of occupational therapist assistants either by licensing, registration, or certification; requirements vary by State.

- Employment is projected to grow much faster than average as demand for occupational therapist services rises and as occupational therapists increasingly use assistants and aides.

- Job prospects should be very good for occupational therapist assistants; jobseekers holding only a high school diploma might face keen competition for occupational therapist aide jobs.

Nature of the Work

Occupational therapist assistants and aides work under the supervision of occupational therapists to provide rehabilitative services to persons with mental, physical, emotional, or developmental impairments. The ultimate goal is to improve clients' quality of life and ability to perform daily activities. For example, occupational therapist assistants help injured workers re-enter the labor force by teaching them how to compensate for lost motor skills or help individuals with learning disabilities increase their independence.

Occupational therapist assistants help clients with rehabilitative activities and exercises outlined in a treatment plan developed in collaboration with an occupational therapist. Activities range from teaching the proper method of moving from a bed into a wheelchair to the best way to stretch and limber the muscles of the hand. Assistants monitor an individual's activities to make sure that they are performed correctly and to provide encouragement. They also record their client's progress for the occupational therapist. If the treatment is not having the intended effect, or the client is not improving as expected, the therapist may alter the treatment program in hopes of obtaining better results. In addition, occupational therapist assistants document the billing of the client's health insurance provider.

Occupational therapist aides typically prepare materials and assemble equipment used during treatment. They are responsible for a range of clerical tasks, including scheduling appointments, answering the telephone, restocking or ordering depleted supplies, and filling out insurance forms or other paperwork. Aides are not regulated by States, so the law does not allow them to perform as wide a range of tasks as occupational therapist assistants.

Work environment. Occupational therapist assistants and aides need to have a moderate degree of strength because of the physical exertion required to assist patients. For example, assistants and aides may need to lift patients. Constant kneeling, stooping, and standing for long periods also are part of the job.

The hours and days that occupational therapist assistants and aides work vary by facility and whether they are full time or part time. For example, many outpatient therapy offices and clinics have evening and weekend hours to coincide with patients' schedules.

Training, Other Qualifications, and Advancement

An associate degree from an accredited academic program is generally required to qualify for occupational therapist assistant jobs. In contrast, occupational therapist aides usually receive most of their training on the job. Many States regulate the practice of occupational therapist assistants either by licensing, registration, or certification; requirements vary by State.

Education and training. Occupational therapist assistants must attend a school accredited by the Accreditation Council for Occupational Therapy Education (ACOTE) in order to sit for the national certifying exam for occupational therapist assistants. There were 135 ACOTE accredited occupational therapist assistant programs in 2009.

The first year of study typically involves an introduction to healthcare, basic medical terminology, anatomy, and physiology. In the second year, courses are more rigorous and usually include occupational therapy courses in areas such as mental health, adult physical disabilities, gerontology, and pediatrics. Students also must complete at least 16 weeks of supervised fieldwork in a clinic or community setting.

Applicants to occupational therapist assistant programs can improve their chances of admission by taking high school courses in biology and health and by performing volunteer

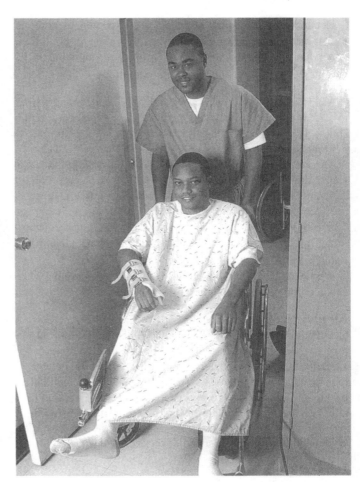

Occupational therapy assistants and aides need a moderate degree of strength because of the physical exertion required to assist patients.

work in nursing care facilities, occupational or physical therapists' offices, or other healthcare settings.

Occupational therapist aides usually receive most of their training on the job. Qualified applicants must have a high school diploma, strong interpersonal skills, and a desire to help people in need. Applicants may increase their chances of getting a job by volunteering their services, thus displaying initiative and aptitude to the employer.

Licensure. Forty States, Guam, Puerto Rico, and the District of Columbia regulate the practice of occupational therapist assistants either by licensing, registration, or certification. In addition, eligibility requirements vary by State. Contact your State's licensing board for specific regulatory requirements on occupational therapist assistants.

Some States have additional requirements for therapist assistants who work in schools or early intervention programs. These requirements may include education-related classes, an education practice certificate, or early intervention certification.

Certification and other qualifications. Certification is voluntary. The National Board for Certifying Occupational Therapy certifies occupational therapist assistants through a national certifying exam. Those who pass the test are awarded the title Certified Occupational Therapy Assistant (COTA). In some States, the national certifying exam meets requirements for regulation, but other States have their own licensing exam.

Occupational therapist assistants are expected to continue their professional development by participating in continuing education courses and workshops in order to maintain certification. A number of States require continuing education as a condition of maintaining licensure.

Assistants and aides must be responsible, patient, and willing to take directions and work as part of a team. Furthermore, they should be caring and want to help people who are not able to help themselves.

Advancement. Occupational therapist assistants may advance into administration positions. They might organize all the assistants in a large occupational therapy department or act as the director for a specific department such as sports medicine. Some assistants go on to teach classes in accredited occupational therapist assistant academic programs or lead health risk reduction classes for the elderly.

With proper formal education, occupational therapist aides can become occupational therapist assistants.

Employment

Occupational therapist assistants and aides held about 34,400 jobs in 2008, with assistants holding about 26,600 jobs and aides holding approximately 7,800 jobs. About 28 percent of jobs for assistants and aides were in offices of other health practitioners, 27 percent were in hospitals, and 20 percent were in nursing care facilities. The rest were primarily in community care facilities for the elderly, home healthcare services, individual and family services, and government agencies.

Job Outlook

Employment is expected to grow much faster than average as demand for occupational therapy services rises and as occupational therapists increasingly use assistants and aides. Job prospects should be very good for occupational therapist assistants. Jobseekers holding only a high school diploma might face keen competition for occupational therapist aide jobs.

Employment change. Employment of occupational therapist assistants and aides is expected to grow by 30 percent from 2008 to 2018, much faster than the average for all occupations. Demand for occupational therapist assistants and aides will continue to rise because of the increasing number of individuals with disabilities or limited function.

The growing elderly population is particularly vulnerable to chronic and debilitating conditions that require therapeutic services. These patients often need additional assistance in their treatment, making the roles of assistants and aides vital. Also, the large baby-boom generation is entering the prime age for heart attacks and strokes, further increasing the demand for cardiac and physical rehabilitation. In addition, future medical developments should permit an increased per-

centage of trauma victims to survive, creating added demand for therapy services. Demand for therapy may be dampened by Federal legislation imposing limits on reimbursement for therapy services.

Demand from adolescents will increase due to expansion of the school-age population and Federal legislation mandating funding for education for the disabled.

Occupational therapists are expected to increasingly employ assistants to reduce the cost of occupational therapy services. Once a patient is evaluated and a treatment plan is designed by the therapist, the occupational therapist assistant can provide many aspects of treatment, as prescribed by the therapist.

Job prospects. Opportunities for occupational therapist assistants should be very good. However, individuals with only a high school diploma may face keen competition for occupational therapist aide jobs. Occupational therapist assistants and aides with prior experience working in an occupational therapy office or other healthcare setting will have the best job opportunities. In addition to employment growth, job openings will result from the need to replace occupational therapist assistants and aides who leave the occupation permanently over the 2008–18 period.

Earnings

Median annual wages of occupational therapist assistants were $48,230 in May 2008. The middle 50 percent earned between $39,240 and $57,810. The lowest 10 percent earned less than $31,150, and the highest 10 percent earned more than $65,160. Median annual wages in the industries employing the largest numbers of occupational therapist assistants in May 2008 were:

Home health care services...$53,090
Offices of other health practitioners............................50,810
Nursing care facilities 50,790
General medical and surgical hospitals........................45,760
Elementary and secondary schools 41,850

Median annual wages of occupational therapist aides were $26,960 in May 2008. The middle 50 percent earned between $21,930 and $33,340. The lowest 10 percent earned less than $17,850, and the highest 10 percent earned more than $46,910. Median annual wages in the industries employing the largest numbers of occupational therapist aides in May 2008 were:

Specialty (except psychiatric and
    substance abuse) hospitals.....................................$30,400
General medical and surgical hospitals........................27,750
Offices of other health practitioners............................26,850
Elementary and secondary schools 26,820
Nursing care facilities 25,790

Projections data from the National Employment Matrix

Occupational Title	SOC Code	Employment, 2008	Projected Employment, 2018	Change, 2008-2018	
				Number	Percent
Occupational therapist assistants and aides	31-2010	34,400	44,800	10,300	30
Occupational therapist assistants	31-2011	26,600	34,600	7,900	30
Occupational therapist aides	31-2012	7,800	10,200	2,400	31

(NOTE) Data in this table are rounded. See the discussion of the employment projections table in the *Handbook* introductory chapter on *Occupational Information Included in the Handbook.*

Related Occupations

Occupational therapist assistants and aides work under the supervision and direction of occupational therapists. Other workers in the healthcare field who work under similar supervision include:

Sources of Additional Information

For information on a career as an occupational therapist assistant or aide, and a list of accredited programs, contact:

➤ American Occupational Therapy Association, 4720 Montgomery Lane, PO Box 31220, Bethesda, MD 20824-1220. Internet: **http://www.aota.org**

The Occupational Information Network (O*NET) provides information on a wide range of occupational characteristics. Links to O*NET appear at the end of the Internet version of this occupational statement, accessible at **http://www.bls.gov/ooh/ocos166.htm**

Physical Therapist Assistants and Aides

Significant Points

- Employment is projected to grow much faster than average.

- Physical therapist assistants should have very good job prospects; on the other hand, aides may face keen competition from the large pool of qualified applicants.

- Aides usually learn skills on the job, while physical therapist assistants have an associate degree; most States require licensing for assistants.

- Most jobs are in offices of other health practitioners and in hospitals.

Nature of the Work

Physical therapist assistants and aides help physical therapists to provide treatment that improves patient mobility, relieves pain, and prevents or lessens physical disabilities of patients. A physical therapist might ask a physical therapist assistant to help patients exercise or learn to use crutches, for example, or an aide to gather and prepare therapy equipment. Patients include accident victims and individuals with disabling conditions such as lower-back pain, arthritis, heart disease, fractures, head injuries, and cerebral palsy.

Physical therapist assistants assist physical therapists in providing care to patients. Under the direction and supervision of physical therapists, they provide exercise, instruction; therapeutic methods like electrical stimulation, mechanical traction, and ultrasound; massage; and gait and balance training. Physical ther-

apist assistants record the patient's responses to treatment and report the outcome of each treatment to the physical therapist.

Physical therapist aides help make therapy sessions productive, under the direct supervision of a physical therapist or physical therapist assistant. They usually are responsible for keeping the treatment area clean and organized and for preparing for each patient's therapy. When patients need assistance moving to or from a treatment area, aides assist in their transport. Because they are not licensed, aides do not perform the clinical tasks of a physical therapist assistant in States where licensure is required.

The duties of aides include some clerical tasks, such as ordering depleted supplies, answering the phone, and filling out insurance forms and other paperwork. The extent to which an aide or an assistant performs clerical tasks depends on the needs and organization of the facility.

Work environment. Physical therapist assistants and aides need a moderate degree of strength because of the physical exertion required in assisting patients with their treatment. In some cases, assistants and aides need to lift patients. Frequent kneeling, stooping, bending, and standing for long periods also are part of the job.

The hours and days that physical therapist assistants and aides work vary with the facility. About 28 percent of all physical therapist assistants and aides work part-time. Many outpatient physical therapy offices and clinics have evening and weekend hours, to coincide with patients' personal schedules.

Training, Other Qualifications, and Advancement

Most physical therapy aides are trained on the job, while almost all physical therapist assistants earn an associate degree from an accredited physical therapist assistant program. Most States require licensing for physical therapist assistants.

Education and training. Employers typically require physical therapy aides to have a high school diploma. They are trained on the job, and most employers provide clinical on-the-job training.

In most States, physical therapist assistants are required by law to hold an associate degree. The American Physical Therapy Association's Commission on Accreditation in Physical

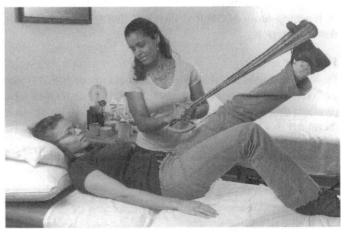

Physical therapist assistants and aides provide treatment that improves patient mobility, relieves pain, and prevents or lessens physical disabilities, under the direction of physical therapists.

Therapy Education accredits postsecondary physical therapy assistant programs. In 2009, there were 223 accredited programs, which usually last 2 years and culminate in an associate degree.

Programs are divided into academic coursework and hands-on clinical experience. Academic coursework includes algebra, English, anatomy and physiology, and psychology. Clinical work includes certifications in cardiopulmonary resuscitation (CPR) and other first aid, and field experience in treatment centers. Both educators and prospective employers view clinical experience as essential to ensuring that students understand the responsibilities of a physical therapist assistant.

Licensure. Licensing is not required to practice as a physical therapy aide. However, most States regulate physical therapist assistants through licensure, registration, or certification. Most States require physical therapist assistants to graduate from an accredited education program and pass the National Physical Therapy Exam. Some States may require physical therapy assistants to pass State exams. Many States also require continuing education credits for physical therapist assistants to maintain licensure. Complete information on regulations can be obtained from State licensing boards.

Other qualifications. Physical therapist assistants and aides should be well-organized, detail oriented, and caring. They should be able to take direction and work well in a team situation. They usually have strong interpersonal skills and a desire to help people in need.

Advancement. Some physical therapist aides advance to become therapist assistants after gaining experience and completing an accredited education program.

Some physical therapist assistants advance their knowledge and skills in a variety of clinical areas after graduation. The American Physical Therapy Association recognizes physical therapist assistants who have gained additional skills in geriatric, pediatric, musculoskeletal, neuromuscular, integumentary, and cardiopulmonary physical therapy. Physical therapist assistants may also advance in non-clinical areas, like administrative positions. These positions might include organizing all the assistants in a large physical therapy organization or acting as the director for a specific department such as aquatic therapy. Physical therapist assistants may also pursue a career in teaching at an accredited physical therapist assistant academic program.

Employment

Physical therapist assistants and aides held about 109,900 jobs in 2008. Physical therapist assistants held about 63,800 jobs; physical therapist aides held 46,100. Both work with physical therapists in a variety of settings. About 72 percent of jobs were in offices of other health practitioners and in hospitals. Others worked primarily in nursing care facilities, home health care services, and outpatient care centers.

Job Outlook

Employment is expected to grow much faster than average because of increasing demand for physical therapy services. Job prospects for physical therapist assistants are expected to be very good. Aides may experience keen competition for jobs.

Employment change. Employment of physical therapist assistants and aides is expected to grow by 35 percent from 2008 through 2018, much faster than the average for all occupations. Changes to restrictions on reimbursement for physical therapy services by third-party payers will increase patient access to services and, thus, increase demand. The increasing number of people who need therapy reflects, in part, the increasing elderly population. The elderly population is particularly vulnerable to chronic and debilitating conditions that require therapeutic services. These patients often need additional assistance in their treatment, making the roles of assistants and aides vital. In addition, the large baby-boom generation is entering the prime age for heart attacks and strokes, further increasing the demand for cardiac and physical rehabilitation.

Medical and technological developments should permit an increased percentage of trauma victims and newborns with birth defects to survive, creating added demand for therapy and rehabilitative services.

Physical therapists are expected to increasingly use assistants and aides to reduce the cost of physical therapy services. Once a patient is evaluated and a treatment plan is designed by the physical therapist, the physical therapist assistant can provide many parts of the treatment, as directed by the therapist.

Job prospects. Opportunities for individuals interested in becoming physical therapist assistants are expected to be very good; with help from physical therapist assistants, physical therapists are able to manage more patients. However, physical therapy aides may face keen competition from the large pool of qualified individuals. In addition to employment growth, job openings will result from the need to replace workers who leave the occupation permanently. Job opportunities should be particularly good in acute hospital, skilled nursing, and orthopedic settings, where the elderly are most often treated. Job prospects should be especially favorable in rural areas, as many physical therapists tend to cluster in highly populated urban and suburban areas.

Earnings

Median annual wages of physical therapist assistants were $46,140 in May 2008. The middle 50 percent earned between

Projections data from the National Employment Matrix

Occupational Title	SOC Code	Employment, 2008	Projected Employment, 2018	Change, 2008-2018	
				Number	Percent
Physical therapist assistants and aides	31-2020	109,900	147,800	37,900	35
Physical therapist assistants	31-2021	63,800	85,000	21,200	33
Physical therapist aides	31-2022	46,100	62,800	16,700	36

(NOTE) Data in this table are rounded. See the discussion of the employment projections table in the *Handbook* introductory chapter on *Occupational Information Included in the Handbook.*

$37,170 and $54,900. The lowest 10 percent earned less than $28,580, and the highest 10 percent earned more than $63,830. Median annual wages in the industries employing the largest numbers of physical therapist assistants in May 2008 were:

Home health care services	$51,950
Nursing care facilities	51,090
General medical and surgical hospitals	45,510
Offices of other health practitioners	44,580
Offices of physicians	43,390

Median annual wages of physical therapist aides were $23,760 in May 2008. The middle 50 percent earned between $19,910 and $28,670. The lowest 10 percent earned less than $17,270, and the highest 10 percent earned more than $33,540. Median annual wages in the industries employing the largest numbers of physical therapy aides in May 2008 were:

Nursing care facilities	$26,530
General medical and surgical hospitals	24,780
Specialty (except psychiatric and substance abuse) hospitals	24,590
Offices of physicians	23,730
Offices of other health practitioners	22,550

Related Occupations

Physical therapist assistants and aides work under the supervision of physical therapists. Other workers in the health care field who work under similar supervision include:

	Page
Dental assistants	447
Medical assistants	455
Nursing and psychiatric aides	460
Occupational therapist assistants and aides	462
Pharmacy technicians and aides	436

Sources of Additional Information

Career information on physical therapist assistants and a list of schools offering accredited programs can be obtained from:
➤ The American Physical Therapy Association, 1111 North Fairfax St., Alexandria, VA 22314-1488. Internet: **http://www.apta.org**

The Occupational Information Network (O*NET) provides information on a wide range of occupational characteristics. Links to O*NET appear at the end of the Internet version of this occupational statement, accessible at **http://www.bls.gov/ooh/ocos167.htm**

Protective Service Occupations

Correctional Officers

Significant Points

- The work can be stressful and hazardous; correctional officers have one of the highest rates of nonfatal on-the-job injuries.

- Most jobs are in State and local government prisons and jails.

- Job opportunities are expected to be favorable.

Nature of the Work

Correctional officers, also known as *detention officers* when they work in pretrial detention facilities, are responsible for overseeing individuals who have been arrested and are awaiting trial or who have been convicted of a crime and sentenced to serve time in a jail, reformatory, or penitentiary.

The jail population changes constantly as some prisoners are released, some are convicted and transferred to prison, and new offenders are arrested and enter the system. Correctional officers in local jails admit and process about 13 million people a year, with nearly 800,000 offenders in jail at any given time. Correctional officers in State and Federal prisons watch over the approximately 1.6 million offenders who are incarcerated there at any given time. Typically, offenders serving time at county jails are sentenced to a year or less. Those serving a year or more are usually housed in state or federal prisons.

Correctional officers maintain security and inmate accountability to prevent disturbances, assaults, and escapes. Officers have no law enforcement responsibilities outside of the institution where they work. (For more information on related occupations, see the statements on police and detectives and on probation officers and correctional treatment specialists, elsewhere in the *Handbook*.)

Regardless of the setting, correctional officers maintain order within the institution and enforce rules and regulations. To help ensure that inmates are orderly and obey rules, correctional officers monitor the activities and supervise the work assignments of inmates. Sometimes, officers must search inmates and their living quarters for contraband like weapons or drugs, settle disputes between inmates, and enforce discipline. Correctional officers periodically inspect the facilities, checking cells and other areas of the institution for unsanitary conditions, contraband, fire hazards, and any evidence of infractions of rules. In addition, they routinely inspect locks, window bars, grilles, doors, and gates for signs of tampering. Finally, officers inspect mail and visitors for prohibited items.

Correctional officers report orally and in writing on inmate conduct and on the quality and quantity of work done by inmates. Officers also report security breaches, disturbances, violations of rules, and any unusual occurrences. They usually keep a daily log or record of their activities. Correctional officers cannot show favoritism and must report any inmate who violates the rules. If a crime is committed within their institution or an inmate escapes, they help the responsible law enforcement authorities investigate or search for the escapee. In jail and prison facilities with direct supervision of cellblocks, officers work unarmed. They are equipped with communications devices so that they can summon help if necessary. These

Correctional officers inspect mail and visitors for prohibited items.

officers often work in a cellblock alone, or with another officer, among the 50 to 100 inmates who reside there. The officers enforce regulations primarily through their interpersonal communication skills and through the use of progressive sanctions, such as the removal of some privileges.

In the highest security facilities, where the most dangerous inmates are housed, correctional officers often monitor the activities of prisoners from a centralized control center with closed-circuit television cameras and a computer tracking system. In such an environment, the inmates may not see anyone but officers for days or weeks at a time and may leave their cells only for showers, solitary exercise time, or visitors. Depending on the offenders' security classification, correctional officers may have to restrain inmates in handcuffs and leg irons to safely escort them to and from cells and other areas and to see authorized visitors. Officers also escort prisoners between the institution and courtrooms, medical facilities, and other destinations.

Bailiffs, also known as *marshals* or *court officers*, are law enforcement officers who maintain safety and order in courtrooms. Their duties, which vary by location, include enforcing courtroom rules, assisting judges, guarding juries from outside contact, delivering court documents, and providing general security for courthouses.

Work environment. Working in a correctional institution can be stressful and hazardous. Every year, correctional officers are injured in confrontations with inmates. Correctional officers and jailers have one of the highest rates of nonfatal on-the-job injuries. First-line supervisors/managers of correctional officers also face the risk of work-related injury. Correctional officers may work indoors or outdoors. Some correctional institutions are well lighted, temperature controlled, and ventilated, but others are old, overcrowded, hot, and noisy. Although both jails and prisons can be dangerous places to work, prison populations are more stable than jail populations, and correctional officers in prisons know the security and custodial requirements of the prisoners with whom they are dealing. Consequently, they tend to be safer places to work.

Correctional officers usually work an 8-hour day, 5 days a week, on rotating shifts. Some correctional facilities have longer shifts and more days off between scheduled work weeks.

Because prison and jail security must be provided around the clock, officers work all hours of the day and night, weekends, and holidays. In addition, officers may be required to work paid overtime.

Training, Other Qualifications, and Advancement

Correctional officers go through a training academy and then are assigned to a facility where they learn most of what they need to know for their work through on-the-job training. Qualifications vary by agency, but all agencies require a high school diploma or equivalent, and some also require some college education or full-time work experience. Military experience is often seen as a plus for corrections employment.

Education and training. A high school diploma or graduation equivalency degree is required by all employers. The Federal Bureau of Prisons requires entry-level correctional officers to have at least a bachelor's degree; 3 years of full-time experience in a field providing counseling, assistance, or supervision to individuals; or a combination of the two. Some State and local corrections agencies require some college credits, but law enforcement or military experience may be substituted to fulfill this requirement.

Federal, State, and some local departments of corrections provide training for correctional officers based on guidelines established by the American Correctional Association and the American Jail Association. Some States have regional training academies that are available to local agencies. At the conclusion of formal instruction, all State and local correctional agencies provide on-the-job training, including training on legal restrictions and interpersonal relations. Many systems require firearms proficiency and self-defense skills. Officer trainees typically receive several weeks or months of training in an actual job setting under the supervision of an experienced officer. However, on-the-job training varies widely from agency to agency.

Academy trainees generally receive instruction in a number of subjects, including institutional policies, regulations, and operations, as well as custody and security procedures. New Federal correctional officers must undergo 200 hours of formal training within the first year of employment. They also must complete 120 hours of specialized training at the U.S. Federal Bureau of Prisons residential training center at Glynco, Georgia, within 60 days of their appointment. Experienced officers receive annual in-service training to keep abreast of new developments and procedures.

Correctional officers that are members of prison tactical response teams are trained to respond to disturbances, riots, hostage situations, forced cell moves, and other potentially dangerous confrontations. Team members practice disarming prisoners wielding weapons, protecting themselves and inmates against the effects of chemical agents, and other tactics.

Other qualifications. All institutions require correctional officers to be at least 18 to 21 years of age, be a U.S. citizen or permanent resident, and have no felony convictions. New applicants for Federal corrections positions must be appointed before they are 37 years old. Some institutions require previous experience in law enforcement or the military, but college credits can be substituted to fulfill this requirement. Others require a record of previous job stability, usually accomplished through

2 years of work experience, which need not be related to corrections or law enforcement.

Correctional officers must be in good health. Candidates for employment are generally required to meet formal standards of physical fitness, eyesight, and hearing. In addition, many jurisdictions use standard tests to determine applicant suitability to work in a correctional environment. Good judgment and the ability to think and act quickly are indispensable. Applicants are typically screened for drug abuse, subject to background checks, and required to pass a written examination.

Advancement. Qualified officers may advance to the position of correctional sergeant. Correctional sergeants supervise correctional officers and usually are responsible for maintaining security and directing the activities of other officers during an assigned shift or in an assigned area. Ambitious and qualified correctional officers can be promoted to supervisory or administrative positions all the way up to warden. In some jurisdictions, corrections officers are given the opportunity to "bid" for a specialty assignment, such as working in correctional industries, correctional health or correctional counseling, and receive additional training. Promotion prospects may be enhanced by attending college. Officers sometimes transfer to related jobs, such as probation officer, parole officer, and correctional treatment specialist.

Employment

Correctional officers and jailors held about 454,500 jobs in 2008, while first-line supervisors and managers of correctional officers held about 43,500 jobs. An additional 20,200 workers were employed as bailiffs. The vast majority of correctional officers and jailors and their supervisors were employed by State and local government in correctional institutions such as prisons, prison camps, and youth correctional facilities.

Job Outlook

Employment growth is expected to be as fast as the average for all occupations, and job opportunities are expected to be favorable.

Employment change. Employment of correctional officers is expected to grow 9 percent between 2008 and 2018, about as fast as the average for all occupations. Increasing demand for correctional officers will stem from population growth and rising rates of incarceration. Mandatory sentencing guidelines calling for longer sentences and reduced parole for inmates are a primary reason for increasing incarceration rates. Some States are reconsidering mandatory sentencing guidelines because of budgetary constraints, court decisions, and doubts about their effectiveness. Some employment opportunities also will arise in the private sector, as public authorities contract with private companies to provide and staff corrections facilities. Both State and Federal corrections agencies are increasingly using private prisons.

Job prospects. Job opportunities for correctional officers are expected to be favorable. The need to replace correctional officers who transfer to other occupations, retire, or leave the labor force, coupled with rising employment demand, will generate job openings. In the past, some local and State corrections agencies have experienced difficulty in attracting and keeping qualified applicants, largely because of low salaries, shift work, and the concentration of jobs in rural locations. This situation is expected to continue.

Earnings

Median annual wages of correctional officers and jailers were $38,380 in May 2008. The middle 50 percent earned between $29,660 and $51,000. The lowest 10 percent earned less than $25,300, and the highest 10 percent earned more than $64,110. Median annual wages in the public sector were $50,830 in the Federal Government, $38,850 in State government, and $37,510 in local government. In the facilities support services industry, where the relatively small number of officers employed by privately operated prisons is classified, median annual wages were $28,790.

Median annual wages of first-line supervisors/managers of correctional officers were $57,380 in May 2008. The middle 50 percent earned between $41,740 and $73,630. The lowest 10 percent earned less than $32,300, and the highest 10 percent earned more than $86,970. Median annual wages were $57,050 in State government and $57,300 in local government.

Median annual wages of bailiffs were $37,820 in May 2008. The middle 50 percent earned between $26,730 and $51,470. The lowest 10 percent earned less than $18,750, and the highest 10 percent earned more than $61,500. Median annual wages were $32,690 in local government.

In March 2009, the average salary for Federal correctional officers was $53,459. Federal salaries were slightly higher in areas where prevailing local pay levels were higher.

In addition to typical benefits, correctional officers employed in the public sector are usually provided with uniforms or a clothing allowance to purchase their own uniforms. Civil service systems or merit boards cover officers employed by the Federal Govern-

Projections data from the National Employment Matrix

Occupational Title	SOC Code	Employment, 2008	Projected Employment, 2018	Change, 2008-2018	
				Number	Percent
Correctional officers..	—	518,200	566,500	48,300	9
First-line supervisors/managers of correctional officers...............	33-1011	43,500	47,200	3,700	9
Bailiffs, correctional officers, and jailers.....................................	33-3010	474,800	519,400	44,600	9
Bailiffs..	33-3011	20,200	21,900	1,700	8
Correctional officers and jailers..	33-3012	454,500	497,500	42,900	9

(NOTE) Data in this table are rounded. See the discussion of the employment projections table in the *Handbook* introductory chapter on *Occupational Information Included in the Handbook.*

ment and most State governments. Their retirement coverage entitles correctional officers to retire at age 50 after 20 years of service or at any age with 25 years of service. Unionized correctional officers often have slightly higher wages and benefits.

Related Occupations

Other protective service occupations:

Sources of Additional Information

Further information about correctional officers is available from:

➤ American Correctional Association, 206 N. Washington St., Suite 200, Alexandria, VA 22314. Internet: **http://www.aca.org**

➤ American Jail Association, 1135 Professional Ct., Hagerstown, MD 21740. Internet: **http://www.corrections.com/aja**

➤ Information on entrance requirements, training, and career opportunities for correctional officers at the Federal level may be obtained from the Federal Bureau of Prisons. Internet: **http://www.bop.gov**

Information on obtaining a position as a correctional officer with the Federal Government is available from the Office of Personnel Management through USAJOBS, the Federal Government's official employment information system. This resource for locating and applying for job opportunities can be accessed through the Internet at **http://www.usajobs.opm.gov** or through an interactive voice response telephone system at (703) 724-1850 or TDD (978) 461-8404. These numbers are not toll free, so charges may result.

The Occupational Information Network (O*NET) provides information on a wide range of occupational characteristics. Links to O*NET appear at the end of the Internet version of this occupational statement, accessible at **http://www.bls.gov/ooh/ocos156.htm**

Fire Fighters

Significant Points

- Fire fighting involves hazardous conditions and long, irregular hours.

- About 9 out of 10 fire fighters were employed by local governments.

- Applicants generally must pass written, physical, and medical examinations, and candidates with some postsecondary education are increasingly preferred.

- Keen competition for jobs is expected because this occupation attracts many qualified candidates.

Nature of the Work

Every year, fires and other emergencies take thousands of lives and destroy property worth billions of dollars. *Fire fighters* help protect the public against these dangers by responding to fires and a variety of other emergencies. Although they put out fires, fire fighters more frequently respond to other emergencies. They are often the first emergency personnel at the scene of a traffic accident or medical emergency and may be called upon to treat injuries or perform other vital functions.

During duty hours, fire fighters must be prepared to respond immediately to a fire or other emergency. Fighting fires is complex and dangerous, and requires organization and teamwork. At every emergency scene, fire fighters perform specific duties assigned by a superior officer. At fires, they connect hose lines to hydrants and operate a pump to send water to high-pressure hoses. Some carry hoses, climb ladders, and enter burning buildings—using systematic and careful procedures—to put out fires. At times, they may need to use tools to make their way through doors, walls, and debris, sometimes with the aid of information about a building's floor plan. Some find and rescue occupants who are unable to leave the building safely without assistance. They also provide emergency medical attention, ventilate smoke-filled areas and attempt to salvage the contents of buildings. Fire fighters' duties may change several times while the company is in action. Sometimes they remain at the site of a disaster for days at a time, rescuing trapped survivors, and assisting with medical treatment.

Fire fighters work in a variety of settings, including metropolitan areas, rural areas, airports, chemical plants and other industrial sites. They also have assumed a range of responsibilities, including providing emergency medical services. In fact, most calls to which fire fighters respond involve medical emergencies. In addition, some fire fighters work in hazardous materials units that are specially trained for the control, prevention, and cleanup of hazardous materials, such as oil spills or accidents involving the transport of chemicals. (For more information, see the *Handbook* section on hazardous materials removal workers.)

Workers specializing in forest fires utilize methods and equipment different from those of other fire fighters. When fires break out, crews of fire fighters are brought in to suppress the blaze with heavy equipment and water hoses. Fighting forest fires, like fighting urban fires, is rigorous work. One of the most effective means of fighting a forest fire is creating fire lines—cutting down trees and digging out grass and all other combustible vegetation in the path of the fire in order to deprive it of fuel. Elite fire fighters called *smoke jumpers* parachute from airplanes to reach otherwise inaccessible areas. This tactic, however, can be extremely hazardous.

When they aren't responding to fires and other emergencies, fire fighters clean and maintain equipment, learn additional skills related to their jobs, conduct practice drills, and participate in physical fitness activities. They also prepare written reports on fire incidents and review fire science literature to stay informed about technological developments and changing administrative practices and policies.

Work environment. Fire fighters spend much of their time at fire stations, which are usually similar to dormitories. When an

Fire fighters help protect the public by responding to fires and a variety of other emergencies.

alarm sounds, fire fighters respond, regardless of the weather or hour. Fire fighting involves a high risk of death or injury. Common causes include floors caving in, walls toppling, traffic accidents, and exposure to flame and smoke. Fire fighters also may come into contact with poisonous, flammable, or explosive gases and chemicals and radioactive materials, all of which may have immediate or long-term effects on their health. For these reasons, they must wear protective gear that can be very heavy and hot.

Work hours of fire fighters are longer and more varied than the hours of most other workers. Many fire fighters work about 50 hours a week, and sometimes they may work longer. In some agencies, fire fighters are on duty for 24 hours, then off for 48 hours, and receive an extra day off at intervals. In others, they work a day shift of 10 hours for 3 or 4 days, work a night shift of 14 hours for 3 or 4 nights, have 3 or 4 days off, and then repeat the cycle. In addition, fire fighters often work extra hours at fires and other emergencies and are regularly assigned to work on holidays. Fire lieutenants and fire captains frequently work the same hours as the fire fighters they supervise.

Training, Other Qualifications, and Advancement

Applicants for fire fighting jobs usually are required to have at least a high school diploma, but candidates with some postsecondary education are increasingly being preferred. Most municipal jobs require passing written and physical tests. All fire fighters receive extensive training after being hired.

Education and training. Most fire fighters have a high school diploma; however, the completion of community college courses or, in some cases, an associate's degree, in fire science may improve an applicant's chances for a job. A number of colleges and universities offer courses leading to 2-year or 4-year degrees in fire engineering or fire science. In recent years, an increasing proportion of new fire fighters have had some education after high school.

As a rule, entry-level workers in large fire departments are trained for several weeks at the department's training center or academy. Through classroom instruction and practical training, the recruits study fire fighting techniques, fire prevention, hazardous materials control, local building codes, and emergency medical procedures,

including first aid and cardiopulmonary resuscitation (CPR). They also learn how to use axes, chain saws, fire extinguishers, ladders, and other fire fighting and rescue equipment. After successfully completing training, the recruits are assigned to a fire company, where they undergo a period of probation.

Many fire departments have accredited apprenticeship programs lasting up to 4 years, including programs in fighting forest fires. These programs combine formal instruction with on-the-job training under the supervision of experienced fire fighters.

Almost all departments require fire fighters to be certified as emergency medical technicians. (For more information, see the section of the *Handbook* on emergency medical technicians and paramedics.) Although most fire departments require the lowest level of certification, Emergency Medical Technician-Basic (EMT-Basic), larger departments in major metropolitan areas increasingly are requiring paramedic certification. Some departments include this training in the fire academy, whereas others prefer that recruits earn EMT certification on their own, but will give them up to 1 year to do it.

In addition to participating in training programs conducted by local fire departments, some fire fighters attend training sessions sponsored by the U.S. National Fire Academy. These training sessions cover topics such as executive development, antiarson techniques, disaster preparedness, hazardous materials control, and public fire safety and education. Some States also have mandatory or voluntary fire fighter training and certification programs. Many fire departments offer fire fighters incentives, such as tuition reimbursement or higher pay, for completing advanced training.

Other qualifications. Applicants for municipal fire fighting jobs usually must pass a written exam; tests of strength, physical stamina, coordination, and agility; and a medical examination that includes a drug screening. Workers may be monitored on a random basis for drug use after accepting employment. Examinations are generally open to people who are at least 18 years of age and have a high school education or its equivalent. Those who receive the highest scores in all phases of testing have the best chances of being hired.

Among the personal qualities fire fighters need are mental alertness, self-discipline, courage, mechanical aptitude, endurance, strength, and a sense of public service. Initiative and good judgment also are extremely important, because fire fighters make quick decisions in emergencies. Members of a crew live and work closely together under conditions of stress and danger for extended periods, so they must be dependable and able to get along well with others. Leadership qualities are necessary for officers, who must establish and maintain discipline and efficiency, as well as direct the activities of the fire fighters in their companies.

Advancement. Most experienced fire fighters continue studying to improve their job performance and prepare for promotion examinations. To progress to higher level positions, they acquire expertise in advanced fire fighting equipment and techniques, building construction, emergency medical technology, writing, public speaking, management and budgeting procedures, and public relations.

Opportunities for promotion depend upon the results of written examinations, as well as job performance, interviews, and seniority. Hands-on tests that simulate real-world job situations also are used by some fire departments.

Usually, fire fighters are first promoted to engineer, then lieutenant, captain, battalion chief, assistant chief, deputy chief, and, finally, chief. For promotion to positions higher than battalion chief, many fire departments now require a bachelor's degree, preferably in fire science, public administration, or a related field. An associate's degree is required for executive fire officer certification from the National Fire Academy.

Employment

In 2008, total paid employment in fire fighting occupations was about 365,600. Fire fighters held about 310,400 jobs, and first-line supervisors/managers of fire fighting and prevention workers held about 55,200. These employment figures include only paid career fire fighters—they do not cover volunteer fire fighters, who perform the same duties and may constitute the majority of fire fighters in a residential area. According to the U.S. Fire Administration, about 70 percent of fire companies were staffed entirely by volunteer fire fighters in 2007.

About 91 percent of fire fighting workers were employed by local governments. Some local and regional fire departments are being consolidated into countywide establishments to reduce administrative staffs, cut costs, and establish consistent training standards and work procedures. Some large cities have thousands of career fire fighters, while many small towns have only a few. Most of the fire fighters not employed by local governments worked in fire departments on Federal and State installations, including airports. Private fire fighting companies employ a small number of fire fighters.

Job Outlook

Although employment is expected to grow faster than the average for all jobs, candidates for these positions are expected to face keen competition because these positions are highly attractive and sought after.

Employment change. Employment of fire fighters is expected to grow by 19 percent over the 2008–18 decade, which is faster than the average for all occupations. Most job growth will stem from volunteer fire fighting positions being converted to paid positions. In recent years, it has become more difficult for volunteer fire departments to recruit and retain volunteers, perhaps because of the considerable amount of training and time commitment required. Furthermore, a trend toward more people living in and around cities has increased the demand for fire fighters. When areas develop and become more densely populated, emergencies and fires affect more buildings and more people and, therefore, require more fire fighters.

Job prospects. Prospective fire fighters are expected to face keen competition for available job openings. Many people are attracted to fire fighting because (1) it is challenging and provides the opportunity to perform an essential public service, (2) a high school education is usually sufficient for entry, and (3) a pension is usually guaranteed after 25 years of service. Consequently, the number of qualified applicants in most areas far exceeds the number of job openings, even though the written examination and physical requirements eliminate many applicants. This situation is expected to persist in coming years. Applicants with the best chances are those who are physically fit and score the highest on physical-conditioning and mechanical aptitude exams. Those who have completed some fire fighter education at a community college and have EMT or paramedic certification will have an additional advantage.

Earnings

Median annual wages of fire fighters were $44,260 in May 2008. The middle 50 percent earned between $31,180 and $58,440. The lowest 10 percent earned less than $22,440, and the highest 10 percent earned more than $72,210. Median annual wages were $44,800 in local government, $45,610 in the Federal Government, $25,300 in other support services, and $37,870 in State governments.

Median annual wages of first-line supervisors/managers of fire fighting and prevention workers were $67,440 in May 2008. The middle 50 percent earned between $53,820 and $86,330. The lowest 10 percent earned less than $40,850, and the highest 10 percent earned more than $108,930. First-line supervisors/managers of fire fighting and prevention workers employed in local government earned a median of about $69,000 a year.

According to the International City-County Management Association, average salaries in 2008 for sworn full-time positions were as follows:

Rank	Minimum annual base salary	Maximum annual base salary
Fire chief	$78,672	$104,780
Deputy chief	69,166	88,571
Battalion chief	66,851	81,710
Assistant fire chief	65,691	83,748
Fire captain	60,605	72,716
Fire lieutenant	50,464	60,772
Engineer	48,307	62,265

Fire fighters who average more than a certain number of work hours per week are required to be paid overtime. The threshold is determined by the department. Fire fighters often work extra

Projections data from the National Employment Matrix

Occupational Title	SOC Code	Employment, 2008	Projected Employment, 2018	Change, 2008-2018 Number	Change, 2008-2018 Percent
Fire fighting occupations...	–	365,600	427,600	62,100	17
First-line supervisors/managers of fire fighting and prevention workers...	33-1021	55,200	59,700	4,500	8
Fire fighters...	33-2011	310,400	367,900	57,500	19

(NOTE) Data in this table are rounded. See the discussion of the employment projections table in the *Handbook* introductory chapter on *Occupational Information Included in the Handbook.*

shifts to maintain minimum staffing levels and during special emergencies.

In 2008, 66 percent of all fire fighters were union members or covered by a union contract. Fire fighters receive benefits that usually include medical and liability insurance, vacation and sick leave, and some paid holidays. Almost all fire departments provide protective clothing (helmets, boots, and coats) and breathing apparatus, and many also provide dress uniforms. Fire fighters generally are covered by pension plans, often offering retirement at half pay after 25 years of service or if the individual is disabled in the line of duty.

Related Occupations

Other occupations that involve protecting the public and property are:

Sources of Additional Information

Information about a career as a fire fighter may be obtained from local fire departments and from either of the following organizations:

➤ International Association of Fire Fighters, 1750 New York Ave. NW., Washington, DC 20006. Internet: **http://www.iaff.org**

➤ U.S. Fire Administration, 16825 South Seton Ave., Emmitsburg, MD 21727. Internet: **http://www.usfa.dhs.gov**

Information about professional qualifications and a list of colleges and universities offering 2-year or 4-year degree programs in fire science or fire prevention may be obtained from:
➤ National Fire Academy, 16825 South Seton Ave., Emmitsburg, MD 21727. Internet: **http://www.usfa.dhs.gov/nfa**

The Occupational Information Network (O*NET) provides information on a wide range of occupational characteristics. Links to O*NET appear at the end of the Internet version of this occupational statement, accessible at **http://www.bls.gov/ooh/ocos329.htm**

Police and Detectives

Significant Points

- Police work can be dangerous and stressful.

- Education requirements range from a high school diploma to a college degree or higher.

- Job opportunities in most local police departments will be favorable for qualified individuals, while competition is expected for jobs in State and Federal agencies.

- Bilingual applicants with college training in police science or with military police experience will have the best opportunities.

Nature of the Work

Police officers and *detectives* protect lives and property. *Law enforcement officer's* duties depend on the size and type of their organizations.

Police and detectives pursue and apprehend individuals who break the law and then issue citations or give warnings. A large proportion of their time is spent writing reports and maintaining records of incidents they encounter. Most police officers patrol their jurisdictions and investigate any suspicious activity they notice. They also respond to calls from individuals. Detectives, who often are called *agents* or *special agents*, perform investigative duties such as gathering facts and collecting evidence.

The daily activities of police and detectives vary with their occupational specialty—such as police officer, *game warden*, or detective—and whether they are working for a local, State, or Federal agency. Duties also differ substantially among various Federal agencies, which enforce different aspects of the law. Regardless of job duties or location, police officers and detectives at all levels must write reports and maintain meticulous records that will be needed if they testify in court.

State and Local Law Enforcement. Uniformed police officers have general law enforcement duties. They maintain regular patrols and respond to calls for service. Much of their time is spent responding to calls and doing paperwork. They may direct traffic at the scene of an accident, investigate a burglary, or give first aid to an accident victim. In large police departments, officers usually are assigned to a specific type of duty.

Many urban police agencies are involved in community policing—a practice in which an officer builds relationships with the citizens of local neighborhoods and mobilizes the public to help fight crime.

Police agencies are usually organized into geographic districts, with uniformed officers assigned to patrol a specific area. *Officers* in large agencies often patrol with a partner. They attempt to become familiar with their patrol area and remain alert for anything unusual. Suspicious circumstances and hazards to public safety are investigated or noted, and officers are dispatched to individual calls for assistance within their district. During their shift, they may identify, pursue, and arrest suspected criminals; resolve problems within the community; and enforce traffic laws.

Some agencies have special geographic jurisdictions and enforcement responsibilities. Public college and university police forces, public school district police, and agencies serving transportation systems and facilities are examples. Most law enforcement workers in special agencies are uniformed officers.

Some police officers specialize in a particular field, such as chemical and microscopic analysis, training and firearms instruction, or handwriting and fingerprint identification. Others work with special units, such as horseback, bicycle, motorcycle, or harbor patrol; canine corps; special weapons and tactics (SWAT); or emergency response teams. A few local and special law enforcement officers primarily perform jail-related duties or work in courts. (For information on other officers who work in jails and prisons, see correctional officers, listed elsewhere in the *Handbook*.)

Sheriffs and *deputy sheriffs* enforce the law on the county level. Sheriffs usually are elected to their posts and perform duties similar to those of a local or county police chief. Sheriffs' departments tend to be relatively small, most having fewer than 50 sworn officers. Deputy sheriffs have law enforcement duties similar to those of officers in urban police departments. Police and sheriffs' deputies who provide security in city and county courts are sometimes called *bailiffs*.

State police officers, sometimes called *State troopers* or *highway patrol officers*, arrest criminals Statewide and patrol highways to enforce motor vehicle laws and regulations. State police officers often issue traffic citations to motorists. At the scene of accidents, they may direct traffic, give first aid, and call for emergency equipment. They also write reports used to determine the cause of the accident. State police officers frequently are called upon to render assistance to other law enforcement agencies, especially those in rural areas or small towns.

State highway patrols operate in every State except Hawaii. Most full-time sworn personnel are uniformed officers who regularly patrol and respond to calls for service. Others work as investigators, perform court-related duties, or carry out administrative or other assignments.

Detectives are plainclothes investigators who gather facts and collect evidence for criminal cases. Some are assigned to interagency task forces to combat specific types of crime. They conduct interviews, examine records, observe the activities of suspects, and participate in raids or arrests. Detectives usually specialize in investigating one type of violation, such as homicide or fraud. They are assigned cases on a rotating basis and work on them until an arrest and conviction is made or until the case is dropped.

Fish and game wardens enforce fishing, hunting, and boating laws. They patrol hunting and fishing areas, conduct search and rescue operations, investigate complaints and accidents, and aid in prosecuting court cases.

Federal Law Enforcement. *Federal Bureau of Investigation (FBI) agents* are the Government's principal investigators, responsible for investigating violations of more than 200 categories of Federal law and conducting sensitive national security investigations. Agents may conduct surveillance, monitor court-authorized wiretaps, examine business records, investigate white-collar crime, or participate in sensitive undercover assignments. The FBI investigates a wide range of criminal activity, including organized crime, public corruption, financial crime, bank robbery, kidnapping, terrorism, espionage, drug trafficking, and cybercrime.

There are many other Federal agencies that enforce particular types of laws. *U.S. Drug Enforcement Administration (DEA) agents* enforce laws and regulations relating to illegal drugs. *U.S. marshals and deputy marshals* provide security for the Federal courts and ensure the effective operation of the judicial system. *Bureau of Alcohol, Tobacco, Firearms, and Explosives agents* enforce and investigate violations of Federal firearms and explosives laws, as well as Federal alcohol and tobacco tax regulations. The U.S. Department of State *Bureau of Diplomatic Security special agents* are engaged in the battle against terrorism.

The *Department of Homeland Security* also employs numerous law enforcement officers within several different agencies, including Customs and Border Protection, Immigration and Customs Enforcement, and the U.S. Secret Service. *U.S. Border Patrol agents* protect more than 8,000 miles of international

The daily activities of police and detectives vary with their occupational specialty.

land and water boundaries. *Immigration inspectors* interview and examine people seeking entry into the United States and its territories. *Customs inspectors* enforce laws governing imports and exports by inspecting cargo, baggage, and articles worn or carried by people, vessels, vehicles, trains, and aircraft entering or leaving the United States. *Federal Air Marshals* provide air security by guarding against attacks targeting U.S. aircraft, passengers, and crews. *U.S. Secret Service special agents* and *U.S. Secret Service uniformed officers* protect the President, the Vice President, their immediate families, and other public officials. Secret Service special agents also investigate counterfeiting, forgery of Government checks or bonds, and fraudulent use of credit cards.

Other Federal agencies employ police and special agents with sworn arrest powers and the authority to carry firearms. These agencies include the Postal Service, the Bureau of Indian Affairs Office of Law Enforcement, the Forest Service, and the National Park Service.

Work environment. Police and detective work can be very dangerous and stressful. Police officers and detectives have one of the highest rates of on-the-job injury and illness. In addition to the obvious dangers of confrontations with criminals, police officers and detectives need to be constantly alert and ready to deal appropriately with a number of other threatening situations. Many law enforcement officers witness death and suffering resulting from accidents and criminal behavior. A career in law enforcement may take a toll on their private lives.

Uniformed officers, detectives, agents, and inspectors usually are scheduled to work 40-hour weeks, but paid overtime is common. Shift work is necessary because protection must be provided around the clock. Junior officers frequently work weekends, holidays, and nights. Police officers and detectives are required to work whenever they are needed and may work long hours during investigations. Officers in most jurisdictions, whether on or off duty, are expected to be armed and to exercise their authority when necessary.

The jobs of some Federal agents, such as U.S. Secret Service and DEA special agents, require extensive travel, often on very short notice. These agents may relocate a number of times over the course of their careers. Some special agents, such as those in the U.S. Border Patrol, may work outdoors in rugged terrain and in all kinds of weather.

Training, Other Qualifications, and Advancement

Education requirements range from a high school diploma to a college degree or higher. Most police and detectives learn much of what they need to know on the job, often in their agency's training academy. Civil service regulations govern the appointment of police and detectives in most States, large municipalities, and special police agencies, as well as in many smaller jurisdictions. Candidates must be U.S. citizens, usually at least 21 years old, and meet rigorous physical and personal qualifications.

Education and training. Applicants usually must have at least a high school education, and some departments require 1 or 2 years of college coursework or, in some cases, a college degree. Physical education classes and participation in sports are also helpful in developing the competitiveness, stamina, and agility needed for many law enforcement positions. Knowledge of a foreign language is an asset in many Federal agencies and urban departments.

State and local agencies encourage applicants to take courses or training related to law enforcement subjects after high school. Many entry-level applicants for police jobs have completed some formal postsecondary education, and a significant number are college graduates. Many junior colleges, colleges, and universities offer programs in law enforcement or administration of justice. Many agencies pay all or part of the tuition for officers to work toward degrees in criminal justice, police science, administration of justice, or public administration and pay higher salaries to those who earn one of those degrees.

Before their first assignments, officers usually go through a period of training. In State and large local police departments, recruits get training in their agency's police academy, often for 12 to 14 weeks. In small agencies, recruits often attend a regional or State academy. Training includes classroom instruction in constitutional law and civil rights, State laws and local ordinances, and accident investigation. Recruits also receive training and supervised experience in patrol, traffic control, use of firearms, self-defense, first aid, and emergency response. Police departments in some large cities hire high school graduates who are still in their teens as police cadets or trainees. They do clerical work and attend classes, usually for 1 to 2 years, until they reach the minimum age requirement and can be appointed to the regular force.

Fish and game wardens also must meet specific requirements. Most States require at least 2 years of college study. Once hired, fish and game wardens attend a training academy lasting from 3 to 12 months, sometimes followed by further training in the field.

Federal agencies require a bachelor's degree, related work experience, or a combination of the two. Federal law enforcement agents undergo extensive training, usually at the U.S. Marine Corps base in Quantico, Virginia, or the Federal Law Enforcement Training Center in Glynco, Georgia. The specific educational requirements, qualifications, and training information for a particular Federal agency can be found on its Web site. Many of these agencies are listed as sources of additional information at the end of this statement.

To be considered for appointment as an FBI agent, an applicant must be a college graduate and have at least 3 years of professional work experience or must have an advanced degree plus 2 years of professional work experience. An applicant who meets these criteria also must have one of the following: a college major in accounting, electrical engineering, information technology, or computer science; fluency in a foreign language; a degree from an accredited law school; or 3 years of related full-time work experience. All new FBI agents undergo 18 weeks of training at the FBI Academy on the U.S. Marine Corps base in Quantico, Virginia.

Other qualifications. Civil service regulations govern the appointment of police and detectives in most States, large municipalities, and special police agencies, as well as in many smaller jurisdictions. Candidates must be U.S. citizens, usually must be at least 21 years old, and must meet rigorous physical and personal qualifications. Physical examinations for entry into law enforcement often include tests of vision, hearing, strength, and agility. Eligibility for appointment usually depends on one's performance in competitive written examinations and previous education and experience.

Candidates should enjoy working with people and meeting the public. Because personal characteristics such as honesty, sound judgment, integrity, and a sense of responsibility are especially important in law enforcement, candidates are interviewed by senior officers and their character traits and backgrounds are investigated. A history of domestic violence may disqualify a candidate. In some agencies, candidates are interviewed by a psychiatrist or a psychologist, or given a personality test. Most applicants are subjected to lie detector examinations or drug testing. Some agencies subject sworn personnel to random drug testing as a condition of continuing employment.

Although similar in nature, the requirements for Federal agents are generally more stringent and the background checks are more thorough. There are polygraph tests as well as interviews with references. Jobs that require security clearances have additional requirements.

Advancement. Police officers usually become eligible for promotion after a probationary period ranging from 6 months to 3 years. In large departments, promotion may enable an officer to become a detective or to specialize in one type of police work, such as working with juveniles. Promotions to corporal, sergeant, lieutenant, and captain usually are made according to a candidate's position on a promotion list, as determined by scores on a written examination and on-the-job performance.

Federal agents often are on the General Services (GS) pay scale. Most begin at the GS-5 or GS-7 level. As agents meet time-in-grade and knowledge and skills requirements, they move up the GS scale. Promotions at and above GS-13 are most often managerial positions. Many agencies hire internally for these supervisory positions. A few agents may be able to enter the Senior Executive Series ranks of upper management.

Continuing training helps police officers, detectives, and special agents improve their job performance. Through police department academies, regional centers for public safety employees established by the States, and Federal agency training centers, instructors provide annual training in self-defense tactics, firearms, use-of-force policies, sensitivity and communications skills, crowd-control techniques, relevant legal developments, and advances in law enforcement equipment.

Employment

Police and detectives held about 883,600 jobs in 2008. About 79 percent were employed by local governments. State police agencies employed about 11 percent. Various Federal agencies employ police and detectives.

According to the U.S. Bureau of Justice Statistics, police and detectives employed by local governments worked primarily in cities with more than 25,000 inhabitants. Some cities have very large police forces, while thousands of small communities employ fewer than 25 officers each.

Job Outlook

Job opportunities in most local police departments will be favorable for qualified individuals, whereas competition is expected for jobs in State and Federal agencies. As fast as average employment growth is expected.

Employment change. Employment of police and detectives is expected to grow 10 percent over the 2008–18 decade, about as fast as the average for all occupations. Population growth is the main source of demand for police services.

Job prospects. Overall opportunities in local police departments will be favorable for individuals who meet the psychological, personal, and physical qualifications. In addition to openings from employment growth, many openings will be created by the need to replace workers who retire and those who leave local agencies for Federal jobs and private-sector security jobs. Jobs in local police departments that offer relatively low salaries, or those in urban communities in which the crime rate is relatively high, may be the easiest to get. Some smaller departments may have fewer opportunities as budgets limit the ability to hire additional officers. Bilingual applicants with military experience or college training in police science will have the best opportunities in local and State departments.

There will be more competition for jobs in Federal and State law enforcement agencies than for jobs in local agencies. Bilingual applicants with a bachelor's degree and several years of law enforcement or military experience, especially investigative experience, will have the best opportunities in Federal agencies.

The level of government spending determines the level of employment for police and detectives. The number of job opportunities, therefore, can vary from year to year and from place to place. Layoffs are rare because retirements enable most staffing cuts to be handled through attrition. Trained law enforcement officers who lose their jobs because of budget cuts usually have little difficulty finding jobs with other agencies.

Earnings

Police and sheriff's patrol officers had median annual wages of $51,410 in May 2008. The middle 50 percent earned between $38,850 and $64,940. The lowest 10 percent earned less than $30,070, and the highest 10 percent earned more than $79,680. Median annual wages were $46,620 in Federal Government, $57,270 in State government, $51,020 in local government and $43,350 in educational services.

In May 2008, median annual wages of police and detective supervisors were $75,490. The middle 50 percent earned between $59,320 and $92,700. The lowest 10 percent earned less than $46,000, and the highest 10 percent earned more than $114,300. Median annual wages were $89,930 in Federal Government, $75,370 in State government, and $74,820 in local government.

In May 2008, median annual wages of detectives and criminal investigators were $60,910. The middle 50 percent earned between $45,930 and $81,490. The lowest 10 percent earned less than $36,500, and the highest 10 percent earned more than $97,870. Median annual wages were $73,170 in Federal Government, $53,910 in State government, and $55,930 in local government.

In May 2008, median annual wages of fish and game wardens were $48,930. The middle 50 percent earned between $37,500 and $61,290. The lowest 10 percent earned less than $30,400, and the highest 10 percent earned more than $81,710. Median annual wages were $48,960 in Federal Government, $50,440 in State government, and $35,810 in local government.

In May 2008, median annual wages of parking enforcement workers were $32,390. The middle 50 percent earned between $25,400 and $42,000. The lowest 10 percent earned less than $20,510, and the highest 10 percent earned more than $50,470. Median annual wages were $33,130 in local government and $27,640 in educational services.

In May 2008, median annual wages of transit and railroad police were $46,670. The middle 50 percent earned between $37,640 and $57,830. The lowest 10 percent earned less than $31,300, and the highest 10 percent earned more than $72,700. Median annual wages were $49,370 in State government, $43,720 in local government, and $56,300 in rail transportation.

Federal law provides special salary rates to Federal employees who serve in law enforcement. Additionally, Federal special agents and inspectors receive law enforcement availability pay (LEAP)—equal to 25 percent of the agent's grade and step—awarded because of the large amount of overtime that these agents are expected to work. Salaries were slightly

Projections data from the National Employment Matrix

Occupational Title	SOC Code	Employment, 2008	Projected Employment, 2018	Change, 2008-2018	
				Number	Percent
Police and detectives..	–	883,600	968,400	84,700	10
First-line supervisors/managers of police and detectives	33-1012	97,300	105,200	7,800	8
Detectives and criminal investigators...	33-3021	112,200	130,900	18,700	17
Fish and game wardens...	33-3031	8,300	9,000	700	8
Police officers..	33-3050	665,700	723,300	57,500	9
Police and sheriff's patrol officers	33-3051	661,500	718,800	57,300	9
Transit and railroad police	33-3052	4,300	4,500	200	5

(NOTE) Data in this table are rounded. See the discussion of the employment projections table in the *Handbook* introductory chapter on *Occupational Information Included in the Handbook.*

higher in selected areas where the prevailing local pay level was higher. Because Federal agents may be eligible for a special law enforcement benefits package, applicants should ask their recruiter for more information.

Total earnings for local, State, and special police and detectives frequently exceed the stated salary because of payments for overtime, which can be significant.

According to the International City-County Management Association's annual Police and Fire Personnel, Salaries, and Expenditures Survey, average salaries for sworn full-time positions in 2008 were as follows:

Rank	Minimum salary	Maximum salary w/o longevity
Police chief	$90,570	$113,930
Deputy chief	74,834	96,209
Police captain	72,761	91,178
Police lieutenant	65,688	79,268
Police sergeant	58,739	70,349
Police corporal	49,421	61,173

In addition to the common benefits—paid vacation, sick leave, and medical and life insurance—most police and sheriffs' departments provide officers with special allowances for uniforms. Many police officers retire at half-pay after 20 years of service; others often are eligible to retire with 30 or fewer years of service.

Related Occupations

Other occupations that help protect and serve people are:

Sources of Additional Information

Information about entry requirements may be obtained from Federal, State, and local law enforcement agencies.

To find Federal, State, and local law enforcement job fairs and other recruiting events across the country, contact:
➤ National Law Enforcement Recruiters Association, PO Box 17132, Arlington, VA 22216. Internet: **http://www.nlera.org**

For general information about sheriffs and to learn more about the National Sheriffs' Association scholarship, contact:
➤ National Sheriffs' Association, 1450 Duke St., Alexandria, VA 22314. Internet: **http://www.sheriffs.org**

For information about chiefs of police, contact:
➤ International Association of Chiefs of Police, 515 N. Washington St., Alexandria, VA 22314. Internet: **http://www.theiacp.org**

Information related to Federal law enforcement:
Information about qualifications for employment as a Federal Bureau of Investigation (FBI) Special Agent is available

from the nearest State FBI office. The address and phone number are listed in the local telephone directory. Internet: **http://www.fbi.gov**

Information on career opportunities, qualifications, and training for U.S. Secret Service Special Agents and Uniformed Officers is available from the Secret Service Personnel Division at (202) 406-5830, (888) 813-8777, (888) 813-USSS, or U.S. Secret Services, Recruitment and Hiring Coordination Center, 245 Murray Dr., Building 410, Washington, DC 20223. Internet: **http://www.secretservice.gov/join**

Information about qualifications for employment as a Drug Enforcement Administration (DEA) Special Agent is available from the nearest DEA office, DEA Office of Personnel, 8701 Morrissette Dr., Springfield, VA 22152, or call (800) DEA-4288. Internet: **http://www.usdoj.gov/dea**

Information about jobs in other Federal law enforcement agencies is available from:
➤ U.S. Marshals Service, Human Resources Division—Law Enforcement Recruiting, Washington, DC 20530-1000. Internet: **http://www.usmarshals.gov**

➤ U.S. Bureau of Alcohol, Tobacco, Firearms, and Explosives, Office of Governmental and Public Affairs, 99 New York Ave. NE. Mail Stop 5S144, Washington, DC 20226. Internet: **http://www.atf.gov**

➤ U.S. Customs and Border Protection, 1300 Pennsylvania Ave. NW., Washington, DC 20229. Internet: **http://www.cbp.gov**

➤ U.S. Department of Homeland Security, Washington, DC 20528. Internet: **http://www.dhs.gov**

The Occupational Information Network (O*NET) provides information on a wide range of occupational characteristics. Links to O*NET appear at the end of the Internet version of this occupational statement, accessible at **http://www.bls.gov/ooh/ocos160.htm**

Private Detectives and Investigators

Significant Points

- Work hours are often irregular, and the work can be dangerous.
- About 21 percent are self-employed.
- Keen competition is expected for most jobs.
- Most private detectives and investigators have some college education and previous experience in investigative work.

Nature of the Work

Private detectives and *investigators* assist individuals, businesses, and attorneys by finding and analyzing information. They connect clues to uncover facts about legal, financial, or personal matters. Private detectives and investigators offer many services, including executive, corporate, and celebrity protection; preemployment verification; and individual background profiles. Some investigate computer crimes, such as identity theft, harassing e-mails, and illegal downloading of copyrighted material. They also provide assistance in criminal and civil liability cases, insurance claims and fraud cases, child custody and protection cases, missing-persons cases, and pre-marital screening. They are sometimes hired to investigate individuals to prove or disprove infidelity.

Private detectives and investigators may use many methods to determine the facts in a case. Much of their work is done with a computer. For example, they often recover deleted e-mails and documents. They also may perform computer database searches or work with someone who does. Computers allow investigators to quickly obtain huge amounts of information, such as records of a subject's prior arrests, convictions, and civil legal judgments; telephone numbers; information about motor vehicle registrations; records of association and club memberships; social networking site details; and even photographs.

Detectives and investigators also perform various other types of surveillance or searches. To verify facts, such as an individual's income or place of employment, they may make phone calls or visit a subject's workplace. In other cases, especially those involving missing persons and background checks, investigators interview people to gather as much information as possible about an individual. Sometimes investigators go undercover, pretending to be someone else in order to get information or to observe a subject inconspicuously. They even arrange to be hired in businesses to observe workers for wrongdoing.

Most detectives and investigators are trained to perform physical surveillance, which may be high tech or low tech. They may observe a site, such as the home of a subject, from an inconspicuous location or a vehicle. Using photographic and video cameras, binoculars, cell phones, and GPS systems, detectives gather information on an individual. Surveillance can be time consuming.

The duties of private detectives and investigators depend on the needs of their clients. In cases that involve fraudulent workers' compensation claims, for example, investigators may carry out long-term covert observation of a person suspected of fraud. If an investigator observes the person performing an activity that contradicts injuries stated in a worker's compensation

Private detectives and investigators may use many methods to determine the facts in a case.

claim, the investigator would take video or still photographs to document the activity and report it to the client.

Detectives and investigators must be mindful of the law in conducting investigations. They keep up with Federal, State, and local legislation, such as privacy laws and other legal issues affecting their work. The legality of certain methods may be unclear, and investigators and detectives must make judgment calls in deciding how to pursue a case. They must also know how to collect evidence properly so that they do not compromise its admissibility in court.

Private detectives and investigators often specialize. Those who focus on intellectual property theft, for example, investigate and document acts of piracy, help clients stop illegal activity, and provide intelligence for prosecution and civil action. Other investigators specialize in developing financial profiles and carrying out asset searches. Their reports reflect information gathered through interviews, investigation and surveillance, and research, including reviews of public documents.

Computer forensic investigators specialize in recovering, analyzing, and presenting data from computers for use in investigations or as evidence. They determine the details of intrusions into computer systems, recover data from encrypted or erased files, and recover e-mails and deleted passwords.

Legal investigators assist in preparing criminal defenses, locating witnesses, serving legal documents, interviewing police and prospective witnesses, and gathering and reviewing evidence. Legal investigators also may collect information on the parties to a litigation, take photographs, testify in court, and assemble evidence and reports for trials. They often work for law firms or lawyers.

Corporate investigators conduct internal and external investigations for corporations. In internal investigations, they may investigate drug use in the workplace, ensure that expense accounts are not abused, or determine whether employees are stealing assets, merchandise, or information. External investigations attempt to thwart criminal schemes from outside the corporation, such as fraudulent billing by a supplier. Investigators may spend months posing as employees of the company in order to find misconduct.

Financial investigators may be hired to develop confidential financial profiles of individuals or companies that are prospective parties to large financial transactions. These investigators often are certified public accountants (CPAs) who work closely with investment bankers and other accountants. They also might search for assets in order to recover damages awarded by a court in fraud or theft cases.

Detectives who work for retail stores or hotels are responsible for controlling losses and protecting assets. *Store detectives*, also known as *loss prevention agents*, safeguard the assets of retail stores by apprehending anyone attempting to steal merchandise or destroy store property. They prevent theft by shoplifters, vendor representatives, delivery personnel, and store employees. Store detectives also conduct periodic inspections of stock areas, dressing rooms, and rest rooms, and sometimes assist in opening and closing the store. They may prepare loss prevention and security reports for management and testify in court against people they apprehend. *Hotel detectives* protect guests of the establishment from theft of their belongings and preserve order in hotel restaurants and bars. They also may keep undesirable individuals, such as known thieves, off the premises.

Work environment. Many detectives and investigators spend time away from their offices conducting interviews or doing surveillance, but some work in the office most of the day conducting computer searches and making phone calls. When an investigator is working on a case, the environment might range from plush boardrooms to seedy bars. Store and hotel detectives work in the businesses that they protect.

Investigators generally work alone, but they sometimes work with others, especially during surveillance or when they follow a subject. Some of the work involves confrontation, so the job can be stressful and dangerous. Some situations, such as certain bodyguard assignments for corporate or celebrity clients, call for the investigator to be armed. In most cases, however, a weapon is not necessary, because the purpose of the work is gathering information and not law enforcement or criminal apprehension. Owners of investigative agencies have the added stress of having to deal with demanding and sometimes distraught clients. Although considered a dangerous occupation, private detectives and investigators have a relatively low incidence of nonfatal work-related injuries.

Private detectives and investigators often work irregular hours because of the need to conduct surveillance and contact people who are not available during normal working hours. Early morning, evening, weekend, and holiday work is common.

Training, Other Qualifications, and Advancement

Most private detectives and investigators have some college education and previous experience in investigative work. In the majority of States, they are required to be licensed.

Education and training. There are no formal education requirements for most private detective and investigator jobs, although many have postsecondary degrees. Courses in criminal justice and police science are helpful to aspiring private detectives and investigators. Although related experience is usually required, some people enter the occupation directly after graduation from college, generally with an associate's or bachelor's degree in criminal justice or police science. Experience in police investigation is viewed favorably.

Most corporate investigators must have a bachelor's degree, preferably in a business-related field. Some corporate investigators have a master's degree in business administration or a law degree; others are CPAs.

For computer forensics work, a computer science or accounting degree is more helpful than a criminal justice degree. An accounting degree provides good background knowledge for investigating computer fraud. Either of these two degrees provides a good starting point, after which investigative techniques can be learned on the job. Alternatively, many colleges and universities now offer certificate programs, requiring from 15 to 21 credits, in computer forensics. These programs are most beneficial to law enforcement officers, paralegals, or others who already are involved in investigative work. A few colleges and universities now offer bachelor's or master's degrees in computer forensics, and others are planning to begin offering such degrees. Most computer forensic investigators learn their trade while working for a law enforcement agency, either as a sworn officer or a civilian computer forensic analyst. They are trained at their agency's computer forensics training program. Many people enter law enforcement specifically to get this training and establish a reputation before moving to the private sector.

Most of the work of private detectives and investigators is learned on the job. New investigators will usually start by learning how to use databases to gather information. The training they receive depends on the type of firm. At an insurance company, a new investigator will learn to recognize insurance fraud. At a firm that specializes in domestic cases, a new worker might observe a senior investigator performing surveillance. Learning by doing, in which new investigators are put on cases and gain skills as they go, is a common approach. Corporate investigators hired by large companies, however, may receive formal training in business practices, management structure, and various finance-related topics.

Because they work with changing technologies, computer forensic investigators never stop training. They learn the latest methods of fraud detection and new software programs and operating systems by attending conferences and courses offered by software vendors and professional associations.

Licensure. Most States and the District of Columbia require private detectives and investigators to be licensed. Licensing requirements vary, however. Seven States—Alabama, Alaska, Colorado, Idaho, Mississippi, South Dakota, and Wyoming—have no Statewide licensing requirements. Some States have few requirements, and many others have stringent regulations. For example, the Bureau of Security and Investigative Services of the California Department of Consumer Affairs requires private investigators to be 18 years of age or older; have a combination of education in police science, criminal law, or justice and experience equaling 3 years (6,000 hours); pass a criminal history background check by the California Department of Justice and the FBI (in most States, convicted felons cannot be issued a license); and receive a qualifying score on a 2-hour written examination covering laws and regulations. In all States, detectives and investigators who carry handguns must meet additional requirements. Because laws change, it is important to verify the licensing laws related to private investigators with the State and locality where work will be performed.

There are no licenses specifically for computer forensic investigators, but some States require them to be licensed private investigators. Even where licensure is not required, a private investigator license is useful to some because it allows them to perform followup or related tasks.

Other qualifications. Private detectives and investigators typically have previous experience in other occupations. Some have worked in other occupations for insurance or collections companies, in the private security industry, or as paralegals. Many investigators enter the field after serving in law enforcement, the military, government auditing and investigative positions, or Federal intelligence jobs. Former law enforcement officers, military investigators, and government agents, who frequently are able to retire after 25 years of service, often become private detectives or investigators in a second career. Others enter from jobs in finance, accounting, commercial credit, investigative reporting, insurance, and law. These individuals often can apply their previous work experience in a related investigative specialty.

For private detective and investigator jobs, most employers look for individuals with ingenuity, persistence, and assertiveness. A candidate must not be afraid of confrontation, should communicate well, and should be able to think on his or her feet. Good interviewing and interrogation skills also are important and usually are acquired in earlier careers in law enforcement or other fields. Because the courts often are the judge of a properly conducted investigation, the investigator must be able to present the facts in a manner that a jury will believe. The screening process for potential employees typically includes a background check for a criminal history.

Certification and advancement. Some investigators receive certification from a professional organization to demonstrate competency in a field. For example, the National Association of Legal Investigators confers the Certified Legal Investigator designation upon licensed investigators who devote a majority of their practice to negligence or criminal defense investigations. To receive the designation, applicants must have 5 years of investigations experience. They also must satisfy educational requirements and continuing-training requirements and must pass written and oral exams.

ASIS International, a trade organization for the security industry, offers the Professional Certified Investigator certification. To qualify, applicants must have a high school diploma or the equivalent; must have 5 years of investigations experience, including 2 years managing investigations; and must pass an exam.

Most private detective agencies are small, with little room for advancement. Usually, there are no defined ranks or steps, so advancement takes the form of increases in salary and assignment status. Many detectives and investigators start their own firms after gaining a few years of experience. Corporate and legal investigators may rise to supervisor or manager of the security or investigations department.

Employment

Private detectives and investigators held about 45,500 jobs in 2008. About 21 percent were self-employed, including many for whom investigative work was a second job. Around 41 percent of detective and investigator jobs were in investigation and security services, including private detective agencies. The rest worked mostly in State and local government, legal services firms, department or other general merchandise stores, employment services companies, insurance agencies, and credit mediation establishments, including banks and other depository institutions.

Job Outlook

Keen competition is expected for most jobs despite much faster than average employment growth.

Employment change. Employment of private detectives and investigators is expected to grow 22 percent over the 2008–18

decade, much faster than the average for all occupations. Increased demand for private detectives and investigators will result from heightened security concerns, increased litigation, and the need to protect confidential information and property of all kinds. The proliferation of criminal activity on the Internet, such as identity theft, spamming, e-mail harassment, and illegal downloading of copyrighted materials, also will increase the demand for private investigators. Employee background checks, conducted by private investigators, have become standard for an increasing number of jobs. Growing financial activity worldwide will increase the demand for investigators to control internal and external financial losses, to monitor competitors, and to prevent industrial spying. More individuals are investigating care facilities, such as childcare providers, hospices, and hospitals.

Job prospects. Keen competition is expected for most jobs because private detective and investigator careers attract many qualified people, including relatively young retirees from law enforcement and military careers. The best opportunities for new jobseekers will be in entry-level jobs in detective agencies. Opportunities are expected to be favorable for qualified computer forensic investigators.

Earnings

Median annual wages of salaried private detectives and investigators were $41,760 in May 2008. The middle 50 percent earned between $30,870 and $59,060. The lowest 10 percent earned less than $23,500, and the highest 10 percent earned more than $76,640. Wages of private detectives and investigators vary greatly by employer, specialty, and geographic area.

Related Occupations

Other occupations whose duties involve collecting information include:

Other occupations whose duties involve property protection include:

Other occupations whose duties involve preparing financial profiles and conducting asset searches include:

Projections data from the National Employment Matrix

Occupational Title	SOC Code	Employment, 2008	Projected Employment, 2018	Change, 2008-2018	
				Number	Percent
Private detectives and investigators	33-9021	45,500	55,500	10,000	22

(NOTE) Data in this table are rounded. See the discussion of the employment projections table in the *Handbook* introductory chapter on *Occupational Information Included in the Handbook.*

Sources of Additional Information

For information on local licensing requirements, contact your State Department of Public Safety, State Division of Licensing, or local or State police headquarters.

For information on a career as a legal investigator and about the Certified Legal Investigator credential, contact:
➤ National Association of Legal Investigators, NALI World Headquarters, 235 N. Pine Street, Lansing, MI. 48933. Internet: **http://www.nalionline.org**

For more information about investigative and other security careers, about the Professional Certified Investigator credential, and for a list of colleges and universities offering security-related courses and majors, contact:
➤ ASIS International, 1625 Prince St., Alexandria, VA 22314-2818. Internet: **http://www.asisonline.org**

The Occupational Information Network (O*NET) provides information on a wide range of occupational characteristics. Links to O*NET appear at the end of the Internet version of this occupational statement, accessible at **http://www.bls.gov/ooh/ocos157.htm**

Security Guards and Gaming Surveillance Officers

Significant Points

- Job opportunities should be favorable, but competition is expected for some higher paying jobs.

- Because of limited formal training requirements and flexible hours, this occupation attracts many individuals seeking a second or part-time job.

- These jobs can be hazardous.

Nature of the Work

Security guards, also called *security officers*, patrol and inspect property to protect against fire, theft, vandalism, terrorism, and illegal activity. They protect their employer's property, enforce laws on the property, deter criminal activity, and other problems. These workers may be armed. They use various forms of telecommunications to call for assistance from police, fire, or emergency medical services. Security guards write comprehensive reports outlining their observations and activities during their assigned shift. They also may interview witnesses or victims, prepare case reports, and testify in court.

Although all security guards perform essentially the same function, their specific tasks depend on whether they work in a "static," or stationary, security position or on a mobile patrol. Guards assigned to static security positions usually stay at one location for a specified length of time. These guards must become closely acquainted with the property and people associated with their station and must often monitor alarms and closed-circuit TV cameras. In contrast, guards assigned to mobile patrol drive or walk from one location to another and conduct security checks within an assigned area. They may detain or arrest criminal violators, answer service calls concerning

Guards assigned to static security positions usually stay at one location for a specified length of time.

criminal activity or other safety concerns, and issue traffic violation warnings.

The security guard's job responsibilities also vary from one employer to another. In department stores, guards protect people, records, merchandise, money, and equipment. They often work with undercover store detectives to prevent theft by customers or employees, and help apprehend shoplifting suspects prior to the arrival of the police. Some shopping centers and theaters have officers who patrol their parking lots to deter assaults, car thefts, and robberies. In office buildings, banks, and hospitals, guards maintain order and protect the institution's customers, staff, and property. At air, sea, and rail terminals and other transportation facilities, guards and *screeners* protect people, freight, property, and equipment. Using metal detectors and other identification equipment, they may screen passengers and visitors for weapons and explosives, ensure that nothing is stolen while a vehicle is being loaded or unloaded, and watch for fires and criminals.

Guards who work in public buildings such as museums or art galleries protect paintings and exhibits by watching people and inspecting packages entering and leaving the building. In factories, laboratories, government buildings, data processing centers, and military bases, security officers protect information, products, computer codes, and defense secrets, and check the credentials of people and vehicles entering and leaving the premises. Guards working at universities, parks, and sports stadiums perform crowd control, supervise parking and seating, and direct traffic. Security guards stationed at the entrance to bars and nightclubs, prevent access by minors, collect cover charges at the door, maintain order among customers, and protect patrons and property.

Armored car guards protect money and valuables during transit. They also protect individuals responsible for making commercial bank deposits from theft or injury. They pick up money or other valuables from businesses and transport them to another location. Carrying money between the truck and the business can be extremely hazardous. As a result, armored car guards usually wear bulletproof vests and often carry firearms.

Gaming surveillance officers, also known as *surveillance agents*, and *gaming investigators* act as security agents for casino employees, managers, and patrons. Using primarily audio and video equipment in an observation room, they observe casino operations for irregular activities, such as cheating or theft, and monitor compliance with rules, regulations, and laws. They maintain and organize recordings from security cameras, since these are sometimes used as evidence in police investigations. Some casinos use a catwalk over one-way mirrors located above the casino floor to augment electronic surveillance equipment. Surveillance agents occasionally leave the surveillance room and walk the casino floor.

All security officers must show good judgment and common sense, follow directions, testify accurately in court, and follow company policy and guidelines. In an emergency, they must be able to take charge and direct others to safety. In larger organizations, a security manager might oversee a group of security officers. In smaller organizations, however, a single worker may be responsible for all security.

Work environment. Most security guards and gaming surveillance officers spend considerable time on their feet, either assigned to a specific post or patrolling buildings and grounds. Guards may be stationed at a guard desk inside a building to monitor electronic security and surveillance devices or to check the credentials of people entering or leaving the premises. They also may be stationed at a guardhouse outside the entrance to a gated facility or community and may use a portable radio or cellular telephone to be in constant contact with a central station. Guards who work during the day may have a great deal of contact with other employees and the public. Gaming surveillance officers often work behind a bank of monitors controlling numerous cameras in a casino and thus can develop eyestrain.

Guards usually work shifts of 8 hours or longer and are often on call in case of an emergency. When employers need 24-hour coverage 7 days a week, guards may rotate work schedules for total coverage. In 2008, about 16 percent of security guards and gaming surveillance officers worked part time, and some held a second job as a guard to supplement their primary earnings.

The work usually is routine, but these jobs can be hazardous. Guards must be constantly alert for threats to themselves and the property they are protecting. In 2008, gaming surveillance workers had one of the highest rates of nonfatal on-the-job injuries.

Training, Other Qualifications, and Advancement

Generally, there are no specific education requirements for security guards, but employers usually prefer to fill armed guard positions with people who have at least a high school diploma. Gaming surveillance officers often need some education beyond high school. In most States, guards must be licensed.

Education and training. Many employers of unarmed guards do not have any specific educational requirements. For armed guards, employers usually prefer individuals who are high school graduates or who hold an equivalent certification.

Many employers give newly hired guards instruction before they start the job and provide on-the-job training. The amount of training guards receive varies. Training is more rigorous for armed guards because their employers are legally responsible for any use of force. Armed guards receive formal training in areas such as weapons retention and laws covering the use of force. They may be periodically tested in the use of firearms.

An increasing number of States are making ongoing training a legal requirement for retention of licensure. Guards may receive training in protection, public relations, report writing, crisis deterrence, first aid, and specialized training relevant to their particular assignment.

ASIS International has written voluntary training guidelines that are intended to provide regulating bodies consistent minimum standards for the quality of security services. These guidelines recommend that security guards receive at least 48 hours of training within the first 100 days of employment. The guidelines also suggest that security guards be required to pass a written or performance examination covering topics such as sharing information with law enforcement, crime prevention, handling evidence, the use of force, court testimony, report writing, interpersonal and communication skills, and emergency response procedures. In addition, they recommend annual retraining and additional firearms training for armed officers.

Some employers prefer to hire security guards with some higher education, such as a police science or criminal justice degree. In addition, there are other programs and courses available at some postsecondary schools that focus specifically on security guards.

Guards who are employed at establishments that place a heavy emphasis on security usually receive extensive formal training. For example, guards at nuclear power plants undergo several months of training before going on duty—and even then, they perform their tasks under close supervision for a significant period of time. They are taught to use firearms, administer first aid, operate alarm systems and electronic security equipment, and spot and deal with security problems.

Gaming surveillance officers and investigators usually need some training beyond high school but not usually a bachelor's degree. Several educational institutes offer certification programs. Classroom training usually is conducted in a casino-like atmosphere and includes the use of surveillance camera equipment. Previous security experience is a plus. Employers prefer either individuals with casino experience and significant knowledge of casino operations or those with law enforcement and investigation experience.

Licensure and certification. Most States require that guards be licensed. To be licensed as a guard, individuals must usually be at least 18 years old, pass a background check, and complete classroom training in such subjects as property rights, emergency procedures, and detention of suspected criminals. Drug testing often is required and may be ongoing and random. Guards who carry weapons must be licensed by the appropriate government authority, and some receive further certification as special police officers, allowing them to make limited types of arrests while on duty. Armed guard positions also have more stringent background checks and entry requirements than those of unarmed guards.

In addition to being licensed, some security guards can become certified. Certifications are not mandatory. ASIS International offers the Certified Protection Professional for security people who want a transferrable validation of their knowledge and skills.

Other qualifications. Most jobs require a driver's license. For positions as armed guards, employers often seek people who have had responsible experience in other occupations or former law enforcement officers.

Rigorous hiring and screening programs consisting of background, criminal record, and fingerprint checks are becoming the norm in the occupation. Applicants are expected to have good character references, no serious police record, and good health. They should be mentally alert, emotionally stable, and physically fit to cope with emergencies. Guards who have frequent contact with the public should have good communication skills.

Like security guards, gaming surveillance officers and gaming investigators must have keen observation skills and excellent verbal and writing abilities to document violations or suspicious behavior. They also need to be physically fit and have quick reflexes because they sometimes must detain individuals until local law enforcement officials arrive.

Advancement. Compared with unarmed security guards, armed guards and special police usually enjoy higher earnings and benefits, greater job security, and more potential for advancement. Because many people do not stay long in this occupation, opportunities for advancement are good for those who make a career in security. Most large organizations use a military type of ranking that offers the possibility of advancement in both position and salary. Some guards may advance to supervisor or security manager positions. Guards with postsecondary education often have an advantage in securing supervisory positions. Guards with management skills may open their own contract security guard agencies. Guards can also move to an organization that needs higher levels of security, which may result in more prestige or higher pay.

Employment

Security guards and gaming surveillance officers held 1.1 million jobs in 2008. About 55 percent of all jobs for security guards were in investigation and security services, including guard and armored car services. These organizations provide security on a contract basis, assigning their guards to buildings and other sites as needed. Most other security officers were employed directly by a wide variety of businesses and governments. Guard jobs are found throughout the country, most commonly in metropolitan areas.

Gaming surveillance officers work primarily in gambling industries; traveler accommodation, which includes casino hotels; and local government. They are employed only in those States and on those Indian reservations where gambling is legal.

A significant number of law enforcement officers work as security guards when they are off duty, in order to supplement their incomes. Often working in uniform and with the official cars assigned to them, they add a high-profile security presence to the establishment with which they have contracted. At construction sites and apartment complexes, for example, their presence often deters crime. (Police and detectives are discussed elsewhere in the *Handbook.*)

Job Outlook

Opportunities for security guards and gaming surveillance officers should be favorable, although competition is expected for some higher paying jobs. Numerous job openings will stem from faster than average employment growth—driven by the demand for increased security—and from the need to replace those who leave this large occupation each year.

Employment change. Employment of security guards is expected to grow by 14 percent between 2008 and 2018, which is faster than the average for all occupations. This occupation will have a very large number of new jobs arise, about 152,500 over the projections decade. Concern about crime, vandalism, and terrorism continues to increase the need for security. Demand for guards also will grow as private security firms increasingly perform duties—such as providing security at public events and in residential neighborhoods—that were formerly handled by police officers. Additionally, private security firms are expected to provide more protection to facilities, such as hospitals and nursing homes.

Employment of gaming surveillance officers and gaming investigators is expected to grow by 12 percent between 2008 and 2018, as fast as the average for all occupations. Casinos will hire more surveillance officers if more States legalize gambling or if the number of casinos increases in States where gambling is already legal. In addition, casino security forces will employ more technically trained personnel as technology becomes increasingly important in thwarting casino cheating and theft.

Job prospects. Job opportunities for security guards should be favorable because of growing demand for these workers and the need to replace experienced workers who leave the occupation. In addition to full-time job opportunities, the limited training requirements and flexible hours attract many people seeking part-time or second jobs. However, competition is expected for higher paying positions that require longer periods of training; these positions usually are found at facilities that require a high level of security, such as nuclear power plants or weapons installations. Applicants with prior experience in the gaming industry should enjoy the best prospects for jobs as gaming surveillance officers.

Projections data from the National Employment Matrix

Occupational Title	SOC Code	Employment, 2008	Projected Employment, 2018	Change, 2008-2018	
				Number	Percent
Security guards and gaming surveillance officers............................	33-9030	1,086,000	1,239,500	153,600	14
Gaming surveillance officers and gaming investigators	33-9031	9,300	10,400	1,100	12
Security guards..	33-9032	1,076,600	1,229,100	152,500	14

(NOTE) Data in this table are rounded. See the discussion of the employment projections table in the *Handbook* introductory chapter on *Occupational Information Included in the Handbook.*

Earnings

Median annual wages of security guards were $23,460 in May 2008. The middle 50 percent earned between $19,150 and $30,100. The lowest 10 percent earned less than $16,680, and the highest 10 percent earned more than $39,360. Median annual wages in the industries employing the largest numbers of security guards were:

General medical and surgical hospitals	$29,020
Elementary and secondary schools	27,980
Local government	27,660
Traveler accommodation	25,660
Investigation and security services	22,170

Gaming surveillance officers and gaming investigators had median annual wages of $28,850 in May 2008. The middle 50 percent earned between $23,000 and $37,690. The lowest 10 percent earned less than $19,290, and the highest 10 percent earned more than $48,310.

Related Occupations

Other security and protective service occupations include:

	Page
Correctional officers	467
Gaming services occupations	520
Police and detectives	473
Private detectives and investigators	477

Sources of Additional Information

Further information about work opportunities for guards is available from local security and guard firms and State employment service offices. Information about licensing requirements for guards may be obtained from the State licensing commission or the State police department. In States where local jurisdictions establish licensing requirements, contact a local government authority such as the sheriff, county executive, or city manager.

For more information about security careers, about the Certified Protection Professional, and for a list of colleges and universities offering security-related courses and majors, contact:

➤ ASIS International, 1625 Prince St., Alexandria, VA 22314-2818. Internet: **http://www.asisonline.org**

For more information related to jobs with the Transportation Security Administration, call the TSA Recruitment Center at (800) 887-1895 or (800) 887-5506 (TTY), or visit their website. Internet: **http://www.tsa.gov/join/careers/careers_security_jobs.shtm**

The Occupational Information Network (O*NET) provides information on a wide range of occupational characteristics. Links to O*NET appear at the end of the Internet version of this occupational statement, accessible at **http://www.bls.gov/ooh/ocos159.htm**

Food Preparation and Serving Related Occupations

Chefs, Head Cooks, and Food Preparation and Serving Supervisors

Significant Points

- Most workers in these occupations have prior experience in the food service or hospitality industries.

- While most workers have some postsecondary training, many experienced workers with less education can still be promoted into these positions.

- Job opportunities are expected to be good, largely because of high turnover; however, keen competition is expected for jobs at upscale restaurants that generally pay more.

Nature of the Work

Chefs, head cooks, and food preparation and serving supervisors oversee the daily food service operation of a restaurant or other food service establishment. *Chefs and head cooks* are usually responsible for directing cooks in the kitchen, dealing with food-related concerns, and providing leadership. They are also the most skilled cooks in the kitchen and use their creativity and knowledge of food to develop and prepare recipes.

Food preparation and serving supervisors oversee the kitchen and non-kitchen staff in a restaurant or food service facility. They may also oversee food preparation workers in fast food, cafeteria, or casual dining restaurants, where the menu is fairly standard from day to day, or in more formal restaurants, where a chef provides specific guidelines and exacting standards on how to prepare each item.

All of these workers—chefs, head cooks, and food preparation and serving supervisors—hire, train, and supervise staff, prepare cost estimates for food and supplies, set work schedules, order supplies, and ensure that the food service establishment runs efficiently and profitably. Additionally, these workers ensure that sanitation and safety standards are observed and comply with local regulations. Fresh food must be stored and cooked properly, work surfaces and dishes clean and sanitary, and staff and customers safe from illness or injury to avoid being closed by the health department or law enforcement.

While all chefs have a role in preparing the food, developing recipes, determining serving sizes, planning menus, ordering food supplies, and overseeing kitchen operations to ensure uniform quality and presentation of meals, different types of chefs may have unique roles to perform or specialize in certain aspects of the job. *Executive chefs, head cooks, and chefs de cuisine*, are primarily responsible for coordinating the work of the cooks and directing the preparation of meals. Executive chefs are in charge of all food service operations and also may supervise several kitchens of a hotel, restaurant or corporate dining operation. A *sous chef*, or sub chef, is the second-in-command and runs the kitchen in the absence of the chef. Many chefs earn fame both for themselves and for their kitchens because of the quality and distinctive nature of the food they serve.

As a greater variety of establishments prepare and serve food, chefs and head cooks and first-line supervisors of food

Chefs, head cooks, and food preparation and serving supervisors work long hours preparing ingredients before cooking.

preparation and serving workers can be found in a greater variety of places. Grocery and specialty food stores employ these workers to develop recipes and prepare meals for customers to carry out. They increasingly work in residential care facilities, such as nursing homes, and in schools and hospitals. Some chefs and head cooks work for individuals rather than for restaurants, cafeterias, or food manufacturers. *Personal chefs* and *private household cooks* plan and prepare meals in private homes according to the client's tastes or dietary needs. They order groceries and supplies, clean the kitchen, and wash dishes and utensils. They also may serve meals. Personal chefs usually prepare a week's worth of meals in the client's home for the client to heat and serve according to directions. They may be self-employed or work as part of a team of personal chefs and employed by a company that provides this service. Private household cooks typically work full time for one client, such as corporate executives, university presidents, or diplomats, who regularly entertain as a part of their official duties.

While the work of chefs and head cooks is concentrated in the kitchen or in providing overall guidance, food preparation and serving supervisors oversee specific areas of operation in food service establishments or the kitchen and counter areas of quick service restaurants. In fast food and casual dining restaurants, they may share many of the same functions with food service managers. They are responsible for dealing with customer complaints, balancing the books at the end of the day, scheduling workers, and ordering supplies. They also supervise and train kitchen and food preparation staff and ensure that these workers know how to gather food supplies, operate equipment, and assemble orders.

Work environment. Restaurants and other food service facilities where these workers are employed are required to be clean and sanitary. Although the seating areas of eating places are often attractive, kitchens can be crowded and hot and filled with potential dangers, such as hot ovens and slippery floors. Job hazards for those working in kitchens include slips and falls, cuts, and burns, but these injuries are seldom serious. Chefs, head cooks, and supervisors are under constant pressure to get meals prepared quickly, while ensuring quality is maintained and safety and sanitation guidelines are observed. Because the pace can be hectic

during peak dining times, workers must be able to communicate clearly so that food orders and service are done correctly.

Work hours in restaurants may include early mornings, late evenings, holidays, and weekends. Schedules for those working in offices, factories and school cafeterias may be more regular. In fine-dining restaurants, work schedules tend to be longer because of the time required to prepare ingredients in advance. Many executive chefs regularly work 12-hour days because they oversee the delivery of foodstuffs early in the day, plan the menu, and prepare those menu items that require the most skill. Depending upon the days of operation, some chefs or other supervisors may take less busy days off to offset the longer hours on other days.

Training, Other Qualifications, and Advancement

Most workers in these occupations have prior experience in the food service or hospitality industries. Most start as food preparation workers or line cooks in a full-service restaurant and work their way up to positions with more responsibility. Some attend cooking school or take vocational training classes and participate in internships or apprenticeship programs to acquire the additional skills needed to create menus and run a business.

Education and training. While most chefs, head cooks, and food preparation and serving supervisors have some postsecondary training, many experienced workers with less education can still be promoted. Formal training may take place at a community college, technical school, culinary arts school, or a 2-year or 4-year college with a degree in hospitality. A growing number of chefs participate in training programs sponsored by independent cooking schools, professional culinary institutes, 2-year or 4-year colleges with a hospitality or culinary arts department, or in the armed forces. Some large hotels and restaurants also operate their own training and job-placement programs for chefs and head cooks. Executive chefs, head cooks, and sous chefs who work in fine-dining restaurants require many years of training and experience.

For students in culinary training programs, most of their time is spent in kitchens learning to prepare meals by practicing cooking skills. They learn knife techniques and proper use and care of kitchen equipment. Training programs also include courses in nutrition, menu planning, portion control, purchasing and inventory methods, proper food storage procedures, and use of leftover food to minimize waste. Students also learn sanitation and public health rules for handling food. Training in food service management, computer accounting and inventory software, and banquet service are featured in some training programs. Most formal training programs also require students to get experience in a commercial kitchen through an internship, apprenticeship, or out-placement program.

Although formal training is an important way to enter the profession, many chefs are trained on the job, receiving real work experience and training from chef-mentors in the restaurants where they work. Others enter the profession through formal apprenticeship programs sponsored by professional culinary institutes, industry associations, and trade unions in coordination with the U.S. Department of Labor. The American Culinary Federation accredits more than 200 formal academic training programs and sponsors apprenticeship programs around the country. Typical apprenticeships last 2 years and combine classroom training and work experience. Accreditation is an indication that a culinary program meets recognized standards regarding course content, facilities, and quality of instruction.

Other qualifications. Chefs, head cooks, and food preparation and serving supervisors must demonstrate strong leadership and communication skills and have the ability to motivate others. Chefs and head cooks also must have an intense desire to cook, be creative, and have a keen sense of taste and smell. Personal cleanliness is essential because most States require health certificates indicating that workers are free from communicable diseases. Knowledge of a foreign language can be an asset because it may improve communication with other restaurant staff, vendors, and the restaurant's clientele.

Certification and advancement. The American Culinary Federation certifies pastry professionals, personal chefs, and culinary educators in addition to various levels of chefs. Certification standards are based primarily on experience and formal training. Although certification is not required, it can help to prove accomplishment and lead to advancement and higher-paying positions.

Advancement opportunities for chefs, head cooks, and food preparation and serving supervisors depend on their training, work experience, ability to perform more responsible and sophisticated tasks, and their leadership abilities.

Food preparation and serving supervisors may advance to become food service managers while some chefs and head cooks may go into business as caterers or personal chefs or open their own restaurant. Others may become instructors in culinary training programs, consultants on kitchen design, or food product or equipment sales representatives. A number of chefs and head cooks advance to executive chef positions or food service management positions. When staying in the restaurant business, advancement usually involves moving to a better, busier, or bigger restaurant or working at the corporate level overseeing several restaurants or food service facilities or testing new recipe, menu, or design concepts. (See the section on food service managers elsewhere in the *Handbook*.)

Employment

Chefs, head cooks, and food preparation and serving supervisors held 941,600 jobs in 2008. Food preparation and serving supervisors held 88 percent of these jobs and chefs and head cooks held the remaining 12 percent. Nearly half of chefs and head cooks were employed at full-service restaurants (those that had table service). About nine percent each were employed by hotels and the special food services industry that includes caterers and food service contractors. Eight percent were self-employed.

Forty-three percent of food preparation and serving supervisors were employed by limited-service eating places, made up mostly of cafeterias and fast food restaurants and other places that offer simple carry-out food items. Another 25 percent were employed by full-service restaurants. Supervisors are also found in schools, the special food services industry, and a wide variety of other places that serve food.

Job Outlook

Job opportunities are expected to be good, despite slower than average employment growth, due to the large numbers of workers who leave the occupation and need to be replaced. However, keen competition is expected for jobs at upscale restaurants that generally pay more.

Employment change. Employment of chefs, head cooks, and food preparation and serving supervisors is expected to increase by 6 percent over the 2008-18 decade, which is more slowly than the average for all occupations. Growth will be generated by increases in population, a growing variety of dining venues, and continued demand for convenience. As more people opt for the time-saving ease of letting others do the cooking, the need for workers to oversee food preparation and serving will increase. Also, there is a growing consumer desire for healthier, made-from-scratch meals that chefs and head cooks can better prepare.

Job prospects. Job openings for chefs, head cooks, and food preparation and serving supervisors are expected to be good through 2018; however, competition should be keen for jobs at the more upscale restaurants that tend to pay more. Workers with a good business sense will have better job prospects, especially at restaurant chains where attention to costs is very important. Although job growth will create many new positions, the majority of job openings will stem from the need to replace workers who leave the occupation. The fast pace, long hours, and high energy levels required for these jobs often lead to high turnover.

Earnings

Earnings of chefs, head cooks, and food preparation and serving supervisors vary greatly by region and the type of employer. Earnings are usually highest in upscale restaurants and hotels, where many executive chefs are employed, and in major metropolitan and resort areas.

Median annual wage-and-salary earnings of chefs and head cooks were $38,770 in May 2008. The middle 50 percent earned between $29,050 and $51,540. The lowest 10 percent earned less than $22,120, and the highest 10 percent earned more than

Projections data from the National Employment Matrix

Occupational Title	SOC Code	Employment, 2008	Projected Employment, 2018	Change, 2008-2018	
				Number	Percent
Supervisors, food preparation and serving workers..........................	35-1000	941,600	997,000	55,400	6
Chefs and head cooks..	35-1011	108,300	108,500	200	0
First-line supervisors/managers of food preparation and serving workers	35-1012	833,300	888,500	55,100	7

(NOTE) Data in this table are rounded. See the discussion of the employment projections table in the *Handbook* introductory chapter on *Occupational Information Included in the Handbook.*

$66,680. Median annual wages in May 2008 in the industries employing the largest number of chefs and head cooks were:

Other amusement and recreation industries $45,650
Traveler accommodation 44,660
Special food services 40,890
Full-service restaurants 36,700
Limited-service eating places 30,060

Median annual wage-and-salary earnings of food preparation and serving supervisors were $28,970 in May 2008. The middle 50 percent earned between $22,530 and $37,290. The lowest 10 percent earned less than $18,530, and the highest 10 percent earned more than $46,810. Median annual wages in May 2008 were $32,560 in full-service restaurants and $25,420 in limited-service eating places, the industries employing the largest numbers of food preparation and serving supervisors.

Some employers provide employees with uniforms and free meals, but Federal law permits employers to deduct from their employees' wages the cost or fair value of any meals or lodging provided, and some employers do so. Chefs, head cooks, and food preparation and serving supervisors who work full time often receive typical benefits, but part-time workers usually do not.

In some large hotels and restaurants, kitchen workers belong to unions. The principal unions are the Hotel Employees and Restaurant Employees International Union and the Service Employees International Union.

Related Occupations

Other people who prepare food items include:

Others who also work closely with these workers in the food service industry include:

Sources of Additional Information

Information about job opportunities may be obtained from local employers and local offices of the State employment service.

Career information about chefs, cooks, and other kitchen workers, including a directory of 2-year and 4-year colleges that offer courses or training programs is available from:
➤ National Restaurant Association, 1200 17th St. NW., Washington, DC 20036. Internet: **http://www.restaurant.org**

Information on the American Culinary Federation's culinary apprenticeship and certification programs and a list of accredited culinary programs is available from:
➤ American Culinary Federation, 180 Center Place Way, St. Augustine, FL 32095. Internet: **http://www.acfchefs.org**

For information about becoming a personal or private chef, contact:
➤ American Personal & Private Chef Association, 4572 Delaware St., San Diego, CA 92116. Internet: **http://www.personalchef.com**

For information about culinary apprenticeship programs registered with the U.S. Department of Labor, contact the local office of your State employment service agency, check the department's apprenticeship web site: **http://www.doleta.gov/OA/eta_default.cfm**, or call the toll free helpline: (877) 872-5627.

The Occupational Information Network (O*NET) provides information on a wide range of occupational characteristics. Links to O*NET appear at the end of the Internet version of this occupational statement, accessible at **http://www.bls.gov/ooh/ocos330.htm**

Cooks and Food Preparation Workers

Significant Points

- Many cooks and food preparation workers are young—35 percent are below the age of 24.

- One-third of these workers are employed part time.

- Job openings are expected to be plentiful because many of these workers will leave the occupation for full-time employment or better wages.

Nature of the Work

Cooks and food preparation workers prepare, season, and cook a wide range of foods—from soups, snacks, and salads to entrees, side dishes, and desserts. They work in a variety of restaurants, as well as other places where food is served, such as grocery stores, schools and hospitals. Cooks prepare and cook meals while food preparation workers assist cooks by performing tasks, such as peeling and cutting vegetables, trimming meat, preparing poultry, and keeping work areas clean and monitoring temperatures of ovens and stovetops.

Specifically, *cooks* measure, mix, and cook ingredients according to recipes, using a variety of equipment, including pots, pans, cutlery, ovens, broilers, grills, slicers, grinders, and blenders. *Food preparation workers* perform routine, repetitive tasks under the direction of chefs, head cooks, or food preparation and serving supervisors. These workers prepare the ingredients for complex dishes by slicing and dicing vegetables, and making salads and cold items. They weigh and measure ingredients, retrieve pots and pans, and stir and strain soups and sauces. Food preparation workers may also cut and grind meats, poultry, and seafood in preparation for cooking. They also clean work areas, equipment, utensils, dishes, and silverware.

Larger restaurants and food service establishments tend to have varied menus and larger kitchen staffs. Teams of restaurant cooks, sometimes called *assistant or line cooks*, each work an assigned station that is equipped with the types of stoves, grills, pans, and ingredients needed for the foods prepared at that station. Job titles often reflect the principal ingredient prepared or the type of cooking performed—*vegetable cook*, *fry cook*, or *grill cook*, for example. Chefs, head cooks, or food preparation and serving supervisors generally direct the work of cooks and food preparation workers (information on chefs, head cooks,

Cooks and food preparation workers must perform their duties quickly to keep up with food orders.

and food preparation and serving supervisors is found elsewhere in the *Handbook*.)

The number, type, and responsibilities of cooks vary depending on where they work, the size of the facility, and the complexity and level of service offered. *Institution and cafeteria cooks*, for example, work in the kitchens of schools, cafeterias, businesses, hospitals, and other institutions. For each meal, they prepare a large quantity of a limited number of entrees, vegetables, and desserts according to preset menus. Meals are generally prepared in advance so diners seldom get the opportunity to special order a meal. *Restaurant cooks* usually prepare a wider selection of dishes, cooking most orders individually. *Short-order cooks* prepare foods in restaurants and coffee shops that emphasize fast service and quick food preparation. They grill and garnish hamburgers, prepare sandwiches, fry eggs, and cook French fries, often working on several orders at the same time. *Fast food cooks* prepare a limited selection of menu items in fast-food restaurants. They cook and package food, such as hamburgers and fried chicken, to be kept warm until served. (Combined food preparation and serving workers, who prepare and serve items in fast-food restaurants, are included with the material on food and beverage serving and related workers elsewhere in the *Handbook*.)

Work environment. Many restaurant and institutional kitchens have modern equipment, convenient work areas, and air conditioning, but kitchens in older and smaller eating places are often not as well designed. Kitchen staffs invariably work in small quarters against hot stoves and ovens. They are under constant pressure to prepare meals quickly, while ensuring quality is maintained and safety and sanitation guidelines are observed. Because the pace can be hectic during peak dining times, workers must be able to communicate clearly so that food orders are completed correctly.

Working conditions vary with the type and quantity of food prepared and the local laws governing food service operations. Workers usually must stand for hours at a time, lifting heavy pots and kettles, and working near hot ovens and grills. The incidence of reported injuries for institution and cafeteria cooks, restaurant cooks, and food preparation workers was comparatively high compared to all occupations, but job hazards, such as falls, cuts, and burns, are seldom serious.

Work hours in restaurants may include early mornings, late evenings, holidays, and weekends. Work schedules of cooks and food preparation workers in factory and school cafeterias may be more regular. In 2008, 31 percent of cooks and almost half of food preparation workers had part-time schedules, compared to 16 percent of workers throughout the economy. Work schedules in fine-dining restaurants, however, tend to be longer because of the time required to prepare ingredients in advance.

The wide range in dining hours and the need for fully-staffed kitchens during all open hours creates work opportunities for students, youth, and other individuals seeking supplemental income, flexible work hours, or variable schedules. Sixteen percent of cooks and food preparation workers were 16 to 19 years old in 2008 and another 18 percent were aged 20 to 24. Kitchen workers employed by schools may work during the school year only, usually for 9 or 10 months. Similarly, resort establishments usually only offer seasonal employment.

Training, Other Qualifications, and Advancement
On-the-job training is the most common method of learning for cooks and food preparation workers; however, restaurant cooks and other cooks who want to take on more advanced cooking duties often attend cooking school. Vocational training programs are available to many high school students and may lead to positions in restaurants. Experience, enthusiasm, and a desire to learn are the most common requirements for advancement to higher skilled cooking jobs or positions in higher paying restaurants.

Education and training. A high school diploma is not required for beginning jobs but is recommended for those planning a career in food services. Most fast-food or short-order cooks and food preparation workers learn their skills on the job. Training generally starts with basic sanitation and workplace safety regulations and continues with instruction on food handling, preparation, and cooking procedures.

Although most cooks and food preparation workers learn on the job, students with an interest in food service may be able to take high school or vocational school courses in kitchen basics and food safety and handling procedures. Additional training opportunities are also offered by many State employment services agencies and local job counseling centers. For example, many school districts, in cooperation with State departments of education, provide on-the-job training and summer workshops for cafeteria kitchen workers who aspire to become cooks.

When hiring restaurant cooks, employers usually prefer applicants who have training after high school. These training programs range from a few months to 2 years or more. Vocational or trade-school programs typically offer basic training in food handling and sanitation procedures, nutrition, slicing and dicing methods for various kinds of meats and vegetables, and basic cooking techniques, such as baking, broiling, and grilling. Longer certificate or degree granting programs, through independent cooking schools, professional culinary institutes, or college degree programs, train cooks who aspire to more responsible positions in fine-dining or upscale restaurants. They offer a wider array of training specialties, such as advanced cooking techniques; cooking for banquets, buffets, or parties; and cuisines and cooking styles from around the world. Some large hotels, restaurants, and the Armed Forces operate their own training and job-placement programs.

Professional culinary institutes, industry associations, and trade unions may also sponsor formal apprenticeship programs for cooks in coordination with the U.S. Department of Labor. The American Culinary Federation accredits more than 200 formal academic training programs and sponsors apprenticeship programs around the country. Typical apprenticeships last 2 years and combine classroom training and work experience. Accreditation is an indication that a culinary program meets recognized standards regarding course content, facilities, and quality of instruction.

Other qualifications. Cooks and food preparation workers must be efficient, quick, and work well as part of a team. Manual dexterity is helpful for cutting, chopping, and plating. These workers also need creativity and a keen sense of taste and smell. Personal cleanliness is essential because most States require health certificates indicating that workers are free from communicable diseases. Knowledge of a foreign language can be an asset because it may improve communication with other restaurant staff, vendors, and the restaurant's clientele.

Certification and advancement. The American Culinary Federation certifies chefs in different skill levels. For cooks seeking certification and advancement to higher-level chef positions, certification can help to demonstrate accomplishment and lead to higher-paying positions.

Advancement opportunities for cooks and food preparation workers depend on their training, work experience, and ability to perform more responsible and sophisticated tasks. Many food preparation workers, for example, may move into assistant or line cook positions or take on more complex food preparation tasks. Cooks who demonstrate an eagerness to learn new cooking skills and to accept greater responsibility may also advance and be asked to train or supervise lesser skilled kitchen staff. Some may become head cooks, chefs, or food preparation and serving supervisors. (See the section on chefs, head cooks, and food preparation and serving supervisors elsewhere in the *Handbook*.) Others may find it necessary to move to other restaurants, often larger or more prestigious ones, in order to advance.

Employment

Cooks and food preparation workers held 3.0 million jobs in 2008. The distribution of jobs among the various types of cooks and food preparation workers was as follows:

Cooks, restaurant 914,200
Food preparation workers 891,900
Cooks, fast food 566,000
Cooks, institution and cafeteria 392,800
Cooks, short order 171,400
Cooks, private household 4,900
Cooks, all other 18,000

Two-thirds of all cooks and food preparation workers were employed in restaurants and other food services and drinking places. About 16 percent worked in institutions such as schools, universities, hospitals, and nursing care facilities. Grocery stores and hotels employed most of the remainder.

Job Outlook

Job opportunities for cooks and food preparation workers are expected to be good because of high turnover and the need to replace the workers who leave these occupations. The enjoyment of eating out and a preference for ready-made meals from a growing population will cause employment of these workers to increase, but slower than the average rate for all occupations over the 2008–18 decade.

Employment change. Employment of cooks and food preparation workers is expected to increase by 6 percent over

Projections data from the National Employment Matrix

Occupational Title	SOC Code	Employment, 2008	Projected Employment, 2018	Change, 2008-2018	
				Number	Percent
Cooks and food preparation workers	35-2000	2,958,100	3,149,600	191,500	6
Cooks	35-2010	2,066,200	2,220,000	153,800	7
Cooks, fast food	35-2011	566,000	608,400	42,400	7
Cooks, institution and cafeteria..	35-2012	391,800	429,700	37,900	10
Cooks, private household	35-2013	4,900	5,100	200	4
Cooks, restaurant...	35-2014	914,200	984,400	70,300	8
Cooks, short order	35-2015	171,400	171,500	100	0
Cooks, all other	35-2019	18,000	20,900	2,900	16
Food preparation workers	35-2021	891,900	929,600	37,800	4

(NOTE) Data in this table are rounded. See the discussion of the employment projections table in the *Handbook* introductory chapter on *Occupational Information Included in the Handbook.*

the 2008–18 decade, more slowly than the average for all occupations. People will continue to enjoy eating out and taking meals home. In response, more restaurants will open and nontraditional food service operations, such as those found inside grocery and convenience stores, will serve more prepared food items. Other places that have dining rooms and cafeterias—such as schools, hospitals, and residential care facilities for the elderly—will open new or expanded food service operations to meet the needs of their growing customer base.

Among food services and drinking places, special food services, which include caterers and food service operators who often provide meals in hospitals, office buildings, or sporting venues on a contract basis, are expected to grow the fastest during the projection period. These companies typically employ large numbers of cafeteria and institution cooks and other cooks who perform cooking duties; employment in these occupations is expected to grow 10 percent and 16 percent, respectively.

Full-service restaurants also will continue to attract patrons and grow in number, but not as fast as the previous decade. As restaurants increase their focus on the carryout business, cooks and food preparation workers will be needed to compete with limited service restaurants and grocery stores. Employment of restaurant cooks is expected to grow by 8 percent.

Limited service eating places, such as fast-food restaurants, sandwich and coffee shops, and other eating places without table service, also are expected to grow during the projection period, as people place greater emphasis on value, quick service, and carryout capability. This will generate greater demand for fast-food cooks. Employment of fast food cooks is expected to increase by 7 percent.

Employment of private household cooks should grow 4 percent, or more slowly than the average for all occupations, and employment of short-order cooks is expected to grow by less than 1 percent, which represents little to no change.

Food preparation workers are expected to grow more slowly than the average for all occupations, or 4 percent. As restaurants and quick service eating places find more efficient ways of preparing meals—such as at central kitchens that may serve multiple outlets or in wholesale and distribution facilities that wash, portion, and season ingredients—food preparation will become simpler, allowing these lower-skilled workers to take on more varied tasks in a growing number of eating places. Additionally, foods requiring simple preparation will increasingly be sold at convenience stores, snack shops, and in grocery stores, which also will employ food preparation workers.

Job prospects. In spite of slower-than-average employment growth, job opportunities for cooks and food preparation workers are expected to be good, primarily because of the very large number of workers that will need to be replaced because of high turnover. Because many of these jobs are part time, people often leave for full-time positions. Individuals seeking full-time positions at high-end restaurants might encounter competition as the number of job applicants exceeds the number of job openings. Generally, there is lower turnover for full-time jobs and at established restaurants that pay well.

Earnings

Earnings of cooks and food preparation workers vary greatly by region and the type of employer. Earnings usually are highest in fine dining restaurants and nicer hotels that have more exacting work standards. These restaurants are usually found in greater numbers in major metropolitan and resort areas.

Median annual wages of cooks, private household were $24,070 in May 2008. The middle 50 percent earned between $19,030 and $36,590. The lowest 10 percent earned less than $16,230, and the highest 10 percent earned more than $56,280.

Median annual wages of institution and cafeteria cooks were $22,210 in May 2008. The middle 50 percent earned between $17,850 and $27,460. The lowest 10 percent earned less than $15,220, and the highest 10 percent earned more than $33,050. Median annual wages in the industries employing the largest numbers of institution and cafeteria cooks were:

General medical and surgical hospitals	$25,070
Special food services	23,550
Community care facilities for the elderly	22,910
Nursing care facilities	22,140
Elementary and secondary schools	20,460

Median annual wages of restaurant cooks were $21,990 in May 2008. The middle 50 percent earned between $18,230 and $26,150. The lowest 10 percent earned less than $15,880, and the highest 10 percent earned more than $31,330. Median annual wages in the industries employing the largest numbers of restaurant cooks were:

Traveler accommodation	$25,570
Other amusement and recreation industries	24,760
Special food services	24,180
Drinking places (alcoholic beverages)	22,210
Full-service restaurants	21,770
Limited-service eating places	19,060

Median annual wages of short-order cooks were $19,260 in May 2008. The middle 50 percent earned between $16,280 and $23,450. The lowest 10 percent earned less than $14,740, and the highest 10 percent earned more than $27,630. Median annual wages in the industries employing the largest numbers of short-order cooks were:

Full-service restaurants	$19,600
Drinking places (alcoholic beverages)	19,550
Grocery stores	19,540
Other amusement and recreation industries	18,720
Limited-service eating places	17,910

Median annual wages of food preparation workers were $18,630 in May 2008. The middle 50 percent earned between $16,180 and $22,500. The lowest 10 percent earned less than $14,730, and the highest 10 percent earned more than $27,440. Median annual wages in the industries employing the largest number of food preparation workers were:

Grocery stores	$19,580
Full-service restaurants	18,580
Limited-service eating places	16,790

Median annual wages of fast-food cooks were $16,880 in May 2008. The middle 50 percent earned between $15,470 and $19,240. The lowest 10 percent earned less than $14,090, and the highest 10 percent earned more than \$22,080. Median annual wages in the industries employing the largest number of fast-food cooks were:

Grocery stores \$19,180
Full-service restaurants 17,250
Limited-service eating places.......................................16,820
Gasoline stations 16,640

Some employers provide employees with uniforms and free meals, but Federal law permits employers to deduct from their employees' wages the cost or fair value of any meals or lodging provided, and some employers do so. Cooks and food preparation workers who work full time often receive typical benefits, but part-time and hourly workers usually do not.

In some large hotels and restaurants, kitchen workers belong to unions. The principal unions are the Hotel Employees and Restaurant Employees International Union and the Service Employees International Union.

Related Occupations

Other occupations in the food service industry include:

Sources of Additional Information

Information about job opportunities may be obtained from local employers and local offices of the State employment service.

Career information for cooks and other kitchen workers, including a directory of 2- and 4-year colleges that offer courses or training programs, is available from:

➤ National Restaurant Association, 1200 17th St. NW., Washington, DC 20036. Internet: **http://www.restaurant.org**

Information on the American Culinary Federation's apprenticeship and certification programs for cooks and a list of accredited culinary programs is available from:

➤ American Culinary Federation, 180 Center Place Way, St. Augustine, FL 32095. Internet: **http://www.acfchefs.org**

For information about culinary apprenticeship programs registered with the U.S. Department of Labor, contact the local office of your State employment service agency or check the department's apprenticeship Web site: **http://www.doleta.gov/atels_bat,** or call the toll free helpline: (877) 872-5627.

The Occupational Information Network (O*NET) provides information on a wide range of occupational characteristics. Links to O*NET appear at the end of the Internet version of this occupational statement, accessible at **http://www.bls.gov/ooh/ocos331.htm**

Food and Beverage Serving and Related Workers

Significant Points

- Most jobs are part time and have few educational requirements, attracting many young people to the occupation—21 percent of these workers were 16 to 19 years old in 2008, about six times the proportion for all workers.

- Job openings are expected to be abundant through 2018, which will create excellent opportunities for jobseekers.

- Tips comprise a major portion of earnings for servers, so keen competition is expected for jobs in fine dining and more popular restaurants where potential tips are greatest.

Nature of the Work

Food and beverage serving and related workers are the front line of customer service in full-service restaurants, casual dining eateries, and other food service establishments. These workers greet customers, escort them to seats and hand them menus, take food and drink orders, and serve food and beverages. They also answer questions, explain menu items and specials, and keep tables and dining areas clean and set for new diners. Most work as part of a team, helping coworkers to improve workflow and customer service.

Waiters and waitresses, also called *servers*, are the largest group of these workers. They take customers' orders, serve food and beverages, prepare itemized checks, and sometimes accept payment. Their specific duties vary considerably, depending on the establishment. In casual-dining restaurants serving routine, straightforward fare, such as salads, soups, and sandwiches, servers are expected to provide fast, efficient, and courteous service. In fine dining restaurants, where more complicated meals are prepared and often served over several courses, waiters and waitresses provide more formal service emphasizing personal, attentive treatment at a more leisurely pace. Waiters

Food and beverage serving workers assist diners at cafeterias.

and waitresses may meet with managers and chefs before each shift to discuss the menu and any new items or specials, review ingredients for potential food allergies, or talk about any food safety concerns. They also discuss coordination between the kitchen and the dining room and any customer service issues from the previous day or shift. In addition, waiters and waitresses usually check the identification of patrons to ensure they meet the minimum age requirement for the purchase of alcohol and tobacco products wherever those items are sold.

Waiters and waitresses sometimes perform the duties of other food and beverage service workers, including escorting guests to tables, serving customers seated at counters, clearing and setting up tables, or operating a cash register. However, full-service restaurants frequently hire other staff, such as hosts and hostesses, cashiers, or dining room attendants, to perform these duties.

Bartenders fill drink orders either taken directly from patrons at the bar or through waiters and waitresses who place drink orders for dining room customers. Bartenders check the identification of customers seated at the bar to ensure they meet the minimum age requirement for the purchase of alcohol and tobacco products. They prepare mixed drinks, serve bottled or draught beer, and pour wine or other beverages. Bartenders must know a wide range of drink recipes and be able to mix drinks accurately, quickly, and without waste. Some establishments, especially those with higher volume, use equipment that automatically measures, pours, and mixes drinks at the push of a button. Bartenders who use this equipment, however, still must work quickly to handle a large volume of drink orders and be familiar with the ingredients for special drink requests. Much of a bartender's work still must be done by hand.

Besides mixing and serving drinks, bartenders stock and prepare garnishes for drinks; maintain an adequate supply of ice, glasses, and other bar supplies; and keep the bar area clean for customers. They also may collect payment, operate the cash register, wash glassware and utensils, and serve food to customers who dine at the bar. Bartenders usually are responsible for ordering and maintaining an inventory of liquor, mixers, and other bar supplies.

Hosts and hostesses welcome guests and maintain reservation and waiting lists. They may direct patrons to coatrooms, restrooms, or to a place to wait until their table is ready. Hosts and hostesses assign guests to tables suitable for the size of their group, escort patrons to their seats, and provide menus. They also enter reservations, arrange parties, and assist with other special requests. In some restaurants, they act as cashiers.

Dining room and cafeteria attendants and bartender helpers— sometimes referred to collectively as the bus staff—assist waiters, waitresses, and bartenders by cleaning and setting tables, removing dirty dishes, and keeping serving areas stocked with supplies. They may also assist waiters and waitresses by bringing meals out of the kitchen, distributing dishes to individual diners, filling water glasses, and delivering condiments. *Cafeteria attendants* stock serving tables with food, trays, dishes, and silverware. They may carry trays to dining tables for patrons. Bartender helpers keep bar equipment clean and glasses washed. Dishwashers clean dishes, cutlery, and kitchen utensils and equipment.

Food also is prepared and served in limited-service eateries, which don't employ servers and specialize in simpler preparations that often are made in advance. Two occupations with large numbers of workers are common in these types of establishments: *combined food preparation and serving workers, including fast food*; and *counter attendants, cafeteria, food concession, and coffee shop*. Combined food preparation and serving workers are employed primarily by fast food restaurants. They take food and beverage orders, retrieve items when ready, fill drink cups, and accept payment. They also may heat food items and assemble salads and sandwiches, which constitutes food preparation. Counter attendants take orders and serve food in snack bars, cafeterias, movie theatres, and coffee shops over a counter or steam table. They may fill cups with coffee, soda, and other beverages and may prepare fountain specialties, such as milkshakes and ice cream sundaes. Counter attendants take carryout orders from diners and wrap or place items in containers. They clean counters, write itemized bills, and sometimes accept payment. Other workers, referred to as *foodservers, nonrestaurant*, serve food to patrons outside of a restaurant environment. They might deliver room service meals in hotels or meals to hospital rooms or act as carhops, bringing orders to parked cars.

Work environment. Food and beverage service workers are on their feet most of the time and often carry heavy trays of food, dishes, and glassware. During busy dining periods, they are under pressure to serve customers quickly and efficiently. The work is relatively safe, but injuries from slips, cuts, and burns often result from hurrying or mishandling sharp tools. Three occupations—food servers, nonrestaurant; dining room and cafeteria attendants and bartender helpers; and dishwashers—reported higher incident rates than many occupations throughout the economy.

Part-time work is more common among food and beverage serving and related workers than among workers in almost any other occupation. In 2008, those on part-time schedules included half of all waiters and waitresses and almost three-fourths of all hosts and hostesses.

Food service and drinking establishments typically maintain long dining hours and offer flexible and varied work opportunities. Many food and beverage serving and related workers work evenings, weekends, and holidays. The long business hours allow for more flexible schedules that appeal to many teenagers who can gain valuable work experience. More than one-fifth of all food and beverage serving and related workers were 16 to 19 years old in 2008—about six times the proportion for all workers.

Training, Other Qualifications, and Advancement
Most food and beverage service jobs are entry level and require a high school diploma or less. Generally, training is received on the job; however, those who wish to work at more upscale restaurants, where income from tips is greater and service standards are higher, may need previous experience or vocational training.

Education and training. There are no specific educational requirements for most food and beverage service jobs. Many employers prefer to hire high school graduates for waiter and waitress, bartender, and host and hostess positions, but completion of high school usually is not required for fast-food workers, counter attendants, dishwashers, and dining room attendants and bartender helpers. Many entrants to these jobs are in their late teens or early twenties and have a high school education or less. Usually, they have little or no work experience. Food and beverage service jobs are a major source of part-time employment for high school and college students, multiple job holders, and those seeking supplemental incomes.

All new employees receive some training from their employer. They learn safe food handling procedures and sanitation practices, for example. Some employers, particularly those in fast-food restaurants, teach new workers using self-study programs, on-line programs, audiovisual presentations, and instructional booklets that explain food preparation and service skills. But most food and beverage serving and related workers pick up their skills by observing and working with more experienced workers. Some full-service restaurants also provide new dining room employees with some form of classroom training that alternates with periods of on-the-job work experience. These training programs communicate the operating philosophy of the restaurant, help establish a personal rapport with other staff, teach formal serving techniques, and instill a desire to work as a team. They also provide an opportunity to discuss customer service situations and the proper ways to handle unpleasant circumstances or unruly patrons.

Some food serving workers can acquire more skills by attending relevant classes offered by public or private vocational schools, restaurant associations, or large restaurant chains. Some bartenders acquire their skills through formal vocational training either by attending a school for bartending or a vocational and technical school where bartending classes are taught. These programs often include instruction on State and local laws and regulations, cocktail recipes, proper attire and conduct, and stocking a bar. Some of these schools help their graduates find jobs. Although few employers require any minimum level of educational attainment, some specialized training is usually needed in food handling and legal issues surrounding serving alcoholic beverages. Employers are more likely to hire and promote employees based on people skills and personal qualities than education.

Other qualifications. Restaurants rely on good food and customer service to retain loyal customers and succeed in a competitive industry. Food and beverage serving and related workers who exhibit excellent personal qualities—such as a neat appearance, an ability to work as part of a team, and a natural rapport with customers—will be highly sought after. Most States require workers who serve alcoholic beverages to be at least 18 years of age, but some States require servers to be older. For bartender jobs, many employers prefer to hire people who are 25 or older. All servers that serve alcohol need to be familiar with State and local laws concerning the sale of alcoholic beverages.

Waiters and waitresses need a good memory to avoid confusing customers' orders and to recall faces, names, and preferences of frequent patrons. Knowledge of a foreign language can be helpful to communicate with a diverse clientele and staff. Restaurants and hotels that have rigid table service standards often offer higher wages and have greater income potential from tips, but they may also have stiffer employment require-

ments, such as prior table service experience or higher education attainment than other establishments.

Advancement. Due to the relatively small size of most food-serving establishments, opportunities for promotion are limited. After gaining experience, some dining room and cafeteria attendants and bartender helpers advance to waiter, waitress, or bartender jobs. For waiters, waitresses, and bartenders, advancement usually is limited to finding a job in a busier or more expensive restaurant or bar where prospects for tip earnings are better. Some bartenders, hosts and hostesses, and waiters and waitresses advance to supervisory jobs, such as dining room supervisor, maitre d', assistant manager, or restaurant general manager. A few bartenders open their own businesses. In larger restaurant chains, food and beverage service workers who excel often are invited to enter the company's formal management training program. (For more information, see food service managers elsewhere in the *Handbook*.)

Employment

Food and beverage serving and related workers held 7.7 million jobs in 2008. The distribution of jobs among the various food and beverage serving occupations was as follows:

Combined food preparation and serving workers, including fast food	2,701,700
Waiters and waitresses	2,381,600
Counter attendants, cafeteria, food concession, and coffee shop	525,400
Dishwashers	522,900
Bartenders	508,700
Dining room and cafeteria attendants and bartender helpers	420,700
Hosts and hostesses, restaurant, lounge, and coffee shop	350,700
Food servers, nonrestaurant	189,800
All other food preparation and serving related workers	50,900

The overwhelming majority of jobs for food and beverage serving and related workers were found in food services and drinking places, such as restaurants, fast food outlets, bars, and catering or contract food service operations. Other jobs were in hotels, motels, and other traveler accommodation establishments; amusement, gambling, and recreation establishments; educational services; nursing care facilities; and civic and social organizations.

Jobs are located throughout the country but are more plentiful in larger cities and tourist areas. Vacation resorts offer seasonal employment.

Job Outlook

Average employment growth is expected, and job opportunities should be excellent for food and beverage serving and related workers as turnover is generally very high among these workers, but job competition is often keen for jobs at upscale restaurants.

Employment change. Overall employment of these workers is expected to increase by 10 percent over the 2008-18 decade, which is about as fast as the average for all occupations. Food and beverage serving and related workers are projected to have one of the largest numbers of new jobs arise, about 761,000,

Projections data from the National Employment Matrix

Occupational Title	SOC Code	Employment, 2008	Projected Employment, 2018	Change, 2008-2018	
				Number	Percent
Food and beverage serving and related workers	–	7,652,400	8,413,100	760,700	10
Food and beverage serving workers..	35-3000	6,307,200	6,962,300	655,100	10
Bartenders	35-3011	508,700	549,500	40,800	8
Fast food and counter workers...	35-3020	3,227,100	3,670,400	443,300	14
Combined food preparation and serving workers, including fast food	35-3021	2,701,700	3,096,000	394,300	15
Counter attendants, cafeteria, food concession, and coffee shop	35-3022	525,400	574,400	49,000	9
Waiters and waitresses	35-3031	2,381,600	2,533,300	151,600	6
Food servers, nonrestaurant	35-3041	189,800	209,100	19,300	10
Other food preparation and serving related workers....................	35-9000	1,345,200	1,450,800	105,600	8
Dining room and cafeteria attendants and bartender helpers.....	35-9011	420,700	444,000	23,300	6
Dishwashers...	35-9021	522,900	583,400	60,400	12
Hosts and hostesses, restaurant, lounge, and coffee shop.........	35-9031	350,700	373,400	22,800	6
Food preparation and serving related workers, all other............	35-9099	50,900	50,000	-900	-2

(NOTE) Data in this table are rounded. See the discussion of the employment projections table in the *Handbook* introductory chapter on *Occupational Information Included in the Handbook.*

over this period. The growth in jobs is expected to increase as the population continues to expand. However, employment will grow more slowly than in the past as people change their dining habits. The growing popularity of take-out food and the growing number and variety of places that offer carryout options, including at many full-service restaurants, will slow the growth of waiters and waitresses and other serving workers.

Projected employment growth will vary by job type. Employment of combined food preparation and serving workers, which includes fast-food workers, is expected to increase faster than the average for all occupations. The limited service segment of the food services and drinking places industry has a low price advantage, fast service, and has been adding healthier foods. Slower than average employment growth is expected for waiters and waitresses, hosts and hostesses, and dining room and cafeteria attendants and bartender helpers, as more people use take-out service. Employment of bartenders, dishwashers, and counter attendants, cafeteria, food concession, and coffee shop will grow about as fast as average. Nonrestaurant servers, such as those who deliver food trays in hotels, hospitals, residential care facilities, or catered events, are expected to have average employment growth.

Job prospects. Job opportunities at most eating and drinking places will be excellent because many people in these occupations change jobs frequently, which creates a large number of openings. Keen competition is expected, however, for jobs in popular restaurants and fine dining establishments, where potential earnings from tips are greatest.

Earnings

Food and beverage serving and related workers derive their earnings from a combination of hourly wages and customer tips. Earnings vary greatly, depending on the type of job and establishment. For example, fast-food workers and hosts and hostesses usually do not receive tips, so their wage rates may be higher than those of waiters and waitresses and bartenders in full-service restaurants, but their overall earnings might be lower. In many full-service restaurants, tips are higher than

wages. In some restaurants, workers contribute all or a portion of their tips to a tip pool, which is distributed among qualifying workers. Tip pools allow workers who don't usually receive tips directly from customers, such as dining room attendants, to feel a part of a team and to share in the rewards of good service.

In May 2008, median hourly wages (including tips) of waiters and waitresses were $8.01. The middle 50 percent earned between $7.32 and $10.35. The lowest 10 percent earned less than $6.73, and the highest 10 percent earned more than $14.26 an hour. For most waiters and waitresses, higher earnings are primarily the result of receiving more in tips rather than higher hourly wages. Tips usually average between 10 percent and 20 percent of guests' checks; waiters and waitresses working in busy or expensive restaurants earn the most.

Bartenders had median hourly wages (including tips) of $8.54. The middle 50 percent earned between $7.53 and $10.98. The lowest 10 percent earned less than $7.00, and the highest 10 percent earned more than $14.93 an hour. Like waiters and waitresses, bartenders employed in public bars may receive more than half of their earnings as tips. Service bartenders often are paid higher hourly wages to offset their lower tip earnings.

Median hourly wages (including tips) of dining room and cafeteria attendants and bartender helpers were $8.05. The middle 50 percent earned between $7.39 and $9.44. The lowest 10 percent earned less than $6.82, and the highest 10 percent earned more than $11.67 an hour. Most received over half of their earnings as wages; the rest of their income was a share of the proceeds from tip pools.

Median hourly wages of hosts and hostesses were $8.42. The middle 50 percent earned between $7.50 and $9.70. The lowest 10 percent earned less than $6.88, and the highest 10 percent earned more than $11.89 an hour. Wages comprised the majority of their earnings. In some cases, wages were supplemented by proceeds from tip pools.

Median hourly wages of combined food preparation and serving workers, including fast food, were $7.90. The middle 50 percent earned between $7.26 and $9.12. The lowest 10 percent earned less than $6.67, and the highest 10 percent earned more than $10.67 an hour. Although some combined food preparation and serving workers receive a part of their earnings as tips, fast-food workers usually do not.

Median hourly wages of counter attendants in cafeterias, food concessions, and coffee shops (including tips) were $8.42. The middle 50 percent earned between $7.57 and $9.64 an hour. The lowest 10 percent earned less than $6.97, and the highest 10 percent earned more than $11.73 an hour.

Median hourly wages of dishwashers were $8.19. The middle 50 percent earned between $7.47 and $9.35. The lowest 10 percent earned less than $6.90, and the highest 10 percent earned more than $10.74 an hour.

Median hourly wages of food servers outside of restaurants were $9.32. The middle 50 percent earned between $7.93 and $11.64. The lowest 10 percent earned less than $7.20, and the highest 10 percent earned more than $14.69 an hour.

Many beginning or inexperienced workers earn the Federal minimum wage ($7.25 per hour as of July 24, 2009), but many States set minimum wages higher than the Federal minimum. Also, various minimum wage exceptions apply under specific circumstances to disabled workers, full-time students, youth under age 20 in their first 90 days of employment, tipped employees, and student-learners. Tipped employees are those who customarily and regularly receive more than $30 a month in tips. The employer may consider tips as part of wages, but the employer must pay at least $2.13 an hour in direct wages.

Many employers provide free meals and furnish uniforms, but some may deduct from wages the cost, or fair value, of any meals or lodging provided. Food and beverage service workers who work full time often receive typical benefits, but part-time workers usually do not. In some large restaurants and hotels, food and beverage serving and related workers belong to unions—principally the Unite HERE and the Service Employees International Union.

Related Occupations

Other workers who prepare or serve food and drink for diners include:

Sources of Additional Information

Information about job opportunities may be obtained from local employers and local offices of State employment services agencies.

A guide to careers in restaurants plus a list of 2- and 4-year colleges offering food service programs and related scholarship information is available from:
➤ National Restaurant Association, 1200 17th St. NW., Washington, DC 20036. Internet: **http://www.restaurant.org**

For general information on hospitality careers, contact:
➤ International Council on Hotel, Restaurant, and Institutional Education, 2810 North Parham Rd., Suite 230, Richmond, VA 23294. Internet: **http://www.chrie.org**

The Occupational Information Network (O*NET) provides information on a wide range of occupational characteristics. Links to O*NET appear at the end of the Internet version of this occupational statement, accessible at **http://www.bls.gov/ooh/ocos162.htm**

Building and Grounds Cleaning and Maintenance Occupations

Building Cleaning Workers

Significant Points

- Entry-level workers need no formal education and learn on the job.

- Most job openings result from the need to replace the many workers who leave this very large occupation.

- Job prospects are expected to be good.

Nature of the Work

Building cleaning workers keep office buildings, hospitals, stores, apartment houses, hotels, and residences clean, sanitary, and in good condition. Some do only cleaning, while others have a wide range of duties.

Janitors and cleaners perform a variety of heavy cleaning duties, such as cleaning floors, shampooing rugs, washing walls and glass, and removing trash. They may fix leaky faucets, empty trash cans, do painting and carpentry, replenish bathroom supplies, mow lawns, and see that heating and air-conditioning equipment works properly. On a typical day, janitors may wet-or-dry-mop floors, clean bathrooms, vacuum carpets, dust furniture, make minor repairs, and exterminate insects and rodents. They may also clean snow or debris from sidewalks in front of buildings and notify management of the need for major repairs. While janitors typically perform most of the duties mentioned, cleaners tend to work for companies that specialize in one type of cleaning activity, such as washing windows.

Maids and housekeeping cleaners perform any combination of light cleaning duties to keep private households or commercial establishments, such as hotels, restaurants, hospitals, and nursing homes, clean and orderly. In private households, they dust and polish furniture; sweep, mop, and wax floors; vacuum; and clean ovens, refrigerators, and bathrooms. They also may wash dishes, polish silver, and change and make beds. Some

Building cleaning workers are employed in hospitals, office buildings, and other settings.

wash, fold, and iron clothes; a few wash windows. General houseworkers also may take clothes and laundry to the cleaners, buy groceries, and perform other errands. In hotels, aside from cleaning and maintaining the premises, maids and housekeeping cleaners may deliver ironing boards, cribs, and rollaway beds to guests' rooms. In hospitals, they also may wash bed frames, make beds, and disinfect and sanitize equipment and supplies with germicides. Janitors, maids, and cleaners use many kinds of equipment, tools, and cleaning materials. For one job, they may need standard cleaning implements; another may require an electric floor polishing machine and a special cleaning solution. Improved building materials, chemical cleaners, and power equipment have made many tasks easier and less time consuming, but cleaning workers must learn the proper use of equipment and cleaners to avoid harming floors, fixtures, building occupants, and themselves.

Cleaning supervisors coordinate, schedule, and supervise the activities of janitors and cleaners. They assign tasks and inspect building areas to see that work has been done properly; they also issue supplies and equipment and inventory stocks to ensure that supplies on hand are adequate. They may be expected to screen and hire job applicants; train new and experienced employees; and recommend promotions, transfers, or dismissals. Supervisors may prepare reports concerning the occupancy of rooms, hours worked, and department expenses. Some also perform cleaning duties.

Building cleaning workers in large office and residential buildings, and more recently in large hotels, often work in teams consisting of workers who specialize in vacuuming, picking up trash, and cleaning restrooms, among other things. Supervisors conduct inspections to ensure that the building is cleaned properly and the team is functioning efficiently. In hotels, one member of the team is responsible for reporting electronically to the supervisor when rooms are cleaned.

Work environment. Because office buildings generally are cleaned while they are empty, many cleaning workers work evening hours. Some, however, such as school and hospital custodians, work in the daytime. When there is a need for 24-hour maintenance, janitors may be assigned to shifts. Many full-time building cleaners worked about 40 hours a week in 2008, but a

substantial number worked part time. Part-time cleaners usually work in the evenings and on weekends.

Most building cleaning workers work indoors, but some work outdoors part of the time, sweeping walkways, mowing lawns, or shoveling snow. Working with machines can be noisy, and some tasks, such as cleaning bathrooms and trash rooms, can be dirty and unpleasant. Building cleaning workers experience injuries more frequently than workers in most other occupations. They may suffer cuts, bruises, and burns from machines, handtools, and chemicals. They spend most of their time on their feet, sometimes lifting or pushing heavy furniture or equipment. Many tasks, such as dusting or sweeping, require constant bending, stooping, and stretching. Lifting the increasingly heavier mattresses at nicer hotels in order to change the linens can cause back injuries and sprains.

Training, Other Qualifications, and Advancement

Most building cleaning workers, except supervisors, do not need any formal education and mainly learn their skills on the job or in informal training sessions sponsored by their employers. Supervisors, though, generally have at least a high school diploma and often some college.

Education and training. No special education is required for most entry-level janitorial or cleaning jobs, but workers should be able to perform simple arithmetic and follow instructions. High school shop courses are helpful for jobs involving repair work. Most building cleaners learn their skills on the job. Beginners usually work with an experienced cleaner, doing routine cleaning. As they gain more experience, they are assigned more complicated tasks. In some cities, programs run by unions, government agencies, or employers teach janitorial skills. Students learn how to clean buildings thoroughly and efficiently; how to select and safely use various cleansing agents; and how to operate and maintain machines, such as wet-and-dry vacuums, buffers, and polishers. Students learn to plan their work, to follow safety and health regulations, to interact positively with people in the buildings they clean, and to work without supervision. Instruction in minor electrical, plumbing, and other repairs also may be given.

Supervisors of building cleaning workers usually need at least a high school diploma, but many have completed some college or earned a degree, especially those who work at places where clean rooms and well-functioning buildings are a necessity, such as in hospitals and hotels. In many establishments, they are required to take some in-service training to improve their housekeeping techniques and procedures and to enhance their supervisory skills.

Other qualifications. Employers usually look for dependable, hard-working individuals who are in good health, follow directions well, and get along with other people.

Certification and advancement. A small number of cleaning supervisors and managers are members of the International Executive Housekeepers Association, which offers two kinds of certification programs for cleaning supervisors and managers: Certified Executive Housekeeper (CEH) and Registered Executive Housekeeper (REH). The CEH designation is offered to those with a high school education, while the REH designation is offered to those who have a 4-year college degree. Both designations are earned by attending courses and passing exams

Projections data from the National Employment Matrix

Occupational Title	SOC Code	Employment, 2008	Projected Employment, 2018	Change, 2008-2018	
				Number	Percent
Building cleaning workers	–	4,139,000	4,343,300	204,300	5
First-line supervisors/managers of housekeeping and janitorial workers..	37-1011	251,100	263,900	12,800	5
Building cleaning workers	37-2010	3,887,900	4,079,400	191,500	5
Janitors and cleaners, except maids and housekeeping cleaners..	37-2011	2,375,300	2,479,400	104,100	4
Maids and housekeeping cleaners..	37-2012	1,498,200	1,583,700	85,600	6
Building cleaning workers, all other...	37-2019	14,500	16,200	1,700	12

(NOTE) Data in this table are rounded. See the discussion of the employment projections table in the *Handbook* introductory chapter on *Occupational Information Included in the Handbook.*

and both must be renewed every 3 years to ensure that workers keep abreast of new cleaning methods. Those with the REH designation usually oversee the cleaning services of hotels, hospitals, casinos, and other large institutions that rely on well-trained experts for their cleaning needs.

Advancement opportunities for workers usually are limited in organizations where they are the only maintenance worker. Where there is a large maintenance staff, however, cleaning workers can be promoted to supervisor or to area supervisor or manager. Some janitors open their own maintenance or cleaning businesses.

Employment

Building cleaning workers held about 4.1 million jobs in 2008. About 299,000 were self-employed.

Janitors and cleaners worked in nearly every type of establishment and held about 2.4 million jobs. Around 33 percent of janitors worked for firms supplying services to buildings and dwellings, about 20 percent were employed in educational services, and 6 percent worked in government. About 132,700 were self employed.

Maids and housekeepers held about 1.5 million jobs. Private households employed about 30 percent of these workers, while hotels, motels, and other traveler accommodations employed 29 percent. Hospitals, nursing homes, and other residential care facilities employed about 17 percent. Although cleaning jobs can be found in all cities and towns, most are located in highly populated areas where there are many office buildings, schools, apartment houses, nursing homes, and hospitals. About 106,900 maids and housekeeping cleaners were self employed in 2008.

First-line supervisors of housekeeping and janitorial workers held 251,100 jobs. Approximately 22 percent worked in firms supplying services to buildings and dwellings, while approximately 15 percent were employed in educational services. About 12 percent worked in hotels, motels, and all other traveler accommodation while about 9 percent worked in healthcare organizations. About 58,400 were self employed.

Job Outlook

Overall employment of building cleaning workers is expected to grow more slowly than the average, and job opportunities are expected to be good.

Employment change. The number of building cleaning workers is expected to grow by 5 percent from 2008 and 2018, more slowly than the average for all occupations. Unlike some occupations, increased productivity is not expected to impact the employment of building cleaning workers. Despite small improvements in cleaning supplies, tools, and processes, roughly the same number of workers will be needed for any given building.

Employment of janitors and cleaners is projected to increase by 4 percent, more slowly than the average for all occupations. As the pace of construction contracts and fewer buildings are built, growth in this occupation should be relatively slow. Many new jobs are expected in healthcare, however, as this industry is expected to grow rapidly, and in administrative support firms as more claiming work is contracted out. Employment of maids and housekeeping cleaners is also expected to increase more slowly than the average, growing by 6 percent from 2008 to 2018. Many new jobs are expected in hotels as demand for accommodations increases, in private households as more people purchase residential cleaning services, and companies that supply maid services on a contract basis, as more of this work is contracted out. Employment of supervisors and managers of these workers, in addition, is expected to grow more slowly than the average, increasing by 5 percent. An increasing number of supervisors will be needed to manage the growing number of janitors, maids, and other cleaning workers.

Job prospects. Job prospects are expected to be good. Most job openings should result from the need to replace the many workers who leave this very large occupation.

Earnings

Median hourly wages of janitors and cleaners, except maids and housekeeping cleaners, were $10.31 in May 2008. The middle 50 percent earned between $8.42 and $13.30. The lowest 10 percent earned less than $7.41and the highest 10 percent earned more than $17.08. Median hourly wages in May 2008 in the industries employing the largest numbers of janitors and cleaners, except maids and housekeeping cleaners, were as follows:

Local government..$12.82
Elementary and secondary schools 12.45
General medical and surgical hospitals..........................11.42
Colleges, universities, and professional schools 11.90
Services to buildings and dwellings 9.31

Median hourly wages of maids and housekeeping cleaners were $9.13 in May 2008. The middle 50 percent earned between $7.92 and $11.10. The lowest 10 percent earned less than $7.09, and the highest 10 percent earned more than $13.72.

Median hourly wages in general medical and surgical hospitals were $10.31, while median hourly wages in the traveler accommodation industry were $8.75 in May 2008.

Median hourly wages of wage-and-salary first-line supervisors and managers of housekeeping and janitorial workers were $16.34 in May 2008. The middle 50 percent earned between $12.82 and $21.07. The lowest 10 percent earned less than $10.33, and the highest 10 percent earned more than $26.29. Median hourly wages in May 2008 in the industries employing the largest numbers of first-line supervisors and managers of housekeeping and janitorial workers were as follows:

Local government 19.65
Elementary and secondary schools 18.84
Nursing care facilities 15.78
Services to buildings and dwellings 15.39
Traveler accommodation 14.07

Related Occupations

Workers who also specialize in one of the many job functions of janitors and cleaners include:

Sources of Additional Information

Information about janitorial jobs may be obtained from State employment service offices.

For information on certification in executive housekeeping, contact:

➤ International Executive Housekeepers Association, Inc., 1001 Eastwind Dr., Suite 301, Westerville, OH 43081-3361. Internet: **http://www.ieha.org**

The Occupational Information Network (O*NET) provides information on a wide range of occupational characteristics. Links to O*NET appear at the end of the Internet version of this occupational statement, accessible at **http://www.bls.gov/ooh/ocos174.htm**

Grounds Maintenance Workers

Significant Points

- Most grounds maintenance workers need no formal education and are trained on the job; however, some workers may require formal education.

- Occupational characteristics include full-time and part-time jobs, seasonal jobs, physically demanding work, and low earnings.

- Job opportunities are expected to be good.

Nature of the Work

Grounds maintenance workers perform a variety of tasks necessary to achieve a pleasant and functional outdoor environment. They mow lawns, rake leaves, trim hedges and trees; plant flowers; and otherwise ensure that the grounds of houses, businesses, and parks are attractive, orderly, and healthy. They also

care for indoor gardens and plantings in commercial and public facilities, such as malls, hotels, and botanical gardens.

These workers use handtools such as shovels, rakes, pruning and handsaws, hedge and brush trimmers, and axes. They also use power lawnmowers, chain saws, leaf blowers, and electric clippers. Some use equipment such as tractors and twin-axle vehicles.

Grounds maintenance workers can be divided into several specialties, including landscaping workers, groundskeeping workers, pesticide handlers, tree trimmers, and grounds maintenance supervisors. In general, these specialties have varying job duties, but in many cases their responsibilities overlap.

Landscaping workers create new functional outdoor areas and upgrade existing landscapes, but also may help maintain landscapes. Their duties include planting bushes, trees, sod, and other forms of vegetation, as well as, edging, trimming, fertilizing, watering, and mulching lawns and grounds. They also grade property by creating or smoothing hills and inclines, install lighting or sprinkler systems, and build walkways, terraces, patios, decks, and fountains. Landscaping workers provide their services in a variety of residential and commercial settings, such as homes, apartment buildings, office buildings, shopping malls, and hotels and motels.

Groundskeeping workers, also called *groundskeepers*, usually focus on maintaining existing grounds. In addition to caring for sod, plants, and trees, they rake and mulch leaves, clear snow from walkways and parking lots, and use irrigation methods to adjust water consumption and prevent waste. These individuals work on athletic fields, golf courses, cemeteries, university campuses, and parks, as well as many of the same settings as landscaping workers. They also see to the proper upkeep and repair of sidewalks, parking lots, groundskeeping equipment, pools, fountains, fences, planters, and benches.

Groundskeeping workers who care for athletic fields keep natural and artificial turf in top condition, mark out boundaries, and paint turf with team logos and names before events. They mow, water, fertilize, and aerate the fields regularly. They must make sure that the underlying soil on fields with natural turf has the required composition to allow proper drainage and to support the grasses used on the field. In sports venues, they vacuum and disinfect synthetic turf after its use to prevent the growth of harmful bacteria, and they remove the turf and replace the cushioning pad periodically.

Groundskeepers in parks and recreation facilities care for lawns, trees, and shrubs; maintain playgrounds; clean buildings; and keep parking lots, picnic areas, and other public spaces free of litter. They also may erect and dismantle snow fences, and maintain swimming pools. These workers inspect buildings and equipment, make needed repairs, and keep everything freshly painted.

Workers who maintain golf courses are called *greenskeepers*. Greenskeepers do many of the same things as other groundskeepers, but they also periodically relocate the holes on putting greens to prevent uneven wear of the turf and to add interest and challenge to the game. Greenskeepers also keep canopies, benches, ball washers, and tee markers repaired and freshly painted.

Some groundskeepers specialize in caring for cemeteries and memorial gardens. They dig graves to specified depths, gener-

Grounds maintenance workers mow lawns and trim hedges and trees.

ally using a backhoe. They mow grass regularly, apply fertilizers and other chemicals, prune shrubs and trees, plant flowers, and remove debris from graves.

Pesticide handlers, sprayers, and applicators, vegetation mix herbicides, fungicides, or insecticides and apply them through sprays, dusts, or vapors into the soil or onto plants. Those working for chemical lawn service firms are more specialized, inspecting lawns for problems and applying fertilizers, pesticides, and other chemicals to stimulate growth and prevent or control weeds, diseases, or insect infestation. Many practice integrated pest-management techniques.

Tree trimmers and pruners, sometimes called *arborists*, cut away dead or excess branches from trees or shrubs to clear roads, sidewalks, or utilities' equipment, or to improve the appearance, health, and value of trees. Some specialize in diagnosing and treating tree diseases, and in performing preventive measures to keep trees healthy. Some may plant trees. Some of these workers also specialize in pruning, trimming and shaping ornamental trees and shrubs for private residences, golf courses, or other institutional grounds. Tree trimmers and pruners use handsaws, pole saws, shears, and clippers. When trimming near power lines, they usually work on truck-mounted lifts and use power pruners.

Supervisors of landscaping and groundskeeping workers oversee grounds maintenance work. They prepare cost estimates, schedule work for crews on the basis of weather conditions or the availability of equipment, perform spot checks to ensure the quality of the service, and suggest changes in work procedures. In addition, supervisors train workers; keep employees' time records and record work performed; and may assist workers when deadlines are near. Supervisors who own their own business are also known as *landscape contractors*. They also often call themselves *landscape designers* if they create landscape design plans. Landscape designers also design exterior floral displays by planting annual or perennial flowers. Some work with landscape architects. (Landscape architects, discussed elsewhere in the *Handbook*, create more technical architectural plans and usually work on larger projects.) Supervisors of workers on golf courses are known as *superintendents*.

Work environment. Many grounds maintenance jobs are seasonal, available mainly in the spring, summer, and fall, when most planting, mowing, trimming, and cleanup are necessary. Most of the work is performed outdoors in all kinds of weather. It can be physically demanding and repetitive, involving bending, lifting, and shoveling. This occupation offers opportunities for both part-time and full-time work.

According to BLS data, full-time landscaping and groundskeeping workers, tree trimmers and pruners, and the supervisors of these workers experienced a much higher than average rate of work-related injury and illness. Those who work with pesticides, fertilizers, and other chemicals, as well as dangerous equipment and tools such as power lawnmowers and chain saws, must exercise safety precautions. Workers who use motorized equipment must take care to protect their hearing.

Training, Other Qualifications, and Advancement

Most grounds maintenance workers need no formal education and are trained on the job. However, some workers may require formal education in areas such as landscape design, horticulture, or business management.

Education and training. There usually are no minimum educational requirements for entry-level positions in grounds maintenance. In 2008, most workers had no education beyond high school. A short period of on-the-job training generally is sufficient to teach new hires the necessary skills, which often include planting and maintenance procedures; the operation of mowers, trimmers, leaf blowers, small tractors and other equipment; and proper safety procedures. Large institutional employers such as golf courses or municipalities may supplement on-the-job training with coursework in subjects like horticulture or small engine repair. A bachelor's degree may be needed for those who want to become specialists.

Supervisors may need a high school diploma, and may receive several months of on-the-job training. Formal training in landscape design, horticulture, arboriculture, or business may improve an applicant's chances for employment. Landscape designers may be required to obtain such training.

Licensure. Most States require licensure or certification for workers who apply pesticides. Requirements vary but usually include passing a test on the proper use and disposal of insecticides, herbicides, and fungicides. Some States also require that landscape contractors be licensed.

Other qualifications. Employers look for responsible, self-motivated individuals because grounds maintenance workers often work with little supervision. Employers want people who can learn quickly and follow instructions accurately so that time is not wasted and plants are not damaged. Driving a vehicle is often needed for these jobs. If driving is required, preference is given to applicants with a driver's license, a good driving record, and experience driving a truck.

Certification and advancement. Laborers who demonstrate a proficiency in the work and have good communication skills may advance to crew leader or other supervisory positions. Becoming a grounds manager or landscape contractor may require some formal education beyond high school in addition to several years of experience. Some workers with groundskeeping backgrounds may start their own businesses after several years of experience.

Certification from a professional organization may improve a worker's chances for advancement. The Professional Grounds Management Society offers voluntary certification to grounds managers who have a bachelor's degree in a relevant major with at least 4 years of experience, including 2 years as a supervisor; an associate degree in a relevant major with 6 years of experience, including 3 years as a supervisor; or 8 years of experience including 4 years as a supervisor, and no degree. Additionally, candidates for certification must pass two examinations covering subjects such as insects and diseases, soils, trees and shrubs, turf management, irrigation, and budgets and finances. This organization also offers certification for grounds technicians. Candidates for this program must have a high school diploma or GED as well as 2 years of work experience as a grounds technician.

The Professional Landcare Network offers six certifications for individuals with varying levels of experience, in landscaping and grounds maintenance. Each of these programs requires applicants to pass an examination, and some require self-study course work. The Tree Care Industry Association offers five levels of credentials. Currently available credentials include Tree Care Apprentice, Ground Operations Specialist, Tree Climber Specialist, Aerial Lift Specialist and Tree Care Specialist, as well as a certification program in safety. These programs are available to individuals with varying levels of experience, and require applicants to pass training courses.

Employment

Grounds maintenance workers held about 1.5 million jobs in 2008. Employment was distributed as follows:

Landscaping and groundskeeping workers 1,205,800
First-line supervisors/managers of landscaping,
    lawn service, and groundskeeping workers............217,900
Tree trimmers and pruners 45,000
Pesticide handlers, sprayers, and
    applicators, vegetation...30,800
Grounds maintenance workers, all other......................21,100

About 36 percent of all grounds maintenance workers were employed in companies providing landscaping services to buildings and dwellings. Others worked for educational institutions, public and private. Some were employed by local governments, installing and maintaining landscaping for parks, hospitals, and other public facilities. Around 402,000 grounds maintenance workers were self-employed, providing landscape maintenance directly to customers on a contract basis.

Job Outlook

Employment is expected to grow faster than average, and job opportunities should be good.

Employment change. Employment of grounds maintenance workers is expected to increase by 18 percent during the 2008–18 decade, which is faster than the average for all occupations. In addition, grounds maintenance workers will be among the occupations with largest numbers of new jobs, with around 269,200. More workers will be needed to keep up with increasing demand for lawn care and landscaping services both from large institutions and from individual homeowners.

Major institutions, such as universities and corporate headquarters, recognize the importance of good landscape design in attracting personnel and clients and are expected to continue to use grounds maintenance services to maintain and upgrade their properties. Homeowners are also a growing source of demand for grounds maintenance workers. Many two-income households lack the time to take care of their lawns so they increasingly hire people to maintain them. Also, as the population ages, more elderly homeowners will require lawn care services to help maintain their yards.

Employment of tree trimmers and pruners should grow by 26 percent from 2008-18, which is much faster than the average for all occupations. In order to improve the environment, mu-

Projections data from the National Employment Matrix

Occupational Title	SOC Code	Employment, 2008	Projected Employment, 2018	Change, 2008-2018	
				Number	Percent
Grounds maintenance workers..	–	1,520,600	1,789,900	269,200	18
First-line supervisors/managers of landscaping,					
lawn service, and groundskeeping workers	37-1012	217,900	250,300	32,400	15
Grounds maintenance workers..	37-3000	1,302,700	1,539,500	236,800	18
Landscaping and groundskeeping workers.................................	37-3011	1,205,800	1,422,900	217,100	18
Pesticide handlers, sprayers, and applicators, vegetation	37-3012	30,800	36,300	5,400	18
Tree trimmers and pruners	37-3013	45,000	56,800	11,800	26
Grounds maintenance workers, all other.................................	37-3019	21,100	23,600	2,500	12

(NOTE) Data in this table are rounded. See the discussion of the employment projections table in the *Handbook* introductory chapter on *Occupational Information Included in the Handbook.*

nicipalities across the country are planting more trees in urban areas, increasing demand for these workers.

Job prospects. Job opportunities are expected to be good. Openings will arise from faster-than-average growth and the need to replace workers who leave this large occupation.

Job opportunities for nonseasonal work are best in regions with temperate climates, where landscaping and lawn services are required all year. Opportunities may vary with local economic conditions.

Earnings

Wages of grounds maintenance workers are low. Median hourly wages of landscaping and groundskeeping workers were $11.13 in May 2008. The middle 50 percent earned between $9.09 and $14.01 per hour. The lowest 10 percent earned less than $7.98 per hour, and the highest 10 percent earned more than $17.57. Median hourly wages in the largest employing industries of landscaping and groundskeeping workers in May 2008 were as follows:

Elementary and secondary schools	$13.70
Local government	12.65
Services to buildings and dwellings	11.11
Other amusement and recreation industries	10.01
Employment services	9.92

Median hourly wages of pesticide handlers, sprayers, and applicators, vegetation were $14.31 in May 2008. The middle 50 percent earned between $11.61 and $17.86 per hour. The lowest 10 percent earned less than $9.53 per hour, and the highest 10 percent earned more than $21.59. Median hourly wages in the services to buildings and dwellings industry were $14.51 in May 2008.

Median hourly wages of tree trimmers and pruners were $14.41 in May 2008. The middle 50 percent earned between $11.50 and $18.18 per hour. The lowest 10 percent earned less than $9.62 per hour, and the highest 10 percent earned more than $22.34. Median hourly wages in the services to buildings and dwellings industry were $14.04 in May 2008.

Median hourly wages of first-line supervisors/manages of landscaping, lawn service, and groundskeeping workers were $19.19 in May 2008. The middle 50 percent earned between $15.22 and $24.90 per hour. The lowest 10 percent earned less than $12.57 per hour, and the highest 10 percent earned more than $31.33. Median hourly wages in the largest employing industries of first-line supervisors/managers of landscaping, lawn service, and groundskeeping workers in May 2008 were as follows:

Local government	$22.89
Other amusement and recreation industries	20.82
Services to buildings and dwellings	18.50

Related Occupations

Other occupations that work with plants and soils include:

	Page
Agricultural workers, other	609
Farmers, ranchers, and agricultural managers	48
Forest and conservation workers	604
Landscape architects	154
Logging workers	606

Sources of Additional Information

For career and certification information on tree trimmers and pruners, contact:
➤ Tree Care Industry Association, 136 Harvey Road, Suite 101, Londonderry, NH 03053. Internet: **http://www.treecareindustry.org**

For information on work as a landscaping and groundskeeping worker, contact the following organizations:
➤ Professional Grounds Management Society, 720 Light St., Baltimore, MD 21230. Internet: **http://www.pgms.org**

➤ Professional Landcare Network, 950 Herndon Pkwy., Suite 450, Herndon, VA 20170. Internet: **http://www.landcarenetwork.org**

For information on becoming a licensed pesticide applicator, contact your State's Department of Agriculture or Department of Environmental Protection or Conservation.

The Occupational Information Network (O*NET) provides information on a wide range of occupational characteristics. Links to O*NET appear at the end of the Internet version of this occupational statement, accessible at **http://www.bls.gov/ooh/ocos172.htm**

Pest Control Workers

Significant Points

- A high school diploma generally is the minimum educational requirement.

- States require pest control workers to be licensed through training and examination.

- Job prospects are expected to be very good.

Nature of the Work

Unwanted creatures that infest buildings or surrounding areas can pose serious risks to health and safety. *Pest control workers* remove these creatures from households, apartment buildings, places of businesses, and other structures, to protect people and maintain structural integrity.

Common pests include roaches, rats, mice, spiders, termites, ants, and bedbugs. Using information about pests' biology and habits, along with an arsenal of pest management techniques, pest control workers locate, identify, and remove pests. They set traps, apply pesticides, and even modify structures at the discretion of the customer.

Many pest problems require pesticide application. Pest control workers use two different types of pesticides—general use and restricted use. General use pesticides are the most widely used and are available in diluted concentrations to the public. Restricted use pesticides are used for the most severe infestations and are available only to licensed professionals. Because of their potential harm to pest control workers, customers, and the environment, restricted-use pesticides are heavily regulated by Federal law.

For some jobs, pest control workers use a combination of pest management techniques, a practice known as integrated pest management. One method involves using proper sanitation and creating physical barriers. Pests cannot survive without food and will not infest a building if they cannot enter it. Another method involves using baits that either destroy the pests or prevent them from reproducing. Yet another method involves using mechanical devices, such as traps, that remove pests from the immediate environment.

Some workers use pest-management technology to make home inspections more efficient. This technology, which uses microchips to identify areas of pest activity, is used most frequently for termites. The chips, which are placed in baiting stations, emit signals that can tell pest control workers if is termites are present. Workers pick up the signals using a device similar to a metal detector, allowing them to quickly evaluate an entire building.

Pest control workers generally can be divided into three categories: technicians, applicators, and supervisors. Position titles and job duties vary by State, however.

Pest control technicians are usually entry-level workers who identify potential pest problems, conduct inspections, and design control strategies. They work directly with the customer and are permitted to apply a limited range of pesticides.

Applicators perform more complex tasks, are able to use a wider range of pesticides, and may specialize in a certain area of pest control. Those that specialize in controlling termites are called *termite control technicians*. They use chemicals and modify structures to eliminate termites and prevent future infestation. To treat infested areas, termite control technicians drill holes and cut openings into buildings to access infestations and install physical barriers or bait systems around the structure. Some termite control technicians even repair structural damage caused by termites.

Applicators that specialize in fumigation are called *Fumigators*. These workers use poisonous gases, called fumigants, to treat serious infestations. Fumigators pre-treat infested buildings by examining, measuring, and sealing the buildings. Then, using cylinders, hoses, and valves, they fill structures with the proper amount and concentration of fumigant. To prevent accidental fumigant exposure, fumigators padlock doors, post warning signs, and monitor buildings closely to detect and stop leaks.

Pest control supervisors, also known as operators, direct technicians and applicators. Supervisors are licensed to apply pesticides, but they usually are more involved in running the business. Many supervisors own their own business. Supervisors are responsible for ensuring that employees obey rules regarding pesticide use and resolving any problems that arise with regulatory officials or customers. Most States require each pest control establishment to have a supervisor.

Work environment. Because work must be done on site, pest control workers travel to visit clients. Pest control workers must kneel, bend, reach, and crawl to inspect and treat structures. They work both indoors and out, in all weather conditions. Applicators must wear heavy protective gear, including respirators, gloves, and goggles, when working with pesticides.

There are health risks associated with pesticide use. Various pest control chemicals are toxic and could be harmful, if not used properly. Health risks are limited by the extensive training required for licensure and the use of recommended protective

Pest control workers help to keep buildings free of insects, rodents, and other animals.

equipment. However, pest control workers still experience injuries more frequently than workers in many other occupations.

Most pest control workers work around 40 hours per week, but about 16 percent worked more than 50 hours per week in 2008. Pest control workers often work evenings and weekends, but many work consistent shifts.

Training, Other Qualifications, and Advancement
State laws require pest control workers to be licensed. Most workers need a high school diploma and receive training on the job.

Education and training. A high school diploma or equivalent is the minimum qualification for most pest control jobs, but some jobs may not require any formal education. A college degree may be required for other jobs. Most pest control workers may begin their careers as technicians. They often receive both formal classroom and on-the-job training provided by the employer, but they also may be required to study on their own. Training usually involves a combination of classroom study and on-the-job experience for each category of work that the pest control worker would like to perform. Categories may include general pest control, rodent control, termite control, fumigation, and ornamental and turf control. In addition, technicians must attend general training in pesticide safety and use. Pest control workers usually can complete this training in fewer than 3 months.

Projections data from the National Employment Matrix

Occupational Title	SOC Code	Employment, 2008	Projected Employment, 2018	Change, 2008-2018	
				Number	Percent
Pest control workers..	37-2021	67,500	77,800	10,300	15

(NOTE) Data in this table are rounded. See the discussion of the employment projections table in the *Handbook* introductory chapter on *Occupational Information Included in the Handbook*.

After completing the required training, workers can provide supervised pest control services. Because pest control methods change, workers often attend continuing education classes, which are frequently provided by product manufacturers.

Licensure. Pest control workers must be licensed. Requirements vary by State, but pest control workers generally must undergo training and pass an examination. Some States also require workers to have a high school diploma or equivalent and pass a background check; some also have additional requirements for applicators and operators. Most pest control firms provide training and help their employees prepare for the examination. In some States, individuals may be able to work as apprentices before becoming licensed.

Other qualifications. Pest control workers must be in good health, because of the physical demands of the job, and they also must be able to withstand uncomfortable conditions—such as the heat of climbing into an attic in the summertime or the chill of sliding into a crawlspace during winter. In addition, many pest control companies require their employees to have a good driving record.

Advancement. Advancement opportunities come with experience in the field. After a designated number of years on the job, technicians may advance to become applicators. Applicators with several years of experience often become supervisors. Some experienced workers may start their own pest management company. Pest control workers in large organizations may advance into administrative positions, although a college degree may be required for such opportunities.

Employment

Pest control workers held about 67,500 jobs in 2008; about 86 percent of workers were employed in the exterminating and pest control services industry. About 7 percent of workers were self-employed. Jobs are concentrated in States with warmer climates and larger cities, due to the greater number of pests in these areas.

Job Outlook

Employment growth is expected to be faster than the average, and job prospects should be very good.

Employment change. Employment of pest control workers is expected to grow by 15 percent between 2008 and 2018, which is faster than the average for all occupations. Demand for pest control workers is projected to increase for a number of reasons. More people are expected to use pest control services as environmental and health concerns and improvements in the standard of living convince more people to hire professionals, rather than attempt pest control work themselves. Growth in the population, particularly in Sunbelt States where pests are more common, also will generate new residential, commercial, and government buildings that will require treatment by pest con-

trol workers. However, if the rate of new building construction moderates, employment growth of pest control workers may slow down.

Job prospects. Job prospects should be very good for qualified applicants, due to the limited number of people seeking work in this occupation. In addition to job growth, opportunities also should arise from the need to replace workers who leave the occupation.

Earnings

Median hourly wages of pest control workers were $14.37 in May 2008. The middle 50 percent earned between $11.68 and $17.67. The lowest 10 percent earned less than $9.45, and the top 10 percent earned over $21.34. Wages may vary by job function.

Related Occupations

Pest control workers visit homes and places of business to provide building services. Other workers who provide services to buildings include:

	Page
Building cleaning workers ..:..	495
Construction laborers	635
Grounds maintenance workers...	498
Heating, air-conditioning, and refrigeration mechanics and installers..	703

Sources of Additional Information

Private employment agencies and State employment services offices have information about available job opportunities for pest control workers.

For information about State licensing requirements, contact your local office of the U.S. Department of Agriculture or your State's environmental protection (or conservation) agency.

For more information about pest control careers and training, contact:

➤ National Pest Management Association, 10460 North St., Fairfax, VA 22030. Internet: **http://www.pestworld.org/Looking-for-a-Career-in-Pest-Management**

The Occupational Information Network (O*NET) provides information on a wide range of occupational characteristics. Links to O*NET appear at the end of the Internet version of this occupational statement, accessible at **http://www.bls.gov/ooh/ocos254.htm**

Personal Care and Service Occupations

Animal Care and Service Workers

Significant Points

- Animal lovers get satisfaction in this occupation, but the work can be unpleasant, physically and emotionally demanding, and sometimes dangerous.

- Most workers are trained on the job, but employers generally prefer to hire people who have experience with animals; some jobs require formal education.

- Most positions will present excellent employment opportunities; however, keen competition is expected for jobs as zookeepers and marine mammal trainers.

- Earnings are relatively low.

Nature of the Work

Many people like animals. But, as pet owners will admit, taking care of them is hard work. *Animal care and service workers*—who include *animal caretakers* and *animal trainers*—train, feed, water, groom, bathe, and exercise animals and clean, disinfect, and repair their cages. They also play with the animals, provide companionship, and observe behavioral changes that could indicate illness or injury. Boarding kennels, pet stores, animal shelters, rescue leagues, veterinary hospitals and clinics, stables, laboratories, aquariums and natural aquatic habitats, and zoological parks all house animals and employ animal care and service workers. Job titles and duties vary by employment setting.

Kennel attendants care for pets while their owners are working or traveling out of town. Beginning attendants perform basic

Animal caretakers who specialize in grooming or maintaining a pet's appearance are called groomers.

tasks, such as cleaning both the cages and the dog runs, filling food and water dishes, and exercising animals. Experienced attendants may provide basic animal health care, as well as bathe animals, trim nails, and attend to other grooming needs. Attendants who work in kennels also may sell pet food and supplies, assist in obedience training, or prepare animals for shipping.

Groomers are animal caretakers who specialize in maintaining a pet's appearance. Most groom dogs and a few groom cats. Some groomers work in kennels, veterinary clinics, animal shelters, or pet supply stores. Others operate their own grooming business, typically at a salon or, increasingly, by making house calls. Such mobile services are growing rapidly because they offer convenience for pet owners, flexibility of schedules for groomers, and minimal trauma for pets resulting from their being in unfamiliar surroundings. Groomers clean and sanitize equipment to prevent the spread of disease, as well as maintaining a clean and safe environment for the animals. Groomers also schedule appointments, discuss pets' grooming needs with clients, and collect general information on the pets' health and behavior. Groomers sometimes are the first to notice a medical problem, such as an ear or skin infection, that requires veterinary care.

Grooming the pet involves several steps: an initial brush-out is followed by a clipping of hair with combs and grooming shears; the groomer then cuts the animal's nails, cleans the ears, bathes and blow-dries the animal, and ends with a final trim and styling.

Animal caretakers in animal shelters work mainly with cats and dogs and perform a variety of duties typically determined by the worker's experience. In addition to attending to the basic needs of the animals, caretakers at shelters keep records of the animals, including information about any tests or treatments performed on them. Experienced caretakers may vaccinate newly admitted animals under the direction of a veterinarian or veterinary technician and euthanize (painlessly put to death) seriously ill, severely injured, or unwanted animals. Animal caretakers in animal shelters also interact with the public, answering telephone inquiries, screening applicants who wish to adopt an animal, or educating visitors on neutering and other animal health issues.

Pet sitters look after one or more animals when their owner is away. They do this by traveling to the pet owner's home to carry out the daily routine. Most pet sitters feed, walk, and play with the animal, but some more experienced sitters also may be required to bathe, train, or groom them. Most watch over dogs and a few take care of cats. By not removing the pet from its normal surroundings, trauma is reduced and the animal can maintain its normal diet and exercise regimen.

Grooms, or caretakers, care for horses in stables. They saddle and unsaddle horses, give them rubdowns, and walk them to cool them off after a ride. They also feed, groom, and exercise the horses; clean out stalls and replenish bedding; polish saddles; clean and organize the tack (harness, saddle, and bridle) room; and store supplies and feed. Experienced grooms may help train horses.

In zoos, animal care and service workers, called *keepers*, prepare the diets and clean the enclosures of animals and sometimes assist in raising them when they are very young. They watch for any signs of illness or injury, monitor eating patterns or any changes in behavior and record their observations. Keepers also may answer questions and ensure that the visiting public behaves responsibly toward the exhibited animals. Depending on the zoo, keepers may be assigned to work with a broad group of animals, such as mammals, birds, or reptiles, or they may work with a limited collection of animals such as primates, large cats, or small mammals.

Animal trainers train animals for riding, security, performance, obedience, or assisting people with disabilities. Animal trainers do this by accustoming the animal to the human voice and human contact and teaching the animal to respond to commands. The three most commonly trained animals are dogs, horses, and marine mammals, including dolphins and sea lions. Trainers use several techniques to help them train animals. One technique, known as a bridge, is a stimulus that a trainer uses to communicate the precise moment an animal does something correctly. When the animal responds correctly, the trainer gives positive reinforcement in a variety of ways: offering food, toys, play, and rubdowns or speaking the word "good." Animal training takes place in small steps and often takes months and even years of repetition. During the teaching process, trainers provide animals with mental stimulation, physical exercise, and husbandry. A relatively new form of training teaches animals to cooperate with workers giving medical care: animals learn "veterinary" behaviors, such as allowing for the collection of blood samples; physical, x-ray, ultrasonic, and dental exams; physical therapy; and the administration of medicines and replacement fluids.

Training also can be a good tool for facilitating the relocation of animals from one habitat to another, easing, for example, the process of loading horses onto trailers. Trainers often work in competitions or shows, such as circuses, marine parks, and aquariums; many others work in animal shelters, dog kennels and salons, or horse farms. Trainers in shows work to display the talent and ability of an animal, such as a dolphin, through interactive programs to educate and entertain the public.

In addition to their hands-on work with the animals, trainers often oversee other aspects of animals' care, such as preparing their diet and providing a safe and clean environment and habitat.

Work environment. People who love animals get satisfaction from working with and helping them. However, some of the work may be unpleasant, physically or emotionally demanding, and, sometimes, dangerous. Data from the U.S. Bureau of Labor Statistics show that full-time animal care and service workers experienced a work-related injury and illness rate that was higher than the national average. Most animal care and service workers have to clean animal cages and lift, hold, or restrain animals, risking exposure to bites or scratches. Their work often involves kneeling, crawling, repeated bending, and, occasionally, lifting heavy supplies such as bales of hay or bags of feed. Animal caretakers must take precautions when treating animals with germicides or insecticides. They may work outdoors in all kinds of weather, and the work setting can be noisy. Caretakers of show and sports animals travel to competitions.

Animal care and service workers who witness abused animals or who assist in euthanizing unwanted, aged, or hopelessly injured animals may experience emotional distress. Those working for private humane societies and municipal animal shelters often deal with the public, some of whom may be hostile. Such workers must maintain a calm and professional demeanor while helping to enforce the laws regarding animal care.

Animal care and service workers often work irregular hours. Most animals are fed every day, so caretakers often work weekend and holiday shifts. In some animal hospitals, research facilities, and animal shelters, an attendant is on duty 24 hours a day, which means night shifts.

Training, Other Qualifications, and Advancement

On-the-job training is the most common way animal care and service workers learn their work; however, employers generally prefer to hire people who have experience with animals. Some jobs require formal education.

Education and training. Animal trainers often need a high school diploma or GED equivalent. Some animal training jobs may require a bachelor's degree and additional skills. For example, marine mammal trainers usually need a bachelor's degree in biology, marine biology, animal science, psychology, or a related field. An animal health technician degree also may qualify trainers for some jobs.

Most equine trainers learn their trade by working as a groom at a stable. Some study at an accredited private training school.

Many dog trainers attend workshops and courses at community colleges and vocational schools. Topics include basic study of canines, learning theory of animals, teaching obedience cues, problem solving methods, and safety. Many such schools also offer business training.

Pet sitters are not required to have any specific training, but knowledge and some form of previous experience with animals often is recommended.

Many zoos require their caretakers to have a bachelor's degree in biology, animal science, or a related field. Most require experience with animals, preferably as a volunteer or paid keeper in a zoo.

Pet groomers typically learn their trade by completing an informal apprenticeship, usually lasting 6 to 10 weeks, under the guidance of an experienced groomer. Prospective groomers also may attend one of the 50 State-licensed grooming schools throughout the country, with programs varying in length from 2 to 18 weeks. Beginning groomers often start by taking on one duty, such as bathing and drying the pet. They eventually assume responsibility for the entire grooming process, from the initial brush-out to the final clipping.

Animal caretakers in animal shelters are not required to have any specialized training, but training programs and workshops are available through the Humane Society of the United States, the American Humane Association, and the National Animal Control Association. Workshop topics include investigations of cruelty, appropriate methods of euthanasia for shelter animals, proper guidelines for capturing animals, techniques for preventing problems with wildlife, and dealing with the public.

Beginning animal caretakers in kennels learn on the job and usually start by cleaning cages and feeding animals.

Certification and other qualifications. Certifications are available in many animal service occupations. For dog trainers, certification by a professional association or one of the hundreds of private vocational or State-approved trade schools can be advantageous. The National Dog Groomers Association of America offers certification for master status as a groomer. To earn certification, applicants must demonstrate their practical skills and pass two exams. The National Association of Professional Pet Sitters offers a two-stage, home-study certification program for those who wish to become pet care professionals. Topics include business management, animal care, and animal health issues, and applicants must pass a written exam to earn certification. The Pet Care Services Association offers a three-stage, home-study program for individuals interested in pet care. Levels I and II focus on basic principles of animal care and customer service, while Level III spotlights management and professional aspects of the pet care business. Those who complete the third stage and pass oral and written examinations become Certified Kennel Operators (CKO).

All animal care and service workers need patience, sensitivity, and problem-solving ability. Those who work in shelters also need tact and communication skills, because they often deal with individuals who abandon their pets. The ability to handle emotional people is vital for workers at shelters.

Animal trainers especially need problem-solving skills and experience in animal obedience. Successful marine mammal trainers also should have good-public speaking skills, because presentations are a large part of the job. Usually four to five trainers work with a group of animals at one time; therefore, trainers should be able to work as part of a team. Marine mammal trainers must also be good swimmers; certification in SCUBA is a plus.

Most horse-training jobs have minimum weight requirements for candidates.

Advancement. With experience and additional training, caretakers in animal shelters may become adoption coordinators, animal control officers, emergency rescue drivers, assistant shelter managers, or shelter directors. Pet groomers who work in large retail establishments or kennels may, with experience, move into supervisory or managerial positions. Experienced groomers often choose to open their own salons or mobile grooming business. Advancement for kennel caretakers takes the form of promotion to kennel supervisor, assistant manager, and manager; those with enough capital and experience may open up their own kennels. Zookeepers may advance to senior keeper, assistant head keeper, head keeper, and assistant curator, but very few openings occur, especially for the higher level positions.

Employment

Animal care and service workers held 220,400 jobs in 2008. Nearly 4 out of 5 worked as nonfarm animal caretakers; the remainder worked as animal trainers. Nonfarm animal caretakers often worked in boarding kennels, animal shelters, rescue leagues, stables, grooming shops, pet stores, animal hospi-

tals, and veterinary offices. A significant number of caretakers worked for animal humane societies, racing stables, dog and horse racetrack operators, zoos, theme parks, circuses, and other amusement and recreation services.

Employment of animal trainers is concentrated in animal services that specialize in training and in commercial sports, where racehorses and dogs are trained. About 54 percent of animal trainers were self-employed.

Job Outlook

Because many workers leave this occupation each year, there will be excellent job opportunities for most positions. Much faster than average employment growth also will add to job openings. However, keen competition is expected for jobs as zookeepers and marine mammal trainers.

Employment change. Employment of animal care and service workers is expected to grow 21 percent over the 2008–18 decade, much faster than the average for all occupations. The companion pet population, which drives employment of animal caretakers in kennels, grooming shops, animal shelters, and veterinary clinics and hospitals, is anticipated to increase. Pet owners—including a large number of baby boomers, whose disposable income is expected to increase as they age—are expected to increasingly purchase grooming services, daily and overnight boarding services, training services, and veterinary services, resulting in more jobs for animal care and service workers. As more pet owners consider their pets part of the family, demand for luxury animal services and the willingness to spend greater amounts of money on pets should continue to grow. Demand for marine mammal trainers, on the other hand, should grow slowly.

Demand for animal care and service workers in animal shelters is expected to grow as communities increasingly recognize the connection between animal abuse and abuse toward humans and continue to commit private funds to animal shelters, many of which are working hand in hand with social service agencies and law enforcement teams.

Job prospects. Due to employment growth and the need to replace workers who leave the occupation, job opportunities for most positions should be excellent. The need to replace pet sitters, dog walkers, kennel attendants, and animal control and shelter workers leaving the field will create the overwhelming majority of job openings. Many animal caretaker jobs require little or no training and have flexible work schedules, making them suitable for people seeking a first job or for temporary or part-time work. Prospective groomers also will face excellent opportunities as the companion dog population is expected to grow and services such as mobile grooming continue to grow in popularity. The outlook for caretakers in zoos and aquari-

Projections data from the National Employment Matrix

Occupational Title	SOC Code	Employment, 2008	Projected Employment, 2018	Change, 2008-2018	
				Number	Percent
Animal care and service workers	39-2000	220,400	265,900	45,500	21
Animal trainers	39-2011	47,100	56,700	9,600	20
Nonfarm animal caretakers	39-2021	173,300	209,100	35,900	21

(NOTE) Data in this table are rounded. See the discussion of the employment projections table in the *Handbook* introductory chapter on *Occupational Information Included in the Handbook.*

ums, however, is not favorable, due to slow job growth and keen competition for the few positions.

Prospective mammal trainers also will face keen competition as the number of applicants greatly exceeds the number of available positions. Prospective horse trainers should anticipate an equally challenging labor market because the number of entry-level positions is limited. Dog trainers, however, should experience conditions that are more favorable, driven by their owners' desire to instill obedience in their pet. Opportunities for dog trainers should be best in large metropolitan areas.

Job opportunities for animal care and service workers may vary from year to year because the strength of the economy affects demand for these workers. Pet owners tend to spend more on animal services when the economy is strong.

Earnings

Wages are relatively low. Median annual wages of nonfarm animal caretakers were $19,360 in May 2008. The middle 50 percent earned between $16,720 and $24,300. The bottom 10 percent earned less than $15,140, and the top 10 percent earned more than $31,590. Median annual wages in the industries employing the largest numbers of nonfarm animal caretakers in May 2008 were as follows:

Spectator sports	$20,520
Other personal services	19,530
Social advocacy organizations	18,640
Veterinary services	18,380
Other miscellaneous store retailers	18,320

Median annual wages of animal trainers were $27,270 in May 2008. The middle 50 percent earned between $19,880 and $38,280. The lowest 10 percent earned less than $16,700, and the top 10 percent earned more than $51,400.

Related Occupations

Others who work extensively with animals include

	Page
Agricultural workers, other	609
Animal control workers	825
Biological scientists	181
Farmers, ranchers, and agricultural managers	48
Veterinarians	402
Veterinary assistants and laboratory animal caretakers	826
Veterinary technologists and technicians	443

Sources of Additional Information

For career information and information on training, certification, and earnings of a related occupation—animal control officers—contact:
➤ National Animal Control Association, P.O. Box 480851, Kansas City, MO 64148-0851. Internet: **http://www.nacanet.org**

For information on becoming an advanced pet care technician at a kennel, contact:
➤ Pet Care Services Association, 2760 N. Academy Blvd., Suite 120, Colorado Springs, CO 80917. Internet: **http://www.petcareservices.org**

For general information on pet grooming careers, including workshops and certification information, contact:
➤ National Dog Groomers Association of America, P.O. Box 101, Clark, PA 16113. Internet: **http://www.nationaldoggroomers.com**

For information on pet sitting, including certification information, contact:
➤ National Association of Professional Pet Sitters, 15000 Commerce Parkway, Suite C, Mount Laurel, NJ 08054. Internet: **http://www.petsitters.org**

The Occupational Information Network (O*NET) provides information on a wide range of occupational characteristics. Links to O*NET appear at the end of the Internet version of this occupational statement, accessible at **http://www.bls.gov/ooh/ocos168.htm**

Barbers, Cosmetologists, and Other Personal Appearance Workers

Significant Points

- Employment is expected to grow much faster than the average for all occupations.

- A State license is required for barbers, cosmetologists, and most other personal appearance workers, although qualifications vary by State.

- About 44 percent of workers are self employed; many also work flexible schedules.

Nature of the Work

Barbers and *cosmetologists* focus on providing hair care services to enhance the appearance of customers. Other personal appearance workers, such as *manicurists and pedicurists*, *shampooers*, and *skin care specialists*, provide specialized beauty services that help clients look and feel their best.

Barbers cut, trim, shampoo, and style hair mostly for male clients. They also may fit hairpieces and offer scalp treatments and facial shaving. In many States, barbers are licensed to color,

Nail technicians work in salons and provide various services including manicures.

bleach, and highlight hair, and to offer permanent-wave services. Barbers also may provide skin care and nail treatments.

Hairdressers, hairstylists, and cosmetologists offer a wide range of beauty services, such as shampooing, cutting, coloring, and styling of hair. They may advise clients on how to care for their hair at home. In addition, cosmetologists may be trained to give manicures, pedicures, and scalp and facial treatments; provide makeup analysis; and clean and style wigs and hairpieces.

A number of workers offer specialized services. Manicurists and pedicurists, called *nail technicians* in some States, work exclusively on nails and provide manicures, pedicures, polishing, and nail extensions to clients. Another group of specialists is skin care specialists, or *estheticians*, who cleanse and beautify the skin by giving facials, full-body treatments, and head and neck massages, as well as apply makeup. They also may remove hair through waxing or, if properly trained, with laser treatments. Finally, in larger salons, shampooers specialize in shampooing and conditioning hair.

In addition to working with clients, personal appearance workers may keep records of hair color or skin care regimens used by their regular clients. A growing number actively sell hair, skin, and nail care products. Barbers, cosmetologists, and other personal appearance workers who operate their own salons have managerial duties that may include hiring, supervising, and firing workers, as well as keeping business and inventory records, ordering supplies, and arranging for advertising.

Work environment. Many full-time barbers, cosmetologists, and other personal appearance workers put in a 40-hour week, but longer hours are common, especially among self-employed workers. Work schedules may include evenings and weekends, the times when beauty salons and barbershops are busiest. Many workers, especially those who are self-employed, determine their own schedules. In 2008, about 29 percent of barbers, hairstylists and cosmetologists worked part time, and 14 percent had variable schedules.

Barbers, cosmetologists, and other personal appearance workers usually work in clean, pleasant surroundings with good lighting and ventilation. Most work in a salon or barbershop, although some may work in a spa, hotel, or resort. Good health and stamina are important, because these workers are on their feet for most of their shift. Prolonged exposure to some hair and nail chemicals may cause irritation, so protective clothing, such as plastic gloves or aprons, may be worn.

Training, Other Qualifications, and Advancement

All States require barbers, cosmetologists, and other personal appearance workers to be licensed, with the exceptions of shampooers. To qualify for a license, most job seekers are required to graduate from a State-licensed barber or cosmetology school.

Education and training. A high school diploma or GED is required for some personal appearance workers in some States. In addition, most States require that barbers and cosmetologists complete a program in a State-licensed barber or cosmetology school. Programs in hairstyling, skin care, and other personal appearance services can be found in both high schools and in public or private postsecondary vocational schools.

Full-time programs in barbering and cosmetology usually last 9 months or more and may lead to an associate degree, but

training for manicurists and pedicurists and skin care specialists requires significantly less time. Shampooers generally do not need formal training. Most professionals take advanced courses in hairstyling or other personal appearance services to keep up with the latest trends. They also may take courses in sales and marketing.

Licensure. All States require barbers, cosmetologists, and other personal appearance workers to be licensed, with the exception of shampooers. Qualifications for a license vary by State, but generally a person must have a high school diploma or GED, be at least 16 years old, and have graduated from a State-licensed barber or cosmetology school. After graduating from a State approved training program, students take a State licensing examination. The exam consists of a written test and, in some cases, a practical test of styling skills or an oral examination. In many States, cosmetology training may be credited toward a barbering license, and vice versa, and a few States combine the two licenses. Most States require separate licensing examinations for manicurists, pedicurists, and skin care specialists. A fee is usually required upon application for a license, and periodic license renewals may be necessary.

Some States have reciprocity agreements that allow licensed barbers and cosmetologists to obtain a license in another State without additional formal training, but such agreements are uncommon. Consequently, persons who wish to work in a particular State should review the laws of that State before entering a training program.

Other qualifications. Successful personal appearance workers should have an understanding of fashion, art, and technical design. They also must keep a neat personal appearance and a clean work area. Interpersonal skills, image, and attitude play an important role in career success. As client retention and retail sales become an increasingly important part of salons' revenue, the ability to be an effective salesperson becomes ever more vital for salon workers. Some cosmetology schools consider "people skills" to be such an integral part of the job that they require coursework in that area. Business skills are important for those who plan to operate their own salons.

Advancement. Advancement usually takes the form of higher earnings, as barbers and cosmetologists gain experience and build a steady clientele. Some barbers and cosmetologists manage salons, lease booth space in salons, or open their own salons after several years of experience. Others teach in barber or cosmetology schools or provide training through vocational schools. Still others advance to other related occupations, such as sales representatives for companies that sell salon-related products, image or fashion consultants, or examiners for State licensing boards.

Employment

Barbers, cosmetologists, and other personal appearance workers held about 821,900 jobs in 2008. Of these, barbers and cosmetologists held 684,200 jobs, manicurists and pedicurists 76,000, skin care specialists 38,800, and shampooers 22,900.

Most of these workers are employed in personal care services establishments, such as beauty salons, barber shops, nail salons, day and resort spas. Others were employed in nursing and other residential care homes. Nearly every town has a barbershop or

Projections data from the National Employment Matrix

Occupational Title	SOC Code	Employment, 2008	Projected Employment, 2018	Change, 2008-2018	
				Number	Percent
Barbers, cosmetologists, and other personal appearance workers	–	821,900	987,400	165,500	20
Barbers and cosmetologists...	39-5010	684,200	817,400	133,200	19
Barbers	39-5011	53,500	59,700	6,200	12
Hairdressers, hairstylists, and cosmetologists...........................	39-5012	630,700	757,700	127,000	20
Manicurists and pedicurists..	39-5092	76,000	90,200	14,300	19
Shampooers...	39-5093	22,900	26,300	3,400	15
Skin care specialists	39-5094	38,800	53,500	14,700	38

(NOTE) Data in this table are rounded. See the discussion of the employment projections table in the *Handbook* introductory chapter on *Occupational Information Included in the Handbook.*

beauty salon, but employment in this occupation is concentrated in the most populous cities and States.

About 44 percent of all barbers, cosmetologists, and other personal appearance workers are self-employed. Many of these workers own their own salon, but a growing number of the self-employed lease booth space or a chair from the salon's owner. In this case, workers provide their own supplies, and are responsible for paying their own taxes and benefits. They may pay a monthly or weekly fee to the salon owner, who is responsible for utilities and maintenance of the building.

Job Outlook
Overall employment of barbers, cosmetologists, and other personal appearance workers is projected to grow much faster than the average for all occupations. Opportunities for entry-level workers should be favorable, while job candidates at high-end establishments will face keen competition.

Employment change. Personal appearance workers will grow by 20 percent from 2008 to 2018, which is much faster than the average for all occupations.

Employment trends are expected to vary among the different occupational specialties. Employment of hairdressers, hairstylists, and cosmetologists will increase by about 20 percent, while the number of barbers will increase by 12 percent. This growth will primarily come from an increasing population, which will lead to greater demand for basic hair services. Additionally, the demand for hair coloring and other advanced hair treatments has increased in recent years, particularly among baby boomers and young people. This trend is expected to continue, leading to a favorable outlook for hairdressers, hairstylists, and cosmetologists. Employment of shampooers will grow by 15 percent, as many cosmetologists and barbers are able to perform shampooing services, as well.

Continued growth in the number full-service spas and nail salons will also generate numerous job openings for manicurists, pedicurists, and skin care specialists. Estheticians and other skin care specialists will see large gains in employment, and are expected to grow almost 38 percent, primarily due to the popularity of skin treatments for relaxation and medical well-being. Manicurists and pedicurists meanwhile will grow by 19 percent.

Job prospects. Job opportunities generally should be good, particularly for licensed personal appearance workers seeking entry-level positions. A large number of job openings will come about from the need to replace workers who transfer to other occupations, retire, or leave the labor force for other reasons. However, workers can expect keen competition for jobs

and clients at higher paying salons, as these positions are relatively few and require applicants to compete with a large pool of licensed and experienced cosmetologists. Opportunities will generally be best for those with previous experience and for those licensed to provide a broad range of services.

Earnings
Median hourly wages in May 2008 for hairdressers, hairstylists, and cosmetologists, including tips and commission, were $11.13. The middle 50 percent earned between $8.57 and $15.03. The lowest 10 percent earned less than $7.47, and the highest 10 percent earned more than $20.41.

Median hourly wages in May 2008 for barbers, including tips, were $11.56. The middle 50 percent earned between $8.93 and $14.69. The lowest 10 percent earned less than $7.56, and the highest 10 percent earned more than $19.51.

Among skin care specialists, median hourly wages, including tips, were $13.81, for manicurists and pedicurists $9.46, and for shampooers $8.32.

While earnings for entry-level workers usually are low, earnings can be considerably higher for those with experience. A number of factors, such as the size and location of the salon, determine the total income of personal appearance workers. They may receive commissions based on the price of the service, or a salary based on the number of hours worked, and many receive commissions on the products they sell. In addition, some salons pay bonuses to employees who bring in new business. For many personal appearance workers, the ability to attract and hold regular clients is a key factor in determining earnings.

Although some salons offer paid vacations and medical benefits, many self-employed and part-time workers in this occupation do not enjoy such benefits. Some personal appearance workers receive free trail products from manufacturers in the hope that they will recommend the products to clients.

Related Occupations

	Page
Fitness workers..	513
Makeup artists, theatrical and performance	526
Massage therapists	452

Sources of Additional Information
For details on State licensing requirements and approved barber or cosmetology schools, contact your State boards of barber or cosmetology examiners.

State licensing board requirements and a list of licensed training schools for cosmetologists may be obtained from:
➤ National Accrediting Commission of Cosmetology Arts and Sciences, 4401 Ford Ave., Suite 1300, Alexandria, VA 22302. Internet: **http://www.naccas.org**

Information about a career in cosmetology is available from:
➤ National Cosmetology Association, 401 N. Michigan Ave., Chicago, IL 60611. Internet: **http://www.ncacares.org**

For information on a career as a barber, contact:
➤ National Association of Barber Boards of America, 2703 Pine Street, Arkadelphia, AR 71923. Internet: **http://www.nationalbarberboards.com**

The Occupational Information Network (O*NET) provides information on a wide range of occupational characteristics. Links to O*NET appear at the end of the Internet version of this occupational statement, accessible at **http://www.bls.gov/ooh/ocos332.htm**

Child Care Workers

Significant Points

- About 33 percent of child care workers are self-employed, most of whom provided child care in their homes.

- Training requirements range from a high school diploma to a college degree, although some jobs require less than a high school diploma.

- Many workers leave these jobs every year, creating good job opportunities.

Nature of the Work

Child care workers nurture, teach, and care for children who have not yet entered kindergarten. They also supervise older children before and after school. These workers play an important role in children's development by caring for them when their parents are at work or are away for other reasons or when the parents place their children in care to help them socialize with children their age. In addition to attending to children's health, safety, and nutrition, child care workers organize activities and implement curricula that stimulate children's physical, emotional, intellectual, and social growth. They help children explore individual interests, develop talents and independence, build self-esteem, learn how to get along with others, and prepare for more formal schooling.

Child care workers generally are classified into three different groups based on where they work: private household workers, who care for children at the children's homes; family child care providers, who care for children in the providers' homes; and child care workers who work at child care centers, which include Head Start, Early Head Start, full-day and part-day preschool, and other early childhood programs.

Private household workers who are employed on an hourly basis usually are called babysitters. These child care workers bathe, dress, and feed children; supervise their play; wash their clothes; and clean their rooms. Babysitters also may put children to bed and wake them, read to them, involve them in educational games, take them for doctors' visits, and discipline them. Those who are in charge of infants prepare bottles and change diapers. Babysitters may work for many different families. Workers who are employed by one family are often called nannies. They generally take care of children from birth to age 12, tending to the child's early education, nutrition, health, and other needs. They also may perform the duties of a housekeeper, including cleaning and doing the laundry.

Family child care providers often work alone with a small group of children, although some work in larger settings they work in groups or teams. Child care centers generally have more than one adult per group of children; in groups of children aged 3 to 5 years, a child care worker may assist a more experienced preschool teacher.

Most child care workers perform a combination of basic care and teaching duties, but the majority of their time is spent on caregiving activities. However, there is an increasing focus on preparing children aged 3 to 5 years for school. Workers whose primary responsibility is teaching are classified as preschool teachers. (Preschool teachers are covered elsewhere in the *Handbook*.) However, many basic care activities also are opportunities for children to learn. For example, a worker who shows a child how to tie a shoelace teaches the child while providing for that child's basic needs.

Child care workers spend most of their day working with children. However, they do maintain contact with parents or guardians through informal meetings or scheduled conferences to discuss each child's progress and needs. Many child care workers keep records of each child's progress and suggest ways in which parents can stimulate their child's learning and development at home. Some child care centers and before- and afterschool programs actively recruit parent volunteers to work with the children and participate in administrative decisions and program planning.

Young children learn mainly through playing, solving problems, questioning, and experimenting. Child care workers recognize that fact and capitalize on children's play and other experiences to further their language development (through storytelling and acting games), improve their social skills (by having them work together to build a neighborhood in a sandbox), and introduce scientific and mathematical concepts (by balancing and counting blocks when building a bridge or mixing colors when painting). Often, a less structured approach, including small-group lessons; one-on-one instruction; and creative activities such as art, dance, and music, is used to teach young children. Child care workers play a vital role in preparing children to build the skills they will need in school.

Child care workers in child care centers, schools, or family child care homes greet young children as they arrive, help them with their jackets, and select an activity of interest. When caring for infants, they feed and change them. To ensure a well-balanced program, child care workers prepare daily and long-term schedules of activities. Each day's activities balance individual and group play, as well as quiet time and time for physical activity. Children are given some freedom to participate in activities they are interested in. As children age, child care workers may provide

Child care workers nurture, teach, and care for children who have not yet entered kindergarten and older children before and after school.

more guided learning opportunities, particularly in the areas of math and reading.

Concern over school-aged children being home alone before and after school has spurred many parents to seek alternative ways for their children to spend their time constructively. The purpose of before- and after-school programs is to watch over school-aged children during the gap between school hours and the end of their parents' daily work hours. These programs also may operate during the summer and on weekends. Workers in before- and after-school programs may help students with their homework or engage them in extracurricular activities, including field trips, sports, learning about computers, painting, photography, and other subjects. Some child care workers are responsible for taking children to school in the morning and picking them up from school in the afternoon. Before- and after-school programs may be operated by public school systems, local community centers, or other private organizations.

Helping to keep children healthy is another important part of the job. Child care workers serve nutritious meals and snacks and teach good eating habits and personal hygiene. They ensure that children have proper rest periods. They identify children who may not feel well, and they may help parents locate programs that will provide basic health services. Child care workers also watch for children who show signs of emotional or developmental problems. Upon identifying such a child, they discuss the child's situation with their supervisor and the child's parents. Early identification of children with special needs—such as those with behavioral, emotional, physical, or learning disabilities—is important in improving their future learning ability. Special education teachers often work with preschool children to provide the individual attention they need. (Special education teachers are discussed elsewhere in the *Handbook.*)

Work environment. Helping children grow, learn, and gain new skills can be very rewarding. The work is sometimes routine, but new activities and challenges mark each day. Child care can be physically and emotionally taxing as workers con-

stantly stand, walk, bend, stoop, and lift to attend to each child's interests and problems. These workers experienced a larger than average number of work-related injuries or illnesses.

States regulate child care facilities, the number of children per child care worker, the qualifications of the staff, and the health and safety of the children. To ensure that children in child care centers receive proper supervision, State or local regulations may require a certain ratio of workers to children. The ratio varies with the age of the children. For infants (children under 1 year old), child care workers may be responsible for 3 or 4 children. For toddler's (children 1 to 2 years old), workers may be responsible for 4 to 10 children, and for preschool-aged children (those between 3 and 5 years old), workers may be responsible for 8 to 25 children. However, these regulations vary greatly from State to State. In before- and after-school programs, workers may be responsible for many school-aged children at a time.

Family child care providers work out of their own homes, an arrangement that provides convenience, but also requires that their homes be accommodating to young children. Private household workers usually work in the homes or apartments of their employers. Most live in their own homes and travel to work, although some live in the home of their employer and generally are provided with their own room and bath. They often come to feel like part of their employer's family.

The work hours of child care workers vary widely. Child care centers usually are open year round, with long hours so that parents can drop off and pick up their children before and after work. Some centers employ full-time and part-time staff with staggered shifts to cover the entire day. Some workers are unable to take regular breaks during the day due to limited staffing. Public and many private preschool programs operate during the typical 9- or 10-month school year, employing both full-time and part-time workers. Family child care providers have flexible hours and daily routines, but they may work long or unusual hours to fit parents' work schedules. Live-in nannies usually work longer hours than do child care workers who live in their own homes. However, although nannies may work evenings or weekends, they usually get other time off. About 36 percent worked part time.

Training, Other Qualifications, and Advancement
Licensure and training requirements vary greatly by State, but some jobs require less than a high school diploma.

Education and training. The training and qualifications required of child care workers vary widely. Each State has its own licensing requirements that regulate caregiver training. These requirements range from less than a high school diploma, to a national Child Development Associate (CDA) credential, to community college courses or a college degree in child development or early childhood education. State requirements are generally higher for workers at child care centers than for family child care providers.

Child care workers in private settings who care for only a few children often are not regulated by States at all. Child care workers generally can obtain some form of employment with less than a high school diploma and little or no experience, but certain private firms and publicly funded programs have more demanding training and education requirements. Different public funding streams may set other education and professional development requirements. For example, many States have separate funding for prekindergarten programs for 4-year-old children. In accordance with the regulations that accompany the funding, these States typically set higher education degree requirements for those workers than do ordinary State child care licensing requirements.

Some employers prefer workers who have taken secondary or postsecondary courses in child development and early childhood education or who have work experience in a child care setting. Other employers require their own specialized training. An increasing number of employers are requiring an associate's degree in early childhood education

Licensure. Many States require child care centers, including those in private homes, to be licensed if they care for more than a few children. In order to obtain their license, child care centers may require child care workers to pass a background check, get immunizations, and meet a minimum training requirement.

Other qualifications. Child care workers must anticipate and prevent problems, deal with disruptive children, provide fair but firm discipline, and be enthusiastic and constantly alert. They must communicate effectively with the children and their parents, as well as with teachers and other child care workers. Workers should be mature, patient, understanding, and articulate and have energy and physical stamina. Skills in music, art, drama, and storytelling also are important. Self-employed child care workers must have business sense and management abilities.

Certification and advancement. Some employers prefer to hire child care workers who have earned a nationally recognized Child Development Associate (CDA) credential or the Child Care Professional (CCP) designation from the Council for Professional Recognition and the National Child Care Association, respectively. Requirements include child care experience and coursework, such as college courses or employer-provided seminars.

Opportunities for advancement are limited. However, as child care workers gain experience, some may advance to supervisory or administrative positions in large child care centers or preschools. Often, these positions require additional training, such as a bachelor's or master's degree. Other workers move on to work in resource and referral agencies, consulting with parents on available child care services. A few workers become involved in policy or advocacy work related to child care and early childhood education. With a bachelor's degree, workers may become preschool teachers or become certified to teach in public or private schools. Some workers set up their own child care businesses.

Employment

Child care workers held about 1.3 million jobs in 2008. About 33 percent of child care workers were self-employed; most of these were family child care providers.

Child day care services employed about 19 percent of all child care workers, and about 19 percent worked for private households. The remainder worked primarily in educational services; nursing and residential care facilities; amusement and recreation industries; civic and social organizations; and individual and family services. Some child care programs are for-profit centers, which may be affiliated with a local or national company. A very small percentage of private-industry establishments operate onsite child care centers for the children of their employees.

Job Outlook

Child care workers are expected to experience job growth that is about as fast as the average for all occupations. Job prospects will be good because of the many workers who leave the occupation and need to be replaced.

Employment change. Employment of child care workers is projected to increase by 11 percent between 2008 and 2018, which is about as fast as the average for all occupations. An increasing emphasis on early childhood education programs will increase demand for these workers. Child care workers often work alongside preschool teachers as assistants. Therefore, increased demand for formal preschool programs will create growth for child care workers. Although only a few States currently provide targeted or universal preschool programs, many more are considering or starting such programs. A rise in enrollment in private preschools is likely as the value of formal education before kindergarten becomes more widely accepted. More States moving toward universal preschool education could increase employment growth for child care workers. However, growth will be moderated by relatively slow growth in the population of children under the age of five, who are generally cared for by these workers.

Job prospects. High replacement needs should create good job opportunities for child care workers. Qualified persons who are interested in this work should have little trouble finding and keeping a job. Many child care workers must be replaced each year as they leave the occupation to fulfill family responsibilities, to study, or for other reasons. Others leave because they are interested in pursuing other occupations or because of low wages.

Earnings

Pay depends on the educational attainment of the worker and the type of establishment. Although the pay generally is very low, more education usually means higher earnings. Median hourly wages of child care workers were $9.12 in May 2008. The mid-

Projections data from the National Employment Matrix

Occupational Title	SOC Code	Employment, 2008	Projected Employment, 2018	Change, 2008-2018	
				Number	Percent
Child care workers	39-9011	1,301,900	1,443,900	142,100	11

(NOTE) Data in this table are rounded. See the discussion of the employment projections table in the *Handbook* introductory chapter on *Occupational Information Included in the Handbook.*

dle 50 percent earned between $7.75 and $11.30. The lowest 10 percent earned less than $7.04, and the highest 10 percent earned more than $13.98. Median hourly wages in the industries employing the largest numbers of child care workers in May 2008 were:

Other residential care facilities	$10.56
Elementary and secondary schools	10.53
Civic and social organizations	8.53
Other amusement and recreation industries	8.41
Child day care services	8.39

Earnings of self-employed child care workers vary with the number of hours worked, the number and ages of the children, and the geographic location.

Benefits vary, but are minimal for most child care workers. Many employers offer free or discounted child care to employees. Some offer a full benefits package, including health insurance and paid vacations, but others offer no benefits at all. Some employers offer seminars and workshops to help workers learn new skills. A few are willing to cover the cost of courses taken at community colleges or technical schools. Live-in nannies receive free room and board.

Related Occupations

Child care work requires patience; creativity; an ability to nurture, motivate, teach, and influence children; and leadership, organizational, and administrative skills. Others who work with children and need these qualities and skills include:

	Page
Teacher assistants	276
Teachers—kindergarten, elementary, middle, and secondary	288
Teachers—preschool, except special education	286
Teachers—special education	294

Sources of Additional Information

For an electronic question-and-answer service on child care, for information on becoming a child care provider, and for information on other resources, contact:

➤ National Child Care Information Center, 10530 Rosehaven St., Suite 400 Fairfax, VA 22030. Internet: **http://www.nccic.org**

For eligibility requirements and a description of the Child Development Associate credential, contact:

➤ Council for Professional Recognition, 2460 16th St., NW., Washington, DC 20009-3547. Internet: **http://www.cdacouncil.org**

For eligibility requirements and a description of the Child Care Professional designation, contact:

➤ National Child Care Association, 1325 G St., NW., Suite 500, Washington, DC 20005. Internet: **http://www.nccanet.org**

For information about early childhood education, contact:

➤ National Association for the Education of Young Children, 1313 L St., NW., Suite 500 Washington, DC 20005. Internet: **http://www.naeyc.org**

For information about a career as a nanny, contact:

➤ International Nanny Association, PO Box 1299, Hyannis, MA 02601. Internet: **http://www.nanny.org**

State departments of human services or social services can supply State regulations and training requirements for child care workers.

The Occupational Information Network (O*NET) provides information on a wide range of occupational characteristics. Links to O*NET appear at the end of the Internet version of this occupational statement, accessible at **http://www.bls.gov/ooh/ocos170.htm**

Fitness Workers

Significant Points

- Many fitness and personal training jobs are part time, but many workers increase their hours by working at several different facilities or at clients' homes.

- Most fitness workers need to be certified.

- Employment is expected to grow much faster than the average.

- Job prospects are expected to be good.

Nature of the Work

Fitness workers lead, instruct, and motivate individuals or groups in exercise activities, including cardiovascular exercise, strength training, and stretching. They work in health clubs, country clubs, hospitals, universities, yoga and Pilates studios, resorts, and clients' homes. Fitness workers also are found in workplaces, where they organize and direct health and fitness programs for employees. Although gyms and health clubs offer a variety of exercise activities, such as weight lifting, yoga, cardiovascular training, and karate, fitness workers typically specialize in only a few areas.

Personal trainers work one-on-one or with two or three clients, either in a gym or in the clients' homes. They help clients assess their level of physical fitness and set and reach fitness

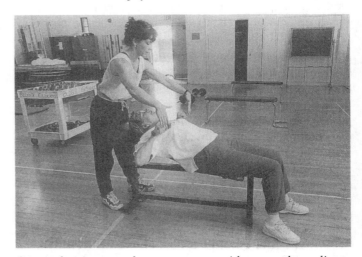

Personal trainers work one-on-one or with two or three clients, either in a gym or in the client's home.

goals. *Trainers* also demonstrate various exercises and help clients improve their exercise techniques. They may keep records of their clients' exercise sessions to monitor the clients' progress toward physical fitness. They also may advise their clients on how to modify their lifestyles outside of the gym to improve their fitness.

Group exercise instructors conduct group exercise sessions that usually include aerobic exercise, stretching, and muscle conditioning. Cardiovascular conditioning classes often are set to music. *Instructors* select the music and choreograph a corresponding exercise sequence. Two increasingly popular conditioning methods taught in exercise classes are Pilates and yoga. In these classes, instructors demonstrate the different moves and positions of the particular method; they also observe students and correct those who are doing the exercises improperly. Group exercise instructors are responsible for ensuring that their classes are motivating, safe, and challenging, yet not too difficult for the participants.

Fitness directors oversee the fitness-related aspects of a health club or fitness center. They create and oversee programs that meet the needs of the club's members, including new-member orientations, fitness assessments, and workout incentive programs. They also select fitness equipment; coordinate personal training and group exercise programs; hire, train, and supervise fitness staff; and carry out administrative duties.

Fitness workers in smaller facilities with few employees may perform a variety of functions in addition to their fitness duties, such as tending the front desk, signing up new members, giving tours of the fitness center, writing newsletter articles, creating posters and flyers, and supervising the weight-training and cardiovascular equipment areas. In larger commercial facilities, personal trainers often are required to sell their services to members and to make a specified number of sales. Some fitness workers may combine the duties of group exercise instructors and personal trainers; in smaller facilities, the fitness director may teach classes and do personal training.

Work environment. Most fitness workers spend their time indoors at fitness or recreation centers and health clubs. Fitness directors and supervisors, however, typically spend most of their time in an office. In some fitness centers, workers may split their time among doing office work, engaging in personal training, and teaching classes. Nevertheless, fitness workers at all levels risk suffering injuries during physical activities.

Since most fitness centers are open long hours, fitness workers often work nights and weekends and even occasional holidays. In 2008, about 40 percent of fitness workers were part-time employees. Some may travel from place to place throughout the day, to different gyms or to clients' homes, to maintain a full work schedule.

Fitness workers generally enjoy a lot of autonomy. Group exercise instructors choreograph or plan their own classes, and personal trainers have the freedom to design and implement their clients' workout routines.

Training, Other Qualifications, and Advancement

For most fitness workers, certification is critical. Personal trainers usually must be certified to begin working with clients or

with members of a fitness facility. Group fitness instructors may begin without a certification, but they are often encouraged or required by their employers to become certified.

Education and training. The education and training required depends on the specific type of fitness work: personal training, group fitness, and a specialization such as Pilates or yoga each need different preparation. Personal trainers often start out by taking classes to become certified. Then they may begin by working alongside an experienced trainer before being allowed to train clients alone. Group fitness instructors often get started by participating in exercise classes until they are ready to audition as instructors and, if the audition is successful, begin teaching classes. They also may improve their skills by taking training courses or attending fitness conventions. Most employers require instructors to work toward becoming certified.

Fitness workers usually do not receive much on-the-job training; they are expected to know how to do their jobs when they are hired. Workers may receive some organizational training to learn about the operations of their new employer. Occasionally, they receive specialized training if they are expected to teach or lead a specific method of exercise or focus on a particular age or ability group. Because requirements vary from employer to employer, before pursuing training it may be helpful to contact local fitness centers or other potential employers to find out what background they prefer.

An increasing number of employers are requiring fitness workers to have a bachelor's degree in a field related to health or fitness, such as exercise science or physical education. Some employers allow workers to substitute a college degree for certification, but most employers who require a bachelor's degree also require certification.

Training for *Pilates* and *yoga instructors* has changed. When interest in these forms of exercise exploded, the demand for teachers grew faster than the ability to train them properly. Inexperienced teachers contributed to student injuries, leading to a push toward more standardized, rigorous requirements for teacher training.

Pilates and *yoga teachers* now need specialized training in their particular method of exercise. For Pilates, training options range from weekend-long workshops to yearlong programs, but the trend is toward requiring even more training. The Pilates Method Alliance has established training standards that recommend at least 200 hours of training; the group also has standards for training schools and maintains a list of training schools that meet the requirements. However, some Pilates teachers are certified group exercise instructors who attend short Pilates workshops; currently, many fitness centers hire people with minimal Pilates training if the applicants have a fitness certification and group fitness experience.

Training requirements for yoga teachers are similar to those for Pilates teachers. Training programs range from a few days to more than 2 years. Many people get their start by taking yoga; eventually, their teachers may consider them ready to assist or to substitute teach. Some students may begin teaching their own classes when their yoga teachers think that they are ready; the teachers may even provide letters of recommendation. Those who wish to pursue teaching more seriously usually seek formal teacher training.

Currently, there are many training programs throughout the yoga community, as well as programs throughout the fitness industry. The Yoga Alliance has established training standards requiring at least 200 training hours, with a specified number of hours in techniques, teaching methodology, anatomy, physiology, philosophy, and other areas. The Yoga Alliance also registers schools that train students to its standards. Because some schools may meet the standards but not be registered, prospective students should check the requirements and decide whether particular schools meet them.

Certification and other qualifications. The most important characteristic that an employer looks for in a new fitness instructor is the ability to plan and lead a class that is motivating and safe. Group fitness instructors do not necessarily require certification to begin working. However, most organizations encourage their group instructors to become certified over time, and many require it.

In the fitness field, there are many organizations that offer certification. Getting certified by one of the top certification organizations is becoming increasingly important, especially for personal trainers. One way to ensure that a certifying organization is reputable is to make sure that it is accredited by the National Commission for Certifying Agencies.

Most certifying organizations require candidates to have a high school diploma, be certified in cardiopulmonary resuscitation (CPR), and pass an exam. All certification exams have a written component, and some also have a practical component. The exams measure knowledge of human physiology, understanding of proper exercise techniques, assessment of client fitness levels, and development of appropriate exercise programs. There is no particular training program required for certification; candidates may prepare however they prefer. Certifying organizations do offer study materials, including books, CD-ROMs, other audio and visual materials, and exam preparation workshops and seminars, but candidates are not required to purchase materials to take exams.

Certification generally is good for 2 years, after which workers must become recertified by attending continuing education classes or conferences, writing articles, or giving presentations. Some organizations offer more advanced certification that requires an associate's or bachelor's degree in an exercise-related subject for individuals who are interested in training athletes, working with people who are injured or ill, or advising clients on general health.

Pilates and yoga instructors usually do not need group exercise certification to maintain their employment. It is more important that they have specialized training in their particular method of exercise. However, the Pilates Method Alliance does offer certification. Pilates certification requires 450 hours of documented training or 720 hours of full-time work the previous 12 months.

People planning fitness careers should be outgoing, excellent communicators, good at motivating people, and sensitive to the needs of others. Excellent health and physical fitness are important because of the physical nature of the job. Those who wish to be personal trainers in a large commercial fitness center should have strong sales skills. All personal trainers should have the personality and motivation to attract and retain clients.

Advancement. A bachelor's degree in exercise science, physical education, kinesiology (the study of the mechanics of human motion, including the role of the muscles), or a related area, along with experience, usually is required to advance to management positions in a health club or fitness center. Some organizations require a master's degree. As in other occupations, managerial skills also are needed to advance to supervisory or managerial positions. College courses in management, business administration, accounting, and personnel management may be helpful, but many fitness companies have corporate universities in which they train employees for management positions.

Personal trainers may advance to head trainer, with responsibility for hiring and overseeing the personal training staff and for bringing in new personal-training clients. Group fitness instructors may be promoted to group exercise director, a position responsible for hiring instructors and coordinating exercise classes. Later, a worker might become the fitness director of an organization, managing the fitness budget and staff. A worker also might become the general manager, whose main focus is the financial aspects of the organization, particularly setting and achieving sales goals; in a small fitness center, however, the general manager usually is involved with all aspects of running the facility. Some workers go into business for themselves and open their own fitness centers.

Employment

Fitness workers held about 261,100 jobs in 2008. About 61 percent of all personal trainers and group exercise instructors worked in fitness and recreational sports centers, including health clubs. Another 13 percent worked in civic and social organizations. About 9 percent of fitness workers were self-employed; many of these were personal trainers, while others were group fitness instructors working on a contract basis with fitness centers. Many fitness jobs are part time, and many workers hold multiple jobs, teaching or doing personal training at several different fitness centers and at clients' homes.

Job Outlook

Jobs for fitness workers are expected to increase much faster than the average for all occupations. Fitness workers should

Projections data from the National Employment Matrix

Occupational Title	SOC Code	Employment, 2008	Projected Employment, 2018	Change, 2008-2018	
				Number	Percent
Fitness trainers and aerobics instructors	39-9031	261,100	337,900	76,800	29

(NOTE) Data in this table are rounded. See the discussion of the employment projections table in the *Handbook* introductory chapter on *Occupational Information Included in the Handbook.*

have good opportunities because of continued job growth in health clubs, fitness facilities, and other settings in which fitness workers are concentrated.

Employment change. Employment of fitness workers is expected to increase 29 percent over the 2008–18 decade, which is much faster than the average for all occupations. These workers are expected to gain jobs because an increasing number of people are spending time and money on fitness and more businesses are recognizing the benefits of health and fitness programs for their employees.

Aging baby boomers, one group that increasingly is becoming concerned with staying healthy and physically fit, will be the main driver of employment growth in fitness workers. An additional factor is the combination of a reduction in the number of physical education programs in schools with parents' growing concern about childhood obesity. This factor will increase the need for fitness workers to work with children in nonschool settings, such as health clubs. Increasingly, parents also are hiring personal trainers for their children, and the number of weight-training gyms for children is expected to continue to grow. Health club membership among young adults has grown steadily as well, driven by concern with physical fitness and by rising incomes.

As health clubs strive to provide more personalized service to keep their members motivated, they will continue to offer personal training and a wide variety of group exercise classes. Participation in yoga and Pilates is expected to continue to increase, driven partly by the aging population, which demands low-impact forms of exercise and seeks relief from arthritis and other ailments.

Job prospects. Opportunities are expected to be good for fitness workers because demand for these workers is expected to remain strong in health clubs, fitness facilities, and other settings in which fitness workers are concentrated. In addition, many job openings will stem from the need to replace the large numbers of workers who leave these occupations each year. Part-time jobs will be easier to find than full-time jobs. People with degrees in fitness-related subjects will have better opportunities because clients prefer to work with people they perceive as higher quality trainers. Trainers who incorporate new technology and wellness issues as part of their services may be in more demand.

Earnings

Median annual wages of fitness trainers and aerobics instructors in May 2008 were $29,210. The middle 50 percent earned between $19,610 and $44,420. The bottom 10 percent earned less than $16,120, while the top 10 percent earned $60,760 or more. These figures do not include the earnings of the self-employed. Earnings of successful self-employed personal trainers can be much higher. Median annual wages in the industries employing the largest numbers of fitness workers in May 2008 were as follows:

General medical and surgical hospitals	$32,140
Fitness and recreational sports centers	30,610
Local government	30,200
Civic and social organizations	25,110
Other schools and instruction	24,230

Because many fitness workers work part time, they often do not receive benefits such as health insurance or retirement plans from their employers. They are able to use fitness facilities at no cost, however.

Related Occupations

Other occupations that focus on health and physical fitness include the following:

	Page
Athletes, coaches, umpires, and related workers	321
Dietitians and nutritionists	366
Physical therapists	377
Recreation workers	522

Sources of Additional Information

For more information about fitness careers and about universities and other institutions offering programs in health and fitness, contact:

➤ National Strength and Conditioning Association, 1885 Bob Johnson Drive, Colorado Springs, CO 80906. Internet: **http://www.nsca-lift.org**

For information about personal trainer and group fitness instructor certifications, contact:

➤ American College of Sports Medicine, P.O. Box 1440, Indianapolis, IN 46206-1440. Internet: **http://www.acsm.org**

➤ American Council on Exercise, 4851 Paramount Dr., San Diego, CA 92123. Internet: **http://www.acefitness.org**

➤ National Academy of Sports Medicine, 26632 Agoura Rd., Calabasas, CA 91302. Internet: **http://www.nasm.org**

➤ NSCA Certification Commission, 1885 Bob Johnson Drive, Colorado Springs, CO 80906. Internet: **http://www.nsca-cc.org**

For information about Pilates certification and training programs, contact:

➤ Pilates Method Alliance, P.O. Box 37096, Miami, FL 33137-0906. Internet: **http://www.pilatesmethodalliance.org**

For information on yoga teacher training programs, contact:

➤ Yoga Alliance, 1701 Clarendon Boulevard, Suite 110, Arlington, VA 22209. Internet: **http://www.yogaalliance.org**

For information about health clubs and sports clubs, contact:

➤ International Health, Racquet, and Sportsclub Association, Seaport Center, 70 Fargo Street, Boston, MA 02210. Internet: **http://cms.ihrsa.org**

The Occupational Information Network (O*NET) provides information on a wide range of occupational characteristics. Links to O*NET appear at the end of the Internet version of this occupational statement, accessible at

http://www.bls.gov/ooh/ocos296.htm

Flight Attendants

Significant Points

- Competition for positions is expected to remain keen because the opportunity for travel attracts more applicants than there are jobs.

- Job duties are learned through formal on-the-job training at a flight training center.

- A high school diploma is the minimum educational requirement, but airlines prefer applicants with a college degree and with experience in dealing with the public.

Nature of the Work

Major airlines are required by law to provide *flight attendants* for the safety and security of the traveling public. Although the primary job of the flight attendants is to ensure that security and safety regulations are followed, attendants also try to make flights comfortable and enjoyable for passengers.

At least 1 hour before takeoff, attendants are briefed by the captain—the pilot in command—on such things as emergency evacuation procedures, coordination of the crew, the length of the flight, expected weather conditions, and any special issues having to do with passengers. Flight attendants make sure that first-aid kits and other emergency equipment are aboard and in working order and that the passenger cabin is in order, with adequate supplies of food, beverages, and any other amenities. As passengers board the plane, flight attendants greet them, check their tickets, and tell them where to store carry-on items.

Before the plane takes off, flight attendants instruct all passengers in the use of emergency equipment and check to see that seatbelts are fastened, seat backs are in upright positions, and all carry-on items are properly stowed. In the air, helping passengers in the event of an emergency is the most important responsibility of a flight attendant. Safety-related actions range from reassuring passengers during rough weather to directing passengers who must evacuate a plane following an emergency landing. Flight attendants also answer questions about the flight, and help small children, elderly or disabled persons, and any others needing assistance. Flight attendants may administer first aid to passengers who become ill. Flight attendants generally serve beverages and on many flights sell precooked meals or snacks. Prior to landing, flight attendants take inventory of headsets, alcoholic beverages, and moneys collected. They also report any medical problems passengers may have had, the condition of cabin equipment, and any lost-and-found articles.

Lead, or first, flight attendants, sometimes known as *pursers,* oversee the work of the other attendants aboard the aircraft, while performing most of the same duties.

Work environment. Because airlines operate around the clock and year round, flight attendants can work nights, holidays, and weekends. In most cases, agreements between the airline and the employees' union determine the total daily and monthly working time. Scheduled on-duty time usually is limited to 12 hours per day, however flight attendants can be scheduled up to 14 hours per day, with somewhat greater maximums

Flight attendants spend a great deal of time away from home.

for international flying. The Federal Aviation Administration (FAA) requires that flight attendants receive 9 consecutive hours of rest following any duty period.

Attendants usually fly 65 to 90 hours a month and generally spend another 50 hours a month on the ground preparing planes for flights, writing reports following completed flights, and waiting for planes to arrive. Most airlines guarantee a minimum of 65 to 85 flight hours per month, with the option to work additional hours. Flight attendants receive extra compensation for additional hours.

Flight attendants may be away from their home base at least one-third of the time. During this period, the airlines provide hotel accommodations and an allowance for meal expenses.

Flight attendants must be flexible and willing to relocate. However, many flight attendants elect to live in one place and commute to their assigned home base. Home bases and routes worked are bid for and awarded on a seniority basis, so the longer the flight attendant has been employed, the more likely he or she is to work on their preferred flights. Almost all flight attendants start out working on reserve status, or on call. Flight attendants on reserve status usually live near their home base, because they are required to be able to report to their home base on short notice. On small corporate airlines, flight attendants often work on an as-needed basis and must adapt to varying environments and passengers.

The combination of free time and free or discounted airfares provides flight attendants the opportunity to travel. However, the work can be strenuous and trying. Flight attendants stand during much of the flight and must remain pleasant and efficient, regardless of how tired they are or how demanding passengers may be. Occasionally, flight attendants must deal with turbulent flights which can cause difficulties regarding service and cause anxiety among passengers that flight attendants must address.

Working in a moving aircraft leaves flight attendants susceptible to injuries. According to BLS data, full-time flight attendants experienced a much higher than average work-related injury and illness rate. Various physical injuries can occur when opening overhead compartments or while pushing heavy service carts. In addition, medical problems can arise from irregular sleeping and eating patterns, dealing with stressful passengers, working in a pressurized environment, and breathing recycled air.

Training, Other Qualifications, and Advancement

Flight attendants must be certified by the FAA. A high school diploma or its equivalent is the minimum educational requirement, but airlines increasingly prefer applicants who have a college degree. Experience in dealing with the public is important, because flight attendants must be able to interact comfortably with strangers and remain calm under duress.

Education and training. A high school diploma or its equivalent is the minimum educational requirement. However, airlines increasingly prefer applicants with a college degree. Applicants who attend schools or colleges that offer flight attendant training may have an advantage over other applicants. Highly desirable areas of concentration include people-oriented disciplines, such as communications, psychology, nursing, travel and tourism, hospitality, and education. Flight attendants for international airlines generally must speak a foreign language fluently. For their international flights, some of the major airlines prefer candidates who can speak two major foreign languages.

Once hired, all candidates must undergo a period of formal training. The length of training, ranging from 3 to 6 weeks, depends on the size and type of carrier and takes place at the airline's flight training center. Airlines that do not operate training centers generally send new employees to the center of another airline. Some airlines may provide transportation to the training centers and an allowance for room, board, and school supplies, while other airlines charge individuals for training. New trainees are not considered employees of the airline until they successfully complete the training program. Trainees learn emergency procedures, such as evacuating an airplane, operating emergency systems and equipment, administering first aid, and surviving in the water. In addition, trainees are taught how to deal with disruptive passengers and with hijacking and terrorist situations. New hires learn flight regulations and duties, gain knowledge of company operations and policies, and receive instruction on personal grooming and weight control. Trainees for international routes get additional instruction in passport and customs regulations. Trainees must perform many drills and duties unaided, in front of the training staff. Throughout training, they also take tests designed to eliminate unsuccessful trainees. Toward the end of their training, students go on practice flights. Upon successful completion of training, flight attendants receive the FAA Certificate of Demonstrated Proficiency. Flight attendants also are required to go through periodic retraining and pass an FAA safety examination to continue flying.

Licensure and certification. All flight attendants must be certified by the FAA. To be certified, flight attendants are required to successfully complete training requirements, such as

evacuation, fire fighting, medical emergency, and security procedures established by the FAA and the Transportation Security Administration. They also must perform the assigned duties of a cabin crew member and complete an approved proficiency check. Flight attendants are certified for specific types of aircraft, regardless of the carrier. Therefore, only 1-day or 2-day recurrent training, with the new carrier, is needed for those flight attendants who change airlines, as long as the type of aircraft remains the same.

Other qualifications. Airlines prefer to hire poised, tactful, and resourceful people who can speak clearly and interact comfortably with strangers and remain calm under duress. Applicants with previous experience in dealing with the public are preferred by airlines. Additionally, airlines usually have age, physical, and appearance requirements. Applicants usually must be at least 18 to 21 years old, although some carriers may have higher minimum-age requirements. Applicants must meet height requirements for reaching overhead bins, which often contain emergency equipment, and most airlines want candidates with weight proportionate to height. Flight attendants must be in excellent health, and a medical evaluation is required. Vision is required to be correctable to 20/30 or better with glasses or contact lenses (uncorrected no worse than 20/200). Men must have their hair cut above the collar and be clean shaven. Airlines prefer applicants with no visible tattoos, body piercing, or unusual hairstyles or makeup.

In addition to education and training, airlines conduct a thorough background check, which goes back as many as 10 years, as required by the FAA,. Everything about an applicant is investigated, including date of birth, employment history, criminal record, school records, and any gaps in employment. Employment is contingent on a successful background check. An applicant will not be offered a job or will be immediately dismissed if his or her background check shows any discrepancies. All U.S. airlines require that applicants be citizens of the United States or registered aliens with legal rights to obtain employment in the United States.

Advancement. After completing initial training, flight attendants are assigned to one of their airline's bases. New flight attendants are placed on reserve status and are called either to staff extra flights or to fill in for crewmembers that are sick, on vacation, or rerouted. When they are not on duty, reserve flight attendants must be available to report for flights on short notice. They usually remain on reserve for at least 1 year but, in some cities, it may take 5 to 10 years—or longer—to advance from reserve status. Flight attendants who no longer are on reserve bid monthly for regular assignments. Because assignments are based on seniority, usually only the most experienced attendants get their choice of assignments. Advancement takes longer today than in the past, because experienced flight attendants are remaining in this career longer than in the past.

Some flight attendants become supervisors, moving from senior or lead flight attendant, to check flight attendant, to flight attendant supervisor, then on to base manager, and finally to manager or vice president of in-flight operations. They may take on additional duties, such as recruiting, instructing, or developing in-flight products. Their experience also may qualify

Projections data from the National Employment Matrix

Occupational Title	SOC Code	Employment, 2008	Projected Employment, 2018	Change, 2008-2018	
				Number	Percent
Flight attendants..	39-6031	98,700	106,700	8,000	8

(NOTE) Data in this table are rounded. See the discussion of the employment projections table in the *Handbook* introductory chapter on *Occupational Information Included in the Handbook.*

them for numerous airline-related jobs involving contact with the public, such as reservation ticket agent or public relations specialist. Flight attendants who do not want to travel often for various reasons may move to a position as an administrative assistant. With additional education, some flight attendants may decide to transfer to other areas of the airline for which they work, such as risk management or human resources.

Employment

Flight attendants held about 98,700 jobs in 2008. Commercial airlines employed the vast majority of flight attendants, and most attendants lived near major metropolitan airports or airports operating as hubs for the major airlines. A small number of flight attendants worked for companies that offered chartered flights.

Job Outlook

Employment of flight attendants is projected to grow about as fast as average. Competition for jobs is expected to remain keen because the opportunity for travel attracts more applicants than there are jobs.

Employment change. Employment of flight attendants is expected to grow by 8 percent, which is about as fast as the average for all occupations over the 2008–18 period. Population growth and an improving economy are expected to boost the number of airline passengers. As airlines expand their capacity to meet rising demand by increasing the number and size of planes in operation and the number of flights offered, more flight attendants will be needed.

Job prospects. Despite growing demand for flight attendants, competition is expected to be keen because this job usually attracts more applicants than there are jobs, with only the most qualified eventually being hired. College graduates who have experience dealing with the public should have the best chance of being hired. Job opportunities may be better with the faster growing regional and commuter, low-cost, and charter airlines. There also are job opportunities for professionally trained flight attendants to work for companies operating private aircraft for their executives.

The majority of job opportunities through the year 2018 will arise from the need to replace flight attendants who leave the labor force or transfer to other occupations, often for higher earnings or a more stable lifestyle. With the job now viewed increasingly as a profession, however, fewer flight attendants leave their jobs, and job turnover is not as high as in the past. According to the Association of Flight Attendants, the average job tenure of attendants is currently 16 years and is increasing.

In the long run, opportunities for persons seeking flight attendant jobs should improve as the airline industry expands. Over the next decade, however, demand for flight attendants

will fluctuate with the demand for air travel, which is highly sensitive to swings in the economy. During downturns, as air traffic declines, the hiring of flight attendants declines, and some experienced attendants may be laid off until traffic recovers.

Earnings

Median annual wages of flight attendants were $35,930 in May 2008. The middle 50 percent earned between $28,420 and $49,910. The lowest 10 percent earned less than $20,580, and the highest 10 percent earned more than $65,350.

According to data from the Association of Flight Attendants, beginning attendants had median earnings of $16,191 a year in 2009. Beginning pay scales for flight attendants vary by carrier, however. New hires usually begin at the same pay scale, regardless of experience; all flight attendants receive the same future pay increases based on an established pay scale.

Some airlines offer incentive pay for working holidays, night and international flights, or taking positions that require additional responsibility or paperwork.

Flight attendants and their immediate families are entitled to free or discounted fares on their own airline and reduced fares on most other airlines. Some airlines require that the flight attendant be with an airline for 3 to 6 months before taking advantage of this benefit. Other benefits may include medical, dental, and life insurance; 401K or other retirement plan; sick leave; paid holidays; stock options; paid vacations; and tuition reimbursement. Flight attendants also receive a "per diem" allowance for meal expenses while on duty away from home. Flight attendants are required to purchase uniforms and wear them while on duty. The airlines usually pay for uniform replacement items, and may provide a small allowance to cover cleaning and upkeep of the uniforms.

The majority of flight attendants hold union membership, primarily with the Association of Flight Attendants. Other unions that represent flight attendants include the Transport Workers Union of America and the International Brotherhood of Teamsters.

Related Occupations

Other jobs that involve helping people as a safety professional, while requiring the ability to be calm even under trying circumstances, include:

Sources of Additional Information

Information about job opportunities and qualifications required for work at a particular airline may be obtained by writing to the airline's human resources office.

For further information on flight attendants, contact:
➤ Association of Flight Attendants-CWA, 501 Third St. NW., Washington, DC 20001. Internet: **http://www.afanet.org**

The Occupational Information Network (O*NET) provides information on a wide range of occupational characteristics. Links to O*NET appear at the end of the Internet version of this occupational statement, accessible at **http://www.bls.gov/ooh/ocos171.htm**

Gaming Services Occupations

Significant Points

- Workers need a license issued by a regulatory agency, such as a State casino control board or commission.

- Competition for jobs is expected to be keen.

- Job prospects will be best for those with previous casino gaming experience, a degree or technical or vocational training in gaming or a hospitality-related field, and strong customer service skills.

Nature of the Work

Legalized gambling in the United States today includes casino gaming, State lotteries, pari-mutuel wagering on contests such as horse or dog racing, and charitable gaming. There are a number of service occupations that are unique to the multibillion-dollar world of gaming, the playing of games of chance.

The majority of *gaming services workers* are employed in casinos. Duties and titles may vary within occupations from one establishment to another. Some positions are associated with oversight and direction—supervision, surveillance, and investigation—while others involve working with the games or patrons themselves by tending slot machines, dealing cards or running games, handling money, writing and running tickets,

Gaming service employees must have excellent customer service skills.

and other activities. In most gaming jobs, workers interact directly with patrons, and part of their responsibility is to make those interactions enjoyable.

Like nearly every business establishment, casinos have workers who direct and oversee day-to-day operations. *Gaming supervisors* and *gaming managers* oversee the gaming operations and personnel in an assigned area. They circulate among the tables and observe the operations to ensure that all of the stations and games are covered for each shift and that workers and gamblers adhere to the rules of the games. Gaming supervisors and gaming managers often interpret or explain the operating rules of the house to patrons who may have difficulty understanding the rules. Periodically, they address complaints about service.

Gaming managers also have additional responsibilities beyond those of supervisors. For example, gaming managers prepare work schedules and station assignments for their subordinates. They are responsible for interviewing, hiring, training, and evaluating new workers.

Slot key persons coordinate and supervise the slot machine department and its workers. Their duties include verifying and paying off jackpots to patrons, resetting slot machines after completing the payoff, and refilling machines with tickets or money. Slot key persons must be familiar with a variety of slot machines and be able to make minor repairs and adjustments to the machines as needed. If major repairs are required, slot key persons determine whether the slot machine should be removed from the floor. They also enforce safety rules and report hazards within their assigned areas.

Gaming and sports book writers and runners assist in the operations of games such as bingo and keno, in addition to taking bets on sporting events. They scan tickets presented by patrons and calculate and distribute winnings. Some writers and runners operate the equipment that randomly selects the numbers. Others may announce numbers selected, pick up tickets from patrons, collect bets, or receive, verify, and record patrons' cash wagers.

Gaming dealers operate table games such as craps, blackjack, and roulette. Standing or sitting behind the table, dealers provide dice, dispense cards to players, or run the equipment. Dealers also monitor the patrons for infractions of casino rules. Gaming dealers must be skilled in customer service and in executing their game. Dealers determine winners, calculate and pay winning bets, and collect losing bets. Most gaming dealers are competent in at least two games, one usually being blackjack or craps.

Work environment. Most casinos are open 24 hours a day, 7 days a week. Employees can be expected to work nights, weekends, and holidays. Casino work can be physically demanding. Most occupations require that workers stand for long periods; some require the lifting of heavy items. The atmosphere in casinos exposes workers to certain hazards, such as cigarette, cigar, and pipe smoke. Noise from slot machines, gaming tables, and talking workers and patrons may be distracting to some, although workers wear protective headgear in areas where loud machinery is used to count money.

Training, Other Qualifications, and Advancement

Each casino establishes its own education, training, and experience requirements, but all gaming service workers must obtain a license from a regulatory agency, such as a State casino control board or commission.

Education and training. There usually are no minimum educational requirements for entry-level gaming jobs, although most employers prefer workers with at least a high school diploma or GED.

Each casino establishes its own requirements for education, training, and experience. Some of the major casinos and slot machine manufacturers run their own training schools, and almost all provide some form of in-house training in addition to requiring certification. The type and quantity of classes needed may vary. Many institutions of higher learning offer training or classes toward certificates in gaming, as well as offering associate's, bachelor's, or master's degrees in a variety of hospitality-related fields, such as hospitality management, hospitality administration, or hotel management. Some schools offer training in games, gaming supervision, slot attendant and slot repair technician work, slot department management, and surveillance and security.

Slot key persons do not need to meet formal educational requirements to enter the occupation, but completion of slot attendant or slot technician training is helpful. As with most other gaming workers, slot key persons receive on-the-job training during the first several weeks of employment.

Gaming and sports book writers and runners usually have at least a high school diploma or GED. Most of these workers receive on-the-job training.

Most gaming dealers acquire their skills by attending a dealer school or a vocational and technical school. Such schools teach the rules and procedures of the games, as well as State and local laws and regulations. Although beneficial, graduation from one of these schools does not guarantee a job at a casino, because most casinos also require prospective dealers to audition for open positions. During the audition, personal qualities are assessed along with knowledge of the games.

For most gaming supervisor and gaming manager positions, an associate's or bachelor's degree is beneficial, but not required. Most employees in these occupations have experience in other gaming occupations, typically as dealers, and have a broad knowledge of casino rules, regulations, procedures, and games.

Licensure. Gaming services workers are required to be licensed by a regulatory agency, such as a State casino control board or commission. Applicants for a license must provide photo identification and pay a fee. Some States may require gaming service workers to be residents of that State. Age requirements vary by State. The licensing application process also includes a background investigation and drug test.

Other qualifications. In addition to possessing a license, gaming services workers need superior customer service skills. Casino gaming workers provide entertainment and hospitality to patrons, and the quality of their service contributes to an establishment's success or failure. Therefore, gaming workers need good communication skills, an outgoing personality, and the ability to maintain their composure even when dealing with angry or demanding patrons. Personal integrity also is important because workers handle large amounts of money.

Gaming services workers who manage money should have some experience handling cash or using calculators or computers. For such positions, most casinos administer a math test to assess an applicant's level of competency.

Gaming supervisors and gaming managers must have strong leadership, organizational, and communication skills. Excellent customer service and employee relations skills also are necessary.

Advancement. Advancement opportunities in casino gaming depend less on workers' previous casino duties and titles than on their ability and eagerness to learn new jobs. For example, an entry-level gaming worker eventually might advance to become a dealer or card room manager or to assume some other supervisory position.

Employment

Gaming services occupations provided 178,700 jobs in 2008. Employment among occupational specialties was distributed as follows:

Gaming dealers	91,100
Gaming supervisors	40,900
Slot key persons	24,400
Gaming and sports book writers and runners	16,200
Gaming managers	6,200

Gaming services workers are found mainly in the traveler accommodation and gambling industries. Most are employed in commercial casinos, including riverboat casinos, casino hotels,

Projections data from the National Employment Matrix

Occupational Title	SOC Code	Employment, 2008	Projected Employment, 2018	Change, 2008-2018	
				Number	Percent
Gaming services occupations	–	178,700	204,400	25,700	14
Gaming managers	11-9071	6,200	6,900	700	12
First-line supervisors/managers of gaming workers	39-1010	65,300	70,800	5,500	8
Gaming supervisors	39-1011	40,900	45,700	4,800	12
Slot key persons	39-1012	24,400	25,100	700	3
Gaming dealers	39-3011	91,100	108,400	17,300	19
Gaming and sports book writers and runners	39-3012	16,200	18,300	2,100	13

(NOTE) Data in this table are rounded. See the discussion of the employment projections table in the *Handbook* introductory chapter on *Occupational Information Included in the Handbook.*

and pari-mutuel racetracks with casinos—known as "racinos," which are legal in 20 states. In addition, there are 29 States with Indian casinos. The largest number of gaming services workers work in casinos in Nevada. Legal lotteries are held in 43 States and the District of Columbia, and pari-mutuel wagering is legal in 40 States. Forty-seven States and the District of Columbia also allow charitable gaming.

Job Outlook

Employment of gaming service workers is expected to grow faster than the average for all occupations. Opportunities will be best for those with previous casino gaming experience, a degree or technical or vocational training in gaming or a hospitality-related field, and strong customer service skills.

Employment change. Employment in gaming services occupations is projected to grow by 14 percent between 2008 and 2018, which is faster than the average for all occupations. The increasing popularity and prevalence of Indian casinos and racinos will provide new job openings. States that have recently legalized gaming in the form of electronic gaming devices or table games will provide growth as more gaming facilities are opened. With many States benefiting from casino gambling in the form of tax revenue or agreements with Indian tribes, additional States are reconsidering their opposition to legalized gambling and will likely approve the construction of more casinos and other gaming establishments during the next decade. Additional job growth will occur as popular tourist destinations, such as Las Vegas, continue to expand their gaming operations.

The increase in gaming reflects growth in the population and in its disposable income, both of which are expected to continue. Higher expectations for customer service among gaming patrons also should result in more jobs for gaming services workers. Because of increasing demand in gaming establishments for additional table games, particularly poker, the largest growth is expected among gaming dealers. However, new automated electronic table games, which eliminate the need for dealers, will moderate growth.

Advancements in slot machine technology, such as coinless slot machines—known as "ticket-in, ticket-out machines"—will cause employment of slot key persons to grow by 3 percent from 2008 to 2018, which is slower than the average for all occupations. Ticket-in, ticket-out technology reduces the need for slot key persons to pay out jackpots, fill hoppers, and reset machines. Additionally, slot machines linked to a network allow adjustments to be made from a central computer server rather than from the floor by a slot key person.

Job prospects. In addition to job openings arising from employment growth, opportunities will result from the need to replace workers transferring to other occupations or leaving the labor force.

Keen competition for gaming services jobs is expected, because there generally are more applicants than jobs. Job prospects in gaming services occupations will be best for those with previous casino gaming experience, a degree or technical or vocational training in gaming or a hospitality-related field, and strong interpersonal and customer service skills.

Earnings

Wages for gaming services workers vary according to occupation, level of experience, training, location, and the size of the gaming establishment. The following were median annual wages for various gaming services occupations in May 2008:

Gaming managers	$68,290
Gaming supervisors	45,500
Slot key persons	25,460
Gaming and sports book writers and runners	19,690
Gaming dealers	16,310

Gaming dealers generally receive a large portion of their earnings from tips in the form of tokens received from players. Earnings from tips vary with the table games the dealer operates, the personal traits of the dealer, and the pooling policies of the casino.

Related Occupations

Other occupations that provide hospitality and customer service include:

	Page
Cashiers	530
Gaming cage workers	565
Retail salespersons	543
Sales worker supervisors	551
Security guards and gaming surveillance officers	481
Tellers	599

Sources of Additional Information

For additional information on careers in gaming, visit your public library and your State gaming regulatory agency or casino control commission.

Information on careers in gaming also is available from:
➤ American Gaming Association, 1299 Pennsylvania Ave. NW., Suite 1175, Washington, DC 20004. Internet: **http://www.americangaming.org**

The Occupational Information Network (O*NET) provides information on a wide range of occupational characteristics. Links to O*NET appear at the end of the Internet version of this occupational statement, accessible at **http://www.bls.gov/ooh/ocos275.htm**

Recreation Workers

Significant Points

- The recreation field offers an unusually large number of part-time and seasonal job opportunities.

- Opportunities for part-time, seasonal, and temporary recreation jobs will be good, but competition will remain keen for full-time career positions.

- Many recreation workers spend most of their time outdoors and may work in a variety of weather conditions.

Many recreation workers spend most of their time outdoors in various weather conditions.

Nature of the Work

As participation in organized recreational activities grows, *recreation workers* will be needed to plan, organize, and direct these activities in local playgrounds and recreation areas, parks, community and senior centers, nursing homes and other senior housing, camps, and tourist attractions. These workers lead groups in activities such as arts and crafts, sports, performing arts, camping, and other special interests. They make sure that participants abide by the rules of the camps and recreational facilities and that safety practices are adhered to so that no one gets injured. Recreation workers also are found in some businesses or business groups, where they direct leisure activities for employees, such as softball or bowling, and organize sports leagues.

Recreation workers hold a variety of positions at different levels of responsibility. Those who work directly with children in residential or day camps are called *camp counselors*. These workers lead and instruct children and teenagers in a variety of outdoor recreation activities, such as swimming, hiking, horseback riding, and camping. In addition, counselors who specialize may teach campers special subjects, such as archery, boating, music, drama, gymnastics, tennis, and computers. In residential camps, counselors also provide guidance and supervise daily living and socialization. *Camp directors* typically supervise camp counselors, plan camp activities or programs, and perform the various administrative functions of a camp.

Workers who provide instruction and coaching primarily in one activity, such as art, music, drama, swimming, or tennis, are called *activity specialists*. These workers can work in camps or anywhere else where there is interest in a single activity.

Recreation leaders are responsible for a recreation program's daily operation. They primarily organize and direct participants, schedule the use of facilities, keep records of equipment use, and ensure that recreation facilities and equipment are used properly. In addition, they may lead classes and provide instruction in a recreational activity.

Recreation supervisors oversee recreation leaders and plan, organize, and manage recreational activities to meet the needs of a variety of populations. These workers often serve as liaisons between the director of the park or recreation center and the recreation leaders. Recreation supervisors with more specialized responsibilities also may direct special activities or events or oversee a major activity, such as aquatics, gymnastics, or one or more performing arts.

Directors of recreation and parks develop and manage comprehensive recreation programs in parks, playgrounds, and other settings. Directors usually serve as technical advisors to State and local recreation and park commissions and may be responsible for recreation and park budgets.

Work environment. Recreation workers work in a variety of settings—for example, a cruise ship, a nature park, a summer camp, or a playground in the center of an urban community. Many recreation workers spend most of their time outdoors and may work in a variety of weather conditions. Recreation directors and supervisors, however, typically spend most of their time in an office, planning programs and special events. Directors and supervisors generally engage in less physical activity than do lower level recreation workers. Nevertheless, recreation workers at all levels risk suffering injuries during physical activities.

Some recreation workers work about 40 hours a week. However, many people entering this field, such as camp counselors, may have some night and weekend work, irregular hours, and seasonal employment. In 2008, about 40 percent of these workers worked part time.

Training, Other Qualifications, and Advancement

The educational and training requirements for recreation workers vary widely with on the type of job. Full-time career positions usually require a college degree. Many jobs, however, require demonstrated knowledge of the activity or can be learned with only a short period of on-the-job training.

Education and training. The educational needs for people entering into this occupational field vary widely depending on the job and level of responsibility. For activity specialists, it is more important to have experience and demonstrated competence in a particular activity, such as art or kayaking, than to have a degree. Camp counselors often are older teenagers or young adults who have experienced camping as a child and enjoy the camping experience. A degree is less important than the counselor's maturity level, ability to work well with children and teens, and ability to make sure that they stay safe.

Those working in administrative positions for large organizations or public recreation systems may need a bachelor's degree or higher. Full-time career professional positions usually require a college degree with a major in parks and recreation or leisure studies, but a bachelor's degree in any liberal arts field may be sufficient for some jobs in the private sector. In industrial recreation, or "employee services" as it is more commonly called, companies that offer recreational activities for their employees prefer to hire those with a bachelor's degree in recreation or leisure studies and a background in business administration.

Employers seeking candidates for some administrative positions favor those with at least a master's degree in parks and recreation, business administration, or public administration. Most require at least an associate's degree in recreation studies or a related field.

An associate's or bachelor's degree in a recreation-related discipline, along with experience, is preferred for most recreation supervisor jobs and is required for most higher level administrative jobs. Graduates of associate's degree programs in parks and recreation, social work, and other human services disciplines also can enter some career recreation positions. High school graduates occasionally enter career positions, but doing so is not common.

Programs leading to an associate's or bachelor's degree in parks and recreation, leisure studies, or related fields are offered at several hundred colleges and universities. Many also offer master's or doctoral degrees in the field. In 2009, 89 bachelor's degree programs in parks and recreation were accredited by the National Recreation and Park Association (NRPA). Accredited programs provide broad exposure to the history, theory, and practice of park and recreation management. Courses offered include community organization; supervision and administration; recreational needs of special populations, such as the elderly or disabled; and supervised fieldwork. Students may specialize in areas such as therapeutic recreation, park management, outdoor recreation, industrial or commercial recreation, and camp management.

Specialized training or experience in a particular field, such as art, music, drama, or athletics, is an asset for many jobs. Some jobs also require certification. For example, a lifesaving certificate is a prerequisite for teaching or coaching water-related activities.

The large number of seasonal and part-time workers learn through on-the-job training.

Licensure and certification. The NRPA certifies individuals for professional and technical jobs. Certified park and recreation professionals must pass an exam. In order to qualify to take the exam, individuals need to (1) have earned a bachelor's degree in a major such as recreation, park resources, or leisure services from a program accredited by the NRPA or have at least 1 year of experience if the program is not accredited; (2) have earned any other bachelor's degree and have at least 3 years of relevant full-time work experience; or (3) have at least 5 years of full-time experience in the field. Continuing education is necessary to remain certified.

Many cities and localities require lifeguards to be certified. Training and certification details vary from State to State and county to county. Information on lifeguards is available from local parks and recreation departments.

Other qualifications. People planning careers in recreation should be outgoing, good at motivating people, and sensitive to the needs of others. Excellent health and physical fitness often are required, due to the physical nature of some jobs. Time management and the ability to manage others also is important.

Advancement. Recreation workers start their careers working with people. As they gain experience, they may get promoted to positions with greater responsibilities. Recreation workers with experience and managerial skills may advance to supervisory or managerial positions. Eventually, they may become the director of a recreation department.

Employment

Recreation workers held about 327,500 jobs in 2008, and many additional workers held summer jobs in the occupation. About 31 percent of recreation workers worked for local governments, primarily in park and recreation departments. About 16 percent of recreation workers were employed by nursing and residential care facilities, and another 10 percent were employed in civic and social organizations, such as the Boy Scouts or Girl Scouts or the YMCA and YWCA.

Job Outlook

Faster than average growth is expected. Jobs opportunities for part-time, seasonal, and temporary recreation workers will be good, but competition will remain keen for career positions as recreation workers.

Employment change. Overall employment of recreation workers is projected to increase by 15 percent between 2008 and 2018, which is faster than the average for all occupations. Although people will spend more time and money on recreation, budget restrictions in State and local government will limit the number of jobs added. Many of the new jobs will be in social assistance organizations and in nursing and residential care facilities. Civic and social organizations and fitness and sports centers will also contribute to growth.

Growth will be driven by the growing numbers of young and older Americans. The large numbers of births in recent years likely will increase the demand for recreation services for children, and retiring baby boomers are expected to have more leisure time, higher disposable incomes, and more concern for health and fitness than previous generations had. The latter fac-

Projections data from the National Employment Matrix

Occupational Title	SOC Code	Employment, 2008	Projected Employment, 2018	Change, 2008-2018	
				Number	Percent
Recreation workers	39-9032	327,500	375,700	48,200	15

(NOTE) Data in this table are rounded. See the discussion of the employment projections table in the *Handbook* introductory chapter on *Occupational Information Included in the Handbook.*

tors should lead to an increasing demand for recreation services for baby boomers.

Job prospects. Applicants for part-time, seasonal, and temporary recreation jobs should have good opportunities, but competition will remain keen for career positions because the recreation field attracts many applicants and because the number of career positions is limited compared with the number of lower level seasonal jobs. Opportunities for staff positions should be best for people with formal training and experience in part-time or seasonal recreation jobs. Volunteer experience, part-time work during school, and a summer job are viewed favorably. Those with graduate degrees should have the best opportunities for supervisory or administrative positions. Job openings will stem from growth and the need to replace the large numbers of workers who leave the occupation each year.

Earnings

In May 2008, median annual wages of recreation workers who worked full time were $21,960. The middle 50 percent earned between $17,680 and $28,810. The lowest paid 10 percent earned less than $15,630, while the highest paid 10 percent earned $37,730 or more. However, earnings of recreation directors and others in supervisory or managerial positions can be substantially higher. Most public and private recreation agencies provide full-time recreation workers with typical benefits; part-time workers receive few, if any, benefits. In May 2008, median annual wages in the industries employing the largest numbers of recreation workers were as follows:

Nursing care facilities	$23,100
Individual and family services	22,260
Local government	21,890
Civic and social organizations	19,800
Other amusement and recreation industries	19,670

The large numbers of temporary, seasonal jobs in the recreation field typically are filled by high school or college students, generally do not have formal education requirements, and are open to anyone with the desired personal qualities. Employers compete for a share of the vacationing student labor force, and although salaries in recreation often are lower than those in other fields, the nature of the work and the opportunity to work outdoors are attractive to many.

Part-time, seasonal, and volunteer jobs in recreation include summer camp counselors, craft specialists, and afterschool and weekend recreation program leaders. In addition, many teachers and college students accept jobs as recreation workers when school is not in session. The vast majority of volunteers serve as activity leaders at local day camp programs or in youth organizations, camps, nursing homes, hospitals, senior centers, and other settings.

Related Occupations

Other occupations that require leadership skills, as well as a desire to work with and help others, include the following:

	Page
Athletes, coaches, umpires, and related workers	321
Counselors	234
Fitness workers	513
Probation officers and correctional treatment specialists	241
Psychologists	215
Recreational therapists	389
Social workers	246
Teachers—self enrichment education	292

Sources of Additional Information

For information on jobs in recreation, contact employers such as local government departments of parks and recreation, nursing homes and other residential facilities, the Boy Scouts or Girl Scouts, and other local social or religious organizations.

For information on careers, certification, and academic programs in parks and recreation, contact:

➤ National Recreation and Park Association, 22377 Belmont Ridge Rd., Ashburn, VA 20148-4501. Internet: **http://www.nrpa.org**

For information about a career as a camp counselor, contact:

➤ American Camp Association, 5000 State Road 67 North, Martinsville, IN 46151-7902. Internet: **http://www.acacamps.org**

The Occupational Information Network (O*NET) provides information on a wide range of occupational characteristics. Links to O*NET appear at the end of the Internet version of this occupational statement, accessible at **http://www.bls.gov/ooh/ocos058.htm**

Other Service Occupations

Fire Inspectors and Investigators

Nature of the Work

Fire inspectors visit and inspect businesses and other places of assembly each year to ensure that these places meet State and local fire codes. These inspectors may also work with developers and planners to check and approve plans for new buildings and to inspect buildings under construction. *Fire investigators* determine the causes of fires. They collect evidence, interview witnesses, and prepare reports on fires in cases in which the cause may be arson or criminal negligence. In national forests and parks, *forest fire inspectors* and *prevention specialists* spot fires from watchtowers and report the fires to headquarters by telephone or radio. They also patrol to ensure that travelers and campers comply with fire regulations.

Education and Training

Most fire inspectors and investigators have experience in fire suppression in addition to a high school diploma. They get on-the-job training in inspection or investigation or attend training academies.

Job Outlook

Current and projected employment:

2008 Employment	16,600
2018 Employment	18,100
Employment change	1,500
Growth rate	9%

Employment change. Fire inspectors and investigators are expected to grow as fast as the average for all occupations. As cities and other areas grow, there are more buildings to inspect and fires to investigate. Employment of fire inspectors and investigators should grow along with the population.

Job prospects. Jobseekers should expect keen competition. Those who have completed some fire suppression education at a community college, have experience in fire suppression, or have experience and training related to criminal investigation should have an advantage.

Earnings

Median annual wages in May 2008 were as follows:

Fire inspectors and investigators	$53,030
Forest fire inspectors and prevention specialists	31,380

Related Occupations

	Page
Firefighters	470
Police and detectives	473
Private detectives and investigators	477

Sources of Additional Information

For additional information related to training for fire inspectors and investigators, contact State or local code enforcement officials, fire departments, fire marshals, or:

➤ National Fire Academy, 16825 South Seton Ave., Emmitsburg, MD 21727. Internet: **http://www.usfa.dhs.gov/nfa/**

The Occupational Information Network (O*NET) provides information on a wide range of occupational characteristics. Links to O*NET appear at the end of the Internet version of this occupational statement, accessible at **http://www.bls.gov/ooh/ocos328.htm**

Makeup Artists, Theatrical and Performance

Nature of the Work

Theatrical and performance makeup artists apply makeup to enhance performing artists' appearances for movie, television, or stage performances. They may be self-employed or work directly for a theater, television station, or production company.

Education and Training

Most theatrical and performance makeup artists undergo post-secondary training at a school of cosmetology or other specialized institute. Such programs may last several months to a year, and may require a high school diploma for admission. Depending on the State and specific work being performed, makeup artists who also style hair usually require a State license. A background or courses in art and design may be helpful.

Job Outlook

Current and projected employment:

2008 Employment	2,800
2018 Employment	3,300
Employment change	500
Growth rate	17%

Employment change. Employment is expected to grow faster than the average for all occupations. Continued increases in the demand for television programs, movies, and other entertainment will lead to new openings for theatrical and performance makeup artists. At the same time, the increasing use of computer-generated effects in films and the popularity of reality television have limited growth for this occupation. As this is a small occupation, the number of new jobs will be few, despite the faster than average growth.

Job prospects. Theatrical and performance makeup artists will face keen competition. Entry-level workers should expect few opportunities, while those with experience will have more work. Job openings will be greatest in areas with many media production companies, particularly Los Angeles and New York City.

Earnings

Median hourly wages for makeup artists, theatrical and performance, were $12.63 in May 2008.

Related Occupations

	Page
Barbers, cosmetologists, and other personal appearance workers	507

Sources of Additional Information

The Occupational Information Network (O*NET) provides information on a wide range of occupational characteristics. Links to O*NET appear at the end of the Internet version of this occupational statement, accessible at **http://www.bls.gov/ooh/ocos333.htm**

Sales and Related Occupations

Advertising Sales Agents

Significant Points

- Applicants who have sales experience and a college degree should have the best opportunities, but keen competition for jobs is expected during downturns in spending on advertising.

- Educational requirements vary; the ability to communicate effectively and persuasively is important for entry-level candidates.

- Performance-based pay, including bonuses and commissions, can make up a large portion of an advertising sales agent's earnings.

- Pressure to meet monthly sales quotas can be stressful.

Nature of the Work

Advertising sales agents—often referred to as *account executives* or *advertising sales representatives*—sell or solicit advertising primarily for newspapers and periodicals, television and radio, websites, telephone directories, and direct mail and outdoor advertisers. Because such a large share of revenue for many of these media outlets is generated from advertising, advertising sales agents play an important role in their success.

More than half of all advertising sales agents work in the information sector, mostly for media firms including television and radio broadcasters, print and Internet publishers, and cable program distributors. Firms that are regionally based often need the help of two types of advertising sales agents, one to handle local clients and one to solicit advertising from national advertisers. Print publications and radio and television stations employ local sales agents, who are responsible for sales in an immediate territory, while separate companies known as media representative firms sell advertising space or time for media owners at the national level. Sales agents employed in media representation work exclusively through executives at advertising agencies, called media buyers, who purchase advertising space for their clients who want to initiate national advertising campaigns. When a local television broadcaster, radio station, newspaper, or online publisher is working with a media representative firm, the media company normally employs a national sales manager to coordinate efforts with the media representative.

Most advertising sales agents work outside the office occasionally, calling on clients and prospective clients at their places of business. These agents may have an appointment, or they may practice cold calling—arriving without an appointment. Obtaining new accounts is an important part of the job, and they may spend much of their time traveling to and visiting prospective advertisers and current clients. Sales agents also may work on their employer's premises and handle sales for customers who walk in or telephone the firm to inquire about advertising.

Some may make telephone sales calls as well—calling prospects, attempting to sell the media firm's advertising space or time, and arranging followup appointments between interested prospects and sales agents.

A critical part of building relationships with clients is learning about their needs. Before the first meeting with a client, a sales agent gathers background information on the client's products, current customers, prospective customers, and the geographic area of the target market. The sales agent then meets with the clients to explain how specific types of advertising will help promote the client's products or services most effectively. If a client wishes to proceed, the advertising sales agent prepares an advertising proposal to present to the client. Preparation of the proposal entails determining the advertising medium to be used, preparing sample advertisements, and providing the client with cost estimates for the project. Because consolidation among media industries has brought the sales of different types of advertising under one roof, advertising sales increasingly are in the form of integrated packages. This means that advertising sales agents may sell packages that include print and online ad space and time slots with a broadcast subsidiary. Technological innovations also have created more products to sell, meaning that a local television sales agent might sell ad space on a station's Web site and mobile service, in addition to selling commercials.

After a contract has been established, advertising sales agents serve as the main contact between the advertiser or ad agency and the media firm. They handle communication between the parties and assist in developing sample artwork or radio and television spots if needed. For radio and television advertisements, they also may arrange for commercial taping sessions and accompany clients to the sessions.

In addition to maintaining sales and overseeing clients' accounts, advertising sales agents' other duties include analyzing sales statistics and audience demographics, preparing reports on clients' accounts, and scheduling and keeping appointments and work hours. They read about new and existing products and monitor the sales, prices, and products of their competitors. In many firms, the advertising sales agent handles the drafting of contracts specifying the advertising work to be performed and its cost, and may undertake customer service responsibilities such as answering questions or addressing any problems the client may have with the proposal. Sales agents also are responsible for developing sales tools, promotional plans, and media kits, which they use to help make a sale.

Work environment. Selling can be stressful because income and job security depend directly on the agent's ability to maintain and expand his or her clientele. Companies generally set monthly sales quotas and place considerable pressure on advertising sales agents to meet those quotas. The added stress of rejection places more pressure on the agent.

Although most agents work long and often irregular hours, some have the freedom to determine their own schedules. The Internet and other electronic tools allow agents to do more work from home or while on the road, enabling them to send messages and documents to clients and coworkers, keep up with industry news, and access databases that help them target potential customers. Advertising sales agents use e-mail to conduct much of the business with their clients.

Many advertising sales agents work more than 40 hours per week, frequently involving irregular hours and work on weekends and holidays. However, many advertising sales agents are able to set their own schedules. Ten percent of advertising sales agents were employed part time in 2008.

Training, Other Qualifications, and Advancement

For sales positions that require meeting clients, large employers prefer applicants with a college degree. Smaller companies generally are more willing to hire individuals with a high school degree. Successful sales experience and the ability to communicate effectively become more important than educational attainment once the candidate is hired. Most training for advertising sales agents takes place informally on the job.

Education and training. Although a high school diploma may be sufficient for an entry-level advertising sales position, some employers prefer applicants with a college degree, particularly for sales positions that require meeting clients. Courses in marketing, leadership, communication, business, and advertising are helpful. For those who have a proven record of successfully selling other products, educational requirements are not likely to be strict.

Most training, however, takes place on the job, and can be formal or informal in nature. In most cases, an experienced sales manager instructs a newly hired advertising sales agent who lacks sales experience. In this one-on-one environment, supervisors typically coach new hires and observe them as they make sales calls and contact clients. Supervisors then advise the new hires on ways to improve their interaction with clients. Employers may bring in consultants to lead formal training sessions when agents sell to a specialized market segment, such as automotive dealers or real estate professionals.

Other qualifications. Employers look for applicants who are honest and who possess a pleasant personality and neat professional appearance. After gaining entry into the occupation, the advertising sales agent will find that successful sales experience and the ability to communicate effectively become more important than educational attainment. In fact, when the agent is selling or soliciting ad space, personality traits are equally, if not more, important than one's academic background. In general, smaller companies are more willing to hire unproven individuals.

Because they represent their employers to the executives of client organizations, advertising sales agents must have excellent interpersonal and written communication skills. Being multilingual, particularly in English and Spanish, is another skill that will benefit prospective advertising agents as media increasingly seek to market to Hispanics and foreign-born persons. Self-motivation, organization, persistence, independence, and the ability to multitask are required because advertising sales agents set their own schedules and perform their duties without much supervision. Creativity also is an invaluable trait for advertising sales agents, who must come up with new ways to attract clients and to serve existing ones.

Bringing in new clients is an important part of an advertising sales agent's job.

Advancement. Advancement in the occupation means taking on bigger, more lucrative clients. Agents with proven leadership ability and a strong sales record may advance to supervisory and managerial positions, such as sales supervisor, sales manager, or vice president of sales. Frequent contact with managers of other departments and people in other firms provides sales agents with leads about job openings, enhancing their advancement opportunities. Successful advertising sales agents also may advance to positions in other industries, such as corporate sales. In small firms, where the number of supervisory and management positions is limited, advancement may come slowly. Promotion may occur more quickly in larger media firms and in media representative firms.

Employment

Advertising sales agents held about 166,800 jobs in 2008. Workers were concentrated in three industries: 33 percent were in advertising, public relations, and related services; about 32 percent were employed in newspaper, periodical, book, and directory publishers; and 17 percent were in radio and television broadcasting. Media representative firms are in the advertising and related services industry. A relatively small number of jobs were found in cable and other program distribution.

Employment is spread around the country, but jobs in radio and television stations and large, well-known publications are concentrated in metropolitan areas. Media representative firms also are concentrated in large cities with many advertising agencies, such as New York City.

Job Outlook

Employment is projected to increase about as fast as average. Growth in new media outlets, such as the Internet, will be partially offset by a decline in print media. Applicants who have sales experience and a college degree should have the best opportunities, but keen competition for jobs is expected during downturns in advertising spending.

Projections data from the National Employment Matrix

Occupational Title	SOC Code	Employment, 2008	Projected Employment, 2018	Change, 2008-2018	
				Number	Percent
Advertising sales agents...	41-3011	166,800	178,900	12,100	7

(NOTE) Data in this table are rounded. See the discussion of the employment projections table in the *Handbook* introductory chapter on *Occupational Information Included in the Handbook.*

Employment change. Employment of advertising sales agents is expected to increase by 7 percent from 2008 to 2018, about as fast as the average for all occupations. Fast growth in the number of cable channels, online advertisers, and other advertising media will create many new opportunities for advertisers. This growth will be partially offset by the decline in print media, which will decrease the demand for advertising sales agents in these industries.

Advertising as an industry is expected to grow over the 2008–18 period. Changes in technology will create new and more efficient ways for advertisers to reach customers, which will increase the need for advertising sales agents. Growth should be particularly high in online advertising sales, in cable television, and for consolidated media firms.

At the same time, the industries employing large shares of advertising sales agents, particularly the newspaper, periodical, and directory publishing industries, have suffered significant declines in recent years. As a result, there are likely to be fewer opportunities for advertising sales agents within these areas compared to other industries over the next decade.

Although advances in technology have made advertising sales agents more productive, allowing agents to take on additional duties and improve the quality of the services they provide, technological advances have not substantially decreased overall demand for these workers. Productivity gains have had the largest effect on the miscellaneous services that these workers provide, such as accounting, the formulation of proposals, and customer service duties, allowing them to provide faster, improved services to their clients. For example, the use of e-mail has considerably shortened the time it takes to negotiate a sale and place an ad. Sales agents may accomplish more in less time, but many work more hours than in the past, spending additional time on followup and service calls. Thus, although productivity gains will temper the growth of advertising sales agents, who can now manage more accounts, the increasing growth in advertising across all industries will ensure that new advertising sales agents will continue to be needed in the future.

Job prospects. Applicants who have sales experience and a college degree should have the best opportunities. For those with a proven sales record in advertising sales, opportunities should be excellent. In addition to the job openings generated by employment growth, openings will occur each year because of the need to replace sales representatives who transfer to other occupations or leave the labor force. Each year, many advertising sales agents discover that they are unable to earn enough money; as a result, they leave the occupation. Advertising revenues are sensitive to economic downturns, which cause the industries and companies that advertise to reduce both the frequency of campaigns and the overall level of spending on advertising. Advertising sales agents must work hard to get the most out of every dollar spent on advertising under these conditions. Therefore, the number of opportunities for advertising sales agents fluctuates with the business cycle. Applicants can expect keen competition for job openings during downturns in advertising spending.

Earnings

Including commissions, median annual wages for all advertising sales agents were $43,480 per year in May 2008. The middle 50 percent earned between $30,750 and $64,320 a year. The lowest 10 percent earned less than $22,620, and the highest 10 percent earned more than $93,600 a year. Median annual wages for sales agents in the industries in which they were concentrated were as follows:

Motion picture and video industries...........................	$62,600
Cable and other subscription programming.................	50,740
Advertising, public relations, and related services.......	48,550
Radio and television broadcasting..............................	41,750
Newspaper, periodical, book, and directory publishers...	38,100

Performance-based pay, including bonuses and commissions, can make up a large portion of an advertising sales agent's earnings. Most employers pay some combination of salaries, commissions, and bonuses. Commissions are usually based on individual sales numbers, whereas bonuses may depend on individual performance, on the performance of all sales workers in a group or district, or on the performance of the entire company. For agents covering multiple areas or regions, commissions also may be based on the difficulty in making a sale in that particular area. Sales revenue is affected by the economic conditions and business expectations facing the industries that tend to advertise. Earnings from commissions are likely to be high when these industries are doing well and low when companies decide not to advertise as frequently.

In addition to their earnings, advertising sales agents are usually reimbursed for entertaining clients and for other business expenses, such as the costs of transportation, meals, and hotel stays. They often receive benefits such as health and life insurance, pension plans, vacation and sick leave, personal use of a company car, and frequent-flier mileage. Some companies offer incentives such as free vacation trips or gifts for outstanding sales workers.

Related Occupations

Advertising sales agents market services to clients in order to increase sales revenue. Other workers with similar duties include:

Sources of Additional Information

To learn about opportunities for employment as an advertising sales agent, contact local broadcasters, radio stations, and publishers for advertising sales representative positions or look for media representative firms in your area.

For information about advertising sales careers in newspaper publishing, contact:

➤ The Newspaper Association of America, 4401 Wilson Boulevard, Suite 900, Arlington, Va. 22203. Internet: **http://www.naa.org**

The Occupational Information Network (O*NET) provides information on a wide range of occupational characteristics. Links to O*NET appear at the end of the Internet version of this occupational statement, accessible at **http://www.bls.gov/ooh/ocos297.htm**

Cashiers

Significant Points

- Cashiers need little or no work experience; they are trained on the job.

- Opportunities for full-time and part-time jobs are expected to be good because of the need to replace the large number of workers who leave cashier jobs.

- Many cashiers start at the minimum wage.

Nature of the Work

Supermarkets, department stores, gasoline service stations, movie theaters, restaurants, and many other businesses employ cashiers to register the sale of their goods and services. Although specific job duties vary by employer, cashiers usually are assigned to a register at the beginning of their shifts and are given a drawer containing a specific amount of money with which to start—their "till." They must count their till to ensure that it contains the correct amount of money and adequate supplies of change. Some cashiers also handle returns and exchanges. When they do, they must ensure that returned merchandise is in good condition, and determine where and when it was purchased and what type of payment was used.

After entering charges for all items and subtracting the value of any coupons or special discounts, cashiers total the customer's bill and take payment. Forms of payment include cash, personal checks, and gift, credit, and debit cards. Cashiers must know the store's policies and procedures for each type of payment the store accepts. For checks and credit and debit card charges, they may request additional identification from the customer or call in for an authorization. They must verify the age of customers purchasing alcohol or tobacco. When the sale is complete, cashiers issue a receipt to the customer and return the appropriate change. They may also wrap or bag the purchase.

At the end of their shifts, cashiers once again count the drawers' contents and compare the totals with sales data. An occasional shortage of small amounts may be overlooked but, in many establishments, repeated shortages are grounds for

Cashiers must be friendly and courteous when interacting with customers.

dismissal. In addition to counting the contents of their drawers at the end of their shifts, cashiers usually separate and total charge forms, return slips, coupons, and any other non-cash items.

Most cashiers use scanners and computers, but some establishments still require price and product information to be entered manually. In a store with scanners, a cashier passes a product's Universal Product Code over the scanning device, which transmits the code number to a computer. The computer identifies the item and its price. In other establishments, cashiers manually enter codes into computers and then descriptions of the items and their prices appear on the screen.

Depending on the type of establishment, cashiers may have other duties as well. In many supermarkets, for example, cashiers weigh produce and bulk food, as well as return unwanted items to the shelves. In convenience stores, cashiers may be required to know how to use a variety of machines other than cash registers, and how to furnish money orders and sell lottery tickets. Operating ticket-dispensing machines and answering customers' questions are common duties for cashiers who work at movie theaters and ticket agencies.

Work environment. Most cashiers work indoors, usually standing in booths or behind counters. Often, they are not allowed to leave their workstations without supervisory approval because they are responsible for large sums of money. The work of cashiers can be very repetitious, but improvements in workstation design in many stores are alleviating problems caused by repetitive motion. In addition, the work can sometimes be dangerous; the risk from robberies and homicides is much higher for cashiers than for other workers, although more safety precautions are being taken to help deter robbers.

About 47 percent of all cashiers worked part time in 2008. Hours of work often vary depending on the needs of the employer. Generally, cashiers are expected to work weekends, evenings, and holidays to accommodate customers' needs. However, many employers offer flexible schedules. Because the holiday season is the busiest time for most retailers, many employers restrict the use of vacation time from Thanksgiving through the beginning of January.

Training, Other Qualifications, and Advancement

Cashier jobs usually are entry-level positions requiring little or no previous work experience. They require good customer service skills.

Education and training. Although there are no specific educational requirements, employers filling full-time jobs often prefer applicants with high school diplomas.

Nearly all cashiers are trained on the job. In small businesses, an experienced worker often trains beginners. The trainee spends the first day observing the operation and becoming familiar with the store's equipment, policies, and procedures. After this, trainees are assigned to a register—frequently under the supervision of an experienced worker. In larger businesses, trainees spend several days in classes before being placed at cash registers. Topics typically covered in class include a description of the industry and the company, store policies and procedures, equipment operation, and security.

Training for experienced workers is not common, except when new equipment is introduced or when procedures change. In these cases, the employer or a representative of the equipment manufacturer trains workers on the job.

Other qualifications. People who want to become cashiers should be able to do repetitious work accurately. They also need basic mathematics skills and good manual dexterity. Because cashiers deal constantly with the public, they should be neat in appearance and able to deal tactfully and pleasantly with customers. In addition, some businesses prefer to hire workers who can operate specialized equipment or who have business experience, such as typing, selling, or handling money.

Advancement. Advancement opportunities for cashiers vary. For those working part time, promotion may be to a full-time position. Others advance to head cashier or cash-office clerk. In addition, this job offers a good opportunity to learn about an employer's business and can serve as a steppingstone to a more responsible position.

Employment

Cashiers held about 3.55 million jobs in 2008. Although cashiers are employed in almost every industry, 24 percent of all jobs were in grocery stores. Gasoline stations, department stores, and other retail establishments also employed large numbers of these workers. Outside of retail establishments, many cashiers worked in food services and drinking places.

Job Outlook

Cashiers are expected to grow more slowly than the average for all occupations. Opportunities for full-time and part-time jobs are expected to be good because of the need to replace the large number of workers who leave this occupation.

Employment change. Employment of cashiers is expected to grow by 4 percent between 2008 and 2018 which is slower than the average for all occupations. Continued growth in retail sales is expected, but the rising popularity of purchasing goods online will limit the employment growth of cashiers, although many customers still prefer the traditional method of purchasing goods at stores. Also, the growing use of self-service checkout systems in retail trade, especially at grocery stores, should have an adverse effect on employment of cashiers. These self-checkout systems may outnumber checkouts with cashiers in the future in many establishments. The impact on job growth for cashiers will largely depend on the public's acceptance of this self-service technology.

Job prospects. Opportunities for full-time and part-time cashier jobs should continue to be good because of the need to replace the large number of workers who transfer to other occupations or leave the labor force. There is substantial movement into and out of the occupation because education and training requirements are minimal and the predominance of part-time jobs is attractive to people seeking a short-term source of income rather than a full-time career. Historically, workers under the age of 25 have filled many of the openings in this occupation. In 2008, about 47 percent of all cashiers were 24 years of age or younger.

Because cashiers are needed in businesses and organizations of all types and sizes, job opportunities are found throughout the country. However, job opportunities may vary from year to year because the strength of the economy affects demand for cashiers. Companies tend to hire more cashiers when the economy is strong. Seasonal demand for cashiers also causes fluctuations in employment.

Earnings

Many cashiers start at the Federal minimum wage, which was $7.25 an hour as of July 2009. Some State laws set the minimum wage higher, and establishments must pay at least that amount. Wages tend to be higher in areas where there is intense competition for workers.

Median hourly wages of cashiers, except gaming in May 2008 were $8.49. The middle 50 percent earned between $7.50 and $9.72 an hour. The lowest 10 percent earned less than $6.88, and the highest 10 percent earned more than $12.02 an hour. Median hourly wages in the industries employing the largest numbers of cashiers in May 2008 were:

Health and personal care stores	$8.71
Other general merchandise stores	8.60
Grocery stores	8.59
Department stores	8.38
Gasoline stations	8.16

Similar to other occupations, benefits for full-time cashiers tend to be better than those for cashiers working part time. In addition to typical benefits, those working in retail establishments

Projections data from the National Employment Matrix

Occupational Title	SOC Code	Employment, 2008	Projected Employment, 2018	Change, 2008-2018	
				Number	Percent
Cashiers, except gaming	41-2011	3,550,000	3,675,500	125,500	4

(NOTE) Data in this table are rounded. See the discussion of the employment projections table in the *Handbook* introductory chapter on *Occupational Information Included in the Handbook.*

often receive discounts on purchases, and cashiers in restaurants may receive free or low-cost meals. Some employers also offer employee stock option plans and education reimbursement plans.

Related Occupations

Cashiers accept payment for the purchase of goods and services. Other workers with similar duties include:

Sources of Additional Information

General information on careers in grocery stores is available from:
➤ Food Marketing Institute, 2345 Crystal Dr., Suite 800, Arlington, VA 22202. Internet: **http://www.fmi.org**

For information about employment opportunities as a cashier, contact:
➤ The Association for Convenience and Petroleum Retailing, 1600 Duke St., Alexandria, VA 22314. Internet: **http://www.nacsonline.com**

➤ United Food and Commercial Workers International Union, Education Office, 1775 K St. NW., Washington, DC 20006.

The Occupational Information Network (O*NET) provides information on a wide range of occupational characteristics. Links to O*NET appear at the end of the Internet version of this occupational statement, accessible at **http://www.bls.gov/ooh/ocos335.htm**

Demonstrators and Product Promoters

Significant Points

- Job openings should be plentiful.

- Most jobs are part time or short term or have variable work schedules, and many jobs require frequent travel.

- On-the-job training is provided and education beyond high school is not required.

Nature of the Work

Demonstrators and *product promoters* create public interest in buying products such as cosmetics, food, and housewares. The information they provide helps consumers make choices among the wide variety of products and services they can buy.

Demonstrators and product promoters encourage people and stores to buy a product by demonstrating it to prospective customers and answering their questions. They may sell the demonstrated merchandise or gather names of prospects to contact later or pass on to sales staff. Demonstrators promote sales of a product to consumers, while product promoters encourage sales to retail stores and help them market products effectively.

Demonstrators and product promoters generate sales of both sophisticated and simple products, ranging from computer software to mops. They attract an audience by offering samples, administering contests, distributing prizes and coupons, and using direct-mail advertising. They must greet and catch the attention of possible customers and quickly identify those who are interested and able to buy. They inform and educate customers about the features of products and demonstrate their use with apparent ease in order to inspire confidence in the product and its manufacturer. They also distribute information, such as brochures and order forms. Some demonstrations are intended to generate immediate sales through impulse buying, whereas others increase the likelihood of future sales by increasing brand awareness.

Demonstrations and product promotions are conducted in retail and grocery stores, shopping malls, trade shows, and outdoor fairs. Locations are selected on the basis of the nature of the product and the type of audience. Demonstrations at large events may require teams of demonstrators to handle large crowds efficiently. Some demonstrators promote products on videotape or on television programs, such as "infomercials" or home shopping programs.

Demonstrators and product promoters may prepare the content of a presentation and alter it to target a specific audience or to keep it current. They may participate in the design of an exhibit or customize the exhibit for particular audiences. Results obtained by demonstrators and product promoters are analyzed, and presentations are adjusted to make them more effective. Demonstrators and product promoters also may be involved in transporting, assembling, and disassembling materials used in demonstrations.

A demonstrator's presentation may include visuals, models, case studies, testimonials, test results, and surveys. The equipment used for a demonstration varies with the product being demonstrated. A food product demonstration might require the use of cooking utensils, while a software demonstration could require the use of a multimedia computer. Demonstrators must be familiar with the product to be able to relate detailed

Demonstrators and product promoters encourage people and stores to buy a product by showing it to prospective customers and answering their questions.

Projections data from the National Employment Matrix

Occupational Title	SOC Code	Employment, 2008	Projected Employment, 2018	Change, 2008-2018	
				Number	Percent
Demonstrators and product promoters...	41-9011	102,800	110,100	7,300	7

(NOTE) Data in this table are rounded. See the discussion of the employment projections table in the *Handbook* introductory chapter on *Occupational Information Included in the Handbook.*

information to customers and to answer any questions that arise before, during, or after a demonstration. In order to do so, they may research the product presented, the products of competitors, and the interests and concerns of the target audience before conducting a demonstration. Demonstrations of complex products often need practice.

Work environment. About 54 percent of all demonstrators and product promoters work part time and about 22 percent have variable work schedules. Many positions may last 6 months or less.

Demonstrators and product promoters may work long hours while standing or walking, with little opportunity to rest. Some of them travel frequently, and night and weekend work often is required. The atmosphere of a crowded trade show or State fair frequently is hectic, and demonstrators and product promoters may feel pressure to influence the greatest number of consumers possible in a very limited amount of time. However, many enjoy the opportunity to interact with a variety of people.

Training, Other Qualifications, and Advancement
On-the-job training is provided and education beyond high school is not required.

Education and training. Demonstrators and product promoters usually receive on-the-job training, and formal postsecondary education is not required. Training is primarily product oriented, because a demonstrator must be familiar with the product to demonstrate it properly. The length of training varies with the complexity of the product. Experience with the product or familiarity with similar products may be required for the demonstration of complex products, such as computers. During the training process, demonstrators may be introduced to the manufacturer's corporate philosophy and preferred methods for dealing with customers.

Other qualifications. Employers look for demonstrators and product promoters with good communication skills and a pleasant appearance and personality. Demonstrators and product promoters must be comfortable with public speaking. They should be able to entertain an audience and use humor, spontaneity, and personal interest in the product as promotional tools. Foreign language skills are helpful.

Advancement. Demonstrators and product promoters who perform well and show leadership abilities may advance to other marketing and sales occupations or open their own business.

Employment
Demonstrators and product promoters held about 102,800 jobs in 2008. About 23 percent of all salaried jobs for demonstrators and product promoters were in retail trade, especially general merchandise stores, and 18 percent were in advertising, public relations, and related services. Other jobs were found in administrative and support services, including employment services.

Job Outlook
Employment of demonstrators and product promoters is expected to grow as fast as average for all occupations through 2018. Job openings should be plentiful over the next decade.

Employment change. Demonstrators and product promoters are expected to experience 7 percent growth between 2008 and 2018, as fast as the average for all occupations. Job growth should be driven by increases in the number and size of trade shows and greater use of these workers in department stores and various retail shops for in-store promotions. Product demonstration is considered a highly effective marketing tool. New jobs should arise as firms devote a greater percentage of marketing budgets to product demonstration. However, it is also an expensive method of marketing, which will somewhat limit growth.

Job prospects. Job openings should be plentiful for demonstrators and product promoters. Employers may have difficulty finding qualified demonstrators who are willing to fill part-time, short-term positions.

Employment of demonstrators and product promoters is affected by downturns in the business cycle. Many firms tend to reduce advertising budgets during recessions.

Earnings
Demonstrators and product promoters had median hourly wages of $11.18 in May 2008. The middle 50 percent earned between $9.06 and $14.88. The lowest 10 percent earned less than $8.14, and the highest 10 percent earned more than $19.94. Employers of demonstrators and product promoters generally pay for job-related travel expenses.

Related Occupations
Other jobs related to sales and product promotion include:

Sources of Additional Information
For information about careers in product promotion marketing, contact:

➤ Association for Integrated Marketing, 257 Park Avenue South, Suite 1102, New York, NY 10010. Internet: **http://www.pmalink.org**

➤ Promotional Products Association International, 3125 Skyway Circle North, Irving, Texas 75038. Internet: **http://www.ppa.org**

The Occupational Information Network (O*NET) provides information on a wide range of occupational characteristics. Links to O*NET appear at the end of the Internet version of this occupational statement, accessible at **http://www.bls.gov/ooh/ocos336.htm**

Insurance Sales Agents

Significant Points

- In addition to offering insurance policies, agents increasingly sell mutual funds, annuities, and securities and offer comprehensive financial planning services, including retirement and estate planning services, some designed specifically for the elderly.

- Agents must obtain a license in the States where they sell.

- Job opportunities should be best for college graduates who have sales ability, excellent interpersonal skills, and expertise in a wide range of insurance and financial services.

Nature of the Work

Most people have their first contact with an insurance company through an insurance sales agent. These workers help individuals, families, and businesses select insurance policies that provide the best protection for their lives, health, and property.

Insurance sales agents, commonly referred to as "producers" in the insurance industry, sell one or more types of insurance, such as property and casualty, life, health, disability, and long-term care. Property and casualty insurance agents sell policies that protect individuals and businesses from financial loss resulting from automobile accidents, fire, theft, storms, and other events that can damage property. For businesses, property and casualty insurance can also cover injured workers' compensation, product liability claims, or medical malpractice claims.

Life insurance agents specialize in selling policies that pay beneficiaries when a policyholder dies. Depending on the policyholder's circumstances, a cash-value policy can be designed to provide retirement income, funds for the education of children, and other benefits, as well. Life insurance agents also sell annuities that promise a retirement income. Health insurance agents sell health insurance policies that cover the costs of medical care and loss of income due to illness or injury. They also may sell dental insurance and short-term and long-term-disability insurance policies. Agents may specialize in any one of these products, or function as generalists, providing multiple products to a single customer.

An increasing number of insurance sales agents offer their clients advice on how to minimize risk as well as comprehensive financial planning services, especially to those approaching retirement. These services include retirement planning, estate planning, and assistance in setting up pension plans for businesses. As a result, many insurance agents are involved in

"cross-selling" or "total account development." Besides offering insurance, these agents may become licensed to sell mutual funds, variable annuities, and other securities. This practice is most common with life insurance agents who already sell annuities, but many property and casualty agents also sell financial products. (See the statement on securities, commodities, and financial services sales agents elsewhere in the *Handbook*.)

Insurance sales agents also prepare reports, maintain records, and seek out new clients. In the event that policy holders experience a loss, agents help them settle their insurance claims. Insurance sales agents working exclusively for one insurance company are referred to as *captive agents*. These agents typically have a contractual agreement with the carrier, and are usually an employee of the carrier. Independent insurance agents, or *brokers*, are mostly facilitators who represent several companies. They match insurance policies for their clients with the company that offers the best rate and coverage.

Technology—specifically, the Internet—has greatly affected the insurance business, making the tasks of obtaining price quotes and processing applications and service requests faster and easier. The Internet has made it easier for agents to take on more clients and to be better informed about new products. It has also altered the relationship between agent and client. Agents formerly used to devote much of their time to marketing and selling products to new clients. Now, clients are increasingly obtaining insurance quotes from a company's Web site and then contacting the company directly to purchase policies. This interaction gives the client a more active role in selecting their policy, while reducing the amount of time agents spend seeking new clients. Insurance sales agents also obtain many new accounts through referrals, so it is important that they maintain regular contact with their clients to ensure that the client's financial needs are being met. Developing a satisfied clientele that will recommend an agent's services to other potential customers is a key to success for agents.

Increasing competition in the insurance industry has spurred carriers to find new ways to keep their clients satisfied. One solution is hiring customer service representatives who are accessible 24 hours a day, 7 days a week to handle routine tasks such as answering questions, making changes in policies, processing claims, and selling more products to clients. The opportunity to cross-sell new products to clients will help an agent's business grow. The use of customer service representatives also allows agents to concentrate their efforts on seeking out new clients and maintaining relationships with old ones. (See the statements on customer service representatives; and claims adjusters, appraisers, examiners, and investigators elsewhere in the *Handbook*.)

Work environment. Most insurance sales agents work in offices. Since some agencies are small, agents may work alone or with only a few others. Some independent agents, or brokers, however, may spend much of their time traveling to meet with clients, close sales, or investigate claims. Agents usually determine their own hours of work and often schedule evening and weekend appointments for the convenience of clients. Some sales agents meet with clients during business hours and then spend evenings doing paperwork and preparing presentations

An increasing number of insurance sales agents offer comprehensive financial planning services to their clients.

for prospective clients. Although most agents work a 40-hour week, some may work much longer.

Training, Other Qualifications, and Advancement

Every sales agent involved in the solicitation, selling, or negotiation of insurance must have a State-issued license. Licensure requirements vary by State but typically require some insurance-related coursework and the passing of several exams. Although some agents are hired right out of college, many are hired by insurance companies as customer service representatives and are later promoted to sales agent.

Education and training. For insurance sales agent jobs, many companies and independent agencies prefer to hire college graduates—especially those who have majored in business, finance, or economics. High school graduates may be hired if they have proven sales ability or have been successful in other types of work.

College training can help agents grasp the technical aspects of insurance policies as well as the fundamentals of the insurance industry. Many colleges and universities offer courses in insurance, and a few schools offer a bachelor's degree in the field. College courses in finance, mathematics, accounting, economics, business law, marketing, and business administration enable insurance sales agents to understand how social and economic conditions relate to the insurance industry. Courses in psychology, sociology, and public speaking can prove useful in improving sales techniques. In addition, familiarity with

popular software packages has become very important because computers provide instantaneous information on a wide variety of financial products and greatly improve an agent's efficiency.

Agents learn many of their job duties on the job from other agents. Many employers have their new agents shadow an experienced agent for a period of time. This allows the agent to learn how to conduct their business, how the agency interacts with clients, and how to write policies.

Employers also are placing greater emphasis on continuing professional education as the diversity of financial products sold by insurance agents increases. It is important for insurance agents to keep up to date on issues concerning clients. Changes in tax laws, government benefits programs, and other State and Federal regulations can affect the insurance needs of clients and the way in which agents conduct business. Agents can enhance their selling skills and broaden their knowledge of insurance and other financial services by taking courses at colleges and universities and by attending institutes, conferences, and seminars sponsored by insurance organizations.

Licensure. Insurance sales agents must obtain a license in the States where they plan to work. Separate licenses are required for agents to sell life and health insurance and property and casualty insurance. In most States, licenses are issued only to applicants who complete specified prelicensing courses and who pass State examinations covering insurance fundamentals and State insurance laws. Most State licensing authorities also have mandatory continuing education requirements every 2 years, focusing on insurance laws, consumer protection, ethics, and the technical details of various insurance policies.

As the demand for financial products and financial planning increases, many insurance agents choose to gain the proper licensing and certification to sell securities and other financial products. Doing so, however, requires substantial study and passing an additional examination—either the Series 6 or Series 7 licensing exam, both of which are administered by the National Association of Securities Dealers (NASD). The Series 6 exam is for individuals who wish to sell only mutual funds and variable annuities, whereas the Series 7 exam is the main NASD series license that qualifies agents as general securities sales representatives.

Other qualifications. Previous experience in sales or insurance jobs can be very useful in becoming an insurance sales agent. In selling commercial insurance, technical experience in a particular field can help sell policies to those in the same profession. As a result, these agents tend to be older than entrants in many other occupations.

Insurance sales agents should be flexible, enthusiastic, confident, disciplined, hard working, and willing to solve problems. They should communicate effectively and inspire customer confidence. Because they usually work without supervision, sales agents must have good time-management skills and the initiative to locate new clients.

Certification and advancement. A number of organizations offer professional designation programs that certify an agent's expertise in specialties such as life, health, and property and casualty insurance, as well as financial consulting. For example, The National Alliance for Insurance Education and Research offers a wide variety of courses in health, life and property, and casualty insurance for independent insurance agents. Although voluntary, such programs assure clients and employers that an agent has a thorough understanding of the relevant specialty. Agents who complete certification are usually required to fulfill a specified number of hours of continuing education to retain their designation, as determined by the Alliance.

In the area of financial planning, many agents find it worthwhile to demonstrate competency by earning the certified financial planner or chartered financial consultant designation. The Certified Financial Planner credential, issued by the Certified Financial Planner Board of Standards, requires relevant experience, completion of education requirements, passing a comprehensive examination, and adherence to an enforceable code of ethics. The exam tests the candidate's knowledge of the financial planning process, insurance and risk management, employee benefits planning, taxes and retirement planning, and investment and estate planning.

The Chartered Financial Consultant (ChFC) and the Chartered Life Underwriter (CLU) designations, issued by the American College in Bryn Mawr, Pennsylvania, typically require professional experience and the completion of an eight-course program of study. For those new to the industry, however, the American College offers the Life Underwriter Training Council Fellow (FUTCF), an introductory course that teaches basic insurance concepts. Many property and casualty insurance agents obtain the Chartered Property Casualty Underwriter (CPCU) designation, offered by the American Institute for Chartered Property Casualty Underwriter. The majority of professional designations in insurance have continuing education requirements.

An insurance sales agent who shows ability and leadership may become a sales manager in a local office. A few advance to managerial or executive positions. However, many who have established a client base prefer to remain in sales work. Some—particularly in the property and casualty field—launch their own independent agencies or brokerage firms.

Employment

Insurance sales agents held about 434,800 jobs in 2008. About 51 percent of insurance sales agents work for insurance agencies and brokerages. About 21 percent work directly for insurance carriers. Although most insurance agents specialize in life and health insurance or property and casualty insurance, a growing number of "multiline" agents sell all lines of insurance. A small number of agents work for banks and securities brokerages as a result of the increasing integration of the finance and insurance industries. Approximately 22 percent of insurance sales agents are self employed.

The majority of insurance sales agents are employed in local offices or independent agencies, but some work in the headquarters of insurance companies.

Job Outlook

Employment is expected to grow about as fast as average for all occupations. Opportunities will be best for college graduates who have sales ability, excellent interpersonal skills, and expertise in a wide range of insurance and financial services.

Employment change. Employment of insurance sales agents is expected to increase by 12 percent over the 2008–18 period, which is about as fast as average for all occupations. Future demand for insurance sales agents depends largely on the variety of financial products and volume of sales. Sales of health insurance, long-term-care insurance, and other comprehensive financial planning services designed specifically for the elderly are expected to rise sharply as the population ages. In addition, a growing population will increase demand for insurance for automobiles, homes, and high-priced valuables and equipment. As new businesses emerge and existing firms expand their insurance coverage, sales of commercial insurance also should increase, including coverage such as product liability, workers' compensation, employee benefits, and pollution liability insurance.

Employment of agents will not keep up with the rising level of insurance sales, however. Many insurance carriers are trying to contain costs and are shedding their captive agents—those agents working directly for insurance carriers. Instead carriers are relying more on independent agents or brokers.

It is unlikely that the Internet will threaten the jobs of these agents. The automation of policy and claims processing allows insurance agents to take on more clients. Most clients value their relationship with their agent and prefer personal service, discussing their policies directly with their agents, rather than through a computer. Insurance law and investments are becoming more complex, and many people and businesses lack the time and expertise to buy insurance without the advice of an agent.

Job prospects. College graduates who have sales ability, excellent interpersonal skills, and expertise in a wide range of insurance and financial services should enjoy the best prospects. Multilingual agents should have an advantage, because they can serve a wider range of customers. Additionally, insurance language tends to be quite technical, so agents who have a firm understanding of relevant technical and legal terms will also be desirable to employers. Many beginning agents fail to earn enough from commissions to meet their income goals and eventually transfer to other careers. Many job openings are likely to result from the need to replace agents who leave the occupation or retire.

Agents may face some competition from traditional securities brokers and bankers, as they also sell insurance policies. Insurance sales agents will need to expand the products and services they offer as consolidation increases among insurance companies, banks, and brokerage firms and as demands increase from clients for more comprehensive financial planning.

Independent agents who incorporate new technology into their existing businesses will remain competitive. Agents who

Projections data from the National Employment Matrix

Occupational Title	SOC Code	Employment, 2008	Projected Employment, 2018	Change, 2008-2018	
				Number	Percent
Insurance sales agents..	41-3021	434,800	486,400	51,600	12

(NOTE) Data in this table are rounded. See the discussion of the employment projections table in the *Handbook* introductory chapter on *Occupational Information Included in the Handbook.*

use the Internet to market their products will reach a broader client base and expand their business. Agents who offer better customer service also will remain competitive.

Earnings

The median annual wages of wage and salary insurance sales agents were $45,430 in May 2008. The middle 50 percent earned between $33,070 and $68,730. The lowest 10 percent had earnings of $26,120 or less, while the highest 10 percent earned more than $113,930. Median annual wages in May 2008 in the two industries employing the largest number of insurance sales agents were $48,150 for insurance carriers, and $44,450 for agencies, brokerages, and other insurance related activities.

Many independent agents are paid by commission only, whereas sales workers who are employees of an agency or an insurance carrier may be paid in one of three ways: salary only, salary plus commission, or salary plus bonus. In general, commissions are the most common form of compensation, especially for experienced agents. The amount of the commission depends on the type and amount of insurance sold and on whether the transaction is a new policy or a renewal. Bonuses usually are awarded when agents meet their sales goals or when an agency meets its profit goals. Some agents involved with financial planning receive a fee for their services, rather than a commission.

Company-paid benefits to insurance sales agents usually include continuing education, training to qualify for licensing, group insurance plans, office space, and clerical support services. Some companies also may pay for automobile and transportation expenses, attendance at conventions and meetings, promotion and marketing expenses, and retirement plans. Independent agents working for insurance agencies receive fewer benefits, but their commissions may be higher to help them pay for marketing and other expenses.

Related Occupations

Other workers who provide or sell financial products or services include:

Sources of Additional Information

Occupational information about insurance sales agents is available from the home office of many insurance companies. Information on State licensing requirements may be obtained from the department of insurance at any State capital.

For information about insurance sales careers and training, contact:
➤ National Association of Professional Insurance Agents, 400 N. Washington St., Alexandria, VA 22314. Internet: **http://www.pianet.org**

For information about health insurance sales careers, contact:
➤ National Association of Health Underwriters, 2000 N. 14th St., Suite 450, Arlington, VA 22201. Internet: **http://www.nahu.org**

For general information on the property and casualty field, contact:
➤ Insurance Information Institute, 110 William St., New York, NY 10038. Internet: **http://www.iii.org**

For information about professional designation programs, contact:
➤ The American Institute for Chartered Property and Casualty Underwriters/Insurance Institute of America, 720 Providence Rd., Suite 100, Malvern, PA 19355-3433. Internet: **http://www.aicpcu.org**

➤ The American College, 270 S. Bryn Mawr Ave., Bryn Mawr, PA 19010-2195. Internet: **http://www.theamericancollege.edu**

For information on financial planning careers, contact:
➤ Certified Financial Planner Board of Standards, Inc., 1425 K St. NW., Suite 500, Washington, DC 20005. Internet: **http://www.cfp.net**

The Occupational Information Network (O*NET) provides information on a wide range of occupational characteristics. Links to O*NET appear at the end of the Internet version of this occupational statement, accessible at **http://www.bls.gov/ooh/ocos118.htm**

Models

Significant Points

- Despite faster than average growth, keen competition is expected for modeling jobs.

- Most jobs are part time or have variable work schedules, and many jobs require frequent travel.

- Formal training is limited and education beyond high school usually is not required.

Nature of the Work

Models create public interest in buying products such as clothing, cosmetics, food, and housewares. The information they provide helps consumers make choices among the wide variety of products and services they can buy.

Models pose for photos, paintings, or sculptures. They display clothing such as dresses, coats, underclothing, swimwear, and suits, for a variety of audiences and in various types of media. They model accessories, such as handbags, shoes, and jewelry, and promote beauty products, including fragrances and cosmetics. The most successful models, called supermodels, hold celebrity status and often use their image to sell books, calendars, fitness videos, and other products. In addition to modeling, they may appear in movies and television shows.

Models appear in printed publications, at live modeling events, and on television to advertise and promote products and services. Most modeling jobs are for printed publications, and models usually do a combination of editorial, commercial, and catalog work. Editorial print modeling uses still photographs of models for fashion magazine covers and to accompany feature articles. Commercial print modeling includes work for advertisements in magazines, newspapers, and billboards. Models advertise merchandise and appear in department-store catalogs, mail-order catalogs, and on the Internet.

During a photo shoot, a model poses to demonstrate the features of clothing and other products. Models make small changes in posture and facial expression to capture the look desired by the client. Photographers instruct models to pose in certain positions and to interact with their physical surroundings. Models work closely with photographers, hair and clothing stylists, makeup artists, and clients to produce the desired look and to finish the photo shoot on schedule. Stylists and makeup artists prepare the model for the photo shoot, provide touchups, and change the look of models throughout the day. If stylists are not provided, models must apply their own makeup and bring their own clothing.

Live modeling is done in a variety of locations. Live models stand, turn, and walk to demonstrate clothing to a variety of audiences. At fashion shows and in showrooms, garment buyers are the primary audience. Runway models display clothes that are intended for direct sale to consumers or are the artistic expressions of the designer. High fashion, or haute couture, runway models walk a runway before an audience of photographers, journalists, designers, and garment buyers. Live modeling also is done in apparel marts, department stores, and fitting rooms of clothing designers. In retail establishments, models display clothing directly for shoppers and may be required to describe the features and prices of the clothing. Other models pose for sketch artists, painters, and sculptors.

Because advertisers often need to target specific segments of the population, models may specialize in a certain area. For example, petite and plus-size fashions are modeled by women whose size is smaller or larger than that worn by the typical model. Models who are disabled may be used to model fashions or products for disabled consumers. "Parts" models have a body part, such as a hand or foot, which is particularly well suited to model products such as fingernail polish or shoes.

Almost all models work through agents who provide a link between models and clients. Agents scout for new faces, advise and train new models, and promote them to clients. Clients pay models, and the agency receives a portion of the model's earnings for its services. A typical modeling job lasts only 1 day, so modeling agencies differ from other employment agencies in that they maintain an ongoing relationship with the model.

With the help of agents, models spend a considerable amount of time promoting and developing themselves. Models assemble and maintain portfolios, print composite cards, and travel to check out potential clients, or "go-sees." A portfolio is a collection of a model's previous work that is carried to all go-sees and bookings. A composite card contains the

Models appear in printed publications, at live modeling events, and on television to advertise and promote products and services.

best photographs from a model's portfolio, along with his or her measurements. Increasingly, composite cards are being sent electronically to clients and printed portfolios are being replaced with digital portfolios.

Models must gather information before a job. From an agent, they learn the pay, date, time, and length of the shoot. Also, models need to ask if hair, makeup, and clothing stylists will be provided. It is helpful for models to know what product is being promoted and what image they should project. Some models research the client and the product being modeled to prepare for a shoot. Once a job is completed, models must check in with their agency and plan for the next appointment.

Work environment. Many models work part time, often with variable work schedules.

Models work under a variety of conditions varying from difficult to glamorous. Models can work in a comfortable, climate-controlled studio or outdoors in adverse weather conditions. Schedules can be demanding and sometimes stressful. Yet, successful models interact with a variety of people and enjoy frequent travel. They may meet potential clients at several go-sees in one day and often travel to work in distant cities, foreign countries, and exotic locations.

Training, Other Qualifications, and Advancement
Formal training is limited and education beyond high school usually is not required.

Education and training. Some aspiring models opt to attend modeling schools. Modeling schools provide training in posing, walking, makeup application, and other basic tasks, but attending such schools does not necessarily lead to job opportunities. Agents continually scout for fresh faces at modeling schools, and many models are discovered in this way. Most agencies review snapshots or have "open calls," during which models are seen in person; this service usually is provided free of charge. Some agencies sponsor modeling contests and searches. Very few people who send in snapshots or attend open calls are offered contracts.

Agencies advise models on how to dress, wear makeup, and conduct themselves properly during go-sees and bookings. Because models' advancement depends on their previous work, development of a good portfolio is key to getting assignments. The higher the quality of the photos in the portfolio and the more current they are, the more likely it is that the model will find work.

Other qualifications. Models should be photogenic and have a basic knowledge of hair styling, makeup, and clothing. A model should have flawless skin, healthy hair, and attractive facial features. Specific requirements depend on the client, but most models must be within certain ranges for height, weight, and clothing size in order to meet the practical needs of fashion designers, photographers, and advertisers. Requirements may change slightly from time to time along with common perceptions of physical beauty. However, most fashion designers believe that their clothing looks best on tall, thin models. Although physical requirements may be relaxed for some types of modeling jobs, opportunities are limited for those who do not meet these basic requirements.

A model's career depends on preservation of his or her physical characteristics, so models must control their diet, exercise regularly, and get enough sleep in order to stay healthy. Haircuts, pedicures, and manicures are necessary work-related expenses for models.

The ability to relate to the camera in order to capture the desired look on film is essential; agents test prospective models using snapshots or professional photographs. For photographic and runway work, models must be able to move gracefully and confidently. Training in acting, voice, and dance is useful and allows a model to be considered for television work. Foreign language skills are useful because successful models travel frequently to foreign countries.

Models must interact with a large number of people, so personality plays an important role in success. Models must be professional, polite, and prompt because every contact could lead to future employment. Organizational skills are necessary to manage personal lives, financial matters, and work and travel schedules. Competition for jobs is keen and clients' needs are very specific, so patience and persistence are essential. State and local governments require models under the age of 18 to hold a work permit.

Advancement. Models advance by working more regularly and being selected for assignments that have higher pay. They may begin to appear in magazines, print campaigns, commercials, or runway shows with higher profiles. They may begin to work with clients who will provide them with more widespread exposure. A model's selection of an agency is an important factor for advancement in the occupation. The better the reputation and skill of the agency, the more assignments a model is likely to get. Prospective clients prefer to work with agents, which makes it very difficult for a model to pursue a freelance career. Modeling careers are relatively short.

Employment

Models held about 2,200 jobs in 2008. About 18 percent were self-employed.

Job Outlook

Employment of models is expected to grow faster than average for all occupations through 2018. Nonetheless, models should face keen competition for a small number of openings.

Employment change. Employment of models is expected to grow by 16 percent between 2008 and 2018, which is faster than the average for all occupations. Growth in the employment of models will be driven by their continued use in advertising products. Advertisers will continue to use models in fashion shows, catalogs, and print campaigns as a method to increase awareness of their product.

Job prospects. Modeling is considered a glamorous occupation, and it has few formal entry requirements. Consequently, those who wish to pursue a modeling career can expect keen competition for jobs. The modeling profession typically attracts many more jobseekers than there are job openings. The increasing diversity of the general population should boost demand for models more representative of diverse racial and ethnic groups. Work for male models also should increase as society becomes more receptive to the marketing of men's fashions. Because fashions change frequently, demand for a model's look may fluctuate. Most models experience periods of unemployment.

Employment of models, which is often irregular to begin with, is also affected by downturns in the business cycle. Many firms tend to reduce advertising budgets during recessions.

Earnings

Median hourly wages of models were $13.18 in May 2008. The middle 50 percent earned between $10.09 and $17.23. The lowest 10 percent earned less than $8.32, and the highest 10 percent earned more than $21.10. Wages vary for different types of modeling, and they depend on the experience and reputation of the model. Female models typically earn more than male models for similar work. Hourly wages can be relatively high, particularly for supermodels and others in high demand, but models may not work every day and jobs may last only a few hours. Models occasionally receive free or discounted clothing instead of, or in addition to, regular wages. Almost all models work with an agent and pay a percentage of their earnings in return for the agent's services. Models who do not find immediate work may receive payments, called advances, from agents to cover promotional and living expenses. Models usually provide their own health and retirement benefits.

Projections data from the National Employment Matrix

Occupational Title	SOC Code	Employment, 2008	Projected Employment, 2018	Change, 2008-2018	
				Number	Percent
Models..	41-9012	2,200	2,600	400	16

(NOTE) Data in this table are rounded. See the discussion of the employment projections table in the *Handbook* introductory chapter on *Occupational Information Included in the Handbook.*

Related Occupations

Models create interest in buying clothing and other products and services by performing before the public eye. Other people who create interest in a product or service or who perform in public include:

Sources of Additional Information

For information about modeling schools and agencies in your area, contact a local consumer affairs organization such as the Better Business Bureau.

The Occupational Information Network (O*NET) provides information on a wide range of occupational characteristics. Links to O*NET appear at the end of the Internet version of this occupational statement, accessible at **http://www.bls.gov/ooh/ocos337.htm**

Real Estate Brokers and Sales Agents

Significant Points

- A license is required in every State and the District of Columbia.

- Residential real estate brokers and sales agents often work evenings and weekends.

- Although gaining a job may be relatively easy, beginning workers face competition from well-established, more experienced agents and brokers.

- Employment is sensitive to swings in the economy, as well as interest rates; during periods of declining economic activity or rising interest rates, the volume of sales and the resulting demand for sales workers fall.

Nature of the Work

One of the most complex and significant financial events in peoples' lives is the purchase or sale of a home or investment property. Because of the complexity and importance of this transaction, people typically seek the help of *real estate brokers* and *sales agents* when buying or selling real estate.

Real estate brokers and sales agents have a thorough knowledge of the real estate market in their communities. They know which neighborhoods will best fit clients' needs and budgets. They are familiar with local zoning and tax laws and know where to obtain financing for the purchase of property.

Brokers and agents do the same type of work, but brokers are licensed to manage their own real estate businesses. Agents must work with a broker. They usually provide their services to a licensed real estate broker on a contract basis. In return, the broker pays the agent a portion of the commission earned from the agent's sale of the property. Brokers, as independent businesspeople, often sell real estate owned by others; they also may rent or manage properties for a fee.

When selling property, brokers and agents arrange for title searches to verify ownership and for meetings between buyers and sellers during which they agree to the details of the transactions. In a final meeting, the new owners take possession of the property. Agents and brokers also act as intermediaries in price negotiations between buyers and sellers. They may help to arrange financing from a lender for the prospective buyer, which may make the difference between success and failure in closing a sale. In some cases, brokers and agents assume primary responsibility for finalizing, or closing, sales, but typically this function is done by lenders or lawyers.

Agents and brokers spend a significant amount of time looking for properties to buy or sell. They obtain listings—agreements by owners to place properties for sale with the firm. When listing a property for sale, agents and brokers compare the listed property with similar properties that recently sold, to determine a competitive market price for the property. Following the sale of the property, both the agent who sold it and the agent who obtained the listing receive a portion of the commission. Thus, agents who sell a property that they themselves have listed can increase their commission.

Before showing residential properties to potential buyers, agents meet with them to get an idea of the type of home the buyers would like, and how much the buyers can afford to spend. They may also ask buyers to sign a loyalty contract, which states that the agent will be the only one to show houses to the buyer. An agent or broker then generates lists of properties for sale, their location and description, and available sources of financing. In some cases, agents and brokers use computers to give buyers a virtual tour of properties that interest them.

Agents may meet numerous times with prospective buyers to discuss and visit available properties. Agents identify and emphasize the most pertinent selling details. To a young family looking for a house, for example, they may emphasize the convenient floor plan, the area's low crime rate, and the proximity to schools and shopping. To a potential investor, they may point out the tax advantages of owning a rental property and finding a renter. If negotiation over price becomes necessary, agents must follow their client's instructions thoroughly and may present counteroffers to reach the final sales price.

Once the buyer and seller have signed a contract, the real estate broker or agent must ensure that all terms of the contract are met before the closing date. If the seller agrees to any repairs, the broker or agent ensures they are made. Increasingly, brokers and agents must deal with environmental issues as well, such as advising buyers about lead paint on the walls. In addition, the agent must make sure that any legally mandated or agreed-upon inspections, such as termite and radon inspections, take place. Loan officers, attorneys, and other people handle many details, but the agent must ensure that they are carried out.

Most real estate brokers and sales agents sell residential property. A small number—usually employed in large or specialized firms—sell commercial, industrial, agricultural, or other types of real estate. Every specialty requires knowledge of that particular type of property and clientele. Selling, buying, or leasing business property requires an understanding of leasing practices, business trends, and the location of the property. Agents who sell, buy, or lease industrial properties must know about the

Most real estate brokers and sales agents sell residential property.

region's transportation, utilities, and labor supply. Whatever the type of property, the agent or broker must know how to meet the client's particular requirements.

Work environment. Real estate agents and brokers often work more than a standard 40-hour week, often working evenings and weekends for the convenience of clients. Although the hours are long and frequently irregular, most agents and brokers have the freedom to determine their own schedule.

Advances in telecommunications and the ability to retrieve data about properties over the Internet allow many real estate brokers and sales agents to work out of their homes instead of real estate offices. Even with this convenience, workers spend much of their time away from their desks—showing properties to customers, analyzing properties for sale, meeting with prospective clients, or researching the real estate market.

Training, Other Qualifications, and Advancement

In every State and the District of Columbia, real estate brokers and sales agents must be licensed. Prospective agents must be high school graduates, be at least 18 years old, and pass a written test administered by the State.

Education and training. Agents and brokers must be high school graduates. In fact, as real estate transactions have become more legally complex, many firms have turned to college graduates to fill positions. A large number of agents and brokers have some college training.

Most universities, colleges, and community colleges offer various courses in real estate. Some offer associate and bachelor's degrees in real estate, but mostly they offer certificate programs. Additionally, college courses in finance, business administration, statistics, economics, law, and English are also helpful. For those who intend to start their own company, business courses such as marketing and accounting are as important as courses in real estate or finance.

Many local real estate associations that are members of the National Association of Realtors sponsor courses covering the fundamentals and legal aspects of the field. Advanced courses in mortgage financing, property development and management, and other subjects also are available. Also, some brokerage firms offer formal training programs for both beginners and experienced agents. In addition, much of the training needed to learn the practical aspects of the trade happens on the job, under

the direction of an experienced agent, who may demonstrate how to use a computer to locate or list available properties and identify sources of financing.

Licensure. In every State and the District of Columbia, real estate brokers and sales agents must be licensed. Prospective brokers and agents must pass a written examination. The examination—more comprehensive for brokers than for agents—includes questions on basic real estate transactions and the laws affecting the sale of property. Most States require candidates for the general sales license to complete between 30 and 90 hours of classroom instruction. To get a broker's license an individual needs between 60 and 90 hours of formal training and a specific amount of experience selling real estate, usually 1 to 3 years. Some States waive the experience requirements for the broker's license for applicants who have a bachelor's degree in real estate.

State licenses typically must be renewed every 1 or 2 years; usually, no examination is needed. However, many States require continuing education for license renewals. Prospective agents and brokers should contact the real estate licensing commission of the State in which they wish to work to verify the exact licensing requirements.

Other qualifications. Personality traits are as important as academic background. Brokers look for agents who have a pleasant personality and a neat appearance. They must be at least 18 years old. Maturity, good judgment, trustworthiness, honesty, and enthusiasm for the job are required to attract prospective customers in this highly competitive field. Agents should be well organized, be detail oriented, and have a good memory for names, faces, and business particulars. A good knowledge of the local area and its neighborhoods is a clear advantage.

Advancement. As agents gain knowledge and expertise, they become more efficient in closing a greater number of transactions and increase their income. In many large firms, experienced agents can advance to sales manager or general manager. People who earn their broker's license may open their own offices. Others with experience and training in estimating property values may become real estate appraisers, and people familiar with operating and maintaining rental properties may become property managers. (See the *Handbook* statements on property, real estate, and community association managers; and appraisers and assessors of real estate.) Experienced agents and brokers with a thorough knowledge of business conditions and property values in their localities may enter mortgage financing or real estate investment counseling.

Employment

In 2008, real estate brokers and sales agents held about 517,800 jobs; real estate sales agents held approximately 76 percent of these jobs.

Many real estate brokers and sales agents worked part time, combining their real estate activities with other careers. About 59 percent of real estate brokers and sales agents were self-employed. Real estate is sold in all areas, but employment is concentrated in large urban areas and in rapidly growing communities.

Most real estate firms are relatively small; indeed, some are one-person businesses. By contrast, some large real estate firms have several hundred agents operating out of numerous branch offices. Many brokers have franchise agreements with

Projections data from the National Employment Matrix

Occupational Title	SOC Code	Employment, 2008	Projected Employment, 2018	Change, 2008-2018	
				Number	Percent
Real estate brokers and sales agents	41-9020	517,800	592,100	74,300	14
Real estate brokers	41-9021	123,400	134,000	10,600	9
Real estate sales agents	41-9022	394,400	458,200	63,700	16

(NOTE) Data in this table are rounded. See the discussion of the employment projections table in the *Handbook* introductory chapter on *Occupational Information Included in the Handbook.*

national or regional real estate organizations. Under this type of arrangement, the broker pays a fee in exchange for the privilege of using the more widely known name of the parent organization. Although franchised brokers often receive help in training sales staff and running their offices, they bear the ultimate responsibility for the success or failure of their firms.

Job Outlook

Employment of real estate brokers and agents is expected to grow faster than average. Beginning agents and brokers, however, will face competition from their well-established, more experienced counterparts.

Employment change. Employment of real estate brokers and sales agents is expected to grow 14 percent during the 2008-18 decade, faster than average for all occupations. A growing population, particularly young adults who will be forming households in greater numbers, will require the services of real estate agents and brokers to buy their homes. Home sales will be sparked by the continuing desire for people to own their own homes and their perception that real estate will be a good investment over the long run. However, job growth will be somewhat limited by the increasing use of the Internet, which is improving the productivity of agents and brokers, and transforming the way they do business. For example, prospective customers often can perform their own searches for properties that meet their criteria by accessing real estate information on the Internet.

Job prospects. In addition to job growth, a large number of job openings will arise from the need to replace workers who transfer to other occupations or leave the labor force. Real estate brokers and sales agents are older, on average, than most other workers, and many are expected to leave the occupation over the next decade.

Employment of real estate brokers and sales agents is sensitive to swings in the economy, such as a recession. During periods of declining economic activity or rising interest rates, the volume of sales and the resulting demand for sales workers fall. As a result, the income of agents and brokers declines, and many work fewer hours or leave the occupation altogether. Over the coming decade, the opportunity for part-time work is expected to decline. Although the occupation is relatively easy to enter, increasingly complex legal and technological requirements are raising startup costs associated with becoming an agent and making it more difficult for part-time workers to enter the occupation.

Well-trained, ambitious people who enjoy selling—particularly those with extensive social and business connections in their communities—should have the best chance for success. However, beginning agents and brokers often face competition from their well-established, more experienced counterparts in obtaining listings and in closing an adequate number of sales.

Earnings

The median annual wages, including commissions, of salaried real estate sales agents were $40,150 in May 2008. The middle 50 percent earned between $27,390 and $64,820 a year. The lowest 10 percent earned less than $21,120, and the highest 10 percent earned more than $101,860. Median annual wages in the industries employing the largest number of real estate sales agents in May 2008 were:

Residential building construction	$49,620
Land subdivision	44,410
Offices of real estate agents and brokers	41,320
Activities related to real estate	36,410
Lessors of real estate	32,150

Median annual wages, including commissions, of salaried real estate brokers were $57,500 in May 2008. The middle 50 percent earned between $36,420 and $93,970 a year. Median annual wages in the industries employing the largest number of real estate brokers in May 2008 were:

Residential building construction	$63,280
Offices of real estate agents and brokers	59,710
Activities related to credit Intermediation	57,740
Activities related to real estate	56,140
Lessors of real estate	47,230

Commissions on sales are the main source of earnings of real estate agents and brokers. The rate of commission varies according to whatever the agent and broker agree on, the type of property, and its value. The percentage paid on the sale of farm and commercial properties or unimproved land is typically higher than the percentage paid for selling a home.

Commissions may be divided among several agents and brokers. The broker or agent who obtains a listing usually shares the commission with the broker or agent who sells the property and with the firms that employ each of them. Although an agent's share varies greatly from one firm to another, often it is about half of the total amount received by the firm. Agents who both list and sell a property maximize their commission.

Income usually increases as an agent gains experience, but individual motivation, economic conditions, and the type and location of the property also can affect income. Sales workers who are active in community organizations and in local real estate associations can broaden their contacts and increase their income. A beginner's earnings often are irregular because a few weeks or even months may go by without a sale. Although some brokers allow an agent to draw against future income from a special account, the practice is not common with new employees. The beginner, therefore, should have enough money to live for about 6 months or until commissions increase.

Related Occupations

Other occupations requiring knowledge of real estate include:

Sources of Additional Information

Information on licensing requirements for real estate brokers and sales agents is available from most local real estate organizations or from the State real estate commission or board.

More information about opportunities in real estate is available on the Internet site of the following organization:

➤ National Association of Realtors. Internet: **http://www.realtor.org**

The Occupational Information Network (O*NET) provides information on a wide range of occupational characteristics. Links to O*NET appear at the end of the Internet version of this occupational statement, accessible at **http://www.bls.gov/ooh/ocos120.htm**

Retail Salespersons

Significant Points

- Good employment opportunities are expected because of the need to replace the large number of workers who leave the occupation each year.

- Many salespersons work evenings and weekends, particularly during peak retail periods.

- Employers look for people who enjoy working with others and who have good communication skills, an interest in sales work, a neat appearance, and a courteous demeanor.

- Although advancement opportunities are limited, having a college degree or a great deal of experience may help retail salespersons move into management positions.

Nature of the Work

Whether selling shoes, computer equipment, or automobiles, retail salespersons assist customers in finding what they are looking for. They also try to increase sales by describing a product's features, demonstrating its uses, and promoting its value.

In addition to selling, many retail salespersons—especially those who work in department and apparel stores—conduct financial transactions with their customers. This usually involves receiving payments by cash, check, debit card, or credit card; operating cash registers; and bagging or packaging purchases. Depending on the hours they work, retail salespersons may have to open or close cash registers. This work may in-

Retail salespersons work in various settings, including clothing stores, automobile dealers, and electronics and appliance stores.

clude counting the money in the register and separating charge slips, coupons, and exchange vouchers. Retail salespersons also may have to make deposits at a cash office. (Cashiers, who have similar duties, are discussed elsewhere in the *Handbook*.) In addition, retail salespersons may help stock shelves or racks, arrange for mailing or delivery of purchases, mark price tags, take inventory, and prepare displays.

For some sales jobs, particularly those involving expensive and complex items, retail salespersons need special knowledge or skills. For example, salespersons who sell automobiles must be able to explain the features of various models, the manufacturers' specifications, the types of options and financing available, and the details of associated warranties. In addition, all retail salespersons must recognize security risks and thefts and understand their organization's procedure for handling such situations—procedures that may include notifying security guards or calling police.

Work environment. Most retail salespersons work in clean, comfortable, well-lit stores. However, they often stand for long periods and may need supervisory approval to leave the sales floor. They also may work outdoors if they sell items such as cars, plants, or lumber yard materials.

The Monday-through-Friday, 9-to-5 workweek is the exception rather than the rule for retail salespersons. Many salespersons work evenings and weekends, particularly during holidays and other peak sales periods. The end-of-year holiday season often is the busiest time, and as a result, many employers limit the use of vacation time between Thanksgiving and the beginning of January.

This occupation offers opportunities for both full-time and part-time work. About 34 percent of retail salespersons worked part time in 2008. Part-time opportunities may vary by setting, however, as many who sell big-ticket items are required to work full time.

Training, Other Qualifications, and Advancement

Retail salespersons typically learn their skills through on-the-job training. Although advancement opportunities are limited, having a college degree or a great deal of experience may help retail salespersons move into management positions.

Education and training. There usually are no formal education requirements for retail sales positions, but employers often prefer applicants with a high school diploma or its equivalent. This may be especially important for those who sell technical products or "big-ticket" items, such as electronics or automobiles. A college degree may be required for management trainee positions, especially in larger retail establishments.

Most retail salespersons receive on-the-job training, which usually lasts anywhere from a few days to a few months. In small stores, newly hired workers usually are trained by an experienced employee. In large stores, training programs are more formal and generally are conducted over several days. Topics often include customer service, security, the store's policies and procedures, and cash register operation. Depending on the type of product they are selling, employees may be given additional specialized training. For example, those working in cosmetics receive instruction on the types of products the store offers and for whom the cosmetics would be most beneficial. Likewise, those who sell computers may be instructed in the technical differences between computer products. Because providing the best possible service to customers is a high priority for many employers, employees often are given periodic training to update and refine their skills.

Other qualifications. Employers look for people who enjoy working with others and who possess good communication skills. Employers also value workers who have the tact and patience to deal with difficult customers. Among other desirable characteristics are an interest in sales work, a neat appearance, and a courteous demeanor. The ability to speak more than one language may be helpful for employment in communities where people from various cultures live and shop. Before hiring a salesperson, some employers conduct a background check, especially for a job selling high-priced items.

Advancement. Opportunities for advancement vary. In some small establishments, advancement is limited because one person—often the owner—does most of the managerial work. In others, some salespersons can be promoted to assistant manager. Large retail businesses usually prefer to hire college graduates as management trainees, making a college education increasingly important. However, motivated and capable employees without college degrees still may advance to administrative or supervisory positions in large establishments.

As salespersons gain experience and seniority, they often move into positions with greater responsibility and may be given their choice of departments in which to work. This opportunity often means moving to areas with higher potential earnings and commissions. The highest earnings potential usually lies in selling "big-ticket" items—such as cars, jewelry, furniture, and electronic equipment—although doing so often requires extensive knowledge of the product and an excellent talent for persuasion.

Previous sales experience may be an asset when one is applying for positions with larger retailers or in nonretail industries, such as financial services, wholesale trade, or manufacturing.

Employment

Retail salespersons held about 4.5 million jobs in 2008. The largest employers were clothing and clothing accessories stores, department stores, building material and supplies dealers, motor vehicle and parts dealers, and general merchandise stores such as warehouse clubs and supercenters. In addition, about 156,500 retail salespersons were self-employed.

Because retail stores are found in every city and town, employment is distributed geographically in much the same way as the population.

Job Outlook

Employment is expected to grow about as fast as average. Due to the frequency with which people leave this occupation, job opportunities are expected to be good.

Employment change. Employment is expected to grow by 8 percent over the 2008–18 decade, about as fast as the average for all occupations. In addition, given the size of this occupation, about 374,700 new retail salesperson jobs will arise over the projections decade—more jobs than will be generated in almost any other occupation.

Employment growth among retail salespersons reflects rising retail sales stemming from a growing population. Many retail establishments will continue to expand in size and number, leading to new retail sales positions. Growth will be fastest in general merchandise stores, many of which sell a wide assortment of goods at low prices. As consumers continue to prefer these stores other establishments with higher prices, growth in this industry will be rapid. Employment of retail sales persons is expected to decline in department stores and automobile dealers as these industries see a reduction in store locations.

Despite the growing popularity of electronic commerce, the impact of online shopping on the employment of retail salespersons is expected to be minimal. Internet sales have not decreased the need for retail salespersons. Retail stores commonly use an online presence to complement their in-store sales, and many consumers prefer to buy merchandise in person. Retail salespersons will remain important in assisting customers, providing specialized service, and increasing customer satisfaction.

Job prospects. Employment opportunities for retail salespersons are expected to be good because of the need to replace the large number of workers who transfer to other occupations or leave the labor force each year. In addition, many new jobs will be created for retail salespersons as businesses seek to expand operations and enhance customer service. A substantial number of these openings should occur in warehouse clubs and supercenters as a result of strong growth among these establishments.

Projections data from the National Employment Matrix

Occupational Title	SOC Code	Employment, 2008	Projected Employment, 2018	Change, 2008-2018	
				Number	Percent
Retail salespersons	41-2031	4,489,200	4,863,900	374,700	8

(NOTE) Data in this table are rounded. See the discussion of the employment projections table in the *Handbook* introductory chapter on *Occupational Information Included in the Handbook.*

Opportunities for part-time work should be abundant, and demand is expected be strong for temporary workers during peak selling periods, such as the end-of-year holiday season between Thanksgiving and the beginning of January.

During economic downturns, sales volumes and the resulting demand for sales workers usually decline. Consequently, retail sales jobs generally are more susceptible to fluctuations in the economy than are many other occupations.

Earnings

Median hourly wages of wage-and-salary retail salespersons, including commissions, were $9.86 in May 2008. The middle 50 percent earned between $8.26 and $13.35 an hour. The lowest 10 percent earned less than $7.37, and the highest 10 percent earned more than $19.14 an hour. Median hourly wages in the industries employing the largest numbers of retail salespersons in May 2008 were as follows:

Automobile dealers	$18.91
Building material and supplies dealers	11.95
Other general merchandise stores	9.22
Department stores	9.14
Clothing stores	8.94

Many beginning or inexperienced workers earn the Federal minimum wage of $7.25 an hour, but many States set minimum wages higher than the Federal minimum. In areas where employers have difficulty attracting and retaining workers, wages tend to be higher than the legislated minimum.

Compensation systems can vary by type of establishment and merchandise sold. Salespersons receive hourly wages, commissions, or a combination of the two. Under a commission system, salespersons receive a percentage of the sales they make. This system offers sales workers the opportunity to increase their earnings considerably, but they may find that their earnings depend strongly on their ability to sell their product and on the ups and downs of the economy.

Benefits may be limited in smaller stores, but benefits in large establishments usually are considerable. In addition, nearly all salespersons are able to buy their store's merchandise at a discount, with the savings depending on the type of merchandise. Also, to bolster revenue, employers may use incentive programs such as awards, bonuses, and profit-sharing plans to the sales staff.

Related Occupations

Other occupations that provide customer service, sell items, or operate cash registers include the following:

Sources of Additional Information

Information on careers in retail sales may be obtained from the personnel offices of local stores or from State merchants' associations.

General information about retailing is available from:

➤ National Retail Federation, 325 7th St. NW., Suite 1100, Washington, DC 20004. Internet: **http://www.nrf.com**

Information about training for a career in automobile sales is available from:

➤ National Automobile Dealers Association, Public Relations Department, 8400 Westpark Dr., McLean, VA 22102-3591. Internet: **http://www.nada.org**

The Occupational Information Network (O*NET) provides information on a wide range of occupational characteristics. Links to O*NET appear at the end of the Internet version of this occupational statement, accessible at **http://www.bls.gov/ooh/ocos121.htm**

Sales Engineers

Significant Points

- A bachelor's degree in engineering usually is required; many sales engineers have previous work experience in an engineering specialty.

- Competition for jobs is expected.

- Earnings typically are based on a combination of salary and commission.

Nature of the Work

Many products and services, especially those purchased by large companies and institutions, are highly complex. Sales engineers—also called *technical sales support workers*—determine how products and services could be designed or modified to suit customers' needs. They also may advise customers on how best to use the products or services provided.

Sales engineers specialize in technologically and scientifically advanced products. They possess extensive knowledge of these products, including knowledge about their components, functions, and the scientific processes that make them work. They use their technical skills to explain the benefits of their products to potential customers and to demonstrate how their products are better than the products of their competitors. Often, they modify and adjust products to meet customers' specific needs. Some sales engineers work for the companies that design and build technical products, while others work for independent sales firms.

Many of the duties of sales engineers are similar to those of other salespersons. They must interest the client in purchasing their products, negotiate a price, and complete the sale. Some sales engineers, however, are teamed with other salespersons who concentrate on marketing and selling the product, enabling the sales engineer to concentrate on the technical aspects of the job. By working on a sales team, each member is able to focus on his or her strengths and expertise. (Information on other sales occupations, including sales representatives, wholesale and manufacturing, appears elsewhere in the *Handbook*.)

Sales engineers use scientific knowledge to help their customers choose the right technical products.

Sales engineers tend to employ selling techniques that are different from those used by most other sales workers. They generally use a "consultative" style; that is, they focus on the client's problem and show how it can be solved or mitigated with their product or service. This selling style differs from the "benefits and features" method, whereby the salesperson describes the product and leaves the customer to decide how it would be useful.

In addition to retaining current clients and attracting new ones, sales engineers help clients solve any problems that arise when the product is installed. Afterward, they may continue to serve as a liaison between the client and their company. Increasingly, sales engineers are asked to undertake additional tasks related to sales, such as market research, because of their familiarity with clients' purchasing needs. Drawing on this same familiarity, sales engineers may help identify and develop new products.

Work environment. Workers in this occupation can encounter pressure and stress because their income and job security often depend directly on their success in sales and customer service. Many work more than 40 hours per week to meet sales goals and client needs. Although the hours may be long and often irregular, many sales engineers have the freedom to determine their own schedules. Consequently, they often can arrange their appointments so that they can have time off when they want it.

Some sales engineers have large territories and travel extensively. Because sales regions may cover several States, sales engineers may be away from home for several days or even weeks at a time, often traveling by airplane. Others cover a smaller region and travel mostly by car, spending few nights away from home. International travel to secure contracts with foreign clients is becoming more common.

Training, Other Qualifications, and Advancement
Sales engineers generally are required to posses a bachelor's degree in engineering, and many have previous work experience in an engineering specialty. New sales engineers may need some on-the-job training in sales or may work closely with a sales mentor before they can work on their own.

Education and training. A bachelor's degree in engineering usually is required for a person to become a sales engineer. However, workers without a degree, but with previous experience in sales and technical experience or training, sometimes hold the title of sales engineer. Also, workers who have a degree in a science, such as chemistry, or even a degree in business with little or no previous sales experience, may be called sales engineers.

University engineering programs generally require 4 years of study. They vary in content, but all contain courses in math and the physical sciences, as well as general education courses such as English and communications. In addition, most require the development of computer skills. Some programs offer a general engineering curriculum; students then specialize on the job or in graduate school. Most programs, however, require students to choose an area of specialization. The most common majors are electrical, mechanical, and civil engineering, but some programs offer additional majors, such as chemical, biomedical, and computer hardware engineering.

New graduates with engineering degrees may need sales experience and training before they can work independently as sales engineers. Training may involve teaming with a sales mentor who is familiar with the employer's business practices, customers, procedures, and company culture. After the training period has been completed, sales engineers may continue to partner with someone who lacks technical skills, yet excels in the art of sales.

It is important for sales engineers to continue their engineering and sales education throughout their careers. Much of their value to their employers depends on their knowledge of, and ability to sell, the latest technologies. Sales engineers in high-technology fields, such as information technology and advanced electronics, may find that their technical knowledge rapidly becomes obsolete, requiring frequent retraining.

Other qualifications. Many sales engineers first work as engineers. For some, engineering experience is necessary to obtain the technical background that is needed to sell their employers' products or services effectively.

These workers must possess excellent communication skills, because interacting with customers is one of their main job functions. They also must be strong in math and have an aptitude for science as they work with complex, technical products.

Advancement. Promotion may include a higher commission rate, a larger sales territory, or elevation to the position of supervisor or marketing manager. Alternatively, sales engineers may move into different occupations, such as consulting.

Employment
Sales engineers held about 78,000 jobs in 2008. About 34 percent were employed in wholesale trade establishments, and another 24 percent were employed in manufacturing establishments. Smaller numbers of sales engineers worked in computer systems design and related services organizations, as well as telecommunications firms. Unlike workers in many other sales occupations, very few sales engineers are self-employed.

Job Outlook
Job growth for sales engineers is projected to be about as fast as average, and competition for jobs is expected.

Employment change. Employment of sales engineers is expected to grow by 9 percent between 2008 and 2018, about

Projections data from the National Employment Matrix

Occupational Title	SOC Code	Employment, 2008	Projected Employment, 2018	Change, 2008-2018	
				Number	Percent
Sales engineers...	41-9031	78,000	84,900	6,900	9

(NOTE) Data in this table are rounded. See the discussion of the employment projections table in the *Handbook* introductory chapter on *Occupational Information Included in the Handbook.*

as fast as the average for all occupations. Job growth will stem from the increasing variety and technical nature of the goods and services to be sold. Competitive pressures and advancing technology will force companies to improve and update product designs more frequently and to optimize their manufacturing, sales processes, and general business processes, thus requiring the services of sales engineers.

Growth will be fastest in technology companies, such as software publishers and computer systems design firms. Increasing demand for the latest, most sophisticated technological products will spur demand for sales engineers with expertise in the field. Conversely, as manufacturing organizations continue to outsource their sales functions to independent companies, employment in the manufacturing industry will fall.

Job prospects. Competition for jobs is expected because the relatively high earnings potential of this occupation creates significant interest in sales engineer positions. Prospects will be best for those with the personal traits necessary for successful sales work. In addition to new positions created as companies expand their sales forces, some openings will arise each year from the need to replace sales engineers who transfer to other occupations or leave the labor force.

Earnings

Median annual wages, including commissions, of sales engineers were $83,100 in May 2008. The middle 50 percent earned between $63,340 and $108,470 a year. The lowest 10 percent earned less than $49,640, and the highest 10 percent earned more than $136,770 a year. Median annual wages of sales engineers employed by the computer systems design and related services industry were $95,580.

Compensation varies significantly by the type of firm and the product sold. Most employers offer a combination of salary and commission payments or a salary plus a bonus. Those working in independent sales companies may just earn commissions. Commissions usually are based on the value of sales, whereas bonuses may depend on individual performance, on the performance of all workers in the group or district, or on the company's performance. Earnings from commissions and bonuses may vary greatly from year to year, depending on sales ability, the demand for the company's products or services, and the overall economy.

In addition to receiving their earnings, sales engineers who work for manufacturers usually are reimbursed for expenses such as transportation, meals, hotels, and customer entertainment. Besides receiving typical benefits, sales engineers may get personal use of a company car and frequent-flyer mileage. Some companies offer incentives such as free vacation trips or gifts for outstanding performance. Sales engineers who work in independent firms may have higher, but less stable, earnings and, often, relatively few benefits. For example, most inde-

pendent sales engineers do not get paid vacations, a common benefit for many other workers.

Related Occupations

Other occupations that perform technical duties or sell products and services include the following:

Sources of Additional Information

Information on careers for manufacturers' representatives and agents is available from:
➤ Manufacturers' Agents National Association, 16 A Journey, Suite 200, Aliso Viejo, CA 92656-3317. Internet: **http://www.manaonline.org**

➤ Manufacturers' Representatives Educational Research Foundation, 8329 Cole St., Arvada, CO 80005. Internet: **http://www.mrerf.org**

The Occupational Information Network (O*NET) provides information on a wide range of occupational characteristics. Links to O*NET appear at the end of the Internet version of this occupational statement, accessible at **http://www.bls.gov/ooh/ocos123.htm**

Sales Representatives, Wholesale and Manufacturing

Significant Points

- Job prospects will be best for those with a college degree, the appropriate technical expertise, and the personal traits necessary for successful selling.

- Earnings usually are based on a combination of salary and commission.

- Employment opportunities and earnings may fluctuate from year to year because sales are affected by changing economic conditions.

Nature of the Work

Sales representatives are an important part of manufacturers' and wholesalers' success. Regardless of the type of products they sell, sales representatives' primary duties are to make customers interested in their merchandise and to arrange the sale of that merchandise.

The process of promoting and selling a product can be extensive, at times taking up to several months. Whether in person or over the phone, sales representatives describe their products, conduct demonstrations, explain the benefits that their products convey, and answer any questions that their customers may have.

Sales representatives—sometimes called *manufacturers' representatives* or *manufacturers' agents*—generally work for manufacturers, wholesalers, or technical companies. Some work for a single organization, while others represent several companies and sell a range of products. Rather than selling goods directly to consumers, sales representatives deal with businesses, government agencies, and other organizations. (Retail salespersons, who sell directly to consumers, and sales engineers, who specialize in sales of technical products and services, are discussed elsewhere in the *Handbook*.)

Some sales representatives specialize in technical and scientific products ranging from agricultural and mechanical equipment to computer and pharmaceutical goods. Other representatives deal with all other types of goods, including food, office supplies, and apparel.

Sales representatives stay abreast of new products and the changing needs of their customers in a variety of ways. They attend trade shows at which new products and technologies are showcased. They also attend conferences and conventions to meet other sales representatives and clients and discuss new product developments. In addition, the entire sales force may participate in company-sponsored meetings to review the firm's sales performance, product development, sales goals, and profitability.

Frequently, sales representatives who lack the necessary expertise about a given product may team with a technical expert. In this arrangement, the technical expert—sometimes a sales engineer—attends the sales presentation to explain the product and answer questions or concerns. The sales representative makes the preliminary contact with customers, introduces the company's product, and closes the sale. Under such an arrangement, the representative is able to spend more time maintaining and soliciting accounts and less time acquiring technical knowledge. After the sale, representatives may make follow up visits to ensure that the equipment is functioning properly and may even help train customers' employees to operate and maintain new equipment. Those selling technical goods also may arrange for the product to be installed. Those selling consumer goods often suggest how and where merchandise should be displayed. When working with retailers, they may help arrange promotional programs, store displays, and advertising.

Sales representatives have several duties beyond selling products. They analyze sales statistics, prepare reports, and handle administrative duties such as filing expense accounts, scheduling appointments, and making travel plans. They also read about new and existing products and monitor the sales, prices, and products of their competitors.

Sales representatives generally work in either inside sales, interacting with customers over the phone from an office location, or outside "field" sales, traveling to meet clients in person.

Inside sales representatives may spend a lot of their time on the phone, selling goods, taking orders, and resolving problems or complaints about the merchandise. These sales representatives typically do not leave the office. Frequently, they are responsible for acquiring new clients by "cold calling" various organizations—calling potential customers to establish an initial contact. They also may be responsible for arranging meetings for outside sales representatives.

Outside sales representatives spend much of their time traveling to, and visiting with, current clients and prospective buyers. During a sales call, they discuss the client's needs and suggest how their merchandise or services can meet those needs. They may show samples or catalogs that describe items their company provides, and they may inform customers about prices, availability, and ways in which their products can save money and boost productivity. Because many sales representatives sell several complementary products made by different manufacturers, they may take a broad approach to their customers' business. For example, sales representatives may help install new equipment and train employees in its use.

Work environment. Some sales representatives have large territories and travel considerably. Because a sales region may cover several States, representatives may be away from home for several days or weeks at a time, often traveling by airplane. Others cover a smaller region and travel mostly by car, spending few nights away from home. Sales representatives frequently are on their feet for long periods and may carry heavy sample products, requiring some physical stamina.

In 2008, about 48 percent of sales representatives worked around 40 hours per week, but about 24 percent worked more than 50 hours per week. Since sales calls take place during regular working hours, much of the planning and paperwork involved with sales must be completed during the evening and on weekends. Although the hours are often irregular, many sales representatives have the freedom to determine their own schedules.

Workers in this occupation can encounter pressure and stress because their income and job security often depend directly on the amount of merchandise they sell and their companies usually set goals or quotas that they are expected to meet. Sales

Sales representatives may travel extensively to meet with clients.

representatives also deal with many different types of people, which can be stimulating but demanding.

Training, Other Qualifications, and Advancement

There generally is no formal educational requirement for sales representative positions, but many jobs require some postsecondary education. Regardless of educational background, factors such as communication skills, the ability to sell, and familiarity with brands are essential to being a successful sales representative.

Education and training. There usually is no formal educational requirement for sales representatives. Some positions, especially those which deal with scientific and technical products, require a bachelor's degree. For other jobs, however, applicants can be fully qualified with a high school diploma or its equivalent. For these positions, previous sales experience may be desirable.

Many sales representatives attend seminars in sales techniques or take courses in marketing, economics, communication, or even a foreign language to provide the extra edge needed to make sales. Often, companies have formal training programs for beginning sales representatives that last up to 2 years. However, most businesses accelerate these programs to much shorter timeframes in order to reduce costs and expedite the returns from training. In some programs, trainees rotate among jobs in plants and offices to learn all phases of production, installation, and distribution of the product. In others, trainees take formal classroom instruction at the plant, followed by on-the-job training under the supervision of a field sales manager.

Regardless of where they work, new employees may be trained by accompanying experienced workers on their sales calls. As they gain familiarity with the firm's products and clients, the new workers are given increasing responsibility, until they are eventually assigned their own territory. As businesses experience greater competition, representatives face more pressure to produce sales.

Other qualifications. For sales representative jobs, companies seek individuals who have excellent communication skills and the desire to sell. Those who want to become sales representatives should be goal oriented, persuasive, and able to work well both independently and as part of a team. A pleasant personality and appearance and problem-solving skills are highly valued. Patience and perseverance also are keys to completing a sale, which can take up to several months.

Manufacturers' representatives who operate a sales agency also must manage their business. Doing so requires organizational and general business skills, as well as knowledge of accounting, marketing, and administration.

Certification and advancement. Certifications are available that provide formal recognition of the skills of sales representatives. Many in this profession have either the Certified Professional Manufacturers' Representative (CPMR) certification or the Certified Sales Professional (CSP) certification, offered by the Manufacturers' Representatives Education Research Foundation. Certification typically involves completing formal training and passing an examination.

Frequently, promotion takes the form of an assignment to a larger account or territory, where commissions are likely to be greater. Those who have good sales records and leadership ability may advance to higher level positions such as sales supervisor, district manager, or vice president of sales. Others find opportunities in purchasing, advertising, or marketing research.

Advancement opportunities typically depend on whether the sales representatives are working directly for a manufacturer or wholesaler or whether they are working with an independent sales agency. Experienced sales representatives working directly for a manufacturer or wholesaler may move into jobs as sales trainers and instruct new employees on selling techniques and company policies and procedures. Some leave their organization and start their own independent sales company.

Employment

Manufacturing and wholesale sales representatives held about 2 million jobs in 2008. About 432,900 of these worked with technical and scientific products. Around 61 percent of all representatives worked for wholesale companies. Others were employed in manufacturing establishments, retail organizations, and professional, technical, and scientific firms. Because of the diversity of products and services sold, employment opportunities are available throughout the country. About 73,800 sales representatives were self-employed.

Job Outlook

Job growth is expected to be about as fast as average. Job prospects will be best for those with a college degree, the appropriate technical expertise, and the personal traits necessary for successful selling.

Employment change. Employment of sales representatives, wholesale and manufacturing, is expected to grow by 7 percent between 2008 and 2018, about as fast as the average for all occupations. Given the size of this occupation, a large number of new jobs, about 143,200, will arise over the projection period. Job growth will result from the continued expansion in the variety and number of goods sold throughout the economy. Because they play an important role in the transfer of goods between organizations, sales representatives will be needed to accommodate this expansion. In addition, as technology continues to

Projections data from the National Employment Matrix

Occupational Title	SOC Code	Employment, 2008	Projected Employment, 2018	Change, 2008-2018	
				Number	Percent
Sales representatives, wholesale and manufacturing	41-4000	1,973,200	2,116,400	143,200	7
Sales representatives, wholesale and manufacturing, technical and scientific products	41-4011	432,900	475,000	42,000	10
Sales representatives, wholesale and manufacturing, except technical and scientific products...................................	41-4012	1,540,300	1,641,400	101,100	7

(NOTE) Data in this table are rounded. See the discussion of the employment projections table in the *Handbook* introductory chapter on *Occupational Information Included in the Handbook.*

progress, sales representatives can help ensure that retailers offer the latest products to their customers and that businesses acquire the tools they need to increase their efficiency in operations.

Employment growth will be greatest in independent sales companies as manufacturers continue to outsource sales activities to independent agents rather than using in-house sales workers. Independent sales agents generally are more efficient, reducing the overhead cost to their clients. Also, by using agents who contract their services to more than one company, companies can share costs of the agents with each other.

Job prospects. Job prospects will be best for those with a college degree, the appropriate technical expertise, and the personal traits necessary for successful selling. Opportunities will be better in independent sales companies than with manufacturers, who are expected to continue contracting out field sales duties.

Employment opportunities and earnings may fluctuate from year to year because sales are affected by changing economic conditions and businesses' preferences. In addition, many job openings will result from the need to replace workers who transfer to other occupations or leave the labor force.

Earnings

Median annual wages of sales representatives, wholesale and manufacturing, technical and scientific products, were $70,200, including commissions, in May 2008. The middle 50 percent earned between $48,540 and $99,570 a year. The lowest 10 percent earned less than $34,980, and the highest 10 percent earned more than $133,040 a year. Median annual wages in the industries employing the largest numbers of sales representatives, wholesale and manufacturing, technical and scientific products, were as follows:

Computer systems design and related services	$80,060
Wholesale electronic markets and agents and brokers	77,190
Drugs and druggists' sundries merchant wholesalers	74,840
Professional and commercial equipment and supplies merchant wholesalers	70,140
Electrical and electronic goods merchant wholesalers	63,050

Median annual wages of sales representatives, wholesale and manufacturing, except technical and scientific products, were $51,330, including commission, in May 2008. The middle 50 percent earned between $36,460 and $75,120 a year. The lowest 10 percent earned less than $26,950, and the highest 10 percent earned more than $106,040 a year. Median annual wages in the industries employing the largest numbers of sales representatives, wholesale and manufacturing, except technical and scientific products, were as follows:

Wholesale electronic markets and agents and brokers	$57,100
Machinery equipment and supplies merchant wholesalers	50,310
Professional and commercial equipment and supplies merchant wholesalers	49,750
Grocery and related product merchant wholesalers	47,980
Miscellaneous nondurable goods merchant wholesalers	44,680

Compensation methods for representatives vary significantly by the type of firm and the product sold. Most employers use a combination of salary and commissions or salary plus bonus. Commissions usually are based on the value of sales, whereas bonuses may depend on individual performance, on the performance of all sales workers in the group or district, or on the company's performance. Unlike those working directly for a manufacturer or wholesaler, sales representatives working for an independent sales company usually are not reimbursed for expenses. Depending on the type of product or products they are selling, their experience in the field, and the number of clients they have, they can earn significantly more or less than those working in direct sales for a manufacturer or wholesaler.

In addition to receiving their earnings, sales representatives working directly for a manufacturer or wholesaler usually are reimbursed for expenses such as the costs of transportation, meals, hotels, and entertaining customers. They often receive benefits, including personal use of a company car and frequent flyer mileage. Some companies offer incentives such as free vacation trips or gifts for achieving an outstanding sales performance.

Related Occupations

Sales representatives, wholesale and manufacturing, must have sales ability and knowledge of the products they sell. Other occupations that require similar skills include the following:

	Page
Advertising sales agents	527
Insurance sales agents	534
Purchasing managers, buyers, and purchasing agents	79
Real estate brokers and sales agents	540
Retail salespersons	543
Sales engineers	545
Sales worker supervisors	551
Securities, commodities, and financial services sales agents	553

Sources of Additional Information

Information on careers for manufacturers' representatives and sales agents is available from:

➤ Manufacturers' Agents National Association, 16 A Journey, Ste. 200, Aliso Viejo, CA 92656-3317. Internet: **http://www.manaonline.org**

➤ Manufacturers' Representatives Educational Research Foundation, 8329 Cole St., Arvada, CO 80005. Internet: **http://www.mrerf.org**

The Occupational Information Network (O*NET) provides information on a wide range of occupational characteristics. Links to O*NET appear at the end of the Internet version of this occupational statement, accessible at

http://www.bls.gov/ooh/ocos119.htm

Sales Worker Supervisors

Significant Points

- Employment is projected to increase more slowly than the average for all occupations.

- Competition is expected for jobs; applicants with a college degree or sales experience should have the best opportunities.

- Long, irregular hours, including evenings and weekends, are common.

Nature of the Work

Sales worker supervisors oversee the work of sales and related workers, such as retail salespersons, cashiers, customer service representatives, stock clerks and order fillers, sales engineers, and wholesale sales representatives. Sales worker supervisors are responsible for interviewing, hiring, and training employees. They also may prepare work schedules and assign workers to specific duties. Many of these supervisors hold job titles such as *sales manager, department manager,* or *shift supervisor.*

In retail establishments, sales worker supervisors ensure that customers receive satisfactory service and quality goods. They also answer customers' inquiries, deal with complaints, and sometimes handle purchasing, budgeting, and accounting.

Responsibilities vary with the size and type of establishment. As the size of retail stores grows and the variety of goods and services increases, supervisors tend to specialize in one department or one aspect of merchandising. Sales worker supervisors in large retail establishments are often referred to as department supervisors or managers. They provide day-to-day oversight of individual departments, such as shoes, cosmetics, or housewares in department stores; produce or meat in grocery stores; and car sales in automotive dealerships. Department supervisors establish and implement policies, goals, and procedures for their specific departments; coordinate activities with other department heads; and strive for smooth operations within their departments. They supervise employees whose responsibilities may include pricing and ticketing goods and placing them on display; cleaning and organizing shelves, displays, and inventories in stockrooms; and inspecting merchandise to ensure that nothing is outdated. Sales worker supervisors review inventory and sales records, develop merchandising techniques, and coordinate sales promotions. In addition, they may greet and assist customers and promote sales and good public relations.

Sales worker supervisors in non-retail establishments oversee and coordinate the activities of sales workers who sell industrial products, insurance policies, or services such as advertising, financial, or Internet services. Sales worker supervisors may prepare budgets, make personnel decisions, devise sales-incentive programs, and approve sales contracts.

In small or independent companies and retail stores, sales worker supervisors not only directly supervise sales associates, but they also are responsible for the operation of the entire company or store. Some are self-employed business or store owners.

Work environment. Most sales worker supervisors have offices. In retail trade, their offices are within the stores, usually close to the areas they oversee. Although they spend some time in the office completing merchandise orders or arranging work schedules, a large portion of their workday is spent on the sales floor, supervising employees or selling merchandise.

Work hours of supervisors vary greatly among establishments because work schedules usually depend on the needs of the customer. Supervisors generally work at least 40 hours a week. Long, irregular hours are common, particularly during sales, holidays, busy shopping seasons, and at times when inventory is recorded. Supervisors are expected to work some evenings and weekends but usually are given a day off during the week. Hours can change weekly, and supervisors sometimes must report to work on short notice, especially when employees are absent. Independent owners often can set their own schedules, but hours must be convenient to customers.

Training, Other Qualifications, and Advancement

Sales worker supervisors usually gain knowledge of management principles and practices through work experience. Many supervisors begin their careers as salespersons, cashiers, or customer service representatives. These workers should be patient, decisive, and sales-oriented.

Education and training. There is no standard educational requirement for sales worker supervisors, and the educational backgrounds of these workers vary widely. For some jobs, a college degree is required. Supervisors who have college degrees often hold associate or bachelor's degrees in liberal arts, social sciences, business, or management. College graduates usually can enter directly into management training programs sponsored by their company, without much experience. Many supervisors, however, are hired without postsecondary education. For these workers, previous experience in a sales occupation is essential. Most sales worker supervisors have retail sales experience or experience as a customer service representative. In these positions, they learn merchandising, customer service, and the basic policies and procedures of the company.

Regardless of education level or major area of study, recommended high school or college courses include those related to business, such as accounting, marketing, management, and sales, as well as those related to social science, such as psychology, sociology, and communication. To gain experience, many

Sales worker supervisors often have extensive experience in a related sales occupation.

college students participate in internship programs that usually are developed jointly by schools and businesses.

The type and amount of training available to supervisors varies by company. Many national retail chains and companies have formal training programs for management trainees that include both classroom and on-site training. Training time may be as brief as 1 week or may last more than 1 year, giving trainees experience during all sales seasons.

Ordinarily, classroom training includes topics such as interviewing, customer service skills, inventory management, employee relations, and scheduling. Training programs for retail franchises are generally extensive, covering all functions of the company's operation, including budgeting, marketing, management, finance, purchasing, product preparation, human resource management, and compensation.

Other qualifications. Sales worker supervisors must possess good communication skills and get along with all types of people. They need initiative, self-discipline, good judgment, and decisiveness. Patience and a conciliatory temperament are necessary when dealing with demanding customers. Supervisors also must be able to motivate, organize, and direct the work of their employees. Supervisors who own their own establishment need good business skills and strong customer service and public relations skills.

Advancement. Supervisors who display leadership and team-building skills, motivation, and decisiveness may become candidates for promotion to assistant manager or manager. A postsecondary degree may speed their advancement into management. In many retail establishments, managers are promoted from within the company. In small retail establishments, where the number of positions is limited, advancement to a higher management position also may be limited. Large establishments often have extensive career ladder programs and may offer supervisors the opportunity to transfer to another store in the chain or to the central office. Although promotions may occur more rapidly in large establishments, some managers may need to relocate every several years to be able to advance.

Supervisors also can become advertising, marketing, promotions, public relations, and sales managers—workers who coordinate marketing plans, monitor sales, and propose advertisements and promotions. They may also become purchasing managers, buyers, or purchasing agents—workers who purchase goods and supplies for their organization or for resale. (These occupations are covered elsewhere in the *Handbook*.)

Some supervisors who have worked in their industry for a long time open their own stores or sales firms. However, retail trade and sales occupations are highly competitive, and although many independent owners succeed, some fail to cover expenses and eventually go out of business.

Employment

Sales worker supervisors held about 2.2 million jobs in 2008. Approximately 34 percent were self-employed, many of whom were store owners. About 48 percent of sales worker supervisors were wage and salary workers employed in the retail sector. Some of the largest employers were grocery stores, department stores, clothing and clothing accessory stores, and general merchandise stores such as warehouse clubs and supercenters. The remaining sales worker supervisors worked in nonretail establishments.

Job Outlook

Employment is projected to grow more slowly than average. Competition for jobs is expected; applicants with a college degree or sales experience should have the best opportunities.

Employment change. Employment of sales worker supervisors is expected to grow by 5 percent between 2008 and 2018, more slowly than the average for all occupations. Job growth will be limited as retail companies increase the responsibilities of retail salespersons and existing sales worker supervisors, and as the retail industry, overall, grows at a slow rate.

Projected employment growth of sales worker supervisors will mirror, in part, the patterns of employment growth in the industries in which they work. For example, faster growth is expected in the professional, scientific, and technical services industry, as a result of strong demand for the services that this industry provides. Conversely, growth of sales worker supervisors will increase more slowly in the retail sector, in-line with overall industry growth.

Job prospects. Similar to other supervisor positions, competition is expected for sales worker supervisor jobs over the 2008-18 period. Candidates who have a college degree, and those with experience—as a sales representative, cashier, or customer service representative, for example—will have the best opportunities.

Some job openings over the next decade will occur as experienced supervisors move into higher levels of management, transfer to other occupations, or leave the labor force. However, these job openings will not be great in number since movement into upper management is also competitive.

Earnings

Wages of sales worker supervisors vary substantially, depending on a worker's level of responsibility, length of service, and the type, size, and location of the firm.

Median annual wages of supervisors of retail sales workers were $35,310, including commissions, in May 2008. The middle 50 percent earned between $27,520 and $46,450. The

Projections data from the National Employment Matrix

Occupational Title	SOC Code	Employment, 2008	Projected Employment, 2018	Change, 2008-2018	
				Number	Percent
Supervisors, sales workers	41-1000	2,192,300	2,305,100	112,800	5
First-line supervisors/managers of retail sales workers	41-1011	1,685,500	1,773,900	88,400	5
First-line supervisors/managers of non-retail sales workers	41-1012	506,800	531,200	24,400	5

(NOTE) Data in this table are rounded. See the discussion of the employment projections table in the *Handbook* introductory chapter on *Occupational Information Included in the Handbook.*

lowest 10 percent earned less than $22,210, and the highest 10 percent earned more than $61,970. Median annual wages in the industries employing the largest numbers of wage and salary supervisors of retail sales workers were as follows:

Building material and supplies dealers $37,710
Grocery stores 35,140
Clothing stores 34,180
Other general merchandise stores 30,590
Department stores..30,480

Median annual wages of supervisors of non-retail sales workers were $68,100, including commissions, in May 2008. The middle 50 percent earned between $51,380 and $98,080. The lowest 10 percent earned less than $36,830, and the highest 10 percent earned more than $136,180. Median annual wages in the industries employing the largest numbers of wage and salary supervisors of non-retail sales workers were as follows:

Professional and commercial equipment
    and supplies merchant wholesalers $82,880
Wholesale electronic markets and agents
    and brokers 81,100
Machinery equipment and supplies
    merchant wholesalers...68,260
Grocery and related product merchant wholesalers.....66,470
Postal Service...60,730

Compensation systems vary by type of establishment and by merchandise sold. Many supervisors receive a commission or a combination of salary and commission. Under a commission system, supervisors receive a percentage of department or store sales. Thus, these supervisors' earnings depend on their ability to sell their product and the condition of the economy. Those who sell large amounts of merchandise or exceed sales goals often receive bonuses or other awards.

Related Occupations

Sales worker supervisors serve customers, supervise workers, and direct and coordinate the operations of an establishment. Workers with similar responsibilities include:

	Page
Administrative services managers..	29
Advertising, marketing, promotions, public relations, and sales managers	32
Food service managers..	55
Lodging managers..	70
Office and administrative support worker supervisors and managers..	594

Sources of Additional Information

Information on employment opportunities for sales worker supervisors may be obtained from the employment offices of various retail establishments or from State employment service offices.

General information on management careers in retail establishments is available from:

➤ National Retail Federation, 325 7th St. NW., Suite 1100, Washington, DC 20004. Internet: **http://www.nrf.com**

Information about management careers and training programs in the motor vehicle dealers industry is available from:
➤ National Automobile Dealers Association, Public Relations Dept., 8400 Westpark Dr., McLean, VA 22102-3591. Internet: **http://www.nada.org**

The Occupational Information Network (O*NET) provides information on a wide range of occupational characteristics. Links to O*NET appear at the end of the Internet version of this occupational statement, accessible at **http://www.bls.gov/ooh/ocos025.htm**

Securities, Commodities, and Financial Services Sales Agents

Significant Points

- Most positions require a bachelor's degree in business, finance, accounting, or economics; a master's degree in business or professional certification is helpful for advancement.

- Applicants face keen competition for jobs, especially in investment banks.

- Turnover is high for newcomers, but those who are successful have a very strong attachment to their occupation because of high earnings and considerable investment in training.

Nature of the Work

Each day, hundreds of billions of dollars change hands on the major United States securities exchanges. This money is used to invest in securities, such as stocks, bonds, or mutual funds, which are bought and sold by large institutional investors, mutual funds, pension plans, and the general public. Most securities trades are arranged through *securities, commodities, and financial services sales agents*, whether they are between individuals with a few hundred dollars or large institutions with hundreds of millions of dollars. The duties of sales agents vary greatly depending on their specialty.

The most common type of securities sales agent is called a *broker* or *stock broker*. Stock brokers advise everyday people, or retail investors, on appropriate investments based on their needs and financial ability. Once the client and broker agree on the best investment, the broker electronically sends the order to the floor of the securities exchange to complete the transaction. After the transaction is finalized, the broker charges a commission for the service.

The most important part of a broker's job is finding clients and building a customer base. Thus, beginning securities and commodities sales agents spend much of their time searching for clients, often relying heavily on telephone solicitation, or "cold calling," from a list of potential clients. Some agents network by joining civic organizations or social groups, while others may rely on referrals from satisfied customers.

Investment bankers are sales agents who connect businesses that need money to finance their operations or expansion plans

People increasingly seek the advice and services of securities, commodities, and financial services sales agents to realize their financial goals.

with investors who are interested in providing that funding in exchange for debt (in the form of bonds) or equity (in the form of stock). This process is called underwriting, and it is the main function of the investment bank. Investment bankers have to sell twice: first, they sell their advisory services to help companies issue new stock or bonds, and second, they sell the securities issued to investors.

Perhaps the most important advisory service provided by investment banks is to help companies new to the public investment arena issue stock for the first time. This process, known as an initial public offering, or IPO, can take a great deal of effort because private companies must meet stringent financial requirements to become publicly owned companies. Corporate finance departments also help private companies sell stock to institutional investors or wealthy individuals. They also advise companies that are interested in funding their operations by taking on debt—often issued in the form of bonds. Unlike a stock, which entitles its holder to partial ownership of a company, a bond entitles its holder to be repaid with a predetermined rate of interest.

Another important advisory service is provided by the mergers and acquisitions department. Investment bankers in this area advise companies that are interested in being acquired, or interested in merging with or purchasing other companies. Once a potential seller or buyer is found, bankers advise their client on how to execute the agreement. Generally both buyers and sellers have investment banks working for them to make sure that the transaction goes smoothly.

Investment banking sales agents and *traders* sell stocks and bonds to investors. Instead of selling their services to companies for fees, salespeople and traders sell securities to customers for commissions. These sales agents generally contact customers and their agents to discuss new stock and bond issues. When an investor decides to make a purchase, the order goes to the trading floor. Traders execute buy and sell orders from clients and make trades on behalf of the bank itself. Because markets fluctuate so much, trading is a split-second decision-making process. If a trader cannot secure the promised price on an exchange, millions of dollars could potentially be lost. On the other hand, if a trader finds a better deal, the bank could make millions more.

A small but powerful group of sales agents work directly on the floor of a stock or commodities exchange. When a firm or investor wishes to buy or sell a security or commodity, sales agents relay the order through their firm's computers to the floor of the exchange. There, *floor brokers* negotiate the price with other floor brokers, make the sale, and forward the purchase price to the sales agents. In addition to floor brokers, who work for individual securities dealers, there are also *independent brokers*. These are similar to floor brokers, except that they are not buyers for specific firms. Instead, they can buy and sell stocks for their own accounts, or corporate accounts that they manage, or they can sell their services to floor brokers who are too busy to execute all of the trades they are responsible for making. *Specialists* or *market makers* also work directly on the exchange floor, and there is generally one for each security or commodity being traded. They facilitate the trading process by quoting prices and by buying or selling shares when there are too many or too few available.

Financial services sales agents consult on a wide variety of banking, securities, insurance, and other related services to individuals and businesses, often catering the services to meet the client's financial needs. They contact potential customers to explain their services which may include checking accounts, loans, certificate of deposits, individual retirement accounts, credit cards, and estate and retirement planning.

Work environment. Most securities and commodities sales agents work in offices under somewhat stressful conditions. The pace of work is fast, and managers tend to be very demanding of their workers since both commissions and advancement are tied to sales.

Stock brokers and investment advisors usually work more than 40 hours a week, including evenings and weekends, as many of their clients work during the day. A growing number of securities sales agents, employed mostly by discount or online brokerage firms, work in call-center environments. In these centers, hundreds of agents spend much of the day on the telephone taking orders from clients or offering assistance and information on their accounts. Often, such call centers operate 24 hours a day, requiring agents to work in shifts.

Investment bankers in corporate finance or mergers and acquisitions typically work long hours and endure extreme stress, especially at the junior levels. Because banks work with companies all over the world, extensive travel is often part of the job, as is evening and weekend work. With some experience, the workload becomes more manageable, but since higher-level workers generally have more contact with clients, they also tend to travel more.

Sales and trading departments typically work more than 40 hours a week, but not nearly as much as their counterparts in investment banking. They also travel less, usually for conferences or training. On the other hand, their jobs are incredibly stressful. For sales agents, every minute of the day that is wasted means they might have made another sale. Since both commissions and advancement are tied to sales, this can be very stressful. Traders have perhaps the most stressful jobs of all, as split second decisions can lead to millions of dollars being won or lost. Trading floors are very busy and often very loud. Exchange workers, much like traders, have highly stressful jobs because the bulk of their work takes place on the floor of the exchanges. However, exchange traders and workers typically work shorter hours than many other agents since most of their work is done while the market is open.

Financial services sales agents normally work 40 hours a week in a comfortable office environment. They may spend considerable time outside the office, meeting with current and prospective clients, and attending civic functions. Some financial services sales agents work exclusively inside banks, providing service to walk-in customers.

Training, Other Qualifications, and Advancement

Most positions require a bachelor's degree in business, finance, accounting, or economics. An MBA or professional certification is helpful for advancement.

Education and training. A bachelor's degree in business, finance, accounting, or economics is important for securities and commodities sales agents, especially in larger firms. Many firms hire summer interns before their last year of college and those who are most successful are offered full-time jobs after they graduate.

Numerous agents eventually get a master's degree in business administration (MBA), which is often a requirement for high-level positions in the securities industry. Because the MBA is a professional degree designed to expose students to real-world business practices, it is considered to be a major asset for job-seekers. Employers often reward MBA holders with higher-level positions, better compensation, and even large signing bonuses.

Most employers provide intensive on-the-job training, teaching employees the specifics of the firm, such as the products and services offered. Trainees in large firms may receive classroom instruction in securities analysis, effective speaking, and the finer points of selling. Firms often rotate their trainees among various departments, to give them a broad perspective of the securities business. In small firms, sales agents often receive training at outside institutions and on the job.

Securities and commodities sales agents must keep up with new products and services and other developments. Because of this, brokers regularly attend conferences and training seminars.

Licensure. Brokers and investment advisors must register as representatives of their firm with the Financial Industry Regulatory Authority (FINRA). Before beginners can qualify as registered representatives, they must be an employee of a registered firm for at least 4 months and pass the General Securities Registered Representative Examination—known as the Series 7 Exam—administered by FINRA. The exam takes 6 hours and contains 250 multiple-choice questions; a passing score is above 70 percent.

Most States require a second examination—the Uniform Securities Agents State Law Examination (Series 63 or 66). This test measures a candidate's knowledge of the securities business in general, customer protection requirements, and recordkeeping procedures. Most firms offer training to help their employees pass these exams.

There are many other licenses available, each of which gives the holder the right to sell different investment products and services. Traders and some other sales representatives also need licenses, although these vary greatly by firm and specialization. Financial services sales agents may also need to be licensed, especially if they sell securities or insurance.

Registered representatives must attend continuing education classes to maintain their licenses. Courses consist of computer-based training in regulatory matters and company training on new products and services.

Other qualifications. Many employers consider personal qualities and skills more important than academic training. Employers seek applicants who have excellent interpersonal and communication skills, a strong work ethic, the ability to work in a team environment, and a desire to succeed. The ability to understand and analyze numbers is also important. Because securities, commodities, and financial services sales agents are entrusted with large sums of money and personal information, employers also make sure that applicants have a good credit history and a clean record. Self-confidence and the ability to handle frequent rejection are important ingredients for success.

Most firms prefer candidates with sales experience, particularly those who have worked on commission in areas such as real estate or insurance. Other firms prefer to hire workers right out of college, with the intention of molding them to their corporate image.

Certification and advancement. Although not always required, certifications enhance professional standing and are recommended by employers. Brokers, investment advisors, and financial services sales agents can earn the Chartered Financial Analyst (CFA) designation, sponsored by the CFA Institute. To qualify for this designation, applicants need a bachelor's degree, four years of related work experience, and must pass three exams which requires several hundred hours of self-study. Exams cover subjects in accounting, economics, securities analysis, financial markets and instruments, corporate finance, asset valuation, and portfolio management, and applicants can take the exams while they are obtaining the required work experience.

Brokers, investment advisors, and financial services sales agents usually advance by accumulating a greater number of accounts. Although beginners often service the accounts of individual investors, they may eventually handle very large institutional accounts, such as those of banks and pension funds. After taking a series of tests, some brokers become portfolio managers and have greater authority to make investment decisions regarding an account. Some experienced sales agents become branch office managers and supervise other sales agents while continuing to provide services for their own customers. A few agents advance to top management positions or become partners in their firms.

Investment bankers who enter the occupation directly after college generally start as analysts. At this level, employees receive intensive training and have little contact with clients as they spend most of their time producing "pitchbooks"–information booklets used to sell products. After 2 to 3 years, top analysts may be promoted to an associate position or asked to leave. Recent graduates from MBA programs can start as associates, which is similar to the analyst position, but with more responsibilities, such as leading a group of analysts and having contact with clients. After 2 to 3 years, associates are promoted or terminated. Successful associates can become vice presidents, and vice presidents may advance to become directors, sometimes called executive directors.

Employment

Securities, commodities, and financial services sales agents held about 317,200 jobs in 2008. About 49 percent of jobs were in the securities, commodity contracts, and other financial investments and related activities industry. About 15 percent of all workers were self-employed.

Because of their close relationship to stock exchanges and large banking operations, most of the major investment banks in the United States are based in New York metropolitan area. Smaller investment banks can be found in many major American cities and some major investment banks have operations in other cities, although most of their business remains in New York.

Job Outlook

Employment is projected to grow as fast as the average. Keen competition is expected as the number of applicants will continue to far exceed the number of job openings in this high-paying occupation.

Employment change. Employment of securities, commodities, and financial services sales agents is expected to grow 9 percent during the 2008–18 decade, about as fast as the average for all occupations. Consolidation of the financial industry, mainly stemming from recent global financial problems, will be the largest inhibitor of employment growth. Increased levels of industry consolidation often result in duplicated tasks among workers, a scenario that is expected to result in layoffs of many broker, sales, and investment banking positions. Additionally, the deregulation of financial markets in past decades has broken down the barriers between investment activities and banking, resulting in competition between traditional banks and securities companies on all levels. However, many of the major investment banks are now owned by large banks and most major banks also have brokerages, which allow their customers to quickly and easily transfer money between their personal banking and investment accounts. The ability of customers to access accounts online, as well as manage their personal investments through the Internet, will result in fewer brokers as well.

Job prospects. Competition for jobs will continue to be keen with more applicants than available openings. Additionally, the recent financial crisis has resulted in mass consolidation in the financial industry, a scenario that will likely result in fewer positions as companies attempt to streamline operations by eliminating duplicate tasks.

Entry-level sales agents, particularly those with previous sales experience, should face better prospects in smaller firms, as opposed to larger firms, where many positions have recently been eliminated. Investment banking is especially known for its competitive hiring process and candidates will face particularly keen competition for the relatively few openings. Having a degree from a prestigious undergraduate institution is very helpful, as are excellent grades in finance, economics, accounting, and business courses. Certifications and graduate degrees, such as a CFA certification or a master's degree in business or finance, can also significantly improve an applicant's prospects. Competition is even greater for positions working in exchanges.

Employment in the securities industry is closely connected with market conditions and the state of the overall economy and is highly volatile during recessionary periods. Turnover is high for newcomers, who face difficult prospects no matter when they join the industry. Once established, however, securities and commodities sales agents have a very strong attachment to their profession because of their high earnings and considerable investment in training.

Earnings

The median annual wage-and-salary wages of securities, commodities, and financial services sales agents were $68,680 in May 2008. The middle half earned between $40,480 and $122,270.

Median annual wages in the industries employing the largest numbers of securities, commodities, and financial services sales agents were:

Other financial investment activities	$94,960
Security and commodity contracts intermediation and brokerage	85,580
Management of companies and enterprises	81,940
Activities related to credit intermediation	52,890
Nondepository credit intermediation	47,760

Because this is a sales occupation, many workers are paid a commission based on the amount of stocks, bonds, mutual funds, insurance, and other products they sell. Most firms provide sales agents with a steady income by paying a "draw against commission"—a minimum salary based on commissions they

Projections data from the National Employment Matrix

Occupational Title	SOC Code	Employment, 2008	Projected Employment, 2018	Change, 2008-2018	
				Number	Percent
Securities, commodities, and financial services sales agents............	41-3031	317,200	346,700	29,600	9

(NOTE) Data in this table are rounded. See the discussion of the employment projections table in the *Handbook* introductory chapter on *Occupational Information Included in the Handbook.*

can be expected to earn. Trainee brokers usually are paid a salary until they develop a client base. The salary gradually decreases in favor of commissions as the broker gains clients.

Investment bankers in corporate finance and mergers and acquisitions are generally paid a base salary with the opportunity to earn a substantial bonus. At the higher levels, bonuses far exceed base salary. This arrangement works similarly to commissions but gives banks greater flexibility to reward members of the team who were more effective. Since investment bankers in sales and trading departments work alone, they generally work on commissions.

Brokers who work for discount brokerage firms that promote the use of telephone and online trading services usually are paid a salary, sometimes boosted by bonuses that reflect the profitability of the office. Financial services sales agents are also paid a salary, although bonuses or commissions from sales are starting to account for a larger share of their income.

Benefits in the securities industry are generally very good. They commonly include healthcare, retirement, and life insurance. Securities firms may also give discounts to employees on financial services that they sell to customers. Other benefits may include paid lunches with clients, paid dinners for employees who work late, and often extensive travel opportunities.

Related Occupations

Other jobs requiring knowledge of finance and an ability to sell include:

	Page
Financial analysts	103
Insurance sales agents	534
Loan officers	109
Personal financial advisors	118
Real estate brokers and sales agents	540

Sources of Additional Information

For information on securities industry employment, contact:
➤ American Academy of Financial Management, 245 Glendale Dr., Suite 1, Metairie, LA 70001. Internet: **http://www.financialanalyst.org**

➤ Securities Industry and Financial Markets Association, 120 Broadway, 35th Floor, New York, NY 10271. Internet: **http://www.sifma.org**

For information on licensing, contact:
➤ Financial Industry Regulatory Authority (FINRA), 1735 K St. NW., Washington, DC 20006. Internet: **http://www.finra.org**

For information on CFA certification, contact:
➤ CFA Institute, P.O. Box 3668, 560 Ray C. Hunt Dr., Charlottesville, VA 22903. Internet: **http://www.cfainstitute.org**

The Occupational Information Network (O*NET) provides information on a wide range of occupational characteristics. Links to O*NET appear at the end of the Internet version of this occupational statement, accessible at **http://www.bls.gov/ooh/ocos122.htm**

Travel Agents

Significant Points

- Many people are attracted to this occupation because of the travel benefits, such as reduced rates for transportation and lodging.

- Applicants with formal training should have the best opportunities to get a job as a travel agent.

- Travel agents who specialize in specific destinations or in certain types of travel or travelers should have the best chance for success.

- Job opportunities and earnings may decline during economic downturns and international crises, when travel plans are likely to be deferred.

Nature of the Work

Travel agents assist travelers by sorting through vast amounts of information to help their clients make the best possible travel arrangements. Travel agents offer advice on destinations and make arrangements for transportation, hotel accommodations, car rentals, and tours for their clients. In addition, resorts and specialty travel groups use travel agents to promote travel packages to their clients.

Travel agents are expected to be able to advise travelers about their destinations, such as the weather conditions, local ordinances and customs, attractions, and exhibitions. For those traveling internationally, agents also provide information on customs regulations, required documents (passports, visas, and certificates of vaccination), travel advisories, and currency exchange rates. In the event of changes in itinerary in the middle of a trip, travel agents intercede on the traveler's behalf to make alternate booking arrangements.

Travel agents use a variety of published and computer-based sources for information on departure and arrival times, fares, quality of hotel accommodations, and group discounts. They may also visit hotels, resorts, and restaurants themselves to evaluate the comfort, cleanliness, and the quality of specific hotels and restaurants so that they can base recommendations on their own experiences or those of colleagues or clients. Many travel agents specialize in specific destinations or regions; others specialize in travel targeted to particular demographic groups, such as senior citizens.

Travel agents who primarily work for tour operators and other travel arrangers may help develop, arrange, and sell the company's own package tours and travel services. They may promote these services, using telemarketing, direct mail, and the Internet. They make presentations to social and special-interest groups, arrange advertising displays, and suggest company-sponsored trips to business managers.

Work environment. Travel agents spend most of their time behind a desk conferring with clients, completing paperwork, contacting airlines and hotels to make travel arrangements, and promoting tours. They also spend a considerable amount of time either on the telephone or on the computer researching travel itineraries or updating reservations and travel documents.

Travel agents help clients plan personal and business trips.

Agents sometimes have to face a great deal of pressure during travel emergencies or when they need to reschedule missed reservations. They are especially busy during peak vacation times, such as summer and holiday travel periods. Many agents, especially those who are self-employed, frequently work more than 40 hours per week, although technology now allows a growing number of agents to work from home.

Training, Other Qualifications, and Advancement

Employers prefer to hire travel agents who have formal training in this field. Superb communication and computer skills are essential for talking with clients and making travel reservations.

Education and training. Most travel agencies prefer applicants who have received training specific to becoming a travel agent. Many vocational schools offer full-time travel agent programs. Travel agent courses also are offered in public adult education programs, online, and in community colleges. These programs teach students about geography, sales, marketing, and travel industry forms and procedures for ticketing and reservations.

A few colleges offer a bachelor's or master's degree in travel and tourism that can benefit prospective agents. Backgrounds in geography, foreign languages, or world history can also be useful for job applicants because they suggest an existing interest in travel and culture, which could help agents develop a rapport with clients.

Continuing education is critical for travel agents because the abundance of travel information readily available through the Internet and other sources has resulted in more informed consumers who expect travel agents to be experts in their field.

Other qualifications. Travel agents must be well-organized, accurate, and detail oriented in order to compile information from various sources and to plan and organize travel itineraries. Agents must have excellent communication skills and must be professional and courteous when dealing with travel representatives and clients.

Personal travel experience is an asset because knowledge about a city or foreign country often helps influence a client's travel plans. Business experience or training is important for self-employed agents who run their own business. In addition, computer skills are necessary and essential, because most travel arrangements are now made using the Internet or electronic reservation systems.

Certification and advancement. Some employees start as reservation clerks or receptionists in travel agencies. With experience and some formal training, they can take on greater responsibilities and eventually assume travel agent duties. In agencies with many offices, travel agents may advance to busier offices or to office manager or other managerial positions.

Those who start their own agencies generally have experience in an established agency. These agents must gain formal approval from suppliers or corporations, such as airlines, ship lines, or rail lines, to extend credit on reservations and to ensure payment. The Airlines Reporting Corporation and the International Airlines Travel Agency Network, for example, are the approving bodies for airlines. To gain approval, an agency must be financially sound and employ at least one experienced manager or travel agent.

Employment

Travel agents held about 105,300 jobs in May 2008 and are found in every part of the country. About 76 percent worked for travel arrangement and reservation services with 60 percent in travel agencies. Another 17 percent were self-employed.

Job Outlook

Little or no change in employment is expected over the 2008–18 period. Applicants with formal training should have the best opportunities to get a job as a travel agent. Travel agents who

Projections data from the National Employment Matrix

Occupational Title	SOC Code	Employment, 2008	Projected Employment, 2018	Change, 2008-2018	
				Number	Percent
Travel agents	41-3041	105,300	104,100	-1,200	-1

(NOTE) Data in this table are rounded. See the discussion of the employment projections table in the *Handbook* introductory chapter on *Occupational Information Included in the Handbook.*

specialize in specific destinations or in certain types of travel or travelers should have the best chance for success.

Employment change. Employment of travel agents is expected to decline by 1 percent over the 2008–18 period. The ease of Internet use and the ready availability of travel and airline Web sites that allow people to research and plan their own trips, make their own reservations, and purchase their own tickets will result in less demand for travel agents for routine travel arrangements. However, as more travelers take exotic and customized trips, the demand for some of the specialized services offered by travel agents will grow. Additionally, the increasing number of international visitors to the United States represents a growing market for travel agents who organize and sell tours to these international visitors.

Job prospects. Applicants with formal training should have the best opportunities to get a job as a travel agent. Agents who specialize in specific destinations, luxury travel, or particular types of travelers, such as ethnic groups or groups with a special interest or hobby, should have the best chance for success.

The demand for travel agents may decline during economic downturns and international crises, when travel plans are likely to be deferred. Thus, job opportunities for travel agents will fluctuate with changing economic and global conditions. Many openings, though, are expected to occur as agents leave for other occupations or retire.

Earnings

Experience, sales ability, and the size and location of the agency determine the salary of a travel agent. Median annual wages of travel agents were $30,570 in May 2008. The middle 50 percent earned between $23,940 and $38,390. The lowest 10 percent earned less than $18,770, while the top 10 percent earned more than $47,860. Median wages in May 2008 for travel agents employed in the travel arrangement and reservation services industry were $30,470.

Salaried agents usually enjoy standard employer-paid benefits that self-employed agents must provide for themselves. When traveling for personal reasons, agents usually get reduced rates for transportation and accommodations. In addition, agents sometimes take "familiarization" trips, at lower cost or no cost to themselves, to learn about various vacation sites. These benefits often attract people to this occupation.

Earnings of travel agents who own their agencies depend mainly on commissions and service fees they charge clients for trip planning. Often it takes time to acquire clients, so it is not unusual for new self-employed agents to have low earnings. Established agents may have lower earnings during economic downturns.

Related Occupations

Travel agents organize and schedule business, educational, or recreational travel or activities. Other workers with similar responsibilities are found in the following occupations:

Sources of Additional Information

For further information on training opportunities, contact:
➤ American Society of Travel Agents, Education Department, 1101 King St., Suite 200, Alexandria, VA 22314. Internet: **http://www.asta.org**

The Occupational Information Network (O*NET) provides information on a wide range of occupational characteristics. Links to O*NET appear at the end of the Internet version of this occupational statement, accessible at **http://www.bls.gov/ooh/ocos124.htm**

Other Sales and Related Occupations

Counter and Rental Clerks

Nature of the Work

Counter and rental clerks receive orders for repairs, rentals, and services. They discuss available options with the customer, write-up details of the purchase, compute the cost, and accept payment.

Education and Training

Most counter and rental clerk jobs are entry-level positions that require little or no experience and minimal formal education. In most companies, counter and rental clerks are trained on the job by more experienced workers and sometimes through the use of videos and other instruction manuals.

Job Outlook

Current and projected employment:

2008 Employment	448,200
2018 Employment	461,900
Employment change	13,700
Growth rate	3%

Employment change. Employment is projected to grow at 3 percent, slower than the average for all occupations. As this occupation usually requires personal contact with the customer, it is difficult to completely automate. Growth in the occupation will reflect growth in the rental business, including apartment rentals, and growth in the purchasing of services, such as dry cleaning and auto repairs, and the desire by companies to provide greater customer service. Trends, such as videos provided by mail and online, may reduce the need for some of these clerks at video rental stores.

Job prospects. Job opportunities are expected to be favorable. Entry-level jobs typically experience high turnover and generate numerous job openings, leading to favorable job opportunities as workers who leave this occupation will need to be replaced.

Earnings

Median annual wages for counter and rental clerks were $20,900 in May 2008.

Related Occupations

	Page
Cashiers	530
Postal service clerks	596
Retail salespersons	543
Tellers	599

Sources of Additional Information

➤ American Rental Association, 1900 19th St., Moline, IL 61265. Internet: **http://www.ararental.org**

The Occupational Information Network (O*NET) provides information on a wide range of occupational characteristics. Links to O*NET appear at the end of the Internet version of this occupational statement, accessible at **http://www.bls.gov/ooh/ocos117.htm**

Office and Administrative Support Occupations

Financial Clerks

Bill and Account Collectors

Significant Points

- Employment of bill and account collectors is projected to grow by about 19 percent over the 2008-18 decade, which is faster than average for all occupations.

- Most jobs in this occupation require only a high school diploma, though many employers prefer workers with some customer service experience.

- Job prospects should be favorable, especially for those with related work experience.

Nature of the Work

Bill and account collectors, often called *collectors*, attempt to collect payment on overdue bills. Some are employed by third-party collection agencies, while others—known as *in-house collectors*—work directly for the original creditors, such as mortgage and credit card companies, health care providers, and utilities.

The duties of bill and account collectors are similar across the many different organizations in which they work. First, collectors are called upon to locate and notify consumers or businesses with delinquent accounts, usually over the telephone, but sometimes by letter. When debtors move without leaving a forwarding address, collectors may check with the post office, telephone companies, credit bureaus, or former neighbors to obtain the new address. This is called "skip tracing." Computer systems assist in tracing by automatically tracking when individuals or companies change their addresses or contact information on any of their open accounts.

Once collectors find debtors, they inform them of the overdue accounts and solicit payment. If necessary, they review terms of sale, or credit contracts. Good collectors use their listening skills to attempt to learn the cause of delinquencies. They generally have the authority to offer repayment plans or other assistance to make it easier for debtors to pay their bills. In many cases, they are able to find payment solutions that will allow the debtor to pay off their accounts. They may also offer simple advice or refer customers to debt counselors.

If a consumer agrees to pay, the collector records this commitment and checks later to verify that the payment was made. If a consumer fails to pay, the collector prepares a statement indicating the consumer's delinquency for the credit department of the establishment. In more extreme cases, collectors may initiate repossession proceedings, disconnect service, or hand the account over to an attorney for legal action. Most collectors handle other administrative functions for the accounts assigned to them, including recording changes of address and purging the records of the deceased.

Because people are very sensitive about their financial problems, collectors must be careful to follow applicable Federal and State laws that govern their work. The Federal Trade Commission requires that a collector positively identify the delinquent account holder before announcing that the purpose of the call is to collect a debt. The collector must then issue a statement—often called a "mini-Miranda"—that lets the customer know that he or she is a collector. Collectors also face many State laws that govern how they must proceed in doing their work. Most companies use electronic systems to help collectors remember all laws and regulations governing each call.

Collectors use computers and a variety of automated systems in their jobs. Companies keep records of their accounts using computers, and collectors can keep track of previous collection attempts and other information in computerized notes. Using this information puts them at an advantage when trying to negotiate with consumers. As with most call-center workers, they use headsets instead of regular telephones. Many also use automatic dialing, which allows collectors to make calls quickly and efficiently, without the chance of dialing incorrectly.

Work environment. In-house bill and account collectors typically are employed in an office environment, and those who work for third-party collection agencies may work in a call-center environment. Workers spend most of their time on the phone tracking down and contacting people with debts. The work can be stressful, as many consumers are confrontational when pressed about their debts. Successful collectors must face regular rejection and still be ready to make the next call in a polite and positive voice. Fortunately, some consumers appreciate assistance in resolving their outstanding debts, and can be quite grateful.

As in most jobs where workers spend most of their time on the phone, collectors usually have goals they are expected to meet. Typically these include calls per hour and success rate goals. Additionally, because most workers are offered incentives for collecting, they may rely on a certain level of success to meet their own budgetary needs.

Bill and account collectors sometimes must work evenings and weekends. While some collectors work part-time, the majority work 40 hours per week. Flexible work schedules are common.

Training, Other Qualifications, and Advancement

Most employers require collectors to have at a least a high school diploma and prefer applicants with postsecondary education or customer service experience. Employers provide on-the-job training to new employees.

Bill and account collectors must have good communication and people skills as their work requires daily interactions with customers.

Education and training.   Most bill and account collectors are required to have at least a high school diploma. However, employers prefer workers who have completed some college or who have experience in other occupations that involve contact with the public. Previous experience working in a call center is especially helpful.

Once hired, workers receive on-the-job training. New employees learn company procedures under the guidance of a supervisor or other senior worker. Some formal classroom training may also be necessary, such as training in specific computer software. Additional training topics usually include telephone techniques and negotiation skills. Workers also learn the laws governing the collection of debt as mandated by the Fair Debt Collection Practices Act and various State laws.

Other qualifications.   Workers should have good communication and people skills because they need to speak to consumers daily, some of whom may be in stressful financial situations. They should be comfortable talking on the telephone with people they have never met. They must be mature and able to handle rejection. Computer literacy and experience with advanced telecommunications equipment is also useful.

Advancement.   As collectors gain experience, their success rates generally go up, leading them to earn more money in commissions. Successful collectors are usually given larger accounts with higher earning opportunities. Some become team leaders or supervisors. Workers who acquire additional skills, experience, and training improve their advancement opportunities.

Employment

Bill and account collectors held about 411,000 jobs in 2008. About one quarter of collectors worked in business support services. Another 19 percent worked in finance and insurance, and 18 percent worked for health care and social assistance providers.

Job Outlook

Employment of bill and account collectors is expected to grow faster than the average for all occupations. Job prospects are expected to be favorable, especially for those with related work experience.

Employment change.   Employment of bill and account collectors is projected to grow by about 19 percent over the 2008-18 decade, which is faster than average for all occupations. New jobs should be created in key industries such as health care and financial services, which often have delinquent accounts. In-house bill collectors will take on some of these collections, while others will be sold to third-party collection agencies. In both cases, bill and account collectors will be responsible for recovering these debts, causing the occupation to grow.

Job growth will be tempered somewhat by continued outsourcing of collections work to offshore call centers. In recent years, many companies have chosen to use these call centers for some of their debt recovery efforts. Nevertheless, creditors will continue to hire collectors in the United States, as domestic workers tend to have greater success in negotiating with clients.

The occupation should see large growth in the health care industry. The rapid growth projected in this industry, in combination with increasing prices, should result in many collections opportunities. This will affect both collectors who work in the health care industry itself and those who work for collections agencies that accept accounts from health care providers.

Job prospects.   Opportunities for job seekers who are looking for bill and account collector jobs should be favorable due to continued job growth and the need to replace workers who leave the occupation. Those who have experience in a related occupation should have the best prospects. Companies prefer to hire workers who have worked in a call center before, or in another job that requires regular phone-based negotiations.

Unlike most occupations, the number of collections jobs tends to remain stable and even grow during economic downturns. When the economy suffers, individuals and businesses struggle to meet their financial obligations. While this increases the number of debts that must be collected, it also means that fewer people are able to pay their outstanding debt. Companies decide how many collectors to hire based on expected success rates. As a result, the number of collectors does not necessarily increase proportionally to the number of delinquent accounts. Nevertheless, the number of collections jobs tends to remain stable during downturns, although prospective employees may face increased competition for these jobs.

Earnings

Median hourly wages of bill and account collectors were $14.73 in May 2008. The middle 50 percent earned between $12.14 and $18.12. The lowest 10 percent earned less than $10.17, and the highest 10 percent earned more than $22.07. Most bill and

Projections data from the National Employment Matrix

Occupational Title	SOC Code	Employment, 2008	Projected Employment, 2018	Change, 2008-2018	
				Number	Percent
Bill and account collectors...	43-3011	411,000	490,500	79,500	19

(NOTE) Data in this table are rounded. See the discussion of the employment projections table in the *Handbook* introductory chapter on *Occupational Information Included in the Handbook.*

account collectors earn commissions based on the amount of debt they recover.

Related Occupations

Bill and account collectors review and collect information on accounts. Other occupations with similar responsibilities include:

Collectors spend most of their time on the telephone, speaking with customers. Other jobs that require regular telephone interaction include:

Sources of Additional Information

Career information on bill and account collectors is available from:

➤ ACA International, The Association of Credit and Collection Professionals, P.O. Box 390106, Minneapolis, MN 55439. Internet: **http://www.acainternational.org**

The Occupational Information Network (O*NET) provides information on a wide range of occupational characteristics. Links to O*NET appear at the end of the Internet version of this occupational statement, accessible at **http://www.bls.gov/ooh/ocos143.htm**

Bookkeeping, Accounting, and Auditing Clerks

Significant Points

- Bookkeeping, accounting, and auditing clerks held about 2.1 million jobs in 2008 and are employed in nearly every industry.

- A high school degree is the minimum requirement; however, postsecondary education is increasingly important, and an associate degree in business or accounting is required for some positions.

- The large size of this occupation ensures plentiful job openings, including many opportunities for temporary and part-time work.

Nature of the Work

Bookkeeping, accounting, and auditing clerks are financial recordkeepers. They update and maintain accounting records, including those which calculate expenditures, receipts, accounts payable and receivable, and profit and loss. These workers have a wide range of skills from full-charge bookkeepers, who can maintain an entire company's books, to accounting clerks who handle specific tasks. All these clerks make numerous computations each day and must be comfortable using computers to calculate and record data.

In small businesses, *bookkeepers and bookkeeping clerks* often have responsibility for some or all the accounts, known as the general ledger. They record all transactions and post debits (costs) and credits (income). They also produce financial statements and prepare reports and summaries for supervisors and managers. Bookkeepers prepare bank deposits by compiling data from cashiers, verifying and balancing receipts, and sending cash, checks, or other forms of payment to the bank. Additionally, they may handle payroll, make purchases, prepare invoices, and keep track of overdue accounts.

In large companies, *accounting clerks* have more specialized tasks. Their titles, such as *accounts payable clerk* or *accounts receivable clerk*, often reflect the type of accounting they do. In addition, their responsibilities vary by level of experience. Entry-level accounting clerks post details of transactions, total accounts, and compute interest charges. They also may monitor loans and accounts to ensure that payments are up to date. More advanced accounting clerks may total, balance, and reconcile billing vouchers; ensure the completeness and accuracy of data on accounts; and code documents according to company procedures.

Auditing clerks verify records of transactions posted by other workers. They check figures, postings, and documents to ensure that they are mathematically accurate, and properly coded. They also correct or note errors for accountants or other workers to fix.

As organizations continue to computerize their financial records, many bookkeeping, accounting, and auditing clerks use specialized accounting software, spreadsheets, and databases. Most clerks now enter information from receipts or bills into computers, and the information is then stored electronically. The widespread use of computers also has enabled bookkeeping, accounting, and auditing clerks to take on additional responsibilities, such as payroll, procurement, and billing. Many of these functions require these clerks to write letters and make phone calls to customers or clients.

Work environment. Bookkeeping, accounting, and auditing clerks work in an office environment. They may experience eye and muscle strain, backaches, headaches, and repetitive motion

Bookkeeping, accounting, and auditing clerks handle financial records for many small businesses.

injuries from using computers on a daily basis. Clerks may have to sit for extended periods while reviewing detailed data.

Many bookkeeping, accounting, and auditing clerks work regular business hours and a standard 40-hour week, although some may work occasional evenings and weekends. About 1 out of 4 clerks worked part time in 2008.

Bookkeeping, accounting, and auditing clerks may work longer hours to meet deadlines at the end of the fiscal year, during tax time, or when monthly or yearly accounting audits are performed. Additionally, those who work in hotels, restaurants, and stores may put in overtime during peak holiday and vacation seasons.

Training, Other Qualifications, and Advancement

Employers usually require bookkeeping, accounting, and auditing clerks to have at least a high school diploma and some accounting coursework or relevant work experience. Clerks should also have good communication skills, be detail oriented, and trustworthy.

Education and training. Most bookkeeping, accounting, and auditing clerks are required to have a high school degree at a minimum. However, having some postsecondary education is increasingly important and an associate degree in business or accounting is required for some positions. Although a bachelor's degree is rarely required, graduates may accept bookkeeping, accounting, and auditing clerk positions to get into a particular company or to enter the accounting or finance field with the hope of eventually being promoted.

Once hired, bookkeeping, accounting, and auditing clerks usually receive on-the-job training. Under the guidance of a supervisor or another experienced employee, new clerks learn company procedures. Some formal classroom training also may be necessary, such as training in specialized computer software.

Other qualifications. Bookkeeping, accounting, and auditing clerks must be careful, orderly, and detail-oriented to avoid making errors and to recognize errors made by others. These workers also should be discreet and trustworthy, because they frequently come in contact with confidential material. They should also have good communication skills, because they increasingly work with customers. In addition, all bookkeeping, accounting, and auditing clerks should have a strong aptitude for numbers.

Experience in a related job and working in an office environment is recommended. Workers must be able to use computers, and knowledge of specialized bookkeeping or accounting software is especially valuable.

Certification and advancement. Bookkeeping, accounting, and auditing clerks, particularly those who handle all the recordkeeping for a company, may find it beneficial to become certified. The Certified Bookkeeper (CB) designation, awarded by the American Institute of Professional Bookkeepers, demonstrates that individuals have the skills and knowledge needed to carry out all bookkeeping functions, including overseeing payroll and balancing accounts, according to accepted accounting procedures. For cer-

tification, candidates must have at least 2 years of bookkeeping experience, pass a four-part examination, and adhere to a code of ethics. Several colleges and universities offer a preparatory course for certification; some offer courses online. Additionally, certified bookkeepers are required to meet a continuing education requirement every 3 years to maintain certification.

Bookkeeping, accounting, and auditing clerks usually advance by taking on more duties for higher pay or by transferring to a closely related occupation. Most companies fill office and administrative support supervisory and managerial positions by promoting individuals from within their organizations, so clerks who acquire additional skills, experience, and training improve their advancement opportunities. With appropriate experience and education, some bookkeeping, accounting, and auditing clerks may become accountants or auditors.

Employment

Bookkeeping, accounting, and auditing clerks held about 2.1 million jobs in 2008. They work in nearly all industries and at all levels of government. State and local government, educational services, health care, and the accounting, tax preparation, bookkeeping, and payroll services industries are among the individual industries employing the largest numbers of these clerks.

Job Outlook

Job growth is projected to be about as fast as the average. The large size of this occupation ensures plentiful job opportunities, as many bookkeeping, accounting, and auditing clerks are expected to retire or transfer to other occupations.

Employment change. Employment of bookkeeping, accounting, and auditing clerks is projected to grow by 10 percent during the 2008–18 decade, which is about as fast as the average for all occupations. This occupation is one of the largest growth occupations in the economy, with about 212,400 new jobs expected over the projections decade.

A growing economy will result in more financial transactions and other activities that require recordkeeping by these workers. Additionally, an increased emphasis on accuracy, accountability, and transparency in the reporting of financial data for public companies will increase the demand for these workers. Also, new regulations and reporting methods, including the use of International Financial Reporting Standards, should result in additional demand for clerks involved in accounting and auditing. However, growth will be limited by improvements in accounting software and document-scanning technology that make it easier to record, track, audit, and file financial information, including transactions and reports. Moreover, companies will continue to outsource their bookkeeping, accounting, and, in some cases, auditing functions to third party contractors located both domestically and abroad.

Job prospects. While many job openings are expected to result from job growth, even more openings will stem from

Projections data from the National Employment Matrix

Occupational Title	SOC Code	Employment, 2008	Projected Employment, 2018	Change, 2008-2018	
				Number	Percent
Bookkeeping, accounting, and auditing clerks	43-3031	2,063,800	2,276,200	212,400	10

(NOTE) Data in this table are rounded. See the discussion of the employment projections table in the *Handbook* introductory chapter on *Occupational Information Included in the Handbook.*

the need to replace existing workers who leave. Each year, numerous jobs will become available, as clerks transfer to other occupations or leave the labor force. The large size of this occupation ensures plentiful job openings, including many opportunities for temporary and part-time work.

Clerks who can carry out a wider range of bookkeeping and accounting activities will be in greater demand than specialized clerks. For example, demand for full-charge bookkeepers is expected to increase, because they can perform a wider variety of financial transactions, including payroll and billing. Certified Bookkeepers (CBs) and those with several years of accounting or bookkeeping experience who have demonstrated that they can handle a range of tasks will have the best job prospects.

Earnings

In May 2008, the median annual wages of bookkeeping, accounting, and auditing clerks were $32,510. The middle half of the occupation earned between $26,350 and $40,130. The top 10 percent of bookkeeping, accounting, and auditing clerks earned more than $49,260, and the bottom 10 percent earned less than $20,950.

Related Occupations

Bookkeeping, accounting, and auditing clerks work with financial records. Other workers who perform similar duties include:

	Page
Accountants and auditors	86
Billing and posting clerks and machine operators	587
Brokerage clerks	588
Credit authorizers, checkers, and clerks	589
Payroll and timekeeping clerks	595
Procurement clerks	597

Sources of Additional Information

For information on the Certified Bookkeeper designation, contact:

➤ American Institute of Professional Bookkeepers, 6001 Montrose Rd., Suite 500, Rockville, MD 20852. Internet: **http://www.aipb.org**

The Occupational Information Network (O*NET) provides information on a wide range of occupational characteristics. Links to O*NET appear at the end of the Internet version of this occupational statement, accessible at **http://www.bls.gov/ooh/ocos144.htm**

Gaming Cage Workers

Significant Points

- Most employers prefer applicants who have at least a high school diploma and experience in handling money or previous casino employment.

- Workers need a license, which requires a background investigation.

- Employment is projected to decline rapidly.

- Jobseekers are expected to face competition.

Nature of the Work

Gaming cage workers and *gaming change persons and booth cashiers* work in casinos and other gaming establishments. The "cage" where these workers can be found is the central depository for money, gaming chips, and paperwork necessary to support casino play.

Gaming cage workers and gaming change persons and booth cashiers carry out a wide range of financial transactions and handle any paperwork that may be required. Gaming cage workers, known as *cage cashiers*, exchange patrons' chips, tickets, and tokens for cash. Gaming change persons and booth cashiers work in booths and process credit card cash advances and wire transfers and cash checks for patrons. Both cage workers and booth cashiers may sell gambling chips, tokens, or tickets to patrons or to other workers for resale to patrons. Additionally, some cage workers may perform credit checks and verify credit references for people who want to open a house credit account. They may use cash registers, adding machines, or computers to calculate and record transactions. At the end of their shift, cage workers and booth cashiers must balance the books.

Because gaming establishments are closely scrutinized, cage workers and booth cashiers must follow a number of rules and regulations related to their handling of money. For example, they monitor large cash transactions and report these transactions to the Internal Revenue Service to help enforce tax regulations and prevent money laundering. Also, in determining when to extend credit or cash a check, cage workers must follow detailed procedures.

Work environment. The atmosphere in casinos is often considered glamorous. However, casino work also can be physically demanding. The occupation requires workers to stand for long periods, with constant reaching and grabbing for money, chips, and tickets. Sometimes cage workers and booth cashiers may be expected to lift and carry relatively heavy items. The casino atmosphere exposes workers to certain hazards, such as cigarette, cigar, and pipe smoke. Noise from slot machines, gaming tables, and talking workers and patrons may be distracting to some, although workers wear protective headgear in areas where loud machinery is used to count money.

Gaming cage workers exchange tickets and chips for money.

Most casinos are open 24 hours a day, 7 days a week, and offer three staggered shifts. Casinos typically require cage workers to work nights, weekends, and holidays.

Training, Other Qualifications, and Advancement

Although there are no mandatory education requirements, gaming cage workers and gaming change persons and booth cashiers typically receive on-the-job training and are licensed by a regulatory agency, such as a State casino control board or commission.

Education and training. There usually are no minimum educational requirements, although most employers prefer at least a high school diploma or the equivalent.

Once hired gaming cage workers and gaming change persons and booth cashiers usually receive on-the-job training. Under the guidance of a supervisor or other senior worker, new employees learn company procedures. Some formal classroom training also may be necessary, such as training in specific gaming regulations and procedures.

Licensure. All gaming workers are required to have a license issued by a regulatory agency, such as a State casino control board or commission. Applicants for a license must provide photo identification and pay a fee. Some States may require gaming cage workers to be residents of that State. Age requirements vary by State. The licensing application process also includes a background investigation and drug test.

Other qualifications. Experience in handling money or previous casino employment is preferred. Prospective workers are sometimes required to pass a basic math test, and they must be careful, orderly, and detail oriented in order to avoid making errors and to recognize errors made by others. These workers also should be discreet and trustworthy because they frequently come in contact with confidential material such as a patron's credit information. Good customer service skills and computer proficiency also are necessary for this occupation. Each casino establishes its own requirements for education, training, and experience.

Advancement. Advancement opportunities in casino gaming depend less on workers' previous casino duties and titles than on their ability and eagerness to learn new jobs. For example, in addition to advancement opportunities available in the cage, such as promotion to head cage cashier or supervisor, cage workers and booth cashiers may advance onto the floor and become dealers or supervisors.

Employment

Gaming cage workers held about 16,900 jobs, and gaming change persons and booth cashiers held about 22,300 jobs, in 2008. All of these individuals work in establishments that offer gaming; employment is concentrated in Nevada, California, Washington, and Mississippi. However, numerous States have legalized gambling, and gaming establishments can now be found in many parts of the country.

Job Outlook

Employment of gaming cage workers and gaming change persons and booth cashiers is projected to decline rapidly through 2018. Jobseekers are expected to face competition because the number of applicants is likely to exceed the number of openings.

Employment change. Employment of gaming cage workers and gaming change persons and booth cashiers is expected to decrease rapidly by about 10 percent between 2008 and 2018. Gaming cage workers and gaming change persons and booth cashiers will experience employment declines as casinos increasingly automate transactions, reducing the amount of cash handled by employees. For example, self-serve cashout and change machines are common, along with automated teller machines. In addition, most slot machines are now able to make payouts in tickets instead of coins. Tickets can be read by other slot machines and the amount on the ticket transferred to the new machine, or tickets can be read by self-serve machines that allow players to cash out without ever going to the cage. Known as ticket-in, ticket-out game play, these technologies reduce the number of cash transactions needed to play and speed up the exchange process, which means that fewer workers are needed to handle the cage than in the past. In addition, such machines have eliminated the need to have booths and change persons on the slots floor at many casinos. However, many gaming cage workers and gaming change persons and booth cashiers likely will be given opportunities by their employers to transfer to other occupations related to customer service.

Job prospects. Some openings will result from high turnover in these occupations caused by the high level of scrutiny workers receive and the need to be accurate. However, jobseekers are expected to face competition because the number of applicants is likely to exceed the number of openings. People with good mathematics abilities, previous casino experience, some background in accounting or bookkeeping, and good customer service skills should have the best opportunities.

Earnings

Wages for gaming cage workers and gaming change persons and booth cashiers vary according to level of experience, training, location, and size of the gaming establishment. Median hourly wages of gaming cage workers were $11.97 in May 2008. The middle 50 percent earned between $10.09 and $14.66 an hour. The lowest 10 percent earned less than $8.66, and the highest 10 percent earned more than $17.35 an hour.

Projections data from the National Employment Matrix

Occupational Title	SOC Code	Employment, 2008	Projected Employment, 2018	Change, 2008-2018	
				Number	Percent
Gaming cage workers...	–	39,200	35,100	-4,100	-10
Gaming change persons and booth cashiers	41-2012	22,300	20,000	-2,300	-10
Gaming cage workers...	43-3041	16,900	15,100	-1,800	-10

(NOTE) Data in this table are rounded. See the discussion of the employment projections table in the *Handbook* introductory chapter on *Occupational Information Included in the Handbook.*

Median hourly wages of gaming change persons and booth cashiers were $10.57 in May 2008. The middle 50 percent earned between $8.60 and $13.11 an hour. The lowest 10 percent earned less than $7.48, and the highest 10 percent earned more than $15.41 an hour.

Related Occupations

Other workers who provide hospitality and customer service while handling financial transactions include:

Sources of Additional Information

Information on employment opportunities for gaming cage workers and gaming change persons and booth cashiers is available from local offices of the State employment service.

Information on careers in gaming also is available from:

➤ American Gaming Association, 1299 Pennsylvania Ave. NW., Suite 1175, Washington, DC 20004. Internet: **http://www.americangaming.org**

The Occupational Information Network (O*NET) provides information on a wide range of occupational characteristics. Links to O*NET appear at the end of the Internet version of this occupational statement, accessible at **http://www.bls.gov/ooh/ocos338.htm**

Information and Record Clerks

Customer Service Representatives

Significant Points

- Customer service representatives held about 2.3 million jobs in 2008, ranking among the largest occupations.

- Most companies require a high school diploma and will provide job training.

- Employment is projected to grow faster than average, and job prospects should be good.

Nature of the Work

Customer service representatives provide a valuable link between customers and the companies who produce the products they buy and the services they use. They are responsible for responding to customer inquiries and making sure that any problems they are experiencing are resolved. Although most customer service representatives do their work by telephone in call centers, some interact with customers by e-mail, fax, post, or face-to-face.

Many customer service inquiries involve simple questions or requests. For instance, a customer may want to know the status of an order or wish to change his or her address in the company's file. However, some questions may be somewhat more difficult, and may require additional research or help from an expert. In some cases, a representative's main function may be to determine who in the organization is best suited to answer a customer's questions.

Some customer inquiries are complaints, which generally must be handled in accordance with strict company policies. In some cases, representatives may try to fix problems or suggest solutions. They may have the authority to reverse erroneous fees or send replacement products. Other representatives act as gatekeepers who make sure that complaints are valid before accepting customer returns.

Although selling products and services is not the primary function of a customer service representative, some customer services representatives may provide information that helps customers to make purchasing decisions. For instance, a representative may

point out a product or service that would fulfill a customer's needs. (For information on workers whose primary function is sales, see the statement on retail salespersons elsewhere in the *Handbook*).

Customer service representatives use computers, telephones, and other technology extensively in their work. When the customer has an account with the company, a representative will usually open his or her file in the company's computer system. Representatives use this information to solve problems and may be able to make specific changes as necessary. They also have access to responses for the most commonly asked questions and specific guidelines for dealing with requests or complaints. In the event that the representative does not know the answer or is unable to solve a specific problem, a supervisor or other experienced worker may provide assistance.

Many customer service workers are located in call centers, where they spend the entire day speaking on the telephone. Companies usually keep statistics on their workers to make sure they are working efficiently. This helps them to keep up with their call volume and ensures that customers do not have to wait on hold for extended periods of time. Supervisors may listen in on or tape calls to ensure customers are getting quality service.

Almost every industry employs customer service representatives, and their duties may vary greatly depending on the nature of the organization. For instance, representatives who work in banks may have similar duties to tellers, whereas those in insurance companies may be required to handle paperwork, such as changes to policies or renewals. Those who work for utility and communication companies may assist customers with service problems, such as outages. Representatives who work in retail stores often handle returns and help customers to find items in their stores.

Work environment. Although customer service representatives work in a variety of settings, most work in areas that are clean and well lit. Those who work in call centers generally have their own workstations or cubicle spaces equipped with telephones, headsets, and computers. Because many call centers are open extended hours or are staffed around the clock, these positions may require workers to take on early morning, evening, or late night shifts. Weekend or holiday work is also common. Because peak times may not last for a full shift, many workers are part-time or work a split shift. As a result, the occupation is well suited to flexible work schedules. Many companies hire additional employees at certain times of year when higher call volumes are expected.

Call centers may be crowded and noisy, and work may be repetitious and stressful, with little time between calls. Also, long periods spent sitting, typing, or looking at a computer screen may cause eye and muscle strain, backaches, headaches, and repetitive motion injuries. A growing number of employers are hiring telecommuters, who provide customer service from their own homes. Although this remains somewhat rare, it can be a major advantage for workers who need to remain in their homes during the day.

Customer service representatives working in retail stores may have customers approach them in person or contact them by telephone. They may be required to work later in the evenings or on weekends, as stores are generally open during those times. Evenings and weekends tend to be peak hours for customer traffic.

Customer service representatives may have to deal with difficult or irate customers, which can be challenging. However, the ability to resolve customers' problems has the potential to be very rewarding.

Training, Other Qualifications, and Advancement

Most jobs require at least a high school diploma. Employers provide training to workers before they begin serving customers.

Education and training. Most customer service representative jobs require a high school diploma. However, because employers are demanding a more skilled workforce, some customer service jobs now require associate or bachelor's degrees. High school and college level courses in computers, English, or business are helpful in preparing for a job in customer service.

Training requirements vary by industry. Almost all customer service representatives are provided with some training prior to beginning work. This training generally focuses on the company and its products, the most commonly asked questions, the computer and telephone systems they will be using, and basic people skills. Length of training varies, but often lasts several weeks. Some customer service representatives are expected to update their training regularly. This is particularly true of workers in industries such as banking, in which regulations and products are continually changing.

Other qualifications. Because customer service representatives constantly interact with the public, good communication and problem-solving skills are essential. Verbal communication and listening skills are especially important. Companies prefer to hire individuals who have a pleasant speaking voice and are easy to understand. For workers who communicate through e-mail, good typing, spelling, and grammar skills are necessary. Basic to intermediate computer knowledge and good interpersonal skills are also important.

Customer service representatives play a critical role in providing an interface between customers and companies. As a result, employers seek out people who are friendly and possess a professional manner. The ability to deal patiently with problems and complaints and to remain courteous when faced with difficult or angry people is critical. Also, a customer service representative often must be able to work independently within specified time constraints.

Good communication and problem-solving skills are essential for customer service representatives.

Advancement. Customer service jobs are often good introductory positions into a company or an industry. In some cases, experienced workers can move into supervisory or managerial positions or they may move into areas such as product development, in which they can use their knowledge to improve products and services. Some people work in call centers with the hope of transferring to a position in another department.

Employment

Customer service representatives held about 2.3 million jobs in 2008, ranking among the largest occupations. They can be found in almost every industry, although about 23 percent worked in the finance and insurance industry. Another 15 percent worked in the administrative and support services industry, which includes third party telephone call centers.

Job Outlook

Customer service representatives are expected to experience faster than average growth. Furthermore, job prospects should be good as many workers who leave this very large occupation will need to be replaced.

Employment change. Employment of customer service representatives is expected to grow by about 18 percent over the 2008-18 period, faster than the average for all occupations.

Projections data from the National Employment Matrix

Occupational Title	SOC Code	Employment, 2008	Projected Employment, 2018	Change, 2008-2018	
				Number	Percent
Customer service representatives..	43-4051	2,252,400	2,651,900	399,500	18

(NOTE) Data in this table are rounded. See the discussion of the employment projections table in the *Handbook* introductory chapter on *Occupational Information Included in the Handbook.*

Providing quality customer service is important to nearly every company in the economy; in addition, companies are expected to place increasing emphasis on customer relationships, resulting in increased demand for customer service representatives. This very large occupation is projected to provide about 400,000 new jobs over the next decade.

Customer service representatives are especially prevalent in the finance and insurance industry, as many customer interactions do not require physical contact. Employment of customer service representatives in this industry is expected to increase 9 percent over the 2008-18 period.

Although technology has tempered growth of this occupation to some degree, it has also created many opportunities for growth. For instance, online banking has reduced the need for telephone banking services. At the same time, however, it has increased the need for customer service representatives who assist users with banking Web sites. Additionally, online services create many new opportunities for customer support representatives as companies that operate on the Internet provide customer service by telephone.

In the past, many companies chose to relocate their customer service call centers in foreign countries, which led to layoffs in some industries. Although many companies continue to offshore some of their customer service jobs, this is becoming less prevalent than in the past. While it continues to be less expensive to hire workers overseas, many companies have found that foreign workers do not have the same cultural sensitivity as those located within the United States.

Job prospects. Prospects for obtaining a job in this field are expected to be good, with more job openings than jobseekers. In particular, bilingual jobseekers should enjoy excellent opportunities. Rapid job growth, coupled with a large number of workers who leave the occupation each year, should make finding a job as a customer service representative relatively easy.

While jobs in some industries may be affected by economic downturns, customer service representatives are not as vulnerable to layoffs as some other workers. This is, in part, because many customer service representatives work in industries where customers have accounts. While customers may have less money to spend, and as a result may choose to purchase fewer goods or services, they continue to have customer service needs. For instance, during an economic downturn, individuals may have less money in their bank accounts, but they continue to need banking services and customer service from their banks. Nevertheless, companies do attempt to cut costs during such times, so downsizing is still a possibility.

Earnings

In May 2008, median hourly wages of customer service representatives were $14.36. The middle 50 percent earned between $11.34 and $18.27. The lowest 10 percent earned less than $9.15, and the highest 10 percent earned more than $23.24.

Earnings for customer service representatives vary according to level of skill required, experience, training, location, and size of firm. Median hourly wages in the industries employing the largest numbers of these workers in May 2008 were:

Insurance carriers	$15.74
Agencies, brokerages, and other insurance related activities..	15.28
Depository credit intermediation....................................	14.56
Employment services	12.73
Business support services..	11.56

In addition to receiving an hourly wage, full-time customer service representatives who work evenings, nights, weekends, or holidays may receive shift differential pay. Also, because call centers are often open during extended hours, or even 24 hours a day, some customer service representatives have the benefit of being able to work a schedule that does not conform to the traditional workweek. Other benefits can include life and health insurance, pensions, bonuses, employer-provided training, and discounts on the products and services the company offers.

Related Occupations

Customer service representatives interact with customers to provide information in response to inquiries about products and services and to handle and resolve complaints. Other occupations in which workers have similar dealings with customers and the public include:

	Page
Bill and account collectors..	561
Computer support specialists	138
Insurance sales agents..	534
Retail salespersons...	543
Securities, commodities, and financial services sales agents...	553
Tellers...	599

Sources of Additional Information

For more information on customer service positions, contact your State employment office or:

➤ International Customer Service Association. 24 Wernik Pl., Metuchen, NJ 08840. Internet: **http://www.icsatoday.org**

The Occupational Information Network (O*NET) provides information on a wide range of occupational characteristics. Links to O*NET appear at the end of the Internet version of this occupational statement, accessible at **http://www.bls.gov/ooh/ocos280.htm**

Receptionists and Information Clerks

Significant Points

- Good interpersonal skills are critical.
- A high school diploma or its equivalent is the most common educational requirement.
- A large number of job openings are expected.
- Opportunities should be best for persons with a wide range of clerical and technical skills, particularly those with related work experience.

Nature of the Work

Receptionists and information clerks are charged with a responsibility that may affect the success of an organization: making a good first impression. Receptionists and information clerks answer telephones, route and screen calls, greet visitors, respond to inquiries from the public, and provide information about the organization. Some are responsible for the coordination of all mail into and out of the office. In addition, they contribute to the security of an organization by helping to monitor the access of visitors—a function that has become increasingly important.

Whereas some tasks are common to most receptionists and information clerks, their specific responsibilities vary with the type of establishment in which they work. For example, receptionists and information clerks in hospitals and in doctors' offices may gather patients' personal and insurance information and direct them to the proper waiting rooms. In corporate headquarters, they may greet visitors and manage the scheduling of the board room or common conference area. In beauty or hair salons, they arrange appointments, direct customers to the hairstylist, and may serve as cashiers. In factories, large corporations, and government offices, receptionists and information clerks may provide identification cards and arrange for escorts to take visitors to the proper office. Those working for bus and train companies respond to inquiries about departures, arrivals, stops, and other related matters.

Receptionists and information clerks use the telephone, personal computers, and other electronic devices to send e-mail and fax documents, for example. Despite the widespread use of automated answering systems or voice mail, many receptionists and clerks still take messages and inform other employees of visitors' arrivals or cancellation of an appointment. When they are not busy with callers, most workers are expected to assist other administrative employees by performing a variety of office duties, including opening and sorting mail, collecting and distributing parcels, transmitting and delivering facsimiles, and performing Internet search tasks. Other duties include updating appointment calendars, preparing travel vouchers, and performing basic bookkeeping, word processing, and filing.

Companies sometimes hire off-site receptionists and information clerks called, virtual receptionists, to perform, or supplement, many of the duties done by the traditional receptionist. Virtual receptionists use software integrated into their phone system to instantly track their employer's location, in-form them of every call, and relay vital information to their callers. Using fax mailbox services, employers can retrieve faxes from any location at any time. The service receives them for the employer in special mailboxes and then transfers them when the line is free.

Work environment. Receptionists and information clerks who greet customers and visitors usually work in areas that are highly visible and designed and furnished to make a good impression. Most work stations are clean, well lighted, and relatively quiet. Virtual receptionists work from home or at an off-site office building. The work performed by some receptionists and information clerks may be tiring, repetitious, and stressful as they may spend all day answering continuously ringing telephones and sometimes encounter difficult or irate callers. The work environment, however, may be very friendly and motivating for individuals who enjoy greeting customers face to face and making them feel comfortable. About 30 percent of receptionists and information clerks worked part time.

Training, Other Qualifications, and Advancement

A high school diploma or its equivalent is the most common educational requirement, although hiring requirements for receptionists and information clerks vary by industry and employer. Good interpersonal skills and being technologically proficient also are important to employers.

Education and training. Receptionists and information clerks generally need a high school diploma or equivalent as most of their training is received on the job. However, employers often look for applicants who already possess certain skills, such as knowledge of spreadsheet and word processing software or answering telephones. Some employers also may prefer some formal office education or training. On the job, they learn how to operate the telephone system and computers. They also learn the proper procedures for greeting visitors and for distributing mail, fax messages, and parcels. While many of these skills can be learned quickly, those who are charged with relaying information to visitors or customers may need several months to learn details about the organization.

Receptionists and information clerks answer telephones, route and screen calls, greet visitors, respond to inquiries from the public, and provide information about the organization.

Projections data from the National Employment Matrix

Occupational Title	SOC Code	Employment, 2008	Projected Employment, 2018	Change, 2008-2018	
				Number	Percent
Receptionists and information clerks..	43-4171	1,139,200	1,312,100	172,900	15

(NOTE) Data in this table are rounded. See the discussion of the employment projections table in the *Handbook* introductory chapter on *Occupational Information Included in the Handbook*.

Other qualifications. Good interpersonal and customer service skills—being courteous, professional, and helpful—are critical for this job. Being an active listener often is a key quality needed by receptionists and information clerks that requires the ability to listen patiently to the points being made, to wait to speak until others have finished, and to ask appropriate questions when necessary. In addition, the ability to relay information accurately to others is important.

The ability to operate a wide range of office technology also is helpful, as receptionists and information clerks are often asked to work on other assignments during the day.

Advancement. Advancement for receptionists generally comes about either by transferring to an occupation with more responsibility or by being promoted to a supervisory position. Receptionists with especially strong computer skills, a bachelor's degree, and several years of experience may advance to a better paying job as a secretary or an administrative assistant.

Employment

Receptionists and information clerks held about 1.1 million jobs in 2008. The healthcare and social assistance industries—including offices of physicians, hospitals, nursing homes, and outpatient care facilities—employed about 36 percent of all receptionists and information clerks. Wholesale and retail trade, personal services, educational services, finance and insurance, employment services, religious organizations, and real estate industries also employed large numbers of receptionists and information clerks.

Job Outlook

Employment is projected to grow faster than the average for all occupations. Job growth, coupled with the need to replace workers who transfer to other occupations or leave the labor force, will generate a large number of job openings for receptionists and information clerks.

Employment change. Employment of receptionists and information clerks is expected to increase by 15 percent from 2008 to 2018, which is faster than the average for all occupations. Employment growth will result from growth in industries such as offices of physicians and in other health practitioners, legal services, personal care services, construction, and management and technical consulting.

Technology will have conflicting effects on employment growth for receptionists and information clerks. The increasing use of voice mail and other telephone automation reduces the need for receptionists by allowing one receptionist to perform work that formerly required several. At the same time, however, the increasing use of other technology has caused a consolidation of clerical responsibilities and growing demand for workers with diverse clerical and technical

skills, such as virtual receptionists. Because receptionists and information clerks may perform a wide variety of clerical tasks, they should continue to be in demand. Further, they perform many tasks that are interpersonal in nature and are not easily automated, ensuring continued demand for their services in a variety of establishments.

Job prospects. In addition to job growth, numerous job opportunities will be created as receptionists and information clerks transfer to other occupations or leave the labor force altogether. Opportunities should be best for persons with a wide range of clerical and technical skills, particularly those with related work experience.

Earnings

Median hourly wages of receptionists and information clerks in May 2008 were $11.80. The middle 50 percent earned between $9.69 and $14.44. The lowest 10 percent earned less than $8.09, and the highest 10 percent earned more than $17.07. Median hourly wages in the industries employing the largest number of receptionists and information clerks in May 2008 were:

Offices of dentists...	$13.78
Offices of physicians	12.20
Employment services	11.63
Offices of other health practitioners..............................	11.45
Personal care services	9.35

Related Occupations

Receptionists deal with the public and often direct people to others who can assist them. Other workers who perform similar duties include:

	Page
Customer service representatives...	567
Dispatchers, except police, fire, and ambulance	590
Secretaries and administrative assistants	583

Sources of Additional Information

State employment offices can provide information on job openings for receptionists.

For information related to administrative occupations, including educational programs and certified designations, contact:
➤ International Association of Administrative Professionals, P.O. Box 20404, Kansas City, MO 64195-0404. Internet: **http://www.iaap-hq.org**

The Occupational Information Network (O*NET) provides information on a wide range of occupational characteristics. Links to O*NET appear at the end of the Internet version of this occupational statement, accessible at **http://www.bls.gov/ooh/ocos134.htm**

Material Recording, Scheduling, Dispatching, and Distributing Occupations

Cargo and Freight Agents

Significant Points

- Cargo and freight agents need no more than a high school diploma and learn their duties informally on the job.

- Much faster than average employment growth is expected.

- Job prospects are expected to be good.

Nature of the Work

Cargo and freight agents help transportation companies manage incoming and outgoing shipments in airline, train, or trucking terminals or on shipping docks. Agents expedite shipments by determining a route, preparing all necessary documents, and arranging for the pickup of freight or cargo and its delivery to loading platforms. They may also keep records of the cargo, including its amount, type, weight, dimensions, destination, and time of shipment. They also keep a tally of missing items and record the condition of damaged items.

Cargo and freight agents arrange cargo according to destination. They also determine any shipping rates and other applicable charges. For imported or exported freight, they verify that the proper customs paperwork is in order. Cargo and freight agents often track shipments electronically, using bar codes, and answer customers' questions about the status of their shipments.

Employment of cargo and freight agents is expected to grow much faster than average.

Work environment. Cargo and freight agents work in a wide variety of environments. Some work in warehouses, stockrooms, or shipping and receiving rooms that may not be temperature controlled. Others may spend time in cold storage rooms or outside on loading platforms, where they are exposed to the weather.

Most jobs for cargo and freight agents involve frequent standing, bending, walking, and stretching. Some lifting and carrying of small items may be involved. Although automated devices have lessened the physical demands of this occupation, not every employer has these devices. The work still can be strenuous, even though mechanical material-handling equipment is used to move heavy items.

The typical workweek is Monday through Friday. However, evening and weekend hours are common in jobs involving large shipments.

Training, Other Qualifications, and Advancement

Cargo and freight agents need no more than a high school diploma and learn their duties informally on the job.

Education and training. Many jobs are entry level and most require a high school diploma. Cargo and freight agents undergo informal on-the-job training. For example, they may start out by checking items to be shipped and making sure that addresses are correct.

Other qualifications. Employers prefer to hire people who are comfortable using computers. Typing, filing, recordkeeping, and other clerical skills also are important.

Advancement. Advancement opportunities for cargo and freight agents are usually limited, but some agents may become team leaders or use their experience to switch to other clerical occupations in the businesses where they work. Some may move to higher paying transportation industry jobs, such as freight brokering.

Employment

Cargo and freight agents held about 85,900 jobs in 2008. Most agents were employed in transportation. Approximately 52 percent worked for firms engaged in support activities for the transportation industry, 19 percent were in the air transportation industry, 8 percent worked for courier businesses, and 7 percent were in the truck transportation industry.

Job Outlook

Employment is expected to grow much faster than average; job prospects are expected to be good.

Employment change. Employment of cargo and freight agents is expected to increase by 24 percent during the 2008-18 decade, which is much faster than the average for all occupations. As the overall economy continues to grow, more agents will be needed to handle the growing number of shipments resulting from increases in cargo traffic. Additionally, as shipments require multiple modes of transportation to reach their final destinations, such as freight trucking and air, a greater number

Projections data from the National Employment Matrix

Occupational Title	SOC Code	Employment, 2008	Projected Employment, 2018	Change, 2008-2018	
				Number	Percent
Cargo and freight agents	43-5011	85,900	106,500	20,600	24

(NOTE) Data in this table are rounded. See the discussion of the employment projections table in the *Handbook* introductory chapter on *Occupational Information Included in the Handbook.*

of agents will be needed to manage the process. The growing popularity of online shopping and same day delivery may also spur employment growth.

Job prospects. A combination of job growth and turnover are expected to result in good job prospects for cargo and freight agents. However, employment of cargo and freight agents is sensitive to the fluctuations of the economy, and workers may experience high levels of unemployment when the overall level of economic activity falls.

Earnings

Median hourly wages of cargo and freight agents in May 2008 were $17.92. The middle 50 percent earned between $13.67 and $22.92. The lowest 10 percent earned less than $10.65, and the highest 10 percent earned more than $27.70. Median hourly wages in the industries employing the largest numbers of cargo and freight agents in May 2008 were:

Scheduled air transportation...$18.39
Freight transportation arrangement................................18.34
Couriers and express delivery services 18.08
General freight trucking...17.99
Support activities for air transportation..........................11.48

These workers usually receive the same benefits as most other workers. If uniforms are required, employers generally provide them or offer an allowance to purchase them.

Related Occupations

Cargo and freight agents coordinate shipments of cargo by airlines, trains, and trucks. Others who do similar work are:

	Page
Postal Service clerks	596
Postal Service mail sorters, processors, and processing machine operators	596
Shipping, receiving, and traffic clerks....................................	577
Weighers, measurers, checkers, and samplers, recordkeeping	599

Sources of Additional Information

Information about the freight and cargo industry, including training opportunities, is available from:

➤ Transportation Intermediaries Association (TIA). 1625 Prince Street, Suite 200, Alexandria, VA 22314. Internet: **http://www.tianet.org**

The Occupational Information Network (O*NET) provides information on a wide range of occupational characteristics. Links to O*NET appear at the end of the Internet version of this occupational statement, accessible at **http://www.bls.gov/ooh/ocos281.htm**

Couriers and Messengers

Significant Points

- A high school diploma is sufficient for most positions; those operating a vehicle require a valid State driver's license.

- Little or no change in employment is expected over the 2008-2018 period.

Nature of the Work

Couriers and *messengers* move and distribute documents and packages for individuals, businesses, institutions, and government agencies. They pick up documents and packages from customers and deliver them to their final destinations, usually within a local area. Because they only travel to nearby locations, couriers and messengers often specialize in same-day delivery. Some offer faster service, such as delivery within one hour. Couriers and messengers also deliver items that senders are unwilling to entrust to other means of delivery, such as important legal or financial documents, passports, airline tickets, medical specimens, and occasionally donated organs.

Couriers and messengers receive their instructions either in person or by mobile telephone, two-way radio, or wireless data service. They then use that information to pick up items and deliver them to their destinations. They may take payment upon pickup, and are often responsible for obtaining signatures upon delivery.

Some couriers and messengers carry items only for their employers, often law firms, banks, medical laboratories, or financial institutions. Others act as part of organizations' internal mail system and carry items mainly within an organization's buildings or entirely within one building. Many couriers and messengers work for messenger or courier services. Those with experience may open their own courier and messenger business and work as independent contractors.

Couriers and messengers reach their destination by several methods. Most drive vans or trucks, but some drive cars or ride motorcycles. In congested urban areas, messengers sometimes use bicycles to make deliveries. Some may travel by foot.

Work environment. Couriers and messengers spend most of their time making deliveries alone and are not closely supervised. Those who deliver by bicycle must be physically fit and be able to cope with all weather conditions and the hazards of heavy traffic. Car, van, and truck couriers must sometimes carry heavy loads, either manually or with the aid of a hand truck. They also have to deal with difficult parking situations, traffic jams, and road construction.

Couriers and messengers are responsible for the items they deliver until they are in the hands of the customer. Often, deliveries contain valuable or sensitive information and with it, expectations of safe and timely delivery making the job stressful at times. The pressure of making as many deliveries as possible to increase one's earnings can also be stressful and may lead to unsafe driving or cycling practices.

The typical workweek is Monday through Friday; however, evening and weekend hours are common.

Training, Other Qualifications, and Advancement

Most couriers and messengers train on the job and are not required to hold more than a high school diploma. Communication skills, a good driving record, and good sense of direction are helpful.

Education and training. Most courier and messenger jobs do not have formal education requirements; however, a high school diploma may be helpful in getting a job. Couriers and messengers usually learn as they work, sometimes training with an experienced worker for a short time.

Those who deal with hazardous or sensitive packages such as medical samples or donated organs may need to take a course in safely and effectively handling these items.

Licensure. Almost all couriers and messengers are required to have valid State driver's license. Having a clean driving record is usually helpful.

Other qualifications. Couriers and messengers need good knowledge of the area in which they travel and a good sense of direction. In addition, good oral and written communication skills are important because communicating with customers and dispatchers is an integral part of some courier and messenger jobs.

Many couriers and messengers are required to provide and maintain their own vehicles, especially those who work as independent contractors. Almost all two-wheeled couriers own their own bicycle, moped, or motorcycle.

Those who own their own courier and messenger business must be able to keep basic accounting records and pay their own taxes.

Advancement. Couriers and messengers have limited advancement opportunities. However, some companies may offer experienced workers preference when assigning jobs, which means they receive higher-paying contracts and more work when business is slow.

Some independent contractors become master contractors. Master contractors organize routes for multiple independent contractors for courier agencies.

Employment

Couriers and messengers held about 122,400 jobs in 2008. About 17 percent worked in healthcare; 12 percent worked in

A good sense of direction is essential for couriers and messengers, who often work under tight time constraints.

the local messengers and local delivery industry; 12 percent were employed by couriers and express delivery services; and 9 percent worked in legal services. About 19 percent were self-employed independent contractors; they provide their own vehicles and, to a certain extent, set their own schedules. However, they are like employees in some respects, because they often contract with one company.

Job Outlook

Little or no employment change is expected through 2018. The need to replace workers who leave the occupation will create the majority of job openings.

Employment change. Little or no change is expected over the 2008-18 decade. Although individuals and businesses continue to value package delivery services, the need for document delivery services has been greatly reduced due to the widespread use of computers and the Internet. Many documents, forms, and other materials that were once hand-

Projections data from the National Employment Matrix

Occupational Title	SOC Code	Employment, 2008	Projected Employment, 2018	Change, 2008-2018	
				Number	Percent
Couriers and messengers...	43-5021	122,400	122,000	-400	0

(NOTE) Data in this table are rounded. See the discussion of the employment projections table in the *Handbook* introductory chapter on *Occupational Information Included in the Handbook.*

delivered are now transferred in digital format. Wider acceptance of digital signatures has reduced the number of legal and financial documents that need to be moved from place to place.

Nonetheless, some demand for courier and messenger services will continue to arise, especially for items that cannot be sent electronically, such as blueprints and other oversized materials, securities, and passports. Couriers will also be required by medical and dental laboratories to pick up and deliver medical specimens and other materials.

Job prospects. Job opportunities will arise out of the need to replace couriers and messengers who leave the occupation. Additionally, a continued need for parcel delivery, both within urban areas and between cities, will result in some jobs for couriers and messengers. The vast majority of openings are expected to be in large urban areas.

Earnings

Median hourly wages of couriers and messengers in May 2008 were $11.22 per hour. The middle 50 percent earned between $9.08 and $14.10. The lowest 10 percent earned less than $7.88, and the highest 10 percent earned more than $17.77. Median hourly wages in the industries employing the largest numbers of couriers and messengers in May 2008 were:

Medical and diagnostic laboratories	$12.05
General medical and surgical hospitals	11.85
Legal services	10.83
Couriers and express delivery services	10.75
Local messengers and local delivery	10.00

Couriers and messengers who are full-time employees usually receive the same benefits as most other workers. About 21 percent are union members, which may lead to higher earnings, better benefits and more job stability. Most independent contractors do not receive benefits, but may have higher earnings. If uniforms are required, employers generally provide them or offer an allowance to purchase them.

Related Occupations

Messengers and couriers deliver letters, parcels, and other items. Others who do similar work include:

Sources of Additional Information

Local employers and local offices of the State employment service can provide additional information about job opportunities. People interested in courier and messenger jobs also may contact local courier and messenger services.

Information on careers as couriers and messengers is available from:

➤ Messenger Courier Association of the Americas, 750 National Press Building, 529 14th St., NW, Washington, DC 20045. Internet: **http://www.mcaa.com/**

The Occupational Information Network (O*NET) provides information on a wide range of occupational characteristics. Links to O*NET appear at the end of the Internet version of this occupational statement, accessible at **http://www.bls.gov/ooh/ocos136.htm**

Postal Service Mail Carriers

Significant Points

- Little or no change in employment is projected over the 2008-18 period.

- Keen competition for jobs is expected.

- Qualification is based on an examination.

- Applicants customarily wait 1 to 2 years or more after passing the examination before being hired.

Nature of the Work

Postal Service mail carriers deliver mail to residences and businesses in cities, towns, and rural areas. Although carriers are classified by their type of route—either city or rural—duties of *city and rural carriers* are similar. Most travel established routes, delivering and collecting mail. Mail carriers start work at the post office early in the morning, when they arrange the mail in delivery sequence. Automated equipment has reduced the time that carriers need to sort the mail, allowing them to spend more of their time delivering it.

Mail carriers cover their routes on foot, by vehicle, or by a combination of both. On foot, they carry a heavy load of mail in a satchel or push it on a cart. In most urban and rural areas, they use a car or small truck. The Postal Service provides vehicles to city carriers; most rural carriers use their own vehicles and are reimbursed for that use. Deliveries are made to houses, to roadside mailboxes, and to large buildings such as offices or apartments, which generally have all of their tenants' mailboxes in one location.

Besides delivering and collecting mail, carriers collect money for postage-due and COD (cash-on-delivery) fees and obtain signed receipts for registered, certified, and insured mail. If a customer is not home, the carrier leaves a notice that tells where special mail is being held. After completing their routes, carriers return to the post office with mail gathered from homes, businesses, and sometimes street collection boxes, and turn in the mail, receipts, and money collected during the day.

Some city carriers may have specialized duties such as delivering only parcels or picking up mail only from mail collection boxes. In comparison with city carriers, rural carriers perform a wider range of postal services, in addition to delivering and picking up mail. For example, rural carriers may sell stamps and money orders and register, certify, and insure parcels and letters. All carriers, however, must be able to answer customers' questions about postal regulations and services and provide change-of-address cards and other postal forms when requested.

Work environment. Most carriers begin work early in the morning—those with routes in a business district can start as early as 4 a.m. Overtime hours are frequently required for urban carriers. Carriers spend most of their time outdoors, delivering mail in all kinds of weather. Though carriers face many natural hazards, such as extreme temperatures and wet and icy roads and sidewalks, serious injuries are often due to the nature of the work, which requires repetitive arm and hand movements, as well as constant lifting and bending. These activities can lead to repetitive stress injuries in various joints and muscles.

Training, Other Qualifications, and Advancement

All applicants for Postal Service mail carrier jobs are required to take an examination. After passing the exam, it may take 1 to 2 years or longer before being hired because the number of applicants generally exceeds the number of job openings.

Education and training. There are no specific education requirements to become a Postal Service mail carrier; however, all applicants must have a good command of the English language. Upon being hired, new carriers are trained on the job by experienced workers. Many post offices offer classroom instruction on safety and defensive driving. Workers receive additional instruction when new equipment or procedures are introduced. In these cases, usually another postal employee or a training specialist trains the workers.

Other qualifications. Postal Service mail carriers must be at least 18 years old. They must be U.S. citizens or have been granted permanent resident-alien status in the United States, and males must have registered with the Selective Service upon reaching age 18.

All applicants must pass a written examination that measures speed and accuracy at checking names and numbers and the ability to memorize mail distribution procedures. Jobseekers should contact the post office or mail processing center where they wish to work to determine when an exam will be given. Applicants' names are listed in order of their examination scores. Five points are added to the score of an honorably discharged veteran and 10 points are added to the score of a veteran who was wounded in combat or is disabled. When a vacancy occurs, the appointing officer chooses one of the top three applicants; the rest of the names remain on the list to be considered for future openings until their eligibility expires—usually 2 years after the examination date.

When accepted, applicants must undergo a criminal-history check and pass a physical examination and a drug test. Applicants also may be asked to show that they can lift and handle mail sacks weighing 70 pounds. A safe driving record is required for mail carriers who drive at work, and applicants must receive a passing grade on a road test.

Good interpersonal skills are important because mail carriers must be courteous and tactful when dealing with the public, especially when answering questions or receiving complaints. A good memory and the ability to read rapidly and accurately are also important.

Advancement. Postal Service mail carriers may begin on a casual, transitional, part-time, or flexible basis and become regular or full-time employees in order of seniority, as vacancies occur. Carriers can look forward to obtaining preferred routes

Postal Service mail carriers receive good benefits.

as their seniority increases. Postal Service mail carriers can advance to supervisory positions on a competitive basis.

Employment

The U.S. Postal Service employed 343,300 mail carriers in 2008. The majority of mail carriers work in cities and suburbs, while the rest work in rural areas.

Postal Service mail carriers are classified as casual, transitional, part-time flexible, part-time regular, or full time. Casuals are hired for 90 days at a time to help process and deliver mail during peak mailing or vacation periods in rural areas. Transitional carriers are hired on a temporary basis in cities for a period of one year. Part-time, flexible workers do not have a regular work schedule or weekly guarantee of hours but are called as the need arises. Part-time regulars have a set work schedule of fewer than 40 hours per week, often replacing regular full-time workers on their scheduled day off. Few carriers are classified as part-time employees, especially among rural carriers. Full-time postal employees work a 40-hour week over a 5-day period and made up 85 percent of mail carriers in 2008.

Job Outlook

Employment of Postal Service mail carriers is expected to experience little or no change through 2018. Keen competition is

Projections data from the National Employment Matrix

Occupational Title	SOC Code	Employment, 2008	Projected Employment, 2018	Change, 2008-2018	
				Number	Percent
Postal service mail carriers	43-5052	343,300	339,400	-3,900	-1

(NOTE) Data in this table are rounded. See the discussion of the employment projections table in the *Handbook* introductory chapter on *Occupational Information Included in the Handbook.*

expected for mail carrier jobs because of the attractive wages and benefits and relatively low entry requirements.

Employment change. Employment of mail carriers is expected to decline by about 1 percent through 2018. Employment will be adversely affected by several factors. The use of automated "delivery point sequencing" systems to sort letter mail and flat mail directly, according to the order of delivery, reduces the amount of time that carriers spend sorting their mail, allowing them to spend more time on the streets delivering mail. The amount of time carriers save on sorting letter mail and flat mail will allow them to increase the size of their routes, which will reduce the need to hire more carriers. Additionally, the Postal Service is moving toward more centralized mail delivery, such as the use of cluster mailboxes, to cut down on the number of door-to-door deliveries. However, as the population continues to rise and the number of addresses to which mail must be delivered increases the demand for mail carriers in some areas of the country will grow.

Employment and schedules in the Postal Service fluctuate with the demand for its services. When mail volume is high, such as during holidays, full-time employees work overtime, part-time workers get additional hours, and casual workers may be hired.

Job prospects. Those seeking jobs as Postal Service mail carriers can expect to encounter keen competition. The number of applicants usually exceeds the number of job openings because of the occupation's low entry requirements and attractive wages and benefits. The best employment opportunities for mail carriers are expected to be in areas of the country with significant population growth as the number of addresses to which mail must be delivered continues to grow.

Earnings

Median annual wages of Postal Service mail carriers were $49,800 in May 2008. The middle 50 percent earned between $41,270 and 51,250. The lowest 10 earned less than $37,400, while the top 10 percent earned more than $52,400. Rural mail carriers are reimbursed for mileage put on their own vehicles while delivering mail.

Postal Service mail carriers enjoy a variety of employer-provided benefits similar to those enjoyed by other Federal Government workers. The National Association of Letter Carriers and the National Rural Letter Carriers Association together represent most of these workers.

Related Occupations

Other occupations with duties similar to those of Postal Service mail carriers include:

Sources of Additional Information

Information on job requirements, entrance examinations, and specific employment opportunities for Postal Service mail carriers is available from local post offices and State employment service offices. This information also is available from the United States Post Office online at **http://www.usps.com.**

The Occupational Information Network (O*NET) provides information on a wide range of occupational characteristics. Links to O*NET appear at the end of the Internet version of this occupational statement, accessible at **http://www.bls.gov/ooh/ocos345.htm**

Shipping, Receiving, and Traffic Clerks

Significant Points

- Shipping, receiving, and traffic clerks generally are entry-level workers who need no more than a high school diploma.

- Employers prefer to hire those familiar with computers and other electronic office and business equipment.

- Employment is expected to decline moderately as a result of increasing automation; however, job openings will result from the need to replace workers who leave the occupation.

Nature of the Work

Shipping, receiving, and traffic clerks keep records of all goods shipped and received. Their duties depend on the size of the establishment they work for and the level of automation used. Larger companies typically are more able to finance the purchase of computers, scanners, and other equipment to handle some or all of a clerk's responsibilities. In smaller companies, a clerk maintains records, prepares shipments, sorts packages, and accepts deliveries.

Shipping clerks keep records of all outgoing shipments. They prepare shipping documents and mailing labels and make sure that orders have been filled correctly. Also, they record items taken from inventory and note when orders were filled. Sometimes they fill the order themselves, taking merchandise from the stockroom, noting when inventories run low, and wrapping or packing the goods in shipping containers. They also address and label packages, look up and compute freight or postal rates, and record the weight and cost of each shipment. In addition, shipping clerks may prepare invoices and furnish information about shipments to other parts of the company, such as the accounting department. In modern warehouses, the recording of

Shipping clerks weigh orders for shipment.

this shipping information and the printing of mailing labels can be automated with the use of a computer and barcode scanner. Once a shipment is checked and ready to go, shipping clerks may sort and move the goods from the warehouse to the shipping dock or truck terminal and direct their loading.

Receiving clerks perform tasks similar to those of shipping clerks. They determine whether orders have been filled correctly by verifying incoming shipments against the original order and the accompanying bill of lading or invoice. They make a record of the shipment and the condition of its contents. In many firms, receiving clerks either use hand-held scanners to record barcodes on incoming products or manually enter the information into a computer. These data then can be transferred to the appropriate departments. An increasing number of clerks at larger, more modern companies are using radio-frequency identification (RFID) scanners, which store and remotely retrieve data by using tags or transponders. Clerks then check the shipment for any discrepancies in quantity, price, and discounts. Receiving clerks may route or move shipments to the proper department, warehouse section, or stockroom. They also may arrange for adjustments with shippers if merchandise is lost or damaged. Receiving clerks in small businesses may perform some duties similar to those of stock clerks. In larger establishments, receiving clerks may control all receiving platform operations, such as the scheduling of trucks, recording of shipments, and handling of damaged goods.

Traffic clerks maintain records on the destination, weight, and charges for all incoming and outgoing freight. They verify rate charges by comparing the classification of materials with rate charts. In many companies, this work may be automated. Information either is scanned or is entered by hand into a computer for use by the accounting department or other departments within the company. Traffic clerks also keep a file of claims for overcharges and for damage to goods in transit.

It is common, especially in smaller companies, for workers to perform the functions of all three positions. These workers are responsible for incoming and outgoing packages, as well as the logistical details of shipping them. Some shipping, receiving, and traffic clerks share responsibilities with material moving workers (see statement found elsewhere in the *Handbook*) and must sort, load, unload or store items. Clerks with these additional responsibilities may use machinery, such as forklifts, to transport items in a warehouse.

Work environment. Shipping, receiving, and traffic clerks often work in offices inside manufacturing plants or warehouses. Most jobs involve frequent standing, bending, walking, and stretching. Lifting and carrying smaller items also may be involved, especially at small companies with less automation. Although automated devices have lessened the physical demands of this occupation, their use remains somewhat limited. The work still can be strenuous, even though mechanical material handling equipment, such as computerized conveyor systems, may be used to move heavy items.

The typical workweek is Monday through Friday; however, evening and weekend hours are common in some jobs and may be required when large shipments are involved or during major holiday periods.

Training, Other Qualifications, and Advancement
Shipping, receiving, and traffic clerks generally are entry-level workers who need no more than a high school diploma. Because of increasing automation, however, employers prefer to hire those familiar with computers and other electronic office and business equipment.

Education and training. Shipping, receiving, and traffic clerks typically learn the job by doing routine tasks under close supervision. They first learn how to count and mark stock, and then start keeping records and taking inventory.

Training in the use of automated equipment usually is done informally on the job. As these occupations become more automated, however, workers may need longer periods of training to master the use of the equipment and technology. Many employers prefer to hire workers experienced with computers and other electronic equipment.

Other qualifications. Strength, stamina, communication skills, attention to detail, and an ability to work at repetitive tasks, sometimes under pressure, are important characteristics.

Advancement. Shipping, receiving, and traffic clerks may be promoted to supervisory roles, and those with an understanding of other tasks in their firm can move into other positions, such as purchasing managers or logisticians.

Employment
Shipping, receiving, and traffic clerks held about 750,500 jobs in 2008. About 71 percent were employed in manufacturing or by wholesale and retail establishments. Although jobs for shipping,

Projections data from the National Employment Matrix

Occupational Title	SOC Code	Employment, 2008	Projected Employment, 2018	Change, 2008-2018	
				Number	Percent
Shipping, receiving, and traffic clerks	43-5071	750,500	701,200	-49,300	-7

(NOTE) Data in this table are rounded. See the discussion of the employment projections table in the *Handbook* introductory chapter on *Occupational Information Included in the Handbook.*

receiving, and traffic clerks are found throughout the country, many clerks work in urban areas, where shipping depots in factories and wholesale establishments usually are located.

Job Outlook

Employment is expected to decline moderately as a result of increasing automation. However, job openings will result from the need to replace shipping, receiving, and traffic clerks who leave the occupation.

Employment change. Employment of shipping, receiving, and traffic clerks is expected to decline moderately by 7 percent between 2008 and 2018. As companies increasingly use computers and high-technology scanners to store and retrieve shipping and receiving records, fewer clerks will be needed to oversee these activities.

Methods of handling materials have changed significantly in recent years. Large warehouses increasingly are becoming automated, with equipment such as automatic sorting systems, robots, computer-directed trucks, and automated identification and data collection (AIDC) systems. This automation, coupled with the growing use of hand-held barcode and RFID scanners in shipping and receiving departments, should increase the productivity of shipping, receiving, and traffic clerks.

Job prospects. Despite the projected employment decline, many job openings will occur because of the need to replace shipping, receiving, and traffic clerks who leave the occupation. This is a large entry-level occupation, and many vacancies are created as workers leave as part of their normal career progression. Because smaller warehouses, distribution centers, and trucking terminals will continue to rely on sorting and moving goods by hand, job opportunities at those facilities may be better than at larger, more automated centers.

Earnings

Median annual wages of shipping, receiving, and traffic clerks in May 2008 were $27,660. The middle 50 percent earned between $21,900 and $34,640. The lowest 10 percent earned less than $18,000, and the highest 10 percent earned more than $42,990.

These workers usually receive the same benefits as most other workers. If uniforms are required, employers generally provide them or offer an allowance to purchase them.

Related Occupations

Shipping, receiving, and traffic clerks record, check, and often store materials that a company receives. They also process and pack goods for shipment. Other workers who perform similar duties are:

Sources of Additional Information

Additional information about job opportunities may be obtained from local employers and local offices of the State employment service.

The Occupational Information Network (O*NET) provides information on a wide range of occupational characteristics. Links to O*NET appear at the end of the Internet version of this occupational statement, accessible at **http://www.bls.gov/ooh/ocos140.htm**

Miscellaneous Office and Administrative Support Occupations

Desktop Publishers

Significant Points

- About 38 percent work for newspaper, periodical, book, and directory publishers; another 21 percent work in the printing industry.

- Employment is expected to decline rapidly.

- Most employers prefer to hire experienced desktop publishers; among persons without experience, opportunities should be best for those with certificates or degrees in desktop publishing or graphic design.

Nature of the Work

Desktop publishers use computer software to format and combine text, data, photographs, charts, and other graphic art or illustrations into prototypes of pages and other documents that are to be printed. They then may print the document on a high-resolution printer or send the materials to a commercial printer. Examples of materials produced by desktop publishers include books, brochures, calendars, magazines, newsletters, newspapers, and forms.

Desktop publishers typically design and create the graphics that accompany text, find and edit photographs and other digital images, and manipulate the text and images to display information in an attractive and readable format. They design page layouts, develop presentations and advertising campaigns, and do color separation of pictures and graphics material. Some desktop publishers may write some of the text or headlines used in newsletters or brochures.

Desktop publishers use the appropriate software to enter and select formatting properties, such as the size and style of type, column width, and spacing. Print formats are stored in the computer and displayed on its monitor. New information, such as charts, pictures, or more text, can be added. An entire newspaper, catalog, or book page, complete with artwork and graphics, can be created on the screen exactly as it will appear in print. Then, digital files are used to produce printing plates.

Desktop publishers format text, data, photographs, and other graphics into documents that are to be printed.

Like photographers and multimedia artists and animators, desktop publishers can create special effects or other visual images with the use of film, video, computers, or other electronic media. (Separate statements on photographers and on artists and related workers appear elsewhere in the *Handbook*.)

Computer software and printing technology continue to advance, making desktop publishing more economical and efficient than before. Other innovations in the occupation include digital color page-makeup systems, electronic page-layout systems, and off-press color proofing systems. In addition, most materials are reproduced on the Internet as well as printed; therefore, desktop publishers may need to know electronic publishing software, such as Hypertext Markup Language (HTML), and may be responsible for converting text and graphics to an Internet-ready format.

Some desktop publishers may write and edit, as well as layout and design pages. For example, in addition to laying out articles for a newsletter, desktop publishers may be responsible for copyediting content or for writing original content themselves. Desktop publisher's writing and editing responsibilities may vary widely from project to project and employer to employer. Smaller firms typically use desktop publishers to perform a wide range of tasks, while desktop publishers at larger firms may specialize in a certain part of the publishing process. (Writers and editors are discussed elsewhere in the *Handbook*.)

Desktop publishers also may be called publications specialists, electronic publishers, DTP operators, desktop publishing editors, electronic prepress technicians, electronic publishing specialists, image designers, typographers, compositors, layout artists, and Web publications designers. The exact name may vary with the specific tasks performed or simply by personal preference.

Work environment. Desktop publishers usually work in clean, air-conditioned office areas with little noise. They generally work a standard workweek; however, some may work night shifts, weekends, or holidays, depending upon the production schedule for the project or to meet deadlines.

These workers often are subject to stress and the pressures of short deadlines and tight work schedules. Like other workers who spend long hours working in front of a computer monitor, desktop publishers may be susceptible to eyestrain, back discomfort, and hand and wrist problems.

Training, Other Qualifications, and Advancement

Most desktop publishers learn their skills on the job. Experience is the best training, and many desktop publishers get started just by experimenting with the software and developing a knack for designing and laying out material for publication.

Education and training. There is generally no educational requirement for the job of desktop publisher. Most people learn on the job or by taking classes online or through local learning centers that teach the latest software. For those who are interested in pursuing a career in desktop publishing, an associate's degree or a bachelor's degree in graphic arts, graphic communications, or graphic design is preferred. Graphic arts programs are a good way to learn about the desktop publishing software used to format pages, assign type characteristics, and import text and graphics into electronic page layouts. Courses in other aspects of printing also are available at vocational institutes and private trade and technical schools.

Other qualifications. Although formal training is not always required, those with certificates or degrees will have the best job opportunities. Most employers prefer to hire people who have at least a high school diploma and who possess good communication abilities, basic computer skills, and a strong work ethic. Desktop publishers should be able to deal courteously with people, because they have to interact with customers and clients and be able to express design concepts and layout options with them. In addition, they may have to do simple math calculations and compute ratios to scale graphics and artwork and estimate job costs. A basic understanding of, and facility with, computers, printers, scanners, and other office equipment and technologies also is needed to work as a desktop publisher.

Desktop publishers need good manual dexterity, and they must be able to pay attention to detail and work independently. In addition, good eyesight, including visual acuity, depth perception, a wide field of view, color vision, and the ability to focus quickly, are assets. Artistic ability often is a plus. Employers also seek persons who are even tempered and adaptable—important qualities for workers who frequently must meet deadlines and learn how to operate new equipment.

Advancement. Workers with limited training and experience assist more experienced staff on projects while they learn the software and gain practical experience. They advance on the basis of their demonstrated mastery of skills. Some may move into supervisory or management positions. Other desktop publishers may start their own companies or work as independent consultants, while those with more artistic talent and further education may find job opportunities in graphic design or commercial art.

Employment

Desktop publishers held about 26,400 jobs in 2008. Approximately 38 percent worked for newspaper, periodical, book, and directory publishers, while 21 percent worked in the printing and related support activities industry. Other desktop publishers work for professional, scientific, and technical services firms and in many other industries that produce printed or published materials.

Projections data from the National Employment Matrix

Occupational Title	SOC Code	Employment, 2008	Projected Employment, 2018	Change, 2008-2018	
				Number	Percent
Desktop publishers..	43-9031	26,400	20,400	-5,900	-23

(NOTE) Data in this table are rounded. See the discussion of the employment projections table in the *Handbook* introductory chapter on *Occupational Information Included in the Handbook.*

The printing and publishing industries are two of the most geographically dispersed industries in the United States, and desktop publishing jobs are found throughout the country. Although most jobs are in large metropolitan cities, electronic communication networks and the Internet allow some desktop publishers to work from other locations.

Job Outlook

Employment is expected to decline rapidly because more people are learning basic desktop publishing skills as a part of their regular job functions in other occupations and because more organizations are formatting materials for display on the Internet rather than designing pages for print publication.

Employment change. Employment of desktop publishers is expected to decline 23 percent between 2008 and 2018. Desktop publishing has become a frequently used and common tool for designing and laying out printed matter, such as advertisements, brochures, newsletters, and forms. However, increased computer-processing capacity and the widespread availability of more elaborate desktop publishing software will make it easier and more affordable for nonprinting professionals to use. As a result, there will be less need for people to specialize in desktop publishing.

In addition, organizations are increasingly moving their published material to the Internet to save the cost of printing and distributing materials. This change will slow the growth of desktop publishers, especially in smaller membership and trade organizations, which publish newsletters and brief reports. Companies that produce more extensive reports and rely on high-quality, high-resolution color and graphics within their publications, however, will continue to use desktop publishers to lay out publications for offset printing.

Job prospects. There will be some job opportunities for desktop publishers because of the need to replace workers who move into managerial positions, transfer to other occupations, or leave the labor force. However, job prospects will be better for those with experience; many employers prefer to hire experienced desktop publishers because of the long time it takes to become good at this type of work. Among individuals with little or no experience, opportunities should be best for those with computer backgrounds, those with certification in desktop publishing, or those who have completed a postsecondary program in desktop publishing, graphic design, or Web design.

Earnings

Wages for desktop publishers vary according to level of experience, training, geographic location, and company size. Median annual wages of desktop publishers were $36,600 in May 2008. The middle 50 percent earned between $28,140 and $47,870. The lowest 10 percent earned less than $21,860, and the highest 10 percent earned more than $59,210 a year. Median annual wages of desktop publishers in May 2008 were $39,870 in printing and related support services and $33,130 in newspaper, periodical, book, and directory publishers.

Related Occupations

Desktop publishers use artistic and editorial skills in their work. These skills also are essential for the following workers:

	Page
Artists and related workers.......................................	301
Commercial and industrial designers......................	304
Graphic designers..	312
Prepress technicians and workers...........................	748

Sources of Additional Information

Details about training programs may be obtained from local employers, such as newspapers and printing shops, or from local offices of the State employment service.

For information on careers and training in printing, desktop publishing, and graphic arts, write to:

➤ Graphic Arts Education and Research Foundation, 1899 Preston White Dr., Reston, VA 20191-4367. Internet: **http://www.gaerf.org**

➤ Graphic Arts Information Network, 200 Deer Run Rd., Sewickley, PA 15143-2324. Internet: **http://www.gain.net**

The Occupational Information Network (O*NET) provides information on a wide range of occupational characteristics. Links to O*NET appear at the end of the Internet version of this occupational statement, accessible at **http://www.bls.gov/ooh/ocos276.htm**

Office Clerks, General

Significant Points

- Employment growth and high replacement needs in this large occupation will result in numerous job openings.

- Prospects should be best for those with knowledge of basic computer applications and office machinery.

- Part-time and temporary positions are common.

Nature of the Work

Rather than performing a single specialized task, *general office clerks* have responsibilities that often change daily with the needs of the specific job and the employer. Some clerks spend their days filing or keyboarding. Others enter data at a computer terminal. They also operate photocopiers, fax machines, and

General office clerks operate photocopiers, fax machines, and other office equipment.

other office equipment; prepare mailings; proofread documents; and answer telephones and deliver messages.

The specific duties assigned to clerks vary significantly, depending on the type of office in which they work. An office clerk in a doctor's office, for example, would not perform the same tasks that a clerk in a large financial institution or in the office of an auto parts wholesaler would. Although all clerks may sort checks, keep payroll records, take inventory, and access information, they also perform duties unique to their employer. For example, a clerk in a doctor's office may organize medications, a corporate office clerk may help prepare materials for presentations, and a clerk employed by a wholesaler may fill merchandise orders.

Clerks' duties also vary by level of experience. Inexperienced employees may make photocopies, stuff envelopes, or record inquiries. Experienced clerks are usually given additional responsibilities. For example, they may maintain financial or other records, set up spreadsheets, verify statistical reports for accuracy and completeness, handle and adjust customer complaints, work with vendors, make travel arrangements, take inventory of equipment and supplies, answer questions on departmental services and functions, or help prepare invoices or budgetary requests. Senior office clerks may also be expected to monitor and direct the work of lower-level clerks.

Work environment. For the most part, general office clerks work in comfortable office settings. Those on full-time sched-ules usually work a standard 40-hour week; however, some work shifts or overtime during busy periods. About 24 percent of clerks worked part time in 2008. Many clerks also work in temporary positions.

Training, Other Qualifications, and Advancement
General office clerks often need to know how to use computers, word processing, and other business software and office equipment. Experience working in an office is helpful, but office clerks also learn skills on the job.

Education and training. Employers usually require a high school diploma or equivalent, and some require basic computer skills, including familiarity with word processing software, as well as other general office skills. Although most general office clerk jobs are entry-level positions, employers may prefer or require previous office or business experience.

Training for this occupation is available through business education programs offered in high schools, community and junior colleges, and postsecondary vocational schools. Courses in office practices, word processing, and other computer applications are particularly helpful.

Other qualifications. Because general office clerks usually work with other office staff, they should be cooperative and able to work as part of a team. Employers prefer individuals who can perform a variety of tasks and satisfy the needs of the many departments within a company. In addition, applicants should have good writing and other communication skills, be detail oriented, and be adaptable.

Advancement. General office clerks who exhibit strong communication, interpersonal, and analytical skills may be promoted to supervisory positions. Others may move into different, more senior administrative jobs, such as receptionist, secretary, or administrative assistant. After gaining some work experience or specialized skills, many workers transfer to jobs with higher pay or greater advancement potential. Advancement to professional occupations within an organization normally requires additional formal education, such as a college degree.

Employment
General office clerks held about 3.0 million jobs in 2008. Most are employed in relatively small businesses. Although they work in every sector of the economy, about one quarter worked in educational services and in health care and social assistance.

Job Outlook
Employment growth and high replacement needs in this large occupation are expected to result in numerous job openings for general office clerks. Prospects should be best for those with knowledge of basic computer applications and office machinery.

Employment change. Employment of general office clerks is expected to grow by 12 percent between 2008 and 2018, which is about as fast as the average for all occupations. The employment outlook for these workers will continue to be affected by the increasing use of technology, expanding office automation, and the consolidation of administrative support tasks. These factors will lead to a consolidation of administrative support staffs and a diversification of job responsibilities. However, this consolidation will increase the demand for general office clerks because they perform a variety of administrative support tasks,

Projections data from the National Employment Matrix

Occupational Title	SOC Code	Employment, 2008	Projected Employment, 2018	Change, 2008-2018	
				Number	Percent
Office clerks, general	43-9061	3,024,400	3,383,100	358,700	12

(NOTE) Data in this table are rounded. See the discussion of the employment projections table in the *Handbook* introductory chapter on *Occupational Information Included in the Handbook.*

as opposed to clerks with very specific functions. It will become increasingly common within businesses, especially those smaller in size, to find only general office clerks in charge of all administrative support work.

Job prospects. In addition to many full-time job openings for general office clerks, part-time and temporary positions are common. Prospects should be best for those who have knowledge of basic computer applications and office machinery—such as computers, fax machines, telephone systems, and scanners—and good writing and other communication skills. Office clerks with previous business or office experience should also have good job prospects. As general administrative support duties continue to be consolidated, employers will increasingly seek well-rounded individuals with highly developed communication skills and the ability to perform multiple tasks.

Job opportunities may vary from year to year because the strength of the economy affects demand for general office clerks. Companies tend to employ more workers when the economy is strong. Industries least likely to be affected by economic fluctuations tend to be the most stable places for employment.

Earnings

Median annual wages of general office clerks were $25,320 in May 2008; the middle 50 percent earned between $19,620 and $31,980 annually. The lowest 10 percent earned less than $16,030, and the highest 10 percent earned more than $39,880. Median annual wages in the industries employing the largest numbers of general office clerks in May 2008 were:

Local government..$28,750
General medical and surgical hospitals........................27,700
Elementary and secondary schools 25,690
Colleges, universities, and professional schools 25,400
Employment services 23,840

Related Occupations

The duties of general office clerks can include a combination of bookkeeping, keyboarding, office machine operation, and filing. Other office and administrative support workers who perform similar duties include:

Non-clerical entry-level workers who perform these duties include:

Sources of Additional Information

State employment service offices and agencies can provide information about job openings for general office clerks.

For information related to administrative occupations, including educational programs and certified designations, contact:

➤ International Association of Administrative Professionals, P.O. Box 20404, Kansas City, MO 64195-0404. Internet: **http://www.iaap-hq.org**

➤ American Management Association, 1601 Broadway, New York, NY 10019. Internet: **http://www.amanet.org**

➤ Association of Professional Office Managers, P.O. Box 1926, Rockville, MD 20849. Internet: **http://www.apomonline.org**

The Occupational Information Network (O*NET) provides information on a wide range of occupational characteristics. Links to O*NET appear at the end of the Internet version of this occupational statement, accessible at **http://www.bls.gov/ooh/ocos130.htm**

Secretaries and Administrative Assistants

Significant Points

- This occupation ranks among those with the largest number of job openings.

- Opportunities should be best for applicants with extensive knowledge of computer software applications.

- Secretaries and administrative assistants are increasingly assuming responsibilities once reserved for managerial and professional staff.

Nature of the Work

As the reliance on technology continues to expand in offices, the role of the office professional has greatly evolved. Office automation and organizational restructuring have led *secretaries and administrative assistants* to increasingly assume responsibilities once reserved for managerial and professional staff. In spite of these changes, however, the core responsibilities for secretaries and administrative assistants have remained much the same: performing and coordinating an office's administrative

Secretaries and administrative assistants often use computers to create spreadsheets, compose correspondence, manage databases, and create presentations and reports.

activities and storing, retrieving, and integrating information for dissemination to staff and clients.

Secretaries and administrative assistants perform a variety of administrative and clerical duties necessary to run an organization efficiently. They serve as information and communication managers for an office; plan and schedule meetings and appointments; organize and maintain paper and electronic files; manage projects; conduct research; and disseminate information by using the telephone, mail services, Web sites, and e-mail. They may also handle travel and guest arrangements.

Secretaries and administrative assistants use a variety of office equipment, such as fax machines, photocopiers, scanners, and videoconferencing and telephone systems. In addition, secretaries and administrative assistants often use computers to do tasks previously handled by managers and professionals; they create spreadsheets, compose correspondence, manage databases, and create presentations, reports, and documents using desktop publishing software and digital graphics. They may also negotiate with vendors, maintain and examine leased equipment, purchase supplies, manage areas such as stockrooms or corporate libraries, and retrieve data from various sources. At the same time, managers and professionals have assumed many tasks traditionally assigned to secretaries and administrative assistants, such as keyboarding and answering the telephone. Because secretaries and administrative assistants do less dictation and word processing, they now have time to support more members of the executive staff. In a number of organizations, secretaries and administrative assistants work in teams to work flexibly and share their expertise.

Many secretaries and administrative assistants provide training and orientation for new staff, conduct research on the Internet, and operate and troubleshoot new office technologies.

Specific job duties vary with experience and titles. *Executive secretaries and administrative assistants* provide high-level administrative support for an office and for top executives of an organization. Generally, they perform fewer clerical tasks than do secretaries and more information management. In addition to arranging conference calls and supervising other clerical staff, they may handle more complex responsibilities such as reviewing incoming memos, submissions, and reports in order to determine their significance and to plan for their distribution. They also prepare agendas and make arrangements for meetings of committees and executive boards. They may also conduct research and prepare statistical reports.

Some secretaries and administrative assistants, such as *legal* and *medical secretaries*, perform highly specialized work requiring knowledge of technical terminology and procedures. For instance, legal secretaries prepare correspondence and legal papers such as summonses, complaints, motions, responses, and subpoenas under the supervision of an attorney or a paralegal. They may also review legal journals and assist with legal research—for example, by verifying quotes and citations in legal briefs. Additionally, legal secretaries often teach newly minted lawyers how to prepare documents for submission to the courts. Medical secretaries transcribe dictation, prepare correspondence, and assist physicians or medical scientists with reports, speeches, articles, and conference proceedings. They also record simple medical histories, arrange for patients to be hospitalized, and order supplies. Most medical secretaries need to be familiar with insurance rules, billing practices, and hospital or laboratory procedures. Other technical secretaries who assist engineers or scientists may prepare correspondence, maintain their organization's technical library, and gather and edit materials for scientific papers.

Secretaries employed in elementary schools and high schools perform important administrative functions for the school. They are responsible for handling most of the communications between parents, the community, and teachers and administrators who work at the school. As such, they are required to know details about registering students, immunizations, and bus schedules, for example. They schedule appointments, keep track of students' academic records, and make room assignments for classes. Those who work directly for principals screen inquiries from parents and handle those matters not needing a principal's attention. They may also set a principal's calendar to help set her or his priorities for the day.

Some secretaries and administrative assistants, also known as *virtual assistants*, are freelancers who work at a home office. They use the Internet, e-mail, fax, and the phone to communicate with clients. Other duties include medical or legal transcription, writing and editing reports and business correspondence, answering e-mail, data entry, setting appointments, making travel arrangements, bookkeeping, and desktop publishing.

Work environment. Secretaries and administrative assistants usually work in schools, hospitals, corporate settings, government agencies, or legal and medical offices. Virtual assistants work from a home office. Their jobs often involve sitting for long periods. If they spend a lot of time keyboarding, particularly at a computer monitor, they may encounter problems of eyestrain, stress, and repetitive motion ailments such as carpal tunnel syndrome.

The majority of secretaries and administrative assistants are full-time employees who work a standard 40-hour week. About 18 percent of secretaries work part time and many others work in temporary positions. A few are self-employed, freelance (such as virtual assistants), or participate in job-sharing arrangements, in which two people divide responsibility for a single job.

Training, Other Qualifications, and Advancement

Word processing, writing, and communication skills are essential for all secretaries and administrative assistants. Employers increasingly require extensive knowledge of computer software applications, such as desktop publishing, project management, spreadsheets, and database management.

Education and training. High school graduates who have basic office skills may qualify for entry-level secretarial positions. They can acquire these skills in various ways. Training ranges from high school vocational education programs that teach office skills and typing to 1-year and 2-year programs in office administration offered by business and vocational-technical schools, and community colleges. Many temporary placement agencies also provide formal training in computer and office skills. Most medical and legal secretaries must go through specialized training programs that teach them the language of the industry. Virtual assistant training programs are available at many community colleges in transcription, bookkeeping, website design, project management, and computer technology. There are also online training and coaching programs.

Employers of executive secretaries increasingly are seeking candidates with a college degree, as these secretaries work closely with top executives. A degree related to the business or industry in which a person is seeking employment may provide the jobseeker with an advantage in the application process.

Most secretaries and administrative assistants, once hired, tend to acquire more advanced skills through on-the-job instruction by other employees or by equipment and software vendors. Others may attend classes or participate in online education to learn how to operate new office technologies, such as information storage systems, scanners, or new updated software packages. As office automation continues to evolve, retraining and continuing education will remain integral parts of secretarial jobs.

Other qualifications. Secretaries and administrative assistants should be proficient in typing and good at spelling, punctuation, grammar, and oral communication. Employers also look for good customer service and interpersonal skills because secretaries and administrative assistants must be tactful in their dealings with people. Discretion, good judgment, organizational or management ability, initiative, and the ability to work independently are especially important for higher-level administrative positions. Changes in the office environment have increased the demand for secretaries and administrative assistants who are adaptable and versatile.

Certification and advancement. Testing and certification for proficiency in office skills are available through organizations such as the International Association of Administrative Professionals; National Association of Legal Secretaries (NALS), Inc.; Legal Secretaries International, Inc; and International Virtual Assistants Association (IVAA). As secretaries and administrative assistants gain experience, they can earn several different designations. Prominent designations include the Certified Professional Secretary (CPS) and the Certified Administrative Professional (CAP), which can be earned by meeting certain experience or educational requirements and passing an examination. Similarly, those with 1 year of experience in the legal field, or who have concluded

an approved training course and who want to be certified as a legal support professional, can acquire the Accredited Legal Secretary (ALS) designation through a testing process administered by NALS. NALS offers two additional designations: Professional Legal Secretary (PLS), considered an advanced certification for legal support professionals, and a designation for proficiency as a paralegal. Legal Secretaries International confers the Certified Legal Secretary Specialist (CLSS) designation in areas such as intellectual property, criminal law, civil litigation, probate, and business law to those who have 5 years of legal experience and pass an examination. In some instances, certain requirements may be waived. There is currently no set standard of certification for virtual assistants. A number of certifications exist which involve passing a written test covering areas of core competencies and business ethics. The IVAA has three certifications available: Certified Virtual Assistant, Ethics Checked Virtual Assistant; and the Real Estate Virtual Assistant.

Secretaries and administrative assistants generally advance by being promoted to other administrative positions with more responsibilities. Qualified administrative assistants who broaden their knowledge of a company's operations and enhance their skills may be promoted to senior or executive secretary or administrative assistant, clerical supervisor, or office manager. Secretaries with word processing or data entry experience can advance to jobs as word processing or data entry trainers, supervisors, or managers within their own firms or in a secretarial, word processing, or data entry service bureau. Secretarial and administrative support experience also can lead to jobs such as instructor or sales representative with manufacturers of software or computer equipment. With additional training, many legal secretaries become paralegals.

Employment

Secretaries and administrative assistants held about 4.3 million jobs in 2008, ranking it among the largest occupations in the U.S. economy. The following tabulation shows the distribution of employment by secretarial specialty:

Secretaries, except legal, medical, and executive....2,020,000
Executive secretaries and administrative assistants.... 1,594,400
Medical secretaries..471,100
Legal secretaries...262,600

Secretaries and administrative assistants are employed in organizations of every type. Around 90 percent are employed in service-providing industries, ranging from education and healthcare to government and retail trade. Most of the rest work for firms engaged in manufacturing or construction.

Job Outlook

Employment is projected to grow about as fast as the average. Secretaries and administrative assistants will have among the largest number of job openings due to growth and the need to replace workers who transfer to other occupations or leave this occupation. Opportunities should be best for applicants with extensive knowledge of computer software applications.

Employment change. Employment of secretaries and administrative assistants is expected to increase by 11 percent, which is

Projections data from the National Employment Matrix

Occupational Title	SOC Code	Employment, 2008	Projected Employment, 2018	Change, 2008-2018	
				Number	Percent
Secretaries and administrative assistants	43-6000	4,348,100	4,819,700	471,600	11
Executive secretaries and administrative assistants	43-6011	1,594,400	1,798,800	204,400	13
Legal secretaries...	43-6012	262,600	311,000	48,400	18
Medical secretaries..	43-6013	471,100	596,600	125,500	27
Secretaries, except legal, medical, and executive	43-6014	2,020,000	2,113,300	93,300	5

(NOTE) Data in this table are rounded. See the discussion of the employment projections table in the *Handbook* introductory chapter on *Occupational Information Included in the Handbook.*

about as fast as the average for all occupations, between 2008 and 2018. Projected employment varies by occupational specialty. Above average employment growth in the health care and social assistance industry should lead to much faster than the average growth for medical secretaries, while moderate growth in legal services is projected to lead to faster than average growth in employment of legal secretaries. Employment of executive secretaries and administrative assistants is projected to grow as fast as the average for all occupations. Growing industries—such as construction; educational services; health care and social assistance; and professional, scientific, and technical services—will continue to generate the most new jobs. Slower than average growth is expected for secretaries, except legal, medical, or executive, who account for about 46 percent of all secretaries and administrative assistants.

Increasing office automation and organizational restructuring will continue to make secretaries and administrative assistants more productive in coming years. Computers, e-mail, scanners, and voice message systems will allow secretaries and administrative assistants to accomplish more in the same amount of time. The use of automated equipment is also changing the distribution of work in many offices. In some cases, traditional secretarial duties as typing, filing, photocopying, and bookkeeping are being done by clerks in other departments or by the professionals themselves. For example, professionals and managers increasingly do their own word processing and data entry, and handle much of their own correspondence. In some law and medical offices, paralegals and medical assistants are assuming some tasks formerly done by secretaries. Also, many small and medium-sized organizations are outsourcing key administrative functions, such as data entry, bookkeeping, and Internet research, to virtual assistants.

Developments in office technology are certain to continue. However, many secretarial and administrative duties are of a personal, interactive nature and, therefore, are not easily automated. Responsibilities such as planning conferences, working with clients, and instructing staff require tact and communication skills. Because technology cannot substitute for these personal skills, secretaries and administrative assistants will continue to play a key role in most organizations.

As paralegals and medical assistants assume more of the duties traditionally assigned to secretaries, offices will continue to replace the traditional arrangement of one secretary per manager with secretaries and administrative assistants who support the work of systems, departments, or units. This approach means that secretaries and administrative assistants will assume added responsibilities and will be seen as valuable members of a team.

Job prospects. In addition to jobs created from growth, numerous job opportunities will arise from the need to replace secretaries and administrative assistants who transfer to other occupations, including exceptionally skilled executive secretaries and administrative assistants who often move into professional occupations. Job opportunities should be best for applicants with extensive knowledge of computer software applications, with experience as a secretary or administrative assistant, or with advanced communication and computer skills. Applicants with a bachelor's degree will be in great demand to act more as managerial assistants and to perform more complex tasks.

Earnings

Median annual wages of secretaries, except legal, medical, and executive, were $29,050 in May 2008. The middle 50 percent earned between $23,160 and $36,020. The lowest 10 percent earned less than $18,440, and the highest 10 percent earned more than $43,240. Median annual wages in the industries employing the largest numbers of secretaries, except legal, medical, and executive in May 2008 were:

Local government...$32,610
Colleges, universities, and professional schools 31,530
General medical and surgical hospitals........................30,960
Elementary and secondary schools 29,850
Employment services 28,340

Median annual wages of executive secretaries and administrative assistants were $40,030 in May 2008. The middle 50 percent earned between $32,410 and $50,280. The lowest 10 percent earned less than $27,030, and the highest 10 percent earned more than $62,070. Median annual wages in the industries employing the largest numbers of executive secretaries and administrative assistants in May 2008 were:

Management of companies and enterprises $45,190
Local government...41,880
Colleges, universities, and professional schools 39,220
State government..35,540
Employment services 33,820

Median annual wages of legal secretaries were $39,860 in May 2008. The middle 50 percent earned between $30,870 and $50,930. The lowest 10 percent earned less than $25,580, and the highest 10 percent earned more than $62,290. Medical secretaries earned median annual wages of $29,680 in May 2008. The middle 50 percent earned between $24,530 and $36,090. The lowest 10 percent earned less than $20,870, and the highest 10 percent earned more than $42,660.

Virtual assistants set their own rate structure and billing terms based on the type of work, skill level, cost of living in their area, experience, and personal financial needs. Those who bill using an hourly rate can range anywhere from $25 to $100 per hour. Some also bill on a per page or project rate.

Related Occupations

Workers in a number of other occupations also type, record information, and process paperwork. Among them are:

A growing number of secretaries and administrative assistants share in managerial and human resource responsibilities. Occupations requiring these skills include:

Sources of Additional Information

State employment offices provide information about job openings for secretaries and administrative assistants.

For information on the latest trends in the profession, career development advice, and the CPS or CAP designations, contact:
➤ International Association of Administrative Professionals, P.O. Box 20404, Kansas City, MO 64195-0404. Internet: **http://www.iaap-hq.org**

➤ Association of Executive and Administrative Professionals, 900 South Washington St., Suite G-13, Falls Church, VA 22046. Internet: **http://www.theaeap.com**

Information on the CLSS designation can be obtained from:
➤ Legal Secretaries International Inc., 2302 Fannin St., Suite 500, Houston, TX 77002-9136. Internet: **http://www.legalsecretaries.org**

Information on the ALS, PLS, and paralegal certifications is available from:
➤ National Association of Legal Secretaries, Inc., 8159 East 41st. St., Tulsa, OK 74145. Internet: **http://www.nals.org**

Information on virtual assistant certification can be obtained from:
➤ International Virtual Assistants Association, 561 Keystone Ave., Suite 309, Reno, NV 89503. Internet: **http://www.ivaa.org**

The Occupational Information Network (O*NET) provides information on a wide range of occupational characteristics. Links to O*NET appear at the end of the Internet version of this occupational statement, accessible at **http://www.bls.gov/ooh/ocos151.htm**

Other Office and Administrative Support Occupations

Billing and Posting Clerks and Machine Operators

Nature of the Work

Billing and posting clerks and *machine operators*—commonly called *billing clerks*—calculate charges, develop bills, and prepare them to be mailed to customers.

Education and Training

Many billing clerks are hired at entry level. They generally need at least a high school diploma and basic software skills.

Job Outlook

Current and Projected Employment:

2008 Employment	528,800
2018 Employment	609,600
Employment change	80,800
Growth rate	15%

Employment change. Employment is expected to grow faster than average. Automated and electronic billing processes have streamlined billing departments, but job growth is expected due to an increasing number of transactions, especially in the rapidly growing health care industry.

Job prospects. Prospects should be good. Many job openings will occur as workers transfer to other occupations or leave the labor force.

Earnings

Median annual wages for billing and posting clerks and machine operators were $30,950 in May 2008.

Related Occupations

Sources of Additional Information

Information on employment opportunities for billing clerks is available from State job banks.

The Occupational Information Network (O*NET) provides information on a wide range of occupational characteristics. Links to O*NET appear at the end of the Internet version of this occupational statement, accessible at **http://www.bls.gov/ooh/ocos277.htm**

Brokerage Clerks

Nature of the Work

Brokerage clerks perform a number of clerical duties pertaining to transactions involving securities, such as stocks, bonds, commodities, and other kinds of investments. Duties include writing orders for stock purchases and sales, computing transfer taxes, verifying stock transactions, accepting and delivering securities, distributing dividends, and keeping records of daily transactions and holdings.

Education and Training

Brokerage clerk positions usually require only a high school diploma, but graduates from 2- and 4-year college degree programs are increasingly preferred. Short term on-the-job training is common.

Job Outlook

Current and projected employment:

2008 Employment	67,600
2018 Employment	65,800
Employment change	-1,800
Growth rate	-3%

Employment change. Employment of brokerage clerks is expected to decline slowly. Industry consolidation and increased automation of securities transactions through electronic networks will reduce the need for brokerage clerks. Additionally, clerks are often seen as reducing profits as they don't bring in customers, thus making them particularly susceptible to layoffs and downsizing.

Job prospects. Keen competition is expected for most jobs as the financial services industry undergoes further consolidation and the number of applicants is expected to exceed the number of job openings. Those with job related experience or a 2-year or 4-year degree should have the best opportunities.

Earnings

Median annual wages for brokerage clerks were $38,710 in May 2008.

Related Occupations

	Page
Bill and account collectors	561
Billing and posting clerks and machine operators	587
Bookkeeping, accounting, and auditing clerks	563
Tellers	599

Sources of Additional Information

➤ Securities Industry and Financial Markets Association, 120 Broadway, 35th Floor, New York, NY 10271. Internet: **http://www.sifma.org**

The Occupational Information Network (O*NET) provides information on a wide range of occupational char-

acteristics. Links to O*NET appear at the end of the Internet version of this occupational statement, accessible at **http://www.bls.gov/ooh/ocos145.htm**

Communications Equipment Operators

Nature of the Work

Most communications equipment operators work as *switchboard operators* or *telephone operators* for a wide variety of businesses. They may relay incoming, outgoing, and interoffice calls, or assist customers with clerical duties, such as offer directory information, take messages, greet and announce visitors or, in some cases, handle billing requests or emergency calls.

Education and Training

Communications equipment operators generally receive informal on the job training, so a high school diploma is sufficient for most positions.

Job Outlook

Current and projected employment:

2008 Employment	181,600
2018 Employment	163,400
Employment change	-18,200
Growth rate	-10%

Employment change. Employment of communications equipment operators is expected to decline rapidly due to new labor-saving communications technologies, such as voice recognition technology and internet directory assistance services. The movement of jobs to foreign countries, proliferation of cell phones, and consolidation of telephone operator jobs into fewer locations also will continue to negatively impact employment growth.

Job prospects. Despite declining employment, job prospects should be favorable as occupational turnover is expected to remain high.

Earnings

Switchboard operators, including answering service	$24,220
Telephone operators	31,670
Communications equipment operators, all other	35,050

Related Occupations

	Page
Customer service representatives	567
Dispatchers, except police, fire, and ambulance	590
Hotel, motel, and resort desk clerks	592
Police, fire, and ambulance dispatchers	595
Receptionists and information clerks	570

Sources of Additional Information

For information on employment opportunities, contact companies in the industries that employ communications equipment operators.

The Occupational Information Network (O*NET) provides information on a wide range of occupational characteristics. Links to O*NET appear at the end of the Internet version of this occupational statement, accessible at **http://www.bls.gov/ooh/ocos154.htm**

Computer Operators

Nature of the Work

Computer operators oversee the operation of computer hardware systems, ensuring that these machines are used as efficiently and securely as possible. They control the console of either a mainframe digital computer or a group of minicomputers and set controls on the computers and peripheral devices required to run computer tasks or "jobs." Operators maintain logbooks or operating records for each job run and list any events, such as malfunctions, that occur during their shift. Other computer operators perform and monitor routine tasks, such as tape backup, virus checking, software upgrading, and basic maintenance or help programmers and systems analysts test and debug new programs. Computer processing operations regularly run around-the-clock, allowing opportunities for evening, night, or weekend work. However, increased automation and telecommunication systems lessen the need for full-time coverage of operations and permits many operators to monitor systems remotely.

Education and Training

Computer operators generally require a high school degree and are trained by employers on the job. Most computer operators expect to advance to other positions in the information technology field within a few years.

Job Outlook

Current and projected employment:
2008 Employment	110,000
2018 Employment	89,500
Employment change	-20,500
Growth rate	-19%

Employment change. Employment of computer operators is projected to decline rapidly because advances in technology are making many of the duties performed by these workers obsolete. The expanding use of software that automates computer operations gives companies the option of making systems more efficient, but greatly reduces the need for operators.

Job prospects. Experienced operators are expected to face competition for the few job openings that will arise each year to replace workers who transfer to other occupations or leave the labor force. Opportunities will be best for operators who have formal computer education, familiarity with a variety of operating systems, and knowledge of the latest technology.

Earnings

Median annual wages for computer operators were $35,600 in May 2008.

Related Occupations

	Page
Computer software engineers and computer programmers	134
Computer systems analysts	140

Sources of Additional Information

The Occupational Information Network (O*NET) provides information on a wide range of occupational characteristics. Links to O*NET appear at the end of the Internet version of this occupational statement, accessible at **http://www.bls.gov/ooh/ocos128.htm**

Credit Authorizers, Checkers, and Clerks

Nature of the Work

Credit authorizers, checkers, and clerks review credit history and obtain the information needed to determine the creditworthiness of individuals or businesses applying for credit.

Education and Training

Employers may hire clerks with only a high school diploma, but some prefer workers with an accounting education from a trade school or community college. Most employers provide on-the-job training.

Job Outlook

Current and projected employment:
2008 Employment	63,800
2018 Employment	65,600
Employment change	1,800
Growth rate	3%

Employment change. Slower than average growth is expected. While technology continues to improve the efficiency of credit application processing, jobs will continue to arise as a result of increased risk aversion and closer attention to credit policies by lenders.

Job prospects. Prospects should be good. Openings will arise from the need to replace workers who leave the occupation for various reasons, such as advancement to another position.

Earnings

Median annual wages for credit authorizers, checkers, and clerks were $30,390 in May 2008.

Related Occupations

	Page
Bill and account collectors	561
Loan interviewers and clerks	593
Loan officers	109

Sources of Additional Information

State employment offices can provide information about job openings for credit authorizers, checkers, and clerks.

The Occupational Information Network (O*NET) provides information on a wide range of occupational characteristics. Links to O*NET appear at the end of the Internet version of this occupational statement, accessible at **http://www.bls.gov/ooh/ocos129.htm**

Data Entry and Information Processing Workers

Nature of the Work
Data entry and information processing workers enter data into a computer, operate a variety of office machines, and perform other clerical or administrative duties. Data entry and information processing workers also are known as word processors, typists, and data entry keyers, or, less commonly, electronic data processors, keypunch technicians, and transcribers. *Word processors and typists* set up and prepare reports, letters, mailing labels, and other text material. Some may work with highly technical material, plan and key complicated statistical tables, combine and rearrange materials from different sources, or prepare master copies. *Data entry keyers* input lists of items, numbers, or other data, *e.g.*, customers' personal information, medical records, or membership lists, into computers or complete forms that appear on a computer screen. They also may reformat existing data, edit current information, or proofread new entries for accuracy. Data entry keyers may use scanners, electronically transmitted files, or other forms of character recognition systems. Generally, these employees work standard workdays, but technology allows many to work from remote locations, including home, or during off hours when processing demands are less.

Education and Training
Many data entry and information processing workers are hired right out of high school and trained on the job. Spelling, punctuation, and grammar skills are important, as is familiarity with standard office equipment and procedures. Students may acquire skills in keyboarding and in the use of word processing, spreadsheet, and database management software in high schools, community colleges, business schools, temporary help agencies, or using self-teaching aids such as books, tapes, and Internet tutorials.

Job Outlook
Current and projected employment:

2008 Employment	426,200
2018 Employment	400,700
Employment change	-25,500
Growth rate	-6%

Employment change. Employment of data entry and information processing workers is expected to decline moderately. Improved technologies and greater social acceptance of workers performing their own data entry and information processing work will lessen the need for these workers, except for highly detailed or sophisticated work.

Job prospects. The need to replace workers who transfer to other occupations or leave this large occupation for other reasons will produce numerous job openings each year. Job prospects will be most favorable for those with the best technical skills and be willing to upgrade their skills continuously in order to remain marketable.

Earnings
Median annual wages in May 2008 were as follows:

Word processors and typists	$31,390
Data entry keyers	26,120

Related Occupations

	Page
Computer operators	589
Dispatchers, except police, fire, and ambulance	590
Medical records and health information technicians	423
Police, fire, and ambulance dispatchers	595
Secretaries and administrative assistants	583

Sources of Additional Information
➤ International Association of Administrative Professionals, P.O. Box 20404, Kansas City, MO 64195. Internet: **http://www.iaap-hq.org**

The Occupational Information Network (O*NET) provides information on a wide range of occupational characteristics. Links to O*NET appear at the end of the Internet version of this occupational statement, accessible at **http://www.bls.gov/ooh/ocos155.htm**

Dispatchers, Except Police, Fire, and Ambulance

Nature of the Work
Dispatchers schedule and dispatch workers, equipment, or service vehicles to carry materials or passengers. They keep records, logs, and schedules of the calls that they receive and of the transportation vehicles that they monitor and control. Many dispatchers employ computer-aided dispatch systems to accomplish these tasks.

Education and Training
Workers usually have a high school degree and learn the skills needed to do their jobs through a few months of on-the-job training.

Job Outlook
Current and projected employment:

2008 Employment	195,700
2018 Employment	190,700
Employment change	-5,000
Growth rate	-3%

Employment change. Employment is expected to decline slowly. Increasing worker productivity may cause an employment decline; however population growth and economic expansion may limit the decline.

Job prospects. Favorable opportunities are expected, largely due to job openings arising from the need to replace workers who transfer to other occupations or leave the labor force. As the equipment becomes more complex, individuals with computer skills and experience should have the best prospects for employment.

Earnings
Median annual wages for dispatchers, except police, fire, and ambulance, were $33,850 in May 2008.

Related Occupations

Sources of Additional Information
Information about work opportunities for dispatchers is available from local employers and State employment service offices.

The Occupational Information Network (O*NET) provides information on a wide range of occupational characteristics. Links to O*NET appear at the end of the Internet version of this occupational statement, accessible at **http://www.bls.gov/ooh/ocos342.htm**

Eligibility Interviewers, Government Programs

Nature of the Work
Eligibility interviewers, government programs interview applicants for government services and determine if they qualify for government assistance, such as welfare, unemployment benefits, Social Security benefits, and public housing. They prepare case files, determine the appropriate amount of payment, and follow up with recipients to determine their eligibility for services after a certain period.

Education and Training
Most employees are trained on the job and learn from more-experienced workers. Good interpersonal and communication skills and organizational ability are needed for this job.

Job Outlook
Current and projected employment:

2008 Employment	119,500
2018 Employment	130,500
Employment change	11,000
Growth rate	9%

Employment change. Employment is projected to grow about as fast as the average for all occupations. The increase in the number of retiring baby boomers becoming eligible for Social Security and other government entitlement programs will be the main cause of growth in this occupation. However, automation should reduce employment growth for some eligibility interviewers, as more government programs allow people to apply for assistance online.

Job prospects. Job opportunities are expected to be favorable. Prospects will be best for those with a broad range of job skills, such as good customer service, math, and telephone skills.

Earnings
Median annual wages for eligibility interviewers, government programs were $39,310 in May 2008.

Related Occupations

Sources of Additional Information
Information about work opportunities in this occupation is available from local and State Government employment offices.

The Occupational Information Network (O*NET) provides information on a wide range of occupational characteristics. Links to O*NET appear at the end of the Internet version of this occupational statement, accessible at **http://www.bls.gov/ooh/ocos339.htm**

File Clerks

Nature of the Work
File clerks classify, store, retrieve, track, and update records and information.

Education and Training
Most employers prefer applicants with a high school diploma or its equivalent. Most training occurs on the job, and can be learned in a short period of time.

Job Outlook
Current and projected employment:

2008 Employment	212,200
2018 Employment	162,600
Employment change	-49,600
Growth rate	-23%

Employment change. Employment is expected to decline rapidly. Employment is expected to decline due to productivity gains from office automation and the consolidation of clerical jobs. Additionally, most files are stored digitally and can be retrieved electronically, reducing the demand for file clerks.

Job prospects. Favorable opportunities are expected. Despite employment declines, job opportunities should arise from the need to replace workers who leave the labor force or transfer to other occupations. Job prospects will be best for those who have typing and other secretarial skills and who are familiar with a wide range of office machines, especially personal computers.

Earnings
Median annual wages for file clerks were $23,800 in May 2008.

Related Occupations

Sources of Additional Information

The Occupational Information Network (O*NET) provides information on a wide range of occupational characteristics. Links to O*NET appear at the end of the Internet version of this occupational statement, accessible at **http://www.bls.gov/ooh/ocos146.htm**

Hotel, Motel, and Resort Desk Clerks

Nature of the Work

Hotel, motel, and resort desk clerks are the first line of customer service for a lodging property. They register arriving guests, assign rooms, and answer guests' questions on hotel services and other matters. At other times, they check out guests and report problems with guest rooms or public areas to the housekeeping or maintenance staff. Night and weekend work is common and approximately 1 in 4 desk clerks works part time.

Education and Training

Most hotel, motel, and resort desk clerks learn their job through short-term on-the-job training, which describes their job duties, familiarizes them with the hotel's facilities, and provides instruction on how to use the computerized reservation, room assignment, and billing systems. Postsecondary education is not required for this job, but some background or coursework in hospitality is helpful. Most importantly, employers look for people who are friendly and customer-service oriented, well groomed, and display maturity and good judgment.

Job Outlook

Current and projected employment:

2008 Employment	230,200
2018 Employment	261,700
Employment change	31,500
Growth rate	14%

Employment change. Employment of hotel, motel, and resort desk clerks is expected to grow faster than the average. As developers open new hotels, jobs for hotel, motel, and resort desk clerks should become available. The recent trend toward smaller limited-service hotels, which are more efficient to operate and require less staff, however, will mean fewer desk clerks for each hotel. In addition, jobs will be created as consumers begin traveling again after the hiatus brought on by the recent economic downturn.

Job prospects. During recessions, vacation and business travel declines, and hotels and motels need fewer desk clerks; however, newly opened hotels and the need to replace the many desk clerks who leave this occupation each year will offer some new opportunities.

Earnings

Median annual wages for hotel, motel, and resort desk clerks were $19,480 in May 2008.

Related Occupations

Sources of Additional Information

➤ American Hotel & Lodging Association, 1201 New York Ave., NW, Suite 600 Washington, DC 20005. Internet: **http://www.ahla.com**

The Occupational Information Network (O*NET) provides information on a wide range of occupational characteristics. Links to O*NET appear at the end of the Internet version of this occupational statement, accessible at **http://www.bls.gov/ooh/ocos132.htm**

Human Resources Assistants, Except Payroll and Timekeeping

Nature of the Work

Human resources assistants maintain the human resource records of an organization's employees. These records include such information as name, address, job title, and earnings; benefits such as health and life insurance; and tax withholdings.

Education and Training

Employers prefer to hire people who have a high school diploma or its equivalent. Computer, communication, and interpersonal skills are also important.

Job Outlook

Current and projected employment:

2008 Employment	169,700
2018 Employment	160,000
Employment change	-9,700
Growth rate	-6%

Employment change. Employment is expected to decline slowly. Productivity gains from office automation and increases in the use of electronic files will lead to declines in the demand for human resources assistants to do data entry and recordkeeping.

Job prospects. Applicants may face competition. Job opportunities should be best for those with excellent communication and computer skills and a broad based knowledge of general office functions.

Earnings

Median annual wages for human resource assistants, except payroll and timekeeping, were $35,750 in May 2008.

Related Occupations

Sources of Additional Information

➤ Society for Human Resource Management, 1800 Duke St., Alexandria, VA 22314. Internet: **http://www.shrm.org**

The Occupational Information Network (O*NET) provides information on a wide range of occupational characteristics. Links to O*NET appear at the end of the Internet version of this occupational statement, accessible at **http://www.bls.gov/ooh/ocos150.htm**

Interviewers, Except Eligibility and Loan

Nature of the Work

Interviewers obtain and verify information from individuals and businesses by mail, telephone, or in person for the purpose of completing forms, applications, and questionnaires, such as market research surveys, Census forms, college admission applications, and medical histories. They review the answers for completeness and accuracy and record the information.

Education and Training

Most employers prefer applicants with a high school diploma or its equivalent or a mix of education and related experience. New employees generally are trained on the job.

Job Outlook

Current and projected employment:

2008 Employment 233,400
2018 Employment 269,900
Employment change..36,400
Growth rate.. 16%

Employment change. Employment is projected to grow faster than the average for all occupations. Rapid growth in the healthcare and market research industries that employ the majority of these workers will generate jobs for interviewers. However, the expanding use of online surveys and questionnaires to conduct market research and the increasing use of digital health records will impede growth.

Job prospects. Job prospects are expected to be good. Turnover is generally high for this occupation where over a quarter of the jobs are part time. Applicants with good customer service and communications skills and those that are detail oriented should have the best prospects.

Earnings

Median annual wages for interviewers, except eligibility and loan, were $28,140 in May 2008.

Related Occupations

Sources of Additional Information

The Occupational Information Network (O*NET) provides information on a wide range of occupational characteristics. Links to O*NET appear at the end of the Internet version of this occupational statement, accessible at **http://www.bls.gov/ooh/ocos340.htm**

Loan Interviewers and Clerks

Nature of the Work

Loan interviewers, also called *loan processors* or *loan clerks*, interview applicants and others to obtain and verify personal and financial information for the purposes of completing loan applications. They also prepare the documents that go to the appraiser and are issued at closing.

Education and Training

A high school diploma or equivalent is generally the minimum needed to get into the occupation; some college coursework is usually preferred. Once hired, new interviewers receive short-term on-the-job-training to learn about pricing loans and about the rules and regulations regarding the issuing of loans. Excellent written and verbal communication skills are essential.

Job Outlook

Current and projected employment:

2008 Employment 210,400
2018 Employment 219,400
Employment change..9,100
Growth rate.. 4%

Employment change. Employment is projected to grow slower than the average for all occupations. A growing population will, over time, spur demand for home loans and, thus, for loan interviewers to verify and process financial data on the application and to assemble documents and prepare them for settlement. However, the increasing use of online applications will limit demand for loan interviewers.

Job prospects. Prospects will be best for applicants with a broad range of job skills, including good customer service, math, and telephone skills. The job outlook for loan interviewers and clerks is sensitive to overall economic activity.

Earnings

Median annual wages for loan interviewers and clerks were $32,470 in May 2008.

Related Occupations

Sources of Additional Information

➤ Mortgage Bankers Association, 1331 L St., NW., Washington, DC 20005. Internet: **http://www.mortgagebankers.org**

The Occupational Information Network (O*NET) provides information on a wide range of occupational characteristics. Links to O*NET appear at the end of the Internet version of this occupational statement, accessible at **http://www.bls.gov/ooh/ocos341.htm**

Meter Readers, Utilities

Nature of the Work

Meter readers read electric, gas, water, or steam consumption meters and record the volume used. They also inspect the meters and their connections for any defects or damage and supply repair and maintenance workers with the information necessary to fix damaged meters.

Education and Training

Most meter reader jobs require a high school diploma and a valid driver's license. Many people start utility careers in this occupation with the goal of advancing to positions with more responsibility.

Job Outlook

Current and projected employment:

2008 Employment	45,300
2018 Employment	36,300
Employment change	-9,100
Growth rate	-20%

Employment change. Employment is expected to decline rapidly. New Automatic Meter Reader (AMR) systems allow meters to be monitored and billed from a central point, reducing the need for meter readers.

Job prospects. Jobseekers can expect competition. Although this is a declining occupation, job opportunities are expected to be good because of the need to replace workers leaving the occupation.

Earnings

Median annual wages for meter readers, utilities were $32,950 in May 2008.

Related Occupations

	Page
Line installers and repairers	713
Power plant operators, distributors, and dispatchers	760

Sources of Additional Information

➤ International Brotherhood of Electrical Workers, 900 Seventh St. NW, Washington, DC 20001. Internet: **http://www.ibew.org**

The Occupational Information Network (O*NET) provides information on a wide range of occupational characteristics. Links to O*NET appear at the end of the Internet version of this occupational statement, accessible at **http://www.bls.gov/ooh/ocos282.htm**

Office and Administrative Support Worker Supervisors and Managers

Nature of the Work

Office and administrative support supervisors and managers plan or supervise support staff to ensure that they can work efficiently. After allocating work assignments and issuing deadlines, office and administrative support supervisors and managers oversee the work to ensure that it is proceeding on schedule and meeting established quality standards.

Education and Training

Many employers require office and administrative support supervisors and managers to have postsecondary training—and in some cases, an associate or even a bachelor's degree. Most firms fill office and administrative support supervisory and managerial positions by promoting office or administrative support workers from within their organizations.

Job Outlook

Current and projected employment:

2008 Employment	1,457,200
2018 Employment	1,617,500
Employment change	160,300
Growth rate	11%

Employment change. Employment of office and administrative support supervisors and managers is expected to grow about as fast as the average for all occupations through the year 2018. Continuing advances in technology should increase office and administrative support workers' productivity and allow a wider variety of tasks to be performed by people in professional positions.

Job prospects. Keen competition is expected for jobs as the number of applicants greatly exceeds the number of job openings. Opportunities will continue to be best for those office and administrative support worker supervisors and managers who show leadership and team building skills, and who are able to multitask, communicate well, and keep abreast of technological advances.

Earnings

Median annual wages for office and administrative support worker supervisors and managers were $45,790 in May 2008.

Related Occupations

	Page
Administrative services managers	29
Education administrators	41
Office clerks, general	581
Secretaries and administrative assistants	583

Sources of Additional Information

➤ International Association of Administrative Professionals, P.O. Box 20404, Kansas City, MO 64195-0404. Internet: **http://www.iaap-hq.org**

The Occupational Information Network (O*NET) provides information on a wide range of occupational characteristics. Links to O*NET appear at the end of the Internet version of this occupational statement, accessible at **http://www.bls.gov/ooh/ocos127.htm**

Order Clerks

Nature of the Work

Order clerks receive and process orders for a variety of goods or services and inform customers of receipt, prices, shipping dates, and delays. Order clerks also prepare simple contracts and handle customer complaints.

Education and Training

Most order clerks are trained on the job. Employers prefer workers with a high school diploma or its equivalent, and who are computer literate and proficient in word-processing and spreadsheet software.

Job Outlook

Current and projected employment:

2008 Employment 245,700
2018 Employment 181,500
Employment change.. -64,200
Growth rate..-26%

Employment change. Employment is expected to decline rapidly. Improvements in technology and office automation continue to increase worker productivity and decrease the need for order clerks.

Job prospects. Favorable opportunities are expected. Despite employment declines, numerous openings will occur each year to replace order clerks who transfer to other occupations or leave the labor force. Many of these openings will be for seasonal work, especially in catalog companies or online retailers catering to holiday gift buyers.

Earnings

Median annual wages for order clerks were $27,990 in May 2008.

Related Occupations

	Page
Cargo and freight agents	572
Customer service representatives	567
Stock clerks and order fillers	598

Sources of Additional Information

The Occupational Information Network (O*NET) provides information on a wide range of occupational characteristics. Links to O*NET appear at the end of the Internet version of this occupational statement, accessible at **http://www.bls.gov/ooh/ocos148.htm**

Payroll and Timekeeping Clerks

Nature of the Work

Payroll and timekeeping clerks compile and post employee time and payroll data. They ensure that employees are paid on time and that their paychecks are accurate.

Education and Training

Payroll and timekeeping clerks typically learn the skills they need on the job. Employers prefer high school graduates who have computer skills.

Job Outlook

Current and projected employment:

2008 Employment 208,700
2018 Employment 197,700
Employment change.. -10,900
Growth rate..-5%

Employment change. Employment is projected to decline slowly. Increased automation of the payroll and timekeeping process, and the use of computer software that allows employees to update and record their own payroll and timekeeping information, will decrease the need for payroll and timekeeping clerks.

Job prospects. Favorable opportunities are expected. Despite the projected employment decline, job openings will arise each year as payroll and timekeeping clerks leave the labor force or transfer to other occupations. Those who have completed a certification program, indicating that they can handle more complex payroll issues, will have an advantage in the job market.

Earnings

Median annual wages for payroll and timekeeping clerks were $34,810 in May 2008.

Related Occupations

	Page
Bill and account collectors	561
Billing and posting clerks and machine operators	587
Bookkeeping, accounting, and auditing clerks	563

Sources of Additional Information

➤ American Payroll Association, 660 North Main Ave., Suite 100, San Antonio, TX 78205. Internet: **http://www.americanpayroll.org**

The Occupational Information Network (O*NET) provides information on a wide range of occupational characteristics. Links to O*NET appear at the end of the Internet version of this occupational statement, accessible at**http://www.bls.gov/ooh/ocos149.htm**

Police, Fire, and Ambulance Dispatchers

Nature of the Work

Police, fire, and ambulance dispatchers, also called 911 operators, monitor the location of emergency services personnel from their jurisdiction's emergency services departments. These workers dispatch the appropriate type and number of units in response to calls for assistance.

Education and Training

Workers usually have a high school degree and develop the necessary skills in about 3 to 6 months of on-the-job training. Many States require specific types of training or certification from a professional association.

Job Outlook

Current and projected employment:

2008 Employment	99,900
2018 Employment	117,700
Employment change	17,800
Growth rate	18%

Employment change. Employment is expected to grow faster than average. The growing and aging population will increase demand for emergency services and create new jobs for police, fire, and ambulance dispatchers. Growth may be slowed in some places, as some municipalities consolidate their call centers.

Job prospects. Favorable opportunities are expected, largely due to job openings arising from the need to replace workers who transfer to other occupations or leave the labor force. As the equipment dispatchers use becomes more complex, individuals with computer skills should have the best opportunities.

Earnings

Median annual wages for police, fire, and ambulance dispatchers were $33,670 in May 2008.

Related Occupations

	Page
Air traffic controllers	784
Communications equipment operators	588
Customer service representatives	567
Dispatchers, except police, fire, and ambulance	590
Reservation and transportation ticket agents and travel clerks	598

Sources of Additional Information

➤ Association of Public Safety Communications Officials, International, 351 N. Williamson Blvd., Daytona Beach, FL 32114. Internet: **http://www.apco911.org**

The Occupational Information Network (O*NET) provides information on a wide range of occupational characteristics. Links to O*NET appear at the end of the Internet version of this occupational statement, accessible at **http://www.bls.gov/ooh/ocos343.htm**

Postal Service Clerks

Nature of the Work

Postal Service clerks sell stamps, money orders, postal stationery, and mailing envelopes and boxes in post offices throughout the country. These workers register, certify, and insure mail, calculate and collect postage, and answer questions about other postal matters.

Education and Training

All applicants for Postal Service jobs are required to take an examination. Additionally, they must be at least 18 years of age and a U.S. citizen or have been granted permanent resident-alien status in the United States. Males must have registered with the Selective Service upon reaching age 18. A good command of the English language is also required.

Job Outlook

Current and projected employment:

2008 Employment	75,800
2018 Employment	62,100
Employment change	-13,700
Growth rate	-18%

Employment change. Employment is projected to decline rapidly. Postal Service clerks will be adversely affected by the decline in first-class mail volume because of the increasing use of electronic mail and automated bill pay.

Job prospects. Keen competition for jobs is expected. The number of applicants usually exceeds the number of job openings because of the occupation's low entry requirements and attractive wages and benefits.

Earnings

Median annual wages of postal service clerks were $51,040 in May 2008.

Related Occupations

	Page
Counter and rental clerks	560
Postal Service mail carriers	575
Postal Service mail sorters, processors, and processing machine operators	596
Shipping, receiving, and traffic clerks	577

Sources of Additional Information

➤ United States Postal Service. Contact your local post office. Internet: **http://www.usps.com**

The Occupational Information Network (O*NET) provides information on a wide range of occupational characteristics. Links to O*NET appear at the end of the Internet version of this occupational statement, accessible at **http://www.bls.gov/ooh/ocos344.htm**

Postal Service Mail Sorters, Processors, and Processing Machine Operators

Nature of the Work

Postal Service mail sorters, processors, and processing machine operators prepare incoming and outgoing mail for distribution at post offices and at mail processing centers. They load and unload postal trucks and move mail around mail processing centers. They also load and operate mail processing, sorting, and canceling machinery.

Education and Training

All applicants for Postal Service jobs are required to take a Postal Service examination. Additionally, they must be at least 18 years of age, and be a U.S. citizen or have been granted permanent resident-alien status in the United States. Males must have registered with the Selective Service upon reaching age 18. A good command of the English language also is required.

Job Outlook

Current and projected employment:
2008 Employment 179,900
2018 Employment 125,300
Employment change... -54,500
Growth rate..-30%

Employment change. Employment is projected to decline rapidly. Increased use of automated equipment for sorting and processing mail reduces the need for employees in this occupation. Employment also will be negatively affected by companies increasingly presorting their own mail before it arrives at the Post Office to qualify for postage rate reductions.

Job prospects. Keen competition for jobs is expected. The number of applicants usually exceeds the number of job openings because of the occupation's low entry requirements and attractive wages and benefits.

Earnings

Median annual wages for Postal Service mail sorters, processors, and processing machine operators were $50,020 in May 2008.

Related Occupations

Sources of Additional Information

➤ United States Postal Service. Contact your local post office. Internet: **http://www.usps.com**

The Occupational Information Network (O*NET) provides information on a wide range of occupational characteristics. Links to O*NET appear at the end of the Internet version of this occupational statement, accessible at **http://www.bls.gov/ooh/ocos346.htm**

Procurement Clerks

Nature of the Work

Procurement clerks compile requests for materials, prepare purchase orders, keep track of purchases and supplies, and handle inquiries about orders. They make sure that what was purchased arrives on schedule and meets the purchaser's specifications.

Education and Training

Most employers prefer applicants who have a high school diploma or its equivalent. Most procurement clerks are trained on the job under close supervision of more experienced employees.

Job Outlook

Current and projected employment:
2008 Employment 81,500
2018 Employment 86,200
Employment change..4,800
Growth rate... 6%

Employment change. Employment is expected to grow more slowly than the average. The need for procurement clerks will be reduced, as the use of computers to place orders directly with suppliers and as ordering over the Internet becomes more prevalent.

Job prospects. Job prospects are expected to be favorable. Job openings will arise out of the need to replace workers who transfer to other occupations or leave the labor force.

Earnings

Median hourly wages for procurement clerks were $16.72 in May 2008.

Related Occupations

Sources of Additional Information

The Occupational Information Network (O*NET) provides information on a wide range of occupational characteristics. Links to O*NET appear at the end of the Internet version of this occupational statement, accessible at **http://www.bls.gov/ooh/ocos279.htm**

Production, Planning, and Expediting Clerks

Nature of the Work

Production and planning clerks compile records and reports on various aspects of production, such as materials and parts used, products produced, machine and instrument readings, and frequency of defects. Expediting clerks contact vendors and shippers to ensure that merchandise, supplies, and equipment are forwarded on the specified shipping dates.

Education and Training

Many production, planning, and expediting jobs are at the entry level and do not require more than a high school diploma. These clerks usually learn the job by doing routine tasks under close supervision. Computer skills are very important.

Job Outlook

Current and projected employment:
2008 Employment 283,500
2018 Employment 287,800
Employment change..4,300
Growth rate... 2%

Employment change. Employment of production, planning, and expediting clerks is projected to show little or no growth over the 2008–2018 projection period. As greater emphasis is placed on the timely delivery of goods and services throughout the economy, there will be increasing need for production, planning, and expediting clerks at all levels of the supply chain. However, the expected employment declines in manufacturing will limit the growth of this occupation.

Job prospects. In addition to new jobs, job openings will arise from the need to replace production, planning, and expediting clerks who leave the labor force or transfer to other occupations. Opportunities will be better in industries that are experiencing faster growth, such as wholesale trade and warehousing.

Earnings

Median annual wages for production, planning, and expediting clerks were $40,480 in May 2008.

Related Occupations

	Page
Cargo and freight agents	572
Shipping, receiving, and traffic clerks	577
Stock clerks and order fillers	598
Weighers, measurers, checkers, and samplers, recordkeeping	599

Sources of Additional Information

The Occupational Information Network (O*NET) provides information on a wide range of occupational characteristics. Links to O*NET appear at the end of the Internet version of this occupational statement, accessible at **http://www.bls.gov/ooh/ocos283.htm**

Reservation and Transportation Ticket Agents and Travel Clerks

Nature of the Work

Reservation and transportation ticket agents and travel clerks make and confirm travel reservations and sell tickets to passengers. They may check baggage and direct passengers to designated departure areas, or provide tourists with travel information, such as points of interest, restaurants, rates, and emergency services. Some work at transportation center ticket counters and travel offices, while others answer telephones and e-mail at reservation call centers or at individual properties. Most work a standard 40-hour week in locations that typically operate around the clock.

Education and Training

Most workers in this occupation need only a high school diploma or its equivalent. Much of the training comes from company-sponsored programs where they learn about the company's reservation system and ticketing procedures and travel-related information.

Job Outlook

Current and projected employment:

2008 Employment	168,300
2018 Employment	181,900
Employment change	13,600
Growth rate	8%

Employment change. Employment of reservation and transportation ticket agents and travel clerks is expected to grow as fast as average. Increased use of online reservations systems and self-service ticketing machines will reduce the number of people necessary to provide these services.

Job prospects. Applicants for these jobs are likely to encounter competition in part because of the low entry requirements and good travel benefits offered by many companies in the travel industry. Employment opportunities may fluctuate with the economy which often has a strong impact on travel industry employment.

Earnings

Median annual wages for reservation and transportation ticket agents and travel clerks were $31,070 in May 2008.

Related Occupations

	Page
Hotel, motel, and resort desk clerks	592
Receptionists and information clerks	570
Travel agents	557

Sources of Additional Information

The Occupational Information Network (O*NET) provides information on a wide range of occupational characteristics. Links to O*NET appear at the end of the Internet version of this occupational statement, accessible at **http://www.bls.gov/ooh/ocos135.htm**

Stock Clerks and Order Fillers

Nature of the Work

Stock clerks receive merchandise in stores, warehouses, stockrooms, and other storage facilities; unpack it; mark items with identifying codes, such as price, stock, or inventory control codes; stock shelves; and help customers with their packages. Order fillers complete customers mail, Web, and phone orders by retrieving the ordered merchandise, computing the prices and recording the sale, and preparing it for shipment. Most jobs are physically demanding and may result in minor muscle ailments, scrapes, or other injuries. In retail establishments, evening and weekend hours are common.

Education and Training

A high school diploma or GED is usually sufficient for this occupation. Most stock clerks and order fillers learn their jobs through short-term on-the-job training.

Job Outlook

Current and projected employment:

2008 Employment	1,858,800
2018 Employment	1,993,300
Employment change	134,400
Growth rate	7%

Employment change. Average growth in the employment of stock clerks and order fillers is expected. Most stock clerks and order fillers work in retail trade, most notably in grocery and department stores, stocking shelves and retrieving items for customers. These tasks, which usually require handling small quantities of items, are difficult to automate.

Job prospects. Numerous job openings will occur due to the need to replace workers who leave the occupation, a characteristic of very large occupations with minimal training requirements. Job openings in grocery, general merchandise, clothing, and department stores will be greater than in other industries, because much of the work is done manually and is difficult to automate.

Earnings

Median annual wages for stock clerks and order fillers were $20,800 in May 2008.

Related Occupations

Sources of Additional Information

The Occupational Information Network (O*NET) provides information on a wide range of occupational characteristics. Links to O*NET appear at the end of the Internet version of this occupational statement, accessible at **http://www.bls.gov/ooh/ocos139.htm**

Tellers

Nature of the Work

Bank tellers are responsible for quickly and accurately processing routine transactions that customers conduct at banks. Routine transactions include cashing checks and making deposits, loan payments, and withdrawals.

Education and Training

Most teller jobs require a high school diploma and a background check. Tellers are usually trained on the job.

Job Outlook

Current and projected employment:

2008 Employment	600,500
2018 Employment	638,000
Employment change	37,500
Growth rate	6%

Employment change. Employment of tellers is expected to grow more slowly than average. To attract customers, banks are opening new branch offices in a variety of locations, such as grocery stores, and keeping their branches open longer during the day and on weekends. Both of these trends are expected to result in some job growth for tellers, particularly those who work part time.

Job prospects. Job prospects for tellers are expected to be favorable. Most job openings will arise from growth and from the need to replace the many tellers who transfer to other occupations.

Earnings

Median annual wages for tellers were $23,610 in May 2008.

Related Occupations

Sources of Additional Information

Contact your local bank for additional information.

The Occupational Information Network (O*NET) provides information on a wide range of occupational characteristics. Links to O*NET appear at the end of the Internet version of this occupational statement, accessible at **http://www.bls.gov/ooh/ocos126.htm**

Weighers, Measurers, Checkers, and Samplers, Recordkeeping

Nature of the Work

Weighers, measurers, checkers, and samplers weigh, measure, and check materials, supplies, and equipment to keep accurate records. Most of their duties are clerical. They verify the quantity, quality, and overall value of the items they are responsible for and check the condition of items purchased, sold, or produced against records, bills, invoices, or receipts.

Education and Training

Most jobs do not require more than a high school diploma or its equivalent. However, preference is given to applicants familiar with computers. Typing, filing, recordkeeping, and other clerical skills are important.

Job Outlook

Current and projected employment:

2008 Employment	71,900
2018 Employment	62,400
Employment change	-9,400
Growth rate	-13%

Employment change. Employment is projected to decline rapidly. Increased use of automated equipment that performs the functions of these workers will lessen the need for weighers, checkers, measurers, and samplers.

Job prospects. Favorable opportunities are expected. Despite employment declines, job opportunities should arise from the need to replace workers who leave the labor force or transfer to other occupations.

Earnings

Median annual wages for weighers, measurers, checkers, and samplers, recordkeeping were $26,940 in May 2008.

Related Occupations

Sources of Additional Information

The Occupational Information Network (O*NET) provides information on a wide range of occupational characteristics. Links to O*NET appear at the end of the Internet version of this occupational statement, accessible at **http://www.bls.gov/ooh/ocos284.htm**

Farming, Fishing, and Forestry Occupations

Fishers and Fishing Vessel Operators

Significant Points

- This occupation is characterized by strenuous work, long hours, seasonal employment, and some of the most hazardous conditions in the workforce.

- About 56 percent of all workers are self-employed, among the highest proportions in the workforce.

- Fishers usually begin as deckhands and acquire their occupational skills on the job.

- Employment is projected to decline moderately.

Nature of the Work

Fishers and fishing vessel operators catch and trap various types of marine life for human consumption, animal feed, bait, and other uses. (Aquaculture—the raising and harvesting, under controlled conditions, of fish and other aquatic life in ponds or confined bodies of water—is covered in the *Handbook* statement on farmers, ranchers, and agricultural managers.)

Fishing hundreds of miles from shore with commercial fishing vessels—large boats capable of hauling a catch of tens of thousands of pounds of fish—requires a crew that includes a captain, or skipper, a first mate and sometimes a second mate, a boatswain (called a deckboss on some smaller boats), and deckhands with specialized skills.

The *fishing boat captain* plans and oversees the fishing operation, the fish to be sought, the location of the best fishing grounds, the method of capture, the duration of the trip, and the sale of the catch.

The captain ensures that the fishing vessel is seaworthy; oversees the purchase of supplies, gear, and equipment, such as fuel, netting, and cables; obtains the required fishing permits and licenses; and hires qualified crew members and assigns their duties. The captain plots the vessel's course using compasses, charts, and electronic navigational equipment, such as loran systems or GPS navigation systems. Captains also use radar and sonar to avoid obstacles above and below the water and to detect fish. Sophisticated tracking technology allows captains to better locate schools of fish. The captain directs the fishing operation through subordinate officers' and records daily activities in the ship's log. In port, the captain sells the catch to wholesalers, food processors, or through a fish auction and ensures that each crew member receives the prearranged portion of the proceeds. Captains increasingly use the Internet to bypass processors and sell fish directly to consumers, grocery stores, and restaurants often even before they return to port.

The *first mate* is the captain's assistant and assumes control of the vessel when the captain is off duty. Duty shifts, called watches, usually last 6 hours. In this role, the first mate must be familiar with navigation requirements and the operation of all electronic equipment. The mate's regular duty though, with the help of the boatswain and under the captain's oversight, is to direct the fishing operations and sailing responsibilities of the deckhands, including the operation, maintenance, and repair of the vessel and the gathering, preservation, stowing, and unloading of the catch.

The *boatswain*, a highly experienced deckhand with supervisory responsibilities, directs the *deckhands* as they carry out the sailing and fishing operations. Before departure, the deckhands load equipment and supplies. When necessary, boatswains repair fishing gear, equipment, nets, and accessories. They operate the fishing gear, letting out and pulling in nets and lines, and extract the catch, such as cod, flounder, and tuna, from the nets or the lines' hooks. Deckhands use dip nets to prevent the escape of small fish and gaffs to facilitate the landing of large fish. They then wash, salt, ice, and stow away the catch. Deckhands also must ensure that decks are clear and clean at all times and that the vessel's engines and equipment are kept in good working order. Unless "lumpers" (laborers or longshore workers) are hired, the deckhands unload the catch.

Large fishing vessels that operate in deep water generally have technologically advanced equipment, and some may have facilities on board where the fish are processed and prepared for sale. Such vessels are equipped for long stays at sea and can perform the work of several smaller boats.

Some fishers work on small boats in relatively shallow waters, often in sight of land. Navigation and communication needs are vital and constant for almost all types of boats. On these small boats, crews often consist of one or two members who are involved in all aspects of the fishing operation. Their work might include placing gill nets across the mouths of rivers or inlets, entrapment nets in bays and lakes, or pots and traps for fish or shellfish such as lobsters and crabs. Dredges and scrapes are sometimes used to gather shellfish such as oysters and scallops. A very small proportion of commercial fishing is conducted as diving operations. Depending upon the water's depth, divers wearing regulation diving suits with an umbilical (air line) or a scuba outfit and equipment use spears to catch fish and use nets and other equipment to gather shellfish, coral, sea urchins, abalone, and sponges. In very shallow waters, fish are caught from small boats with an outboard motor, from rowboats, or by wading from shore. Fishers use a wide variety of hand-operated equipment, including nets, tongs, rakes, hoes, hooks, and shovels, to gather fish and shellfish; to catch amphibians and reptiles such as frogs and turtles; and to harvest marine vegetation such as Irish moss and kelp.

Although most fishers are involved in commercial fishing, some captains and deckhands use their expertise in fishing for sport or recreational purposes. For this type of fishing, a group of people charter a fishing vessel with a captain, and possibly several

A fisher tends to his equipment on his fishing boat.

deckhands, for periods ranging from several hours to a number of days and embark upon sportfishing, socializing, and relaxation.

Work environment. Fishing operations are conducted under various environmental conditions, depending on the region, body of water, and the kind of species sought. Storms, fog, and wind may hamper fishing vessels or cause them to suspend fishing operations and return to port. In relatively busy fisheries, boats have to take care to avoid collisions.

Fishers and fishing vessel operators work under some of the most hazardous conditions of any occupation, and transportation to a hospital or doctor often is not readily available when injuries occur. The crew must be on guard against the danger of injury from malfunctioning fishing gear, entanglement in fishing nets and gear, slippery decks, ice formation in the winter, or being swept overboard by a large wave. Malfunctioning navigation or communication equipment may lead to collisions or shipwrecks.

Fishers and fishing vessel operators endure strenuous outdoor work and long hours. Commercial fishing trips may require a stay of several weeks, or even months, hundreds of miles away from one's home port. The pace of work may vary, but even during travel between the home port and the fishing grounds deckhands on smaller boats usually try to finish their cleaning and maintenance duties so that there are no chores remaining to be done at port. However, lookout watches are a regular responsibility, and crew members must be prepared to stand watch at prearranged times of the day or night. Although fishing gear has improved, and operations have become more mechanized, netting and processing fish are strenuous activities. Newer vessels have improved living quarters and amenities such as television and shower stalls, but crews still experience the aggravations of confined quarters, continuous close personal contact, and the absence of family.

Training, Other Qualifications, and Advancement

Fishers usually acquire their occupational skills on the job. There are no formal academic training requirements.

Education and training. Most fishers begin as deckhands and learn their trade on the job. Deckhands normally start by finding work through family, friends, or simply walking around the docks and asking for employment. Some larger trawlers

and processing ships are run by larger companies, where new workers can apply through the companies' human resources department. Operators of large commercial fishing vessels are required to complete a Coast Guard-approved training course. Students can expedite their entrance into these occupations by enrolling in 2-year vocational-technical programs offered by secondary schools. In addition, some community colleges and universities offer fishery technology and related programs that include courses in seamanship, vessel operations, marine safety, navigation, vessel repair and maintenance, health emergencies, and fishing gear technology. Secondary and postsecondary programs are normally offered in or near coastal areas, and usually include hands-on experience.

Experienced fishers may find short-term workshops especially useful. These generally are offered through various postsecondary institutions and provide a good working knowledge of electronic equipment used in navigation and communication and offer information on the latest improvements in fishing gear.

Licensure. Captains and mates on large fishing vessels of at least 200 gross tons must be licensed. Captains of sportfishing boats used for charter, regardless of the boats' size, must also be licensed. Crew members on certain fish-processing vessels may need a merchant mariner's document. The U.S. Coast Guard issues these documents and licenses to individuals who meet the stipulated health, physical, and academic requirements. (For information about merchant marine occupations, see the section on water transportation occupations elsewhere in the *Handbook*.) States set licensing requirements for boats operating in State waters, defined as inland waters and waters within 3 miles of the coast.

Fishers need a permit to fish in almost any water. Permits are distributed by States for State waters and by regional fishing councils for Federal waters. The permits specify the season when fishing is allowed, the type of fish that may be caught, and sometimes the type of fishing gear that is permissible.

Other qualifications. Fishers must be in good health and possess physical strength. Good coordination, mechanical aptitude, and the ability to work under difficult or dangerous conditions are necessary to operate, maintain, and repair equipment and fishing gear. Fishers need stamina to work long hours at sea, often under difficult conditions. On large vessels, they must be able to work as members of a team. Fishers must be patient, yet always alert, to overcome the boredom of long watches when they are not engaged in fishing operations. The ability to assume any deckhand's functions on short notice is important. As supervisors, mates must be able to assume all duties, including the captain's, when necessary. The captain must be highly experienced, mature, and decisive and also must possess the skills needed to run business operations.

Advancement. On fishing vessels, most fishers begin as deckhands. Experienced, reliable deckhands who display supervisory qualities may become boatswains, who, in turn, may become second mates, first mates, and, finally, captains. Deckhands who acquire experience and whose interests are in ship engineering—the maintenance and repair of ship engines and equipment—can eventually become licensed chief engineers on large commercial vessels after meeting the Coast Guard's experience, physical, and academic requirements. Almost all captains become self-employed, and the overwhelming majority eventually own, or have an interest in, one or more fishing ships. Some may choose to run a sport or recreational fishing operation.

Employment

Fishers and fishing vessel operators held an estimated 35,600 jobs in 2008. Over half were self-employed. Most fishing takes place off the coasts, particularly off Alaska, the Gulf Coast, Virginia, California, and New England. Alaska ranks the highest in total volume of fish caught, according to the National Marine Fisheries Service. Many fishers are seasonal workers and positions are usually filled by people who work primarily in other occupations, such as teachers, or by students. For example, salmon season causes employment of fishers in Alaska to more than double during the summer. Because fishing is mostly seasonal and workers are often self-employed, measuring total employment is difficult.

Job Outlook

Employment of fishers and fishing vessel operators is projected to decline moderately as regulations relating to the replenishment of fish stocks reduce allowable fishing.

Employment change. Employment of fishers and fishing vessel operators is expected to decline moderately by 8 percent through the year 2018. Fishers and fishing vessel operators depend on the natural ability of fish stocks to replenish themselves through growth and reproduction, as well as on governmental regulation to promote replenishment of fisheries. As the use of sophisticated electronic equipment for navigation, communication, and locating fish has raised the efficiency of finding fish stocks, the need for setting limits to catches also has risen. Additionally, improvements in fishing gear and the use of highly automated floating processors, where the catch is processed aboard the vessel, have greatly increased fish hauls.

Fisheries councils issue various types of restrictions to prevent over-harvesting and to allow stocks of fish and shellfish to naturally replenish. Fishing councils are shifting to an individual quota system that tends to reduce employment. Nonetheless, such a system is beneficial for those who remain in the industry because it allows for longer fishing seasons, better investment returns, and steadier employment.

In addition, rising seafood imports and increasing competition from farm-raised fish are adversely affecting fishing income and is also causing some fishers to leave the industry. However, competition from farm-raised and imported seafood tends to be concentrated in specific species and thus should have more of an impact in some regions than others.

Governmental efforts to replenish stocks are having some positive results, which should increase the stock of fish in the future. Furthermore, efforts by private fishers' associations

on the West Coast to increase government monitoring of the fisheries may help to prevent the type of decline in fish stocks found in waters off the East Coast. Nevertheless, pollution is now being recognized as a new factor affecting the reproduction of fish, a scenario that may take years to mitigate. Consequently, fewer fishers and fishing vessel operators are expected to make their living from the Nation's waters in the years ahead.

Job prospects. The vast majority of job openings will result from the need to replace fishers and fishing vessel operators who leave the occupation because of the strenuous and hazardous nature of the job and the lack of steady, year-round income. The best prospects should be with large fishing operations, while opportunities with small independent fishers are expected to be limited. Sportfishing boats may provide some job opportunities.

Earnings

In May 2008, median annual wages of wage-and-salary fishers were $27,950. The middle 50 percent earned between $19,510 and $33,580. The bottom 10 percent earned less than $16,080, while the top 10 percent earned more than $45,930. Earnings of fishers and fishing vessel operators normally are highest in the summer and fall when demand for their catch and environmental conditions are favorable and lowest during the winter. Many full-time and most part-time workers supplement their income by working in other activities during the off-season.

Earnings of fishers vary widely, depending upon their position, their ownership percentage of the vessel, the size of their ship, and the amount and value of the catch. The costs of the fishing operation such as fuel, repair and maintenance of gear and equipment, and the crew's supplies are deducted from the sale of the catch. Net proceeds are distributed among the crew members in accordance with a prearranged percentage. Generally, the ship's owner, usually its captain, receives half of the net proceeds. From this amount, the owner pays for depreciation, maintenance and repair, and replacement and insurance costs of the ship and its equipment; the money that remains is the owner's profit.

Related Occupations

Other occupations that involve outdoor work with fish and watercraft include:

	Page
Fish and game wardens	473
Water transportation occupations	805

Many ships not only catch the fish but also cut, trim, and preserve it. Seafood processing work done on land is performed by meat, poultry, and fish cutters and trimmers.

Projections data from the National Employment Matrix

Occupational Title	SOC Code	Employment, 2008	Projected Employment, 2018	Change, 2008-2018	
				Number	Percent
Fishers and related fishing workers	45-3011	35,600	32,900	-2,700	-8

(NOTE) Data in this table are rounded. See the discussion of the employment projections table in the *Handbook* introductory chapter on *Occupational Information Included in the Handbook.*

Sources of Additional Information

Information on licensing of fishing vessel captains and mates and on requirements for merchant mariner documentation is available from the U.S. Coast Guard Marine Inspection Office or Marine Safety Office in your State. Or contact either of the following agencies:

➤ National Maritime Center, Coast Guard Headquarters, 2100 Second Street, SW., Washington, DC. 20593-0005. Internet: **http://www.uscg.mil/nmc/**

➤ Commanding Officer (MSC), 2100 Second St. SW, Stop 7102, Washington, DC 20593-7102. Internet: **http://www.uscg.mil/hq/msc/**

The Occupational Information Network (O*NET) provides information on a wide range of occupational characteristics. Links to O*NET appear at the end of the Internet version of this occupational statement, accessible at **http://www.bls.gov/ooh/ocos177.htm**

Forest and Conservation Workers

Significant Points

- Most forest and conservation workers develop skills through on-the-job training.

- Seasonal demand for forest and conservation workers can vary by region and time of year.

- The best employment opportunities should continue to be in Maine, the Southeast, and the Pacific Northwest.

Nature of the Work

The Nation's forests are a rich natural resource, providing beauty, tranquility, and varied recreational benefits, as well as wood for commercial use. Managing and harvesting the forests and woodlands require many different kinds of workers. Forest and conservation workers help develop, maintain, and protect the forests by growing and planting new seedlings, fighting insects and diseases that attack trees, and helping to control soil erosion.

Forest and conservation workers perform a variety of tasks to reforest and conserve timberlands and to maintain forest facilities, such as roads and campsites. Some forest workers, called tree planters, use digging and planting tools called "dibbles" and "hoedads" to plant seedlings to reforest timberland areas. Forest workers also remove diseased or undesirable trees with power saws or handsaws, spray trees with insecticides and fungicides to kill insects and to protect against disease, and apply herbicides on undesirable brush to reduce competing vegetation. Those who work for State and local governments or who are under contract with them also clear away brush and debris from camp trails, roadsides, and camping areas. Some forest workers clean kitchens and rest rooms at recreational facilities and campgrounds. In private industry, forest workers usually working under the direction of professional foresters, may paint boundary lines, assist with controlled burning, aid

in marking and measuring trees, and keep tallies of examined and counted trees.

Other forest and conservation workers work in forest nurseries, sorting out tree seedlings and discarding those not meeting standards of root formation, stem development, and condition of foliage.

Some forest workers are employed on tree farms, where they plant, cultivate, and harvest many different kinds of trees. Their duties vary with the type of farm. Those who work on specialty farms, such as farms growing Christmas or ornamental trees for nurseries, are responsible for shearing treetops and limbs to control the growth of the trees under their care, to increase the density of limbs, and to improve the shapes of the trees. In addition, these workers' duties include planting the seedlings, spraying to control surrounding weed growth and insects, and harvesting the trees.

Other forest workers gather, by hand or with the use of handtools, products from the woodlands, such as decorative greens, tree cones and barks, moss, and other wild plant life. Some may tap trees for sap to make syrup or chemicals.

Work environment. Most of these jobs are physically demanding. Workers spend all their time outdoors, sometimes in poor weather and often in isolated areas. It may be necessary for some forestry aides or forest workers to walk long distances

Forest and conservation workers strive to promote growth of individual trees and entire forests.

through densely wooded areas to accomplish their work tasks. The increased use of enclosed machines has decreased some of the discomforts caused by inclement weather and has generally made tasks much safer.

Still, workers must be careful and use proper safety measures and equipment such as hardhats, eye protection, safety clothing, and boots to reduce the risk of injury. Data from the U.S. Bureau of Labor Statistics show that full-time forest and conservation workers experienced a work-related injury and illness rate that was higher than the national average. But the jobs of forest and conservation workers generally are much less hazardous than those of logging workers, who work in a similar environment.

Training, Other Qualifications, and Advancement

Most forest and conservation workers develop skills through on-the-job training, learning from experienced workers.

Education and training. Generally, a high school diploma is sufficient for most forest and conservation occupations. Many forest worker jobs offer only seasonal employment during warm-weather months, so students are often hired to perform short-term, labor-intensive tasks, such as planting tree seedlings or conducting pre-commercial tree thinning.

Training programs for forest and conservation workers are common in many States. These training programs typically take place in the field, encouraging the health and productivity of the Nation's forests through programs such as the Sustainable Forest Initiative.

Some vocational and technical schools and community colleges offer courses leading to a 2-year technical degree in forest management technology, wildlife management, conservation, and forest harvesting, all of which are helpful in obtaining a job. A curriculum that includes field trips to observe or participate in forestry or logging activities provides a particularly good background. Additionally, a few community colleges offer training for equipment operators.

Other qualifications. Forest and conservation workers must be in good health and able to work outdoors every day. They also must be able to work as part of a team. Maturity and good judgment are important in making quick, intelligent decisions when hazards arise. Mechanical aptitude and coordination are necessary for operators of machinery and equipment, who often are responsible for repair and maintenance.

Advancement. Advancement generally takes place by obtaining a bachelor's degree in forestry or related field. A bachelor's degree may also qualify candidates to become a forester. (See the section on conservation scientists and foresters elsewhere in the *Handbook*.)

Employment

Forest and conservation workers held about 12,900 jobs in 2008 in the following industries:

State government	5,900
Forestry	2,000
Local government	1,600

About 58 percent of all forest and conservation workers work for government, primarily at the State and local level. Those employed in forest management services may work on a contract basis for the U.S. Department of Agriculture's Forest Service. Self-employed forest and conservation workers make up around 1 percent of the occupation.

Although forest and conservation workers are located in every State, employment is concentrated in the West and Southeast, where many national and private forests and parks are located. Seasonal demand for forest and conservation workers can vary by region and time of year. For northern States, in particular, winter weather can interrupt forestry operations.

Job Outlook

Employment is expected to experience average growth. Most job openings will result from the large number of workers who leave these jobs on a seasonal basis and from an increase in retirements.

Employment change. Employment of forest and conservation workers is expected to grow 9 percent over the 2008-18 decade, as fast as the average for all occupations. Demand for forest and conservation workers will increase as more land is set aside to protect natural resources or wildlife habitats. In addition, more jobs may be created by recent Federal legislation designed to prevent destructive wildfires by thinning the forests and by setting controlled burns in dry regions susceptible to forest fires.

Recent developments in Western forests may result in the conversion of unused roads into forestland, thus creating some new jobs. Additionally, increasing pressure from a growing number of stakeholders for the United States Forest Service to undertake major road repair may also result in higher levels of employment. Employment growth will, nonetheless, be largely determined by each of these programsí ability to obtain necessary funding.

Job prospects. Some opportunities will stem from employment growth, but most openings will arise from the large number of workers who leave these jobs on a seasonal basis and from an increase in retirements expected over the next decade. The best employment opportunities should continue to be in Maine, the Southeast, and the Pacific Northwest.

Employment of forest and conservation workers can sometimes be unsteady. During the muddy spring season and the cold winter months, weather often can curtail the work, depending on the geographic region.

Projections data from the National Employment Matrix

Occupational Title	SOC Code	Employment, 2008	Projected Employment, 2018	Change, 2008-2018	
				Number	Percent
Forest and conservation workers	45-4011	12,900	14,000	1,100	9

(NOTE) Data in this table are rounded. See the discussion of the employment projections table in the *Handbook* introductory chapter on *Occupational Information Included in the Handbook.*

Earnings

In May 2008, median hourly wages of wage and salary forest and conservation workers were $10.98. The middle 50 percent earned between $8.98 and $14.75. The lowest 10 percent earned less than $8.02, and the highest 10 percent earned more than $20.04.

Many beginning or inexperienced workers earn the Federal minimum wage of $7.25 per hour as of July 24, 2009, but many States may set minimum wages higher than the Federal minimum.

Forest and conservation workers who work for State and local governments or for large, private firms generally enjoy more generous benefits than do workers in smaller firms.

Related Occupations

Other occupations concerned with the care of trees and their environment include:

Sources of Additional Information

For information about timber-cutting and logging careers and about secondary and postsecondary programs offering training for logging occupations, contact:

➤ Forest Resources Association, Inc., 600 Jefferson Plaza, Suite 350, Rockville, MD 20852-1157. Internet: **http://www.forestresources.org**

For information on the Sustainable Forestry Initiative training programs, contact:

➤ American Forest and Paper Association, 1111 19th St. NW., Suite 800, Washington, DC 20036-3652. Internet: **http://www.afandpa.org**

A list of State forestry associations and other forestry-related State associations is available at most public libraries. Schools of Forestry at State land-grant colleges or universities also can be useful sources of information.

The Occupational Information Network (O*NET) provides information on a wide range of occupational characteristics. Links to O*NET appear at the end of the Internet version of this occupational statement, accessible at **http://www.bls.gov/ooh/ocos350.htm**

Logging Workers

Significant Points

- Workers spend all their time outdoors, sometimes in poor weather and often in isolated areas.

- Most jobs are physically demanding and can be hazardous.

- Employment is projected to grow 6 percent, which is slower than the average.

- Despite slower than average employment growth, job opportunities should be good because of the need to replace workers who leave the occupation for other jobs that are less physically demanding, dangerous, and prone to layoffs.

Nature of the Work

Logging workers harvest thousands of acres of forests each year for the timber that provides the raw material for countless consumer and industrial products. The timber-cutting and logging process is carried out by a logging crew. A typical crew might consist of one or two tree fallers or one tree harvesting machine operator to cut down trees, one bucker to cut logs, two logging skidder operators to drag cut trees to the loading deck, and one equipment operator to load the logs onto trucks.

Fallers, commonly known as *tree fallers,* cut down trees with hand-held power chain saws or mobile felling machines. Using gas-powered chain saws, *buckers* trim off the tops and branches and buck (cut) the resulting logs into specified lengths. *Choke setters* fasten chokers (steel cables or chains) around logs to be skidded (dragged) by tractors or forwarded by the cable-yarding system to the landing or deck area, where the logs are separated by species and type of product, such as pulpwood, saw logs, or veneer logs, and loaded onto trucks. *Rigging slingers* and *chasers* set up and dismantle the cables and guy wires of the yarding system. *Log sorters, markers, movers,* and *chippers* sort, mark, and move logs, based on species, size, and ownership, and tend machines that chip up logs.

Logging equipment operators use tree harvesters to fell the trees, shear the limbs off, and then cut the logs into desired lengths. They drive tractors mounted on crawler tracks and operate self-propelled machines called skidders or forwarders, which drag or transport logs from the felling site in the woods to the log landing area for loading. They also operate grapple loaders, which lift and load logs into trucks. Some logging equipment operators, usually at a sawmill or a pulp-mill woodyard, use a tracked or wheeled machine similar to a forklift to unload logs and pulpwood off of trucks or gondola railroad cars. Some newer, more efficient logging equipment has state-of-the-art computer technology, requiring skilled operators with more training.

Log graders and *scalers* inspect logs for defects, measure logs to determine their volume, and estimate the marketable content or value of logs or pulpwood. These workers often use hand-held data collection devices to enter data about individual trees; later, the data can be downloaded to a central computer.

A logging worker cuts a log into smaller lengths.

Other timber-cutting and logging workers have a variety of responsibilities. Some hike through forests to assess logging conditions. Some clear areas of brush and other growth to prepare for logging activities or to promote the growth of desirable species of trees.

Most crews work for self-employed logging contractors who have substantial logging experience, the capital to purchase equipment, and the skills needed to run a small business successfully. Many contractors work alongside their crews as supervisors and often operate one of the logging machines, such as the grapple loader or the tree harvester. Some manage more than one crew and function as owner-supervisors.

Although timber-cutting and logging equipment has greatly improved and operations are becoming increasingly mechanized, many logging jobs still are dangerous and very labor intensive. These jobs require various levels of skill, ranging from the unskilled task of manually moving logs, branches, and equipment to skillfully using chain saws to fell trees, and heavy equipment to skid and load logs onto trucks. To keep costs down, many timber-cutting and logging workers maintain and repair the equipment they use. A skillful, experienced logging worker is expected to handle a variety of logging operations.

Work environment. Logging jobs are physically demanding and can be hazardous. Workers spend all their time outdoors, sometimes in poor weather and often in isolated areas. The increased use of enclosed machines has decreased some of the discomforts caused by inclement weather and has generally made logging much safer. Workers in some sparsely populated western States and northern Maine commute long distances between their homes and logging sites. A few logging camps in Alaska and Maine house workers in bunkhouses. In the more densely populated eastern and southern States, commuting distances are shorter.

Most logging occupations involve lifting, climbing, and other strenuous activities, although machinery has eliminated some heavy labor. Loggers work under unusually hazardous conditions. Falling branches, vines, and rough terrain are constant hazards, as are the dangers associated with tree-felling and log-handling operations. Special care must be taken during strong winds, which can even halt logging operations. Slippery or muddy ground, hidden roots, or vines not only reduce efficiency, but also present a constant danger, especially in the presence of moving vehicles and machinery. Poisonous plants, brambles, insects, snakes, heat, humidity, and extreme cold are common conditions where loggers work. The use of hearing protection devices is required on logging operations because the high noise level of felling and skidding operations over long periods may impair one's hearing. Workers must be careful and use proper safety measures and equipment such as hardhats, eye and ear protection, safety clothing, and boots to reduce the risk of injury.

Training, Other Qualifications, and Advancement
Most logging workers develop skills through on-the-job training, learning from experienced workers.

Education and training. Generally, a high school diploma is sufficient for most logging occupations. Through on-the-job training, logging workers become familiar with the character and dangers of the forest environment and the operation of logging machinery and equipment.

Safety training is a vital and required part of the instruction of all logging workers. Many State forestry or logging associations provide training sessions for tree fallers, whose job duties require more skill and experience than do other positions on the logging team. Sessions may take place in the field, where trainees, under the supervision of an experienced logger, have the opportunity to practice various felling techniques. Fallers learn how to manually cut down extremely large or expensive trees safely and with minimal damage to the felled or surrounding trees.

Training programs for loggers are common in many States. Although specific coursework may vary by State, most programs usually include classroom or field training in a number of areas, including best management practices, environmental compliance, wetlands, safety, endangered species, reforestation, and business management. Some programs lead to logger certification.

Logging companies and trade associations, such as the Northeastern Loggers Association, the American Loggers Council, and the Forest Resources Association, Inc., also offer training programs for workers who operate large, expensive machinery and equipment. Often, a representative of the equipment manufacturer spends several days in the field explaining and overseeing the operation of newly purchased machinery.

Some vocational and technical schools and community colleges offer courses leading to a 2-year technical degree in forest harvesting, which may be helpful in obtaining a job. A curriculum that includes field trips to observe or participate in logging activities provides a particularly good background. Additionally, a few community colleges offer training for equipment operators.

Other qualifications. Logging workers must be in good health and able to work outdoors every day. They also must be able to work as part of a team. Many logging occupations require physical strength and stamina. Maturity and good judgment are important in making quick, intelligent decisions when hazards arise. Mechanical aptitude and coordination are necessary for machinery and equipment operators, who often are responsible for repair and maintenance. Self-employed loggers need initiative and managerial and business skills to be successful as logging contractors.

Advancement. Logging workers generally advance from tasks requiring a lot of manual labor to those involving the operation of expensive, sometimes complicated logging equipment. Inexperienced entrants usually begin as laborers, carrying tools and equipment, clearing brush, performing equipment maintenance, and loading and unloading logs and brush. For some, familiarization with logging operations may lead to jobs such as log-handling equipment operator. Further experience may lead to jobs involving the operation of more complicated machinery and yarding towers to transport, load, and unload logs. Those who have the skills required for the efficient use of power saws and other equipment may become fallers and buckers.

Some experienced logging workers start their own logging contractor businesses, but to do so they also need some basic business skills, which are essential in logging's difficult business climate.

Projections data from the National Employment Matrix

Occupational Title	SOC Code	Employment, 2008	Projected Employment, 2018	Change, 2008-2018	
				Number	Percent
Logging workers	45-4020	66,100	70,000	3,900	6
Fallers...	45-4021	11,000	10,700	-300	-3
Logging equipment operators	45-4022	41,700	44,900	3,200	8
Log graders and scalers..	45-4023	5,500	5,400	-100	-2
Logging workers, all other...	45-4029	8,000	9,100	1,100	14

(NOTE) Data in this table are rounded. See the discussion of the employment projections table in the *Handbook* introductory chapter on *Occupational Information Included in the Handbook.*

Employment

Logging workers held about 66,100 jobs in 2008 in the following occupations:

Logging equipment operators 41,700
Fallers...11,000
Log graders and scalers...5,500
Logging workers, all others...8,000

About half of all logging workers work for the logging industry. Another 31 percent are self-employed, who mostly work under contract to landowners and the logging industry. About 10 percent work in the wood product manufacturing industry, mainly in sawmills.

Seasonal demand for logging workers can vary by region and time of year. For northern States in particular, winter weather can interrupt logging operations, although some logging can be done in winter.

Job Outlook

Employment of logging workers is projected to grow more slowly than the average over the 2008–18 decade. Despite slower than average employment growth, job opportunities should be good because of the need to replace workers who leave the occupation for jobs that are less hazardous.

Employment change. Employment of logging workers is expected to grow 6 percent from 2008 to 2018, which is slower than the average for all occupations. New policies allowing some access to Federal timberland may result in some logging jobs, and Federal legislation designed to prevent destructive wildfires by proactively thinning forests in susceptible regions also may result in additional jobs. Foreign and domestic demand for new wood products, such as wood pellets, is expected to result in some employment growth as well. Nonetheless, domestic timber producers continue to face increasing competition from foreign producers, who can harvest the same amount of timber at lower cost. The logging industry is expected to continue to consolidate in order to reduce costs, which may offset the creation of most new jobs.

Increased mechanization of logging operations and improvements in logging equipment will continue to depress demand for many manual timber-cutting and logging workers. Employment of fallers, buckers, choke setters, and other workers whose jobs are labor intensive should decline as more laborsaving equipment is used. Employment of machinery and equipment operators, such as tree harvesting, skidding, and log-handling equipment operators, will be less adversely affected and should rise as logging companies switch away from manual tree felling.

Job prospects. Despite slower than average employment growth, job opportunities should be good because of the need to replace workers who leave the occupation for other jobs that are less physically demanding, dangerous, and prone to layoffs. Employment of logging workers can sometimes be unsteady as changes in the level of construction, particularly residential construction, can cause slowdowns in logging activities in the short term. In addition, logging operations must be relocated when timber in a particular area has been harvested. During prolonged periods of inactivity, some workers may stay on the job to maintain or repair logging machinery and equipment, but others are laid off or forced to find jobs in other occupations.

Earnings

Earnings of logging workers vary by size of establishment and by geographic area. Workers in the largest establishments earn more than those in the smallest ones. Workers in Alaska and the Northwest earn more than those in the South, where the cost of living is generally lower. Median hourly wages in May 2008 for logging occupations were as follows:

Log graders and scalers...$15.64
Logging equipment operators 15.18
Fallers..14.66
Logging workers, all others...15.96

Small logging contractor firms generally offer timber-cutting and logging workers few benefits beyond vacation days. However, some employers offer full-time workers basic benefits, such as medical coverage, and provide safety apparel and equipment.

Related Occupations

Other occupations concerned with the care of trees and their environment include:

Sources of Additional Information

For information about timber-cutting and logging careers and about secondary and postsecondary programs offering training for logging occupations, contact:

➤ Forest Resources Association, Inc., 600 Jefferson Plaza, Suite 350, Rockville, MD 20852-1157. Internet: **http://www.forestresources.org**

➤ American Loggers Council, P.O. Box 966, Hemphill, TX 75948-0966. Internet: **http://www.americanloggers.org**

For information on the Sustainable Forestry Initiative training programs, contact:

➤ American Forest & Paper Association, 1111 19th St. NW., Suite 800, Washington, DC 20036-3652. Internet: **http://www.afandpa.org**

A list of State forestry associations and other forestry-related State associations is available at most public libraries. Schools of Forestry at State land-grant colleges or universities also can be useful sources of information.

The Occupational Information Network (O*NET) provides information on a wide range of occupational characteristics. Links to O*NET appear at the end of the Internet version of this occupational statement, accessible at **http://www.bls.gov/ooh/ocos351.htm**

Agricultural Workers, Other

Significant Points

- Duties vary widely—from raising plants and livestock to operating large farm equipment.

- The majority of agricultural workers learn their skills on the job in less than a month; animal breeders require more work experience or a college degree.

- Job openings are expected to be numerous; opportunities for agricultural equipment operators, and crop, greenhouse, and nursery farmworkers should be particularly plentiful.

Nature of the Work

Agricultural workers play a large role in getting food, plants, and other agricultural products to market. Working mostly on farms or ranches, but also in nurseries and slaughterhouses, these workers have numerous and diverse duties. Among their activities are planting and harvesting crops, installing irrigation, and delivering animals. While most agricultural workers have relatively few technical skills, some have college degrees that train them to breed animals with specific traits.

Crop, nursery, and greenhouse farmworkers and laborers—the largest specialty by far—perform numerous activities related to growing and harvesting grains, fruits, vegetables, nuts, fiber, trees, shrubs, and other crops. They plant and seed, prune, irrigate, harvest, and pack and load crops for shipment. Farmworkers also apply pesticides, herbicides, and fertilizers to crops and repair fences and some farm equipment. Nursery and greenhouse workers prepare land or greenhouse beds for growing horticultural products, such as trees, plants, flowers, and sod. Their duties include planting, watering, pruning, weeding, and spraying the plants. They may cut, roll, and stack sod; stake trees; tie, wrap, and pack plants to fill orders; and dig up or move field-grown and containerized shrubs and trees.

Farm and ranch animal farmworkers—the second largest specialty—care for live farm, ranch, or water animals that may include cattle, sheep, swine, goats, horses, poultry, finfish, shellfish, and bees. The animals are usually raised to supply meat, fur, skins, feathers, eggs, milk, or honey. Duties may include feeding, watering, herding, grazing, castrating, branding, debeaking, weighing, catching, and loading animals; they also maintain records on animals, examine animals to detect diseases and injuries, assist in delivering animals at their birth, and administer medications, vaccinations, or insecticides. Many workers clean and maintain animal housing areas every day. On dairy farms, farmworkers operate milking machines.

Other agricultural workers known as *agricultural equipment operators* use a variety of farm equipment to plow, sow seeds, and maintain and harvest crops. Equipment may include tractors, fertilizer spreaders, haybines, raking equipment, balers, combines, threshers, and trucks. These workers also operate machines, such as conveyor belts, loading machines, separators, cleaners, and dryers, used in moving and treating crops after their harvest. As part of the job, workers may make adjustments and minor repairs to equipment.

Animal breeders select and breed animals using their knowledge of genetics and animal science to produce offspring with desired traits and characteristics, such as chickens that lay more eggs, pigs that produce leaner meat, and sheep with more desirable wool. Other animal breeders breed and raise cats, dogs, and other household pets. Larger and more expensive animals, such as horses and cattle, are usually bred through artificial insemination, a specialized technique which requires taking semen from the male and then inseminating the female. This process ensures better results than conventional mating and also enables one prized male to sire many more offspring. To know which animals to breed and when, animal breeders keep detailed records, including the health of the animals, their size and weight, and the amount and quality of the product produced by them. They also keep track of the traits of the offspring. Some animal breeders work as consultants for a number of farmers, but others breed and raise their own animals for sale or future breeding. For those who raise animals, tasks might include fixing and cleaning animal shelters, feeding and watering the animals, and overseeing animals' health. Some breeders supervise others who perform these tasks. Animal breeders also read journals and newsletters to learn the latest information on breeding and veterinary practices.

Work environment. Working conditions for agricultural workers vary widely. Much of the work of farmworkers and laborers on farms and ranches is physically strenuous and takes place outdoors in all kinds of weather. Harvesting fruits and vegetables, for example, may require much bending, stooping, and lifting. Workers may have limited access to sanitation facilities while working in the field and drinking water may also be limited. Nevertheless, many agricultural workers enjoy the variety of their work, the rural setting, the satisfaction of working the land, and raising animals.

Farm work does not lend itself to a regular 40-hour work-week. In fact, about 16 percent of all agricultural workers have a variable schedule. Work cannot be delayed when crops must be planted or harvested or when animals must be sheltered and fed. Long hours and weekend work is common in these jobs. For example, farmworkers and agricultural equipment operators may work 6 or 7 days a week during planting and harvesting seasons.

Many agricultural worker jobs are seasonal in nature, so some workers also do other jobs during slow seasons. Migrant farmworkers, who move from location to location as crops ripen, live an unsettled lifestyle, which can be stressful. Work also is seasonal for farmworkers in nurseries; spring and summer are the busiest times of the year. Greenhouse workers enjoy relatively comfortable working conditions while tending plants indoors. However, during the busy seasons, when landscape contractors need plants, work schedules may be more demanding, often requiring weekend work. Moreover, the transition from warm weather to cold weather means that nursery workers might have to work overtime with little notice in order to move plants indoors to protect them from frost. Farmworkers who work with animals usually have a more regular schedule; their work is steadier and year round, but they sometimes must come to work on short notice to help handle emergencies.

Farmworkers risk exposure to pesticides and other hazardous chemicals sprayed on crops or plants. However, exposure can be minimal if safety procedures are followed. Those who work on mechanized farms must take precautions to avoid injury when working with tools and heavy equipment. Those who work directly with animals risk being bitten or kicked.

Animal breeders spend most of their time outdoors around animals but can also work in offices or laboratories. Breeders who consult may travel from farm to farm. If they need to sell offspring, breeders may travel to attend shows and meet potential buyers. While tending to the animals, breeders may be bitten or kicked.

Training, Other Qualifications, and Advancement
The majority of agricultural workers learn their skills on the job in less than a month; animal breeders require more work experience or a college degree.

Education and training. Most farmworkers learn their jobs quickly as they work; many do not have a high school diploma. People without a high school diploma are particularly common in the crop production sector, which is more labor-intensive and employs numerous migrant farmworkers. Other agricultural workers may require a month to a year of training on the job, depending on their responsibilities.

Other qualifications. Experience working on a farm or around animals is helpful but not necessary to qualify for many jobs. For those who operate equipment on the road or drive a truck as part their job, a driver's license or commercial driver's license is required.

Nursery workers who deal directly with customers must be friendly and tactful. Employers also look for responsible, self-motivated individuals because nursery workers sometimes work with little supervision.

Advancement. Farmworkers who work hard, have good communication skills, and take an interest in the business may advance to crew leader or other supervisory positions. The ability to speak both English and Spanish is quite helpful in supervisory work as well.

Some agricultural workers aspire to become farm, ranch, or other agricultural managers, or own farms or ranches themselves. (Farmers, ranchers, and agricultural managers are discussed elsewhere in the *Handbook*.) In addition, their knowledge of raising and harvesting produce may provide an excellent background for becoming purchasing agents and buyers of farm products. Knowledge of working a farm as a business can also help agricultural workers become farm and home management advisors. Those who earn a college degree in agricultural science could become agricultural and food scientists. (Agricultural and food scientists are discussed elsewhere in the *Handbook*.)

Employment
Agricultural workers held about 821,700 jobs in 2008. About one third was employed in animal production; some found employment in support activities for agriculture and forestry.

Arizona, California, Colorado, Texas, and New Mexico employ approximately one quarter of all crop workers; California, Florida, and Oregon employ the most nursery workers.

Job Outlook
Job opportunities for agricultural workers occupations should be abundant because large numbers of workers leave these jobs due to their low wages and physical demands. Little or no

A nursery worker waters flowers in a greenhouse.

Projections data from the National Employment Matrix

Occupational Title	SOC Code	Employment, 2008	Projected Employment, 2018	Change, 2008-2018	
				Number	Percent
Agricultural workers, all other..	—	821,700	804,400	17,400	-2
Animal breeders..	45-2021	14,700	15,500	800	6
Miscellaneous agricultural workers...	45-2090	807,000	788,800	-18,200	-2

(NOTE) Data in this table are rounded. See the discussion of the employment projections table in the *Handbook* introductory chapter on *Occupational Information Included in the Handbook*.

change in employment is expected over the 2008–18 decade, reflecting in large part the outlook for farmworkers in crops, nurseries, and greenhouses, who make up the largest majority of all agricultural workers.

Employment change. Overall employment is expected to show little or no change in employment. Fewer agricultural workers will be needed overall because of continued consolidation of farms and technological advancements in farm equipment that is raising output per farm worker. The agriculture industry also is expected to face increased competition from foreign countries and rising imports, particularly from Central America and China because of trade agreements with those regions. Nursery and greenhouse workers might experience some job growth in this period, if the demand for landscaping plants resumes its growth pattern.

Job prospects. Job openings should be plentiful because of relatively large numbers of workers who leave these jobs for other occupations. This is especially true for jobs as agricultural equipment operators, and crop, greenhouse, and nursery farmworkers. Those who work with animals tend to have a more settled lifestyle, as the work does not require them to follow crops for harvest.

Earnings

Agricultural workers had the following median hourly wages in May 2008:

Animal breeders $13.02
Agricultural equipment operators 10.92
Farmworkers, farm and ranch animals...........................10.13
Farmworkers and laborers, crop, nursery,
    and greenhouse..8.64
Agricultural workers, all others....................................12.00

Farmworkers in crop production often are paid piece rates, with earnings based on how much they do instead of how many hours they work. Farmworkers tend to receive fewer benefits

than those in many other occupations. Some employers supply seasonal workers with room and board.

Related Occupations

The duties of farmworkers who perform outdoor labor are similar to the duties of:

                                                        Page
Fishers and fishing vessel operators..601
Forest and conservation workers..604
Grounds maintenance workers..498

Farmworkers who work with farm and ranch animals perform tasks similar to those of:
Animal care and service workers..504

Animal breeders may perform some work similar to those of:
Veterinarians..402
Veterinary technologists and technicians 443

Sources of Additional Information

Information on agricultural worker jobs is available from:
➤ United Farm Workers, P.O. Box 62, Keene, CA 93531-0062. Internet: **http://www.ufw.org/**

Information on training is available from:
➤ New England Small Farm Institute, 275 Jackson Street, Belchertown, MA 01007-9818. Internet: **http://www.growingnewfarmers.org/**

The Occupational Information Network (O*NET) provides information on a wide range of occupational characteristics. Links to O*NET appear at the end of the Internet version of this occupational statement, accessible at **http://www.bls.gov/ooh/ocos349.htm**

Other Farming, Fishing, and Forestry Occupations

Agricultural Inspectors

Nature of the Work
Agricultural inspectors are employed by Federal and State governments to ensure compliance with laws and regulations governing the health, safety, and quality of agricultural commodities, processing equipment and facilities, and fish and logging operations.

Education and Training
Most jobs require work experience in a related field, such as food processing, or some college coursework in biology, agricultural science, or a related subject.

Job Outlook
Current and projected employment:

2008 Employment 16,600
2018 Employment 18,700
Employment change...2,100
Growth rate.. 13%

Employment change. Average employment growth is expected as Federal and State governments, the largest employers of these workers, are not expected to hire a significant number of new inspectors. However, demand for agricultural inspectors may increase significantly if pending legislation requiring greater scrutiny of the food industry by the Food and Drug Administration is passed.

Job prospects. Prospects should be good as a large number of government inspectors are expected to retire in the coming decade.

Earnings
Median annual wages of agricultural inspectors were $41,170 in May 2008.

Related Occupations

	Page
Food scientists and technologists	177
Purchasing agents and buyers, farm products	79

Sources of Additional Information
Information on obtaining positions as an agricultural inspector with the Federal Government is available from the Office of Personnel Management through USAJOBS, the Federal Government's official employment information system. This resource for locating and applying for job opportunities can be accessed through the Internet at **http://www.usajobs.opm.gov** or through an interactive voice response telephone system at (703) 724-1850 or TDD (978) 461-8404. These numbers are not toll free, and charges may result.

The Occupational Information Network (O*NET) provides information on a wide range of occupational characteristics. Links to O*NET appear at the end of the Internet version of this occupational statement, accessible at **http://www.bls.gov/ooh/ocos347.htm**

Graders and Sorters, Agricultural Products

Nature of the Work
Graders and sorters grade, sort, or classify unprocessed food and other agricultural products by size, weight, color, or condition and discard inferior or defective products.

Education and Training
While some jobs require a high school diploma, simple jobs that need mostly visual inspection might be filled by those with work-related experience.

Job Outlook
Current and projected employment:

2008 Employment 33,400
2018 Employment 33,500
Employment change...100
Growth rate.. 0%

Employment change. Little or no change in employment is expected. Increased use of electronic sorters, higher levels of imported agricultural products, and growth of produce with less waste will result in decreased demand for these workers.

Job prospects. Most job openings will arise from the need to replace workers who leave the occupation each year. There may be competition for positions.

Earnings
Median hourly wages for graders and sorters of agricultural products were $9.06 per hour in May 2008.

Related Occupations

	Page
Agricultural inspectors	612

Sources of Additional Information
Information on obtaining positions as an agricultural inspector with the Federal Government is available from the Office of Personnel Management through USAJOBS, the Federal Government's official employment information system. This resource for locating and applying for job opportunities can be accessed through the Internet at **http://www.usajobs.opm.gov** or through an interactive voice response telephone system at (703) 724-1850 or TDD (978) 461-8404. These numbers are not toll free, and charges may result.

The Occupational Information Network (O*NET) provides information on a wide range of occupational characteristics. Links to O*NET appear at the end of the Internet version of this occupational statement, accessible at **http://www.bls.gov/ooh/ocos348.htm**

Construction Trades and Related Workers

Boilermakers

Significant Points

- Most boilermakers learn their job through a formal apprenticeship; people with a welding certification or other welding training get priority in selection to boilermaker apprenticeship programs.

- Boilermakers use potentially dangerous equipment and the work is physically demanding.

- Job opportunities are expected to be favorable.

Nature of the Work

Boilermakers and *boilermaker mechanics* make, install, and repair boilers, closed vats, and other large vessels or containers that hold liquids and gases. Boilers heat water or other fluids under extreme pressure for use in generating electric power and to provide heat and power in buildings, factories, and ships. Tanks and vats are used to store and process chemicals, oil, beer, and hundreds of other products.

In addition to installing and maintaining boilers and other vessels, boilermakers also help erect and repair air pollution equipment, blast furnaces, water treatment plants, storage and process tanks, and smoke stacks. Boilermakers also install refractory brick and other heat-resistant materials in fireboxes or pressure vessels. Some install and maintain the huge pipes used in dams to send water to and from hydroelectric power generation turbines.

Boilers and other high-pressure vessels used to hold liquids and gases usually are made in sections by casting each piece out of steel, iron, copper, or stainless steel. Manufacturers increasingly are automating this process to improve the quality of these vessels. Boilermakers weld sections of the boiler together, often using robotic welding systems or automated welding machines. Small boilers may be assembled in the manufacturing plant; larger boilers usually are prefabricated in numerous pieces and assembled on site, although they may be temporarily assembled in a fabrication shop to ensure a proper fit before final assembly at the permanent site.

Because boilers last a long time—sometimes 50 years or more—boilermakers need to regularly maintain them and upgrade components, such as boiler tubes, heating elements, and ductwork, to increase efficiency. They frequently inspect fittings, feed pumps, safety and check valves, water and pressure gauges, boiler controls, and auxiliary machinery. For closed vats and other large vessels, boilermakers clean or supervise cleaning of the vats using scrapers, wire brushes, and cleaning solvents. They repair or replace defective parts using hand and power tools, gas torches, and welding equipment, and may operate metalworking machinery to repair or make parts. They also dismantle leaky boilers, patch weak spots with metal stock, replace defective sections, and strengthen joints.

Before making or repairing a fabricated metal product, a boilermaker studies design drawings and creates full size patterns or templates, using straightedges, squares, transits, and tape measures. After the various sized shapes and pieces are marked out on metal, boilermakers use hand and power tools or flame cutting torches to make the cuts. The sections of metal are then bent into shape and accurately lined up before they are welded together. If the plate sections are very large, heavy cranes are used to lift the parts into place. Boilermakers align sections using plumb bobs, levels, wedges, and turnbuckles. They use metalworking machinery and other tools to remove irregular edges so that metal pieces fit together properly. They then join them by bolting, welding, or riveting. Boilermakers also align and attach water tubes, stacks and liners, safety and check valves, water and pressure gauges, and other parts, and test complete vessels for leaks or other defects.

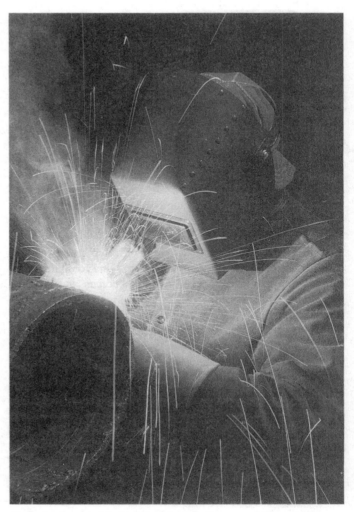

Boilermakers weld sections of the boiler together.

Work environment. Boilermakers often use potentially dangerous equipment, such as acetylene torches and power grinders, handle heavy parts and tools, and work on ladders or on top of large vessels. Dams, boilers, storage tanks, and pressure vessels are usually of substantial size, thus a major portion of boilermaker work is performed at great heights, sometimes hundreds of feet above the ground in the case of dams. The work is physically demanding and may be done in cramped quarters inside boilers, vats, or tanks that are often dark, damp, and poorly ventilated. Field construction work is performed outside so exposure to all types of weather conditions, including extreme heat and cold, is common. To reduce the chance of injuries, boilermakers often wear hardhats, harnesses, protective clothing, ear plugs, safety glasses and shoes, and respirators.

Boilermakers may experience extended periods of overtime when equipment is shut down for maintenance. Overtime work also may be necessary to meet construction or production deadlines. However, since most field construction and repair work is contract work, there may be periods of unemployment when a contract is complete. Many boilermakers must travel to a project and live away from home for long periods of time.

Training, Other Qualifications, and Advancement

Most boilermakers learn this trade through a formal apprenticeship. People with a welding certification or other welding training get priority in selection to boilermaker apprenticeship programs.

Education and training. Boilermakers learn their trade through formal apprenticeships offered through unions or employers or from a combination of trade and technical school training and employer-provided training. Training usually includes both boilermaking and structural fabrication. Apprenticeship programs usually consist of 6,000 hours or 4 years of paid on-the-job training, supplemented by a minimum of 144 hours of classroom instruction each year in subjects such as set-up and assembly rigging, plate and pressure welding, blueprint reading, and layout. Those who finish registered apprenticeships are certified as fully qualified journey-level workers.

Most apprentices must be at least 18 years old, a high school graduate or holder of a GED, and be legally authorized to work in the United States. Those with welding training or a welding certification will have an advantage in applying for apprenticeship programs. When an apprenticeship becomes available, the local union usually publicizes the opportunity by notifying local vocational schools and high school vocational programs. Education often continues throughout a boilermaker's career as they often attend classes or seminars to learn about new equipment, procedures, and technology.

Other qualifications. The work of boilermakers requires a high degree of technical skill, knowledge, and dedication. Because the tools and equipment used by boilermakers are typically heavier and more cumbersome than those in other construction trades, having physical strength and stamina is important. Good manual dexterity is also important.

Advancement. Some boilermakers advance to supervisory positions. Because of their extensive training, those qualified through apprenticeships usually have an advantage in getting promoted over those who have not gone through the complete program.

Employment

Boilermakers held about 20,200 jobs in 2008. About 21 percent worked in the nonresidential building construction industry, assembling and erecting boilers and other vessels. Another 21 percent worked in manufacturing.

Job Outlook

Employment is projected to grow faster than average. Favorable job opportunities are expected.

Employment change. Employment of boilermakers is expected to grow by 19 percent between 2008 and 2018. Growth will be driven by the need to maintain and upgrade, rather than replace, the many existing boilers that are getting older, and by the need to meet the growing population's demand for electric power. While boilers historically have lasted over 50 years, the need to replace components, such as boiler tubes, heating elements, and ductwork, is an ongoing process that will continue to spur demand for boilermakers. To meet the requirements of the Clean Air Act, utility companies also will need to continue upgrading their boiler systems.

Federal policies are also encouraging the construction of more environmentally sound and higher efficiency clean-burning coal, wind, and solar power plants, which will spur demand for boilermakers.

Installation of new boilers and pressure vessels, air pollution equipment, water treatment plants, storage and process tanks, electric static precipitators, and stacks and liners, will further drive growth of boilermakers, although to a lesser extent than repairs will.

Job prospects. Job prospects should be favorable because the work of a boilermaker remains hazardous and physically demanding, leading some qualified applicants to seek other types of work. Job growth will generate some new openings, but an even greater number of openings will arise from the numerous boilermakers expected to retire.

People who have welding training or a welding certificate should have the best opportunities for being selected for boilermaker apprenticeship programs.

Many industries that purchase boilers are sensitive to economic conditions. Therefore, during economic downturns, boilermakers in the construction industry may be temporarily laid off. However, maintenance and repairs of boilers must continue even during economic downturns so boilermaker mechanics in

Projections data from the National Employment Matrix

Occupational Title	SOC Code	Employment, 2008	Projected Employment, 2018	Change, 2008-2018	
				Number	Percent
Boilermakers	47-2011	20,200	24,000	3,800	19

(NOTE) Data in this table are rounded. See the discussion of the employment projections table in the *Handbook* introductory chapter on *Occupational Information Included in the Handbook.*

manufacturing and other industries generally have more stable employment.

Earnings

In May 2008, the median annual wage and salary of boiler-makers was about $52,260. The middle 50 percent earned between $41,210 and $64,300. The lowest 10 percent earned less than $32,480, and the highest 10 percent earned more than $76,160. Apprentices generally start at about half of journey-level wages, with wages gradually increasing to the journey wage as workers gain skills.

Many boilermakers belong to labor unions, most to the International Brotherhood of Boilermakers. Other boilermakers are members of the International Association of Machinists, the United Automobile Workers, or the United Steelworkers of America.

Related Occupations

Workers in other occupations that fabricate, assemble, install, or repair metal equipment or machines include:

	Page
Assemblers and fabricators	723
Industrial machinery mechanics and millwrights	709
Machinists	737
Plumbers, pipelayers, pipefitters, and steamfitters	659
Sheet metal workers	665
Tool and die makers	740
Welding, soldering, and brazing workers	743

Sources of Additional Information

For more information about boilermaking apprenticeships or other training opportunities, contact local offices of the unions previously mentioned, local construction companies and boiler manufacturers, or the local office of your State employment service. You can also find information on the registered apprenticeships together with links to State apprenticeship programs on the U.S. Department of Labor's Web site: **http://www.doleta.gov/atels_bat.** Apprenticeship information is also available from the U.S. Department of Labor's toll free helpline: (877) 872-5627.

For information on apprenticeships and the boilermaking occupation, contact:

➤ International Brotherhood of Boilermakers, Iron Ship Builders, Blacksmiths, Forgers, and Helpers, 753 State Ave., Suite 570, Kansas City, KS 66101. Internet: **http://www.boilermakers.org**

For general information on apprenticeships and how to get them, see the *Occupational Outlook Quarterly* article "Apprenticeships: Career training, credentials—and a paycheck in your pocket," online at **http://www.bls.gov/opub/ooq/2002/summer/art01.pdf** and in print at many libraries and career centers.

The Occupational Information Network (O*NET) provides information on a wide range of occupational characteristics. Links to O*NET appear at the end of the Internet version of this occupational statement, accessible at **http://www.bls.gov/ooh/ocos221.htm**

Brickmasons, Blockmasons, and Stonemasons

Significant Points

- Job opportunities are expected to be good, especially for those with restoration skills.
- Some entrants learn informally on the job, but apprenticeship programs provide the most thorough training.
- The work is usually outdoors and involves lifting heavy materials and working on scaffolds.
- About 27 percent of brickmasons, blockmasons, and stonemasons were self-employed.

Nature of the Work

Brickmasons, blockmasons, and *stonemasons* create attractive, durable surfaces and structures. For thousands of years, these workers have built buildings, fences, roads, walkways, and walls using bricks, concrete blocks, and natural stone. The structures that they build will continue to be in demand for years to come.

The work varies in complexity, from laying a simple masonry walkway to installing an ornate exterior on a highrise building. Workers cut or break the materials used to create walls, floors, and other structures. Once their building materials are properly sized, they are laid with or without a binding material. Workers use their own perceptions and a variety of tools to ensure that the structure meets the desired standards. After they finish laying the bricks, blocks, or stone, the workers clean the finished product with a variety of cleaning agents.

Brickmasons and blockmasons—who often are called simply *bricklayers*—build and repair walls, floors, partitions, fireplaces, chimneys, and other structures with brick, precast masonry panels, concrete block, and other masonry materials. Some brickmasons specialize in installing firebrick linings in industrial furnaces.

When building a structure, brickmasons usually start in the corners. Because of the precision needed, corners are time-consuming to erect and require the skills of experienced brick-layers. To lay the brick, brickmasons spread a bed of mortar (a mixture of cement, lime, sand, and water) with a trowel (a flat, bladed metal tool with a handle), place the brick on the mortar bed, and press and tap the brick into place. Depending on blueprint specifications, brickmasons either cut bricks with a hammer and chisel or saw them to fit around windows, doors, and other openings. Mortar joints are then finished with jointing tools for a sealed, neat, uniform appearance. Although brickmasons typically use steel supports, or lintels, at window and door openings, they sometimes build brick arches, which support and enhance the beauty of the brickwork.

Refractory masons are brickmasons who specialize in installing firebrick and refractory tile in high-temperature boilers, furnaces, cupolas, ladles, and soaking pits in industrial establishments. Most of these workers are employed in steel mills, where molten materials flow on refractory beds from furnaces to rolling machines. They also are employed at oil refineries, glass furnaces, incinerators, and other locations requiring high temperatures during the manufacturing process.

After a structure is completed there is often work that still needs to be done. *Pointing*, *cleaning*, and *caulking workers* can be the final workers on a job or the primary workers on a restoration project. These workers usually replace bricks or make repairs to brickwork on older structures where mortar has come loose. Special care is taken not to damage the main structural integrity or the bricks, blocks, or stone. Depending on how much mortar is being replaced, it may take several applications to allow the new mortar to cure properly. After laying the new bricks, the workers use chemicals to clean the brick and stone to give the structure a finished appearance.

Stonemasons build stone walls, as well as set stone exteriors and floors. They work with two types of stone—natural-cut stone, such as marble, granite, and limestone; and artificial stone, made from concrete, marble chips, or other masonry materials. Masons use a special hammer and chisel to cut stone. They cut stone along the grain to make various shapes and sizes, and valuable pieces are often cut with a saw that has a diamond blade. Stonemasons often work from a set of drawings in which each stone has been numbered for identification. Helpers may locate and carry these prenumbered stones to the masons. A derrick operator using a hoist may be needed to lift large stone pieces into place.

A blockmason sets concrete blocks.

When building a stone wall, masons set the first course of stones into a shallow bed of mortar. They then align the stones with wedges, plumb lines, and levels, and work them into position with various tools. Masons continue to build the wall by alternating layers of mortar and courses of stone. As the work progresses, masons remove the wedges, fill the joints between stones, and use a pointed metal tool, called a tuck pointer, to smooth the mortar to an attractive finish. To hold large stones in place, stonemasons attach brackets to the stones and weld or bolt these brackets to anchors in the wall. Finally, masons wash the stones with a cleansing solution to remove stains and dry the mortar.

When setting stone floors, which often consist of large and heavy pieces of stone, masons first use a trowel to spread a layer of damp mortar over the surface to be covered. They then use crowbars and hard rubber mallets for aligning and leveling to set the stone in the mortar bed. To finish, workers fill the joints and clean the stone slabs.

Some masons specialize in setting marble, which, in many respects, is similar to setting large pieces of stone. Brickmasons and stonemasons also repair imperfections and cracks and replace broken or missing masonry units in walls and floors.

Most nonresidential buildings are now built with walls made of some combination of any of the following: concrete block, brick veneer, stone, granite, marble, tile, and glass. In the past, masons doing nonresidential interior work mainly built block partition walls and elevator shafts, but because many types of masonry and stone are used in the interiors of today's nonresidential structures, these workers now must be more versatile. For example, some brickmasons and blockmasons now install structural insulated concrete units and wall panels. They also install a variety of masonry anchors and other masonry-associated accessories used in many highrise buildings.

Work environment. Brickmasons, blockmasons, and stonemasons usually work outdoors; in contrast to the past when work slowed down in the winter months, new processes and materials are allowing these masons to work in a greater variety of weather conditions. Masons stand, kneel, and bend for long periods and often have to lift heavy materials. Common hazards include injuries from tools and falls from scaffolds, but these can often be avoided when proper safety equipment, such as a hardhat, is used and when proper safety practices are followed.

Many workers work a standard 40-hour week. Some, however, do work more. Earnings for workers in the construction trades can be reduced on occasion when poor weather and slowdowns in construction activity decrease the amount of time the laborers can work.

Training, Other Qualifications, and Advancement

Some brickmasons, blockmasons, and stonemasons pick up their skills informally, observing and learning from experienced workers. Many others receive initial training in vocational education schools or from industry-based programs common throughout the country. Others complete an apprenticeship, which provides the most thorough training.

Education and training. Individuals who learn the trade on the job usually start as helpers, laborers, or mason tenders. These workers carry materials, move or assemble scaffolds, and mix mortar. When the opportunity arises, they learn from experienced craftworkers how to mix and spread mortar, lay brick and block, or set stone. They also may learn restoration skills such as cleaning, pointing, and repointing. As they gain experience, they learn more difficult tasks and make the transition to full-fledged craftworkers. The learning period usually lasts longer for workers who learn the trade on the job than for those who have already been trained in an apprenticeship program. Registered apprenticeship programs usually last between 3 and 4 years.

Some workers learn the trade at technical schools that offer masonry courses. Entrance requirements and fees vary depending on the school and who is funding the program. Some people take courses before being hired, and some take them later as part of on-the-job training.

Apprenticeships for brickmasons, blockmasons, and stonemasons usually are sponsored by local union-management joint apprenticeship and training committees, local contractors, or trade associations. Apprenticeship programs usually require 3 to 4 years of on-the-job training, in addition to a minimum of 144 hours of classroom instruction each year in blueprint reading, mathematics, layout work, sketching, and other subjects. In the coming years, the focus of apprenticeships is likely to change from time served to demonstrated competence. This may result in apprenticeships of shorter average duration. Applicants for apprenticeships must be at least 17 years old and in good physical condition. A high school diploma is preferable, especially with courses in mathematics, mechanical drawing, and general shop.

Apprentices often start by working with laborers: carrying materials, mixing mortar, and building scaffolds for about a month. Next, apprentices learn to lay, align, and join brick and block. They may also learn to work with stone and concrete, which is important when using other masonry materials.

Bricklayers who work in nonresidential construction usually work for large contractors and receive well-rounded training—normally through an apprenticeship in all phases of brick or stone work. Those who work in residential construction usually work for small contractors and specialize in only one or two aspects of the job.

Other qualifications. The most desired qualities in workers are dependability and a strong work ethic. Knowledge of basic math, including measurement, volume, mixing proportions, algebra, plane geometry, and mechanical drawing are important in this trade.

Advancement. With additional training and experience, brickmasons, blockmasons, and stonemasons may become supervisors for masonry contractors. Some eventually become owners of businesses and may spend most of their time as managers. Others move into closely related areas such as construction management or building inspection. Many unionized Joint Apprenticeship and Training Committees offer "lifelong learning" through continuing education courses that help those members who want to advance their technical knowledge and their careers.

Employment

Brickmasons, blockmasons, and stonemasons held 160,200 jobs in 2008. The vast majority were brickmasons and blockmasons. Workers in these crafts are employed in building construction or by specialty trade contractors.

About 27 percent of brickmasons, blockmasons, and stonemasons were self-employed. Many of the self-employed are contractors who work on small jobs, such as patios, walkways, and fireplaces.

Job Outlook

Brickmasons, blockmasons, and stonemasons should see as fast as average growth as the construction industry responds to the needs of a growing population. Job prospects should be better for workers with more thorough training who can work on complex structures.

Employment change. Jobs for brickmasons, blockmasons, and stonemasons are expected to increase by 12 percent over the 2008–18 decade, as fast as the average for all occupations, as the rising population will create a need for schools, hospitals, apartment buildings, and other structures. Also stimulating demand for workers will be the need to build more energy-efficient industrial facilities and office buildings (some of which may be made from brick) and to restore a growing number of old brick buildings. Moreover, the Federal Government has indicated a willingness to spend more on repairing schools and on making government buildings more energy efficient, which should have a positive impact on the construction industry in general.

Because of demographic forces, the residential housing market is expected to eventually pick up again. Brick exteriors and, particularly, stone should remain popular, reflecting a growing preference for durable exterior materials requiring little maintenance. There is also an increased demand for durable homes that incorporate brick or stone in hurricane-prone areas.

Job prospects. Job opportunities for brickmasons, blockmasons, and stonemasons are expected to be in rough balance over the 2008–18 period as laid-off workers and a reduced level of construction help balance out a need for skilled brickmasons, blockmasons, and stonemasons. The masonry workforce is growing older, and a large number of masons are expected to retire over the next decade, which will create many job openings. Applicants who take masonry-related courses at technical schools will improve their job prospects.

Projections data from the National Employment Matrix

Occupational Title	SOC Code	Employment, 2008	Projected Employment, 2018	Change, 2008-2018	
				Number	Percent
Brickmasons, blockmasons, and stonemasons................................	47-2020	160,200	178,600	18,500	12
Brickmasons and blockmasons..	47-2021	135,800	151,500	15,600	12
Stonemasons	47-2022	24,300	27,100	2,800	12

(NOTE) Data in this table are rounded. See the discussion of the employment projections table in the *Handbook* introductory chapter on *Occupational Information Included in the Handbook.*

Employment of brickmasons, blockmasons, and stonemasons, like that of many other construction workers, is sensitive to changes in the economy. When the level of construction activity falls, workers in these trades can experience periods of unemployment. On the other hand, shortages of workers may occur in some areas during peak periods of building activity. Ongoing, however, is the need to repair and restore a large number of aging masonry buildings. This work will increase opportunities for workers with these types of skills.

New concerns over the costs of heating and cooling buildings of all types has led to a need to train construction workers of all types, including brickmasons, blockmasons, and stonemasons, in the emerging field of green construction. Contractors familiar with this burgeoning area will have better job opportunities in the future.

Earnings

Median hourly wages of brickmasons and blockmasons in May 2008 were $21.94. The middle 50 percent earned between $16.77 and $28.46. The lowest 10 percent earned less than $13.26, and the highest 10 percent earned more than $35.63. In the two industries employing the largest numbers of brickmasons and blockmasons in May 2008—the foundation, structure, and building exterior contractors industry and the nonresidential building industry—median hourly wages were $21.71 and $23.84, respectively.

Median hourly wages of wage and salary stonemasons in May 2008 were $18.17. The middle 50 percent earned between $14.31 and $23.72. The lowest 10 percent earned less than $11.63, and the highest 10 percent earned more than $31.87.

Apprentices or helpers usually start at about 50 percent of the wage rate paid to experienced workers. Pay increases as apprentices gain experience and learn new skills. Employers usually increase apprentices' wages about every 6 months on the basis of specific advancement criteria.

About 18 percent of brickmasons, blockmasons, and stonemasons were members of unions, mainly the International Union of Bricklayers and Allied Craftsworkers.

Related Occupations

Brickmasons, blockmasons, and stonemasons combine a thorough knowledge of brick, concrete block, stone, and marble with manual skill to erect attractive, yet highly durable, structures. Workers in other occupations with similar skills include:

	Page
Carpenters	618
Carpet, floor, and tile installers and finishers	621
Cement masons, concrete finishers, segmental pavers, and terrazzo workers	625
Drywall and ceiling tile installers, tapers, plasterers, and stucco masons	638

Sources of Additional Information

For details about apprenticeships or other work opportunities in these trades, contact local bricklaying, stonemasonry, or marble-setting contractors; the Associated Builders and Contractors; a local office of the International Union of Bricklayers and Allied Craftsworkers; a local joint union-management apprenticeship committee; or the nearest office of a State employment service or apprenticeship agency. Apprenticeship information is also available from the U.S. Department of Labor's toll-free helpline: (877) 872-5627 and online at: **http://www.doleta.gov/OA/eta_default.cfm**

For general information on apprenticeships and how to get them, see the *Occupational Outlook Quarterly* article "Apprenticeships: Career training, credentials—and a paycheck in your pocket," online at **http://www.bls.gov/opub/ooq/2002/summer/art01.pdf** and in print in many libraries and career centers.

For information on training for brickmasons, blockmasons, and stonemasons, contact:

➤ Mason Contractors Association of America, 33 South Roselle Rd., Schaumburg, IL 60193. Internet: **http://www.masoncontractors.org**

➤ National Association of Home Builders, Home Builders Institute, 1201 15th St. NW., Washington, DC 20005. Internet: **http://www.hbi.org**

For information about training, including a credential in green construction, contact:

➤ International Union of Bricklayers and Allied Craftworkers, 620 F St. NW., Washington, DC 20004. Internet: **http://www.bacweb.org**

➤ National Center for Construction Education and Research, 3600 NW. 43rd St., Bldg. G, Gainesville, FL 32606. Internet: **http://www.nccer.org**

For general information about the work of bricklayers, contact:

➤ International Masonry Institute National Training Center, The James Brice House, 42 East St., Annapolis, MD 21401. Internet: **http://www.imiweb.org**

➤ Associated General Contractors of America, Inc., 2300 Wilson Blvd., Suite 400, Arlington, VA 22201. Internet: **http://www.agc.org**

➤ National Concrete Masonry Association, 13750 Sunrise Valley Dr., Herndon, VA 20171-4662. Internet: **http://www.ncma.org**

The Occupational Information Network (O*NET) provides information on a wide range of occupational characteristics. Links to O*NET appear at the end of the Internet version of this occupational statement, accessible at **http://www.bls.gov/ooh/ocos201.htm**

Carpenters

Significant Points

- About 32 percent of all carpenters are self-employed.

- Job opportunities should be best for those with the most training and skills.

- Carpenters can learn their craft through on-the-job training, vocational schools or technical colleges, or formal apprenticeship programs, which often takes 3 to 4 years.

Nature of the Work

Carpenters construct, erect, install, and repair structures and fixtures made from wood and other materials. Carpenters are involved in many different kinds of construction, from the building of highways and bridges to the installation of kitchen cabinets.

Each carpentry task is somewhat different, but most involve the same basic steps. Working from blueprints or instructions from supervisors, carpenters first do the layout—measuring, marking, and arranging materials—in accordance with local building codes. They cut and shape wood, plastic, fiberglass, or drywall using hand and power tools, such as chisels, planes, saws, drills, and sanders. They then join the materials with nails, screws, staples, or adhesives. In the last step, carpenters do a final check of the accuracy of their work with levels, rules, plumb bobs, framing squares, and surveying equipment, and make any necessary adjustments. Some materials come prefabricated, allowing for easier and faster installation.

Carpenters may do many different carpentry tasks, or they may specialize in one or two. Carpenters who remodel homes and other structures, for example, need a broad range of carpentry skills. As part of a single job, they might frame walls and partitions, put in doors and windows, build stairs, install cabinets and molding, and complete many other tasks. Well-trained carpenters are able to switch from residential building to commercial construction or remodeling work, depending on which offers the best work opportunities.

Carpenters who work for large construction contractors or specialty contractors may perform only a few regular tasks, such as constructing wooden forms for pouring concrete, or erecting scaffolding. Some carpenters build tunnel bracing, or brattices, in underground passageways and mines to control the circulation of air through the passageways and to worksites. Others build concrete forms for tunnel, bridge, or sewer construction projects.

Carpenters employed outside the construction industry perform a variety of installation and maintenance work. They may replace panes of glass, ceiling tiles, and doors, as well as repair desks, cabinets, and other furniture. Depending on the employer, carpenters install partitions, doors, and windows; change locks; and repair broken furniture. In manufacturing firms, carpenters may assist in moving or installing machinery.

A carpenter uses a pneumatic gun for hammering nails.

(For more information on workers who install machinery, see the discussion of industrial machinery mechanics and millwrights, as well as maintenance and repair workers, general, elsewhere in the *Handbook*.)

Work environment. As is true of other building trades, carpentry work is sometimes strenuous. Prolonged standing, climbing, bending, and kneeling often are necessary. Carpenters risk injury working with sharp or rough materials, using sharp tools and power equipment, and working in situations where they might slip or fall. Consequently, workers in this occupation experience a very high incidence of nonfatal injuries and illnesses. Additionally, carpenters who work outdoors are subject to variable weather conditions.

Many carpenters work a standard 40 hour week; however, some work more. About 7 percent worked part time.

Training, Other Qualifications, and Advancement

Carpenters can learn their craft through on-the-job training, vocational schools or technical colleges, or formal apprenticeship programs, which often takes 3 to 4 years.

Education and training. Learning to be a carpenter can start in high school. Classes in English, algebra, geometry, physics, mechanical drawing, blueprint reading, and general shop will prepare students for the further training they will need.

After high school, there are a number of different ways to obtain the necessary training. Some people get a job as a carpenter's helper, assisting more experienced workers. At the same time, the helper might attend a trade or vocational school, or community college to receive further trade-related training and eventually become a carpenter.

Some employers offer employees formal apprenticeships. These programs combine on-the-job training with related classroom instruction. Apprentices usually must be at least 18 years old and meet local requirements. Apprenticeship programs usually last 3 to 4 years, but new rules may allow apprentices to complete programs sooner as competencies are demonstrated.

On the job, apprentices learn elementary structural design and become familiar with common carpentry jobs, such as layout, form building, rough framing, and outside and inside finishing. They also learn to use the tools, machines, equipment, and materials of the trade. In the classroom, apprentices learn safety, first aid, blueprint reading, freehand sketching, basic mathematics, and various carpentry techniques. Both in the classroom and on the job, they learn the relationship between carpentry and the other building trades.

The number of apprenticeship programs is limited, however, so only a small proportion of carpenters learn their trade through these programs. Most apprenticeships are offered by commercial and industrial building contractors, along with construction unions.

Some people who are interested in carpentry careers choose to receive classroom training before seeking a job. There are a number of public and private vocational-technical schools and training academies affiliated with unions and contractors that offer training to become a carpenter. Employers often look favorably upon these students and usually start them at a higher level than those without this training.

Other qualifications. Carpenters need manual dexterity, good eye-hand coordination, physical fitness, and a good sense of balance. The ability to solve mathematical problems quickly and accurately also is required. In addition, military service or a good work history is viewed favorably by employers.

Certification and advancement. Carpenters who complete formal apprenticeship programs receive certification as journeypersons. Some carpenters earn other certifications in scaffold building, high torque bolting, or pump work. These certifications prove that carpenters are able to perform these tasks, which can lead to additional responsibilities.

Carpenters usually have more opportunities than most other construction workers to become general construction supervisors, because carpenters are exposed to the entire construction process. For those who would like to advance, it is increasingly important to be able to communicate in both English and Spanish in order to relay instructions and safety precautions to workers; Spanish-speaking workers make up a large part of the construction workforce in many areas. Carpenters may advance to carpentry supervisor or general construction supervisor positions. Others may become independent contractors. Supervisors and contractors need good communication skills to deal with clients and subcontractors. They also should be able to identify and estimate the quantity of materials needed to complete a job and accurately estimate how long a job will take to complete and what it will cost.

Employment

Carpenters are employed throughout the country in almost every community and make up the second largest building trades occupation. They held about 1.3 million jobs in 2008.

About 32 percent worked in the construction of buildings industry, and about 22 percent worked for specialty trade contractors. Most of the rest of wage and salary carpenters worked for manufacturing firms, government agencies, retail establishments, and a wide variety of other industries. About 32 percent of all carpenters were self-employed. Some carpenters change employers each time they finish a construction job. Others alternate between working for a contractor and working as contractors themselves on small jobs, depending on where the work is available.

Job Outlook

As fast as average job growth, coupled with replacement needs, will create a large number of openings each year. Job opportunities should be best for those with the most training and skills.

Employment change. Employment of carpenters is expected to increase by 13 percent during the 2008–18 decade, as fast as the average for all occupations. Population growth over the next decade will stimulate some growth in the construction industry over the long run to meet people's housing and other basic needs. Energy conservation will also stimulate demand for buildings that are more energy efficient, particularly in the industrial sector. The home remodeling market also will create demand for carpenters. Moreover, construction of roads and bridges should

increase the demand for carpenters in the coming decade. Much will depend on spending by the Federal and State governments, as they attempt to upgrade and repair existing infrastructure, such as highways, bridges, and public buildings.

Some of the demand for carpenters, however, will be offset by expected productivity gains resulting from the increasing use of prefabricated components and improved fasteners and tools. Prefabricated wall panels, roof assemblies, and stairs, as well as prehung doors and windows can be installed very quickly. Instead of having to be built on the worksite, prefabricated walls, partitions, and stairs can be lifted into place in one operation; beams and, in some cases, entire roof assemblies, are lifted into place using a crane. As prefabricated components become more standardized, builders will use them more often. New and improved tools, equipment, techniques, and materials also are making carpenters more versatile, allowing them to perform more carpentry tasks.

Job prospects. Job opportunities will be good for those with the most training and skills. The need to replace carpenters who retire or leave the occupation for other reasons should result in a large number of openings. Carpenters with specialized or all-around skills will have better opportunities for steady work than carpenters who can perform only a few relatively simple, routine tasks.

Employment of carpenters, like that of many other construction workers, is sensitive to the fluctuations of the economy. Workers in these trades may experience periods of unemployment when the overall level of construction falls. On the other hand, shortages of these workers may occur in some areas during peak periods of building activity.

Job opportunities for carpenters also vary by geographic area. Construction activity parallels the movement of people and businesses and reflects differences in local economic conditions. The areas with the largest population increases will also provide the best opportunities for jobs as carpenters and for apprenticeships for people seeking to become carpenters.

Earnings

In May 2008, median hourly wages of wage and salary carpenters were $18.72. The middle 50 percent earned between $14.42 and $25.37. The lowest 10 percent earned less than $11.66, and the highest 10 percent earned more than $33.34. Median hourly wages in the industries employing the largest numbers of carpenters were as follows:

Nonresidential building construction $21.08
Building finishing contractors 19.37
Residential building construction 18.24
Foundation, structure, and building
    exterior contractors 17.67
Employment services 15.81

Projections data from the National Employment Matrix

Occupational Title	SOC Code	Employment, 2008	Projected Employment, 2018	Change, 2008-2018	
				Number	Percent
Carpenters	47-2031	1,284,900	1,450,300	165,400	13

(NOTE) Data in this table are rounded. See the discussion of the employment projections table in the *Handbook* introductory chapter on *Occupational Information Included in the Handbook.*

Earnings can be reduced on occasion, because carpenters lose worktime in bad weather and during recessions when jobs are unavailable. Earnings may be increased by overtime during busy periods.

Some carpenters are members of the United Brotherhood of Carpenters and Joiners of America. About 19 percent of all carpenters were members of unions or covered by union contracts, higher than the average for all occupations.

Related Occupations

Carpenters are skilled construction workers. Other skilled construction occupations include:

Sources of Additional Information

For information about carpentry apprenticeships or other work opportunities in this trade, contact local carpentry contractors, locals of the union mentioned above, local joint union-contractor apprenticeship committees, or the nearest office of the State employment service or apprenticeship agency. You can also find information on the registered apprenticeship system with links to State apprenticeship programs on the U.S. Department of Labor Web site: **http://www.doleta.gov/OA/eta_default.cfm.** Apprenticeship information is also available from the U.S. Department of Labor toll-free helpline: (877) 872-5627.

For information on training opportunities and carpentry in general, contact:

➤ Associated Builders and Contractors, 4250 North Fairfax Dr., 9th Floor, Arlington, VA 22203-1607. Internet: **http://www.trytools.org**

➤ Associated General Contractors of America, Inc., 2300 Wilson Blvd., Suite 400, Arlington, VA 22201-5426. Internet: **http://www.agc.org**

➤ National Center for Construction Education and Research, 3600 NW. 43rd St., Bldg. G, Gainesville, FL, 32606-8134. Internet: **http://www.nccer.org**

➤ National Association of Home Builders, Home Builders Institute, 1201 15th St. NW., Washington, DC 20005-2842. Internet: **http://www.hbi.org**

➤ United Brotherhood of Carpenters and Joiners of America, Carpenters Training Fund, 101 Constitution Ave. NW, Washington, DC 20001-2192. Internet: **http://www.carpenters.org**

For general information on apprenticeships and how to get them, see the *Occupational Outlook Quarterly* article "Apprenticeships: Career training, credentials—and a paycheck in your pocket," online at **http://www.bls.gov/opub/ooq/2002/summer/art01.pdf** and in print at many libraries and career centers.

The Occupational Information Network (O*NET) provides information on a wide range of occupational characteristics. Links to O*NET appear at the end of the Internet version of this occupational statement, accessible at **http://www.bls.gov/ooh/ocos202.htm**

Carpet, Floor, and Tile Installers and Finishers

Significant Points

- Most workers learn on the job.
- About 35 percent of carpet, floor, and tile installers and finishers are self-employed.
- Projected job growth varies by specialty; for example, tile and marble setters are expected to grow by 14 percent, while carpet installers is projected to decline by 1 percent.
- Employment of carpet, floor, and tile installers and finishers is less sensitive to fluctuations in construction activity than is employment of workers in other construction trades.

Nature of the Work

Carpet, floor, and tile installers and finishers lay floor coverings in homes, offices, hospitals, stores, restaurants, and many other types of buildings. Tile also may be installed on walls and ceilings. Carpet, tile, and other types of floor coverings not only serve an important basic function in buildings, but their decorative qualities also contribute to the appeal of the buildings.

Before installing carpet, carpet installers first inspect the surface to be covered to determine its condition and, when necessary, correct any imperfections that could show through the carpet or cause the carpet to wear unevenly. They measure the area to be carpeted and plan the layout, keeping in mind likely traffic patterns and placement of seams for best appearance and maximum wear.

When installing wall-to-wall carpet without tacks, installers first fasten a tackless strip to the floor, next to the wall. They then install the padded cushion, or underlay. Next, they roll out, measure, mark, and cut the carpet, allowing for 2 to 3 inches of extra carpet for the final fitting. Using a device called a "knee kicker," they position the carpet, stretching it to fit evenly on the floor and snugly against each wall and door threshold. They then cut off the excess carpet. Finally, using a power stretcher, they stretch the carpet, hooking it to the tackless strip to hold it in place. The installers then finish the edges using a wall trimmer.

Because most carpet comes in 12-foot widths, wall-to-wall installations require installers to join carpet sections together for large rooms. The installers join the sections using heat-taped seams—seams held together by a special plastic tape that is activated by heat.

In commercial installations, carpet often is glued directly to the floor or to padding that has been glued to the floor. For special upholstery work, such as installing carpet on stairs, carpet may be held in place with staples.

Carpet installers use hand tools such as hammers, drills, staple guns, carpet knives, and rubber mallets. They also may use carpet-laying tools, such as carpet shears, knee kickers, wall trimmers, loop pile cutters, heat irons, and power stretchers.

Floor installers and *floor layers* lay floor coverings such as laminate, linoleum, vinyl, cork, and rubber for decorative purposes or to reduce noise, absorb shocks, or create air-tight environments. Although these workers also may install carpet, wood, or tile, that is not their main job. Before installing the floor, floor layers inspect the surface to be covered and, if necessary, correct any defects, such as a sub-floor that is unleveled or contains rotted wood, in order to start with a strong, smooth, clean foundation. Then they measure and cut flooring materials. When installing linoleum or vinyl, they may use an adhesive to glue the material directly to the floor. For laminate floor installation, workers may unroll and install a polyethylene film that acts as a moisture barrier, along with a thicker, padded underlayer that helps reduce noise. Cork and rubber floors can often be installed directly on top of the sub-floor without an underlayer. Finally, floor layers install the floor covering to form a tight fit.

After a carpenter installs a new hardwood floor or when a customer wants to refinish an old wood floor, floor sanders and finishers are called in to smooth any imperfections in the wood and apply coats of varnish or polyurethane. To remove imperfections and smooth the surface, they scrape and sand wood floors using floor-sanding machines. After sanding, they then examine the floor and remove excess glue from joints using a knife or wood chisel and may further sand the wood surfaces by hand, using sandpaper. Finally, they apply sealant using brushes or rollers, often applying multiple coats.

Tile installers, *tilesetters*, and *marble setters* apply hard tile and marble to floors, walls, ceilings, countertops, patios, and

Carpet, floor, and tile installers and finishers lay floor coverings in homes and other types of buildings.

roof decks. Tile and marble are durable, impervious to water, and easy to clean, making them a popular building material in bathrooms, kitchens, hospitals, and commercial buildings.

Prior to installation, tilesetters use measuring devices, spacers, and levels to ensure that the tile is placed in a consistent manner. Tiles vary in color, shape, and size, with their sides ranging from 1 inch to 24 or more inches in length, so tilesetters sometimes prearrange tiles on a dry floor according to the planned design. This allows them to examine the pattern, check that they have enough of each type of tile, and determine where they will have to cut tiles to fit the design in the available space. Tilesetters cut tiles with a machine saw or a special cutting tool to cover all exposed areas, including corners and around pipes, tubs, and wash basins. To set tile on a flat, solid surface, such as drywall, concrete, plaster, or wood, tilesetters first use a tooth-edged trowel to spread a "thin set"—a thin layer of either cement adhesive or "mastic," which is a very sticky paste. They then properly position the tile and gently tap the surface with the trowel handle, a rubber mallet, or a small block of wood to set the tile evenly and firmly. Spacers are used to maintain exact distance between tiles, and any excess thin set is wiped off the tile immediately after placement.

To apply tile to an area that lacks a solid surface, tilesetters nail a support of metal mesh or tile backer board to the wall or ceiling to be tiled. They use a trowel to apply a cement mortar—called a "scratch coat"—onto the metal screen, and scratch the surface of the soft mortar with a small tool similar to a rake. After the scratch coat has dried, tilesetters apply a brown coat of mortar to level the surface, and then apply mortar to the brown coat and begin to place tile onto the surface. Hard backer board also is used in areas where there is excess moisture, such as a shower stall.

When the cement or mastic has set, tilesetters fill the joints with "grout," which is very fine cement. Grout that is used for joints 1/8th of an inch and larger typically has sand in it. Tilesetters then apply the grout to the surface with a rubber-edged device called a "float" or a grouting trowel to fill the joints and remove excess grout. Before the grout sets, they wipe the tiles and smooth the joints with a wet sponge for a uniform appearance.

Marble setters cut and set marble slabs on floors and walls of buildings. They trim and cut marble to specified sizes using a power wet saw, other electric cutting equipment, or handtools. After setting the marble in place, the workers polish the marble to a high luster using power tools or by hand.

Work environment. Carpet, floor, and tile installers and finishers usually work indoors and have regular daytime hours. However, when floor covering installers need to work in occupied stores or offices, they may work evenings and weekends to avoid disturbing customers or employees. By the time workers install carpets, flooring, or tile in a new structure, the majority of construction has been completed and the work area is relatively clean and uncluttered. Installing these materials is labor intensive; workers spend much of their time bending, kneeling, and reaching—activities that require endurance. The work can be very hard on workers' knees; therefore, safety regulations often require that they wear kneepads. Carpet installers frequently lift heavy rolls of carpet and may move heavy furniture, which requires strength and can be physically exhausting and hard on workers' backs. Carpet and floor layers may be exposed to fumes from various kinds of glue and to fibers of certain types of carpet. Tile and floor installers are usually required to wear safety goggles when using certain equipment.

Workers are subject to cuts from tools or materials, falls from ladders, and strained muscles. Data from the U.S. Bureau of Labor Statistics show that full-time carpet, floor, and tile installers and finishers experienced a work-related injury and illness rate that was higher than the national average.

Training, Other Qualifications, and Advancement

The vast majority of carpet, floor, and tile installers and finishers learn their trade informally on the job. Some workers, mostly tile setters, learn through formal apprenticeship programs, which include classroom instruction and paid on-the-job training.

Education and training. Most carpet installers receive short-term on-the-job training, often sponsored by individual contractors; therefore, a high school diploma usually is not required. Workers start as helpers and begin with simple assignments, such as installing stripping and padding, or helping to stretch newly installed carpet. With experience, helpers take on more difficult assignments, such as cutting and fitting.

Tile and marble setters learn their craft mostly through long-term on-the-job training. They start by helping carry materials and learning about the tools of the trade, and later they take on more difficult tasks, such as preparing the subsurface for tile or marble. As tile and marble setters progress, they learn to cut the tile and marble to fit the job. They also learn to apply grout and sealants to give the product its final appearance. Apprenticeship programs and some contractor-sponsored programs provide comprehensive training in all phases of the tilesetting and floor layer trades.

Other floor layers also learn on the job and begin by learning how to use the tools of the trade. As they progress, they learn how to cut and install the various floor coverings.

Other qualifications. Good manual dexterity, eye-hand coordination, physical fitness, and sense of balance and color are some of the skills needed to become carpet, floor, and tile installers and finishers. The ability to solve basic arithmetic problems quickly and accurately also is required. In addition, reliability and a good work history are viewed favorably by contractors.

Advancement. Carpet, floor, and tile installers and finishers sometimes advance to become supervisors, salespersons, or estimators. In these positions, they must be able to estimate the time, money, and quantity of materials needed to complete a job.

Some carpet installers may become managers for large installation firms. For those interested in advancement, it is increasingly important to be able to communicate in both English and Spanish because Spanish-speaking workers make up a large part of the construction workforce in many areas. Workers who want to advance to supervisor jobs or become independent contractors also need good English skills to deal with clients and subcontractors.

Many carpet, floor, and tile installers and finishers who begin working for someone else eventually go into business for themselves as independent contractors.

Employment

Carpet, floor, and tile installers and finishers held about 160,500 jobs in 2008. About 35 percent of all carpet, floor, and tile installers and finishers were self-employed. The following tabulation shows 2008 total employment by specialty:

Tile and marble setters	76,000
Carpet installers	51,100
Floor layers, except carpet, wood, and hard tiles	21,200
Floor sanders and finishers	12,200

Many carpet installers work for flooring contractors or floor covering retailers. Most salaried tilesetters are employed by tile-setting contractors who work mainly on nonresidential construction projects, such as schools, hospitals, and office buildings. Most self-employed tilesetters work on residential projects.

Although carpet, floor, and tile installers and finishers are employed throughout the Nation, they tend to be concentrated in populated areas where there are high levels of construction activity.

Job Outlook

Employment of carpet, floor, and tile installers and finishers is expected to grow as fast as the average for all occupations. Job growth and opportunities, however, will differ among the individual occupations in this category.

Employment change. Overall employment is expected to grow by 7 percent between 2008 and 2018, about as fast as the average. Tile and marble setting, the largest specialty, will experience faster than average employment growth because population and business growth will result in more construction of shopping malls, hospitals, schools, restaurants, and other structures in which tile is used extensively. Tiles, including those made of glass, slate, and mosaic, and other less traditional materials, are also becoming more popular, particularly in the growing number of more expensive homes.

Employment of carpet installers, the second-largest specialty, will decline by 1 percent as residential investors and homeowners increasingly choose hardwood and tile floors because of their durability, neutral colors, and low maintenance, and because owners feel these floors will add to the value of their

Projections data from the National Employment Matrix

Occupational Title	SOC Code	Employment, 2008	Projected Employment, 2018	Change, 2008-2018	
				Number	Percent
Carpet, floor, and tile installers and finishers	47-2040	160,500	171,900	11,400	7
Carpet installers	47-2041	51,100	50,500	-600	-1
Floor layers, except carpet, wood, and hard tiles	47-2042	21,200	21,000	-200	-1
Floor sanders and finishers	47-2043	12,200	13,600	1,400	11
Tile and marble setters	47-2044	76,000	86,800	10,800	14

(NOTE) Data in this table are rounded. See the discussion of the employment projections table in the *Handbook* introductory chapter on *Occupational Information Included in the Handbook.*

homes. Carpets, on the other hand, stain and wear out faster than wood or tile, which contributes to the decreased demand for carpet installation. Nevertheless, carpet will continue to be used in nonresidential structures such as schools, offices, and hospitals. Also, many multifamily structures will require or recommend carpet because it provides sound dampening.

Workers who install other types of flooring, including laminate, cork, bamboo, rubber, and vinyl, should have little or no job growth because these materials are used less frequently and are often laid by other types of construction workers. Employment of floor sanders and finishers—a small specialty—is projected to grow by 11 percent because of the increasing use of prefinished hardwood flooring and because their work is heavily concentrated in the relatively small niche market of residential remodeling. There should also be some employment growth resulting from restoration of damaged hardwood floors, a procedure that is typically more cost effective than installing new floors.

Job prospects. In addition to employment growth, numerous job openings are expected for carpet, floor, and tile installers and finishers because of the need to replace workers who leave the occupation. The strenuous nature of the work leads to high replacement needs; many of these workers do not stay in the occupation long.

Few openings will arise for vinyl and linoleum floor installers because the number of these jobs is comparatively small and because homeowners can increasingly take advantage of easy application products, such as self-adhesive vinyl tiles.

Employment of carpet, floor, and tile installers and finishers is less sensitive to changes in construction activity than most other construction occupations because much of the work involves replacing worn carpet and other flooring in existing buildings. However, workers in these trades may still experience periods of unemployment when the overall level of construction falls. On the other hand, shortages of these workers may occur in some areas during peak periods of building activity.

Earnings

In May 2008, median hourly wages of carpet installers were $17.80. The middle 50 percent earned between $12.82 and $25.35. The lowest 10 percent earned less than $10.23, and the top 10 percent earned more than $34.10. Median hourly wages of carpet installers working for building finishing contractors were $18.25, and $16.92 for those working in home furnishings stores. Carpet installers are paid either on an hourly basis or by the number of yards of carpet installed.

Median hourly wages of wage and salary floor layers except carpet, wood, and hard tiles were $17.50 in May 2008. The middle 50 percent earned between $13.34 and $23.33. The lowest 10 percent earned less than $10.55, and the top 10 percent earned more than $30.84.

Median hourly wages of floor sanders and finishers were $15.41 in May 2008. The middle 50 percent earned between $12.79 and $20.16. The lowest 10 percent earned less than $10.54, and the top 10 percent earned more than $25.96.

Median hourly wages of tile and marble setters were $18.85 in May 2008. The middle 50 percent earned between $13.71 and $25.19. The lowest 10 percent earned less than $10.65, and the top 10 percent earned more than $32.40.

Earnings of carpet, floor, and tile installers and finishers vary greatly by geographic location and by union membership status. Some carpet, floor, and tile installers and finishers belong to the United Brotherhood of Carpenters and Joiners of America. Some tilesetters belong to the International Union of Bricklayers and Allied Craftsmen, and some carpet installers belong to the International Brotherhood of Painters and Allied Trades.

Apprentices and other trainees usually start out earning about half of what an experienced worker earns; their wage rates increase as they advance through the training program.

Related Occupations

Carpet, floor, and tile installers and finishers measure, cut, and fit materials to cover a space. Workers in other occupations involving similar skills, but using different materials, include:

	Page
Brickmasons, blockmasons, and stonemasons	615
Carpenters	618
Cement masons, concrete finishers, segmental pavers, and terrazzo workers	625
Drywall and ceiling tile installers, tapers, plasterers, and stucco masons	638
Painters and paperhangers	656
Roofers	662
Sheet metal workers	665

Sources of Additional Information

For details about apprenticeships or work opportunities, contact local flooring or tilesetting contractors or retailers, locals of the unions previously mentioned, or the nearest office of the State apprenticeship agency or employment service. Apprenticeship information is also available from the U.S. Department of Labor's toll-free helpline: 1 (877) 872–5627.

Additional information on training for carpet installers and floor layers is available from:
➤ Finishing Trades Institute International, 7230 Parkway Drive, Hanover, MD 21076. Internet: **http://www.finishingtradesinstitute.org**

For general information about the work of tile installers and finishers, contact:
➤ National Association of Home Builders, Home Builders Institute, 1201 15th St. NW., Washington, DC 20005. Internet: **http://www.hbi.org** and **http://www.nahb.org**

For more information about tile setting and tile training, contact:
➤ National Tile Contractors Association, P.O. Box 13629, Jackson, MS 39236. Internet: **http://www.tile-assn.com**

For general information on apprenticeships and how to get them, see the *Occupational Outlook Quarterly* article "Apprenticeships: Career training, credentials—and a paycheck in your pocket," online at **http://www.bls.gov/opub/ooq/2002/summer/art01.pdf** and in print at many libraries and career centers.

The Occupational Information Network (O*NET) provides information on a wide range of occupational characteristics. Links to O*NET appear at the end of the Internet version of this occupational statement, accessible at **http://www.bls.gov/ooh/ocos203.htm**

Cement Masons, Concrete Finishers, Segmental Pavers, and Terrazzo Workers

Significant Points

- Job opportunities are expected to be good, especially for those with the most experience and skills.

- Most workers learn on the job or through a combination of classroom and on-the-job training that can take 3 to 4 years.

- Cement masons often have variable schedules and work overtime, with premium pay, because once concrete has been placed, the job must be completed quickly.

Nature of the Work

Cement masons, concrete finishers, and terrazzo workers all work with concrete, one of the most common and durable materials used in construction. Once set, concrete—a mixture of Portland cement, sand, gravel, and water—becomes the foundation for everything from decorative patios and floors to huge dams or miles of roadways.

Cement masons and *concrete finishers* place and finish concrete. They also may color concrete surfaces, expose aggregate (small stones) in walls and sidewalks, or fabricate concrete beams, columns, and panels. In preparing a site to place concrete, cement masons first set the forms for holding the concrete and properly align them. They then direct the casting of the concrete and supervise laborers who use shovels or special tools to spread it. Masons then guide a straightedge back and forth across the top of the forms to "screed," or level, the freshly placed concrete. Immediately after leveling the concrete, masons carefully float it—which means to smooth the concrete surface with a "bull float," a long-handled tool of about 8 by 48 inches that covers the coarser materials in the concrete and brings a rich mixture of fine cement paste to the surface.

After the concrete has been leveled and floated, concrete finishers press an edger between the forms and the concrete and guide it along the edge and the surface. This produces slightly rounded edges and helps prevent chipping or cracking. Concrete finishers use a special tool called a "groover" to make joints or grooves at specific intervals that help control cracking. Next, they smooth the surface using either a powered or hand trowel, which is a small, smooth, rectangular metal tool.

Sometimes, cement masons perform all the steps of laying concrete, including the finishing. As the final step, they retrowel the concrete surface back and forth with powered or hand trowels to create a smooth finish. For a coarse, nonskid finish, masons brush the surface with a broom or stiff-bristled brush. For a pebble finish, they embed small gravel chips into the surface. They then wash any excess cement from the exposed chips with a mild acid solution. For color, they use colored premixed concrete.

Throughout the entire process, cement masons must monitor how the wind, heat, or cold affects the curing of the concrete.

They must have a thorough knowledge of concrete characteristics so that, by using sight and touch, they can determine what is happening to the concrete and take measures to prevent defects.

Segmental pavers lay out, cut, and install pavers—flat pieces of masonry made from compacted concrete or brick. This masonry is typically installed in patios, sidewalks, plazas, streets, crosswalks, parking lots, and driveways. Installers usually begin their work by preparing a base that has been graded to the proper depth and filled and leveled with a layer of sand. Installers then place the pavers in a pattern, normally by hand but sometimes by machine. Sand is then added to fill the joints between the pavers.

Terrazzo workers and *finishers* create attractive walkways, floors, patios, and panels by exposing marble chips and other fine aggregates on the surface of finished concrete. Much of the preliminary work of terrazzo workers is similar to that of cement masons. Depending on the type of terrazzo, they usually first build a solid, level concrete foundation that is 3 to 4 inches deep. Second, after the forms are removed from the foundation, workers add a 1-inch layer of sandy concrete. Terrazzo workers partially embed, or attach with adhesive, metal divider strips in the concrete wherever there is to be a joint or change of color in the terrazzo. For the third and final layer, terrazzo workers blend and place into each of the panels a fine marble chip mixture that may be color-pigmented. While the mixture is still wet, workers add additional marble chips of various colors into each panel and roll a lightweight roller over the entire surface.

When the terrazzo is thoroughly set, helpers grind it with a terrazzo grinder, which is somewhat like a floor polisher, only much heavier. Any depressions left by the grinding are filled with a matching grout material and hand-troweled for a smooth, uniform surface. Terrazzo workers then clean, polish, and seal the dry surface for a lustrous finish.

Work environment. Concrete, segmental paving, and terrazzo work is fast paced and strenuous, and requires continuous physical effort. A work week of 40 hours is the most common, although the number of hours can be increased or decreased by outside factors, such as the need to coordinate work with other jobs being done on the construction site. As a result, about 17 percent of workers have a variable schedule.

Because most finishing is done at floor level, workers must bend and kneel often. Many jobs are outdoors, and work is

Concrete workers direct the concrete to a desired location.

generally halted during inclement weather. The work, either indoors or outdoors, may be in areas that are muddy, dusty, or dirty. To avoid chemical burns from uncured concrete and sore knees from frequent kneeling, many workers wear kneepads. Workers usually also wear water-repellent boots while working with wet concrete.

Training, Other Qualifications, and Advancement

Most cement masons, concrete finishers, segmental pavers, and terrazzo workers learn their trades through on-the-job training, either as helpers or in apprenticeship programs. Some workers also learn their jobs by attending trade or vocational-technical schools.

Education and training. Many masons and finishers first gain experience as construction laborers. (See the section on construction laborers elsewhere in the *Handbook*.) Most on-the-job training programs consist of informal instruction, in which experienced workers teach helpers to use the tools, equipment, machines, and materials of the trade. Trainees begin with tasks such as edging, jointing, and using a straightedge on freshly placed concrete. As training progresses, assignments become more complex, and trainees can usually do finishing work within a short time.

Some workers train in formal apprenticeship programs usually sponsored by local contractors, trade associations, or local union-management committees. These programs combine on-the-job training with a recommended minimum of 144 hours of classroom instruction each year. In the classroom, apprentices learn applied mathematics, blueprint reading, and safety. Apprentices generally receive special instruction in layout work and cost estimation. Apprenticeships may take 3 to 4 years to complete, although completion times are increasingly variable as apprenticeship progression based on demonstrated competence instead of time is gaining popularity. Applying for an apprenticeship may require a written test and a physical exam.

Many States have technical schools that offer courses in masonry which improve employment and advancement opportunities. Entrance requirements and fees vary depending on the school and who is funding the program. These schools may offer courses before hiring or after hiring as part of the on-the-job training.

Other qualifications. The most important qualities employers look for are dependability and a strong work ethic. When hiring helpers and apprentices, employers prefer high school graduates who are at least 18 years old, possess a driver's license, and are in good physical condition. The ability to get along with others is also important because cement masons frequently work in teams. High school courses in general science, mathematics, and vocational-technical subjects—such as blueprint reading and mechanical drawing—provide a helpful background. Cement masons, concrete finishers, segmental pavers, and terrazzo workers should enjoy doing demanding work. They should take pride in craftsmanship and be able to work without close supervision.

Advancement. With additional training, cement masons, concrete finishers, segmental pavers, or terrazzo workers may become supervisors for masonry contractors or move into construction management, building inspection, or contract estimation. Certification programs offered through the National Concrete Masonry Association may allow workers to advance more quickly as they document higher levels of skill in working with concrete. Some workers eventually become owners of businesses, where they may spend most of their time managing rather than practicing their original trade. For those who want to own their own business, taking business classes will help to prepare.

Employment

Cement masons, concrete finishers, segmental pavers, and terrazzo workers held about 207,800 jobs in 2008; segmental pavers and terrazzo workers accounted for only a small portion of the total. Most cement masons and concrete finishers worked for specialty trade contractors, primarily foundation, structure, and building exterior contractors. They also worked for contractors in nonresidential and residential building construction and in heavy and civil engineering construction on projects such as highways, bridges, shopping malls, or large buildings such as factories, schools, and hospitals. A small number were employed by firms that manufacture concrete products. Most segmental pavers and terrazzo workers worked for specialty trade contractors who install decorative floors and wall panels.

Only about 5 percent of cement masons, concrete finishers, segmental pavers, and terrazzo workers were self-employed, a smaller proportion than in other building trades. Most self-employed masons specialize in small jobs, such as driveways, sidewalks, and patios.

Job Outlook

Average employment growth is expected, and job prospects are expected to be good, especially for those with the most experience and skills.

Employment change. Employment of cement masons, concrete finishers, segmental pavers, and terrazzo workers is

Projections data from the National Employment Matrix

Occupational Title	SOC Code	Employment, 2008	Projected Employment, 2018	Change, 2008-2018	
				Number	Percent
Cement masons, concrete finishers, segmental pavers, and terrazzo workers..	–	207,800	234,500	26,700	13
Cement masons, concrete finishers, and terrazzo workers............	47-2050	206,600	233,200	26,600	13
Cement masons and concrete finishers....................................	47-2051	201,000	226,800	25,900	13
Terrazzo workers and finishers..	47-2053	5,600	6,300	700	13
Segmental pavers...	47-4091	1,200	1,300	100	7

(NOTE) Data in this table are rounded. See the discussion of the employment projections table in the *Handbook* introductory chapter on *Occupational Information Included in the Handbook.*

expected to grow approximately 13 percent over the 2008–18 decade, about as fast as the average for all occupations. Over the long run, more workers will likely be needed to build new highways, bridges, factories, and other residential and nonresidential structures to meet the demands of a growing population. Additionally, cement masons will be needed to repair and renovate existing highways and bridges and other aging structures. Additional funds for these projects are expected to come from the Federal Government, which plans to spend money on construction to stimulate the national economy by addressing necessary infrastructure repairs and renovating schools and other government buildings.

The use of concrete for buildings is increasing because its strength is an important asset in areas prone to severe weather. For example, residential construction in Florida is using more concrete as building requirements are changed in reaction to the increased frequency and intensity of hurricanes. Concrete use is likely to expand into other hurricane-prone areas as the durability of the Florida homes is demonstrated.

Job prospects. Opportunities for cement masons, concrete finishers, segmental pavers, and terrazzo workers are expected to be good, particularly for those with the most experience and skills. Employers report difficulty in finding workers with the right skills, as many qualified jobseekers often prefer work that is less strenuous and has more comfortable working conditions. There are also expected to be a significant number of retirements over the next decade, which will create more job openings. Applicants who take masonry-related courses at technical schools will have better opportunities than those without these courses.

Employment of cement masons, concrete finishers, segmental pavers, and terrazzo workers, like that of many other construction workers, is sensitive to the fluctuations of the economy. Workers in these trades may experience periods of unemployment when the overall level of construction falls. On the other hand, shortages of these workers may occur in some areas during peak periods of building activity.

Earnings

In May 2008, the median hourly wage of cement masons and concrete finishers was $16.87. The middle 50 percent earned between $13.46 and $22.71. The bottom 10 percent earned less than $11.02, and the top 10 percent earned more than $30.30. Median hourly wages in the industries employing the largest numbers of cement masons and concrete finishers were as follows:

Nonresidential building construction	$17.82
Other specialty trade contractors	17.26
Highway, street, and bridge construction	17.12
Residential building construction	16.68
Foundation, structure, and building exterior contractors	16.67

In May 2008, the median hourly wage of terrazzo workers and finishers was $17.25. The middle 50 percent earned between $13.65 and $23.12. The bottom 10 percent earned less than $10.82, and the top 10 percent earned more than $30.12.

In May 2008, the median hourly wage of segmental pavers was $13.17. The middle 50 percent earned between $10.77 and

$16.41. The bottom 10 percent earned less than $9.14, and the top 10 percent earned more than $19.33.

Like other construction trades workers who are paid by the hour, earnings of cement masons, concrete finishers, segmental pavers, and terrazzo workers may be reduced on occasion because poor weather and slowdowns in construction activity limit the amount of time they can work. Nonunion workers generally have lower wage rates than union workers. Apprentices usually start at 50 to 60 percent of the rate paid to experienced workers, and increases are generally achieved by meeting specified advancement requirements every 6 months. Cement masons often work overtime, with premium pay, because once concrete has been placed, the job must be completed.

About 14 percent of cement masons, concrete finishers, segmental pavers, and terrazzo workers belong to unions, the largest of which are the Operative Plasterers' and Cement Masons' International Association of the United States and Canada, and the International Union of Bricklayers and Allied Craftworkers. A few terrazzo workers belong to the United Brotherhood of Carpenters and Joiners of the United States.

Related Occupations

Other construction-related occupations requiring similar skills and knowledge include:

	Page
Brickmasons, blockmasons, and stonemasons	615
Carpet, floor, and tile installers and finishers	621
Drywall and ceiling tile installers, tapers, plasterers, and stucco masons	638

An additional occupation in which workers use cement, segmental pavers, and terazzo in their work is:

Grounds maintenance workers	498

Sources of Additional Information

For information about apprenticeships and work opportunities, contact local concrete or terrazzo contractors, local offices of unions previously mentioned, a local joint union-management apprenticeship committee, or the nearest office of a State employment service or apprenticeship agency. Apprenticeship information is also available from the U.S. Department of Labor's toll-free helpline: (877) 872-5627. You may also check the U.S. Department of Labor's Web site for information on apprenticeships and links to State apprenticeship programs. Internet: **http://www.doleta.gov/OA/eta_default.cfm**

For general information about cement masons, concrete finishers, segmental pavers, and terrazzo workers, contact:

➤ Associated Builders and Contractors, Workforce Development Division, 4250 North Fairfax Dr., 9th Floor, Arlington, VA 22203-1607. Internet: **http://www.trytools.org**

➤ Associated General Contractors of America, Inc., 2300 Wilson Blvd., Suite 400, Arlington, VA 22201-5426. Internet: **http://www.agc.org**

➤ International Union of Bricklayers and Allied Craftworkers, International Masonry Institute, The James Brice House, 42 East St., Annapolis, MD 21401-1731. Internet: **http://www.imiweb.org**

➤ National Center for Construction Education and Research, 3600 NW. 43rd St., Bldg. G, Gainesville, FL 32606-8127. Internet: **http://www.nccer.org**

➤ National Concrete Masonry Association, 13750 Sunrise Valley Dr., Herndon, VA 20171-4662. Internet: **http://www.ncma.org**

➤ National Terrazzo and Mosaic Association, 201 North Maple, Suite 208, Purcellville, VA 20132-6102. Internet: **http://www.ntma.com**

➤ Operative Plasterers' and Cement Masons' International Association of the United States and Canada, 11720 Beltsville Dr., Suite 700, Beltsville, MD 20705-3104. Internet: **http://www.opcmia.org**

➤ Portland Cement Association, 5420 Old Orchard Rd., Skokie, IL 60077-1083. Internet: **http://www.cement.org**

For more information about careers and training as a mason, contact:

➤ Mason Contractors Association of America, 33 South Roselle Rd., Schaumburg, IL 60193-1646. Internet: **http://www.masoncontractors.org**

For general information on apprenticeships and how to get them, see the *Occupational Outlook Quarterly* article "Apprenticeships: Career training, credentials—and a paycheck in your pocket," online at **http://www.bls.gov/opub/ooq/2002/summer/art01.pdf** and in print at many libraries and career centers.

The Occupational Information Network (O*NET) provides information on a wide range of occupational characteristics. Links to O*NET appear at the end of the Internet version of this occupational statement, accessible at **http://www.bls.gov/ooh/ocos204.htm**

Construction and Building Inspectors

Significant Points

- About 44 percent of inspectors worked for local governments, primarily municipal or county building departments.

- Many home inspectors are self-employed.

- Training requirements vary widely; some States require a license or certificate.

- Opportunities should be best for those with construction-related work experience; training in engineering, architecture, construction technology, or related fields; or certification as a construction inspector.

Nature of the Work

Construction and building inspectors examine buildings, highways and streets, sewer and water systems, dams, bridges, and other structures. They ensure that their construction, alteration, or repair complies with building codes and ordinances, zoning regulations, and contract specifications. Building codes and standards are the primary means by which building construction is regulated in the United States for the health and safety of the general public. National model building and construction codes are published by the International Code Council (ICC), although many localities have additional ordinances and codes that modify or add to the National model codes. To monitor compliance with regulations, inspectors make an initial inspection during the first phase of construction and follow up with further inspections throughout the construction project. However, no inspection is ever exactly the same. In areas where certain types of severe weather or natural disasters—such as earthquakes or hurricanes—are more common, inspectors monitor compliance with additional safety regulations designed to protect structures and occupants during those events.

There are many types of inspectors. *Building inspectors* inspect the structural quality and general safety of buildings. Some specialize in for example, structural steel or reinforced-concrete structures. Before construction begins, *plan examiners* determine whether the plans for the building or other structure comply with building codes and whether they are suited to the engineering and environmental demands of the building site. To inspect the condition of the soil and the positioning and depth of the footings, inspectors visit the worksite before the foundation is poured. Later, they return to the site to inspect the foundation after it has been completed. The size and type of structure, as well as the rate at which it proceeds toward completion, determine the number of other site visits they must make. Upon completion of the project, they make a final, comprehensive inspection.

In addition to structural characteristics, a primary concern of building inspectors is fire safety. They inspect structures' fire sprinklers, alarms, smoke control systems, and fire exits. Inspectors assess the type of construction, the building's contents, adequacy of fire protection equipment, and any risks posed by adjoining buildings. (For additional information on *fire inspectors*, see the statement on fire inspectors and investigators elsewhere in the *Handbook*.)

Electrical inspectors examine the installation of electrical systems and equipment to ensure that they function properly and comply with electrical codes and standards. They visit worksites to inspect new and existing sound and security systems, wiring, lighting, motors, and generating equipment. They also inspect the installation of the electrical wiring for heating and air-conditioning systems, appliances, and other components.

Elevator inspectors examine lifting and conveying devices such as elevators, escalators, moving sidewalks, lifts and hoists, inclined railways, ski lifts, and amusement rides.

Home inspectors conduct inspections of newly built or previously owned homes, condominiums, town homes, manufactured homes, apartments, and commercial buildings. Home inspection has become a standard practice in the home-purchasing process. Home inspectors are most often hired by prospective home buyers to inspect and report on the condition of a home's systems, components, and structure. Although they look for and report violations of building codes, they do not have the power to enforce compliance with the codes. Typically, they are hired either immediately prior to a purchase offer on a home or as a contingency to a sales contract. In addition to examining structural quality, home inspectors inspect all home systems and features, including roofing as well as the exterior, attached garage or carport, foundation, interior, plumbing, and electrical, heating, and cooling systems. Some home inspections are done for homeowners who want an evaluation of their home's condition, for example, prior to putting the home on the market or as a way to diagnose problems.

Mechanical inspectors examine the installation of heating, ventilation, air conditioning, and refrigeration systems and equipment to insure they are installed and function properly. This may include the inspection of commercial kitchen equipment, gas-fired appliances, and boilers.

Plumbing inspectors examine the installation of piping systems to insure the safety and health of the drinking water system, chemical process piping for industrial uses, and the sanitary disposal of waste. On most construction sites this will involve at least three inspections, including the piping layout, venting, backflow protection, and setting of fixtures.

Public works inspectors ensure that Federal, State, and local government water and sewer system, highway, street, bridge, and dam construction conforms to detailed contract specifications. They inspect excavation and fill operations, the placement of forms for concrete, concrete mixing and pouring, asphalt paving, and grading operations. They record the work and materials used so that contract payments can be calculated. Public

Although inspections are primarily visual, inspectors may use tape measures, survey instruments, and metering devices.

works inspectors may specialize in highways, structural steel, reinforced concrete, or ditches. Others specialize in dredging operations required for bridges and dams or for harbors.

The owner of a building or structure under construction employs *specification inspectors* to ensure that work is done according to design specifications. Specification inspectors represent the owner's interests, not those of the general public. Insurance companies and financial institutions also may use their services.

Details concerning construction projects, building and occupancy permits, and other documentation generally are stored on computers so that they can easily be retrieved and updated. For example, inspectors may use laptop computers to record their findings while inspecting a site. Most inspectors use computers to help them monitor the status of construction inspection activities and keep track of permits issued, and some can access all construction and building codes from their computers on the job site, decreasing the need for paper binders. However, many inspectors continue to use a paper checklist to detail their findings.

Although inspections are primarily visual, inspectors may use tape measures, survey instruments, metering devices, and equipment such as concrete strength measurers. They keep a log of their work, take photographs, and file reports. Many inspectors also use laptops or other portable electronic devices onsite to facilitate the accuracy of their written reports, as well as e-mail and fax machines to send out the results. If necessary, they act on their findings. For example, government and construction inspectors notify the construction contractor, superintendent, or supervisor when they discover a violation of a code or ordinance or something that does not comply with the contract specifications or approved plans. If the problem is not corrected within a reasonable or otherwise specified period, government inspectors have authority to issue a "stop-work" order.

Many inspectors also investigate construction or alterations being done without proper permits. Inspectors who are employees of municipalities enforce laws pertaining to the proper design, construction, and use of buildings. They direct violators of permit laws to obtain permits and to submit to inspection.

Work environment. Construction and building inspectors usually work alone. However, several may be assigned to large, complex projects, particularly because inspectors tend to specialize in different areas of construction. Although they spend considerable time inspecting construction worksites, inspectors also spend time in a field office reviewing blueprints, answering letters or telephone calls, writing reports, and scheduling inspections.

Many construction sites are dirty and may be cluttered with tools, materials, or debris. Inspectors may have to climb ladders or many flights of stairs or crawl around in tight spaces. Although their work generally is not considered hazardous, inspectors, like other construction workers, wear hardhats and adhere to other safety requirements while at a construction site.

Inspectors normally work regular hours. However, they may work additional hours during periods when a lot of construction is taking place. Also, if an accident occurs at a construction site, inspectors must respond immediately and may work additional hours to complete their report. Non-government inspectors—especially those who are self-employed—may have a varied work schedule, at times working evenings and weekends.

Training, Other Qualifications, and Advancement

Although requirements vary considerably, construction and building inspectors should have a thorough knowledge of construction materials and practices. In some States, construction and building inspectors are required to obtain a special license or certification, so it is important to check with the appropriate State agency.

Education and training. Most employers require at least a high school diploma or the equivalent, even for workers with considerable experience. More often, employers look for persons who have studied engineering or architecture or who have a degree from a community or junior college with courses in building inspection, home inspection, construction technology, drafting, and mathematics. Many community colleges offer certificate or associate degree programs in building inspection technology. Courses in blueprint reading, algebra, geometry, and English also are useful. A growing number of construction and building inspectors are entering the occupation with a college degree, which often can substitute for previous experience.

The level of training requirements varies by type of inspector and State. In general, construction and building inspectors receive much of their training on the job, although they must learn building codes and standards on their own. Working with an experienced inspector, they learn about inspection techniques; codes, ordinances, and regulations; contract specifications; and recordkeeping and reporting duties. Supervised onsite inspections also may be a part of the training. Other requirements can include various courses and assigned reading. Some courses and instructional material are available online as well as through formal venues.

Licensure and certification. Many States and local jurisdictions require some type of license or certification for employment as a construction and building inspector. Requirements may vary by State or local municipality. Typical requirements for licensure or certification include previous experience, a minimum educational attainment level, such as a high school diploma, and passing a State-approved examination. Some States have individual licensing programs for inspectors, while others may require certification by such associations as the International Code Council, International Association of Plumbing and Mechanical Officials, and National Fire Protection Association.

Similarly, some States require home inspectors to obtain a State-issued license or certification. Currently, 34 States have regulations affecting home inspectors. Requirements for a license or certification vary by State, but may include obtaining a minimum level of education, having a set amount of experience with inspections, purchasing liability insurance of a certain amount, and the passing of an examination. Renewal is usually every few years and annual continuing education is almost always required.

Other qualifications. Because inspectors must possess the right mix of technical knowledge, experience, and education, employers prefer applicants who have both formal training and experience. For example, many inspectors previously worked as carpenters, electricians, or plumbers. Home inspectors combine knowledge of multiple specialties, so many of them come

into the occupation having a combination of certifications and previous experience in various construction trades.

Construction and building inspectors must be in good physical condition in order to walk and climb about construction and building sites. They also must have a driver's license so that they can get to scheduled appointments.

Advancement. Being a member of a nationally recognized inspection association enhances employment opportunities and may be required by some employers. Even if it is not required, certification can enhance an inspector's opportunities for employment and advancement to more responsible positions. To become certified, inspectors with substantial experience and education must pass examinations on topics including code requirements, construction techniques and materials, standards of practice, and codes of ethics. The International Code Council offers multiple voluntary certifications, as do many other professional associations. Many categories of certification are awarded for inspectors and plan examiners in a variety of specialties, including the Certified Building Official (CBO) certification, for code compliance, and the Residential Building Inspector (RBI) certification, for home inspectors. In a few cases, there are no education or experience prerequisites, and certification consists of passing an examination in a designated field either at a regional location or online. In addition, Federal, State, and many local governments may require inspectors to pass a civil service exam.

Because they advise builders and the general public on building codes, construction practices, and technical developments, construction and building inspectors must keep abreast of changes in these areas. Continuing education is required by many States and certifying organizations. Numerous employers provide formal training to broaden inspectors' knowledge of construction materials, practices, and techniques. Inspectors who work for agencies or firms that do not conduct their own training programs can expand their knowledge and upgrade their skills by attending State-sponsored training programs, by taking college or correspondence courses, or by attending seminars and conferences sponsored by various related organizations, including professional organizations. An engineering or architectural degree often is required for advancement to supervisory positions.

Employment

Construction and building inspectors held about 106,400 jobs in 2008. Local governments—primarily municipal or county building departments—employed 44 percent. Employment of local government inspectors is concentrated in cities and in suburban areas undergoing rapid growth. Local governments in larger jurisdictions may employ large inspection staffs, including many plan examiners or inspectors who specialize in structural steel, reinforced concrete, and boiler, electrical, and elevator inspection. In smaller jurisdictions, only one or a few inspectors with generalist skills in multiple areas may be on staff.

Another 27 percent of construction and building inspectors worked for architectural and engineering services firms, conducting inspections for a fee or on a contract basis. Many of these were home inspectors working on behalf of potential real estate purchasers. Most of the remaining inspectors were employed in other service-providing industries or by State governments.

Projections data from the National Employment Matrix

Occupational Title	SOC Code	Employment, 2008	Projected Employment, 2018	Change, 2008-2018	
				Number	Percent
Construction and building inspectors..	47-4011	106,400	124,200	17,900	17

(NOTE) Data in this table are rounded. See the discussion of the employment projections table in the *Handbook* introductory chapter on *Occupational Information Included in the Handbook.*

About 8 percent of construction and building inspectors were self-employed; many of these were home inspectors.

Job Outlook

Inspectors should experience faster than average employment growth. Opportunities should be best for those with construction-related work experience; training in engineering, architecture, construction technology, or related fields; or certification as a construction inspector.

Employment change. Employment of construction and building inspectors is expected to grow 17 percent over the 2008-2018 decade, faster than the average for all occupations. Concern for public safety and a desire for improvement in the quality of construction should continue to stimulate demand for construction and building inspectors in government as well as in firms specializing in architectural, engineering, and related services. As the result of new technology such as building information modeling (BIM), the availability of a richer set of buildings data in a more timely and transparent manner will make it easier to conduct plan reviews. This will lead to more time and resources spent on inspections. In addition, the growing focus on natural and manmade disasters is increasing the level of interest in and need for qualified inspectors. Issues such as green and sustainable design are new areas of focus that will also drive the demand for construction and building inspectors.

The routine practice of obtaining home inspections is a relatively recent development, causing employment of home inspectors to increase rapidly. Although employment of home inspectors is expected to continue to increase, the attention given to this specialty, combined with the desire of some construction workers to move into less strenuous and potentially higher paying work, may result in reduced growth of home inspectors in some areas. In addition, increasing State regulations are starting to limit entry into the specialty only to those who have a given level of previous experience and who are certified.

Job prospects. Those with construction-related work experience; training in engineering, architecture, construction technology, or related fields; or certification as a construction inspector will have the best prospects. Inspectors are involved in all phases of construction, including maintenance and repair work, and are therefore less likely than many construction workers to lose their jobs when new construction slows during recessions. Those who are self-employed, such as home inspectors, are more likely to be affected by economic downturns or fluctuations in the real estate market. However, those with a thorough knowledge of construction practices and skills in areas such as reading and evaluating blueprints and plans will be better off. In addition to openings stemming from the expected employment growth, some job openings will arise from the need to replace inspectors who transfer to other occupations or leave the labor force.

Earnings

Median annual wages of wage and salary construction and building inspectors were $50,180 in May 2008. The middle 50 percent earned between $39,070 and $63,360. The lowest 10 percent earned less than $31,270, and the highest 10 percent earned more than $78,070. Median annual wages in the industries employing the largest numbers of construction and building inspectors were:

Federal Executive Branch $62,120	
Management, scientific, and technical consulting services 58,520	
Local government..50,330	
Architectural, engineering, and related services 49,320	
State government...45,700	

Building inspectors, including plan examiners, generally earn the highest salaries. Salaries in large metropolitan areas are substantially higher than those in small jurisdictions.

Benefits vary by place of employment. Those working for the government and private companies typically receive standard benefits, including health and medical insurance, a retirement plan, and paid annual leave. Those who are self-employed may have to provide their own benefits.

About 25 percent of all construction and building inspectors belonged to a union or were covered by a union contract in 2008.

Related Occupations

Because construction and building inspectors are familiar with construction principles, the most closely related occupations are construction occupations, especially:

Construction and building inspectors also combine knowledge of construction principles and law with an ability to coordinate data, diagnose problems, and communicate with people. Workers in other occupations using a similar combination of skills include:

Sources of Additional Information

Information about building codes, certification, and a career as a construction or building inspector is available from:
➤ International Code Council, 500 New Jersey Ave. NW., 6th Floor, Washington, DC 20001-2070. Internet: **http://www.iccsafe.org**

➤ National Fire Protection Association, 1 Batterymarch Park, Quincy, MA 02169-7471. Internet: **http://www.nfpa.org**

For more information about construction inspectors, contact:
➤ Association of Construction Inspectors, 810N Farrell Dr. Palm Springs, CA 92262. Internet: **http://www.aci-assoc.org**

For more information about electrical inspectors, contact:
➤ International Association of Electrical Inspectors, 901 Waterfall Way, Suite 602, Richardson, TX 75080-7702. Internet: **http://www.iaei.org**

For more information about elevator inspectors, contact:
➤ National Association of Elevator Safety Authorities International, 6957 Littlerock Rd. SW., Ste A, Tumwater, WA 98512. Internet: **http://www.naesai.org**

For more information about education and training for mechanical and plumbing inspectors, contact:
➤ International Association for Plumbing and Mechanical Officials, 5001 E. Philadelphia St., Ontario, CA 91761. Internet: **http://www.iapmo.org**

For information about becoming a home inspector, contact any of the following organizations:
➤ American Society of Home Inspectors, 932 Lee St., Suite 101, Des Plaines, IL 60016. Internet: **http://www.ashi.org**

➤ National Association of Home Inspectors, 4248 Park Glen Rd., Minneapolis, MN 55416. Internet: **http://www.nahi.org**

For information about a career as a State or local government construction or building inspector, contact your State or local employment service.

The Occupational Information Network (O*NET) provides information on a wide range of occupational characteristics. Links to O*NET appear at the end of the Internet version of this occupational statement, accessible at **http://www.bls.gov/ooh/ocos004.htm**

Construction Equipment Operators

Significant Points

- Construction equipment operators are trained either through a formal apprenticeship program, through on-the-job training, through a paid training program, or a combination of these programs.

- Job opportunities are expected to be good.

- Hourly pay is relatively high, but operators of some types of equipment cannot work in inclement weather, so total annual earnings may be reduced.

Nature of the Work

Construction equipment operators use machinery to move construction materials, earth, and other heavy materials at construction sites and mines. They operate equipment that clears and grades land to prepare it for construction of roads, buildings, and bridges, as well as airport runways, power generation facilities, dams, levees, and other structures. They use machines to dig trenches to lay or repair sewer and other utilities, and hoist heavy construction materials. They even may work offshore constructing oil rigs. Construction equipment operators also operate machinery that spreads asphalt and concrete on roads and other structures.

These workers also help set up and inspect the equipment, make adjustments, and perform some maintenance and minor repairs. Construction equipment is more technologically advanced than it was in the past. For example, global positioning system (GPS) technology is now being used to help with grading and leveling activities.

Included in the construction equipment operator occupation are operating engineers and other construction equipment operators; paving and surfacing equipment operators; and piledriver operators. *Operating engineers* and *other construction equipment operators* work with one or several types of power construction equipment. They may operate excavation and loading machines equipped with scoops, shovels, or buckets that dig sand, gravel, earth, or similar materials and load it into trucks or onto conveyors. In addition operating to the familiar bulldozers, they operate trench excavators, road graders, and similar equipment. Sometimes, they may drive and control industrial trucks or tractors equipped with forklifts or booms for lifting materials or with hitches for pulling trailers. They also may operate and maintain air compressors, pumps, and other power equipment at construction sites.

Paving and surfacing equipment operators operate machines that spread and level asphalt or spread and smooth concrete for roadways or other structures. *Asphalt spreader operators* turn valves to regulate the temperature and flow of asphalt onto the roadbed. They must take care that the machine distributes the paving material evenly and without voids, and they must make sure that there is a constant flow of asphalt going into the hopper. Concrete paving machine operators control levers and turn handwheels to move attachments that spread, vibrate, and level wet concrete in forms. They must observe the surface of the concrete to identify low spots into which workers must add concrete. They use other attachments to smooth the surface of the concrete, spray on a curing compound, and cut expansion joints. Tamping equipment operators operate tamping machines that compact earth and other fill materials for roadbeds or other construction sites. They also may operate machines with interchangeable hammers to cut or break up old pavement and drive guardrail posts into the earth.

Piledriver operators use large machines mounted on skids, barges, or cranes to hammer piles into the ground. Piles are long, heavy beams of wood or steel driven into the ground to support retaining walls, bulkheads, bridges, piers, or building foundations. Some piledriver operators work on offshore oil rigs. Piledriver operators move hand and foot levers and turn valves to activate, position, and control the pile-driving equipment.

Work environment. Construction equipment operators work outdoors in nearly every type of climate and weather condition, although in many areas of the country some types of

Construction equipment operators level the surface of a construction site.

construction operations must be suspended in winter. Bulldozers, scrapers, and especially piledrivers are noisy and shake or jolt the operator. Operating heavy construction equipment can be dangerous, and this occupation incurs injuries and illnesses at a higher-than-average rate. As with most machinery, accidents generally can be avoided by observing proper operating procedures and safety practices. Construction equipment operators often get dirty, greasy, muddy, or dusty. Some operators work in remote locations on large construction projects, such as highways and dams, or in factory or mining operations.

Operators may have irregular hours because work on some construction projects continues around the clock or must be performed late at night or early in the morning.

Training, Other Qualifications, and Advancement
Construction equipment operators are trained either through a formal apprenticeship program, through on-the-job training, through a paid training program, or a combination of these programs.

Education and training. Employers of construction equipment operators generally prefer to hire high school graduates, although some employers may train nongraduates to operate some types of equipment. High school courses in automobile mechanics are helpful because workers may perform maintenance on their machines. Also useful are courses in science and mechanical drawing. With the development of GPS, construction equipment operators need more experience with computers than in the past.

On the job, workers may start by operating light equipment under the guidance of an experienced operator. Later, they may operate heavier equipment, such as bulldozers. Technologically advanced construction equipment with computerized controls and improved hydraulics and electronics requires more skill to operate. Operators of such equipment may need more training and some understanding of electronics.

It is generally accepted that formal training provides more comprehensive skills. Some construction equipment operators train in formal operating engineer apprenticeship programs administered by union-management committees of the International Union of Operating Engineers (IUOE). Because apprentices learn to operate a wider variety of machines than do other beginners, they usually have better job opportunities. Apprenticeship programs consist of at least 3 years, or 6,000 hours, of paid on-the-job training together with 144 hours of related classroom instruction each year.

Private vocational schools offer instruction in the operation of certain types of construction equipment. Completion of such programs may help a person get a job. However, people considering this kind of training should check the school's reputation among employers in the area and find out if the school offers the opportunity to work on actual machines in realistic situations. A large amount of information can be learned in classrooms, but to become a skilled construction equipment operator, a worker needs to actually perform the various tasks. Many training facilities, including IUOE apprenticeship programs, incorporate sophisticated simulators into their training, allowing beginners to familiarize themselves with the equipment in a controlled environment.

Certification and other qualifications. Mechanical aptitude and experience operating related mobile equipment, such as farm tractors or heavy equipment, in the Armed Forces or elsewhere is an asset. Construction equipment operators often need a commercial driver's license to haul their equipment to the various jobsites. Commercial driver's licenses are issued by States according to each State's rules and regulations. Operators also need to be in good physical condition and have a good sense of balance, the ability to judge distance, and eye-hand-foot coordination. Some operator positions require the ability to work at heights.

Certification or training from the right school can improve opportunities for jobseekers; some employers may require operators to be certified. While attending some vocational schools, or by fulfilling the requirements of related professional associations, operators can qualify for various certifications. These certifications prove to potential employers that an operator is able to handle specific types of equipment.

Advancement. Construction equipment operators can advance to become supervisors. Some operators choose to pass on their knowledge and teach in training facilities. Other operators start their own contracting businesses, although doing so may be difficult because of high startup costs.

Employment
Construction equipment operators held about 469,300 jobs in 2008. Jobs were found in every section of the country and were distributed among various types of operators as follows:

Operating engineers and other construction equipment operators	404,500
Paving, surfacing, and tamping equipment operators	60,200
Pile-driver operators	4,600

About 63 percent of construction equipment operators worked in the construction industry. Many equipment operators worked in heavy and civil engineering construction, building highways, bridges, or railroads. About 16 percent of construction equipment operators worked in local government. Others—mostly grader, bulldozer, and scraper operators—worked in mining. Some also worked for manufacturing or utility companies. About 3 percent of construction equipment operators were self-employed.

Projections data from the National Employment Matrix

Occupational Title	SOC Code	Employment, 2008	Projected Employment, 2018	Change, 2008-2018	
				Number	Percent
Construction equipment operators	47-2070	469,300	525,500	56,200	12
Paving, surfacing, and tamping equipment operators	47-2071	60,200	67,200	6,900	12
Pile-driver operators...	47-2072	4,600	5,200	600	13
Operating engineers and other construction equipment operators.....	47-2073	404,500	453,200	48,700	12

(NOTE) Data in this table are rounded. See the discussion of the employment projections table in the *Handbook* introductory chapter on *Occupational Information Included in the Handbook*.

Job Outlook

Average job growth is projected. The need to fill jobs and re-place workers who leave the occupation should result in good job opportunities for construction equipment operators.

Employment change. Employment of construction equipment operators is expected to increase 12 percent between 2008 and 2018, about as fast as the average for all occupations. The likelihood of increased spending by the Federal Government on infrastructure to improve roads and bridges, railroads, the electric transmission system, and water and sewer systems, which are in great need of repair across the country, will generate numerous jobs for construction equipment operators who work primarily in these areas. In addition, population increases and the need for construction projects, such as new roads and sewer lines to service the increased population, will generate more jobs. However, without the extra spending on infrastructure by the Federal Government, employment may be flat as States and localities struggle with reduced taxes and budget shortfalls to pay for road and other improvements.

An expected rise in energy production is expected to increase work on oil rigs, smart grids, windmill farms, pipeline construction, and other types of power-generating facilities. Also, increased output of mines and rock and gravel quarries will generate jobs in the mining industry.

Job prospects. Job opportunities for construction equipment operators are expected to be good because the occupation often does not attract enough qualified candidates to fill jobs. Some workers' reluctance to work in construction makes it easier for willing workers to get operator jobs.

In addition, many job openings will arise from job growth and from the need to replace experienced construction equipment operators who transfer to other occupations, retire, or leave the job for other reasons. Construction equipment operators who can use a wide variety of equipment will have the best prospects. Operators with pipeline experience will have especially good opportunities if, as expected, natural-gas companies expand work on their infrastructure.

Employment of construction equipment operators, like that of many other construction workers, is sensitive to fluctuations in the economy. Workers in these trades may experience periods of unemployment when the overall level of construction falls. However, shortages of these workers may occur in some areas during peak periods of building activity.

Earnings

Wages for construction equipment operators vary. In May 2008, median hourly wages of wage and salary operating engineers and other construction equipment operators were $18.88. The middle 50 percent earned between $14.78 and $25.49. The lowest 10 percent earned less than $12.47, and the highest 10 percent earned more than $33.34. Median hourly wages in the industries employing the largest numbers of operating engineers were as follows:

Nonresidential building construction $21.45
Highway, street, and bridge construction.......................21.20
Utility system construction 19.79
Other specialty trade contractors...................................18.61
Local government...17.19

Median hourly wages of wage and salary paving, surfacing, and tamping equipment operators were $16.00 in May 2008. The middle 50 percent earned between $12.94 and $20.75. The lowest 10 percent earned less than $10.77, and the highest 10 percent earned more than $26.70. Median hourly wages in the industries employing the largest numbers of paving, surfacing, and tamping equipment operators were as follows:

Other specialty trade contractors..................................$16.16
Highway, street, and bridge construction.......................16.13
Local government...15.94

In May 2008, median hourly wages of wage and salary pile-driver operators were $23.01. The middle 50 percent earned between $17.52 and $32.94. The lowest 10 percent earned less than $14.25, and the highest 10 percent earned more than $38.01. Median hourly wages in the industries employing the largest numbers of piledriver operators were as follows:

Other specialty trade contractors..................................$26.07
Other heavy and civil engineering construction..............23.24
Nonresidential building construction 20.46
Utility system construction 19.54

Hourly pay is relatively high, particularly in large metropolitan areas. However, annual earnings of some workers may be lower than hourly rates would indicate because worktime may be limited by bad weather. About 27 percent of construction equipment operators belong to a union.

Related Occupations

Other workers who operate mechanical equipment include the following:

Sources of Additional Information

For further information about apprenticeships or work opportunities for construction equipment operators, contact a local of the International Union of Operating Engineers, a local apprenticeship committee, or the nearest office of the State apprenticeship agency or employment service. You also can find information on the registered apprenticeship system, with links to State apprenticeship programs, on the U.S. Department of Labor's Web site: **http://www.doleta.gov/OA/eta_default.cfm.** In addition, apprenticeship information is available from the U.S. Department of Labor's toll free help line: (877) 872-5627.

For general information about the work of construction equipment operators, contact:

➤ Associated General Contractors of America, 2300 Wilson Blvd., Suite 400, Arlington, VA 22201-5426. Internet: **http://www.agc.org**

➤ International Union of Operating Engineers, 1125 17th St. NW., Washington, DC 20036-4786. Internet: **http://www.iuoe.org**

➤ National Center for Construction Education and Research, 3600 NW. 43rd St., Bldg. G, Gainesville, FL 32606-8134. Internet: **http://www.nccer.org**

➤ Pile Driving Contractors Association, P.O. Box 66208, Orange Park, FL 32065-0021. Internet: **http://www.piledrivers.org**

For general information on apprenticeships and how to get them, see the *Occupational Outlook Quarterly* article "Apprenticeships: Career training, credentials—and a paycheck in your pocket," online at **http://www.bls.gov/opub/ooq/2002/summer/art01.pdf** and in print at many libraries and career centers.

The Occupational Information Network (O*NET) provides information on a wide range of occupational characteristics. Links to O*NET appear at the end of the Internet version of this occupational statement, accessible at **http://www.bls.gov/ooh/ocos255.htm**

Construction Laborers

Significant Points

- Many construction laborer jobs require a variety of basic skills, but others require specialized training and experience.

- Most construction laborers learn on the job, but formal apprenticeship programs provide the most thorough preparation.

- Job opportunities vary by locality, but in many areas there will be competition, especially for jobs requiring limited skills.

- Laborers who have specialized skills or who can relocate near new construction projects should have the best opportunities.

Nature of the Work

Construction laborers can be found on almost all construction sites, performing a wide range of tasks from the very easy to the hazardous. They can be found at building, highway, and heavy construction sites; residential and commercial sites; tunnel and shaft excavations; and demolition sites. Many of the jobs they perform require physical strength, training, and experience. Other jobs require little skill and can be learned quickly. Although most construction laborers specialize in a type of construction, such as highway or tunnel construction, some are generalists who perform many different tasks during all stages of construction. Construction laborers who work in underground construction, such as in tunnels, or in demolition are more likely to specialize in only those areas.

Construction laborers clean and prepare construction sites. They remove trees and debris; tend pumps, compressors, and generators; and erect and disassemble scaffolding and other temporary structures. They load, unload, identify, and distribute building materials to the appropriate location according to project plans and specifications. Laborers also tend machines; for example, they may use a portable mixer to mix concrete or tend a machine that pumps concrete, grout, cement, sand, plaster, or stucco through a spray gun for application to ceilings and walls. They often help other craftworkers, including carpenters, plasterers, operating engineers, and masons.

Construction laborers are responsible for the installation and maintenance of traffic control devices and patterns. At highway construction sites, this work may include clearing and preparing highway work zones and rights-of-way; installing traffic barricades, cones, and markers; and controlling traffic passing near, in, and around work zones. Construction laborers also dig trenches; install sewer, water, and storm drainpipes; and place concrete and asphalt on roads. Other highly specialized tasks include operating laser guidance equipment to place pipes; operating air, electric, and pneumatic drills; and transporting and setting explosives for the construction of tunnels, shafts, and roads.

Some construction laborers help with the removal of hazardous materials, such as asbestos, lead, or chemicals. (Workers who specialize in, and are certified for, the removal of hazardous materials are discussed in the *Handbook* statement on hazardous materials removal workers.)

Construction laborers operate a variety of equipment, including pavement breakers; jackhammers; earth tampers; concrete, mortar, and plaster mixers; electric and hydraulic boring machines; torches; small mechanical hoists; laser beam equipment; and surveying and measuring equipment. They may use computers and other high-tech input devices to control robotic pipe cutters and cleaners. To perform their jobs effectively, construction laborers must be familiar with the duties of other craftworkers and with the materials, tools, and machinery they use, as all of these workers work as part of a team, jointly carrying out assigned construction tasks.

Work environment. Most construction laborers do physically demanding work. Some work at great heights or outdoors in all weather conditions. Some jobs expose workers to harmful materials or chemicals, fumes, odors, loud noises, or dangerous machinery. Some laborers may be exposed to

A construction laborer performs work on a scale too small for a large piece of equipment.

lead-based paint, asbestos, or other hazardous substances during their work, especially when they work in confined spaces. Workers in this occupation experience one of the highest rates of nonfatal injuries and illnesses; consequently, the work requires constant attention to safety on the job. To avoid injury, workers in these jobs wear safety clothing, such as gloves, hardhats, protective chemical suits, and devices to protect their eyes, respiratory system, or hearing. While working underground, construction laborers must be especially alert in order to follow procedures safely and must deal with a variety of hazards.

A standard 40 hour work week is the most common work week for construction laborers. About 1 in 7 has a variable schedule, as overnight work may be required in highway work. In some parts of the country, construction laborers may work only during certain seasons. They also may experience weather-related work stoppages at any time of the year.

Training, Other Qualifications, and Advancement

Many construction laborer jobs require a variety of basic skills, but others require specialized training and experience. Most construction laborers learn on the job, but formal apprenticeship programs provide the most thorough preparation.

Education and training. Although some construction laborer jobs have no specific educational qualifications or entry-level training, apprenticeships for laborers usually require a high school diploma or the equivalent. High school classes in English, mathematics, physics, mechanical drawing, blueprint reading, welding, and general shop can be helpful.

Most workers start by getting a job with a contractor who provides on-the-job training. Increasingly, construction laborers are finding work through temporary-help agencies that send laborers to construction sites for short-term work. Entry-level workers generally help more experienced workers, by performing routine tasks such as cleaning and preparing the worksite and unloading materials. When the opportunity arises, they learn from experienced construction trades workers how to do more difficult tasks, such as operating tools and equipment. Construction laborers also may choose or be required to attend a trade or vocational school, association

training class, or community college to receive further trade-related training.

Some laborers receive more formal training in the form of an apprenticeship. These programs include between 2 and 4 years of classroom and on-the-job training. In the first 200 hours, workers learn basic construction skills, such as blueprint reading, the correct use of tools and equipment, and safety and health procedures. The remainder of the curriculum consists of specialized skills training in three of the largest segments of the construction industry: building construction, heavy and high-way construction, and environmental remediation, such as lead or asbestos abatement and mold or hazardous waste remediation. Training in "green," energy-efficient construction, an area of growth in the construction industry, is now available and can help workers find employment.

Workers who use dangerous equipment or handle toxic chemicals usually receive specialized safety training. Laborers who remove hazardous materials are required to take union- or employer-sponsored Occupational Safety and Health Administration safety training.

Apprenticeship applicants usually must be at least 18 years old and meet local requirements. Because the number of apprenticeship programs is limited, however, only a small proportion of laborers learn their trade in this way.

Other qualifications. Laborers need manual dexterity, eye-hand coordination, good physical fitness, a good sense of balance, and an ability to work as a member of a team. The ability to solve arithmetic problems quickly and accurately may be required. In addition, military service or a good work history is viewed favorably by contractors.

Certification and advancement. Laborers may earn certifications in welding, scaffold erecting, and concrete finishing. These certifications help workers prove that they have the knowledge to perform more complex tasks.

Through training and experience, laborers can move into other construction occupations. Laborers may also advance to become construction supervisors or general contractors. For those who would like to advance, it is increasingly important to be able to communicate in both English and Spanish in order to relay instructions and safety precautions to workers with limited understanding of English; Spanish-speaking workers make up a large part of the construction workforce in many areas. Supervisors and contractors need good communication skills to deal with clients and subcontractors.

In addition, supervisors and contractors should be able to identify and estimate the quantity of materials needed to complete a job and accurately estimate how long a job will take to complete and what it will cost. Computer skills also are important for advancement as construction becomes increasingly mechanized and computerized.

Employment

Construction laborers held about 1.2 million jobs in 2008. They worked throughout the country, but like the general population, were concentrated in metropolitan areas. About 62 percent of construction laborers worked in the construction industry, including 27 percent who worked for specialty trade contractors. About 21 percent were self-employed in 2008.

Projections data from the National Employment Matrix

Occupational Title	SOC Code	Employment, 2008	Projected Employment, 2018	Change, 2008-2018	
				Number	Percent
Construction laborers	47-2061	1,248,700	1,504,600	255,900	20

(NOTE) Data in this table are rounded. See the discussion of the employment projections table in the *Handbook* introductory chapter on *Occupational Information Included in the Handbook.*

Job Outlook

Employment is expected to grow much faster than the average. In many areas, there will be competition for jobs, especially those requiring limited skills. Laborers who have specialized skills or who can relocate near new construction projects should have the best opportunities.

Employment change. Employment of construction laborers is expected to grow by 20 percent between 2008 and 2018, much faster than the average for all occupations. Because of the large variety of tasks that laborers perform, demand for laborers will mirror the level of overall construction activity. However, some jobs may be adversely affected by automation as they are replaced by new machinery and equipment that improves productivity and quality.

Increasing job prospects for construction laborers, however, is the expected additional government funding for the repair and reconstruction of the Nation's infrastructure, such as roads, bridges, public buildings, and water lines. The occupation should experience an increase in demand because laborers make up a significant portion of workers on these types of projects.

New emphasis on green construction also should help lead to better employment prospects as many green practices require more labor on construction sites. Additional duties resulting from practicing green construction include having to segregate materials that can be used again from those which cannot, and the actual reuse of such materials. In addition, these workers will be needed for the construction of any new projects to harness wind or solar power.

Job prospects. In many geographic areas, construction laborers—especially for those with limited skills—will experience competition because of a plentiful supply of workers who are willing to work as day laborers. Overall opportunities will be best for those with experience and specialized skills and for those who can relocate to areas with new construction projects. Opportunities also will be better for laborers specializing in road construction.

Employment of construction laborers, like that of many other construction workers, is sensitive to the fluctuations of the economy. On the one hand, workers in these trades may experience periods of unemployment when the overall level of construction falls. On the other hand, shortages of these workers may occur in some areas during peak periods of building activity.

Earnings

Median hourly wages of wage and salary construction laborers in May 2008 were $13.71. The middle 50 percent earned between $10.74 and $18.57. The lowest 10 percent earned less than $8.67, and the highest 10 percent earned more than $25.98. Median hourly wages in the industries employing the largest number of construction laborers were as follows:

Nonresidential building construction	$14.95
Other specialty trade contractors	13.81
Residential building construction	13.79
Foundation, structure, and building exterior contractors	13.35
Employment services	10.80

Earnings for construction laborers can be reduced by poor weather or by downturns in construction activity, which sometimes result in layoffs. Apprentices or helpers usually start out earning about 60 percent of the wage paid to experienced workers. Pay increases as apprentices gain experience and learn new skills.

Some laborers—about 14 percent—belong to a union, mainly the Laborers' International Union of North America.

Related Occupations

The work of construction laborers is closely related to that of other construction occupations, as well as that of others who perform similar physical work, such as the following:

	Page
Assemblers and fabricators	723
Brickmasons, blockmasons, and stonemasons	615
Forest and conservation workers	604
Grounds maintenance workers	498
Highway maintenance workers	829
Logging workers	606
Material moving occupations	809
Refractory materials repairers, except brickmasons	830
Roustabouts, oil and gas	829
Structural metal fabricators and fitters	723

Sources of Additional Information

For information about jobs as a construction laborer, contact local building or construction contractors, local joint labor-management apprenticeship committees, apprenticeship agencies, or the local office of your State Employment Service. You also can find information on the registered apprenticeships, together with links to State apprenticeship programs, on the U.S. Department of Labor's Web site: **http://www.doleta.gov/OA/eta_default.cfm.** Apprenticeship information also is available from the U.S. Department of Labor's toll-free help line: (877) 872-5627.

For general information on apprenticeships and how to get them, see the *Occupational Outlook Quarterly* article "Apprenticeships: Career training, credentials—and a paycheck in your pocket," online at **http://www.bls.gov/opub/ooq/2002/summer/art01.pdf** and in print at many libraries and career centers.

For information on education programs for laborers, contact:

➤ Laborers-AGC Education and Training Fund, 37 Deerfield Rd., P.O. Box 37, Pomfret Center, CT 06258-0037.

➤ National Center for Construction Education and Research, 3600 NW. 43rd St., Bldg. G, Gainesville, FL 32606. Internet: **http://www.nccer.org**

The Occupational Information Network (O*NET) provides information on a wide range of occupational characteristics. Links to O*NET appear at the end of the Internet version of this occupational statement, accessible at **http://www.bls.gov/ooh/ocos248.htm**

Drywall and Ceiling Tile Installers, Tapers, Plasterers, and Stucco Masons

Significant Points

- Most workers learn their trade through informal training programs or through an apprenticeship.

- Work is physically demanding.

- Job prospects are expected to be good.

- Workers may be idled when downturns in the economy slow construction activity.

Nature of the Work

Drywall and *ceiling tile installers*, *tapers*, *plasterers*, and *stucco masons* are specialty construction workers who build, apply, or fasten interior and exterior wallboards or wall coverings in residential, commercial, and other structures. Specifically, drywall and ceiling tile installers and tapers work indoors, installing wallboards to ceilings or to interior walls of buildings; plasterers and stucco masons, on the other hand, work both indoors and outdoors—applying plaster to interior walls and cement or stucco to exterior walls. While most work is performed for functionality, such as fireproofing and sound dampening, some applications are intended purely for decorative purposes.

Drywall consists of a thin layer of gypsum between two layers of heavy paper. It is used to make walls and ceilings in most buildings today because it is faster and cheaper to install than plaster.

There are two kinds of drywall workers—installers and tapers—although many workers do both types of work. Installers, also called *framers* or *hangers*, fasten drywall panels to the inside framework of houses and other buildings. Tapers or *finishers*, prepare these panels for painting by taping and finishing joints and imperfections. In addition to drywall workers, ceiling tile installers also help to build walls and ceilings.

Because drywall panels are manufactured in standard sizes—usually 4 feet by 8 feet—drywall installers must measure, cut, fit, and fasten them to the inside framework of buildings. Installers saw, drill, or cut holes in panels for electrical outlets, air-conditioning units, and plumbing. After making these alterations, installers typically screw the wallboard panels to the wood or metal framework, called studs. Because drywall is

heavy and cumbersome, another worker usually helps the installer to position and secure the panel. Installers often use a lift when placing ceiling panels.

After the drywall is installed, tapers fill joints between panels with a joint compound, also called spackle or "mud." Using the wide, flat tip of a special trowel, they spread the compound into and along each side of the joint. They immediately use the trowel to press a paper tape—used to reinforce the drywall and to hide imperfections—into the wet compound and to smooth away excess material. Nail and screw depressions also are covered with this compound, as are imperfections caused by the installation of air-conditioning vents and other fixtures. Using increasingly wider trowels, tapers apply second and third coats of the compound, sanding the treated areas after each coat to make them smooth and devoid of seams.

Ceiling tile installers, or *acoustical carpenters*, apply or mount acoustical tiles or blocks, strips, or sheets of shock-absorbing materials to ceilings and walls of buildings to reduce deflection of sound or to decorate rooms. First, they measure and mark the surface according to blueprints and drawings. Then, they nail or screw moldings to the wall to support and seal the joint between the ceiling tile and the wall. Finally, they mount the tile, either by applying a cement adhesive to the back of the tile and then pressing the tile into place, or by nailing, screwing, or wire-tying the lath directly to the structural framework.

Plasterers apply plaster to interior walls and ceilings to form fire-resistant and relatively soundproof surfaces. They also apply plaster veneer over drywall to create smooth or textured abrasion-resistant finishes. In addition, plasterers install pre-fabricated exterior insulation systems over existing walls—for good insulation and interesting architectural effects—and cast ornamental designs in plaster. Stucco masons apply durable plasters, such as polymer-based acrylic finishes and stucco, to exterior surfaces.

Plasterers can plaster either solid surfaces, such as concrete block, or supportive wire mesh called lath. When plasterers work with hard interior surfaces, such as concrete block and concrete, they first apply a brown coat of gypsum plaster that provides a base, which is followed by a second, or finish coat, also called "white coat." When plastering metal-mesh lath foundations, they apply a preparatory, or "scratch coat" with a trowel. They spread this rich plaster mixture into and over the metal lath. Before the plaster sets, plasterers scratch its surface with a rake-like tool to produce ridges, so that the subsequent brown coat will bond tightly. They then apply the brown coat and the white finish coat.

When plastering on non-solid surfaces, *lathers* are needed to help build supportive walls out of wire. This support base is put on walls, ceilings, ornamental frameworks, and partitions of buildings before plaster and other coatings are added.

Applying different types of plaster coating requires different techniques. When applying the brown coat, plasterers spray or trowel the mixture onto the surface, then smooth it to an even, level surface. For the finish, or white coat, plasterers usually prepare a mixture of plaster and water. They quickly apply this using a "hawk," that is a light, metal plate with a handle, along with a trowel, brush, and water. This mixture, which sets very quickly, produces a very smooth, durable finish.

ing. Some workers need to use stilts; others may have to lift and maneuver heavy, cumbersome materials, such as oversized wallboards. The work also can be dusty and dirty, irritating the skin, eyes, and lungs, unless protective masks, goggles, and gloves are used. Hazards include falls from ladders and scaffolds, and injuries from power tools and from working with sharp tools, such as utility knives.

Most work indoors, except for the relatively few stucco masons who apply exterior finishes.

Training, Other Qualifications, and Advancement

Most workers learn their trade through informal training programs or through an apprenticeship. It can take 3 to 4 years of paid on-the-job training to become a fully skilled worker, but many skills can be learned within the first year. In general, the more formal the training process, the more skilled the individual becomes, and the more in demand by employers.

Education and training. A high school education, or its equivalent, is helpful, as are courses basic math, mechanical drawing, and blueprint reading. The most common way to get a first job is to find an employer who will provide on-the-job training. Entry-level workers generally start as helpers, assisting more experienced workers. Employers may also send new employees to a trade or vocational school or community college to receive classroom training.

Some employers, particularly large nonresidential construction contractors with unionized workforces, offer employees formal apprenticeships. These programs combine on-the-job training with related classroom instruction—at least 144 hours of instruction each year for drywall and ceiling tile installers and tapers, and 166 hours for plasterers and stucco masons. The length of the apprenticeship program, usually 3 to 4 years, varies with the apprentice's skill. Because the number of apprenticeship programs is limited, however, only a small proportion of these workers learn their trade this way.

Helpers and apprentices start by carrying materials, lifting and cleaning up debris. They also learn to use the tools, machines, equipment, and materials of the trade. Within a few weeks, they learn to measure, cut, apply, and install materials. Eventually, they become fully experienced workers. At the end of their training, workers learn to estimate the cost of completing a job.

Other jobseekers may choose to obtain their training before seeking a job. There are a number of vocational-technical schools and training academies affiliated with the industry's unions and contractors that offer training in these occupations. Employers often look favorably upon graduates of these training programs and usually start them at a higher level than those without the training.

Other qualifications. Workers need to be in good physical condition and have good eye-hand coordination, a sense of balance and manual dexterity. For drywall and ceiling tile installers and tapers, the ability to solve basic arithmetic problems quickly and accurately is required. They also should be able to identify and estimate the quantity of materials needed to complete a job, and accurately estimate how long a job will take to complete and at what cost.

Drywall and ceiling tile installers, tapers, plasterers, and stucco masons learn their trade through informal training programs or through apprenticeships.

Plasterers create decorative interior surfaces as well. One way that they do this is by pressing a brush or trowel firmly against a wet plaster surface and using a circular hand motion to create decorative swirls. Plasterers sometimes do more complex decorative and ornamental work that requires special skill and creativity. For example, they may mold intricate wall and ceiling designs, such as cornice pieces and chair rails. Following an architect's blueprint, plasterers pour or spray a special plaster into a mold and allow it to set. Workers then remove the molded plaster and put it in place, according to the plan.

Stucco masons usually apply stucco—a mixture of Portland cement, lime, and sand—over cement, concrete, masonry or wire lath. Stucco also may be applied directly to a wire lath with a scratch coat, followed by a brown coat, and then a finish coat. Stucco masons may also embed marble or gravel chips into the finish coat to achieve a pebble-like, decorative finish.

When required, stucco masons apply insulation to the exteriors of new and old buildings. They cover the outer wall with rigid foam insulation board and reinforcing mesh, and then trowel on a base coat. They may apply an additional coat of this material with a decorative finish.

Work environment. As in many other construction trades, this work is physically demanding. Drywall and ceiling tile installers, tapers, plasterers, and stucco masons spend most of the day on their feet, either standing, bending, stretching, or kneel-

Artistic creativity is helpful for plasterers and stucco masons who apply decorative finishes. In addition, a good work history is viewed favorably by contractors.

Apprentices usually must be at least 18 years old and have a high school diploma or GED. Those who complete apprenticeships registered with the Federal or State Government receive a journey worker certificate that is recognized Nationwide.

Certification and advancement. Some organizations related to masonry trades offer training and certification intended to enhance the skills of their members. For example, the International Union of Bricklayers and Allied Craftworkers International Masonry Institute confers designations in several areas of specialization, including one for plastering. Candidates who complete a 12-week certification program can earn a designation as a "journey level plasterer" by passing a competency-based exam. Experienced candidates can become trainers and earn a designation as "Certified Instructor or Journeyworkers and Apprentices in the Trowel Trades."

Drywall and ceiling tile installers, tapers, plasterers, and stucco masons may advance to supervisor or general construction supervisor positions. However, it is increasingly important to be able to communicate in both English and Spanish in order to relay instructions and safety precautions to workers with limited understanding of English because Spanish-speaking workers make up a large part of the construction workforce in many areas. Knowing English well also makes it easier to advance. Many workers become independent contractors. Others become building inspectors.

Employment

Drywall and ceiling tile installers, tapers, plasterers, and stucco masons held about 237,700 jobs in 2008. About 19 percent were self-employed independent contractors. The following tabulation shows 2008 wage-and-salary employment by specialty:

Drywall and ceiling tile installers 151,300
Plasterers and stucco masons 49,000
Tapers 37,400

Most workers are employed in populous areas. In other areas, where there may not be enough work to keep them employed full time, carpenters and painters usually do the work.

Job Outlook

Employment of drywall and ceiling tile installers, tapers, plasterers, and stucco masons is expected to grow about as fast as average for all occupations. Job growth, however, will differ among the individual occupations in this category. Good job prospects are expected overall.

Employment change. Overall employment is expected to grow by 12 percent between 2008 and 2018. Employment of drywall and ceiling tile installers—the largest specialty—is expected to grow 14 percent, reflecting growth of new construction and remodeling projects. New residential construction projects are expected to provide the majority of jobs during the projection decade, but home improvement and renovation projects are also expected to create jobs because existing residential and nonresidential buildings are getting old and need repair.

Employment of tapers is expected to grow 13 percent, which is as fast as the average. Demand for tapers, which often mirrors demand for drywall installers, also will be driven by the overall growth of construction activity.

Employment of plasterers and stucco masons, on the other hand, is expected to grow 7 percent. Despite an increased appreciation for the attractiveness and durability that plaster provides, growing use of cheaper and easier to install alternatives, such as drywall, will impede employment growth for these workers. Nonetheless, stucco masons will experience some employment growth due to demand for new polymer-based exterior insulating finishes that are gaining popularity, particularly in the South and Southwest regions of the country.

Job prospects. Job opportunities for drywall and ceiling tile installers, tapers, plasterers, and stucco masons are expected to be good overall. Many potential workers are not attracted to this occupation because they prefer work that is less strenuous and has more comfortable working conditions. Experienced workers will have especially favorable opportunities.

Besides opportunities resulting from job growth, many drywall and ceiling tile installer and taper jobs will open up each year because of the need to replace workers who transfer to other occupations or leave the labor force. Skilled, experienced plasterers with artistic ability should have excellent opportunities, especially with restoration projects. Decorative custom finishes, expensive homes, and large-scale restoration projects will further result in opportunities for plasterers in the Northeast, particularly in urban areas. For stucco masons, the best employment opportunities should continue to be in Florida, California, and the Southwest, where the use of stucco is expected to remain popular.

Like many other construction workers, employment in these occupations is sensitive to the fluctuations of the economy. Workers in these trades may experience periods of

Projections data from the National Employment Matrix

Occupational Title	SOC Code	Employment, 2008	Projected Employment, 2018	Change, 2008-2018	
				Number	Percent
Drywall and ceiling tile installers, tapers, plasterers, and stucco masons..	–	237,700	266,200	28,500	12
Drywall installers, ceiling tile installers, and tapers	47-2080	188,700	214,000	25,300	13
Drywall and ceiling tile installers	47-2081	151,300	171,700	20,500	14
Tapers..	47-2082	37,400	42,300	4,900	13
Plasterers and stucco masons..	47-2161	49,000	52,200	3,200	7

(NOTE) Data in this table are rounded. See the discussion of the employment projections table in the *Handbook* introductory chapter on *Occupational Information Included in the Handbook.*

unemployment when the overall level of construction falls. On the other hand, shortages of these workers may occur in some areas during peak periods of building activity.

Earnings

The median hourly wages of wage and salary drywall and ceiling tile installers were $18.12 in May 2008. The middle 50 percent earned between $14.23 and $23.80. The lowest 10 percent earned less than $11.64, and the highest 10 percent earned more than $31.72.

Median hourly wages of wage and salary tapers were $21.03 in May 2008. The middle 50 percent earned between $15.45 and $28.27. The lowest 10 percent earned less than $12.62, and the highest 10 percent earned more than $34.91.

Median hourly wages of wage and salary plasterers and stucco masons were $18.01 in May 2008. The middle 50 percent earned between $14.36 and $22.94. The lowest 10 percent earned less than $12.01, and the top 10 percent earned more than $29.59.

Related Occupations

Drywall and ceiling tile installers, tapers, plasterers, and stucco masons combine strength and dexterity with precision and accuracy to make materials fit according to a plan. Other occupations that require similar abilities include:

Sources of Additional Information

For information about work opportunities in this field, contact local drywall installation, ceiling tile installation, plaster and stucco mason contractors, a local joint union-management apprenticeship committee, a State or local chapter of the Associated Builders and Contractors, or the nearest office of the State employment service or apprenticeship agency. You can also find information on the registered apprenticeship system with links to State apprenticeship programs on the U.S. Department of Labor's Web site: **http://www.doleta.gov/atels_bat.** Apprenticeship information is also available from the U.S. Department of Labor's toll free helpline: (877) 282-5627.

For details about job qualifications and training programs in drywall application and finishing and ceiling tile installation, contact:

➤ Associated Builders and Contractors, 4250 North Fairfax Dr., 9th Floor, Arlington, VA 22203. Internet: **http://www.abc.org/**

➤ Association of Wall and Ceiling Industries International, 513 West Broad St., Suite 210, Falls Church, VA 22046. Internet: **http://www.awci.org**

➤ Finishing Trades Institute, International Union of Painters and Allied Trades, 1750 New York Ave. NW., Washington, DC 20006. Internet: **http://www.finishingtradesinstitute.org**

➤ National Association of Home Builders, Home Builders Institute, 1201 15th St. NW., 6th Floor, Washington, DC 20005. Internet: **http://www.hbi.org**

➤ National Center for Construction Education and Research, 3600 NW. 43rd St., Building G, Gainesville, FL 32606. Internet: **http://www.nccer.org**

For information about plasterers, contact:
➤ Operative Plasterers' and Cement Masons' International Association of the United States and Canada, 11720 Beltsville Dr., Suite 700, Beltsville, MD 20705. Internet: **http://www.opcmia.org**

For general information on apprenticeships and how to get them, see the *Occupational Outlook Quarterly* article "Apprenticeships: Career training, credentials—and a paycheck in your pocket," online at **http://www.bls.gov/opub/ooq/2002/summer/art01.pdf** and in print at many libraries and career centers.

The Occupational Information Network (O*NET) provides information on a wide range of occupational characteristics. Links to O*NET appear at the end of the Internet version of this occupational statement, accessible at **http://www.bls.gov/ooh/ocos352.htm**

Electricians

Significant Points

- Job opportunities should be good, especially for those with the broadest range of skills.

- Most electricians acquire their skills by completing an apprenticeship program usually lasting 4 years.

- About 79 percent of electricians work in the construction industry or are self-employed, but there also will be opportunities for electricians in other industries.

Nature of the Work

Electricians install and maintain all of the electrical and power systems for our homes, businesses, and factories. They install and maintain the wiring and control equipment through which electricity flows. They also install and maintain electrical equipment and machines in factories and a wide range of other businesses.

Electricians generally focus on either construction or maintenance, although many do both. Electricians specializing in construction primarily install wiring systems into factories, businesses, and new homes. Electricians specializing in maintenance fix and upgrade existing electrical systems and repair electrical equipment. All electricians must follow State and local building codes and the National Electrical Code when performing their work.

Electricians usually start their work by reading blueprints—technical diagrams that show the locations of circuits, outlets, load centers, panel boards, and other equipment. After determining where all the wires and components will go, electricians install and connect the wires to circuit breakers, transformers, outlets, or other components and systems.

When installing wiring, electricians use handtools such as conduit benders, screwdrivers, pliers, knives, hacksaws, and wire strippers, as well as power tools such as drills and saws. Later, they use ammeters, ohmmeters, voltmeters, harmonics testers, and other equipment to test connections and ensure the compatibility and safety of components.

Maintenance electricians repair or replace electric and electronic equipment when it breaks. They make needed repairs as quickly as possible in order to minimize inconvenience. They may replace items such as circuit breakers, fuses, switches, electrical and electronic components, or wire.

Electricians also periodically inspect all equipment to ensure that it is operating properly and to correct problems before breakdowns occur.

Maintenance work varies greatly, depending on where an electrician works. Electricians who focus on residential work perform a wide variety of electrical work for homeowners. They may rewire a home and replace an old fuse box with a new circuit breaker box to accommodate additional appliances, or they may install new lighting and other electric household items, such as ceiling fans. These electricians also might do some construction and installation work.

Electricians in large factories usually do maintenance work that is more complex. These kinds of electricians may repair motors, transformers, generators, and electronic controllers on machine tools and industrial robots. They also advise management as to whether the continued operation of certain equipment could be hazardous. When working with complex electronic devices, they may consult with engineers, engineering technicians, line installers and repairers, or industrial machinery mechanics and maintenance workers. (Statements on these occupations appear elsewhere in the *Handbook*.)

Work environment. Electricians work indoors and out, at construction sites, in homes, and in businesses or factories. The work may be strenuous at times and may include bending conduit, lifting heavy objects, and standing, stooping, and kneeling for long periods. Electricians risk injury from electrical shock, falls, and cuts, and must follow strict safety procedures to avoid injuries. Data from the U.S. Bureau of Labor Statistics show that full-time electricians experienced a work-related injury and illness rate that was higher than the national average. When working outdoors, they may be subject to inclement weather. Some electricians may have to travel long distances to jobsites.

Most electricians work a standard 40-hour week, although overtime may be required. Those who do maintenance work may work nights or weekends and be on call to go to the worksite when needed. Electricians in industrial settings may have periodic extended overtime during scheduled maintenance or retooling periods. Companies that operate 24 hours a day may employ three shifts of electricians.

Training, Other Qualifications, and Advancement

Most electricians learn their trade through apprenticeship programs that combine on-the-job training with related classroom instruction.

Education and training. Apprenticeship programs combine paid on-the-job training with related classroom instruction. Joint training committees made up of local unions of the International Brotherhood of Electrical Workers and local chapters of the National Electrical Contractors Association; individual electrical contracting companies; or local chapters of the Associated Builders and Contractors and the Independent Electrical Contractors Association usually sponsor apprenticeship programs.

Because of the comprehensive training received, those who complete apprenticeship programs qualify to do both maintenance and construction work. Apprenticeship programs usually last 4 years. Each year includes at least 144 hours of classroom instruction and 2,000 hours of on-the-job training. In the classroom, apprentices learn electrical theory, blueprint reading, mathematics, electrical code requirements, and safety and first aid practices. They also may receive specialized training in soldering, communications, fire alarm systems, and cranes and elevators.

On the job, apprentices work under the supervision of experienced electricians. At first, they drill holes, set anchors and attach conduit. Later, they measure, fabricate, and install conduit and install, connect, and test wiring, outlets, and switches. They also learn to set up and draw diagrams for entire electrical systems. Eventually, they practice and master all of an electrician's main tasks.

Some people start their classroom training before seeking an apprenticeship. A number of public and private vocational-technical schools and training academies offer training to become an electrician. Employers often hire students who complete these programs and usually start them at a more advanced level than

An electrician prepares the wiring for an interior room.

those without this training. A few people become electricians by first working as helpers—assisting electricians by setting up job sites, gathering materials, and doing other nonelectrical work—before entering an apprenticeship program. All apprentices need a high school diploma or a General Equivalency Diploma (G.E.D.). Electricians also may need additional classes in mathematics because they solve mathematical problems on the job.

Education continues throughout an electrician's career. Electricians may need to take classes to learn about changes to the National Electrical Code, and they often complete regular safety programs, manufacturer-specific training, and management training courses. Classes on such topics as low-voltage voice and data systems, telephone systems, video systems, and alternative energy systems such as solar energy and wind energy increasingly are being given as these systems become more prevalent. Other courses teach electricians how to become contractors.

Licensure. Most States and localities require electricians to be licensed. Although licensing requirements vary from State to State, electricians usually must pass an examination that tests their knowledge of electrical theory, the National Electrical Code, and local and State electric and building codes.

Electrical contractors who do electrical work for the public, as opposed to electricians who work for electrical contractors, often need a special license. In some States, electrical contractors need certification as master electricians. Most States require master electricians to have at least 7 years of experience as an electrician or a bachelor's degree in electrical engineering or a related field.

Other qualifications. Applicants for apprenticeships usually must be at least 18 years old and have a high school diploma or a G.E.D. They also may have to pass a test and meet other requirements.

Other skills needed to become an electrician include manual dexterity, eye-hand coordination, physical fitness, and a good sense of balance. Electricians also need good color vision because workers frequently must identify electrical wires by color. In addition, apprenticeship committees and employers view a good work history or military service favorably.

Advancement. Experienced electricians can advance to jobs as supervisors. In construction, they also may become project managers or construction superintendents. Those with sufficient capital and management skills can start their own contracting business, although doing so often requires a special electrical contractor's license. Supervisors and contractors should be able to identify and estimate costs and prices and the time and materials needed to complete a job. Many electricians also become electrical inspectors.

For those who seek to advance, it is increasingly important to be able to communicate in both English and Spanish in order to relay instructions and safety precautions to workers with limited understanding of English; Spanish-speaking workers make up a large part of the construction workforce in many areas. Spanish-speaking workers who want to advance in this occupation need very good English skills to understand electrician classes and installation instructions, which are usually written in English and are highly technical.

Employment

Electricians held about 694,900 jobs in 2008. About 65 percent of wage and salary workers were employed by electrical contracting firms, and the remainder worked as electricians in a variety of other industries. In addition, about 9 percent of electricians were self-employed.

Job Outlook

Average employment growth is expected. Job prospects should be good, particularly for workers with the widest range of skills, including voice, data, and video wiring.

Employment change. Employment of electricians should increase 12 percent between 2008 and 2018, about as fast as the average for all occupations. As the population grows, electricians will be needed to wire new homes, restaurants, schools, and other structures that will be built to accommodate the growing population. In addition, older buildings will require improvements to their electrical systems to meet modern codes and accommodate higher electricity consumption due to the greater use of electronic equipment in houses and workplaces.

New technologies also are expected to continue to spur demand for these workers. Robots and other automated manufacturing systems in factories will require the installation and maintenance of more complex wiring systems. In addition, efforts to boost conservation of energy in public buildings and in new construction will boost demand for electricians because electricians are key to installing some of the latest energy savers, such as solar panels and motion sensors for turning on lights.

Job prospects. In addition to jobs created by the increased demand for electrical work, openings are expected over the next decade as electricians retire. This will create good job opportunities, especially for those with the widest range of skills, including voice, data, and video wiring. Job openings for electricians will vary by location and specialty, however, and will be best in the fastest growing regions of the country.

Employment of electricians, like that of many other construction workers, is sensitive to the fluctuations of the economy. On the one hand, workers in these trades may experience periods of unemployment when the overall level of construction falls. On the other hand, shortages of these workers may occur in some areas during peak periods of building activity.

Although employment of maintenance electricians is steadier than that of construction electricians, those working in the automotive and other manufacturing industries that are sensitive to cyclical swings in the economy may experience layoffs during

Projections data from the National Employment Matrix

Occupational Title	SOC Code	Employment, 2008	Projected Employment, 2018	Change, 2008-2018	
				Number	Percent
Electricians..	47-2111	694,900	777,900	83,000	12

(NOTE) Data in this table are rounded. See the discussion of the employment projections table in the *Handbook* introductory chapter on *Occupational Information Included in the Handbook.*

recessions. In addition, in many industries opportunities for maintenance electricians may be limited by increased contracting out for electrical services in an effort to reduce operating costs. However, increased job opportunities for electricians in electrical contracting firms should partially offset job losses in other industries.

Earnings

In May 2008, median hourly wages of wage and salary electricians were $22.32. The middle 50 percent earned between $17.00 and $29.88. The lowest 10 percent earned less than $13.54, and the highest 10 percent earned more than $38.18. Median hourly wages in the industries employing the largest numbers of electricians were as follows:

Electric power generation, transmission and distribution	$28.15
Local government	25.66
Nonresidential building construction	22.21
Building equipment contractors	21.72
Employment services	18.32

Apprentices usually start at between 30 and 50 percent of the rate paid to fully trained electricians, depending on experience. As apprentices become more skilled, they receive periodic pay increases throughout their training.

About 32 percent of all electricians are members of a union, especially the International Brotherhood of Electrical Workers. Among unions representing maintenance electricians are the International Brotherhood of Electrical Workers; the International Union of Electronic, Electrical, Salaried, Machine, and Furniture Workers; the International Association of Machinists and Aerospace Workers; the International Union, United Automobile, Aircraft and Agricultural Implement Workers of America; and the United Steelworkers of America.

Related Occupations

Other occupations that combine manual skill and knowledge of electrical materials and concepts include the following:

	Page
Computer, automated teller, and office machine repairers	672
Electrical and electronics drafters	170
Electrical and electronics Engineering technicians	173
Electrical and electronics installers and repairers	675
Electronic home entertainment equipment installers and repairers	678
Elevator installers and repairers	644
Heating, air-conditioning, and refrigeration mechanics and installers	703
Line installers and repairers	713

Sources of Additional Information

For details about apprenticeships or other work opportunities in this trade, contact the offices of the State employment service, the State apprenticeship agency, local electrical contractors or firms that employ maintenance electricians, or local union-management electrician apprenticeship committees. Apprenticeship information is available from the U.S. Department of Labor's toll free help line: (877) 872-5627. Internet: **http://www.doleta.gov/OA/eta_default.cfm**

Information may be available as well from local chapters of the Independent Electrical Contractors, Inc.; the National Electrical Contractors Association; the Home Builders Institute; the Associated Builders and Contractors trade association; and the International Brotherhood of Electrical Workers.

For information about union apprenticeship and training programs, contact:

➤ National Joint Apprenticeship Training Committee, 301 Prince George's Blvd., Upper Marlboro, MD 20774-7410. Internet: **http://www.njatc.org**

➤ National Electrical Contractors Association, 3 Bethesda Metro Center, Suite 1100, Bethesda, MD 20814-6302. Internet: **http://www.necanet.org**

➤ International Brotherhood of Electrical Workers, 900 Seventh St. NW., Washington, DC 20001-3886. Internet: **http://www.ibew.org**

For information about independent apprenticeship programs, contact:

➤ Associated Builders and Contractors, Workforce Development Department, 4250 North Fairfax Dr., 9th Floor, Arlington, VA 22203-1607. Internet: **http://www.trytools.org**

➤ Independent Electrical Contractors, Inc., 4401 Ford Ave., Suite 1100, Alexandria, VA 22302-1464. Internet: **http://www.ieci.org**

➤ National Association of Home Builders, Home Builders Institute, 1201 15th St. NW, 6th Floor, Washington, DC 20005-2842. Internet: **http://www.hbi.org**

➤ National Center for Construction Education and Research, 3600 NW. 43rd St., Bldg. G, Gainesville, FL 32606-8134. Internet: **http://www.nccer.org**

For general information on apprenticeships and how to get them, see the *Occupational Outlook Quarterly* article "Apprenticeships: Career training, credentials—and a paycheck in your pocket," online at **http://www.bls.gov/opub/ooq/2002/summer/art01.pdf** and in print at many libraries and career centers.

The Occupational Information Network (O*NET) provides information on a wide range of occupational characteristics. Links to O*NET appear at the end of the Internet version of this occupational statement, accessible at **http://www.bls.gov/ooh/ocos206.htm**

Elevator Installers and Repairers

Significant Points

- Most workers belong to a union and enter the occupation through a 4-year apprenticeship program.

- Excellent employment opportunities are expected.

- Elevator installers and repairers are less affected by seasonality and downturns in the economy than most other construction trades workers because much of the work involves maintenance and repair.

Nature of the Work

Elevator installers and repairers—also called *elevator constructors* or *elevator mechanics*—assemble, install, and replace elevators, escalators, chairlifts, dumbwaiters, moving walkways, and similar equipment in new and old buildings. Once the equipment is in service, they maintain and repair it as well. They also are responsible for modernizing older equipment.

To install, repair, and maintain modern elevators, which are almost all electronically controlled, elevator installers and repairers must have a thorough knowledge of electronics, hydraulics, and electricity. Many elevators are controlled with microprocessors, which are programmed to dispatch elevators in the most efficient manner. With these controls, it is possible to get the greatest amount of service with the smallest number of cars.

Elevator installers and repairers usually specialize in installation, maintenance, or repair work. Maintenance and repair workers generally need greater knowledge of electronics and electricity than do installers because a large part of maintenance and repair work is troubleshooting.

When installing a new elevator, installers and repairers begin by studying blueprints to determine the equipment needed to install rails, machinery, car enclosures, motors, pumps, cylinders, and plunger foundations. Then, they begin equipment installation. Working on scaffolding or platforms, installers bolt or weld steel rails to the walls of the shaft to guide the elevator.

Elevator installers put in electrical wires and controls by running tubing, called conduit, along a shaft's walls from floor to floor. Once the conduit is in place, mechanics pull plastic-covered electrical wires through it. They then install electrical components and related devices required at each floor and at the main control panel in the machine room.

Installers bolt or weld together the steel frame of an elevator car at the bottom of the shaft; install the car's platform, walls, and doors; and attach guide shoes and rollers to minimize the lateral motion of the car as it travels through the shaft. They also install the outer doors and door frames at the elevator entrances on each floor.

For cabled elevators, workers install geared or gearless machines with a traction drive wheel that guides and moves heavy steel cables connected to the elevator car and counterweight. (The counterweight moves in the opposite direction from the car and balances most of the weight of the car to reduce the weight that the elevator's motor must lift.) Elevator installers also install elevators in which a car sits on a hydraulic plunger that is driven by a pump. The plunger pushes the elevator car up from underneath, similar to a hydraulic lift in an auto service station.

Installers and repairers also install escalators. They place the steel framework, the electrically powered stairs, and the tracks and install associated motors and electrical wiring. In addition to elevators and escalators, installers and repairers also may install devices such as dumbwaiters and material lifts—which are similar to elevators in design—as well as moving walkways, stair lifts, and wheelchair lifts.

Once an elevator is operating correctly, it must be maintained and serviced regularly to keep it in safe working condition. Elevator installers and repairers generally do preventive maintenance—such as oiling and greasing moving parts, replacing worn parts, testing equipment with meters and gauges, and adjusting equipment for optimal performance. They ensure that the equipment and rooms are clean. They also troubleshoot and may be called to do emergency repairs. Unlike most elevator installers, people who specialize in elevator maintenance work independently most of the day and typically service many of the same elevators on multiple occasions over time.

A service crew usually handles major repairs—for example, replacing cables, elevator doors, or machine bearings. These tasks may require the use of cutting torches or rigging equipment—tools that an elevator repairer would not normally carry. Service crews also do major modernization and alteration work, such as moving and replacing electrical motors, hydraulic pumps, and control panels.

The most highly skilled elevator installers and repairers, called "adjusters," specialize in fine-tuning all the equipment after installation. Adjusters make sure that an elevator works according to specifications and stops correctly at each floor within a specified time. Adjusters need a thorough knowledge of electronics, electricity, and computers to ensure that newly installed elevators operate properly.

Work environment. Elevator installers lift and carry heavy equipment and parts, and they may work in cramped spaces or awkward positions. Potential hazards include falls, electrical shock, muscle strains, and other injuries related to handling heavy equipment. To prevent injury, workers often are required to wear hardhats, harnesses, ear plugs, safety glasses, protective clothing and shoes, and occasionally, respirators. Data from the U.S. Bureau of Labor Statistics show that full-time elevator installers and repairers experienced a work-related injury and illness rate that was much higher than the national average.

Most elevator installers and repairers work a 40-hour week. However, overtime is required when essential equipment must be repaired, and some workers are on 24-hour call. Because most of their work is performed indoors in buildings, elevator installers and repairers lose less work time because of inclement weather than do most other workers in the construction trades.

Employment of elevator installers and repairers is less affected by economic downturns and seasonality than employment in other construction trades.

Training, Other Qualifications, and Advancement

Most elevator installers receive their education through an apprenticeship program. High school classes in mathematics, science, and shop may help applicants compete for apprenticeship openings.

Education and training. Most elevators installers and repairers learn their trade in an apprenticeship program administered by local joint educational committees representing the employers and the union—the International Union of Elevator Constructors. In nonunion shops, workers may complete training programs sponsored by independent contractors.

Apprenticeship programs teach a range of skills and usually last 4 years. Programs combine paid on-the-job training with classroom instruction in blueprint reading, electrical and electronic theory, mathematics, applications of physics, and safety.

Most apprentices assist experienced elevator installers and repairers. Beginners carry materials and tools, bolt rails to walls, and assemble elevator cars. Eventually, apprentices learn more difficult tasks, such as wiring.

Applicants for apprenticeship positions must have a high school diploma or the equivalent. High school courses in electricity, mathematics, and physics provide a useful background. As elevators become increasingly sophisticated, workers may need to get more advanced education—for example, a certificate or associate degree in electronics. Workers with education beyond high school usually advance more quickly than their counterparts without a degree.

Many elevator installers and repairers receive additional training on their particular company's equipment.

Licensure. Many cities and States require elevator installers and repairers to pass a licensing examination. However, other requirements for licensure may vary.

Certification and other qualifications. Workers who also complete an apprenticeship registered by the U.S. Department of Labor or their State board earn a journeyworker certificate recognized nationwide. Applicants for apprenticeship positions must be at least 18 years old, have a high school diploma or equivalent, and pass an aptitude test and a drug test. Good physical condition and mechanical skills also are important.

Jobs with many employers require membership in the union. To be considered fully qualified by the union, workers must complete an apprenticeship and pass a standard exam administered by the National Elevator Industry Educational Program.

The National Association of Elevator Contractors also offers certification as a Certified Elevator Technician (CET) or Certified Accessibility and Private Residence Lift Technician (CAT).

Advancement. Ongoing training is very important for a worker to keep up with technological developments in elevator repair. In fact, union elevator installers and repairers typically receive training throughout their careers, through correspondence courses, seminars, or formal classes. This training greatly improves one's chances for promotion and retention.

Some installers may receive additional training in specialized areas and advance to the position of mechanic-in-charge, adjuster, supervisor, or elevator inspector. Adjusters, for example, may be picked for their position because they possess particular skills or are electronically inclined. Other workers may move into management, sales, or product-design jobs.

Employment

Elevator installers and repairers held about 24,900 jobs in 2008. Most were employed by specialty trades contractors, particularly other building equipment contractors.

Job Outlook

Even with average job growth, excellent job opportunities are expected in this occupation.

Employment change. Employment of elevator installers and repairers is expected to increase 9 percent during the 2008–18 decade. Demand for additional elevator installers depends greatly on growth in nonresidential construction, such as commercial office buildings and stores that have elevators and escalators. This sector of the construction industry is expected to grow during the decade as the economy expands. In addition, the need to continually maintain, update and repair old equipment, provide access to the disabled, and install increasingly sophisticated equipment and controls should add to the demand for elevator installers and repairers. Another factor causing the demand for elevator installers and repairers to increase is a growing number of elderly people who require easier access to their homes through stair lifts and residential elevators.

Job prospects. Workers who seek to enter this occupation should have excellent opportunities. Elevator installer and repairer jobs have relatively high earnings and good benefits. However, it is the dangerous and physically challenging nature of this occupation and the significant training it requires that reduce the number of applicants and create better opportunities for those who apply. Job prospects should be best for those with postsecondary education in electronics or experience in the military.

Elevators, escalators, lifts, moving walkways, and related equipment need to be kept in good working condition year round every year, so employment of elevator repairers is less affected by economic downturns and seasonality than employment in other construction trades. Although elevator installers and repairers are employed throughout the Nation, the majority of positions tend to be concentrated in the Northeast because of its high concentration of tall office and residential structures.

Projections data from the National Employment Matrix

Occupational Title	SOC Code	Employment, 2008	Projected Employment, 2018	Change, 2008-2018	
				Number	Percent
Elevator installers and repairers	47-4021	24,900	27,100	2,300	9

(NOTE) Data in this table are rounded. See the discussion of the employment projections table in the *Handbook* introductory chapter on *Occupational Information Included in the Handbook.*

Earnings

Wages of elevator installers and repairers are among the highest of all construction trades. Median hourly wages of elevator installers and repairers were $33.35 in May 2008. The middle 50 percent earned between $25.79 and $39.41. The lowest 10 percent earned less than $19.38, and the top 10 percent earned more than $46.78. Median hourly wages in the building equipment contractors industry were $33.46.

Wages for members of the International Union of Elevator Constructors vary on the basis of locale and specialty. Check with a local chapter in your area for average wages.

Over half of all elevator installers and repairers were members of unions or covered by a union contract, one of the highest proportions of all occupations. Of those in a union, the largest number were members of the International Union of Elevator Constructors. In addition to free continuing education, elevator installers and repairers receive the basic benefits enjoyed by most other workers.

Related Occupations

Elevator installers and repairers combine electrical and mechanical skills with construction skills, such as welding, rigging, measuring, and blueprint reading. Other occupations that require many of these skills are:

	Page
Boilermakers	613
Electrical and electronics installers and repairers	675
Electricians	641
Industrial machinery mechanics and millwrights	709
Sheet metal workers	665
Structural and reinforcing iron and metal workers	668

Sources of Additional Information

For information about apprenticeships or job opportunities as an elevator mechanic, contact local contractors, a local chapter of the International Union of Elevator Constructors, a local joint union-management apprenticeship committee, or the nearest office of your State employment service or apprenticeship agency. You can also find information on the registered apprenticeship system with links to State apprenticeship programs on the U.S. Department of Labor's Web site: **http://www.doleta.gov/atels_bat.** Apprenticeship information is also available from the U.S. Department of Labor's toll-free helpline: (877) 872–5627.

For further information on opportunities as an elevator installer and repairer, contact:

➤ International Union of Elevator Constructors, 7154 Columbia Gateway Dr., Columbia, MD 21046. Internet: **http://www.iuec.org**

For additional information about the Certified Elevator Technician (CET) program or the Certified Accessibility and Private Residence Lift Technician (CAT) program, contact:

➤ National Association of Elevator Contractors, 1298 Wellbrook Circle, Conyers, GA 30012. Internet: **http://www.naec.org**

For general information on apprenticeships and how to get them, see the *Occupational Outlook Quarterly* article

"Apprenticeships: Career training, credentials—and a paycheck in your pocket," online at **http://www.bls.gov/opub/ooq/2002/summer/art01.pdf** and in print at many libraries and career centers.

The Occupational Information Network (O*NET) provides information on a wide range of occupational characteristics. Links to O*NET appear at the end of the Internet version of this occupational statement, accessible at **http://www.bls.gov/ooh/ocos189.htm**

Glaziers

Significant Points

- Glaziers generally learn the trade by helping experienced workers, sometimes with supplemental classroom training.

- Job opportunities are expected to be good.

- Employment is expected to grow 8 percent, about as fast as the average for all occupations.

Nature of the Work

Glass serves many uses in modern life. Insulated and specially treated glass keeps in warmed or cooled air and provides good condensation and sound control. Tempered and laminated glass makes doors and windows more secure. In large commercial buildings, glass panels give office buildings a distinctive look, while reducing the need for artificial lighting. The creative use of large windows, glass doors, skylights, and sunroom additions makes homes bright, airy, and inviting.

Glaziers are responsible for selecting, cutting, installing, replacing, and removing all types of glass. They generally work on one of several types of projects.

Residential glazing involves work, such as replacing glass in home windows; installing glass mirrors, shower doors, and bathtub enclosures; and fitting glass for tabletops and display cases. On commercial interior projects, glaziers install items such as heavy, often etched, decorative room dividers or security windows. Glazing projects also may involve replacement of storefront windows for establishments such as supermarkets, auto dealerships, or banks. In the construction of large commercial buildings, glaziers, after reading and interpreting blueprints and specifications, build metal framework extrusions and install glass panels or curtain walls. (Workers who replace and repair glass in motor vehicles are not covered in this statement. See the statement on automotive body and related repairers elsewhere in the *Handbook*.)

Besides working with glass, glaziers also may work with plastics, granite, marble, and other similar materials used as glass substitutes and with films or laminates that improve the durability or safety of the glass. They may mount steel and aluminum sashes or frames and attach locks and hinges to glass doors.

For most jobs, the glass is precut and mounted in frames at a factory or a contractor's shop. It arrives at the jobsite ready for glaziers to position and secure it in place. They may use a crane or hoist with suction cups to lift large, heavy pieces of glass. They then gently guide the glass into position by hand.

Once glaziers have the glass in place, they secure it with mastic, putty, or other paste-like cement, or with bolts, rubber gaskets, glazing compound, metal clips, or metal or wood moldings. When they secure glass using a rubber gasket—a thick, molded rubber half-tube with a split running its length—they first secure the gasket around the perimeter within the opening, then set the glass into the split side of the gasket, causing it to clamp to the edges and hold the glass firmly in place.

When they use metal clips and wood moldings, glaziers first secure the molding to the opening, place the glass in the molding, and then force springlike metal clips between the glass and the molding. The clips exert pressure and keep the glass firmly in place.

When a glazing compound is used, glaziers first spread it neatly against and around the edges of the molding on the inside of the opening. Next, they install the glass. Pressing it against the compound on the inside molding, workers screw or nail outside molding that loosely holds the glass in place. To hold it firmly, they pack the space between the molding and the glass with glazing compound and then trim any excess material with a glazing knife.

For some jobs, the glazier must cut the glass manually at the jobsite. To prepare the glass for cutting, glaziers rest it either on edge on a rack, or "A-frame," or flat against a cutting table. They then measure and mark the glass for the cut.

Glaziers cut glass with a special tool that has a small, very hard metal wheel. Using a straightedge as a guide, the glazier presses the cutter's wheel firmly on the glass, guiding and rolling it carefully to make a score just below the surface. To help the cutting tool move smoothly across the glass, workers brush a thin layer of oil along the line of the intended cut or dip the cutting tool in oil. Immediately after cutting, the glazier presses on the shorter end of the glass to break it cleanly along the cut.

In addition to handtools such as glasscutters, suction cups, and glazing knives, glaziers use power tools such as saws, drills, cutters, and grinders. An increasing number of glaziers use computers in the shop or at the jobsite to improve their layout work and reduce the amount of wasted glass.

Work environment. Glaziers often work outdoors, sometimes in inclement weather. They typically work with sharp tools and are often around broken glass. As a result, the rate of nonfatal injuries and illnesses for glaziers is among the highest of any occupation. For these reasons, constant attention to safety is crucial in this occupation.

Glaziers' work is quite physical, and so they must be prepared to lift heavy glass panels and work on scaffolding, sometimes at great heights. In addition, glaziers do a considerable amount of bending, kneeling, lifting, and standing during the installation process.

Most glaziers work a standard 40 hour workweek. During construction boom times, however, they may be required to work 50 or even 60 hours per week.

Training, Other Qualifications, and Advancement

Glaziers generally learn their trade by helping experienced workers, sometimes with supplemental classroom training. A few formal apprenticeship programs are available.

Education and training. Glaziers learn their trade through formal and informal training programs. Usually 3 years of classroom and on-the-job training are required to become a skilled glazier. There are a number of different avenues that one can take to obtain the necessary training. Most glaziers start by obtaining a job with a contractor who then provides on-the-job training. Entry-level workers generally start as helpers, assisting more experienced workers. During this time, employers may send the employee to a trade or vocational school or community college to receive further classroom training.

Some employers offer formal apprenticeships. These programs combine paid on-the-job training with related classroom instruction. Apprenticeship applicants usually must be at least 18 years old and meet local requirements. The length of the program is usually 3 years but varies with the apprentice's skill. Because the number of apprenticeship programs is limited, however, only a small proportion of glaziers learn their trade through these programs.

On the job, apprentices or helpers often start by carrying glass and cleaning up debris in glass shops. They often practice cutting on discarded glass. Later, they are given an opportunity to cut glass for a job and assist experienced workers on simple installation jobs. By working with experienced glaziers, they eventually acquire the skills of a fully qualified glazier. On the job, they learn to use the tools and equipment of the trade; handle, measure, cut, and install glass and metal framing; cut and fit moldings; and install and balance glass doors. In the classroom, they are taught about glass and installation techniques as well as basic mathematics, blueprint reading and sketching, general construction techniques, safety practices, and first aid.

Manufacturers have often worked with unions to ensure that workers know everything they need to know in order to install manufacturers' products safely and properly. In line with the architectural push for green construction, trade associations, unions, and partnerships between the two are now offering training to construction workers on the latest energy efficient products and green building techniques.

Licensure. Only the State of Connecticut currently requires glaziers to have a license. In addition to passing a test, workers need education, experience, and an apprenticeship to be licensed. There is a voluntary license in Florida. Other States may require licenses in the future.

Other qualifications. Skills needed to become a glazier include manual dexterity, good eye-hand coordination, physical

Glaziers cut class to lengths specified by the customer.

fitness, and a good sense of balance. The ability to solve arithmetic problems quickly and accurately also is required. In addition, a good work history or military service is viewed favorably by employers.

Certification and advancement. Glaziers who learn the trade through a formal registered apprenticeship program become certified journeyworkers. Some associations offer other certifications. The National Glass Association, for example, offers a series of written examinations that certify an individual's competency to perform glazier work at three progressively difficult levels of proficiency: Level I Glazier; Level II Commercial Interior or Residential Glazier, or Storefront or Curtainwall Glazier; and Level III Master Glazier.

Advancement for glaziers generally consists of increases in pay; some advance to glazier supervisors, general construction supervisors, independent contractors, or cost estimators. For those who would like to advance, it is increasingly important to be able to communicate in both English and Spanish to relay instructions and safety precautions to workers with limited understanding of English, because Spanish-speaking workers make up a large part of the construction workforce in many areas. Supervisors and contractors need good communication skills to deal with clients and subcontractors and should be able to identify and estimate the quantity of materials needed to complete a job and accurately estimate how long a job will take to complete and at what cost.

Employment

Glaziers held 54,100 jobs in 2008. About 61 percent of glaziers worked for foundation, structure, and building exterior contractors. About 14 percent of glaziers worked in building material and supplies dealers that install or replace glass. A small amount—about 7 percent—were self-employed.

Job Outlook

Average employment growth is projected. Good job opportunities are expected, especially for those with a range of skills.

Employment change. Employment is expected to grow 8 percent from 2008-2018, about as fast as average for all occupations. Job growth will stem from increasing demand for new commercial construction emphasizing glass exteriors. As manufacturers of glass products continue to improve the energy efficiency of glass windows, architects are designing more buildings with glass exteriors, especially in the South. In addition, the continuing need to modernize and repair existing structures, including residences, often involves installing new windows. Demand for specialized safety glass and glass coated with protective laminates is also growing, in response to a higher need for security and the need to withstand hurricanes, particularly in many commercial and government buildings.

Counteracting these factors, however, is the ability of other workers, such as carpenters to install windows of simple design and low cost, which reduces employment growth for glaziers.

Job prospects. In addition to growth, job openings will arise from the need to replace glaziers who leave the occupation, resulting in good job opportunities. Since employers prefer workers who can do a variety of tasks, glaziers with a range of skills will have the best opportunities.

Like other construction trades workers, glaziers employed in the construction industry should expect to experience periods of unemployment, because of the limited duration of construction projects and the cyclical nature of the construction industry. During downturns in the economy, job openings for glaziers are reduced, as the level of construction declines. However, construction activity varies from area to area, so job openings fluctuate with local economic conditions. Employment opportunities should be greatest in metropolitan areas, where most glazing contractors and glass shops are located.

Earnings

In May 2008, median hourly wages of wage and salary glaziers were $17.11. The middle 50 percent earned between $13.37 and $22.66. The lowest 10 percent earned less than $10.65, and the highest 10 percent earned more than $30.47. Median hourly wages in the foundation, structure, and building exterior contractors industry were $17.79. Median hourly wages for glaziers employed by building materials and supply dealers, where most glass shops are found, were $14.90.

Glaziers covered by union contracts generally earn more than their nonunion counterparts. Apprentice wage rates usually start at 40 to 50 percent of the rate paid to experienced glaziers and increase as workers gain experience. Because glaziers can lose work time because of weather conditions and fluctuations in construction activity, their overall earnings may be lower than their hourly wages suggest.

Related Occupations

Glaziers use their knowledge of construction materials and techniques to install glass. Other construction workers whose jobs also involve skilled, custom work include:

	Page
Brickmasons, blockmasons, and stonemasons	615
Carpenters	618
Carpet, floor, and tile installers and finishers	621
Cement masons, concrete finishers, segmental pavers, and terrazzo workers	625
Painters and paperhangers	656
Sheet metal workers	665

Other workers who repair and install automobile glass are:
Automotive body and related repairers 687

Projections data from the National Employment Matrix

Occupational Title	SOC Code	Employment, 2008	Projected Employment, 2018	Change, 2008-2018	
				Number	Percent
Glaziers	47-2121	54,100	58,300	4,200	8

(NOTE) Data in this table are rounded. See the discussion of the employment projections table in the *Handbook* introductory chapter on *Occupational Information Included in the Handbook.*

Sources of Additional Information

For more information about glazier apprenticeships or work opportunities, contact local glazing or general contractors, a local of the International Union of Painters and Allied Trades, a local joint union-management apprenticeship agency, or the nearest office of the State employment service or State apprenticeship agency. You can also find information on the registered apprenticeships together with links to State apprenticeship programs on the U.S. Department of Labor Web site: **http://www.doleta.gov/atels_bat.** Apprenticeship information is also available from the U.S. Department of Labor toll-free helpline: 1 (877) 872-5627.

For general information about the work of glaziers, contact:
➤ International Union of Painters and Allied Trades, 1750 New York Ave. NW., Washington, DC 20006. Internet: **http://www.iupat.org**

For information concerning training for glaziers, contact:
➤ Associated Builders and Contractors, Workforce Development Department, 4250 North Fairfax Dr., 9th Floor, Arlington, VA 22203-1607. Internet: **http://www.trytools.org**

➤ Finishing Trades Institute, 7230 Parkway Dr., Hanover, MD 21076-1307. Internet: **http://www.finishingtradesinstitute.org**

➤ National Glass Association, Education and Training Department, 8200 Greensboro Dr., Suite 302, McLean, VA 22102-3881. Internet: **http://www.glass.org**

For general information on apprenticeships and how to get them, see the *Occupational Outlook Quarterly* article "Apprenticeships: Career training, credentials—and a paycheck in your pocket," online at **http://www.bls.gov/opub/ooq/2002/summer/art01.pdf** and in print at many libraries and career centers.

The Occupational Information Network (O*NET) provides information on a wide range of occupational characteristics. Links to O*NET appear at the end of the Internet version of this occupational statement, accessible at **http://www.bls.gov/ooh/ocos207.htm**

Hazardous Materials Removal Workers

Significant Points

- Formal education beyond high school is not required, but government standards require specific types of on-the-job training.

- Good job opportunities are expected, mainly due to the need to replace workers who leave the occupation.

- Working conditions can be hazardous.

Nature of the Work

Hazardous materials removal workers identify, remove, package, transport, and dispose of asbestos, radioactive and nuclear waste, arsenic, lead, and mercury—or any materials that typically possess at least one of four characteristics—ignitability, corrosivity, reactivity, or toxicity. These workers often respond to emergencies where harmful substances are present, and are sometimes called abatement, remediation, or decontamination specialists. Increased public awareness and Federal and State regulations are resulting in the removal of hazardous materials from buildings, facilities, and the environment to prevent contamination of natural resources and to promote public health and safety.

Hazardous materials removal workers use a variety of tools and equipment, depending on the work at hand. Equipment ranges from brooms to personal protective suits that completely isolate workers from the hazardous material. Because of the threat of contamination, workers often wear disposable or reusable coveralls, gloves, hardhats, shoe covers, safety glasses or goggles, chemical-resistant clothing, face shields, and devices to protect one's hearing. Most workers are also required to wear respirators while working, to protect them from airborne particles or noxious gases. The respirators range from simple versions that cover only the mouth and nose to self-contained suits with their own air supply. Recent improvements to respiratory equipment allows for greater comfort, enabling workers to wear the equipment for a longer period of time.

Asbestos and lead are two of the most common contaminants that hazardous materials removal workers encounter. Through the 1970s, asbestos was used to fireproof roofing and flooring, for heat insulation, and for a variety of other purposes. It was durable, fire retardant, corrosion resistant, and insulated well, making it ideal for such applications. Embedded in materials, asbestos is fairly harmless; airborne as a particulate, however, can cause several deadly lung diseases, including lung cancer and asbestosis. Today, asbestos is rarely used in buildings, but there are still structures that contain this material that must be remediated. Similarly, lead was a common building element found in paint and plumbing fixtures and pipes until the late 1970s. Because lead is easily absorbed into the bloodstream, often from breathing lead dust or from eating chips of paint containing lead, it can cause serious health risks, especially in children. Due to these risks, it has become necessary to remove lead-based products from buildings and structures.

Asbestos abatement workers and *lead abatement workers* remove asbestos, lead, and other materials from buildings scheduled to be renovated or demolished. Using a variety of hand and power tools, such as vacuums and scrapers, these workers remove the asbestos and lead from surfaces. A typical residential lead abatement project involves the use of a chemical to strip the lead-based paint from the walls of the home. Lead abatement workers apply the compound with a putty knife and allow it to dry. Then they scrape the hazardous material into an impregnable container for transport and storage. They also use sandblasters and high-pressure water sprayers to remove lead from larger structures. The vacuums utilized by asbestos abatement workers have special, highly efficient filters designed to trap the asbestos, which later is disposed of or stored. During the abatement, special monitors measure the amount of asbestos and lead in the air, to protect the workers; in addition, lead abatement workers wear a personal air monitor that indicates the amount of lead to which a worker has been exposed. Workers also use monitoring devices to identify the asbestos, lead, and other materials that need to be removed from the surfaces of walls and structures.

Transportation of hazardous materials is safer today than it was in the past, but accidents still occur. *Emergency and disaster response workers* clean up hazardous materials after train derailments and trucking accidents. These workers also are needed when an immediate cleanup is required, as would be the case after an attack by biological or chemical weapons.

Some hazardous materials removal workers specialize in radioactive substances. These substances range from low-level-contaminated protective clothing, tools, filters, and medical equipment, to highly radioactive nuclear reactor fuels. *Decontamination technicians* perform duties similar to those of janitors and cleaners, but the items and areas they clean are radioactive. They use brooms, mops, and other tools to clean exposed areas and remove exposed items for decontamination or disposal. Some of these jobs are now being done by robots controlled by people away from the contamination site. Increasingly, many of these remote devices are being used to automatically monitor and survey surfaces, such as floors and walls, for contamination.

With experience, decontamination technicians can advance to *radiation-protection technician* jobs and use radiation survey meters and other remote devices to locate and assess radiated materials, operate high-pressure cleaning equipment for decontamination, and package radioactive materials for transportation or disposal.

Some hazardous materials removal workers specialize in radioactive substances.

Decommissioning and decontamination workers remove and treat radioactive materials generated by nuclear facilities and power plants. With a variety of handtools, they break down contaminated items such as "gloveboxes," which are used to process radioactive materials. At decommissioning sites, the workers clean and decontaminate the facility, as well as remove any radioactive or contaminated materials.

Treatment, storage, and disposal workers transport and prepare materials for treatment or disposal. To ensure proper treatment of materials, laws enforced by the U.S. Environmental Protection Agency (EPA) or Occupational Safety and Health Administration (OSHA) require these workers to be able to verify shipping manifests. At incinerator facilities, treatment, storage, and disposal workers transport materials from the customer or service center to the incinerator. At landfills, they follow a strict procedure for the processing and storage of hazardous materials. They organize and track the location of items in the landfill and may help change the state of a material from liquid to solid in preparation for its storage. These workers typically operate heavy machinery, such as forklifts, earthmoving machinery, and large trucks and rigs.

To help clean up the Nation's hazardous waste sites, a Federal program, called Superfund, was created in 1980. Under the Superfund program, abandoned, accidentally spilled, or illegally dumped hazardous waste that poses a current or future threat to human health or the environment is cleaned up. In doing so, the EPA along with potentially responsible parties, communities, local, State, and Federal authorities, identify hazardous waste sites, test site conditions, devise cleanup plans, and clean up the sites.

Mold remediation is a new aspect of some hazardous materials removal work. Some types of mold can cause harsh allergic reactions, especially in people who are susceptible to them. Although mold is present in almost all structures and is not usually defined as a hazardous material, some mold—especially the types that cause allergic reactions—can infest a building to such a degree that extensive efforts must be taken to remove it safely. Molds are fungi that typically grow in warm, damp conditions both indoors and outdoors year round. They can be found in heating and air-conditioning ducts, within walls, and in showers, attics, and basements. Although mold remediation is often undertaken by other construction workers, large scale mold removal is usually handled by hazardous materials removal workers, who take special precautions to protect themselves and surrounding areas from being contaminated.

Hazardous materials removal workers may also be required to construct scaffolding or erect containment areas prior to abatement or decontamination. In most cases, government regulation dictates that hazardous materials removal workers be closely supervised on the worksite. The standard usually is 1 supervisor to every 10 workers. The work is highly structured, sometimes planned years in advance, and usually team oriented. There is a great deal of cooperation among supervisors and workers. Because of the hazard presented by the materials being removed, work areas are restricted to licensed hazardous materials removal workers, thus minimizing exposure to the public.

Work environment. Hazardous materials removal workers function in a highly structured environment to minimize the danger they face. Each phase of an operation is planned in advance, and workers are trained to deal with hazardous situations. Crews and supervisors take every safety measure to ensure that the worksite is safe. Whether they work with asbestos, mold, lead abatement, or in radioactive decontamination, hazardous materials removal workers must stand, stoop, and kneel for long periods. Some must wear fully enclosed personal protective suits for several hours at a time; these suits may be hot and uncomfortable and may cause some individuals to experience claustrophobia.

Hazardous materials removal workers face different working conditions, depending on their area of expertise. Although many work a standard 40-hour week, overtime and shift work are common, especially for emergency and disaster response workers. Asbestos and lead abatement workers usually work in structures such as office buildings, schools, or historic buildings under renovation. Because they are under pressure to complete their work within certain deadlines, workers may experience fatigue. Completing projects frequently requires night and weekend work, because hazardous materials removal workers often work around the schedules of others. Treatment, storage, and disposal workers are employed primarily at facilities such as landfills, incinerators, boilers, and industrial furnaces. These facilities often are located in remote areas, due to the kinds of work being done, so workers may have to commute long distances to their jobs.

Decommissioning and decontamination workers, decontamination technicians, and radiation protection technicians work at nuclear facilities and electric power plants. Like treatment, storage, and disposal facilities, these sites are often far from urban areas. Workers who perform jobs in cramped conditions may need to use sharp tools to dismantle contaminated objects. A hazardous materials removal worker must have great self-control and a level head to cope with the daily stress associated with handling hazardous materials.

Hazardous materials removal workers may be required to travel outside their normal working areas in order to respond to emergency cleanups, which sometimes take several days or weeks to complete. During the cleanup, workers may be away from home for the entire time.

Training, Other Qualifications, and Advancement

No formal education beyond a high school diploma is required for a person to become a hazardous materials removal worker. However, Federal, State, and local government standards require specific types of on-the-job training. Regulations vary by specialty and sometimes by State or locality. Employers are responsible for employee training.

Education and training. Hazardous materials removal workers usually need at least 40 hours of formal on-the-job training. For most specialties, this training must meet specific requirements set by the Federal Government or individual States.

Licensure. Workers who treat asbestos and lead, the most common contaminants, must complete a training program through their employer that meets Occupational Safety and Health Administration (OSHA) standards. Employer-sponsored training is usually performed in-house, and the employer is responsible for covering all technical and safety subjects outlined by OSHA.

To become an emergency and disaster response worker and treatment, storage, and disposal worker, candidates must obtain a Federal license as mandated by OSHA. Employers are responsible for ensuring that employees complete a formal 40-hour training program, given either in house or in OSHA-approved training centers. The program covers health hazards, personal protective equipment and clothing, site safety, recognition and identification of hazards, and decontamination.

In some cases, workers may discover one hazardous material while abating another. If workers are not licensed to handle the newly discovered material, they cannot continue to work with it. Many experienced workers opt to take courses in additional types of hazardous material removal to avoid this situation.

Mold removal is not regulated by OSHA, but is regulated by each State. For decommissioning and decontamination workers employed at nuclear facilities, training is most extensive. In addition to obtaining licensure through the standard 40-hour training course in hazardous waste removal, workers must take courses dealing with regulations governing nuclear materials and radiation safety as mandated by the Nuclear Regulatory Commission. These courses add up to approximately 3 months of training, although most are not taken consecutively. Many agencies, organizations, and companies throughout the country provide training programs that are approved by the U.S. Environmental Protection Agency, the U.S. Department of Energy, and other regulatory bodies. To maintain their license, workers in all fields are required to take continuing education courses as a refresher, every year.

Other qualifications. Workers must be able to perform basic mathematical conversions and calculations when mixing solutions that neutralize contaminants and should have good physical strength and manual dexterity. Because of the nature of the work and the time constraints sometimes involved, employers prefer people who are dependable, prompt, and detail-oriented. Since much of the work is done in buildings, a background in construction is helpful.

Employment

Hazardous materials removal workers held about 42,500 jobs in 2008. About 79 percent were employed in waste management and remediation services. Another 5 percent were employed in construction.

Job Outlook

Employment is expected to grow faster than average. Good job opportunities are expected because of the need to replace the large number of workers who leave the occupation each year.

Employment change. Employment of hazardous materials removal workers is expected to grow 15 percent between 2008 and 2018, faster than the average for all occupations. The need for decontamination technicians, radiation safety technicians, and decommissioning workers, in response to increased pressure for cleaner electric generation facilities, is expected to drive employment growth. Furthermore, renewed interest in nuclear power production could lead to the reactivation of additional facilities, resulting in the need for many new remediation workers.

Numerous Superfund projects will require cleanup of hazardous materials waste sites, also spurring demand for hazardous materials removal workers. However, employment growth will largely be determined by Federal funding.

Since the 1970s, asbestos and lead-based paints and plumbing fixtures and pipes have not been used and much of the re-

Projections data from the National Employment Matrix

Occupational Title	SOC Code	Employment, 2008	Projected Employment, 2018	Change, 2008-2018	
				Number	Percent
Hazardous materials removal workers	47-4041	42,500	48,800	6,300	15

(NOTE) Data in this table are rounded. See the discussion of the employment projections table in the *Handbook* introductory chapter on *Occupational Information Included in the Handbook.*

mediation stemming from those products has taken place. With the continuing decline in the number of structures that contain asbestos and lead, demand for asbestos and lead abatement workers will be somewhat limited. Some demand, however, will result from the need to abate lead and asbestos from Federal and historic buildings.

Job prospects. In addition to job openings from employment growth, many openings are expected for hazardous materials removal workers because of the need to replace workers who leave the occupation, leading to good opportunities. Job opportunities for radiation safety technicians and decontamination workers should be plentiful as a number of new workers will be needed to replace those who retire or leave the occupation for other reasons. Additional openings may result for remediation workers if nuclear power is more widely adopted in the next decade.

Lead and asbestos workers will have some opportunities at specialty remediation companies as restoration of Federal buildings and historic structures continues, although at a slower pace than in the past. The best employment opportunities for mold remediation workers will be in Southeast, and parts of the Northeast and Northwest, where mold tends to thrive.

Many of these workers are not greatly affected by economic fluctuations because the facilities in which they work must operate, regardless of the state of the economy.

Earnings

Median hourly wages of hazardous materials removal workers were $17.94 in May 2008. The middle 50 percent earned between $14.09 and $24.09 per hour. The lowest 10 percent earned less than $11.41 per hour, and the highest 10 percent earned more than $30.42 per hour. Median hourly wages in remediation and other waste management services, the largest industry employing hazardous materials removal workers, were $18.10.

Related Occupations

Workers who perform similar tasks to those of hazardous materials removal workers include:

Other workers who commonly respond to emergencies involving hazardous materials include:

Sources of Additional Information

For more information on hazardous materials removal workers in the construction industry, including information on training, contact:

➤ Laborers-AGC Education and Training Fund, 37 Deerfield Rd., Pomfret, CT 06259.

The Occupational Information Network (O*NET) provides information on a wide range of occupational characteristics. Links to O*NET appear at the end of the Internet version of this occupational statement, accessible at **http://www.bls.gov/ooh/ocos256.htm**

Insulation Workers

Significant Points

- Workers must follow strict safety guidelines to protect themselves from insulating irritants.
- Most insulation workers learn their work informally on the job; mechanical insulators usually complete formal apprenticeship programs.
- Job opportunities are expected to be excellent.

Nature of the Work

Properly insulated buildings reduce energy consumption by keeping heat in during the winter and out in the summer. Vats, tanks, vessels, boilers, steam and hot-water pipes, and refrigerated storage rooms also are insulated to prevent the wasteful loss of heat or cold and to prevent burns. Insulation also helps to reduce the noise that passes through walls and ceilings. Insulation workers install the materials used to insulate buildings and mechanical equipment.

Insulation workers, mechanical, apply insulating materials to pipes and ductwork, or other mechanical systems, in order to help control and maintain temperature. When covering a steam pipe, for example, these insulation workers measure and cut sections of insulation to the proper length, stretch it open along a cut that runs the length of the material, and slip it over the pipe. They then fasten the insulation with adhesive, staples, tape, or wire bands. Sometimes, they wrap a cover of aluminum, plastic, or canvas over the insulation and cement or band the cover in place. Finally, mechanical insulation workers may screw on metal around insulated pipes to protect the insulation from the weather or physical abuse.

Insulation workers, floor, ceiling, and wall, apply or blow in insulation in attics and exterior walls. When blowing-in loose-fill insulation, a helper feeds a machine with fiberglass, cellulose, or rock-wool insulation, while another worker blows the insulation with a compressor hose into the space being filled.

When covering a wall or other flat surface, these insulation workers may use a hose to spray foam insulation onto a wire mesh that provides a rough surface to which the foam can cling and that adds strength to the finished surface. Workers may then install drywall or apply a final coat of plaster for a finished appearance. In new construction or on major renovations, insulation workers staple fiberglass or rock-wool batts to exterior walls and ceilings before drywall, paneling, or plaster walls are put in place.

In making major renovations to old buildings or when putting new insulation around pipes and industrial machinery, insulation workers often must first remove the old insulation. In the past, asbestos—now known to cause cancer in humans—was used extensively in walls and ceilings and to cover pipes, boilers, and various industrial equipment. Because of this danger, U.S. Environmental Protection Agency regulations require that asbestos be removed before a building undergoes major renovations or is demolished. When asbestos is present, specially trained workers must remove it before insulation workers can install the new insulating materials. (See the statement on hazardous materials removal workers elsewhere in the *Handbook*.)

Insulation workers use common handtools, including trowels, brushes, knives, scissors, saws, pliers, and stapling guns. They may use power saws to cut insulating materials, welding

Insulation workers should have excellent job opportunities.

machines to join metal or secure clamps, and compressors to blow or spray insulation.

Work environment. Insulation workers generally work indoors in residential and industrial settings. They spend most of the workday on their feet, either standing, bending, or kneeling. They also work from ladders or in confined spaces. Their work usually requires more coordination than strength. In industrial settings, these workers often insulate pipes and vessels at temperatures that may cause burns. Minute particles from insulation materials, especially when blown, can irritate the eyes, skin, and respiratory system.

Insulation workers who install insulation on floors, ceilings, and walls experience a high rate of injuries and illnesses. Consequently, workers must follow strict safety guidelines to protect themselves from insulating irritants. They must keep work areas well ventilated; wear protective suits, masks, and respirators; and take decontamination showers when necessary. Most insulation is applied after buildings are enclosed, so weather conditions have less effect on the employment of insulation workers than some other construction workers.

Training, Other Qualifications, and Advancement

Most insulation workers learn their trade informally on the job, although most mechanical insulators complete formal apprenticeship programs.

Education and training. Employers prefer to hire high school graduates. High school courses in blueprint reading, shop mathematics, science, pattern layout, woodworking, and general construction provide a helpful background.

Most new workers receive instruction and supervision from experienced insulation workers. Trainees begin with simple tasks, such as carrying insulation or holding material while it is fastened in place. On-the-job training can take up to 4 years. Learning to install insulation in homes generally requires less training than does learning to apply insulation in commercial and industrial settings. As they gain experience, trainees receive less supervision, more responsibility, and higher pay.

Trainees in formal apprenticeship programs receive in-depth instruction in all phases of insulation. Apprenticeships are generally offered by contractors that install and maintain mechanical industrial insulation. Apprenticeship programs may be provided by a joint committee of local insulation contractors and the local union of the International Association of Heat and Frost Insulators and Allied Workers, to which some insulation workers belong. Programs normally consist of 4 or 5 years of on-the-job training coupled with classroom instruction, and apprentices must pass practical and written tests to demonstrate their knowledge of the trade.

Licensure. The Environmental Protection Agency offers mandatory certification for insulation workers who remove and handle asbestos.

Other qualifications. For entry-level jobs, insulation contractors prefer to hire workers who are in good physical condition and licensed to drive. Applicants seeking apprenticeship positions are advised to have a high school diploma or its equivalent and be at least 18 years old. Supervisors and contractors, especially, need good communication skills to deal with clients and subcontractors.

Certification and advancement. Voluntary certification programs have been developed by insulation contractor organizations to help workers prove their skills and knowledge of residential and industrial insulation. The National Insulation Association also offers a certification in performing an energy appraisal to determine if and how insulation can benefit industrial customers.

Skilled insulation workers may advance to supervisor, shop superintendent, or insulation contract estimator, or they may set up their own insulation business.

For those who would like to advance, it is increasingly important to be able to relay instructions and safety precautions to workers in both English and Spanish because Spanish-speaking workers make up a large part of the construction workforce in many areas.

Employment

Insulation workers held about 57,300 jobs in 2008. About 92 percent were employed in the construction industry, with 50 percent working for drywall and insulation contractors. In less populated areas, plumbers and pipefitters, carpenters, heating and air-conditioning installers, or drywall installers may do insulation work.

Job Outlook

Insulation workers should have excellent opportunities due to faster than average job growth, coupled with the need to replace many workers who leave this occupation.

Employment change. Employment of insulation workers is expected to increase 17 percent during the 2008-18 decade, faster than the average for all occupations. Demand for insulation workers will be spurred by the need to make existing buildings more energy efficient, as well as to the anticipated construction of new power plants—a big user of piping and equipment. Modest increases in the housing stock over the decade will also generate jobs for insulation workers.

Job prospects. Job opportunities for insulation workers are expected to be excellent. In addition to opportunities created by growth, job openings will arise from the need to replace workers who retire or leave the labor force for other reasons. The irritating nature of many insulation materials, combined with the often difficult working conditions, causes many insulation workers to leave the occupation each year.

Insulation workers in the construction industry may experience periods of unemployment because of the short duration of many construction projects and the cyclical nature of construction activity. However, as the occupation focuses more and more on weatherization, energy efficiency, and green house gas reduction, the occupation should become more protected against such cyclical ups and downs in construction overall. Workers employed to perform industrial plant maintenance generally have more stable employment because maintenance and repair must be done continually.

Earnings

In May 2008, median hourly wages of wage and salary insulation workers, floor, ceiling, and wall, were $15.34. The middle 50 percent earned between $12.04 and $19.64. The lowest 10 percent earned less than $9.61, and the highest 10 percent earned more than $26.53. Median hourly wages of insulation workers, mechanical, were $17.95. The middle 50 percent earned between $14.01 and $24.58. The lowest 10 percent earned less than $11.46, and the highest 10 percent earned more than $32.82. Median hourly wages in the industries employing the largest numbers of insulation workers were:

Insulation workers, mechanical
  Building equipment contractors $17.87
  Building finishing contractors 17.53
Insulation workers, floor, ceiling, and wall
  Building finishing contractors 15.11

Union workers tend to earn more than nonunion workers. Apprentices start at about one-half of the journey worker's wage. Insulation workers doing commercial and industrial work earn substantially more than those working in residential construction, which does not require as much skill.

Related Occupations

Insulation workers combine their knowledge of insulation materials with the skills of cutting, fitting, and installing materials. Workers in occupations involving similar skills include:

Sources of Additional Information

For information about training programs or other work opportunities in this trade, contact a local insulation contractor, the nearest office of the State employment service or apprenticeship agency, or the following organizations:

➤ National Insulation Association, 12100 Sunset Hills Rd., Suite 330, Reston, VA 20190-3295. Internet: **http://www.insulation.org**

Projections data from the National Employment Matrix

Occupational Title	SOC Code	Employment, 2008	Projected Employment, 2018	Change, 2008-2018	
				Number	Percent
Insulation workers	47-2130	57,300	67,300	9,900	17
Insulation workers, floor, ceiling, and wall	47-2131	27,600	31,700	4,200	15
Insulation workers, mechanical	47-2132	29,800	35,500	5,800	19

(NOTE) Data in this table are rounded. See the discussion of the employment projections table in the *Handbook* introductory chapter on *Occupational Information Included in the Handbook.*

➤ International Association of Heat and Frost Insulators and Allied Workers, 9602 Martin Luther King, Jr. Highway, Lanham, MD 20706-1839. Internet: **http://www.insulators.org**

➤ North American Insulation Manufacturers' Association, 44 Canal Center Plaza, Suite 310, Alexandria, VA 22314-1548. Internet: **http://www.naima.org/pages/resources/training.html**

You can also find information on the registered apprenticeships together with links to State apprenticeship programs on the U.S. Department of Labor's Web site: **http://www.doleta.gov/OA/eta_default.cfm.** Apprenticeship information is also available from the U.S. Department of Labor's toll free helpline: (877) 872-5627.

For general information on apprenticeships and how to get them, see the *Occupational Outlook Quarterly* article "Apprenticeships: Career training, credentials—and a paycheck in your pocket," online at **http://www.bls.gov/opub/ooq/2002/summer/art01.pdf** and in print at many libraries and career centers.

The Occupational Information Network (O*NET) provides information on a wide range of occupational characteristics. Links to O*NET appear at the end of the Internet version of this occupational statement, accessible at **http://www.bls.gov/ooh/ocos208.htm**

Painters and Paperhangers

Significant Points

- Most workers learn informally on the job as helpers, but some experts recommend completion of an apprenticeship program.

- Employment prospects for painters should be excellent due to the large numbers of workers who leave the occupation for other jobs; paperhangers will face very limited opportunities.

- About 45 percent of painters and paperhangers are self-employed.

Nature of the Work

Paint and indoor wall coverings make surfaces clean, attractive, and vibrant. In addition, paints and other sealers protect exterior surfaces from erosion caused by exposure to the weather.

Painters apply paint, stain, varnish, and other finishes to buildings and other structures. They select the right paint or finish for the surface to be covered, taking into account durability, ease of handling, method of application, and customers' wishes. Painters first prepare the surfaces to be coated, so that the paint will adhere properly. This may require removing the old coat of paint by sanding, wire brushing, burning, or water and abrasive blasting. Painters also fill nail holes and cracks, sandpaper rough spots, and wash walls and trim to remove dirt, grease, and dust. On new surfaces, they apply a primer or sealer to prepare the surface for the top coat. Painters also mix paints and match colors, relying on knowledge of paint composition and color harmony. In most paint shops or hardware stores, mixing and matching are automated.

There are several ways to apply paint and similar coverings. Therefore, painters must be able to choose the appropriate paint applicator for each job, depending on the surface to be covered, the characteristics of the finish, and other factors. Some jobs need only a good bristle brush with a soft, tapered edge; others require a dip or fountain pressure roller; still, others are best done using a paint sprayer. Many jobs need several types of applicators. In fact, painters may use an assortment of brushes, edgers, and rollers for a single job. The right tools speed the painter's work and produce the most attractive finish.

Some painting artisans specialize in creating distinctive finishes by using one of many decorative techniques. These techniques frequently involve "broken color," a process created by applying one or more colors in broken layers over a different base coat to produce a speckled or textured effect. Often these techniques employ glazes or washes applied over a solid colored background. Glazes are made of oil-based paints and give a sleek glow to walls. Washes are made of latex-based paints that have been thinned with water which adds a greater sense of depth and texture. Other decorative painting techniques include sponging, rag-rolling, stippling, sheen striping, dragging, distressing, color blocking, marbling, and faux finishes.

Some painters specialize in painting industrial structures to prevent deterioration. One example is applying a protective coating to oil rigs or steel bridges to fight corrosion. The coating most commonly used is a waterborne acrylic solvent that is easy to apply and environmentally friendly, but other specialized and sometimes difficult-to-apply coatings may be used. Painters may also coat interior and exterior manufacturing facilities and equipment such as storage tanks, plant buildings, lockers, piping, structural steel, and ships.

When painting any industrial structure, workers must take necessary safety precautions depending on their project. Those who specialize in interior applications such as painting the inside of storage tanks, for example, must wear a full-body protective suit. When working on bridges, painters are often suspended by cables and may work at extreme heights. When working on tall buildings, painters erect scaffolding, including "swing stages," scaffolds suspended by ropes, or cables attached to roof hooks. When painting steeples and other pointed structures, they use a bosun's chair, a swing-like device.

Paperhangers cover walls with decorative coverings made of paper, vinyl, or fabric. They first prepare the surface to be covered by applying a compound, which seals the surface and makes the covering adhere better. When redecorating, they may first remove the old covering by soaking, steaming, or applying solvents. When necessary, they patch holes and take care of other imperfections before hanging the new wall covering.

After preparing the surface, paperhangers mix the adhesive unless they are using pretreated paper. They then measure the area to be covered, check the covering for flaws, cut the covering into strips of the proper size, and closely examine the pattern in order to match it when the strips are hung. A great deal of this process can now be handled by specialized equipment.

The next step is to brush or roll the adhesive onto the back of the covering, if needed, and to then place the strips on the wall, making sure the pattern is matched, the strips are straight, and the edges are butted together to make tight, closed seams. Finally, paperhangers smooth the strips to remove bubbles and wrinkles, trim the top and bottom with a utility knife, and wipe off any excess adhesive.

Work environment. Most painters and paperhangers work 40 hours a week or less; about 25 percent have variable schedules or work part time. Painters and paperhangers must stand for long periods, often working from scaffolding and ladders. Their jobs also require a considerable amount of climbing, bending, kneeling, and stretching. These workers must have good stamina because much of the work is done with their arms raised overhead. Painters, especially industrial painters, often work outdoors, almost always in dry, warm weather. Those who paint bridges or building infrastructure may be exposed to extreme heights and uncomfortable positions; some painters work suspended with ropes or cables.

Some painting jobs can leave a worker covered with paint. Drywall dust created by electric sanders prior to painting requires workers to wear protective safety glasses and a dust mask. Painters and paperhangers occasionally work with materials that are hazardous or toxic, such as when they are required to remove lead-based paints. In the most dangerous

Painters and paperhangers must stand for long periods, often working from scaffolding and ladders.

situations, painters work in a sealed self-contained suit to prevent inhalation of or contact with hazardous materials. Data from the U.S. Bureau of Labor Statistics show that full-time painters and paperhangers experienced a work-related injury and illness rate that was higher than the national average.

Training, Other Qualifications, and Advancement

Painting and paperhanging is learned mostly on the job, but some experts recommend completion of an apprenticeship program.

Education and training. Most painters and paperhangers learn through on-the-job training and by working as a helper for an experienced painter. However, there are a number of formal and informal training programs that provide more thorough instruction and a better career foundation. In general, the more formal the training received, the more likely the individual will enter the profession at a higher level and earn a higher salary. There are limited informal training opportunities for paperhangers because there are fewer paperhangers and helpers are usually not required.

A high school education or its equivalent usually is required to enter an apprenticeship program. Apprenticeships for painters and paperhangers consist of 2 to 4 years of paid on-the-job training, supplemented by a minimum of 144 hours of related classroom instruction each year. Apprentices receive instruction in color harmony, use and care of tools and equipment, surface preparation, application techniques, paint mixing and matching, characteristics of different finishes, blueprint reading, wood finishing, and safety.

Besides apprenticeships, some workers gain skills by attending technical or vocational schools that offer training prior to employment. These schools can take about a year to complete.

Whether a painter learns the trade through a formal apprenticeship or informally as a helper, on-the-job instruction covers similar skill areas. Under the direction of experienced workers, trainees carry supplies, erect scaffolds, and do simple painting and surface preparation tasks while they learn about paint and painting equipment. As they gain experience, trainees learn to prepare surfaces for painting and paperhanging, to mix paints, and to apply paint and wall coverings efficiently and neatly. Near the end of their training, they may learn decorating concepts, color coordination, and cost-estimating techniques. In addition to learning craft skills, painters must become familiar with safety and health regulations so that their work complies with the law.

Other qualifications. Painters and paperhangers should have good manual dexterity, vision, and color sense. They also need physical stamina and balance to work on ladders and platforms. Apprentices or helpers generally must be at least 18 years old, in addition to the high school diploma or GED that most apprentices need.

Certification and advancement. Some organizations offer training and certification to enhance the skills of their members. People interested in industrial painting, for example, can earn several designations from the National Association of Corrosion Engineers in several areas of specialization, including one for coating applicators, called

Protective Coating Specialist. Courses range from 1 day to several weeks depending on the certification program and specialty, and applicants must usually satisfy work experience requirements.

Painters and paperhangers may advance to supervisory or estimating jobs with painting and decorating contractors. Many establish their own painting and decorating businesses. For those who would like to advance, it is increasingly important to be able to communicate in both English and Spanish in order to relay instructions and safety precautions to workers with limited English skills; Spanish-speaking workers make up a large segment of the construction workforce in many areas. Painting contractors need good English skills to deal with clients and subcontractors.

Employment

Painters and paperhangers held about 450,100 jobs in 2008 of which 98 percent were painters. Around 36 percent of painters and paperhangers work for painting and wall covering contractors engaged in new construction, repair, restoration, or remodeling work. In addition, organizations that own or manage large buildings—such as apartment complexes—may employ painters, as do some schools, hospitals, factories, and government agencies.

Job Outlook

Overall employment is expected to grow 7 percent, reflecting as fast as average growth among painters but a rapid decline in the number of paperhangers. Excellent employment opportunities are expected for painters due to the need to replace the large number of workers who leave the occupation; paperhangers will have very limited opportunities.

Employment change. Overall employment is expected to grow by 7 percent between 2008 and 2018, about as fast as the average for all occupations. Employment of painters will grow 7 percent, as retiring baby boomers either purchase second homes or otherwise leave their existing homes that then require interior painting. Investors who sell properties or rent them out will also require the services of painters prior to completing a transaction. The relatively short life of exterior paints in residential homes as well as changing color and application trends will continue to support demand for painters. Painting is labor-intensive and not susceptible to technological changes that might make workers more productive and slow employment growth.

Growth of industrial painting will be driven by the need to prevent corrosion and deterioration of the many industrial structures by painting or coating them. Applying a protective coating to steel bridges, for example, is cost-effective and can add years to the life expectancy of a bridge.

Employment of paperhangers, on the other hand, should decline rapidly as many homeowners take advantage of easy application materials and resort to cheaper alternatives, such as painting.

Job prospects. Job prospects for painters should be excellent because of the need to replace workers who leave the occupation for other jobs. There are no strict training requirements for entry into these jobs, so many people with limited skills work as painters or helpers for a relatively short time and then move on to other types of work with higher pay or better working conditions.

Opportunities for industrial painters should be excellent as the positions available should be greater than the pool of qualified individuals to fill them. While industrial structures that require painting are located throughout the Nation, the best employment opportunities should be in the Gulf Coast region, where strong demand and the largest concentration of workers exists.

Very few openings will arise for paperhangers because the number of these jobs is comparatively small and cheaper, more modern decorative finishes such as faux effects and sponge painting have gained in popularity at the expense of paper, vinyl, or fabric wall coverings.

Jobseekers considering these occupations should expect some periods of unemployment, especially until they gain experience. Many construction projects are of short duration, and construction activity is cyclical in nature. Remodeling, restoration, and maintenance projects, however, should continue as homeowners undertake renovation projects and hire painters even in economic downturns. Nonetheless, workers in these trades may experience periods of unemployment when the overall level of construction falls. On the other hand, a shortage of these workers may occur in some areas during peak periods of building activity.

Earnings

In May 2008, median hourly wages of wage and salary painters, construction and maintenance, were $15.85, not including the earnings of the self-employed. The middle 50 percent earned between $13.13 and $20.55. The lowest 10 percent earned less than $10.75, and the highest 10 percent earned more than $27.16. Median hourly wages in the industries employing the largest numbers of painters were as follows:

Nonresidential building construction $16.72
Building finishing contractors..15.48
Residential building construction...................................14.87

Projections data from the National Employment Matrix

Occupational Title	SOC Code	Employment, 2008	Projected Employment, 2018	Change, 2008-2018	
				Number	Percent
Painters and paperhangers...	47-2140	450,100	479,900	29,800	7
Painters, construction and maintenance	47-2141	442,800	473,600	30,900	7
Paperhangers	47-2142	7,400	6,300	-1,100	-14

(NOTE) Data in this table are rounded. See the discussion of the employment projections table in the *Handbook* introductory chapter on *Occupational Information Included in the Handbook.*

In May 2008, median hourly wages for wage and salary paperhangers were $16.76. The middle 50 percent earned between $13.64 and $23.08. The lowest 10 percent earned less than $10.82, and the highest 10 percent earned more than $33.48.

Earnings for painters may be reduced on occasion because of bad weather and the short-term nature of many construction jobs. Hourly wage rates for apprentices usually start at 40 to 50 percent of the rate for experienced workers and increase periodically.

Some painters and paperhangers are members of the International Brotherhood of Painters and Allied Trades. Some painters are members of other unions.

Related Occupations

Painters and paperhangers apply various coverings to decorate and protect wood, drywall, metal, and other surfaces. Other construction workers who do finishing work include:

Sources of Additional Information

For details about painting and paperhanging apprenticeships or work opportunities, contact local painting and decorating contractors, local trade organizations, a local of the International Union of Painters and Allied Trades, a local joint union-management apprenticeship committee, or an office of the State apprenticeship agency or employment service.

For information about the work of painters and paperhangers and training opportunities, contact:

➤ Associated Builders and Contractors, Workforce Development Department, 4250 North Fairfax Dr., 9th Floor, Arlington, VA 22203. Internet: **http://www.trytools.org**

➤ International Union of Painters and Allied Trades, 1750 New York Ave. NW., Washington, DC 20006. Internet: **http://www.iupat.org**

➤ National Center for Construction Education and Research, 3600 NW 43rd St., Bldg. G, Gainesville, FL 32606. Internet: **http://www.nccer.org**

➤ Painting and Decorating Contractors of America, 1801 Park 270 Dr., Suite 220, St. Louis, MO 63146. Internet: **http://www.pdca.org**

For general information about the work of industrial painters and opportunities for training and certification as a protective coating specialist, contact:

➤ National Association of Corrosion Engineers, 1440 South Creek Dr., Houston, TX 77084. Internet: **http://www.nace.org**

The Occupational Information Network (O*NET) provides information on a wide range of occupational characteristics. Links to O*NET appear at the end of the Internet version of this occupational statement, accessible at **http://www.bls.gov/ooh/ocos209.htm**

Plumbers, Pipelayers, Pipefitters, and Steamfitters

Significant Points

- Job opportunities should be very good.
- These workers constitute one of the largest and highest paid construction occupations.
- Most States and localities require plumbers to be licensed.
- Most workers train in apprenticeship programs and in career or technical schools or community colleges.

Nature of the Work

Most people are familiar with plumbers who come to their home to unclog a drain or fix a leaking toilet. Plumbers, pipelayers, pipefitters, and steamfitters install, maintain, and repair many different types of pipe systems. Some of these systems move water from reservoirs to municipal water treatment plants and then to residential, commercial, and public buildings. Other systems dispose of waste, supply gas to stoves and furnaces, or provide for heating and cooling needs. Pipe systems in powerplants carry the steam that powers huge turbines. Pipes also are used in manufacturing plants to move material through the production process. Specialized piping systems are very important in both pharmaceutical and computer-chip manufacturing.

Although plumbing, pipelaying, pipefitting, and steamfitting are sometimes considered a single trade, workers generally specialize in one of five areas. *Plumbers* install and repair the water, waste disposal, drainage, and gas systems in homes and commercial and industrial buildings. Plumbers also install plumbing fixtures—bathtubs, showers, sinks, and toilets—and appliances such as dishwashers, waste disposers, and water heaters. *Pipelayers* lay clay, concrete, plastic, or cast-iron pipe for drains, sewers, water mains, and oil or gas lines. Before laying the pipe, pipelayers prepare and grade the trenches either manually or with machines. After laying the pipe, they weld,

Pipelayers install pipe to be buried underground on huge construction projects.

glue, cement, or otherwise join the pieces together. *Pipefitters* install and repair both high-pressure and low-pressure pipe systems used in manufacturing, in the generation of electricity, and in the heating and cooling of buildings. They also install automatic controls that are increasingly being used to regulate these systems. *Steamfitters* install pipe systems that move liquids or gases under high pressure. *Sprinklerfitters* install automatic fire sprinkler systems in buildings. Plumbers, pipelayers, pipefitters, and steamfitters use many different materials and construction techniques, depending on the type of project. Residential water systems, for example, incorporate copper, steel, and plastic pipe that can be handled and installed by one or two plumbers. Municipal sewerage systems, by contrast, are made of large cast-iron pipes; installation normally requires crews of pipefitters. Despite these differences, all plumbers, pipelayers, pipefitters, and steamfitters must be able to follow building plans or blueprints and instructions from supervisors, lay out the job, and work efficiently with the materials and tools of their trade. When plumbers working construction install piping in a new house, they work from blueprints or drawings that show the planned location of pipes, plumbing fixtures, and appliances. Recently, plumbers have become more involved in the design process. Their knowledge of codes and the operation of plumbing systems can cut costs. First they lay out the job to fit the piping into the structure of the house with the least waste of material. Then they measure and mark areas in which pipes will be installed and connected. Construction plumbers also check for obstructions such as electrical wiring and, if necessary, plan the pipe installation around the problem.

Sometimes, plumbers have to cut holes in walls, ceilings, and floors of a house. With some systems, they may hang steel supports from ceiling joists to hold the pipe in place. To assemble a system, plumbers—using saws, pipe cutters, and pipe-bending machines—cut and bend lengths of pipe. They connect the lengths of pipe with fittings, using methods that depend on the type of pipe used. For plastic pipe, plumbers connect the sections and fittings with adhesives. For copper pipe, they slide a fitting over the end of the pipe and solder it in place with a torch.

After the piping is in place in the house, plumbers install the fixtures and appliances and connect the system to the outside water or sewer lines. Finally, using pressure gauges, they check the system to ensure that the plumbing works properly.

Work environment. Plumbers work in commercial and residential settings where water and septic systems need to be installed and maintained. Pipefitters and steamfitters most often work in industrial and power plants. Pipelayers work outdoors, sometimes in remote areas, laying pipes that connect sources of oil, gas, and chemicals with the users of these resources. Sprinklerfitters work in all buildings that require the use of fire sprinkler systems.

Because plumbers, pipelayers, pipefitters, and steamfitters frequently must lift heavy pipes, stand for long periods, and sometimes work in uncomfortable or cramped positions, they need physical strength and stamina. They also may have to work outdoors in inclement weather. In addition, they are subject to possible falls from ladders, cuts from sharp tools, and burns from hot pipes or soldering equipment. Consequently, this occupation experiences rates of nonfatal injuries and illnesses that are much higher than average.

Plumbers, pipelayers, pipefitters, and steamfitters often work more than 40 hours per week and can be on call for emergencies nights and weekends. Some pipelayers may need to travel to and from worksites.

Training, Other Qualifications, and Advancement

Most plumbers, pipelayers, pipefitters, and steamfitters train on the job through jointly administered apprenticeships and in career or technical schools or community colleges.

Education and training. Plumbers, pipelayers, pipefitters, and steamfitters enter into the occupation in a variety of ways. Most plumbers, pipefitters, and steamfitters get their training in jointly administered apprenticeships or in technical schools and community colleges. Pipelayers typically receive their training on the job.

Apprenticeship programs generally provide the most comprehensive training available for these jobs. Such programs are, for the most part, administered jointly by union locals and their affiliated companies or by nonunion contractor organizations. Organizations that sponsor apprenticeships include the United Association of Journeymen and Apprentices of the Plumbing and Pipefitting Industry of the United States and Canada; local employers of either the Mechanical Contractors Association of America or the National Association of Plumbing-Heating-Cooling Contractors; a union associated with a member of the National Fire Sprinkler Association; the Associated Builders and Contractors; the National Association of Plumbing-Heating-Cooling Contractors; the American Fire Sprinkler Association; and the Home Builders Institute of the National Association of Home Builders.

Apprenticeships—both union and nonunion—consist of 4 or 5 years of paid on-the-job training and at least 144 hours of related classroom instruction per year. Classroom subjects include drafting and blueprint reading, mathematics, applied physics and chemistry, safety, and local plumbing codes and regulations. On the job, apprentices first learn basic skills, such as identifying grades and types of pipe, using the tools of the trade, and unloading materials safely. As apprentices gain experience, they learn how to work with various types of pipe and how to install different piping systems and plumbing fixtures. Apprenticeship gives trainees a thorough knowledge of all aspects of the trade. Although most plumbers, pipefitters, and steamfitters are trained through apprenticeships, some still learn their skills informally on the job or by taking classes on their own.

Licensure. Although there are no uniform national licensing requirements, most States and communities require plumbers to be licensed. Licensing requirements vary, but most localities require workers to have 2 to 5 years of experience and to pass an examination that tests their knowledge of the trade and of local plumbing codes before they are permitted to work independently. Several States require a special license to work on gas lines. A few States require pipefitters to be licensed. Licenses usually require a test, experience, or both.

Other qualifications. Applicants for union or nonunion apprentice jobs must be at least 18 years old and in good physical condition. A drug test may be required. Apprenticeship committees may require applicants to have a high school diploma or its equivalent. For jointly administered apprenticeships approved by the U.S. Department of Labor, a high school diploma is mandatory, because these programs can earn credit from community colleges and, in some cases, from 4-year colleges. Armed Forces training in plumbing, pipefitting, and steamfitting is considered very good preparation. In fact, people with this background may be given credit for previous experience when they enroll in a civilian apprenticeship program. High school or postsecondary courses in shop, plumbing, general mathematics, drafting, blueprint reading, computers, and physics also are good preparation.

Certification and advancement. With additional training, some plumbers, pipefitters, and steamfitters become supervisors for mechanical and plumbing contractors. Others, especially plumbers, go into business for themselves, often starting as a self-employed plumber working from home. Some eventually become owners of businesses employing many workers and may spend most of their time as managers rather than as plumbers. Others move into closely related areas such as construction management or building inspection.

For those who would like to advance, it is becoming increasingly important to be able to communicate in both English and Spanish in order to relay instructions and safety precautions to workers with limited understanding of English; Spanish-speaking workers make up a large part of the construction workforce in many areas. Supervisors and contractors need good communication skills to deal with clients and subcontractors.

In line with new opportunities arising from the growing need to conserve water, the Plumbing-Heating-Cooling Contractors—National Association has formed a partnership with GreenPlumbers USA to train and certify plumbers across the Nation on water-saving technologies and energy efficiency. Attainment of this certification may help people trained in this area to get more jobs and advance more quickly.

Employment

Plumbers, pipelayers, pipefitters, and steamfitters constitute one of the largest construction occupations, holding about 555,900 jobs in 2008. About 56 percent worked for plumbing, heating, and air-conditioning contractors engaged in new construction, repair, modernization, or maintenance work. Others were employed by a variety of industrial, commercial, and government employers. Pipefitters, for example, were employed in the petroleum and chemical industries to maintain the pipes that carry industrial liquids and gases. About 12 percent of plumbers, pipelayers, pipefitters, and steamfitters were self-employed.

Job Outlook

Faster than average employment growth is projected. Job opportunities are expected to be very good.

Employment change. Employment of plumbers, pipelayers, pipefitters, and steamfitters is expected to grow 16 percent between 2008 and 2018, faster than the average for all occupations. Demand for plumbers will stem from new construction and from renovation of buildings. In addition, repair and maintenance of existing residential systems will keep plumbers employed. A growing emphasis on water conservation, particularly in dryer parts of the country, that will require retrofitting in order to conserve water in new ways will increase demand for plumbers. Demand for pipefitters and steamfitters will be driven by maintenance and construction of places such as powerplants, water and wastewater treatment plants, office buildings, and factories, all of which have extensive pipe systems. The stimulus package aimed at repairing the Nation's infrastructure should help the employment picture immediately; long-term growth of pipelayer jobs will stem from the building of new water and sewer lines and of pipelines to new oil and gas fields. Demand for sprinklerfitters also should also increase, because of proposed changes to construction codes, set to take effect in 2011, that will require the installation of fire sprinkler systems in residential buildings where these systems had previously never been required.

Job prospects. Job opportunities are expected to be very good, with demand for skilled plumbers, pipelayers, pipefitters, and steamfitters expected to outpace the supply of well-trained workers in this craft. Some employers report difficulty finding workers with the right qualifications. In addition, many people currently working in these trades are expected to retire over the next 10 years, which will create additional job openings. Workers with welding experience should have especially good opportunities.

Traditionally, many organizations with extensive pipe systems have employed their own plumbers or pipefitters to maintain equipment and keep systems running smoothly. But, to reduce labor costs, a large number of these firms no longer employ full-time, in-house plumbers or pipefitters. Instead, when they need a plumber, they increasingly are relying on workers provided under service contracts by plumbing and pipefitting contractors.

Construction projects generally provide only temporary employment. When a project ends, some plumbers, pipelayers, pipefitters, and steamfitters may be unemployed until they can begin work on a new project, although most companies are trying to limit these periods of unemployment in order to retain workers. In addition, the jobs of plumbers, pipelayers, pipefitters, and steamfitters are generally less sensitive to changes in economic conditions than are jobs in other construction trades. Moreover, the coming emphasis on conservation of energy and water is opening up opportunities for those

Projections data from the National Employment Matrix

Occupational Title	SOC Code	Employment, 2008	Projected Employment, 2018	Change, 2008-2018	
				Number	Percent
Pipelayers, plumbers, pipefitters, and steamfitters.............................	47-2150	555,900	642,100	86,300	16
Pipelayers..	47-2151	61,200	71,700	10,500	17
Plumbers, pipefitters, and steamfitters	47-2152	494,700	570,500	75,800	15

(NOTE) Data in this table are rounded. See the discussion of the employment projections table in the *Handbook* introductory chapter on *Occupational Information Included in the Handbook.*

plumbers, pipefitters, and steamfitters who become proficient in new green technologies.

Earnings

Plumbers, pipelayers, pipefitters, and steamfitters are among the highest paid workers in construction occupations. Median hourly wages of wage and salary plumbers, pipefitters, and steamfitters were $21.94 in May 2008. The middle 50 percent earned between $16.63 and $29.66. The lowest 10 percent earned less than $13.22, and the highest 10 percent earned more than $37.93. Median hourly wages in the industries employing the largest numbers of plumbers, pipefitters, and steamfitters were as follows:

Natural gas distribution	$26.27
Nonresidential building construction	23.14
Building equipment contractors	21.86
Utility system construction	21.15
Local government	20.65

In May 2008, median hourly wages of wage and salary pipelayers were $15.72. The middle 50 percent earned between $12.84 and $20.85. The lowest 10 percent earned less than $10.74, and the highest 10 percent earned more than $27.43.

Apprentices usually begin at about 50 percent of the wage rate paid to experienced workers. Wages increase periodically as skills improve. After an initial waiting period, apprentices receive the same benefits as experienced plumbers, pipelayers, pipefitters, and steamfitters.

About 31 percent of plumbers, pipelayers, pipefitters, and steamfitters belonged to a union. Many of these workers are members of the United Association of Journeymen and Apprentices of the Plumbing and Pipefitting Industry of the United States and Canada.

Related Occupations

Other workers who install and repair mechanical systems in buildings include the following:

	Page
Boilermakers	613
Electricians	641
Elevator installers and repairers	644
Heating, air-conditioning, and refrigeration mechanics and installers	703
Industrial machinery mechanics and millwrights	709
Sheet metal workers	665
Stationary engineers and boiler operators	763

Other construction-related workers who need to know plumbing requirements include the following:

Construction and building inspectors	628
Construction managers	38

Sources of Additional Information

For information about apprenticeships or work opportunities in plumbing, pipelaying, pipefitting, and steamfitting, contact local plumbing, heating, and air-conditioning contractors; a local or State chapter of the Plumbing-Heating-Cooling Contractors; a local chapter of the Mechanical Contractors Association; a local chapter of the United Association of Journeymen and Ap-

prentices of the Plumbing and Pipefitting Industry of the United States and Canada; or the nearest office of your State employment service or apprenticeship agency.

Apprenticeship information also is available from the U.S. Department of Labor's toll-free help line: (877) 872-5627.

For information about apprenticeship opportunities for plumbers, pipefitters, and steamfitters, contact:

➤ United Association of Journeymen and Apprentices of the Plumbing and Pipefitting Industry, Three Park Place, Annapolis, MD 21401-3687. Internet: **http://www.ua.org**

For general information about the work of pipelayers, plumbers, and pipefitters, contact:

➤ Mechanical Contractors Association of America, 1385 Piccard Dr., Rockville, MD 20850-4329. Internet: **http://www.mcaa.org**

➤ National Center for Construction Education and Research, 3600 NW. 43rd St., Bldg. G, Gainesville, FL 32606-8134. Internet: **http://www.nccer.org**

➤ Plumbing-Heating-Cooling Contractors—National Association, 180 S. Washington St, Falls Church, VA 22046-2935. Internet: **http://www.phccweb.org**

For general information about the work of sprinklerfitters, contact:

➤ American Fire Sprinkler Association, Inc., 12750 Merit Dr., Suite 350, Dallas, TX 75251-1273. Internet: **http://www.firesprinkler.org**

➤ National Fire Sprinkler Association, 40 Jon Barrett Rd., Patterson, NY 12563-2164. Internet: **http://www.nfsa.org**

For general information on apprenticeships and how to get them, see the *Occupational Outlook Quarterly* article "Apprenticeships: Career training, credentials—and a paycheck in your pocket," online at **http://www.bls.gov/opub/ooq/2002/summer/art01.pdf** and in print at many libraries and career centers.

The Occupational Information Network (O*NET) provides information on a wide range of occupational characteristics. Links to O*NET appear at the end of the Internet version of this occupational statement, accessible at **http://www.bls.gov/ooh/ocos211.htm**

Roofers

Significant Points

- Most roofers learn their skills on the job; some train through 3-year apprenticeships.

- Demand for roofers is less vulnerable to downturns in the economy than demand for other construction trades because most roofing work consists of repair and reroofing.

- Most job openings will occur from the need to replace those who leave the occupation because the work can be hot, strenuous, and dirty, causing many people to switch to jobs in other construction trades.

Nature of the Work

Roofers repair and install roofs made from a combination of some of the following: tar, asphalt, gravel, rubber, thermoplastic, metal, and shingles—all of which protect buildings and their contents from water damage. A leaky roof can damage ceilings, walls, and furnishings. Repair and reroofing—replacing old roofs on existing buildings—make up the majority of work for roofers.

There are two types of roofs—low-slope and steep-slope. Low-slope roofs rise 4 inches or less per horizontal foot and are installed in layers. Steep-slope roofs rise more than 4 inches per horizontal foot and are usually covered in shingles. Most commercial, industrial, and apartment buildings contain low-slope roofs, while the majority of residential houses have steep-slope roofs. Some roofers work on both types; others specialize.

Most low-slope roofs are covered with several layers of materials. Roofers begin by installing a layer of insulation on the roof deck, followed by applying a tarlike substance called molten bitumen on top of it. Next, they install overlapping layers of roofing felt—a fabric soaked in bitumen—over the surface. Roofers use a mop to spread hot bitumen over the felt before adding another layer of felt. This seals the seams and makes the surface waterproof. Roofers repeat these steps to build up the desired number of layers, called "plies." The top layer is then glazed to make a smooth finish or has gravel embedded in the hot bitumen to create a rough surface.

An increasing number of low-slope roofs are covered with single-ply membranes of waterproof rubber or thermoplastic compounds. Roofers roll these sheets over the roof's insulation and seal the seams. Adhesive, mechanical fasteners, or stone ballast hold the sheets in place. Roofers must make sure the building is strong enough to hold the stone ballast.

A small but increasing number of buildings now have "green" roofs that incorporate landscape roofing systems. A landscape roofing system begins with a single or multiply waterproof layer. After it is proven to be leak free, roofers put a root barrier over it, and then layers of soil, in which trees and grass are planted. Roofers are responsible for making sure the roof is watertight and can endure the weight and water needs of the plants.

Most residential steep-slope roofs are covered with shingles. To apply shingles, roofers first lay, cut, and tack 3-foot strips of roofing felt over the entire roof. Starting from the bottom edge, roofers then nail overlapping rows of shingles to the roof. Roofers measure and cut the felt and shingles to fit intersecting roof surfaces and to fit around vent pipes and chimneys. Wherever two sections of the roof meet each other at an angle or where shingles reach a vent pipe or chimney, roofers cement or nail flashing-strips of metal or shingle over the joints to make them watertight. Finally, roofers cover exposed nail-heads with roofing cement or caulking to prevent water leakage. A similar process is used when installing tile, metal shingles, or shakes (rough wooden shingles).

Some roofers specialize in waterproofing or dampproofing masonry and concrete walls, floors, and foundations. To prepare surfaces for waterproofing, they hammer and chisel away rough spots or remove them with a rubbing brick before applying a coat of liquid waterproofing compound. They also may paint or spray surfaces with a waterproofing material or attach waterproofing membrane to surfaces. Roofers usually spray a bitumen-based coating on interior or exterior surfaces when dampproofing.

Work environment. Roofing work is strenuous. It involves heavy lifting, as well as climbing, bending, and kneeling. Roofers work outdoors in all types of weather, particularly when making repairs. However, they rarely work when it rains or in very cold weather because ice can be dangerous. In northern States, roofing work is generally not performed during winter months. During the summer, roofers may work overtime to complete jobs quickly, especially before forecasted rainfall.

Workers risk slips or falls from scaffolds, ladders, or roofs, and burns from hot bitumen, but safety precautions can prevent most accidents. In addition, roofs can become extremely hot during the summer, causing heat-related illnesses. Data from the U.S. Bureau of Labor Statistics show that full-time roofers experienced a work-related injury and illness rate that was much higher than the national average.

Training, Other Qualifications, and Advancement

Most roofers learn their skills on the job by working as helpers for experienced roofers and by taking classes, including safety training offered by their employers; some complete 3-year apprenticeships.

Education and training. A high school education, or its equivalent, is helpful and so are courses in mechanical drawing and basic mathematics. Although most workers learn roofing as helpers for experienced workers, some roofers train through 3-year apprenticeship programs administered by local union-management committees representing roofing contractors and locals of the United Union of Roofers, Waterproofers, and Allied Workers. Apprenticeship programs usually include at least 2,000 hours of paid long-term on-the-job training each year, plus a minimum of 144 hours of classroom instruction a year in tools and their use, arithmetic, safety, and other topics. On-the-job training for apprentices is similar to the training given to helpers, but an apprenticeship program is more structured and comprehensive. Apprentices, for example, also learn to dampproof and waterproof walls.

Trainees start by carrying equipment and material and erecting scaffolds and hoists. Within 2 or 3 months, they are taught to measure, cut, and fit roofing materials and, later, to lay asphalt or fiberglass shingles. Because some roofing materials are used infrequently, such as solar tiles, it can take several years to get experience working on all types of roofing.

Other qualifications. Physical condition and strength, along with good balance, are essential for roofers. They cannot be afraid of heights. Experience with metal-working is helpful for workers who install metal roofing. Usually, apprentices must be at least 18 years old.

Advancement. Roofers may advance to become supervisors or estimators for a roofing contractor or become independent contractors themselves.

Employment

Roofers held about 148,900 jobs in 2008. About 70 percent of all salaried roofers worked for roofing contractors, while only

Roofers need good physical condition, strength, and balance.

21 percent were self-employed. Many self-employed roofers specialized in residential work.

Job Outlook

Most job openings will occur from turnover because the work is hot, strenuous, and dirty, causing many people to switch to jobs in other construction trades. Employment is projected to grow slower than the average.

Employment change. Employment of roofers is expected to grow 4 percent between 2008 and 2018, slower than the average for all occupations. Roofs deteriorate faster than most other parts of buildings and, as a result, they need to be repaired or replaced more often. In addition to repair work, the need to install roofs on new buildings may result in some job growth. So as building construction increases, some demand for roofers can be expected.

Employment growth, nonetheless, may be impeded because a greater proportion of roofing work may be completed by other construction workers as opposed to traditional roofing contractors.

Job prospects. Job opportunities for roofers will occur primarily because of the need to replace workers who leave the occupation. The proportion of roofers who leave the occupation each year is higher than in most construction trades—roofing work is hot, strenuous, and dirty, and a considerable number of workers treat roofing as a temporary job until they find other work. Some roofers leave the occupation to go into other construction trades. Jobs should be easier to find during spring and summer.

Employment of roofers who install new roofs, like that of many other construction workers, is sensitive to fluctuations of the economy. Workers may experience periods of unemployment when the overall level of construction falls. On the other hand, shortages of these workers may occur in some areas during peak periods of building activity. Nevertheless, roofing work is more heavily concentrated in repair and replacement rather than new installation, making demand for roofing less vulnerable to downturns than demand for some other construction trades.

Earnings

In May 2008, median hourly wages of roofers were $16.17. The middle 50 percent earned between $12.97 and $21.98. The lowest 10 percent earned less than $10.63, and the highest 10 percent earned more than $28.46. Median hourly wages of roofers in the foundation, structure, and building exterior contractors industry were $16.26. Earnings may be less on occasions when poor weather limits the time roofers can work.

Apprentices usually begin earning about 40 percent to 50 percent of the rate paid to experienced roofers. They receive periodic raises as they master the skills of the trade.

Some roofers are members of United Union of Roofers, Waterproofers, and Allied Workers. Hourly wages and fringe benefits are generally higher for union workers.

Related Occupations

Roofers use shingles, tile, bitumen and gravel, single-ply plastic or rubber sheets, or other materials to protect and waterproof building surfaces. Workers in other occupations who cover surfaces with special materials for protection and decoration include:

Projections data from the National Employment Matrix

Occupational Title	SOC Code	Employment, 2008	Projected Employment, 2018	Change, 2008-2018	
				Number	Percent
Roofers	47-2181	148,900	154,600	5,700	4

(NOTE) Data in this table are rounded. See the discussion of the employment projections table in the *Handbook* introductory chapter on *Occupational Information Included in the Handbook.*

Sources of Additional Information

For information about apprenticeships or job opportunities in roofing, contact local roofing contractors, a local chapter of the roofers union, a local joint union-management apprenticeship committee, or the nearest office of your State employment service or apprenticeship agency. You can also find information on the registered apprenticeship system with links to State apprenticeship programs on the U.S. Department of Labor's Web site at **http://www.doleta.gov/atels_bat.** Apprenticeship information is also available from the U.S. Department of Labor's toll-free helpline: 1 (877) 872–5627.

For information about the work of roofers, contact:

➤ National Roofing Contractors Association, 10255 W. Higgins Rd., Suite 600, Rosemont, IL 60018-5607. Internet: **http://www.nrca.net**

➤ United Union of Roofers, Waterproofers, and Allied Workers, 1660 L St. NW., Suite 800, Washington, DC 20036. Internet: **http://www.unionroofers.com**

For general information on apprenticeships and how to get them, see the *Occupational Outlook Quarterly* article "Apprenticeships: Career training, credentials—and a paycheck in your pocket," online at **http://www.bls.gov/opub/ooq/2002/summer/art01.pdf** and in print at many libraries and career centers.

The Occupational Information Network (O*NET) provides information on a wide range of occupational characteristics. Links to O*NET appear at the end of the Internet version of this occupational statement, accessible at **http://www.bls.gov/ooh/ocos212.htm**

Sheet Metal Workers

Significant Points

- Sheet metal workers are primarily employed in construction and manufacturing industries.

- Workers learn through informal on-the-job training or formal apprenticeship programs.

- Job opportunities in construction should be good, particularly for individuals who have apprenticeship training or who are certified welders; applicants for jobs in manufacturing will experience competition.

Nature of the Work

Sheet metal workers make, install, and maintain heating, ventilation, and air-conditioning duct systems; roofs; siding; rain gutters; downspouts; skylights; restaurant equipment; outdoor signs; railroad cars; tailgates; customized precision equipment; and many other products made from metal sheets. They also may work with fiberglass and plastic materials. Although some workers specialize in fabrication, installation, or maintenance, most do all three jobs. Sheet metal workers do both construction-related work and mass production of sheet metal products in manufacturing.

Sheet metal workers first study plans and specifications to determine the kind and quantity of materials they will need. They

A sheet metal worker is using a torch to heat a sheet of metal.

measure, cut, bend, shape, and fasten pieces of sheet metal to make ductwork, countertops, and other custom products. Sheet metal workers program and operate computerized metalworking equipment. They cut, drill, and form parts with computer-controlled saws, lasers, shears, and presses.

In shops without computerized equipment, and for products that cannot be made with such equipment, sheet metal workers make the required calculations and use tapes, rulers, and other measuring devices for layout work. They then cut or stamp the parts with machine tools.

Before assembling pieces, sheet metal workers use measuring instruments such as tape measures, calipers, and micrometers to check each part for accuracy. If necessary, they use hand, rotary, or squaring shears and hacksaws to finish pieces. After inspecting the pieces, workers fasten seams and joints together with welds, bolts, cement, rivets, solder, or other connecting devices. They then take the parts constructed in the shop and assemble the pieces further as they install them. These workers install ducts, pipes, and tubes by joining them end to end and hanging them with metal hangers secured to a ceiling or a wall. They also use shears, hammers, punches, and drills to make parts at the worksite or to alter parts made in the shop.

Some jobs are done completely at the jobsite. When installing a metal roof, for example, sheet metal workers usually measure and cut the roofing panels onsite. They secure the first panel in place and interlock and fasten the grooved edge of the next panel into the grooved edge of the first. Then they nail or weld the free edge of the panel to the structure. This two-step process is repeated for each additional panel. Finally, the workers fasten machine-made molding at joints, along corners, and around windows and doors, for a neat, finished effect.

In addition to installation, some sheet metal workers specialize in testing, balancing, adjusting, and servicing existing air-conditioning and ventilation systems to make sure they are functioning properly and to improve their energy efficiency. Properly installed duct systems are a key component of heating, ventilation, and air-conditioning (HVAC) systems; sometimes duct installers are called HVAC technicians. A growing activity for sheet metal workers is the commissioning of a building—a complete mechanical inspection of the building's HVAC, water, and lighting systems.

Sheet metal workers in manufacturing plants make sheet metal parts for products such as aircraft or industrial equipment. Although some of the fabrication techniques used in large-scale manufacturing are similar to those used in smaller shops, the work may be highly automated and repetitive. Sheet metal workers doing such work may be responsible for reprogramming the computer control systems of the equipment they operate.

Work environment.   Sheet metal workers usually work a 40-hour week. Those who fabricate sheet metal products work in small shops and manufacturing plants that are usually well lighted and well ventilated. However, they stand for long periods and lift heavy materials and finished pieces. Those performing installation at construction sites or inside buildings do considerable bending, lifting, standing, climbing, and squatting, sometimes in close quarters or awkward positions. Working outdoors exposes sheet metal workers to various kinds of weather.

Sheet metal workers must follow safety practices, because this occupation has a relatively high rate of nonfatal injuries. Some sheet metal workers work around high-speed machines, which can be dangerous. Others are subject to cuts from sharp metal, burns from soldering or welding, and falls from ladders or scaffolds. They often are required to wear safety glasses and must not wear jewelry or loose-fitting clothing that could easily be caught in a machine. To avoid repetitive-type injuries, they may work at a variety of different production stations.

Training, Other Qualifications, and Advancement
Sheet metal workers learn their trade through both formal apprenticeships and informal on-the-job training programs. Formal apprenticeships are more likely to be found in construction.

Education and training.   To become a skilled sheet metal construction worker usually takes between 4 and 5 years of both classroom and on-the-job training. Although there are a number of different ways to obtain this training, generally the more formalized the training received by an individual, the more thoroughly skilled the person becomes and the more likely he or she is to be in demand by employers. For some, this training begins in a high school, where classes in English, algebra, geometry, physics, mechanical drawing and blueprint reading, and general shop are recommended.

After high school, there are a number of different ways to train. One way is to get a job with a contractor who will provide training on the job. Entry-level workers generally start as helpers, assisting more experienced workers. Most begin by carrying metal and cleaning up debris in a metal shop, learning about materials, tools, and their uses as they go about their tasks. Later, they learn to operate machines that bend or cut metal. In time, helpers go to the jobsite to learn installation. Employers may send their employees to a trade or vocational school to take courses or to a community college to receive further formal training. Helpers may be promoted to the journeyman level if they show the requisite knowledge and skills. Most sheet metal workers in large-scale manufacturing receive on-the-job training, with additional classwork or in-house training as necessary. The training needed to become proficient in manufacturing takes less time than the training for proficiency in construction.

Apprenticeship programs combine paid on-the-job training with related classroom instruction. Usually, apprenticeship applicants must be at least 18 years old and meet local requirements. The length of the program, typically 4 to 5 years, varies with the apprentice's skill. Apprenticeship programs provide comprehensive instruction in both sheet metal fabrication and sheet metal installation. They may be administered by local joint committees composed of the Sheet Metal Workers' International Association and local chapters of the Sheet Metal and Air-Conditioning Contractors National Association.

Sheet metal workers can choose one of many specialties. Workers can specialize in commercial and residential HVAC installation and maintenance, industrial welding and fabrication, exterior or architectural sheet metal installation, sign fabrication, service and refrigeration, and testing and balancing of building systems.

On the job, apprentices receive first safety training and then training in tasks that allow them to begin work immediately. They use materials such as fiberglass, plastics, and other nonmetallic materials. Workers focus on a particular sheet metal career path. In the classroom, apprentices learn computer aided drafting; reading of plans and specifications; trigonometry and geometry applicable to layout work; welding; the use of computerized equipment; the principles of heating, air-conditioning, and ventilation systems. In addition, apprentices learn the relationship between sheet metal work and other construction work.

Other qualifications.   Sheet metal workers need to be in good physical condition and have mechanical and mathematical aptitude and good reading skills. Good eye-hand coordination, accurate perception of spaces and forms, and manual dexterity also are important. Courses in algebra, trigonometry, geometry, mechanical drawing, and shop provide a helpful background for learning the trade, as does related work experience obtained in the U.S. Armed Services.

Certification and advancement.   It is important for experienced sheet metal workers to keep abreast of new technological developments, such as the use of computerized layout and laser-cutting machines. In addition, new software, called B.I.M., which stands for "building information modeling," allows contractors, architects, and engineers to coordinate their efforts and increase efficiency at worksites.

Certifications in one of the specialties also can be beneficial to workers. Certifications related to sheet metal specialties are offered by a wide variety of associations, several of which are listed in the sources of additional information at the end of this statement.

Sheet metal workers in construction may advance to supervisory jobs. Some of these workers take additional training in welding and do more specialized work. Workers who perform building and system testing are able to move into construction and building inspection. Others go into the contracting business for themselves. Because a sheet metal contractor must have a shop with equipment to fabricate products, this type of contracting business is more expensive to start than other types of construction contracting.

Sheet metal workers in manufacturing may advance to positions as supervisors or quality inspectors. Some of these workers may move into other management positions.

Employment

Sheet metal workers held about 170,700 jobs in 2008. About 63 percent of all sheet metal workers were in the construction industry, including 46 percent who worked for plumbing, heating, and air-conditioning contractors; most of the rest in construction worked for roofing contractors and for building finishing contractors. Some worked for general contractors engaged in residential and commercial building and for other special trade contractors.

About 23 percent of all sheet metal workers were in manufacturing industries, such as the fabricated metal products, machinery, and aerospace products and parts industries. Some sheet metal workers work for the Federal Government.

Compared with workers in most construction craft occupations, relatively few sheet metal workers are self-employed.

Job Outlook

Slower than average employment growth is projected. Job opportunities should be best for individuals who have apprenticeship training or who are certified welders. Applicants for jobs in manufacturing will experience competition.

Employment change. Employment of sheet metal workers is expected to increase by 6 percent between 2008 and 2018, slower than the average for all occupations. This change reflects anticipated growth in the number of industrial, commercial, and residential structures to be built over the decade. In addition, it reflects the need to install energy-efficient air-conditioning, heating, and ventilation systems in older buildings and to perform other types of renovation and maintenance work on these systems. Also, the popularity of decorative sheet metal products and increased architectural restoration are expected to add to the demand for sheet metal workers.

Sheet metal workers in manufacturing, however, are expected to experience a moderate decline in employment as the industry becomes more automated and some of the work is done in other countries.

Job prospects. Job opportunities are expected to be good for sheet metal workers in the construction industry, reflecting both employment growth and openings arising each year as experienced sheet metal workers leave the occupation. Opportunities should be particularly good for individuals who have apprenticeship training or who are certified welders. Applicants for jobs in manufacturing will experience competition.

Sheet metal workers in construction may experience periods of unemployment, particularly when construction projects end and economic conditions dampen construction activity. However, because maintenance of existing equipment makes up a large part of the work done by sheet metal workers, they are less affected by construction downturns than are some other construction occupations. Installation of new air-conditioning and heating systems in existing buildings is expected to continue as individuals and businesses adopt more energy-efficient equipment to cut utility bills. In addition, a large proportion of sheet metal installation and maintenance is done indoors, so sheet metal workers usually lose less worktime because of bad weather than do other construction workers.

Earnings

In May 2008, median hourly wages of sheet metal workers were $19.37. The middle 50 percent earned between $14.39 and $27.03. The lowest 10 percent of all sheet metal workers earned less than $11.43, and the highest 10 percent earned more than $35.36. The median hourly wages of the largest industries employing sheet metal workers were as follows:

Federal Government	$23.37
Building finishing contractors	21.35
Building equipment contractors	19.98
Foundation, structure, and building exterior contractors	17.67
Architectural and structural metals manufacturing	17.32

Apprentices normally start at about 40 to 50 percent of the rate paid to experienced workers. As apprentices acquire more skills, they receive periodic pay increases, until their pay approaches that of experienced workers.

About 32 percent of all sheet metal workers belong to a union. Union workers in some areas receive supplemental wages from the union when they are laid off or experience shortened workweeks.

Projections data from the National Employment Matrix

Occupational Title	SOC Code	Employment, 2008	Projected Employment, 2018	Change, 2008-2018	
				Number	Percent
Sheet metal workers	47-2211	170,700	181,800	11,100	6

(NOTE) Data in this table are rounded. See the discussion of the employment projections table in the *Handbook* introductory chapter on *Occupational Information Included in the Handbook.*

Related Occupations

To fabricate and install sheet metal products, sheet metal workers combine metalworking skills and knowledge of construction materials and techniques. Other occupations in which workers lay out and fabricate metal products include the following:

Sources of Additional Information

For more information about apprenticeships or other work opportunities, contact local sheet metal contractors or heating, refrigeration, and air-conditioning contractors; a local of the Sheet Metal Workers International Association; a local of the Sheet Metal and Air-Conditioning Contractors National Association; a local joint union-management apprenticeship committee; or the nearest office of your State employment service or apprenticeship agency. You also can find information on the registered apprenticeship system with links to State apprenticeship programs on the U.S. Department of Labor's Web site: **http://www.doleta.gov/OA/eta_default.cfm.** Apprenticeship information is available as well from the U.S. Department of Labor's toll-free help line: (877) 872-5627.

For general and training information about sheet metal workers, contact:

➤ Fabricators and Manufacturers Association, International, 833 Featherstone Road, Rockford, IL 61107-6301. Internet: **http://www.fmanet.org**

➤ International Training Institute for the Sheet Metal and Air-Conditioning Industry, 601 North Fairfax St., Suite 240, Alexandria, VA 22314-2083. Internet: **http://www.sheetmetal-iti.org**

➤ National Center for Construction Education and Research, 3600 NW 43rd St., Bldg. G, Gainesville, FL 32606-8134. Internet: **http://www.nccer.org**

➤ Sheet Metal and Air Conditioning Contractors' National Association, 4201 Lafayette Center Dr., Chantilly, VA 20151-1209. Internet: **http://www.smacna.org**

➤ Sheet Metal Workers International Association, 1750 New York Ave. NW., 6th Floor, Washington, DC 20006-5301. Internet: **http://www.smwia.org**

For general information on apprenticeships and how to get them, see the *Occupational Outlook Quarterly* article "Apprenticeships: Career training, credentials—and a paycheck in your pocket," online at **http://www.bls.gov/opub/ooq/2002/summer/art01.pdf** and in print at many libraries and career centers.

The Occupational Information Network (O*NET) provides information on a wide range of occupational characteristics. Links to O*NET appear at the end of the Internet version of this occupational statement, accessible at **http://www.bls.gov/ooh/ocos214.htm**

Structural and Reinforcing Iron and Metal Workers

Significant Points

- Workers must be in good physical condition and have no fear of heights.

- Most employers recommend completion of a formal 3-year or 4-year paid apprenticeship, but some workers learn on the job.

- In most areas of the country, job opportunities should be favorable.

Nature of the Work

Structural and reinforcing iron and metal workers place and install iron or steel girders, columns, and other construction materials to form buildings, bridges, and other structures. They also position and secure steel bars or mesh in concrete forms in order to reinforce the concrete used in highways, buildings, bridges, tunnels, and other structures. In addition, they repair and renovate older buildings and structures. Even though the primary metal involved in this work is steel, these workers often are known as *ironworkers* or *erectors*. Some ironworkers make structural metal in fabricating shops, which are usually located away from the construction site. (These workers are covered in the statement on assemblers and fabricators found elsewhere in the *Handbook*.)

Before construction can begin, ironworkers must erect steel frames and assemble the cranes and derricks that move structural steel, reinforcing bars, buckets of concrete, lumber, and other materials and equipment around the construction site. Once this job has been completed, workers begin to connect

Workers hammer large structural steel into the ground at a construction site.

steel columns, beams, and girders according to blueprints and instructions from supervisors and superintendents. Structural steel, reinforcing rods, and ornamental iron generally come to the construction site ready for erection—cut to the proper size, with holes drilled for bolts and numbered for assembly.

Ironworkers at the construction site unload and stack the prefabricated steel so that it can be hoisted easily when needed. To hoist the steel, ironworkers attach cables (slings) to the steel and to the crane or derrick. One worker directs the hoist operator with hand signals while another worker holds a rope (tag line) attached to the steel to prevent it from swinging. The crane or derrick hoists steel into place in the framework, whereupon two ironworkers, called connectors, position the steel with connecting bars and spud wrenches—a long wrench with a pointed handle. Workers using driftpins or the handle of a spud wrench align the holes in the steel with the holes in the framework. Ironworkers check vertical and horizontal alignment with plumb bobs, laser equipment, transits, or levels; then they bolt or weld the piece permanently in place.

Reinforcing iron and rebar workers, sometimes called *rod busters*, set reinforcing bars (often called rebar) in the forms that hold concrete, following blueprints showing the location, size, and number of bars. They then fasten the bars together by tying wire around them with pliers. When reinforcing floors, ironworkers place spacers under the rebar to hold the bars off the deck. Although these materials usually arrive ready to use, ironworkers occasionally must cut bars with metal shears or acetylene torches, bend them by hand or machine, or weld them with arc-welding equipment. Some concrete is reinforced with welded wire fabric that ironworkers put into position using hooked rods. Post-tensioning is another technique used to reinforce concrete. In this technique, workers substitute cables for rebar. When the concrete is poured, the ends of the cables are left exposed. After the concrete cures, ironworkers tighten the cables with jacking equipment specially designed for the purpose. Post-tensioning allows designers to create larger open areas in a building, because supports can be placed further apart. This technique is commonly employed in parking garages and arenas.

Ornamental ironworkers install stairs, handrails, curtain walls (the nonstructural walls and window frames of many large buildings), and other miscellaneous metal after the structure of the building has been completed. As they hoist pieces into position, ornamental ironworkers make sure that the pieces are properly fitted and aligned before bolting or welding them for a secure fit.

Work environment. Structural and reinforcing iron and metal workers usually work outside in all kinds of weather. However, those who work at great heights do not work during wet, icy, or extremely windy conditions. Because the danger of injuries from falls is great, ironworkers use safety devices such as safety harnesses, scaffolding, and nets to reduce risk. Nevertheless, this occupation does experience an above average rate of nonfatal injuries.

Training, Other Qualifications, and Advancement
Many workers learn to be ironworkers through formal apprenticeships, but others learn on the job. Certifications in welding and rigging can increase a worker's usefulness on the job site.

Education and training. Most employers recommend a 3-year to 4-year apprenticeship consisting of a combination of paid on-the-job training and classroom instruction as the best way to learn this trade. Apprenticeship programs are administered by committees made up of representatives of local unions of the International Association of Bridge, Structural, Ornamental and Reinforcing Iron Workers or the local chapters of contractors' associations. To be accepted into an apprenticeship program, most employers and local apprenticeship committees prefer that applicants have a high school diploma. In addition, high school courses in general mathematics, mechanical drawing, English, and welding are considered helpful.

Classroom study for apprentices consists of blueprint reading; mathematics, the basics of structural erecting, rigging, reinforcing, welding, assembling, and safety training. Apprentices also study the care and safe use of tools and materials. On the job, apprentices work in all aspects of the trade, such as unloading and storing materials at the job site, rigging materials for movement by crane, connecting structural steel, and welding.

Some ironworkers learn the trade informally on the job, without completing an apprenticeship. On-the-job trainees usually begin by assisting experienced ironworkers on simple jobs, such as carrying various materials. With experience, trainees perform more difficult tasks, such as cutting and fitting different parts.

Other qualifications. Ironworkers must be at least 18 years old. Because materials used in iron working are heavy and bulky, ironworkers must be in good physical condition. They also need good agility, balance, eyesight, and depth perception to work safely at great heights on narrow beams and girders. Ironworkers should not be afraid of heights or suffer from dizziness.

Certification and advancement. Ironworkers who complete apprenticeships are certified at the journey level, which often make them more competitive candidates for jobs and promotions. Those who meet education and experience requirements can become welders certified by the American Welding Society. Apprenticeship programs often provide trainees the opportunity to become welder-certified as part of their coursework because welding skills are useful for many ironworker tasks.

Some experienced workers are promoted to supervisor. Others may go into the contracting business for themselves. The ability to communicate in both English and Spanish will improve opportunities for advancement.

Employment
Ironworkers held about 97,800 jobs in 2008; structural iron and steel workers held about 70,200 jobs, and reinforcing iron and rebar workers held about 27,700 jobs. About 88 percent worked in construction, with 51 percent working for foundation, structure, and building exterior contractors. Most of the remaining ironworkers worked for contractors specializing in the construction of various structures, such as bridges, buildings, and factories.

Structural and reinforcing iron and metal workers are employed in all parts of the country, but most work in metropolitan areas, where the bulk of commercial and industrial construction takes place.

Projections data from the National Employment Matrix

Occupational Title	SOC Code	Employment, 2008	Projected Employment, 2018	Change, 2008-2018	
				Number	Percent
Structural and reinforcing iron and metal workers	–	97,800	110,000	12,200	12
Reinforcing iron and rebar workers	47-2171	27,700	31,100	3,500	13
Structural iron and steel workers	47-2221	70,200	78,900	8,700	12

(NOTE) Data in this table are rounded. See the discussion of the employment projections table in the *Handbook* introductory chapter on *Occupational Information Included in the Handbook.*

Job Outlook

Average job growth is projected. In most areas of the country, job opportunities should be favorable.

Employment change. Employment of structural and reinforcing iron and metal workers is expected to grow 12 percent between 2008 and 2018, about as fast as the average for all occupations. The rehabilitation, maintenance, and replacement of a growing number of older buildings, powerplants, highways, and bridges also are expected to create employment opportunities. State and Federal legislatures will likely continue to call for road construction and related infrastructure projects, which will secure jobs for the near future. However, a lack of qualified applicants challenges the education and retraining needs of the industry to meet the demands of employment growth.

Job prospects. In addition to new jobs from employment growth, many job openings will result from the need to replace experienced ironworkers who leave the occupation or retire. In most areas, job opportunities should be favorable, although the number of job openings can fluctuate from year to year with economic conditions and the level of construction activity.

Employment of structural and reinforcing iron and metal workers, like that of many other construction workers, is sensitive to the fluctuations of the economy. Workers in these trades may experience periods of unemployment when the overall level of construction falls. On the other hand, shortages of these workers may occur in some areas during peak periods of building activity. Similarly, job opportunities for ironworkers may vary widely by geographic area. Population growth in the South and West should create more job opportunities than elsewhere as bridges, buildings, and roads are constructed. Job openings for ironworkers usually are more abundant during the spring and summer months, when the level of construction activity increases. Workers who are willing to relocate are often able to find work in another area.

Earnings

In May 2008, median hourly wages of structural iron and steel workers were $20.68. The middle 50 percent earned between $15.18 and $29.15. The lowest 10 percent earned less than $12.25, and the highest 10 percent earned more than $37.04.

In May 2008, median hourly wages of reinforcing iron and rebar workers were $19.18. The middle 50 percent earned between $14.35 and $27.29. The lowest 10 percent earned less than $11.78, and the highest 10 percent earned more than $35.26.

In May 2008, median hourly wages of structural iron and steel workers in foundation, structure, and building exterior contractors were $21.51 and in nonresidential building con-

struction, $18.53. Reinforcing iron and rebar workers earned median hourly wages of $19.37 in foundation, structure, and building exterior contractors.

About 40 percent of the workers in this trade are union members. According to International Association of Bridge, Structural, Ornamental, and Reinforcing Iron Workers, average hourly compensation, including benefits, for structural and reinforcing metal workers who belonged to a union and worked full time were higher than the hourly earnings of nonunion workers. Structural and reinforcing iron and metal workers in New York, Boston, San Francisco, Chicago, Los Angeles, Philadelphia, and other large cities received the highest wages.

Apprentices generally start at about 60 percent of the rate paid to experienced journey level workers. Throughout the course of the apprenticeship program, as they acquire skills they receive periodic increases until their pay approaches that of experienced workers.

Earnings for ironworkers may be reduced on occasion because work can be limited by bad weather and economic downturns.

Related Occupations

Structural and reinforcing iron and metal workers play an essential role in erecting buildings, bridges, highways, power lines, and other structures. Others who work on these construction jobs include:

Sources of Additional Information

For more information on apprenticeships or other work opportunities, contact local general contractors; a local of the International Association of Bridge, Structural, Ornamental, and Reinforcing Iron Workers Union; a local ironworkers' joint union-management apprenticeship committee; a local or State chapter of the Associated Builders and Contractors or the Associated General Contractors; or the nearest office of your State employment service or apprenticeship agency. You can also find information on the registered apprenticeship system with links to State apprenticeship programs on the U.S. Department of Labor's

Web site: **http://www.doleta.gov/OA/eta_default.cfm.** Apprenticeship information is also available from the U.S. Department of Labor's toll free helpline: (877) 872-5627.

For apprenticeship information, contact:

➤ International Association of Bridge, Structural, Ornamental, and Reinforcing Iron Workers, Apprenticeship Department, 1750 New York Ave. NW., Suite 400, Washington, DC 20006-5315. Internet: **http://www.ironworkers.org/organization/Apprenticeship.aspx**

For general information about ironworkers, contact:

➤ Associated Builders and Contractors, Workforce Development Department, 4250 North Fairfax Dr., 9th Floor, Arlington, VA 22203-1607. Internet: **http://www.trytools.org**

➤ Associated General Contractors of America, Inc., 2300 Wilson Blvd., Suite 400., Arlington, VA 22201-5426. Internet: **http://www.agc.org**

For general information on apprenticeships and how to get them, see the *Occupational Outlook Quarterly* article "Apprenticeships: Career training, credentials—and a paycheck in your pocket," online at **http://www.bls.gov/opub/ooq/2002/summer/art01.pdf** and in print at many libraries and career centers.

The Occupational Information Network (O*NET) provides information on a wide range of occupational characteristics. Links to O*NET appear at the end of the Internet version of this occupational statement, accessible at **http://www.bls.gov/ooh/ocos215.htm**

Installation, Maintenance, and Repair Occupations

Electrical and Electronic Equipment Mechanics, Installers, and Repairers

Computer, Automated Teller, and Office Machine Repairers

Significant Points

- Employment is expected to decline slowly.

- Job prospects will be best for applicants with knowledge of electronics, certification, formal training, and repair experience.

- Workers qualify for these jobs by receiving training in electronics from associate degree programs, the military, vocational schools, equipment manufacturers, or employers.

Nature of the Work

Computer, automated teller, and office machine repairers install, fix, and maintain many of the machines that are used by businesses, households, and consumers. For large or stationary machines, repairers frequently perform the work on site. These workers—known as *field technicians*—often have assigned areas where they perform preventive maintenance on a regular basis. *Bench technicians* commonly repair smaller equipment and often work in repair shops located in stores, factories, or service centers. In small companies, repairers may work both in repair shops and at customer locations.

Computer repairers, also known as *computer service technicians* or *data processing equipment repairers*, service mainframe, server, and personal computers; printers; and auxiliary computer equipment. These workers primarily perform hands-on repair, maintenance, and installation of computers and related equipment. Workers who provide technical assistance, in person or by telephone, to computer system users are known as computer support specialists or computer support technicians. (See the section on computer support specialists and systems administrators elsewhere in the *Handbook*.)

Computer repairers typically replace subsystems instead of repairing them. Commonly replaced subsystems include video cards, which transmit signals from the computer to the monitor; hard drives, which store data; and network cards, which allow communication over the network. Replacement is common because subsystems are usually inexpensive and businesses are reluctant to shut down their computers for time-consuming repairs. Defective modules may be given to bench technicians, who use software programs to diagnose the problem and who may repair the modules, if possible.

Office machine and *cash register servicers* work on photocopiers, cash registers, and fax machines. Newer models of office machinery include computerized components that allow them to function more reliably than earlier models and, therefore, require less maintenance.

Office machine repairers usually work on machinery at the customer's workplace. However, if the machines are small enough, customers may bring them to a repair shop for repair. Common malfunctions include paper jams caused by worn or dirty parts, and poor-quality copy resulting from problems with lamps, lenses, or mirrors. These malfunctions often can be resolved simply by cleaning the relevant components. Breakdowns also may result from the general wear and tear of commonly used parts. For example, heavy use of a photocopier may wear down the printhead, which applies ink to the final copy. In such cases, the repairer usually replaces the part instead of repairing it.

Automated teller machine servicers install and repair automated teller machines (ATMs) and, increasingly, electronic kiosks. In addition to performing bank transactions without the assistance of a teller, electric kiosks are being used for a variety of non-traditional services, including stamp, phone card, and ticket sales. A growing number of electronic kiosks also allow consumers to redeem movie tickets or airline and train boarding passes.

When ATMs malfunction, computer networks often recognize the problem and alert repairers. Common problems include worn magnetic heads on card readers, which prevent the equipment from recognizing customers' bankcards, and "pick failures," which prevent the equipment from dispensing the correct amount of cash. In such cases, field technicians travel to the locations of ATMs and repair equipment by removing and replacing defective components. Broken components may be taken to a repair shop, where bench technicians make the necessary repairs. Field technicians perform routine maintenance on a regular basis, replacing worn parts and running diagnostic tests to ensure that the equipment operates properly.

To install large equipment, such as mainframe computers and ATMs, repairers connect the equipment to power sources and communication lines that allow the transmission of information over computer networks. For example, when an ATM dispenses cash, it transmits the withdrawal information to the customer's bank. Workers may also install operating software and peripheral equipment, checking that all components are configured to operate together correctly.

Computer, automated teller, and office machine repairers use a variety of tools for diagnostic tests and repair. To

Computer, automated teller, and office machine repairers use a variety of tools for diagnostic tests and repair.

diagnose malfunctions, they use multimeters to measure voltage, current, resistance, and other electrical properties; signal generators to provide test signals; and oscilloscopes to monitor equipment signals. To diagnose computerized equipment, repairers use software programs. To repair or adjust equipment, workers use handtools, such as pliers, screwdrivers, and soldering irons.

Work environment. Repairers usually work in clean, well-lighted surroundings. Because computers and office machines are sensitive to extreme temperatures and humidity, repair shops usually are air-conditioned and well ventilated. Field repairers must travel frequently to various locations to install, maintain, or repair customers' equipment. ATM repairers may have to perform their jobs in small, confined spaces that house the equipment.

Because computers and ATMs are critical for many organizations to function efficiently, data processing equipment repairers and ATM field technicians often work around the clock. Their schedules may include evening, weekend, and holiday shifts, sometimes assigned on the basis of seniority. Office machine and cash register servicers usually work regular business hours because the equipment they repair is not

as critical. Most repairers work about 40 hours per week, but about 9 percent work more than 50 hours per week. Although their jobs are not strenuous, repairers often must lift equipment and work in a variety of postures. Repairers of computer monitors need to discharge voltage from the equipment to avoid electrocution.

Training, Other Qualifications, and Advancement

Knowledge of electronics is required, and employers prefer workers with formal training. Office machine and ATM repairers usually have an associate degree. Certification is available for entry-level workers and experienced workers seeking advancement.

Education and training. Knowledge of electronics is necessary for employment as a computer, automated teller, or office machine repairer. Employers prefer workers who are certified or who have training in electronics from an associate degree program, the military, a vocational school, or an equipment manufacturer. Employers generally provide some training to new repairers on specific equipment; however, workers are expected to arrive on the job with a basic understanding of equipment repair. Employers may send experienced workers to training sessions to keep up with changes in technology and service procedures.

Most office machine and ATM repairer positions require an associate degree in electronics. A basic understanding of mechanical equipment is also important because many of the parts that fail in office machines and ATMs, such as paper loaders, are mechanical. Entry-level employees at large companies normally receive on-the-job training lasting several months. Such training may include a week of classroom instruction, followed by a period of 2 weeks to several months assisting an experienced repairer.

Other qualifications. Field technicians work closely with customers and must have good communications skills and a neat appearance. Employers may require that field technicians have a driver's license.

Certification and advancement. Various organizations offer certification. For instance, the Electronics Technicians Association (ETA) offers more than 50 certification programs in numerous electronics specialties for varying levels of competence. The International Society of Certified Electronics Technicians also offers certification for several levels of competence, focusing on a broad range of topics, including basic electronics, multimedia systems, electronic systems, and appliance service. To become certified, applicants must meet several prerequisites and pass a comprehensive written or online examination. Certification demonstrates a level of competency. It can make an applicant more attractive to employers or increase an employee's opportunities for advancement.

Newly hired computer repairers may possibly work on personal computers or peripheral equipment. With experience, they can advance to positions maintaining more sophisticated systems, such as networking equipment and servers. Field repairers of ATMs may advance to bench technician positions responsible for more complex repairs. Experienced workers may become specialists who assist other repairers diagnose difficult problems or who work with engineers in designing equipment and developing maintenance procedures. Experienced workers may also move into management positions responsible for supervising other repairers.

Because of their familiarity with equipment, experienced repairers may also move into customer service or sales positions. Some experienced workers open their own repair shops or become wholesalers or retailers of electronic equipment.

Employment

Computer, automated teller, and office machine repairers held about 152,900 jobs in 2008. Wholesale trade establishments employed about 29 percent of the workers in this occupation; most of these establishments were wholesalers of professional and commercial equipment and supplies. Many workers also were employed in electronics and appliance stores and office supply stores. Others worked in electronic and precision equipment repair shops and computer systems design firms. About 20 percent of computer, automated teller, and office machine repairers were self-employed.

Job Outlook

Employment is expected to decline slowly. Opportunities will be best for applicants with knowledge of electronics, formal training, and repair experience. Employers increasingly prefer applicants who are certified.

Employment change. Employment of computer, automated teller, and office machine repairers is expected to decline by 4 percent from 2008 to 2018. Less expensive and more reliable computer equipment is expected to result in fewer computer repairers. Nonetheless, some computer repairers will be needed as malfunctions still occur and can cause severe problems for users, most of whom lack the knowledge to make repairs. Additionally, computers are critical to most businesses today and will become even more so as companies increasingly engage in electronic commerce, and as individuals continue to bank, shop, and pay bills online.

Employment growth of ATM repairers will be impeded as a result of newer technology which allows for the testing and resetting of machines remotely. The relatively slow rate at which new ATMs are installed will also limit demand for ATM repairers, despite a greater reliance on these machines by consumers.

Fewer office machine repairers will be needed as office equipment is often inexpensive and increasingly replaced instead of repaired. However, digital copiers and some newer office machines are more costly and complex. This equipment is often computerized, designed to work on a network, and capable of performing multiple functions. But because this equipment is becoming more reliable, the need for repairers will continue to decline.

Job prospects. Job prospects are expected to be limited as newer equipment continues to require less maintenance and repair. As a result, the vast majority of job openings will stem from the need to replace workers who retire or leave the occupation for other reasons. Those with knowledge of electronics, certification, formal training, and repair experience will have the best prospects.

A growing number of new ATMs called electronic kiosks offer non-traditional retail services, such as employee information processing and ticket redemption, in addition to banking transactions. Candidates who have expertise in the installation, maintenance, and repair of such equipment will also have better job prospects.

Earnings

Median hourly wages of computer, automated teller, and office machine repairers were $18.18 in May 2008. The middle 50 percent earned between $14.17 and $23.20. The lowest 10 percent earned less than $11.14, and the highest 10 percent earned more than $28.41. Median hourly wages in the industries employing the largest numbers of computer, automated teller, and office machine repairers in May 2008 were:

Computer systems design and related services	$19.87
Professional and commercial equipment and supplies merchant wholesalers	19.12
Office supplies, stationery, and gift stores	17.40
Electronic and precision equipment repair and maintenance	17.03
Electronics and appliance stores	15.67

Related Occupations

Workers in other occupations who repair and maintain electronic equipment include:

	Page
Broadcast and sound engineering technicians and radio operators	337
Coin, vending, and amusement machine servicers and repairers	720
Electrical and electronics installers and repairers	675
Electricians	641
Electronic home entertainment equipment installers and repairers	678
Home appliance repairers	707
Maintenance and repair workers, general	716
Radio and telecommunications equipment installers and repairers	680

Sources of Additional Information

For information on electronics careers and certification, contact:
➤ Electronics Technicians Association International, 5 Depot St., Greencastle, IN 46135. Internet: **http://eta-i.org/**

Projections data from the National Employment Matrix

Occupational Title	SOC Code	Employment, 2008	Projected Employment, 2018	Change, 2008-2018	
				Number	Percent
Computer, automated teller, and office machine repairers	49-2011	152,900	146,200	-6,700	-4

(NOTE) Data in this table are rounded. See the discussion of the employment projections table in the *Handbook* introductory chapter on *Occupational Information Included in the Handbook.*

➤ International Society of Certified Electronics Technicians, 3608 Pershing Ave., Fort Worth, TX 76107-4527. Internet: **http://www.iscet.org**

The Occupational Information Network (O*NET) provides information on a wide range of occupational characteristics. Links to O*NET appear at the end of the Internet version of this occupational statement, accessible at **http://www.bls.gov/ooh/ocos186.htm**

Electrical and Electronics Installers and Repairers

Significant Points

- Knowledge of electrical equipment and electronics is necessary for employment; employers often prefer applicants with an associate degree in electronics, and professional certification often is required.

- Job opportunities will be best for applicants with an associate degree, certification, or related experience.

- Overall employment is projected to grow more slowly than the average for all occupations.

Nature of the Work

Businesses and other organizations depend on complex electronic equipment for a variety of functions. Industrial controls automatically monitor and direct production processes on the factory floor. Transmitters and antennae provide communication links for many organizations. Electric power companies use electronic equipment to operate and control generating plants, substations, and monitoring equipment. The Federal Government uses radar and missile control systems to provide for the national defense and to direct commercial air traffic. Such complex pieces of electronic equipment are installed, maintained, and repaired by *electrical and electronics installers and repairers.*

Installers and repairers, known as *field technicians*, often travel to factories or other locations to repair equipment. These workers usually have assigned areas in which they perform preventive maintenance on a regular basis. When equipment breaks down, field technicians go to a customer's site to repair the equipment. *Bench technicians* work in repair shops located in factories and service centers, fixing components that cannot be repaired on the factory floor.

Electrical and electronic equipment are two distinct types of industrial equipment, although a great deal of equipment contains both electrical and electronic components. In general, electrical parts provide the power for the equipment, whereas electronic components control the device.

Some industrial electronic equipment is self-monitoring and alerts repairers to malfunctions. When equipment breaks down, repairers will first check for common causes of trouble, such as loose connections or obviously defective components. If routine checks do not locate the trouble, repairers may refer to schematics and manufacturers' specifications that show connections and provide instructions on how to trace problems. Automated electronic control systems are becoming increasingly complex, making diagnosis more challenging. With these systems, repairers use software programs and testing equipment to diagnose malfunctions. Among their diagnostic tools are multimeters, which measure voltage, current, and resistance, and advanced multimeters, which measure capacitance, inductance, and current gain of transistors. Repairers also use signal generators, which provide test signals, and oscilloscopes, which display signals graphically. Finally, repairers use handtools such as pliers, screwdrivers, soldering irons, and wrenches to replace faulty parts and adjust equipment.

Because repairing components is a complex activity and factories cannot allow production equipment to stand idle, repairers on the factory floor usually remove and replace defective units, such as circuit boards, instead of fixing them. Defective units are discarded or returned to the manufacturer or a specialized shop for repair. Bench technicians at these locations have the training, tools, and parts needed to thoroughly diagnose and repair circuit boards or other complex components. These workers also locate and repair circuit defects, such as poorly soldered joints, blown fuses, or malfunctioning transistors.

Electrical and electronics installers often retrofit older manufacturing equipment with new automated control devices. Older manufacturing machines are frequently in good working order, but are limited by inefficient control systems for which replacement parts are no longer available. As a result, installers sometimes replace old electronic control units with new programming logic controls (PLCs). Setting up and installing a new PLC involves connecting it to different sensors and electrically powered devices (electric motors, switches, and pumps) and writing a computer program to operate the PLC. Electronics installers often coordinate their efforts with those of other workers who are installing and maintaining equipment. (See the section on industrial machinery mechanics and millwrights elsewhere in the *Handbook.*)

Electrical and electronics installers and repairers, transportation equipment install, adjust, or maintain mobile electronic communication equipment, including sound, sonar, security, navigation, and surveillance systems on trains, watercraft, or other vehicles. *Electrical and electronics repairers, powerhouse, substation, and relay* inspect, test, maintain, or repair electrical equipment used in generating stations, substations, and in-service relays. These workers may be known as powerhouse electricians, relay technicians, or power transformer repairers. *Electric motor, power tool, and related repairers*—such as armature winders, generator mechanics, and electric golf cart repairers—specialize in installing, maintaining, and repairing electric motors, wiring, or switches.

Electronic equipment installers and repairers, motor vehicles have a significantly different job. They install, diagnose, and repair communication, sound, security, and navigation equipment in motor vehicles. Most installation work involves either new alarm or sound systems. New sound systems vary significantly in cost and complexity of installation. For instance, replacing a head unit (radio) with a new CD player is simple, requiring the removal of a few screws and the connection of a few wires. Installing a new sound system with a subwoofer, amplifier, and fuses is far more complicated. The

Motor vehicle electronic equipment installers and repairers normally work indoors in well-ventilated and well-lighted repair shops.

installer builds a custom fiberglass or wood box designed to hold the subwoofer and to fit inside the unique dimensions of the automobile. Installing sound-deadening material, which often is necessary with more powerful speakers, requires an installer to remove many parts of a car (for example, seats, carpeting, or interiors of doors), add sound-absorbing material in empty spaces, and reinstall the interior parts. The installer also runs new speaker and electrical cables. The new system may require additional fuses, a new electrical line to be run from the battery through a newly drilled hole in the firewall into the interior of the vehicle, or a more powerful alternator or battery. Motor vehicle installers and repairers work with an increasingly complex range of electronic equipment, including DVD players, satellite navigation equipment, passive security systems, and active security systems.

Work environment. Many electrical and electronics installers and repairers work on factory floors, where they are subject to noise, dirt, vibration, and heat. Bench technicians primarily work in repair shops, where the surroundings are reasonably quiet, comfortable, and well lighted.

Installers and repairers may have to do heavy lifting and work in a variety of positions. They must follow safety guidelines and often wear protective goggles and hardhats. When working on ladders or on elevated equipment, repairers must wear harnesses to avoid falls. Before repairing a piece of machinery, these workers must follow procedures to ensure that others cannot start the equipment during the repair process. They also must take precautions against electric shock by locking off power to the unit under repair.

Motor vehicle electronic equipment installers and repairers normally work indoors in well-ventilated and well-lighted repair shops. Minor cuts and bruises are common, but serious accidents usually are avoided when safety practices are observed.

Training, Other Qualifications, and Advancement
Applicants with an associate degree in electronics are preferred, and professional certification often is required.

Education and training. Knowledge of electrical equipment and electronics is necessary for employment. Employers often prefer applicants with an associate degree from a community college or technical school, although a high school diploma may be sufficient for some jobs. Entry-level repairers may begin by working with experienced technicians who provide technical guidance, and work independently only after developing the necessary skills.

Other qualifications. Installers and repairers should have good eyesight and color perception to work with the intricate components used in electronic equipment. Field technicians work closely with customers and should have good communication skills and a neat appearance. Employers also may require that field technicians have a driver's license.

Certification and advancement. Various organizations offer certification. For instance, the Electronics Technicians Association (ETA) offers over 50 certification programs in numerous electronics specialties for varying levels of competence. The International Society of Certified Electronics Technicians also offers certification for several levels of competence, focusing on a broad range of topics, including basic electronics, electronic systems, and appliance service. To become certified, applicants must meet several prerequisites and pass a comprehensive written or online examination. Certification demonstrates a level of competency and can make an applicant more attractive to employers, as well as increase one's opportunities for advancement.

Experienced repairers with advanced training may become specialists or troubleshooters who assist other repairers diagnose difficult problems. Workers with leadership skills may become supervisors of other repairers. Some experienced workers open their own repair shops.

Employment
Electrical and electronics installers and repairers held about 160,900 jobs in 2008. The following tabulation breaks down their employment by occupational specialty:

Electrical and electronics installers and repairers, commercial and industrial equipment	78,000
Electric motor, power tool, and related repairers	23,700
Electrical and electronics repairers, powerhouse, substation, and relay	23,400
Electrical equipment installers and repairers, motor vehicles	19,700
Electrical and electronics installers and repairers, transportation equipment	16,100

Many repairers worked for repair and maintenance establishments.

Job Outlook
Overall employment is expected to grow more slowly than the average through the year 2018. Job prospects should be best for applicants with an associate degree, certification, and related experience.

Employment change. Overall employment of electrical and electronics installers and repairers is expected to grow by 5 percent through the year 2018, which is slower than the average for all occupations. Growth rates, however, will vary by occupational specialty.

Projections data from the National Employment Matrix

Occupational Title	SOC Code	Employment, 2008	Projected Employment, 2018	Change, 2008-2018	
				Number	Percent
Electrical and electronics installers and repairers...............................	–	160,900	168,400	7,500	5
Electric motor, power tool, and related repairers..........................	49-2092	23,700	24,900	1,200	5
Electrical and electronics installers and repairers, transportation equipment	49-2093	16,100	16,700	700	4
Electrical and electronics repairers, commercial and industrial equipment...	49-2094	78,000	81,000	2,900	4
Electrical and electronics repairers, powerhouse, substation, and relay..	49-2095	23,400	26,100	2,700	12
Electronic equipment installers and repairers, motor vehicles	49-2096	19,700	19,700	0	0

(NOTE) Data in this table are rounded. See the discussion of the employment projections table in the *Handbook* introductory chapter on *Occupational Information Included in the Handbook.*

Employment of electrical and electronics installers and repairers of commercial and industrial equipment is expected to grow 4 percent, which is slower than the average for all occupations. As equipment becomes more sophisticated, businesses will strive to lower costs by increasing and improving automation. Companies will install electronic controls, robots, sensors, and other equipment to automate processes such as assembly and testing. Improved reliability of equipment, however, may constrain employment growth of installers; on the other hand, companies will increasingly rely on repairers because malfunctions that idle commercial and industrial equipment will continue to be costly.

Little or no employment change is expected for motor vehicle electronic equipment installers and repairers. As motor vehicle manufacturers install more and better sound, security, entertainment, and navigation systems in new vehicles, and as newer electronic systems require progressively less maintenance, employment growth for aftermarket electronic equipment installers will be limited.

Employment of electric motor, power tool, and related repairers is expected to grow 5 percent, which is slower than the average for all occupations. Retrofitting electrical generators in public buildings to reduce emissions and energy consumption will spur some employment growth. However, improvements in electrical and electronic equipment design, as well as the increased use of disposable tool parts should suppress job growth.

Employment of electrical and electronic installers and repairers of transportation equipment is expected to grow 4 percent, which is slower than the average for all occupations. Declining employment in the rail transportation industry will dampen growth in this occupational specialty.

Employment of electrical and electronics installers and repairers, powerhouse, substation, and relay is also expected to grow 12 percent, about as fast as the average for all occupations. While privatization in utilities industries should improve productivity and hinder employment growth, installation of newer, energy efficient green technologies will spur demand for employment.

Job prospects. Job opportunities should be best for applicants with an associate degree in electronics, certification, and related experience. In addition to employment growth, the need to replace workers who transfer to other occupations or leave the labor force will result in some job openings.

Earnings

Median hourly wages of electrical and electronics repairers, commercial and industrial equipment were $23.29 in May 2008. The middle 50 percent earned between $18.40 and $28.73. The lowest 10 percent earned less than $14.39, and the highest 10 percent earned more than $33.81. In May 2008, median hourly wages were $25.31 in the Federal Government and $22.46 in building equipment contractors, the industries employing the largest numbers of electrical and electronics repairers, commercial and industrial equipment.

Median hourly wages of electric motor, power tool, and related repairers were $16.96 in May 2008. The middle 50 percent earned between $13.48 and $21.57. The lowest 10 percent earned less than $10.47, and the highest 10 percent earned more than $26.40. In May 2008, median hourly wages were $16.57 in commercial and industrial machinery and equipment (except automotive and electronic) repair, the industry employing the largest number of electronic motor, power tool, and related repairers.

Median hourly wages of electrical and electronics repairers, powerhouse, substation, and relay were $29.34 in May 2008. The middle 50 percent earned between $25.68 and $33.72. The lowest 10 percent earned less than $20.91, and the highest 10 percent earned more than $38.43. In May 2008, median hourly wages were $29.66 in electric power generation, transmission, and distribution, the industry employing the largest number of these repairers.

Median hourly wages of electronics installers and repairers, motor vehicles were $13.29 in May 2008. The middle 50 percent earned between $10.79 and $16.89. The lowest 10 percent earned less than $8.85, and the highest 10 percent earned more than $21.07.

Median hourly wages of electrical and electronics repairers, transportation equipment were $21.37 in May 2008. The middle 50 percent earned between $16.86 and $25.73. The lowest 10 percent earned less than $13.42, and the highest 10 percent earned more than $30.32.

Related Occupations

Workers in other occupations who install and repair electronic equipment include:

Sources of Additional Information

For information on careers and certification, contact any of the following organizations:

➤ ACES International, 5381 Chatham Lake Drive, Virginia Beach, VA 23464. Internet: **http://www.acesinternational.org**

➤ Electronics Technicians Association International, 5 Depot St., Greencastle, IN 46135. Internet: **http://eta-i.org/**

➤ International Society of Certified Electronics Technicians, 3608 Pershing Ave., Fort Worth, TX 76107. Internet: **http://www.iscet.org**

The Occupational Information Network (O*NET) provides information on a wide range of occupational characteristics. Links to O*NET appear at the end of the Internet version of this occupational statement, accessible at **http://www.bls.gov/ooh/ocos184.htm**

Electronic Home Entertainment Equipment Installers and Repairers

Significant Points

- Employers increasingly prefer applicants who are certified.

- Job opportunities will be best for applicants with knowledge of electronics, related hands-on experience, and good customer service skills.

- Employment is expected to grow as fast as average, due in large part to the rising sales of home entertainment equipment.

Nature of the Work

Electronic home entertainment equipment installers and repairers—also called *service technicians*—repair a variety of audio and video equipment. They may specialize in one type of product, or may be trained in many different ones. The most common products include televisions and radios, stereo components, digital video disc players, and video cameras. They also install and repair satellite television dishes and home theater systems, which consist of large-screen televisions and sophisticated surround-sound audio components.

Customers usually bring small, portable equipment to repair shops for servicing. Repairers at these locations, known as *bench technicians*, are equipped with a full array of electronic tools and parts. When larger, less mobile equipment breaks down, customers may pay repairers to come to their homes.

These repairers, known as *field technicians*, travel with a limited set of tools and parts, and attempt to complete the repair at the customer's location. If the job is complex, technicians may bring defective components back to the shop for diagnosis and repair.

When equipment breaks down, repairers check for defective components. If routine checks fail to locate the trouble, repairers may refer to schematics and manufacturers' specifications that provide instructions on how to locate problems. Repairers may also use a variety of test equipment to diagnose and identify malfunctions. For example, multimeters detect short circuits, failed capacitors, and blown fuses by measuring voltage, current, and resistance. Color-bar and dot generators provide onscreen test patterns, and oscilloscopes and digital storage scopes measure complex waveforms produced by electronic equipment. Repairs may involve removing and replacing a failed transistor or fuse, often with hand tools, such as pliers, screwdrivers, soldering irons, and wrenches. Repairers also make adjustments to equipment, such as fine tuning the picture quality of a television set or the sound on a surround-sound system.

Improvements in technology have miniaturized and digitized many audio and video recording devices. Miniaturization has made repair work significantly more difficult because both the components and the acceptable tolerances are smaller. Also, components now are mounted on the surface of circuit boards, instead of plugged into slots, requiring more precise soldering when a new part is installed. Improved technologies have lowered the price of electronic home entertainment equipment to the point where customers often replace broken equipment instead of repairing it.

Work environment. Most repairers work in well-lighted electrical repair shops. Field technicians, however, spend much time traveling in service vehicles and working in customers' residences.

Repairers may have to work in a variety of positions and carry heavy equipment. Although the work of repairers is comparatively safe, they must take precautions against minor burns and electric shock. Because television monitors carry high voltage even when they are turned off, repairers need to discharge the voltage before servicing such equipment.

When equipment breaks down, electronic home entertainment equipment installers and repairers check for defective components.

Training, Other Qualifications, and Advancement

Employers prefer applicants who have knowledge of electronics, good problem-solving skills, and previous repair experience. Good customer service skills are essential for field technicians, as they spend a majority of their time working in customers' homes. Certification is available for entry-level workers and experienced workers seeking advancement.

Education and training. Employers prefer applicants who have knowledge and skills in electronics as well as previous repair experience. Many applicants gain these skills at vocational training programs and community colleges. Training programs should include both hands-on experience and theoretical education in digital consumer electronics. Entry-level repairers may work closely with more experienced technicians, who provide technical guidance.

Other qualifications. Field technicians work closely with customers and must have good communication skills and a neat appearance. Repairers also must have good problem solving skills, as their main duty is to diagnose and solve problems. For home entertainment system installers, excellent vision and a keen sense of sound are important for fine-tuning the installed product. Employers usually require that field technicians have a driver's license.

Certification and advancement. A growing number of employers require applicants to be certified. Various organizations offer certification for electronic home entertainment equipment installers and repairers. For instance, the Electronics Technicians Association (ETA) offers certification programs in numerous electronics specialties, including Residential Electronics Systems Integrator. The International Society of Certified Electronics Technicians also offers certification in multimedia systems and electronic systems. To become certified, applicants must meet several prerequisites and pass a comprehensive written or online examination. Certification demonstrates a level of competency. It can make an applicant more attractive to employers or increase an employee's opportunities for advancement. Experienced repairers with advanced training may become specialists or troubleshooters, helping other repairers to diagnose difficult problems. Workers with leadership ability may become supervisors of other repairers. Some experienced workers open their own repair shops.

Employment

Electronic home entertainment equipment installers and repairers held about 51,200 jobs in 2008. Many repairers—about 33 percent—worked in the retail trade industry. About 26 percent of electronic home entertainment equipment installers and repairers were self-employed.

Job Outlook

Employment is expected to increase about as fast as average for all occupations. Job prospects will be best for applicants with certification, knowledge of electronics, related work experience, and good customer service skills.

Employment change. Employment of electronic home entertainment equipment installers and repairers is expected to grow by 11 percent from 2008 to 2018, which is as fast as the average for all occupations. Demand will be driven by the rising sales of home entertainment equipment.

Employment growth of home entertainment installers will be driven by consumer demand for sophisticated digital equipment, such as high definition televisions, video recorders, cameras, and camcorders. Home entertainment systems continue to grow in popularity and consumers' desire for state-of-the-art sound and picture quality will further spur the need for installers.

The need for repairers, however, is expected to grow slowly because home entertainment equipment is less expensive than in the past. As technological developments have lowered the price and improved the reliability of equipment, the demand for repair services has decreased. When a malfunction does occur, it is often cheaper for consumers to replace equipment than to pay for repairs.

Job prospects. Job openings will arise from employment growth and from the need to replace workers who retire or who leave the occupation. Opportunities will be best for applicants with certification, knowledge of electronics, related hands-on experience, and good customer-service skills.

Earnings

Median hourly wages of wage-and-salary electronic home entertainment equipment installers and repairers were $15.42 in May 2008. The middle 50 percent earned between $12.09 and $19.64. The lowest 10 percent earned less than $9.90, and the highest 10 percent earned more than $24.13. In May 2008, median hourly wages of electronic home entertainment equipment installers and repairers in electrical and electronic goods merchant wholesalers were $17.19, and $16.17 in building equipment contractors.

Related Occupations

Other workers who install, repair, and maintain electronic equipment include:

Projections data from the National Employment Matrix

Occupational Title	SOC Code	Employment, 2008	Projected Employment, 2018	Change, 2008-2018	
				Number	Percent
Electronic home entertainment equipment installers and repairers	49-2097	51,200	56,800	5,500	11

(NOTE) Data in this table are rounded. See the discussion of the employment projections table in the *Handbook* introductory chapter on *Occupational Information Included in the Handbook.*

Sources of Additional Information

For information on careers and certification, contact:

➤ Electronics Technicians Association International, 5 Depot St., Greencastle, IN 46135. Internet: **http://www.eta-i.org**

➤ International Society of Certified Electronics Technicians, 3608 Pershing Ave., Fort Worth, TX 76107. Internet: **http://www.iscet.org**

The Occupational Information Network (O*NET) provides information on a wide range of occupational characteristics. Links to O*NET appear at the end of the Internet version of this occupational statement, accessible at **http://www.bls.gov/ooh/ocos187.htm**

Radio and Telecommunications Equipment Installers and Repairers

Significant Points

- Little or no change in employment is projected.

- Job opportunities vary by specialty; good opportunities are expected for central office installers and repairers, but station installers and repairers can expect keen competition.

- Applicants with computer skills and postsecondary electronics training should have the best opportunities.

- Repairers may be on-call around the clock in case of emergencies; therefore, night, weekend, and holiday hours are common.

Nature of the Work

Telephones, computers, and radios depend on a variety of equipment to transmit communications signals and connect to the Internet. From electronic and optical switches that route telephone calls and packets of data to their destinations to radio transmitters and receivers that relay signals from radios in airplanes, boats, and emergency vehicles, complex equipment is needed to keep the country communicating. The workers who set up and maintain this sophisticated equipment are called radio and telecommunications equipment installers and repairers.

Telecommunications equipment installers and repairers have a range of skills and abilities, which vary by the type of work they do and where it is performed. Most work indoors. (Equipment installers who work mainly outdoors are classified as telecommunications line installers and repairers—a separate occupation discussed elsewhere in the *Handbook*.)

Central office installers and repairers—telecommunications equipment installers and repairers who work at switching hubs called central offices—do some of the most complex work. Switching hubs contain the switches and routers that direct packets of information to their destinations. Installers and repairers set up those switches and routers, as well as cables and other equipment.

Although most telephone lines connecting houses to central offices and switching stations are still copper, the lines connecting central hubs to each other are fiber optic. Fiber optic lines,

along with newer packet switching equipment, have greatly increased the transmission capacity of each line, allowing an ever increasing amount of information to pass through the lines. Switches and routers are used to transmit, process, amplify, and direct a massive amount of information. Installing and maintaining this equipment requires a high level of technical knowledge.

Nonetheless, the increasing reliability of switches and routers has simplified maintenance as new self-monitoring telecommunications switches can now alert central office repairers to malfunctions. Some switches allow repairers to diagnose and correct problems from remote locations. When faced with a malfunction, the repairer may refer to manufacturers' manuals that provide maintenance instructions.

As cable television and telecommunications technology converge, the equipment used in both technologies is becoming more similar. The distribution centers for cable television companies, which are similar to central offices in the telecommunications sector, are called headends. *Headend technicians* perform essentially the same work as central office technicians, but they work in the cable television industry.

When problems with telecommunications equipment arise, telecommunications equipment repairers diagnose the source of the problem by testing each part of the equipment—a process that requires understanding how the software and hardware interact. To locate the problem, repairers often use spectrum analyzers, network analyzers, or both, to detect any distortion in the signal. To fix the equipment, repairers may use small hand tools, including pliers and screwdrivers, to remove and replace defective components such as circuit boards or wiring. Newer equipment is easier to repair because whole boards and parts are designed to be quickly removed and replaced. Repairers also may install updated software or programs that maintain existing software.

Another type of telecommunications installer and repairer, *PBX installers and repairers*, set up private branch exchange (PBX) switchboards, which relay incoming, outgoing, and interoffice telephone calls within a single location or organization. To install switches and switchboards, installers first connect the equipment to power lines and communications cables and install frames and supports. They test the connections to ensure that adequate power is available and that the communication links work properly. They also install equipment such as power systems, alarms, and telephone sets. New switches and switchboards are computerized and workers often need to install software or program the equipment to provide specific features. Finally, the installer performs tests to verify that the newly installed equipment functions properly. If a problem arises, PBX repairers determine whether it is located within the PBX system or whether it stems from the telephone lines maintained by the local telephone company. Newer installations may use voice-over Internet protocol (VoIP) systems—systems that operate like PBX, but they use a company's computer wiring to run Internet access, network applications, and telephone communications.

Station installers and repairers, telephone—commonly known as *home installers and repairers* or *telecommunications service technicians*—install and repair telecommunications wiring and equipment in customers' home or business premises. They install telephone, VoIP, Internet, and other communications services by installing wiring inside the home or connecting existing wiring to outside service lines. Depending on the service required, they may set up television capability or connect modems and install software on a customer's computer. To complete the connection to an outside service line, the installer may need to climb telephone poles or ladders and test the line. Later on, if a maintenance problem occurs, station repairers test the customer's lines to determine if the problem is located in the customer's premises or in the outside service lines and attempt to fix the problem if it is inside. If the problem is with the outside service lines, telecommunications line repairers usually are called to fix it.

Radio mechanics install and maintain radio transmitting and receiving equipment, excluding cellular communications systems. This includes stationary equipment mounted on transmission towers or tall buildings and mobile equipment, such as two-way radio communications systems in taxis, airplanes, ships, and emergency vehicles. Aviation and marine radio mechanics also may work on other electronic equipment, in addition to radios. Newer radio equipment is self-monitoring and may alert mechanics to potential malfunctions. When malfunctions occur, these mechanics examine equipment for damaged components and either fix them, replace the part, or make a software modification. They may use electrical measuring instruments to monitor signal strength, transmission capacity, interference, and signal delay, as well as hand tools to replace defective components and adjust equipment so that it performs within required specifications.

Work environment. Radio and telecommunications equipment installers and repairers generally work in clean, well-lighted, air-conditioned surroundings, such as a telecommunications company's central office, a customer's location, or an electronic service center. Traveling to the site of the installation or repair is common among station installers and repairers, PBX and VoIP installers and repairers, and radio mechanics. Installation may require access to rooftops, attics, ladders, and telephone poles to complete the repair. Radio mechanics may need to work on transmission towers, which may be located on top of tall buildings or mountains, as well as aboard airplanes and ships.

The work of most repairers involves lifting, reaching, stooping, crouching, and crawling. Adherence to safety precautions is important in order to guard against work hazards. These hazards include falls, minor burns, and electrical shock. Data from the U.S. Bureau of Labor Statistics show that telecommunications equipment installers and repairers, except line installers, experienced a work-related injury and illness rate that was higher than the national average.

Nearly all radio and telecommunications equipment installers and repairers work full time during regular business hours to meet the demand for repair services during the workday. Schedules are more irregular at employers that provide repair services 24 hours a day, such as for police radio communications operations or where installation and maintenance must take place after normal business hours. At these locations, mechanics work a variety of shifts, including weekend and holiday hours. Repairers may be on call around the clock, in case of emergencies, and may have to work overtime.

Training, Other Qualifications, and Advancement

Postsecondary education in electronics and computer technology is increasingly required for radio and telecommunications equipment installers and repairer jobs, and a few employers even prefer people with a bachelor's degree for some of the most complex types of work.

Education and training. As telecommunications technology becomes more complex, the education required for radio and telecommunications equipment installers and repairer jobs has increased. Most employers prefer applicants with postsecondary training in electronics and familiarity with computers. The education needed for these jobs may vary from certification to a 2- or 4-year degree in electronics or a related subject. Sources of training include 2- and 4-year college programs in electronics or communications technology, military experience in radios and electronics, trade schools, and programs offered by equipment and software manufacturers. Educational requirements are higher for central office installers and repairers and for those working in nonresidential settings.

Many in the telecommunications industry work their way up into this occupation by gaining experience at less difficult jobs. Experience as a telecommunications line installer or station installer is helpful before moving up to the job of central office installer and other more complex jobs, for example. Military experience with communications equipment is also valued by many employers in both telecommunications and radio repair.

Newly hired repairers usually receive some training from their employers. This may include formal classroom training in electronics, communications systems, or software and informal hands-on training assisting an experienced repairer. Large companies may send repairers to outside training sessions to learn about new equipment and service procedures. As networks have become more sophisticated—often including equipment from a variety of companies—the knowledge needed for installation and maintenance also has increased.

Licensure. Aviation and marine radio mechanics are required to have a license from the Federal Communications

Radio and telecommunications equipment installers often use computers to diagnose problems with telecommunications switching equipment.

Commission before they can work on these types of radios. This requires passing several exams on radio law, electronics fundamentals, and maintenance practices.

Other qualifications. Familiarity with computers, being mechanically inclined, and being able to solve problems are traits that are highly regarded by employers. Repairers must also be able to distinguish colors, because wires are typically color-coded. For positions that require climbing poles and towers, workers must be in good physical shape and not afraid of heights. Repairers who handle assignments alone at a customer's site must be able to work without close supervision. For workers who frequently contact customers, a pleasant personality, neat appearance, and good communications skills also are important.

Certification and advancement. This is an occupation where the technology is changing rapidly. Workers must keep abreast of the latest equipment available and know how to repair it. Telecommunications equipment installers and repairers often need to be certified to perform certain tasks or to work on specific equipment. Certification usually requires taking classes. Some certifications are needed to enter the occupation; others are meant to improve one's current abilities or to advance in the occupation.

The Society of Cable and Telecommunications Engineers and the Telecommunications Industry Association offer certifications to workers in this field. Telecommunications equipment manufacturers also provide training on specific equipment.

Experienced repairers with advanced training may become specialists or troubleshooters who help other repairers diagnose difficult problems, or may work with engineers in designing equipment and developing maintenance procedures. Home installers may advance to wiring computer networks or working as a central office installer and repairer. Because of their familiarity with equipment, repairers are particularly well qualified to become manufacturers' sales workers. Workers with leadership ability also may become maintenance supervisors or service managers. Some experienced workers open their own repair service shops, or become wholesalers or retailers of electronic equipment.

Employment

Radio and telecommunications equipment installers and repairers held about 208,800 jobs in 2008. About 203,100 were telecommunications equipment installers and repairers, except line installers. The remaining 5,700 were radio mechanics.

Telecommunications equipment installers and repairers work mostly in the telecommunications industry. Increasingly, however, they can be found in the construction industry working as contractors to the telecommunications industry.

Radio mechanics work in the electronic and precision equipment repair and maintenance industry, the telecommunications industry, electronics and appliance stores, government, and other industries.

Job Outlook

Little or no change in employment of radio and telecommunications equipment installers and repairers is projected. Job opportunities vary by specialty; good opportunities are expected for central office installers and repairers, but station installers and repairers can expect keen competition. Job prospects are best for those with computer skills and postsecondary training in electronics.

Employment change. Little or no change in employment of radio and telecommunications equipment installers and repairers is expected during the 2008-18 period. Over the next decade, telecommunications companies will provide faster Internet connections, provide video-on-demand, add hundreds of television stations, and many services that haven't even been invented yet. Although building the new networks required to provide these services will create jobs, these gains will be offset by a decline in maintenance work. The new equipment requires much less maintenance work because it is newer, more reliable, easier to repair, and more resistant to damage from the elements.

The increased reliability of radio equipment and the use of self-monitoring systems also will continue to lessen the need for radio mechanics. However, technological changes are also creating new wireless applications that create jobs for radio mechanics.

Job prospects. Applicants with computer skills and postsecondary training in electronics should have the best opportunities for radio and telecommunications equipment installer and repairer jobs, but opportunities will vary by specialty. Good opportunities should be available for central office and PBX installers and repairers experienced in current technology, as the growing popularity of VoIP, expanded multimedia offerings such as video on demand, and other telecommunications services continue to place additional demand on telecommunications networks. These new services require high data transfer rates, which can be achieved only by installing new optical switching and routing equipment. Extending high-speed communications from central offices to customers also will require telecommunications equipment installers to put in place more advanced switching and routing equipment,

Projections data from the National Employment Matrix

Occupational Title	SOC Code	Employment, 2008	Projected Employment, 2018	Change, 2008-2018	
				Number	Percent
Radio and telecommunications equipment installers and repairers	49-2020	208,800	208,100	-700	0
Radio mechanics	49-2021	5,700	5,500	-200	-4
Telecommunications equipment installers and repairers, except line installers..	49-2022	203,100	202,600	-500	0

(NOTE) Data in this table are rounded. See the discussion of the employment projections table in the *Handbook* introductory chapter on *Occupational Information Included in the Handbook.*

but opportunities for repairers will be limited by the increased reliability and automation of the new switching equipment.

Station installers and repairers can expect keen competition. Prewired buildings and the increasing reliability of telephone equipment will reduce the need for installation and maintenance of customers' telephones, as will the declining number of pay telephones in operation as use of cellular telephones grows. However, some of these losses should be offset by the need to upgrade internal lines in businesses and the wiring of new homes and businesses with fiber optic lines.

Radio mechanics should find good opportunities if they have a strong background in electronics and an ability to work independently. Increasing competition from cellular services is limiting the growth of radio services, but employers report difficulty finding adequate numbers of qualified radio mechanics to perform repair work.

Earnings

In May 2008, median annual wages of telecommunications equipment installers and repairers, except line installers, were $55,600. The middle 50 percent earned between $42,930 and $63,030. The bottom 10 percent earned less than $31,330, whereas the top 10 percent earned more than $69,470. Median annual wages of these workers in the wired telecommunications carriers industry were $57,160 in May 2008.

Median annual wages of radio mechanics in May 2008 were $40,260. The middle 50 percent earned between $30,680 and $51,560. The bottom 10 percent earned less than $24,610, whereas the top 10 percent earned more than $63,600.

About 32 percent of radio and telecommunication equipment installers and repairers are members of unions, such as the Communications Workers of America (CWA) and the International Brotherhood of Electrical Workers (IBEW.)

Telecommunications equipment installers and repairers employed by large telecommunications companies who also belong to unions often have very good benefits, including health, dental, vision, and life insurance. They also usually have good retirement and leave policies. Those working for small independent companies and contractors may get fewer benefits.

Radio mechanics tend to work for small electronics firms or government. Benefits vary widely depending upon the type of work and size of firm. Government jobs usually have good benefits.

Related Occupations

Other occupations that involve work with electronic and telecommunications equipment includes:

Sources of Additional Information

For information on career and training opportunities, contact:
➤ International Brotherhood of Electrical Workers, Telecommunications Department, 900 7th St. NW. Washington, DC 20001.

➤ Communications Workers of America, 501 3rd St. NW. Washington, DC 20001. Internet: **http://www.cwa-union.org/jobs**

➤ National Coalition for Telecommunications Education and Learning, CAEL, 6021 South Syracuse Way, Suite 213 Greenwood Village, CO 80111. Internet: **http://www.nactel.org**

For information on training and professional certifications in broadband telecommunications, contact:
➤ Society of Cable Telecommunications Engineers, Certification Department, 140 Philips Rd., Exton, PA 19341-1318. **Internet: http://www.scte.org**

For information on training and licensing for aviation and marine radio mechanics, contact:
➤ The Federal Communications Commission (FCC), 445 12th St. SW. Washington, DC 20554. Internet: **http://wireless.fcc.gov/commoperators**

For more information on employers, education, and training in marine electronics and radios, contact:
➤ National Marine Electronics Association, 7 Riggs Ave., Severna Park, MD 21164. Internet: **http://www.nmea.org**

The Occupational Information Network (O*NET) provides information on a wide range of occupational characteristics. Links to O*NET appear at the end of the Internet version of this occupational statement, accessible at **http://www.bls.gov/ooh/ocos188.htm**

Vehicle and Mobile Equipment Mechanics, Installers, and Repairers

Aircraft and Avionics Equipment Mechanics and Service Technicians

Significant Points

- Most workers learn their jobs in 1 of about 170 schools certified by the Federal Aviation Administration (FAA).

- Job opportunities should be favorable for persons who have completed an aircraft mechanic training program, but keen competition is likely for jobs at major airlines, which offer the best pay and benefits.

- Job opportunities are likely to continue to be best at small commuter and regional airlines, at FAA repair stations, and in general aviation.

Nature of the Work

Today's airplanes are highly complex machines with parts that must function within extreme tolerances for them to operate safely. To keep aircraft in peak operating condition, *aircraft and avionics equipment mechanics and service technicians* perform scheduled maintenance, make repairs, and complete inspections required by the FAA.

Many aircraft mechanics specialize in preventive maintenance. They inspect aircraft engines, landing gear, instruments, pressurized sections, accessories—brakes, valves, pumps, and air-conditioning systems, for example—and other parts of the aircraft, and do the necessary maintenance and replacement of parts. They also keep records related to the maintenance performed on the aircraft. Mechanics and technicians conduct inspections following a schedule based on the number of hours the aircraft has flown, calendar days since the last inspection, cycles of operation, or a combination of these factors. In large, sophisticated planes equipped with aircraft monitoring systems, mechanics can gather valuable diagnostic information from electronic boxes and consoles that monitor the aircraft's basic operations. In planes of all sorts, aircraft mechanics examine engines by working through specially designed openings while standing on ladders or scaffolds or by using hoists or lifts to remove the entire engine from the craft. After taking an engine apart, mechanics use precision instruments to measure parts for wear and use x-ray and magnetic inspection equipment to check for invisible cracks. They repair or replace worn or defective parts. Mechanics also may repair sheet metal or composite surfaces; measure the tension of control cables; and check for corrosion, distortion, and cracks in the fuselage, wings, and tail. After completing all repairs, they must test the equipment to ensure that it works properly.

Other mechanics specialize in repair work rather than inspection. They find and fix problems that pilots describe. For example, during a preflight check, a pilot may discover that the aircraft's fuel gauge does not work. To solve the problem, mechanics may troubleshoot the electrical system, using electrical test equipment to make sure that no wires are broken or shorted out, and replace any defective electrical or electronic components. Mechanics work as fast as safety permits so that the aircraft can be put back into service quickly.

Some mechanics work on one or many different types of aircraft, such as jets, propeller-driven airplanes, and helicopters. Others specialize in one section of a particular type of aircraft, such as the engine, hydraulics, or electrical system. In small, independent repair shops, mechanics usually inspect and repair many different types of aircraft.

Airframe mechanics are authorized to work on any part of the aircraft except the instruments, power plants, and propellers. *Powerplant mechanics* are authorized to work on engines and do limited work on propellers. Combination airframe-and-powerplant mechanics—called *A&P mechanics*—work on all parts of the plane except the instruments. Most mechanics working on civilian aircraft today are A&P mechanics.

Avionics systems—components used for aircraft navigation and radio communications, weather radar systems, and other instruments and computers that control flight, engine, and other primary functions—are now an integral part of aircraft design and have vastly increased aircraft capability. *Avionics technicians* repair and maintain these systems. Because of the increasing use of technology, more time is spent repairing electronic systems, such as computerized controls. Technicians also may be required to analyze and develop solutions to complex electronic problems.

Work environment. Mechanics work in hangars, repair stations, or out on the airfield on the "flight lines" where aircraft park. Mechanics often work under time pressure to maintain flight schedules or, in general aviation, to keep from inconveniencing customers. At the same time, mechanics have a tre-

Avionics technicians are responsible for repairing an aircraft's electronics systems.

mendous responsibility to maintain safety standards, and this can cause the job to be stressful.

Frequently, mechanics must lift or pull objects weighing more than 70 pounds. They often stand, lie, or kneel in awkward positions and occasionally must work in precarious positions, such as on scaffolds or ladders. Noise and vibration are common when engines are being tested, so ear protection is necessary. According to BLS data, full-time aircraft mechanics and service technicians experienced a higher than average work-related injury and illness rate. Aircraft mechanics usually work 40 hours a week on 8-hour shifts around the clock. Overtime and weekend work is frequent.

Training, Other Qualifications, and Advancement

Most mechanics who work on civilian aircraft are certified by the FAA, which requires mechanics to be at least 18 years of age, fluent in English, and have a high school diploma or its equivalent in addition to having the needed technical skills. Most mechanics learn their skills in an FAA-certified Aviation Maintenance Technician School

Education and training. Although a few people become mechanics through on-the-job training, most learn the skills needed to do their jobs in 1 of about 170 Aviation Maintenance Technician schools certified by the FAA. By law, FAA standards require that certified mechanic schools offer students a minimum of 1,900 class-hours. Coursework in schools normally lasts from 12 to 24 months and provides training with the tools and equipment used on the job. About one-third of these schools award 2-year and 4-year degrees in avionics, aviation technology, or aviation maintenance management.

Aircraft trade schools are placing more emphasis on technologies such as turbine engines, composite materials, and aviation electronics, which are increasingly being used in the construction of new aircraft. Technological advances have also affected aircraft maintenance, meaning mechanics must have an especially strong background in computers and electronics to get or keep jobs in this field.

Courses in mathematics, physics, chemistry, electronics, computer science, and mechanical drawing are helpful because they demonstrate many of the principles involved in the operation of aircraft, and knowledge of these principles is often necessary to make repairs. Courses that develop writing skills also are important because mechanics are often required to submit reports. Mechanics must be able to read, write, and understand English.

A few mechanics are trained on the job by experienced mechanics. Their work must be supervised and documented by certified mechanics until they have FAA certificates.

Licensure. The FAA requires that all maintenance work on aircraft be performed by certified mechanics or under the supervision of a certified mechanic. As a result, most airlines hire mechanics that have FAA certification. The FAA offers certification for airframe mechanics and powerplant mechanics, although most airlines prefer to hire mechanics with a combined A&P certificate.

Mechanics need at least 18 months of work experience before applying for an airframe or powerplant certificate, and 30 months of experience working with both engines and air-

frames for a combined A&P certificate, although completion of a program at an FAA-certified school can be substituted for theses work experience requirements.

In addition to having experience or formal training, applicants for all certificates must pass written, oral, and practical tests that demonstrate that they can do the work authorized by the certificate. Written tests are administered at one of the many designated computer testing facilities worldwide, while the oral and practical tests are administered by a Designated Mechanic Examiner of the FAA. All tests must be passed within a 24- month period to receive certification.

FAA regulations require current work experience to keep certificates valid. Applicants must have at least 1,000 hours of work experience in the previous 24 months or take a refresher course. Mechanics also must take at least 16 hours of training every 24 months to keep their certificates current. Many mechanics take training courses offered by manufacturers or employers, usually through outside contractors.

The FAA allows certified airframe mechanics who are trained and qualified and who have the proper tools to work on avionics equipment. However, avionics technicians are not required to have FAA certification if they have avionics repair experience from the military or from working for avionics manufacturers. Avionics technicians who work on communications equipment must obtain a restricted radio-telephone operator license from the Federal Communications Commission.

Other qualifications. Aircraft mechanics must do careful and thorough work that requires a high degree of mechanical aptitude. Employers seek applicants who are self-motivated, hard-working, enthusiastic, and able to diagnose and solve complex mechanical problems. Additionally, employers prefer mechanics who can perform a variety of tasks. Agility is important for the reaching and climbing necessary to do the job. Because they may work on the tops of wings and fuselages on large jet planes, aircraft mechanics must not be afraid of heights.

Advances in computer technology, aircraft systems, and the materials used to manufacture airplanes have made mechanics' jobs more highly technical. Aircraft mechanics must possess the skills necessary to troubleshoot and diagnose complex aircraft systems. They also must continually update their skills with and knowledge of new technology and advances in aircraft technology.

Some aircraft mechanics in the Armed Forces acquire enough general experience to satisfy the work experience requirements for the FAA certificate. With additional study, they may pass the certifying exam. In general, however, jobs in the military services are too specialized to provide the broad experience required by the FAA. Most Armed Forces mechanics have to complete the entire FAA training program, although a few receive some credit for the material they learned in the service. In any case, military experience is a great advantage when seeking employment; employers consider applicants with formal training to be the most desirable applicants.

Advancement. As aircraft mechanics gain experience, they may advance to lead mechanic (or crew chief), inspector, lead inspector, or shop supervisor positions. Opportunities are best for those who have an aircraft inspector's authorization. To obtain an

Projections data from the National Employment Matrix

Occupational Title	SOC Code	Employment, 2008	Projected Employment, 2018	Change, 2008-2018	
				Number	Percent
Aircraft and avionics equipment mechanics and service technicians	–	140,300	150,100	9,800	7
Avionics technicians	49-2091	18,800	20,800	2,000	11
Aircraft mechanics and service technicians..................................	49-3011	121,500	129,300	7,800	6

(NOTE) Data in this table are rounded. See the discussion of the employment projections table in the *Handbook* introductory chapter on *Occupational Information Included in the Handbook.*

inspector's authorization, a mechanic must have held an A&P certificate for at least 3 years, with 24 months of hands-on experience.

In the airlines, where promotion often is determined by examination, supervisors sometimes advance to executive positions. Those with broad experience in maintenance and overhaul might become inspectors with the FAA. With additional business and management training, some open their own aircraft maintenance facilities. Mechanics with the necessary pilot licenses and flying experience may take the FAA examination for the position of flight engineer, with opportunities to become pilots.

Mechanics and technicians learn many different skills in their training that can be applied to other jobs, and some transfer to other skilled repairer occupations or electronics technician jobs. For example, some avionics technicians continue their education and become aviation engineers, electrical engineers (specializing in circuit design and testing), or communication engineers. Others become repair consultants, in-house electronics designers, or join research groups that test and develop products.

Employment

Aircraft and avionics equipment mechanics and service technicians held about 140,300 jobs in 2008; about 87 percent of these workers were aircraft mechanics and service technicians; the rest were avionics technicians.

Employment of aircraft and avionics equipment mechanics and service technicians primarily is concentrated in a small number of industries. Almost half of aircraft and avionics equipment mechanics and service technicians worked in air transportation and support activities for air transportation. About 21 percent worked in aerospace product and parts manufacturing and about 15 percent worked for the Federal Government. Most of the rest worked for companies that operate their own planes to transport executives and cargo.

Most airline mechanics and service technicians work at major airports near large cities. Civilian mechanics employed by the U.S. Armed Forces work at military installations.

Job Outlook

Job growth for aircraft and avionics equipment mechanics and service technicians is expected to be about as fast as the average for all occupations. Job opportunities should be favorable for people who have completed an aircraft mechanic training program, but keen competition is likely for jobs at major airlines.

Employment change. Employment is expected to increase by 7 percent during the 2008-18 period, which is about as fast as the average for all occupations. Passenger air traffic is expected to increase as the result of an expanding economy and a growing population, and the need for aircraft mechanics and service technicians will grow accordingly. Although there is an increasing trend for some large airlines to outsource aircraft and avionics equipment mechanic jobs overseas, most airline companies still prefer that aircraft maintenance be performed in the U.S. because overseas contractors may not comply with more stringent U.S. safety regulations.

Job prospects. Most job openings for aircraft mechanics through the year 2018 will stem from the need to replace the many mechanics expected to retire over the next decade. In addition, some mechanics will leave to work in related fields, such as automobile repair, as their skills are largely transferable to other maintenance and repair occupations.

Also contributing to favorable future job opportunities for mechanics is the long-term trend toward fewer students entering technical schools to learn skilled maintenance and repair trades. Many of the students who have the ability and aptitude to work on planes are choosing to go to college, work in computer-related fields, or go into other repair and maintenance occupations with better working conditions. If this trend continues, the supply of trained aviation mechanics may not keep up with the needs of the air transportation industry.

Job opportunities will continue to be the best at small commuter and regional airlines, at FAA repair stations, and in general aviation. Commuter and regional airlines is the fastest growing segment of the air transportation industry, but wages in these airlines tend to be lower than those in the major airlines, so they attract fewer job applicants. Also, some jobs will become available as experienced mechanics leave for higher paying jobs with the major airlines or transfer to other occupations. Mechanics will face more competition for jobs with large airlines because the high wages and travel benefits that these jobs offer generally attract more qualified applicants than there are openings.

Nonetheless, job opportunities with the airlines are expected to be better than they have been in the past. In general, prospects will be best for applicants with experience and an A&P certification. Mechanics who keep abreast of technological advances in electronics, composite materials, and other areas will be in greatest demand. Also, mechanics who are willing to relocate to smaller rural areas will have better job opportunities.

Avionics technicians who are trained to work with complex aircraft systems, performing some duties normally performed by certified A&P mechanics, should have the best job prospects. Additionally, technicians with licensing that enables them to work on the airplane, either removing or reinstalling equipment, are expected to be in especially high demand.

Earnings

Median hourly wages of aircraft mechanics and service technicians were about $24.71 in May 2008. The middle 50 percent earned between $20.25 and $29.25. The lowest 10 percent earned less than $15.85, and the highest 10 percent earned more than $33.19. Median hourly wages in the industries employing the largest numbers of aircraft mechanics and service technicians in May 2008 were:

Scheduled air transportation	$27.96
Federal Executive Branch	24.98
Aerospace product and parts manufacturing	24.47
Nonscheduled air transportation	24.27
Support activities for air transportation	20.95

Median hourly wages of avionics technicians were about $23.71 in May 2008. The middle 50 percent earned between $20.10 and $28.02. The lowest 10 percent earned less than $16.45, and the highest 10 percent earned more than $30.87.

Mechanics who work on jets for the major airlines generally earn more than those working on other aircraft. Those who graduate from an aviation maintenance technician school often earn higher starting salaries than individuals who receive training in the Armed Forces or on the job. Airline mechanics and their immediate families receive reduced-fare transportation on their own and most other airlines.

Almost 3 in 10 aircraft and avionics equipment mechanics and service technicians are members of unions or covered by union agreements. The principal unions are the International Association of Machinists and Aerospace Workers and the Transport Workers Union of America. Some mechanics are represented by the International Brotherhood of Teamsters.

Related Occupations

Workers in some other occupations that involve similar mechanical and electrical work include:

	Page
Automotive service technicians and mechanics	690
Electrical and electronics installers and repairers	675
Electricians	641
Elevator installers and repairers	644

Sources of Additional Information

Information about jobs with a particular airline can be obtained by writing to the personnel manager of the company.

For general information about aircraft and avionics equipment mechanics and service technicians, contact:

➤ Professional Aviation Maintenance Association, 400 North Washington St., Suite 300. Alexandria, VA 22314. Internet: **http://www.pama.org**

For information on jobs in a particular area, contact employers at local airports or local offices of the State employment service.

Information on obtaining positions as aircraft and avionics equipment mechanics and service technicians with the Federal Government is available from the Office of Personnel Management through USAJOBS, the Federal Government's official employment information system. This resource for locating and applying for job opportunities can be accessed through the Internet at **http://www.usajobs.opm.gov** or through an interactive voice response telephone system at (703) 724-1850 or TDD (978) 461-8404. These numbers are not toll free, and charges may result.

The Occupational Information Network (O*NET) provides information on a wide range of occupational characteristics. Links to O*NET appear at the end of the Internet version of this occupational statement, accessible at **http://www.bls.gov/ooh/ocos179.htm**

Automotive Body and Related Repairers

Significant Points

- Little or no change in the overall number of jobs is expected.

- Repairers need good reading ability and basic mathematics and computer skills to use print and digital technical manuals.

- Many repairers, particularly in urban areas, need a national certification to advance past entry-level work.

Nature of the Work

Most of the damage resulting from everyday vehicle collisions can be repaired, and vehicles can be refinished to look and drive like new. This damage may be relatively minor, such as scraped paint or a dented panel, or major, requiring the complex replacement of parts. Such repair services are performed by trained workers.

Automotive body and related repairers, often called *collision repair technicians*, straighten bent bodies, remove dents, and replace crumpled parts that cannot be fixed. They repair all types of vehicles, and although some work on large trucks, buses, or tractor-trailers, most work on cars and small trucks. They can work alone, with only general direction from supervisors, or as specialists on a repair team. In some shops, helpers or apprentices assist experienced repairers.

Each damaged vehicle presents different challenges for repairers. Using their broad knowledge of automotive construction and repair techniques, automotive body repairers must decide how to handle each job based on what the vehicle is made of and what needs to be fixed. They must first determine the extent of the damage and decide which parts can be repaired or need to be replaced.

If the car is heavily damaged, an automotive body repairer might start by measuring the frame to determine if there has been structural damage. Repairers would then attach or clamp frames and sections to structural machines that use hydraulic pressure to align damaged components. "Unibody" vehicles—designs built without frames—must be restored to precise factory specifications for the vehicle to operate correctly. For these vehicles, repairers use bench systems to accurately measure how much each section is out of alignment, and hydraulic machinery to return the vehicle to its original shape.

Automotive body repairers must carefully restore cars to given specifications following an accident.

Only once the frame is aligned properly can repairers begin to fix or replace other damaged body parts. If the vehicle or part is made of metal, body repairers will use a pneumatic metal-cutting gun or a plasma cutter to remove badly damaged sections of body panels and then weld or otherwise attach replacement sections. Less serious dents are pulled out with a hydraulic jack or hand prying bar or knocked out with hand tools or pneumatic hammers. Small dents and creases in the metal are smoothed by holding a small anvil against one side of the damaged area while hammering the opposite side. Repairers may also remove very small pits and dimples with pick hammers and punches in a process called metal finishing. Body repairers then use plastic or solder to fill small dents that cannot be worked out of plastic or metal panels. On metal panels, they sculpt the hardened filler to the original shape by filing, grinding and sanding the repair back to the shape that is desired.

Body repairers may also repair or replace the plastic body parts that are increasingly used on new vehicles. They remove damaged panels and identify the type and properties of the plastic used. Some types of plastic allow repairers to apply heat from a hot-air welding gun or immerse the panel in hot water and press the softened section back into shape by hand. In most cases, it is more cost effective for the plastic parts to be replaced rather than to be repaired. A few body repairers specialize in fixing fiberglass car bodies.

Some body repairers specialize in installing and repairing glass in automobiles and other vehicles. *Automotive glass installers and repairers* remove broken, cracked, or pitted windshields and window glass. Glass installers apply a moisture-proofing compound along the edges of the glass, place the glass in the vehicle, and install rubber strips around the sides of the windshield or window to make it secure and weatherproof.

Many large shops make repairs using an assembly-line approach where vehicles are fixed by a team of repairers who each specialize in several types of repair. One worker might straighten frames while another repairs doors and fenders, for example. In most shops, automotive painters do the priming and refinishing, but in small shops, workers often do both body repairing and painting. (Automotive painters are discussed in the section on painting and coating workers, except construction and maintenance elsewhere in the *Handbook*.)

Work environment. Repairers work indoors in body shops where noise from the clatter of hammers against metal and the whine of power tools is prevalent. Most shops are well ventilated to disperse dust and paint fumes. Body repairers may also be required to work in awkward or cramped positions, and much of their work can be physically challenging. Hazards include cuts from sharp metal edges, burns from torches and heated metal, and injuries from power tools. However, serious accidents usually are avoided when the shop is kept clean and orderly and safety practices are observed.

Most automotive body repairers work a standard 40-hour week. More than 40 hours a week may be required when there is a backlog of repair work to be completed. This may include working on weekends.

Training, Other Qualifications, and Advancement

As automotive technology rapidly becomes more sophisticated, most employers prefer applicants who have completed a formal training program in automotive body repair or refinishing. Most new repairers complete at least part of this training on the job, while continuing to receive training from industry vendors or suppliers throughout their careers. Many repairers, particularly in urban areas, need a national certification to advance past entry-level work.

Education and training. A high school diploma or GED is often all that is required to enter this occupation, but more specific education and training is needed to learn how to repair newer automobiles. Collision repair programs may be offered in high school or in postsecondary vocational schools and community colleges. Courses in electronics, physics, chemistry, English, computers, and mathematics provide a good background for a career as an automotive body repairer. Training programs combine classroom instruction and hands-on practice.

Trade and technical school programs typically award certificates to graduates after 6 months to a year of collision repair study. Some community colleges offer 2-year programs in collision repair. Many of these schools also offer certificates for individual courses, so that students are able to take classes incrementally or as needed.

New repairers begin by assisting experienced body repairers in tasks such as removing damaged parts and sanding body panels. Novices learn to remove small dents and make other minor repairs. They then progress to more difficult tasks, such as straightening body parts and installing either repaired or replaced bolt-on parts. Generally, it takes 3 to 4 years of hands-on training to become skilled in all aspects of body repair, some of which may be completed as part of a formal education program. Basic automotive glass installation and repair can be learned in as little as 6 months, but becoming fully qualified can take several years.

Continuing education and training are needed throughout a career in automotive body repair. Automotive parts composition, body materials, electronics, and airbags and other new safety components continue to change and to become more complex. To keep up with these technological advances, repairers must continue to gain new skills by reading technical manuals and furthering their education with classes and seminars. Many companies within the automotive body repair industry

Projections data from the National Employment Matrix

Occupational Title	SOC Code	Employment, 2008	Projected Employment, 2018	Change, 2008-2018	
				Number	Percent
Automotive body and related repairers..	–	185,900	187,000	1,100	1
Automotive body and related repairers..	49-3021	166,400	167,200	800	0
Automotive glass installers and repairers	49-3022	19,500	19,900	400	2

(NOTE) Data in this table are rounded. See the discussion of the employment projections table in the *Handbook* introductory chapter on *Occupational Information Included in the Handbook.*

send employees to advanced training programs to brush up on old skills or to learn new techniques.

Other qualifications. Fully skilled automotive body repairers must have good reading ability and basic mathematics, including geometry, physics, and computer skills. Restoring unibody automobiles to their original specification requires repairers to follow instructions and diagrams in print and digital technical manuals and to make precise three-dimensional measurements of the position of one body section relative to another. In addition, repairers should enjoy working with their hands and be able to pay attention to detail while they work.

Certification and advancement. Certification by the National Institute for Automotive Service Excellence (ASE), although voluntary, is the pervasive industry credential for experienced automotive body repairers. Many repairers, particularly in urban areas, need a national certification to advance past entry-level work. Repairers may take up to four ASE Master Collision Repair and Refinish Exams. Repairers who pass at least one exam and have 2 years of hands-on work experience earn ASE certification. The completion of a postsecondary program in automotive body repair may be substituted for 1 year of work experience. Those who pass all four exams become ASE Master Collision Repair and Refinish Technicians. Automotive body repairers must retake the examination at least every 5 years to retain their certification. Ongoing training through the Inter-Industry Conference on Auto Collision Repair (I-CAR) can lead to additional recognition as a Platinum technician. Finally, many vehicle manufacturers and paint manufacturers also have product certification programs that can advance a repairer's career.

As beginners increase their skills, learn new techniques, earn certifications, and complete work more rapidly, their pay increases. An experienced automotive body repairer with managerial ability may advance to shop supervisor, and some workers open their own body repair shops. Other repairers become automobile damage appraisers for insurance companies.

Employment

Automotive body and related repairers held about 185,900 jobs in 2008; about 10 percent specialized in automotive glass installation and repair. Around 62 percent of repairers worked for automotive repair and maintenance shops, while 17 percent worked for automobile dealers. A small number worked for wholesalers of motor vehicles, parts, and supplies. About 12 percent of automotive body repairers were self-employed.

Job Outlook

Employment is projected to see little or no change. Job opportunities will be excellent for people with formal training in automotive body repair and refinishing as older workers retire and

need to be replaced; those without any training or experience will face competition.

Employment change. Employment of automotive body repairers is expected to grow by 1 percent over the 2008-18 decade. The number of vehicles on the road is expected to continue increasing over the next decade. This will lead to overall growth in the demand for collision repair services. The increasing role of technology in vehicles also will mean new opportunities for workers with expertise or training in repairing particular makes and models of cars or working with specific materials.

However, several factors will limit the number of new jobs for automotive body repairers. The increasingly advanced technology used in vehicles has led to significant increases in the prices of new and replacement parts. Collision repair shop owners, in an effort to stay profitable, have adopted productivity enhancing techniques. The result of this has also been consolidation within the industry, or a decreasing number of collision repair shops and limited total employment growth. In some cases, the use of new technology like airbags has led to more cars that are involved in accidents to be declared a total loss – where repairing a car costs more than the value of the vehicle. High insurance deductibles have meant that an increasing number of cars suffering minor collision damage are going unrepaired.

Job prospects. Although few jobs are expected to arise due to growth, the need to replace experienced repairers who transfer to other occupations or who retire or stop working for other reasons will provide many job openings over the next 10 years. Opportunities will be excellent for people with formal training in automotive body repair and refinishing. Those without any training or experience in automotive body refinishing or collision repair will face competition for these jobs.

Earnings

Median hourly wages of automotive body and related repairers, including incentive pay, were $17.81 in May 2008. The middle 50 percent earned between $13.74 and $23.57 an hour. The lowest 10 percent earned less than $10.75, and the highest 10 percent earned more than $30.17 an hour. Median hourly wages of automotive body and related repairers were $18.95 in automobile dealers and $17.40 in automotive repair and maintenance.

Median hourly wages of automotive glass installers and repairers, including incentive pay, were $15.44 in May 2008. The middle 50 percent earned between $12.40 and $18.88 an hour. The lowest 10 percent earned less than $9.71 and the highest 10 percent earned more than $23.39 an hour. Median hourly wages in automotive repair and maintenance shops, the industry employing most automotive glass installers and repairers, were $15.34.

The majority of body repairers employed by independent repair shops and automotive dealers are paid on an incentive basis. Under this system, body repairers are paid a set amount for various tasks, and earnings depend on both the amount of work assigned and how fast it is completed. Employers frequently guarantee workers a minimum weekly salary. Body repairers who work for trucking companies, buslines, and other organizations that maintain their own vehicles usually receive an hourly wage.

Helpers and trainees typically earn between 30 percent and 60 percent of the earnings of skilled workers. They are paid by the hour until they are skilled enough to be paid on an incentive basis.

Employee benefits vary widely from business to business. However, industry sources report that benefits such as paid leave, health insurance, and retirement assistance are increasingly common in the collision repair industry. Automotive dealerships are the most likely to offer such incentives.

Related Occupations

Other occupations associated with vehicle maintenance and repair includes:

Sources of Additional Information

Additional details about work opportunities may be obtained from automotive body repair shops, automobile dealers, or local offices of your State employment service. State employment service offices also are a source of information about training programs.

For general information about automotive body repairer careers, contact any of the following sources:

➤ Automotive Careers Today, 8400 Westpark Dr., MS #2, McLean, VA 22102. Internet: **http://www.autocareerstoday.org**

➤ Automotive Service Association, P.O. Box 929, Bedford, TX 76095. Internet: **http://www.asashop.org**

➤ Inter-Industry Conference on Auto Collision Repair Education Foundation (I-CAR), 5125 Trillium Blvd., Hoffman Estates, IL 60192. Internet: **http://www.collisioncareers.org**

➤ Society of Collision Repair Specialists, P.O. Box 909 Prosser, WA 99350. Internet: **http://www.scrs.com**

For general information about careers in automotive glass installation and repair, contact:

➤ National Glass Association, 8200 Greensboro Dr., Suite 302, McLean, VA 22102. Internet: **http://www.myglassclass.com**

For information on how to become a certified automotive body repairer, write to:

➤ National Institute for Automotive Service Excellence (ASE), 101 Blue Seal Dr. SE., Suite 101, Leesburg, VA 20175. Internet: **http://www.asecert.org**

For a directory of certified automotive body repairer programs, contact:

➤ National Automotive Technician Education Foundation, 101 Blue Seal Dr. SE., Suite 101, Leesburg, VA 20175. Internet: **http://www.natef.org**

For a directory of accredited private trade and technical schools that offer training programs in automotive body repair, contact:

➤ Accrediting Commission of Career Schools and Colleges, 2101 Wilson Blvd., Suite 302, Arlington, VA 22201. Internet: **http://www.accsc.org**

The Occupational Information Network (O*NET) provides information on a wide range of occupational characteristics. Links to O*NET appear at the end of the Internet version of this occupational statement, accessible at **http://www.bls.gov/ooh/ocos180.htm**

Automotive Service Technicians and Mechanics

Significant Points

- Automotive service technicians and mechanics must continually adapt to changing technology and repair techniques.

- Formal automotive technician training is the best preparation.

- Opportunities should be very good for those who complete postsecondary automotive training programs; those without formal automotive training are likely to face competition for entry-level jobs.

Nature of the Work

Automotive service technicians inspect, maintain, and repair automobiles and light trucks that run on gasoline, electricity, or alternative fuels, such as ethanol. They perform basic care maintenance, such as oil changes and tire rotations, diagnose more complex problems, and plan and execute vehicle repairs. (Service technicians who work on diesel-powered trucks, buses, and equipment are discussed in the *Handbook* section on diesel service technicians and mechanics. Motorcycle technicians—who repair and service motorcycles, motor scooters, mopeds, and small all-terrain vehicles—are discussed in the *Handbook* section on small engine mechanics.)

Automotive service technicians' and mechanics' responsibilities have evolved from simple mechanical repairs to high-level technology-related work. Today, integrated electronic systems and complex computers regulate vehicles and their performance while on the road. This increasing sophistication of automobiles requires workers who can use computerized shop equipment and work with electronic components while maintaining their skills with traditional hand tools. Technicians must have an increasingly broad knowledge of how vehicles' complex components work and interact. They also must be able to work with electronic diagnostic equipment and digital manuals and reference materials.

When mechanical or electrical troubles occur, technicians first get a description of the problem from the owner or, in a large shop, from the repair service estimator or service advisor who wrote the repair order. To locate the problem, technicians use a diagnostic approach. First, they test to see whether components and systems are secure and working properly. Then, they isolate the components or systems that might be the cause of the problem. For example, if an air-conditioner malfunctions, the technician might check for a simple problem, such as a low coolant level, or a more complex issue, such as a bad drive-train connection that has shorted out the air conditioner. As part of their investigation, technicians may test drive the vehicle or use a variety of testing equipment, including onboard and hand-held diagnostic computers or compression gauges. These tests may indicate whether a component is salvageable or whether a new one is required. Accuracy and efficiency are critical in diagnosing and repairing vehicles, as parts are increasingly expensive, and timely repairs allow shops to take on more business.

During routine service inspections, technicians test and lubricate engines and other major components. Sometimes, technicians repair or replace worn parts before they cause breakdowns or damage the vehicle. Technicians usually follow a checklist to ensure that they examine every critical part. Belts, hoses, plugs, brakes, fuel systems, and other potentially troublesome items are watched closely.

Service technicians use a variety of tools in their work. They use power tools, such as pneumatic wrenches, to remove bolts quickly; machine tools like lathes and grinding machines to rebuild brakes; welding and flame-cutting equipment to remove and repair exhaust systems; and jacks and hoists to lift cars and engines. They also use common hand tools, such as screwdrivers, pliers, and wrenches, to work on small parts and in hard-to-reach places. Technicians usually provide their own hand tools, and many experienced workers have thousands of dollars invested in them. Employers furnish expensive power tools, engine analyzers, and other diagnostic equipment.

Computers are also commonplace in modern repair shops. Service technicians compare the readouts from computerized diagnostic testing devices with benchmarked standards given by the manufacturer. Deviations outside of acceptable levels tell the technician to investigate that part of the vehicle more closely. Through the Internet or from software packages, most shops receive automatic updates to technical manuals and access to manufacturers' service information, technical service bulletins, and other databases that allow technicians to keep up with common problems and to learn new procedures.

High technology tools are needed to fix the computer equipment that operates everything from the engine to the radio in many cars. In fact, today, most automotive systems, such as braking, transmission, and steering systems, are controlled primarily by computers and electronic components. Additionally, luxury vehicles often have integrated global positioning systems, accident-avoidance systems, and other new features with which technicians will need to become familiar. Also, as more alternate-fuel vehicles are purchased, more automotive service technicians will need to learn the science behind these automobiles and how to repair them.

Automotive service technicians in large shops often specialize in certain types of repairs. For example, *transmission technicians and rebuilders* work on gear trains, couplings, hydraulic pumps, and other parts of transmissions. Extensive knowledge of computer controls, the ability to diagnose electrical and hydraulic problems, and other specialized skills are needed to work on these complex components, which employ some of the most sophisticated technology used in vehicles. *Tune-up technicians* adjust ignition timing and valves and adjust or replace spark plugs and other parts to ensure efficient engine performance. They often use electronic testing equipment to isolate and adjust malfunctions in fuel, ignition, and emissions control systems.

Automotive air-conditioning repairers install and repair air-conditioners and service their components, such as compressors, condensers, and controls. These workers require special training in Federal and State regulations governing the handling and disposal of refrigerants. *Front-end mechanics* align and balance wheels and repair steering mechanisms and suspension systems. They frequently use special alignment equipment and wheel-balancing machines. *Brake repairers* adjust brakes, replace brake linings and pads, and make other repairs on brake systems. Some technicians specialize in both brake and front-end work.

Work environment. While in 2008, most automotive service technicians worked a standard 40 hour week, 24 percent

Automotive service technicians and mechanics perform routine vehicle maintenance as well as major repairs.

worked longer hours. Some may work evenings and weekends to satisfy customer service needs. Generally, service technicians work indoors in well-ventilated and well-lighted repair shops. However, some shops are drafty and noisy. Although many problems can be fixed with simple computerized adjustments, technicians frequently work with dirty and greasy parts and in awkward positions. They often lift heavy parts and tools. As a result, minor workplace injuries are not uncommon, but technicians usually can avoid serious accidents if safe practices are observed.

Training, Other Qualifications, and Advancement

Automotive technology is rapidly growing in sophistication, and employers are increasingly looking for workers who have completed a formal training program in high school or in a postsecondary vocational school or community college. Acquiring National Institute for Automotive Service Excellence (ASE) certification is important for those seeking work in large, urban areas.

Education and training. Most employers regard the successful completion of a vocational training program in automotive service technology as the best preparation for trainee positions. High school programs, while an asset, vary greatly in scope. Graduates of these programs may need further training to become qualified. Some of the more extensive high school programs participate in Automotive Youth Education Service (AYES), a partnership between high school automotive repair programs, automotive manufacturers, and franchised automotive dealers. All AYES high school programs are certified by the National Institute for Automotive Service Excellence. Students who complete these programs are well prepared to enter entry-level technician positions or to advance their technical education. Courses in automotive repair, electronics, physics, chemistry, English, computers, and mathematics provide a good educational background for a career as a service technician.

Postsecondary automotive technician training programs usually provide intensive career preparation through a combination of classroom instruction and hands-on practice. Schools update their curriculums frequently to reflect changing technology and equipment. Some trade and technical school programs provide concentrated training for 6 months to a year, depending on how many hours the student attends each week, and upon completion, award a certificate. Community college programs usually award a certificate or an associate degree. Some students earn repair certificates in a particular skill and leave to begin their careers. Associate degree programs, however, usually take 2 years to complete and include classes in English, basic mathematics, computers, and other subjects, as well as automotive repair. Recently, some programs have added classes on customer service, stress management, and other employability skills. Some formal training programs have alliances with tool manufacturers that help entry-level technicians accumulate tools during their training period.

Various automobile manufacturers and participating franchised dealers also sponsor 2-year associate degree programs at postsecondary schools across the Nation. Students in these programs typically spend alternate 6-week to 12-week periods attending classes full time and working full time in the service departments of sponsoring dealers. At these dealerships, students work with an experienced worker who provides hands-on instruction and timesaving tips.

Those new to automotive service usually start as trainee technicians, technicians' helpers, or lubrication workers, and gradually acquire and practice their skills by working with experienced mechanics and technicians. In many cases, on-the-job training may be a part of a formal education program. With a few months' experience, beginners perform many routine service tasks and make simple repairs. While some graduates of postsecondary automotive training programs often are able to earn promotion to the journey level after only a few months on the job, it typically takes 2 to 5 years of experience to become a fully qualified service technician, who is expected to quickly perform the more difficult types of routine service and repairs. An additional 1 to 2 years of experience familiarizes technicians with all types of repairs. Complex specialties, such as transmission repair, require another year or two of training and experience. In contrast, brake specialists may learn their jobs in considerably less time because they do not need complete knowledge of automotive repair.

Employers increasingly send experienced automotive service technicians to manufacturer training centers to learn to repair new models or to receive special training in the repair of components, such as electronic fuel injection or air-conditioners. Motor vehicle dealers and other automotive service providers may send promising beginners or experienced technicians to manufacturer-sponsored technician training programs to upgrade or maintain employees' skills. Factory representatives also visit many shops to conduct short training sessions.

Other qualifications. The ability to diagnose the source of a problem quickly and accurately requires good reasoning ability and a thorough knowledge of automobiles. Many technicians consider diagnosing hard-to-find troubles one of their most challenging and satisfying duties. For trainee automotive service technician jobs, employers look for people with strong communication and analytical skills. Technicians need good reading, mathematics, and computer skills to study technical manuals. They must also read to keep up with new technology and learn new service and repair procedures and specifications.

Training in electronics is vital because electrical components, or a series of related components, account for nearly all malfunctions in modern vehicles. Trainees must possess mechanical aptitude and knowledge of how automobiles work. Experience working on motor vehicles in the Armed Forces or as a hobby can be very valuable.

Certification and advancement. ASE certification has become a standard credential for automotive service technicians. While not mandatory for work in automotive service, certification is common for all experienced technicians in large, urban areas. Certification is available in eight different areas of automotive service, such as electrical systems, engine repair, brake systems, suspension and steering, and heating and air-conditioning. For certification in each area, technicians must have at least 2 years of experience and pass the examination. Completion of an automotive training program in high school, vocational or trade school, or community or junior college may be substituted for 1 year of experience. For ASE certification as a Master Automobile Technician, technicians must pass all eight examinations.

Projections data from the National Employment Matrix

Occupational Title	SOC Code	Employment, 2008	Projected Employment, 2018	Change, 2008-2018	
				Number	Percent
Automotive service technicians and mechanics..............................	49-3023	763,700	799,600	35,900	5

(NOTE) Data in this table are rounded. See the discussion of the employment projections table in the *Handbook* introductory chapter on *Occupational Information Included in the Handbook.*

By becoming skilled in multiple auto repair services, technicians can increase their value to their employer and their pay. Experienced technicians who have administrative ability sometimes advance to shop supervisor or service manager. Those with sufficient funds many times open independent automotive repair shops. Technicians who work well with customers may become automotive repair service estimators. They may also find work as educators.

Employment

Automotive service technicians and mechanics held about 763,700 jobs in 2008. Automotive repair and maintenance shops and automobile dealers employed the majority of these workers, with 31 percent working in shops and 28 percent employed by dealers. In addition, automotive parts, accessories, and tire stores employed 7 percent of automotive service technicians. Others worked in gasoline stations; automotive equipment rental and leasing companies; Federal, State, and local governments; and other organizations. About 16 percent of service technicians were self-employed, compared with 7 percent of all installation, maintenance, and repair occupations.

Job Outlook

The number of jobs for automotive service technicians and mechanics is projected to grow slower than the average for all occupations, although many job openings will arise as experienced technicians retire. Opportunities should be good for those who complete postsecondary automotive training programs, as some employers report difficulty finding workers with the right skills; those without formal automotive training are likely to face competition for entry-level jobs.

Employment change. Employment of automotive service technicians and mechanics is expected to increase by 5 percent between 2008 and 2018, slower than the average for all occupations. Continued growth in the number of vehicles in use in the United States will lead to new jobs for workers performing basic car maintenance and repair. More entry-level workers will be needed to perform these services, such as oil changes and replacing worn brakes. Additionally, the average lifespan of vehicles is increasing, which will further increase the demand for repair services, especially post-warranty work. The increasing use of advanced technology in automobiles will also lead to new opportunities for repair technicians, especially those with specialized skills or certifications. Workers with expertise in certain makes or models of vehicles, or with an advanced understanding of certain systems, such as hybrid-fuel technology, will be in demand. At the same time, consolidation in the automobile dealer industry, a significant employer of technicians, will limit the need for new workers.

Job prospects. In addition to openings from growth, many job openings will be created by the need to replace retiring technicians. Job opportunities are expected to be very good for those who complete postsecondary automotive training programs and who earn ASE certification. Some employers report difficulty in finding workers with the right skills. People with good diagnostic and problem-solving abilities, training in electronics, and computer skills are expected to have the best opportunities. Those without formal automotive training are likely to face competition for entry-level jobs.

Most new job openings will be in automobile dealerships and independent repair shops where most automobile service technicians currently work. However, the large-scale restructuring and closing of many automobile dealerships will lead to fewer openings in dealer service centers for the initial part of the next decade.

Earnings

Median hourly wages of automotive service technicians and mechanics, including commission, were $16.88 in May 2008. The middle 50 percent earned between $12.44 and $22.64 per hour. The lowest 10 percent earned less than $9.56, and the highest 10 percent earned more than $28.71 per hour. Median annual wages in the industries employing the largest numbers of service technicians were as follows:

Local government...$20.07
Automobile dealers 19.61
Automotive repair and maintenance 15.26
Gasoline stations 15.22
Automotive parts, accessories, and tire stores...............14.90

Many experienced technicians employed by automobile dealers and independent repair shops receive a commission related to the labor cost charged to the customer. Under this system, weekly earnings depend on the amount of work completed. Employers frequently guarantee commissioned technicians a minimum weekly salary. Some employees offer health and retirement benefits, but such compensation packages are not universal and can vary widely.

Related Occupations

Other workers who repair and service motor vehicles include:

Page
Automotive body and related repairers 687
Diesel service technicians and mechanics 694
Heavy vehicle and mobile equipment service
  technicians and mechanics 697
Small engine mechanics...700

Sources of Additional Information

For more details about work opportunities, contact local automobile dealers and repair shops or local offices of the State employment service. The State employment service also may have information about training programs.

For general information about a career as an automotive service technician, contact:

➤ Automotive Careers Today, 8400 Westpark Dr., MS #2, McLean, VA 22102. Internet: **http://www.autocareerstoday.org**

➤ Career Voyages, U.S. Department of Labor, 200 Constitution Ave., NW., Washington, DC 20210. Internet: **http://www.careervoyages.gov/automotive-main.cfm**

A list of certified automotive service technician training programs can be obtained from:

➤ National Automotive Technicians Education Foundation, 101 Blue Seal Dr. SE., Suite 101, Leesburg, VA 20175. Internet: **http://www.natef.org**

For a directory of accredited private trade and technical schools that offer programs in automotive service technician training, contact:

➤ Accrediting Commission of Career Schools and Colleges, 2101 Wilson Blvd., Suite 302, Arlington, VA 22201. Internet: **http://www.accsc.org**

Information on automobile manufacturer-sponsored programs in automotive service technology can be obtained from:

➤ Automotive Youth Educational Systems (AYES), 101 Blue Seal Dr. SE, Suite 101, Leesburg, VA, 20175. Internet: **http://www.ayes.org**

Information on how to become a certified automotive service technician is available from:

➤ National Institute for Automotive Service Excellence (ASE), 101 Blue Seal Dr. SE., Suite 101, Leesburg, VA 20175. Internet: **http://www.asecert.org**

The Occupational Information Network (O*NET) provides information on a wide range of occupational characteristics. Links to O*NET appear at the end of the Internet version of this occupational statement, accessible at **http://www.bls.gov/ooh/ocos181.htm**

Diesel Service Technicians and Mechanics

Significant Points

- In addition to high school course offerings in automotive repair and electronics, programs in diesel engine repair are offered by many community colleges and trade and technical schools.

- Opportunities are expected to be very good for people who complete formal training programs; applicants without formal training will face competition for jobs.

- National certification, the recognized standard of achievement, enhances a diesel service technician's advancement opportunities.

Nature of the Work

Diesel-powered engines are more efficient and durable than their gasoline-burning counterparts. These powerful engines are standard in our Nation's trucks, locomotives, and buses and are becoming more prevalent in light vehicles, including passenger vehicles, pickups, and other work trucks.

Diesel service technicians and mechanics, including *bus and truck mechanics* and *diesel engine specialists*, repair and maintain the diesel engines that power transportation equipment. Other diesel technicians and mechanics work on other heavy vehicles and mobile equipment, including bulldozers, cranes, road graders, farm tractors, and combines. Others repair diesel-powered passenger automobiles, light trucks, or boats. (For information on technicians and mechanics working primarily on gasoline-powered automobiles, heavy vehicles and mobile equipment, or boat engines, see the *Handbook* sections on automotive service technicians, heavy vehicle and mobile equipment service technicians and mechanics, and small engine mechanics.)

Increasingly, diesel technicians must be versatile enough to adapt to customers' needs and to new technologies. It is common for technicians to handle all kinds of repairs, working on a vehicle's electrical system one day and doing major engine repairs the next. Diesel maintenance is becoming increasingly complex, as more electronic components are used to control the operation of an engine. For example, microprocessors now regulate and manage fuel injection and engine timing, increasing the engine's efficiency. Also, new emissions standards may require mechanics to retrofit engines with emissions control systems, such as emission filters and catalysts, to comply with pollution regulations. In modern shops, diesel service technicians use hand-held or laptop computers to diagnose problems and adjust engine functions.

Technicians who work for organizations that maintain their own vehicles spend most of their time doing preventive maintenance. During a routine maintenance check, technicians follow a checklist that includes inspecting brake systems, steering mechanisms, wheel bearings, and other important parts. Following inspection, technicians repair or adjust parts that do not work properly or remove and replace parts that cannot be fixed.

Diesel service technicians and mechanics repair large trucks to keep them running smoothly.

Diesel service technicians use a variety of tools in their work, including power tools, such as pneumatic wrenches that remove bolts quickly; machine tools, such as lathes and grinding machines to rebuild brakes; welding and flame-cutting equipment to remove and repair exhaust systems; and jacks and hoists to lift and move large parts. Common hand tools—screwdrivers, pliers, and wrenches—are used to work on small parts and get at hard-to-reach places. Diesel service technicians and mechanics also use a variety of computerized testing equipment to pinpoint and analyze malfunctions in electrical systems and engines. Employers typically furnish expensive power tools, computerized engine analyzers, and other diagnostic equipment, but workers usually accumulate their own hand tools over time.

Work environment. Technicians normally work in well-lighted and ventilated areas. However, some shops are drafty and noisy. Many employers provide lockers and shower facilities. Diesel technicians usually work indoors, although they occasionally repair vehicles on the road or at the jobsite. Diesel technicians may lift heavy parts and tools, handle greasy and dirty parts, and stand or lie in awkward positions while making repairs. Minor cuts, burns, and bruises are common, although serious accidents can usually be avoided when safety procedures are followed. Technicians may work as a team or be assisted by an apprentice or helper when doing heavy work, such as removing engines and transmissions.

Most service technicians work a standard 40-hour week, although some work longer hours, particularly if they are self-employed. A growing number of shops have expanded their hours to speed repairs and offer more convenience to customers. Some truck and bus firms provide maintenance and repair service around the clock and on weekends.

Training, Other Qualifications, and Advancement

Employers prefer to hire graduates of formal training programs because those workers are able to advance quickly to the journey level of diesel service. Other workers who learn diesel engine repair through on-the-job training need 3 to 4 years of experience before becoming journey-level technicians.

Education and training. High school courses in automotive repair, electronics, English, mathematics, and physics provide a strong educational background for a career as a diesel service technician or mechanic. Many mechanics have additional training after high school.

A large number of community colleges and trade and vocational schools offer programs in diesel engine repair. These programs usually last from 6 months to 2 years and may lead to a certificate of completion or an associate degree. Some offer about 30 hours per week of hands-on training with equipment; others offer more lab or classroom instruction. Formal training provides a foundation in the latest diesel technology and

instruction in the service and repair of the equipment that technicians will encounter on the job. Training programs also teach technicians to interpret technical manuals and to communicate well with co-workers and customers. Increasingly, employers work closely with representatives of educational programs, providing instructors with the latest equipment, techniques, and tools and offering jobs to graduates.

Although formal training programs lead to the best prospects, some technicians and mechanics learn through on-the-job training. Unskilled beginners generally are assigned tasks such as cleaning parts, fueling and lubricating vehicles, and driving vehicles into and out of the shop. Beginners are usually promoted to trainee positions as they gain experience and as vacancies become available.

After a few months' experience, most trainees can perform routine service tasks and make minor repairs. These workers advance to increasingly difficult jobs as they improve their ability and competence. After technicians master the repair and service of diesel engines, they learn to work on related components, such as brakes, transmissions, and electrical systems. Generally, technicians with at least 3 to 4 years of on-the-job experience will qualify as journey-level diesel technicians.

Employers often send experienced technicians and mechanics to special training classes conducted by manufacturers and vendors, in which workers learn about the latest technology and repair techniques.

Other qualifications. Employers usually look for applicants who have mechanical aptitude and strong problem-solving skills and who are at least 18 years old and in good physical condition. Technicians need a State commercial driver's license to test-drive trucks or buses on public roads. Many companies also require applicants to pass a drug test. Practical experience in automobile repair at an automotive service station, in the Armed Forces, or as a hobby is valuable as well.

Certification and advancement. Experienced diesel service technicians and mechanics with leadership ability may advance to shop supervisor or service manager, and some open their own repair shops. Technicians and mechanics with sales ability sometimes become sales representatives.

Although national certification is not required for employment, many diesel engine technicians and mechanics find that it increases their ability to advance. Certification by the National Institute for Automotive Service Excellence (ASE) is the recognized industry credential for diesel and other automotive service technicians and mechanics. Diesel service technicians may be certified in specific areas of truck repair, such as drivetrains, brakes, suspension and steering, electrical and electronic systems, or preventive maintenance and inspection. For certification in each area, a technician must pass one or more of the ASE-administered exams and present proof of 2 years of relevant work experience. To become what's known as a master

Projections data from the National Employment Matrix

Occupational Title	SOC Code	Employment, 2008	Projected Employment, 2018	Change, 2008-2018	
				Number	Percent
Bus and truck mechanics and diesel engine specialists	49-3031	263,100	278,000	14,900	6

(NOTE) Data in this table are rounded. See the discussion of the employment projections table in the *Handbook* introductory chapter on *Occupational Information Included in the Handbook.*

technician, all the tests in a given series must be passed. To remain certified, technicians must be retested every 5 years.

Employment
Diesel service technicians and mechanics held about 263,100 jobs in 2008. These workers were employed in almost every industry, particularly those that use trucks, buses, and equipment to haul, deliver, and transport materials, goods, and people. The largest employer, the truck transportation industry, employed about 17 percent of diesel service technicians and mechanics. About 8 percent were employed by automotive repair and maintenance facilities. The rest were employed throughout the economy, including construction, manufacturing, retail and wholesale trade, and automotive leasing. About 6 percent were self-employed. Nearly every area of the country employs diesel service technicians and mechanics, although most work is found in towns and cities where trucking companies, bus lines, and other fleet owners have large operations.

Job Outlook
The number of jobs for diesel service technicians and mechanics is projected to grow slower than the average for all occupations. Opportunities should be very good for people who complete formal training in diesel mechanics; applicants without formal training will face competition for jobs.

Employment change. Employment of diesel service technicians and mechanics is expected to grow by 6 percent from 2008 to 2018, slower than the average for all occupations. The diesel engine, because of its durability and fuel efficiency, is the preferred engine for heavy-duty trucks, buses, and other large vehicles. As more freight is shipped across the country, additional trucks, and corresponding truck repairers, will be needed. Despite this trend, the increasing durability of new vehicles will limit the need for additional workers. Most new jobs will continue to be in the freight trucking and automotive repair and maintenance industries. Beyond the growth in the number of vehicles that need to be serviced, there will be additional demand for diesel engines mechanics to retrofit and modernize existing vehicles to comply with environmental regulations.

Due to higher fuel efficiency requirements for automakers, diesel engines are expected to be used in a small but increasing number of cars and light trucks. This will create additional jobs for diesel service technicians, specifically in the automotive repair and maintenance and automobile dealer industries.

Job prospects. People who enter diesel engine repair will find favorable opportunities, especially as the need to replace workers who retire increases over the next decade. Opportunities should be very good for people with strong technical skills and who complete formal training in diesel mechanics at community colleges or vocational schools. Applicants without formal training will face competition for jobs.

Earnings
Median hourly wages of bus and truck mechanics and diesel engine specialists, including incentive pay, were $18.94 in May 2008. The middle 50 percent earned between $15.25 and $23.58 an hour. The lowest 10 percent earned less than $12.50, and the highest 10 percent earned more than $28.41 an hour. Median hourly wages in the industries employing the largest numbers of bus and truck mechanics and diesel engine specialists in May 2008 were as follows:

Automotive equipment rental and leasing	$19.27
Motor vehicle and motor vehicle parts and supplies merchant wholesalers	19.04
General freight trucking	18.00
Automotive repair and maintenance	17.83
Specialized freight trucking	16.99

Because many experienced technicians employed by truck fleet dealers and independent repair shops receive a commission related to the labor cost charged to the customer, weekly earnings depend on the amount of work completed. Beginners usually earn from 50 to 75 percent of the rate of skilled workers and receive increases as they become more skilled.

About 23 percent of diesel service technicians and mechanics are members of labor unions, including the International Association of Machinists and Aerospace Workers; the Amalgamated Transit Union; the International Union, United Automobile, Aerospace and Agricultural Implement Workers of America; the Transport Workers Union of America; the Sheet Metal Workers' International Association; and the International Brotherhood of Teamsters. Labor unions may provide additional benefits for their members.

Related Occupations
Diesel service technicians and mechanics repair trucks, buses, and other diesel-powered equipment. Related technician and mechanic occupations include:

	Page
Aircraft and avionics equipment mechanics and service technicians	684
Automotive body and related repairers	687
Automotive service technicians and mechanics	690
Heavy vehicle and mobile equipment service technicians and mechanics	697
Small engine mechanics	700

Sources of Additional Information
More details about work opportunities for diesel service technicians and mechanics may be obtained from local employers such as trucking companies, truck dealers, or bus lines; locals of the unions previously mentioned; and local offices of your State employment service. Local State employment service offices also may have information about training programs. State boards of postsecondary career schools have information on licensed schools with training programs for diesel service technicians and mechanics.

General information about a career as a diesel service technician or mechanic is available from:

➤ Association of Diesel Specialists, 400 Admiral Blvd., Kansas City, MO 64106. Internet: **http://www.diesel.org**

Information on how to become a certified diesel technician of medium to heavy-duty vehicles or a certified bus technician is available from:

➤ National Institute for Automotive Service Excellence (ASE), 101 Blue Seal Dr. SE., Suite 101, Leesburg, VA 20175. Internet: **http://www.asecert.org**

For a directory of accredited private trade and technical schools with training programs for diesel service technicians and mechanics, contact:

➤ Accrediting Commission of Career Schools and Colleges, 2101 Wilson Blvd., Suite 302, Arlington, VA 22201. Internet: **http://www.accsc.org**

➤ National Automotive Technicians Education Foundation, 101 Blue Seal Dr. SE., Suite 101, Leesburg, VA 20175. Internet: **http://www.natef.org**

The Occupational Information Network (O*NET) provides information on a wide range of occupational characteristics. Links to O*NET appear at the end of the Internet version of this occupational statement, accessible at **http://www.bls.gov/ooh/ocos182.htm**

Heavy Vehicle and Mobile Equipment Service Technicians and Mechanics

Significant Points

- Opportunities should be excellent for people with formal postsecondary training in heavy equipment repair; those without formal training will face competition.

- Generally, a service technician with at least 3 to 4 years of on-the-job experience is accepted as fully qualified.

- Wages for mobile heavy equipment mechanics are higher than the average for all installation, maintenance, and repair workers.

Nature of the Work

Heavy vehicles and mobile equipment are indispensable to many industrial activities, from construction to railroad transportation. Various types of equipment move materials, till land, lift beams, and dig earth to pave the way for development and production.

Heavy vehicle and mobile equipment service technicians and mechanics often work on hydraulic equipment, performing needed repairs.

Heavy vehicle and mobile equipment service technicians and mechanics repair and maintain engines and hydraulic, transmission, and electrical systems for this equipment. Farm machinery, cranes, bulldozers, and railcars are all examples of heavy vehicles that require such service. (For information on service technicians specializing in diesel engines, see the section on diesel service technicians and mechanics elsewhere in the *Handbook*.)

Service technicians perform routine maintenance checks on agricultural, industrial, construction, and rail equipment. They service fuel, brake, and transmission systems to ensure peak performance, safety, and longevity of the equipment. Maintenance checks and comments from equipment operators usually alert technicians to problems. After locating the problem, these technicians rely on their training and experience to use the best possible technique to solve it.

With many types of modern equipment, technicians can use diagnostic computers to diagnose components needing adjustment or repair. If necessary, they may partially dismantle affected components to examine parts for damage or excessive wear. Then, using hand-held tools, they repair, replace, clean, and lubricate parts as necessary. In some cases, technicians re-calibrate systems by typing codes into the onboard computer. After reassembling the component and testing it for safety, they put it back into the equipment and return the equipment to the field.

Many types of heavy and mobile equipment use hydraulic systems to raise and lower movable parts. When hydraulic components malfunction, technicians examine them for fluid leaks, ruptured hoses, or worn gaskets on fluid reservoirs. Occasionally, the equipment requires extensive repairs, as when a defective hydraulic pump needs replacing.

Service technicians diagnose electrical problems and adjust or replace defective components. They also disassemble and repair undercarriages and track assemblies. Occasionally, technicians weld broken equipment frames and structural parts, using electric or gas welders.

Technicians use a variety of tools in their work: power tools, such as pneumatic wrenches to remove bolts quickly, machine tools, like lathes and grinding machines, to rebuild brakes, welding and flame-cutting equipment to remove and repair exhaust systems, and jacks and hoists to lift and move large parts. Service technicians also use common hand tools—screwdrivers, pliers, and wrenches—to work on small parts and to get at hard-to-reach places. They may use a variety of computerized testing equipment to pinpoint and analyze malfunctions in electrical systems and other essential systems. Tachometers and dynamometers, for example, can be used to locate engine malfunctions. Service technicians also use ohmmeters, ammeters, and voltmeters when working on electrical systems. Employers typically furnish expensive power tools, computerized engine analyzers, and other diagnostic equipment, but hand tools are normally accumulated with experience, and many experienced technicians have thousands of dollars invested in them.

It is common for technicians in large shops to specialize in one or two types of repair. For example, a shop may have individual specialists in major engine repair, transmission work, electrical systems, and suspension or brake systems. Technicians in smaller shops, on the other hand, generally perform multiple functions.

Technicians also specialize in types of equipment. *Mobile heavy equipment mechanics and service technicians,* for example, keep construction and surface mining equipment, such as bulldozers, cranes, graders, and excavators in working order. Typically, these workers are employed by equipment wholesale distribution and leasing firms, large construction and mining companies, local and Federal governments, and other organizations operating and maintaining heavy machinery and equipment fleets. Service technicians employed by the Federal Government may work on tanks and other armored military equipment.

Farm equipment mechanics service, maintain, and repair farm equipment, as well as smaller lawn and garden tractors sold to homeowners. What once was a general repairer's job around the farm has evolved into a specialized technical career. Farmers have increasingly turned to farm equipment dealers to service and repair their equipment because the machinery has grown in complexity. Modern equipment uses more computers, electronics, and hydraulics, making it difficult to perform repairs without specialized training and tools.

Railcar repairers specialize in servicing railroad locomotives and other rolling stock, streetcars and subway cars, or mine cars. Most railcar repairers work for railroads, public and private transit companies, and railcar manufacturers.

Work environment. Heavy vehicle and mobile equipment service technicians usually work indoors. To repair vehicles and equipment, technicians often lift heavy parts and tools, handle greasy and dirty parts, and stand or lie in awkward positions. Minor cuts, burns, and bruises are common. However, serious accidents normally can be avoided as long as safety practices are observed. Although some shops are drafty and noisy, technicians usually work in well-lighted and ventilated areas. Many employers provide uniforms, locker rooms, and shower facilities. Mobile heavy equipment mechanics and railcar repairers generally work a standard 40-hour week.

When heavy or mobile equipment breaks down at a construction site, it may be too difficult or expensive to bring into a repair shop, so the shop will send a field service technician to the site to make repairs. Field service technicians work outdoors and spend much of their time away from the shop. Generally, more experienced service technicians specialize in field service. They drive trucks specially equipped with replacement parts and tools. On occasion, they must travel many miles to reach disabled machinery.

The hours of work for farm equipment mechanics vary according to the season of the year. During the busy planting and harvesting seasons, farm equipment mechanics often work 6 or 7 days a week, 10 to 12 hours daily. In slow winter months, however, they may work fewer than 40 hours a week.

Training, Other Qualifications, and Advancement

Although industry experts recommend that applicants complete a formal diesel or heavy equipment mechanic training program after graduating from high school, many people qualify for service technician jobs by training on the job. Employers seek people with mechanical aptitude who are knowledgeable about diesel engines, transmissions, electrical systems, computers, and hydraulics.

Education and training. High school courses in automobile repair, physics, chemistry, and mathematics provide a strong foundation for a career as a service technician or mechanic. After high school, those interested in heavy vehicle repair can choose to attend community colleges or vocational schools that offer programs in diesel technology. Some of these schools tailor programs to heavy equipment mechanics. These programs teach the basics of analytical and diagnostic techniques, electronics, and hydraulics. The increased use of electronics and computers makes training in electronics essential for new heavy and mobile equipment mechanics. Some 1-year to 2-year programs lead to a certificate of completion, while others lead to an associate degree in diesel or heavy equipment mechanics. Formal training programs enable trainee technicians to advance to the journey, or experienced worker, level sooner than with informal ones.

Entry-level workers with no formal background in heavy vehicle repair begin to perform routine service tasks and make minor repairs after a few months of on-the-job training. As they prove their ability and competence, workers advance to harder jobs. Generally, a service technician with at least 3 to 4 years of on-the-job experience is accepted as fully qualified.

Many employers send trainee technicians to training sessions conducted by heavy equipment manufacturers. The sessions, which typically last up to 1 week, provide intensive instruction in the repair of the manufacturer's equipment. Some sessions focus on particular components found in the equipment, such as diesel engines, transmissions, axles, or electrical systems. Other sessions focus on particular types of equipment, such as crawler-loaders and crawler-dozers. When appropriate, experienced technicians attend training sessions to gain familiarity with new technology or equipment.

Other qualifications. Technicians must read and interpret service manuals, so reading ability and communication skills are both important. The technology used in heavy equipment is becoming more sophisticated, and technicians should feel comfortable with computers and electronics because hand-held diagnostic computers are often used to make engine adjustments and diagnose problems. Experience in the Armed Forces working on diesel engines and heavy equipment provides valuable background for these positions.

Certification and advancement. There is no one certification that is recognized throughout the various industries that employ heavy vehicle mobile equipment service technicians. Rather, graduation or completion of an accredited postsecondary program in heavy vehicle repair is seen as the best credential for employees to have. Manufacturers also offer certificates in specific repairs or working with particular equipment. Such credentials allow employees to take on more responsibilities and advance faster.

Experienced technicians may advance to field service jobs, where they have a greater opportunity to tackle problems independently and earn additional pay. Field positions may require a commercial driver's license and a clean driving record. Technicians with administrative ability may become shop supervisors or service managers. Some technicians open their own repair shops or invest in a franchise.

Projections data from the National Employment Matrix

Occupational Title	SOC Code	Employment, 2008	Projected Employment, 2018	Change, 2008-2018	
				Number	Percent
Heavy vehicle and mobile equipment service technicians and mechanics..	49-3040	190,700	206,100	15,500	8
Farm equipment mechanics	49-3041	31,200	33,400	2,100	7
Mobile heavy equipment mechanics, except engines	49-3042	136,300	148,100	11,800	9
Rail car repairers	49-3043	23,100	24,600	1,500	7

(NOTE) Data in this table are rounded. See the discussion of the employment projections table in the *Handbook* introductory chapter on *Occupational Information Included in the Handbook.*

Employment

Heavy vehicle and mobile equipment service technicians and mechanics held about 190,700 jobs in 2008. Approximately 136,300 were mobile heavy equipment mechanics, 31,200 were farm equipment mechanics, and 23,100 were railcar repairers.

About 29 percent were employed by machinery, equipment, and supplies merchant wholesalers. About 13 percent worked in construction, primarily for specialty trade contractors and highway, street, and bridge construction companies; another 11 percent were employed by Federal, State, and local governments. Other service technicians worked in mining; rail transportation; and commercial and industrial machinery and equipment rental, leasing, and repair. A small number repaired equipment for machinery and railroad rolling stock manufacturers. About 6 percent of service technicians were self-employed.

Nearly every area of the country employs heavy and mobile equipment service technicians and mechanics, although most work in towns and cities where equipment dealers, equipment rental and leasing companies, and construction companies have repair facilities.

Job Outlook

The number of heavy vehicle and mobile equipment service technicians and mechanics is expected to grow about as fast as the average for all occupations. Those who have completed postsecondary training programs should find excellent opportunities, as employers report difficulty finding candidates with this training to fill available positions. Those without a formal background in diesel engine or heavy vehicle repair will face competition.

Employment change. Employment of heavy vehicle and mobile equipment service technicians and mechanics is expected to grow by 8 percent through the year 2018, about as fast as the average for all occupations. Demand will be driven primarily by growth in the use of heavy equipment in the construction industry, although growth will be slower in this industry than in recent years. In addition, the increasing sophistication of the technology used in heavy vehicles and mechanics should lead to greater demand for technicians and mechanics with specialized skills.

Growth in other industries that use heavy equipment, such as energy exploration and mining, will also contribute to the need for new workers. The need to feed a growing population, and the increased use of agriculture products to make biofuels, will lead to additional farm mechanic jobs, while the continued expansion of railways for freight shipping and transportation will lead to new openings for railcar repairers. Many new mobile heavy equipment and farm equipment mechanic positions are expected be in firms that sell, rent, or lease such machines, as their repair services make up an important part of their business. Employment of mobile heavy equipment mechanics is expected to grow by 9 percent from 2008-18, while jobs for farm equipment mechanics and rail car repairers are expected to increase by 7 percent.

Job prospects. Opportunities for heavy vehicle and mobile equipment service technicians and mechanics should be excellent for those who have completed formal training programs in diesel or heavy equipment mechanics. Employers report difficulty finding candidates with formal postsecondary training to fill available service technician positions. People without formal training are expected to encounter growing difficulty entering these jobs. Most job openings for mobile, rail, and farm equipment technicians will arise from the need to replace experienced repairers who retire or change occupations.

Construction and mining operations, which use large numbers of heavy vehicles and mobile equipment, are particularly sensitive to changes in the level of economic activity. While the increased use of such equipment increases the need for periodic service and repair, heavy and mobile equipment may be idle during downturns. As a result, opportunities for service technicians who work on construction and mining equipment may fluctuate with the cyclical nature of these industries. In addition, opportunities for farm equipment mechanics are seasonal and are best in warmer months.

Earnings

Median hourly wages of mobile heavy equipment mechanics were $20.59 in May 2008, higher than the $18.60 per hour median for all installation, maintenance, and repair occupations. The middle 50 percent earned between $16.71 and $24.85. The lowest 10 percent earned less than $13.61, and the highest 10 percent earned more than $30.57. Median hourly wages in the industries employing the largest numbers of mobile heavy equipment mechanics were as follows:

Local government..$21.93
Machinery, equipment, and supplies
    merchant wholesalers 20.49
Other specialty trade contractors....................................19.83
Commercial and industrial machinery and
    equipment rental and leasing.....................................19.39
Commercial and industrial machinery and
    equipment (except automotive and electronic)
    repair and maintenance..18.93

Median hourly wages of farm equipment mechanics were $15.32 in May 2008. The middle 50 percent earned between $12.54 and $18.61. The lowest 10 percent earned less than $10.28, and the highest 10 percent earned more than $22.37. In machinery, equipment, and supplies merchant wholesalers, the industry employing the largest number of farm equipment mechanics, median wages were $15.64.

Median hourly wages of railcar repairers were $21.48 in May 2008. The middle 50 percent earned between $16.83 and $25.84. The lowest 10 percent earned less than $13.49, and the highest 10 percent earned more than $30.23. Median hourly wages were $23.82 in rail transportation, the industry employing the largest number of railcar repairers.

About 23 percent of heavy vehicle and mobile equipment service technicians and mechanics are members of unions, including the International Association of Machinists and Aerospace Workers, the International Union of Operating Engineers, and the International Brotherhood of Teamsters. Members may enjoy job benefits in addition to what employers provide.

Related Occupations

Workers in related repair occupations include:

Sources of Additional Information

More details about job openings for heavy vehicle and mobile equipment service technicians and mechanics may be obtained from local heavy and mobile equipment dealers and distributors, construction contractors, and government agencies. Local offices of the State employment service also may have information on job openings and training programs.

For general information about a career as a heavy vehicle and mobile equipment service technician or mechanic, contact:
➤ Associated Equipment Distributors, 615 W. 22nd St., Oak Brook, IL 60523. Internet: **http://www.aedcareers.com**

A list of certified diesel service technician training programs can be obtained from:
➤ National Automotive Technician Education Foundation (NATEF), 101 Blue Seal Dr. SE., Suite 101, Leesburg, VA 20175. Internet: **http://www.natef.org**

Information on certification as a heavy-duty diesel service technician is available from:
➤ National Institute for Automotive Service Excellence (ASE), 101 Blue Seal Dr. SE., Suite 101, Leesburg, VA 20175. Internet: **http://www.asecert.org**

The Occupational Information Network (O*NET) provides information on a wide range of occupational characteristics. Links to O*NET appear at the end of the Internet version of this occupational statement, accessible at **http://www.bls.gov/ooh/ocos197.htm**

Small Engine Mechanics

Significant Points

- Job prospects should be excellent for people who complete formal training programs.
- Average job growth is expected.
- Use of motorcycles, motorboats, and outdoor power equipment is seasonal in many areas, so mechanics may service other types of equipment or work reduced hours in the winter.

Nature of the Work

Small engine mechanics repair and service power equipment ranging from jet skis to chainsaws. Mechanics usually specialize in the service and repair of one type of equipment, such as motorcycles, motorboats, and outdoor power equipment, although they may work on closely related products.

When a piece of equipment breaks down, mechanics use various techniques to diagnose the source and extent of the problem. The mark of a skilled mechanic is the ability to diagnose mechanical, fuel, and electrical problems and to make repairs quickly. Quick and accurate diagnosis requires problem-solving ability and a thorough knowledge of the equipment's operation.

Some jobs require minor adjustments or the replacement of a single item, but a complete engine overhaul could require hours to disassemble the engine and replace worn valves, pistons, bearings, and other internal parts. Some highly skilled mechanics use specialized components and the latest computerized equipment to customize and tune motorcycles and motorboats for racing.

Hand tools are the most important work-related possessions of mechanics. Small engine mechanics use wrenches, pliers, and screwdrivers on a regular basis. Mechanics usually provide their own tools, although employers will furnish expensive power tools, computerized engine analyzers, and other diagnostic equipment. Computerized engine analyzers, compression gauges, ammeters and voltmeters, and other testing devices help mechanics locate faulty parts and tune engines. This equipment provides a systematic performance report of

Motorcycle mechanics use hand tools to make needed adjustments and repairs.

various components to compare against normal ratings. After pinpointing the problem, the mechanic makes the needed adjustments, repairs, or replacements.

Small engines also require periodic service to minimize the chance of breakdowns and to keep them operating at peak performance. During routine maintenance, mechanics follow a checklist that includes the inspection and cleaning of brakes, electrical systems, fuel injection systems, plugs, carburetors, and other parts. Following inspection, mechanics usually repair or adjust parts that do not work properly or replace unfixable parts.

Motorcycle mechanics specialize in the repair and overhaul of motorcycles, motor scooters, mopeds, dirt bikes, and all-terrain vehicles. Besides repairing engines, they may work on transmissions, brakes, and ignition systems and make minor body repairs. Mechanics often service just a few makes and models of motorcycles because most work for dealers that service only the products they sell.

Motorboat mechanics and *marine equipment mechanics* repair and adjust the electrical and mechanical equipment of inboard and outboard boat engines. Most small boats have portable outboard engines that are removed and brought into the repair shop. Larger craft, such as cabin cruisers and commercial fishing boats, are powered by diesel or gasoline inboard or inboard-outboard engines, which are removed only for major overhauls. Most of these repairs, therefore, are performed at docks or marinas. Motorboat mechanics also may work on propellers, steering mechanisms, marine plumbing, and other boat equipment.

Outdoor power equipment and other small engine mechanics service and repair outdoor power equipment such as lawnmowers, garden tractors, edge trimmers, and chain saws. They also may occasionally work on portable generators and go-carts. In addition, small engine mechanics in certain parts of the country may work on snowblowers and snowmobiles, but demand for this type of repair is both seasonal and regional.

Work environment. Small engine mechanics usually work in repair shops that are well lighted and ventilated but are sometimes noisy when engines are tested. Motorboat mechanics may work outdoors in poor weather conditions when making repairs aboard boats. They may also work in cramped or awkward positions to reach a boat's engine. Outdoor power equipment mechanics face similar conditions when they need to make on-site repairs.

During the winter months in the northern United States, mechanics may work fewer than 40 hours a week because the amount of repair and service work declines when lawnmowers, motorboats, and motorcycles are not in use. Many mechanics work full time only during the busy spring and summer seasons. However, they often schedule time-consuming engine overhauls

or work on snowmobiles and snowblowers during winter downtime. Mechanics may work considerably more than 40 hours a week when demand is strong.

Training, Other Qualifications, and Advancement

Due to the increasing complexity of motorcycles and motorboats, employers prefer to hire mechanics who have graduated from formal training programs. However, because the number of these specialized postsecondary programs is limited, most mechanics still learn their skills on the job or while working in related occupations.

Education and training. Employers prefer to hire high school graduates for trainee mechanic positions, but many will accept applicants with less education if they possess adequate reading, writing, and math skills. Helpful high school courses include small engine repair, automobile mechanics, science, and business math. Many equipment dealers employ high school students part time and during the summer to help assemble new equipment and perform minor repairs.

Once employed, trainees learn routine service tasks under the guidance of experienced mechanics by replacing ignition points and spark plugs or by taking apart, assembling, and testing new equipment. As they gain experience and proficiency, trainees progress to more difficult tasks, such as advanced computerized diagnosis and engine overhauls. Anywhere from several months to 3 years of on-the-job training may be necessary before a novice worker becomes competent in all aspects of the repair of motorcycle and motorboat engines. Repair of outdoor equipment, because of fewer moving parts, requires less on-the-job training.

A growing number of motorcycle and marine equipment mechanics graduate from formal motorcycle and motorboat postsecondary programs. Employers prefer to hire these workers for their advanced knowledge of small engine repair. These workers also need far less on-the-job training and tend to advance quickly to more demanding small engine repair jobs.

Employers often send mechanics and trainees to courses conducted by motorcycle, motorboat, and outdoor power equipment manufacturers or distributors. These courses, which can last up to 2 weeks, upgrade workers' skills and provide information on repairing new models. Manufacturer classes are usually a prerequisite for any mechanic who performs warranty work for manufacturers or insurance companies.

Other qualifications. For trainee jobs, employers hire people with mechanical aptitude who are knowledgeable about the fundamentals of small engines. Many trainees get their start by working on automobiles, motorcycles, motorboats, or outdoor power equipment as a hobby. Knowledge of basic electronics is essential because many parts of small vehicles and engines are electric.

Projections data from the National Employment Matrix

Occupational Title	SOC Code	Employment, 2008	Projected Employment, 2018	Change, 2008-2018	
				Number	Percent
Small engine mechanics..	49-3050	70,400	75,100	4,800	7
Motorboat mechanics..	49-3051	22,100	23,400	1,200	6
Motorcycle mechanics	49-3052	18,800	20,500	1,600	9
Outdoor power equipment and other small engine mechanics	49-3053	29,400	31,300	1,900	6

(NOTE) Data in this table are rounded. See the discussion of the employment projections table in the *Handbook* introductory chapter on *Occupational Information Included in the Handbook.*

Advancement. The skills needed for small engine repair can transfer to other occupations, such as automobile, diesel, or heavy vehicle and mobile equipment mechanics. Experienced mechanics with leadership ability may advance to shop supervisor or service manager jobs. Mechanics with sales ability sometimes become sales representatives or open their own repair shops or dealerships.

Employment

Small engine mechanics held about 70,400 jobs in 2008. Motorcycle mechanics held around 18,800 jobs, motorboat mechanics held approximately 22,100 jobs, and outdoor power equipment and other small engine mechanics held about 29,400 jobs. Thirty-seven percent of small engine mechanics worked for motor vehicle and parts dealers, while 13 percent were employed in retail lawn and garden equipment and supplies stores. Nine percent were employed by repair and maintenance shops. Most of the remainder worked in wholesale distributors, equipment rental and leasing companies, and landscaping services. About 13 percent were self-employed, compared to about 7 percent of workers in all installation, maintenance, and repair occupations.

Job Outlook

Average employment growth is projected for small engine mechanics. Job prospects should be excellent for people who complete formal training programs. Use of motorcycles, motorboats, and outdoor power equipment is seasonal in many areas, so mechanics may service other types of equipment or work reduced hours in the winter.

Employment change. Employment of small engine mechanics is expected to grow by 7 percent between 2008 and 2018, about as fast as the average for all occupations. Growth will vary by the type of equipment these mechanics repair.

The number of registered motorcycles has increased steadily in recent years, leading to corresponding greater demand for motorcycle repair services. This trend is expected to continue, leading to new opportunities for motorcycle mechanics. Most new jobs will continue to be in the motorcycle dealer industry, as service operations are an important aspect of business for many firms in this industry. The increasing sophistication of motorcycles will create new opportunities for specialists in independent repair shops as well, however. Overall, motorcycle mechanics will grow by 9 percent.

By contrast, the number of additional motorboats in use has been limited in recent years. The retail boat industry, the primary employer of repair technicians, has consolidated, creating fewer new opportunities for mechanics. As such, motorboat mechanics are expected to grow by 6 percent.

Outdoor equipment mechanics will also grow by 6 percent. Demand for repair services is expected to rise over time as outdoor machines become more complex. Growth is also projected in the landscaping services industry, which frequently uses small engine equipment that needs regular servicing. Most new jobs in this in this occupation will continue to be in outdoor small engine equipment retail shops.

Job prospects. Job prospects should be excellent for people who complete formal training programs. Employers prefer mechanics that have knowledge of multiple types of engines and emissions-reducing technology as the government increases regulation of the emissions produced by small engines. Many of the job openings for small engine mechanics will result from the need to replace the many experienced small engine mechanics who are expected to transfer to other occupations, retire, or stop working for other reasons.

Earnings

Median wages of motorcycle mechanics were $15.08 an hour in May 2008, as compared to $18.60 for all installation, maintenance, and repair occupations. The middle 50 percent earned between $12.10 and $19.20. The lowest 10 percent earned less than $9.76, and the highest 10 percent earned more than $24.27. Median hourly wages in the industry employing the largest number of motorcycle mechanics, other motor vehicle dealers, or retail shops selling vehicles other than cars and trucks, were $15.13.

Median wages of motorboat mechanics were $16.60 an hour in May 2008. The middle 50 percent earned between $13.31 and $20.68. The lowest 10 percent earned less than $10.74, and the highest 10 percent earned more than $25.41. Median hourly wages in other motor vehicle dealers, the industry employing the largest number of motorboat mechanics, were $16.48.

Median wages of outdoor power equipment and other small engine mechanics were $13.91 an hour in May 2008. The middle 50 percent earned between $11.24 and $17.03. The lowest 10 percent earned less than $9.12, and the highest 10 percent earned more than $20.40. Median hourly wages in lawn and garden equipment and supplies stores, the industry employing the largest number of outdoor power equipment and other small engine mechanics, were $13.66.

Small engine mechanics in small shops usually receive few benefits, but those employed in larger shops often receive typical benefits such as paid vacations, sick leave, and health insurance. Some employers also pay for work-related training, provide uniforms, and help mechanics purchase new tools.

Related Occupations

Mechanics and repairers who work on durable equipment other than small engines include:

Sources of Additional Information

To learn about work opportunities, contact local motorcycle, motorboat, and lawn and garden equipment dealers, boatyards, and marinas. Local offices of the State employment service also may have information about employment and training opportunities.

The Occupational Information Network (O*NET) provides information on a wide range of occupational characteristics. Links to O*NET appear at the end of the Internet version of this occupational statement, accessible at **http://www.bls.gov/ooh/ocos198.htm**

Miscellaneous Installation, Maintenance, and Repair Occupations

Heating, Air-conditioning, and Refrigeration Mechanics and Installers

Significant Points

- Job prospects are expected to be excellent.

- Employment is projected to grow much faster than the average.

- Employers prefer to hire those who have completed technical school training or a formal apprenticeship.

Nature of the Work

Heating and air-conditioning systems control the temperature, humidity, and the total air quality in residential, commercial, industrial, and other buildings. By providing a climate controlled environment, refrigeration systems make it possible to store and transport food, medicine, and other perishable items. *Heating, air-conditioning, and refrigeration mechanics and installers*—also called *technicians*—install, maintain, and repair such systems. Because heating, ventilation, air-conditioning, and refrigeration systems often are referred to as HVACR systems, these workers also may be called HVACR technicians.

Heating, air-conditioning, and refrigeration systems consist of many mechanical, electrical, and electronic components, such as motors, compressors, pumps, fans, ducts, pipes, thermostats, and switches. In central forced air heating systems, for example, a furnace heats air, which is then distributed through a system of metal or fiberglass ducts. Technicians maintain, diagnose, and correct problems throughout the entire system. To do this, they adjust system controls to recommended settings and test the performance of the system using special tools and test equipment.

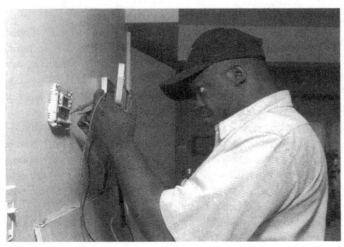

A heating, air-conditioning, and refrigeration mechanic works on a thermostat for a heating and air-conditioning system.

Technicians often specialize in either installation or maintenance and repair, although they are trained to do both. They also may specialize in doing heating work or air-conditioning or refrigeration work. Some specialize in one type of equipment—for example, hydronics (water-based heating systems), solar panels, or commercial refrigeration.

Technicians are often required to sell service contracts to their clients. Service contracts provide for regular maintenance of the heating and cooling systems, and they help to reduce the seasonal fluctuations of this type of work.

Technicians follow blueprints or other specifications to install oil, gas, electric, solid-fuel, and multiple-fuel heating systems and air-conditioning systems. After putting the equipment in place, they install fuel and water supply lines, air ducts and vents, pumps, and other components. They may connect electrical wiring and controls and check the unit for proper operation. To ensure the proper functioning of the system, furnace installers often use combustion test equipment, such as carbon dioxide testers, carbon monoxide testers, combustion analyzers, and oxygen testers. These tests ensure that the system will operate safely and at peak efficiency.

After a furnace or air-conditioning unit has been installed, technicians often perform routine maintenance and repair work to keep the systems operating efficiently. They may adjust burners and blowers and check for leaks. If the system is not operating properly, technicians check the thermostat, burner nozzles, controls, or other parts to diagnose and correct the problem.

Technicians also install and maintain heat pumps, which are similar to air conditioners but can be reversed so that they both heat and cool a home. Because of the added complexity, and the fact that they run both in summer and winter, these systems often require more maintenance and need to be replaced more frequently than traditional furnaces and air conditioners.

During the summer, when heating systems are not being used, heating equipment technicians do maintenance work, such as replacing filters, ducts, and other parts of the system that may accumulate dust and impurities during the operating season. During the winter, air-conditioning mechanics inspect the systems and do required maintenance, such as overhauling compressors.

Refrigeration mechanics install, service, and repair industrial and commercial refrigerating systems and a variety of refrigeration equipment. They follow blueprints, design specifications, and manufacturers' instructions to install motors, compressors, condensing units, evaporators, piping, and other components. They connect this equipment to the ductwork, refrigerant lines, and electrical power source. After making the connections, refrigerator mechanics charge the system with refrigerant, check it for proper operation and leaks, and program control systems.

When air-conditioning and refrigeration technicians service equipment, they must use care to conserve, recover, and recycle the refrigerants used in air-conditioning and refrigeration systems. The release of these refrigerants can be harmful to the environment. Technicians conserve the refrigerant by making sure that there are no leaks in the system; they recover it by venting the refrigerant into proper cylinders; they recycle it for reuse with special filter-dryers; or they ensure that the refrigerant is properly disposed of.

Heating, air-conditioning, and refrigeration mechanics and installers are adept at using a variety of tools to work with refrigerant lines and air ducts, including hammers, wrenches, metal snips, electric drills, pipe cutters and benders, measurement gauges, and acetylene torches. They use voltmeters, thermometers, pressure gauges, manometers, and other testing devices to check airflow, refrigerant pressure, electrical circuits, burners, and other components.

Other craft workers sometimes install or repair cooling and heating systems. For example, on a large air-conditioning installation job, especially where workers are covered by union contracts, ductwork might be done by sheet metal workers and duct installers; electrical work by electricians; and installation of piping, condensers, and other components by pipelayers, plumbers, pipefitters, and steamfitters. Home appliance repairers usually service room air-conditioners and household refrigerators. (Additional information about each of these occupations appears elsewhere in the *Handbook*.)

Work environment.   Heating, air-conditioning, and refrigeration mechanics and installers work in homes, retail establishments, hospitals, office buildings, and factories—anywhere there is climate-control equipment that needs to be installed, repaired, or serviced. They may be assigned to specific job sites at the beginning of each day or may be dispatched to a variety of locations if they are making service calls.

Technicians may work outside in cold or hot weather, or in buildings that are uncomfortable because the air-conditioning or heating equipment is broken. In addition, technicians might work in awkward or cramped positions, and sometimes they are required to work in high places. Hazards include electrical shock, burns, muscle strains, and other injuries from handling heavy equipment. Appropriate safety equipment is necessary when handling refrigerants because contact can cause skin damage, frostbite, or blindness. When working in tight spaces, inhalation of refrigerant is a possible hazard.

The majority of mechanics and installers work at least 40 hours per week. During peak seasons, they often work overtime or irregular hours. Maintenance workers, including those who provide maintenance services under contract, often work evening or weekend shifts and are on call. Most employers try to provide a full workweek year-round by scheduling both installation and maintenance work, and many manufacturers and contractors now provide or even require year-round service contracts. In most shops that service both heating and air-conditioning equipment, employment is stable throughout the year.

Training, Other Qualifications, and Advancement

Because of the increasing sophistication of heating, air-conditioning, and refrigeration systems, employers prefer to hire those who have completed technical school training or a formal apprenticeship. Some mechanics and installers, however, still learn the trade informally on the job.

Education and training.   Many heating, air-conditioning, and refrigeration mechanics and installers receive their primary training in secondary and postsecondary technical and trade schools and junior and community colleges that offer programs in heating, air-conditioning, and refrigeration. These programs can take between 6 months and 2 years to complete. Others get their training in the Armed Forces.

High school students interested in some initial training for this industry should take courses in shop math, mechanical drawing, applied physics and chemistry, electronics, blueprint reading, and computer applications. Some knowledge of plumbing or electrical work and a basic understanding of electronics are beneficial for an HVACR technician. Secondary and postsecondary students studying HVACR learn about theory of temperature control, equipment design and construction, and electronics. They also learn the basics of installation, maintenance, and repair.

Three accrediting agencies have set academic standards for HVACR programs: HVAC Excellence; the National Center for Construction Education and Research; and the Partnership for Air-Conditioning, Heating, and Refrigeration Accreditation. After completing these programs, new technicians generally need between 6 months to 2 years of field experience before they are considered proficient.

Many other technicians train through apprenticeships. Apprenticeship programs frequently are run by joint committees representing local chapters of the Air-Conditioning Contractors of America, the Mechanical Contractors Association of America, Plumbing-Heating-Cooling Contractors—National Association, and locals of the Sheet Metal Workers' International Association or the United Association of Journeymen and Apprentices of the Plumbing and Pipefitting Industry of the United States and Canada. Local chapters of the Associated Builders and Contractors and the National Association of Home Builders sponsor other apprenticeship programs. Formal apprenticeship programs normally last 3 to 5 years and combine paid on-the-job training with classroom instruction. Classes include subjects such as safety practices, the use and care of tools, blueprint reading, and the theory and design of heating, ventilation, air-conditioning, and refrigeration systems. In addition to understanding how systems work, technicians must learn about refrigerant products and the legislation and regulations that govern their use.

Applicants for apprenticeships must have a high school diploma or equivalent. Math and reading skills are essential. After completing an apprenticeship program, technicians are considered skilled trades workers and capable of working alone. These programs are also a pathway to certification and, in some cases, college credits.

Those who acquire their skills on the job usually begin by assisting experienced technicians. They may begin by performing simple tasks such as carrying materials, insulating refrigerant lines, or cleaning furnaces. In time, they move on to more difficult tasks, such as cutting and soldering pipes and sheet metal and checking electrical and electronic circuits.

Licensure.   Heating, air-conditioning, and refrigeration mechanics and installers are required to be licensed by some States and localities. Requirements for licensure vary greatly, but all States or localities that require a license have a test that must be passed. The contents of these tests vary by State or locality, with some requiring extensive knowledge of electrical codes and others focusing more on HVACR-specific knowledge. Completion of an apprenticeship program or 2 to 5 years of experience are also common requirements.

In addition, all technicians who purchase or work with refrigerants must be certified in their proper handling. To become certified to purchase and handle refrigerants, technicians must pass a written examination specific to the type of work in which they specialize. The three possible areas of certification are: Type I—servicing small appliances; Type II—high-pressure refrigerants; and Type III—low-pressure refrigerants. Exams are administered by organizations approved by the U.S. Environmental Protection Agency, such as trade schools, unions, contractor associations, or building groups.

Other qualifications. Because technicians frequently deal directly with the public, they should be courteous and tactful, especially when dealing with an aggravated customer. They should be in good physical condition because they sometimes have to lift and move heavy equipment.

Certification and advancement. Throughout the learning process, technicians may have to take a number of tests that measure their skills. For those with relevant coursework and less than 2 years of experience, the industry has developed a series of exams to test basic competency in residential heating and cooling, light commercial heating and cooling, and commercial refrigeration. These are referred to as "Entry-level" certification exams and are commonly conducted at both secondary and postsecondary technical and trade schools.

Additionally, HVACR technicians who have at least 1 year of experience performing installations and 2 years of experience performing maintenance and repair can take a number of different tests to certify their competency in working with specific types of equipment, such as oil-burning furnaces. The Air Conditioning, Heating, and Refrigeration Institute offers an Industry Competency Exam; HVAC Excellence offers both a Secondary Employment Ready Exam and a Secondary Heat and Heat Plus exams; and National Occupational Competency Testing Institute offers a secondary exam; and the Refrigeration Service Engineers Society offers two levels of certification, as well. Employers increasingly recommend taking and passing these tests and obtaining certification; doing so may increase advancement opportunities.

Another way to increase advancement opportunities is to take advantage of any courses that will improve competency with computers; these courses are useful because of the increasing complexity of automated computer controls in larger buildings.

Advancement usually takes the form of higher wages. Some technicians, however, may advance to positions as supervisor or service manager. Others may move into sales and marketing. Still others may become building superintendents, cost estimators, system test and balance specialists, or, with the necessary certification, teachers. Those with sufficient money and managerial skill can open their own contracting business.

Employment

Heating, air-conditioning, and refrigeration mechanics and installers held about 308,200 jobs in 2008; about 54 percent worked for plumbing, heating, and air-conditioning contractors. The rest were employed in a variety of industries throughout the country, reflecting a widespread dependence on climate-control systems. Some worked for refrigeration and air-conditioning service and repair shops, schools, and stores that sell heating and air-conditioning systems. Local governments, the Federal Government, hospitals, office buildings, and other organizations that operate large air-conditioning, refrigeration, or heating systems also employed these workers. About 16 percent of these workers were self-employed.

Job Outlook

With much faster than average job growth and numerous expected retirements, heating, air-conditioning, and refrigeration mechanics and installers should have excellent employment opportunities.

Employment change. Employment of heating, air-conditioning, and refrigeration mechanics and installers is projected to increase 28 percent during the 2008-18 decade, much faster than the average for all occupations. As the population and stock of buildings grows, so does the demand for residential, commercial, and industrial climate-control systems. Residential HVACR systems generally need replacement after 10 to 15 years; the large number of homes built in recent years will enter this replacement timeframe by 2018. The increased complexity of HVACR systems, which increases the possibility that equipment may malfunction, also will create opportunities for service technicians. A growing focus on improving indoor air quality and the increasing use of refrigerated equipment by a rising number of stores and gasoline stations that sell food should also create more jobs for heating, air-conditioning, and refrigeration technicians.

Concern for the environment and the need to reduce energy consumption overall has prompted the development of new energy-saving heating and air-conditioning systems. This emphasis on better energy management is expected to lead to the replacement of older systems and the installation of newer, more efficient systems in existing homes and buildings. Also, demand for maintenance and service work should rise as businesses and homeowners strive to keep increasingly complex systems operating at peak efficiency. Regulations prohibiting the discharge and production of older types of refrigerants that pollute the atmosphere should continue to result in

Projections data from the National Employment Matrix

Occupational Title	SOC Code	Employment, 2008	Projected Employment, 2018	Change, 2008-2018	
				Number	Percent
Heating, air conditioning, and refrigeration mechanics and installers	49-9021	308,200	394,800	86,600	28

(NOTE) Data in this table are rounded. See the discussion of the employment projections table in the *Handbook* introductory chapter on *Occupational Information Included in the Handbook*.

the need to replace many existing air conditioning systems or to modify them to use new environmentally safe refrigerants. The pace of replacement in the commercial and industrial sectors will quicken if Congress or individual States change tax rules designed to encourage companies to buy new HVACR equipment.

Job prospects. Job prospects for heating, air-conditioning, and refrigeration mechanics and installers are expected to be excellent, particularly for those who have completed training from an accredited technical school or a formal apprenticeship. A growing number of retirements of highly skilled technicians are expected to generate many more job openings. Many contractors have reported problems finding enough workers to meet the demand for service and installation of HVACR systems.

Technicians who specialize in installation work may experience periods of unemployment when the level of new construction activity declines, but maintenance and repair work usually remains relatively stable. People and businesses depend on their climate-control or refrigeration systems and must keep them in good working order, regardless of economic conditions.

In light of the complexity of new computer-controlled HVACR systems in modern high-rise buildings, prospects should be best for those who can acquire and demonstrate computer competency. Training in new techniques that improve energy efficiency will also make it much easier to enter the occupation.

Earnings

Median hourly wages of heating, air-conditioning, and refrigeration mechanics and installers were $19.08 in May 2008. The middle 50 percent earned between $14.94 and $24.84 an hour. The lowest 10 percent earned less than $12.19, and the top 10 percent earned more than $30.59. Median hourly wages in the industries employing the largest numbers of heating, air-conditioning, and refrigeration mechanics and installers were:

Local government	$22.79
Hardware, and plumbing and heating equipment and supplies merchant wholesalers	22.18
Commercial and industrial machinery and equipment (except automotive and electronic) repair and maintenance	20.83
Direct selling establishments	20.03
Building equipment contractors	18.26

Apprentices usually earn about 50 percent of the wage rate paid to experienced workers. As they gain experience and improve their skills, they receive periodic increases until they reach the wage rate of experienced workers.

Heating, air-conditioning, and refrigeration mechanics and installers generally receive a variety of employer-sponsored benefits. In addition to typical benefits such as health insurance and pension plans, some employers pay for work-related training and provide uniforms, company vans, and tools.

About 15 percent of heating, air-conditioning, and refrigeration mechanics and installers are members of a union. The unions to which the greatest numbers of mechanics and installers belong are the Sheet Metal Workers International Association and the United Association of Journeymen and Apprentices of the Plumbing and Pipefitting Industry of the United States and Canada.

Related Occupations

Heating, air-conditioning, and refrigeration mechanics and installers work with sheet metal and piping, and repair machinery, such as electrical motors, compressors, and burners. Other workers who have similar duties include:

Sources of Additional Information

For more information about opportunities for training, certification, and employment in this trade, contact local vocational and technical schools; local heating, air-conditioning, and refrigeration contractors; a local of the unions or organizations previously mentioned; a local joint union-management apprenticeship committee; or the nearest office of the State employment service or apprenticeship agency. You can also find information on the registered apprenticeship system with links to State apprenticeship programs on the U.S. Department of Labor's Web site: **http://www.doleta.gov/OA/eta_default.cfm.** Apprenticeship information is also available from the U.S. Department of Labor's toll free helpline: (877) 872-5627.

For information on career opportunities, training, and technician certification, contact:

➤ Air-Conditioning Contractors of America, 2800 Shirlington Rd., Suite 300, Arlington, VA 22206-3607. Internet: **http://www.acca.org**

➤ Air-Conditioning, Heating, and Refrigeration Institute, 2111 Wilson Blvd., Suite 500, Arlington, VA 22201-3001. Internet: **http://www.ahrinet.org**

➤ Associated Builders and Contractors, Workforce Development Department, 4250 North Fairfax Dr., 9th Floor, Arlington, VA 22203-1607. Internet: **http://www.trytools.org**

➤ Carbon Monoxide Safety Association, P.O. Box 669, Eastlake, CO 80614-0669. Internet: **http://www.cosafety.org**

➤ Green Mechanical Council 1701 Pennsylvania, Ave. NW, Suite 300 Washington, DC 20006-5813. Internet: **http://www.greenmech.org**

➤ Home Builders Institute, National Association of Home Builders, 1201 15th St. NW., 6th Floor, Washington, DC 20005-2842. Internet: **http://www.hbi.org**

➤ HVAC Excellence, P.O. Box 491, Mt. Prospect, IL 60056-0521. Internet: **http://www.hvacexcellence.org**

➤ Mechanical Contractors Association of America, Mechanical Service Contractors of America, 1385 Piccard Dr., Rockville, MD 20850-4329. Internet: **http://www.mcaa.org**

➤ National Center for Construction Education and Research, 3600 NW 43rd Street, Bldg. G, Gainesville, FL 32606-8134. Internet: **http://www.nccer.org**

➤ National Occupational Competency Testing Institute, 500 North Bronson Ave., Big Rapids, MI 49307-2737. Internet: **http://www.nocti.org**

➤ North American Technician Excellence, 2111 Wilson Blvd., Suite 510, Arlington, VA 22201-3051. Internet: **http://www.natex.org**

➤ Plumbing-Heating-Cooling Contractors, 180 S. Washington St., P.O. Box 6808, Falls Church, VA 22046-6808. Internet: **http://www.phccweb.org**

➤ Radiant Panel Association, P.O. Box 717, Loveland, CO 80539-0717. Internet: **http://www.radiantpanelassociation.org**

➤ Refrigeration Service Engineers Society, 1666 Rand Rd., Des Plaines, IL 60016-3552. Internet: **http://www.rses.org**

➤ Sheet Metal and Air-Conditioning Contractors National Association, 4201 Lafayette Center Dr., Chantilly, VA 20151-1209. Internet: **http://www.smacna.org**

➤ United Association of Journeymen and Apprentices of the Plumbing and Pipefitting Industry, United Association Bldg., 3 Park Place, Annapolis, MD 21401-3687. Internet: **http://www.ua.org**

The Occupational Information Network (O*NET) provides information on a wide range of occupational characteristics. Links to O*NET appear at the end of the Internet version of this occupational statement, accessible at **http://www.bls.gov/ooh/ocos192.htm**

Home Appliance Repairers

Significant Points

• Little or no change in employment is projected; however, excellent job opportunities are expected, particularly for those with formal training in appliance repair and electronics.

• Good customer service skills and a driver's license are essential.

Nature of the Work

Home appliance repairers, more commonly referred to as home appliance repair technicians, install and repair home appliances such as refrigerators, dishwashers, washers and dryers, ranges, microwave ovens, and window air-conditioning units. This work is typically done on site. (Workers whose primary responsibility is the installation and repair of heating and central air-conditioning units are covered in a separate *Handbook* statement on heating, air-conditioning, and refrigeration mechanics and installers.) A small number of home appliance repair technicians service small appliances such as vacuum cleaners, small kitchen appliances, and microwaves that are portable and usually repaired in a central repair shop rather than in the home.

When installing major appliances such as refrigerators, washing machines, and cooking products, technicians may have to connect the appliances to a gas or water line. In these cases, once the connections are in place, they turn on the gas or water and check for leaks. When complete, they may show the customer how to work the appliance and answer customers' questions about the care and use of the appliance.

When problems with major home appliances occur, home appliance repair technicians will usually make a site visit to visually inspect the appliance and make the repair. To determine the cause of the failure, they will check for unusual noises, excessive vibration, leakage of fluid, or loose parts. Technicians disassemble the appliance to examine its internal parts for signs of wear or corrosion. They follow service manual diagnostic procedures and use testing devices such as ammeters, voltmeters, and wattmeters to check electrical systems for shorts and faulty connections.

After identifying problems, home appliance repair technicians replace or repair defective belts, motors, heating elements, switches, gears, or other items. They tighten, align, clean, and lubricate parts as necessary. Technicians use common handtools, including screwdrivers, wrenches, files, and pliers, as well as soldering guns and tools designed for specific appliances. Appliances with electronic parts often require new circuit boards or other electronic components.

When repairing refrigerators and window air-conditioners, repairers must take care to conserve, recover, and recycle chlorofluorocarbon (CFC) and hydrochlorofluorocarbon (HCFC) refrigerants used in the cooling systems, as is required by law. Federal regulations also require that home appliance repair technicians document the capture and disposal of refrigerants.

In addition to making repairs, technicians keep records of parts used and hours worked, prepare bills, and collect payments. If an appliance is under warranty, a technician may need to confer with the manufacturer of the appliance to recoup monetary claims for work performed.

Work environment. When they are fully qualified to work alone, home appliance repair technicians usually work with little or no direct supervision and spend much of the day on the road driving to and from appointments and emergency calls. Those who work on portable appliances generally work in service center repair shops. Although many home appliance repair technicians work a standard 40-hour week, some work weekends and early morning or evening shifts to cover hours as needed and some remain on call for emergencies. In summer, demand for repairs to refrigerators and window air conditioners go up and may cause additional work and overtime.

Technicians sometimes work in cramped and uncomfortable positions when they are replacing parts in hard-to-reach areas of appliances, but the jobs are generally not hazardous as long as workers exercise care and follow safety precautions to avoid electrical shocks and gas leaks, and use safety measures when lifting and moving large appliances.

Training, Other Qualifications, and Advancement

Most entry-level workers in this profession enter without any specific training or experience and learn on the job, although employers prefer to hire those who have completed programs in electronics

Most home appliance repairers enter the occupation with a high school diploma and little or no training repairing appliances.

or appliance repair. A driver's license and good customer service skills are essential to work on appliances in customer's homes.

Education and training. Most home appliance repair technicians enter the occupation with a high school diploma or its equivalent and little training in repairing appliances. Most learn their jobs while working with more experienced workers and by attending in-house classes sponsored by the employer. Some appliance manufacturers and employers have formal training programs that include home study and shop classes, in which trainees work with demonstration appliances and other training equipment. Many technicians also receive supplemental instruction through 2- or 3-week seminars conducted by appliance manufacturers. Technicians authorized for warranty work by manufacturers are required to attend periodic training sessions. Training can last from several months to a few years.

In businesses that fix portable appliances in a repair shop, trainees work on a single type of appliance, such as a vacuum cleaner, until they master its repair. Then they move on to others, until they can work on all appliances repaired by the shop.

While on-the-job training is the most common method of training, employers prefer to hire workers that have attended high school or postsecondary vocational or technical programs in electronics or appliance repair. These programs can last 1 to 2 years and include courses in basic electricity and electronics as most home appliances contain electronic components. These programs can help reduce the amount of on-the-job training required for entry-level workers.

Most home appliance repair technicians will need to take periodic classes throughout their careers to keep their skills up to date and to be able to repair the latest home appliance models.

Licensure. The U.S. Environmental Protection Agency (EPA) has mandated that all repair technicians who buy or work with refrigerants pass a written examination to become certified in proper refrigerant handling. Exams are administered by EPA-approved organizations, such as trade schools, unions, and employer associations. There also are EPA-approved take-home certification exams. Although no formal training is required for certification, many of these organizations offer training programs designed to prepare workers for the certification examination.

Certification and other qualifications. A helpful manner with customers and good communication skills are essential for those who work in clients' homes. Technicians must be courteous and tactful. They must also be dependable. A driver's license with a clean driving record is also usually required to drive to customers' homes, and some employers may require a background check and drug test. Mechanical and electrical aptitudes are desirable. Those who are self-employed need good business and financial skills to maintain a business. Membership in a trade association can help business owners learn from others in the field.

Home appliance repair technicians may demonstrate their competence by passing one of several certification examinations offered by various organizations. Although voluntary, such certifications can be helpful when seeking employment. The National Appliance Service Technician Certification (NASTeC), which is administered by the International Society of Certified Electronics Technicians (ISCET), requires technicians to pass a comprehensive examination that tests their competence in the diagnosis, repair, and maintenance of major home appliances. The Professional Service Association (PSA) administers a similar certification program based on skill competencies developed by the industry and updated annually. Those who pass the PSA examination can earn the Master Certified Appliance Professional (MCAP) designation.

Advancement. Technicians in large shops or service centers may be promoted to supervisor, assistant service manager, or service manager. Some technicians advance to managerial positions such as regional service manager or parts manager for

Projections data from the National Employment Matrix

Occupational Title	SOC Code	Employment, 2008	Projected Employment, 2018	Change, 2008-2018	
				Number	Percent
Home appliance repairers	49-9031	49,600	50,600	1,100	2

(NOTE) Data in this table are rounded. See the discussion of the employment projections table in the *Handbook* introductory chapter on *Occupational Information Included in the Handbook.*

appliance or tool manufacturers. Experienced technicians who have sufficient funds and knowledge of small-business management frequently open their own repair shops.

Employment

Home appliance repair technicians are employed throughout the country, but a higher concentration of jobs can be found in more populated areas. Home appliance repair technicians held 49,600 jobs in 2008. About 32 percent of salaried technicians worked for retail trade establishments, mainly electronics and appliance stores. Another 21 percent worked in the personal and household goods repair and maintenance industry. About 27 percent of repairers were self-employed.

Job Outlook

Little to no change in employment of home appliance repairers is projected. However, excellent job opportunities are projected, particularly for individuals with formal training in appliance repair and electronics.

Employment change. Employment of home appliance repairers will increase by 2 percent between 2008 and 2018, reflecting the difficulty of employers in finding qualified applicants. Although the number of home appliances in use is expected to increase with growth in the numbers of households, companies report difficulty in hiring repair technicians. In addition, the decision to repair an appliance often depends on the price to replace the appliance versus the cost to make the repairs. So while higher priced major appliances designed to have a long life are more likely to be repaired, small and cheaper appliances are increasingly being discarded rather than be repaired. With sales of high-end appliances growing, demand for major appliance repair technicians should be strong into the future, but weaker for those specializing in small, portable appliances.

Job prospects. Job opportunities for home appliance repair technicians are expected to be excellent over the 2008-18 period, with job openings continuing to outnumber jobseekers. Companies report numerous unfilled vacancies and the expected retirement of many older technicians. Opportunities will be best in metropolitan areas. Individuals with formal training in appliance repair and electronics should have the best opportunities.

Jobs are expected to be increasingly concentrated in larger household goods repair services companies as stores increasingly outsource repair work to companies that specialize in maintenance and repair. Employment is relatively steady and workers are rarely laid off because demand for major appliance repair services is fairly constant.

Earnings

Median hourly wages, including commissions, of home appliance repairers were $16.30 in May 2008. The middle 50 percent earned between $12.87 and $20.92 an hour. The lowest 10 percent earned less than $9.98, and the highest 10 percent earned more than $25.92 an hour. In May 2008, median hourly wages of home appliance repairer technicians in the largest employing industries were $15.05 in electronics and appliance stores and $17.58 in personal and household goods repair and maintenance.

Earnings of home appliance repairer technicians vary with skill level, geographic location, and type of equipment repaired.

Many repairers receive a commission along with their salary, therefore earnings increase with the number of jobs a repairer can complete in a day.

Many larger dealers, manufacturers, and service stores offer typical benefits such as health insurance coverage, sick leave, and retirement and pension programs. Some provide company vehicles.

Related Occupations

Other workers who repair electrical and electronic equipment include:

Sources of Additional Information

For general information on home appliance repair technicians and the Certified Appliance Professional program, contact:
➤ Professional Service Association, 71 Columbia St., Cohoes, NY 12047. Internet: **http://www.psaworld.com**

For information on the National Appliance Service Technician Certification program, contact:
➤ International Society of Certified Electronics Technicians, 3608 Pershing Ave., Fort Worth, TX 76107. Internet: **http://www.nastec.org**

For general information on home appliance repair technicians, contact:
➤ United Servicers Association, 1 Presidential Way, Suite 106, Woburn, MA 01801. Internet: **http://www.unitedservicers.com**

The Occupational Information Network (O*NET) provides information on a wide range of occupational characteristics. Links to O*NET appear at the end of the Internet version of this occupational statement, accessible at **http://www.bls.gov/ooh/ocos193.htm**

Industrial Machinery Mechanics and Millwrights

Significant Points

- Most workers are employed in manufacturing.

- Machinery maintenance workers learn on the job, industrial machinery mechanics usually need some education after high school, and millwrights typically learn through formal apprenticeship programs.

- Applicants with broad skills in machine repair and maintenance should have favorable job prospects.

Nature of the Work

Imagine an automobile assembly line: a large conveyor system moves unfinished automobiles down the line, giant robotic welding arms bond the different body panels together, hydraulic lifts move the motor into the body of the car, and giant presses stamp body parts from flat sheets of steel. All these complex machines need workers to install them and service them to make sure they function properly. Assembling and setting up these machines on the factory floor is the job of millwrights, while industrial machinery mechanics and machinery maintenance workers maintain and repair these machines.

Millwrights are the highly skilled workers who install, assemble, and, when necessary, dismantle machinery in factories, power plants, and construction sites. These workers consult with engineers and managers to determine the best location to place a machine. Millwrights then transport the machine parts to the desired location, using fork lifts, hoists, winches, cranes and other equipment. Machines do not arrive in one piece, and millwrights need to assemble them from their component parts. Millwrights must understand how a machine functions to assemble and disassemble it properly; this may involve knowledge of electronics, pneumatics, and computer systems. They use complex instruction books that detail the assembly of the machinery and use tools such as levels, welding machines, and hydraulic torque wrenches. Millwrights use micrometers, precision measuring devices, to achieve the extreme tolerances required by modern machines. On large projects, the use of cranes and trucks is common.

Assembly of a machine can take a few days or several weeks. Aside from assembly, millwrights are also involved in major repairs and disassembly of machines. If a manufacturing plant needs to clear floor space for new machinery, it can sell or trade-in old equipment. The breaking down of a machine is normally just as complicated as assembling it; all parts must be carefully taken apart, categorized and packaged for shipping.

While major repairs may require the assistance of a millwright, keeping machines in good working order is the primary responsibility of *industrial machinery mechanics,* also called industrial machinery repairers or maintenance machinists. To do this effectively, these workers must be able to detect minor problems and correct them before they become larger problems. Machinery mechanics use technical manuals, their understanding of the equipment, and careful observation to discover the cause of the problem. For example, after hearing a vibration from a machine, the mechanic must decide whether it is due to worn belts, weak motor bearings, or some other problem. Mechanics often need years of training and experience to fully diagnose all problems, but computerized diagnostic systems and vibration analysis techniques provide aid in determining the nature of the problem.

After diagnosing the problem, the industrial machinery mechanic may disassemble the equipment to repair or replace the necessary parts. Increasingly, mechanics are expected to have the electrical, electronics, and computer programming skills to repair sophisticated equipment on their own. Once a repair is made, mechanics perform tests to ensure that the machine is running smoothly. Primary responsibilities of industrial machinery mechanics also include preventive maintenance; for

example, they adjust and calibrate automated manufacturing equipment, such as industrial robots.

The most basic maintenance and repair tasks are performed by *machinery maintenance workers.* These employees are responsible for cleaning and lubricating machinery, performing basic diagnostic tests, checking performance, and testing damaged machine parts to determine whether major repairs are necessary. In carrying out these tasks, maintenance workers must follow machine specifications and adhere to maintenance schedules. Maintenance workers may perform minor repairs, but major repairs generally are left to machinery mechanics.

Industrial machinery mechanics and machinery maintenance workers use a variety of tools to perform repairs and preventive maintenance. They may use handtools to adjust a motor or a chain hoist to lift a heavy printing press off the ground. When replacements for broken or defective parts are not readily available, or when a machine must be returned quickly to production, mechanics may create a new part using lathes, grinders, or drill presses. Mechanics use catalogs to order replacement parts and often follow blueprints, technical manuals, and engineering specifications to maintain and fix equipment. By keeping complete and up-to-date records, mechanics try to anticipate trouble and service equipment before factory production is interrupted. If an industrial machinery mechanic is unable to repair a machine and a major overhaul is needed, a millwright with expertise on the machine may be hired to make the repair.

Work environment. In production facilities, these workers are subject to common shop injuries such as cuts, bruises, and strains. In the construction setting, workers must be careful of heavy equipment. They also may work in awkward positions, including on top of ladders or in cramped conditions under large machinery, which exposes them to additional hazards. To avoid injuries, workers must follow safety precautions and use protective equipment, such as hardhats, safety glasses, steel-tipped shoes, hearing protectors, and belts.

Because factories and other facilities cannot afford to have industrial machinery out of service for long periods, mechanics may be on call or assigned to work nights or on weekends. Overtime is common among these occupations, as about 30 percent of employees worked over 40 hours per week, on average, in 2008.

Millwrights are typically employed on a contract basis and may only spend a few days or weeks at a single site. As a result, schedules of work can be unpredictable, and workers may experience down time in between jobs.

Training, Other Qualifications, and Advancement

Millwrights typically go through formal apprenticeship programs that last a few years and involve both classroom and on-the-job training. Industrial machinery mechanics usually need some education after high school plus experience working on specific machines before they can be considered a mechanic. Machinery maintenance workers can usually get a job with little more than a high school diploma or its equivalent; most workers learn on the job.

Education and training. All machinery maintenance and millwright worker positions generally require a high school diploma, GED, or its equivalent. However, employers increasingly prefer to hire machinery maintenance workers with some training in industrial technology. Employers also prefer to hire

Millwrights install and inspect power generating turbines.

those who have taken high school or postsecondary courses in mechanical drawing, mathematics, blueprint reading, computer programming, or electronics.

Most millwrights, and some industrial machinery mechanics, enter the occupation through an apprenticeship program that typically lasts about 4 years. Apprenticeships can be sponsored by local union chapters, employers, or the State labor department. Training in these apprenticeships involves a combination of on-the-job training and classroom learning. Jobseekers can apply for union apprenticeships, and qualified applicants may begin training in local training facilities and factories.

Industrial machinery mechanics usually need a year or more of formal education and training after high school to learn the growing range of mechanical and technical skills that they need. While mechanics used to specialize in one area, such as hydraulics or electronics, many factories now require every mechanic to have knowledge of electricity, electronics, hydraulics, and computer programming.

Workers can get this training in a number of different ways. A 2-year associate degree program in industrial maintenance provides good preparation. Other mechanics may start as helpers or in other factory jobs and learn the skills of the trade informally and by taking courses offered through their employer. It is common for experienced production workers to move into maintenance positions if they show good mechanical abili-

ties. Employers may offer on-site classroom training or send workers to local technical schools while they receive on-the-job training. Classroom instruction focuses on subjects such as shop mathematics, blueprint reading, welding, electronics, and computer training. In addition to classroom training, it is important that mechanics train on the specific machines they will repair. They can get this training on the job, through dealer or manufacturer's representatives, or in a classroom.

Machinery maintenance workers typically receive on-the-job training lasting a few months to a year to perform routine tasks, such as setting up, cleaning, lubricating, and starting machinery. This training may be offered by experienced workers, professional trainers, or representatives of equipment manufacturers.

Other qualifications. Machinery mechanics must have good problem-solving abilities, as it is important for them to be able to discover the cause of a problem to repair it. Mechanical aptitude and manual dexterity are also important. Good reading comprehension is necessary to understand the technical manuals of a wide range of machines; and good communications skills are also essential in order for millwrights, mechanics and maintenance workers to understand the needs of other workers and managers. In addition, good physical conditioning and agility are necessary because repairers sometimes have to lift heavy objects or climb to reach equipment.

Advancement. Opportunities for advancement vary by specialty. Machinery maintenance workers, if they take classes and gain additional skills, may advance to industrial machinery mechanic or supervisor. Industrial machinery mechanics also advance by working with more complicated equipment and gaining additional repair skills. The most highly skilled repairers can be promoted to supervisor, master mechanic, or millwright. Experienced millwrights can advance into team leading roles.

Employment

Industrial machinery mechanics, machinery maintenance workers and millwrights held about 408,300 jobs in 2008. 45,200 of these jobs were held by millwrights, with the largest concentration of workers in manufacturing and construction industries. In manufacturing, many of these workers are employed in the transportation equipment, wood product, and paper manufacturing industries. In construction, most workers were employed in the nonresidential building, and building equipment contractors, industries. Also, some millwrights work in the utilities industry.

Industrial machinery mechanics held about 287,700 jobs, while machinery maintenance workers accounted for 75,400 jobs. Many of both types of workers were employed in the manufacturing sector in industries such as food processing and chemical, fabricated metal product, machinery, and motor

Projections data from the National Employment Matrix

Occupational Title	SOC Code	Employment, 2008	Projected Employment, 2018	Change, 2008-2018	
				Number	Percent
Industrial machinery mechanics and millwrights	–	408,300	433,300	25,000	6
Industrial machinery mechanics	49-9041	287,700	308,600	20,900	7
Maintenance workers, machinery	49-9043	75,400	78,800	3,400	5
Millwrights..	49-9044	45,200	45,900	600	1

(NOTE) Data in this table are rounded. See the discussion of the employment projections table in the *Handbook* introductory chapter on *Occupational Information Included in the Handbook.*

vehicle and parts manufacturing. Additionally, about 10 percent work in wholesale trade, mostly for dealers of industrial equipment. Manufacturers often rely on these dealers to make complex repairs to specific machines. About 9 percent of mechanics work for the commercial and industrial machinery and equipment repair and maintenance industry, often making site visits to companies to repair equipment.

Job Outlook

Employment is projected to grow more slowly than average, and applicants with broad skills in machine repair and maintenance should have favorable job prospects.

Employment change. Employment of industrial machinery mechanics and millwrights is expected to grow 6 percent from 2008 to 2018, more slowly than the average for all occupations. The increased use of machinery in manufacturing will require more millwrights to install this equipment and more mechanics and maintenance workers to keep it in good working order.

Employment of millwrights is expected to grow 1 percent from 2008 to 2018. The demand for millwrights is driven by the purchasing of machinery in the construction and manufacturing industries. Cost-cutting pressures will drive manufacturers to further automate production and increase machinery presence on the factory floor. The growth of the power industry will also generate work for millwrights, as they install and repair turbines on wind mills, coal plants, and hydroelectric dams.

Employment of industrial machinery mechanics and maintenance workers is expected to grow 7 percent from 2008 to 2018. As factories become increasingly automated, these workers will be needed to maintain and repair the automated equipment. However, many new computer-controlled machines are capable of diagnosing problems quickly, resulting in faster and easier repair, which somewhat slows the growth of these occupations.

Job prospects. Applicants with broad skills in machine repair and maintenance should have favorable job prospects. In addition to job openings from growth, there will be a need to replace the many older workers who are expected to retire, and those who leave the occupation for other reasons. Some employers have reported difficulty in recruiting young workers with the necessary skills.

Mechanics and millwrights are not as affected by changes in production levels as other manufacturing workers, as mechanics and millwrights often are retained during production downtime to complete major equipment overhaul and to keep expensive machinery in working order.

Earnings

Median hourly wages of millwrights were $22.87 in May 2008. The middle 50 percent earned between $17.85 and $30.53. The lowest 10 percent earned less than $14.37, and the highest 10 percent earned more than $37.02.

Median hourly wages of industrial machinery mechanics were $20.99 in May 2008. The middle 50 percent earned between $16.87 and $25.82. The lowest 10 percent earned less than $13.63, and the highest 10 percent earned more than $31.40.

Machinery maintenance workers earned somewhat less than the higher skilled industrial machinery mechanics. Median hourly wages of machinery maintenance workers were $17.69 in May 2008. The middle 50 percent earned between $13.75 and $22.82. The lowest 10 percent earned less than $10.83, and the highest 10 percent earned more than $28.10.

Earnings vary by industry and geographic region. Median hourly wages in the industries employing the largest numbers of industrial machinery mechanics are:

Motor vehicle parts manufacturing $24.04
Machinery, equipment, and supplies
    merchant wholesalers 20.17
Plastics product manufacturing 20.05
Commercial and industrial machinery and
    equipment (except automotive and electronic)
    repair and maintenance..18.65
Animal slaughtering and processing 16.65

In 2008, almost half of all millwrights belonged to unions, while about 19 percent of industrial machinery mechanics were union members.

Related Occupations

Other workers do installation, maintenance, and repair, including:

                                                        Page
Electrical and electronics installers and repairers 675
Electricians.. 641
Machinists 737
Maintenance and repair workers, general 716
Plumbers, pipelayers, pipefitters, and steamfitters.................. 659
Welding, soldering, and brazing workers............................... 743

Sources of Additional Information

For information about millwright training and apprenticeships, contact:

➤ United Brotherhood of Carpenters/Millwrights, 6801 Placid St., Las Vegas, NV 89119. Internet: **www.ubcmillwrights.org**

For further information on apprenticeship programs, write to the Apprenticeship Council of your State's labor department or local firms that employ machinery mechanics and repairers. You can also find information on registered apprenticeships, together with links to State apprenticeship programs, on the U.S. Department of Labor Web site: **www.doleta.gov/OA/eta_default.cfm**. Apprenticeship information is also available from the U.S. Department of Labor toll-free helpline: (877) 872-5627.

The Occupational Information Network (O*NET) provides information on a wide range of occupational characteristics. Links to O*NET appear at the end of the Internet version of this occupational statement, accessible at **http://www.bls.gov/ooh/ocos353.htm**

Line Installers and Repairers

Significant Points

- Earnings are higher in this occupation than in many other occupations that do not require postsecondary education.

- A growing number of retirements should create very good job opportunities, especially for electrical power-line installers and repairers.

- Line installers and repairers often work outdoors, and conditions can be hazardous.

- Most positions require several years of long-term on-the-job training.

Nature of the Work

Every time you turn on your lights, call someone on the phone, watch cable television, or access the Internet, you are connecting to complex networks of lines and cables that provide you with electricity and connect you with the outside world. *Line installers and repairers*, also known as *line workers* or *linemen,* are the people who install and maintain these networks.

Because these systems are so complicated, most line workers specialize in certain skill areas; the areas in which they specialize depend on their employers and on what part of the network the workers service. Line workers can be divided into two categories: *electrical power-line installers and repairers,* and *telecommunications line installers and repairers.* Workers can further specialize in either installation or repair. Electrical line workers can also be divided into workers who install and maintain the multistate power grids, and those who work for local utilities. Similarly, telecommunications line workers specialize in telephone, cable, fiber-optic, and other networks. Each of these specializations requires specific skills, and it may be difficult to transfer skills learned in one area to another. In many cases, two or more skills sets will be combined, especially for experienced workers and supervisors.

Electrical power-line installers and repairers install and maintain the power grid—the network of power lines that moves electricity from generating plants to customers. They routinely work with high voltage electricity, which requires extreme caution. This can range from hundreds of thousands of volts for long-distance transmission lines that make up the power grid to less than 10,000 volts for distribution lines that supply electricity to homes and businesses. Line workers who maintain the interstate power grid work in crews that travel to work locations throughout a large region to maintain transmission lines and towers. Workers employed by local utilities work mainly with lower voltage distribution lines, maintaining equipment such as transformers, voltage regulators, and switches. They may also work on traffic lights and streetlights.

In contrast, telecommunications line installers and repairers install and maintain the lines and cables used by local and long-distance telephone services, cable television, the Internet, and other communications networks. These services use a variety of different types of cables, including fiber-optic cables. Un-like metallic cables that carry electricity, fiber optic cables are made of glass or plastic and transmit signals using light. Working with fiber optics requires special skills, such as splicing and terminating optical cables. Additionally, workers must be able to test and troubleshoot cables and networking equipment.

Line installers are workers who install new cable. They may work for construction contractors, utilities, or telecommunications companies. They generally start a new job by digging underground trenches or erecting utility poles and towers to carry the wires and cables. They use a variety of construction equipment, including digger derricks, which are trucks equipped with augers and cranes used to dig holes in the ground and set poles in place. Line installers also use trenchers, cable plows, and borers, which are used to cut openings in the earth for the laying of underground cables. Once the infrastructure is in place, line installers string cable along poles and towers or through tunnels and trenches.

Line repairers are employed by utilities and telecommunications companies that maintain existing power and telecommunications lines. Maintenance needs may be identified in a variety of ways, including remote monitoring equipment, inspections by airplane or helicopter, and customer reports of service outages. Workers may also replace aging or outdated equipment. Many of these workers have installation duties in addition to their repair duties.

When a problem is reported, line repairers must identify its cause and fix it. This usually involves testing equipment and replacing it as necessary. In order to work on poles, line installers usually use bucket trucks to elevate themselves to the top of the structure, although all line workers must be adept at climbing poles when necessary. Workers use special safety equipment to keep them from falling when climbing utility poles. Storms and other natural disasters can cause extensive damage to networks of lines. When a connection goes out, line repairers must work quickly to restore service to customers.

Work environment. The work of line installers and repairers can be very physically demanding. Line installers must be comfortable working both at heights and in confined spaces. While bucket trucks have reduced the amount of climbing workers must do, all line workers must be able to climb utility poles and balance while working on them. They must also be able to lift equipment and work in a variety of positions, such as stoop-

Most line installers need several years of on-the-job training.

ing or kneeling. Their work often requires that they drive utility vehicles, travel long distances, and work outdoors under poor weather conditions.

Line workers encounter serious hazards on their jobs and must follow safety procedures to minimize potential danger. They wear safety equipment when entering utility holes and test for the presence of gas before going underground. Electric power-line workers have somewhat hazardous jobs. High-voltage power lines can instantly electrocute a worker who comes in contact with a live cable. When possible, workers arrange for lines to be de-energized and test to make sure that any remaining voltage has been neutralized. When workers must work with live wires, they use electrically insulated protective devices and tools to ensure their safety. Power lines are typically higher than telephone and cable television lines, increasing the risk of severe injury due to falls. To prevent injuries, line installers must use fall-protection equipment when working on poles or towers.

While safety procedures and training have significantly reduced the danger that line workers face, the job is still among the most dangerous jobs in the American economy. Both tele-communications and electrical line workers have relatively high rates of nonfatal occupational injuries. In the early days of electricity, one in four line workers suffered fatal injuries on the job. Today, however, fatalities are extremely rare.

Workers on the interstate power grid or on long-distance communications systems are often required to travel extensively as part of their jobs. Since line installers and repairers fix damage from storms, they may be asked to work long and irregular hours during unpleasant weather. They can expect to frequently be on-call and work overtime. When performing normal maintenance and constructing new lines, line installers work more traditional hours.

Training, Other Qualifications, and Advancement

Most line installers and repairers require several years of long-term on-the-job training and some classroom work to become proficient. Formal apprenticeships are common.

Education and training. Most companies require that line installers and repairers have a high school diploma or the equivalent. Employers look for people with basic knowledge of algebra and trigonometry and good reading and writing skills. Technical knowledge of electricity or electronics obtained through military service, vocational programs or community colleges can be helpful, but it is rarely required for new employees.

Many community colleges offer programs in telecommunications, electronics, or electricity. Some programs work with local companies to offer 1-year certificates that emphasize hands-on field work. More advanced 2-year associate degree programs provide students with a broader knowledge of the technology used in telecommunications and electrical utilities. They offer courses in electricity, electronics, fiber optics, and microwave transmission.

Line installers and repairers receive most of their training on the job. Electrical line installers and repairers often must complete formal apprenticeships or other employer training programs. These programs, which can last up to 5 years, combine on-the-job training with formal classroom courses and are sometimes administered jointly by the employer and the union representing the workers. Safety regulations strictly define the training and educational requirements for apprentice electrical line installers, but licensure is not required.

Line installers and repairers working for telephone and cable television companies receive several years of on-the-job training. They also may attend training or take online courses provided by equipment manufacturers, schools, unions, or industry training organizations.

Other qualifications. Physical fitness is important because line workers must be able to climb, lift heavy objects (many employers require applicants to be able to lift at least 50 pounds), and do other physical activity that requires stamina, strength, and coordination. They often must work at a considerable height above the ground, so they cannot be afraid of heights. They must also work underground and in bucket trucks, so they must also be comfortable working in confined spaces. Normal ability to distinguish colors is necessary because wires and cables are often color coded. In addition, line workers usually need commercial driver's licenses to operate company-owned vehicles, and a good driving record is important.

Line installers and repairers must also be able to read instructions, write reports, and solve problems. They should also be mechanically inclined and like working with computers and new technology. Workers often rely on their fellow crew members for their safety, so teamwork is critical. Being able to get along with other people is very important in this job.

Advancement. Entry-level line workers generally begin with classroom training and begin an apprenticeship. Their on-the-job training begins with basic tasks, such as ground work and tree trimming. As they continue to learn additional skills from more experienced workers, they may advance to stringing cable and performing service installations. In time, they advance to more sophisticated maintenance and repair positions in which they are responsible for increasingly larger portions of the network.

After about 3 to 5 years of working, qualified line workers reach the journeyman level. A journeyman line worker is no longer considered apprenticed, and can do most tasks without supervision. Journeyman line workers may also qualify for positions at other companies. Workers with many years of ex-

Projections data from the National Employment Matrix

Occupational Title	SOC Code	Employment, 2008	Projected Employment, 2018	Change, 2008-2018	
				Number	Percent
Line installers and repairers	49-9050	284,900	291,600	6,600	2
Electrical power-line installers and repairers	49-9051	113,900	119,000	5,100	4
Telecommunications line installers and repairers	49-9052	171,000	172,600	1,600	1

(NOTE) Data in this table are rounded. See the discussion of the employment projections table in the *Handbook* introductory chapter on *Occupational Information Included in the Handbook.*

perience may become first-line supervisors or may advance to trainer positions.

Employment

Line installers and repairers held about 284,900 jobs in 2008. Approximately 171,000 were telecommunications line installers and repairers while the remaining 113,900 were electrical power-line installers and repairers. Nearly all line installers worked for telecommunications companies, including both cable television distribution and telecommunications companies; construction contractors; and electric power generation, transmission, and distribution companies.

Job Outlook

Little or no change in employment is expected. Retirements are expected to create very good job opportunities for new workers, particularly for electrical power-line installers and repairers.

Employment change. Overall employment of line installers and repairers will grow by 2 percent between 2008 and 2018. Despite employment declines in some of the major industries that employ these workers, some growth will occur as population growth and expansion of cities create increased need for power and communications lines. Further, the emphasis of both the electrical power and telecommunications industries on reliability will lead to reinforcement of these networks, which will require more workers.

Employment of telecommunications line installers and repairers will grow by about 1 percent over the 2008–2018 decade. As the population grows, installers will continue to be needed to provide new telephone, cable, and Internet services for new developments. Additionally, the exponential growth of the Internet will require more long-distance fiber-optic lines, including interstate and undersea cables.

Employment of electrical power-line installers and repairers is expected to grow by about 4 percent between 2008 and 2018. As with telecommunications line installers and repairers, growth will be largely attributable to the growing population and expansion of cities. With each new development, new lines are installed which will require maintenance. In addition, the interstate power grid will continue to grow in complexity to ensure reliability.

Job prospects. Very good job opportunities are expected, especially for electrical power-line installers and repairers. Because of layoffs in the 1990s, more of the electrical power industry is near retirement age than in most industries. This is of special concern for electrical line workers, who must be in good physical shape and cannot necessarily put off retirement in response to incentives. Telecommunications line workers face a similar demographic challenge. Additionally, technically skilled workers who do not have a college degree have an increasing number of employment opportunities, creating competition among employers. As a result, opportunities for new entrants should be very good.

Earnings

Earnings for line installers and repairers are above the average for occupations that do not require postsecondary education. In May 2008, median annual wages for electrical power-line installers and repairers were $55,100. The middle 50 percent earned between $41,340 and $66,030. The lowest 10 percent earned less than $31,420, and the highest 10 percent earned more than $78,780. Median annual wages in the industries employing the largest numbers of electrical power-line installers and repairers in May 2008 are shown below:

Natural gas distribution	$84,350
Electric power generation, transmission and distribution	58,530
Local government	52,900
Building equipment contractors	52,870
Utility system construction	45,420

Median annual wages for telecommunications line installers and repairers were $48,090 in May 2008. The middle 50 percent earned between $33,680 and $60,670. The lowest 10 percent earned less than $25,790, and the highest 10 percent earned more than $67,990. Median annual wages in the industries employing the largest numbers of telecommunications line installers and repairers in May 2008 are shown below:

Other telecommunications	$58,100
Wired telecommunications carriers	54,860
Cable and other subscription programming	39,970
Building equipment contractors	37,760
Utility system construction	34,580

Many line installers and repairers belong to unions, principally the Communications Workers of America, the International Brotherhood of Electrical Workers, and the Utility Workers Union of America. For these workers, union contracts set wage rates and wage increases and determine the time needed to advance from one wage level to the next.

Good health, education, and vacation benefits are common in the occupation.

Related Occupations

Other workers who install and repair electrical and electronic equipment include:

	Page
Electrical and electronics installers and repairers	675
Electricians	641
Power plant operators, distributors, and dispatchers	760
Radio and telecommunications equipment installers and repairers	680

Sources of Additional Information

For more details about employment opportunities, contact the telephone, cable television, or electrical power companies in your community. For general information and educational resources on line installer and repairer jobs, contact:

➤ American Public Power Association, 1875 Connecticut Ave. NW, Suite 1200, Washington, DC 20009-5715. Internet: **http://www.appanet.org**

➤ Center for Energy Workforce Development, 701 Pennsylvania Ave. NW., Washington, DC 20004-2696. Internet: **http://www.cewd.org**

➤ The Fiber Optic Association, 1119 S Mission Rd #355, Fallbrook, CA 92028. Internet: **http://www.thefoa.org**

➤ International Brotherhood of Electrical Workers, 900 Seventh St. NW, Washington, DC 20001. Internet: **http://www.ibew.org**

➤ National Joint Apprenticeship and Training Committee (NJATC), 301 Prince Georges Blvd., Suite D, Upper Marlboro, MD 20774. Internet: **http://www.njatc.org**

The Occupational Information Network (O*NET) provides information on a wide range of occupational characteristics. Links to O*NET appear at the end of the Internet version of this occupational statement, accessible at **http://www.bls.gov/ooh/ocos195.htm**

Maintenance and Repair Workers, General

Significant Points

- General maintenance and repair workers are employed in almost every industry.

- Many workers learn their skills informally on the job; obtaining certification may result in better advancement opportunities in higher paying industries.

- Job growth and turnover in this large occupation should result in excellent job opportunities, especially for people with experience in maintenance and related fields.

Nature of the Work

Most craft workers specialize in one kind of work, such as plumbing or carpentry. *General maintenance and repair workers*, however, have skills in many different crafts. They repair and maintain machines, mechanical equipment, and buildings and work on plumbing, electrical, and air-conditioning and heating systems. They build partitions, make plaster or drywall repairs, and fix or paint roofs, windows, doors, floors, woodwork, and other parts of building structures. They also maintain and repair specialized equipment and machinery found in cafeterias, laundries, hospitals, stores, offices, and factories.

Maintenance and repair workers need to know about computer controls of various building systems.

Typical duties include troubleshooting and fixing faulty electrical switches, repairing air-conditioning motors, and unclogging drains. New buildings sometimes have computer-controlled systems that allow maintenance workers to make adjustments in building settings and monitor for problems from a central location. For example, they can remotely control light sensors that turn off lights automatically after a set amount of time or identify a broken ventilation fan that needs to be replaced.

General maintenance and repair workers inspect and diagnose problems and determine the best way to correct them, frequently checking blueprints, repair manuals, and parts catalogs. They obtain supplies and repair parts from distributors or storerooms. Using common hand and power tools such as screwdrivers, saws, drills, wrenches, and hammers, as well as specialized equipment and electronic testing devices, these workers replace or fix worn or broken parts, where necessary, or make adjustments to correct malfunctioning equipment and machines.

General maintenance and repair workers also perform routine preventive maintenance and ensure that machines continue to run smoothly, building systems operate efficiently, and the physical condition of buildings does not deteriorate. Following a checklist, they may inspect drives, motors, and belts, check fluid levels, replace filters, and perform other maintenance actions. Maintenance and repair workers keep records of their work.

Employees in small establishments, where they are often the only maintenance worker, make all repairs, except for very large or difficult jobs. In larger establishments, duties may be limited to the maintenance of everything in a single workshop or a particular area.

Work environment. General maintenance and repair workers often carry out many different tasks in a single day, at any number of locations, including indoor and outdoor. They may work inside a single building, such as a hotel or hospital, or be responsible for the maintenance of many buildings, such as those in an apartment complex or college campus. They may have to stand for long periods, lift heavy objects, and work in uncomfortably hot or cold environments, in awkward and cramped positions, or on ladders. Those employed in small establishments often work with only limited supervision. Those in larger establishments frequently work under the direct supervision of an experienced worker. Some tasks put workers at risk of electrical shock, burns, falls, cuts, and bruises. Data from the U.S. Bureau of Labor Statistics show that full-time general maintenance workers experienced a work-related injury and illness rate that was much higher than the national average. Most general maintenance workers work a 40-hour week. Some work evening, night, or weekend shifts or are on call for emergency repairs.

Training, Other Qualifications, and Advancement

Many general maintenance and repair workers learn their skills informally on the job as helpers to other repairers or to carpenters, electricians, and other construction workers. Certification is available for entry-level workers, as well as experienced workers seeking advancement.

Education and training. General maintenance and repair workers often learn their skills informally on the job. They start as helpers, watching and learning from skilled maintenance

Projections data from the National Employment Matrix

Occupational Title	SOC Code	Employment, 2008	Projected Employment, 2018	Change, 2008-2018	
				Number	Percent
Maintenance and repair workers, general	49-9042	1,361,300	1,509,200	147,900	11

(NOTE) Data in this table are rounded. See the discussion of the employment projections table in the *Handbook* introductory chapter on *Occupational Information Included in the Handbook.*

workers. Helpers begin by performing simple jobs, such as fixing leaky faucets and replacing light bulbs, and progress to more difficult tasks, such as overhauling machinery or building walls. Some learn their skills by working as helpers to other types of repair or construction workers, including machinery repairers, carpenters, or electricians.

Several months of on-the-job training are required to become fully qualified, depending on the skill level required. Some jobs require a year or more to become fully qualified. Because a growing number of new buildings rely on computers to control their systems, general maintenance and repair workers may need basic computer skills, such as how to log onto a central computer system and navigate through a series of menus. Companies that install computer-controlled equipment usually provide on-site training for general maintenance and repair workers.

Many employers prefer to hire high school graduates. High school courses in mechanical drawing, electricity, woodworking, blueprint reading, science, mathematics, and computers are useful. Because of the wide variety of tasks performed by maintenance and repair workers, technical education is an important part of their training. Maintenance and repair workers often need to do work that involves electrical, plumbing, and heating and air- conditioning systems, or painting and roofing tasks. Although these basic tasks may not require a license to do the work, a good working knowledge of many repair and maintenance tasks is required. Many maintenance and repair workers learn some of these skills in high school shop classes and postsecondary trade or vocational schools or community colleges.

Licensure. Licensing requirements vary by State and locality. In some cases, workers may need to be licensed in a particular specialty such as electrical or plumbing work.

Other qualifications. Technical and mechanical aptitude, the ability to use shop mathematics, and manual dexterity are important attributes. Good health is necessary because the job involves much walking, climbing, standing, reaching, and heavy lifting. Difficult jobs require problem-solving ability, and many positions require the ability to work without direct supervision.

Certification and advancement. The International Management Institute (IMI) offers certification for three levels of competence, focusing on a broad range of topics, including blueprints, mathematics, basic electricity, piping systems, landscape maintenance, and troubleshooting skills. The lowest level of certification is Certified Maintenance Technician, the second level is Certified Maintenance Professional, and the highest level of certification is Certified Maintenance Manager. To become certified, applicants must meet several prerequisites and pass a comprehensive written examination.

Many general maintenance and repair workers in large organizations advance to maintenance supervisor or become craftwork-

ers such as electricians, heating and air-conditioning mechanics, or plumbers. Within small organizations, promotion opportunities may be limited. Obtaining IMI certification may lead to better advancement opportunities in higher paying industries.

Employment

General maintenance and repair workers held about 1.4 million jobs in 2008. They were employed in almost every industry. Around 18 percent worked in manufacturing industries, while about 11 percent worked for Government. Others worked for wholesale and retail firms and for real estate firms that operate office and apartment buildings.

Job Outlook

Average employment growth is expected. Job growth and the need to replace those who leave this large occupation should result in excellent job opportunities, especially for those with experience in maintenance and related fields.

Employment change. Employment of general maintenance and repair workers is expected to grow 11 percent during the 2008-18 decade, about as fast as the average for all occupations. Employment is related to the number of buildings—for example, office and apartment buildings, stores, schools, hospitals, hotels, and factories—and the amount of equipment needing maintenance and repair. One factor limiting job growth is that computers allow buildings to be monitored more efficiently, partially reducing the need for workers.

Job prospects. Job opportunities should be excellent, especially for those with experience in maintenance or related fields. Those who obtain certification will also face excellent opportunities. General maintenance and repair is a large occupation, generating many job openings due to growth and the need to replace those who leave the occupation. Many job openings are expected to result from the retirement of experienced maintenance workers over the next decade.

Earnings

Median hourly wages of general maintenance and repair workers were $16.21 in May 2008. The middle 50 percent earned between $12.44 and $21.09. The lowest 10 percent earned less than $9.78, and the highest 10 percent earned more than $25.94. Median hourly wages in the industries employing the largest numbers of general maintenance and repair workers in May 2008 are shown in the following tabulation:

Local government	$17.11
Elementary and secondary schools	16.86
Activities related to real estate	14.41
Lessors of real estate	13.91
Traveler accommodation	12.65

About 15 percent of general maintenance and repair workers are members of unions, including the American Federation of State, County, and Municipal Employees and the United Auto Workers.

Related Occupations

Some duties of general maintenance and repair workers are similar to those of:

Sources of Additional Information

Information about job opportunities may be obtained from local employers and local offices of the State.

For information related to training and certification, contact:
➤ International Maintenance Institute, P.O. Box 751896, Houston, TX 77275-1896. Internet: **http://www.imionline.org**

➤ Society for Maintenance and Reliability Professionals, 8400 Westpark Drive, 2nd Floor, McLean, VA 22102-3570. Internet: **http://www.smrp.org/**

The Occupational Information Network (O*NET) provides information on a wide range of occupational characteristics. Links to O*NET appear at the end of the Internet version of this occupational statement, accessible at **http://www.bls.gov/ooh/ocos194.htm**

Medical Equipment Repairers

Significant Points

- Employment is projected to grow 27 percent, which is much faster than the average for all occupations.

- Excellent job opportunities are expected.

- Employers generally prefer applicants with an associate's degree in biomedical equipment technology or engineering; a bachelor's degree often is needed for advancement.

- Repairers may be on-call around the clock in case of emergencies.

Nature of the Work

Medical equipment repairers, also known as *biomedical equipment technicians* (BMET), maintain, adjust, calibrate, and repair a wide variety of electronic, electromechanical, and hydraulic equipment used in hospitals and other medical environments, including health practitioners' offices. They may work on patient monitors, defibrillators, medical imaging equipment (x rays, CAT scanners, and ultrasound equipment), voice-controlled operating tables, electric wheelchairs, as well as other sophisticated dental, optometric, and ophthalmic equipment.

Medical equipment repairers use a wide variety of tools to conduct their work, including multimeters, specialized software, and computers designed to communicate with specific pieces of hardware. They may also use hand tools, soldering irons, and other electronic tools to fix or adjust malfunctioning equipment, such as a broken wheelchair. If a machine is not functioning to its potential, the repairer may have to adjust the mechanical or hydraulic components, or adjust the software to bring the equipment back into calibration. Most medical equipment is powered by electricity, but because many also have mechanical and hydraulic components, being familiar with all of these systems is critical.

In some cases, medical equipment repairers perform routine scheduled maintenance to ensure that all equipment is in good working order. Since many doctors, particularly specialty practitioners, regularly use complex medical devices to run tests and diagnose patients, they must be guaranteed that the readings are accurate. For less complicated equipment, such as electric hospital beds, many repairs may take place on an as-needed-basis.

In a hospital setting, specialists must be comfortable working around patients because repairs occasionally must take place while equipment is being used. When this is the case, the repairer must take great care to ensure that repairs do not disturb patients.

Many medical equipment repairers are employed in hospitals. Some, however, work for electronic equipment repair and maintenance companies that service medical equipment used by other health practitioners, including gynecologists, orthodontists, veterinarians, and other diagnostic medical professionals. Whereas some medical equipment repairers are trained to fix a wide variety of equipment, others specialize and become proficient at repairing one or a small number of machines.

Work environment. Medical equipment repairers usually work daytime hours, but are often expected to be on call. Still, like other hospital employees, some repairers work irregular hours and may be required to work overtime if an important piece of medical equipment malfunctions. Medical equipment repairers often must work in a patient environment, which has the potential to expose them to diseases and other health risks. Because medical equipment is often used in life-saving therapies, diagnosing and repairing equipment can be urgent. Although this may be gratifying, it can also be very stressful. Those who work as contractors often have to travel—sometimes long distances—to perform needed repairs.

Training, Other Qualifications, and Advancement

Employers generally prefer candidates with an associate's degree in biomedical technology or engineering; a bachelor's degree often is needed for advancement.

In some cases, medical equipment repairs must be performed while equipment is in use.

Education and training. Although education requirements vary depending on a worker's experience and area of specialization, the most common education path for repairers is an associate degree in biomedical equipment technology or engineering. Those who repair less complicated equipment, such as hospital beds or electric wheelchairs, may learn entirely through on-the-job training. Others, particularly those who work on more sophisticated equipment such as CAT scanners and defibrillators, may need a bachelor's degree. New workers generally start by observing and assisting experienced repairers over a period of 3 to 6 months, learning a single piece of equipment at a time. Gradually, they begin working more independently, while still under close supervision. Each piece of equipment is different, and medical equipment repairers must learn each one separately. In some cases, this requires careful study of a machine's technical specifications and manual. Medical device manufacturers also may provide training courses in a classroom or online.

Because medical equipment technology is rapidly evolving and new devices are frequently introduced, repairers must constantly update their skills and knowledge of equipment. As a result, they must constantly learn new technologies and equipment through seminars, self-study, and certification exams.

Certification and other qualifications. Medical equipment repairers are problem solvers—diagnosing and repairing equipment, often under time constraints—therefore, being able to work under pressure is critical. As in most repair occupations, having mechanical and technical aptitude, as well as manual dexterity, is important.

Some associations offer certifications for medical equipment repairers. For example, the Association for the Advancement of Medical Instrumentation (AAMI) offers certification in three specialty areas—Certified Biomedical Equipment Technician (CBET), Certified Radiology Equipment Specialists (CRES), and Certified Laboratory Equipment Specialist (CLEB). Those who wish to become certified must satisfy a combination of education and experience requirements prior to taking the AAMI examination. Candidates who meet the necessary criteria can begin pursuing the desired certification on the basis of their qualifications. Certification demonstrates a level of competency and can make an applicant more attractive to employers, as well as increase one's opportunities for advancement. Most employers, particularly hospitals, often pay for their in-house medical repairers to become certified.

Advancement. Most medical equipment repairers advance by demonstrating competency at lower levels, which allows them to repair more complex equipment. Some may become supervisors or managers, but these positions usually require a bachelor's degree. Experienced repairers also may serve as mentors for new employees or teach training courses on specific products.

Employment

Medical equipment repairers held 41,400 jobs in May 2008. Industries employing the largest number of medical equipment repairers in 2008 were:

Professional and commercial equipment and supplies merchant wholesalers	9,400
Hospitals, public and private	7,100
Electronic and precision equipment repair and maintenance	5,700
Health and personal care stores	2,300
Consumer goods rental	2,300

Job Outlook

Medical equipment repairers are projected to grow much faster than average between 2008 and 2018. Opportunities should be excellent for qualified job seekers.

Employment change. Employment of medical equipment repairers is expected to grow 27 percent over the 2008-18 decade, which is much faster than the average for all occupations. As the proportion of people in older age groups will grow faster than the total population between 2008 and 2018, demand for overall healthcare will increase. Increased demand for healthcare services and increasing complexity of the medical equipment used in hospitals and by private practitioners will result in a greater need for repairers. For example, a growing number of hospital diagnostic, electromedical, and patient monitoring equipment including CAT scans, electrocardiogram, magnetic resonance imaging, ultrasound, and x-ray machines, as well as hospital furniture, such as full electric beds and wheelchairs, will all need to be maintained and repaired. Additionally, machines used by private practitioners and technicians to diagnose and treat vision, teeth, and other parts of the human body also are becoming increasingly sophisticated, and will further spur growth of medical equipment repairers.

Job prospects. A combination of employment growth and the need to replace workers leaving the occupation will result

Projections data from the National Employment Matrix

Occupational Title	SOC Code	Employment, 2008	Projected Employment, 2018	Change, 2008-2018	
				Number	Percent
Medical equipment repairers	49-9062	41,400	52,600	11,300	27

(NOTE) Data in this table are rounded. See the discussion of the employment projections table in the *Handbook* introductory chapter on *Occupational Information Included in the Handbook.*

in excellent job prospects over the next decade. The number of job openings is expected to outnumber the number of qualified applicants; therefore, applicants should have little difficulty finding jobs. Candidates with an associate's degree in biomedical equipment technology or engineering should have the best prospects. Opportunities should be even more abundant for those who are willing to relocate because relatively few qualified applicants can be found in rural areas.

Earnings

Median annual wages for medical equipment repairers in May 2008 were $41,520. The middle 50 percent earned between $31,590 and $53,720. The lowest 10 percent earned less than $25,860, and the highest 10 percent earned more than $65,930.

Median annual wages for medical equipment repairers in the largest industries were:

General medical and surgical hospitals	$45,990
Electronic and precision equipment repair and maintenance	44,740
Professional and commercial equipment and supplies merchant wholesalers	42,950
Health and personal care stores	32,770
Consumer goods rental	29,020

Related Occupations

Other workers who repair precision mechanical and electronic equipment include:

	Page
Coin, vending, and amusement machine servicers and repairers	720
Computer, automated teller, and office machine repairers	672
Medical, dental, and ophthalmic laboratory technicians	774

Sources of Additional Information

For information about medical equipment technicians and a list of schools with related programs of study, contact:

➤ Association for the Advancement of Medical Instrumentation (AAMI), 1110 North Glebe Rd., Suite 220, Arlington, VA 22201-4795. Internet: **http://www.aami.org**

The Occupational Information Network (O*NET) provides information on a wide range of occupational characteristics. Links to O*NET appear at the end of the Internet version of this occupational statement, accessible at **http://www.bls.gov/ooh/ocos355.htm**

Other Installation, Maintenance, and Repair Occupations

Camera and Photographic Equipment Repairers

Nature of the Work

Camera and photographic equipment repairers fix broken film and digital cameras and other optical devices.

Education and Training

Most camera repairers undergo internships or apprenticeships; these usually last about 2 years.

Job Outlook

Current and projected employment:

2008 Employment	4,600
2018 Employment	3,900
Employment change	-700
Growth rate	-15%

Employment change. Employment is expected to decline rapidly. Technological improvements mean that most consumers prefer to replace broken cameras with newer models, even at the high end, saving on the high cost of repair.

Job prospects. Competition for jobs is expected. Decline of the occupation is expected to make job opportunities scarce, although there continue to be some positions working for warranty repair centers.

Earnings

Median annual wages for camera and photographic equipment repairers were $34,300 in May 2008.

Related Occupations

	Page
Electrical and electronics installers and repairers	675
Electronic home entertainment equipment installers and repairers	678
Watch repairers	721

Sources of Additional Information

➤ PMA, The Worldwide Community of Imaging Associations, 3000 Picture Place, Jackson, MI 49201. Internet: **http://www.pmai.org/**

The Occupational Information Network (O*NET) provides information on a wide range of occupational characteristics. Links to O*NET appear at the end of the Internet version of this occupational statement, accessible at **http://www.bls.gov/ooh/ocos354.htm**

Coin, Vending, and Amusement Machine Servicers and Repairers

Nature of the Work

Coin, vending, and amusement machine servicers and repairers install, service, adjust, or repair machines, including arcade games, food and beverage machines, slot machines, jukeboxes, and other similar machines that dispense games or merchandise for money or credit. Servicers usually stock the machines and record the items sold and money collected. Repairers ensure the machines are operating correctly and make repairs as needed.

Education and Training
Most workers learn their skills on the job, but employers increasingly prefer to hire applicants with some high school or vocational school courses in electronics, refrigeration, and machine repair. A driver's license is required for those who need to drive to stock or repair machines.

Job Outlook
Current and projected employment:
2008 Employment 43,800
2018 Employment 46,900
Employment change..3,100
Growth rate.. 7%

Employment change. Average growth is expected. While the number of vending and slot machines are expected to rise, they are also becoming easier to service and require fewer repairs. There will be fewer video arcade machines as people play more of these games at home.

Job prospects. Job opportunities should be excellent for repairers who have training in electronics, and who are willing to travel and work at times outside regular business hours. Opportunities will be fair for servicers, or route drivers.

Earnings
Median annual wages of coin, vending, and amusement machine servicers and repairers were $29,930 in May 2008.

Related Occupations

Sources of Additional Information
The Occupational Information Network (O*NET) provides information on a wide range of occupational characteristics. Links to O*NET appear at the end of the Internet version of this occupational statement, accessible at **http://www.bls.gov/ooh/ocos200.htm**

Musical Instrument Repairers and Tuners

Nature of the Work
Musical instrument repairers and *tuners* are craft workers who use a variety of techniques and tools to bring damaged or out-of-tune instruments into proper working order. They often specialize by type of instrument and in either tuning or repair.

Education and Training
Most musical instrument repairers and tuners learn their craft through trade schools or apprenticeships. A basic ability to play the instruments being repaired is normally required.

Job Outlook
Current and projected employment:
2008 Employment 6,100
2018 Employment 6,100
Employment change..0
Growth rate.. 0%

Employment change. Musical instrument repairers and tuners are expected to experience little or no change in employment from 2008-18. Band and orchestra programs in high schools provide most of the business for repairers, and they are not as prevalent as they once were, but this has been offset somewhat by population growth.

Job prospects. Job prospects should be excellent. As the baby boomer generation retires and many skilled workers leave the workforce, new workers will be needed to replace them.

Earnings
Median annual wages for musical instrument repairers and tuners were $33,080 in May 2008.

Related Occupations

Sources of Additional Information
➤ National Association of Professional Band Instrument Repair Technicians (NAPBIRT), P.O. Box 51, Normal, IL 61761. Internet: **http://www.napbirt.org**

The Occupational Information Network (O*NET) provides information on a wide range of occupational characteristics. Links to O*NET appear at the end of the Internet version of this occupational statement, accessible at **http://www.bls.gov/ooh/ocos356.htm**

Watch Repairers

Nature of the Work
Watch repairers, also known as *watchmakers* or *horologists*, use precision tools to fix expensive and antique timepieces. They diagnose problems and repair, clean, adjust, and replace parts as necessary to return watches to proper working condition.

Education and Training
Developing proficiency in watch repair requires several years of education and experience. Some workers take advanced train-

ing courses and earn certifications, such as the Certified Watch-maker (CW) title.

Job Outlook

Current and projected employment:

2008 Employment	3,200
2018 Employment	2,800
Employment change	-400
Growth rate	-14%

Employment change. Employment of watch repairers is expected to decline rapidly. The high cost of repairs will compel many consumers to replace their watches rather than have them fixed.

Job prospects. Good job prospects are expected. There will be many openings for new entrants as baby boomers retire.

Earnings

Median annual wages for watch repairers were $34,660 in May 2008.

Related Occupations

Sources of Additional Information

➤ American Watchmakers-Clockmakers Institute (AWCI), 701 Enterprise Dr., Harrison, OH 45030-1696. Internet: **http://www.awi-net.org**

The Occupational Information Network (O*NET) provides information on a wide range of occupational characteristics. Links to O*NET appear at the end of the Internet version of this occupational statement, accessible at **http://www.bls.gov/ooh/ocos357.htm**

Production Occupations

Assemblers and Fabricators

Significant Points

- Most assemblers work on teams, making good communication skills and the ability to get along with others important.

- A high school diploma is sufficient for most jobs, but experience and extra training is needed for more advanced assembly work.

- Employment is projected to experience little or no change between 2008 and 2018.

- Job opportunities are expected to be good in the manufacturing sector, particularly in growing, high-technology industries.

Nature of the Work

Assemblers and fabricators play an important role in the manufacturing process. They assemble both finished products and the pieces that go into them. The products they assemble using tools, machines, and their hands range from entire airplanes to children's toys. They fabricate and assemble household appliances, automobiles, computers, electronic devices, and more.

Changes in technology have transformed the manufacturing and assembly process. Modern manufacturing systems use robots, computers, programmable motion control devices, and various sensing technologies. These systems change the way in which goods are made and affect the jobs of those who make them. The more advanced assemblers must be able to work with these new technologies and use them to produce goods.

The job of an assembler or fabricator ranges from very easy to very complicated, requiring a range of knowledge and skills. Skilled assemblers putting together complex machines, for example, begin by reading detailed schematics or blueprints that show how to assemble the machine. After determining how parts should connect, they use hand or power tools to trim, shim, cut, and make other adjustments to fit components together and align properly. Once the parts are properly aligned, they connect them with bolts and screws or by welding or soldering pieces together.

Careful quality control is important throughout the assembly process, so assemblers look for faulty components and mistakes in the assembly process. They help to fix problems before more defective products are produced.

Manufacturing techniques are evolving away from traditional assembly line systems toward "lean" manufacturing systems, which are causing the nature of assemblers' work to change. Lean manufacturing uses teams of workers to produce entire products or components. *Team assemblers* may still work on an assembly line, but they rotate through different tasks, rather than specializing in a single task. The team also may decide how the work is assigned and how different tasks are performed.

This worker flexibility helps companies cover for absent workers, improves productivity, and increases companies' ability to respond to changes in demand by shifting labor from one product line to another. For example, if demand for a product drops, companies may reduce the total number of workers producing it, asking the remaining workers to perform more stages of the assembly process. Some aspects of lean production, such as rotating tasks and seeking worker input on improving the assembly process, are common to all assembly and fabrication occupations.

Although most assemblers and fabricators are classified as team assemblers, others specialize in producing one type of product or perform the same or similar tasks throughout the assembly process. These workers are classified according to the products they assemble or produce. *Electrical and electronic equipment assemblers*, for example, build products such as electric motors, computers, electronic control devices, and sensing equipment. Automated systems have been put in place as many small electronic parts are too small or fragile for human assembly. Much of the remaining work of electrical and electronic assemblers is manual assembly during the small-scale production of electronic devices used in avionic systems, military systems, and medical equipment. Manual production requires these workers to use devices such as soldering irons. *Electromechanical equipment assemblers* assemble and modify electromechanical devices such as household appliances, CT scanners, or vending machines. The workers use a variety of tools, such as rulers, rivet guns and soldering irons. *Coil winders, tapers, and finishers* wind wire coil used in a variety of electric and electronic products, including resistors, transformers, generators, and electric motors.

Engine and other machine assemblers construct, assemble, or rebuild engines and turbines, and machines used in automobiles, construction and mining equipment, and power generators. *Aircraft structure, surfaces, rigging, and systems assemblers* assemble, fit, fasten, and install parts of airplanes, space vehicles, or missiles, including tails and wings, landing gear, and heating and ventilation systems. *Structural metal fabricators and fitters* cut, align, and fit together structural metal parts and may assist in welding or riveting the parts together. *Fiberglass laminators and fabricators* develop products made of fiberglass, mainly boat decks and hulls. *Timing device assemblers, adjusters, and calibrators* perform precision assembling or adjusting of timing devices within very narrow tolerances.

It has become more common to involve assemblers and fabricators in product development. Designers and engineers consult manufacturing workers during the design stage to improve product reliability and manufacturing efficiency. For example, an assembler may tell a designer that the dashboard of a new car design will be too difficult to install quickly and consistently. The designer could then redesign it to make it easier to install.

Some experienced assemblers work with designers and engineers to build prototypes or test products. These assemblers must be able to read and interpret complex engineering specifications from text, drawings, and computer-aided drafting systems. They also may need to use a variety of tools and precision measuring instruments.

Work environment.   Most assemblers and manufacturers work in manufacturing plants. The working environment is improving, but varies by plant and by industry. Many physically difficult tasks have been automated or made easier through the use of power tools, such as tightening massive bolts or moving heavy parts into position. Assembly work, however, may still involve long periods of standing or sitting.

Most factories today are generally clean, well-lit, and well-ventilated; and depending on what type of work is being performed, they may also need to be dirt and dust-free. Electronic and electromechanical assemblers particularly must work in environments free of dust that could affect the operation of the products they build. Some assemblers may come into contact with potentially harmful chemicals or fumes, but ventilation systems and other safety precautions normally minimize any harmful effects. Other assemblers may come in contact with oil and grease, and their working areas may be quite noisy. Fiberglass laminators and fabricators are exposed to fiberglass, which may irritate the skin; these workers wear gloves and long sleeves and must use respirators for safety.

Most full-time assemblers work a 40-hour week, although overtime and shift work are common in some industries. Work schedules of assemblers may vary at plants with more than one shift.

Training, Other Qualifications, and Advancement
The education level and qualifications needed to enter these jobs vary depending on the industry and employer. While a high school diploma or GED is sufficient for most jobs, experience and extra training is needed for more advanced assembly work.

Education and training.   Most applicants for assembler positions need only a high school diploma or GED, with workers learning the skills they need through on-the-job training, sometimes including employer-sponsored classroom instruction. Some employers may require specialized training or an associate degree for the most skilled assembly jobs. For example, jobs with electrical, electronic, and aircraft and motor vehicle products manufacturers typically require more formal education through technical schools.

Certification and other qualifications.   Assembly workers must be able to follow instructions carefully, which may require some basic reading skills and the ability to follow diagrams and pictures. Manual dexterity and the ability to carry out complex, repetitive tasks quickly and methodically also are important. For some positions, the ability to lift heavy objects may be needed. Team assemblers also need good interpersonal and communication skills to be able to work well with their teammates. Good eyesight and manual dexterity is necessary for assemblers and fabricators who work with small parts. Plants that make electrical and electronic products may test applicants for color vision, because their products often contain many differently colored wires.

Certifications are not common for most types of assemblers and fabricators. However, many employers that hire electrical

Assemblers test circuits in electronic devices.

and electronic assembly workers, especially those in the aerospace and defense industries, require certifications in soldering, such as those offered by the IPC.

Advancement.   As assemblers and fabricators become more experienced, they may progress to jobs that require greater skill and may be given more responsibility. Experienced assemblers may become product repairers, if they have learned the many assembly operations and understand the construction of a product. These workers fix assembled pieces that operators or inspectors have identified as defective. Assemblers also can advance to quality control jobs or be promoted to supervisor. Experienced assemblers and fabricators also may become members of research and development teams, working with engineers and other project designers to design, develop, and build prototypes, and test new product models.

Employment
Assemblers and fabricators held about 2.0 million jobs in 2008. They worked in many industries, but over 75 percent worked in manufacturing. Within the manufacturing sector, assembly of transportation equipment, such as aircraft, autos, trucks, and buses, accounted for 20 percent of all jobs. Assembly of computers and electronic products accounted for another 11 percent of all jobs. Other industries that employ many assemblers and fabricators are machinery manufacturing and electrical equipment, appliance, and component manufacturing.

Projections data from the National Employment Matrix

Occupational Title	SOC Code	Employment, 2008	Projected Employment, 2018	Change, 2008-2018	
				Number	Percent
Assemblers and fabricators...	51-2000	1,950,900	1,913,100	-37,800	-2
Aircraft structure, surfaces, rigging, and systems assemblers	51-2011	44,100	48,200	4,100	9
Electrical, electronics, and electromechanical assemblers	51-2020	297,500	254,200	-43,200	-15
Coil winders, tapers, and finishers...	51-2021	22,100	16,500	-5,600	-25
Electrical and electronic equipment assemblers	51-2022	213,300	182,000	-31,300	-15
Electromechanical equipment assemblers	51-2023	62,100	55,700	-6,400	-10
Engine and other machine assemblers	51-2031	39,900	36,700	-3,200	-8
Structural metal fabricators and fitters.....................................	51-2041	114,100	113,700	-400	0
Miscellaneous assemblers and fabricators	51-2090	1,455,400	1,460,200	4,900	0
Fiberglass laminators and fabricators	51-2091	30,300	28,900	-1,400	-5
Team assemblers	51-2092	1,112,300	1,112,700	400	0
Timing device assemblers, adjusters, and calibrators	51-2093	2,700	2,600	-100	-4
All other assemblers and fabricators...	51-2099	309,900	316,000	6,000	2

(NOTE) Data in this table are rounded. See the discussion of the employment projections table in the *Handbook* introductory chapter on *Occupational Information Included in the Handbook.*

The following tabulation shows the employment of assemblers and fabricators in the manufacturing industries that employed the most workers in 2008:

Motor vehicle parts manufacturing 134,900	
Semiconductor and other electronic component manufacturing.......................................94,800	
Motor vehicle manufacturing.....................................85,000	
Navigational, measuring, electromedical, and control instruments manufacturing....................72,400	
Architectural and structural metals manufacturing......71,700	

Assemblers and fabricators also work in many other nonmanufacturing industries. Twelve percent were employed by employment services firms, mostly as temporary workers; these temporary workers were mostly assigned to manufacturing plants. Wholesale and retail trade firms employed the next highest number of assemblers and fabricators. Many of these assemblers perform the final assembly of goods before the item is delivered to the customer. For example, most imported furniture is shipped in pieces and assemblers for furniture wholesalers and retailers put together the furniture prior to delivery.

Team assemblers, the largest specialty, accounted for 57 percent of assembler and fabricator jobs. The distribution of employment among the various types of assemblers was as follows in 2008:

Team assemblers 1,112,300	
Electrical and electronic equipment assemblers 213,300	
Structural metal fabricators and fitters 114,100	
Electromechanical equipment assemblers....................62,100	
Aircraft structure, surfaces, rigging, and systems assemblers...44,100	
Engine and other machine assemblers 39,900	
Fiberglass laminators and fabricators...........................30,300	
Coil winders, tapers, and finishers 22,100	
Timing device assemblers, adjusters, and calibrators 2,700	
Assemblers and fabricators, all other.........................309,900	

Job Outlook

Employment is projected to experience little or no change, primarily reflecting productivity growth and strong foreign competition in manufacturing. Job opportunities are expected to be good for qualified applicants in the manufacturing sector, particularly in growing, high-technology industries.

Employment change. Employment of assemblers and fabricators is expected to experience little or no change between 2008 and 2018, declining by 2 percent. Within the manufacturing sector, employment of assemblers and fabricators will be determined largely by the growth or decline in the production of certain manufactured goods. In general, despite projected growth in the output of manufactured goods, overall employment is not expected to grow as the whole sector becomes more efficient and is able to produce more with fewer workers. However, some individual industries are projected to have more jobs than others. The aircraft products and parts industry is projected to gain jobs over the decade as demand for new commercial planes grows significantly. Thus, the need for aircraft structure, surfaces, rigging, and systems assemblers is expected to grow. Also, industries such as electromedical product manufacturing, which includes magnetic resonance imaging (MRI) machines, pacemakers, and other devices, should grow with an aging population requiring additional medical technology.

In most other manufacturing industries, employment of assemblers and fabricators will be negatively affected by increasing productivity, which will come from improved processes, tools, and, in some cases, automation. Automation is limited in assembly by intricate products and complicated techniques. Automation will replace workers in operations with a large volume of simple, repetitive work. Automation will have less effect on the assembly of products that are low in volume or very complicated.

The use of team production techniques has been one factor in the continuing success of the manufacturing sector, boosting productivity and improving the quality of goods. Thus, while the number of assemblers overall is expected to decline in manufacturing, the number of team assemblers should grow as more manufacturing plants convert to using team production techniques.

Some manufacturers have sent their assembly functions to countries where labor costs are lower. Decisions by U.S. corporations to move manufacturing to other nations may limit employment growth for assemblers in some industries.

The largest increase in the number of assemblers and fabricators is projected to be in the employment services industry, which supplies temporary workers to various industries. Temporary workers are gaining in importance in the manufacturing sector and elsewhere, as companies facing cost pressures strive for a more flexible workforce to meet fluctuations in the market.

Job prospects. Job opportunities for assemblers are expected to be good for qualified applicants in the manufacturing sector, particularly in growing, high-technology industries, such as aerospace and electromedical devices. Some employers report difficulty finding qualified applicants looking for manufacturing employment. Many job openings will result from the need to replace workers leaving or retiring from this large occupational group.

Earnings
Wages vary by industry, geographic region, skill, educational level, and complexity of the machinery operated. Median hourly wages of team assemblers were $12.32 in May 2008. The middle 50 percent earned between $9.75 and $15.60. The lowest 10 percent earned less than $8.20, and the highest 10 percent earned more than $19.69. Median hourly wages in the manufacturing industries employing the largest numbers of team assemblers were as follows:

Motor vehicle manufacturing......................................$24.91
Motor vehicle body and trailer manufacturing...............14.13
Motor vehicle parts manufacturing 13.76
Plastics product manufacturing 11.31
Employment services 9.61

Median hourly wages of electrical and electronic equipment assemblers were $13.22 in May 2008. The middle 50 percent earned between $10.52 and $16.85. The lowest 10 percent earned less than $8.77, and the highest 10 percent earned more than $21.15. Median hourly wages in the manufacturing industries employing the largest numbers of electrical and electronic equipment assemblers were as follows:

Navigational, measuring, electromedical,
   and control instruments manufacturing....................$14.76
Electrical equipment manufacturing 13.25
Other electrical equipment and
   component manufacturing...12.62
Semiconductor and other electronic
   component manufacturing...12.59
Employment services 10.68

In May 2008, other assemblers and fabricators had the following median hourly wages:

Aircraft structure, surfaces, rigging,
   and systems assemblers...$21.22
Engine and other machine assemblers 15.70
Structural metal fabricators and fitters 15.58
Electromechanical equipment assemblers......................14.11
Timing device assemblers, adjusters, and calibrators 13.73
Fiberglass laminators and fabricators............................13.48
Coil winders, tapers, and finishers 13.33
Assemblers and fabricators, all other 13.37

Some assemblers and fabricators are members of labor unions. These unions include the International Association of Machinists and Aerospace Workers; the United Automobile, Aerospace and Agricultural Implement Workers of America; the International Brotherhood of Electrical Workers; and the United Steelworkers of America.

Related Occupations
Other occupations that involve operating machines and tools and assembling and checking products include:

	Page
Industrial machinery mechanics and millwrights	709
Inspectors, testers, sorters, samplers, and weighers................	768
Machine setters, operators, and tenders—metal and plastic ...	734
Welding, soldering, and brazing workers...............................	743

Sources of Additional Information
For information on certifications in electronics soldering, contact:
➤ IPC, 3000 Lakeside Dr., 309 S, Bannockburn, IL 60015 Internet: **http://www.ipc.org**

The Occupational Information Network (O*NET) provides information on a wide range of occupational characteristics. Links to O*NET appear at the end of the Internet version of this occupational statement, accessible at **http://www.bls.gov/ooh/ocos217.htm**

Food Processing Occupations

Significant Points

- Most workers in manual food processing jobs require little or no training prior to being hired.

- As more jobs involving cutting and processing meat shift from retail stores to food processing plants, job growth will be concentrated among lesser skilled workers, who are employed primarily in manufacturing.

- Highly skilled bakers should be in demand.

Nature of the Work
Food processing occupations include many different types of workers who process raw food products into the finished goods sold by grocers, wholesalers, restaurants, or institutional food services. These workers perform a variety of tasks and are responsible for producing many of the food products found in every household. Some of these workers are bakers, others slaughter or process meat, and still others operate food processing equipment.

Bakers mix and bake ingredients according to recipes to produce varying types and quantities of breads, pastries, and other baked goods. Bakers commonly are employed in commercial bakeries that distribute breads and pastries through established wholesale and retail outlets, mail order, or manufacturers' outlets. In these manufacturing facilities, bakers produce mostly standardized baked goods in large quantities, using high-volume mixing machines, ovens, and other equipment. Grocery stores and specialty shops produce smaller quantities of breads, pastries, and other baked goods for consumption on their premises or for sale as specialty baked goods. Although the quantities prepared and sold in these stores are often small, they often come in a wide variety of flavors and sizes.

Other food processing workers convert animal carcasses into manageable pieces of meat, known as boxed meat or case-ready meat, suitable for sale to wholesalers and retailers. The nature of their jobs varies significantly depending on the stage of the process in which they are involved. In animal slaughtering and processing plants, slaughterers and meat packers slaughter cattle, hogs, and sheep, and cut carcasses into large wholesale cuts, such as rounds, loins, ribs, tenders, and chucks, to facilitate the handling, distribution, marketing, and sale of meat. In most plants, some *slaughterers and meat packers* further process the large parts into case-ready cuts that are ready for retail stores. Retailers and grocers increasingly prefer such prepackaged meat products because a butcher isn't needed to further portion the cuts for sale. Slaughterers and meat packers also produce hamburger meat and meat trimmings, and prepare sausages, luncheon meats, and other fabricated meat products. They usually work on assembly lines, with each individual responsible for only a few of the many cuts needed to process a carcass. Depending on the type of cut, these workers use knives; cleavers; meat saws; bandsaws; or other potentially dangerous equipment.

Poultry cutters and trimmers slaughter and cut up chickens, turkeys, and other types of poultry. Although the packaging end of the poultry processing industry is becoming increasingly automated, many jobs, such as slaughtering, trimming, and deboning, are still done manually. Most poultry cutters and trimmers perform routine cuts on poultry as it moves along production lines.

Meat, poultry, and fish cutters and trimmers also prepare ready-to-cook foods, often at processing plants, but increasingly at grocery and specialty food stores. This preparation often entails filleting meat, poultry, or fish; cutting it into bite-sized pieces or tenders; preparing and adding vegetables; and applying sauces and flavorings, marinades, or breading. These case-ready products are gaining in popularity as they offer quick and easy preparation for consumers while, in many cases, also offering healthier options.

Manufacturing and retail establishments are both likely to employ fish cutters and trimmers, also called fish cleaners. These workers primarily scale, cut, and dress fish by removing the head, scales, and other inedible portions and then cut the fish into steaks or fillets. In retail markets, these workers also may wait on customers and clean fish to order. Some fish processing is done aboard ships where fish can be caught, processed, and often flash frozen to preserve freshness.

Butchers and meat cutters generally process meat at later stages of production, although some are employed at meat processing plants. Most work for grocery stores, wholesale establishments that supply meat to restaurants, or institutional food service facilities that separate wholesale cuts of meat into retail cuts or smaller pieces, known as primals. These butchers cut meat into steaks and chops, shape and tie roasts, and grind beef for sale as chopped meat. Boneless cuts are prepared using knives, slicers, or power cutters, while bandsaws and cleavers are required to cut bone-in pieces of meat. Butchers and meat cutters in retail food stores also may weigh, wrap, and label the cuts of meat; arrange them in refrigerated cases for display; and prepare special cuts to fill orders by customers.

Others who work in food processing include *food batchmakers,* who set up and operate equipment that mixes, blends, or cooks ingredients used in the manufacture of food products according to formulas or recipes; *food cooking machine operators and tenders,* who operate or tend cooking equipment, such as steam-cooking vats, deep-fry cookers, pressure cookers, kettles, and boilers to prepare a wide range of cooked food products, and *food and tobacco roasting, baking, and drying machine operators and tenders,* who use equipment to reduce the moisture content of food or tobacco products or to prepare food for canning. The machines they use include hearth ovens, kiln driers, roasters, char kilns, steam ovens, and vacuum drying equipment. These workers monitor equipment for temperature, humidity, or

Food processing workers cut meat into smaller sizes and wrap them for sale.

other factors and make the appropriate adjustments to ensure proper cooking and processing.

All workers who work with food must regularly clean and sanitize utensils, work surfaces, and equipment used to process food to comply with health and sanitation guidelines to prevent the spread of disease.

Work environment. Working conditions vary by occupation and by type and size of establishment, but all employees are required to maintain good personal hygiene and keep equipment clean. Facilities that process food, regardless of industry or location, are regularly inspected to ensure that equipment and employees comply with health and sanitation regulations.

Most bakers work in bakeries, grocery stores, and restaurants. Bakeries are often hot and noisy. Bakers typically work under strict order deadlines and critical time-sensitive baking requirements, both of which can induce stress. Bakers usually work odd hours and may work early mornings, evenings, weekends, and holidays.

Butchers and meat cutters in animal slaughtering and processing plants and in large grocery stores, work in large meat cutting rooms equipped with power machines, extremely sharp knives, and conveyors. In smaller retail shops, butchers or fish cleaners may work in a cramped space behind the meat or fish counter where they also can keep track of customers.

Butchers and meat cutters, poultry and fish cutters and trimmers, and slaughterers and meatpackers often work in cold, damp rooms where meat is kept to prevent spoiling. In addition, long periods of standing and repetitive physical tasks make the work tiring. Working with sharp knives on slippery floors makes butchers and meat cutters more susceptible to injury than almost all other workers in the economy; however, injury rates for the animal slaughtering and processing industry have been declining. Injuries include cuts and occasional amputations, which occur when knives, cleavers, or power tools are used improperly. Also, repetitive slicing and lifting often lead to cumulative trauma injuries, such as carpal tunnel syndrome and back strains. To reduce the incidence of cumulative trauma injuries, some employers have reduced employee workloads, added prescribed rest periods, redesigned jobs and tools, and promoted increased awareness of early warning signs as steps to prevent further injury. Nevertheless, workers in the occupation still face the potential threat that some injuries may be disabling.

Workers who operate food processing machinery typically work in production areas that are specially designed for food preservation or processing. Food batchmakers, in particular, work in kitchen-type, assembly-line production facilities. The ovens, as well as the motors of blenders, mixers, and other equipment, often make work areas very warm and noisy. Hazards created by the equipment that these workers use can cause injuries such as cuts and scrapes from cleaning and handling sharp tools and utensils and burns from being in contact with hot surfaces and liquids.

Food batchmakers; food and tobacco roasting, baking, and drying machine operators; and food cooking machine operators and tenders spend a great deal of time on their feet and generally work a regular 40-hour week that may include night and early morning shifts.

Training, Other Qualifications, and Advancement

No formal education is required for most food processing jobs. Employers generally provide most of the training for these occupations upon being hired.

Education and training. Bakers need to become skilled in baking, icing, and decorating. They often start their careers as apprentices or trainees. Apprentice bakers usually start in craft bakeries, while trainees usually begin in store bakeries, such as those in supermarkets. Many apprentice bakers participate in correspondence study and may work towards a certificate in baking.

The skills needed to be a baker are often underestimated. Bakers need to learn how to combine ingredients and to learn how ingredients are affected by heat. They need to learn how to operate and maintain a range of equipment used in the production process. Courses in nutrition are helpful for those selling baked goods or developing new recipes. If running a small business, they need to know how to operate a business. All bakers must follow government health and sanitation regulations.

Most butchers and meat, poultry, and fish cutters and trimmers acquire their skills through on-the-job training programs. The length of training varies significantly. Simple cutting operations require a few days to learn, while more complicated tasks, such as eviscerating slaughtered animals, generally require several months of training. The training period for highly skilled butchers at the retail level may be 1 or 2 years.

Generally, trainees begin by doing less difficult jobs, such as making simple cuts or removing bones. Under the guidance of experienced workers, trainees learn the proper use and care of tools and equipment, while also learning how to prepare various cuts of meat. After demonstrating skill with various meat cutting tools, trainees learn to divide carcasses into wholesale cuts and wholesale cuts into retail and individual portions. Trainees also may learn to roll and tie roasts, prepare sausage, and cure meat. Those employed in retail food establishments often are taught to perform basic business operations, such as inventory control, meat buying, and recordkeeping. In addition, growing concern about food-borne pathogens in meats has led employers to offer numerous safety seminars and extensive training in food safety to employees.

On-the-job training is common among food machine operators and tenders. They learn to run the different types of equipment by watching and helping other workers. Training can last anywhere from a month to a year, depending on the complexity of the tasks and the number of products involved. A degree in an appropriate area—dairy processing for those working in dairy product operations, for example—is helpful for advancement to a lead worker or a supervisory role. Most food batchmakers participate in on-the-job training, usually from about a month to a year. Some food batchmakers learn their trade through an approved apprenticeship program.

Other qualifications. Bakers need to be able to follow instructions, have an eye for detail, and communicate well with others. Meat, poultry, and fish cutters and trimmers need manual dexterity, good depth perception, color discrimination, and good hand-eye coordination. They also need physical strength to lift and move heavy pieces of meat. Butchers and fish cleaners who wait on customers should have a pleasant personality, a neat

Projections data from the National Employment Matrix

Occupational Title	SOC Code	Employment, 2008	Projected Employment, 2018	Change, 2008-2018	
				Number	Percent
Food processing occupations	51-3000	706,700	734,000	27,400	4
Bakers	51-3011	151,600	151,900	300	0
Butchers and other meat, poultry, and fish processing workers....	51-3020	397,100	413,900	16,800	4
Butchers and meat cutters	51-3021	129,100	131,000	1,900	1
Meat, poultry, and fish cutters and trimmers.............................	51-3022	169,600	180,400	10,800	6
Slaughterers and meat packers...	51-3023	98,400	102,500	4,100	4
Miscellaneous food processing workers	51-3090	157,900	168,200	10,300	7
Food and tobacco roasting, baking, and drying machine operators and tenders	51-3091	18,100	18,200	100	0
Food batchmakers	51-3092	100,500	109,200	8,800	9
Food cooking machine operators and tenders..........................	51-3093	39,300	40,800	1,500	4

(NOTE) Data in this table are rounded. See the discussion of the employment projections table in the *Handbook* introductory chapter on *Occupational Information Included in the Handbook.*

appearance, and the ability to communicate clearly. In some States, a health certificate is required for employment.

Certification and advancement. Bakers have the option of obtaining certification through the Retail Bakers of America. While not mandatory, obtaining certification assures the public and prospective employers that the baker has sufficient skills and knowledge to work at a retail baking establishment.

The Retail Bakers of America offers certification for four levels of competence with a focus on several broad areas, including baking sanitation, management, retail sales, and staff training. Those who wish to become certified must satisfy a combination of education and experience requirements prior to taking an examination. The education and experience requirements vary by the level of certification desired. For example, a certified journey baker requires no formal education but a minimum of 1 year of work experience. By contrast, a certified master baker must have earned the certified baker designation, and must have completed 30 hours of sanitation coursework approved by a culinary school or government agency, 30 hours of professional development courses or workshops, and a minimum of 8 years of commercial or retail baking experience.

Food processing workers in retail or wholesale establishments may progress to supervisory jobs, such as department managers or team leaders in supermarkets. A few of these workers may become buyers for wholesalers or supermarket chains. Some food processing workers go on to open their own markets or bakeries. In processing plants, workers may advance to supervisory positions or become team leaders.

Employment

Food processing workers held 706,700 jobs in 2008. Employment among the various types of food processing occupations was distributed as follows:

Meat, poultry, and fish cutters and trimmers..............169,600
Bakers...151,600
Butchers and meat cutters 129,100
Food batchmakers 100,500
Slaughterers and meat packers...98,400
Food cooking machine operators and tenders..............39,300
Food and tobacco roasting, baking, and drying machine operators and tenders 18,100

Fifty-eight percent of all food processing workers were employed in food manufacturing, including animal slaughtering and processing plants, the largest industry component. Food and beverage stores, which include grocery and specialty food stores, employed another 27 percent. Butchers, meat cutters, and bakers are employed in stores in almost every city and town in the Nation, while most other food processing jobs are concentrated in communities with food processing plants.

Job Outlook

Increased demand for processed food and meat by a growing population will increase the need for food processing workers; however, processing plant and distribution efficiencies will offset growing output and cause employment of these workers to grow more slowly than the average between 2008 and 2018. In addition, job opportunities should be good as the need to replace experienced workers who transfer to other occupations or leave the labor force should generate additional job openings.

Employment change. Overall employment in the food processing occupations is projected to increase 4 percent during the 2008–18 decade, more slowly than the average for all occupations. As the Nation's population grows, the demand for meat, poultry, and seafood, baked goods, and other processed foods will increase requiring additional people to work in these occupations. Additionally, consumers are increasingly seeking out more convenient methods of preparing meals, which is driving up demand for convenient ready-to-eat or heat foods. These foods are increasingly being prepared at the factory, as well as the local grocery store for carry-out, thus increasing the need for workers in both locations. However, increasing productivity at meat and food processing plants should offset some of the need for more workers at these plants.

Slaughterers and meat packers, meat, poultry, and fish cutters and trimmers, and butchers and meat cutters are all expected to experience some growth in employment. For these occupations in particular, faster growth will take place at the processing plant and away from retail stores, as meats are increasingly processed at processing plants or centralized facilities for delivery to stores. This shift from retail stores to food processing plants will cause demand for lesser skilled workers, who are employed primarily in meat packing manufacturing plants, to be greater than for butchers and meat cutters.

Many of these same reasons apply to employment in food processing jobs; however, these jobs are more automated than the meat processing occupations, thus productivity improvements will likely impact these workers more. Food batchmakers will experience average employment growth largely due to improved packaging and distribution operations; employment of food cooking machine operators and tenders will grow more slowly than the average; and food and tobacco roasting, baking, and drying machine operators and tenders will show little or no growth.

A growing number of stores that sell cookies, bread, and other specialty baked goods, will spur demand for bakers, particularly in grocery and other specialty stores, but increased use of off-site contract bakers with larger baking capacities will off-set increased demand and cause employment to show little or no change.

Job prospects. Jobs should be available in all food processing specialties because of the need to replace experienced workers who transfer to other occupations or leave the labor force. Highly skilled bakers should be especially in demand because of growing demand for specialty products and the time it takes to learn to make these products.

Earnings

Earnings vary by industry, skill, geographic region, and educational level. Median annual wages of bakers were $23,290 in May 2008. The middle 50 percent earned between $18,760 and $29,720. The lowest 10 percent earned less than $16,420, and the highest 10 percent earned more than $37,250. Median annual wages in the industries employing the largest numbers of bakers in May 2008 were:

Bakeries and tortilla manufacturing	$23,860
Grocery stores	23,700
Other general merchandise stores	23,610
Full-service restaurants	22,300
Limited-service eating places	20,500

Median annual wages of butchers and meat cutters were $28,290 in May 2008. The middle 50 percent earned between $21,700 and $36,670. The lowest 10 percent earned less than $17,600, and the highest 10 percent earned more than $45,060. Butchers and meat cutters employed at the retail level typically earned more than those in manufacturing. Median annual wages in the industries employing the largest numbers of butchers and meat cutters in May 2008 were:

Other general merchandise stores	$33,830
Grocery stores	29,090
Grocery and related products merchant wholesalers	28,710
Specialty food stores	25,830
Animal slaughtering and processing	24,060

Meat, poultry, and fish cutters and trimmers typically earn less than butchers and meat cutters. In May 2008, median annual wages for these lower skilled workers were $21,810. The middle 50 percent earned between $18,520 and $25,130. The lowest 10 percent earned less than $16,640, while the highest 10 percent earned more than $30,070. Median annual wages in the industries employing the largest numbers of meat, poultry, and fish cutters and trimmers in May 2008 were:

Grocery and related product merchant holesalers	$23,030
Animal slaughtering and processing	22,100
Grocery stores	21,360
Specialty food stores	19,490
Seafood product preparation and packaging	18,600

In May 2008, median annual wages for slaughterers and meat packers were $23,030. The middle 50 percent earned between $19,700 and $26,450. The lowest 10 percent earned less than $17,130, and the highest 10 percent earned more than $30,740. Median annual wages in animal slaughtering and processing, the industry employing the largest number of slaughterers and meat packers, were $23,040 in May 2008.

In May 2008, median annual wages for food and tobacco roasting, baking, and drying machine operators and tenders were $26,640. The middle 50 percent earned between $21,100 and $35,470. The lowest 10 percent earned less than $17,610, and the highest 10 percent earned more than $42,370. Median annual wages in bakeries and tortilla manufacturing, the industry employing the largest number of food and tobacco roasting, baking, and drying machine operators and tenders, were $29,700 in May 2008.

Median annual earnings of food batchmakers were $24,170 in May 2008. The middle 50 percent earned between $18,820 and $31,980. The lowest 10 percent earned less than $16,260, and the highest 10 percent earned more than $40,210. Median annual wages in the industries employing the largest numbers of food batchmakers in May 2008 were:

Dairy product manufacturing	$31,840
Other food manufacturing	25,780
Fruit and vegetable preserving and specialty food manufacturing	24,190
Sugar and confectionery product manufacturing	23,310
Bakeries and tortilla manufacturing	22,800

Median annual wages for food cooking machine operators and tenders were $22,880 in May 2008. The middle 50 percent earned between $18,650 and $28,680. The lowest 10 percent earned less than $16,370, and the highest 10 percent earned more than $34,330. Median annual wages in the industries employing the largest numbers of food cooking machine operators and tenders in May 2008 were:

Other food manufacturing	$26,820
Fruit and vegetable preserving and specialty food manufacturing	25,520
Bakeries and tortilla manufacturing	22,900
Animal slaughtering and processing	22,090
Grocery stores	19,710

Food processing workers generally received typical benefits, including pension plans for union members or those employed by grocery stores. However, poultry workers rarely earned substantial benefits. In 2008, 16 percent of all food processing workers were union members or were covered by a union contract. Many food processing workers are members of the United Food and Commercial Workers International Union.

Related Occupations

Food processing workers must be skilled at both hand and machine work and must have some knowledge of processes and techniques that are involved in handling and preparing food. Other occupations that require similar skills and knowledge include

Sources of Additional Information

See your State employment service offices for information about job openings for food processing occupations.

For information on various levels of certification as a baker, contact:

➤ Retail Bakers of America, 8400 Westpark Drive, 2nd Floor, McLean, VA, 22102

The Occupational Information Network (O*NET) provides information on a wide range of occupational characteristics. Links to O*NET appear at the end of the Internet version of this occupational statement, accessible at **http://www.bls.gov/ooh/ocos219.htm**

Metal Workers and Plastic Workers

Computer Control Programmers and Operators

Significant Points

- Manufacturing industries employ almost all of these workers.

- Workers learn in apprenticeship programs, informally on the job, and in secondary, vocational, or postsecondary schools; many entrants have previously worked as machinists or machine setters, operators, and tenders.

- Applicants are expected to face competition for jobs.

Nature of the Work

Computer control programmers and operators use computer numerically controlled (CNC) machines to produce a wide variety of products, from automobile engines to computer keyboards. CNC machines operate by reading the code included in a computer-controlled module, which drives the machine tool and performs the functions of forming and shaping a part formerly done by machine operators. CNC machines include tools such as lathes, laser cutting machines, roll forms, press brakes and printing presses. CNC machines use the same techniques as many other mechanical manufacturing machines but are controlled by a central computer instead of a human operator or electric switchboard. Many old-fashioned machines can be retrofitted with a computer control, which can greatly improve the productivity of a machine. Computer control programmers and operators normally produce large quantities of one part, although they may produce small batches or one-of-a-kind items. These machines are most commonly used in metalworking industries where precision is imperative, because computers can be more accurate than humans in this work.

CNC programmers—also referred to as *numerical tool and process control programmers*—develop the programs that run the machine tools. They often review three-dimensional computer-aided/automated design (CAD) blueprints of a part and determine the sequence of events that will be needed to make the part. This may involve calculating where to cut or bore into the workpiece, how fast to feed the metal into the machine, and how much metal to remove.

Next, CNC programmers turn the planned machining operations into a set of instructions. These instructions are translated into a computer aided/automated manufacturing (CAM) program containing a set of commands for the machine to follow. On a CNC machine, commands normally are a series of numbers (hence, numerical control) that may describe where cuts should occur, where a roll should bend a piece, or the speed of the feed into the machine. After the program is developed, CNC programmers and operators check the programs to ensure that the machinery will function properly and that the output will meet specifications. Because a problem with the program could damage costly machinery and cutting tools or simply waste valuable time and materials, computer simulations may be used to check the program before a trial run. If errors are found, the program must be changed and retested until the problem is resolved. In addition, growing connectivity between CAD/CAM software and CNC machine tools is raising productivity by automatically translating designs into instructions for the computer controller on the machine tool. Many new machines take advantage of easy-to-use graphical user interface programs that use pictures and buttons, instead of long strings of a computer programming language. This improvement in usability has pushed many manufacturing companies to combine the jobs of CNC programmers and machine operators.

After the programming work is completed, *CNC setup operators*—also referred to as *computer-controlled machine tool operators, metal and plastic*—set up the machine for the job. They download the program into the machine, load the proper tools into the machine, position the workpiece on the CNC machine tool—spindle, lathe, milling machine, or other machine—and then start the machine. During the test run of a new program, the setup operator, who may also have some programming skills, or the CNC programmer closely monitors the machine for signs of problems, such as a vibrating work piece, the breakage of cutting tools, or an out-of-specification final product. If a problem is detected, a setup operator or CNC programmer will modify the program using the control module to eliminate the problems or to improve the speed and accuracy of the program.

Once a program is completed, the operation of the CNC machine may move from the more experienced setup operator to a less-skilled machine operator. Operators load workpieces and

Applicants for computer control programmer and operator jobs are expected to face competition.

tools into a machine, press the start button, monitor the machine for problems, and measure the parts produced to check that they match specifications. If they encounter a problem that requires modification to the cutting program, they shut down the machine and wait for a more experienced CNC setup operator to fix the problem. Many CNC operators start at this basic level and gradually perform more setup tasks as they gain experience.

Regardless of skill level, all CNC operators detect some problems by listening for specific sounds—for example, a dull cutting tool that needs changing or excessive vibration. Machine tools rotate at high speeds, which can create problems with harmonic vibrations in the workpiece. Vibrations cause the machine tools to make minor cutting errors, hurting the quality of the product. Operators listen for vibrations and then adjust the cutting speed to compensate. For common errors in the machine, programmers write code that displays an error code to help operators, who are expected to make minor repairs, and machine mechanics fix a problem quickly. CNC operators also ensure that the workpiece is being properly lubricated and cooled, since the machining of metal products generates a significant amount of heat.

Since CNC machines can operate with limited input from the operator, a single operator may monitor several machines simultaneously. Typically, an operator might monitor two machines cutting relatively simple parts from softer materials, while devoting most of his or her attention to a third machine cutting a much more difficult part from hard metal, such as stainless steel. Operators are often expected to carefully schedule their work so that all of the machines are always operating.

Work environment. Most machine shops are clean, well lit, and ventilated. Most modern CNC machines are partially or totally enclosed, minimizing the exposure of workers to noise, debris, and the lubricants used to cool workpieces during machining. People working in this occupation report fewer injuries than most other manufacturing jobs; nevertheless, working around machine tools can be noisy and presents certain dangers, and workers must follow safety precautions to minimize injuries. Computer-controlled machine tool operators, metal and plastic, wear protective equipment, such as safety glasses to shield against bits of flying metal and earplugs to dampen

machinery noise. They also must exercise caution when handling hazardous coolants and lubricants. The job requires stamina, because operators stand most of the day and, at times, may need to lift moderately heavy workpieces.

Numerical tool and process control programmers work on desktop computers that may be in offices or on the shop floor. The office areas usually are clean, well lit, and free of machine noise. On the shop floor, CNC programmers encounter the same hazards and exercise the same safety precautions as do CNC operators.

Many computer control programmers and operators work a 40-hour week. CNC operators increasingly work evening and weekend shifts as companies justify investments in more expensive machinery by extending hours of operation. Overtime is common during peak production periods.

Training, Other Qualifications, and Advancement
Computer control programmers and operators train in various ways—in apprenticeship programs, informally on the job, and in secondary, vocational, or postsecondary schools. In general, the more skills needed for the job, the more education and training are needed to qualify. Many entrants have previously worked as machinists or machine setters, operators, and tenders.

Education and training. The amount and type of education and training needed depends on the type of job. Entry-level CNC machine operators may need at least a few months of on-the-job training to reach proficiency. Setup operators and programmers, however, may need years of experience or formal training to write or modify programs. Programmers and operators can receive their training in various ways—in apprenticeship programs, informally on the job, and in secondary, vocational, or postsecondary schools. A growing number of computer control programmers and more skilled operators receive their formal training from community or technical colleges. For some specialized types of programming, such as that needed to produce complex parts for the aerospace or shipbuilding industries, employers may prefer individuals with a degree in engineering.

For those interested in becoming computer control programmers or operators, high school or vocational school courses in mathematics (trigonometry and algebra), blueprint reading, computer programming, metalworking, and drafting are recommended. Apprenticeship programs consist of shop training and related classroom instruction. In shop training, apprentices learn filing, handtapping, and dowel fitting, as well as the operation of various machine tools. Classroom instruction includes math, physics, programming, blueprint reading, CAD software, safety, and shop practices. Skilled computer control programmers and operators need an understanding of the machining process, including the complex physics that occur at the cutting point. Thus, most training programs teach CNC operators and programmers to perform operations on manual machines prior to operating CNC machines.

As new technology is introduced, computer control programmers and operators normally receive additional training to update their skills. This training usually is provided by a representative of the equipment manufacturer or a local technical school. Many employers offer tuition reimbursement for job-related courses.

Projections data from the National Employment Matrix

Occupational Title	SOC Code	Employment, 2008	Projected Employment, 2018	Change, 2008-2018	
				Number	Percent
Computer control programmers and operators	51-4010	157,800	164,500	6,700	4
Computer-controlled machine tool operators, metal and plastic.....	51-4011	141,000	150,300	9,300	7
Numerical tool and process control programmers	51-4012	16,800	14,200	-2,600	-15

(NOTE) Data in this table are rounded. See the discussion of the employment projections table in the *Handbook* introductory chapter on *Occupational Information Included in the Handbook.*

Certification and other qualifications. Employers prefer to hire workers who have a basic knowledge of computers and electronics and experience with machine tools. In fact, many entrants to these occupations have experience working as machine setters, operators, and tenders or machinists. Persons interested in becoming computer control programmers or operators should be mechanically inclined and able to work independently and do highly accurate work.

To boost the skill level of all metalworkers and to create a more uniform standard of competency, a number of training facilities and colleges have formed certification programs. Employers may pay for training and certification tests after hiring an entry-level worker.

Advancement. Computer control programmers and operators can advance in several ways. Experienced CNC operators may become CNC programmers or machinery mechanics, and some are promoted to supervisory or administrative positions in their firms. Some highly skilled workers move into tool and die making, and a few open their own shops.

Employment

Computer control programmers and operators held about 157,800 jobs in 2008. About 90 percent were computer-controlled machine tool operators, metal and plastic, and about 10 percent were numerical tool and process control programmers. The manufacturing industry employs almost all these workers. Employment was concentrated in fabricated metal products manufacturing, machinery manufacturing, plastics products manufacturing, and transportation equipment manufacturing making mostly aerospace and automobile parts. Although computer control programmers and operators work in all parts of the country, jobs are most plentiful in the areas where manufacturing is concentrated.

Job Outlook

Despite the projected increase in employment, applicants are expected to face competition for jobs, as there are more trained workers than available jobs.

Employment change. Overall employment of computer control programmers and operators is expected to increase by 4 percent over the 2008–18 period, which is slower than average for all occupations. Employment of computer controlled machine tool operators, metal and plastic is expected to increase by 7 percent, which is about as fast as the average for all occupations. The increasing use of CNC machine tools in all sectors of the manufacturing industry, replacing older mechanical metal and plastic working machines, will increase demand for computer-controlled machine tool operators. However, the demand for computer control programmers will be negatively affected by the increasing use of software (CAD/CAM) that automatically translates part and product designs into CNC machine tool instructions, and by simpler interfaces that allow machine operators to program the machines themselves. As a result, employment of numerical tool and process control programmers will decline by 15 percent over the projection period.

Job prospects. Computer control programmers and operators should face competition for jobs, as many workers currently operating mechanical machines will be retrained to operate computer controlled machines and programming activities are increasingly done by these operators; however, workers with the ability to operate multiple CNC machine types should have better opportunities, as companies are increasingly demanding more versatile workers.

Earnings

Median hourly wages of computer-controlled machine tool operators, metal and plastic, were $16.03 in May 2008. The middle 50 percent earned between $12.83 and $19.45. The lowest 10 percent earned less than $10.49, whereas the top 10 percent earned more than $23.84. Median hourly wages in the manufacturing industries employing the largest numbers of computer-controlled machine tool operators, metal and plastic, in May 2008 were:

Aerospace product and parts manufacturing	$18.89
Metalworking machinery manufacturing	18.08
Machine shops; turned product; and screw, nut, and bolt manufacturing	15.57
Motor vehicle parts manufacturing	15.18
Plastics product manufacturing	14.19

Median hourly wages of numerical tool and process control programmers were $21.30 in May 2008. The middle 50 percent earned between $16.94 and $26.55. The lowest 10 percent earned less than $13.65, while the top 10 percent earned more than $32.59.

Many employers, especially those with formal apprenticeship programs, offer tuition assistance for training classes.

Related Occupations

Occupations most closely related to computer control programmers and operators are other metal and plastic working occupations, which include:

Sources of Additional Information

For more information on training and new technology for computer control programmers and operators, contact:

➤ Fabricators and Manufacturers Association, 833 Featherstone Rd., Rockford, IL 61107 Internet: **http://www.fmanet.org**

The Occupational Information Network (O*NET) provides information on a wide range of occupational characteristics. Links to O*NET appear at the end of the Internet version of this occupational statement, accessible at **http://www.bls.gov/ooh/ocos286.htm**

Machine Setters, Operators, and Tenders—Metal and Plastic

Significant Points

- Manufacturing industries employ over 90 percent of workers.

- A few weeks of on-the-job training is sufficient for most workers to learn basic machine tending operations, but a year or more is required to become a highly skilled operator or setter.

- Employment is projected to decline rapidly.

- Those who can operate multiple machines will have the best opportunities for advancement and for gaining jobs with more long-term potential.

Nature of the Work

Consider the parts of a toaster, such as the metal or plastic housing or the lever that lowers the toast. These parts, and many other metal and plastic products, are produced by machines that are controlled by machine setters, operators, and tenders—metal and plastic. In fact, machine operators in the metalworking and plastics industries play a major role in producing most of the consumer products on which we rely daily.

In general, these workers can be separated into two groups—those who set up machines for operation and those who operate the machines during production. *Machine setters*, or setup workers, prepare the machines prior to production, perform initial test runs producing a part, and may adjust and make minor repairs to the machinery during its operation. *Machine operators and tenders* primarily monitor the machinery during its operation; sometimes they load or unload the machine or make minor adjustments to the controls. Many workers both set up and operate equipment.

Setup workers prepare machines for production runs. Most machines can make a variety of products, and these different items are made by using different inputs or tooling. For instance, a single machine may use different sized tools to produce both large and small wheels for cars. The tools inside the machine must be changed and maintained by setup workers. On some machines, tools may become dull after extended use and must be sharpened. It is common for a setter to remove the tool, use a grinder or file to sharpen the tool, and place the tool back in the machine. New tools are produced by tool and die makers. (See

statement on tool and die makers elsewhere in the *Handbook*.) After installing the tools into a machine, setup workers often produce the initial batch of goods, inspect the products, and turn the machine over to an operator.

Machine operators and tenders are responsible for running machines in manufacturing plants. After a setter prepares a machine for production, an operator observes the machine and the objects it produces. Operators may have to load the machine with materials for production or adjust machine speeds during production. Operators must periodically inspect the parts a machine produces by comparing the parts to blueprint using rulers, micrometers, and other specialized measuring devices. If the products do not meet design parameters, the machine is shut down; if it is a common, minor error the operator may fix the machine, but if it is more serious an industrial machinery mechanic is called to make a repair. (See the statement on industrial machinery mechanics and millwrights elsewhere in the *Handbook*.) Some machines don't require constant input or attention, so the operator may oversee multiple machines at a given time. In many cases, operators must document production numbers in a notebook or computer database at the end of every hour or shift.

Setters, operators, and tenders usually are identified by the type of machine with which they work. Some examples of specific titles are drilling-machine and boring-machine setup workers, milling-machine and planing-machine tenders, and lathe-machine and turning-machine tool operators. Job duties usually vary with the size of the firm and the type of machine being operated. Although some workers specialize in one or two types of machinery, many are trained to set up or operate a variety of machines. Increasing automation allows machine setters to operate multiple machines simultaneously. In addition, newer production techniques, such as team-oriented "lean" manufacturing, require machine operators to rotate between different machines. Rotating assignments results in more varied work, but also requires workers to have a wider range of skills.

Work environment. Most machine setters, operators, and tenders—metal and plastic work in areas that are clean, well lit, and well ventilated. Nevertheless, stamina is required, because machine operators and setters are on their feet much of the

Machine operators stop production when faulty parts are produced.

day and may do moderately heavy lifting. Also, these workers operate powerful, high-speed machines that can be dangerous if strict safety rules are not observed. Most operators wear protective equipment, such as safety glasses, earplugs, and steel-toed boots, to protect against flying particles of metal or plastic, noise from the machines, and heavy objects that could be dropped. Many modern machines are enclosed, minimizing the exposure of workers to noise, dust, and lubricants used during machining. Other required safety equipment varies by work setting and machine. For example, those in the plastics industry who work near materials that emit dangerous fumes or dust must wear respirators.

Overtime is common during periods of increased production for most machine setters, operators, and tenders—metal and plastic, but they usually work a 40-hour week. Because many metalworking and plastics working shops operate more than one shift daily, some operators work nights and weekends.

Training, Other Qualifications, and Advancement

A few weeks of on-the-job training is sufficient for most workers to learn basic machine operations, but a year or more is required to become a highly skilled operator or setter.

Education and training. Employers generally prefer workers who have a high school diploma or equivalent for jobs as machine setters, operators, and tenders. Those interested in this occupation can improve their employment opportunities by completing high school courses in shop and blueprint reading and by gaining a working knowledge of the properties of metals and plastics. A solid math background, including courses in algebra, geometry, trigonometry, and basic statistics, also is useful, along with experience working with computers.

Machine operator trainees begin by observing and assisting experienced workers, sometimes in formal training programs or apprenticeships. Under supervision, they may start by supplying materials, starting and stopping the machine, or removing finished products from it. Then they advance to the more difficult tasks performed by operators, such as adjusting feed speeds, changing cutting tools, or inspecting a finished product for defects. Eventually, some develop the skills and experience to set up machines and assist newer operators.

The complexity of the equipment largely determines the time required to become an operator. Most operators learn the basic machine operations and functions in a few weeks, but a year or more may be needed to become skilled operators or to advance to the more highly skilled job of setter. Although many operators learn on the job, some community colleges and other educational institutions offer courses and certifications in operating metal and plastics machines. In addition to providing on-the-job training, some employers send promising machine operators to classes. Other employers prefer to hire workers who have completed, or currently are enrolled in, a training program.

Setters or technicians often plan the sequence of work, make the first production run, and determine which adjustments need to be made. As a result, these workers need a thorough knowledge of the machinery and of the products being manufactured. Strong analytical abilities are particularly important for this job. Some companies have formal training programs for operators and setters, which often combine classroom instruction with on-the-job training.

Other qualifications. As the machinery in manufacturing plants becomes more complex and with changes to shop-floor organization that require more teamwork among employees, employers increasingly look for persons with good communication and interpersonal skills. Mechanical aptitude, manual dexterity, and experience working with machinery also are helpful.

Certification and advancement. Job opportunities and advancement can be enhanced by becoming certified in a particular machine skill. There are many trade groups that offer certification for machine operators and setup workers, and certifications vary greatly depending upon the skill level involved. Certifications may allow operators and setters to switch jobs more easily because they can prove their skills to a potential employer.

Advancement usually takes the form of higher pay and a wider range of responsibilities. With experience and expertise, workers can become trainees for more highly skilled positions; for instance, it is common for machine operators to move into setup or machinery maintenance positions. Setup workers may also move into maintenance, machinist, or tool and die maker roles. (See the statements on industrial machinery mechanics and millwrights, machinists, and tool and die makers elsewhere in the *Handbook*.) Skilled workers with good communication and analytical skills can move into supervisory positions.

Employment

Machine setters, operators, and tenders, metal and plastic held about 1.0 million jobs in 2008. About 9 out of 10 jobs were found in manufacturing—primarily in fabricated metal products, plastics and rubber products, primary metal, machinery, and motor vehicle parts manufacturing.

Job Outlook

Employment is expected to decline rapidly. Those who can operate multiple machines will have the best opportunities for advancement and for gaining jobs with more long-term potential.

Employment change. Employment in the various machine setter, operator, and tender occupations is expected to decline rapidly by 13 percent from 2008 to 2018. Employment will be affected by technological advances, changing demand for the goods they produce, foreign competition, and the reorganization of production processes.

One of the most important factors influencing employment change in this occupation is the implementation of labor-saving machinery. Many firms are adopting new technologies, such as computer-controlled machine tools and robots in order to improve quality, lower production costs, and remain competitive. The switch to computer-controlled machinery requires the employment of computer control programmers and operators (see this statement elsewhere in the *Handbook*) instead of machine setters, operators and tenders. The lower-skilled manual machine tool operators and tenders jobs are more likely to be eliminated by these new technologies, because the functions they perform may be more effectively completed with computer-controlled machinery.

The demand for machine setters, operators, and tenders—metal and plastic is also affected by the demand for the parts they

Projections data from the National Employment Matrix

Occupational Title	SOC Code	Employment, 2008	Projected Employment, 2018	Change, 2008-2018	
				Number	Percent
Machine setters, operators, and tenders—metal and plastic	–	1,028,400	899,000	-129,400	-13
Forming machine setters, operators, and tenders, metal and lastic	51-4020	153,200	137,700	-15,500	-10
Extruding and drawing machine setters, operators, and tenders, metal and plastic	51-4021	90,700	86,000	-4,700	-5
Forging machine setters, operators, and tenders, metal and plastic	51-4022	28,100	22,600	-5,500	-19
Rolling machine setters, operators, and tenders, metal and plastic	51-4023	34,400	29,000	-5,300	-16
Machine tool cutting setters, operators, and tenders, metal and plastic	51-4030	444,300	368,400	-75,900	-17
Cutting, punching, and press machine setters, operators, and tenders, metal and plastic	51-4031	236,800	203,500	-33,300	-14
Drilling and boring machine tool setters, operators, and tenders, metal and plastic	51-4032	33,000	24,200	-8,900	-27
Grinding, lapping, polishing, and buffing machine tool setters, operators, and tenders, metal and plastic	51-4033	92,700	77,900	-14,800	-16
Lathe and turning machine tool setters, operators, and tenders, metal and plastic	51-4034	55,700	40,800	-14,900	-27
Milling and planing machine setters, operators, and tenders, metal and plastic	51-4035	26,200	22,000	-4,100	-16
Metal furnace and kiln operators and tenders	51-4050	34,100	31,000	-3,100	-9
Metal-refining furnace operators and tenders	51-4051	19,100	17,400	-1,600	-9
Pourers and casters, metal	51-4052	15,100	13,600	-1,500	-10
Model makers and patternmakers, metal and plastic	51-4060	17,100	16,100	-1,000	-6
Model makers, metal and plastic	51-4061	10,100	9,500	-600	-6
Patternmakers, metal and plastic...	51-4062	7,000	6,600	-400	-6
Molders and molding machine setters, operators, and tenders, metal and plastic	51-4070	158,800	150,700	-8,200	-5
Foundry mold and coremakers..	51-4071	15,000	13,200	-1,800	-12
Molding, coremaking, and casting machine setters, operators, and tenders, metal and plastic	51-4072	143,800	137,400	-6,400	-4
Multiple machine tool setters, operators, and tenders, metal and plastic	51-4081	86,000	73,400	-12,600	-15
Miscellaneous metalworkers and plastic workers........................	51-4190	134,900	121,800	-13,100	-10
Heat treating equipment setters, operators, and tenders, metal and plastic	51-4191	23,200	20,700	-2,500	-11
Lay-out workers, metal and plastic..	51-4192	8,300	7,300	-1,000	-12
Plating and coating machine setters, operators, and tenders, metal and plastic	51-4193	39,500	34,600	-4,900	-12
Tool grinders, filers, and sharpeners	51-4194	18,800	17,400	-1,400	-7
All other metal workers and plastic workers	51-4199	45,000	41,700	-3,300	-7

(NOTE) Data in this table are rounded. See the discussion of the employment projections table in the *Handbook* introductory chapter on *Occupational Information Included in the Handbook.*

produce. Both the plastic and metal manufacturing industries face stiff foreign competition that is limiting the demand for domestically produced parts. Some domestic firms have outsourced their production to foreign countries, which has limited employment of machine setters and operators. Another way domestic manufacturers compete with low-wage foreign competition is by increasing their use of automated systems, which can make manufacturing establishments more competitive by improving their productivity. This increased automation also limits employment growth.

Job prospects. Despite the overall projected employment decline, a number of machine setter, operator, and tender jobs will become available because of an expected surge in retirements, primarily baby boomers, in the coming years. Workers with a thorough background in machine operations, certifications from industry associations, exposure to a variety of machines, and a good working knowledge of the properties of metals and plastics will be better able to adjust to the changing environment. In addition, new shop-floor arrangements will reward workers with good basic mathematics and reading skills, good communication skills, and the ability and willingness to learn new tasks. As workers adapt to team-oriented production methods, those who can operate multiple machines will have the best opportunities for advancement and for gaining jobs with more long-term potential.

Earnings

Wages for machine operators can vary by size of the company, union status, industry, and skill level and experience of the operator. Also, temporary employees, who are being hired in greater numbers, usually get paid less than permanently employed workers. The median hourly wages in May 2008 for a variety of machine setters, operators, and tenders—metal and plastic were:

Model makers, metal and plastic	$19.55
Patternmakers, metal and plastic	17.75
Metal-refining furnace operators and tenders	17.47
Lay-out workers, metal and plastic	16.79
Rolling machine setters, operators, and tenders, metal and plastic	16.40
Milling and planing machine setters, operators, and tenders, metal and plastic	16.00
Lathe and turning machine tool setters, operators, and tenders, metal and plastic	15.84
Pourers and casters, metal	15.66
Heat treating equipment setters, operators, and tenders, metal and plastic	15.40
Tool grinders, filers, and sharpeners	15.37
Forging machine setters, operators, and tenders, metal and plastic	14.90
Multiple machine tool setters, operators, and tenders, metal and plastic	14.87
Drilling and boring machine tool setters, operators, and tenders, metal and plastic	14.83
Extruding and drawing machine setters, operators, and tenders, metal and plastic	14.31
Grinding, lapping, polishing, and buffing machine tool setters, operators, and tenders, metal and plastic	14.16
Foundry mold and coremakers	14.13
Plating and coating machine setters, operators, and tenders, metal and plastic	13.65
Cutting, punching, and press machine setters, operators, and tenders, metal and plastic	13.54
Molding, coremaking, and casting machine setters, operators, and tenders, metal and plastic	13.17
Metal workers and plastic workers, all other	15.61

Related Occupations

Workers whose duties are closely related to machine setters, operators, and tenders—metal and plastic include:

Sources of Additional Information

For general information about careers and companies employing metal machine setters, operators, and tenders, contact:

➤ Fabricators and Manufacturers Association, 833 Featherstone Rd., Rockford, IL 61107 Internet: **http://www.fmanet.org**

The Occupational Information Network (O*NET) provides information on a wide range of occupational characteristics. Links to O*NET appear at the end of the Internet version of this occupational statement, accessible at **http://www.bls.gov/ooh/ocos224.htm**

Machinists

Significant Points

- Machinists learn their job skills in apprenticeship programs, informally on the job, in vocational high schools, and in community or technical colleges.

- Many entrants previously have worked as machine setters, operators, or tenders.

- Employment is projected to decline slowly, but job opportunities are expected to be good.

Nature of the Work

Machinists use machine tools, such as lathes, milling machines, and grinders, to produce precision metal parts. Although they may produce large quantities of one part, precision machinists often produce small batches or one-of-a-kind items. They use their knowledge of the working properties of metals and their skill with machine tools to plan and carry out the operations needed to make machined products that meet precise specifications. The parts that machinists make range from bolts to automobile pistons.

Machinists first review electronic or written blueprints or specifications for a job before they machine a part. Next, they calculate where to cut or bore into the workpiece—the piece of steel, aluminum, titanium, plastic, silicon, or any other material that is being shaped. They determine how fast to feed the workpiece into the machine and how much material to remove. They then select tools and materials for the job, plan the sequence of cutting and finishing operations, and mark the workpiece to show where cuts should be made.

After this layout work is completed, machinists perform the necessary machining operations. They position the workpiece on the machine tool—drill press, lathe, milling machine, or other type of machine—set the controls, and make the cuts. During the machining process, they must constantly monitor the feed rate and speed of the machine. Machinists also ensure that the workpiece is properly lubricated and cooled, because the machining of metal products generates a significant amount of heat. The temperature of the workpiece is a key concern, because most metals expand when heated; machinists must adjust the size of their cuts relative to the temperature.

During the cutting process, machinists detect problems by listening for specific sounds—for example, that of a dull cutting tool or excessive vibration. Dull cutting tools are removed and replaced. Cutting speeds are adjusted to compensate for harmonic vibrations, which can decrease the accuracy of cuts, particularly on newer high-speed spindles and lathes. After the work is completed, machinists use both simple and highly sophisticated

Machinists remove and replace worn-out machine tools.

measuring tools to check the accuracy of their work against the blueprints.

Some machinists, often called *production machinists*, may produce large quantities of one part, especially parts requiring the use of complex operations and great precision. Many modern machine tools are computer numerically controlled (CNC). CNC machines, following a computer program, control the cutting tool speed, change dull tools, and perform all necessary cuts to create a part. Frequently, machinists work with computer control programmers to determine how the automated equipment will cut a part. (See the section on computer control programmers and operators elsewhere in the *Handbook*.) The machinist determines the cutting path, speed of the cut and the feed rate, and the programmer converts path, speed, and feed information into a set of instructions for the CNC machine tool. Many machinists must be able to use both manual and computer-controlled machinery in their job.

Because most machinists train in CNC programming, they may write basic programs themselves and often modify programs in response to problems encountered during test runs. Modifications, called offsets, not only fix problems, but they also improve efficiency by reducing manufacturing time and tool wear. After the production process is designed, computer control operators implement it by performing relatively simple and repetitive operations.

Some manufacturing techniques employ automated parts loaders, automatic tool changers, and computer controls, allowing machines to operate without anyone present. One production machinist, working 8 hours a day, might monitor equipment, replace worn cutting tools, check the accuracy of parts being produced, adjust offsets, and perform other tasks on several CNC machines that operate 24 hours a day. In the off-hours, during what is known as "lights out manufacturing," which is the practice of running machines while the operators are not present, a factory may need only a few workers to monitor the entire factory.

Maintenance machinists repair or make new parts for existing machinery. After an industrial machinery mechanic or maintenance worker discovers the broken part of a machine, they give the broken part to the machinist. (See the section on industrial machinery mechanics and millwrights elsewhere in the *Handbook*.) To replace broken parts, maintenance machinists refer to blueprints and perform the same machining operations that were needed to create the original part. While production machinists are concentrated in a few industries, maintenance machinists work in many manufacturing industries.

Because the technology of machining is changing rapidly, machinists must learn to operate a wide range of machines. Some newer machines use lasers, water jets, or electrified wires to cut the workpiece. While some of the computer controls are similar to other machine tools, machinists must understand the unique cutting properties of these different machines. As engineers create new types of machine tools and new materials to machine, machinists must constantly learn new machining properties and techniques.

Work environment. Today, many machine shops are relatively clean, well lit, and ventilated. Computer-controlled machines often are partially or totally enclosed, minimizing the exposure of workers to noise, debris, and the lubricants used to cool workpieces during machining. Nevertheless, working around machine tools presents certain dangers, and workers must follow safety precautions. Machinists wear protective equipment, such as safety glasses to shield against bits of flying metal, and earplugs to dampen machinery noise. They also must exercise caution when handling hazardous coolants and lubricants, although many common water-based lubricants present little hazard. The job requires stamina, because machinists stand most of the day and, at times, may need to lift moderately heavy workpieces. Modern factories use autoloaders and overhead cranes to reduce heavy lifting.

Many machinists work a 40-hour week. Evening and weekend shifts are becoming more common, as companies extend hours of operation to make better use of expensive machines. However, this trend is somewhat offset by lights-out manufacturing that uses fewer machinists and the use of machine operators for less desirable shifts. Overtime work is common during peak production periods.

Training, Other Qualifications, and Advancement

Machinists train in apprenticeship programs, vocational schools, or community or technical colleges, or informally on the job. Many entrants previously have worked as machine setters, operators, or tenders.

Education and training. There are many different ways to become a skilled machinist. Many entrants previously have worked as machine setters, operators, or tenders. In high school, students should take math courses, especially trigonometry and geometry and, if available, courses in blueprint reading, metalworking, and drafting. Some advanced positions, such as those in the aircraft manufacturing industry, require the use of advanced applied calculus and physics. Due to the increasing use of computer controlled machinery, basic computer skills are needed before entering a training program. After high school, some machinists learn entirely on the job, but most acquire their skills in a mix of classroom and on-the-job training. Formal apprenticeship programs, typically sponsored by a union or manufacturer, are an excellent way to learn the job of machinist, but are often hard

Projections data from the National Employment Matrix

Occupational Title	SOC Code	Employment, 2008	Projected Employment, 2018	Change, 2008-2018	
				Number	Percent
Machinists	51-4041	421,500	402,200	-19,300	-5

(NOTE) Data in this table are rounded. See the discussion of the employment projections table in the *Handbook* introductory chapter on *Occupational Information Included in the Handbook.*

to get into. Apprentices usually must have a high school diploma, GED, or the equivalent; and most have taken algebra and trigonometry classes.

Apprenticeship programs consist of paid shop training and related classroom instruction lasting up to 4 years. In shop training, apprentices work almost full time and are supervised by an experienced machinist, while learning to operate various machine tools. Classroom instruction includes math, physics, materials science, blueprint reading, mechanical drawing, and quality and safety practices. In addition, as machine shops have increased their use of computer-controlled equipment, training in the operation and programming of CNC machine tools has become essential. Apprenticeship classes are often taught in cooperation with local community colleges or vocational-technical schools. A growing number of machinists are learning the trade through 2-year associate degree programs at community or technical colleges. Graduates of these programs still need significant on-the-job experience as machinists' assistants before they are fully qualified.

Certification and other qualifications. People interested in becoming machinists should be mechanically inclined, have good problem-solving abilities, be able to work independently, and be able to do highly accurate work (tolerances may reach 50/1,000,000ths of an inch) that requires concentration and physical effort. Experience working with machine tools is helpful. In fact, many entrants have worked as machine setters, operators, or tenders.

To boost the skill level of machinists and to create a more uniform standard of competency, a number of training facilities, State apprenticeship boards, and colleges offer certification programs. Completing a recognized certification program provides a machinist with better career opportunities and helps employers better judge the abilities of new hires. Journeyworker certification can be obtained from State apprenticeship boards after completing an apprenticeship; this certification is recognized by many employers and often leads to better career opportunities.

As new automation is introduced, machinists normally receive additional training to update their skills. This training usually is provided by a representative of the equipment manufacturer or a local technical school. Some employers offer tuition reimbursement for job-related courses.

Advancement. Machinists can advance in several ways. Experienced machinists may become CNC programmers, tool and die makers, or mold makers, or be promoted to supervisory or administrative positions in their firms. A few open their own machine shops.

Employment

Machinists held about 421,500 jobs in 2008. About 78 percent of machinists work in manufacturing industries, such as machine shops and machinery, motor vehicle and parts, aerospace products and parts, and other transportation equipment manufacturing. Maintenance machinists work in most industries that use production machinery.

Job Outlook

Although employment of machinists is projected to decline slowly, job prospects are expected to be good.

Employment change. Employment of machinists is projected to decline by 5 percent over the 2008–18 decade, due to rising productivity among these workers and strong foreign competition in the manufacture of goods. Machinists are becoming more efficient as a result of the expanded use of and improvements in technologies such as CNC machine tools, autoloaders, high-speed machining, and lights out manufacturing. This allows fewer machinists to accomplish the same amount of work. Technology is not expected to affect the employment of machinists as significantly as that of some other production workers, however, because machinists monitor and maintain many automated systems. Due to modern production techniques, employers prefer workers, such as machinists, who have a wide range of skills and are capable of performing almost any task in a machine shop.

Job prospects. Despite the projected decline in employment, job opportunities for machinists should continue to be good, as employers value the wide-ranging skills of these workers. Also, many young people with the necessary educational and personal qualifications needed to become machinists prefer to attend college or may not wish to enter production occupations. Therefore, the number of workers learning to be machinists is expected to be less than the number of job openings arising each year from the need to replace experienced machinists who retire or transfer to other occupations. Employment levels in this occupation are influenced by economic cycles—as the demand for machined goods falls, machinists involved in production may be laid off or forced to work fewer hours.

Earnings

Median hourly wages of machinists were $17.41 in May 2008. The middle 50 percent earned between $13.66 and $21.85. The lowest 10 percent earned less than $10.79, while the top 10 percent earned more than $26.60. Median hourly wages in the manufacturing industries employing the largest number of machinists were:

Aerospace product and parts manufacturing $19.49
Metalworking machinery manufacturing 17.90
Motor vehicle parts manufacturing 17.06
Machine shops; turned product; and screw, nut,
    and bolt manufacturing...16.93
Employment services 12.94

Apprentices earn much less than experienced machinists, but earnings increase quickly as they improve their skills. Also, most employers pay for apprentices' training classes.

Related Occupations

Machinists share similar duties with these other manufacturing occupations:

Sources of Additional Information

For information on training and new technology for machinists, contact:

➤ Fabricators and Manufacturers Association, 833 Featherstone Rd., Rockford, IL 61107 Internet: **http://www.fmanet.org**

Information on the registered apprenticeship system with links to State apprenticeship programs may also be found on the U.S. Department of Labor Web site: **http://www.doleta.gov/OA/eta_default.cfm.** Apprenticeship information is also available from the U.S. Department of Labor toll-free helpline: (877) 872-5627.

The Occupational Information Network (O*NET) provides information on a wide range of occupational characteristics. Links to O*NET appear at the end of the Internet version of this occupational statement, accessible at **http://www.bls.gov/ooh/ocos223.htm**

Tool and Die Makers

Significant Points

- Tool and die makers are one of the highest paid and most highly skilled production occupations.

- Most tool and die makers need 4 or 5 years of classroom instruction and on-the-job training to become fully qualified.

- Employment is projected to decline moderately, but job opportunities should be excellent, as many employers report difficulty finding qualified applicants.

Nature of the Work

Tool and die makers are among the most highly skilled workers in manufacturing. These workers produce and repair tools, dies, and special guiding and holding devices that enable machines to produce a variety of products we use daily—from clothing and furniture to heavy equipment and parts for aircraft. They may work in manufacturing plants that produce tools in house, or in machine shops that only produce specialized machine tools for other manufacturers.

Toolmakers craft precision tools and machines that are used to cut, shape, and form metal and other materials. They also produce jigs and fixtures—devices that hold metal while it is bored, stamped, or drilled—and gauges and other measuring devices. *Die makers* construct metal forms, called dies, that are used to shape metal in stamping and forging operations. They also make metal molds for diecasting and for molding plastics, ceramics, and composite materials. Some tool and die makers craft prototypes of parts, and then, working with engineers and designers, determine how best to manufacture the part. In addition to developing, designing, and producing new tools and dies, these workers also may repair worn or damaged tools, dies, gauges, jigs, and fixtures.

To perform these functions, tool and die makers employ many types of machine tools and precision measuring instruments. They also must be familiar with the machining properties, such as hardness and heat tolerance of a wide variety of common metals, alloys, plastics, ceramics, and other composite materials. Tool and die makers are knowledgeable in machining operations, mathematics, and blueprint reading. In fact, tool and die makers often are considered highly specialized machinists. Machinists typically produce less elaborate parts for machinery, while tool and die makers craft very durable, complex machine tools. As a result, tool and die makers must have a general understanding of the mechanics of machinery. (See the section on machinists elsewhere in the *Handbook*.)

While many tools and dies are designed by engineers or tool designers, tool and die makers are also trained to design tools and often do. They may travel to a customer's plant to observe the operation and suggest ways in which a new tool could improve the manufacturing process.

Once a tool or die is designed, tool and die makers, working from blueprints, plan the sequence of operations necessary to manufacture the tool or die. They measure and mark the pieces of metal that will be cut to form parts of the final product. At this point, tool and die makers cut, drill, or bore the part as required, checking to ensure that the final product meets specifications. Finally, these workers assemble the parts and perform finishing jobs, such as filing, grinding, and polishing surfaces. While manual machining has declined, it is still used for unique parts and sharpening of used tools.

Many tool and die makers use computer-aided design (CAD) to develop products and parts. Specifications entered into computer programs can be used to electronically develop blueprints for the required tools and dies. Numerical tool and process control programmers use CAD or computer-aided manufacturing (CAM) programs to convert electronic drawings into CAM-based computer programs that contain instructions for a sequence of cutting tool operations. (See the section on computer control programmers and operators elsewhere in the *Handbook*.) Once these programs are developed, computer numerically controlled (CNC) machines follow the set of instructions contained in the program to produce the part. Computer-controlled machine tool operators or machinists normally operate CNC machines, but tool and die makers are often trained in both operating CNC machines and writing CNC programs; and they may perform either task. CNC programs are stored electronically for future use, saving time and increasing worker productivity.

After machining the parts, tool and die makers carefully check the accuracy of the parts using many tools, including coordinate measuring machines, which use sensor arms and software to compare the dimensions of the part to electronic blueprints. Next, they assemble the different parts into a functioning machine. They file, grind, shim, and adjust the different parts to properly fit them together. Finally, tool and die makers set up a test run, using the tools or dies they have made to make sure that the manufactured parts meet specifications. If problems occur, they compensate by adjusting the tools or dies.

Work environment. Tool and die makers may either work in toolrooms or manufacturing production floors. Toolrooms are generally kept clean and cool to minimize heat-related expansion of metal workpiece, while specialty machine shops have a factory floor covered with machinery. To minimize the exposure of workers to moving parts, machines have guards and shields. Most computer-controlled machines are totally enclosed, minimizing workers' exposure to noise, dust, and the lubricants used to cool workpieces during machining. Working around this machinery can still be dangerous, so tool and die makers must follow safety rules and wear protective equipment, such as safety glasses to shield against bits of flying metal, earplugs to protect against noise, and gloves and masks to reduce exposure to hazardous lubricants and cleaners. These workers also need stamina, because they often spend much of the day on their feet and may do moderately heavy lifting. Companies employing tool and die makers have traditionally operated only one shift per day. Overtime and weekend work are common, especially during peak production periods.

Training, Other Qualifications, and Advancement

It usually takes 4 or 5 years of classroom and paid on-the-job training to become a fully trained tool and die maker. Good math, problem-solving, and computer skills are important requirements for these workers.

Education and training. Most tool and die makers learn their trade through 4 or 5 years of education and training in formal apprenticeships or in other postsecondary programs offered at local community colleges or technical schools. These programs often include a mix of classroom instruction and paid hands-on experience. According to most employers, apprenticeship programs are the best way to learn all aspects of tool and die making. Most apprentices must have a high school diploma, GED, or equivalent. In high school, students should take courses in physics and mathematics, including trigonometry and geometry.

Traditional apprenticeships usually require that the apprentice complete a specific number of work and classroom hours to complete the program, which typically takes 4 or 5 years. Some companies and State apprenticeship programs, however, are now shifting from time-based programs to competency-based programs. Under competency-based programs, apprentices can move ahead more quickly by passing a series of exams and demonstrating competency in a particular job skill.

While formal apprenticeship programs may be the best way to learn the job, many tool and die makers receive most of their formal classroom training from community and technical colleges, while working for a company that often supports the employee's training goals and provides the needed on-the-job training less formally. Apprentices usually work 40 hours per week and attend technical college courses at night. These trainees often begin as machine operators and gradually take on more difficult assignments. Many machinists become tool and die makers.

During their training, tool and die maker trainees learn to operate milling machines, lathes, grinders, laser and water cutting machines, wire electrical discharge machines, and other machine tools. They also learn to use handtools for fitting and assembling gauges and other mechanical and metalforming equipment. In addition, they study metalworking processes, such as heat treating and plating. Classroom training usually consists of tool designing, tool programming, blueprint reading, and mathematics courses, including algebra, geometry, calculus, trigonometry, and statistics. Tool and die makers must have good computer skills to work with CAD/CAM technology, CNC machine tools, and computerized measuring machines.

Even after completing a formal training program, tool and die makers still need years of experience to become highly skilled. Most specialize in making certain types of tools, molds, or dies.

Certification and other qualifications. State apprenticeship boards certify tool and die makers as journey workers after they have completed a licensed program. While a State certification is not necessary to work as a tool and die maker, it gives workers more flexibility in employment, as many employers require this certification. Apprentices usually must be at least 18 years old, in addition to having a high school education and high school mathematics classes.

Because tools and dies must meet strict specifications—precision to one ten-thousandth of an inch is common—the work of tool and die makers requires skill with precision measuring devices and a high degree of patience and attention to detail. Good eyesight is essential. People entering this occupation also should be mechanically inclined, able to work and solve problems independently, have strong mathematical skills, and be capable of doing work that requires concentration and physical effort. Tool and die makers who visit customers' plants need good communication, interpersonal, and sales skills.

Tool and die makers wear safety glasses for eye protection.

Employers generally look for someone with a strong educational background, as they desire intelligent, dependable workers. Problem-solving skills are also a must in this occupation, as technologies and skills are constantly changing in this profession. As automation continues to change the way tools and dies are made, workers regularly need to update their skills to learn how to operate new equipment. Also, as materials such as alloys, ceramics, polymers, and plastics are increasingly used, tool and die makers need to learn new machining techniques to deal with these new materials.

Advancement. There are several ways for skilled workers to advance. Some move into supervisory and administrative positions in their firms or they start their own shop. Others may take computer courses and become computer-controlled machine tool programmers. With a college degree, a tool and die maker can go into engineering or tool design.

Employment

Tool and die makers held about 84,300 jobs in 2008. Most worked in industries that manufacture metalworking machinery, transportation equipment, such as motor vehicle parts, fabricated metal products, and plastics products. Although they are found throughout the country, jobs are most plentiful in the Midwest and the Northeast, where many metalworking companies are located.

Job Outlook

Employment is projected to decline moderately. However, excellent job opportunities are expected, as many employers report difficulty finding qualified applicants.

Employment change. Employment of tool and die makers is projected to decline by 8 percent over the 2008–18 decade, due to foreign competition in manufacturing and advances in automation, including CNC machine tools and computer-aided design, that should improve worker productivity. On the other hand, tool and die makers play a key role in building and maintaining advanced automated manufacturing equipment, which makes them less susceptible to lay-offs from automation than other less skilled production workers. As firms invest in new equipment, modify production techniques, and implement product design changes more rapidly, they will continue to rely heavily on skilled tool and die makers for retooling.

Job prospects. Despite declining employment, excellent job opportunities are expected as many openings will result from workers retiring or leaving the occupation for other reasons. Employers in certain parts of the country report difficulty attracting skilled workers and apprenticeship candidates with the necessary abilities to fill openings. The number of workers receiving training in this occupation is expected to continue to be fewer than the number of openings created each year by tool and die makers who retire or transfer to other occupations. A major factor limiting the number of people entering the occupation is that many young people who have the educational and personal qualifications necessary to learn tool and die making usually prefer to attend college or do not wish to enter production occupations.

Earnings

Median hourly wages of tool and die makers were $22.32 in May 2008. The middle 50 percent earned between $18.00 and $27.99. The lowest 10 percent had earnings of less than $14.69, while the top 10 percent earned more than $34.76. Median hourly wages in the manufacturing industries employing the largest numbers of tool and die makers were as follows:

Motor vehicle parts manufacturing	$27.99
Forging and stamping	21.80
Plastics product manufacturing	21.55
Machine shops; turned product; and screw, nut, and bolt manufacturing	20.73
Metalworking machinery manufacturing	20.46

The pay of apprentices is tied to their skill level. As they gain more skills and reach specific levels of performance and experience, their pay increases. About 22 percent of tool and die makers belong to unions.

Related Occupations

Some manufacturing occupations similar to tool and die makers are:

	Page
Computer control programmers and operators	731
Industrial machinery mechanics and millwrights	709
Machine setters, operators, and tenders—metal and plastic	734
Machinists	737
Welding, soldering, and brazing workers	743

Sources of Additional Information

For more information on education and technology for tool and die makers, contact:

➤ Fabricators and Manufacturers Association, 833 Featherstone Rd., Rockford, IL 61107 Internet: **http://www.fmanet.org**

Information on the registered apprenticeship system with links to State apprenticeship programs can be found on the U.S. Department of Labor Web site: **http://www.doleta. gov/OA/eta_default.cfm**. Apprenticeship information is also available from the U.S. Department of Labor toll free helpline: (877) 872-5627.

The Occupational Information Network (O*NET) provides information on a wide range of occupational charac-

Projections data from the National Employment Matrix

Occupational Title	SOC Code	Employment, 2008	Projected Employment, 2018	Change, 2008-2018	
				Number	Percent
Tool and die makers	51-4111	84,300	77,600	-6,700	-8

(NOTE) Data in this table are rounded. See the discussion of the employment projections table in the *Handbook* introductory chapter on *Occupational Information Included in the Handbook.*

teristics. Links to O*NET appear at the end of the Internet version of this occupational statement, accessible at **http://www.bls.gov/ooh/ocos225.htm**

Welding, Soldering, and Brazing Workers

Significant Points

- About 2 out of 3 jobs in this occupation are in manufacturing industries.

- Training ranges from a few weeks to several years of school and on-the-job training.

- Employment is projected to experience little or no change.

- Job prospects should be good for skilled welders because employers are reporting difficulty finding enough qualified people.

Nature of the Work
Welding is the most common way of permanently joining metal parts. In this process, heat is applied to metal pieces, melting and fusing them to form a permanent bond. Because of its strength, welding is used in shipbuilding, automobile manufacturing and repair, aerospace applications, and thousands of other manufacturing activities. Welding also is used to join beams in the construction of buildings, bridges, and other structures and to join pipes in pipelines, power-plants, and refineries.

Welders may work in a wide variety of industries, from car racing to manufacturing. The work done in the different industries and the equipment used may vary greatly. The most common and simplest type of welding today is arc welding, which uses electrical currents to create heat and bond metals together, but there are over 100 different processes that a welder can employ. The type of weld used is normally determined by the types of metals being joined and the conditions under which the welding is to take place. Steel, for instance, can be welded more easily than titanium. Some of these processes involve manually using a rod and heat to join metals, while others are semiautomatic, with a welding machine feeding wire to bond materials. Automated welding, done completely by robots, is increasingly being used in the manufacturing industry.

Like welders, *soldering and brazing workers* use molten metal to join two pieces of metal. However, the metal added during the soldering and brazing process has a melting point lower than that of the piece, so only the added metal is melted, not the piece. Soldering uses metals with a melting point below 840 degrees Fahrenheit; brazing uses metals with a higher melting point. Because soldering and brazing do not melt the pieces being joined, these processes normally do not create the distortions or weaknesses in the pieces that can occur with welding. Soldering commonly is used to make electrical and electronic circuit boards, such as computer chips. Soldering workers tend to work with small pieces

that must be precisely positioned. Brazing often is used to connect copper plumbing pipes and thinner metals that the higher temperatures of welding would warp. Brazing also can be used to apply coatings to parts to reduce wear and protect against corrosion.

Skilled welding, soldering, and brazing workers generally plan work from drawings, called blueprints, or specifications and use their knowledge of welding processes and base metals to determine how best to join the parts. The difficulty of the weld is determined by its position—horizontal, vertical, over-head, or 6G (circular, as in large pipes)—and by the type of metals to be fused. Highly skilled welders often are trained to work with a wide variety of materials, such as titanium, aluminum, or plastics, in addition to steel. Welders then select and set up welding equipment, execute the planned welds, and examine the welds to ensure that they meet standards or specifications.

Automated welding is being used in an increasing number of production processes. In these instances, a machine or robot performs the welding tasks while being monitored by a welding machine operator. *Welding, soldering, and brazing machine setters, operators, and tenders* follow specified layouts, work orders, or blueprints. Operators must load parts correctly and monitor the machine constantly to ensure that it produces the desired bond. About 12 percent of all welding, soldering, and brazing workers operate automated machinery.

Welders inspect the placement of parts before bonding metals.

The work of *arc, plasma, and oxy-gas cutters* is closely related to that of welders. However, instead of joining metals, cutters use the heat from an electric arc, a stream of ionized gas called plasma, or burning gases to cut and trim metal objects to specific dimensions. Cutters also dismantle large objects, such as ships, railroad cars, automobiles, buildings, or aircraft. Some operate and monitor cutting machines similar to those used by welding machine operators.

Work environment. Welding, soldering, and brazing workers often are exposed to a number of hazards, including very hot materials and the intense light created by the arc. They wear safety shoes, goggles, masks with protective lenses, and other devices designed to prevent burns and eye injuries and to protect them from falling objects. The Occupational Safety and Health Administration (OSHA) requires that welders work in safely ventilated areas to avoid the danger from inhalation of gases and particulates that can result from welding processes. Because of these hazards, welding, soldering, and brazing workers suffer more work-related injuries than do workers in most occupations, but injuries can be minimized if proper safety procedures are followed. Automated welding, soldering, and brazing machine operators are not exposed to as many dangers, and a face shield or goggles usually provide adequate protection for these workers.

Welders and cutters may work outdoors, often in inclement weather, or indoors, sometimes in a confined area designed to contain sparks and glare. Outdoors, they may work on a scaffold or platform high off the ground. In addition, they may be required to lift heavy objects and work in a variety of awkward positions while bending, stooping, or standing to perform work overhead.

Although about 50 percent of welders, solderers, and brazers work a 40-hour week, overtime is common, and about 1 out of 5 welder works 50 hours per week or more. Many manufacturing firms offer two or three shifts, ranging from 8 to 12 hours, which allows them to continue production around the clock if needed.

Training, Other Qualifications, and Advancement

Training for welding, soldering, and brazing workers can range from a few weeks of school or on-the-job training for low-skilled positions to several years of combined school and on-the-job training for highly skilled jobs.

Education and training. Formal training is available in high schools and postsecondary institutions, such as vocational-technical institutes, community colleges, and private welding, soldering, and brazing schools. The U.S. Armed Forces operate welding and soldering schools as well. Some employers are willing to hire inexperienced entry-level workers and train them on the job, but many prefer to hire workers who have been through formal training programs. Courses in blueprint reading, shop mathematics, mechanical drawing, physics, chemistry, and metallurgy are helpful. An understanding of electricity also is very helpful, and knowledge of computers is gaining importance, especially for welding, soldering, and brazing machine operators, who are becoming more responsible for programming robots and other computer-controlled machines. Because understand-

ing the welding process and inspecting welds is important for both welders and welding machine operators, companies hiring machine operators prefer workers with a background in welding.

Certification and other qualifications. Some welding positions require general certifications in welding or certifications in specific skills such as inspection or robotic welding. The American Welding Society certification courses are offered at many welding schools. Some employers have developed their own internal certification tests. Some employers are willing to pay training and testing costs for employees, while others require workers to pay for classes and certification themselves.

The Institute for Printed Circuits offers certifications and training in soldering. In industries such as aerospace and defense, where highly accurate and skilled work is required, many employers require these certifications. In addition, the increasing use of lead-free soldering techniques, which require more skill than traditional lead-based soldering techniques, has increased the importance of certification to employers.

Welding, soldering, and brazing workers need good eyesight, hand-eye coordination, and manual dexterity, along with good math, problem-solving, and communication skills. They should be able to concentrate on detailed work for long periods and be able to bend, stoop, and work in awkward positions. In addition, welders increasingly must be willing to receive training and perform tasks required in other production jobs.

Advancement. Welders can advance to more skilled welding jobs with additional training and experience. For example, they may become welding technicians, supervisors, inspectors, or instructors. Some experienced welders open their own repair shops. Other welders, especially those who obtain a bachelor's degree or have many years of experience, may become welding engineers.

Employment

In 2008, welders, cutters, solderers, and brazers held about 412,300 jobs and welding, soldering, and brazing machine setters, operators, and tenders held about 54,100 jobs. About 65 percent of welding jobs were found in manufacturing. Jobs were concentrated in fabricated metal product manufacturing, transportation equipment manufacturing, machinery manufacturing, architectural and structural metals manufacturing, and construction.

Job Outlook

Employment is projected to experience little or no change over the next decade. Good job opportunities are expected for skilled welders because some employers are reporting difficulty finding qualified workers.

Employment change. Employment of welders, cutters, solderers, and brazers is expected to experience little or no change, declining by about 2 percent over the 2008–18 decade, while employment of welding, soldering, and brazing machine setters, operators, and tenders is expected to decline about 7 percent over the same decade. Continued enhancements in productivity and increased automation will reduce the need for welders, although the outlook for welders in man-

Projections data from the National Employment Matrix

Occupational Title	SOC Code	Employment, 2008	Projected Employment, 2018	Change, 2008-2018	
				Number	Percent
Welding, soldering, and brazing workers..	51-4120	466,400	455,900	-10,500	-2
Welders, cutters, solderers, and brazers	51-4121	412,300	405,600	-6,700	-2
Welding, soldering, and brazing machine setters, operators, and tenders	51-4122	54,100	50,300	-3,800	-7

(NOTE) Data in this table are rounded. See the discussion of the employment projections table in the *Handbook* introductory chapter on *Occupational Information Included in the Handbook*.

ufacturing is stronger than that for other occupations in this industry because of the importance and versatility of welding as a manufacturing process. The basic skills of welding are the same across industries, so welders can easily shift from one industry to another, depending on where they are needed most. For example, welders laid off in the automotive manufacturing industry may be able to find work in the oil and gas industry, although the shift may require relocating.

Automation will affect welders and welding machine operators differently than other manufacturing occupations. Semiautomated and automated welding machines can be used for many types of welds, but welders still are needed to operate the machines and to inspect the weld and make adjustments. In addition, much of the work in custom applications is difficult or impossible to automate. This type of work includes manufacturing small batches of items, construction work, and making repairs in factories.

Job prospects. Job prospects for welders will vary with the welder's skill level. Prospects should be good for welders trained in the latest technologies. Welding schools report that graduates have little difficulty finding work, and many welding employers report difficulty finding properly skilled welders. However, welders without up-to-date training may face competition for job openings. For all welders, prospects will be better for workers who are willing to relocate to different parts of the country.

Earnings

Median wages of welders, cutters, solderers, and brazers were $16.13 an hour in May 2008. The middle 50 percent earned between $13.20 and $19.61. The lowest 10 percent earned less than $10.85, and the top 10 percent earned more than $24.38. The range of wages of welders reflects the wide range of skill levels in the occupation. Median hourly wages of welders, cutters, solderers, and brazers in the industries employing the largest numbers of them were as follows:

Other general purpose machinery manufacturing	$16.34
Agriculture, construction, and mining machinery manufacturing..	16.28
Commercial and industrial machinery and equipment (except automotive and electronic) repair and maintenance..	15.93
Architectural and structural metals manufacturing........	15.05
Motor vehicle body and trailer manufacturing..............	14.73

Median wages of welding, soldering, and brazing machine setters, operators, and tenders were $15.20 an hour in May 2008. The middle 50 percent earned between $12.62 and $18.63. The lowest 10 percent earned less than $10.47, and the top 10 percent earned more than $23.92. Median wages in motor vehicle parts manufacturing, the industry employing these workers in the largest numbers, were $15.34 an hour in May 2008.

About 20 percent of welders belong to labor unions; the particular unions that welders belong to depend on the industry and company in which the welder is employed.

Related Occupations

Other skilled metal workers include the following:

	Page
Assemblers and fabricators	723
Boilermakers	613
Computer control programmers and operators	731
Jewelers and precious stone and metal workers.....................	770
Machine setters, operators, and tenders— metal and plastic..	734
Machinists	737
Plumbers, pipelayers, pipefitters, and steamfitters..................	659
Sheet metal workers	665
Tool and die makers	740

Sources of Additional Information

For information on training opportunities and jobs for welding, soldering, and brazing workers, contact local employers, the local office of the State employment service, or schools providing welding, soldering, or brazing training.

Information on careers, certifications, and educational opportunities in welding is available from:

➤ American Welding Society, 550 N.W. LeJeune Rd., Miami, FL 33126. Internet: **http://www.aws.org**

➤ Fabricators and Manufacturers Association, 833 Featherstone Rd., Rockford, IL 61107 Internet: **http://www.fmanet.org**

The Occupational Information Network (O*NET) provides information on a wide range of occupational characteristics. Links to O*NET appear at the end of the Internet version of this occupational statement, accessible at **http://www.bls.gov/ooh/ocos226.htm**

Printing Occupations

Bookbinders and Bindery Workers

Significant Points

- Employment is expected to decline rapidly, reflecting the use of more productive machinery and the growth of electronic media.

- Opportunities for hand bookbinders are limited because of the declining demand for this highly specialized work and the resulting decline in the number of establishments that do this work.

- Most bookbinders and bindery workers train on the job.

Nature of the Work

The process of combining printed sheets into finished products such as books, magazines, catalogs, folders, and directories is known as "binding." When publications or advertising supplements have been printed, they must then be folded, glued, stitched, stapled, trimmed, or otherwise turned into the finished product that will be seen by the public. *Bindery workers* set up, operate, and maintain the machines that perform these various tasks, while *bookbinders* perform highly skilled hand finishing operations.

Job duties depend on the material being bound. Some types of binding and finishing jobs consist of only one step. Preparing leaflets or newspaper inserts, for example, requires only folding and trimming. Binding books and magazines, on the other hand, requires a number of steps. Bindery workers first assemble the books and magazines from large, flat, printed sheets of paper. They then operate machines that first fold printed sheets into "signatures," which are groups of pages arranged sequentially. They then assemble the signatures in sequence and join them by means of a saddle-stitch process or perfect binding (where no stitches are used).

Bookbinders and bindery workers use automated binding machines to finish printed reports.

In firms that do "edition binding," workers bind books produced in large numbers, or "runs."

Bookbinders also do repair work on rare books, such as sewing, stitching, or gluing the assembled printed sheets. They also shape book bodies with presses and trimming machines and reinforce them with glued fabric strips. Covers are created separately and glued, pasted, or stitched onto the book bodies. The books then undergo a variety of finishing operations, often including wrapping in paper jackets. In establishments that print new books, this work is done mechanically.

A small number of bookbinders work in hand binderies. These highly skilled workers design original or special bindings for limited editions, or restore and rebind rare books. Some binders repair books and provide other specialized binding services to libraries.

Bookbinders and bindery workers in small shops may perform many binding tasks, while those in large shops tend to specialize. Tasks may include performing perfect binding or operating laminating machinery. Others specialize as folder operators or cutter operators, and may perform adjustments and minor repairs to equipment as needed.

Work environment. Binderies often are noisy and jobs can be strenuous, requiring considerable lifting, standing, and carrying. Binding often resembles an assembly line on which workers perform repetitive tasks. The jobs also may require stooping, kneeling, and crouching. Equipment and protective clothing that help minimize injuries is available; however, minor injuries occur frequently in the occupation.

Bookbinders and bindery workers normally work 40 hours per week, although weekend and holiday hours may be necessary to meet production schedules. Some bindery workers may work on shifts for larger printers that operate around the clock. Part-time and on-call schedules are common to meet fluctuating demand or impending deadlines.

Training, Other Qualifications, and Advancement

On-the-job training remains the most common form of training for entry level bindery workers, but new technology will require workers to obtain more formal training. Attention to detail and mechanical aptitude are important for these jobs.

Education and training. High school students interested in bindery careers should take shop courses or attend a vocational-technical high school. Occupational skill centers also provide an introduction to bindery work and bookbinding. For entry-level positions, most employers look for high school graduates or those with associate degrees.

Training in graphic communications also can be an asset. Vocational-technical institutes offer postsecondary programs in the graphic arts, as do some skill-updating or retraining programs and community colleges. Other programs are made available by unions to their members. Four-year colleges also offer programs related to printing and publishing, but their emphasis is on preparing people for careers as graphic artists, educators, or managers in the graphic arts field.

While postsecondary education is available, most bookbinders and bindery workers learn the craft through on-the-job training. Inexperienced workers may start out as helpers and perform simpler tasks, such as moving paper from cutting machines to folding machines or catching stock as it comes off machines. They learn basic binding skills, including the characteristics of paper and how to cut large sheets of paper into different sizes with the least amount of waste. Usually, it takes one to three months to learn to operate simpler machines but it can take up to one year to become completely familiar with more complex equipment, such as computerized binding machines. As workers gain experience, they learn to operate more types of equipment. To keep pace with changing technology, retraining is increasingly important for bindery workers.

Formal apprenticeships are not as common as they used to be, but still are offered by some employers. Apprenticeships allow beginners to acquire skills by working alongside skilled workers while also taking classes. The more structured apprenticeship programs enable workers to acquire the high levels of specialization and skill needed for some bindery and bookbinding jobs.

Other qualifications. Bindery work requires careful attention to detail. Accuracy, patience, neatness, and good eyesight are all important. Mechanical aptitude is necessary to operate automated equipment, and workers with computer skills will increasingly be in demand. Manual dexterity is needed in order to count, insert, and fold. In addition, creativity and artistic ability are necessary for hand bookbinding.

Certification and advancement. With experience, binders can expect increased salaries and more responsibility. Completion of a formal certification program can further advancement opportunities. Without additional training, advancement opportunities outside of bindery work are limited. In large binderies, experienced bookbinders or bindery workers may advance to supervisory positions.

Employment

In 2008, bookbinders and bindery workers held about 66,500 jobs, including 6,100 as bookbinders and 60,400 as bindery workers. More than 8 out of 10 bookbinding and bindery jobs were in printing and related support activities. Traditionally, the largest employers of bindery workers were bindery trade shops, which are companies that specialize in providing binding services for printers without binderies or whose printing production exceeds their binding capabilities. However, this type of binding is now being done increasingly in-house, and is now called "in-line finishing." The publishing industry employed 5 percent of bookbinders and bindery workers.

Job Outlook

Employment of bookbinders and bindery workers is projected to decline rapidly between 2008 and 2018, but opportunities for skilled, specialized bindery workers should be good because of their experience and expertise. Many job openings also will be created by bindery workers who transfer to other occupations.

Employment change. Overall employment of bookbinders and bindery workers is expected to decline rapidly by 19 percent between 2008 and 2018. Over this period, demand for bindery workers will slow as distribution of advertising supplements shifts from print to electronic media even as print productivity increases. Employment declines, however, may be ameliorated somewhat, because the demand for quick turnaround of print work, typical for most commercial printing work, makes work less amenable to being outsourced to foreign countries. To a great extent, sophisticated equipment has automated much of the mechanical bindery work, allowing more companies to perform bindery services in-house rather than send work to specialized binding shops. Also, more efficient and flexible binding machinery will slow the growth in demand for workers to do specialized binding.

Job prospects. Experienced workers will continue to have the best opportunities for skilled jobs. Prospects for all bindery jobs will be best for workers who have completed training or certification programs, internships, or who have experience in a related production occupation.

Earnings

Median hourly wages of bookbinders were $14.92 in May 2008, compared to $13.99 per hour for all production occupations. The middle 50 percent earned between $10.34 and $19.46 an hour. The lowest 10 percent earned less than $8.35, and the highest 10 percent earned more than $27.68.

Median hourly wages of bindery workers were $13.17 in May 2008. The middle 50 percent earned between $10.23 and $17.02 an hour. The lowest 10 percent earned less than $8.42, and the highest 10 percent earned more than $21.31.

Related Occupations

Other workers who set up and operate production machinery include:

Sources of Additional Information

Information about apprenticeships and other training opportunities may be obtained from local printing industry associations,

Projections data from the National Employment Matrix

Occupational Title	SOC Code	Employment, 2008	Projected Employment, 2018	Change, 2008-2018	
				Number	Percent
Bookbinders and bindery workers	51-5010	66,500	53,600	-12,900	-19
Bindery workers	51-5011	60,400	48,200	-12,100	-20
Bookbinders	51-5012	6,100	5,400	-700	-12

(NOTE) Data in this table are rounded. See the discussion of the employment projections table in the *Handbook* introductory chapter on *Occupational Information Included in the Handbook.*

local binderies, local offices of the Graphic Communications Conference or local offices of the State employment service. Apprenticeship information is also available from the U.S. Department of Labor's toll-free helpline: 1 (877) 282-5627.

For information on careers and training programs in printing and the graphic arts, contact:

➤ Graphic Arts Education and Research Foundation, 1899 Preston White Dr., Reston, VA 20191. Internet: **http://www.gaerf.org/**

➤ Printing Industries of America 200 Deer Run Rd., Sewickley, PA 15143. Internet: **http://www.printing.org/**

➤ NPES The Association for Suppliers of Printing Publishing, and Converting Technologies, 1899 Preston White Dr., Reston, VA 20191. Internet: **http://www.npes.org/education/index.html**

➤ National Association of Printing Leadership , 75 West Century Road, Suite 100, Paramus, NJ 07652. Internet: **http://www.napl.org/**

The Occupational Information Network (O*NET) provides information on a wide range of occupational characteristics. Links to O*NET appear at the end of the Internet version of this occupational statement, accessible at **http://www.bls.gov/ooh/ocos232.htm**

Prepress Technicians and Workers

Significant Points

- Most prepress technician jobs now require formal postsecondary graphic communications training in the various types of computer software used in digital imaging.

- Employment is projected to decline rapidly as the increased use of computers in typesetting and page layout requires fewer prepress technicians.

Nature of the Work

The printing process has three stages: prepress, press, and binding or finishing. While workers in small print shops are usually responsible for all three stages, in most printing firms, formatting print jobs and correcting layout errors before the job goes to print is the responsibility of a specialized group of workers. *Prepress technicians and workers* are responsible for this prepress work. They perform a variety of tasks to help transform text and pictures into finished pages and prepare the pages for print.

Some prepress technicians, known as "preflight technicians," take images from graphic designers, customer service staff, team leaders, or directly from customers and check them for completeness. They review job specifications and design either from submitted sketches or clients' electronic files to ensure that everything is correct and all files and photos are included. Once clients and preflight technicians agree that everything is in order, preflight technicians forward the files to prepress technicians to set up printers.

Offset printing plates are thin sheets of metal that carry the final image to be printed. Printing presses use this plate to copy the image to the final printed products. Once a printing plate has been created, prepress technicians collaborate with printing press operators to check for any potential printing problems. Several plates may be needed if a job requires color, but advanced printing technology generally does not require plates.

Prepress workers generally use a photographic process to make offset printing plates. This is a complex process involving ultraviolet light and chemical exposure through which the text and images of a print job harden on a metal plate and become water repellent. These hard, water repellent portions of the metal plate are in the form of the text and images that will be printed. More recently, however, the printing industry has moved to technology known as "direct-to-plate," by which the prepress technicians send the data directly to a plating system, bypassing the need for the photographic technique. The direct-to-plate technique is just one example of digital imaging technology that has largely replaced cold-type print technology.

Using direct-to-plate technology, the technicians produce an electronic image of the printed pages. The electronic image is used to create a "proof" which is printed and delivered or mailed to the customer. Alternatively, the electronic file can be e-mailed to the client for a final check. Once the customer approves the proofs, technicians use laser "imagesetters" to expose digital images of the pages directly onto the thin metal printing plates or directly to a digital press and skip the plate-making process altogether.

Advances in computer software and printing technology continue to change prepress work. Prepress workers often receive files from customers on a computer disk, via e-mail, or through an Internet site that contains typeset material already laid out in pages. This work is usually done by desktop publishers or graphic designers who have knowledge of publishing software. (Sections on desktop publishers and graphic designers appear elsewhere in the Handbook.) Despite the shortcuts that technological advancements allow, workers still need to understand the basic processes behind prepress, press, and finishing operations. Some workers, known as job printers, perform prepress and print operations.

Prepress technicians and workers ensure that printing presses are set correctly and that images and colors are correct before the full job order is printed.

Job printers often are found in small establishments where work combines several job skills.

Work environment. Prepress technicians and workers usually work in clean, air-conditioned areas with little noise. Some workers may develop eyestrain from working in front of a video display terminal or other problems, such as muscle aches or back pain. Workers are often subject to stress and the pressures of deadlines and tight work schedules.

Prepress employees usually work an 8-hour day. Some workers—particularly those employed by newspapers—work night shifts. Weekend and holiday work may be required, particularly when a print job is behind schedule. Part-time job printers and prepress technicians made up about 14 percent of this occupation in 2008.

Training, Other Qualifications, and Advancement

Employers prefer workers with formal training in printing or publishing. Familiarity with the printing process, including the technology used, and attention to detail are the qualities that employers will seek most in job applicants.

Education and training. Many employers consider the best candidates for prepress jobs to be individuals with a combination of work experience in the printing industry and formal training in new digital technology. The experience of these applicants provides them with an understanding of how printing plants operate and demonstrates their interest in advancing within the industry.

Traditionally, prepress technicians and workers started as helpers and were trained on the job. Some of these jobs required years of experience performing detailed manual work to become skillful enough to perform the most difficult tasks. Today, however, employers expect workers to have some formal postsecondary graphic communications training in the various types of computer software used in digital imaging and will train workers on the job as needed.

For beginners, 2-year associate degree programs offered by community colleges, junior colleges, and technical schools teach the latest prepress skills and allow students to practice applying them. There are also 4-year bachelor's degree programs in graphic design aimed primarily at students who plan to move into management positions in printing or design. For workers who do not wish to enroll in a degree program, prepress-related courses are offered at many community colleges, junior colleges, 4-year colleges and universities, vocational-technical institutes, and private trade and technical schools. Workers with experience in other printing techniques can take a few college-level graphic communications courses to upgrade their skills and qualify for prepress jobs.

Other qualifications. Employers prefer workers with good communication skills, both oral and written. When prepress problems arise, prepress technicians should be able to deal courteously with customers to resolve them. In small shops, they may take customer orders and provide pricing information. Persons interested in working for firms using advanced printing technology need to be comfortable with electronics and computers. At times, prepress personnel may have to perform computations in order to estimate job costs or operate many of the machines used to run modern printing equipment.

Prepress technicians and workers need manual dexterity and accurate eyesight. Good color vision helps workers find mistakes and locate potential problems. It is essential for prepress workers to be able to pay attention to detail and work independently. Artistic ability is often a plus. Employers also seek persons who are comfortable with the pressures of meeting deadlines, using new software, and operating new equipment.

Advancement. Employers may send experienced technicians to industry-sponsored programs to update or develop new skills. Retraining due to technology and equipment changes is a constant as printing firms continually seek ways to improve efficiency and lower production costs. This kind of prepress training is sometimes offered in-house or through equipment makers and unions in the printing industry.

Employment

Prepress technicians and workers overall held about 106,900 jobs in 2008. Most prepress jobs are found in the printing and related support activities industry, while newspaper publishers employ the second largest number of prepress technicians and workers.

The printing and publishing industries are among the most geographically dispersed in the United States. While prepress jobs thus are found throughout the country, large numbers are concentrated in large printing centers such as the Chicago, Los Angeles–Long Beach, New York City, Minneapolis–St. Paul, Philadelphia, Boston, and Washington, DC metropolitan areas.

Job Outlook

Employment of prepress technicians and workers is projected to decline rapidly through 2018, because of improvements in printing technology that require fewer of these workers. Despite this, job prospects are good for prepress technicians with good computer and customer service skills.

Employment change. Overall employment of prepress technicians and workers is expected to decline by 13 percent over

Projections data from the National Employment Matrix

Occupational Title	SOC Code	Employment, 2008	Projected Employment, 2018	Change, 2008-2018	
				Number	Percent
Prepress technicians and workers	–	106,900	92,600	-14,300	-13
Job printers..	51-5021	45,700	42,200	-3,500	-8
Prepress technicians and workers	51-5022	61,200	50,400	-10,800	-18

(NOTE) Data in this table are rounded. See the discussion of the employment projections table in the *Handbook* introductory chapter on *Occupational Information Included in the Handbook.*

the 2008–2018 period. Demand for printed material, especially product packaging, should grow, reflecting an increase in consumer demand for manufactured goods and an expanding population. But the growing use of computers and publishing software by even the smallest of printing shops will result in rising productivity of prepress technicians, offsetting the growth of new jobs.

Computer software now allows office workers to specify text typeface and style and to format pages. This development shifts traditional prepress functions away from printing plants into advertising and public relations agencies, graphic design firms, and large corporations. As page layout and graphic design capabilities of computer software become less expensive and more user-friendly, many companies are turning to in-house desktop publishing. Some organizations also find it less costly to prepare their own newsletters and other reports. At some publishing companies, writers and editors do more composition of their stories using publishing software to gauge layout needs, but generally rely on prepress technicians to perform the actual layout. The rapid growth in the use of digital printing and desktop publishing has eliminated many prepress technician jobs associated with older printing technologies. In addition, new technologies are increasing the amount of automation in printing companies, requiring fewer prepress workers to do the same work.

Job prospects. Despite a decline in the number of new prepress positions, opportunities will be favorable for workers with strong computer and customer service skills, such as pre-flight technicians who electronically check materials prepared by clients and adapt them for printing. Electronic prepress technicians, digital proofers, platemakers, and graphic designers are using new equipment and ever-improving software to design and lay out publications and complete their printing more quickly.

To remain competitive and profitable, commercial printing companies are offering other services in addition to printing to increase the value of their core service and provide customers with a one-stop option. For example, printers are looking for database administrators, Web site developers, and information technology specialists to assist with providing e-mail distribution and graphic design services. Individuals who are technologically savvy can pick up sales or customer service functions; those who have completed postsecondary programs in printing technology or graphic communications will have the best opportunities.

Earnings

Wage rates for prepress technicians and workers depend on basic factors such as employer, education, and location. Median hourly wages of prepress technicians and workers were $16.84 in May 2008, compared to $13.99 per hour for all production occupations. The middle 50 percent earned between $12.74 and $21.80 an hour. The lowest 10 percent earned less than $10.01, and the highest 10 percent earned more than $26.30 an hour. Median hourly wages in printing and related support activities were $17.39 in May 2008, while workers at newspaper, periodical, book, and directory publishers earned $15.82 an hour.

For job printers, median hourly wages were $16.21 in May 2008. The middle 50 percent earned between $12.59 and $20.57 an hour. The lowest 10 percent earned less than $9.91, and the highest 10 percent earned more than $25.38 an hour. Median hourly wages in the industries employing the largest numbers of job printers in May 2008 were $16.77 in printing and related support activities, and $15.18 in the newspaper, periodical, book, and directory publishers industry.

Related Occupations

Other printing workers and those who use artistic skills in their work include:

Sources of Additional Information

Details about training programs may be obtained from local employers, such as newspapers and printing shops, or from local offices of the State employment service.

Information on careers and training in printing and the graphic arts is available from:

➤ Graphic Arts Education and Research Foundation, 1899 Preston White Dr., Reston, VA 20191. Internet: **http://www.gaerf.org**

➤ Printing Industries of America, 200 Deer Run Rd., Sewickley, PA 15143. Internet: **http://www.printing.org/**

➤ NPES The Association for Suppliers of Printing Publishing, and Converting Technologies, 1899 Preston White Dr., Reston, VA 20191. Internet: **http://www.npes.org/education/index.html**

➤ NAPL National Association of Printing Leadership, 75 West Century Road, Suite 100, Paramus, NJ 07652. Internet: **http://www.napl.org/**

The Occupational Information Network (O*NET) provides information on a wide range of occupational characteristics. Links to O*NET appear at the end of the Internet version of this occupational statement, accessible at **http://www.bls.gov/ooh/ocos230.htm**

Printing Machine Operators

Significant Points

- Most printing machine operators are trained on the job.

- Retirements among older press operators are expected to create openings for skilled workers.

- Rising demand for customized print jobs will mean those skilled in digital printing operations will have the best job opportunities.

Nature of the Work

Printing machine operators, also known as *press operators*, prepare, operate, and maintain printing presses. Duties vary according to the type of press they operate. Traditional printing methods, such as offset lithography, gravure, flexography, and letterpress, use a plate or roller that carries the final image that is to be printed and copies the image to paper. In addition to the traditional printing processes, plateless or nonimpact processes are coming into general use. Plateless processes—including digital, electrostatic, and ink-jet printing—are used for copying, duplicating, and document and specialty printing, usually by quick printing shops and smaller in-house printing shops. Digital presses with longer run capabilities are increasingly being used by commercial printers for short-run or customized printing jobs. Digital presses also allow printers to transfer files, blend colors, and proof images electronically, thus avoiding the costly and time-consuming steps of making printing plates that are common to lithographic or off-set printing.

Printing machine operators' jobs differ from one shop to another because of differences in the types and sizes of presses. Small commercial shops with relatively small presses, those that print only one or two colors at a time, can be operated by one person, often an owner or manager who performs all business activities. To attract a wider range of clients, larger commercial print shops may run several presses with different size and color capacities. Press operators typically specialize in operating one type of press but may operate more than one press at a time. However, press operators who are trained on more than one type of printing press are valuable because they can work on multiple types of printing jobs. Large newspaper, magazine, and book printers use giant "in-line web" presses that require a crew of several press operators and press assistants.

After working with prepress technicians (who are covered elsewhere in the Handbook) to identify and resolve any potential problems with a job, press operators prepare machines for printing. To prepare presses, operators install the printing plate with the images to be printed and adjust the pressure at which the machine prints. They then ink the presses, load paper, and adjust the press to the paper size. Operators ensure that paper and ink meet specifications, and adjust the flow of ink to the inking rollers accordingly. They then feed paper through the press cylinders and adjust feed and tension controls. New digital technology, in contrast, is able to automate much of this work.

While printing presses are running, press operators monitor their operation and keep the paper feeders well stocked. They make adjustments to manage ink distribution, speed, and temperature in the drying chamber, if the press has one. If paper tears or jams and the press stops, which can happen with some offset presses, operators quickly correct the problem to minimize downtime. Similarly, operators working with other high-speed presses constantly look for problems, and when necessary make quick corrections to avoid expensive losses of paper and ink. Throughout the run, operators must regularly pull sheets to check for any printing imperfections. Most printers have, or will soon have, presses with computers and sophisticated instruments to control press operations, making it possible to complete printing jobs in less time. With this equipment, press operators set up, monitor, and adjust the printing process on a control panel or computer monitor, which allows them to control the press electronically.

In most shops, press operators also perform preventive maintenance. They oil and clean the presses and make minor repairs.

Work environment. Operating a press can be physically and mentally demanding, and sometimes tedious. Press operators are on their feet most of the time. Operators often work under pressure to meet deadlines. Most printing presses are capable of high printing speeds, and adjustments must be made quickly to avoid waste. Pressrooms are noisy, and workers in certain areas wear ear protection. Working with press machinery can be hazardous, but the threat of serious accidents has decreased. Newer computerized presses are equipped with safety features and allow operators to make most adjustments from a control panel.

Many press operators, particularly those who work for newspapers, work weekends, nights, and holidays as many presses operate continuously. They also may work overtime to meet deadlines. Most operators worked 40 hours per week in 2008.

Training, Other Qualifications, and Advancement

Although employers prefer that beginners complete a formal apprenticeship or a postsecondary program in printing equipment operation, many press operators are trained on the job. Attention to detail and familiarity with electronics and computers are essential for operators.

Printing machine operators monitor each print job to ensure proper printer maintenance and to minimize malfunctions.

Education and training. Beginning press operators load, unload, and clean presses. With time and training, they may become fully qualified to operate that type of press. Operators can gain experience on more than one kind of printing press during the course of their career.

Experienced operators will periodically receive retraining and skill updating. For example, printing plants that change from sheet-fed offset presses to digital presses have to retrain the entire press crew because skill requirements for the two types of presses are different.

Apprenticeships for press operators, once the dominant method for preparing for this occupation, are becoming less prevalent. When they are offered by the employer, they include on-the-job instruction and related classroom training or correspondence school courses.

Formal postsecondary programs in printing equipment operation offered by technical and trade schools, community colleges, and universities are growing in importance. Postsecondary courses in printing provide the theoretical and technical knowledge needed to operate advanced equipment. Some postsecondary school programs require two years of study and award an associate degree.

Because of technical developments in the printing industry, courses in chemistry, electronics, color theory, and physics are helpful.

Other qualifications. Persons who wish to become press operators need mechanical aptitude to make press adjustments and repairs. Workers need good vision and attention to detail to locate and fix problems with print jobs. Oral and written communication skills also are required. Operators should possess the mathematical skills necessary to compute percentages, weights, and measures, and to calculate the amount of ink and paper needed to do a job. Operators now also need basic computer skills to work with newer printing presses.

Certification and advancement. As press operators gain experience, they may advance in pay and responsibility by working on more complex printing presses. For example, operators who have demonstrated their ability to work with one-color sheet-fed presses may be trained to operate four-color sheet-fed presses. Voluntarily earning formal certification may also help press operators advance. Operators also may advance to pressroom supervisors and become responsible for an entire press crew. In addition, press operators can draw on their knowledge of press operations to become cost estimators, providing estimates of printing jobs to potential customers, sales representatives, and instructors of printing-related courses, or move into other administrative or executive occupations.

Employment

Printing machine operators held about 195,600 jobs in 2008. Over half of all press operator jobs were in printing and related sup-

port activities. Paper manufacturing and newspaper publishers also were large employers. Additional jobs were in advertising, public relations, and related services and plastics product manufacturing.

The printing and newspaper publishing industries are two of the most geographically dispersed in the United States. While printing machine operators thus can find jobs throughout the country, large numbers of jobs are concentrated in large printing centers such as the Chicago, Los Angeles-Long Beach, New York, Minneapolis-St. Paul, Philadelphia, Boston, and Washington, DC metropolitan areas.

Job Outlook

Employment of printing machine operators is projected to decline moderately through 2018, as newer printing presses require fewer operators. Despite this, job opportunities are expected to be favorable because a large number of these workers are expected to retire or leave the occupation over the next decade. The best opportunities will be available to skilled press operators.

Employment change. Employment of press operators is expected to decline by 5 percent over the 2008-18 period. Employment will fall because increasing printer speed and automation require fewer press operators to maintain production levels. This will be especially true among the large printing press operations such as those used by the newspaper industry. Expansion of digital printing technologies and related increases in production cost efficiencies, however, will allow printers to print smaller quantities more profitably and meet the growing interest in the print-on-demand and electronic publishing markets. This should widen the market for printed materials, offsetting some of the employment loss from increased productivity. Short-run print capabilities will permit printers to distribute a wider variety of catalogs, direct mail enclosures, newspaper inserts, and other kinds of print as advertisers are better able to identify the specific interests of a targeted market or audience.

Job prospects. Opportunities for employment in printing press operations should be favorable. Retirements of older printing machine operators and the need for workers trained on computerized printing equipment will create many job openings. For example, small printing jobs will increasingly be run on sophisticated high-speed digital printing equipment that requires a complex set of skills, such as knowledge of database management software. Those who complete postsecondary training programs in printing and who are comfortable with computers will have the best employment opportunities.

Earnings

Median hourly wages of printing machine operators were $15.46 in May 2008, compared to $13.99 per hour for all production occupations. The middle 50 percent earned between $11.65 and $20.08 an hour. The lowest 10 percent earned less than $9.13,

Projections data from the National Employment Matrix

Occupational Title	SOC Code	Employment, 2008	Projected Employment, 2018	Change, 2008-2018	
				Number	Percent
Printing machine operators	51-5023	195,600	185,000	-10,700	-5

(NOTE) Data in this table are rounded. See the discussion of the employment projections table in the *Handbook* introductory chapter on *Occupational Information Included in the Handbook.*

and the highest 10 percent earned more than $24.98 an hour. Median hourly wages in May 2008 were $17.70 in newspaper, periodical, book and directory publishers and $15.85 in printing and related support activities, industries employing among the largest numbers of printing machine operators.

The basic wage rate for a printing machine operator depends on the geographic area in which the work is located and on the size and complexity of the printing press being operated.

Related Occupations

Other workers who set up and operate production machinery include:

	Page
Bookbinders and bindery workers	746
Machine setters, operators, and tenders—metal and plastic	734
Prepress technicians and workers	748

Sources of Additional Information

Details about apprenticeships and other training opportunities may be obtained from local employers, such as newspapers and printing shops, local offices of the Graphic Communications Conference of the International Brotherhood of Teamsters, local affiliates of Printing Industries of America, or local offices of the State employ-ment service. Apprenticeship information is also available from the U.S. Department of Labor's toll-free helpline: 1 (877) 282-5627.

For information on careers and training in printing and the graphic arts contact:

➤ NPES The Association for Suppliers of Printing Publishing, and Converting Technologies, 1899 Preston White Dr., Reston, VA 20191. Internet: **http://www.npes.org/education/index.html**

➤ Printing Industries of America, 200 Deer Run Rd., Sewickley, PA 15143. Internet: **http://www.printing.org/**

➤ Graphic Arts Education and Research Foundation, 1899 Preston White Dr., Reston, VA 20191. Internet: **http://www.gaerf.org**

➤ NAPL National Association of Printing Leadership, 75 West Century Road, Suite 100, Paramus, NJ 07652. Internet: **http://www.napl.org/**

The Occupational Information Network (O*NET) pro-vides information on a wide range of occupational charac-teristics. Links to O*NET appear at the end of the Inter-net version of this occupational statement, accessible at **http://www.bls.gov/ooh/ocos231.htm**

Textile, Apparel, and Furnishings Occupations

Significant Points

- Most workers learn their skills informally on the job, working alongside more experienced workers.

- International competition and greater worker pro-ductivity will result in rapidly declining employ-ment for most occupations; upholsterers and laundry and dry-cleaning workers, however, are expected to experience some employment growth.

- The need to replace workers who retire or leave the occupation for other reasons will lead to numerous job openings.

- Earnings of most workers are relatively low.

Nature of the Work

Textile, apparel, and furnishings workers produce fibers, cloth, and upholstery, and fashion them into a wide range of products that we use in our daily lives. Textiles are the basis of towels, bed linens, hosiery and socks, and nearly all clothing, but they also are a key ingredient in products ranging from roofing to tires. This statement covers a wide variety of occupations related to the production and care of textiles, apparel, and furnishings, ranging from heavy industrial machine operators to craft workers who make custom clothing and upholster furniture.

Laundry and dry-cleaning workers, the largest specialty, clean garments, linens, draperies, blankets, and other articles. They also may clean leather, suede, furs, and rugs. Laundry and dry-cleaning workers ensure proper cleaning by adjusting machine settings for a given fabric or article, as determined by the cleaning instructions on each item of clothing. When necessary, workers treat spots and stains on articles before laundering or dry-cleaning. They tend machines during cleaning and ensure that items are not lost or misplaced with those of another customer.

Closely related to dry-cleaning workers are *pressers, tex-tile, garment, and related materials*. These workers often work in dry-cleaning establishments and are responsible for starching, steaming and ironing clothing and other items to remove wrinkles. When finished, they assemble each custom-er's items, bag or box the articles, and prepare an itemized bill for the customer.

Tailors, dressmakers, and custom sewers alter and repair garments in local neighborhood shops, department stores, or dry-cleaning establishments. Alterations may include hemming pants or dresses, and repairs commonly consist of patching or sewing a torn article of clothing. Some workers may be required to make elaborate custom clothing for special occasions or other unique events.

Most workers in apparel occupations, however, are found in manufacturing, performing specialized tasks in the production of large numbers of garments that are shipped to retail estab-lishments for sale. *Fabric and apparel patternmakers* convert a clothing designer's original model of a garment into sepa-rate parts that can be laid out on a length of fabric. They use computers to outline the parts and draw in details to indicate the position of pleats, buttonholes, and other features. They then alter the size of the pieces in the pattern to produce garments of various sizes and, in doing so, determine the best layout of pieces to minimize waste of material. Once a pattern has been created, mass production of the garment begins.

The first step in manufacturing textiles is preparing the fibers. *Extruding and forming machine setters, operators, and tenders, synthetic and glass fibers*, set up and operate machines that extrude or force liquid synthetic material, such as rayon, fiberglass, or liquid polymers through small holes and draw out filaments. Other operators put natural fibers such as cotton or wool through carding and combing machines that clean and align them into short lengths. *Textile winding, twisting, and drawing-out machine setters, operators, and tenders* make yarn from this material, taking care to repair any breaks. *Textile bleaching and dyeing machine operators and tenders* control machines that wash, bleach, and dye yarn or finished fabrics.

When the yarn or fiber has been prepared, the next step is to produce fabric. *Textile knitting and weaving machine setters, operators, and tenders* put the yarn on machines that weave, knit, loop, or tuft it into a product. Different types of machines are used for these processes, but operators may perform similar tasks, repairing breaks in the yarn and monitoring the yarn supply. Some products, such as hosiery and carpeting, emerge nearly finished. In other cases, the fabric goes on to the next step in the manufacturing process.

Textile cutting machine setters, operators, and tenders use patterns—those from patternmakers—to prepare the pieces from which finished apparel will be made. *Sewing machine operators* then join these pieces together, reinforce seams, and attach buttons, hooks, zippers, and accessories. In some cases, *hand sewers* may be employed to make adjustments and perform specialty work. After the product is sewn, other workers remove lint and loose threads, inspect, and package the garments.

Shoe machine operators and tenders tend machines used in making footwear. They perform a variety of duties including cutting, joining, decorating, reinforcing, and finishing shoes and shoe parts. *Shoe and leather workers and repairers* may finish work that cannot be done by machine. Most repairers are employed in cobbler shops, where they fix shoes and other leather products, such as luggage and saddles.

Upholsterers make, fix, and restore furniture that is covered with fabric. Those who produce new furniture typically start with bare wooden frames. First, they install webbing, tacking it to one side of the frame, stretching it tight, and tacking it to the other side. They then tie each spring to the webbing and its neighboring springs, covering it with filler, such as foam or polyester batting. Next, they measure and cut pieces of fabric for the arms, backs, seats, sides, and other surfaces, leaving as little waste as possible. Finally, they sew the fabric pieces together and attach them to frames with tacks, staples, or glue, while also affixing any ornaments, such as fringes, buttons, or rivets. Some upholsterers work with used furniture, often repairing or replacing fabric that is in poor condition.

Work environment. Most people in textile, apparel, and furnishings occupations work a standard 5-day, 35- to 40-hour week. Working on evenings and weekends is common for shoe and leather workers, laundry and dry-cleaning workers, and tailors, dressmakers, and sewers, who often are employed in retail stores. Many textile and fiber mills often use rotating schedules of shifts so that employees do not continuously work nights or days.

Upholsterers make, fix, and restore furniture that is covered with fabric.

Working conditions vary by establishment and by occupation. For example, machinery in textile mills is often noisy, as are areas in which sewing and pressing are performed in apparel factories; patternmaking and spreading areas tend to be much quieter. Older factories are cluttered, hot, and poorly lit and ventilated, but more modern facilities usually have more workspace and are well lit and ventilated. Textile machinery operators use protective glasses and masks that cover their noses and mouths to protect against airborne particles. Many machines operate at high speeds, and textile machinery workers must be careful not to wear clothing or jewelry that could get caught in moving parts. In addition, extruding and forming machine operators wear protective shoes and clothing when working with certain chemical compounds.

Work in apparel production can be physically demanding. Some workers sit for long periods, and others spend many hours on their feet, leaning over tables and operating machinery. Operators must be attentive while running sewing machines, pressers, automated cutters, and the like. A few workers may need to wear protective clothing, such as gloves. Data from the U.S. Bureau of Labor Statistics show that full-time shoe machine operators and tenders experienced a work-related injury and illness rate that was higher than the national average.

Laundries and dry-cleaning establishments are often hot and noisy. Employees also may be exposed to harsh solvents, but newer environmentally-friendly and less-toxic cleaning solvents are improving the work environment in these establishments. Areas in which shoe and leather workers make or repair shoes and other leather items can be noisy, and odors from leather dyes and stains frequently are present. Workers must take care to avoid punctures, lacerations, and abrasions.

Upholstery work can be dangerous, and upholsterers usually wear protective gloves and clothing when using sharp tools and lifting and handling furniture or springs. During most of the workday, upholsterers stand and may do a lot of bending and heavy lifting. They also may work in awkward positions for short periods. Full-time upholsterers also experienced a work-related injury and illness rate that was much higher than the national average.

Training, Other Qualifications, and Advancement

Most textile, apparel, and furnishings workers learn their skills informally on the job, working alongside more experienced workers.

Education and training. Most workers in these jobs have a high school diploma or less education. However, applicants with postsecondary vocational training or previous work experience may have a better chance of getting a more skilled job and advancing to a supervisory position.

Machine operators usually are trained on the job by more experienced employees or by machinery manufacturers' representatives. Operators begin with simple tasks and are assigned more difficult operations as they gain experience.

Precision shoe and leather workers and repairers also learn their skills on the job. Manual dexterity and mechanical aptitude are important in shoe repair and leatherworking. Beginners start as helpers for experienced workers, but in manufacturing, they may attend more formal in-house training programs. Beginners gradually take on more tasks until they are fully qualified, a process that takes about 2 years in an apprenticeship program or as a helper in a shop. Other workers spend 6 months to a year in a vocational training program.

Custom tailors, dressmakers, and sewers often have previous experience in apparel production, design, or alteration. Knowledge of fabrics, design, and construction is very important. Custom tailors sometimes learn these skills through courses in high school or a community college. Tailors who perform alterations usually learn informally by observing other, more experienced workers.

Laundry and dry-cleaning workers, including pressers, usually learn on the job. Although laundries and dry-cleaners prefer entrants with previous work experience, they routinely hire inexperienced workers.

Most upholsterers learn their skills on the job, but a few do so through apprenticeships. Inexperienced persons also may take training in basic upholstery in vocational schools and some community colleges. The length of training may vary from 6 weeks to 3 years. Upholsterers who work on custom-made pieces may train for 8 to 10 years.

Other qualifications. In manufacturing, textile and apparel workers need good hand-eye coordination, manual dexterity, physical stamina, and the ability to perform repetitive tasks for long periods. As machinery in the industry continues to become more complex, knowledge of the basics of computers and electronics will increasingly be an asset. In addition, the trends toward cross-training of operators and working in teams will increase the time needed to become fully trained on all machines and require interpersonal skills to work effectively with others.

Upholsterers should have manual dexterity, good coordination, and the strength to tightly stretch fabric and lift heavy furniture. An eye for detail, a flair for color, and the ability to use fabrics creatively also are helpful.

Advancement. Some production workers may become first-line supervisors. A small number or workers in shoemaking and leatherworking occupations begin as workers or repairers and advance to salaried supervisory and managerial positions. Some open their own shops. These workers are more likely to succeed if they understand business practices and management

and offer good customer service, in addition to their technical skills.

Upholsterers, too, can open their own shops. However, the upholstery business is highly competitive, and successfully operating a shop is difficult. Some experienced or highly skilled upholsterers may become supervisors or sample makers in large shops and factories.

Employment

Textile, apparel, and furnishings workers held 787,500 jobs in 2008. Employment in the detailed occupations that make up this group was distributed as follows:

Laundry and dry-cleaning workers 235,400
Sewing machine operators 212,400
Pressers, textile, garment, and related materials 66,600
Tailors, dressmakers, and custom sewers.....................54,600
Upholsters 52,700
Textile winding, twisting, and drawing out
    machine setters, operators, and tenders.....................34,900
Textile knitting and weaving machine setters,
    operators, and tenders...29,200
Textile cutting machine setters, operators,
    and tenders...19,400
Textile bleaching and dyeing machine
    operators and tenders..16,000
Extruding and forming machine setters, operators,
    and tenders, synthetic and glass fibers......................14,100
Sewers, hand..12,200
Shoe and leather workers and repairers.........................9,200
Fabric and apparel patternmakers 8,200
Shoe machine operators and tenders.............................4,800
All other textile, apparel, and furnishings workers 17,900

Many manufacturing jobs can be found in California, New York, North Carolina, Texas, and Pennsylvania. Jobs in reupholstery, shoe repair and custom leatherwork, and laundry and dry-cleaning establishments are found in cities and towns throughout the Nation. Overall, about 11 percent of all workers in textile, apparel, and furnishings occupations were self-employed; however, about 43 percent of all tailors, dressmakers, and sewers and about 29 percent of all upholsterers were self-employed.

Job Outlook

Overall employment of textile, apparel, and furnishings workers is expected to decline rapidly through 2018, but outlook varies by detailed occupation. In addition to some employment growth in a few specialties, the vast majority of openings will stem from the need to replace workers who leave the occupation each year.

Employment change. Employment in textile, apparel, and furnishing occupations is expected to decline by 15 percent between 2008 and 2018. Apparel workers have been among the most rapidly declining occupational groups in the economy. Increasing imports, the growing use of offshore assembly, and greater productivity through automation will contribute to additional job losses. Also, many new textiles require less production and processing.

Domestic production of apparel and textiles will continue to move abroad, and imports to the U.S. market are expected to increase. Fierce competition in the market for apparel will

Projections data from the National Employment Matrix

Occupational Title	SOC Code	Employment, 2008	Projected Employment, 2018	Change, 2008-2018	
				Number	Percent
Textile, apparel, and furnishings occupations....................................	51-6000	787,500	667,600	-119,900	-15
Laundry and dry-cleaning workers	51-6011	235,400	242,000	6,600	3
Pressers, textile, garment, and related materials	51-6021	66,600	61,100	-5,500	-8
Sewing machine operators	51-6031	212,400	140,900	-71,500	-34
Shoe and leather workers	51-6040	14,000	11,000	-3,000	-21
Shoe and leather workers and repairers	51-6041	9,200	7,900	-1,300	-14
Shoe machine operators and tenders.......................................	51-6042	4,800	3,100	-1,700	-35
Tailors, dressmakers, and sewers	51-6050	66,800	64,700	-2,100	-3
Sewers, hand	51-6051	12,200	11,200	-1,000	-8
Tailors, dressmakers, and custom sewers................................	51-6052	54,600	53,600	-1,100	-2
Textile machine setters, operators, and tenders...........................	51-6060	99,500	60,600	-38,800	-39
Textile bleaching and dyeing machine operators and tenders.....	51-6061	16,000	8,800	-7,200	-45
Textile cutting machine setters, operators, and tenders	51-6062	19,400	13,400	-6,000	-31
Textile knitting and weaving machine setters, operators, and tenders	51-6063	29,200	17,700	-11,500	-39
Textile winding, twisting, and drawing out machine setters, operators, and tenders.................................	51-6064	34,900	20,700	-14,200	-41
Miscellaneous textile, apparel, and furnishings workers	51-6090	92,900	87,200	-5,700	-6
Extruding and forming machine setters, operators, and tenders, synthetic and glass fibers	51-6091	14,100	9,300	-4,800	-34
Fabric and apparel patternmakers	51-6092	8,200	6,000	-2,200	-27
Upholsterers	51-6093	52,700	56,300	3,600	7
All other textile, apparel, and furnishings workers...................	51-6099	17,900	15,600	-2,300	-13

(NOTE) Data in this table are rounded. See the discussion of the employment projections table in the *Handbook* introductory chapter on *Occupational Information Included in the Handbook.*

keep domestic apparel and textile firms under intense pressure to cut costs and produce more with fewer workers. Although the textile industry already is highly automated, it will continue to seek to increase worker productivity through the introduction of labor-saving machinery and the invention of new fibers and fabrics that reduce production costs. Technological developments, such as computer-aided marking and grading, computer-controlled cutters, semiautomatic sewing and pressing machines, and automated material-handling systems have increased output while reducing the need for some workers in larger firms.

Despite advances in technology, the apparel industry has had difficulty utilizing automated equipment for assembly tasks because of the delicate properties of many textiles. Also, the industry produces a wide variety of apparel items that change frequently with changes in style and season. Even so, increasing numbers of sewing machine operator jobs are expected to be lost to workers abroad. Employment of sewing machine operators is expected to decline rapidly by 34 percent.

Tailors, dressmakers, and custom sewers—the most skilled apparel workers—are expected to experience little or no change in employment. Most of these workers are self-employed or work in clothing stores. The demand for custom home furnishings and tailored clothes is diminishing in general, but remains steady in upscale stores and by certain clients. Designer apparel and other handmade goods also appeal to people looking for one-of-a-kind items.

Employment of shoe and leather workers and repairers is expected to decline by 14 percent through 2018 as a result of growing imports of less expensive shoes and leather goods and of increasing productivity of U.S. manufacturers. Also, buying new shoes often is cheaper than repairing worn or damaged ones.

Employment of laundry and dry-cleaning workers is expected to grow 3 percent, slower than the average for all occupations. Many of these jobs continue to be locally-based, thus an expanding population will result in some employment growth.

Employment of upholsterers is expected to grow 7 percent, which is about as fast as the average for all occupations. Employment growth will be driven by custom upholstery services, which is expected to increase as consumers seek to restore antique furniture and items with sentimental or intrinsic value.

The following table shows the projected growth rates from 2008 to 2018 for detailed textile and apparel manufacturing occupations:

Upholsters 7
Laundry and dry-cleaning workers 3
Tailors, dressmakers, and custom sewers...........................-2
Pressers, textile, garment, and related materials ....-8
Sewers, hand..-8
Shoe and leather workers and repairers...........................-14
Fabric and apparel patternmakers ....-27
Textile cutting machine setters, operators, and tenders.....-31
Extruding and forming machine setters, operators, and tenders, synthetic and glass fibers..........................-34
Sewing machine operators ....-34
Shoe machine operators and tenders...............................-35
Textile knitting and weaving machine setters, operators, and tenders..-39
Textile winding, twisting, and drawing out machine setters, operators, and tenders........................-41
Textile bleaching and dyeing machine operators and tenders..-45
All other textile, apparel, and furnishings workers ....-13

Job prospects. Despite a rapid decline in overall employment, the need to replace workers who transfer to other occupations, retire, or leave the occupation for other reasons will lead to numerous job openings. Relatively low earnings and poor working conditions will continue to result in a high job turnover.

Earnings

Earnings of textile, apparel, and furnishings workers vary by occupation. Because many production workers in apparel manufacturing are paid according to the number of acceptable pieces they produce, their total earnings depend on skill, speed, and accuracy. Workers covered by union contracts tend to have higher earnings. Median hourly wages by occupation in May 2008 were as follows:

Fabric and apparel patternmakers	$18.15
Extruding and forming machine setters, operators, and tenders, synthetic and glass fibers	14.98
Upholsters	13.94
Textile knitting and weaving machine setters, operators, and tenders	12.21
Shoe machine operators and tenders	12.06
Tailors, dressmakers, and custom sewers	12.01
Textile winding, twisting, and drawing out machine setters, operators, and tenders	11.53
Textile bleaching and dyeing machine operators and tenders	11.38
Shoe and leather workers and repairers	11.00
Textile cutting machine setters, operators, and tenders	10.88
Sewers, hand	10.58
Sewing machine operators	9.55
Pressers, textile, garment, and related materials	9.15
Laundry and dry-cleaning workers	9.14
All other textile, apparel, and furnishings workers	11.85

Benefits vary by size of company and work that is done. Apparel workers in retail trade also may receive a discount on their purchases from the company for which they work. In addition, some of the larger manufacturers operate company stores from which employees can purchase apparel products at significant discounts. Some small firms and dry-cleaning establishments, however, offer only limited benefits. Self-employed workers generally have to purchase their own insurance.

In the manufacturing industry, many workers are union members. Workers who are covered by union contracts often have higher pay and better benefits.

Related Occupations

Textile, apparel, and furnishings workers are primarily light manufacturing workers. Similar occupations include:

Sources of Additional Information

Information about job opportunities in textile, apparel, and furnishings occupations is available from local employers and local offices of State employment services.

For information on dry-cleaning occupations, contact:
➤ Drycleaning & Laundry Institute, 14700 Sweitzer Ln., Laurel, MD 20707. Internet: **http://www.ifi.org**

For information on textile and apparel manufacturing occupations, contact:
➤ American Apparel & Footwear Association, 1601 No. Kent Street, 12th floor, Arlington, VA 22209. Internet: **http://www.apparelandfootwear.org**

The Occupational Information Network (O*NET) provides information on a wide range of occupational characteristics. Links to O*NET appear at the end of the Internet version of this occupational statement, accessible at **http://www.bls.gov/ooh/ocos233.htm**

Woodworkers

Significant Points

- Most woodworkers are trained on the job; becoming a skilled woodworker often requires several years of experience.

- Job prospects should be excellent for highly skilled woodworkers who are proficient users of computerized numerical control machines.

- Employment is highly sensitive to economic cycles; during economic downturns, workers are subject to layoffs or reductions in hours.

Nature of the Work

Despite the abundance of plastics, metals, and other materials, wood products continue to be an important part of our daily lives. Many of these products are mass produced, including most furniture, kitchen cabinets, and musical instruments. Other products are custom-crafted in shops using specialized tools. The people who design, produce, and test these products are called *woodworkers*.

Although the term woodworker may evoke the image of a craftsman who builds ornate furniture using hand tools, the modern woodworking trade is highly technical and relies on advanced equipment and highly-skilled operators. Workers use automated machinery, such as computerized numerical control (CNC) machines to do much of the work. Even specialized artisans generally use a variety of power tools in their work. Much of the work is often done in a high production assembly line facility, but there is also some work that is customized and does not lend itself to assembly line fabrication. Woodworkers are employed in every part of the secondary wood products industry—from sawmill to finished product—and their activities vary greatly.

Woodworkers set up, operate and tend all types of machines, such as drill presses, lathes, shapers, routers, sanders, planers, and wood-nailing machines. Operators set up the equipment, cut and shape wooden parts, and verify dimensions using a template, caliper, or rule. After wood parts are made, woodworkers add fasteners and adhesives and connect the pieces to form a complete unit. Products are then sanded, stained, and, if necessary, coated with a sealer, such as a lacquer or varnish.

In some cases, these tasks are managed by different workers with specialized training. For instance, *woodworking machine setters, operators, and tenders* may specialize in operating specific pieces of woodworking machinery. *Furniture finishers* stain and seal wood products; they often work with antiques and must make judgments about how to best preserve and repair them.

On the other hand, some woodworkers are less specialized, and must know how to complete many stages of the process. *Cabinetmakers* and *bench carpenters* often design and create sets of cabinets that are customized for particular spaces. In some cases, their duties could begin with designing a set of cabinets to particular specifications and end with installing them. *Architectural woodworkers* design and create customized wooden furniture and accents that are part of a building. This might include a desk that is built into a hotel lobby, a bar in

Woodworkers set up equipment, verify dimensions, and cut and shape wooden parts.

a pub, or booths in a restaurant. Other woodworkers, such as *model makers*, create scale models of products or buildings that are used in construction; *patternmakers* construct dies that are used for castings.

Work environment. Working conditions vary greatly, depending on specific job duties. Workers may have to handle heavy, bulky materials and often encounter excessive noise and dust. Workers must often wear earplugs, gloves, and goggles to protect themselves. These occupations tend to have relatively high non-fatal injury rates, since woodworkers spend much of their time using power tools, which can be dangerous. Data from the U.S. Bureau of Labor Statistics show that sawing machine operators experienced a work-related injury and illness rate that was much higher than the national average.

Training, Other Qualifications, and Advancement
Becoming a fully-trained woodworker requires many skills, and generally takes several years of on-the-job training. Skill with computers and computer-controlled machinery is increasingly important.

Education and training. Many employers seek applicants with a high school diploma or the equivalent because of the growing sophistication of machinery and the constant need for retraining. People seeking woodworking jobs can enhance their employment and advancement prospects by completing high school and receiving training in mathematics and computer applications.

Some woodworkers acquire skills through technical schools or community college courses. Others may attend universities that offer training in wood technology, furniture manufacturing, wood engineering, and production management. These programs prepare students for positions in production, supervision, engineering, and management and are increasingly important as woodworking technology advances.

While education is helpful, woodworkers are primarily trained on the job, where they learn skills from experienced workers. Beginning workers are assigned basic tasks, such as putting a piece of wood through a machine or catching the wood at the end of the process. As they gain experience, they perform more complex jobs with less supervision. They can learn basic machine operations and job tasks in about a year. Skilled workers learn to read blueprints, set up machines, and plan work sequences. Becoming a skilled woodworker often requires 3 or more years.

Other qualifications. In addition to training, woodworkers need mechanical ability, manual dexterity, and the ability to pay attention to detail and safety. They should be comfortable working with geometric concepts; for example, they must be able to visualize how shapes will fit together in three dimensions. Skill with computers and computer-controlled machinery is increasingly important in this high-tech occupation.

Advancement. Advancement opportunities depend on education and training, seniority, and a worker's skills and initiative. Experienced woodworkers often become supervisors responsible for the work of a group of woodworkers. Others may become full-time CNC operators, designing woodwork using computer aided design software. Still others become inspectors, making sure that products are built to proper specifications. Production workers can advance into these positions by assuming additional responsibilities and attending workshops, seminars, or college programs. Those who are highly skilled may set up their own woodworking shops.

Employment

Woodworkers held about 323,300 jobs in 2008. Self-employed woodworkers accounted for 12 percent of these jobs. About 76 percent of woodworkers were employed in manufacturing. About 39 percent worked in establishments manufacturing furniture and related products, and 32 percent worked in wood product manufacturing, producing a variety of raw, intermediate, and finished woodstock. Wholesale and retail lumber dealers, furniture stores, reupholstery and furniture repair shops, and construction firms also employ woodworkers.

Woodworking jobs are found throughout the country. However, lumber and wood products-related production jobs are concentrated in the Southeast, Midwest, and Northwest, close to the supply of wood. Furniture-making jobs are more prevalent in the Southeast. Custom shops can be found everywhere, but generally are concentrated in or near highly populated areas.

Job Outlook

Employment of woodworkers is expected to grow more slowly than the average for all occupations. Job prospects will be excellent for highly qualified workers

Employment change. Employment of woodworkers is expected to grow by 6 percent during the 2008-18 decade, which is slower than the average for all occupations. Increased automation in the wood products manufacturing industry has led to slow job growth for some time, but this has been tempered in recent years by increased demand for domestic wood products. Technology has become very important to this industry, and automation has greatly reduced the number of people required to produce a finished product. While this has slowed employment growth somewhat, improved efficiency has made domestic wood products more competitive with imports.

Demand for these workers will stem from increases in population, personal income, and business expenditures and from the continuing need for repair and renovation of residential and commercial properties. Therefore, opportunities should be available for workers who specialize in items such as moldings, cabinets, stairs, and windows. Firms that focus on custom woodwork will be best able to compete against imports without transferring jobs offshore.

Employment in all woodworking specialties is highly sensitive to economic cycles. During economic downturns, workers are subject to layoffs or reductions in hours.

Job prospects. Prospects should be excellent for highly qualified workers. In general, opportunities for more highly skilled woodworkers will be better than for woodworkers in specialties susceptible to automation and competition from imported wood products. The need for woodworkers with technical skills to operate their increasingly advanced computerized machinery will be especially great. Workers who know how to create and execute custom designs on a computer will be in strong demand. These jobs require an understanding of wood and a strong understanding of computers—a combination that can be somewhat difficult to find.

The number of new workers entering these occupations has declined greatly in recent years, as training programs become less available or popular. Opportunities should be best for woodworkers who, through vocational education or experience, develop highly specialized woodworking skills or knowledge of CNC machine tool operation.

Earnings

Median hourly wages of cabinetmakers and bench carpenters were $13.93 in May 2008. The middle 50 percent earned between $11.14 and $17.40. The lowest 10 percent earned less than $9.22, and the highest 10 percent earned more than $21.73.

Median hourly wages of sawing machine setters, operators, and tenders, wood were $12.41. The middle 50 percent earned between $9.96 and $15.24. The lowest 10 percent earned less than $8.35, and the highest 10 percent earned more than $18.92.

Median hourly wages of woodworking machine setters, operators, and tenders, except sawing were $11.89. The middle 50 percent earned between $9.69 and $14.73. The lowest 10 percent earned less than $8.28, and the highest 10 percent earned more than $17.89.

Median hourly wages were $12.93 for furniture finishers and $11.57 for all other woodworkers.

Projections data from the National Employment Matrix

Occupational Title	SOC Code	Employment, 2008	Projected Employment, 2018	Change, 2008-2018	
				Number	Percent
Woodworkers	51-7000	323,300	344,000	20,600	6
Cabinetmakers and bench carpenters..	51-7011	131,700	143,700	11,900	9
Furniture finishers...	51-7021	26,500	27,700	1,200	4
Model makers and patternmakers, wood	51-7030	3,500	3,500	0	-1
Model makers, wood...	51-7031	1,700	1,700	0	2
Patternmakers, wood...	51-7032	1,900	1,800	-100	-3
Woodworking machine setters, operators, and tenders.................	51-7040	138,400	145,100	6,700	5
Sawing machine setters, operators, and tenders, wood............	51-7041	52,600	53,400	800	1
Woodworking machine setters, operators, and tenders, except sawing..	51-7042	85,700	91,700	6,000	7
All other woodworkers...	51-7099	23,300	24,000	800	3

(NOTE) Data in this table are rounded. See the discussion of the employment projections table in the *Handbook* introductory chapter on *Occupational Information Included in the Handbook.*

Related Occupations

Occupations that require similar skills include:

Sources of Additional Information

For information about careers and education and training programs in woodworking, contact:

➤ Architectural Woodwork Institute, 46179 Westlake Drive, Suite 120, Potomac Falls, VA 20165. Internet: **http://www.awinet.org**

➤ WoodIndustryEd.org, c/o AWFS, 500 Citadel Dr., Suite 200, Commerce, CA 90040. Internet: **http://www.woodindustryed.org**

➤ WoodLINKS USA, P.O. Box 445, Tuscola, IL 61953. Internet: **http://www.woodlinksusa.org**

The Occupational Information Network (O*NET) provides information on a wide range of occupational characteristics. Links to O*NET appear at the end of the Internet version of this occupational statement, accessible at **http://www.bls.gov/ooh/ocos237.htm**

Plant and System Operators

Power Plant Operators, Distributors, and Dispatchers

Significant Points

- Overall employment is projected to experience little or no change over the next decade, but job prospects are expected to be excellent for qualified applicants as many workers retire.

- Several years of classroom and on-the-job training are required to become fully qualified.

- Familiarity with computers and a basic understanding of science and math are helpful for those entering the field.

Nature of the Work

Electricity is one of our nation's most vital resources. It powers everything from light bulbs and appliances that you use around your house to supercomputers that power the Internet. From the moment you flip the first switch each morning, you are connecting to a huge network of people, electric lines, and generating equipment. *Power plant operators* control the machinery that generates electricity. *Power plant distributors and dispatchers* control the flow of electricity as it travels through a network of transmission lines from the power plant to industrial plants and substations, and then flows through distribution lines to residential users.

Power plant operators control and monitor boilers, turbines, generators, and auxiliary equipment in power-generating plants. They distribute power among generators, regulate the output from several generators, and monitor instruments to maintain voltage and regulate electricity flows from the plant. When demand changes, power plant operators communicate with dispatchers at distribution centers to match production with system the load. On the basis of this communication, they start and stop generators, altering the amount of electricity

output. They also go on rounds to check that everything in the plant is operating correctly and keep records of switching operations and loads on generators, lines, and transformers. In all of these tasks, they use computers to report unusual incidents, malfunctioning equipment, or maintenance performed during their shifts.

Nuclear power reactor operators perform similar tasks at a nuclear power plant. Most start working as equipment operators or auxiliary operators. At this stage, they help the more senior workers with equipment maintenance and operation while learning the basics of plant operation. With experience and training they may be licensed by the Nuclear Regulatory Commission as reactor operators, making them authorized to control equipment that affects the power of the reactor in a nuclear power plant. Senior reactor operators supervise the operation of all controls in the control room. At least one senior operator must be on duty during each shift to act as the plant supervisor.

Power distributors and dispatchers, also called load dispatchers or systems operators, work for utility companies, nonutility generators, and other companies that access the power grid. They control the flow of electricity through transmission lines to industrial plants and substations that supply residential and commercial needs for electricity. They monitor and operate current converters, voltage transformers, and circuit breakers. Dispatchers also monitor other distribution equipment and record readings at a map board—a diagram of the transmission grid system showing the status of transmission circuits and connections with substations and industrial plants. In doing this, they communicate closely with power plant operators, energy traders, and local utilities to route energy from generating stations to customers.

Dispatchers anticipate changes in power needs caused by weather, such as increased demand for power on a hot day or outages during a thunderstorm. They also react to changes in the structure of the grid due to transformer or transmission line failures and route current around affected areas. In substations, they operate and monitor equipment that increases or decreases voltage and they operate switchboard levers to control the flow of electricity in and out of the substations.

Work environment. Operators, distributors, and dispatchers who work in control rooms generally sit or stand at a control station. The work is not physically strenuous, but it does require constant attention. When operators are on rounds or performing other work outside of the control room, they may be exposed to danger from electric shock, falls, and burns. In addition, nuclear reactor operators may be exposed to small amounts of ionizing radiation during the course of their work.

Because power transmission is both vitally important and sensitive to attacks, security is a major concern for energy companies. Nuclear power plants and transmission stations have especially high security, and workers should be prepared to work in secured environments.

Because electricity is provided around the clock, operators, distributors, and dispatchers usually work one of three 8-hour shifts or one of two 12-hour shifts on a rotating basis. Shift assignments may change periodically so that all operators share less desirable shifts. Work on rotating shifts can be stressful and fatiguing because of the constant changes in living and sleeping patterns.

Training, Other Qualifications, and Advancement

Power plant operators, dispatchers, and distributors generally need a combination of education, on-the-job training, and experience. Candidates with strong mechanical, technical and computer skills are generally preferred.

Both operators and dispatchers are subject to random drug and alcohol tests. Nuclear reactor operators must pass a medical examination every 2 years.

Education and training. Operator and dispatcher jobs require at least a high school diploma. Workers with college or vocational school degrees will have advantages in finding a job, as well as more advancement opportunities, especially in nuclear power plants. Although it is not a prerequisite, many nuclear power reactor operators have bachelor's degrees in engineering or the physical sciences.

Workers selected for training as power plant operators or distributors undergo extensive on-the-job training and classroom

Power plant operators use computers to report unusual incidents, malfunctioning equipment, or maintenance performed during their shifts.

instruction. Several years of training and experience are necessary to become fully qualified.

In addition to receiving initial training, a power plant operator, distributor, or dispatcher, is required to spend a certain number of hours each year taking refresher courses. Operators train on plant simulators designed to replicate situations that could occur at the plant. Similarly, dispatchers and system operators train extensively on power system simulators to keep skills sharp to prevent blackouts.

Licensure and certification. Some power plant operators, distributors and dispatchers must earn and maintain licenses. The specific requirements vary by job function and jurisdiction.

Power plant operators not working in a nuclear facility are often licensed as engineers or firemen by State licensing boards. Requirements vary from State to State and also depend on the specific job function of the operator and the license needed.

Nuclear power reactor operators must pass an examination and maintain licenses administered by the Nuclear Regulatory Commission (NRC). Before beginning training, a nuclear power plant operator must have 3 years of power plant experience. At least 1 of the 3 years must be at the nuclear power plant where the operator is to be licensed, and 6 months should be as a nonlicensed operator at the plant. Training generally takes at least 1 year, after which the worker must take an NRC-administered written examination and operating test. To maintain their licenses, reactor operators must pass an annual practical plant-operating exam and a biennial written exam administered by their employers. Reactor operators can upgrade their licenses to the senior-reactor-operator level after a year of licensed experience at the plant by taking another examination given by the NRC. Individuals with a bachelor's degree in engineering or the equivalent may apply for senior operator's licenses directly if they have 3 years of nuclear power plant experience, with at least 6 months at the site. Training includes simulator and on-the-job training, classroom instruction, and individual study. Experience in other power plants or with Navy nuclear-propulsion plants also is helpful. Although waivers are possible, licensed nuclear power reactor operators and senior operators generally have to pass a new written examination and operating test administered by the NRC if they transfer to another facility.

Power distributors and dispatchers who are in positions in which they could affect the power grid must be certified by the North American Energy Reliability Corporation (NERC). There are three types of certification offered by NERC: reliability coordinator, transmission operator, and balancing authority. Each of these qualifies a worker to handle a different job function. Distributors and dispatchers who distribute power within local utilities generally do not need to be licensed or certified.

Other qualifications. Electric company recruiters generally look for individuals with strong math and science backgrounds for these highly technical jobs. Understanding electricity and math—especially algebra and trigonometry—are important, although workers learn many of these concepts and skills in specialized training courses. Workers should also be good at working with tools. Problem solving is an important part of most electrical workers' jobs, so recruiters usually look for people who can easily figure out how things work. Successful utility workers are generally good with mechanics and enjoy fixing things.

In order to measure these aptitudes, many companies require that their workers take the Power Plant Maintenance (MASS) and Plant Operator (POSS) exams administered by the Edison Electrical Institute. These tests measure reading comprehension, understanding of mechanical concepts, spatial ability, and mathematical ability.

Advancement. After finishing work in the classroom, most entry-level workers start as helpers or laborers and advance to more responsible positions as they become comfortable in the plant. Workers are generally classified into 3-5 levels based on experience. For each level, there are training requirements, mandatory waiting times, and exams. With sufficient training and experience, workers can become shift supervisors, trainers, or consultants.

Because power plants have different systems and safety mechanisms, it can sometimes be difficult to advance by moving to a different company, although this is not always the case. Most power companies promote from within and most workers advance within a particular plant or by moving to another plant owned by the same utility.

Employment

Power plant operators, distributors, and dispatchers held about 50,400 jobs in 2008, of which 5,000 were nuclear power reactor operators, 10,000 were power distributors and dispatchers, and 35,400 were power plant operators. Jobs were located throughout the country.

Job Outlook

Overall employment of power plant operators, distributors, and dispatchers is projected to experience little or no change, but job opportunities are expected to be excellent because of the large number of retiring workers who must be replaced, an increased demand for energy, and recent legislation that paves the way for a number of new plants.

Employment change. Between 2008 and 2018, overall employment of power plant operators, distributors, and dispatchers is expected to experience little or no change. Although Americans' energy use continues to grow annually, the intense competition among generators resulting from deregulation will temper that growth.

Power plant operators in non-nuclear power plants are expected to decline by 2 percent between 2008 and 2018, representing little or no change, as energy companies continue to promote efficiency and build more efficient plants. While most

of the major employment effects of deregulation have already occurred, generators continue to focus on cost cutting. As older, less efficient plants are retired, they are being replaced with new plants that have higher capacities and require fewer workers. Because the capacity of the new plants is higher, fewer are needed to produce the same amount of electricity.

Employment of nuclear power reactor operators is expected to grow by 19 percent between 2008 and 2018, faster than the average for all occupations, because of plant construction and new rules on operator fatigue. Although no new plants have been licensed since the 1990s, many sites have applied for permits which will need to be staffed before the end of the projections decade. Further, newly enacted NRC regulations on fatigue limit the length of shifts, meaning that nuclear facilities may need more operators.

On the other hand, power distributor and dispatcher employment is expected to experience little or no change, declining by 2 percent between 2008 and 2018, reflecting further industry consolidation.

Job prospects. Job opportunities are expected to be excellent for well-qualified applicants because of a large number of retirements in the electric power industry. During the 1990s, the emphasis on cost cutting among utilities led to hiring freezes and the laying off of younger workers. The result is that many power plant operators, distributors, and dispatchers are nearing retirement age. Utilities have responded by setting up new education programs at community colleges and high schools throughout the country. While many individuals are showing interest in these high-paying jobs, prospects will be best for workers with strong technical and mechanical skills and an understanding of science and mathematics.

Earnings

Median annual wages of power plant operators were $58,470 in May 2008. The middle 50 percent earned between $47,850 and $68,250. The lowest 10 percent earned less than $38,020, and the highest 10 percent earned more than $80,390.

Median annual wages of nuclear power reactor operators were $73,320 in May 2008. The middle 50 percent earned between $63,440 and $82,540. The lowest 10 percent earned less than $55,730, and the highest 10 percent earned more than $96,480.

Median annual wages of power distributors and dispatchers were $65,890 in May 2008. The middle 50 percent earned between $55,520 and $77,780. The lowest 10 percent earned less than $45,010, and the highest 10 percent earned more than $88,500.

About 40 percent of power plant operators, distributors, and dispatchers were members of unions in 2008.

Projections data from the National Employment Matrix

Occupational Title	SOC Code	Employment, 2008	Projected Employment, 2018	Change, 2008-2018	
				Number	Percent
Power plant operators, distributors, and dispatchers.........................	51-8010	50,400	50,600	200	0
Nuclear power reactor operators...	51-8011	5,000	6,000	1,000	19
Power distributors and dispatchers...	51-8012	10,000	9,800	-200	-2
Power plant operators..	51-8013	35,400	34,800	-600	-2

(NOTE) Data in this table are rounded. See the discussion of the employment projections table in the *Handbook* introductory chapter on *Occupational Information Included in the Handbook.*

Related Occupations

Other workers who monitor and operate plant and system equipment include:

Sources of Additional Information

For general information about power plant operators, nuclear power reactor operators, and power plant distributors and dispatchers, contact:

➤ American Public Power Association, 1875 Connecticut Ave. NW., Suite 1200, Washington, DC 20009-5715. Internet: **http://www.appanet.org**

➤ Center for Energy Workforce Development, 701 Pennsylvania Ave. NW., Washington, DC 20004-2696. Internet: **http://www.cewd.org**

➤ International Brotherhood of Electrical Workers, 900 Seventh St NW., Washington, DC 20001. Internet: **http://www.ibew.org**

Information on licensing for nuclear reactor operators and senior reactor operators is available from:

➤ U.S. Nuclear Regulatory Commission, Washington, DC 20555-0001. Internet: **http://www.nrc.gov**

Information on certification for power distributors and dispatchers is available from:

➤ North American Electric Reliability Corporation, 116-390 Village Blvd., Princeton, NJ 08540-5721. Internet: **http://www.nerc.com**

The Occupational Information Network (O*NET) provides information on a wide range of occupational characteristics. Links to O*NET appear at the end of the Internet version of this occupational statement, accessible at **http://www.bls.gov/ooh/ocos227.htm**

Stationary Engineers and Boiler Operators

Significant Points

- Workers usually acquire their skills through a formal apprenticeship program or through on-the-job training.

- Licensure is required in many States and is a prerequisite for many job openings.

- Employment is projected to grow more slowly than average, and applicants may face competition for jobs.

Nature of the Work

Most large office buildings, malls, warehouses, and other commercial facilities have extensive heating, ventilation, and air-conditioning systems that keep them comfortable all year long. Industrial plants often have additional facilities to provide electrical power, steam, or other services. *Stationary engineers* and *boiler operators* control and maintain these systems, which include boilers, chillers, air-conditioning and refrigeration equipment, diesel engines, turbines, generators, pumps, condensers, and compressors. The equipment that stationary engineers and boiler operators control is similar to equipment operated by locomotive or marine engineers, except that it is used to generate heat or electricity rather than to move a train or ship.

Stationary engineers and boiler operators start up, regulate, repair, and shut down equipment. They ensure that the equipment operates safely, economically, and within established limits by monitoring meters, gauges, and computerized controls. When necessary, they control equipment manually and make adjustments using hand and power tools. They watch and listen to machinery and routinely check safety devices, record data in logs, and identify any potential problems.

Routine maintenance is a regular part of the work of stationary engineers and boiler operators. Engineers use tools to perform repairs ranging from a complete overhaul to replacing defective valves, gaskets, or bearings. They lubricate moving parts, replace filters, and remove soot and corrosion that can reduce the boiler's operating efficiency. They also test the water in the boiler and add chemicals to prevent corrosion and harmful deposits.

In most facilities, stationary engineers are responsible for the maintenance and balancing of air systems, as well as hydronic systems that heat or cool buildings by circulating fluid (such as water or water vapor) in a closed system of pipes. They may check the air quality of the ventilation system and make adjustments to keep the operation of the boiler within mandated guidelines. Servicing, troubleshooting, repairing, and monitoring modern systems all require the use of sophisticated electrical and electronic test equipment.

In a large building or industrial plant, a senior stationary engineer may be in charge of all mechanical systems in the building and may supervise a team of assistant stationary engineers, turbine operators, boiler tenders, and air-conditioning and refrigeration operators and mechanics. In small buildings, there may be only one stationary engineer who operates and maintains all of the systems.

Work environment. Engine rooms, power plants, boiler rooms, mechanical rooms, and electrical rooms are usually clean and well lit. Even under the most favorable conditions, however, some stationary engineers and boiler operators are exposed to high temperatures, dust, dirt, and high noise levels from the equipment. Maintenance duties also may require contact with oil, grease, or smoke. Workers spend much of the time on their feet. They also may have to crawl inside boilers and work while crouched or kneeling to inspect, clean, or repair equipment.

Safety is a major concern for these workers. Stationary engineers and boiler operators work around hazardous machinery, and must follow procedures to guard against burns, electric shock, noise, dangerous moving parts, and exposure to hazardous materials. Despite these precautions, however, sta-

Stationary engineers and boiler operators control and maintain equipment that is used to generate heat or electricity.

tionary engineers and boiler operators have a relatively high rate of occupational injuries.

Stationary engineers and boiler operators generally have steady, year-round employment. The average workweek is 40 hours. In facilities that operate around the clock, engineers and operators usually work one of three daily 8-hour shifts on a rotating basis. Weekend and holiday work are often required, as many buildings are open 365 days a year.

Training, Other Qualifications, and Advancement

Many stationary engineers and boiler operators begin their careers in mechanic or helper positions and are trained on the job by more experienced engineers. Others begin by entering formal apprenticeships or training programs. Licensure is required in many States and jurisdictions, and is a prerequisite for many job openings.

Education and training. Most employers prefer to hire people with at least a high school diploma or the equivalent for stationary engineers and boiler operator jobs. Workers acquire their skills primarily on the job and usually start as apprentices or helpers. This practical experience may be supplemented by postsecondary vocational training in subjects such as computerized controls and instrumentation. Becoming an engineer or operator without completing a formal apprenticeship program usually requires many years of work experience.

The International Union of Operating Engineers sponsors apprenticeship programs and is the principal union for stationary engineers and boiler operators. Apprenticeships usually last 4 years and include 6,000 hours of on-the-job training. Apprentices learn to operate boilers, generators, compressors, motors, and air-conditioning and refrigerating equipment.

Apprentices also receive 600 hours of classroom instruction, studying elementary physics, practical chemistry, blueprint reading, instrumentation, and other technical subjects.

Continuing education—such as vocational school or college courses—is becoming increasingly important for stationary engineers and boiler operators, in part because of the growing complexity of the equipment with which engineers and operators now work.

Most large and some small employers encourage and pay for skill-improvement training for their employees. Training is almost always provided when new equipment is introduced or when regulations concerning some aspect of the workers' duties change.

Licensure. Many State and local governments have licensing requirements for stationary engineers and boiler operators. Applicants for licensure usually must be at least 18 years of age, reside for a specified period in the State or locality in which they wish to work, meet experience requirements, and pass a written examination. A stationary engineer or boiler operator who moves from one State or city to another may have to pass an examination for a new license because of regional differences in licensing requirements.

There are generally four or five classes of stationary engineer licenses. Each class specifies the type and size of equipment the engineer is permitted to operate without supervision. A top-level stationary engineer is qualified to run a large facility, supervise others, and operate equipment of all types and capacities. An applicant for this license may be required to have a high school education, have completed an apprenticeship or lengthy on-the-job training, and have several years of experience working with a lower class license. Engineers with licenses below this level are limited in the types or capacities of equipment they may operate without supervision.

Many job openings require that workers be licensed before starting the job, although some jobs may offer apprenticeships.

Other qualifications. In addition to training, stationary engineers and boiler operators need mechanical aptitude and manual dexterity. Most employers of entry-level workers and apprenticeship committees prefer applicants with a basic understanding of mathematics, science, computers, mechanical drawing, machine shop practice, and chemistry. Being in good physical condition is also important.

Advancement. Generally, engineers advance as they obtain higher class licenses. These licenses permit boiler operators to work with larger, more powerful, or more varied equipment. In jurisdictions where licenses are not required, workers generally advance by taking company-administered exams. Some stationary engineers and boiler operators advance to become boiler inspectors, chief plant engineers, building and plant superintendents, or building managers. A few obtain jobs as examining engineers or technical instructors.

Because most stationary engineering staffs are relatively small, workers may find it difficult to advance, especially within a company. Most high-level positions are held by experienced workers with seniority. Workers wishing to move up to these positions must often change employers or wait for older workers to retire before they can advance.

Employment

Stationary engineers and boiler operators held about 41,600 jobs in 2008. They worked throughout the country, generally in the more heavily populated areas in which large industrial and commercial establishments are located. Jobs were dispersed throughout a variety of industries. The majority of jobs were in manufacturing, Government, public and private educational services, and public and private hospitals.

Job Outlook

Employment in this occupation is expected to grow more slowly than average through 2018. Applicants may face competition for jobs. Employment opportunities will be best for those who have apprenticeship training and are licensed in their jurisdictions.

Employment change. Employment of stationary engineers and boiler operators is expected to grow by 5 percent between 2008 and 2018, which is slower than the average for all occupations. Continuing commercial and industrial development will increase the amount of equipment to be operated and maintained. Although automated systems and computerized controls are making newly installed equipment more efficient, experienced workers will increasingly be needed to maintain and repair these complex systems.

While employment of stationary engineers and boiler operators is spread across all industries, some industries will experience more growth than others. The largest employment growth will occur in industries with the need for precise temperature control, such as hospitals.

Job prospects. People interested in working as stationary engineers and boiler operators should expect to face competition for these relatively high-paying positions. Although many opportunities will be created by the retirement of the baby-boomer generation, finding an entry-level job can be difficult—especially for inexperienced and unlicensed workers. While there are workers employed in most establishments with large buildings, the typical engineering staff is relatively small. The tendency of experienced workers to stay in a job for decades can make it difficult for entry-level workers to find a job.

Workers who have completed a training course or apprenticeship will have the best prospects. Additionally, in States and jurisdictions where licenses are required, workers who are licensed prior to beginning employment will have better opportunities.

Earnings

Median annual wages of stationary engineers and boiler operators were $49,790 in May 2008. The middle 50 percent earned between $39,390 and $61,670. The lowest 10 percent earned less than $30,630, and the highest 10 percent earned more than $74,500.

Related Occupations

Workers who monitor and operate stationary machinery include:

Other workers who maintain the equipment and machinery in a building or plant are:

Sources of Additional Information

Information about apprenticeships, vocational training, and work opportunities is available from State employment service offices, local chapters of the International Union of Operating Engineers, vocational schools, and State and local licensing agencies. Apprenticeship information is also available from the U.S. Department of Labor's toll-free helpline: (877) 872-5627

Specific questions about this occupation should be addressed to:
➤ International Union of Operating Engineers, 1125 17th St. NW., Washington, DC 20036. Internet: **http://www.iuoe.org**

➤ National Association of Power Engineers, Inc., 1 Springfield St., Chicopee, MA 01013. Internet: **http://www.napenational.org**

The Occupational Information Network (O*NET) provides information on a wide range of occupational characteristics. Links to O*NET appear at the end of the Internet version of this occupational statement, accessible at **http://www.bls.gov/ooh/ocos228.htm**

Water and Liquid Waste Treatment Plant and System Operators

Significant Points

- Employment is concentrated in local government and water, sewage, and other systems utilities.

- Because of expected much faster than average employment growth and a large number of upcoming retirements, job opportunities will be excellent.

- Completion of an associate degree or a 1-year certificate program in environmental studies or a related field may help applicants to find jobs and advance more quickly.

Nature of the Work

Water is one of our society's most important resources. While most people take it for granted, it takes a lot of work to get water from natural sources—reservoirs, streams, and groundwater—into our taps. Similarly, it is a complicated process to convert the wastewater in our drains and sewers into a form that is safe to release into the environment. *Water treatment plant and system operators* run the equipment, control the processes, and monitor the plants that treat water so that it is safe to drink.

Liquid waste treatment plant and system operators do similar work to remove pollutants from domestic and industrial waste.

Fresh water is pumped from wells, rivers, streams, and reservoirs to water treatment plants, where it is treated and distributed to customers. Used water, also known as wastewater, travels through sewage pipes to treatment plants where it is treated and either returned to streams, rivers, and oceans, or reused for irrigation. Operators in both types of plants control equipment and monitor processes that remove or destroy harmful materials, chemicals, and microorganisms from the water. They also run tests to make sure that the processes are working correctly and keep records of water quality and other indicators.

Water and wastewater treatment plant operators operate and maintain the pumps and motors that move water and wastewater through filtration systems. They monitor the indicators at their plants and make adjustments as necessary. They read meters and gauges to make sure that plant equipment is working properly. They take samples and run tests to determine the quality of the water being produced. At times, they may adjust the amount of chemicals, such as chlorine and fluorine, being added to the water.

The specific duties of plant operators depend on the type and size of the plant. In a small plant, one operator may be responsible for maintaining all of the systems. This operator would most likely work during the day and be on call during nights and weekends. In medium-size plants, operators may work in shifts to monitor the plant at all hours of the day. In large plants, multiple operators work the same shifts and are more specialized in their duties, often relying on computerized systems to help monitor plant processes.

Occasionally, operators must work during emergencies. Weather conditions may cause large amounts of storm water and wastewater to flow into sewers, exceeding a plant's capacity. Emergencies also may be caused by malfunctions within a plant, such as chemical leaks or oxygen deficiencies. Operators are trained in emergency management procedures and use safety equipment to protect their health, as well as that of the public.

Both tap water and wastewater are highly regulated by the U.S. Environmental Protection Agency. Plant operators must be familiar with these regulations and ensure that their high standards are met. Operators are also responsible for keeping records that document compliance and for being aware of new regulations that are enacted.

Work environment. Water and wastewater treatment plant and system operators work both indoors and outdoors and may be exposed to noise from machinery and to unpleasant odors. Operators' work is physically demanding and often is performed in locations that are difficult to access or unclean. They must pay close attention to safety procedures because of the presence of hazardous conditions, such as slippery walkways, dangerous gases, and malfunctioning equipment. As a result, operators have a higher-than-average occupational injury rate.

Plants operate 24 hours a day, 7 days a week. In small plants, operators may work during the day and be on call in the evening, at night, and on weekends. Medium-size and large plants that require constant monitoring may employ workers in three 8-hour shifts. Because larger plants require constant monitoring, weekend and holiday work is generally required. Operators may be required to work overtime.

Water and liquid waste treatment plant and system operators read meters and gauges to make sure that plant equipment is working properly.

Training, Other Qualifications, and Advancement

Employers usually hire high school graduates who are trained on the job. Completion of a training program may enhance an applicant's competitiveness in the job market.

Education and training. A high school diploma is usually required for an individual to become a water or wastewater treatment plant operator. Some applicants complete certificate or associate degree programs in water-quality and wastewater-treatment technology. Employers prefer to hire such candidates, because completion of a program minimizes the training needed at the plant and also shows a commitment to working in the industry. These programs are offered by community colleges, technical schools, and trade associations, and can be found throughout the country. In some cases, a degree or certificate program can be substituted for experience, allowing a worker to become licensed at a higher level more quickly.

Trainees usually start as attendants or operators-in-training and learn their skills on the job under the direction of an experienced operator. They learn by observing and doing routine tasks such as recording meter readings, taking samples of wastewater and sludge, and performing simple maintenance and repair work on pumps, electric motors, valves, and other plant equipment. Larger treatment plants generally combine this on-the-job training with formal classroom or self-paced study programs.

Licensure and certification. Both water and liquid waste plant and system operators must be certified by their States. Requirements and standards vary widely depending on the State. Most States have four different levels of certification, depending on the operator's experience and training. Although some States will honor licenses from other States, operators who move may have to take a new set of exams to become certified in a different State. The Association of Boards of Certification (ABC) offers a certificate program that may be helpful for operators who plan to move to a different State.

Other qualifications. Water and wastewater treatment plant operators need mechanical aptitude and the ability to solve problems intuitively. They also should be competent in basic mathematics, chemistry, and biology. They must have the ability to apply data to formulas that determine treatment requirements, flow levels, and concentration levels. Some basic familiarity with computers also is necessary, because operators generally use them to record data. Some plants also use computer-controlled equipment and instrumentation.

Advancement. Most States have four levels of certification for water and liquid waste treatment plant and system operators. On the basis of criteria such as the size of the plant and the treatment processes employed, each plant is given a corresponding level. A small system may only require the lowest level of certification. An operator who has that certification would be able to operate the plant without any supervision. In some States, operators in small plants can earn higher certifications through knowledge tests, while in other States, experience in a larger plant is required. Either way, operators in these plants will find it difficult to advance in their careers without moving to a larger plant.

As plants get larger and more complicated, operators need more skills before they are allowed to work without supervision. At the largest plants, operators who have the highest level of certification work as shift supervisors and may be in charge of large teams of operators. Operators in these plants can start as trainees and work through the different levels of certification until they advance to the level of shift supervisor.

Some experienced operators get jobs as technicians with State drinking-water-control or water-pollution- control agencies. In that capacity, they monitor and provide technical assistance to plants throughout the State. Vocational-technical school or community-college training generally is preferred for technician jobs. Experienced operators may transfer to related jobs with industrial liquid-waste treatment plants, water or liquid waste treatment equipment and chemical companies, engineering consulting firms, or vocational-technical schools.

Employment

Water and wastewater treatment plant and system operators held about 113,400 jobs in 2008. About 78 percent of all operators worked for local governments. Others worked primarily for water, sewage, and other systems utilities and for waste treatment and disposal and waste management services. Jobs were located throughout the country.

Job Outlook

Water and wastewater treatment plant and system operator jobs are expected to grow much faster than the average for all occupations. Job opportunities should be excellent for qualified workers.

Employment change. Employment of water and liquid waste treatment plant and system operators is expected to grow by 20 percent between 2008 and 2018, which is much faster than the average for all occupations. A growing population and the increasingly suburban geography of the United States are expected to boost demand for water and wastewater-treatment services. As new plants are constructed to meet this demand,

new water and wastewater treatment plant and system operator jobs will arise.

Local governments are the largest employers of water and wastewater treatment plant and system operators. Employment in privately owned facilities will grow faster, because Federal certification requirements have increased utilities' reliance on private firms specializing in the operation and management of water- and wastewater-treatment facilities.

Job prospects. Job opportunities should be excellent, both because of the expected much faster than average employment growth and because the retirement of the baby-boomer generation will require that many operators be replaced. Further, the number of applicants for these jobs is normally low, primarily because of the physically demanding and unappealing nature of some of the work. Opportunities should be best for people with mechanical aptitude and problem-solving skills.

Earnings

Median annual wages of water and wastewater treatment plant and system operators were $38,430 in May 2008. The middle 50 percent earned between $30,040 and $48,640. The lowest 10 percent earned less than $23,710, and the highest 10 percent earned more than $59,860. Median annual wages of water and liquid waste treatment plant and systems operators in May 2008 were $38,510 in local government and $37,620 in water, sewage, and other systems.

In addition to their annual salaries, water and wastewater treatment plant and system operators usually receive benefits that may include health and life insurance, a retirement plan, and educational reimbursement for job-related courses.

Related Occupations

Other workers whose main activity consists of operating a system of machinery to process or produce materials include:

	Page
Chemical plant and system operators	831
Gas plant operators	831
Petroleum pump system operators, refinery operators, and gaugers	832
Power plant operators, distributors, and dispatchers	760
Stationary engineers and boiler operators	763

Sources of Additional Information

For information on employment opportunities, contact State or local water pollution control agencies, State water and liquid waste operator associations, State environmental training centers, or local offices of the State employment service.

For information on certification, contact:

➤ Association of Boards of Certification, 208 Fifth St., Suite 201, Ames, IA 50010-6259. Internet: **http://www.abccert.org**

Projections data from the National Employment Matrix

Occupational Title	SOC Code	Employment, 2008	Projected Employment, 2018	Change, 2008-2018	
				Number	Percent
Water and liquid waste treatment plant and system operators	51-8031	113,400	135,900	22,500	20

(NOTE) Data in this table are rounded. See the discussion of the employment projections table in the *Handbook* introductory chapter on *Occupational Information Included in the Handbook.*

For educational information related to a career as a water or liquid waste treatment plant and system operator, contact:

➤ American Water Works Association, 6666 West Quincy Ave., Denver, CO 80235. Internet: **http://www.awwa.org**

➤ National Rural Water Association, 2915 S. 13th St., Duncan, OK 73533. Internet: **http://www.nrwa.org**

➤ Water Environment Federation, 601 Wythe St., Alexandria, VA 22314-1994. Internet: **http://www.wef.org**

The Occupational Information Network (O*NET) provides information on a wide range of occupational characteristics. Links to O*NET appear at the end of the Internet version of this occupational statement, accessible at **http://www.bls.gov/ooh/ocos229.htm**

Miscellaneous Production Occupations

Inspectors, Testers, Sorters, Samplers, and Weighers

Significant Points

- About 69 percent are employed in manufacturing establishments.

- Although a high school diploma is sufficient for the basic testing of products, complex precision-inspecting positions are filled by experienced workers.

- Employment is expected to decline slowly.

Nature of the Work

Inspectors, testers, sorters, samplers, and weighers, often called *quality-control inspectors* or another, similar name, ensure that your food will not make you sick, that your car will run properly, and that your pants will not split the first time you wear them. These workers monitor or audit quality standards for virtually all manufactured products, including foods, textiles, clothing, glassware, motor vehicles, electronic components, computers, and structural steel. As product quality becomes increasingly important to the success of many manufacturing firms, daily duties of inspectors place more focus on this aspect of their jobs.

Regardless of title, all inspectors, testers, sorters, samplers, and weighers work to guarantee the quality of the goods their firms produce. Specific job duties vary across the wide range of industries in which these workers are found. Materials inspectors may check products by sight, sound, feel, smell, or even taste to locate imperfections such as cuts, scratches, missing pieces, or crooked seams. These workers may verify dimensions, color, texture, strength, or other physical characteristics of objects. Mechanical inspectors generally verify that parts fit, move correctly, and are properly lubricated; check the pressure of gases and the level of liquids; test the flow of electricity; and do a test run to check for proper operation of a machine or piece of equipment. Some jobs involve only a quick visual inspection; others require a longer, detailed one. Sorters may separate goods according to length, size, fabric type, or color, while samplers test or inspect a sample taken from a batch or production run for malfunctions or defects. Weighers weigh quantities of materials for use in production. Testers repeatedly test existing products or prototypes under real-world conditions. Through these tests, companies determine how long a product will last, what parts will break down first, and how to improve durability.

Quality-control workers are involved at every stage of the production process. Some examine materials received from a supplier before sending them to the production line. Others inspect components and assemblies or perform a final check on the finished product. Depending on their skill level, inspectors also may set up and test equipment, calibrate precision instruments, repair defective products, or record data.

These workers rely on a number of tools to perform their jobs. Although some still use hand-held measurement devices such as micrometers, calipers, and alignment gauges, it is more common for them to operate electronic inspection equipment, such as coordinate-measuring machines (CMMs). These machines use sensitive probes to measure a part's dimensional accuracy and allow the inspector to analyze the results with computer software. Inspectors testing electrical devices may use voltmeters, ammeters, and ohmmeters to test potential difference, current flow, and resistance, respectively. All the tools that inspectors use are maintained by calibration technicians, who ensure that they work properly and generate accurate readings.

Inspectors mark, tag, or note problems. They may reject defective items outright, send them for repair, or fix minor problems themselves. If the product is acceptable, the inspector will certify it. Quality-control workers record the results of their inspections, compute the percentage of defects and other statistical measures, and prepare inspection and test reports. Some electronic inspection equipment automatically provides test reports containing these inspection results. When defects are found, inspectors notify supervisors and help to analyze and correct the production problems.

The emphasis on finding the root cause of defects is a basic tenet of modern management and production philosophies. Current philosophies emphasize constant quality improvement through analysis and correction of the causes of defects. The nature of inspectors' work has changed from merely checking for defects to determining the cause of those defects.

This increased emphasis on quality means that companies now have integrated teams of inspection and production workers who jointly review and improve product quality. In addition, many companies use self-monitoring production machines to ensure that the output is produced within quality standards. These machines not only can alert inspectors to production problems, but also sometimes automatically repair defects.

Some firms have completely automated inspection with the help of advanced vision inspection systems using machinery installed at one or several points in the production process.

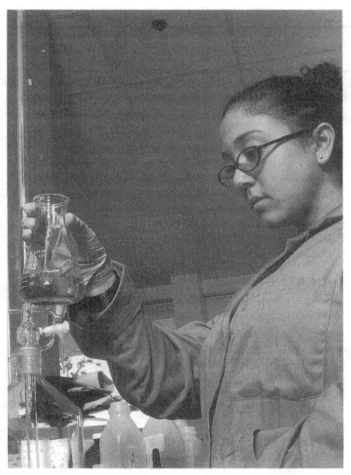

Working conditions for inspectors, testers, sorters, samplers and weighers vary by industry and establishment size.

Inspectors in these firms monitor the equipment, review output, and perform random product checks.

Work environment. Working conditions vary by industry and establishment size. As a result, some inspectors examine similar products for an entire shift, whereas others examine a variety of items.

In manufacturing, it is common for most inspectors to remain at one workstation. Inspectors in some industries may be on their feet all day and may have to lift heavy objects, whereas in other industries they sit during most of their shift and read electronic printouts of data. Workers in heavy manufacturing plants may be exposed to the noise and grime of machinery; in other plants, inspectors work in clean, air-conditioned environments suitable for carrying out controlled tests. As a result of these varied working conditions, injuries are not uncommon for this occupation, and workers must follow proper procedures to minimize risks.

Some inspectors work evenings, nights, or weekends. Shift assignments generally are made on the basis of seniority. Overtime may be required to meet production goals.

Training, Other Qualifications, and Advancement

Although a high school diploma is sufficient for the basic testing of products, complex precision-inspecting positions are filled by experienced workers.

Education and training. Training requirements vary with the responsibilities of the quality-control worker. For workers who perform simple "pass/fail" tests of products, a high school diploma generally is sufficient, together with limited in-house training. Training for new inspectors may cover the use of special meters, gauges, computers, and other instruments; quality-control techniques; blueprint reading; safety; and reporting requirements. There are some postsecondary training programs, but many employers prefer to train inspectors on the job.

The chances of finding work in this occupation can be improved by studying industrial trades, including computer-aided design, in high school or in a postsecondary vocational program. Laboratory work in the natural or biological sciences also may improve one's analytical skills and increase one's chances of finding work in medical or pharmaceutical labs, where many of these workers are employed.

As companies implement more automated inspection techniques that require less manual inspection, workers in this occupation will have to learn to operate and program more sophisticated equipment and learn software applications. Because these operations require additional skills, the need for higher education may be necessary. To address this need, some colleges are offering associate's degrees in fields such as quality control management.

Other qualifications. In general, inspectors, testers, sorters, samplers, and weighers need mechanical aptitude, math and communication skills, and good hand-eye coordination and vision. Another important skill is the ability to analyze and interpret blueprints, data, manuals, and other material to determine specifications, inspection procedures, formulas, and methods for making adjustments.

Certification and advancement. The American Society for Quality offers 15 different types of certifications for workers in quality control. These certifications may assist workers in advancing within the occupation. They generally require a certain number of years of experience in the field and passage of an exam.

Advancement for workers with the necessary skills frequently takes the form of additional duties and responsibilities. Complex inspection positions are filled by experienced assemblers, machine operators, or mechanics who already have a thorough knowledge of the products and production processes. To advance to these positions, experienced workers may need training in statistical process control, new automation, or the company's quality assurance policies. Because automated inspection equipment and electronic recording of results are becoming common, computer skills also are important.

Employment

Inspectors, testers, sorters, samplers, and weighers held about 464,700 jobs in 2008. About 69 percent worked in manufacturing establishments that produced such products as motor vehicle parts, plastics products, semiconductor and other electronic components, and aerospace products and parts. Inspectors, testers, sorters, samplers, and weighers also were found in employment services; wholesale trade; and professional, scientific, and technical services.

Projections data from the National Employment Matrix

Occupational Title	SOC Code	Employment, 2008	Projected Employment, 2018	Change, 2008-2018	
				Number	Percent
Inspectors, testers, sorters, samplers, and weighers.........................	51-9061	464,700	447,800	-16,900	-4

(NOTE) Data in this table are rounded. See the discussion of the employment projections table in the *Handbook* introductory chapter on *Occupational Information Included in the Handbook.*

Job Outlook

Like many other occupations concentrated in manufacturing industries, employment is expected to decline slowly, primarily because of the growing use of automated inspection and the redistribution of some quality-control responsibilities from inspectors to production workers.

Employment change. Employment of inspectors, testers, sorters, samplers, and weighers is expected to decline by 4 percent between 2008 and 2018. Because the majority of these employees work in the manufacturing sector, their outlook is greatly affected by what happens to manufacturing companies. The emphasis on improving quality and productivity has led many manufacturers to invest in automated inspection equipment and to take a more systematic approach to quality inspection. Continued improvements in technologies allow firms to automate inspection tasks, increasing workers' productivity and reducing the demand for inspectors.

In addition, work in many manufacturing companies continues to move abroad. As more production moves offshore, the number of quality-control workers is expected to decline as well.

Firms increasingly are integrating quality control into the production process. Many inspection duties are being redistributed from specialized inspectors to fabrication and assembly workers, who monitor quality at every stage of the production process. In addition, the growing implementation of statistical process control is resulting in "smarter" inspection. Using this system, firms survey the sources and incidence of defects so that they can better focus their efforts on reducing the number of defective products manufactured.

In some industries, however, automation is not a feasible alternative to manual inspection. Where key inspection elements are oriented toward size, such as length, width, or thickness, automation will become more important in the future. But where taste, smell, texture, appearance, complexity of fabric, or performance of the product is important, inspection will continue to be done by workers.

Job prospects. Although numerous job openings will arise through the need to replace workers who move out of this large occupation, many of these jobs will be open only to experienced workers with advanced skills. There will be better opportunities in the employment services industry, as more manufacturers use contract inspection workers, and in growing manufacturing industries, such as medical equipment and pharmaceuticals.

Earnings

Median hourly wages of inspectors, testers, sorters, samplers, and weighers were $15.02 in May 2008. The middle 50 percent earned between $11.58 and $19.52 an hour. The lowest 10 percent earned less than $9.28 an hour, and the highest 10 percent earned more than $25.47 an hour. Median hourly wages in the industries

employing the largest numbers of inspectors, testers, sorters, samplers, and weighers in May 2008 were as follows:

Aerospace product and parts manufacturing................$22.10
Motor vehicle parts manufacturing 16.39
Semiconductor and other electronic component manufacturing...14.22
Plastics product manufacturing 13.87
Employment services 11.64

Related Occupations

Other workers who conduct inspections include the following:

Sources of Additional Information

For general information about inspection, testing, and certification, contact:

➤ American Society for Quality, 600 North Plankinton Ave., Milwaukee, WI 53203. Internet: **http://www.asq.org**

The Occupational Information Network (O*NET) provides information on a wide range of occupational characteristics. Links to O*NET appear at the end of the Internet version of this occupational statement, accessible at **http://www.bls.gov/ooh/ocos220.htm**

Jewelers and Precious Stone and Metal Workers

Significant Points

- About 54 percent of all jewelers and precious stone and metal workers are self-employed.

- Jewelers usually learn their trade in vocational or technical schools, through distance-learning centers, or on the job.

- Prospects for bench jewelers and other skilled jewelers should be favorable; keen competition is expected for lower skilled manufacturing jobs, such as assemblers and polishers.

Nature of the Work

Jewelers and precious stone and metal workers use a variety of common and specialized equipment to design and manufacture new pieces of jewelry; cut, set, and polish gem stones; repair or adjust rings, necklaces, bracelets, earrings, and other jewelry; and appraise jewelry, precious metals, and gems. Jewelers usually specialize in one or more of these areas and may work for large jewelry manufacturing firms, for small retail jewelry shops, or as owners of their own businesses. Regardless of the type of work done or the work setting, jewelers need a high degree of skill, precision, and attention to detail.

Some jewelers design or make their own jewelry. Following their own designs or those created by designers or customers, they begin by shaping the metal or by carving wax to make a model for casting the metal. Individual parts then are soldered together, and the jeweler may mount a diamond or other gem or may engrave a design into the metal. Other jewelers do finishing work, such as setting stones, polishing, or engraving, or make repairs. Typical repair work includes enlarging or reducing ring sizes, resetting stones, and replacing broken clasps and mountings.

Bench jewelers usually work in jewelry retailers. They perform a wide range of tasks, from simple jewelry cleaning and repair to moldmaking and fabricating pieces from scratch. In larger manufacturing businesses, jewelers usually specialize in a single operation. *Mold and model makers* create models or tools for the jewelry that is to be produced. *Assemblers* solder or fuse jewelry and their parts; they also may set stones. *Engravers* etch designs into metal with specialized tools, and *polishers* bring a finished luster to the final product.

Jewelers typically do the handiwork required to produce a piece of jewelry, while *gemologists* and laboratory graders analyze, describe, and certify the quality and characteristics of gem stones. Gemologists may work in gemological laboratories or as quality control experts for retailers, importers, or manufacturers. After using microscopes, computerized tools, and other grading instruments to examine gem stones or finished pieces of jewelry, they write reports certifying that the items are of a particular quality. Many jewelers also study gemology to become familiar with the physical properties of the gem stones with which they work.

Jewelry appraisers carefully examine jewelry to determine its value, after which they write appraisal documents. They determine the value of a piece by researching the jewelry market and by using reference books, auction catalogs, price lists, and the Internet. They may work for jewelry stores, appraisal firms, auction houses, pawnbrokers, or insurance companies. Many gemologists also become appraisers.

In small retail stores or repair shops, jewelers and appraisers may be involved in all aspects of the work. Those who own or manage stores or shops also hire and train employees; order, market, and sell merchandise; and perform other managerial duties.

New technology is helping to produce jewelry of high quality at a reduced cost and in a shorter amount of time. For example, lasers are often used for cutting and improving the quality of stones, for applying intricate engraving or design work, and for inscribing personal messages or identification on jewelry. Jewelers also use lasers to weld metals together in milliseconds with no seams or blemishes, improving the quality and appearance of jewelry.

Some manufacturing firms use computer-aided design and manufacturing (CAD/CAM) to facilitate product design and automate some steps in the moldmaking and modelmaking process. CAD allows jewelers to create a virtual-reality model of a piece of jewelry. Using CAD, jewelers can modify the design, change the stone, or try a different setting and see the contemplated changes on a computer screen before cutting a stone or performing other costly steps. Once they are satisfied with the model, they use CAM to produce a mold. After the mold is made, it is easier for manufacturing firms to produce numerous copies of a given piece of jewelry, which can be distributed to retail establishments across the country. Similar techniques may be used in the retail setting, allowing customers to review their jewelry designs with the jeweler and make modifications before committing themselves to the expense of a customized piece of jewelry.

Work environment. A jeweler's work involves a great deal of concentration and attention to detail. Trying to satisfy customers' and employers' demands for speed and quality while working on precious stones and metal can cause fatigue and stress. However, the use of more ergonomically correct jewelers' benches has eliminated most of the strain and discomfort caused by spending long periods over a workbench.

Jewelers need a high degree of skill and must pay attention to detail.

Lasers require both careful handling to avoid injury and steady hands to direct precision tasks. In larger manufacturing plants and some smaller repair shops, chemicals, sharp or pointed tools, and jewelers' torches pose safety threats and may cause injury if proper care is not taken. Most dangerous chemicals, however, have been replaced with synthetic, less toxic products to meet safety requirements.

In repair shops, jewelers usually work alone with little supervision. In retail stores, they may talk with customers about repairs, perform custom design work, and even do some selling. Because many of their materials are valuable, jewelers must observe strict security procedures, including working behind locked doors that are opened only by a buzzer, working on the other side of barred windows, making use of burglar alarms, and, in larger jewelry establishments, working in the presence of armed guards.

Training, Other Qualifications, and Advancement

Jewelers usually learn their trade on-the-job over the course of several months; however, vocational or technical schools or distance-learning centers are becoming more common ways for workers to learn their skills. Formal training enhances employment and advancement opportunities.

Education and training. Jewelers have traditionally learned their trade through several months of on-the-job training; while this method is still common, particularly in manufacturing plants, many are also learning their skills in vocational or technical schools or through distance-learning centers. Computer-aided design is becoming increasingly important to retail jewelers and students may wish to obtain training in it. This skill can usually be obtained through technical school; however, some employers may provide training in it, as well.

In jewelry manufacturing plants, workers traditionally develop their skills through informal apprenticeships and on-the-job training. The apprenticeship or training period lasts up to 1 year, depending on the difficulty of the specialty. Training usually focuses on casting, setting stones, making models, or engraving.

There are also many technical schools offering training designed for jewelers. Some manufacturers prefer graduates because they require less on-the-job training. Course topics can include blueprint reading, math, and shop theory.

For jewelers who work in retail stores or repair shops, vocational training or college courses offer the best job preparation. These programs may vary in length from 6 months to a year and teach jewelry making and repairing skills, such as designing, casting, setting and polishing stones, as well as the use and care of jeweler's tools and equipment.

There are various institutes that offer courses and programs in gemology. These programs cover a wide range of topics, including the identification and grading of diamonds and gem stones.

While it is not required, some students may wish to obtain a higher level degree. For them, art and design schools offer programs leading to the degree of bachelor of fine arts or master of fine arts in jewelry design.

Other qualifications. The precise and delicate nature of jewelry work requires finger and hand dexterity, good hand-eye coordination, patience, and concentration. Artistic ability and fashion consciousness are major assets, particularly in jewelry design and jewelry shops, because jewelry must be stylish and attractive. Those who work in jewelry stores have frequent contact with customers and should be neat, personable, and knowledgeable about the merchandise. In addition, employers require workers of good character because jewelers work with valuable materials.

Certification and advancement. Jewelers of America offers four credentials, ranging from Certified Bench Jeweler Technician to Certified Master Bench Jeweler, for bench jewelers who pass a written and practical exam. Certification is not required to work as a bench jeweler, but it may help jewelers to show expertise and to advance.

Advancement opportunities are limited and depend greatly on an individual's skill and initiative. In manufacturing, some jewelers advance to supervisory jobs, such as master jeweler or head jeweler. Jewelers who work in jewelry stores or repair shops may become managers; some open their own businesses.

Those interested in starting their own business should first establish themselves and build a reputation for their work within the jewelry trade. Once they obtain sufficient credit from jewelry suppliers and wholesalers, they can acquire the necessary inventory. Also, because the jewelry business is highly competitive, jewelers who plan to open their own store should have sales experience and knowledge of marketing and business management. Courses in these subjects often are available from technical schools and community colleges.

Employment

Jewelers and precious stone and metal workers held about 52,100 jobs in 2008. About 54 percent of these workers were self-employed; many operated their own store or repair shop, and some specialized in designing and creating custom jewelry.

About 21 percent of salaried jobs for jewelers and precious stone and metal workers were in retail trade, primarily in jewelry, luggage, and leather goods stores. Another 15 percent of jobs were in jewelry and silverware manufacturing. A small number of jobs were with merchant wholesalers of miscellaneous durable goods and in repair shops providing repair and maintenance of personal and household goods. Although jewelry stores and repair shops were found in every city and in many small towns, most jobs were in larger metropolitan areas.

Projections data from the National Employment Matrix

Occupational Title	SOC Code	Employment, 2008	Projected Employment, 2018	Change, 2008-2018	
				Number	Percent
Jewelers and precious stone and metal workers...............................	51-9071	52,100	54,800	2,800	5

(NOTE) Data in this table are rounded. See the discussion of the employment projections table in the *Handbook* introductory chapter on *Occupational Information Included in the Handbook.*

Job Outlook

Employment is expected to grow more slowly than average. Prospects for bench jewelers and other skilled jewelers should be favorable; keen competition is expected for lower skilled manufacturing jobs, such as assemblers and polishers.

Employment change. Employment of jewelers and precious stone and metal workers is expected to grow by 5 percent between 2008 and 2018, more slowly than the average for all occupations. Most jewelry is currently imported, and continued growth in imports will limit demand, particularly for lower-skilled workers. However, demand for bench jewelers or other skilled jewelers will grow as consumers seek more customized jewelry.

Additionally, the consolidation and increased online presence of many jewelry outlets will constrain employment growth in the near future. Although nontraditional jewelry marketers, such as Internet retailers and discount stores, have expanded in recent years, many traditional retailers have countered with their own successful online presence. Since nontraditional retailers require fewer sales staff, which limits employment opportunities for jewelers, any slowdown in their expansion at the expense of jewelry shops is a positive sign for employment growth.

Traditional jewelers may continue to lose some of their market share to nontraditional outlets, but they will maintain a large customer base. Many buyers prefer to see and try on jewelry before purchasing it, or to enjoy the experience of shopping in a store. Jewelry stores also have the advantage of being able to offer personalized service and build client relationships. Additionally, new jewelry sold by nontraditional retailers will create demand for skilled jewelers for sizing, cleaning, and repair work.

Job prospects. Despite limited employment growth, opportunities should be favorable for bench jewelers and other skilled jewelers. New jewelers will be needed to replace those who retire or who leave the occupation for other reasons. When master jewelers retire, they take with them years of experience that require substantial time and financial resources to replace. Many employers have difficulty finding and retaining jewelers with the right skills and the necessary knowledge. Opportunities in jewelry stores and repair shops will be best for graduates from training programs for jewelers or gemologists and for those workers with training in CAD/CAM.

Keen competition is expected for lower skilled manufacturing jobs that are amenable to automation, such as assemblers and polishers. Jewelry designers who wish to create their own jewelry lines should expect intense competition. Although demand for customized and boutique jewelry is strong, it is difficult for independent designers to establish themselves.

The jewelry industry can be cyclical. During economic downturns, demand for jewelry products and for jewelers tends to decrease. However, demand for repair workers should remain strong even during economic slowdowns because maintaining and repairing jewelry is an ongoing process. In fact, demand for jewelry repair may increase during recessions, as people repair or restore existing pieces rather than purchase new ones.

Earnings

Median annual wages for jewelers and precious stone and metal workers were $32,940 in May 2008. The middle 50 percent earned between $24,370 and $43,440. The lowest 10 percent earned less than $19,000, and the highest 10 percent earned more than $55,130.

Most jewelers start out with a base salary, but once they become more proficient, they may begin charging by the number of pieces completed. Jewelers who work in retail stores may earn a commission for each piece of jewelry sold. Many jewelers also enjoy a variety of benefits, including reimbursement from their employers for work-related courses and discounts on jewelry purchases.

Related Occupations

Jewelers and precious stone and metal workers do precision handwork. Other skilled workers who do similar jobs include:

	Page
Welding, soldering, and brazing workers	743
Woodworkers	757

Some jewelers and precious stone and metal workers create their own jewelry designs. Other occupations that require visual arts abilities include:

Artists and related workers	301
Commercial and industrial designers	304
Fashion designers	307

Some jewelers and precious stone and metal workers are involved in the buying and selling of stones, metals, or finished pieces of jewelry. Similar occupations include:

Retail salespersons	543
Sales representatives, wholesale and manufacturing	547

Sources of Additional Information

Information on job opportunities and training programs for jewelers and gemologists is available from:

➤ Gemological Institute of America, 5345 Armada Dr., Carlsbad, CA 92008. Internet: **http://www.gia.edu**

For more information about bench jeweler certification and careers in jewelry design and retail, including different career paths, training options, and schools, contact:

➤ Jewelers of America, 52 Vanderbilt Ave., 19th Floor, New York, NY 10017. Internet: **http://www.jewelers.org**

For information on jewelry design and manufacturing, training, and schools offering jewelry-related programs and degrees by State, contact:

➤ Manufacturing Jewelers and Suppliers of America, 57 John L. Dietsch Square Attleboro Falls, MA 02763. Internet: **http://www.mjsa.org**

To receive a list of accredited technical schools that have programs in gemology, contact:

➤ Accrediting Commission of Career Schools and Colleges, 2101 Wilson Blvd., Suite 302, Arlington, VA 22201. Internet: **http://www.accsc.org**

The Occupational Information Network (O*NET) provides information on a wide range of occupational characteristics. Links to O*NET appear at the end of the Internet version of this occupational statement, accessible at **http://www.bls.gov/ooh/ocos222.htm**

Medical, Dental, and Ophthalmic Laboratory Technicians

Significant Points

- Around 58 percent of jobs were in medical equipment and supplies manufacturing, usually in small, privately owned businesses.

- Most technicians learn their craft on the job, but many employers prefer to hire those with formal training.

- Faster than average employment growth is expected for dental and ophthalmic laboratory technicians, while average employment growth is expected for medical appliance technicians.

- Job opportunities should be favorable because few people seek these positions.

Nature of the Work

When patients require a medical device to help them see clearly, chew and speak well, or walk, their healthcare providers send requests to medical, dental, and ophthalmic laboratory technicians. These technicians produce a variety of implements to help patients.

Medical appliance technicians construct, fit, maintain, and repair braces, artificial limbs, joints, arch supports, and other surgical and medical appliances. They follow prescriptions or detailed instructions from podiatrists, orthotists, prosthetists or other healthcare professionals for patients who need them because of a birth defect, disease, accident, or amputation. Podiatrists or orthotists request orthoses—braces, supports, corrective shoes, or other devices; while prosthetists order prostheses—replacement limbs, such as an arm, leg, hand, or foot. Medical appliance technicians who work with these types of devices are called *orthotic and prosthetic (O&P) technicians*. Other medical appliance technicians work with appliances, such as hearing aids, that help correct other medical problems.

For O&P technicians, creating orthoses and prostheses takes several steps. First, technicians construct or receive a plaster cast of the patient's limb or foot to use as a pattern. Increasingly, technicians are using digital files sent by the prescribing practitioner who uses a scanner and uploads the images using computer software. When fabricating artificial limbs or braces, O&P technicians utilize many different materials including plaster, thermoplastics, carbon fiber, acrylic and epoxy resins. More advanced prosthetic devices are electronic, using information technology. Next, O&P technicians carve, cut, or grind the material using hand or power tools. Then they weld the parts together and use grinding and buffing wheels to smooth and polish the devices. Next, they may cover or pad the devices with leather, felt, plastic, or another material. Finally, technicians may mix pigments according to formulas to match the patient's skin color and apply the mixture to create a cosmetic cover for the artificial limb.

After fabrication, medical appliance technicians test devices for proper alignment, movement, and biomechanical stability using meters and alignment fixtures. Over time the appliance will wear down, so technicians must repair and maintain the device. They also may service and repair the machinery used for the fabrication of orthotic and prosthetic devices.

Dental laboratory technicians fill prescriptions from dentists for crowns, bridges, dentures, and other dental prosthetics. First, dentists send a prescription or work authorization for each item to be manufactured, along with an impression or mold of the patient's mouth or teeth. With new technology, a technician may receive a digital impression rather than a physical mold. Then dental laboratory technicians, also called dental technicians, create a model of the patient's mouth by pouring plaster into the impression and allowing it to set. They place the model on an apparatus that mimics the bite and movement of the patient's jaw. The model serves as the basis of the prosthetic device. Technicians examine the model, noting the size and shape of the adjacent teeth, as well as gaps within the gumline. Based upon these observations and the dentist's specifications, technicians build and shape a wax tooth or teeth model, using small hand instruments called wax spatulas and wax carvers. The wax model is used to cast the metal framework for the prosthetic device.

After the wax tooth has been formed, dental technicians pour the cast and form the metal and, using small hand-held tools, prepare the surface to allow the metal and porcelain to bond. They then apply porcelain in layers to mimic the precise shape and color of a tooth. Technicians place the tooth in a porcelain furnace to bake the porcelain onto the metal framework, and then they adjust the shape and color with subsequent grinding and addition of porcelain to achieve a sealed finish. The final product is a nearly exact replica of the lost tooth or teeth.

In some laboratories, technicians perform all stages of the work, whereas in other labs, each technician does only a few. Dental laboratory technicians can specialize in one of five areas—orthodontic appliances, crowns and bridges, complete dentures, partial dentures, or ceramics. Job titles can reflect specialization in these areas. For example, technicians who make porcelain and acrylic restorations are called *dental ceramists*.

Ophthalmic laboratory technicians—also known as manufacturing opticians, optical mechanics, or optical goods workers—make prescription eyeglass or contact lenses. Ophthalmic laboratory technicians cut, grind, edge, polish, and finish lenses according to specifications provided by dispensing opticians, optometrists, or ophthalmologists. Although some lenses still are produced by hand, technicians are increasingly using automated equipment to make lenses. To make a pair of glasses, typically the technician cuts the prescription lenses, bevels the edges to fit the frame, dips each lens into dye if the prescription calls for tinted or coated lenses, polishes the edges, and combines the lenses and frame parts. Some ophthalmic laboratory technicians manufacture lenses for other optical instruments, such as telescopes and binoculars.

In small laboratories, technicians usually handle every phase of the operation. In large ones, in which virtually every phase of the operation is automated, technicians may be responsible for operating computerized equipment. Technicians also inspect the final product for quality and accuracy.

Ophthalmic laboratory technicians should not be confused with workers in other vision care occupations, such as ophthalmologists, optometrists, and dispensing opticians. (See the

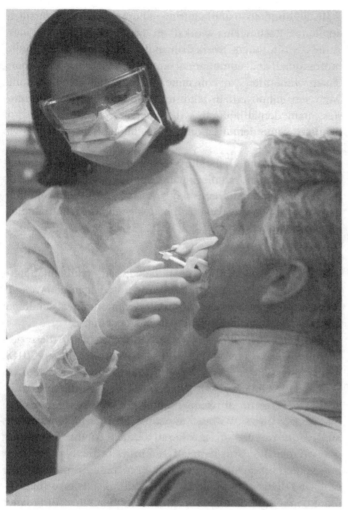

Dental laboratory technicians create crowns, bridges, dentures, and other dental prosthetics.

statement on physicians and surgeons, which includes ophthalmologists, as well as the statements on optometrists and opticians, dispensing, elsewhere in the *Handbook*.)

Work environment. Medical, dental, and ophthalmic laboratory technicians generally work in clean, well-lighted, and well-ventilated laboratories. They have limited contact with the public. Most salaried laboratory technicians work 40 hours a week, but a few work part time. At times, technicians wear goggles to protect their eyes, gloves to handle hot objects, or masks to avoid inhaling dust. They may spend a great deal of time standing. Medical appliance technicians should be particularly careful when working with tools because there is a risk of injury.

Dental technicians usually have their own workbenches, which can be equipped with Bunsen burners, grinding and polishing equipment, and hand instruments, such as wax spatulas and wax carvers. Some dental technicians have computer-aided milling equipment to assist them with creating artificial teeth.

Training, Other Qualifications, and Advancement
Most medical, dental, and ophthalmic laboratory technicians learn their craft on the job. Many employers prefer to hire those with formal training or at least a high school diploma.

Education and training. Although there are no formal education or training requirements to become a medical, dental, or ophthalmic laboratory technician, having a high school diploma is typically the standard requirement for obtaining a job. High school students interested in becoming medical, dental, or ophthalmic laboratory technicians should take courses in mathematics and science. Courses in metal and wood shop, art, drafting, and computers are recommended. Courses in management and business may help those wishing to operate their own laboratories.

Most medical, dental, and ophthalmic laboratory technicians are hired with a high school diploma and learn their tasks through on-the-job training. They usually begin as helpers and gradually learn new skills as they gain experience. For example, dental laboratory technicians begin by pouring plaster into an impression, and progress to more complex procedures, such as making porcelain crowns and bridges. Ophthalmic laboratory technicians may start by marking or blocking lenses for grinding and move onto grinding, cutting, edging, and beveling lenses as they progress.

The length of time spent in on-the-job training varies for each of these occupations. For example, medical appliance technicians usually receive long-term training, while ophthalmic laboratory technicians usually spend less time in training. The length of the training period also varies by the laboratory where the technician is employed, since each laboratory operates differently.

Formal training also is available. In 2008, there were 5 orthotic- and prosthetic-technician programs accredited by the National Commission on Orthotic and Prosthetic Education (NCOPE). These programs offer either an associate degree or a 1-year certificate for orthotic or prosthetic technicians.

Training in dental laboratory technology is available through universities, community and junior colleges, vocational-technical institutes, and the Armed Forces. In 2008, 20 programs in dental laboratory technology were accredited by the Commission on Dental Accreditation in conjunction with the American Dental Association. Accredited programs normally take 2 years to complete, although a few programs can take up to 4 years to complete.

A few ophthalmic laboratory technicians learn their trade in the Armed Forces or in the few programs in optical technology offered by vocational-technical institutes or trade schools. In 2008, there were two programs in ophthalmic technology accredited by the Commission on Opticianry Accreditation (COA).

Licensure and certification. Three States–Kentucky, South Carolina, and Texas–require a dental laboratory to employ at least one Certified Dental Technician in order to operate. This certification is administered by the National Board for Certification in Dental Laboratory Technology (NBC) and the requirements are discussed under Certification and Advancement. In Florida, laboratories must register with the State and at least one dental technician in each dental laboratory must complete 18 hours of continuing education every two years.

Other qualifications. A high degree of manual dexterity, good vision, and the ability to recognize very fine color shadings and variations in shape are necessary for medical, dental, and ophthalmic laboratory technicians. An artistic aptitude for detailed work also is important. Computer skills are valuable for technicians using automated systems.

Certification and advancement. Certification may increase chances of advancement. Voluntary certification for orthotic and prosthetic technicians is available through the American Board for Certification in Orthotics and Prosthetics (ABC). Applicants are eligible for an exam after completing a program accredited by NCOPE or obtaining 2 years of experience as a technician under the direct supervision of an ABC-certified practitioner. After successfully passing the appropriate exam, technicians receive the Registered Orthotic Technician, Registered Prosthetic Technician, or Registered Prosthetic-Orthotic Technician credential.

With additional formal education, medical appliance technicians who make orthotics and prostheses can advance to become orthotists or prosthetists—practitioners who work with patients who need braces, prostheses, or related devices and help to determine the specifications for those devices.

Dental laboratory technicians may obtain the Certified Dental Technician designation from the National Board for Certification in Dental Laboratory Technology (NBC), an independent board established by the National Association of Dental Laboratories. Certification, which is voluntary except in three States, can be obtained in five specialty areas: crowns and bridges, ceramics, partial dentures, complete dentures, and orthodontic appliances. To qualify for the CDT credential, technicians must meet educational requirements and pass two written exams and one practical exam. The educational requirement may be obtained through graduation from a dental technology program or at least 5 years of experience as a dental laboratory technician. CDT's must complete twelve hours of continuing education each year to maintain their certification. Dental technicians who only perform certain tasks in a laboratory can take a written and practical exam in modules of dental technology. These result in a Certificate of Competency in a specific skill area and do not require continuing education.

In large dental laboratories, dental technicians may become supervisors or managers. Experienced technicians may teach or take jobs with dental suppliers in such areas as product development, marketing, and sales. Opening one's own laboratory is another, and more common, way to advance and earn more.

Ophthalmic laboratory technicians also can become supervisors and managers. Some become dispensing opticians, although further education or training is generally required to advance.

Employment

Medical, dental, and ophthalmic laboratory technicians held about 95,200 jobs in 2008. About 58 percent of jobs were in medical equipment and supplies manufacturing, which usually are small, privately owned businesses with fewer than five employees. However, some laboratories are large; a few employ more than 1,000 workers. The following tabulation shows employment by occupation:

Dental laboratory technicians......................................46,000
Opthalmic laboratory technicians 35,200
Medical appliance technicians 13,900

In addition to manufacturing laboratories, many medical appliance technicians worked in health and personal care stores, while others worked in public and private hospitals, professional and commercial equipment and supplies merchant wholesalers, or consumer goods rental centers. Some were self-employed. In addition to manufacturing laboratories, many dental laboratory technicians worked in offices of dentists. Some dental laboratory technicians open their own offices.

Most ophthalmic laboratory technician jobs were in medical equipment and supplies manufacturing laboratories. Others worked in health and personal care stores, offices of optometrists, and professional and commercial equipment and supplies merchant wholesalers.

Job Outlook

Overall employment of medical, dental, and ophthalmic laboratory technicians is expected to grow faster than the average, but varies by detailed occupation. Job opportunities should be favorable because few people seek these positions.

Employment change. Overall employment for these occupations is expected to grow 14 percent from 2008 to 2018, which is faster than the average for all occupations. Medical appliance technicians will grow at 11 percent, about as fast as the average for all occupations, because of the increasing prevalence of the two leading causes of limb loss—diabetes and cardiovascular disease—and because of the increasing rate of obesity. The demand for orthotic devices, such as braces and orthopedic footwear, will increase as more people will need these support devices. In addition, advances in technology may spur demand for prostheses that allow for greater movement.

Employment of dental laboratory technicians is expected to grow 14 percent, which is faster than the average for all occupations. During the last few years, increased demand has arisen from an aging public that is growing increasingly interested in cosmetic prostheses. For example, many dental laboratories are filling orders for composite fillings that are the same shade of white as natural teeth to replace older, less attractive fillings. Additionally, the growing and aging population will require more dental products fabricated by dental technicians, such as bridges and crowns, since more people are retaining their original teeth. This job growth will be limited, however, by productivity gains stemming from continual technological advancements in laboratories.

Ophthalmic laboratory technicians are expected to experience employment growth of 15 percent, faster than the average for all occupations. Demographic trends make it likely that many more Americans will need vision care in the years ahead. Not only will the population grow, but also the proportion of middle-aged and older adults is projected to increase rapidly. Middle age is a time when many people use corrective lenses for the first time, and the need for vision care continues to increase with age. However, the increasing use of automated machinery will temper job growth for ophthalmic laboratory technicians.

Projections data from the National Employment Matrix

Occupational Title	SOC Code	Employment, 2008	Projected Employment, 2018	Change, 2008-2018	
				Number	Percent
Medical, dental, and ophthalmic laboratory technicians	51-9080	95,200	108,300	13,100	14
Dental laboratory technicians	51-9081	46,000	52,400	6,400	14
Medical appliance technicians...	51-9082	13,900	15,400	1,500	11
Ophthalmic laboratory technicians..	51-9083	35,200	40,400	5,200	15

(NOTE) Data in this table are rounded. See the discussion of the employment projections table in the *Handbook* introductory chapter on *Occupational Information Included in the Handbook.*

Job prospects. Job opportunities for medical, dental, and ophthalmic laboratory technicians should be favorable, due to expected faster than average growth. Few people seek these jobs, reflecting the relatively limited public awareness and low starting wages. Those with formal training in a medical, dental, or ophthalmic laboratory technology program will have the best job prospects. In addition to openings from job growth, many job openings also will arise from the need to replace technicians who transfer to other occupations or who leave the labor force.

Earnings

Median annual wages of wage and salary medical appliance technicians were $34,460 in May 2008. The middle 50 percent earned between $26,600 and $47,210. The lowest 10 percent earned less than $21,720, and the highest 10 percent earned more than $63,750.

Median annual wages of wage and salary dental laboratory technicians were $34,170 in May 2008. The middle 50 percent earned between $26,260 and $44,790. The lowest 10 percent earned less than $20,740, and the highest 10 percent earned more than $58,140. In the two industries that employed the most dental laboratory technicians—medical equipment and supplies manufacturing and offices of dentists—median annual wages were $33,700 and $35,000, respectively.

Median annual wages of wage and salary ophthalmic laboratory technicians were $27,210 in May 2008. The middle 50 percent earned between $21,580 and $34,810. The lowest 10 percent earned less than $18,080, and the highest 10 percent earned more than $42,890. Median annual wages were $25,250 in medical equipment and supplies manufacturing and $25,580 in health and personal care stores, the two industries that employ the most ophthalmic laboratory technicians.

Related Occupations

Medical, dental, and ophthalmic laboratory technicians manufacture and work with the same devices that are used by:

Other occupations that work with or manufacture goods using similar tools and skills include:

Sources of Additional Information

For information on careers in orthotics and prosthetics, contact:
➤ American Academy of Orthotists and Prosthetists, 1331 H St. NW., Suite 501, Washington, DC 20005. Internet: **http://www.opcareers.org**

For a list of accredited programs for orthotic and prosthetic technicians, contact:
➤ National Commission on Orthotic and Prosthetic Education, 330 John Carlyle St., Suite 200, Alexandria, VA 22314. Internet: **http://www.ncope.org**

For information on requirements for certification of orthotic and prosthetic technicians, contact:
➤ American Board for Certification in Orthotics, Prosthetics, and Pedorthics, 330 John Carlyle St., Suite 210, Alexandria, VA 22314. Internet: **http://www.abcop.org**

For a list of accredited programs in dental laboratory technology, contact:
➤ Commission on Dental Accreditation, American Dental Association, 211 E. Chicago Ave., Chicago, IL 60611. Internet: **http://www.ada.org/prof/ed/accred/commission/index.asp**

For information on requirements for certification of dental laboratory technicians, contact:
➤ National Board for Certification in Dental Laboratory Technology, 325 John Knox Rd., L103, Tallahassee, FL 32303. Internet: **http://www.nbccert.org**

For information on career opportunities in commercial dental laboratories, contact:
➤ National Association of Dental Laboratories, 325 John Knox Rd., L103, Tallahassee, FL 32303. Internet: **http://www.nadl.org**

For information on an accredited program in ophthalmic laboratory technology, contact:
➤ Commission on Opticianry Accreditation, P.O. Box 142 Florence, IN 47020. Internet: **http://www.coaccreditation.com**

General information on grants and scholarships is available from individual schools. State employment service offices can provide information about job openings for medical, dental, and ophthalmic laboratory technicians.

The Occupational Information Network (O*NET) provides information on a wide range of occupational characteristics. Links to O*NET appear at the end of the Internet version of this occupational statement, accessible at **http://www.bls.gov/ooh/ocos238.htm**

Painting and Coating Workers, except Construction and Maintenance

Significant Points

- About 2 out of 3 jobs are in manufacturing establishments.

- Most workers acquire their skills on the job; training usually lasts from a few days to several months, but becoming skilled in all aspects of painting can require 1 to 2 years of experience and training.

- Overall employment is projected to grow.

- Good job prospects are expected for skilled workers with painting experience.

Nature of the Work

Millions of items ranging from cars to candy are covered by paint, plastic, varnish, chocolate, or some other type of coating solution. Painting or coating is used to make a product more attractive or protect it from the elements. The paint finish on an automobile, for example, makes the vehicle more attractive and provides protection from corrosion. Achieving this end result is the work of *painting and coating workers*.

Before painting and coating workers can begin to apply the paint or other coating, they often need to prepare the surface. A metal, wood, or plastic part may need to be sanded or ground to correct imperfections or rough up a surface so that paint will stick to it. After preparing the surface, the product is carefully cleaned to prevent any dust or dirt from becoming trapped under the paint. Metal parts are often washed or dipped in chemical baths to prepare the surface for painting and protect against corrosion. If the product has more than one color or has unpainted parts, masking is required. Masking normally involves carefully covering portions of the product with tape and paper.

After the product is prepared for painting, coating, or varnishing, a number of techniques may be used to apply the paint. Perhaps the most straightforward technique is simply dipping an item in a large vat of paint or other coating. This is the technique used by *dippers*, who immerse racks or baskets of articles in vats of paint, liquid plastic, or other solutions by means of a power hoist. This technique is commonly used for small parts in electronic equipment, such as cell phones.

Spraying products with a solution of paint or some other coating is also quite common. *Spray machine operators* use spray guns to coat metal, wood, ceramic, fabric, paper, and food products with paint and other coating solutions. Following a formula, operators fill the machine's tanks with a mixture of paints or chemicals, adding prescribed amounts of solution. Then they adjust nozzles on the spray guns to obtain the proper dispersion of the spray and hold or position the guns to direct the spray onto the article. Operators also check the flow and viscosity of the paint or solution and visually inspect the quality of the coating. When products are drying, these workers often must regulate the temperature and air circulation in drying ovens.

Some factories use automated painting systems that are operated by *coating*, *painting*, and *spraying machine setters*, *operators*, *and tenders*. When setting up these systems, opera-

tors position the automatic spray guns, set the nozzles, and synchronize the action of the guns with the speed of the conveyor carrying articles through the machine and drying ovens. The operator also may add solvents or water to the paint vessel to prepare the paint for application. During the operation of the painting machines, these workers tend the equipment, observe gauges on the control panel, and check articles for evidence of any variation from specifications. The operator uses a manual spray gun to "touch up" flaws.

Individuals who paint, coat, or decorate articles such as furniture, glass, pottery, toys, cakes, and books are known as *painting, coating, and decorating workers*. Some workers coat confectionery, bakery, and other food products with melted chocolate, cheese, oils, sugar, or other substances. Paper is often coated to give it its gloss or finish and silver, tin, and copper solutions are often sprayed on glass to make mirrors.

The best known group of painting and coating workers are those who refinish old or damaged cars, trucks, and buses in automotive body repair and paint shops. *Transportation equipment painters* who work in repair shops are among the most highly skilled manual spray operators, because they perform intricate, detailed work and mix paints to match the original color, a task that is especially difficult if the color has faded. The preparation work on an old car is similar to painting other metal objects. The paint is normally applied with a manually controlled spray gun.

Transportation equipment painters who work on new cars oversee several automated steps. A modern car is first dipped in an anti-corrosion bath, then coated with colored paint, and then painted in several coats of clear paint, which prevents scratches from damaging the colored paint.

Most other transportation equipment painters either paint equipment too large to paint automatically—such as ships or giant construction equipment—or perform touch-up work to

Automotive painters wear ventilators to ensure safety.

repair flaws in the paint caused either by damage during assembly or flaws during the automated painting process.

With all types of coating, it is common for the painting process to be repeated several times to achieve a thick, smooth, protective coverage.

Work environment. Painting and coating workers typically work indoors and may be exposed to dangerous fumes from paint and coating solutions, although in general, workers' exposure to hazardous chemicals has decreased because of regulations limiting emissions of volatile organic compounds and other hazardous air pollutants. Painting usually is done in special ventilated booths with workers typically wearing masks or respirators that cover their noses and mouths. More sophisticated paint booths and fresh-air systems are increasingly used to provide a safer work environment.

Operators have to stand for long periods, and when using a spray gun, they may have to bend, stoop, or crouch in uncomfortable positions to reach different parts of the products.

Most painting and coating workers work a normal 40-hour week, but automotive painters in repair shops can work more than 50 hours a week, depending on the number of vehicles that need repainting.

Training, Other Qualifications, and Advancement

A high school diploma or equivalent is required for most workers; training for new workers usually lasts from a few days to several months, but becoming skilled in all aspects of painting can require 1 to 2 years of experience.

Education and training. Painting and coating workers employed in the manufacturing sector are usually required to have a high school degree or equivalent; employers in other sectors may be willing to hire workers without a high school diploma. Training for beginning painting and coating machine setters, operators, and tenders and for painting, coating, and decorating workers, may last from a few days to a couple of months. Coating, painting, and spraying machine setters, operators, and tenders who modify the operation of computer-controlled equipment may require additional training in computer operations and minor programming. Transportation equipment painters typically learn their jobs through either apprenticeships as helpers or postsecondary education in painting.

Becoming skilled in all aspects of painting usually requires 1 to 2 years of experience and sometimes requires some formal classroom instruction and on-the-job training. Beginning helpers usually remove trim, clean, and sand surfaces to be painted; mask surfaces they do not want painted; and polish finished work. As helpers gain experience, they progress to more complicated tasks, such as mixing paint to achieve a good match and using spray guns to apply primer coats or final coats to small areas.

Additional instruction in safety, equipment, and techniques is offered at some community colleges and vocational or technical schools. Employers also sponsor training programs to help their workers become more productive. Additional training is available from manufacturers of chemicals, paints, or equipment, explaining their products and giving tips about techniques.

Other qualifications. Painting and coating workers in factories need to be able to read and follow detailed plans or blueprints. Some workers also need artistic talent to paint furniture, decorate cakes, or make sure that the paint on a car or other object is the right color. Applicants should be able to breathe comfortably wearing a respirator.

Certification and advancement. Voluntary certification by the National Institute for Automotive Service Excellence (ASE) is recognized as the standard of achievement for automotive painters. For certification, painters must pass a written examination and have at least 2 years of experience in the field. High school, trade or vocational school, or community or junior college training in automotive refinishing that meets ASE standards may substitute for up to 1 year of experience. To retain the certification, painters must retake the examination at least every 5 years. Outside of automobile painters, few receive certifications.

Some automotive painters go to technical schools to learn the intricacies of mixing and applying different types of paint. Such programs can improve employment prospects and speed up promotion. Experienced painting and coating workers with leadership ability may become team leaders or supervisors. Many become paint and coating inspectors. Those who get practical experience or formal training may become sales or technical representatives for chemical or paint companies. Some automotive painters eventually open their own shops.

Employment

Painting and coating workers held about 192,700 jobs in 2008. Coating, painting, and spraying machine setters, operators, and tenders accounted for about 107,800 jobs, while transportation equipment painters constituted about 52,200. Another 32,700 jobs were held by painting, coating, and decorating workers.

Approximately 2 out of 3 workers were employed by manufacturing establishments, particularly those that manufacture fabricated metal products, transportation equipment, industrial machines, household and office furniture, and plastic, wood, and paper products. Outside manufacturing, workers were

Projections data from the National Employment Matrix

Occupational Title	SOC Code	Employment, 2008	Projected Employment, 2018	Change, 2008-2018	
				Number	Percent
Painting workers	51-9120	192,700	199,900	7,300	4
Coating, painting, and spraying machine setters, operators, and tenders	51-9121	107,800	111,300	3,500	3
Painters, transportation equipment.................................	51-9122	52,200	52,600	400	1
Painting, coating, and decorating workers	51-9123	32,700	36,000	3,300	10

(NOTE) Data in this table are rounded. See the discussion of the employment projections table in the *Handbook* introductory chapter on *Occupational Information Included in the Handbook.*

employed by independent automotive repair shops and by motor vehicle dealers. About 6 percent were self-employed.

Job Outlook

Overall employment is expected to grow slower than the average for all occupations, but employment change will vary by specialty. Good job prospects are expected for skilled workers with painting experience.

Employment change. Overall employment of painting and coating workers is expected to increase by 4 percent from 2008-2018, which is slower than the average for all occupations. This growth will be driven primarily by the increasing number of goods requiring painting or coating. However, growth will be limited by gains in efficiency from automation and other processes. For example, operators will be able to coat goods more rapidly as sophisticated industrial machinery moves and aims spray guns more efficiently. Much of the growth in these occupations will be seen in the retail sector, as automation is less common in this industry.

Job prospects. Like many manufacturing occupations, employers report difficulty finding qualified workers. Opportunities should be good for those with painting experience. Job openings will result from the need to replace workers who leave the occupation and from increased specialization in manufacturing.

Earnings

Median hourly wages coating, painting, and spraying machine setters, operators, and tenders were $13.66 in May 2008. The middle 50 percent earned between $11.00 and $16.97 an hour. The lowest 10 percent earned less than $9.18, and the highest 10 percent earned more than $20.35 an hour.

Median hourly wages transportation equipment painters were $17.86 in May 2008. The middle 50 percent earned between $13.99 and $24.01 an hour. The lowest 10 percent earned less than $11.31, and the highest 10 percent earned more than $29.93 an hour. Median hourly wages of transportation equipment painters were $17.86 in automotive repair and maintenance shops and $26.61 in motor vehicle manufacturing.

Median hourly wages of painting, coating, and decorating workers were $11.57 in May 2008. The middle 50 percent earned between $9.46 and $14.60 an hour. The lowest 10 percent earned less than $8.15, and the highest 10 percent earned more than $18.55 an hour.

Many automotive painters employed by motor vehicle dealers and independent automotive repair shops receive a commission, based on the labor cost charged to the customer. Under this method, earnings depend largely on the amount of work a painter does and how fast it is completed. Employers frequently guarantee commissioned painters a minimum weekly salary. Helpers and trainees usually receive an hourly rate until they become sufficiently skilled to work on commission. Trucking companies, bus lines, and other organizations that repair and refinish their own vehicles usually pay by the hour.

Some painting and coating machine operators belong to unions, including the United Auto Workers and the International Brotherhood of Teamsters. Most union operators work for manufacturers and large motor vehicle dealers.

Related Occupations

The work performed by the following occupations is similar to the duties of painting and coating workers:

	Page
Automotive body and related repairers	687
Machine setters, operators, and tenders—metal and plastic	734
Painters and paperhangers	656

Sources of Additional Information

For more details about work opportunities, contact local manufacturers, automotive body repair shops, motor vehicle dealers, vocational schools, locals of unions representing painting and coating workers, or the local offices of your State employment service. The State employment service also may be a source of information about training programs.

For a directory of certified automotive painting programs, contact:

➤ National Automotive Technician Education Foundation, 101 Blue Seal Dr., Suite 101, Leesburg, VA 20175. Internet: **http://www.natef.org**

The Occupational Information Network (O*NET) provides information on a wide range of occupational characteristics. Links to O*NET appear at the end of the Internet version of this occupational statement, accessible at **http://www.bls.gov/ooh/ocos240.htm**

Semiconductor Processors

Significant Points

- Employment is expected to decline rapidly over the next 10 years, despite increased demand for semiconductor products.

- Opportunities will be best for applicants who have an associate degree in a relevant subject and work experience in high-tech manufacturing.

- Although applicants may face competition, many skills learned in this occupation are transferable to other high-tech manufacturing jobs.

Nature of the Work

Semiconductors are unique substances, which, under different conditions, can act as either conductors or insulators of electricity. Semiconductor processors turn one of these substances—silicon—into integrated circuits, also known as microchips. These integrated circuits contain anywhere from dozens to millions of tiny electronic components, and are used in a wide range of products, from personal computers and cellular telephones to airplanes and missile guidance systems.

Semiconductor processors—often referred to in the industry as *technicians* or *process technicians*—oversee the manufacturing process of microchips. This process begins with the production of cylinders of silicon called ingots. The ingots then are sliced into thin wafers. Using automated equipment, robots polish the wafers, imprint precise microscopic patterns of the circuitry onto them using photolithography, etch out patterns with acids, and replace the patterns with conductors, such as aluminum or copper. The wafers then receive a chemical bath to make them smooth, and the imprint process begins again on a new layer with the next pattern. A complex chip may contain more than 20 layers of circuitry. Once the process is complete, wafers are then cut into individual chips, which are enclosed in a casing and shipped to equipment manufacturers.

The manufacturing and slicing of wafers to create semiconductors takes place in clean rooms—production areas that are kept free of all airborne matter, because the circuitry on a chip is so small that even microscopic particles can make it unusable. All semiconductor processors working in clean rooms must wear special lightweight outer garments known as "bunny suits." These garments fit over clothing to prevent lint and other particles from contaminating the clean room.

Semiconductor processors troubleshoot production problems and make equipment adjustments and repairs. They take the lead in assuring quality control and in maintaining equipment. They also test completed chips to make sure they work properly. To keep equipment repairs to a minimum, technicians perform diagnostic analyses and run computations. For example, technicians may determine if a flaw in a chip is due to contamination and peculiar to that wafer, or if the flaw is inherent in the manufacturing process.

Work environment. Workers begin their shift by putting on a bunny suit. For new workers, this often can take as much as 40 minutes, but experienced workers can generally do it in 5 minutes or less. The work pace in clean rooms is deliberately slow. Limited movement keeps the air in clean rooms as free as possible of dust and other particles, which can destroy microchips during their production. Because the machinery sets the operators' rate of work, workers maintain a relaxed pace. Technicians are on their feet most of the day, walking through the clean room to oversee production activities.

The temperature in the clean rooms must be kept within a narrow range and generally is comfortable for workers. Although bunny suits cover virtually the entire body, their lightweight fabric keeps the temperature inside fairly comfortable. Entry

Semiconductor processors troubleshoot problems in the production of microchips and make equipment adjustments and repairs.

and exit of workers from the clean room are controlled to minimize contamination, and workers must be reclothed in a clean bunny suit and decontaminated each time they return to the clean room.

Semiconductor fabricating plants operate around the clock. Night and weekend work is common. In some plants, workers maintain standard 8-hour shifts, 5 days a week. In other plants, employees are on duty for 12-hour shifts to minimize the disruption of clean room operations brought about by changes. Managers also may allow workers to alternate schedules, thereby distributing the overnight shift equitably.

Training, Other Qualifications, and Advancement
Semiconductor processors typically have associate degrees or technical school certificates, as well as math and science skills.

Education and training. For semiconductor processor jobs, employers prefer applicants who have completed associate degrees in highly automated systems, electromechanical automation, or electronics. However, completion of a 1-year certificate program in semiconductor technology or high-tech manufacturing, offered by some community colleges, may be sufficient. Some semiconductor technology programs at community colleges include internships at semiconductor fabricating plants. Hands-on training is an important part of degree and certificate programs.

To ensure that operators and technicians keep their skills current, employers provide regular on-the-job training. Some employers also provide financial assistance to employees who want to earn associate or bachelor's degrees, especially if the employee is working toward becoming a technician.

Other qualifications. People interested in becoming semiconductor processors—either operators or technicians—need strong technical skills, an ability to solve problems intuitively, and an ability to work in teams. Mathematics, including statistics, and physical science knowledge are useful. Communication skills and an understanding of manufacturing principles also are very important.

Advancement. Workers advance as they become more comfortable with the equipment and better understand the manufacturing process. Employees train workers for several months, after which they become entry-level operators or technicians. After a few years, as they become more knowledgeable about the operations of the plant, they generally advance to the intermediate level. This entails greater responsibilities. Over time, usually 7 to 10 years, workers may become senior technicians, who lead teams of technicians and work directly with engineers to develop processes in the plant.

Employment
Semiconductor processors held approximately 31,600 jobs in 2008. Nearly all of them were employed in the computer and electronic product manufacturing industry.

Job Outlook
Employment of semiconductor processors is projected to decline rapidly through 2018. Opportunities will be best for those with associate degrees and experience working in high-tech manufacturing.

Projections data from the National Employment Matrix

Occupational Title	SOC Code	Employment, 2008	Projected Employment, 2018	Change, 2008-2018	
				Number	Percent
Semiconductor processors	51-9141	31,600	21,600	-10,000	-32

(NOTE) Data in this table are rounded. See the discussion of the employment projections table in the *Handbook* introductory chapter on *Occupational Information Included in the Handbook.*

Employment change. Employment of semiconductor processors is projected to decline by 32 percent between 2008 and 2018. This reflects a changing manufacturing environment in which technological advances have reduced the need for workers.

Most of the microchips produced in the United States are highly complex. The success of these chips depends chiefly on their speed and flexibility. Meeting both of these goals requires smaller individual components, which are now measured in nanometers (one millionth of a millimeter). Because the components are so small, it is now impossible for humans to handle chips in production, since these chips are so sensitive to dust and other particles. As a result, there has been a decline in semiconductor processor employment for many years, despite a strong domestic industry. As technology advances, the decline in employment is expected to continue.

Job prospects. Jobseekers can expect competition for these positions, in response to the rapid decline in employment. Nonetheless, some jobs will open up due to the need to replace workers who leave the occupation. Prospects will be best for applicants with associate degrees and experience in high-tech manufacturing. Like most manufacturing industries, the semiconductor industry is highly sensitive to economic downturns.

Despite competition for these jobs, however, people who are interested in this type of work should be aware that the duties of semiconductor processors closely resemble those of other high-tech manufacturing jobs. Many of the skills learned in an associate degree or technical school program—as well as on the job—are transferable to other occupations.

Earnings

Median annual wages of wage-and-salary semiconductor processors were $32,230 in May 2008. The middle 50 percent earned between $26,650 and $40,220. The lowest 10 percent earned less than $21,980, and the top 10 percent earned more than $50,400.

Technicians with associate degrees in a related field generally start at higher salaries than those with less education.

Semiconductor processors generally received good benefits packages, including healthcare, disability plans and life insurance, stock options and retirement.

Related Occupations

Other occupations involved in high-tech manufacturing production include:

	Page
Assemblers and fabricators	723
Electrical engineers	161
Engineering technicians	173
Inspectors, testers, sorters, samplers, and weighers................	768
Science technicians	230
Tool and die makers	740

Sources of Additional Information

For more information on semiconductor processor careers, contact:

➤ Maricopa Advanced Technology Education Center, 4110 E. Wood St., Suite 1, Phoenix, AZ 85040. Internet: **http://www.matec.org**

➤ SEMI, 3081 Zanker Rd., San Jose, CA 95134. Internet: **http://www.semi.org**

➤ Semiconductor Industry Association, 181 Metro Dr., Suite 450, San Jose, CA 95110. Internet: **http://www.sia-online.org**

The Occupational Information Network (O*NET) provides information on a wide range of occupational characteristics. Links to O*NET appear at the end of the Internet version of this occupational statement, accessible at **http://www.bls.gov/ooh/ocos257.htm**

Other Production Occupations

Photographic Process Workers and Processing Machine Operators

Nature of the Work

Photographic processing machine operators use various machines to create prints from film or digital photographs. Most digital processing is done automatically by computer software. *Photographic process workers* perform more delicate tasks, such as retouching photographic negatives, prints, and images to emphasize or correct specific features.

Education and Training

Most skills needed for these jobs can be learned on-the-job in a few months.

Job Outlook

Current and projected employment:

2008 Employment	73,000
2018 Employment	61,200
Employment change	-11,800
Growth rate	-16%

Employment change. Employment is expected to decline rapidly. Self-service machines, home printers, and online ordering services will be able to meet most of the demand for digital prints, but there still will be some demand for professionals to operate the machines, and to develop and print photos from people who continue to use film cameras. Using digital cameras and technology, consumers who have a personal computer are able to edit and to retouch pictures on their computers.

Job prospects. Job opportunities will be best for individuals with experience using computers and digital technology.

Earnings

Median annual wages in May 2008 were as follows:

Photographic process workers.....................................$26,010
Photographic processing machine operators................20,360

Related Occupations

Sources of Additional Information

➤ Photo Marketing Association International, 3000 Picture Pl, Jackson, MI 49201. Internet: **http://www.pmai.org**

The Occupational Information Network (O*NET) provides information on a wide range of occupational characteristics. Links to O*NET appear at the end of the Internet version of this occupational statement, accessible at **http://www.bls.gov/ooh/ocos241.htm**

Transportation and Material Moving Occupations

Air Transportation Occupations

Air Traffic Controllers

Significant Points

- The vast majority of air traffic controllers are employed by the Federal Aviation Administration (FAA), an agency of the Federal Government.

- Applicants without prior air traffic control experience must be 30 years of age or younger.

- Replacement needs will continue to account for most job openings, reflecting the large number of air traffic controllers who will be eligible to retire over the next decade.

- Competition for jobs will remain keen.

Nature of the Work

The National Airspace System (NAS) is a vast network of people and equipment that ensures the safe operation of commercial and private aircraft. *Air traffic controllers* work within the NAS to coordinate the movement of air traffic to make certain that planes stay a safe distance apart. Their immediate concern is safety, but controllers also must direct planes efficiently to minimize delays. Some regulate airport traffic through designated airspaces; others regulate airport arrivals and departures.

Terminal controllers watch over all planes traveling in an airport's airspace. Their main responsibility is to organize the flow of aircraft into and out of the airport. They work in either the control tower or the terminal radar approach control (TRACON) room or building. Relying on visual observation, the *tower local controllers* sequence arrival aircraft for landing and issue departure clearances for those departing from the airport. Other controllers in the tower control the movement of aircraft on the taxiways, handle flight data, and provide flight plan clearances. *Terminal radar controllers* manage aircraft departing from or arriving to an airport by monitoring each aircraft's movement on radar to ensure that a safe distance is maintained between all aircraft under their control. In addition, terminal controllers keep pilots informed about weather and runway conditions.

Many different controllers are involved in the departure of an airplane. If the plane is flying under instrument flight rule conditions, a flight plan is filed prior to departure. The *tower flight data controller* receives the flight plan in the form of a flight strip, which is output from a computer, and arranges it in sequence. When an aircraft calls for clearance the *clearance delivery controller* issues the clearance and moves the strip over

to the *ground controller* who manages the movement of aircraft on the airport surface, except the active runway. When the aircraft arrives at the active runway the strip is moved to the local controller who issues the departure clearance, observes the takeoff and turns the plane over to the departure controller. The TRACON departure controller identifies the plane on radar, climbs it, and directs it on course.

After each plane departs, terminal controllers notify *en route controllers*, who take charge next. There are 20 air route traffic control centers located around the country, each employing 300 to 700 controllers, with more than 150 on duty during peak hours at the busiest facilities. Airplanes usually fly along designated routes; each center is assigned a certain airspace containing many different routes. En route controllers work either individually or in teams of two, depending on how heavy traffic is; each team is responsible for a sector of the center's airspace.

As the plane proceeds on its flight plan to its destination it is handed off from sector to sector both within the center and to adjoining centers. To prepare for planes about to enter the team's sector, the *radar associate controller* organizes flight plans output from a printer into strip bays. If two planes are scheduled to enter the team's sector in conflict, the controller may arrange with the preceding sector unit for one plane to change its flight path or altitude. As a plane approaches a team's airspace, the radar controller accepts responsibility for the plane from the previous sector. The controller also delegates responsibility for the plane to the next sector when the plane leaves the team's airspace.

When the plane is approximately 50 miles from the destination airport, it is handed off to that airport's *terminal radar arrival controller* who sequences it with other arrivals, and issues an approach clearance. As the plane nears the runway, the pilot is issued a clearance to contact the tower. The local controller issues the landing clearance. Once the plane has landed, the ground controller directs it along the taxiways to its assigned gate. The local and ground controllers usually work entirely by sight, but may use airport surface radar if visibility is very poor.

Both airport tower and en route controllers usually control several planes at a time, often making quick decisions about completely different activities. For example, a controller might direct a plane on its landing approach and at the same time provide pilots entering the airport's airspace with information about conditions at the airport. While instructing these pilots, the controller also might observe other planes in the vicinity, such as those in a holding pattern waiting for permission to land, to ensure that they remain well separated.

In addition to airport towers and en route centers, air traffic controllers also work in flight service stations at 17 locations in Alaska. These *flight service specialists* provide pilots with

Competition for air traffic controller jobs is expected to remain keen.

preflight and in-flight weather information, suggested routes, and other aeronautical information important to the safety of a flight. Flight service specialists relay air traffic control clearances to pilots not in direct communications with a tower or center, assist pilots in emergency situations, and initiate and coordinate searches for missing or overdue aircraft. At certain locations where there is no airport tower or the tower has closed for the day, flight service specialists provide airport advisory services to landing and departing aircraft. However, they are not involved in actively managing and separating air traffic.

Some air traffic controllers work at the FAA's Air Traffic Control Systems Command Center in Herndon, VA, where they oversee the entire system. They look for situations that will create bottlenecks or other problems in the system and then respond with a management plan for traffic into and out of the troubled sector. The objective is to keep traffic levels in the trouble spots manageable for the controllers working at en route centers.

Work environment. During busy times, controllers must work rapidly and efficiently. Total concentration is required to keep track of several planes at the same time and to make certain that all pilots receive correct instructions. The mental stress of being responsible for the safety of several aircraft and their passengers can be exhausting. Unlike tower controllers, radar controllers also have the extra stress of having to work in semi-darkness, never seeing the actual aircraft they control except as a small "blip" on the radarscope. Controllers who work in flight service stations work in offices close to the communications and computer equipment.

Controllers work a basic 40-hour week; however, they may work additional hours, for which they receive overtime, or premium pay, or equal time off. Because most control towers and centers operate 24 hours a day, 7 days a week, controllers rotate night and weekend shifts. Contract towers and flight service station working conditions may vary somewhat from the FAA.

Training, Other Qualifications, and Advancement

To become an air traffic controller with the FAA, a person must achieve a qualifying score on the FAA-authorized pre-employment test and meet the basic qualification requirements

in accordance with Federal law. Those without prior air traffic control experience must be 30 years of age or younger.

Education and training. There are three main pathways to become an air traffic controller with the FAA. The first is air traffic controllers with prior experience through either the FAA or the Department of Defense as a civilian or veteran. Second are applicants from the general public. These applicants must have 3 years of progressively responsible full-time work experience, have completed a full 4 years of college, or a combination of both. In combining education and experience, 1 year of undergraduate study—30 semester or 45 quarter hours—is equivalent to 9 months of work experience. The third way is for an applicant to have successfully completed an aviation-related program of study through the FAA's Air Traffic-Collegiate Training Initiative (AT-CTI) program. In 2008, there were 31 schools in the AT-CTI program.

AT-CTI program schools offer 2–year or 4-year non-engineering degrees that teach basic courses in aviation and air traffic control. In addition to graduation, AT-CTI candidates need a recommendation from their school before being considered for employment as an air traffic controller by the FAA.

Candidates with prior experience as air traffic controllers are automatically qualified for FAA air traffic controller positions. However, applicants from the general public and the AT-CTI program must pass the FAA-authorized pre-employment test that measures their ability to learn the duties of a controller. The test is administered by computer and takes about 8 hours to complete. To take the test, an applicant must apply under an open advertisement for air traffic control positions and be chosen to take the examination. When there are many more applicants than available testing positions, applicants are selected randomly. However, the FAA guarantees that all AT-CTI students in good standing in their programs will be given the FAA pre-employment test. Those who achieve a qualifying score on the test become eligible for employment as an air traffic controller. Candidates must be granted security and medical clearance and are subject to drug screening. Additionally, applicants must meet other basic qualification requirements in accordance with Federal law. These requirements include United States citizenship and the ability to speak English.

Upon selection, employees attend the FAA Academy in Oklahoma City, OK, for 12 weeks of training, during which they learn the fundamentals of the airway system, FAA regulations, controller equipment, and aircraft performance characteristics, as well as more specialized tasks. Graduates of the AT-CTI program are eligible to bypass the Air Traffic Basics Course, which is the first 5 weeks of qualification training at the FAA Academy.

After graduation from the FAA Academy in Oklahoma City, candidates are assigned to an air traffic control facility and are classified as "developmental controllers" until they complete all requirements to be certified for all of the air traffic control positions within a defined area of a given facility. Generally, it takes new controllers with only initial controller training between 2 and 4 years, depending on the facility and the availability of facility staff or contractors to provide on-the-job training, to complete all the certification requirements to become certified professional controllers. Individuals who have had prior controller experience normally take less time to become fully certified. Controllers who fail to complete either the academy or the on-the-job portions of the training usually are dismissed. Controllers must pass a physical examination each year and a job performance examination twice each year. Failure to become certified in any position at a facility within a specified time also may result in dismissal. Controllers also are subject to drug screenings as a condition of continuing employment.

Other qualifications. Air traffic controllers must be articulate to give pilots directions quickly and clearly. Intelligence and a good memory also are important because controllers constantly receive information that they must immediately grasp, interpret, and remember. Decisiveness also is required because controllers often have to make quick decisions. The ability to concentrate is crucial because controllers must make these decisions in the midst of noise and other distractions.

Advancement. At airports, new controllers begin by supplying pilots with basic flight data and airport information. They then advance to the position of ground controller, local controller, departure controller, and, finally, arrival controller. At an air route traffic control center, new controllers first deliver printed flight plans to teams, gradually advancing to radar associate controller and then to radar controller.

Controllers can transfer to jobs at different locations or advance to supervisory positions, including management or staff jobs—such as air traffic control data systems computer specialist—in air traffic control, and top administrative jobs in the FAA. However, there are only limited opportunities for a controller to switch from a position in an en route center to a tower.

Employment

Air traffic controllers held about 26,200 jobs in 2008. The vast majority were employed by the FAA, while a small number of civilian controllers also work for the U.S. Department of Defense. In addition to controllers employed by the Federal Government, some work for private air traffic control companies providing service to non-FAA towers and contract flight service stations.

Job Outlook

Air traffic controllers should experience about as fast as average employment growth, but most opportunities are expected to result from the need to replace workers who retire or leave the occupation for other reasons. Keen competition is expected for air traffic controller positions.

Employment change. Employment of air traffic controllers is projected to grow by 13 percent from 2008 to 2018, which is about as fast as the average for all occupations. Increasing air traffic will require more controllers to handle the additional work. Job growth, however, is not expected to keep pace with the increasing number of aircraft flying due to advances in technology.

The FAA is implementing an automated air traffic control system that will allow controllers to more efficiently deal with the demands of increased air traffic. It includes the replacement of aging equipment and the introduction of new systems, technologies, and procedures to enhance safety and security and support future aviation growth. Future developments will include the use of the Global Positioning System (GPS) to eliminate radar-based air traffic control and give controllers real-time displays of aircraft locations. This will allow for more efficient flight paths and reduced air traffic congestion, and it will also allow controllers to handle more traffic, increasing their productivity.

Job prospects. Most job opportunities are expected as the result of replacement needs from workers leaving the occupation. The majority of today's air traffic controllers will be eligible to retire over the next decade, although not all are expected to do so. Despite the increasing number of job openings for air traffic controllers, competition to get into the FAA Academy is expected to remain keen, as there generally are many more test applicants than there are openings.

Air traffic controllers who continue to meet the proficiency and medical requirements enjoy more job security than do most workers. While demand for air transportation declines during recessions, controllers are rarely laid off.

Earnings

Air traffic controllers earn relatively high pay and have good benefits. Median annual wages of air traffic controllers in May 2008 were $111,870. The middle 50 percent earned between $71,050 and $143,780. The lowest 10 percent earned less than $45,020, and the highest 10 percent earned more than $161,010. The average annual salary, excluding overtime earnings, for air traffic controllers in the Federal Government—which employs 90 percent of all controllers—was $109,218 in March 2009.

The Air Traffic Control pay system classifies each air traffic facility into one of eight levels with corresponding pay bands. Under this pay system, controllers' salaries are determined by the rating of the facility. Higher ratings usually mean higher controller salaries and greater demands on the controller's judgment, skill, and decision-making ability.

Depending on length of service, air traffic controllers receive 13 to 26 days of paid vacation and 13 days of paid sick leave each year, in addition to life insurance and health benefits. Controllers also can retire at an earlier age and with fewer years of service than other Federal employees. Air traffic controllers are eligible to retire at age 50 with 20 years of service as an active air traffic controller or after 25 years of active service at any age. There is a mandatory retirement age of 56 for controllers who manage air traffic. However, Federal law provides for exemptions to the mandatory age of 56, up to age 61 in certain cases, but controllers must have exceptional skills and experience. Earnings and benefits for controllers working in contract towers or flight service stations

Projections data from the National Employment Matrix

Occupational Title	SOC Code	Employment, 2008	Projected Employment, 2018	Change, 2008-2018	
				Number	Percent
Air traffic controllers..	53-2021	26,200	29,600	3,400	13

(NOTE) Data in this table are rounded. See the discussion of the employment projections table in the *Handbook* introductory chapter on *Occupational Information Included in the Handbook.*

may vary. Many air traffic controllers hold union membership, primarily with the National Air Traffic Controllers Association.

Related Occupations

Another occupation involved in the direction and control of traffic in air transportation is:

Sources of Additional Information

For further information on how to qualify and apply for a job as an air traffic controller, contact the FAA:

➤ Federal Aviation Administration, 800 Independence Ave. SW., Washington, DC 20591. Internet: **http://www.faa.gov**

For further information on air traffic controllers, contact:
➤ National Air Traffic Controllers Association, 1325 Massachusetts Ave. NW., Washington, DC 20005. Internet: **http://www.natca.org/**

The Occupational Information Network (O*NET) provides information on a wide range of occupational characteristics. Links to O*NET appear at the end of the Internet version of this occupational statement, accessible at **http://www.bls.gov/ooh/ocos108.htm**

Aircraft Pilots and Flight Engineers

Significant Points

- Regional and low-cost airlines offer the best opportunities; pilots face strong competition for jobs at the major airlines, which offer better pay and benefits.

- Many pilots have learned to fly in the military, but growing numbers have college degrees with flight training from civilian flying schools that are certified by the Federal Aviation Administration (FAA).

- Newly hired pilots at major airlines typically have about 4,000 hours of flight experience.

Nature of the Work

Pilots are highly trained professionals who fly airplanes or helicopters to carry out a wide variety of tasks. Most are *airline pilots, copilots,* and *flight engineers* who transport passengers and cargo. However, 34 percent are commercial pilots involved in dusting crops, spreading seed for reforestation, testing aircraft, flying passengers and cargo to areas not served by regular airlines, directing firefighting efforts, tracking criminals, monitoring traffic, and rescuing and evacuating injured persons.

Except on small aircraft, two pilots usually make up the cockpit crew. Generally, the most experienced pilot, the *captain,* is in command and supervises all other crew members. The pilot and the copilot, often called the *first officer,* share flying and other duties, such as communicating with air traffic controllers and monitoring the instruments. Some large aircraft have a third crewmember, the flight engineer, who assists the pilots by monitoring and operating many of the instruments and systems, making minor in-flight repairs, and watching for other aircraft. The flight engineer also assists the pilots with the company, air

traffic control, and cabin crew communications. New technology can perform many flight tasks, however, and virtually all new aircraft now fly with only two pilots, who rely more heavily on computerized controls.

Before departure, pilots plan their flights carefully. They thoroughly check their aircraft to make sure that the engines, controls, instruments, and other systems are functioning properly. They also make sure that baggage or cargo has been loaded correctly. They confer with flight dispatchers and aviation weather forecasters to find out about weather conditions en route and at their destination. Based on this information, they choose a route, altitude, and speed that will provide the safest, most economical, and smoothest flight. When flying under instrument flight rules—procedures governing the operation of the aircraft when there is poor visibility—the pilot in command, or the company dispatcher, normally files an instrument flight plan with air traffic control so that the flight can be coordinated with other air traffic.

Takeoff and landing are the most difficult parts of the flight, and require close coordination between the two pilots. For example, as the plane accelerates for takeoff, the pilot concentrates on the runway while the copilot, scans the instrument panel. To calculate the speed they must attain to become airborne, pilots consider the altitude of the airport, outside temperature, weight of the plane, and speed and direction of the wind. The moment the plane reaches takeoff speed, the copilot informs the pilot, who then pulls back on the controls to raise the nose of the plane. Captains and first officers usually alternate flying each leg from takeoff to landing.

Unless the weather is bad, the flight itself is relatively routine. Airplane pilots, with the assistance of autopilot and the flight management computer, steer the plane along their planned route and are monitored by the air traffic control stations they pass along the way. They regularly scan the instrument panel to check their fuel supply; the condition of their engines; and the air-conditioning, hydraulic, and other systems. Pilots may request a change in altitude or route if circumstances dictate. For example, if the ride is rougher than expected, pilots may ask air traffic control if pilots flying at other altitudes have reported better conditions; if so, they may request an altitude change. This procedure also may be used to find a stronger tailwind or a weaker headwind to save fuel and increase speed. In contrast, because helicopters are used for short trips at relatively low altitude, helicopter pilots must be constantly on the lookout for trees, bridges, power lines, transmission towers, and other dangerous obstacles as well as low-flying general aviation aircraft. Regardless of the type of aircraft, all pilots must monitor warning devices designed to help detect sudden shifts in wind conditions that can cause crashes.

Pilots must rely completely on their instruments when visibility is poor. On the basis of altimeter readings, they know how high above ground they are and whether they can fly safely over mountains and other obstacles. Special navigation radios give pilots precise information that, with the help of special charts, tells them their exact position. Other very sophisticated equipment provides directions to a point just above the end of a runway and enables pilots to land completely without an outside visual reference. Once on the ground, pilots must complete

Before every flight, pilots inspect the aircraft.

records on their flight and the aircraft maintenance status for their company and the FAA.

The number of nonflying duties that pilots have depends on the employment setting. Airline pilots have the services of large support staffs and, consequently, perform few nonflying duties. However, because of the large numbers of passengers, airline pilots may be called upon to coordinate handling of disgruntled or disruptive passengers. Also, under the Federal Flight Deck Officer program airline pilots who undergo rigorous training and screening are deputized as Federal law enforcement officers and are issued firearms to protect the cockpit against intruders and hijackers. Pilots employed by other organizations, such as charter operators or businesses, have many other duties. They may load the aircraft, handle all passenger luggage to ensure a balanced load, and supervise refueling; other nonflying responsibilities include keeping records, scheduling flights, arranging for major maintenance, and performing minor aircraft maintenance and repairs.

Some pilots are flight instructors. They teach their students in ground-school classes, in simulators, and in dual-controlled planes and helicopters. A few specially trained pilots are examiners or check pilots. They periodically fly with other pilots or pilot's license applicants to make sure that they are proficient.

Work environment. Most pilots spend a considerable amount of time away from home because the majority of flights involve overnight layovers. According to the Airline Pilot's Association, pilots spend approximately 360 hours a month away from their home base. When pilots are away from home, the airlines provide hotel accommodations, transportation between the hotel and airport, and an allowance for meals and other expenses.

Airline pilots, especially those on international routes, often experience jet lag—fatigue caused by many hours of flying through different time zones. To guard against pilot fatigue, which could result in unsafe flying conditions, the FAA requires airlines to allow pilots at least 8 hours of uninterrupted rest in the 24 hours before finishing their flight duty.

Commercial pilots face other types of job hazards. The work of test pilots, who check the flight performance of new and experimental planes, may be dangerous. Pilots who are crop dusters may be exposed to toxic chemicals and seldom have the benefit of a regular landing strip. Helicopter pilots involved in rescue and police work may be subject to personal injury. All pilots face the potential risk of hearing loss due to prolonged exposure to the constant noise coming from an aircraft's engines.

Although flying does not involve much physical effort, the mental stress of being responsible for a safe flight, regardless of the weather, can be tiring. Pilots must be alert and quick to react if something goes wrong, particularly during takeoff and landing.

FAA regulations limit flying time of airline pilots of large aircraft to a maximum of 100 hours a month and 1,000 hours a year. Most airline pilots fly an average of 75 hours a month and work an additional 140 hours a month performing nonflying duties, which includes waiting for delays to clear and their aircraft to arrive. Most pilots have variable work schedules, working several days on, then several days off. Airlines operate flights at all hours of the day and night, so work schedules often are irregular. Flight assignments are based on seniority; the sooner pilots are hired, the stronger their bidding power is for preferred assignments.

Commercial pilots also may have irregular schedules, flying 30 hours one month and 90 hours the next. Because these pilots frequently have many nonflying responsibilities, they have much less free time than do airline pilots. Except for corporate flight department pilots, most commercial pilots do not remain away from home overnight, although they may work odd hours. However, if the company owns a fleet of planes, pilots may fly a regular schedule.

Flight instructors may have irregular and seasonal work schedules, depending on their students' available time and the weather. Instructors frequently work in the evening or on weekends.

Training, Other Qualifications, and Advancement

Many pilots have learned to fly in the military, but growing numbers have college degrees with flight training from civilian flying schools that are certified by the FAA. All pilots who are paid to transport passengers or cargo must have a commercial pilot's license.

Education and training. Although some small airlines hire high school graduates, most airlines require at least 2 years of college and prefer to hire college graduates. In fact, most entrants to this occupation have a college degree. Because the number of college-educated applicants continues to increase, many employers are making a college degree an educational requirement. Preferred courses in preparation for a career as an airline pilot include English, mathematics, physics, and aeronautical engineering.

Pilots also need flight experience to qualify for a license. The U.S. Armed Forces have always been an important source of experienced pilots because of the extensive flying time and experience on jet aircraft and helicopters. However, an increasing number of people are becoming pilots by attending flight schools or by taking lessons from FAA-certified flight instructors. Completing classes at a flight school approved by the FAA can reduce the amount of flight experience required for a pilot's license. In 2009, the FAA certified about 600 civilian flying schools, including some colleges and universities that offer degree credit for pilot training. Initial training for airline pilots typically includes a week of company indoctrination; 3 to 6 weeks of ground school and simulator training; and 25 hours of initial operating experience, including a check-ride with an

FAA aviation safety inspector. Once trained, pilots are required to attend recurrent training and simulator checks once or twice a year throughout their career.

Licensure. To qualify for FAA licensure, applicants must be at least 18 years old and have at least 250 hours of flight experience. Applicants also must pass a strict physical examination to make sure that they are in good health and have 20/20 vision with or without corrective lenses, good hearing, and no physical handicaps that could impair their performance. They must pass a written test that includes questions on the principles of safe flight, navigation techniques, and FAA regulations, and must demonstrate their flying ability to FAA or designated examiners.

To fly during periods of low visibility, pilots must be rated by the FAA to fly by instruments. Pilots may qualify for this rating by having the required hours of flight experience, including 40 hours of experience in flying by instruments; they also must pass a written examination on procedures and FAA regulations covering instrument flying and demonstrate to an examiner their ability to fly by instruments. Requirements for the instrument rating vary depending on the certification level of flight school.

Airline pilots must fulfill additional requirements. Captains must have an air transport pilot's license. Applicants for this license must be at least 23 years old and have a minimum of 1,500 hours of flying experience, including cross country, night, and instrument flying, and must pass FAA written and flight examinations. Usually, they also have one or more advanced ratings depending on the requirements of their particular job. Because pilots must be able to make quick decisions and accurate judgments under pressure, many airline companies reject applicants who do not pass required psychological and aptitude tests. All licenses are valid so long as a pilot can pass the periodic physical and eye examinations and tests of flying skills required by the FAA and company regulations.

Other qualifications. Depending on the type of aircraft, new airline pilots start as first officers or flight engineers. Although some airlines favor applicants who already have a flight engineer's license, they may provide flight engineer training for those who have only the commercial license. Many pilots begin with smaller regional or commuter airlines, where they obtain experience flying passengers on scheduled flights into busy airports in all weather conditions. These jobs often lead to higher paying jobs with bigger, national or major airlines. Newly hired pilots at major airlines typically have about 4,000 hours of flight experience.

Companies other than airlines usually require less flying experience. However, a commercial pilot's license is a minimum requirement, and employers prefer applicants who have experience in the type of craft they will be flying. New employees usually start as first officers, or fly less sophisticated equipment.

Advancement. Advancement for pilots usually is limited to other flying jobs. Many pilots start as flight instructors, building up their flying hours while they earn money teaching. As they become more experienced, these pilots occasionally fly charter planes or perhaps get jobs with small air transportation firms, such as air-taxi companies. Some advance to flying corporate planes. A small number get flight engineer jobs with the airlines.

In the airlines, advancement usually depends on seniority provisions of union contracts. After 1 to 5 years, flight engineers advance according to seniority to first officer and, after 5 to 15 years, to captain. Seniority also determines which pilots get the more desirable routes. In a nonairline job, a first officer may advance to captain and, in large companies, to chief pilot or director of aviation in charge of aircraft scheduling, maintenance, and flight procedures.

Employment

Civilian aircraft pilots and flight engineers held about 116,000 jobs in 2008. About 76,800 worked as airline pilots, copilots, and flight engineers. The rest were commercial pilots who worked as flight instructors at local airports or for large businesses that fly company cargo and executives in their own airplanes or helicopters. Some commercial pilots flew small planes for air-taxi companies, usually to or from lightly traveled airports not served by major airlines. Others worked for a variety of businesses, performing tasks such as dusting crops, inspecting pipelines, or conducting sightseeing trips.

Pilots are located across the country, but airline pilots usually are based near major metropolitan airports or airports operating as hubs for the major airlines.

Job Outlook

Aircraft pilots and flight engineers are expected to grow about as fast as the average for all occupations. Regional airlines and low-cost carriers will present the best opportunities; pilots attempting to get jobs at the major airlines will face strong competition.

Employment change. Employment of aircraft pilots and flight engineers is projected to grow 12 percent from 2008 to 2018, which is about as fast as the average for all occupations. Population growth and an expanding economy in the long run are expected to boost the demand for air travel, contributing to job growth. New jobs will be created as airlines expand their capacity to meet this rising demand by increasing the number of planes in operation and the number of flights offered.

Job prospects. Job opportunities are expected to be best for experienced pilots with the regional airlines and low-cost carriers, which are expected to grow faster than the major air-

Projections data from the National Employment Matrix

Occupational Title	SOC Code	Employment, 2008	Projected Employment, 2018	Change, 2008-2018	
				Number	Percent
Aircraft pilots and flight engineers	53-2010	116,000	129,700	13,700	12
Airline pilots, copilots, and flight engineers	53-2011	76,800	83,300	6,400	8
Commercial pilots	53-2012	39,200	46,500	7,300	19

(NOTE) Data in this table are rounded. See the discussion of the employment projections table in the *Handbook* introductory chapter on *Occupational Information Included in the Handbook.*

lines. Opportunities with air cargo carriers also should arise because of increasing security requirements for shipping freight on passenger airlines, growth in electronic commerce, and increased demand for global freight. Business, commuter, corporate, and on-demand air taxi travel also should provide some new jobs for pilots.

Pilots attempting to get jobs at the major airlines will face strong competition, as those firms tend to attract many more applicants than the number of job openings. Applicants also will have to compete with laid-off pilots for any available jobs. Pilots who have logged the greatest number of flying hours using sophisticated equipment typically have the best prospects. For this reason, military pilots often have an advantage over other applicants.

In addition to job openings arising from employment growth, opportunities will result from the need to replace workers transferring to other occupations or leaving the labor force. Additional openings will result from the mandatory retirement of commercial airline pilots at age 65.

Employment of pilots is sensitive to cyclical swings in the economy. During recessions, when a decline in the demand for air travel forces airlines to ground planes and curtail the number of flights, airlines may temporarily furlough some pilots.

Earnings

Earnings of aircraft pilots and flight engineers vary greatly depending whether they work as airline or commercial pilots. Earnings also depend on factors such as rank, seniority, and the size and type of aircraft flown. For example, pilots who fly jet aircraft usually earn higher salaries than pilots who fly turboprops. Airline pilots and flight engineers may earn extra pay for night and international flights. In May 2008, median annual wages of airline pilots, copilots, and flight engineers were $111,680. The middle 50 percent earned between $81,580 and $150,480.

Median annual wages of commercial pilots were $65,340 in May 2008. The middle 50 percent earned between $45,680 and $89,540. The lowest 10 percent earned less than $32,020, and the highest 10 percent earned more than $129,580.

Airline pilots usually are eligible for life and health insurance plans. They also receive retirement benefits and, if they fail the FAA physical examination at some point in their careers, they get disability payments. In addition, pilots receive an expense allowance, or "per diem," for every hour they are away from home. Some airlines also provide allowances to pilots for purchasing and cleaning their uniforms. As an additional benefit, pilots and their immediate families usually are entitled to free or reduced-fare transportation on their own and other airlines.

More than half of all aircraft pilots are members of unions. Most of the pilots who fly for the major airlines are members of the Air Line Pilots Association, International, but those employed by one major airline are members of the Allied Pilots Association.

Related Occupations

Although they are not in the cockpit, other occupations that also play an important role in making sure flights are safe and on schedule, and participate in many of the decisions that pilots must make, include:

	Page
Air traffic controllers	784
Airfield operations specialists	832

Sources of Additional Information

For information about job opportunities, salaries, and qualifications, write to the personnel manager of the particular airline.

For information on pilots, contact:
➤ Federal Aviation Administration, 800 Independence Ave. SW., Washington, DC 20591. Internet: **http://www.faa.gov**

For information on airline pilots, contact:
➤ Air Line Pilots Association, International, 1625 Massachusetts Ave. NW., Washington, DC 20036. Internet: **http://www.clearedtodream.org**

For information on helicopter pilots, contact:
➤ Helicopter Association International, 1635 Prince St., Alexandria, VA 22314. Internet: **http://www.rotor.com**

For information about job opportunities in companies other than airlines, consult the classified section of aviation trade magazines and apply to companies that operate aircraft at local airports.

The Occupational Information Network (O*NET) provides information on a wide range of occupational characteristics. Links to O*NET appear at the end of the Internet version of this occupational statement, accessible at **http://www.bls.gov/ooh/ocos107.htm**

Motor Vehicle Operators

Bus Drivers

Significant Points

- Opportunities should be good, although applicants for higher paying public transit bus driver positions may encounter competition.

- State and Federal governments establish bus driver qualifications and standards, which include a commercial driver's license.

- Work schedules vary considerably among various types of bus drivers.

- Bus drivers must possess strong customer service skills, including communication skills and the ability to manage large groups of people with varying needs.

Nature of the Work

Bus drivers provide transportation for millions of people, from commuters to school children to vacationers. There are two major kinds of bus drivers. *Transit and intercity bus drivers* transport people within or across States, along routes run within a metropolitan area or county, or on chartered excursions and tours. *School bus drivers* take children to and from schools and school-related activities.

Bus drivers pick up and drop off passengers at bus stops, stations, or—in the case of students—at regularly scheduled neighborhood locations and school, all according to strict time schedules. Drivers must operate vehicles safely, sometimes in heavy traffic. They also cannot let light traffic put them ahead of schedule so that they miss passengers. Bus drivers drive a range of vehicles from 15-passenger buses to 60-foot articulated buses that can carry more than 100 passengers.

Transit and intercity bus drivers can be further divided into those who work for local transportation agencies, those who drive on regularly scheduled intercity routes, and those who op-

Bus drivers must be alert, especially in heavy traffic or in bad weather, to prevent accidents.

erate motor coaches. Both transit and regularly scheduled intercity service drivers begin a day's work at their garage or bus terminal. There, they may stock up on tickets or transfers and prepare trip reports before starting their first scheduled routes. In some transportation firms, maintenance departments are responsible for keeping vehicles in good condition; in others, drivers check their vehicles' tires, brakes, windshield wipers, lights, oil, fuel, and water supplies before beginning their routes. Drivers usually verify that buses have proper safety equipment, such as fire extinguishers, first aid kits, and emergency reflectors.

Local transit and intercity bus drivers collect fares; answer questions about schedules, routes, and transfer points; and sometimes announce stops. Intercity bus drivers may make only one to two stops between distant cities, or they may stop at towns just a few miles apart. Local transit bus drivers usually cover several routes each day over the same city and suburban streets, stopping as frequently as every few blocks or whenever passengers request stops.

Local transit bus drivers submit daily trip reports with a record of trips, significant schedule delays, and mechanical problems. Intercity drivers who drive across State or national boundaries must comply with U.S. Department of Transportation reporting regulations, including vehicle inspection reports, distances traveled and the time they spend driving.

Motor coach operators transport passengers on chartered trips and sightseeing tours. Whereas other bus drivers make predetermined stops on a schedule, these drivers work at the convenience of the groups they transport. Drivers routinely interact with customers and tour guides to make the trip as comfortable and informative as possible. They are directly responsible for making sure tours stay on-time and ensuring the overall success of each trip. These drivers act as customer service representatives, tour guides, program directors, and safety guides. Trips frequently last more than a day, so coach operators may spend extended periods away from home.

School bus drivers usually drive the same routes each day, stopping to pick up pupils in the morning and returning them to their homes in the afternoon. Some school bus drivers also transport students and teachers on field trips or to sporting events. In addition to driving, some school bus drivers work part time in the school system as janitors, mechanics, or classroom assistants, when not driving buses.

Bus drivers must be alert, especially in heavy traffic or in bad weather to prevent accidents, and to avoid sudden stops or swerves that jar passengers. School bus drivers must exercise particular caution when children are getting on or off the bus. They must maintain order on their bus and enforce school safety standards by allowing only students to board. In addition, they must know and enforce the school system's rules regarding student conduct. As the number of students with physical or behavioral disabilities increases, school bus drivers must learn how to accommodate their special needs.

Some school bus drivers can take their bus home or park it in a more convenient area, rather than reporting to an assigned terminal or garage. School bus drivers do not collect fares. Instead, they prepare weekly reports on the number of students, trips or "runs," work hours, miles, and fuel consumption. Their supervisors set time schedules and routes for the day or week.

Work environment. Driving a bus through heavy traffic while dealing with passengers is more stressful and fatiguing than physically strenuous. Many drivers enjoy the opportunity to work without direct supervision, with full responsibility for their bus and passengers. To improve working conditions and retain drivers, many bus lines provide ergonomically designed seats and controls for drivers.

Transit and intercity bus drivers are often at high risk, mainly because they work alone and some passengers may be dangerous. Data from the U.S. Bureau of Labor Statistics show that transit and intercity bus drivers experienced a work-related injury and illness rate that was higher than the national average. School bus drivers, in contrast, have an average rate of non-fatal occupational injuries similar to all other occupations.

About 35 percent of all bus drivers worked part time in 2008. School bus drivers work only when schools are in session. Some work 20 hours a week or less, driving one or two routes in the morning and afternoon. Drivers taking field or athletic trips, or who also have midday kindergarten routes, may work more hours a week.

Regular local transit and intercity bus drivers usually have a 5 or 6 day workweek. They may have to work one or both weekend days on a regular basis. Some drivers work in the early morning, in the evening, or after midnight. To accommodate commuters, many work "split shifts"—for example, 6 a.m. to 10 a.m. and 3 p.m. to 7 p.m., with time off in between. Depending on the length of their routes, intercity bus drivers may spend one or more nights away from home at a time. Others may make a round-trip (or several round-trips) during a single day and come home at the end of each shift.

Motor coach operators may work any day and all hours of the day, including weekends and holidays. Their hours are dictated by the destinations, schedules, and itineraries of chartered tours. Like all commercial drivers, their weekly hours must be consistent with the Department of Transportation's rules and regulations concerning hours of service and they are required to document their time in a logbook.

Training, Other Qualifications, and Advancement

State and Federal governments establish bus driver qualifications and standards, which include a commercial driver's license (CDL) with the proper endorsements. Many employers provide several weeks of training and help new employees obtain their CDL.

Education and training. Some employers prefer high school graduates and require a written test of ability to follow complex bus schedules, but the ability to drive and a clean license are usually more important.

Most companies give driver trainees 2 to 8 weeks of classroom and behind-the-wheel instruction. In the classroom, trainees learn Department of Transportation and company work rules, safety regulations, State and municipal driving regulations, and safe driving practices. They also learn to read schedules, determine fares, keep records, and deal courteously with passengers.

During training, all bus drivers practice driving on set courses. They practice turns and zigzag maneuvers, backing up, and driving in narrow lanes. Then, they drive in light traffic and, eventually, on congested highways and city streets. They also make trial runs without passengers to improve their driving skills and learn the routes. Local transit trainees memorize and drive each of the runs operating out of their assigned garage. New drivers make regularly scheduled trips with passengers, accompanied by an experienced driver who gives helpful tips, answers questions, and evaluates the new driver's performance. Most bus drivers get brief supplemental training periodically to stay informed of safety issues and regulatory changes.

Licensure. All bus drivers must obtain commercial driver's licenses (CDL) with the proper endorsements. Qualifications and standards for drivers are established by State and Federal regulations. Bus drivers are responsible for complying with regulations within their own States, as well as those of other States (or countries) where they operate.

To qualify for a commercial driver's license, applicants must pass a knowledge test on rules and regulations and then demonstrate in a skills test that they can operate a bus safely. The Department of Transportation keeps a national database of all driving violations incurred by CDL holders, and a State may not issue a license to a person who has already had a license suspended or revoked in another State. Drivers may only hold one license at a time, and must surrender all other driver's licenses upon receiving their new CDLs.

Bus drivers must also have passenger endorsements for their licenses. Transit, intercity, and motor coach operators must have a passenger vehicle (P) endorsement, while school bus drivers must have both a passenger (P) and a school bus (S) endorsement. Both of these endorsements require a passing score on knowledge and skills tests administered by the State licensing agency or partner institution. The knowledge test is a written exam that covers laws of the road, whereas the skills test is administered by a certified examiner in the appropriate commercial vehicle. Information on how to apply for a commercial driver's license and each type of endorsement can be obtained from State motor vehicle administrations and the Federal Motor Carrier Safety Administration.

Although many States allow those who are 18 years of age and older to drive buses within State borders, the U.S. Department of Transportation establishes minimum qualifications for bus drivers engaged in interstate commerce. Federal Motor Carrier Safety Regulations require drivers to be at least 21 years old and to pass a physical examination once every 2 years. All drivers also must be able to read and speak English well enough to read road signs, prepare reports, and communicate with law enforcement officers and the public.

The main physical requirements include good hearing, at least 20/40 vision with or without glasses or corrective lenses, and a 70-degree field of vision in each eye. Drivers must also be able to distinguish the colors on a traffic light and hear a forced whisper in one ear at not less than 5 feet (with a hearing aid, if necessary). Drivers must have normal blood pressure and normal use of their arms and legs. They may not use any controlled substances, unless prescribed by a licensed physician.

People with epilepsy or with diabetes controlled by insulin are not permitted to be interstate bus drivers.

Federal regulations also require employers to test their drivers for alcohol and drug use as a condition of employment and require periodic random tests of the drivers while they are on duty. In addition, a driver must not have been convicted of a felony involving the use of a motor vehicle or a crime involving drugs, driving under the influence of drugs or alcohol, refusing to submit to an alcohol test required by a State or its implied consent laws or regulations, leaving the scene of a crime, or causing a fatality through negligent operation of a commercial vehicle.

Other qualifications. Many employers prefer applicants who are at least 24 years old. Because bus drivers deal with passengers, they must be courteous. They need an even temperament and emotional stability because driving in heavy, fast-moving, or stop-and-go traffic and dealing with passengers can be stressful. Drivers must have strong customer service skills, including communication skills and the ability to coordinate and manage large groups of people. In some States, school bus drivers must pass a background investigation to uncover any criminal record or history of mental problems.

Advancement. New intercity and local transit drivers usually are placed on an "extra" list to drive chartered runs, extra buses on regular runs, and special runs, such as those during morning and evening rush hours and to sports events. New drivers also substitute for regular drivers who are ill or on vacation. New drivers remain on the extra list and may work only part time, perhaps for several years, until they have enough seniority to get a regular run.

Senior drivers may bid for the runs that they prefer, such as those with more work hours, lighter traffic, weekends off, or— in the case of intercity bus drivers—higher earnings or fewer workdays per week.

Opportunities for promotion are generally limited, but experienced drivers may become supervisors or dispatchers. In transit agencies with rail systems, drivers may become train operators or station attendants. Some bus drivers become either instructors of new bus drivers or master-instructors, who train new instructors. Few drivers become managers. Promotion in publicly owned bus systems is often determined by competitive civil service examination. Some motor coach drivers purchase their own equipment and open their own business.

Employment

Bus drivers held about 647,500 jobs in 2008. Around 70 percent of all bus drivers were school bus drivers working primarily for school systems or for companies providing school bus services under contract. Most of the remainder worked for private and local government transit systems; some also worked for intercity and charter bus lines.

Job Outlook

Bus drivers should expect average job growth and good employment opportunities. Those seeking higher paying public transit bus driver positions may encounter competition. Individuals who have clean driving records and who are willing to work part-time or irregular schedules will have the best job prospects.

Employment change. Overall employment of bus drivers is expected to grow by 7 percent between 2008 and 2018, which is about as fast as the average for all occupations. This growth will be spread among the various occupational specialties.

Employment growth for local transit and intercity bus drivers is projected to be 8 percent over the 2008-18 decade, about as fast as the average for all occupations, mainly as a result of a changing attitude toward public transit in the U.S. High gas prices in recent years have convinced many people to use public transportation. At the same time, public transportation is seen as an environmentally friendly alternative to driving. As a result, many State and local governments have increased funding for public transportation. This trend is expected to continue, and will lead to incrementally higher employment of transit bus drivers over the course of the projections decade. At the same time, however, inexpensive airline tickets and competition from train services will limit the growth of intercity bus travel.

Employment of school bus drivers is expected to grow by 6 percent over the 2008-18 decade, which is slower than the average for all occupations. The growth that does occur will be in response to an increase in the number of school-age children in the U.S. While enrollment continues to increase, however, growth will be tempered by budget cuts by local school districts, which has led to service reductions and greater emphasis on route efficiency.

Job prospects. People seeking jobs as bus drivers likely will have good opportunities. New jobs will be created, but most job openings are expected because of the need to replace workers who take jobs in other occupations or retire. School bus driving jobs, particularly in rapidly growing suburban areas, should be plentiful because most are part-time positions with high turnover. Those seeking higher paying public transit bus driver positions may encounter competition.

Individuals who have clean driving records and who are willing to work a part-time or irregular schedule probably will have the best job prospects. Opportunities for intercity driving positions should be good, although employment prospects for motor coach drivers will depend on tourism, which fluctuates with the economy.

Projections data from the National Employment Matrix

Occupational Title	SOC Code	Employment, 2008	Projected Employment, 2018	Change, 2008-2018	
				Number	Percent
Bus drivers	53-3020	647,500	691,400	43,900	7
Bus drivers, transit and intercity	53-3021	193,900	209,900	16,000	8
Bus drivers, school..................	53-3022	453,600	481,500	27,900	6

(NOTE) Data in this table are rounded. See the discussion of the employment projections table in the *Handbook* introductory chapter on *Occupational Information Included in the Handbook.*

Full-time bus drivers rarely are laid off during recessions, but competition for jobs increases significantly during periods of high unemployment. The majority of workers in this occupation are employed by local governments and schools. The number of students who need transportation to school does not change during times of economic distress, and mass transit ridership often goes up. However, during recessions, when workers in other industries lose their jobs, many try to become bus drivers, as it is a relatively high-paying job given that it requires so little training. As a result, people who want to become bus drivers during such times may face keen competition for jobs. In contrast, during times when unemployment is low, employers may have difficulty attracting enough people to this occupation.

Earnings

Median hourly wages for wage-and-salary transit and intercity bus drivers were $16.32 in May 2008. The middle 50 percent earned between $12.44 and $21.58 per hour. The lowest 10 percent earned less than $9.82, and the highest 10 percent earned more than $26.74 per hour.

Median hourly wages of wage-and-salary school bus drivers were $12.79 in May 2008. The middle 50 percent earned between $9.61 and $15.78 per hour. The lowest 10 percent earned less than $7.38, and the highest 10 percent earned more than $19.11 per hour.

Bus drivers generally receive good benefits from their employers. Most intercity and local transit bus drivers receive paid health and life insurance, sick leave, vacation leave, and free bus rides on any of the regular routes of their line or system. School bus drivers receive sick leave, and many are covered by health and life insurance and pension plans. Because they generally do not work when school is not in session, they do not get vacation leave.

About 38 percent of bus drivers were members of unions or were covered by union contracts in 2008. Many intercity and local transit bus drivers are members of the Amalgamated Transit Union or Transport Workers Union of America.

Related Occupations

Other occupations that involve driving a vehicle include:

Sources of Additional Information

For information on employment opportunities, contact local transit systems, intercity bus lines, school systems, or the local offices of the State employment service.

Information on Federal regulations for drivers of commercial vehicles can be obtained from:
➤ Federal Motor Carrier Safety Administration, 1200 New Jersey Ave. SE., Washington, DC 20590. Internet: **http://www.fmcsa.dot.gov**

Information on school bus driving is available from:
➤ National Association of State Directors of Pupil Transportation Services, P.O. Box 5446, Steamboat Springs, CO 80477. Internet: **http://www.nasdpts.org**

➤ National School Transportation Association, 113 South West St., 4th Floor, Alexandria, VA 22314. Internet: **http://www.yellowbuses.org**

Information on public transit bus driving is available from:
➤ American Public Transportation Association, 1666 K St. NW., Washington DC 20006. Internet: **http://www.apta.com**

General information on motor coach driving is available from:
➤ United Motorcoach Association, 113 South West St., 4th Floor, Alexandria, VA 22314. Internet: **http://www.uma.org**

The Occupational Information Network (O*NET) provides information on a wide range of occupational characteristics. Links to O*NET appear at the end of the Internet version of this occupational statement, accessible at **http://www.bls.gov/ooh/ocos242.htm**

Taxi Drivers and Chauffeurs

Significant Points

- Taxi drivers and chauffeurs may work any schedule, including full time, part time, night, evening, weekend, and on a seasonal basis.

- Very few drivers are paid an hourly wage; most rent their vehicles from a cab fleet, although many own their vehicles.

- Local taxi commissions set licensing standards for driving experience and training.

- Job opportunities should be plentiful.

Nature of the Work

Taxi and limousine services make it easy for customers to get around when driving their own cars or using public transportation is inconvenient. *Taxi drivers* and *chauffeurs* take passengers to and from their homes, workplaces, and recreational pursuits, such as dining, entertainment, and shopping, and to and from business-related events. These professional drivers help both residents and out-of-town guests get around a city or urban area. In addition to regular point-to-point services, some drivers offer sight-seeing services around their cities.

Drivers must be alert to conditions on the road, especially in heavy and congested traffic or in bad weather. They must take precautions to prevent accidents and avoid sudden stops, turns, and other driving maneuvers that would jar passengers.

The majority of people in this occupation work as taxi drivers. Typically, taxi drivers own their vehicles or rent them from a company called a fleet. Drivers who rent their vehicles usually report to a garage where they are assigned a vehicle, most frequently a large, conventional automobile modified for commercial passenger transport. Drivers check their cabs' fuel and oil levels and make sure that the lights, brakes, and windshield wipers are in good working order. If anything is not working properly, the driver who discovers the problem reports it to a dispatcher or company mechanic. Some drivers own their own cabs. Generally, they park at their homes overnight, so they simply drive to their first pickup when they start working. Like other car owners, they are responsible for their own insurance, maintenance, and for making sure that the car is in good working order.

Taxi drivers usually find fares in one of three ways. Most commonly, they work with dispatch services, which allow customers to call in a request for a cab. Dispatchers relay the information to drivers by two-way radio, cellular telephone, or onboard computer. This is the most common method in smaller cities, late at night, or in low-traffic areas. Drivers may also pick up passengers waiting at cabstands or in taxi lines at airports, train stations, hotels, restaurants, and other places where people frequently seek taxis. In major cities, drivers "cruise" the streets looking for fares, although this is not legal in all jurisdictions.

Good drivers are familiar with streets in the areas they serve so they can choose the most efficient route to destinations and avoid traffic. They know the locations of frequently requested destinations, such as airports, bus and railroad terminals, convention centers, hotels, and other points of interest. In case of emergency, drivers should know the location of fire and police stations, as well as hospitals.

Upon arrival at the final destination, the driver determines the fare and announces it to the passenger. Each jurisdiction has its own regulations that set the structure of the fare system covering licensed taxis. In most areas, a taximeter measures the fare based on the distance covered and the amount of time spent in traffic. Drivers start their meters when passengers enter the cab and turn them off when they reach their final destinations. The fare may also include surcharges, such as base fares, dispatcher fees, or fees for additional passengers, tolls, luggage, or other services. Passengers usually add a tip or gratuity to the fare. The amount of the gratuity depends, in part, on the passengers' satisfaction with the quality and efficiency of the ride and the courtesy of the driver. Drivers issue receipts upon request. They may also fill out logs for use by their fleets.

Chauffeurs operate limousines, vans, and private cars. They may work for hire, as taxicabs do; or they may work for private businesses, government agencies, or wealthy individuals. Chauffeur services differ from taxi services in that all trips are prearranged. Many chauffeurs transport customers in large vans between hotels and airports, bus terminals, or train stations. Others drive luxury automobiles, such as private cars or limousines.

At the beginning of each workday, chauffeurs prepare their automobiles or vans for use. They inspect their vehicles for cleanliness and, when needed, clean the interior and wash the exterior body, windows, and mirrors. They check fuel and oil levels and make sure the lights, tires, brakes, and windshield wipers work. Chauffeurs may perform routine maintenance and make minor repairs, such as changing tires or adding oil and other fluids. If a vehicle requires a more complicated repair, they take it to a professional mechanic.

Chauffeurs cater to passengers by providing attentive customer service and paying attention to detail. They help riders into the car by holding open doors, holding umbrellas when it is raining, and loading packages and luggage into the trunk of the car. Chauffeurs may perform errands for their employers such as delivering packages or picking up clients arriving at airports. To ensure a pleasurable ride in their limousines, many chauffeurs offer conveniences and luxuries such as newspapers, magazines, music, drinks, televisions, and telephones. Increasingly, chauffeurs work as full-service executive assistants, simultaneously acting as driver, secretary, and itinerary planner.

Some drivers transport individuals with special needs, such as those with disabilities and the elderly. These drivers, known as *paratransit drivers*, operate specially equipped vehicles designed to accommodate a variety of needs in non-emergency situations. Although special certification is not necessary, some additional training on the equipment and passenger needs may be required.

Work environment. Driving for long periods can be tiring and stressful, especially in densely populated urban areas. Being seated in the same position for most of the day can also be very uncomfortable. Taxi drivers and chauffeurs often have to load and unload heavy luggage and packages. They are also at high risk for robbery, because they work alone and often carry large amounts of cash. Data from the U.S. Bureau of Labor Statistics show that taxi drivers and chauffeurs experienced a work-related injury and illness rate that was much higher than the national average.

Work hours of taxi drivers and chauffeurs vary greatly. Some jobs offer full-time or part-time employment with work hours that can change from day to day or remain the same. It is often necessary for drivers to report to work on short notice. Chauffeurs who work for a single employer may be on call much of the time. Evening and weekend work is common for drivers and chauffeurs employed by limousine and taxicab services.

Whereas the needs of the client or employer dictate the work schedule for chauffeurs, the work of taxi drivers is much less structured. Working free of supervision, they may break for a meal or a rest whenever their vehicle is unoccupied. Many taxi drivers like the independent, unsupervised work of driving.

This occupation is attractive to individuals, such as college and postgraduate students, seeking flexible work schedules and to anyone seeking a second source of income. Other service workers, such as ambulance drivers and police officers, sometimes moonlight as taxi drivers or chauffeurs.

Full-time taxi drivers usually work one shift a day, which may last 8 to 12 hours. Part-time drivers may work half a shift

Job opportunities for taxi drivers and chauffeurs should be plentiful.

Projections data from the National Employment Matrix

Occupational Title	SOC Code	Employment, 2008	Projected Employment, 2018	Change, 2008-2018	
				Number	Percent
Taxi drivers and chauffeurs	53-3041	232,300	268,400	36,100	16

(NOTE) Data in this table are rounded. See the discussion of the employment projections table in the *Handbook* introductory chapter on *Occupational Information Included in the Handbook.*

each day, or work a full shift once or twice a week. Drivers may work shifts at all times of the day and night, because most taxi companies offer services 24 hours a day. Early morning and late night shifts are not uncommon. Drivers work long hours during holidays, weekends, and other special times when demand for their services is heavier. Independent drivers set their own hours and schedules.

Training, Other Qualifications, and Advancement

Local governments set licensing standards and requirements for taxi drivers and chauffeurs, which may include minimum amounts of driving experience and training.

Education and training. Little formal education is needed for taxi drivers or chauffeurs, but many have at least a high school diploma, GED, or its equivalent. Drivers need to be able to communicate effectively, read maps, and use basic math. A basic understanding of auto mechanics can also be very useful.

Most taxi and limousine companies give new drivers on-the-job training. This training generally only lasts about a week or two, and is required by law in some jurisdictions. Companies show drivers how to operate the taximeter and communications equipment and how to complete paperwork. Other topics covered include driver safety, customer service, and the best routes to popular sightseeing and entertainment destinations.

Many companies have contracts with social service agencies and transportation services to transport elderly and disabled citizens in non-emergency situations. To support these services, new drivers may get special training in how to handle wheelchair lifts and other mechanical devices.

Licensure. Taxicab or limousine drivers must first have a regular automobile driver's license. In many States, applicants must get a taxi driver or chauffeur's license, commonly called a "hack" license. The Federal Motor Carrier Safety Administration requires a commercial driver's license (CDL) with a passenger (P) endorsement for drivers transporting 16 or more passengers (including the driver). While this is not a concern for taxi drivers, some stretch limousines and other such vehicles may be large enough to require a CDL.

While States set licensing requirements, local regulatory bodies set other terms and conditions. Most cities and urban areas have taxi commissions. These commissions set requirements for drivers, license vehicles to be used as cabs, and even set the rates that drivers are allowed to charge. In many cases, these regulations do not affect chauffeurs.

In most areas, taxis must have medallions that certify them as legally recognized cabs. Passengers generally prefer cars with medallions, as they are guaranteed to be law-abiding by local commissions. Drivers who receive too many complaints can lose their medallions, which discourages unethical behavior.

Regulations can vary greatly among localities. Some areas require new drivers to enroll in up to 80 hours of classroom

instruction, to take an exam, or both before they are allowed to work. Some localities require an English proficiency test, usually in the form of listening comprehension; applicants who do not pass the English exam must take an English course, in addition to any formal driving programs.

Other qualifications. Taxi drivers and chauffeurs work almost exclusively with the public, and should be able to get along with many different types of people. They must be patient when waiting for passengers and when dealing with rude customers. It also is helpful for drivers to be tolerant and level-headed when driving in heavy and congested traffic. Drivers should be dependable, since passengers expect to be picked up at a prearranged time and taken to the correct destinations. Drivers must be responsible and self-motivated, because they work with little supervision. Increasingly, companies encourage drivers to develop loyal customers to improve their business.

Many municipalities and taxicab and chauffeur companies require drivers to have a neat appearance. Many chauffeurs wear formal attire, such as tuxedos, suits, dresses, or uniforms.

Advancement. Taxi drivers and chauffeurs have limited advancement opportunities. Experienced drivers may obtain preferred routes or shifts. Some advance to become lead drivers, who help to train new drivers. Others take dispatching and managerial positions. Some drivers become managers at taxi or limousine fleets. Some people start their own taxi or limousine companies.

In many communities, drivers can purchase their own taxis or limousines and go into business for themselves. Independent owner-drivers need an additional permit allowing them to operate as a business. Some big cities limit the number of operating permits, which keeps many owner-drivers out of the market. In these cities, drivers become owner-drivers by buying or renting permits from owner-drivers who leave the business. Although many owner-drivers are successful, some fail to cover expenses and eventually lose their permits and automobiles. Individuals starting their own taxi companies face many obstacles because of the difficulty in running a small fleet. The lack of dispatch and maintenance facilities often is hard for an owner to overcome. Chauffeurs often have a good deal of success as owner-drivers and many companies begin as individually owned and operated businesses.

For both taxi and limousine service owners, good business sense and courses in accounting, business, and business arithmetic can help an owner-driver be successful. Knowledge of mechanics enables owner-drivers to perform their own routine maintenance and minor repairs to cut expenses.

Employment

Taxi drivers and chauffeurs held about 232,300 jobs in 2008. About 26 percent of taxi drivers and chauffeurs were self-employed. Jobs were located throughout the country, but were concentrated in large cities. Metropolitan areas with the largest employment of taxi drivers and chauffeurs in May 2008 were:

New York-Northern New Jersey-Long Island,
   NY-NJ-PA...16,360
Las Vegas-Paradise, NV 10,160
Los Angeles-Long Beach-Santa Ana, CA 7,510
Chicago-Naperville-Joliet, IL-IN-WI 5,300
Boston-Cambridge-Quincy, MA-NH............................5,040

Job Outlook

Employment of taxi drivers and chauffeurs is expected to grow faster than the average for all occupations. Job opportunities should be plentiful. Applicants with good driving records, good customer service instincts, and the ability to work flexible schedules should have the best prospects.

Employment change. Employment of taxi drivers and chauffeurs is expected to grow 16 percent during the 2008–18 projection period, faster than the average for all occupations. Drivers should see increased business as a result of growth in tourism and business travel. Also, as the number of elderly people increases, taxis will be needed to take them around town. Some growth will stem from Federal legislation requiring increased services for people with disabilities.

Because the demand for taxi and limousine services is very sensitive to economic cycles, drivers may see declining demand for their services during economic downturns. This is especially true for chauffeurs, as expensive limousine services are considered a luxury. Chauffeurs who work for private companies or individuals may face layoffs or reduced hours during times of economic distress.

Job prospects. Opportunities for taxi drivers and chauffeurs are expected to be plentiful, because of the need to replace the many people who work in this occupation for short periods and then leave. Also, the occupation has very low barriers to entry. Because most drivers are paid strictly based on fares, companies take on very little risk when they hire a new driver. Applicants who have clean driving records and who are willing to work flexible schedules should have the best prospects. People who are easy going and make their passengers comfortable will be most likely to succeed, as a significant part of drivers' salaries come from the tips they receive.

Opportunities fluctuate significantly with the overall movements of the economy, because the demand for transportation depends on business travel and tourism. Because most drivers own or rent their vehicles, taxi drivers are seldom laid off, but they may have to increase their work hours, and earnings may decline. When the economy is strong, many drivers transfer to other occupations, which often leads to fewer cabs on the road. Extra drivers may be hired during holiday seasons, as well as during peak travel and tourist times.

Rapidly growing metropolitan areas and cities experiencing economic growth should offer the best job opportunities.

Earnings

Earnings of taxi drivers and chauffeurs vary greatly, depending on factors such as the number of hours worked, regulatory conditions, customer tips, and geographic location. Hybrid vehicles, which have improved gas mileage, offer taxi drivers better earnings, because drivers pay for their gas out of pocket. Median annual wages of wage and salary taxi drivers and chauffeurs, including tips, were $21,550 in May 2008. The middle 50 percent earned between $17,770 and $26,800. The lowest 10 percent earned less than $15,620, and the highest 10 percent earned more than $34,210.

Many taxi drivers pay a daily, weekly, or monthly fee to the company allowing them to lease their vehicles and depend on fares for their livelihood. The fee also may include charges for vehicle maintenance, insurance, and a deposit on the vehicle. This occupation includes many self-employed drivers. BLS does not have data on earnings for self-employed taxi and limousine drivers.

Most taxi drivers and chauffeurs do not receive benefits. Drivers may wish to purchase private health insurance.

Related Occupations

Other workers who have similar jobs include:

	Page
Bus drivers	791
Truck drivers and driver/sales workers	797

Sources of Additional Information

Information on necessary permits and the registration of taxi drivers and chauffeurs is available from local taxi commissions. Questions regarding licensing should be directed to your State motor vehicle administration. For information about work opportunities as a taxi driver or chauffeur, contact local taxi or limousine companies or State employment service offices in your area.

For general information about the work of taxi drivers, chauffeurs, and paratransit drivers, contact:

➤ Taxicab, Limousine and Paratransit Association, 3200 Tower Oaks Blvd., Suite 220, Rockville, MD 20852. Internet: **http://www.tlpa.org**

For general information about the work of limousine drivers, contact:

➤ National Limousine Association, 49 South Maple Ave., Marlton, NJ 08053. Internet: **http://www.limo.org**

The Occupational Information Network (O*NET) provides information on a wide range of occupational characteristics. Links to O*NET appear at the end of the Internet version of this occupational statement, accessible at **http://www.bls.gov/ooh/ocos245.htm**

Truck Drivers and Driver/Sales Workers

Significant Points

- Truck drivers and driver/sales workers comprise one of the largest occupations, holding 3.2 million jobs.

- Overall job opportunities should be favorable, especially for long-haul drivers.

- A commercial driver's license is the most important qualification for most jobs.

Nature of the Work

Almost every product sold in the United States spends at least some time in a truck. While planes, trains, and ships are also used to transport goods, no other form of transportation has the same level of flexibility as a truck. As a result, trucks are used to transport everything from canned food to automobiles. *Truck drivers* and *driver/sales workers* operate these vehicles.

Drivers are responsible for picking up and delivering freight from one place to another. This may be from a manufacturer to a distribution center, from a distribution center to a customer, or between distribution centers. In addition, drivers may be responsible for loading and unloading their cargo. They are also responsible for following applicable laws, keeping logs of their activities, and making sure that their equipment is in good working condition.

Heavy truck and tractor-trailer drivers operate trucks or vans with a capacity of at least 26,001 pounds gross vehicle weight (GVW). The vast majority of these are *over-the-road* or *long-haul drivers*, meaning they deliver goods over intercity routes that may span several States. Some drivers have regular routes or regions where they drive the most, while others take on routes throughout the country or even to Canada and Mexico.

Long-haul drivers are often responsible for planning their own routes. In most cases, operators are given a delivery location and deadline, and they must determine how to get the shipment to its destination on time. This can be difficult, as drivers must find routes that allow large trucks, and must work within the rules imposed by the U.S. Department of Transportation. Drivers must fill out logs to show that they have followed these rules, which mandate maximum driving times and rest periods between shifts. Companies sometimes use two drivers on long runs to minimize downtime. On these "sleeper" runs, one driver sleeps in a berth behind the cab while the other operates the truck.

Light or *delivery services truck drivers*, often called *pick-up and delivery* or *P&D drivers* deliver goods within an urban area or small region. In most cases, they carry shipments from distribution centers to businesses or households. Drivers who work for package delivery services may have a single load and make many stops over the course of the day, while other drivers might have several loads in the course of a day. Depending on the load, drivers may have helpers who load and unload their vehicles. When making deliveries, they may accept payments for cash-on-delivery shipments, or handle paperwork, such as delivery confirmations and receipts.

Specialized truck drivers work with unusual loads. While most trucks carry freight loads in semi-trailers or vans, some carry liquids, oversized loads, or cars. Others carry hazardous materials, such as dangerous chemicals needed for industrial purposes, or waste from chemical processes that must be stored in approved facilities. Drivers who work with these types of loads must follow strict procedures to make sure their loads are delivered safely.

Some drivers, called *driver/sales workers* or *route drivers*, have sales responsibilities. For example, many driver/sales workers deliver and arrange goods to be sold in grocery stores. They may recommend that a store increase their inventory or encourage store managers to sell new products. Companies that

Heavy truck and tractor-trailer drivers are often responsible for planning their own routes to their shipment destinations.

rent linens, towels, or uniforms employ driver/sales workers to visit businesses regularly to replace soiled laundry. Driver/sales workers may also be responsible for soliciting new customers along their routes.

Work environment. Despite new technologies such as power steering, driving a truck is still a physically demanding job. Driving for many hours at a stretch, loading and unloading cargo, and making many deliveries can be tiring. Making the decision to work as a long-haul driver is a major lifestyle choice—drivers may be away from home for days or weeks at a time, and they often spend a great deal of time alone. Local truck drivers usually return home in the evening.

The U.S. Department of Transportation regulates work hours and other working conditions of truck drivers engaged in interstate commerce. A long-distance driver may drive for no more than 11 hours per day, and work a total of no more than 14 hours—including driving and non-driving duties. Between working periods, a driver must have at least 10 hours off duty. Drivers also cannot work more than 60 hours in a week without being off-duty for at least 34 hours straight. Drivers are required to document their time in a log, which shows working hours and mileage by day. Many drivers, particularly on long runs, work close to the maximum time permitted because they are usually compensated according to the number of miles they drive. Drivers on long runs face boredom, loneliness, and fatigue. Drivers often travel nights, holidays, and weekends.

Local truck drivers frequently work 50 or more hours a week. Drivers who handle food for chain grocery stores, produce markets, or bakeries typically work long hours—often late at night or early in the morning. Most drivers have regular routes, although some have different routes each day. Many local truck drivers—particularly driver/sales workers—do a considerable amount of lifting, carrying, and walking.

Training, Other Qualifications, and Advancement

Drivers who operate trucks with a gross vehicle weight of 26,001 pounds, or who operate a vehicle carrying hazardous materials or oversized loads, need a commercial driver's license (CDL). Training for the CDL is offered by many private and public vocational-technical schools. A standard driver's license is required to drive all other trucks. Many jobs driving smaller trucks require only brief on-the-job training.

Education and training. Most prospective truck drivers take driver-training courses at a technical or vocational school to prepare for CDL testing. Driver-training courses teach students how to maneuver large vehicles on crowded streets and in highway traffic. These courses also train drivers how to properly inspect trucks and freight for compliance with regulations.

Some States require prospective drivers to complete a training course in basic truck driving before getting their CDL. Some companies have similar requirements. People interested in attending a driving school should check with local trucking companies to make sure the school's training is acceptable. The Professional Truck Driver Institute (PTDI) certifies driver-training courses at truck driver training schools that meet industry standards and Federal Highway Administration guidelines for training tractor-trailer drivers.

Employers usually have training programs for new drivers who have already earned their CDL. This is often informal and may consist of only a few hours of instruction from an experienced driver. Some companies give 1 to 2 days of classroom instruction covering general duties, the operation and loading of a truck, company policies, and the preparation of delivery forms and company records. New drivers may also ride with and observe experienced drivers before getting their own assignments. Drivers receive additional training to drive special types of trucks or handle hazardous materials. Driver/sales workers receive training on the various types of products their company carries so that they can effectively answer questions about the products and more easily market them to their customers.

Licensure. Federal and State regulations govern the qualifications and standards for truck drivers. Drivers must comply with all Federal regulations and any State regulations that are in excess of those Federal requirements when under that State's jurisdiction.

Truck drivers must have a driver's license issued by the State in which they live. Drivers of trucks with a GVW of 26,001 pounds or more—including most tractor-trailers, as well as bigger straight trucks—must obtain a CDL. All drivers who operate trucks transporting hazardous materials or oversized loads must obtain a CDL and a special endorsement, regardless of truck capacity. In order to receive the hazardous materials endorsement, a driver must be fingerprinted and submit to a criminal background check by the Transportation Security Administration. In many States, a regular driver's license is sufficient for driving light trucks and vans.

To qualify for a CDL, applicants must have clean driving records, pass written tests on rules and regulations, and demonstrate that they can operate commercial trucks safely. A national database permanently records all driving violations committed by those with a CDL, and issuing authorities reject applicants who have suspended or revoked licenses in other States. Licensed drivers must accompany trainees until they get their own CDLs. A person may not hold more than one driver's license at a time and must surrender any other licenses when issued a CDL. Information on how to apply for a CDL may be obtained from State motor vehicle administrations.

Although many States allow 18 year-olds to drive trucks within their borders, a driver must be at least 21 years of age to cross State lines or get special endorsements. Regulations also require drivers to pass a physical examination every 2 years. Physical qualifications include good hearing, at least 20/40 vision with glasses or corrective lenses, and a 70-degree field of vision in each eye. They must also be able to distinguish between colors on traffic lights. Drivers must also have normal use of arms and legs and normal blood pressure. People with epilepsy or diabetes controlled by insulin are not permitted to be interstate truck drivers.

Other qualifications. Federal regulations require employers to test their drivers for alcohol and drug use as a condition of employment and require periodic random tests of the drivers while they are on duty. Drivers may not use any controlled substances, unless prescribed by a licensed physician. A driver must not have been convicted of a felony involving the use of a motor vehicle or a crime involving drugs, driving under the influence of drugs or alcohol, refusing to submit to an alcohol test required by a State or its implied consent laws or regulations, leaving the scene of a crime, or causing a fatality through negligent operation of a motor vehicle. All drivers must be able to read and speak English well enough to read road signs, prepare reports, and communicate with law enforcement officers and the public.

Many trucking companies have higher standards than those required by Federal and State regulations. For example, firms often require that drivers be at least 22 years old, be able to lift heavy objects, and have driven trucks for 3 to 5 years. They may also prefer to hire high school graduates and require annual physical examinations.

Drivers must get along well with people because they often deal directly with customers. Employers seek driver/sales workers who speak well and have self-confidence, initiative, tact, and a neat appearance. Employers also look for responsible, self-motivated individuals who are able to work well with little supervision.

Advancement. Although most new truck drivers are assigned to regular driving jobs immediately, some start as extra drivers—substituting for regular drivers who are ill or on vacation. Extra drivers receive a regular assignment when an opening occurs.

Truck drivers can advance to jobs that provide higher earnings, preferred schedules, or better working conditions. Long-haul truck drivers primarily look for new contracts that offer better pay per mile or higher bonuses. Because companies entrust drivers with millions of dollars worth of equipment and freight, drivers who have a long record of safe driving earn far more than new drivers. Local truck drivers may advance to driving heavy or specialized trucks or transfer to long-distance truck driving. Truck drivers occasionally advance to become dispatchers or managers.

Some long-haul truck drivers—called owner-operators—purchase or lease trucks and go into business for themselves.

Although some are successful, others fail to cover expenses and go out of business. Owner-operators should have good business sense as well as truck driving experience. Courses in accounting, business, and business mathematics are helpful. Knowledge of truck mechanics can enable owner-operators to perform their own routine maintenance and minor repairs.

Employment

Truck drivers and driver/sales workers held about 3.2 million jobs in 2008. Of these workers, 56 percent were heavy truck and tractor-trailer drivers; 31 percent were light or delivery services truck drivers; and 13 percent were driver/sales workers. Most truck drivers find employment in large metropolitan areas or along major interstate roadways where trucking, retail, and wholesale companies tend to have their distribution outlets. Some drivers work in rural areas, providing specialized services such as delivering newspapers to customers.

The truck transportation industry employed 27 percent of all truck drivers and driver/sales workers in the United States. Another 26 percent worked for companies engaged in wholesale or retail trade. The remaining truck drivers and driver/sales workers were distributed across many industries, including construction and manufacturing.

Around 8 percent of all truck drivers and driver/sales workers were self-employed. Of these, a significant number were owner-operators who either served a variety of businesses independently or leased their services and trucks to a trucking company.

Job Outlook

Overall job opportunities should be favorable for truck drivers, especially for long-haul drivers. However, opportunities may vary greatly in terms of earnings, weekly work hours, number of nights spent on the road, and quality of equipment. Competition is expected for jobs offering the highest earnings or most favorable work schedules. Average employment growth is expected.

Employment change. Overall employment of truck drivers and driver/sales workers is expected to grow 9 percent over the 2008-18 decade, which is about as fast as the average for all occupations. As the economy grows, the demand for goods will increase, which will lead to more job opportunities. Because it is such a large occupation, 291,900 new jobs will be created over the 2008-18 period.

The number of heavy and tractor-trailer truck drivers is expected to grow 13 percent between 2008 and 2018, which is about as fast as average, mainly as a result of increasing demand for goods in the U.S. As the economy continues to grow, companies and households will continue to increase their spending on these products, many of which must be shipped over long distances.

Employment of light or delivery services truck drivers should grow 4 percent over the projections decade, which is more slowly than average. Though experiencing slower growth than heavy trucking, light and delivery trucking will similarly be closely tied to the state of the economy. As economic growth occurs, there will be an increasing need for light trucking services, from the distribution of goods from warehouses to the package delivery to households. The number of driver/sales workers is also expected to grow 4 percent between 2008 and 2018, more slowly than average, for the same basic reasons.

Job prospects. Job opportunities should be favorable for truck drivers, especially for long-haul drivers. In addition to occupational growth, numerous job openings will occur as experienced drivers leave this large occupation to transfer to other fields of work, retire, or leave the labor force. As workers leave these jobs, employers work hard to recruit experienced drivers from other companies. As a result, there may be competition for the jobs with the highest earnings and most favorable work schedules. Jobs with local carriers are often more competitive than those with long-distance carriers because of the more desirable working conditions of local carriers.

Despite projected employment growth, the demand for workers may vary greatly depending on the performance of the American economy. During times of expansion, companies may be forced to pay premiums to attract drivers, while during recessions even experienced drivers may find difficulty keeping steady work. Independent owner-operators will be particularly vulnerable to slowdowns. Industries least likely to be affected by economic fluctuation, such as grocery stores, will be the most stable employers of truck drivers and driver/sales workers.

Earnings

Median hourly wages of heavy truck and tractor-trailer drivers were $17.92 in May 2008. The middle 50 percent earned between $14.21 and $22.56. The lowest 10 percent earned less than $11.63, and the highest 10 percent earned more than $27.07.

Median hourly wages of light or delivery services truck drivers were $13.27 in May 2008. The middle 50 percent earned between $10.07 and $17.74. The lowest 10 percent earned less than $8.10, and the highest 10 percent earned more than $24.15.

Median hourly wages of driver/sales workers, including commissions, were $10.70 in May 2008. The middle 50 percent earned between $7.74 and $15.82. The lowest 10 percent earned less than $7.09, and the highest 10 percent earned more than $21.32.

Projections data from the National Employment Matrix

Occupational Title	SOC Code	Employment, 2008	Projected Employment, 2018	Change, 2008-2018	
				Number	Percent
Driver/sales workers and truck drivers...	53-3030	3,189,300	3,481,200	291,900	9
Driver/sales workers..	53-3031	406,400	424,100	17,700	4
Truck drivers, heavy and tractor-trailer..	53-3032	1,798,400	2,031,300	232,900	13
Truck drivers, light or delivery services.......................................	53-3033	984,500	1,025,900	41,400	4

(NOTE) Data in this table are rounded. See the discussion of the employment projections table in the *Handbook* introductory chapter on *Occupational Information Included in the Handbook.*

Employers typically pay long-haul drivers by the mile, with bonus opportunities available for drivers who save the company money. Local truck drivers tend to be paid by the hour, with extra pay for working overtime. The per-mile rate can vary greatly from employer to employer and may even depend on the type of cargo being hauled. Some long-distance drivers—especially owner-operators—are paid a share of the revenue from shipping. Typically, pay increases with experience, seniority, and the size and type of truck driven. Most driver/sales workers receive commissions based on their sales in addition to their wages.

Many truck drivers are members of the International Brotherhood of Teamsters. Some truck drivers employed by companies outside the trucking industry are members of unions representing the plant workers of the companies for which they work. In 2008, about 16 percent of truck drivers and driver/sales workers were union members or covered by union contracts.

Related Occupations
Other driving occupations include:

Sources of Additional Information
Information on truck driver employment opportunities is available from local trucking companies and local offices of the State employment service.

Information on career opportunities in truck driving may be obtained from:
➤ American Trucking Associations, Inc., 950 North Glebe Rd., Suite 210, Arlington, VA 22203. Internet: **http://www.truckline.com**

Information on becoming a truck driver may be obtained from the American Trucking Associations, Inc. industry recruiting page: **http://www.gettrucking.com**

Information on Federal regulations for drivers of commercial vehicles can be obtained from:
➤ Federal Motor Carrier Safety Administration, 1200 New Jersey Ave. SE, Washington, DC 20590. Internet: **http://www.fmcsa.dot.gov**

A list of certified tractor-trailer driver training courses may be obtained from:
➤ Professional Truck Driver Institute, 555 E. Braddock Rd., Alexandria, VA 22314. Internet: **http://www.ptdi.org**

Information on union truck driving can be obtained from:
➤ The International Brotherhood of Teamsters, 25 Louisiana Ave. NW, Washington, DC 20001. Internet: **http://www.teamster.org**

The Occupational Information Network (O*NET) provides information on a wide range of occupational characteristics. Links to O*NET appear at the end of the Internet version of this occupational statement, accessible at **http://www.bls.gov/ooh/ocos246.htm**

Rail Transportation Occupations

Significant Points
- Opportunities are expected to be good for qualified applicants since a large number of workers are expected to retire or leave these occupations from 2008 to 2018.
- 76 percent of these workers are members of unions, and earnings are relatively high.

Nature of the Work
Rail transportation workers are employed by three types of railroads: freight, passenger, and urban transit (subway and light rail). Freight railroads transport billions of tons of goods to destinations within the United States and to ports to be shipped abroad. Passenger railroads deliver millions of passengers and long-distance commuters to destinations throughout the country. Subways and light-rail systems move passengers within metropolitan areas and their surrounding suburbs. All of these modes of rail transportation require employees to operate, oversee, and assist in rail operations. Rail transportation workers not only work on trains, but also can be found working in rail yards where railcars are inspected, repaired, coupled, and uncoupled.

Locomotive engineers operate large trains carrying cargo or passengers between stations. Most engineers run diesel-electric locomotives, although a few operate locomotives powered by battery or externally supplied electricity. Before each run, engineers check the mechanical condition of their locomotives, making any necessary minor adjustments and documenting issues that require more thorough inspection. While trains are in motion, engineers move controls such as throttles and airbrakes. They also monitor instruments that measure speed, amperage, battery charge, and air pressure, both in the brake lines and in the main reservoir. Engineers must have thorough knowledge of their routes and must be constantly aware of the condition and makeup of their train, because trains react differently to the grade and condition of the rail, the number of cars, the ratio of empty cars to loaded cars, and the amount of slack in the train.

Railroad conductors coordinate all activities of freight or passenger train crews. Conductors assigned to freight trains review schedules, switching orders, waybills, and shipping records to obtain loading and unloading information regarding their cargo.

In addition, they are responsible for the distribution of tonnage in the train and the operation of freight cars within rail yards and terminals that use remote control locomotive technology. Conductors assigned to passenger trains also ensure passenger safety and comfort as they go about collecting tickets and fares, making announcements for the benefit of passengers, and coordinating the activities of the crew.

Before trains leave a terminal, the conductor and the engineer discuss any concerns regarding the train's route, timetable, and cargo. During runs and in rail yards, engineers and conductors interface with traffic-control-center personnel, dispatchers, and personnel on other trains to issue or receive information concerning stops, delays, and the locations of trains. While engineers interpret and comply with orders, signals, speed limits, and railroad rules and regulations, conductors use dispatch or electronic monitoring devices to relay information about equipment problems on the train or the rails. Conductors may arrange for the removal of defective cars from the train for repairs at the nearest station or stop, and discuss alternative routes with the engineer and dispatcher if there is a defect in, or obstruction on, the rails.

Railroad brake operators assist with the coupling and uncoupling of cars and operate some switches. In an effort to reduce costs, most railroads have phased out brake operators, and many trains use only an engineer and a conductor. *Signal operators* install, maintain, and repair the signals on tracks and in yards.

Yardmasters, where present, coordinate the activities of workers engaged in railroad yard operations. These activities, which are also performed by conductors, include making up or breaking up trains and switching inbound or outbound traffic to a specific section of the line. Some cars are sent to unload their cargo on special tracks, while others are moved to different tracks to await assembly into new trains on the basis of their destinations. Yardmasters tell yard engineers or other personnel where to move the cars to fit the planned train configuration. Switches—many of them operated remotely by computer—divert trains or railcars to the proper track for coupling and uncoupling.

Also included in rail transportation occupations are several less prevalent occupations. *Switch operators* control the track switches within a rail yard. In rail yards without remote control technology, *rail yard engineers* operate engines within the rail yard. Similarly, *hostlers* operate engines—without attached cars—within the yard, and drive them to and from maintenance shops.

In contrast to other rail transportation workers, subway and streetcar operators generally work for public transit authorities instead of railroads. *Subway operators* control trains that transport passengers through cities and their suburbs. The trains run in underground tunnels, on the surface, or on elevated tracks. Operators must stay alert to observe signals along the track that indicate when they must start, slow, or stop their trains. They also make announcements to riders, may open and close the doors of the train, and ensure that passengers get on and off the subway safely. Increasingly, the train's speed and the amount of time spent at each station are controlled by computers and not by the operator. During breakdowns or emergencies, operators contact their dispatcher or supervisor and may have to evacuate cars.

Streetcar operators drive electric-powered streetcars, trolleys, or light-rail vehicles that transport passengers around metropolitan areas. Some tracks may be built directly into street

Many rail transportation employees work more than 40 hours per week, although minimum rest hours are mandated by Federal regulations.

pavement or have grade crossings, so operators must observe traffic signals and cope with car and truck traffic. Operators start, slow, and stop their cars so that passengers may get on and off easily. Operators may collect fares and issue change and transfers. They also interact with passengers who have questions about fares, schedules, or routes.

Work environment. Rail transportation employees work nights, weekends, and holidays to operate trains that run 24 hours a day, 7 days a week. Many work more than 40 hours per week, although minimum rest hours are mandated by Federal regulations. Engineers and conductors may be placed on an "extra board" on which workers receive assignments only when a railroad needs substitutes for workers who are absent because of vacation, illness, or other reasons. Seniority usually dictates who receives the more desirable shifts, as do union agreements at large unionized railroads. Working conditions also vary by the mode of rail transport.

Freight trains generally are dispatched according to the needs of customers. As a result, train crews may have irregular schedules. It is common for workers to place their name on a list and wait for their turn to work. Jobs usually are assigned on short notice and often at odd hours. Working weekends is common in freight train transportation. Those who work on trains operating between

Projections data from the National Employment Matrix

Occupational Title	SOC Code	Employment, 2008	Projected Employment, 2018	Change, 2008-2018	
				Number	Percent
Rail transportation occupations...	–	130,500	86,200	6,900	9
Locomotive engineers and operators	53-4010	51,100	56,200	5,100	10
Railroad brake, signal, and switch operators	53-4021	25,600	28,000	2,400	9
Railroad conductors and yardmasters	53-4031	41,300	44,100	2,800	7
Subway and streetcar operators	53-4041	7,700	9,100	1,400	19
Rail transportation workers, all other..	53-4099	4,800	5,000	200	4

(NOTE) Data in this table are rounded. See the discussion of the employment projections table in the *Handbook* introductory chapter on *Occupational Information Included in the Handbook.*

points hundreds of miles apart may spend consecutive nights away from home. Because of the distances involved on some routes, many railroad employees work without direct supervision.

Workers on passenger trains ordinarily have regular and reliable shifts. Also, the appearance, temperature, and accommodations of passenger trains are more comfortable than those of freight trains.

Rail yard workers spend most of their time outdoors and work regardless of weather conditions. These workers climb up and down equipment, which can be strenuous and can also be dangerous if safety rules are not followed. The work of conductors and engineers on local runs, on which trains frequently stop at stations or local rail yards to pick up and deliver cars, is also physically demanding.

Training, Other Qualifications, and Advancement

Rail transportation workers start out in a variety of positions as they gain the experience needed for more demanding assignments. Rail transportation workers generally must begin training to become a conductor before they may be considered for an engineer position; engineer positions also require Federal licensure. Nearly all rail transportation workers complete formal classroom and hands-on training before beginning work. Most applicants must pass a drug screening, background check, and physical examination before being hired.

Education and training. Railroads require that applicants have a minimum of a high school diploma or equivalent, and most training is done through a company's formal training program and on-the-job training. Rail yard jobs usually require the successful completion of a company training program before workers are allowed to begin. For brake and signal operator jobs, railroad firms train applicants either in a company program or—especially with smaller railroads—at an outside training facility. Typical training programs combine classroom and on-site training lasting from a few weeks to a few months. Entry-level conductors are either trained by their employers or are required to complete a formal conductor training program through a community college.

Most transit systems that operate subways and streetcars also operate buses. In these systems, subway and streetcar operators usually gain experience by first driving buses. New operators then complete training programs that last from a few weeks to 6 months. After finishing classroom and on-the-job training, operators usually must pass qualifying examinations covering the operating system, troubleshooting, and evacuation and emergency procedures.

Licensure. Locomotive engineers must be federally licensed to operate freight and passenger trains. Federal regulations require beginning engineers to complete a formal engineer train-

ing program, including classroom, simulator, and hands-on instruction in locomotive operation. At the end of the training period, candidates must pass a hearing and visual acuity test, a safety conduct background check, a railroad operation knowledge test, and a skills performance test before receiving an engineer's license. Engineers must periodically pass an operational rules efficiency test to maintain their licensure. The test is an unannounced event requiring engineers to take active or responsive action in certain situations, such as maintaining a particular speed through a curve or yard or complying with a signal.

Because of recent legislation, conductors will soon be subject to Federal licensing requirements similar to those of railroad engineers. For yard occupations, a commercial driver's license may be required because these workers often operate trucks and other heavy vehicles.

Other qualifications. Rail transportation workers must have good hearing, eyesight, and color vision, as well as good hand-eye coordination, manual dexterity, and mechanical aptitude. Physical stamina is required for most rail transportation jobs. Applicants for locomotive engineer jobs and some conductor jobs must be at least 21 years old.

All applicants must have good communication skills and be able to make quick, responsible judgments. Employers require railroad transportation job applicants to pass a physical examination, drug and alcohol screening, and a criminal background check. Under Federal regulation, all people licensed to operate engines are subject to random drug and alcohol testing while on duty; engineers also must undergo periodic physical examinations.

Advancement. Most railroad transportation workers begin as laborers, brake operators, or conductors after completing training on signals, timetables, operating rules, and related subjects. Although new employees may be hired as conductors, seniority determines whether an employee may hold a conductor position full time. Employers almost always fill engineer positions with workers who have experience in other railroad-operating occupations. Subway and streetcar operators with sufficient seniority can advance to station manager or another supervisory position.

Employment

Rail transportation workers held 130,500 jobs in 2008. Employment was distributed as follows:

Locomotive engineers and operators............................51,100
Railroad conductors and yardmasters 41,300
Railroad brake, signal, and switch operators 25,600
Subway and streetcar operators.....................................7,700
Rail transportation workers, all other............................4,800

Most rail transportation workers were employed in the rail transportation industry or in support activities for the industry. Rail transportation and rail transportation support activities made up 87 percent jobs in 2008. The rest worked primarily for local governments that operate subway or streetcar systems.

Job Outlook

Employment in most railroad transportation occupations is expected to grow about as fast as average through the year 2018. Opportunities are expected to be good for qualified applicants, in large part because of the number of workers expected to retire or leave these occupations through 2018.

Employment change. Employment is expected to increase by 9 percent from 2008 through 2018, which is about as fast as the average for all occupations. This will largely be the result of expected increases in the demand for freight and passenger rail transportation as fuel costs increase and rail becomes a cheaper alternative to trucks and automobiles. Despite the slowdown in the economy, in the long term freight transportation should continue to expand as global trade expands and rail freight benefits from the shipment of more goods. However, advances such as remote control locomotive technology, discussed previously, and positive train control technology, which allows for the electronic monitoring of mechanical difficulties and track problems, will allow railroads to improve productivity and consolidate duties. To some extent, this will offset the need for new employees in occupations not essential for railroad operations.

Although demand for passenger rail service is anticipated to increase with the growing population, as is demand for public transit authorities, employment growth for workers in passenger rail will be slow because the addition of new service will be limited by the lack of track, which is not expected to increase by any great extent over the 2008–18 period. Employment of subway and streetcar operators is expected to increase modestly because more commuter and light-rail transportation systems are being proposed around the country.

A law recently passed by the U.S. Congress may have a positive impact on employment in rail transportation occupations. The Rail Safety Improvement Act of 2008 increases the number of hours that train crews must rest between shifts. It also requires more safety improvements to railroad crossings. This law may generate more jobs for engineers and conductors as well as signal operators.

Job prospects. Opportunities for rail transportation workers will be good for workers who meet basic qualifications, because a large number of older workers are expected to retire over the next decade, particularly at freight railroads. Prospects will be best for those positions that are also expected to see growth, like locomotive engineers and conductors.

Entry-level occupations such as brake operator and conductor should be plentiful for applicants with clean drug and criminal records. Opportunities for long-distance train crews are also expected to be good because many of those working in the yards prefer not to travel long distances. Subway and streetcar operators will have the best opportunities in cities where the construction of commuter or light-rail transit systems is underway.

Earnings

Median hourly wages of rail transportation occupations in May 2008 are indicated in the tabulation below. These wages were relatively high compared with $13.14 per hour, the median wage for all transportation occupations.

Subway and streetcar operators	$25.59
Railroad conductors and yardmasters	25.40
Railroad brake, signal, and switch operators	22.94
Locomotive engineers and operators	22.54
Rail tranporation workers, all other	21.12

Most railroad transportation workers are paid according to miles traveled or hours worked, whichever leads to higher earnings. Factors such as seniority, job assignments, and location affect potential earnings.

76 percent of railroad transportation workers are members of unions, compared with 12 percent for all occupations. There are many different railroad unions, and they represent various crafts on the railroads. Among the largest of the railroad employee unions are the United Transportation Union and the Brotherhood of Locomotive Engineers and Trainmen. Many subway operators are members of the Amalgamated Transit Union, while others belong to the Transport Workers Union of North America.

Related Occupations

Other transportation workers include:

	Page
Bus drivers	791
Truck drivers and driver/sales workers	797
Water transportation occupations	805

Workers who repair and maintain railroad rolling stock are included in the occupation:

Heavy vehicle and mobile equipment service technicians and mechanics	697

Workers who load and unload freight from rail cars are included in:

Material moving occupations	809

Sources of Additional Information

To obtain information on employment opportunities, contact either the employment offices of railroads and rail transit systems or State employment service offices.

General information about the rail transportation industry is available from:

➤ Association of American Railroads, 425 3rd St. SW, Suite 1000, Washington, DC 20024. Internet: **http://www.aar.org**

General information about career opportunities in passenger transportation is available from:

➤ National Railroad Passenger Corporation, 60 Massachusetts Ave. NE, 4th floor, Washington, DC 20002. Internet: **http://www.amtrak.com**

General information on career opportunities as a locomotive engineer is available from:

➤ Brotherhood of Locomotive Engineers and Trainmen, 1370 Ontario St. Mezzanine, Cleveland, OH 44113. Internet: **http://www.ble.org**

General information on career opportunities as a conductor, yardmaster, or brake operator is available from:

➤ United Transportation Union, 14600 Detroit Ave., Cleveland, OH 44107. Internet: **http://www.utu.org**

The Occupational Information Network (O*NET) provides information on a wide range of occupational characteristics. Links to O*NET appear at the end of the Internet version of this occupational statement, accessible at **http://www.bls.gov/ooh/ocos244.htm**

Water Transportation Occupations

Significant Points

- Some merchant mariners spend extended periods at sea; others operate boats close to port and go home at night.

- Entry, training, and educational requirements for many water transportation occupations are established and regulated by the U.S. Coast Guard.

- Excellent job opportunities are expected, especially for marine officers.

Nature of the Work

The movement of huge amounts of cargo, as well as passengers, in and out of U.S. waters and sometimes over the oceans depends on workers in water transportation occupations, also known as *merchant mariners.* They operate and maintain civilian-owned deep-sea merchant ships, tugboats, towboats, ferries, barges, offshore supply vessels, cruise ships, and other waterborne craft on the oceans, the Great Lakes, rivers, canals, and other waterways, as well as in harbors. (Workers who operate watercraft used in commercial fishing are described in the section on fishers and fishing vessel operators elsewhere in the *Handbook.*)

Captains, mates, and pilots of water vessels operating on domestic waterways or on U.S.-flagged deep sea ships command or supervise the operations of these ships and water vessels. *Captains* or *masters* are in overall command of the operation of a vessel, and they supervise the work of all other officers and crew. Together with their department heads, captains ensure that proper procedures and safety practices are followed, check to make sure that machinery and equipment are in good working order, and oversee the loading and discharging of cargo or passengers. They also maintain logs and other records tracking the ships' movements, efforts at controlling pollution, and cargo and passengers carried.

Deck officers or *mates* direct the routine operation of the vessel for the captain during the shifts when they are on watch. On smaller vessels, there may be only one mate (called a *pilot* on some inland towing vessels), who alternates watches with the captain. The mate would assume command of the ship if the captain became incapacitated. When more than one mate is necessary aboard a ship, they typically are designated chief mate or first mate, second mate, third mate, etc. Mates also supervise and coordinate activities of the crew aboard the ship.

Captains and mates determine the course and speed of the vessel, maneuvering to avoid hazards and continuously monitoring the vessel's position with charts and navigational aides. Captains and mates oversee crew members who steer the vessel, determine its location, operate engines, communicate with other vessels, perform maintenance, handle lines, and operate equipment on the vessel. They inspect the cargo holds during loading to ensure that the load is stowed according to specifications and regulations. Captains and mates also supervise crew members engaged in maintenance and the primary upkeep of the vessel.

Pilots guide ships in and out of harbors, through straits, and on rivers and other confined waterways where a familiarity with local water depths, winds, tides, currents, and hazards such as reefs and shoals are of prime importance. Pilots on river and canal vessels usually are regular crew members, like mates. Harbor pilots are generally independent contractors who accompany vessels while they enter or leave port. *Harbor pilots* may pilot many ships in a single day.

Ship engineers operate, maintain, and repair propulsion engines, boilers, generators, pumps, and other machinery. Merchant marine vessels usually have four engineering officers: A chief engineer and a first, second, and third assistant engineer. Assistant engineers stand periodic watches, overseeing the safe operation of engines and machinery.

Work schedules for water transportation workers vary based upon the type of ship and length of voyage.

Marine oilers and more experienced *qualified members of the engine department*, or QMEDs, assist the engineers to maintain the vessel in proper running order in the engine spaces below decks. These workers lubricate gears, shafts, bearings, and other moving parts of engines and motors; read pressure and temperature gauges; record data; and sometimes assist with repairs and adjust machinery.

Sailors or deckhands operate the vessel and its deck equipment under the direction of the ship's officers and keep the non-engineering areas in good condition. They stand watch, looking out for other vessels and obstructions in the ship's path, as well as for navigational aids such as buoys and lighthouses. They also steer the ship, measure water depth in shallow water, and maintain and operate deck equipment such as lifeboats, anchors, and cargo-handling gear. When docking or departing, they handle lines. They also perform routine maintenance chores, such as repairing lines, chipping rust, and painting and cleaning decks or other areas. On vessels handling liquid cargo, mariners designated as *pumpmen* hook up hoses, operate pumps, and clean tanks; on tugboats or tow vessels, they tie barges together into tow units, inspect them periodically, and disconnect them when the destination is reached. Experienced sailors are designated *able seamen* on oceangoing vessels, but may be called simply deckhands on inland waters; larger vessels usually have a *boatswain*, or *head seaman*.

A typical deep-sea merchant ship has a captain, three deck officers or mates, a chief engineer and three assistant engineers, plus six or more seamen, such as able seamen, oilers, QMEDs, and a cook. The size and service of the ship determine the number of crewmembers for a particular voyage. Small vessels operating in harbors, on rivers, or along the coast may have a crew comprising only a captain and one deckhand. On smaller vessels the cooking responsibilities usually fall under the deckhands' duties.

On larger coastal ships, the crew may include a captain, a mate or pilot, an engineer, and seven or eight seamen. Unlicensed positions on a large ship may include a full-time cook, an electrician, and machinery mechanics. Some ships may have special unlicensed positions for entry-level apprentice trainees.

Motorboat operators operate small, motor-driven boats that carry six or fewer passengers. They may operate fishing charters, serve as liaisons between ships or between ship and shore, or perform area patrol.

Work environment. Water transportation workers' schedules vary based upon the type of ship and length of voyage. While on the water, crews are normally on duty for half of the day, 7 days a week.

Merchant mariners on survey and long distance cargo vessels can spend extended periods at sea. Most deep-sea mariners are hired for one or more voyages that last for several months; there is no job security after that. The length of time between voyages varies depending on job availability and personal preference.

Workers on supply vessels transport workers, supplies (water, drilling mud, fuel, and food), and equipment to oil and gas drilling platforms mostly in the Gulf of Mexico. Their voyages can last a few hours to a couple of weeks. As oil and gas exploration pushes into deeper waters, these trips take more time.

Workers on tugs and barges operate on the rivers, lakes, inland waterways, and along the coast. Most tugs have two crews

and operate constantly. The crews will alternate, each working for 2-3 weeks and then taking 2-3 weeks off.

Many of those employed on Great Lakes ships work 60 days and have 30 days off, but do not work in the winter when the lakes are frozen. Others work steadily for a week or a month and then have an extended period off. Those on smaller vessels, such as tugs, supply boats and Great Lakes ships, are normally assigned to one vessel and have steady employment.

Workers on ferries transporting commuters work on weekdays in the morning and evening. Other ferries make frequent trips lasting a few hours. Ferries servicing vacation destinations often operate on seasonal schedules. Workers in harbors generally have year-round work. Work in harbors and on ferries is highly sought after because workers return home every day.

People holding water transportation jobs work in all kinds of weather, except when frozen waters make travel impossible. Although merchant mariners try to avoid severe storms while at sea, working in damp and cold conditions often is inevitable. While it is uncommon for vessels to suffer disasters such as fire, explosion, or sinking, workers face the possibility that they may have to abandon their craft on short notice if it collides with another vessel or runs aground. They also risk injury or death from falling overboard and hazards associated with working with machinery, heavy loads, and dangerous cargo. However, modern safety management procedures, advanced emergency communications, and effective international rescue systems have greatly improved mariner safety.

Many companies are working to improve the living conditions on vessels to reduce employee turnover. Most of the Nation's newest vessels are air conditioned, soundproofed to reduce machinery noise, and equipped with comfortable living quarters. Some companies have added improved entertainment systems and hired full-time cooks. These amenities lessen the difficulty of spending long periods away from home. Advances in communications, particularly e-mail, better link mariners to their families. Nevertheless, some mariners dislike the long periods away from home and the confinement aboard ship and consequently leave the occupation.

Training, Other Qualifications, and Advancement

Entry, training, and experience requirements for many water transportation occupations are established and regulated by the U.S. Coast Guard. As of April 15, 2009, mariners on board most ships have to obtain two credentials, a Transportation Worker Identification Credential (TWIC) and a Merchant Mariner Credential (MMC).

Education and training. Entry-level workers are classified as ordinary seamen or deckhands. Workers take some basic training, lasting a few days, in areas such as first aid and firefighting.

There are two paths of education and training for a deck officer or an engineer: applicants must either accumulate thousands of hours of experience while working as a deckhand, or graduate from one of seven merchant marine academies in the United States. In both cases, applicants must pass a written examination. It is difficult to pass the examination without substantial formal schooling or independent study. The academies offer a 4-year academic program leading to a bachelor-of-science degree, a MMC endorsement (issued only by the Coast Guard) as a third mate (deck officer) or third assistant engineer (engineering officer), and, if the person chooses, a commission as ensign in the U.S. Naval Reserve, Merchant Marine Reserve, or Coast Guard Reserve. With experience and additional training, third officers may qualify for higher rank. Generally officers on deep water vessels are academy graduates and those in supply boats, inland waterways, and rivers rose to their positions through years of experience.

Harbor pilot training usually consists of an extended apprenticeship with a towing company or a harbor pilots' association. Entrants may be able seamen or licensed officers.

In recent years, to generate interest in the maritime industry, 18 high schools have been designated "maritime high schools" with a curriculum created by the U.S. Maritime Administration. Graduation from one of these schools can help one's entry in the academies or with jobs elsewhere in the industry.

Licensure. All mariners that are required to obtain Coast Guard credentials are required to obtain a TWIC from the U.S. Department of Homeland Security. This credential states that you are a U.S. citizen or a permanent resident and have passed a security screening.

In addition, with few exceptions, the Coast Guard requires that mariners applying for a credential after April 15, 2009, obtain a MMC. Entry level seamen or deckhands on vessels operating in harbors or on rivers or other waterways do not need a MMC. The MMC replaces the Merchant Mariner Document, the license, and Standards of Training, Certification, and Watchkeeping for Seafarers endorsement. The MMC incorporates the licenses into the credential, which varies by occupational specialty, type of vessel, and by body of water (river, inland waterway, Great Lakes, and oceans). Requirements for the credential increase as the skill level of the occupational specialty and the size of the vessel increase and applicants must pass a test in order qualify. Applicants for the credential must also pass a drug screen, take a medical exam, and meet the minimum age requirements. For more information on credentialing requirements see the Coast Guard's Web site listed in the sources of additional information.

Radio operators are licensed by the Federal Communications Commission.

Other qualifications. Most positions require excellent health, good vision, and color perception. Good general physical condition is needed because many jobs require the ability to lift heavy objects, withstand heat and cold, stand or stoop for long periods of time, dexterity to maneuver through tight spaces, and good balance on uneven and wet surfaces and in rough water.

Advancement. Experience and passing exams are required to advance. Deckhands who wish to advance must decide whether they want to work in the wheelhouse or the engine room. They

will then assist the engineers or deck officers. With experience, assistant engineers and deck officers can advance to become chief engineers or captains. On smaller boats, such as tugs, a captain may choose to become self-employed by buying a boat and working as an owner-operator.

Employment

Water transportation workers held more than 81,100 jobs in 2008. The total number who worked at some point in the year was significantly larger because many merchant marine officers and seamen work only part of the year. The following tabulation shows employment in the occupations that make up this group:

Captains, mates, and pilots of water vessels 33,100
Sailors and marine oilers...32,900
Ship engineers 11,500
Motorboat operators..3,700

About 40 percent of all workers were employed in water transportation services. Another 26 percent worked in establishments related to port and harbor operations, marine cargo handling, or navigational services to shipping. Governments employed 11 percent of all water transportation workers, many of whom worked on supply ships and are civilian mariners of the Navy Department's Military Sealift Command.

Job Outlook

Employment in water transportation occupations is projected to grow faster than average. Excellent job opportunities are expected as demand for people working in the shipping industry, particularly officers, is expected to be greater than the number of people wishing to enter these occupations.

Employment change. Employment in water transportation occupations is projected to grow 15 percent over the 2008-2018 period, faster than the average for all occupations. Job growth will stem from increasing tourism and growth in offshore oil and gas production. Employment will also rise in and around major port cities due to increasing international trade.

Employment in deep-sea shipping for American mariners is expected to remain stable. A fleet of deep-sea U.S.-flagged ships is considered vital to the Nation's defense, so some receive Federal support through a maritime security subsidy and other provisions in laws that limit certain Federal cargoes to ships that fly the U.S. flag.

Employment growth also is expected in passenger cruise ships within U.S. waters. Vessels that operate between U.S. ports are required by law to be U.S.-flagged vessels. The staff-

Projections data from the National Employment Matrix

Occupational Title	SOC Code	Employment, 2008	Projected Employment, 2018	Change, 2008-2018	
				Number	Percent
Water transportation occupations......................................	53-5000	81,100	93,100	12,000	15
Sailors and marine oilers...	53-5011	32,900	36,700	3,800	12
Ship and boat captains and operators.............................	53-5020	36,800	42,800	6,000	16
Captains, mates, and pilots of water vessels	53-5021	33,100	38,800	5,700	17
Motorboat operators...	53-5022	3,700	4,000	300	8
Ship engineers..	53-5031	11,500	13,600	2,100	19

(NOTE) Data in this table are rounded. See the discussion of the employment projections table in the *Handbook* introductory chapter on *Occupational Information Included in the Handbook.*

ing needs for several new U.S. flagged cruise ships that will travel to the Hawaiian Islands will create new opportunities for employment. In addition, a small, but growing interest in using ferries to handle commuter traffic around major metropolitan areas should create some opportunities.

Some growth in water transportation occupations is projected in vessels operating in the Great Lakes and inland waterways as the economy recovers from the recession. Growth will be driven by demand for bulk products, such as coal, iron ore, petroleum, sand and gravel, grain, and chemicals. Since current pipelines cannot transport ethanol, some growth will come from shipping ethanol. Problems with congestion in the rail transportation system will increase demand for inland water transportation.

Job prospects. Excellent job opportunities are anticipated over the next decade as the need to replace workers, particularly officers, will generate many job openings. High turnover, the prospect of many retirements in the water transportation industry as a whole, and growth in the level of trade occurring worldwide will cause more jobs to be created than there will be people interested in taking them. The number of graduates from maritime academies has not kept up with the demand for officers on board ships. In addition, higher regulatory and security requirements has limited the pool of potential seamen. And a limited number of berths (beds) on board ships also is making it difficult for potential seamen to get the required number of hours on board ships to qualify for certain credentials. However, as the industry acknowledges these problems, living conditions, training, and opportunities for advancement should go up to attract more people to the occupations.

Earnings

Earnings vary widely with the particular water transportation position and the worker's experience. Earnings are higher than most other occupations with similar educational requirements for entry-level positions. While wages are lower for sailors than for mates and engineers, sailors' on-board experience is important for advancing into those higher paying positions. Workers are normally paid by the day. Since companies provide food and housing at sea and it is difficult to spend money while working, sailors are able to save a large portion of their pay.

Median annual wages of captains, mates, and pilots of water vessels were $61,960 in May 2008. The middle 50 percent earned between $42,810 and $83,590. The lowest 10 percent had wages of less than $29,330, while the top 10 percent earned over $108,120. Annual pay for captains of larger vessels, such as container ships, oil tankers, or passenger ships may exceed $100,000, but only after many years of experience. Similarly, earnings of captains of tugboats are dependent on the port and the nature of the cargo.

Median annual wages of sailors and marine oilers were $34,390 in May 2008. The middle 50 percent earned between $26,550 and $44,080. The lowest 10 percent had wages of less than $21,110, while the top 10 percent earned over $51,890.

Median annual wages of ship engineers were $60,690 in May 2008. The middle 50 percent earned between $45,520 and

$79,800. The lowest 10 percent had wages of less than $34,420, while the top 10 percent earned over $102,850.

Median annual wages of motorboat operators were $31,910 in May 2008. The middle 50 percent earned between $26,600 and 48,310. The lowest 10 percent had wages of less than $20,420, while the top 10 percent earned over $59,120.

The rate of unionization for these workers is about 12 percent. Unionization rates vary by region. In unionized areas, merchant marine officers and seamen, both veterans and beginners, are hired for voyages through union hiring halls or directly by shipping companies. Hiring halls rank the candidates by the length of time the person has been out of work and fill open slots accordingly. Most major seaports have hiring halls.

Related Occupations

Other occupations that make their living on the seas and coastal waters include:

Fishers and fishing vessel operators 601

Other technicians and mechanics that perform work similar to shipboard engineers, include:

Heavy vehicle and mobile equipment service
  technicians and mechanics 697

Employment opportunities in the Navy and Coast guard are discussed in:

Job opportunities in the armed forces 813

Sources of Additional Information

Information on a career as a mariner, including a substantial listing of training and employment information and contacts in the U.S., may be obtained through:
➤ Maritime Administration, U.S. Department of Transportation, 1200 New Jersey Ave. SE, Washington, DC 20590. Internet: **http://www.marad.dot.gov**

Information on merchant marine careers, training, and licensing requirements is available from:
➤ U.S. Coast Guard National Maritime Center, 2100 Second St. SW, Washington, DC 20593. Internet: **http://www.uscg.mil/nmc**

For information on jobs on inland and coastal waterways aboard tugboats and towboats, contact:
➤ The American Waterways Operators, 801 North Quincy St., Suite 200, Arlington, VA 22203. Internet: **http://www.americanwaterways.com**

The Occupational Information Network (O*NET) provides information on a wide range of occupational characteristics. Links to O*NET appear at the end of the Internet version of this occupational statement, accessible at **http://www.bls.gov/ooh/ocos247.htm**

Material Moving Occupations

Significant Points

- Despite little or no change in employment, numerous job openings will be created by the need to replace workers who leave this very large occupation.

- Most jobs require little work experience or training.

- Pay is low for many positions, and the seasonal nature of the work may reduce earnings.

Nature of the Work

Think about a common bicycle; over the course of its creation many workers have to transport a variety of materials to get it to your local store. First, the raw metal must be produced, either from a mine where an *excavator operator* digs into the earth to gather rocks with the proper minerals and places them on a conveyor operated by a *conveyor tender;* or by a *recyclable material collector* that picks up unwanted metal household goods. Next, the metal is refined in a foundry, at which point a *crane operator* or *hoist and winch operator* may place it on a trailer for shipping. After arriving at a factory, an *industrial truck operator* unloads the metal and a *machine feeder* loads it into a machine for production. After being assembled, the bicycle is placed into a box by a *hand packager* and then moved into a tractor trailer by a *truck loader.* Many products, like this bicycle, are handled by a variety of workers because, even with the use of machinery, moving goods and materials around worksites still requires significant human effort. Material moving workers are generally categorized into two groups—operators, who control the machines that move materials, and laborers, who move materials by hand.

Operators use machinery to move construction materials, earth, petroleum products, and other heavy materials. Generally, they move materials over short distances—around construction sites, factories, or warehouses. Some move materials onto or off of trucks and ships. Operators control equipment by moving levers, wheels, or foot pedals; operating switches; or turning dials. They also may set up and inspect equipment, make adjustments, and perform minor maintenance or repairs.

Laborers and hand material movers move freight, stock, or other materials by hand; clean vehicles, machinery, and other equipment; feed materials into or remove materials from machines or equipment; and pack or package products and materials.

Industrial truck and tractor operators drive and control industrial trucks or tractors that move materials around warehouses, storage yards, factories, construction sites, or other worksites. A typical industrial truck, often called a forklift or lift truck, has a hydraulic lifting mechanism and forks for moving heavy and large objects. Industrial truck and tractor operators also may operate tractors that pull trailers loaded with materials, goods, or equipment within factories and warehouses or around outdoor storage areas.

Excavating and loading machine and dragline operators tend or operate machinery equipped with scoops, shovels, or buck-

ets to dig and load sand, gravel, earth, or similar materials into trucks or onto conveyors. These machines are primarily used in the construction and mining industries. *Dredge operators* excavate waterways, removing sand, gravel, rock, or other materials from harbors, lakes, rivers, and streams. Dredges are used primarily to maintain navigable channels but also are used to restore wetlands and other aquatic habitats; reclaim land; and create and maintain beaches. *Underground mining loading machine operators* load coal, ore, or rock into shuttles and mine cars or onto conveyors. Loading equipment may include power shovels, hoisting engines equipped with cable-drawn scrapers or scoops, and machines equipped with gathering arms and conveyors.

Crane and tower operators use mechanical boom and cable or tower and cable equipment to lift and move materials, machinery, and other heavy objects. Operators extend and retract horizontally mounted booms and lower and raise hooks attached to load lines. Most operators are guided by other workers using hand signals or a radio. Operators position loads from an onboard console or from a remote console at the site. Although crane and tower operators are noticeable at office building and other construction sites, the biggest group works in manufacturing industries that use heavy, bulky materials. Operators also work at major ports, loading and unloading large containers on and off ships. *Hoist and winch operators* control movement of cables, cages, and platforms to move workers and materials for manufacturing, logging, and other industrial operations. They work in positions such as derrick operators and hydraulic boom operators. Many hoist and winch operators are found in manufacturing or construction industries.

Pump operators tend, control, and operate pump and manifold systems that transfer gases, oil, or other materials to vessels or equipment. They maintain the equipment and regulate the flow of materials according to a schedule set up by petroleum engineers or production supervisors. *Gas compressor and gas pumping station operators* operate steam, gas, electric motor, or internal combustion engine-driven compressors. They transmit, compress, or recover gases, such as butane, nitrogen, hydrogen,

Material movers often work in the construction industry.

and natural gas. *Wellhead pumpers* operate pumps and auxiliary equipment to produce flows of oil or gas from extraction sites.

Tank car, truck, and ship loaders operate ship-loading and ship-unloading equipment, conveyors, hoists, and other specialized material-handling equipment such as railroad tank car-unloading equipment. They may gauge or sample shipping tanks and test them for leaks. *Conveyor operators and tenders* control and tend conveyor systems that move materials to or from stockpiles, processing stations, departments, or vehicles. *Shuttle car operators* run diesel or electric-powered shuttle cars in underground mines, transporting materials to mine cars or conveyors.

Laborers and hand freight, stock, and *material movers* manually move materials and perform other unskilled, general labor. These workers move freight, stock, and other materials to and from storage and production areas, loading docks, delivery vehicles, ships, and containers. Their specific duties vary by industry and work setting. In factories, they may move raw materials or finished goods between loading docks, storage areas, and work areas, as well as sort materials and supplies and prepare them according to their work orders. Specialized workers within this group include baggage and cargo handlers—who work in transportation industries—and truck loaders and unloaders.

Hand packers and packagers manually pack, package, or wrap a variety of materials. They may label cartons, inspect items for defects, stamp information on products, keep records of items packed, and stack packages on loading docks. This group also includes order fillers, who pack materials for shipment, as well as gift wrappers. In grocery stores, they may bag groceries, carry packages to customers' cars, and return shopping carts to designated areas.

Machine feeders and offbearers feed materials into or remove materials from equipment or machines tended by other workers.

Cleaners of vehicles and equipment clean machinery, vehicles, storage tanks, pipelines, and similar equipment using water and cleaning agents, vacuums, hoses, brushes, or cloths.

Refuse and recyclable material collectors gather refuse and recyclables from homes and businesses into their trucks for transport to a dump, landfill, or recycling center. They lift and empty garbage cans or recycling bins by hand or, using hydraulic lifts on their vehicles, pick up and empty dumpsters. Some in this group drive the large garbage or recycling truck along the scheduled routes.

(For information on operating engineers; paving, surfacing, and tamping equipment operators; and pile-driver operators, see the statement on construction equipment operators elsewhere in the *Handbook*.)

Work environment. Material moving work tends to be repetitive and physically demanding. Workers may lift and carry heavy objects and stoop, kneel, crouch, or crawl in awkward positions. Some work at great heights and some work outdoors—regardless of weather and climate. Some jobs expose workers to fumes, odors, loud noises, harmful materials and chemicals, or dangerous machinery. To protect their eyes, respiratory systems, and hearing, these workers wear safety clothing, such as gloves, hardhats, and other safety devices such as respirators. These jobs have become less dangerous as safety equipment—such as overhead guards on lift trucks—has become common. Accidents usually can be avoided by observing proper operating procedures and safety practices.

Material movers generally work 8-hour shifts—though longer shifts are not uncommon. In industries that work around the clock, material movers may work overnight shifts. Some do

Projections data from the National Employment Matrix

Occupational Title	SOC Code	Employment, 2008	Projected Employment, 2018	Change, 2008-2018	
				Number	Percent
Material moving occupations...	53-7000	4,583,700	4,537,200	-46,500	-1
Conveyor operators and tenders.................................	53-7011	41,000	37,200	-3,800	-9
Crane and tower operators	53-7021	43,900	40,900	-3,000	-7
Dredge, excavating, and loading machine operators	53-7030	82,300	88,600	6,300	8
Dredge operators..	53-7031	2,200	2,400	200	7
Excavating and loading machine and dragline operators..........	53-7032	75,700	82,100	6,500	9
Loading machine operators, underground mining....................	53-7033	4,400	4,100	-300	-7
Hoist and winch operators	53-7041	2,800	2,600	-200	-8
Industrial truck and tractor operators................................	53-7051	610,300	627,000	16,700	3
Laborers and material movers, hand...................................	53-7060	3,565,700	3,485,400	-80,200	-2
Cleaners of vehicles and equipment................................	53-7061	348,900	352,500	3,600	1
Laborers and freight, stock, and material movers, hand...........	53-7062	2,317,300	2,298,600	-18,700	-1
Machine feeders and offbearers...................................	53-7063	140,600	109,500	-31,200	-22
Packers and packagers, hand......................................	53-7064	758,800	724,800	-34,000	-4
Pumping station operators..	53-7070	32,500	24,500	-8,000	-25
Gas compressor and gas pumping station operators.................	53-7071	4,300	3,400	-900	-21
Pump operators, except wellhead pumpers............................	53-7072	9,700	7,800	-1,900	-20
Wellhead pumpers..	53-7073	18,600	13,300	-5,300	-28
Refuse and recyclable material collectors................................	53-7081	149,000	176,700	27,800	19
Shuttle car operators	53-7111	3,100	3,000	-100	-4
Tank car, truck, and ship loaders....................................	53-7121	12,000	11,200	-900	-7
Material moving workers, all other....................................	53-7199	41,000	40,000	-1,000	-2

(NOTE) Data in this table are rounded. See the discussion of the employment projections table in the *Handbook* introductory chapter on *Occupational Information Included in the Handbook.*

this because their employers do not want to disturb customers during normal business hours. Refuse and recyclable material collectors often work shifts starting at 5 or 6 a.m. Some material movers work only during certain seasons, such as when the weather permits construction activity.

Training, Other Qualifications, and Advancement

Many material moving occupations require little or no formal training. Most training for these occupations is done on the job. For those jobs requiring physical exertion, employers may require that applicants pass a physical exam.

Education and training. Material movers generally learn skills informally, on the job, from more experienced workers or their supervisors. Many employers prefer applicants with a high school diploma or GED, but most simply require workers to be at least 18 years old and physically able to perform the work.

Workers who handle toxic chemicals or use industrial trucks or other dangerous equipment must receive specialized training in safety awareness and procedures. Many of the training requirements are standardized through the Occupational Safety and Health Administration (OSHA), but training for workers in mining is regulated by the Mine Safety and Health Administration (MSHA). This training is usually provided by the employer. Employers also must certify that each operator has received the training and evaluate each operator at least once every 3 years.

For other operators, such as crane operators and those working with specialized loads, there are some training and apprenticeship programs available, such as that offered by the International Union of Operating Engineers. Apprenticeships combine paid on-the-job training with classroom instruction.

Licensure. Seventeen States and 6 cities have laws requiring crane operators to be licensed. Licensing requirements typically include a written test as well as a skills test to demonstrate that the licensee can operate a crane safely.

Certification and other qualifications. Some types of equipment operators can become certified by professional associations, such as the National Commission for the Certification of Crane Operators, and some employers may require operators to be certified.

Material moving equipment operators need a good sense of balance, the ability to judge distances, and eye-hand-foot coordination. For jobs that involve dealing with the public, such as baggers or grocery store courtesy clerks, workers should be pleasant and courteous. Most jobs require basic arithmetic skills, the ability to read procedural manuals, and the capacity to understand orders and other billing documents. Experience operating mobile equipment—such as tractors on farms or heavy equipment in the Armed Forces—is an asset. As material moving equipment becomes more advanced, workers will need to be increasingly comfortable with technology.

Advancement. In many of these occupations, experience may allow workers to qualify or become trainees for jobs such as construction trades workers; assemblers or other production workers; or motor vehicle operators. In many workplaces, new employees gain experience in a material moving position before being promoted to a better paying and more highly skilled job. Some may eventually advance to become supervisors.

Employment

Material movers held 4.6 million jobs in 2008. They were distributed among the detailed occupations as follows:

Laborers and freight, stock, and material movers, hand	2,317,300
Packers and packagers, hand	758,800
Industrial truck and tractor operators	610,300
Cleaners of vehicles and equipment	348,900
Refuse and recyclable material collectors	149,000
Machine feeders and offbearers	140,600
Excavating and loading machine and dragline operators	75,700
Crane and tower operators	43,900
Conveyor operators and tenders	41,000
Wellhead pumpers	18,600
Tank car, truck, and ship loaders	12,000
Pump operators, except wellhead pumpers	9,700
Loading machine operators, underground mining	4,400
Gas compressor and gas pumping station operators	4,300
Shuttle car operators	3,100
Hoist and winch operators	2,800
Dredge operators	2,200
Material moving workers, all other	41,000

About 29 percent of all material movers worked in the wholesale trade or retail trade industries. Another 20 percent worked in manufacturing; 17 percent were in transportation and warehousing; 4 percent were in construction and mining; and 12 percent worked in the employment services industry, on a temporary or contract basis. For example, companies that need workers for only a few days, to move materials or to clean up a site, may contract with temporary help agencies specializing in providing suitable workers on a short-term basis. A small proportion of material movers were self-employed.

Material movers work in every part of the country. Some work in remote locations on large construction projects such as highways and dams, while others work in factories, warehouses, or mining operations.

Job Outlook

Despite little or no change in employment, numerous job openings will be created by the need to replace workers who leave this very large occupation.

Employment change. Employment in material moving occupations is projected to decline by 1 percent between 2008 and 2018. Improvements in equipment, such as automated storage and retrieval systems and conveyors, and in supply management processes, such as automatic identification and data collection (AIDC), will continue to raise productivity and reduce the demand for material movers.

Job growth for material movers depends on the growth or decline of employing industries and the type of equipment the workers operate or the materials they handle. Employment should grow in the warehousing and storage industry as more firms contract out their warehousing functions to this industry. Opportunities for material movers should decline in manufacturing due to productivity improvements and outsourcing of warehousing and other activities that depend on material movers. Opportunities will vary by establishment size as well, as large establishments are more likely to have the resources to invest in automated systems for their material moving needs. Although increasing automation will eliminate some routine tasks, many jobs will remain to meet the need to operate and maintain new equipment.

Job prospects. Despite the projected employment decline, a relatively high number of job openings will be created by the need to replace workers who transfer to other occupations, retire, or leave this very large occupation for other reasons—characteristic of occupations requiring little prior or formal training. Many industries where material moving workers are employed are sensitive to changes in economic conditions, so the number of job openings fluctuates with the economy.

Earnings
Median hourly wages of material moving workers in May 2008 were relatively low, as indicated by the following tabulation:

Gas compressor and gas pumping station operators $21.45
Loading machine operators, underground mining 20.54
Shuttle car operators..20.29
Crane and tower operators..20.13
Pump operators, except wellhead pumpers....................18.81
Wellhead pumpers..18.20
Tank car truck and ship loaders.....................................18.14
Hoist and winch operators...17.50
Excavating and loading machine and
    dragline operators..16.93
Dredge operators 16.70
Refuse and recyclable material collectors......................14.93
Industrial truck and tractor operators 13.98
Conveyor operators and tenders 13.95
Machine feeders and offbearers 12.29
Laborers and freight stock and material movers, hand 10.89
Cleaners of vehicles and equipment................................9.35
Packers and packagers, hand..9.16
Material moving workers, all other 15.68

Wages vary according to experience and job responsibilities. Wages usually are higher in metropolitan areas. Seasonal peaks and lulls in workload can affect the number of hours scheduled, which affects earnings. Some crane operators, such as those unloading containers from ships at major ports, earn substantially more then their counterparts in other industries or establish-ments. Some material movers are union members, and these workers tend to earn higher wages.

Related Occupations
Other entry-level workers who perform physical work or operate machinery:

	Page
Agricultural workers, other	609
Building cleaning workers	495
Construction equipment operators	632
Construction laborers	635
Grounds maintenance workers	498
Logging workers	606

Sources of Additional Information
Information on training and apprenticeships for industrial truck operators is available from:
➤ International Union of Operating Engineers, 1125 17th St. NW., Washington, DC 20036. Internet: **http://www.iuoe.org**

Information on crane and derrick operator certification and licensure is available from:
➤ National Commission for the Certification of Crane Operators, 2750 Prosperity Ave., Suite 505, Fairfax, VA 22031. Internet: **http://www.nccco.org**

Information on safety and training requirements is available from:
➤ U.S. Department of Labor, Occupational Safety and Health Administration (OSHA), 200 Constitution Ave. NW., Washington, DC 20210. Internet: **http://www.osha.gov**

➤ Mine Safety and Health Administration, 1100 Wilson Blvd., Arlington, VA 22209-3939. Internet: **http://www.msha.gov**

For information about job opportunities and training programs, contact local State employment service offices, building or construction contractors, manufacturers, and wholesale and retail establishments.

The Occupational Information Network (O*NET) provides information on a wide range of occupational characteristics. Links to O*NET appear at the end of the Internet version of this occupational statement, accessible at **http://www.bls.gov/ooh/ocos243.htm**

Job Opportunities in the Armed Forces

Significant Points

- Some training and duty assignments are hazardous, even in peacetime; hours and working conditions can be arduous and vary substantially, and personnel must strictly conform to military rules at all times.

- Requirements vary by branch of service, but enlisted personnel need at least a high school diploma or its equivalent while officers need a bachelor's or graduate degree.

- Opportunities should be excellent in all branches of the Armed Forces for applicants who meet designated standards.

- Military personnel are eligible for retirement after 20 years of service.

Nature of the Work

Maintaining a strong national defense requires workers who can do such diverse tasks as run a hospital, command a tank, program a computer system, operate a nuclear reactor, or repair and maintain a helicopter. The military provides training and work experience in these and many other fields for more than 2.4 million people. More than 1.4 million people serve in the active Army, Navy, Marine Corps, and Air Force, and more than 1.0 million serve in their Reserve components and the Air and Army National Guard. (The Coast Guard, which also is discussed in this *Handbook* statement, is part of the Department of Homeland Security.)

The military distinguishes between enlisted and officer careers. Enlisted personnel, who make up about 82 percent of the Armed Forces, carry out the fundamental operations of the

The military provides training and work experience in many fields for more than 2.4 million people.

military in combat, administration, construction, engineering, healthcare, human services, and other areas. Officers, who make up the remaining 18 percent of the Armed Forces, are the leaders of the military, supervising and managing activities in every occupational specialty.

The sections that follow discuss the major occupational groups for enlisted personnel and officers.

Enlisted occupational groups. Administrative careers include a wide variety of positions. The military must keep accurate information for planning and managing its operations. Both paper and electronic records are kept on personnel and on equipment, funds, supplies, and all other aspects of the military. Administrative personnel record information, prepare reports, maintain files, and review information to assist military officers. Personnel may work in a specialized area, such as finance, accounting, legal affairs, maintenance, supply, or transportation.

Combat specialty occupations include enlisted specialties, such as infantry, artillery, and Special Forces, whose members operate weapons or execute special missions during combat. People in these occupations normally specialize by type of weapon system or combat operation. They maneuver against enemy forces and positions, and fire artillery, guns, mortars, and missiles to destroy enemy positions. They also may operate tanks and amphibious assault vehicles in combat or on scouting missions. When the military has especially difficult or specialized missions to perform, it calls upon Special Forces teams. These elite combat forces maintain a constant state of readiness to strike anywhere in the world on a moment's notice. Team members from the Special Forces conduct offensive raids, demolitions, intelligence, search-and-rescue missions, and other operations from aboard aircraft, helicopters, ships, or submarines.

Construction occupations in the military include personnel who build or repair buildings, airfields, bridges, foundations, dams, bunkers, and the electrical and plumbing components of these structures. Personnel in construction occupations operate bulldozers, cranes, graders, and other heavy equipment. Construction specialists also may work with engineers and other building specialists as part of military construction teams. Some personnel specialize in areas such as plumbing or electrical wiring. Plumbers and pipefitters install and repair the plumbing and pipe systems needed in buildings and on aircraft and ships. Building electricians install and repair electrical-wiring systems in offices, airplane hangars, and other buildings on military bases.

Electronic and electrical equipment repair personnel repair and maintain electronic and electrical equipment used in the military. Repairers normally specialize by type of equipment, such as avionics, computers, optical equipment, communications, or weapons systems. For example, electronic instrument repairers install, test, maintain, and repair a wide variety of elec-

Construction specialists may work with engineers and other building specialists as part of military construction teams.

tronic systems, including navigational controls and biomedical instruments. Weapons maintenance technicians maintain and repair weapons used by combat forces; most of these weapons have electronic components and systems that assist in locating targets and in aiming and firing the weapon.

Engineering, science, and technical personnel in the military require specific knowledge to operate technical equipment, solve complex problems, or provide and interpret information. Personnel normally specialize in one area, such as space operations, information technology, environmental health and safety, or intelligence. Space operations specialists use and repair ground-control command equipment related to spacecraft, including electronic systems that track the location and operation of a craft. Information technology specialists develop software programs and operate computer systems. Environmental health and safety specialists inspect military facilities and food supplies for the presence of disease, germs, or other conditions hazardous to health and the environment. Intelligence specialists gather and study aerial photographs and use various types of radar and surveillance systems to discover information needed by the military.

Healthcare personnel assist medical professionals in treating and providing services for men and women in the military. They may work as part of a patient-service team in close contact with doctors, dentists, nurses, and physical therapists. Some specialize in providing emergency medical treatment, operating diagnostic tools such as x-ray and ultrasound equipment, laboratory testing of tissue and blood samples, maintaining pharmacy supplies or patients' records, constructing and repairing dental equipment or eyeglasses, or some other healthcare task.

Human resources development specialists recruit qualified personnel, place them in suitable occupations, and provide training programs. Personnel in this career area normally specialize by activity. For example, recruiting specialists provide information about military careers to young people, parents, schools, and local communities, and explain the Armed Service's employment and training opportunities, pay and benefits, and service life. Personnel specialists collect and store information about the people in the military, including information on their previous and current training, job assignments, promotions, and health. Training specialists and instructors teach classes, give demonstrations, and instruct military personnel on how to perform their jobs.

Machine operator and production personnel operate industrial equipment, machinery, and tools to fabricate and repair parts for a variety of items and structures. They may operate engines, turbines, nuclear reactors, and water pumps. Often, they specialize by type of work performed. Welders and metalworkers, for instance, work with various types of metals to repair or form the structural parts of ships, submarines, buildings, or other equipment. Survival equipment specialists inspect, maintain, and repair survival equipment such as parachutes and aircraft life support equipment.

Media and public affairs personnel assist with the public presentation and interpretation of military information and events. They take photographs; film, record, and edit audio and video programs; present news and music programs; and produce artwork, drawings, and other visual displays. Other public affairs specialists act as interpreters and translators to convert written or spoken foreign languages into English or other languages.

Protective service personnel include those who enforce military laws and regulations and provide emergency responses to natural and human-made disasters. For example, military police control traffic, prevent crime, and respond to emergencies. Other law enforcement and security specialists investigate crimes committed on military property and guard inmates in military correctional facilities. Firefighters put out, control, and help prevent fires in buildings, on aircraft, and aboard ships.

Support service personnel provide subsistence services and support the morale and well-being of military personnel and their families. Food service specialists prepare all types of food in dining halls, hospitals, and ships. Counselors help military personnel and their families deal with personal issues. They work as part of a team that may include social workers, psychologists, medical officers, chaplains, personnel specialists, and commanders. Religious program specialists assist chaplains with religious services, religious education programs, and related administrative duties.

Transportation and material-handling specialists ensure the safe transport of people and cargo. Most personnel within this occupational group are classified according to mode of transportation, such as aircraft, motor vehicle, or ship. Aircrew members operate equipment on aircraft. Vehicle drivers operate all types of heavy military vehicles, including fuel or water tank trucks, semitrailers, heavy troop transports, and passenger buses. Quartermasters and boat operators navigate and pilot many types of small watercraft, including tugboats, gunboats, and barges. Cargo specialists load and unload military supplies, using equipment such as forklifts and cranes.

Vehicle and machinery mechanics conduct preventive and corrective maintenance on aircraft, automotive and heavy equipment, heating and cooling systems, marine engines, and power-house station equipment. These workers typically specialize by the type of equipment that they maintain. For example, aircraft mechanics inspect, service, and repair helicopters, airplanes, and drones. Automotive and heavy equipment mechanics maintain and repair vehicles, such as humvees, trucks, tanks, self-propelled missile launchers, and other combat vehicles. They also repair bulldozers, power shovels, and other construction equipment. Heating and cooling mechanics install and repair air-conditioning, refrigeration, and heating equipment. Marine engine mechanics repair and maintain gasoline and diesel engines on ships, boats, and other watercraft. They also repair shipboard mechanical and electrical equipment. Powerhouse mechanics install, maintain, and repair electrical and mechanical equipment in power-generating stations.

Officer occupational groups. Combat specialty officers plan and direct military operations, oversee combat activities, and serve as combat leaders. This category includes officers in charge of tanks and other armored assault vehicles, artillery systems, Special Forces, and infantry. Combat specialty officers normally specialize by the type of unit they lead. Within the unit, they may further specialize by type of weapon system. Artillery and missile system officers, for example, direct personnel as they target, launch, test, and maintain various types of missiles and artillery. Special operations officers lead their units in offensive raids, demolitions, intelligence gathering, and search-and-rescue missions.

Engineering, science, and technical officers have a wide range of responsibilities based on their area of expertise. They lead or perform activities in areas such as space operations, environmental health and safety, and engineering. These officers may direct the operations of communications centers or the development of complex computer systems. Environmental health and safety officers study the air, ground, and water to identify and analyze sources of pollution and its effects. They also direct programs to control safety and health hazards in the workplace. Other personnel work as aerospace engineers, designing and directing the development of military aircraft, missiles, and spacecraft.

Executive, administrative, and managerial officers oversee and direct military activities in key functional areas, such as finance, accounting, health administration, international relations, and supply. Health services administrators, for instance, are responsible for the overall quality of care provided at the hospitals and clinics they operate. They must ensure that all of the departments work together. As another example, purchasing and contracting managers negotiate and monitor contracts for the purchase of the billions of dollars worth of equipment, supplies, and services that the military buys from private industry each year.

Healthcare officers provide health services at military facilities on the basis of their area of specialization. Officers who examine, diagnose, and treat patients with illness, injury, or disease include physicians, registered nurses, and dentists. Other officers provide therapy, rehabilitative treatment, and additional healthcare services for patients. Physical and occupational therapists plan and administer therapy to help patients adjust to disabilities, regain independence, and return to work. Speech therapists evaluate and treat patients with hearing and speech problems. Dietitians manage food service facilities and plan meals for hospital patients and for outpatients who need special diets. Pharmacists manage the purchase, storage, and dispensing of drugs and medicines. Physicians and surgeons in this occupational group provide the majority of medical services to the military and their families. Dentists treat diseases, disorders, and injuries of the mouth. Optometrists treat vision problems by prescribing eyeglasses or contact lenses. Psychologists provide mental healthcare and also conduct research on behavior and emotions.

Human resource development officers manage recruitment, placement, and training strategies and programs in the military. Recruiting managers direct recruiting efforts and provide information about military careers to young people, parents, schools, and local communities. Personnel managers direct military personnel functions, such as job assignment, staff promotion, and career counseling. Training and education directors identify training needs and develop and manage educational programs designed to keep military personnel current in the skills they need.

Media and public affairs officers oversee the development, production, and presentation of information or events for the public. These officers may produce and direct motion pictures, videos, and television and radio broadcasts that are used for training, news, and entertainment. Some plan, develop, and direct the activities of military bands. Public information officers respond to inquiries about military activities and prepare news releases and reports to keep the public informed.

Protective service officers are responsible for the safety and protection of individuals and property on military bases and vessels. Emergency management officers plan and prepare for all types of natural and human-made disasters by developing warning, control, and evacuation procedures to be used in the event of a disaster. Law enforcement and security officers enforce all applicable laws on military bases and investigate crimes when the law has been broken.

Support services officers manage food service activities and perform services in support of the morale and well-being of military personnel and their families. Food services managers oversee the preparation and delivery of food services within dining facilities located on military installations and vessels. Social workers focus on improving conditions that cause social problems, such as drug and alcohol abuse, racism, and sexism. Chaplains conduct worship services for military personnel and perform other spiritual duties according to the beliefs and practices of various religious faiths.

Transportation officers manage and perform activities related to the safe transport of military personnel and material by air and water. These officers normally specialize by mode of transportation or area of expertise, because, in many cases, they must meet licensing and certification requirements. Pilots in the military fly various types of specialized airplanes and helicopters to execute combat missions and to carry troops and equipment. Navigators use radar, radio, and other navigation equipment to determine their position and plan their route of travel. Officers on ships and submarines work as a team to manage the various departments aboard their vessels. Ships' engineers direct engineering departments aboard ships and submarines, including engine operations, maintenance, repair, heating, and power generation.

Work environment. Specific work environments and conditions depend on the branch of service, the occupational specialty, and other factors. Most military personnel live and work on or near military bases and facilities throughout the United States and the world. These bases and facilities usually offer comfortable housing and amenities, such as stores and recreation centers. Service members move regularly to complete their training or to meet the needs of their branch of service. Some are deployed to defend national interests. Military personnel must be physically fit, mentally stable, and ready to participate in or support combat missions that may be difficult and dangerous and involve time away from family. Some personnel are never deployed near combat areas.

In many circumstances, military personnel work standard hours, but personnel must be prepared to work long hours to fulfill missions, and they must conform to strict military rules at all times. Work hours depend on the occupational specialty and mission.

Training, Other Qualifications, and Advancement

To join the military, applicants must meet age, educational, aptitude, physical, and character requirements. These requirements vary by branch of service and vary between officers, who usu-

Some military personnel are deployed to defend national interests.

ally have a college degree, and enlisted personnel, who often do not. People are assigned an occupational specialty based on their aptitude, former training, and the needs of the military. All service members must sign a contract and commit to a minimum term of service. After joining the military, all enlistees receive general and occupation-specific training.

Those considering enlisting in the military should learn as much as they can about military life before making a decision. Doing so is especially important when one is thinking about making the military a career. Speaking to friends and relatives with military experience is a good idea, as is comparing the pros and cons. The next step is talking to a recruiter, who can determine whether the applicant qualifies for enlistment, explain the various enlistment options, and tell which military occupational specialties currently have openings. Applicants must bear in mind that the recruiter's job is to recruit promising applicants into his or her branch of military service, so the information that the recruiter gives is likely to stress the positive aspects of military life in the branch in which he or she serves.

Applicants should ask their recruiter for the branch they have chosen to assess their chances of being accepted for training in the occupation of their choice or, better still, take the aptitude exam to see how well they score. The military uses this exam as a placement exam, and test scores largely determine an individual's chances of being accepted into a particular training program. Selection for a particular type of training depends on the needs of the service and the applicant's general and technical aptitudes and personal preferences. Because all prospective recruits are required to take the exam, those who do so before committing themselves to enlisting have the advantage of knowing in advance whether they stand a good chance of being accepted for training in a particular specialty. The recruiter can schedule applicants to take the Armed Services Vocational Aptitude Battery without any obligation to join. Many high schools offer the exam as an easy way for students to explore the possibility of a military career, and the test also affords an insight into career areas in which the student has demonstrated aptitudes and interests. The exam is not part of the process of joining the military as an officer.

If an applicant decides to join the military, the next step is to pass the physical examination and sign an enlistment contract. Negotiating the contract involves choosing, qualifying for, and agreeing on a number of enlistment options, such as the length of active-duty time, which may vary according to the option. Most active-duty programs have first-term enlistments of 4 years, although there are some 2-year, 3-year, and 6-year programs. The contract also will state the date of enlistment and other options—for example, bonuses and the types of training to be received. If the service is unable to fulfill any of its obligations under the contract, such as providing a certain kind of training, the contract may become null and void.

All branches of the Armed Services offer a delayed entry program (DEP) by which an individual can delay entry into active duty for up to 1 year after enlisting. High school students can enlist during their senior year and enter a service after graduation. Others choose this program because the job training they desire is not currently available, but will be within the coming year, or because they need time to arrange their personal affairs.

The process of joining the military as an officer is different: officers must meet educational, physical, and character requirements, but they do not take an aptitude test. The education and training section that follows includes more information.

Education and training. All branches of the Armed Forces usually require their members to be high school graduates or have equivalent credentials, such as a GED. In 2008, more than 98 percent of recruits were high school graduates. Officers usually need a bachelor's or graduate degree. Training varies for enlisted and officer personnel and varies by occupational specialty. Currently, the U.S. Military is working with several different certifying bodies to ensure that soldiers who separate from the Armed Forces receive formal recognition in the private sector for their military-based technical training.

Enlisted personnel training. Following enlistment, new members of the Armed Forces undergo initial-entry training, better known as "basic training" or "boot camp." Through courses in military skills and protocol, recruit training provides a 6- to 13-week introduction to military life. Days and nights are carefully structured and include rigorous physical exercise designed to improve strength and endurance and build each unit's cohesion.

Following basic training, most recruits take additional training at technical schools that prepare them for a particular military occupational specialty. The formal training period generally lasts from 10 to 20 weeks, although training for certain occupations—nuclear power plant operator, for example—may take as long as a year. Recruits not assigned to classroom instruction receive on-the-job training at their first duty assignment.

Many service people get college credit for the technical training they receive on duty. Combined with off-duty courses, such training can lead to an associate's degree through programs in community colleges such as the Community College of the Air Force. In addition to receiving on-duty training, military personnel may choose from a variety of educational programs. Most military installations have tuition assistance programs for people wishing to take courses during off-duty hours. The courses may be correspondence courses or courses in degree programs offered by local colleges or universities. Tuition assistance pays up to 100 percent of college costs, up to a credit-hour and annual limit. Each branch of the service provides opportunities for full-time study to a limited number of exceptional applicants. Military personnel accepted into these highly competitive programs receive full pay, allowances, tuition, and related fees. In return, they must agree to serve an additional amount of time in the service. Other highly selective programs enable enlisted personnel to qualify as commissioned officers through additional military training.

Warrant officer training. Warrant officers are technical and tactical leaders who specialize in a specific technical area; for example, Army aviators make up one group of warrant officers. The Army Warrant Officer Corps constitutes less than 5 percent of the total Army. Although the Corps is small in size, its level of responsibility is high. Its members receive extended career opportunities, worldwide leadership assignments, and increased pay and retirement benefits. Selection to attend Warrant Officer Candidate School is highly competitive and restricted to those who meet rank and length-of-service requirements. The only exception is for Army aviator warrant officer, which has no requirement of prior military service.

Officer training. Officer training in the Armed Forces is provided through the Federal service academies (Military, Naval, Air Force, and Coast Guard); the Reserve Officers Training Corps (ROTC) program offered at many colleges and universities; Officer Candidate School (OCS) or Officer Training School (OTS); the National Guard (State Officer Candidate School programs); the Uniformed Services University of Health Sciences; and other programs. All are highly selective and are good options for those wishing to make the military a career. Some personnel are directly appointed to attend one of these academies or programs. People interested in obtaining training through the Federal service academies must be unmarried and without dependents in order to enter and graduate, while those seeking training through OCS, OTS, or ROTC need not be single.

Federal service academies provide a 4-year college program leading to a bachelor-of-science (B.S.) degree. Midshipmen or cadets are provided free room and board, tuition, medical and dental care, and a monthly allowance. Graduates receive regular or reserve commissions and have a 5-year active-duty obligation, or more if they are entering flight training.

To become a candidate for appointment as a cadet or midshipman in one of the service academies, applicants are required to obtain a nomination from an authorized source, usually a member of Congress. Candidates do not need to personally know a member of Congress to request a nomination. Nominees must have an academic record of the requisite quality, college aptitude test scores above an established minimum, and recommendations from teachers or school officials; they also must pass a medical examination. Appointments are made from the list of eligible nominees. Appointments to the Coast Guard Academy, however, are based strictly on merit and do not require a nomination.

ROTC programs train students in approximately 270 Army, 130 Navy and Marine Corps, and 140 Air Force units at participating colleges and universities. In addition to taking regular college courses, trainees take 3 to 5 hours of military instruction a week. After graduation, they may serve as officers on active duty for a stipulated period. Some may serve their obligation in the Reserves or National Guard. In the last 2 years of an ROTC program, students typically receive a monthly allowance while attending school, as well as additional pay for summer training. ROTC scholarships for 2, 3, and 4 years are available on a competitive basis. All scholarships pay for tuition and have allowances for textbooks, supplies, and other costs.

College graduates can earn a commission in the Armed Forces through OCS or OTS programs in the Army, Navy, Air Force, Marine Corps, Coast Guard, and National Guard. These programs consist of several weeks of intensive academic, physical, and leadership training. Those who graduate as officers generally must serve their obligation on active duty.

Personnel with training in certain health professions may qualify for direct appointment as officers. In the case of people studying for the health professions, financial assistance and internship opportunities are available from the military in return for specified periods of military service. Prospective medical students can apply to the Uniformed Services University of Health Sciences, which offers a salary and free tuition in a program leading to a doctor-of-medicine (M.D.) degree. In return, graduates must serve for 7 years in either the military or the Public Health Service. Direct appointments also are available for those qualified to serve in other specialty areas, such as the judge advocate general (legal) or chaplain corps. Flight training is available to commissioned officers in each branch of the Armed Forces. In addition, the Army has a direct enlistment option to become a warrant officer aviator.

Other qualifications. In order to join the services, enlisted personnel must sign a legal agreement called an enlistment contract, which usually involves a commitment of up to 8 years of service. Depending on the terms of the contract, 2 to 6 years are spent on active duty and the balance is spent in the National Guard or Reserves. The enlistment contract obligates the service to provide the agreed-upon job, rating, pay, cash bonuses for enlistment in certain occupations, medical and other benefits, occupational training, and continuing education. In return, enlisted personnel must serve satisfactorily for the period specified.

Requirements for each service vary, but certain qualifications for enlistment are common to all branches. In order to enlist, usually one must be at least 17 years old, be a U.S. citizen or an alien holding permanent resident status, not have a felony record, and possess a birth certificate. Applicants who are 17 years old must have the consent of a parent or legal guardian before entering the service. For active service in the Army, the maximum age is 42; for the Navy, 34; for the Air Force and Coast Guard, 27; and for the Marine Corps, 29. All applicants must pass a written examination—the Armed Services Vocational Aptitude Battery—and meet certain minimum physical standards—for example, for height, weight, vision, and overall health. Officers must meet different age and physical standards, depending on their branch of service.

Women are eligible to enter most military specialties; for example, they may become mechanics, missile maintenance technicians, heavy equipment operators, and fighter pilots, or they may enter into medical care, administrative support, and intelligence specialties. Generally, only occupations involving direct exposure to combat are excluded.

Advancement. Each service has different criteria for promoting personnel. Generally, the first few promotions for both enlisted personnel and officers come easily; subsequent promotions are much more competitive. Criteria for promotion may include time in service and in grade, job performance, a fitness

Table 1. Military rank and employment for active duty personnel, January 2009

Grade	Rank and title				Total Employment
	Army	Navy	Air Force	Marine Corps	
Commissioned officers:					
O-10	General	Admiral	General	General	38
O-9	Lieutenant General	Vice Admiral	Lieutenant General	Lieutenant General	151
O-8	Major General	Rear Admiral (U)	Major General	Major General	304
O-7	Brigadier General	Rear Admiral (L)	Brigadier General	Brigadier General	476
O-6	Colonel	Captain	Colonel	Colonel	12,137
O-5	Lieutenant Colonel	Commander	Lieutenant Colonel	Lieutenant Colonel	29,131
O-4	Major	Lieutenant Commander	Major	Major	44,861
O-3	Captain	Lieutenant	Captain	Captain	72,397
O-2	1st Lieutenant	Lieutenant (JG)	1st Lieutenant	1st Lieutenant	27,492
O-1	2nd Lieutenant	Ensign	2nd Lieutenant	2nd Lieutenant	25,762
Warrant officers:					
W-5	Chief Warrant Officer	Chief Warrant Officer	—	Chief Warrant Officer	679
W-4	Chief Warrant Officer	Chief Warrant Officer	—	Chief Warrant Officer	3,401
W-3	Chief Warrant Officer	Chief Warrant Officer	—	Chief Warrant Officer	5,213
W-2	Chief Warrant Officer	Chief Warrant Officer	—	Chief Warrant Officer	7,255
W-1	Warrant Officer	Warrant Officer	—	Warrant Officer	3,312
Enlisted personnel:					
E-9	Sergeant Major	Master Chief Petty Officer	Chief Master Sergeant	Sergeant Major/ Master Gunnery Sergeant	10,891
E-8	1st Sergeant/Master Sergeant	Senior Chief Petty Officer	Senior Master Sergeant	1st Sergeant/Master Sergeant	28,134
E-7	Sergeant 1st Class	Chief Petty Officer	Master Sergeant	Gunnery Sergeant	101,351
E-6	Staff Sergeant	Petty Officer 1st Class	Technical Sergeant	Staff Sergeant	181,051
E-5	Sergeant	Petty Officer 2nd Class	Staff Sergeant	Sergeant	259,328
E-4	Corporal	Petty Officer 3rd Class	Senior Airman	Corporal	274,336
E-3	Private 1st Class	Seaman	Airman 1st Class	Lance Corporal	206,444
E-2	Private	Seaman Apprentice	Airman	Private 1st Class	93,184
E-1	Private	Seaman Recruit	Airman Basic	Private	71,618

SOURCE: U.S. Department of Defense, Defense Manpower Data Center

report (supervisor's recommendation), and passing scores on written examinations. Table 1 shows the officers, warrant officers, and enlisted ranks by service.

People planning to apply the skills they gained through military training to a civilian career should first determine how good the prospects are for civilian employment in jobs related to the military specialty that interests them. Second, they should know the prerequisites for the related civilian job. Because many civilian occupations require a license, certification, or minimum level of education, it is important to determine whether military training is sufficient for a person to enter the civilian equivalent occupation or, if not, what additional training will be required. Other *Handbook* statements discuss the job outlook, training requirements, and other aspects of civilian occupations for which military training and experience are helpful. Additional information often can be obtained from school counselors.

Employment

In 2009, more than 2.4 million people served in the Armed Forces. More than 1.4 million were on active duty—about 561,000 in the Army, 327,000 in the Navy, 325,000 in the Air Force, and 202,000 in the Marine Corps. In addition, more than 1.0 million people served in their Reserve components and in the Air and Army National Guard, and 41,000 individuals served in the Coast Guard, which is now part of the Department of Homeland Security. Table 2 shows the occupational composition of the active-duty and Coast Guard enlisted personnel in January 2009; table 3 presents similar information for active-duty and Coast Guard officers, including noncommissioned warrant officers.

Military personnel are stationed throughout the United States and in many countries around the world. About half of all military jobs in the U.S. are located in California, Texas, North Carolina, Virginia, Florida, and Georgia. Approximately 265,000 service members were deployed in support of Operations Enduring Freedom and Iraqi Freedom as of June 1, 2009. An additional 378,000 individuals were stationed outside the United States, including 160,000 assigned to ships at sea. About 95,000 were stationed in Europe, mainly in Germany, and an-

In 2009, 41,000 individuals served in the Coast Guard, which is now part of the Department of Homeland Security.

other 71,000 were assigned to East Asia and the Pacific area, mostly in Japan and the Republic of Korea.

Job Outlook

Opportunities should be excellent for qualified individuals in all branches of the Armed Forces.

Employment change. The United States spends a significant portion of its overall budget on national defense. The num-

Table 2. Military enlisted personnel by broad occupational category and branch of military service, January 2009

Occupational Group - Enlisted	Army	Air Force	Coast Guard	Marine Corps	Navy	Total, all services
Administrative occupations	6,727	17,537	1,621	9,219	22,147	57,251
Combat specialty occupations	132,079	480	904	52,445	7,595	193,503
Construction occupations	20,872	4,689	—	6,759	5,521	37,841
Electronic and electrical repair occupations	37,466	34,751	4,663	16,199	47,985	141,064
Engineering, science, and technical occupations	42,770	41,328	1,212	26,940	38,778	151,028
Healthcare occupations	30,945	16,420	772	—	23,960	72,097
Human resource development occupations	20,251	11,321	1	7,134	5,300	44,007
Machine operator and production occupations	6,372	6,181	1,816	2,575	8,596	25,540
Media and public affairs occupations	8,233	6,910	152	2,518	3,659	21,472
Protective service occupations	29,076	34,099	2,816	7,156	12,555	85,702
Support services occupations	13,554	6,071	1,263	2,765	9,188	32,841
Transportation and material handling occupations	69,454	31,396	11,748	25,909	45,176	183,683
Vehicle and machinery mechanic occupations	54,771	43,409	6,119	22,068	45,209	171,576
Non-occupation coded personnel	1,081	6,681	326	12	755	8,855
Total, by service	473,651	261,273	33,413	181,699	276,424	1,226,460

SOURCE: U.S. Department of Defense, Defense Manpower Data Center

Table 3. Military officer personnel by broad occupational category and branch of service, January 2009

Occupational Group - Officer	Army	Air Force	Coast Guard	Marine Corps	Navy	Total, all services
Combat specialty occupations	20,201	2,611	77	5,315	1,125	29,329
Engineering, science, and technical occupations	21,676	17,800	210	4,006	7,616	51,308
Executive, administrative, and managerial occupations	13,104	7,327	197	2,725	5,442	28,795
Healthcare occupations	10,626	8,661	1	—	7,468	26,756
Human resource development occupations	2,676	2,293	151	279	520	5,919
Media and public affairs occupations	310	305	15	175	290	1,095
Protective service occupations	2,867	1,131	60	353	284	4,695
Support services occupations	1,741	758	3	38	857	3,397
Transportation occupations	12,519	22,828	580	7,345	27,340	70,612
Non-occupation coded personnel	2,597	866	6,769	88	386	10,706
Total, by service	88,317	64,580	8,063	20,324	51,328	232,612

SOURCE: U.S. Department of Defense, Defense Manpower Data Center

ber of active-duty personnel is expected to remain roughly constant through 2018. However, recent conflicts and the resulting strain on the military may lead to an increase in the number of active-duty personnel. The current goal of the Armed Forces is to maintain a force sufficient to fight and win two major regional conflicts at the same time. Political events, however, could lead to a significant restructuring with or without an increase in size.

Job prospects. Opportunities should be excellent for qualified individuals in all branches of the Armed Forces through 2018. Many military personnel retire with a pension after 20 years of service, while they still are young enough to start a new career. About 184,000 personnel must be recruited each year to replace those who complete their commitment or retire. Since the end of the draft in 1973, the military has met its personnel requirements with volunteers. When the economy is good and civilian employment opportunities generally are more favorable, it is more difficult for all the services to meet their recruitment quotas. When there are economic downturns, recruits may face more competition for various occupational specialties. It

is also more difficult to meet these goals during times of war, when recruitment goals typically rise.

Educational requirements will continue to rise as military jobs become more technical and complex. High school graduates and applicants with a college background will be sought to fill the ranks of enlisted personnel, while virtually all officers will need at least a bachelor's degree and, in some cases, a graduate degree as well.

Earnings

The earnings structure for military personnel is shown in table 4. Most enlisted personnel started as recruits at Grade E-1 in 2009; however, those with special skills or above-average education started as high as Grade E-4. Most warrant officers started at Grade W-1 or W-2, depending upon their occupational and academic qualifications and the branch of service of which they were a member, but warrant officer typically is not an entry-level occupation and, consequently, most of these individuals had previous military service. Most commissioned officers started at Grade O-1; some with advanced education started at Grade O-2, and some highly trained officers—for example, physicians and dentists—started as high as Grade O-3. Pay varies by total years of service as well as rank. Because it usually takes many years to reach the higher ranks, most personnel in higher ranks receive the higher pay rates awarded to those with many years of service.

In addition to receiving their basic pay, military personnel are provided with free room and board (or a tax-free housing and subsistence allowance), free medical and dental care, a military clothing allowance, military supermarket and department store shopping privileges, 30 days of paid vacation a year (referred to as leave), and travel opportunities. In many duty stations, military personnel may receive a housing allowance that can be used for off-base housing. This allowance can be substantial, but varies greatly by rank and duty station. For example, in fiscal year 2009, the basic allowance for housing for an E-4 with dependents was $681.90 per month; for a comparable individual without dependents, it was $511.50. The allowance for an O-4 with dependents was $1,297.80 per month; for a comparable individual without dependents, it was $1,128.60. Other allowances are paid for foreign duty, hazardous duty, submarine and flight duty, and employment as a medical officer. Athletic and other facilities—such as gymnasiums, tennis courts, golf courses, bowling centers, libraries, and movie theaters—are

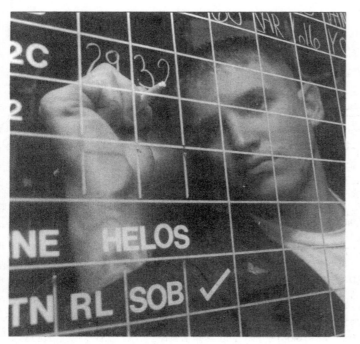

Educational requirements will continue to rise as military jobs become more technical and complex.

Table 4. Military basic monthly pay by grade for active duty personnel, April 2009

Grade	Years of service					
	Less than 2	Over 4	Over 8	Over 12	Over 16	Over 20
Commissioned officers:						
O-10	—	—	—	—	—	14,689
O-9	—	—	—	—	—	12,847
O-8	9,090	9,641	10,299	10,786	11,235	12,172
O-7	7,553	8,195	8,660	9,193	10,299	11,007
O-6	5,598	6,554	6,861	6,898	7,983	8,797
O-5	4,667	5,690	6,053	6,571	7,287	7,697
O-4	4,027	5,042	5,640	6,326	6,654	6,723
O-3	3,540	4,723	5,197	5,622	5,760	5,760
O-2	3,059	4,148	4,233	4,233	4,233	4,233
O-1	2,655	3,341	3,341	3,341	3,341	3,341
Warrant officers:						
W-5	—	—	—	—	—	6,506
W-4	3,659	4,160	4,541	5,021	5,515	5,903
W-3	3,341	3,670	4,114	4,565	4,904	5,422
W-2	2,957	3,382	3,871	4,164	4,481	4,757
W-1	2,595	3,108	3,573	3,882	4,199	4,484
Enlisted personnel:						
E-9	—	—	—	4,521	4,796	5,185
E-8	—	—	3,619	3,878	4,125	4,475
E-7	2,516	2,990	3,285	3,578	3,839	3,995
E-6	2,176	2,602	2,951	3,226	3,323	3,370
E-5	1,994	2,335	2,671	2,828	2,828	2,828
E-4	1,828	2,128	2,219	2,219	2,219	2,219
E-3	1,650	1,860	1,860	1,860	1,860	1,860
E-2	1,569	1,569	1,569	1,569	1,569	1,569
E-1 4 months+	1,400	—	—	—	—	—
E-1 Less than 4 months	1,295	—	—	—	—	—

SOURCE: U.S. Department of Defense—Defense Finance and Accounting Service

available on many military installations. Military personnel are eligible for retirement benefits after 20 years of service.

The Veterans Administration (VA) provides numerous benefits to those who have served at least 24 months of continuous active duty in the Armed Forces. Veterans are eligible for free care in VA hospitals for all service-related disabilities, regardless of time served; those with other medical problems are eligible for free VA care if they are unable to pay the cost of hospitalization elsewhere. Admission to a VA medical center depends on the availability of beds, however. Veterans also are eligible for certain loans, including loans to purchase a home. Regardless of their health, veterans can convert a military life insurance policy to an individual policy with any participating company upon separation from the military. In addition, job counseling, testing, and placement services are available.

Veterans who participate in the Montgomery GI Bill Program receive education benefits. Under this program, Armed Forces personnel may elect to deduct up to $100 a month from their pay during the first 12 months of active duty, putting the money toward their future education. In fiscal year 2009, veterans who served on active duty for 3 or more years or who spent 2 years in active duty plus 4 years in the Selected Reserve received $1,321 a month in basic benefits for 36 months of full-time institutional training. Those who enlisted and served less than 3 years received $1,073 a month for 36 months of the same. In addition, each service provides its own contributions to the enlistee's future education. The sum of the amounts from all these sources becomes the service member's educational fund. Upon separation from active duty, the fund can be used to finance educational costs at any VA-approved institution. Among those institutions which are approved by the VA are many vocational, correspondence, certification, business, technical, and flight training schools; community and junior colleges; and colleges and universities. The new Post-9/11 GI Bill is an alternative education benefit. There is no deductable for service personnel. The size of the benefit is scaled to the State and to the institution that the veteran is attending. Service personnel must carefully choose which program will be of the most benefit to them in their planned educational future.

Sources of Additional Information

Each of the military services publishes handbooks, fact sheets, and pamphlets describing its entrance requirements, its training and advancement opportunities, and other aspects of military careers. These publications are widely available at all recruiting stations, at most State employment service offices, and in high schools, colleges, and public libraries. Information on educational and other veterans' benefits is available from VA offices located throughout the country.

In addition, the Defense Manpower Data Center, an agency of the Department of Defense, publishes *Military Career Guide Online*, a compendium of military occupational, training, and career information designed for use by students and jobseekers. This information is available on the Internet at **http://www.todaysmilitary.com**.

The Occupational Outlook Quarterly also provides information about military careers and training; see the spring 2007 article "Military training for civilian careers (Or: How to gain practical experience while serving your country)," available online at **http://www.bls.gov/opub/ooq/2007/spring/art02.pdf.**

The Occupational Information Network (O*NET) provides information on a wide range of occupational characteristics. Links to O*NET appear at the end of the Internet version of this occupational statement, accessible at **http://www.bls.gov/ooh/ocos249.htm**

Data for Occupations Not Covered in Detail

Employment in the hundreds of occupations covered in detail in the main body of the *Handbook* accounts for more than 134 million, or 89 percent, of all jobs in the economy. Although occupations covering the full spectrum of work are included, those requiring lengthy education or training generally are given the most attention.

This chapter presents summary data on 127 additional occupations, for which employment projections are prepared, but for which detailed occupational information is not developed. These occupations account for about 7 percent of all jobs. For each occupation, the Occupational Information Network (O*NET) code, a brief description of the nature of the work, the number of jobs in 2008, a phrase describing the projected employment change from 2008 to 2018, and the most significant source of postsecondary education or training are presented. For a complete list of O*NET codes cited in the *Handbook*, refer to a later chapter, *Occupational Information Network* (O*NET) *Coverage*. For guidelines on interpreting the description of projected employment change, refer to a chapter in the front of the *Handbook*, Occupational Information Included in the *Handbook*.

The approximately 4 percent of all jobs not covered either in the detailed occupational descriptions in the main body of the *Handbook* or in the summary data presented in this chapter are mainly residual categories, such as "all other managers," for which little meaningful information could be developed.

Management, business, and financial occupations

Agents and business managers of artists, performers, and athletes

Represent and promote artists, performers, and athletes to prospective employers. May handle contract negotiations and other business matters for clients.

2008 Employment: 22, 700
Projected 2008-18 employment change: Much faster than average
Most significant source of postsecondary education or training: Bachelor's or higher degree, plus work experience

Compliance officers, except agriculture, construction, health and safety, and transportation

Examine, evaluate, and investigate eligibility for or conformity with laws and regulations governing contract compliance of licenses and permits, and other compliance and enforcement inspection activities not classified elsewhere. Exclude tax examiners, collectors, and revenue agents and financial examiners.

2008 Employment: 260,200
Projected 2008-18 employment change: Much faster than average
Most significant source of postsecondary education or training: Long-term on-the-job training

Credit analysts

Analyze current credit data and financial statements of individuals or firms to determine the degree of risk involved in extending credit or lending money. Prepare reports with this credit information for use in decision-making.

2008 Employment: 73,200
Projected 2008-18 employment change: Faster than average
Most significant source of postsecondary education or training: Bachelor's degree

Emergency management specialists

Coordinate disaster response or crisis management activities, provide disaster preparedness training and prepare emergency plans and procedures for natural (e.g. hurricanes, floods, earthquakes), wartime, or technological (e.g., nuclear power plant emergencies, hazardous materials spills) disasters or hostage situations.

2008 Employment: 12,800
Projected 2008-18 employment change: Much faster than average
Most significant source of postsecondary education or training: Work experience in a related occupation

Financial examiners

Enforce or ensure compliance with laws and regulations governing financial and securities institutions and financial and real estate transactions. May examine, verify correctness of, or establish authenticity of records.

2008 Employment: 27,000
Projected 2008-18 employment change: Much faster than average
Most significant source of postsecondary education or training: Bachelor's degree

Legislators

Develop laws and statutes at the Federal, State, or local level. Includes only elected officials.

2008 Employment: 67,600
Projected 2008-18 employment change: Little or no change
Most significant source of postsecondary education or training: Bachelor's or higher degree, plus work experience

Loan counselors

Provide guidance to prospective loan applicants who have problems qualifying for traditional loans. Guidance may include determining the best type of loan and explaining loan requirements or restrictions.

2008 Employment: 32,400
Projected 2008-18 employment change: Faster than average
Most significant source of postsecondary education or training: Bachelor's degree

Logisticians

Analyze and coordinate the logistical functions of a firm or organization. Responsible for the entire life cycle of a product, including acquisition, distribution, internal allocation, delivery, and final disposal of resources.

2008 Employment: 100,400
Projected 2008-18 employment change: Much faster than average
Most significant source of postsecondary education or training: Bachelor's degree

Postmasters and mail superintendents

Direct and coordinate operational, administrative, management, and supportive services of a U.S. post office; or coordinate activities of workers engaged in postal and related work in assigned post office.

2008 Employment: 25,600
Projected 2008-18 employment change: Decline rapidly
Most significant source of postsecondary education or training: Work experience in a related occupation

Social and community service managers

Plan, organize, or coordinate the activities of a social service program or community outreach organization. Oversee the program or organization's budget and polices regarding participant involvement, program requirement, and benefits. Work may involve directing social workers, counselors, or probation officers.

2008 Employment: 130,600
Projected 2008-18 employment change: Faster than average
Most significant source of postsecondary education or training: Bachelor's degree

Tax preparers

Prepare tax returns for individuals or small businesses but do not have the background or responsibilities of an accredited or certified public accountant.

2008 Employment: 95,800
Projected 2008-18 employment change: More slowly than average
Most significant source of postsecondary education or training: Moderate-term on-the-job training

Transportation, storage, and distribution managers

Plan, direct, or coordinate transportation, storage, or distribution activities in accordance with governmental policies and regulations. Includes logistics managers.

2008 Employment: 99,700
Projected 2008-18 employment change: Decline slowly
Most significant source of postsecondary education or training: Work experience in a related occupation

Professional and related occupations

Audio-visual collections specialists

Prepare, plan, and operate audio-visual teaching aids for use in education. May record, catalogue, and file audio-visual materials.

2008 Employment: 6,800
Projected 2008-18 employment change: About as fast as average
Most significant source of postsecondary education or training: Bachelor's degree

Clergy

Conduct religious worship and perform other spiritual functions associated with beliefs and practices of religious faith or denomination. Provide spiritual and moral guidance and assistance to members.

2008 Employment: 670,100
Projected 2008-18 employment change: About as fast as average
Most significant source of postsecondary education or training: Master's degree

Dietetic technicians

Assist dieticians in the provision of food service and nutritional programs. Under the supervision of dieticians, may plan and produce meals based on established guidelines, teach principles of food and nutrition, or counsel individuals.

2008 Employment: 25,200
Projected 2008-18 employment change: Faster than average
Most significant source of postsecondary education or training: Postsecondary vocational award

Directors, religious activities and education

Direct and coordinate activities of a denominational group to meet religious needs of students. Plan, direct, or coordinate church school programs designed to promote religious education among church membership. May provide counseling and guidance relative to marital, health, financial, or religious problems.

2008 Employment: 80,400
Projected 2008-18 employment change: About as fast as average
Most significant source of postsecondary education or training: Bachelor's degree

Farm and home management advisors

Advise, instruct, and assist individuals and families engaged in agriculture, agricultural-related processes, or home economics activities. Demonstrate procedures and apply research findings to solve problems; instruct and train in product development, sales, and the utilization of machinery and equipment to promote general welfare. Include county agricultural agents, feed and farm management advisors, home economists, and extension service advisors.

2008 Employment: 13,100
Projected 2008-18 employment change: Little or no change
Most significant source of postsecondary education or training: Bachelor's degree

Law clerks

Assist lawyers or judges by researching or preparing legal documents. May meet with clients or assist lawyers and judges in court. Excludes lawyers, and paralegal and legal assistants.

2008 Employment: 37,700
Projected 2008-18 employment change: Faster than average
Most significant source of postsecondary education or training: Bachelor's degree

Mathematical technicians

Apply standardized mathematical formulas, principles, and methodology to technological problems in engineering and physical sciences in relation to specific industrial and research objectives, processes, equipment, and products.

2008 Employment: 1,200
Projected 2008-18 employment change: About as fast as average
Most significant source of postsecondary education or training: Associate degree

Merchandise displayers and window trimmers

Plan and erect commercial displays, such as those in windows and interiors of retail stores and at trade exhibitions.

2008 Employment: 85,200
Projected 2008-18 employment change: About as fast as average
Most significant source of postsecondary education or training: Moderate-term on-the-job training

Orthotists and prosthetists

Assist patients with disabling conditions of limbs and spine or with partial or total absence of limb by fitting and preparing orthopedic braces and prostheses.

2008 Employment: 5,900
Projected 2008-18 employment change: Faster than average
Most significant source of postsecondary education or training: Bachelor's degree

Psychiatric technicians

Care for mentally impaired or emotionally disturbed individuals, following physician instructions and hospital procedures. Monitor patients' physical and emotional well-being and report to medical staff. May participate in rehabilitation and treatment programs, help with personal hygiene, and administer oral medications and hypodermic injections.

2008 Employment: 57,100
Projected 2008-18 employment change: More slowly than average
Most significant source of postsecondary education or training: Postsecondary vocational award

Set and exhibit designers

Design special exhibits and movie, television, and theater sets. May study scripts, confer with directors, and conduct research to determine appropriate architectural styles.

2008 Employment: 10,900
Projected 2008-18 employment change: Faster than average
Most significant source of postsecondary education or training: Bachelor's degree

Social science research assistants

Assist social scientists in laboratory, survey, and other social research. May perform publication activities, laboratory analysis, quality control, or data management. Normally these individuals work under the direct supervision of a social scientist and assist in those activities which are more routine. Excludes graduate teaching assistants, who both teach and do research.

2008 Employment: 21,000
Projected 2008-18 employment change: Faster than average
Most significant source of postsecondary education or training: Associate degree

Title examiners, abstractors, and searchers

Search real estate records, examine titles, or summarize pertinent legal or insurance details for a variety of purposes. May compile lists of mortgages, contracts, and other instruments pertaining to titles by searching public and private records for law firms, real estate agencies, or title insurance companies.

2008 Employment: 69,500
Projected 2008-18 employment change: Little or no change
Most significant source of postsecondary education or training: Moderate-term on-the-job training

---

Service occupations

Amusement and recreation attendants

Perform a variety of attending duties at amusement or recreation facilities. May schedule use of recreations facilities, maintain and provide equipment to participants of sporting events or recreational pursuits, or operate amusement concessions and rides.

2008 Employment: 263,000
Projected 2008-18 employment change: About as fast as average
Most significant source of postsecondary education or training: Short-term on-the-job training

Animal control workers

Handle animals for the purpose of investigations of mistreatment, or control of abandoned, dangerous, or unattended animals.

2008 Employment: 16,100
Projected 2008-18 employment change: About as fast as average
Most significant source of postsecondary education or training: Moderate-term on-the-job training

Baggage porters and bellhops

Handle baggage for travelers at transportation terminals or for guests at hotels or similar establishments.

2008 Employment: 50,500
Projected 2008-18 employment change: About as fast as average
Most significant source of postsecondary education or training: Short-term on-the-job training

Concierges

Assist patrons at hotel, apartment or office building with personal services. May take messages, arrange or give advice on transportation, business services or entertainment, or monitor guest requests for housekeeping and maintenance.

2008 Employment: 20,800
Projected 2008-18 employment change: Faster than average
Most significant source of postsecondary education or training: Moderate-term on-the-job training

Costume attendants

Select, fit and take care of costumes for cast members, and aid entertainers.

2008 Employment: 5,100
Projected 2008-18 employment change: Faster than average
Most significant source of postsecondary education or training: Short-term on-the-job training

Crossing guards

Guide or control vehicular or pedestrian traffic at such places as streets, schools, railroad crossings, or construction sites.

2008 Employment: 69,900
Projected 2008-18 employment change: About as fast as average
Most significant source of postsecondary education or training: Short-term on-the-job training

Embalmers

Prepare bodies for interment in conformity with legal requirements.

2008 Employment: 8,500
Projected 2008-18 employment change: More slowly than average
Most significant source of postsecondary education or training: Postsecondary vocational award

First-line supervisors/managers of personal service workers

Supervise and coordinate activities of personal service workers, such as supervisors of flight attendants, hairdressers, or caddies.

2008 Employment: 213,200
Projected 2008-18 employment change: Faster than average
Most significant source of postsecondary education or training: Work experience in a related occupation

Funeral attendants

Perform a variety of tasks during a funeral, such as placing casket in parlor or chapel prior to service; arranging floral offerings or lights around casket; directing or escorting mourners; closing casket; and issuing and storing funeral equipment.

2008 Employment: 34,500
Projected 2008-18 employment change: Much faster than average
Most significant source of postsecondary education or training: Short-term on-the-job training

Lifeguards, ski patrol, and other recreational protective service workers

Monitor recreational areas, such as pools, beaches, or ski slopes to provide assistance and protection to participants.

2008 Employment: 115,200
Projected 2008-18 employment change: About as fast as average
Most significant source of postsecondary education or training: Short-term on-the-job-training

Locker room, coatroom, and dressing room attendants

Provide personal items to patrons or customers in locker rooms, dressing rooms, or coatrooms.

2008 Employment: 18,500
Projected 2008-18 employment change: About as fast as average
Most significant source of postsecondary education or training: Short-term on-the-job training

Medical equipment preparers

Prepare, sterilize, install, or clean laboratory or healthcare equipment. May perform routine laboratory tasks and operate or inspect equipment.

2008 Employment: 46,800
Projected 2008-18 employment change: About as fast as average
Most significant source of postsecondary education or training: Short-term on-the-job training

Motion picture projectionists

Set up and operate motion picture projection and related sound reproduction equipment.

2008 Employment: 10,800
Projected 2008-18 employment change: Little or no change
Most significant source of postsecondary education or training: Short-term on-the-job training

Parking enforcement workers

Patrol assigned area, such as public parking lot or section of city to issue tickets to overtime parking violators and illegally parked vehicles.

2008 Employment: 10,000
Projected 2008-18 employment change: Little or no change
Most significant source of postsecondary education or training: Short-term on-the-job training

Residential advisors

Coordinate activities for residents of boarding schools, college fraternities or sororities, college dormitories, or similar establishments. Order supplies and determine need to maintenance, repairs, and furnishings. May maintain household records and assign rooms. May refer residents to counseling resources if needed.

2008 Employment: 56,900
Projected 2008-18 employment change: About as fast as average
Most significant source of postsecondary education or training: Short-term on-the-job training

Tour guides and escorts

Escort individuals or groups on sightseeing tours or through places of interest, such as industrial establishments, public buildings, and art galleries.

2008 Employment: 38,400
Projected 2008-18 employment change: About as fast as average
Most significant source of postsecondary education or training: Moderate-term on-the-job training

Transportation attendants, except flight attendants and baggage porters

Provide services to ensure the safety and comfort of passengers aboard ships, buses, trains, or within the station or terminal. Perform duties, such as greeting passengers, explaining the use of safety equipment, serving meals or beverages, or answering questions related to travel.

2008 Employment: 21,700
Projected 2008-18 employment change: About as fast as average
Most significant source of postsecondary education or training: Short-term on-the-job training

Travel guides

Plan, organize, and conduct long distance cruises, tours, and expeditions for individuals or groups.

2008 Employment: 5,600
Projected 2008-18 employment change: Little or no change
Most significant source of postsecondary education or training: Moderate-term on-the-job training

Ushers, lobby attendants, and ticket takers

Assist patrons at entertainment events by performing duties, such as collecting admission tickets and passes from patrons, assisting in finding seats, searching for lost articles, and locating such facilities as rest rooms and telephones.

2008 Employment: 106,100
Projected 2008-18 employment change: Faster than average
Most significant source of postsecondary education or training: Short-term on-the-job training

Veterinary assistants and laboratory animal caretakers

Feed, water, and examine pets and other nonfarm animals for signs of illness, disease, or injury in laboratories and animal hospitals and clinics. Clean and disinfect cages and work areas, and sterilize laboratory and surgical equipment. May provide routine postoperative care, administer medication orally or topically, or prepare samples for laboratory examination under the supervision of veterinary or laboratory animal technologists or technicians, veterinarians, or scientists. Excludes nonfarm animal caretakers.

2008 Employment: 75,200
Projected 2008-18 employment change: Much faster than average
Most significant source of postsecondary education or training: Short-term on-the-job training

Sales and related occupations

Door-to-door sales workers, news and street vendors, and related workers

Sell goods or services door-to-door or on the street.

2008 Employment: 181,600
Projected 2008-18 employment change: Decline rapidly
Most significant source of postsecondary education or training: Short-term on-the-job training

Parts salespersons

Sell spare and replacement parts and equipment in repair shop or parts store.

2008 Employment: 227,500
Projected 2008-18 employment change: Little or no change
Most significant source of postsecondary education or training: Moderate-term on-the-job training

Telemarketers

Solicit orders for goods and services over the telephone.

2008 Employment: 341,600
Projected 2008-18 employment change: Decline rapidly
Most significant source of postsecondary education or training: Short-term on-the-job training

Office and administrative support occupations

Correspondence clerks

Compose letters in reply to request for merchandise, damage claims, credit and other information, delinquent accounts, incorrect billings, or unsatisfactory services. Duties may include gathering data to formulate reply and typing correspondence.

2008 Employment: 14,200
Projected 2008-18 employment change: Decline rapidly
Most significant source of postsecondary education or training: Short-term-on-the-job training

Court, municipal, and license clerks

Perform clerical duties in courts of law, municipalities, and governmental licensing agencies and bureaus. May prepare docket of cases to be called; secure information for judges and court; prepare draft agendas or bylaws for town or city council; answer official correspondence; keep fiscal records and accounts; issue licenses or permits; record data, administer tests, or collect fees.

2008 Employment: 122,100
Projected 2008-18 employment change: About as fast as average
Most significant source of postsecondary education or training: Short-term-on-the-job training

Insurance claims and policy processing clerks

Process new insurance policies, modifications to existing policies, and claims forms. Obtain information from policyholders to verify the accuracy and completeness of information on claims forms, applications and related documents, and company records. Update existing policies and company records to reflect changes requested by policyholders and insurance company representatives. Excludes claims adjusters, examiners, and investigators.

2008 Employment: 253,800
Projected 2008-18 employment change: Little or no change
Most significant source of postsecondary education or training: Moderate-term on-the-job training

Mail clerks and mail machine operators, except Postal Service

Prepare incoming and outgoing mail for distribution. Use hand or mail handling machines to time, stamp, open, read, sort, and route incoming mail; and address, seal, stamp, fold, stuff, and affix postage to outgoing mail or packages. Duties may also include keeping necessary records and completed forms.

2008 Employment: 141,400
Projected 2008-18 employment change: Decline rapidly
Most significant source of postsecondary education or training: Short-term on-the-job training

New accounts clerks

Interview persons desiring to open bank accounts. Explain banking services available to prospective customers and assist them in preparing application form.

2008 Employment: 87,300
Projected 2008-18 employment change: Little or no change
Most significant source of postsecondary education or training: Work experience in a related occupation

Office machine operators, except computer

Operate one or more of a variety of office machines, such as photocopying, photographic, and duplicating machines, or other office machines. Excludes computer operators; mail clerks and mail machine operators; and billing and posting clerks and machine operators.

2008 Employment: 79,900
Projected 2008-18 employment change: Decline slowly
Most significant source of postsecondary education or training: Short-term on-the-job training

Proofreaders and copy markers

Read transcript or proof type setup to detect and mark for correction any grammatical, typographical, or compositional errors. Excludes workers whose primary duty is editing copy. Includes proofreaders of Braille.

2008 Employment: 18,200
Projected 2008-18 employment change: Decline slowly
Most significant source of postsecondary education or training: Short-term on-the-job training

Statistical assistants

Compile and compute data according to statistical formulas for use in statistical studies. May perform actuarial computations and compile charts and graphs for use by actuaries. Includes actuarial clerks.

2008 Employment: 17,900
Projected 2008-18 employment change: More slowly than average
Most significant source of postsecondary education or training: Moderate-term on-the-job training

Farming, fishing, and forestry occupations

Supervisors, farming, fishing, and forestry workers

This broad occupation includes two detailed occupations—first-line supervisors/managers of farming, fishing, and forestry workers; and farm labor contractors. First-line supervisors/managers of farming, fishing, and forestry workers directly supervise and coordinate the activities of agricultural, forestry, aquacultural, and related workers. Farm labor contractors recruit, hire, furnish, and supervise seasonal or temporary agricultural laborers for a fee. May transport, house, and provide meals for workers. Excludes first-line supervisors/managers of landscaping, lawn service, and groundskeeping workers.

2008 Employment: 48,600
Projected 2008-18 employment change: About as fast as average
Most significant source of postsecondary education or training: Work experience in a related occupation

Construction and extraction occupations

Continuous mining machine operators
Operate self-propelled mining machines that rip coal, metal and non-metal ores, rock, stone, or sand form the face and load it onto conveyors or into shuttle cars in a continuous operation.

2008 Employment: 11,200
Projected 2008-18 employment change: Decline slowly
Most significant source of postsecondary education or training: Moderate-term on-the-job training

Derrick operators, oil and gas
Rig derrick equipment and operate pumps to circulate mud through drill hole.

2008 Employment: 25,000
Projected 2008-18 employment change: Decline rapidly
Most significant source of postsecondary education or training: Moderate-term on-the-job training

Earth drillers, except oil and gas
Operate a variety of drills—such as rotary, churn, and pneumatic—to tap subsurface water and salt deposits, to remove core samples during mineral exploration or soil testing, and to facilitate the use of explosives in mining or construction. May use explosives. Includes horizontal and earth boring machine operators.

2008 Employment: 23,300
Projected 2008-18 employment change: About as fast as average
Most significant source of postsecondary education or training: Moderate-term on-the-job training

Explosives workers, ordnance handling experts, and blasters
Place and detonate explosives to demolish structures or to loosen, remove, or displace earth, rock, or other materials. May perform specialized handling, storage, and accounting procedures. Includes seismograph shooters. Excludes earth drillers, except oil and gas who may also work with explosives.

2008 Employment: 6,300
Projected 2008-18 employment change: More slowly than average
Most significant source of postsecondary education or training: Moderate-term on-the-job training

Fence erectors
Erect and repair metal and wooden fences and fence gates around highways, industrial establishments, residences, or farms, using hand and power tools.

2008 Employment: 33,600
Projected 2008-18 employment change: Faster than average
Most significant source of postsecondary education or training: Moderate-term on-the-job training

First-line supervisors/managers of construction trades and extraction workers
Directly supervise and coordinate activities of construction or extraction workers.

2008 Employment: 698,100
Projected 2008-18 employment change: Faster than average
Most significant source of postsecondary education or training: Work experience in a related occupation

Helpers—brickmasons, blockmasons, stonemasons, and tile and marble setters
Help brickmasons, blockmasons, stonemasons, or tile and marble setters by performing duties of lesser skill. Duties include using, supplying, or holding materials or tools, and cleaning work area and equipment. Excludes apprentice workers and report them with the appropriate skilled construction trade occupation. Excludes construction laborers who do not primarily assist brickmasons, blockmasons, and stonemasons or tile and marble setters.

2008 Employment: 50,800
Projected 2008-18 employment change: Faster than average
Most significant source of postsecondary education or training: Short-term on-the-job training

Helpers—carpenters
Help carpenters by performing duties of lesser skill. Duties include using, supplying, or holding materials or tools, and cleaning work area and equipment. Excludes apprentice workers and report them with the appropriate skilled construction trade occupation. Excludes construction laborers who do not primarily assist carpenters.

2008 Employment: 79,800
Projected 2008-18 employment change: Much faster than average
Most significant source of postsecondary education or training: Short-term on-the-job training

Helpers—electricians
Help electricians by performing duties of lesser skill. Duties include using, supplying, or holding materials or tools, and cleaning work area and equipment. Excludes apprentice workers and report them with them with the appropriate skilled construction trade occupation. Excludes construction laborers who do not primarily assist electricians.

2008 Employment: 105,600
Projected 2008-18 employment change: Much faster than average
Most significant source of postsecondary education or training: Short-term on-the-job training

Helpers—extraction workers
Help extraction craft workers, such as earth drillers, blasters and explosives workers, derrick operators, and mining machine operators, by performing duties of lesser skill. Duties include supplying equipment or cleaning work area. Excludes apprentice workers.

2008 Employment: 26,200
Projected 2008-18 employment change: Decline rapidly
Most significant source of postsecondary education or training: Short-term on-the-job training

Helpers—painters, paperhangers, plasterers, and stucco masons
Help painters, paperhangers, plasterers, or stucco masons by performing duties of lesser skill. Duties including using, supplying, or holding materials or tools, and cleaning work area and equipment. Excludes apprentice workers and report them with the appropriate skilled construction trade occupation. Excludes construction laborers who do not primarily assist painters, paperhangers, plasterers, or stucco masons.

2008 Employment: 19,400
Projected 2008-18 employment change: Decline slowly
Most significant source of postsecondary education or training: Short-term on-the-job training

Helpers—pipelayers, plumbers, pipefitters, and steamfitters

Help pipelayers, plumbers, pipefitters, or steamfitters by performing duties of lesser skill. Duties including using, supplying, or holding materials or tools, and cleaning work area and equipment. Excludes apprentice workers and report them with the appropriate skilled construction trade occupation. Excludes construction laborers who do not primarily assist pipelayers, plumbers, pipefitters or steamfitters.

2008 Employment: 80,300
Projected 2008-18 employment change: Much faster than average
Most significant source of postsecondary education or training: Short-term on-the-job training

Helpers—roofers

Help roofers by performing duties of lesser skill. Duties include using, supplying, or holding materials or tools, and cleaning work area and equipment. Excludes apprentice workers and report them with the appropriate skilled construction trade occupation. Excludes construction laborers who do not primarily assist roofers.

2008 Employment: 18,700
Projected 2008-18 employment change: Decline slowly
Most significant source of postsecondary education or training: Short-term on-the-job training

Highway maintenance workers

Maintain highways, municipal and rural roads, airport runways, and rights-of-way. Duties include patching broken or eroded pavement, repairing guard rails, highway markers, and snow fences. May also mow or clear brush from along road or plow snow from roadway. Excludes tree trimmers and pruners.

2008 Employment: 145,900
Projected 2008-18 employment change: About as fast as average
Most significant source of postsecondary education or training: Moderate-term on-the-job training

Mine cutting and channeling machine operators

Operate machinery—such as longwall shears, plows, and cutting machines—to cut or channel along the face or seams of coal mines, stone quarries, or other mining surfaces to facilitate blasting, separating, or removing minerals or materials from mines or from the earth's surface. Includes shale planers.

2008 Employment: 9,400
Projected 2008-18 employment change: More slowly than average
Most significant source of postsecondary education or training: Moderate-term on-the-job training

Rail-track laying and maintenance equipment operators

Lay, repair, and maintain track for standard or narrow-gauge railroad equipment used in regular railroad service or in plant yards, quarries, sand and gravel pits, and mines. Includes ballast cleaning machine operators and railroad bed tamping machine operators.

2008 Employment: 15,500
Projected 2008-18 employment change: Faster than average
Most significant source of postsecondary education or training: Moderate-term on-the-job training

Rock splitters, quarry

Separate blocks of rough dimension stone from quarry mass using jackhammer and wedges.

2008 Employment: 4,400
Projected 2008-18 employment change: Little or no change
Most significant source of postsecondary education or training: Moderate-term on-the-job training

Roof bolters, mining

Operate machinery to install roof support bolts in underground mine.

2008 Employment: 5,100
Projected 2008-18 employment change: Decline slowly
Most significant source of postsecondary education or training: Moderate-term on-the-job training

Rotary drill operators, oil and gas

Set up or operate a variety of drills to remove petroleum products from the earth and to find and remove core samples for testing during oil and gas exploration.

2008 Employment: 28,600
Projected 2008-18 employment change: Decline rapidly
Most significant source of postsecondary education or training: Moderate-term on-the-job training

Roustabouts, oil and gas

Assemble or repair oil field equipment using hand and power tools. Perform other tasks as needed.

2008 Employment: 65,700
Projected 2008-18 employment change: Decline rapidly
Most significant source of postsecondary education or training: Moderate-term on-the-job training

Septic tank servicers and sewer pipe cleaners

Clean and repair septic tanks, sewer lines, or drains. May patch walls and partitions of tank, replace damaged drain tile, or repair breaks in underground piping.

2008 Employment: 25,900
Projected 2008-18 employment change: Much faster than average
Most significant source of postsecondary education or training: Moderate-term on-the-job training

Service unit operators, oil, gas, and mining

Operate equipment to increase oil flow from producing wells or to remove stick pipe, casing, tools, or other obstructions from drilling wells. May also perform similar services in mining exploration operations. Includes fishing-tool technicians.

2008 Employment: 39,100
Projected 2008-18 employment change: Decline rapidly
Most significant source of postsecondary education or training: Moderate-term on-the-job training

Installation, maintenance, and repair occupations

Bicycle repairers

Repair and service bicycles.

2008 Employment: 10,100
Projected 2008-18 employment change: Faster than average
Most significant source of postsecondary education or training: Moderate-term on-the-job training

Commercial divers

Work below surface of water, using scuba gear to inspect, repair, remove, or install equipment and structures. May use a variety of power and hand tools, such as drills, sledgehammers, torches, and welding equipment. May conduct tests or experiments, rig explosives, or photograph structures or marine life. Excludes fishers and related fishing workers, athletes and sports competitors, and police and sheriff's patrol officers.

2008 Employment: 2,400
Projected 2008-18 employment change: More slowly than average
Most significant source of postsecondary education or training: Post-secondary vocational award

Control and valve installers and repairers, except mechanical door

Install, repair, and maintain mechanical regulating and controlling devices, such as electric meters, gas regulators, thermostats, safety and flow valves, and other mechanical governors.

2008 Employment: 44,500
Projected 2008-18 employment change: Little or no change
Most significant source of postsecondary education or training: Moderate-term on-the-job training

Fabric menders, except garment

Repair tears, holes, and other defects in fabrics, such as draperies, linens, parachutes, and tents.

2008 Employment: 1,100
Projected 2008-18 employment change: Decline rapidly
Most significant source of postsecondary education or training: Moderate-term on-the-job training

First-line supervisors/managers of mechanics, installers, and repairers

Supervise and coordinate the activities of mechanics, installers, and repairers. Excludes team or work leaders.

2008 Employment: 448,500
Projected 2008-18 employment change: More slowly than average
Most significant source of postsecondary education or training: Work experience in a related occupation

Helpers—installation, maintenance, and repair workers

Help installation, maintenance, and repair workers in maintenance, parts replacement, and repair of vehicles, industrial machinery, and electrical and electronic equipment. Perform duties, such as furnishing tools, materials, and supplies to other workers; cleaning work area, machines, and tools; and holding materials or tools for other workers.

2008 Employment: 150,900
Projected 2008-18 employment change: About as fast as average
Most significant source of postsecondary education or training: Short-term on-the-job training

Locksmiths and safe repairers

Repair and open locks; make keys; change locks and safe combinations; and install and repair safes.

2008 Employment: 22,100
Projected 2008-18 employment change: About as fast as average
Most significant source of postsecondary education or training: Moderate-term on-the-job training

Manufactured building and mobile home installers

Move or install mobile homes or prefabricated buildings.

2008 Employment: 10,300
Projected 2008-18 employment change: More slowly than average
Most significant source of postsecondary education or training: Moderate-term on-the-job training

Mechanical door repairers

Install, service, or repair opening and closing mechanisms of automatic doors and hydraulic door closers. Includes garage door mechanics.

2008 Employment: 17,100
Projected 2008-18 employment change: About as fast as average
Most significant source of postsecondary education or training: Moderate-term on-the-job training

Recreational vehicle service technicians

Diagnose, inspect, adjust, repair, or overhaul recreational vehicles including travel trailers. May specialize in maintaining gas, electrical, hydraulic, plumbing, or chassis/towing systems as well as repairing generators, appliances, and interior components. Includes workers who perform customized van conversions. Excludes automotive service technicians and mechanics, and bus and truck mechanics and diesel engine specialists who also work on recreation vehicles.

2008 Employment: 13,700
Projected 2008-18 employment change: About as fast average
Most significant source of postsecondary education or training: Long-term on-the-job training

Refractory materials repairers, except brickmasons

Build or repair furnaces, kilns, cupolas, boilers, converters, ladles, soaking pits, ovens, etc., using refractory materials.

2008 Employment: 2,500
Projected 2008-18 employment change: Decline slowly
Most significant source of postsecondary education or training: Moderate-term on-the-job training

Riggers

Set up or repair rigging for construction projects, manufacturing plants, logging yards, ships and shipyards, or for the entertainment industry.

2008 Employment: 13,500
Projected 2008-18 employment change: Little or no change
Most significant source of postsecondary education or training: Short-term on-the-job training

Security and fire alarm systems installers

Install, program, maintain, and repair security and fire alarm wiring and equipment. Ensure that work is in accordance with relevant codes. Excludes electricians who do a broad range of electrical wiring.

2008 Employment: 66,200
Projected 2008-18 employment change: Much faster than average
Most significant source of postsecondary education or training: Post-secondary vocational award

Signal and track switch repairers

Install, inspect, test, maintain, or repair electric gate crossings, signals, signal equipment, track switches, section lines, or intercommunications systems within a railroad system.

2008 Employment: 6,800
Projected 2008-18 employment change: Little or no change
Most significant source of postsecondary education or training: Moderate-term on-the-job training

Tire repairers and changers

Repair and replace tires.

2008 Employment: 103,200
Projected 2008-18 employment change: Little or no change
Most significant source of postsecondary education or training: Short-term on-the-job training

Production occupations

Cementing and gluing machine operators and tenders

Operate or tend cementing and gluing machines to join items for further processing or to form a completed product. Processes include joining veneer sheets into plywood; gluing paper; joining rubber and rubberized fabric parts, plastic, simulated leather, or other materials. Excludes shoe machine operators and tenders.

2008 Employment: 19,800
Projected 2008-18 employment change: Decline rapidly
Most significant source of postsecondary education or training: Moderate-term on-the-job training

Chemical equipment operators and tenders

Operate or tend equipment to control chemical changes or reactions in the processing of industrial or consumer products. Equipment used includes devulcanizers, steam-jacketed kettles, and reactor vessels. Excludes chemical plant and system operators.

2008 Employment: 53,000
Projected 2008-18 employment change: Decline rapidly
Most significant source of postsecondary education or training: Moderate-term on-the-job training

Chemical plant and system operators

Control or operate an entire chemical process or system of machines.

2008 Employment: 45,100
Projected 2008-18 employment change: Decline rapidly
Most significant source of postsecondary education or training: Long-term on-the-job training

Cleaning, washing, and metal pickling equipment operators and tenders

Operate or tend machines to wash or clean products, such as barrels or kegs, glass items, tin plate, food, pulp, coal, plastic, or rubber, to remove impurities.

2008 Employment: 18,000
Projected 2008-18 employment change: Decline slowly
Most significant source of postsecondary education or training: Moderate-term on-the-job training

Cooling and freezing equipment operators and tenders

Operate or tend equipment, such as cooling and freezing units, refrigerators, batch freezers, and freezing tunnels, to cool or freeze products, food, blood plasma, and chemicals.

2008 Employment: 9,900
Projected 2008-18 employment change: Little or no change
Most significant source of postsecondary education or training: Moderate-term on-the-job training

Crushing, grinding, and polishing machine setters, operators, and tenders

Set up, operate, or tend machines to crush, grind, or polish materials, such as coal, glass, grain, stone, food, or rubber.

2008 Employment: 41,200
Projected 2008-18 employment change: Little or no change
Most significant source of postsecondary education or training: Moderate-term on-the-job training

Cutters and trimmers, hand

Use hand tools or hand-held power tools to cut and trim a variety of manufactured items, such as carpet, fabric, stone, glass, or rubber.

2008 Employment: 24,200
Projected 2008-18 employment change: Decline rapidly
Most significant source of postsecondary education or training: Short-term on-the-job training

Cutting and slicing machine setters, operators, and tenders

Set up, operate, or tend machines that cut or slice materials, such as glass, stone, cork, rubber, tobacco, food, paper, or insulating material. Excludes woodworking machines setters, operators, and tenders; cut-

ting, punching, and press machine setters, operators, and tenders, metal and plastic; and textile cutting machine setters, operators, and tenders.

2008 Employment: 75,200
Projected 2008-18 employment change: Decline slowly
Most significant source of postsecondary education or training: Moderate-term on-the-job training

Etchers and engravers

Engrave or etch metal, wood, rubber, or other materials for identification or decorative purposes. Includes such workers as etcher-circuit processors, pantograph engravers, and silk screen etchers. Includes photoengravers with prepress technicians and workers.

2008 Employment: 12,000
Projected 2008-18 employment change: Little or no change
Most significant source of postsecondary education or training: Long-term on-the-job training

Extruding, forming, pressing, and compacting machine setters, operators, and tenders

Set up, operate, or tend machines, such as glass forming machines, plodder machines, and tuber machines, to shape and form products, such as glassware, food, rubber, soap, brick, tile, clay, wax, tobacco, or cosmetics. Excludes paper goods machine setters, operators, and tenders; and shoe machine operators and tenders.

2008 Employment: 83,300
Projected 2008-18 employment change: Faster than average
Most significant source of postsecondary education or training: Moderate-term on-the-job training

First-line supervisors/managers of production and operating workers

Supervise and coordinate the activities of production and operating workers, such as inspectors, precision workers, machine setters, and operators, assemblers, fabricators, and plant and system operators. Excludes team or work leaders.

2008 Employment: 681,200
Projected 2008-18 employment change: Decline slowly
Most significant source of postsecondary education or training: Work experience in a related occupation

Furnace, kiln, oven, drier, and kettle operators and tenders

Operate or tend heating equipment other than basic metal, plastic or food processing equipment. Includes activities, such as annealing glass, drying lumber, curing rubber, removing moisture from materials, or boiling soap.

2008 Employment: 24,500
Projected 2008-18 employment change: Decline slowly
Most significant source of postsecondary education or training: Moderate-term on-the-job training

Gas plant operators

Distribute or process gas for utility companies and others by controlling compressors to maintain specified pressures on main pipelines.

2008 Employment: 14,900
Projected 2008-18 employment change: Decline slowly
Most significant source of postsecondary education or training: Long-term on-the-job training

Grinding and polishing workers, hand

Grind, sand, or polish, using hand tools or hand-held power tools, a variety of metal, wood, stone, clay, plastic, or glass objects. Includes chippers, buffers, and finishers.

2008 Employment: 40,100
Projected 2008-18 employment change: About as fast as average
Most significant source of postsecondary education or training: Moderate-term on-the-job training

Helpers—production workers

Help production workers by performing duties of lesser skill. Duties include supplying or holding materials or tools, and cleaning work area and equipment. Excludes apprentice workers.

2008 Employment: 484,000
Projected 2008-18 employment change: Little or no change
Most significant source of postsecondary education or training: Short-term on-the-job training

Mixing and blending machine setters, operators, and tenders

Set up, operate, or tend machines to mix or blend materials, such as chemicals, tobacco, liquids, color pigments, or explosive ingredients. Excludes food batchmakers.

2008 Employment: 141,500
Projected 2008-18 employment change: Faster than average
Most significant source of postsecondary education or training: Moderate-term on-the-job training

Molders, shapers, and casters, except metal and plastic

Mold, shape, form, cast, or carve products such as food products, figurines, tile, pipes, and candles consisting of clay, glass, plaster, concrete, stone, or combinations of materials.

2008 Employment: 48,200
Projected 2008-18 employment change: More slowly than average
Most significant source of postsecondary education or training: Moderate-term on-the-job training

Packaging and filling machine operators and tenders

Operate or tend machines to prepare industrial or consumer products for storage or shipment. Includes cannery workers who pack food products.

2008 Employment: 349,000
Projected 2008-18 employment change: Little or no change
Most significant source of postsecondary education or training: Short-term on-the-job training

Paper goods machine setters, operators, and tenders

Set up, operate, or tend paper goods machines that perform a variety of functions, such as converting, sawing, corrugating, banding, wrapping, boxing, stitching, forming, or sealing paper or paperboard sheets into products.

2008 Employment: 103,300
Projected 2008-18 employment change: Decline rapidly
Most significant source of postsecondary education or training: Moderate-term on-the-job training

Petroleum pump system operators, refinery operators, and gaugers

Control the operation of petroleum refining or processing units. May specialize in controlling manifold and pumping systems, gauging or testing oil in storage tanks, or regulating the flow of oil into pipelines.

2008 Employment: 47,100
Projected 2008-18 employment change: Decline rapidly
Most significant source of postsecondary education or training: Long-term on-the-job training

Separating, filtering, clarifying, precipitating, and still machine setters, operators, and tenders

Set up, operate, or tend continuous flow or vat-type equipment; filter presses; shaker screens; centrifuges; condenser tubes; precipitating, fermenting, or evaporating tanks; scrubbing towers; or batch stills. These machines extract, sort, or separate liquids, gases, or solids from other materials to recover a refined product. Includes dairy processing equipment operators. Excludes chemical equipment operators and tenders.

2008 Employment: 40,800
Projected 2008-18 employment change: About as fast as average
Most significant source of postsecondary education or training: Moderate-term on-the-job training

Tire builders

Operate machines to build tires from rubber components.

2008 Employment: 21,400
Projected 2008-18 employment change: Decline rapidly
Most significant source of postsecondary education or training: Moderate-term on-the-job training

Transportation and material moving occupations

Aircraft cargo handling supervisors

Direct ground crew in the loading, unloading, securing, and staging of aircraft cargo and baggage. Determine the quantity and orientation of cargo and compute aircraft center of gravity. May accompany aircraft as member of flight crew and monitor and handle cargo in flight, and assist and brief passengers on safety and emergency procedures. Includes loadmasters.

2008 Employment: 4,900
Projected 2008-18 employment change: About as fast as average
Most significant source of postsecondary education or training: Work experience in a related occupation

Airfield operations specialists

Ensure the safe takeoff and landing of commercial and military aircraft. Duties include coordination between air-traffic control and maintenance personnel; dispatching; using airfield landing and navigational aids; implementing airfield safety procedures; monitoring and maintaining flight records; and applying knowledge of weather information.

2008 Employment: 8,100
Projected 2008-18 employment change: About as fast as average
Most significant source of postsecondary education or training: Long-term on-the-job training

Ambulance drivers and attendants, except emergency medical technicians

Drive ambulance or assist ambulance drivers in transporting sick, injured, or convalescent persons. Assist in lifting patients.

2008 Employment: 22,200
Projected 2008-18 employment change: About as fast as average
Most significant source of postsecondary education or training: Moderate-term on-the-job training

Bridge and lock tenders

Operate and tend bridges, canal locks, and lighthouses to permit marine passage on inland waterways, near shores, and at danger points in waterway passages. May supervise such operations. Includes drawbridge operators, lock tenders and operators, and slip bridge operators.

2008 Employment: 4,700
Projected 2008-18 employment change: About as fast as average
Most significant source of postsecondary education or training: Short-term on-the-job training

First-line supervisors/managers of helpers, laborers, and material movers, hand

Supervise and coordinate the activities of helpers, laborers, or material movers.

2008 Employment: 183,500
Projected 2008-18 employment change: More slowly than average
Most significant source of postsecondary education or training: Work experience in a related occupation

First-line supervisors/managers of transportation and material moving machine and vehicle operators

Directly supervise and coordinate activities of transportation and material-moving machine and vehicle operators and helpers.

2008 Employment: 217,600
Projected 2008-18 employment change: Decline slowly
Most significant source of postsecondary education or training: Work experience in a related occupation

Parking lot attendants

Park automobiles or issue tickets for customers in parking lot or garage. May collect fee.

2008 Employment: 136,200
Projected 2008-18 employment change: More slowly than average
Most significant source of postsecondary education or training: Short-term on-the-job training

Service station attendants

Service automobiles, buses, trucks, boats, and other automotive or marine vehicles with fuel, lubricants, and accessories. Collect payment for services and supplies. May lubricate vehicle, change motor oil, install antifreeze, or replace lights or other accessories, such as windshield wiper blades or fan belts. May repair or replace tires.

2008 Employment: 83,300
Projected 2008-18 employment change: Little or no change
Most significant source of postsecondary education or training: Short-term on-the-job training

Traffic technicians

Conduct field studies to determine traffic volume, speed, effectiveness of signals, adequacy of lighting, and other factors influencing traffic conditions, under direction of traffic engineer.

2008 Employment: 7,400
Projected 2008-18 employment change: About as fast as average
Most significant source of postsecondary education or training: Short-term on-the-job training

Transportation inspectors

Inspect equipment or goods in connection with the safe transport of cargo or people. Includes rail transport inspectors, such as freight inspectors, car inspectors, rail inspectors, and other nonprecision inspectors of other types of transportation vehicles.

2008 Employment: 26,900
Projected 2008-18 employment change: Faster than average
Most significant source of postsecondary education or training: Work experience in a related occupation

Assumptions and Methods Used in Preparing Employment Projections

Occupational statements in the *Handbook* include numerical projections of the change in employment between 2008 and 2018. These projections are developed using the Bureau of Labor Statistics (BLS) employment projections model system. Projections of occupational employment are the final step in the system; these steps are listed in the discussion of methods below. A discussion of projections methods also is accessible on the Internet at **http://www.bls.gov/opub/hom/homch13_a.htm**. The November 2009 *Monthly Labor Review* presents a comprehensive discussion of the 2008-18 projections of the economy, labor force, and industry and occupation employment. The winter 2009-10 *Occupational Outlook Quarterly* presents the projections in a series of charts.

The projections reflect the knowledge and judgment of staff in the BLS Office of Occupational Statistics and Employment Projections and of knowledgeable people from other BLS offices, other government agencies, colleges and universities, industries, unions, professional societies, and trade associations, who furnished data and information, prepared reports, or reviewed the projections. BLS takes full responsibility, however, for the projections.

Assumptions. The information in the *Handbook* is based on an economic projection which, in turn, is based on assumptions about several key variables that affect the U.S. economy. The United States entered a severe recession in December 2007, leading to declining output and high unemployment. However, BLS expects the economy to return to its long-term trend rate of growth over the next decade. Consequently, the employment projections are based on an anticipated growth rate of 2.4 percent of Gross Domestic Product (GDP) per year from 2008 to 2018.

Other key assumptions include slower growth in the labor force (0.8 percent annually from 2008 to 2018 compared with 1.1 percent annually over the past 10-year period, 1998–2008) as a large number of workers retire, and a slowdown in labor productivity (1.8 percent average annual growth compared with 2.6 percent annually over the 1998–2008 period). The projections model also assumes an unemployment rate of 5.1 percent in 2018.

Growth in personal consumption expenditures, the largest single component of GDP, is expected to slow to 2.5 percent annually from 2008-18, down from the 3 percent annual average from 1998–2008. Underlying this assumption is an expected slowdown in the growth of spending on non-durable goods (defined as goods lasting less than three years) and durable goods (such as cars and large appliances). Growth in spending on consumer services is anticipated to be stronger than overall personal consumption growth, however, driven in part by continued increases in medical care spending.

Residential investment (the construction of new homes and dwellings) is expected to increase 5.1 percent annually over the projections period, reflecting the severe housing slump

downturn that began in 2006 and the historically low starting point. Non-residential investment, which includes purchases by firms of equipment and software as well as construction of non-residential structures, should see 3.0 percent growth per year from 2008 to 2018, similar to the 3.1 percent annual growth from 1998-2008. Underlying this assumption is an anticipated slowdown (compared to the prior decade) in non-residential structure investment. Total investment, consisting of residential plus non-residential investment, is expected to increase by 3.9 percent annually from 2008-18, reaching 15.7 percent of GDP in 2018, higher than the 14.0 percent mark of 2008.

BLS expects the trade deficit to be 4.4 percent of GDP in 2018, below the 2004 peak of 5.6 percent, but still equivalent to about $650 billion. Inflation is expected to average 1.9 percent from 2008 to 2018, reflecting low levels of inflation during the initial years due to the recession, followed by a return to the long-term trend.

Although BLS considers these assumptions reasonable, the economy may follow a different course, resulting in a different pattern of occupational growth. Real growth also could be different because most occupations are sensitive to a much wider variety of factors than those considered in the various projections models. Unforeseen changes in consumer, business, or government spending patterns and in the ways in which goods and services are produced as well as advances in technology could greatly alter the growth of individual occupations.

Methods. This section summarizes the steps involved in BLS projections of employment by occupation. BLS uses U.S. Census Bureau projections of the population by age, gender, ethnicity, and race, combined with projections of labor force participation rates—the percent of the specified group of the population working or seeking work—to arrive at estimates of the civilian labor force for the projected year.

BLS projections are developed in a series of steps, each of which is based on separate projections procedures, models, and various related assumptions. These steps, or system components, deal with:

1. Size and demographic composition of the labor force
2. Growth of the aggregate economy (GDP)
3. Inter-industry relationships (input-output) used to allocate components of final demand to commodities
4. Industry output and employment
5. Occupational employment

These components provide the overall analytical framework needed to develop detailed employment projections. Each component is developed in order, with the results of each used as input for successive components and with some results feeding back into earlier steps. Each step is repeated a number of times to ensure internal consistency as assumptions and results are reviewed and revised.

The projections of the labor force and assumptions about other demographic variables, fiscal and monetary policies, foreign economic activity, and energy prices form the input to the macroeconomic model. This model projects GDP (all final sales in the economy) and the distribution of GDP by its major demand components (consumer expenditures, investment, government consumption and gross investment, and exports and imports).

Estimating the intermediate flows of goods and services—for example, the steel incorporated into automobiles—is the next step in the projections process. The resulting estimates of demand for goods and services are used to project industry output of final products as well as total output by industry.

Industry output of goods and services is then used to estimate industry employment. Trends in productivity are used to evaluate the future output per worker hour, and additional analysis is used to calculate worker hours. These estimates, along with output projections, are used to develop the final industry employment projections.

An industry-occupation matrix, also known as the National Employment Matrix, is used to project employment for wage and salary workers. The matrix shows occupational staffing patterns—each occupation as a percent of employment in every industry. The matrix covering the 2008-18 period includes 276 detailed industries and 750 detailed occupations. Data for current staffing patterns in the matrix come from the BLS Occupational Employment Statistics (OES) survey, which collects data from employers on a 3-year cycle.

The occupational staffing patterns for each industry were projected based on anticipated changes in the ways in which goods and services are produced, and were then applied to projected industry employment. The resulting employment was summed across industries to derive total wage and salary employment by occupation. Using this method, rapid employment growth is projected for healthcare workers, such as pharmacists and physical therapists, while employment of newspaper publishing workers, such as reporters and correspondents, is expected to decline, reflecting the projected changes in the healthcare and newspaper publishing industries, respectively.

Employment in an occupation also may grow or decline as a result of many other factors. For example, relatively fast growth is expected among computer systems analysts and software engineers as organizations continue to adopt increasingly sophisticated technology. On the other hand, automation, the expanding use of computers, and developments in computer software will result in declining employment among procurement clerks, order clerks, and word processors and typists. The projected-year matrix incorporates these expected changes.

Data on self-employed workers in each occupation come from the Current Population Survey (CPS). Numbers of self-employed workers were projected separately.

Replacement needs. In most occupations, replacement needs provide more job openings than growth. Replacement openings occur as people leave occupations. Some individuals transfer to other occupations as a step up the career ladder or to change careers; some stop working temporarily, perhaps to return to school or care for a family; other workers—retirees for example—leave the labor force permanently. A discussion of replacements and the methods used to prepare estimates is presented on the Bureau's Employment Projections homepage at **http://www.bls.gov/emp**.

Occupational Information Network Coverage

The *Occupational Information Network* (O*NET), which replaced the *Dictionary of Occupational Titles,* is used by public employment service offices to classify and place job-seekers. O*NET was developed by job analysts. The information on job duties, knowledge and skills, education and training, and other occupational characteristics comes directly from workers and employers. Information on O*NET is available from O*NET Project, U.S. Department of Labor/ETA, 200 Constitution Ave. NW., Room S-4231, Washington, DC 20210-0001. Telephone (202) 693-3660. Internet: **http://www.doleta.gov/programs/onet**.

The structure of O*NET reflects the *Standard Occupational Classification* (SOC) system, and represents the Federal Government's effort to analyze the occupational structure in the United States and to provide a national occupational classification system. The 2000 SOC includes about 820 detailed occupations. The Government is developing the 2010 SOC. Information on the SOC, including its occupational structure, is available on the Internet: **http://www.bls.gov/soc**.

Occupational statements in this 2010-11 edition of the *Handbook* are based on the 2000 SOC, which relates to or matches the definitions used in the Bureau's Occupational Employment Statistics (OES) survey—the principal source of occupational employment data in the *Handbook*. The table below lists O*NET codes and titles that are related to occupations in the *Handbook*.

Index

C

F

J

K

L

M

N

O

Q

R

T

U

V

W

X

Y

Z

BLS Employment Projections Online

http://www.bls.gov/emp

Federal Government's Premier Career Guidance Publications

- Occupational Outlook Handbook
- Career Guide to Industries
- Occupational Outlook Quarterly

People Are Asking

- Which occupations and industries will grow the fastest?
- Which occupations and industries will add the most new jobs?
- How does BLS develop employment projections?

Projections-Related Articles

- Occupational employment projections to 2018
- Charting the projections
- The job outlook in brief

Searchable Databases

- Occupational Employment, Training, and Earnings
- National Employment Matrix
- Tables created by BLS

Related Links

- BLS career information for young people
- State employment projections
- Standard Occupational Classification (SOC) system

Contacts

Telephone listings for industry and occupational experts in the Office of Occupational Statistics and Employment Projections

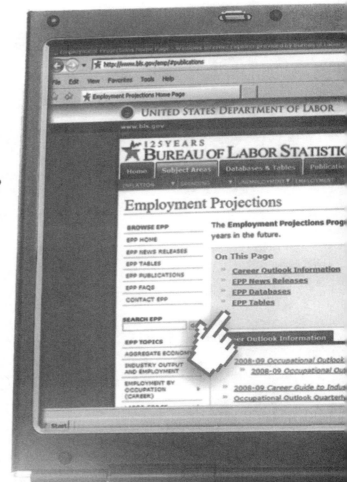